Bender's
2015
TAX RETURN
MANUAL

Special Forms Supplement

by
Bobbi Halpin, J.D.

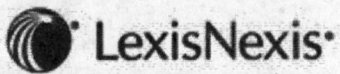

ISBN 978-1-6328-1641-2

EDITORIAL OFFICES
630 CENTRAL AVENUE, NEW PROVIDENCE, NJ 07974 (908) 464-6800
201 MISSION STREET, SAN FRANCISCO, CA 94105 (415) 908-3200

BENDER'S 2015 TAX RETURN MANUAL

FORMS SUPPLEMENT

TABLE OF CONTENTS

BLANK FORMS

Form 706   United States Estates (and Generation-Skipping Transfer) Tax Return

        Instructions to Form 706

Form 1040   U.S. Individual Income Tax Return

Schedule A	Itemized Deductions
Schedule B	Interest and Ordinary Dividends
Schedule C	Profit or Loss From Business (Sole Proprietorship)
Schedule C-EZ	Net Profit From Business
Schedule D	Capital Gains and Losses
Schedule E	Supplemental Income and Loss (From rental real estate, royalties, partnerships, S corporations, estates, trusts, REMICs, etc.)
Schedule EIC	Earned Income Credit (Qualifying Child Information)
Schedule F	Profit or Loss From Farming
Schedule H	Household Employment Taxes
Schedule J	Income Averaging for Farmers and Fishermen
Schedule R	Credit for the Elderly or the Disabled
Schedule SE	Self-Employment Tax
Schedule 8812	Child Tax Credit

        Instructions to Form 1040 and Schedules

Form 1040A   U.S. Individual Income Tax Return

        Instructions to Form 1040A

Schedule B	Interest and Ordinary Dividends
Schedule EIC	Earned Income Credit (Qualifying Child Information)
Schedule R	Credit for the Elderly or the Disabled

        Instructions to Schedule R

Schedule 8812	Child Tax Credit

        Instructions to Schedule 8812

Form 1040EZ   Income Tax Return for Single and Joint Filers With No Dependents

        Instructions to Form 1040EZ

Form 1040-V   Payment Voucher

Form 1040X   Amended U.S. Individual Tax Return

TAX FORMS
FINDING LIST

TAX FORMS FINDING LIST

PART 1 of the Manual includes filled-in tax forms with line-by-line instructions. Each filled-in tax form is located at a specific section number in PART 1. When filled-in tax forms are not available from the IRS when the Main Volume goes to print, a cautionary note appears at that section in the Main Volume. These filled-in tax forms can be found in forms supplements.

PART 2 of the Manual includes reproducible blank tax forms and instructions. The blank tax forms and instructions are organized in numerical order. Any blank tax forms that are not available when the Main Volume goes to print may be included in forms supplements.

The following Tax Forms Finding List helps you locate both filled-in and blank reproducible tax forms in the Manual. The Tax Forms Finding List is located before PART 1 and in PART 2 of the Main Volume. For each tax form, the list tells you:

(1) the name and number of the tax form;

(2) whether the tax form is included as a blank reproducible form only or also as a filled-in form;

(3) the section of the Manual where the filled-in form appears; and

(4) whether the blank or filled-in tax form is located in the Main Volume or was not released by the IRS when the Main Volume went to print.

Form	Title		Blank/Filled-In	Location
706	United States Estate (and Generation-Skipping Transfer) Tax Return		Blank	Supplement 1
			Filled-In (§ 7.20)	Supplement 1
	Instructions to Form 706			Supplement 1
709	United States Gift (and Generation-Skipping Transfer) Tax Return		Blank	Main Volume
			Filled-In (§ 8.20)	Main Volume
	Instructions to Form 709			Main Volume
712	Life Insurance Statement		Blank	Main Volume
851	Affiliations Schedule		Blank	Main Volume
926	Return by a U.S. Transferor of Property to a Foreign Corporation		Blank	Main Volume
	Instructions to Form 926			Main Volume
966	Corporate Dissolution or Liquidation		Blank	Main Volume
970	Application To Use LIFO Inventory Method		Blank	Main Volume
1040	U.S. Individual Income Tax Return		Blank	Supplement 1
			Filled-In (§ 2.1320)	Supplement 1
	Schedule A	Itemized Deductions	Blank	Supplement 1
			Filled-In (§ 2.1340)	Supplement 1
	Schedule B	Interest and Ordinary Dividends	Blank	Supplement 1
			Filled-In (§ 2.1360)	
	Schedule C	Profit or Loss From Business (Sole Proprietorship)	Blank	Supplement 1
			Filled-In (§§ 2.1381, 2.1382)	Supplement 1
	Schedule C-EZ	Net Profit From Business	Blank	Supplement 1
			Filled-In (§ 2.3160)	Supplement 1
	Schedule D	Capital Gains and Losses	Blank	Supplement 1
			Filled-In (§ 2.1400)	Supplement 1
	Schedule E	Supplemental Income and Loss (From rental real estate, royalties, partnerships, S corporations, estates, trusts, REMICs, etc.)	Blank	Supplement 1
			Filled-In (§§ 2.1420, 6.23)	Supplement 1
	Schedule EIC	Earned Income Credit (Qualifying Child Information)	Blank	Supplement 1
	Schedule F	Profit or Loss From Farming	Blank	Supplement 1
			Filled-In (§ 2.1440)	Supplement 1
	Schedule H	Household Employment Taxes	Blank	Supplement 1
	Schedule J	Income Averaging for Farmers and Fishermen	Blank	Supplement 1
	Schedule R	Credit for the Elderly or the Disabled	Blank	Supplement 1
			Filled-In (§ 2.3220)	Main Volume
	Schedule SE	Self-Employment Tax	Blank	Supplement 1
			Filled-In (§ 2.1460)	Supplement 1

TAX INCREASE PREVENTION ACT OF 2014

Tax Increase Prevention Act of 2014
Pub L No 113-295, 113th Cong, 2d Sess (Dec 19, 2014)

On December 19, 2014, after the main volume of this *Manual* went to print, President Obama signed into law the Tax Increase and Prevention Act of 2014. The Act retroactively extends a number of tax breaks for businesses and individuals through 2014. Following are highlights of selected provisions.

<u>BUSINESS-RELATED CREDITS AND ISSUES</u>

Alternative fuel and alternative fuel mixture credits. The alternative fuel credit and the alternative fuel mixture excise tax credits have been extended to apply to sales or uses for any period through December 31, 2014. (IRC §§ 6426(d)(5), 6426(e)(3), 6427(e)(6)(C); Pub L No 113-295, 113th Cong, 2d Sess, § 160(b) (Dec 19, 2014))

American Samoa economic development credit. The American Samoa economic development credit has been extended to apply to the 2014 tax year. (Tax Relief and Health Care Act of 2006, § 119(d); American Taxpayer Relief Act of 2012, § 330; Pub L No 113-295, 113th Cong, 2d Sess, § 141 (Dec 19, 2014))

Employer wage credit for military employees. The employer wage credit for employees who are active duty members of the uniformed services has been extended through 2014. The credit is available to eligible small business employers and generally equals 20% of the wage differential payments made to qualified military employees. (IRC § 45P(f); Pub L No 113-295, 113th Cong, 2d Sess, § 118 (Dec 19, 2014))

Empowerment zone tax incentives. Tax incentives through empowerment zones have generally been extended through 2014. (IRC § 1391(d)(1)(A)(i); Pub L No 113-295, 113th Cong, 2d Sess, § 139 (Dec 19, 2014))

Excise tax credit for alcohol fuel, biodiesel, and alternative fuels. The biodiesel mixture credit has been extended to sales, uses, or removals for any period through December 31, 2014. (IRC §§ 6426(c)(6), 6427(e)(6)(B); Pub L No 113-295, 113th Cong, 2d Sess, § 160(a) (Dec 19, 2014))

Indian employment credit. The Indian employment credit has been extended to qualified wages and health insurance expenses incurred through December 31, 2014. (IRC § 45A(f); Pub L No 113-295, 113th Cong, 2d Sess, § 114 (Dec 19, 2014))

Low-income housing credit rate. The temporary minimum low-income tax credit rate for non-federally subsidized new buildings has been extended to apply to housing dollar amount allocations made through December 31, 2014. (IRC § 42(b)(2)(A); Pub L No 113-295, 113th Cong, 2d Sess, § 112 (Dec 19, 2014))

Mine rescue team training credit. The mine rescue team training credit has been extended through 2014. Available only to eligible employers, the credit is limited to the lesser of $10,000 or 20% of the amount of actual training expenses incurred for qualified mine rescue team employees. (IRC § 45N(e); Pub L No 113-295, 113th Cong, 2d Sess, § 117 (Dec 19, 2014))

New markets tax credit. The new markets tax credit for holders of qualified equity investments has been extended through 2014. (IRC § 45D(f)(1)(G); Pub L No 113-295, 113th Cong, 2d Sess, § 115 (Dec 19, 2014))

Railroad track maintenance credit. The railroad track maintenance credit has been extended and is available for qualified railroad track maintenance expenditures paid or incurred in tax years ending prior to January 1, 2015. (IRC § 45G(f); Pub L No 113-295, 113th Cong, 2d Sess, § 116 (Dec 19, 2014))

Research credit. The credit for increasing research activities has been extended to qualified research expenses paid or incurred on or before December 31, 2014. (IRC §§ 41(a), (h)(1), 45C(b)(1)(D); Pub L No 113-295, 113th Cong, 2d Sess, § 111 (Dec 19, 2014))

Work opportunity credit. The work opportunity credit has been extended to wages paid through December 31, 2014. The work opportunity tax credit benefits employers who hire employees that are members of targeted groups, including veterans, ex-felons, SSI recipients, and others. (IRC § 51(c)(4); Pub L No 113-295, 113th Cong, 2d Sess, § 119 (Dec 19, 2014))

CAPITAL GAINS

Small business stock: temporary exclusion of 100% of gain. The temporary exclusion of 100% of the gain on disposition of small business stock is extended through 2014. The extension applies to stock acquired before January 1, 2015. (IRC § 1202(a)(4); Pub L No 113-295, 113th Cong, 2d Sess, § 136 (Dec 19, 2014))

CHARITABLE CONTRIBUTIONS, DISTRIBUTIONS, AND DEDUCTION

Capital gain real property contributed for conservation purposes. Extension is available for contributions of property made by December 31, 2014, including contribution by certain corporate farmers and ranchers. (IRC § 170(b)(1)(E)(vi), (b)(2)(B)(iii); Pub L No 113-295, 113th Cong, 2d Sess, § 106 (Dec 19, 2014))

Charitable distributions from individual retirement account. IRA owners aged 70½ and older can continue to distribute up to $100,000 of IRA funds tax-free to charitable organizations, in order to satisfy required minimum IRA distributions. This provision has been extended, applicable to distributions made on or before December 31, 2014. (IRC § 408(d)(8)(F); Pub L No 113-295, 113th Cong, 2d Sess, § 108 (Dec 19, 2014))

Enhanced charitable deduction for contributions of food inventory. The enhanced charitable deduction for contributions of food inventory has been extended to apply to contributions made through December 31, 2014. (IRC § 170(e)(3)(C)(iv); Pub L No 113-295, 113th Cong, 2d Sess, § 126 (Dec 19, 2014))

DEPRECIATION

Bonus depreciation. Bonus depreciation of 50% for qualified property has been extended through tax year 2014. Bonus depreciation is taken prior to the Section 179 expensing deduction and the normal amount of depreciation allowed for that property, and is an addition to such deductions. Bonus depreciation is available for the first year in which the property is placed in service. Bonus depreciation is not available for ADS property but has the advantage of not being an AMT preference item. Bonus depreciation is subject to recapture as ordinary income. (IRC §§ 168(k), 179, 1245; Pub L No 113-295, 113th Cong, 2d Sess, § 125(a) (Dec 19, 2014)) The taxpayer may continue to elect to accelerate the AMT credit in lieu of bonus depreciation through tax year 2014. (IRC § 168(k)(4)(D)(iii)(II); Pub L No 113-295, 113th Cong, 2d Sess, § 125(c) (Dec 19, 2014))

Fifteen-year straight line cost recovery for qualified leasehold improvements, qualified restaurant buildings and improvements, and qualified retail improvements. The provision allowing for 15-year straight line cost recovery for specified items has been extended to property placed in service in tax years ending before January 1, 2015. (IRC § 168(e)(3)(E); Pub L No 113-295, 113th Cong, 2d Sess, § 122 (Dec 19, 2014))

Classification of certain race horses as three-year property. The provision that allows race horses to be classified as three-year property has been extended to tax years ending before January 1, 2015. (IRC § 168(e)(3)(A)(i); Pub L No 113-295, 113th Cong, 2d Sess, § 121 (Dec 19, 2014))

Energy efficient commercial buildings deduction. The depreciation deduction for energy efficient commercial buildings has been extended to apply to property placed in service on or before December 31, 2014. (IRC § 179D(h); Pub L No 113-295, 113th Cong, 2d Sess, § 158 (Dec 19, 2014))

Indian reservation property—accelerated depreciation. Accelerated depreciation may be claimed for business property located on an Indian reservation. This provision has been extended to property placed in service on or before December 31, 2014. (IRC § 168(j)(8); Pub L No 113-295, 113th Cong, 2d Sess, § 124 (Dec 19, 2014))

Mine safety equipment—election to expense. The election to expense advanced mine safety equipment at 50% of cost has been extended through tax year 2014. The extension applies to property placed in service on or before December 31, 2014. (IRC § 179E(g); Pub L No 113-295, 113th Cong, 2d Sess, § 128 (Dec 19, 2014))

Motorsports entertainment complexes allowed seven-year recovery period. The seven-year recovery period allowed for motorsports entertainment complexes is extended for properties placed in service before January 1, 2015. (IRC § 168(i)(15)(D); Pub L No 113-295, 113th Cong, 2d Sess, § 123 (Dec 19, 2014))

Second generation biofuel plant property. The special allowance for second generation biofuel plant property has been extended through tax year 2014, applicable to property placed in service before January 1, 2015. (IRC § 168(I)(2)(D); Pub L No 113-295, 113th Cong, 2d Sess, § 157 (Dec 19, 2014))

Section 179 expensing limitations; computer software; treatment of certain real property as Section 179 property. The Section 179 maximum expensing deduction is once again $500,000, as it has been since 2010. The planned reduction of that amount to $25,000 has been put off for at least one more tax year. (IRC § 179(b)(1); Pub L No 113-295, 113th Cong, 2d Sess, § 127(a)(1) (Dec 19, 2014)) The deduction continues to be reduced by the excess of the cost over $2,000,000, the threshold amount that was scheduled to be reduced to $200,000 but has now been rescheduled to take place in 2015. (IRC § 179(b)(2); Pub L No 113-295, 113th Cong, 2d Sess, § 127(a)(2) (Dec 19, 2014)) Computer software continues to apply for expensing under Section 179 for the 2014 tax year. (IRC § 179(d)(1)(A)(ii); Pub L No 113-295, 113th Cong, 2d Sess, § 127(b) (Dec 19, 2014)) Qualified business real property continues to be eligible for Section 179 expensing, as the provision has been extended through the 2014 tax year. (IRC § 179(f)(1); Pub L No 113-295, 113th Cong, 2d Sess, § 127(d)(1) (Dec 19, 2014)) The Section 179 carryover provisions have also been extended. (IRC § 179(f)(4); Pub L No 113-295, 113th Cong, 2d Sess, § 127(d)(2) (Dec 19, 2014))

EDUCATION AND TEACHING EXPENSES AND DEDUCTIONS

Deduction for certain expenses of elementary and secondary school teachers. Elementary and secondary school teachers may deduct expenses incurred for teaching supplies and other materials up to a maximum of $250, even if they do not itemize deductions. This deduction has been extended through tax year 2014. (IRC § 62(a)(2)(D); Pub L No 113-295, 113th Cong, 2d Sess, § 101 (Dec 19, 2014))

Deduction for qualified tuition and related expenses. The above-the-line deduction for tuition and related expenses has been extended for otherwise qualifying expenses incurred through December 31, 2014. (IRC § 222(e); Pub L No 113-295, 113th Cong, 2d Sess, § 107 (Dec 19, 2014))

EMPLOYER-PROVIDED BENEFITS

Qualified transportation fringe benefit. For 2014, employers may provide employees with excludable qualified transportation fringe benefits in the maximum amount of $130 per month for commuter vehicle expenses or for a transit pass; the maximum exclusion for qualified parking fees is $250. This legislation reflects the rule in the applicable 2013 revenue procedure. Parity is extended for benefits provided before January 1, 2015. (IRC § 132(f)(2); Pub L No 113-295, 113th Cong, 2d Sess, § 103 (Dec 19, 2014). See also Rev Proc 2013-35, § 3.16, 2013-2 CB 537)

Alcohol, etc., used as fuel—second generation biofuel producer credit. The credit for second generation biofuel producers has been extended through tax year 2014. The extension applies to qualified second generation biofuel produced before January 1, 2015. (IRC § 40(b)(6)(J)(i); Pub L No 113-295, 113th Cong, 2d Sess, § 152 (Dec 19, 2014))

Biodiesel and renewable diesel. The credit for biodiesel and renewable diesel used as fuel has been extended to apply to fuels sold or used on or before December 31, 2014. (IRC § 40A(g); Pub L No 113-295, 113th Cong, 2d Sess, § 153 (Dec 19, 2014))

Energy credit: election to treat qualified facilities as energy property. The election to treat qualified facilities as energy property for purposes of the energy credit has been extended through tax year 2014. (IRC § 48(a)(5)(C)(ii); Pub L No 113-295, 113th Cong, 2d Sess, § 155(b) (Dec 19, 2014))

Energy produced from certain renewable resources credit. The credits for energy produced from certain renewable resources have been extended through 2014 for the following types of qualified facilities: (IRC § 45(d); Pub L No 113-295, 113th Cong, 2d Sess, § 155(a) (Dec 19, 2014))

- Wind facilities (IRC § 45(d)(1))
- Closed-loop biomass facilities (IRC § 45(d)(2)(A))
- Open-loop biomass facilities (IRC § 45(d)(3)(A))
- Geothermal or solar energy facilities (IRC § 45(d)(4))
- Landfill gas facilities (IRC § 45(d)(6))
- Trash facilities (IRC § 45(d)(7))
- Qualified hydropower facilities (IRC § 45(d)(9))
- Marine and hydrokinetic renewable energy facilities (IRC § 45(d)(11)(B))

New energy efficient home credit. The new energy efficient home credit has been extended for tax years through 2014, applicable to energy efficient new homes acquired on or before December 31, 2014. (IRC § 45L(g); Pub L No 113-295, 113th Cong, 2d Sess, § 156 (Dec 19, 2014))

Nonbusiness energy property. The credit for nonbusiness energy property has been extended through tax year 2014. The extension applies to property placed in service on or before December 31, 2014. (IRC § 25C(g)(2); Pub L No 113-295, 113th Cong, 2d Sess, § 151 (Dec 19, 2014))

Production credit for Indian coal facilities placed in service before 2009. The provision extends the availability of the production credit for nine years, over the previous eight-year period. (IRC § 45(e)(10)(A); Pub L No 113-295, 113th Cong, 2d Sess, § 154 (Dec 19, 2014))

MORTGAGE INTEREST AND DISCHARGE OF MORTGAGE INDEBTEDNESS

Exclusion from gross income of discharged qualified principal residence indebtedness. The exclusion from gross income of the amount of discharged qualified principal residence indebtedness (up to $2,000,000) has been extended to apply to amounts discharged by a bank prior to January 1, 2015. (IRC § 108(a)(1)(E); Pub L No 113-295, 113th Cong, 2d Sess, § 102 (Dec 19, 2014)) Unless a specific exclusion such as this one applies, the cancellation of indebtedness on a principal residence is otherwise included in gross income. This exclusion has been available since 2007.

Mortgage insurance premiums treated as qualified residence interest. Mortgage insurance premiums continue to be treated as qualified residence interest, deductible for taxpayers who itemize. The provision applies to mortgage insurance premiums paid through December 31, 2014. (IRC § 163(h)(3)(E)(iv)(I); Pub L No 113-295, 113th Cong, 2d Sess, § 104 (Dec 19, 2014))

QUALIFIED PRODUCTION ACTIVITIES INCOME

Puerto Rico: Qualified production activities deduction. The deduction for qualified production activities with respect to activities within Puerto Rico has been extended to include the first nine tax years of the production (up from eight) and to include tax years ending before January 1, 2015. (IRC § 199(d)(8)(C); Pub L No 113-295, 113th Cong, 2d Sess, § 130 (Dec 19, 2014))

S CORPORATION ISSUES

S corporation stock basis adjustment for charitable contributions of property. The stock basis adjustment allowed for S corporation stock that is subject of a charitable donation has been extended to apply to contributions made in tax years ending on or before December 31, 2014. (IRC § 1367(a)(2); Pub L No 113-295, 113th Cong, 2d Sess, § 137 (Dec 19, 2014))

S corporation built-in gains tax reduced recognition period. The reduced recognition period for the S corporation built-in gains tax has been extended through 2014. (IRC § 1374(d)(7)(C); Pub L No 113-295, 113th Cong, 2d Sess, § 138 (Dec 19, 2014))

SALES TAX DEDUCTION

Option to deduct sales tax in lieu of state and local income taxes. The deductibility of state and local general sales taxes, in lieu of state and local income taxes, has been extended to apply to amounts paid before January 1, 2015. (IRC § 164(b)(5)(I); Pub L No 113-295, 113th Cong, 2d Sess, § 105 (Dec 19, 2014))

FILLED-IN FORMS

§ 1.120 Filled-In Form 1040A

| Form **1040A** | Department of the Treasury—Internal Revenue Service **U.S. Individual Income Tax Return** (99) | **2014** | IRS Use Only—Do not write or staple in this space. |

Your first name and initial	Last name	OMB No. 1545-0074
John M.	Best	**Your social security number** 1 2 3 0 9 6 7 4 3
If a joint return, spouse's first name and initial	Last name	**Spouse's social security number**
Ellen G.	Best	4 3 7 6 1 4 2 3 8

Home address (number and street). If you have a P.O. box, see instructions.   Apt. no.

1930 Loring Place

▲ Make sure the SSN(s) above and on line 6c are correct.

City, town or post office, state, and ZIP code. If you have a foreign address, also complete spaces below (see instructions).

Bronx, NY 10453

Presidential Election Campaign
Check here if you, or your spouse if filing jointly, want $3 to go to this fund. Checking a box below will not change your tax or refund. ☑ You ☐ Spouse

Foreign country name   Foreign province/state/county   Foreign postal code

Filing status
Check only one box.

1 ☐ Single
2 ☑ Married filing jointly (even if only one had income)
3 ☐ Married filing separately. Enter spouse's SSN above and full name here. ▶
4 ☐ Head of household (with qualifying person). (See instructions.) If the qualifying person is a child but not your dependent, enter this child's name here. ▶
5 ☐ Qualifying widow(er) with dependent child (see instructions)

Exemptions

If more than six dependents, see instructions.

6a ☑ **Yourself.** If someone can claim you as a dependent, **do not** check box 6a.
b ☑ **Spouse**

Boxes checked on 6a and 6b	2

c **Dependents:**

(1) First name Last name	(2) Dependent's social security number	(3) Dependent's relationship to you	(4) ✔ if child under age 17 qualifying for child tax credit (see instructions)
Hilda Best	823-53-1064	Daughter	☑
Jack Best	822-92-1158	Son	☑
Jane Best	628-21-6299	Mother	☐
			☐
			☐
			☐

No. of children on 6c who:
• lived with you — **2**
• did not live with you due to divorce or separation (see instructions)
Dependents on 6c not entered above — **1**

Add numbers on lines above ▶ **5**

d Total number of exemptions claimed.

Income

Attach Form(s) W-2 here. Also attach Form(s) 1099-R if tax was withheld.

If you did not get a W-2, see instructions.

7	Wages, salaries, tips, etc. Attach Form(s) W-2.	7	58,000
8a	**Taxable** interest. Attach Schedule B if required.	8a	424
b	**Tax-exempt** interest. **Do not** include on line 8a. 8b 500		
9a	Ordinary dividends. Attach Schedule B if required.	9a	115
b	Qualified dividends (see instructions). 9b 115		
10	Capital gain distributions (see instructions).	10	
11a	IRA distributions. 11a	11b Taxable amount (see instructions). 11b	
12a	Pensions and annuities. 12a 2,000	12b Taxable amount (see instructions). 12b	0
13	Unemployment compensation and Alaska Permanent Fund dividends.	13	2,000
14a	Social security benefits. 14a	14b Taxable amount (see instructions). 14b	
15	Add lines 7 through 14b (far right column). This is your **total income.** ▶	15	60,539

Adjusted gross income

16	Educator expenses (see instructions). 16		
17	IRA deduction (see instructions). 17 2,000		
18	Student loan interest deduction (see instructions). 18		
19	Tuition and fees. Attach Form 8917. 19		
20	Add lines 16 through 19. These are your **total adjustments.**	20	2,000
21	Subtract line 20 from line 15. This is your **adjusted gross income.** ▶	21	58,539

For Disclosure, Privacy Act, and Paperwork Reduction Act Notice, see separate instructions.   Cat. No. 11327A   Form **1040A** (2014)

Tax, credits, and payments	22	Enter the amount from line 21 (adjusted gross income).		22	58,539
	23a	Check if: ☐ **You** were born before January 2, 1950, ☐ Blind **Total boxes** ☐ **Spouse** was born before January 2, 1950, ☐ Blind checked ▶ 23a			
	b	If you are married filing separately and your spouse itemizes deductions, check here ▶ 23b ☐			

Standard Deduction for—
• People who check any box on line 23a or 23b **or** who can be claimed as a dependent, see instructions.
• All others:
Single or Married filing separately, $6,200
Married filing jointly or Qualifying widow(er), $12,400
Head of household, $9,100

	24	Enter your **standard deduction**.		24	12,400
	25	Subtract line 24 from line 22. If line 24 is more than line 22, enter -0-.		25	46,139
	26	**Exemptions.** Multiply $3,950 by the number on line 6d.		26	19,750
	27	Subtract line 26 from line 25. If line 26 is more than line 25, enter -0-. This is your **taxable income.** ▶		27	26,389
	28	**Tax,** including any alternative minimum tax (see instructions).	28	3,034	
	29	Excess advance premium tax credit repayment. Attach Form 8962.	29		
	30	Add lines 28 and 29.		30	3,034
	31	Credit for child and dependent care expenses. Attach Form 2441.	31		
	32	Credit for the elderly or the disabled. Attach Schedule R.	32		
	33	Education credits from Form 8863, line 19.	33		
	34	Retirement savings contributions credit. Attach Form 8880.	34		
	35	Child tax credit. Attach Schedule 8812, if required.	35	2,000	
	36	Add lines 31 through 35. These are your **total credits.**		36	2,000
	37	Subtract line 36 from line 30. If line 36 is more than line 30, enter -0-.		37	1,034
	38	Health care: individual responsibility (see instructions). Full-year coverage ☑		38	
	39	Add line 37 and line 38. This is your **total tax.**		39	1,034
	40	Federal income tax withheld from Forms W-2 and 1099.	40	850	
If you have a qualifying child, attach Schedule EIC.	41	2014 estimated tax payments and amount applied from 2013 return.	41		
	42a	**Earned income credit (EIC).**	42a		
	b	Nontaxable combat pay election. 42b			
	43	Additional child tax credit. Attach Schedule 8812.	43		
	44	American opportunity credit from Form 8863, line 8.	44		
	45	Net premium tax credit. Attach Form 8962.	45		
	46	Add lines 40, 41, 42a, 43, 44, and 45. These are your **total payments.** ▶		46	850

Refund	47	If line 46 is more than line 39, subtract line 39 from line 46. This is the amount you **overpaid.**		47	
Direct deposit? See instructions and fill in 48b, 48c, and 48d or Form 8888.	48a	Amount of line 47 you want **refunded to you.** If Form 8888 is attached, check here ▶ ☐ 48a			
	▶ b	Routing number ⬜⬜⬜⬜⬜⬜⬜⬜⬜ ▶ c Type: ☐ Checking ☐ Savings			
	▶ d	Account number ⬜⬜⬜⬜⬜⬜⬜⬜⬜⬜⬜⬜⬜⬜⬜⬜⬜			
	49	Amount of line 47 you want **applied to your 2015 estimated tax.**	49		

Amount you owe	50	**Amount you owe.** Subtract line 46 from line 39. For details on how to pay, see instructions. ▶		50	184
	51	Estimated tax penalty (see instructions).	51		

Third party designee

Do you want to allow another person to discuss this return with the IRS (see instructions)? ☐ **Yes.** Complete the following. ☐ **No**

Designee's name ▶	Phone no. ▶	Personal identification number (PIN) ▶ ⬜⬜⬜⬜⬜

Sign here

Joint return? See instructions.
Keep a copy for your records.

Under penalties of perjury, I declare that I have examined this return and accompanying schedules and statements, and to the best of my knowledge and belief, they are true, correct, and accurately list all amounts and sources of income I received during the tax year. Declaration of preparer (other than the taxpayer) is based on all information of which the preparer has any knowledge.

Your signature	Date	Your occupation	Daytime phone number
John Best	4/15/2015	Sales	
Spouse's signature. If a joint return, **both** must sign.	Date	Spouse's occupation	If the IRS sent you an Identity Protection PIN, enter it here (see inst.) ⬜⬜⬜⬜⬜⬜
Ellen Best	4/15/2015	Homemaker	

Paid preparer use only

Print/type preparer's name	Preparer's signature	Date	Check ▶ ☑ if self-employed	PTIN
Alan Young	*Alan Young*	4/15/2015		
Firm's name ▶ Alan Young, CPA			Firm's EIN ▶	
Firm's address ▶ 391 Loring Place, Bronx, NY 10453			Phone no.	

Qualified Dividends and Capital Gain Tax Worksheet—Line 28

Before you begin: ✓ Be sure you do not have to file Form 1040 (see the Instructions for Form 1040A, line 10).

1.	Enter the amount from Form 1040A, line 27 . . . . **1.**	26,389
2.	Enter the amount from Form 1040A, line 9b **2.** 115	
3.	Enter the amount from Form 1040A, line 10 . . . . **3.** _____	
4.	Add lines 2 and 3 . . . . **4.**	115
5.	Subtract line 4 from line 1. If zero or less, enter -0- . . . . **5.**	26,274
6.	Enter the **smaller** of:	
	• The amount on line 1, or	
	• $36,900 if single or married filing separately,	
	$73,800 if married filing jointly or qualifying widow(er), or } . . . . **6.**	26,389
	$49,400 if head of household.	
7.	Enter the smaller of line 5 or line 6 . . . . **7.**	26,274
8.	Subtract line 7 from line 6. This amount is taxed at 0% . . . . **8.**	115
9.	Enter the smaller of line 1 or line 4 . . . . **9.**	115
10.	Enter the amount from line 8 . . . . **10.**	115
11.	Subtract line 10 from line 9 . . . . **11.**	0
12.	Multiply line 11 by 15% (.15) . . . . **12.**	0
13.	Use the Tax Table to figure the tax on the amount on line 5. Enter the tax here . . . . **13.**	3,034
14.	Add lines 12 and 13 . . . . **14.**	3,034
15.	Use the Tax Table to figure the tax on the amount on line 1. Enter the tax here . . . . **15.**	3,051
16.	**Tax on all taxable income.** Enter the **smaller** of line 14 or line 15 here and on Form 1040A, line 28 . . . . **16.**	3,034

2014 Child Tax Credit Worksheet—Line 35

1. To be a qualifying child for the child tax credit, the child must be your dependent, **under age 17** at the end of 2014, and meet all the conditions in Steps 1 through 3 in the instructions for line 6c. Make sure you check the box on Form 1040A, line 6c, column (4), for each qualifying child.
2. If you do not have a qualifying child, you cannot claim the child tax credit.
3. If your qualifying child has an ITIN instead of an SSN, file Schedule 8812.

Part 1

1. Number of qualifying children: ___2___ × $1,000. Enter the result.

   | 1 | 2,000 |

2. Enter the amount from Form 1040A, line 22.

   | 2 | 58,539 |

3. Enter the amount shown below for your filing status.

   • Married filing jointly — $110,000

   • Single, head of household, or qualifying widow(er) — $75,000

   • Married filing separately — $55,000

   | 3 | 110,000 |

4. Is the amount on line 2 more than the amount on line 3?

   ☒ **No.** Leave line 4 blank. Enter -0- on line 5, and go to line 6.

   ☐ **Yes.** Subtract line 3 from line 2.
   If the result is not a multiple of $1,000, increase it to the next multiple of $1,000. For example, increase $425 to $1,000, increase $1,025 to $2,000, etc.

   | 4 | |

5. Multiply the amount on line 4 by 5% (.05). Enter the result.

   | 5 | 0 |

6. Is the amount on line 1 more than the amount on line 5?

   ☐ **No.** (STOP)
   You cannot take the child tax credit on Form 1040A, line 35. You also cannot take the additional child tax credit on Form 1040A, line 43. Complete the rest of your Form 1040A.

   ☒ **Yes.** Subtract line 5 from line 1. Enter the result.
   Go to Part 2.

   | 6 | 2,000 |

§ 1.160 Filled-In Form 1040EZ

Form **1040EZ**

Department of the Treasury—Internal Revenue Service

Income Tax Return for Single and Joint Filers With No Dependents (99) **2014**

OMB No. 1545-0074

Your first name and initial	Last name	Your social security number
Patricia	Taylor	9 8 7 6 5 4 3

If a joint return, spouse's first name and initial	Last name	Spouse's social security number

Home address (number and street). If you have a P.O. box, see instructions.
4 Devon Place

Apt. no.

▲ Make sure the SSN(s) above are correct.

City, town or post office, state, and ZIP code. If you have a foreign address, also complete spaces below (see instructions).
Peekskill, NY 10566

Foreign country name	Foreign province/state/county	Foreign postal code

Presidential Election Campaign
Check here if you, or your spouse if filing jointly, want $3 to go to this fund. Checking a box below will not change your tax or refund. ☑ You ☐ Spouse

Income

Attach Form(s) W-2 here.

Enclose, but do not attach, any payment.

1 Wages, salaries, and tips. This should be shown in box 1 of your Form(s) W-2. Attach your Form(s) W-2. **1** 21,840

2 Taxable interest. If the total is over $1,500, you cannot use Form 1040EZ. **2** 120

3 Unemployment compensation and Alaska Permanent Fund dividends (see instructions). **3**

4 Add lines 1, 2, and 3. This is your **adjusted gross income.** **4** 21,960

5 If someone can claim you (or your spouse if a joint return) as a dependent, check the applicable box(es) below and enter the amount from the worksheet on back.
☐ You ☐ Spouse
If no one can claim you (or your spouse if a joint return), enter $10,150 if **single**; $20,300 if **married filing jointly.** See back for explanation. **5** 10,150

6 Subtract line 5 from line 4. If line 5 is larger than line 4, enter -0-. This is your **taxable income.** ▶ **6** 11,810

Payments, Credits, and Tax

7 Federal income tax withheld from Form(s) W-2 and 1099. **7** 2,100

8a **Earned income credit (EIC)** (see instructions) **8a**

b Nontaxable combat pay election. **8b**

9 Add lines 7 and 8a. These are your **total payments and credits.** ▶ **9** 2,100

10 **Tax.** Use the amount on **line 6 above** to find your tax in the tax table in the instructions. Then, enter the tax from the table on this line. **10** 1,318

11 Health care: individual responsibility (see instructions) Full-year coverage ☑ **11**

12 Add lines 10 and 11. This is your **total tax.** **12** 1,318

Refund

Have it directly deposited! See instructions and fill in 13b, 13c, and 13d, or Form 8888.

13a If line 9 is larger than line 12, subtract line 12 from line 9. This is your **refund.**
If Form 8888 is attached, check here ▶ ☐ **13a** 782

▶ b Routing number [ ] ▶ c Type: ☐ Checking ☐ Savings

▶ d Account number [ ]

Amount You Owe

14 If line 12 is larger than line 9, subtract line 9 from line 12. This is the **amount you owe.** For details on how to pay, see instructions. ▶ **14**

Third Party Designee

Do you want to allow another person to discuss this return with the IRS (see instructions)? ☐ **Yes.** Complete below. ☐ **No**

Designee's name ▶
Phone no. ▶
Personal identification number (PIN) ▶ [ ]

Sign Here

Under penalties of perjury, I declare that I have examined this return and, to the best of my knowledge and belief, it is true, correct, and accurately lists all amounts and sources of income I received during the tax year. Declaration of preparer (other than the taxpayer) is based on all information of which the preparer has any knowledge.

Joint return? See instructions.

Keep a copy for your records.

Your signature *Patricia Taylor*
Date 4/15/2015
Your occupation Editorial Assistant
Daytime phone number 201-222-2222

Spouse's signature. If a joint return, **both** must sign.
Date
Spouse's occupation

If the IRS sent you an Identity Protection PIN, enter it here (see inst.) [ ]

Paid Preparer Use Only

Print/Type preparer's name	Preparer's signature	Date	Check ☐ if self-employed	PTIN

Firm's name ▶
Firm's EIN ▶

Firm's address ▶
Phone no.

For Disclosure, Privacy Act, and Paperwork Reduction Act Notice, see instructions.

Cat. No. 11329W

Form **1040EZ** (2014)

Use this form if

- Your filing status is single or married filing jointly. If you are not sure about your filing status, see instructions.
- You (and your spouse if married filing jointly) were under age 65 and not blind at the end of 2014. If you were born on January 1, 1950, you are considered to be age 65 at the end of 2014.
- You do not claim any dependents. For information on dependents, see Pub. 501.
- Your taxable income (line 6) is less than $100,000.
- You do not claim any adjustments to income. For information on adjustments to income, use the TeleTax topics listed under *Adjustments to Income* at *www.irs.gov/taxtopics* (see instructions).
- The only tax credit you can claim is the earned income credit (EIC). The credit may give you a refund even if you do not owe any tax. You do not need a qualifying child to claim the EIC. For information on credits, use the TeleTax topics listed under *Tax Credits* at *www.irs.gov/taxtopics* (see instructions). If you received a Form 1098-T or paid higher education expenses, you may be eligible for a tax credit or deduction that you must claim on Form 1040A or Form 1040. For more information on tax benefits for education, see Pub. 970. If you can claim the premium tax credit or you received any advance payment of the premium tax credit in 2014, you must use Form 1040A or Form 1040.
- You had only wages, salaries, tips, taxable scholarship or fellowship grants, unemployment compensation, or Alaska Permanent Fund dividends, and your taxable interest was not over $1,500. But if you earned tips, including allocated tips, that are not included in box 5 and box 7 of your Form W-2, you may not be able to use Form 1040EZ (see instructions). If you are planning to use Form 1040EZ for a child who received Alaska Permanent Fund dividends, see instructions.

Filling in your return

If you received a scholarship or fellowship grant or tax-exempt interest income, such as on municipal bonds, see the instructions before filling in the form. Also, see the instructions if you received a Form 1099-INT showing federal income tax withheld or if federal income tax was withheld from your unemployment compensation or Alaska Permanent Fund dividends.

For tips on how to avoid common mistakes, see instructions.

Remember, you must report all wages, salaries, and tips even if you do not get a Form W-2 from your employer. You must also report all your taxable interest, including interest from banks, savings and loans, credit unions, etc., even if you do not get a Form 1099-INT.

Worksheet for Line 5 — Dependents Who Checked One or Both Boxes

Use this worksheet to figure the amount to enter on line 5 if someone can claim you (or your spouse if married filing jointly) as a dependent, even if that person chooses not to do so. To find out if someone can claim you as a dependent, see Pub. 501.

A. Amount, if any, from line 1 on front . . . .　　+　　350.00　Enter total ▶　A. _____

B. Minimum standard deduction . . . . B. ___1,000___

C. Enter the **larger** of line A or line B here . . . . C. _____

D. Maximum standard deduction. If **single,** enter $6,200; if **married filing jointly,** enter $12,400 . D. _____

E. Enter the **smaller** of line C or line D here. This is your standard deduction . . . . E. _____

F. Exemption amount.
- If single, enter -0-.
- If married filing jointly and —
  —both you and your spouse can be claimed as dependents, enter -0-.
  —only one of you can be claimed as a dependent, enter $3,950.　　　　　　　　　　　　　F. _____

G. Add lines E and F. Enter the total here and on line 5 on the front . . . . G. _____

(keep a copy for your records)

If you did not check any boxes on line 5, enter on line 5 the amount shown below that applies to you.
- Single, enter $10,150. This is the total of your standard deduction ($6,200) and your exemption ($3,950).
- Married filing jointly, enter $20,300. This is the total of your standard deduction ($12,400), your exemption ($3,950), and your spouse's exemption ($3,950).

Mailing Return

Mail your return by **April 15, 2015.** Mail it to the address shown on the last page of the instructions.

§ 2.480 Social Security Benefits Worksheet

Social Security Benefits Worksheet—Lines 20a and 20b

Keep for Your Records

Before you begin:
- ✓ Complete Form 1040, lines 21 and 23 through 32, if they apply to you.
- ✓ Figure any write-in adjustments to be entered on the dotted line next to line 36 (see the instructions for line 36).
- ✓ If you are married filing separately and you lived apart from your spouse for all of 2014, enter "D" to the right of the word "benefits" on line 20a. If you do not, you may get a math error notice from the IRS.
- ✓ Be sure you have read the **Exception** in the line 20a and 20b instructions to see if you can use this worksheet instead of a publication to find out if any of your benefits are taxable.

1. Enter the total amount from **box 5** of **all** your **Forms SSA-1099** and **Forms RRB-1099.** Also, enter this amount on Form 1040, line 20a .... **1.** _____

2. Enter one-half of line 1 .... **2.** _____

3. Combine the amounts from Form 1040, lines 7, 8a, 9a, 10 through 14, 15b, 16b, 17 through 19, and 21 .... **3.** _____

4. Enter the amount, if any, from Form 1040, line 8b .... **4.** _____

5. Combine lines 2, 3, and 4 .... **5.** _____

6. Enter the total of the amounts from Form 1040, lines 23 through 32, plus any write-in adjustments you entered on the dotted line next to line 36 .... **6.** _____

7. Is the amount on line 6 less than the amount on line 5?

   ☐ **No.** 🛑 None of your social security benefits are taxable. Enter -0- on Form 1040, line 20b.

   ☐ **Yes.** Subtract line 6 from line 5 .... **7.** _____

8. If you are:
   - Married filing jointly, enter $32,000
   - Single, head of household, qualifying widow(er), or married filing separately and you **lived apart** from your spouse for all of 2014, enter $25,000
   - Married filing separately and you lived with your spouse at any time in 2014, skip lines 8 through 15; multiply line 7 by 85% (.85) and enter the result on line 16. Then go to line 17

   .... **8.** _____

9. Is the amount on line 8 less than the amount on line 7?

   ☐ **No.** 🛑 None of your social security benefits are taxable. Enter -0- on Form 1040, line 20b. If you are married filing separately and you **lived apart** from your spouse for all of 2014, be sure you entered "D" to the right of the word "benefits" on line 20a.

   ☐ **Yes.** Subtract line 8 from line 7 .... **9.** _____

10. Enter: $12,000 if married filing jointly; $9,000 if single, head of household, qualifying widow(er), or married filing separately and you **lived apart** from your spouse for all of 2014 .... **10.** _____

11. Subtract line 10 from line 9. If zero or less, enter -0- .... **11.** _____

12. Enter the **smaller** of line 9 or line 10 .... **12.** _____

13. Enter one-half of line 12 .... **13.** _____

14. Enter the **smaller** of line 2 or line 13 .... **14.** _____

15. Multiply line 11 by 85% (.85). If line 11 is zero, enter -0- .... **15.** _____

16. Add lines 14 and 15 .... **16.** _____

17. Multiply line 1 by 85% (.85) .... **17.** _____

18. **Taxable social security benefits.** Enter the **smaller** of line 16 or line 17. Also enter this amount on Form 1040, line 20b .... **18.** _____

TIP *If any of your benefits are taxable for 2014 **and** they include a lump-sum benefit payment that was for an earlier year, you may be able to reduce the taxable amount. See* Lump-Sum Election *in Pub. 915 for details.*

§ 2.1320   Filled-In Form 1040

Form 1040

Department of the Treasury—Internal Revenue Service   (99)

U.S. Individual Income Tax Return   **2014**   OMB No. 1545-0074   IRS Use Only—Do not write or staple in this space.

For the year Jan. 1–Dec. 31, 2014, or other tax year beginning _____, 2014, ending _____, 20 ___   See separate instructions.

Your first name and initial	Last name	Your social security number
Tom E.	Dodd	1 2 3 4 5 6 7 8 9
If a joint return, spouse's first name and initial	Last name	Spouse's social security number
Mary A.	Dodd	9 8 7 6 5 4 3 2 1

Home address (number and street). If you have a P.O. box, see instructions.   Apt. no.

987 Main Street

▲ Make sure the SSN(s) above and on line 6c are correct.

City, town or post office, state, and ZIP code. If you have a foreign address, also complete spaces below (see instructions).

Pleasanttown, NY 01234

Foreign country name   Foreign province/state/county   Foreign postal code

Presidential Election Campaign

Check here if you, or your spouse if filing jointly, want $3 to go to this fund. Checking a box below will not change your tax or refund.   ☐ You   ☑ Spouse

Filing Status

Check only one box.

1 ☐ Single
2 ☑ Married filing jointly (even if only one had income)
3 ☐ Married filing separately. Enter spouse's SSN above and full name here. ▶
4 ☐ Head of household (with qualifying person). (See instructions.) If the qualifying person is a child but not your dependent, enter this child's name here. ▶
5 ☐ Qualifying widow(er) with dependent child

Exemptions

6a ☑ **Yourself.** If someone can claim you as a dependent, **do not** check box 6a . . . . .
b ☑ **Spouse** . . . .

c Dependents:	(2) Dependent's social security number	(3) Dependent's relationship to you	(4) ✓ if child under age 17 qualifying for child tax credit (see instructions)
(1) First name Last name			
Jay T. Dodd	3 3 3 3 3 3 3 3 3		☑
John A. Dodd	4 4 4 4 4 4 4 4 4		☑
Sarah J. Dodd	9 9 9 9 9 9 9 9 9		☐
			☐

If more than four dependents, see instructions and check here ▶ ☐

d   Total number of exemptions claimed . . . .

Boxes checked on 6a and 6b   **2**
No. of children on 6c who:
• lived with you   **2**
• did not live with you due to divorce or separation (see instructions)
Dependents on 6c not entered above   **1**
Add numbers on lines above ▶   **5**

Income

Attach Form(s) W-2 here. Also attach Forms W-2G and 1099-R if tax was withheld.

If you did not get a W-2, see instructions.

7	Wages, salaries, tips, etc. Attach Form(s) W-2	7	84,900
8a	**Taxable** interest. Attach Schedule B if required	8a	4,075
b	**Tax-exempt** interest. **Do not** include on line 8a . . .	8b	2,000		
9a	Ordinary dividends. Attach Schedule B if required	9a	1,300
b	Qualified dividends	9b	1,300		
10	Taxable refunds, credits, or offsets of state and local income taxes	10	275
11	Alimony received	11	0
12	Business income or (loss). Attach Schedule C or C-EZ	12	1,944
13	Capital gain or (loss). Attach Schedule D if required. If not required, check here ▶ ☐	13	27,165
14	Other gains or (losses). Attach Form 4797	14	8,175
15a	IRA distributions . 15a	b Taxable amount	15b	0
16a	Pensions and annuities 16a	b Taxable amount	16b	0
17	Rental real estate, royalties, partnerships, S corporations, trusts, etc. Attach Schedule E	17	(15,615)
18	Farm income or (loss). Attach Schedule F	18	(2,775)
19	Unemployment compensation	19	
20a	Social security benefits 20a	b Taxable amount . . .	20b	
21	Other income. List type and amount _____	21	650
22	Combine the amounts in the far right column for lines 7 through 21. This is your **total income** ▶	22	110,094

Adjusted Gross Income

23	Educator expenses	23	
24	Certain business expenses of reservists, performing artists, and fee-basis government officials. Attach Form 2106 or 2106-EZ	24	
25	Health savings account deduction. Attach Form 8889 .	25	
26	Moving expenses. Attach Form 3903	26	
27	Deductible part of self-employment tax. Attach Schedule SE .	27	371
28	Self-employed SEP, SIMPLE, and qualified plans .	28	
29	Self-employed health insurance deduction	29	
30	Penalty on early withdrawal of savings	30	425
31a	Alimony paid b Recipient's SSN ▶	31a	
32	IRA deduction	32	
33	Student loan interest deduction	33	
34	Tuition and fees. Attach Form 8917	34	
35	Domestic production activities deduction. Attach Form 8903	35	
36	Add lines 23 through 35	36	796
37	Subtract line 36 from line 22. This is your **adjusted gross income** . . . . . ▶	37	109,298

For Disclosure, Privacy Act, and Paperwork Reduction Act Notice, see separate instructions.   Cat. No. 11320B   Form **1040** (2014)

Tax and Credits	38	Amount from line 37 (adjusted gross income)	38	109,298
	39a	Check if: ☐ **You** were born before January 2, 1950, ☐ **Blind.** ☐ **Spouse** was born before January 2, 1950, ☐ **Blind.** } Total boxes checked ▶ 39a		
	b	If your spouse itemizes on a separate return or you were a dual-status alien, check here▶ 39b☐		

	40	**Itemized deductions** (from Schedule A) **or** your **standard deduction** (see left margin)	40	28,948
	41	Subtract line 40 from line 38	41	80,350
	42	**Exemptions.** If line 38 is $152,525 or less, multiply $3,950 by the number on line 6d. Otherwise, see instructions	42	19,750
	43	**Taxable income.** Subtract line 42 from line 41. If line 42 is more than line 41, enter -0-	43	60,600
	44	**Tax** (see instructions). Check if any from: **a** ☐ Form(s) 8814 **b** ☐ Form 4972 **c** ☐	44	3,911
	45	**Alternative minimum tax** (see instructions). Attach Form 6251	45	0
	46	Excess advance premium tax credit repayment. Attach Form 8962	46	0
	47	Add lines 44, 45, and 46 ▶	47	3,911
	48	Foreign tax credit. Attach Form 1116 if required	48	
	49	Credit for child and dependent care expenses. Attach Form 2441	49	600
	50	Education credits from Form 8863, line 19	50	
	51	Retirement savings contributions credit. Attach Form 8880	51	
	52	Child tax credit. Attach Schedule 8812, if required	52	2,000
	53	Residential energy credits. Attach Form 5695	53	
	54	Other credits from Form: **a** ☐ 3800 **b** ☐ 8801 **c** ☐	54	
	55	Add lines 48 through 54. These are your **total credits**	55	2,600
	56	Subtract line 55 from line 47. If line 55 is more than line 47, enter -0- ▶	56	1,311
Other Taxes	57	Self-employment tax. Attach Schedule SE	57	742
	58	Unreported social security and Medicare tax from Form: **a** ☐ 4137 **b** ☐ 8919	58	
	59	Additional tax on IRAs, other qualified retirement plans, etc. Attach Form 5329 if required	59	
	60a	Household employment taxes from Schedule H	60a	
	b	First-time homebuyer credit repayment. Attach Form 5405 if required	60b	
	61	Health care: individual responsibility (see instructions) Full-year coverage ☑	61	
	62	Taxes from: **a** ☐ Form 8959 **b** ☐ Form 8960 **c** ☐ Instructions; enter code(s)	62	
	63	Add lines 56 through 62. This is your **total tax** ▶	63	2,053
Payments	64	Federal income tax withheld from Forms W-2 and 1099	64	7,800
	65	2014 estimated tax payments and amount applied from 2013 return	65	
If you have a qualifying child, attach Schedule EIC.	66a	**Earned income credit (EIC)**	66a	
	b	Nontaxable combat pay election 66b		
	67	Additional child tax credit. Attach Schedule 8812	67	
	68	American opportunity credit from Form 8863, line 8	68	
	69	Net premium tax credit. Attach Form 8962	69	
	70	Amount paid with request for extension to file	70	
	71	Excess social security and tier 1 RRTA tax withheld	71	
	72	Credit for federal tax on fuels. Attach Form 4136	72	
	73	Credits from Form: **a** ☐ 2439 **b** ☐ Reserved **c** ☐ Reserved **d** ☐	73	
	74	Add lines 64, 65, 66a, and 67 through 73. These are your **total payments** ▶	74	7,800
Refund	75	If line 74 is more than line 63, subtract line 63 from line 74. This is the amount you **overpaid**	75	5,747
	76a	Amount of line 75 you want **refunded to you.** If Form 8888 is attached, check here ▶☐	76a	5,747
Direct deposit? See instructions.	b	Routing number		
		▶c Type: ☐ Checking ☐ Savings		
	d	Account number		
	77	Amount of line 75 you want **applied to your 2015 estimated tax** ▶ 77		
Amount You Owe	78	**Amount you owe.** Subtract line 74 from line 63. For details on how to pay, see instructions ▶	78	
	79	Estimated tax penalty (see instructions) 79		

Third Party Designee

Do you want to allow another person to discuss this return with the IRS (see instructions)? ☐ **Yes.** Complete below.   ☐ **No**

Designee's name ▶	Phone no. ▶	Personal identification number (PIN) ▶	

Sign Here

Joint return? See instructions.
Keep a copy for your records.

Under penalties of perjury, I declare that I have examined this return and accompanying schedules and statements, and to the best of my knowledge and belief, they are true, correct, and complete. Declaration of preparer (other than taxpayer) is based on all information of which preparer has any knowledge.

Your signature	Date	Your occupation	Daytime phone number
Tom Dodd	4/15/2015	Accountant	
Spouse's signature. If a joint return, **both** must sign.	Date	Spouse's occupation	If the IRS sent you an Identity Protection PIN, enter it here (see inst.)
Mary Dodd	4/15/2015	Secretary	

Paid Preparer Use Only

Print/Type preparer's name	Preparer's signature	Date	Check ☑ if self-employed	PTIN
Alan Young	*Alan Young*	4/15/2015		
Firm's name ▶ Alan Young, CPA			Firm's EIN ▶	
Firm's address ▶ 789 Main Street, Pleasanttown, NY 01234			Phone no.	

§ 2.1340 Filled-In Schedule A, Form 1040

SCHEDULE A
(Form 1040)

Department of the Treasury
Internal Revenue Service (99)

Itemized Deductions

▶ Information about Schedule A and its separate instructions is at *www.irs.gov/schedulea*.
▶ **Attach to Form 1040.**

OMB No. 1545-0074

2014

Attachment
Sequence No. **07**

Name(s) shown on Form 1040

Tom E. and Mary A. Dodd

Your social security number

123-45-6789

Medical and Dental Expenses		**Caution.** Do not include expenses reimbursed or paid by others.				
	1	Medical and dental expenses (see instructions)	**1**	4,725		
	2	Enter amount from Form 1040, line 38 **2** 109,298				
	3	Multiply line 2 by 10% (.10). But if either you or your spouse was born before January 2, 1950, multiply line 2 by 7.5% (.075) instead	**3**	10,930		
	4	Subtract line 3 from line 1. If line 3 is more than line 1, enter -0-			**4**	0
Taxes You Paid	5	State and local (**check only one box**):				
		a ☑ Income taxes, **or**	**5**	3,853		
		b ☐ General sales taxes				
	6	Real estate taxes (see instructions)	**6**	1,080		
	7	Personal property taxes	**7**	450		
	8	Other taxes. List type and amount ▶	**8**			
	9	Add lines 5 through 8			**9**	5,383
Interest You Paid	10	Home mortgage interest and points reported to you on Form 1098	**10**	9,765		
	11	Home mortgage interest not reported to you on Form 1098. If paid to the person from whom you bought the home, see instructions and show that person's name, identifying no., and address ▶	**11**			
Note. Your mortgage interest deduction may be limited (see instructions).	12	Points not reported to you on Form 1098. See instructions for special rules	**12**			
	13	Mortgage insurance premiums (see instructions)	**13**			
	14	Investment interest. Attach Form 4952 if required. (See instructions.)	**14**	6,000		
	15	Add lines 10 through 14			**15**	15,765
Gifts to Charity	16	Gifts by cash or check. If you made any gift of $250 or more, see instructions	**16**	4,300		
If you made a gift and got a benefit for it, see instructions.	17	Other than by cash or check. If any gift of $250 or more, see instructions. You **must** attach Form 8283 if over $500	**17**	3,250		
	18	Carryover from prior year	**18**			
	19	Add lines 16 through 18			**19**	7,550
Casualty and Theft Losses	20	Casualty or theft loss(es). Attach Form 4684. (See instructions.)			**20**	0
Job Expenses and Certain Miscellaneous Deductions	21	Unreimbursed employee expenses—job travel, union dues, job education, etc. Attach Form 2106 or 2106-EZ if required. (See instructions.) ▶	**21**	1,350		
	22	Tax preparation fees	**22**			
	23	Other expenses—investment, safe deposit box, etc. List type and amount ▶	**23**	800		
	24	Add lines 21 through 23	**24**	2,150		
	25	Enter amount from Form 1040, line 38 **25** 109,298				
	26	Multiply line 25 by 2% (.02)	**26**	2,186		
	27	Subtract line 26 from line 24. If line 26 is more than line 24, enter -0-			**27**	0
Other Miscellaneous Deductions	28	Other—from list in instructions. List type and amount ▶			**28**	250
Total Itemized Deductions	29	Is Form 1040, line 38, over $152,525?				
		☑ **No.** Your deduction is not limited. Add the amounts in the far right column for lines 4 through 28. Also, enter this amount on Form 1040, line 40.			**29**	28,948
		☐ **Yes.** Your deduction may be limited. See the Itemized Deductions Worksheet in the instructions to figure the amount to enter.				
	30	If you elect to itemize deductions even though they are less than your standard deduction, check here ▶ ☐				

For Paperwork Reduction Act Notice, see Form 1040 instructions.

Cat. No. 17145C

Schedule A (Form 1040) 2014

SCHEDULE B (Form 1040A or 1040) Department of the Treasury Internal Revenue Service (99)	**Interest and Ordinary Dividends** ► Attach to Form 1040A or 1040. ► Information about Schedule B and its instructions is at *www.irs.gov/scheduleb*.

OMB No. 1545-0074

2014

Attachment
Sequence No. **08**

Name(s) shown on return

Tom E. and Mary A. Dodd

Your social security number

123-45-6789

Part I

Interest

(See instructions on back and the instructions for Form 1040A, or Form 1040, line 8a.)

Note. If you received a Form 1099-INT, Form 1099-OID, or substitute statement from a brokerage firm, list the firm's name as the payer and enter the total interest shown on that form.

1 List name of payer. If any interest is from a seller-financed mortgage and the buyer used the property as a personal residence, see instructions on back and list this interest first. Also, show that buyer's social security number and address ►

	Amount
John Q. Smith, Installment Sale 2012	1,000
First National Bank Savings	250
Series E-EE Bonds	1,100
Big Blue, Inc.	550
Bond interest	450
Low Rent Ltd Ptp	50
Big Time Hotel S corp	25

2 Add the amounts on line 1 — **2** 4,075

3 Excludable interest on series EE and I U.S. savings bonds issued after 1989. Attach Form 8815 — **3**

4 Subtract line 3 from line 2. Enter the result here and on Form 1040A, or Form 1040, line 8a — ► **4**

Note. If line 4 is over $1,500, you must complete Part III.

Part II

Ordinary Dividends

(See instructions on back and the instructions for Form 1040A, or Form 1040, line 9a.)

Note. If you received a Form 1099-DIV or substitute statement from a brokerage firm, list the firm's name as the payer and enter the ordinary dividends shown on that form.

5 List name of payer ►

	Amount
GrantCo	750
Newcorp	250
Pioneer Gas & Electric	300

6 Add the amounts on line 5. Enter the total here and on Form 1040A, or Form 1040, line 9a — ► **6** 1,300

Note. If line 6 is over $1,500, you must complete Part III.

Part III

Foreign Accounts and Trusts

(See instructions on back.)

You must complete this part if you **(a)** had over $1,500 of taxable interest or ordinary dividends; **(b)** had a foreign account; or **(c)** received a distribution from, or were a grantor of, or a transferor to, a foreign trust.

		Yes	No
7a	At any time during 2014, did you have a financial interest in or signature authority over a financial account (such as a bank account, securities account, or brokerage account) located in a foreign country? See instructions		✓
	If "Yes," are you required to file FinCEN Form 114, Report of Foreign Bank and Financial Accounts (FBAR), to report that financial interest or signature authority? See FinCEN Form 114 and its instructions for filing requirements and exceptions to those requirements		
b	If you are required to file FinCEN Form 114, enter the name of the foreign country where the financial account is located ►		
8	During 2014, did you receive a distribution from, or were you the grantor of, or transferor to, a foreign trust? If "Yes," you may have to file Form 3520. See instructions on back		✓

For Paperwork Reduction Act Notice, see your tax return instructions.   Cat. No. 17146N   Schedule B (Form 1040A or 1040) 2014

§ 2.1380 Filled-In Schedules C, Form 1040

§ 2.1381 Filled-In Schedule C, Form 1040--Tom Dodd

SCHEDULE C
(Form 1040)

Department of the Treasury
Internal Revenue Service (99)

Profit or Loss From Business
(Sole Proprietorship)

▶ Information about Schedule C and its separate instructions is at *www.irs.gov/schedulec*.
▶ Attach to Form 1040, 1040NR, or 1041; partnerships generally must file Form 1065.

OMB No. 1545-0074

2014

Attachment
Sequence No. **09**

Name of proprietor	Social security number (SSN)
Tom E. Dodd	123-45-6789

A Principal business or profession, including product or service (see instructions)
Tax Preparation Services

B Enter code from instructions
▶ 5 4 1 2 1 3

C Business name. If no separate business name, leave blank.

D Employer ID number (EIN), (see instr.)

E Business address (including suite or room no.) ▶ 987 Main Street
City, town or post office, state, and ZIP code   Pleasanttown, NY 01234

F Accounting method: **(1)** ☑ Cash **(2)** ☐ Accrual **(3)** ☐ Other (specify) ▶ _____

G Did you "materially participate" in the operation of this business during 2014? If "No," see instructions for limit on losses . ☑ Yes ☐ No

H If you started or acquired this business during 2014, check here . . . . ▶ ☐

I Did you make any payments in 2014 that would require you to file Form(s) 1099? (see instructions) . . . . . . ☐ Yes ☑ No

J If "Yes," did you or will you file required Forms 1099? . . . . ☐ Yes ☐ No

Part I Income

1	Gross receipts or sales. See instructions for line 1 and check the box if this income was reported to you on Form W-2 and the "Statutory employee" box on that form was checked . . . . ▶ ☐	**1**	24,000
2	Returns and allowances	**2**	
3	Subtract line 2 from line 1	**3**	24,000
4	Cost of goods sold (from line 42)	**4**	
5	**Gross profit.** Subtract line 4 from line 3	**5**	24,000
6	Other income, including federal and state gasoline or fuel tax credit or refund (see instructions)	**6**	
7	**Gross income.** Add lines 5 and 6 . . . . ▶	**7**	24,000

Part II Expenses. Enter expenses for business use of your home **only** on line 30.

8	Advertising	**8**	250	18	Office expense (see instructions)	**18**	300
9	Car and truck expenses (see instructions).	**9**		19	Pension and profit-sharing plans .	**19**	
10	Commissions and fees .	**10**		20	Rent or lease (see instructions):		
11	Contract labor (see instructions)	**11**		a	Vehicles, machinery, and equipment	**20a**	
12	Depletion	**12**		b	Other business property . . .	**20b**	
13	Depreciation and section 179 expense deduction (not included in Part III) (see instructions).	**13**	3,550	21	Repairs and maintenance . . .	**21**	
				22	Supplies (not included in Part III) .	**22**	
				23	Taxes and licenses	**23**	685
				24	Travel, meals, and entertainment:		
14	Employee benefit programs (other than on line 19) . .	**14**	350	a	Travel	**24a**	
15	Insurance (other than health)	**15**		b	Deductible meals and entertainment (see instructions)	**24b**	400
16	Interest:			25	Utilities	**25**	600
a	Mortgage (paid to banks, etc.)	**16a**		26	Wages (less employment credits) .	**26**	6,000
b	Other	**16b**	1,125	27a	Other expenses (from line 48) . .	**27a**	735
17	Legal and professional services	**17**		b	**Reserved for future use** . . .	**27b**	

28	**Total expenses** before expenses for business use of home. Add lines 8 through 27a . . . . . . ▶	**28**	13,995
29	Tentative profit or (loss). Subtract line 28 from line 7	**29**	10,005
30	Expenses for business use of your home. Do not report these expenses elsewhere. Attach Form 8829 unless using the simplified method (see instructions). **Simplified method filers only:** enter the total square footage of: (a) your home: _____ and (b) the part of your home used for business: _____ . Use the Simplified Method Worksheet in the instructions to figure the amount to enter on line 30	**30**	1,981
31	**Net profit or (loss).** Subtract line 30 from line 29. • If a profit, enter on both **Form 1040, line 12** (or **Form 1040NR, line 13**) and on **Schedule SE, line 2.** (If you checked the box on line 1, see instructions). Estates and trusts, enter on **Form 1041, line 3.** • If a loss, you **must** go to line 32.	**31**	8,024
32	If you have a loss, check the box that describes your investment in this activity (see instructions). • If you checked 32a, enter the loss on both **Form 1040, line 12,** (or **Form 1040NR, line 13**) and on **Schedule SE, line 2.** (If you checked the box on line 1, see the line 31 instructions). Estates and trusts, enter on **Form 1041, line 3.** • If you checked 32b, you **must** attach **Form 6198.** Your loss may be limited.	**32a** ☑ All investment is at risk. **32b** ☐ Some investment is not at risk.	

For Paperwork Reduction Act Notice, see the separate instructions.   Cat. No. 11334P   Schedule C (Form 1040) 2014

Part III Cost of Goods Sold (see instructions)

33 Method(s) used to value closing inventory: **a** ☐ Cost **b** ☐ Lower of cost or market **c** ☐ Other (attach explanation)

34 Was there any change in determining quantities, costs, or valuations between opening and closing inventory?
If "Yes," attach explanation . . . . ☐ Yes ☐ No

35	Inventory at beginning of year. If different from last year's closing inventory, attach explanation . . .	35
36	Purchases less cost of items withdrawn for personal use	36
37	Cost of labor. Do not include any amounts paid to yourself	37
38	Materials and supplies	38
39	Other costs	39
40	Add lines 35 through 39	40
41	Inventory at end of year	41
42	**Cost of goods sold.** Subtract line 41 from line 40. Enter the result here and on line 4 . . .	42

Part IV Information on Your Vehicle. Complete this part **only** if you are claiming car or truck expenses on line 9 and are not required to file Form 4562 for this business. See the instructions for line 13 to find out if you must file Form 4562.

43 When did you place your vehicle in service for business purposes? (month, day, year) ▶ / /

44 Of the total number of miles you drove your vehicle during 2014, enter the number of miles you used your vehicle for:

a Business _____ **b** Commuting (see instructions) _____ **c** Other _____

45 Was your vehicle available for personal use during off-duty hours? . . . . ☐ Yes ☐ No

46 Do you (or your spouse) have another vehicle available for personal use? . . . . ☐ Yes ☐ No

47a Do you have evidence to support your deduction? . . . . ☐ Yes ☐ No

 b If "Yes," is the evidence written? . . . . ☐ Yes ☐ No

Part V Other Expenses. List below business expenses not included on lines 8–26 or line 30.

Bank service charges	35
Dues and publications	50
Outside services	650
48 **Total other expenses.** Enter here and on line 27a **48**	735

§ 2.1382 Filled-In Schedule C, Form 1040--Mary Dodd

SCHEDULE C
(Form 1040)

Department of the Treasury
Internal Revenue Service (99)

Profit or Loss From Business
(Sole Proprietorship)

▶ Information about Schedule C and its separate instructions is at *www.irs.gov/schedulec*.
▶ Attach to Form 1040, 1040NR, or 1041; partnerships generally must file Form 1065.

OMB No. 1545-0074

2014

Attachment
Sequence No. **09**

Name of proprietor	Social security number (SSN)
Mary A. Dodd	987-65-4321

A Principal business or profession, including product or service (see instructions)

Oil and gas

B Enter code from instructions ▶ 2 1 1 1 1 0

C Business name. If no separate business name, leave blank.

D Employer ID number (EIN), (see instr.)

E Business address (including suite or room no.) ▶ 987 Main Street
City, town or post office, state, and ZIP code   Pleasanttown, NY 01234

F Accounting method: **(1)** ☑ Cash **(2)** ☐ Accrual **(3)** ☐ Other (specify) ▶

G Did you "materially participate" in the operation of this business during 2014? If "No," see instructions for limit on losses ☑ Yes ☐ No

H If you started or acquired this business during 2014, check here . . . . ▶ ☐

I Did you make any payments in 2014 that would require you to file Form(s) 1099? (see instructions) . . . . . ☐ Yes ☑ No

J If "Yes," did you or will you file required Forms 1099? . . . . ☐ Yes ☑ No

Part I   Income

1	Gross receipts or sales. See instructions for line 1 and check the box if this income was reported to you on Form W-2 and the "Statutory employee" box on that form was checked . . . . . . ▶ ☐	**1**	4,000
2	Returns and allowances	**2**	
3	Subtract line 2 from line 1	**3**	4,000
4	Cost of goods sold (from line 42)	**4**	
5	**Gross profit.** Subtract line 4 from line 3	**5**	4,000
6	Other income, including federal and state gasoline or fuel tax credit or refund (see instructions) . . .	**6**	
7	**Gross income.** Add lines 5 and 6 . . . . ▶	**7**	4,000

Part II   Expenses. Enter expenses for business use of your home **only** on line 30.

8	Advertising	**8**		18	Office expense (see instructions)	**18**	
9	Car and truck expenses (see instructions)	**9**		19	Pension and profit-sharing plans	**19**	
10	Commissions and fees	**10**		20	Rent or lease (see instructions):		
11	Contract labor (see instructions)	**11**		a	Vehicles, machinery, and equipment	**20a**	
12	Depletion	**12**	600	b	Other business property . . .	**20b**	
13	Depreciation and section 179 expense deduction (not included in Part III) (see instructions)	**13**		21	Repairs and maintenance . .	**21**	
				22	Supplies (not included in Part III)	**22**	
				23	Taxes and licenses	**23**	280
14	Employee benefit programs (other than on line 19) . .	**14**		24	Travel, meals, and entertainment:		
				a	Travel	**24a**	
15	Insurance (other than health)	**15**		b	Deductible meals and entertainment (see instructions) .	**24b**	
16	Interest:			25	Utilities	**25**	
a	Mortgage (paid to banks, etc.)	**16a**		26	Wages (less employment credits) .	**26**	
b	Other	**16b**		27a	Other expenses (from line 48) . .	**27a**	9,200
17	Legal and professional services	**17**		b	**Reserved for future use** . . .	**27b**	

28	**Total expenses** before expenses for business use of home. Add lines 8 through 27a . . . . . . ▶	**28**	10,080
29	Tentative profit or (loss). Subtract line 28 from line 7	**29**	(6,080)
30	Expenses for business use of your home. Do not report these expenses elsewhere. Attach Form 8829 unless using the simplified method (see instructions). **Simplified method filers only:** enter the total square footage of: (a) your home: _____ and (b) the part of your home used for business: _____. Use the Simplified Method Worksheet in the instructions to figure the amount to enter on line 30	**30**	
31	**Net profit or (loss).** Subtract line 30 from line 29.		
	• If a profit, enter on both **Form 1040, line 12** (or **Form 1040NR, line 13**) and on **Schedule SE, line 2**. (If you checked the box on line 1, see instructions). Estates and trusts, enter on **Form 1041, line 3**. • If a loss, you **must** go to line 32.	**31**	(6,080)
32	If you have a loss, check the box that describes your investment in this activity (see instructions). • If you checked 32a, enter the loss on both **Form 1040, line 12,** (or **Form 1040NR, line 13**) and on **Schedule SE, line 2.** (If you checked the box on line 1, see the line 31 instructions). Estates and trusts, enter on **Form 1041, line 3.** • If you checked 32b, you **must** attach **Form 6198.** Your loss may be limited.	**32a** ☑ All investment is at risk. **32b** ☐ Some investment is not at risk.	

For Paperwork Reduction Act Notice, see the separate instructions.   Cat. No. 11334P   Schedule C (Form 1040) 2014

Schedule C (Form 1040) 2014   Page **2**

Part III   Cost of Goods Sold (see instructions)

33 Method(s) used to
value closing inventory: **a** ☐ Cost   **b** ☐ Lower of cost or market   **c** ☐ Other (attach explanation)

34 Was there any change in determining quantities, costs, or valuations between opening and closing inventory?
If "Yes," attach explanation . . . .   ☐ Yes   ☐ No

35 Inventory at beginning of year. If different from last year's closing inventory, attach explanation . . .	**35**	
36 Purchases less cost of items withdrawn for personal use	**36**	
37 Cost of labor. Do not include any amounts paid to yourself	**37**	
38 Materials and supplies	**38**	
39 Other costs	**39**	
40 Add lines 35 through 39	**40**	
41 Inventory at end of year	**41**	
42 **Cost of goods sold.** Subtract line 41 from line 40. Enter the result here and on line 4	**42**	

Part IV   Information on Your Vehicle. Complete this part **only** if you are claiming car or truck expenses on line 9 and are not required to file Form 4562 for this business. See the instructions for line 13 to find out if you must file Form 4562.

43 When did you place your vehicle in service for business purposes? (month, day, year) ▶ ___ / ___ / ___

44 Of the total number of miles you drove your vehicle during 2014, enter the number of miles you used your vehicle for:

a Business _____   **b** Commuting (see instructions) _____   **c** Other _____

45 Was your vehicle available for personal use during off-duty hours? . . . .   ☐ Yes   ☐ No

46 Do you (or your spouse) have another vehicle available for personal use? . . . .   ☐ Yes   ☐ No

47a Do you have evidence to support your deduction? . . . .   ☐ Yes   ☐ No

b If "Yes," is the evidence written? . . . .   ☐ Yes   ☐ No

Part V   Other Expenses. List below business expenses not included on lines 8–26 or line 30.

IDC	7,500
LOE	1,700
48 Total other expenses. Enter here and on line 27a **48**	9,200

Schedule C (Form 1040) 2014

SCHEDULE D		
(Form 1040)		

Capital Gains and Losses

OMB No. 1545-0074

2014

Department of the Treasury
Internal Revenue Service (99)

► Attach to Form 1040 or Form 1040NR.
► Information about Schedule D and its separate instructions is at *www.irs.gov/scheduled*.
► Use Form 8949 to list your transactions for lines 1b, 2, 3, 8b, 9, and 10.

Attachment
Sequence No. **12**

Name(s) shown on return
Tom E. and Mary A. Dodd

Your social security number
123-45-6789

Part I	Short-Term Capital Gains and Losses—Assets Held One Year or Less			

See instructions for how to figure the amounts to enter on the lines below. This form may be easier to complete if you round off cents to whole dollars.	**(d)** Proceeds (sales price)	**(e)** Cost (or other basis)	**(g)** Adjustments to gain or loss from Form(s) 8949, Part I, line 2, column (g)	**(h) Gain or (loss)** Subtract column (e) from column (d) and combine the result with column (g)
1a Totals for all short-term transactions reported on Form 1099-B for which basis was reported to the IRS and for which you have no adjustments (see instructions). However, if you choose to report all these transactions on Form 8949, leave this line blank and go to line 1b .				
1b Totals for all transactions reported on Form(s) 8949 with **Box A** checked				
2 Totals for all transactions reported on Form(s) 8949 with **Box B** checked	4,000	(7,250)		(3,250)
3 Totals for all transactions reported on Form(s) 8949 with **Box C** checked				

4 Short-term gain from Form 6252 and short-term gain or (loss) from Forms 4684, 6781, and 8824 .	**4**	
5 Net short-term gain or (loss) from partnerships, S corporations, estates, and trusts from Schedule(s) K-1	**5**	
6 Short-term capital loss carryover. Enter the amount, if any, from line 8 of your **Capital Loss Carryover Worksheet** in the instructions	**6** (	2,100)
7 Net short-term capital gain or (loss). Combine lines 1a through 6 in column (h). If you have any long-term capital gains or losses, go to Part II below. Otherwise, go to Part III on the back	**7**	(5,350)

Part II	Long-Term Capital Gains and Losses—Assets Held More Than One Year			

See instructions for how to figure the amounts to enter on the lines below. This form may be easier to complete if you round off cents to whole dollars.	**(d)** Proceeds (sales price)	**(e)** Cost (or other basis)	**(g)** Adjustments to gain or loss from Form(s) 8949, Part II, line 2, column (g)	**(h) Gain or (loss)** Subtract column (e) from column (d) and combine the result with column (g)
8a Totals for all long-term transactions reported on Form 1099-B for which basis was reported to the IRS and for which you have no adjustments (see instructions). However, if you choose to report all these transactions on Form 8949, leave this line blank and go to line 8b .				
8b Totals for all transactions reported on Form(s) 8949 with **Box D** checked				
9 Totals for all transactions reported on Form(s) 8949 with **Box E** checked	1,080	(600)		480
10 Totals for all transactions reported on Form(s) 8949 with **Box F** checked.				

11 Gain from Form 4797, Part I; long-term gain from Forms 2439 and 6252; and long-term gain or (loss) from Forms 4684, 6781, and 8824	**11**	31,815
12 Net long-term gain or (loss) from partnerships, S corporations, estates, and trusts from Schedule(s) K-1	**12**	
13 Capital gain distributions. See the instructions	**13**	700
14 Long-term capital loss carryover. Enter the amount, if any, from line 13 of your **Capital Loss Carryover Worksheet** in the instructions	**14** (	)
15 **Net long-term capital gain or (loss).** Combine lines 8a through 14 in column (h). Then go to Part III on the back	**15**	32,515

For Paperwork Reduction Act Notice, see your tax return instructions.   Cat. No. 11338H   Schedule D (Form 1040) 2014

Part III	**Summary**	

| 16 | Combine lines 7 and 15 and enter the result . . . . | **16** | 27,165 |

- If line 16 is a **gain,** enter the amount from line 16 on Form 1040, line 13, or Form 1040NR, line 14. Then go to line 17 below.
- If line 16 is a **loss,** skip lines 17 through 20 below. Then go to line 21. Also be sure to complete line 22.
- If line 16 is **zero,** skip lines 17 through 21 below and enter -0- on Form 1040, line 13, or Form 1040NR, line 14. Then go to line 22.

17 Are lines 15 and 16 **both** gains?

☑ **Yes.** Go to line 18.

☐ **No.** Skip lines 18 through 21, and go to line 22.

| 18 | Enter the amount, if any, from line 7 of the **28% Rate Gain Worksheet** in the instructions . . ▶ | **18** | 0 |

| 19 | Enter the amount, if any, from line 18 of the **Unrecaptured Section 1250 Gain Worksheet** in the instructions . . . . ▶ | **19** | 0 |

20 Are lines 18 and 19 **both** zero or blank?

☑ **Yes.** Complete the **Qualified Dividends and Capital Gain Tax Worksheet** in the instructions for Form 1040, line 44 (or in the instructions for Form 1040NR, line 42). **Do not** complete lines 21 and 22 below.

☐ **No.** Complete the **Schedule D Tax Worksheet** in the instructions. **Do not** complete lines 21 and 22 below.

21 If line 16 is a loss, enter here and on Form 1040, line 13, or Form 1040NR, line 14, the **smaller** of:

- The loss on line 16 or
- ($3,000), or if married filing separately, ($1,500) } . . . . | **21** ( )

Note. When figuring which amount is smaller, treat both amounts as positive numbers.

22 Do you have qualified dividends on Form 1040, line 9b, or Form 1040NR, line 10b?

☐ **Yes.** Complete the **Qualified Dividends and Capital Gain Tax Worksheet** in the instructions for Form 1040, line 44 (or in the instructions for Form 1040NR, line 42).

☐ **No.** Complete the rest of Form 1040 or Form 1040NR.

28% Rate Gain Worksheet—Line 18

1.	Enter the total of all collectibles gain or (loss) from items you reported on Form 8949, Part II .... **1.**	480

2.	Enter as a positive number the total of:
	  • Any section 1202 exclusion you reported in column (g) of Form 8949, Part II, with code "Q" in column (f), for which you excluded 50% of the gain;
	  • ⅔ of any section 1202 exclusion you reported in column (g) of Form 8949, Part II, with code "Q" in column (f), for which you excluded 60% of the gain; and
	  • ⅓ of any section 1202 exclusion you reported in column (g) of Form 8949, Part II, with code "Q" in column (f), for which you excluded 75% of the gain. .... **2.**
		0

3.	Enter the total of all collectibles gain or (loss) from Form 4684, line 4 (but only if Form 4684, line 15, is more than zero); Form 6252; Form 6781, Part II; and Form 8824 .... **3.**	0

4.	Enter the total of any collectibles gain reported to you on:
	  • Form 1099-DIV, box 2d;
	  • Form 2439, box 1d; and
	  • Schedule K-1 from a partnership, S corporation, estate, or trust. .... **4.**
		0

5.	Enter your long-term capital loss carryovers from Schedule D, line 14, and Schedule K-1 (Form 1041), box 11, code C .... **5.**	(0)
6.	If Schedule D, line 7, is a (loss), enter that (loss) here. Otherwise, enter -0- .... **6.**	(5,350)
7.	Combine lines 1 through 6. If zero or less, enter -0-. If more than zero, also enter this amount on Schedule D, line 18 .... **7.**	0

Unrecaptured Section 1250 Gain Worksheet—Line 19

Keep for Your Records

If you are not reporting a gain on Form 4797, line 7, skip lines 1 through 9 and go to line 10.

1. If you have a section 1250 property in Part III of Form 4797 for which you made an entry in Part I of Form 4797 (but not on Form 6252), enter the **smaller** of line 22 or line 24 of Form 4797 for that property. If you did not have any such property, go to line 4. If you had more than one such property, see instructions .... **1.** _____

2. Enter the amount from Form 4797, line 26g, for the property for which you made an entry on line 1 .... **2.** _____

3. Subtract line 2 from line 1 .... **3.** _____

4. Enter the total unrecaptured section 1250 gain included on line 26 or line 37 of Form(s) 6252 from installment sales of trade or business property held more than 1 year (see instructions) .... **4.** _____

5. Enter the total of any amounts reported to you on a Schedule K-1 from a partnership or an S corporation as "unrecaptured section 1250 gain" .... **5.** _____

6. Add lines 3 through 5 .... **6.** _____

7. Enter the **smaller** of line 6 or the gain from Form 4797, line 7 .... **7.** _____

8. Enter the amount, if any, from Form 4797, line 8 .... **8.** _____

9. Subtract line 8 from line 7. If zero or less, enter -0- .... **9.** _____

10. Enter the amount of any gain from the sale or exchange of an interest in a partnership attributable to unrecaptured section 1250 gain (see instructions) **10.** 0

11. Enter the total of any amounts reported to you as "unrecaptured section 1250 gain" on a Schedule K-1, Form 1099-DIV, or Form 2439 from an estate, trust, real estate investment trust, or mutual fund (or other regulated investment company) or in connection with a Form 1099-R **11.** 0

12. Enter the total of any unrecaptured section 1250 gain from sales (including installment sales) or other dispositions of section 1250 property held more than 1 year for which you did not make an entry in Part I of Form 4797 for the year of sale (see instructions) **12.** 0

13. Add lines 9 through 12 .... **13.** 0

14. If you had any section 1202 gain or collectibles gain or (loss), enter the total of lines 1 through 4 of the **28% Rate Gain Worksheet**. Otherwise, enter -0- **14.** 0

15. Enter the (loss), if any, from Schedule D, line 7. If Schedule D, line 7, is zero or a gain, enter -0- **15.** (5,350)

16. Enter your long-term capital loss carryovers from Schedule D, line 14, and Schedule K-1 (Form 1041), box 11, code C* **16.** (0)

17. Combine lines 14 through 16. If the result is a (loss), enter it as a positive amount. If the result is zero or a gain, enter -0- **17.** 5,350

18. **Unrecaptured section 1250 gain.** Subtract line 17 from line 13. If zero or less, enter -0-. If more than zero, enter the result here and on Schedule D, line 19 .... **18.** 0

*If you are filing Form 2555 or 2555-EZ (relating to foreign earned income), see the footnote in the Foreign Earned Income Tax Worksheet in the Form 1040 instructions before completing this line.

Qualified Dividends and Capital Gain Tax Worksheet—Line 44

Keep for Your Records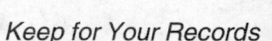

Before you begin:
  ✓ See the earlier instructions for line 44 to see if you can use this worksheet to figure your tax.
  ✓ Before completing this worksheet, complete Form 1040 through line 43.
  ✓ If you do not have to file Schedule D and you received capital gain distributions, be sure you checked the box on line 13 of Form 1040.

1. Enter the amount from Form 1040, line 43. However, if you are filing Form 2555 or 2555-EZ (relating to foreign earned income), enter the amount from line 3 of the Foreign Earned Income Tax Worksheet .... **1.** | 60,600

2. Enter the amount from Form 1040, line 9b* .... **2.** | 1,300

3. Are you filing Schedule D?*
  ☐ **Yes.** Enter the **smaller** of line 15 or 16 of Schedule D. If either line 15 or line 16 is blank or a loss, enter -0-
  ☐ **No.** Enter the amount from Form 1040, line 13 } **3.** | 27,165

4. Add lines 2 and 3 .... **4.** | 28,465

5. If filing Form 4952 (used to figure investment interest expense deduction), enter any amount from line 4g of that form. Otherwise, enter -0- .... **5.** | 0

6. Subtract line 5 from line 4. If zero or less, enter -0- .... **6.** | 28,465

7. Subtract line 6 from line 1. If zero or less, enter -0- .... **7.** | 32,135

8. Enter:
  $36,900 if single or married filing separately,
  $73,800 if married filing jointly or qualifying widow(er),
  $49,400 if head of household. } .... **8.** | 73,800

9. Enter the smaller of line 1 or line 8 .... **9.** | 60,600

10. Enter the smaller of line 7 or line 9 .... **10.** | 32,135

11. Subtract line 10 from line 9. This amount is taxed at 0% .... **11.** | 28,465

12. Enter the smaller of line 1 or line 6 .... **12.** | 28,465

13. Enter the amount from line 11 .... **13.** | 28,465

14. Subtract line 13 from line 12 .... **14.** | 0

15. Enter:
  $406,750 if single,
  $228,800 if married filing separately,
  $457,600 if married filing jointly or qualifying widow(er), } .... **15.** | 457,600
  $432,200 if head of household.

16. Enter the smaller of line 1 or line 15 .... **16.** | 60,600

17. Add lines 7 and 11 .... **17.** | 60,600

18. Subtract line 17 from line 16. If zero or less, enter -0- .... **18.** | 0

19. Enter the smaller of line 14 or line 18 .... **19.** | 0

20. Multiply line 19 by 15% (.15) .... **20.** | 0

21. Add lines 11 and 19 .... **21.** | 28,465

22. Subtract line 21 from line 12 .... **22.** | 0

23. Multiply line 22 by 20% (.20) .... **23.** | 0

24. Figure the tax on the amount on line 7. If the amount on line 7 is less than $100,000, use the Tax Table to figure the tax. If the amount on line 7 is $100,000 or more, use the Tax Computation Worksheet .... **24.** | 3,911

25. Add lines 20, 23, and 24 .... **25.** | 3,911

26. Figure the tax on the amount on line 1. If the amount on line 1 is less than $100,000, use the Tax Table to figure the tax. If the amount on line 1 is $100,000 or more, use the Tax Computation Worksheet .... **26.** | 8,186

27. **Tax on all taxable income.** Enter the **smaller** of line 25 or line 26. Also include this amount on Form 1040, line 44. If you are filing Form 2555 or 2555-EZ, do not enter this amount on Form 1040, line 44. Instead, enter it on line 4 of the Foreign Earned Income Tax Worksheet .... **27.** | 3,911

*If you are filing Form 2555 or 2555-EZ, see the footnote in the Foreign Earned Income Tax Worksheet before completing this line.

SCHEDULE E (Form 1040) Department of the Treasury Internal Revenue Service (99)	**Supplemental Income and Loss** (From rental real estate, royalties, partnerships, S corporations, estates, trusts, REMICs, etc.) ▶ Attach to Form 1040, 1040NR, or Form 1041. ▶ Information about Schedule E and its separate instructions is at *www.irs.gov/schedulee*.	OMB No. 1545-0074 2014 Attachment Sequence No. 13

Name(s) shown on return	Your social security number
Tom E. and Mary A. Dodd	123-45-6789

Part I   **Income or Loss From Rental Real Estate and Royalties**   **Note.** If you are in the business of renting personal property, use **Schedule C or C-EZ** (see instructions). If you are an individual, report farm rental income or loss from **Form 4835** on page 2, line 40.

A Did you make any payments in 2014 that would require you to file Form(s) 1099? (see instructions)		☐ Yes	☑ No
B If "Yes," did you or will you file required Forms 1099?		☐ Yes	☐ No

1a Physical address of each property (street, city, state, ZIP code)

A	First St Duplex, 200 E 1st St, Pleasanttown, NY 01111
B	Oil and Gas royalties
C	

1b	Type of Property (from list below)	2 For each rental real estate property listed above, report the number of fair rental and personal use days. Check the **QJV** box only if you meet the requirements to file as a qualified joint venture. See instructions.		Fair Rental Days	Personal Use Days	QJV
A	2		A	365		☐
B	6		B			☐
C			C			☐

Type of Property:

1 Single Family Residence	3 Vacation/Short-Term Rental	5 Land 7 Self-Rental
2 Multi-Family Residence	4 Commercial	6 Royalties 8 Other (describe)

Income:	Properties:		A	B	C
3	Rents received	3	9,200		
4	Royalties received	4		4,000	
Expenses:					
5	Advertising	5			
6	Auto and travel (see instructions)	6			
7	Cleaning and maintenance	7			
8	Commissions.	8			
9	Insurance	9	600		
10	Legal and other professional fees	10			
11	Management fees	11			
12	Mortgage interest paid to banks, etc. (see instructions)	12	6,300		
13	Other interest.	13			
14	Repairs.	14	1,050		
15	Supplies	15			
16	Taxes	16	1,200	315	
17	Utilities.	17	250		
18	Depreciation expense or depletion	18	4,000	600	
19	Other (list) ▶ HOA dues	19	125		
20	Total expenses. Add lines 5 through 19	20	13,525	915	
21	Subtract line 20 from line 3 (rents) and/or 4 (royalties). If result is a (loss), see instructions to find out if you must file **Form 6198**	21	(4,325)	3,085	
22	Deductible rental real estate loss after limitation, if any, on **Form 8582** (see instructions)	22	(4,325)	( )	( )

23a	Total of all amounts reported on line 3 for all rental properties	23a	9,200	
b	Total of all amounts reported on line 4 for all royalty properties	23b	4,000	
c	Total of all amounts reported on line 12 for all properties	23c	6,300	
d	Total of all amounts reported on line 18 for all properties	23d	4,600	
e	Total of all amounts reported on line 20 for all properties	23e	14,440	
24	**Income.** Add positive amounts shown on line 21. **Do not** include any losses	24	3,085
25	**Losses.** Add royalty losses from line 21 and rental real estate losses from line 22. Enter total losses here	25	(4,325)
26	**Total rental real estate and royalty income or (loss).** Combine lines 24 and 25. Enter the result here. If Parts II, III, IV, and line 40 on page 2 do not apply to you, also enter this amount on Form 1040, line 17, or Form 1040NR, line 18. Otherwise, include this amount in the total on line 41 on page 2	26	(1,240)

For Paperwork Reduction Act Notice, see the separate instructions.   Cat. No. 11344L   Schedule E (Form 1040) 2014

Name(s) shown on return. Do not enter name and social security number if shown on other side.	Your social security number
Tom E. and Mary A. Dodd	123-45-6789

Caution. The IRS compares amounts reported on your tax return with amounts shown on Schedule(s) K-1.

Part II — Income or Loss From Partnerships and S Corporations

Note. If you report a loss from an at-risk activity for which **any** amount is **not** at risk, you **must** check the box in column (e) on line 28 and attach **Form 6198**. See instructions.

27 Are you reporting any loss not allowed in a prior year due to the at-risk, excess farm loss, or basis limitations, a prior year unallowed loss from a passive activity (if that loss was not reported on Form 8582), or unreimbursed partnership expenses? If you answered "Yes," see instructions before completing this section.   ☐ **Yes**   ☑ **No**

28	(a) Name	(b) Enter P for partnership; S for S corporation	(c) Check if foreign partnership	(d) Employer identification number	(e) Check if any amount is not at risk
A	Low Rent Ltd	P	☐	73-1234567	☐
B	Red Oaks Ltd	P	☐	73-8888888	☐
C	Big Time Hotel Inc.	S	☐	01-3456789	☐
D			☐		☐

	Passive Income and Loss		Nonpassive Income and Loss		
	(f) Passive loss allowed (attach **Form 8582** if required)	(g) Passive income from **Schedule K–1**	(h) Nonpassive loss from **Schedule K–1**	(i) Section 179 expense deduction from **Form 4562**	(j) Nonpassive income from **Schedule K–1**
A			12,000		
B	875				
C	4,500				
D					
29a Totals					
b Totals	5,375		12,000		

30	Add columns (g) and (j) of line 29a	30	
31	Add columns (f), (h), and (i) of line 29b	31	(17,375)
32	**Total partnership and S corporation income or (loss).** Combine lines 30 and 31. Enter the result here and include in the total on line 41 below	32	(17,375)

Part III — Income or Loss From Estates and Trusts

33	(a) Name	(b) Employer identification number
A	Mary Dodd Trust	99-0011223
B		

	Passive Income and Loss		Nonpassive Income and Loss	
	(c) Passive deduction or loss allowed (attach **Form 8582** if required)	(d) Passive income from **Schedule K–1**	(e) Deduction or loss from **Schedule K–1**	(f) Other income from **Schedule K–1**
A				3,000
B				
34a Totals				3,000
b Totals				

35	Add columns (d) and (f) of line 34a	35	3,000
36	Add columns (c) and (e) of line 34b	36	( )
37	**Total estate and trust income or (loss).** Combine lines 35 and 36. Enter the result here and include in the total on line 41 below	37	3,000

Part IV — Income or Loss From Real Estate Mortgage Investment Conduits (REMICs)—Residual Holder

38	(a) Name	(b) Employer identification number	(c) Excess inclusion from Schedules Q, line 2c (see instructions)	(d) Taxable income (net loss) from Schedules Q, line 1b	(e) Income from Schedules Q, line 3b

39	Combine columns (d) and (e) only. Enter the result here and include in the total on line 41 below	39	

Part V — Summary

40	Net farm rental income or (loss) from **Form 4835**. Also, complete line 42 below	40	
41	Total income or (loss). Combine lines 26, 32, 37, 39, and 40. Enter the result here and on Form 1040, line 17, or Form 1040NR, line 18 ▶	41	(15,615)

42 **Reconciliation of farming and fishing income.** Enter your **gross** farming and fishing income reported on Form 4835, line 7; Schedule K-1 (Form 1065), box 14, code B; Schedule K-1 (Form 1120S), box 17, code V; and Schedule K-1 (Form 1041), box 14, code F (see instructions) . . | 42 | |

43 **Reconciliation for real estate professionals.** If you were a real estate professional (see instructions), enter the net income or (loss) you reported anywhere on Form 1040 or Form 1040NR from all rental real estate activities in which you materially participated under the passive activity loss rules . . | 43 | |

§ 2.1440 Filled-In Schedule F, Form 1040

SCHEDULE F (Form 1040) Department of the Treasury Internal Revenue Service (99)	**Profit or Loss From Farming** ▶ Attach to Form 1040, Form 1040NR, Form 1041, Form 1065, or Form 1065-B. ▶ Information about Schedule F and its separate instructions is at *www.irs.gov/schedulef*.	OMB No. 1545-0074 20**14** Attachment Sequence No. **14**

Name of proprietor	Social security number (SSN)
Tom E. Dodd	123-45-6789

A Principal crop or activity	**B** Enter code from Part IV	**C** Accounting method:	**D** Employer ID number (EIN), (see instr)
Beef Cattle	▶ 1 1 2 1 1 1	☑ Cash ☐ Accrual	

E Did you "materially participate" in the operation of this business during 2014? If "No," see instructions for limit on passive losses ☐ Yes ☐ No

F Did you make any payments in 2014 that would require you to file Form(s) 1099 (see instructions)? . . . . ☐ Yes ☐ No

G If "Yes," did you or will you file required Forms 1099? . . . . ☐ Yes ☐ No

Part I — Farm Income—Cash Method. Complete Parts I and II (Accrual method. Complete Parts II and III, and Part I, line 9.)

1a	Sales of livestock and other resale items (see instructions)	**1a**	18,000			
b	Cost or other basis of livestock or other items reported on line 1a	**1b**	12,000			
c	Subtract line 1b from line 1a			**1c**		6,000
2	Sales of livestock, produce, grains, and other products you raised			**2**		6,500
3a	Cooperative distributions (Form(s) 1099-PATR)	**3a**	350	**3b** Taxable amount	**3b**	350
4a	Agricultural program payments (see instructions) .	**4a**		**4b** Taxable amount	**4b**	
5a	Commodity Credit Corporation (CCC) loans reported under election			**5a**		
b	CCC loans forfeited	**5b**	3,000	**5c** Taxable amount	**5c**	3,000
6	Crop insurance proceeds and federal crop disaster payments (see instructions)					
a	Amount received in 2014	**6a**	1,250	**6b** Taxable amount	**6b**	0
c	If election to defer to 2015 is attached, check here ▶ ☐			**6d** Amount deferred from 2013	**6d**	
7	Custom hire (machine work) income			**7**		2,500
8	Other income, including federal and state gasoline or fuel tax credit or refund (see instructions)			**8**		
9	**Gross income.** Add amounts in the right column (lines 1c, 2, 3b, 4b, 5a, 5c, 6b, 6d, 7, and 8). If you use the accrual method, enter the amount from Part III, line 50 (see instructions) . . . . ▶			**9**		18,350

Part II — Farm Expenses—Cash and Accrual Method. Do not include personal or living expenses (see instructions).

10	Car and truck expenses (see instructions). Also attach **Form 4562**	**10**		**23**	Pension and profit-sharing plans	**23**		
11	Chemicals	**11**		**24**	Rent or lease (see instructions)			
12	Conservation expenses (see instructions)	**12**		**a**	Vehicles, machinery, equipment	**24a**		
13	Custom hire (machine work) .	**13**		**b**	Other (land, animals, etc.) . .	**24b**		650
14	Depreciation and section 179 expense (see instructions)	**14**		**25**	Repairs and maintenance . .	**25**		800
15	Employee benefit programs other than on line 23 . . .	**15**		**26**	Seeds and plants	**26**		1,150
16	Feed	**16**	2,750	**27**	Storage and warehousing . .	**27**		
17	Fertilizers and lime . . .	**17**	1,100	**28**	Supplies	**28**		450
18	Freight and trucking . . .	**18**		**29**	Taxes	**29**		400
19	Gasoline, fuel, and oil . . .	**19**	1,400	**30**	Utilities	**30**		600
20	Insurance (other than health)	**20**	600	**31**	Veterinary, breeding, and medicine	**31**		650
21	Interest:			**32**	Other expenses (specify):			
a	Mortgage (paid to banks, etc.)	**21a**	6,000	**a**	contract labor	**32a**		3,200
b	Other	**21b**	1,200	**b**		**32b**		
22	Labor hired (less employment credits)	**22**		**c**		**32c**		
				d		**32d**		
				e		**32e**		
				f		**32f**		

33	**Total expenses.** Add lines 10 through 32f. If line 32f is negative, see instructions . . . . ▶		**33**	21,125
34	**Net farm profit or (loss).** Subtract line 33 from line 9		**34**	(2,775)

If a profit, stop here and see instructions for where to report. If a loss, complete lines 35 and 36.

35 Did you receive an applicable subsidy in 2014? (see instructions) . . . . ☐ Yes ☑ No

36 Check the box that describes your investment in this activity and see instructions for where to report your loss.

a ☑ All investment is at risk. **b** ☐ Some investment is not at risk.

Cat. No. 11346H Schedule F (Form 1040) 2014

Part III — Farm Income—Accrual Method (see instructions).

37	Sales of livestock, produce, grains, and other products (see instructions)	**37**	
38a	Cooperative distributions (Form(s) 1099-PATR) . **38a**	**38b** Taxable amount **38b**	
39a	Agricultural program payments **39a**	**39b** Taxable amount **39b**	
40	Commodity Credit Corporation (CCC) loans:		
a	CCC loans reported under election	**40a**	
b	CCC loans forfeited **40b**	**40c** Taxable amount **40c**	
41	Crop insurance proceeds	**41**	
42	Custom hire (machine work) income	**42**	
43	Other income (see instructions)	**43**	
44	Add amounts in the right column for lines 37 through 43 (lines 37, 38b, 39b, 40a, 40c, 41, 42, and 43) .	**44**	
45	Inventory of livestock, produce, grains, and other products at beginning of the year. Do not include sales reported on Form 4797	**45**	
46	Cost of livestock, produce, grains, and other products purchased during the year	**46**	
47	Add lines 45 and 46	**47**	
48	Inventory of livestock, produce, grains, and other products at end of year .	**48**	
49	Cost of livestock, produce, grains, and other products sold. Subtract line 48 from line 47*	**49**	
50	**Gross income.** Subtract line 49 from line 44. Enter the result here and on Part I, line 9 . . . . . ▶	**50**	

*If you use the unit-livestock-price method or the farm-price method of valuing inventory and the amount on line 48 is larger than the amount on line 47, subtract line 47 from line 48. Enter the result on line 49. Add lines 44 and 49. Enter the total on line 50 and on Part I, line 9.

Part IV — Principal Agricultural Activity Codes

⚠️ **CAUTION**

Do not file Schedule F (Form 1040) to report the following.

• *Income from providing agricultural services such as soil preparation, veterinary, farm labor, horticultural, or management for a fee or on a contract basis. Instead file Schedule C (Form 1040) or Schedule C-EZ (Form 1040).*

• *Income from breeding, raising, or caring for dogs, cats, or other pet animals. Instead file Schedule C (Form 1040) or Schedule C-EZ (Form 1040).*

• *Sales of livestock held for draft, breeding, sport, or dairy purposes. Instead file Form 4797.*

These codes for the Principal Agricultural Activity classify farms by their primary activity to facilitate the administration of the Internal Revenue Code. These six-digit codes are based on the North American Industry Classification System (NAICS).

Select the code that best identifies your primary farming activity and enter the six-digit number on line B.

Crop Production
111100   Oilseed and grain farming
111210   Vegetable and melon farming
111300   Fruit and tree nut farming
111400   Greenhouse, nursery, and floriculture production
111900   Other crop farming

Animal Production
112111   Beef cattle ranching and farming
112112   Cattle feedlots
112120   Dairy cattle and milk production
112210   Hog and pig farming
112300   Poultry and egg production
112400   Sheep and goat farming
112510   Aquaculture
112900   Other animal production

Forestry and Logging
113000   Forestry and logging (including forest nurseries and timber tracts)

§ 2.1460 Filled-In Schedule SE, Form 1040

SCHEDULE SE
(Form 1040)

Department of the Treasury
Internal Revenue Service (99)

Self-Employment Tax

▶ Information about Schedule SE and its separate instructions is at *www.irs.gov/schedulese.*

▶ Attach to Form 1040 or Form 1040NR.

OMB No. 1545-0074

2014

Attachment
Sequence No. **17**

Name of person with **self-employment** income (as shown on Form 1040 or Form 1040NR)	Social security number of person with **self-employment** income ▶
Tom E. Dodd	123-45-6789

Before you begin: To determine if you must file Schedule SE, see the instructions.

May I Use Short Schedule SE or Must I Use Long Schedule SE?

Note. Use this flowchart **only if** you must file Schedule SE. If unsure, see *Who Must File Schedule SE* in the instructions.

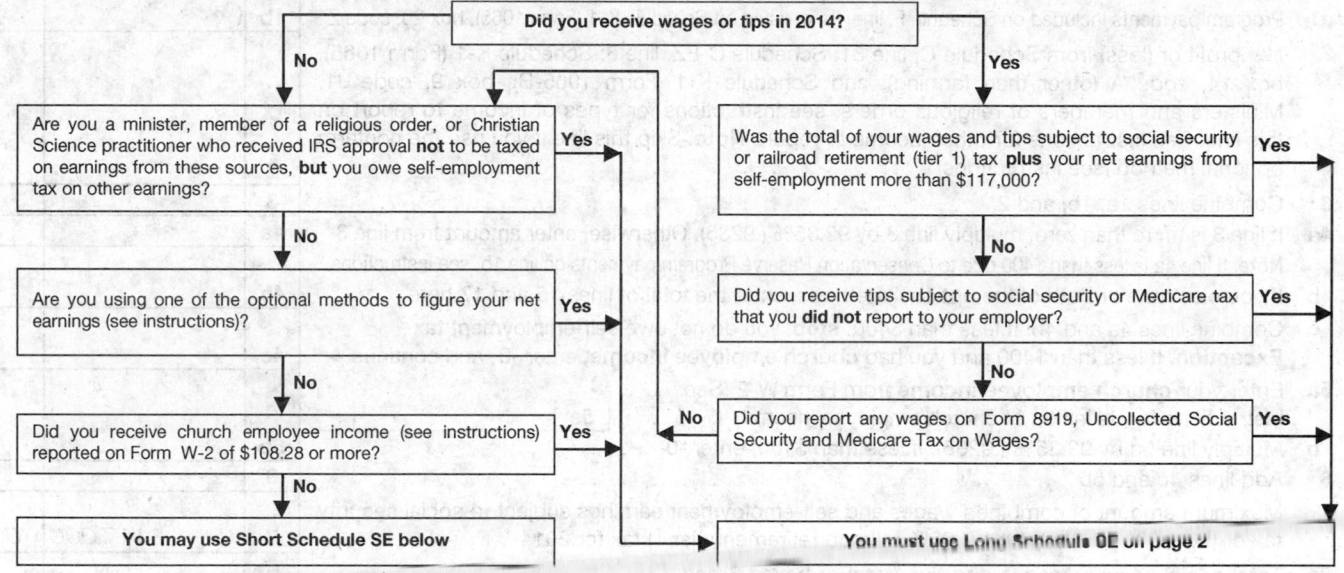

Section A—Short Schedule SE. **Caution.** Read above to see if you can use Short Schedule SE.

1a	Net farm profit or (loss) from Schedule F, line 34, and farm partnerships, Schedule K-1 (Form 1065), box 14, code A	**1a**	(2,775)
b	If you received social security retirement or disability benefits, enter the amount of Conservation Reserve Program payments included on Schedule F, line 4b, or listed on Schedule K-1 (Form 1065), box 20, code Z	**1b** (	)
2	Net profit or (loss) from Schedule C, line 31; Schedule C-EZ, line 3; Schedule K-1 (Form 1065), box 14, code A (other than farming); and Schedule K-1 (Form 1065-B), box 9, code J1. Ministers and members of religious orders, see instructions for types of income to report on this line. See instructions for other income to report	**2**	8,024
3	Combine lines 1a, 1b, and 2	**3**	5,249
4	Multiply line 3 by 92.35% (.9235). If less than $400, you do not owe self-employment tax; do **not** file this schedule unless you have an amount on line 1b . . . . ▶	**4**	4,847
	Note. If line 4 is less than $400 due to Conservation Reserve Program payments on line 1b, see instructions.		
5	**Self-employment tax.** If the amount on line 4 is:		
	• $117,000 or less, multiply line 4 by 15.3% (.153). Enter the result here and on **Form 1040, line 57,** or **Form 1040NR, line 55**		
	• More than $117,000, multiply line 4 by 2.9% (.029). Then, add $14,508 to the result. Enter the total here and on **Form 1040, line 57,** or **Form 1040NR, line 55**	**5**	742
6	**Deduction for one-half of self-employment tax.** Multiply line 5 by 50% (.50). Enter the result here and on **Form 1040, line 27,** or **Form 1040NR, line 27**	**6**	371	

For Paperwork Reduction Act Notice, see your tax return instructions.   Cat. No. 11358Z   **Schedule SE (Form 1040) 2014**

Attachment Sequence No. **17**

Name of person with **self-employment** income (as shown on Form 1040 or Form 1040NR)	Social security number of person with **self-employment** income ▶

Section B—Long Schedule SE

Part I Self-Employment Tax

Note. If your only income subject to self-employment tax is **church employee income,** see instructions. Also see instructions for the definition of church employee income.

A If you are a minister, member of a religious order, or Christian Science practitioner **and** you filed Form 4361, but you had $400 or more of **other** net earnings from self-employment, check here and continue with Part I . . . . ▶ ☐

1a Net farm profit or (loss) from Schedule F, line 34, and farm partnerships, Schedule K-1 (Form 1065), box 14, code A. **Note.** Skip lines 1a and 1b if you use the farm optional method (see instructions) | **1a** | |

b If you received social security retirement or disability benefits, enter the amount of Conservation Reserve Program payments included on Schedule F, line 4b, or listed on Schedule K-1 (Form 1065), box 20, code Z | **1b** (|) |

2 Net profit or (loss) from Schedule C, line 31; Schedule C-EZ, line 3; Schedule K-1 (Form 1065), box 14, code A (other than farming); and Schedule K-1 (Form 1065-B), box 9, code J1. Ministers and members of religious orders, see instructions for types of income to report on this line. See instructions for other income to report. **Note.** Skip this line if you use the nonfarm optional method (see instructions) . . . . | **2** | |

3 Combine lines 1a, 1b, and 2 . . . . | **3** | |

4a If line 3 is more than zero, multiply line 3 by 92.35% (.9235). Otherwise, enter amount from line 3 | **4a** | |
Note. If line 4a is less than $400 due to Conservation Reserve Program payments on line 1b, see instructions.

b If you elect one or both of the optional methods, enter the total of lines 15 and 17 here . . | **4b** | |

c Combine lines 4a and 4b. If less than $400, **stop;** you do not owe self-employment tax. **Exception.** If less than $400 and you had **church employee income,** enter -0- and continue ▶ | **4c** | |

5a Enter your **church employee income** from Form W-2. See instructions for definition of church employee income . . . | **5a** | |

b Multiply line 5a by 92.35% (.9235). If less than $100, enter -0- . . . . | **5b** | |

6 Add lines 4c and 5b . . . . | **6** | |

7 Maximum amount of combined wages and self-employment earnings subject to social security tax or the 6.2% portion of the 7.65% railroad retirement (tier 1) tax for 2014 . . . . . | **7** | 117,000 | 00 |

8a Total social security wages and tips (total of boxes 3 and 7 on Form(s) W-2) and railroad retirement (tier 1) compensation. If $117,000 or more, skip lines 8b through 10, and go to line 11 | **8a** | |

b Unreported tips subject to social security tax (from Form 4137, line 10) | **8b** | |

c Wages subject to social security tax (from Form 8919, line 10) | **8c** | |

d Add lines 8a, 8b, and 8c . . . . | **8d** | |

9 Subtract line 8d from line 7. If zero or less, enter -0- here and on line 10 and go to line 11 . ▶ | **9** | |

10 Multiply the **smaller** of line 6 or line 9 by 12.4% (.124) . . . . | **10** | |

11 Multiply line 6 by 2.9% (.029) . . . . | **11** | |

12 **Self-employment tax.** Add lines 10 and 11. Enter here and on **Form 1040, line 57,** or **Form 1040NR, line 55** | **12** | |

13 **Deduction for one-half of self-employment tax.** Multiply line 12 by 50% (.50). Enter the result here and on **Form 1040, line 27,** or **Form 1040NR, line 27** . . . . . | **13** | |

Part II Optional Methods To Figure Net Earnings (see instructions)

Farm Optional Method. You may use this method **only** if **(a)** your gross farm income[1] was not more than $7,200, **or (b)** your net farm profits[2] were less than $5,198.

14 Maximum income for optional methods . . . . | **14** | 4,800 | 00 |

15 Enter the **smaller** of: two-thirds (2/3) of gross farm income[1] (not less than zero) or $4,800. Also include this amount on line 4b above . . . . | **15** | |

Nonfarm Optional Method. You may use this method **only** if **(a)** your net nonfarm profits[3] were less than $5,198 and also less than 72.189% of your gross nonfarm income,[4] **and (b)** you had net earnings from self-employment of at least $400 in 2 of the prior 3 years. **Caution.** You may use this method no more than five times.

16 Subtract line 15 from line 14 . . . . | **16** | |

17 Enter the **smaller** of: two-thirds (2/3) of gross nonfarm income[4] (not less than zero) **or** the amount on line 16. Also include this amount on line 4b above . . . . | **17** | |

[1] From Sch. F, line 9, and Sch. K-1 (Form 1065), box 14, code B.
[2] From Sch. F, line 34, and Sch. K-1 (Form 1065), box 14, code A—minus the amount you would have entered on line 1b had you not used the optional method.
[3] From Sch. C, line 31; Sch. C-EZ, line 3; Sch. K-1 (Form 1065), box 14, code A; and Sch. K-1 (Form 1065-B), box 9, code J1.
[4] From Sch. C, line 7; Sch. C-EZ, line 1; Sch. K-1 (Form 1065), box 14, code C; and Sch. K-1 (Form 1065-B), box 9, code J2.

§ 2.1480 Filled-In Form 2106

Form **2106**	**Employee Business Expenses**	OMB No. 1545-0074

Department of the Treasury
Internal Revenue Service (99)

▶ **Attach to Form 1040 or Form 1040NR.**
▶ **Information about Form 2106 and its separate instructions is available at** *www.irs.gov/form2106.*

20**14**

Attachment
Sequence No. **129**

Your name	Occupation in which you incurred expenses	Social security number
Tom E. Dodd	Executive	123 : 45 : 6789

Part I **Employee Business Expenses and Reimbursements**

Step 1 Enter Your Expenses

		Column A Other Than Meals and Entertainment	Column B Meals and Entertainment
1	Vehicle expense from line 22 or line 29. (Rural mail carriers: See instructions.) **1**		
2	Parking fees, tolls, and transportation, including train, bus, etc., that **did not** involve overnight travel or commuting to and from work . **2**		
3	Travel expense while away from home overnight, including lodging, airplane, car rental, etc. **Do not** include meals and entertainment . **3**		
4	Business expenses not included on lines 1 through 3. **Do not** include meals and entertainment **4**	1,350	
5	Meals and entertainment expenses (see instructions) **5**		
6	**Total expenses.** In Column A, add lines 1 through 4 and enter the result. In Column B, enter the amount from line 5 . . . . . **6**	1,350	

Note. *If you were not reimbursed for any expenses in Step 1, skip line 7 and enter the amount from line 6 on line 8.*

Step 2 Enter Reimbursements Received From Your Employer for Expenses Listed in Step 1

7	Enter reimbursements received from your employer that were **not** reported to you in box 1 of Form W-2. Include any reimbursements reported under code "L" in box 12 of your Form W-2 (see instructions). **7**		

Step 3 Figure Expenses To Deduct on Schedule A (Form 1040 or Form 1040NR)

8	Subtract line 7 from line 6. If zero or less, enter -0-. However, if line 7 is greater than line 6 in Column A, report the excess as income on Form 1040, line 7 (or on Form 1040NR, line 8) **8**	1,350	

Note. *If both columns of line 8 are zero, you cannot deduct employee business expenses. Stop here and attach Form 2106 to your return.*

9	In Column A, enter the amount from line 8. In Column B, multiply line 8 by 50% (.50). (Employees subject to Department of Transportation (DOT) hours of service limits: Multiply meal expenses incurred while away from home on business by 80% (.80) instead of 50%. For details, see instructions.) **9**	1,350	
10	Add the amounts on line 9 of both columns and enter the total here. **Also, enter the total on Schedule A (Form 1040), line 21** (or on **Schedule A (Form 1040NR), line 7**). (Armed Forces reservists, qualified performing artists, fee-basis state or local government officials, and individuals with disabilities: See the instructions for special rules on where to enter the total.) . . . . . ▶ **10**		1,350

For Paperwork Reduction Act Notice, see your tax return instructions.   Cat. No. 11700N   Form **2106** (2014)

Part II　Vehicle Expenses

Section A—General Information (You must complete this section if you are claiming vehicle expenses.)

			(a) Vehicle 1	(b) Vehicle 2
11	Enter the date the vehicle was placed in service	11	/ /	/ /
12	Total miles the vehicle was driven during 2014	12	miles	miles
13	Business miles included on line 12	13	miles	miles
14	Percent of business use. Divide line 13 by line 12	14	%	%
15	Average daily roundtrip commuting distance	15	miles	miles
16	Commuting miles included on line 12	16	miles	miles
17	Other miles. Add lines 13 and 16 and subtract the total from line 12	17	miles	miles
18	Was your vehicle available for personal use during off-duty hours?		☐ Yes	☐ No
19	Do you (or your spouse) have another vehicle available for personal use?		☐ Yes	☐ No
20	Do you have evidence to support your deduction?		☐ Yes	☐ No
21	If "Yes," is the evidence written?		☐ Yes	☐ No

Section B—Standard Mileage Rate (See the instructions for Part II to find out whether to complete this section or Section C.)

22	Multiply line 13 by 56¢ (.56). Enter the result here and on line 1	22	

Section C—Actual Expenses

			(a) Vehicle 1		(b) Vehicle 2	
23	Gasoline, oil, repairs, vehicle insurance, etc.	23				
24a	Vehicle rentals	24a				
b	Inclusion amount (see instructions)	24b				
c	Subtract line 24b from line 24a	24c				
25	Value of employer-provided vehicle (applies only if 100% of annual lease value was included on Form W-2—see instructions)	25				
26	Add lines 23, 24c, and 25	26				
27	Multiply line 26 by the percentage on line 14	27				
28	Depreciation (see instructions)	28				
29	Add lines 27 and 28. Enter total here and on line 1	29				

Section D—Depreciation of Vehicles (Use this section only if you owned the vehicle and are completing Section C for the vehicle.)

			(a) Vehicle 1		(b) Vehicle 2	
30	Enter cost or other basis (see instructions)	30				
31	Enter section 179 deduction (see instructions)	31				
32	Multiply line 30 by line 14 (see instructions if you claimed the section 179 deduction)	32				
33	Enter depreciation method and percentage (see instructions)	33				
34	Multiply line 32 by the percentage on line 33 (see instructions)	34				
35	Add lines 31 and 34	35				
36	Enter the applicable limit explained in the line 36 instructions	36				
37	Multiply line 36 by the percentage on line 14	37				
38	Enter the **smaller** of line 35 or line 37. If you skipped lines 36 and 37, enter the amount from line 35. Also enter this amount on line 28 above	38				

§ 2.1520 Filled-In Form 2441

Form **2441**	**Child and Dependent Care Expenses**			OMB No. 1545-0074

Department of the Treasury
Internal Revenue Service (99)

► Attach to Form 1040, Form 1040A, or Form 1040NR.

► Information about Form 2441 and its separate instructions is at *www.irs.gov/form2441.*

1040
1040A
1040NR

2441

2014

Attachment Sequence No. **21**

Name(s) shown on return

Tom E. and Mary A. Dodd

Your social security number

123-45-6789

Part I **Persons or Organizations Who Provided the Care**—You **must** complete this part.
(If you have more than two care providers, see the instructions.)

1	(a) Care provider's name	(b) Address (number, street, apt. no., city, state, and ZIP code)	(c) Identifying number (SSN or EIN)	(d) Amount paid (see instructions)
	ABC Care	3 East 4th Street Pleasanttown, NY 01234	01-3335555	4,700

Did you receive **dependent care benefits?**

No ——► Complete only Part II below.

Yes ——► Complete Part III on the back next.

Caution. If the care was provided in your home, you may owe employment taxes. If you do, you cannot file Form 1040A. For details, see the instructions for Form 1040, line 60a, or Form 1040NR, line 59a.

Part II **Credit for Child and Dependent Care Expenses**

2 Information about your **qualifying person(s).** If you have more than two qualifying persons, see the instructions.

(a) Qualifying person's name		(b) Qualifying person's social security number	(c) **Qualified expenses** you incurred and paid in 2014 for the person listed in column (a)
First	Last		
John	Dodd	444-44-4444	4,700

3	Add the amounts in column (c) of line 2. **Do not** enter more than $3,000 for one qualifying person or $6,000 for two or more persons. If you completed Part III, enter the amount from line 31	**3**	3,000
4	Enter your **earned income.** See instructions	**4**	78,524
5	If married filing jointly, enter your spouse's earned income (if you or your spouse was a student or was disabled, see the instructions); **all others,** enter the amount from line 4 .	**5**	8,320
6	Enter the **smallest** of line 3, 4, or 5	**6**	3,000
7	Enter the amount from Form 1040, line 38; Form 1040A, line 22; or Form 1040NR, line 37. . . . . . **7**	109,298		

8 Enter on line 8 the decimal amount shown below that applies to the amount on line 7

If line 7 is:				If line 7 is:		
Over	But not over	Decimal amount is		Over	But not over	Decimal amount is
$0—15,000		.35		$29,000—31,000		.27
15,000—17,000		.34		31,000—33,000		.26
17,000—19,000		.33		33,000—35,000		.25
19,000—21,000		.32		35,000—37,000		.24
21,000—23,000		.31		37,000—39,000		.23
23,000—25,000		.30		39,000—41,000		.22
25,000—27,000		.29		41,000—43,000		.21
27,000—29,000		.28		43,000—No limit		.20

8	X . 20

9	Multiply line 6 by the decimal amount on line 8. If you paid 2013 expenses in 2014, see the instructions	**9**	600
10	Tax liability limit. Enter the amount from the Credit Limit Worksheet in the instructions. **10**	4,061	
11	**Credit for child and dependent care expenses.** Enter the **smaller** of line 9 or line 10 here and on Form 1040, line 49; Form 1040A, line 31; or Form 1040NR, line 47	**11**	600

For Paperwork Reduction Act Notice, see your tax return instructions. Cat. No. 11862M Form **2441** (2014)

Form **4562**	**Depreciation and Amortization**	OMB No. 1545-0172
	(Including Information on Listed Property)	**2014**
Department of the Treasury Internal Revenue Service (99)	▶ Attach to your tax return. ▶ Information about Form 4562 and its separate instructions is at *www.irs.gov/form4562.*	Attachment Sequence No. **179**

Name(s) shown on return	Business or activity to which this form relates	Identifying number
Tom E. Dodd	Schedule C - Tax Preparation Services	123-45-678

Part I **Election To Expense Certain Property Under Section 179**

Note: *If you have any listed property, complete Part V before you complete Part I.*

1	Maximum amount (see instructions)	**1**	500,000
2	Total cost of section 179 property placed in service (see instructions)	**2**	2,500
3	Threshold cost of section 179 property before reduction in limitation (see instructions)	**3**	2,000,000
4	Reduction in limitation. Subtract line 3 from line 2. If zero or less, enter -0-	**4**	0
5	Dollar limitation for tax year. Subtract line 4 from line 1. If zero or less, enter -0-. If married filing separately, see instructions	**5**	500,000

6	(a) Description of property	(b) Cost (business use only)	(c) Elected cost		

7	Listed property. Enter the amount from line 29 . . . . **7** 2,500		
8	Total elected cost of section 179 property. Add amounts in column (c), lines 6 and 7	**8**	2,500
9	Tentative deduction. Enter the **smaller** of line 5 or line 8	**9**	2,500
10	Carryover of disallowed deduction from line 13 of your 2013 Form 4562	**10**	0
11	Business income limitation. Enter the smaller of business income (not less than zero) or line 5 (see instructions)	**11**	2,500
12	Section 179 expense deduction. Add lines 9 and 10, but do not enter more than line 11	**12**	2,500
13	Carryover of disallowed deduction to 2015. Add lines 9 and 10, less line 12 ▶ **13**		

Note: *Do not use Part II or Part III below for listed property. Instead, use Part V.*

Part II **Special Depreciation Allowance and Other Depreciation (Do not** include listed property.) (See instructions.)

14	Special depreciation allowance for qualified property (other than listed property) placed in service during the tax year (see instructions)	**14**	1,800
15	Property subject to section 168(f)(1) election	**15**	
16	Other depreciation (including ACRS)	**16**	160

Part III **MACRS Depreciation (Do not include listed property.) (See instructions.)**

Section A

17	MACRS deductions for assets placed in service in tax years beginning before 2014	**17**	1,050
18	If you are electing to group any assets placed in service during the tax year into one or more general asset accounts, check here . . . . ▶ ☐		

Section B—Assets Placed in Service During 2014 Tax Year Using the General Depreciation System

(a) Classification of property	(b) Month and year placed in service	(c) Basis for depreciation (business/investment use only—see instructions)	(d) Recovery period	(e) Convention	(f) Method	(g) Depreciation deduction
19a 3-year property						
b 5-year property						
c 7-year property						
d 10-year property						
e 15-year property						
f 20-year property						
g 25-year property			25 yrs.		S/L	
h Residential rental property			27.5 yrs.	MM	S/L	
			27.5 yrs.	MM	S/L	
i Nonresidential real property	1-2014	8,900	39 yrs.	MM	S/L	194
				MM	S/L	

Section C—Assets Placed in Service During 2014 Tax Year Using the Alternative Depreciation System

20a Class life					S/L	
b 12-year			12 yrs.		S/L	
c 40-year			40 yrs.	MM	S/L	

Part IV **Summary** (See instructions.)

21	Listed property. Enter amount from line 28	**21**	
22	**Total.** Add amounts from line 12, lines 14 through 17, lines 19 and 20 in column (g), and line 21. Enter here and on the appropriate lines of your return. Partnerships and S corporations—see instructions .	**22**	3,744
23	For assets shown above and placed in service during the current year, enter the portion of the basis attributable to section 263A costs **23**		

For Paperwork Reduction Act Notice, see separate instructions.   Cat. No. 12906N   Form **4562** (2014)

Part V **Listed Property** (Include automobiles, certain other vehicles, certain aircraft, certain computers, and property used for entertainment, recreation, or amusement.)

Note: *For any vehicle for which you are using the standard mileage rate or deducting lease expense, complete **only** 24a, 24b, columns (a) through (c) of Section A, all of Section B, and Section C if applicable.*

Section A—Depreciation and Other Information (Caution: *See the instructions for limits for passenger automobiles.*)

24a Do you have evidence to support the business/investment use claimed? ☑ **Yes** ☐ **No**   **24b** If "Yes," is the evidence written? ☑ **Yes** ☐ **No**

(a) Type of property (list vehicles first)	(b) Date placed in service	(c) Business/ investment use percentage	(d) Cost or other basis	(e) Basis for depreciation (business/investment use only)	(f) Recovery period	(g) Method/ Convention	(h) Depreciation deduction	(i) Elected section 179 cost
25 Special depreciation allowance for qualified listed property placed in service during the tax year and used more than 50% in a qualified business use (see instructions) .					**25**			
26 Property used more than 50% in a qualified business use:								
Computer	6-5-2014	100 %	2,500	2,500				2,500
		%						
		%						
27 Property used 50% or less in a qualified business use:								
		%				S/L –		
		%				S/L –		
		%				S/L –		
28 Add amounts in column (h), lines 25 through 27. Enter here and on line 21, page 1 .					**28**			
29 Add amounts in column (i), line 26. Enter here and on line 7, page 1							**29**	2,500

Section B—Information on Use of Vehicles

Complete this section for vehicles used by a sole proprietor, partner, or other "more than 5% owner," or related person. If you provided vehicles to your employees, first answer the questions in Section C to see if you meet an exception to completing this section for those vehicles.

	(a) Vehicle 1		(b) Vehicle 2		(c) Vehicle 3		(d) Vehicle 4		(e) Vehicle 5		(f) Vehicle 6	
30 Total business/investment miles driven during the year (**do not** include commuting miles) .												
31 Total commuting miles driven during the year												
32 Total other personal (noncommuting) miles driven												
33 Total miles driven during the year. Add lines 30 through 32												
34 Was the vehicle available for personal use during off-duty hours?	Yes	No	Yes	No	Yes	No	Yes	No	Yes	No	Yes	No
35 Was the vehicle used primarily by a more than 5% owner or related person? . .												
36 Is another vehicle available for personal use?												

Section C—Questions for Employers Who Provide Vehicles for Use by Their Employees

Answer these questions to determine if you meet an exception to completing Section B for vehicles used by employees who **are not** more than 5% owners or related persons (see instructions).

	Yes	No
37 Do you maintain a written policy statement that prohibits all personal use of vehicles, including commuting, by your employees?		
38 Do you maintain a written policy statement that prohibits personal use of vehicles, except commuting, by your employees? See the instructions for vehicles used by corporate officers, directors, or 1% or more owners . .		
39 Do you treat all use of vehicles by employees as personal use?		
40 Do you provide more than five vehicles to your employees, obtain information from your employees about the use of the vehicles, and retain the information received?		
41 Do you meet the requirements concerning qualified automobile demonstration use? (See instructions.) . . .		

Note: *If your answer to 37, 38, 39, 40, or 41 is "Yes," do not complete Section B for the covered vehicles.*

Part VI **Amortization**

(a) Description of costs	(b) Date amortization begins	(c) Amortizable amount	(d) Code section	(e) Amortization period or percentage	(f) Amortization for this year
42 Amortization of costs that begins during your 2014 tax year (see instructions):					
43 Amortization of costs that began before your 2014 tax year				**43**	
44 **Total.** Add amounts in column (f). See the instructions for where to report				**44**	

§ 2.1560 Filled-In Form 4684

Form 4684

Department of the Treasury
Internal Revenue Service

Casualties and Thefts

▶ Information about Form 4684 and its separate instructions is at *www.irs.gov/form4684*.
▶ Attach to your tax return.
▶ Use a separate Form 4684 for each casualty or theft.

OMB No. 1545-0177

2014

Attachment
Sequence No. **26**

Name(s) shown on tax return	Identifying number
Tom E. Dodd	123-45-6789

SECTION A—Personal Use Property (Use this section to report casualties and thefts of property **not** used in a trade or business or for income-producing purposes.)

1 Description of properties (show type, location, and date acquired for each property). Use a separate line for each property lost or damaged from the same casualty or theft.

Property **A** Pleasure boat

Property **B**

Property **C**

Property **D**

		Properties			
		A	**B**	**C**	**D**
2 Cost or other basis of each property	**2**	9,000			
3 Insurance or other reimbursement (whether or not you filed a claim) (see instructions)	**3**	0			
Note: *If line 2 is more than line 3, skip line 4.*					
4 Gain from casualty or theft. If line 3 is **more** than line 2, enter the difference here and skip lines 5 through 9 for that column. See instructions if line 3 includes insurance or other reimbursement you did not claim, or you received payment for your loss in a later tax year	**4**				
5 Fair market value **before** casualty or theft	**5**	6,500			
6 Fair market value **after** casualty or theft	**6**	0			
7 Subtract line 6 from line 5	**7**	6,500			
8 Enter the **smaller** of line 2 or line 7	**8**	6,500			
9 Subtract line 3 from line 8. If zero or less, enter -0-	**9**	6,500			

10 Casualty or theft loss. Add the amounts on line 9 in columns A through D	**10**	6,500
11 Enter the **smaller** of line 10 or $100	**11**	100
12 Subtract line 11 from line 10	**12**	6,400
Caution: *Use only one Form 4684 for lines 13 through 18.*		
13 Add the amounts on line 12 of all Forms 4684	**13**	6,400
14 Add the amounts on line 4 of all Forms 4684	**14**	0
15 • If line 14 is **more** than line 13, enter the difference here and on Schedule D. **Do not** complete the rest of this section (see instructions). • If line 14 is **less** than line 13, enter -0- here and go to line 16. • If line 14 is **equal** to line 13, enter -0- here. **Do not** complete the rest of this section.	**15**	0
16 If line 14 is **less** than line 13, enter the difference	**16**	6,400
17 Enter 10% of your adjusted gross income from Form 1040, line 38, or Form 1040NR, line 37. Estates and trusts, see instructions	**17**	10,930
18 Subtract line 17 from line 16. If zero or less, enter -0-. Also enter the result on Schedule A (Form 1040), line 20, or Form 1040NR, Schedule A, line 6. Estates and trusts, enter the result on the "Other deductions" line of your tax return	**18**	0

For Paperwork Reduction Act Notice, see instructions.   Cat. No. 12997O   Form **4684** (2014)

§ 2.1580 Filled-In Form 4797

Form **4797**	**Sales of Business Property**	OMB No. 1545-0184

Form **4797**

Sales of Business Property
(Also Involuntary Conversions and Recapture Amounts
Under Sections 179 and 280F(b)(2))
▶ Attach to your tax return.
▶ Information about Form 4797 and its separate instructions is at *www.irs.gov/form4797.*

OMB No. 1545-0184

2014

Department of the Treasury
Internal Revenue Service

Attachment
Sequence No. **27**

Name(s) shown on return	Identifying number
Tom E. and Mary A. Dodd	123-45-6789

1 Enter the gross proceeds from sales or exchanges reported to you for 2014 on Form(s) 1099-B or 1099-S (or substitute statement) that you are including on line 2, 10, or 20 (see instructions) . . . . | **1** |

Part I **Sales or Exchanges of Property Used in a Trade or Business and Involuntary Conversions From Other Than Casualty or Theft—Most Property Held More Than 1 Year** (see instructions)

2	**(a)** Description of property	**(b)** Date acquired (mo., day, yr.)	**(c)** Date sold (mo., day, yr.)	**(d)** Gross sales price	**(e)** Depreciation allowed or allowable since acquisition	**(f)** Cost or other basis, plus improvements and expense of sale	**(g)** Gain or (loss) Subtract (f) from the sum of (d) and (e)
From Schedule K-1,						450	450
Form 1120S							

3	Gain, if any, from Form 4684, line 39	**3**	
4	Section 1231 gain from installment sales from Form 6252, line 26 or 37	**4**	
5	Section 1231 gain or (loss) from like-kind exchanges from Form 8824	**5**	
6	Gain, if any, from line 32, from other than casualty or theft	**6**	29,865
7	Combine lines 2 through 6. Enter the gain or (loss) here and on the appropriate line as follows:	**7**	30,315

Partnerships (except electing large partnerships) and S corporations. Report the gain or (loss) following the instructions for Form 1065, Schedule K, line 10, or Form 1120S, Schedule K, line 9. Skip lines 8, 9, 11, and 12 below.

Individuals, partners, S corporation shareholders, and all others. If line 7 is zero or a loss, enter the amount from line 7 on line 11 below and skip lines 8 and 9. If line 7 is a gain and you did not have any prior year section 1231 losses, or they were recaptured in an earlier year, enter the gain from line 7 as a long-term capital gain on the Schedule D filed with your return and skip lines 8, 9, 11, and 12 below.

8	Nonrecaptured net section 1231 losses from prior years (see instructions)	**8**	
9	Subtract line 8 from line 7. If zero or less, enter -0-. If line 9 is zero, enter the gain from line 7 on line 11 below. If line 9 is more than zero, enter the amount from line 8 on line 12 below and enter the gain from line 9 as a long-term capital gain on the Schedule D filed with your return (see instructions)	**9**	30,315

Part II **Ordinary Gains and Losses** (see instructions)

10	Ordinary gains and losses not included on lines 11 through 16 (include property held 1 year or less):

11	Loss, if any, from line 7	**11**	( )
12	Gain, if any, from line 7 or amount from line 8, if applicable	**12**	
13	Gain, if any, from line 31	**13**	8,175
14	Net gain or (loss) from Form 4684, lines 31 and 38a	**14**	
15	Ordinary gain from installment sales from Form 6252, line 25 or 36	**15**	
16	Ordinary gain or (loss) from like-kind exchanges from Form 8824	**16**	
17	Combine lines 10 through 16	**17**	8,175

18 For all except individual returns, enter the amount from line 17 on the appropriate line of your return and skip lines a and b below. For individual returns, complete lines a and b below:

a If the loss on line 11 includes a loss from Form 4684, line 35, column (b)(ii), enter that part of the loss here. Enter the part of the loss from income-producing property on Schedule A (Form 1040), line 28, and the part of the loss from property used as an employee on Schedule A (Form 1040), line 23. Identify as from "Form 4797, line 18a." See instructions . . | **18a** | |

b Redetermine the gain or (loss) on line 17 excluding the loss, if any, on line 18a. Enter here and on Form 1040, line 14 | **18b** | 8,175 |

For Paperwork Reduction Act Notice, see separate instructions.	Cat. No. 13086I	Form **4797** (2014)

Part III   Gain From Disposition of Property Under Sections 1245, 1250, 1252, 1254, and 1255
(see instructions)

19	(a) Description of section 1245, 1250, 1252, 1254, or 1255 property:		(b) Date acquired (mo., day, yr.)	(c) Date sold (mo., day, yr.)
A	Lease and well equipment		6-1-2010	8-15-2014
B	Lease and well equipment		2-15-2010	7-15-2014
C	Office building		2-15-2001	6-2-2014
D				

	These columns relate to the properties on lines 19A through 19D. ▶		Property A	Property B	Property C	Property D
20	Gross sales price (**Note:** *See line 1 before completing.*)	20	7,500	6,000	125,000	
21	Cost or other basis plus expense of sale	21	10,000	4,500	150,000	
22	Depreciation (or depletion) allowed or allowable	22	7,120	3,555	53,365	
23	Adjusted basis. Subtract line 22 from line 21	23	2,880	945	96,635	
24	Total gain. Subtract line 23 from line 20	24	4,620	5,055	28,365	
25	**If section 1245 property:**					
a	Depreciation allowed or allowable from line 22	25a	7,120	3,555		
b	Enter the **smaller** of line 24 or 25a	25b	4,620	3,555		
26	**If section 1250 property:** If straight line depreciation was used, enter -0- on line 26g, except for a corporation subject to section 291.					
a	Additional depreciation after 1975 (see instructions)	26a				
b	Applicable percentage multiplied by the **smaller** of line 24 or line 26a (see instructions)	26b				
c	Subtract line 26a from line 24. If residential rental property **or** line 24 is not more than line 26a, skip lines 26d and 26e	26c				
d	Additional depreciation after 1969 and before 1976	26d				
e	Enter the **smaller** of line 26c or 26d	26e				
f	Section 291 amount (corporations only)	26f				
g	Add lines 26b, 26e, and 26f	26g			0	
27	**If section 1252 property:** Skip this section if you did not dispose of farmland or if this form is being completed for a partnership (other than an electing large partnership).					
a	Soil, water, and land clearing expenses	27a				
b	Line 27a multiplied by applicable percentage (see instructions)	27b				
c	Enter the **smaller** of line 24 or 27b	27c				
28	**If section 1254 property:**					
a	Intangible drilling and development costs, expenditures for development of mines and other natural deposits, mining exploration costs, and depletion (see instructions)	28a				
b	Enter the **smaller** of line 24 or 28a	28b				
29	**If section 1255 property:**					
a	Applicable percentage of payments excluded from income under section 126 (see instructions)	29a				
b	Enter the **smaller** of line 24 or 29a (see instructions)	29b				

Summary of Part III Gains. Complete property columns A through D through line 29b before going to line 30.

30	Total gains for all properties. Add property columns A through D, line 24	30	38,040
31	Add property columns A through D, lines 25b, 26g, 27c, 28b, and 29b. Enter here and on line 13	31	8,175
32	Subtract line 31 from line 30. Enter the portion from casualty or theft on Form 4684, line 33. Enter the portion from other than casualty or theft on Form 4797, line 6	32	29,865

Part IV   Recapture Amounts Under Sections 179 and 280F(b)(2) When Business Use Drops to 50% or Less
(see instructions)

			(a) Section 179	(b) Section 280F(b)(2)
33	Section 179 expense deduction or depreciation allowable in prior years	33		
34	Recomputed depreciation (see instructions)	34		
35	Recapture amount. Subtract line 34 from line 33. See the instructions for where to report	35		

§ 2.1620 Filled-In Form 6251

Form 6251

Department of the Treasury
Internal Revenue Service (99)

Alternative Minimum Tax—Individuals

▶ Information about Form 6251 and its separate instructions is at *www.irs.gov/form6251*.
▶ Attach to Form 1040 or Form 1040NR.

OMB No. 1545-0074

2014

Attachment
Sequence No. **32**

Name(s) shown on Form 1040 or Form 1040NR

Tom E. and Mary A. Dodd

Your social security number

123-45-6789

Part I — Alternative Minimum Taxable Income (See instructions for how to complete each line.)

1	If filing Schedule A (Form 1040), enter the amount from Form 1040, line 41, and go to line 2. Otherwise, enter the amount from Form 1040, line 38, and go to line 7. (If less than zero, enter as a negative amount.) **1**	80,350
2	Medical and dental. If you or your spouse was 65 or older, enter the **smaller** of Schedule A (Form 1040), line 4, **or** 2.5% (.025) of Form 1040, line 38. If zero or less, enter -0- **2**	0
3	Taxes from Schedule A (Form 1040), line 9 . . . . **3**	5,383
4	Enter the home mortgage interest adjustment, if any, from line 6 of the worksheet in the instructions for this line **4**	0
5	Miscellaneous deductions from Schedule A (Form 1040), line 27 . . . . **5**	0
6	If Form 1040, line 38, is $152,525 or less, enter -0-. Otherwise, see instructions **6**	(0)
7	Tax refund from Form 1040, line 10 or line 21 . . . . **7**	(275)
8	Investment interest expense (difference between regular tax and AMT) **8**	
9	Depletion (difference between regular tax and AMT) **9**	
10	Net operating loss deduction from Form 1040, line 21. Enter as a positive amount . . . **10**	
11	Alternative tax net operating loss deduction **11**	(0)
12	Interest from specified private activity bonds exempt from the regular tax **12**	2,000
13	Qualified small business stock (7% of gain excluded under section 1202) **13**	
14	Exercise of incentive stock options (excess of AMT income over regular tax income) . . . **14**	2,000
15	Estates and trusts (amount from Schedule K-1 (Form 1041), box 12, code A) **15**	
16	Electing large partnerships (amount from Schedule K-1 (Form 1065-B), box 6) **16**	
17	Disposition of property (difference between AMT and regular tax gain or loss) **17**	
18	Depreciation on assets placed in service after 1986 (difference between regular tax and AMT) **18**	1,750
19	Passive activities (difference between AMT and regular tax income or loss) **19**	
20	Loss limitations (difference between AMT and regular tax income or loss) **20**	
21	Circulation costs (difference between regular tax and AMT) **21**	
22	Long-term contracts (difference between AMT and regular tax income) **22**	
23	Mining costs (difference between regular tax and AMT) **23**	
24	Research and experimental costs (difference between regular tax and AMT) **24**	
25	Income from certain installment sales before January 1, 1987 . . . . **25**	( )
26	Intangible drilling costs preference **26**	
27	Other adjustments, including income-based related adjustments **27**	750
28	**Alternative minimum taxable income.** Combine lines 1 through 27. (If married filing separately and line 28 is more than $242,450, see instructions.) **28**	91,958

Part II — Alternative Minimum Tax (AMT)

29 Exemption. (If you were under age 24 at the end of 2014, see instructions.)

IF your filing status is . . .	AND line 28 is not over . . .	THEN enter on line 29 . . .		
Single or head of household	$117,300	$52,800		
Married filing jointly or qualifying widow(er)	156,500	82,100		
Married filing separately	78,250	41,050	**29**	82,100
If line 28 is **over** the amount shown above for your filing status, see instructions.				

30	Subtract line 29 from line 28. If more than zero, go to line 31. If zero or less, enter -0- here and on lines 31, 33, and 35, and go to line 34 . . . . **30**		9,858
31	• If you are filing Form 2555 or 2555-EZ, see instructions for the amount to enter. • If you reported capital gain distributions directly on Form 1040, line 13; you reported qualified dividends on Form 1040, line 9b; **or** you had a gain on both lines 15 and 16 of Schedule D (Form 1040) (as refigured for the AMT, if necessary), complete Part III on the back and enter the amount from line 64 here. • **All others:** If line 30 is $182,500 or less ($91,250 or less if married filing separately), multiply line 30 by 26% (.26). Otherwise, multiply line 30 by 28% (.28) and subtract $3,650 ($1,825 if married filing separately) from the result. **31**		0
32	Alternative minimum tax foreign tax credit (see instructions) **32**		0
33	Tentative minimum tax. Subtract line 32 from line 31 . . . . **33**		0
34	Add Form 1040, line 44 (minus any tax from Form 4972), and Form 1040, line 46. Subtract from the result any foreign tax credit from Form 1040, line 48. If you used Schedule J to figure your tax on Form 1040, line 44, refigure that tax without using Schedule J before completing this line (see instructions) **34**		3,911
35	**AMT.** Subtract line 34 from line 33. If zero or less, enter -0-. Enter here and on Form 1040, line 45 . . . . **35**		0

For Paperwork Reduction Act Notice, see your tax return instructions.   Cat. No. 13600G   Form **6251** (2014)

Part III Tax Computation Using Maximum Capital Gains Rates

Complete Part III only if you are required to do so by line 31 or by the Foreign Earned Income Tax Worksheet in the instructions.

36	Enter the amount from Form 6251, line 30. If you are filing Form 2555 or 2555-EZ, enter the amount from line 3 of the worksheet in the instructions for line 31	**36**	9,858
37	Enter the amount from line 6 of the Qualified Dividends and Capital Gain Tax Worksheet in the instructions for Form 1040, line 44, or the amount from line 13 of the Schedule D Tax Worksheet in the instructions for Schedule D (Form 1040), whichever applies (as refigured for the AMT, if necessary) (see instructions). If you are filing Form 2555 or 2555-EZ, see instructions for the amount to enter	**37**	28,465
38	Enter the amount from Schedule D (Form 1040), line 19 (as refigured for the AMT, if necessary) (see instructions). If you are filing Form 2555 or 2555-EZ, see instructions for the amount to enter	**38**	0
39	If you did not complete a Schedule D Tax Worksheet for the regular tax or the AMT, enter the amount from line 37. Otherwise, add lines 37 and 38, and enter the **smaller** of that result or the amount from line 10 of the Schedule D Tax Worksheet (as refigured for the AMT, if necessary). If you are filing Form 2555 or 2555-EZ, see instructions for the amount to enter	**39**	28,465
40	Enter the **smaller** of line 36 or line 39	**40**	9,858
41	Subtract line 40 from line 36	**41**	0
42	If line 41 is $182,500 or less ($91,250 or less if married filing separately), multiply line 41 by 26% (.26). Otherwise, multiply line 41 by 28% (.28) and subtract $3,650 ($1,825 if married filing separately) from the result . . . ▶	**42**	0
43	Enter: • $73,800 if married filing jointly or qualifying widow(er), • $36,900 if single or married filing separately, or • $49,400 if head of household.	**43**	73,800
44	Enter the amount from line 7 of the Qualified Dividends and Capital Gain Tax Worksheet in the instructions for Form 1040, line 44, or the amount from line 14 of the Schedule D Tax Worksheet in the instructions for Schedule D (Form 1040), whichever applies (as figured for the regular tax). If you did not complete either worksheet for the regular tax, enter the amount from Form 1040, line 43; if zero or less, enter -0-. If you are filing Form 2555 or 2555-EZ, see instructions for the amount to enter	**44**	32,135
45	Subtract line 44 from line 43. If zero or less, enter -0-	**45**	41,665
46	Enter the **smaller** of line 36 or line 37	**46**	9,858
47	Enter the **smaller** of line 45 or line 46. This amount is taxed at 0%	**47**	9,858
48	Subtract line 47 from line 46	**48**	0
49	Enter: • $406,750 if single • $228,800 if married filing separately • $457,600 if married filing jointly or qualifying widow(er) • $432,200 if head of household	**49**	457,600
50	Enter the amount from line 45	**50**	41,665
51	Enter the amount from line 7 of the Qualified Dividends and Capital Gain Tax Worksheet in the instructions for Form 1040, line 44, or the amount from line 19 of the Schedule D Tax Worksheet, whichever applies (as figured for the regular tax). If you did not complete either worksheet for the regular tax, enter the amount from Form 1040, line 43; if zero or less, enter -0-. If you are filing Form 2555 or Form 2555-EZ, see instructions for the amount to enter	**51**	32,135
52	Add line 50 and line 51	**52**	73,800
53	Subtract line 52 from line 49. If zero or less, enter -0-	**53**	383,800
54	Enter the smaller of line 48 or line 53	**54**	0
55	Multiply line 54 by 15% (.15) . . . . ▶	**55**	0
56	Add lines 47 and 54	**56**	9,858
	If lines 56 and 36 are the same, skip lines 57 through 61 and go to line 62. Otherwise, go to line 57.		
57	Subtract line 56 from line 46	**57**	
58	Multiply line 57 by 20% (.20) . . . . ▶	**58**	
	If line 38 is zero or blank, skip lines 59 through 61 and go to line 62. Otherwise, go to line 59.		
59	Add lines 41, 56, and 57	**59**	
60	Subtract line 59 from line 36	**60**	
61	Multiply line 60 by 25% (.25) . . . . ▶	**61**	
62	Add lines 42, 55, 58, and 61	**62**	0
63	If line 36 is $182,500 or less ($91,250 or less if married filing separately), multiply line 36 by 26% (.26). Otherwise, multiply line 36 by 28% (.28) and subtract $3,650 ($1,825 if married filing separately) from the result	**63**	2,563
64	Enter the **smaller** of line 62 or line 63 here and on line 31. If you are filing Form 2555 or 2555-EZ, do not enter this amount on line 31. Instead, enter it on line 4 of the worksheet in the instructions for line 31 . . .	**64**	0

§ 2.1700 Filled-In Form 8606

Form **8606**	**Nondeductible IRAs**	OMB No. 1545-0074

Department of the Treasury
Internal Revenue Service (99)

▶ Information about Form 8606 and its separate instructions is at *www.irs.gov/form8606.*
▶ Attach to Form 1040, Form 1040A, or Form 1040NR.

2014
Attachment
Sequence No. **48**

Name. If married, file a separate form for each spouse required to file Form 8606. See instructions.

Tom E. Dodd

Your social security number

123-45-6789

Fill in Your Address Only If You Are Filing This Form by Itself and Not With Your Tax Return ▶

Home address (number and street, or P.O. box if mail is not delivered to your home)

987 Main Street

Apt. no.

City, town or post office, state, and ZIP code. If you have a foreign address, also complete the spaces below.

Pleasanttown, NY 01234

Foreign country name	Foreign province/state/county	Foreign postal code

Part I **Nondeductible Contributions to Traditional IRAs and Distributions From Traditional, SEP, and SIMPLE IRAs**

Complete this part only if one or more of the following apply.

- You made nondeductible contributions to a traditional IRA for 2014.
- You took distributions from a traditional, SEP, or SIMPLE IRA in 2014 **and** you made nondeductible contributions to a traditional IRA in 2014 or an earlier year. For this purpose, a distribution does not include a rollover, one-time distribution to fund an HSA, conversion, recharacterization, or return of certain contributions.
- You converted part, but not all, of your traditional, SEP, and SIMPLE IRAs to Roth IRAs in 2014 (excluding any portion you recharacterized) **and** you made nondeductible contributions to a traditional IRA in 2014 or an earlier year.

1	Enter your nondeductible contributions to traditional IRAs for 2014, including those made for 2014 from January 1, 2015, through April 15, 2015 (see instructions)	**1**	1,000
2	Enter your total basis in traditional IRAs (see instructions)	**2**	0
3	Add lines 1 and 2	**3**	1,000

In 2014, did you take a distribution from traditional, SEP, or SIMPLE IRAs, or make a Roth IRA conversion? — **No** ▶ Enter the amount from line 3 on line 14. Do not complete the rest of Part I.
— **Yes** ▶ Go to line 4.

4	Enter those contributions included on line 1 that were made from January 1, 2015, through April 15, 2015	**4**	0
5	Subtract line 4 from line 3	**5**	1,000
6	Enter the value of **all** your traditional, SEP, and SIMPLE IRAs as of December 31, 2014, plus any outstanding rollovers (see instructions)	**6**	1,000
7	Enter your distributions from traditional, SEP, and SIMPLE IRAs in 2014. **Do not** include rollovers, a one-time distribution to fund an HSA, conversions to a Roth IRA, certain returned contributions, or recharacterizations of traditional IRA contributions (see instructions)	**7**	0
8	Enter the net amount you converted from traditional, SEP, and SIMPLE IRAs to Roth IRAs in 2014. **Do not** include amounts converted that you later recharacterized (see instructions). Also enter this amount on line 16	**8**	0
9	Add lines 6, 7, and 8	**9**	1,000
10	Divide line 5 by line 9. Enter the result as a decimal rounded to at least 3 places. If the result is 1.000 or more, enter "1.000"	**10**	× 1 . 00
11	Multiply line 8 by line 10. This is the nontaxable portion of the amount you converted to Roth IRAs. Also enter this amount on line 17	**11**	0
12	Multiply line 7 by line 10. This is the nontaxable portion of your distributions that you did not convert to a Roth IRA	**12**	0
13	Add lines 11 and 12. This is the nontaxable portion of all your distributions	**13**	0
14	Subtract line 13 from line 3. This is **your total basis in traditional IRAs for 2014 and earlier years**	**14**	1,000
15	**Taxable amount.** Subtract line 12 from line 7. If more than zero, also include this amount on Form 1040, line 15b; Form 1040A, line 11b; or Form 1040NR, line 16b	**15**	0

Note. You may be subject to an additional 10% tax on the amount on line 15 if you were under age 59½ at the time of the distribution (see instructions).

For Privacy Act and Paperwork Reduction Act Notice, see separate instructions.   Cat. No. 63966F   Form **8606** (2014)

§ 2.1705   Filled-In Form 8949

Form **8949**	**Sales and Other Dispositions of Capital Assets**	OMB No. 1545-0074

Department of the Treasury
Internal Revenue Service

▶ Information about Form 8949 and its separate instructions is at *www.irs.gov/form8949*.
▶ File with your Schedule D to list your transactions for lines 1b, 2, 3, 8b, 9, and 10 of Schedule D.

2014
Attachment
Sequence No. **12A**

Name(s) shown on return	Social security number or taxpayer identification number
Tom E. and Mary A. Dodd	123-45-6789

Before you check Box A, B, or C below, see whether you received any Form(s) 1099-B or substitute statement(s) from your broker. A substitute statement will have the same information as Form 1099-B. Either may show your basis (usually your cost) even if your broker did not report it to the IRS. Brokers must report basis to the IRS for most stock you bought in 2011 or later (and for certain debt instruments you bought in 2014 or later).

Part I   **Short-Term.** Transactions involving capital assets you held 1 year or less are short term. For long-term transactions, see page 2.

Note. You may aggregate all short-term transactions reported on Form(s) 1099-B showing basis was reported to the IRS and for which no adjustments or codes are required. Enter the total directly on Schedule D, line 1a; you are not required to report these transactions on Form 8949 (see instructions).

You *must* check Box A, B, *or* C below. Check only one box. If more than one box applies for your short-term transactions, complete a separate Form 8949, page 1, for each applicable box. If you have more short-term transactions than will fit on this page for one or more of the boxes, complete as many forms with the same box checked as you need.

- ☐ **(A)** Short-term transactions reported on Form(s) 1099-B showing basis was reported to the IRS (see **Note** above)
- ☑ **(B)** Short-term transactions reported on Form(s) 1099-B showing basis was **not** reported to the IRS
- ☐ **(C)** Short-term transactions not reported to you on Form 1099-B

1 (a) Description of property (Example: 100 sh. XYZ Co.)	(b) Date acquired (Mo., day, yr.)	(c) Date sold or disposed (Mo., day, yr.)	(d) Proceeds (sales price) (see instructions)	(e) Cost or other basis. See the **Note** below and see *Column (e)* in the separate instructions	(f) Code(s) from instructions	(g) Amount of adjustment	(h) Gain or (loss). Subtract column (e) from column (d) and combine the result with column (g)
300 shares MBI	2-15-2014	9-15-2014	4,000	3,250			750
Nonbusiness bad debt			0	4,000			(4,000)
2 Totals. Add the amounts in columns (d), (e), (g), and (h) (subtract negative amounts). Enter each total here and include on your Schedule D, **line 1b** (if **Box A** above is checked), **line 2** (if **Box B** above is checked), or **line 3** (if **Box C** above is checked) ▶			4,000	7,250			(3,250)

Note. If you checked Box A above but the basis reported to the IRS was incorrect, enter in column (e) the basis as reported to the IRS, and enter an adjustment in column (g) to correct the basis. See *Column (g)* in the separate instructions for how to figure the amount of the adjustment.

For Paperwork Reduction Act Notice, see your tax return instructions.   Cat. No. 37768Z   Form **8949** (2014)

Name(s) shown on return. Name and SSN or taxpayer identification no. not required if shown on other side	Social security number or taxpayer identification number
Tom E. and Mary A. Dodd	123-45-6789

Before you check Box D, E, or F below, see whether you received any Form(s) 1099-B or substitute statement(s) from your broker. A substitute statement will have the same information as Form 1099-B. Either may show your basis (usually your cost) even if your broker did not report it to the IRS. Brokers must report basis to the IRS for most stock you bought in 2011 or later (and for certain debt instruments you bought in 2014 or later).

Part II   **Long-Term.** Transactions involving capital assets you held more than 1 year are long term. For short-term transactions, see page 1.

Note. You may aggregate all long-term transactions reported on Form(s) 1099-B showing basis was reported to the IRS and for which no adjustments or codes are required. Enter the total directly on Schedule D, line 8a; you are not required to report these transactions on Form 8949 (see instructions).

You **must** check Box D, E, **or** F below. **Check only one box.** If more than one box applies for your long-term transactions, complete a separate Form 8949, page 2, for each applicable box. If you have more long-term transactions than will fit on this page for one or more of the boxes, complete as many forms with the same box checked as you need.

- ☐ **(D)** Long-term transactions reported on Form(s) 1099-B showing basis was reported to the IRS (see **Note** above)
- ☑ **(E)** Long-term transactions reported on Form(s) 1099-B showing basis was **not** reported to the IRS
- ☐ **(F)** Long-term transactions not reported to you on Form 1099-B

1 (a) Description of property (Example: 100 sh. XYZ Co.)	(b) Date acquired (Mo., day, yr.)	(c) Date sold or disposed (Mo., day, yr.)	(d) Proceeds (sales price) (see instructions)	(e) Cost or other basis. See the **Note** below and see *Column (e)* in the separate instructions	Adjustment, if any, to gain or loss. If you enter an amount in column (g), enter a code in column (f). See the separate instructions.		(h) Gain or (loss). Subtract column (e) from column (d) and combine the result with column (g)
					(f) Code(s) from instructions	(g) Amount of adjustment	
200 shares TA&T	8-15-2008	8-15-2014	1,080	600			
2 Totals. Add the amounts in columns (d), (e), (g), and (h) (subtract negative amounts). Enter each total here and include on your Schedule D, **line 8b** (if **Box D** above is checked), **line 9** (if **Box E** above is checked), or **line 10** (if **Box F** above is checked) ▶			1,080	600			480

Note. If you checked Box D above but the basis reported to the IRS was incorrect, enter in column (e) the basis as reported to the IRS, and enter an adjustment in column (g) to correct the basis. See *Column (g)* in the separate instructions for how to figure the amount of the adjustment.

2014 Child Tax Credit Worksheet—Line 52

Keep for Your Records

1. To be a qualifying child for the child tax credit, the child must be your dependent, **under age 17** at the end of 2014, and meet all the conditions in Steps 1 through 3 in the instructions for line 6c. Make sure you checked the box on Form 1040, line 6c, column (4), for each qualifying child.

2. If you do not have a qualifying child, you cannot claim the child tax credit.

3. If your qualifying child has an ITIN instead of an SSN, file Schedule 8812.

4. Do **not** use this worksheet, but use Pub. 972 instead, if:
   a. You are claiming the adoption credit, mortgage interest credit, District of Columbia first-time homebuyer credit, or residential energy efficient property credit,
   b. You are excluding income from Puerto Rico, or
   c. You are filing Form 2555, 2555-EZ, or 4563.

Part 1

1. Number of qualifying children: ___2___ × $1,000. Enter the result.

   1 | 2,000

2. Enter the amount from Form 1040, line 38.

   2 | 109,298

3. Enter the amount shown below for your filing status.

   - Married filing jointly — $110,000
   - Single, head of household, or qualifying widow(er) — $75,000
   - Married filing separately — $55,000

   3 | 110,000

4. Is the amount on line 2 more than the amount on line 3?

   ☒ **No.** Leave line 4 blank. Enter -0- on line 5, and go to line 6.

   ☐ **Yes.** Subtract line 3 from line 2.
   If the result is not a multiple of $1,000, increase it to the next multiple of $1,000. For example, increase $425 to $1,000, increase $1,025 to $2,000, etc.

   4 |

5. Multiply the amount on line 4 by 5% (.05). Enter the result.

   5 | 0

6. Is the amount on line 1 more than the amount on line 5?

   ☐ **No.** (STOP)
   You cannot take the child tax credit on Form 1040, line 52. You also cannot take the additional child tax credit on Form 1040, line 67. Complete the rest of your Form 1040.

   ☒ **Yes.** Subtract line 5 from line 1. Enter the result. *Go to Part 2.*

   6 | 2,000

2014 Child Tax Credit Worksheet—Continued

Keep for Your Records

Before you begin Part 2: ✓ Figure the amount of any credits you are claiming on Form 5695, Part II; Form 8910; Form 8936; or Schedule R.

Part 2		

7. Enter the amount from Form 1040, line 47.

7 | 3,911

8. Add any amounts from:

Form 1040, line 48 _____

Form 1040, line 49 + ___600___

Form 1040, line 50 + _____

Form 1040, line 51 + _____

Form 5695, line 30 + _____

Form 8910, line 15 + _____

Form 8936, line 23 + _____

Schedule R, line 22 + _____

Enter the total. **8** | 600

9. Are the amounts on lines 7 and 8 the same?

☐ **Yes.** 🛑
You cannot take this credit because there is no tax to reduce. However, you may be able to take the **additional child tax credit.** See the **TIP** below.

9 | 3,311

☐ **No.** Subtract line 8 from line 7.

10. Is the amount on line 6 more than the amount on line 9?

☐ **Yes.** Enter the amount from line 9. Also, you may be able to take the **additional child tax credit.** See the **TIP** below.

☒ **No.** Enter the amount from line 6.

} **This is your child tax credit.**

10 | 2,000

Enter this amount on Form 1040, line 52.

TIP

You may be able to take the **additional child tax credit** on Form 1040, line 67, if you answered "Yes" on line 9 **or** line 10 above.

● First, complete your Form 1040 through lines 66a and 66b.

● Then, use Schedule 8812 to figure any additional child tax credit.

Form 8960

Department of the Treasury
Internal Revenue Service (99)

Net Investment Income Tax—
Individuals, Estates, and Trusts

▶ Attach to your tax return.
▶ **Information about Form 8960 and its separate instructions is at** *www.irs.gov/form8960.*

OMB No. 1545-2227

2014

Attachment
Sequence No. **72**

Name(s) shown on your tax return

Tom E. and Mary A. Dodd

Your social security number or EIN

123-45-6789

Part I   Investment Income

☐ Section 6013(g) election (see instructions)
☐ Section 6013(h) election (see instructions)
☐ Regulations section 1.1411-10(g) election (see instructions)

1	Taxable interest (see instructions)		**1**	4,075
2	Ordinary dividends (see instructions)		**2**	1,300
3	Annuities (see instructions)		**3**	0
4a	Rental real estate, royalties, partnerships, S corporations, trusts, etc. (see instructions)	**4a** (15,615)		
b	Adjustment for net income or loss derived in the ordinary course of a non-section 1411 trade or business (see instructions)	**4b** 0		
c	Combine lines 4a and 4b		**4c**	(15,615)
5a	Net gain or loss from disposition of property (see instructions)	**5a** 35,340		
b	Net gain or loss from disposition of property that is not subject to net investment income tax (see instructions)	**5b**		
c	Adjustment from disposition of partnership interest or S corporation stock (see instructions)	**5c**		
d	Combine lines 5a through 5c		**5d**	35,340
6	Adjustments to investment income for certain CFCs and PFICs (see instructions)		**6**	0
7	Other modifications to investment income (see instructions)		**7**	(3,000)
8	Total investment income. Combine lines 1, 2, 3, 4c, 5d, 6, and 7		**8**	22,100

Part II   Investment Expenses Allocable to Investment Income and Modifications

9a	Investment interest expenses (see instructions)	**9a** 2,160		
b	State, local, and foreign income tax (see instructions)	**9b** 1,387		
c	Miscellaneous investment expenses (see instructions)	**9c** 0		
d	Add lines 9a, 9b, and 9c		**9d**	3,547
10	Additional modifications (see instructions)		**10**	425
11	Total deductions and modifications. Add lines 9d and 10		**11**	3,972

Part III   Tax Computation

12	Net investment income. Subtract Part II, line 11 from Part I, line 8. Individuals complete lines 13–17. Estates and trusts complete lines 18a–21. If zero or less, enter -0-		**12**	18,128

Individuals:

13	Modified adjusted gross income (see instructions)	**13** 109,298		
14	Threshold based on filing status (see instructions)	**14** 250,000		
15	Subtract line 14 from line 13. If zero or less, enter -0-	**15** 0		
16	Enter the smaller of line 12 or line 15		**16**	0
17	Net investment income tax for individuals. Multiply line 16 by 3.8% (.038). **Enter here and include on your tax return** (see instructions)		**17**	0

Estates and Trusts:

18a	Net investment income (line 12 above)	**18a**		
b	Deductions for distributions of net investment income and deductions under section 642(c) (see instructions)	**18b**		
c	Undistributed net investment income. Subtract line 18b from 18a (see instructions). If zero or less, enter -0-	**18c**		
19a	Adjusted gross income (see instructions)	**19a**		
b	Highest tax bracket for estates and trusts for the year (see instructions)	**19b**		
c	Subtract line 19b from line 19a. If zero or less, enter -0-	**19c**		
20	Enter the smaller of line 18c or line 19c		**20**	
21	Net investment income tax for estates and trusts. Multiply line 20 by 3.8% (.038). **Enter here and include on your tax return** (see instructions)		**21**	

For Paperwork Reduction Act Notice, see your tax return instructions.   Cat. No. 59474M   Form **8960** (2014)

§ 2.3201 Filled-In Form 8615

Form **8615**	**Tax for Certain Children Who Have Unearned Income**	OMB No. 1545-0074
Department of the Treasury Internal Revenue Service (99)	▶ Attach only to the child's Form 1040, Form 1040A, or Form 1040NR. ▶ Information about Form 8615 and its separate instructions is at *www.irs.gov/form8615*.	**2014** Attachment Sequence No. **33**

Child's name shown on return	Child's social security number
Butler T. Enright III	561-13-2444

Before you begin: If the child, the parent, or any of the parent's other children for whom Form 8615 must be filed must use the Schedule D Tax Worksheet or has income from farming or fishing, see **Pub. 929**, Tax Rules for Children and Dependents. It explains how to figure the child's tax using the **Schedule D Tax Worksheet** or **Schedule J** (Form 1040).

A Parent's name (first, initial, and last). **Caution:** *See instructions before completing.*	**B** Parent's social security number
Butler T. Enright III	175-49-5123

C Parent's filing status (check one):

☐ Single   ☑ Married filing jointly   ☐ Married filing separately   ☐ Head of household   ☐ Qualifying widow(er)

Part I   Child's Net Unearned Income

1	Enter the child's unearned income (see instructions)	**1**	3,736
2	If the child **did not** itemize deductions on **Schedule A** (Form 1040 or Form 1040NR), enter $2,000. Otherwise, see instructions	**2**	2,000
3	Subtract line 2 from line 1. If zero or less, **stop;** do not complete the rest of this form but **do** attach it to the child's return	**3**	1,736
4	Enter the child's **taxable income** from Form 1040, line 43; Form 1040A, line 27; or Form 1040NR, line 41. If the child files Form 2555 or 2555-EZ, see the instructions	**4**	2,736
5	Enter the **smaller** of line 3 or line 4. If zero, **stop;** do not complete the rest of this form but **do** attach it to the child's return	**5**	1,736

Part II   Tentative Tax Based on the Tax Rate of the Parent

6	Enter the parent's **taxable income** from Form 1040, line 43; Form 1040A, line 27; Form 1040EZ, line 6; Form 1040NR, line 41; or Form 1040NR-EZ, line 14. If zero or less, enter -0-. If the parent files Form 2555 or 2555-EZ, see the instructions	**6**	40,000
7	Enter the total, if any, from Forms 8615, line 5, of **all other** children of the parent named above. **Do not** include the amount from line 5 above	**7**	
8	Add lines 5, 6, and 7 (see instructions)	**8**	41,736
9	Enter the tax on the amount on line 8 based on the **parent's** filing status above (see instructions). If the Qualified Dividends and Capital Gain Tax Worksheet, Schedule D Tax Worksheet, or Schedule J (Form 1040) is used to figure the tax, check here . . . . ▶ ☐	**9**	5,368
10	Enter the parent's tax from Form 1040, line 44; Form 1040A, line 28, minus any alternative minimum tax; Form 1040EZ, line 10; Form 1040NR, line 42; or Form 1040NR-EZ, line 15. **Do not** include any tax from **Form 4972** or **8814** or any tax from recapture of an education credit. If the parent files Form 2555 or 2555-EZ, see the instructions. If the Qualified Dividends and Capital Gain Tax Worksheet, Schedule D Tax Worksheet, or Schedule J (Form 1040) was used to figure the tax, check here . . . . ▶ ☐	**10**	5,108
11	Subtract line 10 from line 9 and enter the result. If line 7 is blank, also enter this amount on line 13 and go to **Part III**	**11**	260
12a	Add lines 5 and 7 . . . . **12a** 1,736		
b	Divide line 5 by line 12a. Enter the result as a decimal (rounded to at least three places) . . .	**12b**	× 1.00
13	Multiply line 11 by line 12b	**13**	260

Part III   Child's Tax—If lines 4 and 5 above are the same, enter -0- on line 15 and go to line 16.

14	Subtract line 5 from line 4 . . . . **14** 1,000		
15	Enter the tax on the amount on line 14 based on the **child's** filing status (see instructions). If the Qualified Dividends and Capital Gain Tax Worksheet, Schedule D Tax Worksheet, or Schedule J (Form 1040) is used to figure the tax, check here . . . . ▶ ☐	**15**	100
16	Add lines 13 and 15	**16**	360
17	Enter the tax on the amount on line 4 based on the **child's** filing status (see instructions). If the Qualified Dividends and Capital Gain Tax Worksheet, Schedule D Tax Worksheet, or Schedule J (Form 1040) is used to figure the tax, check here . . . . ▶ ☐	**17**	274
18	Enter the **larger** of line 16 or line 17 here and on the **child's** Form 1040, line 44; Form 1040A, line 28; or Form 1040NR, line 42. If the child files Form 2555 or 2555-EZ, see the instructions . .	**18**	360

For Paperwork Reduction Act Notice, see your tax return instructions.   Cat. No. 64113U   Form **8615** (2014)

Form 1116

Department of the Treasury
Internal Revenue Service (99)

Foreign Tax Credit

(Individual, Estate, or Trust)

▶ Attach to Form 1040, 1040NR, 1041, or 990-T.

▶ Information about Form 1116 and its separate instructions is at *www.irs.gov/form1116*.

OMB No. 1545-0121

2014

Attachment
Sequence No. **19**

Name	Identifying number as shown on page 1 of your tax return
Jean Ross	398-21-5555

Use a separate Form 1116 for each category of income listed below. See **Categories of Income** in the instructions. Check only one box on each Form 1116. Report all amounts in U.S. dollars except where specified in Part II below.

- **a** ☐ Passive category income
- **b** ☑ General category income
- **c** ☐ Section 901(j) income
- **d** ☐ Certain income re-sourced by treaty
- **e** ☐ Lump-sum distributions

f Resident of (name of country) ▶ Country A

Note: *If you paid taxes to only one foreign country or U.S. possession, use column A in Part I and line A in Part II. If you paid taxes to more than one foreign country or U.S. possession, use a separate column and line for each country or possession.*

Part I   Taxable Income or Loss From Sources Outside the United States (for Category Checked Above)

		Foreign Country or U.S. Possession			Total (Add cols. A, B, and C.)
		A	**B**	**C**	
g	Enter the name of the foreign country or U.S. possession ▶	Country A			
1a	Gross income from sources within country shown above and of the type checked above (see instructions):	25,000			**1a** 25,000
b	Check if line 1a is compensation for personal services as an employee, your total compensation from all sources is $250,000 or more, and you used an alternative basis to determine its source (see instructions) ▶ ☐				
Deductions and losses (*Caution: See instructions*):					
2	Expenses **definitely related** to the income on line 1a (attach statement)	443			
3	Pro rata share of other deductions not definitely related.				
a	Certain itemized deductions or standard deduction (see instructions)	4,325			
b	Other deductions (attach statement)				
c	Add lines 3a and 3b	4,325			
d	Gross foreign source income (see instructions)	124,200			
e	Gross income from all sources (see instructions)	124,200			
f	Divide line 3d by line 3e (see instructions)	1			
g	Multiply line 3c by line 3f	4,325			
4	Pro rata share of interest expense (see instructions):				
a	Home mortgage interest (use the Worksheet for Home Mortgage Interest in the instructions)				
b	Other interest expense				
5	Losses from foreign sources				
6	Add lines 2, 3g, 4a, 4b, and 5	4,768			**6** 4,768
7	Subtract line 6 from line 1a. Enter the result here and on line 15, page 2 ▶				**7** 20,232

Part II   Foreign Taxes Paid or Accrued (see instructions)

Country	Credit is claimed for taxes (you must check one)		Foreign taxes paid or accrued									
	(h) ☐ Paid		In foreign currency				In U.S. dollars					
	(i) ☐ Accrued		Taxes withheld at source on:			**(n)** Other foreign taxes paid or accrued	Taxes withheld at source on:			**(r)** Other foreign taxes paid or accrued	**(s)** Total foreign taxes paid or accrued (add cols. (o) through (r))
	(j) Date paid or accrued	**(k)** Dividends	**(l)** Rents and royalties	**(m)** Interest			**(o)** Dividends	**(p)** Rents and royalties	**(q)** Interest			
A	Dec 15, 2014										1,900	1,900
B												
C												
8	Add lines A through C, column (s). Enter the total here and on line 9, page 2 ▶										**8**	1,900

For Paperwork Reduction Act Notice, see instructions.   Cat. No. 11440U   Form **1116** (2014)

Part III	Figuring the Credit		
9	Enter the amount from line 8. These are your total foreign taxes paid or accrued for the category of income checked above Part I	**9**	1,900
10	Carryback or carryover (attach detailed computation)	**10**	
11	Add lines 9 and 10	**11**	1,900
12	Reduction in foreign taxes (see instructions)	**12** (	1,518)
13	Taxes reclassified under high tax kickout (see instructions)	**13**	
14	Combine lines 11, 12, and 13. This is the total amount of foreign taxes available for credit	**14**	382
15	Enter the amount from line 7. This is your taxable income or (loss) from sources outside the United States (before adjustments) for the category of income checked above Part I (see instructions)	**15**	20,232
16	Adjustments to line 15 (see instructions)	**16**	
17	Combine the amounts on lines 15 and 16. This is your net foreign source taxable income. (If the result is zero or less, you have no foreign tax credit for the category of income you checked above Part I. Skip lines 18 through 22. However, if you are filing more than one Form 1116, you must complete line 20.)	**17**	20,232
18	**Individuals:** Enter the amount from Form 1040, line 41, or Form 1040NR, line 39. **Estates and trusts:** Enter your taxable income without the deduction for your exemption	**18**	20,232
	Caution: *If you figured your tax using the lower rates on qualified dividends or capital gains, see instructions.*		
19	Divide line 17 by line 18. If line 17 is more than line 18, enter "1"	**19**	1
20	**Individuals:** Enter the amounts from Form 1040, lines 44 and 46. If you are a nonresident alien, enter the amounts from Form 1040NR, lines 42 and 44. **Estates and trusts:** Enter the amount from Form 1041, Schedule G, line 1a, or the total of Form 990-T, lines 36 and 37	**20**	2,865
	Caution: *If you are completing line 20 for separate category e (lump-sum distributions), see instructions.*		
21	Multiply line 20 by line 19 (maximum amount of credit)	**21**	2,865
22	Enter the **smaller** of line 14 or line 21. If this is the only Form 1116 you are filing, skip lines 23 through 27 and enter this amount on line 28. Otherwise, complete the appropriate line in Part IV (see instructions) ▶	**22**	382

Part IV	Summary of Credits From Separate Parts III (see instructions)		
23	Credit for taxes on passive category income	**23**	
24	Credit for taxes on general category income	**24**	
25	Credit for taxes on certain income re-sourced by treaty	**25**	
26	Credit for taxes on lump-sum distributions	**26**	
27	Add lines 23 through 26	**27**	
28	Enter the **smaller** of line 20 or line 27	**28**	382
29	Reduction of credit for international boycott operations. See instructions for line 12	**29**	
30	Subtract line 29 from line 28. This is your **foreign tax credit.** Enter here and on Form 1040, line 48; Form 1040NR, line 46; Form 1041, Schedule G, line 2a; or Form 990-T, line 40a ▶	**30**	382

Form **1116** (2014)

§ 2.3280 Filled-In Form 5329

Form **5329**	**Additional Taxes on Qualified Plans (Including IRAs) and Other Tax-Favored Accounts**	OMB No. 1545-0074
	▶ **Attach to Form 1040 or Form 1040NR.**	20**14**
Department of the Treasury Internal Revenue Service (99)	▶ **Information about Form 5329 and its separate instructions is at** *www.irs.gov/form5329*.	Attachment Sequence No. **29**

Name of individual subject to additional tax. If married filing jointly, see instructions.	Your social security number
Harry Hanes	058-84-1957

Fill in Your Address Only If You Are Filing This Form by Itself and Not With Your Tax Return ▶

Home address (number and street), or P.O. box if mail is not delivered to your home	Apt. no.
436 Retirement Lane	

City, town or post office, state, and ZIP code. If you have a foreign address, also complete the spaces below (see instructions).	If this is an amended return, check here ▶ ☐
New York, NY 10001	

Foreign country name	Foreign province/state/county	Foreign postal code

If you **only** owe the additional 10% tax on early distributions, you may be able to report this tax directly on Form 1040, line 59, or Form 1040NR, line 57, without filing Form 5329. See the instructions for Form 1040, line 59, or for Form 1040NR, line 57.

Part I	**Additional Tax on Early Distributions**			
	Complete this part if you took a taxable distribution before you reached age 59½ from a qualified retirement plan (including an IRA) or modified endowment contract (unless you are reporting this tax directly on Form 1040 or Form 1040NR—see above). You may also have to complete this part to indicate that you qualify for an exception to the additional tax on early distributions or for certain Roth IRA distributions (see instructions).			
1	Early distributions included in income. For Roth IRA distributions, see instructions	**1**		
2	Early distributions included on line 1 that are not subject to the additional tax (see instructions). Enter the appropriate exception number from the instructions: _____	**2**		
3	Amount subject to additional tax. Subtract line 2 from line 1	**3**		
4	**Additional tax.** Enter 10% (.10) of line 3. Include this amount on Form 1040, line 59, or Form 1040NR, line 57	**4**		
	Caution: *If any part of the amount on line 3 was a distribution from a SIMPLE IRA, you may have to include 25% of that amount on line 4 instead of 10% (see instructions).*			

Part II	**Additional Tax on Certain Distributions From Education Accounts**			
	Complete this part if you included an amount in income, on Form 1040 or Form 1040NR, line 21, from a Coverdell education savings account (ESA) or a qualified tuition program (QTP).			
5	Distributions included in income from Coverdell ESAs and QTPs	**5**		
6	Distributions included on line 5 that are not subject to the additional tax (see instructions)	**6**		
7	Amount subject to additional tax. Subtract line 6 from line 5	**7**		
8	**Additional tax.** Enter 10% (.10) of line 7. Include this amount on Form 1040, line 59, or Form 1040NR, line 57	**8**		

Part III	**Additional Tax on Excess Contributions to Traditional IRAs**			
	Complete this part if you contributed more to your traditional IRAs for 2014 than is allowable or you had an amount on line 17 of your 2013 Form 5329.			
9	Enter your excess contributions from line 16 of your 2013 Form 5329 (see instructions). If zero, go to line 15	**9**		
10	If your traditional IRA contributions for 2014 are less than your maximum allowable contribution, see instructions. Otherwise, enter -0-	**10**		
11	2014 traditional IRA distributions included in income (see instructions)	**11**		
12	2014 distributions of prior year excess contributions (see instructions)	**12**		
13	Add lines 10, 11, and 12	**13**		
14	Prior year excess contributions. Subtract line 13 from line 9. If zero or less, enter -0-	**14**		
15	Excess contributions for 2014 (see instructions)	**15**	664	
16	Total excess contributions. Add lines 14 and 15	**16**	664	
17	**Additional tax.** Enter 6% (.06) of the **smaller** of line 16 **or** the value of your traditional IRAs on December 31, 2014 (including 2014 contributions made in 2015). Include this amount on Form 1040, line 59, or Form 1040NR, line 57	**17**	39	84

Part IV	**Additional Tax on Excess Contributions to Roth IRAs**			
	Complete this part if you contributed more to your Roth IRAs for 2014 than is allowable or you had an amount on line 25 of your 2013 Form 5329.			
18	Enter your excess contributions from line 24 of your 2013 Form 5329 (see instructions). If zero, go to line 23	**18**		
19	If your Roth IRA contributions for 2014 are less than your maximum allowable contribution, see instructions. Otherwise, enter -0-	**19**		
20	2014 distributions from your Roth IRAs (see instructions)	**20**		
21	Add lines 19 and 20	**21**		
22	Prior year excess contributions. Subtract line 21 from line 18. If zero or less, enter -0-	**22**		
23	Excess contributions for 2014 (see instructions)	**23**		
24	Total excess contributions. Add lines 22 and 23	**24**		
25	**Additional tax.** Enter 6% (.06) of the **smaller** of line 24 **or** the value of your Roth IRAs on December 31, 2014 (including 2014 contributions made in 2015). Include this amount on Form 1040, line 59, or Form 1040NR, line 57	**25**		

For Privacy Act and Paperwork Reduction Act Notice, see your tax return instructions. Cat. No. 13329Q Form **5329** (2014)

Form 2210

Department of the Treasury
Internal Revenue Service

Underpayment of Estimated Tax by Individuals, Estates, and Trusts

▶ Information about Form 2210 and its separate instructions is at *www.irs.gov/form2210*.
▶ Attach to Form 1040, 1040A, 1040NR, 1040NR-EZ, or 1041.

OMB No. 1545-0074

2014

Attachment Sequence No. **06**

Name(s) shown on tax return	Identifying number
Bill Adams	123-45-6789

Do You Have To File Form 2210?

Complete lines 1 through 7 below. Is line 7 less than $1,000? — **Yes** → **Do not file Form 2210.** You do not owe a penalty.

↓ **No**

Complete lines 8 and 9 below. Is line 6 equal to or more than line 9? — **Yes** → You do not owe a penalty. **Do not file Form 2210** (but if box **E** in Part II applies, you must file page 1 of Form 2210).

↓ **No**

You may owe a penalty. Does any box in Part II below apply? — **Yes** → You **must** file Form 2210. Does box **B, C,** or **D** in Part II apply?

↓ **No** ↓ **No** | **Yes** → You must figure your penalty.

Do not file Form 2210. You are not required to figure your penalty because the IRS will figure it and send you a bill for any unpaid amount. If you want to figure it, you may use Part III or Part IV as a worksheet and enter your penalty amount on your tax return, but **do not file Form 2210.**

You are **not** required to figure your penalty because the IRS will figure it and send you a bill for any unpaid amount. If you want to figure your penalty, you may use Part III or Part IV as a worksheet and enter your penalty amount on your tax return, but **file only page 1 of Form 2210.**

Part I — Required Annual Payment

1	Enter your 2014 tax after credits from Form 1040, line 56 (see instructions if not filing Form 1040)	**1**	2,996
2	Other taxes, including self-employment tax and, if applicable, Additional Medicare Tax and/or Net Investment Income Tax (see instructions)	**2**	3,250
3	Refundable credits, including the premium tax credit (see instructions)	**3**	( )
4	**Current year tax.** Combine lines 1, 2, and 3. If less than $1,000, **stop;** you do not owe a penalty. **Do not** file Form 2210	**4**	6,246
5	Multiply line 4 by 90% (.90) **5** 5,621		
6	Withholding taxes. **Do not** include estimated tax payments (see instructions)	**6**	
7	Subtract line 6 from line 4. If less than $1,000, **stop;** you do not owe a penalty. **Do not** file Form 2210	**7**	6,246
8	Maximum required annual payment based on prior year's tax (see instructions)	**8**	6,258
9	**Required annual payment.** Enter the **smaller** of line 5 or line 8	**9**	5,621

Next: Is line 9 more than line 6?

☐ **No.** You **do not** owe a penalty. **Do not** file Form 2210 unless box **E** below applies.

☑ **Yes.** You may owe a penalty, but **do not** file Form 2210 unless one or more boxes in Part II below applies.

• If box **B, C,** or **D** applies, you must figure your penalty and file Form 2210.

• If box **A** or **E** applies (but not **B, C,** or **D**) file only page 1 of Form 2210. You are **not** required to figure your penalty; the IRS will figure it and send you a bill for any unpaid amount. If you want to figure your penalty, you may use Part III or IV as a worksheet and enter your penalty on your tax return, but **file only page 1 of Form 2210.**

Part II — Reasons for Filing. Check applicable boxes. If none apply, **do not** file Form 2210.

A ☑ You request a **waiver** (see instructions) of your entire penalty. You must check this box and file page 1 of Form 2210, but you are not required to figure your penalty.

B ☐ You request a **waiver** (see instructions) of part of your penalty. You must figure your penalty and waiver amount and file Form 2210.

C ☐ Your income varied during the year and your penalty is reduced or eliminated when figured using the **annualized income installment method.** You must figure the penalty using Schedule AI and file Form 2210.

D ☐ Your penalty is lower when figured by treating the federal income tax withheld from your income as paid on the dates it was actually withheld, instead of in equal amounts on the payment due dates. You must figure your penalty and file Form 2210.

E ☐ You filed or are filing a joint return for either 2013 or 2014, but not for both years, and line 8 above is smaller than line 5 above. You must file page 1 of Form 2210, but you are **not** required to figure your penalty (unless box **B, C,** or **D** applies).

For Paperwork Reduction Act Notice, see separate instructions.	Cat. No. 11744P	Form **2210** (2014)

Part III	Short Method

Can You Use the Short Method?	You can use the short method if: • You made no estimated tax payments (or your only payments were withheld federal income tax), **or** • You paid the same amount of estimated tax on each of the four payment due dates.
Must You Use the Regular Method?	You must use the regular method (Part IV) instead of the short method if: • You made any estimated tax payments late, • You checked box **C** or **D** in Part II, **or** • You are filing Form 1040NR or 1040NR-EZ and you did not receive wages as an employee subject to U.S. income tax withholding.

Note. *If any payment was made earlier than the due date, you can use the short method, but using it may cause you to pay a larger penalty than the regular method. If the payment was only a few days early, the difference is likely to be small.*

10 Enter the amount from Form 2210, line 9		**10**	5,621
11 Enter the amount, if any, from Form 2210, line 6	**11**		
12 Enter the total amount, if any, of estimated tax payments you made .	**12** 5,000		
13 Add lines 11 and 12		**13**	5,000
14 Total underpayment for year. Subtract line 13 from line 10. If zero or less, **stop;** you do not owe a penalty. **Do not file Form 2210 unless you checked box E in Part II**		**14**	621
15 Multiply line 14 by .01995		**15**	12 | 39

16 • If the amount on line 14 was paid **on or after** 4/15/15, enter -0-.
• If the amount on line 14 was paid **before** 4/15/15, make the following computation to find the amount to enter on line 16.
     Amount on   Number of days paid
     line 14   ×   before 4/15/15   × .00008 . . . .
		16	0

17 Penalty. Subtract line 16 from line 15. Enter the result here and on Form 1040, line 79; Form 1040A, line 51; Form 1040NR, line 76; Form 1040NR-EZ, line 26; or Form 1041, line 26. **Do not file Form 2210 unless you checked a box in Part II** . . . . ▶		**17**	12 | 39

Form **2210** (2014)

Part IV	**Regular Method** (See the instructions if you are filing Form 1040NR or 1040NR-EZ.)					

Section A—Figure Your Underpayment		**Payment Due Dates**			
		(a) 4/15/14	**(b)** 6/15/14	**(c)** 9/15/14	**(d)** 1/15/15
18	**Required installments.** If box C in Part II applies, enter the amounts from Schedule AI, line 25. Otherwise, enter 25% (.25) of line 9, Form 2210, in each column **18**				
19	Estimated tax paid and tax withheld (see the instructions). For column (a) only, also enter the amount from line 19 on line 23. If line 19 is equal to or more than line 18 for all payment periods, stop here; you do not owe a penalty. **Do not file Form 2210 unless you checked a box in Part II** **19**				
	Complete lines 20 through 26 of one column before going to line 20 of the next column.				
20	Enter the amount, if any, from line 26 in the previous column **20**				
21	Add lines 19 and 20 . . . . **21**				
22	Add the amounts on lines 24 and 25 in the previous column **22**				
23	Subtract line 22 from line 21. If zero or less, enter -0-. For column (a) only, enter the amount from line 19 . . . . **23**				
24	If line 23 is zero, subtract line 21 from line 22. Otherwise, enter -0- **24**				
25	**Underpayment.** If line 18 is equal to or more than line 23, subtract line 23 from line 18. Then go to line 20 of the next column. Otherwise, go to line 26 . ▶ **25**				
26	**Overpayment.** If line 23 is more than line 18, subtract line 18 from line 23. Then go to line 20 of the next column **26**				

Section B—Figure the Penalty (Use the Worksheet for Form 2210, Part IV, Section B—Figure the Penalty in the instructions.)

27	**Penalty.** Enter the total penalty from line 14 of the Worksheet for Form 2210, Part IV, Section B—Figure the Penalty. Also include this amount on Form 1040, line 79; Form 1040A, line 51; Form 1040NR, line 76; Form 1040NR-EZ, line 26; or Form 1041, line 26. **Do not file Form 2210 unless you checked a box in Part II** . . . . ▶	**27**	

Schedule AI—Annualized Income Installment Method (See the instructions.)

Estates and trusts, **do not** use the period ending dates shown to the right. Instead, use the following: 2/28/14, 4/30/14, 7/31/14, and 11/30/14.

		(a) 1/1/14–3/31/14	(b) 1/1/14–5/31/14	(c) 1/1/14–8/31/14	(d) 1/1/14–12/31/14

Part I   Annualized Income Installments

		(a)	(b)	(c)	(d)
1	Enter your adjusted gross income for each period (see instructions). (Estates and trusts, enter your taxable income without your exemption for each period.) . . **1**				
2	Annualization amounts. (Estates and trusts, see instructions) **2**	4	2.4	1.5	1
3	Annualized income. Multiply line 1 by line 2 . . . **3**				
4	If you itemize, enter itemized deductions for the period shown in each column. All others enter -0-, and skip to line 7. **Exception:** Estates and trusts, skip to line 9 and enter amount from line 3 **4**				
5	Annualization amounts **5**	4	2.4	1.5	1
6	Multiply line 4 by line 5 (see instructions if line 3 is more than $152,525) **6**				
7	In each column, enter the full amount of your standard deduction from Form 1040, line 40, or Form 1040A, line 24. (Form 1040NR or 1040NR-EZ filers, enter -0-. **Exception:** Indian students and business apprentices, see instructions.) . **7**				
8	Enter the **larger** of line 6 or line 7 . . . . . . **8**				
9	Subtract line 8 from line 3 . . . . **9**				
10	In each column, multiply $3,950 by the total number of exemptions claimed (see instructions if line 3 is more than $152,525). (Estates, trusts, and Form 1040NR or 1040NR-EZ filers, see instructions.) . . **10**				
11	Subtract line 10 from line 9. If zero or less, enter -0- **11**				
12	Figure your tax on the amount on line 11 (see instructions) **12**				
13	Self-employment tax from line 34 (complete Part II below) **13**				
14	Enter other taxes for each payment period including, if applicable, Additional Medicare Tax and/or Net Investment Income Tax (see instructions) **14**				
15	Total tax. Add lines 12, 13, and 14 . . . . . . **15**				
16	For each period, enter the same type of credits as allowed on Form 2210, Part I, lines 1 and 3 (see instructions) . . **16**				
17	Subtract line 16 from line 15. If zero or less, enter -0- . **17**				
18	Applicable percentage **18**	22.5%	45%	67.5%	90%
19	Multiply line 17 by line 18 . . . . **19**				
	Complete lines 20–25 of one column before going to line 20 of the next column.				
20	Enter the total of the amounts in all previous columns of line 25 **20**	▓▓▓			
21	Subtract line 20 from line 19. If zero or less, enter -0- . **21**				
22	Enter 25% (.25) of line 9 on page 1 of Form 2210 in each column **22**				
23	Subtract line 25 of the previous column from line 24 of that column. **23**	▓▓▓			
24	Add lines 22 and 23 . . . . **24**				
25	Enter the **smaller** of line 21 or line 24 here and on Form 2210, Part IV, line 18 . . . . ▶ **25**				

Part II   Annualized Self-Employment Tax (Form 1040 and Form 1040NR filers only)

		(a)	(b)	(c)	(d)
26	Net earnings from self-employment for the period (see instructions) **26**				
27	Prorated social security tax limit **27**	$29,250	$48,750	$78,000	$117,000
28	Enter actual wages for the period subject to social security tax or the 6.2% portion of the 7.65% railroad retirement (tier 1) tax. **Exception:** If you filed Form 4137 or Form 8919, see instructions **28**				
29	Subtract line 28 from line 27. If zero or less, enter -0- . **29**				
30	Annualization amounts **30**	0.496	0.2976	0.186	0.124
31	Multiply line 30 by the **smaller** of line 26 or line 29 . **31**				
32	Annualization amounts **32**	0.116	0.0696	0.0435	0.029
33	Multiply line 26 by line 32 . . . . **33**				
34	Add lines 31 and 33. Enter here and on line 13 above ▶ **34**				

2014 Tax Table

 CAUTION

See the instructions for line 44 to see if you must use the Tax Table below to figure your tax.

Example. Mr. and Mrs. Brown are filing a joint return. Their taxable income on Form 1040, line 43, is $25,300. First, they find the $25,300-25,350 taxable income line. Next, they find the column for married filing jointly and read down the column. The amount shown where the taxable income line and filing status column meet is $2,891. This is the tax amount they should enter on Form 1040, line 44.

Sample Table

At Least	But Less Than	Single	Married filing jointly*	Married filing separately	Head of a household
			Your tax is—		
25,200	25,250	3,330	2,876	3,330	3,136
25,250	25,300	3,338	2,884	3,338	3,144
25,300	25,350	3,345	2,891	3,345	3,151
25,350	25,400	3,353	2,899	3,353	3,159

At least	But less than	Single	Married filing jointly *	Married filing separately	Head of a household
			Your tax is—		
0	5	0	0	0	0
5	15	1	1	1	1
15	25	2	2	2	2
25	50	4	4	4	4
50	75	6	6	6	6
75	100	9	9	9	9
100	125	11	11	11	11
125	150	14	14	14	14
150	175	16	16	16	16
175	200	19	19	19	19
200	225	21	21	21	21
225	250	24	24	24	24
250	275	26	26	26	26
275	300	29	29	29	29
300	325	31	31	31	31
325	350	34	34	34	34
350	375	36	36	36	36
375	400	39	39	39	39
400	425	41	41	41	41
425	450	44	44	44	44
450	475	46	46	46	46
475	500	49	49	49	49
500	525	51	51	51	51
525	550	54	54	54	54
550	575	56	56	56	56
575	600	59	59	59	59
600	625	61	61	61	61
625	650	64	64	64	64
650	675	66	66	66	66
675	700	69	69	69	69
700	725	71	71	71	71
725	750	74	74	74	74
750	775	76	76	76	76
775	800	79	79	79	79
800	825	81	81	81	81
825	850	84	84	84	84
850	875	86	86	86	86
875	900	89	89	89	89
900	925	91	91	91	91
925	950	94	94	94	94
950	975	96	96	96	96
975	1,000	99	99	99	99

1,000

At least	But less than	Single	Married filing jointly *	Married filing separately	Head of a household
			Your tax is—		
1,000	1,025	101	101	101	101
1,025	1,050	104	104	104	104
1,050	1,075	106	106	106	106
1,075	1,100	109	109	109	109
1,100	1,125	111	111	111	111
1,125	1,150	114	114	114	114
1,150	1,175	116	116	116	116
1,175	1,200	119	119	119	119
1,200	1,225	121	121	121	121
1,225	1,250	124	124	124	124
1,250	1,275	126	126	126	126
1,275	1,300	129	129	129	129
1,300	1,325	131	131	131	131
1,325	1,350	134	134	134	134
1,350	1,375	136	136	136	136
1,375	1,400	139	139	139	139
1,400	1,425	141	141	141	141
1,425	1,450	144	144	144	144
1,450	1,475	146	146	146	146
1,475	1,500	149	149	149	149
1,500	1,525	151	151	151	151
1,525	1,550	154	154	154	154
1,550	1,575	156	156	156	156
1,575	1,600	159	159	159	159
1,600	1,625	161	161	161	161
1,625	1,650	164	164	164	164
1,650	1,675	166	166	166	166
1,675	1,700	169	169	169	169
1,700	1,725	171	171	171	171
1,725	1,750	174	174	174	174
1,750	1,775	176	176	176	176
1,775	1,800	179	179	179	179
1,800	1,825	181	181	181	181
1,825	1,850	184	184	184	184
1,850	1,875	186	186	186	186
1,875	1,900	189	189	189	189
1,900	1,925	191	191	191	191
1,925	1,950	194	194	194	194
1,950	1,975	196	196	196	196
1,975	2,000	199	199	199	199

2,000

At least	But less than	Single	Married filing jointly *	Married filing separately	Head of a household
			Your tax is—		
2,000	2,025	201	201	201	201
2,025	2,050	204	204	204	204
2,050	2,075	206	206	206	206
2,075	2,100	209	209	209	209
2,100	2,125	211	211	211	211
2,125	2,150	214	214	214	214
2,150	2,175	216	216	216	216
2,175	2,200	219	219	219	219
2,200	2,225	221	221	221	221
2,225	2,250	224	224	224	224
2,250	2,275	226	226	226	226
2,275	2,300	229	229	229	229
2,300	2,325	231	231	231	231
2,325	2,350	234	234	234	234
2,350	2,375	236	236	236	236
2,375	2,400	239	239	239	239
2,400	2,425	241	241	241	241
2,425	2,450	244	244	244	244
2,450	2,475	246	246	246	246
2,475	2,500	249	249	249	249
2,500	2,525	251	251	251	251
2,525	2,550	254	254	254	254
2,550	2,575	256	256	256	256
2,575	2,600	259	259	259	259
2,600	2,625	261	261	261	261
2,625	2,650	264	264	264	264
2,650	2,675	266	266	266	266
2,675	2,700	269	269	269	269
2,700	2,725	271	271	271	271
2,725	2,750	274	274	274	274
2,750	2,775	276	276	276	276
2,775	2,800	279	279	279	279
2,800	2,825	281	281	281	281
2,825	2,850	284	284	284	284
2,850	2,875	286	286	286	286
2,875	2,900	289	289	289	289
2,900	2,925	291	291	291	291
2,925	2,950	294	294	294	294
2,950	2,975	296	296	296	296
2,975	3,000	299	299	299	299

(Continued)

* This column must also be used by a qualifying widow(er).

3,000

At least	But less than	Single	Married filing jointly *	Married filing separately	Head of a household
3,000	3,050	303	303	303	303
3,050	3,100	308	308	308	308
3,100	3,150	313	313	313	313
3,150	3,200	318	318	318	318
3,200	3,250	323	323	323	323
3,250	3,300	328	328	328	328
3,300	3,350	333	333	333	333
3,350	3,400	338	338	338	338
3,400	3,450	343	343	343	343
3,450	3,500	348	348	348	348
3,500	3,550	353	353	353	353
3,550	3,600	358	358	358	358
3,600	3,650	363	363	363	363
3,650	3,700	368	368	368	368
3,700	3,750	373	373	373	373
3,750	3,800	378	378	378	378
3,800	3,850	383	383	383	383
3,850	3,900	388	388	388	388
3,900	3,950	393	393	393	393
3,950	4,000	398	398	398	398

4,000

At least	But less than	Single	Married filing jointly *	Married filing separately	Head of a household
4,000	4,050	403	403	403	403
4,050	4,100	408	408	408	408
4,100	4,150	413	413	413	413
4,150	4,200	418	418	418	418
4,200	4,250	423	423	423	423
4,250	4,300	428	428	428	428
4,300	4,350	433	433	433	433
4,350	4,400	438	438	438	438
4,400	4,450	443	443	443	443
4,450	4,500	448	448	448	448
4,500	4,550	453	453	453	453
4,550	4,600	458	458	458	458
4,600	4,650	463	463	463	463
4,650	4,700	468	468	468	468
4,700	4,750	473	473	473	473
4,750	4,800	478	478	478	478
4,800	4,850	483	483	483	483
4,850	4,900	488	488	488	488
4,900	4,950	493	493	493	493
4,950	5,000	498	498	498	498

5,000

At least	But less than	Single	Married filing jointly *	Married filing separately	Head of a household
5,000	5,050	503	503	503	503
5,050	5,100	508	508	508	508
5,100	5,150	513	513	513	513
5,150	5,200	518	518	518	518
5,200	5,250	523	523	523	523
5,250	5,300	528	528	528	528
5,300	5,350	533	533	533	533
5,350	5,400	538	538	538	538
5,400	5,450	543	543	543	543
5,450	5,500	548	548	548	548
5,500	5,550	553	553	553	553
5,550	5,600	558	558	558	558
5,600	5,650	563	563	563	563
5,650	5,700	568	568	568	568
5,700	5,750	573	573	573	573
5,750	5,800	578	578	578	578
5,800	5,850	583	583	583	583
5,850	5,900	588	588	588	588
5,900	5,950	593	593	593	593
5,950	6,000	598	598	598	598

6,000

At least	But less than	Single	Married filing jointly *	Married filing separately	Head of a household
6,000	6,050	603	603	603	603
6,050	6,100	608	608	608	608
6,100	6,150	613	613	613	613
6,150	6,200	618	618	618	618
6,200	6,250	623	623	623	623
6,250	6,300	628	628	628	628
6,300	6,350	633	633	633	633
6,350	6,400	638	638	638	638
6,400	6,450	643	643	643	643
6,450	6,500	648	648	648	648
6,500	6,550	653	653	653	653
6,550	6,600	658	658	658	658
6,600	6,650	663	663	663	663
6,650	6,700	668	668	668	668
6,700	6,750	673	673	673	673
6,750	6,800	678	678	678	678
6,800	6,850	683	683	683	683
6,850	6,900	688	688	688	688
6,900	6,950	693	693	693	693
6,950	7,000	698	698	698	698

7,000

At least	But less than	Single	Married filing jointly *	Married filing separately	Head of a household
7,000	7,050	703	703	703	703
7,050	7,100	708	708	708	708
7,100	7,150	713	713	713	713
7,150	7,200	718	718	718	718
7,200	7,250	723	723	723	723
7,250	7,300	728	728	728	728
7,300	7,350	733	733	733	733
7,350	7,400	738	738	738	738
7,400	7,450	743	743	743	743
7,450	7,500	748	748	748	748
7,500	7,550	753	753	753	753
7,550	7,600	758	758	758	758
7,600	7,650	763	763	763	763
7,650	7,700	768	768	768	768
7,700	7,750	773	773	773	773
7,750	7,800	778	778	778	778
7,800	7,850	783	783	783	783
7,850	7,900	788	788	788	788
7,900	7,950	793	793	793	793
7,950	8,000	798	798	798	798

8,000

At least	But less than	Single	Married filing jointly *	Married filing separately	Head of a household
8,000	8,050	803	803	803	803
8,050	8,100	808	808	808	808
8,100	8,150	813	813	813	813
8,150	8,200	818	818	818	818
8,200	8,250	823	823	823	823
8,250	8,300	828	828	828	828
8,300	8,350	833	833	833	833
8,350	8,400	838	838	838	838
8,400	8,450	843	843	843	843
8,450	8,500	848	848	848	848
8,500	8,550	853	853	853	853
8,550	8,600	858	858	858	858
8,600	8,650	863	863	863	863
8,650	8,700	868	868	868	868
8,700	8,750	873	873	873	873
8,750	8,800	878	878	878	878
8,800	8,850	883	883	883	883
8,850	8,900	888	888	888	888
8,900	8,950	893	893	893	893
8,950	9,000	898	898	898	898

9,000

At least	But less than	Single	Married filing jointly *	Married filing separately	Head of a household
9,000	9,050	903	903	903	903
9,050	9,100	908	908	908	908
9,100	9,150	915	913	915	913
9,150	9,200	923	918	923	918
9,200	9,250	930	923	930	923
9,250	9,300	938	928	938	928
9,300	9,350	945	933	945	933
9,350	9,400	953	938	953	938
9,400	9,450	960	943	960	943
9,450	9,500	968	948	968	948
9,500	9,550	975	953	975	953
9,550	9,600	983	958	983	958
9,600	9,650	990	963	990	963
9,650	9,700	998	968	998	968
9,700	9,750	1,005	973	1,005	973
9,750	9,800	1,013	978	1,013	978
9,800	9,850	1,020	983	1,020	983
9,850	9,900	1,028	988	1,028	988
9,900	9,950	1,035	993	1,035	993
9,950	10,000	1,043	998	1,043	998

10,000

At least	But less than	Single	Married filing jointly *	Married filing separately	Head of a household
10,000	10,050	1,050	1,003	1,050	1,003
10,050	10,100	1,058	1,008	1,058	1,008
10,100	10,150	1,065	1,013	1,065	1,013
10,150	10,200	1,073	1,018	1,073	1,018
10,200	10,250	1,080	1,023	1,080	1,023
10,250	10,300	1,088	1,028	1,088	1,028
10,300	10,350	1,095	1,033	1,095	1,033
10,350	10,400	1,103	1,038	1,103	1,038
10,400	10,450	1,110	1,043	1,110	1,043
10,450	10,500	1,118	1,048	1,118	1,048
10,500	10,550	1,125	1,053	1,125	1,053
10,550	10,600	1,133	1,058	1,133	1,058
10,600	10,650	1,140	1,063	1,140	1,063
10,650	10,700	1,148	1,068	1,148	1,068
10,700	10,750	1,155	1,073	1,155	1,073
10,750	10,800	1,163	1,078	1,163	1,078
10,800	10,850	1,170	1,083	1,170	1,083
10,850	10,900	1,178	1,088	1,178	1,088
10,900	10,950	1,185	1,093	1,185	1,093
10,950	11,000	1,193	1,098	1,193	1,098

11,000

At least	But less than	Single	Married filing jointly *	Married filing separately	Head of a household
11,000	11,050	1,200	1,103	1,200	1,103
11,050	11,100	1,208	1,108	1,208	1,108
11,100	11,150	1,215	1,113	1,215	1,113
11,150	11,200	1,223	1,118	1,223	1,118
11,200	11,250	1,230	1,123	1,230	1,123
11,250	11,300	1,238	1,128	1,238	1,128
11,300	11,350	1,245	1,133	1,245	1,133
11,350	11,400	1,253	1,138	1,253	1,138
11,400	11,450	1,260	1,143	1,260	1,143
11,450	11,500	1,268	1,148	1,268	1,148
11,500	11,550	1,275	1,153	1,275	1,153
11,550	11,600	1,283	1,158	1,283	1,158
11,600	11,650	1,290	1,163	1,290	1,163
11,650	11,700	1,298	1,168	1,298	1,168
11,700	11,750	1,305	1,173	1,305	1,173
11,750	11,800	1,313	1,178	1,313	1,178
11,800	11,850	1,320	1,183	1,320	1,183
11,850	11,900	1,328	1,188	1,328	1,188
11,900	11,950	1,335	1,193	1,335	1,193
11,950	12,000	1,343	1,198	1,343	1,198

(Continued)

* This column must also be used by a qualifying widow(er).

12,000 / 13,000 / 14,000

At least	But less than	Single	Married filing jointly *	Married filing separately	Head of a household
12,000					
12,000	12,050	1,350	1,203	1,350	1,203
12,050	12,100	1,358	1,208	1,358	1,208
12,100	12,150	1,365	1,213	1,365	1,213
12,150	12,200	1,373	1,218	1,373	1,218
12,200	12,250	1,380	1,223	1,380	1,223
12,250	12,300	1,388	1,228	1,388	1,228
12,300	12,350	1,395	1,233	1,395	1,233
12,350	12,400	1,403	1,238	1,403	1,238
12,400	12,450	1,410	1,243	1,410	1,243
12,450	12,500	1,418	1,248	1,418	1,248
12,500	12,550	1,425	1,253	1,425	1,253
12,550	12,600	1,433	1,258	1,433	1,258
12,600	12,650	1,440	1,263	1,440	1,263
12,650	12,700	1,448	1,268	1,448	1,268
12,700	12,750	1,455	1,273	1,455	1,273
12,750	12,800	1,463	1,278	1,463	1,278
12,800	12,850	1,470	1,283	1,470	1,283
12,850	12,900	1,478	1,288	1,478	1,288
12,900	12,950	1,485	1,293	1,485	1,293
12,950	13,000	1,493	1,298	1,493	1,299
13,000					
13,000	13,050	1,500	1,303	1,500	1,306
13,050	13,100	1,508	1,308	1,508	1,314
13,100	13,150	1,515	1,313	1,515	1,321
13,150	13,200	1,523	1,318	1,523	1,329
13,200	13,250	1,530	1,323	1,530	1,336
13,250	13,300	1,538	1,328	1,538	1,344
13,300	13,350	1,545	1,333	1,545	1,351
13,350	13,400	1,553	1,338	1,553	1,359
13,400	13,450	1,560	1,343	1,560	1,366
13,450	13,500	1,568	1,348	1,568	1,374
13,500	13,550	1,575	1,353	1,575	1,381
13,550	13,600	1,583	1,358	1,583	1,389
13,600	13,650	1,590	1,363	1,590	1,396
13,650	13,700	1,598	1,368	1,598	1,404
13,700	13,750	1,605	1,373	1,605	1,411
13,750	13,800	1,613	1,378	1,613	1,419
13,800	13,850	1,620	1,383	1,620	1,426
13,850	13,900	1,628	1,388	1,628	1,434
13,900	13,950	1,635	1,393	1,635	1,441
13,950	14,000	1,643	1,398	1,643	1,449
14,000					
14,000	14,050	1,650	1,403	1,650	1,456
14,050	14,100	1,658	1,408	1,658	1,464
14,100	14,150	1,665	1,413	1,665	1,471
14,150	14,200	1,673	1,418	1,673	1,479
14,200	14,250	1,680	1,423	1,680	1,486
14,250	14,300	1,688	1,428	1,688	1,494
14,300	14,350	1,695	1,433	1,695	1,501
14,350	14,400	1,703	1,438	1,703	1,509
14,400	14,450	1,710	1,443	1,710	1,516
14,450	14,500	1,718	1,448	1,718	1,524
14,500	14,550	1,725	1,453	1,725	1,531
14,550	14,600	1,733	1,458	1,733	1,539
14,600	14,650	1,740	1,463	1,740	1,546
14,650	14,700	1,748	1,468	1,748	1,554
14,700	14,750	1,755	1,473	1,755	1,561
14,750	14,800	1,763	1,478	1,763	1,569
14,800	14,850	1,770	1,483	1,770	1,576
14,850	14,900	1,778	1,488	1,778	1,584
14,900	14,950	1,785	1,493	1,785	1,591
14,950	15,000	1,793	1,498	1,793	1,599

15,000 / 16,000 / 17,000

At least	But less than	Single	Married filing jointly *	Married filing separately	Head of a household
15,000					
15,000	15,050	1,800	1,503	1,800	1,606
15,050	15,100	1,808	1,508	1,808	1,614
15,100	15,150	1,815	1,513	1,815	1,621
15,150	15,200	1,823	1,518	1,823	1,629
15,200	15,250	1,830	1,523	1,830	1,636
15,250	15,300	1,838	1,528	1,838	1,644
15,300	15,350	1,845	1,533	1,845	1,651
15,350	15,400	1,853	1,538	1,853	1,659
15,400	15,450	1,860	1,543	1,860	1,666
15,450	15,500	1,868	1,548	1,868	1,674
15,500	15,550	1,875	1,553	1,875	1,681
15,550	15,600	1,883	1,558	1,883	1,689
15,600	15,650	1,890	1,563	1,890	1,696
15,650	15,700	1,898	1,568	1,898	1,704
15,700	15,750	1,905	1,573	1,905	1,711
15,750	15,800	1,913	1,578	1,913	1,719
15,800	15,850	1,920	1,583	1,920	1,726
15,850	15,900	1,928	1,588	1,928	1,734
15,900	15,950	1,935	1,593	1,935	1,741
15,950	16,000	1,943	1,598	1,943	1,749
16,000					
16,000	16,050	1,950	1,603	1,950	1,756
16,050	16,100	1,958	1,608	1,958	1,764
16,100	16,150	1,965	1,613	1,965	1,771
16,150	16,200	1,973	1,618	1,973	1,779
16,200	16,250	1,980	1,623	1,980	1,786
16,250	16,300	1,988	1,628	1,988	1,794
16,300	16,350	1,995	1,633	1,995	1,801
16,350	16,400	2,003	1,638	2,003	1,809
16,400	16,450	2,010	1,643	2,010	1,816
16,450	16,500	2,018	1,648	2,018	1,824
16,500	16,550	2,025	1,653	2,025	1,831
16,550	16,600	2,033	1,658	2,033	1,839
16,600	16,650	2,040	1,663	2,040	1,846
16,650	16,700	2,048	1,668	2,048	1,854
16,700	16,750	2,055	1,673	2,055	1,861
16,750	16,800	2,063	1,678	2,063	1,869
16,800	16,850	2,070	1,683	2,070	1,876
16,850	16,900	2,078	1,688	2,078	1,884
16,900	16,950	2,085	1,693	2,085	1,891
16,950	17,000	2,093	1,698	2,093	1,899
17,000					
17,000	17,050	2,100	1,703	2,100	1,906
17,050	17,100	2,108	1,708	2,108	1,914
17,100	17,150	2,115	1,713	2,115	1,921
17,150	17,200	2,123	1,718	2,123	1,929
17,200	17,250	2,130	1,723	2,130	1,936
17,250	17,300	2,138	1,728	2,138	1,944
17,300	17,350	2,145	1,733	2,145	1,951
17,350	17,400	2,153	1,738	2,153	1,959
17,400	17,450	2,160	1,743	2,160	1,966
17,450	17,500	2,168	1,748	2,168	1,974
17,500	17,550	2,175	1,753	2,175	1,981
17,550	17,600	2,183	1,758	2,183	1,989
17,600	17,650	2,190	1,763	2,190	1,996
17,650	17,700	2,198	1,768	2,198	2,004
17,700	17,750	2,205	1,773	2,205	2,011
17,750	17,800	2,213	1,778	2,213	2,019
17,800	17,850	2,220	1,783	2,220	2,026
17,850	17,900	2,228	1,788	2,228	2,034
17,900	17,950	2,235	1,793	2,235	2,041
17,950	18,000	2,243	1,798	2,243	2,049

18,000 / 19,000 / 20,000

At least	But less than	Single	Married filing jointly *	Married filing separately	Head of a household
18,000					
18,000	18,050	2,250	1,803	2,250	2,056
18,050	18,100	2,258	1,808	2,258	2,064
18,100	18,150	2,265	1,813	2,265	2,071
18,150	18,200	2,273	1,819	2,273	2,079
18,200	18,250	2,280	1,826	2,280	2,086
18,250	18,300	2,288	1,834	2,288	2,094
18,300	18,350	2,295	1,841	2,295	2,101
18,350	18,400	2,303	1,849	2,303	2,109
18,400	18,450	2,310	1,856	2,310	2,116
18,450	18,500	2,318	1,864	2,318	2,124
18,500	18,550	2,325	1,871	2,325	2,131
18,550	18,600	2,333	1,879	2,333	2,139
18,600	18,650	2,340	1,886	2,340	2,146
18,650	18,700	2,348	1,894	2,348	2,154
18,700	18,750	2,355	1,901	2,355	2,161
18,750	18,800	2,363	1,909	2,363	2,169
18,800	18,850	2,370	1,916	2,370	2,176
18,850	18,900	2,378	1,924	2,378	2,184
18,900	18,950	2,385	1,931	2,385	2,191
18,950	19,000	2,393	1,939	2,393	2,199
19,000					
19,000	19,050	2,400	1,946	2,400	2,206
19,050	19,100	2,408	1,954	2,408	2,214
19,100	19,150	2,415	1,961	2,415	2,221
19,150	19,200	2,423	1,969	2,423	2,229
19,200	19,250	2,430	1,976	2,430	2,236
19,250	19,300	2,438	1,984	2,438	2,244
19,300	19,350	2,445	1,991	2,445	2,251
19,350	19,400	2,453	1,999	2,453	2,259
19,400	19,450	2,460	2,006	2,460	2,266
19,450	19,500	2,468	2,014	2,468	2,274
19,500	19,550	2,475	2,021	2,475	2,281
19,550	19,600	2,483	2,029	2,483	2,289
19,600	19,650	2,490	2,036	2,490	2,296
19,650	19,700	2,498	2,044	2,498	2,304
19,700	19,750	2,505	2,051	2,505	2,311
19,750	19,800	2,513	2,059	2,513	2,319
19,800	19,850	2,520	2,066	2,520	2,326
19,850	19,900	2,528	2,074	2,528	2,334
19,900	19,950	2,535	2,081	2,535	2,341
19,950	20,000	2,543	2,089	2,543	2,349
20,000					
20,000	20,050	2,550	2,096	2,550	2,356
20,050	20,100	2,558	2,104	2,558	2,364
20,100	20,150	2,565	2,111	2,565	2,371
20,150	20,200	2,573	2,119	2,573	2,379
20,200	20,250	2,580	2,126	2,580	2,386
20,250	20,300	2,588	2,134	2,588	2,394
20,300	20,350	2,595	2,141	2,595	2,401
20,350	20,400	2,603	2,149	2,603	2,409
20,400	20,450	2,610	2,156	2,610	2,416
20,450	20,500	2,618	2,164	2,618	2,424
20,500	20,550	2,625	2,171	2,625	2,431
20,550	20,600	2,633	2,179	2,633	2,439
20,600	20,650	2,640	2,186	2,640	2,446
20,650	20,700	2,648	2,194	2,648	2,454
20,700	20,750	2,655	2,201	2,655	2,461
20,750	20,800	2,663	2,209	2,663	2,469
20,800	20,850	2,670	2,216	2,670	2,476
20,850	20,900	2,678	2,224	2,678	2,484
20,900	20,950	2,685	2,231	2,685	2,491
20,950	21,000	2,693	2,239	2,693	2,499

* This column must also be used by a qualifying widow(er).

(Continued)

21,000

At least	But less than	Single	Married filing jointly *	Married filing separately	Head of a household
		Your tax is—			
21,000	21,050	2,700	2,246	2,700	2,506
21,050	21,100	2,708	2,254	2,708	2,514
21,100	21,150	2,715	2,261	2,715	2,521
21,150	21,200	2,723	2,269	2,723	2,529
21,200	21,250	2,730	2,276	2,730	2,536
21,250	21,300	2,738	2,284	2,738	2,544
21,300	21,350	2,745	2,291	2,745	2,551
21,350	21,400	2,753	2,299	2,753	2,559
21,400	21,450	2,760	2,306	2,760	2,566
21,450	21,500	2,768	2,314	2,768	2,574
21,500	21,550	2,775	2,321	2,775	2,581
21,550	21,600	2,783	2,329	2,783	2,589
21,600	21,650	2,790	2,336	2,790	2,596
21,650	21,700	2,798	2,344	2,798	2,604
21,700	21,750	2,805	2,351	2,805	2,611
21,750	21,800	2,813	2,359	2,813	2,619
21,800	21,850	2,820	2,366	2,820	2,626
21,850	21,900	2,828	2,374	2,828	2,634
21,900	21,950	2,835	2,381	2,835	2,641
21,950	22,000	2,843	2,389	2,843	2,649

22,000

At least	But less than	Single	Married filing jointly *	Married filing separately	Head of a household
22,000	22,050	2,850	2,396	2,850	2,656
22,050	22,100	2,858	2,404	2,858	2,664
22,100	22,150	2,865	2,411	2,865	2,671
22,150	22,200	2,873	2,419	2,873	2,679
22,200	22,250	2,880	2,426	2,880	2,686
22,250	22,300	2,888	2,434	2,888	2,694
22,300	22,350	2,895	2,441	2,895	2,701
22,350	22,400	2,903	2,449	2,903	2,709
22,400	22,450	2,910	2,456	2,910	2,716
22,450	22,500	2,918	2,464	2,918	2,724
22,500	22,550	2,925	2,471	2,925	2,731
22,550	22,600	2,933	2,479	2,933	2,739
22,600	22,650	2,940	2,486	2,940	2,746
22,650	22,700	2,948	2,494	2,948	2,754
22,700	22,750	2,955	2,501	2,955	2,761
22,750	22,800	2,963	2,509	2,963	2,769
22,800	22,850	2,970	2,516	2,970	2,776
22,850	22,900	2,978	2,524	2,978	2,784
22,900	22,950	2,985	2,531	2,985	2,791
22,950	23,000	2,993	2,539	2,993	2,799

23,000

At least	But less than	Single	Married filing jointly *	Married filing separately	Head of a household
23,000	23,050	3,000	2,546	3,000	2,806
23,050	23,100	3,008	2,554	3,008	2,814
23,100	23,150	3,015	2,561	3,015	2,821
23,150	23,200	3,023	2,569	3,023	2,829
23,200	23,250	3,030	2,576	3,030	2,836
23,250	23,300	3,038	2,584	3,038	2,844
23,300	23,350	3,045	2,591	3,045	2,851
23,350	23,400	3,053	2,599	3,053	2,859
23,400	23,450	3,060	2,606	3,060	2,866
23,450	23,500	3,068	2,614	3,068	2,874
23,500	23,550	3,075	2,621	3,075	2,881
23,550	23,600	3,083	2,629	3,083	2,889
23,600	23,650	3,090	2,636	3,090	2,896
23,650	23,700	3,098	2,644	3,098	2,904
23,700	23,750	3,105	2,651	3,105	2,911
23,750	23,800	3,113	2,659	3,113	2,919
23,800	23,850	3,120	2,666	3,120	2,926
23,850	23,900	3,128	2,674	3,128	2,934
23,900	23,950	3,135	2,681	3,135	2,941
23,950	24,000	3,143	2,689	3,143	2,949

24,000

At least	But less than	Single	Married filing jointly *	Married filing separately	Head of a household
24,000	24,050	3,150	2,696	3,150	2,956
24,050	24,100	3,158	2,704	3,158	2,964
24,100	24,150	3,165	2,711	3,165	2,971
24,150	24,200	3,173	2,719	3,173	2,979
24,200	24,250	3,180	2,726	3,180	2,986
24,250	24,300	3,188	2,734	3,188	2,994
24,300	24,350	3,195	2,741	3,195	3,001
24,350	24,400	3,203	2,749	3,203	3,009
24,400	24,450	3,210	2,756	3,210	3,016
24,450	24,500	3,218	2,764	3,218	3,024
24,500	24,550	3,225	2,771	3,225	3,031
24,550	24,600	3,233	2,779	3,233	3,039
24,600	24,650	3,240	2,786	3,240	3,046
24,650	24,700	3,248	2,794	3,248	3,054
24,700	24,750	3,255	2,801	3,255	3,061
24,750	24,800	3,263	2,809	3,263	3,069
24,800	24,850	3,270	2,816	3,270	3,076
24,850	24,900	3,278	2,824	3,278	3,084
24,900	24,950	3,285	2,831	3,285	3,091
24,950	25,000	3,293	2,839	3,293	3,099

25,000

At least	But less than	Single	Married filing jointly *	Married filing separately	Head of a household
25,000	25,050	3,300	2,846	3,300	3,106
25,050	25,100	3,308	2,854	3,308	3,114
25,100	25,150	3,315	2,861	3,315	3,121
25,150	25,200	3,323	2,869	3,323	3,129
25,200	25,250	3,330	2,876	3,330	3,136
25,250	25,300	3,338	2,884	3,338	3,144
25,300	25,350	3,345	2,891	3,345	3,151
25,350	25,400	3,353	2,899	3,353	3,159
25,400	25,450	3,360	2,906	3,360	3,166
25,450	25,500	3,368	2,914	3,368	3,174
25,500	25,550	3,375	2,921	3,375	3,181
25,550	25,600	3,383	2,929	3,383	3,189
25,600	25,650	3,390	2,936	3,390	3,196
25,650	25,700	3,398	2,944	3,398	3,204
25,700	25,750	3,405	2,951	3,405	3,211
25,750	25,800	3,413	2,959	3,413	3,219
25,800	25,850	3,420	2,966	3,420	3,226
25,850	25,900	3,428	2,974	3,428	3,234
25,900	25,950	3,435	2,981	3,435	3,241
25,950	26,000	3,443	2,989	3,443	3,249

26,000

At least	But less than	Single	Married filing jointly *	Married filing separately	Head of a household
26,000	26,050	3,450	2,996	3,450	3,256
26,050	26,100	3,458	3,004	3,458	3,264
26,100	26,150	3,465	3,011	3,465	3,271
26,150	26,200	3,473	3,019	3,473	3,279
26,200	26,250	3,480	3,026	3,480	3,286
26,250	26,300	3,488	3,034	3,488	3,294
26,300	26,350	3,495	3,041	3,495	3,301
26,350	26,400	3,503	3,049	3,503	3,309
26,400	26,450	3,510	3,056	3,510	3,316
26,450	26,500	3,518	3,064	3,518	3,324
26,500	26,550	3,525	3,071	3,525	3,331
26,550	26,600	3,533	3,079	3,533	3,339
26,600	26,650	3,540	3,086	3,540	3,346
26,650	26,700	3,548	3,094	3,548	3,354
26,700	26,750	3,555	3,101	3,555	3,361
26,750	26,800	3,563	3,109	3,563	3,369
26,800	26,850	3,570	3,116	3,570	3,376
26,850	26,900	3,578	3,124	3,578	3,384
26,900	26,950	3,585	3,131	3,585	3,391
26,950	27,000	3,593	3,139	3,593	3,399

27,000

At least	But less than	Single	Married filing jointly *	Married filing separately	Head of a household
27,000	27,050	3,600	3,146	3,600	3,406
27,050	27,100	3,608	3,154	3,608	3,414
27,100	27,150	3,615	3,161	3,615	3,421
27,150	27,200	3,623	3,169	3,623	3,429
27,200	27,250	3,630	3,176	3,630	3,436
27,250	27,300	3,638	3,184	3,638	3,444
27,300	27,350	3,645	3,191	3,645	3,451
27,350	27,400	3,653	3,199	3,653	3,459
27,400	27,450	3,660	3,206	3,660	3,466
27,450	27,500	3,668	3,214	3,668	3,474
27,500	27,550	3,675	3,221	3,675	3,481
27,550	27,600	3,683	3,229	3,683	3,489
27,600	27,650	3,690	3,236	3,690	3,496
27,650	27,700	3,698	3,244	3,698	3,504
27,700	27,750	3,705	3,251	3,705	3,511
27,750	27,800	3,713	3,259	3,713	3,519
27,800	27,850	3,720	3,266	3,720	3,526
27,850	27,900	3,728	3,274	3,728	3,534
27,900	27,950	3,735	3,281	3,735	3,541
27,950	28,000	3,743	3,289	3,743	3,549

28,000

At least	But less than	Single	Married filing jointly *	Married filing separately	Head of a household
28,000	28,050	3,750	3,296	3,750	3,556
28,050	28,100	3,758	3,304	3,758	3,564
28,100	28,150	3,765	3,311	3,765	3,571
28,150	28,200	3,773	3,319	3,773	3,579
28,200	28,250	3,780	3,326	3,780	3,586
28,250	28,300	3,788	3,334	3,788	3,594
28,300	28,350	3,795	3,341	3,795	3,601
28,350	28,400	3,803	3,349	3,803	3,609
28,400	28,450	3,810	3,356	3,810	3,616
28,450	28,500	3,818	3,364	3,818	3,624
28,500	28,550	3,825	3,371	3,825	3,631
28,550	28,600	3,833	3,379	3,833	3,639
28,600	28,650	3,840	3,386	3,840	3,646
28,650	28,700	3,848	3,394	3,848	3,654
28,700	28,750	3,855	3,401	3,855	3,661
28,750	28,800	3,863	3,409	3,863	3,669
28,800	28,850	3,870	3,416	3,870	3,676
28,850	28,900	3,878	3,424	3,878	3,684
28,900	28,950	3,885	3,431	3,885	3,691
28,950	29,000	3,893	3,439	3,893	3,699

29,000

At least	But less than	Single	Married filing jointly *	Married filing separately	Head of a household
29,000	29,050	3,900	3,446	3,900	3,706
29,050	29,100	3,908	3,454	3,908	3,714
29,100	29,150	3,915	3,461	3,915	3,721
29,150	29,200	3,923	3,469	3,923	3,729
29,200	29,250	3,930	3,476	3,930	3,736
29,250	29,300	3,938	3,484	3,938	3,744
29,300	29,350	3,945	3,491	3,945	3,751
29,350	29,400	3,953	3,499	3,953	3,759
29,400	29,450	3,960	3,506	3,960	3,766
29,450	29,500	3,968	3,514	3,968	3,774
29,500	29,550	3,975	3,521	3,975	3,781
29,550	29,600	3,983	3,529	3,983	3,789
29,600	29,650	3,990	3,536	3,990	3,796
29,650	29,700	3,998	3,544	3,998	3,804
29,700	29,750	4,005	3,551	4,005	3,811
29,750	29,800	4,013	3,559	4,013	3,819
29,800	29,850	4,020	3,566	4,020	3,826
29,850	29,900	4,028	3,574	4,028	3,834
29,900	29,950	4,035	3,581	4,035	3,841
29,950	30,000	4,043	3,589	4,043	3,849

(Continued)

* This column must also be used by a qualifying widow(er).

30,000

If line 43 (taxable income) is— At least	But less than	Single	Married filing jointly *	Married filing separately	Head of a household
30,000	30,050	4,050	3,596	4,050	3,856
30,050	30,100	4,058	3,604	4,058	3,864
30,100	30,150	4,065	3,611	4,065	3,871
30,150	30,200	4,073	3,619	4,073	3,879
30,200	30,250	4,080	3,626	4,080	3,886
30,250	30,300	4,088	3,634	4,088	3,894
30,300	30,350	4,095	3,641	4,095	3,901
30,350	30,400	4,103	3,649	4,103	3,909
30,400	30,450	4,110	3,656	4,110	3,916
30,450	30,500	4,118	3,664	4,118	3,924
30,500	30,550	4,125	3,671	4,125	3,931
30,550	30,600	4,133	3,679	4,133	3,939
30,600	30,650	4,140	3,686	4,140	3,946
30,650	30,700	4,148	3,694	4,148	3,954
30,700	30,750	4,155	3,701	4,155	3,961
30,750	30,800	4,163	3,709	4,163	3,969
30,800	30,850	4,170	3,716	4,170	3,976
30,850	30,900	4,178	3,724	4,178	3,984
30,900	30,950	4,185	3,731	4,185	3,991
30,950	31,000	4,193	3,739	4,193	3,999

31,000

At least	But less than	Single	Married filing jointly *	Married filing separately	Head of a household
31,000	31,050	4,200	3,746	4,200	4,006
31,050	31,100	4,208	3,754	4,208	4,014
31,100	31,150	4,215	3,761	4,215	4,021
31,150	31,200	4,223	3,769	4,223	4,029
31,200	31,250	4,230	3,776	4,230	4,036
31,250	31,300	4,238	3,784	4,238	4,044
31,300	31,350	4,245	3,791	4,245	4,051
31,350	31,400	4,253	3,799	4,253	4,059
31,400	31,450	4,260	3,806	4,260	4,066
31,450	31,500	4,268	3,814	4,268	4,074
31,500	31,550	4,275	3,821	4,275	4,081
31,550	31,600	4,283	3,829	4,283	4,089
31,600	31,650	4,290	3,836	4,290	4,096
31,650	31,700	4,298	3,844	4,298	4,104
31,700	31,750	4,305	3,851	4,305	4,111
31,750	31,800	4,313	3,859	4,313	4,119
31,800	31,850	4,320	3,866	4,320	4,126
31,850	31,900	4,328	3,874	4,328	4,134
31,900	31,950	4,335	3,881	4,335	4,141
31,950	32,000	4,343	3,889	4,343	4,149

32,000

At least	But less than	Single	Married filing jointly *	Married filing separately	Head of a household
32,000	32,050	4,350	3,896	4,350	4,156
32,050	32,100	4,358	3,904	4,358	4,164
32,100	32,150	4,365	3,911	4,365	4,171
32,150	32,200	4,373	3,919	4,373	4,179
32,200	32,250	4,380	3,926	4,380	4,186
32,250	32,300	4,388	3,934	4,388	4,194
32,300	32,350	4,395	3,941	4,395	4,201
32,350	32,400	4,403	3,949	4,403	4,209
32,400	32,450	4,410	3,956	4,410	4,216
32,450	32,500	4,418	3,964	4,418	4,224
32,500	32,550	4,425	3,971	4,425	4,231
32,550	32,600	4,433	3,979	4,433	4,239
32,600	32,650	4,440	3,986	4,440	4,246
32,650	32,700	4,448	3,994	4,448	4,254
32,700	32,750	4,455	4,001	4,455	4,261
32,750	32,800	4,463	4,009	4,463	4,269
32,800	32,850	4,470	4,016	4,470	4,276
32,850	32,900	4,478	4,024	4,478	4,284
32,900	32,950	4,485	4,031	4,485	4,291
32,950	33,000	4,493	4,039	4,493	4,299

33,000

At least	But less than	Single	Married filing jointly *	Married filing separately	Head of a household
33,000	33,050	4,500	4,046	4,500	4,306
33,050	33,100	4,508	4,054	4,508	4,314
33,100	33,150	4,515	4,061	4,515	4,321
33,150	33,200	4,523	4,069	4,523	4,329
33,200	33,250	4,530	4,076	4,530	4,336
33,250	33,300	4,538	4,084	4,538	4,344
33,300	33,350	4,545	4,091	4,545	4,351
33,350	33,400	4,553	4,099	4,553	4,359
33,400	33,450	4,560	4,106	4,560	4,366
33,450	33,500	4,568	4,114	4,568	4,374
33,500	33,550	4,575	4,121	4,575	4,381
33,550	33,600	4,583	4,129	4,583	4,389
33,600	33,650	4,590	4,136	4,590	4,396
33,650	33,700	4,598	4,144	4,598	4,404
33,700	33,750	4,605	4,151	4,605	4,411
33,750	33,800	4,613	4,159	4,613	4,419
33,800	33,850	4,620	4,166	4,620	4,426
33,850	33,900	4,628	4,174	4,628	4,434
33,900	33,950	4,635	4,181	4,635	4,441
33,950	34,000	4,643	4,189	4,643	4,449

34,000

At least	But less than	Single	Married filing jointly *	Married filing separately	Head of a household
34,000	34,050	4,650	4,196	4,650	4,456
34,050	34,100	4,658	4,204	4,658	4,464
34,100	34,150	4,665	4,211	4,665	4,471
34,150	34,200	4,673	4,219	4,673	4,479
34,200	34,250	4,680	4,226	4,680	4,486
34,250	34,300	4,688	4,234	4,688	4,494
34,300	34,350	4,695	4,241	4,695	4,501
34,350	34,400	4,703	4,249	4,703	4,509
34,400	34,450	4,710	4,256	4,710	4,516
34,450	34,500	4,718	4,264	4,718	4,524
34,500	34,550	4,725	4,271	4,725	4,531
34,550	34,600	4,733	4,279	4,733	4,539
34,600	34,650	4,740	4,286	4,740	4,546
34,650	34,700	4,748	4,294	4,748	4,554
34,700	34,750	4,755	4,301	4,755	4,561
34,750	34,800	4,763	4,309	4,763	4,569
34,800	34,850	4,770	4,316	4,770	4,576
34,850	34,900	4,778	4,324	4,778	4,584
34,900	34,950	4,785	4,331	4,785	4,591
34,950	35,000	4,793	4,339	4,793	4,599

35,000

At least	But less than	Single	Married filing jointly *	Married filing separately	Head of a household
35,000	35,050	4,800	4,346	4,800	4,606
35,050	35,100	4,808	4,354	4,808	4,614
35,100	35,150	4,815	4,361	4,815	4,621
35,150	35,200	4,823	4,369	4,823	4,629
35,200	35,250	4,830	4,376	4,830	4,636
35,250	35,300	4,838	4,384	4,838	4,644
35,300	35,350	4,845	4,391	4,845	4,651
35,350	35,400	4,853	4,399	4,853	4,659
35,400	35,450	4,860	4,406	4,860	4,666
35,450	35,500	4,868	4,414	4,868	4,674
35,500	35,550	4,875	4,421	4,875	4,681
35,550	35,600	4,883	4,429	4,883	4,689
35,600	35,650	4,890	4,436	4,890	4,696
35,650	35,700	4,898	4,444	4,898	4,704
35,700	35,750	4,905	4,451	4,905	4,711
35,750	35,800	4,913	4,459	4,913	4,719
35,800	35,850	4,920	4,466	4,920	4,726
35,850	35,900	4,928	4,474	4,928	4,734
35,900	35,950	4,935	4,481	4,935	4,741
35,950	36,000	4,943	4,489	4,943	4,749

36,000

At least	But less than	Single	Married filing jointly *	Married filing separately	Head of a household
36,000	36,050	4,950	4,496	4,950	4,756
36,050	36,100	4,958	4,504	4,958	4,764
36,100	36,150	4,965	4,511	4,965	4,771
36,150	36,200	4,973	4,519	4,973	4,779
36,200	36,250	4,980	4,526	4,980	4,786
36,250	36,300	4,988	4,534	4,988	4,794
36,300	36,350	4,995	4,541	4,995	4,801
36,350	36,400	5,003	4,549	5,003	4,809
36,400	36,450	5,010	4,556	5,010	4,816
36,450	36,500	5,018	4,564	5,018	4,824
36,500	36,550	5,025	4,571	5,025	4,831
36,550	36,600	5,033	4,579	5,033	4,839
36,600	36,650	5,040	4,586	5,040	4,846
36,650	36,700	5,048	4,594	5,048	4,854
36,700	36,750	5,055	4,601	5,055	4,861
36,750	36,800	5,063	4,609	5,063	4,869
36,800	36,850	5,070	4,616	5,070	4,876
36,850	36,900	5,078	4,624	5,078	4,884
36,900	36,950	5,088	4,631	5,088	4,891
36,950	37,000	5,100	4,639	5,100	4,899

37,000

At least	But less than	Single	Married filing jointly *	Married filing separately	Head of a household
37,000	37,050	5,113	4,646	5,113	4,906
37,050	37,100	5,125	4,654	5,125	4,914
37,100	37,150	5,138	4,661	5,138	4,921
37,150	37,200	5,150	4,669	5,150	4,929
37,200	37,250	5,163	4,676	5,163	4,936
37,250	37,300	5,175	4,684	5,175	4,944
37,300	37,350	5,188	4,691	5,188	4,951
37,350	37,400	5,200	4,699	5,200	4,959
37,400	37,450	5,213	4,706	5,213	4,966
37,450	37,500	5,225	4,714	5,225	4,974
37,500	37,550	5,238	4,721	5,238	4,981
37,550	37,600	5,250	4,729	5,250	4,989
37,600	37,650	5,263	4,736	5,263	4,996
37,650	37,700	5,275	4,744	5,275	5,004
37,700	37,750	5,288	4,751	5,288	5,011
37,750	37,800	5,300	4,759	5,300	5,019
37,800	37,850	5,313	4,766	5,313	5,026
37,850	37,900	5,325	4,774	5,325	5,034
37,900	37,950	5,338	4,781	5,338	5,041
37,950	38,000	5,350	4,789	5,350	5,049

38,000

At least	But less than	Single	Married filing jointly *	Married filing separately	Head of a household
38,000	38,050	5,363	4,796	5,363	5,056
38,050	38,100	5,375	4,804	5,375	5,064
38,100	38,150	5,388	4,811	5,388	5,071
38,150	38,200	5,400	4,819	5,400	5,079
38,200	38,250	5,413	4,826	5,413	5,086
38,250	38,300	5,425	4,834	5,425	5,094
38,300	38,350	5,438	4,841	5,438	5,101
38,350	38,400	5,450	4,849	5,450	5,109
38,400	38,450	5,463	4,856	5,463	5,116
38,450	38,500	5,475	4,864	5,475	5,124
38,500	38,550	5,488	4,871	5,488	5,131
38,550	38,600	5,500	4,879	5,500	5,139
38,600	38,650	5,513	4,886	5,513	5,146
38,650	38,700	5,525	4,894	5,525	5,154
38,700	38,750	5,538	4,901	5,538	5,161
38,750	38,800	5,550	4,909	5,550	5,169
38,800	38,850	5,563	4,916	5,563	5,176
38,850	38,900	5,575	4,924	5,575	5,184
38,900	38,950	5,588	4,931	5,588	5,191
38,950	39,000	5,600	4,939	5,600	5,199

* This column must also be used by a qualifying widow(er).

(Continued)

If line 43 (taxable income) is—		And you are—			
At least	But less than	Single	Married filing jointly *	Married filing separately	Head of a household
		Your tax is—			

39,000

At least	But less than	Single	Married filing jointly *	Married filing separately	Head of a household
39,000	39,050	5,613	4,946	5,613	5,206
39,050	39,100	5,625	4,954	5,625	5,214
39,100	39,150	5,638	4,961	5,638	5,221
39,150	39,200	5,650	4,969	5,650	5,229
39,200	39,250	5,663	4,976	5,663	5,236
39,250	39,300	5,675	4,984	5,675	5,244
39,300	39,350	5,688	4,991	5,688	5,251
39,350	39,400	5,700	4,999	5,700	5,259
39,400	39,450	5,713	5,006	5,713	5,266
39,450	39,500	5,725	5,014	5,725	5,274
39,500	39,550	5,738	5,021	5,738	5,281
39,550	39,600	5,750	5,029	5,750	5,289
39,600	39,650	5,763	5,036	5,763	5,296
39,650	39,700	5,775	5,044	5,775	5,304
39,700	39,750	5,788	5,051	5,788	5,311
39,750	39,800	5,800	5,059	5,800	5,319
39,800	39,850	5,813	5,066	5,813	5,326
39,850	39,900	5,825	5,074	5,825	5,334
39,900	39,950	5,838	5,081	5,838	5,341
39,950	40,000	5,850	5,089	5,850	5,349

40,000

At least	But less than	Single	Married filing jointly *	Married filing separately	Head of a household
40,000	40,050	5,863	5,096	5,863	5,356
40,050	40,100	5,875	5,104	5,875	5,364
40,100	40,150	5,888	5,111	5,888	5,371
40,150	40,200	5,900	5,119	5,900	5,379
40,200	40,250	5,913	5,126	5,913	5,386
40,250	40,300	5,925	5,134	5,925	5,394
40,300	40,350	5,938	5,141	5,938	5,401
40,350	40,400	5,950	5,149	5,950	5,409
40,400	40,450	5,963	5,156	5,963	5,416
40,450	40,500	5,975	5,164	5,975	5,424
40,500	40,550	5,988	5,171	5,988	5,431
40,550	40,600	6,000	5,179	6,000	5,439
40,600	40,650	6,013	5,186	6,013	5,446
40,650	40,700	6,025	5,194	6,025	5,454
40,700	40,750	6,038	5,201	6,038	5,461
40,750	40,800	6,050	5,209	6,050	5,469
40,800	40,850	6,063	5,216	6,063	5,476
40,850	40,900	6,075	5,224	6,075	5,484
40,900	40,950	6,088	5,231	6,088	5,491
40,950	41,000	6,100	5,239	6,100	5,499

41,000

At least	But less than	Single	Married filing jointly *	Married filing separately	Head of a household
41,000	41,050	6,113	5,246	6,113	5,506
41,050	41,100	6,125	5,254	6,125	5,514
41,100	41,150	6,138	5,261	6,138	5,521
41,150	41,200	6,150	5,269	6,150	5,529
41,200	41,250	6,163	5,276	6,163	5,536
41,250	41,300	6,175	5,284	6,175	5,544
41,300	41,350	6,188	5,291	6,188	5,551
41,350	41,400	6,200	5,299	6,200	5,559
41,400	41,450	6,213	5,306	6,213	5,566
41,450	41,500	6,225	5,314	6,225	5,574
41,500	41,550	6,238	5,321	6,238	5,581
41,550	41,600	6,250	5,329	6,250	5,589
41,600	41,650	6,263	5,336	6,263	5,596
41,650	41,700	6,275	5,344	6,275	5,604
41,700	41,750	6,288	5,351	6,288	5,611
41,750	41,800	6,300	5,359	6,300	5,619
41,800	41,850	6,313	5,366	6,313	5,626
41,850	41,900	6,325	5,374	6,325	5,634
41,900	41,950	6,338	5,381	6,338	5,641
41,950	42,000	6,350	5,389	6,350	5,649

42,000

At least	But less than	Single	Married filing jointly *	Married filing separately	Head of a household
42,000	42,050	6,363	5,396	6,363	5,656
42,050	42,100	6,375	5,404	6,375	5,664
42,100	42,150	6,388	5,411	6,388	5,671
42,150	42,200	6,400	5,419	6,400	5,679
42,200	42,250	6,413	5,426	6,413	5,686
42,250	42,300	6,425	5,434	6,425	5,694
42,300	42,350	6,438	5,441	6,438	5,701
42,350	42,400	6,450	5,449	6,450	5,709
42,400	42,450	6,463	5,456	6,463	5,716
42,450	42,500	6,475	5,464	6,475	5,724
42,500	42,550	6,488	5,471	6,488	5,731
42,550	42,600	6,500	5,479	6,500	5,739
42,600	42,650	6,513	5,486	6,513	5,746
42,650	42,700	6,525	5,494	6,525	5,754
42,700	42,750	6,538	5,501	6,538	5,761
42,750	42,800	6,550	5,509	6,550	5,769
42,800	42,850	6,563	5,516	6,563	5,776
42,850	42,900	6,575	5,524	6,575	5,784
42,900	42,950	6,588	5,531	6,588	5,791
42,950	43,000	6,600	5,539	6,600	5,799

43,000

At least	But less than	Single	Married filing jointly *	Married filing separately	Head of a household
43,000	43,050	6,613	5,546	6,613	5,806
43,050	43,100	6,625	5,554	6,625	5,814
43,100	43,150	6,638	5,561	6,638	5,821
43,150	43,200	6,650	5,569	6,650	5,829
43,200	43,250	6,663	5,576	6,663	5,836
43,250	43,300	6,675	5,584	6,675	5,844
43,300	43,350	6,688	5,591	6,688	5,851
43,350	43,400	6,700	5,599	6,700	5,859
43,400	43,450	6,713	5,606	6,713	5,866
43,450	43,500	6,725	5,614	6,725	5,874
43,500	43,550	6,738	5,621	6,738	5,881
43,550	43,600	6,750	5,629	6,750	5,889
43,600	43,650	6,763	5,636	6,763	5,896
43,650	43,700	6,775	5,644	6,775	5,904
43,700	43,750	6,788	5,651	6,788	5,911
43,750	43,800	6,800	5,659	6,800	5,919
43,800	43,850	6,813	5,666	6,813	5,926
43,850	43,900	6,825	5,674	6,825	5,934
43,900	43,950	6,838	5,681	6,838	5,941
43,950	44,000	6,850	5,689	6,850	5,949

44,000

At least	But less than	Single	Married filing jointly *	Married filing separately	Head of a household
44,000	44,050	6,863	5,696	6,863	5,956
44,050	44,100	6,875	5,704	6,875	5,964
44,100	44,150	6,888	5,711	6,888	5,971
44,150	44,200	6,900	5,719	6,900	5,979
44,200	44,250	6,913	5,726	6,913	5,986
44,250	44,300	6,925	5,734	6,925	5,994
44,300	44,350	6,938	5,741	6,938	6,001
44,350	44,400	6,950	5,749	6,950	6,009
44,400	44,450	6,963	5,756	6,963	6,016
44,450	44,500	6,975	5,764	6,975	6,024
44,500	44,550	6,988	5,771	6,988	6,031
44,550	44,600	7,000	5,779	7,000	6,039
44,600	44,650	7,013	5,786	7,013	6,046
44,650	44,700	7,025	5,794	7,025	6,054
44,700	44,750	7,038	5,801	7,038	6,061
44,750	44,800	7,050	5,809	7,050	6,069
44,800	44,850	7,063	5,816	7,063	6,076
44,850	44,900	7,075	5,824	7,075	6,084
44,900	44,950	7,088	5,831	7,088	6,091
44,950	45,000	7,100	5,839	7,100	6,099

45,000

At least	But less than	Single	Married filing jointly *	Married filing separately	Head of a household
45,000	45,050	7,113	5,846	7,113	6,106
45,050	45,100	7,125	5,854	7,125	6,114
45,100	45,150	7,138	5,861	7,138	6,121
45,150	45,200	7,150	5,869	7,150	6,129
45,200	45,250	7,163	5,876	7,163	6,136
45,250	45,300	7,175	5,884	7,175	6,144
45,300	45,350	7,188	5,891	7,188	6,151
45,350	45,400	7,200	5,899	7,200	6,159
45,400	45,450	7,213	5,906	7,213	6,166
45,450	45,500	7,225	5,914	7,225	6,174
45,500	45,550	7,238	5,921	7,238	6,181
45,550	45,600	7,250	5,929	7,250	6,189
45,600	45,650	7,263	5,936	7,263	6,196
45,650	45,700	7,275	5,944	7,275	6,204
45,700	45,750	7,288	5,951	7,288	6,211
45,750	45,800	7,300	5,959	7,300	6,219
45,800	45,850	7,313	5,966	7,313	6,226
45,850	45,900	7,325	5,974	7,325	6,234
45,900	45,950	7,338	5,981	7,338	6,241
45,950	46,000	7,350	5,989	7,350	6,249

46,000

At least	But less than	Single	Married filing jointly *	Married filing separately	Head of a household
46,000	46,050	7,363	5,996	7,363	6,256
46,050	46,100	7,375	6,004	7,375	6,264
46,100	46,150	7,388	6,011	7,388	6,271
46,150	46,200	7,400	6,019	7,400	6,279
46,200	46,250	7,413	6,026	7,413	6,286
46,250	46,300	7,425	6,034	7,425	6,294
46,300	46,350	7,438	6,041	7,438	6,301
46,350	46,400	7,450	6,049	7,450	6,309
46,400	46,450	7,463	6,056	7,463	6,316
46,450	46,500	7,475	6,064	7,475	6,324
46,500	46,550	7,488	6,071	7,488	6,331
46,550	46,600	7,500	6,079	7,500	6,339
46,600	46,650	7,513	6,086	7,513	6,346
46,650	46,700	7,525	6,094	7,525	6,354
46,700	46,750	7,538	6,101	7,538	6,361
46,750	46,800	7,550	6,109	7,550	6,369
46,800	46,850	7,563	6,116	7,563	6,376
46,850	46,900	7,575	6,124	7,575	6,384
46,900	46,950	7,588	6,131	7,588	6,391
46,950	47,000	7,600	6,139	7,600	6,399

47,000

At least	But less than	Single	Married filing jointly *	Married filing separately	Head of a household
47,000	47,050	7,613	6,146	7,613	6,406
47,050	47,100	7,625	6,154	7,625	6,414
47,100	47,150	7,638	6,161	7,638	6,421
47,150	47,200	7,650	6,169	7,650	6,429
47,200	47,250	7,663	6,176	7,663	6,436
47,250	47,300	7,675	6,184	7,675	6,444
47,300	47,350	7,688	6,191	7,688	6,451
47,350	47,400	7,700	6,199	7,700	6,459
47,400	47,450	7,713	6,206	7,713	6,466
47,450	47,500	7,725	6,214	7,725	6,474
47,500	47,550	7,738	6,221	7,738	6,481
47,550	47,600	7,750	6,229	7,750	6,489
47,600	47,650	7,763	6,236	7,763	6,496
47,650	47,700	7,775	6,244	7,775	6,504
47,700	47,750	7,788	6,251	7,788	6,511
47,750	47,800	7,800	6,259	7,800	6,519
47,800	47,850	7,813	6,266	7,813	6,526
47,850	47,900	7,825	6,274	7,825	6,534
47,900	47,950	7,838	6,281	7,838	6,541
47,950	48,000	7,850	6,289	7,850	6,549

(Continued)

* This column must also be used by a qualifying widow(er).

48,000

At least	But less than	Single	Married filing jointly *	Married filing separately	Head of a household
		Your tax is—			
48,000	48,050	7,863	6,296	7,863	6,556
48,050	48,100	7,875	6,304	7,875	6,564
48,100	48,150	7,888	6,311	7,888	6,571
48,150	48,200	7,900	6,319	7,900	6,579
48,200	48,250	7,913	6,326	7,913	6,586
48,250	48,300	7,925	6,334	7,925	6,594
48,300	48,350	7,938	6,341	7,938	6,601
48,350	48,400	7,950	6,349	7,950	6,609
48,400	48,450	7,963	6,356	7,963	6,616
48,450	48,500	7,975	6,364	7,975	6,624
48,500	48,550	7,988	6,371	7,988	6,631
48,550	48,600	8,000	6,379	8,000	6,639
48,600	48,650	8,013	6,386	8,013	6,646
48,650	48,700	8,025	6,394	8,025	6,654
48,700	48,750	8,038	6,401	8,038	6,661
48,750	48,800	8,050	6,409	8,050	6,669
48,800	48,850	8,063	6,416	8,063	6,676
48,850	48,900	8,075	6,424	8,075	6,684
48,900	48,950	8,088	6,431	8,088	6,691
48,950	49,000	8,100	6,439	8,100	6,699

49,000

At least	But less than	Single	Married filing jointly *	Married filing separately	Head of a household
49,000	49,050	8,113	6,446	8,113	6,706
49,050	49,100	8,125	6,454	8,125	6,714
49,100	49,150	8,138	6,461	8,138	6,721
49,150	49,200	8,150	6,469	8,150	6,729
49,200	49,250	8,163	6,476	8,163	6,736
49,250	49,300	8,175	6,484	8,175	6,744
49,300	49,350	8,188	6,491	8,188	6,751
49,350	49,400	8,200	6,499	8,200	6,759
49,400	49,450	8,213	6,506	8,213	6,766
49,450	49,500	8,225	6,514	8,225	6,781
49,500	49,550	8,238	6,521	8,238	6,794
49,550	49,600	8,250	6,529	8,250	6,806
49,600	49,650	8,263	6,536	8,263	6,819
49,650	49,700	8,275	6,544	8,275	6,831
49,700	49,750	8,288	6,551	8,288	6,844
49,750	49,800	8,300	6,559	8,300	6,856
49,800	49,850	8,313	6,566	8,313	6,869
49,850	49,900	8,325	6,574	8,325	6,881
49,900	49,950	8,338	6,581	8,338	6,894
49,950	50,000	8,350	6,589	8,350	6,906

50,000

At least	But less than	Single	Married filing jointly *	Married filing separately	Head of a household
50,000	50,050	8,363	6,596	8,363	6,919
50,050	50,100	8,375	6,604	8,375	6,931
50,100	50,150	8,388	6,611	8,388	6,944
50,150	50,200	8,400	6,619	8,400	6,956
50,200	50,250	8,413	6,626	8,413	6,969
50,250	50,300	8,425	6,634	8,425	6,981
50,300	50,350	8,438	6,641	8,438	6,994
50,350	50,400	8,450	6,649	8,450	7,006
50,400	50,450	8,463	6,656	8,463	7,019
50,450	50,500	8,475	6,664	8,475	7,031
50,500	50,550	8,488	6,671	8,488	7,044
50,550	50,600	8,500	6,679	8,500	7,056
50,600	50,650	8,513	6,686	8,513	7,069
50,650	50,700	8,525	6,694	8,525	7,081
50,700	50,750	8,538	6,701	8,538	7,094
50,750	50,800	8,550	6,709	8,550	7,106
50,800	50,850	8,563	6,716	8,563	7,119
50,850	50,900	8,575	6,724	8,575	7,131
50,900	50,950	8,588	6,731	8,588	7,144
50,950	51,000	8,600	6,739	8,600	7,156

51,000

At least	But less than	Single	Married filing jointly *	Married filing separately	Head of a household
		Your tax is—			
51,000	51,050	8,613	6,746	8,613	7,169
51,050	51,100	8,625	6,754	8,625	7,181
51,100	51,150	8,638	6,761	8,638	7,194
51,150	51,200	8,650	6,769	8,650	7,206
51,200	51,250	8,663	6,776	8,663	7,219
51,250	51,300	8,675	6,784	8,675	7,231
51,300	51,350	8,688	6,791	8,688	7,244
51,350	51,400	8,700	6,799	8,700	7,256
51,400	51,450	8,713	6,806	8,713	7,269
51,450	51,500	8,725	6,814	8,725	7,281
51,500	51,550	8,738	6,821	8,738	7,294
51,550	51,600	8,750	6,829	8,750	7,306
51,600	51,650	8,763	6,836	8,763	7,319
51,650	51,700	8,775	6,844	8,775	7,331
51,700	51,750	8,788	6,851	8,788	7,344
51,750	51,800	8,800	6,859	8,800	7,356
51,800	51,850	8,813	6,866	8,813	7,369
51,850	51,900	8,825	6,874	8,825	7,381
51,900	51,950	8,838	6,881	8,838	7,394
51,950	52,000	8,850	6,889	8,850	7,406

52,000

At least	But less than	Single	Married filing jointly *	Married filing separately	Head of a household
52,000	52,050	8,863	6,896	8,863	7,419
52,050	52,100	8,875	6,904	8,875	7,431
52,100	52,150	8,888	6,911	8,888	7,444
52,150	52,200	8,900	6,919	8,900	7,456
52,200	52,250	8,913	6,926	8,913	7,469
52,250	52,300	8,925	6,934	8,925	7,481
52,300	52,350	8,938	6,941	8,938	7,494
52,350	52,400	8,950	6,949	8,950	7,506
52,400	52,450	8,963	6,956	8,963	7,519
52,450	52,500	8,975	6,964	8,975	7,531
52,500	52,550	8,988	6,971	8,988	7,544
52,550	52,600	9,000	6,979	9,000	7,556
52,600	52,650	9,013	6,986	9,013	7,569
52,650	52,700	9,025	6,994	9,025	7,581
52,700	52,750	9,038	7,001	9,038	7,594
52,750	52,800	9,050	7,009	9,050	7,606
52,800	52,850	9,063	7,016	9,063	7,619
52,850	52,900	9,075	7,024	9,075	7,631
52,900	52,950	9,088	7,031	9,088	7,644
52,950	53,000	9,100	7,039	9,100	7,656

53,000

At least	But less than	Single	Married filing jointly *	Married filing separately	Head of a household
53,000	53,050	9,113	7,046	9,113	7,669
53,050	53,100	9,125	7,054	9,125	7,681
53,100	53,150	9,138	7,061	9,138	7,694
53,150	53,200	9,150	7,069	9,150	7,706
53,200	53,250	9,163	7,076	9,163	7,719
53,250	53,300	9,175	7,084	9,175	7,731
53,300	53,350	9,188	7,091	9,188	7,744
53,350	53,400	9,200	7,099	9,200	7,756
53,400	53,450	9,213	7,106	9,213	7,769
53,450	53,500	9,225	7,114	9,225	7,781
53,500	53,550	9,238	7,121	9,238	7,794
53,550	53,600	9,250	7,129	9,250	7,806
53,600	53,650	9,263	7,136	9,263	7,819
53,650	53,700	9,275	7,144	9,275	7,831
53,700	53,750	9,288	7,151	9,288	7,844
53,750	53,800	9,300	7,159	9,300	7,856
53,800	53,850	9,313	7,166	9,313	7,869
53,850	53,900	9,325	7,174	9,325	7,881
53,900	53,950	9,338	7,181	9,338	7,894
53,950	54,000	9,350	7,189	9,350	7,906

54,000

At least	But less than	Single	Married filing jointly *	Married filing separately	Head of a household
		Your tax is—			
54,000	54,050	9,363	7,196	9,363	7,919
54,050	54,100	9,375	7,204	9,375	7,931
54,100	54,150	9,388	7,211	9,388	7,944
54,150	54,200	9,400	7,219	9,400	7,956
54,200	54,250	9,413	7,226	9,413	7,969
54,250	54,300	9,425	7,234	9,425	7,981
54,300	54,350	9,438	7,241	9,438	7,994
54,350	54,400	9,450	7,249	9,450	8,006
54,400	54,450	9,463	7,256	9,463	8,019
54,450	54,500	9,475	7,264	9,475	8,031
54,500	54,550	9,488	7,271	9,488	8,044
54,550	54,600	9,500	7,279	9,500	8,056
54,600	54,650	9,513	7,286	9,513	8,069
54,650	54,700	9,525	7,294	9,525	8,081
54,700	54,750	9,538	7,301	9,538	8,094
54,750	54,800	9,550	7,309	9,550	8,106
54,800	54,850	9,563	7,316	9,563	8,119
54,850	54,900	9,575	7,324	9,575	8,131
54,900	54,950	9,588	7,331	9,588	8,144
54,950	55,000	9,600	7,339	9,600	8,156

55,000

At least	But less than	Single	Married filing jointly *	Married filing separately	Head of a household
55,000	55,050	9,613	7,346	9,613	8,169
55,050	55,100	9,625	7,354	9,625	8,181
55,100	55,150	9,638	7,361	9,638	8,194
55,150	55,200	9,650	7,369	9,650	8,206
55,200	55,250	9,663	7,376	9,663	8,219
55,250	55,300	9,675	7,384	9,675	8,231
55,300	55,350	9,688	7,391	9,688	8,244
55,350	55,400	9,700	7,399	9,700	8,256
55,400	55,450	9,713	7,406	9,713	8,269
55,450	55,500	9,725	7,414	9,725	8,281
55,500	55,550	9,738	7,421	9,738	8,294
55,550	55,600	9,750	7,429	9,750	8,306
55,600	55,650	9,763	7,436	9,763	8,319
55,650	55,700	9,775	7,444	9,775	8,331
55,700	55,750	9,788	7,451	9,788	8,344
55,750	55,800	9,800	7,459	9,800	8,356
55,800	55,850	9,813	7,466	9,813	8,369
55,850	55,900	9,825	7,474	9,825	8,381
55,900	55,950	9,838	7,481	9,838	8,394
55,950	56,000	9,850	7,489	9,850	8,406

56,000

At least	But less than	Single	Married filing jointly *	Married filing separately	Head of a household
56,000	56,050	9,863	7,496	9,863	8,419
56,050	56,100	9,875	7,504	9,875	8,431
56,100	56,150	9,888	7,511	9,888	8,444
56,150	56,200	9,900	7,519	9,900	8,456
56,200	56,250	9,913	7,526	9,913	8,469
56,250	56,300	9,925	7,534	9,925	8,481
56,300	56,350	9,938	7,541	9,938	8,494
56,350	56,400	9,950	7,549	9,950	8,506
56,400	56,450	9,963	7,556	9,963	8,519
56,450	56,500	9,975	7,564	9,975	8,531
56,500	56,550	9,988	7,571	9,988	8,544
56,550	56,600	10,000	7,579	10,000	8,556
56,600	56,650	10,013	7,586	10,013	8,569
56,650	56,700	10,025	7,594	10,025	8,581
56,700	56,750	10,038	7,601	10,038	8,594
56,750	56,800	10,050	7,609	10,050	8,606
56,800	56,850	10,063	7,616	10,063	8,619
56,850	56,900	10,075	7,624	10,075	8,631
56,900	56,950	10,088	7,631	10,088	8,644
56,950	57,000	10,100	7,639	10,100	8,656

If line 43 (taxable income) is— / *And you are—*

* This column must also be used by a qualifying widow(er).

(Continued)

If line 43 (taxable income) is—		And you are—			
At least	But less than	Single	Married filing jointly *	Married filing separately	Head of a household
		Your tax is—			

57,000

At least	But less than	Single	Married filing jointly *	Married filing separately	Head of a household
57,000	57,050	10,113	7,646	10,113	8,669
57,050	57,100	10,125	7,654	10,125	8,681
57,100	57,150	10,138	7,661	10,138	8,694
57,150	57,200	10,150	7,669	10,150	8,706
57,200	57,250	10,163	7,676	10,163	8,719
57,250	57,300	10,175	7,684	10,175	8,731
57,300	57,350	10,188	7,691	10,188	8,744
57,350	57,400	10,200	7,699	10,200	8,756
57,400	57,450	10,213	7,706	10,213	8,769
57,450	57,500	10,225	7,714	10,225	8,781
57,500	57,550	10,238	7,721	10,238	8,794
57,550	57,600	10,250	7,729	10,250	8,806
57,600	57,650	10,263	7,736	10,263	8,819
57,650	57,700	10,275	7,744	10,275	8,831
57,700	57,750	10,288	7,751	10,288	8,844
57,750	57,800	10,300	7,759	10,300	8,856
57,800	57,850	10,313	7,766	10,313	8,869
57,850	57,900	10,325	7,774	10,325	8,881
57,900	57,950	10,338	7,781	10,338	8,894
57,950	58,000	10,350	7,789	10,350	8,906

58,000

At least	But less than	Single	Married filing jointly *	Married filing separately	Head of a household
58,000	58,050	10,363	7,796	10,363	8,919
58,050	58,100	10,375	7,804	10,375	8,931
58,100	58,150	10,388	7,811	10,388	8,944
58,150	58,200	10,400	7,819	10,400	8,956
58,200	58,250	10,413	7,826	10,413	8,969
58,250	58,300	10,425	7,834	10,425	8,981
58,300	58,350	10,438	7,841	10,438	8,994
58,350	58,400	10,450	7,849	10,450	9,006
58,400	58,450	10,463	7,856	10,463	9,019
58,450	58,500	10,475	7,864	10,475	9,031
58,500	58,550	10,488	7,871	10,488	9,044
58,550	58,600	10,500	7,879	10,500	9,056
58,600	58,650	10,513	7,886	10,513	9,069
58,650	58,700	10,525	7,894	10,525	9,081
58,700	58,750	10,538	7,901	10,538	9,094
58,750	58,800	10,550	7,909	10,550	9,106
58,800	58,850	10,563	7,916	10,563	9,119
58,850	58,900	10,575	7,924	10,575	9,131
58,900	58,950	10,588	7,931	10,588	9,144
58,950	59,000	10,600	7,939	10,600	9,156

59,000

At least	But less than	Single	Married filing jointly *	Married filing separately	Head of a household
59,000	59,050	10,613	7,946	10,613	9,169
59,050	59,100	10,625	7,954	10,625	9,181
59,100	59,150	10,638	7,961	10,638	9,194
59,150	59,200	10,650	7,969	10,650	9,206
59,200	59,250	10,663	7,976	10,663	9,219
59,250	59,300	10,675	7,984	10,675	9,231
59,300	59,350	10,688	7,991	10,688	9,244
59,350	59,400	10,700	7,999	10,700	9,256
59,400	59,450	10,713	8,006	10,713	9,269
59,450	59,500	10,725	8,014	10,725	9,281
59,500	59,550	10,738	8,021	10,738	9,294
59,550	59,600	10,750	8,029	10,750	9,306
59,600	59,650	10,763	8,036	10,763	9,319
59,650	59,700	10,775	8,044	10,775	9,331
59,700	59,750	10,788	8,051	10,788	9,344
59,750	59,800	10,800	8,059	10,800	9,356
59,800	59,850	10,813	8,066	10,813	9,369
59,850	59,900	10,825	8,074	10,825	9,381
59,900	59,950	10,838	8,081	10,838	9,394
59,950	60,000	10,850	8,089	10,850	9,406

60,000

At least	But less than	Single	Married filing jointly *	Married filing separately	Head of a household
60,000	60,050	10,863	8,096	10,863	9,419
60,050	60,100	10,875	8,104	10,875	9,431
60,100	60,150	10,888	8,111	10,888	9,444
60,150	60,200	10,900	8,119	10,900	9,456
60,200	60,250	10,913	8,126	10,913	9,469
60,250	60,300	10,925	8,134	10,925	9,481
60,300	60,350	10,938	8,141	10,938	9,494
60,350	60,400	10,950	8,149	10,950	9,506
60,400	60,450	10,963	8,156	10,963	9,519
60,450	60,500	10,975	8,164	10,975	9,531
60,500	60,550	10,988	8,171	10,988	9,544
60,550	60,600	11,000	8,179	11,000	9,556
60,600	60,650	11,013	8,186	11,013	9,569
60,650	60,700	11,025	8,194	11,025	9,581
60,700	60,750	11,038	8,201	11,038	9,594
60,750	60,800	11,050	8,209	11,050	9,606
60,800	60,850	11,063	8,216	11,063	9,619
60,850	60,900	11,075	8,224	11,075	9,631
60,900	60,950	11,088	8,231	11,088	9,644
60,950	61,000	11,100	8,239	11,100	9,656

61,000

At least	But less than	Single	Married filing jointly *	Married filing separately	Head of a household
61,000	61,050	11,113	8,246	11,113	9,669
61,050	61,100	11,125	8,254	11,125	9,681
61,100	61,150	11,138	8,261	11,138	9,694
61,150	61,200	11,150	8,269	11,150	9,706
61,200	61,250	11,163	8,276	11,163	9,719
61,250	61,300	11,175	8,284	11,175	9,731
61,300	61,350	11,188	8,291	11,188	9,744
61,350	61,400	11,200	8,299	11,200	9,756
61,400	61,450	11,213	8,306	11,213	9,769
61,450	61,500	11,225	8,314	11,225	9,781
61,500	61,550	11,238	8,321	11,238	9,794
61,550	61,600	11,250	8,329	11,250	9,806
61,600	61,650	11,263	8,336	11,263	9,819
61,650	61,700	11,275	8,344	11,275	9,831
61,700	61,750	11,288	8,351	11,288	9,844
61,750	61,800	11,300	8,359	11,300	9,856
61,800	61,850	11,313	8,366	11,313	9,869
61,850	61,900	11,325	8,374	11,325	9,881
61,900	61,950	11,338	8,381	11,338	9,894
61,950	62,000	11,350	8,389	11,350	9,906

62,000

At least	But less than	Single	Married filing jointly *	Married filing separately	Head of a household
62,000	62,050	11,363	8,396	11,363	9,919
62,050	62,100	11,375	8,404	11,375	9,931
62,100	62,150	11,388	8,411	11,388	9,944
62,150	62,200	11,400	8,419	11,400	9,956
62,200	62,250	11,413	8,426	11,413	9,969
62,250	62,300	11,425	8,434	11,425	9,981
62,300	62,350	11,438	8,441	11,438	9,994
62,350	62,400	11,450	8,449	11,450	10,006
62,400	62,450	11,463	8,456	11,463	10,019
62,450	62,500	11,475	8,464	11,475	10,031
62,500	62,550	11,488	8,471	11,488	10,044
62,550	62,600	11,500	8,479	11,500	10,056
62,600	62,650	11,513	8,486	11,513	10,069
62,650	62,700	11,525	8,494	11,525	10,081
62,700	62,750	11,538	8,501	11,538	10,094
62,750	62,800	11,550	8,509	11,550	10,106
62,800	62,850	11,563	8,516	11,563	10,119
62,850	62,900	11,575	8,524	11,575	10,131
62,900	62,950	11,588	8,531	11,588	10,144
62,950	63,000	11,600	8,539	11,600	10,156

63,000

At least	But less than	Single	Married filing jointly *	Married filing separately	Head of a household
63,000	63,050	11,613	8,546	11,613	10,169
63,050	63,100	11,625	8,554	11,625	10,181
63,100	63,150	11,638	8,561	11,638	10,194
63,150	63,200	11,650	8,569	11,650	10,206
63,200	63,250	11,663	8,576	11,663	10,219
63,250	63,300	11,675	8,584	11,675	10,231
63,300	63,350	11,688	8,591	11,688	10,244
63,350	63,400	11,700	8,599	11,700	10,256
63,400	63,450	11,713	8,606	11,713	10,269
63,450	63,500	11,725	8,614	11,725	10,281
63,500	63,550	11,738	8,621	11,738	10,294
63,550	63,600	11,750	8,629	11,750	10,306
63,600	63,650	11,763	8,636	11,763	10,319
63,650	63,700	11,775	8,644	11,775	10,331
63,700	63,750	11,788	8,651	11,788	10,344
63,750	63,800	11,800	8,659	11,800	10,356
63,800	63,850	11,813	8,666	11,813	10,369
63,850	63,900	11,825	8,674	11,825	10,381
63,900	63,950	11,838	8,681	11,838	10,394
63,950	64,000	11,850	8,689	11,850	10,406

64,000

At least	But less than	Single	Married filing jointly *	Married filing separately	Head of a household
64,000	64,050	11,863	8,696	11,863	10,419
64,050	64,100	11,875	8,704	11,875	10,431
64,100	64,150	11,888	8,711	11,888	10,444
64,150	64,200	11,900	8,719	11,900	10,456
64,200	64,250	11,913	8,726	11,913	10,469
64,250	64,300	11,925	8,734	11,925	10,481
64,300	64,350	11,938	8,741	11,938	10,494
64,350	64,400	11,950	8,749	11,950	10,506
64,400	64,450	11,963	8,756	11,963	10,519
64,450	64,500	11,975	8,764	11,975	10,531
64,500	64,550	11,988	8,771	11,988	10,544
64,550	64,600	12,000	8,779	12,000	10,556
64,600	64,650	12,013	8,786	12,013	10,569
64,650	64,700	12,025	8,794	12,025	10,581
64,700	64,750	12,038	8,801	12,038	10,594
64,750	64,800	12,050	8,809	12,050	10,606
64,800	64,850	12,063	8,816	12,063	10,619
64,850	64,900	12,075	8,824	12,075	10,631
64,900	64,950	12,088	8,831	12,088	10,644
64,950	65,000	12,100	8,839	12,100	10,656

65,000

At least	But less than	Single	Married filing jointly *	Married filing separately	Head of a household
65,000	65,050	12,113	8,846	12,113	10,669
65,050	65,100	12,125	8,854	12,125	10,681
65,100	65,150	12,138	8,861	12,138	10,694
65,150	65,200	12,150	8,869	12,150	10,706
65,200	65,250	12,163	8,876	12,163	10,719
65,250	65,300	12,175	8,884	12,175	10,731
65,300	65,350	12,188	8,891	12,188	10,744
65,350	65,400	12,200	8,899	12,200	10,756
65,400	65,450	12,213	8,906	12,213	10,769
65,450	65,500	12,225	8,914	12,225	10,781
65,500	65,550	12,238	8,921	12,238	10,794
65,550	65,600	12,250	8,929	12,250	10,806
65,600	65,650	12,263	8,936	12,263	10,819
65,650	65,700	12,275	8,944	12,275	10,831
65,700	65,750	12,288	8,951	12,288	10,844
65,750	65,800	12,300	8,959	12,300	10,856
65,800	65,850	12,313	8,966	12,313	10,869
65,850	65,900	12,325	8,974	12,325	10,881
65,900	65,950	12,338	8,981	12,338	10,894
65,950	66,000	12,350	8,989	12,350	10,906

(Continued)

* This column must also be used by a qualifying widow(er).

If line 43 (taxable income) is—		And you are—			
At least	But less than	Single	Married filing jointly *	Married filing separately	Head of a household
		Your tax is—			

66,000

At least	But less than	Single	Married filing jointly *	Married filing separately	Head of a household
66,000	66,050	12,363	8,996	12,363	10,919
66,050	66,100	12,375	9,004	12,375	10,931
66,100	66,150	12,388	9,011	12,388	10,944
66,150	66,200	12,400	9,019	12,400	10,956
66,200	66,250	12,413	9,026	12,413	10,969
66,250	66,300	12,425	9,034	12,425	10,981
66,300	66,350	12,438	9,041	12,438	10,994
66,350	66,400	12,450	9,049	12,450	11,006
66,400	66,450	12,463	9,056	12,463	11,019
66,450	66,500	12,475	9,064	12,475	11,031
66,500	66,550	12,488	9,071	12,488	11,044
66,550	66,600	12,500	9,079	12,500	11,056
66,600	66,650	12,513	9,086	12,513	11,069
66,650	66,700	12,525	9,094	12,525	11,081
66,700	66,750	12,538	9,101	12,538	11,094
66,750	66,800	12,550	9,109	12,550	11,106
66,800	66,850	12,563	9,116	12,563	11,119
66,850	66,900	12,575	9,124	12,575	11,131
66,900	66,950	12,588	9,131	12,588	11,144
66,950	67,000	12,600	9,139	12,600	11,156

67,000

At least	But less than	Single	Married filing jointly *	Married filing separately	Head of a household
67,000	67,050	12,613	9,146	12,613	11,169
67,050	67,100	12,625	9,154	12,625	11,181
67,100	67,150	12,638	9,161	12,638	11,194
67,150	67,200	12,650	9,169	12,650	11,206
67,200	67,250	12,663	9,176	12,663	11,219
67,250	67,300	12,675	9,184	12,675	11,231
67,300	67,350	12,688	9,191	12,688	11,244
67,350	67,400	12,700	9,199	12,700	11,256
67,400	67,450	12,713	9,206	12,713	11,269
67,450	67,500	12,725	9,214	12,725	11,281
67,500	67,550	12,738	9,221	12,738	11,294
67,550	67,600	12,750	9,229	12,750	11,306
67,600	67,650	12,763	9,236	12,763	11,319
67,650	67,700	12,775	9,244	12,775	11,331
67,700	67,750	12,788	9,251	12,788	11,344
67,750	67,800	12,800	9,259	12,800	11,356
67,800	67,850	12,813	9,266	12,813	11,369
67,850	67,900	12,825	9,274	12,825	11,381
67,900	67,950	12,838	9,281	12,838	11,394
67,950	68,000	12,850	9,289	12,850	11,406

68,000

At least	But less than	Single	Married filing jointly *	Married filing separately	Head of a household
68,000	68,050	12,863	9,296	12,863	11,419
68,050	68,100	12,875	9,304	12,875	11,431
68,100	68,150	12,888	9,311	12,888	11,444
68,150	68,200	12,900	9,319	12,900	11,456
68,200	68,250	12,913	9,326	12,913	11,469
68,250	68,300	12,925	9,334	12,925	11,481
68,300	68,350	12,938	9,341	12,938	11,494
68,350	68,400	12,950	9,349	12,950	11,506
68,400	68,450	12,963	9,356	12,963	11,519
68,450	68,500	12,975	9,364	12,975	11,531
68,500	68,550	12,988	9,371	12,988	11,544
68,550	68,600	13,000	9,379	13,000	11,556
68,600	68,650	13,013	9,386	13,013	11,569
68,650	68,700	13,025	9,394	13,025	11,581
68,700	68,750	13,038	9,401	13,038	11,594
68,750	68,800	13,050	9,409	13,050	11,606
68,800	68,850	13,063	9,416	13,063	11,619
68,850	68,900	13,075	9,424	13,075	11,631
68,900	68,950	13,088	9,431	13,088	11,644
68,950	69,000	13,100	9,439	13,100	11,656

69,000

At least	But less than	Single	Married filing jointly *	Married filing separately	Head of a household
69,000	69,050	13,113	9,446	13,113	11,669
69,050	69,100	13,125	9,454	13,125	11,681
69,100	69,150	13,138	9,461	13,138	11,694
69,150	69,200	13,150	9,469	13,150	11,706
69,200	69,250	13,163	9,476	13,163	11,719
69,250	69,300	13,175	9,484	13,175	11,731
69,300	69,350	13,188	9,491	13,188	11,744
69,350	69,400	13,200	9,499	13,200	11,756
69,400	69,450	13,213	9,506	13,213	11,769
69,450	69,500	13,225	9,514	13,225	11,781
69,500	69,550	13,238	9,521	13,238	11,794
69,550	69,600	13,250	9,529	13,250	11,806
69,600	69,650	13,263	9,536	13,263	11,819
69,650	69,700	13,275	9,544	13,275	11,831
69,700	69,750	13,288	9,551	13,288	11,844
69,750	69,800	13,300	9,559	13,300	11,856
69,800	69,850	13,313	9,566	13,313	11,869
69,850	69,900	13,325	9,574	13,325	11,881
69,900	69,950	13,338	9,581	13,338	11,894
69,950	70,000	13,350	9,589	13,350	11,906

70,000

At least	But less than	Single	Married filing jointly *	Married filing separately	Head of a household
70,000	70,050	13,363	9,596	13,363	11,919
70,050	70,100	13,375	9,604	13,375	11,931
70,100	70,150	13,388	9,611	13,388	11,944
70,150	70,200	13,400	9,619	13,400	11,956
70,200	70,250	13,413	9,626	13,413	11,969
70,250	70,300	13,425	9,634	13,425	11,981
70,300	70,350	13,438	9,641	13,438	11,994
70,350	70,400	13,450	9,649	13,450	12,006
70,400	70,450	13,463	9,656	13,463	12,019
70,450	70,500	13,475	9,664	13,475	12,031
70,500	70,550	13,488	9,671	13,488	12,044
70,550	70,600	13,500	9,679	13,500	12,056
70,600	70,650	13,513	9,686	13,513	12,069
70,650	70,700	13,525	9,694	13,525	12,081
70,700	70,750	13,538	9,701	13,538	12,094
70,750	70,800	13,550	9,709	13,550	12,106
70,800	70,850	13,563	9,716	13,563	12,119
70,850	70,900	13,575	9,724	13,575	12,131
70,900	70,950	13,588	9,731	13,588	12,144
70,950	71,000	13,600	9,739	13,600	12,156

71,000

At least	But less than	Single	Married filing jointly *	Married filing separately	Head of a household
71,000	71,050	13,613	9,746	13,613	12,169
71,050	71,100	13,625	9,754	13,625	12,181
71,100	71,150	13,638	9,761	13,638	12,194
71,150	71,200	13,650	9,769	13,650	12,206
71,200	71,250	13,663	9,776	13,663	12,219
71,250	71,300	13,675	9,784	13,675	12,231
71,300	71,350	13,688	9,791	13,688	12,244
71,350	71,400	13,700	9,799	13,700	12,256
71,400	71,450	13,713	9,806	13,713	12,269
71,450	71,500	13,725	9,814	13,725	12,281
71,500	71,550	13,738	9,821	13,738	12,294
71,550	71,600	13,750	9,829	13,750	12,306
71,600	71,650	13,763	9,836	13,763	12,319
71,650	71,700	13,775	9,844	13,775	12,331
71,700	71,750	13,788	9,851	13,788	12,344
71,750	71,800	13,800	9,859	13,800	12,356
71,800	71,850	13,813	9,866	13,813	12,369
71,850	71,900	13,825	9,874	13,825	12,381
71,900	71,950	13,838	9,881	13,838	12,394
71,950	72,000	13,850	9,889	13,850	12,406

72,000

At least	But less than	Single	Married filing jointly *	Married filing separately	Head of a household
72,000	72,050	13,863	9,896	13,863	12,419
72,050	72,100	13,875	9,904	13,875	12,431
72,100	72,150	13,888	9,911	13,888	12,444
72,150	72,200	13,900	9,919	13,900	12,456
72,200	72,250	13,913	9,926	13,913	12,469
72,250	72,300	13,925	9,934	13,925	12,481
72,300	72,350	13,938	9,941	13,938	12,494
72,350	72,400	13,950	9,949	13,950	12,506
72,400	72,450	13,963	9,956	13,963	12,519
72,450	72,500	13,975	9,964	13,975	12,531
72,500	72,550	13,988	9,971	13,988	12,544
72,550	72,600	14,000	9,979	14,000	12,556
72,600	72,650	14,013	9,986	14,013	12,569
72,650	72,700	14,025	9,994	14,025	12,581
72,700	72,750	14,038	10,001	14,038	12,594
72,750	72,800	14,050	10,009	14,050	12,606
72,800	72,850	14,063	10,016	14,063	12,619
72,850	72,900	14,075	10,024	14,075	12,631
72,900	72,950	14,088	10,031	14,088	12,644
72,950	73,000	14,100	10,039	14,100	12,656

73,000

At least	But less than	Single	Married filing jointly *	Married filing separately	Head of a household
73,000	73,050	14,113	10,046	14,113	12,669
73,050	73,100	14,125	10,054	14,125	12,681
73,100	73,150	14,138	10,061	14,138	12,694
73,150	73,200	14,150	10,069	14,150	12,706
73,200	73,250	14,163	10,076	14,163	12,719
73,250	73,300	14,175	10,084	14,175	12,731
73,300	73,350	14,188	10,091	14,188	12,744
73,350	73,400	14,200	10,099	14,200	12,756
73,400	73,450	14,213	10,106	14,213	12,769
73,450	73,500	14,225	10,114	14,225	12,781
73,500	73,550	14,238	10,121	14,238	12,794
73,550	73,600	14,250	10,129	14,250	12,806
73,600	73,650	14,263	10,136	14,263	12,819
73,650	73,700	14,275	10,144	14,275	12,831
73,700	73,750	14,288	10,151	14,288	12,844
73,750	73,800	14,300	10,159	14,300	12,856
73,800	73,850	14,313	10,169	14,313	12,869
73,850	73,900	14,325	10,181	14,325	12,881
73,900	73,950	14,338	10,194	14,338	12,894
73,950	74,000	14,350	10,206	14,350	12,906

74,000

At least	But less than	Single	Married filing jointly *	Married filing separately	Head of a household
74,000	74,050	14,363	10,219	14,363	12,919
74,050	74,100	14,375	10,231	14,375	12,931
74,100	74,150	14,388	10,244	14,388	12,944
74,150	74,200	14,400	10,256	14,400	12,956
74,200	74,250	14,413	10,269	14,413	12,969
74,250	74,300	14,425	10,281	14,425	12,981
74,300	74,350	14,438	10,294	14,438	12,994
74,350	74,400	14,450	10,306	14,450	13,006
74,400	74,450	14,463	10,319	14,463	13,019
74,450	74,500	14,475	10,331	14,477	13,031
74,500	74,550	14,488	10,344	14,491	13,044
74,550	74,600	14,500	10,356	14,505	13,056
74,600	74,650	14,513	10,369	14,519	13,069
74,650	74,700	14,525	10,381	14,533	13,081
74,700	74,750	14,538	10,394	14,547	13,094
74,750	74,800	14,550	10,406	14,561	13,106
74,800	74,850	14,563	10,419	14,575	13,119
74,850	74,900	14,575	10,431	14,589	13,131
74,900	74,950	14,588	10,444	14,603	13,144
74,950	75,000	14,600	10,456	14,617	13,156

(Continued)

* This column must also be used by a qualifying widow(er).

If line 43 (taxable income) is—		And you are—				If line 43 (taxable income) is—		And you are—				If line 43 (taxable income) is—		And you are—			
At least	But less than	Single	Married filing jointly *	Married filing separately	Head of a household	At least	But less than	Single	Married filing jointly *	Married filing separately	Head of a household	At least	But less than	Single	Married filing jointly *	Married filing separately	Head of a household
		Your tax is—						Your tax is—						Your tax is—			
75,000						**78,000**						**81,000**					
75,000	75,050	14,613	10,469	14,631	13,169	78,000	78,050	15,363	11,219	15,471	13,919	81,000	81,050	16,113	11,969	16,311	14,669
75,050	75,100	14,625	10,481	14,645	13,181	78,050	78,100	15,375	11,231	15,485	13,931	81,050	81,100	16,125	11,981	16,325	14,681
75,100	75,150	14,638	10,494	14,659	13,194	78,100	78,150	15,388	11,244	15,499	13,944	81,100	81,150	16,138	11,994	16,339	14,694
75,150	75,200	14,650	10,506	14,673	13,206	78,150	78,200	15,400	11,256	15,513	13,956	81,150	81,200	16,150	12,006	16,353	14,706
75,200	75,250	14,663	10,519	14,687	13,219	78,200	78,250	15,413	11,269	15,527	13,969	81,200	81,250	16,163	12,019	16,367	14,719
75,250	75,300	14,675	10,531	14,701	13,231	78,250	78,300	15,425	11,281	15,541	13,981	81,250	81,300	16,175	12,031	16,381	14,731
75,300	75,350	14,688	10,544	14,715	13,244	78,300	78,350	15,438	11,294	15,555	13,994	81,300	81,350	16,188	12,044	16,395	14,744
75,350	75,400	14,700	10,556	14,729	13,256	78,350	78,400	15,450	11,306	15,569	14,006	81,350	81,400	16,200	12,056	16,409	14,756
75,400	75,450	14,713	10,569	14,743	13,269	78,400	78,450	15,463	11,319	15,583	14,019	81,400	81,450	16,213	12,069	16,423	14,769
75,450	75,500	14,725	10,581	14,757	13,281	78,450	78,500	15,475	11,331	15,597	14,031	81,450	81,500	16,225	12,081	16,437	14,781
75,500	75,550	14,738	10,594	14,771	13,294	78,500	78,550	15,488	11,344	15,611	14,044	81,500	81,550	16,238	12,094	16,451	14,794
75,550	75,600	14,750	10,606	14,785	13,306	78,550	78,600	15,500	11,356	15,625	14,056	81,550	81,600	16,250	12,106	16,465	14,806
75,600	75,650	14,763	10,619	14,799	13,319	78,600	78,650	15,513	11,369	15,639	14,069	81,600	81,650	16,263	12,119	16,479	14,819
75,650	75,700	14,775	10,631	14,813	13,331	78,650	78,700	15,525	11,381	15,653	14,081	81,650	81,700	16,275	12,131	16,493	14,831
75,700	75,750	14,788	10,644	14,827	13,344	78,700	78,750	15,538	11,394	15,667	14,094	81,700	81,750	16,288	12,144	16,507	14,844
75,750	75,800	14,800	10,656	14,841	13,356	78,750	78,800	15,550	11,406	15,681	14,106	81,750	81,800	16,300	12,156	16,521	14,856
75,800	75,850	14,813	10,669	14,855	13,369	78,800	78,850	15,563	11,419	15,695	14,119	81,800	81,850	16,313	12,169	16,535	14,869
75,850	75,900	14,825	10,681	14,869	13,381	78,850	78,900	15,575	11,431	15,709	14,131	81,850	81,900	16,325	12,181	16,549	14,881
75,900	75,950	14,838	10,694	14,883	13,394	78,900	78,950	15,588	11,444	15,723	14,144	81,900	81,950	16,338	12,194	16,563	14,894
75,950	76,000	14,850	10,706	14,897	13,406	78,950	79,000	15,600	11,456	15,737	14,156	81,950	82,000	16,350	12,206	16,577	14,906
76,000						**79,000**						**82,000**					
76,000	76,050	14,863	10,719	14,911	13,419	79,000	79,050	15,613	11,469	15,751	14,169	82,000	82,050	16,363	12,219	16,591	14,919
76,050	76,100	14,875	10,731	14,925	13,431	79,050	79,100	15,625	11,481	15,765	14,181	82,050	82,100	16,375	12,231	16,605	14,931
76,100	76,150	14,888	10,744	14,939	13,444	79,100	79,150	15,638	11,494	15,779	14,194	82,100	82,150	16,388	12,244	16,619	14,944
76,150	76,200	14,900	10,756	14,953	13,456	79,150	79,200	15,650	11,506	15,793	14,206	82,150	82,200	16,400	12,256	16,633	14,956
76,200	76,250	14,913	10,769	14,967	13,469	79,200	79,250	15,663	11,519	15,807	14,219	82,200	82,250	16,413	12,269	16,647	14,969
76,250	76,300	14,925	10,781	14,981	13,481	79,250	79,300	15,675	11,531	15,821	14,231	82,250	82,300	16,425	12,281	16,661	14,981
76,300	76,350	14,938	10,794	14,995	13,494	79,300	79,350	15,688	11,544	15,835	14,244	82,300	82,350	16,438	12,294	16,675	14,994
76,350	76,400	14,950	10,806	15,009	13,506	79,350	79,400	15,700	11,556	15,849	14,256	82,350	82,400	16,450	12,306	16,689	15,006
76,400	76,450	14,963	10,819	15,023	13,519	79,400	79,450	15,713	11,569	15,863	14,269	82,400	82,450	16,463	12,319	16,703	15,019
76,450	76,500	14,975	10,831	15,037	13,531	79,450	79,500	15,725	11,581	15,877	14,281	82,450	82,500	16,475	12,331	16,717	15,031
76,500	76,550	14,988	10,844	15,051	13,544	79,500	79,550	15,738	11,594	15,891	14,294	82,500	82,550	16,488	12,344	16,731	15,044
76,550	76,600	15,000	10,856	15,065	13,556	79,550	79,600	15,750	11,606	15,905	14,306	82,550	82,600	16,500	12,356	16,745	15,056
76,600	76,650	15,013	10,869	15,079	13,569	79,600	79,650	15,763	11,619	15,919	14,319	82,600	82,650	16,513	12,369	16,759	15,069
76,650	76,700	15,025	10,881	15,093	13,581	79,650	79,700	15,775	11,631	15,933	14,331	82,650	82,700	16,525	12,381	16,773	15,081
76,700	76,750	15,038	10,894	15,107	13,594	79,700	79,750	15,788	11,644	15,947	14,344	82,700	82,750	16,538	12,394	16,787	15,094
76,750	76,800	15,050	10,906	15,121	13,606	79,750	79,800	15,800	11,656	15,961	14,356	82,750	82,800	16,550	12,406	16,801	15,106
76,800	76,850	15,063	10,919	15,135	13,619	79,800	79,850	15,813	11,669	15,975	14,369	82,800	82,850	16,563	12,419	16,815	15,119
76,850	76,900	15,075	10,931	15,149	13,631	79,850	79,900	15,825	11,681	15,989	14,381	82,850	82,900	16,575	12,431	16,829	15,131
76,900	76,950	15,088	10,944	15,163	13,644	79,900	79,950	15,838	11,694	16,003	14,394	82,900	82,950	16,588	12,444	16,843	15,144
76,950	77,000	15,100	10,956	15,177	13,656	79,950	80,000	15,850	11,706	16,017	14,406	82,950	83,000	16,600	12,456	16,857	15,156
77,000						**80,000**						**83,000**					
77,000	77,050	15,113	10,969	15,191	13,669	80,000	80,050	15,863	11,719	16,031	14,419	83,000	83,050	16,613	12,469	16,871	15,169
77,050	77,100	15,125	10,981	15,205	13,681	80,050	80,100	15,875	11,731	16,045	14,431	83,050	83,100	16,625	12,481	16,885	15,181
77,100	77,150	15,138	10,994	15,219	13,694	80,100	80,150	15,888	11,744	16,059	14,444	83,100	83,150	16,638	12,494	16,899	15,194
77,150	77,200	15,150	11,006	15,233	13,706	80,150	80,200	15,900	11,756	16,073	14,456	83,150	83,200	16,650	12,506	16,913	15,206
77,200	77,250	15,163	11,019	15,247	13,719	80,200	80,250	15,913	11,769	16,087	14,469	83,200	83,250	16,663	12,519	16,927	15,219
77,250	77,300	15,175	11,031	15,261	13,731	80,250	80,300	15,925	11,781	16,101	14,481	83,250	83,300	16,675	12,531	16,941	15,231
77,300	77,350	15,188	11,044	15,275	13,744	80,300	80,350	15,938	11,794	16,115	14,494	83,300	83,350	16,688	12,544	16,955	15,244
77,350	77,400	15,200	11,056	15,289	13,756	80,350	80,400	15,950	11,806	16,129	14,506	83,350	83,400	16,700	12,556	16,969	15,256
77,400	77,450	15,213	11,069	15,303	13,769	80,400	80,450	15,963	11,819	16,143	14,519	83,400	83,450	16,713	12,569	16,983	15,269
77,450	77,500	15,225	11,081	15,317	13,781	80,450	80,500	15,975	11,831	16,157	14,531	83,450	83,500	16,725	12,581	16,997	15,281
77,500	77,550	15,238	11,094	15,331	13,794	80,500	80,550	15,988	11,844	16,171	14,544	83,500	83,550	16,738	12,594	17,011	15,294
77,550	77,600	15,250	11,106	15,345	13,806	80,550	80,600	16,000	11,856	16,185	14,556	83,550	83,600	16,750	12,606	17,025	15,306
77,600	77,650	15,263	11,119	15,359	13,819	80,600	80,650	16,013	11,869	16,199	14,569	83,600	83,650	16,763	12,619	17,039	15,319
77,650	77,700	15,275	11,131	15,373	13,831	80,650	80,700	16,025	11,881	16,213	14,581	83,650	83,700	16,775	12,631	17,053	15,331
77,700	77,750	15,288	11,144	15,387	13,844	80,700	80,750	16,038	11,894	16,227	14,594	83,700	83,750	16,788	12,644	17,067	15,344
77,750	77,800	15,300	11,156	15,401	13,856	80,750	80,800	16,050	11,906	16,241	14,606	83,750	83,800	16,800	12,656	17,081	15,356
77,800	77,850	15,313	11,169	15,415	13,869	80,800	80,850	16,063	11,919	16,255	14,619	83,800	83,850	16,813	12,669	17,095	15,369
77,850	77,900	15,325	11,181	15,429	13,881	80,850	80,900	16,075	11,931	16,269	14,631	83,850	83,900	16,825	12,681	17,109	15,381
77,900	77,950	15,338	11,194	15,443	13,894	80,900	80,950	16,088	11,944	16,283	14,644	83,900	83,950	16,838	12,694	17,123	15,394
77,950	78,000	15,350	11,206	15,457	13,906	80,950	81,000	16,100	11,956	16,297	14,656	83,950	84,000	16,850	12,706	17,137	15,406

(Continued)

* This column must also be used by a qualifying widow(er).

If line 43 (taxable income) is— At least	But less than	Single	Married filing jointly *	Married filing separately	Head of a household
					Your tax is—
84,000					
84,000	84,050	16,863	12,719	17,151	15,419
84,050	84,100	16,875	12,731	17,165	15,431
84,100	84,150	16,888	12,744	17,179	15,444
84,150	84,200	16,900	12,756	17,193	15,456
84,200	84,250	16,913	12,769	17,207	15,469
84,250	84,300	16,925	12,781	17,221	15,481
84,300	84,350	16,938	12,794	17,235	15,494
84,350	84,400	16,950	12,806	17,249	15,506
84,400	84,450	16,963	12,819	17,263	15,519
84,450	84,500	16,975	12,831	17,277	15,531
84,500	84,550	16,988	12,844	17,291	15,544
84,550	84,600	17,000	12,856	17,305	15,556
84,600	84,650	17,013	12,869	17,319	15,569
84,650	84,700	17,025	12,881	17,333	15,581
84,700	84,750	17,038	12,894	17,347	15,594
84,750	84,800	17,050	12,906	17,361	15,606
84,800	84,850	17,063	12,919	17,375	15,619
84,850	84,900	17,075	12,931	17,389	15,631
84,900	84,950	17,088	12,944	17,403	15,644
84,950	85,000	17,100	12,956	17,417	15,656
85,000					
85,000	85,050	17,113	12,969	17,431	15,669
85,050	85,100	17,125	12,981	17,445	15,681
85,100	85,150	17,138	12,994	17,459	15,694
85,150	85,200	17,150	13,006	17,473	15,706
85,200	85,250	17,163	13,019	17,487	15,719
85,250	85,300	17,175	13,031	17,501	15,731
85,300	85,350	17,188	13,044	17,515	15,744
85,350	85,400	17,200	13,056	17,529	15,756
85,400	85,450	17,213	13,069	17,543	15,769
85,450	85,500	17,225	13,081	17,557	15,781
85,500	85,550	17,238	13,094	17,571	15,794
85,550	85,600	17,250	13,106	17,585	15,806
85,600	85,650	17,263	13,119	17,599	15,819
85,650	85,700	17,275	13,131	17,613	15,831
85,700	85,750	17,288	13,144	17,627	15,844
85,750	85,800	17,300	13,156	17,641	15,856
85,800	85,850	17,313	13,169	17,655	15,869
85,850	85,900	17,325	13,181	17,669	15,881
85,900	85,950	17,338	13,194	17,683	15,894
85,950	86,000	17,350	13,206	17,697	15,906
86,000					
86,000	86,050	17,363	13,219	17,711	15,919
86,050	86,100	17,375	13,231	17,725	15,931
86,100	86,150	17,388	13,244	17,739	15,944
86,150	86,200	17,400	13,256	17,753	15,956
86,200	86,250	17,413	13,269	17,767	15,969
86,250	86,300	17,425	13,281	17,781	15,981
86,300	86,350	17,438	13,294	17,795	15,994
86,350	86,400	17,450	13,306	17,809	16,006
86,400	86,450	17,463	13,319	17,823	16,019
86,450	86,500	17,475	13,331	17,837	16,031
86,500	86,550	17,488	13,344	17,851	16,044
86,550	86,600	17,500	13,356	17,865	16,056
86,600	86,650	17,513	13,369	17,879	16,069
86,650	86,700	17,525	13,381	17,893	16,081
86,700	86,750	17,538	13,394	17,907	16,094
86,750	86,800	17,550	13,406	17,921	16,106
86,800	86,850	17,563	13,419	17,935	16,119
86,850	86,900	17,575	13,431	17,949	16,131
86,900	86,950	17,588	13,444	17,963	16,144
86,950	87,000	17,600	13,456	17,977	16,156
87,000					
87,000	87,050	17,613	13,469	17,991	16,169
87,050	87,100	17,625	13,481	18,005	16,181
87,100	87,150	17,638	13,494	18,019	16,194
87,150	87,200	17,650	13,506	18,033	16,206
87,200	87,250	17,663	13,519	18,047	16,219
87,250	87,300	17,675	13,531	18,061	16,231
87,300	87,350	17,688	13,544	18,075	16,244
87,350	87,400	17,700	13,556	18,089	16,256
87,400	87,450	17,713	13,569	18,103	16,269
87,450	87,500	17,725	13,581	18,117	16,281
87,500	87,550	17,738	13,594	18,131	16,294
87,550	87,600	17,750	13,606	18,145	16,306
87,600	87,650	17,763	13,619	18,159	16,319
87,650	87,700	17,775	13,631	18,173	16,331
87,700	87,750	17,788	13,644	18,187	16,344
87,750	87,800	17,800	13,656	18,201	16,356
87,800	87,850	17,813	13,669	18,215	16,369
87,850	87,900	17,825	13,681	18,229	16,381
87,900	87,950	17,838	13,694	18,243	16,394
87,950	88,000	17,850	13,706	18,257	16,406
88,000					
88,000	88,050	17,863	13,719	18,271	16,419
88,050	88,100	17,875	13,731	18,285	16,431
88,100	88,150	17,888	13,744	18,299	16,444
88,150	88,200	17,900	13,756	18,313	16,456
88,200	88,250	17,913	13,769	18,327	16,469
88,250	88,300	17,925	13,781	18,341	16,481
88,300	88,350	17,938	13,794	18,355	16,494
88,350	88,400	17,950	13,806	18,369	16,506
88,400	88,450	17,963	13,819	18,383	16,519
88,450	88,500	17,975	13,831	18,397	16,531
88,500	88,550	17,988	13,844	18,411	16,544
88,550	88,600	18,000	13,856	18,425	16,556
88,600	88,650	18,013	13,869	18,439	16,569
88,650	88,700	18,025	13,881	18,453	16,581
88,700	88,750	18,038	13,894	18,467	16,594
88,750	88,800	18,050	13,906	18,481	16,606
88,800	88,850	18,063	13,919	18,495	16,619
88,850	88,900	18,075	13,931	18,509	16,631
88,900	88,950	18,088	13,944	18,523	16,644
88,950	89,000	18,100	13,956	18,537	16,656
89,000					
89,000	89,050	18,113	13,969	18,551	16,669
89,050	89,100	18,125	13,981	18,565	16,681
89,100	89,150	18,138	13,994	18,579	16,694
89,150	89,200	18,150	14,006	18,593	16,706
89,200	89,250	18,163	14,019	18,607	16,719
89,250	89,300	18,175	14,031	18,621	16,731
89,300	89,350	18,188	14,044	18,635	16,744
89,350	89,400	18,201	14,056	18,649	16,756
89,400	89,450	18,215	14,069	18,663	16,769
89,450	89,500	18,229	14,081	18,677	16,781
89,500	89,550	18,243	14,094	18,691	16,794
89,550	89,600	18,257	14,106	18,705	16,806
89,600	89,650	18,271	14,119	18,719	16,819
89,650	89,700	18,285	14,131	18,733	16,831
89,700	89,750	18,299	14,144	18,747	16,844
89,750	89,800	18,313	14,156	18,761	16,856
89,800	89,850	18,327	14,169	18,775	16,869
89,850	89,900	18,341	14,181	18,789	16,881
89,900	89,950	18,355	14,194	18,803	16,894
89,950	90,000	18,369	14,206	18,817	16,906
90,000					
90,000	90,050	18,383	14,219	18,831	16,919
90,050	90,100	18,397	14,231	18,845	16,931
90,100	90,150	18,411	14,244	18,859	16,944
90,150	90,200	18,425	14,256	18,873	16,956
90,200	90,250	18,439	14,269	18,887	16,969
90,250	90,300	18,453	14,281	18,901	16,981
90,300	90,350	18,467	14,294	18,915	16,994
90,350	90,400	18,481	14,306	18,929	17,006
90,400	90,450	18,495	14,319	18,943	17,019
90,450	90,500	18,509	14,331	18,957	17,031
90,500	90,550	18,523	14,344	18,971	17,044
90,550	90,600	18,537	14,356	18,985	17,056
90,600	90,650	18,551	14,369	18,999	17,069
90,650	90,700	18,565	14,381	19,013	17,081
90,700	90,750	18,579	14,394	19,027	17,094
90,750	90,800	18,593	14,406	19,041	17,106
90,800	90,850	18,607	14,419	19,055	17,119
90,850	90,900	18,621	14,431	19,069	17,131
90,900	90,950	18,635	14,444	19,083	17,144
90,950	91,000	18,649	14,456	19,097	17,156
91,000					
91,000	91,050	18,663	14,469	19,111	17,169
91,050	91,100	18,677	14,481	19,125	17,181
91,100	91,150	18,691	14,494	19,139	17,194
91,150	91,200	18,705	14,506	19,153	17,206
91,200	91,250	18,719	14,519	19,167	17,219
91,250	91,300	18,733	14,531	19,181	17,231
91,300	91,350	18,747	14,544	19,195	17,244
91,350	91,400	18,761	14,556	19,209	17,256
91,400	91,450	18,775	14,569	19,223	17,269
91,450	91,500	18,789	14,581	19,237	17,281
91,500	91,550	18,803	14,594	19,251	17,294
91,550	91,600	18,817	14,606	19,265	17,306
91,600	91,650	18,831	14,619	19,279	17,319
91,650	91,700	18,845	14,631	19,293	17,331
91,700	91,750	18,859	14,644	19,307	17,344
91,750	91,800	18,873	14,656	19,321	17,356
91,800	91,850	18,887	14,669	19,335	17,369
91,850	91,900	18,901	14,681	19,349	17,381
91,900	91,950	18,915	14,694	19,363	17,394
91,950	92,000	18,929	14,706	19,377	17,406
92,000					
92,000	92,050	18,943	14,719	19,391	17,419
92,050	92,100	18,957	14,731	19,405	17,431
92,100	92,150	18,971	14,744	19,419	17,444
92,150	92,200	18,985	14,756	19,433	17,456
92,200	92,250	18,999	14,769	19,447	17,469
92,250	92,300	19,013	14,781	19,461	17,481
92,300	92,350	19,027	14,794	19,475	17,494
92,350	92,400	19,041	14,806	19,489	17,506
92,400	92,450	19,055	14,819	19,503	17,519
92,450	92,500	19,069	14,831	19,517	17,531
92,500	92,550	19,083	14,844	19,531	17,544
92,550	92,600	19,097	14,856	19,545	17,556
92,600	92,650	19,111	14,869	19,559	17,569
92,650	92,700	19,125	14,881	19,573	17,581
92,700	92,750	19,139	14,894	19,587	17,594
92,750	92,800	19,153	14,906	19,601	17,606
92,800	92,850	19,167	14,919	19,615	17,619
92,850	92,900	19,181	14,931	19,629	17,631
92,900	92,950	19,195	14,944	19,643	17,644
92,950	93,000	19,209	14,956	19,657	17,656

* This column must also be used by a qualifying widow(er).

(Continued)

If line 43 (taxable income) is—		And you are—			
At least	But less than	Single	Married filing jointly *	Married filing separately	Head of a household
		Your tax is—			

93,000

At least	But less than	Single	Married filing jointly *	Married filing separately	Head of a household
93,000	93,050	19,223	14,969	19,671	17,669
93,050	93,100	19,237	14,981	19,685	17,681
93,100	93,150	19,251	14,994	19,699	17,694
93,150	93,200	19,265	15,006	19,713	17,706
93,200	93,250	19,279	15,019	19,727	17,719
93,250	93,300	19,293	15,031	19,741	17,731
93,300	93,350	19,307	15,044	19,755	17,744
93,350	93,400	19,321	15,056	19,769	17,756
93,400	93,450	19,335	15,069	19,783	17,769
93,450	93,500	19,349	15,081	19,797	17,781
93,500	93,550	19,363	15,094	19,811	17,794
93,550	93,600	19,377	15,106	19,825	17,806
93,600	93,650	19,391	15,119	19,839	17,819
93,650	93,700	19,405	15,131	19,853	17,831
93,700	93,750	19,419	15,144	19,867	17,844
93,750	93,800	19,433	15,156	19,881	17,856
93,800	93,850	19,447	15,169	19,895	17,869
93,850	93,900	19,461	15,181	19,909	17,881
93,900	93,950	19,475	15,194	19,923	17,894
93,950	94,000	19,489	15,206	19,937	17,906

94,000

At least	But less than	Single	Married filing jointly *	Married filing separately	Head of a household
94,000	94,050	19,503	15,219	19,951	17,919
94,050	94,100	19,517	15,231	19,965	17,931
94,100	94,150	19,531	15,244	19,979	17,944
94,150	94,200	19,545	15,256	19,993	17,956
94,200	94,250	19,559	15,269	20,007	17,969
94,250	94,300	19,573	15,281	20,021	17,981
94,300	94,350	19,587	15,294	20,035	17,994
94,350	94,400	19,601	15,306	20,049	18,006
94,400	94,450	19,615	15,319	20,063	18,019
94,450	94,500	19,629	15,331	20,077	18,031
94,500	94,550	19,643	15,344	20,091	18,044
94,550	94,600	19,657	15,356	20,105	18,056
94,600	94,650	19,671	15,369	20,119	18,069
94,650	94,700	19,685	15,381	20,133	18,081
94,700	94,750	19,699	15,394	20,147	18,094
94,750	94,800	19,713	15,406	20,161	18,106
94,800	94,850	19,727	15,419	20,175	18,119
94,850	94,900	19,741	15,431	20,189	18,131
94,900	94,950	19,755	15,444	20,203	18,144
94,950	95,000	19,769	15,456	20,217	18,156

95,000

At least	But less than	Single	Married filing jointly *	Married filing separately	Head of a household
95,000	95,050	19,783	15,469	20,231	18,169
95,050	95,100	19,797	15,481	20,245	18,181
95,100	95,150	19,811	15,494	20,259	18,194
95,150	95,200	19,825	15,506	20,273	18,206
95,200	95,250	19,839	15,519	20,287	18,219
95,250	95,300	19,853	15,531	20,301	18,231
95,300	95,350	19,867	15,544	20,315	18,244
95,350	95,400	19,881	15,556	20,329	18,256
95,400	95,450	19,895	15,569	20,343	18,269
95,450	95,500	19,909	15,581	20,357	18,281
95,500	95,550	19,923	15,594	20,371	18,294
95,550	95,600	19,937	15,606	20,385	18,306
95,600	95,650	19,951	15,619	20,399	18,319
95,650	95,700	19,965	15,631	20,413	18,331
95,700	95,750	19,979	15,644	20,427	18,344
95,750	95,800	19,993	15,656	20,441	18,356
95,800	95,850	20,007	15,669	20,455	18,369
95,850	95,900	20,021	15,681	20,469	18,381
95,900	95,950	20,035	15,694	20,483	18,394
95,950	96,000	20,049	15,706	20,497	18,406

96,000

At least	But less than	Single	Married filing jointly *	Married filing separately	Head of a household
96,000	96,050	20,063	15,719	20,511	18,419
96,050	96,100	20,077	15,731	20,525	18,431
96,100	96,150	20,091	15,744	20,539	18,444
96,150	96,200	20,105	15,756	20,553	18,456
96,200	96,250	20,119	15,769	20,567	18,469
96,250	96,300	20,133	15,781	20,581	18,481
96,300	96,350	20,147	15,794	20,595	18,494
96,350	96,400	20,161	15,806	20,609	18,506
96,400	96,450	20,175	15,819	20,623	18,519
96,450	96,500	20,189	15,831	20,637	18,531
96,500	96,550	20,203	15,844	20,651	18,544
96,550	96,600	20,217	15,856	20,665	18,556
96,600	96,650	20,231	15,869	20,679	18,569
96,650	96,700	20,245	15,881	20,693	18,581
96,700	96,750	20,259	15,894	20,707	18,594
96,750	96,800	20,273	15,906	20,721	18,606
96,800	96,850	20,287	15,919	20,735	18,619
96,850	96,900	20,301	15,931	20,749	18,631
96,900	96,950	20,315	15,944	20,763	18,644
96,950	97,000	20,329	15,956	20,777	18,656

97,000

At least	But less than	Single	Married filing jointly *	Married filing separately	Head of a household
97,000	97,050	20,343	15,969	20,791	18,669
97,050	97,100	20,357	15,981	20,805	18,681
97,100	97,150	20,371	15,994	20,819	18,694
97,150	97,200	20,385	16,006	20,833	18,706
97,200	97,250	20,399	16,019	20,847	18,719
97,250	97,300	20,413	16,031	20,861	18,731
97,300	97,350	20,427	16,044	20,875	18,744
97,350	97,400	20,441	16,056	20,889	18,756
97,400	97,450	20,455	16,069	20,903	18,769
97,450	97,500	20,469	16,081	20,917	18,781
97,500	97,550	20,483	16,094	20,931	18,794
97,550	97,600	20,497	16,106	20,945	18,806
97,600	97,650	20,511	16,119	20,959	18,819
97,650	97,700	20,525	16,131	20,973	18,831
97,700	97,750	20,539	16,144	20,987	18,844
97,750	97,800	20,553	16,156	21,001	18,856
97,800	97,850	20,567	16,169	21,015	18,869
97,850	97,900	20,581	16,181	21,029	18,881
97,900	97,950	20,595	16,194	21,043	18,894
97,950	98,000	20,609	16,206	21,057	18,906

98,000

At least	But less than	Single	Married filing jointly *	Married filing separately	Head of a household
98,000	98,050	20,623	16,219	21,071	18,919
98,050	98,100	20,637	16,231	21,085	18,931
98,100	98,150	20,651	16,244	21,099	18,944
98,150	98,200	20,665	16,256	21,113	18,956
98,200	98,250	20,679	16,269	21,127	18,969
98,250	98,300	20,693	16,281	21,141	18,981
98,300	98,350	20,707	16,294	21,155	18,994
98,350	98,400	20,721	16,306	21,169	19,006
98,400	98,450	20,735	16,319	21,183	19,019
98,450	98,500	20,749	16,331	21,197	19,031
98,500	98,550	20,763	16,344	21,211	19,044
98,550	98,600	20,777	16,356	21,225	19,056
98,600	98,650	20,791	16,369	21,239	19,069
98,650	98,700	20,805	16,381	21,253	19,081
98,700	98,750	20,819	16,394	21,267	19,094
98,750	98,800	20,833	16,406	21,281	19,106
98,800	98,850	20,847	16,419	21,295	19,119
98,850	98,900	20,861	16,431	21,309	19,131
98,900	98,950	20,875	16,444	21,323	19,144
98,950	99,000	20,889	16,456	21,337	19,156

99,000

At least	But less than	Single	Married filing jointly *	Married filing separately	Head of a household
99,000	99,050	20,903	16,469	21,351	19,169
99,050	99,100	20,917	16,481	21,365	19,181
99,100	99,150	20,931	16,494	21,379	19,194
99,150	99,200	20,945	16,506	21,393	19,206
99,200	99,250	20,959	16,519	21,407	19,219
99,250	99,300	20,973	16,531	21,421	19,231
99,300	99,350	20,987	16,544	21,435	19,244
99,350	99,400	21,001	16,556	21,449	19,256
99,400	99,450	21,015	16,569	21,463	19,269
99,450	99,500	21,029	16,581	21,477	19,281
99,500	99,550	21,043	16,594	21,491	19,294
99,550	99,600	21,057	16,606	21,505	19,306
99,600	99,650	21,071	16,619	21,519	19,319
99,650	99,700	21,085	16,631	21,533	19,331
99,700	99,750	21,099	16,644	21,547	19,344
99,750	99,800	21,113	16,656	21,561	19,356
99,800	99,850	21,127	16,669	21,575	19,369
99,850	99,900	21,141	16,681	21,589	19,381
99,900	99,950	21,155	16,694	21,603	19,394
99,950	100,000	21,169	16,706	21,617	19,406

$100,000 or over use the Tax Computation Worksheet

* This column must also be used by a qualifying widow(er).

2014 Tax Rate Schedules

The Tax Rate Schedules are shown so you can see the tax rate that applies to all levels of taxable income. Do not use them to figure your tax. Instead, see the instructions for line 44.

Schedule X—If your filing status is **Single**

If your taxable income is: Over—	But not over—	The tax is:	of the amount over—
$0	$9,075	.... 10%	$0
9,075	36,900	$907.50 + 15%	9,075
36,900	89,350	5,081.25 + 25%	36,900
89,350	186,350	18,193.75 + 28%	89,350
186,350	405,100	45,353.75 + 33%	186,350
405,100	406,750	117,541.25 + 35%	405,100
406,750	....	118,118.75 + 39.6%	406,750

Schedule Y-1—If your filing status is **Married filing jointly** or **Qualifying widow(er)**

If your taxable income is: Over—	But not over—	The tax is:	of the amount over—
$0	$18,150	.... 10%	$0
18,150	73,800	$1,815.00 + 15%	18,150
73,800	148,850	10,162.50 + 25%	73,800
148,850	226,850	28,925.00 + 28%	148,850
226,850	405,100	50,765.00 + 33%	226,850
405,100	457,600	109,587.50 + 35%	405,100
457,600	....	127,962.50 + 39.6%	457,600

Schedule Y-2—If your filing status is **Married filing separately**

If your taxable income is: Over—	But not over—	The tax is:	of the amount over—
$0	$9,075	.... 10%	$0
9,075	36,900	$907.50 + 15%	9,075
36,900	74,425	5,081.25 + 25%	36,900
74,425	113,425	14,462.50 + 28%	74,425
113,425	202,550	25,382.50 + 33%	113,425
202,550	228,800	54,793.75 + 35%	202,550
228,800	....	63,981.25 + 39.6%	228,800

Schedule Z—If your filing status is **Head of household**

If your taxable income is: Over—	But not over—	The tax is:	of the amount over—
$0	$12,950	.... 10%	$0
12,950	49,400	$1,295.00 + 15%	12,950
49,400	127,550	6,762.50 + 25%	49,400
127,550	206,600	26,300.00 + 28%	127,550
206,600	405,100	48,434.00 + 33%	206,600
405,100	432,200	113,939.00 + 35%	405,100
432,200	....	123,424.00 + 39.6%	432,200

2014 Earned Income Credit (EIC) Table
Caution. This is **not** a tax table.

1. To find your credit, read down the "At least - But less than" columns and find the line that includes the amount you were told to look up from your EIC Worksheet.

2. Then, go to the column that includes your filing status and the number of qualifying children you have. Enter the credit from that column on your EIC Worksheet.

Example. If your filing status is single, you have one qualifying child, and the amount you are looking up from your EIC Worksheet is $2,455, you would enter $842.

If the amount you are looking up from the worksheet is—		And your filing status is— Single, head of household, or qualifying widow(er) and the number of children you have is—			
		0	1	2	3
At least	But less than	Your credit is—			
2,400	2,450	186	825	970	1,091
2,450	2,500	189	842	990	1,114

If the amount you are looking up from the worksheet is—		Single, head of household, or qualifying widow(er) and the number of children you have is—				Married filing jointly and the number of children you have is—			
At least	But less than	0	1	2	3	0	1	2	3
$1	$50	$2	$9	$10	$11	$2	$9	$10	$11
50	100	6	26	30	34	6	26	30	34
100	150	10	43	50	56	10	43	50	56
150	200	13	60	70	79	13	60	70	79
200	250	17	77	90	101	17	77	90	101
250	300	21	94	110	124	21	94	110	124
300	350	25	111	130	146	25	111	130	146
350	400	29	128	150	169	29	128	150	169
400	450	33	145	170	191	33	145	170	191
450	500	36	162	190	214	36	162	190	214
500	550	40	179	210	236	40	179	210	236
550	600	44	196	230	259	44	196	230	259
600	650	48	213	250	281	48	213	250	281
650	700	52	230	270	304	52	230	270	304
700	750	55	247	290	326	55	247	290	326
750	800	59	264	310	349	59	264	310	349
800	850	63	281	330	371	63	281	330	371
850	900	67	298	350	394	67	298	350	394
900	950	71	315	370	416	71	315	370	416
950	1,000	75	332	390	439	75	332	390	439
1,000	1,050	78	349	410	461	78	349	410	461
1,050	1,100	82	366	430	484	82	366	430	484
1,100	1,150	86	383	450	506	86	383	450	506
1,150	1,200	90	400	470	529	90	400	470	529
1,200	1,250	94	417	490	551	94	417	490	551
1,250	1,300	98	434	510	574	98	434	510	574
1,300	1,350	101	451	530	596	101	451	530	596
1,350	1,400	105	468	550	619	105	468	550	619
1,400	1,450	109	485	570	641	109	485	570	641
1,450	1,500	113	502	590	664	113	502	590	664
1,500	1,550	117	519	610	686	117	519	610	686
1,550	1,600	120	536	630	709	120	536	630	709
1,600	1,650	124	553	650	731	124	553	650	731
1,650	1,700	128	570	670	754	128	570	670	754
1,700	1,750	132	587	690	776	132	587	690	776
1,750	1,800	136	604	710	799	136	604	710	799
1,800	1,850	140	621	730	821	140	621	730	821
1,850	1,900	143	638	750	844	143	638	750	844
1,900	1,950	147	655	770	866	147	655	770	866
1,950	2,000	151	672	790	889	151	672	790	889
2,000	2,050	155	689	810	911	155	689	810	911
2,050	2,100	159	706	830	934	159	706	830	934
2,100	2,150	163	723	850	956	163	723	850	956
2,150	2,200	166	740	870	979	166	740	870	979
2,200	2,250	170	757	890	1,001	170	757	890	1,001
2,250	2,300	174	774	910	1,024	174	774	910	1,024
2,300	2,350	178	791	930	1,046	178	791	930	1,046
2,350	2,400	182	808	950	1,069	182	808	950	1,069
2,400	2,450	186	825	970	1,091	186	825	970	1,091
2,450	2,500	189	842	990	1,114	189	842	990	1,114
2,500	2,550	193	859	1,010	1,136	193	859	1,010	1,136
2,550	2,600	197	876	1,030	1,159	197	876	1,030	1,159
2,600	2,650	201	893	1,050	1,181	201	893	1,050	1,181
2,650	2,700	205	910	1,070	1,204	205	910	1,070	1,204
2,700	2,750	208	927	1,090	1,226	208	927	1,090	1,226
2,750	2,800	212	944	1,110	1,249	212	944	1,110	1,249

If the amount you are looking up from the worksheet is—		Single, head of household, or qualifying widow(er) and the number of children you have is—				Married filing jointly and the number of children you have is—			
At least	But less than	0	1	2	3	0	1	2	3
2,800	2,850	216	961	1,130	1,271	216	961	1,130	1,271
2,850	2,900	220	978	1,150	1,294	220	978	1,150	1,294
2,900	2,950	224	995	1,170	1,316	224	995	1,170	1,316
2,950	3,000	228	1,012	1,190	1,339	228	1,012	1,190	1,339
3,000	3,050	231	1,029	1,210	1,361	231	1,029	1,210	1,361
3,050	3,100	235	1,046	1,230	1,384	235	1,046	1,230	1,384
3,100	3,150	239	1,063	1,250	1,406	239	1,063	1,250	1,406
3,150	3,200	243	1,080	1,270	1,429	243	1,080	1,270	1,429
3,200	3,250	247	1,097	1,290	1,451	247	1,097	1,290	1,451
3,250	3,300	251	1,114	1,310	1,474	251	1,114	1,310	1,474
3,300	3,350	254	1,131	1,330	1,496	254	1,131	1,330	1,496
3,350	3,400	258	1,148	1,350	1,519	258	1,148	1,350	1,519
3,400	3,450	262	1,165	1,370	1,541	262	1,165	1,370	1,541
3,450	3,500	266	1,182	1,390	1,564	266	1,182	1,390	1,564
3,500	3,550	270	1,199	1,410	1,586	270	1,199	1,410	1,586
3,550	3,600	273	1,216	1,430	1,609	273	1,216	1,430	1,609
3,600	3,650	277	1,233	1,450	1,631	277	1,233	1,450	1,631
3,650	3,700	281	1,250	1,470	1,654	281	1,250	1,470	1,654
3,700	3,750	285	1,267	1,490	1,676	285	1,267	1,490	1,676
3,750	3,800	289	1,284	1,510	1,699	289	1,284	1,510	1,699
3,800	3,850	293	1,301	1,530	1,721	293	1,301	1,530	1,721
3,850	3,900	296	1,318	1,550	1,744	296	1,318	1,550	1,744
3,900	3,950	300	1,335	1,570	1,766	300	1,335	1,570	1,766
3,950	4,000	304	1,352	1,590	1,789	304	1,352	1,590	1,789
4,000	4,050	308	1,369	1,610	1,811	308	1,369	1,610	1,811
4,050	4,100	312	1,386	1,630	1,834	312	1,386	1,630	1,834
4,100	4,150	316	1,403	1,650	1,856	316	1,403	1,650	1,856
4,150	4,200	319	1,420	1,670	1,879	319	1,420	1,670	1,879
4,200	4,250	323	1,437	1,690	1,901	323	1,437	1,690	1,901
4,250	4,300	327	1,454	1,710	1,924	327	1,454	1,710	1,924
4,300	4,350	331	1,471	1,730	1,946	331	1,471	1,730	1,946
4,350	4,400	335	1,488	1,750	1,969	335	1,488	1,750	1,969
4,400	4,450	339	1,505	1,770	1,991	339	1,505	1,770	1,991
4,450	4,500	342	1,522	1,790	2,014	342	1,522	1,790	2,014
4,500	4,550	346	1,539	1,810	2,036	346	1,539	1,810	2,036
4,550	4,600	350	1,556	1,830	2,059	350	1,556	1,830	2,059
4,600	4,650	354	1,573	1,850	2,081	354	1,573	1,850	2,081
4,650	4,700	358	1,590	1,870	2,104	358	1,590	1,870	2,104
4,700	4,750	361	1,607	1,890	2,126	361	1,607	1,890	2,126
4,750	4,800	365	1,624	1,910	2,149	365	1,624	1,910	2,149
4,800	4,850	369	1,641	1,930	2,171	369	1,641	1,930	2,171
4,850	4,900	373	1,658	1,950	2,194	373	1,658	1,950	2,194
4,900	4,950	377	1,675	1,970	2,216	377	1,675	1,970	2,216
4,950	5,000	381	1,692	1,990	2,239	381	1,692	1,990	2,239
5,000	5,050	384	1,709	2,010	2,261	384	1,709	2,010	2,261
5,050	5,100	388	1,726	2,030	2,284	388	1,726	2,030	2,284
5,100	5,150	392	1,743	2,050	2,306	392	1,743	2,050	2,306
5,150	5,200	396	1,760	2,070	2,329	396	1,760	2,070	2,329
5,200	5,250	400	1,777	2,090	2,351	400	1,777	2,090	2,351
5,250	5,300	404	1,794	2,110	2,374	404	1,794	2,110	2,374
5,300	5,350	407	1,811	2,130	2,396	407	1,811	2,130	2,396
5,350	5,400	411	1,828	2,150	2,419	411	1,828	2,150	2,419
5,400	5,450	415	1,845	2,170	2,441	415	1,845	2,170	2,441
5,450	5,500	419	1,862	2,190	2,464	419	1,862	2,190	2,464
5,500	5,550	423	1,879	2,210	2,486	423	1,879	2,210	2,486
5,550	5,600	426	1,896	2,230	2,509	426	1,896	2,230	2,509

(Continued)

Earned Income Credit (EIC) Table - Continued

(Caution. This is not a tax table.)

If the amount you are looking up from the worksheet is—		Single, head of household, or qualifying widow(er) and the number of children you have is—				Married filing jointly and the number of children you have is—			
At least	But less than	0	1	2	3	0	1	2	3
		Your credit is—				Your credit is—			
5,600	5,650	430	1,913	2,250	2,531	430	1,913	2,250	2,531
5,650	5,700	434	1,930	2,270	2,554	434	1,930	2,270	2,554
5,700	5,750	438	1,947	2,290	2,576	438	1,947	2,290	2,576
5,750	5,800	442	1,964	2,310	2,599	442	1,964	2,310	2,599
5,800	5,850	446	1,981	2,330	2,621	446	1,981	2,330	2,621
5,850	5,900	449	1,998	2,350	2,644	449	1,998	2,350	2,644
5,900	5,950	453	2,015	2,370	2,666	453	2,015	2,370	2,666
5,950	6,000	457	2,032	2,390	2,689	457	2,032	2,390	2,689
6,000	6,050	461	2,049	2,410	2,711	461	2,049	2,410	2,711
6,050	6,100	465	2,066	2,430	2,734	465	2,066	2,430	2,734
6,100	6,150	469	2,083	2,450	2,756	469	2,083	2,450	2,756
6,150	6,200	472	2,100	2,470	2,779	472	2,100	2,470	2,779
6,200	6,250	476	2,117	2,490	2,801	476	2,117	2,490	2,801
6,250	6,300	480	2,134	2,510	2,824	480	2,134	2,510	2,824
6,300	6,350	484	2,151	2,530	2,846	484	2,151	2,530	2,846
6,350	6,400	488	2,168	2,550	2,869	488	2,168	2,550	2,869
6,400	6,450	492	2,185	2,570	2,891	492	2,185	2,570	2,891
6,450	6,500	496	2,202	2,590	2,914	496	2,202	2,590	2,914
6,500	6,550	496	2,219	2,610	2,936	496	2,219	2,610	2,936
6,550	6,600	496	2,236	2,630	2,959	496	2,236	2,630	2,959
6,600	6,650	496	2,253	2,650	2,981	496	2,253	2,650	2,981
6,650	6,700	496	2,270	2,670	3,004	496	2,270	2,670	3,004
6,700	6,750	496	2,287	2,690	3,026	496	2,287	2,690	3,026
6,750	6,800	496	2,304	2,710	3,049	496	2,304	2,710	3,049
6,800	6,850	496	2,321	2,730	3,071	496	2,321	2,730	3,071
6,850	6,900	496	2,338	2,750	3,094	496	2,338	2,750	3,094
6,900	6,950	496	2,355	2,770	3,116	496	2,355	2,770	3,116
6,950	7,000	496	2,372	2,790	3,139	496	2,372	2,790	3,139
7,000	7,050	496	2,389	2,810	3,161	496	2,389	2,810	3,161
7,050	7,100	496	2,406	2,830	3,184	496	2,406	2,830	3,184
7,100	7,150	496	2,423	2,850	3,206	496	2,423	2,850	3,206
7,150	7,200	496	2,440	2,870	3,229	496	2,440	2,870	3,229
7,200	7,250	496	2,457	2,890	3,251	496	2,457	2,890	3,251
7,250	7,300	496	2,474	2,910	3,274	496	2,474	2,910	3,274
7,300	7,350	496	2,491	2,930	3,296	496	2,491	2,930	3,296
7,350	7,400	496	2,508	2,950	3,319	496	2,508	2,950	3,319
7,400	7,450	496	2,525	2,970	3,341	496	2,525	2,970	3,341
7,450	7,500	496	2,542	2,990	3,364	496	2,542	2,990	3,364
7,500	7,550	496	2,559	3,010	3,386	496	2,559	3,010	3,386
7,550	7,600	496	2,576	3,030	3,409	496	2,576	3,030	3,409
7,600	7,650	496	2,593	3,050	3,431	496	2,593	3,050	3,431
7,650	7,700	496	2,610	3,070	3,454	496	2,610	3,070	3,454
7,700	7,750	496	2,627	3,090	3,476	496	2,627	3,090	3,476
7,750	7,800	496	2,644	3,110	3,499	496	2,644	3,110	3,499
7,800	7,850	496	2,661	3,130	3,521	496	2,661	3,130	3,521
7,850	7,900	496	2,678	3,150	3,544	496	2,678	3,150	3,544
7,900	7,950	496	2,695	3,170	3,566	496	2,695	3,170	3,566
7,950	8,000	496	2,712	3,190	3,589	496	2,712	3,190	3,589
8,000	8,050	496	2,729	3,210	3,611	496	2,729	3,210	3,611
8,050	8,100	496	2,746	3,230	3,634	496	2,746	3,230	3,634
8,100	8,150	496	2,763	3,250	3,656	496	2,763	3,250	3,656
8,150	8,200	491	2,780	3,270	3,679	496	2,780	3,270	3,679
8,200	8,250	487	2,797	3,290	3,701	496	2,797	3,290	3,701
8,250	8,300	483	2,814	3,310	3,724	496	2,814	3,310	3,724
8,300	8,350	479	2,831	3,330	3,746	496	2,831	3,330	3,746
8,350	8,400	475	2,848	3,350	3,769	496	2,848	3,350	3,769
8,400	8,450	472	2,865	3,370	3,791	496	2,865	3,370	3,791
8,450	8,500	468	2,882	3,390	3,814	496	2,882	3,390	3,814
8,500	8,550	464	2,899	3,410	3,836	496	2,899	3,410	3,836
8,550	8,600	460	2,916	3,430	3,859	496	2,916	3,430	3,859
8,600	8,650	456	2,933	3,450	3,881	496	2,933	3,450	3,881
8,650	8,700	452	2,950	3,470	3,904	496	2,950	3,470	3,904
8,700	8,750	449	2,967	3,490	3,926	496	2,967	3,490	3,926
8,750	8,800	445	2,984	3,510	3,949	496	2,984	3,510	3,949
8,800	8,850	441	3,001	3,530	3,971	496	3,001	3,530	3,971
8,850	8,900	437	3,018	3,550	3,994	496	3,018	3,550	3,994
8,900	8,950	433	3,035	3,570	4,016	496	3,035	3,570	4,016
8,950	9,000	430	3,052	3,590	4,039	496	3,052	3,590	4,039
9,000	9,050	426	3,069	3,610	4,061	496	3,069	3,610	4,061
9,050	9,100	422	3,086	3,630	4,084	496	3,086	3,630	4,084
9,100	9,150	418	3,103	3,650	4,106	496	3,103	3,650	4,106
9,150	9,200	414	3,120	3,670	4,129	496	3,120	3,670	4,129
9,200	9,250	410	3,137	3,690	4,151	496	3,137	3,690	4,151
9,250	9,300	407	3,154	3,710	4,174	496	3,154	3,710	4,174
9,300	9,350	403	3,171	3,730	4,196	496	3,171	3,730	4,196
9,350	9,400	399	3,188	3,750	4,219	496	3,188	3,750	4,219
9,400	9,450	395	3,205	3,770	4,241	496	3,205	3,770	4,241
9,450	9,500	391	3,222	3,790	4,264	496	3,222	3,790	4,264
9,500	9,550	387	3,239	3,810	4,286	496	3,239	3,810	4,286
9,550	9,600	384	3,256	3,830	4,309	496	3,256	3,830	4,309
9,600	9,650	380	3,273	3,850	4,331	496	3,273	3,850	4,331
9,650	9,700	376	3,290	3,870	4,354	496	3,290	3,870	4,354
9,700	9,750	372	3,305	3,890	4,376	496	3,305	3,890	4,376
9,750	9,800	368	3,305	3,910	4,399	496	3,305	3,910	4,399
9,800	9,850	365	3,305	3,930	4,421	496	3,305	3,930	4,421
9,850	9,900	361	3,305	3,950	4,444	496	3,305	3,950	4,444
9,900	9,950	357	3,305	3,970	4,466	496	3,305	3,970	4,466
9,950	10,000	353	3,305	3,990	4,489	496	3,305	3,990	4,489
10,000	10,050	349	3,305	4,010	4,511	496	3,305	4,010	4,511
10,050	10,100	345	3,305	4,030	4,534	496	3,305	4,030	4,534
10,100	10,150	342	3,305	4,050	4,556	496	3,305	4,050	4,556
10,150	10,200	338	3,305	4,070	4,579	496	3,305	4,070	4,579
10,200	10,250	334	3,305	4,090	4,601	496	3,305	4,090	4,601
10,250	10,300	330	3,305	4,110	4,624	496	3,305	4,110	4,624
10,300	10,350	326	3,305	4,130	4,646	496	3,305	4,130	4,646
10,350	10,400	322	3,305	4,150	4,669	496	3,305	4,150	4,669
10,400	10,450	319	3,305	4,170	4,691	496	3,305	4,170	4,691
10,450	10,500	315	3,305	4,190	4,714	496	3,305	4,190	4,714
10,500	10,550	311	3,305	4,210	4,736	496	3,305	4,210	4,736
10,550	10,600	307	3,305	4,230	4,759	496	3,305	4,230	4,759
10,600	10,650	303	3,305	4,250	4,781	496	3,305	4,250	4,781
10,650	10,700	299	3,305	4,270	4,804	496	3,305	4,270	4,804
10,700	10,750	296	3,305	4,290	4,826	496	3,305	4,290	4,826
10,750	10,800	292	3,305	4,310	4,849	496	3,305	4,310	4,849
10,800	10,850	288	3,305	4,330	4,871	496	3,305	4,330	4,871
10,850	10,900	284	3,305	4,350	4,894	496	3,305	4,350	4,894
10,900	10,950	280	3,305	4,370	4,916	496	3,305	4,370	4,916
10,950	11,000	277	3,305	4,390	4,939	496	3,305	4,390	4,939
11,000	11,050	273	3,305	4,410	4,961	496	3,305	4,410	4,961
11,050	11,100	269	3,305	4,430	4,984	496	3,305	4,430	4,984
11,100	11,150	265	3,305	4,450	5,006	496	3,305	4,450	5,006
11,150	11,200	261	3,305	4,470	5,029	496	3,305	4,470	5,029
11,200	11,250	257	3,305	4,490	5,051	496	3,305	4,490	5,051
11,250	11,300	254	3,305	4,510	5,074	496	3,305	4,510	5,074
11,300	11,350	250	3,305	4,530	5,096	496	3,305	4,530	5,096
11,350	11,400	246	3,305	4,550	5,119	496	3,305	4,550	5,119
11,400	11,450	242	3,305	4,570	5,141	496	3,305	4,570	5,141
11,450	11,500	238	3,305	4,590	5,164	496	3,305	4,590	5,164
11,500	11,550	234	3,305	4,610	5,186	496	3,305	4,610	5,186
11,550	11,600	231	3,305	4,630	5,209	496	3,305	4,630	5,209
11,600	11,650	227	3,305	4,650	5,231	496	3,305	4,650	5,231
11,650	11,700	223	3,305	4,670	5,254	496	3,305	4,670	5,254
11,700	11,750	219	3,305	4,690	5,276	496	3,305	4,690	5,276
11,750	11,800	215	3,305	4,710	5,299	496	3,305	4,710	5,299
11,800	11,850	212	3,305	4,730	5,321	496	3,305	4,730	5,321
11,850	11,900	208	3,305	4,750	5,344	496	3,305	4,750	5,344
11,900	11,950	204	3,305	4,770	5,366	496	3,305	4,770	5,366
11,950	12,000	200	3,305	4,790	5,389	496	3,305	4,790	5,389
12,000	12,050	196	3,305	4,810	5,411	496	3,305	4,810	5,411
12,050	12,100	192	3,305	4,830	5,434	496	3,305	4,830	5,434
12,100	12,150	189	3,305	4,850	5,456	496	3,305	4,850	5,456
12,150	12,200	185	3,305	4,870	5,479	496	3,305	4,870	5,479
12,200	12,250	181	3,305	4,890	5,501	496	3,305	4,890	5,501
12,250	12,300	177	3,305	4,910	5,524	496	3,305	4,910	5,524
12,300	12,350	173	3,305	4,930	5,546	496	3,305	4,930	5,546
12,350	12,400	169	3,305	4,950	5,569	496	3,305	4,950	5,569
12,400	12,450	166	3,305	4,970	5,591	496	3,305	4,970	5,591
12,450	12,500	162	3,305	4,990	5,614	496	3,305	4,990	5,614
12,500	12,550	158	3,305	5,010	5,636	496	3,305	5,010	5,636
12,550	12,600	154	3,305	5,030	5,659	496	3,305	5,030	5,659
12,600	12,650	150	3,305	5,050	5,681	496	3,305	5,050	5,681
12,650	12,700	146	3,305	5,070	5,704	496	3,305	5,070	5,704
12,700	12,750	143	3,305	5,090	5,726	496	3,305	5,090	5,726
12,750	12,800	139	3,305	5,110	5,749	496	3,305	5,110	5,749

(Continued)

Earned Income Credit (EIC) Table - Continued

(**Caution.** This is **not** a tax table.)

If the amount you are looking up from the worksheet is—		Single, head of household, or qualifying widow(er) and the number of children you have is—				Married filing jointly and the number of children you have is—			
At least	But less than	0	1	2	3	0	1	2	3
		Your credit is—				Your credit is—			
12,800	12,850	135	3,305	5,130	5,771	496	3,305	5,130	5,771
12,850	12,900	131	3,305	5,150	5,794	496	3,305	5,150	5,794
12,900	12,950	127	3,305	5,170	5,816	496	3,305	5,170	5,816
12,950	13,000	124	3,305	5,190	5,839	496	3,305	5,190	5,839
13,000	13,050	120	3,305	5,210	5,861	496	3,305	5,210	5,861
13,050	13,100	116	3,305	5,230	5,884	496	3,305	5,230	5,884
13,100	13,150	112	3,305	5,250	5,906	496	3,305	5,250	5,906
13,150	13,200	108	3,305	5,270	5,929	496	3,305	5,270	5,929
13,200	13,250	104	3,305	5,290	5,951	496	3,305	5,290	5,951
13,250	13,300	101	3,305	5,310	5,974	496	3,305	5,310	5,974
13,300	13,350	97	3,305	5,330	5,996	496	3,305	5,330	5,996
13,350	13,400	93	3,305	5,350	6,019	496	3,305	5,350	6,019
13,400	13,450	89	3,305	5,370	6,041	496	3,305	5,370	6,041
13,450	13,500	85	3,305	5,390	6,064	496	3,305	5,390	6,064
13,500	13,550	81	3,305	5,410	6,086	496	3,305	5,410	6,086
13,550	13,600	78	3,305	5,430	6,109	493	3,305	5,430	6,109
13,600	13,650	74	3,305	5,450	6,131	489	3,305	5,450	6,131
13,650	13,700	70	3,305	5,460	6,143	485	3,305	5,460	6,143
13,700	13,750	66	3,305	5,460	6,143	482	3,305	5,460	6,143
13,750	13,800	62	3,305	5,460	6,143	478	3,305	5,460	6,143
13,800	13,850	59	3,305	5,460	6,143	474	3,305	5,460	6,143
13,850	13,900	55	3,305	5,460	6,143	470	3,305	5,460	6,143
13,900	13,950	51	3,305	5,460	6,143	466	3,305	5,460	6,143
13,950	14,000	47	3,305	5,460	6,143	462	3,305	5,460	6,143
14,000	14,050	43	3,305	5,460	6,143	459	3,305	5,460	6,143
14,050	14,100	39	3,305	5,460	6,143	455	3,305	5,460	6,143
14,100	14,150	36	3,305	5,460	6,143	451	3,305	5,460	6,143
14,150	14,200	32	3,305	5,460	6,143	447	3,305	5,460	6,143
14,200	14,250	28	3,305	5,460	6,143	443	3,305	5,460	6,143
14,250	14,300	24	3,305	5,460	6,143	439	3,305	5,460	6,143
14,300	14,350	20	3,305	5,460	6,143	436	3,305	5,460	6,143
14,350	14,400	16	3,305	5,460	6,143	432	3,305	5,460	6,143
14,400	14,450	13	3,305	5,460	6,143	428	3,305	5,460	6,143
14,450	14,500	9	3,305	5,460	6,143	424	3,305	5,460	6,143
14,500	14,550	5	3,305	5,460	6,143	420	3,305	5,460	6,143
14,550	14,600	*	3,305	5,460	6,143	417	3,305	5,460	6,143
14,600	14,650	0	3,305	5,460	6,143	413	3,305	5,460	6,143
14,650	14,700	0	3,305	5,460	6,143	409	3,305	5,460	6,143
14,700	14,750	0	3,305	5,460	6,143	405	3,305	5,460	6,143
14,750	14,800	0	3,305	5,460	6,143	401	3,305	5,460	6,143
14,800	14,850	0	3,305	5,460	6,143	397	3,305	5,460	6,143
14,850	14,900	0	3,305	5,460	6,143	394	3,305	5,460	6,143
14,900	14,950	0	3,305	5,460	6,143	390	3,305	5,460	6,143
14,950	15,000	0	3,305	5,460	6,143	386	3,305	5,460	6,143
15,000	15,050	0	3,305	5,460	6,143	382	3,305	5,460	6,143
15,050	15,100	0	3,305	5,460	6,143	378	3,305	5,460	6,143
15,100	15,150	0	3,305	5,460	6,143	374	3,305	5,460	6,143
15,150	15,200	0	3,305	5,460	6,143	371	3,305	5,460	6,143
15,200	15,250	0	3,305	5,460	6,143	367	3,305	5,460	6,143
15,250	15,300	0	3,305	5,460	6,143	363	3,305	5,460	6,143
15,300	15,350	0	3,305	5,460	6,143	359	3,305	5,460	6,143
15,350	15,400	0	3,305	5,460	6,143	355	3,305	5,460	6,143
15,400	15,450	0	3,305	5,460	6,143	352	3,305	5,460	6,143
15,450	15,500	0	3,305	5,460	6,143	348	3,305	5,460	6,143
15,500	15,550	0	3,305	5,460	6,143	344	3,305	5,460	6,143
15,550	15,600	0	3,305	5,460	6,143	340	3,305	5,460	6,143
15,600	15,650	0	3,305	5,460	6,143	336	3,305	5,460	6,143
15,650	15,700	0	3,305	5,460	6,143	332	3,305	5,460	6,143
15,700	15,750	0	3,305	5,460	6,143	329	3,305	5,460	6,143
15,750	15,800	0	3,305	5,460	6,143	325	3,305	5,460	6,143
15,800	15,850	0	3,305	5,460	6,143	321	3,305	5,460	6,143
15,850	15,900	0	3,305	5,460	6,143	317	3,305	5,460	6,143
15,900	15,950	0	3,305	5,460	6,143	313	3,305	5,460	6,143
15,950	16,000	0	3,305	5,460	6,143	309	3,305	5,460	6,143
16,000	16,050	0	3,305	5,460	6,143	306	3,305	5,460	6,143
16,050	16,100	0	3,305	5,460	6,143	302	3,305	5,460	6,143
16,100	16,150	0	3,305	5,460	6,143	298	3,305	5,460	6,143
16,150	16,200	0	3,305	5,460	6,143	294	3,305	5,460	6,143
16,200	16,250	0	3,305	5,460	6,143	290	3,305	5,460	6,143
16,250	16,300	0	3,305	5,460	6,143	286	3,305	5,460	6,143
16,300	16,350	0	3,305	5,460	6,143	283	3,305	5,460	6,143
16,350	16,400	0	3,305	5,460	6,143	279	3,305	5,460	6,143
16,400	16,450	0	3,305	5,460	6,143	275	3,305	5,460	6,143
16,450	16,500	0	3,305	5,460	6,143	271	3,305	5,460	6,143
16,500	16,550	0	3,305	5,460	6,143	267	3,305	5,460	6,143
16,550	16,600	0	3,305	5,460	6,143	264	3,305	5,460	6,143
16,600	16,650	0	3,305	5,460	6,143	260	3,305	5,460	6,143
16,650	16,700	0	3,305	5,460	6,143	256	3,305	5,460	6,143
16,700	16,750	0	3,305	5,460	6,143	252	3,305	5,460	6,143
16,750	16,800	0	3,305	5,460	6,143	248	3,305	5,460	6,143
16,800	16,850	0	3,305	5,460	6,143	244	3,305	5,460	6,143
16,850	16,900	0	3,305	5,460	6,143	241	3,305	5,460	6,143
16,900	16,950	0	3,305	5,460	6,143	237	3,305	5,460	6,143
16,950	17,000	0	3,305	5,460	6,143	233	3,305	5,460	6,143
17,000	17,050	0	3,305	5,460	6,143	229	3,305	5,460	6,143
17,050	17,100	0	3,305	5,460	6,143	225	3,305	5,460	6,143
17,100	17,150	0	3,305	5,460	6,143	221	3,305	5,460	6,143
17,150	17,200	0	3,305	5,460	6,143	218	3,305	5,460	6,143
17,200	17,250	0	3,305	5,460	6,143	214	3,305	5,460	6,143
17,250	17,300	0	3,305	5,460	6,143	210	3,305	5,460	6,143
17,300	17,350	0	3,305	5,460	6,143	206	3,305	5,460	6,143
17,350	17,400	0	3,305	5,460	6,143	202	3,305	5,460	6,143
17,400	17,450	0	3,305	5,460	6,143	199	3,305	5,460	6,143
17,450	17,500	0	3,305	5,460	6,143	195	3,305	5,460	6,143
17,500	17,550	0	3,305	5,460	6,143	191	3,305	5,460	6,143
17,550	17,600	0	3,305	5,460	6,143	187	3,305	5,460	6,143
17,600	17,650	0	3,305	5,460	6,143	183	3,305	5,460	6,143
17,650	17,700	0	3,305	5,460	6,143	179	3,305	5,460	6,143
17,700	17,750	0	3,305	5,460	6,143	176	3,305	5,460	6,143
17,750	17,800	0	3,305	5,460	6,143	172	3,305	5,460	6,143
17,800	17,850	0	3,305	5,460	6,143	168	3,305	5,460	6,143
17,850	17,900	0	3,298	5,451	6,133	164	3,305	5,460	6,143
17,900	17,950	0	3,290	5,440	6,122	160	3,305	5,460	6,143
17,950	18,000	0	3,282	5,429	6,112	156	3,305	5,460	6,143
18,000	18,050	0	3,274	5,419	6,101	153	3,305	5,460	6,143
18,050	18,100	0	3,266	5,408	6,091	149	3,305	5,460	6,143
18,100	18,150	0	3,258	5,398	6,080	145	3,305	5,460	6,143
18,150	18,200	0	3,250	5,387	6,070	141	3,305	5,460	6,143
18,200	18,250	0	3,242	5,377	6,059	137	3,305	5,460	6,143
18,250	18,300	0	3,234	5,366	6,049	133	3,305	5,460	6,143
18,300	18,350	0	3,226	5,356	6,038	130	3,305	5,460	6,143
18,350	18,400	0	3,218	5,345	6,028	126	3,305	5,460	6,143
18,400	18,450	0	3,210	5,335	6,017	122	3,305	5,460	6,143
18,450	18,500	0	3,202	5,324	6,007	118	3,305	5,460	6,143
18,500	18,550	0	3,194	5,314	5,996	114	3,305	5,460	6,143
18,550	18,600	0	3,186	5,303	5,986	111	3,305	5,460	6,143
18,600	18,650	0	3,178	5,293	5,975	107	3,305	5,460	6,143
18,650	18,700	0	3,170	5,282	5,965	103	3,305	5,460	6,143
18,700	18,750	0	3,162	5,272	5,954	99	3,305	5,460	6,143
18,750	18,800	0	3,154	5,261	5,943	95	3,305	5,460	6,143
18,800	18,850	0	3,146	5,250	5,933	91	3,305	5,460	6,143
18,850	18,900	0	3,138	5,240	5,922	88	3,305	5,460	6,143
18,900	18,950	0	3,130	5,229	5,912	84	3,305	5,460	6,143
18,950	19,000	0	3,122	5,219	5,901	80	3,305	5,460	6,143
19,000	19,050	0	3,114	5,208	5,891	76	3,305	5,460	6,143
19,050	19,100	0	3,106	5,198	5,880	72	3,305	5,460	6,143
19,100	19,150	0	3,098	5,187	5,870	68	3,305	5,460	6,143
19,150	19,200	0	3,090	5,177	5,859	65	3,305	5,460	6,143

* If the amount you are looking up from the worksheet is at least $14,550 but less than $14,590, and you have no qualifying children, your credit is $2.
If the amount you are looking up from the worksheet is $14,590 or more, and you have no qualifying children, you cannot take the credit.

(Continued)

Earned Income Credit (EIC) Table - *Continued*

(Caution. This is not a tax table.)

If the amount you are looking up from the worksheet is—		Single, head of household, or qualifying widow(er) and the number of children you have is—				Married filing jointly and the number of children you have is—				If the amount you are looking up from the worksheet is—		Single, head of household, or qualifying widow(er) and the number of children you have is—				Married filing jointly and the number of children you have is—			
At least	But less than	0	1	2	3	0	1	2	3	At least	But less than	0	1	2	3	0	1	2	3
		Your credit is—				Your credit is—						Your credit is—				Your credit is—			
19,200	19,250	0	3,082	5,166	5,849	61	3,305	5,460	6,143	22,400	22,450	0	2,571	4,492	5,175	0	3,305	5,460	6,143
19,250	19,300	0	3,074	5,156	5,838	57	3,305	5,460	6,143	22,450	22,500	0	2,563	4,482	5,164	0	3,305	5,460	6,143
19,300	19,350	0	3,066	5,145	5,828	53	3,305	5,460	6,143	22,500	22,550	0	2,555	4,471	5,154	0	3,305	5,460	6,143
19,350	19,400	0	3,058	5,135	5,817	49	3,305	5,460	6,143	22,550	22,600	0	2,547	4,461	5,143	0	3,305	5,460	6,143
19,400	19,450	0	3,050	5,124	5,807	46	3,305	5,460	6,143	22,600	22,650	0	2,539	4,450	5,133	0	3,305	5,460	6,143
19,450	19,500	0	3,042	5,114	5,796	42	3,305	5,460	6,143	22,650	22,700	0	2,531	4,440	5,122	0	3,305	5,460	6,143
19,500	19,550	0	3,034	5,103	5,786	38	3,305	5,460	6,143	22,700	22,750	0	2,523	4,429	5,112	0	3,305	5,460	6,143
19,550	19,600	0	3,026	5,093	5,775	34	3,305	5,460	6,143	22,750	22,800	0	2,515	4,419	5,101	0	3,305	5,460	6,143
19,600	19,650	0	3,018	5,082	5,764	30	3,305	5,460	6,143	22,800	22,850	0	2,507	4,408	5,091	0	3,305	5,460	6,143
19,650	19,700	0	3,010	5,071	5,754	26	3,305	5,460	6,143	22,850	22,900	0	2,499	4,398	5,080	0	3,305	5,460	6,143
19,700	19,750	0	3,002	5,061	5,743	23	3,305	5,460	6,143	22,900	22,950	0	2,491	4,387	5,069	0	3,305	5,460	6,143
19,750	19,800	0	2,994	5,050	5,733	19	3,305	5,460	6,143	22,950	23,000	0	2,483	4,376	5,059	0	3,305	5,460	6,143
19,800	19,850	0	2,986	5,040	5,722	15	3,305	5,460	6,143	23,000	23,050	0	2,475	4,366	5,048	0	3,305	5,460	6,143
19,850	19,900	0	2,978	5,029	5,712	11	3,305	5,460	6,143	23,050	23,100	0	2,467	4,355	5,038	0	3,305	5,460	6,143
19,900	19,950	0	2,970	5,019	5,701	7	3,305	5,460	6,143	23,100	23,150	0	2,459	4,345	5,027	0	3,305	5,460	6,143
19,950	20,000	0	2,962	5,008	5,691	3	3,305	5,460	6,143	23,150	23,200	0	2,451	4,334	5,017	0	3,305	5,460	6,143
20,000	20,050	0	2,954	4,998	5,680	*	3,305	5,460	6,143	23,200	23,250	0	2,443	4,324	5,006	0	3,305	5,460	6,143
20,050	20,100	0	2,946	4,987	5,670	0	3,305	5,460	6,143	23,250	23,300	0	2,435	4,313	4,996	0	3,305	5,460	6,143
20,100	20,150	0	2,938	4,977	5,659	0	3,305	5,460	6,143	23,300	23,350	0	2,427	4,303	4,985	0	3,294	5,446	6,129
20,150	20,200	0	2,930	4,966	5,649	0	3,305	5,460	6,143	23,350	23,400	0	2,419	4,292	4,975	0	3,286	5,436	6,118
20,200	20,250	0	2,922	4,956	5,638	0	3,305	5,460	6,143	23,400	23,450	0	2,411	4,282	4,964	0	3,278	5,425	6,108
20,250	20,300	0	2,914	4,945	5,628	0	3,305	5,460	6,143	23,450	23,500	0	2,403	4,271	4,954	0	3,270	5,415	6,097
20,300	20,350	0	2,906	4,935	5,617	0	3,305	5,460	6,143	23,500	23,550	0	2,395	4,261	4,943	0	3,262	5,404	6,087
20,350	20,400	0	2,898	4,924	5,607	0	3,305	5,460	6,143	23,550	23,600	0	2,387	4,250	4,933	0	3,254	5,394	6,076
20,400	20,450	0	2,890	4,913	5,596	0	3,305	5,460	6,143	23,600	23,650	0	2,379	4,240	4,922	0	3,246	5,383	6,066
20,450	20,500	0	2,882	4,903	5,585	0	3,305	5,460	6,143	23,650	23,700	0	2,371	4,229	4,912	0	3,238	5,373	6,055
20,500	20,550	0	2,874	4,892	5,575	0	3,305	5,460	6,143	23,700	23,750	0	2,363	4,219	4,901	0	3,230	5,362	6,045
20,550	20,600	0	2,866	4,882	5,564	0	3,305	5,460	6,143	23,750	23,800	0	2,355	4,208	4,890	0	3,223	5,352	6,034
20,600	20,650	0	2,858	4,871	5,554	0	3,305	5,460	6,143	23,800	23,850	0	2,347	4,197	4,880	0	3,215	5,341	6,024
20,650	20,700	0	2,850	4,861	5,543	0	3,305	5,460	6,143	23,850	23,900	0	2,339	4,187	4,869	0	3,207	5,330	6,013
20,700	20,750	0	2,842	4,850	5,533	0	3,305	5,460	6,143	23,900	23,950	0	2,331	4,176	4,859	0	3,199	5,320	6,002
20,750	20,800	0	2,834	4,840	5,522	0	3,305	5,460	6,143	23,950	24,000	0	2,323	4,166	4,848	0	3,191	5,309	5,992
20,800	20,850	0	2,826	4,829	5,512	0	3,305	5,460	6,143	24,000	24,050	0	2,315	4,155	4,838	0	3,183	5,299	5,981
20,850	20,900	0	2,818	4,819	5,501	0	3,305	5,460	6,143	24,050	24,100	0	2,307	4,145	4,827	0	3,175	5,288	5,971
20,900	20,950	0	2,810	4,808	5,491	0	3,305	5,460	6,143	24,100	24,150	0	2,299	4,134	4,817	0	3,167	5,278	5,960
20,950	21,000	0	2,802	4,798	5,480	0	3,305	5,460	6,143	24,150	24,200	0	2,291	4,124	4,806	0	3,159	5,267	5,950
21,000	21,050	0	2,794	4,787	5,470	0	3,305	5,460	6,143	24,200	24,250	0	2,283	4,113	4,796	0	3,151	5,257	5,939
21,050	21,100	0	2,786	4,777	5,459	0	3,305	5,460	6,143	24,250	24,300	0	2,275	4,103	4,785	0	3,143	5,246	5,929
21,100	21,150	0	2,778	4,766	5,449	0	3,305	5,460	6,143	24,300	24,350	0	2,267	4,092	4,775	0	3,135	5,236	5,918
21,150	21,200	0	2,770	4,756	5,438	0	3,305	5,460	6,143	24,350	24,400	0	2,259	4,082	4,764	0	3,127	5,225	5,908
21,200	21,250	0	2,762	4,745	5,428	0	3,305	5,460	6,143	24,400	24,450	0	2,251	4,071	4,754	0	3,119	5,215	5,897
21,250	21,300	0	2,754	4,734	5,417	0	3,305	5,460	6,143	24,450	24,500	0	2,243	4,061	4,743	0	3,111	5,204	5,887
21,300	21,350	0	2,746	4,724	5,406	0	3,305	5,460	6,143	24,500	24,550	0	2,235	4,050	4,733	0	3,103	5,194	5,876
21,350	21,400	0	2,738	4,713	5,396	0	3,305	5,460	6,143	24,550	24,600	0	2,227	4,040	4,722	0	3,095	5,183	5,866
21,400	21,450	0	2,730	4,703	5,385	0	3,305	5,460	6,143	24,600	24,650	0	2,219	4,029	4,711	0	3,087	5,173	5,855
21,450	21,500	0	2,722	4,692	5,375	0	3,305	5,460	6,143	24,650	24,700	0	2,211	4,018	4,701	0	3,079	5,162	5,845
21,500	21,550	0	2,714	4,682	5,364	0	3,305	5,460	6,143	24,700	24,750	0	2,203	4,008	4,690	0	3,071	5,151	5,834
21,550	21,600	0	2,706	4,671	5,354	0	3,305	5,460	6,143	24,750	24,800	0	2,195	3,997	4,680	0	3,063	5,141	5,823
21,600	21,650	0	2,698	4,661	5,343	0	3,305	5,460	6,143	24,800	24,850	0	2,187	3,987	4,669	0	3,055	5,130	5,813
21,650	21,700	0	2,690	4,650	5,333	0	3,305	5,460	6,143	24,850	24,900	0	2,179	3,976	4,659	0	3,047	5,120	5,802
21,700	21,750	0	2,682	4,640	5,322	0	3,305	5,460	6,143	24,900	24,950	0	2,171	3,966	4,648	0	3,039	5,109	5,792
21,750	21,800	0	2,674	4,629	5,312	0	3,305	5,460	6,143	24,950	25,000	0	2,163	3,955	4,638	0	3,031	5,099	5,781
21,800	21,850	0	2,666	4,619	5,301	0	3,305	5,460	6,143	25,000	25,050	0	2,155	3,945	4,627	0	3,023	5,088	5,771
21,850	21,900	0	2,658	4,608	5,291	0	3,305	5,460	6,143	25,050	25,100	0	2,147	3,934	4,617	0	3,015	5,078	5,760
21,900	21,950	0	2,650	4,598	5,280	0	3,305	5,460	6,143	25,100	25,150	0	2,139	3,924	4,606	0	3,007	5,067	5,750
21,950	22,000	0	2,642	4,587	5,270	0	3,305	5,460	6,143	25,150	25,200	0	2,131	3,913	4,596	0	2,999	5,057	5,739
22,000	22,050	0	2,634	4,577	5,259	0	3,305	5,460	6,143	25,200	25,250	0	2,123	3,903	4,585	0	2,991	5,046	5,729
22,050	22,100	0	2,626	4,566	5,249	0	3,305	5,460	6,143	25,250	25,300	0	2,115	3,892	4,575	0	2,983	5,036	5,718
22,100	22,150	0	2,618	4,555	5,238	0	3,305	5,460	6,143	25,300	25,350	0	2,107	3,882	4,564	0	2,975	5,025	5,708
22,150	22,200	0	2,610	4,545	5,227	0	3,305	5,460	6,143	25,350	25,400	0	2,099	3,871	4,554	0	2,967	5,015	5,697
22,200	22,250	0	2,602	4,534	5,217	0	3,305	5,460	6,143	25,400	25,450	0	2,091	3,860	4,543	0	2,959	5,004	5,687
22,250	22,300	0	2,594	4,524	5,206	0	3,305	5,460	6,143	25,450	25,500	0	2,083	3,850	4,532	0	2,951	4,994	5,676
22,300	22,350	0	2,586	4,513	5,196	0	3,305	5,460	6,143	25,500	25,550	0	2,075	3,839	4,522	0	2,943	4,983	5,665
22,350	22,400	0	2,579	4,503	5,185	0	3,305	5,460	6,143	25,550	25,600	0	2,067	3,829	4,511	0	2,935	4,972	5,655

* If the amount you are looking up from the worksheet is at least $20,000 but less than $20,020, and you have no qualifying children, your credit is $1.
If the amount you are looking up from the worksheet is $20,020 or more, and you have no qualifying children, you cannot take the credit.

(Continued)

Earned Income Credit (EIC) Table - Continued

(Caution. This is not a tax table.)

If the amount you are looking up from the worksheet is—		Single, head of household, or qualifying widow(er) and the number of children you have is—				Married filing jointly and the number of children you have is—			
At least	But less than	0	1	2	3	0	1	2	3
		Your credit is—				Your credit is—			
25,600	25,650	0	2,059	3,818	4,501	0	2,927	4,962	5,644
25,650	25,700	0	2,051	3,808	4,490	0	2,919	4,951	5,634
25,700	25,750	0	2,043	3,797	4,480	0	2,911	4,941	5,623
25,750	25,800	0	2,035	3,787	4,469	0	2,903	4,930	5,613
25,800	25,850	0	2,027	3,776	4,459	0	2,895	4,920	5,602
25,850	25,900	0	2,019	3,766	4,448	0	2,887	4,909	5,592
25,900	25,950	0	2,011	3,755	4,438	0	2,879	4,899	5,581
25,950	26,000	0	2,003	3,745	4,427	0	2,871	4,888	5,571
26,000	26,050	0	1,995	3,734	4,417	0	2,863	4,878	5,560
26,050	26,100	0	1,987	3,724	4,406	0	2,855	4,867	5,550
26,100	26,150	0	1,979	3,713	4,396	0	2,847	4,857	5,539
26,150	26,200	0	1,971	3,703	4,385	0	2,839	4,846	5,529
26,200	26,250	0	1,963	3,692	4,375	0	2,831	4,836	5,518
26,250	26,300	0	1,955	3,681	4,364	0	2,823	4,825	5,508
26,300	26,350	0	1,947	3,671	4,353	0	2,815	4,815	5,497
26,350	26,400	0	1,939	3,660	4,343	0	2,807	4,804	5,486
26,400	26,450	0	1,931	3,650	4,332	0	2,799	4,793	5,476
26,450	26,500	0	1,923	3,639	4,322	0	2,791	4,783	5,465
26,500	26,550	0	1,915	3,629	4,311	0	2,783	4,772	5,455
26,550	26,600	0	1,907	3,618	4,301	0	2,775	4,762	5,444
26,600	26,650	0	1,899	3,608	4,290	0	2,767	4,751	5,434
26,650	26,700	0	1,891	3,597	4,280	0	2,759	4,741	5,423
26,700	26,750	0	1,883	3,587	4,269	0	2,751	4,730	5,413
26,750	26,800	0	1,875	3,576	4,259	0	2,743	4,720	5,402
26,800	26,850	0	1,867	3,566	4,248	0	2,735	4,709	5,392
26,850	26,900	0	1,859	3,555	4,238	0	2,727	4,699	5,381
26,900	26,950	0	1,851	3,545	4,227	0	2,719	4,688	5,371
26,950	27,000	0	1,843	3,534	4,217	0	2,711	4,678	5,360
27,000	27,050	0	1,835	3,524	4,206	0	2,703	4,667	5,350
27,050	27,100	0	1,827	3,513	4,196	0	2,695	4,657	5,339
27,100	27,150	0	1,819	3,502	4,185	0	2,687	4,646	5,329
27,150	27,200	0	1,811	3,492	4,174	0	2,679	4,636	5,318
27,200	27,250	0	1,803	3,481	4,164	0	2,671	4,625	5,307
27,250	27,300	0	1,795	3,471	4,153	0	2,663	4,614	5,297
27,300	27,350	0	1,787	3,460	4,143	0	2,655	4,604	5,286
27,350	27,400	0	1,780	3,450	4,132	0	2,647	4,593	5,276
27,400	27,450	0	1,772	3,439	4,122	0	2,639	4,583	5,265
27,450	27,500	0	1,764	3,429	4,111	0	2,631	4,572	5,255
27,500	27,550	0	1,756	3,418	4,101	0	2,623	4,562	5,244
27,550	27,600	0	1,748	3,408	4,090	0	2,615	4,551	5,234
27,600	27,650	0	1,740	3,397	4,080	0	2,607	4,541	5,223
27,650	27,700	0	1,732	3,387	4,069	0	2,599	4,530	5,213
27,700	27,750	0	1,724	3,376	4,059	0	2,591	4,520	5,202
27,750	27,800	0	1,716	3,366	4,048	0	2,583	4,509	5,192
27,800	27,850	0	1,708	3,355	4,038	0	2,575	4,499	5,181
27,850	27,900	0	1,700	3,345	4,027	0	2,567	4,488	5,171
27,900	27,950	0	1,692	3,334	4,016	0	2,559	4,478	5,160
27,950	28,000	0	1,684	3,323	4,006	0	2,551	4,467	5,150
28,000	28,050	0	1,676	3,313	3,995	0	2,543	4,456	5,139
28,050	28,100	0	1,668	3,302	3,985	0	2,535	4,446	5,128
28,100	28,150	0	1,660	3,292	3,974	0	2,527	4,435	5,118
28,150	28,200	0	1,652	3,281	3,964	0	2,519	4,425	5,107
28,200	28,250	0	1,644	3,271	3,953	0	2,511	4,414	5,097
28,250	28,300	0	1,636	3,260	3,943	0	2,503	4,404	5,086
28,300	28,350	0	1,628	3,250	3,932	0	2,495	4,393	5,076
28,350	28,400	0	1,620	3,239	3,922	0	2,487	4,383	5,065
28,400	28,450	0	1,612	3,229	3,911	0	2,479	4,372	5,055
28,450	28,500	0	1,604	3,218	3,901	0	2,471	4,362	5,044
28,500	28,550	0	1,596	3,208	3,890	0	2,463	4,351	5,034
28,550	28,600	0	1,588	3,197	3,880	0	2,455	4,341	5,023
28,600	28,650	0	1,580	3,187	3,869	0	2,447	4,330	5,013
28,650	28,700	0	1,572	3,176	3,859	0	2,439	4,320	5,002
28,700	28,750	0	1,564	3,166	3,848	0	2,431	4,309	4,992
28,750	28,800	0	1,556	3,155	3,837	0	2,424	4,299	4,981
28,800	28,850	0	1,548	3,144	3,827	0	2,416	4,288	4,971
28,850	28,900	0	1,540	3,134	3,816	0	2,408	4,277	4,960
28,900	28,950	0	1,532	3,123	3,806	0	2,400	4,267	4,949
28,950	29,000	0	1,524	3,113	3,795	0	2,392	4,256	4,939
29,000	29,050	0	1,516	3,102	3,785	0	2,384	4,246	4,928
29,050	29,100	0	1,508	3,092	3,774	0	2,376	4,235	4,918
29,100	29,150	0	1,500	3,081	3,764	0	2,368	4,225	4,907
29,150	29,200	0	1,492	3,071	3,753	0	2,360	4,214	4,897
29,200	29,250	0	1,484	3,060	3,743	0	2,352	4,204	4,886
29,250	29,300	0	1,476	3,050	3,732	0	2,344	4,193	4,876
29,300	29,350	0	1,468	3,039	3,722	0	2,336	4,183	4,865
29,350	29,400	0	1,460	3,029	3,711	0	2,328	4,172	4,855
29,400	29,450	0	1,452	3,018	3,701	0	2,320	4,162	4,844
29,450	29,500	0	1,444	3,008	3,690	0	2,312	4,151	4,834
29,500	29,550	0	1,436	2,997	3,680	0	2,304	4,141	4,823
29,550	29,600	0	1,428	2,987	3,669	0	2,296	4,130	4,813
29,600	29,650	0	1,420	2,976	3,658	0	2,288	4,120	4,802
29,650	29,700	0	1,412	2,965	3,648	0	2,280	4,109	4,792
29,700	29,750	0	1,404	2,955	3,637	0	2,272	4,098	4,781
29,750	29,800	0	1,396	2,944	3,627	0	2,264	4,088	4,770
29,800	29,850	0	1,388	2,934	3,616	0	2,256	4,077	4,760
29,850	29,900	0	1,380	2,923	3,606	0	2,248	4,067	4,749
29,900	29,950	0	1,372	2,913	3,595	0	2,240	4,056	4,739
29,950	30,000	0	1,364	2,902	3,585	0	2,232	4,046	4,728
30,000	30,050	0	1,356	2,892	3,574	0	2,224	4,035	4,718
30,050	30,100	0	1,348	2,881	3,564	0	2,216	4,025	4,707
30,100	30,150	0	1,340	2,871	3,553	0	2,208	4,014	4,697
30,150	30,200	0	1,332	2,860	3,543	0	2,200	4,004	4,686
30,200	30,250	0	1,324	2,850	3,532	0	2,192	3,993	4,676
30,250	30,300	0	1,316	2,839	3,522	0	2,184	3,983	4,665
30,300	30,350	0	1,308	2,829	3,511	0	2,176	3,972	4,655
30,350	30,400	0	1,300	2,818	3,501	0	2,168	3,962	4,644
30,400	30,450	0	1,292	2,807	3,490	0	2,160	3,951	4,634
30,450	30,500	0	1,284	2,797	3,479	0	2,152	3,941	4,623
30,500	30,550	0	1,276	2,786	3,469	0	2,144	3,930	4,612
30,550	30,600	0	1,268	2,776	3,458	0	2,136	3,919	4,602
30,600	30,650	0	1,260	2,765	3,448	0	2,128	3,909	4,591
30,650	30,700	0	1,252	2,755	3,437	0	2,120	3,898	4,581
30,700	30,750	0	1,244	2,744	3,427	0	2,112	3,888	4,570
30,750	30,800	0	1,236	2,734	3,416	0	2,104	3,877	4,560
30,800	30,850	0	1,228	2,723	3,406	0	2,096	3,867	4,549
30,850	30,900	0	1,220	2,713	3,395	0	2,088	3,856	4,539
30,900	30,950	0	1,212	2,702	3,385	0	2,080	3,846	4,528
30,950	31,000	0	1,204	2,692	3,374	0	2,072	3,835	4,518
31,000	31,050	0	1,196	2,681	3,364	0	2,064	3,825	4,507
31,050	31,100	0	1,188	2,671	3,353	0	2,056	3,814	4,497
31,100	31,150	0	1,180	2,660	3,343	0	2,048	3,804	4,486
31,150	31,200	0	1,172	2,650	3,332	0	2,040	3,793	4,476
31,200	31,250	0	1,164	2,639	3,322	0	2,032	3,783	4,465
31,250	31,300	0	1,156	2,628	3,311	0	2,024	3,772	4,455
31,300	31,350	0	1,148	2,618	3,300	0	2,016	3,762	4,444
31,350	31,400	0	1,140	2,607	3,290	0	2,008	3,751	4,433
31,400	31,450	0	1,132	2,597	3,279	0	2,000	3,740	4,423
31,450	31,500	0	1,124	2,586	3,269	0	1,992	3,730	4,412
31,500	31,550	0	1,116	2,576	3,258	0	1,984	3,719	4,402
31,550	31,600	0	1,108	2,565	3,248	0	1,976	3,709	4,391
31,600	31,650	0	1,100	2,555	3,237	0	1,968	3,698	4,381
31,650	31,700	0	1,092	2,544	3,227	0	1,960	3,688	4,370
31,700	31,750	0	1,084	2,534	3,216	0	1,952	3,677	4,360
31,750	31,800	0	1,076	2,523	3,206	0	1,944	3,667	4,349
31,800	31,850	0	1,068	2,513	3,195	0	1,936	3,656	4,339
31,850	31,900	0	1,060	2,502	3,185	0	1,928	3,646	4,328
31,900	31,950	0	1,052	2,492	3,174	0	1,920	3,635	4,318
31,950	32,000	0	1,044	2,481	3,164	0	1,912	3,625	4,307
32,000	32,050	0	1,036	2,471	3,153	0	1,904	3,614	4,297
32,050	32,100	0	1,028	2,460	3,143	0	1,896	3,604	4,286
32,100	32,150	0	1,020	2,449	3,132	0	1,888	3,593	4,276
32,150	32,200	0	1,012	2,439	3,121	0	1,880	3,583	4,265
32,200	32,250	0	1,004	2,428	3,111	0	1,872	3,572	4,254
32,250	32,300	0	996	2,418	3,100	0	1,864	3,561	4,244
32,300	32,350	0	988	2,407	3,090	0	1,856	3,551	4,233
32,350	32,400	0	981	2,397	3,079	0	1,848	3,540	4,223
32,400	32,450	0	973	2,386	3,069	0	1,840	3,530	4,212
32,450	32,500	0	965	2,376	3,058	0	1,832	3,519	4,202
32,500	32,550	0	957	2,365	3,048	0	1,824	3,509	4,191
32,550	32,600	0	949	2,355	3,037	0	1,816	3,498	4,181
32,600	32,650	0	941	2,344	3,027	0	1,808	3,488	4,170
32,650	32,700	0	933	2,334	3,016	0	1,800	3,477	4,160
32,700	32,750	0	925	2,323	3,006	0	1,792	3,467	4,149
32,750	32,800	0	917	2,313	2,995	0	1,784	3,456	4,139

(Continued)

Earned Income Credit (EIC) Table - Continued

(Caution. This is not a tax table.)

If the amount you are looking up from the worksheet is—		Single, head of household, or qualifying widow(er) and the number of children you have is—				Married filing jointly and the number of children you have is—			
At least	But less than	0	1	2	3	0	1	2	3
		Your credit is—				Your credit is—			
32,800	32,850	0	909	2,302	2,985	0	1,776	3,446	4,128
32,850	32,900	0	901	2,292	2,974	0	1,768	3,435	4,118
32,900	32,950	0	893	2,281	2,963	0	1,760	3,425	4,107
32,950	33,000	0	885	2,270	2,953	0	1,752	3,414	4,097
33,000	33,050	0	877	2,260	2,942	0	1,744	3,403	4,086
33,050	33,100	0	869	2,249	2,932	0	1,736	3,393	4,075
33,100	33,150	0	861	2,239	2,921	0	1,728	3,382	4,065
33,150	33,200	0	853	2,228	2,911	0	1,720	3,372	4,054
33,200	33,250	0	845	2,218	2,900	0	1,712	3,361	4,044
33,250	33,300	0	837	2,207	2,890	0	1,704	3,351	4,033
33,300	33,350	0	829	2,197	2,879	0	1,696	3,340	4,023
33,350	33,400	0	821	2,186	2,869	0	1,688	3,330	4,012
33,400	33,450	0	813	2,176	2,858	0	1,680	3,319	4,002
33,450	33,500	0	805	2,165	2,848	0	1,672	3,309	3,991
33,500	33,550	0	797	2,155	2,837	0	1,664	3,298	3,981
33,550	33,600	0	789	2,144	2,827	0	1,656	3,288	3,970
33,600	33,650	0	781	2,134	2,816	0	1,648	3,277	3,960
33,650	33,700	0	773	2,123	2,806	0	1,640	3,267	3,949
33,700	33,750	0	765	2,113	2,795	0	1,632	3,256	3,939
33,750	33,800	0	757	2,102	2,784	0	1,625	3,246	3,928
33,800	33,850	0	749	2,091	2,774	0	1,617	3,235	3,918
33,850	33,900	0	741	2,081	2,763	0	1,609	3,224	3,907
33,900	33,950	0	733	2,070	2,753	0	1,601	3,214	3,896
33,950	34,000	0	725	2,060	2,742	0	1,593	3,203	3,886
34,000	34,050	0	717	2,049	2,732	0	1,585	3,193	3,875
34,050	34,100	0	709	2,039	2,721	0	1,577	3,182	3,865
34,100	34,150	0	701	2,028	2,711	0	1,569	3,172	3,854
34,150	34,200	0	693	2,018	2,700	0	1,561	3,161	3,844
34,200	34,250	0	685	2,007	2,690	0	1,553	3,151	3,833
34,250	34,300	0	677	1,997	2,679	0	1,545	3,140	3,823
34,300	34,350	0	669	1,986	2,669	0	1,537	3,130	3,812
34,350	34,400	0	661	1,976	2,658	0	1,529	3,119	3,802
34,400	34,450	0	653	1,965	2,648	0	1,521	3,109	3,791
34,450	34,500	0	645	1,955	2,637	0	1,513	3,098	3,781
34,500	34,550	0	637	1,944	2,627	0	1,505	3,088	3,770
34,550	34,600	0	629	1,934	2,616	0	1,497	3,077	3,760
34,600	34,650	0	621	1,923	2,605	0	1,489	3,067	3,749
34,650	34,700	0	613	1,912	2,595	0	1,481	3,056	3,739
34,700	34,750	0	605	1,902	2,584	0	1,473	3,045	3,728
34,750	34,800	0	597	1,891	2,574	0	1,465	3,035	3,717
34,800	34,850	0	589	1,881	2,563	0	1,457	3,024	3,707
34,850	34,900	0	581	1,870	2,553	0	1,449	3,014	3,696
34,900	34,950	0	573	1,860	2,542	0	1,441	3,003	3,686
34,950	35,000	0	565	1,849	2,532	0	1,433	2,993	3,675
35,000	35,050	0	557	1,839	2,521	0	1,425	2,982	3,665
35,050	35,100	0	549	1,828	2,511	0	1,417	2,972	3,654
35,100	35,150	0	541	1,818	2,500	0	1,409	2,961	3,644
35,150	35,200	0	533	1,807	2,490	0	1,401	2,951	3,633
35,200	35,250	0	525	1,797	2,479	0	1,393	2,940	3,623
35,250	35,300	0	517	1,786	2,469	0	1,385	2,930	3,612
35,300	35,350	0	509	1,776	2,458	0	1,377	2,919	3,602
35,350	35,400	0	501	1,765	2,448	0	1,369	2,909	3,591
35,400	35,450	0	493	1,754	2,437	0	1,361	2,898	3,581
35,450	35,500	0	485	1,744	2,426	0	1,353	2,888	3,570
35,500	35,550	0	477	1,733	2,416	0	1,345	2,877	3,559
35,550	35,600	0	469	1,723	2,405	0	1,337	2,866	3,549
35,600	35,650	0	461	1,712	2,395	0	1,329	2,856	3,538
35,650	35,700	0	453	1,702	2,384	0	1,321	2,845	3,528
35,700	35,750	0	445	1,691	2,374	0	1,313	2,835	3,517
35,750	35,800	0	437	1,681	2,363	0	1,305	2,824	3,507
35,800	35,850	0	429	1,670	2,353	0	1,297	2,814	3,496
35,850	35,900	0	421	1,660	2,342	0	1,289	2,803	3,486
35,900	35,950	0	413	1,649	2,332	0	1,281	2,793	3,475
35,950	36,000	0	405	1,639	2,321	0	1,273	2,782	3,465

If the amount you are looking up from the worksheet is—		Single, head of household, or qualifying widow(er) and the number of children you have is—				Married filing jointly and the number of children you have is—			
At least	But less than	0	1	2	3	0	1	2	3
		Your credit is—				Your credit is—			
36,000	36,050	0	397	1,628	2,311	0	1,265	2,772	3,454
36,050	36,100	0	389	1,618	2,300	0	1,257	2,761	3,444
36,100	36,150	0	381	1,607	2,290	0	1,249	2,751	3,433
36,150	36,200	0	373	1,597	2,279	0	1,241	2,740	3,423
36,200	36,250	0	365	1,586	2,269	0	1,233	2,730	3,412
36,250	36,300	0	357	1,575	2,258	0	1,225	2,719	3,402
36,300	36,350	0	349	1,565	2,247	0	1,217	2,709	3,391
36,350	36,400	0	341	1,554	2,237	0	1,209	2,698	3,380
36,400	36,450	0	333	1,544	2,226	0	1,201	2,687	3,370
36,450	36,500	0	325	1,533	2,216	0	1,193	2,677	3,359
36,500	36,550	0	317	1,523	2,205	0	1,185	2,666	3,349
36,550	36,600	0	309	1,512	2,195	0	1,177	2,656	3,338
36,600	36,650	0	301	1,502	2,184	0	1,169	2,645	3,328
36,650	36,700	0	293	1,491	2,174	0	1,161	2,635	3,317
36,700	36,750	0	285	1,481	2,163	0	1,153	2,624	3,307
36,750	36,800	0	277	1,470	2,153	0	1,145	2,614	3,296
36,800	36,850	0	269	1,460	2,142	0	1,137	2,603	3,286
36,850	36,900	0	261	1,449	2,132	0	1,129	2,593	3,275
36,900	36,950	0	253	1,439	2,121	0	1,121	2,582	3,265
36,950	37,000	0	245	1,428	2,111	0	1,113	2,572	3,254
37,000	37,050	0	237	1,418	2,100	0	1,105	2,561	3,244
37,050	37,100	0	229	1,407	2,090	0	1,097	2,551	3,233
37,100	37,150	0	221	1,396	2,079	0	1,089	2,540	3,223
37,150	37,200	0	213	1,386	2,068	0	1,081	2,530	3,212
37,200	37,250	0	205	1,375	2,058	0	1,073	2,519	3,201
37,250	37,300	0	197	1,365	2,047	0	1,065	2,508	3,191
37,300	37,350	0	189	1,354	2,037	0	1,057	2,498	3,180
37,350	37,400	0	182	1,344	2,026	0	1,049	2,487	3,170
37,400	37,450	0	174	1,333	2,016	0	1,041	2,477	3,159
37,450	37,500	0	166	1,323	2,005	0	1,033	2,466	3,149
37,500	37,550	0	158	1,312	1,995	0	1,025	2,456	3,138
37,550	37,600	0	150	1,302	1,984	0	1,017	2,445	3,128
37,600	37,650	0	142	1,291	1,974	0	1,009	2,435	3,117
37,650	37,700	0	134	1,281	1,963	0	1,001	2,424	3,107
37,700	37,750	0	126	1,270	1,953	0	993	2,414	3,096
37,750	37,800	0	118	1,260	1,942	0	985	2,403	3,086
37,800	37,850	0	110	1,249	1,932	0	977	2,393	3,075
37,850	37,900	0	102	1,239	1,921	0	969	2,382	3,065
37,900	37,950	0	94	1,228	1,910	0	961	2,372	3,054
37,950	38,000	0	86	1,217	1,900	0	953	2,361	3,044
38,000	38,050	0	78	1,207	1,889	0	945	2,350	3,033
38,050	38,100	0	70	1,196	1,879	0	937	2,340	3,022
38,100	38,150	0	62	1,186	1,868	0	929	2,329	3,012
38,150	38,200	0	54	1,175	1,858	0	921	2,319	3,001
38,200	38,250	0	46	1,165	1,847	0	913	2,308	2,991
38,250	38,300	0	38	1,154	1,837	0	905	2,298	2,980
38,300	38,350	0	30	1,144	1,826	0	897	2,287	2,970
38,350	38,400	0	22	1,133	1,816	0	889	2,277	2,959
38,400	38,450	0	14	1,123	1,805	0	881	2,266	2,949
38,450	38,500	0	6	1,112	1,795	0	873	2,256	2,938
38,500	38,550	0	*	1,102	1,784	0	865	2,245	2,928
38,550	38,600	0	0	1,091	1,774	0	857	2,235	2,917
38,600	38,650	0	0	1,081	1,763	0	849	2,224	2,907
38,650	38,700	0	0	1,070	1,753	0	841	2,214	2,896
38,700	38,750	0	0	1,060	1,742	0	833	2,203	2,886
38,750	38,800	0	0	1,049	1,731	0	826	2,193	2,875
38,800	38,850	0	0	1,038	1,721	0	818	2,182	2,865
38,850	38,900	0	0	1,028	1,710	0	810	2,171	2,854
38,900	38,950	0	0	1,017	1,700	0	802	2,161	2,843
38,950	39,000	0	0	1,007	1,689	0	794	2,150	2,833
39,000	39,050	0	0	996	1,679	0	786	2,140	2,822
39,050	39,100	0	0	986	1,668	0	778	2,129	2,812
39,100	39,150	0	0	975	1,658	0	770	2,119	2,801
39,150	39,200	0	0	965	1,647	0	762	2,108	2,791

* If the amount you are looking up from the worksheet is at least $38,500 but less than $38,511, and you have one qualifying child, your credit is $1. If the amount you are looking up from the worksheet is $38,511 or more, and you have one qualifying child, you cannot take the credit.

(Continued)

Earned Income Credit (EIC) Table - *Continued*

(Caution. This is not a tax table.)

If the amount you are looking up from the worksheet is—		Single, head of household, or qualifying widow(er) and the number of children you have is—				Married filing jointly and the number of children you have is—			
At least	But less than	0	1	2	3	0	1	2	3
		Your credit is—				Your credit is—			
39,200	39,250	0	0	954	1,637	0	754	2,098	2,780
39,250	39,300	0	0	944	1,626	0	746	2,087	2,770
39,300	39,350	0	0	933	1,616	0	738	2,077	2,759
39,350	39,400	0	0	923	1,605	0	730	2,066	2,749
39,400	39,450	0	0	912	1,595	0	722	2,056	2,738
39,450	39,500	0	0	902	1,584	0	714	2,045	2,728
39,500	39,550	0	0	891	1,574	0	706	2,035	2,717
39,550	39,600	0	0	881	1,563	0	698	2,024	2,707
39,600	39,650	0	0	870	1,552	0	690	2,014	2,696
39,650	39,700	0	0	859	1,542	0	682	2,003	2,686
39,700	39,750	0	0	849	1,531	0	674	1,992	2,675
39,750	39,800	0	0	838	1,521	0	666	1,982	2,664
39,800	39,850	0	0	828	1,510	0	658	1,971	2,654
39,850	39,900	0	0	817	1,500	0	650	1,961	2,643
39,900	39,950	0	0	807	1,489	0	642	1,950	2,633
39,950	40,000	0	0	796	1,479	0	634	1,940	2,622
40,000	40,050	0	0	786	1,468	0	626	1,929	2,612
40,050	40,100	0	0	775	1,458	0	618	1,919	2,601
40,100	40,150	0	0	765	1,447	0	610	1,908	2,591
40,150	40,200	0	0	754	1,437	0	602	1,898	2,580
40,200	40,250	0	0	744	1,426	0	594	1,887	2,570
40,250	40,300	0	0	733	1,416	0	586	1,877	2,559
40,300	40,350	0	0	723	1,405	0	578	1,866	2,549
40,350	40,400	0	0	712	1,395	0	570	1,856	2,538
40,400	40,450	0	0	701	1,384	0	562	1,845	2,528
40,450	40,500	0	0	691	1,373	0	554	1,835	2,517
40,500	40,550	0	0	680	1,363	0	546	1,824	2,506
40,550	40,600	0	0	670	1,352	0	538	1,813	2,496
40,600	40,650	0	0	659	1,342	0	530	1,803	2,485
40,650	40,700	0	0	649	1,331	0	522	1,792	2,475
40,700	40,750	0	0	638	1,321	0	514	1,782	2,464
40,750	40,800	0	0	628	1,310	0	506	1,771	2,454
40,800	40,850	0	0	617	1,300	0	498	1,761	2,443
40,850	40,900	0	0	607	1,289	0	490	1,750	2,433
40,900	40,950	0	0	596	1,279	0	482	1,740	2,422
40,950	41,000	0	0	586	1,268	0	474	1,729	2,412
41,000	41,050	0	0	575	1,258	0	466	1,719	2,401
41,050	41,100	0	0	565	1,247	0	458	1,708	2,391
41,100	41,150	0	0	554	1,237	0	450	1,698	2,380
41,150	41,200	0	0	544	1,226	0	442	1,687	2,370
41,200	41,250	0	0	533	1,216	0	434	1,677	2,359
41,250	41,300	0	0	522	1,205	0	426	1,666	2,349
41,300	41,350	0	0	512	1,194	0	418	1,656	2,338
41,350	41,400	0	0	501	1,184	0	410	1,645	2,327
41,400	41,450	0	0	491	1,173	0	402	1,634	2,317
41,450	41,500	0	0	480	1,163	0	394	1,624	2,306
41,500	41,550	0	0	470	1,152	0	386	1,613	2,296
41,550	41,600	0	0	459	1,142	0	378	1,603	2,285
41,600	41,650	0	0	449	1,131	0	370	1,592	2,275
41,650	41,700	0	0	438	1,121	0	362	1,582	2,264
41,700	41,750	0	0	428	1,110	0	354	1,571	2,254
41,750	41,800	0	0	417	1,100	0	346	1,561	2,243
41,800	41,850	0	0	407	1,089	0	338	1,550	2,233
41,850	41,900	0	0	396	1,079	0	330	1,540	2,222
41,900	41,950	0	0	386	1,068	0	322	1,529	2,212
41,950	42,000	0	0	375	1,058	0	314	1,519	2,201
42,000	42,050	0	0	365	1,047	0	306	1,508	2,191
42,050	42,100	0	0	354	1,037	0	298	1,498	2,180
42,100	42,150	0	0	343	1,026	0	290	1,487	2,170
42,150	42,200	0	0	333	1,015	0	282	1,477	2,159
42,200	42,250	0	0	322	1,005	0	274	1,466	2,148
42,250	42,300	0	0	312	994	0	266	1,455	2,138
42,300	42,350	0	0	301	984	0	258	1,445	2,127
42,350	42,400	0	0	291	973	0	250	1,434	2,117
42,400	42,450	0	0	280	963	0	242	1,424	2,106
42,450	42,500	0	0	270	952	0	234	1,413	2,096
42,500	42,550	0	0	259	942	0	226	1,403	2,085
42,550	42,600	0	0	249	931	0	218	1,392	2,075
42,600	42,650	0	0	238	921	0	210	1,382	2,064
42,650	42,700	0	0	228	910	0	202	1,371	2,054
42,700	42,750	0	0	217	900	0	194	1,361	2,043
42,750	42,800	0	0	207	889	0	186	1,350	2,033
42,800	42,850	0	0	196	879	0	178	1,340	2,022
42,850	42,900	0	0	186	868	0	170	1,329	2,012
42,900	42,950	0	0	175	857	0	162	1,319	2,001
42,950	43,000	0	0	164	847	0	154	1,308	1,991
43,000	43,050	0	0	154	836	0	146	1,297	1,980
43,050	43,100	0	0	143	826	0	138	1,287	1,969
43,100	43,150	0	0	133	815	0	130	1,276	1,959
43,150	43,200	0	0	122	805	0	122	1,266	1,948
43,200	43,250	0	0	112	794	0	114	1,255	1,938
43,250	43,300	0	0	101	784	0	106	1,245	1,927
43,300	43,350	0	0	91	773	0	98	1,234	1,917
43,350	43,400	0	0	80	763	0	90	1,224	1,906
43,400	43,450	0	0	70	752	0	82	1,213	1,896
43,450	43,500	0	0	59	742	0	74	1,203	1,885
43,500	43,550	0	0	49	731	0	66	1,192	1,875
43,550	43,600	0	0	38	721	0	58	1,182	1,864
43,600	43,650	0	0	28	710	0	50	1,171	1,854
43,650	43,700	0	0	17	700	0	42	1,161	1,843
43,700	43,750	0	0	7	689	0	34	1,150	1,833
43,750	43,800	0	0	*	678	0	27	1,140	1,822
43,800	43,850	0	0	0	668	0	19	1,129	1,812
43,850	43,900	0	0	0	657	0	11	1,118	1,801
43,900	43,950	0	0	0	647	0	**	1,108	1,790
43,950	44,000	0	0	0	636	0	0	1,097	1,780
44,000	44,050	0	0	0	626	0	0	1,087	1,769
44,050	44,100	0	0	0	615	0	0	1,076	1,759
44,100	44,150	0	0	0	605	0	0	1,066	1,748
44,150	44,200	0	0	0	594	0	0	1,055	1,738
44,200	44,250	0	0	0	584	0	0	1,045	1,727
44,250	44,300	0	0	0	573	0	0	1,034	1,717
44,300	44,350	0	0	0	563	0	0	1,024	1,706
44,350	44,400	0	0	0	552	0	0	1,013	1,696
44,400	44,450	0	0	0	542	0	0	1,003	1,685
44,450	44,500	0	0	0	531	0	0	992	1,675
44,500	44,550	0	0	0	521	0	0	982	1,664
44,550	44,600	0	0	0	510	0	0	971	1,654
44,600	44,650	0	0	0	499	0	0	961	1,643
44,650	44,700	0	0	0	489	0	0	950	1,633
44,700	44,750	0	0	0	478	0	0	939	1,622
44,750	44,800	0	0	0	468	0	0	929	1,611
44,800	44,850	0	0	0	457	0	0	918	1,601
44,850	44,900	0	0	0	447	0	0	908	1,590
44,900	44,950	0	0	0	436	0	0	897	1,580
44,950	45,000	0	0	0	426	0	0	887	1,569
45,000	45,050	0	0	0	415	0	0	876	1,559
45,050	45,100	0	0	0	405	0	0	866	1,548
45,100	45,150	0	0	0	394	0	0	855	1,538
45,150	45,200	0	0	0	384	0	0	845	1,527
45,200	45,250	0	0	0	373	0	0	834	1,517
45,250	45,300	0	0	0	363	0	0	824	1,506
45,300	45,350	0	0	0	352	0	0	813	1,496
45,350	45,400	0	0	0	342	0	0	803	1,485
45,400	45,450	0	0	0	331	0	0	792	1,475
45,450	45,500	0	0	0	320	0	0	782	1,464
45,500	45,550	0	0	0	310	0	0	771	1,453
45,550	45,600	0	0	0	299	0	0	760	1,443

* If the amount you are looking up from the worksheet is at least $43,750 but less than $43,756, and you have two qualifying children, your credit is $1.
If the amount you are looking up from the worksheet is $43,756 or more, and you have two qualifying children, you cannot take the credit.

** If the amount you are looking up from the worksheet is at least $43,900 but less than $43,941, and you have one qualifying child, your credit is $3.
If the amount you are looking up from the worksheet is $43,941 or more, and you have one qualifying child, you cannot take the credit.

(Continued)

Earned Income Credit (EIC) Table - *Continued*

(Caution. This is not a tax table.)

If the amount you are looking up from the worksheet is—		Single, head of household, or qualifying widow(er) and the number of children you have is—				Married filing jointly and the number of children you have is—			
At least	But less than	0	1	2	3	0	1	2	3
		Your credit is—				Your credit is—			
45,600	45,650	0	0	0	289	0	0	750	1,432
45,650	45,700	0	0	0	278	0	0	739	1,422
45,700	45,750	0	0	0	268	0	0	729	1,411
45,750	45,800	0	0	0	257	0	0	718	1,401
45,800	45,850	0	0	0	247	0	0	708	1,390
45,850	45,900	0	0	0	236	0	0	697	1,380
45,900	45,950	0	0	0	226	0	0	687	1,369
45,950	46,000	0	0	0	215	0	0	676	1,359
46,000	46,050	0	0	0	205	0	0	666	1,348
46,050	46,100	0	0	0	194	0	0	655	1,338
46,100	46,150	0	0	0	184	0	0	645	1,327
46,150	46,200	0	0	0	173	0	0	634	1,317
46,200	46,250	0	0	0	163	0	0	624	1,306
46,250	46,300	0	0	0	152	0	0	613	1,296
46,300	46,350	0	0	0	141	0	0	603	1,285
46,350	46,400	0	0	0	131	0	0	592	1,274
46,400	46,450	0	0	0	120	0	0	581	1,264
46,450	46,500	0	0	0	110	0	0	571	1,253
46,500	46,550	0	0	0	99	0	0	560	1,243
46,550	46,600	0	0	0	89	0	0	550	1,232
46,600	46,650	0	0	0	78	0	0	539	1,222
46,650	46,700	0	0	0	68	0	0	529	1,211
46,700	46,750	0	0	0	57	0	0	518	1,201
46,750	46,800	0	0	0	47	0	0	508	1,190
46,800	46,850	0	0	0	36	0	0	497	1,180
46,850	46,900	0	0	0	26	0	0	487	1,169
46,900	46,950	0	0	0	15	0	0	476	1,159
46,950	47,000	0	0	0	*	0	0	466	1,148
47,000	47,050	0	0	0	0	0	0	455	1,138
47,050	47,100	0	0	0	0	0	0	445	1,127
47,100	47,150	0	0	0	0	0	0	434	1,117
47,150	47,200	0	0	0	0	0	0	424	1,106
47,200	47,250	0	0	0	0	0	0	413	1,095
47,250	47,300	0	0	0	0	0	0	402	1,085
47,300	47,350	0	0	0	0	0	0	392	1,074
47,350	47,400	0	0	0	0	0	0	381	1,064
47,400	47,450	0	0	0	0	0	0	371	1,053
47,450	47,500	0	0	0	0	0	0	360	1,043
47,500	47,550	0	0	0	0	0	0	350	1,032
47,550	47,600	0	0	0	0	0	0	339	1,022
47,600	47,650	0	0	0	0	0	0	329	1,011
47,650	47,700	0	0	0	0	0	0	318	1,001
47,700	47,750	0	0	0	0	0	0	308	990
47,750	47,800	0	0	0	0	0	0	297	980
47,800	47,850	0	0	0	0	0	0	287	969
47,850	47,900	0	0	0	0	0	0	276	959
47,900	47,950	0	0	0	0	0	0	266	948
47,950	48,000	0	0	0	0	0	0	255	938
48,000	48,050	0	0	0	0	0	0	244	927
48,050	48,100	0	0	0	0	0	0	234	916
48,100	48,150	0	0	0	0	0	0	223	906
48,150	48,200	0	0	0	0	0	0	213	895
48,200	48,250	0	0	0	0	0	0	202	885
48,250	48,300	0	0	0	0	0	0	192	874
48,300	48,350	0	0	0	0	0	0	181	864
48,350	48,400	0	0	0	0	0	0	171	853
48,400	48,450	0	0	0	0	0	0	160	843
48,450	48,500	0	0	0	0	0	0	150	832
48,500	48,550	0	0	0	0	0	0	139	822
48,550	48,600	0	0	0	0	0	0	129	811
48,600	48,650	0	0	0	0	0	0	118	801
48,650	48,700	0	0	0	0	0	0	108	790
48,700	48,750	0	0	0	0	0	0	97	780
48,750	48,800	0	0	0	0	0	0	87	769
48,800	48,850	0	0	0	0	0	0	76	759
48,850	48,900	0	0	0	0	0	0	65	748
48,900	48,950	0	0	0	0	0	0	55	737
48,950	49,000	0	0	0	0	0	0	44	727
49,000	49,050	0	0	0	0	0	0	34	716
49,050	49,100	0	0	0	0	0	0	23	706
49,100	49,150	0	0	0	0	0	0	13	695
49,150	49,200	0	0	0	0	0	0	**	685
49,200	49,250	0	0	0	0	0	0	0	674
49,250	49,300	0	0	0	0	0	0	0	664
49,300	49,350	0	0	0	0	0	0	0	653
49,350	49,400	0	0	0	0	0	0	0	643
49,400	49,450	0	0	0	0	0	0	0	632
49,450	49,500	0	0	0	0	0	0	0	622
49,500	49,550	0	0	0	0	0	0	0	611
49,550	49,600	0	0	0	0	0	0	0	601
49,600	49,650	0	0	0	0	0	0	0	590
49,650	49,700	0	0	0	0	0	0	0	580
49,700	49,750	0	0	0	0	0	0	0	569
49,750	49,800	0	0	0	0	0	0	0	558
49,800	49,850	0	0	0	0	0	0	0	548
49,850	49,900	0	0	0	0	0	0	0	537
49,900	49,950	0	0	0	0	0	0	0	527
49,950	50,000	0	0	0	0	0	0	0	516
50,000	50,050	0	0	0	0	0	0	0	506
50,050	50,100	0	0	0	0	0	0	0	495
50,100	50,150	0	0	0	0	0	0	0	485
50,150	50,200	0	0	0	0	0	0	0	474
50,200	50,250	0	0	0	0	0	0	0	464
50,250	50,300	0	0	0	0	0	0	0	453
50,300	50,350	0	0	0	0	0	0	0	443
50,350	50,400	0	0	0	0	0	0	0	432
50,400	50,450	0	0	0	0	0	0	0	422
50,450	50,500	0	0	0	0	0	0	0	411
50,500	50,550	0	0	0	0	0	0	0	400
50,550	50,600	0	0	0	0	0	0	0	390
50,600	50,650	0	0	0	0	0	0	0	379
50,650	50,700	0	0	0	0	0	0	0	369
50,700	50,750	0	0	0	0	0	0	0	358
50,750	50,800	0	0	0	0	0	0	0	348
50,800	50,850	0	0	0	0	0	0	0	337
50,850	50,900	0	0	0	0	0	0	0	327
50,900	50,950	0	0	0	0	0	0	0	316
50,950	51,000	0	0	0	0	0	0	0	306
51,000	51,050	0	0	0	0	0	0	0	295
51,050	51,100	0	0	0	0	0	0	0	285
51,100	51,150	0	0	0	0	0	0	0	274
51,150	51,200	0	0	0	0	0	0	0	264
51,200	51,250	0	0	0	0	0	0	0	253
51,250	51,300	0	0	0	0	0	0	0	243
51,300	51,350	0	0	0	0	0	0	0	232
51,350	51,400	0	0	0	0	0	0	0	221
51,400	51,450	0	0	0	0	0	0	0	211
51,450	51,500	0	0	0	0	0	0	0	200
51,500	51,550	0	0	0	0	0	0	0	190
51,550	51,600	0	0	0	0	0	0	0	179
51,600	51,650	0	0	0	0	0	0	0	169
51,650	51,700	0	0	0	0	0	0	0	158
51,700	51,750	0	0	0	0	0	0	0	148
51,750	51,800	0	0	0	0	0	0	0	137
51,800	51,850	0	0	0	0	0	0	0	127
51,850	51,900	0	0	0	0	0	0	0	116
51,900	51,950	0	0	0	0	0	0	0	106
51,950	52,000	0	0	0	0	0	0	0	95

* If the amount you are looking up from the worksheet is at least $46,950 but less than $46,997, and you have three qualifying children, your credit is $5.
If the amount you are looking up from the worksheet is $46,997 or more, and you have three qualifying children, you cannot take the credit.

** If the amount you are looking up from the worksheet is at least $49,150 but less than $49,186, and you have two qualifying children, your credit is $4.
If the amount you are looking up from the worksheet is $49,186 or more, and you have two qualifying children, you cannot take the credit.

(Continued)

Earned Income Credit (EIC) Table - *Continued*

(Caution. This is not a tax table.)

If the amount you are looking up from the worksheet is–		Single, head of household, or qualifying widow(er) and the number of children you have is–				Married filing jointly and the number of children you have is–				If the amount you are looking up from the worksheet is–		Single, head of household, or qualifying widow(er) and the number of children you have is–				Married filing jointly and the number of children you have is–			
		0	1	2	3	0	1	2	3			0	1	2	3	0	1	2	3
At least	But less than	Your credit is–				Your credit is–				At least	But less than	Your credit is–				Your credit is–			
52,000	52,050	0	0	0	0	0	0	0	85	52,400	52,427	0	0	0	0	0	0	0	3
52,050	52,100	0	0	0	0	0	0	0	74										
52,100	52,150	0	0	0	0	0	0	0	64										
52,150	52,200	0	0	0	0	0	0	0	53										
52,200	52,250	0	0	0	0	0	0	0	42										
52,250	52,300	0	0	0	0	0	0	0	32										
52,300	52,350	0	0	0	0	0	0	0	21										
52,350	52,400	0	0	0	0	0	0	0	11										

§ 3.400 Filled-In Form 1120

Form **1120**	**U.S. Corporation Income Tax Return**	OMB No. 1545-0123
Department of the Treasury Internal Revenue Service	For calendar year 2014 or tax year beginning _____, 2014, ending _____, 20 ____ ▶ Information about Form 1120 and its separate instructions is at *www.irs.gov/form1120.*	**2014**

A Check if:
1a Consolidated return (attach Form 851) ☐
 b Life/nonlife consolidated return . . ☐
2 Personal holding co. (attach Sch. PH) . ☐
3 Personal service corp. (see instructions) . . ☐
4 Schedule M-3 attached ☐

TYPE OR PRINT

Name
James Brothers' Mens' Wear, Inc.

Number, street, and room or suite no. If a P.O. box, see instructions.
4321 S. Main Street

City or town, state, or province, country and ZIP or foreign postal code
Atlanta, GA 63284

B Employer identification number
73-0068478

C Date incorporated
4-1-1965

D Total assets (see instructions)
$ 685,553

E Check if: (1) ☐ Initial return (2) ☐ Final return (3) ☐ Name change (4) ☐ Address change

Income	1a	Gross receipts or sales	1a	1,025,550
	b	Returns and allowances	1b	43,970
	c	Balance. Subtract line 1b from line 1a	1c	981,580
	2	Cost of goods sold (attach Form 1125-A)	2	768,780
	3	Gross profit. Subtract line 2 from line 1c	3	212,800
	4	Dividends (Schedule C, line 19)	4	8,000
	5	Interest	5	261,000
	6	Gross rents	6	
	7	Gross royalties	7	
	8	Capital gain net income (attach Schedule D (Form 1120))	8	8,250
	9	Net gain or (loss) from Form 4797, Part II, line 17 (attach Form 4797)	9	3,200
	10	Other income (see instructions—attach statement)	10	
	11	**Total income.** Add lines 3 through 10 . . . . . ▶	11	493,250
Deductions (See instructions for limitations on deductions.)	12	Compensation of officers (see instructions—attach Form 1125-E) . . . . . ▶	12	90,000
	13	Salaries and wages (less employment credits)	13	112,800
	14	Repairs and maintenance	14	1,200
	15	Bad debts	15	
	16	Rents	16	52,500
	17	Taxes and licenses	17	41,000
	18	Interest	18	33,000
	19	Charitable contributions	19	10,000
	20	Depreciation from Form 4562 not claimed on Form 1125-A or elsewhere on return (attach Form 4562)	20	24,800
	21	Depletion	21	
	22	Advertising	22	24,000
	23	Pension, profit-sharing, etc., plans	23	
	24	Employee benefit programs	24	7,200
	25	Domestic production activities deduction (attach Form 8903)	25	
	26	Other deductions (attach statement)	26	26,000
	27	**Total deductions.** Add lines 12 through 26 . . . . . ▶	27	422,500
	28	Taxable income before net operating loss deduction and special deductions. Subtract line 27 from line 11.	28	70,750
	29a	Net operating loss deduction (see instructions)	29a	
	b	Special deductions (Schedule C, line 20)	29b	6,400
	c	Add lines 29a and 29b	29c	6,400
Tax, Refundable Credits, and Payments	30	**Taxable income.** Subtract line 29c from line 28 (see instructions)	30	64,350
	31	Total tax (Schedule J, Part I, line 11)	31	16,776
	32	Total payments and refundable credits (Schedule J, Part II, line 21)	32	100,000
	33	Estimated tax penalty (see instructions). Check if Form 2220 is attached . . . . ▶ ☐	33	
	34	**Amount owed.** If line 32 is smaller than the total of lines 31 and 33, enter amount owed	34	
	35	**Overpayment.** If line 32 is larger than the total of lines 31 and 33, enter amount overpaid	35	83,224
	36	Enter amount from line 35 you want: **Credited to 2015 estimated tax** ▶ **Refunded** ▶	36	83,224

Sign Here

Under penalties of perjury, I declare that I have examined this return, including accompanying schedules and statements, and to the best of my knowledge and belief, it is true, correct, and complete. Declaration of preparer (other than taxpayer) is based on all information of which preparer has any knowledge.

▶ *Tom James*
Signature of officer   Date

▶ President
Title

May the IRS discuss this return with the preparer shown below (see instructions)? ☑ Yes ☐ No

Paid Preparer Use Only

Print/Type preparer's name	Preparer's signature	Date	Check ☑ if self-employed	PTIN
Alan Young	*Alan Young*			

Firm's name ▶ Alan Young, CPA   Firm's EIN ▶

Firm's address ▶ 1234 S. Main Street, Atlanta, GA 63284   Phone no.

For Paperwork Reduction Act Notice, see separate instructions.   Cat. No. 11450Q   Form **1120** (2014)

Schedule C	Dividends and Special Deductions (see instructions)	(a) Dividends received	(b) %	(c) Special deductions (a) × (b)
1	Dividends from less-than-20%-owned domestic corporations (other than debt-financed stock)		70	
2	Dividends from 20%-or-more-owned domestic corporations (other than debt-financed stock)	8,000	80	6,400
3	Dividends on debt-financed stock of domestic and foreign corporations		see instructions	
4	Dividends on certain preferred stock of less-than-20%-owned public utilities . . .		42	
5	Dividends on certain preferred stock of 20%-or-more-owned public utilities		48	
6	Dividends from less-than-20%-owned foreign corporations and certain FSCs . . .		70	
7	Dividends from 20%-or-more-owned foreign corporations and certain FSCs . . .		80	
8	Dividends from wholly owned foreign subsidiaries		100	
9	**Total.** Add lines 1 through 8. See instructions for limitation			6,400
10	Dividends from domestic corporations received by a small business investment company operating under the Small Business Investment Act of 1958		100	
11	Dividends from affiliated group members		100	
12	Dividends from certain FSCs		100	
13	Dividends from foreign corporations not included on lines 3, 6, 7, 8, 11, or 12 . . .			
14	Income from controlled foreign corporations under subpart F (attach Form(s) 5471) .			
15	Foreign dividend gross-up			
16	IC-DISC and former DISC dividends not included on lines 1, 2, or 3			
17	Other dividends			
18	Deduction for dividends paid on certain preferred stock of public utilities			
19	**Total dividends.** Add lines 1 through 17. Enter here and on page 1, line 4 . . . ▶			
20	**Total special deductions.** Add lines 9, 10, 11, 12, and 18. Enter here and on page 1, line 29b . . . . ▶			6,400

Schedule J	Tax Computation and Payment (see instructions)						

Part I—Tax Computation

1	Check if the corporation is a member of a controlled group (attach Schedule O (Form 1120))			▶ ☐			
2	Income tax. Check if a qualified personal service corporation (see instructions)			▶ ☐	**2**		11,088
3	Alternative minimum tax (attach Form 4626)				**3**		5,688
4	Add lines 2 and 3				**4**		16,776
5a	Foreign tax credit (attach Form 1118)	**5a**					
b	Credit from Form 8834 (see instructions)	**5b**					
c	General business credit (attach Form 3800)	**5c**					
d	Credit for prior year minimum tax (attach Form 8827) . .	**5d**					
e	Bond credits from Form 8912	**5e**					
6	**Total credits.** Add lines 5a through 5e				**6**		
7	Subtract line 6 from line 4				**7**		16,776
8	Personal holding company tax (attach Schedule PH (Form 1120))				**8**		
9a	Recapture of investment credit (attach Form 4255)	**9a**					
b	Recapture of low-income housing credit (attach Form 8611)	**9b**					
c	Interest due under the look-back method—completed long-term contracts (attach Form 8697)	**9c**					
d	Interest due under the look-back method—income forecast method (attach Form 8866)	**9d**					
e	Alternative tax on qualifying shipping activities (attach Form 8902)	**9e**					
f	Other (see instructions—attach statement)	**9f**					
10	**Total.** Add lines 9a through 9f				**10**		
11	**Total tax.** Add lines 7, 8, and 10. Enter here and on page 1, line 31				**11**		16,776

Part II—Payments and Refundable Credits

12	2013 overpayment credited to 2014				**12**		
13	2014 estimated tax payments				**13**		100,000
14	2014 refund applied for on Form 4466				**14**	(	)
15	Combine lines 12, 13, and 14				**15**		100,000
16	Tax deposited with Form 7004				**16**		
17	Withholding (see instructions)				**17**		
18	**Total payments.** Add lines 15, 16, and 17				**18**		100,000
19	Refundable credits from:						
a	Form 2439	**19a**					
b	Form 4136	**19b**					
c	Form 8827, line 8c	**19c**					
d	Other (attach statement—see instructions).	**19d**					
20	**Total credits.** Add lines 19a through 19d				**20**		
21	**Total payments and credits.** Add lines 18 and 20. Enter here and on page 1, line 32				**21**		100,000

Schedule K	Other Information (see instructions)					Yes	No
1	Check accounting method: **a** ☐ Cash **b** ☑ Accrual **c** ☐ Other (specify) ▶ _____						
2	See the instructions and enter the:						
a	Business activity code no. ▶ _____ 448110 _____						
b	Business activity ▶ _____						
c	Product or service ▶ _____						
3	Is the corporation a subsidiary in an affiliated group or a parent-subsidiary controlled group?						✓
	If "Yes," enter name and EIN of the parent corporation ▶ _____						
	_____						
4	At the end of the tax year:						
a	Did any foreign or domestic corporation, partnership (including any entity treated as a partnership), trust, or tax-exempt organization own directly 20% or more, or own, directly or indirectly, 50% or more of the total voting power of all classes of the corporation's stock entitled to vote? If "Yes," complete Part I of Schedule G (Form 1120) (attach Schedule G)						✓
b	Did any individual or estate own directly 20% or more, or own, directly or indirectly, 50% or more of the total voting power of all classes of the corporation's stock entitled to vote? If "Yes," complete Part II of Schedule G (Form 1120) (attach Schedule G) .						✓

Form **1120** (2014)

Schedule K	**Other Information** *continued* (see instructions)			Yes	No

5 At the end of the tax year, did the corporation:

a Own directly 20% or more, or own, directly or indirectly, 50% or more of the total voting power of all classes of stock entitled to vote of any foreign or domestic corporation not included on **Form 851,** Affiliations Schedule? For rules of constructive ownership, see instructions.   ✓

If "Yes," complete (i) through (iv) below.

(i) Name of Corporation	**(ii)** Employer Identification Number (if any)	**(iii)** Country of Incorporation	**(iv)** Percentage Owned in Voting Stock

b Own directly an interest of 20% or more, or own, directly or indirectly, an interest of 50% or more in any foreign or domestic partnership (including an entity treated as a partnership) or in the beneficial interest of a trust? For rules of constructive ownership, see instructions.   ✓

If "Yes," complete (i) through (iv) below.

(i) Name of Entity	**(ii)** Employer Identification Number (if any)	**(iii)** Country of Organization	**(iv)** Maximum Percentage Owned in Profit, Loss, or Capital

6 During this tax year, did the corporation pay dividends (other than stock dividends and distributions in exchange for stock) in excess of the corporation's current and accumulated earnings and profits? (See sections 301 and 316.) . . . . ✓

If "Yes," file **Form 5452,** Corporate Report of Nondividend Distributions.

If this is a consolidated return, answer here for the parent corporation and on Form 851 for each subsidiary.

7 At any time during the tax year, did one foreign person own, directly or indirectly, at least 25% of **(a)** the total voting power of all classes of the corporation's stock entitled to vote or **(b)** the total value of all classes of the corporation's stock? . . . . ✓

For rules of attribution, see section 318. If "Yes," enter:

(i) Percentage owned ▶ _____ and **(ii)** Owner's country ▶ _____

(c) The corporation may have to file **Form 5472,** Information Return of a 25% Foreign-Owned U.S. Corporation or a Foreign Corporation Engaged in a U.S. Trade or Business. Enter the number of Forms 5472 attached ▶ _____

8 Check this box if the corporation issued publicly offered debt instruments with original issue discount . . . . ▶ ☐

If checked, the corporation may have to file **Form 8281,** Information Return for Publicly Offered Original Issue Discount Instruments.

9 Enter the amount of tax-exempt interest received or accrued during the tax year ▶ $ _____

10 Enter the number of shareholders at the end of the tax year (if 100 or fewer) ▶ _____ 3

11 If the corporation has an NOL for the tax year and is electing to forego the carryback period, check here . . . . ▶ ☐

If the corporation is filing a consolidated return, the statement required by Regulations section 1.1502-21(b)(3) must be attached or the election will not be valid.

12 Enter the available NOL carryover from prior tax years (do not reduce it by any deduction on line 29a.) ▶ $ _____

13 Are the corporation's total receipts (page 1, line 1a, plus lines 4 through 10) for the tax year **and** its total assets at the end of the tax year less than $250,000? . . . . ✓

If "Yes," the corporation is not required to complete Schedules L, M-1, and M-2. Instead, enter the total amount of cash distributions and the book value of property distributions (other than cash) made during the tax year ▶ $ _____

14 Is the corporation required to file Schedule UTP (Form 1120), Uncertain Tax Position Statement (see instructions)? . . . ✓

If "Yes," complete and attach Schedule UTP.

15a Did the corporation make any payments in 2014 that would require it to file Form(s) 1099? . . . . ✓

  b If "Yes," did or will the corporation file required Forms 1099? . . . . . . ✓

16 During this tax year, did the corporation have an 80% or more change in ownership, including a change due to redemption of its own stock?   ✓

17 During or subsequent to this tax year, but before the filing of this return, did the corporation dispose of more than 65% (by value) of its assets in a taxable, non-taxable, or tax deferred transaction?   ✓

18 Did the corporation receive assets in a section 351 transfer in which any of the transferred assets had a fair market basis or fair market value of more than $1 million?   ✓

Schedule L — Balance Sheets per Books

	Assets	Beginning of tax year (a)	Beginning of tax year (b)	End of tax year (c)	End of tax year (d)
1	Cash		21,870		36,910
2a	Trade notes and accounts receivable	47,680		83,070	
b	Less allowance for bad debts	( )	47,680	( )	83,070
3	Inventories		356,925		321,830
4	U.S. government obligations				
5	Tax-exempt securities (see instructions)				116,618
6	Other current assets (attach statement)				
7	Loans to shareholders				
8	Mortgage and real estate loans				
9	Other investments (attach statement)		16,010		94,800
10a	Buildings and other depreciable assets	89,500		93,500	
b	Less accumulated depreciation	(56,750)	32,750	(66,179)	27,325
11a	Depletable assets				
b	Less accumulated depletion	( )		( )	
12	Land (net of any amortization)		5,000		5,000
13a	Intangible assets (amortizable only)				
b	Less accumulated amortization	( )		( )	
14	Other assets (attach statement)		4,000		
15	Total assets		484,235		685,553
	Liabilities and Shareholders' Equity				
16	Accounts payable		83,450		46,540
17	Mortgages, notes, bonds payable in less than 1 year		76,412		288,600
18	Other current liabilities (attach statement)				
19	Loans from shareholders				
20	Mortgages, notes, bonds payable in 1 year or more				
21	Other liabilities (attach statement)				
22	Capital stock: a Preferred stock				
	b Common stock	30,000	30,000	30,000	30,000
23	Additional paid-in capital		10,000		10,000
24	Retained earnings—Appropriated (attach statement)				
25	Retained earnings—Unappropriated		284,373		310,413
26	Adjustments to shareholders' equity (attach statement)				
27	Less cost of treasury stock		( )		( )
28	Total liabilities and shareholders' equity		484,235		685,553

Schedule M-1 — Reconciliation of Income (Loss) per Books With Income per Return

Note: The corporation may be required to file Schedule M-3 (see instructions).

1	Net income (loss) per books	26,040	7	Income recorded on books this year not included on this return (itemize):		
2	Federal income tax per books	69,710				
3	Excess of capital losses over capital gains			Tax-exempt interest $ _____		
4	Income subject to tax not recorded on books this year (itemize): _____			_____		12,000
	_____		8	Deductions on this return not charged against book income this year (itemize):		
5	Expenses recorded on books this year not deducted on this return (itemize):		a	Depreciation $ _____		
a	Depreciation $ _____		b	Charitable contributions $ _____		
b	Charitable contributions $ _____			_____		8,000
c	Travel and entertainment $ _____		9	Add lines 7 and 8		20,000
	_____	1,000				
6	Add lines 1 through 5	96,750	10	Income (page 1, line 28)—line 6 less line 9		76,750

Schedule M-2 — Analysis of Unappropriated Retained Earnings per Books (Line 25, Schedule L)

1	Balance at beginning of year	284,373	5	Distributions: a Cash		
2	Net income (loss) per books	26,040		b Stock		
3	Other increases (itemize): _____			c Property		
	_____		6	Other decreases (itemize): _____		
	_____		7	Add lines 5 and 6		
4	Add lines 1, 2, and 3	310,413	8	Balance at end of year (line 4 less line 7)		310,413

§ 3.420 Filled-In Schedule D (Form 1120) and Form 8949

SCHEDULE D	Capital Gains and Losses	OMB No. 1545-0123
(Form 1120)		
Department of the Treasury Internal Revenue Service	▶ Attach to Form 1120, 1120-C, 1120-F, 1120-FSC, 1120-H, 1120-IC-DISC, 1120-L, 1120-ND, 1120-PC, 1120-POL, 1120-REIT, 1120-RIC, 1120-SF, or certain Forms 990-T. ▶ Information about Schedule D (Form 1120) and its separate instructions is at *www.irs.gov/form1120.*	2014

Name	Employer identification number
James Brothers' Men's Wear, Inc.	73-0068478

Part I — Short-Term Capital Gains and Losses—Assets Held One Year or Less

See instructions for how to figure the amounts to enter on the lines below. This form may be easier to complete if you round off cents to whole dollars.	**(d)** Proceeds (sales price)	**(e)** Cost (or other basis)	**(g)** Adjustments to gain or loss from Form(s) 8949, Part I, line 2, column (g)	**(h) Gain or (loss)** Subtract column (e) from column (d) and combine the result with column (g)
1a Totals for all short-term transactions reported on Form 1099-B for which basis was reported to the IRS and for which you have no adjustments (see instructions). However, if you choose to report all these transactions on Form 8949, leave this line blank and go to line 1b				
1b Totals for all transactions reported on Form(s) 8949 with **Box A** checked				
2 Totals for all transactions reported on Form(s) 8949 with **Box B** checked				
3 Totals for all transactions reported on Form(s) 8949 with **Box C** checked				

4 Short-term capital gain from installment sales from Form 6252, line 26 or 37	**4**	
5 Short-term capital gain or (loss) from like-kind exchanges from Form 8824	**5**	
6 Unused capital loss carryover (attach computation)	**6** ( )	
7 Net short-term capital gain or (loss). Combine lines 1a through 6 in column h	**7**	

Part II — Long-Term Capital Gains and Losses—Assets Held More Than One Year

See instructions for how to figure the amounts to enter on the lines below. This form may be easier to complete if you round off cents to whole dollars.	**(d)** Proceeds (sales price)	**(e)** Cost (or other basis)	**(g)** Adjustments to gain or loss from Form(s) 8949, Part II, line 2, column (g)	**(h) Gain or (loss)** Subtract column (e) from column (d) and combine the result with column (g)
8a Totals for all long-term transactions reported on Form 1099-B for which basis was reported to the IRS and for which you have no adjustments (see instructions). However, if you choose to report all these transactions on Form 8949, leave this line blank and go to line 8b				
8b Totals for all transactions reported on Form(s) 8949 with **Box D** checked				
9 Totals for all transactions reported on Form(s) 8949 with **Box E** checked	15,250	7,000		8,250
10 Totals for all transactions reported on Form(s) 8949 with **Box F** checked				

11 Enter gain from Form 4797, line 7 or 9	**11**	
12 Long-term capital gain from installment sales from Form 6252, line 26 or 37	**12**	
13 Long-term capital gain or (loss) from like-kind exchanges from Form 8824	**13**	
14 Capital gain distributions (see instructions)	**14**	
15 Net long-term capital gain or (loss). Combine lines 8a through 14 in column h	**15**	8,250

Part III — Summary of Parts I and II

16 Enter excess of net short-term capital gain (line 7) over net long-term capital loss (line 15)	**16**	
17 Net capital gain. Enter excess of net long-term capital gain (line 15) over net short-term capital loss (line 7)	**17**	8,250
18 Add lines 16 and 17. Enter here and on Form 1120, page 1, line 8, or the proper line on other returns . .	**18**	8,250

Note. *If losses exceed gains, see **Capital losses** in the instructions.*

For Paperwork Reduction Act Notice, see the Instructions for Form 1120.   Cat. No. 11460M   Schedule D (Form 1120) (2014)

Form **8949**

Department of the Treasury
Internal Revenue Service

Sales and Other Dispositions of Capital Assets

▶ Information about Form 8949 and its separate instructions is at *www.irs.gov/form8949*.
▶ File with your Schedule D to list your transactions for lines 1b, 2, 3, 8b, 9, and 10 of Schedule D.

OMB No. 1545-0074

2014

Attachment
Sequence No. **12A**

Name(s) shown on return	Social security number or taxpayer identification number
James Brothers' Men's Wear, Inc.	73-0068478

Before you check Box A, B, or C below, see whether you received any Form(s) 1099-B or substitute statement(s) from your broker. A substitute statement will have the same information as Form 1099-B. Either may show your basis (usually your cost) even if your broker did not report it to the IRS. Brokers must report basis to the IRS for most stock you bought in 2011 or later (and for certain debt instruments you bought in 2014 or later).

Part I   **Short-Term.** Transactions involving capital assets you held 1 year or less are short term. For long-term transactions, see page 2.

Note. You may aggregate all short-term transactions reported on Form(s) 1099-B showing basis was reported to the IRS and for which no adjustments or codes are required. Enter the total directly on Schedule D, line 1a; you are not required to report these transactions on Form 8949 (see instructions).

You *must* check Box A, B, *or* C below. Check only one box. If more than one box applies for your short-term transactions, complete a separate Form 8949, page 1, for each applicable box. If you have more short-term transactions than will fit on this page for one or more of the boxes, complete as many forms with the same box checked as you need.

- ☐ **(A)** Short-term transactions reported on Form(s) 1099-B showing basis was reported to the IRS (see **Note** above)
- ☐ **(B)** Short-term transactions reported on Form(s) 1099-B showing basis was **not** reported to the IRS
- ☐ **(C)** Short-term transactions not reported to you on Form 1099-B

1 (a) Description of property (Example: 100 sh. XYZ Co.)	(b) Date acquired (Mo., day, yr.)	(c) Date sold or disposed (Mo., day, yr.)	(d) Proceeds (sales price) (see instructions)	(e) Cost or other basis. See the **Note** below and see *Column (e)* in the separate instructions	Adjustment, if any, to gain or loss. If you enter an amount in column (g), enter a code in column (f). See the separate instructions. (f) Code(s) from instructions	(g) Amount of adjustment	(h) Gain or (loss). Subtract column (e) from column (d) and combine the result with column (g)
200 shares of Flowers & Co. stock	9-15-2010	4-15-2014	4,250	2,000			2,250
Land	6-20-2006	5-1-2014	11,000	5,000			6,000
2 Totals. Add the amounts in columns (d), (e), (g), and (h) (subtract negative amounts). Enter each total here and include on your Schedule D, **line 1b** (if **Box A** above is checked), **line 2** (if **Box B** above is checked), or **line 3** (if **Box C** above is checked) ▶			15,250	7,000			8,250

Note. If you checked Box A above but the basis reported to the IRS was incorrect, enter in column (e) the basis as reported to the IRS, and enter an adjustment in column (g) to correct the basis. See *Column (g)* in the separate instructions for how to figure the amount of the adjustment.

For Paperwork Reduction Act Notice, see your tax return instructions.   Cat. No. 37768Z   Form **8949** (2014)

Name(s) shown on return. Name and SSN or taxpayer identification no. not required if shown on other side	Social security number or taxpayer identification number

Before you check Box D, E, or F below, see whether you received any Form(s) 1099-B or substitute statement(s) from your broker. A substitute statement will have the same information as Form 1099-B. Either may show your basis (usually your cost) even if your broker did not report it to the IRS. Brokers must report basis to the IRS for most stock you bought in 2011 or later (and for certain debt instruments you bought in 2014 or later).

Part II **Long-Term.** Transactions involving capital assets you held more than 1 year are long term. For short-term transactions, see page 1.

Note. You may aggregate all long-term transactions reported on Form(s) 1099-B showing basis was reported to the IRS and for which no adjustments or codes are required. Enter the total directly on Schedule D, line 8a; you are not required to report these transactions on Form 8949 (see instructions).

You *must* check Box D, E, *or* F below. Check only one box. If more than one box applies for your long-term transactions, complete a separate Form 8949, page 2, for each applicable box. If you have more long-term transactions than will fit on this page for one or more of the boxes, complete as many forms with the same box checked as you need.

☐ **(D)** Long-term transactions reported on Form(s) 1099-B showing basis was reported to the IRS (see **Note** above)
☐ **(E)** Long-term transactions reported on Form(s) 1099-B showing basis was **not** reported to the IRS
☐ **(F)** Long-term transactions not reported to you on Form 1099-B

1 (a) Description of property (Example: 100 sh. XYZ Co.)	(b) Date acquired (Mo., day, yr.)	(c) Date sold or disposed (Mo., day, yr.)	(d) Proceeds (sales price) (see instructions)	(e) Cost or other basis. See the **Note** below and see *Column (e)* in the separate instructions	(f) Code(s) from instructions	(g) Amount of adjustment	(h) Gain or (loss). Subtract column (e) from column (d) and combine the result with column (g)

Adjustment, if any, to gain or loss. If you enter an amount in column (g), enter a code in column (f). **See the separate instructions.**

2 Totals. Add the amounts in columns (d), (e), (g), and (h) (subtract negative amounts). Enter each total here and include on your Schedule D, **line 8b** (if **Box D** above is checked), **line 9** (if **Box E** above is checked), or **line 10** (if **Box F** above is checked) ▶

Note. If you checked Box D above but the basis reported to the IRS was incorrect, enter in column (e) the basis as reported to the IRS, and enter an adjustment in column (g) to correct the basis. See *Column (g)* in the separate instructions for how to figure the amount of the adjustment.

§ 3.440 Filled-In Form 4562

Form **4562**	**Depreciation and Amortization**	OMB No. 1545-0172
	(Including Information on Listed Property)	**2014**
Department of the Treasury Internal Revenue Service (99)	▶ Attach to your tax return. ▶ Information about Form 4562 and its separate instructions is at *www.irs.gov/form4562.*	Attachment Sequence No. **179**

Name(s) shown on return	Business or activity to which this form relates	Identifying number
James Brothers' Men's Wear, Inc.	Retail Sales	73-0068478

Part I Election To Expense Certain Property Under Section 179

Note: *If you have any listed property, complete Part V before you complete Part I.*

1	Maximum amount (see instructions)	1	500,000
2	Total cost of section 179 property placed in service (see instructions)	2	22,000
3	Threshold cost of section 179 property before reduction in limitation (see instructions)	3	2,000,000
4	Reduction in limitation. Subtract line 3 from line 2. If zero or less, enter -0-	4	0
5	Dollar limitation for tax year. Subtract line 4 from line 1. If zero or less, enter -0-. If married filing separately, see instructions	5	500,000

6	(a) Description of property	(b) Cost (business use only)	(c) Elected cost	
	5-year equipment	22,000	22,000	

7	Listed property. Enter the amount from line 29 . . . . **7**		
8	Total elected cost of section 179 property. Add amounts in column (c), lines 6 and 7	8	22,000
9	Tentative deduction. Enter the **smaller** of line 5 or line 8	9	22,000
10	Carryover of disallowed deduction from line 13 of your 2013 Form 4562	10	
11	Business income limitation. Enter the smaller of business income (not less than zero) or line 5 (see instructions)	11	22,000
12	Section 179 expense deduction. Add lines 9 and 10, but do not enter more than line 11	12	22,000
13	Carryover of disallowed deduction to 2015. Add lines 9 and 10, less line 12 ▶ **13**		

Note: *Do not use Part II or Part III below for listed property. Instead, use Part V.*

Part II Special Depreciation Allowance and Other Depreciation (Do not include listed property.) (See instructions.)

14	Special depreciation allowance for qualified property (other than listed property) placed in service during the tax year (see instructions)	14	1,800
15	Property subject to section 168(f)(1) election	15	
16	Other depreciation (including ACRS)	16	160

Part III MACRS Depreciation (Do not include listed property.) (See instructions.)

Section A

17	MACRS deductions for assets placed in service in tax years beginning before 2014	17	
18	If you are electing to group any assets placed in service during the tax year into one or more general asset accounts, check here ▶ ☐		

Section B—Assets Placed in Service During 2014 Tax Year Using the General Depreciation System

(a) Classification of property	(b) Month and year placed in service	(c) Basis for depreciation (business/investment use only—see instructions)	(d) Recovery period	(e) Convention	(f) Method	(g) Depreciation deduction
19a 3-year property						
b 5-year property		4,200	5 years	1/2 year	DOB	840
c 7-year property						
d 10-year property						
e 15-year property						
f 20-year property						
g 25-year property			25 yrs.		S/L	
h Residential rental property			27.5 yrs.	MM	S/L	
			27.5 yrs.	MM	S/L	
i Nonresidential real property			39 yrs.	MM	S/L	
				MM	S/L	

Section C—Assets Placed in Service During 2014 Tax Year Using the Alternative Depreciation System

20a Class life					S/L	
b 12-year			12 yrs.		S/L	
c 40-year			40 yrs.	MM	S/L	

Part IV Summary (See instructions.)

21	Listed property. Enter amount from line 28	21	
22	**Total.** Add amounts from line 12, lines 14 through 17, lines 19 and 20 in column (g), and line 21. Enter here and on the appropriate lines of your return. Partnerships and S corporations—see instructions	22	24,800
23	For assets shown above and placed in service during the current year, enter the portion of the basis attributable to section 263A costs **23**		

For Paperwork Reduction Act Notice, see separate instructions.   Cat. No. 12906N   Form **4562** (2014)

Part V **Listed Property** (Include automobiles, certain other vehicles, certain aircraft, certain computers, and property used for entertainment, recreation, or amusement.)

　　　Note: *For any vehicle for which you are using the standard mileage rate or deducting lease expense, complete **only** 24a, 24b, columns (a) through (c) of Section A, all of Section B, and Section C if applicable.*

Section A—Depreciation and Other Information (Caution: *See the instructions for limits for passenger automobiles.*)

24a Do you have evidence to support the business/investment use claimed? ☐ **Yes** ☐ **No**　**24b** If "Yes," is the evidence written? ☐ **Yes** ☐ **No**

(a) Type of property (list vehicles first)	(b) Date placed in service	(c) Business/ investment use percentage	(d) Cost or other basis	(e) Basis for depreciation (business/investment use only)	(f) Recovery period	(g) Method/ Convention	(h) Depreciation deduction	(i) Elected section 179 cost
25 Special depreciation allowance for qualified listed property placed in service during the tax year and used more than 50% in a qualified business use (see instructions) . **25**								
26 Property used more than 50% in a qualified business use:								
		%						
		%						
		%						
27 Property used 50% or less in a qualified business use:								
		%				S/L –		
		%				S/L –		
		%				S/L –		
28 Add amounts in column (h), lines 25 through 27. Enter here and on line 21, page 1 . **28**								
29 Add amounts in column (i), line 26. Enter here and on line 7, page 1							**29**	

Section B—Information on Use of Vehicles

Complete this section for vehicles used by a sole proprietor, partner, or other "more than 5% owner," or related person. If you provided vehicles to your employees, first answer the questions in Section C to see if you meet an exception to completing this section for those vehicles.

	(a) Vehicle 1		(b) Vehicle 2		(c) Vehicle 3		(d) Vehicle 4		(e) Vehicle 5		(f) Vehicle 6	
30 Total business/investment miles driven during the year (**do not** include commuting miles) .												
31 Total commuting miles driven during the year												
32 Total other personal (noncommuting) miles driven												
33 Total miles driven during the year. Add lines 30 through 32												
34 Was the vehicle available for personal use during off-duty hours?	Yes	No	Yes	No	Yes	No	Yes	No	Yes	No	Yes	No
35 Was the vehicle used primarily by a more than 5% owner or related person? . .												
36 Is another vehicle available for personal use?												

Section C—Questions for Employers Who Provide Vehicles for Use by Their Employees

Answer these questions to determine if you meet an exception to completing Section B for vehicles used by employees who **are not** more than 5% owners or related persons (see instructions).

		Yes	No
37	Do you maintain a written policy statement that prohibits all personal use of vehicles, including commuting, by your employees?		
38	Do you maintain a written policy statement that prohibits personal use of vehicles, except commuting, by your employees? See the instructions for vehicles used by corporate officers, directors, or 1% or more owners . .		
39	Do you treat all use of vehicles by employees as personal use?		
40	Do you provide more than five vehicles to your employees, obtain information from your employees about the use of the vehicles, and retain the information received?		
41	Do you meet the requirements concerning qualified automobile demonstration use? (See instructions.) . . .		

Note: *If your answer to 37, 38, 39, 40, or 41 is "Yes," do not complete Section B for the covered vehicles.*

Part VI **Amortization**

(a) Description of costs	(b) Date amortization begins	(c) Amortizable amount	(d) Code section	(e) Amortization period or percentage	(f) Amortization for this year
42 Amortization of costs that begins during your 2014 tax year (see instructions):					
43 Amortization of costs that began before your 2014 tax year **43**					
44 **Total.** Add amounts in column (f). See the instructions for where to report **44**					

Form **4797**	**Sales of Business Property** (Also Involuntary Conversions and Recapture Amounts Under Sections 179 and 280F(b)(2)) ▶ Attach to your tax return. ▶ Information about Form 4797 and its separate instructions is at *www.irs.gov/form4797.*	OMB No. 1545-0184 **2014**
Department of the Treasury Internal Revenue Service		Attachment Sequence No. **27**

Name(s) shown on return	Identifying number
James Brothers' Men's Wear, Inc.	73-0068478

1 Enter the gross proceeds from sales or exchanges reported to you for 2014 on Form(s) 1099-B or 1099-S (or substitute statement) that you are including on line 2, 10, or 20 (see instructions) **1**

Part I Sales or Exchanges of Property Used in a Trade or Business and Involuntary Conversions From Other Than Casualty or Theft—Most Property Held More Than 1 Year (see instructions)

2	**(a)** Description of property	**(b)** Date acquired (mo., day, yr.)	**(c)** Date sold (mo., day, yr.)	**(d)** Gross sales price	**(e)** Depreciation allowed or allowable since acquisition	**(f)** Cost or other basis, plus improvements and expense of sale	**(g)** Gain or (loss) Subtract (f) from the sum of (d) and (e)

3 Gain, if any, from Form 4684, line 39	**3**	
4 Section 1231 gain from installment sales from Form 6252, line 26 or 37	**4**	
5 Section 1231 gain or (loss) from like-kind exchanges from Form 8824	**5**	
6 Gain, if any, from line 32, from other than casualty or theft.	**6**	
7 Combine lines 2 through 6. Enter the gain or (loss) here and on the appropriate line as follows:	**7**	

Partnerships (except electing large partnerships) and S corporations. Report the gain or (loss) following the instructions for Form 1065, Schedule K, line 10, or Form 1120S, Schedule K, line 9. Skip lines 8, 9, 11, and 12 below.

Individuals, partners, S corporation shareholders, and all others. If line 7 is zero or a loss, enter the amount from line 7 on line 11 below and skip lines 8 and 9. If line 7 is a gain and you did not have any prior year section 1231 losses, or they were recaptured in an earlier year, enter the gain from line 7 as a long-term capital gain on the Schedule D filed with your return and skip lines 8, 9, 11, and 12 below.

8 Nonrecaptured net section 1231 losses from prior years (see instructions)	**8**	
9 Subtract line 8 from line 7. If zero or less, enter -0-. If line 9 is zero, enter the gain from line 7 on line 12 below. If line 9 is more than zero, enter the amount from line 8 on line 12 below and enter the gain from line 9 as a long-term capital gain on the Schedule D filed with your return (see instructions)	**9**	

Part II Ordinary Gains and Losses (see instructions)

10 Ordinary gains and losses not included on lines 11 through 16 (include property held 1 year or less):

11 Loss, if any, from line 7	**11** ( )
12 Gain, if any, from line 7 or amount from line 8, if applicable	**12**
13 Gain, if any, from line 31	**13** 3,200
14 Net gain or (loss) from Form 4684, lines 31 and 38a	**14**
15 Ordinary gain from installment sales from Form 6252, line 25 or 36	**15**
16 Ordinary gain or (loss) from like-kind exchanges from Form 8824.	**16**
17 Combine lines 10 through 16	**17** 3,200

18 For all except individual returns, enter the amount from line 17 on the appropriate line of your return and skip lines a and b below. For individual returns, complete lines a and b below:

a If the loss on line 11 includes a loss from Form 4684, line 35, column (b)(ii), enter that part of the loss here. Enter the part of the loss from income-producing property on Schedule A (Form 1040), line 28, and the part of the loss from property used as an employee on Schedule A (Form 1040), line 23. Identify as from "Form 4797, line 18a." See instructions . . | **18a**

b Redetermine the gain or (loss) on line 17 excluding the loss, if any, on line 18a. Enter here and on Form 1040, line 14 | **18b**

For Paperwork Reduction Act Notice, see separate instructions.	Cat. No. 13086I	Form **4797** (2014)

Part III Gain From Disposition of Property Under Sections 1245, 1250, 1252, 1254, and 1255
(see instructions)

19	(a) Description of section 1245, 1250, 1252, 1254, or 1255 property:		(b) Date acquired (mo., day, yr.)	(c) Date sold (mo., day, yr.)
A	Equipment		4-15-2010	7-18-2014
B				
C				
D				

	These columns relate to the properties on lines 19A through 19D. ▶		Property A	Property B	Property C	Property D
20	Gross sales price (**Note:** See line 1 before completing.)	**20**	5,825			
21	Cost or other basis plus expense of sale	**21**	12,500			
22	Depreciation (or depletion) allowed or allowable.	**22**	9,875			
23	Adjusted basis. Subtract line 22 from line 21.	**23**	2,625			
24	Total gain. Subtract line 23 from line 20	**24**	3,200			
25	**If section 1245 property:**					
a	Depreciation allowed or allowable from line 22	**25a**	9,875			
b	Enter the **smaller** of line 24 or 25a	**25b**	3,200			
26	**If section 1250 property:** If straight line depreciation was used, enter -0- on line 26g, except for a corporation subject to section 291.					
a	Additional depreciation after 1975 (see instructions)	**26a**				
b	Applicable percentage multiplied by the **smaller** of line 24 or line 26a (see instructions)	**26b**				
c	Subtract line 26a from line 24. If residential rental property **or** line 24 is not more than line 26a, skip lines 26d and 26e	**26c**				
d	Additional depreciation after 1969 and before 1976.	**26d**				
e	Enter the **smaller** of line 26c or 26d	**26e**				
f	Section 291 amount (corporations only)	**26f**				
g	Add lines 26b, 26e, and 26f.	**26g**				
27	**If section 1252 property:** Skip this section if you did not dispose of farmland or if this form is being completed for a partnership (other than an electing large partnership).					
a	Soil, water, and land clearing expenses	**27a**				
b	Line 27a multiplied by applicable percentage (see instructions)	**27b**				
c	Enter the **smaller** of line 24 or 27b	**27c**				
28	**If section 1254 property:**					
a	Intangible drilling and development costs, expenditures for development of mines and other natural deposits, mining exploration costs, and depletion (see instructions)	**28a**				
b	Enter the **smaller** of line 24 or 28a	**28b**				
29	**If section 1255 property:**					
a	Applicable percentage of payments excluded from income under section 126 (see instructions)	**29a**				
b	Enter the **smaller** of line 24 or 29a (see instructions)	**29b**				

Summary of Part III Gains. Complete property columns A through D through line 29b before going to line 30.

30	Total gains for all properties. Add property columns A through D, line 24	**30**	3,200
31	Add property columns A through D, lines 25b, 26g, 27c, 28b, and 29b. Enter here and on line 13	**31**	3,200
32	Subtract line 31 from line 30. Enter the portion from casualty or theft on Form 4684, line 33. Enter the portion from other than casualty or theft on Form 4797, line 6	**32**	

Part IV Recapture Amounts Under Sections 179 and 280F(b)(2) When Business Use Drops to 50% or Less
(see instructions)

			(a) Section 179	(b) Section 280F(b)(2)
33	Section 179 expense deduction or depreciation allowable in prior years.	**33**		
34	Recomputed depreciation (see instructions)	**34**		
35	Recapture amount. Subtract line 34 from line 33. See the instructions for where to report	**35**		

Form **4626**

Department of the Treasury
Internal Revenue Service

Alternative Minimum Tax—Corporations

► Attach to the corporation's tax return.
► Information about Form 4626 and its separate instructions is at *www.irs.gov/form4626*.

OMB No. 1545-0123

20**14**

Name	Employer identification number
James Brothers' Men's Wear, Inc.	73-0068478

Note: *See the instructions to find out if the corporation is a small corporation exempt from the alternative minimum tax (AMT) under section 55(e).*

1	Taxable income or (loss) before net operating loss deduction	**1**	70,750
2	**Adjustments and preferences:**		
a	Depreciation of post-1986 property	**2a**	325
b	Amortization of certified pollution control facilities.	**2b**	
c	Amortization of mining exploration and development costs	**2c**	
d	Amortization of circulation expenditures (personal holding companies only)	**2d**	
e	Adjusted gain or loss	**2e**	
f	Long-term contracts	**2f**	
g	Merchant marine capital construction funds.	**2g**	
h	Section 833(b) deduction (Blue Cross, Blue Shield, and similar type organizations only)	**2h**	
i	Tax shelter farm activities (personal service corporations only)	**2i**	
j	Passive activities (closely held corporations and personal service corporations only)	**2j**	
k	Loss limitations	**2k**	
l	Depletion	**2l**	
m	Tax-exempt interest income from specified private activity bonds	**2m**	6,000
n	Intangible drilling costs	**2n**	
o	Other adjustments and preferences	**2o**	
3	Pre-adjustment alternative minimum taxable income (AMTI). Combine lines 1 through 2o.	**3**	77,075

4	**Adjusted current earnings (ACE) adjustment:**			
a	ACE from line 10 of the ACE worksheet in the instructions	**4a**	86,150	
b	Subtract line 3 from line 4a. If line 3 exceeds line 4a, enter the difference as a negative amount (see instructions).	**4b**	9,075	
c	Multiply line 4b by 75% (.75). Enter the result as a positive amount	**4c**	6,806	
d	Enter the excess, if any, of the corporation's total increases in AMTI from prior year ACE adjustments over its total reductions in AMTI from prior year ACE adjustments (see instructions). **Note:** *You **must** enter an amount on line 4d (even if line 4b is positive).*	**4d**	0	
e	ACE adjustment.			
	• If line 4b is zero or more, enter the amount from line 4c	**4e**		6,806
	• If line 4b is less than zero, enter the **smaller** of line 4c or line 4d as a negative amount			
5	Combine lines 3 and 4e. If zero or less, stop here; the corporation does not owe any AMT	**5**		83,881
6	Alternative tax net operating loss deduction (see instructions).	**6**		
7	**Alternative minimum taxable income.** Subtract line 6 from line 5. If the corporation held a residual interest in a REMIC, see instructions	**7**		83,881

8	**Exemption phase-out** (if line 7 is $310,000 or more, skip lines 8a and 8b and enter -0- on line 8c):		
a	Subtract $150,000 from line 7 (if completing this line for a member of a controlled group, see instructions). If zero or less, enter -0- **8a**		
b	Multiply line 8a by 25% (.25). **8b**		
c	Exemption. Subtract line 8b from $40,000 (if completing this line for a member of a controlled group, see instructions). If zero or less, enter -0-	**8c**	0
9	Subtract line 8c from line 7. If zero or less, enter -0-	**9**	83,881
10	Multiply line 9 by 20% (.20)	**10**	16,776
11	Alternative minimum tax foreign tax credit (AMTFTC) (see instructions)	**11**	
12	Tentative minimum tax. Subtract line 11 from line 10.	**12**	16,776
13	Regular tax liability before applying all credits except the foreign tax credit	**13**	11,088
14	**Alternative minimum tax.** Subtract line 13 from line 12. If zero or less, enter -0-. Enter here and on Form 1120, Schedule J, line 3, or the appropriate line of the corporation's income tax return	**14**	5,688

For Paperwork Reduction Act Notice, see separate instructions.   Cat. No. 12955I   Form **4626** (2014)

Adjusted Current Earnings (ACE) Worksheet

Keep for Your Records

► See ACE Worksheet Instructions.

1	Pre-adjustment AMTI . Enter the amount from line 3 of Form 4626		**1**	
2	ACE depreciation adjustment:			
a	AMT depreciation	**2a**		
b	ACE depreciation:			
	(1) Post-1993 property .... **2b(1)**			
	(2) Post-1989, pre-1994 property .... **2b(2)**			
	(3) Pre-1990 MACRS property .... **2b(3)**			
	(4) Pre-1990 original ACRS property .... **2b(4)**			
	(5) Property described in sections 168(f)(1) through (4) ...... **2b(5)**			
	(6) Other property .... **2b(6)**			
	(7) Total ACE depreciation. Add lines 2b(1) through 2b(6) .... **2b(7)**			
c	ACE depreciation adjustment. Subtract line 2b(7) from line 2a		**2c**	
3	Inclusion in ACE of items included in earnings and profits (E&P):			
a	Tax-exempt interest income **3a**			
b	Death benefits from life insurance contracts **3b**			
c	All other distributions from life insurance contracts (including surrenders) **3c**			
d	Inside buildup of undistributed income in life insurance contracts **3d**			
e	Other items (see Regulations sections 1.56(g)-1(c)(6)(iii) through (ix) for a partial list) **3e**			
f	Total increase to ACE from inclusion in ACE of items included in E&P. Add lines 3a through 3e		**3f**	
4	Disallowance of items not deductible from E&P:			
a	Certain dividends received **4a**			
b	Dividends paid on certain preferred stock of public utilities that are deductible under section 247 .... **4b**			
c	Dividends paid to an ESOP that are deductible under section 404(k) **4c**			
d	Nonpatronage dividends that are paid and deductible under section 1382(c) **4d**			
e	Other items (see Regulations sections 1.56(g)-1(d)(3)(i) and (ii) for a partial list) **4e**			
f	Total increase to ACE because of disallowance of items not deductible from E&P. Add lines 4a through 4e		**4f**	
5	Other adjustments based on rules for figuring E&P:			
a	Intangible drilling costs **5a**			
b	Circulation expenditures **5b**			
c	Organizational expenditures **5c**			
d	LIFO inventory adjustments **5d**			
e	Installment sales **5e**			
f	Total other E&P adjustments. Combine lines 5a through 5e		**5f**	
6	Disallowance of loss on exchange of debt pools		**6**	
7	Acquisition expenses of life insurance companies for qualified foreign contracts		**7**	
8	Depletion		**8**	
9	Basis adjustments in determining gain or loss from sale or exchange of pre-1994 property		**9**	
10	**Adjusted current earnings.** Combine lines 1, 2c, 3f, 4f, and 5f through 9. Enter the result here and on line 4a of Form 4626		**10**	

Form **2220**	**Underpayment of Estimated Tax by Corporations**	OMB No. 1545-0123
Department of the Treasury Internal Revenue Service	▶ **Attach to the corporation's tax return.** ▶ **Information about Form 2220 and its separate instructions is at** *www.irs.gov/form2220.*	20**14**

Name	Employer identification number
Premco	73-1234567

Note: *Generally, the corporation is not required to file Form 2220 (see Part II below for exceptions) because the IRS will figure any penalty owed and bill the corporation. However, the corporation may still use Form 2220 to figure the penalty. If so, enter the amount from page 2, line 38 on the estimated tax penalty line of the corporation's income tax return, but* **do not** *attach Form 2220.*

Part I	Required Annual Payment			

1	Total tax (see instructions)		**1**	90,000
2a	Personal holding company tax (Schedule PH (Form 1120), line 26) included on line 1	**2a**	0	
b	Look-back interest included on line 1 under section 460(b)(2) for completed long-term contracts or section 167(g) for depreciation under the income forecast method . .	**2b**	0	
c	Credit for federal tax paid on fuels (see instructions)	**2c**	0	
d	**Total.** Add lines 2a through 2c		**2d**	0
3	Subtract line 2d from line 1. If the result is less than $500, **do not** complete or file this form. The corporation does not owe the penalty		**3**	90,000
4	Enter the tax shown on the corporation's 2013 income tax return (see instructions). **Caution:** *If the tax is zero or the tax year was for less than 12 months, skip this line and enter the amount from line 3 on line 5* . .		**4**	81,000
5	**Required annual payment.** Enter the **smaller** of line 3 or line 4. If the corporation is required to skip line 4, enter the amount from line 3		**5**	81,000

Part II	Reasons for Filing—Check the boxes below that apply. If any boxes are checked, the corporation **must** file Form 2220 even if it does not owe a penalty (see instructions).

6	☐ The corporation is using the adjusted seasonal installment method.
7	☐ The corporation is using the annualized income installment method.
8	☐ The corporation is a "large corporation" figuring its first required installment based on the prior year's tax.

Part III	Figuring the Underpayment				

			(a)	(b)	(c)	(d)
9	**Installment due dates.** Enter in columns (a) through (d) the 15th day of the 4th (**Form 990-PF filers:** Use 5th month), 6th, 9th, and 12th months of the corporation's tax year	**9**	4/15/14	6/15/14	9/15/14	12/15/14
10	**Required installments.** If the box on line 6 and/or line 7 above is checked, enter the amounts from Schedule A, line 38. If the box on line 8 (but not 6 or 7) is checked, see instructions for the amounts to enter. If none of these boxes are checked, enter 25% of line 5 above in each column	**10**	20,250	20,250	20,250	20,250
11	Estimated tax paid or credited for each period (see instructions). For column (a) only, enter the amount from line 11 on line 15	**11**	17,500	17,500	17,500	17,500
	Complete lines 12 through 18 of one column before going to the next column.					
12	Enter amount, if any, from line 18 of the preceding column	**12**		0	0	0
13	Add lines 11 and 12	**13**		17,500	17,500	17,500
14	Add amounts on lines 16 and 17 of the preceding column	**14**		2,750	5,500	8,250
15	Subtract line 14 from line 13. If zero or less, enter -0-	**15**	17,500	14,750	12,000	9,250
16	If the amount on line 15 is zero, subtract line 13 from line 14. Otherwise, enter -0-	**16**		0	0	
17	**Underpayment.** If line 15 is less than or equal to line 10, subtract line 15 from line 10. Then go to line 12 of the next column. Otherwise, go to line 18	**17**	2,750	5,500	8,250	11,000
18	**Overpayment.** If line 10 is less than line 15, subtract line 10 from line 15. Then go to line 12 of the next column	**18**	0	0	0	

Go to Part IV on page 2 to figure the penalty. Do not go to Part IV if there are no entries on line 17—no penalty is owed.

For Paperwork Reduction Act Notice, see separate instructions. Cat. No. 11746L Form **2220** (2014)

Part IV Figuring the Penalty

		(a)	(b)	(c)	(d)
19	Enter the date of payment or the 15th day of the 3rd month after the close of the tax year, whichever is earlier (see instructions). *(Form 990-PF and Form 990-T filers:* Use 5th month instead of 3rd month.) **19**	6/15/2014	9/15/2014	12/15/2014	3/15/2014
20	Number of days from due date of installment on line 9 to the date shown on line 19 . . . . **20**	61	92	91	90
21	Number of days on line 20 after 4/15/2014 and before 7/1/2014 **21**	61	15	0	0
22	Underpayment on line 17 × $\frac{\text{Number of days on line 21}}{365}$ × 3% **22**	$ 13.79	$ 6.78	$ 0	$
23	Number of days on line 20 after 6/30/2014 and before 10/1/2014 **23**		77	15	
24	Underpayment on line 17 × $\frac{\text{Number of days on line 23}}{365}$ × 3% **24**	$	$ 34.81	$ 10.17	$
25	Number of days on line 20 after 9/30/2014 and before 1/1/2015 **25**			76	16
26	Underpayment on line 17 × $\frac{\text{Number of days on line 25}}{365}$ × 3% **26**	$	$	$ 51.53	$ 14.47
27	Number of days on line 20 after 12/31/2014 and before 4/1/2015 **27**				74
28	Underpayment on line 17 × $\frac{\text{Number of days on line 27}}{365}$ × 3% **28**	$	$	$	$ 66.90
29	Number of days on line 20 after 3/31/2015 and before 7/1/2015 **29**				
30	Underpayment on line 17 × $\frac{\text{Number of days on line 29}}{365}$ × *% **30**	$	$	$	$
31	Number of days on line 20 after 6/30/2015 and before 10/1/2015 **31**				
32	Underpayment on line 17 × $\frac{\text{Number of days on line 31}}{365}$ × *% **32**	$	$	$	$
33	Number of days on line 20 after 9/30/2015 and before 1/1/2016 **33**				
34	Underpayment on line 17 × $\frac{\text{Number of days on line 33}}{365}$ × *% **34**	$	$	$	$
35	Number of days on line 20 after 12/31/2015 and before 2/16/2016 **35**				
36	Underpayment on line 17 × $\frac{\text{Number of days on line 35}}{366}$ × *% **36**	$	$	$	$
37	Add lines 22, 24, 26, 28, 30, 32, 34, and 36 . . . . **37**	$ 13.79	$ 41.59	$ 61.70	$ 81.37
38	**Penalty.** Add columns (a) through (d) of line 37. Enter the total here and on Form 1120, line 33; or the comparable line for other income tax returns **38**				$ 198.45

*Use the penalty interest rate for each calendar quarter, which the IRS will determine during the first month in the preceding quarter. These rates are published quarterly in an IRS News Release and in a revenue ruling in the Internal Revenue Bulletin. To obtain this information on the Internet, access the IRS website at *www.irs.gov*. You can also call 1-800-829-4933 to get interest rate information.

Schedule A Adjusted Seasonal Installment Method and Annualized Income Installment Method
(see instructions)

Form 1120S filers: *For lines 1, 2, 3, and 21, below, "taxable income" refers to excess net passive income or the amount on which tax is imposed under section 1374(a), whichever applies.*

Part I Adjusted Seasonal Installment Method (Caution: *Use this method only if the base period percentage for any 6 consecutive months is at least 70%. See instructions.*)

		(a) First 3 months	(b) First 5 months	(c) First 8 months	(d) First 11 months
1	Enter taxable income for the following periods:				
a	Tax year beginning in 2011	1a			
b	Tax year beginning in 2012	1b			
c	Tax year beginning in 2013	1c			
2	Enter taxable income for each period for the tax year beginning in 2014 (see instructions for the treatment of extraordinary items) .	2			

		First 4 months	First 6 months	First 9 months	Entire year
3	Enter taxable income for the following periods:				
a	Tax year beginning in 2011	3a			
b	Tax year beginning in 2012	3b			
c	Tax year beginning in 2013	3c			
4	Divide the amount in each column on line 1a by the amount in column (d) on line 3a	4			
5	Divide the amount in each column on line 1b by the amount in column (d) on line 3b	5			
6	Divide the amount in each column on line 1c by the amount in column (d) on line 3c	6			
7	Add lines 4 through 6	7			
8	Divide line 7 by 3.0	8			
9a	Divide line 2 by line 8	9a			
b	Extraordinary items (see instructions)	9b			
c	Add lines 9a and 9b	9c			
10	Figure the tax on the amount on line 9c using the instructions for Form 1120, Schedule J, line 2 (or comparable line of corporation's return)	10			
11a	Divide the amount in columns (a) through (c) on line 3a by the amount in column (d) on line 3a	11a			
b	Divide the amount in columns (a) through (c) on line 3b by the amount in column (d) on line 3b	11b			
c	Divide the amount in columns (a) through (c) on line 3c by the amount in column (d) on line 3c	11c			
12	Add lines 11a through 11c	12			
13	Divide line 12 by 3.0	13			
14	Multiply the amount in columns (a) through (c) of line 10 by columns (a) through (c) of line 13. In column (d), enter the amount from line 10, column (d)	14			
15	Enter any alternative minimum tax for each payment period (see instructions)	15			
16	Enter any other taxes for each payment period (see instructions)	16			
17	Add lines 14 through 16	17			
18	For each period, enter the same type of credits as allowed on Form 2220, lines 1 and 2c (see instructions)	18			
19	Total tax after credits. Subtract line 18 from line 17. If zero or less, enter -0-	19			

Part II — Annualized Income Installment Method

		(a) First months	(b) First months	(c) First months	(d) First months
20	Annualization periods (see instructions) **20**				
21	Enter taxable income for each annualization period (see instructions for the treatment of extraordinary items) . . . **21**				
22	Annualization amounts (see instructions) **22**				
23a	Annualized taxable income. Multiply line 21 by line 22 . . . **23a**				
b	Extraordinary items (see instructions) **23b**				
c	Add lines 23a and 23b **23c**				
24	Figure the tax on the amount on line 23c using the instructions for Form 1120, Schedule J, line 2 (or comparable line of corporation's return) **24**				
25	Enter any alternative minimum tax for each payment period (see instructions) **25**				
26	Enter any other taxes for each payment period (see instructions) **26**				
27	Total tax. Add lines 24 through 26 . . . . **27**				
28	For each period, enter the same type of credits as allowed on Form 2220, lines 1 and 2c (see instructions) **28**				
29	Total tax after credits. Subtract line 28 from line 27. If zero or less, enter -0- **29**				
30	Applicable percentage **30**	25%	50%	75%	100%
31	Multiply line 29 by line 30 . . . . **31**				

Part III — Required Installments

Note: *Complete lines 32 through 38 of one column before completing the next column.*

		1st installment	2nd installment	3rd installment	4th installment
32	If only Part I or Part II is completed, enter the amount in each column from line 19 or line 31. If both parts are completed, enter the **smaller** of the amounts in each column from line 19 or line 31 . . **32**				
33	Add the amounts in all preceding columns of line 38 (see instructions) **33**				
34	**Adjusted seasonal or annualized income installments.** Subtract line 33 from line 32. If zero or less, enter -0- . . . **34**				
35	Enter 25% of line 5 on page 1 of Form 2220 in each column. **Note:** *"Large corporations," see the instructions for line 10 for the amounts to enter* **35**				
36	Subtract line 38 of the preceding column from line 37 of the preceding column **36**				
37	Add lines 35 and 36 . . . . **37**				
38	**Required installments.** Enter the **smaller** of line 34 or line 37 here and on page 1 of Form 2220, line 10 (see instructions) . **38**				

§ 4.30 Filled-In Form 1120S

Form 1120S

U.S. Income Tax Return for an S Corporation

Department of the Treasury
Internal Revenue Service

► Do not file this form unless the corporation has filed or is attaching Form 2553 to elect to be an S corporation.
► Information about Form 1120S and its separate instructions is at *www.irs.gov/form1120s*.

OMB No. 1545-0123

2014

For calendar year 2014 or tax year beginning _____, 2014, ending _____, 20____

A S election effective date		Name	**D** Employer identification number
12-18-1987	**TYPE**	Wilson Distributors	70-0084678
B Business activity code number (see instructions)	**OR**	Number, street, and room or suite no. If a P.O. box, see instructions.	**E** Date incorporated
	PRINT	1000 East Jefferson Street	6-4-1986
442990		City or town, state or province, country, and ZIP or foreign postal code	**F** Total assets (see instructions)
C Check if Sch. M-3 attached ☐		Detroit, Michigan 48236	$ 848,726

G Is the corporation electing to be an S corporation beginning with this tax year? ☐ Yes ☑ No · If "Yes," attach Form 2553 if not already filed

H Check if: **(1)** ☐ Final return **(2)** ☐ Name change **(3)** ☐ Address change **(4)** ☐ Amended return **(5)** ☐ S election termination or revocation

I Enter the number of shareholders who were shareholders during any part of the tax year . . . . ► 3

Caution. Include **only** trade or business income and expenses on lines 1a through 21. See the instructions for more information.

Income

1a	Gross receipts or sales	**1a**	1,831,308			
b	Returns and allowances	**1b**	5,860			
c	Balance. Subtract line 1b from line 1a			**1c**	1,825,448	
2	Cost of goods sold (attach Form 1125-A)			**2**	1,409,783	
3	Gross profit. Subtract line 2 from line 1c			**3**	415,665	
4	Net gain (loss) from Form 4797, line 17 (attach Form 4797)			**4**		
5	Other income (loss) (see instructions—attach statement)			**5**	11,724	
6	**Total income (loss).** Add lines 3 through 5 . . . . ►			**6**	427,389	

Deductions (see instructions for limitations)

7	Compensation of officers (see instructions—attach Form 1125-E) . .	**7**	79,824	
8	Salaries and wages (less employment credits)	**8**	120,878	
9	Repairs and maintenance	**9**	4,818	
10	Bad debts	**10**	2,100	
11	Rents	**11**	26,173	
12	Taxes and licenses	**12**	20,723	
13	Interest	**13**	44,000	
14	Depreciation not claimed on Form 1125-A or elsewhere on return (attach Form 4562) . .	**14**	26,614	
15	Depletion **(Do not deduct oil and gas depletion.)**	**15**		
16	Advertising	**16**	9,827	
17	Pension, profit-sharing, etc., plans	**17**	2,000	
18	Employee benefit programs	**18**	16,048	
19	Other deductions (attach statement)	**19**	67,489	
20	**Total deductions.** Add lines 7 through 19 . . . . ►	**20**	420,494	
21	**Ordinary business income (loss).** Subtract line 20 from line 6 . . .	**21**	6,895	

Tax and Payments

22a	Excess net passive income or LIFO recapture tax (see instructions) . .	**22a**			
b	Tax from Schedule D (Form 1120S)	**22b**			
c	Add lines 22a and 22b (see instructions for additional taxes) . . .			**22c**	
23a	2014 estimated tax payments and 2013 overpayment credited to 2014	**23a**			
b	Tax deposited with Form 7004	**23b**			
c	Credit for federal tax paid on fuels (attach Form 4136)	**23c**			
d	Add lines 23a through 23c			**23d**	
24	Estimated tax penalty (see instructions). Check if Form 2220 is attached . . . . . ► ☐			**24**	
25	**Amount owed.** If line 23d is smaller than the total of lines 22c and 24, enter amount owed . .			**25**	
26	**Overpayment.** If line 23d is larger than the total of lines 22c and 24, enter amount overpaid .			**26**	
27	Enter amount from line 26 **Credited to 2015 estimated tax** ► _____ **Refunded** ►			**27**	

Sign Here

Under penalties of perjury, I declare that I have examined this return, including accompanying schedules and statements, and to the best of my knowledge and belief, it is true, correct, and complete. Declaration of preparer (other than taxpayer) is based on all information of which preparer has any knowledge.

► *Jane Wilson*
Signature of officer   Date   ► Title

May the IRS discuss this return with the preparer shown below (see instructions)? ☑ Yes ☐ No

Paid Preparer Use Only

Print/Type preparer's name	Preparer's signature	Date	Check ☑ if self-employed	PTIN
Alan Young	*Alan Young*			
Firm's name ► Alan Young, CPA			Firm's EIN ►	
Firm's address ► 100 East Jefferson Street, Detroit, Michigan 48236			Phone no.	

For Paperwork Reduction Act Notice, see separate instructions.   Cat. No. 11510H   Form **1120S** (2014)

Schedule B	**Other Information** (see instructions)				Yes	No

1 Check accounting method: **a** ☑ Cash **b** ☐ Accrual
  c ☐ Other (specify) ▶ _____

2 See the instructions and enter the:
  a Business activity ▶ Distribution   **b** Product or service ▶ Perfume/Cosmetics

3 At any time during the tax year, was any shareholder of the corporation a disregarded entity, a trust, an estate, or a nominee or similar person? If "Yes," attach Schedule B-1, Information on Certain Shareholders of an S Corporation . . — ✓

4 At the end of the tax year, did the corporation:

a Own directly 20% or more, or own, directly or indirectly, 50% or more of the total stock issued and outstanding of any foreign or domestic corporation? For rules of constructive ownership, see instructions. If "Yes," complete (i) through (v) below . . . . — ✓

(i) Name of Corporation	**(ii)** Employer Identification Number (if any)	**(iii)** Country of Incorporation	**(iv)** Percentage of Stock Owned	**(v)** If Percentage in (iv) is 100%, Enter the Date (if any) a Qualified Subchapter S Subsidiary Election Was Made

b Own directly an interest of 20% or more, or own, directly or indirectly, an interest of 50% or more in the profit, loss, or capital in any foreign or domestic partnership (including an entity treated as a partnership) or in the beneficial interest of a trust? For rules of constructive ownership, see instructions. If "Yes," complete (i) through (v) below . . . . — ✓

(i) Name of Entity	**(ii)** Employer Identification Number (if any)	**(iii)** Type of Entity	**(iv)** Country of Organization	**(v)** Maximum Percentage Owned in Profit, Loss, or Capital

5 a At the end of the tax year, did the corporation have any outstanding shares of restricted stock? . . . . — ✓
  If "Yes," complete lines (i) and (ii) below.
  (i) Total shares of restricted stock . . . . ▶ _____
  (ii) Total shares of non-restricted stock . . . . ▶ _____

b At the end of the tax year, did the corporation have any outstanding stock options, warrants, or similar instruments? . — ✓
  If "Yes," complete lines (i) and (ii) below.
  (i) Total shares of stock outstanding at the end of the tax year ▶ _____
  (ii) Total shares of stock outstanding if all instruments were executed ▶ _____

6 Has this corporation filed, or is it required to file, **Form 8918,** Material Advisor Disclosure Statement, to provide information on any reportable transaction? . . . . — ✓

7 Check this box if the corporation issued publicly offered debt instruments with original issue discount . . . ▶ ☐
  If checked, the corporation may have to file **Form 8281,** Information Return for Publicly Offered Original Issue Discount Instruments.

8 If the corporation: **(a)** was a C corporation before it elected to be an S corporation **or** the corporation acquired an asset with a basis determined by reference to the basis of the asset (or the basis of any other property) in the hands of a C corporation **and (b)** has net unrealized built-in gain in excess of the net recognized built-in gain from prior years, enter the net unrealized built-in gain reduced by net recognized built-in gain from prior years (see instructions) . . . . ▶ $ _____

9 Enter the accumulated earnings and profits of the corporation at the end of the tax year. $ _____

10 Does the corporation satisfy **both** of the following conditions?
a The corporation's total receipts (see instructions) for the tax year were less than $250,000 . . . .
b The corporation's total assets at the end of the tax year were less than $250,000 . . . . — ✓
  If "Yes," the corporation is not required to complete Schedules L and M-1.

11 During the tax year, did the corporation have any non-shareholder debt that was canceled, was forgiven, or had the terms modified so as to reduce the principal amount of the debt? . . . . — ✓
  If "Yes," enter the amount of principal reduction $ _____

12 During the tax year, was a qualified subchapter S subsidiary election terminated or revoked? If "Yes," see instructions . — ✓

13 a Did the corporation make any payments in 2014 that would require it to file Form(s) 1099? . . . . — ✓
  b If "Yes," did the corporation file or will it file required Forms 1099? . . . .

Schedule K		Shareholders' Pro Rata Share Items			Total amount	

Income (Loss)

	1	Ordinary business income (loss) (page 1, line 21)			**1**	6,895
	2	Net rental real estate income (loss) (attach Form 8825)			**2**	3,990
	3a	Other gross rental income (loss)	**3a**			
	b	Expenses from other rental activities (attach statement)	**3b**			
	c	Other net rental income (loss). Subtract line 3b from line 3a			**3c**	
	4	Interest income			**4**	11,590
	5	Dividends: a Ordinary dividends			**5a**	4,990
		b Qualified dividends	**5b**	4,990		
	6	Royalties			**6**	
	7	Net short-term capital gain (loss) (attach Schedule D (Form 1120S))			**7**	
	8a	Net long-term capital gain (loss) (attach Schedule D (Form 1120S))			**8a**	2,250
	b	Collectibles (28%) gain (loss)	**8b**			
	c	Unrecaptured section 1250 gain (attach statement)	**8c**			
	9	Net section 1231 gain (loss) (attach Form 4797)			**9**	(1,428)
	10	Other income (loss) (see instructions)　Type ▶			**10**	

Deductions

	11	Section 179 deduction (attach Form 4562)			**11**	6,500
	12a	Charitable contributions			**12a**	1,200
	b	Investment interest expense			**12b**	
	c	Section 59(e)(2) expenditures (1) Type ▶ ____ (2) Amount ▶			**12c(2)**	
	d	Other deductions (see instructions)　Type ▶			**12d**	

Credits

	13a	Low-income housing credit (section 42(j)(5))			**13a**	
	b	Low-income housing credit (other)			**13b**	
	c	Qualified rehabilitation expenditures (rental real estate) (attach Form 3468, if applicable)			**13c**	
	d	Other rental real estate credits (see instructions)　Type ▶			**13d**	
	e	Other rental credits (see instructions)　Type ▶			**13e**	
	f	Biofuel producer credit (attach Form 6478)			**13f**	
	g	Other credits (see instructions)　Type ▶			**13g**	

Foreign Transactions

	14a	Name of country or U.S. possession ▶				
	b	Gross income from all sources			**14b**	
	c	Gross income sourced at shareholder level			**14c**	
		Foreign gross income sourced at corporate level				
	d	Passive category			**14d**	
	e	General category			**14e**	
	f	Other (attach statement)			**14f**	
		Deductions allocated and apportioned at shareholder level				
	g	Interest expense			**14g**	
	h	Other			**14h**	
		Deductions allocated and apportioned at corporate level to foreign source income				
	i	Passive category			**14i**	
	j	General category			**14j**	
	k	Other (attach statement)			**14k**	
		Other information				
	l	Total foreign taxes (check one): ▶ ☐ Paid ☐ Accrued			**14l**	
	m	Reduction in taxes available for credit (attach statement)			**14m**	
	n	Other foreign tax information (attach statement)				

Alternative Minimum Tax (AMT) Items

	15a	Post-1986 depreciation adjustment			**15a**	1,020
	b	Adjusted gain or loss			**15b**	
	c	Depletion (other than oil and gas)			**15c**	
	d	Oil, gas, and geothermal properties—gross income			**15d**	
	e	Oil, gas, and geothermal properties—deductions			**15e**	
	f	Other AMT items (attach statement)			**15f**	

Items Affecting Shareholder Basis

	16a	Tax-exempt interest income			**16a**	5,215
	b	Other tax-exempt income			**16b**	
	c	Nondeductible expenses			**16c**	4,002
	d	Distributions (attach statement if required) (see instructions)			**16d**	3,000
	e	Repayment of loans from shareholders			**16e**	

Schedule K	Shareholders' Pro Rata Share Items (continued)		Total amount	

17a	Investment income	**17a**		
b	Investment expenses	**17b**		
c	Dividend distributions paid from accumulated earnings and profits	**17c**		
d	Other items and amounts (attach statement)			
18	**Income/loss reconciliation.** Combine the amounts on lines 1 through 10 in the far right column. From the result, subtract the sum of the amounts on lines 11 through 12d and 14l	**18**	20,587	

Schedule L	Balance Sheets per Books	Beginning of tax year		End of tax year	
	Assets	**(a)**	**(b)**	**(c)**	**(d)**
1	Cash		82,525		89,574
2a	Trade notes and accounts receivable . . .	231,102		276,483	
b	Less allowance for bad debts	( )	231,102	( )	276,483
3	Inventories		121,549		124,757
4	U.S. government obligations		201,500		230,000
5	Tax-exempt securities (see instructions) . .				
6	Other current assets (attach statement) . . .				
7	Loans to shareholders				
8	Mortgage and real estate loans				
9	Other investments (attach statement) . . .		13,760		6,000
10a	Buildings and other depreciable assets . . .	178,649		181,389	
b	Less accumulated depreciation	(45,828)	132,821	(83,198)	98,191
11a	Depletable assets				
b	Less accumulated depletion	( )		( )	
12	Land (net of any amortization)		22,471		22,471
13a	Intangible assets (amortizable only)	2,500		2,500	
b	Less accumulated amortization	(750)	1,750	(1,250)	1,250
14	Other assets (attach statement)				
15	Total assets		807,478		848,726
	Liabilities and Shareholders' Equity				
16	Accounts payable		55,826		92,746
17	Mortgages, notes, bonds payable in less than 1 year				
18	Other current liabilities (attach statement) . .				
19	Loans from shareholders		400,000		400,000
20	Mortgages, notes, bonds payable in 1 year or more		22,000		19,850
21	Other liabilities (attach statement)				
22	Capital stock		2,000		2,000
23	Additional paid-in capital		277,825		277,825
24	Retained earnings		49,827		56,305
25	Adjustments to shareholders' equity (attach statement)				
26	Less cost of treasury stock		( )		( )
27	Total liabilities and shareholders' equity . .		807,478		848,726

Form **1120S** (2014)

Schedule M-1	Reconciliation of Income (Loss) per Books With Income (Loss) per Return

Note. The corporation may be required to file Schedule M-3 (see instructions)

1	Net income (loss) per books	28,300	5	Income recorded on books this year not included on Schedule K, lines 1 through 10 (itemize):		
2	Income included on Schedule K, lines 1, 2, 3c, 4, 5a, 6, 7, 8a, 9, and 10, not recorded on books this year (itemize)_____		a	Tax-exempt interest $ _____ 5,215		5,215
3	Expenses recorded on books this year not included on Schedule K, lines 1 through 12 and 14l (itemize):		6	Deductions included on Schedule K, lines 1 through 12 and 14l, not charged against book income this year (itemize):		
a	Depreciation $ _____		a	Depreciation $ _____ 6,500		
b	Travel and entertainment $ _____			_____		6,500
	_____	4,002	7	Add lines 5 and 6		11,715
4	Add lines 1 through 3	32,302	8	Income (loss) (Schedule K, line 18). Line 4 less line 7		20,587

Schedule M-2	Analysis of Accumulated Adjustments Account, Other Adjustments Account, and Shareholders' Undistributed Taxable Income Previously Taxed (see instructions)

		(a) Accumulated adjustments account	(b) Other adjustments account	(c) Shareholders' undistributed taxable income previously taxed
1	Balance at beginning of tax year	7,894	3,100	
2	Ordinary income from page 1, line 21 . . .	6,895		
3	Other additions	22,820	5,215	
4	Loss from page 1, line 21	( )		
5	Other reductions	(14,954)	( )	
6	Combine lines 1 through 5	22,655	8,315	
7	Distributions other than dividend distributions	(3,000)		
8	Balance at end of tax year. Subtract line 7 from line 6	19,655	8,315	

Form **1120S** (2014)

Form **8949**	**Sales and Other Dispositions of Capital Assets**	OMB No. 1545-0074
Department of the Treasury Internal Revenue Service	▶ Information about Form 8949 and its separate instructions is at *www.irs.gov/form8949*. ▶ File with your Schedule D to list your transactions for lines 1b, 2, 3, 8b, 9, and 10 of Schedule D.	2014 Attachment Sequence No. **12A**

Name(s) shown on return	Social security number or taxpayer identification number
Wilson Distributors	70-0084678

Before you check Box A, B, or C below, see whether you received any Form(s) 1099-B or substitute statement(s) from your broker. A substitute statement will have the same information as Form 1099-B. Either may show your basis (usually your cost) even if your broker did not report it to the IRS. Brokers must report basis to the IRS for most stock you bought in 2011 or later (and for certain debt instruments you bought in 2014 or later).

Part I | **Short-Term.** Transactions involving capital assets you held 1 year or less are short term. For long-term transactions, see page 2.

Note. You may aggregate all short-term transactions reported on Form(s) 1099-B showing basis was reported to the IRS and for which no adjustments or codes are required. Enter the total directly on Schedule D, line 1a; you are not required to report these transactions on Form 8949 (see instructions).

You *must* check Box A, B, *or* C below. Check only one box. If more than one box applies for your short-term transactions, complete a separate Form 8949, page 1, for each applicable box. If you have more short-term transactions than will fit on this page for one or more of the boxes, complete as many forms with the same box checked as you need.

☐ **(A)** Short-term transactions reported on Form(s) 1099-B showing basis was reported to the IRS (see **Note** above)

☐ **(B)** Short-term transactions reported on Form(s) 1099-B showing basis was **not** reported to the IRS

☐ **(C)** Short-term transactions not reported to you on Form 1099-B

1 (a) Description of property (Example: 100 sh. XYZ Co.)	(b) Date acquired (Mo., day, yr.)	(c) Date sold or disposed (Mo., day, yr.)	(d) Proceeds (sales price) (see instructions)	(e) Cost or other basis. See the **Note** below and see *Column (e)* in the separate instructions	(f) Code(s) from instructions	(g) Amount of adjustment	(h) Gain or (loss). Subtract column (e) from column (d) and combine the result with column (g)

Column headers for the adjustment section: **Adjustment, if any, to gain or loss.** If you enter an amount in column (g), enter a code in column (f). **See the separate instructions.**

2 Totals. Add the amounts in columns (d), (e), (g), and (h) (subtract negative amounts). Enter each total here and include on your Schedule D, **line 1b** (if **Box A** above is checked), **line 2** (if **Box B** above is checked), or **line 3** (if **Box C** above is checked) ▶

Note. If you checked Box A above but the basis reported to the IRS was incorrect, enter in column (e) the basis as reported to the IRS, and enter an adjustment in column (g) to correct the basis. See *Column (g)* in the separate instructions for how to figure the amount of the adjustment.

For Paperwork Reduction Act Notice, see your tax return instructions.   Cat. No. 37768Z   Form **8949** (2014)

Name(s) shown on return. Name and SSN or taxpayer identification no. not required if shown on other side	Social security number or taxpayer identification number
Wilson Distributors	70-0084678

Before you check Box D, E, or F below, see whether you received any Form(s) 1099-B or substitute statement(s) from your broker. A substitute statement will have the same information as Form 1099-B. Either may show your basis (usually your cost) even if your broker did not report it to the IRS. Brokers must report basis to the IRS for most stock you bought in 2011 or later (and for certain debt instruments you bought in 2014 or later).

Part II	**Long-Term.** Transactions involving capital assets you held more than 1 year are long term. For short-term transactions, see page 1.

Note. You may aggregate all long-term transactions reported on Form(s) 1099-B showing basis was reported to the IRS and for which no adjustments or codes are required. Enter the total directly on Schedule D, line 8a; you are not required to report these transactions on Form 8949 (see instructions).

You *must* check Box D, E, *or* F below. Check only one box. If more than one box applies for your long-term transactions, complete a separate Form 8949, page 2, for each applicable box. If you have more long-term transactions than will fit on this page for one or more of the boxes, complete as many forms with the same box checked as you need.

- ☐ **(D)** Long-term transactions reported on Form(s) 1099-B showing basis was reported to the IRS (see **Note** above)
- ☑ **(E)** Long-term transactions reported on Form(s) 1099-B showing basis was **not** reported to the IRS
- ☐ **(F)** Long-term transactions not reported to you on Form 1099-B

1 (a) Description of property (Example: 100 sh. XYZ Co.)	(b) Date acquired (Mo., day, yr.)	(c) Date sold or disposed (Mo., day, yr.)	(d) Proceeds (sales price) (see instructions)	(e) Cost or other basis. See the **Note** below and see *Column (e)* in the separate instructions	(f) Code(s) from instructions	(g) Amount of adjustment	(h) Gain or (loss). Subtract column (e) from column (d) and combine the result with column (g)
200 shares of Revlon Inc.	9-18-2007	6-8-2014	16,010	13,760			2,250
2 Totals. Add the amounts in columns (d), (e), (g), and (h) (subtract negative amounts). Enter each total here and include on your Schedule D, **line 8b** (if **Box D** above is checked), **line 9** (if **Box E** above is checked), or **line 10** (if **Box F** above is checked) ▶			16,010	13,760			2,250

Note. If you checked Box D above but the basis reported to the IRS was incorrect, enter in column (e) the basis as reported to the IRS, and enter an adjustment in column (g) to correct the basis. See *Column (g)* in the separate instructions for how to figure the amount of the adjustment.

§ 4.60 Filled-In Form 4562

Form **4562**	**Depreciation and Amortization**	OMB No. 1545-0172
	(Including Information on Listed Property)	**2014**
Department of the Treasury Internal Revenue Service (99)	▶ Attach to your tax return. ▶ Information about Form 4562 and its separate instructions is at *www.irs.gov/form4562*.	Attachment Sequence No. **179**

Name(s) shown on return	Business or activity to which this form relates	Identifying number

Part I **Election To Expense Certain Property Under Section 179**
Note: *If you have any listed property, complete Part V before you complete Part I.*

1	Maximum amount (see instructions)	1	500,000
2	Total cost of section 179 property placed in service (see instructions)	2	6,500
3	Threshold cost of section 179 property before reduction in limitation (see instructions)	3	2,000,000
4	Reduction in limitation. Subtract line 3 from line 2. If zero or less, enter -0-	4	0
5	Dollar limitation for tax year. Subtract line 4 from line 1. If zero or less, enter -0-. If married filing separately, see instructions	5	500,000

6	**(a)** Description of property	**(b)** Cost (business use only)	**(c)** Elected cost		
	Equipment	6,500	6,500		

7	Listed property. Enter the amount from line 29	7		
8	Total elected cost of section 179 property. Add amounts in column (c), lines 6 and 7	8	6,500
9	Tentative deduction. Enter the **smaller** of line 5 or line 8	9	6,500
10	Carryover of disallowed deduction from line 13 of your 2013 Form 4562	10	
11	Business income limitation. Enter the smaller of business income (not less than zero) or line 5 (see instructions)	11	6,500
12	Section 179 expense deduction. Add lines 9 and 10, but do not enter more than line 11	12	6,500
13	Carryover of disallowed deduction to 2015. Add lines 9 and 10, less line 12 ▶	13	

Note: *Do not use Part II or Part III below for listed property. Instead, use Part V.*

Part II **Special Depreciation Allowance and Other Depreciation (Do not** include listed property.**)** (See instructions.)

14	Special depreciation allowance for qualified property (other than listed property) placed in service during the tax year (see instructions)	14	
15	Property subject to section 168(f)(1) election	15	
16	Other depreciation (including ACRS)	16	

Part III **MACRS Depreciation (Do not** include listed property.**)** (See instructions.)

Section A

17	MACRS deductions for assets placed in service in tax years beginning before 2014	17	23,724
18	If you are electing to group any assets placed in service during the tax year into one or more general asset accounts, check here ▶ ☐		

Section B—Assets Placed in Service During 2014 Tax Year Using the General Depreciation System

(a) Classification of property	**(b)** Month and year placed in service	**(c)** Basis for depreciation (business/investment use only—see instructions)	**(d)** Recovery period	**(e)** Convention	**(f)** Method	**(g)** Depreciation deduction
19a 3-year property						
b 5-year property						
c 7-year property						
d 10-year property						
e 15-year property						
f 20-year property						
g 25-year property			25 yrs.		S/L	
h Residential rental property			27.5 yrs.	MM	S/L	
			27.5 yrs.	MM	S/L	
i Nonresidential real property			39 yrs.	MM	S/L	
				MM	S/L	

Section C—Assets Placed in Service During 2014 Tax Year Using the Alternative Depreciation System

20a Class life					S/L	
b 12-year			12 yrs.		S/L	
c 40-year			40 yrs.	MM	S/L	

Part IV **Summary** (See instructions.)

21	Listed property. Enter amount from line 28	21	
22	**Total.** Add amounts from line 12, lines 14 through 17, lines 19 and 20 in column (g), and line 21. Enter here and on the appropriate lines of your return. Partnerships and S corporations—see instructions	22	30,224
23	For assets shown above and placed in service during the current year, enter the portion of the basis attributable to section 263A costs	23	

For Paperwork Reduction Act Notice, see separate instructions.   Cat. No. 12906N   Form **4562** (2014)

Part V **Listed Property** (Include automobiles, certain other vehicles, certain aircraft, certain computers, and property used for entertainment, recreation, or amusement.)

Note: *For any vehicle for which you are using the standard mileage rate or deducting lease expense, complete only 24a, 24b, columns (a) through (c) of Section A, all of Section B, and Section C if applicable.*

Section A—Depreciation and Other Information (Caution: *See the instructions for limits for passenger automobiles.*)

24a Do you have evidence to support the business/investment use claimed? ☐ Yes ☐ No **24b** If "Yes," is the evidence written? ☐ Yes ☐ No

(a) Type of property (list vehicles first)	(b) Date placed in service	(c) Business/ investment use percentage	(d) Cost or other basis	(e) Basis for depreciation (business/investment use only)	(f) Recovery period	(g) Method/ Convention	(h) Depreciation deduction	(i) Elected section 179 cost
25 Special depreciation allowance for qualified listed property placed in service during the tax year and used more than 50% in a qualified business use (see instructions) . **25**								
26 Property used more than 50% in a qualified business use:								
		%						
		%						
		%						
27 Property used 50% or less in a qualified business use:								
		%			S/L –			
		%			S/L –			
		%			S/L –			
28 Add amounts in column (h), lines 25 through 27. Enter here and on line 21, page 1 . **28**								
29 Add amounts in column (i), line 26. Enter here and on line 7, page 1 . . . . **29**								

Section B—Information on Use of Vehicles

Complete this section for vehicles used by a sole proprietor, partner, or other "more than 5% owner," or related person. If you provided vehicles to your employees, first answer the questions in Section C to see if you meet an exception to completing this section for those vehicles.

	(a) Vehicle 1		(b) Vehicle 2		(c) Vehicle 3		(d) Vehicle 4		(e) Vehicle 5		(f) Vehicle 6	
30 Total business/investment miles driven during the year (**do not** include commuting miles) .												
31 Total commuting miles driven during the year												
32 Total other personal (noncommuting) miles driven												
33 Total miles driven during the year. Add lines 30 through 32												
34 Was the vehicle available for personal use during off-duty hours?	Yes	No	Yes	No	Yes	No	Yes	No	Yes	No	Yes	No
35 Was the vehicle used primarily by a more than 5% owner or related person? . .												
36 Is another vehicle available for personal use?												

Section C—Questions for Employers Who Provide Vehicles for Use by Their Employees

Answer these questions to determine if you meet an exception to completing Section B for vehicles used by employees who **are not** more than 5% owners or related persons (see instructions).

		Yes	No
37	Do you maintain a written policy statement that prohibits all personal use of vehicles, including commuting, by your employees?		
38	Do you maintain a written policy statement that prohibits personal use of vehicles, except commuting, by your employees? See the instructions for vehicles used by corporate officers, directors, or 1% or more owners . .		
39	Do you treat all use of vehicles by employees as personal use?		
40	Do you provide more than five vehicles to your employees, obtain information from your employees about the use of the vehicles, and retain the information received?		
41	Do you meet the requirements concerning qualified automobile demonstration use? (See instructions.) . .		

Note: *If your answer to 37, 38, 39, 40, or 41 is "Yes," do not complete Section B for the covered vehicles.*

Part VI **Amortization**

(a) Description of costs	(b) Date amortization begins	(c) Amortizable amount	(d) Code section	(e) Amortization period or percentage	(f) Amortization for this year
42 Amortization of costs that begins during your 2014 tax year (see instructions):					
43 Amortization of costs that began before your 2014 tax year **43**					
44 Total. Add amounts in column (f). See the instructions for where to report **44**					

§ 4.80 Filled In Form 4797

Form **4797**	**Sales of Business Property**	OMB No. 1545-0184

Form 4797

(Also Involuntary Conversions and Recapture Amounts
Under Sections 179 and 280F(b)(2))

2014

Department of the Treasury
Internal Revenue Service

▶ Attach to your tax return.
▶ Information about Form 4797 and its separate instructions is at *www.irs.gov/form4797*.

Attachment
Sequence No. **27**

Name(s) shown on return: Wilson Distributors

Identifying number: 70-0084678

1 Enter the gross proceeds from sales or exchanges reported to you for 2014 on Form(s) 1099-B or 1099-S (or substitute statement) that you are including on line 2, 10, or 20 (see instructions) **1**

Part I Sales or Exchanges of Property Used in a Trade or Business and Involuntary Conversions From Other Than Casualty or Theft—Most Property Held More Than 1 Year (see instructions)

2	(a) Description of property	(b) Date acquired (mo., day, yr.)	(c) Date sold (mo., day, yr.)	(d) Gross sales price	(e) Depreciation allowed or allowable since acquisition	(f) Cost or other basis, plus improvements and expense of sale	(g) Gain or (loss) Subtract (f) from the sum of (d) and (e)
	Computer	7-1-2011	1-2-2014	2,998	3,642	8,068	(1,428)

3 Gain, if any, from Form 4684, line 39 . . . . **3**

4 Section 1231 gain from installment sales from Form 6252, line 26 or 37 . . . . **4**

5 Section 1231 gain or (loss) from like-kind exchanges from Form 8824 . . . . **5**

6 Gain, if any, from line 32, from other than casualty or theft **6**

7 Combine lines 2 through 6. Enter the gain or (loss) here and on the appropriate line as follows: **7** (1,428)

Partnerships (except electing large partnerships) and S corporations. Report the gain or (loss) following the instructions for Form 1065, Schedule K, line 10, or Form 1120S, Schedule K, line 9. Skip lines 8, 9, 11, and 12 below.

Individuals, partners, S corporation shareholders, and all others. If line 7 is zero or a loss, enter the amount from line 7 on line 11 below and skip lines 8 and 9. If line 7 is a gain and you did not have any prior year section 1231 losses, or they were recaptured in an earlier year, enter the gain from line 7 as a long-term capital gain on the Schedule D filed with your return and skip lines 8, 9, 11, and 12 below.

8 Nonrecaptured net section 1231 losses from prior years (see instructions) . . . . **8** SCorp

9 Subtract line 8 from line 7. If zero or less, enter -0-. If line 9 is zero, enter the gain from line 7 on line 12 below. If line 9 is more than zero, enter the amount from line 8 on line 12 below and enter the gain from line 9 as a long-term capital gain on the Schedule D filed with your return (see instructions) **9**

Part II Ordinary Gains and Losses (see instructions)

10 Ordinary gains and losses not included on lines 11 through 16 (include property held 1 year or less):

11 Loss, if any, from line 7 . . . . **11** ( )

12 Gain, if any, from line 7 or amount from line 8, if applicable **12**

13 Gain, if any, from line 31 . . . . **13**

14 Net gain or (loss) from Form 4684, lines 31 and 38a **14**

15 Ordinary gain from installment sales from Form 6252, line 25 or 36 . . . . **15**

16 Ordinary gain or (loss) from like-kind exchanges from Form 8824 . . . . **16**

17 Combine lines 10 through 16 . . . . **17**

18 For all except individual returns, enter the amount from line 17 on the appropriate line of your return and skip lines a and b below. For individual returns, complete lines a and b below:

a If the loss on line 11 includes a loss from Form 4684, line 35, column (b)(ii), enter that part of the loss here. Enter the part of the loss from income-producing property on Schedule A (Form 1040), line 28, and the part of the loss from property used as an employee on Schedule A (Form 1040), line 23. Identify as from "Form 4797, line 18a." See instructions . . . **18a**

b Redetermine the gain or (loss) on line 17 excluding the loss, if any, on line 18a. Enter here and on Form 1040, line 14 **18b**

For Paperwork Reduction Act Notice, see separate instructions.

Cat. No. 13086I

Form **4797** (2014)

Part III	**Gain From Disposition of Property Under Sections 1245, 1250, 1252, 1254, and 1255** (see instructions)			

19	(a) Description of section 1245, 1250, 1252, 1254, or 1255 property:		**(b)** Date acquired (mo., day, yr.)	**(c)** Date sold (mo., day, yr.)
A				
B				
C				
D				

	These columns relate to the properties on lines 19A through 19D. ▶		**Property A**	**Property B**	**Property C**	**Property D**
20	Gross sales price (**Note:** *See line 1 before completing.*)	**20**				
21	Cost or other basis plus expense of sale	**21**				
22	Depreciation (or depletion) allowed or allowable	**22**				
23	Adjusted basis. Subtract line 22 from line 21	**23**				
24	Total gain. Subtract line 23 from line 20	**24**				
25	**If section 1245 property:**					
a	Depreciation allowed or allowable from line 22	**25a**				
b	Enter the **smaller** of line 24 or 25a	**25b**				
26	**If section 1250 property:** If straight line depreciation was used, enter -0- on line 26g, except for a corporation subject to section 291.					
a	Additional depreciation after 1975 (see instructions)	**26a**				
b	Applicable percentage multiplied by the **smaller** of line 24 or line 26a (see instructions)	**26b**				
c	Subtract line 26a from line 24. If residential rental property **or** line 24 is not more than line 26a, skip lines 26d and 26e	**26c**				
d	Additional depreciation after 1969 and before 1976	**26d**				
e	Enter the **smaller** of line 26c or 26d	**26e**				
f	Section 291 amount (corporations only)	**26f**				
g	Add lines 26b, 26e, and 26f	**26g**				
27	**If section 1252 property:** Skip this section if you did not dispose of farmland or if this form is being completed for a partnership (other than an electing large partnership).					
a	Soil, water, and land clearing expenses	**27a**				
b	Line 27a multiplied by applicable percentage (see instructions)	**27b**				
c	Enter the **smaller** of line 24 or 27b	**27c**				
28	**If section 1254 property:**					
a	Intangible drilling and development costs, expenditures for development of mines and other natural deposits, mining exploration costs, and depletion (see instructions)	**28a**				
b	Enter the **smaller** of line 24 or 28a	**28b**				
29	**If section 1255 property:**					
a	Applicable percentage of payments excluded from income under section 126 (see instructions)	**29a**				
b	Enter the **smaller** of line 24 or 29a (see instructions)	**29b**				

Summary of Part III Gains. Complete property columns A through D through line 29b before going to line 30.

30	Total gains for all properties. Add property columns A through D, line 24	**30**	
31	Add property columns A through D, lines 25b, 26g, 27c, 28b, and 29b. Enter here and on line 13	**31**	
32	Subtract line 31 from line 30. Enter the portion from casualty or theft on Form 4684, line 33. Enter the portion from other than casualty or theft on Form 4797, line 6	**32**	

Part IV	**Recapture Amounts Under Sections 179 and 280F(b)(2) When Business Use Drops to 50% or Less** (see instructions)			

			(a) Section 179	**(b)** Section 280F(b)(2)
33	Section 179 expense deduction or depreciation allowable in prior years	**33**		
34	Recomputed depreciation (see instructions)	**34**		
35	Recapture amount. Subtract line 34 from line 33. See the instructions for where to report	**35**		

§ 4.120 Filled-In Schedules K-1, Form 1120S

671113

☐ Final K-1   ☐ Amended K-1   OMB No. 1545-0123

Schedule K-1
(Form 1120S)
Department of the Treasury
Internal Revenue Service

2014

For calendar year 2014, or tax
year beginning _____ , 2014
ending _____ , 20 _____

Shareholder's Share of Income, Deductions, Credits, etc.
▶ See back of form and separate instructions.

Part I	Information About the Corporation

A Corporation's employer identification number
70-0084678

B Corporation's name, address, city, state, and ZIP code

Wilson Distributors
1000 East Jefferson Street
Detroit, Michigan 48236

C IRS Center where corporation filed return
Cincinnati, Ohio

Part II	Information About the Shareholder

D Shareholder's identifying number
243-84-3576

E Shareholder's name, address, city, state, and ZIP code

Jane Wilson
790 Lakeshore Drive
Grosse Pointe, Michigan 48236

F Shareholder's percentage of stock
ownership for tax year . . . .   50 %

For IRS Use Only

Part III	Shareholder's Share of Current Year Income, Deductions, Credits, and Other Items		
1 Ordinary business income (loss) **3,448**	13 Credits		
2 Net rental real estate income (loss) **1,996**			
3 Other net rental income (loss)			
4 Interest income **5,795**			
5a Ordinary dividends **2,495**			
5b Qualified dividends **2,495**	14 Foreign transactions		
6 Royalties			
7 Net short-term capital gain (loss)			
8a Net long-term capital gain (loss) **1,125**			
8b Collectibles (28%) gain (loss)			
8c Unrecaptured section 1250 gain			
9 Net section 1231 gain (loss) **(714)**			
10 Other income (loss)	15 Alternative minimum tax (AMT) items		
	A **510**		
11 Section 179 deduction **3,250**	16 Items affecting shareholder basis		
12 Other deductions	A **2,607**		
A **600**	C **2,001**		
	D **1,500**		
	17 Other information		

* See attached statement for additional information.

For Paperwork Reduction Act Notice, see Instructions for Form 1120S.   IRS.gov/form1120s   Cat. No. 11520D   **Schedule K-1 (Form 1120S) 2014**

671113

Schedule K-1
(Form 1120S)
Department of the Treasury
Internal Revenue Service

2014

For calendar year 2014, or tax
year beginning _____, 2014
ending _____, 20 ___

Shareholder's Share of Income, Deductions, Credits, etc.
▶ See back of form and separate instructions.

Part III	**Shareholder's Share of Current Year Income, Deductions, Credits, and Other Items**		
1	Ordinary business income (loss) 1,724	13	Credits
2	Net rental real estate income (loss) 997		
3	Other net rental income (loss)		
4	Interest income 2,898		
5a	Ordinary dividends		
5b	Qualified dividends 1,247	14	Foreign transactions
6	Royalties 1,247		
7	Net short-term capital gain (loss)		
8a	Net long-term capital gain (loss) 562		
8b	Collectibles (28%) gain (loss)		
8c	Unrecaptured section 1250 gain		
9	Net section 1231 gain (loss) (357)		
10	Other income (loss)	15	Alternative minimum tax (AMT) items
		A	255
11	Section 179 deduction 1,625	16	Items affecting shareholder basis
12	Other deductions	A	1,304
A	300	C	1,000
		D	750
		17	Other information

Part I   Information About the Corporation

A Corporation's employer identification number
70-0084678

B Corporation's name, address, city, state, and ZIP code

Wilson Distributors
1000 East Jefferson Street
Detroit, Michigan 48236

C IRS Center where corporation filed return
Cincinnati, Ohio

Part II   Information About the Shareholder

D Shareholder's identifying number
501-78-9874

E Shareholder's name, address, city, state, and ZIP code

Bob Smith
128 Canterbury Drive
Rochester, Michigan 48250

F Shareholder's percentage of stock
ownership for tax year . . . . __25__ %

For IRS Use Only

* See attached statement for additional information.

671113

☐ Final K-1   ☐ Amended K-1   OMB No. 1545-0123

Schedule K-1 **(Form 1120S)** Department of the Treasury Internal Revenue Service	**2014** For calendar year 2014, or tax year beginning _____ , 2014 ending _____ , 20 _____

Shareholder's Share of Income, Deductions, Credits, etc.   ▶ See back of form and separate instructions.

Part I	**Information About the Corporation**

A Corporation's employer identification number
70-0084678

B Corporation's name, address, city, state, and ZIP code

Wilson Distributors
1000 East Jefferson Street
Detroit, Michigan 48236

C IRS Center where corporation filed return
Cincinnati, Ohio

Part II	**Information About the Shareholder**

D Shareholder's identifying number
501-78-9874

E Shareholder's name, address, city, state, and ZIP code

Mary Cox
101 Hillside Road
Auburn Hills, Michigan 48289

F Shareholder's percentage of stock
ownership for tax year . . . . _____ 25 %

For IRS Use Only

Part III	**Shareholder's Share of Current Year Income, Deductions, Credits, and Other Items**		
1	Ordinary business income (loss) 1,724	13	Credits
2	Net rental real estate income (loss) 997		
3	Other net rental income (loss)		
4	Interest income 2,897		
5a	Ordinary dividends 1,248		
5b	Qualified dividends 1,248	14	Foreign transactions
6	Royalties		
7	Net short-term capital gain (loss)		
8a	Net long-term capital gain (loss) 563		
8b	Collectibles (28%) gain (loss)		
8c	Unrecaptured section 1250 gain		
9	Net section 1231 gain (loss) (357)		
10	Other income (loss)	15	Alternative minimum tax (AMT) items
		A	255
11	Section 179 deduction 1,625	16	Items affecting shareholder basis
12	Other deductions	A	1,304
A	300	C	1,001
		D	750
		17	Other information

* See attached statement for additional information.

For Paperwork Reduction Act Notice, see Instructions for Form 1120S.   IRS.gov/form1120s   Cat. No. 11520D   **Schedule K-1 (Form 1120S) 2014**

Form 1065

Department of the Treasury Internal Revenue Service

U.S. Return of Partnership Income

For calendar year 2014, or tax year beginning _____, 2014, ending _____, 20 _____.

▶ Information about Form 1065 and its separate instructions is at *www.irs.gov/form1065*.

OMB No. 1545-0123

2014

A Principal business activity Manufacturing	Name of partnership B&J Computers	**D** Employer identification number 38-0801478
B Principal product or service Computer Equipment	**Type or Print** — Number, street, and room or suite no. If a P.O. box, see the instructions. 20 Michigan Avenue	**E** Date business started 1-1-2001
C Business code number 334110	City or town, state or province, country, and ZIP or foreign postal code Ann Arbor, Michigan 48239	**F** Total assets (see the instructions) $ 2,977,525

G Check applicable boxes: **(1)** ☐ Initial return **(2)** ☐ Final return **(3)** ☐ Name change **(4)** ☐ Address change **(5)** ☐ Amended return
(6) ☐ Technical termination - also check (1) or (2)

H Check accounting method: **(1)** ☐ Cash **(2)** ☑ Accrual **(3)** ☐ Other (specify) ▶ _____

I Number of Schedules K-1. Attach one for each person who was a partner at any time during the tax year ▶ 3

J Check if Schedules C and M-3 are attached . . . . ☐

Caution. *Include only trade or business income and expenses on lines 1a through 22 below. See the instructions for more information.*

Income	**1a** Gross receipts or sales	**1a**	8,869,212	
	b Returns and allowances	**1b**	10,500	
	c Balance. Subtract line 1b from line 1a	**1c**		8,858,712
	2 Cost of goods sold (attach Form 1125-A)	**2**		5,825,892
	3 Gross profit. Subtract line 2 from line 1c	**3**		3,032,820
	4 Ordinary income (loss) from other partnerships, estates, and trusts (attach statement) . .	**4**		14,561
	5 Net farm profit (loss) (attach Schedule F (Form 1040))	**5**		
	6 Net gain (loss) from Form 4797, Part II, line 17 (attach Form 4797)	**6**		3,000
	7 Other income (loss) (attach statement) *consulting income*	**7**		100,000
	8 **Total income (loss).** Combine lines 3 through 7	**8**		3,150,381
Deductions (see the instructions for limitations)	**9** Salaries and wages (other than to partners) (less employment credits)	**9**		1,526,104
	10 Guaranteed payments to partners	**10**		403,000
	11 Repairs and maintenance	**11**		76,341
	12 Bad debts	**12**		25,000
	13 Rent	**13**		301,000
	14 Taxes and licenses	**14**		194,088
	15 Interest	**15**		89,335
	16a Depreciation (if required, attach Form 4562)	**16a**	97,047	
	b Less depreciation reported on Form 1125-A and elsewhere on return	**16b**	94,905	**16c** 2,142
	17 Depletion (**Do not deduct oil and gas depletion.**)	**17**		
	18 Retirement plans, etc.	**18**		60,000
	19 Employee benefit programs	**19**		88,975
	20 Other deductions (attach statement)	**20**		225,313
	21 **Total deductions.** Add the amounts shown in the far right column for lines 9 through 20 .	**21**		2,991,298
	22 **Ordinary business income (loss).** Subtract line 21 from line 8	**22**		159,083

Sign Here

Under penalties of perjury, I declare that I have examined this return, including accompanying schedules and statements, and to the best of my knowledge and belief, it is true, correct, and complete. Declaration of preparer (other than general partner or limited liability company member manager) is based on all information of which preparer has any knowledge.

▶ *Bill Benson*

Signature of general partner or limited liability company member manager   Date ▶

May the IRS discuss this return with the preparer shown below (see instructions)? ☑ Yes ☐ No

Paid Preparer Use Only

Print/Type preparer's name Alan Young	Preparer's signature *Alan Young*	Date	Check ☑ if self-employed	PTIN
Firm's name ▶ Alan Young, CPA			Firm's EIN ▶	
Firm's address ▶ 2 Michigan Avenue, Ann Arbor, Michigan 48239			Phone no.	

For Paperwork Reduction Act Notice, see separate instructions.   Cat. No. 11390Z   Form **1065** (2014)

Schedule B   Other Information

		Yes	No
1	What type of entity is filing this return? Check the applicable box:		

a ☑ Domestic general partnership   **b** ☐ Domestic limited partnership

c ☐ Domestic limited liability company   **d** ☐ Domestic limited liability partnership

e ☐ Foreign partnership   **f** ☐ Other ▶

		Yes	No
2	At any time during the tax year, was any partner in the partnership a disregarded entity, a partnership (including an entity treated as a partnership), a trust, an S corporation, an estate (other than an estate of a deceased partner), or a nominee or similar person?		✓
3	At the end of the tax year:		
a	Did any foreign or domestic corporation, partnership (including any entity treated as a partnership), trust, or tax-exempt organization, or any foreign government own, directly or indirectly, an interest of 50% or more in the profit, loss, or capital of the partnership? For rules of constructive ownership, see instructions. If "Yes," attach Schedule B-1, Information on Partners Owning 50% or More of the Partnership		✓
b	Did any individual or estate own, directly or indirectly, an interest of 50% or more in the profit, loss, or capital of the partnership? For rules of constructive ownership, see instructions. If "Yes," attach Schedule B-1, Information on Partners Owning 50% or More of the Partnership		✓
4	At the end of the tax year, did the partnership:		
a	Own directly 20% or more, or own, directly or indirectly, 50% or more of the total voting power of all classes of stock entitled to vote of any foreign or domestic corporation? For rules of constructive ownership, see instructions. If "Yes," complete (i) through (iv) below		✓

(i) Name of Corporation	(ii) Employer Identification Number (if any)	(iii) Country of Incorporation	(iv) Percentage Owned in Voting Stock

		Yes	No
b	Own directly an interest of 20% or more, or own, directly or indirectly, an interest of 50% or more in the profit, loss, or capital in any foreign or domestic partnership (including an entity treated as a partnership) or in the beneficial interest of a trust? For rules of constructive ownership, see instructions. If "Yes," complete (i) through (v) below		✓

(i) Name of Entity	(ii) Employer Identification Number (if any)	(iii) Type of Entity	(iv) Country of Organization	(v) Maximum Percentage Owned in Profit, Loss, or Capital

		Yes	No
5	Did the partnership file Form 8893, Election of Partnership Level Tax Treatment, or an election statement under section 6231(a)(1)(B)(ii) for partnership-level tax treatment, that is in effect for this tax year? See Form 8893 for more details	✓	
6	Does the partnership satisfy **all four** of the following conditions?		
a	The partnership's total receipts for the tax year were less than $250,000.		
b	The partnership's total assets at the end of the tax year were less than $1 million.		
c	Schedules K-1 are filed with the return and furnished to the partners on or before the due date (including extensions) for the partnership return.		
d	The partnership is not filing and is not required to file Schedule M-3		✓
	If "Yes," the partnership is not required to complete Schedules L, M-1, and M-2; Item F on page 1 of Form 1065; or Item L on Schedule K-1.		
7	Is this partnership a publicly traded partnership as defined in section 469(k)(2)?		✓
8	During the tax year, did the partnership have any debt that was cancelled, was forgiven, or had the terms modified so as to reduce the principal amount of the debt?		✓
9	Has this partnership filed, or is it required to file, Form 8918, Material Advisor Disclosure Statement, to provide information on any reportable transaction?		✓
10	At any time during calendar year 2014, did the partnership have an interest in or a signature or other authority over a financial account in a foreign country (such as a bank account, securities account, or other financial account)? See the instructions for exceptions and filing requirements for FinCEN Form 114, Report of Foreign Bank and Financial Accounts (FBAR). If "Yes," enter the name of the foreign country. ▶		✓

Schedule B	Other Information *(continued)*		
		Yes	**No**
11	At any time during the tax year, did the partnership receive a distribution from, or was it the grantor of, or transferor to, a foreign trust? If "Yes," the partnership may have to file Form 3520, Annual Return To Report Transactions With Foreign Trusts and Receipt of Certain Foreign Gifts. See instructions		✓
12a	Is the partnership making, or had it previously made (and not revoked), a section 754 election?		✓
	See instructions for details regarding a section 754 election.		
b	Did the partnership make for this tax year an optional basis adjustment under section 743(b) or 734(b)? If "Yes," attach a statement showing the computation and allocation of the basis adjustment. See instructions		✓
c	Is the partnership required to adjust the basis of partnership assets under section 743(b) or 734(b) because of a substantial built-in loss (as defined under section 743(d)) or substantial basis reduction (as defined under section 734(d))? If "Yes," attach a statement showing the computation and allocation of the basis adjustment. See instructions		✓
13	Check this box if, during the current or prior tax year, the partnership distributed any property received in a like-kind exchange or contributed such property to another entity (other than disregarded entities wholly owned by the partnership throughout the tax year) . . . . ▶ ☐		
14	At any time during the tax year, did the partnership distribute to any partner a tenancy-in-common or other undivided interest in partnership property?		✓
15	If the partnership is required to file Form 8858, Information Return of U.S. Persons With Respect To Foreign Disregarded Entities, enter the number of Forms 8858 attached. See instructions ▶		
16	Does the partnership have any foreign partners? If "Yes," enter the number of Forms 8805, Foreign Partner's Information Statement of Section 1446 Withholding Tax, filed for this partnership. ▶		✓
17	Enter the number of Forms 8865, Return of U.S. Persons With Respect to Certain Foreign Partnerships, attached to this return. ▶ 0		
18a	Did you make any payments in 2014 that would require you to file Form(s) 1099? See instructions	✓	
b	If "Yes," did you or will you file required Form(s) 1099?	✓	
19	Enter the number of Form(s) 5471, Information Return of U.S. Persons With Respect To Certain Foreign Corporations, attached to this return. ▶ 0		
20	Enter the number of partners that are foreign governments under section 892. ▶ 0		

Designation of Tax Matters Partner (see instructions)

Enter below the general partner or member manager designated as the tax matters partner (TMP) for the tax year of this return:

Name of designated TMP ▶	Bill Benson	Identifying number of TMP ▶	502-80-3458
If the TMP is an entity, name of TMP representative ▶	12 Ann Arbor Blvd	Phone number of TMP ▶	
Address of designated TMP ▶	Ann Arbor, Michigan 48239		

Schedule K		**Partners' Distributive Share Items**			**Total amount**
Income (Loss)	**1**	Ordinary business income (loss) (page 1, line 22)		**1**	159,083
	2	Net rental real estate income (loss) (attach Form 8825)		**2**	6,405
	3a	Other gross rental income (loss)	**3a**		
	b	Expenses from other rental activities (attach statement)	**3b**		
	c	Other net rental income (loss). Subtract line 3b from line 3a		**3c**	
	4	Guaranteed payments		**4**	403,000
	5	Interest income		**5**	12,560
	6	Dividends: **a** Ordinary dividends		**6a**	8,900
		b Qualified dividends	**6b**	8,900	
	7	Royalties		**7**	
	8	Net short-term capital gain (loss) (attach Schedule D (Form 1065))		**8**	
	9a	Net long-term capital gain (loss) (attach Schedule D (Form 1065))		**9a**	111,000
	b	Collectibles (28%) gain (loss)	**9b**		
	c	Unrecaptured section 1250 gain (attach statement)	**9c**		
	10	Net section 1231 gain (loss) (attach Form 4797)		**10**	
	11	Other income (loss) (see instructions) Type ▶		**11**	
Deductions	**12**	Section 179 deduction (attach Form 4562)		**12**	
	13a	Contributions		**13a**	2,950
	b	Investment interest expense		**13b**	2,000
	c	Section 59(e)(2) expenditures: **(1)** Type ▶ _____ **(2)** Amount ▶		**13c(2)**	
	d	Other deductions (see instructions) Type ▶ med. insurance 55% ptr.		**13d**	3,000
Self-Employ-ment	**14a**	Net earnings (loss) from self-employment		**14a**	104,561
	b	Gross farming or fishing income		**14b**	
	c	Gross nonfarm income		**14c**	
Credits	**15a**	Low-income housing credit (section 42(j)(5))		**15a**	
	b	Low-income housing credit (other)		**15b**	
	c	Qualified rehabilitation expenditures (rental real estate) (attach Form 3468, if applicable)		**15c**	
	d	Other rental real estate credits (see instructions) Type ▶ _____		**15d**	
	e	Other rental credits (see instructions) Type ▶ _____		**15e**	
	f	Other credits (see instructions) Type ▶ _____		**15f**	
Foreign Transactions	**16a**	Name of country or U.S. possession ▶ _____			
	b	Gross income from all sources		**16b**	
	c	Gross income sourced at partner level		**16c**	
		Foreign gross income sourced at partnership level			
	d	Passive category ▶ _____ **e** General category ▶ _____ **f** Other ▶		**16f**	
		Deductions allocated and apportioned at partner level			
	g	Interest expense ▶ _____ **h** Other		**16h**	
		Deductions allocated and apportioned at partnership level to foreign source income			
	i	Passive category ▶ _____ **j** General category ▶ _____ **k** Other ▶		**16k**	
	l	Total foreign taxes (check one): ▶ Paid ☐ Accrued ☐		**16l**	
	m	Reduction in taxes available for credit (attach statement)		**16m**	
	n	Other foreign tax information (attach statement)			
Alternative Minimum Tax (AMT) Items	**17a**	Post-1986 depreciation adjustment		**17a**	9,000
	b	Adjusted gain or loss		**17b**	
	c	Depletion (other than oil and gas)		**17c**	
	d	Oil, gas, and geothermal properties—gross income		**17d**	
	e	Oil, gas, and geothermal properties—deductions		**17e**	
	f	Other AMT items (attach statement)		**17f**	
Other Information	**18a**	Tax-exempt interest income		**18a**	
	b	Other tax-exempt income		**18b**	
	c	Nondeductible expenses		**18c**	
	19a	Distributions of cash and marketable securities		**19a**	220,000
	b	Distributions of other property		**19b**	
	20a	Investment income		**20a**	
	b	Investment expenses		**20b**	
	c	Other items and amounts (attach statement)			

Analysis of Net Income (Loss)

1	Net income (loss). Combine Schedule K, lines 1 through 11. From the result, subtract the sum of Schedule K, lines 12 through 13d, and 16l					**1**	692,998	

2	Analysis by partner type:	(i) Corporate	(ii) Individual (active)	(iii) Individual (passive)	(iv) Partnership	(v) Exempt Organization	(vi) Nominee/Other
a	General partners	363,400	209,848	120,750			
b	Limited partners						

Schedule L — Balance Sheets per Books

	Assets	Beginning of tax year (a)	(b)	End of tax year (c)	(d)
1	Cash		38,989		275,960
2a	Trade notes and accounts receivable . . .	284,512		313,586	
b	Less allowance for bad debts		284,512		313,586
3	Inventories		383,097		247,865
4	U.S. government obligations		100,000		125,000
5	Tax-exempt securities				74,000
6	Other current assets (attach statement) . .		96,000		64,561
7a	Loans to partners (or persons related to partners)				
b	Mortgage and real estate loans				
8	Other investments (attach statement) . . .				
9a	Buildings and other depreciable assets . .	960,000		1,240,000	
b	Less accumulated depreciation	98,200	861,800	162,247	1,077,753
10a	Depletable assets				
b	Less accumulated depletion				
11	Land (net of any amortization)		420,000		770,000
12a	Intangible assets (amortizable only) . .			36,000	
b	Less accumulated amortization			7,200	28,800
13	Other assets (attach statement)		50,000		
14	Total assets		2,234,398		2,977,525
	Liabilities and Capital				
15	Accounts payable		428,698		
16	Mortgages, notes, bonds payable in less than 1 year		125,000		
17	Other current liabilities (attach statement) .				
18	All nonrecourse loans				900,000
19a	Loans from partners (or persons related to partners)				
b	Mortgages, notes, bonds payable in 1 year or more				
20	Other liabilities (attach statement)				
21	Partners' capital accounts		1,680,700		1,753,698
22	Total liabilities and capital		2,234,398		2,977,525

Schedule M-1 — Reconciliation of Income (Loss) per Books With Income (Loss) per Return

Note. The partnership may be required to file Schedule M-3 (see instructions).

1	Net income (loss) per books	292,998	6	Income recorded on books this year not included on Schedule K, lines 1 through 11 (itemize):		
2	Income included on Schedule K, lines 1, 2, 3c, 5, 6a, 7, 8, 9a, 10, and 11, not recorded on books this year (itemize): _____		a	Tax-exempt interest $ _____		
3	Guaranteed payments (other than health insurance)	400,000	7	Deductions included on Schedule K, lines 1 through 13d, and 16l, not charged against book income this year (itemize):		
4	Expenses recorded on books this year not included on Schedule K, lines 1 through 13d, and 16l (itemize):		a	Depreciation $ _____		
a	Depreciation $ _____		8	Add lines 6 and 7		0
b	Travel and entertainment $ _____		9	Income (loss) (Analysis of Net Income (Loss), line 1. Subtract line 8 from line 5 .		
5	Add lines 1 through 4	692,998				692,998

Schedule M-2 — Analysis of Partners' Capital Accounts

1	Balance at beginning of year . . .	1,680,700	6	Distributions: a Cash		220,000
2	Capital contributed: **a** Cash . . .	0		**b** Property		
	b Property . .		7	Other decreases (itemize): _____		
3	Net income (loss) per books	292,998				
4	Other increases (itemize): _____		8	Add lines 6 and 7		220,000
5	Add lines 1 through 4	1,973,698	9	Balance at end of year. Subtract line 8 from line 5		1,753,698

SCHEDULE D (Form 1065) Department of the Treasury Internal Revenue Service	Capital Gains and Losses ► Attach to Form 1065 or Form 8865. ► Use Form 8949 to list your transactions for lines 1b, 2, 3, 8b, 9, and 10. ► Information about Schedule D (Form 1065) and its separate instructions is at *www.irs.gov/form1065*.	OMB No. 1545-0123 2014

Name of partnership	Employer identification number
B&J Computers	38-0801478

Part I Short-Term Capital Gains and Losses—Assets Held One Year or Less

See instructions for how to figure the amounts to enter on the lines below. This form may be easier to complete if you round off cents to whole dollars.	(d) Proceeds (sales price)	(e) Cost (or other basis)	(g) Adjustments to gain or loss from Form(s) 8949, Part I, line 2, column (g)	(h) Gain or (loss) Subtract column (e) from column (d) and combine the result with column (g)
1a Totals for all short-term transactions reported on Form 1099-B for which basis was reported to the IRS and for which you have no adjustments (see instructions). However, if you choose to report all these transactions on Form 8949, leave this line blank and go to line 1b .				
1b Totals for all transactions reported on Form(s) 8949 with **Box A** checked				
2 Totals for all transactions reported on Form(s) 8949 with **Box B** checked				
3 Totals for all transactions reported on Form(s) 8949 with **Box C** checked				

4 Short-term capital gain from installment sales from Form 6252, line 26 or 37	**4**	
5 Short-term capital gain or (loss) from like-kind exchanges from Form 8824	**5**	
6 Partnership's share of net short-term capital gain (loss), including specially allocated short-term capital gains (losses), from other partnerships, estates, and trusts	**0**	
7 Net short-term capital gain or (loss). Combine lines 1a through 6 in column (h). Enter here and on Form 1065, Schedule K, line 8 or 11; or Form 8865, Schedule K, line 8 or 11	**7**	

Part II Long-Term Capital Gains and Losses—Assets Held More Than One Year

See instructions for how to figure the amounts to enter on the lines below. This form may be easier to complete if you round off cents to whole dollars.	(d) Proceeds (sales price)	(e) Cost (or other basis)	(g) Adjustments to gain or loss from Form(s) 8949, Part II, line 2, column (g)	(h) Gain or (loss) Subtract column (e) from column (d) and combine the result with column (g)
8a Totals for all long-term transactions reported on Form 1099-B for which basis was reported to the IRS and for which you have no adjustments (see instructions). However, if you choose to report all these transactions on Form 8949, leave this line blank and go to line 8b .				
8b Totals for all transactions reported on Form(s) 8949 with **Box D** checked				
9 Totals for all transactions reported on Form(s) 8949 with **Box E** checked	283,000	172,000		111,000
10 Totals for all transactions reported on Form(s) 8949 with **Box F** checked				

11 Long-term capital gain from installment sales from Form 6252, line 26 or 37	**11**	
12 Long-term capital gain or (loss) from like-kind exchanges from Form 8824	**12**	
13 Partnership's share of net long-term capital gain (loss), including specially allocated long-term capital gains (losses), from other partnerships, estates, and trusts	**13**	
14 Capital gain distributions (see instructions)	**14**	
15 **Net long-term capital gain or (loss).** Combine lines 8a through 14 in column (h). Enter here and on Form 1065, Schedule K, line 9a or 11; or Form 8865, Schedule K, line 9a or 11	**15**	111,000

For Paperwork Reduction Act Notice, see the Instructions for Form 1065.   Cat. No. 11393G   Schedule D (Form 1065) 2014

Form **8949**

Department of the Treasury
Internal Revenue Service

Sales and Other Dispositions of Capital Assets

▶ Information about Form 8949 and its separate instructions is at *www.irs.gov/form8949*.
▶ File with your Schedule D to list your transactions for lines 1b, 2, 3, 8b, 9, and 10 of Schedule D.

OMB No. 1545-0074

2014

Attachment
Sequence No. **12A**

Name(s) shown on return	Social security number or taxpayer identification number
B&J Computers	38-0801478

Before you check Box A, B, or C below, see whether you received any Form(s) 1099-B or substitute statement(s) from your broker. A substitute statement will have the same information as Form 1099-B. Either may show your basis (usually your cost) even if your broker did not report it to the IRS. Brokers must report basis to the IRS for most stock you bought in 2011 or later (and for certain debt instruments you bought in 2014 or later).

Part I **Short-Term.** Transactions involving capital assets you held 1 year or less are short term. For long-term transactions, see page 2.

Note. You may aggregate all short-term transactions reported on Form(s) 1099-B showing basis was reported to the IRS and for which no adjustments or codes are required. Enter the total directly on Schedule D, line 1a; you are not required to report these transactions on Form 8949 (see instructions).

You *must* check Box A, B, *or* C below. Check only one box. If more than one box applies for your short-term transactions, complete a separate Form 8949, page 1, for each applicable box. If you have more short-term transactions than will fit on this page for one or more of the boxes, complete as many forms with the same box checked as you need.

- ☐ **(A)** Short-term transactions reported on Form(s) 1099-B showing basis was reported to the IRS (see **Note** above)
- ☐ **(B)** Short-term transactions reported on Form(s) 1099-B showing basis was **not** reported to the IRS
- ☐ **(C)** Short-term transactions not reported to you on Form 1099-B

1 (a) Description of property (Example: 100 sh. XYZ Co.)	(b) Date acquired (Mo., day, yr.)	(c) Date sold or disposed (Mo., day, yr.)	(d) Proceeds (sales price) (see instructions)	(e) Cost or other basis. See the **Note** below and see *Column (e)* in the separate instructions	Adjustment, if any, to gain or loss. If you enter an amount in column (g), enter a code in column (f). See the separate instructions. — (f) Code(s) from instructions	(g) Amount of adjustment	(h) Gain or (loss). Subtract column (e) from column (d) and combine the result with column (g)

2 Totals. Add the amounts in columns (d), (e), (g), and (h) (subtract negative amounts). Enter each total here and include on your Schedule D, **line 1b** (if **Box A** above is checked), **line 2** (if **Box B** above is checked), or **line 3** (if **Box C** above is checked) ▶

Note. If you checked Box A above but the basis reported to the IRS was incorrect, enter in column (e) the basis as reported to the IRS, and enter an adjustment in column (g) to correct the basis. See *Column (g)* in the separate instructions for how to figure the amount of the adjustment.

For Paperwork Reduction Act Notice, see your tax return instructions.　　Cat. No. 37768Z　　Form **8949** (2014)

Name(s) shown on return. Name and SSN or taxpayer identification no. not required if shown on other side	Social security number or taxpayer identification number
B&J Computers	38-0801478

Before you check Box D, E, or F below, see whether you received any Form(s) 1099-B or substitute statement(s) from your broker. A substitute statement will have the same information as Form 1099-B. Either may show your basis (usually your cost) even if your broker did not report it to the IRS. Brokers must report basis to the IRS for most stock you bought in 2011 or later (and for certain debt instruments you bought in 2014 or later).

Part II   **Long-Term.** Transactions involving capital assets you held more than 1 year are long term. For short-term transactions, see page 1.

Note. You may aggregate all long-term transactions reported on Form(s) 1099-B showing basis was reported to the IRS and for which no adjustments or codes are required. Enter the total directly on Schedule D, line 8a; you are not required to report these transactions on Form 8949 (see instructions).

You *must* check Box D, E, *or* F below. Check only one box. If more than one box applies for your long-term transactions, complete a separate Form 8949, page 2, for each applicable box. If you have more long-term transactions than will fit on this page for one or more of the boxes, complete as many forms with the same box checked as you need.

- ☐ **(D)** Long-term transactions reported on Form(s) 1099-B showing basis was reported to the IRS (see **Note** above)
- ☑ **(E)** Long-term transactions reported on Form(s) 1099-B showing basis was **not** reported to the IRS
- ☐ **(F)** Long-term transactions not reported to you on Form 1099-B

1 (a) Description of property (Example: 100 sh. XYZ Co.)	(b) Date acquired (Mo., day, yr.)	(c) Date sold or disposed (Mo., day, yr.)	(d) Proceeds (sales price) (see instructions)	(e) Cost or other basis. See the **Note** below and see *Column (e)* in the separate instructions	(f) Code(s) from instructions	(g) Amount of adjustment	(h) Gain or (loss). Subtract column (e) from column (d) and combine the result with column (g)
6.8 acres in Bad Axe, Michigan	2-15-2002	3-23-2014	225,000	150,000			75,000
10,000 shares Abinion Modem, Inc.	3-3-1999	4-2-2014	58,000	22,000			36,000
2 Totals. Add the amounts in columns (d), (e), (g), and (h) (subtract negative amounts). Enter each total here and include on your Schedule D, **line 8b** (if **Box D** above is checked), **line 9** (if **Box E** above is checked), or **line 10** (if **Box F** above is checked) ▶			283,000	172,000			111,000

Note. If you checked Box D above but the basis reported to the IRS was incorrect, enter in column (e) the basis as reported to the IRS, and enter an adjustment in column (g) to correct the basis. See *Column (g)* in the separate instructions for how to figure the amount of the adjustment.

§ 5.60 Filled-In Schedules K-1, Form 1065

651113

| Final K-1 | Amended K-1 | OMB No. 1545-0123 |

Schedule K-1 (Form 1065)

2014

Department of the Treasury
Internal Revenue Service

For calendar year 2014, or tax
year beginning _____ , 2014
ending _____ , 20 ___

Partner's Share of Income, Deductions, Credits, etc. ▶ See back of form and separate instructions.

Part III	Partner's Share of Current Year Income, Deductions, Credits, and Other Items

Part I	**Information About the Partnership**

A Partnership's employer identification number
38-0801478

B Partnership's name, address, city, state, and ZIP code

B&J Computers
20 Michigan Ave
Ann Arbor, Michigan 48239

C IRS Center where partnership filed return

D ☐ Check if this is a publicly traded partnership (PTP)

Part II	**Information About the Partner**

E Partner's identifying number
502-80-3458

F Partner's name, address, city, state, and ZIP code

Bill Benson
12 Arbor Blvd
Ann Arbor, Michigan 48239

G ☒ General partner or LLC member-manager ☐ Limited partner or other LLC member

H ☒ Domestic partner ☐ Foreign partner

I1 What type of entity is this partner? Individual

I2 If this partner is a retirement plan (IRA/SEP/Keogh/etc.), check here ☐

J Partner's share of profit, loss, and capital (see instructions):

	Beginning	Ending
Profit	%	55 %
Loss	%	55 %
Capital	%	55 %

K Partner's share of liabilities at year end:

Nonrecourse	$	495,000
Qualified nonrecourse financing	$	
Recourse	$	178,105

L Partner's capital account analysis:

Beginning capital account	$	312,200
Capital contributed during the year	$	
Current year increase (decrease)	$	146,848
Withdrawals & distributions	$ (	121,000)
Ending capital account	$	338,048

☐ Tax basis ☐ GAAP ☐ Section 704(b) book
☐ Other (explain)

M Did the partner contribute property with a built-in gain or loss?
☐ Yes ☒ No
If "Yes," attach statement (see instructions)

1	Ordinary business income (loss)		87,496	15	Credits
2	Net rental real estate income (loss)		3,522		
3	Other net rental income (loss)			16	Foreign transactions
4	Guaranteed payments		63,000		
5	Interest income		6,908		
6a	Ordinary dividends		4,895		
6b	Qualified dividends		4,895		
7	Royalties				
8	Net short-term capital gain (loss)				
9a	Net long-term capital gain (loss)		41,250	17	Alternative minimum tax (AMT) items 4,950
9b	Collectibles (28%) gain (loss)				
9c	Unrecaptured section 1250 gain				
10	Net section 1231 gain (loss)			18	Tax-exempt income and nondeductible expenses
11	Other income (loss)				
12	Section 179 deduction			19	Distributions 121,000
13	Other deductions		1,623	20	Other information
			3,000		
			1,100		
14	Self-employment earnings (loss)		72,147		

*See attached statement for additional information.

For IRS Use Only

For Paperwork Reduction Act Notice, see Instructions for Form 1065.   IRS.gov/form1065   Cat. No. 11394R   Schedule K-1 (Form 1065) 2014

☐ Final K-1	☐ Amended K-1	OMB No. 1545-0123

Schedule K-1
(Form 1065) 2014

Department of the Treasury
Internal Revenue Service

For calendar year 2014, or tax
year beginning _____, 2014
ending _____, 20_____

Partner's Share of Income, Deductions,
Credits, etc. ▶ See back of form and separate instructions.

Part III — Partner's Share of Current Year Income, Deductions, Credits, and Other Items

1	Ordinary business income (loss)	15	Credits
	31,817		
2	Net rental real estate income (loss)		
	1,281		
3	Other net rental income (loss)	16	Foreign transactions
4	Guaranteed payments		
	310,000		
5	Interest income		
	2,512		
6a	Ordinary dividends		
	1,780		
6b	Qualified dividends		
	1,780		
7	Royalties		
8	Net short-term capital gain (loss)		
9a	Net long-term capital gain (loss)	17	Alternative minimum tax (AMT) items
	15,000		1,800
9b	Collectibles (28%) gain (loss)		
9c	Unrecaptured section 1250 gain		
10	Net section 1231 gain (loss)	18	Tax-exempt income and nondeductible expenses
11	Other income (loss)		
		19	Distributions
12	Section 179 deduction		44,000
13	Other deductions		
A	590	20	Other information
I	400		
14	Self-employment earnings (loss)		
	*corporate taxpayer		

*See attached statement for additional information.

Part I — Information About the Partnership

A Partnership's employer identification number
38-0801478

B Partnership's name, address, city, state, and ZIP code

B&J Computers
20 Michigan Ave
Ann Arbor, Michigan 48239

C IRS Center where partnership filed return

D ☐ Check if this is a publicly traded partnership (PTP)

Part II — Information About the Partner

E Partner's identifying number
70-0809172

F Partner's name, address, city, state, and ZIP code

Premier Capital
1020 Mason Street
Fargo, North Dakota 58211

G ☒ General partner or LLC member-manager ☐ Limited partner or other LLC member

H ☒ Domestic partner ☐ Foreign partner

I1 What type of entity is this partner? Corporation

I2 If this partner is a retirement plan (IRA/SEP/Keogh/etc.), check here ☐

J Partner's share of profit, loss, and capital (see instructions):

	Beginning	Ending
Profit	%	20 %
Loss	%	20 %
Capital	%	20 %

K Partner's share of liabilities at year end:

Nonrecourse	$	180,000
Qualified nonrecourse financing	$	
Recourse	$	64,765

L Partner's capital account analysis:

Beginning capital account	$	1,240,000
Capital contributed during the year	$	
Current year increase (decrease)	$	53,400
Withdrawals & distributions	$ (	44,000)
Ending capital account	$	1,249,400

☐ Tax basis ☐ GAAP ☐ Section 704(b) book
☐ Other (explain)

M Did the partner contribute property with a built-in gain or loss?
☐ Yes ☒ No
If "Yes," attach statement (see instructions)

For IRS Use Only

For Paperwork Reduction Act Notice, see Instructions for Form 1065.   IRS.gov/form1065   Cat. No. 11394R   **Schedule K-1 (Form 1065) 2014**

651113

☐ Final K-1   ☐ Amended K-1   OMB No. 1545-0123

Schedule K-1
(Form 1065)

Department of the Treasury
Internal Revenue Service

2014

For calendar year 2014, or tax

year beginning _____ , 2014

ending _____ , 20 _____

Partner's Share of Income, Deductions, Credits, etc.
► See back of form and separate instructions.

Part I Information About the Partnership

A Partnership's employer identification number
38-0801478

B Partnership's name, address, city, state, and ZIP code

B&J Computers
20 Michigan Ave
Ann Arbor, Michigan 48239

C IRS Center where partnership filed return

D ☐ Check if this is a publicly traded partnership (PTP)

Part II Information About the Partner

E Partner's identifying number
309-89-8675

F Partner's name, address, city, state, and ZIP code

John Jackson
318 Pontiac
Novi, Michigan 48250

G ☒ General partner or LLC member-manager   ☐ Limited partner or other LLC member

H ☒ Domestic partner   ☐ Foreign partner

I1 What type of entity is this partner? Individual

I2 If this partner is a retirement plan (IRA/SEP/Keogh/etc.), check here . . . . ☐

J Partner's share of profit, loss, and capital (see instructions):

	Beginning	Ending
Profit	%	25 %
Loss	%	25 %
Capital	%	25 %

K Partner's share of liabilities at year end:

Nonrecourse . . . . . . $ 225,000
Qualified nonrecourse financing . $
Recourse . . . . $ 80,957

L Partner's capital account analysis:

Beginning capital account . . . $ 128,500
Capital contributed during the year $
Current year increase (decrease) . $ 92,750
Withdrawals & distributions . . $ (55,000)
Ending capital account . . . . $ 166,250

☐ Tax basis   ☐ GAAP   ☐ Section 704(b) book
☐ Other (explain)

M Did the partner contribute property with a built-in gain or loss?
☐ Yes   ☒ No
If "Yes," attach statement (see instructions)

Part III Partner's Share of Current Year Income, Deductions, Credits, and Other Items

#	Item	Amount	#	Item	Amount
1	Ordinary business income (loss)	39,770	15	Credits	
2	Net rental real estate income (loss)	1,602			
3	Other net rental income (loss)		16	Foreign transactions	
4	Guaranteed payments	30,000			
5	Interest income	3,140			
6a	Ordinary dividends	2,225			
6b	Qualified dividends	2,225			
7	Royalties				
8	Net short-term capital gain (loss)				
9a	Net long-term capital gain (loss)	54,750	17	Alternative minimum tax (AMT) items	
9b	Collectibles (28%) gain (loss)		A		2,250
9c	Unrecaptured section 1250 gain				
10	Net section 1231 gain (loss)		18	Tax-exempt income and nondeductible expenses	
11	Other income (loss)				
12	Section 179 deduction		19	Distributions	55,000
13	Other deductions				
	A	737	20	Other information	
	I	500			
14	Self-employment earnings (loss)	32,414			

*See attached statement for additional information.

For IRS Use Only

For Paperwork Reduction Act Notice, see Instructions for Form 1065.   IRS.gov/form1065   Cat. No. 11394R   Schedule K-1 (Form 1065) 2014

§ 5.80 Filled-In Form 4562

Form **4562**	**Depreciation and Amortization**	OMB No. 1545-0172
Department of the Treasury Internal Revenue Service (99)	**(Including Information on Listed Property)** ▶ Attach to your tax return. ▶ Information about Form 4562 and its separate instructions is at *www.irs.gov/form4562*.	**2014** Attachment Sequence No. **179**

Name(s) shown on return	Business or activity to which this form relates	Identifying number
B&J Computers	Manufacturing computer equipment	38-0801478

Part I Election To Expense Certain Property Under Section 179
Note: *If you have any listed property, complete Part V before you complete Part I.*

1	Maximum amount (see instructions)	1
2	Total cost of section 179 property placed in service (see instructions)	2
3	Threshold cost of section 179 property before reduction in limitation (see instructions)	3
4	Reduction in limitation. Subtract line 3 from line 2. If zero or less, enter -0-	4
5	Dollar limitation for tax year. Subtract line 4 from line 1. If zero or less, enter -0-. If married filing separately, see instructions	5

6	(a) Description of property	(b) Cost (business use only)	(c) Elected cost

7	Listed property. Enter the amount from line 29 . . . . [7]	
8	Total elected cost of section 179 property. Add amounts in column (c), lines 6 and 7	8
9	Tentative deduction. Enter the **smaller** of line 5 or line 8	9
10	Carryover of disallowed deduction from line 13 of your 2013 Form 4562	10
11	Business income limitation. Enter the smaller of business income (not less than zero) or line 5 (see instructions)	11
12	Section 179 expense deduction. Add lines 9 and 10, but do not enter more than line 11	12
13	Carryover of disallowed deduction to 2015. Add lines 9 and 10, less line 12 ▶ [13]	

Note: *Do not use Part II or Part III below for listed property. Instead, use Part V.*

Part II Special Depreciation Allowance and Other Depreciation (Do not include listed property.) (See instructions.)

14	Special depreciation allowance for qualified property (other than listed property) placed in service during the tax year (see instructions)	14	9,680
15	Property subject to section 168(f)(1) election	15	
16	Other depreciation (including ACRS)	16	

Part III MACRS Depreciation (Do not include listed property.) (See instructions.)

Section A

17	MACRS deductions for assets placed in service in tax years beginning before 2014	17	87,367
18	If you are electing to group any assets placed in service during the tax year into one or more general asset accounts, check here . . . . ▶ ☐		

Section B—Assets Placed in Service During 2014 Tax Year Using the General Depreciation System

(a) Classification of property	(b) Month and year placed in service	(c) Basis for depreciation (business/investment use only—see instructions)	(d) Recovery period	(e) Convention	(f) Method	(g) Depreciation deduction
19a 3-year property						
b 5-year property						
c 7-year property						
d 10-year property						
e 15-year property						
f 20-year property						
g 25-year property			25 yrs.		S/L	
h Residential rental property			27.5 yrs.	MM	S/L	
			27.5 yrs.	MM	S/L	
i Nonresidential real property			39 yrs.	MM	S/L	
				MM	S/L	

Section C—Assets Placed in Service During 2014 Tax Year Using the Alternative Depreciation System

20a Class life					S/L	
b 12-year			12 yrs.		S/L	
c 40-year			40 yrs.	MM	S/L	

Part IV Summary (See instructions.)

21	Listed property. Enter amount from line 28	21	
22	**Total.** Add amounts from line 12, lines 14 through 17, lines 19 and 20 in column (g), and line 21. Enter here and on the appropriate lines of your return. Partnerships and S corporations—see instructions	22	97,047
23	For assets shown above and placed in service during the current year, enter the portion of the basis attributable to section 263A costs . . . . . . [23]		

For Paperwork Reduction Act Notice, see separate instructions. Cat. No. 12906N Form **4562** (2014)

Part V **Listed Property** (Include automobiles, certain other vehicles, certain aircraft, certain computers, and property used for entertainment, recreation, or amusement.)

Note: *For any vehicle for which you are using the standard mileage rate or deducting lease expense, complete only 24a, 24b, columns (a) through (c) of Section A, all of Section B, and Section C if applicable.*

Section A—Depreciation and Other Information (Caution: *See the instructions for limits for passenger automobiles.***)**

24a Do you have evidence to support the business/investment use claimed? ☐ Yes ☐ No				24b If "Yes," is the evidence written? ☐ Yes ☐ No				
(a) Type of property (list vehicles first)	**(b)** Date placed in service	**(c)** Business/ investment use percentage	**(d)** Cost or other basis	**(e)** Basis for depreciation (business/investment use only)	**(f)** Recovery period	**(g)** Method/ Convention	**(h)** Depreciation deduction	**(i)** Elected section 179 cost
25 Special depreciation allowance for qualified listed property placed in service during the tax year and used more than 50% in a qualified business use (see instructions) . **25**								
26 Property used more than 50% in a qualified business use:								
		%						
		%						
		%						
27 Property used 50% or less in a qualified business use:								
		%				S/L –		
		%				S/L –		
		%				S/L –		
28 Add amounts in column (h), lines 25 through 27. Enter here and on line 21, page 1 . **28**								
29 Add amounts in column (i), line 26. Enter here and on line 7, page 1 . . . . **29**								

Section B—Information on Use of Vehicles

Complete this section for vehicles used by a sole proprietor, partner, or other "more than 5% owner," or related person. If you provided vehicles to your employees, first answer the questions in Section C to see if you meet an exception to completing this section for those vehicles.

		(a) Vehicle 1		**(b)** Vehicle 2		**(c)** Vehicle 3		**(d)** Vehicle 4		**(e)** Vehicle 5		**(f)** Vehicle 6	
30	Total business/investment miles driven during the year (**do not** include commuting miles) .												
31	Total commuting miles driven during the year												
32	Total other personal (noncommuting) miles driven												
33	Total miles driven during the year. Add lines 30 through 32												
34	Was the vehicle available for personal use during off-duty hours?	**Yes**	**No**	**Yes**	**No**	**Yes**	**No**	**Yes**	**No**	**Yes**	**No**	**Yes**	**No**
35	Was the vehicle used primarily by a more than 5% owner or related person? . .												
36	Is another vehicle available for personal use?												

Section C—Questions for Employers Who Provide Vehicles for Use by Their Employees

Answer these questions to determine if you meet an exception to completing Section B for vehicles used by employees who **are not** more than 5% owners or related persons (see instructions).

		Yes	No
37	Do you maintain a written policy statement that prohibits all personal use of vehicles, including commuting, by your employees?		
38	Do you maintain a written policy statement that prohibits personal use of vehicles, except commuting, by your employees? See the instructions for vehicles used by corporate officers, directors, or 1% or more owners . .		
39	Do you treat all use of vehicles by employees as personal use?		
40	Do you provide more than five vehicles to your employees, obtain information from your employees about the use of the vehicles, and retain the information received?		
41	Do you meet the requirements concerning qualified automobile demonstration use? (See instructions.) . . .		

Note: *If your answer to 37, 38, 39, 40, or 41 is "Yes," do not complete Section B for the covered vehicles.*

Part VI **Amortization**

(a) Description of costs	**(b)** Date amortization begins	**(c)** Amortizable amount	**(d)** Code section	**(e)** Amortization period or percentage	**(f)** Amortization for this year
42 Amortization of costs that begins during your 2014 tax year (see instructions):					
43 Amortization of costs that began before your 2014 tax year **43**					
44 **Total.** Add amounts in column (f). See the instructions for where to report **44**					

§ 5.100   Filled-In Form 4797

Form **4797**	**Sales of Business Property** (Also Involuntary Conversions and Recapture Amounts Under Sections 179 and 280F(b)(2)) ▶ Attach to your tax return. ▶ Information about Form 4797 and its separate instructions is at *www.irs.gov/form4797.*	OMB No. 1545-0184 **2014**
Department of the Treasury Internal Revenue Service		Attachment Sequence No. **27**

Name(s) shown on return	Identifying number
B&J Computers	38-0801478

| 1 | Enter the gross proceeds from sales or exchanges reported to you for 2014 on Form(s) 1099-B or 1099-S (or substitute statement) that you are including on line 2, 10, or 20 (see instructions) . . . . | **1** | |

Part I **Sales or Exchanges of Property Used in a Trade or Business and Involuntary Conversions From Other Than Casualty or Theft—Most Property Held More Than 1 Year** (see instructions)

2	(a) Description of property	(b) Date acquired (mo., day, yr.)	(c) Date sold (mo., day, yr.)	(d) Gross sales price	(e) Depreciation allowed or allowable since acquisition	(f) Cost or other basis, plus improvements and expense of sale	(g) Gain or (loss) Subtract (f) from the sum of (d) and (e)

3	Gain, if any, from Form 4684, line 39	**3**	
4	Section 1231 gain from installment sales from Form 6252, line 26 or 37	**4**	
5	Section 1231 gain or (loss) from like-kind exchanges from Form 8824	**5**	
6	Gain, if any, from line 32, from other than casualty or theft.	**6**	
7	Combine lines 2 through 6. Enter the gain or (loss) here and on the appropriate line as follows:	**7**	

> **Partnerships (except electing large partnerships) and S corporations.** Report the gain or (loss) following the instructions for Form 1065, Schedule K, line 10, or Form 1120S, Schedule K, line 9. Skip lines 8, 9, 11, and 12 below.
>
> **Individuals, partners, S corporation shareholders, and all others.** If line 7 is zero or a loss, enter the amount from line 7 on line 11 below and skip lines 8 and 9. If line 7 is a gain and you did not have any prior year section 1231 losses, or they were recaptured in an earlier year, enter the gain from line 7 as a long-term capital gain on the Schedule D filed with your return and skip lines 8, 9, 11, and 12 below.

| 8 | Nonrecaptured net section 1231 losses from prior years (see instructions) . . . . | **8** | |
| 9 | Subtract line 8 from line 7. If zero or less, enter 0 . If line 9 is zero, enter the gain from line 7 on line 12 below. If line 9 is more than zero, enter the amount from line 8 on line 12 below and enter the gain from line 9 as a long-term capital gain on the Schedule D filed with your return (see instructions) . . . . | **9** | |

Part II **Ordinary Gains and Losses** (see instructions)

10	Ordinary gains and losses not included on lines 11 through 16 (include property held 1 year or less):						

11	Loss, if any, from line 7	**11**	( )
12	Gain, if any, from line 7 or amount from line 8, if applicable	**12**	
13	Gain, if any, from line 31	**13**	3,000
14	Net gain or (loss) from Form 4684, lines 31 and 38a	**14**	
15	Ordinary gain from installment sales from Form 6252, line 25 or 36	**15**	
16	Ordinary gain or (loss) from like-kind exchanges from Form 8824.	**16**	
17	Combine lines 10 through 16	**17**	3,000

18	For all except individual returns, enter the amount from line 17 on the appropriate line of your return and skip lines a and b below. For individual returns, complete lines a and b below:		
a	If the loss on line 11 includes a loss from Form 4684, line 35, column (b)(ii), enter that part of the loss here. Enter the part of the loss from income-producing property on Schedule A (Form 1040), line 28, and the part of the loss from property used as an employee on Schedule A (Form 1040), line 23. Identify as from "Form 4797, line 18a." See instructions . .	**18a**	
b	Redetermine the gain or (loss) on line 17 excluding the loss, if any, on line 18a. Enter here and on Form 1040, line 14	**18b**	

For Paperwork Reduction Act Notice, see separate instructions.   Cat. No. 13086I   Form **4797** (2014)

Part III **Gain From Disposition of Property Under Sections 1245, 1250, 1252, 1254, and 1255**
(see instructions)

19	(a) Description of section 1245, 1250, 1252, 1254, or 1255 property:		(b) Date acquired (mo., day, yr.)	(c) Date sold (mo., day, yr.)
A	Automatic Assembly Robot		1-13-2011	6-18-2014
B				
C				
D				

	These columns relate to the properties on lines 19A through 19D. ▶		Property A	Property B	Property C	Property D
20	Gross sales price (**Note:** *See line 1 before completing.*)	20	95,400			
21	Cost or other basis plus expense of sale	21	220,000			
22	Depreciation (or depletion) allowed or allowable	22	127,600			
23	Adjusted basis. Subtract line 22 from line 21	23	92,400			
24	Total gain. Subtract line 23 from line 20	24	3,000			
25	**If section 1245 property:**					
a	Depreciation allowed or allowable from line 22	25a	127,600			
b	Enter the **smaller** of line 24 or 25a	25b	3,000			
26	**If section 1250 property:** If straight line depreciation was used, enter -0- on line 26g, except for a corporation subject to section 291.					
a	Additional depreciation after 1975 (see instructions)	26a				
b	Applicable percentage multiplied by the **smaller** of line 24 or line 26a (see instructions)	26b				
c	Subtract line 26a from line 24. If residential rental property or line 24 is not more than line 26a, skip lines 26d and 26e	26c				
d	Additional depreciation after 1969 and before 1976.	26d				
e	Enter the **smaller** of line 26c or 26d	26e				
f	Section 291 amount (corporations only)	26f				
g	Add lines 26b, 26e, and 26f.	26g				
27	**If section 1252 property:** Skip this section if you did not dispose of farmland or if this form is being completed for a partnership (other than an electing large partnership).					
a	Soil, water, and land clearing expenses	27a				
b	Line 27a multiplied by applicable percentage (see instructions)	27b				
c	Enter the **smaller** of line 24 or 27b	27c				
28	**If section 1254 property:**					
a	Intangible drilling and development costs, expenditures for development of mines and other natural deposits, mining exploration costs, and depletion (see instructions)	28a				
b	Enter the **smaller** of line 24 or 28a	28b				
29	**If section 1255 property:**					
a	Applicable percentage of payments excluded from income under section 126 (see instructions)	29a				
b	Enter the **smaller** of line 24 or 29a (see instructions)	29b				

Summary of Part III Gains. Complete property columns A through D through line 29b before going to line 30.

30	Total gains for all properties. Add property columns A through D, line 24	30	3,000
31	Add property columns A through D, lines 25b, 26g, 27c, 28b, and 29b. Enter here and on line 13	31	3,000
32	Subtract line 31 from line 30. Enter the portion from casualty or theft on Form 4684, line 33. Enter the portion from other than casualty or theft on Form 4797, line 6	32	0

Part IV **Recapture Amounts Under Sections 179 and 280F(b)(2) When Business Use Drops to 50% or Less**
(see instructions)

			(a) Section 179	(b) Section 280F(b)(2)
33	Section 179 expense deduction or depreciation allowable in prior years	33		
34	Recomputed depreciation (see instructions)	34		
35	Recapture amount. Subtract line 34 from line 33. See the instructions for where to report	35		

§ 6.20 Filled-In Form 1041

Form **1041**
Department of the Treasury—Internal Revenue Service
U.S. Income Tax Return for Estates and Trusts
2014
OMB No. 1545-0092

▶ Information about Form 1041 and its separate instructions is at *www.irs.gov/form1041.*

A Check all that apply:

For calendar year 2014 or fiscal year beginning _____ , 2014, and ending _____ , 20 ____

A Check all that apply:		
☐ Decedent's estate		
☐ Simple trust	Name of estate or trust (If a grantor type trust, see the instructions.)	**C** Employer identification number
☑ Complex trust	Samuel Johnson Trust	32-0014568
☐ Qualified disability trust	Name and title of fiduciary	**D** Date entity created
☐ ESBT (S portion only)	First National Bank, Trustee	6-23-2000
☐ Grantor type trust	Number, street, and room or suite no. (If a P.O. box, see the instructions.)	**E** Nonexempt charitable and split-interest trusts, check applicable box(es), see instructions.
☐ Bankruptcy estate-Ch. 7	200 N.W. Second Street	☐ Described in sec. 4947(a)(1). Check here if not a private foundation . . ▶ ☐
☐ Bankruptcy estate-Ch. 11	City or town, state or province, country, and ZIP or foreign postal code	
☐ Pooled income fund	Red Fox, Montana 41614	☐ Described in sec. 4947(a)(2)

B Number of Schedules K-1 attached (see instructions) ▶ 1

F Check applicable boxes:
☐ Initial return ☐ Final return ☐ Amended return ☐ Net operating loss carryback
☐ Change in trust's name ☐ Change in fiduciary ☐ Change in fiduciary's name ☐ Change in fiduciary's address

G Check here if the estate or filing trust made a section 645 election . . . . . . ▶ ☐ Trust TIN ▶

Income

1	Interest income	**1**	12,147
2a	Total ordinary dividends	**2a**	2,405
b	Qualified dividends allocable to: **(1)** Beneficiaries _____ **(2)** Estate or trust _____ 2,405		
3	Business income or (loss). Attach Schedule C or C-EZ (Form 1040) . . .	**3**	
4	Capital gain or (loss). Attach Schedule D (Form 1041)	**4**	8,210
5	Rents, royalties, partnerships, other estates and trusts, etc. Attach Schedule E (Form 1040)	**5**	9,985
6	Farm income or (loss). Attach Schedule F (Form 1040)	**6**	
7	Ordinary gain or (loss). Attach Form 4797	**7**	
8	Other income. List type and amount _____	**8**	
9	**Total income.** Combine lines 1, 2a, and 3 through 8 . . . . ▶	**9**	32,747

Deductions

10	Interest. Check if Form 4952 is attached ▶ ☐	**10**	1,680
11	Taxes	**11**	490
12	Fiduciary fees	**12**	1,004
13	Charitable deduction (from Schedule A, line 7)	**13**	2,000
14	Attorney, accountant, and return preparer fees	**14**	
15a	Other deductions **not** subject to the 2% floor (attach schedule) . . .	**15a**	
b	Net operating loss deduction (see instructions)	**15b**	
c	Allowable miscellaneous itemized deductions subject to the 2% floor . . .	**15c**	727
16	Add lines 10 through 15c . . . . ▶	**16**	5,901
17	Adjusted total income or (loss). Subtract line 16 from line 9 . . . | **17** | 26,846		
18	Income distribution deduction (from Schedule B, line 15). Attach Schedules K-1 (Form 1041)	**18**	15,997
19	Estate tax deduction including certain generation-skipping taxes (attach computation) . . .	**19**	
20	Exemption	**20**	100
21	Add lines 18 through 20 . . . . ▶	**21**	16,097

Tax and Payments

22	Taxable income. Subtract line 21 from line 17. If a loss, see instructions	**22**	10,749
23	**Total tax** (from Schedule G, line 7)	**23**	1,815
24	**Payments: a** 2014 estimated tax payments and amount applied from 2013 return	**24a**	540
b	Estimated tax payments allocated to beneficiaries (from Form 1041-T)	**24b**	0
c	Subtract line 24b from line 24a	**24c**	540
d	Tax paid with Form 7004 (see instructions)	**24d**	
e	Federal income tax withheld. If any is from Form(s) 1099, check ▶ ☐	**24e**	
	Other payments: **f** Form 2439 _____ ; **g** Form 4136 _____ ; Total ▶	**24h**	
25	**Total payments.** Add lines 24c through 24e, and 24h	**25**	540
26	Estimated tax penalty (see instructions)	**26**	0
27	**Tax due.** If line 25 is smaller than the total of lines 23 and 26, enter amount owed	**27**	1,275
28	**Overpayment.** If line 25 is larger than the total of lines 23 and 26, enter amount overpaid . .	**28**	
29	Amount of line 28 to be: **a Credited to 2015 estimated tax** ▶ _____ ; **b Refunded** ▶	**29**	

Sign Here

Under penalties of perjury, I declare that I have examined this return, including accompanying schedules and statements, and to the best of my knowledge and belief, it is true, correct, and complete. Declaration of preparer (other than taxpayer) is based on all information of which preparer has any knowledge.

▶ _____ Signature of fiduciary or officer representing fiduciary   Date   ▶ 46-8358724 EIN of fiduciary if a financial institution

May the IRS discuss this return with the preparer shown below (see instr.)? ☑ Yes ☐ No

Paid Preparer Use Only

Print/Type preparer's name	Preparer's signature	Date	Check ☑ if self-employed	PTIN
Alan Young	*Alan Young*			

Firm's name ▶ Alan Young, CPA   Firm's EIN ▶

Firm's address ▶ 100 N.W. Second Street, Red Fox, Montana 41614   Phone no.

For Paperwork Reduction Act Notice, see the separate instructions.   Cat. No. 11370H   Form **1041** (2014)

Schedule A	Charitable Deduction. Do not complete for a simple trust or a pooled income fund.		
1	Amounts paid or permanently set aside for charitable purposes from gross income (see instructions)	1	2,000
2	Tax-exempt income allocable to charitable contributions (see instructions)	2	
3	Subtract line 2 from line 1	3	2,000
4	Capital gains for the tax year allocated to corpus and paid or permanently set aside for charitable purposes	4	
5	Add lines 3 and 4	5	2,000
6	Section 1202 exclusion allocable to capital gains paid or permanently set aside for charitable purposes (see instructions)	6	
7	**Charitable deduction.** Subtract line 6 from line 5. Enter here and on page 1, line 13	7	2,000

Schedule B	Income Distribution Deduction		
1	Adjusted total income (see instructions)	1	26,846
2	Adjusted tax-exempt interest	2	4,944
3	Total net gain from Schedule D (Form 1041), line 19, column (1) (see instructions)	3	
4	Enter amount from Schedule A, line 4 (minus any allocable section 1202 exclusion)	4	
5	Capital gains for the tax year included on Schedule A, line 1 (see instructions)	5	
6	Enter any gain from page 1, line 4, as a negative number. If page 1, line 4, is a loss, enter the loss as a positive number	6	(8,210)
7	**Distributable net income.** Combine lines 1 through 6. If zero or less, enter -0-	7	23,580
8	If a complex trust, enter accounting income for the tax year as determined under the governing instrument and applicable local law **8** 38,162		
9	Income required to be distributed currently	9	18,000
10	Other amounts paid, credited, or otherwise required to be distributed	10	2,250
11	Total distributions. Add lines 9 and 10. If greater than line 8, see instructions	11	20,250
12	Enter the amount of tax-exempt income included on line 11	12	4,253
13	Tentative income distribution deduction. Subtract line 12 from line 11	13	15,997
14	Tentative income distribution deduction. Subtract line 2 from line 7. If zero or less, enter -0-	14	18,636
15	**Income distribution deduction.** Enter the smaller of line 13 or line 14 here and on page 1, line 18	15	15,997

Schedule G	Tax Computation (see instructions)			
1	**Tax: a** Tax on taxable income (see instructions)	1a	1,257	
	b Tax on lump-sum distributions. Attach Form 4972	1b		
	c Alternative minimum tax (from Schedule I (Form 1041), line 56)	1c	0	
	d Total. Add lines 1a through 1c	1d		1,257
2a	Foreign tax credit. Attach Form 1116	2a		
b	General business credit. Attach Form 3800	2b		
c	Credit for prior year minimum tax. Attach Form 8801	2c		
d	Bond credits. Attach Form 8912	2d		
e	**Total credits.** Add lines 2a through 2d	2e		0
3	Subtract line 2e from line 1d. If zero or less, enter -0-	3		1,257
4	Net investment income tax from Form 8960, line 21	4		558
5	Recapture taxes. Check if from: ☐ Form 4255 ☐ Form 8611	5		
6	Household employment taxes. Attach Schedule H (Form 1040)	6		
7	**Total tax.** Add lines 3 through 6. Enter here and on page 1, line 23	7		1,815

	Other Information	Yes	No
1	Did the estate or trust receive tax-exempt income? If "Yes," attach a computation of the allocation of expenses. Enter the amount of tax-exempt interest income and exempt-interest dividends ▶ $ _____ 5,415	✓	
2	Did the estate or trust receive all or any part of the earnings (salary, wages, and other compensation) of any individual by reason of a contract assignment or similar arrangement?		✓
3	At any time during calendar year 2014, did the estate or trust have an interest in or a signature or other authority over a bank, securities, or other financial account in a foreign country?		✓
	See the instructions for exceptions and filing requirements for FinCEN Form 114. If "Yes," enter the name of the foreign country ▶ _____		
4	During the tax year, did the estate or trust receive a distribution from, or was it the grantor of, or transferor to, a foreign trust? If "Yes," the estate or trust may have to file Form 3520. See instructions		✓
5	Did the estate or trust receive, or pay, any qualified residence interest on seller-provided financing? If "Yes," see the instructions for required attachment		✓
6	If this is an estate or a complex trust making the section 663(b) election, check here (see instructions) ▶ ☐		
7	To make a section 643(e)(3) election, attach Schedule D (Form 1041), and check here (see instructions) ▶ ☐		
8	If the decedent's estate has been open for more than 2 years, attach an explanation for the delay in closing the estate, and check here ▶ ☐		
9	Are any present or future trust beneficiaries skip persons? See instructions		✓

§ 6.21 Filled-In Schedule I, Form 1041

SCHEDULE I (Form 1041) Department of the Treasury Internal Revenue Service	**Alternative Minimum Tax—Estates and Trusts** ► Attach to Form 1041. ► Information about Schedule I (Form 1041) and its separate instructions is at *www.irs.gov/form1041*.	OMB No. 1545-0092 2014

Name of estate or trust	Employer identification number
Samuel Johnson Trust	32-0014568

Part I — Estate's or Trust's Share of Alternative Minimum Taxable Income

1	Adjusted total income or (loss) (from Form 1041, line 17)	**1**	26,846
2	Interest	**2**	
3	Taxes	**3**	490
4	Miscellaneous itemized deductions (from Form 1041, line 15c)	**4**	727
5	Refund of taxes	**5**	( )
6	Depletion (difference between regular tax and AMT)	**6**	
7	Net operating loss deduction. Enter as a positive amount	**7**	
8	Interest from specified private activity bonds exempt from the regular tax	**8**	
9	Qualified small business stock (see instructions)	**9**	
10	Exercise of incentive stock options (excess of AMT income over regular tax income)	**10**	
11	Other estates and trusts (amount from Schedule K-1 (Form 1041), box 12, code A)	**11**	
12	Electing large partnerships (amount from Schedule K-1 (Form 1065-B), box 6)	**12**	
13	Disposition of property (difference between AMT and regular tax gain or loss)	**13**	
14	Depreciation on assets placed in service after 1986 (difference between regular tax and AMT)	**14**	
15	Passive activities (difference between AMT and regular tax income or loss)	**15**	
16	Loss limitations (difference between AMT and regular tax income or loss)	**16**	
17	Circulation costs (difference between regular tax and AMT)	**17**	
18	Long-term contracts (difference between AMT and regular tax income)	**18**	
19	Mining costs (difference between regular tax and AMT)	**19**	
20	Research and experimental costs (difference between regular tax and AMT)	**20**	
21	Income from certain installment sales before January 1, 1987	**21**	( )
22	Intangible drilling costs preference	**22**	
23	Other adjustments, including income-based related adjustments	**23**	
24	Alternative tax net operating loss deduction (See the instructions for the limitation that applies.)	**24**	( )
25	Adjusted alternative minimum taxable income. Combine lines 1 through 24	**25**	28,063
	Note: *Complete Part II below before going to line 26.*		
26	Income distribution deduction from Part II, line 44	**26** 15,997	
27	Estate tax deduction (from Form 1041, line 19)	**27**	
28	Add lines 26 and 27	**28**	15,997
29	Estate's or trust's share of alternative minimum taxable income. Subtract line 28 from line 25	**29**	12,066

If line 29 is:
- $23,500 or less, stop here and enter -0- on Form 1041, Schedule G, line 1c. The estate or trust is not liable for the alternative minimum tax.
- Over $23,500, but less than $172,250, go to line 45.
- $172,250 or more, enter the amount from line 29 on line 51 and go to line 52.

Part II — Income Distribution Deduction on a Minimum Tax Basis

30	Adjusted alternative minimum taxable income (see instructions)	**30**	28,063
31	Adjusted tax-exempt interest (other than amounts included on line 8)	**31**	4,944
32	Total net gain from Schedule D (Form 1041), line 19, column (1). If a loss, enter -0-	**32**	
33	Capital gains for the tax year allocated to corpus and paid or permanently set aside for charitable purposes (from Form 1041, Schedule A, line 4)	**33**	
34	Capital gains paid or permanently set aside for charitable purposes from gross income (see instructions)	**34**	
35	Capital gains computed on a minimum tax basis included on line 25	**35**	(8,210)
36	Capital losses computed on a minimum tax basis included on line 25. Enter as a positive amount	**36**	
37	Distributable net alternative minimum taxable income (DNAMTI). Combine lines 30 through 36. If zero or less, enter -0-	**37**	24,797
38	Income required to be distributed currently (from Form 1041, Schedule B, line 9)	**38**	18,000
39	Other amounts paid, credited, or otherwise required to be distributed (from Form 1041, Schedule B, line 10)	**39**	2,250
40	Total distributions. Add lines 38 and 39	**40**	20,250
41	Tax-exempt income included on line 40 (other than amounts included on line 8)	**41**	4,253
42	Tentative income distribution deduction on a minimum tax basis. Subtract line 41 from line 40	**42**	15,997

For Paperwork Reduction Act Notice, see the Instructions for Form 1041.　　　Cat. No. 51517Q　　　Schedule I (Form 1041) (2014)

Part II	Income Distribution Deduction on a Minimum Tax Basis *(continued)*			
43	Tentative income distribution deduction on a minimum tax basis. Subtract line 31 from line 37. If zero or less, enter -0-		**43**	19,853
44	**Income distribution deduction on a minimum tax basis.** Enter the smaller of line 42 or line 43. Enter here and on line 26		**44**	15,997

Part III	Alternative Minimum Tax				
45	Exemption amount			**45**	$23,500 00
46	Enter the amount from line 29	**46**	12,066		
47	Phase-out of exemption amount	**47**	$78,250 00		
48	Subtract line 47 from line 46. If zero or less, enter -0-	**48**	0		
49	Multiply line 48 by 25% (.25)			**49**	0
50	Subtract line 49 from line 45. If zero or less, enter -0-			**50**	23,500
51	Subtract line 50 from line 46			**51**	0
52	Go to Part IV of Schedule I to figure line 52 if the estate or trust has qualified dividends or has a gain on lines 18a and 19 of column (2) of Schedule D (Form 1041) (as refigured for the AMT, if necessary). Otherwise, if line 51 is—				
	• $182,500 or less, multiply line 51 by 26% (.26).				
	• Over $182,500, multiply line 51 by 28% (.28) and subtract $3,650 from the result			**52**	0
53	Alternative minimum foreign tax credit (see instructions)			**53**	
54	Tentative minimum tax. Subtract line 53 from line 52			**54**	0
55	Enter the tax from Form 1041, Schedule G, line 1a (minus any foreign tax credit from Schedule G, line 2a)			**55**	1,257
56	**Alternative minimum tax.** Subtract line 55 from line 54. If zero or less, enter -0-. Enter here and on Form 1041, Schedule G, line 1c			**56**	0

Part IV	Line 52 Computation Using Maximum Capital Gains Rates				
	Caution: *If you did not complete Part V of Schedule D (Form 1041), the Schedule D Tax Worksheet, or the Qualified Dividends Tax Worksheet in the Instructions for Form 1041, see the instructions before completing this part.*				
57	Enter the amount from line 51			**57**	0
58	Enter the amount from Schedule D (Form 1041), line 26, line 13 of the Schedule D Tax Worksheet, or line 4 of the Qualified Dividends Tax Worksheet in the Instructions for Form 1041, whichever applies (as refigured for the AMT, if necessary)	**58**	10,615		
59	Enter the amount from Schedule D (Form 1041), line 18b, column (2) (as refigured for the AMT, if necessary). If you did not complete Schedule D for the regular tax or the AMT, enter -0-	**59**	0		
60	If you did not complete a Schedule D Tax Worksheet for the regular tax or the AMT, enter the amount from line 58. Otherwise, add lines 58 and 59 and enter the **smaller** of that result or the amount from line 10 of the Schedule D Tax Worksheet (as refigured for the AMT, if necessary)	**60**	10,615		
61	Enter the **smaller** of line 57 or line 60			**61**	0
62	Subtract line 61 from line 57			**62**	0
63	If line 62 is $182,500 or less, multiply line 62 by 26% (.26). Otherwise, multiply line 62 by 28% (.28) and subtract $3,650 from the result ▶			**63**	0
64	Maximum amount subject to the 0% rate	**64**	$2,500 00		
65	Enter the amount from line 27 of Schedule D (Form 1041), line 14 of the Schedule D Tax Worksheet, or line 5 of the Qualified Dividends Tax Worksheet in the Instructions for Form 1041, whichever applies (as figured for the regular tax). If you did not complete Schedule D or either worksheet for the regular tax, enter the amount from Form 1041, line 22; if zero or less, enter -0-	**65**	134		
66	Subtract line 65 from line 64. If zero or less, enter -0-	**66**	2,316		
67	Enter the **smaller** of line 57 or line 58	**67**	0		
68	Enter the **smaller** of line 66 or line 67. This amount is taxed at 0%	**68**	0		
69	Subtract line 68 from line 67	**69**	0		

Part IV	Line 52 Computation Using Maximum Capital Gains Rates *(continued)*			
70	Maximum amount subject to rates below 20%	**70**	$12,150	00
71	Enter the amount from line 66	**71**	2,316	
72	Enter the amount from line 27 of Schedule D (Form 1041), line 18 of the Schedule D Tax Worksheet, or line 5 of the Qualified Dividends Tax Worksheet, whichever applies (as figured for the regular tax). If you did not complete Schedule D or either worksheet for the regular tax, enter the amount from Form 1041, line 22; if zero or less, enter -0- . ▶	**72**	134	
73	Add line 71 and line 72	**73**	2,450	
74	Subtract line 73 from line 70. If zero or less, enter -0-	**74**	9,700	
75	Enter the **smaller** of line 69 or 74	**75**	0	
76	Multiply line 75 by 15% (.15) . . . . ▶	**76**	0	
77	Add lines 68 and 75	**77**	0	
	If lines 77 and 57 are the same, skip lines 78 through 82 and go to line 83. Otherwise, go to line 78.			
78	Subtract line 77 from line 67	**78**		
79	Multiply line 78 by 20% (.20) . . . . ▶	**79**		
	If line 59 is zero or blank, skip lines 80 through 82 and go to line 83. Otherwise, go to line 80.			
80	Add lines 62, 77, and 78	**80**		
81	Subtract line 80 from line 57	**81**		
82	Multiply line 81 by 25% (.25) . . . . ▶	**82**		
83	Add lines 63, 76, 79, and 82	**83**	0	
84	If line 57 is $182,500 or less, multiply line 57 by 26% (.26). Otherwise, multiply line 57 by 28% (.28) and subtract $3,650 from the result	**84**	0	
85	Enter the **smaller** of line 83 or line 84 here and on line 52	**85**	0	

§ 6.22 Filled-In Schedule K-1, Form 1041

661113

☐ Final K-1   ☐ Amended K-1   OMB No. 1545-0092

**Schedule K-1
(Form 1041)**
Department of the Treasury
Internal Revenue Service

2014

For calendar year 2014,
or tax year beginning _____ , 2014,
and ending _____ , 20 _____

Beneficiary's Share of Income, Deductions, Credits, etc.

▶ **See back of form and instructions.**

Part I	Information About the Estate or Trust

A Estate's or trust's employer identification number

32-0014568

B Estate's or trust's name

Samuel Johnson Trust

C Fiduciary's name, address, city, state, and ZIP code

First National Bank, Trustee
200 N.W. 2nd Street
Red Fox, Montana 41614

D ☐ Check if Form 1041-T was filed and enter the date it was filed

_____

E ☒ Check if this is the final Form 1041 for the estate or trust

Part II	Information About the Beneficiary

F Beneficiary's identifying number

463-97-0923

G Beneficiary's name, address, city, state, and ZIP code

Samuel Johnson
200 Briarwood Lane
Sun Valley Farms, Idaho 65891

H ☒ Domestic beneficiary   ☐ Foreign beneficiary

Part III	Beneficiary's Share of Current Year Income, Deductions, Credits, and Other Items
1 Interest income	**11** Final year deductions
7,695	
2a Ordinary dividends	
405	
2b Qualified dividends	
405	
3 Net short-term capital gain	
4a Net long-term capital gain	
4b 28% rate gain	**12** Alternative minimum tax adjustment
4c Unrecaptured section 1250 gain	
5 Other portfolio and nonbusiness income	
2,430	
6 Ordinary business income	
7 Net rental real estate income	
5,467	**13** Credits and credit recapture
8 Other rental income	
9 Directly apportioned deductions	
	14 Other information
10 Estate tax deduction	A 4,253

*See attached statement for additional information.

Note. A statement must be attached showing the beneficiary's share of income and directly apportioned deductions from each business, rental real estate, and other rental activity.

For IRS Use Only

For Paperwork Reduction Act Notice, see the Instructions for Form 1041.   IRS.gov/form1041   Cat. No. 11380D   Schedule K-1 (Form 1041) 2014

§ 6.23 Filled-In Schedule E, Form 1040

SCHEDULE E (Form 1040) Department of the Treasury Internal Revenue Service (99)	**Supplemental Income and Loss** (From rental real estate, royalties, partnerships, S corporations, estates, trusts, REMICs, etc.) ► Attach to Form 1040, 1040NR, or Form 1041. ►Information about Schedule E and its separate instructions is at *www.irs.gov/schedulee*.	OMB No. 1545-0074 20**14** Attachment Sequence No. **13**

Name(s) shown on return	Your social security number
Samuel Johnson Trust	32-0014568

Part I Income or Loss From Rental Real Estate and Royalties Note. If you are in the business of renting personal property, use Schedule C or C-EZ (see instructions). If you are an individual, report farm rental income or loss from Form 4835 on page 2, line 40.

A Did you make any payments in 2014 that would require you to file Form(s) 1099? (see instructions) ☐ Yes ☑ No

B If "Yes," did you or will you file required Forms 1099? ☐ Yes ☐ No

1a	Physical address of each property (street, city, state, ZIP code)
A	Red Fox Mall, Red Fox, Montana 41614
B	
C	

1b	Type of Property (from list below)	2	For each rental real estate property listed above, report the number of fair rental and personal use days. Check the **QJV** box only if you meet the requirements to file as a qualified joint venture. See instructions.		Fair Rental Days	Personal Use Days	QJV
A	4			A	365	0	☐
B				B			☐
C				C			☐

Type of Property:

1 Single Family Residence 3 Vacation/Short-Term Rental 5 Land 7 Self-Rental
2 Multi-Family Residence 4 Commercial 6 Royalties 8 Other (describe)

Income:	Properties:		A	B	C
3	Rents received	3	29,820		
4	Royalties received	4	0		
Expenses:					
5	Advertising	5	645		
6	Auto and travel (see instructions)	6	144		
7	Cleaning and maintenance	7	1,040		
8	Commissions.	8			
9	Insurance	9	2,180		
10	Legal and other professional fees	10			
11	Management fees	11	1,200		
12	Mortgage interest paid to banks, etc. (see instructions)	12			
13	Other interest.	13			
14	Repairs.	14	1,611		
15	Supplies	15	553		
16	Taxes	16	3,000		
17	Utilities.	17	2,467		
18	Depreciation expense or depletion	18	10,000		
19	Other (list) ► _____	19			
20	Total expenses. Add lines 5 through 19	20	22,840		
21	Subtract line 20 from line 3 (rents) and/or 4 (royalties). If result is a (loss), see instructions to find out if you must file **Form 6198**	21	6,980		
22	Deductible rental real estate loss after limitation, if any, on **Form 8582** (see instructions)	22	( )	( )	( )

23a	Total of all amounts reported on line 3 for all rental properties	23a	29,820	
b	Total of all amounts reported on line 4 for all royalty properties	23b	0	
c	Total of all amounts reported on line 12 for all properties	23c	0	
d	Total of all amounts reported on line 18 for all properties	23d	10,000	
e	Total of all amounts reported on line 20 for all properties	23e	22,840	

24	**Income.** Add positive amounts shown on line 21. **Do not** include any losses	24	6,980
25	**Losses.** Add royalty losses from line 21 and rental real estate losses from line 22. Enter total losses here	25	( )
26	**Total rental real estate and royalty income or (loss).** Combine lines 24 and 25. Enter the result here. If Parts II, III, IV, and line 40 on page 2 do not apply to you, also enter this amount on Form 1040, line 17, or Form 1040NR, line 18. Otherwise, include this amount in the total on line 41 on page 2	26	6,980

For Paperwork Reduction Act Notice, see the separate instructions. Cat. No. 11344L Schedule E (Form 1040) 2014

Name(s) shown on return. Do not enter name and social security number if shown on other side.	Your social security number
Samuel Johnson Trust	32-0014568

Caution. The IRS compares amounts reported on your tax return with amounts shown on Schedule(s) K-1.

Part II   Income or Loss From Partnerships and S Corporations

Note. If you report a loss from an at-risk activity for which **any** amount is **not** at risk, you **must** check the box in column **(e)** on line 28 and attach **Form 6198.** See instructions.

27   Are you reporting any loss not allowed in a prior year due to the at-risk, excess farm loss, or basis limitations, a prior year unallowed loss from a passive activity (if that loss was not reported on Form 8582), or unreimbursed partnership expenses? If you answered "Yes," see instructions before completing this section.   ☐ **Yes**   ☐ **No**

28

(a) Name	(b) Enter P for partnership; S for S corporation	(c) Check if foreign partnership	(d) Employer identification number	(e) Check if any amount is not at risk
A BKB Ltd. Domestic Partnership	P	☐	01-3386924	☐
B		☐		☐
C		☐		☐
D		☐		☐

	Passive Income and Loss		Nonpassive Income and Loss		
	(f) Passive loss allowed (attach **Form 8582** if required)	(g) Passive income from **Schedule K-1**	(h) Nonpassive loss from **Schedule K-1**	(i) Section 179 expense deduction from **Form 4562**	(j) Nonpassive income from **Schedule K-1**
A		3,005			
B					
C					
D					
29a Totals		3,005			
b Totals					

30	Add columns (g) and (j) of line 29a	**30**	3,005
31	Add columns (f), (h), and (i) of line 29b	**31** (	0)
32	**Total partnership and S corporation income or (loss).** Combine lines 30 and 31. Enter the result here and include in the total on line 41 below	**32**	3,005

Part III   Income or Loss From Estates and Trusts

33

(a) Name	(b) Employer identification number
A	
B	

	Passive Income and Loss		Nonpassive Income and Loss	
	(c) Passive deduction or loss allowed (attach **Form 8582** if required)	(d) Passive income from **Schedule K-1**	(e) Deduction or loss from **Schedule K-1**	(f) Other income from **Schedule K-1**
A				
B				
34a Totals				
b Totals				

35	Add columns (d) and (f) of line 34a	**35**	
36	Add columns (c) and (e) of line 34b	**36** (	)
37	**Total estate and trust income or (loss).** Combine lines 35 and 36. Enter the result here and include in the total on line 41 below	**37**	

Part IV   Income or Loss From Real Estate Mortgage Investment Conduits (REMICs)—Residual Holder

38

(a) Name	(b) Employer identification number	(c) Excess inclusion from Schedules Q, line 2c (see instructions)	(d) Taxable income (net loss) from Schedules Q, line 1b	(e) Income from Schedules Q, line 3b

39	Combine columns (d) and (e) only. Enter the result here and include in the total on line 41 below	**39**	

Part V   Summary

40	Net farm rental income or (loss) from **Form 4835.** Also, complete line 42 below	**40**	
41	Total income or (loss). Combine lines 26, 32, 37, 39, and 40. Enter the result here and on Form 1040, line 17, or Form 1040NR, line 18 ▶	**41**	9,985
42	**Reconciliation of farming and fishing income.** Enter your **gross** farming and fishing income reported on Form 4835, line 7; Schedule K-1 (Form 1065), box 14, code B; Schedule K-1 (Form 1120S), box 17, code V; and Schedule K-1 (Form 1041), box 14, code F (see instructions) . .	**42**	
43	**Reconciliation for real estate professionals.** If you were a real estate professional (see instructions), enter the net income or (loss) you reported anywhere on Form 1040 or Form 1040NR from all rental real estate activities in which you materially participated under the passive activity loss rules . .	**43**	

SCHEDULE D (Form 1041) Department of the Treasury Internal Revenue Service	**Capital Gains and Losses** ► Attach to Form 1041, Form 5227, or Form 990-T. ► Use Form 8949 to list your transactions for lines 1b, 2, 3, 8b, 9 and 10. ► Information about Schedule D and its separate instructions is at *www.irs.gov/form1041.*	OMB No. 1545-0092 20**14**

Name of estate or trust	Employer identification number
Samuel Johnson Trust	32-0014568

Note: *Form 5227 filers need to complete **only** Parts I and II.*

Part I Short-Term Capital Gains and Losses—Assets Held One Year or Less

	(d) Proceeds (sales price)	**(e)** Cost (or other basis)	**(g)** Adjustments to gain or loss from Form(s) 8949, Part I, line 2, column (g)	**(h) Gain or (loss)** Subtract column (e) from column (d) and combine the result with column (g)
See instructions for how to figure the amounts to enter on the lines below. This form may be easier to complete if you round off cents to whole dollars.				
1a Totals for all short-term transactions reported on Form 1099-B for which basis was reported to the IRS and for which you have no adjustments (see instructions). However, if you choose to report all these transactions on Form 8949, leave this line blank and go to line 1b .				
1b Totals for all transactions reported on Form(s) 8949 with **Box A** checked				
2 Totals for all transactions reported on Form(s) 8949 with **Box B** checked				
3 Totals for all transactions reported on Form(s) 8949 with **Box C** checked				

4 Short-term capital gain or (loss) from Forms 4684, 6252, 6781, and 8824	**4**	
5 Net short-term gain or (loss) from partnerships, S corporations, and other estates or trusts . . .	**5**	
6 Short-term capital loss carryover. Enter the amount, if any, from line 9 of the 2013 Capital Loss Carryover Worksheet	**6** (	)
7 **Net short-term capital gain or (loss).** Combine lines 1a through 6 in column (h). Enter here and on line 17, column (3) on the back . . . . ►	**7**	

Part II Long-Term Capital Gains and Losses—Assets Held More Than One Year

	(d) Proceeds (sales price)	**(e)** Cost (or other basis)	**(g)** Adjustments to gain or loss from Form(s) 8949, Part II, line 2, column (g)	**(h) Gain or (loss)** Subtract column (e) from column (d) and combine the result with column (g)
See instructions for how to figure the amounts to enter on the lines below. This form may be easier to complete if you round off cents to whole dollars.				
8a Totals for all long-term transactions reported on Form 1099-B for which basis was reported to the IRS and for which you have no adjustments (see instructions). However, if you choose to report all these transactions on Form 8949, leave this line blank and go to line 8b .				
8b Totals for all transactions reported on Form(s) 8949 with **Box D** checked				
9 Totals for all transactions reported on Form(s) 8949 with **Box E** checked	15,860	7,650		8,210
10 Totals for all transactions reported on Form(s) 8949 with **Box F** checked				

11 Long-term capital gain or (loss) from Forms 2439, 4684, 6252, 6781, and 8824	**11**	
12 Net long-term gain or (loss) from partnerships, S corporations, and other estates or trusts . . .	**12**	
13 Capital gain distributions	**13**	
14 Gain from Form 4797, Part I	**14**	
15 Long-term capital loss carryover. Enter the amount, if any, from line 14 of the 2013 Capital Loss Carryover Worksheet	**15** (	)
16 **Net long-term capital gain or (loss).** Combine lines 8a through 15 in column (h). Enter here and on line 18a, column (3) on the back . . . . ►	**16**	8,210

For Paperwork Reduction Act Notice, see the Instructions for Form 1041.   Cat. No. 11376V   Schedule D (Form 1041) 2014

Part III	**Summary of Parts I and II** Caution: *Read the instructions before completing this part.*		**(1) Beneficiaries'** (see instr.)	**(2) Estate's** or trust's	**(3) Total**
17	Net short-term gain or (loss)	17			
18	Net long-term gain or (loss):				
a	Total for year	18a		8,210	8,210
b	Unrecaptured section 1250 gain (see line 18 of the wrksht.) .	18b			
c	28% rate gain	18c			
19	**Total net gain or (loss).** Combine lines 17 and 18a . . ▶	19		8,210	8,210

Note: *If line 19, column (3), is a net gain, enter the gain on Form 1041, line 4 (or Form 990-T, Part I, line 4a). If lines 18a and 19, column (2), are net gains, go to Part V, and **do not** complete Part IV. If line 19, column (3), is a net loss, complete Part IV and the **Capital Loss Carryover Worksheet,** as necessary.*

Part IV	**Capital Loss Limitation**			
20	Enter here and enter as a (loss) on Form 1041, line 4 (or Form 990-T, Part I, line 4c, if a trust), the **smaller** of:			
a	The loss on line 19, column (3) **or b** $3,000		20 (	)

Note: *If the loss on line 19, column (3), is more than $3,000, or if Form 1041, page 1, line 22 (or Form 990-T, line 34), is a loss, complete the **Capital Loss Carryover Worksheet** in the instructions to figure your capital loss carryover.*

Part V	**Tax Computation Using Maximum Capital Gains Rates**

Form 1041 filers. Complete this part **only** if both lines 18a and 19 in column (2) are gains, or an amount is entered in Part I or Part II and there is an entry on Form 1041, line 2b(2), **and** Form 1041, line 22, is more than zero.

Caution: *Skip this part and complete the **Schedule D Tax Worksheet** in the instructions if:*

- *Either line 18b, col. (2) or line 18c, col. (2) is more than zero, or*
- *Both Form 1041, line 2b(1), and Form 4952, line 4g are more than zero.*

Form 990-T trusts. Complete this part **only** if both lines 18a and 19 are gains, or qualified dividends are included in income in Part I of Form 990-T, **and** Form 990-T, line 34, is more than zero. Skip this part and complete the **Schedule D Tax Worksheet** in the instructions if either line 18b, col. (2) or line 18c, col. (2) is more than zero.

21	Enter taxable income from Form 1041, line 22 (or Form 990-T, line 34) . .	21	10,749		
22	Enter the **smaller** of line 18a or 19 in column (2) but not less than zero	22	8,210		
23	Enter the estate's or trust's qualified dividends from Form 1041, line 2b(2) (or enter the qualified dividends included in income in Part I of Form 990-T)	23	2,405		
24	Add lines 22 and 23	24	10,615		
25	If the estate or trust is filing Form 4952, enter the amount from line 4g; otherwise, enter -0- . . ▶	25	0		
26	Subtract line 25 from line 24. If zero or less, enter -0-	26	10,615		
27	Subtract line 26 from line 21. If zero or less, enter -0-	27	134		
28	Enter the **smaller** of the amount on line 21 or $2,500	28	2,500		
29	Enter the **smaller** of the amount on line 27 or line 28	29	134		
30	Subtract line 29 from line 28. If zero or less, enter -0-. This amount is taxed at 0% . . . . . ▶	30			2,366
31	Enter the **smaller** of line 21 or line 26	31	10,615		
32	Subtract line 30 from line 26	32	8,249		
33	Enter the **smaller** of line 21 or $12,150	33	10,749		
34	Add lines 27 and 30	34	2,500		
35	Subtract line 34 from line 33. If zero or less, enter -0-	35	8,249		
36	Enter the **smaller** of line 32 or line 35	36	8,249		
37	Multiply line 36 by 15% . . . . ▶	37			1,237
38	Enter the amount from line 31	38	10,615		
39	Add lines 30 and 36	39	10,615		
40	Subtract line 39 from line 38. If zero or less, enter -0-	40	0		
41	Multiply line 40 by 20% . . . . ▶	41			0
42	Figure the tax on the amount on line 27. Use the 2014 Tax Rate Schedule for Estates and Trusts (see the Schedule G instructions in the instructions for Form 1041) . .	42	20		
43	Add lines 37, 41, and 42	43	1,257		
44	Figure the tax on the amount on line 21. Use the 2014 Tax Rate Schedule for Estates and Trusts (see the Schedule G instructions in the instructions for Form 1041) . .	44	2,678		
45	**Tax on all taxable income.** Enter the **smaller** of line 43 or line 44 here and on Form 1041, Schedule G, line 1a (or Form 990-T, line 36) . . . . ▶	45			1,257

Form **8949**

Department of the Treasury
Internal Revenue Service

Sales and Other Dispositions of Capital Assets

▶ Information about Form 8949 and its separate instructions is at *www.irs.gov/form8949.*
▶ File with your Schedule D to list your transactions for lines 1b, 2, 3, 8b, 9, and 10 of Schedule D.

OMB No. 1545-0074

2014

Attachment
Sequence No. **12A**

Name(s) shown on return	Social security number or taxpayer identification number
Samuel Johnson Trust	32-0014568

Before you check Box A, B, or C below, see whether you received any Form(s) 1099-B or substitute statement(s) from your broker. A substitute statement will have the same information as Form 1099-B. Either may show your basis (usually your cost) even if your broker did not report it to the IRS. Brokers must report basis to the IRS for most stock you bought in 2011 or later (and for certain debt instruments you bought in 2014 or later).

Part I   **Short-Term.** Transactions involving capital assets you held 1 year or less are short term. For long-term transactions, see page 2.

Note. You may aggregate all short-term transactions reported on Form(s) 1099-B showing basis was reported to the IRS and for which no adjustments or codes are required. Enter the total directly on Schedule D, line 1a; you are not required to report these transactions on Form 8949 (see instructions).

You *must* check Box A, B, *or* C below. Check only one box. If more than one box applies for your short-term transactions, complete a separate Form 8949, page 1, for each applicable box. If you have more short-term transactions than will fit on this page for one or more of the boxes, complete as many forms with the same box checked as you need.

- ☐ **(A)** Short-term transactions reported on Form(s) 1099-B showing basis was reported to the IRS (see **Note** above)
- ☐ **(B)** Short-term transactions reported on Form(s) 1099-B showing basis was **not** reported to the IRS
- ☐ **(C)** Short-term transactions not reported to you on Form 1099-B

1 **(a)** Description of property (Example: 100 sh. XYZ Co.)	**(b)** Date acquired (Mo., day, yr.)	**(c)** Date sold or disposed (Mo., day, yr.)	**(d)** Proceeds (sales price) (see instructions)	**(e)** Cost or other basis. See the **Note** below and see *Column (e)* in the separate instructions	Adjustment, if any, to gain or loss. If you enter an amount in column (g), enter a code in column (f). **See the separate instructions.**		**(h)** Gain or (loss). Subtract column (e) from column (d) and combine the result with column (g)
					(f) Code(s) from instructions	**(g)** Amount of adjustment	
2 Totals. Add the amounts in columns (d), (e), (g), and (h) (subtract negative amounts). Enter each total here and include on your Schedule D, **line 1b** (if **Box A** above is checked), **line 2** (if **Box B** above is checked), or **line 3** (if **Box C** above is checked) ▶							

Note. If you checked Box A above but the basis reported to the IRS was incorrect, enter in column (e) the basis as reported to the IRS, and enter an adjustment in column (g) to correct the basis. See *Column (g)* in the separate instructions for how to figure the amount of the adjustment.

For Paperwork Reduction Act Notice, see your tax return instructions.   Cat. No. 37768Z   Form **8949** (2014)

Name(s) shown on return. Name and SSN or taxpayer identification no. not required if shown on other side	Social security number or taxpayer identification number
Samuel Johnson Trust	32-0014568

Before you check Box D, E, or F below, see whether you received any Form(s) 1099-B or substitute statement(s) from your broker. A substitute statement will have the same information as Form 1099-B. Either may show your basis (usually your cost) even if your broker did not report it to the IRS. Brokers must report basis to the IRS for most stock you bought in 2011 or later (and for certain debt instruments you bought in 2014 or later).

Part II   **Long-Term.** Transactions involving capital assets you held more than 1 year are long term. For short-term transactions, see page 1.

Note. You may aggregate all long-term transactions reported on Form(s) 1099-B showing basis was reported to the IRS and for which no adjustments or codes are required. Enter the total directly on Schedule D, line 8a; you are not required to report these transactions on Form 8949 (see instructions).

You *must* check Box D, E, *or* F below. Check only one box. If more than one box applies for your long-term transactions, complete a separate Form 8949, page 2, for each applicable box. If you have more long-term transactions than will fit on this page for one or more of the boxes, complete as many forms with the same box checked as you need.

- ☐ **(D)** Long-term transactions reported on Form(s) 1099-B showing basis was reported to the IRS (see **Note** above)
- ☑ **(E)** Long-term transactions reported on Form(s) 1099-B showing basis was **not** reported to the IRS
- ☐ **(F)** Long-term transactions not reported to you on Form 1099-B

1 **(a)** Description of property (Example: 100 sh. XYZ Co.)	**(b)** Date acquired (Mo., day, yr.)	**(c)** Date sold or disposed (Mo., day, yr.)	**(d)** Proceeds (sales price) (see instructions)	**(e)** Cost or other basis. See the **Note** below and see *Column (e)* in the separate instructions	**(f)** Code(s) from instructions	**(g)** Amount of adjustment	**(h)** Gain or (loss). Subtract column (e) from column (d) and combine the result with column (g)
2.2-acre land located in Red Fox, Montana	6-23-1993	1-15-2014	15,860	7,650			8,210
2 Totals. Add the amounts in columns (d), (e), (g), and (h) (subtract negative amounts). Enter each total here and include on your Schedule D, **line 8b** (if **Box D** above is checked), **line 9** (if **Box E** above is checked), or **line 10** (if **Box F** above is checked) ▶			15,860	7,650			8,210

Note. If you checked Box D above but the basis reported to the IRS was incorrect, enter in column (e) the basis as reported to the IRS, and enter an adjustment in column (g) to correct the basis. See *Column (g)* in the separate instructions for how to figure the amount of the adjustment.

Form **2210**	Underpayment of Estimated Tax by Individuals, Estates, and Trusts	OMB No. 1545-0074
Department of the Treasury Internal Revenue Service	▶ Information about Form 2210 and its separate instructions is at *www.irs.gov/form2210.* ▶ Attach to Form 1040, 1040A, 1040NR, 1040NR-EZ, or 1041.	**20**14 Attachment Sequence No. **06**

Name(s) shown on tax return	Identifying number
Samuel Johnson Trust	32-0014568

Do You Have To File Form 2210?

Complete lines 1 through 7 below. Is line 7 less than $1,000? → **Yes** → **Do not file Form 2210.** You do not owe a penalty.

↓ **No**

Complete lines 8 and 9 below. Is line 6 equal to or more than line 9? → **Yes** → You do not owe a penalty. **Do not file Form 2210** (but if box E in Part II applies, you must file page 1 of Form 2210).

↓ **No**

You may owe a penalty. Does any box in Part II below apply? → **Yes** → You **must** file Form 2210. Does box **B, C,** or **D** in Part II apply?

↓ **No** → **No** / **Yes** → You must figure your penalty.

Do not file Form 2210. You are not required to figure your penalty because the IRS will figure it and send you a bill for any unpaid amount. If you want to figure it, you may use Part III or Part IV as a worksheet and enter your penalty amount on your tax return, but **do not file Form 2210.**

You are **not** required to figure your penalty because the IRS will figure it and send you a bill for any unpaid amount. If you want to figure it, you may use Part III or Part IV as a worksheet and enter your penalty amount on your tax return, but **file only page 1 of Form 2210.**

Part I	Required Annual Payment		
1	Enter your 2014 tax after credits from Form 1040, line 56 (see instructions if not filing Form 1040)	**1**	1,815
2	Other taxes, including self-employment tax and, if applicable, Additional Medicare Tax and/or Net Investment Income Tax (see instructions)	**2**	0
3	Refundable credits, including the premium tax credit (see instructions)	**3** (	0)
4	Current year tax. Combine lines 1, 2, and 3. If less than $1,000, **stop;** you do not owe a penalty. **Do not** file Form 2210	**4**	1,815
5	Multiply line 4 by 90% (.90) **5**	1,634	
6	Withholding taxes. **Do not** include estimated tax payments (see instructions)	**6**	0
7	Subtract line 6 from line 4. If less than $1,000, **stop;** you do not owe a penalty. **Do not** file Form 2210	**7**	1,815
8	Maximum required annual payment based on prior year's tax (see instructions)	**8**	540
9	**Required annual payment.** Enter the **smaller** of line 5 or line 8	**9**	540

Next: Is line 9 more than line 6?

☐ **No.** You **do not** owe a penalty. **Do not** file Form 2210 unless box **E** below applies.

☑ **Yes.** You may owe a penalty, but **do not** file Form 2210 unless one or more boxes in Part II below applies.

- If box **B, C,** or **D** applies, you must figure your penalty and file Form 2210.
- If box **A** or **E** applies (but not **B, C,** or **D**) file only page 1 of Form 2210. You are **not** required to figure your penalty; the IRS will figure it and send you a bill for any unpaid amount. If you want to figure your penalty, you may use Part III or IV as a worksheet and enter your penalty on your tax return, but **file only page 1 of Form 2210.**

Part II	Reasons for Filing. Check applicable boxes. If none apply, **do not** file Form 2210.

A ☐ You request a **waiver** (see instructions) of your entire penalty. You must check this box and file page 1 of Form 2210, but you are not required to figure your penalty.

B ☐ You request a **waiver** (see instructions) of part of your penalty. You must figure your penalty and waiver amount and file Form 2210.

C ☐ Your income varied during the year and your penalty is reduced or eliminated when figured using the **annualized income installment method.** You must figure the penalty using Schedule AI and file Form 2210.

D ☐ Your penalty is lower when figured by treating the federal income tax withheld from your income as paid on the dates it was actually withheld, instead of in equal amounts on the payment due dates. You must figure your penalty and file Form 2210.

E ☐ You filed or are filing a joint return for either 2013 or 2014, but not for both years, and line 8 above is smaller than line 5 above. You must file page 1 of Form 2210, but you are **not** required to figure your penalty (unless box **B, C,** or **D** applies).

For Paperwork Reduction Act Notice, see separate instructions.   Cat. No. 11744P   Form **2210** (2014)

Part III | Short Method

Can You Use the Short Method?	You can use the short method if: • You made no estimated tax payments (or your only payments were withheld federal income tax), **or** • You paid the same amount of estimated tax on each of the four payment due dates.
Must You Use the Regular Method?	You must use the regular method (Part IV) instead of the short method if: • You made any estimated tax payments late, • You checked box **C** or **D** in Part II, **or** • You are filing Form 1040NR or 1040NR-EZ and you did not receive wages as an employee subject to U.S. income tax withholding.

Note. *If any payment was made earlier than the due date, you can use the short method, but using it may cause you to pay a larger penalty than the regular method. If the payment was only a few days early, the difference is likely to be small.*

10	Enter the amount from Form 2210, line 9 . . .	**10**	540
11	Enter the amount, if any, from Form 2210, line 6 . . . . **11** 0		
12	Enter the total amount, if any, of estimated tax payments you made . **12** 540		
13	Add lines 11 and 12 . . .	**13**	540
14	**Total underpayment for year.** Subtract line 13 from line 10. If zero or less, **stop;** you do not owe a penalty. **Do not file Form 2210 unless you checked box E in Part II** . . .	**14**	0
15	Multiply line 14 by .01995 . . .	**15**	
16	• If the amount on line 14 was paid **on or after** 4/15/15, enter -0-. • If the amount on line 14 was paid **before** 4/15/15, make the following computation to find the amount to enter on line 16. Amount on Number of days paid line 14 × before 4/15/15 × .00008 . . .	**16**	
17	**Penalty.** Subtract line 16 from line 15. Enter the result here and on Form 1040, line 79; Form 1040A, line 51; Form 1040NR, line 76; Form 1040NR-EZ, line 26; or Form 1041, line 26. **Do not file Form 2210 unless you checked a box in Part II** . . . ▶	**17**	

Form **2210** (2014)

Part IV Regular Method (See the instructions if you are filing Form 1040NR or 1040NR-EZ.)

Section A—Figure Your Underpayment		Payment Due Dates			
		(a) 4/15/14	**(b)** 6/15/14	**(c)** 9/15/14	**(d)** 1/15/15
18 Required installments. If box C in Part II applies, enter the amounts from Schedule AI, line 25. Otherwise, enter 25% (.25) of line 9, Form 2210, in each column	**18**				
19 Estimated tax paid and tax withheld (see the instructions). For column (a) only, also enter the amount from line 19 on line 23. If line 19 is equal to or more than line 18 for all payment periods, stop here; you do not owe a penalty. **Do not file Form 2210 unless you checked a box in Part II**	**19**				
Complete lines 20 through 26 of one column before going to line 20 of the next column.					
20 Enter the amount, if any, from line 26 in the previous column	**20**				
21 Add lines 19 and 20	**21**				
22 Add the amounts on lines 24 and 25 in the previous column	**22**				
23 Subtract line 22 from line 21. If zero or less, enter -0-. For column (a) only, enter the amount from line 19	**23**				
24 If line 23 is zero, subtract line 21 from line 22. Otherwise, enter -0-	**24**				
25 **Underpayment.** If line 18 is equal to or more than line 23, subtract line 23 from line 18. Then go to line 20 of the next column. Otherwise, go to line 26 . ▶	**25**				
26 Overpayment. If line 23 is more than line 18, subtract line 18 from line 23. Then go to line 20 of the next column	**26**				

Section B—Figure the Penalty (Use the Worksheet for Form 2210, Part IV, Section B—Figure the Penalty in the instructions.)

27 **Penalty.** Enter the total penalty from line 14 of the Worksheet for Form 2210, Part IV, Section B—Figure the Penalty. Also include this amount on Form 1040, line 79; Form 1040A, line 51; Form 1040NR, line 76; Form 1040NR-EZ, line 26; or Form 1041, line 26. **Do not file Form 2210 unless you checked a box in Part II** . . . . ▶		**27**	

Schedule AI—Annualized Income Installment Method (See the instructions.)

Estates and trusts, **do not** use the period ending dates shown to the right. Instead, use the following: 2/28/14, 4/30/14, 7/31/14, and 11/30/14.

		(a) 1/1/14–3/31/14	(b) 1/1/14–5/31/14	(c) 1/1/14–8/31/14	(d) 1/1/14–12/31/14
Part I	**Annualized Income Installments**				
1	Enter your adjusted gross income for each period (see instructions). (Estates and trusts, enter your taxable income without your exemption for each period.) **1**				
2	Annualization amounts. (Estates and trusts, see instructions) **2**	4	2.4	1.5	1
3	Annualized income. Multiply line 1 by line 2 **3**				
4	If you itemize, enter itemized deductions for the period shown in each column. All others enter -0-, and skip to line 7. **Exception:** Estates and trusts, skip to line 9 and enter amount from line 3 **4**				
5	Annualization amounts **5**	4	2.4	1.5	1
6	Multiply line 4 by line 5 (see instructions if line 3 is more than $152,525) **6**				
7	In each column, enter the full amount of your standard deduction from Form 1040, line 40, or Form 1040A, line 24. (Form 1040NR or 1040NR-EZ filers, enter -0-. **Exception:** Indian students and business apprentices, see instructions.) **7**				
8	Enter the **larger** of line 6 or line 7 **8**				
9	Subtract line 8 from line 3 **9**				
10	In each column, multiply $3,950 by the total number of exemptions claimed (see instructions if line 3 is more than $152,525). (Estates, trusts, and Form 1040NR or 1040NR-EZ filers, see instructions.) **10**				
11	Subtract line 10 from line 9. If zero or less, enter -0- **11**				
12	Figure your tax on the amount on line 11 (see instructions) **12**				
13	Self-employment tax from line 34 (complete Part II below) **13**				
14	Enter other taxes for each payment period including, if applicable, Additional Medicare Tax and/or Net Investment Income Tax (see instructions) **14**				
15	Total tax. Add lines 12, 13, and 14 **15**				
16	For each period, enter the same type of credits as allowed on Form 2210, Part I, lines 1 and 3 (see instructions) **16**				
17	Subtract line 16 from line 15. If zero or less, enter -0- **17**				
18	Applicable percentage **18**	22.5%	45%	67.5%	90%
19	Multiply line 17 by line 18 **19**				
	Complete lines 20–25 of one column before going to line 20 of the next column.				
20	Enter the total of the amounts in all previous columns of line 25 **20**				
21	Subtract line 20 from line 19. If zero or less, enter -0- **21**				
22	Enter 25% (.25) of line 9 on page 1 of Form 2210 in each column **22**				
23	Subtract line 25 of the previous column from line 24 of that column **23**				
24	Add lines 22 and 23 **24**				
25	Enter the **smaller** of line 21 or line 24 here and on Form 2210, Part IV, line 18 ▶ **25**				
Part II	**Annualized Self-Employment Tax** (Form 1040 and Form 1040NR filers only)				
26	Net earnings from self-employment for the period (see instructions) **26**				
27	Prorated social security tax limit **27**	$29,250	$48,750	$78,000	$117,000
28	Enter actual wages for the period subject to social security tax or the 6.2% portion of the 7.65% railroad retirement (tier 1) tax. **Exception:** If you filed Form 4137 or Form 8919, see instructions **28**				
29	Subtract line 28 from line 27. If zero or less, enter -0- **29**				
30	Annualization amounts **30**	0.496	0.2976	0.186	0.124
31	Multiply line 30 by the **smaller** of line 26 or line 29 **31**				
32	Annualization amounts **32**	0.116	0.0696	0.0435	0.029
33	Multiply line 26 by line 32 **33**				
34	Add lines 31 and 33. Enter here and on line 13 above ▶ **34**				

§ 6.26 Filled-In Form 4562

Form **4562**	**Depreciation and Amortization**	OMB No. 1545-0172
	(Including Information on Listed Property)	**2014**
Department of the Treasury Internal Revenue Service (99)	▶ Attach to your tax return. ▶ Information about Form 4562 and its separate instructions is at *www.irs.gov/form4562*.	Attachment Sequence No. **179**

Name(s) shown on return	Business or activity to which this form relates	Identifying number
Samuel Johnson Trust	Rental Property	32-0014568

Part I — Election To Expense Certain Property Under Section 179
Note: *If you have any listed property, complete Part V before you complete Part I.*

1	Maximum amount (see instructions)	**1**
2	Total cost of section 179 property placed in service (see instructions)	**2**
3	Threshold cost of section 179 property before reduction in limitation (see instructions)	**3**
4	Reduction in limitation. Subtract line 3 from line 2. If zero or less, enter -0-	**4**
5	Dollar limitation for tax year. Subtract line 4 from line 1. If zero or less, enter -0-. If married filing separately, see instructions	**5**

6	(a) Description of property	(b) Cost (business use only)	(c) Elected cost

7	Listed property. Enter the amount from line 29 . . . . . . **7**	
8	Total elected cost of section 179 property. Add amounts in column (c), lines 6 and 7	**8**
9	Tentative deduction. Enter the **smaller** of line 5 or line 8	**9**
10	Carryover of disallowed deduction from line 13 of your 2013 Form 4562	**10**
11	Business income limitation. Enter the smaller of business income (not less than zero) or line 5 (see instructions)	**11**
12	Section 179 expense deduction. Add lines 9 and 10, but do not enter more than line 11	**12**
13	Carryover of disallowed deduction to 2015. Add lines 9 and 10, less line 12 ▶ **13**	

Note: *Do not use Part II or Part III below for listed property. Instead, use Part V.*

Part II — Special Depreciation Allowance and Other Depreciation (Do not include listed property.) (See instructions.)

14	Special depreciation allowance for qualified property (other than listed property) placed in service during the tax year (see instructions)	**14**
15	Property subject to section 168(f)(1) election	**15**
16	Other depreciation (including ACRS)	**16** 10,000

Part III — MACRS Depreciation (Do not include listed property.) (See instructions.)

Section A

17	MACRS deductions for assets placed in service in tax years beginning before 2014	**17**
18	If you are electing to group any assets placed in service during the tax year into one or more general asset accounts, check here ▶ ☐	

Section B—Assets Placed in Service During 2014 Tax Year Using the General Depreciation System

(a) Classification of property	(b) Month and year placed in service	(c) Basis for depreciation (business/investment use only—see instructions)	(d) Recovery period	(e) Convention	(f) Method	(g) Depreciation deduction
19a 3-year property						
b 5-year property						
c 7-year property						
d 10-year property						
e 15-year property						
f 20-year property						
g 25-year property			25 yrs.		S/L	
h Residential rental property			27.5 yrs.	MM	S/L	
			27.5 yrs.	MM	S/L	
i Nonresidential real property			39 yrs.	MM	S/L	
				MM	S/L	

Section C—Assets Placed in Service During 2014 Tax Year Using the Alternative Depreciation System

20a Class life					S/L	
b 12-year			12 yrs.		S/L	
c 40-year			40 yrs.	MM	S/L	

Part IV — Summary (See instructions.)

21	Listed property. Enter amount from line 28	**21**
22	**Total.** Add amounts from line 12, lines 14 through 17, lines 19 and 20 in column (g), and line 21. Enter here and on the appropriate lines of your return. Partnerships and S corporations—see instructions	**22** 10,000
23	For assets shown above and placed in service during the current year, enter the portion of the basis attributable to section 263A costs **23**	

For Paperwork Reduction Act Notice, see separate instructions. Cat. No. 12906N Form **4562** (2014)

Part V Listed Property (Include automobiles, certain other vehicles, certain aircraft, certain computers, and property used for entertainment, recreation, or amusement.)

Note: *For any vehicle for which you are using the standard mileage rate or deducting lease expense, complete **only** 24a, 24b, columns (a) through (c) of Section A, all of Section B, and Section C if applicable.*

Section A—Depreciation and Other Information (Caution: *See the instructions for limits for passenger automobiles.*)

24a Do you have evidence to support the business/investment use claimed? ☐ **Yes** ☐ **No**   **24b** If "Yes," is the evidence written? ☐ **Yes** ☐ **No**

(a) Type of property (list vehicles first)	(b) Date placed in service	(c) Business/investment use percentage	(d) Cost or other basis	(e) Basis for depreciation (business/investment use only)	(f) Recovery period	(g) Method/ Convention	(h) Depreciation deduction	(i) Elected section 179 cost
25 Special depreciation allowance for qualified listed property placed in service during the tax year and used more than 50% in a qualified business use (see instructions) . **25**								
26 Property used more than 50% in a qualified business use:								
		%						
		%						
		%						
27 Property used 50% or less in a qualified business use:								
		%				S/L –		
		%				S/L –		
		%				S/L –		

28 Add amounts in column (h), lines 25 through 27. Enter here and on line 21, page 1 . **28**

29 Add amounts in column (i), line 26. Enter here and on line 7, page 1 . . . . **29**

Section B—Information on Use of Vehicles

Complete this section for vehicles used by a sole proprietor, partner, or other "more than 5% owner," or related person. If you provided vehicles to your employees, first answer the questions in Section C to see if you meet an exception to completing this section for those vehicles.

		(a) Vehicle 1		(b) Vehicle 2		(c) Vehicle 3		(d) Vehicle 4		(e) Vehicle 5		(f) Vehicle 6	
30 Total business/investment miles driven during the year (**do not** include commuting miles) .													
31 Total commuting miles driven during the year													
32 Total other personal (noncommuting) miles driven													
33 Total miles driven during the year. Add lines 30 through 32													
34 Was the vehicle available for personal use during off-duty hours?	Yes	No	Yes	No	Yes	No	Yes	No	Yes	No	Yes	No
35 Was the vehicle used primarily by a more than 5% owner or related person? . .													
36 Is another vehicle available for personal use?													

Section C—Questions for Employers Who Provide Vehicles for Use by Their Employees

Answer these questions to determine if you meet an exception to completing Section B for vehicles used by employees who **are not** more than 5% owners or related persons (see instructions).

	Yes	No
37 Do you maintain a written policy statement that prohibits all personal use of vehicles, including commuting, by your employees?		
38 Do you maintain a written policy statement that prohibits personal use of vehicles, except commuting, by your employees? See the instructions for vehicles used by corporate officers, directors, or 1% or more owners . .		
39 Do you treat all use of vehicles by employees as personal use?		
40 Do you provide more than five vehicles to your employees, obtain information from your employees about the use of the vehicles, and retain the information received?		
41 Do you meet the requirements concerning qualified automobile demonstration use? (See instructions.) . . .		

Note: *If your answer to 37, 38, 39, 40, or 41 is "Yes," do not complete Section B for the covered vehicles.*

Part VI Amortization

(a) Description of costs	(b) Date amortization begins	(c) Amortizable amount	(d) Code section	(e) Amortization period or percentage	(f) Amortization for this year
42 Amortization of costs that begins during your 2014 tax year (see instructions):					

43 Amortization of costs that began before your 2014 tax year **43**

44 **Total.** Add amounts in column (f). See the instructions for where to report **44**

Form **706**	United States Estate (and Generation-Skipping Transfer) Tax Return	

(Rev. August 2013)

▶ **Estate of a citizen or resident of the United States (see instructions). To be filed for decedents dying after December 31, 2012.**

▶ **Information about Form 706 and its separate instructions is at www.irs.gov/form706.**

Department of the Treasury
Internal Revenue Service

OMB No. 1545-0015

Part 1—Decedent and Executor

1a Decedent's first name and middle initial (and maiden name, if any)	1b Decedent's last name	2 Decedent's social security no.
Dan J.	Brown	801 : 76 : 0274

3a City, town, or post office; county; state or province; country; and ZIP or foreign postal code.	3b Year domicile established	4 Date of birth	5 Date of death
1221 N. Everglade, Pomano Beach, Florida 38923	1973	02/01/1951	07/18/2014

6b Executor's address (number and street including apartment or suite no.; city, town, or post office; state or province; country; and ZIP or foreign postal code) and phone no.

6a Name of executor (see instructions)	
Kevin Allen	801 North Cypress Street

6c Executor's social security number (see instructions)	Pomano Beach, Florida
501 : 72 : 0526	Phone no.

6d If there are multiple executors, check here ☐ and attach a list showing the names, addresses, telephone numbers, and SSNs of the additional executors.

7a Name and location of court where will was probated or estate administered	7b Case number
Florida County Court, Pasino Beach, Florida 38925	582/2014

8 If decedent died testate, check here ▶ ☑ and attach a certified copy of the will. **9** If you extended the time to file this Form 706, check here ▶ ☐

10 If Schedule R-1 is attached, check here ▶ ☐ **11** If you are estimating the value of assets included in the gross estate on line 1 pursuant to the special rule of Reg. section 20.2010-2T(a) (7)(ii), check here ▶ ☐

Part 2—Tax Computation

1	Total gross estate less exclusion (from Part 5—Recapitulation, item 13)	1	5,536,449
2	Tentative total allowable deductions (from Part 5—Recapitulation, item 24)	2	3,870,893
3a	Tentative taxable estate (subtract line 2 from line 1)	3a	1,665,556
b	State death tax deduction	3b	16,622
c	Taxable estate (subtract line 3b from line 3a)	3c	1,648,934
4	Adjusted taxable gifts (see instructions)	4	0
5	Add lines 3c and 4	5	1,648,934
6	Tentative tax on the amount on line 5 from Table A in the instructions	6	605,374
7	Total gift tax paid or payable (see instructions)	7	0
8	Gross estate tax (subtract line 7 from line 6)	8	605,374
9a	Basic exclusion amount	9a	2,081,800
9b	Deceased spousal unused exclusion (DSUE) amount from predeceased spouse(s), if any (from Section D, Part 6—Portability of Deceased Spousal Unused Exclusion)	9b	0
9c	Applicable exclusion amount (add lines 9a and 9b)	9c	2,081,800
9d	Applicable credit amount (tentative tax on the amount in 9c from Table A in the instructions)	9d	778,520
10	Adjustment to applicable credit amount (May not exceed $6,000. See instructions.)	10	0
11	Allowable applicable credit amount (subtract line 10 from line 9d)	11	778,520
12	Subtract line 11 from line 8 (but do not enter less than zero)	12	0
13	Credit for foreign death taxes (from Schedule P). (Attach Form(s) 706-CE.)	13	0
14	Credit for tax on prior transfers (from Schedule Q)	14	0
15	Total credits (add lines 13 and 14)	15	0
16	Net estate tax (subtract line 15 from line 12)	16	0
17	Generation-skipping transfer (GST) taxes payable (from Schedule R, Part 2, line 10)	17	0
18	Total transfer taxes (add lines 16 and 17)	18	0
19	Prior payments (explain in an attached statement)	19	0
20	Balance due (or overpayment) (subtract line 19 from line 18)	20	0

Under penalties of perjury, I declare that I have examined this return, including accompanying schedules and statements, and to the best of my knowledge and belief, it is true, correct, and complete. Declaration of preparer other than the executor is based on all information of which preparer has any knowledge.

Sign Here	▶ *Kevin Allen*	▶ 3/12/2015
	Signature of executor	Date
	▶	▶
	Signature of executor	Date

Paid Preparer Use Only	Print/Type preparer's name	Preparer's signature	Date	Check ☑ if self-employed	PTIN
	Fred Johnson	*Fred Johnson*	3/12/2015		
	Firm's name ▶			Firm's EIN ▶	
	Firm's address ▶ 21 NW 2d Street, Pomano Beach, FL 38923			Phone no.	

For Privacy Act and Paperwork Reduction Act Notice, see instructions.   Cat. No. 20548R   Form **706** (Rev. 8-2013)

	Decedent's social security number
Estate of: Dan J. Brown	801 : 76 : 0274

Part 3—Elections by the Executor

Note. For information on electing portability of the decedent's DSUE amount, including how to opt out of the election, see Part 6— Portability of Deceased Spousal Unused Exclusion.

Note. Some of the following elections may require the posting of bonds or liens.

Please check "Yes" or "No" box for each question (see instructions).

			Yes	No
1	Do you elect alternate valuation?	1		✓
2	Do you elect special-use valuation? If "Yes," you must complete and attach Schedule A-1	2		✓
3	Do you elect to pay the taxes in installments as described in section 6166? . . . . If "Yes," you must attach the additional information described in the instructions. **Note. By electing section 6166 installment payments, you may be required to provide security for estate tax deferred under section 6166 and interest in the form of a surety bond or a section 6324A lien.**	3		✓
4	Do you elect to postpone the part of the taxes due to a reversionary or remainder interest as described in section 6163? .	4		✓

Part 4—General Information

Note. Please attach the necessary supplemental documents. **You must attach the death certificate.** (See instructions)

Authorization to receive confidential tax information under Reg. section 601.504(b)(2)(i); to act as the estate's representative before the IRS; and to make written or oral presentations on behalf of the estate:

Name of representative (print or type)	State	Address (number, street, and room or suite no., city, state, and ZIP code)
Fred Johnson	FL	21 NW 2d Street, Pomano Beach, FL 38923

I declare that I am the ☑ attorney/ ☐ certified public accountant/ ☐ enrolled agent (check the applicable box) for the executor. I am not under suspension or disbarment from practice before the Internal Revenue Service and am qualified to practice in the state shown above.

Signature	CAF number	Date	Telephone number
Fred Johnson	4526	*3/12/2015*	222-555-1212

1 Death certificate number and issuing authority (attach a copy of the death certificate to this return).

#28462 Florida County Municipal Hospital

2 Decedent's business or occupation. If retired, check here ▶ ☐ and state decedent's former business or occupation.

Land development, Triad Development Inc.

3a Marital status of the decedent at time of death:

☑ Married ☐ Widow/widower ☐ Single ☐ Legally separated ☐ Divorced

3b For all prior marriages, list the name and SSN of the former spouse, the date the marriage ended, and whether the marriage ended by annulment, divorce, or death. Attach additional statements of the same size if necessary.

4a Surviving spouse's name	4b Social security number	4c Amount received (see instructions)
Ellen Brown	8 0 0 : 0 1 0 : 7 4 2	$2,800,000

5 Individuals (other than the surviving spouse), trusts, or other estates who receive benefits from the estate (do not include charitable beneficiaries shown in Schedule O) (see instructions).

Name of individual, trust, or estate receiving $5,000 or more	Identifying number	Relationship to decedent	Amount (see instructions)
Joey Brown	904-26-0897	son	$190,200
Bill Brown	904-26-0898	son	$190,200
Danny Brown, Jr	502-42-0678	grandson	$100,000

All unascertainable beneficiaries and those who receive less than $5,000 . . . . ▶ | |

| Total . . . . | $480,400 |

If you answer "Yes" to any of the following questions, you must attach additional information as described.

		Yes	No
6	Is the estate filing a protective claim for refund? . . . . If "Yes," complete and attach two copies of Schedule PC for each claim.		✓
7	Does the gross estate contain any section 2044 property (qualified terminable interest property (QTIP) from a prior gift or estate) (see instructions)		✓
8a	Have federal gift tax returns ever been filed? . . . . If "Yes," attach copies of the returns, if available, and furnish the following information:		✓
b	Period(s) covered	c Internal Revenue office(s) where filed		
9a	Was there any insurance on the decedent's life that is not included on the return as part of the gross estate?	✓	
b	Did the decedent own any insurance on the life of another that is not included in the gross estate?		✓

Page 2

		Decedent's social security number		
Estate of: Dan J. Brown		801	76	0274

Part 4—General Information (continued)

	If you answer "Yes" to any of the following questions, you must attach additional information as described.	Yes	No
10	Did the decedent at the time of death own any property as a joint tenant with right of survivorship in which **(a)** one or more of the other joint tenants was someone other than the decedent's spouse, and **(b)** less than the full value of the property is included on the return as part of the gross estate? If "Yes," you must complete and attach Schedule E		✓
11a	Did the decedent, at the time of death, own any interest in a partnership (for example, a family limited partnership), an unincorporated business, or a limited liability company; or own any stock in an inactive or closely held corporation?	✓	
b	If "Yes," was the value of **any** interest owned (from above) discounted on this estate tax return? If "Yes," see the instructions on reporting the total accumulated or effective discounts taken on Schedule F or G		✓
12	Did the decedent make any transfer described in sections 2035, 2036, 2037, or 2038? (see instructions) If "Yes," you must complete and attach Schedule G		✓
13a	Were there in existence at the time of the decedent's death any trusts created by the decedent during his or her lifetime? . .		✓
b	Were there in existence at the time of the decedent's death any trusts not created by the decedent under which the decedent possessed any power, beneficial interest, or trusteeship?	✓	
c	Was the decedent receiving income from a trust created after October 22, 1986, by a parent or grandparent?		✓
	If "Yes," was there a GST taxable termination (under section 2612) on the death of the decedent?		
d	If there was a GST taxable termination (under section 2612), attach a statement to explain. Provide a copy of the trust or will creating the trust, and give the name, address, and phone number of the current trustee(s).		
e	Did the decedent at any time during his or her lifetime transfer or sell an interest in a partnership, limited liability company, or closely held corporation to a trust described in lines 13a or 13b?		✓
	If "Yes," provide the EIN for this transferred/sold item. ▶		
14	Did the decedent ever possess, exercise, or release any general power of appointment? If "Yes," you must complete and attach Schedule H	✓	
15	Did the decedent have an interest in or a signature or other authority over a financial account in a foreign country, such as a bank account, securities account, or other financial account?		✓
16	Was the decedent, immediately before death, receiving an annuity described in the "General" paragraph of the instructions for Schedule I or a private annuity? If "Yes," you must complete and attach Schedule I		✓
17	Was the decedent ever the beneficiary of a trust for which a deduction was claimed by the estate of a predeceased spouse under section 2056(b)(7) and which is not reported on this return? If "Yes," attach an explanation		✓

Part 5—Recapitulation. Note. If estimating the value of one or more assets pursuant to the special rule of Reg. section 20.2010-2T(a)(7)(ii), enter on both lines 10 and 23 the amount noted in the instructions for the corresponding range of values. (See instructions for details.)

Item no.	Gross estate		Alternate value	Value at date of death
1	Schedule A—Real Estate	1		1,075,000
2	Schedule B—Stocks and Bonds	2		1,585,142
3	Schedule C—Mortgages, Notes, and Cash	3		31,225
4	Schedule D—Insurance on the Decedent's Life (attach Form(s) 712) . . .	4		1,250,000
5	Schedule E—Jointly Owned Property (attach Form(s) 712 for life insurance) .	5		371,804
6	Schedule F—Other Miscellaneous Property (attach Form(s) 712 for life insurance)	6		765,528
7	Schedule G—Transfers During Decedent's Life (att. Form(s) 712 for life insurance)	7		0
8	Schedule H—Powers of Appointment	8		135,500
9	Schedule I—Annuities	9		322,250
10	Estimated value of assets subject to the special rule of Reg. section 20.2010-2T(a)(7)(ii)	10		
11	Total gross estate (add items 1 through 10)	11		5,536,449
12	Schedule U—Qualified Conservation Easement Exclusion	12		0
13	Total gross estate less exclusion (subtract item 12 from item 11). Enter here and on line 1 of Part 2—Tax Computation	13		5,536,449

Item no.	Deductions		Amount
14	Schedule J—Funeral Expenses and Expenses Incurred in Administering Property Subject to Claims	14	148,300
15	Schedule K—Debts of the Decedent	15	156,793
16	Schedule K—Mortgages and Liens	16	660,800
17	Total of items 14 through 16	17	965,893
18	Allowable amount of deductions from item 17 (see the instructions for item 18 of the Recapitulation)	18	965,893
19	Schedule L—Net Losses During Administration	19	45,000
20	Schedule L—Expenses Incurred in Administering Property Not Subject to Claims	20	0
21	Schedule M—Bequests, etc., to Surviving Spouse	21	2,800,000
22	Schedule O—Charitable, Public, and Similar Gifts and Bequests	22	60,000
23	Estimated value of deductible assets subject to the special rule of Reg. section 20.2010-2T(a)(7)(ii) . . .	23	0
24	Tentative total allowable deductions (add items 18 through 23). Enter here and on line 2 of the Tax Computation	24	3,870,893

Estate of: Dan J. Brown	Decedent's social security number
	801 76 0274

Part 6—Portability of Deceased Spousal Unused Exclusion (DSUE)

Portability Election

A decedent with a surviving spouse elects portability of the deceased spousal unused exclusion (DSUE) amount, if any, by completing and timely-filing this return. No further action is required to elect portability of the DSUE amount to allow the surviving spouse to use the decedent's DSUE amount.

Section A. Opting Out of Portability

The estate of a decedent with a surviving spouse may opt out of electing portability of the DSUE amount. Check here and do not complete Sections B and C of Part 6 only if the estate opts **NOT** to elect portability of the DSUE amount. ☑

Section B. QDOT

	Yes	No
Are any assets of the estate being transferred to a qualified domestic trust (QDOT)?		

If "Yes," the DSUE amount portable to a surviving spouse (calculated in Section C, below) is preliminary and shall be redetermined at the time of the final distribution or other taxable event imposing estate tax under section 2056A. See instructions for more details.

Section C. DSUE Amount Portable to the Surviving Spouse (To be completed by the estate of a decedent making a portability election.)

Complete the following calculation to determine the DSUE amount that can be transferred to the surviving spouse.

1	Enter the amount from line 9c, Part 2—Tax Computation	**1**	
2	Reserved	**2**	
3	Enter the value of the cumulative lifetime gifts on which tax was paid or payable (see instructions) . . .	**3**	
4	Add lines 1 and 3	**4**	
5	Enter amount from line 10, Part 2—Tax Computation	**5**	
6	Divide amount on line 5 by 40% (0.40) (do not enter less than zero)	**6**	
7	Subtract line 6 from line 4	**7**	
8	Enter the amount from line 5, Part 2– Tax Computation	**8**	
9	Subtract line 8 from line 7 (do not enter less than zero)	**9**	
10	DSUE amount portable to surviving spouse (Enter lesser of line 9 or line 9a, Part 2 – Tax Computation) . .	**10**	

Section D. DSUE Amount Received from Predeceased Spouse(s) (To be completed by the estate of a deceased surviving spouse with DSUE amount from predeceased spouse(s))

Provide the following information to determine the DSUE amount received from deceased spouses.

A Name of Deceased Spouse (dates of death after December 31, 2010, only)	B Date of Death (enter as mm/dd/yy)	C Portability Election Made?		D If "Yes," DSUE Amount Received from Spouse	E DSUE Amount Applied by Decedent to Lifetime Gifts	F Year of Form 709 Reporting Use of DSUE Amount Listed in col E	G Remaining DSUE Amount, if any (subtract col. E from col. D)
		Yes	No				
Part 1 — DSUE RECEIVED FROM LAST DECEASED SPOUSE							
Part 2 — DSUE RECEIVED FROM OTHER PREDECEASED SPOUSE(S) AND USED BY DECEDENT							
Total (for all DSUE amounts from predeceased spouse(s) applied)							

Add the amount from Part 1, column D and the total from Part 2, column E. Enter the result on line 9b, Part 2—Tax Computation . . . . ▶ _____

Estate of: Dan J. Brown

Decedent's social security number		
801	76	0274

SCHEDULE A—Real Estate

- For jointly owned property that must be disclosed on Schedule E, see instructions.
- Real estate that is part of a sole proprietorship should be shown on Schedule F.
- Real estate that is included in the gross estate under sections 2035, 2036, 2037, or 2038 should be shown on Schedule G.
- Real estate that is included in the gross estate under section 2041 should be shown on Schedule H.
- If you elect section 2032A valuation, you must complete Schedule A and Schedule A-1.

Note. If the value of the gross estate, together with the amount of adjusted taxable gifts, is less than the basic exclusion amount and the Form 706 is being filed solely to elect portability of the DSUE amount, consideration should be given as to whether you are required to report the value of assets eligible for the marital or charitable deduction on this schedule. See the instructions and Reg. section 20.2010-2T (a)(7)(ii) for more information. If you are not required to report the value of an asset, identify the property but make no entries in the last three columns.

Item number	Description	Alternate valuation date	Alternate value	Value at date of death
1	3.8 acre tract of unimproved land located on the corner of 2nd Streed and Maple in Edmond, Oklahoma. Land is zoned for commercial office building. Legal description is Lot 24, 25, 26, and 27 of Block 10 in City of Edmond, Oklahoma. Value per attached appraisal by B&K Appraisal, 200 N 2nd Street, Edmond, OK 73108. Land was purchased by decedent 2 months prior to death. Land is subject to a land contract mortgage payable to Edmond Savings and Loan, Edmond, Oklahoma. Balance on mortgage is $600,000, including $10,800 of accrued interest. Reflected on Schedule K.			$1,075,000
	Total from continuation schedules or additional statements attached to this schedule . . .			
	TOTAL. (Also enter on Part 5—Recapitulation, page 3, at item 1.)			$1,075,000

(If more space is needed, attach the continuation schedule from the end of this package or additional statements of the same size.)

Estate of:	Dan J. Brown	**Decedent's social security number**
		801 : 76 : 0274

SCHEDULE A-1—Section 2032A Valuation

Part 1. Type of election (Before making an election, see the checklist in the instructions):

☐ **Protective election (Regulations section 20.2032A-8(b)).** Complete Part 2, line 1, and column A of lines 3 and 4. (see instructions)

☐ **Regular election.** Complete all of Part 2 (including line 11, if applicable) and Part 3. (see instructions)

Before completing Schedule A-1, see the instructions for the information and documents that must be included to make a valid election.

The election is not valid unless the agreement (that is, *Part 3. Agreement to Special Valuation Under Section 2032A):*

• Is signed by each qualified heir with an interest in the specially valued property and

• Is attached to this return when it is filed.

Part 2. Notice of election (Regulations section 20.2032A-8(a)(3))

Note. All real property entered on lines 2 and 3 must also be entered on Schedules A, E, F, G, or H, as applicable.

1   Qualified use—check one ▶ ☐ Farm used for farming, or
    ☐ Trade or business other than farming

2   Real property used in a qualified use, passing to qualified heirs, and to be specially valued on this Form 706.

A Schedule and item number from Form 706	B Full value (without section 2032A(b)(3)(B) adjustment)	C Adjusted value (with section 2032A (b)(3)(B) adjustment)	D Value based on qualified use (without section 2032A(b)(3)(B) adjustment)
Totals			

Attach a legal description of all property listed on line 2.

Attach copies of appraisals showing the column B values for all property listed on line 2.

3   Real property used in a qualified use, passing to qualified heirs, but not specially valued on this Form 706.

A Schedule and item number from Form 706	B Full value (without section 2032A(b)(3)(B) adjustment)	C Adjusted value (with section 2032A (b)(3)(B) adjustment)	D Value based on qualified use (without section 2032A(b)(3)(B) adjustment)
Totals			

If you checked "Regular election," you must attach copies of appraisals showing the column B values for all property listed on line 3.

(continued on next page)

4 Personal property used in a qualified use and passing to qualified heirs.

A Schedule and item number from Form 706	B Adjusted value (with section 2032A (b)(3)(B) adjustment)	A (continued) Schedule and item number from Form 706	B (continued) Adjusted value (with section 2032A (b)(3)(B) adjustment)
		"Subtotal" from Col. B, below left	
Subtotal		**Total adjusted value** . . .	

5 Enter the value of the total gross estate as adjusted under section 2032A(b)(3)(A). ▶ _____

6 **Attach a description of the method used to determine the special value based on qualified use.**

7 Did the decedent and/or a member of his or her family own all property listed on line 2 for at least 5 of the 8 years immediately preceding the date of the decedent's death? . . . . ☐ **Yes** ☐ **No**

8 Were there any periods during the 8-year period preceding the date of the decedent's death during which the decedent or a member of his or her family:

		Yes	No
a	Did not own the property listed on line 2?		
b	Did not use the property listed on line 2 in a qualified use?		
c	Did not materially participate in the operation of the farm or other business within the meaning of section 2032A(e)(6)?		

If you answered "Yes" to any of the above, attach a statement listing the periods. If applicable, describe whether the exceptions of sections 2032A(b)(4) or (5) are met.

9 **Attach affidavits describing the activities constituting material participation and the identity and relationship to the decedent of the material participants.**

10 Persons holding interests. Enter the requested information for each party who received any interest in the specially valued property. **(Each of the qualified heirs receiving an interest in the property must sign the agreement, to be found on Part 3 of this Schedule A-1, and the agreement must be filed with this return.)**

	Name	Address
A		
B		
C		
D		
E		
F		
G		
H		

	Identifying number	Relationship to decedent	Fair market value	Special-use value
A				
B				
C				
D				
E				
F				
G				
H				

You must attach a computation of the GST tax savings attributable to direct skips for each person listed above who is a skip person. (see instructions)

11 **Woodlands election.** Check here ▶ ☐ if you wish to make a Woodlands election as described in section 2032A(e)(13). Enter the schedule and item numbers from Form 706 of the property for which you are making this election ▶ _____

Attach a statement explaining why you are entitled to make this election. The IRS may issue regulations that require more information to substantiate this election. You will be notified by the IRS if you must supply further information.

Schedule A-1—Page 7

Part 3. Agreement to Special Valuation Under Section 2032A

	Decedent's social security number
Estate of: Dan J. Brown	801 76 0274

There cannot be a valid election unless:

• The agreement is executed by each one of the qualified heirs and

• The agreement is included with the estate tax return when the estate tax return is filed.

We (list all qualified heirs)

_____

_____ ,

being all the qualified heirs and (list all other persons having an interest in the property required to sign this agreement)

_____

_____

being all other parties having interests in the property which is qualified real property and which is valued under section 2032A of the Internal Revenue Code, do hereby approve of the election made by _____ ,

Executor/Administrator of the estate of _____ ,

pursuant to section 2032A to value said property on the basis of the qualified use to which the property is devoted and do hereby enter into this agreement pursuant to section 2032A(d).

The undersigned agree and consent to the application of subsection (c) of section 2032A with respect to all the property described on Form 706, Schedule A-1, Part 2, line 2, attached to this agreement. More specifically, the undersigned heirs expressly agree and consent to personal liability under subsection (c) of 2032A for the additional estate and GST taxes imposed by that subsection with respect to their respective interests in the above-described property in the event of certain early dispositions of the property or early cessation of the qualified use of the property. It is understood that if a qualified heir disposes of any interest in qualified real property to any member of his or her family, such member may thereafter be treated as the qualified heir with respect to such interest upon filing a Form 706-A, United States Additional Estate Tax Return, and a new agreement.

The undersigned interested parties who are not qualified heirs consent to the collection of any additional estate and GST taxes imposed under section 2032A(c) from the specially valued property.

If there is a disposition of any interest which passes, or has passed to him or her, or if there is a cessation of the qualified use of any specially valued property which passes or passed to him or her, each of the undersigned heirs agrees to file a Form 706-A, and pay any additional estate and GST taxes due within 6 months of the disposition or cessation.

It is understood by all interested parties that this agreement is a condition precedent to the election of special-use valuation under section 2032A and must be executed by every interested party even though that person may not have received the estate (or GST) tax benefits or be in possession of such property.

Each of the undersigned understands that by making this election, a lien will be created and recorded pursuant to section 6324B of the Code on the property referred to in this agreement for the adjusted tax differences with respect to the estate as defined in section 2032A(c)(2)(C).

As the interested parties, the undersigned designate the following individual as their agent for all dealings with the Internal Revenue Service concerning the continued qualification of the specially valued property under section 2032A and on all issues regarding the special lien under section 6324B. The agent is authorized to act for the parties with respect to all dealings with the Internal Revenue Service on matters affecting the qualified real property described earlier. This includes the authorization:

• To receive confidential information on all matters relating to continued qualification under section 2032A of the specially valued real property and on all matters relating to the special lien arising under section 6324B;

• To furnish the Internal Revenue Service with any requested information concerning the property;

• To notify the Internal Revenue Service of any disposition or cessation of qualified use of any part of the property;

• To receive, but not to endorse and collect, checks in payment of any refund of Internal Revenue taxes, penalties, or interest;

• To execute waivers (including offers of waivers) of restrictions on assessment or collection of deficiencies in tax and waivers of notice of disallowance of a claim for credit or refund; and

• To execute closing agreements under section 7121.

(continued on next page)

Part 3. Agreement to Special Valuation Under Section 2032A *(continued)*

Estate of: Dan J. Brown	**Decedent's social security number**		
	801	76	0274

• Other acts (specify) ▶ _____

By signing this agreement, the agent agrees to provide the Internal Revenue Service with any requested information concerning this property and to notify the Internal Revenue Service of any disposition or cessation of the qualified use of any part of this property.

_____	_____	_____
Name of Agent	Signature	Address

The property to which this agreement relates is listed in Form 706, United States Estate (and Generation-Skipping Transfer) Tax Return, and in the Notice of Election, along with its fair market value according to section 2031 of the Code and its special-use value according to section 2032A. The name, address, social security number, and interest (including the value) of each of the undersigned in this property are as set forth in the attached Notice of Election.

IN WITNESS WHEREOF, the undersigned have hereunto set their hands at _____ ,

this _____ day of _____ .

SIGNATURES OF EACH OF THE QUALIFIED HEIRS:

_____	_____
Signature of qualified heir	Signature of qualified heir

_____	_____
Signature of qualified heir	Signature of qualified heir

_____	_____
Signature of qualified heir	Signature of qualified heir

_____	_____
Signature of qualified heir	Signature of qualified heir

_____	_____
Signature of qualified heir	Signature of qualified heir

_____	_____
Signature of qualified heir	Signature of qualified heir

_____
Signatures of other interested parties

_____
Signatures of other interested parties

Estate of: Dan J. Brown

Decedent's social security number		
801	76	0274

SCHEDULE B—Stocks and Bonds

(For jointly owned property that must be disclosed on Schedule E, see instructions.)

Note. If the value of the gross estate, together with the amount of adjusted taxable gifts, is less than the basic exclusion amount and the Form 706 is being filed solely to elect portability of the DSUE amount, consideration should be given as to whether you are required to report the value of assets eligible for the marital or charitable deduction on this schedule. See the instructions and Reg. section 20.2010-2T (a)(7)(ii) for more information. If you are not required to report the value of an asset, identify the property but make no entries in the last four columns.

Item number	Description, including face amount of bonds or number of shares and par value for identification. Give CUSIP number. If trust, partnership, or closely held entity, give EIN.	Unit value	Alternate valuation date	Alternate value	Value at date of death
		CUSIP number or EIN, where applicable			
1	1,000 shares of Petromark common stock. Stock is traded on NYSE. Mean price of stock on date of death was $165,000. There were no dividends payable to stockholders of record on or before date of death.	234567890	1,000			$165,000
2	2,000 shares of Concor Mutual Growth Fund. Redemption value on date of death was $60.72.	345678901	2,000			$121,440
3	Norman County School District bond, 10.2% par value $50,000. Bond is not actually traded. Fair market value is based on similar sales and present value of yield to maturity. See appraisal from broker attached. Accrued interest on the bond is $482. Value includes accrued interest.	456789012	10.2% $50,000 par			$48,702
4	1,000 shares in Triad Development, Inc. Decedent was 10% shareholder of corporation. Corporation has been in existence 21 years. Fair market value established by Sullivan's Appraisal, Inc., is attached.	567890123	1,000			$1,250,000
	Total from continuation schedules (or additional statements) attached to this schedule . . .				
	TOTAL. (Also enter on Part 5—Recapitulation, page 3, at item 2.)				$1,585,142

(If more space is needed, attach the continuation schedule from the end of this package or additional statements of the same size.)

Estate of: Dan J. Brown

Decedent's social security number		
801	76	0274

SCHEDULE C—Mortgages, Notes, and Cash

(For jointly owned property that must be disclosed on Schedule E, see instructions.)

Note. If the value of the gross estate, together with the amount of adjusted taxable gifts, is less than the basic exclusion amount and the Form 706 is being filed solely to elect portability of the DSUE amount, consideration should be given as to whether you are required to report the value of assets eligible for the marital or charitable deduction on this schedule. See the instructions and Reg. section 20.2010-2T (a)(7)(ii) for more information. If you are not required to report the value of an asset, identify the property but make no entries in the last three columns.

Item number	Description	Alternate valuation date	Alternate value	Value at date of death
1	Cash held by decedent at time of death			$5,600
2	12% demand promissory note of Janet Foster, the decedent's sister-in-law, dated July 2013. Accrued interest to July 18, 2014, is $625.			$25,000 $625
	Total from continuation schedules (or additional statements) attached to this schedule . .			
	TOTAL. (Also enter on Part 5—Recapitulation, page 3, at item 3.)			$31,225

(If more space is needed, attach the continuation schedule from the end of this package or additional statements of the same size.)

	Decedent's social security number
Estate of: Dan J. Brown	801 76 0274

SCHEDULE D—Insurance on the Decedent's Life

You must list all policies on the life of the decedent and attach a Form 712 for each policy.

Note. If the value of the gross estate, together with the amount of adjusted taxable gifts, is less than the basic exclusion amount and the Form 706 is being filed solely to elect portability of the DSUE amount, consideration should be given as to whether you are required to report the value of assets eligible for the marital or charitable deduction on this schedule. See the instructions and Reg. section 20.2010-2T (a)(7)(ii) for more information. If you are not required to report the value of an asset, identify the property but make no entries in the last three columns.

Item number	Description	Alternate valuation date	Alternate value	Value at date of death
1	$1,250,000 whole life insurance policy with Federated Life Insurance Co. in Jacksonville, Florida. Policy # 3287845. The beneficiaries named on the policy were Joey Brown and Bill Brown. Decedent was the owner of the policy.			$1,250,000
2	$500,000 term life policy with U.S. Life Insurance Co. in Tampa, Florida. Decedent did not retain incidents of ownership under IRC § 2042. Ellen Brown was the owner and beneficiary of the policy. Forms 712 are attached.			
	Total from continuation schedules (or additional statements) attached to this schedule . .			
	TOTAL. (Also enter on Part 5—Recapitulation, page 3, at item 4.)			$1,250,000

(If more space is needed, attach the continuation schedule from the end of this package or additional statements of the same size.)

Estate of: Dan J. Brown

Decedent's social security number
801   76   0274

SCHEDULE E—Jointly Owned Property
(If you elect section 2032A valuation, you must complete Schedule E and Schedule A-1.)

PART 1. Qualified Joint Interests—Interests Held by the Decedent and His or Her Spouse as the Only Joint Tenants (Section 2040(b)(2))

Note. If the value of the gross estate, together with the amount of adjusted taxable gifts, is less than the basic exclusion amount and the Form 706 is being filed solely to elect portability of the DSUE amount, consideration should be given as to whether you are required to report the value of assets eligible for the marital or charitable deduction on this schedule. See the instructions and Reg. section 20.2010-2T (a)(7)(ii) for more information. If you are not required to report the value of an asset, identify the property but make no entries in the last three columns.

Item number	Description. For securities, give CUSIP number. If trust, partnership, or closely held entity, give EIN.		Alternate valuation date	Alternate value	Value at date of death
		CUSIP number or EIN, where applicable			
1	Personal family residence located at 1221 Everglade, Pomano Beach, FL. One-story brick with 6 bedrooms on 1.5-acre lot. Legal description is Lot 15, Block 10, Rockford Township in Pompano Beach of Florida County. (See attached appraisal by R.J. Real Estate Appraisers, Inc.)				$642,000
2	Joint savings account at First National Bank of Pompano Beach. Account # 807-8798.				$42,784
	Total from continuation schedules (or additional statements) attached to this schedule					$58,824
1a	Totals **1a**				$743,608
1b	Amounts included in gross estate (one-half of line 1a) **1b**				$371,804

PART 2. All Other Joint Interests

2a State the name and address of each surviving co-tenant. If there are more than three surviving co-tenants, list the additional co-tenants on an attached statement.

	Name	Address (number and street, city, state, and ZIP code)
A.		
B.		
C.		

Item number	Enter letter for co-tenant	Description (including alternate valuation date if any). For securities, give CUSIP number. If trust, partnership, or closely held entity, give EIN		Percentage includible	Includible alternate value	Includible value at date of death
			CUSIP number or EIN, where applicable			
1						
		Total from continuation schedules (or additional statements) attached to this schedule				
2b	Total other joint interests **2b**					
3	**Total includible joint interests** (add lines 1b and 2b). Also enter on Part 5—Recapitulation, page 3, at item 5 . . . . **3**					$371,804

(If more space is needed, attach the continuation schedule from the end of this package or additional statements of the same size.)

		Decedent's social security number		
Estate of: Dan J. Brown		801	76	0274

SCHEDULE F—Other Miscellaneous Property Not Reportable Under Any Other Schedule

(For jointly owned property that must be disclosed on Schedule E, see instructions.)
(If you elect section 2032A valuation, you must complete Schedule F and Schedule A-1.)

Note. If the value of the gross estate, together with the amount of adjusted taxable gifts, is less than the basic exclusion amount and the Form 706 is being filed solely to elect portability of the DSUE amount, consideration should be given as to whether you are required to report the value of assets eligible for the marital or charitable deduction on this schedule. See the instructions and Reg. section 20.2010-2T (a)(7)(ii) for more information. If you are not required to report the value of an asset, identify the property but make no entries in the last three columns.

		Yes	No
1	Did the decedent own any works of art, items, or any collections whose artistic or collectible value at date of death exceeded $3,000?	✓	
	If "Yes," submit full details on this schedule and attach appraisals.		
2	Has the decedent's estate, spouse, or any other person received (or will receive) any bonus or award as a result of the decedent's employment or death?	✓	
	If "Yes," submit full details on this schedule.		
3	Did the decedent at the time of death have, or have access to, a safe deposit box?	✓	

If "Yes," state location, and if held jointly by decedent and another, state name and relationship of joint depositor.

Cooper Savings & Loan, 43 N Main Street, Pompano Beach, Florida
If any of the contents of the safe deposit box are omitted from the schedules in this return, explain fully why omitted.

None

Item number	Description. For securities, give CUSIP number. If trust, partnership, or closely held entity, give EIN	CUSIP number or EIN, where applicable	Alternate valuation date	Alternate value	Value at date of death
1	Life insurance policy on Ellen Brown (#6897548) with Federated Life Insurance Company. Interpolated terminal reserve value of policy, plus prepaid premium cost, establishes value used for estate tax reporting. Form 712 is attached.				$64,578
2	Stamp collection of U.S. postage stamps issued during the Depression years. Appraised value of collection is $400,000. Appraisal was completed by Alfred Benedito, New York, NY. See appraisal attached.				$400,000
3	Automobiles: Kelley Blue Book value or appraisal 2012 Volvo S80 $23,500 2009 Cadillac Escalade $27,450 1957 Ford Thunderbird in need of some $19,500 restoration (appraisal attached)				$70,450
4	Custom Rolex watch				$27,000
5	Fur coats and other salable clothes				$15,000
6	3-carat diamond dinner ring. Purchased two weeks prior to death for $38,000 (VSI1 rating) (from safe deposit box)				$38,500
	Total from continuation schedules (or additional statements) attached to this schedule . .				$150,000
	TOTAL. (Also enter on Part 5—Recapitulation, page 3, at item 6.)				$765,528

(If more space is needed, attach the continuation schedule from the end of this package or additional statements of the same size.)

Estate of: Dan J. Brown

Decedent's social security number		
801	76	0274

SCHEDULE G—Transfers During Decedent's Life

(If you elect section 2032A valuation, you must complete Schedule G and Schedule A-1.)

Note. If the value of the gross estate, together with the amount of adjusted taxable gifts, is less than the basic exclusion amount and the Form 706 is being filed solely to elect portability of the DSUE amount, consideration should be given as to whether you are required to report the value of assets eligible for the marital or charitable deduction on this schedule. See the instructions and Reg. section 20.2010-2T (a)(7)(ii) for more information. If you are not required to report the value of an asset, identify the property but make no entries in the last three columns.

Item number	Description. For securities, give CUSIP number. If trust, partnership, or closely held entity, give EIN	Alternate valuation date	Alternate value	Value at date of death
A.	Gift tax paid or payable by the decedent or the estate for all gifts made by the decedent or his or her spouse within 3 years before the decedent's death (section 2035(b))	X X X X X		
B.	Transfers includible under sections 2035(a), 2036, 2037, or 2038:			
1				
	Total from continuation schedules (or additional statements) attached to this schedule			
	TOTAL. (Also enter on Part 5—Recapitulation, page 3, at item 7.)			

SCHEDULE H—Powers of Appointment

(Include "5 and 5 lapsing" powers (section 2041(b)(2)) held by the decedent.)
(If you elect section 2032A valuation, you must complete Schedule H and Schedule A-1.)

Note. If the value of the gross estate, together with the amount of adjusted taxable gifts, is less than the basic exclusion amount and the Form 706 is being filed solely to elect portability of the DSUE amount, consideration should be given as to whether you are required to report the value of assets eligible for the marital or charitable deduction on this schedule. See the instructions and Reg. section 20.2010-2T (a)(7)(ii) for more information. If you are not required to report the value of an asset, identify the property but make no entries in the last three columns.

Item number	Description	Alternate valuation date	Alternate value	Value at date of death
1	Jane Brown Testamentary Trust created on June 5, 1992. A copy of the trust instrument is attached. Value of assets in trust subject to the power was $135,500.			$135,500
	Total from continuation schedules (or additional statements) attached to this schedule . . .			
	TOTAL. (Also enter on Part 5—Recapitulation, page 3, at item 8.)			$135,500

(If more space is needed, attach the continuation schedule from the end of this package or additional statements of the same size.)

Estate of: Dan J. Brown	**Decedent's social security number**		
	801	76	0274

SCHEDULE I—Annuities

Note. Generally, no exclusion is allowed for the estates of decedents dying after December 31, 1984 (see instructions).

Note. If the value of the gross estate, together with the amount of adjusted taxable gifts, is less than the basic exclusion amount and the Form 706 is being filed solely to elect portability of the DSUE amount, consideration should be given as to whether you are required to report the value of assets eligible for the marital or charitable deduction on this schedule. See the instructions and Reg. section 20.2010-2T (a)(7)(ii) for more information. If you are not required to report the value of an asset, identify the property but make no entries in the last three columns.

A Are you excluding from the decedent's gross estate the value of a lump-sum distribution described in section 2039(f)(2) (as in effect before its repeal by the Deficit Reduction Act of 1984)? . . . . **Yes** | **No** ✓
If "Yes," you must attach the information required by the instructions.

Item number	Description. Show the entire value of the annuity before any exclusions	Alternate valuation date	Includible alternate value	Includible value at date of death
1	Lump-sum distribution payable from Triad Development, Inc.'s qualified profit-sharing plan. The beneficiary of the policy was Ellen Brown.			$228,500
2	Joint survivor annuity with Federated Life Insurance Company in Tampa, Florida. Dan Brown paid 75% of the contract price. The total value of the annuity at Dan Brown's death was $125,000. Since Dan Brown furnished 75% of the contract price, $93,750 is included in the gross estate ($125,000 x 75%).			$93,750
	Total from continuation schedules (or additional statements) attached to this schedule . .			
	TOTAL. (Also enter on Part 5—Recapitulation, page 3, at item 9.)			$322,250

(If more space is needed, attach the continuation schedule from the end of this package or additional statements of the same size.)

Estate of: Dan J. Brown

Decedent's social security number		
801	76	0274

SCHEDULE J—Funeral Expenses and Expenses Incurred in Administering Property Subject to Claims

▶ Use Schedule PC to make a protective claim for refund due to an expense not currently deductible.
For such a claim, report the expense on Schedule J but without a value in the last column.

Note. Do not list expenses of administering property not subject to claims on this schedule. To report those expenses, see instructions.

If executors' commissions, attorney fees, etc., are claimed and allowed as a deduction for estate tax purposes, they are not allowable as a deduction in computing the taxable income of the estate for federal income tax purposes. They are allowable as an income tax deduction on Form 1041, U.S. Income Tax Return for Estates and Trusts, if a waiver is filed to forgo the deduction on Form 706 (see Instructions for Form 1041).

	Yes	No
Are you aware of any actual or potential reimbursement to the estate for any expense claimed as a deduction on this schedule?		✓

If "Yes," attach a statement describing the expense(s) subject to potential reimbursement. (see instructions)

Item number	Description	Expense amount	Total amount
	A. Funeral expenses:		
1	Frederickson Funeral Home in Pompano Beach	$18,500	
2	Peaceful Grounds Cemetery (grave site and maintenance fees)	$7,000	
	Total funeral expenses . . . . ▶		$25,500

B. Administration expenses:

1	Executors' commissions—amount ~~estimated/agreed upon/~~paid. (Strike out the words that do not apply.)		$45,000
2	Attorney fees—amount estimated/~~agreed upon/paid~~. (Strike out the words that do not apply.) . . .		$38,000
3	Accountant fees—amount ~~estimated/agreed upon/~~paid. (Strike out the words that do not apply.) . .		$18,500

	4 Miscellaneous expenses:	Expense amount
4a	Probate court costs	$850
4b	Appraisal fees charged by various appraisers. Fees are noted on each appraisal.	$19,000
4c	Telephone and Federal Express charges incurred by executor for the estate	$1,450
	Total miscellaneous expenses from continuation schedules (or additional statements) attached to this schedule	
	Total miscellaneous expenses . . . . ▶	$21,300
	TOTAL. (Also enter on Part 5—Recapitulation, page 3, at item 14.) . . . . ▶	$148,300

(If more space is needed, attach the continuation schedule from the end of this package or additional statements of the same size.)

Estate of: Dan J. Brown

SCHEDULE K—Debts of the Decedent, and Mortgages and Liens

▶ Use Schedule PC to make a protective claim for refund due to a claim not currently deductible.
For such a claim, report the expense on Schedule K but without a value in the last column.

	Yes	No
Are you aware of any actual or potential reimbursement to the estate for any debt of the decedent, mortgage, or lien claimed as a deduction on this schedule?		✓
If "Yes," attach a statement describing the items subject to potential reimbursement. (see instructions)		
Are any of the items on this schedule deductible under Reg. section 20.2053-4(b) and Reg. section 20.2053-4(c)?		✓
If "Yes," attach a statement indicating the applicable provision and documenting the value of the claim.		

Item number	Debts of the Decedent—Creditor and nature of debt, and allowable death taxes	Amount
1	Last illness expenses of the decedent not reimbursed by insurance	$20,453
2	Unsecured line of credit with Citicorp Trust Bank in New York, NY. Loan No. 234-9706. $110,000 in principal advances, plus unpaid accrued interest of $4,340	$114,340
3	Federal and State of Florida accrued but unpaid income for liabilities	$22,000
	Total from continuation schedules (or additional statements) attached to this schedule	
	TOTAL. (Also enter on Part 5—Recapitulation, page 3, at item 15.)	$156,793

Item number	Mortgages and Liens—Description	Amount
1	Note payable to Edmond Savings & Loan in Edmond, Oklahoma. The balance fo the note at the date of death was $650,000 principal balance and $10,800 in accrued interest. The estate is a guarantor on the note. The proceeds were used to purchase Item 1 on Schedule A. Loan No. 481-420-8.	$660,800
	Total from continuation schedules (or additional statements) attached to this schedule	
	TOTAL. (Also enter on Part 5—Recapitulation, page 3, at item 16.)	$660,800

(If more space is needed, attach the continuation schedule from the end of this package or additional statements of the same size.)

Estate of:	Dan J. Brown	Decedent's social security number
		801 : 76 : 0274

SCHEDULE L—Net Losses During Administration and
Expenses Incurred in Administering Property Not Subject to Claims

▶ **Use Schedule PC to make a protective claim for refund due to an expense not currently deductible.**
For such expenses, report the expense on Schedule L but without a value in the last column.

Item number	Net losses during administration (**Note.** Do not deduct losses claimed on a federal income tax return.)	Amount
1	Tornado damage to parking structure on improved land (see Schedule H) in Edmond, Oklahoma. Date of tornado was December 22, 2014.	$45,000
	Total from continuation schedules (or additional statements) attached to this schedule	
	TOTAL. (Also enter on Part 5—Recapitulation, page 3, at item 19.)	$45,000

Item number	Expenses incurred in administering property not subject to claims. (Indicate whether estimated, agreed upon, or paid.)	Amount
1		
	Total from continuation schedules (or additional statements) attached to this schedule	
	TOTAL. (Also enter on Part 5—Recapitulation, page 3, at item 20.)	

(If more space is needed, attach the continuation schedule from the end of this package or additional statements of the same size.)

Estate of:	Dan J. Brown	**Decedent's social security number**		
		801	76	0274

SCHEDULE M—Bequests, etc., to Surviving Spouse

Note. If the value of the gross estate, together with the amount of adjusted taxable gifts, is less than the basic exclusion amount and the Form 706 is being filed solely to elect portability of the DSUE amount, consideration should be given as to whether you are required to report the value of assets eligible for the marital or charitable deduction on this schedule. See the instructions and Reg. section 20.2010-2T (a)(7)(ii) for more information. If you are not required to report the value of an asset, identify the property but make no entry in the last column.

			Yes	No
1	Did any property pass to the surviving spouse as a result of a qualified disclaimer?	**1**		✓
	If "Yes," attach a copy of the written disclaimer required by section 2518(b).			
2a	In what country was the surviving spouse born? United States			
b	What is the surviving spouse's date of birth? Feb. 20, 1952			
c	Is the surviving spouse a U.S. citizen?	**2c**	✓	
d	If the surviving spouse is a naturalized citizen, when did the surviving spouse acquire citizenship?			
e	If the surviving spouse is not a U.S. citizen, of what country is the surviving spouse a citizen?			
3	**Election Out of QTIP Treatment of Annuities.** Do you elect under section 2056(b)(7)(C)(ii) not to treat as qualified terminable interest property any joint and survivor annuities that are included in the gross estate and would otherwise be treated as qualified terminable interest property under section 2056(b)(7)(C)? (see instructions) . .	**3**		✓

Item number	Description of property interests passing to surviving spouse. For securities, give CUSIP number. If trust, partnership, or closely held entity, give EIN	Amount
	QTIP property:	
A1		
	All other property:	
B1	3.8-acre tract of land located in Edmond, Oklahoma. This property is Item 1 on Schedule A. The value of the land less the mortgage balance (including accrued interest of $414,200).	$369,200
B2	Stocks and bonds listed on Schedule B were bequeathed to Ellen Brown.	$1,585,142
B3	One half of the jointly held property reflected on Schedule E. Property was held as joint tenants with right of survivorship.	$371,804
B4	Annuities reflected on Schedule I consist of a lump-sum distribution and annuity.	$322,250

				Amount
	Total from continuation schedules (or additional statements) attached to this schedule			$151,604
4	**Total** amount of property interests listed on Schedule M	**4**		$2,800,000
5a	Federal estate taxes payable out of property interests listed on Schedule M . . .	**5a**		
b	Other death taxes payable out of property interests listed on Schedule M	**5b**		
c	Federal and state GST taxes payable out of property interests listed on Schedule M	**5c**		
d	Add items 5a, 5b, and 5c		**5d**	
6	Net amount of property interests listed on Schedule M (subtract 5d from 4). Also enter on Part 5—Recapitulation, page 3, at item 21		**6**	$2,800,000

(If more space is needed, attach the continuation schedule from the end of this package or additional statements of the same size.)

Estate of:	Dan J. Brown	Decedent's social security number
		801 : 76 : 0274

SCHEDULE O—Charitable, Public, and Similar Gifts and Bequests

Note. If the value of the gross estate, together with the amount of adjusted taxable gifts, is less than the basic exclusion amount and the Form 706 is being filed solely to elect portability of the DSUE amount, consideration should be given as to whether you are required to report the value of assets eligible for the marital or charitable deduction on this schedule. See the instructions and Reg. section 20.2010-2T (a)(7)(ii) for more information. If you are not required to report the value of an asset, identify the property but make no entry in the last column.

		Yes	No
1a	If the transfer was made by will, has any action been instituted to contest or have interpreted any of its provisions affecting the charitable deductions claimed in this schedule? . . . . If "Yes," full details must be submitted with this schedule.		✓
b	According to the information and belief of the person or persons filing this return, is any such action planned? . If "Yes," full details must be submitted with this schedule.		✓
2	Did any property pass to charity as the result of a qualified disclaimer? . . . . If "Yes," attach a copy of the written disclaimer required by section 2518(b).		✓

Item number	Name and address of beneficiary	Character of institution	Amount
1	First Lutheran Church in Rivertown, Minnesota--cash gift	Church	$50,000
2	University of Arkansas general scholarship fund--cash gift (Copy of letters acknowledging receipt attached.)	College	$10,000
	Total from continuation schedules (or additional statements) attached to this schedule		
3	Total **3**		$60,000
4a	Federal estate tax payable out of property interests listed above **4a**		
b	Other death taxes payable out of property interests listed above **4b**		
c	Federal and state GST taxes payable out of property interests listed above . **4c**		
d	Add items 4a, 4b, and 4c **4d**		
5	Net value of property interests listed above (subtract 4d from 3). Also enter on Part 5—Recapitulation, page 3, at item 22 . . . . **5**		$60,000

(If more space is needed, attach the continuation schedule from the end of this package or additional statements of the same size.)

Schedule O—Page 21

Estate of: Dan J. Brown

Decedent's social security number		
801	76	0274

SCHEDULE P—Credit for Foreign Death Taxes

List all foreign countries to which death taxes have been paid and for which a credit is claimed on this return.

If a credit is claimed for death taxes paid to more than one foreign country, compute the credit for taxes paid to one country on this sheet and attach a separate copy of Schedule P for each of the other countries.

The credit computed on this sheet is for the _____
(Name of death tax or taxes)

_____ imposed in _____
(Name of country)

Credit is computed under the _____
(Insert title of treaty or statute)

Citizenship (nationality) of decedent at time of death

(All amounts and values must be entered in United States money.)

1	Total of estate, inheritance, legacy, and succession taxes imposed in the country named above attributable to property situated in that country, subjected to these taxes, and included in the gross estate (as defined by statute) .	**1**	
2	Value of the gross estate (adjusted, if necessary, according to the instructions)	**2**	
3	Value of property situated in that country, subjected to death taxes imposed in that country, and included in the gross estate (adjusted, if necessary, according to the instructions)	**3**	
4	Tax imposed by section 2001 reduced by the total credits claimed under sections 2010 and 2012 (see instructions)	**4**	
5	Amount of federal estate tax attributable to property specified at item 3. (Divide item 3 by item 2 and multiply the result by item 4.)	**5**	
6	Credit for death taxes imposed in the country named above (the smaller of item 1 or item 5). Also enter on line 13 of Part 2—Tax Computation	**6**	

SCHEDULE Q—Credit for Tax on Prior Transfers

Part 1. Transferor Information

	Name of transferor	Social security number	IRS office where estate tax return was filed	Date of death
A				
B				
C				

Check here ▶ ☐ if section 2013(f) (special valuation of farm, etc., real property) adjustments to the computation of the credit were made (see instructions).

Part 2. Computation of Credit (see instructions)

Item	Transferor			Total A, B, & C
	A	B	C	
1 Transferee's tax as apportioned (from worksheet, (line 7 ÷ line 8) × line 35 for each column) . . .				
2 Transferor's tax (from each column of worksheet, line 20)				
3 Maximum amount before percentage requirement (for each column, enter amount from line 1 or 2, whichever is smaller)				
4 Percentage allowed (each column) (see instructions)	%	%	%	
5 Credit allowable (line 3 × line 4 for each column) .				
6 TOTAL credit allowable (add columns A, B, and C of line 5). Enter here and on line 14 of Part 2—Tax Computation				

SCHEDULE R—Generation-Skipping Transfer Tax

Note. To avoid application of the deemed allocation rules, Form 706 and Schedule R should be filed to allocate the GST exemption to trusts that may later have taxable terminations or distributions under section 2612 even if the form is not required to be filed to report estate or GST tax.

The GST tax is imposed on taxable transfers of interests in property located outside the United States as well as property located inside the United States. (see instructions)

Part 1. GST Exemption Reconciliation (Section 2631) and Special QTIP Election (Section 2652(a)(3))

You no longer need to check a box to make a section 2652(a)(3) (special QTIP) election. If you list qualifying property in Part 1, line 9 below, you will be considered to have made this election. See instructions for details.

1	Maximum allowable GST exemption **1**	5,340,000
2	Total GST exemption allocated by the decedent against decedent's lifetime transfers **2**	
3	Total GST exemption allocated by the executor, using Form 709, against decedent's lifetime transfers **3**	
4	GST exemption allocated on line 6 of Schedule R, Part 2 . . . . **4**	$100,000
5	GST exemption allocated on line 6 of Schedule R, Part 3 . . . . **5**	
6	Total GST exemption allocated on line 4 of Schedule(s) R-1 . . . . **6**	
7	Total GST exemption allocated to *inter vivos* transfers and direct skips (add lines 2–6) **7**	$100,000
8	GST exemption available to allocate to trusts and section 2032A interests (subtract line 7 from line 1) . . . . **U**	5,240,000

9   Allocation of GST exemption to trusts (as defined for GST tax purposes):

A Name of trust	B Trust's EIN (if any)	C GST exemption allocated on lines 2–6, above (see instructions)	D Additional GST exemption allocated (see instructions)	E Trust's inclusion ratio (optional—see instructions)

9D **Total.** May not exceed line 8, above	**9D**		
10	GST exemption available to allocate to section 2032A interests received by individual beneficiaries (subtract line 9D from line 8). You must attach special-use allocation statement (see instructions) .	**10**	5,240,000

Estate of: Dan J. Brown

Decedent's social security number
801 76 0274

Part 2. Direct Skips Where the Property Interests Transferred Bear the GST Tax on the Direct Skips

Name of skip person	Description of property interest transferred	Estate tax value
Danny Brown, Jr.	$100,000 cash	$100,000

1	Total estate tax values of all property interests listed above	1	$100,000
2	Estate taxes, state death taxes, and other charges borne by the property interests listed above . .	2	0
3	GST taxes borne by the property interests listed above but imposed on direct skips other than those shown on this Part 2 (see instructions)	3	0
4	Total fixed taxes and other charges (add lines 2 and 3)	4	0
5	Total tentative maximum direct skips (subtract line 4 from line 1)	5	$100,000
6	GST exemption allocated	6	$100,000
7	Subtract line 6 from line 5	7	0
8	GST tax due (divide line 7 by 3.5)	8	0
9	Enter the amount from line 8 of Schedule R, Part 3	9	0
10	**Total GST taxes payable by the estate** (add lines 8 and 9). Enter here and on line 17 of Part 2— Tax Computation	10	0

Schedule R—Page 24

Estate of: Dan J. Brown

Decedent's social security number		
801	76	0274

Part 3. Direct Skips Where the Property Interests Transferred Do Not Bear the GST Tax on the Direct Skips

Name of skip person	Description of property interest transferred	Estate tax value

1 Total estate tax values of all property interests listed above	1	
2 Estate taxes, state death taxes, and other charges borne by the property interests listed above . .	2	
3 GST taxes borne by the property interests listed above but imposed on direct skips other than those shown on this Part 3 (see instructions)	3	
4 Total fixed taxes and other charges (add lines 2 and 3)	4	
5 Total tentative maximum direct skips (subtract line 4 from line 1)	5	
6 GST exemption allocated	6	
7 Subtract line 6 from line 5	7	
8 GST tax due (multiply line 7 by .40). Enter here and on Schedule R, Part 2, line 9	8	

Schedule R—Page 25

SCHEDULE R-1
(Form 706)
(Rev. August 2013)
Department of the Treasury
Internal Revenue Service

Generation-Skipping Transfer Tax

Direct Skips From a Trust
Payment Voucher

OMB No. 1545-0015

Executor: File one copy with Form 706 and send two copies to the fiduciary. Do not pay the tax shown. See instructions for details.
Fiduciary: See instructions for details. Pay the tax shown on line 6.

Name of trust		**Trust's EIN**
Name and title of fiduciary	Name of decedent	
Address of fiduciary (number and street)	Decedent's SSN	Service Center where Form 706 was filed
City, state, and ZIP or postal code	Name of executor	
Address of executor (number and street)	City, state, and ZIP or postal code	
Date of decedent's death	Filing due date of Schedule R, Form 706 (with extensions)	

Part 1. Computation of the GST Tax on the Direct Skip

Description of property interests subject to the direct skip	Estate tax value

1	Total estate tax value of all property interests listed above	1	
2	Estate taxes, state death taxes, and other charges borne by the property interests listed above	2	
3	Tentative maximum direct skip from trust (subtract line 2 from line 1)	3	
4	GST exemption allocated	4	
5	Subtract line 4 from line 3	5	
6	**GST tax due from fiduciary** (divide line 5 by 3.5). **(See instructions if property will not bear the GST tax.)**	6	

Under penalties of perjury, I declare that I have examined this document, including accompanying schedules and statements, and to the best of my knowledge and belief, it is true, correct, and complete.

Signature(s) of executor(s)   Date

    Date

Signature of fiduciary or officer representing fiduciary   Date

Instructions for the Trustee

Introduction	Schedule R-1 (Form 706) serves as a payment voucher for the Generation-Skipping Transfer (GST) tax imposed on a direct skip from a trust, which you, the trustee of the trust, must pay. The executor completes the Schedule R-1 (Form 706) and gives you two copies. File one copy and keep one for your records.
How to pay	You can pay by check or money order or by electronic funds transfer.
	To pay by check or money order:
	• Make it payable to "United States Treasury."
	• The amount of the check or money order should be the amount on line 6 of Schedule R-1.
	• Write "GST Tax" and the trust's EIN on the check or money order.
	To pay by electronic funds transfer:
	• Funds must be submitted through the Electronic Federal Tax Payment System (EFTPS).
	• Establish an EFTPS account by visiting *www.eftps.gov* or calling 1-800-555-4477.
	• To be considered timely, payments made through EFTPS must be completed no later than 8 p.m. Eastern time the day **before** the due date.
Signature	You must sign the Schedule R-1 in the space provided.
What to mail	Mail your check or money order, if applicable, and the copy of Schedule R-1 that you signed.
Where to mail	Mail to the Department of the Treasury, Internal Revenue Service Center, Cincinnati, OH 45999.
When to pay	The GST tax is due and payable 9 months after the decedent's date of death (shown on the Schedule R-1). You will owe interest on any GST tax not paid by that date.
Automatic extension	You have an automatic extension of time to file Schedule R-1 and pay the GST tax. The automatic extension allows you to file and pay by 2 months after the due date (with extensions) for filing the decedent's Schedule R (shown on the Schedule R-1).
	If you pay the GST tax under the automatic extension, you will be charged interest (but no penalties).
Additional information	For more information, see section 2603(a)(2) and the Instructions for Form 706, United States Estate (and Generation-Skipping Transfer) Tax Return.

Estate of: Dan J. Brown

Decedent's social security number		
801	76	0274

SCHEDULE U—Qualified Conservation Easement Exclusion

Part 1. Election

Note. The executor is deemed to have made the election under section 2031(c)(6) if he or she files Schedule U and excludes any qualifying conservation easements from the gross estate.

Part 2. General Qualifications

1   Describe the land subject to the qualified conservation easement (see instructions) _____

2   Did the decedent or a member of the decedent's family own the land described above during the 3-year period ending on the date of the decedent's death? . . . . ☐ **Yes** ☐ **No**

3   Describe the conservation easement with regard to which the exclusion is being claimed (see instructions).

_____

Part 3. Computation of Exclusion

4	Estate tax value of the land subject to the qualified conservation easement (see instructions) .	**4**	
5	Date of death value of any easements granted prior to decedent's death and included on line 10 below (see instructions)	**5**	
6	Add lines 4 and 5	**6**	
7	Value of retained development rights on the land (see instructions)	**7**	
8	Subtract line 7 from line 6	**8**	
9	Multiply line 8 by 30% (.30)	**9**	
10	Value of qualified conservation easement for which the exclusion is being claimed (see instructions)	**10**	
	Note. If line 10 is less than line 9, continue with line 11. If line 10 is equal to or more than line 9, skip lines 11 through 13, enter ".40" on line 14, and complete the schedule.		
11	Divide line 10 by line 8. Figure to 3 decimal places (for example, ".123")	**11**	
	Note. If line 11 is equal to or less than .100, stop here; the estate does not qualify for the conservation easement exclusion.		
12	Subtract line 11 from .300. Enter the answer in hundredths by rounding any thousandths up to the next higher hundredth (that is, .030 = .03, but .031 = .04)	**12**	
13	Multiply line 12 by 2	**13**	
14	Subtract line 13 from .40	**14**	
15	Deduction under section 2055(f) for the conservation easement (see instructions)	**15**	
16	Amount of indebtedness on the land (see instructions)	**16**	
17	Total reductions in value (add lines 7, 15, and 16)	**17**	
18	Net value of land (subtract line 17 from line 4)	**18**	
19	Multiply line 18 by line 14	**19**	
20	Enter the smaller of line 19 or the exclusion limitation (see instructions). Also enter this amount on item 12, Part 5—Recapitulation, page 3	**20**	

Protective Claim for Refund

▶ **To be used for decedents dying after December 31, 2011. File 2 copies of this schedule with Form 706 for each pending claim or expense under section 2053.**

OMB No. 1545-0015

- Timely filing a protective claim for refund preserves the estate's right to claim a refund based on the amount of an unresolved claim or expense that may not become deductible under section 2053 until after the limitation period ends.

- Schedule PC can be used to file a protective claim for refund and, once the claim or expense becomes deductible, Schedule PC can be used to notify the IRS that a refund is being claimed.

- Schedule PC can be used by the estate of a decedent dying after 2011.

- Schedule PC must be filed with Form 706 and cannot be filed separately. (To file a protective claim for refund or notify the IRS that a refund is being claimed in a form separate from the Form 706, instead use Form 843, Claim for Refund and Request for Abatement.)

- Each separate claim or expense requires a separate Schedule PC (or Form 843, if not filed with Form 706).

- Schedule PC must be filed in duplicate (two copies) for each separate claim or expense.

Part 1. General Information

1. Name of decedent	2. Decedent's social security number
3. Name of fiduciary	4. Date of death
5a. Address (number, street, and room or suite no.)	5b. Room or suite no.
5c. City or town, state, and ZIP or postal code	6. Daytime telephone number

7. Number of Claims. Enter number of Schedules PC being filed with Form 706. _____

If the number is greater than one OR if another Schedule PC or Form 843 was previously filed by or on behalf of the estate, complete Part 3 of this Schedule PC.

8. Fiduciary ☐ Check here if this Schedule PC is being filed with the original Form 706 or is being filed by the same fiduciary who filed the original Form 706 for decedent's estate. If a different fiduciary is filing this Schedule PC, see instructions for establishing the legal authority to pursue the claim for refund on behalf of the estate.

Part 2. Claim Information

Check the box that applies to this claim for refund.

a. ☐ Protective claim for refund made for unresolved claim or expense.

   Amount in contest: _____

b. ☐ Partial refund claimed: partial resolution and/or satisfaction of claim or expense for which a protective claim for refund has been filed previously.

   Date protective claim for refund filed for this claim or expense: _____

   Amount of claim or expense partially resolved and/or satisfied and presently claimed as a deduction under section 2053 (do not include amounts previously deducted): _____

c. ☐ Full and final refund claimed for this claim or expense: resolution and/or satisfaction of claim or expense for which a protective claim for refund has been filed previously.

   Date protective claim for refund filed for this claim or expense: _____

   Amount of claim or expense finally resolved and/or satisfied and presently claimed as a deduction under section 2053 (do not include amounts previously deducted): _____

Estate of: Dan J. Brown				**Decedent's social security number** 801 76 0274	
A Form 706 Schedule and Item number	**B** Identification of the claim • Name or names of the claimant(s) • Basis of the claim or other description of the pending claim or expense • Reasons and contingencies delaying resolution •Status of contested matters •Attach copies of relevant pleadings or other documents	**C** Amount, if any, deducted under Treas. Reg. sections 20.2053-1(d)(4) or 20.2053-4 (b) or (c) for the identified claim or expense	**D** Amount presently claimed as a deduction under section 2053 for the identified claim	**E** Ancillary expenses estimated/ agreed upon/paid (Please indicate)	**F** Amount of tax to be refunded

Part 3. Other Schedules PC and Forms 843 Filed by Estate

If a Schedule PC or Form 843 was previously filed by the estate, complete Part 3 to identify each claim for refund reported.

A Date of death	**B** Internal Revenue office where filed	**C** Date filed	**D** Indicate whether (1) Protective Claim for Refund; (2) Partial Claim for Refund; or (3) Full and Final Claim for Refund	**E** Amount in Contest
1				

To inquire about the receipt and/or processing of the protective claim for refund, please call (866) 699-4083.

(Rev. 8-2013)

(Make copies of this schedule before completing it if you will need more than one schedule.)

Estate of: Dan J. Brown

Decedent's social security number		
801	76	0274

CONTINUATION SCHEDULE

Continuation of Schedule _____

(Enter letter of schedule you are continuing.)

Item number	Description. For securities, give CUSIP number. If trust, partnership, or closely held entity, give EIN.	Unit value (Sch. B, E, or G only)	Alternate valuation date	Alternate value	Value at date of death or amount deductible
	Schedule E Continuation:				Schedule E
3	Joint checking account at Florida County Savings and Loan in Pompano Beach, FL. Account # 805-8124.				$3,824
4	Furniture and fixtures in the decedent's residence at the time of death. See appraisal attached.				$55,000 ------------- $58,824 ========
	Schedule F Continuation:				Schedule F
7	Bonus accrued to Dan at his death of $150,000. This was paid on September 15, 2013 by Triad Development, Inc. to Ellen.				$150,000 ========
	Schedule M Continuation:				Schedule M
B5	Life insurance policy on Ellen Brown's life. Value of policy is listed on Schedule F.				$64,578
B6	Three carat diamond dinner ring. See Schedule F for description of asset and value.				$38,500
B7	Cash in decedent's possession at death, less amount used to pay expenses.				$3,526
B8	Cash in the trust of which Dan Brown held a power of appointment. Remaining assets in the trust passed to decedent's children.				$45,000 ------------- $151,604 ========

TOTAL. (Carry forward to main schedule.) . . . .

BLANK FORMS

Form 706

(Rev. August 2013)

Department of the Treasury
Internal Revenue Service

United States Estate (and Generation-Skipping Transfer) Tax Return

OMB No. 1545-0015

▶ **Estate of a citizen or resident of the United States (see instructions). To be filed for decedents dying after December 31, 2012.**
▶ **Information about Form 706 and its separate instructions is at www.irs.gov/form706.**

Part 1—Decedent and Executor

1a Decedent's first name and middle initial (and maiden name, if any)	**1b** Decedent's last name	**2** Decedent's social security no.
3a City, town, or post office; county; state or province; country; and ZIP or foreign postal code.	**3b** Year domicile established	**4** Date of birth	**5** Date of death

6a Name of executor (see instructions)

6b Executor's address (number and street including apartment or suite no.; city, town, or post office; state or province; country; and ZIP or foreign postal code) and phone no.

6c Executor's social security number (see instructions)

Phone no.

6d If there are multiple executors, check here ☐ and attach a list showing the names, addresses, telephone numbers, and SSNs of the additional executors.

7a Name and location of court where will was probated or estate administered | **7b** Case number

8 If decedent died testate, check here ▶ ☐ and attach a certified copy of the will.   **9** If you extended the time to file this Form 706, check here ▶ ☐

10 If Schedule R-1 is attached, check here ▶ ☐   **11** If you are estimating the value of assets included in the gross estate on line 1 pursuant to the special rule of Reg. section 20.2010-2T(a) (7)(ii), check here ▶ ☐

Part 2—Tax Computation

1	Total gross estate less exclusion (from Part 5—Recapitulation, item 13)	**1**	
2	Tentative total allowable deductions (from Part 5—Recapitulation, item 24)	**2**	
3a	Tentative taxable estate (subtract line 2 from line 1)	**3a**	
b	State death tax deduction	**3b**	
c	Taxable estate (subtract line 3b from line 3a)	**3c**	
4	Adjusted taxable gifts (see instructions)	**4**	
5	Add lines 3c and 4	**5**	
6	Tentative tax on the amount on line 5 from Table A in the instructions	**6**	
7	Total gift tax paid or payable (see instructions)	**7**	
8	Gross estate tax (subtract line 7 from line 6)	**8**	
9a	Basic exclusion amount	**9a**	
9b	Deceased spousal unused exclusion (DSUE) amount from predeceased spouse(s), if any (from Section D, Part 6—Portability of Deceased Spousal Unused Exclusion). .	**9b**	
9c	Applicable exclusion amount (add lines 9a and 9b)	**9c**	
9d	Applicable credit amount (tentative tax on the amount in 9c from Table A in the instructions)	**9d**	
10	Adjustment to applicable credit amount (May not exceed $6,000. See instructions.)	**10**	
11	Allowable applicable credit amount (subtract line 10 from line 9d)	**11**	
12	Subtract line 11 from line 8 (but do not enter less than zero)	**12**	
13	Credit for foreign death taxes (from Schedule P). (Attach Form(s) 706-CE.)	**13**	
14	Credit for tax on prior transfers (from Schedule Q)	**14**	
15	Total credits (add lines 13 and 14)	**15**	
16	Net estate tax (subtract line 15 from line 12)	**16**	
17	Generation-skipping transfer (GST) taxes payable (from Schedule R, Part 2, line 10)	**17**	
18	Total transfer taxes (add lines 16 and 17)	**18**	
19	Prior payments (explain in an attached statement)	**19**	
20	Balance due (or overpayment) (subtract line 19 from line 18)	**20**	

Under penalties of perjury, I declare that I have examined this return, including accompanying schedules and statements, and to the best of my knowledge and belief, it is true, correct, and complete. Declaration of preparer other than the executor is based on all information of which preparer has any knowledge.

Sign Here

▶ Signature of executor _____   Date _____

▶ Signature of executor _____   Date _____

Paid Preparer Use Only

Print/Type preparer's name	Preparer's signature	Date	Check ☐ if self-employed	PTIN
Firm's name ▶				Firm's EIN ▶
Firm's address ▶				Phone no.

For Privacy Act and Paperwork Reduction Act Notice, see instructions.   Cat. No. 20548R   Form **706** (Rev. 8-2013)

	Decedent's social security number

Estate of:

Part 3—Elections by the Executor

			Yes	No
Note. For information on electing portability of the decedent's DSUE amount, including how to opt out of the election, see Part 6—Portability of Deceased Spousal Unused Exclusion. **Note.** Some of the following elections may require the posting of bonds or liens.				
Please check "Yes" or "No" box for each question (see instructions).				
1	Do you elect alternate valuation?	**1**		
2	Do you elect special-use valuation? If "Yes," you must complete and attach Schedule A-1	**2**		
3	Do you elect to pay the taxes in installments as described in section 6166?			
	If "Yes," you must attach the additional information described in the instructions.			
	Note. By electing section 6166 installment payments, you may be required to provide security for estate tax deferred under section 6166 and interest in the form of a surety bond or a section 6324A lien.	**3**		
4	Do you elect to postpone the part of the taxes due to a reversionary or remainder interest as described in section 6163? .	**4**		

Part 4—General Information

Note. Please attach the necessary supplemental documents. **You must attach the death certificate.** (See instructions)

Authorization to receive confidential tax information under Reg. section 601.504(b)(2)(i); to act as the estate's representative before the IRS; and to make written or oral presentations on behalf of the estate:

Name of representative (print or type)	State	Address (number, street, and room or suite no., city, state, and ZIP code)

I declare that I am the ☐ attorney/ ☐ certified public accountant/ ☐ enrolled agent (check the applicable box) for the executor. I am not under suspension or disbarment from practice before the Internal Revenue Service and am qualified to practice in the state shown above.

Signature	CAF number	Date	Telephone number

1 Death certificate number and issuing authority (attach a copy of the death certificate to this return).

2 Decedent's business or occupation. If retired, check here ▶ ☐ and state decedent's former business or occupation.

3a Marital status of the decedent at time of death:

☐ Married ☐ Widow/widower ☐ Single ☐ Legally separated ☐ Divorced

3b For all prior marriages, list the name and SSN of the former spouse, the date the marriage ended, and whether the marriage ended by annulment, divorce, or death. Attach additional statements of the same size if necessary.

4a Surviving spouse's name	4b Social security number	4c Amount received (see instructions)

5 Individuals (other than the surviving spouse), trusts, or other estates who receive benefits from the estate (do not include charitable beneficiaries shown in Schedule O) (see instructions).

Name of individual, trust, or estate receiving $5,000 or more	Identifying number	Relationship to decedent	Amount (see instructions)

All unascertainable beneficiaries and those who receive less than $5,000 . . . . ▶

Total . . . .

If you answer "Yes" to any of the following questions, you must attach additional information as described.		Yes	No
6	Is the estate filing a protective claim for refund? . . . . If "Yes," complete and attach two copies of Schedule PC for each claim.		
7	Does the gross estate contain any section 2044 property (qualified terminable interest property (QTIP) from a prior gift or estate)? (see instructions)		
8a	Have federal gift tax returns ever been filed? . . . . If "Yes," attach copies of the returns, if available, and furnish the following information:		
b	Period(s) covered	c Internal Revenue office(s) where filed		
9a	Was there any insurance on the decedent's life that is not included on the return as part of the gross estate? . .		
b	Did the decedent own any insurance on the life of another that is not included in the gross estate?		

	Decedent's social security number
Estate of:	

Part 4—General Information (continued)

If you answer "Yes" to any of the following questions, you must attach additional information as described.	Yes	No
10 Did the decedent at the time of death own any property as a joint tenant with right of survivorship in which **(a)** one or more of the other joint tenants was someone other than the decedent's spouse, and **(b)** less than the full value of the property is included on the return as part of the gross estate? If "Yes," you must complete and attach Schedule E		
11a Did the decedent, at the time of death, own any interest in a partnership (for example, a family limited partnership), an unincorporated business, or a limited liability company; or own any stock in an inactive or closely held corporation?		
b If "Yes," was the value of **any** interest owned (from above) discounted on this estate tax return? If "Yes," see the instructions on reporting the total accumulated or effective discounts taken on Schedule F or G		
12 Did the decedent make any transfer described in sections 2035, 2036, 2037, or 2038? (see instructions) If "Yes," you must complete and attach Schedule G		
13a Were there in existence at the time of the decedent's death any trusts created by the decedent during his or her lifetime? . . .		
b Were there in existence at the time of the decedent's death any trusts not created by the decedent under which the decedent possessed any power, beneficial interest, or trusteeship?		
c Was the decedent receiving income from a trust created after October 22, 1986, by a parent or grandparent?		
If "Yes," was there a GST taxable termination (under section 2612) on the death of the decedent?		
d If there was a GST taxable termination (under section 2612), attach a statement to explain. Provide a copy of the trust or will creating the trust, and give the name, address, and phone number of the current trustee(s).		
e Did the decedent at any time during his or her lifetime transfer or sell an interest in a partnership, limited liability company, or closely held corporation to a trust described in lines 13a or 13b?		
If "Yes," provide the EIN for this transferred/sold item. ▶		
14 Did the decedent ever possess, exercise, or release any general power of appointment? If "Yes," you must complete and attach Schedule H . . .		
15 Did the decedent have an interest in or a signature or other authority over a financial account in a foreign country, such as a bank account, securities account, or other financial account?		
16 Was the decedent, immediately before death, receiving an annuity described in the "General" paragraph of the instructions for Schedule I or a private annuity? If "Yes," you must complete and attach Schedule I		
17 Was the decedent ever the beneficiary of a trust for which a deduction was claimed by the estate of a predeceased spouse under section 2056(b)(7) and which is not reported on this return? If "Yes," attach an explanation		

Part 5—Recapitulation.

Note. If estimating the value of one or more assets pursuant to the special rule of Reg. section 20.2010-2T(a)(7)(ii), enter on both lines 10 and 23 the amount noted in the instructions for the corresponding range of values. (See instructions for details.)

Item no.	Gross estate		Alternate value	Value at date of death
1	Schedule A—Real Estate	**1**		
2	Schedule B—Stocks and Bonds	**2**		
3	Schedule C—Mortgages, Notes, and Cash	**3**		
4	Schedule D—Insurance on the Decedent's Life (attach Form(s) 712)	**4**		
5	Schedule E—Jointly Owned Property (attach Form(s) 712 for life insurance) .	**5**		
6	Schedule F—Other Miscellaneous Property (attach Form(s) 712 for life insurance)	**6**		
7	Schedule G—Transfers During Decedent's Life (att. Form(s) 712 for life insurance)	**7**		
8	Schedule H—Powers of Appointment	**8**		
9	Schedule I—Annuities	**9**		
10	Estimated value of assets subject to the special rule of Reg. section 20.2010-2T(a)(7)(ii)	**10**		
11	Total gross estate (add items 1 through 10)	**11**		
12	Schedule U—Qualified Conservation Easement Exclusion	**12**		
13	Total gross estate less exclusion (subtract item 12 from item 11). Enter here and on line 1 of Part 2—Tax Computation	**13**		

Item no.	Deductions		Amount
14	Schedule J—Funeral Expenses and Expenses Incurred in Administering Property Subject to Claims	**14**	
15	Schedule K—Debts of the Decedent	**15**	
16	Schedule K—Mortgages and Liens	**16**	
17	Total of items 14 through 16	**17**	
18	Allowable amount of deductions from item 17 (see the instructions for item 18 of the Recapitulation) . .	**18**	
19	Schedule L—Net Losses During Administration	**19**	
20	Schedule L—Expenses Incurred in Administering Property Not Subject to Claims	**20**	
21	Schedule M—Bequests, etc., to Surviving Spouse	**21**	
22	Schedule O—Charitable, Public, and Similar Gifts and Bequests	**22**	
23	Estimated value of deductible assets subject to the special rule of Reg. section 20.2010-2T(a)(7)(ii) . . .	**23**	
24	Tentative total allowable deductions (add items 18 through 23). Enter here and on line 2 of the Tax Computation	**24**	

	Decedent's social security number
Estate of:	

Part 6—Portability of Deceased Spousal Unused Exclusion (DSUE)

Portability Election

A decedent with a surviving spouse elects portability of the deceased spousal unused exclusion (DSUE) amount, if any, by completing and timely-filing this return. No further action is required to elect portability of the DSUE amount to allow the surviving spouse to use the decedent's DSUE amount.

Section A. Opting Out of Portability

The estate of a decedent with a surviving spouse may opt out of electing portability of the DSUE amount. Check here and do not complete Sections B and C of Part 6 only if the estate opts **NOT** to elect portability of the DSUE amount. ☐

Section B. QDOT

	Yes	No
Are any assets of the estate being transferred to a qualified domestic trust (QDOT)?		

If "Yes," the DSUE amount portable to a surviving spouse (calculated in Section C, below) is preliminary and shall be redetermined at the time of the final distribution or other taxable event imposing estate tax under section 2056A. See instructions for more details.

Section C. DSUE Amount Portable to the Surviving Spouse (To be completed by the estate of a decedent making a portability election.)

Complete the following calculation to determine the DSUE amount that can be transferred to the surviving spouse.

1	Enter the amount from line 9c, Part 2—Tax Computation	**1**	
2	Reserved	**2**	
3	Enter the value of the cumulative lifetime gifts on which tax was paid or payable (see instructions) . . .	**3**	
4	Add lines 1 and 3	**4**	
5	Enter amount from line 10, Part 2—Tax Computation	**5**	
6	Divide amount on line 5 by 40% (0.40) (do not enter less than zero)	**6**	
7	Subtract line 6 from line 4	**7**	
8	Enter the amount from line 5, Part 2– Tax Computation	**8**	
9	Subtract line 8 from line 7 (do not enter less than zero)	**9**	
10	DSUE amount portable to surviving spouse (Enter lesser of line 9 or line 9a, Part 2 – Tax Computation) . .	**10**	

Section D. DSUE Amount Received from Predeceased Spouse(s) (To be completed by the estate of a deceased surviving spouse with DSUE amount from predeceased spouse(s))

Provide the following information to determine the DSUE amount received from deceased spouses.

A Name of Deceased Spouse (dates of death after December 31, 2010, only)	B Date of Death (enter as mm/dd/yy)	C Portability Election Made?		D If "Yes," DSUE Amount Received from Spouse	E DSUE Amount Applied by Decedent to Lifetime Gifts	F Year of Form 709 Reporting Use of DSUE Amount Listed in col E	G Remaining DSUE Amount, if any (subtract col. E from col. D)
		Yes	No				
Part 1 — DSUE RECEIVED FROM LAST DECEASED SPOUSE							
Part 2 — DSUE RECEIVED FROM OTHER PREDECEASED SPOUSE(S) AND USED BY DECEDENT							
Total (for all DSUE amounts from predeceased spouse(s) applied)							

Add the amount from Part 1, column D and the total from Part 2, column E. Enter the result on line 9b, Part 2—Tax Computation . . . . ▶ _____

		Decedent's social security number
Estate of:		

SCHEDULE A—Real Estate

- For jointly owned property that must be disclosed on Schedule E, see instructions.
- Real estate that is part of a sole proprietorship should be shown on Schedule F.
- Real estate that is included in the gross estate under sections 2035, 2036, 2037, or 2038 should be shown on Schedule G.
- Real estate that is included in the gross estate under section 2041 should be shown on Schedule H.
- If you elect section 2032A valuation, you must complete Schedule A and Schedule A-1.

Note. If the value of the gross estate, together with the amount of adjusted taxable gifts, is less than the basic exclusion amount and the Form 706 is being filed solely to elect portability of the DSUE amount, consideration should be given as to whether you are required to report the value of assets eligible for the marital or charitable deduction on this schedule. See the instructions and Reg. section 20.2010-2T (a)(7)(ii) for more information. If you are not required to report the value of an asset, identify the property but make no entries in the last three columns.

Item number	Description	Alternate valuation date	Alternate value	Value at date of death
1				
	Total from continuation schedules or additional statements attached to this schedule . . .			
	TOTAL. (Also enter on Part 5—Recapitulation, page 3, at item 1.)			

(If more space is needed, attach the continuation schedule from the end of this package or additional statements of the same size.)

	Decedent's social security number
Estate of:	

SCHEDULE A-1—Section 2032A Valuation

Part 1. Type of election (Before making an election, see the checklist in the instructions):

☐ **Protective election (Regulations section 20.2032A-8(b)).** Complete Part 2, line 1, and column A of lines 3 and 4. (see instructions)

☐ **Regular election.** Complete all of Part 2 (including line 11, if applicable) and Part 3. (see instructions)

Before completing Schedule A-1, see the instructions for the information and documents that must be included to make a valid election.

The election is not valid unless the agreement (that is, *Part 3. Agreement to Special Valuation Under Section 2032A):*

• Is signed by each qualified heir with an interest in the specially valued property and

• Is attached to this return when it is filed.

Part 2. Notice of election (Regulations section 20.2032A-8(a)(3))

Note. All real property entered on lines 2 and 3 must also be entered on Schedules A, E, F, G, or H, as applicable.

1   Qualified use—check one ▶   ☐ Farm used for farming, or

                                   ☐ Trade or business other than farming

2   Real property used in a qualified use, passing to qualified heirs, and to be specially valued on this Form 706.

A Schedule and item number from Form 706	B Full value (without section 2032A(b)(3)(B) adjustment)	C Adjusted value (with section 2032A (b)(3)(B) adjustment)	D Value based on qualified use (without section 2032A(b)(3)(B) adjustment)
Totals			

Attach a legal description of all property listed on line 2.

Attach copies of appraisals showing the column B values for all property listed on line 2.

3   Real property used in a qualified use, passing to qualified heirs, but not specially valued on this Form 706.

A Schedule and item number from Form 706	B Full value (without section 2032A(b)(3)(B) adjustment)	C Adjusted value (with section 2032A (b)(3)(B) adjustment)	D Value based on qualified use (without section 2032A(b)(3)(B) adjustment)
Totals			

If you checked "Regular election," you must attach copies of appraisals showing the column B values for all property listed on line 3.

(continued on next page)

4 Personal property used in a qualified use and passing to qualified heirs.

A Schedule and item number from Form 706	B Adjusted value (with section 2032A (b)(3)(B) adjustment)	A (continued) Schedule and item number from Form 706	B (continued) Adjusted value (with section 2032A (b)(3)(B) adjustment)
		"Subtotal" from Col. B, below left	
Subtotal		**Total adjusted value** . . .	

5 Enter the value of the total gross estate as adjusted under section 2032A(b)(3)(A). ▶ _____

6 **Attach a description of the method used to determine the special value based on qualified use.**

7 Did the decedent and/or a member of his or her family own all property listed on line 2 for at least 5 of the 8 years immediately preceding the date of the decedent's death? . . . . ☐ **Yes** ☐ **No**

8 Were there any periods during the 8-year period preceding the date of the decedent's death during which the decedent or a member of his or her family:

		Yes	No
a	Did not own the property listed on line 2?		
b	Did not use the property listed on line 2 in a qualified use?		
c	Did not materially participate in the operation of the farm or other business within the meaning of section 2032A(e)(6)?		

If you answered "Yes" to any of the above, attach a statement listing the periods. If applicable, describe whether the exceptions of sections 2032A(b)(4) or (5) are met.

9 **Attach affidavits describing the activities constituting material participation and the identity and relationship to the decedent of the material participants.**

10 Persons holding interests. Enter the requested information for each party who received any interest in the specially valued property. **(Each of the qualified heirs receiving an interest in the property must sign the agreement, to be found on Part 3 of this Schedule A-1, and the agreement must be filed with this return.)**

	Name	Address
A		
B		
C		
D		
E		
F		
G		
H		

	Identifying number	Relationship to decedent	Fair market value	Special-use value
A				
B				
C				
D				
E				
F				
G				
H				

You must attach a computation of the GST tax savings attributable to direct skips for each person listed above who is a skip person. (see instructions)

11 **Woodlands election.** Check here ▶ ☐ if you wish to make a Woodlands election as described in section 2032A(e)(13). Enter the schedule and item numbers from Form 706 of the property for which you are making this election ▶ _____

Attach a statement explaining why you are entitled to make this election. The IRS may issue regulations that require more information to substantiate this election. You will be notified by the IRS if you must supply further information.

Schedule A-1—Page 7

Part 3. Agreement to Special Valuation Under Section 2032A

	Decedent's social security number
Estate of:	

There cannot be a valid election unless:

• The agreement is executed by each one of the qualified heirs and

• The agreement is included with the estate tax return when the estate tax return is filed.

We (list all qualified heirs)

_____

_____ ,

being all the qualified heirs and (list all other persons having an interest in the property required to sign this agreement)

_____

_____ ,

being all other parties having interests in the property which is qualified real property and which is valued under section 2032A of the Internal Revenue Code, do hereby approve of the election made by _____ ,
Executor/Administrator of the estate of _____ ,
pursuant to section 2032A to value said property on the basis of the qualified use to which the property is devoted and do hereby enter into this agreement pursuant to section 2032A(d).

The undersigned agree and consent to the application of subsection (c) of section 2032A with respect to all the property described on Form 706, Schedule A-1, Part 2, line 2, attached to this agreement. More specifically, the undersigned heirs expressly agree and consent to personal liability under subsection (c) of 2032A for the additional estate and GST taxes imposed by that subsection with respect to their respective interests in the above-described property in the event of certain early dispositions of the property or early cessation of the qualified use of the property. It is understood that if a qualified heir disposes of any interest in qualified real property to any member of his or her family, such member may thereafter be treated as the qualified heir with respect to such interest upon filing a Form 706-A, United States Additional Estate Tax Return, and a new agreement.

The undersigned interested parties who are not qualified heirs consent to the collection of any additional estate and GST taxes imposed under section 2032A(c) from the specially valued property.

If there is a disposition of any interest which passes, or has passed to him or her, or if there is a cessation of the qualified use of any specially valued property which passes or passed to him or her, each of the undersigned heirs agrees to file a Form 706-A, and pay any additional estate and GST taxes due within 6 months of the disposition or cessation.

It is understood by all interested parties that this agreement is a condition precedent to the election of special-use valuation under section 2032A and must be executed by every interested party even though that person may not have received the estate (or GST) tax benefits or be in possession of such property.

Each of the undersigned understands that by making this election, a lien will be created and recorded pursuant to section 6324B of the Code on the property referred to in this agreement for the adjusted tax differences with respect to the estate as defined in section 2032A(c)(2)(C).

As the interested parties, the undersigned designate the following individual as their agent for all dealings with the Internal Revenue Service concerning the continued qualification of the specially valued property under section 2032A and on all issues regarding the special lien under section 6324B. The agent is authorized to act for the parties with respect to all dealings with the Internal Revenue Service on matters affecting the qualified real property described earlier. This includes the authorization:

• To receive confidential information on all matters relating to continued qualification under section 2032A of the specially valued real property and on all matters relating to the special lien arising under section 6324B;

• To furnish the Internal Revenue Service with any requested information concerning the property;

• To notify the Internal Revenue Service of any disposition or cessation of qualified use of any part of the property;

• To receive, but not to endorse and collect, checks in payment of any refund of Internal Revenue taxes, penalties, or interest;

• To execute waivers (including offers of waivers) of restrictions on assessment or collection of deficiencies in tax and waivers of notice of disallowance of a claim for credit or refund; and

• To execute closing agreements under section 7121.

(continued on next page)

Part 3. Agreement to Special Valuation Under Section 2032A *(continued)*

Estate of:	Decedent's social security number

• Other acts (specify) ▶ _____

By signing this agreement, the agent agrees to provide the Internal Revenue Service with any requested information concerning this property and to notify the Internal Revenue Service of any disposition or cessation of the qualified use of any part of this property.

Name of Agent	Signature	Address

The property to which this agreement relates is listed in Form 706, United States Estate (and Generation-Skipping Transfer) Tax Return, and in the Notice of Election, along with its fair market value according to section 2031 of the Code and its special-use value according to section 2032A. The name, address, social security number, and interest (including the value) of each of the undersigned in this property are as set forth in the attached Notice of Election.

IN WITNESS WHEREOF, the undersigned have hereunto set their hands at _____ ,

this _____ day of _____ .

SIGNATURES OF EACH OF THE QUALIFIED HEIRS:

_____ _____
Signature of qualified heir   Signature of qualified heir

_____ _____
Signature of qualified heir   Signature of qualified heir

_____ _____
Signature of qualified heir   Signature of qualified heir

_____ _____
Signature of qualified heir   Signature of qualified heir

_____ _____
Signature of qualified heir   Signature of qualified heir

_____ _____
Signature of qualified heir   Signature of qualified heir

_____
Signatures of other interested parties

_____
Signatures of other interested parties

Schedule A-1—Page 9

	Decedent's social security number
Estate of:	

SCHEDULE B—Stocks and Bonds

(For jointly owned property that must be disclosed on Schedule E, see instructions.)

Note. If the value of the gross estate, together with the amount of adjusted taxable gifts, is less than the basic exclusion amount and the Form 706 is being filed solely to elect portability of the DSUE amount, consideration should be given as to whether you are required to report the value of assets eligible for the marital or charitable deduction on this schedule. See the instructions and Reg. section 20.2010-2T (a)(7)(ii) for more information. If you are not required to report the value of an asset, identify the property but make no entries in the last four columns.

Item number	Description, including face amount of bonds or number of shares and par value for identification. Give CUSIP number. If trust, partnership, or closely held entity, give EIN.	CUSIP number or EIN, where applicable	Unit value	Alternate valuation date	Alternate value	Value at date of death
1						
	Total from continuation schedules (or additional statements) attached to this schedule . . .					
	TOTAL. (Also enter on Part 5—Recapitulation, page 3, at item 2.)					

(If more space is needed, attach the continuation schedule from the end of this package or additional statements of the same size.)

	Decedent's social security number
Estate of:	

SCHEDULE C—Mortgages, Notes, and Cash

(For jointly owned property that must be disclosed on Schedule E, see instructions.)

Note. If the value of the gross estate, together with the amount of adjusted taxable gifts, is less than the basic exclusion amount and the Form 706 is being filed solely to elect portability of the DSUE amount, consideration should be given as to whether you are required to report the value of assets eligible for the marital or charitable deduction on this schedule. See the instructions and Reg. section 20.2010-2T (a)(7)(ii) for more information. If you are not required to report the value of an asset, identify the property but make no entries in the last three columns.

Item number	Description	Alternate valuation date	Alternate value	Value at date of death
1				
Total from continuation schedules (or additional statements) attached to this schedule . . .				
TOTAL. (Also enter on Part 5—Recapitulation, page 3, at item 3.)				

(If more space is needed, attach the continuation schedule from the end of this package or additional statements of the same size.)

Estate of:	Decedent's social security number

SCHEDULE D—Insurance on the Decedent's Life

You must list all policies on the life of the decedent and attach a Form 712 for each policy.

Note. If the value of the gross estate, together with the amount of adjusted taxable gifts, is less than the basic exclusion amount and the Form 706 is being filed solely to elect portability of the DSUE amount, consideration should be given as to whether you are required to report the value of assets eligible for the marital or charitable deduction on this schedule. See the instructions and Reg. section 20.2010-2T (a)(7)(ii) for more information. If you are not required to report the value of an asset, identify the property but make no entries in the last three columns.

Item number	Description	Alternate valuation date	Alternate value	Value at date of death
1				
	Total from continuation schedules (or additional statements) attached to this schedule . .			
	TOTAL. (Also enter on Part 5—Recapitulation, page 3, at item 4.)			

(If more space is needed, attach the continuation schedule from the end of this package or additional statements of the same size.)

Form 706 (Rev. 8-2013)

Estate of:

	Decedent's social security number

SCHEDULE E—Jointly Owned Property
(If you elect section 2032A valuation, you must complete Schedule E and Schedule A-1.)

PART 1. Qualified Joint Interests—Interests Held by the Decedent and His or Her Spouse as the Only Joint Tenants (Section 2040(b)(2))

Note. If the value of the gross estate, together with the amount of adjusted taxable gifts, is less than the basic exclusion amount and the Form 706 is being filed solely to elect portability of the DSUE amount, consideration should be given as to whether you are required to report the value of assets eligible for the marital or charitable deduction on this schedule. See the instructions and Reg. section 20.2010-2T (a)(7)(ii) for more information. If you are not required to report the value of an asset, identify the property but make no entries in the last three columns.

Item number	Description. For securities, give CUSIP number. If trust, partnership, or closely held entity, give EIN.		Alternate valuation date	Alternate value	Value at date of death
		CUSIP number or EIN, where applicable			
1					
	Total from continuation schedules (or additional statements) attached to this schedule				
1a	Totals	**1a**		
1b	Amounts included in gross estate (one-half of line 1a)	**1b**		

PART 2. All Other Joint Interests

2a State the name and address of each surviving co-tenant. If there are more than three surviving co-tenants, list the additional co-tenants on an attached statement.

	Name	Address (number and street, city, state, and ZIP code)
A.		
B.		
C.		

Item number	Enter letter for co-tenant	Description (including alternate valuation date if any). For securities, give CUSIP number. If trust, partnership, or closely held entity, give EIN		Percentage includible	Includible alternate value	Includible value at date of death
			CUSIP number or EIN, where applicable			
1						
	Total from continuation schedules (or additional statements) attached to this schedule					
2b	Total other joint interests	**2b**		
3	**Total includible joint interests** (add lines 1b and 2b). Also enter on Part 5—Recapitulation, page 3, at item 5	**3**		

(If more space is needed, attach the continuation schedule from the end of this package or additional statements of the same size.)

Schedule E—Page 13

Estate of:	Decedent's social security number

SCHEDULE F—Other Miscellaneous Property Not Reportable Under Any Other Schedule

(For jointly owned property that must be disclosed on Schedule E, see instructions.)

(If you elect section 2032A valuation, you must complete Schedule F and Schedule A-1.)

Note. If the value of the gross estate, together with the amount of adjusted taxable gifts, is less than the basic exclusion amount and the Form 706 is being filed solely to elect portability of the DSUE amount, consideration should be given as to whether you are required to report the value of assets eligible for the marital or charitable deduction on this schedule. See the instructions and Reg. section 20.2010-2T (a)(7)(ii) for more information. If you are not required to report the value of an asset, identify the property but make no entries in the last three columns.

		Yes	No
1	Did the decedent own any works of art, items, or any collections whose artistic or collectible value at date of death exceeded $3,000? . . . . If "Yes," submit full details on this schedule and attach appraisals.		
2	Has the decedent's estate, spouse, or any other person received (or will receive) any bonus or award as a result of the decedent's employment or death? . . . . If "Yes," submit full details on this schedule.		
3	Did the decedent at the time of death have, or have access to, a safe deposit box? . . . . If "Yes," state location, and if held jointly by decedent and another, state name and relationship of joint depositor.		

If any of the contents of the safe deposit box are omitted from the schedules in this return, explain fully why omitted.

Item number	Description. For securities, give CUSIP number. If trust, partnership, or closely held entity, give EIN	CUSIP number or EIN, where applicable	Alternate valuation date	Alternate value	Value at date of death
1					
	Total from continuation schedules (or additional statements) attached to this schedule . .				
	TOTAL. (Also enter on Part 5—Recapitulation, page 3, at item 6.)				

(If more space is needed, attach the continuation schedule from the end of this package or additional statements of the same size.)

Estate of:

	Decedent's social security number

SCHEDULE G—Transfers During Decedent's Life

(If you elect section 2032A valuation, you must complete Schedule G and Schedule A-1.)

Note. If the value of the gross estate, together with the amount of adjusted taxable gifts, is less than the basic exclusion amount and the Form 706 is being filed solely to elect portability of the DSUE amount, consideration should be given as to whether you are required to report the value of assets eligible for the marital or charitable deduction on this schedule. See the instructions and Reg. section 20.2010-2T (a)(7)(ii) for more information. If you are not required to report the value of an asset, identify the property but make no entries in the last three columns.

Item number	Description. For securities, give CUSIP number. If trust, partnership, or closely held entity, give EIN	Alternate valuation date	Alternate value	Value at date of death
A.	Gift tax paid or payable by the decedent or the estate for all gifts made by the decedent or his or her spouse within 3 years before the decedent's death (section 2035(b))	X X X X X		
B.	Transfers includible under sections 2035(a), 2036, 2037, or 2038:			
1				
	Total from continuation schedules (or additional statements) attached to this schedule . .			
	TOTAL. (Also enter on Part 5—Recapitulation, page 3, at item 7.)			

SCHEDULE H—Powers of Appointment

(Include "5 and 5 lapsing" powers (section 2041(b)(2)) held by the decedent.)

(If you elect section 2032A valuation, you must complete Schedule H and Schedule A-1.)

Note. If the value of the gross estate, together with the amount of adjusted taxable gifts, is less than the basic exclusion amount and the Form 706 is being filed solely to elect portability of the DSUE amount, consideration should be given as to whether you are required to report the value of assets eligible for the marital or charitable deduction on this schedule. See the instructions and Reg. section 20.2010-2T (a)(7)(ii) for more information. If you are not required to report the value of an asset, identify the property but make no entries in the last three columns.

Item number	Description	Alternate valuation date	Alternate value	Value at date of death
1				
	Total from continuation schedules (or additional statements) attached to this schedule . . .			
	TOTAL. (Also enter on Part 5—Recapitulation, page 3, at item 8.)			

(If more space is needed, attach the continuation schedule from the end of this package or additional statements of the same size.)

Form 706 (Rev. 8-2013)

| Estate of: | Decedent's social security number |

SCHEDULE I—Annuities

Note. Generally, no exclusion is allowed for the estates of decedents dying after December 31, 1984 (see instructions).

Note. If the value of the gross estate, together with the amount of adjusted taxable gifts, is less than the basic exclusion amount and the Form 706 is being filed solely to elect portability of the DSUE amount, consideration should be given as to whether you are required to report the value of assets eligible for the marital or charitable deduction on this schedule. See the instructions and Reg. section 20.2010-2T (a)(7)(ii) for more information. If you are not required to report the value of an asset, identify the property but make no entries in the last three columns.

A Are you excluding from the decedent's gross estate the value of a lump-sum distribution described in section 2039(f)(2) (as in effect before its repeal by the Deficit Reduction Act of 1984)? . . . .

If "Yes," you must attach the information required by the instructions.

Yes | No

Item number	Description. Show the entire value of the annuity before any exclusions	Alternate valuation date	Includible alternate value	Includible value at date of death
1				
	Total from continuation schedules (or additional statements) attached to this schedule . .			
	TOTAL. (Also enter on Part 5—Recapitulation, page 3, at item 9.)			

(If more space is needed, attach the continuation schedule from the end of this package or additional statements of the same size.)

Estate of:

Decedent's social security number

SCHEDULE J—Funeral Expenses and Expenses Incurred in Administering Property Subject to Claims

▶ Use Schedule PC to make a protective claim for refund due to an expense not currently deductible.
For such a claim, report the expense on Schedule J but without a value in the last column.

Note. Do not list expenses of administering property not subject to claims on this schedule. To report those expenses, see instructions.

If executors' commissions, attorney fees, etc., are claimed and allowed as a deduction for estate tax purposes, they are not allowable as a deduction in computing the taxable income of the estate for federal income tax purposes. They are allowable as an income tax deduction on Form 1041, U.S. Income Tax Return for Estates and Trusts, if a waiver is filed to forgo the deduction on Form 706 (see Instructions for Form 1041).

	Yes	No
Are you aware of any actual or potential reimbursement to the estate for any expense claimed as a deduction on this schedule?		
If "Yes," attach a statement describing the expense(s) subject to potential reimbursement. (see instructions)		

Item number	Description	Expense amount	Total amount
	A. Funeral expenses:		
1			
	Total funeral expenses . . . . ▶		
	B. Administration expenses:		
	1 Executors' commissions—amount estimated/agreed upon/paid. (Strike out the words that do not apply.)		
	2 Attorney fees—amount estimated/agreed upon/paid. (Strike out the words that do not apply.) . . .		
	3 Accountant fees—amount estimated/agreed upon/paid. (Strike out the words that do not apply.) . .		

	4 Miscellaneous expenses:	Expense amount	
	Total miscellaneous expenses from continuation schedules (or additional statements) attached to this schedule		
	Total miscellaneous expenses . . . . ▶		
	TOTAL. (Also enter on Part 5—Recapitulation, page 3, at item 14.) . . . . ▶		

(If more space is needed, attach the continuation schedule from the end of this package or additional statements of the same size.)

Estate of:

	Decedent's social security number

SCHEDULE K—Debts of the Decedent, and Mortgages and Liens

► Use Schedule PC to make a protective claim for refund due to a claim not currently deductible.
For such a claim, report the expense on Schedule K but without a value in the last column.

	Yes	No
Are you aware of any actual or potential reimbursement to the estate for any debt of the decedent, mortgage, or lien claimed as a deduction on this schedule?		
If "Yes," attach a statement describing the items subject to potential reimbursement. (see instructions)		
Are any of the items on this schedule deductible under Reg. section 20.2053-4(b) and Reg. section 20.2053-4(c)? . .		
If "Yes," attach a statement indicating the applicable provision and documenting the value of the claim.		

Item number	Debts of the Decedent—Creditor and nature of debt, and allowable death taxes	Amount
1		
	Total from continuation schedules (or additional statements) attached to this schedule	
	TOTAL. (Also enter on Part 5—Recapitulation, page 3, at item 15.)	

Item number	Mortgages and Liens—Description	Amount
1		
	Total from continuation schedules (or additional statements) attached to this schedule	
	TOTAL. (Also enter on Part 5—Recapitulation, page 3, at item 16.)	

(If more space is needed, attach the continuation schedule from the end of this package or additional statements of the same size.)

Estate of:	Decedent's social security number

SCHEDULE L—Net Losses During Administration and Expenses Incurred in Administering Property Not Subject to Claims

▶ Use Schedule PC to make a protective claim for refund due to an expense not currently deductible.
For such expenses, report the expense on Schedule L but without a value in the last column.

Item number	Net losses during administration (**Note.** Do not deduct losses claimed on a federal income tax return.)	Amount
1		

Total from continuation schedules (or additional statements) attached to this schedule . . . .

TOTAL. (Also enter on Part 5—Recapitulation, page 3, at item 19.) . . . .

Item number	Expenses incurred in administering property not subject to claims. (Indicate whether estimated, agreed upon, or paid.)	Amount
1		

Total from continuation schedules (or additional statements) attached to this schedule . . . .

TOTAL. (Also enter on Part 5—Recapitulation, page 3, at item 20.) . . . .

(If more space is needed, attach the continuation schedule from the end of this package or additional statements of the same size.)

	Decedent's social security number
Estate of:	

SCHEDULE M—Bequests, etc., to Surviving Spouse

Note. If the value of the gross estate, together with the amount of adjusted taxable gifts, is less than the basic exclusion amount and the Form 706 is being filed solely to elect portability of the DSUE amount, consideration should be given as to whether you are required to report the value of assets eligible for the marital or charitable deduction on this schedule. See the instructions and Reg. section 20.2010-2T (a)(7)(ii) for more information. If you are not required to report the value of an asset, identify the property but make no entry in the last column.

			Yes	No
1	Did any property pass to the surviving spouse as a result of a qualified disclaimer?	1		
	If "Yes," attach a copy of the written disclaimer required by section 2518(b).			
2a	In what country was the surviving spouse born? _____			
b	What is the surviving spouse's date of birth? _____			
c	Is the surviving spouse a U.S. citizen?	2c		
d	If the surviving spouse is a naturalized citizen, when did the surviving spouse acquire citizenship? _____			
e	If the surviving spouse is not a U.S. citizen, of what country is the surviving spouse a citizen? _____			
3	**Election Out of QTIP Treatment of Annuities.** Do you elect under section 2056(b)(7)(C)(ii) not to treat as qualified terminable interest property any joint and survivor annuities that are included in the gross estate and would otherwise be treated as qualified terminable interest property under section 2056(b)(7)(C)? (see instructions) . .	3		

Item number	Description of property interests passing to surviving spouse. For securities, give CUSIP number. If trust, partnership, or closely held entity, give EIN	Amount
	QTIP property:	
A1		
	All other property:	
B1		
	Total from continuation schedules (or additional statements) attached to this schedule	
4	**Total** amount of property interests listed on Schedule M **4**	

5a	Federal estate taxes payable out of property interests listed on Schedule M . . .	5a	
b	Other death taxes payable out of property interests listed on Schedule M	5b	
c	Federal and state GST taxes payable out of property interests listed on Schedule M	5c	
d	Add items 5a, 5b, and 5c 5d		
6	Net amount of property interests listed on Schedule M (subtract 5d from 4). Also enter on Part 5— Recapitulation, page 3, at item 21 . . . . **6**		

(If more space is needed, attach the continuation schedule from the end of this package or additional statements of the same size.)

	Decedent's social security number
Estate of:	

SCHEDULE O—Charitable, Public, and Similar Gifts and Bequests

Note. If the value of the gross estate, together with the amount of adjusted taxable gifts, is less than the basic exclusion amount and the Form 706 is being filed solely to elect portability of the DSUE amount, consideration should be given as to whether you are required to report the value of assets eligible for the marital or charitable deduction on this schedule. See the instructions and Reg. section 20.2010-2T (a)(7)(ii) for more information. If you are not required to report the value of an asset, identify the property but make no entry in the last column.

		Yes	No
1a	If the transfer was made by will, has any action been instituted to contest or have interpreted any of its provisions affecting the charitable deductions claimed in this schedule? . . . . If "Yes," full details must be submitted with this schedule.		
b	According to the information and belief of the person or persons filing this return, is any such action planned? . If "Yes," full details must be submitted with this schedule.		
2	Did any property pass to charity as the result of a qualified disclaimer? . . . . If "Yes," attach a copy of the written disclaimer required by section 2518(b).		

Item number	Name and address of beneficiary	Character of institution	Amount
1			

Total from continuation schedules (or additional statements) attached to this schedule				
3	Total		**3**	
4a	Federal estate tax payable out of property interests listed above	**4a**		
b	Other death taxes payable out of property interests listed above	**4b**		
c	Federal and state GST taxes payable out of property interests listed above .	**4c**		
d	Add items 4a, 4b, and 4c		**4d**	
5	Net value of property interests listed above (subtract 4d from 3). Also enter on Part 5—Recapitulation, page 3, at item 22		**5**	

(If more space is needed, attach the continuation schedule from the end of this package or additional statements of the same size.)

Estate of:

SCHEDULE P—Credit for Foreign Death Taxes

List all foreign countries to which death taxes have been paid and for which a credit is claimed on this return.

If a credit is claimed for death taxes paid to more than one foreign country, compute the credit for taxes paid to one country on this sheet and attach a separate copy of Schedule P for each of the other countries.

The credit computed on this sheet is for the _____

(Name of death tax or taxes)

_____ imposed in _____

(Name of country)

Credit is computed under the _____

(Insert title of treaty or statute)

Citizenship (nationality) of decedent at time of death

(All amounts and values must be entered in United States money.)

1	Total of estate, inheritance, legacy, and succession taxes imposed in the country named above attributable to property situated in that country, subjected to these taxes, and included in the gross estate (as defined by statute) .	**1**	
2	Value of the gross estate (adjusted, if necessary, according to the instructions)	**2**	
3	Value of property situated in that country, subjected to death taxes imposed in that country, and included in the gross estate (adjusted, if necessary, according to the instructions)	**3**	
4	Tax imposed by section 2001 reduced by the total credits claimed under sections 2010 and 2012 (see instructions)	**4**	
5	Amount of federal estate tax attributable to property specified at item 3. (Divide item 3 by item 2 and multiply the result by item 4.)	**5**	
6	Credit for death taxes imposed in the country named above (the smaller of item 1 or item 5). Also enter on line 13 of Part 2—Tax Computation	**6**	

SCHEDULE Q—Credit for Tax on Prior Transfers

Part 1. Transferor Information

	Name of transferor	Social security number	IRS office where estate tax return was filed	Date of death
A				
B				
C				

Check here ▶ ☐ if section 2013(f) (special valuation of farm, etc., real property) adjustments to the computation of the credit were made (see instructions).

Part 2. Computation of Credit (see instructions)

Item	Transferor			Total A, B, & C
	A	B	C	
1 Transferee's tax as apportioned (from worksheet, (line 7 ÷ line 8) × line 35 for each column) . .				
2 Transferor's tax (from each column of worksheet, line 20)				
3 Maximum amount before percentage requirement (for each column, enter amount from line 1 or 2, whichever is smaller)				
4 Percentage allowed (each column) (see instructions)	%	%	%	
5 Credit allowable (line 3 × line 4 for each column) .				
6 TOTAL credit allowable (add columns A, B, and C of line 5). Enter here and on line 14 of Part 2—Tax Computation				

SCHEDULE R—Generation-Skipping Transfer Tax

Note. To avoid application of the deemed allocation rules, Form 706 and Schedule R should be filed to allocate the GST exemption to trusts that may later have taxable terminations or distributions under section 2612 even if the form is not required to be filed to report estate or GST tax.

The GST tax is imposed on taxable transfers of interests in property located outside the United States as well as property located inside the United States. (see instructions)

Part 1. GST Exemption Reconciliation (Section 2631) and Special QTIP Election (Section 2652(a)(3))

You no longer need to check a box to make a section 2652(a)(3) (special QTIP) election. If you list qualifying property in Part 1, line 9 below, you will be considered to have made this election. See instructions for details.

1	Maximum allowable GST exemption	**1**	
2	Total GST exemption allocated by the decedent against decedent's lifetime transfers	**2**	
3	Total GST exemption allocated by the executor, using Form 709, against decedent's lifetime transfers	**3**	
4	GST exemption allocated on line 6 of Schedule R, Part 2	**4**	
5	GST exemption allocated on line 6 of Schedule R, Part 3	**5**	
6	Total GST exemption allocated on line 4 of Schedule(s) R-1	**6**	
7	Total GST exemption allocated to *inter vivos* transfers and direct skips (add lines 2–6)	**7**	
8	GST exemption available to allocate to trusts and section 2032A interests (subtract line 7 from line 1)	**8**	

9 Allocation of GST exemption to trusts (as defined for GST tax purposes):

A Name of trust	B Trust's EIN (if any)	C GST exemption allocated on lines 2–6, above (see instructions)	D Additional GST exemption allocated (see instructions)	E Trust's inclusion ratio (optional—see instructions)

9D	**Total.** May not exceed line 8, above	**9D**	

10	GST exemption available to allocate to section 2032A interests received by individual beneficiaries (subtract line 9D from line 8). You must attach special-use allocation statement (see instructions)	**10**

Estate of: | **Decedent's social security number**

Part 2. Direct Skips Where the Property Interests Transferred Bear the GST Tax on the Direct Skips

Name of skip person	Description of property interest transferred	Estate tax value

1	Total estate tax values of all property interests listed above	1	
2	Estate taxes, state death taxes, and other charges borne by the property interests listed above	2	
3	GST taxes borne by the property interests listed above but imposed on direct skips other than those shown on this Part 2 (see instructions)	3	
4	Total fixed taxes and other charges (add lines 2 and 3)	4	
5	Total tentative maximum direct skips (subtract line 4 from line 1)	5	
6	GST exemption allocated	6	
7	Subtract line 6 from line 5	7	
8	GST tax due (divide line 7 by 3.5)	8	
9	Enter the amount from line 8 of Schedule R, Part 3	9	
10	**Total GST taxes payable by the estate** (add lines 8 and 9). Enter here and on line 17 of Part 2—Tax Computation	10	

Estate of:	Decedent's social security number

Part 3. Direct Skips Where the Property Interests Transferred Do Not Bear the GST Tax on the Direct Skips

Name of skip person	Description of property interest transferred	Estate tax value

1	Total estate tax values of all property interests listed above	1	
2	Estate taxes, state death taxes, and other charges borne by the property interests listed above	2	
3	GST taxes borne by the property interests listed above but imposed on direct skips other than those shown on this Part 3 (see instructions)	3	
4	Total fixed taxes and other charges (add lines 2 and 3)	4	
5	Total tentative maximum direct skips (subtract line 4 from line 1)	5	
6	GST exemption allocated	6	
7	Subtract line 6 from line 5	7	
8	GST tax due (multiply line 7 by .40). Enter here and on Schedule R, Part 2, line 9	8	

SCHEDULE R-1
(Form 706)
(Rev. August 2013)
Department of the Treasury
Internal Revenue Service

Generation-Skipping Transfer Tax

Direct Skips From a Trust
Payment Voucher

OMB No. 1545-0015

Executor: File one copy with Form 706 and send two copies to the fiduciary. Do not pay the tax shown. See instructions for details.
Fiduciary: See instructions for details. Pay the tax shown on line 6.

Name of trust		Trust's EIN
Name and title of fiduciary	Name of decedent	
Address of fiduciary (number and street)	Decedent's SSN	Service Center where Form 706 was filed
City, state, and ZIP or postal code	Name of executor	
Address of executor (number and street)	City, state, and ZIP or postal code	
Date of decedent's death	Filing due date of Schedule R, Form 706 (with extensions)	

Part 1. Computation of the GST Tax on the Direct Skip

Description of property interests subject to the direct skip	Estate tax value

1	Total estate tax value of all property interests listed above	1	
2	Estate taxes, state death taxes, and other charges borne by the property interests listed above . .	2	
3	Tentative maximum direct skip from trust (subtract line 2 from line 1)	3	
4	GST exemption allocated	4	
5	Subtract line 4 from line 3	5	
6	**GST tax due from fiduciary** (divide line 5 by 3.5). **(See instructions if property will not bear the GST tax.)**	6	

Under penalties of perjury, I declare that I have examined this document, including accompanying schedules and statements, and to the best of my knowledge and belief, it is true, correct, and complete.

_____
Signature(s) of executor(s)   Date

_____
                                                              Date

_____
Signature of fiduciary or officer representing fiduciary   Date

Schedule R-1—Page 26

Instructions for the Trustee

Introduction

Schedule R-1 (Form 706) serves as a payment voucher for the Generation-Skipping Transfer (GST) tax imposed on a direct skip from a trust, which you, the trustee of the trust, must pay. The executor completes the Schedule R-1 (Form 706) and gives you two copies. File one copy and keep one for your records.

How to pay

You can pay by check or money order or by electronic funds transfer.

To pay by check or money order:

- Make it payable to "United States Treasury."
- The amount of the check or money order should be the amount on line 6 of Schedule R-1.
- Write "GST Tax" and the trust's EIN on the check or money order.

To pay by electronic funds transfer:

- Funds must be submitted through the Electronic Federal Tax Payment System (EFTPS).
- Establish an EFTPS account by visiting *www.eftps.gov* or calling 1-800-555-4477.
- To be considered timely, payments made through EFTPS must be completed no later than 8 p.m. Eastern time the day **before** the due date.

Signature

You must sign the Schedule R-1 in the space provided.

What to mail

Mail your check or money order, if applicable, and the copy of Schedule R-1 that you signed.

Where to mail

Mail to the Department of the Treasury, Internal Revenue Service Center, Cincinnati, OH 45999.

When to pay

The GST tax is due and payable 9 months after the decedent's date of death (shown on the Schedule R-1). You will owe interest on any GST tax not paid by that date.

Automatic extension

You have an automatic extension of time to file Schedule R-1 and pay the GST tax. The automatic extension allows you to file and pay by 2 months after the due date (with extensions) for filing the decedent's Schedule R (shown on the Schedule R-1).

If you pay the GST tax under the automatic extension, you will be charged interest (but no penalties).

Additional information

For more information, see section 2603(a)(2) and the Instructions for Form 706, United States Estate (and Generation-Skipping Transfer) Tax Return.

Estate of:

SCHEDULE U—Qualified Conservation Easement Exclusion

Part 1. Election

Note. The executor is deemed to have made the election under section 2031(c)(6) if he or she files Schedule U and excludes any qualifying conservation easements from the gross estate.

Part 2. General Qualifications

1   Describe the land subject to the qualified conservation easement (see instructions) _____

2   Did the decedent or a member of the decedent's family own the land described above during the 3-year period ending on the date of the decedent's death? . . . . ☐ **Yes** ☐ **No**

3   Describe the conservation easement with regard to which the exclusion is being claimed (see instructions).

_____

Part 3. Computation of Exclusion

4	Estate tax value of the land subject to the qualified conservation easement (see instructions) .	**4**		
5	Date of death value of any easements granted prior to decedent's death and included on line 10 below (see instructions)	**5**		
6	Add lines 4 and 5	**6**		
7	Value of retained development rights on the land (see instructions)	**7**		
8	Subtract line 7 from line 6	**8**		
9	Multiply line 8 by 30% (.30)	**9**		
10	Value of qualified conservation easement for which the exclusion is being claimed (see instructions)	**10**		

Note. If line 10 is less than line 9, continue with line 11. If line 10 is equal to or more than line 9, skip lines 11 through 13, enter ".40" on line 14, and complete the schedule.

11	Divide line 10 by line 8. Figure to 3 decimal places (for example, ".123")	**11**		

Note. If line 11 is equal to or less than .100, stop here; the estate does not qualify for the conservation easement exclusion.

12	Subtract line 11 from .300. Enter the answer in hundredths by rounding any thousandths up to the next higher hundredth (that is, .030 = .03, but .031 = .04)	**12**		
13	Multiply line 12 by 2	**13**		
14	Subtract line 13 from .40	**14**		
15	Deduction under section 2055(f) for the conservation easement (see instructions)	**15**		
16	Amount of indebtedness on the land (see instructions)	**16**		
17	Total reductions in value (add lines 7, 15, and 16)		**17**	
18	Net value of land (subtract line 17 from line 4)		**18**	
19	Multiply line 18 by line 14		**19**	
20	Enter the smaller of line 19 or the exclusion limitation (see instructions). Also enter this amount on item 12, Part 5—Recapitulation, page 3		**20**	

Schedule **PC**
(Rev. August 2013)
Department of the Treasury
Internal Revenue Service

Protective Claim for Refund

► **To be used for decedents dying after December 31, 2011. File 2 copies of this schedule with Form 706 for each pending claim or expense under section 2053.**

OMB No. 1545-0015

- Timely filing a protective claim for refund preserves the estate's right to claim a refund based on the amount of an unresolved claim or expense that may not become deductible under section 2053 until after the limitation period ends.
- Schedule PC can be used to file a protective claim for refund and, once the claim or expense becomes deductible, Schedule PC can be used to notify the IRS that a refund is being claimed.
- Schedule PC can be used by the estate of a decedent dying after 2011.
- Schedule PC must be filed with Form 706 and cannot be filed separately. (To file a protective claim for refund or notify the IRS that a refund is being claimed in a form separate from the Form 706, instead use Form 843, Claim for Refund and Request for Abatement.)
- Each separate claim or expense requires a separate Schedule PC (or Form 843, if not filed with Form 706).
- Schedule PC must be filed in duplicate (two copies) for each separate claim or expense.

Part 1. General Information

1. Name of decedent	**2.** Decedent's social security number
3. Name of fiduciary	**4.** Date of death
5a. Address (number, street, and room or suite no.)	**5b.** Room or suite no.
5c. City or town, state, and ZIP or postal code	**6.** Daytime telephone number

7. Number of Claims. Enter number of Schedules PC being filed with Form 706. ________

If the number is greater than one OR if another Schedule PC or Form 843 was previously filed by or on behalf of the estate, complete Part 3 of this Schedule PC.

8. Fiduciary ☐ Check here if this Schedule PC is being filed with the original Form 706 or is being filed by the same fiduciary who filed the original Form 706 for decedent's estate. If a different fiduciary is filing this Schedule PC, see instructions for establishing the legal authority to pursue the claim for refund on behalf of the estate.

Part 2. Claim Information

Check the box that applies to this claim for refund.

a. ☐ Protective claim for refund made for unresolved claim or expense.

Amount in contest: ____________________

b. ☐ Partial refund claimed: partial resolution and/or satisfaction of claim or expense for which a protective claim for refund has been filed previously.

Date protective claim for refund filed for this claim or expense: ____________________

Amount of claim or expense partially resolved and/or satisfied and presently claimed as a deduction under section 2053 (do not include amounts previously deducted): ____________________

c. ☐ Full and final refund claimed for this claim or expense: resolution and/or satisfaction of claim or expense for which a protective claim for refund has been filed previously.

Date protective claim for refund filed for this claim or expense: ____________________

Amount of claim or expense finally resolved and/or satisfied and presently claimed as a deduction under section 2053 (do not include amounts previously deducted): ____________________

Decedent's social security number

Estate of:

A Form 706 Schedule and Item number	B Identification of the claim • Name or names of the claimant(s) • Basis of the claim or other description of the pending claim or expense • Reasons and contingencies delaying resolution • Status of contested matters • Attach copies of relevant pleadings or other documents	C Amount, if any, deducted under Treas. Reg. sections 20.2053-1(d)(4) or 20.2053-4 (b) or (c) for the identified claim or expense	D Amount presently claimed as a deduction under section 2053 for the identified claim	E Ancillary expenses estimated/ agreed upon/paid (Please indicate)	F Amount of tax to be refunded

Part 3. Other Schedules PC and Forms 843 Filed by Estate

If a Schedule PC or Form 843 was previously filed by the estate, complete Part 3 to identify each claim for refund reported.

A Date of death	B Internal Revenue office where filed	C Date filed	D Indicate whether (1) Protective Claim for Refund; (2) Partial Claim for Refund; or (3) Full and Final Claim for Refund	E Amount in Contest
1				

To inquire about the receipt and/or processing of the protective claim for refund, please call (866) 699-4083.

(Rev. 8-2013)

(Make copies of this schedule before completing it if you will need more than one schedule.)

Estate of:

Decedent's social security number

CONTINUATION SCHEDULE

Continuation of Schedule _____

(Enter letter of schedule you are continuing.)

Item number	Description. For securities, give CUSIP number. If trust, partnership, or closely held entity, give EIN.	Unit value (Sch. B, E, or G only)	Alternate valuation date	Alternate value	Value at date of death or amount deductible

TOTAL. (Carry forward to main schedule.) . . . .

Instructions for Form 706
(Rev. August 2014)

Department of the Treasury
Internal Revenue Service

For decedents dying after December 31, 2013
United States Estate (and Generation-Skipping Transfer) Tax Return

Section references are to the Internal Revenue Code unless otherwise noted.

Prior Revisions of Form 706

For Decedents Dying		Use Revision of Form 706 Dated
After	and Before	
December 31, 1998	January 1, 2001	July 1999
December 31, 2000	January 1, 2002	November 2001
December 31, 2001	January 1, 2003	August 2002
December 31, 2002	January 1, 2004	August 2003
December 31, 2003	January 1, 2005	August 2004
December 31, 2004	January 1, 2006	August 2005
December 31, 2005	January 1, 2007	October 2006
December 31, 2006	January 1, 2008	September 2007
December 31, 2007	January 1, 2009	August 2008
December 31, 2008	January 1, 2010	September 2009
December 31, 2009	January 1, 2011	July 2011
December 31, 2010	January 1, 2012	August 2011
December 31, 2011	January 1, 2013	August 2012
December 31, 2012	January 1, 2014	August 2013

Future Developments

For the latest information about developments related to Form 706 and its instructions, such as legislation enacted after they were published, go to *www.irs.gov/form706*.

What's New

Various dollar amounts and limitations in the Form 706 are indexed for inflation. For decedents dying in 2014, the following amounts are applicable:
- The basic exclusion amount is $5,340,000.
- The ceiling on special-use valuation is $1,090,000.
- The amount used in figuring the 2% portion of estate tax payable in installments is $1,450,000.

The IRS will publish amounts for future years in annual revenue procedures.

On June 26, 2013, the United States Supreme Court held that Section 3 of the Defense of Marriage Act, which said that the terms "marriage" and "spouse" only apply to heterosexual couples, was unconstitutional. (United States v. Windsor, 570 U.S. 12 (2013)). The ruling impacts a number of federal laws, including those governing the reporting and collection of federal taxes. For federal tax purposes, the IRS recognizes same-sex marriages that are valid in the state where they were entered into, regardless of the married couple's residence. See Rev. Rul. 2013–17, 2013–38 I.R.B. 201, available at *http://www.irs.gov/pub/irs-irbs/irb13-38.pdf*. If you believe the new law may affect your estate or gift tax liability or filing requirement, please continue to monitor *IRS.gov* for additional guidance on the application of Windsor.

Reminders
- Executors must provide documentation of their status.
- The credit for transfers made by lifetime gift has been reunified with the credit against transfers made at death.

The applicable credit amount for 2014 is $2,081,800 (based on the basic exclusion amount of $5,340,000). This does not include any applicable credit resulting from DSUE amount received from a predeceased spouse.

- Portability of Deceased Spousal Unused Exclusion

    1. Line 7 Worksheet in the instructions has been expanded to include the calculation for cumulative lifetime gifts on which tax was paid or payable. This amount is used in Section C of Part 6–Portability of Deceased Spousal Unused Exclusion (DSUE).

    2. Part 6—Portability of Deceased Spousal Unused Exclusion (DSUE) was added to Form 706. The only action required to elect portability of the DSUE amount, if any, is to file a timely and complete Form 706. In this Part, taxpayers can opt out of electing to transfer any DSUE amount to a surviving spouse, calculate the amount of DSUE to be transferred in the event of an election, and/or account for any DSUE amount received from predeceased spouse(s).

    3. Line 9 of Part 2—Tax Computation was replaced with lines 9a through 9d to calculate the applicable exclusion amount and applicable credit amount (formerly unified credit amount), factoring in any DSUE amount received from a predeceased spouse.

    4. Executors of estates who are not required to file Form 706 under section 6018(a) but who are filing to elect portability of DSUE amount to the surviving spouse are not required to report the value of certain property eligible for the marital deduction under section 2056 or 2056A or the charitable deduction under section 2055 under the special rule of Reg. section 20.2010–2T(a)(7)(ii). However, the value of those assets must be estimated and included in the total value of the gross estate. The special rule does not apply to assets whose valuation is required for eligibility under section 2032, 2032A, 2652(a)(3), 6166 or other provision of the Code or Regulations.

- A timely and complete Form 706 must be filed by the executor of any estate who intends to transfer the DSUE amount to the decedent's surviving spouse, regardless of the amount of the gross estate. See instructions for *Part 6—Portability of Deceased Spousal Unused Exclusion*, later.
- Filing a timely and complete Form 706 with a DSUE amount will be

considered an election to transfer the DSUE amount to the surviving spouse. An executor of an estate who files a Form 706 that does not elect to transfer the DSUE amount to the surviving spouse must affirmatively opt out of portability. See *Part 6—Portability of Deceased Spousal Unused Exclusion, Section A.*

General Instructions

Purpose of Form

The executor of a decedent's estate uses Form 706 to figure the estate tax imposed by Chapter 11 of the Internal Revenue Code. This tax is levied on the entire taxable estate and not just on the share received by a particular beneficiary. Form 706 is also used to figure the generation-skipping transfer (GST) tax imposed by Chapter 13 on direct skips (transfers to skip persons of interests in property included in the decedent's gross estate).

Which Estates Must File

For decedents who died in 2014, Form 706 must be filed by the executor of the estate of every U.S. citizen or resident:

    a. Whose gross estate, plus adjusted taxable gifts and specific exemption, is more than $5,340,000; or,

    b. Whose executor elects to transfer the DSUE amount to the surviving spouse, regardless of the size of the decedent's gross estate. See instructions for *Part 6—Portability of Deceased Spousal Unused Exclusion* and sections 2010(c)(4) and (c)(5).

To determine whether you must file a return for the estate under test "a" above, add:

    1. The adjusted taxable gifts (as defined in section 2503) made by the decedent after December 31, 1976;

    2. The total specific exemption allowed under section 2521 (as in effect before its repeal by the Tax Reform Act of 1976) for gifts made by the decedent after September 8, 1976; and

    3. The decedent's gross estate valued as of the date of death.

Gross Estate

The gross estate includes all property in which the decedent had an interest (including real property outside the United States). It also includes:

- Certain transfers made during the decedent's life without an adequate and

full consideration in money or money's worth,
- Annuities,
- The includible portion of joint estates with right of survivorship (see instructions for Schedule E),
- The includible portion of tenancies by the entirety (see instructions for Schedule E),
- Certain life insurance proceeds (even though payable to beneficiaries other than the estate) (see instructions for Schedule D),
- Property over which the decedent possessed a general power of appointment,
- Dower or curtesy (or statutory estate) of the surviving spouse, and
- Community property to the extent of the decedent's interest as defined by applicable law.

Note. Under the special rule of Regulations section 20.2010–2T(a)(7)(ii), executors of estates who are not required to file Form 706 under section 6018(a), but who are filing to elect portability of DSUE amount to the surviving spouse, are not required to report the value of certain property eligible for the marital deduction under section 2056 or 2056A or the charitable deduction under section 2055. However, the value of those assets must be estimated and included in the total value of the gross estate. See instructions for *Part 5—Recapitulation, lines 10 and 23*, for more information.

For more specific information, see the instructions for Schedules A through I.

U.S. Citizens or Residents; Nonresident Noncitizens

File Form 706 for the estates of decedents who were either U.S. citizens or U.S. residents at the time of death. For estate tax purposes, a resident is someone who had a domicile in the United States at the time of death. A person acquires a domicile by living in a place for even a brief period of time, as long as the person had no intention of moving from that place.

Decedents who were neither U.S. citizens nor U.S. residents at the time of death, file Form 706-NA, United States Estate (and Generation-Skipping Transfer) Tax Return, for the estate of nonresident not a citizen of the United States.

Residents of U.S. Possessions

All references to citizens of the United States are subject to the provisions of sections 2208 and 2209, relating to decedents who were U.S. citizens and residents of a U.S. possession on the date of death. If such a decedent became a U.S. citizen only because of his or her connection with a possession, then the decedent is considered a nonresident not a citizen of the United States for estate tax purposes, and you should file Form 706-NA. If such a decedent became a U.S. citizen wholly independently of his or her connection with a possession, then the decedent is considered a U.S. citizen for estate tax purposes, and you should file Form 706.

Executor

The term *executor* includes the executor, personal representative, or administrator of the decedent's estate. If none of these is appointed, qualified, and acting in the United States, every person in actual or constructive possession of any property of the decedent is considered an executor and must file a return.

Executors must provide documentation proving their status. Documentation will vary, but may include documents such as a certified copy of the will or a court order designating the executor(s). A statement by the executor attesting to their status is insufficient.

When To File

You must file Form 706 to report estate and/or GST tax within 9 months after the date of the decedent's death. If you are unable to file Form 706 by the due date, you may receive an extension of time to file. Use Form 4768, Application for Extension of Time To File a Return and/or Pay U.S. Estate (and Generation-Skipping Transfer) Taxes, to apply for an automatic 6-month extension of time to file.

Note. An executor can only elect to transfer the DSUE amount to the surviving spouse if the Form 706 is filed timely; that is, within 9 months of the decedent's date of death or, if you have received an extension of time to file, before the 6-month extension period ends.

Private delivery services. You can use certain private delivery services designated by the IRS to meet the "timely mailing as timely filing/paying" rule for tax returns and payments. These private delivery services include only the following:
• DHL Express (DHL): DHL Same Day Service.

• Federal Express (FedEx): FedEx Priority Overnight, FedEx Standard Overnight, FedEx 2Day, FedEx International Priority, FedEx International First.
• United Parcel Service (UPS): UPS Next Day Air, UPS Next Day Air Saver, UPS 2nd Day Air, UPS 2nd Day Air A.M., UPS Worldwide Express Plus, and UPS Worldwide Express.

The private delivery service can tell you how to get written proof of the mailing date.

Where To File

File Form 706 at the following address:

> Department of the Treasury
> Internal Revenue Service Center
> Cincinnati, OH 45999

Paying the Tax

The estate and GST taxes are due within 9 months of the date of the decedent's death. You may request an extension of time for payment by filing Form 4768. You may also elect under section 6166 to pay in installments or under section 6163 to postpone the part of the tax attributable to a reversionary or remainder interest. These elections are made by checking lines 3 and 4 (respectively) of Part 3—Elections by the Executor, and attaching the required statements.

If the tax paid with the return is different from the balance due as figured on the return, explain the difference in an attached statement. If you have made prior payments to the IRS, attach a statement to Form 706 including these facts.

Paying by check. Make the check payable to the "United States Treasury." Please write the decedent's name, social security number (SSN), and "Form 706" on the check to assist us in posting it to the proper account.

Paying Electronically. Payment of the tax due shown on Form 706 may be submitted electronically through the Electronic Federal Tax Payment System (EFTPS). EFTPS is a free service of the Department of Treasury.

To be considered timely, payments made through EFTPS must be completed no later than 8 p.m. Eastern time the day before the due date. All EFTPS payments must be scheduled in advance of the due date and, if necessary, may be changed or cancelled up to two business days before the scheduled payment date.

To get more information about EFTPS or to enroll, visit *www.eftps.gov* or call 1–800–555–4477. Additional information about EFTPS is available in Publication 966, Electronic Federal Tax Payment System: A Guide to Getting Started.

Signature and Verification

 If there is more than one executor, all listed executors are responsible for the return. However, it is sufficient for only one of the co-executors to sign the return.

All executors are responsible for the return as filed and are liable for penalties imposed for erroneous or false returns.

If two or more persons are liable for filing the return, they should all join together in filing one complete return. However, if they are unable to join in making one complete return, each is required to file a return disclosing all the information the person has about the estate, including the name of every person holding an interest in the property and a full description of the property. If the appointed, qualified, and acting executor is unable to make a complete return, then every person holding an interest in the property must, on notice from the IRS, make a return regarding that interest.

The executor who files the return must, in every case, sign the declaration on page 1 under penalties of perjury.

Generally, anyone who is paid to prepare the return must sign the return in the space provided and fill in the Paid Preparer Use Only area. See section 7701(a)(36)(B) for exceptions.

In addition to signing and completing the required information, the paid preparer must give a copy of the completed return to the executor.

Note. A paid preparer may sign original or amended returns by rubber stamp, mechanical device, or computer software program.

Amending Form 706

If you find that you must change something on a return that has already been filed, you should:
• File another Form 706;
• Enter "Supplemental Information" across the top of page 1 of the form; and
• Attach a copy of pages 1, 2, 3, and 4 of the original Form 706 that has already been filed.

If you have already been notified that the return has been selected for examination, you should provide the additional information directly to the office conducting the examination.

Supplemental Documents

Note. You must attach the death certificate to the return.

If the decedent was a citizen or resident of the United States and died testate (leaving a valid will), attach a certified copy of the will to the return. If you cannot obtain a certified copy, attach a copy of the will and an explanation of why it is not certified. Other supplemental documents may be required as explained later. Examples include Forms 712, Life Insurance Statement; 709, United States Gift (and Generation-Skipping Transfer) Tax Return; and 706-CE, Certificate of Payment of Foreign Death Tax; trust and power of appointment instruments; and state certification of payment of death taxes. If you do not file these documents with the return, the processing of the return will be delayed.

If the decedent was a U.S. citizen but not a resident of the United States, you must attach the following documents to the return:

1. A copy of the inventory of property and the schedule of liabilities, claims against the estate, and expenses of administration filed with the foreign court of probate jurisdiction, certified by a proper official of the court;

2. A copy of the return filed under the foreign inheritance, estate, legacy, succession tax, or other death tax act, certified by a proper official of the foreign tax department, if the estate is subject to such a foreign tax; and

3. If the decedent died testate, a certified copy of the will.

Rounding Off to Whole Dollars

You may show the money items on the return and accompanying schedules as whole-dollar amounts. To do so, drop the cents from any amount with less than 50 cents and increase any amount with 50 to 99 cents to the next dollar. For example, $1.39 becomes $1 and $2.55 becomes $3. If you have to add two or more amounts to compute an item's value, include the cents when adding the amounts and round off only the total.

Penalties

Late filing and late payment. Section 6651 provides for penalties for both late filing and for late payment unless there is reasonable cause for the delay. The law also provides for penalties for willful attempts to evade payment of tax. The late filing penalty will not be imposed if the taxpayer can show that the failure to file a timely return is due to reasonable cause.

Reasonable cause determinations. If you receive a notice about penalties after you file Form 706, send an explanation and we will determine if you meet reasonable cause criteria. Do not attach an explanation when you file Form 706. Explanations attached to the return at the time of filing will not be considered.

Valuation understatement. Section 6662 provides a 20% penalty for the underpayment of estate tax that exceeds $5,000 when the underpayment is attributable to valuation understatements. A valuation understatement occurs when the value of property reported on Form 706 is 65% or less of the actual value of the property.

This penalty increases to 40% if there is a gross valuation understatement. A gross valuation understatement occurs if any property on the return is valued at 40% or less of the value determined to be correct.

Penalties also apply to late filing, late payment, and underpayment of GST taxes.

Return preparer. Estate tax return preparers, who prepare any return or claim for refund which reflects an understatement of tax liability due to willful or reckless conduct, are subject to a penalty of $5,000 or 50% of the income derived (or income to be derived), whichever is greater, for the preparation of each such return. See section 6694(b), the regulations thereunder, and Ann. 2009-15, 2009-11 I.R.B. 687 (available at *www.irs.gov/pub/irs-irbs/irb09-11.pdf*) for more information.

Obtaining Forms and Publications To File or Use

Internet. You can access the IRS website 24 hours a day, 7 days a week at *IRS.gov* to:

● Download forms, instructions, and publications;
● Order IRS products online;

● Research your tax questions online;
● Search publications online by topic or keyword; and
● Sign up to receive local and national tax news by email.

Other forms that may be required.
● Form SS-5, Application for a Social Security Card.
● Form 706-CE, Certificate of Payment of Foreign Death Tax.
● Form 706-NA, United States Estate (and Generation-Skipping Transfer) Tax Return, Estate of nonresident not a citizen of the United States.
● Form 709, United States Gift (and Generation-Skipping Transfer) Tax Return.
● Form 712, Life Insurance Statement.
● Form 2848, Power of Attorney and Declaration of Representative.
● Form 4768, Application for Extension of Time To File a Return and/or Pay U.S. Estate (and Generation-Skipping Transfer) Taxes.
● Form 4808, Computation of Credit for Gift Tax.
● Form 8821, Tax Information Authorization.
● Form 8822, Change of Address.

Additional Information. The following publications may assist you in learning about and preparing Form 706:
● Publication 559, Survivors, Executors, and Administrators.
● Publication 910, IRS Guide to Free Tax Services.

Note. For information about release of nonresident U.S. citizen decedents' assets using transfer certificates under Regulations section 20.6325-1, write to:

Internal Revenue Service
Cincinnati, OH 45999
Stop 824G

Specific Instructions

You must file the first four pages of Form 706 and all required schedules. File Schedules A through I, as appropriate, to support the entries in items 1 through 9 of Part 5—Recapitulation.

 Make sure to complete the required pages and schedules in their entirety. Returns filed without entries in each field will not be processed.

IF . . .	THEN . . .
you enter zero on any item of the Recapitulation,	you need not file the schedule (except for Schedule F) referred to on that item.
you are estimating the value of one or more assets pursuant to the special rule of Regulations section 20.2010–2T(a)(7)(ii),	you must report the asset on the appropriate schedule, but you are not required to enter a value for the asset. Include the estimated value of the asset entered on the totals entered on lines 10 and 23 of Part 5— Recapitulation.
you claim an exclusion on item 12,	complete and attach Schedule U.
you claim any deductions on items 14 through 22 of the Recapitulation,	complete and attach the appropriate schedules to support the claimed deductions.
you claim credits for foreign death taxes or tax on prior transfers,	complete and attach Schedule P or Q.
there is not enough space on a schedule to list all the items,	attach a Continuation Schedule (or additional sheets of the same size) to the back of the schedule (see the Continuation Schedule at the end of Form 706); photocopy the blank schedule before completing it, if you will need more than one copy.

Also consider the following:
- Form 706 has 31 numbered pages. The pages are perforated so that you can remove them for copying and filing.
- Number the items you list on each schedule, beginning with the number "1" each time, or using the numbering convention as indicated on the schedule (for example, Schedule M).
- Total the items listed on the schedule and its attachments, Continuation Schedules, etc.
- Enter the total of all attachments, Continuation Schedules, etc., at the bottom of the printed schedule, but do not carry the totals forward from one schedule to the next.
- Enter the total, or totals, for each schedule on page 3, Part 5—Recapitulation.
- Do not complete the "Alternate valuation date" or "Alternate value" columns of any schedule unless you elected alternate valuation on line 1 of Part 3—Elections by the Executor.

Part Instructions

Table A — Unified Rate Schedule

Column A Taxable amount over	Column B Taxable amount not over	Column C Tax on amount in Column A	Column D Rate of tax on excess over amount in Column A
$0	$10,000	$0	18%
10,000	20,000	1,800	20%
20,000	40,000	3,800	22%
40,000	60,000	8,200	24%
60,000	80,000	13,000	26%
80,000	100,000	18,200	28%
100,000	150,000	23,800	30%
150,000	250,000	38,800	32%
250,000	500,000	70,800	34%
500,000	750,000	155,800	37%
750,000	1,000,000	248,300	39%
1,000,000	- - - -	345,800	40%

- When you complete the return, staple all the required pages together in the proper order.

Part 1—Decedent and Executor

Line 2

Enter the social security number (SSN) assigned specifically to the decedent. You cannot use the SSN assigned to the decedent's spouse. If the decedent did not have an SSN, the executor should obtain one for the decedent by filing Form SS-5, with a local Social Security Administration office.

Line 6a. Name of Executor

If there is more than one executor, enter the name of the executor to be contacted by the IRS and see line 6d.

Line 6b. Executor's Address

Use Form 8822 to report a change of the executor's address.

Line 6c. Executor's Social Security Number

Only one executor should complete this line. If there is more than one executor, see line 6d.

Line 6d. Multiple Executors

Check here if there is more than one executor. On an attached statement, provide the names, addresses, telephone numbers, and SSNs of any executor other than the one named on line 6a.

Line 11. Special Rule

If the estate is estimating the value of assets under the special rule of Regulations section 20.2010–2T(a)(7) (ii), check here and see the instructions for lines 10 and 23 of Part 5—Recapitulation.

Part 2—Tax Computation

In general, the estate tax is figured by applying the unified rates shown in Table A to the total of transfers both during life and at death, and then subtracting the gift taxes, as refigured based on the date of death rates. See *Worksheet TG, Line 4 Worksheet, and Line 7 Worksheet.*

Note. You must complete Part 2—Tax Computation.

Line 1

If you elected alternate valuation on line 1, Part 3—Elections by the Executor, enter the amount you entered in the "Alternate value" column of item 13 of Part 5—Recapitulation. Otherwise, enter the amount from the "Value at date of death" column.

Line 3b. State Death Tax Deduction

You may take a deduction on line 3b for estate, inheritance, legacy, or succession taxes paid as the result of the decedent's death to any state or the District of Columbia.

You may claim an anticipated amount of deduction and figure the federal estate tax on the return before the state death taxes have been paid. However, the deduction cannot be finally allowed unless you pay the state death taxes and claim the deduction within 4 years after the return is filed, or later (see section 2058(b)) if:
- A petition is filed with the Tax Court of the United States,
- You have an extension of time to pay, or

Worksheet TG—Taxable Gifts Reconciliation
(To be used for lines 4 and 7 of the Tax Computation)

	a. Calendar year or calendar quarter	b. Total taxable gifts for period (see Note)	**Note.** For the definition of a taxable gift, see section 2503. Follow Form 709. That is, include only the decedent's one-half of split gifts, whether the gifts were made by the decedent or the decedent's spouse. In addition to gifts reported on Form 709, you must include any taxable gifts in excess of the annual exclusion that were not reported on Form 709.			
Gifts made after June 6, 1932, and before 1977			c. Taxable amount included in col. b for gifts included in the gross estate	d. Taxable amount included in col. b for gifts that qualify for "special treatment of split gifts" described below	e. Gift tax paid by decedent on gifts in col. d	f. Gift tax paid by decedent's spouse on gifts in col. c
	1. Total taxable gifts made before 1977					
Gifts made after 1976						
	2. Totals for gifts made after 1976					

Line 4 Worksheet—Adjusted Taxable Gifts Made After 1976

1. Taxable gifts made after 1976. Enter the amount from Worksheet TG, line 2, column b	**1**	
2. Taxable gifts made after 1976 reportable on Schedule G. Enter the amount from Worksheet TG, line 2, column c.	**2**	
3. Taxable gifts made after 1976 that qualify for "special treatment." Enter the amount from Worksheet TG, line 2, column d	**3**	
4. Add lines 2 and 3	**4**	
5. Adjusted taxable gifts. Subtract line 4 from line 1. Enter here and on Part 2—Tax Computation, line 4.	**5**	

• You file a claim for refund or credit of an overpayment which extends the deadline for claiming the deduction.

Note. The deduction is not subject to dollar limits.

If you make a section 6166 election to pay the federal estate tax in installments and make a similar election to pay the state death tax in installments, see section 2058(b) for exceptions and periods of limitation.

If you transfer property other than cash to the state in payment of state inheritance taxes, the amount you may claim as a deduction is the lesser of the state inheritance tax liability discharged or the fair market value (FMV) of the property on the date of the transfer. For more information on the application of such transfers, see the principles discussed in Rev. Rul. 86-117, 1986-2 C.B. 157, prior to the repeal of section 2011.

Send the following evidence to the IRS:

1. Certificate of the proper officer of the taxing state, or the District of Columbia, showing the:

a. Total amount of tax imposed (before adding interest and penalties and before allowing discount),

b. Amount of discount allowed,

c. Amount of penalties and interest imposed or charged,

d. Total amount actually paid in cash, and

e. Date of payment.

2. Any additional proof the IRS specifically requests.

File the evidence requested above with the return, if possible. Otherwise, send it as soon as possible after the return is filed.

Line 6

To figure the tentative tax on the amount on line 5, use Table A—Unified Rate Schedule, above, and put the result on this line.

Lines 4 and 7

Three worksheets are provided to help you figure the entries for these lines. Worksheet TG—Taxable Gifts Reconciliation allows you to reconcile the decedent's lifetime taxable gifts to figure totals that will be used for the Line 4 Worksheet and the Line 7 Worksheet.

You must have all of the decedent's gift tax returns (Forms 709) before completing Worksheet TG—Taxable Gifts Reconciliation. The amounts needed for Worksheet TG can usually be found on the filed returns that were subject to tax. However, if any of the returns were audited by the IRS, use the amounts that were finally determined as a result of the audits.

In addition, you must make a reasonable effort to discover any gifts in excess of the annual exclusion made by the decedent (or on behalf of the decedent under a power of attorney) for which no Forms 709 were filed. Include the value of such gifts in column b of Worksheet TG. The annual exclusion per donee was $3,000 for 1977 through 1981, $10,000 for 1981 through 2001, $11,000 for 2002 through 2005, $12,000 for 2006 through 2008, and $13,000 for 2009 through 2012. For 2013 and 2014, the annual exclusion for gifts of present interest is $14,000 per donee.

Part Instructions

Line 7 Worksheet – Submit a copy with Form 706

	Line 7 Worksheet Part A- Used to determine Applicable Credit Allowable for Prior Periods after 1976				
(a)	Tax Period[1]	Pre-1977			
(b)	Taxable Gifts for Applicable Period				
(c)	Taxable Gifts for Prior Periods [2]				
(d)	Cumulative Taxable Gifts Including Applicable Period (add Row (b) and Row (c))				
(e)	Tax at Date of Death Rates for Prior Gifts (from Row (c))[3]				
(f)	Tax at Date of Death Rates for Cumulative Gifts including Applicable Period (from Row (d))				
(g)	Tax at Date of Death Rates for Gifts in Applicable Period (subtract Row (e) from Row (f))				
(h)	Total DSUE applied from Prior Periods and Applicable Period (from Line 2 of Schedule C of Applicable Period Form 709)				
(i)	Basic Exclusion for Applicable Period (Enter the amount from the Table of Basic Exclusion Amounts)				
(j)	Basic Exclusion amount plus Total DSUE applied in prior periods and applicable period (add Row (h) and Row (i))				
(k)	Maximum Applicable Credit amount based on Row (j) (Using Table A—Unified Rate Schedule)[4]				
(l)	Applicable Credit amount used in Prior Periods (add Row (l) and Row (n) from prior period)				
(m)	Available Credit in Applicable Period (subtract Row (l) from Row (k))				
(n)	Credit Allowable (lesser of Row (g) or Row (m))				
(o)	Tax paid or payable at Date of Death rates for Applicable Period (subtract Row (n) from Row (g))				
(p)	Tax on Cumulative Gifts less tax paid or payable for Applicable Period (subtract Row (o) from Row (f))				
(q)	Cumulative Taxable Gifts less Gifts in the Applicable Period on which tax was paid or payable based on Row (p) (Using the Taxable Gift Amount Table)				
(r)	Gifts in the Applicable Period on which tax was payable (subtract Row (q) from Row (d))				

Line 7 Worksheet Part B		
1	Total gift taxes payable on gifts after 1976 (sum of amounts in Row (o)).	
2	Gift taxes paid by the decedent on gifts that qualify for "special treatment." Enter the amount from Worksheet TG, line 2, col. (e).	
3	Subtract line 2 from line 1.	
4	Gift tax paid by decedent's spouse on split gifts included on Schedule G. Enter amount from Worksheet TG, line 2, col. (f).	
5	Add lines 3 and 4. Enter here and on Part 2—Tax Computation, line 7.	
6	Cumulative lifetime gifts on which tax was paid or payable. Enter this amount on line 3, Section C, Part 6 of Form 706 (sum of amounts in Row (r)).	

Footnotes:
[1]Row (a): For annual returns, enter the tax period as (YYYY). For quarterly returns enter tax period as (YYYY–Q).
[2]Row (c): Enter amount from Row (d) of the previous column.
[3]Row (e): Enter amount from Row (f) of the previous column.
[4]Row (k): Calculate the applicable credit on the amount in row (j), using Table A — Unified Rate Schedule, and enter here. (For each column in row (k), subtract 20 percent of any amount allowed as a specific exemption for gifts made after September 8, 1976, and before January 1, 1977.)

Taxable Gift Amount Table

Column A	Column B	Column C	Column D
Amount in Row (p) Line 7 Worksheet over...	Amount in Row (p) Line 7 Worksheet not over...	Property Value on Amount in Column A	Rate (Divisor) on excess of amount in Column A
0	1,800	0	18%
1,800	3,800	10,000	20%
3,800	8,200	20,000	22%
8,200	13,000	40,000	24%
13,000	18,200	60,000	26%
18,200	23,800	80,000	28%
23,800	38,800	100,000	30%
38,800	70,800	150,000	32%
70,800	155,800	250,000	34%
155,800	248,300	500,000	37%
248,300	345,800	750,000	39%
345,800	------	1,000,000	40%

Table of Basic Exclusion Amounts

Period	Basic Exclusion Amount	Credit Equivalent at 2014 rates
1977 (Quarters 1 and 2)	$30,000	$6,000
1977 (Quarters 3 and 4)	$120,667	$30,000
1978	$134,000	$34,000
1979	$147,333	$38,000
1980	$161,563	$42,500
1981	$175,625	$47,000
1982	$225,000	$62,800
1983	$275,000	$79,300
1984	$325,000	$96,300
1985	$400,000	$121,800
1986	$500,000	$155,800
1987 through 1997	$600,000	$192,800
1998	$625,000	$202,050
1999	$650,000	$211,300
2000 and 2001	$675,000	$220,550
2002 through 2010	$1,000,000	$345,800
2011	$5,000,000	$1,945,800
2012	$5,120,000	$1,993,800
2013	$5,250,000	$2,045,800
2014	$5,340,000	$2,081,800

How to complete line 7 worksheet.

Row (a). Beginning with the earliest year in which the taxable gifts were made, enter the tax period of prior gifts. If you filed returns for gifts made after 1981, enter the calendar year in Row (a) as (YYYY). If you filed returns for gifts made after 1976 and before 1982, enter the calendar quarters in Row (a) as (YYYY-Q).

Row (b). Enter all taxable gifts made in the specified year. Enter all pre-1977 gifts on the pre-1977 column.

Row (c). Enter the amount from Row (d) of the *previous* column.

Row (d). Enter the sum of Row (b) and Row (c) from the current column.

Row (e). Enter the amount from Row (f) of the *previous* column.

Row (f). Enter the tax based on the amount in Row (d) of the current column using Table A — Unified Rate Schedule, earlier.

Row (g). Subtract the amount in Row (e) from the amount in Row (f) for the current column.

Row (h). Complete this row only if a DSUE amount was received from predeceased spouse(s) and was applied to lifetime gifts. See line 2 of Schedule C on the Form 709 filed for the year listed in Row (a) for the amount to be entered in this row.

Row (i). Enter the applicable amount from the Table of Basic Exclusion Amounts.

Row (j). Enter the sum of Rows (h) and Row (i).

Row (k). Calculate the applicable credit on the amount in Row (j) using Table A — Unified Rate Schedule, and enter here.

Note. The entries in each column of Row (k) must be reduced by 20 percent of the amount allowed as a specific exemption for gifts made after September 8, 1976, and before January 1, 1977 (but no more than $6,000).

Row (l). Add the amounts in Row (l) and Row (n) from the *previous* column.

Row (m). Subtract the amount in Row (l) from the amount in Row (k) to determine the amount of any available credit. Enter result in Row (m).

Row (n). Enter the lesser of the amounts in Row (g) or Row (m).

Row (o). Subtract the amount in Row (n) from the amount in Row (g) for the current column.

Row (p). Subtract the amount in Row (o) from the amount in Row (f) for the current column.

Row (q). Enter the Cumulative Taxable Gift amount based on the amount in Row (p) using the Taxable Gift Amount Table.

Row (r). If Row (o) is greater than zero in the applicable period, subtract Row (q) from Row (d). If Row (o) is not greater than zero, enter -0-.

Repeat for each year in which taxable gifts were made.

 Remember to submit a copy of the Line 7 Worksheet when you file Form 706. If additional space is needed to report prior gifts, please attach additional sheets.

Note. In figuring the line 7 amount, do not include any tax paid or payable on gifts made before 1977. The line 7 amount is a hypothetical figure used to calculate the estate tax.

Special treatment of split gifts.

These special rules apply only if:

• The decedent's spouse predeceased the decedent;

• The decedent's spouse made gifts that were "split" with the decedent under the rules of section 2513;

• The decedent was the "consenting spouse" for those split gifts, as that term is used on Form 709; and

• The split gifts were included in the decedent's spouse's gross estate under section 2035.

If all four conditions above are met, do not include these gifts on line 4 of the Tax Computation and do not include the gift taxes payable on these gifts on line 7 of the Tax Computation. These adjustments are incorporated into the worksheets.

Part Instructions

Lines 9a through 9d. Applicable Credit Amount (formerly Unified Credit Amount)

The *applicable credit amount* is allowable credit against estate and gift taxes. It is calculated by determining the tentative tax on the *applicable exclusion amount*, which is the amount that can be transferred before an estate tax liability will be incurred.

The applicable exclusion amount equals the total of:
- Line 9a: The basic exclusion amount. In 2014, the basic exclusion amount, as adjusted for inflation under 2010(c)(3), is $5,340,000.
- Line 9b: The deceased spousal unused exclusion amount (DSUE). If the decedent had a spouse who died after December 31, 2010, whose estate did not use all of its applicable exclusion against gift or estate tax liability, a DSUE amount may be available for use by the decedent's estate. If the predeceased spouse died in 2011, the DSUE amount was calculated and attached to his or her Form 706. If the predeceased spouse died in 2012 or after, this amount is found in Part 6, Section C of the Form 706 filed by the estate of the decedent's predeceased spouse. The amount to be entered on line 9b is calculated in Part 6, Section D.

Line 10. Adjustment to Applicable Credit

If the decedent made gifts (including gifts made by the decedent's spouse and treated as made by the decedent by reason of gift splitting) after September 8, 1976, and before January 1, 1977, for which the decedent claimed a specific exemption, the applicable credit amount on this estate tax return must be reduced. The reduction is figured by entering 20% of the specific exemption claimed for these gifts.

Note. The specific exemption was allowed by section 2521 for gifts made before January 1, 1977.

If the decedent did not make any gifts between September 8, 1976, and January 1, 1977, or if the decedent made gifts during that period but did not claim the specific exemption, enter zero.

Line 15. Total Credits

Generally, line 15 is used to report the total of credit for foreign death taxes (line 13) and credit for tax on prior transfers (line 14).

However, you may also use line 15 to report credit taken for federal gift taxes imposed by Chapter 12 of the Code,

and the corresponding provisions of prior laws, on certain transfers the decedent made before January 1, 1977, that are included in the gross estate. The credit cannot be more than the amount figured by the following formula:

$$\frac{\text{Gross estate tax minus (the sum of the state death taxes and unified credit)}}{\text{Value of gross estate minus (the sum of the deductions for charitable, public, and similar gifts and bequests and marital deduction)}} \times \text{Value of included gift}$$

When taking the credit for pre-1977 federal gift taxes:
- Include the credit in the amount on line 15 and
- Identify and enter the amount of the credit you are taking on the dotted line to the left of the entry space for line 15 on page 1 of Form 706 with a notation, "section 2012 credit."

For more information, see the regulations under section 2012. This computation may be made using Form 4808. Attach a copy of a completed Form 4808 or the computation of the credit. Also, attach all available copies of Forms 709 filed by the decedent to help verify the amounts entered on lines 4 and 7, and the amount of credit taken (on line 15) for pre-1977 federal gift taxes.

Canadian marital credit. In addition to using line 15 to report credit for federal gift taxes on pre-1977 gifts, you may also use line 15 to claim the Canadian marital credit, where applicable.

When taking the marital credit under the 1995 Canadian Protocol:
- Include the credit in the amount on line 15 and
- Identify and enter the amount of the credit you are taking on the dotted line to the left of the entry space for line 15 on page 1 of Form 706 with a notation, "Canadian marital credit."

Also, attach a statement to the return that refers to the treaty, waives QDOT rights, and shows the computation of the marital credit. See the 1995 Canadian income tax treaty protocol for details on figuring the credit.

Part 3—Elections by the Executor

Note. The election to allow the decedent's surviving spouse to use the decedent's unused exclusion amount is

made by filing a timely and complete Form 706. See instructions for *Part 6—Portability of Deceased Spousal Unused Exclusion*, later, and sections 2010(c)(4) and (c)(5).

Line 1. Alternate Valuation

 See the example showing the use of Schedule B where the alternate valuation is adopted.

Unless you elect at the time the return is filed to adopt alternate valuation as authorized by section 2032, value all property included in the gross estate as of the date of the decedent's death. Alternate valuation cannot be applied to only a part of the property.

You may elect special-use valuation (line 2) in addition to alternate valuation.

You may not elect alternate valuation unless the election will decrease both the value of the gross estate and the sum (reduced by allowable credits) of the estate and GST taxes payable by reason of the decedent's death for the property includible in the decedent's gross estate.

Elect alternate valuation by checking "Yes," on line 1 and filing Form 706. You may make a protective alternate valuation election by checking "Yes," on line 1, writing the word "protective," and filing Form 706 using regular values.

Once made, the election may not be revoked. The election may be made on a late-filed Form 706 provided it is not filed later than 1 year after the due date (including extensions actually granted). Relief under sections 301.9100-1 and 301.9100-3 may be available to make an alternate valuation election or a protective alternate valuation election, provided a Form 706 is filed no later than 1 year after the due date of the return (including extensions actually granted).

If alternate valuation is elected, value the property included in the gross estate as of the following dates as applicable:
- Any property distributed, sold, exchanged, or otherwise disposed of or separated or passed from the gross estate by any method within 6 months after the decedent's death is valued on the date of distribution, sale, exchange, or other disposition. Value this property on the date it ceases to be a part of the gross estate; for example, on the date the title passes as the result of its sale, exchange, or other disposition.
- Any property not distributed, sold, exchanged, or otherwise disposed of within the 6-month period is valued as of

6 months after the date of the decedent's death.

- Any property, interest, or estate that is *affected by mere lapse of time* is valued as of the date of decedent's death or on the date of its distribution, sale, exchange, or other disposition, whichever occurs first. However, you may change the date of death value to account for any change in value that is not due to a "mere lapse of time" on the date of its distribution, sale, exchange, or other disposition.

The property included in the alternate valuation and valued as of 6 months after the date of the decedent's death, or as of some intermediate date (as described above) is the property included in the gross estate on the date of the decedent's death. Therefore, you must first determine what property was part of the gross estate at the decedent's death.

Interest. Interest accrued to the date of the decedent's death on bonds, notes, and other interest-bearing obligations is property of the gross estate on the date of death and is included in the alternate valuation.

Rent. Rent accrued to the date of the decedent's death on leased real or personal property is property of the gross estate on the date of death and is included in the alternate valuation.

Dividends. Outstanding dividends that were declared to stockholders of record on or before the date of the decedent's death are considered property of the gross estate on the date of death, and are included in the alternate valuation. Ordinary dividends declared to stockholders of record after the date of the decedent's death are not included in the gross estate on the date of death and are not eligible for alternate valuation. However, if dividends are declared to stockholders of record after the date of the decedent's death so that the shares of stock at the later valuation date do not reasonably represent the same property at the date of the decedent's death, include those dividends (except dividends paid from earnings of the corporation after the date of the decedent's death) in the alternate valuation.

On Schedules A through I, you must show:

1. What property is included in the gross estate on the date of the decedent's death;

2. What property was distributed, sold, exchanged, or otherwise disposed of within the 6-month period after the

decedent's death, and the dates of these distributions, etc. (These two items should be entered in the "Description" column of each schedule. Briefly explain the status or disposition governing the alternate valuation date, such as: "Not disposed of within 6 months following death," "Distributed," "Sold," "Bond paid on maturity," etc. In this same column, describe each item of principal and includible income);

3. The date of death value, entered in the appropriate value column with items of principal and includible income shown separately; and

4. The alternate value, entered in the appropriate value column with items of principal and includible income shown separately. (In the case of any interest or estate, the value of which is affected by lapse of time, such as patents, leaseholds, estates for the life of another, or remainder interests, the value shown under the heading "Alternate value" must be the adjusted value; for example, the value as of the date of death with an adjustment reflecting any difference in its value as of the later date not due to lapse of time.)

Note. If any property on Schedules A through I is being valued pursuant to the special rule of Regulations section 20.2010–2T(a)(7)(ii), values for those assets are not required to be reported on the Schedule. See *Part 5—Recapitulation, line 10.*

Distributions, sales, exchanges, and other dispositions of the property within the 6-month period after the decedent's death must be supported by evidence. If the court issued an order of distribution during that period, you must submit a certified copy of the order as part of the evidence. The IRS may require you to submit additional evidence, if necessary.

If the alternate valuation method is used, the values of life estates, remainders, and similar interests are figured using the age of the recipient on the date of the decedent's death and the value of the property on the alternate valuation date.

Line 2. Special-Use Valuation of Section 2032A

In general. Under section 2032A, you may elect to value certain farm and closely held business real property at its farm or business use value rather than its FMV. Both special-use valuation and alternate valuation may be elected.

To elect special-use valuation, check "Yes," on line 2 and complete and attach Schedule A-1 and its required additional statements. You must file Schedule A-1 and its required attachments with Form 706 for this election to be valid. You may make the election on a late-filed return so long as it is the first return filed.

The total value of the property valued under section 2032A may not be decreased from FMV by more than $1,090,000 for decedents dying in 2014.

Real property may qualify for the section 2032A election if:

1. The decedent was a U.S. citizen or resident at the time of death;

2. The real property is located in the United States;

3. At the decedent's death, the real property was used by the decedent or a family member for farming or in a trade or business, or was rented for such use by either the surviving spouse or a lineal descendant of the decedent to a family member on a net cash basis;

4. The real property was acquired from or passed from the decedent to a qualified heir of the decedent;

5. The real property was owned and used in a qualified manner by the decedent or a member of the decedent's family during 5 of the 8 years before the decedent's death;

6. There was material participation by the decedent or a member of the decedent's family during 5 of the 8 years before the decedent's death; and

7. The property meets the following percentage requirements:

a. At least 50% of the adjusted value of the gross estate must consist of the adjusted value of real or personal property that was being used as a farm or in a closely-held business and that was acquired from, or passed from, the decedent to a qualified heir of the decedent, and

b. At least 25% of the adjusted value of the gross estate must consist of the adjusted value of qualified farm or closely-held business real property.

For this purpose, adjusted value is the value of property determined without regard to its special-use value. The value is reduced for unpaid mortgages on the property or any indebtedness against the property, if the full value of the decedent's interest in the property (not reduced by such mortgage or indebtedness) is included in the value of the gross estate. The adjusted value of the qualified real and personal property used in different businesses may be combined to meet the 50% and 25% requirements.

Qualified Real Property

Qualified use. *Qualified use* means use of the property as a farm for farming purposes or in a trade or business other than farming. Trade or business applies only to the active conduct of a business. It does not apply to passive investment activities or the mere passive rental of property to a person other than a member of the decedent's family. Also, no trade or business is present in the case of activities not engaged in for profit.

Ownership. To qualify as special-use property, the decedent or a member of the decedent's family must have owned and used the property in a qualified use for 5 of the last 8 years before the decedent's death. Ownership may be direct or indirect through a corporation, a partnership, or a trust.

If the ownership is indirect, the business must qualify as a closely-held business under section 6166. The indirect ownership, when combined with periods of direct ownership, must meet the requirements of section 6166 on the date of the decedent's death and for a period of time that equals at least 5 of the 8 years preceding death.

Directly owned property leased by the decedent to a separate closely-held business, is considered qualified real property if the business entity to which it was rented was a closely-held business (as defined by section 6166) for the decedent on the date of the decedent's death and for sufficient time to meet the "5 in 8 years" test explained above.

Structures and other real property improvements. Qualified real property includes residential buildings and other structures and real property improvements regularly occupied or used by the owner or lessee of real property (or by the employees of the owner or lessee) to operate a farm or other closely-held business. A farm residence which the decedent occupied is considered to have been occupied for the purpose of operating the farm even when a family member and not the decedent was the person materially participating in the operation of the farm.

Qualified real property also includes roads, buildings, and other structures and improvements functionally related to the qualified use.

Elements of value such as mineral rights that are not related to the farm or business use are not eligible for special-use valuation.

Property acquired from the decedent. Property is considered to have been acquired from or to have passed from the decedent if one of the following applies:
• The property is considered to have been acquired from or to have passed from the decedent under section 1014(b) (relating to basis of property acquired from a decedent);
• The property is acquired by any person from the estate; or
• The property is acquired by any person from a trust, to the extent the property is includible in the gross estate.

Qualified heir. A person is a *qualified heir* of property if he or she is a member of the decedent's family and acquired or received the property from the decedent. If a qualified heir disposes of any interest in qualified real property to any member of his or her family, that person will then be treated as the qualified heir for that interest.

A *member of the family* includes only:
• An ancestor (parent, grandparent, etc.) of the individual;
• The spouse of the individual;
• The lineal descendant (child, stepchild, grandchild, etc.) of the individual, the individual's spouse, or a parent of the individual; or
• The spouse, widow, or widower of any lineal descendant described above. A legally adopted child of an individual is treated as a child of that individual by blood.

Material Participation

To elect special-use valuation, either the decedent or a member of his or her family must have materially participated in the operation of the farm or other business for at least 5 of the 8 years ending on the date of the decedent's death. The existence of *material participation* is a factual determination. Passively collecting rents, salaries, draws, dividends, or other income from the farm or other business is not sufficient for material participation, nor is merely advancing capital and reviewing a crop plan and financial reports each season or business year.

In determining whether the required participation has occurred, disregard brief periods (that is, 30 days or less) during which there was no material participation, as long as such periods

were both preceded and followed by substantial periods (more than 120 days) during which there was uninterrupted material participation.

Retirement or disability. If, on the date of death, the time period for material participation could not be met because the decedent was retired or disabled, a substitute period may apply. The decedent must have retired on social security or been disabled for a continuous period ending with death. A person is disabled for this purpose if he or she was mentally or physically unable to materially participate in the operation of the farm or other business.

The substitute time period for material participation for these decedents is a period totaling at least 5 years out of the 8-year period that ended on the earlier of:
• The date the decedent began receiving social security benefits or
• The date the decedent became disabled.

Surviving spouse. A surviving spouse who received qualified real property from the predeceased spouse is considered to have materially participated if he or she was engaged in the active management of the farm or other business. If the surviving spouse died within 8 years of the first spouse's death, you may add the period of material participation of the predeceased spouse to the period of active management by the surviving spouse to determine if the surviving spouse's estate qualifies for special-use valuation. To qualify for this, the property must have been eligible for special-use valuation in the predeceased spouse's estate, though it does not have to have been elected by that estate.

For additional details regarding material participation, see Regulations section 20.2032A-3(e).

Valuation Methods

The primary method of valuing special-use property that is used for farming purposes is the annual gross cash rental method. If comparable gross cash rentals are not available, you can substitute comparable average annual net share rentals. If neither of these is available, or if you so elect, you can use the method for valuing real property in a closely-held business.

Average annual gross cash rental. Generally, the special-use value of property that is used for farming purposes is determined as follows:

1. Subtract the average annual state and local real estate taxes on actual tracts of comparable real property from the average annual gross cash rental for that same comparable property and

2. Divide the result in (1) by the average annual effective interest rate charged for all new Federal Land Bank loans. See *Effective interest rate,* later.

The computation of each average annual amount is based on the 5 most recent calendar years ending before the date of the decedent's death.

Gross cash rental. Generally, gross cash rental is the total amount of cash received in a calendar year for the use of actual tracts of comparable farm real property in the same locality as the property being specially valued. You may not use:
- Appraisals or other statements regarding rental value or areawide averages of rentals, or
- Rents paid wholly or partly in-kind, or
- Property for which the amount of rent is based on production.

The rental must have resulted from an arm's-length transaction and the amount of rent may not be reduced by the amount of any expenses or liabilities associated with the farm operation or the lease.

Comparable property. Comparable property must be situated in the same locality as the qualified real property as determined by generally accepted real property valuation rules. The determination of comparability is based on a number of factors, none of which carries more weight than the others. It is often necessary to value land in segments where there are different uses or land characteristics included in the specially valued land.

The following list contains some of the factors considered in determining comparability:
- Similarity of soil;
- Whether the crops grown would deplete the soil in a similar manner;
- Types of soil conservation techniques that have been practiced on the two properties;
- Whether the two properties are subject to flooding;
- Slope of the land;
- For livestock operations, the carrying capacity of the land;
- For timbered land, whether the timber is comparable;
- Whether the property as a whole is unified or segmented. If segmented, the availability of the means necessary for movement among the different sections;

- Number, types, and conditions of all buildings and other fixed improvements located on the properties and their location as it affects efficient management, use, and value of the property; and
- Availability and type of transportation facilities in terms of costs and of proximity of the properties to local markets.

You must specifically identify on the return the property being used as comparable property. Use the type of descriptions used to list real property on Schedule A.

Effective interest rate. See Tables 1 and 2 of Rev. Rul. 2014–21, 2014–34 I.R.B. 381, available at *www.irs.gov/irb/ 2014-34_IRB/ar08.html*, for the average annual effective interest rates in effect for 2014.

Net share rental. You may use average annual net share rental from comparable land only if there is no comparable land from which average annual gross cash rental can be determined. Net share rental is the difference between the gross value of produce received by the lessor from the comparable land and the cash operating expenses (other than real estate taxes) of growing the produce that, under the lease, are paid by the lessor. The production of the produce must be the business purpose of the farming operation. For this purpose, produce includes livestock.

The gross value of the produce is generally the gross amount received if the produce was disposed of in an arm's-length transaction within the period established by the Department of Agriculture for its price support program. Otherwise, the value is the weighted average price for which the produce sold on the closest national or regional commodities market. The value is figured for the date or dates on which the lessor received (or constructively received) the produce.

Valuing a real property interest in closely held business. Use this method to determine the special-use valuation for qualifying real property used in a trade or business other than farming. You may also use this method for qualifying farm property if there is no comparable land or if you elect to use it. Under this method, the following factors are considered:
- The capitalization of income that the property can be expected to yield for farming or for closely-held business purposes over a reasonable period of

time with prudent management and traditional cropping patterns for the area, taking into account soil capacity, terrain configuration, and similar factors;
- The capitalization of the fair rental value of the land for farming or for closely-held business purposes;
- The assessed land values in a state that provides a differential or use value assessment law for farmland or closely-held business;
- Comparable sales of other farm or closely-held business land in the same geographical area far enough removed from a metropolitan or resort area so that nonagricultural use is not a significant factor in the sales price; and
- Any other factor that fairly values the farm or closely-held business value of the property.

Making the Election

Include the words "section 2032A valuation" in the "Description" column of any Form 706 schedule if section 2032A property is included in the decedent's gross estate.

An election under section 2032A need not include all the property in an estate that is eligible for special-use valuation, but sufficient property to satisfy the threshold requirements of section 2032A(b)(1)(B) must be specially valued under the election.

If joint or undivided interests (that is, interests as joint tenants or tenants in common) in the same property are received from a decedent by qualified heirs, an election for one heir's joint or undivided interest need not include any other heir's interest in the same property if the electing heir's interest plus other property to be specially valued satisfies the requirements of section 2032A(b)(1) (B).

If successive interests (that is, life estates and remainder interests) are created by a decedent in otherwise qualified property, an election under section 2032A is available only for that property (or part) in which qualified heirs of the decedent receive all of the successive interests, and such an election must include the interests of all of those heirs.

For example, if a surviving spouse receives a life estate in otherwise qualified property and the spouse's brother receives a remainder interest in fee, no part of the property may be valued under a section 2032A election.

Where successive interests in specially valued property are created, remainder interests are treated as being received by qualified heirs only if the remainder interests are not contingent on surviving a nonfamily member or are not subject to divestment in favor of a nonfamily member.

Protective Election

You may make a protective election to specially value qualified real property. Under this election, whether or not you may ultimately use special-use valuation depends upon final values (as shown on the return determined following examination of the return) meeting the requirements of section 2032A.

To make a protective election, check "Yes," on line 2 and complete Schedule A-1 according to the instructions for Protective Election.

If you make a protective election, complete the initial Form 706 by valuing all property at its FMV. Do not use special-use valuation. Usually, this will result in higher estate and GST tax liabilities than will be ultimately determined if special-use valuation is allowed. The protective election does not extend the time to pay the taxes shown on the return. If you wish to extend the time to pay the taxes, file Form 4768 in adequate time before the due date of the return. See the instructions for Form 4768.

If the estate qualifies for special-use valuation based on the values as finally determined, you must file an amended Form 706 (with a complete section 2032A election) within 60 days after the date of this determination. Prepare the amended return using special-use values under the rules of section 2032A, complete Schedule A-1, and attach all of the required statements.

Additional information

For definitions and additional information, see section 2032A and the related regulations.

Line 3. Section 6166 Installment Payments

If the gross estate includes an interest in a closely-held business, you may be able to elect to pay part of the estate tax in installments under section 6166.

The maximum amount that can be paid in installments is that part of the estate tax that is attributable to the closely-held business; see *Determine how much of the estate tax may be paid in installments under section 6166*, later. In general, that amount is the amount of tax that bears the same ratio to the total estate tax that the value of the closely-held business included in the gross estate bears to the adjusted gross estate.

Bond or lien. The IRS may require that an estate furnish a surety bond when granting the installment payment election. In the alternative, the executor may consent to elect the special lien provisions of section 6324A, in lieu of the bond. The IRS will contact you regarding the specifics of furnishing the bond or electing the special lien. The IRS will make this determination on a case-by-case basis, and you may be asked to provide additional information.

If you elect the lien provisions, section 6324A requires that the lien be placed on property having a value equal to the total deferred tax plus 4 years of interest. The property must be expected to survive the deferral period, and does not necessarily have to be property of the estate. In addition, all people with an interest in the designated property must consent to the creation of this lien.

Percentage requirements. To qualify for installment payments, the value of the interest in the closely held business that is included in the gross estate must be more than 35% of the adjusted gross estate (the gross estate less expenses, indebtedness, taxes, and losses – Schedules J, K, and L of Form 706 (do not include any portion of the state death tax deduction)).

Interests in two or more closely-held businesses are treated as an interest in a single business if at least 20% of the total value of each business is included in the gross estate. For this purpose, include any interest held by the surviving spouse that represents the surviving spouse's interest in a business held jointly with the decedent as community property or as joint tenants, tenants by the entirety, or tenants in common.

Value. The value used for meeting the percentage requirements is the same value used for determining the gross estate. Therefore, if the estate is valued under alternate valuation or special-use valuation, you must use those values to meet the percentage requirements.

Transfers before death. Generally, gifts made before death are not included in the gross estate. However, the estate must meet the 35% requirement by both including in and excluding from the gross estate any gifts made by the decedent in the 3-year period ending on the date of death.

Passive assets. In determining the value of a closely-held business and whether the 35% requirement is met, do not include the value of any passive assets held by the business. A passive asset is any asset not used in carrying on a trade or business. Any asset used in a qualifying lending and financing business is treated as an asset used in carrying on a trade or business; see section 6166(b)(10) for details. Stock in another corporation is a passive asset unless the stock is treated as held by the decedent because of the election to treat holding company stock as business company stock; see *Holding company stock*, later.

If a corporation owns at least 20% in value of the voting stock of another corporation, or the other corporation had no more than 45 shareholders and at least 80% of the value of the assets of each corporation is attributable to assets used in carrying on a trade or business, then these corporations will be treated as a single corporation, and the stock will not be treated as a passive asset. Stock held in the other corporation is not taken into account in determining the 80% requirement.

Interest in closely held business. For purposes of the installment payment election, an *interest in a closely-held business* means:
• Ownership of a trade or business carried on as a proprietorship,
• An interest as a partner in a partnership carrying on a trade or business if 20% or more of the total capital interest was included in the gross estate of the decedent or the partnership had no more than 45 partners, or
• Stock in a corporation carrying on a trade or business if 20% or more in value of the voting stock of the corporation is included in the gross estate of the decedent or the corporation had no more than 45 shareholders.

The partnership or corporation must be carrying on a trade or business at the time of the decedent's death. For further information on whether certain partnerships or corporations owning real property interests constitute a closely-held business, see Rev. Rul. 2006-34, 2006-26 I.R.B. 1171, available at *www.irs.gov/pub/irs-irbs/irb06-26.pdf*.

In determining the number of partners or shareholders, a partnership or stock interest is treated as owned by one partner or shareholder if it is community property or held by a husband and wife as joint tenants, tenants in common, or as tenants by the entirety.

Property owned directly or indirectly by or for a corporation, partnership, estate, or trust is treated as owned proportionately by or for its shareholders, partners, or beneficiaries. For trusts, only beneficiaries with present interests are considered.

The interest in a closely-held farm business includes the interest in the residential buildings and related improvements occupied regularly by the owners, lessees, and employees operating the farm.

Holding company stock. The executor may elect to treat as business company stock the portion of any holding company stock that represents direct ownership (or indirect ownership through one or more other holding companies) in a business company. A *holding company* is a corporation holding stock in another corporation. A *business company* is a corporation carrying on a trade or business.

In general, this election applies only to stock that is not readily tradable. However, the election can be made if the business company stock is readily tradable, as long as all of the stock of each holding company is not readily tradable.

For purposes of the 20% voting stock requirement, stock is treated as voting stock to the extent the holding company owns voting stock in the business company.

If the executor makes this election, the first installment payment is due when the estate tax return is filed. The 5-year deferral for payment of the tax, as discussed later under *Time for payment,* does not apply. In addition, the 2% interest rate, discussed later under *Interest computation,* will not apply. Also, if the business company stock is readily tradable, as explained above, the tax must be paid in five installments.

Determine how much of the estate tax may be paid in installments under section 6166. To determine whether the election may be made, you must calculate the adjusted gross estate. (See, *Line 3 Worksheet —Adjusted Gross Estate,* later.) To determine the value of the adjusted gross estate, subtract the deductions (Schedules J, K, and L) from the value of the gross estate.

To determine over how many installments the estate tax may be paid, please refer to sections 6166(a), (b)(7), (b)(8), and (b)(10).

Time for payment. Under the installment method, the executor may elect to defer payment of the qualified estate tax, but not interest, for up to 5 years from the original payment due date. After the first installment of tax is paid, you must pay the remaining installments annually by the date 1 year after the due date of the preceding installment. There can be no more than 10 installment payments.

Interest on the unpaid portion of the tax is not deferred and must be paid annually. Interest must be paid at the same time as and as a part of each installment payment of the tax.

Acceleration of payments. If the estate fails to make payments of tax or interest within 6 months of the due date, the IRS may terminate the right to make installment payments and force an acceleration of payment of the tax upon notice and demand.

Generally, if any portion of the interest in the closely-held business which qualifies for installment payments is distributed, sold, exchanged, or otherwise disposed of, or money and other property attributable to such an interest is withdrawn, and the aggregate of those events equals or exceeds 50% of the value of the interest, then the right to make installment payments will be terminated, and the unpaid portion of the tax will be due upon notice and demand. See section 6166(g)(1)(A).

Interest computation. A special interest rate applies to installment payments. For decedents dying in 2014, the interest rate is 2% on the lesser of:
- $580,000 or
- The amount of the estate tax that is attributable to the closely-held business and that is payable in installments.

2% portion. The *2% portion* is an amount equal to the amount of the tentative estate tax (on $1,000,000 plus the applicable exclusion amount in effect) minus the applicable credit amount in effect. However, if the amount of estate tax extended under section 6166 is less than the amount figured above, the 2% portion is the lesser amount.

Inflation adjustment. The $1,000,000 amount used to calculate the 2% portion is indexed for inflation for the estates of decedents who died in a calendar year after 1998. For an estate of a decedent who died in 2014, the dollar amount used to determine the "2% portion" of the estate tax payable in installments under section 6166 is $1,450,000.

Computation. Interest on the portion of the tax in excess of the 2% portion is figured at 45% of the annual rate of interest on underpayments. This rate is based on the federal short-term rate and is announced quarterly by the IRS in the Internal Revenue Bulletin.

If you elect installment payments and the estate tax due is more than the maximum amount to which the 2% interest rate applies, each installment payment is deemed to comprise both tax subject to the 2% interest rate and tax subject to 45% of the regular underpayment rate. The amount of each

Line 3 Worksheet—Adjusted Gross Estate

1	What is the value of the decedent's interest in closely-held business(es) included in the gross estate (less value of passive assets, as mentioned in section 6166(b)(9))? . . . .
2	What is the value of the gross estate (Form 706, page 3, Part 5, line 13)? . . . .
3	Add lines 18, 19, and 20 from Form 706, page 3, Part 5. . . . .
4	Subtract line 3 from line 2 to calculate the adjusted gross estate. . . .
5	Divide line 1 by line 4 to calculate the value the business interest bears to the value of the adjusted gross estate. For purposes of this calculation, carry the decimal to the sixth place; the IRS will make this adjustment for purposes of determining the correct amount. If this amount is less than 0.350000, the estate does not qualify to make the election under section 6166.
6	Multiply line 5 by the amount on line 16 of Form 706, page 1, Part 2. This is the maximum amount of estate tax that may be paid in installments under section 6166. (Certain GST taxes may be deferred as well; see section 6166(i) for more information.) . . . .

Part Instructions

installment that is subject to the 2% rate is the same as the percentage of total tax payable in installments that is subject to the 2% rate.

 The interest paid on installment payments is not deductible as an administrative expense of the estate.

Making the election. If you check this line to make a final election, you must attach the notice of election described in Regulations section 20.6166-1(b). If you check this line to make a protective election, you must attach a notice of protective election as described in Regulations section 20.6166-1(d). Regulations section 20.6166-1(b) requires that the notice of election is made by attaching to a timely filed estate tax return the following information:
• The decedent's name and taxpayer identification number as they appear on the estate tax return;
• The amount of tax that is to be paid in installments;
• The date selected for payment of the first installment;
• The number of annual installments, including first installment, in which the tax is to be paid;
• The properties shown on the estate tax return that are the closely-held business interest (identified by schedule and item number); and
• The facts that formed the basis for the executor's conclusion that the estate qualifies for payment of the estate tax in installments.

You may also elect to pay certain GST taxes in installments. See section 6166(i).

Line 4. Reversionary or Remainder Interests

For details of this election, see section 6163 and the related regulations.

Part 4—General Information

Authorization

Completing the authorization will authorize one attorney, accountant, or enrolled agent to represent the estate and receive confidential tax information, but will not authorize the representative to enter into closing agreements for the estate. If you would like to authorize your representative to enter into agreements or perform other designated acts on behalf of the estate, you must file Form 2848 with Form 706.

Note. If you intend for the representative to represent the estate before the IRS, he or she must complete and sign this authorization.

Complete and attach Form 2848 if you would like to authorize:
• Persons other than attorneys, accountants, or enrolled agents to represent the estate, or
• More than one person to receive confidential information or represent the estate, or
• Someone to sign agreements, consents, waivers or other documents for the estate.
Filing a completed Form 2848 with this return may expedite processing of the Form 706.

If you wish only to authorize someone to inspect and/or receive confidential tax information (but not to represent you before the IRS), complete and file Form 8821.

Line 3

Enter the marital status of the decedent at the time of death by checking the appropriate box on line 3a. If the decedent was married at the time of death, complete line 4. If the decedent had one or more prior marriages, complete line 3b by providing the name and SSN of each former spouse, the date(s) the marriage ended, and specify whether the marriage ended by annulment, divorce decree, or death of spouse. If the prior marriage ended in death and the predeceased spouse died after December 31, 2010, complete Part 6 — Portability of Deceased Spousal Unused Exclusion, Section D if the estate of the predeceased spouse elected to allow the decedent to use any unused exclusion amount. For more information, see section 2010(c)(4) and related regulations.

Line 4

Complete line 4 whether or not there is a surviving spouse and whether or not the surviving spouse received any benefits from the estate. If there was no surviving spouse on the date of decedent's death, enter "None" in line 4a and leave lines 4b and 4c blank. The value entered in line 4c need not be exact. See the instructions for "Amount" under line 5 later.

Note. Do not include any DSUE amount transferred to the surviving spouse in the total entered on line 4c.

Line 5

Name. Enter the name of each individual, trust, or estate that received (or will receive) benefits of $5,000 or more from the estate directly as an heir, next-of-kin, devisee, or legatee; or indirectly (for example, as beneficiary of an annuity or insurance policy, shareholder of a corporation, or partner of a partnership that is an heir, etc.).

Identifying number. Enter the SSN of each individual beneficiary listed. If the number is unknown, or the individual has no number, please indicate "unknown" or "none." For trusts and other estates, enter the Employer Identification Number (EIN).

Relationship. For each individual beneficiary, enter the relationship (if known) to the decedent by reason of blood, marriage, or adoption. For trust or estate beneficiaries, indicate "TRUST" or "ESTATE."

Amount. Enter the amount actually distributed (or to be distributed) to each beneficiary including transfers during the decedent's life from Schedule G required to be included in the gross estate. The value to be entered need not be exact. A reasonable estimate is sufficient. For example, where precise values cannot readily be determined, as with certain future interests, a reasonable approximation should be entered. The total of these distributions should approximate the amount of gross estate reduced by funeral and administrative expenses, debts and mortgages, bequests to surviving spouse, charitable bequests, and any federal and state estate and GST taxes paid (or payable) relating to the benefits received by the beneficiaries listed on lines 4 and 5.

All distributions of less than $5,000 to specific beneficiaries may be included with distributions to unascertainable beneficiaries on the line provided.

Line 6. Protective Claim for Refund

If you answered "Yes," complete Schedule PC for each claim. Two copies of each Schedule PC must be filed with the return.

A protective claim for refund may be filed when there is an unresolved claim or expense that will not be deductible under section 2053 before the expiration of the period of limitation under section 6511(a). To preserve the estate's right to a refund once the claim or expense has been finally determined, the protective claim must be filed before the end of the limitations period. For more information on how to file a protective claim for refund with this Form 706, see the instructions for *Schedule PC,* later.

Line 7. Section 2044 Property

If you answered "Yes," these assets must be shown on Schedule F.

Section 2044 property is property for which a previous section 2056(b)(7) election (QTIP election) has been made, or for which a similar gift tax election (section 2523) has been made. For more information, see the instructions for Schedule F, later.

Line 9. Insurance Not Included in the Gross Estate

If you answered "Yes," to either line 9a or 9b, for each policy you must complete and attach Schedule D, Form 712, and an explanation of why the policy or its proceeds are not includible in the gross estate.

Line 11. Partnership Interests and Stock in Close Corporations

If you answered "Yes," on line 11a, you must include full details for partnerships (including family limited partnerships), unincorporated businesses, and limited liability companies on Schedule F (Schedule E if the partnership interest is jointly owned). Also include full details for fractional interests in real estate on Schedule A and for stock of inactive or close corporations on Schedule B.

Value these interests using the rules of Regulations section 20.2031-2 (stocks) or 20.2031-3 (other business interests).

A *close corporation* is a corporation whose shares are owned by a limited number of shareholders. Often, one family holds the entire stock issue. As a result, little, if any, trading of the stock takes place. There is, therefore, no established market for the stock, and those sales that do occur are at irregular intervals and seldom reflect all the elements of a representative transaction as defined by FMV.

Line 13. Trusts

If you answered "Yes," on either line 13a or line 13b, attach a copy of the trust instrument for each trust.

Complete Schedule G if you answered "Yes," on line 13a and Schedule F if you answered "Yes," on line 13b.

Line 15. Foreign Accounts

Check "Yes," on line 15 if the decedent at the time of death had an interest in or signature or other authority over a financial account in a foreign country, such as a bank account, securities account, an offshore trust, or other financial account.

Part 5—Recapitulation

Gross Estate—Items 1 through 11

Items 1 through 9. You must make an entry in each of items 1 through 9.

If the gross estate does not contain any assets of the type specified by a given item, enter zero for that item. Entering zero for any of items 1 through 9 is a statement by the executor, made under penalties of perjury, that the gross estate does not contain any includible assets covered by that item.

Do not enter any amounts in the "Alternate value" column unless you elected alternate valuation on line 1 of Part 3—Elections by the Executor.

Note. If estimating the value of one or more assets pursuant to the special rule of Regulations section 20.2010–2T(a)(7)(ii), do not enter values for those assets in items 1 through 9. Total the estimated values for those assets and follow the instructions for item 10.

Which schedules to attach for items 1 through 9. You must attach:
• Schedule F. Answer its questions even if you report no assets on it;
• Schedules A, B, and C, if the gross estate includes any (1) Real Estate, (2) Stocks and Bonds, or (3) Mortgages, Notes, and Cash, respectively;
• Schedule D, if the gross estate includes any life insurance or if you answered "Yes," to question 9a of Part 4—General Information;
• Schedule E, if the gross estate contains any jointly-owned property or if you answered "Yes," to question 10 of Part 4;
• Schedule G, if the decedent made any of the lifetime transfers to be listed on that schedule or if you answered "Yes," to question 12 or 13a of Part 4;
• Schedule H, if you answered "Yes," to question 14 of Part 4; and
• Schedule I, if you answered "Yes," to question 16 of Part 4.

Item 10. Under Regulations section 20.2010-2T(a)(7)(ii), if the total value of the gross estate and adjusted taxable gifts is less than the basic exclusion

amount (see section 6018(a)) and Form 706 is being filed only to elect portability of the DSUE amount, the estate is not required to report the value of certain property eligible for the marital or charitable deduction. For this property being reported on Schedules A, B, C, D, E, F, G, H, and I, the executor must calculate his or her best estimate of the value. Do not include the estimated value on the line corresponding to the schedule on which the property was reported. Instead, total the estimated value of the assets subject to the special rule and enter on line 10 the amount from the Table of Estimated Values, later, that corresponds to that total.

Note. The special rule does not apply if the valuation of the asset is needed to determine the estate's eligibility for the provisions of sections 2032, 2032A, 2652(a)(3), 6166, or any other provision of the Code or Regulations.

Note. As applies to all other values reported on Form 706, estimates of the value of property subject to the special rule of Regulations section 20.2010-2T(a)(7)(ii) must result from the executor's exercise of due diligence and are subject to penalties of perjury.

Exclusion — Item 12

Item 12. Conservation easement exclusion. Complete and attach Schedule U (along with any required attachments) to claim the exclusion on this line.

Deductions — Items 14 through 23

Items 14 through 22. Attach the appropriate schedules for the deductions claimed.

Item 18. If item 17 is less than or equal to the value (at the time of the decedent's death) of the property subject to claims, enter the amount from item 17 on item 18.

If the amount on item 17 is more than the value of the property subject to claims, enter the greater of:
• The value of the property subject to claims or
• The amount actually paid at the time the return is filed.

In no event should you enter more on item 18 than the amount on item 17. See section 2053 and the related regulations for more information.

Item 23. Under Regulations section 20.2010-2T(a)(7)(ii), if the total value of the gross estate and adjusted taxable

Table of Estimated Values

If the total estimated value of the assets eligible for the special rule under Reg. section 20.2010–2T(a)(7)(ii) is more than	But less than or equal to	Include this amount on lines 10 and 23:
$0	$250,000	$250,000
$250,000	$500,000	$500,000
$500,000	$750,000	$750,000
$750,000	$1,000,000	$1,000,000
$1,000,000	$1,250,000	$1,250,000
$1,250,000	$1,500,000	$1,500,000
$1,500,000	$1,750,000	$1,750,000
$1,750,000	$2,000,000	$2,000,000
$2,000,000	$2,250,000	$2,250,000
$2,250,000	$2,500,000	$2,500,000
$2,500,000	$2,750,000	$2,750,000
$2,750,000	$3,000,000	$3,000,000
$3,000,000	$3,250,000	$3,250,000
$3,250,000	$3,500,000	$3,500,000
$3,500,000	$3,750,000	$3,750,000
$3,750,000	$4,000,000	$4,000,000
$4,000,000	$4,250,000	$4,250,000
$4,250,000	$4,500,000	$4,500,000
$4,500,000	$4,750,000	$4,750,000
$4,750,000	$5,000,000	$5,000,000
$5,000,000	$5,250,000	$5,250,000
$5,250,000	$5,340,000	$5,340,000

gifts is less than the basic exclusion amount (see section 6018(a)) and Form 706 is being filed only to elect portability of the DSUE amount, the estate is not required to report the value of certain property eligible for the marital or charitable deduction. For this property being reported on Schedule M or O, enter on line 23 the amount from line 10.

Part 6—Portability of Deceased Spousal Unused Exclusion (DSUE)

Section 303 of the Tax Relief, Unemployment Insurance Reauthorization, and Job Creation Act of 2010 authorized estates of decedents dying after December 31, 2010, to elect to transfer any unused exclusion to the surviving spouse. The amount received by the surviving spouse is called the *deceased spousal unused exclusion*, or DSUE, amount. If the executor of the decedent's estate elects transfer, or portability, of the DSUE amount, the surviving spouse can apply the DSUE amount received from the estate of his

or her last deceased spouse (defined later) against any tax liability arising from subsequent lifetime gifts and transfers at death.

Note. A nonresident surviving spouse who is not a citizen of the United States may not take into account the DSUE amount of a deceased spouse, except to the extent allowed by treaty with his or her country of citizenship.

Last Deceased Spouse Limitation

The *last deceased spouse* is the most recently deceased person who was married to the surviving spouse at the time of that person's death. The identity of the last deceased spouse is determined as of the day a taxable gift is made, or in the case of a transfer at death, the date of the surviving spouse's death. The identity of the last deceased spouse is not impacted by whether the decedent's estate elected portability or whether the last deceased spouse had any DSUE amount available. Remarriage also does not affect the

designation of the last deceased spouse and does not prevent the surviving spouse from applying the DSUE amount to taxable transfers.

When a taxable gift is made, the DSUE amount received from the last deceased spouse is applied before the surviving spouse's basic exclusion amount. A surviving spouse may use the DSUE amount of the last deceased spouse to offset the tax on any taxable transfer made after the deceased spouse's death. A surviving spouse who has more than one predeceased spouse is not precluded from using the DSUE amount of each spouse in succession. A surviving spouse may not use the sum of DSUE amounts from multiple predeceased spouses at one time nor may the DSUE amount of a predeceased spouse be applied after the death of a subsequent spouse.

Making the Election

A timely-filed and complete Form 706 is required to elect portability of the DSUE amount to a surviving spouse. The filing requirement applies to all estates of decedents choosing to elect portability of the DSUE amount, regardless of the size of the estate. A timely-filed return is one that is filed on or before the due date of the return, including extensions.

The timely filing of a complete Form 706 with DSUE will be deemed a portability election if there is a surviving spouse. The election is effective as of the decedent's date of death, so the DSUE amount received by a surviving spouse may be applied to any transfer occurring after the decedent's death. A portability election is irrevocable, unless an adjustment or amendment to the election is made on a subsequent return filed on or before the due date.

Note. Under Regulations section 20.2010-2T(a)(5), the executor of an estate of a nonresident decedent who was not a citizen of the United States at the time of death cannot make a portability election.

If an executor is appointed, qualified, and acting with the United States on behalf of the decedent's estate, only that executor may make or opt out of a portability election. If there is no executor, see Regulations section 20.2010-2T(a)(6)(ii).

Opting Out

If an estate files a Form 706 but does not wish to make the portability election, the executor can opt out of the portability election by checking the box indicated in Section A of this Part. If no return is required under section 6018(a), not filing Form 706 will avoid making the election.

Computing the DSUE Amount

Regulations section 20.2010-2T(b)(1) requires that a decedent's DSUE be computed on the estate tax return. The DSUE amount is the lesser of (A) the basic exclusion amount in effect on the date of death of the decedent whose DSUE is being computed, or (B) the decedent's applicable exclusion amount less the amount on line 5 of Part 2–Tax Computation on the Form 706 for the estate of the decedent. Amounts on which gift taxes were paid are excluded from adjusted taxable gifts for the purpose of this computation.

When a surviving spouse applies the DSUE amount to a lifetime gift or bequest at death, the IRS may examine any return of a predeceased spouse whose executor elected portability to verify the allowable DSUE amount. The DSUE amount may be adjusted or eliminated as a result of the examination; however, the IRS may only make an assessment of additional tax on the return of the predeceased spouse within the applicable limitations period under section 6501.

Special Rule Where Value of Certain Property Not Required to Be Reported on Form 706

The temporary regulations provide that executors of estates who are not otherwise required to file Form 706 under section 6018(a) do not have to report the value of certain property qualifying for the marital or charitable deduction. For such property, the executor may estimate the value in good faith and with the due diligence to be afforded all assets includible in the gross estate. The amount reported on Form 706 will correspond to a range of dollar values and will be included in the value of the gross estate shown on line 1 of Part 2-Tax Computation. See instructions for lines 10 and 23 of *Part 5-Recapitulation*, above, for more details.

Specific Instructions

Portability Election. If you intend to elect portability of the DSUE amount, timely filing a complete Form 706 is all that is required. Complete section B if any assets of the estate are being transferred to a qualified domestic trust and complete section C of this Part to calculate the DSUE amount that will be transferred to the surviving spouse.

Section A. Opting Out of Portability. If you are filing Form 706 and do not wish to elect portability, then check the box indicated. Do not complete sections B or C.

Section B. Portability and Qualified Domestic Trusts. A *qualified domestic trust* (QDOT) allows the estate of a decedent to bequeath property to surviving spouse who is not a citizen of the United States and still receive a marital deduction. When property passes to a QDOT, estate tax is imposed under section 2056A as distributions are made from the trust. When a QDOT is established and there is a DSUE amount, the executor of the decedent's estate will determine a preliminary DSUE amount for the purpose of electing portability. This amount will decrease as section 2056A distributions are made. In estates with a QDOT, the DSUE amount generally may not be applied against tax arising from lifetime gifts because it will not be available to the surviving spouse until it is finally determined, usually upon the death of the surviving spouse or when the QDOT is terminated.

Check the appropriate box in this section and see the instructions for Schedule M if more information is needed about qualified domestic trusts.

Section C. DSUE Amount Portable to Decedent's Surviving Spouse. Complete section C only if electing portability of the DSUE amount to the surviving spouse.

On line 1, enter the decedent's applicable exclusion amount from Part 2—Tax Computation, line 9c. Under section 2010(c)(2), the *applicable exclusion amount* is the sum of the basic exclusion amount for the year of death and any DSUE amount received from a predeceased spouse, if applicable.

Line 2 is reserved.

On line 3, enter the value of the cumulative lifetime gifts on which gift tax was paid or payable. This amount is figured on line 6 of the Line 7 Worksheet Part B as the total of Row (r) from Line 7 Worksheet Part A. Enter the amount as it appears on line 6 of the Line 7 Worksheet Part B

Figure the unused exclusion amount on line 9. The DSUE amount available to the surviving spouse will be the lesser of this amount or the basic exclusion amount shown on line 9a of Part 2—Tax Computation. Enter the DSUE amount as determined on line 10.

Section D. DSUE Amount Received from Predeceased Spouse(s). Complete section D if the decedent was a surviving spouse who received a DSUE amount from one or more predeceased spouse(s).

Section D requests information on all DSUE amounts received from the decedent's last deceased spouse and any previously deceased spouses. Each line in the chart should reflect a different predeceased spouse; enter the calendar year(s) in column F. In Part 1, provide information on the decedent's last deceased spouse. In Part 2, provide information as requested if the decedent had any other predeceased spouse whose executor made the portability election. Any remaining DSUE amount which was not used prior to the death of a subsequent spouse is not considered in this calculation and cannot be applied against any taxable transfer. In column E, total only the amounts of DSUE received and used from spouses who died before the decedent's last deceased spouse. Add this amount to the amount from Part 1, column D, if any, to determine the decedent's total DSUE amount.

Schedule A—Real Estate

 If any assets to which the special rule of Regulations section 20.2010-2T(a)(7)(ii) applies are reported on this schedule, do not enter any value in the last three columns. See instructions for line 10 of Part 5–Recapitulation for information on how to estimate and report the value of these assets.

If the total gross estate contains any real estate, complete Schedule A and file it with the return. On Schedule A, list real estate the decedent owned or had contracted to purchase. Number each parcel in the left-hand column.

Describe the real estate in enough detail so that the IRS can easily locate it for inspection and valuation. For each parcel of real estate, report the area and, if the parcel is improved, describe the improvements. For city or town property, report the street and number, ward, subdivision, block and lot, etc. For rural property, report the township, range, landmarks, etc.

If any item of real estate is subject to a mortgage for which the decedent's estate is liable, that is, if the indebtedness may be charged against other property of the estate that is not subject to that mortgage, or if the decedent was personally liable for that

Schedule A–Example 1

In this example, alternate valuation is not adopted; the date of death is January 1, 2014.

Item number	Description	Alternate valuation date	Alternate value	Value at date of death
1	House and lot, 1921 William Street, NW, Washington, DC (lot 6, square 481). Rent of $8,100 due at the end of each quarter, February 1, May 1, August 1, and November 1. Value based on appraisal, copy of which is attached			$550,000
	Rent due on item 1 for quarter ending November 1, 2013, but not collected at date of death . . .			8,100
	Rent accrued on Item 1 for November and December 2013			5,400
2	House and lot, 304 Jefferson Street, Alexandria, VA (lot 18, square 40). Rent of $1,800 payable monthly. Value based on appraisal, copy of which is attached			375,000
	Rent due on Item 2 for December 2013, but not collected at death			1,800

Schedule A–Example 2

In this example, alternate valuation is adopted; the date of death is January 1, 2014.

Item number	Description	Alternate valuation date	Alternate value	Value at date of death
1	House and lot, 1921 William Street, NW, Washington, DC (lot 6, square 481). Rent of $8,100 due at the end of each quarter, February 1, May 1, August 1, and November 1. Value based on appraisal, copy of which is attached. Not disposed of within 6 months of date of death	7/1/14	$535,000	$550,000
	Rent due on item 1 for quarter ending November 1, 2013, but not collected until February 1, 2014 . . .	2/1/14	8,100	8,100
	Rent accrued on Item 1 for November and December 2013, collected on February 1, 2014 . . .	2/1/14	5,400	5,400
2	House and lot, 304 Jefferson Street, Alexandria, VA (lot 18, square 40). Rent of $1,800 payable monthly. Value based on appraisal, copy of which is attached. Property exchanged for farm on May 1, 2014	5/1/14	369,000	375,000
	Rent due on Item 2 for December 2013, but not collected until February 1, 2014	2/1/14	1,800	1,800

mortgage, you must report the full value of the property in the value column. Enter the amount of the mortgage under "Description" on this schedule. The unpaid amount of the mortgage may be deducted on Schedule K.

If the decedent's estate is not liable for the amount of the mortgage, report only the value of the equity of redemption (or value of the property less the indebtedness) in the value column as part of the gross estate. Do not enter any amount less than zero. Do not deduct the amount of indebtedness on Schedule K.

Also list on Schedule A real property the decedent contracted to purchase. Report the full value of the property and not the equity in the value column. Deduct the unpaid part of the purchase price on Schedule K.

Report the value of real estate without reducing it for homestead or other exemption, or the value of dower, curtesy, or a statutory estate created instead of dower or curtesy.

Explain how the reported values were determined and attach copies of any appraisals.

Schedule A-1—Section 2032A Valuation

The election to value certain farm and closely-held business property at its special-use value is made by checking "Yes," on Form 706, Part 3—Elections by the Executor, line 2. Schedule A-1 is used to report the additional information that must be submitted to support this election. In order to make a valid election, you must complete Schedule A-1 and attach all of the required statements and appraisals.

For definitions and additional information concerning special-use valuation, see section 2032A and the related regulations.

Part 1. Type of Election

Estate and GST tax elections. If you elect special-use valuation for the estate tax, you must also elect special-use valuation for the Generation-Skipping Transfer (GST) tax and vice versa.

Protective election. To make the protective election described in the separate instructions for Part 3—Elections by the Executor, line 2, you must check the box in Part 1. Type of Election, enter the decedent's name

and social security number in the spaces provided at the top of Schedule A-1, and complete Part 2. Notice of Election, line 1 and lines 3 and 4, column A. For purposes of the protective election, list on line 3 all of the real property that passes to the qualified heirs even though some of the property will be shown on line 2 when the additional notice of election is subsequently filed. You need not complete columns B through D of lines 3 and 4. You need not complete any other line entries on Schedule A-1. Completing Schedule A-1 as described above constitutes a Notice of Protective Election as described in Regulations section 20.2032A-8(b).

Part 2. Notice of Election

Line 10. Because the special-use valuation election creates a potential tax liability for the recapture tax of section 2032A(c), you must list each person who receives an interest in the specially valued property on Schedule A-1. If there are more than eight persons who receive interests, use an additional sheet that follows the format of line 10. In the columns "Fair market value" and "Special-use value," enter the total.

respective values of all the specially valued property interests received by each person.

GST Tax Savings

To figure the additional GST tax due upon disposition (or cessation of qualified use) of the property, each "skip person" (as defined in the instructions to Schedule R) who receives an interest in the specially valued property must know the total GST tax savings all interests in specially valued property received. The GST tax savings is the difference between the total GST tax that was imposed on all interests in specially valued property received by the skip person valued at their special-use value and the total GST tax that would have been imposed on the same interests received by the skip person had they been valued at their FMV.

Because the GST tax depends on the executor's allocation of the GST exemption and the grandchild exclusion, the skip person who receives the interests is unable to figure this GST tax savings. Therefore, for each skip person who receives an interest in specially valued property, you must attach a calculation of the total GST tax savings attributable to that person's interests in specially valued property.

How to figure the GST tax savings. Before figuring each skip person's GST tax savings, complete Schedules R and R-1 for the entire estate (using the special-use values).

For each skip person, complete two Schedules R (Parts 2 and 3 only) as worksheets, one showing the interests in specially valued property received by the skip person at their special-use value and one showing the same interests at their FMV.

If the skip person received interests in specially valued property that were shown on Schedule R-1, show these interests on the Schedule R, Parts 2 and 3 worksheets, as appropriate. Do not use Schedule R-1 as a worksheet.

Completing the special-use value worksheets. On Schedule R, Parts 2 and 3, lines 2 through 4 and 6, enter -0-.

Completing the fair market value worksheets.
- *Schedule R, Parts 2 and 3, lines 2 and 3, fixed taxes and other charges.* If valuing the interests at FMV (instead of special-use value) causes any of these taxes and charges to increase, enter the increased amount (only) on these lines and attach an explanation of the increase. Otherwise, enter -0-.

- *Schedule R, Parts 2 and 3, line 6—GST exemption allocation.* If you completed Schedule R, Part 1, line 10, enter on line 6 the amount shown for the skip person on the line 10 special-use allocation schedule you attached to Schedule R. If you did not complete Schedule R, Part 1, line 10, enter -0- on line 6.

Total GST tax savings. For each skip person, subtract the tax amount on line 10, Part 2 of the special-use value worksheet from the tax amount on line 10, Part 2 of the fair market value worksheet. This difference is the skip person's total GST tax savings.

Part 3. Agreement to Special Valuation Under Section 2032A

The agreement to special valuation is required under sections 2032A(a)(1)(B) and (d)(2) and must be signed by all parties who have any interest in the property being valued based on its qualified use as of the date of the decedent's death.

An interest in property is an interest that, as of the date of the decedent's death, can be asserted under applicable law so as to affect the disposition of the specially valued property by the estate. Any person who at the decedent's death has any such interest in the property, whether present, future, vested, or contingent, must enter into the agreement. Included are owners of remainder and executory interests; the holders of general or special powers of appointment; beneficiaries of a gift over in default of exercise of any such power; joint tenants and holders of similar undivided interests when the decedent held only a joint or undivided interest in the property or when only an undivided interest is specially valued; and trustees of trusts and representatives of other entities holding title to or any interests in the property. An heir who has the power under local law to challenge a will and thereby affect disposition of the property is not, however, considered to be a person with an interest in property under section 2032A solely by reason of that right. Likewise, creditors of an estate are not such persons solely by reason of their status as creditors.

If any person required to enter into the agreement either desires that an agent act for him or her or cannot legally bind himself or herself due to infancy or other incompetency, or due to death before the election under section 2032A is timely exercised, a representative authorized by local law to bind the person in an agreement of this nature

may sign the agreement on his or her behalf.

The IRS will contact the agent designated in the agreement on all matters relating to continued qualification under section 2032A of the specially valued real property and on all matters relating to the special lien arising under section 6324B. It is the duty of the agent as attorney-in-fact for the parties with interests in the specially valued property to furnish the IRS with any requested information and to notify the IRS of any disposition or cessation of qualified use of any part of the property.

Checklist for Section 2032A Election

 When making the special-use valuation election on Schedule A-1, please use this checklist to ensure that you are providing everything necessary to make a valid election.

To have a valid special-use valuation election under section 2032A, you must file, in addition to the federal estate tax return, (a) a notice of election (Schedule A-1, Part 2), and (b) a fully executed agreement (Schedule A-1, Part 3). You must include certain information in the notice of election. To ensure that the notice of election includes all of the information required for a valid election, use the following checklist. The checklist is for your use only. Do not file it with the return.

☐ Does the notice of election include the decedent's name and social security number as they appear on the estate tax return?

☐ Does the notice of election include the relevant qualified use of the property to be specially valued?

☐ Does the notice of election describe the items of real property shown on the estate tax return that are to be specially valued and identify the property by the Form 706 schedule and item number?

Part Instructions

☐ Does the notice of election include the FMV of the real property to be specially valued and also include its value based on the qualified use (determined without the adjustments provided in section 2032A(b)(3)(B))?

☐ Does the notice of election include the adjusted value (as defined in section 2032A(b)(3)(B)) of (a) all real property that both passes from the decedent and is used in a qualified use, without regard to whether it is to be specially valued, and (b) all real property to be specially valued?

☐ Does the notice of election include (a) the items of personal property shown on the estate tax return that pass from the decedent to a qualified heir and that are used in qualified use and (b) the total value of such personal property adjusted under section 2032A(b)(3)(B)?

☐ Does the notice of election include the adjusted value of the gross estate? (See section 2032A(b)(3)(A).)

☐ Does the notice of election include the method used to determine the special-use value?

☐ Does the notice of election include copies of written appraisals of the FMV of the real property?

☐ Does the notice of election include a statement that the decedent and/or a member of his or her family has owned all of the specially valued property for at least 5 years of the 8 years immediately preceding the date of the decedent's death?

☐ Does the notice of election include a statement as to whether there were any periods during the 8-year period preceding the decedent's date of death during which the decedent or a member of his or her family did not (a) own the property to be specially valued, (b) use it in a qualified use, or (c) materially participate in the operation of the farm or other business? (See section 2032A(e)(6).)

☐ Does the notice of election include, for each item of specially valued property, the name of every person who has an interest in that item of specially valued property and the following information about each such person: (a) the person's address, (b) the person's taxpayer identification number, (c) the person's relationship to the decedent, and (d) the value of the property interest passing to that person based on both FMV and qualified use?

☐ Does the notice of election include affidavits describing the activities constituting material participation and the identity of the material participants?

☐ Does the notice of election include a legal description of each item of specially valued property?

(In the case of an election made for qualified woodlands, the information included in the notice of election must include the reason for entitlement to the Woodlands election.)

Any election made under section 2032A will not be valid unless a properly executed agreement (Schedule A-1, Part 3) is filed with the estate tax return. To ensure that the agreement satisfies the requirements for a valid election, use the following checklist:

☐ Has the agreement been signed by each qualified heir having an interest in the property being specially valued?

☐ Has every qualified heir expressed consent to personal liability under section 2032A(c) in the event of an early disposition or early cessation of qualified use?

☐ Is the agreement that is actually signed by the qualified heirs in a form that is binding on all of the qualified heirs having an interest in the specially valued property?

☐ Does the agreement designate an agent to act for the parties to the agreement in all dealings with the IRS on matters arising under section 2032A?

☐ Has the agreement been signed by the designated agent and does it give the address of the agent?

Schedule B—Stocks and Bonds

⚠️ **CAUTION** *If any assets to which the special rule of Regulations section 20.2010-2T(a)(7)(ii) applies are reported on this schedule, do not enter any value in the last three columns. See instructions for line 10 of Part 5–Recapitulation for information on how to estimate and report the value of these assets.*

TIP *Before completing Schedule B, see the examples illustrating the alternate valuation dates being adopted and not being adopted, later.*

If the total gross estate contains any stocks or bonds, you must complete Schedule B and file it with the return.

On Schedule B, list the stocks and bonds included in the decedent's gross estate. Number each item in the left-hand column.

Note. Unless specifically exempted by an estate tax provision of the Code, bonds that are exempt from federal income tax are not exempt from estate

Schedule B Examples

Example showing use of Schedule B where the alternate valuation is not adopted; date of death, January 1, 2014

Item number	Description, including face amount of bonds or number of shares and par value where needed for identification. Give CUSIP number. If trust, partnership, or closely-held entity, give EIN.	CUSIP number or EIN, where applicable	Unit value	Alternate valuation date	Alternate value	Value at date of death
1	$60,000-Arkansas Railroad Co. first mortgage 4%, 20-year bonds, due 2015. Interest payable quarterly on Feb. 1, May 1, Aug. 1, and Nov. 1; N.Y. Exchange	XXXXXXXXX	100	-------	$-------	$ 60,000
	Interest coupons attached to bonds, item 1, due and payable on Nov. 1, 2013, but not cashed at date of death		-------	-------	-------	600
	Interest accrued on item 1, from Nov. 1, 2013, to Jan. 1, 2014		-------	-------	-------	400
2	500 shares Public Service Corp., common; N.Y. Exchange . .	XXXXXXXXX	110	-------	-------	55,000
	Dividend on item 2 of $2 per share declared Dec. 10, 2013, payable on Jan. 9, 2014, to holders of record on Dec. 30, 2013		-------	-------	-------	1,000

Example showing use of Schedule B where the alternate valuation is adopted; date of death, January 1, 2014

Item number	Description, including face amount of bonds or number of shares and par value where needed for identification. Give CUSIP number. If trust, partnership, or closely-held entity, give EIN.	CUSIP number or EIN, where applicable	Unit value	Alternate valuation date	Alternate value	Value at date of death
1	$60,000-Arkansas Railroad Co. first mortgage 4%, 20-year bonds, due 2015. Interest payable quarterly on Feb. 1, May 1, Aug. 1, and Nov. 1; N.Y. Exchange	XXXXXXXXX	100	------	$------	$ 60,000
	$30,000 of item 1 distributed to legatees on Apr. 1, 2014		99	4/1/14	29,700	------
	$30,000 of item 1 sold by executor on May 1, 2014		98	5/1/14	29,400	------
	Interest coupons attached to bonds, item 1, due and payable on Nov. 1, 2013, but not cashed at date of death. Cashed by executor on Feb. 2, 2014		------	2/2/14	600	600
	Interest accrued on item 1, from Nov. 1, 2013, to Jan. 1, 2014. Cashed by executor on Feb. 2, 2014		------	2/2/14	400	400
2	500 shares Public Service Corp., common; N.Y. Exchange . .	XXXXXXXXX	110	------	------	55,000
	Not disposed of within 6 months following death		90	7/1/14	45,000	------
	Dividend on item 2 of $2 per share declared Dec. 10, 2013, paid on Jan. 9, 2014, to holders of record on Dec. 30, 2013		------	1/9/14	1,000	1,000

tax. You should list these bonds on Schedule B.

Public housing bonds includible in the gross estate must be included at their full value.

If you paid any estate, inheritance, legacy, or succession tax to a foreign country on any stocks or bonds included in this schedule, group those stocks and bonds together and label them "Subjected to Foreign Death Taxes."

List interest and dividends on each stock or bond on a separate line.

Indicate as a separate item dividends that have not been collected at death

and are payable to the decedent or the estate because the decedent was a stockholder of record on the date of death. However, if the stock is being traded on an exchange and is selling ex-dividend on the date of the decedent's death, do not include the amount of the dividend as a separate item. Instead, add it to the ex-dividend quotation in determining the FMV of the stock on the date of the decedent's death. Dividends declared on shares of stock before the death of the decedent but payable to stockholders of record on a date after the decedent's death are not includible in the gross estate for

federal estate tax purposes and should not be listed here.

Description

Stocks. For stocks, indicate:
- Number of shares;
- Whether common or preferred;
- Issue;
- Par value where needed for identification;
- Price per share;
- Exact name of corporation;
- Principal exchange upon which sold, if listed on an exchange; and
- Nine-digit CUSIP number (defined later).

Part Instructions

Bonds. For bonds, indicate:
- Quantity and denomination;
- Name of obligor;
- Date of maturity;
- Interest rate;
- Interest due date;
- Principal exchange, if listed on an exchange; and
- Nine-digit CUSIP number.

If the stock or bond is unlisted, show the company's principal business office.

If the gross estate includes any interest in a trust, partnership, or closely-held entity, provide the employer identification number (EIN) of the entity in the description column on Schedules B, E, F, G, M, and O. You must also provide the EIN of an estate (if any) in the description column on the above-noted schedules, where applicable.

The CUSIP (Committee on Uniform Security Identification Procedure) number is a nine-digit number that is assigned to all stocks and bonds traded on major exchanges and many unlisted securities. Usually, the CUSIP number is printed on the face of the stock certificate. If you do not have a stock certificate, the CUSIP may be found on the broker's or custodian's statement or by contacting the company's transfer agent.

Valuation

List the FMV of the stocks or bonds. The FMV of a stock or bond (whether listed or unlisted) is the mean between the highest and lowest selling prices quoted on the valuation date. If only the closing selling prices are available, then the FMV is the mean between the quoted closing selling price on the valuation date and on the trading day before the valuation date.

If there were no sales on the valuation date, figure the FMV as follows:

1. Find the mean between the highest and lowest selling prices on the nearest trading date before and the nearest trading date after the valuation date. Both trading dates must be reasonably close to the valuation date.

2. Prorate the difference between the mean prices to the valuation date.

3. Add or subtract (whichever applies) the prorated part of the difference to or from the mean price figured for the nearest trading date before the valuation date.

If no actual sales were made reasonably close to the valuation date,

make the same computation using the mean between the bona fide bid and asked prices instead of sales prices. If actual sales prices or bona fide bid and asked prices are available within a reasonable period of time before the valuation date but not after the valuation date, or vice versa, use the mean between the highest and lowest sales prices or bid and asked prices as the FMV.

For example, assume that sales of stock nearest the valuation date (June 15) occurred 2 trading days before (June 13) and 3 trading days after (June 18). On those days, the mean sale prices per share were $10 and $15, respectively. Therefore, the price of $12 is considered the FMV of a share of stock on the valuation date. If, however, on June 13 and 18, the mean sale prices per share were $15 and $10, respectively, the FMV of a share of stock on the valuation date is $13.

If only closing prices for bonds are available, see Regulations section 20.2031-2(b).

Apply the rules in the section 2031 regulations to determine the value of inactive stock and stock in close corporations. Attach to Schedule B complete financial and other data used to determine value, including balance sheets (particularly the one nearest to the valuation date) and statements of the net earnings or operating results and dividends paid for each of the 5 years immediately before the valuation date.

Securities reported as of no value, of nominal value, or obsolete should be listed last. Include the address of the company and the state and date of the incorporation. Attach copies of correspondence or statements used to determine the "no value."

If the security was listed on more than one stock exchange, use either the records of the exchange where the security is principally traded or the composite listing of combined exchanges, if available, in a publication of general circulation. In valuing listed stocks and bonds, you should carefully check accurate records to obtain values for the applicable valuation date.

If you get quotations from brokers, or evidence of the sale of securities from the officers of the issuing companies, attach to the schedule copies of the letters furnishing these quotations or evidence of sale.

Schedule C—Mortgages, Notes, and Cash

 If any assets to which the special rule of Regulations section 20.2010-2T(a)(7)(ii) applies are reported on this schedule, do not enter any value in the last three columns. See instructions for line 10 of Part 5–Recapitulation for information on how to estimate and report the value of these assets.

Complete Schedule C and file it with your return if the total gross estate contains any:
- Mortgages,
- Notes, or
- Cash.

List on Schedule C:
- Mortgages and notes payable **to the decedent** at the time of death.
- Cash the decedent had at the date of death.

Note. Do not list mortgages and notes payable **by the decedent** on Schedule C. (If these are deductible, list them on Schedule K.)

List the items on Schedule C in the following order:

1. Mortgages;
2. Promissory notes;
3. Contracts by decedent to sell land;
4. Cash in possession; and
5. Cash in banks, savings and loan associations, and other types of financial organizations.

What to enter in the "Description" column:
For mortgages, list:
- Face value,
- Unpaid balance,
- Date of mortgage,
- Name of maker,
- Property mortgaged,
- Date of maturity,
- Interest rate, and
- Interest date.

Example to enter in "Description" column: "Bond and mortgage of $50,000, unpaid balance: $17,000; dated: January 1, 1992; John Doe to Richard Roe; premises: 22 Clinton Street, Newark, NJ; due: January 1, 2014; interest payable at 10% a year—January 1 and July 1."

For promissory notes, list in the same way as mortgages.

For contracts by the decedent to sell land, list:

- Name of purchaser,
- Contract date,
- Property description,
- Sale price,
- Initial payment,
- Amounts of installment payment,
- Unpaid balance of principal, and
- Interest rate.

For cash on hand, list such cash separately from bank deposits.

For cash in banks, savings and loan associations, and other types of financial organizations, list:
- Name and address of each financial organization,
- Amount in each account,
- Serial or account number,
- Nature of account—checking, savings, time deposit, etc., and
- Unpaid interest accrued from date of last interest payment to the date of death.

Note. If you obtain statements from the financial organizations, keep them for IRS inspection.

Schedule D—Insurance on the Decedent's Life

 If any assets to which the special rule of Regulations section 20.2010-2T(a)(7)(ii) applies are reported on this schedule, do not enter any value in the last three columns.. See instructions for line 10 of Part 5–Recapitulation for information on how to estimate and report the value of these assets.

If you are required to file Form 706 and there was any insurance on the decedent's life, whether or not included in the gross estate, you must complete Schedule D and file it with the return.

Insurance you must include on Schedule D. Under section 2042, you must include in the gross estate:
- Insurance on the decedent's life receivable by or for the benefit of the estate; and
- Insurance on the decedent's life receivable by beneficiaries other than the estate, as described below.

The term "insurance" refers to life insurance of every description, including death benefits paid by fraternal beneficiary societies operating under the lodge system, and death benefits paid under no-fault automobile insurance policies if the no-fault insurer was unconditionally bound to pay the benefit in the event of the insured's death.

Insurance in favor of the estate. Include on Schedule D the full amount of the proceeds of insurance on the life of the decedent receivable by the executor or otherwise payable to or for the benefit of the estate. Insurance in favor of the estate includes insurance used to pay the estate tax, and any other taxes, debts, or charges that are enforceable against the estate. The manner in which the policy is drawn is immaterial as long as there is an obligation, legally binding on the beneficiary, to use the proceeds to pay taxes, debts, or charges. You must include the full amount even though the premiums or other consideration may have been paid by a person other than the decedent.

Insurance receivable by beneficiaries other than the estate. Include on Schedule D the proceeds of all insurance on the life of the decedent not receivable by, or for the benefit of, the decedent's estate if the decedent possessed at death any of the following incidents of ownership, exercisable either alone or in conjunction with any person or entity.

Incidents of ownership in a policy include:
- The right of the insured or estate to its economic benefits;
- The power to change the beneficiary;
- The power to surrender or cancel the policy;
- The power to assign the policy or to revoke an assignment;
- The power to pledge the policy for a loan;
- The power to obtain from the insurer a loan against the surrender value of the policy; and
- A reversionary interest if the value of the reversionary interest was more than 5% of the value of the policy immediately before the decedent died. (An interest in an insurance policy is considered a reversionary interest if, for example, the proceeds become payable to the insured's estate or payable as the insured directs if the beneficiary dies before the insured.)

Life insurance not includible in the gross estate under section 2042 may be includible under some other section of the Code. For example, a life insurance policy could be transferred by the decedent in such a way that it would be includible in the gross estate under section 2036, 2037, or 2038. See the instructions to Schedule G for a description of these sections.

Completing the Schedule

You must list every insurance policy on the life of the decedent, whether or not it is included in the gross estate.

Under "Description," list:
- The name of the insurance company, and
- The number of the policy.

For every life insurance policy listed on the schedule, request a statement on Form 712, Life Insurance Statement, from the company that issued the policy. Attach the Form 712 to Schedule D.

If the policy proceeds are paid in one sum, enter the net proceeds received (from Form 712, line 24) in the value (and alternate value) columns of Schedule D. If the policy proceeds are not paid in one sum, enter the value of the proceeds as of the date of the decedent's death (from Form 712, line 25).

If part or all of the policy proceeds are not included in the gross estate, explain why they were not included.

Schedule E—Jointly Owned Property

 If any assets to which the special rule of Regulations section 20.2010-2T(a)(7)(ii) applies are reported on this schedule, do not enter any value in the last three columns. See instructions for line 10 of Part 5–Recapitulation for information on how to estimate and report the value of these assets.

If you are required to file Form 706, complete Schedule E and file it with the return if the decedent owned any joint property at the time of death, whether or not the decedent's interest is includible in the gross estate.

Enter on this schedule all property of whatever kind or character, whether real estate, personal property, or bank accounts, in which the decedent held at the time of death an interest either as a joint tenant with right to survivorship or as a tenant by the entirety.

Do not list on this schedule property that the decedent held as a tenant in common, but report the value of the interest on Schedule A if real estate, or on the appropriate schedule if personal property. Similarly, community property held by the decedent and spouse should be reported on the appropriate Schedules A through I. The decedent's interest in a partnership should not be entered on this schedule unless the partnership interest itself is jointly-owned. Solely owned partnership interests should be reported on Schedule F, "Other Miscellaneous Property Not Reportable Under Any Other Schedule."

Part 1. Qualified joint interests held by decedent and spouse. Under section 2040(b)(2), a joint interest is a qualified joint interest if the decedent and the surviving spouse held the interest as:

• Tenants by the entirety, or
• Joint tenants with right of survivorship if the decedent and the decedent's spouse are the only joint tenants.

Interests that meet either of the two requirements above should be entered in Part 1. Joint interests that do not meet either of the two requirements above should be entered in Part 2.

Under "Description," describe the property as required in the instructions for Schedules A, B, C, and F for the type of property involved. For example, jointly held stocks and bonds should be described using the rules given in the instructions to Schedule B.

Under "Alternate value" and "Value at date of death," enter the full value of the property.

Note. You cannot claim the special treatment under section 2040(b) for property held jointly by a decedent and a surviving spouse who is not a U.S. citizen. Report these joint interests on Part 2 of Schedule E, not Part 1.

Part 2. All other joint interests. All joint interests that were not entered in Part 1 must be entered in Part 2.

For each item of property, enter the appropriate letter A, B, C, etc., from line 2a to indicate the name and address of the surviving co-tenant.

Under "Description," describe the property as required in the instructions for Schedules A, B, C, and F for the type of property involved.

In the "Percentage includible" column, enter the percentage of the total value of the property included in the gross estate.

Generally, you must include the full value of the jointly-owned property in the gross estate. However, the full value should not be included if you can show that a part of the property originally belonged to the other tenant or tenants and was never received or acquired by the other tenant or tenants from the decedent for less than adequate and full consideration in money or money's

worth. Full value of jointly-owned property also does not have to be included in the gross estate if you can show that any part of the property was acquired with consideration originally belonging to the surviving joint tenant or tenants. In this case, you may exclude from the value of the property an amount proportionate to the consideration furnished by the other tenant or tenants. Relinquishing or promising to relinquish dower, curtesy, or statutory estate created instead of dower or curtesy, or other marital rights in the decedent's property or estate is not consideration in money or money's worth. See the Schedule A instructions for the value to show for real property that is subject to a mortgage.

If the property was acquired by the decedent and another person or persons by gift, bequest, devise, or inheritance as joint tenants, and their interests are not otherwise specified by law, include only that part of the value of the property that is figured by dividing the full value of the property by the number of joint tenants.

If you believe that less than the full value of the entire property is includible in the gross estate for tax purposes, you must establish the right to include the smaller value by attaching proof of the extent, origin, and nature of the decedent's interest and the interest(s) of the decedent's co-tenant or co-tenants.

In the "Includible alternate value" and "Includible value at date of death" columns, enter only the values that you believe are includible in the gross estate.

Schedule F—Other Miscellaneous Property

 If any assets to which the special rule of Regulations section 20.2010-2T(a)(7)(ii) applies are reported on this schedule, do not enter any value in the last three columns. See instructions for line 10 of Part 5–Recapitulation for information on how to estimate and report the value of these assets.

You must complete Schedule F and file it with the return.

On Schedule F, list all items that must be included in the gross estate that are not reported on any other schedule, including:

• Debts due the decedent (other than notes and mortgages included on Schedule C);
• Interests in business;

• Any interest in an Archer medical savings account (MSA) or health savings account (HSA), unless such interest passes to the surviving spouse; and
• Insurance on the life of another (obtain and attach Form 712, for each policy).

Note (for single premium or paid-up policies). In certain situations (for example, where the surrender value of the policy exceeds its replacement cost), the true economic value of the policy will be greater than the amount shown on line 59 of Form 712. In these situations, report the full economic value of the policy on Schedule F. See Rev. Rul. 78-137, 1978-1 C.B. 280 for details.

• Section 2044 property (see *Decedent Who Was a Surviving Spouse,* later);
• Claims (including the value of the decedent's interest in a claim for refund of income taxes or the amount of the refund actually received);
• Rights;
• Royalties;
• Leaseholds;
• Judgments;
• Reversionary or remainder interests;
• Shares in trust funds (attach a copy of the trust instrument);
• Household goods and personal effects, including wearing apparel;
• Farm products and growing crops;
• Livestock;
• Farm machinery; and
• Automobiles.

Interests. If the decedent owned any interest in a partnership or unincorporated business, attach a statement of assets and liabilities for the valuation date and for the 5 years before the valuation date. Also, attach statements of the net earnings for the same 5 years. Be sure to include the EIN of the entity. You must account for goodwill in the valuation. In general, furnish the same information and follow the methods used to value close corporations. See the instructions for Schedule B.

All partnership interests should be reported on Schedule F unless the partnership interest, itself, is jointly-owned. Jointly-owned partnership interests should be reported on Schedule E.

If real estate is owned by a sole proprietorship, it should be reported on Schedule F and not on Schedule A. Describe the real estate with the same detail required for Schedule A.

Valuation discounts. If you answered "Yes," to Part 4—General Information, line 11b for any interest in a partnership, an unincorporated business, a limited liability company, or stock in a closely-held corporation, attach a statement that lists the item number from Schedule F and identifies the total effective discount taken (that is, XX.XX%) on such interest.

Example of effective discount:

a	Pro-rata value of limited liability company (before any discounts)	$100.00
b	Minus: 10% discounts for lack of control	(10.00)
c	Marketable minority interest value (as if freely traded minority interest value)	$90.00
d	Minus: 15% discount for lack of marketability	(13.50)
e	Non-marketable minority interest value	$76.50

Calculation of effective discount:

(**a** minus **e**) divided by **a** = effective discount
($100.00 - $76.50) ÷ $100.00 = 23.50%

Note. The amount of discounts are based on the factors pertaining to a specific interest and those discounts shown in the example are for demonstration purposes only.

If you answered "Yes," to line 11b for any transfer(s) described in (1) through (5) in the Schedule G instructions (and made by the decedent), **attach a statement to Schedule G** which lists the item number from that schedule and identifies the total effective discount taken (that is, XX.XX%) on such transfer(s).

Line 1. If the decedent owned at the date of death works of art or items with collectible value (for example, jewelry, furs, silverware, books, statuary, vases, oriental rugs, coin or stamp collections), check the "Yes," box on line 1 and provide full details. If any item or collection of similar items is valued at more than $3,000, attach an appraisal by an expert under oath and the required statement regarding the appraiser's qualifications (see Regulations section 20.2031-6(b)).

Decedent Who Was a Surviving Spouse

If the decedent was a surviving spouse, he or she may have received qualified terminable interest property (QTIP) from the predeceased spouse for which the marital deduction was elected either on the predeceased spouse's estate tax return or on a gift tax return, Form 709. The election is available for transfers made and decedents dying after December 31, 1981. List such property on Schedule F.

If this election was made and the surviving spouse retained his or her interest in the QTIP property at death, the full value of the QTIP property is includible in his or her estate, even though the qualifying income interest terminated at death. It is valued as of the date of the surviving spouse's death, or alternate valuation date, if applicable. Do not reduce the value by any annual exclusion that may have applied to the transfer creating the interest.

The value of such property included in the surviving spouse's gross estate is treated as passing from the surviving spouse. It therefore qualifies for the charitable and marital deductions on the surviving spouse's estate tax return if it meets the other requirements for those deductions.

For additional details, see Regulations section 20.2044-1.

Schedule G—Transfers During Decedent's Life

 If any assets to which the special rule of Regulations section 20.2010-2T(a)(7)(ii) applies are reported on this schedule, do not enter any value in the last three columns. See instructions for line 10 of Part 5–Recapitulation for information on how to estimate and report the value of these assets.

Complete Schedule G and file it with the return if the decedent made any of the transfers described in (1) through (5) later, or if you answered "Yes," to question 12 or 13a of Part 4—General Information.

Report the following types of transfers on this schedule:

IF...	AND...	THEN...
the decedent made a transfer from a trust,	at the time of the transfer, the transfer was from a portion of the trust that was owned by the grantor under section 676 (other than by reason of section 672(e)) by reason of a power in the grantor,	for purposes of sections 2035 and 2038, treat the transfer as made directly by the decedent.
	Any such transfer within the annual gift tax exclusion is not includible in the gross estate.	

1. **Certain gift taxes (section 2035(b)).** Enter at item A of Schedule G the total value of the gift taxes that were paid by the decedent or the estate on gifts made by the decedent or the decedent's spouse within 3 years of death.

The date of the gift, not the date of payment of the gift tax, determines whether a gift tax paid is included in the gross estate under this rule. Therefore, you should carefully examine the Forms 709 filed by the decedent and the decedent's spouse to determine what part of the total gift taxes reported on them was attributable to gifts made within 3 years of death.

For example, if the decedent died on July 10, 2013, you should examine gift tax returns for 2013, 2012, 2011, and 2010. However, the gift taxes on the 2010 return that are attributable to gifts made on or before July 10, 2010, are not included in the gross estate.

Explain how you figured the includible gift taxes if the entire gift taxes shown on any Form 709 filed for gifts made within 3 years of death are not included in the gross estate. Also attach copies of any relevant gift tax returns filed by the decedent's spouse for gifts made within 3 years of death.

2. **Other transfers within 3 years of death (section 2035(a)).** These transfers include only the following:
• Any transfer by the decedent with respect to a life insurance policy within 3 years of death; or

- Any transfer within 3 years of death of a retained section 2036 life estate, section 2037 reversionary interest, or section 2038 power to revoke, etc., if the property subject to the life estate, interest, or power would have been included in the gross estate had the decedent continued to possess the life estate, interest, or power until death.

These transfers are reported on Schedule G, regardless of whether a gift tax return was required to be filed for them when they were made. However, the amount includible and the information required to be shown for the transfers are determined:
- For insurance on the life of the decedent using the instructions to Schedule D (attach Forms 712);
- For insurance on the life of another using the instructions to Schedule F (attach Forms 712); and
- For sections 2036, 2037, and 2038 transfers, using paragraphs (3), (4), and (5) of these instructions.

3. Transfers with retained life estate (section 2036). These are transfers by the decedent in which the decedent retained an interest in the transferred property. The transfer can be in trust or otherwise, but excludes bona fide sales for adequate and full consideration.

Interests or rights. Section 2036 applies to the following retained interests or rights:
- The right to income from the transferred property;
- The right to the possession or enjoyment of the property; and
- The right, either alone or with any person, to designate the persons who shall receive the income from, possess, or enjoy, the property.

Retained annuity, unitrust, and other income interests in trusts. If a decedent transferred property into a trust and retained or reserved the right to use the property, or the right to an annuity, unitrust, or other interest in such trust for the property for decedent's life, any period not ascertainable without reference to the decedent's death, or for a period that does not, in fact, end before the decedent's death, then the decedent's right to use the property or the retained annuity, unitrust, or other interest (whether payable from income and/or principal) is the retention of the possession or enjoyment of, or the right to the income from, the property for purposes of section 2036. See Regulations section 20.2036-1(c)(2).

Retained voting rights. Transfers with a retained life estate also include transfers of stock in a controlled corporation after June 22, 1976, if the decedent retained or acquired voting rights in the stock. If the decedent retained direct or indirect voting rights in a controlled corporation, the decedent is considered to have retained enjoyment of the transferred property. A corporation is a *controlled corporation* if the decedent owned (actually or constructively) or had the right (either alone or with any other person) to vote at least 20% of the total combined voting power of all classes of stock. See section 2036(b)(2). If these voting rights ceased or were relinquished within 3 years of the decedent's death, the corporate interests are included in the gross estate as if the decedent had actually retained the voting rights until death.

The amount includible in the gross estate is the value of the transferred property at the time of the decedent's death. If the decedent kept or reserved an interest or right to only a part of the transferred property, the amount includible in the gross estate is a corresponding part of the entire value of the property.

A retained life estate does not have to be legally enforceable. What matters is that a substantial economic benefit was retained. For example, if a mother transferred title to her home to her daughter but with the informal understanding that she was to continue living there until her death, the value of the home would be includible in the mother's estate even if the agreement would not have been legally enforceable.

4. **Transfers taking effect at death (section 2037).** A transfer that takes effect at the decedent's death is one under which possession or enjoyment can be obtained only by surviving the decedent. A transfer is not treated as one that takes effect at the decedent's death unless the decedent retained a reversionary interest (defined later) in the property that immediately before the decedent's death had a value of more than 5% of the value of the transferred property. If the transfer was made before October 8, 1949, the reversionary interest must have arisen by the express terms of the instrument of transfer.

A *reversionary interest* is, generally, any right under which the transferred property will or may be returned to the decedent or the decedent's estate. It also includes the possibility that the transferred property may become subject to a power of disposition by the decedent. It does not matter if the right arises by the express terms of the instrument of transfer or by operation of law. For this purpose, reversionary interest does not include the possibility that the income alone from the property may return to the decedent or become subject to the decedent's power of disposition.

5. **Revocable transfers (section 2038).** The gross estate includes the value of any transferred property which was subject to the decedent's power to alter, amend, revoke, or terminate the transfer at the time of the decedent's death. A decedent's power to change beneficiaries and to increase any beneficiary's enjoyment of the property are examples of this.

It does not matter whether the power was reserved at the time of the transfer, whether it arose by operation of law, or whether it was later created or conferred. The rule applies regardless of the source from which the power was acquired, and regardless of whether the power was exercisable by the decedent alone or with any person (and regardless of whether that person had a substantial adverse interest in the transferred property).

The capacity in which the decedent could use a power has no bearing. If the decedent gave property in trust and was the trustee with the power to revoke the trust, the property would be included in his or her gross estate. For transfers or additions to an irrevocable trust after October 28, 1979, the transferred property is includible if the decedent reserved the power to remove the trustee at will and appoint another trustee.

If the decedent relinquished within 3 years of death any of the includible powers described above, figure the gross estate as if the decedent had actually retained the powers until death.

Only the part of the transferred property that is subject to the decedent's power is included in the gross estate.

For more detailed information on which transfers are includible in the gross estate, see Regulations section 20.2038-1.

Special Valuation Rules for Certain Lifetime Transfers

Sections 2701 through 2704 provide rules for valuing certain transfers to family members.

Section 2701 deals with the transfer of an interest in a corporation or partnership while retaining certain distribution rights, or a liquidation, put, call, or conversion right.

Section 2702 deals with the transfer of an interest in a trust while retaining any interest other than a qualified interest. In general, a *qualified interest* is a right to receive certain distributions from the trust at least annually, or a noncontingent remainder interest if all of the other interests in the trust are distribution rights specified in section 2702.

Section 2703 provides rules for the valuation of property transferred to a family member but subject to an option, agreement, or other right to acquire or use the property at less than FMV. It also applies to transfers subject to restrictions on the right to sell or use the property.

Finally, section 2704 provides that in certain cases, the lapse of a voting or liquidation right in a family-owned corporation or partnership will result in a deemed transfer.

These rules have potential consequences for the valuation of property in an estate. If the decedent (or any member of his or her family) was involved in any such transactions, see sections 2701 through 2704 and the related regulations for additional details.

How To Complete Schedule G

All transfers (other than outright transfers not in trust and bona fide sales) made by the decedent at any time during life must be reported on Schedule G, regardless of whether you believe the transfers are subject to tax. If the decedent made any transfers not described in these instructions, the transfers should not be shown on Schedule G. Instead, attach a statement describing these transfers by listing:
- The date of the transfer,
- The amount or value of the transferred property, and
- The type of transfer.

Complete the schedule for each transfer that is included in the gross estate under sections 2035(a), 2036, 2037, and 2038 as described in the Instructions for Schedule G.

In the "Item number" column, number each transfer consecutively beginning with "1." In the "Description" column, list the name of the transferee and the date of the transfer, and give a complete description of the property. Transfers

included in the gross estate should be valued on the date of the decedent's death or, if alternate valuation is elected, according to section 2032.

If only part of the property transferred meets the terms of section 2035(a), 2036, 2037, or 2038, then only a corresponding part of the value of the property should be included in the value of the gross estate. If the transferee makes additions or improvements to the property, the increased value of the property at the valuation date should not be included on Schedule G. However, if only a part of the value of the property is included, enter the value of the whole under the column headed "Description" and explain what part was included.

Attachments. If a transfer, by trust or otherwise, was made by a written instrument, attach a copy of the instrument to Schedule G. If the copy of the instrument is of public record, it should be certified; if not of public record, the copy should be verified.

Schedule H—Powers of Appointment

 If any assets to which the special rule of Regulations section 20.2010-2T(a)(7)(ii) applies are reported on this schedule, do not enter any value in the last three columns. See instructions for line 10 of Part 5–Recapitulation for information on how to estimate and report the value of these assets.

Complete Schedule H and file it with the return if you answered "Yes," to question 14 of Part 4—General Information.

On Schedule H, include in the gross estate:
- The value of property for which the decedent possessed a general power of appointment (defined later) on the date of his or her death and
- The value of property for which the decedent possessed a general power of appointment that he or she exercised or released before death by disposing of it in such a way that if it were a transfer of property owned by the decedent, the property would be includible in the decedent's gross estate as a transfer with a retained life estate, a transfer taking effect at death, or a revocable transfer.

With the above exceptions, property subject to a power of appointment is not includible in the gross estate if the decedent released the power

completely and the decedent held no interest in or control over the property.

If the failure to exercise a general power of appointment results in a lapse of the power, the lapse is treated as a release only to the extent that the value of the property that could have been appointed by the exercise of the lapsed power is more than the greater of $5,000 or 5% of the total value, at the time of the lapse, of the assets out of which, or the proceeds of which, the exercise of the lapsed power could have been satisfied.

Powers of Appointment

A *power of appointment* determines who will own or enjoy the property subject to the power and when they will own or enjoy it. The power must be created by someone other than the decedent. It does not include a power created or held on property transferred by the decedent.

A power of appointment includes all powers which are, in substance and effect, powers of appointment regardless of how they are identified and regardless of local property laws. For example, if a settlor transfers property in trust for the life of his wife, with a power in the wife to appropriate or consume the principal of the trust, the wife has a power of appointment.

Some powers do not in themselves constitute a power of appointment. For example, a power to amend only administrative provisions of a trust that cannot substantially affect the beneficial enjoyment of the trust property or income is not a power of appointment. A power to manage, invest, or control assets, or to allocate receipts and disbursements, when exercised only in a fiduciary capacity, is not a power of appointment.

General power of appointment. A *general power of appointment* is a power that is exercisable in favor of the decedent, the decedent's estate, the decedent's creditors, or the creditors of the decedent's estate, except:

1. A power to consume, invade, or appropriate property for the benefit of the decedent that is limited by an ascertainable standard relating to health, education, support, or maintenance of the decedent.

2. A power exercisable by the decedent only in conjunction with:

a. the creator of the power or

b. a person who has a substantial interest in the property subject to the power, which is adverse to the exercise of the power in favor of the decedent.

A part of a power is considered a general power of appointment if the power:

1. May only be exercised by the decedent in conjunction with another person and

2. Is also exercisable in favor of the other person (in addition to being exercisable in favor of the decedent, the decedent's creditors, the decedent's estate, or the creditors of the decedent's estate).

When there is a partial power, figure the amount included in the gross estate by dividing the value of the property by the number of persons (including the decedent) in favor of whom the power is exercisable.

Date power was created. Generally, a power of appointment created by will is considered created on the date of the testator's death.

A power of appointment created by an inter vivos instrument is considered created on the date the instrument takes effect. If the holder of a power exercises it by creating a second power, the second power is considered as created at the time of the exercise of the first.

Attachments

If the decedent ever possessed a power of appointment, attach a certified or verified copy of the instrument granting the power and a certified or verified copy of any instrument by which the power was exercised or released. You must file these copies even if you contend that the power was not a general power of appointment, and that the property is not otherwise includible in the gross estate.

Schedule I—Annuities

 If any assets to which the special rule of Regulations section 20.2010-2T(a)(7)(ii) applies are reported on this schedule, do not enter any value in the last three columns. See instructions for line 10 of Part 5–Recapitulation for information on how to estimate and report the value of these assets.

Complete Schedule I and file it with the return if you answered "Yes," to question 16 of Part 4—General Information.

Enter on Schedule I every annuity that meets all of the conditions under General, later, and every annuity

described in paragraphs (a) through (h) of *Annuities Under Approved Plans,* even if the annuities are wholly or partially excluded from the gross estate.

For a discussion regarding the QTIP treatment of certain joint and survivor annuities, see the Schedule M, line 3 instructions.

General

These rules apply to all types of annuities, including pension plans, individual retirement arrangements, purchased commercial annuities, and private annuities.

In general, you must include in the gross estate all or part of the value of any annuity that meets the following requirements:
- It is receivable by a beneficiary following the death of the decedent and by reason of surviving the decedent;
- The annuity is under a contract or agreement entered into after March 3, 1931;
- The annuity was payable to the decedent (or the decedent possessed the right to receive the annuity) either alone or in conjunction with another, for the decedent's life or for any period not ascertainable without reference to the decedent's death or for any period that did not in fact end before the decedent's death; and
- The contract or agreement is not a policy of insurance on the life of the decedent.

Note. A *private annuity* is an annuity issued by a party not engaged in the business of writing annuity contracts, typically a junior generation family member or a family trust.

An annuity contract that provides periodic payments to a person for life and ceases at the person's death is not includible in the gross estate. Social security benefits are not includible in the gross estate even if the surviving spouse receives benefits.

An annuity or other payment that is not includible in the decedent's or the survivor's gross estate as an annuity may still be includible under some other applicable provision of the law. For example, see *Powers of Appointment and the instructions for Schedule G—Transfers During Decedent's Life,* earlier. See also Regulations section 20.2039-1(e).

If the decedent retired before January 1, 1985, see *Annuities Under Approved Plans,* later, for rules that allow the exclusion of part or all of certain annuities.

Part Includible

If the decedent contributed only part of the purchase price of the contract or agreement, include in the gross estate only that part of the value of the annuity receivable by the surviving beneficiary that the decedent's contribution to the purchase price of the annuity or agreement bears to the total purchase price.

For example, if the value of the survivor's annuity was $20,000 and the decedent had contributed three-fourths of the purchase price of the contract, the amount includible is $15,000 ($^{3}/_{4}$ × $20,000).

Except as provided under *Annuities Under Approved Plans,* contributions made by the decedent's employer to the purchase price of the contract or agreement are considered made by the decedent if they were made by the employer because of the decedent's employment. For more information, see section 2039(b).

Definitions

Annuity. An *annuity* consists of one or more payments extending over any period of time. The payments may be equal or unequal, conditional or unconditional, periodic or sporadic.

Examples. The following are examples of contracts (but not necessarily the only forms of contracts) for annuities that must be included in the gross estate:

1. A contract under which the decedent immediately before death was receiving or was entitled to receive, for the duration of life, an annuity with payments to continue after death to a designated beneficiary, if surviving the decedent.

2. A contract under which the decedent immediately before death was receiving or was entitled to receive, together with another person, an annuity payable to the decedent and the other person for their joint lives, with payments to continue to the survivor following the death of either.

3. A contract or agreement entered into by the decedent and employer under which the decedent immediately before death and following retirement was receiving, or was entitled to receive, an annuity payable to the decedent for life. After the decedent's death, if survived by a designated beneficiary, the annuity was payable to the beneficiary with payments either

fixed by contract or subject to an option or election exercised or exercisable by the decedent. However, see *Annuities Under Approved Plans,* later.

4. A contract or agreement entered into by the decedent and the decedent's employer under which at the decedent's death, before retirement, or before the expiration of a stated period of time, an annuity was payable to a designated beneficiary, if surviving the decedent. However, see *Annuities Under Approved Plans,* later.

5. A contract or agreement under which the decedent immediately before death was receiving, or was entitled to receive, an annuity for a stated period of time, with the annuity to continue to a designated beneficiary, surviving the decedent, upon the decedent's death and before the expiration of that period of time.

6. An annuity contract or other arrangement providing for a series of substantially equal periodic payments to be made to a beneficiary for life or over a period of at least 36 months after the date of the decedent's death under an individual retirement account, annuity, or bond as described in section 2039(e) (before its repeal by P.L. 98-369).

Payable to the decedent. An annuity or other payment was payable to the decedent if, at the time of death, the decedent was in fact receiving an annuity or other payment, with or without an enforceable right to have the payments continued.

Right to receive an annuity. The decedent had the right to receive an annuity or other payment if, immediately before death, the decedent had an enforceable right to receive payments at some time in the future, whether or not at the time of death the decedent had a present right to receive payments.

Annuities Under Approved Plans

The following rules relate to whether part or all of an otherwise includible annuity may be excluded. These rules have been repealed and apply only if the decedent either:
• On December 31, 1984, was both a participant in the plan and in pay status (for example, had received at least one benefit payment on or before December 31, 1984) and had irrevocably elected the form of the benefit before July 18, 1984, or
• Had separated from service before January 1, 1985, and did not change the form of benefit before death.

The amount excluded cannot exceed $100,000 unless either of the following conditions is met:
• On December 31, 1982, the decedent was both a participant in the plan and in pay status (for example, had received at least one benefit payment on or before December 31, 1982) and the decedent irrevocably elected the form of the benefit before January 1, 1983, or
• The decedent separated from service before January 1, 1983, and did not change the form of benefit before death.

Approved Plans

Approved plans may be separated into two categories:
• Pension, profit-sharing, stock bonus, and other similar plans and
• Individual retirement arrangements (IRAs), and retirement bonds.

Different exclusion rules apply to the two categories of plans.

Pension, etc., plans. The following plans are approved plans for the exclusion rules:

a. An employees' trust (or a contract purchased by an employees' trust) forming part of a pension, stock bonus, or profit-sharing plan that met all the requirements of section 401(a), either at the time of the decedent's separation from employment (whether by death or otherwise) or at the time of the termination of the plan (if earlier);

b. A retirement annuity contract purchased by the employer (but not by an employees' trust) under a plan that, at the time of the decedent's separation from employment (by death or otherwise), or at the time of the termination of the plan (if earlier), was a plan described in section 403(a);

c. A retirement annuity contract purchased for an employee by an employer that is an organization referred to in section 170(b)(1)(A)(ii) or (vi), or that is a religious organization (other than a trust), and that is exempt from tax under section 501(a);

d. Chapter 73 of Title 10 of the United States Code; or

e. A bond purchase plan described in section 405 (before its repeal by P.L. 98-369, effective for obligations issued after December 31, 1983).

Exclusion rules for pension, etc., plans. If an annuity under an *approved plan* described in (a) through (e) above is receivable by a beneficiary other than the executor and the decedent made no

contributions under the plan toward the cost, no part of the value of the annuity, subject to the $100,000 limitation (if applicable), is includible in the gross estate.

If the decedent made a contribution under a plan described in (a) through (e) above toward the cost, include in the gross estate on this schedule that proportion of the value of the annuity which the amount of the decedent's contribution under the plan bears to the total amount of all contributions under the plan. The remaining value of the annuity is excludable from the gross estate subject to the $100,000 limitation (if applicable). For the rules to determine whether the decedent made contributions to the plan, see Regulations section 20.2039-1(c).

IRAs and retirement bonds. The following plans are approved plans for the exclusion rules:

f. An individual retirement account described in section 408(a),

g. An individual retirement annuity described in section 408(b), or

h. A retirement bond described in section 409(a) (before its repeal by P.L. 98-369).

Exclusion rules for IRAs and retirement bonds. These plans are approved plans only if they provide for a series of substantially equal periodic payments made to a beneficiary for life, or over a period of at least 36 months after the date of the decedent's death.

Subject to the $100,000 limitation (if applicable), if an annuity under a "plan" described in (f) through (h) above is receivable by a beneficiary other than the executor, the entire value of the annuity is excludable from the gross estate even if the decedent made a contribution under the plan.

However, if any payment to or for an account or annuity described in paragraph (f), (g), or (h) earlier was not allowable as an income tax deduction under section 219 (and was not a rollover contribution as described in section 2039(e) before its repeal by P.L. 98-369), include in the gross estate on this schedule that proportion of the value of the annuity which the amount not allowable as a deduction under section 219 and not a rollover contribution bears to the total amount paid to or for such account or annuity. For more information, see Regulations section 20.2039-5.

Rules applicable to all approved plans. The following rules apply to all

Part Instructions

approved plans described in paragraphs (a) through (h) earlier.

If any part of an annuity under a "plan" described in (a) through (h) earlier is receivable by the executor, it is generally includible in the gross estate to the extent that it is receivable by the executor in that capacity. In general, the annuity is receivable by the executor if it is to be paid to the executor or if there is an agreement (expressed or implied) that it will be applied by the beneficiary for the benefit of the estate (such as in discharge of the estate's liability for death taxes or debts of the decedent, etc.) or that its distribution will be governed to any extent by the terms of the decedent's will or the laws of descent and distribution.

If data available to you does not indicate whether the plan satisfies the requirements of section 401(a), 403(a), 408(a), 408(b), or 409(a), you may obtain that information from the IRS office where the employer's principal place of business is located.

Line A. Lump Sum Distribution Election

Note. The following rules have been repealed and apply only if the decedent:
- On December 31, 1984, was both a participant in the plan and in pay status (for example, had received at least one benefit payment on or before December 31, 1984) and had irrevocably elected the form of the benefit before July 18, 1984, or
- Had separated from service before January 1, 1985, and did not change the form of benefit before death.

Generally, the entire amount of any lump sum distribution is included in the decedent's gross estate. However, under this special rule, all or part of a lump sum distribution from a qualified (approved) plan will be excluded if the lump sum distribution is included in the recipient's income for income tax purposes.

If the decedent was born before 1936, the recipient may be eligible to elect special "10-year averaging" rules (under repealed section 402(e)) and capital gain treatment (under repealed section 402(a)(2)) in figuring the income tax on the distribution. For more information, see Pub. 575, Pension and Annuity Income. If this option is available, the estate tax exclusion cannot be claimed unless the recipient elects to forego the "10-year averaging" and capital gain treatment in figuring the income tax on the distribution. The recipient elects to forego this treatment

by treating the distribution as taxable on his or her income tax return as described in Regulations section 20.2039-4(d). The election is irrevocable.

The amount excluded from the gross estate is the portion attributable to the employer contributions. The portion, if any, attributable to the employee-decedent's contributions is always includible. Also, you may not figure the gross estate in accordance with this election unless you check "Yes" on line A and attach the name, address, and identifying number of the recipients of the lump sum distributions. See Regulations section 20.2039-4(d) (2).

How To Complete Schedule I

In describing an annuity, give the name and address of the grantor of the annuity. Specify if the annuity is under an approved plan.

IF . . .	THEN . . .
the annuity is under an approved plan,	state the ratio of the decedent's contribution to the total purchase price of the annuity.
the decedent was employed at the time of death and an annuity as described in Definitions, Annuity, Example 4, above, became payable to any beneficiary because the beneficiary survived the decedent,	state the ratio of the decedent's contribution to the total purchase price of the annuity.
an annuity under an individual retirement account or annuity became payable to any beneficiary because that beneficiary survived the decedent and is payable to the beneficiary for life or for at least 36 months following the decedent's death,	state the ratio of the amount paid for the individual retirement account or annuity that was not allowable as an income tax deduction under section 219 (other than a rollover contribution) to the total amount paid for the account or annuity.
the annuity is payable out of a trust or other fund,	the description should be sufficiently complete to fully identify it.
the annuity is payable for a term of years,	include the duration of the term and the date on which it began.

IF . . .	THEN . . .
the annuity is payable for the life of a person other than the decedent,	include the date of birth of that person.
the annuity is wholly or partially excluded from the gross estate,	enter the amount excluded under "Description" and explain how you figured the exclusion.

Schedule J—Funeral Expenses and Expenses Incurred in Administering Property Subject to Claims

 Use Schedule PC to make a protective claim for refund for expenses which are not currently deductible under section 2053. For such a claim, report the expense on Schedule J but without a value in the last column.

General. Complete and file Schedule J if you claim a deduction on item 14 of Part 5—Recapitulation.

On Schedule J, itemize funeral expenses and expenses incurred in administering property subject to claims. List the names and addresses of persons to whom the expenses are payable and describe the nature of the expense. **Do not list expenses incurred in administering property not subject to claims on this schedule. List them on Schedule L instead.**

The deduction is limited to the amount paid for these expenses that is allowable under local law but may not exceed:

1. The value of property subject to claims included in the gross estate, plus

2. The amount paid out of property included in the gross estate but not subject to claims. This amount must actually be paid by the due date of the estate tax return.

The applicable local law under which the estate is being administered determines which property is and is not subject to claims. If under local law a particular property interest included in the gross estate would bear the burden for the payment of the expenses, then the property is considered property subject to claims.

Unlike certain claims against the estate for debts of the decedent (see the instructions for Schedule K), you cannot deduct expenses incurred in administering property subject to claims on both the estate tax return and the estate's income tax return. If you choose to deduct them on the estate tax return, you cannot deduct them on a Form 1041, U.S. Income Tax Return for Estate and Trusts, filed for the estate. Funeral expenses are only deductible on the estate tax return.

Funeral expenses. Itemize funeral expenses on line A. Deduct from the expenses any amounts that were reimbursed, such as death benefits payable by the Social Security Administration or the Veterans Administration.

Executors' commissions. When you file the return, you may deduct commissions that have actually been paid to you or that you expect will be paid. Do not deduct commissions if none will be collected. If the amount of the commissions has not been fixed by decree of the proper court, the deduction will be allowed on the final examination of the return, provided that:
• The Estate and Gift Tax Territory Manager is reasonably satisfied that the commissions claimed will be paid;
• The amount entered as a deduction is within the amount allowable by the laws of the jurisdiction where the estate is being administered; and
• It is in accordance with the usually accepted practice in that jurisdiction for estates of similar size and character.

If you have not been paid the commissions claimed at the time of the final examination of the return, you must support the amount you deducted with an affidavit or statement signed under the penalties of perjury that the amount has been agreed upon and will be paid.

You may not deduct a bequest or devise made to you instead of commissions. If, however, the decedent fixed by will the compensation payable to you for services to be rendered in the administration of the estate, you may deduct this amount to the extent it is not more than the compensation allowable by the local law or practice.

Do not deduct on this schedule amounts paid as trustees' commissions whether received by you acting in the capacity of a trustee or by a separate trustee. If such amounts were paid in administering property not subject to claims, deduct them on Schedule L.

Note. Executors' commissions are taxable income to the executors. Therefore, be sure to include them as income on your individual income tax return.

Attorney fees. Enter the amount of attorney fees that have actually been paid or that you reasonably expect to be paid. If, on the final examination of the return, the fees claimed have not been awarded by the proper court and paid, the deduction will be allowed provided the Estate and Gift Tax Territory Manager is reasonably satisfied that the amount claimed will be paid and that it does not exceed a reasonable payment for the services performed, taking into account the size and character of the estate and the local law and practice. If the fees claimed have not been paid at the time of final examination of the return, the amount deducted must be supported by an affidavit, or statement signed under the penalties of perjury, by the executor or the attorney stating that the amount has been agreed upon and will be paid.

Do not deduct attorney fees incidental to litigation incurred by the beneficiaries. These expenses are charged against the beneficiaries personally and are not administration expenses authorized by the Code.

Interest expense. Interest expenses incurred after the decedent's death are generally allowed as a deduction if they are reasonable, necessary to the administration of the estate, and allowable under local law.

Interest incurred as the result of a federal estate tax deficiency is a deductible administrative expense. Penalties are not deductible even if they are allowable under local law.

Note. If you elect to pay the tax in installments under section 6166, you may not deduct the interest payable on the installments.

Miscellaneous expenses. Miscellaneous administration expenses necessarily incurred in preserving and distributing the estate are deductible. These expenses include appraiser's and accountant's fees, certain court costs, and costs of storing or maintaining assets of the estate.

The expenses of selling assets are deductible only if the sale is necessary to pay the decedent's debts, the expenses of administration, or taxes, or to preserve the estate or carry out distribution.

Schedule K—Debts of the Decedent and Mortgages and Liens

 Use Schedule PC to make a protective claim for refund for expenses which are not currently deductible under section 2053. For such a claim, report the expense on Schedule K but without a value in the last column.

You must complete and attach Schedule K if you claimed deductions on either item 15 or item 16 of Part 5—Recapitulation.

Income vs. estate tax deduction. Taxes, interest, and business expenses accrued at the date of the decedent's death are deductible both on Schedule K and as deductions in respect of the decedent on the income tax return of the estate.

If you choose to deduct medical expenses of the decedent only on the estate tax return, they are fully deductible as claims against the estate. If, however, they are claimed on the decedent's final income tax return under section 213(c), they may not also be claimed on the estate tax return. In this case, you also may not deduct on the estate tax return any amounts that were not deductible on the income tax return because of the percentage limitations.

Debts of the Decedent

List under "Debts of the Decedent" only valid debts the decedent owed at the time of death. List any indebtedness secured by a mortgage or other lien on property of the gross estate under the heading "Mortgages and Liens." If the amount of the debt is disputed or the subject of litigation, deduct only the amount the estate concedes to be a valid claim.

Generally, if the claim against the estate is based on a promise or agreement, the deduction is limited to the extent that the liability was contracted bona fide and for an adequate and full consideration in money or money's worth. However, any enforceable claim based on a promise or agreement of the decedent to make a contribution or gift (such as a pledge or a subscription) to or for the use of a charitable, public, religious, etc., organization is deductible to the extent that the deduction would be allowed as a bequest under the statute that applies.

Certain claims of a former spouse against the estate based on the relinquishment of marital rights are deductible on Schedule K. For these claims to be deductible, all of the following conditions must be met:

• The decedent and the decedent's spouse must have entered into a written agreement relative to their marital and property rights.

• The decedent and the spouse must have been divorced before the decedent's death and the divorce must have occurred within the 3-year period beginning on the date 1 year before the agreement was entered into. It is not required that the agreement be approved by the divorce decree.

• The property or interest transferred under the agreement must be transferred to the decedent's spouse in settlement of the spouse's marital rights.

You may not deduct a claim made against the estate by a remainderman relating to section 2044 property. Section 2044 property is described in the instructions to line 7 in Part 4—General Information.

Include in this schedule notes unsecured by mortgage or other lien and give full details, including:
• Name of payee,
• Face and unpaid balance,
• Date and term of note,
• Interest rate, and
• Date to which interest was paid before death.

Include the exact nature of the claim as well as the name of the creditor. If the claim is for services performed over a period of time, state the period covered by the claim.

Example. Edison Electric Illuminating Co., for electric service during December 2013, $150.

If the amount of the claim is the unpaid balance due on a contract for the purchase of any property included in the gross estate, indicate the schedule and item number where you reported the property. If the claim represents a joint and separate liability, give full facts and explain the financial responsibility of the co-obligor.

Property and income taxes. The deduction for property taxes is limited to the taxes accrued before the date of the decedent's death. Federal taxes on income received during the decedent's lifetime are deductible, but taxes on income received after death are not deductible.

Keep all vouchers or original records for inspection by the IRS.

Allowable death taxes. If you elect to take a deduction for foreign death taxes

under section 2053(d) rather than a credit under section 2014, the deduction is subject to the limitations described in section 2053(d) and its regulations. If you have difficulty figuring the deduction, you may request a computation of it. Send your request within a reasonable amount of time before the due date of the return to:

Department of the Treasury
Commissioner of Internal Revenue
Washington, DC 20224.

Attach to your request a copy of the will and relevant documents, a statement showing the distribution of the estate under the decedent's will, and a computation of the state or foreign death tax showing any amount payable by a charitable organization.

Mortgages and Liens

Under "Mortgages and Liens" list only obligations secured by mortgages or other liens on property included in the gross estate at its full value or at a value that was undiminished by the amount of the mortgage or lien. If the debt is enforceable against other property of the estate not subject to the mortgage or lien, or if the decedent was personally liable for the debt, include the full value of the property subject to the mortgage or lien in the gross estate under the appropriate schedule and deduct the mortgage or lien on the property on this schedule.

However, if the decedent's estate is not liable, include in the gross estate only the value of the equity of redemption (or the value of the property less the amount of the debt), and do not deduct any portion of the indebtedness on this schedule.

Notes and other obligations secured by the deposit of collateral, such as stocks, bonds, etc., also should be listed under "Mortgages and Liens."

Description

Include under the "Description" column the particular schedule and item number where the property subject to the mortgage or lien is reported in the gross estate.

Include the name and address of the mortgagee, payee, or obligee, and the date and term of the mortgage, note, or other agreement by which the debt was established. Also include the face amount, the unpaid balance, the rate of interest, and date to which the interest was paid before the decedent's death.

Schedule L—Net Losses During Administration and Expenses Incurred in Administering Property Not Subject to Claims

 Use Schedule PC to make a protective claim for refund for expenses which are not currently deductible under section 2053. For such a claim, report the expense on Schedule L but without a value in the last column.

Complete Schedule L and file it with the return if you claim deductions on either item 19 or item 20 of Part 5—Recapitulation.

Net Losses During Administration

You may deduct only those losses from thefts, fires, storms, shipwrecks, or other casualties that occurred during the settlement of the estate. Deduct only the amount not reimbursed by insurance or otherwise.

Describe in detail the loss sustained and the cause. If you received insurance or other compensation for the loss, state the amount collected. Identify the property for which you are claiming the loss by indicating the schedule and item number where the property is included in the gross estate.

If you elect alternate valuation, do not deduct the amount by which you reduced the value of an item to include it in the gross estate.

Do not deduct losses claimed as a deduction on a federal income tax return or depreciation in the value of securities or other property.

Expenses Incurred in Administering Property Not Subject to Claims

You may deduct expenses incurred in administering property that is included in the gross estate but that is not subject to claims. Only deduct these expenses if they were paid before the section 6501 period of limitations for assessment expired.

The expenses deductible on this schedule are usually expenses incurred in the administration of a trust established by the decedent before death. They may also be incurred in the collection of other assets or the transfer or clearance of title to other property included in the decedent's gross estate for estate tax purposes, but not included in the decedent's probate estate.

The expenses deductible on this schedule are limited to those that are the result of settling the decedent's interest in the property or of vesting good title to the property in the beneficiaries. Expenses incurred on behalf of the transferees (except those described earlier) are not deductible. Examples of deductible and nondeductible expenses are provided in Regulations section 20.2053-8(d).

List the names and addresses of the persons to whom each expense was payable and the nature of the expense. Identify the property for which the expense was incurred by indicating the schedule and item number where the property is included in the gross estate. If you do not know the exact amount of the expense, you may deduct an estimate, provided that the amount may be verified with reasonable certainty and will be paid before the period of limitations for assessment (referred to earlier) expires. Keep all vouchers and receipts for inspection by the IRS.

Schedule M—Bequests, etc., to Surviving Spouse (Marital Deduction)

 If any assets to which the special rule of Regulations section 20.2010-2T(a)(7)(ii) applies are reported on this schedule, do not enter any value in the last three columns. See instructions for line 23 of Part 5–Recapitulation for information on how to estimate and report the value of these assets.

General

You must complete Schedule M and file it with the return if you claim a deduction on Part 5—Recapitulation, item 21.

The marital deduction is authorized by section 2056 for certain property interests that pass from the decedent to the surviving spouse. You may claim the deduction only for property interests that are included in the decedent's gross estate (Schedules A through I).

Note. The marital deduction is generally not allowed if the surviving spouse is not a U.S. citizen. The marital deduction is allowed for property passing to such a surviving spouse in a qualified domestic trust (QDOT) or if such property is transferred or irrevocably assigned to such a trust before the estate tax return is filed. The executor must elect QDOT status on the return. See the instructions that follow for details on the election.

Property Interests That You May List on Schedule M

Generally, you may list on Schedule M all property interests that pass from the decedent to the surviving spouse and are included in the gross estate. However, do not list any *nondeductible terminable interests* (described later) on Schedule M unless you are making a QTIP election. The property for which you make this election must be included on Schedule M. See *Qualified terminable interest property,* later.

For the rules on common disaster and survival for a limited period, see section 2056(b)(3).

You may list on Schedule M only those interests that the surviving spouse takes:

1. As the decedent's legatee, devisee, heir, or donee;

2. As the decedent's surviving tenant by the entirety or joint tenant;

3. As an appointee under the decedent's exercise of a power or as a taker in default at the decedent's nonexercise of a power;

4. As a beneficiary of insurance on the decedent's life;

5. As the surviving spouse taking under dower or curtesy (or similar statutory interest); and

6. As a transferee of a transfer made by the decedent at any time.

Property Interests That You May Not List on Schedule M

Do not list on Schedule M:

1. The value of any property that does not pass from the decedent to the surviving spouse;

2. Property interests that are not included in the decedent's gross estate;

3. The full value of a property interest for which a deduction was claimed on Schedules J through L. The value of the property interest should be reduced by the deductions claimed with respect to it;

4. The full value of a property interest that passes to the surviving spouse subject to a mortgage or other encumbrance or an obligation of the surviving spouse. Include on Schedule M only the net value of the interest after reducing it by the amount of the mortgage or other debt;

5. Nondeductible terminable interests (described later); or

6. Any property interest disclaimed by the surviving spouse.

Terminable Interests

Certain interests in property passing from a decedent to a surviving spouse are referred to as *terminable interests.* These are interests that will terminate or fail after the passage of time, or on the occurrence or nonoccurrence of a designated event. Examples are: life estates, annuities, estates for terms of years, and patents.

The ownership of a bond, note, or other contractual obligation, which when discharged would not have the effect of an annuity for life or for a term, is not considered a terminable interest.

Nondeductible terminable interests. Unless you are making a QTIP election, do not enter a terminable interest on Schedule M if:

1. Another interest in the same property passed from the decedent to some other person for less than adequate and full consideration in money or money's worth; and

2. By reason of its passing, the other person or that person's heirs may enjoy part of the property after the

Example—Listing Property Interests on Schedule M

Item number	Description of property interests passing to surviving spouse. For securities, give CUSIP number. If trust, partnership, or closely-held entity, give EIN.	Amount
	All other property:	
B1	One-half the value of a house and lot, 256 South West Street, held by decedent and surviving spouse as joint tenants with right of survivorship under deed dated July 15, 1975 (Schedule E, Part I, item 1)	$182,500
B2	Proceeds of Metropolitan Life Insurance Company policy No. 104729, payable in one sum to surviving spouse (Schedule D, item 3)	200,000
B3	Cash bequest under Paragraph Six of will	100,000

termination of the surviving spouse's interest.

This rule applies even though the interest that passes from the decedent to a person other than the surviving spouse is not included in the gross estate, and regardless of when the interest passes. The rule also applies regardless of whether the surviving spouse's interest and the other person's interest pass from the decedent at the same time.

Property interests that are considered to pass to a person other than the surviving spouse are any property interest that: (a) passes under a decedent's will or intestacy; (b) was transferred by a decedent during life; or (c) is held by or passed on to any person as a decedent's joint tenant, as appointee under a decedent's exercise of a power, as taker in default at a decedent's release or nonexercise of a power, or as a beneficiary of insurance on the decedent's life. See Regulations section 20.2056(c)-3.

For example, a decedent devised real property to his wife for life, with remainder to his children. The life interest that passed to the wife does not qualify for the marital deduction because it will terminate at her death and the children will thereafter possess or enjoy the property.

However, if the decedent purchased a joint and survivor annuity for himself and his wife who survived him, the value of the survivor's annuity, to the extent that it is included in the gross estate, qualifies for the marital deduction because even though the interest will terminate on the wife's death, no one else will possess or enjoy any part of the property.

The marital deduction is not allowed for an interest that the decedent directed the executor or a trustee to convert, after death, into a terminable interest for the surviving spouse. The marital deduction is not allowed for such an interest even if there was no interest in the property passing to another person and even if the terminable interest would otherwise have been deductible under the exceptions described later for life estates, life insurance, and annuity payments with powers of appointment. For more information, see Regulations sections 20.2056(b)-1(f) and 20.2056(b)-1(g), Example (7).

If any property interest passing from the decedent to the surviving spouse may be paid or otherwise satisfied out of any of a group of assets, the value of the property interest is, for the entry on Schedule M, reduced by the value of any asset or assets that, if passing from the decedent to the surviving spouse, would be nondeductible terminable interests. Examples of property interests that may be paid or otherwise satisfied out of any of a group of assets are a bequest of the residue of the decedent's estate, or of a share of the residue, and a cash legacy payable out of the general estate.

Example. A decedent bequeathed $100,000 to the surviving spouse. The general estate includes a term for years (valued at $10,000 in determining the value of the gross estate) in an office building, which interest was retained by the decedent under a deed of the building by gift to a son. Accordingly, the value of the specific bequest entered on Schedule M is $90,000.

Life estate with power of appointment in the surviving spouse. A property interest, whether or not in trust, will be treated as passing to the surviving spouse, and will not be treated as a nondeductible terminable interest if: (a) the surviving spouse is entitled for life to all of the income from the entire interest; (b) the income is payable annually or at more frequent intervals; (c) the surviving spouse has the power, exercisable in favor of the surviving spouse or the estate of the surviving spouse, to appoint the entire interest; (d) the power is exercisable by the surviving spouse alone and (whether exercisable by will or during life) is exercisable by the surviving spouse in all events; and (e) no part of the entire interest is subject to a power in any other person to appoint any part to any person other than the surviving spouse (or the surviving spouse's legal representative or relative if the surviving spouse is disabled. See Regulations section 20.2056(b)-5(a) and Rev. Rul. 85-35, 1985-1 C.B. 328). If these five conditions are satisfied only for a specific portion of the entire interest, see Regulations sections 20.2056(b)-5(b) and -5(c) to determine the amount of the marital deduction.

Life insurance, endowment, or annuity payments, with power of appointment in surviving spouse. A property interest consisting of the entire proceeds under a life insurance, endowment, or annuity contract is treated as passing from the decedent to the surviving spouse, and will not be treated as a nondeductible terminable interest if: (a) the surviving spouse is entitled to receive the proceeds in installments, or is entitled to interest on them, with all amounts payable during the life of the spouse, payable only to the surviving spouse; (b) the installment or interest payments are payable annually, or more frequently, beginning not later than 13 months after the decedent's death; (c) the surviving spouse has the power, exercisable in favor of the surviving spouse or of the estate of the surviving spouse, to appoint all amounts payable under the contract; (d) the power of appointment is exercisable by the surviving spouse alone and (whether exercisable by will or during life) is exercisable by the surviving spouse in all events; and (e) no part of the amount payable under the contract is subject to a power in any other person to appoint any part to any person other than the surviving spouse. If these five conditions are satisfied only for a specific portion of the proceeds, see Regulations section 20.2056(b)-6(b) to determine the amount of the marital deduction.

Charitable remainder trusts. An interest in a charitable remainder trust will not be treated as a nondeductible terminable interest if:

1. The interest in the trust passes from the decedent to the surviving spouse, and

2. The surviving spouse is the only beneficiary of the trust other than charitable organizations described in section 170(c).

A *charitable remainder trust* is either a charitable remainder annuity trust or a charitable remainder unitrust. (See section 664 for descriptions of these trusts.)

Election To Deduct Qualified Terminable Interests (QTIP)

You may elect to claim a marital deduction for qualified terminable interest property or property interests. You make the QTIP election simply by listing the qualified terminable interest property on Part A of Schedule M and inserting its value. You are presumed to have made the QTIP election if you list the property and insert its value on Schedule M. If you make this election, the surviving spouse's gross estate will include the value of the qualified terminable interest property. See the instructions for *Part 4—General Information, line 7,* for more details. **The election is irrevocable.**

If you file a Form 706 in which you do not make this election, you may not file an amended return to make the election unless you file the amended return on or before the due date for filing the original Form 706.

The effect of the election is that the property (interest) will be treated as passing to the surviving spouse and will not be treated as a nondeductible terminable interest. All of the other marital deduction requirements must still be satisfied before you may make this election. For example, you may not make this election for property or property interests that are not included in the decedent's gross estate.

Qualified terminable interest property. *Qualified terminable interest property* is property (a) that passes from the decedent, (b) in which the surviving spouse has a qualifying income interest for life, and (c) for which election under section 2056(b)(7) has been made.

The surviving spouse has a *qualifying income interest for life* if the surviving spouse is entitled to all of the income from the property payable annually or at more frequent intervals, or has a usufruct interest for life in the property, and during the surviving spouse's lifetime no person has a power to appoint any part of the property to any person other than the surviving spouse. An annuity is treated as an income interest regardless of whether the property from which the annuity is payable can be separately identified.

Regulations sections 20.2044-1 and 20.2056(b)-7(d)(3) state that an interest in property is eligible for QTIP treatment if the income interest is contingent upon the executor's election even if that portion of the property for which no election is made will pass to or for the benefit of beneficiaries other than the surviving spouse.

The QTIP election may be made for all or any part of qualified terminable interest property. A partial election must relate to a fractional or percentile share of the property so that the elective part will reflect its proportionate share of the increase or decline in the whole of the property when applying section 2044 or 2519. Thus, if the interest of the surviving spouse in a trust (or other property in which the spouse has a qualified life estate) is qualified terminable interest property, you may make an election for a part of the trust (or other property) only if the election relates to a defined fraction or percentage of the entire trust (or other property). The fraction or percentage may be defined by means of a formula.

Election to Deduct Qualified Terminable Interest Property Under Section 2056(b)(7). If a trust (or other property) meets the requirements of qualified terminable interest property under section 2056(b)(7), and

1. The trust or other property is listed on Schedule M, and

2. The value of the trust (or other property) is entered in whole or in part as a deduction on Schedule M,

then unless the executor specifically identifies the trust (all or a fractional portion or percentage) or other property to be excluded from the election, the executor shall be deemed to have made an election to have such trust (or other property) treated as qualified terminable interest property under section 2056(b)(7).

If less than the entire value of the trust (or other property) that the executor has included in the gross estate is entered as a deduction on Schedule M, the executor shall be considered to have made an election only as to a fraction of the trust (or other property). The numerator of this fraction is equal to the amount of the trust (or other property) deducted on Schedule M. The denominator is equal to the total value of the trust (or other property).

Qualified Domestic Trust Election (QDOT)

The marital deduction is allowed for transfers to a surviving spouse who is not a U.S. citizen only if the property passes to the surviving spouse in a *qualified domestic trust (QDOT)* or if such property is transferred or irrevocably assigned to a QDOT before the decedent's estate tax return is filed.

A *QDOT* is any trust:

1. That requires at least one trustee to be either a citizen of the United States or a domestic corporation;

2. That requires that no distribution of corpus from the trust can be made unless such a trustee has the right to withhold from the distribution the tax imposed on the QDOT;

3. That meets the requirements of any applicable regulations; and

4. For which the executor has made an election on the estate tax return of the decedent.

Note. For trusts created by an instrument executed before November 5, 1990, paragraphs 1 and 2 above will be treated as met if the trust instrument

requires that all trustees be individuals who are citizens of the United States or domestic corporations.

You make the QDOT election simply by listing the qualified domestic trust or the entire value of the trust property on Schedule M and deducting its value. You are presumed to have made the QDOT election if you list the trust or trust property and insert its value on Schedule M. **Once made, the election is irrevocable.**

If an election is made to deduct qualified domestic trust property under section 2056A(d), provide the following information for each qualified domestic trust on an attachment to this schedule:

1. The name and address of every trustee;

2. A description of each transfer passing from the decedent that is the source of the property to be placed in trust; and

3. The employer identification number (EIN) for the trust.

The election must be made for an entire QDOT trust. In listing a trust for which you are making a QDOT election, **unless you specifically identify the trust as not subject to the election, the election will be considered made for the entire trust.**

The determination of whether a trust qualifies as a QDOT will be made as of the date the decedent's Form 706 is filed. If, however, judicial proceedings are brought before the Form 706's due date (including extensions) to have the trust revised to meet the QDOT requirements, then the determination will not be made until the court-ordered changes to the trust are made.

Election to Deduct Qualified Domestic Trust Property Under Section 2056A. If a trust meets the requirement of a qualified domestic trust under section 2056A(a), the return is filed no later than 1 year after the time prescribed by law (including extensions), and the entire value of the trust or trust property is listed and entered as a deduction on Schedule M, then unless the executor specifically identifies the trust to be excluded from the election, the executor shall be deemed to have made an election to have the entire trust treated as qualified domestic trust property.

Line 1

If property passes to the surviving spouse as the result of a qualified disclaimer, check "Yes," and attach a copy of the written disclaimer required by section 2518(b).

Line 3

Section 2056(b)(7)(C)(ii) creates an automatic QTIP election for certain joint and survivor annuities that are includible in the estate under section 2039. To qualify, only the surviving spouse can have the right to receive payments before the death of the surviving spouse.

The executor can elect out of QTIP treatment, however, by checking the "Yes," box on line 3. **Once made, the election is irrevocable.** If there is more than one such joint and survivor annuity, you are not required to make the election for all of them.

If you make the election out of QTIP treatment by checking "Yes," on line 3, you cannot deduct the amount of the annuity on Schedule M. If you do not elect out, you must list the joint and survivor annuities on Schedule M.

Listing Property Interests on Schedule M

List each property interest included in the gross estate that passes from the decedent to the surviving spouse and for which a marital deduction is claimed. This includes otherwise nondeductible terminable interest property for which you are making a QTIP election. Number each item in sequence and describe each item in detail. Describe the instrument (including any clause or paragraph number) or provision of law under which each item passed to the surviving spouse. Indicate the schedule and item number of each asset.

In listing otherwise nondeductible property for which you are making a QTIP election, unless you specifically identify a fractional portion of the trust or other property as not subject to the election, the election will be considered made for the entire interest.

Enter the value of each interest before taking into account the federal estate tax or any other death tax. The valuation dates used in determining the value of the gross estate apply also on Schedule M.

If Schedule M includes a bequest of the residue or a part of the residue of the decedent's estate, attach a copy of the computation showing how the value of the residue was determined. Include a statement showing:
- The value of all property that is included in the decedent's gross estate (Schedules A through I) but is not a part

of the decedent's probate estate, such as lifetime transfers, jointly-owned property that passed to the survivor on decedent's death, and the insurance payable to specific beneficiaries;
- The values of all specific and general legacies or devises, with reference to the applicable clause or paragraph of the decedent's will or codicil. (If legacies are made to each member of a class, for example, $1,000 to each of decedent's employees, only the number in each class and the total value of property received by them need be furnished);
- The date of birth of all persons, the length of whose lives may affect the value of the residuary interest passing to the surviving spouse; and
- Any other important information such as that relating to any claim to any part of the estate not arising under the will.

Lines 5a, 5b, and 5c. The total of the values listed on Schedule M must be reduced by the amount of the federal estate tax, the federal GST tax, and the amount of state or other death and GST taxes paid out of the property interest involved. If you enter an amount for state or other death or GST taxes on line 5b or 5c, identify the taxes and attach your computation of them.

Attachments. If you list property interests passing by the decedent's will on Schedule M, attach a certified copy of the order admitting the will to probate. If, when you file the return, the court of probate jurisdiction has entered any decree interpreting the will or any of its provisions affecting any of the interests listed on Schedule M, or has entered any order of distribution, attach a copy of the decree or order. In addition, the IRS may request other evidence to support the marital deduction claimed.

Schedule O—Charitable, Public, and Similar Gifts and Bequests

 If any assets to which the special rule of Regulations section 20.2010-2T(a)(7)(ii) applies are reported on this schedule, do not enter any value in the last three columns. See instructions for line 23 of Part 5–Recapitulation for information on how to estimate and report the value of these assets.

General

You must complete Schedule O and file it with the return if you claim a deduction on item 22 of Part 5—Recapitulation.

You can claim the charitable deduction allowed under section 2055 for the value of property in the decedent's gross estate that was transferred by the decedent during life or by will to or for the use of any of the following:
- The United States, a state, a political subdivision of a state, or the District of Columbia, for exclusively public purposes;
- Any corporation or association organized and operated exclusively for religious, charitable, scientific, literary, or educational purposes, including the encouragement of art, or to foster national or international amateur sports competition (but only if none of its activities involve providing athletic facilities or equipment, unless the organization is a qualified amateur sports organization) and the prevention of cruelty to children and animals. No part of the net earnings may benefit any private individual and no substantial activity may be undertaken to carry on propaganda, or otherwise attempt to influence legislation or participate in any political campaign on behalf of any candidate for public office;
- A trustee or a fraternal society, order or association operating under the lodge system, if the transferred property is to be used exclusively for religious, charitable, scientific, literary, or educational purposes, or for the prevention of cruelty to children or animals. No substantial activity may be undertaken to carry on propaganda or otherwise attempt to influence legislation, or participate in any political campaign on behalf of any candidate for public office;
- Any veterans organization incorporated by an Act of Congress or any of its departments, local chapters, or posts, for which none of the net earnings benefits any private individual; or
- Employee stock ownership plans, if the transfer qualifies as a *qualified gratuitous transfer of qualified employer securities* within the meaning provided in section 664(g).

For this purpose, certain Indian tribal governments are treated as states and transfers to them qualify as deductible charitable contributions. See section 7871 and Rev. Proc. 2008-55, 2008-39 I.R.B. 768, available at *www.irs.gov/ pub/irs-irbs/irb08-39.pdf*, as modified and supplemented by subsequent revenue procedures, for a list of qualifying Indian tribal governments.

You may also claim a charitable contribution deduction for a qualifying conservation easement granted after the decedent's death under the provisions of section 2031(c)(9).

The charitable deduction is allowed for amounts that are transferred to charitable organizations as a result of either a qualified disclaimer (see *Line 2. Qualified Disclaimer,* later) or the complete termination of a power to consume, invade, or appropriate property for the benefit of an individual. It does not matter whether termination occurs because of the death of the individual or in any other way. The termination must occur within the period of time (including extensions) for filing the decedent's estate tax return and before the power has been exercised.

The deduction is limited to the amount actually available for charitable uses. Therefore, if under the terms of a will or the provisions of local law, or for any other reason, the federal estate tax, the federal GST tax, or any other estate, GST, succession, legacy, or inheritance tax is payable in whole or in part out of any bequest, legacy, or devise that would otherwise be allowed as a charitable deduction, the amount you may deduct is the amount of the bequest, legacy, or devise reduced by the total amount of the taxes.

If you elected to make installment payments of the estate tax, and the interest is payable out of property transferred to charity, you must reduce the charitable deduction by an estimate of the maximum amount of interest that will be paid on the deferred tax.

For split-interest trusts or pooled income funds, only the figure that is passing to the charity should be entered in the "Amount" column. Do not enter the entire amount that passes to the trust or fund.

If you are deducting the value of the residue or a part of the residue passing to charity under the decedent's will, attach a copy of the computation showing how you determined the value, including any reduction for the taxes described earlier.

Also include:
• A statement that shows the values of all specific and general legacies or devises for both charitable and noncharitable uses. For each legacy or devise, indicate the paragraph or section of the decedent's will or codicil that applies. If legacies are made to each member of a class (for example,

$1,000 to each of the decedent's employees), show only the number of each class and the total value of property they received;
• The date of birth of all life tenants or annuitants, the length of whose lives may affect the value of the interest passing to charity under the decedent's will;
• A statement showing the value of all property that is included in the decedent's gross estate but does not pass under the will, such as transfers, jointly-owned property that passed to the survivor on decedent's death, and insurance payable to specific beneficiaries; and
• Any other important information such as that relating to any claim, not arising under the will, to any part of the estate (that is, a spouse claiming dower or curtesy, or similar rights).

Line 2. Qualified Disclaimer

The charitable deduction is allowed for amounts that are transferred to charitable organizations as a result of a qualified disclaimer. To be a *qualified disclaimer*, a refusal to accept an interest in property must meet the conditions of section 2518. These are explained in Regulations sections 25.2518-1 through 25.2518-3. If property passes to a charitable beneficiary as the result of a qualified disclaimer, check the "Yes," box on line 2 and attach a copy of the written disclaimer required by section 2518(b).

Attachments

If the charitable transfer was made by will, attach a certified copy of the order admitting the will to probate, in addition to the copy of the will. If the charitable transfer was made by any other written instrument, attach a copy. If the instrument is of record, the copy should be certified; if not, the copy should be verified.

Value

The valuation dates used in determining the value of the gross estate apply also on Schedule O.

Schedule P—Credit for Foreign Death Taxes

General

If you claim a credit on line 13 of Part 2—Tax Computation, complete Schedule P and file it with the return. Attach Form(s) 706-CE to Form 706 to support any credit you claim.

If the foreign government refuses to certify Form 706-CE, file it directly with

the IRS as instructed on the Form 706-CE. See Form 706-CE for instructions on how to complete the form and a description of the items that must be attached to the form when the foreign government refuses to certify it.

The credit for foreign death taxes is allowable only if the decedent was a citizen or resident of the United States. However, see section 2053(d) and the related regulations for exceptions and limitations if the executor has elected, in certain cases, to deduct these taxes from the value of the gross estate. For a resident, not a citizen, who was a citizen or subject of a foreign country for which the President has issued a proclamation under section 2014(h), the credit is allowable only if the country of which the decedent was a national allows a similar credit to decedents who were U.S. citizens residing in that country.

The credit is authorized either by statute or by treaty. If a credit is authorized by a treaty, whichever of the following is the most beneficial to the estate is allowed:
• The credit figured under the treaty;
• The credit figured under the statute; or
• The credit figured under the treaty, plus the credit figured under the statute for death taxes paid to each political subdivision or possession of the treaty country that are not directly or indirectly creditable under the treaty.

Under the statute, the credit is authorized for all death taxes (national and local) imposed in the foreign country. Whether local taxes are the basis for a credit under a treaty depends upon the provisions of the particular treaty.

If a credit for death taxes paid in more than one foreign country is allowable, a separate computation of the credit must be made for each foreign country. The copies of Schedule P on which the additional computations are made should be attached to the copy of Schedule P provided in the return.

The total credit allowable for any property, whether subjected to tax by one or more than one foreign country, is limited to the amount of the federal estate tax attributable to the property. The anticipated amount of the credit may be figured on the return, but the credit cannot finally be allowed until the foreign tax has been paid and a Form 706-CE evidencing payment is filed. Section 2014(g) provides that for credits for foreign death taxes, each U.S.

possession is deemed a foreign country.

Convert death taxes paid to the foreign country into U.S. dollars by using the rate of exchange in effect at the time each payment of foreign tax is made.

If a credit is claimed for any foreign death tax that is later recovered, see Regulations section 20.2016-1 for the notice required within 30 days.

Limitation Period

The credit for foreign death taxes is limited to those taxes that were actually paid and for which a credit was claimed within the later of 4 years after the filing of the estate tax return, before the date of expiration of any extension of time for payment of the federal estate tax, or 60 days after a final decision of the Tax Court on a timely filed petition for a redetermination of a deficiency.

Credit Under the Statute

For the credit allowed by the statute, the question of whether particular property is situated in the foreign country imposing the tax is determined by the same principles that would apply in determining whether similar property of a nonresident not a U.S. citizen is situated within the United States for purposes of the federal estate tax. See the instructions for Form 706-NA.

Computation of Credit Under the Statute

Item 1. Enter the amount of the estate, inheritance, legacy, and succession taxes paid to the foreign country and its possessions or political subdivisions, attributable to property that is:
- Situated in that country,
- Subjected to these taxes, and
- Included in the gross estate.

The amount entered at item 1 should not include any tax paid to the foreign country for property not situated in that country and should not include any tax paid to the foreign country for property not included in the gross estate. If only a part of the property subjected to foreign taxes is both situated in the foreign country and included in the gross estate, it will be necessary to determine the portion of the taxes attributable to that part of the property. Also, attach the computation of the amount entered at item 1.

Item 2. Enter the value of the gross estate, less the total of the deductions on items 21 and 22 of Part 5—Recapitulation.

Item 3. Enter the value of the property situated in the foreign country that is subjected to the foreign taxes and included in the gross estate, less those portions of the deductions taken on Schedules M and O that are attributable to the property.

Item 4. Subtract any credit claimed on line 15 for federal gift taxes on pre-1977 gifts (section 2012) from line 12 of Part 2—Tax Computation, and enter the balance at item 4 of Schedule P.

Credit Under Treaties

If you are reporting any items on this return based on the provisions of a death tax treaty, you may have to attach a statement to this return disclosing the return position that is treaty based. See Regulations section 301.6114-1 for details.

In general. If the provisions of a treaty apply to the estate of a U.S. citizen or resident, a credit is authorized for payment of the foreign death tax or taxes specified in the treaty. Treaties with death tax conventions are in effect with the following countries: Australia, Austria, Canada, Denmark, Finland, France, Germany, Greece, Ireland, Italy, Japan, Netherlands, Norway, South Africa, Switzerland, and the United Kingdom.

A credit claimed under a treaty is in general figured on Schedule P in the same manner as the credit is figured under the statute with the following principal exceptions:
- The situs rules contained in the treaty apply in determining whether property was situated in the foreign country;
- The credit may be allowed only for payment of the death tax or taxes specified in the treaty (but see the instructions earlier for credit under the statute for death taxes paid to each political subdivision or possession of the treaty country that are not directly or indirectly creditable under the treaty);
- If specifically provided, the credit is proportionately shared for the tax applicable to property situated outside both countries, or that was deemed in some instances situated within both countries; and
- The amount entered at item 4 of Schedule P is the amount shown on line 12 of Part 2—Tax Computation, less the total of the credits claimed for federal gift taxes on pre-1977 gifts (section 2012) and for tax on prior transfers (line 14 of Part 2—Tax Computation). (If a credit is claimed for tax on prior transfers, it will be necessary to complete Schedule Q

before completing Schedule P.) For examples of computation of credits under the treaties, see the applicable regulations.

Computation of credit in cases where property is situated outside both countries or deemed situated within both countries. See the appropriate treaty for details.

Schedule Q—Credit for Tax on Prior Transfers

General

Complete Schedule Q and file it with the return if you claim a credit on Part 2—Tax Computation, line 14.

The term *transferee* means the decedent for whose estate this return is filed. If the transferee received property from a transferor who died within 10 years before, or 2 years after, the transferee, a credit is allowable on this return for all or part of the federal estate tax paid by the transferor's estate for the transfer. There is no requirement that the property be identified in the estate of the transferee or that it exist on the date of the transferee's death. It is sufficient for the allowance of the credit that the transfer of the property was subjected to federal estate tax in the estate of the transferor and that the specified period of time has not elapsed. A credit may be allowed for property received as the result of the exercise or nonexercise of a power of appointment when the property is included in the gross estate of the donee of the power.

If the transferee was the transferor's surviving spouse, no credit is allowed for property received from the transferor to the extent that a marital deduction was allowed to the transferor's estate for the property. There is no credit for tax on prior transfers for federal gift taxes paid in connection with the transfer of the property to the transferee.

If you are claiming a credit for tax on prior transfers on Form 706-NA, you should first complete and attach Part 5—Recapitulation from Form 706 before figuring the credit on Schedule Q from Form 706.

Section 2056(d)(3) contains specific rules for allowing a credit for certain transfers to a spouse who was not a U.S. citizen where the property passed outright to the spouse, or to a qualified domestic trust.

Property

The term *property* includes any interest (legal or equitable) of which the transferee received the beneficial ownership. The transferee is considered the beneficial owner of property over which the transferee received a general power of appointment. Property does not include interests to which the transferee received only a bare legal title, such as that of a trustee. Neither does it include an interest in property over which the transferee received a power of appointment that is not a general power of appointment. In addition to interests in which the transferee received the complete ownership, the credit may be allowed for annuities, life estates, terms for years, remainder interests (whether contingent or vested), and any other interest that is less than the complete ownership of the property, to the extent that the transferee became the beneficial owner of the interest.

Maximum Amount of the Credit

The *maximum amount of the credit* is the smaller of:

1. The amount of the estate tax of the transferor's estate attributable to the transferred property or

2. The amount by which:

a. An estate tax on the transferee's estate determined without the credit for tax on prior transfers exceeds

b. An estate tax on the transferee's estate determined by excluding from the gross estate the net value of the transfer.

If credit for a particular foreign death tax may be taken under either the statute or a death duty convention, and on this return the credit actually is taken under the convention, then no credit for that foreign death tax may be taken into consideration in figuring estate tax (a) or estate tax (b), above.

Percent Allowable

Where transferee predeceased the transferor. If not more than 2 years elapsed between the dates of death, the credit allowed is 100% of the maximum

amount. If more than 2 years elapsed between the dates of death, no credit is allowed.

Where transferor predeceased the transferee. The percent of the maximum amount that is allowed as a credit depends on the number of years that elapsed between dates of death. It is determined using the following table:

Period of Time Exceeding	Not Exceeding	Percent Allowable
- - - - -	2 years	100
2 years	4 years	80
4 years	6 years	60
6 years	8 years	40
8 years	10 years	20
10 years	- - - - -	none

How To Figure the Credit

A worksheet for Schedule Q is provided to allow you to figure the limits before completing Schedule Q. Transfer the appropriate amounts from the worksheet to Schedule Q as indicated on the schedule. You do not need to file the worksheet with Form 706, but keep it for your records.

Cases involving transfers from two or more transferors. Part I of the worksheet and Schedule Q enable you to figure the credit for as many as three transferors. The number of transferors is irrelevant to Part II of the worksheet. If you are figuring the credit for more than three transferors, use more than one worksheet and Schedule Q, Part I, and combine the totals for the appropriate lines.

Section 2032A additional tax. If the transferor's estate elected special-use valuation and the additional estate tax of section 2032A(c) was imposed at any time up to 2 years after the death of the decedent for whom you are filing this return, check the box on Schedule Q. On lines 1 and 9 of the worksheet, include the property subject to the additional estate tax at its FMV rather

than its special-use value. On line 10 of the worksheet, include the additional estate tax paid as a federal estate tax paid.

How To Complete the Schedule Q Worksheet

Most of the information to complete Part I of the worksheet should be obtained from the transferor's Form 706.

Line 5. Enter on line 5 the applicable marital deduction claimed for the transferor's estate (from the transferor's Form 706).

Lines 10 through 18. Enter on these lines the appropriate taxes paid by the transferor's estate.

If the transferor's estate elected to pay the federal estate tax in installments, enter on line 10 only the total of the installments that have actually been paid at the time you file this Form 706. See Rev. Rul. 83-15, 1983-1 C.B. 224, for more details.

Line 21. Add lines 11 (allowable applicable credit) and 13 (foreign death taxes credit) of Part 2—Tax Computation to the amount of any credit taken (on line 15) for federal gift taxes on pre-1977 gifts (section 2012). Subtract this total from Part 2—Tax Computation, line 8. Enter the result on line 21 of the worksheet.

Line 26. If you figured the marital deduction using the unlimited marital deduction in effect for decedents dying after 1981, for purposes of determining the marital deduction for the reduced gross estate, see Rev. Rul. 90-2, 1990-1 C.B. 169. To determine the "reduced adjusted gross estate," subtract the amount on line 25 of the Schedule Q Worksheet from the amount on line 24 of the worksheet. If community property is included in the amount on line 24 of the worksheet, figure the reduced adjusted gross estate using the rules of Regulations section 20.2056(c)-2 and Rev. Rul. 76-311, 1976-2 C.B. 261.

Worksheet for Schedule Q—Credit for Tax on Prior Transfers

Part I — Transferor's tax on prior transfers

Item	Transferor (From Schedule Q) A	Transferor (From Schedule Q) B	Transferor (From Schedule Q) C	Total for all transfers (line 8 only)
1. Gross value of prior transfer to this transferee				
2. Death taxes payable from prior transfer				
3. Encumbrances allocable to prior transfer				
4. Obligations allocable to prior transfer. .				
5. Marital deduction applicable to line 1 above, as shown on transferor's Form 706 . . .				
6. **TOTAL.** Add lines 2, 3, 4, and 5 . . .				
7. **Net value of transfers.** Subtract line 6 from line 1.				
8. **Net value of transfers.** Add columns A, B, and C of line 7.				
9. Transferor's taxable estate.				
10. Federal estate tax paid				
11. State death taxes paid				
12. Foreign death taxes paid				
13. Other death taxes paid				
14. **TOTAL taxes paid.** Add lines 10, 11, 12, and 13				
15. **Value of transferor's estate.** Subtract line 14 from line 9				
16. Net federal estate tax paid on transferor's estate				
17. Credit for gift tax paid on transferor's estate with respect to pre-1977 gifts (section 2012)				
18. Credit allowed transferor's estate for tax on prior transfers from prior transfer(s) who died within 10 years before death of decedent . .				
19. **Tax on transferor's estate.** Add lines 16, 17, and 18				
20. Transferor's tax on prior transfers ((line 7 ÷ line 15) × line 19 of respective estates). .				

Part II — Transferee's tax on prior transfers

Item		Amount
21. Transferee's actual tax before allowance of credit for prior transfers (see instructions) . . .	21	
22. Total gross estate of transferee from line 1 of the Tax Computation, page 1, Form 706.	22	
23. Net value of all transfers from line 8 of this worksheet	23	
24. Transferee's reduced gross estate. Subtract line 23 from line 22	24	
25. Total debts and deductions (not including marital and charitable deductions) (line 3b of Part 2—Tax Computation, page 1 and items 18, 19, and 20 of the Recapitulation, page 3, Form 706)	25	
26. Marital deduction from item 21, Recapitulation, page 3, Form 706 (see instructions).	26	
27. Charitable bequests from item 22, Recapitulation, page 3, Form 706 . .	27	
28. Charitable deduction proportion ([line 23 ÷ (line 22 − line 25)] × line 27)	28	
29. Reduced charitable deduction. Subtract line 28 from line 27.	29	
30. Transferee's deduction as adjusted. Add lines 25, 26, and 29	30	
31. (a) Transferee's reduced taxable estate. Subtract line 30 from line 24	31(a)	
(b) Adjusted taxable gifts	31(b)	
(c) Total reduced taxable estate. Add lines 31(a) and 31(b)	31(c)	
32. Tentative tax on reduced taxable estate.	32	
33. (a) Post-1976 gift taxes paid	33(a)	
(b) Unified credit (applicable credit amount)	33(b)	
(c) Section 2012 gift tax credit. . . .	33(c)	
(d) Section 2014 foreign death tax credit .	33(d)	
(e) Total credits. Add lines 33(a) through 33(d)	33(e)	
34. Net tax on reduced taxable estate. Subtract line 33(e) from line 32	34	
35. Transferee's tax on prior transfers. Subtract line 34 from line 21	35	

Part Instructions

Schedules R and R-1 – Generation-Skipping Transfer Tax

Introduction and Overview

Schedule R is used to figure the generation-skipping transfer (GST) tax that is payable by the estate. Schedule R-1 is used to figure the GST tax that is payable by certain trusts that are includible in the gross estate.

The GST tax reported on Form 706 is imposed only on direct skips occurring at death. Unlike the estate tax, which is imposed on the value of the entire taxable estate regardless of who receives it, the GST tax is imposed only on the value of interests in property, wherever located, that actually pass to certain transferees, who are referred to as *skip persons* (defined later).

For purposes of Form 706, the property interests transferred must be includible in the gross estate before they are subject to the GST tax. Therefore, the first step in figuring the GST tax liability is to determine the property interests includible in the gross estate by completing Schedules A through I of Form 706.

The second step is to determine who the skip persons are. To do this, assign each transferee to a generation and determine whether each transferee is a *natural person* or a *trust* for GST purposes. See section 2613 and Regulations section 26.2612–1(d) for details.

The third step is to determine which skip persons are transferees of *interests in property.* If the skip person is a natural person, anything transferred is an interest in property. If the skip person is a trust, make this determination using the rules under Interest in property, later. These first three steps are described in detail under the main heading, *Determining Which Transfers Are Direct Skips,* later.

The fourth step is to determine whether to enter the transfer on Schedule R or on Schedule R-1. See the rules under the main heading, Dividing Direct Skips Between Schedules R and R-1.

The fifth step is to complete Schedules R and R-1 using the How To Complete instructions for each schedule.

Determining Which Transfers Are Direct Skips

Effective dates. The rules below apply only for the purpose of determining if a transfer is a direct skip that should be reported on Schedule R or R-1 of Form 706.

In general. The GST tax is effective for the estates of decedents dying after October 22, 1986.

Irrevocable trusts. The GST tax will not apply to any transfer under a trust that was irrevocable on September 25, 1985, but only to the extent that the transfer was not made out of corpus added to the trust after September 25, 1985. An addition to the corpus after that date will cause a proportionate part of future income and appreciation to be subject to the GST tax. For more information, see Regulations section 26.2601-1(b)(1).

Mental disability. If, on October 22, 1986, the decedent was under a mental disability to change the disposition of his or her property and did not regain the competence to dispose of property before death, the GST tax will not apply to any property included in the gross estate (other than property transferred on behalf of the decedent during life and after October 21, 1986). The GST tax will also not apply to any transfer under a trust to the extent that the trust consists of property included in the gross estate (other than property transferred on behalf of the decedent during life and after October 21, 1986).

Under a mental disability means the decedent lacked the competence to execute an instrument governing the disposition of his or her property, regardless of whether there was an adjudication of incompetence or an appointment of any other person charged with the care of the person or property of the transferor.

If the decedent had been adjudged mentally incompetent, a copy of the judgment or decree must be filed with this return.

If the decedent had not been adjudged mentally incompetent, the executor must file with the return a certification from a qualified physician stating that in his opinion the decedent had been mentally incompetent at all times on and after October 22, 1986, and that the decedent had not regained the competence to modify or revoke the terms of the trust or will prior to his death or a statement as to why no such certification may be obtained from a physician.

Direct skip. The GST tax reported on Form 706 and Schedule R-1 is imposed only on direct skips. For purposes of Form 706, a *direct skip* is a transfer that is:

- Subject to the estate tax,
- Of an interest in property, and
- To a skip person.

All three requirements must be met before the transfer is subject to the GST tax. A transfer is subject to the estate tax if you are required to list it on any of Schedules A through I of Form 706. To determine if a transfer is of an interest in property and to a skip person, you must first determine if the transferee is a natural person or a trust as defined later.

Trust. For purposes of the GST tax, a *trust* includes not only an ordinary trust (as defined in *Special rule for trusts other than ordinary trusts,* later), but also any other arrangement (other than an estate) which, although not explicitly a trust, has substantially the same effect as a trust. For example, a trust includes life estates with remainders, terms for years, and insurance and annuity contracts.

Substantially separate and independent shares of different beneficiaries in a trust are treated as separate trusts.

Interest in property. If a transfer is made to a natural person, it is always considered a transfer of *an interest in property* for purposes of the GST tax.

If a transfer is made to a trust, a person will have an interest in the property transferred to the trust if that person either has a present right to receive income or corpus from the trust (such as an income interest for life) or is a permissible current recipient of income or corpus from the trust (that is, may receive income or corpus at the discretion of the trustee).

Skip person. A transferee who is a natural person is a *skip person* if that transferee is assigned to a generation that is two or more generations below the generation assignment of the decedent. See *Determining the generation of a transferee,* later.

A transferee who is a trust is a skip person if all the interests in the property (as defined above) transferred to the trust are held by skip persons. Thus, whenever a non-skip person has an interest in a trust, the trust will not be a skip person even though a skip person also has an interest in the trust.

A trust will also be a skip person if there are no interests in the property transferred to the trust held by any person, and future distributions or terminations from the trust can be made only to skip persons.

Non-skip person. A *non-skip person* is any transferee who is not a skip person.

Determining the generation of a transferee. Generally, a generation is determined along family lines as follows:

1. Where the beneficiary is a lineal descendant of a grandparent of the decedent (that is, the decedent's cousin, niece, nephew, etc.), the number of generations between the decedent and the beneficiary is determined by subtracting the number of generations between the grandparent and the decedent from the number of generations between the grandparent and the beneficiary.

2. Where the beneficiary is a lineal descendant of a grandparent of a spouse (or former spouse) of the decedent, the number of generations between the decedent and the beneficiary is determined by subtracting the number of generations between the grandparent and the spouse (or former spouse) from the number of generations between the grandparent and the beneficiary.

3. A person who at any time was married to a person described in (1) or (2) above is assigned to the generation of that person. A person who at any time was married to the decedent is assigned to the decedent's generation.

4. A relationship by adoption or half-blood is treated as a relationship by whole-blood.

5. A person who is not assigned to a generation according to (1), (2), (3), or (4) above is assigned to a generation based on his or her birth date, as follows:

a. A person who was born not more than 12½ years after the decedent is in the decedent's generation.

b. A person born more than 12½ years, but not more than 37½ years, after the decedent is in the first generation younger than the decedent.

c. A similar rule applies for a new generation every 25 years.

If more than one of the rules for assigning generations applies to a transferee, that transferee is generally assigned to the youngest of the generations that would apply.

If an estate, trust, partnership, corporation, or other entity (other than certain charitable organizations and trusts described in sections 511(a)(2)

and 511(b)(2)) is a transferee, then each person who indirectly receives the property interests through the entity is treated as a transferee and is assigned to a generation as explained in the above rules. However, this look-through rule does not apply for the purpose of determining whether a transfer to a trust is a direct skip.

Generation assignment where intervening parent is deceased. A special rule may apply in the case of the death of a parent of the transferee. For terminations, distributions, and transfers after December 31, 1997, the existing rule that applied to grandchildren of the decedent has been extended to apply to other lineal descendants.

If property is transferred to an individual who is a descendant of a parent of the transferor, and that individual's parent (who is a lineal descendant of the parent of the transferor) is deceased at the time the transfer is subject to gift or estate tax, then for purposes of generation assignment, the individual is treated as if he or she is a member of the generation that is one generation below the lower of:
- The transferor's generation or
- The generation assignment of the youngest living ancestor of the individual, who is also a descendant of the parent of the transferor.

The same rules apply to the generation assignment of any descendant of the individual.

This rule does not apply to a transfer to an individual who is not a lineal descendant of the transferor if the transferor has any living lineal descendants.

If any transfer of property to a trust would have been a direct skip except for this generation assignment rule, then the rule also applies to transfers from the trust attributable to such property.

See examples in Regulations section 26.2651–1(c).

Ninety-day rule. For purposes of determining if an individual's parent is deceased at the time of a testamentary transfer, an individual's parent who dies no later than 90 days after a transfer occurring by reason of the death of the transferor is treated as having predeceased the transferor. The 90-day rule applies to transfers occurring on or after July 18, 2005. See Regulations section 26.2651-1, for more information.

Charitable organizations.
Charitable organizations and trusts

described in sections 511(a)(2) and 511(b)(2) are assigned to the decedent's generation. Transfers to such organizations are therefore not subject to the GST tax.

Charitable remainder trusts.
Transfers to or in the form of charitable remainder annuity trusts, charitable remainder unitrusts, and pooled income funds are not considered made to skip persons and, therefore, are not direct skips even if all of the life beneficiaries are skip persons.

Estate tax value. Estate tax value is the value shown on Schedules A through I of this Form 706.

Examples. The rules above can be illustrated by the following examples:

1. Under the will, the decedent's house is transferred to the decedent's daughter for her life with the remainder passing to her children. This transfer is made to a "trust" even though there is no explicit trust instrument. The interest in the property transferred (the present right to use the house) is transferred to a non-skip person (the decedent's daughter). Therefore, the trust is not a skip person because there is an interest in the transferred property that is held by a non-skip person. The transfer is not a direct skip.

2. The will bequeaths $100,000 to the decedent's grandchild. This transfer is a direct skip that is not made in trust and should be shown on Schedule R.

3. The will establishes a trust that is required to accumulate income for 10 years and then pay its income to the decedent's grandchildren for the rest of their lives and, upon their deaths, distribute the corpus to the decedent's great-grandchildren. Because the trust has no current beneficiaries, there are no present interests in the property transferred to the trust. All of the persons to whom the trust can make future distributions (including distributions upon the termination of interests in property held in trust) are skip persons (for example, the decedent's grandchildren and great-grandchildren). Therefore, the trust itself is a skip person and you should show the transfer on Schedule R.

4. The will establishes a trust that is to pay all of its income to the decedent's grandchildren for 10 years. At the end of 10 years, the corpus is to be distributed to the decedent's children. All of the present interests in this trust are held by skip persons. Therefore, the trust is a skip person and you should show this

transfer on Schedule R. You should show the estate tax value of all the property transferred to the trust even though the trust has some ultimate beneficiaries who are non-skip persons.

Dividing Direct Skips Between Schedules R and R-1

 Report all generation-skipping transfers on Schedule R unless the rules below specifically provide that they are to be reported on Schedule R-1.

Under section 2603(a)(2), the GST tax on direct skips from a trust (as defined for GST tax purposes) is to be paid by the trustee and not by the estate. Schedule R-1 serves as a notification from the executor to the trustee that a GST tax is due.

For a direct skip to be reportable on Schedule R-1, the trust must be includible in the decedent's gross estate.

If the decedent was a surviving spouse receiving benefits for his or her lifetime from a marital deduction power of appointment (or QTIP) trust created by the decedent's spouse, then transfers caused by reason of the decedent's death from that trust to skip persons are direct skips required to be reported on Schedule R-1.

If a direct skip is made "from a trust" under these rules, it is reportable on Schedule R-1 even if it is also made "to a trust" rather than to an individual.

Similarly, if property in a trust (as defined for GST tax purposes) is included in the decedent's gross estate under sections 2035, 2036, 2037, 2038, 2039, 2041, or 2042 and such property is, by reason of the decedent's death, transferred to skip persons, the transfers are direct skips required to be reported on Schedule R-1.

Special rule for trusts other than ordinary trusts. An *ordinary trust* is defined in Regulations section 301.7701-4(a) as "an arrangement created by a will or by an inter vivos declaration whereby trustees take title to property for the purpose of protecting or conserving it for the beneficiaries under the ordinary rules applied in chancery or probate courts." Direct skips from ordinary trusts are required to be reported on Schedule R-1 regardless of their size unless the executor is also a trustee (see *Executor as trustee,* below).

Direct skips from trusts that are trusts for GST tax purposes but are not

ordinary trusts are to be shown on Schedule R-1 only if the total of all tentative maximum direct skips from the entity is $250,000 or more. If this total is less than $250,000, the skips should be shown on Schedule R. For purposes of the $250,000 limit, *tentative maximum direct skips* is the amount you would enter on line 5 of Schedule R-1 if you were to file that schedule.

A liquidating trust (such as a bankruptcy trust) under Regulations section 301.7701-4(d) is not treated as an ordinary trust for the purposes of this special rule.

If the proceeds of a life insurance policy are includible in the gross estate and are payable to a beneficiary who is a skip person, the transfer is a direct skip from a trust that is not an ordinary trust. It should be reported on Schedule R-1 if the total of all the tentative maximum direct skips from the company is $250,000 or more. Otherwise, it should be reported on Schedule R.

Similarly, if an annuity is includible on Schedule I and its survivor benefits are payable to a beneficiary who is a skip person, then the estate tax value of the annuity should be reported as a direct skip on Schedule R-1 if the total tentative maximum direct skips from the entity paying the annuity is $250,000 or more.

Executor as trustee. If any of the executors of the decedent's estate are trustees of the trust, then all direct skips for that trust must be shown on Schedule R and not on Schedule R-1, even if they would otherwise have been required to be shown on Schedule R-1. This rule applies even if the trust has other trustees who are not executors of the decedent's estate.

How To Complete Schedules R and R-1

Valuation. Enter on Schedules R and R-1 the estate tax value of the property interests subject to the direct skips. If you elected alternate valuation (section 2032) and/or special-use valuation (section 2032A), you must use the alternate and/or special-use values on Schedules R and R-1.

How To Complete Schedule R

Part 1. GST Exemption Reconciliation

Part 1, line 6 of both Parts 2 and 3, and line 4 of Schedule R-1 are used to allocate the decedent's GST exemption. This allocation is made by filing Form

706 and attaching a completed Schedule R and/or R-1. Once made, the allocation is irrevocable. You are not required to allocate all of the decedent's GST exemption. However, the portion of the exemption that you do not allocate will be allocated by the IRS under the deemed allocation of unused GST exemption rules of section 2632(e).

For transfers made through 1998, the GST exemption was $1 million. The current GST exemption is $5,340,000. The exemption amounts for 1999 through 2013 are as follows:

Year of transfer	GST exemption
1999	$1,010,000
2000	$1,030,000
2001	$1,060,000
2002	$1,100,000
2003	$1,120,000
2004 and 2005	$1,500,000
2006, 2007, and 2008	$2,000,000
2009	$3,500,000
2010 and 2011	$5,000,000
2012	$5,120,000
2013	$5,250,000

The amount of each increase can only be allocated to transfers made (or appreciation that occurred) during or after the year of the increase. The following example shows the application of this rule:

Example. In 2003, G made a direct skip of $1,120,000 and applied her full $1,120,000 of GST exemption to the transfer. G made a $450,000 taxable direct skip in 2004 and another of $90,000 in 2006. For 2004, G can only apply $380,000 of exemption ($380,000 inflation adjustment from 2004) to the $450,000 transfer in 2004. For 2006, G can apply $90,000 of exemption to the 2006 transfer, but nothing to the transfer made in 2004. At the end of 2006, G would have $410,000 of unused exemption that she can apply to future transfers (or appreciation) starting in 2007.

Special QTIP election. In the case of property for which a marital deduction is allowed to the decedent's estate under section 2056(b)(7) (QTIP election), section 2652(a)(3) allows you to treat such property for purposes of the GST tax as if the election to be treated as qualified terminable interest property had not been made.

The 2652(a)(3) election must include the value of all property in the trust for which a QTIP election was allowed under section 2056(b)(7).

If a section 2652(a)(3) election is made, then the decedent will, for GST tax purposes, be treated as the transferor of all the property in the trust for which a marital deduction was allowed to the decedent's estate under section 2056(b)(7). In this case, the executor of the decedent's estate may allocate part or all of the decedent's GST exemption to the property.

You make the election simply by listing qualifying property on line 9 of Part 1.

Line 2. These allocations will have been made either on Forms 709 filed by the decedent or on Notices of Allocation made by the decedent for inter vivos transfers that were not direct skips but to which the decedent allocated the GST exemption. These allocations by the decedent are irrevocable.

Also include on this line allocations deemed to have been made by the decedent under the rules of section 2632. Unless the decedent elected out of the deemed allocation rules, allocations are deemed to have been made in the following order:

1. To inter vivos direct skips and

2. Beginning with transfers made after December 31, 2000, to lifetime transfers to certain trusts, by the decedent, that constituted indirect skips that were subject to the gift tax.

For more information, see section 2632 and related regulations.

Line 3. Make an entry on this line if you are filing Form(s) 709 for the decedent and wish to allocate any exemption.

Lines 4, 5, and 6. These lines represent your allocation of the GST exemption to direct skips made by reason of the decedent's death. Complete Parts 2 and 3 and Schedule R-1 before completing these lines.

Line 9. Line 9 is used to allocate the remaining unused GST exemption (from line 8) and to help you figure the trust's inclusion ratio. Line 9 is a Notice of Allocation for allocating the GST exemption to trusts as to which the decedent is the transferor and from which a generation-skipping transfer could occur after the decedent's death.

If line 9 is not completed, the deemed allocation at death rules will apply to allocate the decedent's remaining unused GST exemption. The exemption will be first allocated to property that is

the subject of a direct skip occurring at the decedent's death, and then to trusts as to which the decedent is the transferor. To avoid the application of the deemed allocation rules, you should enter on line 9 every trust (except certain trusts entered on Schedule R-1, as described later) to which you wish to allocate any part of the decedent's GST exemption. Unless you enter a trust on line 9, the unused GST exemption will be allocated to it under the deemed allocation rules.

If a trust is entered on Schedule R-1, the amount you entered on line 4 of Schedule R-1 serves as a Notice of Allocation and you need not enter the trust on line 9 unless you wish to allocate more than the Schedule R-1, line 4 amount to the trust. However, you must enter the trust on line 9 if you wish to allocate any of the unused GST exemption amount to it. Such an additional allocation would not ordinarily be appropriate in the case of a trust entered on Schedule R-1 when the trust property passes outright (rather than to another trust) at the decedent's death. However, where section 2032A property is involved, it may be appropriate to allocate additional exemption amounts to the property. See the instructions for line 10 later.

 To avoid application of the deemed allocation rules, Form 706 and Schedule R should be filed to allocate the exemption to trusts that may later have taxable terminations or distributions under section 2612 even if the form is not required to be filed to report estate or GST tax.

Line 9, column C. Enter the GST exemption, included on lines 2 through 6 of Part 1 of Schedule R (discussed above), that was allocated to the trust.

Line 9, column D. Allocate the amount on line 8 of Part 1 of Schedule R in line 9, column D. This amount may be allocated to transfers into trusts that are not otherwise reported on Form 706. For example, the line 8 amount may be allocated to an inter vivos trust established by the decedent during his or her lifetime and not included in the gross estate. This allocation is made by identifying the trust on line 9 and making an allocation to it using column D. If the trust is not included in the gross estate, value the trust as of the date of death. Inform the trustee of each trust listed on line 9 of the total GST exemption you allocated to the trust. The trustee will need this information to figure the GST

tax on future distributions and terminations.

Line 9, column E. Trust's inclusion ratio. The trustee must know the trust's inclusion ratio to figure the trust's GST tax for future distributions and terminations. You are not required to inform the trustee of the inclusion ratio and may not have enough information to figure it. Therefore, you are not required to make an entry in column E. However, column E and the worksheet later are provided to assist you in figuring the inclusion ratio for the trustee if you wish to do so.

Inform the trustee of the amount of the GST exemption you allocated to the trust. Line 9, columns C and D may be used to figure this amount for each trust.

Note. This worksheet will figure an accurate inclusion ratio only if the decedent was the only settlor of the trust. Use a separate worksheet for each trust (or separate share of a trust that is treated as a separate trust).

WORKSHEET (inclusion ratio):

1 Total estate and gift tax value of all of the property interests that passed to the trust . . . . _____
2 Estate taxes, state death taxes, and other charges actually recovered from the trust . . . _____
3 GST taxes imposed on direct skips to skip persons other than this trust and borne by the property transferred to this trust . . . . _____
4 GST taxes actually recovered from this trust (from Schedule R, Part 2, line 8 or Schedule R-1, line 6) . . . . _____
5 Add lines 2 through 4 . . . . . _____
6 Subtract line 5 from line 1 . . _____
7 Add columns C and D of line 9 . . . . _____
8 Divide line 7 by line 6 . . . . . _____
9 Trust's inclusion ratio. Subtract line 8 from 1.000 . . . . _____

Line 10. Special-use allocation. For skip persons who receive an interest in section 2032A special-use property, you may allocate more GST exemption than the direct skip amount to reduce the additional GST tax that would be due when the interest is later disposed of or qualified use ceases. See Schedule A-1, above, for more details about this additional GST tax.

Enter on line 10 the total additional GST exemption available to allocate to all skip persons who received any interest in section 2032A property. Attach a special-use allocation statement listing each such skip person and the amount of the GST exemption allocated to that person.

If you do not allocate the GST exemption, it will be automatically allocated under the deemed allocation at death rules. To the extent any amount is not so allocated, it will be automatically allocated to the earliest disposition or cessation that is subject to the GST tax. Under certain circumstances, post-death events may cause the decedent to be treated as a transferor for purposes of Chapter 13.

Line 10 may be used to set aside an exemption amount for such an event. Attach a statement listing each such event and the amount of exemption allocated to that event.

Parts 2 and 3.

Use Part 2 to figure the GST tax on transfers in which the property interests transferred are to bear the GST tax on the transfers. Use Part 3 to report the GST tax on transfers in which the property interests transferred do not bear the GST tax on the transfers.

Section 2603(b) requires that unless the governing instrument provides otherwise, the GST tax is to be charged to the property constituting the transfer. Therefore, you will usually enter all of the direct skips on Part 2.

You may enter a transfer on Part 3 only if the will or trust instrument directs, by specific reference, that the GST tax is not to be paid from the transferred property interests.

Part 2, Line 3. Enter zero on this line unless the will or trust instrument specifies that the GST taxes will be paid by property other than that constituting the transfer (as described above). Enter on line 3 the total of the GST taxes shown on Part 3 and Schedule(s) R-1 that are payable out of the property interests shown on Part 2, line 1.

Part 2, Line 6. Do not enter more than the amount on line 5. Additional allocations may be made using Part 1.

Part 3, Line 3. See the instructions to Part 2, line 3 above. Enter only the total of the GST taxes shown on Schedule(s) R-1 that are payable out of the property interests shown on Part 3, line 1.

Part 3, Line 6. See the instructions to Part 2, line 6 above.

How To Complete Schedule R-1

Filing due date. Enter the due date of Form 706. You must send the copies of Schedule R-1 to the fiduciary before this date.

Line 4. Do not enter more than the amount on line 3. If you wish to allocate an additional GST exemption, you must use Schedule R, Part 1. Making an entry on line 4 constitutes a Notice of Allocation of the decedent's GST exemption to the trust.

Line 6. If the property interests entered on line 1 will not bear the GST tax, multiply line 6 by 40% (0.40).

Signature. The executor(s) must sign Schedule R-1 in the same manner as Form 706. See *Signature and Verification,* above.

Filing Schedule R-1. Attach to Form 706 one copy of each Schedule R-1 that you prepare. Send two copies of each Schedule R-1 to the fiduciary.

Schedule U—Qualified Conservation Easement Exclusion

 If at the time of the contribution of the conservation easement, the value of the easement, the value of the land subject to the easement, or the value of any retained development right was different than the estate tax value, you must complete a separate computation in addition to completing Schedule U.

Use a copy of Schedule U as a worksheet for this separate computation. Complete lines 4 through 14 of the worksheet Schedule U. However, the value you use on lines 4, 5, 7, and 10 of the worksheet is the value for these items as of the date of the contribution of the easement, not the estate tax value. If the date of contribution and the estate tax values are the same, you do not need to do a separate computation.

After completing the worksheet, enter the amount from line 14 of the worksheet on line 14 of Schedule U. Finish completing Schedule U by entering amounts on lines 4, 7, and 15 through 20, following the instructions later for those lines. At the top of Schedule U, enter "worksheet attached." Attach the worksheet to the return.

Under section 2031(c), you may elect to exclude a portion of the value of land that is subject to a qualified

conservation easement. You make the election by filing Schedule U with all of the required information and excluding the applicable value of the land that is subject to the easement on Part 5—Recapitulation, at item 12. To elect the exclusion, include on Schedule A, B, E, F, G, or H, as appropriate, the decedent's interest in the land that is subject to the exclusion. You must make the election on a timely filed Form 706, including extensions.

The exclusion is the lesser of:
- The applicable percentage of the value of land (after certain reductions) subject to a qualified conservation easement or
- $500,000.

Once made, the election is irrevocable.

General Requirements

Qualified Land

Land may qualify for the exclusion if all of the following requirements are met:
- The decedent or a member of the decedent's family must have owned the land for the 3-year period ending on the date of the decedent's death.
- No later than the date the election is made, a qualified conservation easement on the land has been made by the decedent, a member of the decedent's family, the executor of the decedent's estate, or the trustee of a trust that holds the land.
- The land is located in the United States or one of its possessions.

Member of Family

Members of the decedent's family include the decedent's spouse; ancestors; lineal descendants of the decedent, of the decedent's spouse, and of the parents of the decedent; and the spouse of any lineal descendant. A legally adopted child of an individual is considered a child of the individual by blood.

Indirect Ownership of Land

The qualified conservation easement exclusion applies if the land is owned indirectly through a partnership, corporation, or trust, if the decedent owned (directly or indirectly) at least 30% of the entity. For the rules on determining ownership of an entity, see *Ownership rules,* later.

Ownership rules. An interest in property owned, directly or indirectly, by or for a corporation, partnership, or trust is considered proportionately owned by or for the entity's shareholders, partners, or beneficiaries. A person is the beneficiary of a trust only if he or she has a present interest in the trust. For additional information, see the ownership rules in section 2057(e)(3).

Qualified Conservation Easement

A *qualified conservation easement* is one that would qualify as a qualified conservation contribution under section 170(h). It must be a contribution:
• Of a qualified real property interest,
• To a qualified organization, and
• Exclusively for conservation purposes.

Qualified real property interest. A *qualified real property interest* is any of the following:
• The entire interest of the donor, other than a qualified mineral interest;
• A remainder interest; or
• A restriction granted in perpetuity on the use that may be made of the real property. The restriction must include a prohibition on more than a de minimis use for commercial recreational activity.

Qualified organization. A *qualified organization* includes:
• Corporations and any community chest, fund, or foundation, organized and operated exclusively for religious, charitable, scientific, testing for public safety, literary, or educational purposes, or to foster national or international amateur sports competition, or for the prevention of cruelty to children or animals, without net earnings benefitting any individual shareholder and without activity with the purpose of influencing legislation or political campaigning, which

  a. Receives more than one-third of its support from gifts, contributions, membership fees, or receipts from sales, admissions fees, or performance of services, or

  b. Is controlled by such an organization.
• Any entity that qualifies under section 170(b)(1)(A)(v) or (vi).

Conservation purpose. An easement has a *conservation purpose* if it is for:
• The preservation of land areas for outdoor recreation by, or for the education of, the public;
• The protection of a relatively natural habitat of fish, wildlife, or plants, or a similar ecosystem; or
• The preservation of open space (including farmland and forest land) where such preservation is for the scenic enjoyment of the general public,

or under a clearly delineated federal, state, or local conservation policy and will yield a significant public benefit.

Specific Instructions

Line 1

If the land is reported as one or more item numbers on a Form 706 schedule, simply list the schedule and item numbers. If the land subject to the easement is only part of an item, however, list the schedule and item number and describe the part subject to the easement. See the Instructions for *Schedule A — Real Estate* for information on how to describe the land.

Line 3

Using the general rules for describing real estate, provide enough information so the IRS can value the easement. Give the date the easement was granted and by whom it was granted.

Line 4

Enter on this line the gross value at which the land was reported on the applicable asset schedule on this Form 706. Do not reduce the value by the amount of any mortgage outstanding. Report the estate tax value even if the easement was granted by the decedent (or someone other than the decedent) prior to the decedent's death.

Note. If the value of the land reported on line 4 was different at the time the easement was contributed than that reported on Form 706, see the *Caution* at the beginning of the Schedule U Instructions.

Line 5

The amount on line 5 should be the date of death value of any qualifying conservation easements granted prior to the decedent's death, whether granted by the decedent or someone other than the decedent, for which the exclusion is being elected.

Note. If the value of the easement reported on line 5 was different at the time the easement was contributed than at the date of death, see the *Caution* at the beginning of the Schedule U Instructions.

Line 7

You must reduce the land value by the value of any development rights retained by the donor in the conveyance of the easement. A *development right* is any right to use the land for any

commercial purpose that is not subordinate to or directly supportive of the use of the land as a farm for farming purposes.

Note. If the value of the retained development rights reported on line 7 was different at the time the easement was contributed than at the date of death, see the *Caution* at the beginning of the Schedule U Instructions.

You do not have to make this reduction if everyone with an interest in the land (regardless of whether in possession) agrees to permanently extinguish the retained development right. The agreement must be filed with this return and must include the following information and terms:

  1. A statement that the agreement is made under section 2031(c)(5);

  2. A list of all persons in being holding an interest in the land that is subject to the qualified conservation easement. Include each person's name, address, tax identifying number, relationship to the decedent, and a description of their interest;

  3. The items of real property shown on the estate tax return that are subject to the qualified conservation easement (identified by schedule and item number);

  4. A description of the retained development right that is to be extinguished;

  5. A clear statement of consent that is binding on all parties under applicable local law:

  a. To take whatever action is necessary to permanently extinguish the retained development rights listed in the agreement and

  b. To be personally liable for additional taxes under section 2031(c)(5)(C) if this agreement is not implemented by the earlier of:

    • The date that is 2 years after the date of the decedent's death or
    • The date of sale of the land subject to the qualified conservation easement;

  6. A statement that in the event this agreement is not timely implemented, that they will report the additional tax on whatever return is required by the IRS and will file the return and pay the additional tax by the last day of the 6th month following the applicable date described above.

All parties to the agreement must sign the agreement.

Line 10

Enter the total value of the qualified conservation easements on which the exclusion is based. This could include easements granted by the decedent (or someone other than the decedent) prior to the decedent's death, easements granted by the decedent that take effect at death, easements granted by the executor after the decedent's death, or some combination of these.

 Use the value of the easement as of the date of death, even if the easement was granted prior to the date of death. But, if the value of the easement was different at the time the easement was contributed than at the date of death, see the Caution *at the beginning of the Schedule U Instructions.*

Explain how this value was determined and attach copies of any appraisals. Normally, the appropriate way to value a conservation easement is to determine the FMV of the land both before and after the granting of the easement, with the difference being the value of the easement.

Reduce the reported value of the easement by the amount of any consideration received for the easement. If the date of death value of the easement is different from the value at the time the consideration was received, reduce the value of the easement by the same proportion that the consideration received bears to the value of the easement at the time it was granted. For example, assume the value of the easement at the time it was granted was $100,000 and $10,000 was received in consideration for the easement. If the easement was worth $150,000 at the date of death, you must reduce the value of the easement by $15,000 ($10,000/$100,000 × $150,000) and report the value of the easement on line 10 as $135,000.

Line 15

If a charitable contribution deduction for this land has been taken on Schedule O, enter the amount of the deduction here. If the easement was granted after the decedent's death, a contribution deduction may be taken on Schedule O, if it otherwise qualifies, as long as no income tax deduction was or

will be claimed for the contribution by any person or entity.

Line 16

Reduce the value of the land by the amount of any acquisition indebtedness on the land at the date of the decedent's death. Acquisition indebtedness includes the unpaid amount of:
• Any indebtedness incurred by the donor in acquiring the property;
• Any indebtedness incurred before the acquisition if the indebtedness would not have been incurred but for the acquisition;
• Any indebtedness incurred after the acquisition if the indebtedness would not have been incurred but for the acquisition and the incurrence of the indebtedness was reasonably foreseeable at the time of the acquisition; and
• The extension, renewal, or refinancing of acquisition indebtedness.

Schedule PC—Protective Claim for Refund

A *protective claim for refund* preserves the estate's right to a refund of tax paid on any amount included in the gross estate which would be deductible under section 2053 but has not been paid or otherwise will not meet the requirements of section 2053 until after the limitations period for filing the claim has passed. See section 6511(a).

 Only use Schedule PC for section 2053 protective claims for refund being filed with Form 706. If the initial notice of the protective claim for refund is being submitted after Form 706 has been filed, use Form 843, Claim for Refund and Request for Abatement, to file the claim.

Schedule PC may be used to file a section 2053 protective claim for refund by estates of decedents who died after December 31, 2011. It will also be used to inform the IRS when the contingency leading to the protective claim for refund is resolved and the refund due the estate is finalized. The estate must indicate whether the Schedule PC being filed is the initial notice of protective claim for refund, notice of partial claim for refund, or notice of the final resolution of the claim for refund.

Because each separate claim or expense requires a separate Schedule PC, more than one Schedule PC may be included with Form 706, if applicable. Two copies of

each Schedule PC must be included with Form 706.

Note. Filing a section 2053 protective claim for refund on Schedule PC will not suspend the IRS' review and examination of Form 706, nor will it delay the issuance of a closing letter for the estate.

Initial Notice of Claim

The first Schedule PC to be filed is the initial notice of protective claim for refund. The estate will receive a written acknowledgment of receipt of the claim from the IRS. If the acknowledgment is not received within 180 days of filing the protective claim for refund on Schedule PC, the fiduciary should contact the IRS at (866) 699-4083 to inquire about the receipt and processing of the claim. A certified mail receipt or other evidence of delivery is not sufficient to confirm receipt and processing of the protective claim for refund.

Note. The written acknowledgment of receipt does not constitute a determination that all requirements for a valid protective claim for refund have been met.

In general, the claim will not be subject to substantive review until the amount of the claim has been established. However, a claim can be disallowed at the time of filing. For example, the claim for refund will be rejected if:
• The claim was not timely filed;
• The claim was not filed by the fiduciary or other person with authority to act on behalf of the estate;
• The acknowledgment of the penalties of perjury statement (on page 1 of Form 706) was not signed; or,
• The claim is not adequately described.

If the IRS does not raise such a defect when the claim is filed, it will not be precluded from doing so in the later substantive review.

The estate may be given an opportunity to cure any defects in the initial notice by filing a corrected and signed protective claim for refund before the expiration of the limitations period in section 6511(a) or within 45 days of notice of the defect, whichever is later.

Related Ancillary Expenses

If a Section 2053 protective claim for refund has been adequately identified on Schedule PC, the IRS will presume that the claim includes certain expenses related to resolving, defending or satisfying the claim. These ancillary expenses may include attorneys' fees, court costs, appraisal fees, and accounting fees. The estate is not required to separately identify or substantiate these expenses; however, each expense must meet the requirements of section 2053 to be deductible.

Notice of Final Resolution of Claim

When an expense that was the subject of a section 2053 protective claim for refund is finally determined, the estate must notify the IRS that the claim for refund is ready for consideration. The notification should provide facts and evidence substantiating the deduction under section 2053 and the resulting recomputation of the estate tax liability. A separate notice of final resolution must be filed with the IRS for each resolved section 2053 protective claim for refund.

There are two means by which the estate may notify the IRS of the resolution of the uncertainty that deprived the estate of the deduction when Form 706 was filed. The estate may file a supplemental Form 706 with an updated Schedule PC and including each schedule affected by the allowance of the deduction under section 2053. Page 1 of Form 706 should contain the notation "Supplemental Information – Notification of Consideration of Section 2053 Protective Claim(s) for Refund" and include the filing date of the initial notice of protective claim for refund. A copy of the initial notice of claim should also be submitted.

Alternatively, the estate may notify the IRS by filing an updated Form 843, Claim for Refund and Request for Abatement. Form 843 must contain the notation "Notification of Consideration of Section 2053 Protective Claim(s) for Refund," including the filing date of the initial notice of protective claim for refund, on page 1. A copy of the initial notice of claim must also be submitted.

The estate should notify the IRS of resolution within 90 days of the date the claim or expense is paid or the date on which the amount of the claim becomes certain and no longer subject to contingency, whichever is later. Separate notifications must be submitted for every section 2053 protective claim for refund that was filed.

If the final section 2053 claim or expense involves multiple or recurring payments, the 90-day period begins on the date of the last payment. The estate may also notify the IRS (not more than annually) as payments are being made and possibly qualify for a partial refund based on the amounts paid through the date of the notice.

Specific Instructions

Part 1. General Information

Complete Part 1 by providing information that is correct and complete as of the time Schedule PC is filed. If filing an updated Schedule PC with a supplemental Form 706 or as notice of final resolution of the protective claim for refund, be sure to update the information from the original filing to ensure that it is accurate. Be particularly careful to verify that contact information (addresses and telephone numbers) and the reason for filing Schedule PC are indicated correctly. If the fiduciary is different from the executor identified on page 1 of Form 706 or has changed since the initial notice of protective claim for refund was filed, attach letters testamentary, letters of administration, or similar documentation evidencing the fiduciary's authority to file the protective claim for refund on behalf of the estate. Include a copy of Form 56, Notice Concerning Fiduciary Relationship, if it has been filed.

Part 2. Claim Information

For a protective claim for refund to be properly filed and considered, the claim or expense forming the basis of the potential 2053 deduction must be clearly identified. Using the check boxes provided, indicate whether you are filing the initial claim for refund, a claim for partial refund or a final claim. On the chart in Part 2, give the Form 706 schedule and item number of the claim or expense. List any amounts claimed under exceptions for ascertainable amounts (Regulations section 20.2053-1(d)(4)), claims and counterclaims in related matters (Regulations section 20.2053-4(b)), or claims under $500,000 (Regulations section 20.2053-4(c)). Provide all relevant information as described including, most importantly, an explanation of the reasons and contingencies delaying the actual payment to be made in satisfaction of the claim or expense. Complete columns E and F only if filing a notice of partial or final resolution. Show the amount of ancillary or related expenses to be included in the claim for refund and indicate whether this amount is estimated, agreed upon, or has been paid. Also show the amount being claimed for refund.

Note. If you made partial claims for a recurring expense, the amount presently claimed as a deduction under section 2053 will only include the amount presently claimed, not the cumulative amount.

Part 3. Other Schedules PC and Forms 843 Filed by the Estate

On the chart in Part 3, provide information on other protective claims for refund that have been previously filed on behalf of the estate (if any), whether on other Schedules PC or on Form 843. When the initial claim for refund is filed, only information from Form(s) 843 need be included in Part 3. However, when filing a partial or final claim for refund, complete Part 3 by including the status of all claims filed by or on behalf of the estate, including those filed on other Schedules PC with Form 706. For each such claim, give the place of filing, date of filing and amount of the claim.

Continuation Schedule

When you need to list more assets or deductions than you have room for on one of the main schedules, use the Continuation Schedule at the end of Form 706. It provides a uniform format for listing additional assets from Schedules A through I and additional deductions from Schedules J, K, L, M, and O.

Please remember to:

- Use a separate Continuation Schedule for each main schedule you are continuing. Do not combine assets or deductions from different schedules on one Continuation Schedule.
- Make copies of the blank schedule before completing it if you expect to need more than one.
- Use as many Continuation Schedules as needed to list all the assets or deductions.
- Enter the letter of the schedule you are continuing in the space at the top of the Continuation Schedule.
- Use the Unit value column **only** if continuing Schedule B, E, or G. For all other schedules, use this space to continue the description.
- Carry the total from the Continuation Schedules forward to the appropriate line on the main schedule.

If continuing	Report	Where on Continuation Schedule
Schedule E, Pt. 2	*Percentage includible*	*Alternate valuation date*
Schedules J, L, M	*Continued description of deduction*	*Alternate valuation date **and** Alternate value*
Schedule O	*Character of institution*	*Alternate valuation date **and** Alternate value*
Schedule O	*Amount of each deduction*	*Amount deductible*

Instructions for Schedules

Index

Checklists for Completing Form 706

To ensure a complete return, review the following checklists before filing Form 706.

Attachments . . .

☐   Death Certificate

☐   Certified copy of the will—if decedent died testate, you must attach a certified copy of the will. If not certified, explain why.

☐   Appraisals—attach any appraisals used to value property included on the return.

☐   Copies of all trust documents where the decedent was a grantor or a beneficiary.

☐   Form 2848 or 8821, if applicable.

☐   Copy of any Form(s) 709 filed by the decedent.

☐   Copy of Line 7 worksheet, if applicable.

☐   Form 712, if any policies of life insurance are included on the return.

☐   Form 706-CE, if claiming a foreign death tax credit.

Have you . . .

☐ Signed the return at the bottom of page 1?

☐ Had the preparer sign, if applicable?

☐ Obtained the signature of your authorized representative on Part 4, page 2?

☐ Entered a Total on all schedules filed?

☐ Made an entry on every line of the Recapitulation, even if it is a zero?

☐ Included the CUSIP number for all stocks and bonds?

☐ Included the EIN of trusts, partnerships, and closely held entities?

☐ Included the first 4 pages of the return and all required schedules?

☐ Completed Schedule F? It must be filed with all returns.

☐ Completed Part 4, line 4, on page 2, if there is a surviving spouse?

☐ Completed and attached Schedule D to report insurance on the life of the decedent, even if its value is not included in the estate?

☐ Included any QTIP property received from a predeceased spouse?

☐ Entered the decedent's name, SSN, and "Form 706" on your check or money order?

☐ Completed Part 6, section A if the estate elects not to transfer any deceased spousal unused exclusion (DSUE) amount to the surviving spouse?

☐ Completed Part 6, section C if the estate elects portability of any DSUE amount?

☐ Completed Part 6, section D and included a copy of the Form 706 of any predeceased spouse(s) from whom a deceased spousal unused exclusion (DSUE) amount was received and applied?

Form **1040**

Department of the Treasury—Internal Revenue Service   (99)

U.S. Individual Income Tax Return **2014** OMB No. 1545-0074 | IRS Use Only—Do not write or staple in this space.

For the year Jan. 1–Dec. 31, 2014, or other tax year beginning _____ , 2014, ending _____ , 20 ___ | See separate instructions.

| Your first name and initial | Last name | | Your social security number |

| If a joint return, spouse's first name and initial | Last name | | Spouse's social security number |

Home address (number and street). If you have a P.O. box, see instructions. | Apt. no. |

▲ Make sure the SSN(s) above and on line 6c are correct.

City, town or post office, state, and ZIP code. If you have a foreign address, also complete spaces below (see instructions).

Foreign country name | Foreign province/state/county | Foreign postal code

Presidential Election Campaign
Check here if you, or your spouse if filing jointly, want $3 to go to this fund. Checking a box below will not change your tax or refund. ☐ You ☐ Spouse

Filing Status

Check only one box.

1 ☐ Single
2 ☐ Married filing jointly (even if only one had income)
3 ☐ Married filing separately. Enter spouse's SSN above and full name here. ▶
4 ☐ Head of household (with qualifying person). (See instructions.) If the qualifying person is a child but not your dependent, enter this child's name here. ▶
5 ☐ Qualifying widow(er) with dependent child

Exemptions

6a ☐ **Yourself.** If someone can claim you as a dependent, **do not** check box 6a . . . . . .
b ☐ **Spouse** . . . .

Boxes checked on 6a and 6b

c **Dependents:**

(1) First name Last name	(2) Dependent's social security number	(3) Dependent's relationship to you	(4) ✓ if child under age 17 qualifying for child tax credit (see instructions)
			☐
			☐
			☐
			☐

If more than four dependents, see instructions and check here ▶ ☐

No. of children on 6c who:
• lived with you
• did not live with you due to divorce or separation (see instructions)

Dependents on 6c not entered above

d Total number of exemptions claimed . . . .

Add numbers on lines above ▶

Income

Attach Form(s) W-2 here. Also attach Forms W-2G and 1099-R if tax was withheld.

If you did not get a W-2, see instructions.

7	Wages, salaries, tips, etc. Attach Form(s) W-2	7	
8a	**Taxable** interest. Attach Schedule B if required	8a	
b	**Tax-exempt** interest. **Do not** include on line 8a . .	8b	
9a	Ordinary dividends. Attach Schedule B if required	9a	
b	Qualified dividends	9b	
10	Taxable refunds, credits, or offsets of state and local income taxes	10	
11	Alimony received	11	
12	Business income or (loss). Attach Schedule C or C-EZ	12	
13	Capital gain or (loss). Attach Schedule D if required. If not required, check here ▶ ☐	13	
14	Other gains or (losses). Attach Form 4797	14	
15a	IRA distributions . 15a _____	b Taxable amount . . .	15b	
16a	Pensions and annuities 16a _____	b Taxable amount . . .	16b	
17	Rental real estate, royalties, partnerships, S corporations, trusts, etc. Attach Schedule E	17	
18	Farm income or (loss). Attach Schedule F	18	
19	Unemployment compensation	19	
20a	Social security benefits 20a _____	b Taxable amount . . .	20b	
21	Other income. List type and amount _____	21	
22	Combine the amounts in the far right column for lines 7 through 21. This is your **total income** ▶	22	

Adjusted Gross Income

23	Educator expenses	23	
24	Certain business expenses of reservists, performing artists, and fee-basis government officials. Attach Form 2106 or 2106-EZ	24	
25	Health savings account deduction. Attach Form 8889 .	25	
26	Moving expenses. Attach Form 3903	26	
27	Deductible part of self-employment tax. Attach Schedule SE .	27	
28	Self-employed SEP, SIMPLE, and qualified plans .	28	
29	Self-employed health insurance deduction .	29	
30	Penalty on early withdrawal of savings	30	
31a	Alimony paid b Recipient's SSN ▶ _____	31a	
32	IRA deduction	32	
33	Student loan interest deduction	33	
34	Tuition and fees. Attach Form 8917	34	
35	Domestic production activities deduction. Attach Form 8903	35	
36	Add lines 23 through 35	36	
37	Subtract line 36 from line 22. This is your **adjusted gross income** . . . . ▶	37	

For Disclosure, Privacy Act, and Paperwork Reduction Act Notice, see separate instructions. Cat. No. 11320B Form **1040** (2014)

Tax and Credits	38	Amount from line 37 (adjusted gross income)		38	
	39a	Check if: ☐ **You** were born before January 2, 1950, ☐ Blind. **Total boxes** ☐ **Spouse** was born before January 2, 1950, ☐ Blind. ☐ checked ▶ 39a			
	b	If your spouse itemizes on a separate return or you were a dual-status alien, check here ▶ 39b ☐			

<table>
<tr><td rowspan="12">Standard Deduction for—
• People who check any box on line 39a or 39b or who can be claimed as a dependent, see instructions.
• All others:
Single or Married filing separately, $6,200
Married filing jointly or Qualifying widow(er), $12,400
Head of household, $9,100</td></tr>
<tr><td>40</td><td colspan="2">Itemized deductions (from Schedule A) or your standard deduction (see left margin) . .</td><td>40</td><td></td></tr>
<tr><td>41</td><td colspan="2">Subtract line 40 from line 38 . . . .</td><td>41</td><td></td></tr>
<tr><td>42</td><td colspan="2">Exemptions. If line 38 is $152,525 or less, multiply $3,950 by the number on line 6d. Otherwise, see instructions</td><td>42</td><td></td></tr>
<tr><td>43</td><td colspan="2">Taxable income. Subtract line 42 from line 41. If line 42 is more than line 41, enter -0- . .</td><td>43</td><td></td></tr>
<tr><td>44</td><td colspan="2">Tax (see instructions). Check if any from: a ☐ Form(s) 8814   b ☐ Form 4972 c ☐ _____</td><td>44</td><td></td></tr>
<tr><td>45</td><td colspan="2">Alternative minimum tax (see instructions). Attach Form 6251 . . . .</td><td>45</td><td></td></tr>
<tr><td>46</td><td colspan="2">Excess advance premium tax credit repayment. Attach Form 8962 . . . . . .</td><td>46</td><td></td></tr>
<tr><td>47</td><td colspan="2">Add lines 44, 45, and 46 . . . . ▶</td><td>47</td><td></td></tr>
<tr><td>48</td><td>Foreign tax credit. Attach Form 1116 if required . . .</td><td>48</td><td></td><td></td></tr>
<tr><td>49</td><td>Credit for child and dependent care expenses. Attach Form 2441</td><td>49</td><td></td><td></td></tr>
<tr><td>50</td><td>Education credits from Form 8863, line 19 . . . .</td><td>50</td><td></td><td></td></tr>
</table>

	51	Retirement savings contributions credit. Attach Form 8880	51		
	52	Child tax credit. Attach Schedule 8812, if required . . .	52		
	53	Residential energy credits. Attach Form 5695	53		
	54	Other credits from Form: **a** ☐ 3800 **b** ☐ 8801 **c** ☐ _____	54		
	55	Add lines 48 through 54. These are your **total credits**		55	
	56	Subtract line 55 from line 47. If line 55 is more than line 47, enter -0- . . . . . ▶		56	
Other Taxes	57	Self-employment tax. Attach Schedule SE		57	
	58	Unreported social security and Medicare tax from Form: **a** ☐ 4137 **b** ☐ 8919 . .		58	
	59	Additional tax on IRAs, other qualified retirement plans, etc. Attach Form 5329 if required . .		59	
	60a	Household employment taxes from Schedule H		60a	
	b	First-time homebuyer credit repayment. Attach Form 5405 if required		60b	
	61	Health care: individual responsibility (see instructions) Full-year coverage ☐		61	
	62	Taxes from: **a** ☐ Form 8959 **b** ☐ Form 8960 **c** ☐ Instructions; enter code(s) _____		62	
	63	Add lines 56 through 62. This is your **total tax** . . . . ▶		63	

<table>
<tr><td rowspan="11">Payments

If you have a qualifying child, attach Schedule EIC.</td><td>64</td><td>Federal income tax withheld from Forms W-2 and 1099 . .</td><td>64</td><td></td><td></td></tr>
<tr><td>65</td><td>2014 estimated tax payments and amount applied from 2013 return</td><td>65</td><td></td><td></td></tr>
<tr><td>66a</td><td>Earned income credit (EIC) . . . .</td><td>66a</td><td></td><td></td></tr>
<tr><td>b</td><td>Nontaxable combat pay election   66b</td><td></td><td></td><td></td></tr>
<tr><td>67</td><td>Additional child tax credit. Attach Schedule 8812 . . .</td><td>67</td><td></td><td></td></tr>
<tr><td>68</td><td>American opportunity credit from Form 8863, line 8 . . .</td><td>68</td><td></td><td></td></tr>
<tr><td>69</td><td>Net premium tax credit. Attach Form 8962 . . . . .</td><td>69</td><td></td><td></td></tr>
<tr><td>70</td><td>Amount paid with request for extension to file . . . .</td><td>70</td><td></td><td></td></tr>
<tr><td>71</td><td>Excess social security and tier 1 RRTA tax withheld . . .</td><td>71</td><td></td><td></td></tr>
<tr><td>72</td><td>Credit for federal tax on fuels. Attach Form 4136 . . .</td><td>72</td><td></td><td></td></tr>
<tr><td>73</td><td>Credits from Form: a ☐ 2439 b ☐ Reserved c ☐ Reserved d ☐</td><td>73</td><td></td><td></td></tr>
</table>

	74	Add lines 64, 65, 66a, and 67 through 73. These are your **total payments** . . . . . ▶	74	
Refund Direct deposit? See instructions.	75	If line 74 is more than line 63, subtract line 63 from line 74. This is the amount you **overpaid**	75	
	76a	Amount of line 75 you want **refunded to you**. If Form 8888 is attached, check here . ▶ ☐	76a	
	▶ b	Routing number ⬚⬚⬚⬚⬚⬚⬚⬚⬚ ▶ c Type: ☐ Checking ☐ Savings		
	▶ d	Account number ⬚⬚⬚⬚⬚⬚⬚⬚⬚⬚⬚⬚⬚⬚⬚⬚⬚		
	77	Amount of line 75 you want **applied to your 2015 estimated tax** ▶ 77		
Amount You Owe	78	**Amount you owe.** Subtract line 74 from line 63. For details on how to pay, see instructions ▶	78	
	79	Estimated tax penalty (see instructions) 79		

Third Party Designee	Do you want to allow another person to discuss this return with the IRS (see instructions)? ☐ **Yes.** Complete below. ☐ **No**
	Designee's name ▶ _____ Phone no. ▶ _____ Personal identification number (PIN) ▶ ⬚⬚⬚⬚⬚

Sign Here Joint return? See instructions. Keep a copy for your records.	Under penalties of perjury, I declare that I have examined this return and accompanying schedules and statements, and to the best of my knowledge and belief, they are true, correct, and complete. Declaration of preparer (other than taxpayer) is based on all information of which preparer has any knowledge.		
	Your signature	Date	Your occupation Daytime phone number
	Spouse's signature. If a joint return, **both** must sign.	Date	Spouse's occupation If the IRS sent you an Identity Protection PIN, enter it here (see inst.) ⬚⬚⬚⬚⬚⬚

Paid Preparer Use Only	Print/Type preparer's name	Preparer's signature	Date	Check ☐ if self-employed PTIN
	Firm's name ▶			Firm's EIN ▶
	Firm's address ▶			Phone no.

SCHEDULE A (Form 1040)

Department of the Treasury
Internal Revenue Service (99)

Itemized Deductions

▶ Information about Schedule A and its separate instructions is at *www.irs.gov/schedulea*.
▶ Attach to Form 1040.

OMB No. 1545-0074

2014

Attachment Sequence No. **07**

Name(s) shown on Form 1040

Your social security number

Medical and Dental Expenses	**Caution.** Do not include expenses reimbursed or paid by others.	
	1 Medical and dental expenses (see instructions) **1**	
	2 Enter amount from Form 1040, line 38 **2**	
	3 Multiply line 2 by 10% (.10). But if either you or your spouse was born before January 2, 1950, multiply line 2 by 7.5% (.075) instead **3**	
	4 Subtract line 3 from line 1. If line 3 is more than line 1, enter -0-	**4**
Taxes You Paid	**5** State and local (check only one box): 　**a** ☐ Income taxes, **or** 　**b** ☐ General sales taxes **5**	
	6 Real estate taxes (see instructions) **6**	
	7 Personal property taxes **7**	
	8 Other taxes. List type and amount ▶ _____ _____ **8**	
	9 Add lines 5 through 8	**9**
Interest You Paid **Note.** Your mortgage interest deduction may be limited (see instructions).	**10** Home mortgage interest and points reported to you on Form 1098 **10**	
	11 Home mortgage interest not reported to you on Form 1098. If paid to the person from whom you bought the home, see instructions and show that person's name, identifying no., and address ▶ _____ _____ **11**	
	12 Points not reported to you on Form 1098. See instructions for special rules **12**	
	13 Mortgage insurance premiums (see instructions) **13**	
	14 Investment interest. Attach Form 4952 if required. (See instructions.) **14**	
	15 Add lines 10 through 14	**15**
Gifts to Charity If you made a gift and got a benefit for it, see instructions.	**16** Gifts by cash or check. If you made any gift of $250 or more, see instructions. **16**	
	17 Other than by cash or check. If any gift of $250 or more, see instructions. You **must** attach Form 8283 if over $500 . . . **17**	
	18 Carryover from prior year **18**	
	19 Add lines 16 through 18	**19**
Casualty and Theft Losses	**20** Casualty or theft loss(es). Attach Form 4684. (See instructions.)	**20**
Job Expenses and Certain Miscellaneous Deductions	**21** Unreimbursed employee expenses—job travel, union dues, job education, etc. Attach Form 2106 or 2106-EZ if required. (See instructions.) ▶ _____ **21**	
	22 Tax preparation fees **22**	
	23 Other expenses—investment, safe deposit box, etc. List type and amount ▶ _____ **23**	
	24 Add lines 21 through 23 . . . . **24**	
	25 Enter amount from Form 1040, line 38 **25**	
	26 Multiply line 25 by 2% (.02) **26**	
	27 Subtract line 26 from line 24. If line 26 is more than line 24, enter -0-	**27**
Other Miscellaneous Deductions	**28** Other—from list in instructions. List type and amount ▶ _____ _____	**28**
Total Itemized Deductions	**29** Is Form 1040, line 38, over $152,525? 　☐ **No.** Your deduction is not limited. Add the amounts in the far right column for lines 4 through 28. Also, enter this amount on Form 1040, line 40. 　☐ **Yes.** Your deduction may be limited. See the Itemized Deductions Worksheet in the instructions to figure the amount to enter.	**29**
	30 If you elect to itemize deductions even though they are less than your standard deduction, check here . . . . ▶ ☐	

For Paperwork Reduction Act Notice, see Form 1040 instructions.　　Cat. No. 17145C　　Schedule A (Form 1040) 2014

SCHEDULE B
(Form 1040A or 1040)

Department of the Treasury
Internal Revenue Service (99)

Interest and Ordinary Dividends

▶ Attach to Form 1040A or 1040.
▶ Information about Schedule B and its instructions is at *www.irs.gov/scheduleb*.

OMB No. 1545-0074

2014

Attachment
Sequence No. **08**

Name(s) shown on return

Your social security number

Part I **Interest** (See instructions on back and the instructions for Form 1040A, or Form 1040, line 8a.) **Note.** If you received a Form 1099-INT, Form 1099-OID, or substitute statement from a brokerage firm, list the firm's name as the payer and enter the total interest shown on that form.	**1**	List name of payer. If any interest is from a seller-financed mortgage and the buyer used the property as a personal residence, see instructions on back and list this interest first. Also, show that buyer's social security number and address ▶		**Amount**
			1	
	2	Add the amounts on line 1	**2**	
	3	Excludable interest on series EE and I U.S. savings bonds issued after 1989. Attach Form 8815	**3**	
	4	Subtract line 3 from line 2. Enter the result here and on Form 1040A, or Form 1040, line 8a . . . . ▶	**4**	

Note. If line 4 is over $1,500, you must complete Part III.

Part II **Ordinary Dividends** (See instructions on back and the instructions for Form 1040A, or Form 1040, line 9a.) **Note.** If you received a Form 1099-DIV or substitute statement from a brokerage firm, list the firm's name as the payer and enter the ordinary dividends shown on that form.	**5**	List name of payer ▶		**Amount**
			5	
	6	Add the amounts on line 5. Enter the total here and on Form 1040A, or Form 1040, line 9a . . . . ▶	**6**	

Note. If line 6 is over $1,500, you must complete Part III.

Part III **Foreign Accounts and Trusts** (See instructions on back.)	You must complete this part if you **(a)** had over $1,500 of taxable interest or ordinary dividends; **(b)** had a foreign account; or **(c)** received a distribution from, or were a grantor of, or a transferor to, a foreign trust.		**Yes**	**No**
	7a	At any time during 2014, did you have a financial interest in or signature authority over a financial account (such as a bank account, securities account, or brokerage account) located in a foreign country? See instructions		
		If "Yes," are you required to file FinCEN Form 114, Report of Foreign Bank and Financial Accounts (FBAR), to report that financial interest or signature authority? See FinCEN Form 114 and its instructions for filing requirements and exceptions to those requirements		
	b	If you are required to file FinCEN Form 114, enter the name of the foreign country where the financial account is located ▶		
	8	During 2014, did you receive a distribution from, or were you the grantor of, or transferor to, a foreign trust? If "Yes," you may have to file Form 3520. See instructions on back		

For Paperwork Reduction Act Notice, see your tax return instructions.   Cat. No. 17146N   Schedule B (Form 1040A or 1040) 2014

General Instructions

Section references are to the Internal Revenue Code unless otherwise noted.

Future Developments

For the latest information about developments related to Schedule B (Form 1040A or 1040) and its instructions, such as legislation enacted after they were published, go to *www.irs.gov/scheduleb*.

Purpose of Form

Use Schedule B if any of the following applies.

• You had over $1,500 of taxable interest or ordinary dividends.

• You received interest from a seller-financed mortgage and the buyer used the property as a personal residence.

• You have accrued interest from a bond.

• You are reporting original issue discount (OID) in an amount less than the amount shown on Form 1099-OID.

• You are reducing your interest income on a bond by the amount of amortizable bond premium.

• You are claiming the exclusion of interest from series EE or I U.S. savings bonds issued after 1989.

• You received interest or ordinary dividends as a nominee.

• You had a financial interest in, or signature authority over, a financial account in a foreign country or you received a distribution from, or were a grantor of, or transferor to, a foreign trust. Part III of the schedule has questions about foreign accounts and trusts.

Specific Instructions

 *You can list more than one payer on each entry space for lines 1 and 5, but be sure to clearly show the amount paid next to the payer's name. Add the separate amounts paid by the payers listed on an entry space and enter the total in the "Amount" column. If you still need more space, attach separate statements that are the same size as the printed schedule. Use the same format as lines 1 and 5, but show your totals on Schedule B. Be sure to put your name and social security number (SSN) on the statements and attach them at the end of your return.*

Part I. Interest

Line 1. Report on line 1 all of your taxable interest. Taxable interest should be shown on your Forms 1099-INT, Forms 1099-OID, or substitute statements. Include interest from series EE, H, HH, and I U.S. savings bonds. List each payer's name and show the amount. Do not report on this line any tax-exempt interest from box 8 or box 9 of Form 1099-INT. Instead, report the amount from box 8 on line 8b of Form 1040A or 1040. If an amount is shown in box 9 of Form 1099-INT, you generally must report it on line 12 of Form 6251. See the Instructions for Form 6251 for more details.

Seller-financed mortgages. If you sold your home or other property and the buyer used the property as a personal residence, list first any interest the buyer paid you on a mortgage or other form of seller financing. Be sure to show the buyer's name, address, and SSN. You must also let the buyer know your SSN. If you do not show the buyer's name, address, and SSN, or let the buyer know your SSN, you may have to pay a $50 penalty.

Nominees. If you received a Form 1099-INT that includes interest you received as a nominee (that is, in your name, but the interest actually belongs to someone else), report the total on line 1. Do this even if you later distributed some or all of this income to others. Under your last entry on line 1, put a subtotal of all interest listed on line 1. Below this subtotal, enter "Nominee Distribution" and show the total interest you received as a nominee. Subtract this amount from the subtotal and enter the result on line 2.

 *If you received interest as a nominee, you must give the actual owner a Form 1099-INT unless the owner is your spouse. You must also file a Form 1096 and a Form 1099-INT with the IRS. For more details, see the* General Instructions for Certain Information Returns *and the* Instructions for Forms 1099-INT and 1099-OID.

Accrued interest. When you buy bonds between interest payment dates and pay accrued interest to the seller, this interest is taxable to the seller. If you received a Form 1099 for interest as a purchaser of a bond with accrued interest, follow the rules earlier under *Nominees* to see how to report the accrued interest. But identify the amount to be subtracted as "Accrued Interest."

Original issue discount (OID). If you are reporting OID in an amount less than the amount shown on Form 1099-OID, follow the rules earlier under *Nominees* to see how to report the OID. But identify the amount to be subtracted as "OID Adjustment."

Amortizable bond premium. If you are reducing your interest income on a bond by the amount of amortizable bond premium, follow the rules earlier under *Nominees* to see how to report the interest. But identify the amount to be subtracted as "ABP Adjustment."

Line 3. If, during 2014, you cashed series EE or I U.S. savings bonds issued after 1989 and you paid qualified higher education expenses for yourself, your spouse, or your dependents, you may be able to exclude part or all of the interest on those bonds. See Form 8815 for details.

Part II. Ordinary Dividends

 *You may have to file Form 5471 if, in 2014, you were an officer or director of a foreign corporation. You may also have to file Form 5471 if, in 2014, you owned 10% or more of the total (a) value of a foreign corporation's stock, or (b) combined voting power of all classes of a foreign corporation's stock with voting rights. For details, see* Form 5471 *and its instructions.*

Line 5. Report on line 5 all of your ordinary dividends. This amount should be shown in box 1a of your Forms 1099-DIV or substitute statements. List each payer's name and show the amount.

Nominees. If you received a Form 1099-DIV that includes ordinary dividends you received as a nominee (that is, in your name, but the ordinary dividends actually belong to someone else), report the total on line 5. Do this even if you later distributed some or all of this income to others. Under your last entry on line 5, put a subtotal of all ordinary dividends listed on line 5. Below this subtotal, enter "Nominee Distribution" and show the total ordinary dividends you received as a nominee. Subtract this amount from the subtotal and enter the result on line 6.

 *If you received dividends as a nominee, you must give the actual owner a Form 1099-DIV unless the owner is your spouse. You must also file a Form 1096 and a Form 1099-DIV with the IRS. For more details, see the* General Instructions for Certain Information Returns *and the* Instructions for Form 1099-DIV.

Part III. Foreign Accounts and Trusts

 *Regardless of whether you are required to file FinCEN Form 114 (FBAR), you may be required to file Form 8938, Statement of Specified Foreign Financial Assets, with your income tax return. Failure to file Form 8938 may result in penalties and extension of the statute of limitations. See www.irs.gov/form8938 for more information.*

Line 7a–Question 1. Check the "Yes" box if at any time during 2014 you had a financial interest in or signature authority over a financial account located in a foreign country. See the definitions that follow. Check the "Yes" box even if you are not required to file FinCEN Form 114, Report of Foreign Bank and Financial Accounts (FBAR).

Financial account. A financial account includes, but is not limited to, a securities, brokerage, savings, demand, checking, deposit, time deposit, or other account maintained with a financial institution (or other person performing the services of a financial institution). A financial account also includes a commodity futures or options account, an insurance policy with a cash value (such as a whole life insurance policy), an annuity policy with a cash value, and shares in a mutual fund or similar pooled fund (that is, a fund that is available to the general public with a regular net asset value determination and regular redemptions).

Financial account located in a foreign country. A financial account is located in a foreign country if the account is physically located outside of the United States. For example, an account maintained with a branch of a United States bank that is physically located outside of the United States is a foreign financial account. An account maintained with a branch of a foreign bank that is physically located in the United States is not a foreign financial account.

Signature authority. Signature authority is the authority of an individual (alone or in conjunction with another individual) to control the disposition of assets held in a foreign financial account by direct communication (whether in writing or otherwise) to the bank or other financial institution that maintains the financial account. See the FinCEN Form 114 instructions for exceptions. Do not consider the exceptions relating to signature authority in answering Question 1 on line 7a.

Other definitions. For definitions of "financial interest," "United States," and other relevant terms, see the instructions for FinCEN Form 114.

Line 7a–Question 2. See FinCEN Form 114 and its instructions to determine whether you must file the form. Check the "Yes" box if you are required to file the form; check the "No" box if you are not required to file the form.

If you checked the "Yes" box to Question 2 on line 7a, FinCEN Form 114 must be electronically filed with the Financial Crimes Enforcement Network (FinCEN) at the following website: *http://bsaefiling. fincen.treas.gov/main.html*. Do not attach FinCEN Form 114 to your tax return. To be considered timely, FinCEN Form 114 **must be received** by June 30, 2015.

 If you are required to file FinCEN Form 114 but do not properly do so, you may have to pay a civil penalty up to $10,000. A person who willfully fails to report an account or provide account identifying information may be subject to a civil penalty equal to the greater of $100,000 or 50 percent of the balance in the account at the time of the violation. Willful violations may also be subject to criminal penalties.

Line 7b. If you are required to file FinCEN Form 114, enter the name of the foreign country or countries in the space provided on line 7b. Attach a separate statement if you need more space.

Line 8. If you received a distribution from a foreign trust, you must provide additional information. For this purpose, a loan of cash or marketable securities generally is considered to be a distribution. See Form 3520 for details.

If you were the grantor of, or transferor to, a foreign trust that existed during 2014, you may have to file Form 3520.

Do not attach Form 3520 to Form 1040. Instead, file it at the address shown in its instructions.

If you were treated as the owner of a foreign trust under the grantor trust rules, you are also responsible for ensuring that the foreign trust files Form 3520-A. Form 3520-A is due on March 16, 2015, for a calendar year trust. See the instructions for Form 3520-A for more details.

SCHEDULE C (Form 1040)

Department of the Treasury
Internal Revenue Service (99)

Profit or Loss From Business
(Sole Proprietorship)

▶ Information about Schedule C and its separate instructions is at *www.irs.gov/schedulec*.
▶ Attach to Form 1040, 1040NR, or 1041; partnerships generally must file Form 1065.

OMB No. 1545-0074

2014

Attachment
Sequence No. 09

Name of proprietor

Social security number (SSN)

| A | Principal business or profession, including product or service (see instructions) | | B Enter code from instructions ▶ | | | |

| C | Business name. If no separate business name, leave blank. | | D Employer ID number (EIN), (see instr.) | | | |

E Business address (including suite or room no.) ▶
City, town or post office, state, and ZIP code

F Accounting method: **(1)** ☐ Cash **(2)** ☐ Accrual **(3)** ☐ Other (specify) ▶

G Did you "materially participate" in the operation of this business during 2014? If "No," see instructions for limit on losses . ☐ Yes ☐ No

H If you started or acquired this business during 2014, check here . . . . ▶ ☐

I Did you make any payments in 2014 that would require you to file Form(s) 1099? (see instructions) . . . . ☐ Yes ☐ No

J If "Yes," did you or will you file required Forms 1099? . . . . ☐ Yes ☐ No

Part I Income

1	Gross receipts or sales. See instructions for line 1 and check the box if this income was reported to you on Form W-2 and the "Statutory employee" box on that form was checked . . . . ▶ ☐	1	
2	Returns and allowances	2	
3	Subtract line 2 from line 1	3	
4	Cost of goods sold (from line 42)	4	
5	**Gross profit.** Subtract line 4 from line 3	5	
6	Other income, including federal and state gasoline or fuel tax credit or refund (see instructions) . . .	6	
7	**Gross income.** Add lines 5 and 6 . . . . ▶	7	

Part II Expenses. Enter expenses for business use of your home **only** on line 30.

8	Advertising	8		18	Office expense (see instructions)	18	
9	Car and truck expenses (see instructions)	9		19	Pension and profit-sharing plans .	19	
				20	Rent or lease (see instructions):		
10	Commissions and fees .	10		a	Vehicles, machinery, and equipment	20a	
11	Contract labor (see instructions)	11		b	Other business property . . .	20b	
12	Depletion	12		21	Repairs and maintenance . . .	21	
13	Depreciation and section 179 expense deduction (not included in Part III) (see instructions)	13		22	Supplies (not included in Part III) .	22	
				23	Taxes and licenses	23	
				24	Travel, meals, and entertainment:		
14	Employee benefit programs (other than on line 19) . .	14		a	Travel	24a	
15	Insurance (other than health)	15		b	Deductible meals and entertainment (see instructions) .	24b	
16	Interest:			25	Utilities	25	
a	Mortgage (paid to banks, etc.)	16a		26	Wages (less employment credits) .	26	
b	Other	16b		27a	Other expenses (from line 48) . .	27a	
17	Legal and professional services	17		b	**Reserved for future use** . . .	27b	

28	**Total expenses** before expenses for business use of home. Add lines 8 through 27a . . . . . . ▶	28	
29	Tentative profit or (loss). Subtract line 28 from line 7	29	
30	Expenses for business use of your home. Do not report these expenses elsewhere. Attach Form 8829 unless using the simplified method (see instructions). **Simplified method filers only:** enter the total square footage of: (a) your home: _____ and (b) the part of your home used for business: _____ . Use the Simplified Method Worksheet in the instructions to figure the amount to enter on line 30	30	
31	**Net profit or (loss).** Subtract line 30 from line 29. • If a profit, enter on both **Form 1040, line 12** (or **Form 1040NR, line 13**) and on **Schedule SE, line 2.** (If you checked the box on line 1, see instructions). Estates and trusts, enter on **Form 1041, line 3.** • If a loss, you **must** go to line 32.	31	
32	If you have a loss, check the box that describes your investment in this activity (see instructions). • If you checked 32a, enter the loss on both **Form 1040, line 12,** (or **Form 1040NR, line 13**) and on **Schedule SE, line 2.** (If you checked the box on line 1, see the line 31 instructions). Estates and trusts, enter on **Form 1041, line 3.** • If you checked 32b, you **must** attach **Form 6198.** Your loss may be limited.	32a ☐ All investment is at risk. 32b ☐ Some investment is not at risk.	

For Paperwork Reduction Act Notice, see the separate instructions.   Cat. No. 11334P   Schedule C (Form 1040) 2014

| Part III | Cost of Goods Sold | (see instructions) |

33 Method(s) used to
value closing inventory: **a** ☐ Cost **b** ☐ Lower of cost or market **c** ☐ Other (attach explanation)

34 Was there any change in determining quantities, costs, or valuations between opening and closing inventory?
If "Yes," attach explanation . . . . ☐ **Yes** ☐ **No**

35 Inventory at beginning of year. If different from last year's closing inventory, attach explanation . . .	**35**	
36 Purchases less cost of items withdrawn for personal use	**36**	
37 Cost of labor. Do not include any amounts paid to yourself	**37**	
38 Materials and supplies	**38**	
39 Other costs	**39**	
40 Add lines 35 through 39	**40**	
41 Inventory at end of year	**41**	
42 **Cost of goods sold.** Subtract line 41 from line 40. Enter the result here and on line 4	**42**	

| Part IV | Information on Your Vehicle. Complete this part **only** if you are claiming car or truck expenses on line 9 and are not required to file Form 4562 for this business. See the instructions for line 13 to find out if you must file Form 4562. |

43 When did you place your vehicle in service for business purposes? (month, day, year) ▶ _____ / _____ / _____

44 Of the total number of miles you drove your vehicle during 2014, enter the number of miles you used your vehicle for:

a Business _____ **b** Commuting (see instructions) _____ **c** Other _____

45 Was your vehicle available for personal use during off-duty hours? . . . . ☐ **Yes** ☐ **No**

46 Do you (or your spouse) have another vehicle available for personal use? . . . . ☐ **Yes** ☐ **No**

47a Do you have evidence to support your deduction? . . . . ☐ **Yes** ☐ **No**

b If "Yes," is the evidence written? . . . . ☐ **Yes** ☐ **No**

| Part V | Other Expenses. List below business expenses not included on lines 8–26 or line 30. |

--	
--	
--	
--	
--	
--	
--	
--	

48 **Total other expenses.** Enter here and on line 27a	**48**	

SCHEDULE C-EZ
(Form 1040)

Department of the Treasury
Internal Revenue Service (99)

Net Profit From Business
(Sole Proprietorship)

▶ Partnerships, joint ventures, etc., generally must file Form 1065 or 1065-B.
▶ Attach to Form 1040, 1040NR, or 1041. ▶ See instructions on page 2.

OMB No. 1545-0074

2014

Attachment
Sequence No. **09A**

Name of proprietor

Social security number (SSN)

Part I General Information

You May Use Schedule C-EZ Instead of Schedule C Only If You:

- Had business expenses of $5,000 or less.
- Use the cash method of accounting.
- Did not have an inventory at any time during the year.
- Did not have a net loss from your business.
- Had only one business as either a sole proprietor, qualified joint venture, or statutory employee.

And You:

- Had no employees during the year.
- Are not required to file **Form 4562**, Depreciation and Amortization, for this business. See the instructions for Schedule C, line 13, to find out if you must file.
- Do not deduct expenses for business use of your home.
- Do not have prior year unallowed passive activity losses from this business.

A Principal business or profession, including product or service

B Enter business code (see page 2)
▶

C Business name. If no separate business name, leave blank.

D Enter your EIN (see page 2)

E Business address (including suite or room no.). Address not required if same as on page 1 of your tax return.

City, town or post office, state, and ZIP code

F Did you make any payments in 2014 that would require you to file Form(s) 1099? (see the Schedule C Instructions) . . . . ☐ Yes ☐ No

G If "Yes," did you or will you file required Forms 1099? . . . . ☐ Yes ☐ No

---

Part II Figure Your Net Profit

1 **Gross receipts. Caution.** If this income was reported to you on Form W-2 and the "Statutory employee" box on that form was checked, see *Statutory employees* in the instructions for Schedule C, line 1, and check here . . . . ▶ ☐ | **1** |

2 **Total expenses** (see page 2). If more than $5,000, you **must** use Schedule C . . . . | **2** |

3 **Net profit.** Subtract line 2 from line 1. If less than zero, you **must** use Schedule C. Enter on both **Form 1040, line 12,** and **Schedule SE, line 2,** or on **Form 1040NR, line 13** and **Schedule SE, line 2** (see instructions). (Statutory employees **do not** report this amount on Schedule SE, line 2.) Estates and trusts, enter on **Form 1041, line 3** . . . . | **3** |

Part III Information on Your Vehicle. Complete this part **only** if you are claiming car or truck expenses on line 2.

4 When did you place your vehicle in service for business purposes? (month, day, year) ▶ _____ .

5 Of the total number of miles you drove your vehicle during 2014, enter the number of miles you used your vehicle for:

a Business _____ b Commuting (see page 2) _____ c Other _____

6 Was your vehicle available for personal use during off-duty hours? . . . . ☐ Yes ☐ No

7 Do you (or your spouse) have another vehicle available for personal use? . . . . ☐ Yes ☐ No

8a Do you have evidence to support your deduction? . . . . ☐ Yes ☐ No

b If "Yes," is the evidence written? . . . . ☐ Yes ☐ No

For Paperwork Reduction Act Notice, see the separate instructions for Schedule C (Form 1040). Cat. No. 14374D Schedule C-EZ (Form 1040) 2014

Instructions

Future developments. For the latest information about developments related to Schedule C-EZ (Form 1040) and its instructions, such as legislation enacted after they were published, go to *www.irs.gov/schedulecez.*

 Before you begin, see General Instructions *in the 2014 Instructions for Schedule C.*

You can use Schedule C-EZ instead of Schedule C if you operated a business or practiced a profession as a sole proprietorship or qualified joint venture, or you were a statutory employee and you have met all the requirements listed in Schedule C-EZ, Part I.

For more information on electing to be taxed as a qualified joint venture (including the possible social security benefits of this election), see *Qualified Joint Venture* in the instructions for Schedule C. You can also go to IRS.gov and enter "qualified joint venture" in the search box.

Line A

Describe the business or professional activity that provided your principal source of income reported on line 1. Give the general field or activity and the type of product or service.

Line B

Enter the six-digit code that identifies your principal business or professional activity. See the Instructions for Schedule C for the list of codes.

Line D

Enter on line D the employer identification number (EIN) that was issued to you and in your name as a sole proprietor. If you are filing Form 1041, enter the EIN issued to the estate or trust. Do not enter your SSN. Do not enter another taxpayer's EIN (for example, from any Forms 1099-MISC that you received). If you are the sole owner of a limited liability company (LLC), **do not** enter on line D the EIN issued to the LLC, if any. **If you do not have an EIN, leave line D blank.**

You need an EIN only if you have a qualified retirement plan or are required to file an employment, excise, alcohol, tobacco, or firearms tax return, are a payer of gambling winnings, or are filing Form 1041 for an estate or trust. If you need an EIN, see the Instructions for Form SS-4.

Line E

Enter your business address. Show a street address instead of a box number. Include the suite or room number, if any.

Line F

See the instructions for line I in the Instructions for Schedule C to help determine if you are required to file any Forms 1099.

Line 1

Enter gross receipts from your trade or business. Include amounts you received in your trade or business that were properly shown on Form 1099-MISC. If the total amounts that were reported in box 7 of Forms 1099-MISC are more than the total you are reporting on line 1, attach a statement explaining the difference. You must show all items of taxable income actually or constructively received during the year (in cash, property, or services). Income is constructively received when it is credited to your account or set aside for you to use. Do not offset this amount by any losses.

Line 2

Enter the total amount of all deductible business expenses you actually paid during the year. Examples of these expenses include advertising, car and truck expenses, commissions and fees, insurance, interest, legal and professional services, office expenses, rent or lease expenses, repairs and maintenance, supplies, taxes, travel, the allowable percentage of business meals and entertainment, and utilities (including telephone). For details, see the instructions for Schedule C, Parts II and V. You can use the optional worksheet below to record your expenses. Enter on lines **b** through **f** the type and amount of expenses not included on line **a.**

If you claim car or truck expenses, be sure to complete Schedule C-EZ, Part III.

Line 3

Nonresident aliens using Form 1040NR should also enter the total on Schedule SE, line 2, if you are covered under the U.S. social security system due to an international social security agreement currently in effect. See the Instructions for Schedule SE for information on international social security agreements.

Line 5b

Generally, commuting is travel between your home and a work location. If you converted your vehicle during the year from personal to business use (or vice versa), enter your commuting miles only for the period you drove your vehicle for business. For information on certain travel that is considered a business expense rather than commuting, see the Instructions for Form 2106.

Optional Worksheet for Line 2 (keep a copy for your records)

a	Deductible meals and entertainment (see the instructions for Schedule C, line 24b)	**a**	
b	_____	**b**	
c	_____	**c**	
d	_____	**d**	
e	_____	**e**	
f	_____	**f**	
g	**Total.** Add lines **a** through **f.** Enter here and on line 2	**g**	

SCHEDULE D (Form 1040)	Capital Gains and Losses	OMB No. 1545-0074

SCHEDULE D (Form 1040)

Department of the Treasury
Internal Revenue Service (99)

Capital Gains and Losses

▶ Attach to Form 1040 or Form 1040NR.
▶ Information about Schedule D and its separate instructions is at *www.irs.gov/scheduled*.
▶ Use Form 8949 to list your transactions for lines 1b, 2, 3, 8b, 9, and 10.

OMB No. 1545-0074

2014

Attachment
Sequence No. **12**

Name(s) shown on return

Your social security number

Part I   Short-Term Capital Gains and Losses—Assets Held One Year or Less

See instructions for how to figure the amounts to enter on the lines below.

This form may be easier to complete if you round off cents to whole dollars.

	(d) Proceeds (sales price)	**(e)** Cost (or other basis)	**(g)** Adjustments to gain or loss from Form(s) 8949, Part I, line 2, column (g)	**(h) Gain or (loss)** Subtract column (e) from column (d) and combine the result with column (g)
1a Totals for all short-term transactions reported on Form 1099-B for which basis was reported to the IRS and for which you have no adjustments (see instructions). However, if you choose to report all these transactions on Form 8949, leave this line blank and go to line 1b .				
1b Totals for all transactions reported on Form(s) 8949 with **Box A** checked				
2 Totals for all transactions reported on Form(s) 8949 with **Box B** checked				
3 Totals for all transactions reported on Form(s) 8949 with **Box C** checked				

4 Short-term gain from Form 6252 and short-term gain or (loss) from Forms 4684, 6781, and 8824 .	**4**	
5 Net short-term gain or (loss) from partnerships, S corporations, estates, and trusts from Schedule(s) K-1	**5**	
6 Short-term capital loss carryover. Enter the amount, if any, from line 8 of your **Capital Loss Carryover Worksheet** in the instructions	**6** (	)
7 **Net short-term capital gain or (loss).** Combine lines 1a through 6 in column (h). If you have any long-term capital gains or losses, go to Part II below. Otherwise, go to Part III on the back	**7**	

Part II   Long-Term Capital Gains and Losses—Assets Held More Than One Year

See instructions for how to figure the amounts to enter on the lines below.

This form may be easier to complete if you round off cents to whole dollars.

	(d) Proceeds (sales price)	**(e)** Cost (or other basis)	**(g)** Adjustments to gain or loss from Form(s) 8949, Part II, line 2, column (g)	**(h) Gain or (loss)** Subtract column (e) from column (d) and combine the result with column (g)
8a Totals for all long-term transactions reported on Form 1099-B for which basis was reported to the IRS and for which you have no adjustments (see instructions). However, if you choose to report all these transactions on Form 8949, leave this line blank and go to line 8b .				
8b Totals for all transactions reported on Form(s) 8949 with **Box D** checked				
9 Totals for all transactions reported on Form(s) 8949 with **Box E** checked				
10 Totals for all transactions reported on Form(s) 8949 with **Box F** checked.				

11 Gain from Form 4797, Part I; long-term gain from Forms 2439 and 6252; and long-term gain or (loss) from Forms 4684, 6781, and 8824	**11**	
12 Net long-term gain or (loss) from partnerships, S corporations, estates, and trusts from Schedule(s) K-1	**12**	
13 Capital gain distributions. See the instructions	**13**	
14 Long-term capital loss carryover. Enter the amount, if any, from line 13 of your **Capital Loss Carryover Worksheet** in the instructions	**14** (	)
15 **Net long-term capital gain or (loss).** Combine lines 8a through 14 in column (h). Then go to Part III on the back	**15**	

For Paperwork Reduction Act Notice, see your tax return instructions.   Cat. No. 11338H   Schedule D (Form 1040) 2014

Part III **Summary**

16 Combine lines 7 and 15 and enter the result **16**

    • If line 16 is a **gain,** enter the amount from line 16 on Form 1040, line 13, or Form 1040NR, line 14. Then go to line 17 below.

    • If line 16 is a **loss,** skip lines 17 through 20 below. Then go to line 21. Also be sure to complete line 22.

    • If line 16 is **zero,** skip lines 17 through 21 below and enter -0- on Form 1040, line 13, or Form 1040NR, line 14. Then go to line 22.

17 Are lines 15 and 16 **both** gains?
    ☐ **Yes.** Go to line 18.
    ☐ **No.** Skip lines 18 through 21, and go to line 22.

18 Enter the amount, if any, from line 7 of the **28% Rate Gain Worksheet** in the instructions . . ▶ **18**

19 Enter the amount, if any, from line 18 of the **Unrecaptured Section 1250 Gain Worksheet** in the instructions . . . . ▶ **19**

20 Are lines 18 and 19 **both** zero or blank?
    ☐ **Yes.** Complete the **Qualified Dividends and Capital Gain Tax Worksheet** in the instructions for Form 1040, line 44 (or in the instructions for Form 1040NR, line 42). **Do not** complete lines 21 and 22 below.

    ☐ **No.** Complete the **Schedule D Tax Worksheet** in the instructions. **Do not** complete lines 21 and 22 below.

21 If line 16 is a loss, enter here and on Form 1040, line 13, or Form 1040NR, line 14, the **smaller** of:

    • The loss on line 16 or
    • ($3,000), or if married filing separately, ($1,500) }   . . . . **21** (   )

    Note. When figuring which amount is smaller, treat both amounts as positive numbers.

22 Do you have qualified dividends on Form 1040, line 9b, or Form 1040NR, line 10b?

    ☐ **Yes.** Complete the **Qualified Dividends and Capital Gain Tax Worksheet** in the instructions for Form 1040, line 44 (or in the instructions for Form 1040NR, line 42).

    ☐ **No.** Complete the rest of Form 1040 or Form 1040NR.

SCHEDULE E (Form 1040)

Department of the Treasury
Internal Revenue Service (99)

Supplemental Income and Loss

(From rental real estate, royalties, partnerships, S corporations, estates, trusts, REMICs, etc.)

▶ Attach to Form 1040, 1040NR, or Form 1041.
▶ Information about Schedule E and its separate instructions is at *www.irs.gov/schedulee.*

OMB No. 1545-0074

2014

Attachment Sequence No. **13**

Name(s) shown on return

Your social security number

Part I — **Income or Loss From Rental Real Estate and Royalties** Note. If you are in the business of renting personal property, use **Schedule C or C-EZ** (see instructions). If you are an individual, report farm rental income or loss from **Form 4835** on page 2, line 40.

A Did you make any payments in 2014 that would require you to file Form(s) 1099? (see instructions) ☐ Yes ☐ No

B If "Yes," did you or will you file required Forms 1099? ☐ Yes ☐ No

1a Physical address of each property (street, city, state, ZIP code)

A

B

C

1b	Type of Property (from list below)	2	For each rental real estate property listed above, report the number of fair rental and personal use days. Check the **QJV** box only if you meet the requirements to file as a qualified joint venture. See instructions.		Fair Rental Days	Personal Use Days	QJV
A				A			☐
B				B			☐
C				C			☐

Type of Property:

1 Single Family Residence   3 Vacation/Short-Term Rental   5 Land   7 Self-Rental

2 Multi-Family Residence   4 Commercial   6 Royalties   8 Other (describe)

Income:	Properties:		A	B	C
3	Rents received	3			
4	Royalties received	4			
Expenses:					
5	Advertising	5			
6	Auto and travel (see instructions)	6			
7	Cleaning and maintenance	7			
8	Commissions	8			
9	Insurance	9			
10	Legal and other professional fees	10			
11	Management fees	11			
12	Mortgage interest paid to banks, etc. (see instructions)	12			
13	Other interest	13			
14	Repairs	14			
15	Supplies	15			
16	Taxes	16			
17	Utilities	17			
18	Depreciation expense or depletion	18			
19	Other (list) ▶ _____	19			
20	Total expenses. Add lines 5 through 19	20			
21	Subtract line 20 from line 3 (rents) and/or 4 (royalties). If result is a (loss), see instructions to find out if you must file **Form 6198**	21			
22	Deductible rental real estate loss after limitation, if any, on **Form 8582** (see instructions)	22	( )	( )	( )

23a	Total of all amounts reported on line 3 for all rental properties	23a	
b	Total of all amounts reported on line 4 for all royalty properties	23b	
c	Total of all amounts reported on line 12 for all properties	23c	
d	Total of all amounts reported on line 18 for all properties	23d	
e	Total of all amounts reported on line 20 for all properties	23e	

24	**Income.** Add positive amounts shown on line 21. **Do not** include any losses	24	
25	**Losses.** Add royalty losses from line 21 and rental real estate losses from line 22. Enter total losses here	25	( )
26	**Total rental real estate and royalty income or (loss).** Combine lines 24 and 25. Enter the result here. If Parts II, III, IV, and line 40 on page 2 do not apply to you, also enter this amount on Form 1040, line 17, or Form 1040NR, line 18. Otherwise, include this amount in the total on line 41 on page 2	26	

For Paperwork Reduction Act Notice, see the separate instructions.   Cat. No. 11344L   Schedule E (Form 1040) 2014

Name(s) shown on return. Do not enter name and social security number if shown on other side. | **Your social security number**

Caution. The IRS compares amounts reported on your tax return with amounts shown on Schedule(s) K-1.

| **Part II** | **Income or Loss From Partnerships and S Corporations** **Note.** If you report a loss from an at-risk activity for which **any** amount is **not** at risk, you **must** check the box in column **(e)** on line 28 and attach **Form 6198.** See instructions. |

27 Are you reporting any loss not allowed in a prior year due to the at-risk, excess farm loss, or basis limitations, a prior year unallowed loss from a passive activity (if that loss was not reported on Form 8582), or unreimbursed partnership expenses? If you answered "Yes," see instructions before completing this section. ☐ **Yes** ☐ **No**

28

	(a) Name	**(b)** Enter **P** for partnership; **S** for S corporation	**(c)** Check if foreign partnership	**(d)** Employer identification number	**(e)** Check if any amount is not at risk
A			☐		☐
B			☐		☐
C			☐		☐
D			☐		☐

	Passive Income and Loss		Nonpassive Income and Loss		
	(f) Passive loss allowed (attach **Form 8582** if required)	**(g)** Passive income from **Schedule K–1**	**(h)** Nonpassive loss from **Schedule K–1**	**(i)** Section 179 expense deduction from **Form 4562**	**(j)** Nonpassive income from **Schedule K–1**
A					
B					
C					
D					
29a Totals					
b Totals					

30	Add columns (g) and (j) of line 29a	**30**	
31	Add columns (f), (h), and (i) of line 29b	**31** (	)
32	**Total partnership and S corporation income or (loss).** Combine lines 30 and 31. Enter the result here and include in the total on line 41 below	**32**	

| **Part III** | **Income or Loss From Estates and Trusts** |

33

	(a) Name	**(b)** Employer identification number
A		
B		

	Passive Income and Loss		Nonpassive Income and Loss	
	(c) Passive deduction or loss allowed (attach **Form 8582** if required)	**(d)** Passive income from **Schedule K–1**	**(e)** Deduction or loss from **Schedule K–1**	**(f)** Other income from **Schedule K–1**
A				
B				
34a Totals				
b Totals				

35	Add columns (d) and (f) of line 34a	**35**	
36	Add columns (c) and (e) of line 34b	**36** (	)
37	**Total estate and trust income or (loss).** Combine lines 35 and 36. Enter the result here and include in the total on line 41 below	**37**	

| **Part IV** | **Income or Loss From Real Estate Mortgage Investment Conduits (REMICs)—Residual Holder** |

38

(a) Name	**(b)** Employer identification number	**(c)** Excess inclusion from **Schedules Q,** line 2c (see instructions)	**(d)** Taxable income (net loss) from **Schedules Q,** line 1b	**(e)** Income from **Schedules Q,** line 3b

| **39** | Combine columns (d) and (e) only. Enter the result here and include in the total on line 41 below | **39** | |

| **Part V** | **Summary** |

| **40** | Net farm rental income or (loss) from **Form 4835.** Also, complete line 42 below | **40** | |
| **41** | **Total income or (loss).** Combine lines 26, 32, 37, 39, and 40. Enter the result here and on Form 1040, line 17, or Form 1040NR, line 18 ▶ | **41** | |

42 **Reconciliation of farming and fishing income.** Enter your **gross** farming and fishing income reported on Form 4835, line 7; Schedule K-1 (Form 1065), box 14, code B; Schedule K-1 (Form 1120S), box 17, code V; and Schedule K-1 (Form 1041), box 14, code F (see instructions) . . | **42** | |

43 **Reconciliation for real estate professionals.** If you were a real estate professional (see instructions), enter the net income or (loss) you reported anywhere on Form 1040 or Form 1040NR from all rental real estate activities in which you materially participated under the passive activity loss rules . . | **43** | |

SCHEDULE EIC
(Form 1040A or 1040)

Department of the Treasury
Internal Revenue Service (99)

Earned Income Credit
Qualifying Child Information

► **Complete and attach to Form 1040A or 1040 only if you have a qualifying child.**
► Information about Schedule EIC (Form 1040A or 1040) and its instructions is at *www.irs.gov/scheduleeic.*

OMB No. 1545-0074

2014

Attachment
Sequence No. **43**

Name(s) shown on return

Your social security number

Before you begin:
- See the instructions for Form 1040A, lines 42a and 42b, or Form 1040, lines 66a and 66b, to make sure that **(a)** you can take the EIC, and **(b)** you have a qualifying child.
- Be sure the child's name on line 1 and social security number (SSN) on line 2 agree with the child's social security card. Otherwise, at the time we process your return, we may reduce or disallow your EIC. If the name or SSN on the child's social security card is not correct, call the Social Security Administration at 1-800-772-1213.

- *If you take the EIC even though you are not eligible, you may not be allowed to take the credit for up to 10 years. See the instructions for details.*
- *It will take us longer to process your return and issue your refund if you do not fill in all lines that apply for each qualifying child.*

Qualifying Child Information

	Child 1	Child 2	Child 3
1 Child's name If you have more than three qualifying children, you have to list only three to get the maximum credit.	First name Last name	First name Last name	First name Last name
2 Child's SSN The child must have an SSN as defined in the instructions for Form 1040A, lines 42a and 42b, or Form 1040, lines 66a and 66b, unless the child was born and died in 2014. If your child was born and died in 2014 and did not have an SSN, enter "Died" on this line and attach a copy of the child's birth certificate, death certificate, or hospital medical records.			
3 Child's year of birth	Year _ _ _ _ *If born after 1995 and the child is younger than you (or your spouse, if filing jointly), skip lines 4a and 4b; go to line 5.*	Year _ _ _ _ *If born after 1995 and the child is younger than you (or your spouse, if filing jointly), skip lines 4a and 4b; go to line 5.*	Year _ _ _ _ *If born after 1995 and the child is younger than you (or your spouse, if filing jointly), skip lines 4a and 4b; go to line 5.*
4 a Was the child under age 24 at the end of 2014, a student, and younger than you (or your spouse, if filing jointly)?	☐ **Yes.** *Go to line 5.* ☐ **No.** *Go to line 4b.*	☐ **Yes.** *Go to line 5.* ☐ **No.** *Go to line 4b.*	☐ **Yes.** *Go to line 5.* ☐ **No.** *Go to line 4b.*
b Was the child permanently and totally disabled during any part of 2014?	☐ **Yes.** *Go to line 5.* ☐ **No.** The child is not a qualifying child.	☐ **Yes.** *Go to line 5.* ☐ **No.** The child is not a qualifying child.	☐ **Yes.** *Go to line 5.* ☐ **No.** The child is not a qualifying child.
5 Child's relationship to you (for example, son, daughter, grandchild, niece, nephew, foster child, etc.)			
6 Number of months child lived with you in the United States during 2014 • If the child lived with you for more than half of 2014 but less than 7 months, enter "7." • If the child was born or died in 2014 and your home was the child's home for more than half the time he or she was alive during 2014, enter "12."	_ _ _ months *Do not enter more than 12 months.*	_ _ _ months *Do not enter more than 12 months.*	_ _ _ months *Do not enter more than 12 months.*

For Paperwork Reduction Act Notice, see your tax return instructions.

Cat. No. 13339M

Schedule EIC (Form 1040A or 1040) 2014

Purpose of Schedule

After you have figured your earned income credit (EIC), use Schedule EIC to give the IRS information about your qualifying child(ren).

To figure the amount of your credit or to have the IRS figure it for you, see the instructions for Form 1040A, lines 42a and 42b, or Form 1040, lines 66a and 66b.

Taking the EIC when not eligible. If you take the EIC even though you are not eligible and it is determined that your error is due to reckless or intentional disregard of the EIC rules, you will not be allowed to take the credit for 2 years even if you are otherwise eligible to do so. If you fraudulently take the EIC, you will not be allowed to take the credit for 10 years. You may also have to pay penalties.

Future developments. For the latest information about developments related to Schedule EIC (Form 1040A or 1040) and its instructions, such as legislation enacted after they were published, go to *www.irs.gov/scheduleeic.*

 You may also be able to take the additional child tax credit if your child was your dependent and under age 17 at the end of 2014. For more details, see the instructions for line 43 of Form 1040A or line 67 of Form 1040.

Qualifying Child

A qualifying child for the EIC is a child who is your . . .

Son, daughter, stepchild, foster child, brother, sister, stepbrother, stepsister, half brother, half sister, or a descendant of any of them (for example, your grandchild, niece, or nephew)

was . . .

Under age 19 at the end of 2014 and younger than you (or your spouse, if filing jointly)
or
Under age 24 at the end of 2014, a student, and younger than you (or your spouse, if filing jointly)
or
Any age and permanently and totally disabled

Who is not filing a joint return for 2014
or is filing a joint return for 2014 only to claim
a refund of withheld income tax or estimated tax paid

Who lived with you in the United States for more than half of 2014. If the child did not live with you for the required time, see *Exception to time lived with you* in the instructions for Form 1040A, lines 42a and 42b, or Form 1040, lines 66a and 66b.

 *If the child was married or meets the conditions to be a qualifying child of another person (other than your spouse if filing a joint return), special rules apply. For details, see* Married child *or* Qualifying child of more than one person *in the instructions for Form 1040A, lines 42a and 42b, or Form 1040, lines 66a and 66b.*

SCHEDULE F (Form 1040)

Department of the Treasury
Internal Revenue Service (99)

Profit or Loss From Farming

▶ Attach to Form 1040, Form 1040NR, Form 1041, Form 1065, or Form 1065-B.
▶ Information about Schedule F and its separate instructions is at *www.irs.gov/schedulef*.

OMB No. 1545-0074

2014

Attachment Sequence No. **14**

Name of proprietor

Social security number (SSN)

A Principal crop or activity

B Enter code from Part IV ▶

C Accounting method:
☐ Cash ☐ Accrual

D Employer ID number (EIN), (see instr)

E Did you "materially participate" in the operation of this business during 2014? If "No," see instructions for limit on passive losses ☐ Yes ☐ No

F Did you make any payments in 2014 that would require you to file Form(s) 1099 (see instructions)? ☐ Yes ☐ No

G If "Yes," did you or will you file required Forms 1099? ☐ Yes ☐ No

Part I — Farm Income—Cash Method. Complete Parts I and II (Accrual method. Complete Parts II and III, and Part I, line 9.)

1a	Sales of livestock and other resale items (see instructions)	1a		
b	Cost or other basis of livestock or other items reported on line 1a	1b		
c	Subtract line 1b from line 1a		1c	
2	Sales of livestock, produce, grains, and other products you raised		2	
3a	Cooperative distributions (Form(s) 1099-PATR) . 3a	3b Taxable amount	3b	
4a	Agricultural program payments (see instructions) . 4a	4b Taxable amount	4b	
5a	Commodity Credit Corporation (CCC) loans reported under election		5a	
b	CCC loans forfeited 5b	5c Taxable amount	5c	
6	Crop insurance proceeds and federal crop disaster payments (see instructions)			
a	Amount received in 2014 . . . . 6a	6b Taxable amount	6b	
c	If election to defer to 2015 is attached, check here ▶ ☐	6d Amount deferred from 2013	6d	
7	Custom hire (machine work) income		7	
8	Other income, including federal and state gasoline or fuel tax credit or refund (see instructions) . . .		8	
9	**Gross income.** Add amounts in the right column (lines 1c, 2, 3b, 4b, 5a, 5c, 6b, 6d, 7, and 8). If you use the accrual method, enter the amount from Part III, line 50 (see instructions) . . . . ▶		9	

Part II — Farm Expenses—Cash and Accrual Method. Do not include personal or living expenses (see instructions).

10	Car and truck expenses (see instructions). Also attach Form 4562	10		23	Pension and profit-sharing plans	23	
11	Chemicals	11		24	Rent or lease (see instructions)		
12	Conservation expenses (see instructions)	12		a	Vehicles, machinery, equipment	24a	
13	Custom hire (machine work) .	13		b	Other (land, animals, etc.) . .	24b	
14	Depreciation and section 179 expense (see instructions)	14		25	Repairs and maintenance . .	25	
				26	Seeds and plants	26	
15	Employee benefit programs other than on line 23 . . .	15		27	Storage and warehousing . .	27	
				28	Supplies	28	
16	Feed	16		29	Taxes	29	
17	Fertilizers and lime . . .	17		30	Utilities	30	
18	Freight and trucking . . .	18		31	Veterinary, breeding, and medicine	31	
19	Gasoline, fuel, and oil . . .	19		32	Other expenses (specify):		
20	Insurance (other than health) .	20		a	_____	32a	
21	Interest:			b	_____	32b	
a	Mortgage (paid to banks, etc.) .	21a		c	_____	32c	
b	Other	21b		d	_____	32d	
22	Labor hired (less employment credits)	22		e	_____	32e	
				f		32f	

33	**Total expenses.** Add lines 10 through 32f. If line 32f is negative, see instructions . . . . . . ▶	33	
34	**Net farm profit or (loss).** Subtract line 33 from line 9	34	
	If a profit, stop here and see instructions for where to report. If a loss, complete lines 35 and 36.		
35	Did you receive an applicable subsidy in 2014? (see instructions)	☐ Yes ☐ No	
36	Check the box that describes your investment in this activity and see instructions for where to report your loss.		
a	☐ All investment is at risk. b ☐ Some investment is not at risk.		

For Paperwork Reduction Act Notice, see the separate instructions.

Cat. No. 11346H

Schedule F (Form 1040) 2014

Part III Farm Income—Accrual Method (see instructions).

37	Sales of livestock, produce, grains, and other products (see instructions)	37	
38a	Cooperative distributions (Form(s) 1099-PATR) [38a _____] 38b Taxable amount	38b	
39a	Agricultural program payments [39a _____] 39b Taxable amount	39b	
40	Commodity Credit Corporation (CCC) loans:		
a	CCC loans reported under election	40a	
b	CCC loans forfeited [40b _____] 40c Taxable amount	40c	
41	Crop insurance proceeds	41	
42	Custom hire (machine work) income	42	
43	Other income (see instructions)	43	
44	Add amounts in the right column for lines 37 through 43 (lines 37, 38b, 39b, 40a, 40c, 41, 42, and 43)	44	
45	Inventory of livestock, produce, grains, and other products at beginning of the year. Do not include sales reported on Form 4797 [45 _____]		
46	Cost of livestock, produce, grains, and other products purchased during the year [46 _____]		
47	Add lines 45 and 46 [47 _____]		
48	Inventory of livestock, produce, grains, and other products at end of year [48 _____]		
49	Cost of livestock, produce, grains, and other products sold. Subtract line 48 from line 47*	49	
50	**Gross income.** Subtract line 49 from line 44. Enter the result here and on Part I, line 9 ▶	50	

*If you use the unit-livestock-price method or the farm-price method of valuing inventory and the amount on line 48 is larger than the amount on line 47, subtract line 47 from line 48. Enter the result on line 49. Add lines 44 and 49. Enter the total on line 50 and on Part I, line 9.

Part IV Principal Agricultural Activity Codes

CAUTION

Do not file Schedule F (Form 1040) to report the following.

• *Income from providing agricultural services such as soil preparation, veterinary, farm labor, horticultural, or management for a fee or on a contract basis. Instead file Schedule C (Form 1040) or Schedule C-EZ (Form 1040).*

• *Income from breeding, raising, or caring for dogs, cats, or other pet animals. Instead file Schedule C (Form 1040) or Schedule C-EZ (Form 1040).*

• *Sales of livestock held for draft, breeding, sport, or dairy purposes. Instead file Form 4797.*

These codes for the Principal Agricultural Activity classify farms by their primary activity to facilitate the administration of the Internal Revenue Code. These six-digit codes are based on the North American Industry Classification System (NAICS).

Select the code that best identifies your primary farming activity and enter the six-digit number on line B.

Crop Production

111100	Oilseed and grain farming
111210	Vegetable and melon farming
111300	Fruit and tree nut farming
111400	Greenhouse, nursery, and floriculture production
111900	Other crop farming

Animal Production

112111	Beef cattle ranching and farming
112112	Cattle feedlots
112120	Dairy cattle and milk production
112210	Hog and pig farming
112300	Poultry and egg production
112400	Sheep and goat farming
112510	Aquaculture
112900	Other animal production

Forestry and Logging

113000	Forestry and logging (including forest nurseries and timber tracts)

SCHEDULE H
(Form 1040)

Department of the Treasury
Internal Revenue Service (99)

Household Employment Taxes

(For Social Security, Medicare, Withheld Income, and Federal Unemployment (FUTA) Taxes)

▶ **Attach to Form 1040, 1040NR, 1040-SS, or 1041.**

▶ **Information about Schedule H and its separate instructions is at www.irs.gov/scheduleh.**

OMB No. 1545-1971

2014

Attachment
Sequence No. **44**

Name of employer

Social security number

Employer identification number

Calendar year taxpayers having no household employees in 2014 do not have to complete this form for 2014.

A Did you pay **any one** household employee cash wages of $1,900 or more in 2014? (If any household employee was your spouse, your child under age 21, your parent, or anyone under age 18, see the line A instructions before you answer this question.)

☐ **Yes.** Skip lines B and C and go to line 1.
☐ **No.** Go to line B.

B Did you withhold federal income tax during 2014 for any household employee?

☐ **Yes.** Skip line C and go to line 7.
☐ **No.** Go to line C.

C Did you pay **total** cash wages of $1,000 or more in **any** calendar **quarter** of 2013 or 2014 to **all** household employees? (**Do not** count cash wages paid in 2013 or 2014 to your spouse, your child under age 21, or your parent.)

☐ **No. Stop.** Do not file this schedule.
☐ **Yes.** Skip lines 1-9 and go to line 10.

Part I Social Security, Medicare, and Federal Income Taxes

1 Total cash wages subject to social security tax	**1**	
2 Social security tax. Multiply line 1 by 12.4% (.124)		**2**
3 Total cash wages subject to Medicare tax	**3**	
4 Medicare tax. Multiply line 3 by 2.9% (.029)		**4**
5 Total cash wages subject to Additional Medicare Tax withholding . .	**5**	
6 Additional Medicare Tax withholding. Multiply line 5 by 0.9% (.009)		**6**
7 Federal income tax withheld, if any		**7**
8 **Total social security, Medicare, and federal income taxes.** Add lines 2, 4, 6, and 7		**8**

9 Did you pay **total** cash wages of $1,000 or more in **any** calendar **quarter** of 2013 or 2014 to **all** household employees? (**Do not** count cash wages paid in 2013 or 2014 to your spouse, your child under age 21, or your parent.)

☐ **No. Stop.** Include the amount from line 8 above on Form 1040, line 60a. If you are not required to file Form 1040, see the line 9 instructions.

☐ **Yes.** Go to line 10.

For Privacy Act and Paperwork Reduction Act Notice, see the instructions.   Cat. No. 12187K   Schedule H (Form 1040) 2014

Part II Federal Unemployment (FUTA) Tax

		Yes	No
10	Did you pay unemployment contributions to only one state? (If you paid contributions to a credit reduction state, see instructions and check "No.") **10**		
11	Did you pay all state unemployment contributions for 2014 by April 15, 2015? Fiscal year filers see instructions **11**		
12	Were all wages that are taxable for FUTA tax also taxable for your state's unemployment tax? **12**		

Next: If you checked the **"Yes"** box on **all** the lines above, complete Section A.

If you checked the **"No"** box on **any** of the lines above, skip Section A and complete Section B.

Section A

13	Name of the state where you paid unemployment contributions ▶ _____		
14	Contributions paid to your state unemployment fund **14**		
15	Total cash wages subject to FUTA tax **15**		
16	**FUTA tax.** Multiply line 15 by .6% (.006). Enter the result here, skip Section B, and go to line 25 **16**		

Section B

17 Complete all columns below that apply (if you need more space, see instructions):

(a) Name of state	(b) Taxable wages (as defined in state act)	(c) State experience rate period		(d) State experience rate	(e) Multiply col. (b) by .054	(f) Multiply col. (b) by col. (d)	(g) Subtract col. (f) from col. (e). If zero or less, enter -0-.	(h) Contributions paid to state unemployment fund
		From	To					

18	Totals **18**	
19	Add columns (g) and (h) of line 18 . . . . . . **19**	
20	Total cash wages subject to FUTA tax (see the line 15 instructions) **20**	
21	Multiply line 20 by 6.0% (.060) **21**	
22	Multiply line 20 by 5.4% (.054) **22**	
23	Enter the **smaller** of line 19 or line 22	
	(Employers in a credit reduction state must use the worksheet on page H-7 and check here) . ☐ **23**	
24	**FUTA tax.** Subtract line 23 from line 21. Enter the result here and go to line 25 . . . . . **24**	

Part III Total Household Employment Taxes

25	Enter the amount from line 8. If you checked the "Yes" box on line C of page 1, enter -0- . . . **25**	
26	Add line 16 (or line 24) and line 25 . . . . **26**	
27	Are you required to file Form 1040?	

☐ **Yes. Stop.** Include the amount from line 26 above on Form 1040, line 60a. **Do not** complete Part IV below.

☐ **No.** You may have to complete Part IV. See instructions for details.

Part IV Address and Signature— Complete this part **only** if required. See the line 27 instructions.

Address (number and street) or P.O. box if mail is not delivered to street address | Apt., room, or suite no.

City, town or post office, state, and ZIP code

Under penalties of perjury, I declare that I have examined this schedule, including accompanying statements, and to the best of my knowledge and belief, it is true, correct, and complete. No part of any payment made to a state unemployment fund claimed as a credit was, or is to be, deducted from the payments to employees. Declaration of preparer (other than taxpayer) is based on all information of which preparer has any knowledge.

▶ _____ Employer's signature

▶ _____ Date

Paid Preparer Use Only	Print/Type preparer's name	Preparer's signature	Date	Check ☐ if self-employed	PTIN
	Firm's name ▶		Firm's EIN ▶		
	Firm's address ▶		Phone no.		

SCHEDULE J (Form 1040)	Income Averaging for Farmers and Fishermen	OMB No. 1545-0074
Department of the Treasury Internal Revenue Service (99)	▶ Attach to Form 1040 or Form 1040NR. ▶ Information about Schedule J and its separate instructions is at *www.irs.gov/schedulej*.	**2014** Attachment Sequence No. **20**

Name(s) shown on return   Social security number (SSN)

1 Enter the taxable income from your **2014** Form 1040, line 43, or Form 1040NR, line 41 . . . **1**

2a Enter your **elected farm income** (see instructions). **Do not** enter more than the amount on line 1   **2a**

Capital gain included on line 2a:

b Excess, if any, of net long-term capital gain over net short-term capital loss **2b**

c Unrecaptured section 1250 gain **2c**

3 Subtract line 2a from line 1 . . . . **3**

4 Figure the tax on the amount on line 3 using the **2014** tax rates (see instructions) **4**

5 If you used Schedule J to figure your tax for:
- 2013, enter the amount from your 2013 Schedule J, line 11.
- 2012 but not 2013, enter the amount from your 2012 Schedule J, line 15.
- 2011 but not 2012 or 2013, enter the amount from your 2011 Schedule J, line 3.

   Otherwise, enter the taxable income from your **2011** Form 1040, line 43; Form 1040A, line 27; Form 1040EZ, line 6; Form 1040NR, line 41; or Form 1040NR-EZ, line 14. If zero or less, see instructions.   **5**

6 Divide the amount on **line 2a** by 3.0 . . . . **6**

7 Combine lines 5 and 6. If zero or less, enter -0- **7**

8 Figure the tax on the amount on line 7 using the **2011** tax rates (see instructions) **8**

9 If you used Schedule J to figure your tax for:
- 2013, enter the amount from your 2013 Schedule J, line 15.
- 2012 but not 2013, enter the amount from your 2012 Schedule J, line 3.

   Otherwise, enter the taxable income from your **2012** Form 1040, line 43; Form 1040A, line 27; Form 1040EZ, line 6; Form 1040NR, line 41; or Form 1040NR-EZ, line 14. If zero or less, see instructions.   **9**

10 Enter the amount from line 6 . . . . **10**

11 Combine lines 9 and 10. If less than zero, enter as a negative amount   **11**

12 Figure the tax on the amount on line 11 using the **2012** tax rates (see instructions) **12**

13 If you used Schedule J to figure your tax for 2013, enter the amount from your 2013 Schedule J, line 3. Otherwise, enter the taxable income from your **2013** Form 1040, line 43; Form 1040A, line 27; Form 1040EZ, line 6; Form 1040NR, line 41; or Form 1040NR-EZ, line 14. If zero or less, see instructions . . **13**

14 Enter the amount from line 6 . . . . **14**

15 Combine lines 13 and 14. If less than zero, enter as a negative amount   **15**

16 Figure the tax on the amount on line 15 using the **2013** tax rates (see instructions) **16**

17 Add lines 4, 8, 12, and 16 . . . . **17**

18	Amount from line 17	**18**		

19 If you used Schedule J to figure your tax for:

- 2013, enter the amount from your 2013 Schedule J, line 12.

- 2012 but not 2013, enter the amount from your 2012 Schedule J, line 16.

- 2011 but not 2012 or 2013, enter the amount from your 2011 Schedule J, line 4.

Otherwise, enter the tax from your **2011** Form 1040, line 44;* Form 1040A, line 28;* Form 1040EZ, line 10; Form 1040NR, line 42;* or Form 1040NR-EZ, line 15.

19

20 If you used Schedule J to figure your tax for:

- 2013, enter the amount from your 2013 Schedule J, line 16.

- 2012 but not 2013, enter the amount from your 2012 Schedule J, line 4.

Otherwise, enter the tax from your **2012** Form 1040, line 44;* Form 1040A, line 28;* Form 1040EZ, line 10; Form 1040NR, line 42;* or Form 1040NR-EZ, line 15.

20

21 If you used Schedule J to figure your tax for 2013, enter the amount from your 2013 Schedule J, line 4. Otherwise, enter the tax from your **2013** Form 1040, line 44;* Form 1040A, line 28;* Form 1040EZ, line 10; Form 1040NR, line 42;* or Form 1040NR-EZ, line 15 . .

21

*Only include tax reported on this line that is imposed by section 1 of the Internal Revenue Code (see instructions). **Do not** include alternative minimum tax from Form 1040A.

22	Add lines 19 through 21	**22**		
23	**Tax.** Subtract line 22 from line 18. Also include this amount on Form 1040, line 44; or Form 1040NR, line 42	**23**		

Caution. Your tax may be less if you figure it using the 2014 Tax Table, Tax Computation Worksheet, Qualified Dividends and Capital Gain Tax Worksheet, or Schedule D Tax Worksheet. Attach Schedule J only if you are using it to figure your tax.

Schedule J (Form 1040) 2014

Schedule R (Form 1040A or 1040)	**Credit for the Elderly or the Disabled**		OMB No. 1545-0074

Schedule R
(Form 1040A or 1040)

Department of the Treasury
Internal Revenue Service (99)

Credit for the Elderly or the Disabled

▶ Complete and attach to Form 1040A or 1040.
▶ Information about Schedule R and its separate instructions is at *www.irs.gov/scheduler*.

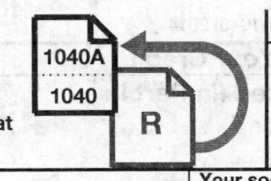

OMB No. 1545-0074

2014

Attachment
Sequence No. **16**

Name(s) shown on Form 1040A or 1040

Your social security number

You may be able to take this credit and reduce your tax if by the end of 2014:

• You were age 65 or older   **or**   • You were under age 65, you retired on **permanent and total** disability, and you received taxable disability income.

But you must also meet other tests. See instructions.

TIP In most cases, the IRS can figure the credit for you. See instructions.

Part I Check the Box for Your Filing Status and Age

If your filing status is:	And by the end of 2014:		Check only one box:
Single, Head of household, or Qualifying widow(er)	**1** You were 65 or older	**1**	☐
	2 You were under 65 and you retired on permanent and total disability . .	**2**	☐
	3 Both spouses were 65 or older	**3**	☐
	4 Both spouses were under 65, but only one spouse retired on permanent and total disability	**4**	☐
Married filing jointly	**5** Both spouses were under 65, and both retired on permanent and total disability	**5**	☐
	6 One spouse was 65 or older, and the other spouse was under 65 and retired on permanent and total disability	**6**	☐
	7 One spouse was 65 or older, and the other spouse was under 65 and **not** retired on permanent and total disability	**7**	☐
Married filing separately	**8** You were 65 or older and you lived apart from your spouse for all of 2014 .	**8**	☐
	9 You were under 65, you retired on permanent and total disability, and you lived apart from your spouse for all of 2014	**9**	☐

Did you check box 1, 3, 7, or 8? ——— **Yes** ——▶ Skip Part II and complete Part III on the back.

——— **No** ——▶ Complete Parts II and III.

Part II Statement of Permanent and Total Disability (Complete **only** if you checked box 2, 4, 5, 6, or 9 above.)

If: 1 You filed a physician's statement for this disability for 1983 or an earlier year, or you filed or got a statement for tax years after 1983 and your physician signed line B on the statement, **and**

2 Due to your continued disabled condition, you were unable to engage in any substantial gainful activity in 2014, check this box . . . . ▶ ☐

• If you checked this box, you do not have to get another statement for 2014.

• If you **did not** check this box, have your physician complete the statement in the instructions. You **must** keep the statement for your records.

Part III   **Figure Your Credit**

10   **If you checked (in Part I):**   **Enter:**

Box 1, 2, 4, or 7 . . . .$5,000

Box 3, 5, or 6 . . . .$7,500   } **10**

Box 8 or 9 . . . .$3,750

| **Did you check box 2, 4, 5, 6, or 9 in Part I?** | → Yes ——————→ You **must** complete line 11. |
| | → No ———————→ Enter the amount from line 10 on line 12 and go to line 13. |

11   **If you checked (in Part I):**

- Box 6, add $5,000 to the taxable disability income of the spouse who was under age 65. Enter the total.
- Box 2, 4, or 9, enter your taxable disability income.   } **11**
- Box 5, add your taxable disability income to your spouse's taxable disability income. Enter the total.

TIP   For more details on what to include on line 11, see *Figure Your Credit* in the instructions.

12   If you completed line 11, enter the **smaller** of line 10 or line 11. **All others,** enter the amount from line 10 . . . . **12**

13   Enter the following pensions, annuities, or disability income that you (and your spouse if filing jointly) received in 2014.

  a Nontaxable part of social security benefits and nontaxable part of railroad retirement benefits treated as social security (see instructions). **13a**

  b Nontaxable veterans' pensions and any other pension, annuity, or disability benefit that is excluded from income under any other provision of law (see instructions). **13b**

  c Add lines 13a and 13b. (Even though these income items are not taxable, they **must** be included here to figure your credit.) If you did not receive any of the types of nontaxable income listed on line 13a or 13b, enter -0- on line 13c **13c**

14   Enter the amount from Form 1040A, line 22, or Form 1040, line 38 . . . . . **14**

15   **If you checked (in Part I):**   **Enter:**

Box 1 or 2 . . . . . . $7,500

Box 3, 4, 5, 6, or 7 . . . $10,000 } **15**

Box 8 or 9 . . . . . . $5,000

16   Subtract line 15 from line 14. If zero or less, enter -0- **16**

17   Enter one-half of line 16 . . . . **17**

18   Add lines 13c and 17 . . . . **18**

19   Subtract line 18 from line 12. If zero or less, **stop; you cannot** take the credit. Otherwise, go to line 20 . . . . **19**

20   Multiply line 19 by 15% (.15). **20**

21   Tax liability limit. Enter the amount from the Credit Limit Worksheet in the instructions . **21**

22   **Credit for the elderly or the disabled.** Enter the **smaller** of line 20 or line 21. Also enter this amount on Form 1040A, line 32, or include on Form 1040, line 54 (check box **c** and enter "Sch R" on the line next to that box) **22**

| SCHEDULE SE
(Form 1040)
Department of the Treasury
Internal Revenue Service (99) | **Self-Employment Tax**
▶ Information about Schedule SE and its separate instructions is at *www.irs.gov/schedulese.*
▶ Attach to Form 1040 or Form 1040NR. | OMB No. 1545-0074
2014
Attachment
Sequence No. **17** |

| Name of person with **self-employment** income (as shown on Form 1040 or Form 1040NR) | Social security number of person
with **self-employment** income ▶ |

Before you begin: To determine if you must file Schedule SE, see the instructions.

May I Use Short Schedule SE or Must I Use Long Schedule SE?

Note. Use this flowchart **only if** you must file Schedule SE. If unsure, see *Who Must File Schedule SE* in the instructions.

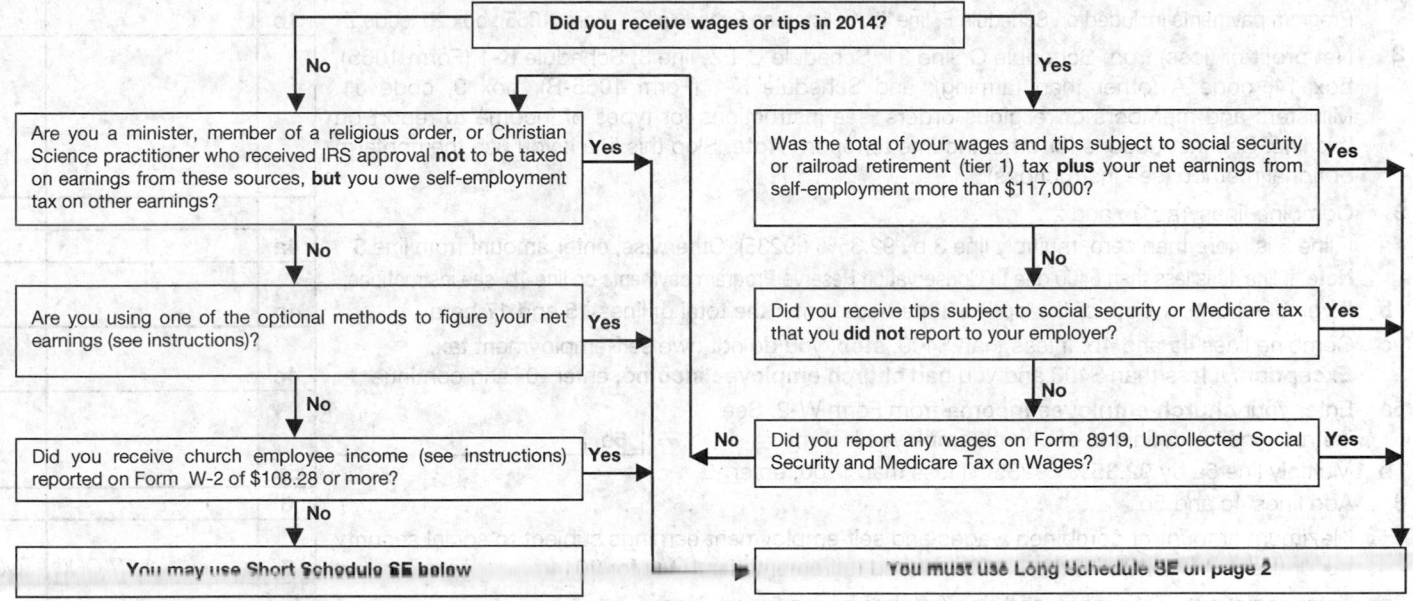

Section A—Short Schedule SE. **Caution.** Read above to see if you can use Short Schedule SE.

1a	Net farm profit or (loss) from Schedule F, line 34, and farm partnerships, Schedule K-1 (Form 1065), box 14, code A	**1a**	
b	If you received social security retirement or disability benefits, enter the amount of Conservation Reserve Program payments included on Schedule F, line 4b, or listed on Schedule K-1 (Form 1065), box 20, code Z	**1b** (	)
2	Net profit or (loss) from Schedule C, line 31; Schedule C-EZ, line 3; Schedule K-1 (Form 1065), box 14, code A (other than farming); and Schedule K-1 (Form 1065-B), box 9, code J1. Ministers and members of religious orders, see instructions for types of income to report on this line. See instructions for other income to report	**2**	
3	Combine lines 1a, 1b, and 2	**3**	
4	Multiply line 3 by 92.35% (.9235). If less than $400, you do not owe self-employment tax; **do not** file this schedule unless you have an amount on line 1b . . . . ▶	**4**	
	Note. If line 4 is less than $400 due to Conservation Reserve Program payments on line 1b, see instructions.		
5	**Self-employment tax.** If the amount on line 4 is: • $117,000 or less, multiply line 4 by 15.3% (.153). Enter the result here and on **Form 1040, line 57,** or **Form 1040NR, line 55** • More than $117,000, multiply line 4 by 2.9% (.029). Then, add $14,508 to the result. Enter the total here and on **Form 1040, line 57,** or **Form 1040NR, line 55**	**5**	
6	**Deduction for one-half of self-employment tax.** Multiply line 5 by 50% (.50). Enter the result here and on **Form 1040, line 27,** or **Form 1040NR, line 27**	**6**	

| For Paperwork Reduction Act Notice, see your tax return instructions. | Cat. No. 11358Z | Schedule SE (Form 1040) 2014 |

Attachment Sequence No. **17**

Name of person with **self-employment** income (as shown on Form 1040 or Form 1040NR)	Social security number of person with **self-employment** income ▶

Section B—Long Schedule SE

Part I Self-Employment Tax

Note. If your only income subject to self-employment tax is **church employee income,** see instructions. Also see instructions for the definition of church employee income.

A If you are a minister, member of a religious order, or Christian Science practitioner **and** you filed Form 4361, but you had $400 or more of **other** net earnings from self-employment, check here and continue with Part I . . . . ▶ ☐

1a	Net farm profit or (loss) from Schedule F, line 34, and farm partnerships, Schedule K-1 (Form 1065), box 14, code A. **Note.** Skip lines 1a and 1b if you use the farm optional method (see instructions)	**1a**		
b	If you received social security retirement or disability benefits, enter the amount of Conservation Reserve Program payments included on Schedule F, line 4b, or listed on Schedule K-1 (Form 1065), box 20, code Z	**1b**	(	)
2	Net profit or (loss) from Schedule C, line 31; Schedule C-EZ, line 3; Schedule K-1 (Form 1065), box 14, code A (other than farming); and Schedule K-1 (Form 1065-B), box 9, code J1. Ministers and members of religious orders, see instructions for types of income to report on this line. See instructions for other income to report. **Note.** Skip this line if you use the nonfarm optional method (see instructions)	**2**		
3	Combine lines 1a, 1b, and 2	**3**		
4a	If line 3 is more than zero, multiply line 3 by 92.35% (.9235). Otherwise, enter amount from line 3 **Note.** If line 4a is less than $400 due to Conservation Reserve Program payments on line 1b, see instructions.	**4a**		
b	If you elect one or both of the optional methods, enter the total of lines 15 and 17 here . .	**4b**		
c	Combine lines 4a and 4b. If less than $400, **stop;** you do not owe self-employment tax. **Exception.** If less than $400 and you had **church employee income,** enter -0- and continue ▶	**4c**		
5a	Enter your **church employee income** from Form W-2. See instructions for definition of church employee income . . . **5a**			
b	Multiply line 5a by 92.35% (.9235). If less than $100, enter -0-	**5b**		
6	Add lines 4c and 5b	**6**		
7	Maximum amount of combined wages and self-employment earnings subject to social security tax or the 6.2% portion of the 7.65% railroad retirement (tier 1) tax for 2014	**7**	117,000	00
8a	Total social security wages and tips (total of boxes 3 and 7 on Form(s) W-2) and railroad retirement (tier 1) compensation. If $117,000 or more, skip lines 8b through 10, and go to line 11 **8a**			
b	Unreported tips subject to social security tax (from Form 4137, line 10) **8b**			
c	Wages subject to social security tax (from Form 8919, line 10) **8c**			
d	Add lines 8a, 8b, and 8c	**8d**		
9	Subtract line 8d from line 7. If zero or less, enter -0- here and on line 10 and go to line 11 . ▶	**9**		
10	Multiply the **smaller** of line 6 or line 9 by 12.4% (.124)	**10**		
11	Multiply line 6 by 2.9% (.029)	**11**		
12	**Self-employment tax.** Add lines 10 and 11. Enter here and on **Form 1040, line 57,** or **Form 1040NR, line 55**	**12**		
13	**Deduction for one-half of self-employment tax.** Multiply line 12 by 50% (.50). Enter the result here and on **Form 1040, line 27,** or **Form 1040NR, line 27** **13**			

Part II Optional Methods To Figure Net Earnings (see instructions)

Farm Optional Method. You may use this method **only** if **(a)** your gross farm income[1] was not more than $7,200, **or (b)** your net farm profits[2] were less than $5,198.

14	Maximum income for optional methods	**14**	4,800	00
15	Enter the **smaller** of: two-thirds (2/3) of gross farm income[1] (not less than zero) or $4,800. Also include this amount on line 4b above	**15**		

Nonfarm Optional Method. You may use this method **only** if **(a)** your net nonfarm profits[3] were less than $5,198 and also less than 72.189% of your gross nonfarm income,[4] **and (b)** you had net earnings from self-employment of at least $400 in 2 of the prior 3 years. **Caution.** You may use this method no more than five times.

16	Subtract line 15 from line 14	**16**	
17	Enter the **smaller** of: two-thirds (2/3) of gross nonfarm income[4] (not less than zero) **or** the amount on line 16. Also include this amount on line 4b above	**17**	

[1] From Sch. F, line 9, and Sch. K-1 (Form 1065), box 14, code B.

[2] From Sch. F, line 34, and Sch. K-1 (Form 1065), box 14, code A—minus the amount you would have entered on line 1b had you not used the optional method.

[3] From Sch. C, line 31; Sch. C-EZ, line 3; Sch. K-1 (Form 1065), box 14, code A; and Sch. K-1 (Form 1065-B), box 9, code J1.

[4] From Sch. C, line 7; Sch. C-EZ, line 1; Sch. K-1 (Form 1065), box 14, code C; and Sch. K-1 (Form 1065-B), box 9, code J2.

SCHEDULE 8812
(Form 1040A or 1040)

Department of the Treasury
Internal Revenue Service (99)

Child Tax Credit

▶ **Attach to Form 1040, Form 1040A, or Form 1040NR.**
▶ **Information about Schedule 8812 and its separate instructions is at**
www.irs.gov/schedule8812.

1040
1040A
1040NR
8812

OMB No. 1545-0074

20**14**

Attachment
Sequence No. 47

Name(s) shown on return

Your social security number

Part I	**Filers Who Have Certain Child Dependent(s) with an ITIN (Individual Taxpayer Identification Number)**

⚠️ **CAUTION**

Complete this part only for each dependent who has an ITIN and for whom you are claiming the child tax credit.
If your dependent is not a qualifying child for the credit, you cannot include that dependent in the calculation of this credit.

Answer the following questions for each dependent listed on Form 1040, line 6c; Form 1040A, line 6c; or Form 1040NR, line 7c, who has an ITIN (Individual Taxpayer Identification Number) and that you indicated is a qualifying child for the child tax credit by checking column (4) for that dependent.

A For the first dependent identified with an ITIN and listed as a qualifying child for the child tax credit, did this child meet the substantial presence test? See separate instructions.

☐ Yes   ☐ No

B For the second dependent identified with an ITIN and listed as a qualifying child for the child tax credit, did this child meet the substantial presence test? See separate instructions.

☐ Yes   ☐ No

C For the third dependent identified with an ITIN and listed as a qualifying child for the child tax credit, did this child meet the substantial presence test? See separate instructions.

☐ Yes   ☐ No

D For the fourth dependent identified with an ITIN and listed as a qualifying child for the child tax credit, did this child meet the substantial presence test? See separate instructions.

☐ Yes   ☐ No

Note. If you have more than four dependents identified with an ITIN and listed as a qualifying child for the child tax credit, see the instructions and check here . . . . ▶ ☐

Part II	**Additional Child Tax Credit Filers**

1   **1040 filers:**   Enter the amount from line 6 of your Child Tax Credit Worksheet (see the Instructions for Form 1040, line 52).

     1040A filers: Enter the amount from line 6 of your Child Tax Credit Worksheet (see the Instructions for Form 1040A, line 35).

     1040NR filers: Enter the amount from line 6 of your Child Tax Credit Worksheet (see the Instructions for Form 1040NR, line 49).

     If you used Pub. 972, enter the amount from line 8 of the Child Tax Credit Worksheet in the publication.

   1

2 Enter the amount from Form 1040, line 52; Form 1040A, line 35; or Form 1040NR, line 49 . . . . . .   **2**

3 Subtract line 2 from line 1. If zero, **stop;** you cannot take this credit **3**

4a Earned income (see separate instructions) **4a**

  b Nontaxable combat pay (see separate instructions) **4b**

5 Is the amount on line 4a more than $3,000?

   ☐ **No.** Leave line 5 blank and enter -0- on line 6.

   ☐ **Yes.** Subtract $3,000 from the amount on line 4a. Enter the result . . .   **5**

6 Multiply the amount on line 5 by 15% (.15) and enter the result **6**

   Next. Do you have three or more qualifying children?

   ☐ **No.** If line 6 is zero, stop; you cannot take this credit. Otherwise, skip Part III and enter the **smaller** of line 3 or line 6 on line 13.

   ☐ **Yes.** If line 6 is equal to or more than line 3, skip Part III and enter the amount from line 3 on line 13. Otherwise, go to line 7.

Part III	**Certain Filers Who Have Three or More Qualifying Children**				

7   Withheld social security, Medicare, and Additional Medicare taxes from Form(s) W-2, boxes 4 and 6. If married filing jointly, include your spouse's amounts with yours. If your employer withheld or you paid Additional Medicare Tax or tier 1 RRTA taxes, see separate instructions **7**

8   **1040 filers:**   Enter the total of the amounts from Form 1040, lines 27 and 58, plus any taxes that you identified using code "UT" and entered on line 62.

       1040A filers: Enter -0-.   **8**

       1040NR filers: Enter the total of the amounts from Form 1040NR, lines 27 and 56, plus any taxes that you identified using code "UT" and entered on line 60.

9   Add lines 7 and 8 . . . .   **9**

10   **1040 filers:**   Enter the total of the amounts from Form 1040, lines 66a and 71.

       1040A filers: Enter the total of the amount from Form 1040A, line 42a, plus any excess social security and tier 1 RRTA taxes withheld that you entered to the left of line 46 (see separate instructions).   **10**

       1040NR filers: Enter the amount from Form 1040NR, line 67.

11   Subtract line 10 from line 9. If zero or less, enter -0- **11**

12   Enter the **larger** of line 6 or line 11 . . . . **12**

      Next, enter the **smaller** of line 3 or line 12 on line 13.

Part IV	**Additional Child Tax Credit**				

13   **This is your additional child tax credit** **13**

1040
1040A
1040NR ◄

Enter this amount on Form 1040, line 67, Form 1040A, line 43, or Form 1040NR, line 64.

1040

THIS BOOKLET DOES NOT CONTAIN INSTRUCTIONS FOR ANY FORM 1040 SCHEDULES

INSTRUCTIONS

2014

 makes doing your taxes faster and easier.

 is the fast, safe, and free way to prepare and *e-file* your taxes. See *www.irs.gov/freefile*.

Get a faster refund, reduce errors, and save paper. For more information on **IRS** *e-file* and Free File, see *Options for e-filing your returns* in these instructions or click on **IRS** *e-file* at IRS.gov.

2014 TAX CHANGES

See *What's New* in these instructions.

FUTURE DEVELOPMENTS

For the latest information about developments related to Form 1040 and its instructions, such as legislation enacted after they were published, go to *www.irs.gov/form1040*.

Department of the Treasury **Internal Revenue Service** IRS.gov

Jan 05, 2015

Cat. No. 24811V

Table of Contents

Department of the Treasury

Internal Revenue Service

The Taxpayer Advocate Service Is Here To Help You

What is the Taxpayer Advocate Service?
The Taxpayer Advocate Service (TAS) is an *independent* organization within the Internal Revenue Service (IRS) that helps taxpayers and protects taxpayer rights. Our job is to ensure that every taxpayer is treated fairly and that you know and understand your rights under the *Taxpayer Bill of Rights*.

What can the Taxpayer Advocate Service do for you?
We can help you resolve problems that you can't resolve with the IRS. And our service is free. If you qualify for our assistance, your advocate will be with you at every turn and do everything possible. TAS can help you if:

- Your problem is causing financial difficulty for you, your family, or your business.
- You face (or your business is facing) an immediate threat of adverse action.
- You've tried repeatedly to contact the IRS but no one has responded, or the IRS hasn't responded by the date promised.

How can you reach us?
We have offices in *every state, the District of Columbia, and Puerto Rico*. Your local advocate's number is at *www.TaxpayerAdvocate.irs.gov*, at *www.irs.gov/advocate*, and in your local directory. You can also call us at 1-877-777-4778.

How can you learn about your taxpayer rights?
The Taxpayer Bill of Rights describes ten basic rights that all taxpayers have when dealing with the IRS. Our Tax Toolkit at *www.TaxpayerAdvocate.irs.gov* can help you understand *what these rights mean to you* and how they apply. These are *your* rights. Know them. Use them.

How else does the Taxpayer Advocate Service help taxpayers?
TAS works to resolve large-scale problems that affect many taxpayers. If you know of one of these broad issues, please report it to us at *www.irs.gov/sams*.

Low Income Taxpayer Clinics Help Taxpayers

Low Income Taxpayer Clinics (LITCs) are independent from the IRS. Some serve individuals whose income is below a certain level and who need to resolve a tax problem. These clinics provide professional representation before the IRS or in court on audits, appeals, tax collection disputes, and other issues for free or for a small fee. Some clinics provide information about taxpayer rights and responsibilities in many different languages for individuals who speak English as a second language. For more information, and to find a clinic near you, read the LITC page on *www.irs.gov/litc* or IRS *Publication 4134, Low Income Taxpayer Clinic List*. You can also get this publication at your local IRS office or by calling 1-800-829-3676.

Suggestions for Improving the IRS

Taxpayer Advocacy Panel

Have a suggestion for improving the IRS and do not know who to contact? The Taxpayer Advocacy Panel (TAP) is a diverse group of citizen volunteers who listen to taxpayers, identify taxpayers' issues, and make suggestions for improving IRS service and customer satisfaction. The panel is demographically and geographically diverse, with at least one member from each state, the District of Columbia, and Puerto Rico. Contact TAP at *www.improveirs.org* or 1-888-912-1227 (toll-free).

Options for *e-filing* your returns—safely, quickly, and easily.

Why do 80% of Americans file their taxes electronically?

- *Security*—The IRS uses the latest encryption technology to safeguard your information.
- *Flexible Payments*—File early; pay by April 15.
- *Greater Accuracy*—Fewer errors mean faster processing.
- *Quick Receipt*—Get an acknowledgment that your return was received and accepted.
- *Go Green*—Reduce the amount of paper used.
- *It's Free*—through Free File.
- *Faster Refunds*—Get your refund faster by *e-filing* using direct deposit.

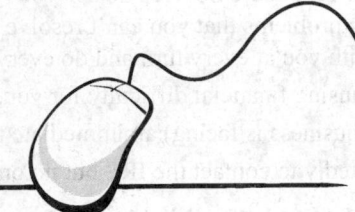

IRS *e-file*: It's Safe. It's Easy. It's Time.

Joining the more than 120 million Americans who already are using *e-file* is easy. Just ask your paid or volunteer tax preparer, use commercial software, or use Free File. IRS *e-file* is the safest, most secure way to transmit your tax return to the IRS. Since 1990, the IRS has processed more than 1 billion *e-filed* tax returns safely and securely. There's no paper return to be lost or stolen.

Most tax return preparers are now required to use IRS *e-file*. If you are asked if you want to *e-file*, just give it a try. IRS *e-file* is now the norm, not the exception. Most states also use electronic filing.

Free *e-file* Help Available Nationwide

Volunteers are available in communities nationwide providing free tax assistance to low to moderate income (generally under $53,000 in adjusted gross income) and elderly taxpayers (age 60 and older). At selected sites, taxpayers can input and electronically file their own tax return with the assistance of an IRS-certified volunteer.

See *How To Get Tax Help* near the end of these instructions for additional information or visit IRS.gov (Keyword: VITA) for a VITA/TCE site near you!

Do Your Taxes for Free

If your adjusted gross income was $60,000 or less in 2014, you can use free tax software to prepare and *e-file* your tax return. Earned more? Use Free File Fillable Forms.

Free File. This public-private partnership, between the IRS and tax software providers, makes approximately 15 brand name commercial software products and *e-file* available for free. Seventy percent of the nation's taxpayers are eligible.

Just visit *www.irs.gov/freefile* for details. Free File combines all the benefits of *e-file* and easy-to-use software at no cost. Guided questions will help ensure you get all the tax credits and deductions you are due. It's fast, safe, and free.

You can review each of the 15 software provider's criteria for free usage or use an online tool to find which free software products match your situation. Some software providers offer state tax return preparation for free. Free File is available in English and Spanish.

Free File Fillable Forms. The IRS offers electronic versions of IRS paper forms that also can be *e-filed* for free. Free File Fillable Forms is best for people experienced in preparing their own tax returns. There are no income limitations. Free File Fillable Forms does basic math calculations. It supports only federal tax forms.

IRS.gov is the gateway to all electronic services offered by the IRS, as well as the spot to download forms at *www.irs.gov/formspubs*.

Make your tax payments electronically—it's easy.

You can make electronic payments online, by phone, or from a mobile device. Paying electronically is safe and secure. The IRS uses the latest encryption technology and does not store banking information. When you use any of the IRS electronic payment options, it puts you in control of paying your tax bill and gives you peace of mind. You determine the payment date, and you will receive an immediate confirmation from the IRS. It's easy, secure, and much quicker than mailing in a check or money order. Go to *www.irs.gov/payments* to see all your electronic payment options.

What's New

Health care: individual responsibility. You must either:

• Indicate on line 61 that you, your spouse (if filing jointly), and your dependents had health care coverage throughout 2014,

• Claim an exemption from the health care coverage requirement for some or all of 2014 and attach Form 8965, or

• Make a shared responsibility payment if, for any month in 2014, you, your spouse (if filing jointly), or your dependents did not have coverage and do not qualify for a coverage exemption. See the instructions for line 61 and Form 8965 for more information.

Premium tax credit. You may be eligible to claim the premium tax credit if you, your spouse, or a dependent enrolled in health insurance through the Health Insurance Marketplace. See the instructions for line 69 and Form 8962 for more information.

Advance payments of the premium tax credit. Advance payments of the premium tax credit may have been made to the health insurer to help pay for the insurance coverage of you, your spouse, or your dependent. If advance payments of the premium tax credit were made, you must file a 2014 tax return and Form 8962. If you enrolled someone who is not claimed as a dependent on your tax return or for more information, see the instructions for Form 8962.

Form 1095-A. If you, your spouse, or a dependent enrolled in health insurance through the Marketplace, you should have received Form(s) 1095-A. If you receive Form(s) 1095-A for 2014, save it. It will help you figure your premium tax credit. If you did not receive a Form 1095-A, contact the Marketplace.

Medicaid waiver payments. If you received certain payments under a Medicaid waiver program for caring for someone who lives in your home with you, you may be able to exclude these payments from your income. See the instructions for line 21.

If you reported these payments on your return for 2013 or an earlier year, see *www.irs.gov/Individuals/Certain-Medicaid-Waiver-Payments-May-Be-Excludable-From-Income*. You may want to file Form 1040X to amend that prior year return.

Pell grants and other scholarships or fellowships. Choosing to include otherwise tax free scholarships or fellowships in your income can increase an education credit and lower your total tax or increase your refund. See the instructions for line 68, the instructions for Form 8863, and Pub. 970 for more information.

Personal exemption amount increased for certain taxpayers. Your personal exemption is increased to $3,950. But the amount is reduced if your adjusted gross income is more than:

• $152,525 if married filing separately,

• $254,200 if single,

• $279,650 if head of household, or

• $305,050 if married filing jointly or qualifying widow(er).

See the instructions for line 42.

Alternative minimum tax worksheet. We have added a worksheet to the instructions for line 45. If you are not sure whether you need to complete Form 6251, you can use this worksheet to see whether you should complete it.

Mailing your return. If you live in Missouri and need to make a payment with your paper return, you will need to mail it to a different address this year. See *Where Do You File?* at the end of these instructions.

Direct deposit. To combat fraud and identity theft, the number of refunds that can be directly deposited to a single financial account or prepaid debit card is now limited to three a year. After this limit is exceeded, paper checks will be sent instead.

Direct Pay. The best way to pay your taxes is with IRS Direct Pay. It's the safe, easy, and free way to pay from your checking or savings account in one online session. Just click "Pay Your Tax Bill" on IRS.gov.

Filing Requirements

These rules apply to all U.S. citizens, regardless of where they live, and resident aliens.

Do You Have To File?

Use Chart A, B, or C to see if you must file a return. U.S. citizens who lived in or had income from a U.S. possession should see Pub. 570. Residents of Puerto Rico can use TeleTax topic 901 to see if they must file.

 Even if you do not otherwise have to file a return, you should file one to get a refund of any federal income tax withheld. You should also file if you are eligible for any of the following credits.
- *Earned income credit.*
- *Additional child tax credit.*
- *American opportunity credit.*
- *Credit for federal tax on fuels.*
- *Premium tax credit.*

See Pub. 501 for details. Also see Pub. 501 if you do not have to file but received a Form 1099-B (or substitute statement).

Premium tax credit. If advance payments of the premium tax credit were made for you, your spouse, or a dependent who enrolled in coverage through the Health Insurance Marketplace, you must file a 2014 return and attach Form 8962.

Exception for certain children under age 19 or full-time students. If certain conditions apply, you can elect to include on your return the income of a child who was under age 19 at the end of 2014 or was a full-time student under age 24 at the end of 2014. To do so, use Form 8814. If you make this election, your child does not have to file a return. For details, use TeleTax topic 553 or see Form 8814.

A child born on January 1, 1991, is considered to be age 24 at the end of 2014. Do not use Form 8814 for such a child.

Resident aliens. These rules also apply if you were a resident alien. Also, you may qualify for certain tax treaty benefits. See Pub. 519 for details.

Nonresident aliens and dual-status aliens. These rules also apply if you were a nonresident alien or a dual-status alien and both of the following apply.
- You were married to a U.S. citizen or resident alien at the end of 2014.
- You elected to be taxed as a resident alien.

See Pub. 519 for details.

 Specific rules apply to determine if you are a resident alien, nonresident alien, or dual-status alien. Most nonresident aliens and dual-status aliens have different filing requirements and may have to file Form 1040NR or Form 1040NR-EZ. Pub. 519 discusses these requirements and other information to help aliens comply with U.S. tax law.

When and Where Should You File?

File Form 1040 by **April 15, 2015.** If you file after this date, you may have to pay interest and penalties. See *Interest and Penalties,* later.

If you were serving in, or in support of, the U.S. Armed Forces in a designated combat zone or contingency operation, you may be able to file later. See Pub. 3 for details.

Filing instructions and addresses are at the end of these instructions.

What if You Cannot File on Time?

You can get an automatic 6-month extension if, no later than the date your return is due, you file Form 4868. For details, see Form 4868.

 An automatic 6-month extension to file does not extend the time to pay your tax. If you do not pay your tax by the original due date of your return, you will owe interest on the unpaid tax and may owe penalties. See Form 4868.

If you are a U.S. citizen or resident alien, you may qualify for an automatic extension of time to file without filing Form 4868. You qualify if, on the due date of your return, you meet one of the following conditions.
- You live outside the United States and Puerto Rico and your main place of business or post of duty is outside the United States and Puerto Rico.
- You are in military or naval service on duty outside the United States and Puerto Rico.

This extension gives you an extra 2 months to file and pay the tax, but interest will be charged from the original due date of the return on any unpaid tax. You must include a statement showing that you meet the requirements. If you are still unable to file your return by the end of the 2-month period, you can get an additional 4 months if, no later than June 15, 2015, you file Form 4868. This 4-month extension of time to file does not extend the time to pay your tax. See Form 4868.

Private Delivery Services

If you *e-file* your return, there is no need to mail it. See the *e-file* page, earlier, or IRS.gov for more information. However, if you choose to mail it, you can use certain private delivery services designated by the IRS to meet the "timely mailing as timely filing/paying" rule for tax returns and payments. These private delivery services include only the following.
- United Parcel Service (UPS): UPS Next Day Air, UPS Next Day Air Saver, UPS 2nd Day Air, UPS 2nd Day Air A.M., UPS Worldwide Express Plus, and UPS Worldwide Express.

- Federal Express (FedEx): FedEx Priority Overnight, FedEx Standard Overnight, FedEx 2Day, FedEx International Priority, and FedEx International First.

For more information, go to IRS.gov and enter "private delivery service" in the search box. The search results will direct you to the IRS mailing address to use if you are using a private delivery service. You will also find any updates to the list of designated private delivery services.

The private delivery service can tell you how to get written proof of the mailing date.

Chart A—For Most People

IF your filing status is . . .	AND at the end of 2014 you were* . . .	THEN file a return if your gross income** was at least . . .
Single (see the instructions for line 1)	under 65 65 or older	$10,150 11,700
Married filing jointly*** (see the instructions for line 2)	under 65 (both spouses) 65 or older (one spouse) 65 or older (both spouses)	$20,300 21,500 22,700
Married filing separately (see the instructions for line 3)	any age	$3,950
Head of household (see the instructions for line 4)	under 65 65 or older	$13,050 14,600
Qualifying widow(er) with dependent child (see the instructions for line 5)	under 65 65 or older	$16,350 17,550

*If you were born on January 1, 1950, you are considered to be age 65 at the end of 2014. (If your spouse died in 2014 or if you are preparing a return for someone who died in 2014, see Pub. 501.)

**Gross Income means all income you received in the form of money, goods, property, and services that is not exempt from tax, including any income from sources outside the United States or from the sale of your main home (even if you can exclude part or all of it). Do not include any social security benefits unless (a) you are married filing a separate return and you lived with your spouse at any time in 2014 or (b) one-half of your social security benefits plus your other gross income and any tax-exempt interest is more than $25,000 ($32,000 if married filing jointly). If (a) or (b) applies, see the instructions for lines 20a and 20b to figure the taxable part of social security benefits you must include in gross income. Gross income includes gains, but not losses, reported on Form 8949 or Schedule D. Gross income from a business means, for example, the amount on Schedule C, line 7, or Schedule F, line 9. But, in figuring gross income, do not reduce your income by any losses, including any loss on Schedule C, line 7, or Schedule F, line 9.

***If you did not live with your spouse at the end of 2014 (or on the date your spouse died) and your gross income was at least $3,950, you must file a return regardless of your age.

Chart B—For Children and Other Dependents (See the instructions for line 6c to find out if someone can claim you as a dependent.)

If your parent (or someone else) can claim you as a dependent, use this chart to see if you must file a return.

In this chart, **unearned income** includes taxable interest, ordinary dividends, and capital gain distributions. It also includes unemployment compensation, taxable social security benefits, pensions, annuities, and distributions of unearned income from a trust. **Earned income** includes salaries, wages, tips, professional fees, and taxable scholarship and fellowship grants. **Gross income** is the total of your unearned and earned income.

Single dependents. Were you **either** age 65 or older **or** blind?

☐ **No.** You must file a return if **any** of the following apply.
- Your unearned income was over $1,000.
- Your earned income was over $6,200.
- Your gross income was more than the **larger** of—
  - $1,000, or
  - Your earned income (up to $5,850) plus $350.

☐ **Yes.** You must file a return if **any** of the following apply.
- Your unearned income was over $2,550 ($4,100 if 65 or older **and** blind).
- Your earned income was over $7,750 ($9,300 if 65 or older **and** blind).
- Your gross income was more than the **larger** of—
  - $2,550 ($4,100 if 65 or older **and** blind), or
  - Your earned income (up to $5,850) plus $1,900 ($3,450 if 65 or older **and** blind).

Married dependents. Were you **either** age 65 or older **or** blind?

☐ **No.** You must file a return if **any** of the following apply.
- Your unearned income was over $1,000.
- Your earned income was over $6,200.
- Your gross income was at least $5 and your spouse files a separate return and itemizes deductions.
- Your gross income was more than the **larger** of—
  - $1,000, or
  - Your earned income (up to $5,850) plus $350.

☐ **Yes.** You must file a return if **any** of the following apply.
- Your unearned income was over $2,200 ($3,400 if 65 or older **and** blind).
- Your earned income was over $7,400 ($8,600 if 65 or older **and** blind).
- Your gross income was at least $5 and your spouse files a separate return and itemizes deductions.
- Your gross income was more than the **larger** of—
  - $2,200 ($3,400 if 65 or older **and** blind), or
  - Your earned income (up to $5,850) plus $1,550 ($2,750 if 65 or older **and** blind).

Chart C—Other Situations When You Must File

You must file a return if any of the five conditions below apply for 2014.

1. You owe any special taxes, including any of the following.

   a. Alternative minimum tax.

   b. Additional tax on a qualified plan, including an individual retirement arrangement (IRA), or other tax-favored account. But if you are filing a return only because you owe this tax, you can file **Form 5329** by itself.

   c. Household employment taxes. But if you are filing a return only because you owe this tax, you can file **Schedule H** by itself.

   d. Social security and Medicare tax on tips you did not report to your employer or on wages you received from an employer who did not withhold these taxes.

   e. Recapture of first-time homebuyer credit. See the instructions for line 60b.

   f. Write-in taxes, including uncollected social security and Medicare or RRTA tax on tips you reported to your employer or on group-term life insurance and additional taxes on health savings accounts. See the instructions for line 62.

   g. Recapture taxes. See the instructions for line 44 and line 62.

2. You (or your spouse, if filing jointly) received HSA, Archer MSA, or Medicare Advantage MSA distributions.

3. You had net earnings from self-employment of at least $400.

4. You had wages of $108.28 or more from a church or qualified church-controlled organization that is exempt from employer social security and Medicare taxes.

5. Advance payments of the premium tax credit were made for you, your spouse, or a dependent who enrolled in coverage through the Health Insurance Marketplace. You should have received Form(s) 1095-A showing the amount of the advance payments, if any.

Where To Report Certain Items From 2014 Forms W-2, 1097, 1098, and 1099

IRS *e-file* IRS *e-file* takes the guesswork out of preparing your return. You may also be eligible to use Free File to file your federal income tax return. Visit *www.irs.gov/efile* for details.

If any federal income tax withheld is shown on these forms, include the tax withheld on Form 1040, line 64. If any state or local income tax withheld is shown on these forms and you deduct state and local income taxes on Schedule A, line 5, include the tax withheld in your deduction on that line.

Form	Item and Box in Which It Should Appear	Where To Report
W-2	Wages, tips, other compensation (box 1)	Form 1040, line 7
	Allocated tips (box 8)	See *Wages, Salaries, Tips, etc.*
	Dependent care benefits (box 10)	Form 2441, Part III
	Adoption benefits (box 12, code T)	Form 8839, line 20
	Employer contributions to an Archer MSA (box 12, code R)	Form 8853, line 1
	Employer contributions to a health savings account (box 12, code W)	Form 8889, line 9
	Uncollected social security and Medicare or RRTA tax (box 12, code A, B, M, or N)	See the instructions for Form 1040, line 62
W-2G	Gambling winnings (box 1)	Form 1040, line 21 (Schedule C or C-EZ for professional gamblers)
1097-BTC	Bond tax credit	See Form 8912 and its instructions
1098	Mortgage interest (box 1) Points (box 2)	Schedule A, line 10, but first see the instructions on Form 1098*
	Refund of overpaid interest (box 3)	Form 1040, line 21, but first see the instructions on Form 1098*
	Mortgage insurance premiums (box 4)	See the instructions for Schedule A, line 13*
1098-C	Contributions of motor vehicles, boats, and airplanes	Schedule A, line 17
1098-E	Student loan interest (box 1)	See the instructions for Form 1040, line 33*
1098-MA	Homeowner mortgage payments (box 3)	Schedule A, but first see the instructions on Form 1098-MA
1098-T	Qualified tuition and related expenses (box 1)	See the instructions for Form 1040, line 34, or Form 1040, line 50; but first see the instructions on Form 1098-T*
1099-A	Acquisition or abandonment of secured property	See Pub. 4681
1099-B	Sales price of stocks, bonds, etc. (box 1d), cost or other basis (box 1e), and adjustments (box 1g)	Form 8949 or Schedule D, whichever applies; see the Instructions for Form 8949
	Aggregate profit or (loss) on contracts (box 11)	Form 6781, line 1
	Bartering (box 13)	See Pub. 525
1099-C	Canceled debt (box 2)	See Pub. 4681
1099-DIV	Total ordinary dividends (box 1a)	Form 1040, line 9a
	Qualified dividends (box 1b)	See the instructions for Form 1040, line 9b
	Total capital gain distributions (box 2a)	Form 1040, line 13, or, if required, Schedule D, line 13
	Unrecaptured section 1250 gain (box 2b)	See the instructions for Schedule D, line 19
	Section 1202 gain (box 2c)	See *Exclusion of Gain on Qualified Small Business (QSB) Stock* in the instructions for Schedule D
	Collectibles (28%) gain (box 2d)	See the instructions for Schedule D, line 18
	Nondividend distributions (box 3)	See the instructions for Form 1040, line 9a
	Investment expenses (box 5)	Schedule A, line 23
	Foreign tax paid (box 6)	Form 1040, line 48, or Schedule A, line 8; but first see the instructions for line 48
	Exempt-interest dividends (box 10)	Form 1040, line 8b
	Specified private activity bond interest dividends (box 11)	Form 6251, line 12
1099-G	Unemployment compensation (box 1)	See the instructions for Form 1040, line 19
	State or local income tax refunds, credits, or offsets (box 2)	See the instructions for Form 1040, line 10, and if box 8 on Form 1099-G is checked, see the box 8 instructions
	RTAA payments (box 5)	Form 1040, line 21
	Taxable grants (box 6)	Form 1040, line 21*
	Agriculture payments (box 7)	See the Instructions for Schedule F or Pub. 225*
	Market gain (box 9)	See the Instructions for Schedule F

*If the item relates to an activity for which you are required to file Schedule C, C-EZ, E, or F or Form 4835, report the taxable or deductible amount allocable to the activity on that schedule or form instead.

Form	Item and Box in Which It Should Appear	Where To Report
1099-INT	Interest income (box 1)	See the instructions on Form 1099-INT
	Early withdrawal penalty (box 2)	Form 1040, line 30
	Interest on U.S. savings bonds and Treasury obligations (box 3)	See the instructions on Form 1099-INT and the instructions for Form 1040, line 8a
	Investment expenses (box 5)	Schedule A, line 23
	Foreign tax paid (box 6)	Form 1040, line 48, or Schedule A, line 8; but first see the instructions for line 48
	Tax-exempt interest (box 8)	Form 1040, line 8b
	Specified private activity bond interest (box 9)	Form 6251, line 12
	Market discount (box 10)	See the instructions on Form 1099-INT and Pub. 550
	Bond premium (box 11)	See the instructions on Form 1099-INT and Pub. 550
1099-K	Payment card and third party network transactions	Schedule C, C-EZ, E, or F
1099-LTC	Long-term care and accelerated death benefits	See Pub. 525 and the Instructions for Form 8853
1099-MISC	Rents (box 1)	See the Instructions for Schedule E*
	Royalties (box 2)	See the Instructions for Schedule E* (for timber, coal, and iron ore royalties, see Pub. 544)*
	Other income (box 3)	Form 1040, line 21*
	Nonemployee compensation (box 7)	Schedule C, C-EZ, or F; but if you were not self-employed, see the instructions on Form 1099-MISC
	Excess golden parachute payments (box 13)	See the instructions for Form 1040, line 62
	Other (boxes 5, 6, 8, 9, 10, 14, and 15b)	See the instructions on Form 1099-MISC
1099-OID	Original issue discount (box 1) Other periodic interest (box 2)	See the instructions on Form 1099-OID
	Early withdrawal penalty (box 3)	Form 1040, line 30
	Market discount (box 5)	See the instructions on Form 1099-OID and Pub. 550
	Acquisition premium (box 6)	See the instructions on Form 1099-OID and Pub. 550
	Original issue discount on U.S. Treasury obligations (box 8)	See the instructions on Form 1099-OID
	Investment expenses (box 9)	Schedule A, line 23
1099-PATR	Patronage dividends and other distributions from a cooperative (boxes 1, 2, 3, and 5)	Schedule C, C-EZ, or F or Form 4835; but first see the instructions on Form 1099-PATR
	Domestic production activities deduction (box 6)	Form 8903, line 23
	Credits and other deductions (boxes 7, 8, and 10)	See the instructions on Form 1099-PATR
	Patron's AMT adjustment (box 9)	Form 6251, line 27
1099-Q	Qualified education program payments	See the instructions for Form 1040, line 21
1099-R	Distributions from IRAs**	See the instructions for Form 1040, lines 15a and 15b
	Distributions from pensions, annuities, etc.	See the instructions for Form 1040, lines 16a and 16b
	Capital gain (box 3)	See the instructions on Form 1099-R
	Disability income with code 3 in box 7	See the instructions for Form 1040, line 7
1099-S	Gross proceeds from real estate transactions (box 2)	Form 4797, Form 6252, Form 8824, or Form 8949
	Buyer's part of real estate tax (box 5)	See the instructions for Schedule A, line 6*
1099-SA	Distributions from health savings accounts (HSAs)	Form 8889, line 14a
	Distributions from MSAs***	Form 8853
SSA-1099	Social security benefits	See the instructions for lines 20a and 20b
RRB-1099	Railroad retirement benefits	See the instructions for lines 20a and 20b

*If the item relates to an activity for which you are required to file Schedule C, C-EZ, E, or F or Form 4835, report the taxable or deductible amount allocable to the activity on that schedule or form instead.

**This includes distributions from Roth, SEP, and SIMPLE IRAs.

***This includes distributions from Archer and Medicare Advantage MSAs.

Need more information or forms? Visit IRS.gov.

Line Instructions for Form 1040

IRS *e-file* takes the guesswork out of preparing your return. You may also be eligible to use Free File to file your federal income tax return. Visit *www.irs.gov/efile* for details.

Section references are to the Internal Revenue Code.

Name and Address

Print or type the information in the spaces provided. If you are married filing a separate return, enter your spouse's name on line 3 instead of below your name.

 If you filed a joint return for 2013 and you are filing a joint return for 2014 with the same spouse, be sure to enter your names and SSNs in the same order as on your 2013 return.

Name Change

If you changed your name because of marriage, divorce, etc., be sure to report the change to the Social Security Administration (SSA) before filing your return. This prevents delays in processing your return and issuing refunds. It also safeguards your future social security benefits.

Address Change

If you plan to move after filing your return, use Form 8822 to notify the IRS of your new address.

P.O. Box

Enter your box number only if your post office does not deliver mail to your home.

Foreign Address

If you have a foreign address, enter the city name on the appropriate line. Do not enter any other information on that line, but also complete the spaces below that line. Do not abbreviate the country name. Follow the country's practice for entering the postal code and the name of the province, county, or state.

Death of a Taxpayer

See *Death of a Taxpayer* under *General Information,* later.

Social Security Number (SSN)

An incorrect or missing SSN can increase your tax, reduce your refund, or delay your refund. To apply for an SSN, fill in Form SS-5 and return it, along with the appropriate evidence documents, to the Social Security Administration (SSA). You can get Form SS-5 online at *www.socialsecurity.gov,* from your local SSA office, or by calling the SSA at 1-800-772-1213. It usually takes about 2 weeks to get an SSN once the SSA has all the evidence and information it needs.

Check that both the name and SSN on your Forms 1040, W-2, and 1099 agree with your social security card. If they do not, certain deductions and credits on your Form 1040 may be reduced or disallowed and you may not receive credit for your social security earnings. If your Form W-2 shows an incorrect SSN or name, notify your employer or the form-issuing agent as soon as possible to make sure your earnings are credited to your social security record. If the name or SSN on your social security card is incorrect, call the SSA.

IRS Individual Taxpayer Identification Numbers (ITINs) for Aliens

If you are a nonresident or resident alien and you do not have and are not eligible to get an SSN, you must apply for an ITIN. For details on how to do so, see Form W-7 and its instructions. It takes 6 to 10 weeks to get an ITIN.

If you already have an ITIN, enter it wherever your SSN is requested on your tax return.

Note. An ITIN is for tax use only. It does not entitle you to social security benefits or change your employment or immigration status under U.S. law.

Nonresident Alien Spouse

If your spouse is a nonresident alien, he or she must have either an SSN or an ITIN if:
- You file a joint return,
- You file a separate return and claim an exemption for your spouse, or
- Your spouse is filing a separate return.

Presidential Election Campaign Fund

This fund helps pay for Presidential election campaigns. The fund reduces candidates' dependence on large contributions from individuals and groups and places candidates on an equal financial footing in the general election. The fund also helps pay for pediatric medical research. If you want $3 to go to this fund, check the box. If you are filing a joint return, your spouse can also have $3 go to the fund. If you check a box, your tax or refund will not change.

Filing Status

Check only the filing status that applies to you. The ones that will usually give you the lowest tax are listed last.
- Married filing separately.
- Single.
- Head of household.
- Married filing jointly.
- Qualifying widow(er) with dependent child.

Same-sex marriage. For federal tax purposes, individuals of the same sex are considered married if they were lawfully married in a state (or foreign country) whose laws authorize the marriage of two individuals of the same sex, even if the state (or foreign country) in which they now live does not recognize same-sex marriage. The term "spouse" includes an individual married to a person of the same sex if the couple is lawfully married under state (or foreign) law. However, individuals who have entered into a registered domestic partnership, civil union, or other similar relationship that is not considered a marriage under state (or foreign) law are not considered married for federal tax purposes. For more details, see Pub. 501.

 More than one filing status can apply to you. You can choose the one that will give you the lowest tax.

Line 1

Single

You can check the box on line 1 if any of the following was true on December 31, 2014.

- You were never married.
- You were legally separated according to your state law under a decree of divorce or separate maintenance. But if, at the end of 2014, your divorce was not final (an interlocutory decree), you are considered married and cannot check the box on line 1.
- You were widowed before January 1, 2014, and did not remarry before the end of 2014. But if you have a dependent child, you may be able to use the qualifying widow(er) filing status. See the instructions for line 5.

Line 2

Married Filing Jointly

You can check the box on line 2 if any of the following apply.

- You were married at the end of 2014, even if you did not live with your spouse at the end of 2014.
- Your spouse died in 2014 and you did not remarry in 2014.
- You were married at the end of 2014, and your spouse died in 2015 before filing a 2014 return.

A married couple filing jointly report their combined income and deduct their combined allowable expenses on one return. They can file a joint return even if only one had income or if they did not

live together all year. However, both persons must sign the return. Once you file a joint return, you cannot choose to file separate returns for that year after the due date of the return.

Joint and several tax liability. If you file a joint return, both you and your spouse are generally responsible for the tax and interest or penalties due on the return. This means that if one spouse does not pay the tax due, the other may have to. Or, if one spouse does not report the correct tax, both spouses may be responsible for any additional taxes assessed by the IRS. You may want to file separately if:

- You believe your spouse is not reporting all of his or her income, or
- You do not want to be responsible for any taxes due if your spouse does not have enough tax withheld or does not pay enough estimated tax.

See the instructions for line 3. Also see *Innocent Spouse Relief* under *General Information,* later.

Nonresident aliens and dual-status aliens. Generally, a married couple cannot file a joint return if either spouse is a nonresident alien at any time during the year. However, if you were a nonresident alien or a dual-status alien and were married to a U.S. citizen or resident alien at the end of 2014, you can elect to be treated as a resident alien and file a joint return. See Pub. 519 for details.

Line 3

Married Filing Separately

If you are married and file a separate return, you generally report only your own income, exemptions, deductions, and credits. Generally, you are responsible only for the tax on your own income. Different rules apply to people in community property states; see Pub. 555.

However, you will usually pay more tax than if you use another filing status for which you qualify. Also, if you file a separate return, you cannot take the student loan interest deduction, the tuition and fees deduction, the education credits, or the earned income credit. You also cannot take the standard deduction if your spouse itemizes deductions.

Be sure to enter your spouse's SSN or ITIN on Form 1040. If your spouse does

not have and is not required to have an SSN or ITIN, enter "NRA."

 You may be able to file as head of household if you had a child living with you and you lived apart from your spouse during the last 6 months of 2014. See Married persons who live apart.

Line 4

Head of Household

This filing status is for unmarried individuals who provide a home for certain other persons. You are considered unmarried for this purpose if any of the following applies.

- You were legally separated according to your state law under a decree of divorce or separate maintenance at the end of 2014. But if, at the end of 2014, your divorce was not final (an interlocutory decree), you are considered married.
- You are married but lived apart from your spouse for the last 6 months of 2014 and you meet the other rules under *Married persons who live apart.*
- You are married to a nonresident alien at any time during the year and you do not choose to treat him or her as a resident alien.

Check the box on line 4 only if you are unmarried (or considered unmarried) and either *Test 1* or *Test 2* applies.

Test 1. You paid over half the cost of keeping up a home that was the main home for all of 2014 of your parent whom you can claim as a dependent on line 6c, except under a multiple support agreement (see the line 6c instructions). Your parent did not have to live with you.

Test 2. You paid over half the cost of keeping up a home in which you lived and in which one of the following also lived for more than half of the year (if half or less, see *Exception to time lived with you*).

1. Any person whom you can claim as a dependent on line 6c. But do not include:

a. Your child whom you claim as your dependent because of the rule for *Children of divorced or separated parents* in the line 6c instructions,

Need more information or forms? Visit IRS.gov.

b. Any person who is your dependent only because he or she lived with you for all of 2014, or

c. Any person you claimed as a dependent under a multiple support agreement. See the line 6c instructions.

2. Your unmarried qualifying child who is not your dependent.

3. Your married qualifying child who is not your dependent only because you can be claimed as a dependent on line 6c of someone else's 2014 return.

4. Your qualifying child who, even though you are the custodial parent, is not your dependent because of the rule for *Children of divorced or separated parents* in the line 6c instructions.

If the child is not claimed as your dependent on line 6c, enter the child's name on line 4. If you do not enter the name, it will take us longer to process your return.

Qualifying child. To find out if someone is your qualifying child, see Step 1 of the line 6c instructions.

Dependent. To find out if someone is your dependent, see the instructions for line 6c.

Exception to time lived with you. Temporary absences by you or the other person for special circumstances, such as school, vacation, business, medical care, military service, or detention in a juvenile facility, count as time lived in the home. Also see *Kidnapped child* in the line 6c instructions, if applicable.

If the person for whom you kept up a home was born or died in 2014, you still may be able to file as head of household. If the person is your qualifying child, the child must have lived with you for more than half the part of the year he or she was alive. If the person is anyone else, see Pub. 501.

Keeping up a home. To find out what is included in the cost of keeping up a home, see Pub. 501.

If you used payments you received under Temporary Assistance for Needy Families (TANF) or other public assistance programs to pay part of the cost of keeping up your home, you cannot count them as money you paid. However, you must include them in the total cost of keeping up your home to figure if you paid over half the cost.

Married persons who live apart. Even if you were not divorced or legally separated at the end of 2014, you are considered unmarried if all of the following apply.

• You lived apart from your spouse for the last 6 months of 2014. Temporary absences for special circumstances, such as for business, medical care, school, or military service, count as time lived in the home.

• You file a separate return from your spouse.

• You paid over half the cost of keeping up your home for 2014.

• Your home was the main home of your child, stepchild, or foster child for more than half of 2014 (if half or less, see *Exception to time lived with you*, earlier).

• You can claim this child as your dependent or could claim the child except that the child's other parent can claim him or her under the rule for *Children of divorced or separated parents* in the line 6c instructions.

Adopted child. An adopted child is always treated as your own child. An adopted child includes a child lawfully placed with you for legal adoption.

Foster child. A foster child is any child placed with you by an authorized placement agency or by judgment, decree, or other order of any court of competent jurisdiction.

Line 5

Qualifying Widow(er) With Dependent Child

You can check the box on line 5 and use joint return tax rates for 2014 if all of the following apply.

1. Your spouse died in 2012 or 2013 and you did not remarry before the end of 2014.

2. You have a child or stepchild you can claim as a dependent on line 6c. This does not include a foster child.

3. This child lived in your home for all of 2014. If the child did not live with you for the required time, see *Exception to time lived with you*, later.

4. You paid over half the cost of keeping up your home.

5. You could have filed a joint return with your spouse the year he or she died, even if you did not actually do so.

If your spouse died in 2014, you cannot file as qualifying widow(er) with dependent child. Instead, see the instructions for line 2.

Adopted child. An adopted child is always treated as your own child. An adopted child includes a child lawfully placed with you for legal adoption.

Dependent. To find out if someone is your dependent, see the instructions for line 6c.

Exception to time lived with you. Temporary absences by you or the child for special circumstances, such as school, vacation, business, medical care, military service, or detention in a juvenile facility, count as time lived in the home. Also see *Kidnapped child* in the line 6c instructions, if applicable.

A child is considered to have lived with you for all of 2014 if the child was born or died in 2014 and your home was the child's home for the entire time he or she was alive.

Keeping up a home. To find out what is included in the cost of keeping up a home, see Pub. 501.

If you used payments you received under Temporary Assistance for Needy Families (TANF) or other public assistance programs to pay part of the cost of keeping up your home, you cannot count them as money you paid. However, you must include them in the total cost of keeping up your home to figure if you paid over half the cost.

Exemptions

You usually can deduct $3,950 on line 42 for each exemption you can take.

Line 6b

Spouse

Check the box on line 6b if either of the following applies.

1. Your filing status is married filing jointly and your spouse cannot be claimed as a dependent on another person's return.

2. You were married at the end of 2014, your filing status is married filing separately or head of household, and both of the following apply.

a. Your spouse had no income and is not filing a return.

b. Your spouse cannot be claimed as a dependent on another person's return.

If your filing status is head of household and you check the box on line 6b, enter the name of your spouse on the dotted line next to line 6b. Also, enter your spouse's social security number in the space provided at the top of your return. If you became divorced or legally separated during 2014, you cannot take an exemption for your former spouse.

Death of your spouse. If your spouse died in 2014 and you did not remarry by the end of 2014, check the box on line 6b if you could have taken an exemption for your spouse on the date of death. For other filing instructions, see *Death of a Taxpayer* under *General Information,* later.

Line 6c—Dependents

Dependents and Qualifying Child for Child Tax Credit

Follow the steps below to find out if a person qualifies as your dependent, qualifies you to take the child tax credit, or both. If you have more than four dependents, check the box to the left of line 6c and include a statement showing the information required in columns (1) through (4).

Step 1 **Do You Have a Qualifying Child?**

A qualifying child is a child who is your...

Son, daughter, stepchild, foster child, brother, sister, stepbrother, stepsister, half brother, half sister, or a descendant of any of them (for example, your grandchild, niece, or nephew)

was ...

Under age 19 at the end of 2014 and younger than you (or your spouse, if filing jointly)

or

Under age 24 at the end of 2014, a student (defined later), and younger than you (or your spouse, if filing jointly)

or

Any age and permanently and totally disabled (defined later)

Who did not provide over half of his or her own support for 2014 (see Pub. 501)

Who is not filing a joint return for 2014 or is filing a joint return for 2014 only to claim a refund of withheld income tax or estimated tax paid (see Pub. 501 for details and examples)

Who lived with you for more than half of 2014. If the child did not live with you for the required time, see *Exception to time lived with you,* later.

 *If the child meets the conditions to be a qualifying child of any other person (other than your spouse if filing jointly) for 2014, see* Qualifying child of more than one person, *later.*

1. Do you have a child who meets the conditions to be your qualifying child?

☐ **Yes.** Go to Step 2. ☐ **No.** Go to Step 4.

Step 2 **Is Your Qualifying Child Your Dependent?**

1. Was the child a U.S. citizen, U.S. national, U.S. resident alien, or a resident of Canada or Mexico? (See Pub. 519 for the definition of a U.S. national or U.S. resident alien. If the child was adopted, see *Exception to citizen test,* later.)

☐ **Yes.** Continue   ☐ **No.** You cannot claim this child as a dependent.

2. Was the child married?

☐ **Yes.** See *Married person,* later. ☐ **No.** Continue

3. Could you, or your spouse if filing jointly, be claimed as a dependent on someone else's 2014 tax return? See Steps 1, 2, and 4.

☐ **Yes.** You cannot claim any dependents. Go to Form 1040, line 7. ☐ **No.** You can claim this child as a dependent. Complete Form 1040, line 6c, columns (1) through (3) for this child. Then, go to Step 3.

Step 3 **Does Your Qualifying Child Qualify You for the Child Tax Credit?**

1. Was the child under age 17 at the end of 2014?

☐ **Yes.** Continue ☐ **No.** This child is not a qualifying child for the child tax credit.

2. Was the child a U.S. citizen, U.S. national, or U.S. resident alien? (See Pub. 519 for the definition of a U.S. national or U.S. resident alien. If the child was adopted, see *Exception to citizen test,* later.)

☐ **Yes.** This child is a qualifying child for the child tax credit. Check the box on Form 1040, line 6c, column (4). ☐ **No.** This child is not a qualifying child for the child tax credit.

Step 4 Is Your Qualifying Relative Your Dependent?

A qualifying relative is a person who is your...

Son, daughter, stepchild, foster child, or a descendant of any of them (for example, your grandchild)

or

Brother, sister, half brother, half sister, or a son or daughter of any of them (for example, your niece or nephew)

or

Father, mother, or an ancestor or sibling of either of them (for example, your grandmother, grandfather, aunt, or uncle)

or

Stepbrother, stepsister, stepfather, stepmother, son-in-law, daughter-in-law, father-in-law, mother-in-law, brother-in-law, or sister-in-law

or

Any other person (other than your spouse) who lived with you all year as a member of your household if your relationship did not violate local law. If the person did not live with you for the required time, see *Exception to time lived with you*, later

AND

Who was not a qualifying child (see Step 1) of any taxpayer for 2014. For this purpose, a person is not a taxpayer if he or she is not required to file a U.S. income tax return **and** either does not file such a return or files only to get a refund of withheld income tax or estimated tax paid. See Pub. 501 for details and examples

AND

Who had gross income of less than $3,950 in 2014. If the person was permanently and totally disabled, see *Exception to gross income test*, later

AND

For whom you provided over half of his or her support in 2014. But see *Children of divorced or separated parents*, *Multiple support agreements*, and *Kidnapped child*, later.

1. Does any person meet the conditions to be your qualifying relative?

☐ **Yes.** Continue   ☐ **No.** (stop)

Go to Form 1040, line 7.

2. Was your qualifying relative a U.S. citizen, U.S. national, U.S. resident alien, or a resident of Canada or Mexico? (See Pub. 519 for the definition of a U.S. national or U.S. resident alien. If your qualifying relative was adopted, see *Exception to citizen test*, later.)

☐ **Yes.** Continue   ☐ **No.** (stop)

You cannot claim this person as a dependent.

3. Was your qualifying relative married?

☐ **Yes.** See *Married person*, later.   ☐ **No.** Continue

4. Could you, or your spouse if filing jointly, be claimed as a dependent on someone else's 2014 tax return? See Steps 1, 2, and 4.

☐ **Yes.** (stop)   ☐ **No.** You can claim this person as a dependent. Complete Form 1040, line 6c, columns (1) through (3). Do not check the box on Form 1040, line 6c, column (4).

You cannot claim any dependents. Go to Form 1040, line 7.

Definitions and Special Rules

Adopted child. An adopted child is always treated as your own child. An adopted child includes a child lawfully placed with you for legal adoption.

Adoption taxpayer identification numbers (ATINs). If you have a dependent who was placed with you for legal adoption and you do not know his or her SSN, you must get an ATIN for the dependent from the IRS. See Form W-7A for details. If the dependent is not a U.S. citizen or resident alien, apply for an ITIN instead, using Form W-7.

Children of divorced or separated parents. A child will be treated as the qualifying child or qualifying relative of his or her noncustodial parent (defined later) if all of the following conditions apply.

1. The parents are divorced, legally separated, separated under a written separation agreement, or lived apart at all times during the last 6 months of 2014 (whether or not they are or were married).

2. The child received over half of his or her support for 2014 from the parents (and the rules on *Multiple support agreements*, later, do not apply). Support of a child received from a parent's spouse is treated as provided by the parent.

3. The child is in custody of one or both of the parents for more than half of 2014.

4. Either of the following applies.

Need more information or forms? Visit IRS.gov.

a. The custodial parent signs Form 8332 or a substantially similar statement that he or she will not claim the child as a dependent for 2014, and the noncustodial parent includes a copy of the form or statement with his or her return. If the divorce decree or separation agreement went into effect after 1984 and before 2009, the noncustodial parent may be able to include certain pages from the decree or agreement instead of Form 8332. See *Post-1984 and pre-2009 decree or agreement* and *Post-2008 decree or agreement*.

b. A pre-1985 decree of divorce or separate maintenance or written separation agreement between the parents provides that the noncustodial parent can claim the child as a dependent, and the noncustodial parent provides at least $600 for support of the child during 2014.

If conditions (1) through (4) apply, only the noncustodial parent can claim the child for purposes of the dependency exemption (line 6c) and the child tax credits (lines 52 and 67). However, this special rule does not apply to head of household filing status, the credit for child and dependent care expenses, the exclusion for dependent care benefits, or the earned income credit. See Pub. 501 for details.

Custodial and noncustodial parents. The custodial parent is the parent with whom the child lived for the greater number of nights in 2014. The noncustodial parent is the other parent. If the child was with each parent for an equal number of nights, the custodial parent is the parent with the higher adjusted gross income. See Pub. 501 for an exception for a parent who works at night, rules for a child who is emancipated under state law, and other details.

Post-1984 and pre-2009 decree or agreement. The decree or agreement must state all three of the following.

1. The noncustodial parent can claim the child as a dependent without regard to any condition, such as payment of support.

2. The other parent will not claim the child as a dependent.

3. The years for which the claim is released.

The noncustodial parent must include all of the following pages from the decree or agreement.
- Cover page (include the other parent's SSN on that page).
- The pages that include all the information identified in (1) through (3) above.
- Signature page with the other parent's signature and date of agreement.

 You must include the required information even if you filed it with your return in an earlier year.

Post-2008 decree or agreement. If the divorce decree or separation agreement went into effect after 2008, the noncustodial parent cannot include pages from the decree or agreement instead of Form 8332. The custodial parent must sign either Form 8332 or a substantially similar statement the only purpose of which is to release the custodial parent's claim to an exemption for a child, and the noncustodial parent must include a copy with his or her return. The form or statement must release the custodial parent's claim to the child without any conditions. For example, the release must not depend on the noncustodial parent paying support.

Release of exemption revoked. A custodial parent who has revoked his or her previous release of a claim to exemption for a child must include a copy of the revocation with his or her return. For details, see Form 8332.

Exception to citizen test. If you are a U.S. citizen or U.S. national and your adopted child lived with you all year as a member of your household, that child meets the requirement to be a U.S. citizen in Step 2, question 1; Step 3, question 2; and Step 4, question 2.

Exception to gross income test. If your relative (including a person who lived with you all year as a member of your household) is permanently and totally disabled (defined later), certain income for services performed at a sheltered workshop may be excluded for this test. For details, see Pub. 501.

Exception to time lived with you. Temporary absences by you or the other person for special circumstances, such as school, vacation, business, medical care, military service, or detention in a juvenile facility, count as time the person lived with you. Also see *Children of divorced or separated parents*, earlier, or *Kidnapped child*, later.

If the person meets all other requirements to be your qualifying child but was born or died in 2014, the person is considered to have lived with you for more than half of 2014 if your home was this person's home for more than half the time he or she was alive in 2014.

Any other person is considered to have lived with you for all of 2014 if the person was born or died in 2014 and your home was this person's home for the entire time he or she was alive in 2014.

Foster child. A foster child is any child placed with you by an authorized placement agency or by judgment, decree, or other order of any court of competent jurisdiction.

Kidnapped child. If your child is presumed by law enforcement authorities to have been kidnapped by someone who is not a family member, you may be able to take the child into account in determining your eligibility for head of household or qualifying widow(er) filing status, the dependency exemption, the child tax credit, and the earned income credit (EIC). For details, see Pub. 501 (Pub. 596 for the EIC).

Married person. If the person is married and files a joint return, you cannot claim that person as your dependent. However, if the person is married but does not file a joint return or files a joint return only to claim a refund of withheld income tax or estimated tax paid, you may be able to claim him or her as a dependent. (See Pub. 501 for details and examples.) In that case, go to Step 2, question 3 (for a qualifying child) or Step 4, question 4 (for a qualifying relative).

Multiple support agreements. If no one person contributed over half of the support of your relative (or a person who lived with you all year as a member of your household) but you and another person(s) provided more than half of your relative's support, special rules may apply that would treat you as having provided over half of the support. For details, see Pub. 501.

Permanently and totally disabled. A person is permanently and totally disabled if, at any time in 2014, the person cannot engage in any substantial gainful activity because of a physical or mental condition and a doctor has determined that this condition has lasted or can be expected to last continuously for at least a year or can be expected to lead to death.

Qualifying child of more than one person. Even if a child meets the conditions to be the qualifying child of more than one person, only one person can claim the child as a qualifying child for all of the following tax benefits, unless the special rule for *Children of divorced or separated parents,* described earlier, applies.

1. Dependency exemption (line 6c).
2. Child tax credits (lines 52 and 67).
3. Head of household filing status (line 4).
4. Credit for child and dependent care expenses (line 49).
5. Exclusion for dependent care benefits (Form 2441, Part III).
6. Earned income credit (lines 66a and 66b).

No other person can take any of the six tax benefits just listed unless he or she has a different qualifying child. If you and any other person can claim the child as a qualifying child, the following rules apply.

- If only one of the persons is the child's parent, the child is treated as the qualifying child of the parent.
- If the parents file a joint return together and can claim the child as a qualifying child, the child is treated as the qualifying child of the parents.
- If the parents do not file a joint return together but both parents claim the child as a qualifying child, the IRS will treat the child as the qualifying child of the parent with whom the child lived for the longer period of time in 2014. If the child lived with each parent for the same amount of time, the IRS will treat the child as the qualifying child of the parent who had the higher adjusted gross income (AGI) for 2014.
- If no parent can claim the child as a qualifying child, the child is treated as the qualifying child of the person who had the highest AGI for 2014.
- If a parent can claim the child as a qualifying child but no parent does so claim the child, the child is treated as the qualify-

ing child of the person who had the highest AGI for 2014, but only if that person's AGI is higher than the highest AGI of any parent of the child who can claim the child.

Example. Your daughter meets the conditions to be a qualifying child for both you and your mother. Your daughter does not meet the conditions to be a qualifying child of any other person, including her other parent. Under the rules just described, you can claim your daughter as a qualifying child for all of the six tax benefits just listed for which you otherwise qualify. Your mother cannot claim any of those six tax benefits unless she has a different qualifying child. However, if your mother's AGI is higher than yours and you do not claim your daughter as a qualifying child, your daughter is the qualifying child of your mother.

For more details and examples, see Pub. 501.

If you will be claiming the child as a qualifying child, go to Step 2. Otherwise, stop; you cannot claim any benefits based on this child.

Social security number. You must enter each dependent's social security number (SSN). Be sure the name and SSN entered agree with the dependent's social security card. Otherwise, at the time we process your return, we may disallow the exemption claimed for the dependent and reduce or disallow any other tax benefits (such as the child tax credit) based on that dependent. If the name or SSN on the dependent's social security card is not correct or you need to get an SSN for your dependent, contact the Social Security Administration. See *Social Security Number (SSN)*, earlier. If your dependent will not have a number by the date your return is due, see *What If You Cannot File on Time?* earlier.

If your dependent child was born and died in 2014 and you do not have an SSN for the child, enter "Died" in column (2) and include a copy of the child's birth certificate, death certificate, or hospital records. The document must show the child was born alive.

Student. A student is a child who during any part of 5 calendar months of 2014 was enrolled as a full-time student at a school, or took a full-time, on-farm training course given by a school or a state, county, or local government agency. A school includes a technical, trade, or mechanical school. It does not include an on-the-job training course, correspondence school, or school offering courses only through the Internet.

Income

Generally, you must report all income except income that is exempt from tax by law. For details, see the following instructions, especially the instructions for lines 7 through 21. Also see Pub. 525.

Foreign-Source Income

You must report unearned income, such as interest, dividends, and pensions, from sources outside the United States unless exempt by law or a tax treaty. You must also report earned income, such as wages and tips, from sources outside the United States.

If you worked abroad, you may be able to exclude part or all of your foreign earned income. For details, see Pub. 54 and Form 2555 or 2555-EZ.

Foreign retirement plans. If you were a beneficiary of a foreign retirement plan, you may have to report the undistributed income earned in your plan. However, if you were the beneficiary of a Canadian registered retirement plan, see Revenue Procedure 2014-55, 2014-44 I.R.B. 753, available at *www.irs.gov//irb/2014-44_IRB/ar10.html*, to find out if you can elect to defer tax on the undistributed income.

Report distributions from foreign pension plans on lines 16a and 16b.

Foreign accounts and trusts. You must complete Part III of Schedule B if you:

- Had a foreign account, or
- Received a distribution from, or were a grantor of, or a transferor to, a foreign trust.

If you had foreign financial assets in 2014, you may have to file Form 8938. See Form 8938 and its instructions.

Chapter 11 Bankruptcy Cases

If you are a debtor in a chapter 11 bankruptcy case, income taxable to the bankruptcy estate and reported on the estate's income tax return includes:

- Earnings from services you performed after the beginning of the case (both wages and self-employment income), and
- Income from property described in section 541 of title 11 of the U.S. Code

that you either owned when the case began or that you acquired after the case began and before the case was closed, dismissed, or converted to a case under a different chapter.

Because this income is taxable to the estate, do not include this income on your own individual income tax return. The only exception is for purposes of figuring your self-employment tax. For that purpose, you must take into account all your self-employment income for the year from services performed both before and after the beginning of the case. Also, you (or the trustee, if one is appointed) must allocate between you and the bankruptcy estate the wages, salary, or other compensation and withheld income tax reported to you on Form W-2. A similar allocation is required for income and withheld income tax reported to you on Forms 1099. You must also include a statement that indicates you filed a chapter 11 case and that explains how income and withheld income tax reported to you on Forms W-2 and 1099 are allocated between you and the estate. For more details, including acceptable allocation methods, see Notice 2006-83, 2006-40 I.R.B. 596, available at *www.irs.gov/irb/2006-40_IRB/ar12.html*.

Community Property States

Community property states are Arizona, California, Idaho, Louisiana, Nevada, New Mexico, Texas, Washington, and Wisconsin. If you and your spouse lived in a community property state, you must usually follow state law to determine what is community income and what is separate income. For details, see Form 8958 and Pub. 555.

Nevada, Washington, and California domestic partners. A registered domestic partner in Nevada, Washington, or California generally must report half the combined community income of the individual and his or her domestic partner. See Form 8958 and Pub. 555.

Rounding Off to Whole Dollars

You can round off cents to whole dollars on your return and schedules. If you do round to whole dollars, you must round all amounts. To round, drop amounts under 50 cents and increase amounts from

50 to 99 cents to the next dollar. For example, $1.39 becomes $1 and $2.50 becomes $3.

If you have to add two or more amounts to figure the amount to enter on a line, include cents when adding the amounts and round off only the total.

Line 7

Wages, Salaries, Tips, etc.

Enter the total of your wages, salaries, tips, etc. If a joint return, also include your spouse's income. For most people, the amount to enter on this line should be shown in box 1 of their Form(s) W-2. But the following types of income must also be included in the total on line 7.

- All wages received as a household employee for which you did not receive a Form W-2 because an employer paid you less than $1,900 in 2014. Also, enter "HSH" and the total amount not reported on Form(s) W-2 on the dotted line next to line 7.
- Tip income you did not report to your employer. This should include any allocated tips shown in box 8 on your Form(s) W-2 unless you can prove that your unreported tips are less than the amount in box 8. Allocated tips are not included as income in box 1. See Pub. 531 for more details. Also include the value of any noncash tips you received, such as tickets, passes, or other items of value. Although you do not report these noncash tips to your employer, you must report them on line 7.

 You may owe social security and Medicare or railroad retirement (RRTA) tax on unreported tips. See the instructions for line 58.

- Dependent care benefits, which should be shown in box 10 of your Form(s) W-2. But first complete Form 2441 to see if you can exclude part or all of the benefits.
- Employer-provided adoption benefits, which should be shown in box 12 of your Form(s) W-2 with code T. But see the Instructions for Form 8839 to find out if you can exclude part or all of the benefits. You may also be able to exclude amounts if you adopted a child with special needs and the adoption became final in 2014.

• Scholarship and fellowship grants not reported on Form W-2. Also, enter "SCH" and the amount on the dotted line next to line 7. However, if you were a degree candidate, include on line 7 only the amounts you used for expenses other than tuition and course-related expenses. For example, amounts used for room, board, and travel must be reported on line 7.

• Excess salary deferrals. The amount deferred should be shown in box 12 of your Form W-2, and the "Retirement plan" box in box 13 should be checked. If the total amount you (or your spouse if filing jointly) deferred for 2014 under all plans was more than $17,500 (excluding catch-up contributions as explained later), include the excess on line 7. This limit is (a) $12,000 if you have only SIMPLE plans, or (b) $20,500 for section 403(b) plans if you qualify for the 15-year rule in Pub. 571. Although designated Roth contributions are subject to this limit, do not include the excess attributable to such contributions on line 7. They are already included as income in box 1 of your Form W-2.

A higher limit may apply to participants in section 457(b) deferred compensation plans for the 3 years before retirement age. Contact your plan administrator for more information.

If you were age 50 or older at the end of 2014, your employer may have allowed an additional deferral (catch-up contributions) of up to $5,500 ($2,500 for section 401(k)(11) and SIMPLE plans). This additional deferral amount is not subject to the overall limit on elective deferrals.

 You cannot deduct the amount deferred. It is not included as income in box 1 of your Form W-2.

• Disability pensions shown on Form 1099-R if you have not reached the minimum retirement age set by your employer. But see *Insurance Premiums for Retired Public Safety Officers* in the instructions for lines 16a and 16b. Disability pensions received after you reach minimum retirement age and other payments shown on Form 1099-R (other than payments from an IRA*) are reported on lines 16a and 16b. Payments from

an IRA are reported on lines 15a and 15b.

• Corrective distributions from a retirement plan shown on Form 1099-R of excess salary deferrals and excess contributions (plus earnings). But do not include distributions from an IRA* on line 7. Instead, report distributions from an IRA on lines 15a and 15b.

• Wages from Form 8919, line 6.

This includes a Roth, SEP, or SIMPLE IRA.

Were You a Statutory Employee?

If you were, the "Statutory employee" box in box 13 of your Form W-2 should be checked. Statutory employees include full-time life insurance salespeople and certain agent or commission drivers, traveling salespeople, and homeworkers. If you have related business expenses to deduct, report the amount shown in box 1 of your Form W-2 on Schedule C or C-EZ along with your expenses.

Missing or Incorrect Form W-2?

Your employer is required to provide or send Form W-2 to you no later than February 2, 2015. If you do not receive it by early February, use TeleTax topic 154 to find out what to do. Even if you do not get a Form W-2, you must still report your earnings on line 7. If you lose your Form W-2 or it is incorrect, ask your employer for a new one.

Line 8a

Taxable Interest

Each payer should send you a Form 1099-INT or Form 1099-OID. Enter your total taxable interest income on line 8a. But you must fill in and attach Schedule B if the total is over $1,500 or any of the other conditions listed at the beginning of the Schedule B instructions apply to you.

Interest credited in 2014 on deposits that you could not withdraw because of the bankruptcy or insolvency of the financial institution may not have to be included in your 2014 income. For details, see Pub. 550.

 If you get a 2014 Form 1099-INT for U.S. savings bond interest that includes amounts you reported before 2014, see Pub. 550.

Line 8b

Tax-Exempt Interest

If you received any tax-exempt interest, such as from municipal bonds, each payer should send you a Form 1099-INT. Your tax-exempt interest should be shown in box 8 of Form 1099-INT. Enter the total on line 8b. Also include on line 8b any exempt-interest dividends from a mutual fund or other regulated investment company. This amount should be shown in box 10 of Form 1099-DIV.

Do not include interest earned on your IRA, health savings account, Archer or Medicare Advantage MSA, or Coverdell education savings account.

Line 9a

Ordinary Dividends

Each payer should send you a Form 1099-DIV. Enter your total ordinary dividends on line 9a. This amount should be shown in box 1a of Form(s) 1099-DIV.

You must fill in and attach Schedule B if the total is over $1,500 or you received, as a nominee, ordinary dividends that actually belong to someone else.

Nondividend Distributions

Some distributions are a return of your cost (or other basis). They will not be taxed until you recover your cost (or other basis). You must reduce your cost (or other basis) by these distributions. After you get back all of your cost (or other basis), you must report these distributions as capital gains on Form 8949. For details, see Pub. 550.

Need more information or forms? Visit IRS.gov.

Dividends on insurance policies are a partial return of the premiums you paid. Do not report them as dividends. Include them in income on line 21 only if they exceed the total of all net premiums you paid for the contract.

Line 9b

Qualified Dividends

Enter your total qualified dividends on line 9b. Qualified dividends are also included in the ordinary dividend total required to be shown on line 9a. Qualified dividends are eligible for a lower tax rate than other ordinary income. Generally, these dividends are shown in box 1b of Form(s) 1099-DIV. See Pub. 550 for the definition of qualified dividends if you received dividends not reported on Form 1099-DIV.

Exception. Some dividends may be reported as qualified dividends in box 1b of Form 1099-DIV but are not qualified dividends. These include:

• Dividends you received as a nominee. See the Schedule B instructions.

• Dividends you received on any share of stock that you held for less than 61 days during the 121-day period that began 60 days before the ex-dividend date. The ex-dividend date is the first date following the declaration of a dividend on which the purchaser of a stock is not entitled to receive the next dividend payment. When counting the number of days you held the stock, include the day you disposed of the stock but not the day you acquired it. See the examples that follow. Also, when counting the number of days you held the stock, you cannot count certain days during which your risk of loss was diminished. See Pub. 550 for more details.

• Dividends attributable to periods totaling more than 366 days that you received on any share of preferred stock held for less than 91 days during the 181-day period that began 90 days before the ex-dividend date. When counting the number of days you held the stock, you cannot count certain days during which your risk of loss was diminished. See Pub. 550 for more details. Preferred dividends attributable to periods totaling less than 367 days are subject to the 61-day holding period rule just described.

• Dividends on any share of stock to the extent that you are under an obligation (including a short sale) to make related payments with respect to positions in substantially similar or related property.

• Payments in lieu of dividends, but only if you know or have reason to know that the payments are not qualified dividends.

Example 1. You bought 5,000 shares of XYZ Corp. common stock on July 8, 2014. XYZ Corp. paid a cash dividend of 10 cents per share. The ex-dividend date was July 16, 2014. Your Form 1099-DIV from XYZ Corp. shows $500 in box 1a (ordinary dividends) and in box 1b (qualified dividends). However, you sold the 5,000 shares on August 11, 2014. You held your shares of XYZ Corp. for only 34 days of the 121-day period (from July 9, 2014, through August 11, 2014). The 121-day period began on May 17, 2014 (60 days before the ex-dividend date), and ended on September 14, 2014. You have no qualified dividends from XYZ Corp. because you held the XYZ stock for less than 61 days.

Example 2. The facts are the same as in Example 1 except that you bought the stock on July 15, 2014 (the day before the ex-dividend date), and you sold the stock on September 16, 2014. You held the stock for 63 days (from July 16, 2014, through September 16, 2014). The $500 of qualified dividends shown in box 1b of Form 1099-DIV are all qualified dividends because you held the stock for 61 days of the 121-day period (from July 16, 2014, through September 14, 2014).

Example 3. You bought 10,000 shares of ABC Mutual Fund common stock on July 8, 2014. ABC Mutual Fund paid a cash dividend of 10 cents a share. The ex-dividend date was July 16, 2014. The ABC Mutual Fund advises you that the portion of the dividend eligible to be treated as qualified dividends equals 2 cents per share. Your Form 1099-DIV from ABC Mutual Fund shows total ordinary dividends of $1,000 and qualified dividends of $200. However, you sold the 10,000 shares on August 11, 2014. You have no qualified dividends from ABC Mutual Fund because you held the ABC Mutual Fund stock for less than 61 days.

 Use the Qualified Dividends and Capital Gain Tax Worksheet or the Schedule D Tax Worksheet, whichever applies, to figure your tax. See the instructions for line 44 for details.

Line 10

Taxable Refunds, Credits, or Offsets of State and Local Income Taxes

 None of your refund is taxable if, in the year you paid the tax, you either (a) did not itemize deductions, or (b) elected to deduct state and local general sales taxes instead of state and local income taxes.

If you received a refund, credit, or offset of state or local income taxes in 2014, you may be required to report this amount. If you did not receive a Form 1099-G, check with the government agency that made the payments to you. Your 2014 Form 1099-G may have been made available to you only in an electronic format, and you will need to get instructions from the agency to retrieve this document. Report any taxable refund you received even if you did not receive Form 1099-G.

If you chose to apply part or all of the refund to your 2014 estimated state or local income tax, the amount applied is treated as received in 2014. If the refund was for a tax you paid in 2013 and you deducted state and local income taxes on line 5 of your 2013 Schedule A, use the State and Local Income Tax Refund Worksheet in these instructions to see if any of your refund is taxable.

Exception. See *Itemized Deduction Recoveries* in Pub. 525 instead of using the State and Local Income Tax Refund Worksheet in these instructions if any of the following applies.

1. You received a refund in 2014 that is for a tax year other than 2013.

2. You received a refund other than an income tax refund, such as a general sales tax or real property tax refund, in

State and Local Income Tax Refund Worksheet—Line 10

Keep for Your Records

Before you begin: ✓ Be sure you have read the **Exception** in the instructions for this line to see if you can use this worksheet instead of Pub. 525 to figure if any of your refund is taxable.

1. Enter the income tax refund from **Form(s) 1099-G** (or similar statement). But **do not** enter more than the amount of your state and local income taxes shown on your 2013 Schedule A, line 5 .... 1. _____

2. Enter your total itemized deductions from your 2013 Schedule A, line 29 .... 2. _____

   Note. If the filing status on your 2013 Form 1040 was married filing separately and your spouse itemized deductions in 2013, skip lines 3 through 5, enter the amount from line 2 on line 6, and go to line 7.

3. Enter the amount shown below for the filing status claimed on your **2013** Form 1040.

   - Single or married filing separately—$6,100
   - Married filing jointly or qualifying widow(er)—$12,200
   - Head of household—$8,950

   } 3. _____

4. Did you fill in line 39a on your 2013 Form 1040?

   ☐ **No.** Enter -0-.

   ☐ **Yes.** Multiply the number in the box on line 39a of your 2013 Form 1040 by $1,200 ($1,500 if your 2013 filing status was single or head of household).

   } 4. _____

5. Add lines 3 and 4 .... 5. _____

6. Is the amount on line 5 less than the amount on line 2?

   ☐ **No.** (STOP) None of your refund is taxable.

   ☐ **Yes.** Subtract line 5 from line 2 .... 6. _____

7. **Taxable part of your refund.** Enter the **smaller** of line 1 or line 6 here and on Form 1040, line 10 .... 7. _____

2014 of an amount deducted or credit claimed in an earlier year.

3. The amount on your 2013 Form 1040, line 42, was more than the amount on your 2013 Form 1040, line 41.

4. You had taxable income on your 2013 Form 1040, line 43, but no tax on your Form 1040, line 44, because of the 0% tax rate on net capital gain and qualified dividends in certain situations.

5. Your 2013 state and local income tax refund is more than your 2013 state and local income tax deduction minus the amount you could have deducted as your 2013 state and local general sales taxes.

6. You made your last payment of 2013 estimated state or local income tax in 2014.

7. You owed alternative minimum tax in 2013.

8. You could not use the full amount of credits you were entitled to in 2013 because the total credits were more than the amount shown on your 2013 Form 1040, line 46.

9. You could be claimed as a dependent by someone else in 2013.

10. You received a refund because of a jointly filed state or local income tax return, but you are not filing a joint 2014 Form 1040 with the same person.

11. You had to use the Itemized Deductions Worksheet in the 2013 Instructions for Schedule A and both of the following apply.

a. You could not deduct all of the amount on the 2013 Itemized Deductions Worksheet, line 1.

b. The amount on line 8 of that 2013 worksheet would be more than the amount on line 4 of that worksheet if the amount on line 4 were reduced by 80% of the refund you received in 2014.

Line 11

Alimony Received

Enter amounts received as alimony or separate maintenance. You must let the person who made the payments know your social security number. If you do not, you may have to pay a penalty. For more details, see Pub. 504.

Line 12

Business Income or (Loss)

If you operated a business or practiced your profession as a sole proprietor, re-

Need more information or forms? Visit IRS.gov.

port your income and expenses on Schedule C or C-EZ.

Line 13

Capital Gain or (Loss)

If you sold a capital asset, such as a stock or bond, you must complete and attach Form 8949 and Schedule D.

Exception 1. You do not have to file Form 8949 or Schedule D if both of the following apply.

1. You have no capital losses, and your only capital gains are capital gain distributions from Form(s) 1099-DIV, box 2a (or substitute statements).

2. None of the Form(s) 1099-DIV (or substitute statements) have an amount in box 2b (unrecaptured section 1250 gain), box 2c (section 1202 gain), or box 2d (collectibles (28%) gain).

Exception 2. You must file Schedule D, but generally do not have to file Form 8949, if *Exception 1* does not apply and your only capital gains and losses are:

- Capital gain distributions,
- A capital loss carryover from 2013,
- A gain from Form 2439 or 6252 or Part I of Form 4797,
- A gain or loss from Form 4684, 6781, or 8824,
- A gain or loss from a partnership, S corporation, estate, or trust, or
- Gains and losses from transactions for which you received a Form 1099-B (or substitute statement) that shows basis was reported to the IRS and for which you do not need to make any adjustments in column (g) of Form 8949 or enter any codes in column (f) of Form 8949.

If *Exception 1* applies, enter your total capital gain distributions (from box 2a of Form(s) 1099-DIV) on line 13 and check the box on that line. If you received capital gain distributions as a nominee (that is, they were paid to you but actually belong to someone else), report on line 13 only the amount that belongs to you. Include a statement showing the full amount you received and the amount you received as a nominee. See the Schedule B instructions for filing requirements for Forms 1099-DIV and 1096.

 If you do not have to file Schedule D, use the Qualified Dividends and Capital Gain Tax Worksheet in the line 44 instructions to figure your tax.

Line 14

Other Gains or (Losses)

If you sold or exchanged assets used in a trade or business, see the Instructions for Form 4797.

Lines 15a and 15b

IRA Distributions

You should receive a Form 1099-R showing the total amount of any distribution from your IRA before income tax or other deductions were withheld. This amount should be shown in box 1 of Form 1099-R. Unless otherwise noted in the line 15a and 15b instructions, an IRA includes a traditional IRA, Roth IRA, simplified employee pension (SEP) IRA, and a savings incentive match plan for employees (SIMPLE) IRA. Except as provided next, leave line 15a blank and enter the total distribution (from Form 1099-R, box 1) on line 15b.

Exception 1. Enter the total distribution on line 15a if you rolled over part or all of the distribution from one:

- IRA to another IRA of the same type (for example, from one traditional IRA to another traditional IRA),
- SEP or SIMPLE IRA to a traditional IRA, or
- IRA to a qualified plan other than an IRA.

Also, enter "Rollover" next to line 15b. If the total distribution was rolled over in a qualified rollover, enter -0- on line 15b. If the total distribution was not rolled over in a qualified rollover, enter the part not rolled over on line 15b unless *Exception 2* applies to the part not rolled over. Generally, a qualified rollover must be made within 60 days after the day you received the distribution. For more details on rollovers, see Pub. 590-A and Pub. 590-B.

If you rolled over the distribution into a qualified plan other than an IRA or you made the rollover in 2015, include a statement explaining what you did.

Exception 2. If any of the following apply, enter the total distribution on line 15a and see Form 8606 and its instructions to figure the amount to enter on line 15b.

1. You received a distribution from an IRA (other than a Roth IRA) and you made nondeductible contributions to any of your traditional or SEP IRAs for 2014 or an earlier year. If you made nondeductible contributions to these IRAs for 2014, also see Pub. 590-A and Pub. 590-B.

2. You received a distribution from a Roth IRA. But if either (a) or (b) below applies, enter -0- on line 15b; you do not have to see Form 8606 or its instructions.

   a. Distribution code T is shown in box 7 of Form 1099-R and you made a contribution (including a conversion) to a Roth IRA for 2009 or an earlier year.

   b. Distribution code Q is shown in box 7 of Form 1099-R.

3. You converted part or all of a traditional, SEP, or SIMPLE IRA to a Roth IRA in 2014.

4. You had a 2013 or 2014 IRA contribution returned to you, with the related earnings or less any loss, by the due date (including extensions) of your tax return for that year.

5. You made excess contributions to your IRA for an earlier year and had them returned to you in 2014.

6. You recharacterized part or all of a contribution to a Roth IRA as a traditional IRA contribution, or vice versa.

Exception 3. If the distribution is a qualified charitable distribution (QCD), enter the total distribution on line 15a. If the total amount distributed is a QCD, enter -0- on line 15b. If only part of the distribution is a QCD, enter the part that is not a QCD on line 15b unless *Exception 2* applies to that part. Enter "QCD" next to line 15b.

A QCD is a distribution made directly by the trustee of your IRA (other than an ongoing SEP or SIMPLE IRA) to an organization eligible to receive tax-deductible contributions (with certain exceptions). You must have been at least age 70½ when the distribution was made.

Generally, your total QCDs for the year cannot be more than $100,000. (On a joint return, your spouse can also have a QCD of up to $100,000.) The amount of the QCD is limited to the amount that would otherwise be included in your income. If your IRA includes nondeductible contributions, the distribution is first considered to be paid out of otherwise taxable income. See Pub. 590-A for details.

 You cannot claim a charitable contribution deduction for any QCD not included in your income.

Exception 4. If the distribution is a health savings account (HSA) funding distribution (HFD), enter the total distribution on line 15a. If the total amount distributed is an HFD and you elect to exclude it from income, enter -0- on line 15b. If only part of the distribution is an HFD and you elect to exclude that part from income, enter the part that is not an HFD on line 15b unless *Exception 2* applies to that part. Enter "HFD" next to line 15b.

An HFD is a distribution made directly by the trustee of your IRA (other than an ongoing SEP or SIMPLE IRA) to your HSA. If eligible, you generally can elect to exclude an HFD from your income once in your lifetime. You cannot exclude more than the limit on HSA contributions or more than the amount that would otherwise be included in your income. If your IRA includes nondeductible contributions, the HFD is first considered to be paid out of otherwise taxable income. See Pub. 969 for details.

 The amount of an HFD reduces the amount you can contribute to your HSA for the year. If you fail to maintain eligibility for an HSA for the 12 months following the month of the HFD, you may have to report the HFD as income and pay an additional tax. See Form 8889, Part III.

More than one exception applies. If more than one exception applies, include a statement showing the amount of each exception, instead of making an entry next to line 15b. For example: "Line 15b – $1,000 Rollover and $500 HFD." But you do not need to attach a statement if

only *Exception 2* and one other exception apply.

More than one distribution. If you (or your spouse if filing jointly) received more than one distribution, figure the taxable amount of each distribution and enter the total of the taxable amounts on line 15b. Enter the total amount of those distributions on line 15a.

 You may have to pay an additional tax if (a) you received an early distribution from your IRA and the total was not rolled over, or (b) you were born before July 1, 1943, and received less than the minimum required distribution from your traditional, SEP, and SIMPLE IRAs. See the instructions for line 59 for details.

More information. For more information about IRAs, see Pub. 590-A and Pub. 590-B.

Lines 16a and 16b

Pensions and Annuities

You should receive a Form 1099-R showing the total amount of your pension and annuity payments before income tax or other deductions were withheld. This amount should be shown in box 1 of Form 1099-R. Pension and annuity payments include distributions from 401(k), 403(b), and governmental 457(b) plans. Rollovers and lump-sum distributions are explained later. Do not include the following payments on lines 16a and 16b. Instead, report them on line 7.

- Disability pensions received before you reach the minimum retirement age set by your employer.
- Corrective distributions (including any earnings) of excess salary deferrals or excess contributions to retirement plans. The plan must advise you of the year(s) the distributions are includible in income.

 Attach Form(s) 1099-R to Form 1040 if any federal income tax was withheld.

Fully Taxable Pensions and Annuities

Your payments are fully taxable if (a) you did not contribute to the cost (see *Cost,* later) of your pension or annuity,

or (b) you got your entire cost back tax free before 2014. But see *Insurance Premiums for Retired Public Safety Officers,* later. If your pension or annuity is fully taxable, enter the total pension or annuity payments (from Form(s) 1099-R, box 1) on line 16b; do not make an entry on line 16a.

Fully taxable pensions and annuities also include military retirement pay shown on Form 1099-R. For details on military disability pensions, see Pub. 525. If you received a Form RRB-1099-R, see Pub. 575 to find out how to report your benefits.

Partially Taxable Pensions and Annuities

Enter the total pension or annuity payments (from Form 1099-R, box 1) on line 16a. If your Form 1099-R does not show the taxable amount, you must use the General Rule explained in Pub. 939 to figure the taxable part to enter on line 16b. But if your annuity starting date (defined later) was after July 1, 1986, see *Simplified Method*, later, to find out if you must use that method to figure the taxable part.

You can ask the IRS to figure the taxable part for you for a $1,000 fee. For details, see Pub. 939.

If your Form 1099-R shows a taxable amount, you can report that amount on line 16b. But you may be able to report a lower taxable amount by using the General Rule or the Simplified Method or if the exclusion for retired public safety officers, discussed next, applies.

Insurance Premiums for Retired Public Safety Officers

If you are an eligible retired public safety officer (law enforcement officer, firefighter, chaplain, or member of a rescue squad or ambulance crew), you can elect to exclude from income distributions made from your eligible retirement plan that are used to pay the premiums for coverage by an accident or health plan or a long-term care insurance contract. You can do this only if you retired because of disability or because you reached normal retirement age. The premiums can be for coverage for you, your spouse, or dependents. The distribution must be from a plan maintained by the

Need more information or forms? Visit IRS.gov.

employer from which you retired as a public safety officer. Also, the distribution must be made directly from the plan to the provider of the accident or health plan or long-term care insurance contract. You can exclude from income the smaller of the amount of the premiums or $3,000. You can make this election only for amounts that would otherwise be included in your income.

An eligible retirement plan is a governmental plan that is a qualified trust or a section 403(a), 403(b), or 457(b) plan.

If you make this election, reduce the otherwise taxable amount of your pension or annuity by the amount excluded. The amount shown in box 2a of Form 1099-R does not reflect the exclusion. Report your total distributions on line 16a and the taxable amount on line 16b. Enter "PSO" next to line 16b.

If you are retired on disability and reporting your disability pension on line 7, include only the taxable amount on that line and enter "PSO" and the amount excluded on the dotted line next to line 7.

Simplified Method

You must use the Simplified Method if either of the following applies.

1. Your annuity starting date was after July 1, 1986, and you used this method last year to figure the taxable part.

2. Your annuity starting date was after November 18, 1996, and both of the following apply.

a. The payments are from a qualified employee plan, a qualified employee annuity, or a tax-sheltered annuity.

b. On your annuity starting date, either you were under age 75 or the number of years of guaranteed payments was fewer than 5. See Pub. 575 for the definition of guaranteed payments.

If you must use the Simplified Method, complete the Simplified Method Worksheet in these instructions to figure the taxable part of your pension or annuity. For more details on the Simplified Method, see Pub. 575 (or Pub. 721 for U.S. Civil Service retirement benefits).

 If you received U.S. Civil Service retirement benefits and you chose the alternative annuity option, see Pub. 721 to figure the taxable part of your annuity. Do not use the Simplified Method Worksheet in these instructions.

Annuity Starting Date

Your annuity starting date is the later of the first day of the first period for which you received a payment or the date the plan's obligations became fixed.

Age (or Combined Ages) at Annuity Starting Date

If you are the retiree, use your age on the annuity starting date. If you are the survivor of a retiree, use the retiree's age on his or her annuity starting date. But if your annuity starting date was after 1997 and the payments are for your life and that of your beneficiary, use your combined ages on the annuity starting date.

If you are the beneficiary of an employee who died, see Pub. 575. If there is more than one beneficiary, see Pub. 575 or Pub. 721 to figure each beneficiary's taxable amount.

Cost

Your cost is generally your net investment in the plan as of the annuity starting date. It does not include pre-tax contributions. Your net investment should be shown in box 9b of Form 1099-R for the first year you received payments from the plan.

Rollovers

Generally, a qualified rollover is a tax-free distribution of cash or other assets from one retirement plan that is contributed to another plan within 60 days of receiving the distribution. However, a qualified rollover to a Roth IRA or a designated Roth account is generally not a tax-free distribution. Use lines 16a and 16b to report a qualified rollover, including a direct rollover, from one qualified employer's plan to another or to an IRA or SEP.

Enter on line 16a the distribution from Form 1099-R, box 1. From this amount, subtract any contributions (usually shown in box 5) that were taxable to

you when made. From that result, subtract the amount of the qualified rollover. Enter the remaining amount on line 16b. If the remaining amount is zero and you have no other distribution to report on line 16b, enter zero on line 16b. Also, enter "Rollover" next to line 16b.

See Pub. 575 for more details on rollovers, including special rules that apply to rollovers from designated Roth accounts, partial rollovers of property, and distributions under qualified domestic relations orders.

Lump-Sum Distributions

If you received a lump-sum distribution from a profit-sharing or retirement plan, your Form 1099-R should have the "Total distribution" box in box 2b checked. You may owe an additional tax if you received an early distribution from a qualified retirement plan and the total amount was not rolled over in a qualified rollover. For details, see the instructions for line 59.

Enter the total distribution on line 16a and the taxable part on line 16b. For details, see Pub 575.

 If you or the plan participant was born before January 2, 1936, you could pay less tax on the distribution. See Form 4972.

Line 19

Unemployment Compensation

You should receive a Form 1099-G showing in box 1 the total unemployment compensation paid to you in 2014. Report this amount on line 19. However, if you made contributions to a governmental unemployment compensation program or to a governmental paid family leave program and you are not itemizing deductions, reduce the amount you report on line 19 by those contributions. If you are itemizing deductions, see the Form 1099-G instructions.

If you received an overpayment of unemployment compensation in 2014 and you repaid any of it in 2014, subtract the amount you repaid from the total amount you received. Enter the result on line 19. Also, enter "Repaid" and the amount you repaid on the dotted line

Simplified Method Worksheet—Lines 16a and 16b

Before you begin: ✓	If you are the beneficiary of a deceased employee or former employee who died **before** August 21, 1996, include any death benefit exclusion that you are entitled to (up to $5,000) in the amount entered on line 2 below.

More than one pension or annuity. If you had more than one partially taxable pension or annuity, figure the taxable part of each separately. Enter the total of the taxable parts on Form 1040, line 16b. Enter the total pension or annuity payments received in 2014 on Form 1040, line 16a.

1. Enter the total pension or annuity payments from Form 1099-R, box 1. Also, enter this amount on Form 1040, line 16a . . . . **1.** _____

2. Enter your cost in the plan at the annuity starting date . . . . **2.** _____

   Note. If you completed this worksheet last year, skip line 3 and enter the amount from line 4 of last year's worksheet on line 4 below (even if the amount of your pension or annuity has changed). Otherwise, go to line 3.

3. Enter the appropriate number from **Table 1** below. **But** if your annuity starting date was **after** 1997 **and** the payments are for your life and that of your beneficiary, enter the appropriate number from **Table 2** below . . . . **3.** _____

4. Divide line 2 by the number on line 3 . . . . **4.** _____

5. Multiply line 4 by the number of months for which this year's payments were made. If your annuity starting date was **before** 1987, skip lines 6 and 7 and enter this amount on line 8. Otherwise, go to line 6 . . . . **5.** _____

6. Enter the amount, if any, recovered tax free in years after 1986. If you completed this worksheet last year, enter the amount from line 10 of last year's worksheet . . . . . **6.** _____

7. Subtract line 6 from line 2 . . . . **7.** _____

8. Enter the **smaller** of line 5 or line 7 . . . . **8.** _____

9. **Taxable amount.** Subtract line 8 from line 1. Enter the result, but not less than zero. Also, enter this amount on Form 1040, line 16b. If your Form 1099-R shows a larger amount, use the amount on this line instead of the amount from Form 1099-R. If you are a retired public safety officer, see *Insurance Premiums for Retired Public Safety Officers* before entering an amount on line 16b . . . . **9.** _____

10. Was your annuity starting date before 1987?

    ☐ **Yes.** (STOP) Do not complete the rest of this worksheet.

    ☐ **No.** Add lines 6 and 8. This is the **amount you have recovered tax free** through 2014. You will need this number if you need to fill out this worksheet next year . . . . **10.** _____

11. **Balance of cost to be recovered.** Subtract line 10 from line 2. If zero, you will not have to complete this worksheet next year. The payments you receive next year will generally be fully taxable . . . . **11.** _____

Table 1 for Line 3 Above

IF the age at annuity starting date was . . .	**AND your annuity starting date was—**	
	before November 19, 1996, enter on line 3 . . .	**after** November 18, 1996, enter on line 3 . . .
55 or under	300	360
56–60	260	310
61–65	240	260
66–70	170	210
71 or older	120	160

Table 2 for Line 3 Above

IF the combined ages at annuity starting date were . . .	THEN enter on line 3 . . .
110 or under	410
111–120	360
121–130	310
131–140	260
141 or older	210

Need more information or forms? Visit IRS.gov.

next to line 19. If, in 2014, you repaid unemployment compensation that you included in gross income in an earlier year, you can deduct the amount repaid on Schedule A, line 23. But if you repaid more than $3,000, see *Repayments* in Pub. 525 for details on how to report the repayment.

Lines 20a and 20b

Social Security Benefits

You should receive a Form SSA-1099 showing in box 3 the total social security benefits paid to you. Box 4 will show the amount of any benefits you repaid in 2014. If you received railroad retirement benefits treated as social security, you should receive a Form RRB-1099.

Use the Social Security Benefits Worksheet in these instructions to see if any of your benefits are taxable.

Exception. Do not use the Social Security Benefits Worksheet in these instructions if any of the following applies.

• You made contributions to a traditional IRA for 2014 and you or your spouse were covered by a retirement plan at work or through self-employment. Instead, use the worksheets in Pub. 590-A to see if any of your social security benefits are taxable and to figure your IRA deduction.

• You repaid any benefits in 2014 and your total repayments (box 4) were more than your total benefits for 2014 (box 3). None of your benefits are taxable for 2014. Also, you may be able to take an itemized deduction or a credit for part of the excess repayments if they were for benefits you included in gross income in an earlier year. For more details, see Pub. 915.

• You file Form 2555, 2555-EZ, 4563, or 8815, or you exclude employer-provided adoption benefits or income from sources within Puerto Rico. Instead, use the worksheet in Pub. 915.

 Benefits for earlier year received in 2014? If any of your benefits are taxable for 2014 and they include a lump-sum benefit payment that was for an earlier year, you may be able to reduce the taxable amount. See Lump-Sum Election *in Pub. 915 for details.*

Line 21

Other Income

 Do not report on this line any income from self-employment or fees received as a notary public. Instead, you must use Schedule C, C-EZ, or F, even if you do not have any business expenses. Also, do not report on line 21 any nonemployee compensation shown on Form 1099-MISC (unless it is not self-employment income, such as income from a hobby or a sporadic activity). Instead, see the instructions on Form 1099-MISC to find out where to report that income.

Taxable income. Use line 21 to report any taxable income not reported elsewhere on your return or other schedules. List the type and amount of income. If necessary, include a statement showing the required information. For more details, see *Miscellaneous Income* in Pub. 525.

Examples of income to report on line 21 include the following.

• Most prizes and awards.

• Jury duty pay. Also see the instructions for line 36.

• Alaska Permanent Fund dividends.

• Reimbursements or other amounts received for items deducted in an earlier year, such as medical expenses, real estate taxes, general sales taxes, or home mortgage interest. See *Recoveries* in Pub. 525 for details on how to figure the amount to report.

• Income from the rental of personal property if you engaged in the rental for profit but were not in the business of renting such property. Also see the instructions for line 36.

• Income from an activity not engaged in for profit. See Pub. 535.

• Taxable distributions from a Coverdell education savings account (ESA) or a qualified tuition program (QTP). Distributions from these accounts may be taxable if (a) they are more than the qualified higher education expenses of the designated beneficiary in 2014, and (b) they were not included in a qualified rollover. See Pub. 970. Nontaxable distributions from these accounts, including rollovers, do not have to be reported on Form 1040.

 You may have to pay an additional tax if you received a taxable distribution from a Coverdell ESA or a QTP. See the Instructions for Form 5329.

• Taxable distributions from a health savings account (HSA) or an Archer MSA. Distributions from these accounts may be taxable if (a) they are more than the unreimbursed qualified medical expenses of the account beneficiary or account holder in 2014, and (b) they were not included in a qualified rollover. See Pub. 969.

 You may have to pay an additional tax if you received a taxable distribution from an HSA or an Archer MSA. See the Instructions for Form 8889 for HSAs or the Instructions for Form 8853 for Archer MSAs.

• Amounts deemed to be income from an HSA because you did not remain an eligible individual during the testing period. See Form 8889, Part III.

• Gambling winnings, including lotteries, raffles, a lump-sum payment from the sale of a right to receive future lottery payments, etc. For details on gambling losses, see the instructions for Schedule A, line 28.

 Attach Form(s) W-2G to Form 1040 if any federal income tax was withheld.

• Reemployment trade adjustment assistance (RTAA) payments. These payments should be shown in box 5 of Form 1099-G.

• Loss on certain corrective distributions of excess deferrals. See *Retirement Plan Contributions* in Pub. 525.

• Dividends on insurance policies if they exceed the total of all net premiums you paid for the contract.

• Recapture of a charitable contribution deduction relating to the contribution of a fractional interest in tangible personal property. See *Fractional Interest in Tangible Personal Property* in Pub. 526. Interest and an additional 10% tax apply to the amount of the recapture. See the instructions for line 62.

• Recapture of a charitable contribution deduction if the charitable organization disposes of the donated property within 3 years of the contribution. See *Recapture if no exempt use* in Pub. 526.

Social Security Benefits Worksheet—Lines 20a and 20b

Keep for Your Records

Before you begin:
- ✓ Complete Form 1040, lines 21 and 23 through 32, if they apply to you.
- ✓ Figure any write-in adjustments to be entered on the dotted line next to line 36 (see the instructions for line 36).
- ✓ If you are married filing separately and you lived apart from your spouse for all of 2014, enter "D" to the right of the word "benefits" on line 20a. If you do not, you may get a math error notice from the IRS.
- ✓ Be sure you have read the **Exception** in the line 20a and 20b instructions to see if you can use this worksheet instead of a publication to find out if any of your benefits are taxable.

1. Enter the total amount from **box 5** of **all** your **Forms SSA-1099** and **Forms RRB-1099.** Also, enter this amount on Form 1040, line 20a .... **1.** _____

2. Enter one-half of line 1 .... **2.** _____

3. Combine the amounts from Form 1040, lines 7, 8a, 9a, 10 through 14, 15b, 16b, 17 through 19, and 21 .... **3.** _____

4. Enter the amount, if any, from Form 1040, line 8b .... **4.** _____

5. Combine lines 2, 3, and 4 .... **5.** _____

6. Enter the total of the amounts from Form 1040, lines 23 through 32, plus any write-in adjustments you entered on the dotted line next to line 36 .... **6.** _____

7. Is the amount on line 6 less than the amount on line 5?

☐ **No.** STOP None of your social security benefits are taxable. Enter -0- on Form 1040, line 20b.

☐ **Yes.** Subtract line 6 from line 5 .... **7.** _____

8. If you are:
   - Married filing jointly, enter $32,000
   - Single, head of household, qualifying widow(er), or married filing separately and you **lived apart** from your spouse for all of 2014, enter $25,000
   - Married filing separately and you lived with your spouse at any time in 2014, skip lines 8 through 15; multiply line 7 by 85% (.85) and enter the result on line 16. Then go to line 17

   8 _____

9. Is the amount on line 8 less than the amount on line 7?

☐ **No.** STOP None of your social security benefits are taxable. Enter -0- on Form 1040, line 20b. If you are married filing separately and you **lived apart** from your spouse for all of 2014, be sure you entered "D" to the right of the word "benefits" on line 20a.

☐ **Yes.** Subtract line 8 from line 7 .... **9.** _____

10. Enter: $12,000 if married filing jointly; $9,000 if single, head of household, qualifying widow(er), or married filing separately and you **lived apart** from your spouse for all of 2014 .... **10.** _____

11. Subtract line 10 from line 9. If zero or less, enter -0- .... **11.** _____

12. Enter the **smaller** of line 9 or line 10 .... **12.** _____

13. Enter one-half of line 12 .... **13.** _____

14. Enter the **smaller** of line 2 or line 13 .... **14.** _____

15. Multiply line 11 by 85% (.85). If line 11 is zero, enter -0- .... **15.** _____

16. Add lines 14 and 15 .... **16.** _____

17. Multiply line 1 by 85% (.85) .... **17.** _____

18. **Taxable social security benefits.** Enter the **smaller** of line 16 or line 17. Also enter this amount on Form 1040, line 20b .... **18.** _____

TIP *If any of your benefits are taxable for 2014 **and** they include a lump-sum benefit payment that was for an earlier year, you may be able to reduce the taxable amount. See Lump-Sum Election in Pub. 915 for details.*

Need more information or forms? Visit IRS.gov.

• **Canceled debts.** These amounts may be shown in box 2 of Form 1099-C. However, part or all of your income from the cancellation of debt may be nontaxable. See Pub. 4681 or go to IRS.gov and enter "canceled debt" or "foreclosure" in the search box.

• **Taxable part of disaster relief payments.** See Pub. 525 to figure the taxable part, if any. If any of your disaster relief payment is taxable, attach a statement showing the total payment received and how you figured the taxable part.

Nontaxable income. Do not report any nontaxable income on line 21. Examples of nontaxable income include the following.

• Child support.

• Payments you received to help you pay your mortgage loan under the HFA Hardest Hit Fund or the Emergency Homeowners' Loan Program or similar state program.

• Any Pay-for-Performance Success Payments that reduce the principal balance of your home mortgage under the Home Affordable Modification Program.

• Life insurance proceeds received because of someone's death (other than from certain employer-owned life insurance contracts).

• Gifts and bequests. However, if you received a gift or bequest from a foreign person of more than $15,358, you may have to report information about it on Form 3520, Part IV. See the Instructions for Form 3520.

Net operating loss (NOL) deduction. Include on line 21 any NOL deduction from an earlier year. Subtract it from any income on line 21 and enter the result. If the result is less than zero, enter it in parentheses. On the dotted line next to line 21, enter "NOL" and show the amount of the deduction in parentheses. See Pub. 536 for details.

Medicaid waiver payments to care provider. Certain Medicaid waiver payments you received for caring for someone living in your home with you may be nontaxable. If these payments were incorrectly reported to you in box 1 of Form(s) W-2, and you cannot get a corrected Form W-2, include the amount on line 7. On line 21, subtract the nontaxable amount of the payments from any income on line 21 and enter the result. If the result is less than zero, enter it in parentheses. Enter "Notice 2014-7" and the nontaxable amount on the dotted line next to line 21. For more information about these payments, see Pub. 525.

Adjusted Gross Income

Line 23

Educator Expenses

If you were an eligible educator in 2014, you can deduct on line 23 up to $250 of qualified expenses you paid in 2014. If you and your spouse are filing jointly and both of you were eligible educators, the maximum deduction is $500. However, neither spouse can deduct more than $250 of his or her qualified expenses on line 23. You may be able to deduct expenses that are more than the $250 (or $500) limit on Schedule A, line 21. An eligible educator is a kindergarten through grade 12 teacher, instructor, counselor, principal, or aide who worked in a school for at least 900 hours during a school year.

Qualified expenses include ordinary and necessary expenses paid in connection with books, supplies, equipment (including computer equipment, software, and services), and other materials used in the classroom. An ordinary expense is one that is common and accepted in your educational field. A necessary expense is one that is helpful and appropriate for your profession as an educator. An expense does not have to be required to be considered necessary.

Qualified expenses do not include expenses for home schooling or for nonathletic supplies for courses in health or physical education.

You must reduce your qualified expenses by the following amounts.

• Excludable U.S. series EE and I savings bond interest from Form 8815.

• Nontaxable qualified tuition program earnings or distributions.

• Any nontaxable distribution of Coverdell education savings account earnings.

• Any reimbursements you received for these expenses that were not reported to you in box 1 of your Form W-2.

For more details, use Teletax topic 458 or see Pub. 529.

Line 24

Certain Business Expenses of Reservists, Performing Artists, and Fee-Basis Government Officials

Include the following deductions on line 24.

• Certain business expenses of National Guard and reserve members who traveled more than 100 miles from home to perform services as a National Guard or reserve member.

• Performing-arts-related expenses as a qualified performing artist.

• Business expenses of fee-basis state or local government officials.

For more details, see Form 2106 or 2106-EZ.

Line 25

Health Savings Account (HSA) Deduction

You may be able to take this deduction if contributions (other than employer contributions, rollovers, and qualified HSA funding distributions from an IRA) were made to your HSA for 2014. See Form 8889.

Line 26

Moving Expenses

If you moved in connection with your job or business or started a new job, you may be able to take this deduction. But your new workplace must be at least 50 miles farther from your old home than your old home was from your old workplace. If you had no former workplace, your new workplace must be at least 50 miles from your old home. Use TeleTax topic 455 or see Form 3903.

Self-Employed Health Insurance Deduction Worksheet—Line 29

Keep for Your Records

Before you begin: ✓ Be sure you have read the **Exception** in the instructions for this line to see if you can use this worksheet instead of Pub. 535 to figure your deduction.

1. Enter the total amount paid in 2014 for health insurance coverage established under your business (or the S corporation in which you were a more-than-2% shareholder) for 2014 for you, your spouse, and your dependents. Your insurance can also cover your child who was under age 27 at the end of 2014, even if the child was not your dependent. But do not include amounts for any month you were eligible to participate in an employer-sponsored health plan or amounts paid from retirement plan distributions that were nontaxable because you are a retired public safety officer .... 1. _____

2. Enter your net profit* and any other earned income** from the business under which the insurance plan is established, minus any deductions on Form 1040, lines 27 and 28. Do not include Conservation Reserve Program payments exempt from self-employment tax .... 2. _____

3. **Self-employed health insurance deduction.** Enter the **smaller** of line 1 or line 2 here and on Form 1040, line 29. **Do not** include this amount in figuring any medical expense deduction on Schedule A .... 3. _____

*If you used either optional method to figure your net earnings from self-employment, do not enter your net profit. Instead, enter the amount from Schedule SE, Section B, line 4b.

Earned income includes net earnings and gains from the sale, transfer, or licensing of property you created. However, it does not include capital gain income. If you were a more-than-2% shareholder in the S corporation under which the insurance plan is established, earned income is your Medicare wages (box 5 of Form W-2) from that corporation.

Line 27

Deductible Part of Self-Employment Tax

If you were self-employed and owe self-employment tax, fill in Schedule SE to figure the amount of your deduction. If you completed Section A of Schedule SE, the deductible part of your self-employment tax is on line 6. If you completed Section B of Schedule SE, it is on line 13.

Line 28

Self-Employed SEP, SIMPLE, and Qualified Plans

If you were self-employed or a partner, you may be able to take this deduction. See Pub. 560 or, if you were a minister, Pub. 517.

Line 29

Self-Employed Health Insurance Deduction

You may be able to deduct the amount you paid for health insurance for yourself, your spouse, and your dependents. The insurance can also cover your child who was under age 27 at the end of 2014, even if the child was not your dependent. A child includes your son, daughter, stepchild, adopted child, or foster child (defined in the line 6c instructions).

One of the following statements must be true.

- You were self-employed and had a net profit for the year reported on Schedule C, C-EZ, or F.
- You were a partner with net earnings from self-employment.
- You used one of the optional methods to figure your net earnings from self-employment on Schedule SE.
- You received wages in 2014 from an S corporation in which you were a more-than-2% shareholder. Health insurance premiums paid or reimbursed by the S corporation are shown as wages on Form W-2.

The insurance plan must be established under your business. Your personal services must have been a material income-producing factor in the business. If you are filing Schedule C, C-EZ, or F, the policy can be either in your name or in the name of the business.

If you are a partner, the policy can be either in your name or in the name of the partnership. You can either pay the premiums yourself or your partnership can pay them and report them as guaranteed payments. If the policy is in your name and you pay the premiums yourself, the partnership must reimburse you and report the premiums as guaranteed payments.

If you are a more-than-2% shareholder in an S corporation, the policy can be either in your name or in the name of the S corporation. You can either pay the premiums yourself or the S corporation can pay them and report them as wages. If the policy is in your name and you pay the premiums yourself, the S corporation must reimburse you. You can deduct the premiums only if the S corporation reports the premiums paid or reimbursed as wages in box 1 of your Form W-2 in 2014 and you also report the premium payments or reimbursements as wages on Form 1040, line 7.

But if you were also eligible to participate in any subsidized health plan maintained by your or your spouse's employer for any month or part of a month in 2014, amounts paid for health insurance coverage for that month cannot be used to figure the deduction. Also, if you were eligible for any month or part of a month to participate in any subsi-

Need more information or forms? Visit IRS.gov.

dized health plan maintained by the employer of either your dependent or your child who was under age 27 at the end of 2014, do not use amounts paid for coverage for that month to figure the deduction.

Example. If you were eligible to participate in a subsidized health plan maintained by your spouse's employer from September 30 through December 31, you cannot use amounts paid for health insurance coverage for September through December to figure your deduction.

Medicare premiums you voluntarily pay to obtain insurance in your name that is similar to qualifying private health insurance can be used to figure the deduction. Amounts paid for health insurance coverage from retirement plan distributions that were nontaxable because you are a retired public safety officer cannot be used to figure the deduction.

For more details, see Pub. 535.

If you qualify to take the deduction, use the Self-Employed Health Insurance Deduction Worksheet to figure the amount you can deduct.

Exceptions. Use Pub. 535 instead of the Self-Employed Health Insurance Deduction Worksheet in these instructions to figure your deduction if any of the following applies.
- You had more than one source of income subject to self-employment tax.
- You file Form 2555 or 2555-EZ.
- You are using amounts paid for qualified long-term care insurance to figure the deduction.

Use Pub. 974 instead of the worksheet in these instructions if the insurance plan established, or considered to be established, under your business was obtained through the Health Insurance Marketplace and you are claiming the premium tax credit.

Line 30

Penalty on Early Withdrawal of Savings

The Form 1099-INT or Form 1099-OID you received will show the amount of any penalty you were charged.

Lines 31a and 31b

Alimony Paid

If you made payments to or for your spouse or former spouse under a divorce or separation instrument, you may be able to take this deduction. Use TeleTax topic 452 or see Pub. 504.

Line 32

IRA Deduction

 If you made any nondeductible contributions to a traditional individual retirement arrangement (IRA) for 2014, you must report them on Form 8606.

If you made contributions to a traditional IRA for 2014, you may be able to take an IRA deduction. But you, or your spouse if filing a joint return, must have had earned income to do so. For IRA purposes, earned income includes alimony and separate maintenance payments reported on line 11. If you were a member of the U.S. Armed Forces, earned income includes any nontaxable combat pay you received. If you were self-employed, earned income is generally your net earnings from self-employment if your personal services were a material income-producing factor. For more details, see Pub. 590-A. A statement should be sent to you by June 1, 2015, that shows all contributions to your traditional IRA for 2014.

Use the IRA Deduction Worksheet to figure the amount, if any, of your IRA deduction. But read the following 11-item list before you fill in the worksheet.

1. If you were age 70½ or older at the end of 2014, you cannot deduct any contributions made to your traditional IRA for 2014 or treat them as nondeductible contributions.

2. You cannot deduct contributions to a Roth IRA. But you may be able to take the retirement savings contributions credit (saver's credit). See the instructions for line 51.

3. If you are filing a joint return and you or your spouse made contributions to both a traditional IRA and a Roth IRA for 2014, do not use the IRA Deduction Worksheet in these instructions. Instead,

see Pub. 590-A to figure the amount, if any, of your IRA deduction.

4. You cannot deduct elective deferrals to a 401(k) plan, 403(b) plan, section 457 plan, SIMPLE plan, or the federal Thrift Savings Plan. These amounts are not included as income in box 1 of your Form W-2. But you may be able to take the retirement savings contributions credit. See the instructions for line 51.

5. If you made contributions to your IRA in 2014 that you deducted for 2013, do not include them in the worksheet.

6. If you received income from a nonqualified deferred compensation plan or nongovernmental section 457 plan that is included in box 1 of your Form W-2, or in box 7 of Form 1099-MISC, do not include that income on line 8 of the worksheet. The income should be shown in (a) box 11 of your Form W-2, (b) box 12 of your Form W-2 with code Z, or (c) box 15b of Form 1099-MISC. If it is not, contact your employer or the payer for the amount of the income.

7. You must file a joint return to deduct contributions to your spouse's IRA. Enter the total IRA deduction for you and your spouse on line 32.

8. Do not include qualified rollover contributions in figuring your deduction. Instead, see the instructions for lines 15a and 15b.

9. Do not include trustees' fees that were billed separately and paid by you for your IRA. These fees can be deducted only as an itemized deduction on Schedule A.

10. Do not include any repayments of qualified reservist distributions. You cannot deduct them. For information on how to report these repayments, see *Qualified reservist repayments* in Pub. 590-A.

11. If the total of your IRA deduction on line 32 plus any nondeductible contribution to your traditional IRAs shown on Form 8606 is less than your total traditional IRA contributions for 2014, see Pub. 590-A for special rules.

TIP *By April 1 of the year after the year in which you turn age 70½, you must start taking minimum required distributions from your traditional IRA. If you do not, you may have to pay a 50% additional tax on the amount that should have been distributed. For details, including how to figure the minimum required distribution, see Pub. 590-B.*

Were You Covered by a Retirement Plan?

If you were covered by a retirement plan (qualified pension, profit-sharing (including 401(k)), annuity, SEP, SIMPLE, etc.) at work or through self-employment, your IRA deduction may be reduced or eliminated. But you can still make contributions to an IRA even if you cannot deduct them. In any case, the income earned on your IRA contributions is not taxed until it is paid to you.

The "Retirement plan" box in box 13 of your Form W-2 should be checked if you were covered by a plan at work even if you were not vested in the plan. You are also covered by a plan if you were self-employed and had a SEP, SIMPLE, or qualified retirement plan.

If you were covered by a retirement plan and you file Form 2555, 2555-EZ, or 8815, or you exclude employer-provided adoption benefits, see Pub. 590-A to figure the amount, if any, of your IRA deduction.

Married persons filing separately. If you were not covered by a retirement plan but your spouse was, you are considered covered by a plan unless you lived apart from your spouse for all of 2014.

 You may be able to take the retirement savings contributions credit. See the line 51 instructions.

IRA Deduction Worksheet—Line 32 *Keep for Your Records* 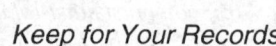

 If you were age 70½ or older at the end of 2014, you cannot deduct any contributions made to your traditional IRA or treat them as nondeductible contributions. Do not complete this worksheet for anyone age 70½ or older at the end of 2014. If you are married filing jointly and only one spouse was under age 70½ at the end of 2014, complete this worksheet only for that spouse.

Before you begin:	✓ Be sure you have read the 11-item list in the instructions for this line. You may not be able to use this worksheet.
	✓ Figure any write-in adjustments to be entered on the dotted line next to line 36 (see the instructions for line 36).
	✓ If you are married filing separately and you lived apart from your spouse for all of 2014, enter "D" on the dotted line next to Form 1040, line 32. If you do not, you may get a math error notice from the IRS.

Your IRA   **Spouse's IRA**

1a. Were you covered by a retirement plan (see *Were You Covered by a Retirement Plan?*)? . . . .   **1a.** ☐ Yes ☐ No

b. If married filing jointly, was your spouse covered by a retirement plan? . . . .   **1b.** ☐ Yes ☐ No

Next. If you checked "No" on line 1a (and "No" on line 1b if married filing jointly), skip lines 2 through 6, enter the applicable amount below on line 7a (and line 7b if applicable), and go to line 8.
- $5,500, if under age 50 at the end of 2014.
- $6,500, if age 50 or older but under age 70½ at the end of 2014.

Otherwise, go to line 2.

2. Enter the amount shown below that applies to you.
- Single, head of household, or married filing separately and you **lived apart** from your spouse for all of 2014, enter $70,000.
- Qualifying widow(er), enter $116,000.   **2a.** _____   **2b.** _____
- Married filing jointly, enter $116,000 in both columns. But if you checked "No" on either line 1a or 1b, enter $191,000 for the person who was not covered by a plan.
- Married filing separately and you lived with your spouse at any time in 2014, enter $10,000.

3. Enter the amount from Form 1040, line 22 . . . .   **3.** _____

4. Enter the total of the amounts from Form 1040, lines 23 through 31a, plus any write-in adjustments you entered on the dotted line next to line 36 . . . .   **4.** _____

5. Subtract line 4 from line 3. If married filing jointly, enter the result in both columns . . . .   **5a.** _____   **5b.** _____

6. Is the amount on line 5 less than the amount on line 2?

☐ **No.** 🛑 None of your IRA contributions are deductible. For details on nondeductible IRA contributions, see Form 8606.

☐ **Yes.** Subtract line 5 from line 2 in each column. Follow the instruction below that applies to you.
- If single, head of household, or married filing separately, and the result is $10,000 or more, enter the applicable amount below on line 7 for that column and go to line 8.
  i. $5,500, if under age 50 at the end of 2014.
  ii. $6,500, if age 50 or older but under age 70½ at the end of 2014.
  If the result is less than $10,000, go to line 7.   **6a.** _____   **6b.** _____
- If married filing jointly or qualifying widow(er), and the result is $20,000 or more ($10,000 or more in the column for the IRA of a person who was not covered by a retirement plan), enter the applicable amount below on line 7 for that column and go to line 8.
  i. $5,500, if under age 50 at the end of 2014.
  ii. $6,500 if age 50 or older but under age 70½ at the end of 2014.
  Otherwise, go to line 7.

IRA Deduction Worksheet—*Continued*

		Your IRA	Spouse's IRA

7. Multiply lines 6a and 6b by the percentage below that applies to you. If the result is not a multiple of $10, increase it to the next multiple of $10 (for example, increase $490.30 to $500). If the result is $200 or more, enter the result. But if it is less than $200, enter $200.

   • Single, head of household, or married filing separately, multiply by 55% (.55) (or by 65% (.65) in the column for the IRA of a person who is age 50 or older at the end of 2014).

   • Married filing jointly or qualifying widow(er), multiply by 27.5% (.275) (or by 32.5% (.325) in the column for the IRA of a person who is age 50 or older at the end of 2014). But if you checked "No" on either line 1a or 1b, then in the column for the IRA of the person who was not covered by a retirement plan, multiply by 55% (.55) (or by 65% (.65) if age 50 or older at the end of 2014).

   7a. _____   **7b.** _____

8. Enter the total of your (and your spouse's if filing jointly):

   • Wages, salaries, tips, etc. Generally, this is the amount reported in box 1 of Form W-2. Exceptions are explained earlier in these instructions for line 32.

   • Alimony and separate maintenance payments reported on Form 1040, line 11.

   • Nontaxable combat pay. This amount should be reported in box 12 of Form W-2 with code Q.

   8. _____

9. Enter the earned income you (and your spouse if filing jointly) received as a self-employed individual or a partner. Generally, this is your (and your spouse's if filing jointly) net earnings from self-employment if your personal services were a material income-producing factor, minus any deductions on Form 1040, lines 27 and 28. If zero or less, enter -0-. For more details, see Pub. 590-A . . . . **9.** _____

10. Add lines 8 and 9 . . . . **10.** _____

   ⚠ **CAUTION** *If married filing jointly and line 10 is less than $11,000 ($12,000 if one spouse is age 50 or older at the end of 2014; $13,000 if both spouses are age 50 or older at the end of 2014),* **stop here** *and use the worksheet in Pub. 590-A to figure your IRA deduction.*

11. Enter traditional IRA contributions made, or that will be made by April 15, 2015, for 2014 to your IRA on line 11a and to your spouse's IRA on line 11b . . . . **11a.** _____ **11b.** _____

12. On line 12a, enter the **smallest** of line 7a, 10, or 11a. On line 12b, enter the **smallest** of line 7b, 10, or 11b. This is the most you can deduct. Add the amounts on lines 12a and 12b and enter the total on Form 1040, line 32. Or, if you want, you can deduct a smaller amount and treat the rest as a nondeductible contribution (see Form 8606) . . . . **12a.** _____ **12b.** _____

Need more information or forms? Visit IRS.gov.

Line 33

Student Loan Interest Deduction

You can take this deduction only if all of the following apply.

• You paid interest in 2014 on a qualified student loan (defined later).

• Your filing status is any status except married filing separately.

• Your modified adjusted gross income (AGI) is less than: $80,000 if single, head of household, or qualifying widow(er); $160,000 if married filing jointly. Use lines 2 through 4 of the worksheet below to figure your modified AGI.

• You, or your spouse if filing jointly, are not claimed as a dependent on someone else's (such as your parent's) 2014 tax return.

Use the worksheet in these instructions to figure your student loan interest deduction.

Exception. Use Pub. 970 instead of the worksheet in these instructions to figure your student loan interest deduction if you file Form 2555, 2555-EZ, or 4563, or you exclude income from sources within Puerto Rico.

Qualified student loan. A qualified student loan is any loan you took out to pay the qualified higher education expenses for any of the following individuals who was an eligible student.

1. Yourself or your spouse.

2. Any person who was your dependent when the loan was taken out.

3. Any person you could have claimed as a dependent for the year the loan was taken out except that:

a. The person filed a joint return,

b. The person had gross income that was equal to or more than the exemption amount for that year ($3,950 for 2014), or

c. You, or your spouse if filing jointly, could be claimed as a dependent on someone else's return.

However, a loan is not a qualified student loan if (a) any of the proceeds were used for other purposes, or (b) the loan was from either a related person or a person who borrowed the proceeds under a qualified employer plan or a contract purchased under such a plan. For details, see Pub. 970.

Qualified higher education expenses. Qualified higher education expenses generally include tuition, fees, room and board, and related expenses such as books and supplies. The expenses must be for education in a degree, certificate, or similar program at an eligible educational institution. An eligible educational institution includes most colleges, universities, and certain vocational schools. For details, see Pub. 970.

Student Loan Interest Deduction Worksheet—Line 33

Keep for Your Records

Before you begin:
✓ Figure any write-in adjustments to be entered on the dotted line next to line 36 (see the instructions for line 36).
✓ Be sure you have read the **Exception** in the instructions for this line to see if you can use this worksheet instead of Pub. 970 to figure your deduction.

1. Enter the total interest you paid in 2014 on qualified student loans (see the instructions for line 33). **Do not** enter more than $2,500 .... **1.** _____

2. Enter the amount from Form 1040, line 22 .... **2.** _____

3. Enter the total of the amounts from Form 1040, lines 23 through 32, plus any write-in adjustments you entered on the dotted line next to line 36 .... **3.** _____

4. Subtract line 3 from line 2 .... **4.** _____

5. Enter the amount shown below for your filing status.
   • Single, head of household, or qualifying widow(er)—$65,000
   • Married filing jointly—$130,000 .... **5.** _____

6. Is the amount on line 4 more than the amount on line 5?
   ☐ **No.** Skip lines 6 and 7, enter -0- on line 8, and go to line 9.
   ☐ **Yes.** Subtract line 5 from line 4 .... **6.** _____

7. Divide line 6 by $15,000 ($30,000 if married filing jointly). Enter the result as a decimal (rounded to at least three places). If the result is 1.000 or more, enter 1.000 .... **7.** _____

8. Multiply line 1 by line 7 .... **8.** _____

9. **Student loan interest deduction.** Subtract line 8 from line 1. Enter the result here and on Form 1040, line 33. **Do not** include this amount in figuring any other deduction on your return (such as on Schedule A, C, E, etc.) .... **9.** _____

Line 34

Tuition and Fees

If you paid qualified tuition and fees for yourself, your spouse, or your dependent(s), you may be able to take this deduction. See Form 8917.

 You may be able to take a credit for your educational expenses instead of a deduction. See the instructions for lines 50 and 68 for details.

Line 35

Domestic Production Activities Deduction

You may be able to deduct up to 9% of your qualified production activities income from the following activities.

1. Construction of real property performed in the United States.

2. Engineering or architectural services performed in the United States for construction of real property in the United States.

3. Any lease, rental, license, sale, exchange, or other disposition of:

a. Tangible personal property, computer software, and sound recordings that you manufactured, produced, grew, or extracted in whole or in significant part in the United States,

b. Any qualified film you produced, or

c. Electricity, natural gas, or potable water you produced in the United States.

Your deduction may be reduced if you had oil-related qualified production activities income.

The deduction does not apply to income derived from:

• The sale of food and beverages you prepared at a retail establishment;

• Property you leased, licensed, or rented for use by any related person;

• The transmission or distribution of electricity, natural gas, or potable water; or

• The lease, rental, license, sale, exchange, or other disposition of land.

For details, see Form 8903 and its instructions.

Line 36

Include in the total on line 36 any of the following write-in adjustments. To find out if you can take the deduction, see the form or publication indicated. On the dotted line next to line 36, enter the amount of your deduction and identify it as indicated.

• Archer MSA deduction (see Form 8853). Identify as "MSA."

• Jury duty pay if you gave the pay to your employer because your employer paid your salary while you served on the jury. Identify as "Jury Pay."

• Deductible expenses related to income reported on line 21 from the rental of personal property engaged in for profit. Identify as "PPR."

• Reforestation amortization and expenses (see Pub. 535). Identify as "RFST."

• Repayment of supplemental unemployment benefits under the Trade Act of 1974 (see Pub. 525). Identify as "Sub-Pay TRA."

• Contributions to section 501(c)(18)(D) pension plans (see Pub. 525). Identify as "501(c)(18)(D)."

• Contributions by certain chaplains to section 403(b) plans (see Pub. 517). Identify as "403(b)."

• Attorney fees and court costs for actions involving certain unlawful discrimination claims, but only to the extent of gross income from such actions (see Pub. 525). Identify as "UDC."

• Attorney fees and court costs you paid in connection with an award from the IRS for information you provided that helped the IRS detect tax law violations, up to the amount of the award includible in your gross income. Identify as "WBF."

Line 37

If line 37 is less than zero, you may have a net operating loss that you can carry to another tax year. See the Instructions for Form 1045 for details.

Tax and Credits

Line 39a

If you were born before January 2, 1950, or were blind at the end of 2014, check the appropriate box(es) on line 39a. If you were married and checked the box on Form 1040, line 6b, and your spouse was born before January 2, 1950, or was blind at the end of 2014, also check the appropriate box(es) for your spouse. Be sure to enter the total number of boxes checked. Do not check any box(es) for your spouse if your filing status is head of household.

Death of spouse in 2014. If your spouse was born before January 2, 1950, but died in 2014 before reaching age 65, do not check the box that says "Spouse was born before January 2, 1950."

A person is considered to reach age 65 on the day before his or her 65th birthday.

Example. Your spouse was born on February 14, 1949, and died on February 13, 2014. Your spouse is considered age 65 at the time of death. Check the appropriate box for your spouse on line 39a. However, if your spouse died on February 12, 2014, your spouse is not considered age 65. Do not check the box.

Death of taxpayer in 2014. If you are preparing a return for someone who died in 2014, see Pub. 501 before completing line 39a.

Blindness

If you were not totally blind as of December 31, 2014, you must get a statement certified by your eye doctor (ophthalmologist or optometrist) that:

• You cannot see better than 20/200 in your better eye with glasses or contact lenses, or

• Your field of vision is 20 degrees or less.

If your eye condition is not likely to improve beyond the conditions listed above, you can get a statement certified by your eye doctor (ophthalmologist or optometrist) to this effect instead.

You must keep the statement for your records.

Line 39b

If your filing status is married filing separately (box 3 is checked), and your spouse itemizes deductions on his or her return, check the box on line 39b. Also check that box if you were a dual-status alien. But if you were a dual-status alien and you file a joint return with your

Need more information or forms? Visit IRS.gov.

spouse who was a U.S. citizen or resident alien at the end of 2014 and you and your spouse agree to be taxed on your combined worldwide income, do not check the box.

Line 40

Itemized Deductions or Standard Deduction

In most cases, your federal income tax will be less if you take the larger of your itemized deductions or standard deduction.

Itemized Deductions

To figure your itemized deductions, fill in Schedule A.

Standard Deduction

Most people can find their standard deduction by looking at the amounts listed under "All others" to the left of line 40.

Exception 1 – dependent. If you, or your spouse if filing jointly, can be claimed as a dependent on someone else's 2014 return, use the Standard Deduction Worksheet for Dependents to figure your standard deduction.

Exception 2 – box on line 39a checked. If you checked any box on line 39a, figure your standard deduction using the Standard Deduction Chart for People Who Were Born Before January 2, 1950, or Were Blind.

Exception 3 – box on line 39b checked. If you checked the box on line 39b, your standard deduction is zero, even if you were born before January 2, 1950, or were blind.

Line 42

Exemptions

If the amount on line 38 is over $152,525, use the Deduction for Exemptions Worksheet to figure your deduction for exemptions.

Standard Deduction Worksheet for Dependents—Line 40

Keep for Your Records

Use this worksheet **only** if someone can claim you, or your spouse if filing jointly, as a dependent.

1. Is your **earned income*** more than $650?
   - ☐ **Yes.** Add $350 to your earned income. Enter the total
   - ☐ **No.** Enter $1,000 ⎫ .... **1.** _____

2. Enter the amount shown below for your filing status.
   - • Single or married filing separately—$6,200
   - • Married filing jointly or qualifying widow(er)—$12,400
   - • Head of household—$9,100 ⎫ .... **2.** _____

3. **Standard deduction.**
   a. Enter the **smaller** of line 1 or line 2. If born after January 1, 1950, and not blind, **stop here** and enter this amount on Form 1040, line 40. Otherwise, go to line 3b .... **3a.** _____
   b. If born before January 2, 1950, or blind, multiply the number on Form 1040, line 39a, by $1,200 ($1,550 if single or head of household) .... **3b.** _____
   c. Add lines 3a and 3b. Enter the total here and on Form 1040, line 40 .... **3c.** _____

** **Earned income** includes wages, salaries, tips, professional fees, and other compensation received for personal services you performed. It also includes any taxable scholarship or fellowship grant. Generally, your earned income is the total of the amount(s) you reported on Form 1040, lines 7, 12, and 18, minus the amount, if any, on line 27.*

Standard Deduction Chart for People Who Were Born Before January 2, 1950, or Were Blind

Do not use this chart if someone can claim you, or your spouse if filing jointly, as a dependent. Instead, use the worksheet above.

Enter the number from the box on
Form 1040, line 39a ....▶    Do not use the number of exemptions from line 6d.

IF your filing status is . . .	AND the number in the box above is . . .	THEN your standard deduction is . . .
Single	1 2	$7,750 9,300
Married filing jointly or Qualifying widow(er)	1 2 3 4	$13,600 14,800 16,000 17,200
Married filing separately	1 2 3 4	$7,400 8,600 9,800 11,000
Head of household	1 2	$10,650 12,200

Need more information or forms? Visit IRS.gov.

Deduction for Exemptions Worksheet—Line 42

Keep for Your Records

1. Is the amount on Form 1040, line 38, more than the amount shown on line 4 below for your filing status?

   ☐ **No.** (STOP) Multiply $3,950 by the total number of exemptions claimed on Form 1040, line 6d, and enter the result on line 42.

   ☐ **Yes. Continue.**

2. Multiply $3,950 by the total number of exemptions claimed on Form 1040, line 6d .... **2.** _____

3. Enter the amount from Form 1040, line 38 .... **3.** _____

4. Enter the amount shown below for your filing status.
   - Single —$254,200
   - Married filing jointly or qualifying widow(er)—$305,050
   - Married filing separately—$152,525
   - Head of household—$279,650

   } .... **4.** _____

5. Subtract line 4 from line 3. If the result is more than $122,500 ($61,250 if married filing separately) , (STOP) Enter -0- on line 42 .... **5.** _____

6. Divide line 5 by $2,500 ($1,250 if married filing separately). If the result is not a whole number, increase it to the next higher whole number (for example, increase .00004 to 1) .... **6.** _____

7. Multiply line 6 by 2% (.02) and enter the result as a decimal .... **7.** _____

8. Multiply line 2 by line 7 .... **8.** _____

9. **Deduction for exemptions.** Subtract line 8 from line 2. Enter the result here and on Form 1040, line 42 .... **9.** _____

Line 44

Tax

Include in the total on line 44 all of the following taxes that apply.

- Tax on your taxable income. Figure the tax using one of the methods described here.
- Tax from Form(s) 8814 (relating to the election to report child's interest or dividends). Check the appropriate box.
- Tax from Form 4972 (relating to lump-sum distributions). Check the appropriate box.
- Tax due to making a section 962 election (the election made by a domestic shareholder of a controlled foreign corporation to be taxed at corporate rates). See section 962 for details. Check box c and enter the amount and "962" in the space next to that box. Attach a statement showing how you figured the tax.

- Recapture of an education credit. You may owe this tax if you claimed an education credit in an earlier year, and either tax-free educational assistance or a refund of qualified expenses was received in 2014 for the student. See Form 8863 for more details. Check box c and enter the amount and "ECR" in the space next to that box.
- Any tax from Form 8621, line 16e, relating to a section 1291 fund. Check box c and enter the amount of the tax and "1291TAX" in the space next to that box.

Do you want the IRS to figure the tax on your taxable income for you?

☐ **Yes.** See chapter 30 of Pub. 17 for details, including who is eligible and what to do. If you have paid too much, we will send you a refund. If you did not pay enough, we will send you a bill.

☐ **No.** Use one of the following methods to figure your tax.

Tax Table or Tax Computation Worksheet. If your taxable income is less than $100,000, you must use the Tax Table, later in these instructions, to figure your tax. Be sure you use the correct column. If your taxable income is $100,000 or more, use the Tax Computation Worksheet right after the Tax Table.

However, do not use the Tax Table or Tax Computation Worksheet to figure your tax if any of the following applies.

Form 8615. Form 8615 generally must be used to figure the tax for any child who had more than $2,000 of unearned income, such as taxable interest, ordinary dividends, or capital gains (including capital gain distributions), and who either:

1. Was under age 18 at the end of 2014,

2. Was age 18 at the end of 2014 and did not have earned income that was more than half of the child's support, or

3. Was a full-time student at least age 19 but under age 24 at the end of 2014 and did not have earned income that was more than half of the child's support.

But if the child files a joint return for 2014 or if neither of the child's parents was alive at the end of 2014, do not use Form 8615 to figure the child's tax.

A child born on January 1, 1997, is considered to be age 18 at the end of 2014; a child born on January 1, 1996, is considered to be age 19 at the end of 2014; a child born on January 1, 1991, is considered to be age 24 at the end of 2014.

Schedule D Tax Worksheet. If you have to file Schedule D, and line 18 or 19 of Schedule D is more than zero, use the Schedule D Tax Worksheet in the Instructions for Schedule D to figure the amount to enter on Form 1040, line 44. But if you are filing Form 2555 or 2555-EZ, you must use the Foreign Earned Income Tax Worksheet instead.

Qualified Dividends and Capital Gain Tax Worksheet. Use the Qualified Dividends and Capital Gain Tax Worksheet, later, to figure your tax if you do not have to use the Schedule D Tax Worksheet and if any of the following applies.

• You reported qualified dividends on Form 1040, line 9b.

• You do not have to file Schedule D and you reported capital gain distributions on Form 1040, line 13.

• You are filing Schedule D and Schedule D, lines 15 and 16, are both more than zero.

But if you are filing Form 2555 or 2555-EZ, you must use the Foreign Earned Income Tax Worksheet instead.

Schedule J. If you had income from farming or fishing (including certain amounts received in connection with the Exxon Valdez litigation), your tax may be less if you choose to figure it using income averaging on Schedule J.

Foreign Earned Income Tax Worksheet. If you claimed the foreign earned income exclusion, housing exclusion, or housing deduction on Form 2555 or 2555-EZ, you must figure your tax using the Foreign Earned Income Tax Worksheet.

Need more information or forms? Visit IRS.gov.

Foreign Earned Income Tax Worksheet—Line 44

Keep for Your Records

> ⚠️ **CAUTION** If Form 1040, line 43, is zero, do not complete this worksheet.

1. Enter the amount from Form 1040, line 43 .... **1.** _____

2a. Enter the amount from your (and your spouse's, if filing jointly) Form 2555, lines 45 and 50, or Form 2555-EZ, line 18 .... **2a.** _____

  b. Enter the total amount of any itemized deductions or exclusions you could not claim because they are related to excluded income .... **b.** _____

  c. Subtract line 2b from line 2a. If zero or less, enter -0- .... **c.** _____

3. Add lines 1 and 2c .... **3.** _____

4. **Tax on the amount on line 3**. Use the Tax Table, Tax Computation Worksheet, Qualified Dividends and Capital Gain Tax Worksheet*, Schedule D Tax Worksheet*, or Form 8615, whichever applies. See the instructions for line 44 to see which tax computation method applies. (Do not use a second Foreign Earned Income Tax Worksheet to figure the tax on this line) .... **4.** _____

5. **Tax on the amount on line 2c**. If the amount on line 2c is less than $100,000, use the Tax Table to figure this tax. If the amount on line 2c is $100,000 or more, use the Tax Computation Worksheet .... **5.** _____

6. Subtract line 5 from line 4. Enter the result. If zero or less, enter -0-. Also include this amount on Form 1040, line 44 .... **6.** _____

*Enter the amount from line 3 above on line 1 of the Qualified Dividends and Capital Gain Tax Worksheet or Schedule D Tax Worksheet if you use either of those worksheets to figure the tax on line 4 above. Complete the rest of that worksheet through line 6 (line 10 if you use the Schedule D Tax Worksheet). Next, you must determine if you have a capital gain excess. To find out if you have a capital gain excess, subtract Form 1040, line 43, from line 6 of your Qualified Dividends and Capital Gain Tax Worksheet (line 10 of your Schedule D Tax Worksheet). If the result is more than zero, that amount is your capital gain excess.

If you do not have a capital gain excess, complete the rest of either of those worksheets according to the worksheet's instructions. Then complete lines 5 and 6 above.

If you have a capital gain excess, complete a second Qualified Dividends and Capital Gain Tax Worksheet or Schedule D Tax Worksheet (whichever applies) as instructed above but in its entirety and with the following additional modifications. Then complete lines 5 and 6 above. These modifications are to be made only for purposes of filling out the Foreign Earned Income Tax Worksheet above.

1. Reduce (but not below zero) the amount you would otherwise enter on line 3 of your Qualified Dividends and Capital Gain Tax Worksheet or line 9 of your Schedule D Tax Worksheet by your capital gain excess.

2. Reduce (but not below zero) the amount you would otherwise enter on line 2 of your Qualified Dividends and Capital Gain Tax Worksheet or line 6 of your Schedule D Tax Worksheet by any of your capital gain excess not used in (1) above.

3. Reduce (but not below zero) the amount on your Schedule D (Form 1040), line 18, by your capital gain excess.

4. Include your capital gain excess as a loss on line 16 of your Unrecaptured Section 1250 Gain Worksheet in the Instructions for Schedule D (Form 1040).

Qualified Dividends and Capital Gain Tax Worksheet—Line 44

Keep for Your Records

Before you begin:
- ✓ See the earlier instructions for line 44 to see if you can use this worksheet to figure your tax.
- ✓ Before completing this worksheet, complete Form 1040 through line 43.
- ✓ If you do not have to file Schedule D and you received capital gain distributions, be sure you checked the box on line 13 of Form 1040.

1. Enter the amount from Form 1040, line 43. However, if you are filing Form 2555 or 2555-EZ (relating to foreign earned income), enter the amount from line 3 of the Foreign Earned Income Tax Worksheet .... **1.** _____

2. Enter the amount from Form 1040, line 9b* .... **2.** _____

3. Are you filing Schedule D?*
   ☐ **Yes.** Enter the **smaller** of line 15 or 16 of Schedule D. If either line 15 or line 16 is blank or a loss, enter -0-
   ☐ **No.** Enter the amount from Form 1040, line 13 **3.** _____

4. Add lines 2 and 3 .... **4.** _____

5. If filing Form 4952 (used to figure investment interest expense deduction), enter any amount from line 4g of that form. Otherwise, enter -0- .... **5.** _____

6. Subtract line 5 from line 4. If zero or less, enter -0- .... **6.** _____

7. Subtract line 6 from line 1. If zero or less, enter -0- .... **7.** _____

8. Enter:
   $36,900 if single or married filing separately,
   $73,800 if married filing jointly or qualifying widow(er),
   $49,400 if head of household. .... **8.** _____

9. Enter the smaller of line 1 or line 8 .... **9.** _____

10. Enter the smaller of line 7 or line 9 .... **10.** _____

11. Subtract line 10 from line 9. This amount is taxed at 0% .... **11.** _____

12. Enter the smaller of line 1 or line 6 .... **12.** _____

13. Enter the amount from line 11 .... **13.** _____

14. Subtract line 13 from line 12 .... **14.** _____

15. Enter:
    $406,750 if single,
    $228,800 if married filing separately,
    $457,600 if married filing jointly or qualifying widow(er),
    $432,200 if head of household. .... **15.** _____

16. Enter the smaller of line 1 or line 15 .... **16.** _____

17. Add lines 7 and 11 .... **17.** _____

18. Subtract line 17 from line 16. If zero or less, enter -0- .... **18.** _____

19. Enter the smaller of line 14 or line 18 .... **19.** _____

20. Multiply line 19 by 15% (.15) .... **20.** _____

21. Add lines 11 and 19 .... **21.** _____

22. Subtract line 21 from line 12 .... **22.** _____

23. Multiply line 22 by 20% (.20) .... **23.** _____

24. Figure the tax on the amount on line 7. If the amount on line 7 is less than $100,000, use the Tax Table to figure the tax. If the amount on line 7 is $100,000 or more, use the Tax Computation Worksheet .... **24.** _____

25. Add lines 20, 23, and 24 .... **25.** _____

26. Figure the tax on the amount on line 1. If the amount on line 1 is less than $100,000, use the Tax Table to figure the tax. If the amount on line 1 is $100,000 or more, use the Tax Computation Worksheet .... **26.** _____

27. **Tax on all taxable income.** Enter the **smaller** of line 25 or line 26. Also include this amount on Form 1040, line 44. If you are filing Form 2555 or 2555-EZ, do not enter this amount on Form 1040, line 44. Instead, enter it on line 4 of the Foreign Earned Income Tax Worksheet .... **27.** _____

If you are filing Form 2555 or 2555-EZ, see the footnote in the Foreign Earned Income Tax Worksheet before completing this line.

Need more information or forms? Visit IRS.gov.

Line 45

Alternative Minimum Tax (AMT)

If you are not sure whether you owe the AMT, complete the Worksheet To See if You Should Fill in Form 6251.

 An electronic version of this worksheet is available on IRS.gov. Enter "AMT Assistant" in the search box.

Exception. Fill in Form 6251 instead of using the worksheet if you claimed or received any of the following items.

- Accelerated depreciation.
- Tax-exempt interest from private activity bonds.
- Intangible drilling, circulation, research, experimental, or mining costs.
- Amortization of pollution-control facilities or depletion.
- Income or (loss) from tax-shelter farm activities, passive activities, partnerships, S corporations, or activities for which you are not at risk.
- Income from long-term contracts not figured using the percentage-of-completion method.
- Interest paid on a home mortgage not used to buy, build, or substantially improve your home.
- Investment interest expense reported on Form 4952.
- Net operating loss deduction.
- Alternative minimum tax adjustments from an estate, trust, electing large partnership, or cooperative.
- Section 1202 exclusion.
- Stock by exercising an incentive stock option and you did not dispose of the stock in the same year.
- Any general business credit claimed on Form 3800 if either line 6 (in Part I) or line 25 of Form 3800 is more than zero.
- Qualified electric vehicle credit.
- Alternative fuel vehicle refueling property tax.
- Credit for prior year minimum tax.
- Foreign tax credit.

 Form 6251 should be filled in for certain children who are under age 24 at the end of 2014. See the Instructions for Form 6251 for more information.

Line 46

Excess Advance Premium Tax Credit Repayment

The premium tax credit helps pay premiums for health insurance purchased from the Health Insurance Marketplace. If advance payments of this credit were made for coverage for you, your spouse, or your dependent, complete Form 8962. If the advance payments were more than the premium tax credit you can claim, enter the amount, if any, from Form 8962, line 29.

If you enrolled someone who is not claimed as a dependent on your return or for more information, see the instructions for Form 8962.

Line 48

Foreign Tax Credit

If you paid income tax to a foreign country or U.S. possession, you may be able to take this credit. Generally, you must complete and attach Form 1116 to do so.

Exception. You do not have to complete Form 1116 to take this credit if all of the following apply.

1. All of your foreign source gross income was from interest and dividends and all of that income and the foreign tax paid on it were reported to you on Form 1099-INT, Form 1099-DIV, or Schedule K-1 (or substitute statement).

2. The total of your foreign taxes was not more than $300 (not more than $600 if married filing jointly).

3. You held the stock or bonds on which the dividends or interest were paid for at least 16 days and were not obligated to pay these amounts to someone else.

4. You are not filing Form 4563 or excluding income from sources within Puerto Rico.

5. All of your foreign taxes were:

a. Legally owed and not eligible for a refund or reduced tax rate under a tax treaty, and

b. Paid to countries that are recognized by the United States and do not support terrorism.

For more details on these requirements, see the Instructions for Form 1116.

Do you meet all five requirements just listed?

☐ **Yes.** Enter on line 48 the smaller of (a) your total foreign taxes, or (b) the total of the amounts on Form 1040, lines 44 and 46.

☐ **No.** See Form 1116 to find out if you can take the credit and, if you can, if you have to file Form 1116.

Line 49

Credit for Child and Dependent Care Expenses

You may be able to take this credit if you paid someone to care for:
- Your qualifying child under age 13 whom you claim as your dependent,
- Your disabled spouse or any other disabled person who could not care for himself or herself, or
- Your child whom you could not claim as a dependent because of the rules for *Children of divorced or separated parents* in the instructions for line 6c.

For details, use TeleTax topic 602 or see Form 2441.

Line 50

Education Credits

If you (or your dependent) paid qualified expenses in 2014 for yourself, your spouse, or your dependent to enroll in or attend an eligible educational institution, you may be able to take an education credit. See Form 8863 for details. However, you cannot take an education credit if any of the following applies.
- You, or your spouse if filing jointly, are claimed as a dependent on someone else's (such as your parent's) 2014 tax return.
- Your filing status is married filing separately.
- The amount on Form 1040, line 38, is $90,000 or more ($180,000 or more if married filing jointly).
- You are taking a deduction for tuition and fees on Form 1040, line 34, for the same student.

Worksheet To See if You Should Fill in Form 6251—Line 45

Keep for Your Records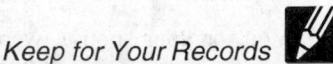

Before you begin: ✓ Be sure you have read the **Exception** in the instructions for this line to see if you must fill in Form 6251 instead of using this worksheet.

1. Are you filing **Schedule A?**

   ☐ **No.** Skip lines 1 through 3; enter on line 4 the amount from Form 1040, line 38, and go to line 5

   ☐ **Yes.** Enter the amount from Form 1040, line 41 . . . . **1.** _____

2. If you or your spouse was age 65 or older, enter the **smaller** of the amount on Schedule A, line 4, or 2.5% (0.25) of the amount on Form 1040, line 38. If zero or less, enter -0- . . . . **2.** _____

3. Enter the total of the amounts from Schedule A, lines 9 and 27 . . . . **3.** _____

4. Add lines 1 through 3 . . . . **4.** _____

5. Enter any tax refund from Form 1040, lines 10 and 21 . . . . **5.** _____

6. If you completed the Itemized Deductions Worksheet in the Instructions for Schedule A, enter the amount from line 9 of that worksheet . . . . **6.** _____

7. Add lines 5 and 6 . . . . **7.** _____

8. Subtract line 7 from line 4 . . . . **8.** _____

9. Enter the amount shown below for your filing status

   • Single or head of household—$52,800

   • Married filing jointly or qualifying widow(er)—$82,100   } . . . .

   • Married filing separately—$41,050   **9.** _____

10. Is the amount on line 8 more than the amount on line 9?

    ☐ **No.** (STOP) You do not need to fill in Form 6251. Do not complete the rest of this worksheet.

    ☐ **Yes.** Subtract line 9 from line 8 . . . . **10.** _____

11. Enter the amount shown below for your filing status.

    • Single or head of household—$117,300

    • Married filing jointly or qualifying widow(er)—$156,500   } . . . .

    • Married filing separately—$78,250   **11.** _____

12. Is the amount on line 8 more than the amount on line 11?

    ☐ **No.** Enter -0-. Skip line 13. Enter on line 14 the amount from line 10, and go to line 15.

    ☐ **Yes.** Subtract line 11 from line 8 . . . . **12.** _____

13. Multiply line 12 by 25% (.25) and enter the **smaller** of the result or line 9 . . . . **13.** _____

14. Add lines 10 and 13 . . . . **14.** _____

15. Is the amount on line 14 more than $182,500 ($91,250 if married filing separately)?

    ☐ **Yes.** (STOP) Fill in Form 6251 to see if you owe the alternative minimum tax.

    ☐ **No.** Multiply line 14 by 26% (.26) . . . . **15.** _____

16. Add Form 1040, line 44 (minus any tax from Form 4972), and Form 1040, line 46. (If you used Schedule J to figure your tax on Form 1040, line 44, refigure that tax without using Schedule J before including it in this calculation) . . . . **16.** _____

Next. Is the amount on line 15 more than the amount on line 16?

   ☐ **Yes.** Fill in Form 6251 to see if you owe the alternative minimum tax.

   ☐ **No.** You do not owe alternative minimum tax and do not need to fill out Form 6251. Leave line 45 blank.

Need more information or forms? Visit IRS.gov.

- You, or your spouse, were a nonresident alien for any part of 2014 unless your filing status is married filing jointly.

You may be able to increase an education credit if the student chooses to include all or part of a Pell grant or certain other scholarships or fellowships in income.

For more information, see Pub. 970, the instructions for line 68, and *www.irs.gov/uac/Am-I-Eligible-to-Claim-an-Education-Credit%3F*.

Line 51

Retirement Savings Contributions Credit (Saver's Credit)

You may be able to take this credit if you, or your spouse if filing jointly, made (a) contributions, other than rollover contributions, to a traditional or Roth IRA; (b) elective deferrals to a 401(k) or 403(b) plan (including designated Roth contributions) or to a governmental 457, SEP, or SIMPLE plan; (c) voluntary employee contributions to a qualified retirement plan (including the federal Thrift Savings Plan); or (d) contributions to a 501(c)(18)(D) plan.

However, you cannot take the credit if either of the following applies.

1. The amount on Form 1040, line 38, is more than $30,000 ($45,000 if head of household; $60,000 if married filing jointly).

2. The person(s) who made the qualified contribution or elective deferral (a) was born after January 1, 1997, (b) is claimed as a dependent on someone else's 2014 tax return, or (c) was a student (defined next).

You were a student if during any part of 5 calendar months of 2014 you:
- Were enrolled as a full-time student at a school, or
- Took a full-time, on-farm training course given by a school or a state, county, or local government agency.

A school includes a technical, trade, or mechanical school. It does not include an on-the-job training course, correspondence school, or school offering courses only through the Internet.

For more details, use TeleTax topic 610 or see Form 8880.

2014 Child Tax Credit Worksheet—Line 52

Keep for Your Records

CAUTION

1. To be a qualifying child for the child tax credit, the child must be your dependent, **under age 17** at the end of 2014, and meet all the conditions in Steps 1 through 3 in the instructions for line 6c. Make sure you checked the box on Form 1040, line 6c, column (4), for each qualifying child.

2. If you do not have a qualifying child, you cannot claim the child tax credit.

3. If your qualifying child has an ITIN instead of an SSN, file Schedule 8812.

4. Do **not** use this worksheet, but use Pub. 972 instead, if:

   a. You are claiming the adoption credit, mortgage interest credit, District of Columbia first-time homebuyer credit, or residential energy efficient property credit,

   b. You are excluding income from Puerto Rico, or

   c. You are filing Form 2555, 2555-EZ, or 4563.

Part 1

1. Number of qualifying children: _____ × $1,000. Enter the result. | **1** |

2. Enter the amount from Form 1040, line 38. | **2** |

3. Enter the amount shown below for your filing status.

   ● Married filing jointly — $110,000

   ● Single, head of household, or qualifying widow(er) — $75,000

   ● Married filing separately — $55,000

   | **3** |

4. Is the amount on line 2 more than the amount on line 3?

   ☐ **No.** Leave line 4 blank. Enter -0- on line 5, and go to line 6.

   ☐ **Yes.** Subtract line 3 from line 2.
   If the result is not a multiple of $1,000, increase it to the next multiple of $1,000. For example, increase $425 to $1,000, increase $1,025 to $2,000, etc.

   | **4** |

5. Multiply the amount on line 4 by 5% (.05). Enter the result. | **5** |

6. Is the amount on line 1 more than the amount on line 5?

   ☐ **No.** (STOP)
   You cannot take the child tax credit on Form 1040, line 52. You also cannot take the additional child tax credit on Form 1040, line 67. Complete the rest of your Form 1040.

   ☐ **Yes.** Subtract line 5 from line 1. Enter the result. *Go to Part 2.*

   | **6** |

Need more information or forms? Visit IRS.gov.

2014 Child Tax Credit Worksheet—*Continued*   *Keep for Your Records*

Before you begin Part 2: √ Figure the amount of any credits you are claiming on Form 5695, Part II; Form 8910; Form 8936; or Schedule R.

Part 2

7. Enter the amount from Form 1040, line 47.   **7**

8. Add any amounts from:

   Form 1040, line 48 _____

   Form 1040, line 49 + _____

   Form 1040, line 50 + _____

   Form 1040, line 51 + _____

   Form 5695, line 30 + _____

   Form 8910, line 15 + _____

   Form 8936, line 23 + _____

   Schedule R, line 22 + _____

   Enter the total. **8**

9. Are the amounts on lines 7 and 8 the same?

   ☐ **Yes.** (STOP)
      You cannot take this credit because there is no tax to reduce. However, you may be able to take the **additional child tax credit.** See the **TIP** below.

   ☐ **No.** Subtract line 8 from line 7.   **9**

10. Is the amount on line 6 more than the amount on line 9?

    ☐ **Yes.** Enter the amount from line 9.
       Also, you may be able to take the **additional child tax credit.** See the **TIP** below.   } **This is your child tax credit.**

    ☐ **No.** Enter the amount from line 6.

    10

    Enter this amount on Form 1040, line 52.

    1040

TIP   You may be able to take the **additional child tax credit** on Form 1040, line 67, if you answered "Yes" on line 9 **or** line 10 above.

- First, complete your Form 1040 through lines 66a and 66b.

- Then, use Schedule 8812 to figure any additional child tax credit.

Line 53

Residential Energy Credits

Residential energy efficient property credit. You may be able to take this credit by completing and attaching Form 5695 if you paid for any of the following during 2014.

- Qualified solar electric property for use in your home located in the United States.
- Qualified solar water heating property for use in your home located in the United States.
- Qualified fuel cell property installed on or in connection with your main home located in the United States.
- Qualified small wind energy property for use in connection with your home located in the United States.
- Qualified geothermal heat pump property installed on or in connection with your home located in the United States.

Nonbusiness energy property credit. You may be able to take this credit by completing and attaching Form 5695 for any of the following improvements to your main home located in the United States in 2014 if they are new and meet certain requirements for energy efficiency.

- Any insulation material or system primarily designed to reduce heat gain or loss in your home.
- Exterior windows (including skylights).
- Exterior doors.
- A metal roof or asphalt roof with pigmented coatings or cooling granules primarily designed to reduce the heat gain in your home.

You may also be able to take this credit for the cost of the following items if the items meet certain performance and quality standards.

- Certain electric heat pump water heaters, electric heat pumps, central air conditioners, and natural gas, propane, or oil water heaters.
- A qualified furnace or hot water boiler that uses natural gas, propane, or oil.
- A stove that burns biomass fuel to heat your home or to heat water for use in your home.

- An advanced main air circulating fan used in a natural gas, propane, or oil furnace.

Condos and co-ops. If you are a member of a condominium management association for a condominium you own or a tenant-stockholder in a cooperative housing corporation, you are treated as having paid your proportionate share of any costs of such association or corporation for purposes of these credits.

More details. For details, see Form 5695.

Line 54

Other Credits

Enter the total of the following credits on line 54 and check the appropriate box(es). Check all boxes that apply. If box c is checked, also enter the applicable form number. To find out if you can take the credit, see the form or publication indicated.

- General business credit. This credit consists of a number of credits that usually apply only to individuals who are partners, shareholders in an S corporation, self-employed, or who have rental property. See Form 3800 or Pub. 334.
- Credit for prior year minimum tax. If you paid alternative minimum tax in a prior year, see Form 8801.
- Mortgage interest credit. If a state or local government gave you a mortgage credit certificate, see Form 8396.
- Credit for the elderly or the disabled. See Schedule R.
- Adoption credit. You may be able to take this credit if you paid expenses to adopt a child or you adopted a child with special needs and the adoption became final in 2014. See the Instructions for Form 8839.
- District of Columbia first-time homebuyer credit. You cannot claim this credit for a home you bought after 2011. You can claim it only if you have a credit carryforward from 2013. See Form 8859.
- Qualified plug-in electric drive motor vehicle credit. See Form 8936.
- Qualified electric vehicle credit. You cannot claim this credit for a vehicle placed in service after 2006. You can claim this credit only if you have an electric vehicle passive activity credit

carried forward from a prior year. See Form 8834.

- Alternative motor vehicle credit. See Form 8910 if you placed a new fuel cell motor vehicle in service during 2014.
- Alternative fuel vehicle refueling property credit. See Form 8911.
- Credit to holders of tax credit bonds. See Form 8912.

Other Taxes

Line 58

Unreported Social Security and Medicare Tax from Forms 4137 and 8919

Enter the total of any taxes from Form 4137 and Form 8919. Check the appropriate box(es).

Form 4137. If you received tips of $20 or more in any month and you did not report the full amount to your employer, you must pay the social security and Medicare or railroad retirement (RRTA) tax on the unreported tips.

Do not include the value of any noncash tips, such as tickets or passes. You do not pay social security and Medicare taxes or RRTA tax on these noncash tips.

To figure the social security and Medicare tax, use Form 4137. If you owe RRTA tax, contact your employer. Your employer will figure and collect the RRTA tax.

 You may be charged a penalty equal to 50% of the social security and Medicare or RRTA tax due on tips you received but did not report to your employer.

Form 8919. If you are an employee who received wages from an employer who did not withhold social security and Medicare tax from your wages, use Form 8919 to figure your share of the unreported tax. Include on line 58 the amount from line 13 of Form 8919. Include the amount from line 6 of Form 8919 on Form 1040, line 7.

Need more information or forms? Visit IRS.gov.

Line 59

Additional Tax on IRAs, Other Qualified Retirement Plans, etc.

If any of the following apply, see Form 5329 and its instructions to find out if you owe this tax and if you must file Form 5329. Also see Form 5329 and its instructions for definitions of the terms used here.

1. You received an early distribution from (a) an IRA or other qualified retirement plan, (b) an annuity, or (c) a modified endowment contract entered into after June 20, 1988, and the total distribution was not rolled over in a qualified rollover contribution.

2. Excess contributions were made to your IRAs, Coverdell education savings accounts (ESAs), Archer MSAs, or health savings accounts (HSAs).

3. You received taxable distributions from Coverdell ESAs or qualified tuition programs.

4. You were born before July 1, 1943, and did not take the minimum required distribution from your IRA or other qualified retirement plan.

Exception. If only item (1) applies and distribution code 1 is correctly shown in box 7 of all your Forms 1099-R, you do not have to file Form 5329. Instead, multiply the taxable amount of the distribution by 10% (.10) and enter the result on line 59. The taxable amount of the distribution is the part of the distribution you reported on Form 1040, line 15b or line 16b, or on Form 4972. Also, enter "No" under the heading *Other Taxes* to the left of line 59 to indicate that you do not have to file Form 5329. But you must file Form 5329 if distribution code 1 is incorrectly shown in box 7 of Form 1099-R or you qualify for an exception, such as the exceptions for qualified medical expenses, qualified higher education expenses, qualified first-time homebuyer distributions, or a qualified reservist distribution.

Line 60a

Household Employment Taxes

Enter the household employment taxes you owe for having a household employee. If any of the following apply, see Schedule H and its instructions to find out if you owe these taxes.

1. You paid any one household employee (defined below) cash wages of $1,900 or more in 2014. Cash wages include wages paid by check, money order, etc. But do not count amounts paid to an employee who was under age 18 at any time in 2014 and was a student.

2. You withheld federal income tax during 2014 at the request of any household employee.

3. You paid total cash wages of $1,000 or more in any calendar quarter of 2013 or 2014 to household employees.

Any person who does household work is a household employee if you can control what will be done and how it will be done. Household work includes work done in or around your home by babysitters, nannies, health aides, housekeepers, yard workers, and similar domestic workers.

Line 60b

First-time Homebuyer Credit Repayment

Enter the first-time homebuyer credit you have to repay if you:
- Disposed of the home within 36 months after buying it,
- Stopped using the home as your main home within 36 months after buying it, or
- Bought the home in 2008.

If you bought the home in 2008 and owned and used it as your main home for all of 2014, you can enter your 2014 repayment on this line without attaching Form 5405.

See the Form 5405 instructions for details and for exceptions to the repayment rule. Also see the Form 5405 instructions if the home you bought was destroyed, condemned, or sold under threat of condemnation and you did not buy a new home within 2 years.

Line 61

Health Care: Individual Responsibility

Beginning in 2014, individuals must have health care coverage, qualify for a health coverage exemption, or make a shared responsibility payment with their tax return.

If you had qualifying health care coverage (called minimum essential coverage) for every month of 2014 for yourself, your spouse (if filing jointly), and anyone you could or did claim as a dependent, check the box on this line and leave the entry space blank.

Otherwise, do not check the box on this line. See the instructions for Form 8965.

If you can be claimed as a dependent, do not check the box on this line. Leave the entry space blank. You do not need to attach Form 8965 or see its instructions.

Minimum essential coverage. Most health care coverage that people have is minimum essential coverage.

Minimum essential coverage includes:
- Health care coverage provided by your employer,
- Health insurance coverage you buy through the Health Insurance Marketplace,
- Many types of government-sponsored health coverage including Medicare, most Medicaid coverage, and most health care coverage provided to veterans and active duty service members, and
- Certain types of coverage you buy directly from an insurance company.

See the instructions for Form 8965 for more information on what qualifies as minimum essential coverage.

Premium tax credit. If you, your spouse, or a dependent enrolled in health insurance through the Marketplace, you may be able to claim the premium tax credit. See the instructions for line 69 and Form 8962.

Line 62

Other Taxes

Use line 62 to report any taxes not reported elsewhere on your return or other schedules. To find out if you owe the tax, see the form or publication indicated. Enter on line 62 the total of all of the following taxes you owe.

Additional Medicare Tax. See Form 8959 and its instructions if the total of your 2014 wages and self-employment income was more than:

- $125,000 if married filing separately,
- $250,000 if married filing jointly, or
- $200,000 if single, head of household, or qualifying widow(er).

Also see Form 8959 if you had railroad retirement (RRTA) compensation that was more than the amount just listed that applies to you.

If you are married filing jointly and either you or your spouse had wages or RRTA compensation of more than $200,000, your employer may have withheld Additional Medicare Tax even if you do not owe the tax. In that case, you may be able to get a refund of the tax withheld. See the Instructions for Form 8959 to find out how to report the withheld tax on Form 8959 and Form 1040.

Check box a if you owe the tax.

Net Investment Income Tax. See Form 8960 and its instructions if the amount on Form 1040, line 38, is more than:

- $125,000 if married filing separately,
- $250,000 if married filing jointly or qualifying widow(er), or
- $200,000 if single or head of household.

If you file Form 2555 or 2555-EZ, see Form 8960 and its instructions if the amount on Form 1040, line 38, is more than:

- $25,800 if married filing separately,
- $150,800 if married filing jointly or qualifying widow(er), or
- $100,800 if single or head of household.

Check box b if you owe the tax.

Other taxes. For the following taxes, check box c and, in the space next to that box, enter the amount of the tax and the code that identifies it. If you need more room, attach a statement listing the amount of each tax and the code.

1. Additional tax on health savings account (HSA) distributions (see Form 8889, Part II). Identify as "HSA."

2. Additional tax on an HSA because you did not remain an eligible individual during the testing period (see Form 8889, Part III). Identify as "HDHP."

3. Additional tax on Archer MSA distributions (see Form 8853). Identify as "MSA."

4. Additional tax on Medicare Advantage MSA distributions (see Form 8853). Identify as "Med MSA."

5. Recapture of the following credits.

   a. Investment credit (see Form 4255). Identify as "ICR."

   b. Low-income housing credit (see Form 8611). Identify as "LIHCR."

   c. Indian employment credit (see Form 8845). Identify as "IECR."

   d. New markets credit (see Form 8874). Identify as "NMCR."

   e. Credit for employer-provided child care facilities (see Form 8882). Identify as "ECCFR."

   f. Alternative motor vehicle credit (see Form 8910). Identify as "AMVCR."

   g. Alternative fuel vehicle refueling property credit (see Form 8911). Identify as "ARPCR."

   h. Qualified plug-in electric drive motor vehicle credit (see Form 8936). Identify as "8936R."

6. Recapture of federal mortgage subsidy. If you sold your home in 2014 and it was financed (in whole or in part) from the proceeds of any tax-exempt qualified mortgage bond or you claimed the mortgage interest credit, see Form 8828. Identify as "FMSR."

7. Section 72(m)(5) excess benefits tax (see Pub. 560). Identify as "Sec. 72(m)(5)."

8. Uncollected social security and Medicare or RRTA tax on tips or group-term life insurance. This tax should be shown in box 12 of Form W-2 with codes A and B or M and N. Identify as "UT."

9. Golden parachute payments. If you received an excess parachute payment (EPP), you must pay a 20% tax on it. This tax should be shown in box 12 of Form W-2 with code K. If you received a Form 1099-MISC, the tax is 20% of the EPP shown in box 13. Identify as "EPP."

10. Tax on accumulation distribution of trusts (see Form 4970). Identify as "ADT."

11. Excise tax on insider stock compensation from an expatriated corporation. See section 4985. Identify as "ISC."

12. Interest on the tax due on installment income from the sale of certain residential lots and timeshares. Identify as "453(l)(3)."

13. Interest on the deferred tax on gain from certain installment sales with a sales price over $150,000. Identify as "453A(c)."

14. Additional tax on recapture of a charitable contribution deduction relating to a fractional interest in tangible personal property. See Pub. 526. Identify as "FITPP."

15. Look-back interest under section 167(g) or 460(b). See Form 8697 or 8866. Identify as "8697" or "8866."

16. Additional tax on income you received from a nonqualified deferred compensation plan that fails to meet the requirements of section 409A. This income should be shown in box 12 of Form W-2 with code Z, or in box 15b of Form 1099-MISC. The tax is 20% of the amount required to be included in income plus an interest amount determined under section 409A(a)(1)(B)(ii). See section 409A(a)(1)(B) for details. Identify as "NQDC."

17. Additional tax on compensation you received from a nonqualified deferred compensation plan described in section 457A if the compensation would have been includible in your income in an earlier year except that the amount was not determinable until 2014. The tax is 20% of the amount required to be included in income plus an interest amount determined under section

Need more information or forms? Visit IRS.gov.

457A(c)(2). See section 457A for details. Identify as "457A."

18. Tax on noneffectively connected income for any part of the year you were a nonresident alien (see the Instructions for Form 1040NR). Identify as "1040NR."

19. Any interest amount from Form 8621, line 16f, relating to distributions from, and dispositions of, stock of a section 1291 fund. Identify as "1291INT."

20. Any interest amount from Form 8621, line 24. Identify as "1294INT."

Payments

Line 64

Federal Income Tax Withheld

Add the amounts shown as federal income tax withheld on your Forms W-2, W-2G, and 1099-R. Enter the total on line 64. The amount withheld should be shown in box 2 of Form W-2 and in box 4 of Form W-2G or 1099-R. Attach Forms W-2G and 1099-R to the front of your return if federal income tax was withheld.

If you received a 2014 Form 1099 showing federal income tax withheld on dividends, taxable or tax-exempt interest income, unemployment compensation, social security benefits, railroad retirement benefits, or other income you received, include the amount withheld in the total on line 64. This should be shown in box 4 of Form 1099, box 6 of Form SSA-1099, or box 10 of Form RRB-1099.

If you had Additional Medicare Tax withheld by your employer(s) in 2014, include the amount shown on Form 8959, line 24, in the total on line 64. Attach Form 8959.

Also include on line 64 any federal income tax withheld that is shown on a Schedule K-1.

Line 65

2014 Estimated Tax Payments

Enter any estimated federal income tax payments you made for 2014. Include any overpayment that you applied to your 2014 estimated tax from:

- Your 2013 return, or
- An amended return (Form 1040X).

If you and your spouse paid joint estimated tax but are now filing separate income tax returns, you can divide the amount paid in any way you choose as long as you both agree. If you cannot agree, you must divide the payments in proportion to each spouse's individual tax as shown on your separate returns for 2014. For an example of how to do this, see Pub. 505. You may want to attach an explanation of how you and your spouse divided the payments. Be sure to show both social security numbers (SSNs) in the space provided on the separate returns. If you or your spouse paid separate estimated tax but you are now filing a joint return, add the amounts you each paid. Follow these instructions even if your spouse died in 2014 or in 2015 before filing a 2014 return.

Divorced taxpayers. If you got divorced in 2014 and you made joint estimated tax payments with your former spouse, enter your former spouse's SSN in the space provided on the front of Form 1040. If you were divorced and remarried in 2014, enter your present spouse's SSN in the space provided on the front of Form 1040. Also, under the heading *Payments* to the left of line 65, enter your former spouse's SSN, followed by "DIV."

Name change. If you changed your name because of marriage, divorce, etc., and you made estimated tax payments using your former name, attach a statement to the front of Form 1040. On the statement, explain all the payments you and your spouse made in 2014 and the name(s) and SSN(s) under which you made them.

Lines 66a and 66b— Earned Income Credit (EIC)

What Is the EIC?

The EIC is a credit for certain people who work. The credit may give you a refund even if you do not owe any tax or did not have any tax withheld.

To Take the EIC:

- Follow the steps below.
- Complete the worksheet that applies to you or let the IRS figure the credit for you.
- If you have a qualifying child, complete and attach Schedule EIC.

For help in determining if you are eligible for the EIC, go to *www.irs.gov/eitc* and click on "EITC Assistant." This service is available in English and Spanish.

 If you take the EIC even though you are not eligible and it is determined that your error is due to reckless or intentional disregard of the EIC rules, you will not be allowed to take the credit for 2 years even if you are otherwise eligible to do so. If you fraudulently take the EIC, you will not be allowed to take the credit for 10 years. See Form 8862, who must file, later. You may also have to pay penalties.

Step 1 All Filers

1. If, in 2014:
   - 3 or more children lived with you, is the amount on Form 1040, line 38, less than $46,997 ($52,427 if married filing jointly)?
   - 2 children lived with you, is the amount on Form 1040, line 38, less than $43,756 ($49,186 if married filing jointly)?
   - 1 child lived with you, is the amount on Form 1040, line 38, less than $38,511 ($43,941 if married filing jointly)?
   - No children lived with you, is the amount on Form 1040, line 38, less than $14,590 ($20,020 if married filing jointly)?

   ☐ **Yes.** Continue ↳   ☐ **No.** (STOP)
                                            You cannot take the credit.

2. Do you, and your spouse if filing a joint return, have a social security number that allows you to work and is valid for EIC purposes (explained later under *Definitions and Special Rules*)?

   ☐ **Yes.** Continue ↳   ☐ **No.** (STOP)
                                            You cannot take the credit. Enter "No" on the dotted line next to line 66a.

3. Is your filing status married filing separately?

   ☐ **Yes.** (STOP)   ☐ **No.** Continue ↳
   You cannot take the credit.

4. Are you filing Form 2555 or 2555-EZ (relating to foreign earned income)?

   ☐ **Yes.** (STOP)   ☐ **No.** Continue ↳
   You cannot take the credit.

5. Were you or your spouse a nonresident alien for any part of 2014?

   ☐ **Yes.** See *Nonresident aliens,* later, under *Definitions and Special Rules.*   ☐ **No.** Go to Step 2.

Step 2 Investment Income

1. Add the amounts from Form 1040:

Line 8a	_____
Line 8b	+ _____
Line 9a	+ _____
Line 13*	+ _____

   Investment Income = [_____]

   *If line 13 is a loss, enter -0-.

2. Is your investment income more than $3,350?

   ☐ **Yes.** Continue ↳   ☐ **No.** Skip question 3; go to question 4.

3. Are you filing Form 4797 (relating to sales of business property)?

   ☐ **Yes.** See *Form 4797 filers,* later, under *Definitions and Special Rules.*   ☐ **No.** (STOP) You cannot take the credit.

4. Do any of the following apply for 2014?
   - You are filing Schedule E.
   - You are reporting income from the rental of personal property not used in a trade or business.
   - You are reporting income on Form 1040, line 21, from Form 8814 (relating to election to report child's interest and dividends).

   ☐ **Yes.** You must use Worksheet 1 in Pub. 596 to see if you can take the credit.   ☐ **No.** Go to Step 3.

Need more information or forms? Visit IRS.gov.

Step 3 Qualifying Child

A qualifying child for the EIC is a child who is your...

Son, daughter, stepchild, foster child, brother, sister, stepbrother, stepsister, half brother, half sister, or a descendant of any of them (for example, your grandchild, niece, or nephew)

was ...

Under age 19 at the end of 2014 and younger than you
(or your spouse, if filing jointly)

or

Under age 24 at the end of 2014, a student (defined later), and younger than you (or your spouse, if filing jointly)

or

Any age and permanently and totally disabled (defined later)

Who is not filing a joint return for 2014
or is filing a joint return for 2014 only to claim a refund of withheld income tax or estimated tax paid (see Pub. 596 for examples)

Who lived with you in the United States for more than half of 2014.
If the child did not live with you for the required time, see *Exception to time lived with you,* later.

⚠️ **CAUTION** *If the child meets the conditions to be a qualifying child of any other person (other than your spouse if filing a joint return) for 2014, see* Qualifying child of more than one person, *later. If the child was married, see* Married child, *later.*

1. Do you have at least one child who meets the conditions to be your qualifying child?

☐ **Yes.** The child must have a valid social security number (SSN) as defined later, unless the child was born and died in 2014. If at least one qualifying child has a valid SSN (or was born or died in 2014), go to question 2. Otherwise, you cannot take the credit.

☐ **No.** Skip questions 2 and 3; go to Step 4.

2. Are you filing a joint return for 2014?

☐ **Yes.** Skip question 3 and Step 4; go to Step 5.

☐ **No.** Continue ↘

3. Could you be a qualifying child of another person for 2014? (Check "No" if the other person is not required to file, and is not filing, a 2014 tax return or is filing a 2014 return only to claim a refund of withheld income tax or estimated tax paid (see Pub. 596 for examples).)

☐ **Yes.** 🛑
You cannot take the credit. Enter "No" on the dotted line next to line 66a.

☐ **No.** Skip Step 4; go to Step 5.

Step 4 Filers Without a Qualifying Child

1. Is the amount on Form 1040, line 38, less than $14,590 ($20,020 if married filing jointly)?

☐ **Yes.** Continue ↓

☐ **No.** 🛑
You cannot take the credit.

2. Were you, or your spouse if filing a joint return, at least age 25 but under age 65 at the end of 2014? (Check "Yes" if you, or your spouse if filing a joint return, were born after December 31, 1949, and before January 2, 1990.) If your spouse died in 2014 or if you are preparing a return for someone who died in 2014, see Pub. 596 before you answer.

☐ **Yes.** Continue ↓

☐ **No.** 🛑
You cannot take the credit.

3. Was your main home, and your spouse's if filing a joint return, in the United States for more than half of 2014? Members of the military stationed outside the United States, see *Members of the military,* later, before you answer.

☐ **Yes.** Continue ↓

☐ **No.** 🛑
You cannot take the credit. Enter "No" on the dotted line next to line 66a.

4. Are you filing a joint return for 2014?

☐ **Yes.** Skip questions 5 and 6; go to Step 5.

☐ **No.** Continue ↘

5. Could you be a qualifying child of another person for 2014? (Check "No" if the other person is not required to file, and is not filing, a 2014 tax return or is filing a 2014 return only to claim a refund of withheld income tax or estimated tax paid (see Pub. 596 for examples).)

☐ **Yes.** 🛑
You cannot take the credit. Enter "No" on the dotted line next to line 66a.

☐ **No.** Continue ↘

6. Can you be claimed as a dependent on someone else's 2014 tax return?

☐ **Yes.** (STOP)   ☐ **No.** Go to Step 5.

You cannot take the credit.

Step 5 Earned Income

1. Are you filing Schedule SE because you were a member of the clergy or you had church employee income of $108.28 or more?

☐ **Yes.** See *Clergy* or *Church employees,* whichever applies.   ☐ **No.** Complete the following worksheet.

1. Enter the amount from Form 1040, line 7 . . . . **1.**_____

2. Enter any amount included on Form 1040, line 7, that is a taxable scholarship or fellowship grant not reported on a Form W-2 . . . . **2.**_____

3. Enter any amount included on Form 1040, line 7, that you received for work performed while an inmate in a penal institution. (Enter "PRI" and the same amount on the dotted line next to Form 1040, line 7) . . . . **3.**_____

4. Enter any amount included on Form 1040, line 7, that you received as a pension or annuity from a nonqualified deferred compensation plan or a nongovernmental section 457 plan. (Enter "DFC" and the same amount on the dotted line next to Form 1040, line 7.) This amount may be shown in box 11 of Form W-2. If you received such an amount but box 11 is blank, contact your employer for the amount received . . . . **4.**_____

5. Enter any amount included on Form 1040, line 7, that is a Medicaid waiver payment you exclude from income. (See the instructions for line 21) . . . . **5.**_____

6. Add lines 2, 3, 4, and 5 . . . . **6.**_____

7. Subtract line 6 from line 1 . . . . **7.**_____

8. Enter all of your nontaxable combat pay if you elect to include it in earned income. Also enter this amount on Form 1040, line 66b. See *Combat pay, nontaxable,* later . . . . **8.**_____

⚠ **CAUTION**   *Electing to include nontaxable combat pay may increase or decrease your EIC. Figure the credit with and without your nontaxable combat pay before making the election.*

9. Add lines 7 and 8. **This is your earned income** . . . . **9.**_____

2. Were you self-employed at any time in 2014, or are you filing Schedule SE because you were a member of the clergy or you had church employee income, or are you filing Schedule C or C-EZ as a statutory employee?

☐ **Yes.** Skip question 3 and Step 6; go to Worksheet B.   ☐ **No.** Continue ↘

3. If you have:
- 3 or more qualifying children, is your earned income less than $46,997 ($52,427 if married filing jointly)?
- 2 qualifying children, is your earned income less than $43,756 ($49,186 if married filing jointly)?
- 1 qualifying child, is your earned income less than $38,511 ($43,941 if married filing jointly)?
- No qualifying children, is your earned income less than $14,590 ($20,020 if married filing jointly)?

☐ **Yes.** Go to Step 6.   ☐ **No.** (STOP)

You cannot take the credit.

Step 6 How To Figure the Credit

1. Do you want the IRS to figure the credit for you?

☐ **Yes.** See *Credit figured by the IRS,* later.   ☐ **No.** Go to Worksheet A.

Definitions and Special Rules

Adopted child. An adopted child is always treated as your own child. An adopted child includes a child lawfully placed with you for legal adoption.

Church employees. Determine how much of the amount on Form 1040, line 7, was also reported on Schedule SE, Section B, line 5a. Subtract that amount from the amount on Form 1040, line 7, and enter the result on line 1 of the worksheet in Step 5 (instead of entering the actual amount from Form 1040, line 7). Be sure to answer "Yes" to question 2 in Step 5.

Clergy. The following instructions apply to ministers, members of religious orders who have not taken a vow of poverty, and Christian Science practitioners. If you are filing Schedule SE and the amount on line 2 of that schedule includes an amount that was also reported on Form 1040, line 7:

1. Enter "Clergy" on the dotted line next to Form 1040, line 66a.

2. Determine how much of the amount on Form 1040, line 7, was also reported on Schedule SE, Section A, line 2, or Section B, line 2.

3. Subtract that amount from the amount on Form 1040, line 7. Enter the result on line 1 of the worksheet in Step 5 (instead of entering the actual amount from Form 1040, line 7).

4. Be sure to answer "Yes" to question 2 in Step 5.

Combat pay, nontaxable. If you were a member of the U.S. Armed Forces who served in a combat zone, certain pay is excluded from your income. See *Combat Zone Exclusion* in Pub. 3. You can elect to include this pay in your earned income when

Need more information or forms? Visit IRS.gov.

figuring the EIC. The amount of your nontaxable combat pay should be shown in box 12 of Form(s) W-2 with code Q. If you are filing a joint return and both you and your spouse received nontaxable combat pay, you can each make your own election. In other words, if one of you makes the election, the other one can also make it but does not have to.

Credit figured by the IRS. To have the IRS figure your EIC:

1. Enter "EIC" on the dotted line next to Form 1040, line 66a.

2. Be sure you enter the nontaxable combat pay you elect to include in earned income on Form 1040, line 66b. See *Combat pay, nontaxable*, earlier.

3. If you have a qualifying child, complete and attach Schedule EIC. If your EIC for a year after 1996 was reduced or disallowed, see *Form 8862, who must file*, later.

Exception to time lived with you. Temporary absences by you or the child for special circumstances, such as school, vacation, business, medical care, military service, or detention in a juvenile facility, count as time the child lived with you. Also see *Kidnapped child* in the instructions for line 6c and *Members of the military*, later. A child is considered to have lived with you for more than half of 2014 if the child was born or died in 2014 and your home was this child's home for more than half the time he or she was alive in 2014.

Form 4797 filers. If the amount on Form 1040, line 13, includes an amount from Form 4797, you must use Worksheet 1 in Pub. 596 to see if you can take the EIC. Otherwise, stop; you cannot take the EIC.

Form 8862, who must file. You must file Form 8862 if your EIC for a year after 1996 was reduced or disallowed for any reason other than a math or clerical error. But do not file Form 8862 if either of the following applies.

• You filed Form 8862 for another year, the EIC was allowed for that year, and your EIC has not been reduced or disallowed again for any reason other than a math or clerical error.

• You are taking the EIC without a qualifying child and the only reason your EIC was reduced or disallowed in the other year was because it was determined that a child listed on Schedule EIC was not your qualifying child.

Also, do not file Form 8862 or take the credit for the:

• 2 years after the most recent tax year for which there was a final determination that your EIC claim was due to reckless or intentional disregard of the EIC rules, or

• 10 years after the most recent tax year for which there was a final determination that your EIC claim was due to fraud.

Foster child. A foster child is any child placed with you by an authorized placement agency or by judgment, decree, or other order of any court of competent jurisdiction. For more details on authorized placement agencies, see Pub. 596.

Married child. A child who was married at the end of 2014 is a qualifying child only if (a) you can claim him or her as your dependent on Form 1040, line 6c, or (b) you could have claimed him or her as your dependent except for the special rule for *Children of divorced or separated parents* in the instructions for line 6c.

Members of the military. If you were on extended active duty outside the United States, your main home is considered to be in the United States during that duty period. Extended active duty is military duty ordered for an indefinite period or for a period of more than 90 days. Once you begin serving extended active duty, you are considered to be on extended active duty even if you do not serve more than 90 days.

Nonresident aliens. If your filing status is married filing jointly, go to Step 2. Otherwise, stop; you cannot take the EIC. Enter "No" on the dotted line next to line 66a.

Permanently and totally disabled. A person is permanently and totally disabled if, at any time in 2014, the person could not engage in any substantial gainful activity because of a physical or mental condition and a doctor has determined that this condition (a) has lasted or can be expected to last continuously for at least a year, or (b) can be expected to lead to death.

Qualifying child of more than one person. Even if a child meets the conditions to be the qualifying child of more than one person, only one person can claim the child as a qualifying child for all of the following tax benefits, unless the special rule for *Children of divorced or separated parents* in the instructions for line 6c applies.

1. Dependency exemption (line 6c).

2. Child tax credits (lines 52 and 67).

3. Head of household filing status (line 4).

4. Credit for child and dependent care expenses (line 49).

5. Exclusion for dependent care benefits (Form 2441, Part III).

6. Earned income credit (lines 66a and 66b).

No other person can take any of the six tax benefits just listed unless he or she has a different qualifying child. If you and any other person can claim the child as a qualifying child, the following rules apply.

• If only one of the persons is the child's parent, the child is treated as the qualifying child of the parent.

• If the parents file a joint return together and can claim the child as a qualifying child, the child is treated as the qualifying child of the parents.

• If the parents do not file a joint return together but both parents claim the child as a qualifying child, the IRS will treat the child as the qualifying child of the parent with whom the child lived for the longer period of time in 2014. If the child lived with each parent for the same amount of time, the IRS will treat the child as the qualifying child of the parent who had the higher adjusted gross income (AGI) for 2014.

• If no parent can claim the child as a qualifying child, the child is treated as the qualifying child of the person who had the highest AGI for 2014.

• If a parent can claim the child as a qualifying child but no parent does so claim the child, the child is treated as the qualifying child of the person who had the highest AGI for 2014, but only if that person's AGI is higher than the highest AGI of any parent of the child who can claim the child.

Example. Your daughter meets the conditions to be a qualifying child for both you and your mother. Your daughter does not meet the conditions to be a qualifying child of any other person, including her other parent. Under the rules just described, you can claim your daughter as a qualifying child for all of the six tax benefits listed here for which you otherwise qualify. Your mother cannot claim any of the six tax benefits listed here unless she has a different qualifying child. However, if your mother's AGI is higher than yours and you do not claim your daughter as a qualifying child, your daughter is the qualifying child of your mother.

For more details and examples, see Pub. 596.

If you will not be taking the EIC with a qualifying child, enter "No" on the dotted line next to line 66a. Otherwise, go to Step 3, question 1.

Social security number (SSN). For the EIC, a valid SSN is a number issued by the Social Security Administration unless "Not Valid for Employment" is printed on the social security card and the number was issued solely to allow the recipient of the SSN to apply for or receive a federally funded benefit. However, if "Valid for Work Only With DHS Authorization" is printed on your social security card, your SSN is valid for EIC purposes only as long as the DHS authorization is still valid.

To find out how to get an SSN, see *Social Security Number (SSN)* near the beginning of these instructions. If you will not have an SSN by the date your return is due, see *What if You Cannot File on Time?*

Student. A student is a child who during any part of 5 calendar months of 2014 was enrolled as a full-time student at a school, or took a full-time, on-farm training course given by a school or a state, county, or local government agency. A school includes a technical, trade, or mechanical school. It does not include an on-the-job training course, correspondence school, or school offering courses only through the Internet.

Welfare benefits, effect of credit on. Any refund you receive as a result of taking the EIC cannot be counted as income when determining if you or anyone else is eligible for benefits or assistance, or how much you or anyone else can receive, under any federal program or under any state or local program financed in whole or in part with federal funds. These programs include Temporary Assistance for Needy Families (TANF), Medicaid, Supplemental Security Income (SSI), and Supplemental Nutrition Assistance Program (food stamps). In addition, when determining eligibility, the refund cannot be counted as a resource for at least 12 months after you receive it. Check with your local benefit coordinator to find out if your refund will affect your benefits.

Need more information or forms? Visit IRS.gov.

Worksheet A—2014 EIC—Lines 66a and 66b

Keep for Your Records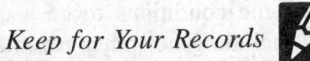

Before you begin: ✓ Be sure you are using the correct worksheet. Use this worksheet only if you answered "No" to Step 5, question 2. Otherwise, use Worksheet B.

Part 1

All Filers Using Worksheet A

1. Enter your earned income from Step 5. **1** _____

2. Look up the amount on line 1 above in the EIC Table (right after Worksheet B) to find the credit. Be sure you use the correct column for your filing status and the number of children you have. Enter the credit here. **2** _____

   If line 2 is zero, (STOP) You cannot take the credit.
   Enter "No" on the dotted line next to line 66a.

3. Enter the amount from Form 1040, line 38. **3** _____

4. Are the amounts on lines 3 and 1 the same?

   ☐ **Yes.** Skip line 5; enter the amount from line 2 on line 6.

   ☐ **No.** Go to line 5.

Part 2

Filers Who Answered "No" on Line 4

5. If you have:
   - No qualifying children, is the amount on line 3 less than $8,150 ($13,550 if married filing jointly)?
   - 1 or more qualifying children, is the amount on line 3 less than $17,850 ($23,300 if married filing jointly)?

   ☐ **Yes.** Leave line 5 blank; enter the amount from line 2 on line 6.

   ☐ **No.** Look up the amount on line 3 in the EIC Table to find the credit. Be sure you use the correct column for your filing status and the number of children you have. Enter the credit here. **5** _____
   Look at the amounts on lines 5 and 2.
   Then, enter the **smaller** amount on line 6.

Part 3

Your Earned Income Credit

6. **This is your earned income credit.** **6** _____

   Enter this amount on Form 1040, line 66a.

   ### Reminder—

   ✓ If you have a qualifying child, complete and attach Schedule EIC.

   ⚠ **CAUTION** *If your EIC for a year after 1996 was reduced or disallowed, see Form 8862, who must file, earlier, to find out if you must file Form 8862 to take the credit for 2014.*

Worksheet **B**—2014 EIC—Lines 66a and 66b

Keep for Your Records

Use this worksheet if you answered "Yes" to Step 5, question 2.

√ Complete the parts below (Parts 1 through 3) that apply to you. Then, continue to Part 4.

√ If you are married filing a joint return, include your spouse's amounts, if any, with yours to figure the amounts to enter in Parts 1 through 3.

Part 1

Self-Employed, Members of the Clergy, and People With Church Employee Income Filing Schedule SE

1a. Enter the amount from Schedule SE, Section A, line 3, or Section B, line 3, whichever applies. | **1a** |

b. Enter any amount from Schedule SE, Section B, line 4b, and line 5a. | + | **1b** |

c. Combine lines 1a and 1b. | = | **1c** |

d. Enter the amount from Schedule SE, Section A, line 6, or Section B, line 13, whichever applies. | − | **1d** |

e. Subtract line 1d from 1c. | = | **1e** |

Part 2

Self-Employed NOT Required To File Schedule SE

For example, your net earnings from self-employment were less than $400.

2. Do not include on these lines any statutory employee income, any net profit from services performed as a notary public, any amount exempt from self-employment tax as the result of the filing and approval of Form 4029 or Form 4361, or any other amounts exempt from self-employment tax.

a. Enter any net farm profit or (loss) from Schedule F, line 34, and from farm partnerships, Schedule K-1 (Form 1065), box 14, code A*. | **2a** |

b. Enter any net profit or (loss) from Schedule C, line 31; Schedule C-EZ, line 3; Schedule K-1 (Form 1065), box 14, code A (other than farming); and Schedule K-1 (Form 1065-B), box 9, code J1*. | + | **2b** |

c. Combine lines 2a and 2b. | = | **2c** |

If you have any Schedule K-1 amounts, complete the appropriate line(s) of Schedule SE, Section A. Reduce the Schedule K-1 amounts as described in the Partner's Instructions for Schedule K-1. Enter your name and social security number on Schedule SE and attach it to your return.

Part 3

Statutory Employees Filing Schedule C or C-EZ

3. Enter the amount from Schedule C, line 1, or Schedule C-EZ, line 1, that you are filing as a statutory employee. | **3** |

Part 4

All Filers Using Worksheet B

Note. If line 4b includes income on which you should have paid self-employment tax but did not, we may reduce your credit by the amount of self-employment tax not paid.

4a. Enter your earned income from Step 5. | **4a** |

b. Combine lines 1e, 2c, 3, and 4a. **This is your total earned income.** | **4b** |

If line 4b is zero or less, (STOP) You cannot take the credit. Enter "No" on the dotted line next to line 66a.

5. If you have:

● 3 or more qualifying children, is line 4b less than $46,997 ($52,427 if married filing jointly)?
● 2 qualifying children, is line 4b less than $43,756 ($49,186 if married filing jointly)?
● 1 qualifying child, is line 4b less than $38,511 ($43,941 if married filing jointly)?
● No qualifying children, is line 4b less than $14,590 ($20,020 if married filing jointly)?

☐ **Yes.** If you want the IRS to figure your credit, see *Credit figured by the IRS,* earlier. If you want to figure the credit yourself, enter the amount from line 4b on line 6 of this worksheet.

☐ **No.** (STOP) You cannot take the credit. Enter "No" on the dotted line next to line 66a.

Need more information or forms? Visit IRS.gov.

Worksheet **B**—2014 EIC—Lines 66a and 66b—*Continued*   *Keep for Your Records*

Part 5

All Filers Using Worksheet B

6. Enter your total earned income from Part 4, line 4b.   **6**

7. Look up the amount on line 6 above in the EIC Table to find the credit. Be sure you use the correct column for your filing status and the number of children you have. Enter the credit here.   **7**

If line 7 is zero, (STOP) You cannot take the credit.
Enter "No" on the dotted line next to line 66a.

8. Enter the amount from Form 1040, line 38.   **8**

9. Are the amounts on lines 8 and 6 the same?

☐ **Yes.** Skip line 10; enter the amount from line 7 on line 11.

☐ **No.** Go to line 10.

Part 6

Filers Who Answered "No" on Line 9

10. If you have:
   ● No qualifying children, is the amount on line 8 less than $8,150 ($13,550 if married filing jointly)?
   ● 1 or more qualifying children, is the amount on line 8 less than $17,850 ($23,300 if married filing jointly)?

☐ **Yes.** Leave line 10 blank; enter the amount from line 7 on line 11.

☐ **No.** Look up the amount on line 8 in the EIC Table to find the credit. Be sure you use the correct column for your filing status and the number of children you have. Enter the credit here.   **10**
   Look at the amounts on lines 10 and 7.
   Then, enter the **smaller** amount on line 11.

Part 7

Your Earned Income Credit

11. **This is your earned income credit.**   **11**

Enter this amount on Form 1040, line 66a.

Reminder—

✓ If you have a qualifying child, complete and attach Schedule EIC.

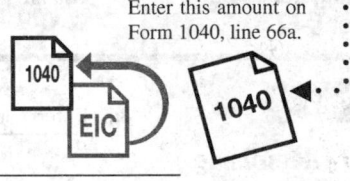

 *If your EIC for a year after 1996 was reduced or disallowed, see Form 8862, who must file, earlier, to find out if you must file Form 8862 to take the credit for 2014.*

2014 Earned Income Credit (EIC) Table
Caution. This is **not** a tax table.

1. To find your credit, read down the "At least - But less than" columns and find the line that includes the amount you were told to look up from your EIC Worksheet.

2. Then, go to the column that includes your filing status and the number of qualifying children you have. Enter the credit from that column on your EIC Worksheet.

Example. If your filing status is single, you have one qualifying child, and the amount you are looking up from your EIC Worksheet is $2,455, you would enter $842.

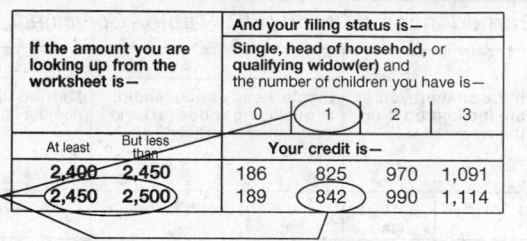

If the amount you are looking up from the worksheet is—		And your filing status is—			
		Single, head of household, or qualifying widow(er) and the number of children you have is—			
		0	1	2	3
At least	But less than	Your credit is—			
2,400	2,450	186	825	970	1,091
2,450	2,500	189	842	990	1,114

If the amount you are looking up from the worksheet is—		And your filing status is—							
		Single, head of household, or qualifying widow(er) and the number of children you have is—				Married filing jointly and the number of children you have is—			
		0	1	2	3	0	1	2	3
At least	But less than	Your credit is—				Your credit is—			
$1	$50	$2	$9	$10	$11	$2	$9	$10	$11
50	100	6	26	30	34	6	26	30	34
100	150	10	43	50	56	10	43	50	56
150	200	13	60	70	79	13	60	70	79
200	250	17	77	90	101	17	77	90	101
250	300	21	94	110	124	21	94	110	124
300	350	25	111	130	146	25	111	130	146
350	400	29	128	150	169	29	128	150	169
400	450	33	145	170	191	33	145	170	191
450	500	36	162	190	214	36	162	190	214
500	550	40	179	210	236	40	179	210	236
550	600	44	196	230	259	44	196	230	259
600	650	48	213	250	281	48	213	250	281
650	700	52	230	270	304	52	230	270	304
700	750	55	247	290	326	55	247	290	326
750	800	59	264	310	349	59	264	310	349
800	850	63	281	330	371	63	281	330	371
850	900	67	298	350	394	67	298	350	394
900	950	71	315	370	416	71	315	370	416
950	1,000	75	332	390	439	75	332	390	439
1,000	1,050	78	349	410	461	78	349	410	461
1,050	1,100	82	366	430	484	82	366	430	484
1,100	1,150	86	383	450	506	86	383	450	506
1,150	1,200	90	400	470	529	90	400	470	529
1,200	1,250	94	417	490	551	94	417	490	551
1,250	1,300	98	434	510	574	98	434	510	574
1,300	1,350	101	451	530	596	101	451	530	596
1,350	1,400	105	468	550	619	105	468	550	619
1,400	1,450	109	485	570	641	109	485	570	641
1,450	1,500	113	502	590	664	113	502	590	664
1,500	1,550	117	519	610	686	117	519	610	686
1,550	1,600	120	536	630	709	120	536	630	709
1,600	1,650	124	553	650	731	124	553	650	731
1,650	1,700	128	570	670	754	128	570	670	754
1,700	1,750	132	587	690	776	132	587	690	776
1,750	1,800	136	604	710	799	136	604	710	799
1,800	1,850	140	621	730	821	140	621	730	821
1,850	1,900	143	638	750	844	143	638	750	844
1,900	1,950	147	655	770	866	147	655	770	866
1,950	2,000	151	672	790	889	151	672	790	889
2,000	2,050	155	689	810	911	155	689	810	911
2,050	2,100	159	706	830	934	159	706	830	934
2,100	2,150	163	723	850	956	163	723	850	956
2,150	2,200	166	740	870	979	166	740	870	979
2,200	2,250	170	757	890	1,001	170	757	890	1,001
2,250	2,300	174	774	910	1,024	174	774	910	1,024
2,300	2,350	178	791	930	1,046	178	791	930	1,046
2,350	2,400	182	808	950	1,069	182	808	950	1,069
2,400	2,450	186	825	970	1,091	186	825	970	1,091
2,450	2,500	189	842	990	1,114	189	842	990	1,114
2,500	2,550	193	859	1,010	1,136	193	859	1,010	1,136
2,550	2,600	197	876	1,030	1,159	197	876	1,030	1,159
2,600	2,650	201	893	1,050	1,181	201	893	1,050	1,181
2,650	2,700	205	910	1,070	1,204	205	910	1,070	1,204
2,700	2,750	208	927	1,090	1,226	208	927	1,090	1,226
2,750	2,800	212	944	1,110	1,249	212	944	1,110	1,249

If the amount you are looking up from the worksheet is—		And your filing status is—							
		Single, head of household, or qualifying widow(er) and the number of children you have is—				Married filing jointly and the number of children you have is—			
		0	1	2	3	0	1	2	3
At least	But less than	Your credit is—				Your credit is—			
2,800	2,850	216	961	1,130	1,271	216	961	1,130	1,271
2,850	2,900	220	978	1,150	1,294	220	978	1,150	1,294
2,900	2,950	224	995	1,170	1,316	224	995	1,170	1,316
2,950	3,000	228	1,012	1,190	1,339	228	1,012	1,190	1,339
3,000	3,050	231	1,029	1,210	1,361	231	1,029	1,210	1,361
3,050	3,100	235	1,046	1,230	1,384	235	1,046	1,230	1,384
3,100	3,150	239	1,063	1,250	1,406	239	1,063	1,250	1,406
3,150	3,200	243	1,080	1,270	1,429	243	1,080	1,270	1,429
3,200	3,250	247	1,097	1,290	1,451	247	1,097	1,290	1,451
3,250	3,300	251	1,114	1,310	1,474	251	1,114	1,310	1,474
3,300	3,350	254	1,131	1,330	1,496	254	1,131	1,330	1,496
3,350	3,400	258	1,148	1,350	1,519	258	1,148	1,350	1,519
3,400	3,450	262	1,165	1,370	1,541	262	1,165	1,370	1,541
3,450	3,500	266	1,182	1,390	1,564	266	1,182	1,390	1,564
3,500	3,550	270	1,199	1,410	1,586	270	1,199	1,410	1,586
3,550	3,600	273	1,216	1,430	1,609	273	1,216	1,430	1,609
3,600	3,650	277	1,233	1,450	1,631	277	1,233	1,450	1,631
3,650	3,700	281	1,250	1,470	1,654	281	1,250	1,470	1,654
3,700	3,750	285	1,267	1,490	1,676	285	1,267	1,490	1,676
3,750	3,800	289	1,284	1,510	1,699	289	1,284	1,510	1,699
3,800	3,850	293	1,301	1,530	1,721	293	1,301	1,530	1,721
3,850	3,900	296	1,318	1,550	1,744	296	1,318	1,550	1,744
3,900	3,950	300	1,335	1,570	1,766	300	1,335	1,570	1,766
3,950	4,000	304	1,352	1,590	1,789	304	1,352	1,590	1,789
4,000	4,050	308	1,369	1,610	1,811	308	1,369	1,610	1,811
4,050	4,100	312	1,386	1,630	1,834	312	1,386	1,630	1,834
4,100	4,150	316	1,403	1,650	1,856	316	1,403	1,650	1,856
4,150	4,200	319	1,420	1,670	1,879	319	1,420	1,670	1,879
4,200	4,250	323	1,437	1,690	1,901	323	1,437	1,690	1,901
4,250	4,300	327	1,454	1,710	1,924	327	1,454	1,710	1,924
4,300	4,350	331	1,471	1,730	1,946	331	1,471	1,730	1,946
4,350	4,400	335	1,488	1,750	1,969	335	1,488	1,750	1,969
4,400	4,450	339	1,505	1,770	1,991	339	1,505	1,770	1,991
4,450	4,500	342	1,522	1,790	2,014	342	1,522	1,790	2,014
4,500	4,550	346	1,539	1,810	2,036	346	1,539	1,810	2,036
4,550	4,600	350	1,556	1,830	2,059	350	1,556	1,830	2,059
4,600	4,650	354	1,573	1,850	2,081	354	1,573	1,850	2,081
4,650	4,700	358	1,590	1,870	2,104	358	1,590	1,870	2,104
4,700	4,750	361	1,607	1,890	2,126	361	1,607	1,890	2,126
4,750	4,800	365	1,624	1,910	2,149	365	1,624	1,910	2,149
4,800	4,850	369	1,641	1,930	2,171	369	1,641	1,930	2,171
4,850	4,900	373	1,658	1,950	2,194	373	1,658	1,950	2,194
4,900	4,950	377	1,675	1,970	2,216	377	1,675	1,970	2,216
4,950	5,000	381	1,692	1,990	2,239	381	1,692	1,990	2,239
5,000	5,050	384	1,709	2,010	2,261	384	1,709	2,010	2,261
5,050	5,100	388	1,726	2,030	2,284	388	1,726	2,030	2,284
5,100	5,150	392	1,743	2,050	2,306	392	1,743	2,050	2,306
5,150	5,200	396	1,760	2,070	2,329	396	1,760	2,070	2,329
5,200	5,250	400	1,777	2,090	2,351	400	1,777	2,090	2,351
5,250	5,300	404	1,794	2,110	2,374	404	1,794	2,110	2,374
5,300	5,350	407	1,811	2,130	2,396	407	1,811	2,130	2,396
5,350	5,400	411	1,828	2,150	2,419	411	1,828	2,150	2,419
5,400	5,450	415	1,845	2,170	2,441	415	1,845	2,170	2,441
5,450	5,500	419	1,862	2,190	2,464	419	1,862	2,190	2,464
5,500	5,550	423	1,879	2,210	2,486	423	1,879	2,210	2,486
5,550	5,600	426	1,896	2,230	2,509	426	1,896	2,230	2,509

(Continued)

Earned Income Credit (EIC) Table - *Continued* **(Caution.** This is **not** a tax table.)

If the amount you are looking up from the worksheet is–		And your filing status is– **Single, head of household,** or **qualifying widow(er)** and the number of children you have is–				**Married filing jointly** and the number of children you have is–			
		0	1	2	3	0	1	2	3
At least	But less than	Your credit is–				Your credit is–			
5,600	5,650	430	1,913	2,250	2,531	430	1,913	2,250	2,531
5,650	5,700	434	1,930	2,270	2,554	434	1,930	2,270	2,554
5,700	5,750	438	1,947	2,290	2,576	438	1,947	2,290	2,576
5,750	5,800	442	1,964	2,310	2,599	442	1,964	2,310	2,599
5,800	5,850	446	1,981	2,330	2,621	446	1,981	2,330	2,621
5,850	5,900	449	1,998	2,350	2,644	449	1,998	2,350	2,644
5,900	5,950	453	2,015	2,370	2,666	453	2,015	2,370	2,666
5,950	6,000	457	2,032	2,390	2,689	457	2,032	2,390	2,689
6,000	6,050	461	2,049	2,410	2,711	461	2,049	2,410	2,711
6,050	6,100	465	2,066	2,430	2,734	465	2,066	2,430	2,734
6,100	6,150	469	2,083	2,450	2,756	469	2,083	2,450	2,756
6,150	6,200	472	2,100	2,470	2,779	472	2,100	2,470	2,779
6,200	6,250	476	2,117	2,490	2,801	476	2,117	2,490	2,801
6,250	6,300	480	2,134	2,510	2,824	480	2,134	2,510	2,824
6,300	6,350	484	2,151	2,530	2,846	484	2,151	2,530	2,846
6,350	6,400	488	2,168	2,550	2,869	488	2,168	2,550	2,869
6,400	6,450	492	2,185	2,570	2,891	492	2,185	2,570	2,891
6,450	6,500	496	2,202	2,590	2,914	496	2,202	2,590	2,914
6,500	6,550	496	2,219	2,610	2,936	496	2,219	2,610	2,936
6,550	6,600	496	2,236	2,630	2,959	496	2,236	2,630	2,959
6,600	6,650	496	2,253	2,650	2,981	496	2,253	2,650	2,981
6,650	6,700	496	2,270	2,670	3,004	496	2,270	2,670	3,004
6,700	6,750	496	2,287	2,690	3,026	496	2,287	2,690	3,026
6,750	6,800	496	2,304	2,710	3,049	496	2,304	2,710	3,049
6,800	6,850	496	2,321	2,730	3,071	496	2,321	2,730	3,071
6,850	6,900	496	2,338	2,750	3,094	496	2,338	2,750	3,094
6,900	6,950	496	2,355	2,770	3,116	496	2,355	2,770	3,116
6,950	7,000	496	2,372	2,790	3,139	496	2,372	2,790	3,139
7,000	7,050	496	2,389	2,810	3,161	496	2,389	2,810	3,161
7,050	7,100	496	2,406	2,830	3,184	496	2,406	2,830	3,184
7,100	7,150	496	2,423	2,850	3,206	496	2,423	2,850	3,206
7,150	7,200	496	2,440	2,870	3,229	496	2,440	2,870	3,229
7,200	7,250	496	2,457	2,890	3,251	496	2,457	2,890	3,251
7,250	7,300	496	2,474	2,910	3,274	496	2,474	2,910	3,274
7,300	7,350	496	2,491	2,930	3,296	496	2,491	2,930	3,296
7,350	7,400	496	2,508	2,950	3,319	496	2,508	2,950	3,319
7,400	7,450	496	2,525	2,970	3,341	496	2,525	2,970	3,341
7,450	7,500	496	2,542	2,990	3,364	496	2,542	2,990	3,364
7,500	7,550	496	2,559	3,010	3,386	496	2,559	3,010	3,386
7,550	7,600	496	2,576	3,030	3,409	496	2,576	3,030	3,409
7,600	7,650	496	2,593	3,050	3,431	496	2,593	3,050	3,431
7,650	7,700	496	2,610	3,070	3,454	496	2,610	3,070	3,454
7,700	7,750	496	2,627	3,090	3,476	496	2,627	3,090	3,476
7,750	7,800	496	2,644	3,110	3,499	496	2,644	3,110	3,499
7,800	7,850	496	2,661	3,130	3,521	496	2,661	3,130	3,521
7,850	7,900	496	2,678	3,150	3,544	496	2,678	3,150	3,544
7,900	7,950	496	2,695	3,170	3,566	496	2,695	3,170	3,566
7,950	8,000	496	2,712	3,190	3,589	496	2,712	3,190	3,589
8,000	8,050	496	2,729	3,210	3,611	496	2,729	3,210	3,611
8,050	8,100	496	2,746	3,230	3,634	496	2,746	3,230	3,634
8,100	8,150	496	2,763	3,250	3,656	496	2,763	3,250	3,656
8,150	8,200	491	2,780	3,270	3,679	496	2,780	3,270	3,679
8,200	8,250	487	2,797	3,290	3,701	496	2,797	3,290	3,701
8,250	8,300	483	2,814	3,310	3,724	496	2,814	3,310	3,724
8,300	8,350	479	2,831	3,330	3,746	496	2,831	3,330	3,746
8,350	8,400	475	2,848	3,350	3,769	496	2,848	3,350	3,769
8,400	8,450	472	2,865	3,370	3,791	496	2,865	3,370	3,791
8,450	8,500	468	2,882	3,390	3,814	496	2,882	3,390	3,814
8,500	8,550	464	2,899	3,410	3,836	496	2,899	3,410	3,836
8,550	8,600	460	2,916	3,430	3,859	496	2,916	3,430	3,859
8,600	8,650	456	2,933	3,450	3,881	496	2,933	3,450	3,881
8,650	8,700	452	2,950	3,470	3,904	496	2,950	3,470	3,904
8,700	8,750	449	2,967	3,490	3,926	496	2,967	3,490	3,926
8,750	8,800	445	2,984	3,510	3,949	496	2,984	3,510	3,949
8,800	8,850	441	3,001	3,530	3,971	496	3,001	3,530	3,971
8,850	8,900	437	3,018	3,550	3,994	496	3,018	3,550	3,994
8,900	8,950	433	3,035	3,570	4,016	496	3,035	3,570	4,016
8,950	9,000	430	3,052	3,590	4,039	496	3,052	3,590	4,039
9,000	9,050	426	3,069	3,610	4,061	496	3,069	3,610	4,061
9,050	9,100	422	3,086	3,630	4,084	496	3,086	3,630	4,084
9,100	9,150	418	3,103	3,650	4,106	496	3,103	3,650	4,106
9,150	9,200	414	3,120	3,670	4,129	496	3,120	3,670	4,129

If the amount you are looking up from the worksheet is–		And your filing status is– **Single, head of household,** or **qualifying widow(er)** and the number of children you have is–				**Married filing jointly** and the number of children you have is–			
		0	1	2	3	0	1	2	3
At least	But less than	Your credit is–				Your credit is–			
9,200	9,250	410	3,137	3,690	4,151	496	3,137	3,690	4,151
9,250	9,300	407	3,154	3,710	4,174	496	3,154	3,710	4,174
9,300	9,350	403	3,171	3,730	4,196	496	3,171	3,730	4,196
9,350	9,400	399	3,188	3,750	4,219	496	3,188	3,750	4,219
9,400	9,450	395	3,205	3,770	4,241	496	3,205	3,770	4,241
9,450	9,500	391	3,222	3,790	4,264	496	3,222	3,790	4,264
9,500	9,550	387	3,239	3,810	4,286	496	3,239	3,810	4,286
9,550	9,600	384	3,256	3,830	4,309	496	3,256	3,830	4,309
9,600	9,650	380	3,273	3,850	4,331	496	3,273	3,850	4,331
9,650	9,700	376	3,290	3,870	4,354	496	3,290	3,870	4,354
9,700	9,750	372	3,305	3,890	4,376	496	3,305	3,890	4,376
9,750	9,800	368	3,305	3,910	4,399	496	3,305	3,910	4,399
9,800	9,850	365	3,305	3,930	4,421	496	3,305	3,930	4,421
9,850	9,900	361	3,305	3,950	4,444	496	3,305	3,950	4,444
9,900	9,950	357	3,305	3,970	4,466	496	3,305	3,970	4,466
9,950	10,000	353	3,305	3,990	4,489	496	3,305	3,990	4,489
10,000	10,050	349	3,305	4,010	4,511	496	3,305	4,010	4,511
10,050	10,100	345	3,305	4,030	4,534	496	3,305	4,030	4,534
10,100	10,150	342	3,305	4,050	4,556	496	3,305	4,050	4,556
10,150	10,200	338	3,305	4,070	4,579	496	3,305	4,070	4,579
10,200	10,250	334	3,305	4,090	4,601	496	3,305	4,090	4,601
10,250	10,300	330	3,305	4,110	4,624	496	3,305	4,110	4,624
10,300	10,350	326	3,305	4,130	4,646	496	3,305	4,130	4,646
10,350	10,400	322	3,305	4,150	4,669	496	3,305	4,150	4,669
10,400	10,450	319	3,305	4,170	4,691	496	3,305	4,170	4,691
10,450	10,500	315	3,305	4,190	4,714	496	3,305	4,190	4,714
10,500	10,550	311	3,305	4,210	4,736	496	3,305	4,210	4,736
10,550	10,600	307	3,305	4,230	4,759	496	3,305	4,230	4,759
10,600	10,650	303	3,305	4,250	4,781	496	3,305	4,250	4,781
10,650	10,700	299	3,305	4,270	4,804	496	3,305	4,270	4,804
10,700	10,750	296	3,305	4,290	4,826	496	3,305	4,290	4,826
10,750	10,800	292	3,305	4,310	4,849	496	3,305	4,310	4,849
10,800	10,850	288	3,305	4,330	4,871	496	3,305	4,330	4,871
10,850	10,900	284	3,305	4,350	4,894	496	3,305	4,350	4,894
10,900	10,950	280	3,305	4,370	4,916	496	3,305	4,370	4,916
10,950	11,000	277	3,305	4,390	4,939	496	3,305	4,390	4,939
11,000	11,050	273	3,305	4,410	4,961	496	3,305	4,410	4,961
11,050	11,100	269	3,305	4,430	4,984	496	3,305	4,430	4,984
11,100	11,150	265	3,305	4,450	5,006	496	3,305	4,450	5,006
11,150	11,200	261	3,305	4,470	5,029	496	3,305	4,470	5,029
11,200	11,250	257	3,305	4,490	5,051	496	3,305	4,490	5,051
11,250	11,300	254	3,305	4,510	5,074	496	3,305	4,510	5,074
11,300	11,350	250	3,305	4,530	5,096	496	3,305	4,530	5,096
11,350	11,400	246	3,305	4,550	5,119	496	3,305	4,550	5,119
11,400	11,450	242	3,305	4,570	5,141	496	3,305	4,570	5,141
11,450	11,500	238	3,305	4,590	5,164	496	3,305	4,590	5,164
11,500	11,550	234	3,305	4,610	5,186	496	3,305	4,610	5,186
11,550	11,600	231	3,305	4,630	5,209	496	3,305	4,630	5,209
11,600	11,650	227	3,305	4,650	5,231	496	3,305	4,650	5,231
11,650	11,700	223	3,305	4,670	5,254	496	3,305	4,670	5,254
11,700	11,750	219	3,305	4,690	5,276	496	3,305	4,690	5,276
11,750	11,800	215	3,305	4,710	5,299	496	3,305	4,710	5,299
11,800	11,850	212	3,305	4,730	5,321	496	3,305	4,730	5,321
11,850	11,900	208	3,305	4,750	5,344	496	3,305	4,750	5,344
11,900	11,950	204	3,305	4,770	5,366	496	3,305	4,770	5,366
11,950	12,000	200	3,305	4,790	5,389	496	3,305	4,790	5,389
12,000	12,050	196	3,305	4,810	5,411	496	3,305	4,810	5,411
12,050	12,100	192	3,305	4,830	5,434	496	3,305	4,830	5,434
12,100	12,150	189	3,305	4,850	5,456	496	3,305	4,850	5,456
12,150	12,200	185	3,305	4,870	5,479	496	3,305	4,870	5,479
12,200	12,250	181	3,305	4,890	5,501	496	3,305	4,890	5,501
12,250	12,300	177	3,305	4,910	5,524	496	3,305	4,910	5,524
12,300	12,350	173	3,305	4,930	5,546	496	3,305	4,930	5,546
12,350	12,400	169	3,305	4,950	5,569	496	3,305	4,950	5,569
12,400	12,450	166	3,305	4,970	5,591	496	3,305	4,970	5,591
12,450	12,500	162	3,305	4,990	5,614	496	3,305	4,990	5,614
12,500	12,550	158	3,305	5,010	5,636	496	3,305	5,010	5,636
12,550	12,600	154	3,305	5,030	5,659	496	3,305	5,030	5,659
12,600	12,650	150	3,305	5,050	5,681	496	3,305	5,050	5,681
12,650	12,700	146	3,305	5,070	5,704	496	3,305	5,070	5,704
12,700	12,750	143	3,305	5,090	5,726	496	3,305	5,090	5,726
12,750	12,800	139	3,305	5,110	5,749	496	3,305	5,110	5,749

(Continued)

- 62 -

Need more information or forms? Visit IRS.gov.

Earned Income Credit (EIC) Table - *Continued*

(Caution. This is not a tax table.)

If the amount you are looking up from the worksheet is–		Single, head of household, or qualifying widow(er) and the number of children you have is–				Married filing jointly and the number of children you have is–			
At least	But less than	0	1	2	3	0	1	2	3
		Your credit is–				Your credit is–			
12,800	12,850	135	3,305	5,130	5,771	496	3,305	5,130	5,771
12,850	12,900	131	3,305	5,150	5,794	496	3,305	5,150	5,794
12,900	12,950	127	3,305	5,170	5,816	496	3,305	5,170	5,816
12,950	13,000	124	3,305	5,190	5,839	496	3,305	5,190	5,839
13,000	13,050	120	3,305	5,210	5,861	496	3,305	5,210	5,861
13,050	13,100	116	3,305	5,230	5,884	496	3,305	5,230	5,884
13,100	13,150	112	3,305	5,250	5,906	496	3,305	5,250	5,906
13,150	13,200	108	3,305	5,270	5,929	496	3,305	5,270	5,929
13,200	13,250	104	3,305	5,290	5,951	496	3,305	5,290	5,951
13,250	13,300	101	3,305	5,310	5,974	496	3,305	5,310	5,974
13,300	13,350	97	3,305	5,330	5,996	496	3,305	5,330	5,996
13,350	13,400	93	3,305	5,350	6,019	496	3,305	5,350	6,019
13,400	13,450	89	3,305	5,370	6,041	496	3,305	5,370	6,041
13,450	13,500	85	3,305	5,390	6,064	496	3,305	5,390	6,064
13,500	13,550	81	3,305	5,410	6,086	496	3,305	5,410	6,086
13,550	13,600	78	3,305	5,430	6,109	493	3,305	5,430	6,109
13,600	13,650	74	3,305	5,450	6,131	489	3,305	5,450	6,131
13,650	13,700	70	3,305	5,460	6,143	485	3,305	5,460	6,143
13,700	13,750	66	3,305	5,460	6,143	482	3,305	5,460	6,143
13,750	13,800	62	3,305	5,460	6,143	478	3,305	5,460	6,143
13,800	13,850	59	3,305	5,460	6,143	474	3,305	5,460	6,143
13,850	13,900	55	3,305	5,460	6,143	470	3,305	5,460	6,143
13,900	13,950	51	3,305	5,460	6,143	466	3,305	5,460	6,143
13,950	14,000	47	3,305	5,460	6,143	462	3,305	5,460	6,143
14,000	14,050	43	3,305	5,460	6,143	459	3,305	5,460	6,143
14,050	14,100	39	3,305	5,460	6,143	455	3,305	5,460	6,143
14,100	14,150	36	3,305	5,460	6,143	451	3,305	5,460	6,143
14,150	14,200	32	3,305	5,460	6,143	447	3,305	5,460	6,143
14,200	14,250	28	3,305	5,460	6,143	443	3,305	5,460	6,143
14,250	14,300	24	3,305	5,460	6,143	439	3,305	5,460	6,143
14,300	14,350	20	3,305	5,460	6,143	436	3,305	5,460	6,143
14,350	14,400	16	3,305	5,460	6,143	432	3,305	5,460	6,143
14,400	14,450	13	3,305	5,460	6,143	428	3,305	5,460	6,143
14,450	14,500	9	3,305	5,460	6,143	424	3,305	5,460	6,143
14,500	14,550	5	3,305	5,460	6,143	420	3,305	5,460	6,143
14,550	14,600	*	3,305	5,460	6,143	417	3,305	5,460	6,143
14,600	14,650	0	3,305	5,460	6,143	413	3,305	5,460	6,143
14,650	14,700	0	3,305	5,460	6,143	409	3,305	5,460	6,143
14,700	14,750	0	3,305	5,460	6,143	405	3,305	5,460	6,143
14,750	14,800	0	3,305	5,460	6,143	401	3,305	5,460	6,143
14,800	14,850	0	3,305	5,460	6,143	397	3,305	5,460	6,143
14,850	14,900	0	3,305	5,460	6,143	394	3,305	5,460	6,143
14,900	14,950	0	3,305	5,460	6,143	390	3,305	5,460	6,143
14,950	15,000	0	3,305	5,460	6,143	386	3,305	5,460	6,143
15,000	15,050	0	3,305	5,460	6,143	382	3,305	5,460	6,143
15,050	15,100	0	3,305	5,460	6,143	378	3,305	5,460	6,143
15,100	15,150	0	3,305	5,460	6,143	374	3,305	5,460	6,143
15,150	15,200	0	3,305	5,460	6,143	371	3,305	5,460	6,143
15,200	15,250	0	3,305	5,460	6,143	367	3,305	5,460	6,143
15,250	15,300	0	3,305	5,460	6,143	363	3,305	5,460	6,143
15,300	15,350	0	3,305	5,460	6,143	359	3,305	5,460	6,143
15,350	15,400	0	3,305	5,460	6,143	355	3,305	5,460	6,143
15,400	15,450	0	3,305	5,460	6,143	352	3,305	5,460	6,143
15,450	15,500	0	3,305	5,460	6,143	348	3,305	5,460	6,143
15,500	15,550	0	3,305	5,460	6,143	344	3,305	5,460	6,143
15,550	15,600	0	3,305	5,460	6,143	340	3,305	5,460	6,143
15,600	15,650	0	3,305	5,460	6,143	336	3,305	5,460	6,143
15,650	15,700	0	3,305	5,460	6,143	332	3,305	5,460	6,143
15,700	15,750	0	3,305	5,460	6,143	329	3,305	5,460	6,143
15,750	15,800	0	3,305	5,460	6,143	325	3,305	5,460	6,143
15,800	15,850	0	3,305	5,460	6,143	321	3,305	5,460	6,143
15,850	15,900	0	3,305	5,460	6,143	317	3,305	5,460	6,143
15,900	15,950	0	3,305	5,460	6,143	313	3,305	5,460	6,143
15,950	16,000	0	3,305	5,460	6,143	309	3,305	5,460	6,143

If the amount you are looking up from the worksheet is–		Single, head of household, or qualifying widow(er) and the number of children you have is–				Married filing jointly and the number of children you have is–			
At least	But less than	0	1	2	3	0	1	2	3
		Your credit is–				Your credit is–			
16,000	16,050	0	3,305	5,460	6,143	306	3,305	5,460	6,143
16,050	16,100	0	3,305	5,460	6,143	302	3,305	5,460	6,143
16,100	16,150	0	3,305	5,460	6,143	298	3,305	5,460	6,143
16,150	16,200	0	3,305	5,460	6,143	294	3,305	5,460	6,143
16,200	16,250	0	3,305	5,460	6,143	290	3,305	5,460	6,143
16,250	16,300	0	3,305	5,460	6,143	286	3,305	5,460	6,143
16,300	16,350	0	3,305	5,460	6,143	283	3,305	5,460	6,143
16,350	16,400	0	3,305	5,460	6,143	279	3,305	5,460	6,143
16,400	16,450	0	3,305	5,460	6,143	275	3,305	5,460	6,143
16,450	16,500	0	3,305	5,460	6,143	271	3,305	5,460	6,143
16,500	16,550	0	3,305	5,460	6,143	267	3,305	5,460	6,143
16,550	16,600	0	3,305	5,460	6,143	264	3,305	5,460	6,143
16,600	16,650	0	3,305	5,460	6,143	260	3,305	5,460	6,143
16,650	16,700	0	3,305	5,460	6,143	256	3,305	5,460	6,143
16,700	16,750	0	3,305	5,460	6,143	252	3,305	5,460	6,143
16,750	16,800	0	3,305	5,460	6,143	248	3,305	5,460	6,143
16,800	16,850	0	3,305	5,460	6,143	244	3,305	5,460	6,143
16,850	16,900	0	3,305	5,460	6,143	241	3,305	5,460	6,143
16,900	16,950	0	3,305	5,460	6,143	237	3,305	5,460	6,143
16,950	17,000	0	3,305	5,460	6,143	233	3,305	5,460	6,143
17,000	17,050	0	3,305	5,460	6,143	229	3,305	5,460	6,143
17,050	17,100	0	3,305	5,460	6,143	225	3,305	5,460	6,143
17,100	17,150	0	3,305	5,460	6,143	221	3,305	5,460	6,143
17,150	17,200	0	3,305	5,460	6,143	218	3,305	5,460	6,143
17,200	17,250	0	3,305	5,460	6,143	214	3,305	5,460	6,143
17,250	17,300	0	3,305	5,460	6,143	210	3,305	5,460	6,143
17,300	17,350	0	3,305	5,460	6,143	206	3,305	5,460	6,143
17,350	17,400	0	3,305	5,460	6,143	202	3,305	5,460	6,143
17,400	17,450	0	3,305	5,460	6,143	199	3,305	5,460	6,143
17,450	17,500	0	3,305	5,460	6,143	195	3,305	5,460	6,143
17,500	17,550	0	3,305	5,460	6,143	191	3,305	5,460	6,143
17,550	17,600	0	3,305	5,460	6,143	187	3,305	5,460	6,143
17,600	17,650	0	3,305	5,460	6,143	183	3,305	5,460	6,143
17,650	17,700	0	3,305	5,460	6,143	179	3,305	5,460	6,143
17,700	17,750	0	3,305	5,460	6,143	176	3,305	5,460	6,143
17,750	17,800	0	3,305	5,460	6,143	172	3,305	5,460	6,143
17,800	17,850	0	3,305	5,460	6,143	168	3,305	5,460	6,143
17,850	17,900	0	3,298	5,451	6,133	164	3,305	5,460	6,143
17,900	17,950	0	3,290	5,440	6,122	160	3,305	5,460	6,143
17,950	18,000	0	3,282	5,429	6,112	156	3,305	5,460	6,143
18,000	18,050	0	3,274	5,419	6,101	153	3,305	5,460	6,143
18,050	18,100	0	3,266	5,408	6,091	149	3,305	5,460	6,143
18,100	18,150	0	3,258	5,398	6,080	145	3,305	5,460	6,143
18,150	18,200	0	3,250	5,387	6,070	141	3,305	5,460	6,143
18,200	18,250	0	3,242	5,377	6,059	137	3,305	5,460	6,143
18,250	18,300	0	3,234	5,366	6,049	133	3,305	5,460	6,143
18,300	18,350	0	3,226	5,356	6,038	130	3,305	5,460	6,143
18,350	18,400	0	3,218	5,345	6,028	126	3,305	5,460	6,143
18,400	18,450	0	3,210	5,335	6,017	122	3,305	5,460	6,143
18,450	18,500	0	3,202	5,324	6,007	118	3,305	5,460	6,143
18,500	18,550	0	3,194	5,314	5,996	114	3,305	5,460	6,143
18,550	18,600	0	3,186	5,303	5,986	111	3,305	5,460	6,143
18,600	18,650	0	3,178	5,293	5,975	107	3,305	5,460	6,143
18,650	18,700	0	3,170	5,282	5,965	103	3,305	5,460	6,143
18,700	18,750	0	3,162	5,272	5,954	99	3,305	5,460	6,143
18,750	18,800	0	3,154	5,261	5,943	95	3,305	5,460	6,143
18,800	18,850	0	3,146	5,250	5,933	91	3,305	5,460	6,143
18,850	18,900	0	3,138	5,240	5,922	88	3,305	5,460	6,143
18,900	18,950	0	3,130	5,229	5,912	84	3,305	5,460	6,143
18,950	19,000	0	3,122	5,219	5,901	80	3,305	5,460	6,143
19,000	19,050	0	3,114	5,208	5,891	76	3,305	5,460	6,143
19,050	19,100	0	3,106	5,198	5,880	72	3,305	5,460	6,143
19,100	19,150	0	3,098	5,187	5,870	68	3,305	5,460	6,143
19,150	19,200	0	3,090	5,177	5,859	65	3,305	5,460	6,143

* If the amount you are looking up from the worksheet is at least $14,550 but less than $14,590, and you have no qualifying children, your credit is $2.
If the amount you are looking up from the worksheet is $14,590 or more, and you have no qualifying children, you cannot take the credit.

(Continued)

Earned Income Credit (EIC) Table - *Continued*

(Caution. This is not a tax table.)

If the amount you are looking up from the worksheet is—		Single, head of household, or qualifying widow(er) and the number of children you have is—				Married filing jointly and the number of children you have is—			
At least	But less than	0	1	2	3	0	1	2	3
		Your credit is—				Your credit is—			
19,200	19,250	0	3,082	5,166	5,849	61	3,305	5,460	6,143
19,250	19,300	0	3,074	5,156	5,838	57	3,305	5,460	6,143
19,300	19,350	0	3,066	5,145	5,828	53	3,305	5,460	6,143
19,350	19,400	0	3,058	5,135	5,817	49	3,305	5,460	6,143
19,400	19,450	0	3,050	5,124	5,807	46	3,305	5,460	6,143
19,450	19,500	0	3,042	5,114	5,796	42	3,305	5,460	6,143
19,500	19,550	0	3,034	5,103	5,786	38	3,305	5,460	6,143
19,550	19,600	0	3,026	5,093	5,775	34	3,305	5,460	6,143
19,600	19,650	0	3,018	5,082	5,764	30	3,305	5,460	6,143
19,650	19,700	0	3,010	5,071	5,754	26	3,305	5,460	6,143
19,700	19,750	0	3,002	5,061	5,743	23	3,305	5,460	6,143
19,750	19,800	0	2,994	5,050	5,733	19	3,305	5,460	6,143
19,800	19,850	0	2,986	5,040	5,722	15	3,305	5,460	6,143
19,850	19,900	0	2,978	5,029	5,712	11	3,305	5,460	6,143
19,900	19,950	0	2,970	5,019	5,701	7	3,305	5,460	6,143
19,950	20,000	0	2,962	5,008	5,691	3	3,305	5,460	6,143
20,000	20,050	0	2,954	4,998	5,680	*	3,305	5,460	6,143
20,050	20,100	0	2,946	4,987	5,670	0	3,305	5,460	6,143
20,100	20,150	0	2,938	4,977	5,659	0	3,305	5,460	6,143
20,150	20,200	0	2,930	4,966	5,649	0	3,305	5,460	6,143
20,200	20,250	0	2,922	4,956	5,638	0	3,305	5,460	6,143
20,250	20,300	0	2,914	4,945	5,628	0	3,305	5,460	6,143
20,300	20,350	0	2,906	4,935	5,617	0	3,305	5,460	6,143
20,350	20,400	0	2,898	4,924	5,607	0	3,305	5,460	6,143
20,400	20,450	0	2,890	4,913	5,596	0	3,305	5,460	6,143
20,450	20,500	0	2,882	4,903	5,585	0	3,305	5,460	6,143
20,500	20,550	0	2,874	4,892	5,575	0	3,305	5,460	6,143
20,550	20,600	0	2,866	4,882	5,564	0	3,305	5,460	6,143
20,600	20,650	0	2,858	4,871	5,554	0	3,305	5,460	6,143
20,650	20,700	0	2,850	4,861	5,543	0	3,305	5,460	6,143
20,700	20,750	0	2,842	4,850	5,533	0	3,305	5,460	6,143
20,750	20,800	0	2,834	4,840	5,522	0	3,305	5,460	6,143
20,800	20,850	0	2,826	4,829	5,512	0	3,305	5,460	6,143
20,850	20,900	0	2,818	4,819	5,501	0	3,305	5,460	6,143
20,900	20,950	0	2,810	4,808	5,491	0	3,305	5,460	6,143
20,950	21,000	0	2,802	4,798	5,480	0	3,305	5,460	6,143
21,000	21,050	0	2,794	4,787	5,470	0	3,305	5,460	6,143
21,050	21,100	0	2,786	4,777	5,459	0	3,305	5,460	6,143
21,100	21,150	0	2,778	4,766	5,449	0	3,305	5,460	6,143
21,150	21,200	0	2,770	4,756	5,438	0	3,305	5,460	6,143
21,200	21,250	0	2,762	4,745	5,428	0	3,305	5,460	6,143
21,250	21,300	0	2,754	4,734	5,417	0	3,305	5,460	6,143
21,300	21,350	0	2,746	4,724	5,406	0	3,305	5,460	6,143
21,350	21,400	0	2,738	4,713	5,396	0	3,305	5,460	6,143
21,400	21,450	0	2,730	4,703	5,385	0	3,305	5,460	6,143
21,450	21,500	0	2,722	4,692	5,375	0	3,305	5,460	6,143
21,500	21,550	0	2,714	4,682	5,364	0	3,305	5,460	6,143
21,550	21,600	0	2,706	4,671	5,354	0	3,305	5,460	6,143
21,600	21,650	0	2,698	4,661	5,343	0	3,305	5,460	6,143
21,650	21,700	0	2,690	4,650	5,333	0	3,305	5,460	6,143
21,700	21,750	0	2,682	4,640	5,322	0	3,305	5,460	6,143
21,750	21,800	0	2,674	4,629	5,312	0	3,305	5,460	6,143
21,800	21,850	0	2,666	4,619	5,301	0	3,305	5,460	6,143
21,850	21,900	0	2,658	4,608	5,291	0	3,305	5,460	6,143
21,900	21,950	0	2,650	4,598	5,280	0	3,305	5,460	6,143
21,950	22,000	0	2,642	4,587	5,270	0	3,305	5,460	6,143
22,000	22,050	0	2,634	4,577	5,259	0	3,305	5,460	6,143
22,050	22,100	0	2,626	4,566	5,249	0	3,305	5,460	6,143
22,100	22,150	0	2,618	4,555	5,238	0	3,305	5,460	6,143
22,150	22,200	0	2,610	4,545	5,227	0	3,305	5,460	6,143
22,200	22,250	0	2,602	4,534	5,217	0	3,305	5,460	6,143
22,250	22,300	0	2,594	4,524	5,206	0	3,305	5,460	6,143
22,300	22,350	0	2,586	4,513	5,196	0	3,305	5,460	6,143
22,350	22,400	0	2,579	4,503	5,185	0	3,305	5,460	6,143
22,400	22,450	0	2,571	4,492	5,175	0	3,305	5,460	6,143
22,450	22,500	0	2,563	4,482	5,164	0	3,305	5,460	6,143
22,500	22,550	0	2,555	4,471	5,154	0	3,305	5,460	6,143
22,550	22,600	0	2,547	4,461	5,143	0	3,305	5,460	6,143
22,600	22,650	0	2,539	4,450	5,133	0	3,305	5,460	6,143
22,650	22,700	0	2,531	4,440	5,122	0	3,305	5,460	6,143
22,700	22,750	0	2,523	4,429	5,112	0	3,305	5,460	6,143
22,750	22,800	0	2,515	4,419	5,101	0	3,305	5,460	6,143
22,800	22,850	0	2,507	4,408	5,091	0	3,305	5,460	6,143
22,850	22,900	0	2,499	4,398	5,080	0	3,305	5,460	6,143
22,900	22,950	0	2,491	4,387	5,069	0	3,305	5,460	6,143
22,950	23,000	0	2,483	4,376	5,059	0	3,305	5,460	6,143
23,000	23,050	0	2,475	4,366	5,048	0	3,305	5,460	6,143
23,050	23,100	0	2,467	4,355	5,038	0	3,305	5,460	6,143
23,100	23,150	0	2,459	4,345	5,027	0	3,305	5,460	6,143
23,150	23,200	0	2,451	4,334	5,017	0	3,305	5,460	6,143
23,200	23,250	0	2,443	4,324	5,006	0	3,305	5,460	6,143
23,250	23,300	0	2,435	4,313	4,996	0	3,305	5,460	6,143
23,300	23,350	0	2,427	4,303	4,985	0	3,294	5,446	6,129
23,350	23,400	0	2,419	4,292	4,975	0	3,286	5,436	6,118
23,400	23,450	0	2,411	4,282	4,964	0	3,278	5,425	6,108
23,450	23,500	0	2,403	4,271	4,954	0	3,270	5,415	6,097
23,500	23,550	0	2,395	4,261	4,943	0	3,262	5,404	6,087
23,550	23,600	0	2,387	4,250	4,933	0	3,254	5,394	6,076
23,600	23,650	0	2,379	4,240	4,922	0	3,246	5,383	6,066
23,650	23,700	0	2,371	4,229	4,912	0	3,238	5,373	6,055
23,700	23,750	0	2,363	4,219	4,901	0	3,230	5,362	6,045
23,750	23,800	0	2,355	4,208	4,890	0	3,223	5,352	6,034
23,800	23,850	0	2,347	4,197	4,880	0	3,215	5,341	6,024
23,850	23,900	0	2,339	4,187	4,869	0	3,207	5,330	6,013
23,900	23,950	0	2,331	4,176	4,859	0	3,199	5,320	6,002
23,950	24,000	0	2,323	4,166	4,848	0	3,191	5,309	5,992
24,000	24,050	0	2,315	4,155	4,838	0	3,183	5,299	5,981
24,050	24,100	0	2,307	4,145	4,827	0	3,175	5,288	5,971
24,100	24,150	0	2,299	4,134	4,817	0	3,167	5,278	5,960
24,150	24,200	0	2,291	4,124	4,806	0	3,159	5,267	5,950
24,200	24,250	0	2,283	4,113	4,796	0	3,151	5,257	5,939
24,250	24,300	0	2,275	4,103	4,785	0	3,143	5,246	5,929
24,300	24,350	0	2,267	4,092	4,775	0	3,135	5,236	5,918
24,350	24,400	0	2,259	4,082	4,764	0	3,127	5,225	5,908
24,400	24,450	0	2,251	4,071	4,754	0	3,119	5,215	5,897
24,450	24,500	0	2,243	4,061	4,743	0	3,111	5,204	5,887
24,500	24,550	0	2,235	4,050	4,733	0	3,103	5,194	5,876
24,550	24,600	0	2,227	4,040	4,722	0	3,095	5,183	5,866
24,600	24,650	0	2,219	4,029	4,711	0	3,087	5,173	5,855
24,650	24,700	0	2,211	4,018	4,701	0	3,079	5,162	5,845
24,700	24,750	0	2,203	4,008	4,690	0	3,071	5,151	5,834
24,750	24,800	0	2,195	3,997	4,680	0	3,063	5,141	5,823
24,800	24,850	0	2,187	3,987	4,669	0	3,055	5,130	5,813
24,850	24,900	0	2,179	3,976	4,659	0	3,047	5,120	5,802
24,900	24,950	0	2,171	3,966	4,648	0	3,039	5,109	5,792
24,950	25,000	0	2,163	3,955	4,638	0	3,031	5,099	5,781
25,000	25,050	0	2,155	3,945	4,627	0	3,023	5,088	5,771
25,050	25,100	0	2,147	3,934	4,617	0	3,015	5,078	5,760
25,100	25,150	0	2,139	3,924	4,606	0	3,007	5,067	5,750
25,150	25,200	0	2,131	3,913	4,596	0	2,999	5,057	5,739
25,200	25,250	0	2,123	3,903	4,585	0	2,991	5,046	5,729
25,250	25,300	0	2,115	3,892	4,575	0	2,983	5,036	5,718
25,300	25,350	0	2,107	3,882	4,564	0	2,975	5,025	5,708
25,350	25,400	0	2,099	3,871	4,554	0	2,967	5,015	5,697
25,400	25,450	0	2,091	3,860	4,543	0	2,959	5,004	5,687
25,450	25,500	0	2,083	3,850	4,532	0	2,951	4,994	5,676
25,500	25,550	0	2,075	3,839	4,522	0	2,943	4,983	5,665
25,550	25,600	0	2,067	3,829	4,511	0	2,935	4,972	5,655

* If the amount you are looking up from the worksheet is at least $20,000 but less than $20,020, and you have no qualifying children, your credit is $1. If the amount you are looking up from the worksheet is $20,020 or more, and you have no qualifying children, you cannot take the credit.

(Continued)

Need more information or forms? Visit IRS.gov.

Earned Income Credit (EIC) Table - *Continued*

(Caution. This is **not** a tax table.)

If the amount you are looking up from the worksheet is—		Single, head of household, or qualifying widow(er) and the number of children you have is—				Married filing jointly and the number of children you have is—			
At least	But less than	0	1	2	3	0	1	2	3
		Your credit is—				Your credit is—			
25,600	25,650	0	2,059	3,818	4,501	0	2,927	4,962	5,644
25,650	25,700	0	2,051	3,808	4,490	0	2,919	4,951	5,634
25,700	25,750	0	2,043	3,797	4,480	0	2,911	4,941	5,623
25,750	25,800	0	2,035	3,787	4,469	0	2,903	4,930	5,613
25,800	25,850	0	2,027	3,776	4,459	0	2,895	4,920	5,602
25,850	25,900	0	2,019	3,766	4,448	0	2,887	4,909	5,592
25,900	25,950	0	2,011	3,755	4,438	0	2,879	4,899	5,581
25,950	26,000	0	2,003	3,745	4,427	0	2,871	4,888	5,571
26,000	26,050	0	1,995	3,734	4,417	0	2,863	4,878	5,560
26,050	26,100	0	1,987	3,724	4,406	0	2,855	4,867	5,550
26,100	26,150	0	1,979	3,713	4,396	0	2,847	4,857	5,539
26,150	26,200	0	1,971	3,703	4,385	0	2,839	4,846	5,529
26,200	26,250	0	1,963	3,692	4,375	0	2,831	4,836	5,518
26,250	26,300	0	1,955	3,681	4,364	0	2,823	4,825	5,508
26,300	26,350	0	1,947	3,671	4,353	0	2,815	4,815	5,497
26,350	26,400	0	1,939	3,660	4,343	0	2,807	4,804	5,486
26,400	26,450	0	1,931	3,650	4,332	0	2,799	4,793	5,476
26,450	26,500	0	1,923	3,639	4,322	0	2,791	4,783	5,465
26,500	26,550	0	1,915	3,629	4,311	0	2,783	4,772	5,455
26,550	26,600	0	1,907	3,618	4,301	0	2,775	4,762	5,444
26,600	26,650	0	1,899	3,608	4,290	0	2,767	4,751	5,434
26,650	26,700	0	1,891	3,597	4,280	0	2,759	4,741	5,423
26,700	26,750	0	1,883	3,587	4,269	0	2,751	4,730	5,413
26,750	26,800	0	1,875	3,576	4,259	0	2,743	4,720	5,402
26,800	26,850	0	1,867	3,566	4,248	0	2,735	4,709	5,392
26,850	26,900	0	1,859	3,555	4,238	0	2,727	4,699	5,381
26,900	26,950	0	1,851	3,545	4,227	0	2,719	4,688	5,371
26,950	27,000	0	1,843	3,534	4,217	0	2,711	4,678	5,360
27,000	27,050	0	1,835	3,524	4,206	0	2,703	4,667	5,350
27,050	27,100	0	1,827	3,513	4,196	0	2,695	4,657	5,339
27,100	27,150	0	1,819	3,502	4,185	0	2,687	4,646	5,329
27,150	27,200	0	1,811	3,492	4,174	0	2,679	4,636	5,318
27,200	27,250	0	1,803	3,481	4,164	0	2,671	4,625	5,307
27,250	27,300	0	1,795	3,471	4,153	0	2,663	4,614	5,297
27,300	27,350	0	1,787	3,460	4,143	0	2,655	4,604	5,286
27,350	27,400	0	1,780	3,450	4,132	0	2,647	4,593	5,276
27,400	27,450	0	1,772	3,439	4,122	0	2,639	4,583	5,265
27,450	27,500	0	1,764	3,429	4,111	0	2,631	4,572	5,255
27,500	27,550	0	1,756	3,418	4,101	0	2,623	4,562	5,244
27,550	27,600	0	1,748	3,408	4,090	0	2,615	4,551	5,234
27,600	27,650	0	1,740	3,397	4,080	0	2,607	4,541	5,223
27,650	27,700	0	1,732	3,387	4,069	0	2,599	4,530	5,213
27,700	27,750	0	1,724	3,376	4,059	0	2,591	4,520	5,202
27,750	27,800	0	1,716	3,366	4,048	0	2,583	4,509	5,192
27,800	27,850	0	1,708	3,355	4,038	0	2,575	4,499	5,181
27,850	27,900	0	1,700	3,345	4,027	0	2,567	4,488	5,171
27,900	27,950	0	1,692	3,334	4,016	0	2,559	4,478	5,160
27,950	28,000	0	1,684	3,323	4,006	0	2,551	4,467	5,150
28,000	28,050	0	1,676	3,313	3,995	0	2,543	4,456	5,139
28,050	28,100	0	1,668	3,302	3,985	0	2,535	4,446	5,128
28,100	28,150	0	1,660	3,292	3,974	0	2,527	4,435	5,118
28,150	28,200	0	1,652	3,281	3,964	0	2,519	4,425	5,107
28,200	28,250	0	1,644	3,271	3,953	0	2,511	4,414	5,097
28,250	28,300	0	1,636	3,260	3,943	0	2,503	4,404	5,086
28,300	28,350	0	1,628	3,250	3,932	0	2,495	4,393	5,076
28,350	28,400	0	1,620	3,239	3,922	0	2,487	4,383	5,065
28,400	28,450	0	1,612	3,229	3,911	0	2,479	4,372	5,055
28,450	28,500	0	1,604	3,218	3,901	0	2,471	4,362	5,044
28,500	28,550	0	1,596	3,208	3,890	0	2,463	4,351	5,034
28,550	28,600	0	1,588	3,197	3,880	0	2,455	4,341	5,023
28,600	28,650	0	1,580	3,187	3,869	0	2,447	4,330	5,013
28,650	28,700	0	1,572	3,176	3,859	0	2,439	4,320	5,002
28,700	28,750	0	1,564	3,166	3,848	0	2,431	4,309	4,992
28,750	28,800	0	1,556	3,155	3,837	0	2,424	4,299	4,981
28,800	28,850	0	1,548	3,144	3,827	0	2,416	4,288	4,971
28,850	28,900	0	1,540	3,134	3,816	0	2,408	4,277	4,960
28,900	28,950	0	1,532	3,123	3,806	0	2,400	4,267	4,949
28,950	29,000	0	1,524	3,113	3,795	0	2,392	4,256	4,939
29,000	29,050	0	1,516	3,102	3,785	0	2,384	4,246	4,928
29,050	29,100	0	1,508	3,092	3,774	0	2,376	4,235	4,918
29,100	29,150	0	1,500	3,081	3,764	0	2,368	4,225	4,907
29,150	29,200	0	1,492	3,071	3,753	0	2,360	4,214	4,897

If the amount you are looking up from the worksheet is—		Single, head of household, or qualifying widow(er) and the number of children you have is—				Married filing jointly and the number of children you have is—			
At least	But less than	0	1	2	3	0	1	2	3
		Your credit is—				Your credit is—			
29,200	29,250	0	1,484	3,060	3,743	0	2,352	4,204	4,886
29,250	29,300	0	1,476	3,050	3,732	0	2,344	4,193	4,876
29,300	29,350	0	1,468	3,039	3,722	0	2,336	4,183	4,865
29,350	29,400	0	1,460	3,029	3,711	0	2,328	4,172	4,855
29,400	29,450	0	1,452	3,018	3,701	0	2,320	4,162	4,844
29,450	29,500	0	1,444	3,008	3,690	0	2,312	4,151	4,834
29,500	29,550	0	1,436	2,997	3,680	0	2,304	4,141	4,823
29,550	29,600	0	1,428	2,987	3,669	0	2,296	4,130	4,813
29,600	29,650	0	1,420	2,976	3,658	0	2,288	4,120	4,802
29,650	29,700	0	1,412	2,965	3,648	0	2,280	4,109	4,792
29,700	29,750	0	1,404	2,955	3,637	0	2,272	4,098	4,781
29,750	29,800	0	1,396	2,944	3,627	0	2,264	4,088	4,770
29,800	29,850	0	1,388	2,934	3,616	0	2,256	4,077	4,760
29,850	29,900	0	1,380	2,923	3,606	0	2,248	4,067	4,749
29,900	29,950	0	1,372	2,913	3,595	0	2,240	4,056	4,739
29,950	30,000	0	1,364	2,902	3,585	0	2,232	4,046	4,728
30,000	30,050	0	1,356	2,892	3,574	0	2,224	4,035	4,718
30,050	30,100	0	1,348	2,881	3,564	0	2,216	4,025	4,707
30,100	30,150	0	1,340	2,871	3,553	0	2,208	4,014	4,697
30,150	30,200	0	1,332	2,860	3,543	0	2,200	4,004	4,686
30,200	30,250	0	1,324	2,850	3,532	0	2,192	3,993	4,676
30,250	30,300	0	1,316	2,839	3,522	0	2,184	3,983	4,665
30,300	30,350	0	1,308	2,829	3,511	0	2,176	3,972	4,655
30,350	30,400	0	1,300	2,818	3,501	0	2,168	3,962	4,644
30,400	30,450	0	1,292	2,807	3,490	0	2,160	3,951	4,634
30,450	30,500	0	1,284	2,797	3,479	0	2,152	3,941	4,623
30,500	30,550	0	1,276	2,786	3,469	0	2,144	3,930	4,612
30,550	30,600	0	1,268	2,776	3,458	0	2,136	3,919	4,602
30,600	30,650	0	1,260	2,765	3,448	0	2,128	3,909	4,591
30,650	30,700	0	1,252	2,755	3,437	0	2,120	3,898	4,581
30,700	30,750	0	1,244	2,744	3,427	0	2,112	3,888	4,570
30,750	30,800	0	1,236	2,734	3,416	0	2,104	3,877	4,560
30,800	30,850	0	1,228	2,723	3,406	0	2,096	3,867	4,549
30,850	30,900	0	1,220	2,713	3,395	0	2,088	3,856	4,539
30,900	30,950	0	1,212	2,702	3,385	0	2,080	3,846	4,528
30,950	31,000	0	1,204	2,692	3,374	0	2,072	3,835	4,518
31,000	31,050	0	1,196	2,681	3,364	0	2,064	3,825	4,507
31,050	31,100	0	1,188	2,671	3,353	0	2,056	3,814	4,497
31,100	31,150	0	1,180	2,660	3,343	0	2,048	3,804	4,486
31,150	31,200	0	1,172	2,650	3,332	0	2,040	3,793	4,476
31,200	31,250	0	1,164	2,639	3,322	0	2,032	3,783	4,465
31,250	31,300	0	1,156	2,628	3,311	0	2,024	3,772	4,455
31,300	31,350	0	1,148	2,618	3,300	0	2,016	3,762	4,444
31,350	31,400	0	1,140	2,607	3,290	0	2,008	3,751	4,433
31,400	31,450	0	1,132	2,597	3,279	0	2,000	3,740	4,423
31,450	31,500	0	1,124	2,586	3,269	0	1,992	3,730	4,412
31,500	31,550	0	1,116	2,576	3,258	0	1,984	3,719	4,402
31,550	31,600	0	1,108	2,565	3,248	0	1,976	3,709	4,391
31,600	31,650	0	1,100	2,555	3,237	0	1,968	3,698	4,381
31,650	31,700	0	1,092	2,544	3,227	0	1,960	3,688	4,370
31,700	31,750	0	1,084	2,534	3,216	0	1,952	3,677	4,360
31,750	31,800	0	1,076	2,523	3,206	0	1,944	3,667	4,349
31,800	31,850	0	1,068	2,513	3,195	0	1,936	3,656	4,339
31,850	31,900	0	1,060	2,502	3,185	0	1,928	3,646	4,328
31,900	31,950	0	1,052	2,492	3,174	0	1,920	3,635	4,318
31,950	32,000	0	1,044	2,481	3,164	0	1,912	3,625	4,307
32,000	32,050	0	1,036	2,471	3,153	0	1,904	3,614	4,297
32,050	32,100	0	1,028	2,460	3,143	0	1,896	3,604	4,286
32,100	32,150	0	1,020	2,449	3,132	0	1,888	3,593	4,276
32,150	32,200	0	1,012	2,439	3,121	0	1,880	3,583	4,265
32,200	32,250	0	1,004	2,428	3,111	0	1,872	3,572	4,254
32,250	32,300	0	996	2,418	3,100	0	1,864	3,561	4,244
32,300	32,350	0	988	2,407	3,090	0	1,856	3,551	4,233
32,350	32,400	0	981	2,397	3,079	0	1,848	3,540	4,223
32,400	32,450	0	973	2,386	3,069	0	1,840	3,530	4,212
32,450	32,500	0	965	2,376	3,058	0	1,832	3,519	4,202
32,500	32,550	0	957	2,365	3,048	0	1,824	3,509	4,191
32,550	32,600	0	949	2,355	3,037	0	1,816	3,498	4,181
32,600	32,650	0	941	2,344	3,027	0	1,808	3,488	4,170
32,650	32,700	0	933	2,334	3,016	0	1,800	3,477	4,160
32,700	32,750	0	925	2,323	3,006	0	1,792	3,467	4,149
32,750	32,800	0	917	2,313	2,995	0	1,784	3,456	4,139

(Continued)

Earned Income Credit (EIC) Table - Continued

(Caution. This is not a tax table.)

If the amount you are looking up from the worksheet is—		Single, head of household, or qualifying widow(er) and the number of children you have is—				Married filing jointly and the number of children you have is—			
At least	But less than	0	1	2	3	0	1	2	3
		Your credit is—				Your credit is—			
32,800	32,850	0	909	2,302	2,985	0	1,776	3,446	4,128
32,850	32,900	0	901	2,292	2,974	0	1,768	3,435	4,118
32,900	32,950	0	893	2,281	2,963	0	1,760	3,425	4,107
32,950	33,000	0	885	2,270	2,953	0	1,752	3,414	4,097
33,000	33,050	0	877	2,260	2,942	0	1,744	3,403	4,086
33,050	33,100	0	869	2,249	2,932	0	1,736	3,393	4,075
33,100	33,150	0	861	2,239	2,921	0	1,728	3,382	4,065
33,150	33,200	0	853	2,228	2,911	0	1,720	3,372	4,054
33,200	33,250	0	845	2,218	2,900	0	1,712	3,361	4,044
33,250	33,300	0	837	2,207	2,890	0	1,704	3,351	4,033
33,300	33,350	0	829	2,197	2,879	0	1,696	3,340	4,023
33,350	33,400	0	821	2,186	2,869	0	1,688	3,330	4,012
33,400	33,450	0	813	2,176	2,858	0	1,680	3,319	4,002
33,450	33,500	0	805	2,165	2,848	0	1,672	3,309	3,991
33,500	33,550	0	797	2,155	2,837	0	1,664	3,298	3,981
33,550	33,600	0	789	2,144	2,827	0	1,656	3,288	3,970
33,600	33,650	0	781	2,134	2,816	0	1,648	3,277	3,960
33,650	33,700	0	773	2,123	2,806	0	1,640	3,267	3,949
33,700	33,750	0	765	2,113	2,795	0	1,632	3,256	3,939
33,750	33,800	0	757	2,102	2,784	0	1,625	3,246	3,928
33,800	33,850	0	749	2,091	2,774	0	1,617	3,235	3,918
33,850	33,900	0	741	2,081	2,763	0	1,609	3,224	3,907
33,900	33,950	0	733	2,070	2,753	0	1,601	3,214	3,896
33,950	34,000	0	725	2,060	2,742	0	1,593	3,203	3,886
34,000	34,050	0	717	2,049	2,732	0	1,585	3,193	3,875
34,050	34,100	0	709	2,039	2,721	0	1,577	3,182	3,865
34,100	34,150	0	701	2,028	2,711	0	1,569	3,172	3,854
34,150	34,200	0	693	2,018	2,700	0	1,561	3,161	3,844
34,200	34,250	0	685	2,007	2,690	0	1,553	3,151	3,833
34,250	34,300	0	677	1,997	2,679	0	1,545	3,140	3,823
34,300	34,350	0	669	1,986	2,669	0	1,537	3,130	3,812
34,350	34,400	0	661	1,976	2,658	0	1,529	3,119	3,802
34,400	34,450	0	653	1,965	2,648	0	1,521	3,109	3,791
34,450	34,500	0	645	1,955	2,637	0	1,513	3,098	3,781
34,500	34,550	0	637	1,944	2,627	0	1,505	3,088	3,770
34,550	34,600	0	629	1,934	2,616	0	1,497	3,077	3,760
34,600	34,650	0	621	1,923	2,605	0	1,489	3,067	3,749
34,650	34,700	0	613	1,912	2,595	0	1,481	3,056	3,739
34,700	34,750	0	605	1,902	2,584	0	1,473	3,045	3,728
34,750	34,800	0	597	1,891	2,574	0	1,465	3,035	3,717
34,800	34,850	0	589	1,881	2,563	0	1,457	3,024	3,707
34,850	34,900	0	581	1,870	2,553	0	1,449	3,014	3,696
34,900	34,950	0	573	1,860	2,542	0	1,441	3,003	3,686
34,950	35,000	0	565	1,849	2,532	0	1,433	2,993	3,675
35,000	35,050	0	557	1,839	2,521	0	1,425	2,982	3,665
35,050	35,100	0	549	1,828	2,511	0	1,417	2,972	3,654
35,100	35,150	0	541	1,818	2,500	0	1,409	2,961	3,644
35,150	35,200	0	533	1,807	2,490	0	1,401	2,951	3,633
35,200	35,250	0	525	1,797	2,479	0	1,393	2,940	3,623
35,250	35,300	0	517	1,786	2,469	0	1,385	2,930	3,612
35,300	35,350	0	509	1,776	2,458	0	1,377	2,919	3,602
35,350	35,400	0	501	1,765	2,448	0	1,369	2,909	3,591
35,400	35,450	0	493	1,754	2,437	0	1,361	2,898	3,581
35,450	35,500	0	485	1,744	2,426	0	1,353	2,888	3,570
35,500	35,550	0	477	1,733	2,416	0	1,345	2,877	3,559
35,550	35,600	0	469	1,723	2,405	0	1,337	2,866	3,549
35,600	35,650	0	461	1,712	2,395	0	1,329	2,856	3,538
35,650	35,700	0	453	1,702	2,384	0	1,321	2,845	3,528
35,700	35,750	0	445	1,691	2,374	0	1,313	2,835	3,517
35,750	35,800	0	437	1,681	2,363	0	1,305	2,824	3,507
35,800	35,850	0	429	1,670	2,353	0	1,297	2,814	3,496
35,850	35,900	0	421	1,660	2,342	0	1,289	2,803	3,486
35,900	35,950	0	413	1,649	2,332	0	1,281	2,793	3,475
35,950	36,000	0	405	1,639	2,321	0	1,273	2,782	3,465

If the amount you are looking up from the worksheet is—		Single, head of household, or qualifying widow(er) and the number of children you have is—				Married filing jointly and the number of children you have is—			
At least	But less than	0	1	2	3	0	1	2	3
		Your credit is—				Your credit is—			
36,000	36,050	0	397	1,628	2,311	0	1,265	2,772	3,454
36,050	36,100	0	389	1,618	2,300	0	1,257	2,761	3,444
36,100	36,150	0	381	1,607	2,290	0	1,249	2,751	3,433
36,150	36,200	0	373	1,597	2,279	0	1,241	2,740	3,423
36,200	36,250	0	365	1,586	2,269	0	1,233	2,730	3,412
36,250	36,300	0	357	1,575	2,258	0	1,225	2,719	3,402
36,300	36,350	0	349	1,565	2,247	0	1,217	2,709	3,391
36,350	36,400	0	341	1,554	2,237	0	1,209	2,698	3,380
36,400	36,450	0	333	1,544	2,226	0	1,201	2,687	3,370
36,450	36,500	0	325	1,533	2,216	0	1,193	2,677	3,359
36,500	36,550	0	317	1,523	2,205	0	1,185	2,666	3,349
36,550	36,600	0	309	1,512	2,195	0	1,177	2,656	3,338
36,600	36,650	0	301	1,502	2,184	0	1,169	2,645	3,328
36,650	36,700	0	293	1,491	2,174	0	1,161	2,635	3,317
36,700	36,750	0	285	1,481	2,163	0	1,153	2,624	3,307
36,750	36,800	0	277	1,470	2,153	0	1,145	2,614	3,296
36,800	36,850	0	269	1,460	2,142	0	1,137	2,603	3,286
36,850	36,900	0	261	1,449	2,132	0	1,129	2,593	3,275
36,900	36,950	0	253	1,439	2,121	0	1,121	2,582	3,265
36,950	37,000	0	245	1,428	2,111	0	1,113	2,572	3,254
37,000	37,050	0	237	1,418	2,100	0	1,105	2,561	3,244
37,050	37,100	0	229	1,407	2,090	0	1,097	2,551	3,233
37,100	37,150	0	221	1,396	2,079	0	1,089	2,540	3,223
37,150	37,200	0	213	1,386	2,068	0	1,081	2,530	3,212
37,200	37,250	0	205	1,375	2,058	0	1,073	2,519	3,201
37,250	37,300	0	197	1,365	2,047	0	1,065	2,508	3,191
37,300	37,350	0	189	1,354	2,037	0	1,057	2,498	3,180
37,350	37,400	0	182	1,344	2,026	0	1,049	2,487	3,170
37,400	37,450	0	174	1,333	2,016	0	1,041	2,477	3,159
37,450	37,500	0	166	1,323	2,005	0	1,033	2,466	3,149
37,500	37,550	0	158	1,312	1,995	0	1,025	2,456	3,138
37,550	37,600	0	150	1,302	1,984	0	1,017	2,445	3,128
37,600	37,650	0	142	1,291	1,974	0	1,009	2,435	3,117
37,650	37,700	0	134	1,281	1,963	0	1,001	2,424	3,107
37,700	37,750	0	126	1,270	1,953	0	993	2,414	3,096
37,750	37,800	0	118	1,260	1,942	0	985	2,403	3,086
37,800	37,850	0	110	1,249	1,932	0	977	2,393	3,075
37,850	37,900	0	102	1,239	1,921	0	969	2,382	3,065
37,900	37,950	0	94	1,228	1,910	0	961	2,372	3,054
37,950	38,000	0	86	1,217	1,900	0	953	2,361	3,044
38,000	38,050	0	78	1,207	1,889	0	945	2,350	3,033
38,050	38,100	0	70	1,196	1,879	0	937	2,340	3,022
38,100	38,150	0	62	1,186	1,868	0	929	2,329	3,012
38,150	38,200	0	54	1,175	1,858	0	921	2,319	3,001
38,200	38,250	0	46	1,165	1,847	0	913	2,308	2,991
38,250	38,300	0	38	1,154	1,837	0	905	2,298	2,980
38,300	38,350	0	30	1,144	1,826	0	897	2,287	2,970
38,350	38,400	0	22	1,133	1,816	0	889	2,277	2,959
38,400	38,450	0	14	1,123	1,805	0	881	2,266	2,949
38,450	38,500	0	6	1,112	1,795	0	873	2,256	2,938
38,500	38,550	0	*	1,102	1,784	0	865	2,245	2,928
38,550	38,600	0	0	1,091	1,774	0	857	2,235	2,917
38,600	38,650	0	0	1,081	1,763	0	849	2,224	2,907
38,650	38,700	0	0	1,070	1,753	0	841	2,214	2,896
38,700	38,750	0	0	1,060	1,742	0	833	2,203	2,886
38,750	38,800	0	0	1,049	1,731	0	826	2,193	2,875
38,800	38,850	0	0	1,038	1,721	0	818	2,182	2,865
38,850	38,900	0	0	1,028	1,710	0	810	2,171	2,854
38,900	38,950	0	0	1,017	1,700	0	802	2,161	2,843
38,950	39,000	0	0	1,007	1,689	0	794	2,150	2,833
39,000	39,050	0	0	996	1,679	0	786	2,140	2,822
39,050	39,100	0	0	986	1,668	0	778	2,129	2,812
39,100	39,150	0	0	975	1,658	0	770	2,119	2,801
39,150	39,200	0	0	965	1,647	0	762	2,108	2,791

* If the amount you are looking up from the worksheet is at least $38,500 but less than $38,511, and you have one qualifying child, your credit is $1.
If the amount you are looking up from the worksheet is $38,511 or more, and you have one qualifying child, you cannot take the credit.

(Continued)

Need more information or forms? Visit IRS.gov.

Earned Income Credit (EIC) Table - Continued

(Caution. This is not a tax table.)

If the amount you are looking up from the worksheet is—		Single, head of household, or qualifying widow(er) and the number of children you have is—				Married filing jointly and the number of children you have is—			
At least	But less than	0	1	2	3	0	1	2	3
		Your credit is—				Your credit is—			
39,200	39,250	0	0	954	1,637	0	754	2,098	2,780
39,250	39,300	0	0	944	1,626	0	746	2,087	2,770
39,300	39,350	0	0	933	1,616	0	738	2,077	2,759
39,350	39,400	0	0	923	1,605	0	730	2,066	2,749
39,400	39,450	0	0	912	1,595	0	722	2,056	2,738
39,450	39,500	0	0	902	1,584	0	714	2,045	2,728
39,500	39,550	0	0	891	1,574	0	706	2,035	2,717
39,550	39,600	0	0	881	1,563	0	698	2,024	2,707
39,600	39,650	0	0	870	1,552	0	690	2,014	2,696
39,650	39,700	0	0	859	1,542	0	682	2,003	2,686
39,700	39,750	0	0	849	1,531	0	674	1,992	2,675
39,750	39,800	0	0	838	1,521	0	666	1,982	2,664
39,800	39,850	0	0	828	1,510	0	658	1,971	2,654
39,850	39,900	0	0	817	1,500	0	650	1,961	2,643
39,900	39,950	0	0	807	1,489	0	642	1,950	2,633
39,950	40,000	0	0	796	1,479	0	634	1,940	2,622
40,000	40,050	0	0	786	1,468	0	626	1,929	2,612
40,050	40,100	0	0	775	1,458	0	618	1,919	2,601
40,100	40,150	0	0	765	1,447	0	610	1,908	2,591
40,150	40,200	0	0	754	1,437	0	602	1,898	2,580
40,200	40,250	0	0	744	1,426	0	594	1,887	2,570
40,250	40,300	0	0	733	1,416	0	586	1,877	2,559
40,300	40,350	0	0	723	1,405	0	578	1,866	2,549
40,350	40,400	0	0	712	1,395	0	570	1,856	2,538
40,400	40,450	0	0	701	1,384	0	562	1,845	2,528
40,450	40,500	0	0	691	1,373	0	554	1,835	2,517
40,500	40,550	0	0	680	1,363	0	546	1,824	2,506
40,550	40,600	0	0	670	1,352	0	538	1,813	2,496
40,600	40,650	0	0	659	1,342	0	530	1,803	2,485
40,650	40,700	0	0	649	1,331	0	522	1,792	2,475
40,700	40,750	0	0	638	1,321	0	514	1,782	2,464
40,750	40,800	0	0	628	1,310	0	506	1,771	2,454
40,800	40,850	0	0	617	1,300	0	498	1,761	2,443
40,850	40,900	0	0	607	1,289	0	490	1,750	2,433
40,900	40,950	0	0	596	1,279	0	482	1,740	2,422
40,950	41,000	0	0	586	1,268	0	474	1,729	2,412
41,000	41,050	0	0	575	1,258	0	466	1,719	2,401
41,050	41,100	0	0	565	1,247	0	458	1,708	2,391
41,100	41,150	0	0	554	1,237	0	450	1,698	2,380
41,150	41,200	0	0	544	1,226	0	442	1,687	2,370
41,200	41,250	0	0	533	1,216	0	434	1,677	2,359
41,250	41,300	0	0	522	1,205	0	426	1,666	2,349
41,300	41,350	0	0	512	1,194	0	418	1,656	2,338
41,350	41,400	0	0	501	1,184	0	410	1,645	2,327
41,400	41,450	0	0	491	1,173	0	402	1,634	2,317
41,450	41,500	0	0	480	1,163	0	394	1,624	2,306
41,500	41,550	0	0	470	1,152	0	386	1,613	2,296
41,550	41,600	0	0	459	1,142	0	378	1,603	2,285
41,600	41,650	0	0	449	1,131	0	370	1,592	2,275
41,650	41,700	0	0	438	1,121	0	362	1,582	2,264
41,700	41,750	0	0	428	1,110	0	354	1,571	2,254
41,750	41,800	0	0	417	1,100	0	346	1,561	2,243
41,800	41,850	0	0	407	1,089	0	338	1,550	2,233
41,850	41,900	0	0	396	1,079	0	330	1,540	2,222
41,900	41,950	0	0	386	1,068	0	322	1,529	2,212
41,950	42,000	0	0	375	1,058	0	314	1,519	2,201
42,000	42,050	0	0	365	1,047	0	306	1,508	2,191
42,050	42,100	0	0	354	1,037	0	298	1,498	2,180
42,100	42,150	0	0	343	1,026	0	290	1,487	2,170
42,150	42,200	0	0	333	1,015	0	282	1,477	2,159
42,200	42,250	0	0	322	1,005	0	274	1,466	2,148
42,250	42,300	0	0	312	994	0	266	1,455	2,138
42,300	42,350	0	0	301	984	0	258	1,445	2,127
42,350	42,400	0	0	291	973	0	250	1,434	2,117

If the amount you are looking up from the worksheet is—		Single, head of household, or qualifying widow(er) and the number of children you have is—				Married filing jointly and the number of children you have is—			
At least	But less than	0	1	2	3	0	1	2	3
		Your credit is—				Your credit is—			
42,400	42,450	0	0	280	963	0	242	1,424	2,106
42,450	42,500	0	0	270	952	0	234	1,413	2,096
42,500	42,550	0	0	259	942	0	226	1,403	2,085
42,550	42,600	0	0	249	931	0	218	1,392	2,075
42,600	42,650	0	0	238	921	0	210	1,382	2,064
42,650	42,700	0	0	228	910	0	202	1,371	2,054
42,700	42,750	0	0	217	900	0	194	1,361	2,043
42,750	42,800	0	0	207	889	0	186	1,350	2,033
42,800	42,850	0	0	196	879	0	178	1,340	2,022
42,850	42,900	0	0	186	868	0	170	1,329	2,012
42,900	42,950	0	0	175	857	0	162	1,319	2,001
42,950	43,000	0	0	164	847	0	154	1,308	1,991
43,000	43,050	0	0	154	836	0	146	1,297	1,980
43,050	43,100	0	0	143	826	0	138	1,287	1,969
43,100	43,150	0	0	133	815	0	130	1,276	1,959
43,150	43,200	0	0	122	805	0	122	1,266	1,948
43,200	43,250	0	0	112	794	0	114	1,255	1,938
43,250	43,300	0	0	101	784	0	106	1,245	1,927
43,300	43,350	0	0	91	773	0	98	1,234	1,917
43,350	43,400	0	0	80	763	0	90	1,224	1,906
43,400	43,450	0	0	70	752	0	82	1,213	1,896
43,450	43,500	0	0	59	742	0	74	1,203	1,885
43,500	43,550	0	0	49	731	0	66	1,192	1,875
43,550	43,600	0	0	38	721	0	58	1,182	1,864
43,600	43,650	0	0	28	710	0	50	1,171	1,854
43,650	43,700	0	0	17	700	0	42	1,161	1,843
43,700	43,750	0	0	7	689	0	34	1,150	1,833
43,750	43,800	0	0	*	678	0	27	1,140	1,822
43,800	43,850	0	0	0	668	0	19	1,129	1,812
43,850	43,900	0	0	0	657	0	11	1,118	1,801
43,900	43,950	0	0	0	647	0	**	1,108	1,790
43,950	44,000	0	0	0	636	0	0	1,097	1,780
44,000	44,050	0	0	0	626	0	0	1,087	1,769
44,050	44,100	0	0	0	615	0	0	1,076	1,759
44,100	44,150	0	0	0	605	0	0	1,066	1,748
44,150	44,200	0	0	0	594	0	0	1,055	1,738
44,200	44,250	0	0	0	584	0	0	1,045	1,727
44,250	44,300	0	0	0	573	0	0	1,034	1,717
44,300	44,350	0	0	0	563	0	0	1,024	1,706
44,350	44,400	0	0	0	552	0	0	1,013	1,696
44,400	44,450	0	0	0	542	0	0	1,003	1,685
44,450	44,500	0	0	0	531	0	0	992	1,675
44,500	44,550	0	0	0	521	0	0	982	1,664
44,550	44,600	0	0	0	510	0	0	971	1,654
44,600	44,650	0	0	0	499	0	0	961	1,643
44,650	44,700	0	0	0	489	0	0	950	1,633
44,700	44,750	0	0	0	478	0	0	939	1,622
44,750	44,800	0	0	0	468	0	0	929	1,611
44,800	44,850	0	0	0	457	0	0	918	1,601
44,850	44,900	0	0	0	447	0	0	908	1,590
44,900	44,950	0	0	0	436	0	0	897	1,580
44,950	45,000	0	0	0	426	0	0	887	1,569
45,000	45,050	0	0	0	415	0	0	876	1,559
45,050	45,100	0	0	0	405	0	0	866	1,548
45,100	45,150	0	0	0	394	0	0	855	1,538
45,150	45,200	0	0	0	384	0	0	845	1,527
45,200	45,250	0	0	0	373	0	0	834	1,517
45,250	45,300	0	0	0	363	0	0	824	1,506
45,300	45,350	0	0	0	352	0	0	813	1,496
45,350	45,400	0	0	0	342	0	0	803	1,485
45,400	45,450	0	0	0	331	0	0	792	1,475
45,450	45,500	0	0	0	320	0	0	782	1,464
45,500	45,550	0	0	0	310	0	0	771	1,453
45,550	45,600	0	0	0	299	0	0	760	1,443

* If the amount you are looking up from the worksheet is at least $43,750 but less than $43,756, and you have two qualifying children, your credit is $1.
  If the amount you are looking up from the worksheet is $43,756 or more, and you have two qualifying children, you cannot take the credit.

** If the amount you are looking up from the worksheet is at least $43,900 but less than $43,941, and you have one qualifying child, your credit is $3.
  If the amount you are looking up from the worksheet is $43,941 or more, and you have one qualifying child, you cannot take the credit.

(Continued)

If the amount you are looking up from the worksheet is—		Single, head of household, or qualifying widow(er) and the number of children you have is—				Married filing jointly and the number of children you have is—				If the amount you are looking up from the worksheet is—		Single, head of household, or qualifying widow(er) and the number of children you have is—				Married filing jointly and the number of children you have is—			
		0	1	2	3	0	1	2	3			0	1	2	3	0	1	2	3
At least	But less than	Your credit is—				Your credit is—				At least	But less than	Your credit is—				Your credit is—			
45,600	45,650	0	0	0	289	0	0	750	1,432	48,800	48,850	0	0	0	0	0	0	76	759
45,650	45,700	0	0	0	278	0	0	739	1,422	48,850	48,900	0	0	0	0	0	0	65	748
45,700	45,750	0	0	0	268	0	0	729	1,411	48,900	48,950	0	0	0	0	0	0	55	737
45,750	45,800	0	0	0	257	0	0	718	1,401	48,950	49,000	0	0	0	0	0	0	44	727
45,800	45,850	0	0	0	247	0	0	708	1,390	49,000	49,050	0	0	0	0	0	0	34	716
45,850	45,900	0	0	0	236	0	0	697	1,380	49,050	49,100	0	0	0	0	0	0	23	706
45,900	45,950	0	0	0	226	0	0	687	1,369	49,100	49,150	0	0	0	0	0	0	13	695
45,950	46,000	0	0	0	215	0	0	676	1,359	49,150	49,200	0	0	0	0	0	0	**	685
46,000	46,050	0	0	0	205	0	0	666	1,348	49,200	49,250	0	0	0	0	0	0	0	674
46,050	46,100	0	0	0	194	0	0	655	1,338	49,250	49,300	0	0	0	0	0	0	0	664
46,100	46,150	0	0	0	184	0	0	645	1,327	49,300	49,350	0	0	0	0	0	0	0	653
46,150	46,200	0	0	0	173	0	0	634	1,317	49,350	49,400	0	0	0	0	0	0	0	643
46,200	46,250	0	0	0	163	0	0	624	1,306	49,400	49,450	0	0	0	0	0	0	0	632
46,250	46,300	0	0	0	152	0	0	613	1,296	49,450	49,500	0	0	0	0	0	0	0	622
46,300	46,350	0	0	0	141	0	0	603	1,285	49,500	49,550	0	0	0	0	0	0	0	611
46,350	46,400	0	0	0	131	0	0	592	1,274	49,550	49,600	0	0	0	0	0	0	0	601
46,400	46,450	0	0	0	120	0	0	581	1,264	49,600	49,650	0	0	0	0	0	0	0	590
46,450	46,500	0	0	0	110	0	0	571	1,253	49,650	49,700	0	0	0	0	0	0	0	580
46,500	46,550	0	0	0	99	0	0	560	1,243	49,700	49,750	0	0	0	0	0	0	0	569
46,550	46,600	0	0	0	89	0	0	550	1,232	49,750	49,800	0	0	0	0	0	0	0	558
46,600	46,650	0	0	0	78	0	0	539	1,222	49,800	49,850	0	0	0	0	0	0	0	548
46,650	46,700	0	0	0	68	0	0	529	1,211	49,850	49,900	0	0	0	0	0	0	0	537
46,700	46,750	0	0	0	57	0	0	518	1,201	49,900	49,950	0	0	0	0	0	0	0	527
46,750	46,800	0	0	0	47	0	0	508	1,190	49,950	50,000	0	0	0	0	0	0	0	516
46,800	46,850	0	0	0	36	0	0	497	1,180	50,000	50,050	0	0	0	0	0	0	0	506
46,850	46,900	0	0	0	26	0	0	487	1,169	50,050	50,100	0	0	0	0	0	0	0	495
46,900	46,950	0	0	0	15	0	0	476	1,159	50,100	50,150	0	0	0	0	0	0	0	485
46,950	47,000	0	0	0	*	0	0	466	1,148	50,150	50,200	0	0	0	0	0	0	0	474
47,000	47,050	0	0	0	0	0	0	455	1,138	50,200	50,250	0	0	0	0	0	0	0	464
47,050	47,100	0	0	0	0	0	0	445	1,127	50,250	50,300	0	0	0	0	0	0	0	453
47,100	47,150	0	0	0	0	0	0	434	1,117	50,300	50,350	0	0	0	0	0	0	0	443
47,150	47,200	0	0	0	0	0	0	424	1,106	50,350	50,400	0	0	0	0	0	0	0	432
47,200	47,250	0	0	0	0	0	0	413	1,095	50,400	50,450	0	0	0	0	0	0	0	422
47,250	47,300	0	0	0	0	0	0	402	1,085	50,450	50,500	0	0	0	0	0	0	0	411
47,300	47,350	0	0	0	0	0	0	392	1,074	50,500	50,550	0	0	0	0	0	0	0	400
47,350	47,400	0	0	0	0	0	0	381	1,064	50,550	50,600	0	0	0	0	0	0	0	390
47,400	47,450	0	0	0	0	0	0	371	1,053	50,600	50,650	0	0	0	0	0	0	0	379
47,450	47,500	0	0	0	0	0	0	360	1,043	50,650	50,700	0	0	0	0	0	0	0	369
47,500	47,550	0	0	0	0	0	0	350	1,032	50,700	50,750	0	0	0	0	0	0	0	358
47,550	47,600	0	0	0	0	0	0	339	1,022	50,750	50,800	0	0	0	0	0	0	0	348
47,600	47,650	0	0	0	0	0	0	329	1,011	50,800	50,850	0	0	0	0	0	0	0	337
47,650	47,700	0	0	0	0	0	0	318	1,001	50,850	50,900	0	0	0	0	0	0	0	327
47,700	47,750	0	0	0	0	0	0	308	990	50,900	50,950	0	0	0	0	0	0	0	316
47,750	47,800	0	0	0	0	0	0	297	980	50,950	51,000	0	0	0	0	0	0	0	306
47,800	47,850	0	0	0	0	0	0	287	969	51,000	51,050	0	0	0	0	0	0	0	295
47,850	47,900	0	0	0	0	0	0	276	959	51,050	51,100	0	0	0	0	0	0	0	285
47,900	47,950	0	0	0	0	0	0	266	948	51,100	51,150	0	0	0	0	0	0	0	274
47,950	48,000	0	0	0	0	0	0	255	938	51,150	51,200	0	0	0	0	0	0	0	264
48,000	48,050	0	0	0	0	0	0	244	927	51,200	51,250	0	0	0	0	0	0	0	253
48,050	48,100	0	0	0	0	0	0	234	916	51,250	51,300	0	0	0	0	0	0	0	243
48,100	48,150	0	0	0	0	0	0	223	906	51,300	51,350	0	0	0	0	0	0	0	232
48,150	48,200	0	0	0	0	0	0	213	895	51,350	51,400	0	0	0	0	0	0	0	221
48,200	48,250	0	0	0	0	0	0	202	885	51,400	51,450	0	0	0	0	0	0	0	211
48,250	48,300	0	0	0	0	0	0	192	874	51,450	51,500	0	0	0	0	0	0	0	200
48,300	48,350	0	0	0	0	0	0	181	864	51,500	51,550	0	0	0	0	0	0	0	190
48,350	48,400	0	0	0	0	0	0	171	853	51,550	51,600	0	0	0	0	0	0	0	179
48,400	48,450	0	0	0	0	0	0	160	843	51,600	51,650	0	0	0	0	0	0	0	169
48,450	48,500	0	0	0	0	0	0	150	832	51,650	51,700	0	0	0	0	0	0	0	158
48,500	48,550	0	0	0	0	0	0	139	822	51,700	51,750	0	0	0	0	0	0	0	148
48,550	48,600	0	0	0	0	0	0	129	811	51,750	51,800	0	0	0	0	0	0	0	137
48,600	48,650	0	0	0	0	0	0	118	801	51,800	51,850	0	0	0	0	0	0	0	127
48,650	48,700	0	0	0	0	0	0	108	790	51,850	51,900	0	0	0	0	0	0	0	116
48,700	48,750	0	0	0	0	0	0	97	780	51,900	51,950	0	0	0	0	0	0	0	106
48,750	48,800	0	0	0	0	0	0	87	769	51,950	52,000	0	0	0	0	0	0	0	95

* If the amount you are looking up from the worksheet is at least $46,950 but less than $46,997, and you have three qualifying children, your credit is $5.
  If the amount you are looking up from the worksheet is $46,997 or more, and you have three qualifying children, you cannot take the credit.

** If the amount you are looking up from the worksheet is at least $49,150 but less than $49,186, and you have two qualifying children, your credit is $4.
   If the amount you are looking up from the worksheet is $49,186 or more, and you have two qualifying children, you cannot take the credit.

(Continued)

Earned Income Credit (EIC) Table - Continued

(Caution. This is not a tax table.)

If the amount you are looking up from the worksheet is—		Single, head of household, or qualifying widow(er) and the number of children you have is—				Married filing jointly and the number of children you have is—				If the amount you are looking up from the worksheet is—		Single, head of household, or qualifying widow(er) and the number of children you have is—				Married filing jointly and the number of children you have is—			
		0	1	2	3	0	1	2	3			0	1	2	3	0	1	2	3
At least	But less than	Your credit is—				Your credit is—				At least	But less than	Your credit is—				Your credit is—			
52,000	52,050	0	0	0	0	0	0	0	85	52,400	52,427	0	0	0	0	0	0	0	3
52,050	52,100	0	0	0	0	0	0	0	74										
52,100	52,150	0	0	0	0	0	0	0	64										
52,150	52,200	0	0	0	0	0	0	0	53										
52,200	52,250	0	0	0	0	0	0	0	42										
52,250	52,300	0	0	0	0	0	0	0	32										
52,300	52,350	0	0	0	0	0	0	0	21										
52,350	52,400	0	0	0	0	0	0	0	11										

Line 67

Additional Child Tax Credit

What Is the Additional Child Tax Credit?

This credit is for certain people who have at least one qualifying child for the child tax credit (as defined in Steps 1, 2, and 3 of the instructions for line 6c). The additional child tax credit may give you a refund even if you do not owe any tax or did not have any tax withheld.

Two Steps To Take the Additional Child Tax Credit!

Step 1. Be sure you figured the amount, if any, of your child tax credit. See the instructions for line 52.

Step 2. Read the TIP at the end of your Child Tax Credit Worksheet. Use Schedule 8812 to see if you can take the additional child tax credit, but only if you meet the condition given in that TIP.

Line 68

American Opportunity Credit

If you meet the requirements to claim an education credit (see the instructions for line 50), enter on line 68 the amount, if any, from Form 8863, line 8. You may be able to increase an education credit and reduce your total tax or increase your tax refund if the student chooses to include all or part of a Pell grant or certain other scholarships or fellowships in income. See Pub. 970 and the instructions for Form 8863 for more information.

Line 69

Net Premium Tax Credit

You may be eligible to claim the premium tax credit if you, your spouse, or a dependent enrolled in health insurance through the Health Insurance Marketplace. The premium tax credit helps pay for this health insurance. Complete Form 8962 to determine the amount of your premium tax credit, if any. Enter the amount, if any, from Form 8962,

line 26. See Pub. 974 and the instructions for Form 8962 for more information.

Line 70

Amount Paid With Request for Extension To File

If you got an automatic extension of time to file Form 1040 by filing Form 4868 or by making a payment, enter the amount of the payment or any amount you paid with Form 4868. If you paid by debit or credit card, do not include on line 70 the convenience fee you were charged. Also, include any amounts paid with Form 2350.

 You may be able to deduct any credit or debit card convenience fees on your 2015 Schedule A.

Line 71

Excess Social Security and Tier 1 RRTA Tax Withheld

If you, or your spouse if filing a joint return, had more than one employer for 2014 and total wages of more than $117,000, too much social security or tier 1 railroad retirement (RRTA) tax may have been withheld. You can take a credit on this line for the amount withheld in excess of $7,254. But if any one employer withheld more than $7,254, you cannot claim the excess on your return. The employer should adjust the tax for you. If the employer does not adjust the overcollection, you can file a claim for refund using Form 843. Figure this amount separately for you and your spouse.

You cannot claim a refund for excess tier 2 RRTA tax on Form 1040. Instead, use Form 843.

For more details, see Pub. 505.

Line 72

Credit for Federal Tax on Fuels

Enter any credit for federal excise taxes paid on fuels that are ultimately used for a nontaxable purpose (for example, an

off-highway business use). Attach Form 4136.

Line 73

Check the box on line 73 to report any credit from Form 2439.

If you are claiming a credit for repayment of amounts you included in your income in an earlier year because it appeared you had a right to the income, include the credit on line 73. Check box d and enter "I.R.C. 1341" in the space next to that box. See Pub. 525 for details about this credit.

If you made a tax payment that does not belong on any other line, include the payment on line 73. Check box d and enter "Tax" in the space next to that box.

If you check more than one box, enter the total of the line 73 credits and payments.

Refund

Line 75

Amount Overpaid

If line 75 is under $1, we will send a refund only on written request.

 If the amount you overpaid is large, you may want to decrease the amount of income tax withheld from your pay by filing a new Form W-4. See Income Tax Withholding and Estimated Tax Payments for 2015 *under* General Information, *later.*

Refund Offset

If you owe past-due federal tax, state income tax, state unemployment compensation debts, child support, spousal support, or certain federal nontax debts, such as student loans, all or part of the overpayment on line 75 may be used (offset) to pay the past-due amount. Offsets for federal taxes are made by the IRS. All other offsets are made by the Treasury Department's Bureau of the Fiscal Service. For federal tax offsets, you will receive a notice from the IRS. For all other offsets, you will receive a notice from the Fiscal Service. To find out if you may have an offset or if you have any questions about it, contact the agency to which you owe the debt.

Injured Spouse

If you file a joint return and your spouse has not paid past-due federal tax, state income tax, state unemployment compensation debts, child support, spousal support, or a federal nontax debt, such as a student loan, part or all of the overpayment on line 75 may be used (offset) to pay the past-due amount. But your part of the overpayment may be refunded to you if certain conditions apply and you complete Form 8379. For details, use TeleTax topic 203 or see Form 8379.

Lines 76a Through 76d
Amount Refunded to You

If you want to check the status of your refund, just use the IRS2Go phone app or go to IRS.gov and click on *Where's My Refund.* See *Refund Information,* later. Information about your return will generally be available within 24 hours after the IRS receives your e-filed return, or 4 weeks after you mail your paper return. If you filed Form 8379 with your return, wait 14 weeks (11 weeks if you filed electronically). Have your 2014 tax return handy so you can enter your social security number, your filing status, and the exact whole dollar amount of your refund.

Where's My Refund? will provide an actual personalized refund date as soon as the IRS processes your tax return and approves your refund.

Effect of refund on benefits. Any refund you receive cannot be counted as income when determining if you or anyone else is eligible for benefits or assistance, or how much you or anyone else can receive, under any federal program or under any state or local program financed in whole or in part with federal funds. These programs include Temporary Assistance for Needy Families (TANF), Medicaid, Supplemental Security Income (SSI), and Supplemental Nutrition Assistance Program (food stamps). In addition, when determining eligibility, the refund cannot be counted as a resource for at least 12 months after you receive it. Check with your local

benefit coordinator to find out if your refund will affect your benefits.

Fast Refunds! Choose direct deposit—a fast, simple, safe, secure way to have your refund deposited automatically to your checking or savings account, including an individual retirement arrangement (IRA). See the information about IRAs later.

If you want us to directly deposit the amount shown on line 76a to your checking or savings account, including an IRA, at a bank or other financial institution (such as a mutual fund, brokerage firm, or credit union) in the United States:

- Complete lines 76b through 76d (if you want your refund deposited to only one account), or
- Check the box on line 76a and attach Form 8888 if you want to split the direct deposit of your refund into more than one account or use all or part of your refund to buy paper series I savings bonds.

If you do not want your refund directly deposited to your account, do not check the box on line 76a. Draw a line through the boxes on lines 76b and 76d. We will send you a check instead.

Do not request a deposit of any part of your refund to an account that is not in your name. Do not allow your tax preparer to deposit any part of your refund into his or her account. The number of direct deposits to a single account or prepaid debit card is limited to three refunds a year. After this limit is exceeded, paper checks will be sent instead. Learn more at IRS.gov.

Why Use Direct Deposit?

- You get your refund faster by direct deposit than you do by check.
- Payment is more secure. There is no check that can get lost or stolen.
- It is more convenient. You do not have to make a trip to the bank to deposit your check.
- It saves tax dollars. It costs the government less to refund by direct deposit.

> *If you file a joint return and check the box on line 76a and attach Form 8888 or fill in lines 76b through 76d, your spouse may get at least part of the refund.*

IRA. You can have your refund (or part of it) directly deposited to a traditional IRA, Roth IRA, or SEP-IRA, but not a SIMPLE IRA. You must establish the IRA at a bank or other financial institution before you request direct deposit. Make sure your direct deposit will be accepted. You must also notify the trustee or custodian of your account of the year to which the deposit is to be applied (unless the trustee or custodian will not accept a deposit for 2014). If you do not, the trustee or custodian can assume the deposit is for the year during which you are filing the return. For example, if you file your 2014 return during 2015 and do not notify the trustee or custodian in advance, the trustee or custodian can assume the deposit to your IRA is for 2015. If you designate your deposit to be for 2014, you must verify that the deposit was actually made to the account by the due date of the return (without regard to extensions). If the deposit is not made by that date, the deposit is not an IRA contribution for 2014. In that case, you must file an amended 2014 return and reduce any IRA deduction and any retirement savings contributions credit you claimed.

> *You and your spouse, if filing jointly, each may be able to contribute up to $5,500 ($6,500 if age 50 or older at the end of 2014) to a traditional IRA or Roth IRA for 2014. You may owe a penalty if your contributions exceed these limits, and the limits may be lower depending on your income. For more information on IRA contributions, see Pub. 590-A. If the limits on IRA contributions change for 2015, Pub. 590-A will have the new 2015 limits.*

For more information on IRAs, see Pub. 590-A and Pub. 590-B.

TreasuryDirect®. You can request a deposit of your refund (or part of it) to a TreasuryDirect® online account to buy U.S. Treasury marketable securities and savings bonds. For more information, go to *www.publicdebt.treas.gov/index1.htm.*

Need more information or forms? Visit IRS.gov.

Form 8888. You can have your refund directly deposited into more than one account or use it to buy up to $5,000 in paper series I savings bonds. You do not need a TreasuryDirect® account to do this. For more information, see the Form 8888 instructions.

Line 76a

You cannot file Form 8888 to split your refund into more than one account or buy paper series I savings bonds if Form 8379 is filed with your return.

Line 76b

The routing number must be nine digits. The first two digits must be 01 through 12 or 21 through 32. On the sample check shown here, the routing number is 250250025. Charles and Mary Ellen Keys would use that routing number unless their financial institution instructed them to use a different routing number for direct deposits.

Ask your financial institution for the correct routing number to enter on line 76b if:

- The routing number on a deposit slip is different from the routing number on your checks,
- Your deposit is to a savings account that does not allow you to write checks, or
- Your checks state they are payable through a financial institution different from the one at which you have your checking account.

Line 76c

Check the appropriate box for the type of account. Do not check more than one box. If the deposit is to an account such as an IRA, health savings account, brokerage account, or other similar account, ask your financial institution whether you should check the "Checking" or "Savings" box. You must check the correct box to ensure your deposit is accepted. For a TreasuryDirect® online account, check the "Savings" box.

Line 76d

The account number can be up to 17 characters (both numbers and letters). Include hyphens but omit spaces and special symbols. Enter the number from left to right and leave any unused boxes

Sample Check—Lines 76b Through 76d

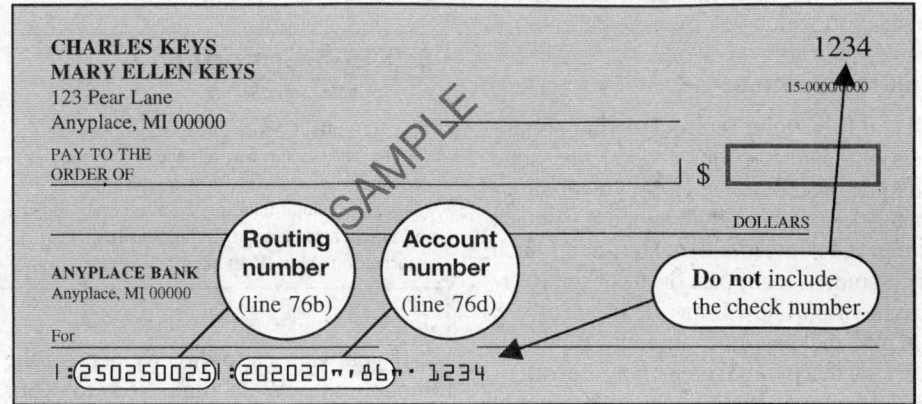

 The routing and account numbers may be in different places on your check.

blank. On the sample check shown here, the account number is 20202086. Do not include the check number.

If the direct deposit to your account(s) is different from the amount you expected, you will receive an explanation in the mail about 2 weeks after your refund is deposited.

Reasons Your Direct Deposit Request May Be Rejected

If any of the following apply, your direct deposit request will be rejected and a check will be sent instead.

- Any numbers or letters on lines 76b through 76d are crossed out or whited out.
- Your financial institution(s) may not allow a joint refund to be deposited to an individual account. The IRS is not responsible if a financial institution rejects a direct deposit.
- You file your 2014 return after December 31, 2015.
- Three direct deposits of tax refunds have already been made to your account or prepaid debit card.
- The name on your account does not match the name on the tax refund.

 The IRS is not responsible for a lost refund if you enter the wrong account information. Check with your financial institution to get the correct routing and account numbers and to make sure your direct deposit will be accepted.

Line 77

Applied to Your 2015 Estimated Tax

Enter on line 77 the amount, if any, of the overpayment on line 75 you want applied to your 2015 estimated tax. We will apply this amount to your account unless you include a statement requesting us to apply it to your spouse's account. Include your spouse's social security number in the statement.

 This election to apply part or all of the amount overpaid to your 2015 estimated tax cannot be changed later.

Amount You Owe

IRS *e-file* offers two electronic payment options. With Electronic Funds Withdrawal, you can pay your current year balance due and also make up to four estimated tax payments. If you file early, you can schedule your payment for withdrawal from your account on a future date, up to and including the due date of the return. Or you can pay using a debit or credit card. Visit *www.irs.gov/payments* for details on both options.

Line 78

Amount You Owe

 To save interest and penalties, pay your taxes in full by April 15, 2015. You do not have to pay if line 78 is under $1.

Include any estimated tax penalty from line 79 in the amount you enter on line 78.

You can pay online, by phone, or by check or money order. Do not include any estimated tax payment for 2015 in this payment. Instead, make the estimated tax payment separately.

Bad check or payment. The penalty for writing a bad check to the IRS is $25 or 2% of the check, whichever is more. However, if the amount of the check is less than $25, the penalty equals the amount of the check. This penalty also applies to other forms of payment if the IRS does not receive the funds. Use TeleTax topic 206.

Pay Online

Paying online is convenient and secure and helps make sure we get your payments on time. You can pay using either of the following electronic payment methods.
- Direct transfer from your bank account. Go to IRS.gov. Click on "Pay Your Tax Bill" and then "Direct Pay."
- Debit or credit card.

To pay your taxes online or for more information, go to *www.irs.gov/payments*. Also see the *e-file* information under *Amount You Owe*, earlier, for information about the Electronic Funds Withdrawal payment option offered when e-filing your return.

Pay by Phone

Paying by phone is another safe and secure method of paying electronically. Use one of the following methods.
- Direct transfer using Electronic Federal Tax Payment System (EFTPS).
- Debit or credit card.

Direct transfer. To use EFTPS, you must be enrolled. You can enroll online or have an enrollment form mailed to you. To make a payment using EFTPS, call 1-800-555-4477 (English) or 1-800-244-4829 (Español). People who are deaf, hard of hearing, or have a speech disability and who have access to TTY/TDD equipment can call 1-800-733-4829. For more information about EFTPS, go to *www.irs.gov/payments*.

Debit or credit card. To pay using a debit or credit card, you can call one of the following service providers. There is a convenience fee charged by these providers that varies by provider, card type, and payment amount.

WorldPay US, Inc.
1-844-729-8298
(1-844-PAY-TAX-8™)
www.payUSAtax.com

Official Payments Corporation
1-888-UPAY-TAX™
(1-888-872-9829)
www.officialpayments.com

Link2Gov Corporation
1-888-PAY-1040™
(1-888-729-1040)
www.PAY1040.com

For the latest details on how to pay by phone, go to *www.irs.gov/payments*.

Pay by Check or Money Order

Make your check or money order payable to "United States Treasury" for the full amount due. Do not send cash. Do not attach the payment to your return. Write "2014 Form 1040" and your name, address, daytime phone number, and social security number (SSN) on your payment. If you are filing a joint return, enter the SSN shown first on your tax return.

To help us process your payment, enter the amount on the right side of the check like this: $ XXX.XX. Do not use dashes or lines (for example, do not enter "$ XXX–" or "$ XXX˟˟/₁₀₀").

Then, complete Form 1040-V following the instructions on that form and enclose it in the envelope with your tax return and payment.

 You may need to (a) increase the amount of income tax withheld from your pay by filing a new Form W-4, (b) increase the tax withheld from other income by filing Form W-4P or W-4V, or (c) make estimated tax payments for 2015. See Income Tax Withholding and Estimated Tax Payments for 2015 under General Information, later.

What If You Cannot Pay?

If you cannot pay the full amount shown on line 78 when you file, you can ask for:
- An installment agreement, or
- An extension of time to pay.

Installment agreement. Under an installment agreement, you can pay all or part of the tax you owe in monthly installments. However, even if your request to pay in installments is granted, you will be charged interest and may be charged a late payment penalty on the tax not paid by April 15, 2015. You must also pay a fee. To limit the interest and penalty charges, pay as much of the tax as possible when you file. But before requesting an installment agreement, you should consider other less costly alternatives, such as a bank loan or credit card payment.

To ask for an installment agreement, you can apply online or use Form 9465. To apply online, go to IRS.gov and click on "Tools" and then "Online Payment Agreement."

Extension of time to pay. If paying the tax when it is due would cause you an undue hardship, you can ask for an extension of time to pay by filing Form 1127 by April 15, 2015. An extension generally will not be granted for more than 6 months. If you pay after April 15, 2015, you will be charged interest on the tax not paid by April 15, 2015. You must pay the tax before the extension runs out. If you do not, penalties may be imposed.

Line 79

Estimated Tax Penalty

You may owe this penalty if:
- Line 78 is at least $1,000 and it is more than 10% of the tax shown on your return, or

Need more information or forms? Visit IRS.gov.

• You did not pay enough estimated tax by any of the due dates. This is true even if you are due a refund.

For most people, the "tax shown on your return" is the amount on your 2014 Form 1040, line 63, minus the total of any amounts shown on lines 61, 66a, 67, 68, 69, and 72 and Forms 8828, 4137, 5329 (Parts III through VIII only), and 8919. Also subtract from line 63 any tax on an excess parachute payment, any excise tax on insider stock compensation of an expatriated corporation, any uncollected social security and Medicare or RRTA tax on tips or group-term life insurance, and any look-back interest due under section 167(g) or 460(b). When figuring the amount on line 63, include household employment taxes only if line 64 is more than zero or you would owe the penalty even if you did not include those taxes.

Exception. You will not owe the penalty if your 2013 tax return was for a tax year of 12 full months and either of the following applies.

1. You had no tax shown on your 2013 return and you were a U.S. citizen or resident for all of 2013.

2. The total of lines 64, 65, and 71 on your 2014 return is at least 100% of the tax shown on your 2013 return (110% of that amount if you are not a farmer or fisherman, and your adjusted gross income (AGI) shown on your 2013 return was more than $150,000 (more than $75,000 if married filing separately for 2014)). Your estimated tax payments for 2014 must have been made on time and for the required amount.

For most people, the "tax shown on your 2013 return" is the amount on your 2013 Form 1040, line 61, minus the total of any amounts shown on lines 64a, 65, 66, and 70 and Forms 8828, 4137, 5329 (Parts III through VIII only), 8885, and 8919. Also subtract from line 61 any tax on an excess parachute payment, any excise tax on insider stock compensation of an expatriated corporation, any uncollected social security and Medicare or RRTA tax on tips or group-term life insurance, any look-back interest due under section 167(g) or 460(b), and any write-in tax included on line 60 from Form 8885. When figuring the amount

on line 61, include household employment taxes only if line 62 is more than zero or you would have owed the estimated tax penalty for 2013 even if you did not include those taxes.

Figuring the Penalty

If the *Exception* just described does not apply and you choose to figure the penalty yourself, use Form 2210 (or 2210-F for farmers and fishermen).

Enter any penalty on line 79. Add the penalty to any tax due and enter the total on line 78.

However, if you have an overpayment on line 75, subtract the penalty from the amount you would otherwise enter on line 76a or line 77. Lines 76a, 77, and 79 must equal line 75.

If the penalty is more than the overpayment on line 75, enter -0- on lines 76a and 77. Then subtract line 75 from line 79 and enter the result on line 78.

Do not file Form 2210 with your return unless Form 2210 indicates that you must do so. Instead, keep it for your records.

 Because Form 2210 is complicated, you can leave line 79 blank and the IRS will figure the penalty and send you a bill. We will not charge you interest on the penalty if you pay by the date specified on the bill. If your income varied during the year, the annualized income installment method may reduce the amount of your penalty. But you must file Form 2210 because the IRS cannot figure your penalty under this method. See the Instructions for Form 2210 for other situations in which you may be able to lower your penalty by filing Form 2210.

Third Party Designee

If you want to allow your preparer, a friend, a family member, or any other person you choose to discuss your 2014 tax return with the IRS, check the "Yes" box in the "Third Party Designee" area of your return. Also, enter the designee's name, phone number, and any five digits the designee chooses as his or her personal identification number (PIN).

If you check the "Yes" box, you, and your spouse if filing a joint return, are authorizing the IRS to call the designee to answer any questions that may arise during the processing of your return. You are also authorizing the designee to:

• Give the IRS any information that is missing from your return,

• Call the IRS for information about the processing of your return or the status of your refund or payment(s),

• Receive copies of notices or transcripts related to your return, upon request, and

• Respond to certain IRS notices about math errors, offsets, and return preparation.

You are not authorizing the designee to receive any refund check, bind you to anything (including any additional tax liability), or otherwise represent you before the IRS. If you want to expand the designee's authorization, see Pub. 947.

The authorization will automatically end no later than the due date (without regard to extensions) for filing your 2015 tax return. This is April 18, 2016, for most people.

Sign Your Return

Form 1040 is not considered a valid return unless you sign it. If you are filing a joint return, your spouse must also sign. If your spouse cannot sign the return, see Pub. 501. Be sure to date your return and enter your occupation(s). If you have someone prepare your return, you are still responsible for the correctness of the return. If your return is signed by a representative for you, you must have a power of attorney attached that specifically authorizes the representative to sign your return. To do this, you can use Form 2848. If you are filing a joint return as a surviving spouse, see *Death of a Taxpayer,* later.

Court-Appointed Conservator, Guardian, or Other Fiduciary

If you are a court-appointed conservator, guardian, or other fiduciary for a mentally or physically incompetent individual who has to file Form 1040, sign your name for the individual and file Form 56.

Child's Return

If your child cannot sign the return, either parent can sign the child's name in the space provided. Then, enter "By (your signature), parent for minor child."

Daytime Phone Number

Providing your daytime phone number may help speed the processing of your return. We may have questions about items on your return, such as the earned income credit or the credit for child and dependent care expenses. If you answer our questions over the phone, we may be able to continue processing your return without mailing you a letter. If you are filing a joint return, you can enter either your or your spouse's daytime phone number.

Electronic Return Signatures!

To file your return electronically, you must sign the return electronically using a personal identification number (PIN). If you are filing online using software, you must use a Self-Select PIN. If you are filing electronically using a tax practitioner, you can use a Self-Select PIN or a Practitioner PIN.

Self-Select PIN. The Self-Select PIN method allows you to create your own PIN. If you are married filing jointly, you and your spouse will each need to create a PIN and enter these PINs as your electronic signatures.

A PIN is any combination of five digits you choose except five zeros. If you use a PIN, there is nothing to sign and nothing to mail—not even your Forms W-2.

To verify your identity, you will be prompted to enter your adjusted gross income (AGI) from your originally filed 2013 federal income tax return, if applicable. Do not use your AGI from an amended return (Form 1040X) or a math error correction made by IRS. AGI is the amount shown on your 2013 Form 1040,

line 38; Form 1040A, line 22; or Form 1040EZ, line 4. If you do not have your 2013 income tax return, call the IRS at 1-800-908-9946 to get a free transcript of your return or visit IRS.gov and click on *Get Transcript of Your Tax Records* under "Tools." (If you filed electronically last year, you may use your prior year PIN to verify your identity instead of your prior year AGI. The prior year PIN is the five digit PIN you used to electronically sign your 2013 return.) You will also be prompted to enter your date of birth (DOB).

 You cannot use the Self-Select PIN method if you are a first-time filer under age 16 at the end of 2014.

 If you cannot locate your prior year AGI or prior year PIN, use the Electronic Filing PIN Request. *This can be found at IRS.gov. Click on* Request an Electronic Filing PIN. *Or you can call 1-866-704-7388.*

Practitioner PIN. The Practitioner PIN method allows you to authorize your tax practitioner to enter or generate your PIN. The practitioner can provide you with details.

Form 8453. You must send in a paper Form 8453 if you have to attach certain forms or other documents that cannot be electronically filed. For details, see Form 8453.

Identity Protection PIN

For 2014, if you received an Identity Protection Personal Identification Number (IP PIN) from the IRS, enter it in the IP PIN spaces provided below your daytime phone number. You must correctly enter all six numbers of your IP PIN. If you did not receive an IP PIN, leave these spaces blank.

 New IP PINs are issued every year. Enter the latest IP PIN you received. IP PINs for 2014 tax returns generally were sent in December 2014.

If you are filing a joint return and both taxpayers receive an IP PIN, only the taxpayer whose social security number (SSN) appears first on the tax return should enter his or her IP PIN. However, if you are filing electronically, both taxpayers must enter their IP PINs.

If you need more information or answers to frequently asked questions on how to use the IP PIN, go to *www.irs.gov/Individuals/Understanding-Your-CP01A-Notice.* If you received an IP PIN but misplaced it, call 1-800-908-4490.

Paid Preparer Must Sign Your Return

Generally, anyone you pay to prepare your return must sign it and include their Preparer Tax Identification Number (PTIN) in the space provided. The preparer must give you a copy of the return for your records. Someone who prepares your return but does not charge you should not sign your return.

Assemble Your Return

Assemble any schedules and forms behind Form 1040 in order of the "Attachment Sequence No." shown in the upper right corner of the schedule or form. If you have supporting statements, arrange them in the same order as the schedules or forms they support and attach them last. Do not attach correspondence or other items unless required to do so. Attach a copy of Forms W-2 and 2439 to the front of Form 1040. If you received a Form W-2c (a corrected Form W-2), attach a copy of your original Forms W-2 and any Forms W-2c. Also attach Forms W-2G and 1099-R to the front of Form 1040 if tax was withheld.

Need more information or forms? Visit IRS.gov.

2014 Tax Table

CAUTION

See the instructions for line 44 to see if you must use the Tax Table below to figure your tax.

Example. Mr. and Mrs. Brown are filing a joint return. Their taxable income on Form 1040, line 43, is $25,300. First, they find the $25,300-25,350 taxable income line. Next, they find the column for married filing jointly and read down the column. The amount shown where the taxable income line and filing status column meet is $2,891. This is the tax amount they should enter on Form 1040, line 44.

Sample Table

At Least	But Less Than	Single	Married filing jointly*	Married filing separately	Head of a household
			Your tax is—		
25,200	25,250	3,330	2,876	3,330	3,136
25,250	25,300	3,338	2,884	3,338	3,144
25,300	25,350	3,345	2,891	3,345	3,151
25,350	25,400	3,353	2,899	3,353	3,159

If line 43 (taxable income) is—		And you are—			
At least	But less than	Single	Married filing jointly *	Married filing separately	Head of a household
			Your tax is—		
0	5	0	0	0	0
5	15	1	1	1	1
15	25	2	2	2	2
25	50	4	4	4	4
50	75	6	6	6	6
75	100	9	9	9	9
100	125	11	11	11	11
125	150	14	14	14	14
150	175	16	16	16	16
175	200	19	19	19	19
200	225	21	21	21	21
225	250	24	24	24	24
250	275	26	26	26	26
275	300	29	29	29	29
300	325	31	31	31	31
325	350	34	34	34	34
350	375	36	36	36	36
375	400	39	39	39	39
400	425	41	41	41	41
425	450	44	44	44	44
450	475	46	46	46	46
475	500	49	49	49	49
500	525	51	51	51	51
525	550	54	54	54	54
550	575	56	56	56	56
575	600	59	59	59	59
600	625	61	61	61	61
625	650	64	64	64	64
650	675	66	66	66	66
675	700	69	69	69	69
700	725	71	71	71	71
725	750	74	74	74	74
750	775	76	76	76	76
775	800	79	79	79	79
800	825	81	81	81	81
825	850	84	84	84	84
850	875	86	86	86	86
875	900	89	89	89	89
900	925	91	91	91	91
925	950	94	94	94	94
950	975	96	96	96	96
975	1,000	99	99	99	99

1,000

If line 43 (taxable income) is—		And you are—			
At least	But less than	Single	Married filing jointly *	Married filing separately	Head of a household
			Your tax is—		
1,000	1,025	101	101	101	101
1,025	1,050	104	104	104	104
1,050	1,075	106	106	106	106
1,075	1,100	109	109	109	109
1,100	1,125	111	111	111	111
1,125	1,150	114	114	114	114
1,150	1,175	116	116	116	116
1,175	1,200	119	119	119	119
1,200	1,225	121	121	121	121
1,225	1,250	124	124	124	124
1,250	1,275	126	126	126	126
1,275	1,300	129	129	129	129
1,300	1,325	131	131	131	131
1,325	1,350	134	134	134	134
1,350	1,375	136	136	136	136
1,375	1,400	139	139	139	139
1,400	1,425	141	141	141	141
1,425	1,450	144	144	144	144
1,450	1,475	146	146	146	146
1,475	1,500	149	149	149	149
1,500	1,525	151	151	151	151
1,525	1,550	154	154	154	154
1,550	1,575	156	156	156	156
1,575	1,600	159	159	159	159
1,600	1,625	161	161	161	161
1,625	1,650	164	164	164	164
1,650	1,675	166	166	166	166
1,675	1,700	169	169	169	169
1,700	1,725	171	171	171	171
1,725	1,750	174	174	174	174
1,750	1,775	176	176	176	176
1,775	1,800	179	179	179	179
1,800	1,825	181	181	181	181
1,825	1,850	184	184	184	184
1,850	1,875	186	186	186	186
1,875	1,900	189	189	189	189
1,900	1,925	191	191	191	191
1,925	1,950	194	194	194	194
1,950	1,975	196	196	196	196
1,975	2,000	199	199	199	199

2,000

If line 43 (taxable income) is—		And you are—			
At least	But less than	Single	Married filing jointly *	Married filing separately	Head of a household
			Your tax is—		
2,000	2,025	201	201	201	201
2,025	2,050	204	204	204	204
2,050	2,075	206	206	206	206
2,075	2,100	209	209	209	209
2,100	2,125	211	211	211	211
2,125	2,150	214	214	214	214
2,150	2,175	216	216	216	216
2,175	2,200	219	219	219	219
2,200	2,225	221	221	221	221
2,225	2,250	224	224	224	224
2,250	2,275	226	226	226	226
2,275	2,300	229	229	229	229
2,300	2,325	231	231	231	231
2,325	2,350	234	234	234	234
2,350	2,375	236	236	236	236
2,375	2,400	239	239	239	239
2,400	2,425	241	241	241	241
2,425	2,450	244	244	244	244
2,450	2,475	246	246	246	246
2,475	2,500	249	249	249	249
2,500	2,525	251	251	251	251
2,525	2,550	254	254	254	254
2,550	2,575	256	256	256	256
2,575	2,600	259	259	259	259
2,600	2,625	261	261	261	261
2,625	2,650	264	264	264	264
2,650	2,675	266	266	266	266
2,675	2,700	269	269	269	269
2,700	2,725	271	271	271	271
2,725	2,750	274	274	274	274
2,750	2,775	276	276	276	276
2,775	2,800	279	279	279	279
2,800	2,825	281	281	281	281
2,825	2,850	284	284	284	284
2,850	2,875	286	286	286	286
2,875	2,900	289	289	289	289
2,900	2,925	291	291	291	291
2,925	2,950	294	294	294	294
2,950	2,975	296	296	296	296
2,975	3,000	299	299	299	299

(Continued)

* This column must also be used by a qualifying widow(er).

If line 43 (taxable income) is— And you are—

Your tax is—

3,000

At least	But less than	Single	Married filing jointly *	Married filing separately	Head of a household
3,000	3,050	303	303	303	303
3,050	3,100	308	308	308	308
3,100	3,150	313	313	313	313
3,150	3,200	318	318	318	318
3,200	3,250	323	323	323	323
3,250	3,300	328	328	328	328
3,300	3,350	333	333	333	333
3,350	3,400	338	338	338	338
3,400	3,450	343	343	343	343
3,450	3,500	348	348	348	348
3,500	3,550	353	353	353	353
3,550	3,600	358	358	358	358
3,600	3,650	363	363	363	363
3,650	3,700	368	368	368	368
3,700	3,750	373	373	373	373
3,750	3,800	378	378	378	378
3,800	3,850	383	383	383	383
3,850	3,900	388	388	388	388
3,900	3,950	393	393	393	393
3,950	4,000	398	398	398	398

4,000

At least	But less than	Single	Married filing jointly *	Married filing separately	Head of a household
4,000	4,050	403	403	403	403
4,050	4,100	408	408	408	408
4,100	4,150	413	413	413	413
4,150	4,200	418	418	418	418
4,200	4,250	423	423	423	423
4,250	4,300	428	428	428	428
4,300	4,350	433	433	433	433
4,350	4,400	438	438	438	438
4,400	4,450	443	443	443	443
4,450	4,500	448	448	448	448
4,500	4,550	453	453	453	453
4,550	4,600	458	458	458	458
4,600	4,650	463	463	463	463
4,650	4,700	468	468	468	468
4,700	4,750	473	473	473	473
4,750	4,800	478	478	478	478
4,800	4,850	483	483	483	483
4,850	4,900	488	488	488	488
4,900	4,950	493	493	493	493
4,950	5,000	498	498	498	498

5,000

At least	But less than	Single	Married filing jointly *	Married filing separately	Head of a household
5,000	5,050	503	503	503	503
5,050	5,100	508	508	508	508
5,100	5,150	513	513	513	513
5,150	5,200	518	518	518	518
5,200	5,250	523	523	523	523
5,250	5,300	528	528	528	528
5,300	5,350	533	533	533	533
5,350	5,400	538	538	538	538
5,400	5,450	543	543	543	543
5,450	5,500	548	548	548	548
5,500	5,550	553	553	553	553
5,550	5,600	558	558	558	558
5,600	5,650	563	563	563	563
5,650	5,700	568	568	568	568
5,700	5,750	573	573	573	573
5,750	5,800	578	578	578	578
5,800	5,850	583	583	583	583
5,850	5,900	588	588	588	588
5,900	5,950	593	593	593	593
5,950	6,000	598	598	598	598

6,000

At least	But less than	Single	Married filing jointly *	Married filing separately	Head of a household
6,000	6,050	603	603	603	603
6,050	6,100	608	608	608	608
6,100	6,150	613	613	613	613
6,150	6,200	618	618	618	618
6,200	6,250	623	623	623	623
6,250	6,300	628	628	628	628
6,300	6,350	633	633	633	633
6,350	6,400	638	638	638	638
6,400	6,450	643	643	643	643
6,450	6,500	648	648	648	648
6,500	6,550	653	653	653	653
6,550	6,600	658	658	658	658
6,600	6,650	663	663	663	663
6,650	6,700	668	668	668	668
6,700	6,750	673	673	673	673
6,750	6,800	678	678	678	678
6,800	6,850	683	683	683	683
6,850	6,900	688	688	688	688
6,900	6,950	693	693	693	693
6,950	7,000	698	698	698	698

7,000

At least	But less than	Single	Married filing jointly *	Married filing separately	Head of a household
7,000	7,050	703	703	703	703
7,050	7,100	708	708	708	708
7,100	7,150	713	713	713	713
7,150	7,200	718	718	718	718
7,200	7,250	723	723	723	723
7,250	7,300	728	728	728	728
7,300	7,350	733	733	733	733
7,350	7,400	738	738	738	738
7,400	7,450	743	743	743	743
7,450	7,500	748	748	748	748
7,500	7,550	753	753	753	753
7,550	7,600	758	758	758	758
7,600	7,650	763	763	763	763
7,650	7,700	768	768	768	768
7,700	7,750	773	773	773	773
7,750	7,800	778	778	778	778
7,800	7,850	783	783	783	783
7,850	7,900	788	788	788	788
7,900	7,950	793	793	793	793
7,950	8,000	798	798	798	798

8,000

At least	But less than	Single	Married filing jointly *	Married filing separately	Head of a household
8,000	8,050	803	803	803	803
8,050	8,100	808	808	808	808
8,100	8,150	813	813	813	813
8,150	8,200	818	818	818	818
8,200	8,250	823	823	823	823
8,250	8,300	828	828	828	828
8,300	8,350	833	833	833	833
8,350	8,400	838	838	838	838
8,400	8,450	843	843	843	843
8,450	8,500	848	848	848	848
8,500	8,550	853	853	853	853
8,550	8,600	858	858	858	858
8,600	8,650	863	863	863	863
8,650	8,700	868	868	868	868
8,700	8,750	873	873	873	873
8,750	8,800	878	878	878	878
8,800	8,850	883	883	883	883
8,850	8,900	888	888	888	888
8,900	8,950	893	893	893	893
8,950	9,000	898	898	898	898

9,000

At least	But less than	Single	Married filing jointly *	Married filing separately	Head of a household
9,000	9,050	903	903	903	903
9,050	9,100	908	908	908	908
9,100	9,150	915	913	915	913
9,150	9,200	923	918	923	918
9,200	9,250	930	923	930	923
9,250	9,300	938	928	938	928
9,300	9,350	945	933	945	933
9,350	9,400	953	938	953	938
9,400	9,450	960	943	960	943
9,450	9,500	968	948	968	948
9,500	9,550	975	953	975	953
9,550	9,600	983	958	983	958
9,600	9,650	990	963	990	963
9,650	9,700	998	968	998	968
9,700	9,750	1,005	973	1,005	973
9,750	9,800	1,013	978	1,013	978
9,800	9,850	1,020	983	1,020	983
9,850	9,900	1,028	988	1,028	988
9,900	9,950	1,035	993	1,035	993
9,950	10,000	1,043	998	1,043	998

10,000

At least	But less than	Single	Married filing jointly *	Married filing separately	Head of a household
10,000	10,050	1,050	1,003	1,050	1,003
10,050	10,100	1,058	1,008	1,058	1,008
10,100	10,150	1,065	1,013	1,065	1,013
10,150	10,200	1,073	1,018	1,073	1,018
10,200	10,250	1,080	1,023	1,080	1,023
10,250	10,300	1,088	1,028	1,088	1,028
10,300	10,350	1,095	1,033	1,095	1,033
10,350	10,400	1,103	1,038	1,103	1,038
10,400	10,450	1,110	1,043	1,110	1,043
10,450	10,500	1,118	1,048	1,118	1,048
10,500	10,550	1,125	1,053	1,125	1,053
10,550	10,600	1,133	1,058	1,133	1,058
10,600	10,650	1,140	1,063	1,140	1,063
10,650	10,700	1,148	1,068	1,148	1,068
10,700	10,750	1,155	1,073	1,155	1,073
10,750	10,800	1,163	1,078	1,163	1,078
10,800	10,850	1,170	1,083	1,170	1,083
10,850	10,900	1,178	1,088	1,178	1,088
10,900	10,950	1,185	1,093	1,185	1,093
10,950	11,000	1,193	1,098	1,193	1,098

11,000

At least	But less than	Single	Married filing jointly *	Married filing separately	Head of a household
11,000	11,050	1,200	1,103	1,200	1,103
11,050	11,100	1,208	1,108	1,208	1,108
11,100	11,150	1,215	1,113	1,215	1,113
11,150	11,200	1,223	1,118	1,223	1,118
11,200	11,250	1,230	1,123	1,230	1,123
11,250	11,300	1,238	1,128	1,238	1,128
11,300	11,350	1,245	1,133	1,245	1,133
11,350	11,400	1,253	1,138	1,253	1,138
11,400	11,450	1,260	1,143	1,260	1,143
11,450	11,500	1,268	1,148	1,268	1,148
11,500	11,550	1,275	1,153	1,275	1,153
11,550	11,600	1,283	1,158	1,283	1,158
11,600	11,650	1,290	1,163	1,290	1,163
11,650	11,700	1,298	1,168	1,298	1,168
11,700	11,750	1,305	1,173	1,305	1,173
11,750	11,800	1,313	1,178	1,313	1,178
11,800	11,850	1,320	1,183	1,320	1,183
11,850	11,900	1,328	1,188	1,328	1,188
11,900	11,950	1,335	1,193	1,335	1,193
11,950	12,000	1,343	1,198	1,343	1,198

(Continued)

* This column must also be used by a qualifying widow(er).

Need more information or forms? Visit IRS.gov.

If line 43 (taxable income) is— At least	But less than	And you are— Single	Married filing jointly *	Married filing sepa-rately	Head of a house-hold
		Your tax is—			
12,000					
12,000	12,050	1,350	1,203	1,350	1,203
12,050	12,100	1,358	1,208	1,358	1,208
12,100	12,150	1,365	1,213	1,365	1,213
12,150	12,200	1,373	1,218	1,373	1,218
12,200	12,250	1,380	1,223	1,380	1,223
12,250	12,300	1,388	1,228	1,388	1,228
12,300	12,350	1,395	1,233	1,395	1,233
12,350	12,400	1,403	1,238	1,403	1,238
12,400	12,450	1,410	1,243	1,410	1,243
12,450	12,500	1,418	1,248	1,418	1,248
12,500	12,550	1,425	1,253	1,425	1,253
12,550	12,600	1,433	1,258	1,433	1,258
12,600	12,650	1,440	1,263	1,440	1,263
12,650	12,700	1,448	1,268	1,448	1,268
12,700	12,750	1,455	1,273	1,455	1,273
12,750	12,800	1,463	1,278	1,463	1,278
12,800	12,850	1,470	1,283	1,470	1,283
12,850	12,900	1,478	1,288	1,478	1,288
12,900	12,950	1,485	1,293	1,485	1,293
12,950	13,000	1,493	1,298	1,493	1,299
13,000					
13,000	13,050	1,500	1,303	1,500	1,306
13,050	13,100	1,508	1,308	1,508	1,314
13,100	13,150	1,515	1,313	1,515	1,321
13,150	13,200	1,523	1,318	1,523	1,329
13,200	13,250	1,530	1,323	1,530	1,336
13,250	13,300	1,538	1,328	1,538	1,344
13,300	13,350	1,545	1,333	1,545	1,351
13,350	13,400	1,553	1,338	1,553	1,359
13,400	13,450	1,560	1,343	1,560	1,366
13,450	13,500	1,568	1,348	1,568	1,374
13,500	13,550	1,575	1,353	1,575	1,381
13,550	13,600	1,583	1,358	1,583	1,389
13,600	13,650	1,590	1,363	1,590	1,396
13,650	13,700	1,598	1,368	1,598	1,404
13,700	13,750	1,605	1,373	1,605	1,411
13,750	13,800	1,613	1,378	1,613	1,419
13,800	13,850	1,620	1,383	1,620	1,426
13,850	13,900	1,628	1,388	1,628	1,434
13,900	13,950	1,635	1,393	1,635	1,441
13,950	14,000	1,643	1,398	1,643	1,449
14,000					
14,000	14,050	1,650	1,403	1,650	1,456
14,050	14,100	1,658	1,408	1,658	1,464
14,100	14,150	1,665	1,413	1,665	1,471
14,150	14,200	1,673	1,418	1,673	1,479
14,200	14,250	1,680	1,423	1,680	1,486
14,250	14,300	1,688	1,428	1,688	1,494
14,300	14,350	1,695	1,433	1,695	1,501
14,350	14,400	1,703	1,438	1,703	1,509
14,400	14,450	1,710	1,443	1,710	1,516
14,450	14,500	1,718	1,448	1,718	1,524
14,500	14,550	1,725	1,453	1,725	1,531
14,550	14,600	1,733	1,458	1,733	1,539
14,600	14,650	1,740	1,463	1,740	1,546
14,650	14,700	1,748	1,468	1,748	1,554
14,700	14,750	1,755	1,473	1,755	1,561
14,750	14,800	1,763	1,478	1,763	1,569
14,800	14,850	1,770	1,483	1,770	1,576
14,850	14,900	1,778	1,488	1,778	1,584
14,900	14,950	1,785	1,493	1,785	1,591
14,950	15,000	1,793	1,498	1,793	1,599
15,000					
15,000	15,050	1,800	1,503	1,800	1,606
15,050	15,100	1,808	1,508	1,808	1,614
15,100	15,150	1,815	1,513	1,815	1,621
15,150	15,200	1,823	1,518	1,823	1,629
15,200	15,250	1,830	1,523	1,830	1,636
15,250	15,300	1,838	1,528	1,838	1,644
15,300	15,350	1,845	1,533	1,845	1,651
15,350	15,400	1,853	1,538	1,853	1,659
15,400	15,450	1,860	1,543	1,860	1,666
15,450	15,500	1,868	1,548	1,868	1,674
15,500	15,550	1,875	1,553	1,875	1,681
15,550	15,600	1,883	1,558	1,883	1,689
15,600	15,650	1,890	1,563	1,890	1,696
15,650	15,700	1,898	1,568	1,898	1,704
15,700	15,750	1,905	1,573	1,905	1,711
15,750	15,800	1,913	1,578	1,913	1,719
15,800	15,850	1,920	1,583	1,920	1,726
15,850	15,900	1,928	1,588	1,928	1,734
15,900	15,950	1,935	1,593	1,935	1,741
15,950	16,000	1,943	1,598	1,943	1,749
16,000					
16,000	16,050	1,950	1,603	1,950	1,756
16,050	16,100	1,958	1,608	1,958	1,764
16,100	16,150	1,965	1,613	1,965	1,771
16,150	16,200	1,973	1,618	1,973	1,779
16,200	16,250	1,980	1,623	1,980	1,786
16,250	16,300	1,988	1,628	1,988	1,794
16,300	16,350	1,995	1,633	1,995	1,801
16,350	16,400	2,003	1,638	2,003	1,809
16,400	16,450	2,010	1,643	2,010	1,816
16,450	16,500	2,018	1,648	2,018	1,824
16,500	16,550	2,025	1,653	2,025	1,831
16,550	16,600	2,033	1,658	2,033	1,839
16,600	16,650	2,040	1,663	2,040	1,846
16,650	16,700	2,048	1,668	2,048	1,854
16,700	16,750	2,055	1,673	2,055	1,861
16,750	16,800	2,063	1,678	2,063	1,869
16,800	16,850	2,070	1,683	2,070	1,876
16,850	16,900	2,078	1,688	2,078	1,884
16,900	16,950	2,085	1,693	2,085	1,891
16,950	17,000	2,093	1,698	2,093	1,899
17,000					
17,000	17,050	2,100	1,703	2,100	1,906
17,050	17,100	2,108	1,708	2,108	1,914
17,100	17,150	2,115	1,713	2,115	1,921
17,150	17,200	2,123	1,718	2,123	1,929
17,200	17,250	2,130	1,723	2,130	1,936
17,250	17,300	2,138	1,728	2,138	1,944
17,300	17,350	2,145	1,733	2,145	1,951
17,350	17,400	2,153	1,738	2,153	1,959
17,400	17,450	2,160	1,743	2,160	1,966
17,450	17,500	2,168	1,748	2,168	1,974
17,500	17,550	2,175	1,753	2,175	1,981
17,550	17,600	2,183	1,758	2,183	1,989
17,600	17,650	2,190	1,763	2,190	1,996
17,650	17,700	2,198	1,768	2,198	2,004
17,700	17,750	2,205	1,773	2,205	2,011
17,750	17,800	2,213	1,778	2,213	2,019
17,800	17,850	2,220	1,783	2,220	2,026
17,850	17,900	2,228	1,788	2,228	2,034
17,900	17,950	2,235	1,793	2,235	2,041
17,950	18,000	2,243	1,798	2,243	2,049
18,000					
18,000	18,050	2,250	1,803	2,250	2,056
18,050	18,100	2,258	1,808	2,258	2,064
18,100	18,150	2,265	1,813	2,265	2,071
18,150	18,200	2,273	1,819	2,273	2,079
18,200	18,250	2,280	1,826	2,280	2,086
18,250	18,300	2,288	1,834	2,288	2,094
18,300	18,350	2,295	1,841	2,295	2,101
18,350	18,400	2,303	1,849	2,303	2,109
18,400	18,450	2,310	1,856	2,310	2,116
18,450	18,500	2,318	1,864	2,318	2,124
18,500	18,550	2,325	1,871	2,325	2,131
18,550	18,600	2,333	1,879	2,333	2,139
18,600	18,650	2,340	1,886	2,340	2,146
18,650	18,700	2,348	1,894	2,348	2,154
18,700	18,750	2,355	1,901	2,355	2,161
18,750	18,800	2,363	1,909	2,363	2,169
18,800	18,850	2,370	1,916	2,370	2,176
18,850	18,900	2,378	1,924	2,378	2,184
18,900	18,950	2,385	1,931	2,385	2,191
18,950	19,000	2,393	1,939	2,393	2,199
19,000					
19,000	19,050	2,400	1,946	2,400	2,206
19,050	19,100	2,408	1,954	2,408	2,214
19,100	19,150	2,415	1,961	2,415	2,221
19,150	19,200	2,423	1,969	2,423	2,229
19,200	19,250	2,430	1,976	2,430	2,236
19,250	19,300	2,438	1,984	2,438	2,244
19,300	19,350	2,445	1,991	2,445	2,251
19,350	19,400	2,453	1,999	2,453	2,259
19,400	19,450	2,460	2,006	2,460	2,266
19,450	19,500	2,468	2,014	2,468	2,274
19,500	19,550	2,475	2,021	2,475	2,281
19,550	19,600	2,483	2,029	2,483	2,289
19,600	19,650	2,490	2,036	2,490	2,296
19,650	19,700	2,498	2,044	2,498	2,304
19,700	19,750	2,505	2,051	2,505	2,311
19,750	19,800	2,513	2,059	2,513	2,319
19,800	19,850	2,520	2,066	2,520	2,326
19,850	19,900	2,528	2,074	2,528	2,334
19,900	19,950	2,535	2,081	2,535	2,341
19,950	20,000	2,543	2,089	2,543	2,349
20,000					
20,000	20,050	2,550	2,096	2,550	2,356
20,050	20,100	2,558	2,104	2,558	2,364
20,100	20,150	2,565	2,111	2,565	2,371
20,150	20,200	2,573	2,119	2,573	2,379
20,200	20,250	2,580	2,126	2,580	2,386
20,250	20,300	2,588	2,134	2,588	2,394
20,300	20,350	2,595	2,141	2,595	2,401
20,350	20,400	2,603	2,149	2,603	2,409
20,400	20,450	2,610	2,156	2,610	2,416
20,450	20,500	2,618	2,164	2,618	2,424
20,500	20,550	2,625	2,171	2,625	2,431
20,550	20,600	2,633	2,179	2,633	2,439
20,600	20,650	2,640	2,186	2,640	2,446
20,650	20,700	2,648	2,194	2,648	2,454
20,700	20,750	2,655	2,201	2,655	2,461
20,750	20,800	2,663	2,209	2,663	2,469
20,800	20,850	2,670	2,216	2,670	2,476
20,850	20,900	2,678	2,224	2,678	2,484
20,900	20,950	2,685	2,231	2,685	2,491
20,950	21,000	2,693	2,239	2,693	2,499

(Continued)

* This column must also be used by a qualifying widow(er).

21,000

At least	But less than	Single	Married filing jointly *	Married filing separately	Head of a household
			Your tax is—		
21,000	21,050	2,700	2,246	2,700	2,506
21,050	21,100	2,708	2,254	2,708	2,514
21,100	21,150	2,715	2,261	2,715	2,521
21,150	21,200	2,723	2,269	2,723	2,529
21,200	21,250	2,730	2,276	2,730	2,536
21,250	21,300	2,738	2,284	2,738	2,544
21,300	21,350	2,745	2,291	2,745	2,551
21,350	21,400	2,753	2,299	2,753	2,559
21,400	21,450	2,760	2,306	2,760	2,566
21,450	21,500	2,768	2,314	2,768	2,574
21,500	21,550	2,775	2,321	2,775	2,581
21,550	21,600	2,783	2,329	2,783	2,589
21,600	21,650	2,790	2,336	2,790	2,596
21,650	21,700	2,798	2,344	2,798	2,604
21,700	21,750	2,805	2,351	2,805	2,611
21,750	21,800	2,813	2,359	2,813	2,619
21,800	21,850	2,820	2,366	2,820	2,626
21,850	21,900	2,828	2,374	2,828	2,634
21,900	21,950	2,835	2,381	2,835	2,641
21,950	22,000	2,843	2,389	2,843	2,649

22,000

At least	But less than	Single	Married filing jointly *	Married filing separately	Head of a household
22,000	22,050	2,850	2,396	2,850	2,656
22,050	22,100	2,858	2,404	2,858	2,664
22,100	22,150	2,865	2,411	2,865	2,671
22,150	22,200	2,873	2,419	2,873	2,679
22,200	22,250	2,880	2,426	2,880	2,686
22,250	22,300	2,888	2,434	2,888	2,694
22,300	22,350	2,895	2,441	2,895	2,701
22,350	22,400	2,903	2,449	2,903	2,709
22,400	22,450	2,910	2,456	2,910	2,716
22,450	22,500	2,918	2,464	2,918	2,724
22,500	22,550	2,925	2,471	2,925	2,731
22,550	22,600	2,933	2,479	2,933	2,739
22,600	22,650	2,940	2,486	2,940	2,746
22,650	22,700	2,948	2,494	2,948	2,754
22,700	22,750	2,955	2,501	2,955	2,761
22,750	22,800	2,963	2,509	2,963	2,769
22,800	22,850	2,970	2,516	2,970	2,776
22,850	22,900	2,978	2,524	2,978	2,784
22,900	22,950	2,985	2,531	2,985	2,791
22,950	23,000	2,993	2,539	2,993	2,799

23,000

At least	But less than	Single	Married filing jointly *	Married filing separately	Head of a household
23,000	23,050	3,000	2,546	3,000	2,806
23,050	23,100	3,008	2,554	3,008	2,814
23,100	23,150	3,015	2,561	3,015	2,821
23,150	23,200	3,023	2,569	3,023	2,829
23,200	23,250	3,030	2,576	3,030	2,836
23,250	23,300	3,038	2,584	3,038	2,844
23,300	23,350	3,045	2,591	3,045	2,851
23,350	23,400	3,053	2,599	3,053	2,859
23,400	23,450	3,060	2,606	3,060	2,866
23,450	23,500	3,068	2,614	3,068	2,874
23,500	23,550	3,075	2,621	3,075	2,881
23,550	23,600	3,083	2,629	3,083	2,889
23,600	23,650	3,090	2,636	3,090	2,896
23,650	23,700	3,098	2,644	3,098	2,904
23,700	23,750	3,105	2,651	3,105	2,911
23,750	23,800	3,113	2,659	3,113	2,919
23,800	23,850	3,120	2,666	3,120	2,926
23,850	23,900	3,128	2,674	3,128	2,934
23,900	23,950	3,135	2,681	3,135	2,941
23,950	24,000	3,143	2,689	3,143	2,949

24,000

At least	But less than	Single	Married filing jointly *	Married filing separately	Head of a household
24,000	24,050	3,150	2,696	3,150	2,956
24,050	24,100	3,158	2,704	3,158	2,964
24,100	24,150	3,165	2,711	3,165	2,971
24,150	24,200	3,173	2,719	3,173	2,979
24,200	24,250	3,180	2,726	3,180	2,986
24,250	24,300	3,188	2,734	3,188	2,994
24,300	24,350	3,195	2,741	3,195	3,001
24,350	24,400	3,203	2,749	3,203	3,009
24,400	24,450	3,210	2,756	3,210	3,016
24,450	24,500	3,218	2,764	3,218	3,024
24,500	24,550	3,225	2,771	3,225	3,031
24,550	24,600	3,233	2,779	3,233	3,039
24,600	24,650	3,240	2,786	3,240	3,046
24,650	24,700	3,248	2,794	3,248	3,054
24,700	24,750	3,255	2,801	3,255	3,061
24,750	24,800	3,263	2,809	3,263	3,069
24,800	24,850	3,270	2,816	3,270	3,076
24,850	24,900	3,278	2,824	3,278	3,084
24,900	24,950	3,285	2,831	3,285	3,091
24,950	25,000	3,293	2,839	3,293	3,099

25,000

At least	But less than	Single	Married filing jointly *	Married filing separately	Head of a household
25,000	25,050	3,300	2,846	3,300	3,106
25,050	25,100	3,308	2,854	3,308	3,114
25,100	25,150	3,315	2,861	3,315	3,121
25,150	25,200	3,323	2,869	3,323	3,129
25,200	25,250	3,330	2,876	3,330	3,136
25,250	25,300	3,338	2,884	3,338	3,144
25,300	25,350	3,345	2,891	3,345	3,151
25,350	25,400	3,353	2,899	3,353	3,159
25,400	25,450	3,360	2,906	3,360	3,166
25,450	25,500	3,368	2,914	3,368	3,174
25,500	25,550	3,375	2,921	3,375	3,181
25,550	25,600	3,383	2,929	3,383	3,189
25,600	25,650	3,390	2,936	3,390	3,196
25,650	25,700	3,398	2,944	3,398	3,204
25,700	25,750	3,405	2,951	3,405	3,211
25,750	25,800	3,413	2,959	3,413	3,219
25,800	25,850	3,420	2,966	3,420	3,226
25,850	25,900	3,428	2,974	3,428	3,234
25,900	25,950	3,435	2,981	3,435	3,241
25,950	26,000	3,443	2,989	3,443	3,249

26,000

At least	But less than	Single	Married filing jointly *	Married filing separately	Head of a household
26,000	26,050	3,450	2,996	3,450	3,256
26,050	26,100	3,458	3,004	3,458	3,264
26,100	26,150	3,465	3,011	3,465	3,271
26,150	26,200	3,473	3,019	3,473	3,279
26,200	26,250	3,480	3,026	3,480	3,286
26,250	26,300	3,488	3,034	3,488	3,294
26,300	26,350	3,495	3,041	3,495	3,301
26,350	26,400	3,503	3,049	3,503	3,309
26,400	26,450	3,510	3,056	3,510	3,316
26,450	26,500	3,518	3,064	3,518	3,324
26,500	26,550	3,525	3,071	3,525	3,331
26,550	26,600	3,533	3,079	3,533	3,339
26,600	26,650	3,540	3,086	3,540	3,346
26,650	26,700	3,548	3,094	3,548	3,354
26,700	26,750	3,555	3,101	3,555	3,361
26,750	26,800	3,563	3,109	3,563	3,369
26,800	26,850	3,570	3,116	3,570	3,376
26,850	26,900	3,578	3,124	3,578	3,384
26,900	26,950	3,585	3,131	3,585	3,391
26,950	27,000	3,593	3,139	3,593	3,399

27,000

At least	But less than	Single	Married filing jointly *	Married filing separately	Head of a household
27,000	27,050	3,600	3,146	3,600	3,406
27,050	27,100	3,608	3,154	3,608	3,414
27,100	27,150	3,615	3,161	3,615	3,421
27,150	27,200	3,623	3,169	3,623	3,429
27,200	27,250	3,630	3,176	3,630	3,436
27,250	27,300	3,638	3,184	3,638	3,444
27,300	27,350	3,645	3,191	3,645	3,451
27,350	27,400	3,653	3,199	3,653	3,459
27,400	27,450	3,660	3,206	3,660	3,466
27,450	27,500	3,668	3,214	3,668	3,474
27,500	27,550	3,675	3,221	3,675	3,481
27,550	27,600	3,683	3,229	3,683	3,489
27,600	27,650	3,690	3,236	3,690	3,496
27,650	27,700	3,698	3,244	3,698	3,504
27,700	27,750	3,705	3,251	3,705	3,511
27,750	27,800	3,713	3,259	3,713	3,519
27,800	27,850	3,720	3,266	3,720	3,526
27,850	27,900	3,728	3,274	3,728	3,534
27,900	27,950	3,735	3,281	3,735	3,541
27,950	28,000	3,743	3,289	3,743	3,549

28,000

At least	But less than	Single	Married filing jointly *	Married filing separately	Head of a household
28,000	28,050	3,750	3,296	3,750	3,556
28,050	28,100	3,758	3,304	3,758	3,564
28,100	28,150	3,765	3,311	3,765	3,571
28,150	28,200	3,773	3,319	3,773	3,579
28,200	28,250	3,780	3,326	3,780	3,586
28,250	28,300	3,788	3,334	3,788	3,594
28,300	28,350	3,795	3,341	3,795	3,601
28,350	28,400	3,803	3,349	3,803	3,609
28,400	28,450	3,810	3,356	3,810	3,616
28,450	28,500	3,818	3,364	3,818	3,624
28,500	28,550	3,825	3,371	3,825	3,631
28,550	28,600	3,833	3,379	3,833	3,639
28,600	28,650	3,840	3,386	3,840	3,646
28,650	28,700	3,848	3,394	3,848	3,654
28,700	28,750	3,855	3,401	3,855	3,661
28,750	28,800	3,863	3,409	3,863	3,669
28,800	28,850	3,870	3,416	3,870	3,676
28,850	28,900	3,878	3,424	3,878	3,684
28,900	28,950	3,885	3,431	3,885	3,691
28,950	29,000	3,893	3,439	3,893	3,699

29,000

At least	But less than	Single	Married filing jointly *	Married filing separately	Head of a household
29,000	29,050	3,900	3,446	3,900	3,706
29,050	29,100	3,908	3,454	3,908	3,714
29,100	29,150	3,915	3,461	3,915	3,721
29,150	29,200	3,923	3,469	3,923	3,729
29,200	29,250	3,930	3,476	3,930	3,736
29,250	29,300	3,938	3,484	3,938	3,744
29,300	29,350	3,945	3,491	3,945	3,751
29,350	29,400	3,953	3,499	3,953	3,759
29,400	29,450	3,960	3,506	3,960	3,766
29,450	29,500	3,968	3,514	3,968	3,774
29,500	29,550	3,975	3,521	3,975	3,781
29,550	29,600	3,983	3,529	3,983	3,789
29,600	29,650	3,990	3,536	3,990	3,796
29,650	29,700	3,998	3,544	3,998	3,804
29,700	29,750	4,005	3,551	4,005	3,811
29,750	29,800	4,013	3,559	4,013	3,819
29,800	29,850	4,020	3,566	4,020	3,826
29,850	29,900	4,028	3,574	4,028	3,834
29,900	29,950	4,035	3,581	4,035	3,841
29,950	30,000	4,043	3,589	4,043	3,849

* This column must also be used by a qualifying widow(er).

(Continued)

Need more information or forms? Visit IRS.gov.

If line 43 (taxable income) is—		And you are—			
At least	But less than	Single	Married filing jointly *	Married filing separately	Head of a household
			Your tax is—		

30,000

At least	But less than	Single	Married filing jointly *	Married filing separately	Head of a household
30,000	30,050	4,050	3,596	4,050	3,856
30,050	30,100	4,058	3,604	4,058	3,864
30,100	30,150	4,065	3,611	4,065	3,871
30,150	30,200	4,073	3,619	4,073	3,879
30,200	30,250	4,080	3,626	4,080	3,886
30,250	30,300	4,088	3,634	4,088	3,894
30,300	30,350	4,095	3,641	4,095	3,901
30,350	30,400	4,103	3,649	4,103	3,909
30,400	30,450	4,110	3,656	4,110	3,916
30,450	30,500	4,118	3,664	4,118	3,924
30,500	30,550	4,125	3,671	4,125	3,931
30,550	30,600	4,133	3,679	4,133	3,939
30,600	30,650	4,140	3,686	4,140	3,946
30,650	30,700	4,148	3,694	4,148	3,954
30,700	30,750	4,155	3,701	4,155	3,961
30,750	30,800	4,163	3,709	4,163	3,969
30,800	30,850	4,170	3,716	4,170	3,976
30,850	30,900	4,178	3,724	4,178	3,984
30,900	30,950	4,185	3,731	4,185	3,991
30,950	31,000	4,193	3,739	4,193	3,999

31,000

At least	But less than	Single	Married filing jointly *	Married filing separately	Head of a household
31,000	31,050	4,200	3,746	4,200	4,006
31,050	31,100	4,208	3,754	4,208	4,014
31,100	31,150	4,215	3,761	4,215	4,021
31,150	31,200	4,223	3,769	4,223	4,029
31,200	31,250	4,230	3,776	4,230	4,036
31,250	31,300	4,238	3,784	4,238	4,044
31,300	31,350	4,245	3,791	4,245	4,051
31,350	31,400	4,253	3,799	4,253	4,059
31,400	31,450	4,260	3,806	4,260	4,066
31,450	31,500	4,268	3,814	4,268	4,074
31,500	31,550	4,275	3,821	4,275	4,081
31,550	31,600	4,283	3,829	4,283	4,089
31,600	31,650	4,290	3,836	4,290	4,096
31,650	31,700	4,298	3,844	4,298	4,104
31,700	31,750	4,305	3,851	4,305	4,111
31,750	31,800	4,313	3,859	4,313	4,119
31,800	31,850	4,320	3,866	4,320	4,126
31,850	31,900	4,328	3,874	4,328	4,134
31,900	31,950	4,335	3,881	4,335	4,141
31,950	32,000	4,343	3,889	4,343	4,149

32,000

At least	But less than	Single	Married filing jointly *	Married filing separately	Head of a household
32,000	32,050	4,350	3,896	4,350	4,156
32,050	32,100	4,358	3,904	4,358	4,164
32,100	32,150	4,365	3,911	4,365	4,171
32,150	32,200	4,373	3,919	4,373	4,179
32,200	32,250	4,380	3,926	4,380	4,186
32,250	32,300	4,388	3,934	4,388	4,194
32,300	32,350	4,395	3,941	4,395	4,201
32,350	32,400	4,403	3,949	4,403	4,209
32,400	32,450	4,410	3,956	4,410	4,216
32,450	32,500	4,418	3,964	4,418	4,224
32,500	32,550	4,425	3,971	4,425	4,231
32,550	32,600	4,433	3,979	4,433	4,239
32,600	32,650	4,440	3,986	4,440	4,246
32,650	32,700	4,448	3,994	4,448	4,254
32,700	32,750	4,455	4,001	4,455	4,261
32,750	32,800	4,463	4,009	4,463	4,269
32,800	32,850	4,470	4,016	4,470	4,276
32,850	32,900	4,478	4,024	4,478	4,284
32,900	32,950	4,485	4,031	4,485	4,291
32,950	33,000	4,493	4,039	4,493	4,299

33,000

At least	But less than	Single	Married filing jointly *	Married filing separately	Head of a household
33,000	33,050	4,500	4,046	4,500	4,306
33,050	33,100	4,508	4,054	4,508	4,314
33,100	33,150	4,515	4,061	4,515	4,321
33,150	33,200	4,523	4,069	4,523	4,329
33,200	33,250	4,530	4,076	4,530	4,336
33,250	33,300	4,538	4,084	4,538	4,344
33,300	33,350	4,545	4,091	4,545	4,351
33,350	33,400	4,553	4,099	4,553	4,359
33,400	33,450	4,560	4,106	4,560	4,366
33,450	33,500	4,568	4,114	4,568	4,374
33,500	33,550	4,575	4,121	4,575	4,381
33,550	33,600	4,583	4,129	4,583	4,389
33,600	33,650	4,590	4,136	4,590	4,396
33,650	33,700	4,598	4,144	4,598	4,404
33,700	33,750	4,605	4,151	4,605	4,411
33,750	33,800	4,613	4,159	4,613	4,419
33,800	33,850	4,620	4,166	4,620	4,426
33,850	33,900	4,628	4,174	4,628	4,434
33,900	33,950	4,635	4,181	4,635	4,441
33,950	34,000	4,643	4,189	4,643	4,449

34,000

At least	But less than	Single	Married filing jointly *	Married filing separately	Head of a household
34,000	34,050	4,650	4,196	4,650	4,456
34,050	34,100	4,658	4,204	4,658	4,464
34,100	34,150	4,665	4,211	4,665	4,471
34,150	34,200	4,673	4,219	4,673	4,479
34,200	34,250	4,680	4,226	4,680	4,486
34,250	34,300	4,688	4,234	4,688	4,494
34,300	34,350	4,695	4,241	4,695	4,501
34,350	34,400	4,703	4,249	4,703	4,509
34,400	34,450	4,710	4,256	4,710	4,516
34,450	34,500	4,718	4,264	4,718	4,524
34,500	34,550	4,725	4,271	4,725	4,531
34,550	34,600	4,733	4,279	4,733	4,539
34,600	34,650	4,740	4,286	4,740	4,546
34,650	34,700	4,748	4,294	4,748	4,554
34,700	34,750	4,755	4,301	4,755	4,561
34,750	34,800	4,763	4,309	4,763	4,569
34,800	34,850	4,770	4,316	4,770	4,576
34,850	34,900	4,778	4,324	4,778	4,584
34,900	34,950	4,785	4,331	4,785	4,591
34,950	35,000	4,793	4,339	4,793	4,599

35,000

At least	But less than	Single	Married filing jointly *	Married filing separately	Head of a household
35,000	35,050	4,800	4,346	4,800	4,606
35,050	35,100	4,808	4,354	4,808	4,614
35,100	35,150	4,815	4,361	4,815	4,621
35,150	35,200	4,823	4,369	4,823	4,629
35,200	35,250	4,830	4,376	4,830	4,636
35,250	35,300	4,838	4,384	4,838	4,644
35,300	35,350	4,845	4,391	4,845	4,651
35,350	35,400	4,853	4,399	4,853	4,659
35,400	35,450	4,860	4,406	4,860	4,666
35,450	35,500	4,868	4,414	4,868	4,674
35,500	35,550	4,875	4,421	4,875	4,681
35,550	35,600	4,883	4,429	4,883	4,689
35,600	35,650	4,890	4,436	4,890	4,696
35,650	35,700	4,898	4,444	4,898	4,704
35,700	35,750	4,905	4,451	4,905	4,711
35,750	35,800	4,913	4,459	4,913	4,719
35,800	35,850	4,920	4,466	4,920	4,726
35,850	35,900	4,928	4,474	4,928	4,734
35,900	35,950	4,935	4,481	4,935	4,741
35,950	36,000	4,943	4,489	4,943	4,749

36,000

At least	But less than	Single	Married filing jointly *	Married filing separately	Head of a household
36,000	36,050	4,950	4,496	4,950	4,756
36,050	36,100	4,958	4,504	4,958	4,764
36,100	36,150	4,965	4,511	4,965	4,771
36,150	36,200	4,973	4,519	4,973	4,779
36,200	36,250	4,980	4,526	4,980	4,786
36,250	36,300	4,988	4,534	4,988	4,794
36,300	36,350	4,995	4,541	4,995	4,801
36,350	36,400	5,003	4,549	5,003	4,809
36,400	36,450	5,010	4,556	5,010	4,816
36,450	36,500	5,018	4,564	5,018	4,824
36,500	36,550	5,025	4,571	5,025	4,831
36,550	36,600	5,033	4,579	5,033	4,839
36,600	36,650	5,040	4,586	5,040	4,846
36,650	36,700	5,048	4,594	5,048	4,854
36,700	36,750	5,055	4,601	5,055	4,861
36,750	36,800	5,063	4,609	5,063	4,869
36,800	36,850	5,070	4,616	5,070	4,876
36,850	36,900	5,078	4,624	5,078	4,884
36,900	36,950	5,088	4,631	5,088	4,891
36,950	37,000	5,100	4,639	5,100	4,899

37,000

At least	But less than	Single	Married filing jointly *	Married filing separately	Head of a household
37,000	37,050	5,113	4,646	5,113	4,906
37,050	37,100	5,125	4,654	5,125	4,914
37,100	37,150	5,138	4,661	5,138	4,921
37,150	37,200	5,150	4,669	5,150	4,929
37,200	37,250	5,163	4,676	5,163	4,936
37,250	37,300	5,175	4,684	5,175	4,944
37,300	37,350	5,188	4,691	5,188	4,951
37,350	37,400	5,200	4,699	5,200	4,959
37,400	37,450	5,213	4,706	5,213	4,966
37,450	37,500	5,225	4,714	5,225	4,974
37,500	37,550	5,238	4,721	5,238	4,981
37,550	37,600	5,250	4,729	5,250	4,989
37,600	37,650	5,263	4,736	5,263	4,996
37,650	37,700	5,275	4,744	5,275	5,004
37,700	37,750	5,288	4,751	5,288	5,011
37,750	37,800	5,300	4,759	5,300	5,019
37,800	37,850	5,313	4,766	5,313	5,026
37,850	37,900	5,325	4,774	5,325	5,034
37,900	37,950	5,338	4,781	5,338	5,041
37,950	38,000	5,350	4,789	5,350	5,049

38,000

At least	But less than	Single	Married filing jointly *	Married filing separately	Head of a household
38,000	38,050	5,363	4,796	5,363	5,056
38,050	38,100	5,375	4,804	5,375	5,064
38,100	38,150	5,388	4,811	5,388	5,071
38,150	38,200	5,400	4,819	5,400	5,079
38,200	38,250	5,413	4,826	5,413	5,086
38,250	38,300	5,425	4,834	5,425	5,094
38,300	38,350	5,438	4,841	5,438	5,101
38,350	38,400	5,450	4,849	5,450	5,109
38,400	38,450	5,463	4,856	5,463	5,116
38,450	38,500	5,475	4,864	5,475	5,124
38,500	38,550	5,488	4,871	5,488	5,131
38,550	38,600	5,500	4,879	5,500	5,139
38,600	38,650	5,513	4,886	5,513	5,146
38,650	38,700	5,525	4,894	5,525	5,154
38,700	38,750	5,538	4,901	5,538	5,161
38,750	38,800	5,550	4,909	5,550	5,169
38,800	38,850	5,563	4,916	5,563	5,176
38,850	38,900	5,575	4,924	5,575	5,184
38,900	38,950	5,588	4,931	5,588	5,191
38,950	39,000	5,600	4,939	5,600	5,199

(Continued)

* This column must also be used by a qualifying widow(er).

If line 43 (taxable income) is—		And you are—			
At least	But less than	Single	Married filing jointly *	Married filing separately	Head of a household
		Your tax is—			

39,000

At least	But less than	Single	Married filing jointly *	Married filing separately	Head of a household
39,000	39,050	5,613	4,946	5,613	5,206
39,050	39,100	5,625	4,954	5,625	5,214
39,100	39,150	5,638	4,961	5,638	5,221
39,150	39,200	5,650	4,969	5,650	5,229
39,200	39,250	5,663	4,976	5,663	5,236
39,250	39,300	5,675	4,984	5,675	5,244
39,300	39,350	5,688	4,991	5,688	5,251
39,350	39,400	5,700	4,999	5,700	5,259
39,400	39,450	5,713	5,006	5,713	5,266
39,450	39,500	5,725	5,014	5,725	5,274
39,500	39,550	5,738	5,021	5,738	5,281
39,550	39,600	5,750	5,029	5,750	5,289
39,600	39,650	5,763	5,036	5,763	5,296
39,650	39,700	5,775	5,044	5,775	5,304
39,700	39,750	5,788	5,051	5,788	5,311
39,750	39,800	5,800	5,059	5,800	5,319
39,800	39,850	5,813	5,066	5,813	5,326
39,850	39,900	5,825	5,074	5,825	5,334
39,900	39,950	5,838	5,081	5,838	5,341
39,950	40,000	5,850	5,089	5,850	5,349

40,000

At least	But less than	Single	Married filing jointly *	Married filing separately	Head of a household
40,000	40,050	5,863	5,096	5,863	5,356
40,050	40,100	5,875	5,104	5,875	5,364
40,100	40,150	5,888	5,111	5,888	5,371
40,150	40,200	5,900	5,119	5,900	5,379
40,200	40,250	5,913	5,126	5,913	5,386
40,250	40,300	5,925	5,134	5,925	5,394
40,300	40,350	5,938	5,141	5,938	5,401
40,350	40,400	5,950	5,149	5,950	5,409
40,400	40,450	5,963	5,156	5,963	5,416
40,450	40,500	5,975	5,164	5,975	5,424
40,500	40,550	5,988	5,171	5,988	5,431
40,550	40,600	6,000	5,179	6,000	5,439
40,600	40,650	6,013	5,186	6,013	5,446
40,650	40,700	6,025	5,194	6,025	5,454
40,700	40,750	6,038	5,201	6,038	5,461
40,750	40,800	6,050	5,209	6,050	5,469
40,800	40,850	6,063	5,216	6,063	5,476
40,850	40,900	6,075	5,224	6,075	5,484
40,900	40,950	6,088	5,231	6,088	5,491
40,950	41,000	6,100	5,239	6,100	5,499

41,000

At least	But less than	Single	Married filing jointly *	Married filing separately	Head of a household
41,000	41,050	6,113	5,246	6,113	5,506
41,050	41,100	6,125	5,254	6,125	5,514
41,100	41,150	6,138	5,261	6,138	5,521
41,150	41,200	6,150	5,269	6,150	5,529
41,200	41,250	6,163	5,276	6,163	5,536
41,250	41,300	6,175	5,284	6,175	5,544
41,300	41,350	6,188	5,291	6,188	5,551
41,350	41,400	6,200	5,299	6,200	5,559
41,400	41,450	6,213	5,306	6,213	5,566
41,450	41,500	6,225	5,314	6,225	5,574
41,500	41,550	6,238	5,321	6,238	5,581
41,550	41,600	6,250	5,329	6,250	5,589
41,600	41,650	6,263	5,336	6,263	5,596
41,650	41,700	6,275	5,344	6,275	5,604
41,700	41,750	6,288	5,351	6,288	5,611
41,750	41,800	6,300	5,359	6,300	5,619
41,800	41,850	6,313	5,366	6,313	5,626
41,850	41,900	6,325	5,374	6,325	5,634
41,900	41,950	6,338	5,381	6,338	5,641
41,950	42,000	6,350	5,389	6,350	5,649

42,000

At least	But less than	Single	Married filing jointly *	Married filing separately	Head of a household
42,000	42,050	6,363	5,396	6,363	5,656
42,050	42,100	6,375	5,404	6,375	5,664
42,100	42,150	6,388	5,411	6,388	5,671
42,150	42,200	6,400	5,419	6,400	5,679
42,200	42,250	6,413	5,426	6,413	5,686
42,250	42,300	6,425	5,434	6,425	5,694
42,300	42,350	6,438	5,441	6,438	5,701
42,350	42,400	6,450	5,449	6,450	5,709
42,400	42,450	6,463	5,456	6,463	5,716
42,450	42,500	6,475	5,464	6,475	5,724
42,500	42,550	6,488	5,471	6,488	5,731
42,550	42,600	6,500	5,479	6,500	5,739
42,600	42,650	6,513	5,486	6,513	5,746
42,650	42,700	6,525	5,494	6,525	5,754
42,700	42,750	6,538	5,501	6,538	5,761
42,750	42,800	6,550	5,509	6,550	5,769
42,800	42,850	6,563	5,516	6,563	5,776
42,850	42,900	6,575	5,524	6,575	5,784
42,900	42,950	6,588	5,531	6,588	5,791
42,950	43,000	6,600	5,539	6,600	5,799

43,000

At least	But less than	Single	Married filing jointly *	Married filing separately	Head of a household
43,000	43,050	6,613	5,546	6,613	5,806
43,050	43,100	6,625	5,554	6,625	5,814
43,100	43,150	6,638	5,561	6,638	5,821
43,150	43,200	6,650	5,569	6,650	5,829
43,200	43,250	6,663	5,576	6,663	5,836
43,250	43,300	6,675	5,584	6,675	5,844
43,300	43,350	6,688	5,591	6,688	5,851
43,350	43,400	6,700	5,599	6,700	5,859
43,400	43,450	6,713	5,606	6,713	5,866
43,450	43,500	6,725	5,614	6,725	5,874
43,500	43,550	6,738	5,621	6,738	5,881
43,550	43,600	6,750	5,629	6,750	5,889
43,600	43,650	6,763	5,636	6,763	5,896
43,650	43,700	6,775	5,644	6,775	5,904
43,700	43,750	6,788	5,651	6,788	5,911
43,750	43,800	6,800	5,659	6,800	5,919
43,800	43,850	6,813	5,666	6,813	5,926
43,850	43,900	6,825	5,674	6,825	5,934
43,900	43,950	6,838	5,681	6,838	5,941
43,950	44,000	6,850	5,689	6,850	5,949

44,000

At least	But less than	Single	Married filing jointly *	Married filing separately	Head of a household
44,000	44,050	6,863	5,696	6,863	5,956
44,050	44,100	6,875	5,704	6,875	5,964
44,100	44,150	6,888	5,711	6,888	5,971
44,150	44,200	6,900	5,719	6,900	5,979
44,200	44,250	6,913	5,726	6,913	5,986
44,250	44,300	6,925	5,734	6,925	5,994
44,300	44,350	6,938	5,741	6,938	6,001
44,350	44,400	6,950	5,749	6,950	6,009
44,400	44,450	6,963	5,756	6,963	6,016
44,450	44,500	6,975	5,764	6,975	6,024
44,500	44,550	6,988	5,771	6,988	6,031
44,550	44,600	7,000	5,779	7,000	6,039
44,600	44,650	7,013	5,786	7,013	6,046
44,650	44,700	7,025	5,794	7,025	6,054
44,700	44,750	7,038	5,801	7,038	6,061
44,750	44,800	7,050	5,809	7,050	6,069
44,800	44,850	7,063	5,816	7,063	6,076
44,850	44,900	7,075	5,824	7,075	6,084
44,900	44,950	7,088	5,831	7,088	6,091
44,950	45,000	7,100	5,839	7,100	6,099

45,000

At least	But less than	Single	Married filing jointly *	Married filing separately	Head of a household
45,000	45,050	7,113	5,846	7,113	6,106
45,050	45,100	7,125	5,854	7,125	6,114
45,100	45,150	7,138	5,861	7,138	6,121
45,150	45,200	7,150	5,869	7,150	6,129
45,200	45,250	7,163	5,876	7,163	6,136
45,250	45,300	7,175	5,884	7,175	6,144
45,300	45,350	7,188	5,891	7,188	6,151
45,350	45,400	7,200	5,899	7,200	6,159
45,400	45,450	7,213	5,906	7,213	6,166
45,450	45,500	7,225	5,914	7,225	6,174
45,500	45,550	7,238	5,921	7,238	6,181
45,550	45,600	7,250	5,929	7,250	6,189
45,600	45,650	7,263	5,936	7,263	6,196
45,650	45,700	7,275	5,944	7,275	6,204
45,700	45,750	7,288	5,951	7,288	6,211
45,750	45,800	7,300	5,959	7,300	6,219
45,800	45,850	7,313	5,966	7,313	6,226
45,850	45,900	7,325	5,974	7,325	6,234
45,900	45,950	7,338	5,981	7,338	6,241
45,950	46,000	7,350	5,989	7,350	6,249

46,000

At least	But less than	Single	Married filing jointly *	Married filing separately	Head of a household
46,000	46,050	7,363	5,996	7,363	6,256
46,050	46,100	7,375	6,004	7,375	6,264
46,100	46,150	7,388	6,011	7,388	6,271
46,150	46,200	7,400	6,019	7,400	6,279
46,200	46,250	7,413	6,026	7,413	6,286
46,250	46,300	7,425	6,034	7,425	6,294
46,300	46,350	7,438	6,041	7,438	6,301
46,350	46,400	7,450	6,049	7,450	6,309
46,400	46,450	7,463	6,056	7,463	6,316
46,450	46,500	7,475	6,064	7,475	6,324
46,500	46,550	7,488	6,071	7,488	6,331
46,550	46,600	7,500	6,079	7,500	6,339
46,600	46,650	7,513	6,086	7,513	6,346
46,650	46,700	7,525	6,094	7,525	6,354
46,700	46,750	7,538	6,101	7,538	6,361
46,750	46,800	7,550	6,109	7,550	6,369
46,800	46,850	7,563	6,116	7,563	6,376
46,850	46,900	7,575	6,124	7,575	6,384
46,900	46,950	7,588	6,131	7,588	6,391
46,950	47,000	7,600	6,139	7,600	6,399

47,000

At least	But less than	Single	Married filing jointly *	Married filing separately	Head of a household
47,000	47,050	7,613	6,146	7,613	6,406
47,050	47,100	7,625	6,154	7,625	6,414
47,100	47,150	7,638	6,161	7,638	6,421
47,150	47,200	7,650	6,169	7,650	6,429
47,200	47,250	7,663	6,176	7,663	6,436
47,250	47,300	7,675	6,184	7,675	6,444
47,300	47,350	7,688	6,191	7,688	6,451
47,350	47,400	7,700	6,199	7,700	6,459
47,400	47,450	7,713	6,206	7,713	6,466
47,450	47,500	7,725	6,214	7,725	6,474
47,500	47,550	7,738	6,221	7,738	6,481
47,550	47,600	7,750	6,229	7,750	6,489
47,600	47,650	7,763	6,236	7,763	6,496
47,650	47,700	7,775	6,244	7,775	6,504
47,700	47,750	7,788	6,251	7,788	6,511
47,750	47,800	7,800	6,259	7,800	6,519
47,800	47,850	7,813	6,266	7,813	6,526
47,850	47,900	7,825	6,274	7,825	6,534
47,900	47,950	7,838	6,281	7,838	6,541
47,950	48,000	7,850	6,289	7,850	6,549

(Continued)

* This column must also be used by a qualifying widow(er).

Need more information or forms? Visit IRS.gov.

If line 43 (taxable income) is—		And you are—			
At least	But less than	Single	Married filing jointly *	Married filing separately	Head of a household
		Your tax is—			

48,000

At least	But less than	Single	Married filing jointly *	Married filing separately	Head of a household
48,000	48,050	7,863	6,296	7,863	6,556
48,050	48,100	7,875	6,304	7,875	6,564
48,100	48,150	7,888	6,311	7,888	6,571
48,150	48,200	7,900	6,319	7,900	6,579
48,200	48,250	7,913	6,326	7,913	6,586
48,250	48,300	7,925	6,334	7,925	6,594
48,300	48,350	7,938	6,341	7,938	6,601
48,350	48,400	7,950	6,349	7,950	6,609
48,400	48,450	7,963	6,356	7,963	6,616
48,450	48,500	7,975	6,364	7,975	6,624
48,500	48,550	7,988	6,371	7,988	6,631
48,550	48,600	8,000	6,379	8,000	6,639
48,600	48,650	8,013	6,386	8,013	6,646
48,650	48,700	8,025	6,394	8,025	6,654
48,700	48,750	8,038	6,401	8,038	6,661
48,750	48,800	8,050	6,409	8,050	6,669
48,800	48,850	8,063	6,416	8,063	6,676
48,850	48,900	8,075	6,424	8,075	6,684
48,900	48,950	8,088	6,431	8,088	6,691
48,950	49,000	8,100	6,439	8,100	6,699

49,000

At least	But less than	Single	Married filing jointly *	Married filing separately	Head of a household
49,000	49,050	8,113	6,446	8,113	6,706
49,050	49,100	8,125	6,454	8,125	6,714
49,100	49,150	8,138	6,461	8,138	6,721
49,150	49,200	8,150	6,469	8,150	6,729
49,200	49,250	8,163	6,476	8,163	6,736
49,250	49,300	8,175	6,484	8,175	6,744
49,300	49,350	8,188	6,491	8,188	6,751
49,350	49,400	8,200	6,499	8,200	6,759
49,400	49,450	8,213	6,506	8,213	6,769
49,450	49,500	8,225	6,514	8,225	6,781
49,500	49,550	8,238	6,521	8,238	6,794
49,550	49,600	8,250	6,529	8,250	6,806
49,600	49,650	8,263	6,536	8,263	6,819
49,650	49,700	8,275	6,544	8,275	6,831
49,700	49,750	8,288	6,551	8,288	6,844
49,750	49,800	8,300	6,559	8,300	6,856
49,800	49,850	8,313	6,566	8,313	6,869
49,850	49,900	8,325	6,574	8,325	6,881
49,900	49,950	8,338	6,581	8,338	6,894
49,950	50,000	8,350	6,589	8,350	6,906

50,000

At least	But less than	Single	Married filing jointly *	Married filing separately	Head of a household
50,000	50,050	8,363	6,596	8,363	6,919
50,050	50,100	8,375	6,604	8,375	6,931
50,100	50,150	8,388	6,611	8,388	6,944
50,150	50,200	8,400	6,619	8,400	6,956
50,200	50,250	8,413	6,626	8,413	6,969
50,250	50,300	8,425	6,634	8,425	6,981
50,300	50,350	8,438	6,641	8,438	6,994
50,350	50,400	8,450	6,649	8,450	7,006
50,400	50,450	8,463	6,656	8,463	7,019
50,450	50,500	8,475	6,664	8,475	7,031
50,500	50,550	8,488	6,671	8,488	7,044
50,550	50,600	8,500	6,679	8,500	7,056
50,600	50,650	8,513	6,686	8,513	7,069
50,650	50,700	8,525	6,694	8,525	7,081
50,700	50,750	8,538	6,701	8,538	7,094
50,750	50,800	8,550	6,709	8,550	7,106
50,800	50,850	8,563	6,716	8,563	7,119
50,850	50,900	8,575	6,724	8,575	7,131
50,900	50,950	8,588	6,731	8,588	7,144
50,950	51,000	8,600	6,739	8,600	7,156

If line 43 (taxable income) is—		And you are—			
At least	But less than	Single	Married filing jointly *	Married filing separately	Head of a household
		Your tax is—			

51,000

At least	But less than	Single	Married filing jointly *	Married filing separately	Head of a household
51,000	51,050	8,613	6,746	8,613	7,169
51,050	51,100	8,625	6,754	8,625	7,181
51,100	51,150	8,638	6,761	8,638	7,194
51,150	51,200	8,650	6,769	8,650	7,206
51,200	51,250	8,663	6,776	8,663	7,219
51,250	51,300	8,675	6,784	8,675	7,231
51,300	51,350	8,688	6,791	8,688	7,244
51,350	51,400	8,700	6,799	8,700	7,256
51,400	51,450	8,713	6,806	8,713	7,269
51,450	51,500	8,725	6,814	8,725	7,281
51,500	51,550	8,738	6,821	8,738	7,294
51,550	51,600	8,750	6,829	8,750	7,306
51,600	51,650	8,763	6,836	8,763	7,319
51,650	51,700	8,775	6,844	8,775	7,331
51,700	51,750	8,788	6,851	8,788	7,344
51,750	51,800	8,800	6,859	8,800	7,356
51,800	51,850	8,813	6,866	8,813	7,369
51,850	51,900	8,825	6,874	8,825	7,381
51,900	51,950	8,838	6,881	8,838	7,394
51,950	52,000	8,850	6,889	8,850	7,406

52,000

At least	But less than	Single	Married filing jointly *	Married filing separately	Head of a household
52,000	52,050	8,863	6,896	8,863	7,419
52,050	52,100	8,875	6,904	8,875	7,431
52,100	52,150	8,888	6,911	8,888	7,444
52,150	52,200	8,900	6,919	8,900	7,456
52,200	52,250	8,913	6,926	8,913	7,469
52,250	52,300	8,925	6,934	8,925	7,481
52,300	52,350	8,938	6,941	8,938	7,494
52,350	52,400	8,950	6,949	8,950	7,506
52,400	52,450	8,963	6,956	8,963	7,519
52,450	52,500	8,975	6,964	8,975	7,531
52,500	52,550	8,988	6,971	8,988	7,544
52,550	52,600	9,000	6,979	9,000	7,556
52,600	52,650	9,013	6,986	9,013	7,569
52,650	52,700	9,025	6,994	9,025	7,581
52,700	52,750	9,038	7,001	9,038	7,594
52,750	52,800	9,050	7,009	9,050	7,606
52,800	52,850	9,063	7,016	9,063	7,619
52,850	52,900	9,075	7,024	9,075	7,631
52,900	52,950	9,088	7,031	9,088	7,644
52,950	53,000	9,100	7,039	9,100	7,656

53,000

At least	But less than	Single	Married filing jointly *	Married filing separately	Head of a household
53,000	53,050	9,113	7,046	9,113	7,669
53,050	53,100	9,125	7,054	9,125	7,681
53,100	53,150	9,138	7,061	9,138	7,694
53,150	53,200	9,150	7,069	9,150	7,706
53,200	53,250	9,163	7,076	9,163	7,719
53,250	53,300	9,175	7,084	9,175	7,731
53,300	53,350	9,188	7,091	9,188	7,744
53,350	53,400	9,200	7,099	9,200	7,756
53,400	53,450	9,213	7,106	9,213	7,769
53,450	53,500	9,225	7,114	9,225	7,781
53,500	53,550	9,238	7,121	9,238	7,794
53,550	53,600	9,250	7,129	9,250	7,806
53,600	53,650	9,263	7,136	9,263	7,819
53,650	53,700	9,275	7,144	9,275	7,831
53,700	53,750	9,288	7,151	9,288	7,844
53,750	53,800	9,300	7,159	9,300	7,856
53,800	53,850	9,313	7,166	9,313	7,869
53,850	53,900	9,325	7,174	9,325	7,881
53,900	53,950	9,338	7,181	9,338	7,894
53,950	54,000	9,350	7,189	9,350	7,906

If line 43 (taxable income) is—		And you are—			
At least	But less than	Single	Married filing jointly *	Married filing separately	Head of a household
		Your tax is—			

54,000

At least	But less than	Single	Married filing jointly *	Married filing separately	Head of a household
54,000	54,050	9,363	7,196	9,363	7,919
54,050	54,100	9,375	7,204	9,375	7,931
54,100	54,150	9,388	7,211	9,388	7,944
54,150	54,200	9,400	7,219	9,400	7,956
54,200	54,250	9,413	7,226	9,413	7,969
54,250	54,300	9,425	7,234	9,425	7,981
54,300	54,350	9,438	7,241	9,438	7,994
54,350	54,400	9,450	7,249	9,450	8,006
54,400	54,450	9,463	7,256	9,463	8,019
54,450	54,500	9,475	7,264	9,475	8,031
54,500	54,550	9,488	7,271	9,488	8,044
54,550	54,600	9,500	7,279	9,500	8,056
54,600	54,650	9,513	7,286	9,513	8,069
54,650	54,700	9,525	7,294	9,525	8,081
54,700	54,750	9,538	7,301	9,538	8,094
54,750	54,800	9,550	7,309	9,550	8,106
54,800	54,850	9,563	7,316	9,563	8,119
54,850	54,900	9,575	7,324	9,575	8,131
54,900	54,950	9,588	7,331	9,588	8,144
54,950	55,000	9,600	7,339	9,600	8,156

55,000

At least	But less than	Single	Married filing jointly *	Married filing separately	Head of a household
55,000	55,050	9,613	7,346	9,613	8,169
55,050	55,100	9,625	7,354	9,625	8,181
55,100	55,150	9,638	7,361	9,638	8,194
55,150	55,200	9,650	7,369	9,650	8,206
55,200	55,250	9,663	7,376	9,663	8,219
55,250	55,300	9,675	7,384	9,675	8,231
55,300	55,350	9,688	7,391	9,688	8,244
55,350	55,400	9,700	7,399	9,700	8,256
55,400	55,450	9,713	7,406	9,713	8,269
55,450	55,500	9,725	7,414	9,725	8,281
55,500	55,550	9,738	7,421	9,738	8,294
55,550	55,600	9,750	7,429	9,750	8,306
55,600	55,650	9,763	7,436	9,763	8,319
55,650	55,700	9,775	7,444	9,775	8,331
55,700	55,750	9,788	7,451	9,788	8,344
55,750	55,800	9,800	7,459	9,800	8,356
55,800	55,850	9,813	7,466	9,813	8,369
55,850	55,900	9,825	7,474	9,825	8,381
55,900	55,950	9,838	7,481	9,838	8,394
55,950	56,000	9,850	7,489	9,850	8,406

56,000

At least	But less than	Single	Married filing jointly *	Married filing separately	Head of a household
56,000	56,050	9,863	7,496	9,863	8,419
56,050	56,100	9,875	7,504	9,875	8,431
56,100	56,150	9,888	7,511	9,888	8,444
56,150	56,200	9,900	7,519	9,900	8,456
56,200	56,250	9,913	7,526	9,913	8,469
56,250	56,300	9,925	7,534	9,925	8,481
56,300	56,350	9,938	7,541	9,938	8,494
56,350	56,400	9,950	7,549	9,950	8,506
56,400	56,450	9,963	7,556	9,963	8,519
56,450	56,500	9,975	7,564	9,975	8,531
56,500	56,550	9,988	7,571	9,988	8,544
56,550	56,600	10,000	7,579	10,000	8,556
56,600	56,650	10,013	7,586	10,013	8,569
56,650	56,700	10,025	7,594	10,025	8,581
56,700	56,750	10,038	7,601	10,038	8,594
56,750	56,800	10,050	7,609	10,050	8,606
56,800	56,850	10,063	7,616	10,063	8,619
56,850	56,900	10,075	7,624	10,075	8,631
56,900	56,950	10,088	7,631	10,088	8,644
56,950	57,000	10,100	7,639	10,100	8,656

(Continued)

* This column must also be used by a qualifying widow(er).

Need more information or forms? Visit IRS.gov.

57,000

If line 43 (taxable income) is— At least	But less than	Single	Married filing jointly *	Married filing sepa-rately	Head of a house-hold
57,000	57,050	10,113	7,646	10,113	8,669
57,050	57,100	10,125	7,654	10,125	8,681
57,100	57,150	10,138	7,661	10,138	8,694
57,150	57,200	10,150	7,669	10,150	8,706
57,200	57,250	10,163	7,676	10,163	8,719
57,250	57,300	10,175	7,684	10,175	8,731
57,300	57,350	10,188	7,691	10,188	8,744
57,350	57,400	10,200	7,699	10,200	8,756
57,400	57,450	10,213	7,706	10,213	8,769
57,450	57,500	10,225	7,714	10,225	8,781
57,500	57,550	10,238	7,721	10,238	8,794
57,550	57,600	10,250	7,729	10,250	8,806
57,600	57,650	10,263	7,736	10,263	8,819
57,650	57,700	10,275	7,744	10,275	8,831
57,700	57,750	10,288	7,751	10,288	8,844
57,750	57,800	10,300	7,759	10,300	8,856
57,800	57,850	10,313	7,766	10,313	8,869
57,850	57,900	10,325	7,774	10,325	8,881
57,900	57,950	10,338	7,781	10,338	8,894
57,950	58,000	10,350	7,789	10,350	8,906

58,000

At least	But less than	Single	Married filing jointly *	Married filing sepa-rately	Head of a house-hold
58,000	58,050	10,363	7,796	10,363	8,919
58,050	58,100	10,375	7,804	10,375	8,931
58,100	58,150	10,388	7,811	10,388	8,944
58,150	58,200	10,400	7,819	10,400	8,956
58,200	58,250	10,413	7,826	10,413	8,969
58,250	58,300	10,425	7,834	10,425	8,981
58,300	58,350	10,438	7,841	10,438	8,994
58,350	58,400	10,450	7,849	10,450	9,006
58,400	58,450	10,463	7,856	10,463	9,019
58,450	58,500	10,475	7,864	10,475	9,031
58,500	58,550	10,488	7,871	10,488	9,044
58,550	58,600	10,500	7,879	10,500	9,056
58,600	58,650	10,513	7,886	10,513	9,069
58,650	58,700	10,525	7,894	10,525	9,081
58,700	58,750	10,538	7,901	10,538	9,094
58,750	58,800	10,550	7,909	10,550	9,106
58,800	58,850	10,563	7,916	10,563	9,119
58,850	58,900	10,575	7,924	10,575	9,131
58,900	58,950	10,588	7,931	10,588	9,144
58,950	59,000	10,600	7,939	10,600	9,156

59,000

At least	But less than	Single	Married filing jointly *	Married filing sepa-rately	Head of a house-hold
59,000	59,050	10,613	7,946	10,613	9,169
59,050	59,100	10,625	7,954	10,625	9,181
59,100	59,150	10,638	7,961	10,638	9,194
59,150	59,200	10,650	7,969	10,650	9,206
59,200	59,250	10,663	7,976	10,663	9,219
59,250	59,300	10,675	7,984	10,675	9,231
59,300	59,350	10,688	7,991	10,688	9,244
59,350	59,400	10,700	7,999	10,700	9,256
59,400	59,450	10,713	8,006	10,713	9,269
59,450	59,500	10,725	8,014	10,725	9,281
59,500	59,550	10,738	8,021	10,738	9,294
59,550	59,600	10,750	8,029	10,750	9,306
59,600	59,650	10,763	8,036	10,763	9,319
59,650	59,700	10,775	8,044	10,775	9,331
59,700	59,750	10,788	8,051	10,788	9,344
59,750	59,800	10,800	8,059	10,800	9,356
59,800	59,850	10,813	8,066	10,813	9,369
59,850	59,900	10,825	8,074	10,825	9,381
59,900	59,950	10,838	8,081	10,838	9,394
59,950	60,000	10,850	8,089	10,850	9,406

60,000

If line 43 (taxable income) is— At least	But less than	Single	Married filing jointly *	Married filing sepa-rately	Head of a house-hold
60,000	60,050	10,863	8,096	10,863	9,419
60,050	60,100	10,875	8,104	10,875	9,431
60,100	60,150	10,888	8,111	10,888	9,444
60,150	60,200	10,900	8,119	10,900	9,456
60,200	60,250	10,913	8,126	10,913	9,469
60,250	60,300	10,925	8,134	10,925	9,481
60,300	60,350	10,938	8,141	10,938	9,494
60,350	60,400	10,950	8,149	10,950	9,506
60,400	60,450	10,963	8,156	10,963	9,519
60,450	60,500	10,975	8,164	10,975	9,531
60,500	60,550	10,988	8,171	10,988	9,544
60,550	60,600	11,000	8,179	11,000	9,556
60,600	60,650	11,013	8,186	11,013	9,569
60,650	60,700	11,025	8,194	11,025	9,581
60,700	60,750	11,038	8,201	11,038	9,594
60,750	60,800	11,050	8,209	11,050	9,606
60,800	60,850	11,063	8,216	11,063	9,619
60,850	60,900	11,075	8,224	11,075	9,631
60,900	60,950	11,088	8,231	11,088	9,644
60,950	61,000	11,100	8,239	11,100	9,656

61,000

At least	But less than	Single	Married filing jointly *	Married filing sepa-rately	Head of a house-hold
61,000	61,050	11,113	8,246	11,113	9,669
61,050	61,100	11,125	8,254	11,125	9,681
61,100	61,150	11,138	8,261	11,138	9,694
61,150	61,200	11,150	8,269	11,150	9,706
61,200	61,250	11,163	8,276	11,163	9,719
61,250	61,300	11,175	8,284	11,175	9,731
61,300	61,350	11,188	8,291	11,188	9,744
61,350	61,400	11,200	8,299	11,200	9,756
61,400	61,450	11,213	8,306	11,213	9,769
61,450	61,500	11,225	8,314	11,225	9,781
61,500	61,550	11,238	8,321	11,238	9,794
61,550	61,600	11,250	8,329	11,250	9,806
61,600	61,650	11,263	8,336	11,263	9,819
61,650	61,700	11,275	8,344	11,275	9,831
61,700	61,750	11,288	8,351	11,288	9,844
61,750	61,800	11,300	8,359	11,300	9,856
61,800	61,850	11,313	8,366	11,313	9,869
61,850	61,900	11,325	8,374	11,325	9,881
61,900	61,950	11,338	8,381	11,338	9,894
61,950	62,000	11,350	8,389	11,350	9,906

62,000

At least	But less than	Single	Married filing jointly *	Married filing sepa-rately	Head of a house-hold
62,000	62,050	11,363	8,396	11,363	9,919
62,050	62,100	11,375	8,404	11,375	9,931
62,100	62,150	11,388	8,411	11,388	9,944
62,150	62,200	11,400	8,419	11,400	9,956
62,200	62,250	11,413	8,426	11,413	9,969
62,250	62,300	11,425	8,434	11,425	9,981
62,300	62,350	11,438	8,441	11,438	9,994
62,350	62,400	11,450	8,449	11,450	10,006
62,400	62,450	11,463	8,456	11,463	10,019
62,450	62,500	11,475	8,464	11,475	10,031
62,500	62,550	11,488	8,471	11,488	10,044
62,550	62,600	11,500	8,479	11,500	10,056
62,600	62,650	11,513	8,486	11,513	10,069
62,650	62,700	11,525	8,494	11,525	10,081
62,700	62,750	11,538	8,501	11,538	10,094
62,750	62,800	11,550	8,509	11,550	10,106
62,800	62,850	11,563	8,516	11,563	10,119
62,850	62,900	11,575	8,524	11,575	10,131
62,900	62,950	11,588	8,531	11,588	10,144
62,950	63,000	11,600	8,539	11,600	10,156

63,000

If line 43 (taxable income) is— At least	But less than	Single	Married filing jointly *	Married filing sepa-rately	Head of a house-hold
63,000	63,050	11,613	8,546	11,613	10,169
63,050	63,100	11,625	8,554	11,625	10,181
63,100	63,150	11,638	8,561	11,638	10,194
63,150	63,200	11,650	8,569	11,650	10,206
63,200	63,250	11,663	8,576	11,663	10,219
63,250	63,300	11,675	8,584	11,675	10,231
63,300	63,350	11,688	8,591	11,688	10,244
63,350	63,400	11,700	8,599	11,700	10,256
63,400	63,450	11,713	8,606	11,713	10,269
63,450	63,500	11,725	8,614	11,725	10,281
63,500	63,550	11,738	8,621	11,738	10,294
63,550	63,600	11,750	8,629	11,750	10,306
63,600	63,650	11,763	8,636	11,763	10,319
63,650	63,700	11,775	8,644	11,775	10,331
63,700	63,750	11,788	8,651	11,788	10,344
63,750	63,800	11,800	8,659	11,800	10,356
63,800	63,850	11,813	8,666	11,813	10,369
63,850	63,900	11,825	8,674	11,825	10,381
63,900	63,950	11,838	8,681	11,838	10,394
63,950	64,000	11,850	8,689	11,850	10,406

64,000

At least	But less than	Single	Married filing jointly *	Married filing sepa-rately	Head of a house-hold
64,000	64,050	11,863	8,696	11,863	10,419
64,050	64,100	11,875	8,704	11,875	10,431
64,100	64,150	11,888	8,711	11,888	10,444
64,150	64,200	11,900	8,719	11,900	10,456
64,200	64,250	11,913	8,726	11,913	10,469
64,250	64,300	11,925	8,734	11,925	10,481
64,300	64,350	11,938	8,741	11,938	10,494
64,350	64,400	11,950	8,749	11,950	10,506
64,400	64,450	11,963	8,756	11,963	10,519
64,450	64,500	11,975	8,764	11,975	10,531
64,500	64,550	11,988	8,771	11,988	10,544
64,550	64,600	12,000	8,779	12,000	10,556
64,600	64,650	12,013	8,786	12,013	10,569
64,650	64,700	12,025	8,794	12,025	10,581
64,700	64,750	12,038	8,801	12,038	10,594
64,750	64,800	12,050	8,809	12,050	10,606
64,800	64,850	12,063	8,816	12,063	10,619
64,850	64,900	12,075	8,824	12,075	10,631
64,900	64,950	12,088	8,831	12,088	10,644
64,950	65,000	12,100	8,839	12,100	10,656

65,000

At least	But less than	Single	Married filing jointly *	Married filing sepa-rately	Head of a house-hold
65,000	65,050	12,113	8,846	12,113	10,669
65,050	65,100	12,125	8,854	12,125	10,681
65,100	65,150	12,138	8,861	12,138	10,694
65,150	65,200	12,150	8,869	12,150	10,706
65,200	65,250	12,163	8,876	12,163	10,719
65,250	65,300	12,175	8,884	12,175	10,731
65,300	65,350	12,188	8,891	12,188	10,744
65,350	65,400	12,200	8,899	12,200	10,756
65,400	65,450	12,213	8,906	12,213	10,769
65,450	65,500	12,225	8,914	12,225	10,781
65,500	65,550	12,238	8,921	12,238	10,794
65,550	65,600	12,250	8,929	12,250	10,806
65,600	65,650	12,263	8,936	12,263	10,819
65,650	65,700	12,275	8,944	12,275	10,831
65,700	65,750	12,288	8,951	12,288	10,844
65,750	65,800	12,300	8,959	12,300	10,856
65,800	65,850	12,313	8,966	12,313	10,869
65,850	65,900	12,325	8,974	12,325	10,881
65,900	65,950	12,338	8,981	12,338	10,894
65,950	66,000	12,350	8,989	12,350	10,906

* This column must also be used by a qualifying widow(er).

(Continued)

Need more information or forms? Visit IRS.gov.

If line 43 (taxable income) is—		And you are—			
At least	But less than	Single	Married filing jointly *	Married filing sepa-rately	Head of a house-hold
		Your tax is—			
66,000					
66,000	66,050	12,363	8,996	12,363	10,919
66,050	66,100	12,375	9,004	12,375	10,931
66,100	66,150	12,388	9,011	12,388	10,944
66,150	66,200	12,400	9,019	12,400	10,956
66,200	66,250	12,413	9,026	12,413	10,969
66,250	66,300	12,425	9,034	12,425	10,981
66,300	66,350	12,438	9,041	12,438	10,994
66,350	66,400	12,450	9,049	12,450	11,006
66,400	66,450	12,463	9,056	12,463	11,019
66,450	66,500	12,475	9,064	12,475	11,031
66,500	66,550	12,488	9,071	12,488	11,044
66,550	66,600	12,500	9,079	12,500	11,056
66,600	66,650	12,513	9,086	12,513	11,069
66,650	66,700	12,525	9,094	12,525	11,081
66,700	66,750	12,538	9,101	12,538	11,094
66,750	66,800	12,550	9,109	12,550	11,106
66,800	66,850	12,563	9,116	12,563	11,119
66,850	66,900	12,575	9,124	12,575	11,131
66,900	66,950	12,588	9,131	12,588	11,144
66,950	67,000	12,600	9,139	12,600	11,156
67,000					
67,000	67,050	12,613	9,146	12,613	11,169
67,050	67,100	12,625	9,154	12,625	11,181
67,100	67,150	12,638	9,161	12,638	11,194
67,150	67,200	12,650	9,169	12,650	11,206
67,200	67,250	12,663	9,176	12,663	11,219
67,250	67,300	12,675	9,184	12,675	11,231
67,300	67,350	12,688	9,191	12,688	11,244
67,350	67,400	12,700	9,199	12,700	11,256
67,400	67,450	12,713	9,206	12,713	11,269
67,450	67,500	12,725	9,214	12,725	11,281
67,500	67,550	12,738	9,221	12,738	11,294
67,550	67,600	12,750	9,229	12,750	11,306
67,600	67,650	12,763	9,236	12,763	11,319
67,650	67,700	12,775	9,244	12,775	11,331
67,700	67,750	12,788	9,251	12,788	11,344
67,750	67,800	12,800	9,259	12,800	11,356
67,800	67,850	12,813	9,266	12,813	11,369
67,850	67,900	12,825	9,274	12,825	11,381
67,900	67,950	12,838	9,281	12,838	11,394
67,950	68,000	12,850	9,289	12,850	11,406
68,000					
68,000	68,050	12,863	9,296	12,863	11,419
68,050	68,100	12,875	9,304	12,875	11,431
68,100	68,150	12,888	9,311	12,888	11,444
68,150	68,200	12,900	9,319	12,900	11,456
68,200	68,250	12,913	9,326	12,913	11,469
68,250	68,300	12,925	9,334	12,925	11,481
68,300	68,350	12,938	9,341	12,938	11,494
68,350	68,400	12,950	9,349	12,950	11,506
68,400	68,450	12,963	9,356	12,963	11,519
68,450	68,500	12,975	9,364	12,975	11,531
68,500	68,550	12,988	9,371	12,988	11,544
68,550	68,600	13,000	9,379	13,000	11,556
68,600	68,650	13,013	9,386	13,013	11,569
68,650	68,700	13,025	9,394	13,025	11,581
68,700	68,750	13,038	9,401	13,038	11,594
68,750	68,800	13,050	9,409	13,050	11,606
68,800	68,850	13,063	9,416	13,063	11,619
68,850	68,900	13,075	9,424	13,075	11,631
68,900	68,950	13,088	9,431	13,088	11,644
68,950	69,000	13,100	9,439	13,100	11,656

If line 43 (taxable income) is—		And you are—			
At least	But less than	Single	Married filing jointly *	Married filing sepa-rately	Head of a house-hold
		Your tax is—			
69,000					
69,000	69,050	13,113	9,446	13,113	11,669
69,050	69,100	13,125	9,454	13,125	11,681
69,100	69,150	13,138	9,461	13,138	11,694
69,150	69,200	13,150	9,469	13,150	11,706
69,200	69,250	13,163	9,476	13,163	11,719
69,250	69,300	13,175	9,484	13,175	11,731
69,300	69,350	13,188	9,491	13,188	11,744
69,350	69,400	13,200	9,499	13,200	11,756
69,400	69,450	13,213	9,506	13,213	11,769
69,450	69,500	13,225	9,514	13,225	11,781
69,500	69,550	13,238	9,521	13,238	11,794
69,550	69,600	13,250	9,529	13,250	11,806
69,600	69,650	13,263	9,536	13,263	11,819
69,650	69,700	13,275	9,544	13,275	11,831
69,700	69,750	13,288	9,551	13,288	11,844
69,750	69,800	13,300	9,559	13,300	11,856
69,800	69,850	13,313	9,566	13,313	11,869
69,850	69,900	13,325	9,574	13,325	11,881
69,900	69,950	13,338	9,581	13,338	11,894
69,950	70,000	13,350	9,589	13,350	11,906
70,000					
70,000	70,050	13,363	9,596	13,363	11,919
70,050	70,100	13,375	9,604	13,375	11,931
70,100	70,150	13,388	9,611	13,388	11,944
70,150	70,200	13,400	9,619	13,400	11,956
70,200	70,250	13,413	9,626	13,413	11,969
70,250	70,300	13,425	9,634	13,425	11,981
70,300	70,350	13,438	9,641	13,438	11,994
70,350	70,400	13,450	9,649	13,450	12,006
70,400	70,450	13,463	9,656	13,463	12,019
70,450	70,500	13,475	9,664	13,475	12,031
70,500	70,550	13,488	9,671	13,488	12,044
70,550	70,600	13,500	9,679	13,500	12,056
70,600	70,650	13,513	9,686	13,513	12,069
70,650	70,700	13,525	9,694	13,525	12,081
70,700	70,750	13,538	9,701	13,538	12,094
70,750	70,800	13,550	9,709	13,550	12,106
70,800	70,850	13,563	9,716	13,563	12,119
70,850	70,900	13,575	9,724	13,575	12,131
70,900	70,950	13,588	9,731	13,588	12,144
70,950	71,000	13,600	9,739	13,600	12,156
71,000					
71,000	71,050	13,613	9,746	13,613	12,169
71,050	71,100	13,625	9,754	13,625	12,181
71,100	71,150	13,638	9,761	13,638	12,194
71,150	71,200	13,650	9,769	13,650	12,206
71,200	71,250	13,663	9,776	13,663	12,219
71,250	71,300	13,675	9,784	13,675	12,231
71,300	71,350	13,688	9,791	13,688	12,244
71,350	71,400	13,700	9,799	13,700	12,256
71,400	71,450	13,713	9,806	13,713	12,269
71,450	71,500	13,725	9,814	13,725	12,281
71,500	71,550	13,738	9,821	13,738	12,294
71,550	71,600	13,750	9,829	13,750	12,306
71,600	71,650	13,763	9,836	13,763	12,319
71,650	71,700	13,775	9,844	13,775	12,331
71,700	71,750	13,788	9,851	13,788	12,344
71,750	71,800	13,800	9,859	13,800	12,356
71,800	71,850	13,813	9,866	13,813	12,369
71,850	71,900	13,825	9,874	13,825	12,381
71,900	71,950	13,838	9,881	13,838	12,394
71,950	72,000	13,850	9,889	13,850	12,406

If line 43 (taxable income) is—		And you are—			
At least	But less than	Single	Married filing jointly *	Married filing sepa-rately	Head of a house-hold
		Your tax is—			
72,000					
72,000	72,050	13,863	9,896	13,863	12,419
72,050	72,100	13,875	9,904	13,875	12,431
72,100	72,150	13,888	9,911	13,888	12,444
72,150	72,200	13,900	9,919	13,900	12,456
72,200	72,250	13,913	9,926	13,913	12,469
72,250	72,300	13,925	9,934	13,925	12,481
72,300	72,350	13,938	9,941	13,938	12,494
72,350	72,400	13,950	9,949	13,950	12,506
72,400	72,450	13,963	9,956	13,963	12,519
72,450	72,500	13,975	9,964	13,975	12,531
72,500	72,550	13,988	9,971	13,988	12,544
72,550	72,600	14,000	9,979	14,000	12,556
72,600	72,650	14,013	9,986	14,013	12,569
72,650	72,700	14,025	9,994	14,025	12,581
72,700	72,750	14,038	10,001	14,038	12,594
72,750	72,800	14,050	10,009	14,050	12,606
72,800	72,850	14,063	10,016	14,063	12,619
72,850	72,900	14,075	10,024	14,075	12,631
72,900	72,950	14,088	10,031	14,088	12,644
72,950	73,000	14,100	10,039	14,100	12,656
73,000					
73,000	73,050	14,113	10,046	14,113	12,669
73,050	73,100	14,125	10,054	14,125	12,681
73,100	73,150	14,138	10,061	14,138	12,694
73,150	73,200	14,150	10,069	14,150	12,706
73,200	73,250	14,163	10,076	14,163	12,719
73,250	73,300	14,175	10,084	14,175	12,731
73,300	73,350	14,188	10,091	14,188	12,744
73,350	73,400	14,200	10,099	14,200	12,756
73,400	73,450	14,213	10,106	14,213	12,769
73,450	73,500	14,225	10,114	14,225	12,781
73,500	73,550	14,238	10,121	14,238	12,794
73,550	73,600	14,250	10,129	14,250	12,806
73,600	73,650	14,263	10,136	14,263	12,819
73,650	73,700	14,275	10,144	14,275	12,831
73,700	73,750	14,288	10,151	14,288	12,844
73,750	73,800	14,300	10,159	14,300	12,856
73,800	73,850	14,313	10,169	14,313	12,869
73,850	73,900	14,325	10,181	14,325	12,881
73,900	73,950	14,338	10,194	14,338	12,894
73,950	74,000	14,350	10,206	14,350	12,906
74,000					
74,000	74,050	14,363	10,219	14,363	12,919
74,050	74,100	14,375	10,231	14,375	12,931
74,100	74,150	14,388	10,244	14,388	12,944
74,150	74,200	14,400	10,256	14,400	12,956
74,200	74,250	14,413	10,269	14,413	12,969
74,250	74,300	14,425	10,281	14,425	12,981
74,300	74,350	14,438	10,294	14,438	12,994
74,350	74,400	14,450	10,306	14,450	13,006
74,400	74,450	14,463	10,319	14,463	13,019
74,450	74,500	14,475	10,331	14,477	13,031
74,500	74,550	14,488	10,344	14,491	13,044
74,550	74,600	14,500	10,356	14,505	13,056
74,600	74,650	14,513	10,369	14,519	13,069
74,650	74,700	14,525	10,381	14,533	13,081
74,700	74,750	14,538	10,394	14,547	13,094
74,750	74,800	14,550	10,406	14,561	13,106
74,800	74,850	14,563	10,419	14,575	13,119
74,850	74,900	14,575	10,431	14,589	13,131
74,900	74,950	14,588	10,444	14,603	13,144
74,950	75,000	14,600	10,456	14,617	13,156

(Continued)

* This column must also be used by a qualifying widow(er).

75,000

At least	But less than	Single	Married filing jointly *	Married filing separately	Head of a household
75,000	75,050	14,613	10,469	14,631	13,169
75,050	75,100	14,625	10,481	14,645	13,181
75,100	75,150	14,638	10,494	14,659	13,194
75,150	75,200	14,650	10,506	14,673	13,206
75,200	75,250	14,663	10,519	14,687	13,219
75,250	75,300	14,675	10,531	14,701	13,231
75,300	75,350	14,688	10,544	14,715	13,244
75,350	75,400	14,700	10,556	14,729	13,256
75,400	75,450	14,713	10,569	14,743	13,269
75,450	75,500	14,725	10,581	14,757	13,281
75,500	75,550	14,738	10,594	14,771	13,294
75,550	75,600	14,750	10,606	14,785	13,306
75,600	75,650	14,763	10,619	14,799	13,319
75,650	75,700	14,775	10,631	14,813	13,331
75,700	75,750	14,788	10,644	14,827	13,344
75,750	75,800	14,800	10,656	14,841	13,356
75,800	75,850	14,813	10,669	14,855	13,369
75,850	75,900	14,825	10,681	14,869	13,381
75,900	75,950	14,838	10,694	14,883	13,394
75,950	76,000	14,850	10,706	14,897	13,406

76,000

At least	But less than	Single	Married filing jointly *	Married filing separately	Head of a household
76,000	76,050	14,863	10,719	14,911	13,419
76,050	76,100	14,875	10,731	14,925	13,431
76,100	76,150	14,888	10,744	14,939	13,444
76,150	76,200	14,900	10,756	14,953	13,456
76,200	76,250	14,913	10,769	14,967	13,469
76,250	76,300	14,925	10,781	14,981	13,481
76,300	76,350	14,938	10,794	14,995	13,494
76,350	76,400	14,950	10,806	15,009	13,506
76,400	76,450	14,963	10,819	15,023	13,519
76,450	76,500	14,975	10,831	15,037	13,531
76,500	76,550	14,988	10,844	15,051	13,544
76,550	76,600	15,000	10,856	15,065	13,556
76,600	76,650	15,013	10,869	15,079	13,569
76,650	76,700	15,025	10,881	15,093	13,581
76,700	76,750	15,038	10,894	15,107	13,594
76,750	76,800	15,050	10,906	15,121	13,606
76,800	76,850	15,063	10,919	15,135	13,619
76,850	76,900	15,075	10,931	15,149	13,631
76,900	76,950	15,088	10,944	15,163	13,644
76,950	77,000	15,100	10,956	15,177	13,656

77,000

At least	But less than	Single	Married filing jointly *	Married filing separately	Head of a household
77,000	77,050	15,113	10,969	15,191	13,669
77,050	77,100	15,125	10,981	15,205	13,681
77,100	77,150	15,138	10,994	15,219	13,694
77,150	77,200	15,150	11,006	15,233	13,706
77,200	77,250	15,163	11,019	15,247	13,719
77,250	77,300	15,175	11,031	15,261	13,731
77,300	77,350	15,188	11,044	15,275	13,744
77,350	77,400	15,200	11,056	15,289	13,756
77,400	77,450	15,213	11,069	15,303	13,769
77,450	77,500	15,225	11,081	15,317	13,781
77,500	77,550	15,238	11,094	15,331	13,794
77,550	77,600	15,250	11,106	15,345	13,806
77,600	77,650	15,263	11,119	15,359	13,819
77,650	77,700	15,275	11,131	15,373	13,831
77,700	77,750	15,288	11,144	15,387	13,844
77,750	77,800	15,300	11,156	15,401	13,856
77,800	77,850	15,313	11,169	15,415	13,869
77,850	77,900	15,325	11,181	15,429	13,881
77,900	77,950	15,338	11,194	15,443	13,894
77,950	78,000	15,350	11,206	15,457	13,906

78,000

At least	But less than	Single	Married filing jointly *	Married filing separately	Head of a household
78,000	78,050	15,363	11,219	15,471	13,919
78,050	78,100	15,375	11,231	15,485	13,931
78,100	78,150	15,388	11,244	15,499	13,944
78,150	78,200	15,400	11,256	15,513	13,956
78,200	78,250	15,413	11,269	15,527	13,969
78,250	78,300	15,425	11,281	15,541	13,981
78,300	78,350	15,438	11,294	15,555	13,994
78,350	78,400	15,450	11,306	15,569	14,006
78,400	78,450	15,463	11,319	15,583	14,019
78,450	78,500	15,475	11,331	15,597	14,031
78,500	78,550	15,488	11,344	15,611	14,044
78,550	78,600	15,500	11,356	15,625	14,056
78,600	78,650	15,513	11,369	15,639	14,069
78,650	78,700	15,525	11,381	15,653	14,081
78,700	78,750	15,538	11,394	15,667	14,094
78,750	78,800	15,550	11,406	15,681	14,106
78,800	78,850	15,563	11,419	15,695	14,119
78,850	78,900	15,575	11,431	15,709	14,131
78,900	78,950	15,588	11,444	15,723	14,144
78,950	79,000	15,600	11,456	15,737	14,156

79,000

At least	But less than	Single	Married filing jointly *	Married filing separately	Head of a household
79,000	79,050	15,613	11,469	15,751	14,169
79,050	79,100	15,625	11,481	15,765	14,181
79,100	79,150	15,638	11,494	15,779	14,194
79,150	79,200	15,650	11,506	15,793	14,206
79,200	79,250	15,663	11,519	15,807	14,219
79,250	79,300	15,675	11,531	15,821	14,231
79,300	79,350	15,688	11,544	15,835	14,244
79,350	79,400	15,700	11,556	15,849	14,256
79,400	79,450	15,713	11,569	15,863	14,269
79,450	79,500	15,725	11,581	15,877	14,281
79,500	79,550	15,738	11,594	15,891	14,294
79,550	79,600	15,750	11,606	15,905	14,306
79,600	79,650	15,763	11,619	15,919	14,319
79,650	79,700	15,775	11,631	15,933	14,331
79,700	79,750	15,788	11,644	15,947	14,344
79,750	79,800	15,800	11,656	15,961	14,356
79,800	79,850	15,813	11,669	15,975	14,369
79,850	79,900	15,825	11,681	15,989	14,381
79,900	79,950	15,838	11,694	16,003	14,394
79,950	80,000	15,850	11,706	16,017	14,406

80,000

At least	But less than	Single	Married filing jointly *	Married filing separately	Head of a household
80,000	80,050	15,863	11,719	16,031	14,419
80,050	80,100	15,875	11,731	16,045	14,431
80,100	80,150	15,888	11,744	16,059	14,444
80,150	80,200	15,900	11,756	16,073	14,456
80,200	80,250	15,913	11,769	16,087	14,469
80,250	80,300	15,925	11,781	16,101	14,481
80,300	80,350	15,938	11,794	16,115	14,494
80,350	80,400	15,950	11,806	16,129	14,506
80,400	80,450	15,963	11,819	16,143	14,519
80,450	80,500	15,975	11,831	16,157	14,531
80,500	80,550	15,988	11,844	16,171	14,544
80,550	80,600	16,000	11,856	16,185	14,556
80,600	80,650	16,013	11,869	16,199	14,569
80,650	80,700	16,025	11,881	16,213	14,581
80,700	80,750	16,038	11,894	16,227	14,594
80,750	80,800	16,050	11,906	16,241	14,606
80,800	80,850	16,063	11,919	16,255	14,619
80,850	80,900	16,075	11,931	16,269	14,631
80,900	80,950	16,088	11,944	16,283	14,644
80,950	81,000	16,100	11,956	16,297	14,656

81,000

At least	But less than	Single	Married filing jointly *	Married filing separately	Head of a household
81,000	81,050	16,113	11,969	16,311	14,669
81,050	81,100	16,125	11,981	16,325	14,681
81,100	81,150	16,138	11,994	16,339	14,694
81,150	81,200	16,150	12,006	16,353	14,706
81,200	81,250	16,163	12,019	16,367	14,719
81,250	81,300	16,175	12,031	16,381	14,731
81,300	81,350	16,188	12,044	16,395	14,744
81,350	81,400	16,200	12,056	16,409	14,756
81,400	81,450	16,213	12,069	16,423	14,769
81,450	81,500	16,225	12,081	16,437	14,781
81,500	81,550	16,238	12,094	16,451	14,794
81,550	81,600	16,250	12,106	16,465	14,806
81,600	81,650	16,263	12,119	16,479	14,819
81,650	81,700	16,275	12,131	16,493	14,831
81,700	81,750	16,288	12,144	16,507	14,844
81,750	81,800	16,300	12,156	16,521	14,856
81,800	81,850	16,313	12,169	16,535	14,869
81,850	81,900	16,325	12,181	16,549	14,881
81,900	81,950	16,338	12,194	16,563	14,894
81,950	82,000	16,350	12,206	16,577	14,906

82,000

At least	But less than	Single	Married filing jointly *	Married filing separately	Head of a household
82,000	82,050	16,363	12,219	16,591	14,919
82,050	82,100	16,375	12,231	16,605	14,931
82,100	82,150	16,388	12,244	16,619	14,944
82,150	82,200	16,400	12,256	16,633	14,956
82,200	82,250	16,413	12,269	16,647	14,969
82,250	82,300	16,425	12,281	16,661	14,981
82,300	82,350	16,438	12,294	16,675	14,994
82,350	82,400	16,450	12,306	16,689	15,006
82,400	82,450	16,463	12,319	16,703	15,019
82,450	82,500	16,475	12,331	16,717	15,031
82,500	82,550	16,488	12,344	16,731	15,044
82,550	82,600	16,500	12,356	16,745	15,056
82,600	82,650	16,513	12,369	16,759	15,069
82,650	82,700	16,525	12,381	16,773	15,081
82,700	82,750	16,538	12,394	16,787	15,094
82,750	82,800	16,550	12,406	16,801	15,106
82,800	82,850	16,563	12,419	16,815	15,119
82,850	82,900	16,575	12,431	16,829	15,131
82,900	82,950	16,588	12,444	16,843	15,144
82,950	83,000	16,600	12,456	16,857	15,156

83,000

At least	But less than	Single	Married filing jointly *	Married filing separately	Head of a household
83,000	83,050	16,613	12,469	16,871	15,169
83,050	83,100	16,625	12,481	16,885	15,181
83,100	83,150	16,638	12,494	16,899	15,194
83,150	83,200	16,650	12,506	16,913	15,206
83,200	83,250	16,663	12,519	16,927	15,219
83,250	83,300	16,675	12,531	16,941	15,231
83,300	83,350	16,688	12,544	16,955	15,244
83,350	83,400	16,700	12,556	16,969	15,256
83,400	83,450	16,713	12,569	16,983	15,269
83,450	83,500	16,725	12,581	16,997	15,281
83,500	83,550	16,738	12,594	17,011	15,294
83,550	83,600	16,750	12,606	17,025	15,306
83,600	83,650	16,763	12,619	17,039	15,319
83,650	83,700	16,775	12,631	17,053	15,331
83,700	83,750	16,788	12,644	17,067	15,344
83,750	83,800	16,800	12,656	17,081	15,356
83,800	83,850	16,813	12,669	17,095	15,369
83,850	83,900	16,825	12,681	17,109	15,381
83,900	83,950	16,838	12,694	17,123	15,394
83,950	84,000	16,850	12,706	17,137	15,406

(Continued)

* This column must also be used by a qualifying widow(er).

Need more information or forms? Visit IRS.gov.

84,000

At least	But less than	Single	Married filing jointly *	Married filing separately	Head of a household
84,000	84,050	16,863	12,719	17,151	15,419
84,050	84,100	16,875	12,731	17,165	15,431
84,100	84,150	16,888	12,744	17,179	15,444
84,150	84,200	16,900	12,756	17,193	15,456
84,200	84,250	16,913	12,769	17,207	15,469
84,250	84,300	16,925	12,781	17,221	15,481
84,300	84,350	16,938	12,794	17,235	15,494
84,350	84,400	16,950	12,806	17,249	15,506
84,400	84,450	16,963	12,819	17,263	15,519
84,450	84,500	16,975	12,831	17,277	15,531
84,500	84,550	16,988	12,844	17,291	15,544
84,550	84,600	17,000	12,856	17,305	15,556
84,600	84,650	17,013	12,869	17,319	15,569
84,650	84,700	17,025	12,881	17,333	15,581
84,700	84,750	17,038	12,894	17,347	15,594
84,750	84,800	17,050	12,906	17,361	15,606
84,800	84,850	17,063	12,919	17,375	15,619
84,850	84,900	17,075	12,931	17,389	15,631
84,900	84,950	17,088	12,944	17,403	15,644
84,950	85,000	17,100	12,956	17,417	15,656

85,000

At least	But less than	Single	Married filing jointly *	Married filing separately	Head of a household
85,000	85,050	17,113	12,969	17,431	15,669
85,050	85,100	17,125	12,981	17,445	15,681
85,100	85,150	17,138	12,994	17,459	15,694
85,150	85,200	17,150	13,006	17,473	15,706
85,200	85,250	17,163	13,019	17,487	15,719
85,250	85,300	17,175	13,031	17,501	15,731
85,300	85,350	17,188	13,044	17,515	15,744
85,350	85,400	17,200	13,056	17,529	15,756
85,400	85,450	17,213	13,069	17,543	15,769
85,450	85,500	17,225	13,081	17,557	15,781
85,500	85,550	17,238	13,094	17,571	15,794
85,550	85,600	17,250	13,106	17,585	15,806
85,600	85,650	17,263	13,119	17,599	15,819
85,650	85,700	17,275	13,131	17,613	15,831
85,700	85,750	17,288	13,144	17,627	15,844
85,750	85,800	17,300	13,156	17,641	15,856
85,800	85,850	17,313	13,169	17,655	15,869
85,850	85,900	17,325	13,181	17,669	15,881
85,900	85,950	17,338	13,194	17,683	15,894
85,950	86,000	17,350	13,206	17,697	15,906

86,000

At least	But less than	Single	Married filing jointly *	Married filing separately	Head of a household
86,000	86,050	17,363	13,219	17,711	15,919
86,050	86,100	17,375	13,231	17,725	15,931
86,100	86,150	17,388	13,244	17,739	15,944
86,150	86,200	17,400	13,256	17,753	15,956
86,200	86,250	17,413	13,269	17,767	15,969
86,250	86,300	17,425	13,281	17,781	15,981
86,300	86,350	17,438	13,294	17,795	15,994
86,350	86,400	17,450	13,306	17,809	16,006
86,400	86,450	17,463	13,319	17,823	16,019
86,450	86,500	17,475	13,331	17,837	16,031
86,500	86,550	17,488	13,344	17,851	16,044
86,550	86,600	17,500	13,356	17,865	16,056
86,600	86,650	17,513	13,369	17,879	16,069
86,650	86,700	17,525	13,381	17,893	16,081
86,700	86,750	17,538	13,394	17,907	16,094
86,750	86,800	17,550	13,406	17,921	16,106
86,800	86,850	17,563	13,419	17,935	16,119
86,850	86,900	17,575	13,431	17,949	16,131
86,900	86,950	17,588	13,444	17,963	16,144
86,950	87,000	17,600	13,456	17,977	16,156

87,000

At least	But less than	Single	Married filing jointly *	Married filing separately	Head of a household
87,000	87,050	17,613	13,469	17,991	16,169
87,050	87,100	17,625	13,481	18,005	16,181
87,100	87,150	17,638	13,494	18,019	16,194
87,150	87,200	17,650	13,506	18,033	16,206
87,200	87,250	17,663	13,519	18,047	16,219
87,250	87,300	17,675	13,531	18,061	16,231
87,300	87,350	17,688	13,544	18,075	16,244
87,350	87,400	17,700	13,556	18,089	16,256
87,400	87,450	17,713	13,569	18,103	16,269
87,450	87,500	17,725	13,581	18,117	16,281
87,500	87,550	17,738	13,594	18,131	16,294
87,550	87,600	17,750	13,606	18,145	16,306
87,600	87,650	17,763	13,619	18,159	16,319
87,650	87,700	17,775	13,631	18,173	16,331
87,700	87,750	17,788	13,644	18,187	16,344
87,750	87,800	17,800	13,656	18,201	16,356
87,800	87,850	17,813	13,669	18,215	16,369
87,850	87,900	17,825	13,681	18,229	16,381
87,900	87,950	17,838	13,694	18,243	16,394
87,950	88,000	17,850	13,706	18,257	16,406

88,000

At least	But less than	Single	Married filing jointly *	Married filing separately	Head of a household
88,000	88,050	17,863	13,719	18,271	16,419
88,050	88,100	17,875	13,731	18,285	16,431
88,100	88,150	17,888	13,744	18,299	16,444
88,150	88,200	17,900	13,756	18,313	16,456
88,200	88,250	17,913	13,769	18,327	16,469
88,250	88,300	17,925	13,781	18,341	16,481
88,300	88,350	17,938	13,794	18,355	16,494
88,350	88,400	17,950	13,806	18,369	16,506
88,400	88,450	17,963	13,819	18,383	16,519
88,450	88,500	17,975	13,831	18,397	16,531
88,500	88,550	17,988	13,844	18,411	16,544
88,550	88,600	18,000	13,856	18,425	16,556
88,600	88,650	18,013	13,869	18,439	16,569
88,650	88,700	18,025	13,881	18,453	16,581
88,700	88,750	18,038	13,894	18,467	16,594
88,750	88,800	18,050	13,906	18,481	16,606
88,800	88,850	18,063	13,919	18,495	16,619
88,850	88,900	18,075	13,931	18,509	16,631
88,900	88,950	18,088	13,944	18,523	16,644
88,950	89,000	18,100	13,956	18,537	16,656

89,000

At least	But less than	Single	Married filing jointly *	Married filing separately	Head of a household
89,000	89,050	18,113	13,969	18,551	16,669
89,050	89,100	18,125	13,981	18,565	16,681
89,100	89,150	18,138	13,994	18,579	16,694
89,150	89,200	18,150	14,006	18,593	16,706
89,200	89,250	18,163	14,019	18,607	16,719
89,250	89,300	18,175	14,031	18,621	16,731
89,300	89,350	18,188	14,044	18,635	16,744
89,350	89,400	18,201	14,056	18,649	16,756
89,400	89,450	18,215	14,069	18,663	16,769
89,450	89,500	18,229	14,081	18,677	16,781
89,500	89,550	18,243	14,094	18,691	16,794
89,550	89,600	18,257	14,106	18,705	16,806
89,600	89,650	18,271	14,119	18,719	16,819
89,650	89,700	18,285	14,131	18,733	16,831
89,700	89,750	18,299	14,144	18,747	16,844
89,750	89,800	18,313	14,156	18,761	16,856
89,800	89,850	18,327	14,169	18,775	16,869
89,850	89,900	18,341	14,181	18,789	16,881
89,900	89,950	18,355	14,194	18,803	16,894
89,950	90,000	18,369	14,206	18,817	16,906

90,000

At least	But less than	Single	Married filing jointly *	Married filing separately	Head of a household
90,000	90,050	18,383	14,219	18,831	16,919
90,050	90,100	18,397	14,231	18,845	16,931
90,100	90,150	18,411	14,244	18,859	16,944
90,150	90,200	18,425	14,256	18,873	16,956
90,200	90,250	18,439	14,269	18,887	16,969
90,250	90,300	18,453	14,281	18,901	16,981
90,300	90,350	18,467	14,294	18,915	16,994
90,350	90,400	18,481	14,306	18,929	17,006
90,400	90,450	18,495	14,319	18,943	17,019
90,450	90,500	18,509	14,331	18,957	17,031
90,500	90,550	18,523	14,344	18,971	17,044
90,550	90,600	18,537	14,356	18,985	17,056
90,600	90,650	18,551	14,369	18,999	17,069
90,650	90,700	18,565	14,381	19,013	17,081
90,700	90,750	18,579	14,394	19,027	17,094
90,750	90,800	18,593	14,406	19,041	17,106
90,800	90,850	18,607	14,419	19,055	17,119
90,850	90,900	18,621	14,431	19,069	17,131
90,900	90,950	18,635	14,444	19,083	17,144
90,950	91,000	18,649	14,456	19,097	17,156

91,000

At least	But less than	Single	Married filing jointly *	Married filing separately	Head of a household
91,000	91,050	18,663	14,469	19,111	17,169
91,050	91,100	18,677	14,481	19,125	17,181
91,100	91,150	18,691	14,494	19,139	17,194
91,150	91,200	18,705	14,506	19,153	17,206
91,200	91,250	18,719	14,519	19,167	17,219
91,250	91,300	18,733	14,531	19,181	17,231
91,300	91,350	18,747	14,544	19,195	17,244
91,350	91,400	18,761	14,556	19,209	17,256
91,400	91,450	18,775	14,569	19,223	17,269
91,450	91,500	18,789	14,581	19,237	17,281
91,500	91,550	18,803	14,594	19,251	17,294
91,550	91,600	18,817	14,606	19,265	17,306
91,600	91,650	18,831	14,619	19,279	17,319
91,650	91,700	18,845	14,631	19,293	17,331
91,700	91,750	18,859	14,644	19,307	17,344
91,750	91,800	18,873	14,656	19,321	17,356
91,800	91,850	18,887	14,669	19,335	17,369
91,850	91,900	18,901	14,681	19,349	17,381
91,900	91,950	18,915	14,694	19,363	17,394
91,950	92,000	18,929	14,706	19,377	17,406

92,000

At least	But less than	Single	Married filing jointly *	Married filing separately	Head of a household
92,000	92,050	18,943	14,719	19,391	17,419
92,050	92,100	18,957	14,731	19,405	17,431
92,100	92,150	18,971	14,744	19,419	17,444
92,150	92,200	18,985	14,756	19,433	17,456
92,200	92,250	18,999	14,769	19,447	17,469
92,250	92,300	19,013	14,781	19,461	17,481
92,300	92,350	19,027	14,794	19,475	17,494
92,350	92,400	19,041	14,806	19,489	17,506
92,400	92,450	19,055	14,819	19,503	17,519
92,450	92,500	19,069	14,831	19,517	17,531
92,500	92,550	19,083	14,844	19,531	17,544
92,550	92,600	19,097	14,856	19,545	17,556
92,600	92,650	19,111	14,869	19,559	17,569
92,650	92,700	19,125	14,881	19,573	17,581
92,700	92,750	19,139	14,894	19,587	17,594
92,750	92,800	19,153	14,906	19,601	17,606
92,800	92,850	19,167	14,919	19,615	17,619
92,850	92,900	19,181	14,931	19,629	17,631
92,900	92,950	19,195	14,944	19,643	17,644
92,950	93,000	19,209	14,956	19,657	17,656

* This column must also be used by a qualifying widow(er).

(Continued)

If line 43 (taxable income) is—		And you are—			
At least	But less than	Single	Married filing jointly *	Married filing separately	Head of a household
		Your tax is—			

93,000

At least	But less than	Single	Married filing jointly *	Married filing separately	Head of a household
93,000	93,050	19,223	14,969	19,671	17,669
93,050	93,100	19,237	14,981	19,685	17,681
93,100	93,150	19,251	14,994	19,699	17,694
93,150	93,200	19,265	15,006	19,713	17,706
93,200	93,250	19,279	15,019	19,727	17,719
93,250	93,300	19,293	15,031	19,741	17,731
93,300	93,350	19,307	15,044	19,755	17,744
93,350	93,400	19,321	15,056	19,769	17,756
93,400	93,450	19,335	15,069	19,783	17,769
93,450	93,500	19,349	15,081	19,797	17,781
93,500	93,550	19,363	15,094	19,811	17,794
93,550	93,600	19,377	15,106	19,825	17,806
93,600	93,650	19,391	15,119	19,839	17,819
93,650	93,700	19,405	15,131	19,853	17,831
93,700	93,750	19,419	15,144	19,867	17,844
93,750	93,800	19,433	15,156	19,881	17,856
93,800	93,850	19,447	15,169	19,895	17,869
93,850	93,900	19,461	15,181	19,909	17,881
93,900	93,950	19,475	15,194	19,923	17,894
93,950	94,000	19,489	15,206	19,937	17,906

94,000

At least	But less than	Single	Married filing jointly *	Married filing separately	Head of a household
94,000	94,050	19,503	15,219	19,951	17,919
94,050	94,100	19,517	15,231	19,965	17,931
94,100	94,150	19,531	15,244	19,979	17,944
94,150	94,200	19,545	15,256	19,993	17,956
94,200	94,250	19,559	15,269	20,007	17,969
94,250	94,300	19,573	15,281	20,021	17,981
94,300	94,350	19,587	15,294	20,035	17,994
94,350	94,400	19,601	15,306	20,049	18,006
94,400	94,450	19,615	15,319	20,063	18,019
94,450	94,500	19,629	15,331	20,077	18,031
94,500	94,550	19,643	15,344	20,091	18,044
94,550	94,600	19,657	15,356	20,105	18,056
94,600	94,650	19,671	15,369	20,119	18,069
94,650	94,700	19,685	15,381	20,133	18,081
94,700	94,750	19,699	15,394	20,147	18,094
94,750	94,800	19,713	15,406	20,161	18,106
94,800	94,850	19,727	15,419	20,175	18,119
94,850	94,900	19,741	15,431	20,189	18,131
94,900	94,950	19,755	15,444	20,203	18,144
94,950	95,000	19,769	15,456	20,217	18,156

95,000

At least	But less than	Single	Married filing jointly *	Married filing separately	Head of a household
95,000	95,050	19,783	15,469	20,231	18,169
95,050	95,100	19,797	15,481	20,245	18,181
95,100	95,150	19,811	15,494	20,259	18,194
95,150	95,200	19,825	15,506	20,273	18,206
95,200	95,250	19,839	15,519	20,287	18,219
95,250	95,300	19,853	15,531	20,301	18,231
95,300	95,350	19,867	15,544	20,315	18,244
95,350	95,400	19,881	15,556	20,329	18,256
95,400	95,450	19,895	15,569	20,343	18,269
95,450	95,500	19,909	15,581	20,357	18,281
95,500	95,550	19,923	15,594	20,371	18,294
95,550	95,600	19,937	15,606	20,385	18,306
95,600	95,650	19,951	15,619	20,399	18,319
95,650	95,700	19,965	15,631	20,413	18,331
95,700	95,750	19,979	15,644	20,427	18,344
95,750	95,800	19,993	15,656	20,441	18,356
95,800	95,850	20,007	15,669	20,455	18,369
95,850	95,900	20,021	15,681	20,469	18,381
95,900	95,950	20,035	15,694	20,483	18,394
95,950	96,000	20,049	15,706	20,497	18,406

If line 43 (taxable income) is—		And you are—			
At least	But less than	Single	Married filing jointly *	Married filing separately	Head of a household
		Your tax is—			

96,000

At least	But less than	Single	Married filing jointly *	Married filing separately	Head of a household
96,000	96,050	20,063	15,719	20,511	18,419
96,050	96,100	20,077	15,731	20,525	18,431
96,100	96,150	20,091	15,744	20,539	18,444
96,150	96,200	20,105	15,756	20,553	18,456
96,200	96,250	20,119	15,769	20,567	18,469
96,250	96,300	20,133	15,781	20,581	18,481
96,300	96,350	20,147	15,794	20,595	18,494
96,350	96,400	20,161	15,806	20,609	18,506
96,400	96,450	20,175	15,819	20,623	18,519
96,450	96,500	20,189	15,831	20,637	18,531
96,500	96,550	20,203	15,844	20,651	18,544
96,550	96,600	20,217	15,856	20,665	18,556
96,600	96,650	20,231	15,869	20,679	18,569
96,650	96,700	20,245	15,881	20,693	18,581
96,700	96,750	20,259	15,894	20,707	18,594
96,750	96,800	20,273	15,906	20,721	18,606
96,800	96,850	20,287	15,919	20,735	18,619
96,850	96,900	20,301	15,931	20,749	18,631
96,900	96,950	20,315	15,944	20,763	18,644
96,950	97,000	20,329	15,956	20,777	18,656

97,000

At least	But less than	Single	Married filing jointly *	Married filing separately	Head of a household
97,000	97,050	20,343	15,969	20,791	18,669
97,050	97,100	20,357	15,981	20,805	18,681
97,100	97,150	20,371	15,994	20,819	18,694
97,150	97,200	20,385	16,006	20,833	18,706
97,200	97,250	20,399	16,019	20,847	18,719
97,250	97,300	20,413	16,031	20,861	18,731
97,300	97,350	20,427	16,044	20,875	18,744
97,350	97,400	20,441	16,056	20,889	18,756
97,400	97,450	20,455	16,069	20,903	18,769
97,450	97,500	20,469	16,081	20,917	18,781
97,500	97,550	20,483	16,094	20,931	18,794
97,550	97,600	20,497	16,106	20,945	18,806
97,600	97,650	20,511	16,119	20,959	18,819
97,650	97,700	20,525	16,131	20,973	18,831
97,700	97,750	20,539	16,144	20,987	18,844
97,750	97,800	20,553	16,156	21,001	18,856
97,800	97,850	20,567	16,169	21,015	18,869
97,850	97,900	20,581	16,181	21,029	18,881
97,900	97,950	20,595	16,194	21,043	18,894
97,950	98,000	20,609	16,206	21,057	18,906

98,000

At least	But less than	Single	Married filing jointly *	Married filing separately	Head of a household
98,000	98,050	20,623	16,219	21,071	18,919
98,050	98,100	20,637	16,231	21,085	18,931
98,100	98,150	20,651	16,244	21,099	18,944
98,150	98,200	20,665	16,256	21,113	18,956
98,200	98,250	20,679	16,269	21,127	18,969
98,250	98,300	20,693	16,281	21,141	18,981
98,300	98,350	20,707	16,294	21,155	18,994
98,350	98,400	20,721	16,306	21,169	19,006
98,400	98,450	20,735	16,319	21,183	19,019
98,450	98,500	20,749	16,331	21,197	19,031
98,500	98,550	20,763	16,344	21,211	19,044
98,550	98,600	20,777	16,356	21,225	19,056
98,600	98,650	20,791	16,369	21,239	19,069
98,650	98,700	20,805	16,381	21,253	19,081
98,700	98,750	20,819	16,394	21,267	19,094
98,750	98,800	20,833	16,406	21,281	19,106
98,800	98,850	20,847	16,419	21,295	19,119
98,850	98,900	20,861	16,431	21,309	19,131
98,900	98,950	20,875	16,444	21,323	19,144
98,950	99,000	20,889	16,456	21,337	19,156

If line 43 (taxable income) is—		And you are—			
At least	But less than	Single	Married filing jointly *	Married filing separately	Head of a household
		Your tax is—			

99,000

At least	But less than	Single	Married filing jointly *	Married filing separately	Head of a household
99,000	99,050	20,903	16,469	21,351	19,169
99,050	99,100	20,917	16,481	21,365	19,181
99,100	99,150	20,931	16,494	21,379	19,194
99,150	99,200	20,945	16,506	21,393	19,206
99,200	99,250	20,959	16,519	21,407	19,219
99,250	99,300	20,973	16,531	21,421	19,231
99,300	99,350	20,987	16,544	21,435	19,244
99,350	99,400	21,001	16,556	21,449	19,256
99,400	99,450	21,015	16,569	21,463	19,269
99,450	99,500	21,029	16,581	21,477	19,281
99,500	99,550	21,043	16,594	21,491	19,294
99,550	99,600	21,057	16,606	21,505	19,306
99,600	99,650	21,071	16,619	21,519	19,319
99,650	99,700	21,085	16,631	21,533	19,331
99,700	99,750	21,099	16,644	21,547	19,344
99,750	99,800	21,113	16,656	21,561	19,356
99,800	99,850	21,127	16,669	21,575	19,369
99,850	99,900	21,141	16,681	21,589	19,381
99,900	99,950	21,155	16,694	21,603	19,394
99,950	100,000	21,169	16,706	21,617	19,406

$100,000
or over
use the Tax
Computation
Worksheet

* This column must also be used by a qualifying widow(er).

Need more information or forms? Visit IRS.gov.

2014 Tax Computation Worksheet—Line 44

See the instructions for line 44 to see if you must use the worksheet below to figure your tax.

Note. If you are required to use this worksheet to figure the tax on an amount from another form or worksheet, such as the Qualified Dividends and Capital Gain Tax Worksheet, the Schedule D Tax Worksheet, Schedule J, Form 8615, or the Foreign Earned Income Tax Worksheet, enter the amount from that form or worksheet in column (a) of the row that applies to the amount you are looking up. Enter the result on the appropriate line of the form or worksheet that you are completing.

Section A—Use if your filing status is **Single.** Complete the row below that applies to you.

Taxable income. If line 43 is—	(a) Enter the amount from line 43	(b) Multiplication amount	(c) Multiply (a) by (b)	(d) Subtraction amount	Tax. Subtract (d) from (c). Enter the result here and on Form 1040, line 44
At least $100,000 but not over $186,350	$	× 28% (.28)	$	$ 6,824.25	$
Over $186,350 but not over $405,100	$	× 33% (.33)	$	$ 16,141.75	$
Over $405,100 but not over $406,750	$	× 35% (.35)	$	$ 24,243.75	$
Over $406,750	$	× 39.6% (.396)	$	$ 42,954.25	$

Section B—Use if your filing status is **Married filing jointly** or **Qualifying widow(er).** Complete the row below that applies to you.

Taxable income. If line 43 is—	(a) Enter the amount from line 43	(b) Multiplication amount	(c) Multiply (a) by (b)	(d) Subtraction amount	Tax. Subtract (d) from (c). Enter the result here and on Form 1040, line 44
At least $100,000 but not over $148,850	$	× 25% (.25)	$	$ 8,287.50	$
Over $148,850 but not over $226,850	$	× 28% (.28)	$	$ 12,753.00	$
Over $226,850 but not over $405,100	$	× 33% (.33)	$	$ 24,095.50	$
Over $405,100 but not over $457,600	$	× 35% (.35)	$	$ 32,197.50	$
Over $457,600	$	× 39.6% (.396)	$	$ 53,247.10	$

Section C—Use if your filing status is **Married filing separately.** Complete the row below that applies to you.

Taxable income. If line 43 is—	(a) Enter the amount from line 43	(b) Multiplication amount	(c) Multiply (a) by (b)	(d) Subtraction amount	Tax. Subtract (d) from (c). Enter the result here and on Form 1040, line 44
At least $100,000 but not over $113,425	$	× 28% (.28)	$	$ 6,376.50	$
Over $113,425 but not over $202,550	$	× 33% (.33)	$	$ 12,047.75	$
Over $202,550 but not over $228,800	$	× 35% (.35)	$	$ 16,098.75	$
Over $228,800	$	× 39.6% (.396)	$	$ 26,623.55	$

Section D—Use if your filing status is **Head of household.** Complete the row below that applies to you.

Taxable income. If line 43 is—	(a) Enter the amount from line 43	(b) Multiplication amount	(c) Multiply (a) by (b)	(d) Subtraction amount	Tax. Subtract (d) from (c). Enter the result here and on Form 1040, line 44
At least $100,000 but not over $127,550	$	× 25% (.25)	$	$ 5,587.50	$
Over $127,550 but not over $206,600	$	× 28% (.28)	$	$ 9,414.00	$
Over $206,600 but not over $405,100	$	× 33% (.33)	$	$ 19,744.00	$
Over $405,100 but not over $432,200	$	× 35% (.35)	$	$ 27,846.00	$
Over $432,200	$	× 39.6% (.396)	$	$ 47,727.20	$

General Information

The IRS Mission. Provide America's taxpayers top-quality service by helping them understand and meet their tax responsibilities and enforce the law with integrity and fairness to all.

How To Avoid Common Mistakes

Mistakes can delay your refund or result in notices being sent to you. One of the best ways to file an accurate return is to use IRS *e-file*. Tax software does the math for you and will help you avoid mistakes. Combining *e-file* with direct deposit is the fastest way to get your refund.

- Make sure you entered the correct name and social security number (SSN) for each dependent you claim on line 6c. Check that each dependent's name and SSN agrees with his or her social security card. For each child under age 17 who is a qualifying child for the child tax credit, make sure you checked the box in line 6c, column (4).
- Check your math, especially for the child tax credit, earned income credit (EIC), taxable social security benefits, total income, itemized deductions or standard deduction, deduction for exemptions, taxable income, total tax, federal income tax withheld, and refund or amount you owe.
- Be sure you used the correct method to figure your tax. See the instructions for line 44.
- Be sure to enter your SSN in the space provided on page 1 of Form 1040. If you are married filing a joint or separate return, also enter your spouse's SSN. Be sure to enter your SSN in the space next to your name. Check that your name and SSN agree with your social security card.
- Make sure your name and address are correct. Enter your (and your spouse's) name in the same order as shown on your last return.
- If you live in an apartment, be sure to include your apartment number in your address.
- If you are taking the standard deduction, see the instructions for line 40 to be sure you entered the correct amount.

- If you received capital gain distributions but were not required to file Schedule D, make sure you checked the box on line 13.
- If you are taking the EIC, be sure you used the correct column of the EIC Table for your filing status and the number of children you have.
- Remember to sign and date Form 1040 and enter your occupation(s).
- Attach your Form(s) W-2 and other required forms and schedules. Put all forms and schedules in the proper order. See *Assemble Your Return*, earlier.
- If you owe tax and are paying by check or money order, be sure to include all the required information on your payment. See the instructions for line 78 for details.
- Do not file more than one original return for the same year, even if you have not gotten your refund or have not heard from the IRS since you filed. Filing more than one original return for the same year, or sending in more than one copy of the same return (unless we ask you to do so), could delay your refund.

Innocent Spouse Relief

Generally, both you and your spouse are each responsible for paying the full amount of tax, interest, and penalties on your joint return. However, you may qualify for relief from liability for tax on a joint return if (a) there is an understatement of tax because your spouse omitted income or claimed false deductions or credits, (b) you are divorced, separated, or no longer living with your spouse, or (c) given all the facts and circumstances, it would not be fair to hold you liable for the tax. You may also qualify for relief if you were a married resident of a community property state but did not file a joint return and are now liable for an unpaid or understated tax. File Form 8857 to request relief. In some cases, Form 8857 may need to be filed within 2 years of the date on which the IRS first attempted to collect the tax from you. Do not file Form 8857 with

your Form 1040. For more information, see Pub. 971 and Form 8857 or you can call the Innocent Spouse office toll-free at 1-855-851-2009.

Income Tax Withholding and Estimated Tax Payments for 2015

If the amount you owe or the amount you overpaid is large, you may want to file a new Form W-4 with your employer to change the amount of income tax withheld from your 2015 pay. For details on how to complete Form W-4, see Pub. 505. If you have pension or annuity income, use Form W-4P. If you receive certain government payments (such as unemployment compensation or social security benefits), you can have tax withheld from those payments by giving the payer Form W-4V.

 You can use the IRS Withholding Calculator *at www.irs.gov/ Individuals/IRS-Withholding-Calculator, instead of Pub. 505 or the worksheets included with Form W-4 or W-4P, to determine whether you need to have your withholding increased or decreased.*

In general, you do not have to make estimated tax payments if you expect that your 2015 Form 1040 will show a tax refund or a tax balance due of less than $1,000. If your total estimated tax for 2015 is $1,000 or more, see Form 1040-ES and Pub. 505 for a worksheet you can use to see if you have to make estimated tax payments. For more details, see Pub. 505.

Secure Your Tax Records from Identity Theft

Identity theft occurs when someone uses your personal information, such as your name, social security number (SSN), or other identifying information, without your permission, to commit fraud or other crimes. An identity thief may use your SSN to get a job or may file a tax return using your SSN to receive a refund.

To reduce your risk:
- Protect your SSN,
- Ensure your employer is protecting your SSN, and
- Be careful when choosing a tax preparer.

If your tax records are affected by identity theft and you receive a notice from the IRS, respond right away to the name and phone number printed on the IRS notice or letter. For more information, see Pub. 4535.

If your SSN has been lost or stolen or you suspect you are a victim of tax-related identity theft, visit *www.irs.gov/identitytheft* to learn what steps you should take.

Victims of identity theft who are experiencing economic harm or a systemic problem, or are seeking help in resolving tax problems that have not been resolved through normal channels, may be eligible for Taxpayer Advocate Service (TAS) assistance. You can reach TAS by calling the National Taxpayer Advocate helpline at 1-877-777-4778. People who are deaf, hard of hearing, or have a speech disability and who have access to TTY/TDD equipment can call 1-800-829-4059. Deaf or hard-of-hearing individuals can also contact the IRS through relay services such as the Federal Relay Service available at *www.gsa.gov/fedrelay*.

Protect yourself from suspicious emails or phishing schemes. Phishing is the creation and use of email and websites designed to mimic legitimate business emails and websites. The most common form is sending an email to a user falsely claiming to be an established legitimate enterprise in an attempt to scam the user into surrendering private information that will be used for identity theft.

The IRS does not initiate contacts with taxpayers via emails. Also, the IRS does not request detailed personal information through email or ask taxpayers for the PIN numbers, passwords, or similar secret access information for their credit card, bank, or other financial accounts.

If you receive an unsolicited email claiming to be from the IRS, forward the message to *phishing@irs.gov*. You may also report misuse of the IRS name, logo, forms, or other IRS property to the Treasury Inspector General for Tax Administration toll-free at 1-800-366-4484. People who are deaf, hard of hearing, or have a speech disability and who have access to TTY/TDD equipment can call 1-800-877-8339. You can forward suspicious emails to the Federal Trade Commission at *spam@uce.gov* or contact them at *www.ftc.gov/idtheft* or 1-877-IDTHEFT (1-877-438-4338). People who are deaf, hard of hearing, or have a speech disability and who have access to TTY/TDD equipment can call 1-866-653-4261.

Visit IRS.gov and enter "identity theft" in the search box to learn more about identity theft and how to reduce your risk.

How Do You Make a Gift To Reduce Debt Held By the Public?

If you wish to do so, make a check payable to "Bureau of the Fiscal Service." You can send it to: Bureau of the Fiscal Service, Attn: Dept G, P.O. Box 2188, Parkersburg, WV 26106-2188. Or you can enclose the check with your income tax return when you file. In the memo section of the check, make a note that it is a gift to reduce the debt held by the public. Do not add your gift to any tax you may owe. See the instructions for line 78 for details on how to pay any tax you owe. Go to *www.publicdebt.treas.gov/index1.htm* for information on how to make this type of gift online.

 You may be able to deduct this gift on your 2015 tax return.

How Long Should Records Be Kept?

Keep a copy of your tax return, worksheets you used, and records of all items appearing on it (such as Forms W-2 and 1099) until the statute of limitations runs out for that return. Usually, this is 3 years from the date the return was due or filed or 2 years from the date the tax was paid, whichever is later. You should keep some records longer. For example, keep property records (including those on your home) as long as they are needed to figure the basis of the original or replacement property. For more details, see chapter 1 of Pub. 17.

Amended Return

File Form 1040X to change a return you already filed. Generally, Form 1040X must be filed within 3 years after the date the original return was filed or within 2 years after the date the tax was paid, whichever is later. But you may have more time to file Form 1040X if you live in a federally declared disaster area or you are physically or mentally unable to manage your financial affairs. See Pub. 556 for details.

Use the *Where's My Amended Return* application on IRS.gov to track the status of your amended return. It can take up to 3 weeks from the date you mailed it to show up in our system.

Need a Copy of Your Tax Return Information?

Tax return transcripts are free and generally are used to validate income and tax filing status for mortgage applications, student and small business loan applications, and during tax preparation. To get a free transcript:
- Visit IRS.gov and click on "Get Transcript of Your Tax Records" under "Tools,"
- Use Form 4506-T or 4506T-EZ, or
- Call us at 1-800-908-9946.

If you need a copy of your actual tax return, use Form 4506. There is a fee for each return requested. See Form 4506 for the current fee. If your main home, principal place of business, or tax records are located in a federally declared disaster area, this fee will be waived.

Death of a Taxpayer

If a taxpayer died before filing a return for 2014, the taxpayer's spouse or personal representative may have to file and sign a return for that taxpayer. A personal representative can be an executor, administrator, or anyone who is in charge of the deceased taxpayer's property. If the deceased taxpayer did not have to file a return but had tax withheld, a return must be filed to get a refund. The person who files the return must enter "Deceased," the deceased taxpayer's name, and the date of death across the top of the return. If this information is not provided, it may delay the processing of the return.

If your spouse died in 2014 and you did not remarry in 2014, or if your spouse died in 2015 before filing a return for 2014, you can file a joint return. A joint return should show your spouse's 2014 income before death and your income for all of 2014. Enter "Filing as surviving spouse" in the area where you sign the return. If someone else is the personal representative, he or she must also sign.

The surviving spouse or personal representative should promptly notify all payers of income, including financial institutions, of the taxpayer's death. This will ensure the proper reporting of income earned by the taxpayer's estate or heirs. A deceased taxpayer's social security number should not be used for tax years after the year of death, except for estate tax return purposes.

Claiming a Refund for a Deceased Taxpayer

If you are filing a joint return as a surviving spouse, you only need to file the tax return to claim the refund. If you are a court-appointed representative, file the return and include a copy of the certificate that shows your appointment. All other filers requesting the deceased taxpayer's refund must file the return and attach Form 1310.

For more details, use TeleTax topic 356 or see Pub. 559.

Past Due Returns

If you or someone you know needs to file past due tax returns, use TeleTax topic 153 or go to *www.irs.gov/ individuals* for help in filing those returns. Send the return to the address that applies to you in the latest Form 1040 instructions. For example, if you are filing a 2011 return in 2015, use the address at the end of these instructions. However, if you got an IRS notice, mail the return to the address in the notice.

How To Get Tax Help

Do you need help with a tax issue or preparing your tax return, or do you need a free publication or form?

Preparing and filing your tax return. Find free options to prepare and file your return on IRS.gov or in your local community if you qualify.
- Go to IRS.gov and click on the Filing tab to see your options.
- Enter "Free File" in the search box to use brand name software to prepare and *e-file* your federal tax return for free.
- Enter "VITA" in the search box, download the free IRS2Go app, or call 1-800-906-9887 to find the nearest Volunteer Income Tax Assistance or Tax Counseling for the Elderly (TCE) location for free tax preparation.
- Enter "TCE" in the search box, download the free IRS2Go app, or call 1-888-227-7669 to find the nearest Tax Counseling for the Elderly location for free tax preparation.

The Volunteer Income Tax Assistance (VITA) program offers free tax help to people who generally make $53,000 or less, persons with disabilities, the elderly, and limited-English-speaking taxpayers who need help preparing their own tax returns. The Tax Counseling for the Elderly (TCE) program offers free tax help for all taxpayers, particularly those who are 60 years of age and older. TCE volunteers specialize in answering questions about pensions and retirement-related issues unique to seniors.

Getting answers to your tax law questions. IRS.gov and IRS2Go are ready when you are—24 hours a day, 7 days a week.
- Enter "ITA" in the search box on IRS.gov for the Interactive Tax Assistant, a tool that will ask you questions on a number of tax law topics and provide answers. You can print the entire interview and the final response.
- Enter "Tax Map" or "Tax Trails" in the search box for detailed information by tax topic.
- Enter "Pub 17" in the search box to get Pub. 17, Your Federal Income Tax for Individuals, which features details on tax-saving opportunities, 2014 tax changes, and thousands of interactive

links to help you find answers to your questions.
- Call TeleTax at 1-800-829-4477 for recorded information on a variety of tax topics. See *What Is TeleTax*, later, for a list of the topics covered.
- Access tax law information in your electronic filing software.
- Go to IRS.gov and click on the Help & Resources tab for more information.

Tax forms and publications. You can download or print all of the forms and publications you may need on *www.irs.gov/formspubs*. Otherwise, you can:
- Go to *www.irs.gov/orderforms* to place an order and have forms mailed to you.
- Call 1-800-829-3676 to order current-year forms, instructions, publications, and prior-year forms and instructions (limited to 5 years).
You should receive your order within 10 business days.

Where to file your tax return.
- Remember, there are many ways to file your return electronically. It's safe, quick and easy. See *Preparing and filing your tax return*, earlier, for more information.
- See *Where Do You File?* at the end of these instructions to determine where to mail your completed paper tax return.

Getting a transcript or copy of a return.
- Go to IRS.gov and click on "Get Transcript of Your Tax Records" under "Tools."
- Download the free IRS2Go app to your smart phone and use it to order transcripts of your tax returns or tax account.
- Call the transcript toll-free line at 1-800-908-9946.
- Mail Form 4506-T or Form 4506T-EZ (both available on IRS.gov).

Using online tools to help prepare your return. Go to IRS.gov and click on the Tools bar to use these and other self-service options.
- The *Earned Income Tax Credit Assistant* determines if you are eligible for the EIC.
- The *First Time Homebuyer Credit Account Look-up* tool provides information on your repayments and account balance.

- The *Alternative Minimum Tax (AMT) Assistant* determines whether you may be subject to AMT.
- The *Online EIN Application* helps you get an Employer Identification Number.
- The *IRS Withholding Calculator* estimates the amount you should have withheld from your paycheck for federal income tax purposes.
- The *Electronic Filing PIN Request* helps to verify your identity when you do not have your prior year AGI or prior year self-selected PIN available.

Understanding identity theft issues.
- Go to *www.irs.gov/uac/Identity-Protection* for information and videos.
- See *Secure Your Tax Records from Identity Theft* under *General Information*, earlier.

Checking on the status of a refund.
- Go to *www.irs.gov/refunds*.
- Download the free IRS2Go app to your smart phone and use it to check your refund status.
- Call the automated refund hotline at 1-800-829-1954. See *Refund Information*, later.

Making a tax payment. You can make electronic payments online, by phone, or from a mobile device. Paying electronically is safe and secure. The IRS uses the latest encryption technology and does not store banking information. It's easy and secure and much quicker than mailing in a check or money order. Go to IRS.gov and click on the Payments tab or the "Pay Your Tax Bill" icon to make a payment using the following options.
- *Direct Pay* (only if you have a checking or savings account).
- Debit or credit card.
- Electronic Federal Tax Payment System.
- Check or money order.

What if I can't pay now? Click on the Payments tab or the "Pay Your Tax Bill" icon on IRS.gov to find more information about these additional options.
- An *online payment agreement* determines if you are eligible to apply for an installment agreement if you cannot pay your taxes in full today. With the needed information, you can complete the application in about 30 minutes, and get immediate approval.

- An offer in compromise allows you to settle your tax debt for less than the full amount you owe. Use the *Offer in Compromise Pre-Qualifier* to confirm your eligibility.

Checking the status of an amended return.
- Go to IRS.gov and click on the Tools tab and then *Where's My Amended Return?*

Understanding an IRS notice or letter.
- Enter "Understanding your notice" in the search box on IRS.gov to find additional information about your IRS notice or letter.

Visiting the IRS. Locate the nearest Taxpayer Assistance Center using the Office Locator tool on IRS.gov. Enter "office locator" in the search box. Or choose the "Contact Us" option on the IRS2Go app and search Local Offices. Before you visit, use the Locator tool to check hours and services available.

Watching IRS videos. The IRS Video portal *www.irsvideos.gov* contains video and audio presentations on topics of interest to individuals, small businesses, and tax professionals. You'll find video clips of tax topics, archived versions of live panel discussions and Webinars, and audio archives of tax practitioner phone forums.

Getting tax information in other languages. For taxpayers whose native language is not English, we have the following resources available.
- Taxpayers can find information on IRS.gov in the following languages.
  - *Spanish*.
  - *Chinese*.
  - *Vietnamese*.
  - *Korean*.
  - *Russian*.
- The IRS Taxpayer Assistance Centers provide over-the-phone interpreter service in over 170 languages, and the service is available free to taxpayers.

Interest and Penalties

You do not have to figure the amount of any interest or penalties you may owe. Because figuring these amounts can be complicated, we will do it for you if you want. We will send you a bill for any amount due.

If you include interest or penalties (other than the estimated tax penalty)

with your payment, identify and enter the amount in the bottom margin of Form 1040, page 2. Do not include interest or penalties (other than the estimated tax penalty) in the amount you owe on line 78.

Interest

We will charge you interest on taxes not paid by their due date, even if an extension of time to file is granted. We will also charge you interest on penalties imposed for failure to file, negligence, fraud, substantial valuation misstatements, substantial understatements of tax, and reportable transaction understatements. Interest is charged on the penalty from the due date of the return (including extensions).

Penalties

Late filing. If you do not file your return by the due date (including extensions), the penalty is usually 5% of the amount due for each month or part of a month your return is late, unless you have a reasonable explanation. If you do, include it with your return. The penalty can be as much as 25% of the tax due. The penalty is 15% per month, up to a maximum of 75%, if the failure to file is fraudulent. If your return is more than 60 days late, the minimum penalty will be $135 (adjusted for inflation) or the amount of any tax you owe, whichever is smaller.

Late payment of tax. If you pay your taxes late, the penalty is usually ½ of 1% of the unpaid amount for each month or part of a month the tax is not paid. The penalty can be as much as 25% of the unpaid amount. It applies to any unpaid tax on the return. This penalty is in addition to interest charges on late payments.

Frivolous return. In addition to any other penalties, the law imposes a penalty of $5,000 for filing a frivolous return. A frivolous return is one that does not contain information needed to figure the correct tax or shows a substantially incorrect tax because you take a frivolous position or desire to delay or interfere with the tax laws. This includes altering or striking out the preprinted language above the space where you sign. For a list of positions identified as frivolous, see Notice 2010-33, 2010-17 I.R.B. 609, available at *www.irs.gov/irb/2010-17_IRB/ar13.html*.

Other. Other penalties can be imposed for negligence, substantial understatement of tax, reportable transaction understatements, filing an erroneous refund claim, and fraud. Criminal penalties may be imposed for willful failure to file, tax evasion, making a false statement, or identity theft. See Pub. 17 for details on some of these penalties.

Taxpayer Bill of Rights

All taxpayers have fundamental rights they should be aware of when dealing with the IRS. The Taxpayer Bill of Rights, which the IRS adopted in June of 2014, takes existing rights in the tax code and groups them into the following 10 broad categories, making them easier to understand. Explore your rights and our obligations to protect them.

The right to be informed. Taxpayers have the right to know what they need to do to comply with the tax laws. They are entitled to clear explanations of the laws and IRS procedures in all tax forms, instructions, publications, notices, and correspondence. They have the right to be informed of IRS decisions about their tax accounts and to receive clear explanations of the outcomes.

The right to quality service. Taxpayers have the right to receive prompt, courteous, and professional assistance in their dealings with the IRS, to be spoken to in a way they can easily understand, to receive clear and easily understandable communications from the IRS, and to speak to a supervisor about inadequate service.

The right to pay no more than the correct amount of tax. Taxpayers have the right to pay only the amount of tax legally due, including interest and penalties, and to have the IRS apply all tax payments properly.

The right to challenge the IRS's position and be heard. Taxpayers have the right to raise objections and provide additional documentation in response to formal IRS actions or proposed actions, to expect that the IRS will consider their timely objections and documentation promptly and fairly, and to receive a response if the IRS does not agree with their position.

The right to appeal an IRS decision in an independent forum. Taxpayers are entitled to a fair and impartial administrative appeal of most IRS decisions, including many penalties, and have the right to receive a written response regarding the Office of Appeals' decision. Taxpayers generally have the right to take their cases to court.

The right to finality. Taxpayers have the right to know the maximum amount of time they have to challenge the IRS's position as well as the maximum amount of time the IRS has to audit a particular tax year or collect a tax debt. Taxpayers have the right to know when the IRS has finished an audit.

The right to privacy. Taxpayers have the right to expect that any IRS inquiry, examination, or enforcement action will comply with the law and be no more intrusive than necessary, and will respect all due process rights, including search and seizure protections and will provide, where applicable, a collection due process hearing.

The right to confidentiality. Taxpayers have the right to expect that any information they provide to the IRS will not be disclosed unless authorized by the taxpayer or by law. Taxpayers have the right to expect appropriate action will be taken against employees, return preparers, and others who wrongfully use or disclose taxpayer return information.

The right to retain representation. Taxpayers have the right to retain an authorized representative of their choice to represent them in their dealings with the IRS. Taxpayers have the right to seek assistance from a _Low Income Taxpayer Clinic_ if they cannot afford representation.

The right to a fair and just tax system. Taxpayers have the right to expect the tax system to consider facts and circumstances that might affect their underlying liabilities, ability to pay, or ability to provide information timely. Taxpayers have the right to receive assistance from the _Taxpayer Advocate Service_ if they are experiencing financial difficulty or if the IRS has not resolved their tax issues properly and timely through its normal channels.

Learn more at _www.irs.gov/taxpayerrights_.

Refund Information

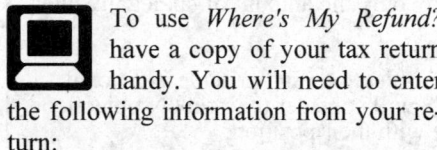 Visit IRS.gov and click on *Where's My Refund?* 24 hours a day, 7 days a week. Information about your return will generally be available within 24 hours after the IRS receives your e-filed return, or 4 weeks after you mail a paper return. But if you filed Form 8379 with your return, allow 14 weeks (11 weeks if you filed electronically) before checking your refund status.

 To use *Where's My Refund?* have a copy of your tax return handy. You will need to enter the following information from your return:

• Your social security number (or individual taxpayer identification number),

• Your filing status, and

• The exact whole dollar amount of your refund.

Where's My Refund? will provide an actual personalized refund date as soon as the IRS processes your tax return and approves your refund.

 Updates to refund status are made once a day - usually at night.

If you do not have Internet access, many services are available by phone:

• You can check the status of your refund on the free IRS2Go phone app.

• You can call 1-800-829-1954 24 hours a day, 7 days a week, for automated refund information. Our phone and walk-in assistors can research the status of your refund only if it's been 21 days or more since you filed electronically or more than 6 weeks since you mailed your paper return.

Do not send in a copy of your return unless asked to do so.

To get a refund, you generally must file your return within 3 years from the date the return was due (including extensions).

Where's My Refund? does not track refunds that are claimed on an amended tax return.

Refund information also is available in Spanish at *www.irs.gov/Spanish* and 1-800-829-1954.

What Is TeleTax?

Recorded Tax Information

Recorded tax information is available 24 hours a day, 7 days a week. Select the number of the topic you want to hear. Then, call 1-800-829-4477. Have paper and pencil handy to take notes.

Topics by Internet

TeleTax topics are also available at www.irs.gov/taxtopics.

TeleTax Topics

All topics are available in Spanish.

Topic No.	Subject
IRS Help Available	
101	IRS services—Volunteer tax assistance, outreach programs, and identity theft
102	Tax assistance for individuals with disabilities
103	Tax help for small businesses and the self-employed
104	Taxpayer Advocate Service—Your voice at the IRS
105	Armed Forces tax information
107	Tax relief in disaster situations
IRS Procedures	
151	Your appeal rights
152	Refund information
153	What to do if you haven't filed your tax return
154	Form W-2 and Form 1099-R (What to do if incorrect or not received)
155	Forms and publications—How to order
156	Copy or transcript of your tax return—How to get one
157	Change your address—How to notify the IRS
158	Ensuring proper credit of payments
159	Prior year(s) Form W-2 (How to get a copy)
161	Returning an erroneous refund—Paper check or direct deposit
Collection	
201	The balance due collection process
202	Tax payment options
203	Refund offsets for unpaid child support, certain federal and state debts, and unemployment compensation debts
204	Offers in compromise
205	Innocent spouse relief (Including separation of liability and equitable relief)
206	Dishonored payments
Alternative Filing Methods	
253	Substitute tax forms

Topic No.	Subject
254	How to choose a tax return preparer
255	Self-select PIN signature method
General Information	
301	When, how, and where to file
303	Checklist of common errors when preparing your tax return
304	Extensions of time to file your tax return
305	Recordkeeping
306	Penalty for underpayment of estimated tax
307	Backup withholding
308	Amended returns
309	Roth IRA contributions
310	Coverdell education savings accounts
311	Power of attorney information
312	Disclosure authorizations
313	Qualified tuition programs (QTPs)
Which Forms to File	
352	Which form—1040, 1040A, or 1040EZ?
356	Decedents
Types of Income	
401	Wages and salaries
403	Interest received
404	Dividends
407	Business income
409	Capital gains and losses
410	Pensions and annuities
411	Pensions—The general rule and the simplified method
412	Lump-sum distributions
413	Rollovers from retirement plans
414	Rental income and expenses
415	Renting residential and vacation property
416	Farming and fishing income
417	Earnings for clergy
418	Unemployment compensation
419	Gambling income and losses
420	Bartering income
421	Scholarships, fellowship grants, and other grants
423	Social security and equivalent railroad retirement benefits
424	401(k) plans
425	Passive activities—Losses and credits

Topic No.	Subject
427	Stock options
429	Traders in securities (information for Form 1040 filers)
430	Receipt of stock in a demutualization
431	Canceled debt—Is it taxable or not?
432	Form 1099-A (Acquisition or Abandonment of Secured Property) and Form 1099-C (Cancellation of Debt)
Adjustments to Income	
451	Individual retirement arrangements (IRAs)
452	Alimony paid
453	Bad debt deduction
455	Moving expenses
456	Student loan interest deduction
457	Tuition and fees deduction
458	Educator expense deduction
Itemized Deductions	
501	Should I itemize?
502	Medical and dental expenses
503	Deductible taxes
504	Home mortgage points
505	Interest expense
506	Charitable contributions
508	Miscellaneous expenses
509	Business use of home
510	Business use of car
511	Business travel expenses
512	Business entertainment expenses
513	Educational expenses
514	Employee business expenses
515	Casualty, disaster, and theft losses (including federally declared disaster areas)
Tax Computation	
551	Standard deduction
552	Tax and credits figured by the IRS
553	Tax on a child's investment income (Kiddie tax)
554	Self-employment tax
556	Alternative minimum tax
557	Additional tax on early distributions from traditional and Roth IRAs

TeleTax Topics

(Continued)

Topic numbers are effective January 1, 2015.

Disclosure, Privacy Act, and Paperwork Reduction Act Notice

The IRS Restructuring and Reform Act of 1998, the Privacy Act of 1974, and the Paperwork Reduction Act of 1980 require that when we ask you for information we must first tell you our legal right to ask for the information, why we are asking for it, and how it will be used. We must also tell you what could happen if we do not receive it and whether your response is voluntary, required to obtain a benefit, or mandatory under the law.

This notice applies to all papers you file with us, including this tax return. It also applies to any questions we need to ask you so we can complete, correct, or process your return; figure your tax; and collect tax, interest, or penalties.

Our legal right to ask for information is Internal Revenue Code sections 6001, 6011, and 6012(a), and their regulations. They say that you must file a return or statement with us for any tax you are liable for. Your response is mandatory under these sections. Code section 6109 requires you to provide your identifying number on the return. This is so we know who you are, and can process your return and other papers. You must fill in all parts of the tax form that apply to you. But you do not have to check the boxes for the Presidential Election Campaign Fund or for the third-party designee. You also do not have to provide your daytime phone number.

You are not required to provide the information requested on a form that is subject to the Paperwork Reduction Act unless the form displays a valid OMB control number. Books or records relating to a form or its instructions must be retained as long as their contents may become material in the administration of any Internal Revenue law.

We ask for tax return information to carry out the tax laws of the United States. We need it to figure and collect the right amount of tax.

If you do not file a return, do not provide the information we ask for, or provide fraudulent information, you may be charged penalties and be subject to criminal prosecution. We may also have to disallow the exemptions, exclusions, credits, deductions, or adjustments shown on the tax return. This could make the tax higher

or delay any refund. Interest may also be charged.

Generally, tax returns and return information are confidential, as stated in Code section 6103. However, Code section 6103 allows or requires the Internal Revenue Service to disclose or give the information shown on your tax return to others as described in the Code. For example, we may disclose your tax information to the Department of Justice to enforce the tax laws, both civil and criminal, and to cities, states, the District of Columbia, and U.S. commonwealths or possessions to carry out their tax laws. We may disclose your tax information to the Department of Treasury and contractors for tax administration purposes; and to other persons as necessary to obtain information needed to determine the amount of or to collect the tax you owe. We may disclose your tax information to the Comptroller General of the United States to permit the Comptroller General to review the Internal Revenue Service. We may disclose your tax information to committees of Congress; federal, state, and local child support agencies; and to other federal agencies for the purposes of determining entitlement for benefits or the eligibility for and the repayment of loans. We may also disclose this information to other countries under a tax treaty, to federal and state agencies to enforce federal nontax criminal laws, or to federal law enforcement and intelligence agencies to combat terrorism.

Please keep this notice with your records. It may help you if we ask you for other information. If you have questions about the rules for filing and giving information, please call or visit any Internal Revenue Service office.

We Welcome Comments on Forms

We try to create forms and instructions that can be easily understood. Often this is difficult to do because our tax laws are very complex. For some people with income mostly from wages, filling in the forms is easy. For others who have businesses, pensions, stocks, rental income, or other investments, it is more difficult.

If you have suggestions for making these forms simpler, we would be happy

to hear from you. You can send us comments from *www.irs.gov/formspubs/*. Click on "More Information" and then on "Give us feedback." Or you can send your comments to Internal Revenue Service, Tax Forms and Publications Division, 1111 Constitution Ave. NW, IR-6526, Washington, DC 20224. Do not send your return to this address. Instead, see the addresses at the end of these instructions.

Although we cannot respond individually to each comment received, we do appreciate your feedback and will consider your comments as we revise our tax forms and instructions.

Estimates of Taxpayer Burden

The following table shows burden estimates based on current statutory requirements as of November 2014, for taxpayers filing a 2014 Form 1040, 1040A, or 1040EZ tax return. Time spent and out-of-pocket costs are presented separately. Time burden is broken out by taxpayer activity, with recordkeeping representing the largest component. Out-of-pocket costs include any expenses incurred by taxpayers to prepare and submit their tax returns. Examples include tax return preparation and submission fees, postage and photocopying costs, and tax preparation software costs. While these estimates do not include burden associated with post-filing activities, IRS operational data indicate that electronically prepared and filed returns have fewer arithmetic errors, implying lower post-filing burden.

Reported time and cost burdens are national averages and do not necessarily reflect a "typical" case. Most taxpayers experience lower than average burden, with taxpayer burden varying considerably by taxpayer type. For instance, the estimated average time burden for all taxpayers filing a Form 1040, 1040A, or 1040EZ is 13 hours, with an average cost of $200 per return. This average includes all associated forms and schedules, across all preparation methods and taxpayer activities. The average burden for taxpayers filing Form 1040 is about 16 hours and $260; the average burden for taxpayers filing Form 1040A is about 8 hours and $80;

and the average for Form 1040EZ filers is about 5 hours and $40.

Within each of these estimates there is significant variation in taxpayer activity. For example, nonbusiness taxpayers are expected to have an average burden of about 8 hours and $110, while business taxpayers are expected to have an average burden of about 24 hours and $410. Similarly, tax preparation fees and other out-of-pocket costs vary extensively depending on the tax situation of the taxpayer, the type of software or professional preparer used, and the geographic location.

If you have comments concerning the time and cost estimates below, you can contact us at either one of the addresses shown under *We Welcome Comments on Forms*.

Estimated Average Taxpayer Burden for Individuals by Activity

Primary Form Filed or Type of Taxpayer	Percentage of Returns	Average Time Burden (Hours)					Average Cost (Dollars)**
		Total Time*	Record Keeping	Tax Planning	Form Completion and Submission	All Other	
All taxpayers	100	13	6	2	4	1	$200
Primary forms filed							
1040	69	16	8	2	5	1	260
1040A	19	8	2	1	3	1	80
1040EZ	12	5	1	***	2	1	40
Type of taxpayer							
Nonbusiness****	68	8	3	1	3	1	110
Business****	32	24	13	3	6	2	410

*Detail may not add to total time due to rounding.
 **Dollars rounded to the nearest $10.
***Rounds to less than 1 hour.
****You are considered a "business" filer if you file one or more of the following with Form 1040: Schedule C, C-EZ, E, or F or Form 2106 or 2106-EZ. You are considered a "nonbusiness" filer if you do not file any of those schedules or forms with Form 1040 or if you file Form 1040A or 1040EZ.

Order Form for Forms and Publications

 You can view and download the tax forms and publications you need at www.irs.gov/formspubs. You can also place an order for forms at www.irs.gov/orderforms to avoid having to complete and mail the order form.

The most frequently ordered forms and publications are listed on the order form. You will receive two copies of each form, one copy of the instructions, and one copy of each publication you order. To help reduce waste, please order only the items you need to prepare your return.

How To Use the Order Form

Circle the items you need on the order form. Use the blank spaces to order items not listed. If you need more space, attach a separate sheet of paper.

Print or type your name and address accurately in the space provided on the order form to ensure delivery of your order. Enclose the order form in an envelope and mail it to the IRS address shown next. You should receive your order within 10 business days after we receive your request.

Do not send your tax return to the address shown here. Instead, see the addresses at the end of these instructions.

Mail Your Order Form To:

Internal Revenue Service
1201 N. Mitsubishi Motorway
Bloomington, IL 61705-6613

---------------------------------- ▲ *Cut here* ▲ ----------------------------------

Save Money and Time by Going Online!
Download or order these and other forms and publications at www.irs.gov/formspubs

Order Form

Please print.

Circle the forms and publications you need. The instructions for any form you order will be included.

Use the **blank spaces** to order items not listed.

Use your QR Reader app on your smartphone to scan this code and get connected to the IRS Forms and Publications homepage.

Name

Postal mailing address | Apt./Suite/Room

City | State | ZIP code

Foreign country | International postal code

Daytime phone number
(   )

1040	Schedule F (1040)	1040-V	4868	8959	Pub. 505	Pub. 551	Pub. 946
Schedule A (1040)	Schedule H (1040)	1040X	5405	8960	Pub. 523	Pub. 554	Pub. 970
Schedule B (1040A or 1040)	Schedule J (1040)	2106	6251	8962	Pub. 525	Pub. 575	Pub. 972
Schedule C (1040)	Schedule R (1040A or 1040)	2441	8283	8965	Pub. 526	Pub. 583	Pub. 4681
Schedule C-EZ (1040)	Schedule SE (1040)	3903	8606	Pub. 1	Pub. 527	Pub. 587	
Schedule D (1040)	Schedule 8812 (1040A or 1040)	4506	8822	Pub. 334	Pub. 529	Pub. 590-A	
Form 8949	1040A	4506-T	8829	Pub. 463	Pub. 535	Pub. 590-B	
Schedule E (1040)	1040EZ	4562	8863	Pub. 501	Pub. 547	Pub. 596	
Schedule EIC (1040A or 1040)	1040-ES (2015)	4684	8917	Pub. 502	Pub. 550	Pub. 915	

Major Categories of Federal Income and Outlays for Fiscal Year 2013

Income and Outlays. These pie charts show the relative sizes of the major categories of federal income and outlays for fiscal year 2013.

Income

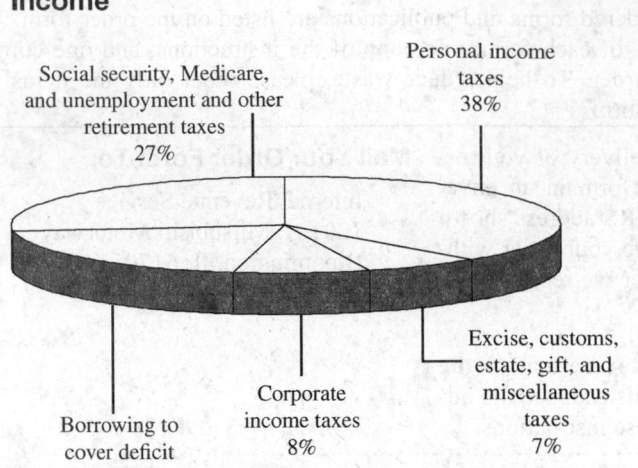

Social security, Medicare, and unemployment and other retirement taxes
27%

Personal income taxes
38%

Borrowing to cover deficit
20%

Corporate income taxes
8%

Excise, customs, estate, gift, and miscellaneous taxes
7%

Outlays

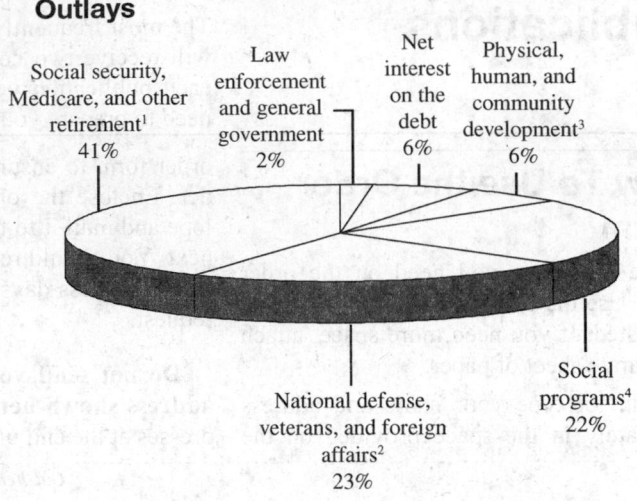

Social security, Medicare, and other retirement[1]
41%

Law enforcement and general government
2%

Net interest on the debt
6%

Physical, human, and community development[3]
6%

National defense, veterans, and foreign affairs[2]
23%

Social programs[4]
22%

On or before the first Monday in February of each year the President is required by law to submit to the Congress a budget proposal for the fiscal year that begins the following October. The budget plan sets forth the President's proposed receipts, spending, and the surplus or deficit for the Federal Government. The plan includes recommendations for new legislation as well as recommendations to change, eliminate, and add programs. After receipt of the President's proposal, the Congress reviews the proposal and makes changes. It first passes a budget resolution setting its own targets for receipts, outlays, and surplus or deficit. Next, individual spending and revenue bills that are consistent with the goals of the budget resolution are enacted.

In fiscal year 2013 (which began on October 1, 2012, and ended on September 30, 2013), Federal income was $2.775 trillion and outlays were $3.455 trillion, leaving a deficit of $680 billion.

Footnotes for Certain Federal Outlays

1. **Social security, Medicare, and other retirement:** These programs provide income support for the retired and disabled and medical care for the elderly.

2. **National defense, veterans, and foreign affairs:** About 18% of outlays were to equip, modernize, and pay our armed forces and to fund national defense activities; about 4% were for veterans benefits and services; and about 1% were for international activities, including military and economic assistance to foreign countries and the maintenance of U.S. embassies abroad.

3. **Physical, human, and community development:** These outlays were for agriculture; natural resources; environment; transportation; aid for elementary and secondary education and direct assistance to college students; job training; deposit insurance, commerce and housing credit, and community development; and space, energy, and general science programs.

4. **Social programs:** About 15% of total outlays were for Medicaid, food stamps, temporary assistance for needy families, supplemental security income, and related programs; and the remaining outlays were for health research and public health programs, unemployment compensation, assisted housing, and social services.

Note. The percentages shown here exclude undistributed offsetting receipts, which were $93 billion in fiscal year 2013. In the budget, these receipts are offset against spending in figuring the outlay totals shown above. These receipts are for the U.S. Government's share of its employee retirement programs, rents and royalties on the Outer Continental Shelf, and proceeds from the sale of assets.

2014
Tax Rate
Schedules

The Tax Rate Schedules are shown so you can see the tax rate that applies to all levels of taxable income. Do not use them to figure your tax. Instead, see the instructions for line 44.

Schedule X—If your filing status is **Single**

If your taxable income is:		The tax is:	of the amount over—
Over—	But not over—		
$0	$9,075	.... 10%	$0
9,075	36,900	$907.50 + 15%	9,075
36,900	89,350	5,081.25 + 25%	36,900
89,350	186,350	18,193.75 + 28%	89,350
186,350	405,100	45,353.75 + 33%	186,350
405,100	406,750	117,541.25 + 35%	405,100
406,750	....	118,118.75 + 39.6%	406,750

Schedule Y-1—If your filing status is **Married filing jointly** or **Qualifying widow(er)**

If your taxable income is:		The tax is:	of the amount over—
Over—	But not over—		
$0	$18,150	.... 10%	$0
18,150	73,800	$1,815.00 + 15%	18,150
73,800	148,850	10,162.50 + 25%	73,800
148,850	226,850	28,925.00 + 28%	148,850
226,850	405,100	50,765.00 + 33%	226,850
405,100	457,000	109,587.50 + 35%	405,100
457,600	....	127,962.50 + 39.6%	457,600

Schedule Y-2—If your filing status is **Married filing separately**

If your taxable income is:		The tax is:	of the amount over—
Over—	But not over—		
$0	$9,075	.... 10%	$0
9,075	36,900	$907.50 + 15%	9,075
36,900	74,425	5,081.25 + 25%	36,900
74,425	113,425	14,462.50 + 28%	74,425
113,425	202,550	25,382.50 + 33%	113,425
202,550	228,800	54,793.75 + 35%	202,550
228,800	....	63,981.25 + 39.6%	228,800

Schedule Z—If your filing status is **Head of household**

If your taxable income is:		The tax is:	of the amount over—
Over—	But not over—		
$0	$12,950	.... 10%	$0
12,950	49,400	$1,295.00 + 15%	12,950
49,400	127,550	6,762.50 + 25%	49,400
127,550	206,600	26,300.00 + 28%	127,550
206,600	405,100	48,434.00 + 33%	206,600
405,100	432,200	113,939.00 + 35%	405,100
432,200	....	123,424.00 + 39.6%	432,200

Where Do You File? Mail your return to the address shown below that applies to you. If you want to use a private delivery service, see *Private Delivery Services* under *Filing Requirements,* earlier.

 Envelopes without enough postage will be returned to you by the post office. Your envelope may need additional postage if it contains more than five pages or is oversized (for example, it is over $^1\!/_4''$ thick). Also, include your complete return address.

IF you live in...	THEN use this address if you:	
	Are requesting a refund or are not enclosing a check or money order...	**Are enclosing a check or money order...**
Florida, Louisiana, Mississippi, Texas	Department of the Treasury Internal Revenue Service Austin, TX 73301-0002	Internal Revenue Service P.O. Box 1214 Charlotte, NC 28201-1214
Alaska, Arizona, California, Colorado, Hawaii, Idaho, Nevada, New Mexico, Oregon, Utah, Washington, Wyoming	Department of the Treasury Internal Revenue Service Fresno, CA 93888-0002	Internal Revenue Service P.O. Box 7704 San Francisco, CA 94120-7704
Arkansas, Illinois, Indiana, Iowa, Kansas, Michigan, Minnesota, Montana, Nebraska, North Dakota, Ohio, Oklahoma, South Dakota, Wisconsin	Department of the Treasury Internal Revenue Service Fresno, CA 93888-0002	Internal Revenue Service P.O. Box 802501 Cincinnati, OH 45280-2501
Alabama, Georgia, Kentucky, New Jersey, North Carolina, South Carolina, Tennessee, Virginia	Department of the Treasury Internal Revenue Service Kansas City, MO 64999-0002	Internal Revenue Service P.O. Box 931000 Louisville, KY 40293-1000
Connecticut, Delaware, District of Columbia, Maine, Maryland, Massachusetts, Missouri, New Hampshire, New York, Pennsylvania, Rhode Island, Vermont, West Virginia	Department of the Treasury Internal Revenue Service Kansas City, MO 64999-0002	Internal Revenue Service P.O. Box 37008 Hartford, CT 06176-7008
A foreign country, U.S. possession or territory*, or use an APO or FPO address, or file Form 2555, 2555-EZ, or 4563, or are a dual-status alien	Department of the Treasury Internal Revenue Service Austin, TX 73301-0215	Internal Revenue Service P.O. Box 1303 Charlotte, NC 28201-1303

*If you live in American Samoa, Puerto Rico, Guam, the U.S. Virgin Islands, or the Northern Mariana Islands, see Pub. 570.

Department of the Treasury
Internal Revenue Service

2014 Instructions for Schedule A (Form 1040)

Itemized Deductions

Use Schedule A (Form 1040) to figure your itemized deductions. In most cases, your federal income tax will be less if you take the larger of your itemized deductions or your standard deduction.

If you itemize, you can deduct a part of your medical and dental expenses and unreimbursed employee business expenses, and amounts you paid for certain taxes, interest, contributions, and miscellaneous expenses. You can also deduct certain casualty and theft losses.

If you and your spouse paid expenses jointly and are filing separate returns for 2014, see Pub. 504 to figure the portion of joint expenses that you can claim as itemized deductions.

 Do not include on Schedule A items deducted elsewhere, such as on Form 1040 or Schedule C, C-EZ, E, or F.

Section references are to the Internal Revenue Code unless otherwise noted.

Future Developments. For the latest information about developments related to Schedule A (Form 1040) and its instructions, such as legislation enacted after they were published, go to *www.irs.gov/schedulea*.

What's New

Limit on itemized deductions. Itemized deductions for taxpayers with adjusted gross incomes above $152,525 may be reduced. See the instructions for line 29.

Standard mileage rates. The standard mileage rate allowed for operating expenses for a car when you use it for medical reasons is 23.5 cents per mile. The business standard mileage rate is 56 cents per mile. The 2014 rate for use of your vehicle to do volunteer work for certain charitable organizations remains at 14 cents per mile.

Medical and Dental Expenses

You generally can deduct only the part of your medical and dental expenses that exceeds 10% of the amount on Form 1040, line 38. However, if either you or your spouse was born before January 2, 1950, you can deduct the part of your medical and dental expenses that exceeds 7.5% of the amount on Form 1040, line 38. See the instructions for line 3.

Pub. 502 discusses the types of expenses you can and cannot deduct. It also explains when you can deduct capital expenses and special care expenses for disabled persons.

 If you received a distribution from a health savings account or a medical savings account in 2014, see Pub. 969 to figure your deduction.

Examples of Medical and Dental Payments You Can Deduct

To the extent you were not reimbursed, you can deduct what you paid for:

- Insurance premiums for medical and dental care, including premiums for qualified long-term care insurance contracts as defined in Pub. 502. But see *Limit on long-term care premiums you can deduct*, later. Reduce the insurance premiums by any self-employed health insurance deduction you claimed on Form 1040, line 29. You cannot deduct insurance premiums paid with pretax dollars because the premiums are not included in box 1 of your Form(s) W-2. If you are a retired public safety officer, you cannot deduct any premiums you paid to the extent they were paid for with a tax-free distribution from your retirement plan.
- Prescription medicines or insulin.
- Acupuncturists, chiropractors, dentists, eye doctors, medical doctors, occupational therapists, osteopathic doctors, physical therapists, podiatrists, psychiatrists, psychoanalysts (medical care only), and psychologists.
- Medical examinations, X-ray and laboratory services, insulin treatment, and whirlpool baths your doctor ordered.
- Diagnostic tests, such as a full-body scan, pregnancy test, or blood sugar test kit.
- Nursing help (including your share of the employment taxes paid). If you paid someone to do both nursing and housework, you can deduct only the cost of the nursing help.
- Hospital care (including meals and lodging), clinic costs, and lab fees.
- Qualified long-term care services (see Pub. 502).
- The supplemental part of Medicare insurance (Medicare B).
- The premiums you pay for Medicare Part D insurance.
- A program to stop smoking and for prescription medicines to alleviate nicotine withdrawal.

Jan 05, 2015

- A weight-loss program as treatment for a specific disease (including obesity) diagnosed by a doctor.
- Medical treatment at a center for drug or alcohol addiction.
- Medical aids such as eyeglasses, contact lenses, hearing aids, braces, crutches, wheelchairs, and guide dogs, including the cost of maintaining them.
- Surgery to improve defective vision, such as laser eye surgery or radial keratotomy.
- Lodging expenses (but not meals) while away from home to receive medical care in a hospital or a medical care facility related to a hospital, provided there was no significant element of personal pleasure, recreation, or vacation in the travel. Do not deduct more than $50 a night for each eligible person.
- Ambulance service and other travel costs to get medical care. If you used your own car, you can claim what you spent for gas and oil to go to and from the place you received the care; or you can claim 23.5 cents per mile. Add parking and tolls to the amount you claim under either method.
- Cost of breast pumps and supplies that assist lactation.

Deceased taxpayer. Certain medical expenses paid out of a deceased taxpayer's estate can be claimed on the deceased taxpayer's final return. See Pub. 502 for details.

Limit on long-term care premiums you can deduct. The amount you can deduct for qualified long-term care insurance contracts (as defined in Pub. 502) depends on the age, at the end of 2014, of the person for whom the premiums were paid. See the following chart for details.

IF the person was, at the end of 2014, age . . .	THEN the most you can deduct is . . .
40 or under	$ 370
41–50	$ 700
51–60	$ 1,400
61–70	$ 3,720
71 or older	$ 4,660

Examples of Medical and Dental Payments You Cannot Deduct

- The cost of diet food.
- Cosmetic surgery unless it was necessary to improve a deformity related to a congenital abnormality, an injury from an accident or trauma, or a disfiguring disease.
- Life insurance or income protection policies.
- The Medicare tax on your wages and tips or the Medicare tax paid as part of the self-employment tax or household employment taxes.

 If you were age 65 or older but not entitled to social security benefits, you can deduct premiums you voluntarily paid for Medicare A coverage.

- Nursing care for a healthy baby. But you may be able to take a credit for the amount you paid. See the instructions for Form 2441.
- Illegal operations or drugs.
- Imported drugs not approved by the U.S. Food and Drug Administration (FDA). This includes foreign-made versions of U.S.-approved drugs manufactured without FDA approval.
- Nonprescription medicines, other than insulin, (including nicotine gum and certain nicotine patches).
- Travel your doctor told you to take for rest or a change.
- Funeral, burial, or cremation costs.

Line 1

Medical and Dental Expenses

Enter the total of your medical and dental expenses, after you reduce these expenses by any payments received from insurance or other sources. See *Reimbursements*, later.

 Do not forget to include insurance premiums you paid for medical and dental care. But if you claimed the self-employed health insurance deduction on Form 1040, line 29, reduce the premiums by the amount on line 29.

Whose medical and dental expenses can you include? You can include medical and dental bills you paid in 2014 for anyone who was one of the following either when the services were provided or when you paid for them.

- Yourself and your spouse.
- All dependents you claim on your return.
- Your child whom you do not claim as a dependent because of the rules for children of divorced or separated parents.
- Any person you could have claimed as a dependent on your return except that person received $3,950 or more of gross income or filed a joint return.
- Any person you could have claimed as a dependent except that you, or your spouse if filing jointly, can be claimed as a dependent on someone else's 2014 return.

Example. You provided over half of your mother's support but cannot claim her as a dependent because she received wages of $3,950 in 2014. You can include on line 1 any medical and dental expenses you paid in 2014 for your mother.

Insurance premiums for certain nondependents. You may have a medical or dental insurance policy that also covers an individual who is not your dependent (for example, a nondependent child under age 27). You cannot deduct any premiums attributable to this individual, unless they are such a person described under *Whose medical and dental expenses can you include*, earlier. However, if you had family coverage when you added this individual to your policy and your premiums did not increase, you can enter on line 1 the full amount of your medical and dental insurance premiums. See Pub. 502 for more information.

Reimbursements. If your insurance company paid the provider directly for part of your expenses, and you paid only the amount that remained, include on line 1 only the amount you paid. If you received a reimbursement in 2014 for medical or dental expenses you paid in 2014, reduce your 2014 expenses by this amount. If you received a reimbursement in 2014 for prior year medical or dental expenses, do not reduce your 2014 expenses by this amount. But if you deducted the expenses in the earlier year and the deduction reduced your tax, you must include the reimbursement in income on Form 1040, line 21. See Pub. 502 for details on how to figure the amount to include.

Cafeteria plans. Do not include on line 1 insurance premiums paid by an employer-sponsored health insurance plan (cafeteria plan) unless the premiums are included in box 1 of your Form(s) W-2. Also, do not include any other medical and dental expenses paid by the plan unless the amount paid is included in box 1 of your Form(s) W-2.

Line 3

Multiply line 2 by 10%. But, if either you or your spouse was born before January 2, 1950, multiply line 2 by 7.5%. The 7.5% rate applies whether you file a joint or separate return as long as one spouse was born before January 2, 1950.

 If you are claiming the 7.5% threshold amount for medical and dental expenses, make sure you check the appropriate box(es) on line 39a of Form 1040 for your situation. If your filing status is married filing separately or head of household, and you were not born before January 2, 1950, attach a statement to your return indicating that you are taking the 7.5% threshold because your spouse meets the requirements.

Death before age 65. A taxpayer is considered to be age 65 on the day before the taxpayer's 65th birthday. If the taxpayer was not age 65 or older at the time of death, the 7.5% threshold does not apply for that taxpayer or the spouse of that taxpayer who is under age 65. For example, a taxpayer who was born on February 14, 1949, dies on February 13, 2014. The taxpayer is considered age 65 at the time of death and the 7.5% threshold applies. However, if the taxpayer died on February 12, 2014, the taxpayer is not considered age 65 and the 7.5% threshold does not apply.

Taxes You Paid

Taxes You Cannot Deduct

- Federal income and most excise taxes.
- Social security, Medicare, federal unemployment (FUTA), and railroad retirement (RRTA) taxes.

- Customs duties.
- Federal estate and gift taxes. But see the instructions for *Line 28*.
- Certain state and local taxes, including: tax on gasoline, car inspection fees, assessments for sidewalks or other improvements to your property, tax you paid for someone else, and license fees (marriage, driver's, dog, etc.).

Line 5

 You can elect to deduct state and local general sales taxes instead of state and local income taxes. You cannot deduct both.

State and Local Income Taxes

If you elect to deduct state and local income taxes, you **must** check **box a** on line 5. Include on this line the state and local income taxes listed next.

- State and local income taxes withheld from your salary during 2014. Your Form(s) W-2 will show these amounts. Forms W-2G, 1099-G, 1099-R, and 1099-MISC may also show state and local income taxes withheld.
- State and local income taxes paid in 2014 for a prior year, such as taxes paid with your 2013 state or local income tax return. Do not include penalties or interest.
- State and local estimated tax payments made during 2014, including any part of a prior year refund that you chose to have credited to your 2014 state or local income taxes.
- Mandatory contributions you made to the California, New Jersey, or New York Nonoccupational Disability Benefit Fund, Rhode Island Temporary Disability Benefit Fund, or Washington State Supplemental Workmen's Compensation Fund.
- Mandatory contributions to the Alaska, California, New Jersey, or Pennsylvania state unemployment fund.
- Mandatory contributions to state family leave programs, such as the New Jersey Family Leave Insurance (FLI) program and the California Paid Family Leave program.

Do not reduce your deduction by any:
- State or local income tax refund or credit you expect to receive for 2014, or
- Refund of, or credit for, prior year state and local income taxes you actually

received in 2014. Instead, see the instructions for Form 1040, line 10.

State and Local General Sales Taxes

If you elect to deduct state and local general sales taxes, you **must** check **box b** on line 5. To figure your deduction, you can use either your actual expenses or the optional sales tax tables.

Actual Expenses

Generally, you can deduct the actual state and local general sales taxes (including compensating use taxes) you paid in 2014 if the tax rate was the same as the general sales tax rate. However, sales taxes on food, clothing, medical supplies, and motor vehicles are deductible as a general sales tax even if the tax rate was less than the general sales tax rate. If you paid sales tax on a motor vehicle at a rate higher than the general sales tax rate, you can deduct only the amount of tax that you would have paid at the general sales tax rate on that vehicle. Motor vehicles include cars, motorcycles, motor homes, recreational vehicles, sport utility vehicles, trucks, vans, and off-road vehicles. Also include any state and local general sales taxes paid for a leased motor vehicle. Do not include sales taxes paid on items used in your trade or business.

 You must keep your actual receipts showing general sales taxes paid to use this method.

Refund of general sales taxes. If you received a refund of state or local general sales taxes in 2014 for amounts paid in 2014, reduce your **actual** 2014 state and local general sales taxes by this amount. If you received a refund of state or local general sales taxes in 2014 for prior year purchases, do not reduce your 2014 state and local general sales taxes by this amount. But if you deducted your **actual** state and local general sales taxes in the earlier year and the deduction reduced your tax, you may have to include the refund in income on Form 1040, line 21. See *Recoveries* in Pub. 525 for details.

Optional Sales Tax Tables

Instead of using your actual expenses, you can use the 2014 Optional State

Sales Tax Table and the 2014 Optional Local Sales Tax Tables for Certain Local Jurisdictions at the end of these instructions to figure your state and local general sales tax deduction. You may also be able to add the state and local general sales taxes paid on certain specified items.

To figure your state and local general sales tax deduction using the tables, complete the State and Local General Sales Tax Deduction Worksheet or use the Sales Tax Deduction Calculator on the IRS website at *www.irs.gov/Individuals/Sales-Tax-Deduction-Calculator*.

 *If your filing status is married filing separately, both you and your spouse elect to deduct sales taxes, **and** your spouse elects to use the optional sales tax tables, you also must use the tables to figure your state and local general sales tax deduction.*

Instructions for the State and Local General Sales Tax Deduction Worksheet

Line 1. If you lived in the same state for all of 2014, enter the applicable amount, based on your 2014 income and exemptions, from the 2014 Optional State Sales Tax Table for your state. Read down the "At least–But less than" columns for your state and find the line that includes your 2014 income. If married filing separately, do not include your spouse's income. Your 2014 income is the amount shown on your Form 1040, line 38, **plus** any nontaxable items, such as the following.
- Tax-exempt interest.
- Veterans' benefits.
- Nontaxable combat pay.
- Workers' compensation.
- Nontaxable part of social security and railroad retirement benefits.
- Nontaxable part of IRA, pension, or annuity distributions. Do not include rollovers.
- Public assistance payments.

The exemptions column refers to the number of exemptions claimed on Form 1040, line 6d.

What if you lived in more than one state? If you lived in more than one state during 2014, look up the table amount for each state using the rules stated earlier. If there is no table for your state, the table amount is considered to be zero. Multiply the table amount for each state you lived in by a fraction. The numerator of the fraction is the number of days you lived in the state during 2014 and the denominator is the total number of days in the year (365). Enter the total of the prorated table amounts for each state on line 1. However, if you also lived in a locality during 2014 that imposed a local general sales tax, do not enter the total on line 1. Instead, complete a separate worksheet for each state you lived in and enter the prorated amount for that state on line 1.

Example. You lived in State A from January 1 through August 31, 2014 (243 days), and in State B from September 1 through December 31, 2014 (122 days). The table amount for State A is $500. The table amount for State B is $400. You would figure your state general sales tax as follows.

State A:	$500 x 243/365 =	$333
State B:	$400 x 122/365 =	134
Total	=	$467

If none of the localities in which you lived during 2014 imposed a local general sales tax, enter $467 on line 1 of your worksheet. Otherwise, complete a separate worksheet for State A and State B. Enter $333 on line 1 of the State A worksheet and $134 on line 1 of the State B worksheet.

Line 2. If you checked the "No" box, enter -0- on line 2, and go to line 3. If you checked the "Yes" box and lived in the same locality for all of 2014, enter the applicable amount, based on your 2014 income and exemptions, from the 2014 Optional Local Sales Tax Tables for Certain Local Jurisdictions for your locality. Read down the "At least–But less than" columns for your locality and find the line that includes your 2014 income. See the instructions for line 1 of the worksheet to figure your 2014 income. The exemptions column refers to the number of exemptions claimed on Form 1040, line 6d.

What if you lived in more than one locality? If you lived in more than one locality during 2014, look up the table amount for each locality using the rules stated earlier. If there is no table for your locality, the table amount is considered to be zero. Multiply the table amount for each locality you lived in by a fraction. The numerator of the fraction is the number of days you lived in the locality during 2014 and the denominator is the total number of days in the year (365). If you lived in more than one locality in the same state and the local general sales tax rate was the same for each locality, enter the total of the prorated table amounts for each locality in that state on line 2. Otherwise, complete a separate worksheet for lines 2 through 6 for each locality and enter each prorated table amount on line 2 of the applicable worksheet.

Example. You lived in Locality 1 from January 1 through August 31, 2014 (243 days), and in Locality 2 from September 1 through December 31, 2014 (122 days). The table amount for Locality 1 is $100. The table amount for Locality 2 is $150. You would figure the amount to enter on line 2 as follows. Note that this amount may not equal your local sales tax deduction, which is figured on line 6 of the worksheet.

Locality 1:	$100 x 243/365 =	$67
Locality 2:	$150 x 122/365 =	50
Total	=	$117

Line 3. If you lived in California, check the "No" box if your combined state and local general sales tax rate is 7.5000%. Otherwise, check the "Yes" box and include on line 3 only the part of the combined rate that is more than 7.5000%.

If you lived in Nevada, check the "No" box if your combined state and local general sales tax rate is 6.8500%. Otherwise, check the "Yes" box and include on line 3 only the part of the combined rate that is more than 6.8500%.

What if your local general sales tax rate changed during 2014? If you checked the "Yes" box and your local general sales tax rate changed during 2014, figure the rate to enter on line 3 as follows. Multiply each tax rate for the period it was in effect by a fraction. The numerator of the fraction is the number of days the rate was in effect during 2014 and the denominator is the total number of days in the year (365). Enter the total of the prorated tax rates on line 3.

Example. Locality 1 imposed a 1% local general sales tax from January 1 through September 30, 2014 (273 days). The rate increased to 1.75% for the peri- od from October 1 through December 31, 2014 (92 days). You would enter "1.189" on line 3, figured as follows.

State and Local General Sales Tax Deduction Worksheet—Line 5b

Keep for Your Records

TIP *Instead of using this worksheet, you can find your deduction by using the Sales Tax Deduction Calculator at IRS.gov.*

Before you begin: See the instructions for line 1 of the worksheet if you:

    ✓ Lived in more than one state during 2014, or
    ✓ Had any **nontaxable** income in 2014.

---

1. Enter your **state** general sales taxes from the 2014 Optional State Sales Tax Table . . . . 1. $ _____

    Next. If, for all of 2014, you lived only in Connecticut, the District of Columbia, Indiana, Kentucky, Maine, Maryland, Massachusetts, Michigan, New Jersey, or Rhode Island, skip lines 2 through 5, enter -0- on line 6, and go to line 7. Otherwise, go to line 2.

2. Did you live in Alaska, Arizona, Arkansas, Colorado, Georgia, Illinois, Louisiana, Missouri, New York, North Carolina, South Carolina, Tennessee, Utah, Virginia, or West Virginia in 2014?

    ☐ **No.** Enter -0-

    ☐ **Yes.** Enter your base **local** general sales taxes from the 2014 Optional Local Sales Tax Tables for Certain Local Jurisdictions   . . . .   2. $ _____

3. Did your locality impose a **local** general sales tax in 2014? Residents of California and Nevada, see the instructions for line 3 of the worksheet.

    ☐ **No.** Skip lines 3 through 5, enter -0- on line 6, and go to line 7.

    ☐ **Yes.** Enter your **local** general sales tax rate, but omit the percentage sign. For example, if your local general sales tax rate was 2.5%, enter 2.5. If your local general sales tax rate changed or you lived in more than one locality in the same state during 2014, see the instructions for line 3 of the worksheet . . . . 3. _____ . _____

4. Did you enter -0- on line 2?

    ☐ **No.** Skip lines 4 and 5 and go to line 6.

    ☐ **Yes.** Enter your **state** general sales tax rate (shown in the table heading for your state), but omit the percentage sign. For example, if your state general sales tax rate is 6%, enter 6.0 . . . . 4. _____ . _____

5. Divide line 3 by line 4. Enter the result as a decimal (rounded to at least three places) . . . . 5. _____ . _____

6. Did you enter -0- on line 2?

    ☐ **No.** Multiply line 2 by line 3

    ☐ **Yes.** Multiply line 1 by line 5. If you lived in more than one locality in the same state during 2014, see the instructions for line 6 of the worksheet   . . . .   6. $ _____

7. Enter your state and local general sales taxes paid on specified items, if any. See the instructions for line 7 of the worksheet . . . . 7. $ _____

8. **Deduction for general sales taxes.** Add lines 1, 6, and 7. Enter the result here and the total from all your state and local general sales tax deduction worksheets, if you completed more than one, on Schedule A, line 5. Be sure to check **box b** on that line . . . . 8. $ _____

January 1 –	
September 30:	1.00 x 273/365 = 0.748
October 1 –	
December 31:	1.75 x 92/365 = 0.441
Total	= 1.189

What if you lived in more than one locality in the same state during 2014? Complete a separate worksheet for lines 2 through 6 for each locality in your state if you lived in more than one locality in the same state during 2014 and each locality did not have the same local general sales tax rate.

To figure the amount to enter on line 3 of the worksheet for each locality in which you lived (except a locality for which you used the 2014 Optional Local Sales Tax Tables for Certain Local Jurisdictions to figure your local general sales tax deduction), multiply the local general sales tax rate by a fraction. The numerator of the fraction is the number of days you lived in the locality during 2014 and the denominator is the total number of days in the year (365).

Example. You lived in Locality 1 from January 1 through August 31, 2014 (243 days), and in Locality 2 from September 1 through December 31, 2014 (122 days). The local general sales tax rate for Locality 1 is 1%. The rate for Locality 2 is 1.75%. You would enter "0.666" on line 3 for the Locality 1 worksheet and "0.585" for the Locality 2 worksheet, figured as follows.

Locality 1:	1.00 x 243/365 = 0.666
Locality 2:	1.75 x 122/365 = 0.585

Line 6. If you lived in more than one locality in the same state during 2014, you should have completed line 1 only on the first worksheet for that state and separate worksheets for lines 2 through 6 for any other locality within that state in which you lived during 2014. If you checked the "Yes" box on line 6 of any of those worksheets, multiply line 5 of that worksheet by the amount that you entered on line 1 for that state on the first worksheet.

Line 7. Enter on line 7 any state and local general sales taxes paid on the following specified items. If you are completing more than one worksheet,

include the total for line 7 on only one of the worksheets.

1. A motor vehicle (including a car, motorcycle, motor home, recreational vehicle, sport utility vehicle, truck, van, and off-road vehicle). Also include any state and local general sales taxes paid for a leased motor vehicle. If the state sales tax rate on these items is higher than the general sales tax rate, only include the amount of tax you would have paid at the general sales tax rate.

2. An aircraft or boat, if the tax rate was the same as the general sales tax rate.

3. A home (including a mobile home or prefabricated home) or substantial addition to or major renovation of a home, but only if the tax rate was the same as the general sales tax rate and any of the following applies.

a. Your state or locality imposes a general sales tax directly on the sale of a home or on the cost of a substantial addition or major renovation.

b. You purchased the materials to build a home or substantial addition or to perform a major renovation and paid the sales tax directly.

c. Under your state law, your contractor is considered your agent in the construction of the home or substantial addition or the performance of a major renovation. The contract must state that the contractor is authorized to act in your name and must follow your directions on construction decisions. In this case, you will be considered to have purchased any items subject to a sales tax and to have paid the sales tax directly.

Do not include sales taxes paid on items used in your trade or business. If you received a refund of state or local general sales taxes in 2014, see *Refund of general sales taxes*, earlier.

Line 6

Real Estate Taxes

 TIP *If you are a homeowner who received assistance under a State Housing Finance Agency Hardest Hit Fund program or an Emergency Homeowners' Loan program, see Pub. 530 for the amount you can deduct on line 6.*

Include taxes (state, local, or foreign) you paid on real estate you own that was not used for business, but only if the taxes are assessed uniformly at a like rate on all real property throughout the community, and the proceeds are used for general community or governmental purposes. Pub. 530 explains the deductions homeowners can take.

Do not include the following amounts on line 6.

- Itemized charges for services to specific property or persons (for example, a $20 monthly charge per house for trash collection, a $5 charge for every 1,000 gallons of water consumed, or a flat charge for mowing a lawn that had grown higher than permitted under a local ordinance).

- Charges for improvements that tend to increase the value of your property (for example, an assessment to build a new sidewalk). The cost of a property improvement is added to the basis of the property. However, a charge is deductible if it is used only to maintain an existing public facility in service (for example, a charge to repair an existing sidewalk, and any interest included in that charge).

If your mortgage payments include your real estate taxes, you can deduct only the amount the mortgage company actually paid to the taxing authority in 2014.

If you sold your home in 2014, any real estate tax charged to the buyer should be shown on your settlement statement and in box 5 of any Form 1099-S you received. This amount is considered a refund of real estate taxes. See *Refunds and rebates*, later. Any real estate taxes you paid at closing should be shown on your settlement statement.

 CAUTION *You must look at your real estate tax bill to decide if any nondeductible itemized charges, such as those listed earlier, are included in the bill. If your taxing authority (or lender) does not furnish you a copy of your real estate tax bill, ask for it.*

Refunds and rebates. If you received a refund or rebate in 2014 of real estate taxes you paid in 2014, reduce your deduction by the amount of the refund or rebate. If you received a refund or rebate in 2014 of real estate taxes you paid in an earlier year, do not reduce your deduction by this amount. Instead, you must include the refund or rebate in income on Form 1040, line 21, if you deducted the real estate taxes in the earlier year and the deduction reduced your tax. See *Recoveries* in Pub. 525 for details on how to figure the amount to include in income.

Line 7

Personal Property Taxes

Enter the state and local personal property taxes you paid, but only if the taxes were based on value alone and were imposed on a yearly basis.

Example. You paid a yearly fee for the registration of your car. Part of the fee was based on the car's value and part was based on its weight. You can deduct only the part of the fee that was based on the car's value.

Line 8

Other Taxes

If you had any deductible tax not listed on line 5, 6, or 7, list the type and amount of tax. Enter only one total on line 8. Include on this line income tax you paid to a foreign country or U.S. possession.

 You may want to take a credit for the foreign tax instead of a deduction. See the instructions for Form 1040, line 48, for details.

Interest You Paid

Whether your interest expense is treated as investment interest, personal interest, or business interest depends on how and when you used the loan proceeds. See Pub. 535 for details.

In general, if you paid interest in 2014 that applies to any period after 2014, you can deduct only amounts that apply for 2014.

Lines 10 and 11

Home Mortgage Interest

 If you are a homeowner who received assistance under a State Housing Finance Agency Hardest Hit Fund program or an Emergency Homeowners' Loan program, see Pub. 530 for the amount you can deduct on line 10 or 11.

A home mortgage is any loan that is secured by your main home or second home. It includes first and second mortgages, home equity loans, and refinanced mortgages.

A home can be a house, condominium, cooperative, mobile home, boat, or similar property. It must provide basic living accommodations including sleeping space, toilet, and cooking facilities.

Limit on home mortgage interest. If you took out any mortgages after October 13, 1987, your deduction may be limited. Any additional amounts borrowed after October 13, 1987, on a line-of-credit mortgage you had on that date are treated as a mortgage taken out after October 13, 1987. If you refinanced a mortgage you had on October 13, 1987, treat the new mortgage as taken out on or before October 13, 1987. But if you refinanced for more than the balance of the old mortgage, treat the excess as a mortgage taken out after October 13, 1987.

See Pub. 936 to figure your deduction if either (1) or (2) next applies. If you had more than one home at the same time, the dollar amounts in (1) and (2) apply to the total mortgages on both homes.

1. You took out any mortgages after October 13, 1987, and used the proceeds for purposes other than to buy, build, or improve your home, and all of these mortgages totaled over $100,000 at any time during 2014. The limit is $50,000 if married filing separately. An example of this type of mortgage is a home equity loan used to pay off credit card bills, buy a car, or pay tuition.

2. You took out any mortgages after October 13, 1987, and used the proceeds to buy, build, or improve your home, and these mortgages plus any mortgages you took out on or before October 13, 1987, totaled over $1 million at any time

during 2014. The limit is $500,000 if married filing separately.

 If the total amount of all mortgages is more than the fair market value of the home, additional limits apply. See Pub. 936.

Line 10

Enter on line 10 mortgage interest and points reported to you on Form 1098. If your Form 1098 shows any refund of overpaid interest, do not reduce your deduction by the refund. Instead, see the instructions for Form 1040, line 21. If you and at least one other person (other than your spouse if filing jointly) were liable for and paid interest on the mortgage, and the interest was reported on the other person's Form 1098, report your share of the interest on line 11 (as explained in the line 11 instructions).

If you paid more interest to the recipient than is shown on Form 1098, see Pub. 936 to find out if you can deduct the additional interest. If you can, attach a statement to your paper return explaining the difference and enter "See attached" to the right of line 10.

 If you are claiming the mortgage interest credit (for holders of qualified mortgage credit certificates issued by state or local governmental units or agencies), subtract the amount shown on Form 8396, line 3, from the total deductible interest you paid on your home mortgage. Enter the result on line 10.

Line 11

If you paid home mortgage insurance interest and it was not reported to you on Form 1098, report your deductible mortgage interest on line 11.

If you paid home mortgage insurance interest to the person from whom you bought the home, write that person's name, identifying number, and address on the dotted lines next to line 11. If the recipient of your home mortgage interest payment(s) is an individual, the identifying number is his or her social security number (SSN). Otherwise, it is the employer identification number. You must also let the recipient know your SSN. If you do not show the required information about the recipient or let the recipient know your SSN, you may have to pay a $50 penalty.

If you and at least one other person (other than your spouse if filing jointly) were liable for and paid interest on the mortgage, and the home mortgage interest paid was reported on the other person's Form 1098, attach a statement to your paper return listing the name and address of that person. To the right of line 11, enter "See attached."

Line 12

Points Not Reported on Form 1098

Points are shown on your settlement statement. Points you paid only to borrow money are generally deductible over the life of the loan. See Pub. 936 to figure the amount you can deduct. Points paid for other purposes, such as for a lender's services, are not deductible.

Refinancing. Generally, you must deduct points you paid to refinance a mortgage over the life of the loan. This is true even if the new mortgage is secured by your main home.

If you used part of the proceeds to improve your main home, you may be able to deduct the part of the points related to the improvement in the year paid. See Pub. 936 for details.

 If you paid off a mortgage early, deduct any remaining points in the year you paid off the mortgage. However, if you refinanced your mortgage with the same lender, see Mortgage ending early *in Pub. 936 for an exception.*

Line 13

Mortgage Insurance Premiums

Enter the qualified mortgage insurance premiums you paid under a mortgage insurance contract issued after December 31, 2006, in connection with home acquisition debt that was secured by your first or second home. Box 4 of Form 1098 may show the amount of premiums you paid in 2014. If you and at least one other person (other than your spouse if filing jointly) were liable for and paid the premiums in connection with the loan, and the premiums were reported on the other person's Form 1098, report

your share of the premiums on line 13. See *Prepaid mortgage insurance premiums*, later, if you paid any premiums allocable to any period after 2014.

Qualified mortgage insurance is mortgage insurance provided by the Department of Veterans Affairs, the Federal Housing Administration, or the Rural Housing Service (or their successor organizations), and private mortgage insurance (as defined in section 2 of the Homeowners Protection Act of 1998 as in effect on December 20, 2006).

Mortgage insurance provided by the Department of Veterans Affairs and the Rural Housing Service is commonly known as a funding fee and guarantee fee respectively. These fees can be deducted fully in 2014 if the mortgage insurance contract was issued in 2014. Contact the mortgage insurance issuer to determine the deductible amount if it is not included in box 4 of Form 1098.

Prepaid mortgage insurance premiums. If you paid qualified mortgage insurance premiums that are allocable to periods after 2014, you must allocate them over the shorter of:
- The stated term of the mortgage, or
- 84 months, beginning with the month the insurance was obtained.

The premiums are treated as paid in the year to which they are allocated. If the mortgage is satisfied before its term, no deduction is allowed for the unamortized balance. See Pub. 936 for details.

The allocation rules, explained earlier, do not apply to qualified mortgage insurance provided by the Department of Veterans Affairs or the Rural Housing Service (or their successor organizations).

Limit on amount you can deduct. You cannot deduct your mortgage insurance premiums if the amount on Form 1040, line 38, is more than $109,000 ($54,500 if married filing separately). If the amount on Form 1040, line 38, is more than $100,000 ($50,000 if married filing separately), your deduction is limited and you must use the Mortgage Insurance Premiums Deduction Worksheet to figure your deduction.

Line 14

Investment Interest

Investment interest is interest paid on money you borrowed that is allocable to property held for investment. It does not include any interest allocable to passive activities or to securities that generate tax-exempt income.

Complete and attach Form 4952 to figure your deduction.

Exception. You do not have to file Form 4952 if all three of the following apply.

1. Your investment interest expense is not more than your investment income from interest and ordinary dividends minus any qualified dividends.

2. You have no other deductible investment expenses.

3. You have no disallowed investment interest expense from 2013.

 Alaska Permanent Fund dividends, including those reported on Form 8814, are not investment income.

For more details, see Pub. 550.

Gifts to Charity

You can deduct contributions or gifts you gave to organizations that are religious, charitable, educational, scientific, or literary in purpose. You can also deduct what you gave to organizations that work to prevent cruelty to children or animals. Certain whaling captains may be able to deduct expenses paid in 2014 for Native Alaskan subsistence bowhead whale hunting activities. See Pub. 526 for details.

To verify an organization's charitable status, you can:
- Check with the organization to which you made the donation. The organization should be able to provide you with verification of its charitable status.
- Use our on-line search tool *Exempt Organizations Select Check* to see if an organization is eligible to receive tax-deductible contributions (Publication 78 data). You can access *Exempt Organizations Select Check* on IRS.gov. Click on *Tools* then on *Exempt Organizations Select Check.*

- Call our Tax Exempt/Government Entities Customer Account Services at 1-877-829-5500.

Examples of Qualified Charitable Organizations

- Churches, mosques, synagogues, temples, etc.
- Boy Scouts, Boys and Girls Clubs of America, CARE, Girl Scouts, Goodwill Industries, Red Cross, Salvation Army, United Way, etc.
- Fraternal orders, if the gifts will be used for the purposes listed under *Gifts to Charity*, earlier.
- Veterans' and certain cultural groups.
- Nonprofit hospitals, and organizations whose purpose is to find a cure for, or help people who have, arthritis, asthma, birth defects, cancer, cerebral palsy, cystic fibrosis, diabetes, heart disease, hemophilia, mental illness or retardation, multiple sclerosis, muscular dystrophy, tuberculosis, etc.
- Most nonprofit educational organizations, such as colleges, but only if your contribution is not a substitute for tuition or other enrollment fees.
- Federal, state, and local governments if the gifts are solely for public purposes.

Amounts You Can Deduct

Contributions can be in cash, property, or out-of-pocket expenses you paid to do volunteer work for the kinds of organizations described earlier. If you drove to and from the volunteer work, you can take the actual cost of gas and oil or 14 cents a mile. Add parking and tolls to the amount you claim under either method. But do not deduct any amounts that were repaid to you.

Gifts from which you benefit. If you made a gift and received a benefit in return, such as food, entertainment, or merchandise, you can generally only deduct the amount that is more than the value of the benefit. But this rule does not apply to certain membership benefits provided in return for an annual payment of $75 or less or to certain items or benefits of token value. For details, see Pub. 526.

Example. You paid $70 to a charitable organization to attend a fund-raising dinner and the value of the dinner was $40. You can deduct only $30.

Gifts of $250 or more. You can deduct a gift of $250 or more only if you have a statement from the charitable organization showing the information in (1) and (2) next.

1. The amount of any money contributed and a description (but not value) of any property donated.

2. Whether the organization did or did not give you any goods or services in return for your contribution. If you did receive any goods or services, a description and estimate of the value must be included. If you received only intangible religious benefits (such as admission to a religious ceremony), the organization must state this, but it does not have to describe or value the benefit.

In figuring whether a gift is $250 or more, do not combine separate donations. For example, if you gave your church $25 each week for a total of $1,300, treat each $25 payment as a separate gift. If you made donations through payroll deductions, treat each deduction from each paycheck as a separate gift. See Pub. 526 if you made a separate gift of $250 or more through payroll deduction.

 You must get the statement by the date you file your return or the due date (including extensions) for filing your return, whichever is earlier. Do not attach the statement to your return. Instead, keep it for your records.

Mortgage Insurance Premiums Deduction Worksheet—Line 13 *Keep for Your Records*

Before you begin: ✓ See the instructions for line 13 to see if you must use this worksheet to figure your deduction.

1. Enter the total premiums you paid in 2014 for qualified mortgage insurance for a contract issued after December 31, 2006 .... 1. _____

2. Enter the amount from Form 1040, line 38 .... 2. _____

3. Enter $100,000 ($50,000 if married filing separately) .... 3. _____

4. Is the amount on line 2 more than the amount on line 3?

    ☐ **No.** Your deduction is not limited. Enter the amount from line 1 of this worksheet on Schedule A, line 13. **Do not** complete the rest of this worksheet.

    ☐ **Yes.** Subtract line 3 from line 2. If the result is not a multiple of $1,000 ($500 if married filing separately), increase it to the next multiple of $1,000 ($500 if married filing separately). For example, increase $425 to $1,000, increase $2,025 to $3,000; or if married filing separately, increase $425 to $500, increase $2,025 to $2,500, etc. .... 4. _____

5. Divide line 4 by $10,000 ($5,000 if married filing separately). Enter the result as a decimal. If the result is 1.0 or more, enter 1.0 .... 5. ___ . ___

6. Multiply line 1 by line 5 .... 6. _____

7. **Mortgage insurance premiums deduction.** Subtract line 6 from line 1. Enter the result here and on Schedule A, line 13 .... 7. _____

Limit on the amount you can deduct. See Pub. 526 to figure the amount of your deduction if any of the following applies.

1. Your cash contributions or contributions of ordinary income property are more than 30% of the amount on Form 1040, line 38.

2. Your gifts of capital gain property are more than 20% of the amount on Form 1040, line 38.

3. You gave gifts of property that increased in value or gave gifts of the use of property.

Amounts You Cannot Deduct

• Travel expenses (including meals and lodging) while away from home, unless there was no significant element of personal pleasure, recreation, or vacation in the travel.

• Political contributions.

• Dues, fees, or bills paid to country clubs, lodges, fraternal orders, or similar groups.

• Cost of raffle, bingo, or lottery tickets. But you may be able to deduct these expenses on line 28. See the instructions for *Line 28* for more information on gambling losses.

• Value of your time or services.

• Value of blood given to a blood bank.

• The transfer of a future interest in tangible personal property (generally, until the entire interest has been transferred).

• Gifts to individuals and groups that are run for personal profit.

• Gifts to foreign organizations. But you may be able to deduct gifts to certain U.S. organizations that transfer funds to foreign charities and certain Canadian, Israeli, and Mexican charities. See Pub. 526 for details.

• Gifts to organizations engaged in certain political activities that are of direct financial interest to your trade or business. See section 170(f)(9).

• Gifts to groups whose purpose is to lobby for changes in the laws.

• Gifts to civic leagues, social and sports clubs, labor unions, and chambers of commerce.

• Value of benefits received in connection with a contribution to a charita-ble organization. See Pub. 526 for exceptions.

• Cost of tuition. But you may be able to deduct this as a job education expense on line 21; as a tuition and fees deduction on Form 1040, line 34; or take an education credit (see Form 8863).

Line 16

Gifts by Cash or Check

Enter on line 16 the total value of gifts you made in cash or by check (including out-of-pocket expenses).

Recordkeeping. For any contribution made in cash, regardless of the amount, you must maintain as a record of the contribution a bank record (such as a canceled check or credit card statement) or a written record from the charity. The written record must include the name of the charity, date, and amount of the contribution. If you made contributions through payroll deduction, see Pub. 526 for information on the records you must keep. Do not attach the record to your tax return. Instead, keep it with your other tax records.

Line 17

Other Than by Cash or Check

Enter on line 17 the total value of your contributions of property other than by cash or check. If you gave used items, such as clothing or furniture, deduct their fair market value at the time you gave them. Fair market value is what a willing buyer would pay a willing seller when neither has to buy or sell and both are aware of the conditions of the sale. For more details on determining the value of donated property, see Pub. 561.

If the amount of your deduction is more than $500, you must complete and attach Form 8283. For this purpose, the "amount of your deduction" means your deduction before applying any income limits that could result in a carryover of contributions. If you deduct more than $500 for a contribution of a motor vehicle, boat, or airplane, you must also attach a statement from the charitable organization to your paper return. The organization may use Form 1098-C to provide the required information. If your total deduction is over $5,000 ($500 for certain contributions of clothing and household items (discussed next)), you may also have to get appraisals of the values of the donated property. See Form 8283 and its instructions for details.

Contributions of clothing and household items. A deduction for these contributions will be allowed only if the items are in good used condition or better. However, this rule does not apply to a contribution of any single item for which a deduction of more than $500 is claimed and for which you include a qualified appraisal and Form 8283 with your tax return.

Recordkeeping. If you gave property, you should keep a receipt or written statement from the organization you gave the property to, or a reliable written record, that shows the organization's name and address, the date and location of the gift, and a description of the property. For each gift of property, you should also keep reliable written records that include:

• How you figured the property's value at the time you gave it. If the value was determined by an appraisal, keep a signed copy of the appraisal.

• The cost or other basis of the property if you must reduce it by any ordinary income or capital gain that would have resulted if the property had been sold at its fair market value.

• How you figured your deduction if you chose to reduce your deduction for gifts of capital gain property.

• Any conditions attached to the gift.

 If your total deduction for gifts of property is over $500, you gave less than your entire interest in the property, or you made a "qualified conservation contribution," your records should contain additional information. See Pub. 526 for details.

Line 18

Carryover From Prior Year

Enter any carryover of contributions that you could not deduct in an earlier year because they exceeded your adjusted gross income limit. See Pub. 526 for details.

Casualty and Theft Losses

Line 20

Complete and attach Form 4684 to figure the amount of your loss to enter on line 20.

You may be able to deduct part or all of each loss caused by theft, vandalism, fire, storm, or similar causes; car, boat, and other accidents; and corrosive drywall. You may also be able to deduct money you had in a financial institution but lost because of the insolvency or bankruptcy of the institution.

You can deduct personal casualty or theft losses only to the extent that:

1. The amount of each separate casualty or theft loss is more than $100, and

2. The total amount of all losses during the year (reduced by the $100 limit discussed in (1)) is more than 10% of the amount on Form 1040, line 38.

Corrosive drywall losses. If you paid for repairs to your personal residence or household appliances because of corrosive drywall, you may be able to deduct on line 20 those amounts paid. See Pub. 547 for details.

Use Schedule A, line 23, to deduct the costs of proving that you had a property loss. Examples of these costs are appraisal fees and photographs used to establish the amount of your loss.

Job Expenses and Certain Miscellaneous Deductions

You can deduct only the part of these expenses that exceeds 2% of the amount on Form 1040, line 38.

Pub. 529 discusses the types of expenses that can and cannot be deducted.

Examples of Expenses You Cannot Deduct

- Political contributions.
- Legal expenses for personal matters that do not produce taxable income.

- Lost or misplaced cash or property.
- Expenses for meals during regular or extra work hours.
- The cost of entertaining friends.
- Commuting expenses. See Pub. 529 for the definition of commuting.
- Travel expenses for employment away from home if that period of employment exceeds 1 year. See Pub. 529 for an exception for certain federal employees.
- Travel as a form of education.
- Expenses of attending a seminar, convention, or similar meeting unless it is related to your employment.
- Club dues.
- Expenses of adopting a child. But you may be able to take a credit for adoption expenses. See Form 8839 and its instructions for details.
- Fines and penalties.
- Expenses of producing tax-exempt income.

Line 21

Unreimbursed Employee Expenses

Enter the total ordinary and necessary job expenses you paid for which you were not reimbursed. (Amounts your employer included in box 1 of your Form W-2 are not considered reimbursements.)

An ordinary expense is one that is common and accepted in your field of trade, business, or profession. A necessary expense is one that is helpful and appropriate for your business. An expense does not have to be required to be considered necessary.

But you must fill in and attach Form 2106 if either (1) or (2), next, applies.

1. You claim any travel, transportation, meal, or entertainment expenses for your job.

2. Your employer paid you for any of your job expenses that you would otherwise report on line 21.

 If you used your own vehicle, are using the standard mileage rate, and (2) earlier, does not apply, you may be able to file Form 2106-EZ instead.

If you do not have to file Form 2106 or 2106-EZ, list the type and amount of

each expense on the dotted line next to line 21. If you need more space, attach a statement to your paper return showing the type and amount of each expense. Enter the total of all these expenses on line 21.

 Do not include on line 21 any educator expenses you deducted on Form 1040, line 23.

Examples of other expenses to include on line 21 are:

- Safety equipment, small tools, and supplies needed for your job.
- Uniforms required by your employer that are not suitable for ordinary wear.
- Protective clothing required in your work, such as hard hats, safety shoes, and glasses.
- Physical examinations required by your employer.
- Dues to professional organizations and chambers of commerce.
- Subscriptions to professional journals.
- Fees to employment agencies and other costs to look for a new job in your present occupation, even if you do not get a new job.
- Certain business use of part of your home. For details, including limits that apply, use TeleTax topic 509 (see the Form 1040 instructions) or see Pub. 587.
- Certain educational expenses. For details, use TeleTax topic 513 (see the Form 1040 instructions) or see Pub. 970. Reduce your educational expenses by any tuition and fees deduction you claimed on Form 1040, line 34.

 You may be able to take a credit for your educational expenses instead of a deduction. See Form 8863 for details.

Line 22

Tax Preparation Fees

Enter the fees you paid for preparation of your tax return, including fees paid for filing your return electronically. If you paid your tax by credit or debit card, include the convenience fee you were charged on line 23 instead of this line.

Line 23

Other Expenses

Enter the total amount you paid to produce or collect taxable income and manage or protect property held for earning income. But do not include any personal expenses. List the type and amount of each expense on the dotted lines next to line 23. If you need more space, attach a statement to your paper return showing the type and amount of each expense. Enter one total on line 23.

Examples of expenses to include on line 23 are:
- Certain legal and accounting fees.
- Clerical help and office rent.
- Custodial (for example, trust account) fees.
- Your share of the investment expenses of a regulated investment company.
- Certain losses on nonfederally insured deposits in an insolvent or bankrupt financial institution. For details, including limits that apply, see Pub. 529.
- Casualty and theft losses of property used in performing services as an employee from Form 4684, lines 32 and 38b, or Form 4797, line 18a.
- Deduction for repayment of amounts under a claim of right if $3,000 or less.
- Convenience fee charged by the card processor for paying your income tax (including estimated tax payments)

by credit or debit card. The deduction is claimed for the year in which the fee was charged to your card.

Other Miscellaneous Deductions

Line 28

Only the expenses listed next can be deducted on this line. List the type and amount of each expense on the dotted lines next to line 28. If you need more space, attach a statement to your paper return showing the type and amount of each expense. Enter one total on line 28.
- Gambling losses (gambling losses include, but are not limited to, the cost of non-winning bingo, lottery, and raffle tickets), but only to the extent of gambling winnings reported on Form 1040, line 21.
- Casualty and theft losses of income-producing property from Form 4684, lines 32 and 38b, or Form 4797, line 18a.
- Loss from other activities from Schedule K-1 (Form 1065-B), box 2.
- Federal estate tax on income in respect of a decedent.
- A deduction for amortizable bond premium (for example, a deduction allowed for a bond premium carryforward or a deduction for amortizable bond pre-

mium on bonds acquired before October 23, 1986).
- An ordinary loss attributable to a contingent payment debt instrument or an inflation-indexed debt instrument (for example, a Treasury Inflation-Protected Security).
- Deduction for repayment of amounts under a claim of right if over $3,000. See Pub. 525 for details.
- Certain unrecovered investment in a pension.
- Impairment-related work expenses of a disabled person.

For more details, see Pub. 529.

Total Itemized Deductions

Line 29

Use the Itemized Deductions Worksheet, to figure the amount to enter on line 29 if the amount on Form 1040, line 38, is over $305,050 if married filing jointly or qualifying widow(er); $279,650 if head of household; $254,200 if single; or $152,525 if married filing separately.

Line 30

If you elect to itemize for state tax or other purposes even though your itemized deductions are less than your standard deduction, check the box on line 30.

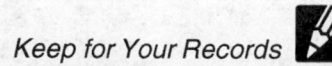
A-13

1. Enter the total of the amounts from Schedule A, lines 4, 9, 15, 19, 20, 27, and 28 .... 1. _____

2. Enter the total of the amount from Schedule A, lines 4, 14, and 20, plus any gambling and casualty or theft losses included on line 28 .... 2. _____

⚠ CAUTION Be sure your total gambling and casualty or theft losses are clearly identified on the dotted lines next to line 28.

3. Is the amount on line 2 less than the amount on line 1?

☐ No. 🛑 Your deduction is not limited. Enter the amount from line 1 of this worksheet on Schedule A, line 29. **Do not** complete the rest of this worksheet.

☐ Yes. Subtract line 2 from line 1 .... 3. _____

4. Multiply line 3 by 80% (.80) .... 4. _____

5. Enter the amount from Form 1040, line 38 .... 5. _____

6. Enter $305,050 if married filing jointly or qualifying widow(er); $279,650 if head of household; $254,200 if single; or $152,525 if married filing separately .... 6. _____

7. Is the amount on line 6 less than the amount on line 5?

☐ No. 🛑 Your deduction is not limited. Enter the amount from line 1 of this worksheet on Schedule A, line 29. **Do not** complete the rest of this worksheet.

☐ Yes. Subtract line 6 from line 5 .... 7. _____

8. Multiply line 7 by 3% (.03) .... 8. _____

9. Enter the **smaller** of line 4 or line 8 .... 9. _____

10. **Total itemized deductions.** Subtract line 9 from line 1. Enter the result here and on Schedule A, line 29 ...... 10. _____

2014 Optional State Sales Tax Tables *(State Sales Tax Rate Shown Next to State Name)*

Income		Exemptions						Exemptions						Exemptions						Exemptions					
At least	But less than	1	2	3	4	5	Over 5	1	2	3	4	5	Over 5	1	2	3	4	5	Over 5	1	2	3	4	5	Over 5
		Alabama			1	**4.0000%**		**Arizona**			2	**5.6000%**		**Arkansas**			2	**6.5000%**		**California**			3	**7.5000%**	
$0	$20,000	223	263	290	310	328	352	214	237	251	262	271	283	283	315	335	350	363	380	267	292	308	321	330	344
$20,000	$30,000	329	387	426	456	481	517	364	403	428	446	462	482	460	513	546	572	592	620	446	488	515	536	552	574
$30,000	$40,000	384	451	496	531	560	601	448	496	527	550	569	595	558	621	662	693	718	753	546	598	631	656	676	703
$40,000	$50,000	431	505	556	595	628	673	524	580	616	644	666	696	644	718	765	801	830	869	635	695	734	763	787	818
$50,000	$60,000	473	554	609	652	687	737	594	658	699	730	755	789	722	805	859	899	931	976	716	785	829	861	888	924
$60,000	$70,000	510	598	657	703	741	795	658	729	775	809	837	875	794	886	945	989	1025	1074	792	867	916	952	981	1021
$70,000	$80,000	545	638	701	750	790	847	719	797	847	884	915	956	862	961	1025	1073	1112	1165	862	945	998	1037	1069	1112
$80,000	$90,000	577	675	742	793	836	896	777	861	915	955	988	1033	925	1032	1100	1152	1194	1251	929	1018	1075	1117	1152	1198
$90,000	$100,000	607	710	780	834	879	942	832	922	979	1023	1058	1106	985	1099	1172	1227	1272	1333	992	1088	1148	1194	1230	1280
$100,000	$120,000	647	757	831	888	936	1003	906	1004	1067	1115	1153	1206	1066	1189	1269	1328	1377	1443	1078	1182	1248	1297	1337	1391
$120,000	$140,000	699	817	896	958	1010	1082	1005	1114	1184	1237	1279	1338	1173	1309	1396	1462	1515	1588	1192	1306	1379	1434	1478	1538
$140,000	$160,000	747	873	957	1023	1078	1155	1099	1218	1295	1353	1399	1464	1274	1421	1516	1588	1646	1726	1299	1424	1504	1564	1612	1677
$160,000	$180,000	792	924	1013	1083	1141	1222	1187	1316	1399	1462	1512	1582	1368	1526	1628	1705	1768	1853	1400	1535	1621	1685	1737	1808
$180,000	$200,000	833	972	1066	1139	1200	1285	1272	1411	1499	1566	1621	1695	1457	1627	1736	1818	1884	1976	1497	1641	1733	1802	1857	1933
$200,000	$225,000	877	1023	1121	1198	1261	1351	1362	1510	1605	1677	1735	1815	1552	1732	1848	1936	2007	2104	1599	1753	1851	1924	1984	2064
$225,000	$250,000	924	1077	1180	1260	1327	1421	1460	1618	1721	1798	1860	1945	1654	1847	1970	2064	2140	2244	1709	1874	1979	2058	2121	2207
$250,000	$275,000	968	1127	1235	1319	1389	1487	1553	1722	1831	1913	1979	2070	1751	1955	2087	2186	2266	2376	1815	1990	2101	2185	2252	2344
$275,000	$300,000	1009	1176	1288	1375	1448	1550	1643	1822	1937	2024	2094	2191	1845	2060	2198	2303	2387	2504	1917	2102	2219	2307	2379	2476
$300,000	or more	1256	1461	1598	1705	1794	1919	2199	2439	2594	2711	2805	2935	2413	2696	2878	3015	3126	3279	2540	2785	2942	3059	3153	3282
Income		**Colorado**			2	**2.9000%**		**Connecticut**			4	**6.3500%**		**District of Columbia**			4	**5.7500%**		**Florida**			1	**6.0000%**	
$0	$20,000	111	124	133	139	144	151	263	289	305	317	327	340	168	181	189	195	200	207	238	261	276	287	296	308
$20,000	$30,000	174	194	207	217	225	236	432	475	502	522	539	561	284	307	322	332	341	353	396	434	459	478	493	513
$30,000	$40,000	208	232	247	259	268	281	526	578	611	636	656	683	350	379	397	410	421	436	483	531	561	584	602	627
$40,000	$50,000	237	264	282	295	306	320	609	670	708	737	760	792	409	443	464	480	493	510	561	616	651	678	699	729
$50,000	$60,000	264	294	313	328	339	356	685	753	797	829	856	891	464	502	526	544	559	579	632	695	734	764	789	822
$60,000	$70,000	288	320	341	357	370	388	755	830	878	914	943	983	514	556	583	604	620	642	698	767	811	844	871	907
$70,000	$80,000	310	345	368	385	399	418	820	902	955	994	1025	1068	561	608	638	660	678	702	759	834	882	918	948	988
$80,000	$90,000	331	368	392	410	425	446	882	970	1027	1069	1103	1149	606	657	689	713	732	759	817	898	950	989	1020	1063
$90,000	$100,000	350	390	415	435	450	472	940	1035	1095	1140	1176	1226	649	704	738	764	784	813	873	959	1014	1056	1090	1136
$100,000	$120,000	377	419	447	467	484	507	1019	1122	1187	1236	1276	1329	708	767	804	833	855	886	947	1041	1101	1147	1183	1233
$120,000	$140,000	411	457	487	510	528	553	1124	1237	1309	1363	1407	1466	785	851	893	924	949	984	1046	1150	1216	1266	1307	1362
$140,000	$160,000	444	493	525	550	569	596	1222	1346	1425	1484	1531	1596	858	931	977	1011	1039	1077	1139	1253	1325	1380	1424	1484
$160,000	$180,000	474	526	561	586	607	636	1315	1448	1533	1596	1647	1717	928	1006	1056	1093	1123	1164	1227	1349	1427	1486	1533	1599
$180,000	$200,000	502	558	594	621	644	674	1403	1545	1636	1704	1758	1833	994	1078	1132	1172	1204	1248	1310	1441	1525	1588	1639	1708
$200,000	$225,000	532	591	629	658	682	714	1496	1648	1745	1817	1875	1955	1064	1155	1212	1255	1290	1337	1399	1538	1628	1695	1749	1824
$225,000	$250,000	564	626	667	698	722	757	1597	1759	1863	1940	2002	2087	1141	1238	1300	1346	1383	1434	1494	1644	1739	1811	1869	1949
$250,000	$275,000	594	660	703	735	761	797	1693	1865	1975	2057	2123	2213	1214	1318	1384	1433	1473	1527	1586	1744	1846	1922	1984	2068
$275,000	$300,000	623	692	737	771	798	836	1785	1967	2083	2170	2240	2335	1285	1395	1465	1517	1559	1617	1674	1841	1949	2029	2094	2184
$300,000	or more	798	885	942	985	1020	1068	2350	2591	2744	2859	2951	3078	1721	1870	1965	2036	2093	2171	2211	2434	2576	2683	2770	2889
Income		**Georgia**			2	**4.0000%**		**Hawaii**			1,7	**4.0000%**		**Idaho**			1	**6.0000%**		**Illinois**			2	**6.2500%**	
$0	$20,000	151	168	179	187	194	203	220	255	279	297	312	333	337	396	436	467	493	529	251	281	301	316	329	346
$20,000	$30,000	241	267	284	297	308	322	356	414	452	482	507	542	501	588	647	692	730	783	389	434	465	488	507	533
$30,000	$40,000	289	321	341	357	369	387	430	501	548	584	614	656	586	687	756	809	852	914	462	516	551	578	601	632
$40,000	$50,000	332	368	391	409	423	443	496	578	632	674	708	757	660	773	849	908	957	1026	525	586	626	657	682	718
$50,000	$60,000	370	411	437	456	472	494	556	647	708	755	794	849	725	849	932	997	1051	1126	582	649	694	728	756	795
$60,000	$70,000	405	449	478	499	517	541	611	711	779	830	873	933	784	917	1007	1077	1135	1216	634	707	755	792	822	864
$70,000	$80,000	438	486	516	540	558	584	662	771	844	900	947	1012	838	980	1076	1150	1212	1298	681	760	812	851	884	929
$80,000	$90,000	468	519	552	577	597	625	711	828	906	966	1016	1086	888	1038	1140	1218	1283	1375	726	809	864	907	941	989
$90,000	$100,000	497	551	586	613	634	663	756	881	964	1029	1082	1156	935	1093	1199	1282	1351	1447	768	856	914	959	995	1046
$100,000	$120,000	536	594	632	660	683	715	818	953	1043	1113	1170	1250	998	1166	1279	1367	1440	1542	824	919	981	1028	1067	1122
$120,000	$140,000	587	651	692	723	748	783	899	1047	1147	1223	1287	1375	1080	1260	1382	1477	1556	1666	898	1000	1068	1119	1162	1221
$140,000	$160,000	635	704	748	782	809	846	975	1136	1244	1328	1396	1493	1155	1348	1478	1579	1663	1781	967	1076	1149	1204	1250	1313
$160,000	$180,000	680	753	801	836	865	905	1047	1220	1335	1425	1499	1602	1225	1429	1567	1673	1762	1886	1030	1147	1224	1283	1331	1398
$180,000	$200,000	722	800	850	888	919	961	1115	1299	1422	1518	1597	1707	1291	1506	1650	1762	1855	1986	1091	1214	1296	1357	1409	1480
$200,000	$225,000	766	849	903	943	975	1020	1186	1383	1514	1616	1699	1817	1360	1585	1737	1855	1952	2090	1154	1284	1369	1435	1489	1564
$225,000	$250,000	814	902	959	1002	1036	1084	1263	1473	1613	1721	1811	1936	1433	1670	1830	1953	2056	2200	1221	1359	1449	1519	1576	1655
$250,000	$275,000	860	952	1012	1057	1094	1144	1337	1559	1707	1822	1916	2049	1503	1750	1917	2046	2154	2305	1285	1429	1525	1598	1658	1741
$275,000	$300,000	903	1001	1064	1111	1149	1202	1407	1641	1798	1918	2018	2158	1569	1826	2000	2135	2247	2404	1347	1497	1597	1673	1736	1823
$300,000	or more	1166	1292	1372	1433	1482	1550	1836	2142	2347	2505	2636	2819	1959	2277	2492	2658	2796	2990	1713	1902	2028	2124	2203	2312
Income		**Indiana**			4	**7.0000%**		**Iowa**			1	**6.0000%**		**Kansas**			1	**6.1500%**		**Kentucky**			4	**6.0000%**	
$0	$20,000	288	322	343	360	373	391	246	273	291	304	315	330	354	413	453	483	509	545	235	262	279	293	303	318
$20,000	$30,000	448	500	533	558	579	607	407	453	483	506	524	549	546	637	698	746	785	840	371	414	441	462	479	502
$30,000	$40,000	533	595	634	664	688	721	497	554	590	618	640	671	648	756	828	884	931	996	445	496	529	553	573	601
$40,000	$50,000	607	677	722	756	783	821	577	644	686	718	744	780	736	859	941	1005	1057	1131	509	567	605	633	656	688
$50,000	$60,000	674	751	801	839	869	911	651	726	774	810	840	880	815	951	1042	1113	1171	1253	568	632	674	705	731	766
$60,000	$70,000	734	818	873	914	947	992	718	801	855	895	927	972	887	1035	1134	1211	1274	1363	621	691	736	771	799	837
$70,000	$80,000	790	881	939	983	1019	1068	782	872	930	974	1010	1059	953	1112	1219	1301	1369	1465	670	746	795	832	862	903
$80,000	$90,000	842	939	1001	1048	1086	1138	842	939	1002	1049	1088	1140	1015	1184	1293	1386	1458	1560	716	797	850	889	921	965
$90,000	$100,000	891	994	1060	1109	1149	1205	899	1003	1070	1121	1162	1218	1074	1252	1372	1465	1542	1649	760	846	901	943	977	1024
$100,000	$120,000	957	1067	1138	1191	1234	1293	976	1089	1162	1217	1262	1323	1152	1343	1472	1571	1654	1769	818	911	970	1015	1052	1103
$120,000	$140,000	1043	1163	1240	1298	1345	1409	1078	1203	1284	1345	1395	1463	1253	1462	1602	1710	1800	1925	895	996	1061	1110	1150	1205
$140,000	$160,000	1123	1252	1335	1398	1448	1518	1175	1312	1400	1467	1521	1595	1348	1573	1723	1839	1936	2071	967	1076	1146	1199	1243	1302
$160,000	$180,000	1198	1335	1424	1490	1544	1618	1265	1413	1508	1580	1638	1719	1436	1675	1835	1959	2062	2205	1034	1150	1226	1282	1328	1392
$180,000	$200,000	1269	1414	1508	1578	1635	1714	1352	1510	1612	1689	1751	1837	1520	1772	1942	2073	2181	2333	1098	1221	1301	1361	1410	1477
$200,000	$225,000	1342	1496	1595	1670	1730	1813	1443	1612	1722	1804	1871	1962	1607	1873	2053	2191	2306	2466	1165	1295	1380	1443	1495	1566
$225,000	$250,000	1422	1585	1689	1768	1832	1920	1542	1724	1840	1928	2000	2098	1700	1982	2172	2318	2440	2610	1237	1375	1464	1532	1587	1662
$250,000	$275,000	1497	1668	1779	1862	1929	2021	1637	1830	1954	2047	2123	2228	1788	2085	2284	2439	2566	2745	1305	1451	1545	1616	1674	1754
$275,000	$300,000	1569	1748	1864	1951	2022	2118	1728	1932	2063	2162	2243	2353	1873	2184	2392	2554	2687	2874	1371	1523	1622	1697	1758	1841
$300,000	or more	1998	2226	2373	2484	2574	2697	2288	2559	2734	2866	2973	3120	2376	2770	3034	3239	3408	3645	1764	1960	2086	2182	2260	2367

(Continued)

2014 Optional State Sales Tax Tables *(Continued)*

Income		Louisiana			2	4.0000%		Maine			4	5.5000%		Maryland			4	6.0000%		Massachusetts			4	6.2500%	
$0	$20,000	161	175	184	191	196	204	146	159	167	173	178	184	208	229	244	255	264	276	201	219	230	239	246	255
$20,000	$30,000	267	291	306	318	327	339	246	267	281	291	299	310	343	380	404	422	437	458	317	345	363	376	387	402
$30,000	$40,000	326	356	374	388	399	415	302	328	345	358	368	381	419	464	493	515	533	559	379	413	434	450	463	481
$40,000	$50,000	379	413	435	451	464	482	352	383	402	417	429	445	486	538	572	598	619	648	434	472	496	514	529	549
$50,000	$60,000	427	466	490	509	523	544	398	433	455	472	485	503	547	606	644	673	697	731	483	525	552	573	589	611
$60,000	$70,000	471	514	541	562	578	600	441	479	504	522	537	557	604	668	711	743	770	806	528	574	603	626	643	668
$70,000	$80,000	513	560	589	612	629	654	480	523	550	570	586	608	656	727	773	808	837	877	569	619	651	675	694	720
$80,000	$90,000	552	603	635	659	678	704	518	564	593	615	632	656	706	782	832	870	901	944	608	661	695	721	741	769
$90,000	$100,000	590	644	678	703	724	752	554	603	634	657	676	701	754	835	888	929	962	1008	645	701	737	764	786	815
$100,000	$120,000	640	699	736	764	786	817	603	656	690	715	736	763	818	906	964	1008	1044	1093	694	755	793	822	846	877
$120,000	$140,000	707	772	813	844	868	902	668	727	764	792	815	845	902	1000	1064	1112	1152	1207	759	825	867	899	924	959
$140,000	$160,000	771	841	886	919	946	983	729	793	834	865	889	923	982	1088	1158	1211	1254	1314	819	891	936	970	997	1035
$160,000	$180,000	830	906	954	990	1020	1059	786	856	900	933	960	996	1057	1171	1247	1304	1350	1415	875	952	1000	1036	1066	1106
$180,000	$200,000	887	968	1020	1058	1090	1132	842	916	963	999	1027	1066	1129	1251	1331	1392	1442	1511	929	1009	1061	1099	1130	1173
$200,000	$225,000	946	1033	1089	1130	1163	1209	900	980	1030	1068	1099	1140	1204	1335	1420	1486	1539	1613	985	1070	1125	1165	1198	1243
$225,000	$250,000	1011	1104	1164	1208	1243	1292	963	1049	1103	1143	1176	1220	1286	1426	1517	1587	1644	1723	1045	1136	1193	1236	1271	1319
$250,000	$275,000	1073	1172	1235	1282	1320	1371	1024	1114	1172	1215	1250	1297	1364	1512	1609	1683	1744	1828	1102	1197	1258	1304	1341	1391
$275,000	$300,000	1133	1237	1304	1353	1393	1448	1082	1178	1239	1285	1321	1371	1439	1596	1698	1776	1840	1929	1157	1257	1321	1368	1407	1460
$300,000	or more	1498	1637	1725	1791	1844	1917	1440	1569	1650	1711	1760	1827	1898	2105	2241	2345	2429	2546	1485	1613	1695	1756	1805	1872

Income		Michigan			4	6.0000%		Minnesota			1	6.8750%		Mississippi			1	7.0000%		Missouri			2	4.2250%	
$0	$20,000	226	251	266	278	288	301	235	254	265	274	281	291	414	476	518	550	576	613	172	195	211	223	233	247
$20,000	$30,000	357	395	419	437	452	473	394	426	446	461	473	489	642	739	803	853	893	950	272	309	334	353	368	390
$30,000	$40,000	427	472	501	523	541	565	483	522	547	566	581	601	763	878	955	1014	1062	1129	325	370	400	422	441	466
$40,000	$50,000	488	540	573	598	618	646	562	609	638	660	677	701	868	1000	1087	1154	1209	1285	373	424	457	483	504	534
$50,000	$60,000	543	601	638	665	688	719	636	688	722	746	766	793	963	1109	1205	1279	1340	1425	415	472	509	538	562	594
$60,000	$70,000	594	656	697	727	751	785	703	762	799	826	848	878	1048	1207	1313	1393	1460	1552	454	516	557	588	614	650
$70,000	$80,000	641	708	751	784	810	847	767	831	871	901	925	958	1128	1299	1412	1499	1570	1670	490	557	601	635	663	701
$80,000	$90,000	685	757	803	837	866	904	827	896	940	972	998	1034	1202	1384	1505	1598	1674	1780	524	595	643	679	708	749
$90,000	$100,000	726	802	851	888	918	959	885	959	1005	1040	1068	1106	1272	1465	1593	1690	1771	1883	556	632	682	720	751	794
$100,000	$120,000	782	863	916	956	988	1032	962	1043	1094	1132	1162	1204	1366	1573	1710	1815	1901	2021	599	680	734	775	809	855
$120,000	$140,000	854	944	1001	1044	1079	1127	1065	1155	1212	1254	1288	1333	1488	1713	1862	1977	2071	2202	655	744	803	847	884	935
$140,000	$160,000	923	1019	1081	1127	1165	1217	1163	1262	1324	1370	1407	1457	1602	1845	2005	2129	2230	2371	708	804	867	915	955	1010
$160,000	$180,000	986	1089	1155	1204	1245	1300	1255	1361	1428	1478	1518	1572	1708	1966	2138	2269	2377	2527	757	859	927	979	1021	1080
$180,000	$200,000	1047	1155	1225	1278	1320	1379	1343	1457	1529	1583	1625	1684	1808	2082	2263	2402	2517	2676	804	912	984	1039	1083	1146
$200,000	$225,000	1110	1225	1299	1355	1400	1462	1436	1559	1636	1693	1739	1801	1913	2202	2394	2541	2662	2831	853	968	1043	1101	1149	1215
$225,000	$250,000	1178	1300	1378	1437	1485	1551	1537	1669	1751	1813	1862	1929	2025	2332	2535	2691	2819	2997	905	1027	1108	1169	1220	1290
$250,000	$275,000	1242	1371	1453	1516	1566	1635	1634	1774	1862	1927	1980	2051	2132	2454	2668	2832	2967	3155	955	1084	1169	1233	1287	1360
$275,000	$300,000	1304	1439	1526	1591	1644	1716	1728	1876	1969	2038	2094	2169	2234	2572	2796	2968	3109	3305	1003	1138	1227	1295	1351	1428
$300,000	or more	1676	1848	1959	2042	2109	2202	2303	2502	2627	2720	2795	2896	2842	3272	3557	3775	3955	4205	1292	1464	1578	1665	1737	1836

Income		Nebraska			1	5.5000%		Nevada			5	6.8500%		New Jersey			4,6	7.0000%		New Mexico			1	5.1250%	
$0	$20,000	223	247	262	273	282	294	265	293	311	324	335	350	248	266	278	286	293	302	195	217	231	241	250	262
$20,000	$30,000	371	410	436	455	470	491	412	456	[illegible]	[illegible]	[illegible]	540	419	449	[illegible]	477	[illegible]	[illegible]	[illegible]	375	[illegible]	419	[illegible]	455
$30,000	$40,000	453	502	533	556	575	601	490	541	574	598	618	646	504	542	566	584	599	618	419	467	498	522	541	567
$40,000	$50,000	527	583	619	647	669	699	558	616	653	681	704	735	586	631	659	680	696	719	492	550	587	614	637	668
$50,000	$60,000	594	658	699	730	755	789	619	683	725	755	780	815	661	712	743	767	786	812	561	626	669	701	727	762
$60,000	$70,000	656	727	772	806	834	872	675	745	789	823	850	888	730	786	822	848	869	898	625	698	745	781	810	850
$70,000	$80,000	714	792	841	878	908	949	727	802	850	886	915	955	795	856	895	924	947	978	685	766	818	857	889	933
$80,000	$90,000	769	853	906	946	979	1023	775	855	906	944	975	1018	857	923	964	995	1020	1054	743	831	887	930	965	1013
$90,000	$100,000	822	911	968	1011	1046	1093	821	905	959	999	1032	1077	915	986	1030	1063	1090	1126	798	892	954	1000	1037	1089
$100,000	$120,000	892	990	1052	1098	1136	1188	881	972	1030	1073	1108	1157	994	1071	1119	1155	1184	1224	873	977	1044	1094	1136	1192
$120,000	$140,000	986	1094	1163	1214	1256	1314	961	1059	1122	1170	1208	1260	1098	1184	1238	1278	1310	1353	973	1089	1165	1221	1267	1331
$140,000	$160,000	1075	1193	1268	1324	1370	1433	1036	1141	1209	1260	1301	1357	1197	1291	1349	1393	1428	1476	1069	1197	1280	1343	1393	1463
$160,000	$180,000	1158	1285	1366	1427	1477	1544	1105	1217	1289	1343	1387	1447	1290	1391	1454	1502	1540	1591	1159	1299	1389	1457	1512	1588
$180,000	$200,000	1238	1374	1461	1526	1579	1651	1171	1289	1365	1423	1469	1533	1379	1487	1555	1606	1646	1702	1247	1397	1494	1568	1627	1709
$200,000	$225,000	1322	1467	1560	1630	1687	1764	1239	1365	1445	1506	1555	1622	1473	1588	1661	1716	1759	1818	1340	1502	1606	1685	1750	1838
$225,000	$250,000	1414	1569	1669	1744	1804	1887	1313	1446	1531	1595	1647	1718	1575	1698	1776	1835	1881	1945	1441	1616	1729	1814	1883	1978
$250,000	$275,000	1501	1666	1772	1852	1916	2004	1383	1522	1612	1679	1734	1808	1672	1803	1887	1948	1998	2066	1538	1725	1846	1937	2012	2113
$275,000	$300,000	1585	1760	1872	1956	2024	2117	1450	1596	1690	1760	1817	1895	1766	1905	1993	2058	2111	2182	1633	1832	1960	2057	2136	2245
$300,000	or more	2100	2334	2483	2596	2686	2811	1850	2035	2154	2243	2315	2414	2340	2526	2644	2731	2802	2897	2222	2496	2672	2806	2915	3064

Income		New York			2	4.0000%		North Carolina			2	4.7500%		North Dakota			1	5.0000%		Ohio			1	5.7500%	
$0	$20,000	144	154	161	166	170	175	221	250	270	285	297	314	188	210	225	237	246	259	225	245	258	268	275	286
$20,000	$30,000	238	256	268	276	283	292	350	398	429	452	472	498	295	330	353	370	385	405	371	404	426	442	455	472
$30,000	$40,000	291	313	327	338	346	357	420	477	514	543	566	598	352	394	421	442	459	483	452	493	519	538	554	576
$40,000	$50,000	338	364	380	392	402	415	481	547	589	622	648	685	402	449	481	505	524	552	523	571	601	624	642	667
$50,000	$60,000	382	411	429	443	454	468	536	609	657	693	723	764	447	500	534	561	583	613	589	642	677	702	723	751
$60,000	$70,000	421	453	474	489	501	518	587	667	719	759	791	836	488	545	583	612	636	669	649	708	746	774	797	828
$70,000	$80,000	459	494	516	532	546	564	634	720	777	819	855	903	527	588	628	660	685	721	705	770	811	841	866	900
$80,000	$90,000	494	532	556	573	588	607	678	770	830	876	914	966	562	628	671	704	731	769	758	828	872	905	932	968
$90,000	$100,000	527	568	593	613	628	649	719	817	881	930	970	1025	596	665	711	746	775	815	809	883	930	965	994	1033
$100,000	$120,000	572	617	645	665	682	705	775	881	950	1002	1045	1104	641	715	764	802	833	876	877	958	1009	1047	1078	1120
$120,000	$140,000	632	681	712	735	754	779	848	964	1039	1097	1144	1209	700	781	835	876	909	956	967	1056	1112	1155	1189	1235
$140,000	$160,000	689	743	776	802	822	849	917	1042	1124	1186	1236	1307	755	842	900	944	981	1031	1052	1149	1210	1256	1294	1344
$160,000	$180,000	742	800	837	864	886	915	981	1114	1202	1268	1323	1398	806	899	961	1008	1047	1101	1132	1236	1302	1352	1392	1446
$180,000	$200,000	793	855	894	923	947	978	1041	1183	1276	1347	1404	1484	855	954	1019	1069	1110	1167	1208	1319	1390	1443	1485	1544
$200,000	$225,000	847	913	955	986	1011	1045	1105	1256	1354	1429	1490	1575	906	1010	1079	1132	1176	1236	1288	1407	1482	1539	1584	1646
$225,000	$250,000	905	976	1021	1054	1081	1117	1174	1334	1438	1518	1583	1673	961	1071	1144	1201	1247	1311	1375	1501	1582	1642	1691	1758
$250,000	$275,000	961	1036	1084	1119	1148	1186	1239	1407	1518	1602	1671	1766	1013	1129	1206	1265	1314	1381	1457	1592	1677	1741	1793	1864
$275,000	$300,000	1014	1094	1144	1182	1212	1253	1301	1478	1594	1683	1755	1855	1063	1185	1265	1327	1378	1448	1537	1679	1769	1837	1891	1966
$300,000	or more	1342	1449	1516	1566	1607	1661	1676	1905	2054	2168	2261	2390	1362	1517	1619	1698	1763	1853	2023	2210	2330	2419	2491	2589

(Continued)

2014 Optional State Sales Tax Tables *(Continued)*

Income		Oklahoma			1	4.5000%		Pennsylvania			1	6.0000%		Rhode Island			4	7.0000%		South Carolina			2	6.0000%	
$0	$20,000	243	279	303	322	338	359	194	210	220	228	234	243	255	278	293	304	313	325	234	257	272	284	293	305
$20,000	$30,000	379	435	473	502	526	560	319	346	363	376	386	400	397	433	455	472	486	504	386	425	450	469	484	505
$30,000	$40,000	452	519	564	598	627	667	388	421	442	458	471	488	472	515	541	562	578	600	470	519	549	572	591	616
$40,000	$50,000	515	591	642	682	714	760	449	488	512	530	545	566	537	586	616	639	658	683	545	601	637	664	685	715
$50,000	$60,000	572	657	713	757	793	844	505	548	576	597	614	637	596	650	684	709	730	758	614	677	718	748	772	805
$60,000	$70,000	624	716	778	826	865	920	557	605	635	658	677	702	650	708	745	773	795	825	677	747	792	825	852	888
$70,000	$80,000	672	771	838	889	931	990	605	657	690	715	736	763	699	762	802	832	855	888	736	812	861	897	926	966
$80,000	$90,000	717	823	894	948	993	1056	650	707	743	770	791	821	745	812	855	886	912	947	792	874	926	965	997	1040
$90,000	$100,000	760	871	946	1004	1052	1119	693	754	792	821	844	876	789	860	905	938	965	1002	845	933	988	1030	1064	1110
$100,000	$120,000	817	936	1017	1079	1130	1202	752	817	859	890	916	950	847	923	971	1007	1036	1076	917	1012	1072	1118	1154	1204
$120,000	$140,000	891	1022	1109	1177	1233	1311	829	901	947	982	1010	1048	923	1006	1059	1098	1130	1173	1011	1117	1183	1233	1274	1329
$140,000	$160,000	960	1101	1195	1268	1328	1412	901	980	1031	1068	1099	1141	994	1084	1140	1182	1216	1263	1101	1216	1288	1343	1387	1447
$160,000	$180,000	1025	1175	1275	1353	1417	1507	969	1054	1109	1150	1182	1228	1060	1155	1216	1261	1297	1346	1185	1308	1387	1445	1493	1557
$180,000	$200,000	1086	1245	1351	1433	1501	1596	1034	1125	1183	1227	1262	1311	1123	1224	1287	1335	1374	1426	1265	1397	1481	1544	1594	1663
$200,000	$225,000	1150	1318	1431	1518	1589	1690	1103	1200	1262	1309	1346	1398	1188	1295	1362	1413	1453	1509	1350	1490	1580	1647	1701	1775
$225,000	$250,000	1219	1397	1516	1608	1684	1790	1177	1281	1347	1397	1438	1493	1258	1371	1443	1496	1539	1598	1441	1592	1687	1759	1817	1896
$250,000	$275,000	1284	1471	1597	1694	1774	1886	1248	1358	1429	1482	1524	1583	1325	1444	1519	1575	1620	1682	1528	1688	1790	1866	1927	2011
$275,000	$300,000	1347	1543	1674	1776	1860	1977	1316	1432	1507	1563	1608	1670	1388	1513	1592	1651	1698	1763	1613	1781	1889	1969	2034	2122
$300,000	or more	1721	1970	2137	2266	2373	2522	1731	1886	1985	2059	2119	2201	1768	1926	2027	2102	2162	2245	2127	2350	2492	2599	2684	2801

Income		South Dakota			1	4.0000%		Tennessee			2	7.0000%		Texas			1	6.2500%		Utah			2	4.7000%	
$0	$20,000	235	271	296	314	330	351	366	416	450	475	496	525	254	283	301	315	326	342	236	267	288	304	317	335
$20,000	$30,000	366	423	461	490	514	548	579	658	711	751	784	830	419	466	497	520	539	565	376	426	459	484	504	533
$30,000	$40,000	437	505	550	584	613	653	693	789	852	900	940	995	510	568	606	634	657	688	452	512	551	581	606	640
$40,000	$50,000	498	575	627	666	699	744	793	903	975	1030	1075	1138	591	658	702	735	762	799	518	587	632	666	695	734
$50,000	$60,000	553	639	696	740	776	827	884	1006	1086	1147	1198	1268	664	741	790	828	858	899	578	655	705	743	775	819
$60,000	$70,000	603	697	759	807	846	901	967	1099	1187	1254	1309	1386	732	817	872	913	946	992	633	717	772	814	848	896
$70,000	$80,000	649	750	817	869	911	971	1043	1187	1281	1354	1413	1495	796	888	948	993	1029	1079	684	774	834	879	917	968
$80,000	$90,000	693	800	872	927	972	1035	1115	1268	1369	1447	1510	1598	856	956	1020	1068	1107	1161	732	829	892	941	981	1036
$90,000	$100,000	733	848	923	982	1030	1097	1183	1345	1453	1535	1602	1695	913	1020	1088	1140	1181	1239	777	880	947	999	1041	1100
$100,000	$120,000	788	911	992	1055	1106	1178	1274	1449	1564	1652	1725	1825	991	1106	1180	1236	1282	1344	838	948	1021	1077	1123	1186
$120,000	$140,000	860	993	1082	1151	1207	1285	1393	1584	1710	1807	1886	1996	1092	1220	1302	1364	1414	1483	917	1039	1118	1179	1229	1299
$140,000	$160,000	927	1071	1167	1240	1301	1385	1505	1712	1848	1952	2037	2156	1189	1328	1417	1485	1540	1615	992	1123	1210	1276	1330	1404
$160,000	$180,000	989	1143	1245	1323	1388	1478	1609	1830	1975	2086	2178	2305	1279	1429	1525	1598	1657	1739	1062	1202	1294	1365	1423	1503
$180,000	$200,000	1048	1211	1319	1402	1471	1566	1708	1942	2096	2214	2311	2446	1365	1525	1629	1707	1770	1857	1128	1277	1375	1450	1511	1596
$200,000	$225,000	1109	1282	1396	1485	1557	1658	1812	2060	2223	2348	2451	2594	1456	1627	1738	1821	1888	1981	1197	1356	1460	1539	1604	1695
$225,000	$250,000	1175	1358	1480	1573	1650	1757	1923	2186	2360	2493	2602	2753	1555	1738	1856	1945	2017	2116	1272	1440	1551	1635	1705	1800
$250,000	$275,000	1238	1431	1559	1657	1738	1851	2029	2307	2490	2630	2745	2904	1649	1843	1968	2063	2139	2245	1343	1521	1638	1727	1800	1901
$275,000	$300,000	1298	1500	1634	1737	1822	1941	2131	2422	2614	2761	2882	3049	1739	1944	2077	2177	2258	2369	1412	1598	1721	1814	1891	1997
$300,000	or more	1657	1915	2086	2218	2326	2478	2740	3114	3361	3550	3705	3920	2292	2564	2740	2872	2979	3127	1822	2063	2221	2342	2441	2578

Income		Vermont			1	6.0000%		Virginia			2	4.3000%		Washington			1	6.5000%		West Virginia			2	6.0000%	
$0	$20,000	163	174	181	186	190	195	178	203	218	230	240	254	260	287	304	316	327	341	250	279	297	311	323	338
$20,000	$30,000	253	270	281	288	294	303	274	310	334	352	367	388	431	476	504	526	543	567	413	461	492	516	535	561
$30,000	$40,000	301	321	334	343	350	360	324	367	395	417	434	459	526	581	616	642	663	693	503	563	601	630	653	686
$40,000	$50,000	343	366	380	390	399	410	368	416	448	472	492	520	611	674	715	746	770	804	584	653	697	731	758	796
$50,000	$60,000	380	406	422	433	442	455	407	460	495	522	544	574	688	760	806	840	868	907	657	735	786	824	855	897
$60,000	$70,000	415	442	459	472	482	496	442	500	538	567	591	624	760	839	889	928	959	1001	725	811	867	909	943	991
$70,000	$80,000	446	476	494	508	519	533	475	537	578	609	634	670	826	912	968	1009	1043	1090	789	883	943	989	1027	1078
$80,000	$90,000	476	507	527	541	553	569	506	572	615	648	675	712	890	982	1042	1087	1123	1173	849	950	1016	1065	1105	1161
$90,000	$100,000	503	537	558	573	585	602	534	604	650	685	713	753	950	1049	1112	1160	1199	1252	906	1014	1084	1137	1180	1239
$100,000	$120,000	540	576	599	615	626	646	573	647	696	733	764	806	1030	1138	1207	1259	1302	1360	983	1101	1177	1234	1281	1345
$120,000	$140,000	589	628	652	670	685	704	623	704	757	797	830	876	1138	1257	1333	1391	1437	1502	1085	1215	1299	1363	1415	1486
$140,000	$160,000	634	677	703	722	738	758	670	757	813	857	892	941	1239	1369	1452	1515	1566	1636	1181	1323	1415	1485	1541	1619
$160,000	$180,000	676	721	749	770	786	809	714	805	866	912	949	1001	1334	1474	1563	1631	1686	1762	1271	1425	1524	1599	1660	1744
$180,000	$200,000	716	764	793	815	833	856	755	852	915	964	1003	1058	1424	1574	1670	1743	1801	1882	1358	1522	1628	1708	1773	1863
$200,000	$225,000	758	808	840	863	881	906	798	900	967	1018	1060	1118	1520	1680	1783	1860	1923	2009	1449	1624	1738	1823	1893	1989
$225,000	$250,000	803	856	889	914	933	959	844	952	1022	1076	1121	1182	1624	1795	1905	1987	2055	2147	1548	1735	1857	1948	2023	2125
$250,000	$275,000	845	901	936	962	982	1010	887	1001	1075	1132	1178	1242	1723	1904	2021	2109	2180	2278	1642	1841	1970	2068	2147	2256
$275,000	$300,000	886	944	981	1008	1029	1059	929	1047	1125	1184	1233	1300	1818	2010	2133	2226	2301	2405	1733	1944	2080	2183	2266	2381
$300,000	or more	1128	1203	1249	1283	1311	1348	1178	1326	1424	1498	1559	1643	2401	2655	2819	2942	3042	3179	2289	2569	2750	2886	2998	3151

Income		Wisconsin			1	5.0000%		Wyoming			1	4.0000%	
$0	$20,000	212	233	247	257	266	277	160	175	184	191	197	204
$20,000	$30,000	347	382	405	422	436	455	266	290	305	317	326	339
$30,000	$40,000	421	465	493	513	530	553	324	354	372	387	398	414
$40,000	$50,000	487	538	570	594	614	640	376	410	432	449	462	480
$50,000	$60,000	547	604	641	668	690	720	423	462	487	506	520	541
$60,000	$70,000	603	666	706	736	760	793	467	510	537	558	574	597
$70,000	$80,000	654	723	767	799	826	862	508	555	585	607	625	649
$80,000	$90,000	703	777	824	859	888	927	547	597	629	653	673	699
$90,000	$100,000	750	828	878	916	946	988	583	637	671	697	718	746
$100,000	$120,000	812	898	952	993	1026	1071	633	691	729	757	779	810
$120,000	$140,000	895	989	1049	1094	1130	1180	698	763	804	835	860	894
$140,000	$160,000	973	1075	1141	1190	1229	1283	760	831	876	909	937	974
$160,000	$180,000	1046	1156	1226	1279	1322	1380	818	894	943	979	1008	1048
$180,000	$200,000	1115	1233	1308	1365	1410	1472	874	955	1007	1046	1077	1119
$200,000	$225,000	1189	1314	1395	1455	1503	1570	932	1019	1074	1116	1149	1195
$225,000	$250,000	1268	1402	1488	1552	1604	1675	996	1089	1148	1192	1227	1276
$250,000	$275,000	1344	1486	1577	1645	1700	1776	1056	1155	1217	1264	1302	1354
$275,000	$300,000	1416	1567	1663	1735	1793	1872	1114	1219	1285	1334	1374	1429
$300,000	or more	1860	2059	2186	2281	2357	2462	1470	1608	1696	1762	1815	1887

Note. Residents of **Alaska** do not have a state sales tax, but should follow the instructions on the next pages to determine their local sales tax amount.

1. Use the Ratio Method to determine your local sales tax deduction, then add that to the appropriate amount in the state table. Your state sales tax rate is provided next to the state name.

2. Follow the instructions on the next pages to determine your local sales tax deduction, then add that to the appropriate amount in the state table.

3. The California table includes the 1.25% uniform local sales tax rate in addition to the 6.25% state sales tax rate for a total of 7.50%. Some California localities impose a larger local sales tax. Taxpayers who reside in those jurisdictions should use the Ratio Method to determine their local sales tax deduction, then add that to the appropriate amount in the state table. The denominator of the correct ratio is 7.50%, and the numerator is the total sales tax rate minus the 7.50% tax rate.

4. This state does not have a local general sales tax, so the amount in the state table is the only amount to be deducted.

5. The Nevada table includes the 2.25% uniform local sales tax rate in addition to the 4.6000% state sales tax rate for a total of 6.85%. Some Nevada localities impose a larger local sales tax. Taypayers who reside in those jurisdictions should use the Ratio Method to determine their local sales tax deduction, then add that to the appropriate amount in the state table. The denominator of the correct ratio is 6.85%, and the numerator is the total sales tax rate minus the 6.85% tax rate.

6. Residents of Salem County, New Jersey should deduct only half of the amount in the state table.

7. The 4.0% rate for Hawaii is actually an excise tax but is treated as a sales tax for purpose of this deduction.

Which Optional Local Sales Tax Table Should I Use?

IF you live in the state of...	AND you live in...	THEN use Local Table...
Alaska	Any locality	C
Arizona	Chandler, Glendale, Gilbert, Mesa, Peoria, Phoenix, Scottsdale, Tempe, Tucson, Yuma, or any other locality	B
Arkansas	Any locality	B
Colorado	Adams County, Arapahoe County, Boulder County, Centennial, Colorado Springs, Denver City/Denver County, El Paso County, Larimer County, Pueblo County, or any other locality	A
	Greeley, Jefferson County, Lakewood, Longmont or Pueblo City	B
	Arvada, Boulder, Fort Collins, Thornton, or Westminster	C
Georgia	Any locality	B
Illinois	City of Aurora	B
	Any other locality	A
Louisiana	Ascension Parish, Bossier Parish, Caddo Parish, Calcasieu Parish, East Baton Rouge Parish, Iberia Parish, Jefferson Parish, Lafayette Parish, Lafourche Parish, Livingston Parish, Orleans Parish, Ouachita Parish, Rapides Parish, St. Bernard Parish, St. Landry Parish, St. Tammany Parish, Tangipahoa Parish, or Terrebonne Parish	C
	Any other locality	B
Missouri	Any locality	B
New York	Counties: Albany, Allegany, Broome, Cattaraugus, Cayuga, Chautauqua, Chemung, Chenango, Clinton, Columbia, Cortland, Delaware, Dutchess, Erie, Essex, Franklin, Fulton, Genesee, Greene, Hamilton, Herkimer, Jefferson, Lewis, Livingston, Madison, Monroe, Montgomery, Nassau, Niagara, Oneida, Onondaga, Ontario, Orange, Orleans, Oswego, Otsego, Putnam, Rensselaer, Rockland, St. Lawrence, Saratoga, Schenectady, Schoharie, Schuyler, Seneca, Steuben, Suffolk, Sullivan, Tioga, Tompkins, Ulster, Warren, Washington, Wayne, Westchester, Wyoming, or Yates New York City or Norwich City	B
	Any other locality	D*
North Carolina	Any locality	A
South Carolina	Aiken County, Horry County, Lexington County, Newberry County, Orangeburg County, York County, or Myrtle Beach	A
	Bamberg County, Charleston County, Cherokee County, Chesterfield County, Darlington County, Dillon County, Florence County, Hampton County, Jasper County, Lee County, Marion County, Marlboro County, or any other locality	B
Tennessee	Any locality	B
Utah	Any locality	A
Virginia	Any locality	B
West Virginia	Any locality	B

*Note. Local Table D is 25% of the NY State table.

2014 Optional Local Sales Tax Tables for Certain Local Jurisdictions

Income		Exemptions						Exemptions					
At least	But less than	1	2	3	4	5	Over 5	1	2	3	4	5	Over 5
		Local Table A						Local Table B					
$0	$20,000	38	43	46	48	50	52	47	53	58	62	64	68
20,000	30,000	60	66	71	74	77	81	71	82	89	94	99	105
30,000	40,000	71	79	84	88	91	96	84	97	105	111	117	124
40,000	50,000	81	90	96	100	104	109	96	110	119	126	132	140
50,000	60,000	89	99	106	111	115	121	106	122	132	140	146	155
60,000	70,000	97	108	115	121	125	131	115	132	143	152	159	169
70,000	80,000	105	117	124	130	135	141	124	142	154	163	170	181
80,000	90,000	112	124	132	139	144	150	132	151	164	173	181	192
90,000	100,000	118	131	140	147	152	159	139	159	173	183	192	203
100,000	120,000	127	141	150	157	163	171	149	171	185	196	205	218
120,000	140,000	138	154	164	171	178	186	162	186	201	213	223	237
140,000	160,000	149	166	176	184	191	200	175	200	216	229	240	254
160,000	180,000	159	176	188	197	204	213	186	212	230	244	255	271
180,000	200,000	168	187	199	208	216	226	196	225	243	258	270	286
200,000	225,000	178	198	210	220	228	239	208	237	257	272	285	302
225,000	250,000	189	209	223	233	241	253	220	251	272	288	301	319
250,000	275,000	199	220	234	245	254	266	231	264	286	303	316	336
275,000	300,000	208	231	246	257	266	279	242	276	299	317	331	351
300,000	or more	265	294	313	327	338	354	306	349	378	400	418	444
		Local Table C						Local Table D					
$0	$20,000	56	64	69	73	77	81	36	39	40	42	43	44
20,000	30,000	87	100	108	114	120	127	60	64	67	69	71	73
30,000	40,000	104	119	129	136	143	151	73	78	82	85	87	89
40,000	50,000	119	136	147	156	163	173	85	91	95	98	101	104
50,000	60,000	132	151	163	173	181	192	96	103	107	111	114	117
60,000	70,000	144	164	178	189	197	209	105	113	119	122	125	130
70,000	80,000	155	177	192	203	212	225	115	124	129	133	137	141
80,000	90,000	165	189	205	217	227	240	124	133	139	143	147	152
90,000	100,000	175	200	217	230	240	255	132	142	148	153	157	162
100,000	120,000	188	215	233	247	258	274	143	154	161	166	171	176
120,000	140,000	205	235	254	269	282	299	158	170	178	184	189	195
140,000	160,000	221	253	274	290	304	322	172	186	194	201	206	212
160,000	180,000	236	270	293	310	324	344	186	200	209	216	222	229
180,000	200,000	250	286	310	328	343	364	198	214	224	231	237	245
200,000	225,000	265	303	329	348	364	386	212	228	239	247	253	261
225,000	250,000	281	322	348	369	385	409	226	244	255	264	270	279
250,000	275,000	296	339	367	388	406	431	240	259	271	280	287	297
275,000	300,000	311	355	385	407	426	452	254	274	286	296	303	313
300,000	or more	397	454	492	520	544	577	336	362	379	392	402	415

Department of the Treasury
Internal Revenue Service

2014 Instructions for Schedule C

Profit or Loss From Business

Use Schedule C (Form 1040) to report income or loss from a business you operated or a profession you practiced as a sole proprietor. An activity qualifies as a business if your primary purpose for engaging in the activity is for income or profit and you are involved in the activity with continuity and regularity. For example, a sporadic activity or a hobby does not qualify as a business. To report income from a nonbusiness activity, see the instructions for Form 1040, line 21, or Form 1040NR, line 21.

Also use Schedule C to report (a) wages and expenses you had as a statutory employee, (b) income and deductions of certain qualified joint ventures, and (c) certain income shown on Form 1099-MISC, Miscellaneous Income. See the *Instructions for Recipient* (back of Copy B of Form 1099-MISC) for the types of income to report on Schedule C.

Small businesses and statutory employees with business expenses of $5,000 or less may be able to file Schedule C-EZ instead of Schedule C. See Schedule C-EZ for details.

You may be subject to state and local taxes and other requirements such as business licenses and fees. Check with your state and local governments for more information.

Section references are to the Internal Revenue Code unless otherwise noted.

Future Developments

For the latest information about developments related to Schedule C and its instructions, such as legislation enacted after they were published, go to *www.irs.gov/schedulec*.

What's New

Standard mileage rate. The business standard mileage rate for 2014 is 56 cents per mile.

Reminders

Simplified method for business use of home deduction. The IRS provides a simplified method to determine your expenses for business use of a home. For more information and to determine if you can use the simplified method, see *Line 30*, later.

General Instructions

Other Schedules and Forms You May Have To File

- Schedule A (Form 1040) to deduct interest, taxes, and casualty losses not related to your business.
- Schedule E (Form 1040) to report rental real estate and royalty income or (loss) that is not subject to self-employment tax.
- Schedule F (Form 1040) to report profit or (loss) from farming.
- Schedule J (Form 1040) to figure your tax by averaging your farming or fishing income over the previous 3 years. Doing so may reduce your tax.
- Schedule SE (Form 1040) to pay self-employment tax on income from any trade or business.
- Form 3800 to claim any of the general business credits.
- Form 4562 to claim depreciation (including the special allowance) on assets placed in service in 2014, to claim amortization that began in 2014, to make an election under section 179 to expense certain property, or to report information on listed property.
- Form 4684 to report a casualty or theft gain or loss involving property used in your trade or business or income-producing property.
- Form 4797 to report sales, exchanges, and involuntary conversions (not from a casualty or theft) of trade or business property.
- Form 6198 to figure your allowable loss if you have a business loss and you have amounts invested in the business for which you are not at risk.
- Form 8582 to figure your allowable loss from passive activities.
- Form 8594 to report certain purchases or sales of groups of assets that constitute a trade or business.
- Form 8824 to report like-kind exchanges.
- Form 8829 to claim actual expenses for business use of your home.
- Form 8903 to take a deduction for income from domestic production activities.

Single-member limited liability company (LLC). Generally, a single-member domestic LLC is not treated as a separate entity for federal income tax purposes. If you are the sole member of a domestic LLC, file Schedule C or C-EZ (or Schedule E or F, if applicable) unless you have elected to treat the domestic LLC as a corporation. See Form 8832 for details on making this election and for information about the tax treatment of a foreign LLC.

Single-member limited liability companies (LLCs) with employees. A single-member LLC must file employment tax returns using the LLC's name and employer identification number (EIN) rather than the owner's name and EIN, even if the LLC is not treated as a separate entity for federal income tax purposes.

Heavy highway vehicle use tax. If you use certain highway trucks, truck-trailers, tractor-trailers, or buses in your trade or business, you may have to pay a federal highway motor vehicle use tax. See the Instructions for Form 2290 to find out if you must pay this tax and visit *www.irs.gov/trucker* for the most recent developments.

Dec 22, 2014

Cat. No. 24329W

Information returns. You may have to file information returns for wages paid to employees, certain payments of fees and other nonemployee compensation, interest, rents, royalties, real estate transactions, annuities, and pensions. See *Line I*, later, and the 2014 General Instructions for Certain Information Returns for details and other payments that may require you to file a Form 1099.

If you received cash of more than $10,000 in one or more related transactions in your trade or business, you may have to file Form 8300. For details, see Pub. 1544.

Business Owned and Operated by Spouses

Generally, if you and your spouse jointly own and operate an unincorporated business and share in the profits and losses, you are partners in a partnership, whether or not you have a formal partnership agreement. You generally have to file Form 1065 instead of Schedule C or C-EZ for your joint business activity; however, you may not have to file Form 1065 if either of the following applies.

• You and your spouse elect to be treated as a qualified joint venture. See *Qualified Joint Venture*, next.

• You and your spouse wholly own the unincorporated business as community property and you treat the business as a sole proprietorship. See *Community Income*, later.

Otherwise, use Form 1065. See Pub. 541 for more details.

Qualified Joint Venture

You and your spouse can elect to treat an unincorporated business as a qualified joint venture instead of a partnership if you:

• Each materially participate in the business (see *Material participation*, later, in the instructions for line G),

• Are the only owners of the business, and

• File a joint return for the tax year.

Making the election will allow you to avoid the complexity of Form 1065, but still give each of you credit for social security earnings on which retirement benefits, disability benefits, survivor benefits, and insurance (Medicare) benefits are based. In most cases, this election will not increase the total tax owed on the joint return.

Jointly owned property. You and your spouse must operate a business to make this election. Do not make the election for jointly owned property that is not a trade or business.

Making the election. To make this election, divide all items of income, gain, loss, deduction, and credit attributable to the business between you and your spouse based on your interests in the business. Each of you must file a separate Schedule C, C-EZ, or F. Enter your share of the applicable income, deduction or loss, on the appropriate lines of your separate Schedule C, C-EZ, or F. Each of you may also need to file a separate Schedule SE to pay self-employment tax. If the business was taxed as a partnership before you made the election, the partnership will be treated as terminating at the end of the preceding tax year. For information on how to report the termination of the partnership, see Pub. 541.

Revoking the election. The election can be revoked only with the permission of the IRS. However, the election remains in effect only for as long as you and your spouse continue to meet the requirements to make the election. If you and your spouse fail to meet the requirements for any year, you will need to make a new election to be treated as a qualified joint venture in any future year.

Employer identification number (EIN). You and your spouse do not need to obtain an EIN to make the election. But you may need an EIN to file other returns, such as employment or excise tax returns. To apply for an EIN, see the Instructions for Form SS-4.

Rental real estate business. If you and your spouse make the election for your rental real estate business, you must each report your share of income and deductions on Schedule E. Rental real estate income generally is not included in net earnings from self-employment subject to self-employment tax and generally is subject to the passive loss limitation rules. Electing qualified joint venture status does not alter the application of the self-employment tax or the passive loss limitation rules.

More information. For more information on qualified joint ventures, go to IRS.gov and enter "qualified joint venture" in the search box.

Community Income

If you and your spouse wholly own an unincorporated business as community property under the community property laws of a state, foreign country, or U.S. possession, you can treat your wholly-owned, unincorporated business as a sole proprietorship, instead of a partnership. Any change in your reporting position will be treated as a conversion of the entity.

Report your income and deductions as follows.

• If only one spouse participates in the business, all of the income from that business is the self-employment earnings of the spouse who carried on the business.

• If both spouses participate, the income and deductions are allocated to the spouses based on their distributive shares.

• If either or both spouses are partners in a partnership, see Pub. 541.

• If both spouses elected to treat the business as a qualifying joint venture, see *Qualified Joint Venture*, earlier.

The only states with community property laws are Arizona, California, Idaho, Louisiana, Nevada, New Mexico, Texas, Washington, and Wisconsin.

Reportable Transaction Disclosure Statement

Use Form 8886 to disclose information for each reportable transaction in which you participated. Form 8886 must be filed for each tax year that your federal income tax liability is affected by your participation in the transaction. You may have to pay a penalty if you are required to file Form 8886 but do not do so. You may also have to pay interest and penalties on any reportable transaction understatements. The following are reportable transactions.

• Any listed transaction that is the same as or substantially similar to tax avoidance transactions identified by the IRS.

• Any transaction offered to you or a related party under conditions of confidentiality for which you paid an advisor a fee of at least $50,000.

• Certain transactions for which you or a related party have contractual protection against disallowance of the tax benefits.

• Certain transactions resulting in a loss of at least $2 million in any single tax year or $4 million in any combination of tax years. (At least $50,000 for a single tax year if the loss arose from a foreign currency transaction defined in section 988(c)(1), whether or not the loss flows through from an S corporation or partnership.)

• Certain transactions of interest entered into after November 1, 2006, that are the same or substantially similar to one of the types of transactions that the IRS has identified by published guidance as a transaction of interest.

See the Instructions for Form 8886 for more details.

Capital Construction Fund

Do not claim on Schedule C or C-EZ the deduction for amounts contributed to a capital construction fund set up under chapter 535 of title 46 of the United States Code. Instead, reduce the amount you would otherwise enter on Form 1040, line 43, by the amount of the deduction. Next to line 43, enter "CCF" and the amount of the deduction. For details, see Pub. 595.

Additional Information

See Pub. 334 for more information for small businesses.

Specific Instructions

Filers of Form 1041. Do not complete the block labeled "Social security number (SSN)." Instead, enter the employer identification number (EIN) issued to the estate or trust on line D.

Line A

Describe the business or professional activity that provided your principal source of income reported on line 1. If you owned more than one business, you must complete a separate Schedule C for each business. Give the general field or activity and the type of product or service. If your general field or activity is wholesale or retail trade, or services connected with production services (mining, construction, or manufacturing), also give the type of customer or client. For example, "wholesale sale of hardware to retailers" or "appraisal of real estate for lending institutions."

Line B

Enter on line B the six-digit code from the *Principal Business or Professional*

Activity Codes chart at the end of these instructions.

Line D

Enter on line D the employer identification number (EIN) that was issued to you on Form SS-4. Do not enter your SSN on this line. Do not enter another taxpayer's EIN (for example, from any Forms 1099-MISC that you received). **If you do not have an EIN, leave line D blank.**

You need an EIN only if you have a qualified retirement plan or are required to file employment, excise, alcohol, tobacco, or firearms returns, or are a payer of gambling winnings. If you need an EIN, see the Instructions for Form SS-4.
Single-member LLCs. If you are the sole owner of an LLC that is not treated as a separate entity for federal income tax purposes, you may have an EIN that was issued to the LLC (in the LLC's legal name) if you are required to file employment tax returns and certain excise tax returns. However, you should **enter on line D only the EIN issued to you and in your name as a sole proprietor.** If you do not have such an EIN, leave line D blank. Do not enter on line D the EIN issued to the LLC.

Line E

Enter your business address. Show a street address instead of a box number. Include the suite or room number, if any. If you conducted the business from your home located at the address shown on Form 1040, page 1, you do not have to complete this line.

Line F

Generally, you can use the cash method, accrual method, or any other method permitted by the Internal Revenue Code. In all cases, the method used must clearly reflect income. Unless you are a qualifying taxpayer or a qualifying small business taxpayer (see the Part III instructions), you must use the accrual method for sales and purchases of inventory items. Special rules apply to long-term contracts (see section 460 for details).

If you use the cash method, show all items of taxable income actually or constructively received during the year (in cash, property, or services). Income is constructively received when it is credited to your account or set aside for you

to use. Also, show amounts actually paid during the year for deductible expenses. However, if the payment of an expenditure creates an asset having a useful life that extends substantially beyond the close of the year, it may not be deductible or may be deductible only in part for the year of the payment. See chapter 1 of Pub. 535.

If you use the accrual method, report income when you earn it and deduct expenses when you incur them even if you do not pay them during the tax year. Accrual-basis taxpayers are put on a cash basis for deducting business expenses owed to a related cash-basis taxpayer. Other rules determine the timing of deductions based on economic performance. See Pub. 538.

To change your accounting method, you generally must file Form 3115. You also may have to make an adjustment to prevent amounts of income or expense from being duplicated or omitted. This is called a section 481(a) adjustment.

Example. You change to the cash method of accounting and choose to account for inventoriable items in the same manner as materials and supplies that are not incidental. You accrued sales in 2013 for which you received payment in 2014. You must report those sales in both years as a result of changing your accounting method and must make a section 481(a) adjustment to prevent duplication of income.

A net negative section 481(a) adjustment is taken into account entirely in the year of the change. A net positive section 481(a) adjustment is generally taken into account over a period of 4 years. Include any net positive section 481(a) adjustments on line 6. If the net section 481(a) adjustment is negative, report it in Part V.

For details on figuring section 481(a) adjustments, see the Instructions for Form 3115, and Rev. Proc. 2006-12, 2006-3 I.R.B. 310, available at *www.irs.gov/irb/2006-03_IRB/ar14.html*. Also see Rev. Proc. 2006-37, 2006-38 I.R.B. 499, available at *www.irs.gov/irb/2006-38_IRB/ar10.html*.

Line G

If your business activity was not a rental activity and you met any of the material participation tests, explained next, or the exception for oil and gas applies (explained later), check the "Yes" box. Otherwise, check the "No" box. If you check the "No" box, this business is a passive activity. If you have a loss from this business, see *Limit on losses*, later. If you have a profit from this business activity but have current year losses from other passive activities or you have prior year unallowed passive activity losses, see the Instructions for Form 8582.

Material participation. For purposes of the seven material participation tests listed later, participation generally includes any work you did in connection with an activity if you owned an interest in the activity at the time you did the work. The capacity in which you did the work does not matter. However, work is not treated as participation if it is work that an owner would not customarily do in the same type of activity and one of your main reasons for doing the work was to avoid the disallowance of losses or credits from the activity under the passive activity rules.

Work you did as an investor in an activity is not treated as participation unless you were directly involved in the day-to-day management or operations of the activity. Work done as an investor includes:

- Studying and reviewing financial statements or reports on the activity,
- Preparing or compiling summaries or analyses of the finances or operations of the activity for your own use, and
- Monitoring the finances or operations of the activity in a nonmanagerial capacity.

Participation by your spouse during the tax year in an activity you own can be counted as your participation in the activity. This rule applies even if your spouse did not own an interest in the activity and whether or not you and your spouse file a joint return. However, this rule does not apply for purposes of determining whether you and your spouse can elect to have your business treated as a qualified joint venture instead of a partnership (see *Qualified Joint Venture*, earlier).

For purposes of the passive activity rules, you materially participated in the operation of this trade or business activity during 2014 if you met any of the following seven tests.

1. You participated in the activity for more than 500 hours during the tax year.

2. Your participation in the activity for the tax year was substantially all of the participation in the activity of all individuals (including individuals who did not own any interest in the activity) for the tax year.

3. You participated in the activity for more than 100 hours during the tax year, and you participated at least as much as any other person for the tax year. This includes individuals who did not own any interest in the activity.

4. The activity is a significant participation activity for the tax year, and you participated in all significant participation activities for more than 500 hours during the year. An activity is a "significant participation activity" if it involves the conduct of a trade or business, you participated in the activity for more than 100 hours during the tax year, and you did not materially participate under any of the material participation tests (other than this test 4).

5. You materially participated in the activity for any 5 of the prior 10 tax years.

6. The activity is a personal service activity in which you materially participated for any 3 prior tax years. A personal service activity is an activity that involves performing personal services in the fields of health, law, engineering, architecture, accounting, actuarial science, performing arts, consulting, or any other trade or business in which capital is not a material income-producing factor.

7. Based on all the facts and circumstances, you participated in the activity on a regular, continuous, and substantial basis for more than 100 hours during the tax year. Your participation in managing the activity does not count in determining if you meet this test if any person (except you) (a) received compensation for performing management services in connection with the activity, or (b) spent more hours during the tax year than you spent performing management services in connection with the activity (regardless of whether the person was compensated for the services).

Rental of property. Generally, a rental activity (such as long-term equipment leasing or rental real estate) is a passive activity even if you materially participated in the activity. However, if you materially participated in a rental real estate activity as a real estate professional, it is not a passive activity. Also, if you met any of the five exceptions listed under

Rental Activities in the Instructions for Form 8582, the rental of the property is not treated as a rental activity and the material participation rules explained earlier apply. See *Activities That Are Not Passive Activities* in the Instructions for Form 8582 for the definition of a real estate professional.

Exception for oil and gas. If you are filing Schedule C to report income and deductions from an oil or gas well in which you own a working interest directly or through an entity that does not limit your liability, check the "Yes" box. The activity of owning a working interest is not a passive activity, regardless of your participation.

Limit on losses. Your loss may be limited if you checked the "No" box on line G. In this case, you may have a loss from a passive activity, and you may have to use Form 8582 to figure your allowable loss, if any, to enter on Schedule C, line 31.

You can deduct losses from passive activities in most cases only to the extent of income from passive activities. For details, see Pub. 925.

Line H

If you started or acquired this business in 2014, check the box on line H. Also check the box if you are reopening or restarting this business after temporarily closing it, and you did not file a 2013 Schedule C or C-EZ for this business.

Line I

If you made any payment in 2014 that would require you to file any Forms 1099, check the "Yes" box. Otherwise, check the "No" box.

You may have to file information returns for wages paid to employees, certain payments of fees and other nonemployee compensation, interest, rents, royalties, real estate transactions, annuities, and pensions. You may also have to file an information return if you sold $5,000 or more of consumer products to a person on a buy-sell, deposit-commission, or other similar basis for resale.

 The Guide to Information Returns *in the 2014 General Instructions for Certain Information Returns identifies which Forms 1099 must be filed, the amounts to report, and the due dates for the required Forms 1099.*

Part I. Income

Except as otherwise provided in the Internal Revenue Code, gross income includes income from whatever source derived. In certain circumstances, however, gross income does not include extraterritorial income that is qualifying foreign trade income. Use Form 8873 to figure the extraterritorial income exclusion. Report it on Schedule C as explained in the Instructions for Form 8873.

If you were a debtor in a chapter 11 bankruptcy case during 2014, see *Chapter 11 Bankruptcy Cases* in the Instructions for Form 1040 (under *Income*) and the Instructions for Schedule SE (Form 1040).

Line 1

Enter gross receipts from your trade or business. Include amounts you received in your trade or business that were properly shown on Forms 1099-MISC. If the total amounts that were reported in box 7 of Forms 1099-MISC are more than the total you are reporting on line 1, attach a statement explaining the difference.

Statutory employees. If you received a Form W-2 and the "Statutory employee" box in box 13 of that form was checked, report your income and expenses related to that income on Schedule C or C-EZ. Enter your statutory employee income from box 1 of Form W-2 on line 1 of Schedule C or C-EZ and check the box on that line. Social security and Medicare tax should have been withheld from your earnings; as a result, you do not owe self-employment tax on these earnings. Statutory employees include full-time life insurance agents, certain agent or commission drivers and traveling salespersons, and certain homeworkers.

If you had both self-employment income and statutory employee income, you must file two Schedules C. You cannot use Schedule C-EZ or combine these amounts on a single Schedule C.

 Qualified joint ventures should report rental real estate income not subject to self-employment tax on Schedule E. See Qualified Joint Venture, *earlier, and the Instructions for Schedule E.*

Installment sales. Generally, the installment method cannot be used to report income from the sale of (a) personal property regularly sold under the installment method, or (b) real property held for resale to customers. But the installment method can be used to report income from sales of certain residential lots and timeshares if you elect to pay interest on the tax due on that income after the year of sale. See section 453(l)(2)(B) for details. If you make this election, include the interest in the total on Form 1040, line 62. Check box c and enter the amount of interest and "453(l)(3)" on the line next to that box.

If you use the installment method, attach a statement to your return. Show separately for 2014 and the 3 preceding years: gross sales, cost of goods sold, gross profit, percentage of gross profit to gross sales, amounts collected, and gross profit on amounts collected.

Line 2

Report your sales returns and allowances as a positive number on line 2. A sales return is a cash or credit refund you gave to customers who returned defective, damaged, or unwanted products. A sales allowance is a reduction in the selling price of products, instead of a cash or credit refund.

Line 6

Report on line 6 amounts from finance reserve income, scrap sales, bad debts you recovered, interest (such as on notes and accounts receivable), state gasoline or fuel tax refunds you received in 2014, any amount of credit for biofuel claimed on line 2 of Form 6478, any amount of credit for biodiesel and renewable diesel fuels claimed on line 8 of Form 8864, credit for federal tax paid on fuels claimed on your 2013 Form 1040, prizes and awards related to your trade or business, and other kinds of miscellaneous business income. Include amounts you received in your trade or business as shown on Form 1099-PATR.

If the business use percentage of any listed property (defined in *Line 13*, later) dropped to 50% or less in 2014, report on this line any recapture of excess depreciation, including any section 179 expense deduction. Use Part IV of Form 4797 to figure the recapture. Also, if the business use percentage drops to 50% or less on leased listed property (other than a vehicle), include on this line any inclu-

sion amount. See chapter 5 of Pub. 946 to figure the amount.

Part II. Expenses

Capitalizing costs of property. If you produced real or tangible personal property or acquired property for resale, certain expenses attributable to the property generally must be included in inventory costs or capitalized. In addition to direct costs, producers of inventory property generally must also include part of certain indirect costs in their inventory. Purchasers of personal property acquired for resale must include part of certain indirect costs in inventory only if the average annual gross receipts for the 3 prior tax years exceed $10 million. Also, you must capitalize part of the indirect costs that benefit real or tangible personal property constructed for use in a trade or business, or noninventory property produced for sale to customers. Reduce the amounts on lines 8 through 26 and Part V by amounts capitalized. See Pub. 538 for a discussion of uniform capitalization rules.

Exception for certain producers. Producers who account for inventoriable items in the same manner as materials and supplies that are not incidental can currently deduct expenditures for direct labor and all indirect costs that would otherwise be included in inventory costs. See *Part III* for more details.

Exception for creative property. If you are a freelance artist, author, or photographer, you may be exempt from the capitalization rules. However, your personal efforts must have created (or reasonably be expected to create) the property. This exception does not apply to any expense related to printing, photographic plates, motion picture films, video tapes, or similar items. These expenses are subject to the capitalization rules. For details, see *Uniform Capitalization Rules* in Pub. 538.

Line 9

You can deduct the actual expenses of operating your car or truck or take the standard mileage rate. This is true even if you used your vehicle for hire (such as a taxicab). You must use actual expenses if you used five or more vehicles simultaneously in your business (such as in fleet operations). You cannot use actual expenses for a leased vehicle if you previously used the standard mileage rate for that vehicle.

You can take the standard mileage rate for 2014 only if you:
- Owned the vehicle and used the standard mileage rate for the first year you placed the vehicle in service, or
- Leased the vehicle and are using the standard mileage rate for the entire lease period.

If you take the standard mileage rate:
- Multiply the number of business miles driven by 56 cents, and
- Add to this amount your parking fees and tolls.

Enter the total on line 9. Do not deduct depreciation, rent or lease payments, or your actual operating expenses.

If you deduct actual expenses:
- Include on line 9 the business portion of expenses for gasoline, oil, repairs, insurance, license plates, etc., and
- Show depreciation on line 13 and rent or lease payments on line 20a.

For details, see chapter 4 of Pub. 463.

Information on your vehicle. If you claim any car and truck expenses, you must provide certain information on the use of your vehicle by completing one of the following.

1. Complete Schedule C, Part IV, or Schedule C-EZ, Part III, if (a) you are claiming the standard mileage rate, you lease your vehicle, or your vehicle is fully depreciated, and (b) you are not required to file Form 4562 for any other reason. If you used more than one vehicle during the year, attach a statement with the information requested in Schedule C, Part IV, or Schedule C-EZ, Part III, for each additional vehicle.

2. Complete Form 4562, Part V, if you are claiming depreciation on your vehicle or you are required to file Form 4562 for any other reason (see *Line 13*, later).

Line 11

Enter the total cost of contract labor for the tax year. Contract labor includes payments to persons you do not treat as employees (for example, independent contractors) for services performed for your trade or business. Do not include contract labor deducted elsewhere on your return, such as contract labor includible on line 17, 21, 26, or 37. Also, do not include salaries and wages paid

to your employees; instead, see *Line 26*, later.

You must file Form 1099-MISC, Miscellaneous Income, to report contract labor payments of $600 or more during the year. See the Instructions for Form 1099-MISC for details.

Line 12

Enter your deduction for depletion on this line. If you have timber depletion, attach Form T (Timber). See chapter 9 of Pub. 535 for details.

Line 13

Depreciation and section 179 expense deduction. Depreciation is the annual deduction allowed to recover the cost or other basis of business or investment property having a useful life substantially beyond the tax year. You can also depreciate improvements made to leased business property. However, stock in trade, inventories, and land are not depreciable. Depreciation starts when you first use the property in your business or for the production of income. It ends when you take the property out of service, deduct all your depreciable cost or other basis, or no longer use the property in your business or for the production of income. You can also elect under section 179 to expense part or all of the cost of certain property you bought in 2014 for use in your business. See the Instructions for Form 4562 and Pub. 946 to figure the amount to enter on line 13.

When to attach Form 4562. You must complete and attach Form 4562 only if you are claiming:
- Depreciation on property placed in service during 2014;
- Depreciation on listed property (defined later), regardless of the date it was placed in service; or
- A section 179 expense deduction.

If you acquired depreciable property for the first time in 2014, see Pub. 946.

Listed property generally includes but is not limited to:
- Passenger automobiles weighing 6,000 pounds or less;
- Any other property used for transportation if the nature of the property lends itself to personal use, such as motorcycles, pickup trucks, etc.;
- Any property used for entertainment or recreational purposes (such as photographic, phonographic, communi-

cation, and video recording equipment); and
- Computers or peripheral equipment.

Exceptions. Listed property does not include photographic, phonographic, communication, or video equipment used exclusively in your trade or business or at your regular business establishment. It also does not include any computer or peripheral equipment used exclusively at a regular business establishment and owned or leased by the person operating the establishment. For purposes of these exceptions, a portion of your home is treated as a regular business establishment only if that portion meets the requirements under section 280A(c)(1) for deducting expenses for the business use of your home.

See *Line 6*, earlier, if the business use percentage of any listed property dropped to 50% or less in 2014.

Line 14

Deduct contributions to employee benefit programs that are not an incidental part of a pension or profit-sharing plan included on line 19. Examples are accident and health plans, group-term life insurance, and dependent care assistance programs. If you made contributions on your behalf as a self-employed person to a dependent care assistance program, complete Form 2441, Parts I and III, to figure your deductible contributions to that program.

You cannot deduct contributions you made on your behalf as a self-employed person for group-term life insurance.

Do not include on line 14 any contributions you made on your behalf as a self-employed person to an accident and health plan. However, you may be able to deduct on Form 1040, line 29, or Form 1040NR, line 29, the amount you paid for health insurance on behalf of yourself, your spouse, and dependents, even if you do not itemize your deductions. See the instructions for Form 1040, line 29, or Form 1040NR, line 29, for details.

You must reduce your line 14 deduction by the amount of any credit for small employer health insurance premiums determined on Form 8941. See Form 8941 and its instructions to determine which expenses are eligible for the credit.

Line 15

Deduct premiums paid for business insurance on line 15. Deduct on line 14 amounts paid for employee accident and health insurance. Do not deduct amounts credited to a reserve for self-insurance or premiums paid for a policy that pays for your lost earnings due to sickness or disability. For details, see chapter 6 of Pub. 535.

Lines 16a and 16b

Interest allocation rules. The tax treatment of interest expense differs depending on its type. For example, home mortgage interest and investment interest are treated differently. "Interest allocation" rules require you to allocate (classify) your interest expense so it is deducted (or capitalized) on the correct line of your return and receives the right tax treatment. These rules could affect how much interest you are allowed to deduct on Schedule C or C-EZ.

Generally, you allocate interest expense by tracing how the proceeds of the loan were used. See chapter 4 of Pub. 535 for details.

If you paid interest on a debt secured by your main home and any of the proceeds from that debt were used in connection with your trade or business, see chapter 4 of Pub. 535 to figure the amount that is deductible on Schedule C or C-EZ.

How to report. If you have a mortgage on real property used in your business (other than your main home), enter on line 16a the interest you paid for 2014 to banks or other financial institutions for which you received a Form 1098 (or similar statement). If you did not receive a Form 1098, enter the interest on line 16b.

If you paid more mortgage interest than is shown on Form 1098, see chapter 4 of Pub. 535 to find out if you can deduct the additional interest. If you can, include the amount on line 16a. Attach a statement to your return explaining the difference and enter "See attached" in the margin next to line 16a.

If you and at least one other person (other than your spouse if you file a joint return) were liable for and paid interest on the mortgage and the other person received the Form 1098, include your share of the interest on line 16b. Attach a statement to your return showing the name and address of the person who received the Form 1098. In the margin next to line 16b, enter "See attached."

If you paid interest in 2014 that also applies to future years, deduct only the part that applies to 2014.

Line 17

Include on this line fees charged by accountants and attorneys that are ordinary and necessary expenses directly related to operating your business.

Include fees for tax advice related to your business and for preparation of the tax forms related to your business. Also include expenses incurred in resolving asserted tax deficiencies relating to your business.

For more information, see Pub. 334 or 535.

Line 18

Include on this line your expenses for office supplies and postage.

Line 19

Enter your deduction for contributions to a pension, profit-sharing, or annuity plan, or plan for the benefit of your employees. If the plan included you as a self-employed person, enter contributions made as an employer on your behalf on Form 1040, line 28, or Form 1040NR, line 28, not on Schedule C.

In most cases, you must file the applicable form listed below if you maintain a pension, profit-sharing, or other funded-deferred compensation plan. The filing requirement is not affected by whether or not the plan qualified under the Internal Revenue Code, or whether or not you claim a deduction for the current tax year. There is a penalty for failure to timely file these forms.

Form 5500-EZ. File this form if you have a one-participant retirement plan that meets certain requirements. A one-participant plan is a plan that covers only you (or you and your spouse).

Form 5500-SF. File this form electronically with the Department of Labor (at *www.efast.dol.gov*) if you have a small plan (fewer than 100 participants in most cases) that meets certain requirements.

Form 5500. File this form electronically with the Department of Labor (at *www.efast.dol.gov*) for a plan that does not meet the requirements for filing Form 5500-EZ or Form 5500-SF.

For details, see Pub. 560.

Lines 20a and 20b

If you rented or leased vehicles, machinery, or equipment, enter on line 20a the business portion of your rental cost. But if you leased a vehicle for a term of 30 days or more, you may have to reduce your deduction by an amount called the inclusion amount. See *Leasing a Car* in chapter 4 of Pub. 463 to figure this amount.

Enter on line 20b amounts paid to rent or lease other property, such as office space in a building.

Line 21

Deduct the cost of incidental repairs and maintenance that do not add to the property's value or appreciably prolong its life. Do not deduct the value of your own labor. Do not deduct amounts spent to restore or replace property; they must be capitalized.

Line 22

In most cases, you can deduct the cost of materials and supplies only to the extent you actually consumed and used them in your business during the tax year (unless you deducted them in a prior tax year). However, if you had incidental materials and supplies on hand for which you kept no inventories or records of use, you can deduct the cost of those you actually purchased during the tax year, provided that method clearly reflects income.

You can also deduct the cost of books, professional instruments, equipment, etc., if you normally use them within a year. However, if their usefulness extends substantially beyond a year, you must generally recover their costs through depreciation.

Line 23

You can deduct the following taxes and licenses on this line.
- State and local sales taxes imposed on you as the seller of goods or services. If you collected this tax from the buyer, you must also include the amount collected in gross receipts or sales on line 1.
- Real estate and personal property taxes on business assets.
- Licenses and regulatory fees for your trade or business paid each year to state or local governments. But some li-

censes, such as liquor licenses, may have to be amortized. See chapter 8 of Pub. 535 for details.

• Social security and Medicare taxes paid to match required withholding from your employees' wages. Reduce your deduction by the amount shown on Form 8846, line 4.

• Federal unemployment tax paid.

• Federal highway use tax.

• Contributions to state unemployment insurance fund or disability benefit fund if they are considered taxes under state law.

Do not deduct the following.

• Federal income taxes, including your self-employment tax. However, you can deduct one-half of your self-employment tax on Form 1040, line 27, (or Form 1040NR, line 27, when covered under the U.S. social security system due to an international social security agreement).

• Estate and gift taxes.

• Taxes assessed to pay for improvements, such as paving and sewers.

• Taxes on your home or personal use property.

• State and local sales taxes on property purchased for use in your business. Instead, treat these taxes as part of the cost of the property.

• State and local sales taxes imposed on the buyer that you were required to collect and pay over to state or local governments. These taxes are not included in gross receipts or sales nor are they a deductible expense. However, if the state or local government allowed you to retain any part of the sales tax you collected, you must include that amount as income on line 6.

• Other taxes and license fees not related to your business.

Line 24a

Enter your expenses for lodging and transportation connected with overnight travel for business while away from your tax home. In most cases, your tax home is your main place of business, regardless of where you maintain your family home. You cannot deduct expenses paid or incurred in connection with employment away from home if that period of employment exceeds 1 year. Also, you cannot deduct travel expenses for your spouse, your dependent, or any other individual unless that person is your employee, the travel is for a *bona fide* business purpose, and the expenses

would otherwise be deductible by that person.

Do not include expenses for meals and entertainment on this line. Instead, see *Line 24b*, later.

Instead of keeping records of your actual incidental expenses, you can use an optional method for deducting incidental expenses only if you did not pay or incur meal expenses on a day you were traveling away from your tax home. The amount of the deduction is $5 a day. Incidental expenses include fees and tips given to porters, baggage carriers, bellhops, hotel maids, stewards or stewardesses and others on ships, and hotel servants in foreign countries. They do not include expenses for laundry, cleaning and pressing of clothing, lodging taxes, or the costs of telegrams or telephone calls. You cannot use this method on any day that you use the standard meal allowance (as explained in *Line 24b*, later).

You cannot deduct expenses for attending a convention, seminar, or similar meeting held outside the North American area unless the meeting is directly related to your trade or business and it is as reasonable for the meeting to be held outside the North American area as within it. These rules apply to both employers and employees. Other rules apply to luxury water travel.

For details on travel expenses, see chapter 1 of Pub. 463.

Line 24b

Enter your total deductible business meal and entertainment expenses. This includes expenses for meals while traveling away from home for business and for meals that are business-related entertainment.

Deductible expenses. Business meal expenses are deductible only if they are (a) directly related to or associated with the active conduct of your trade or business, (b) not lavish or extravagant, and (c) incurred while you or your employee is present at the meal.

You cannot deduct any expense paid or incurred for a facility (such as a yacht or hunting lodge) used for any activity usually considered entertainment, amusement, or recreation.

Also, you cannot deduct membership dues for any club organized for business, pleasure, recreation, or other social purpose. This includes country clubs,

golf and athletic clubs, airline and hotel clubs, and clubs operated to provide meals under conditions favorable to business discussion. But it does not include civic or public service organizations, professional organizations (such as bar and medical associations), business leagues, trade associations, chambers of commerce, boards of trade, and real estate boards, unless a principal purpose of the organization is to entertain, or provide entertainment facilities for, members or their guests.

There are exceptions to these rules as well as other rules that apply to skybox rentals and tickets to entertainment events. See chapters 1 and 2 of Pub. 463.

Standard meal allowance. Instead of deducting the actual cost of your meals while traveling away from home, you can use the standard meal allowance for your daily meals and incidental expenses. Under this method, you deduct a specified amount, depending on where you travel, instead of keeping records of your actual meal expenses. However, you must still keep records to prove the time, place, and business purpose of your travel.

The standard meal allowance is the federal M&IE rate. You can find these rates on the Internet at *www.gsa.gov*. Click on "Per Diem Rates" for links to locations inside and outside the continental United States.

See chapter 1 of Pub. 463 for details on how to figure your deduction using the standard meal allowance, including special rules for partial days of travel.

Amount of deduction. In most cases, you can deduct only 50% of your business meal and entertainment expenses, including meals incurred while away from home on business. However, for individuals subject to the Department of Transportation (DOT) hours of service limits, that percentage is increased to 80% for business meals consumed during, or incident to, any period of duty for which those limits are in effect. Individuals subject to the DOT hours of service limits include the following.

• Certain air transportation workers (such as pilots, crew, dispatchers, mechanics, and control tower operators) who are under Federal Aviation Administration regulations.

• Interstate truck operators who are under DOT regulations.

- Certain merchant mariners who are under Coast Guard regulations.

However, you can fully deduct meals, incidentals, and entertainment furnished or reimbursed to an employee if you properly treat the expense as wages subject to withholding. You can also fully deduct meals, incidentals, and entertainment provided to a nonemployee to the extent the expenses are includible in the gross income of that person and reported on Form 1099-MISC. See Pub. 535 for details and other exceptions.

Daycare providers. If you qualify as a family daycare provider, you can use the standard meal and snack rates, instead of actual costs, to figure the deductible cost of meals and snacks provided to eligible children. See Pub. 587 for details, including recordkeeping requirements.

Line 25

Deduct utility expenses only for your trade or business.

Local telephone service. If you used your home phone for business, do not deduct the base rate (including taxes) of the first phone line into your residence. But you can deduct any additional costs you incurred for business that are more than the base rate of the first phone line. For example, if you had a second line, you can deduct the business percentage of the charges for that line, including the base rate charges.

Line 26

Enter the total salaries and wages for the tax year. Do not include salaries and wages deducted elsewhere on your return or amounts paid to yourself. Reduce your deduction by the amounts claimed on:

- Form 5884, Work Opportunity Credit, line 2;
- Form 8844, Empowerment Zone Employment Credit, line 2;

- Form 8845, Indian Employment Credit, line 4; and
- Form 8932, Credit for Employer Differential Wage Payments, line 2.

Do not reduce your deduction for any portion of a credit that was passed through to you from a pass-through entity.

 If you provided taxable fringe benefits to your employees, such as personal use of a car, do not deduct as wages the amount applicable to depreciation and other expenses claimed elsewhere.

In most cases, you are required to file Form W-2, Wage and Tax Statement, for each employee. See the General Instructions for Forms W-2 and W-3.

Line 30

Business use of your home. You may be able to deduct certain expenses for business use of your home, subject to limitations. To claim a deduction for business use of your home, you can use Form 8829 or you can elect to determine the amount of the deduction using a simplified method.

For additional information about claiming this deduction, see Pub. 587.

 If you are not using the simplified method to determine the amount of expenses you may deduct for business use of a home, do not complete the additional entry spaces on line 30 for total square footage of your home and of the part of the home used for business. Just include the amount from line 35 of your Form 8829 on line 30.

Simplified method. The simplified method is an alternative to the calculation, allocation, and substantiation of actual expenses. In most cases, you will figure your deduction by multiplying the area (measured in square feet) used regularly and exclusively for business, regularly for daycare, or regularly for storage of inventory or product samples, by $5. The area you use to figure your deduction cannot exceed 300 square feet. You cannot use the simplified method to figure a deduction for rental use of your home.

Electing to use the simplified method. You choose whether or not to use the simplified method each tax year. Make the election by using the simplified method to figure the deduction for the qualified business use of a home on a timely-filed, original federal income tax return for that year. An election for a year, once made, is irrevocable. A change from using the simplified method in one year to actual expenses in a succeeding year, or *vice-versa*, is not a change in method of accounting and does not require the consent of the Commissioner.

If you share your home with someone else who uses the home for a separate business that qualifies for this deduction, each of you may make your own election, but not for the same portion of the home.

If you conduct more than one business that qualifies for this deduction in your home, your election to use the simplified method applies to all your qualified business uses of your home. You are limited to a maximum of 300 square feet for all of the businesses you conduct in your home that qualify for this deduction. Allocate the actual square footage used (up to the maximum 300 square feet) among your qualified business uses in any reasonable manner you choose, but you may not allocate more square feet to a qualified business use than you actually use in that business.

Simplified Method Worksheet

1. Enter the amount of the gross income limitation. See Instructions for the Simplified Method Worksheet .... 1. _____

2. Allowable square footage for the qualified business use. Do not enter more than 300 square feet. See Instructions for the Simplified Method Worksheet .... 2. _____

3. Simplified method amount
   a. Maximum allowable amount .... 3a. _____ $5 _____
   b. For daycare facilities not used exclusively for business, enter the decimal amount from the Daycare Facility Worksheet; otherwise, enter 1.0 .... 3b. _____
   c. Multiply line 3a by line 3b and enter result to 2 decimal places .... 3c. _____

4. Multiply line 2 by line 3c .... 4. _____

5. **Allowable expenses using the simplified method.** Enter the smaller of line 1 or line 4 here and include that amount on Schedule C, line 30. If zero or less, enter -0- .... 5. _____

6. **Carryover of unallowed expenses from 2013 that are not allowed in 2014.**
   a. Operating expenses. Enter the amount from your 2013 Form 8829, line 42 .... 6a. _____
   b. Excess casualty losses and depreciation. Enter the amount from your 2013 Form 8829, line 43 .... 6b. _____

Instructions for the Simplified Method Worksheet

Use this worksheet to figure the amount of expenses you may deduct for a qualified business use of a home if you are electing to use the simplified method for that home. If you are not electing to use the simplified method, use Form 8829.

Line 1. If all gross income from your trade or business is from this qualified business use of your home, figure your gross income limitation as follows.

A. Enter the amount from Schedule C, line 29 .... _____
B. Enter any gain derived from the business use of your home and shown on Form 8949 (and included on Schedule D) or Form 4797 ..... _____
C. Add lines A and B .... _____
D. Enter the loss (as a positive number) shown on Form 8949 (and included on Schedule D) or Form 4797 that are allocable to the business, but not allocable to the use of the home .... _____
E. Gross income limitation. Subtract line D from line C. Enter the result here and on line 1 .... _____

If some of the income is from a place of business other than your home, you must first determine the part of your gross income (Schedule C, line 7, and gains from Form 8949, Schedule D, and Form 4797) from the business use of your home. In making this determination, consider the amount of time you spend at each location as well as other facts. After determining the part of your gross income from the business use of your home, subtract from that amount the total expenses shown on Schedule C, line 28, plus any losses shown on Form 8949 (and included in Schedule D) or Form 4797 that are allocable to the business in which you use your home but that are not allocable to the use of the home. Enter the result on Line 1.

Note. If you had more than one home in which you conducted this business during the year, include only the income earned and the deductions attributable to that income during the period you owned the home for which you elected to use the simplified method.

Line 2. If you used the same area for the entire year, enter the smaller of the square feet you actually used and 300. If you and your spouse conducted the business as a qualified joint venture, split the square feet between you and your spouse in the same manner you split your other tax attributes. If you shared space with someone else, used the home for business for only part of the year, or the area you used changed during the year, see *Figuring your allowable expenses for business use of the home* before entering an amount on this line. Do not enter more than 300 square feet or, if applicable, the average monthly allowable square footage on this line. See *Part-year use or area changes (for simplified method only)* for more information on how to figure your average monthly allowable square footage.

Line 3b. If your qualified business use is providing daycare, you may need to account for the time that you used the same part of your home for other purposes. If you used the part of your home exclusively and regularly for providing daycare, enter 1.0 on line 3b. If you did not use the part of your home exclusively for providing daycare, complete the *Daycare Facility Worksheet* to figure what number to enter on line 3b.

Line 6. Since you are using the simplified method this year, you cannot deduct the amounts you entered on lines 6a and 6b this year. If you file Form 8829 next year for your qualified business use of this home, you will be able to include these expenses when you figure your deduction.

Daycare Facility Worksheet (for simplified method)

1. Multiply days used for daycare during the year by hours used per day .... 1. _____

2. Total hours available for use during the year. See Instructions for the Daycare Facility Worksheet .... 2. _____

3. Divide line 1 by line 2. Enter the result as a decimal amount here and on line 3b of the Simplified Method Worksheet .... 3. _____

Instructions for the Daycare Facility Worksheet

Use this worksheet to figure the percentage to use on line 3b of the Simplified Method Worksheet. If you do not use the area of your home exclusively for daycare, you must reduce the prescribed rate before figuring your deduction using the simplified method.

 If you used at least 300 square feet for daycare regularly and exclusively during the year, then you do not need to complete this worksheet. This worksheet is only needed if you did not use the allowable area exclusively for daycare.

Line 1. Enter the total number of hours the facility was used for daycare during the year.

Example. Your home is used Monday through Friday for 12 hours per day for 250 days during the year. It is also used on 50 Saturdays for 8 hours a day. Enter 3,400 hours on line 4 (3,000 hours for weekdays plus 400 hours for Saturdays).

Line 2. If you used your home for daycare during the entire year, multiply 365 days (366 for a leap year) by 24 hours, and enter the result.

If you started or stopped using your home for daycare during the year, you must prorate the number of hours based on the number of days the home was available for daycare. Multiply 24 hours by the number of days available and enter that result.

 If you used your home for more than one business, you will need to file a separate Schedule C for each business. Do not combine your deductions for each business use on a single Schedule C.

Business use of more than one home. You may have used more than one home in your business. If you used more than one home for the same business during 2014, you may elect to use the simplified method for only one home; you must file a Form 8829 to claim a business use of the home deduction for any additional home. If one or more of the homes was not used for the entire year (for example, you moved during the year), see *Part-year use or area changes (for simplified method only)*, later, and *Columns (a) and (b)* in the Instructions for Form 8829.

Other requirements must still be met. You must still meet all the use requirements to claim a deduction for business use of the home. The simplified method is only an alternative to the calculation, allocation, and substantiation of actual expenses. The simplified method is not an alternative to the exclusivity and other tests that must be met in order to qualify for this deduction. For more information about qualifying business uses, see *Qualifying for a Deduction* in Pub. 587.

Gross income limitation. The amount of your deduction is still limited to the gross income derived from qualified business use of the home reduced by the business deductions that are not related to your use of the home. If this limitation reduces the amount of your deduction, you cannot carryover the difference to another tax year.

Carryover of actual expenses from Form 8829. If you used Form 8829 in a prior year, and you had actual expenses that you could carryover to the next year, you cannot claim those expenses if you are using the simplified method. Instead, the actual expenses from Form 8829 that were not allowed will be carried over to the next year that you file Form 8829 for that business use of that home.

Depreciation of home. You cannot deduct any depreciation (including any additional first-year depreciation) or section 179 expense for the portion of your home that is used in a qualified business use if you figure the deduction for the business use of your home using the simplified method. The depreciation deduction allowable for that portion of the home for that year is deemed to be zero.

 Although you cannot deduct any depreciation or section 179 expense for the portion of your home that is a qualified business use because you elect to use the simplified method, you may still claim depreciation or the section 179 expense deduction on other assets (for example, furniture and equipment) used in the qualified business use of your home.

Figuring your allowable expenses for business use of the home. You will figure the deduction using Form 8829 or the simplified method worksheet, or both.

 You may not use the simplified method and also file Form 8829 for the same qualified business use of the same home.

Using Form 8829. Use Form 8829 to figure and claim this deduction for a home if you are not or cannot use the simplified method for that home. For information about claiming this deduction using Form 8829, see the Instructions for Form 8829 and Pub. 587.

Using the simplified method. Use the Simplified Method Worksheet in these instructions to figure your deduction for a qualified business use of your home if you are electing to use the simplified method for that home.

Shared use (for simplified method only). If you share your home with someone else who uses the home for a separate business that also qualifies for this deduction, you may not include the same square feet to figure your deduction as the other person. You must allocate the shared space between you and the other person in a reasonable manner.

Example. Kristen and Lindsey are roommates. Kristen uses 300 square feet of their home for a qualified business use. Lindsey uses 200 square feet of their home for a separate qualified business use. The qualified business uses share 100 square feet. In addition to the portion that they do not share, Kristen and Lindsey can both claim 50 of the 100 square feet or divide the 100 square feet between them in any reasonable manner. If divided evenly, Kristen could claim 250 square feet using the simplified method and Lindsey could claim 150 square feet.

Part-year use or area changes (for simplified method only). If your qualified business use was for a portion of the tax year (for example, a seasonal business, a business that begins during the year, or you moved during the year) or you changed the square footage of your qualified business use, your deduction is limited to the average monthly allowable square footage. You figure the average monthly allowable square footage by adding the amount of allowable square feet you used in each month and dividing the sum by 12.

When determining the average monthly allowable square footage, you cannot take more than 300 square feet into account for any one month. Additionally, if your qualified business use was less than 15 days in a month, you must use -0- for that month.

Example 1. Andy files his federal income tax return on a calendar year basis. On July 20, he began using 400 square feet of his home for a qualified business use. He continued to use the 400 square feet until the end of the year. Andy's average monthly allowable square footage is 125 square feet (300 square feet for August through December divided by the number of months in the year ((0 + 0 + 0 + 0 + 0 + 0 + 0 + 300 + 300 + 300 + 300 + 300)/12)).

Example 2. Roland files his federal income tax return on a calendar year basis. On April 20, he began using 100 square feet of his home for a qualified business use. On August 5, he expanded the area of his qualified business use to 350 square feet. Roland continued to use the 350 square feet until the end of the year. Roland's average monthly allowable square footage is 150 square feet (100 square feet for May through July and 300 square feet for August through December divided by the number of months in the year ((0 + 0 + 0 + 0 + 100 + 100 +100 + 300 + 300 + 300 + 300 + 300)/12)).

Example 3. Donna files her federal income tax return on a calendar year basis. From January 1 through July 16 she used 300 square feet of her home for a qualified business use. On July 17, Donna moved to a new home and immediately began using 200 square feet of the new home for the same qualified business use. While preparing her tax return, Donna used the simplified method to deduct expenses for the qualified business use of her old home. Donna's average monthly allowable square footage is 175 square feet (300 square feet for January through July divided by the number of months in the year ((300 +300 +300 + 300 + 300 + 300 + 300 + 0 + 0 + 0 + 0 + 0)/12)). Donna also prepared Form 8829 to deduct the actual expenses associated with the qualified business use of her new home.

Once you have determined your allowable square footage, enter the result on line 2 of the Simplified Method Worksheet.

 If you moved during the year, your average allowable square footage will generally be less than 300.

 You can use the Area Adjustment Worksheet in Pub. 587 to help you determine the allowable square footage to enter on line 2 of the Simplified Method Worksheet.

Reporting your expenses for business use of the home. If you did not use the simplified method, include the amount from line 35 of Form 8829 on line 30 of the Schedule C you are filing for that business.

If you used the simplified method. If you elect to use the simplified method for the business use of a home, complete the additional entry spaces on line 30 for that home only. Include the amount from line 5 of the Simplified Method Worksheet on line 30.

If you itemize your deductions on Schedule A, you may deduct your mortgage interest, real estate taxes, and casualty losses on Schedule A as if you did not use your home for business. You cannot deduct any excess mortgage interest or excess casualty losses on Schedule C for this home.

Use Part II of Schedule C to deduct business expenses that are unrelated to the qualified business use of the home (for example, expenses for advertising, wages, or supplies, or depreciation of equipment or furniture).

Deduction figured on multiple forms. If you used more than one home for a business during the year, you may use a Form 8829 for each home or you may use the simplified method for one home and Form 8829 for any other home. Combine the amount you figured using the simplified method and the amounts you figured on your Forms 8829, and then enter the total on line 30 of the Schedule C you are filing for that business.

Line 31

Figuring your net profit or allowable loss. If your expenses (including the expenses you report on line 30) are more than your gross income, do not enter your loss on line 31 until you have applied the excess farm loss rules, the at-risk rules, and the passive activity loss rules. To apply these rules, follow the instructions in *Excess farm loss rules*, *Line 32* in these instructions, and the Instructions for Form 8582. After applying those rules, the amount on line 31 will be your allowable loss, and it may be smaller than the amount you figured by subtracting line 30 from line 29.

If your gross income is more than your expenses (including the expenses you report on line 30), and you do not have prior year unallowed passive activity losses, subtract line 30 from line 29. The result is your net profit.

If your gross income is more than your expenses (including the expenses you report on line 30), and you have prior year unallowed passive activity losses, do not enter your net profit on line 31 until you have figured the amount of prior year unallowed passive activity losses you may claim this year for this activity. Use Form 8582 to figure the amount of prior year unallowed passive activity losses you may include on line 31. Make sure to indicate that you are including prior year passive activity losses by entering "PAL" to the left of the entry space.

If you checked the "No" box on line G, see the Instructions for Form 8582; you may need to include information from this schedule on that form, even if you have a net profit.

Rental real estate activity. Unless you are a qualifying real estate professional, a rental real estate activity is a passive activity, even if you materially participated in the activity. If you have a loss, you may need to file Form 8582 to figure your allowable loss. See the Instructions for Form 8582.

Excess farm loss rules. If your Schedule C activity includes processing a farm commodity as part of your farming business, your deductible loss from that activity may be limited if you received certain subsidies. See the Instructions for Schedule F for a list of those subsidies. Use one of the worksheets in the Schedule F instructions to determine if you have an excess farm loss. See the Instructions for Schedule F for more details on how to complete the worksheets.

You must figure and apply your excess farm loss before figuring any limitations to your loss due to the at-risk rules or the passive activity loss rules. Reduce your loss by your excess farm loss before applying the at-risk rules and passive activity loss rules.

Reporting your net profit or allowable loss. Once you have figured your net profit or allowable loss, report it as follows.

Individuals. Enter your net profit or allowable loss on line 31 and include it on Form 1040, line 12. Also, include your net profit or allowable loss on Schedule SE, line 2. However, if you are a statutory employee or notary public, see *Statutory employees* or *Notary public*, later.

Nonresident aliens. Enter your net profit or allowable loss on line 31 and include it on Form 1040NR, line 13. You should also include this amount on Schedule SE, line 2 if you are covered under the U.S. social security system due to an international social security agreement currently in effect. See the Instructions for Schedule SE (Form

1040) for information on international social security agreements. However, if you are a statutory employee or notary public, see *Statutory employees* or *Notary public*, later.

Trusts and estates. Enter the net profit or allowable loss on line 31 and include it on Form 1041, line 3.

Statutory employees. Enter your net profit or allowable loss on line 31 and include it on Form 1040, line 12, or on Form 1040NR, line 13. However, do not report this amount on Schedule SE, line 2. If you were a statutory employee and you are required to file Schedule SE because of other self-employment income, see the Instructions for Schedule SE.

Notary public. Do not enter your net profit from line 31 on Schedule SE, line 2, unless you are required to file Schedule SE because you have other self-employment income. See the Instructions for Schedule SE.

Community income. If you and your spouse had community income and are filing separate returns, see the Instructions for Schedule SE before figuring self-employment tax.

Earned income credit. If you have a net profit on line 31, this amount is earned income and may qualify you for the earned income credit (EIC).

 To figure your EIC, use the instructions for Form 1040, lines 66a and 66b. Complete all applicable steps plus Worksheet B. If you are required to file Schedule SE, remember to enter one-half of your self-employment tax in Part 1, line 1d, of Worksheet B.

Line 32

 You do not need to complete line 32 if line 7 is more than the total of lines 28 and 30.

At-risk rules. In most cases, if you have a business loss and amounts invested in the business for which you are not at risk, you must complete Form 6198 to figure your allowable loss. The at-risk rules generally limit the amount of loss (including loss on the disposition of assets) you can claim to the amount you could actually lose in the business.

Check box 32b if you have amounts invested in this business for which you are not at risk, such as the following.

• Nonrecourse loans used to finance the business, to acquire property used in the business, or to acquire the business that are not secured by your own property (other than property used in the business). However, there is an exception for certain nonrecourse financing borrowed by you in connection with holding real property.

• Cash, property, or borrowed amounts used in the business (or contributed to the business, or used to acquire the business) that are protected against loss by a guarantee, stop-loss agreement, or other similar arrangement (excluding casualty insurance and insurance against tort liability).

• Amounts borrowed for use in the business from a person who has an interest in the business, other than as a creditor, or who is related under section 465(b)(3)(C) to a person (other than you) having such an interest.

Figuring your allowable loss. Before determining your allowable loss, you must check box 32a or 32b to determine if the loss from your business activity is limited by the at-risk rules. Follow the instructions, next, that apply to your box 32 activity.

All investment is at risk. If all amounts are at risk in this business, check box 32a. If you answered "Yes" on line G, your remaining loss (after applying the excess farm loss rules) is your allowable loss. The at-risk rules and the passive activity loss rules do not apply. See *Line 31*, earlier, for how to report your allowable loss.

But if you answered "No" on line G, you may need to complete Form 8582 to figure your allowable loss to enter on line 31. See the Instructions for Form 8582 for details.

Some investment is not at risk. If some investment is not at risk, check box 32b; the at-risk rules apply to your loss. Be sure to attach Form 6198 to your return.

If you answered "Yes" on line G, complete Form 6198 to figure the allowable loss to enter on line 31. The passive activity loss rules do not apply. See *Line 31*, earlier, for how to report your allowable loss.

But if you answered "No" on line G, the passive activity loss rules may apply.

First complete Form 6198 to figure the amount of your profit or loss for the at-risk activity, which may include amounts reported on other forms and schedules, and the at-risk amount for the activity. Follow the Instructions for Form 6198 to determine how much of your Schedule C loss will be allowed. After you figure the amount of your loss that is allowed under the at-risk rules, you may need to complete Form 8582 to figure the allowable loss to enter on line 31. See the Instructions for Form 8582 for details.

 If you checked box 32b because some investment is not at risk and you do not attach Form 6198, the processing of your return may be delayed.

At-risk loss deduction. Any loss from this business not allowed for 2014 only because of the at-risk rules is treated as a deduction allocable to the business in 2015.

More information. For details, see the Instructions for Form 6198 and Pub. 925.

Part III. Cost of Goods Sold

In most cases, if you engaged in a trade or business in which the production, purchase, or sale of merchandise was an income-producing factor, you must take inventories into account at the beginning and end of your tax year.

Exception for certain taxpayers. If you are a qualifying taxpayer or a qualifying small business taxpayer (discussed next), you can account for inventoriable items in the same manner as materials and supplies that are not incidental. Under this accounting method, inventory costs for raw materials purchased for use in producing finished goods and merchandise purchased for resale are deductible in the year the finished goods or merchandise are sold (but not before the year you paid for the raw materials or merchandise, if you are also using the cash method). Enter amounts paid for all raw materials and merchandise during 2014 on line 36. The amount you can deduct for 2014 is figured on line 42.

Qualifying taxpayer. This is a taxpayer (a) whose average annual gross receipts for each tax year ending on or after December 17, 1998, are $1 million or

less, and (b) whose business is not a tax shelter (as defined in section 448(d)(3)). To figure your average annual gross receipts for each tax year, add the gross receipts for that tax year and the 2 preceding tax years. Divide the total by three.

Qualifying small business taxpayer. This is a taxpayer (a) whose average annual gross receipts for each tax year ending on or after December 31, 2000, are $10 million or less, (b) whose business is not a tax shelter (as defined in section 448(d)(3)), and (c) whose principal business activity is not an ineligible activity as explained in Rev. Proc. 2002-28. You can find Rev. Proc. 2002-28 on page 815 of Internal Revenue Bulletin 2002-18 at *www.irs.gov/ pub/irs-irbs/irb02-18.pdf*.

To figure your average annual gross receipts for each tax year, add the gross receipts for that tax year and the 2 preceding tax years. Divide the total by three.

Changing accounting methods. File Form 3115 if you are a qualifying taxpayer or qualifying small business taxpayer and want to change to the cash method or to account for inventoriable items as non-incidental materials and supplies.

Additional information. For additional guidance on this method of accounting for inventoriable items, see the following.
• Pub. 538 discusses both exceptions.
• If you are a qualifying taxpayer, see Rev. Proc. 2001-10, on page 272 of Internal Revenue Bulletin 2001-2 at *www.irs.gov/pub/irs-irbs/irb01-02.pdf*.
• If you are a qualifying small business taxpayer, see Rev. Proc. 2002-28, on page 815 of Internal Revenue Bulletin 2002-18 at *www.irs.gov/pub/irs-irbs/ irb02-18.pdf*.

 Certain direct and indirect expenses may have to be capitalized or included in inventory. See Part II, *earlier. See Pub. 538 for additional information.*

Line 33

Your inventories can be valued at cost, the lower of cost or market, or any other method approved by the IRS. However, you are required to use cost if you are using the cash method of accounting.

Line 35

If you are changing your method of accounting beginning with 2014, refigure last year's closing inventory using your new method of accounting and enter the result on line 35. If there is a difference between last year's closing inventory and the refigured amount, attach an explanation and take it into account when figuring your section 481(a) adjustment. For details, see the example under *Line F*, earlier.

Line 41

If you account for inventoriable items in the same manner as materials and supplies that are not incidental, enter on line 41 the portion of your raw materials and merchandise purchased for resale that is included on line 40 and was not sold during the year.

Part IV. Information on Your Vehicle

Line 44b

In most cases, commuting is travel between your home and a work location. If you converted your vehicle during the year from personal to business use (or *vice versa*), enter your commuting miles only for the period you drove your vehicle for business. For information on certain travel that is considered a business expense rather than commuting, see the Instructions for Form 2106.

Part V. Other Expenses

Include all ordinary and necessary business expenses not deducted elsewhere on Schedule C. List the type and amount of each expense separately in the space provided. Enter the total on lines 48 and 27a. Do not include the cost of business equipment or furniture, replacements or permanent improvements to property, or personal, living, and family expenses. Do not include charitable contributions. Also, you cannot deduct fines or penalties paid to a government for violating any law. For details on business expenses, see Pub. 535.

Amortization. Include amortization in this part. For amortization that begins in

2014, you must complete and attach Form 4562.

You can elect to amortize such costs as:

- The cost of pollution-control facilities;
- Amounts paid for research and experimentation;
- Qualified revitalization expenditures;
- Amounts paid to acquire, protect, expand, register, or defend trademarks or trade names; or
- Goodwill and certain other intangibles.

In most cases, you cannot amortize real property construction period interest and taxes. Special rules apply for allocating interest to real or personal property produced in your trade or business.

For a complete list, see the instructions for Form 4562, Part VI.

At-risk loss deduction. Any loss from this business that was not allowed last year because of the at-risk rules is treated as a deduction allocable to this business in 2014.

Bad debts. Include debts and partial debts from sales or services that were included in income and are definitely known to be worthless. If you later collect a debt that you deducted as a bad debt, include it as income in the year collected. For details, see chapter 10 of Pub. 535.

Business start-up costs. If your business began in 2014, you can elect to deduct up to $5,000 of certain business start-up costs. The $5,000 limit is reduced (but not below zero) by the amount by which your total start-up costs exceed $50,000. Your remaining start-up costs can be amortized over a 180-month period, beginning with the month the business began.

For details, see chapters 7 and 8 of Pub. 535. For amortization that begins in 2014, you must complete and attach Form 4562.

Costs of making commercial buildings energy efficient. You may be able to deduct part or all of the cost of modifying existing commercial buildings to make them energy efficient. For details, see section 179D, Notice 2006-52, Notice 2008-40, and Notice 2012-26. Notice 2006-52, 2006-26 I.R.B. 1175, is available at *www.irs.gov/irb/*

2006–26_IRB/ar11.html. Notice 2008–40, 2008–14 I.R.B. 725, is available at *www.irs.gov/irb/2008–14_IRB/ar12.html.* Notice 2012–26, 2012–17 I.R.B. 847, is available at *www.irs.gov/irb/2012–17_IRB/ar08.html.*

Deduction for removing barriers to individuals with disabilities and the elderly. You may be able to deduct up to $15,000 of costs paid or incurred in 2014 to remove architectural or transportation barriers to individuals with disabilities and the elderly. However, you cannot take both a credit (on Form 8826) and a deduction for the same expenditures.

Excess farm loss deduction. Any loss from this business activity, which includes processing a farm commodity as part of your farming business, that was not allowed last year because of the excess farm loss rules is treated as a deduction allocable to this business activity in 2014.

See the Instructions for Schedule F for a definition of farming business for this purpose and for more information about excess farm losses.

Film and television production expenses. You can elect to deduct costs of certain qualified film and television productions. For details, see chapter 7 of Pub. 535.

Forestation and reforestation costs. Reforestation costs are generally capital expenditures. However, for each qualified timber property, you can elect to expense up to $10,000 ($5,000 if married filing separately) of qualifying reforestation costs paid or incurred in 2014.

You can elect to amortize the remaining costs over 84 months. For amortization that begins in 2014, you must complete and attach Form 4562.

The amortization election does not apply to trusts, and the expense election does not apply to estates and trusts. For details on reforestation expenses, see chapters 7 and 8 of Pub. 535.

Paperwork Reduction Act Notice. We ask for the information on Schedule C (Form 1040) and Schedule C-EZ (Form 1040) to carry out the Internal Revenue laws of the United States. You are required to give us the information. We need it to ensure that you are complying

with these laws and to allow us to figure and collect the right amount of tax.

You are not required to provide the information requested on a form that is subject to the Paperwork Reduction Act unless the form displays a valid OMB control number. Books or records relating to a form or its instructions must be retained as long as their contents may become material in the administration of any Internal Revenue law. Generally, tax returns and return information are confidential, as required by section 6103.

The time needed to complete and file Schedule C (Form 1040) will vary depending on individual circumstances. The estimated burden for individual taxpayers filing this form is included in the estimates shown in the instructions for their individual income tax return. The estimated burden for all other taxpayers who file this form is approved under OMB control number 1545-1974 and is shown next.

Recordkeeping	3 hr., 36 min.
Learning about the law or the form	1 hr., 19 min.
Preparing the form	1 hr., 39 min.
Copying, assembling, and sending the form to the IRS	34 min.

The time needed to complete and file Schedule C-EZ (Form 1040) will vary depending on individual circumstances. The estimated burden for individual taxpayers filing this form is included in the estimates shown in the instructions for their individual income tax return. The estimated burden for all other taxpayers who file this form is approved under OMB control number 1545-1973 and is shown next.

Recordkeeping	45 min.
Learning about the law or the form	3 min.
Preparing the form	35 min.
Copying, assembling, and sending the form to the IRS	20 min.

If you have comments concerning the accuracy of these time estimates or suggestions for making this form simpler, we would be happy to hear from you. See the instructions for the tax return with which this form is filed.

Principal Business or Professional Activity Codes

These codes for the Principal Business or Professional Activity classify sole proprietorships by the type of activity they are engaged in to facilitate the administration of the Internal Revenue Code. These six-digit codes are based on the North American Industry Classification System (NAICS).

Select the category that best describes your primary business activity (for example, Real Estate). Then select the activity that best identifies the principal source of your sales or receipts (for example, real estate agent). Now find the six-digit code assigned to this activity (for example, 531210, the code for offices of real estate agents and brokers) and enter it on Schedule C or C-EZ, line B.

Note. If your principal source of income is from farming activities, you should file Schedule F.

Accommodation, Food Services, & Drinking Places

Accommodation

721310	Rooming & boarding houses
721210	RV (recreational vehicle) parks & recreational camps
721100	Traveler accommodation (including hotels, motels, & bed & breakfast inns)

Food Services & Drinking Places

722514	Cafeterias & buffets
722410	Drinking places (alcoholic beverages)
722511	Full-service restaurants
722513	Limited-service restaurants
722515	Snack & non-alcoholic beverage bars
722300	Special food services (including food service contractors & caterers)

Administrative & Support and Waste Management & Remediation Services

Administrative & Support Services

561430	Business service centers (including private mail centers & copy shops)
561740	Carpet & upholstery cleaning services
561440	Collection agencies
561450	Credit bureaus
561410	Document preparation services
561300	Employment services
561710	Exterminating & pest control services
561210	Facilities support (management) services
561600	Investigation & security services
561720	Janitorial services
561730	Landscaping services
561110	Office administrative services
561420	Telephone call centers (including telephone answering services & telemarketing bureaus)
561500	Travel arrangement & reservation services
561490	Other business support services (including repossession services, court reporting, & stenotype services)
561790	Other services to buildings & dwellings
561900	Other support services (including packaging & labeling services, & convention & trade show organizers)

Waste Management & Remediation Services

562000	Waste management & remediation services

Agriculture, Forestry, Hunting, & Fishing

112900	Animal production (including breeding of cats and dogs)
114110	Fishing
113000	Forestry & logging (including forest nurseries & timber tracts)
114210	Hunting & trapping

Support Activities for Agriculture & Forestry

115210	Support activities for animal production (including farriers)
115110	Support activities for crop production (including cotton ginning, soil preparation, planting, & cultivating)
115310	Support activities for forestry

Arts, Entertainment, & Recreation

Amusement, Gambling, & Recreation Industries

713100	Amusement parks & arcades
713200	Gambling industries
713900	Other amusement & recreation services (including golf courses, skiing facilities, marinas, fitness centers, bowling centers, skating rinks, miniature golf courses)

Museums, Historical Sites, & Similar Institutions

712100	Museums, historical sites, & similar institutions

Performing Arts, Spectator Sports, & Related Industries

711410	Agents & managers for artists, athletes, entertainers, & other public figures
711510	Independent artists, writers, & performers
711100	Performing arts companies
711300	Promoters of performing arts, sports, & similar events
711210	Spectator sports (including professional sports clubs & racetrack operations)

Construction of Buildings

236200	Nonresidential building construction
236100	Residential building construction

Heavy and Civil Engineering Construction

237310	Highway, street, & bridge construction
237210	Land subdivision
237100	Utility system construction
237990	Other heavy & civil engineering construction

Specialty Trade Contractors

238310	Drywall & insulation contractors
238210	Electrical contractors
238350	Finish carpentry contractors
238330	Flooring contractors
238130	Framing carpentry contractors
238150	Glass & glazing contractors
238140	Masonry contractors
238320	Painting & wall covering contractors
238220	Plumbing, heating & air-conditioning contractors
238110	Poured concrete foundation & structure contractors
238160	Roofing contractors
238170	Siding contractors
238910	Site preparation contractors
238120	Structural steel & precast concrete construction contractors
238340	Tile & terrazzo contractors
238290	Other building equipment contractors
238390	Other building finishing contractors
238190	Other foundation, structure, & building exterior contractors
238990	All other specialty trade contractors

Educational Services

611000	Educational services (including schools, colleges, & universities)

Finance & Insurance

Credit Intermediation & Related Activities

522100	Depository credit intermediation (including commercial banking, savings institutions, & credit unions)
522200	Nondepository credit intermediation (including sales financing & consumer lending)
522300	Activities related to credit intermediation (including loan brokers)

Insurance Agents, Brokers, & Related Activities

524210	Insurance agencies & brokerages
524290	Other insurance related activities

Securities, Commodity Contracts, & Other Financial Investments & Related Activities

523140	Commodity contracts brokers
523130	Commodity contracts dealers
523110	Investment bankers & securities dealers
523210	Securities & commodity exchanges
523120	Securities brokers
523900	Other financial investment activities (including investment advice)

Health Care & Social Assistance

Ambulatory Health Care Services

621610	Home health care services
621510	Medical & diagnostic laboratories
621310	Offices of chiropractors
621210	Offices of dentists
621330	Offices of mental health practitioners (except physicians)
621320	Offices of optometrists
621340	Offices of physical, occupational & speech therapists, & audiologists
621111	Offices of physicians (except mental health specialists)
621112	Offices of physicians, mental health specialists
621391	Offices of podiatrists
621399	Offices of all other miscellaneous health practitioners
621400	Outpatient care centers
621900	Other ambulatory health care services (including ambulance services, blood, & organ banks)

Hospitals

622000	Hospitals

Nursing & Residential Care Facilities

623000	Nursing & residential care facilities

Social Assistance

624410	Child day care services
624200	Community food & housing, & emergency & other relief services
624100	Individual & family services
624310	Vocational rehabilitation services

Information

511000	Publishing industries (except Internet)

Broadcasting (except Internet) & Telecommunications

515000	Broadcasting (except Internet)
517000	Telecommunications & Internet service providers

Data Processing Services

518210	Data processing, hosting, & related services
519100	Other information services (including news syndicates & libraries, Internet publishing & broadcasting)

Motion Picture & Sound Recording

512100	Motion picture & video industries (except video rental)
512200	Sound recording industries

Manufacturing

315000	Apparel mfg.
312000	Beverage & tobacco product mfg.
334000	Computer & electronic product mfg.
335000	Electrical equipment, appliance, & component mfg.
332000	Fabricated metal product mfg.
337000	Furniture & related product mfg.
333000	Machinery mfg.
339110	Medical equipment & supplies mfg.
322000	Paper mfg.
324100	Petroleum & coal products mfg.
326000	Plastics & rubber products mfg.
331000	Primary metal mfg.
323100	Printing & related support activities
313000	Textile mills
314000	Textile product mills
336000	Transportation equipment mfg.
321000	Wood product mfg.
339900	Other miscellaneous mfg.

Chemical Manufacturing

325100	Basic chemical mfg.
325500	Paint, coating, & adhesive mfg.
325300	Pesticide, fertilizer, & other agricultural chemical mfg.
325410	Pharmaceutical & medicine mfg.
325200	Resin, synthetic rubber, & artificial & synthetic fibers & filaments mfg.
325600	Soap, cleaning compound, & toilet preparation mfg.
325900	Other chemical product & preparation mfg.

Food Manufacturing

311110	Animal food mfg.
311800	Bakeries, tortilla, & dry pasta mfg.
311500	Dairy product mfg.
311400	Fruit & vegetable preserving & speciality food mfg.
311200	Grain & oilseed milling
311610	Animal slaughtering & processing
311710	Seafood product preparation & packaging
311300	Sugar & confectionery product mfg.
311900	Other food mfg. (including coffee, tea, flavorings, & seasonings)

Leather & Allied Product Manufacturing

316210	Footwear mfg. (including leather, rubber, & plastics)
316110	Leather & hide tanning & finishing
316990	Other leather & allied product mfg.

Nonmetallic Mineral Product Manufacturing
327300 Cement & concrete product mfg.
327100 Clay product & refractory mfg.
327210 Glass & glass product mfg.
327400 Lime & gypsum product mfg.
327900 Other nonmetallic mineral product mfg.

Mining
212110 Coal mining
212200 Metal ore mining
212300 Nonmetallic mineral mining & quarrying
211110 Oil & gas extraction
213110 Support activities for mining

Other Services

Personal & Laundry Services
812111 Barber shops
812112 Beauty salons
812220 Cemeteries & crematories
812310 Coin-operated laundries & drycleaners
812320 Drycleaning & laundry services (except coin-operated) (including laundry & drycleaning drop-off & pickup sites)
812210 Funeral homes & funeral services
812330 Linen & uniform supply
812113 Nail salons
812930 Parking lots & garages
812910 Pet care (except veterinary) services
812920 Photofinishing
812190 Other personal care services (including diet & weight reducing centers)
812990 All other personal services

Repair & Maintenance
811120 Automotive body, paint, interior, & glass repair
811110 Automotive mechanical & electrical repair & maintenance
811190 Other automotive repair & maintenance (including oil change & lubrication shops & car washes)
811310 Commercial & industrial machinery & equipment (except automotive & electronic) repair & maintenance
811210 Electronic & precision equipment repair & maintenance
811430 Footwear & leather goods repair
811410 Home & garden equipment & appliance repair & maintenance
811420 Reupholstery & furniture repair
811490 Other personal & household goods repair & maintenance

Professional, Scientific, & Technical Services
541100 Legal services
541211 Offices of certified public accountants
541214 Payroll services
541213 Tax preparation services
541219 Other accounting services

Architectural, Engineering, & Related Services
541310 Architectural services
541350 Building inspection services
541340 Drafting services
541330 Engineering services
541360 Geophysical surveying & mapping services
541320 Landscape architecture services
541370 Surveying & mapping (except geophysical) services

541380 Testing laboratories

Computer Systems Design & Related Services
541510 Computer systems design & related services

Specialized Design Services
541400 Specialized design services (including interior, industrial, graphic, & fashion design)

Other Professional, Scientific, & Technical Services
541800 Advertising & related services
541600 Management, scientific, & technical consulting services
541910 Market research & public opinion polling
541920 Photographic services
541700 Scientific research & development services
541930 Translation & interpretation services
541940 Veterinary services
541990 All other professional, scientific, & technical services

Real Estate & Rental & Leasing

Real Estate
531100 Lessors of real estate (including miniwarehouses & self-storage units)
531210 Offices of real estate agents & brokers
531320 Offices of real estate appraisers
531310 Real estate property managers
531390 Other activities related to real estate

Rental & Leasing Services
532100 Automotive equipment rental & leasing
532400 Commercial & industrial machinery & equipment rental & leasing
532210 Consumer electronics & appliances rental
532220 Formal wear & costume rental
532310 General rental centers
532230 Video tape & disc rental
532290 Other consumer goods rental

Religious, Grantmaking, Civic, Professional, & Similar Organizations
813000 Religious, grantmaking, civic, professional, & similar organizations

Retail Trade

Building Material & Garden Equipment & Supplies Dealers
444130 Hardware stores
444110 Home centers
444200 Lawn & garden equipment & supplies stores
444120 Paint & wallpaper stores
444190 Other building materials dealers

Clothing & Accessories Stores
448130 Children's & infants' clothing stores
448150 Clothing accessories stores
448140 Family clothing stores
448310 Jewelry stores
448320 Luggage & leather goods stores
448110 Men's clothing stores
448210 Shoe stores
448120 Women's clothing stores
448190 Other clothing stores

Electronic & Appliance Stores
443142 Electronics stores (including audio, video, computer, & camera stores)
443141 Household appliance stores

Food & Beverage Stores
445310 Beer, wine, & liquor stores
445220 Fish & seafood markets
445230 Fruit & vegetable markets
445100 Grocery stores (including supermarkets & convenience stores without gas)
445210 Meat markets
445290 Other specialty food stores

Furniture & Home Furnishing Stores
442110 Furniture stores
442200 Home furnishings stores

Gasoline Stations
447100 Gasoline stations (including convenience stores with gas)

General Merchandise Stores
452000 General merchandise stores

Health & Personal Care Stores
446120 Cosmetics, beauty supplies, & perfume stores
446130 Optical goods stores
446110 Pharmacies & drug stores
446190 Other health & personal care stores

Motor Vehicle & Parts Dealers
441300 Automotive parts, accessories, & tire stores
441222 Boat dealers
441228 Motorcycle, ATV, & all other motor vehicle dealers
441110 New car dealers
441210 Recreational vehicle dealers (including motor home & travel trailer dealers)
441120 Used car dealers

Sporting Goods, Hobby, Book, & Music Stores
451211 Book stores
451120 Hobby, toy, & game stores
451140 Musical instrument & supplies stores
451212 News dealers & newsstands
451130 Sewing, needlework, & piece goods stores
451110 Sporting goods stores

Miscellaneous Store Retailers
453920 Art dealers
453110 Florists
453220 Gift, novelty, & souvenir stores
453930 Manufactured (mobile) home dealers
453210 Office supplies & stationery stores
453910 Pet & pet supplies stores
453310 Used merchandise stores
453990 All other miscellaneous store retailers (including tobacco, candle, & trophy shops)

Nonstore Retailers
454112 Electronic auctions
454111 Electronic shopping
454310 Fuel dealers (including heating oil & liquefied petroleum)
454113 Mail-order houses
454210 Vending machine operators
454390 Other direct selling establishments (including door-to-door retailing, frozen food plan providers, party plan merchandisers, & coffee-break service providers)

Transportation & Warehousing
481000 Air transportation
485510 Charter bus industry
484110 General freight trucking, local
484120 General freight trucking, long distance
485210 Interurban & rural bus transportation

486000 Pipeline transportation
482110 Rail transportation
487000 Scenic & sightseeing transportation
485410 School & employee bus transportation
484200 Specialized freight trucking (including household moving vans)
485300 Taxi & limousine service
485110 Urban transit systems
483000 Water transportation
485990 Other transit & ground passenger transportation
488000 Support activities for transportation (including motor vehicle towing)

Couriers & Messengers
492000 Couriers & messengers

Warehousing & Storage Facilities
493100 Warehousing & storage (except leases of miniwarehouses & self-storage units)

Utilities
221000 Utilities

Wholesale Trade

Merchant Wholesalers, Durable Goods
423200 Furniture & home furnishing
423700 Hardware, & plumbing & heating equipment & supplies
423600 Household appliances & electrical & electronic goods
423940 Jewelry, watch, precious stone, & precious metals
423300 Lumber & other construction materials
423800 Machinery, equipment, & supplies
423500 Metal & mineral (except petroleum)
423100 Motor vehicle & motor vehicle parts & supplies
423400 Professional & commercial equipment & supplies
423930 Recyclable materials
423910 Sporting & recreational goods & supplies
423920 Toy & hobby goods & supplies
423990 Other miscellaneous durable goods

Merchant Wholesalers, Nondurable Goods
424300 Apparel, piece goods, & notions
424800 Beer, wine, & distilled alcoholic beverage
424920 Books, periodicals, & newspapers
424600 Chemical & allied products
424210 Drugs & druggists' sundries
424500 Farm product raw materials
424910 Farm supplies
424930 Flower, nursery stock, & florists' supplies
424400 Grocery & related products
424950 Paint, varnish, & supplies
424100 Paper & paper products
424700 Petroleum & petroleum products
424940 Tobacco & tobacco products
424990 Other miscellaneous nondurable goods

Wholesale Electronic Markets and Agents & Brokers
425110 Business to business electronic markets
425120 Wholesale trade agents & brokers

999999 **Unclassified establishments (unable to classify)**

2014 Instructions for Schedule D

Capital Gains and Losses

These instructions explain how to complete Schedule D (Form 1040). Complete Form 8949 before you complete line 1b, 2, 3, 8b, 9, or 10 of Schedule D.

Use Schedule D:
- To figure the overall gain or loss from transactions reported on Form 8949,
- To report certain transactions you do not have to report on Form 8949,
- To report a gain from Form 2439 or 6252 or Part I of Form 4797,
- To report a gain or loss from Form 4684, 6781, or 8824,
- To report a gain or loss from a partnership, S corporation, estate or trust,
- To report capital gain distributions not reported directly on Form 1040, line 13 (or effectively connected capital gain distributions not reported directly on Form 1040NR, line 14), and
- To report a capital loss carryover from 2013 to 2014.

Additional information. See Pub. 544 and Pub. 550 for more details.

Section references are to the Internal Revenue Code unless otherwise noted.

Future Developments

For the latest information about developments related to Schedule D and its instructions, such as legislation enacted after they were published, go to www.irs.gov/schedule.

What's New

Form 1099-B. Form 1099-B has been redesigned so that the information on it is reported in boxes that are numbered to match the corresponding line and column on Form 8949. A new box has also been added at the top of Form 1099-B to tell you which box to check when completing Form 8949. These changes will make it easier for you to complete Form 8949.

A Form 1099-B (or substitute statement) for transactions involving certain types of debt instruments acquired after 2013 will have more detailed information than a Form 1099-B (or substitute statement) for transactions involving debt instruments acquired before 2014. This is also true for a Form 1099-B (or substitute statement) for options granted or acquired after 2013 or securities futures contracts entered into after 2013. This additional information will help you complete Form 8949 and Schedule D.

General Instructions

Other Forms You May Have To File

Use Form 8949 to report the sale or exchange of a capital asset (defined later) not reported on another form or schedule. Complete all necessary pages of Form 8949 before you complete line 1b, 2, 3, 8b, 9, or 10 of Schedule D. See _Lines 1a and 8a_, later, for more information about when Form 8949 is needed and when it is not.

Use Form 4797 to report the following.

1. The sale or exchange of:

a. Property used in a trade or business;

b. Depreciable and amortizable property;

c. Oil, gas, geothermal, or other mineral property; and

d. Section 126 property.

2. The involuntary conversion (other than from casualty or theft) of property used in a trade or business and capital assets held for business or profit.

3. The disposition of noncapital assets other than inventory or property held primarily for sale to customers in the ordinary course of your trade or business.

4. Ordinary loss on the sale, exchange, or worthlessness of small busi-

ness investment company (section 1242) stock.

5. Ordinary loss on the sale, exchange, or worthlessness of small business (section 1244) stock.

6. Ordinary gain or loss on securities or commodities held in connection with your trading business, if you previously made a mark to market election. See _Traders in Securities_, later.

Use Form 4684 to report involuntary conversions of property due to casualty or theft.

Use Form 6781 to report gains and losses from section 1256 contracts and straddles.

Use Form 8824 to report like-kind exchanges. A like-kind exchange occurs when you exchange business or investment property for property of a like kind.

Capital Asset

Most property you own and use for personal purposes or investment is a capital asset. For example, your house, furniture, car, stocks, and bonds are capital assets. A capital asset is any property owned by you except the following.

1. Stock in trade or other property included in inventory or held mainly for sale to customers. But see the _Tip_ about certain musical compositions or copyrights, later.

2. Accounts or notes receivable for services performed in the ordinary course of your trade or business, for

services rendered as an employee, or from the sale of stock in trade or other property held mainly for sale to customers.

3. Depreciable property used in your trade or business, even if it is fully depreciated.

4. Real estate used in your trade or business.

5. A copyright, a literary, musical, or artistic composition, a letter or memorandum, or similar property that is:

a. Created by your personal efforts,

b. Prepared or produced for you (in the case of a letter, memorandum, or similar property), or

c. Received under circumstances (such as by gift) that entitle you to the basis of the person who created the property or for whom the property was prepared or produced.

But see the *Tip* about certain musical compositions or copyrights, later.

6. A U.S. Government publication, including the Congressional Record, that you received from the Government for less than the normal sales price, or that you received under circumstances that entitle you to the basis of someone who received the publication for less than the normal sales price.

7. Certain commodities derivative financial instruments held by a dealer and connected to the dealer's activities as a dealer. See section 1221(a)(6).

8. Certain hedging transactions entered into in the normal course of your trade or business. See section 1221(a)(7).

9. Supplies regularly used in your trade or business.

 You can elect to treat as capital assets certain musical compositions or copyrights you sold or exchanged. See Pub. 550 for details.

Basis and Recordkeeping

Basis is the amount of your investment in property for tax purposes. The basis of property you buy is usually its cost. You need to know your basis to figure any gain or loss on the sale or other disposition of the property. You must keep accurate records that show the basis and, if applicable, adjusted basis of your property. Your records should show the purchase price, including commissions; increases to basis, such as the cost of improvements; and decreases to basis, such as depreciation, nondividend distributions on stock, and stock splits.

For more information on basis, see *Column (e)–Cost or Other Basis* in the instructions for Form 8949, and the following publications.
- Pub. 551, Basis of Assets.
- Pub. 550, Investment Income and Expenses (Including Capital Gains and Losses).

Short Term or Long Term

Report short-term gains or losses in Part I. Report long-term gains or losses in Part II. The holding period for short-term capital gains and losses is 1 year or less. The holding period for long-term capital gains and losses is more than 1 year.

For more information about holding periods, see the instructions for Form 8949.

Capital Gain Distributions

These distributions are paid by a mutual fund (or other regulated investment company) or real estate investment trust from its net realized long-term capital gains. Distributions of net realized short-term capital gains are not treated as capital gains. Instead, they are included on Form 1099-DIV as ordinary dividends.

Enter on Schedule D, line 13, the total capital gain distributions paid to you during the year, regardless of how long you held your investment. This amount is shown in box 2a of Form 1099-DIV.

If there is an amount in box 2b, include that amount on line 11 of the *Unrecaptured Section 1250 Gain Worksheet* in these instructions if you complete line 19 of Schedule D.

If there is an amount in box 2c, see *Exclusion of Gain on Qualified Small Business (QSB) Stock*, later.

If there is an amount in box 2d, include that amount on line 4 of the *28% Rate Gain Worksheet* in these instructions if you complete line 18 of Schedule D.

If you received capital gain distributions as a nominee (that is, they were paid to you but actually belong to someone else), report on Schedule D, line 13, only the amount that belongs to you. Attach a statement showing the full amount you received and the amount you received as a nominee. See the Instructions for Schedule B to learn about the requirement for you to file Forms 1099-DIV and 1096.

Sale of Your Home

You may not need to report the sale or exchange of your main home. If you must report it, complete Form 8949 before Schedule D.

Report the sale or exchange of your main home on Form 8949 if:
- You cannot exclude all of your gain from income, or
- You received a Form 1099-S for the sale or exchange.

Any gain you cannot exclude is taxable. Generally, if you meet the two following tests, you can exclude up to $250,000 of gain. If both you and your spouse meet these tests and you file a joint return, you can exclude up to $500,000 of gain (but only one spouse needs to meet the ownership requirement in *Test 1*).

Test 1. During the 5-year period ending on the date you sold or exchanged your home, you owned it for 2 years or more (the ownership requirement) and lived in it as your main home for 2 years or more (the use requirement).

Test 2. You have not excluded gain on the sale or exchange of another main home during the 2-year period ending on the date of the sale or exchange of your home.

Reduced exclusion. Even if you do not meet one or both of the above two tests, you still can claim an exclusion if you sold or exchanged the home because of a change in place of employment, health, or certain unforeseen circumstances. In this case, the maximum amount of gain you can exclude is reduced. For more information, see Pub. 523.

Sale of home by surviving spouse. If your spouse died before the sale or exchange, you can still exclude up to $500,000 of gain if:
- The sale or exchange is no later than 2 years after your spouse's death,
- Just before your spouse's death, both spouses met the use requirement of *Test 1*, at least one spouse met the

ownership requirement of *Test 1*, and both spouses met *Test 2*, and

• You did not remarry before the sale or exchange.

Exceptions to Test 1. You can choose to have the 5-year test period for ownership and use in *Test 1* suspended during any period you or your spouse serve outside the United States as a Peace Corps volunteer or serve on qualified official extended duty as a member of the uniformed services or Foreign Service of the United States, as an employee of the intelligence community, or outside the United States as an employee of the Peace Corps. This means you may be able to meet *Test 1* even if, because of your service, you did not actually use the home as your main home for at least the required 2 years during the 5-year period ending on the date of sale. The 5-year period cannot be extended for more than 10 years.

Sale of home acquired in a like-kind exchange. You cannot exclude any gain if:

• You acquired your home in a like-kind exchange in which all or part of the gain was not recognized, and

• You sold or exchanged the home during the 5-year period beginning on the date you acquired it.

How to report the sale of your main home. If you have to report the sale or exchange, report it on Form 8949. If the gain or loss is short term, report it in Part I of Form 8949 with box C checked. If the gain or loss is long term, report it in Part II of Form 8949 with box F checked.

If you had a gain and can exclude part or all of it, enter "H" in column (f). Enter the exclusion as a negative number (in parentheses) in column (g). See the instructions for Form 8949, columns (f), (g), and (h). Complete all columns.

If you had a loss but have to report the sale or exchange because you got a Form 1099-S, see *Nondeductible Losses*, later, for instructions about how to report it.

More information. See Pub. 523 for additional details, including how to figure and report any taxable gain if:

• You (or your spouse if married) used any part of the home for business or rental purposes after May 6, 1997, or

• There was a period of time after 2008 when the home was not your main home.

Partnership Interests

A sale or other disposition of an interest in a partnership may result in ordinary income, collectibles gain (28% rate gain), or unrecaptured section 1250 gain. For details on 28% rate gain, see the instructions for line 18. For details on unrecaptured section 1250 gain, see the instructions for line 19.

Capital Assets Held for Personal Use

Generally, gain from the sale or exchange of a capital asset held for personal use is a capital gain. Report it on Form 8949 with box C checked (if the transaction is short term) or box F checked (if the transaction is long term). However, if you converted depreciable property to personal use, all or part of the gain on the sale or exchange of that property may have to be recaptured as ordinary income. Use Part III of Form 4797 to figure the amount of ordinary income recapture. The recapture amount is included on line 31 (and line 13) of Form 4797. Do not enter any gain from this property on line 32 of Form 4797. If you are not completing Part III for any other properties, enter "N/A" on line 32. If the total gain is more than the recapture amount, enter "From Form 4797" in column (a) of Part I of Form 8949 (if the transaction is short term) or Part II of Form 8949 (if the transaction is long term), and skip columns (b) and (c). In column (d), enter the excess of the total gain over the recapture amount. Leave columns (e) through (g) blank. Complete column (h). Be sure to check box C at the top of Part I or box F at the top of Part II of this Form 8949 (depending on how long you held the asset).

Loss from the sale or exchange of a capital asset held for personal use is not deductible. But if you had a loss from the sale or exchange of real estate held for personal use for which you received a Form 1099-S, you must report the transaction on Form 8949 even though the loss is not deductible. For example, you have a loss on the sale of a vacation home that is not your main home and you received a Form 1099-S for the transaction. Report the transaction in

Part I or Part II of Form 8949, depending on how long you owned the home. Complete all columns. Because the loss is not deductible, enter "L" in column (f). Enter the difference between column (d) and column (e) as a positive amount in column (g). Then complete column (h). For example, if you entered $5,000 in column (d) and $6,000 in column (e), enter $1,000 in column (g). Then enter -0- ($5,000 − $6,000 + $1,000) in column (h). Be sure to check box C at the top of Part I or box F at the top of Part II of this Form 8949 (depending on how long you owned the home).

Capital Losses

You can deduct capital losses up to the amount of your capital gains plus $3,000 ($1,500 if married filing separately). You may be able to use capital losses that exceed this limit in future years. For details, see the instructions for line 21. Be sure to report all of your capital gains and losses even if you cannot use all of your losses in 2014.

Nondeductible Losses

Do not deduct a loss from a sale or exchange between certain related parties. This includes a direct or indirect sale or exchange of property between any of the following.

• Members of a family.

• A corporation and an individual owning more than 50% of the corporation's stock (unless the loss is from a distribution in complete liquidation of a corporation).

• A grantor and a fiduciary of a trust.

• A fiduciary and a beneficiary of the same trust.

• A fiduciary and a fiduciary or beneficiary of another trust created by the same grantor.

• An executor of an estate and a beneficiary of that estate, unless the sale or exchange was to satisfy a pecuniary bequest (that is, a bequest of a sum of money).

• An individual and a tax-exempt organization controlled by the individual or the individual's family.

See Pub. 544 for more details on sales and exchanges between related parties.

Report a transaction that results in a nondeductible loss in Part I or Part II of Form 8949 (depending on how long you held the property). Unless you received a Form 1099-B for the sale or exchange, check box C at the top of Part I or box F at the top of Part II of this Form 8949 (depending on how long you owned the property). Complete all columns. Because the loss is not deductible, enter "L" in column (f). Enter the amount of the nondeductible loss as a positive number in column (g). Complete column (h). See the instructions for Form 8949, columns (f), (g), and (h).

Example 1. You sold land you held as an investment for 5 years to your brother for $10,000. Your basis was $15,000. On Part II of Form 8949, check box F at the top. Enter $10,000 on Form 8949, Part II, column (d). Enter $15,000 in column (e). Because the loss is not deductible, enter "L" in column (f) and $5,000 (the difference between $10,000 and $15,000) in column (g). In column (h), enter -0- ($10,000 − $15,000 + $5,000). If this is your only transaction on this Form 8949, enter $10,000 on Schedule D, line 10, column (d). Enter $15,000 in column (e) and $5,000 in column (g). In column (h), enter -0- ($10,000 − $15,000 + $5,000).

Example 2. You received a Form 1099-B showing proceeds (sales price) of $1,000 and basis of $5,000. Box 7 on Form 1099-B is checked, indicating that your loss of $4,000 ($1,000 − $5,000) is not allowed. On the top of Form 8949, check box A or box B in Part I or box D or box E in Part II (whichever applies). Enter $1,000 in column (d) and $5,000 in column (e). Because the loss is not deductible, enter "L" in column (f) and $4,000 (the difference between $1,000 and $5,000) in column (g). In column (h), enter -0- ($1,000 − $5,000 + $4,000).

At-risk rules. If you disposed of (a) an asset used in an activity to which the at-risk rules apply or (b) any part of your interest in an activity to which the at-risk rules apply, and you have amounts in the activity for which you are not at risk, see the Instructions for Form 6198.

Passive activity rules. If the loss is allowable under the at-risk rules, it then may be subject to the passive activity rules. See Form 8582 and its instructions for details on reporting capital gains and losses from a passive activity.

Items for Special Treatment

• Transactions by a securities dealer. See section 475 and Rev. Rul. 97-39, which begins on page 4 of Internal Revenue Bulletin 1997-39 at *www.irs.gov/ pub/irs-irbs/irb97-39.pdf*.
• Bonds and other debt instruments. See Pub. 550.
• Certain real estate subdivided for sale that may be considered a capital asset. See section 1237.
• Gain on the sale of depreciable property to a more than 50%-owned entity or to a trust of which you are a beneficiary. See Pub. 544.
• Gain on the disposition of stock in an interest charge domestic international sales corporation. See section 995(c).
• Gain on the sale or exchange of stock in certain foreign corporations. See section 1248.
• Transfer of property to a partnership that would be treated as an investment company if it were incorporated. See Pub. 541.
• Sales of stock received under a qualified public utility dividend reinvestment plan. See Pub. 550.
• Transfer of appreciated property to a political organization. See section 84.
• Transfer of property by a U.S. person to a foreign estate or trust. See section 684.
• If you give up your U.S. citizenship, you may be treated as having sold all your property for its fair market value on the day before you gave up your citizenship. This also applies to long-term U.S. residents who cease to be lawful permanent residents. For details, exceptions, and rules for reporting these deemed sales, see Pub. 519 and Form 8854.
• In general, no gain or loss is recognized on the transfer of property from an individual to a spouse or a former spouse if the transfer is incident to a divorce. See Pub. 504.
• Amounts received on the retirement of a debt instrument generally are treated as received in exchange for the debt instrument. See Pub. 550.
• Any loss on the disposition of converted wetland or highly erodible cropland that is first used for farming after March 1, 1986, is reported as a long-term capital loss on Form 8949, but any gain is reported as ordinary income on Form 4797.

• If qualified dividends that you reported on Form 1040, line 9b, or Form 1040NR, line 10b, include extraordinary dividends, any loss on the sale or exchange of the stock is a long-term capital loss to the extent of the extraordinary dividends. An extraordinary dividend is a dividend that equals or exceeds 10% (5% in the case of preferred stock) of your basis in the stock.
• Amounts received by shareholders in corporate liquidations. See Pub. 550.
• Cash received in lieu of fractional shares of stock as a result of a stock split or stock dividend. See Pub. 550.
• Load charges to acquire stock in a regulated investment company (including a mutual fund), which may not be taken into account in determining gain or loss on certain dispositions of the stock if reinvestment rights were exercised. See Pub. 550.
• The sale or exchange of S corporation stock or an interest in a partnership or trust held for more than 1 year, which may result in collectibles gain (28% rate gain). See the instructions for line 18.
• Gain or loss on the disposition of securities futures contracts. See Pub. 550.
• Gain on the constructive sale of certain appreciated financial positions. See Pub. 550.
• Certain constructive ownership transactions. Gain in excess of the gain you would have recognized if you had held a financial asset directly during the term of a derivative contract must be treated as ordinary income. See section 1260. If any portion of the constructive ownership transaction was open in any prior year, you may have to pay interest. See section 1260(b) for details, including how to figure the interest. Include the interest as an additional tax on Form 1040, line 62. Check box c and in the space next to that box, enter "Section 1260(b) interest" and the amount of the interest. If you are filing Form 1040NR, include the interest as an additional tax on line 60. Check box b and, in the space next to that box, enter "Section 1260(b) interest" and the amount of the interest. This interest is not deductible.
• Gain or loss from the disposition of stock or other securities in an investment club. See Pub. 550.
• Certain virtual currencies, such as Bitcoin. See Notice 2014-21, 2014-16

I.R.B. 938, available at *www.irs.gov/irb/ 2014-16_IRB/ar12.html*.

Market Discount Bonds

In general, a capital gain from the disposition of a market discount bond is treated as interest income to the extent of accrued market discount as of the date of disposition. See sections 1276 through 1278 and Pub. 550 for more information on market discount. See the Instructions for Form 8949 for detailed information about how to report the disposition of a market discount bond.

Contingent Payment Debt Instruments

Any gain recognized on the sale, exchange, or retirement of a contingent payment debt instrument subject to the noncontingent bond method is treated as interest income rather than as capital gain. In certain situations, all or a portion of a loss recognized on the sale, exchange, or retirement of a contingent payment debt instrument subject to the noncontingent bond method may be treated as an ordinary loss rather than as a capital loss. See Regulations section 1.1275-4(b) and Pub. 550 for more information on contingent payment debt instruments subject to the noncontingent bond method.

Wash Sales

A wash sale occurs when you sell or otherwise dispose of stock or securities (including a contract or option to acquire or sell stock or securities) at a loss and, within 30 days before or after the sale or disposition, you:

1. Buy substantially identical stock or securities,

2. Acquire substantially identical stock or securities in a fully taxable trade,

3. Enter into a contract or option to acquire substantially identical stock or securities, or

4. Acquire substantially identical stock or securities for your individual retirement arrangement (IRA) or Roth IRA.

You cannot deduct losses from wash sales unless the loss was incurred in the ordinary course of your business as a dealer in stock or securities. The basis of the substantially identical property (or contract or option to acquire such property) is its cost increased by the disallowed loss (except in the case of (4) above).

If you received a Form 1099-B (or substitute statement), boxes 1f and 1g of that form generally will show whether there was any nondeductible wash sale loss and its amount if:

• The stock or securities sold were covered securities (defined in the instructions for Form 8949, column (e)), and

• The substantially identical stock or securities you bought had the same CUSIP number as the stock or securities you sold and were bought in the same account as the stock or securities you sold.

However, you cannot deduct a loss from a wash sale even if it is not reported on Form 1099-B (or substitute statement). For more details on wash sales, see Pub. 550.

Report a wash sale transaction in Part I or Part II (depending on how long you owned the stock or securities) of Form 8949 with the appropriate box checked. Complete all columns. Enter "W" in column (f). Enter as a positive number in column (g) the amount of the loss not allowed. See the instructions for Form 8949, columns (f), (g), and (h).

Traders in Securities

You are a trader in securities if you are engaged in the business of buying and selling securities for your own account. To be engaged in business as a trader in securities, all of the following statements must be true.

• You must seek to profit from daily market movements in the prices of securities and not from dividends, interest, or capital appreciation.

• Your activity must be substantial.

• You must carry on the activity with continuity and regularity.

The following facts and circumstances should be considered in determining if your activity is a business.

• Typical holding periods for securities bought and sold.

• The frequency and dollar amount of your trades during the year.

• The extent to which you pursue the activity to produce income for a livelihood.

• The amount of time you devote to the activity.

You are considered an investor, and not a trader, if your activity does not meet the above definition of a business. It does not matter whether you call yourself a trader or a "day trader."

Like an investor, a trader generally must report each sale of securities (taking into account commissions and any other costs of acquiring or disposing of the securities) on Form 8949 unless one of the exceptions described in the instructions to Form 8949 applies. However, if a trader previously made the mark-to-market election (explained next), each transaction is reported in Part II of Form 4797 instead of on Form 8949. Regardless of whether a trader reports his or her gains and losses on Form 8949 or Form 4797, the gain or loss from the disposition of securities is not taken into account when figuring net earnings from self-employment on Schedule SE. See the Instructions for Schedule SE for an exception that applies to section 1256 contracts.

The limitation on investment interest expense that applies to investors does not apply to interest paid or incurred in a trading business. A trader reports interest expense and other expenses (excluding commissions and other costs of acquiring or disposing of securities) from a trading business on Schedule C (instead of Schedule A).

A trader also may hold securities for investment. The rules for investors generally will apply to those securities. Allocate interest and other expenses between your trading business and your investment securities.

Mark-To-Market Election for Traders

A trader may make an election under section 475(f) to report all gains and losses from securities held in connection with a trading business as ordinary income (or loss), including those from securities held at the end of the year. Securities held at the end of the year are "marked-to-market" by treating them as if they were sold (and reacquired) for fair market value on the last business day of the year. Generally, the election must be made by the due date (not including extensions) of the tax return for the year prior to the year for which the election becomes effective. To be effective for 2014, the election must have been made by April 15, 2014.

Starting with the year the election becomes effective, a trader reports all gains and losses from securities held in connection with the trading business, including securities held at the end of the year, in Part II of Form 4797. If you previously made the election, see the Instructions for Form 4797. For details on making the mark-to-market election for 2015, see Pub. 550 or Rev. Proc. 99-17, 1999-1 C.B. 503. You can find Rev. Proc. 99-17 starting on the bottom of page 52 of Internal Revenue Bulletin 1999-7 at _www.irs.gov/pub/irs-irbs/irb99-07.pdf._

If you hold securities for investment, you must identify them as such in your records on the day you acquired them (for example, by holding the securities in a separate brokerage account). Securities held for investment are not marked-to-market.

Short Sales

A short sale is a contract to sell property you borrowed for delivery to a buyer. At a later date, you either buy substantially identical property and deliver it to the lender or deliver property that you held but did not want to transfer at the time of the sale.

Example. You think the value of XYZ stock will drop. You borrow 10 shares from your broker and sell them for $100. This is a short sale. You later buy 10 shares for $80 and deliver them to your broker to close the short sale. Your gain is $20 ($100 – $80).

Holding period. Usually, your holding period is the amount of time you actually held the property eventually delivered to the broker or lender to close the short sale. However, your gain when closing a short sale is short term if you (a) held substantially identical property for 1 year or less on the date of the short sale, or (b) acquired property substantially identical to the property sold short after the short sale but on or before the date you close the short sale. If you held substantially identical property for more than 1 year on the date of a short sale, any loss realized on the short sale is a long-term capital loss, even if the prop-

erty used to close the short sale was held 1 year or less.

Reporting a short sale. Report any short sale on Form 8949 in the year it closes.

If a short sale closed in 2014 but you did not get a 2014 Form 1099-B (or substitute statement) for it because you entered into it before 2011, report it on Form 8949 in Part I with box C checked or Part II with box F checked (whichever applies). In column (a), enter (for example) "100 sh. XYZ Co.–2010 short sale closed." Fill in the other columns according to their instructions. Report the short sale the same way if you received a 2014 Form 1099-B (or substitute statement) that does not show proceeds (sales price).

Gain or Loss From Options

Report on Form 8949 gain or loss from the closing or expiration of an option that is not a section 1256 contract but is a capital asset in your hands. If an option you purchased expired, enter the expiration date in column (c) and enter "EXPIRED" in column (d). If an option that was granted (written) expired, enter the expiration date in column (b) and enter "EXPIRED" in column (e). Fill in the other columns according to their instructions. See Pub. 550 for details.

If a call option you sold after 2013 was exercised, the option premium you received will be reflected in the proceeds shown in box 1d of the Form 1099-B (or substitute statement) you received. If you sold the call option before 2014, the option premium you received may not be reflected on Form 1099-B. If it is not, enter the premium as a positive number in column (g) of Form 8949. Enter "E" in column (f).

Example. For $10 in 2013, you sold Joe an option to buy one share of XYZ stock for $80. Joe later exercised the option. The Form 1099-B you get shows the proceeds to be $80. Enter $80 in column (d) of Form 8949. Enter "E" in column (f) and $10 in column (g). Complete the other columns according to the instructions.

Floating-NAV Money Market Funds

If you have a capital gain or loss determined under the net asset value (NAV)

method with respect to shares in a floating-NAV money market fund, report the capital gain or loss on Form 8949, Part I, with box C checked. Enter the name of each fund followed by "(NAV)" in column (a). Enter the net gain or loss in column (h). Leave all other columns blank. See the Instructions for Form 8949.

Undistributed Capital Gains

Include on Schedule D, line 11, the amount from box 1a of Form 2439. This represents your share of the undistributed long-term capital gains of the regulated investment company (including a mutual fund) or real estate investment trust.

If there is an amount in box 1b, include that amount on line 11 of the _Unrecaptured Section 1250 Gain Worksheet_ if you complete line 19 of Schedule D.

If there is an amount in box 1c, see _Exclusion of Gain on Qualified Small Business (QSB) Stock,_ later.

If there is an amount in box 1d, include that amount on line 4 of the _28% Rate Gain Worksheet_ if you complete line 18 of Schedule D.

Include on Form 1040, line 73, or Form 1040NR, line 69, the tax paid as shown in box 2 of Form 2439. Also check the box for Form 2439. Add to the basis of your stock the excess of the amount included in income over the amount of the credit for the tax paid. See Pub. 550 for details.

Installment Sales

If you sold property (other than publicly traded stocks or securities) at a gain and you will receive a payment in a tax year after the year of sale, you generally must report the sale on the installment method unless you elect not to. Use Form 6252 to report the sale on the installment method. Also use Form 6252 to report any payment received in 2014 from a sale made in an earlier year that you reported on the installment method.

To elect out of the installment method, report the full amount of the gain on Form 8949 on a timely filed return (including extensions) for the year of the sale. If your original return was filed on time, you can make the election on an amended return filed no later than 6 months after the due date of your return (excluding extensions). Write "Filed pursuant to section 301.9100-2" at the top of the amended return.

Demutualization of Life Insurance Companies

Demutualization of a life insurance company occurs when a mutual life insurance company changes to a stock company. If you were a policyholder or annuitant of the mutual company, you may have received either stock in the stock company or cash in exchange for your equity interest in the mutual company.

If the demutualization transaction qualifies as a tax-free reorganization, no gain or loss is recognized on the exchange of your equity interest in the mutual company for stock. The company can advise you if the transaction is a tax-free reorganization. Your holding period for the new stock includes the period you held an equity interest in the mutual company. If you received cash in exchange for your equity interest, you must recognize any capital gain. If you held the equity interest for more than 1 year, report the gain as a long-term capital gain in Part II of Form 8949. If you held the equity interest for 1 year or less, report the gain as a short-term capital gain in Part I of Form 8949. Be sure the appropriate box is checked at the top of Form 8949.

If the demutualization transaction does not qualify as a tax-free reorganization, you must recognize a capital gain or loss. If you held the equity interest for more than 1 year, report the gain or loss as a long-term capital gain or loss in Part II of Form 8949. If you held the equity interest for 1 year or less, report the gain or loss as a short-term capital gain or loss in Part I of Form 8949. Be sure the appropriate box is checked at the top of Form 8949. Your holding period for the new stock begins on the day after you received the stock.

Small Business (Section 1244) Stock

Report an ordinary loss from the sale, exchange, or worthlessness of small business (section 1244) stock on Form 4797. However, if the total loss is more than the maximum amount that can be treated as an ordinary loss, also report the transaction on Form 8949 as follows.

1. In column (a), enter "Capital portion of section 1244 stock loss."

2. Complete columns (b) and (c) as you normally would.

3. In column (d), enter the entire sales price of the stock sold.

4. In column (e), enter the entire basis of the stock sold.

5. Enter "S" in column (f). See the instructions for Form 8949, columns (f), (g), and (h).

6. In column (g), enter the loss you claimed on Form 4797 for this transaction. Enter it as a positive number.

7. Complete column (h) according to its instructions.

Report the transaction in Part I or Part II of Form 8949 (depending on how long you held the stock) with the appropriate box checked.

Example. You sold section 1244 stock for $1,000. Your basis was $60,000. You had held the stock for 3 years. You can claim $50,000 of your loss as an ordinary loss on Form 4797. To claim the rest of the loss on Form 8949, check the appropriate box at the top. Enter $1,000 on Form 8949, Part II, column (d). Enter $60,000 in column (e). Enter "S" in column (f) and $50,000 (the ordinary loss claimed on Form 4797) in column (g). In column (h), enter ($9,000) ($1,000 − $60,000 + $50,000). Put it in parentheses to show it is a negative amount.

Exclusion of Gain on Qualified Small Business (QSB) Stock

Section 1202 allows you to exclude a portion of the eligible gain on the sale or exchange of QSB stock. The section 1202 exclusion applies only to QSB stock held for more than 5 years. If you acquired the QSB stock on or before February 17, 2009, you can exclude up to 50% of the qualified gain. You can exclude up to 60% of the qualified gain on certain empowerment zone business stock. See *Empowerment Zone Business Stock*, later. If you acquired the QSB stock after February 17, 2009, you can exclude up to 75% of the qualified gain.

To be QSB stock, the stock must meet all of the following tests.

1. It must be stock in a C corporation (that is, not S corporation stock).

2. It must have been originally issued after August 10, 1993.

3. As of the date the stock was issued, the corporation was a domestic C corporation with total gross assets of $50 million or less (a) at all times after August 9, 1993, and before the stock was issued, and (b) immediately after the stock was issued. Gross assets include those of any predecessor of the corporation. All corporations that are members of the same parent-subsidiary controlled group are treated as one corporation.

4. You must have acquired the stock at its original issue (either directly or through an underwriter), either in exchange for money or other property (other than stock) or as pay for services (other than as an underwriter) to the corporation. In certain cases, you may meet this test if you acquired the stock from another person who met the test (such as by gift or inheritance) or through a conversion or exchange of QSB stock you held.

5. During substantially all the time you held the stock:

a. The corporation was a C corporation,

b. At least 80% of the value of the corporation's assets were used in the active conduct of one or more qualified businesses (defined next), and

c. The corporation was not a foreign corporation, DISC, former DISC, regulated investment company, real estate investment trust, REMIC, FASIT, cooperative, or a corporation that has made (or that has a subsidiary that has made) a section 936 election.

 SSBIC. *A specialized small business investment company (SSBIC) is treated as having met test 5b.*

Definition of qualified business. A qualified business is any business that is not one of the following.

• A business involving services performed in the fields of health, law, engineering, architecture, accounting, actuarial science, performing arts, consulting, athletics, financial services, or brokerage services.

- A business whose principal asset is the reputation or skill of one or more employees.
- A banking, insurance, financing, leasing, investing, or similar business.
- A farming business (including the raising or harvesting of trees).
- A business involving the production of products for which percentage depletion can be claimed.
- A business of operating a hotel, motel, restaurant, or similar business.

For more details about limits and additional requirements that may apply, see Pub. 550 or section 1202.

Holding period of stock acquired after February 17, 2009. When you are determining whether your exclusion is limited to 50% or 75% of the gain from this stock, your acquisition date is considered to be the first day you held the stock (determined after applying the holding period rules in section 1223).

Empowerment Zone Business Stock

You generally can exclude up to 60% of your gain if you meet the following additional requirements.

1. The stock you sold or exchanged was stock in a corporation that qualified as an empowerment zone business during substantially all of the time you held the stock.

2. You acquired the stock after December 21, 2000, and before February 18, 2009.

Requirement 1 will still be met if the corporation ceased to qualify after the 5-year period that began on the date you acquired the stock. However, the gain that qualifies for the 60% exclusion cannot be more than the gain you would have had if you had sold the stock on the date the corporation ceased to qualify.

Stock acquired after February 17, 2009. You can exclude up to 75% of your gain if you acquired the stock after February 17, 2009.

More information. For more information about empowerment zone businesses, see section 1397C.

Pass-Through Entities

If you held an interest in a pass-through entity (a partnership, S corporation, common trust fund, or mutual fund or other regulated investment company) that sold QSB stock, to qualify for the exclusion you must have held the interest on the date the pass-through entity acquired the QSB stock and at all times thereafter until the stock was sold.

How To Report

Report the sale or exchange of the QSB stock on Form 8949, Part II, with the appropriate box checked, as you would if you were not taking the exclusion. Then enter "Q" in column (f) and enter the amount of the excluded gain as a negative number in column (g). Put it in parentheses to show it is negative. See the instructions for Form 8949, columns (f), (g), and (h). Complete all remaining columns. If you are completing line 18 of Schedule D, enter as a positive number the amount of your allowable exclusion on line 2 of the 28% Rate Gain Worksheet; if you excluded 60% of the gain, enter ⅔ of the exclusion; if you excluded 75% of the gain, enter ⅓ of the exclusion.

Gain from Form 1099-DIV. If you received a Form 1099-DIV with a gain in box 2c, part or all of that gain (which is also included in box 2a) may be eligible for the section 1202 exclusion. In column (a) of Form 8949, Part II, enter the name of the corporation whose stock was sold. In column (f), enter "Q" and in column (g) enter the amount of the excluded gain as a negative number. See the instructions for Form 8949, columns (f), (g), and (h). If you are completing line 18 of Schedule D, enter as a positive number the amount of your allowable exclusion on line 2 of the 28% Rate Gain Worksheet; if you excluded 60% of the gain, enter ⅔ of the exclusion; if you excluded 75% of the gain, enter ⅓ of the exclusion.

Gain from Form 2439. If you received a Form 2439 with a gain in box 1c, part or all of that gain (which is also included in box 1a) may be eligible for the section 1202 exclusion. In column (a) of Form 8949, Part II, enter the name of the corporation whose stock was sold. In column (f), enter "Q" and in column (g) enter the amount of the excluded gain as

a negative number. See the instructions for Form 8949, columns (f), (g), and (h). If you are completing line 18 of Schedule D, enter as a positive number the amount of your allowable exclusion on line 2 of the 28% Rate Gain Worksheet; if you excluded 60% of the gain, enter ⅔ of the exclusion; if you excluded 75% of the gain, enter ⅓ of the exclusion.

Gain from an installment sale of QSB stock. If all payments are not received in the year of sale, a sale of QSB stock that is not traded on an established securities market generally is treated as an installment sale and is reported on Form 6252. Figure the allowable section 1202 exclusion for the year by multiplying the total amount of the exclusion by a fraction, the numerator of which is the amount of eligible gain to be recognized for the tax year and the denominator of which is the total amount of eligible gain. In column (a) of Form 8949, Part II, enter the name of the corporation whose stock was sold. In column (f), enter "Q" and in column (g) enter the amount of the allowable exclusion for the year as a negative number. See the instructions for Form 8949, columns (f), (g), and (h). If you are completing line 18 of Schedule D, enter as a positive number the amount of your allowable exclusion for the year on line 2 of the 28% Rate Gain Worksheet; if you excluded 60% of the gain, enter ⅔ of the allowable exclusion for the year; if you excluded 75% of the gain, enter ⅓ of the allowable exclusion for the year.

Alternative minimum tax. You must enter 7% of your allowable exclusion for the year on line 13 of Form 6251.

Rollover of Gain From QSB Stock

If you sold QSB stock (defined earlier) that you held for more than 6 months, you can elect to postpone gain if you buy other QSB stock during the 60-day period that began on the date of the sale. A pass-through entity also can make the election to postpone gain. The benefit of the postponed gain applies to your share of the entity's postponed gain if you held an interest in the entity for the entire period the entity held the QSB stock. If a pass-through entity sold QSB stock held for more than 6 months and you held an interest in the entity for the entire period the entity held the stock, you also can elect to postpone gain if you, rather than the pass-through entity, buy the replacement QSB stock within the 60-day period. If you were a partner in a partnership that sold or bought QSB stock, see box 11 of the Schedule K-1 (Form 1065) sent to you by the partnership and Regulations section 1.1045-1.

You must recognize gain to the extent the sale proceeds are more than the cost of the replacement stock. Reduce the basis of the replacement stock by any postponed gain.

You must make the election no later than the due date (including extensions) for filing your tax return for the tax year in which the QSB stock was sold. If your original return was filed on time, you can make the election on an amended return filed no later than 6 months after the due date of your return (excluding extensions). Write "Filed pursuant to section 301.9100-2" at the top of the amended return.

To make the election, report the sale in Part I or Part II (depending on how long you, or the pass-through entity, if applicable, owned the stock) of Form 8949 as you would if you were not making the election. Then enter "R" in column (f). Enter the amount of the postponed gain as a negative number in column (g). Put it in parentheses to show it is negative. See the instructions for Form 8949, columns (f), (g), and (h). Complete all remaining columns.

Rollover of Gain From Empowerment Zone Assets

If you sold a qualified empowerment zone asset that you held for more than 1 year, you may be able to elect to postpone part or all of the gain that you would otherwise include in income. If you make the election, you generally recognize gain on the sale only to the extent, if any, that the amount realized on the sale is more than the cost of qualified empowerment zone assets (replacement property) you purchased during the 60-day period beginning on the date of the sale. The following rules apply.

• No portion of the cost of the replacement property may be taken into account to the extent the cost is taken into account to exclude gain on a different empowerment zone asset.

• The replacement property must qualify as an empowerment zone asset with respect to the same empowerment zone as the asset sold.

• You must reduce the basis of the replacement property by the amount of postponed gain.

• This election does not apply to any gain (a) treated as ordinary income or (b) attributable to real property, or an intangible asset, that is not an integral part of an enterprise zone business.

• The District of Columbia enterprise zone is not treated as an empowerment zone for this purpose.

• The election is irrevocable without IRS consent.

See section 1397C for the definition of empowerment zone and enterprise zone business. You can find out if your business is located within an empowerment zone by using the EZ/RC Address Locator at *www.hud.gov/crlocator*.

Qualified empowerment zone assets are:

1. Tangible property, if:

a. You acquired the property after December 21, 2000,

b. The original use of the property in the empowerment zone began with you, and

c. Substantially all of the use of the property, during substantially all of the time that you held it, was in your enterprise zone business; and

2. Stock in a domestic corporation or a capital or profits interest in a domestic partnership, if:

a. You acquired the stock or partnership interest after December 21, 2000, solely in exchange for cash, from the corporation at its original issue (directly or through an underwriter) or from the partnership;

b. The business was an enterprise zone business (or a new business being organized as an enterprise zone business) as of the time you acquired the stock or partnership interest; and

c. The business qualified as an enterprise zone business during substantially all of the time you held the stock or partnership interest.

See section 1397B for more details.

How to report. Report the sale of empowerment zone stock or an empowerment zone partnership interest on Part II of Form 8949 as you would if you were not making the election. Then enter "R" in column (f), and enter the amount of the postponed gain as a negative number in column (g). Put it in parentheses to show it is negative. See the instructions for Form 8949, columns (f), (g), and (h). Complete all remaining columns.

Report the sale or exchange of empowerment zone business property on Form 4797. See the Form 4797 instructions for details.

Exclusion of Gain From DC Zone Assets

If you sold or exchanged a District of Columbia Enterprise Zone (DC Zone) asset that you acquired after 1997 and held for more than 5 years, you may be able to exclude the amount of qualified capital gain that you would otherwise include in income. The exclusion applies to an interest in, or property of, certain businesses operating in the District of Columbia.

DC Zone asset. A DC Zone asset is any of the following.

• DC Zone business stock.

• DC Zone partnership interest.

• DC Zone business property.

Qualified capital gain. Qualified capital gain is any gain recognized on the sale or exchange of a DC Zone asset that is a capital asset or property used in a trade or business. It does not include any of the following gains.

• Gain treated as ordinary income under section 1245.

• Section 1250 gain figured as if section 1250 applied to all depreciation rather than the additional depreciation.

• Gain attributable to real property, or an intangible asset, that is not an integral part of a DC Zone business.

• Gain from a related-party transaction. See *Sales and Exchanges Between Related Persons* in chapter 2 of Pub. 544.

See section 1400B for more details on DC Zone assets and special rules.

How to report. Report the sale or exchange of DC Zone business stock or a DC Zone partnership interest on Form 8949, Part II, as you would if you were not taking the exclusion. Then enter "X" in column (f). Enter the amount of the exclusion as a negative number in column (g). Put it in parentheses to show it is negative. See the instructions for Form 8949, columns (f), (g), and (h). Complete all remaining columns.

Report the sale or exchange of DC Zone business property on Form 4797. See the Form 4797 instructions for details.

Exclusion of Gain From Qualified Community Assets

If you sold or exchanged a qualified community asset that you acquired after 2001 and before 2010 and held for more than 5 years, you may be able to exclude the qualified capital gain that you would otherwise include in income. The exclusion applies to an interest in, or property of, certain renewal community businesses.

Qualified community asset. A qualified community asset is any of the following.
- Qualified community stock.
- Qualified community partnership interest.
- Qualified community business property.

Qualified capital gain. Qualified capital gain is any gain recognized on the sale or exchange of a qualified community asset but does not include any of the following.
- Gain treated as ordinary income under section 1245.
- Section 1250 gain figured as if section 1250 applied to all depreciation rather than the additional depreciation.
- Gain attributable to real property, or an intangible asset, that is not an integral part of a qualified community business.
- Gain from a related-party transaction. See *Sales and Exchanges Between Related Persons* in chapter 2 of Pub. 544.

See section 1400F for more details on qualified community assets and special rules.

How to report. Report the sale or exchange of qualified community stock or a qualified community partnership interest on Form 8949, Part II, with the appropriate box checked, as you would if you were not taking the exclusion. Then enter "X" in column (f) and enter the amount of the exclusion as a negative number in column (g). Put it in paren-

theses to show it is negative. See the instructions for Form 8949, columns (f), (g), and (h). Complete all remaining columns.

Report the sale or exchange of qualified community business property on Form 4797. See the Form 4797 instructions for details.

Rollover of Gain From Publicly Traded Securities

You can postpone all or part of any gain from the sale of publicly traded securities by buying common stock or a partnership interest in a specialized small business investment company during the 60-day period that began on the date of the sale. See Pub. 550. Also see the instructions for Form 8949, columns (f), (g), and (h).

Rollover of Gain From Stock Sold to ESOPs or Certain Cooperatives

You can postpone all or part of any gain from the sale of qualified securities, held for at least 3 years, to an employee stock ownership plan (ESOP) or eligible worker-owned cooperative, if you buy qualified replacement property. See Pub. 550. Also see the instructions for Form 8949, columns (f), (g), and (h).

Specific Instructions
Rounding Off to Whole Dollars

You can round off cents to whole dollars on your Schedule D. If you do round to whole dollars, you must round all amounts. To round, drop amounts under 50 cents and increase amounts from 50 to 99 cents to the next dollar. For example, $1.39 becomes $1 and $2.50 becomes $3.

If you have to add two or more amounts to figure the amount to enter on a line, include cents when adding the amounts and round off only the total.

Lines 1a and 8a— Transactions Not Reported on Form 8949

You can report on line 1a (for short-term transactions) or line 8a (for long-term transactions) the aggregate totals from

any transactions (except sales of collectibles) for which:
- You received a Form 1099-B (or substitute statement) that shows basis was reported to the IRS and does not show any adjustments in box 1g, and
- You do not need to make any adjustments to the basis or type of gain or loss (short term or long term) reported on Form 1099-B (or substitute statement), or to your gain or loss.

See *How To Complete Form 8949, Columns (f) and (g),* in the Form 8949 instructions for details about possible adjustments to your gain or loss.

If you choose to report these transactions on lines 1a and 8a, do not report them on Form 8949. You do not need to attach a statement to explain the entries on lines 1a and 8a and, if you *e-file* your return, you do not need to file Form 8453.

Figure gain or loss on each line. Subtract the cost or other basis in column (e) from the proceeds (sales price) in column (d). Enter the gain or loss in column (h). Enter negative amounts in parentheses.

Example 1 – basis reported to the IRS. You received a Form 1099-B reporting the sale of stock you held for 3 years. It shows proceeds (in box 1d) of $6,000 and cost or other basis (in box 1e) of $2,000. Box 3 is checked, meaning that basis was reported to the IRS. You do not need to make any adjustments to the amounts reported on Form 1099-B or enter any codes. This was your only 2014 transaction. Instead of reporting this transaction on Form 8949, you can enter $6,000 on Schedule D, line 8a, column (d), $2,000 in column (e), and $4,000 ($6,000 – $2,000) in column (h).

If you had a second transaction that was the same except that the proceeds were $5,000 and the basis was $3,000, combine the two transactions. Enter $11,000 ($6,000 + $5,000) on Schedule D, line 8a, column (d), $5,000 ($2,000 + $3,000) in column (e), and $6,000 ($11,000 - $5,000) in column (h).

Example 2 – basis not reported to the IRS. You received a Form 1099-B showing proceeds (in box 1d) of $6,000 and cost or other basis (in box 1e) of $2,000. Box 3 is not checked, meaning that basis was not reported to the IRS. Do not report this transaction on line 1a or line 8a. Instead, report the transaction on Form 8949. Complete all necessary pages of Form 8949 before completing line 1b, 2, 3, 8b, 9, or 10 of Schedule D.

Example 3 – adjustment. You received a Form 1099-B showing proceeds (in box 1d) of $6,000 and cost or other basis (in box 1e) of $2,000. Box 3 is checked, meaning that basis was reported to the IRS. However, the basis shown in box 1e is incorrect. Do not report this transaction on line 1a or line 8a. Instead, report the transaction on Form 8949. See the instructions for Form 8949, columns (f), (g), and (h). Complete all necessary pages of Form 8949 before completing line 1b, 2, 3, 8b, 9, or 10 of Schedule D.

Lines 1b, 2, 3, 8b, 9, and 10, Column (h)—Transactions Reported on Form 8949

Figure gain or loss on each line. First, subtract the cost or other basis in column (e) from the proceeds (sales price) in column (d). Then combine the result with any adjustments in column (g). Enter the gain or loss in column (h). Enter negative amounts in parentheses.

Example 1 – gain. Column (d) is $6,000 and column (e) is $2,000. Enter $4,000 in column (h).

Example 2 – loss. Column (d) is $6,000 and column (e) is $8,000. Enter ($2,000) in column (h).

Example 3 – adjustment. Column (d) is $6,000, column (e) is $2,000, and column (g) is ($1,000). Enter $3,000 ($6,000 − $2,000 − $1,000) in column (h).

Line 13

See *Capital Gain Distributions*, earlier.

Line 18

If you checked "Yes" on line 17, complete the *28% Rate Gain Worksheet* in these instructions if either of the following apply for 2014.

• You reported in Part II of Form 8949 a section 1202 exclusion from the eligible gain on qualified small business stock (see *Exclusion of Gain on Qualified Small Business (QSB) Stock*, earlier).

• You reported in Part II of Form 8949 a collectibles gain or (loss). A collectibles gain or (loss) is any long-term gain or deductible long-term loss from the sale or exchange of a collectible that is a capital asset.

Collectibles include works of art, rugs, antiques, metals (such as gold, sil-

---

Capital Loss Carryover Worksheet—Lines 6 and 14

 Keep for Your Records

Use this worksheet to figure your capital loss carryovers from 2013 to 2014 if your 2013 Schedule D, line 21, is a loss and **(a)** that loss is a smaller loss than the loss on your 2013 Schedule D, line 16, **or (b)** the amount on your 2013 Form 1040, line 41 (or your 2013 Form 1040NR, line 39, if applicable) is less than zero. Otherwise, you do not have any carryovers.

If you and your spouse once filed a joint return and are filing separate returns for 2014, any capital loss carryover from the joint return can be deducted only on the return of the spouse who actually had the loss.

If you excluded canceled debt from income in 2014, see Pub. 4681.

1. Enter the amount from your 2013 Form 1040, line 41, or your 2013 Form 1040NR, line 39. If a loss, enclose the amount in parentheses .... **1.** _____

2. Enter the loss from your 2013 Schedule D, line 21, as a positive amount .... **2.** _____

3. Combine lines 1 and 2. If zero or less, enter -0- .... **3.** _____

4. Enter the **smaller** of line 2 or line 3 .... **4.** _____

    If line 7 of your 2013 Schedule D is a loss, go to line 5; otherwise, enter -0- on line 5 and go to line 9.

5. Enter the loss from your 2013 Schedule D, line 7, as a positive amount .... **5.** _____

6. Enter any gain from your 2013 Schedule D, line 15. If a loss, enter -0- .... **6.** _____

7. Add lines 4 and 6 .... **7.** _____

8. **Short-term capital loss carryover for 2014.** Subtract line 7 from line 5. If zero or less, enter -0-. If more than zero, also enter this amount on Schedule D, line 6 .... **8.** _____

    If line 15 of your 2013 Schedule D is a loss, go to line 9; otherwise, skip lines 9 through 13.

9. Enter the loss from your 2013 Schedule D, line 15, as a positive amount .... **9.** _____

10. Enter any gain from your 2013 Schedule D, line 7. If a loss, enter -0- .... **10.** _____

11. Subtract line 5 from line 4. If zero or less, enter -0- .... **11.** _____

12. Add lines 10 and 11 .... **12.** _____

13. **Long-term capital loss carryover for 2014.** Subtract line 12 from line 9. If zero or less, enter -0-. If more than zero, also enter this amount on Schedule D, line 14 .... **13.** _____

ver, and platinum bullion), gems, stamps, coins, alcoholic beverages, and certain other tangible property.

Include on the worksheet any gain (but not loss) from the sale or exchange of an interest in a partnership, S corporation, or trust held for more than 1 year and attributable to unrealized appreciation of collectibles. For details, see Regulations section 1.1(h)-1. Also, attach the statement required under Regulations section 1.1(h)-1(e).

Line 19

If you checked "Yes" on line 17, complete the *Unrecaptured Section 1250 Gain Worksheet* in these instructions if any of the following apply for 2014.

• You sold or otherwise disposed of section 1250 property (generally, real property that you depreciated) held more than 1 year.

• You received installment payments for section 1250 property held more than 1 year for which you are reporting gain on the installment method.

• You received a Schedule K-1 from an estate or trust, partnership, or S corporation that shows "unrecaptured section 1250 gain."

• You received a Form 1099-DIV or Form 2439 from a real estate investment trust or regulated investment company (including a mutual fund) that reports "unrecaptured section 1250 gain."

• You reported a long-term capital gain from the sale or exchange of an interest in a partnership that owned section 1250 property.

Instructions for the Unrecaptured Section 1250 Gain Worksheet

Lines 1 through 3. If you had more than one property described on line 1, complete lines 1 through 3 for each property on a separate worksheet. Enter the total of the line 3 amounts for all properties on line 3 and go to line 4.

Line 4. To figure the amount to enter on line 4, follow the steps below for each installment sale of trade or business property held more than 1 year.

Step 1. Figure the smaller of (a) the depreciation allowed or allowable, or (b) the total gain for the sale. This is the smaller of line 22 or line 24 of your 2014 Form 4797 (or the comparable lines of Form 4797 for the year of sale) for the property.

Step 2. Reduce the amount figured in step 1 by any section 1250 ordinary income recapture for the sale. This is the amount from line 26g of your 2014 Form 4797 (or the comparable line of Form 4797 for the year of sale) for the property. The result is your total unrecaptured section 1250 gain that must be allocated to the installment payments received from the sale.

Step 3. Generally, the entire amount of gain from the sale of trade or business property included in each installment payment is treated as unrecaptured section 1250 gain until the total unrecaptured section 1250 gain figured in step 2 has been used in full. Figure the amount of gain treated as unrecaptured section 1250 gain for installment payments received in 2014 as the smaller of (a) the amount from line 26 or line 37 of your 2014 Form 6252, whichever applies, or (b) the amount of unrecaptured section 1250 gain remaining to be reported. This amount is generally the total unrecaptured section 1250 gain for the sale reduced by all gain reported in prior years (excluding section 1250 ordinary income recapture). However, if you chose not to treat all of the gain from payments received after May 6, 1997, and before

28% Rate Gain Worksheet—Line 18

Keep for Your Records

1. Enter the total of all collectibles gain or (loss) from items you reported on Form 8949, Part II	1. _____
2. Enter as a positive number the total of: • Any section 1202 exclusion you reported in column (g) of Form 8949, Part II, with code "Q" in column (f), for which you excluded 50% of the gain; • $2/3$ of any section 1202 exclusion you reported in column (g) of Form 8949, Part II, with code "Q" in column (f), for which you excluded 60% of the gain; and • $1/3$ of any section 1202 exclusion you reported in column (g) of Form 8949, Part II, with code "Q" in column (f), for which you excluded 75% of the gain.	2. _____
3. Enter the total of all collectibles gain or (loss) from Form 4684, line 4 (but only if Form 4684, line 15, is more than zero); Form 6252; Form 6781, Part II; and Form 8824	3. _____
4. Enter the total of any collectibles gain reported to you on: • Form 1099-DIV, box 2d; • Form 2439, box 1d; and • Schedule K-1 from a partnership, S corporation, estate, or trust.	4. _____
5. Enter your long-term capital loss carryovers from Schedule D, line 14, and Schedule K-1 (Form 1041), box 11, code C	5. (_____)
6. If Schedule D, line 7, is a (loss), enter that (loss) here. Otherwise, enter -0-	6. (_____)
7. Combine lines 1 through 6. If zero or less, enter -0-. If more than zero, also enter this amount on Schedule D, line 18	7. _____

Unrecaptured Section 1250 Gain Worksheet—Line 19

 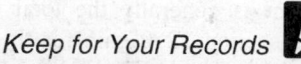

If you are not reporting a gain on Form 4797, line 7, skip lines 1 through 9 and go to line 10.

1. If you have a section 1250 property in Part III of Form 4797 for which you made an entry in Part I of Form 4797 (but not on Form 6252), enter the **smaller** of line 22 or line 24 of Form 4797 for that property. If you did not have any such property, go to line 4. If you had more than one such property, see instructions . . . . **1.** _____

2. Enter the amount from Form 4797, line 26g, for the property for which you made an entry on line 1 . . . . **2.** _____

3. Subtract line 2 from line 1 . . . . **3.** _____

4. Enter the total unrecaptured section 1250 gain included on line 26 or line 37 of Form(s) 6252 from installment sales of trade or business property held more than 1 year (see instructions) . . . . **4.** _____

5. Enter the total of any amounts reported to you on a Schedule K-1 from a partnership or an S corporation as "unrecaptured section 1250 gain" . . . . **5.** _____

6. Add lines 3 through 5 . . . . **6.** _____

7. Enter the **smaller** of line 6 or the gain from Form 4797, line 7 . . . . **7.** _____

8. Enter the amount, if any, from Form 4797, line 8 . . . . **8.** _____

9. Subtract line 8 from line 7. If zero or less, enter -0- . . . . **9.** _____

10. Enter the amount of any gain from the sale or exchange of an interest in a partnership attributable to unrecaptured section 1250 gain (see instructions) . . . . **10.** _____

11. Enter the total of any amounts reported to you as "unrecaptured section 1250 gain" on a Schedule K-1, Form 1099-DIV, or Form 2439 from an estate, trust, real estate investment trust, or mutual fund (or other regulated investment company) or in connection with a Form 1099-R . . . . **11.** _____

12. Enter the total of any unrecaptured section 1250 gain from sales (including installment sales) or other dispositions of section 1250 property held more than 1 year for which you did not make an entry in Part I of Form 4797 for the year of sale (see instructions) . . . . **12.** _____

13. Add lines 9 through 12 . . . . **13.** _____

14. If you had any section 1202 gain or collectibles gain or (loss), enter the total of lines 1 through 4 of the **28% Rate Gain Worksheet**. Otherwise, enter -0- . . . . **14.** _____

15. Enter the (loss), if any, from Schedule D, line 7. If Schedule D, line 7, is zero or a gain, enter -0- . . . . **15.** (_____)

16. Enter your long-term capital loss carryovers from Schedule D, line 14, and Schedule K-1 (Form 1041), box 11, code C* . . . . **16.** (_____)

17. Combine lines 14 through 16. If the result is a (loss), enter it as a positive amount. If the result is zero or a gain, enter -0- . . . . **17.** _____

18. **Unrecaptured section 1250 gain.** Subtract line 17 from line 13. If zero or less, enter -0-. If more than zero, enter the result here and on Schedule D, line 19 . . . . **18.** _____

*If you are filing Form 2555 or 2555-EZ (relating to foreign earned income), see the footnote in the Foreign Earned Income Tax Worksheet in the Form 1040 instructions before completing this line.

August 24, 1999, as unrecaptured section 1250 gain, use only the amount you chose to treat as unrecaptured section 1250 gain for those payments to reduce the total unrecaptured section 1250 gain remaining to be reported for the sale. Include this amount on line 4.

Line 10. Include on line 10 your share of the partnership's unrecaptured section 1250 gain that would result if the partnership had transferred all of its section 1250 property in a fully taxable transaction immediately before you sold or exchanged your interest in that partnership. If you recognized less than all of the realized gain, the partnership will be treated as having transferred only a proportionate amount of each section 1250 property. For details, see Regulations section 1.1(h)-1. Also attach the statement required under Regulations section 1.1(h)-1(e).

Line 12. An example of an amount to include on line 12 is unrecaptured section 1250 gain from the sale of a vacation home you previously used as a rental property but converted to personal use prior to the sale. To figure the amount to enter on line 12, follow the applicable instructions below.

Installment sales. To figure the amount to include on line 12, follow the steps below for each installment sale of property held more than 1 year for which you did not make an entry in Part I of your Form 4797 for the year of sale.

• Step 1. Figure the smaller of (a) the depreciation allowed or allowable, or (b) the total gain for the sale. This is the smaller of line 22 or line 24 of your 2014 Form 4797 (or the comparable lines of Form 4797 for the year of sale) for the property.

• Step 2. Reduce the amount figured in step 1 by any section 1250 ordinary income recapture for the sale. This is the amount from line 26g of your 2014 Form 4797 (or the comparable line of Form 4797 for the year of sale) for the property. The result is your total unrecaptured section 1250 gain that must be allocated to the installment payments received from the sale.

• Step 3. Generally, the amount of capital gain on each installment payment is treated as unrecaptured section 1250 gain until the total unrecaptured section 1250 gain figured in step 2 has been used in full. Figure the amount of gain treated as unrecaptured section 1250 gain for installment payments received in 2014 as the smaller of (a) the amount from line 26 or line 37 of your 2014 Form 6252, whichever applies, or (b) the amount of unrecaptured section 1250 gain remaining to be reported. This amount is generally the total unrecaptured section 1250 gain for the sale reduced by all gain reported in prior years (excluding section 1250 ordinary income recapture). However, if you chose not to treat all of the gain from payments received after May 6, 1997, and before August 24, 1999, as unrecaptured section 1250 gain, use only the amount you chose to treat as unrecaptured section 1250 gain for those payments to reduce the total unrecaptured section 1250 gain remaining to be reported for the sale. Include this amount on line 12.

Other sales or dispositions of section 1250 property. For each sale of property held more than 1 year (for which you did not make an entry in Part I of Form 4797), figure the smaller of (a) the depreciation allowed or allowable, or (b) the total gain for the sale. This is the smaller of line 22 or line 24 of Form 4797 for the property. Next, reduce that amount by any section 1250 ordinary income recapture for the sale. This is the amount from line 26g of Form 4797 for the property. The result is the total unrecaptured section 1250 gain for the sale. Include this amount on line 12.

Line 21

You have a capital loss carryover from 2014 to 2015 if you have a loss on line 16 and either:

- That loss is more than the loss on line 21, or
- The amount on Form 1040, line 41 (or Form 1040NR, line 39, if applicable), is less than zero.

To figure any capital loss carryover to 2015, you will use the Capital Loss Carryover Worksheet in the 2015 Instructions for Schedule D. If you want to figure your carryover to 2015 now, see Pub. 550.

 You will need a copy of your 2014 Form 1040 and Schedule D to figure your capital loss carryover to 2015.

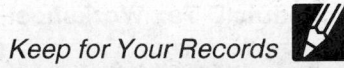
Complete this worksheet only if line 18 or line 19 of Schedule D is more than zero. Otherwise, complete the Qualified Dividends and Capital Gain Tax Worksheet in the Instructions for Form 1040, line 44 (or in the Instructions for Form 1040NR, line 42) to figure your tax. Before completing this worksheet, complete Form 1040 through line 43 (or Form 1040NR through line 41).

Exception: Do not use the Qualified Dividends and Capital Gain Tax Worksheet **or** this worksheet to figure your tax if:
- Line 15 or line 16 of Schedule D is zero or less **and** you have no qualified dividends on Form 1040, line 9b (or Form 1040NR, line 10b); **or**
- Form 1040, line 43 (or Form 1040NR, line 41) is zero or less.

Instead, see the instructions for Form 1040, line 44 (or Form 1040NR, line 42).

1. Enter your taxable income from Form 1040, line 43 (or Form 1040NR, line 41). (However, if you are filing Form 2555 or 2555-EZ (relating to foreign earned income), enter instead the amount from line 3 of the Foreign Earned Income Tax Worksheet in the Instructions for Form 1040, line 44) .... **1.** _____

2. Enter your qualified dividends from Form 1040, line 9b (or Form 1040NR, line 10b) .... **2.** _____

3. Enter the amount from Form 4952 (used to figure investment interest expense deduction), line 4g .... **3.** _____

4. Enter the amount from Form 4952, line 4e* .... **4.** _____

5. Subtract line 4 from line 3. If zero or less, enter -0- .... **5.** _____

6. Subtract line 5 from line 2. If zero or less, enter -0-** .... **6.** _____

7. Enter the **smaller** of line 15 or line 16 of Schedule D .... **7.** _____

8. Enter the **smaller** of line 3 or line 4 .... **8.** _____

9. Subtract line 8 from line 7. If zero or less, enter -0-** .... **9.** _____

10. Add lines 6 and 9 .... **10.** _____

11. Add lines 18 and 19 of Schedule D** .... **11.** _____

12. Enter the **smaller** of line 9 or line 11 .... **12.** _____

13. Subtract line 12 from line 10 .... **13.** _____

14. Subtract line 13 from line 1. If zero or less, enter -0- .... **14.** _____

15. Enter:
    - $36,900 if single or married filing separately;
    - $73,800 if married filing jointly or qualifying widow(er); or
    - $49,400 if head of household .... **15.** _____

16. Enter the **smaller** of line 1 or line 15 .... **16.** _____

17. Enter the **smaller** of line 14 or line 16 .... **17.** _____

18. Subtract line 10 from line 1. If zero or less, enter -0- .... **18.** _____

19. Enter the **larger** of line 17 or line 18 .... **19.** _____

20. Subtract line 17 from line 16. This amount is taxed at 0%. .... **20.** _____

   If lines 1 and 16 are the same, skip lines 21 through 41 and go to line 42. Otherwise, go to line 21.

21. Enter the **smaller** of line 1 or line 13 .... **21.** _____

22. Enter the amount from line 20 (if line 20 is blank, enter -0-) .... **22.** _____

23. Subtract line 22 from line 21. If zero or less, enter -0- .... **23.** _____

24. Enter:
    - $406,750 if single;
    - $228,800 if married filing separately;
    - $457,600 if married filing jointly or qualifying widow(er); or
    - $432,200 if head of household .... **24.** _____

25. Enter the smaller of line 1 or line 24 .... **25.** _____

26. Add lines 19 and 20 .... **26.** _____

27. Subtract line 26 from line 25. If zero or less, enter -0- .... **27.** _____

28. Enter the **smaller** of line 23 or line 27 .... **28.** _____

29. Multiply line 28 by 15% (.15) .... **29.** _____

30. Add lines 22 and 28 .... **30.** _____

   If lines 1 and 30 are the same, skip lines 31 through 41 and go to line 42. Otherwise, go to line 31.

31.	Subtract line 30 from line 21	**31.**	
32.	Multiply line 31 by 20% (.20)	**32.**	

If Schedule D, line 19, is zero or blank, skip lines 33 through 38 and go to line 39. Otherwise, go to line 33.

33.	Enter the **smaller** of line 9 above or Schedule D, line 19	**33.**	
34.	Add lines 10 and 19	**34.**	
35.	Enter the amount from line 1 above	**35.**	
36.	Subtract line 35 from line 34. If zero or less, enter -0-	**36.**	
37.	Subtract line 36 from line 33. If zero or less, enter -0-	**37.**	
38.	Multiply line 37 by 25% (.25)	**38.**	

If Schedule D, line 18, is zero or blank, skip lines 39 through 41 and go to line 42. Otherwise, go to line 39.

39.	Add lines 19, 20, 28, 31, and 37	**39.**	
40.	Subtract line 39 from line 1	**40.**	
41.	Multiply line 40 by 28% (.28)	**41.**	
42.	Figure the tax on the amount on **line 19.** If the amount on line 19 is less than $100,000, use the Tax Table to figure the tax. If the amount on line 19 is $100,000 or more, use the Tax Computation Worksheet	**42.**	
43.	Add lines 29, 32, 38, 41, and 42	**43.**	
44.	Figure the tax on the amount on **line 1.** If the amount on line 1 is less than $100,000, use the Tax Table to figure the tax. If the amount on line 1 is $100,000 or more, use the Tax Computation Worksheet	**44.**	
45.	**Tax on all taxable income (including capital gains and qualified dividends).** Enter the **smaller** of line 43 or line 44. Also include this amount on Form 1040, line 44 (or Form 1040NR, line 42). (If you are filing Form 2555 or 2555-EZ, do not enter this amount on Form 1040, line 44. Instead, enter it on line 4 of the Foreign Earned Income Tax Worksheet in the Form 1040 instructions)	**45.**	

*If applicable, enter instead the smaller amount you entered on the dotted line next to line 4e of Form 4952.

**If you are filing Form 2555 or 2555-EZ, see the footnote in the Foreign Earned Income Tax Worksheet in the Instructions for Form 1040, line 44, before completing this line.

2014 Instructions for Schedule E (Form 1040)

Supplemental Income and Loss

Use Schedule E (Form 1040) to report income or loss from rental real estate, royalties, partnerships, S corporations, estates, trusts, and residual interests in REMICs.

You can attach your own schedule(s) to report income or loss from any of these sources. Use the same format as on Schedule E.

Enter separately on Schedule E the total income and the total loss for each part. Enclose loss figures in (parentheses).

Section references are to the Internal Revenue Code unless otherwise noted.

Future Developments

For the latest information about developments related to Schedule E (Form 1040) and its instructions, such as legislation enacted after they were published, go to *www.irs.gov/schedulee*.

What's New

Standard mileage rate. The standard mileage rate for miles driven in connection with your rental activities is 56 cents a mile.

Reminder

Net Investment Income Tax. Individuals, estates, and trusts may be subject to the Net Investment Income Tax (NIIT). NIIT is a 3.8% tax on the lesser of net investment income or the excess of modified adjusted gross income (MAGI) over the threshold amount. Net investment income may include rental and royalty income, income from partnerships, S corporations and trusts, and income from other passive activities reported on your Schedule E. Use Form 8960, Net Investment Income Tax, to figure this tax. For more information on NIIT, go to IRS.gov and enter "Net Investment Income Tax" in the search box.

General Instructions

Other Schedules and Forms You May Have To File

- Schedule A (Form 1040) to deduct interest, taxes, and casualty losses not related to your business.
- Form 3520 to report certain transactions with foreign trusts and receipt of certain large gifts or bequests from certain foreign persons.
- Form 4562 to claim depreciation (including the special allowance) on assets placed in service in 2014, to claim amortization that began in 2014, to make an election under section 179 to expense certain property, or to report information on listed property.
- Form 4684 to report a casualty or theft gain or loss involving property used in your trade or business or income-producing property.
- Form 4797 to report sales, exchanges, and involuntary conversions (not from a casualty or theft) of trade or business property.
- Form 6198 to figure your allowable loss from an at-risk activity.
- Form 8082 to notify the IRS of any inconsistent tax treatment for an item on your return.
- Form 8582 to figure your allowable loss from passive activities.
- Form 8824 to report like-kind exchanges.
- Form 8826 to claim a credit for expenditures to improve access to your business for individuals with disabilities.
- Form 8873 to figure your extraterritorial income exclusion.
- Form 8910 to claim a credit for placing a new alternative motor vehicle in service for business use.
- Form 8960 to pay Net Investment Income Tax on certain income from your rental and other passive activities.

Single-member limited liability company (LLC). In most cases, a single-member domestic LLC is not treated as a separate entity for federal income tax purposes. If you are the sole member of a domestic LLC, file Schedule E (or Schedule C, C-EZ, or F, if applicable). However, you can elect to treat a domestic LLC as a corporation. See Form 8832 for details on the election and the tax treatment of a foreign LLC.

Information returns. You may have to file information returns for wages paid to employees, certain payments of fees and other nonemployee compensation, interest, rents, royalties, real estate transactions, annuities, and pensions. You generally use Form 1099-MISC, Miscellaneous Income, to report rents and payments of fees and other nonemployee compensation. For details, see *Line A*, later, and the 2014 General Instructions for Certain Information Returns.

If you received cash of more than $10,000 in one or more related transactions in your trade or business, you may have to file Form 8300. For details, see Pub. 1544.

Qualified Joint Venture

If you and your spouse each materially participate (see *Material participation* in the Instructions for Schedule C) as the only members of a jointly owned and operated rental real estate business and you file a joint return for the tax year, you can elect to be treated as a qualified joint venture instead of a partnership. This election, in most cases, will not increase the total tax owed on the joint return. By making the election, you will not be required to file Form 1065 for any year the election is in effect and will instead report the income and deductions directly on your joint return. If you and your spouse filed Form 1065 for the year prior to the election, the partnership terminates at the end of the tax year immediately preceding the year the election takes effect.

Dec 18, 2014

Cat. No. 24332T

Note. Mere joint ownership of property that is not a trade or business does not qualify for the election.

Making the election. To make this election for your rental real estate business, check the "QJV" box on line 2 for each property that is part of the qualified joint venture. You must divide all items of income, gain, loss, deduction, and credit attributable to the rental real estate business between you and your spouse in accordance with your respective interests in the venture. Although you and your spouse will not each file your own Schedule E as part of the qualified joint venture, each of you must report your interest as separate properties on line 1 of Schedule E. On lines 3 through 22 for each separate property interest, you must enter your share of the applicable income, deduction, or loss.

If you have more than three rental real estate or royalty properties, complete and attach as many Schedules E as you need to list them. But fill in lines 23a through 26 on only one Schedule E. The figures on lines 23a through 26 on that Schedule E should be the combined totals for all properties reported on your Schedules E.

Once made, the election can be revoked only with the permission of the IRS. However, the election technically remains in effect only for as long as the spouses filing as a qualified joint venture continue to meet the requirements to be treated as a qualified joint venture. If the spouses fail to meet the qualified joint venture requirements for a year, a new election will be necessary for any future year in which the spouses meet the requirements to be treated as a qualified joint venture.

Rental real estate income generally is not included in net earnings from self-employment subject to self-employment tax and generally is subject to passive loss limitation rules. Electing qualified joint venture status does not alter the application of the self-employment tax or the passive loss limitation rules.

For more information on qualified joint ventures, go to IRS.gov and enter "qualified joint venture" in the search box.

Reportable Transaction Disclosure Statement

Use Form 8886 to disclose information for each reportable transaction in which you participated. Form 8886 must be filed for each tax year that your federal income tax liability is affected by your participation in the transaction. You may have to pay a penalty if you are required to file Form 8886 but do not do so. You may also have to pay interest and penalties on any reportable transaction understatements. The following are reportable transactions.

• Any listed transaction that is the same as or substantially similar to tax avoidance transactions identified by the IRS.

• Any transaction offered to you or a related party under conditions of confidentiality for which you paid an advisor a fee of at least $50,000.

• Certain transactions for which you or a related party have contractual protection against disallowance of the tax benefits.

• Certain transactions resulting in a loss of at least $2 million in any single tax year or $4 million in any combination of tax years. (At least $50,000 for a single tax year if the loss arose from a foreign currency transaction defined in section 988(c)(1), whether or not the loss flows through from an S corporation or partnership.)

• Certain transactions of interest entered into after November 1, 2006, that are the same or substantially similar to transactions that the IRS has identified by notice, regulation, or other form of published guidance as transactions of interest.

See the Instructions for Form 8886 for more details.

At-Risk Rules

In most cases, you must complete Form 6198 to figure your allowable loss if you have:

• A loss from an activity carried on as a trade or business or for the production of income, and

• Amounts in the activity for which you are not at risk.

The at-risk rules in most cases limit the amount of loss (including loss on the disposition of assets) you can claim to the amount you could actually lose in the activity. However, the at-risk rules do not apply to losses from an activity of holding real property placed in service before 1987. They also do not apply to losses from your interest acquired before 1987 in a pass-through entity engaged in such activity. The activity of holding mineral property does not qualify for this exception.

In most cases, you are not at risk for amounts such as the following.

• Nonrecourse loans used to finance the activity, to acquire property used in the activity, or to acquire your interest in the activity that are not secured by your own property (other than property used in the activity). However, there is an exception for certain nonrecourse financing borrowed by you in connection with the activity of holding real property (other than mineral property). See *Qualified nonrecourse financing*, later.

• Cash, property, or borrowed amounts used in the activity (or contributed to the activity, or used to acquire your interest in the activity) that are protected against loss by a guarantee, stop-loss agreement, or other similar arrangement (excluding casualty insurance and insurance against tort liability).

• Amounts borrowed for use in the activity from a person who has an interest in the activity (other than as a creditor) or who is related under section 465(b)(3)(C) to a person (other than you) having such an interest.

Qualified nonrecourse financing. Qualified nonrecourse financing is treated as an amount at risk if it is secured by real property used in an activity of holding real property subject to the at-risk rules. Qualified nonrecourse financing is financing for which no one is personally liable for repayment and is:

• Borrowed by you in connection with the activity of holding real property (other than mineral property),

• Not convertible from a debt obligation to an ownership interest, and

• Loaned or guaranteed by any federal, state, or local government, or borrowed by you from a qualified person.

Qualified person. A qualified person is a person who actively and regularly engages in the business of lending money, such as a bank or savings and loan association. A qualified person cannot be:

- Related to you (unless the nonrecourse financing obtained is commercially reasonable and on substantially the same terms as loans involving unrelated persons),
- The seller of the property (or a person related to the seller), or
- A person who receives a fee due to your investment in real property (or a person related to that person).

For more details about the at-risk rules, see the Instructions for Form 6198 and Pub. 925.

Passive Activity Loss Rules

The passive activity loss rules may limit the amount of losses you can deduct. These rules apply to losses in Parts I, II, and III, and line 40 of Schedule E.

Losses from passive activities may be subject first to the at-risk rules. Losses deductible under the at-risk rules are then subject to the passive activity loss rules.

You can deduct losses from passive activities in most cases only to the extent of income from passive activities. An *exception for certain rental real estate activities* (explained later) may apply.

Passive Activity

A passive activity is any business activity in which you did not materially participate and any rental activity, except as explained later. If you are a limited partner, in most cases, you are not treated as having materially participated in the partnership's activities for the year.

The rental of real or personal property is a rental activity under the passive activity loss rules in most cases, but exceptions apply. If your rental of property is not treated as a rental activity, you must determine whether it is a trade or business activity, and if so, whether you materially participated in the activity for the tax year.

See the Instructions for Form 8582 to determine whether you materially participated in the activity and for the definition of "rental activity."

See Pub. 925 for special rules that apply to rentals of:
- Substantially nondepreciable property,
- Property incidental to development activities, and

- Property related to activities in which you materially participate.

Activities That Are Not Passive Activities

Activities of real estate professionals. If you were a real estate professional for 2014, any rental real estate activity in which you materially participated is not a passive activity. You were a real estate professional for the year only if you met both of the following conditions.
- More than half of the personal services you performed in trades or businesses during the year were performed in real property trades or businesses in which you materially participated.
- You performed more than 750 hours of services during the year in real property trades or businesses in which you materially participated.

If you are married filing jointly, either you or your spouse must meet both of the above conditions without taking into account services performed by the other spouse.

A real property trade or business is any real property development, redevelopment, construction, reconstruction, acquisition, conversion, rental, operation, management, leasing, or brokerage trade or business. Services you performed as an employee are not treated as performed in a real property trade or business unless you owned more than 5% of the stock (or more than 5% of the capital or profits interest) in the employer.

If you qualify as a real estate professional, rental real estate activities in which you materially participated are not passive activities. For purposes of determining whether you materially participated in your rental real estate activities, each interest in rental real estate is a separate activity unless you elect to treat all your interests in rental real estate as one activity. To make this election, attach a statement to your original tax return that declares you are a qualifying taxpayer for the year and you are making the election under section 469(c)(7)(A). The election applies for the year made and all later years in which you are a real estate professional. You can revoke the election only if your facts and circumstances materially change.

 If you did not make this election on your timely filed return, you may be eligible to make a late election to treat all your interest in rental real estate as one activity. See Rev. Proc. 2011-34, 2011-24 I.R.B. 875, available at www.irs.gov/irb/2011-24_IRB/ar07.html.

If you were a real estate professional for 2014, complete Schedule E, line 43.

Other activities. The rental of a dwelling unit that you used as a home is not subject to the passive loss limitation rules. See *Line 2*, later, to see if you used the dwelling unit as a home.

A working interest in an oil or gas well you held directly or through an entity that did not limit your liability is not a passive activity even if you did not materially participate.

Royalty income not derived in the ordinary course of a trade or business reported on Schedule E in most cases is not considered income from a passive activity.

For more details on passive activities, see the Instructions for Form 8582 and Pub. 925.

Exception for Certain Rental Real Estate Activities

If you meet all of the following conditions, your rental real estate losses are not limited by the passive activity loss rules, and you do not need to complete Form 8582. If you do not meet all of these conditions, see the Instructions for Form 8582 to find out if you must complete and attach Form 8582 to figure any losses allowed.

1. Rental real estate activities are your only passive activities.

2. You do not have any prior year unallowed losses from any passive activities.

3. All of the following apply if you have an overall net loss from these activities:

a. You *actively participated* (defined later) in all of the rental real estate activities;

b. If married filing separately, you lived apart from your spouse all year;

c. Your overall net loss from these activities is $25,000 or less ($12,500 or less if married filing separately);

d. You have no current or prior year unallowed credits from passive activities;

e. Your *modified adjusted gross income* (defined later) is $100,000 or less ($50,000 or less if married filing separately); and

f. You do not hold any interest in a rental real estate activity as a limited partner or as a beneficiary of an estate or a trust.

Active participation. You can meet the active participation requirement without regular, continuous, and substantial involvement in real estate activities. But you must have participated in making management decisions or arranging for others to provide services (such as repairs) in a significant and *bona fide* sense. Such management decisions include:

- Approving new tenants,
- Deciding on rental terms,
- Approving capital or repair expenditures, and
- Other similar decisions.

You are not considered to actively participate if, at any time during the tax year, your interest (including your spouse's interest) in the activity was less than 10% by value of all interests in the activity. If you are a limited partner, you are also not treated as actively participating in a partnership's rental real estate activities.

Modified adjusted gross income. This is your adjusted gross income from Form 1040, line 38, or Form 1040NR, line 37, without taking into account:

- Any allowable passive activity loss,
- Rental real estate losses allowed for real estate professionals (see *Activities of real estate professionals*, earlier),
- Taxable social security or tier 1 railroad retirement benefits,
- Deductible contributions to a traditional IRA or certain other qualified retirement plans under section 219,
- The student loan interest deduction,
- The tuition and fees deduction,
- The domestic production activities deduction,
- The deduction for one-half of self-employment tax,
- The exclusion from income of interest from series EE and I U.S. savings

bonds used to pay higher education expenses, and

- Any excluded amounts under an employer's adoption assistance program.

Recordkeeping

You must keep records to support items reported on Schedule E in case the IRS has questions about them. If the IRS examines your tax return, you may be asked to explain the items reported. Good records will help you explain any item and arrive at the correct tax with a minimum of effort. If you do not have records, you may have to spend time getting statements and receipts from various sources. If you cannot produce the correct documents, you may have to pay additional tax and be subject to penalties.

Specific Instructions

Filers of Form 1041. If you are a fiduciary filing Schedule E with Form 1041, enter the estate's or trust's employer identification number (EIN) in the space for "Your social security number."

Part I

 Before you begin, see Line 3 *and* Line 4, *later, to determine if you should report your rental real estate and royalty income on Schedule C, Schedule C-EZ, or Form 4835, instead of Schedule E.*

Line A

If you made any payments in 2014 that would require you to file any Forms 1099, check the "Yes" box. Otherwise, check the "No" box. See the 2014 General Instructions for Certain Information Returns if you are unsure whether you were required to file any Forms 1099. Also see the separate instructions for each Form 1099.

 Generally, you must file Form 1099-MISC if you paid at least $600 in rents, services, prizes, medical and health care payments, and other income payments. The Guide to Information Returns *in the 2014 General Instructions for Certain Information Returns has more information, including*

the due dates for the various information returns. You can find more information at http://www.irs.gov/uac/General-Instructions-for-Certain-Information-Returns.

Income or Loss From Rental Real Estate and Royalties

Use Part I to report the following.

- Income and expenses from rental real estate (including personal property leased with real estate).
- Royalty income and expenses.
- For an estate or trust **only**, farm rental income and expenses based on crops or livestock produced by the tenant. Estates and trusts **do not** use Form 4835 or Schedule F (Form 1040) for this purpose.

If you own a part interest in a rental real estate property, report only your part of the income and expenses on Schedule E.

Complete lines 1 and 2 for each rental real estate property. For royalty properties, line 2 and the address portion on line 1 should be left blank and you should enter code "6" for royalty property.

If you have more than three rental real estate or royalty properties, complete and attach as many Schedules E as you need to list them. But answer lines A and B and fill in lines 23a through 26 on only one Schedule E. The figures on lines 23a through 26 on that Schedule E should be the combined totals for all properties reported on your Schedules E. If you are also using page 2 of Schedule E, use the same Schedule E on which you entered the combined totals for Part I.

Personal property. Do not use Schedule E to report income and expenses from the rental of personal property, such as equipment or vehicles. Instead, use Schedule C or C-EZ if you are in the business of renting personal property. You are in the business of renting personal property if the primary purpose for renting the property is income or profit and you are involved in the rental activity with continuity and regularity.

If your rental of personal property is not a business, see the instructions for

Form 1040, lines 21 and 36, to find out how to report the income and expenses.

Extraterritorial income exclusion. Except as otherwise provided in the Internal Revenue Code, gross income includes all income from whatever source derived. Gross income, however, does not include extraterritorial income that is qualifying foreign trade income under certain circumstances. Use Form 8873 to figure the extraterritorial income exclusion. Report it on Schedule E as explained in the Instructions for Form 8873.

Chapter 11 bankruptcy cases. If you were a debtor in a chapter 11 bankruptcy case, see *Chapter 11 Bankruptcy Cases* under *Income* in the Instructions for Form 1040.

Line 1a

For rental real estate property only, show the street address, city or town, state, and ZIP code. If the property is located in a foreign country, enter the city, province or state, country, and postal code.

Line 1b

Enter one of the codes listed under "Type of Property" in Part I of the form.

Land rental. Enter code "5" for rental of land. For details about the tax treatment of income from this type of rental property, see *Rental of Nondepreciable Property* in Pub. 925.

Self-rental. Enter code "7" for self-rental if you rent property to a trade or business in which you materially participated. See *Rental of Property to a Nonpassive Activity* in Pub. 925 for details about the tax treatment of income from this type of rental property.

Other. Enter code "8" if the property is not one of the other types listed on the form. Attach a statement to your return describing the property.

Line 2

If you rented out a dwelling unit that you also used for personal purposes during the year, you may not be able to deduct all the expenses for the rental part. "Dwelling unit" (unit) means a house, apartment, condominium, mobile home, boat, or similar property.

For each property listed on line 1a, report the number of days in the year each property was rented at fair rental value and the number of days of personal use.

A day of personal use is any day, or part of a day, that the unit was used by:
• You for personal purposes,
• Any other person for personal purposes, if that person owns part of the unit (unless rented to that person under a "shared equity" financing agreement),
• Anyone in your family (or in the family of someone else who owns part of the unit), unless the unit is rented at a fair rental price to that person as his or her main home,
• Anyone who pays less than a fair rental price for the unit, or
• Anyone under an agreement that lets you use some other unit.

Do not count as personal use:
• Any day you spent working substantially full time repairing and maintaining the unit, even if family members used it for recreational purposes on that day, or
• Any days you used the unit as your main home before or after renting it or offering it for rent, if you rented or tried to rent it for at least 12 consecutive months (or for a period of less than 12 consecutive months at the end of which you sold or exchanged it).

Whether or not you can deduct expenses for the unit depends on whether or not you used the unit as a home in 2014. You used the unit as a home if your personal use of the unit was more than the greater of:
• 14 days, or
• 10% of the total days it was rented to others at a fair rental price.

If you did not use the unit as a home, you can deduct all your expenses for the rental part, subject to the *at-risk rules* and the *passive activity loss rules* explained earlier.

If you did use the unit as a home and rented the unit out for fewer than 15 days in 2014, do not report the rental income and do not deduct any rental expenses. If you itemize deductions on Schedule A, you can deduct allowable interest, taxes, and casualty losses.

If you did use the unit as a home and rented the unit out for 15 or more days

in 2014, you may not be able to deduct all your rental expenses. You can deduct all the following expenses for the rental part on Schedule E.

• Mortgage interest.
• Real estate taxes.
• Casualty losses.
• Other rental expenses not related to your use of the unit as a home, such as advertising expenses and rental agents' fees.

If any income is left after deducting these expenses, you can deduct other expenses, including depreciation, up to the amount of remaining income. You can carry over to 2015 the amounts you cannot deduct.

 Regardless of whether you used the unit as a home, expenses related to days of personal use do not qualify as rental expenses. You must allocate your expenses based on the number of days of personal use to total use of the property. For example, you used your property for personal use for 7 days and rented it for 63 days. In most cases, 10% (7÷70) of your expenses are not rental expenses and cannot be deducted on Schedule E.

See Pub. 527 for details.

QJV. Check the box for "QJV" if you owned the property as a member of a qualified joint venture reporting income not subject to self-employment tax. See *Qualified Joint Venture*, earlier.

Line 3

If you received rental income from real estate (including personal property leased with real estate), report the income on line 3. Use a separate column (A, B, or C) for each rental property. Include income received for renting a room or other space.

If you received services or property instead of money as rent, report the fair market value of the services or property as rental income on line 3.

If you provided significant services to the renter, such as maid service, report the rental activity on Schedule C or C-EZ, not on Schedule E. Significant services do not include the furnishing of heat and light, cleaning of public areas, trash collection, or similar services.

If you were a real estate dealer, include only the rent received from real estate (including personal property leased with this real estate) you held for the primary purpose of renting to produce income. Do not use Schedule E to report income and expenses from rentals of real estate you held for sale to customers in the ordinary course of your business as a real estate dealer. Instead use Schedule C or C-EZ for those rentals.

For more details on rental income, use TeleTax topic 414 (see *What is Tele-Tax?* in the Instructions for Form 1040), or see Pub. 527.

Rental income from farm production or crop shares. Report farm rental income and expenses on Form 4835 if:
- You are an individual,
- You received rental income based on crops or livestock produced by the tenant, and
- You did not materially participate in the management or operation of the farm.

Line 4

Report on line 4 royalties from oil, gas, or mineral properties (not including operating interests); copyrights; and patents. Use a separate column (A, B, or C) for each royalty property.

If you received $10 or more in royalties during 2014, the payer should send you a Form 1099-MISC or similar statement by February 2, 2015, showing the amount you received. Report this amount on line 4.

If you are in business as a self-employed writer, inventor, artist, etc., report your royalty income and expenses on Schedule C or C-EZ.

You may be able to treat amounts received as "royalties" for the transfer of a patent or amounts received on the disposal of coal and iron ore as the sale of a capital asset. For details, see Pub. 544.

Enter on line 4 the gross amount of rent and royalty income, even if state or local taxes were withheld from oil or gas payments you received. Include taxes withheld by the producer on line 16.

General Instructions for Lines 5 Through 21

Enter your rental and royalty expenses for each property in the appropriate column. You can deduct all ordinary and necessary expenses, such as taxes, interest, repairs, insurance, management fees, agents' commissions, and depreciation.

Do not deduct the value of your own labor or amounts paid for capital investments or capital improvements.

Enter your total expenses for mortgage interest (line 12), depreciation expenses and depletion (line 18), and total expenses (line 20) on lines 23c through 23e, respectively, even if you have only one property.

Renting out part of your home. If you rent out only part of your home or other property, deduct the part of your expenses that applies to the rented part.

Credit or deduction for access expenditures. You may be able to claim a tax credit for eligible expenditures paid or incurred in 2014 to provide access to your business for individuals with disabilities. See Form 8826 for details.

You can also elect to deduct up to $15,000 of qualified costs paid or incurred in 2014 to remove architectural or transportation barriers to individuals with disabilities and the elderly.

You cannot take both the credit and the deduction for the same expenditures.

Line 6

You can deduct ordinary and necessary auto and travel expenses related to your rental activities, including 50% of meal expenses incurred while traveling away from home. In most cases you can either deduct your actual expenses or take the standard mileage rate. You must use actual expenses if you used more than four vehicles simultaneously in your rental activities (as in fleet operations). You cannot use actual expenses for a leased vehicle if you previously used the standard mileage rate for that vehicle.

You can use the standard mileage rate for 2014 only if you:
- Owned the vehicle and used the standard mileage rate for the first year you placed the vehicle in service, or
- Leased the vehicle and are using the standard mileage rate for the entire

lease period (except the period, if any, before 1998).

If you take the standard mileage rate, multiply the number of miles driven in connection with your rental activities by 56 cents a mile. Include this amount and your parking fees and tolls on line 6.

 You cannot deduct rental or lease payments, depreciation, or your actual auto expenses if you use the standard mileage rate.

If you deduct actual auto expenses:
- Include on line 6 the rental activity portion of the cost of gasoline, oil, repairs, insurance, tires, license plates, etc., and
- Show auto rental or lease payments on line 19 and depreciation on line 18.

If you claim any auto expenses (actual or the standard mileage rate), you must complete Part V of Form 4562 and attach Form 4562 to your tax return.

See Pub. 527 and Pub. 463 for details.

Line 10

Include on line 10 fees for tax advice and the preparation of tax forms related to your rental real estate or royalty properties.

Do not deduct legal fees paid or incurred to defend or protect title to property, to recover property, or to develop or improve property. Instead, you must capitalize these fees and add them to the property's basis.

Lines 12 and 13

In most cases, to determine the interest expense allocable to your rental activities, you must have records to show how the proceeds of each debt were used. Specific tracing rules apply for allocating debt proceeds and repayment. See Pub. 535 for details.

If you have a mortgage on your rental property, enter on line 12 the amount of interest you paid for 2014 to banks or other financial institutions.

Do not deduct prepaid interest when you paid it. You can deduct it only in the year to which it is properly allocable. Points, including loan origination fees, charged only for the use of money must be deducted over the life of the loan.

If you paid $600 or more in interest on a mortgage during 2014, the recipient should send you a Form 1098 or similar statement by February 2, 2015, showing the total interest received from you.

If you paid more mortgage interest than is shown on your Form 1098 or similar statement, see Pub. 535 to find out if you can deduct part or all of the additional interest. If you can, enter the entire deductible amount on line 12. Attach a statement to your return explaining the difference. In the space to the left of line 12, enter "See attached."

Note. If the recipient was not a financial institution or you did not receive a Form 1098 from the recipient, report your deductible mortgage interest on line 13.

If you and at least one other person (other than your spouse if you file a joint return) were liable for and paid interest on the mortgage, and the other person received Form 1098, report your share of the deductible interest on line 13. Attach a statement to your return showing the name and address of the person who received Form 1098. On the dotted line next to line 13, enter "See attached."

Line 14

You can deduct the amounts paid for repairs and maintenance. However, you cannot deduct the cost of improvements. Repairs and maintenance costs are those costs that keep the property in an ordinarily efficient operating condition. Examples are fixing a broken lock or painting a room.

In contrast, improvements are amounts paid to better or restore your property or adapt it to a new or different use. Examples of improvements are adding substantial insulation or replacing an entire HVAC system. Amounts paid to improve your property generally must be capitalized and depreciated (that is, they cannot be deducted in full in the year they are paid or incurred). See *Line 18*, later.

Line 17

You can deduct the cost of ordinary and necessary telephone calls related to your rental activities or royalty income (for example, calls to the renter). However, the base rate (including taxes and other charges) for local telephone service for the first telephone line into your residence is a personal expense and is not deductible.

Line 18

Depreciation is the annual deduction you must take to recover the cost or other basis of business or investment property having a useful life substantially beyond the tax year. Land is not depreciable.

Depreciation starts when you first use the property in your business or for the production of income. It ends when you deduct all your depreciable cost or other basis or no longer use the property in your business or for the production of income.

See the Instructions for Form 4562 to figure the amount of depreciation to enter on line 18.

You must complete and attach Form 4562 only if you are claiming:
• Depreciation on property first placed in service during 2014,
• Depreciation on listed property (defined in the Instructions for Form 4562), including a vehicle, regardless of the date it was placed in service, or
• A section 179 expense deduction or amortization of costs that began in 2014.

See Pub. 527 for more information on depreciation of residential rental property. See Pub. 946 for a more comprehensive guide to depreciation.

If you have an economic interest in mineral property, you may be able to take a deduction for depletion. Mineral property includes oil and gas wells, mines, and other natural deposits (including geothermal deposits). See Pub. 535 for details.

Separating cost of land and buildings. If you buy buildings and your cost includes the cost of the land on which they stand, you must divide the cost between the land and the buildings to figure the basis for depreciation of the buildings. The part of the cost that you allocate to each asset is the ratio of the fair market value of that asset to the fair market value of the whole property at the time you buy it.

If you are not certain of the fair market values of the land and the buildings, you can divide the cost between them based on their assessed values for real estate tax purposes.

Line 19

Enter on line 19 any ordinary and necessary expenses not listed on lines 5 through 18.

Line 21

If you have amounts for which you are not at risk, use Form 6198 to determine the amount of your deductible loss. Enter that amount in the appropriate column of Schedule E, line 21. In the space to the left of line 21, enter "Form 6198." Attach Form 6198 to your return. For details on the at-risk rules, see *At-Risk Rules*, earlier.

Line 22

Do not complete line 22 if the amount on line 21 is from royalty properties.

If you have a rental real estate loss from a *passive activity* (defined earlier), the amount of loss you can deduct may be limited by the passive activity loss rules. You may need to complete Form 8582 to figure the amount of loss, if any, to enter on line 22. See the Instructions for Form 8582 to determine if your loss is limited.

If your rental real estate loss is not from a passive activity or you meet the *exception for certain rental real estate activities* (explained earlier), you do not have to complete Form 8582. Enter the loss from line 21 on line 22.

If you have an unallowed rental real estate loss from a prior year that after completing Form 8582 you can deduct this year, include that loss on line 22.

Parts II and III

If you need more space in Part II or III to list your income or losses, attach a continuation sheet using the same format as shown in Part II or III. However, be sure to complete the "Totals" columns for lines 29a and 29b, or lines 34a and 34b, as appropriate. If you also completed Part I on more than one Schedule E, use the same Schedule E on which you entered the combined totals in Part I.

Tax preference items. If you are a partner, a shareholder in an S corporation, or a beneficiary of an estate or trust, you must take into account your share of preferences and adjustments from these entities for the alternative minimum tax on Form 6251 or Schedule I (Form 1041).

Part II

Income or Loss From Partnerships and S Corporations

If you are a member of a partnership or joint venture or a shareholder in an S corporation, use Part II to report your share of the partnership or S corporation income (even if not received) or loss.

 If you elected to be taxed as a qualified joint venture instead of a partnership, follow the reporting rules under Qualified Joint Venture, *earlier.*

You should receive a Schedule K-1 from the partnership or S corporation. You should also receive a copy of the Partner's or Shareholder's Instructions for Schedule K-1. Your copy of Schedule K-1 and its instructions will tell you where on your return to report your share of the items. If you did not receive these instructions with your Schedule K-1, see the instructions for Form 1040 or Form 1040NR for how to get tax forms, instructions, and publications. Do not attach Schedules K-1 to your return. Keep them for your records.

If you are treating items on your tax return differently from the way the partnership (other than an electing large partnership) or S corporation reported them on its return, you may have to file Form 8082. If you are a partner in an electing large partnership, you must report the items shown on Schedule K-1 (Form 1065-B) on your tax return the same way the partnership reported the items on Schedule K-1.

Special rules that limit losses. Please note the following.

• If you have an interest in a partnership or S corporation that is involved in a farming business, your losses may be limited if the partnership accepted certain subsidies. You will be notified on the Schedule K-1 if the partnership or S corporation received one of these subsidies. Use *Worksheet 1* on the last page of these instructions to determine if you have an excess farm loss for the current year. See the Instructions for Schedule F for more details on how to complete the worksheet. If you had a loss from a partnership or S corporation that was not allowed last year because of the excess farm loss rules, see *Line 27* later, for how to report it.

 If you have other farming businesses requiring you to file Schedule F or any Schedule C activity of processing a farm commodity, use one of the worksheets in the Instructions for Schedule F instead of Worksheet 1 on the last page of these instructions.

• If you have a current year loss, or a prior year unallowed loss, from a partnership or an S corporation, see *At-Risk Rules* and *Passive Activity Loss Rules*, earlier.

Partners and S corporation shareholders should get a separate statement of income, expenses, deductions, and credits for each activity engaged in by the partnership and S corporation. If you are subject to the at-risk rules for any activity, check the box on the appropriate line in Part II, column (e) of Schedule E, and use Form 6198 to figure the amount of any deductible loss. If the activity is nonpassive, enter any deductible loss from Form 6198 on the appropriate line in Part II, column (h) of Schedule E.

• If you have a passive activity loss, in most cases you need to complete Form 8582 to figure the amount of the allowable loss to enter in Part II, column (f), for that activity. But if you are a general partner or an S corporation shareholder reporting your share of a partnership or an S corporation loss from a rental real estate activity and you meet all of the conditions listed earlier under *Exception for Certain Rental Real Estate Activities*, you do not have to complete Form 8582. Instead, enter your allowable loss in Part II, column (f).

If you have passive activity income, complete Part II, column (g), for that activity.

If you have nonpassive income or losses, complete Part II, columns (h) through (j), as appropriate.

Domestic Partnerships

See the Schedule K-1 instructions before entering on your return other partnership items from a passive activity or income or loss from any publicly traded partnership.

You can deduct unreimbursed ordinary and necessary expenses you paid on behalf of the partnership if you were required to pay these expenses under the partnership agreement. See *Line 27*, later, for how to report these expenses.

Report allowable interest expense paid or incurred from debt-financed acquisitions in Part II or on Schedule A depending on the type of expenditure to which the interest is allocated. See Pub. 535 for details.

If you claimed a credit for federal tax on gasoline or other fuels on your 2013 Form 1040 or Form 1040NR based on information received from the partnership, enter as income in column (g) or column (j), whichever applies, the amount of the credit claimed for 2013.

Part or all of your share of partnership income or loss from the operation of the business may be considered net earnings from self-employment that must be reported on Schedule SE. Enter the amount from Schedule K-1 (Form 1065), box 14, code A (or from Schedule K-1 (Form 1065-B), box 9 (code J1)), on Schedule SE, after you reduce this amount by any allowable expenses attributable to that income.

Foreign Partnerships

Follow the instructions below in addition to the instructions earlier for *Domestic Partnerships*.

If you are a U.S. person, you may have received Forms 1099-B, 1099-DIV, and 1099-INT reporting your share of certain partnership income, because payors of income to the foreign partnership in most cases are required to allocate and report payments of that income directly to each of the partners of the foreign partnership. If you received both Schedule K-1 and Form 1099 for the same type and source of partnership income, report only the income shown on Schedule K-1 in accordance with its instructions.

If you are not a U.S. person, you may have received Forms 1042-S reporting your share of certain partnership income, because payors of income to the foreign partnership in most cases are required to allocate and report payments of that income directly to each of the partners of the foreign partnership. If you received both Schedule K-1 and Form 1042-S for the same type and source of partnership income, report the income on your return as follows.

• For all income effectively connected with the conduct of a trade or business in the United States, report only the income shown on Schedule K-1 in accordance with its instructions.

• For all income **not** effectively connected with the conduct of a trade or business in the United States, report on page 4 of Form 1040NR only the income shown on Form 1042-S (if you are required to file Form 1040NR).

Requirement to file Form 8865. If you are a U.S. person, you may have to file Form 8865 if any of the following applies.

1. You controlled a foreign partnership (that is, you owned more than a 50% direct or indirect interest in the partnership).

2. You owned at least a 10% direct or indirect interest in a foreign partnership while U.S. persons controlled that partnership.

3. You had an acquisition, disposition, or change in proportional interest of a foreign partnership that:

a. Increased your direct interest to at least 10% or reduced your direct interest of at least 10% to less than 10%, or

b. Changed your direct interest by at least a 10% interest.

4. You contributed property to a foreign partnership in exchange for a partnership interest if:

a. Immediately after the contribution, you owned, directly or indirectly, at least a 10% interest in the partnership, or

b. The value of the property you contributed, when added to the value of any other property you or any related person contributed to the partnership during the 12-month period ending on the date of transfer, exceeds $100,000.

Also, you may have to file Form 8865 to report certain dispositions by a foreign partnership of property you previously contributed to that partnership if you were a partner at the time of the disposition.

For more details, including penalties for failing to file Form 8865, see Form 8865 and its separate instructions.

S Corporations

If you are a shareholder in an S corporation, your share of the corporation's aggregate losses and deductions (combined income, losses, and deductions) is in most cases limited to the adjusted basis of your corporate stock and any debt the corporation owes you. Any loss or deduction not allowed this year because of the basis limitation can be carried forward and deducted in a later year subject to the basis limitation for that year.

If you are claiming a deduction for your share of an aggregate loss, attach to your return a computation of the adjusted basis of your corporate stock and of any debt the corporation owes you. See the Schedule K-1 instructions for details.

After applying the basis limitation, the deductible amount of your aggregate losses and deductions may be further reduced by the at-risk rules and the passive activity loss rules. See *At-Risk Rules* and *Passive Activity Loss Rules*, earlier.

Distributions of prior year accumulated earnings and profits of S corporations are dividends and are reported on Form 1040, line 9a.

Interest expense relating to the acquisition of shares in an S corporation may be fully deductible on Schedule E. For details, see Pub. 535.

Your share of the net income of an S corporation is not subject to self-employment tax.

Line 27

If you answered "Yes" on line 27, follow the instructions below. If you do not follow these instructions, the IRS may send you a notice of additional tax due because the amounts reported by the partnership or S corporation on Schedule K-1 do not match the amounts you reported on your tax return.

Losses Not Allowed in Prior Years Due to the At-Risk, Excess Farm Loss, or Basis Limitations

• Enter your total prior year unallowed losses that are now deductible on a separate line in column (h) of line 28. Do not combine these losses with, or net them against, any current year amounts from the partnership or S corporation.

• Enter "PYA" in column (a) of the same line.

Prior Year Unallowed Losses From a Passive Activity Not Reported on Form 8582

• Enter on a separate line in column (f) of line 28 your total prior year unallowed losses not reported on Form 8582. Such losses include prior year unallowed losses now deductible because you did not have an overall loss from all passive activities or you disposed of your entire interest in a passive activity in a fully taxable transaction. Do not combine these losses with, or net them against, any current year amounts from the partnership or S corporation.

• Enter "PYA" in column (a) of the same line.

Unreimbursed Partnership Expenses

• You can deduct unreimbursed ordinary and necessary partnership expenses you paid on behalf of the partnership on Schedule E if you were required to pay these expenses under the partnership agreement (except amounts deductible only as itemized deductions, which you must enter on Schedule A).

• Enter unreimbursed partnership expenses from nonpassive activities on a separate line in column (h) of line 28. Do not combine these expenses with, or net them against, any other amounts from the partnership.

• If the expenses are from a passive activity and you are not required to file Form 8582, enter the expenses related to a passive activity on a separate line in column (f) of line 28. Do not combine these expenses with, or net them against, any other amounts from the partnership.

• Enter "UPE" in column (a) of the same line.

Line 28

For nonpassive income or loss (and passive income or losses for which you are not filing Form 8582), enter in the applicable column of line 28 your current year ordinary income or loss from the partnership or S corporation. Report each related item required to be reported on Schedule E (including items of income or loss stated separately on Schedule K-1) in the applicable column of a separate line following the line on which you reported the current year ordinary income or loss. Also enter a description of the related item (for example, depletion) in column (a) of the same line.

If you are required to file Form 8582, see the Instructions for Form 8582 before completing Schedule E.

Part III

Income or Loss From Estates and Trusts

If you are a beneficiary of an estate or trust, use Part III to report your part of the income (even if not received) or loss. You should receive a Schedule K-1 (Form 1041) from the fiduciary. Your copy of Schedule K-1 and its instructions will tell you where on your return to report the items from Schedule K-1. Do not attach Schedule K-1 to your return. Keep it for your records.

If you are treating items on your tax return differently from the way the estate or trust reported them on its return, you may have to file Form 8082.

If you have estimated taxes credited to you from a trust (Form 1041, Schedule K-1, box 13, code A), enter "ES payment claimed" and the amount on the dotted line next to line 37. Do not include this amount in the total on line 37. Instead, enter the amount on Form 1040, line 65, or Form 1040NR, line 63.

A U.S. person who transferred property to a foreign trust may have to report the income received by the trust as a result of the transferred property if, during 2014, the trust had a U.S. beneficiary. See section 679. An individual who received a distribution from, or who was the grantor of or transferor to, a foreign trust must also complete Part III of

Schedule B (Form 1040A or 1040) and may have to file Form 3520. In addition, the owner of a foreign trust must ensure that the trust files an annual information return on Form 3520-A.

Part IV

Income or Loss From Real Estate Mortgage Investment Conduits (REMICs)

If you are the holder of a residual interest in a REMIC, use Part IV to report your total share of the REMIC's taxable income or loss for each quarter included in your tax year. You should receive Schedule Q (Form 1066) and instructions from the REMIC for each quarter. Do not attach Schedule(s) Q to your return. Keep them for your records.

If you are treating REMIC items on your tax return differently from the way the REMIC reported them on its return, you may have to file Form 8082.

If you are the holder of a residual interest in more than one REMIC, attach a continuation sheet using the same format as in Part IV. Enter the combined totals of columns (d) and (e) on Schedule E, line 39. If you also completed Part I on more than one Schedule E, use the same Schedule E on which you entered the combined totals in Part I.

REMIC income or loss is not income or loss from a passive activity.

Note. If you are the holder of a regular interest in a REMIC, do not use Schedule E to report the income you received. Instead, report it on Form 1040, line 8a.

Column (c). Report the total of the amounts shown on Schedule(s) Q, line 2c. This is the smallest amount you are allowed to report as your taxable income (Form 1040, line 43). It is also the smallest amount you are allowed to report as your alternative minimum taxable income (AMTI) on Form 6251, line 28.

If the amount in column (c) is larger than your taxable income would otherwise be, enter the amount from column (c) on Form 1040, line 43, or Form 1040NR, line 41. Similarly, if the amount in column (c) is larger than your AMTI would otherwise be, enter the

amount from column (c) on Form 6251, line 28. Enter "Sch Q" on the dotted line to the left of this amount on Form 1040, line 43 (or Form 1040NR, line 41), and Form 6251, line 28, if applicable.

Note. These rules also apply to estates and trusts that hold a residual interest in a REMIC. Be sure to make the appropriate entries on the comparable lines on Form 1041.

 Do not include the amount shown in column (c) in the total on Schedule E, line 39.

Column (e). Report the total of the amounts shown on Schedule(s) Q, line 3b. If you itemize your deductions, include this amount on Schedule A (Form 1040), line 23.

Part V
Summary

Line 42

You will not be charged a penalty for underpayment of estimated tax if:

1. Your gross farming or fishing income for 2013 or 2014 is at least two-thirds of your gross income, and

2. You file your 2014 tax return and pay the tax due by March 2, 2015.

this form is included in the estimates shown in the instructions for their individual income tax return. The estimated burden for all other taxpayers who file this form is approved under OMB control number 1545-1972 and is shown next.

Recordkeeping	3 hrs., 3 min.
Learning about the law or the form	1 hr., 2 min.
Preparing the form	1 hr., 34 min.
Copying, assembling, and sending the form to the IRS	34 min.

If you have comments concerning the accuracy of these time estimates or suggestions for making this form simpler, we would be happy to hear from you. See the instructions for the tax return with which this form is filed.

Worksheet 1 — Excess farm loss from an interest in a partnership or S corporation involved in farming business(es)

Keep for Your Records

CAUTION: *In determining if you have an excess farm loss, do not take into account any deductions for losses arising by reason of fire, storm, or other casualty, or by reason of disease or drought, involving your farm businesses.*

Note. When instructed in the worksheet below to enter an amount from line 30, 31, or 32 of Schedule E, include only the amount on that line that relates to farming businesses.

1. Enter the amount from your 2014 Schedule(s) E, line 31. If this amount is less than $300,000 ($150,000 if married filing separately), stop here; you do not have an excess farm loss in 2014. If more than $300,000 ($150,000 if married filing separately), continue to line 2 .... **1.** _____

2. Subtract $300,000 ($150,000 if married filing separately) from line 1 .... **2.** _____

3. Enter the amount from your 2014 Schedule(s) E, line 30 .... **3.** _____

4. Is line 3 greater than or equal to line 2? If yes, stop here; you do not have an excess farm loss in 2014. If no, continue to line 5.

5. Enter your net gain/loss from the sale of farming business property reported on Form 4797 .... **5.** _____

6. Enter your net gain/loss from the sale of farming business property reported on Form 8949 .... **6.** _____

7. Combine line 5 and line 6. If zero or less, enter -0- .... **7.** _____

8. Add line 3 and line 7. Is this greater than or equal to line 2? If yes, stop here; you do not have an excess farm loss in 2014. If no, continue to line 9 .... **8.** _____

9. Enter the amount from your 2013 Schedule(s) E, line 32 .... **9.** _____

10. Enter your combined net gain/loss from the sale of farming business property reported on your 2013 Form 4797 and Form 8949. If zero or less, enter -0- .... **10.** _____

11. Enter the amount from your 2012 Schedule(s) E, line 32 .... **11.** _____

12. Enter your combined net gain/loss from the sale of farming business property reported on your 2012 Form 4797 and Form 8949. If zero or less, enter -0- .... **12.** _____

13. Enter the amount from your 2011 Schedule(s) E, line 32 .... **13.** _____

14. Enter your combined net gain/loss from the sale of farming business property reported on your 2011 Form 4797 and Form 8949. If zero or less, enter -0- .... **14.** _____

15. Enter the amount from your 2010 Schedule(s) E, line 32 .... **15.** _____

16. Enter your combined net gain/loss from the sale of farming business property reported on your 2010 Form 4797 and Schedule D. If zero or less, enter -0- .... **16.** _____

17. Enter the amount from your 2009 Schedule(s) E, line 32 .... **17.** _____

18. Enter your combined net gain/loss from the sale of farming business property reported on your 2009 Form 4797 and Schedule D. If zero or less, enter -0- .... **18.** _____

19. Combine lines 9 through 18. If zero or less, enter -0- .... **19.** _____

20. Enter the greater of line 19 or $300,000 ($150,000 if married filing separately) .... **20.** _____

21. Add line 8 and line 20 .... **21.** _____

22. **Excess farm loss.** Subtract line 1 from line 21. If zero or less, you have an excess farm loss that reduces the amount of loss you can deduct this year. If you have more than one farming business with an overall loss this year, allocate the excess farm loss amount on a *pro rata* basis among those farming businesses. .... **22.** _____

2014 Instructions for Schedule F

Profit or Loss From Farming

Use Schedule F (Form 1040) to report farm income and expenses. File it with Form 1040, 1040NR, 1041, 1065, or 1065-B.

Your farming activity may subject you to state and local taxes and other requirements such as business licenses and fees. Check with your state and local governments for more information.

Additional information. Pub. 225 has more information and examples to help you complete your farm tax return. It also lists important dates that apply to farmers.

Section references are to the Internal Revenue Code unless otherwise noted.

Future Developments

For the latest information about developments related to Schedule F (Form 1040) and its instructions, such as legislation enacted after they were published, go to *www.irs.gov/schedulef*.

What's New

Standard mileage rate. The standard mileage rate for business use of your vehicle for 2014 is 56 cents per mile.

General Instructions

Other Schedules and Forms You May Have To File

- Schedule E (Form 1040), Part I, to report rental income from pastureland based on a flat charge. However, report on Schedule F (Form 1040), line 8, pasture income received from taking care of someone else's livestock. Also use Schedule E (Form 1040), Part I, to report farm rental income and expenses of a trust or estate based on crops or livestock produced by a tenant.
- Schedule J (Form 1040) to figure your tax by averaging your farm income over the previous 3 years. Doing so may reduce your tax.
- Schedule SE (Form 1040) to pay self-employment tax on income from your farming business.
- Form 3800 to claim any general business credits.
- Form 4562 to claim depreciation (including the special allowance) on assets placed in service in 2014, to claim amortization that began in 2014, to make an election under section 179 to expense certain property, or to report information on vehicles and other listed property.
- Form 4684 to report a casualty or theft gain or loss involving farm business property, including purchased livestock held for draft, breeding, sport, or dairy purposes. See Pub. 225 for more information on how to report various farm losses, such as losses due to death of livestock or damage to crops or other farm property.

- Form 4797 to report sales, exchanges, or involuntary conversions (other than from a casualty or theft) of certain farm property. Also use this form to report sales of livestock held for draft, breeding, sport, or dairy purposes.
- Form 4835 to report rental income based on crop or livestock shares produced by a tenant if you did not materially participate in the management or operation of a farm. This income is not subject to self-employment tax. See Pub. 225.
- Form 6198 to figure your allowable loss if you have a business loss and you have amounts invested in the business for which you are not at risk.
- Form 8582 to figure your allowable loss from passive activities.
- Form 8824 to report like-kind exchanges.
- Form 8903 to take a deduction for income from domestic production activities.

Single-member limited liability company (LLC). Generally, a single-member domestic LLC is not treated as a separate entity for federal income tax purposes. If you are the sole member of a domestic LLC engaged in the business of farming, file Schedule F (Form 1040). However, you can elect to treat a domestic LLC as a corporation. See Form 8832 for details on the election.

Heavy highway vehicle use tax. If you use certain highway trucks, truck-trailers, tractor trailers, or buses in your farming business, you may have to pay a federal highway motor vehicle use tax. See the Instructions for Form 2290 to find out if you owe this tax and go to *www.irs.gov/trucker* for the latest developments.

Information returns. You may have to file information returns for wages paid to employees, certain payments of fees and other nonemployee compensation, interest, rents, royalties, real estate transactions, annuities, and pensions. For details, see *Line F*, later, and the 2014 General Instructions for Certain Information Returns.

If you received cash of more than $10,000 in one or more related transactions in your farming business, you may have to file Form 8300. For details, see Pub. 1544.

Reportable transaction disclosure statement. If you entered into a reportable transaction in 2014, you must file Form 8886 to disclose information if your federal income tax liability is affected by your participation in the transaction. You may have to pay a penalty if you are required to file Form 8886 but do not do so. You may also have to pay interest and penalties on any reportable transaction understatements. For more information on reportable transactions, see the Instructions for Form 8886.

Farm Owned and Operated By Spouses

If you and your spouse jointly own and operate a farm as an unincorporated business and share in the profits and losses, you can be taxed as a partnership and file Form 1065, or you each can file Schedule F (Form 1040) as a qualified joint venture.

Qualified Joint Venture

If you and your spouse each materially participate as the only members of a jointly owned and operated farm, and you file a joint return for the tax year, you can elect to be treated as a qualified joint venture instead of a partnership. This election in most cases will not increase the total tax owed on the joint return, but it does give each of you credit for social security earnings on which retirement benefits are based and for Medicare coverage without filing a partnership return. For an explanation of "material participation," see the instructions for Schedule C (Form 1040), line G, and *Line E*, later, in these instructions.

Making the election. To make this election, you must divide all items of income, gain, loss, deduction, and credit attributable to the farming business between you and your spouse in accordance with your respective interests in the venture. Each of you must file a separate Schedule F (Form 1040). On each line of your separate Schedule F (Form 1040), you must enter your share of the applicable income, deduction, or loss. Each of you must also file a separate Schedule SE (Form 1040) to pay self-employment tax, as applicable.

As long as you remain qualified, your election cannot be revoked without IRS consent.

For more information on qualified joint ventures, go to IRS.gov and enter "qualified joint venture" in the search box.

Exception—Community Income

If you and your spouse wholly own an unincorporated farming business as community property under the community property laws of a state, foreign country, or U.S. possession, you can treat your wholly-owned, unincorporated business as a sole proprietorship, instead of a partnership. Any change in your reporting position will be treated as a conversion of the entity.

Report your income and deductions as follows.
* If only one spouse participates in the business, all of the income from that business is the self-employment earnings of the spouse who carried on the business.
* If both spouses participate, the income and deductions are allocated to the spouses based on their distributive shares.
* If either or both you and your spouse are partners in a partnership, see Pub. 541.
* If you and your spouse elected to treat the business as a qualifying joint venture, see *Qualified Joint Venture*, earlier, for how to report income and deductions.

The only states with community property laws are Arizona, California, Idaho, Louisiana, Nevada, New Mexico, Texas, Washington, and Wisconsin.

Estimated Tax

If you had to make estimated tax payments for 2014, and you underpaid your estimated tax, you will not be charged a penalty if both of the following apply.
* Your gross farming or fishing income for 2013 or 2014 is at least two-thirds of your gross income, and
* You file your 2014 tax return and pay the tax due by March 2, 2015.

For details, see chapter 15 of Pub. 225.

Specific Instructions

Filers of Forms 1041, 1065, and 1065-B. Do not complete the block labeled "Social security number (SSN)." Instead, enter the employer identification number (EIN) issued to the estate, trust, or partnership on line D.

Line B

On line B, enter one of the 14 principal agricultural activity codes listed in Part IV on page 2 of Schedule F (Form 1040). Select the code that best describes the source of most of your income.

Line C

If you use the cash method, check the box for "Cash." Complete Schedule F (Form 1040), Parts I and II. In most cases, report income in the year in which you actually or constructively received it and deduct expenses in the year you paid them. However, if the payment of an expenditure creates an asset having a useful life that extends substantially beyond the close of the year, it may not be deductible or may be deductible only in part for the year of the payment. See chapter 2 of Pub. 225.

If you use an accrual method, check the box for "Accrual." Complete Schedule F (Form 1040), Parts II, III, and Part I, line 9. Generally, report income in the year in which you earned it and deduct expenses in the year you incurred them, even if you did not pay them in that year. Accrual basis taxpayers are put on a cash basis for deducting business expenses owed to a related cash-basis taxpayer. Other rules determine the timing of deductions based on economic performance. See Pub. 538.

Farming syndicates. Farming syndicates cannot use the cash method of accounting. A farming syndicate may be a partnership, LLC, S corporation, or any other enterprise other than a C corporation if:
* The interests in the business have at any time been offered for sale in a way that would require registration with any federal or state agency, or
* More than 35% of the losses during any tax year are allocable to limited partners or limited entrepreneurs. A limited partner is one who can lose only the amount invested or required to be invested in the partnership. A limited entrepreneur is a person who does not take any active part in managing the business.

Line D

Enter on line D the employer identification number (EIN) that was issued to you on Form SS-4. Do not enter your SSN. Do not enter another taxpayer's EIN (for example, from any Forms 1099-MISC that you received). **If you do not have an EIN, leave line D blank.**

You need an EIN only if you have a qualified retirement plan or are required to file employment, excise, alcohol, tobacco, or firearms returns, or if you are a payer of gambling winnings. If you need an EIN, see the Instructions for Form SS-4.

Single-member LLCs. If you are a sole owner of an LLC that is not treated as a separate entity for federal income tax purposes, you may have an EIN that was issued to the LLC (and in the LLC's legal name) if you are required to file employment tax returns and certain excise tax returns. However, you should **enter on line D only the EIN issued to you and in your name as the sole proprietor of your farming business.** If you do not have such an EIN, leave line D blank. Do not enter on line D the EIN issued to the LLC.

Single-member limited liability companies (LLCs) with employees. Single-member LLCs that are disregarded as entities separate from their owner for federal tax purposes are required to file employment tax returns using the LLC's name and employer identification number (EIN) rather than the LLC owner's name and EIN. For more information, see the Instructions for Form SS-4.

Filers of Forms 1041, 1065, and 1065-B. Enter on line D the EIN issued to the estate, trust, or partnership.

Line E

Material participation. For the definition of material participation for purposes of the passive activity rules, see the instructions for Schedule C (Form 1040), line G. If you meet any of the material participation tests described in those instructions, check the "Yes" box.

If you are a retired or disabled farmer, you are treated as materially participating in a farming business if you materially participated 5 or more of the 8 years preceding your retirement or disability. Also, a surviving spouse is treated as materially participating in a farming activity if he or she actively manages the farm and the real property used for farming meets the estate tax rules for special valuation of farm property passed from a qualifying decedent.

Check the "No" box if you did not materially participate. If you checked "No" and you have a loss from this business, see _Limit on passive losses_, next. If you have a profit from this business activity but have current year losses from other passive activities or prior year unallowed passive activity losses, see the Instructions for Form 8582.

Limit on passive losses. If you checked the "No" box and you have a loss from this business, you may have to use Form 8582 to figure your allowable loss, if any, to enter on Schedule F (Form 1040), line 34. In most cases, you can deduct losses from passive activities only to the extent of income from passive activities. For details, see Pub. 925.

Line F

If you made any payments in 2014 that would require you to file any Forms 1099, check the "Yes" box. Otherwise, check the "No" box. See the 2014 General Instructions for Certain Information Returns if you are unsure whether you are required to file any Forms 1099. Also see the separate specific instructions for each Form 1099.

 Generally, you must file Form 1099-MISC if you paid at least $600 in rents, services, prizes, medical and health care payments, and other income payments. The Guide to Information Returns _in the 2014 General Instructions for Certain Information Returns has more information, including the due dates for the various information returns._

Part I. Farm Income—Cash Method

In Part I, show income received for items listed on lines 1 through 8. In most cases, include both the cash actually or constructively received and the fair market value of goods or other property received for these items. Income is constructively received when it is credited to your account or set aside for you to use. However, direct payments or counter-cyclical payments received under the Food, Conservation, and Energy Act of 2008 and counter-cyclical payments, price loss coverage payments or agricultural risk coverage payments received under the Agricultural Act of 2014 are required to be included in income only in the year of actual receipt.

If you ran the farm yourself and received rents based on crop shares or farm production, report these rents as income on line 2.

Sales of livestock because of weather-related conditions. If you sold livestock because of drought, flood, or other weather-related conditions, you can elect to report the income from the sale in the year after the year of sale if all of the following apply.

- Your main business is farming.
- You can show that you sold the livestock only because of weather-related conditions.
- Your area qualified for federal aid.

See chapter 3 of Pub. 225 for details.

Chapter 11 bankruptcy. If you were a debtor in a chapter 11 bankruptcy case during 2014, see _Chapter 11 Bankruptcy Cases_ in the Instructions for Form 1040 (under _Income_) and the Instructions for Schedule SE (Form 1040).

Forms 1099 or CCC-1099-G. If you received Forms 1099 or CCC-1099-G showing amounts paid to you, first determine if the amounts are to be included with farm income. Then use the following chart to determine where to report the income on Schedule F (Form 1040). Include the Form 1099 or CCC-1099-G amounts in the total amount reported on that line.

Form	Where to report
1099-PATR	Line 3a
1099-A	Line 5b
1099-MISC for crop insurance	Line 6a
1099-G or CCC-1099-G	
• for disaster payments	Line 6a
• for other agricultural program payments	Line 4a

You may receive Form 1099-MISC for other types of income. In this case, report it on whichever line best describes the income. For example, if you receive a Form 1099-MISC for custom farming work, include this amount on line 7.

Lines 3a and 3b

If you received distributions from a cooperative in 2014, you should receive a Form 1099-PATR. On line 3a, show your total distributions from cooperatives. This includes patronage dividends, nonpatronage distributions, per-unit retain allocations, and redemptions of nonqualified written notices of allocation and per-unit retain certificates.

Show patronage dividends received in cash and the dollar amount of qualified written notices of allocation. If you received property as patronage dividends, report the fair market value of the property as income. Include cash advances received from a marketing cooperative. If you received per-unit retains in cash, show the amount of cash. If you received qualified per-unit retain certificates, show the stated dollar amount of the certificates.

Do not include as income on line 3b patronage dividends from buying personal or family items, capital assets, or depreciable assets. Enter these amounts on line 3a only. Because you do not report patronage dividends from these items as income, you must subtract the amount of the dividend from the cost or other basis of these items.

Lines 4a and 4b

Enter on line 4a the total of the following amounts.
   • Direct payments.
   • Counter-cyclical payments.
   • Price loss coverage payments.
   • Agriculture risk coverage payments.
   • Price support payments.
   • Market gain from the repayment of a secured Commodity Credit Corporation (CCC) loan for less than the original loan amount.
   • Diversion payments.
   • Cost-share payments (sight drafts).
   • Payments in the form of materials (such as fertilizer or lime) or services (such as grading or building dams).

These amounts are government payments you received and are usually reported to you on Form 1099-G. You may also receive Form CCC-1099-G from the Department of Agriculture showing the amounts and types of payments made to you.

On line 4b, report only the taxable amount. For example, do not report the market gain shown on Form CCC-1099-G on line 4b if you elected to report CCC loan proceeds as income in the year received (see *Lines 5a Through 5c*, next). No gain results from redemption of the commodity because you previously reported the CCC loan proceeds as income. You are treated as repurchasing the commodity for the amount of the loan repayment. However, if you did not report the CCC loan proceeds under the election, you must report the market gain on line 4b.

If you received a direct or counter-cyclical payment in 2014, your farm losses may be reduced. See *Excess farm loss rules* in *Line 35,* later, for more details.

Lines 5a Through 5c

Commodity Credit Corporation (CCC) loans. In most cases, you do not report CCC loan proceeds as income. However, if you pledge part or all of your production to secure a CCC loan, you can elect to report the loan proceeds as income in the year you receive them. If you make this election (or made the election in a prior year), report loan proceeds you received in 2014 on line 5a. Attach a statement to your return showing the details of the loan(s). See chapter 3 of Pub. 225.

Forfeited CCC loans. Include the full amount forfeited on line 5b, even if you reported the loan proceeds as income. This amount may be reported to you on Form 1099-A.

If you did not elect to report the loan proceeds as income, also include the forfeited amount on line 5c.

If you did elect to report the loan proceeds as income, you generally will not have an entry on line 5c. But if the amount forfeited is different from your basis in the commodity, you may have an entry on line 5c.

See chapter 3 of Pub. 225 for details on the tax consequences of electing to report CCC loan proceeds as income or forfeiting CCC loans.

If you received a CCC loan in 2014, your farm losses may be reduced. See *Excess farm loss rules* in *Line 35,* later, for more details.

Lines 6a Through 6d

In most cases, you must report crop insurance proceeds in the year you receive them. Federal crop disaster payments are treated as crop insurance proceeds. However, if 2014 was the year of damage, you can elect to include certain proceeds in income for 2015. To make this election, check the box on line 6c and attach a statement to your return. See chapter 3 of Pub. 225 for a description of the proceeds for which an election can be made and for what you must include in your statement.

If you elect to defer any eligible crop insurance proceeds, you must defer all such crop insurance proceeds (including federal crop disaster payments) from a single trade or business.

Enter on line 6a the total crop insurance proceeds you received in 2014, even if you elect to include them in income for 2015.

Enter on line 6b the taxable amount of the proceeds you received in 2014. Do not include proceeds you elect to include in income for 2015.

Enter on line 6d the amount, if any, of crop insurance proceeds you received in 2013 and elected to include in income for 2014.

Line 8

Enter on line 8 income not otherwise reportable on lines 1 through 7. This includes the following types of income.

* Illegal federal irrigation subsidies. See chapter 3 of Pub. 225.
* Bartering income.
* Income from cancellation of debt. In most cases, if a debt is canceled or forgiven, you must include the canceled amount in income. If a federal agency, financial institution, or credit union canceled or forgave a debt you owed of $600 or more, it should send you a Form 1099-C, or similar statement, by January 31, 2015, showing the amount of debt canceled in 2014. However, you may be able to exclude the canceled debt from income. See Pub. 4681 for details.
* State gasoline or fuel tax refunds you received in 2014.
* Any amount included in income from line 2 of Form 6478, Biofuel Producer Credit.
* Any amount included in income from line 8 of Form 8864, Biodiesel and Renewable Diesel Fuels Credit.
* The amount of credit for federal tax paid on fuels claimed on your 2013 Form 1040. For information on including the credit in income, see chapter 2 of Pub. 510.
* Any recapture of excess depreciation on any listed property, including any section 179 expense deduction, if the business use percentage of that property decreased to 50% or less in 2014. Use Part IV of Form 4797 to figure the recapture. See the instructions for Schedule C (Form 1040), line 13, for the definition of listed property.
* The inclusion amount on leased listed property (other than vehicles) when the business use percentage drops to 50% or less. See chapter 5 of Pub. 946 to figure the amount.
* Any recapture of the deduction or credit for clean-fuel vehicle refueling property or alternative fuel vehicle refueling property used in your farming business. For details on how to figure recapture, see Regulations section 1.179A-1.
* Any income from breeding fees, or fees from renting teams, machinery, or land that is not reported on Schedule E (Form 1040) or Form 4835.
* The gain or loss on the sale of commodity futures contracts if the contracts were made to protect you from price changes. These are a form of business insurance and are considered hedges. If you had a loss in a closed futures contract, enclose the amount of the loss in parentheses.

 *For property acquired and hedging positions established, you must clearly identify on your books and records both the hedging transaction and the item(s) or aggregate risk being hedged.*

Purchase or sales contracts are not true hedges if they offset losses that already occurred. If you bought or sold commodity futures with the hope of making a profit due to favorable price changes, report the profit or loss on Form 6781 instead of this line.

Part II. Farm Expenses

Do not deduct the following.
* Personal or living expenses (such as taxes, insurance, or repairs on your home) that do not produce farm income.
* Expenses of raising anything you or your family used.
* The value of animals you raised that died.
* Inventory losses.
* Personal losses.

If you were repaid for any part of an expense, you must subtract the amount you were repaid from the deduction.

Capitalizing costs of property. If you produced real or tangible personal property or acquired property for resale, certain expenses must be included in inventory costs or capitalized. These expenses include the direct costs of the property and the share of any indirect costs allocable to that property. However, these rules generally do not apply to expenses of:

1. Producing any plant that has a preproductive period of 2 years or less,

2. Raising animals, or

3. Replanting certain crops if they were lost or damaged by reason of freezing temperatures, disease, drought, pests, or casualty.

 Exceptions (1) and (2) do not apply to tax shelters, farming syndicates, partnerships, or corporations required to use the accrual method of accounting under section 447 or 448(a)(3).

If you capitalize your expenses, do not reduce your deductions on lines 10 through 32e by the capitalized expenses. Instead, enter the total amount capitalized in parentheses on line 32f (to indicate a negative amount) and enter "263A" in the space to the left of the total. See *Preproductive period expenses*, later, for details.

But you may be able to currently deduct rather than capitalize the expenses of producing a plant with a preproductive period of more than 2 years. See *Election to deduct certain preproductive period expenses*, next.

Election to deduct certain preproductive period expenses. If the preproductive period of any plant you produce is more than 2 years, you can elect to currently deduct the expenses rather than capitalize them. But you cannot make this election for the costs of planting or growing citrus or almond groves incurred before the end of the fourth tax year beginning with the tax year you planted them in their permanent grove. You are treated as having made the election by deducting the preproductive period expenses in the first tax year for which you can make this election and by applying the special rules, discussed later.

In the case of a partnership or S corporation, the election must be made by the partner, shareholder, or member. This election cannot be made by tax shelters, farming syndicates, partnerships, or corporations required to use the accrual method of accounting under section 447 or 448(a)(3).

Unless you obtain IRS consent, you must make this election for the first tax year in which you engage in a farming business involving the production of property subject to the capitalization rules. You cannot revoke this election without IRS consent.

Special rules. If you make the election to deduct preproductive expenses for plants:
* Any gain you realize when disposing of the plants is ordinary income up to the amount of the preproductive expenses you deducted, and
* The alternative depreciation rules apply to property placed in service in any tax year your election is in effect.

For details, see *Uniform Capitalization Rules* in chapter 6 of Pub. 225.

Prepaid farm supplies. In most cases, if you use the cash method of accounting and your prepaid farm supplies are more than 50% of your other deductible farm expenses, your deduction for those supplies may be limited. Prepaid farm supplies include expenses for feed, seed, fertilizer, and similar farm supplies not used or consumed during the year.

They also include the cost of poultry that would be allowable as a deduction in a later tax year if you were to:

1. Capitalize the cost of poultry bought for use in your farming business and deduct it ratably over the lesser of 12 months or the useful life of the poultry, and

2. Deduct the cost of poultry bought for resale in the year you sell or otherwise dispose of it.

If the limit applies, you can deduct prepaid farm supplies that do not exceed 50% of your other deductible farm expenses in the year of payment. You can deduct the excess only in the year you use or consume the supplies (other than poultry, which is deductible as explained above). For details and exceptions to these rules, see chapter 4 of Pub. 225.

Whether or not this 50% limit applies, your expenses for livestock feed paid during the year but consumed in a later year may be subject to the rules explained in the line 16 instructions.

Line 10

You can deduct the actual expenses of operating your car or truck or take the standard mileage rate. You must use actual expenses if you used five or more vehicles simultaneously in your farming business (such as in fleet operations). You cannot use actual expenses for a leased vehicle if you previously used the standard mileage rate for that vehicle.

You can take the standard mileage rate for 2014 only if you:
* Owned the vehicle and used the standard mileage rate for the first year you placed the vehicle in service, or
* Leased the vehicle and are using the standard mileage rate for the entire lease period.

If you take the standard mileage rate:
* Multiply the number of business miles driven by 56 cents, and
* Add to this amount your parking fees and tolls, and enter the total on line 10.

Do not deduct depreciation, rent or lease payments, or your actual operating expenses.

If you deduct actual expenses:
* Include on line 10 the business portion of expenses for gasoline, oil, repairs, insurance, license plates, etc., and
* Show depreciation on line 14 and rent or lease payments on line 24a.

If you claim any car or truck expenses (actual or the standard mileage rate), you must provide the information requested on Form 4562, Part V. Be sure to attach Form 4562 to your return.

For details, see chapter 4 of Pub. 463.

Line 12

Deductible conservation expenses generally are those that are paid to conserve soil and water for land used in farming, to prevent erosion of land used for farming, or for endangered species recovery. These expenses include (but are not limited to) costs for the following.
* The treatment or movement of earth, such as leveling, grading, conditioning, terracing, contour furrowing, and the restoration of soil fertility.
* The construction, control, and protection of diversion channels, drainage ditches, irrigation ditches, earthen dams, watercourses, outlets, and ponds.
* The eradication of brush.
* The planting of windbreaks.
* The achievement of site-specific management actions recommended in recovery plans approved pursuant to the Endangered Species Act of 1973.

These expenses can be deducted only if they are consistent with a conservation plan approved by the Natural Resources Conservation Service of the Department of Agriculture or a recovery plan approved pursuant to the Endangered Species Act of 1973, for the area in which your land is located. If no plan exists, the expenses must be consistent with a plan of a comparable state agency. You cannot deduct the expenses if they were paid or incurred for land used in farming in a foreign country.

Do not deduct expenses you paid or incurred to drain or fill wetlands, or to prepare land for center pivot irrigation systems.

Your deduction cannot exceed 25% of your gross income from farming (excluding certain gains from selling assets such as farm machinery and land). If your conservation expenses are more than the limit, the excess can be carried forward and deducted in later tax years. However, the amount deductible for any one year cannot exceed the 25% gross income limit for that year.

For details, see chapter 5 of Pub. 225.

Line 13

Enter amounts paid for custom hire or machine work (the machine operator furnished the equipment).

Do not include amounts paid for rental or lease of equipment you operated yourself. Instead, report those amounts on line 24a.

Line 14

You can deduct depreciation of buildings, improvements, cars and trucks, machinery, and other farm equipment of a permanent nature.

Do not deduct depreciation on your home, furniture or other personal items, land, livestock you bought or raised for resale, or other property in your inventory.

You can also elect under section 179 to expense a portion of the cost of certain property you bought in 2014 for use in your farming business. The section 179 election is made on Form 4562.

For information about depreciation and the section 179 deduction, see Pub. 946 and chapter 7 of Pub. 225. For details on the special depreciation allowance, see chapter 3 of Pub. 946.

See the Instructions for Form 4562 for information on when you must complete and attach Form 4562.

Line 15

Deduct contributions to employee benefit programs that are not an incidental part of a pension or profit sharing plan included on line 23. Examples are accident and health plans, group-term life insurance, and dependent care assistance programs. If you made contributions on your behalf as a self-employed person to a dependent care assistance program, complete Form 2441, Parts I and III, to figure your deductible contributions to that program.

Contributions you made on your behalf as a self-employed person to an accident and health plan or for group-term life insurance are not deductible on Schedule F (Form 1040). However, you may be able to deduct on Form 1040, line 29 (or on Form 1040NR, line 29), the amount you paid for health insurance on behalf of yourself, your spouse, and dependent(s) even if you do not itemize your deductions. See the instructions for Form 1040, line 29, or Form 1040NR, line 29, for details.

You must reduce your line 15 deduction by the amount of any credit for small employer health insurance premiums determined on Form 8941. See Form 8941 and its instructions to determine which expenses are eligible for the credit.

Line 16

If you use the cash method, you cannot deduct when paid the cost of feed your livestock will consume in a later year unless all of the following apply.

• The payment was for the purchase of feed rather than a deposit.

• The prepayment had a business purpose and was not made merely to avoid tax.

• Deducting the prepayment will not materially distort your income.

If all of the above apply, you can deduct the prepaid feed when paid, subject to the overall limit for *Prepaid farm supplies* explained earlier. If all of the above do not apply, you can deduct the prepaid feed only in the year it is consumed.

Line 18

Do not include the cost of transportation incurred in purchasing livestock held for resale as freight paid. Instead, add these costs to the cost of the livestock.

Line 20

Deduct on this line premiums paid for farm business insurance. Deduct on line 15 amounts paid for employee accident and health insurance. Amounts credited to a reserve for self-insurance or premiums paid for a policy that pays for your lost earnings due to sickness or disability are not deductible. For details, see chapter 6 of Pub. 535.

Lines 21a and 21b

Interest allocation rules. The tax treatment of interest expense differs depending on its type. For example, home mortgage interest and investment interest are treated differently. "Interest allocation" rules require you to allocate (classify) your interest expense so it is deducted (or capitalized) on the correct line of your return and receives the right tax treatment. These rules could affect how much interest you are allowed to deduct on Schedule F (Form 1040).

In most cases, you allocate interest expense by tracing how the proceeds of the loan are used. See chapter 4 of Pub. 535 for details.

If you paid interest on a debt secured by your main home and any of the proceeds from that debt were used in your farming business, see chapter 4 of Pub. 535 to figure the amount to include on lines 21a and 21b.

How to report. If you have a mortgage on real property used in your farming business (other than your main home), enter on line 21a the interest you paid for 2014 to banks or other financial institutions for which you received a Form 1098 (or similar statement). If you did not receive a Form 1098, enter the interest on line 21b.

If you paid more mortgage interest than is shown on Form 1098, see chapter 4 of Pub. 535 to find out if you can deduct the additional interest. If you can, include the amount on line 21a. Attach a statement to your return explaining the difference and enter "See attached" in the margin next to line 21a.

If you and at least one other person (other than your spouse if you file a joint return) were liable for and paid interest on the mortgage and the other person received the Form 1098, include your share of the interest on line 21b. Attach a statement to your return showing the name and address of the person who received the Form 1098. In the margin next to line 21b, enter "See attached."

Do not deduct interest you prepaid in 2014 for later years; include only the part that applies to 2014.

Line 22

Enter the amounts you paid for farm labor. Do not include amounts paid to yourself. Reduce your deduction by the amounts claimed on Form 5884, Work Opportunity Credit, line 2.

Include the cost of boarding farm labor but not the value of any products they used from the farm. Include only what you paid household help to care for farm laborers.

 If you provided taxable fringe benefits to your employees, such as personal use of a car, do not include in farm labor the amounts you depreciated or deducted elsewhere.

Line 23

Enter your deduction for contributions to employee pension, profit-sharing, or annuity plans. If the plan included you as a self-employed person, enter contributions made as an employer on your behalf on Form 1040, line 28 (or on Form 1040NR, line 28), not on Schedule F (Form 1040).

In most cases, you must file the applicable form listed next if you maintain a pension, profit-sharing, or other funded-deferred compensation plan. The filing requirement is not affected by whether or not the plan qualified under the Internal Revenue Code, or whether or not you claim a deduction for the current tax year. There is a penalty for failure to timely file these forms.

Form 5500-EZ. File this form if you have a one-participant retirement plan that meets certain requirements. A one-participant plan is a plan that covers only you (or you and your spouse).

Form 5500-SF. File this form electronically with the Department of Labor (at _www.efast.dol.gov_) if you have a small plan (fewer than 100 participants in most cases) that meets certain requirements.

Form 5500. File this form electronically with the Department of Labor (at _www.efast.dol.gov_) for a plan that does not meet the requirements for filing Form 5500-EZ or Form 5500-SF.

For details, see Pub. 560.

Lines 24a and 24b

If you rented or leased vehicles, machinery, or equipment, enter on line 24a the business portion of your rental cost. But if you leased a vehicle for a term of 30 days or more, you may have to reduce your deduction by an inclusion amount. See _Leasing a Car_ in chapter 4 of Pub. 463 to figure this amount.

Enter on line 24b amounts paid to rent or lease other property such as pasture or farmland.

Line 25

Enter amounts you paid for incidental repairs and maintenance of farm buildings, machinery, and equipment that do not add to the property's value or appreciably prolong its life.

Do not deduct repairs or maintenance on your home.

Line 29

You can deduct the following taxes on this line.
- Real estate and personal property taxes on farm business assets.
- Social security and Medicare taxes you paid to match what you are required to withhold from farm employees' wages.
- Federal unemployment tax.
- Federal highway use tax.
- Contributions to state unemployment insurance fund or disability benefit fund if they are considered taxes under state law.

Do not deduct the following taxes on this line.
- Federal income taxes, including your self-employment tax. However, you can deduct one-half of self-employment tax on Form 1040, line 27 or Form 1040NR, line 27.
- Estate and gift taxes.
- Taxes assessed for improvements, such as paving and sewers.
- Taxes on your home or personal use property.
- State and local sales taxes on property purchased for use in your farming business. Instead, treat these taxes as part of the cost of the property.
- Other taxes not related to your farming business.

Line 30

Enter amounts you paid for gas, electricity, water, and other utilities for business use on the farm. Do not include personal utilities. You cannot deduct the base rate (including taxes) of the first telephone line into your residence, even if you use it for your farming business. But you can deduct expenses you paid for your farming business that are more than the cost of the base rate for the first phone line. For example, if you had a second phone line, you can deduct the business percentage of the charges for that line, including the base rate charges.

Lines 32a Through 32f

Include all ordinary and necessary farm expenses not deducted elsewhere on Schedule F (Form 1040), such as advertising, office supplies, etc. Do not include fines or penalties paid to a government for violating any law.

At-risk loss deduction. Any loss from this activity that was not allowed last year because of the at-risk rules is treated as a deduction allocable to this activity in 2014.

Bad debts. See chapter 10 of Pub. 535.

Business start-up costs. If your farming business began in 2014, you can elect to deduct up to $5,000 of certain business start-up costs. The $5,000 limit is reduced (but not below zero) by the amount by which your start-up costs exceed $50,000. Your remaining start-up costs can be amortized over a 180-month period, beginning with the month the farming business began. For details, see chapters 4 and 7 of Pub. 225. For amortization that begins in 2014, you must complete and attach Form 4562.

Business use of your home. You may be able to deduct certain expenses for business use of your home, subject to limitations. You may also be able to use a simplified method to figure your deduction. Use the appropriate worksheets in Pub. 587 to figure your allowable deduction. Do not use Form 8829.

Excess farm loss deduction. Any loss from this activity that was not allowed last year because of the excess farm loss rules is treated as a deduction allocable to this activity in 2014.

Forestation and reforestation costs. Reforestation costs are generally capital expenditures. However, for each qualified timber property, you can elect to expense up to $10,000 ($5,000 if married filing separately) of qualifying reforestation costs paid or incurred in 2014.

You can elect to amortize the remaining costs over 84 months. For amortization that begins in 2014, you must complete and attach Form 4562.

The amortization election does not apply to trusts, and the expense election does not apply to estates and trusts. For details on reforestation expenses, see chapters 4 and 7 of Pub. 225.

Legal and professional fees. You can include on this line fees charged by accountants and attorneys that are ordinary and necessary expenses directly related to your farming business. Include fees for tax advice and for the preparation of tax forms related to your farming business. Also include expenses incurred in resolving asserted tax deficiencies related to your farming business.

Tools. You can deduct the amount you paid for tools that have a short life or cost a small amount, such as shovels and rakes.

Travel, meals, and entertainment. In most cases, you can deduct expenses for farm business travel and 50% of your business meals and entertainment. But there are exceptions and limitations. See the instructions for Schedule C (Form 1040), lines 24a and 24b.

Preproductive period expenses. If you had preproductive period expenses in 2014 that you are capitalizing, enter the total of these expenses in parentheses on line 32f (to indicate a negative amount) and enter "263A" in the space to the left of the total.

For details, see *Capitalizing costs of property*, earlier, and *Uniform Capitalization Rules* in chapter 6 of Pub. 225.

Line 33

If line 32f is a negative amount, subtract it from the total of lines 10 through 32e. Enter the result on line 33.

Line 34

Figuring your net profit or allowable loss. If line 33 is more than line 9, do not enter your loss on line 34 until you have applied the excess farm loss rules, the at-risk rules, and the passive activity loss rules. To apply these rules, follow the instructions for lines 35 and 36, and the Instructions for Form 8582. After applying these rules, the amount on line 34 will be your allowable loss, and it may be smaller than the amount figured by subtracting line 33 from line 9.

If line 9 is more than line 33, and you do not have prior year unallowed passive activity losses, subtract line 33 from line 9. The result is your net profit.

If line 9 is more than line 33, and you have prior year unallowed passive activity losses, do not enter your net profit on line 34 until you have figured the amount of prior year unallowed passive activity losses you may claim this year for this activity. Use Form 8582 to figure the amount of prior year unallowed passive activity losses you may include on line 34. Make sure to indicate that you are including prior year passive activity losses by entering "PAL" to the left of the entry space.

If you checked the "No" box on line E, see the Instructions for Form 8582; you may need to include information from this schedule on that form, even if you have a net profit.

Partnerships. Subtract line 33 from line 9. If the amount is a loss, the partners may need to apply the excess farm loss rules, the at-risk rules, and the passive activity loss rules to determine the amount of their allowable loss.

Reporting your net profit or allowable loss. Once you have figured your net profit or allowable loss, report it as follows.

Individuals. Enter your net profit or allowable loss on line 34 and on Form 1040, line 18, and Schedule SE (Form 1040), line 1a.

Nonresident aliens. Enter the net profit or allowable loss on line 34 and on Form 1040NR, line 19. You should also enter this amount on Schedule SE (Form 1040), line 1a if you are covered under the U.S. social security system due to an international social security agreement currently in effect. See the Instructions for Schedule SE (Form 1040) for information on international social security agreements.

Partnerships. Enter the net profit or loss on line 34 and on Form 1065, line 5 (or Form 1065-B, line 7). Because the excess farm loss rules are applied at the partner level, the partnership will notify each partner on the Schedule K-1 if the partnership received one of the subsidies discussed later. Each partner should complete one of the excess farm loss worksheets to determine if there is an excess farm loss.

Trusts and estates. Enter the net profit or allowable loss on line 34 and on Form 1041, line 6.

Community income. If you and your spouse had community income and are filing separate returns, see the Instructions for Schedule SE (Form 1040) before figuring self-employment tax.

Earned income credit. If you have a net profit on line 34, this amount is earned income and may qualify you for the earned income credit if you meet certain conditions. See the instructions for Form 1040, lines 66a and 66b, for details.

Conservation Reserve Program (CRP) payments. If you received social security retirement or disability benefits in addition to CRP payments, the CRP payments are not subject to self-employment tax. You will deduct these payments from your net farm profit or loss on Schedule SE (Form 1040), line 1b. Do not make any adjustment on Schedule F (Form 1040).

Line 35

Answer line 35 with respect to your <u>farming business</u> (defined later), and not just for the farming activities reported on this Schedule F. You may also have reported farming activities on another Schedule F or on Form 4835.

Check the "Yes" box if you received one of the following subsidies in 2014.
- Any direct or counter-cyclical payments under title I of the Food, Conservation, and Energy Act of 2008 (or any payment you elected instead of this payment).
- Any Commodity Credit Corporation loan.

You are considered to have received one of these subsidies in 2014 if you are a partner or shareholder in a partnership or S corporation that received one of these subsidies during 2014. Check the "No" box if you did not receive one of these subsidies in 2014.

If you checked the "Yes" box, your farm loss may be reduced. You must apply the excess farm loss rules, discussed next.

 If you checked the "No" box, you do not have excess farm loss.

Excess farm loss rules. If you received one of the subsidies listed above, part of your loss may be excess farm loss. Excess farm loss is not an allowable loss. Instead, excess farm loss is carried forward to the next year and treated as a deduction.

Your excess farm loss for a year is the amount by which your total deductions from your farming businesses exceed your total gross income or gain from your farming businesses, plus a threshold amount. The threshold amount is the greater of $300,000 ($150,000 if your filing status is married filing separately) or your total net profit or loss from farming businesses for the last five years (2009 - 2013), including for each of those years any net gain from the sale of property used in your farming businesses.

Farming business defined. A farming business generally is the trade or business of farming, including operating a nursery or sod farm or raising or harvesting of trees bearing fruit, nuts, or other crops, or ornamental trees, such as evergreen trees, if they are cut within the first 6 years.

For purposes of calculating your excess farm loss for the year, a farm business also includes the following.
- A trade or business of processing a farm commodity, even if it is not incidental to your farm.
- Participating in a cooperative that processes a farm commodity.
- Any interest in a partnership or S corporation involved in a farming business.

Figuring your excess farm loss. To figure your excess farm loss, you can use one of the excess farm loss worksheets, later. You may need to adjust your income or deductions before figuring your excess farm loss.

If you file multiple copies of Schedule F (Form 1040), Schedule C (Form 1040), or Schedule E (Form 1040) as part of your farming businesses, you must combine the income, deductions, and net gain/loss for purposes of determining whether you have an excess farm loss on the worksheets. If you sold any property used in your farming businesses, you must include any gain or loss on the sale of that property (reported on Form 4797, Sales of Business Property, Form 8949, Sales and Other Disposition of Capital Assets, or Schedule D (Form 1040), Capital Gains and Losses). Be sure to include the gain or loss attributable to property used in your <u>farming business</u> (defined earlier). Do not include gain or loss attributable to property used in nonfarming businesses or nonbusiness property.

Activities reported on other forms. Because your farming business includes any trade or business of processing a farm commodity that is not incidental to your farm, you may have farming business activities that are reported on Schedule C (Form 1040) that you must also include when figuring your excess farm loss. Any losses from a farming business activity reported on Schedule C (Form 1040) may be limited by the excess farm loss rules.

Because your farming business includes your interest in a partnership or S corporation, you may have farming business activities that are reported on Schedule E (Form 1040) that you must also include when figuring your excess farm loss. Any losses from a farming business activity reported on Schedule E (Form 1040) may be limited by the excess farm loss rules.

Other deductions that must be included. Certain deductions, including the domestic production activities deduction under section 199 and the deduction for one-half of self-employment tax, may need to be included when determining your excess farm loss if the deductions are attributable to your <u>farming business</u> (defined earlier).

In particular, the deduction for one-half of self-employment tax will not be attributable to your farming business on Schedule F (Form 1040) or your business of processing a farm commodity on Schedule C (Form 1040) if the combined amounts on those schedules produce a loss. But the deduction for one-half of self-employment tax should be taken into account when the combined amounts on those schedules produce income (or the farm optional method on Schedule SE (Form 1040) is used) and there is a large loss on Schedule E (Form 1040) passed through from a partnership or S corporation.

Deductions that are not included. Any deduction for losses arising from fire, storm, or other casualty, or from disease or drought involving any farming business should not be included when determining your excess farm loss.

Coordination with at-risk and passive activity loss rules. You must calculate and apply your excess farm loss before calculating any limits due to the at-risk rules or the passive activity loss rules.

Excess farm loss worksheets. You may complete one of these worksheets to determine if you have an excess farm loss in 2014. Do not attach these worksheets to your return; keep them for your records. You will need them next year when any excess farm loss may be deducted. Which worksheet you should use depends on the nature and extent of your farming business.

- Use Worksheet 1 if your farming businesses include only profit or loss reported on one or more Schedules F (Form 1040).
- Use Worksheet 2 if your farming businesses include Schedule F (Form 1040) and any Schedule C (Form 1040) activity of processing a farm commodity.
- Use Worksheet 3 if your farming businesses include Schedule F (Form 1040) and a Schedule E (Form 1040) interest in a partnership or S corporation involved in a farming business.
- Use Worksheet 4 if your farming businesses include Schedule F (Form 1040), Schedule C (Form 1040) activity of processing a farm commodity, a Schedule E (Form 1040) interest in a partnership or S corporation involved in a farming business, and farm rental income or loss reported on Form 4835.
- Use Worksheet 5 if your farming business is limited to only farm rental income or loss reported on Form 4835.

Applying your excess farm loss. You must reduce your loss by the amount of your excess farm loss. Subtract line 33 from line 9 and reduce the number by your excess farm loss. Complete line 36 before entering an amount on line 34.

Example. Subtracting line 33 from line 9 results in ($400,000). You have only one farming business and use Worksheet 1 to figure an excess farm loss of ($100,000). Your allowable loss is reduced to ($300,000). This will be the amount you enter on line 34 unless the at-risk or passive activity loss rules reduce it further.

Any loss from this activity not allowed for 2014 because of the excess farm loss rules is treated as a deduction allocable to the activity in 2015.

At-risk and passive activity loss rules. Use your loss reduced by the excess farm loss to calculate any further limitations due to the at-risk rules or passive activity loss rules.

More than one farming business. If you have more than one farming business with a loss this year, allocate the excess farm loss amount on a *pro rata* basis among those farming businesses. If you have more than one farming business, but only one has a loss, allocate all of the excess farm loss to the farming business with the loss. Do not allocate excess farm loss to a farming business that has a net profit.

Line 36

 You do not need to complete line 36 if line 9 is more than line 33.

At-risk rules. In most cases, if you have a loss from a farming activity and amounts invested in the activity for which you are not at risk, you must complete Form 6198 to figure your allowable loss. The at-risk rules generally limit the amount of loss (including loss on the disposition of assets) you can claim to the amount you could actually lose in the activity.

Check box 36b if you have amounts invested in this activity for which you are not at risk, such as the following.

- Nonrecourse loans used to finance the activity, to acquire property used in the activity, or to acquire the activity that are not secured by your own property (other than property used in the activity). However, there is an exception for certain nonrecourse financing borrowed by you in connection with holding real property.
- Cash, property, or borrowed amounts used in the activity (or contributed to the activity, or used to acquire the activity) that are protected against loss by a guarantee, stop-loss agreement, or other similar arrangement (excluding casualty insurance and insurance against tort liability).
- Amounts borrowed for use in the activity from a person who has an interest in the activity, other than as a creditor, or who is related under section 465(b)(3)(C) to a person (other than you) having such an interest.

Figuring your allowable loss. Before determining your allowable loss, you must check box 36a or 36b to determine if your loss from farming is limited by the at-risk rules. Follow the instructions below that apply to your box 36 activity.

All investment is at risk. If all your investment amounts are at risk in this activity, check box 36a. If you also checked the "Yes" box on line E, your remaining loss (after applying the excess farm loss rules) is your allowable loss. The at-risk rules and the passive activity loss rules do not apply. See *Line 34*, earlier, for how to report your allowable loss.

But if you checked the "No" box on line E, you may need to complete Form 8582 to figure your allowable loss to enter on line 34. See the Instructions for Form 8582.

Some investment is not at risk. If some investment is not at risk, check box 36b; the at-risk rules apply to your loss. Be sure to attach Form 6198 to your return.

If you also checked the "Yes" box on line E, complete Form 6198 to determine the amount of your allowable loss. The passive activity loss rules do not apply. See *Line 34*, earlier, for how to report your allowable loss.

But if you checked the "No" box on line E, the passive activity loss rules may apply. First complete Form 6198 to figure the amount of your profit or loss for the at-risk activity, which may include amounts reported on other forms and schedules, and the at-risk amount for the activity. Follow the Instructions for Form 6198 to determine how much of your Schedule F loss will be allowed. After you figure the amount of your loss that is allowed under the at-risk rules, you may need to complete Form 8582 to figure the allowable loss to enter on line 34. See the Instructions for Form 8582 for details.

 If you checked box 36b because some investment is not at risk and you do not attach Form 6198, the processing of your return may be delayed.

At-risk loss deduction. Any loss from this activity not allowed for 2014 only because of the at-risk rules is treated as a deduction allocable to the activity in 2015.

More information. For details, see Pub. 925 and the Instructions for Form 6198.

Part III. Farm Income—Accrual Method

You may be required to use the accrual accounting method. If you use the accrual method, report farm income when you earn it, not when you receive it. In most cases, you must include animals and crops in your inventory if you use this method. See Pub. 225 for exceptions, inventory methods, how to change methods of accounting, and rules that require certain costs to be capitalized or included in inventory. For information about accounting periods, see Pub. 538, Accounting Periods and Methods.

Chapter 11 bankruptcy. If you were a debtor in a chapter 11 bankruptcy case during 2014, see *Chapter 11 Bankruptcy Cases* in the Instructions for Form 1040 (under *Income*) and the Instructions for Schedule SE (Form 1040).

Lines 38a Through 40c

See the instructions for lines 3a through 5c.

Line 43

See *Line 8*, earlier.

Paperwork Reduction Act Notice. We ask for the information on this form to carry out the Internal Revenue laws of the United States. You are required to give us the information. We need it to ensure that you are complying with these laws and to allow us to figure and collect the right amount of tax.

You are not required to provide the information requested on a form that is subject to the Paperwork Reduction Act unless the form displays a valid OMB control number. Books or records relating to a form or its instructions must be retained as long as their contents may become material in the administration of any Internal Revenue law. Generally, tax returns and return information are confidential, as required by section 6103.

The time needed to complete and file this form will vary depending on individual circumstances. The estimated burden for individual taxpayers filing this form is included in the estimates shown in the instructions for their individual income tax return. The estimated burden for all other taxpayers who file this form is approved under OMB control number 1545-1975 and is shown next.

Recordkeeping	7 hr., 1 min.
Learning about the law or the form	2 hr., 55 min.
Preparing and sending the form to the IRS	1 hr., 46 min.

If you have comments concerning the accuracy of these time estimates or suggestions for making this form simpler, we would be happy to hear from you. See the instructions for the tax return with which this form is filed.

Excess Farm Loss Worksheet 1—Schedule F (Form 1040) farming business only

 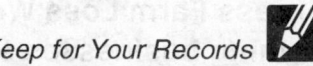

CAUTION: In determining if you have an excess farm loss, do not take into account any deductions for losses arising by reason of fire, storm, or other casualty, or by reason of disease or drought, involving your farming business.

1. Enter the amount from your 2014 Schedule(s) F (Form 1040), line 33. Is this amount less than $300,000 ($150,000 if married filing separately)? If yes, stop here. You do not have an excess farm loss in 2014. If no, continue to line 2 .... 1. _____

2. Subtract $300,000 ($150,000 if married filing separately) from line 1 .... 2. _____

3. Enter the amount from your 2014 Schedule(s) F (Form 1040), line 9 .... 3. _____

4. Is line 3 greater than or equal to line 2? If yes, stop here. You do not have an excess farm loss in 2014. If no, continue to line 5.

5. Enter your net gain/loss from the sale of farming business property reported on Form 4797 .... 5. _____

6. Enter your net gain/loss from the sale of farming business property reported on Form 8949 .... 6. _____

7. Combine line 5 and line 6. If zero or less, enter -0- .... 7. _____

8. Add line 3 and line 7. Is this greater than or equal to line 2? If yes, stop here. You do not have an excess farm loss in 2014. If no, continue to line 9 .... 8. _____

9. Enter the amount from your 2013 Schedule(s) F (Form 1040), line 34 .... 9. _____

10. Enter your combined net gain/loss from the sale of farming business property reported on your 2013 Form 4797 and Form 8949. If zero or less, enter -0- .... 10. _____

11. Enter the amount from your 2012 Schedule(s) F (Form 1040), line 34 .... 11. _____

12. Enter your combined net gain/loss from the sale of farming business property reported on your 2012 Form 4797 and Form 8949. If zero or less, enter -0- .... 12. _____

13. Enter the amount from your 2011 Schedule(s) F (Form 1040), line 34 .... 13. _____

14. Enter your combined net gain/loss from the sale of farming business property reported on your 2011 Form 4797 and Form 8949. If zero or less, enter -0- .... 14. _____

15. Enter the amount from your 2010 Schedule(s) F (Form 1040), line 36 .... 15. _____

16. Enter your combined net gain/loss from the sale of farming business property reported on your 2010 Form 4797 and Schedule D (Form 1040). If zero or less, enter -0- .... 16. _____

17. Enter the amount from your 2009 Schedule(s) F (Form 1040), line 36 .... 17. _____

18. Enter your combined net gain/loss from the sale of farming business property reported on your 2009 Form 4797 and Schedule D (Form 1040). If zero or less, enter -0- .... 18. _____

19. Combine lines 9 through 18. If zero or less, enter -0- .... 19. _____

20. Enter the greater of line 19 or $300,000 ($150,000 if married filing separately) .... 20. _____

21. Add line 8 and line 20 .... 21. _____

22. **Excess farm loss.** Subtract line 1 from line 21. If zero or less, you have an excess farm loss that reduces the amount of loss you can deduct this year. If you have more than one farming business with an overall loss this year, allocate the excess farm loss amount on a *pro rata* basis among those farming businesses .... 22. _____

Excess Farm Loss Worksheet 2—Schedule F (Form 1040) farming businesses and Schedule C (Form 1040) activity of processing a farm commodity

Keep for Your Records

CAUTION: In determining if you have an excess farm loss, do not take into account any deductions for losses arising by reason of fire, storm, or other casualty, or by reason of disease or drought, involving your farming businesses.

1. Enter the amount from your 2014 Schedule(s) F (Form 1040), line 33 .... **1.** _____

2. Enter the total amount from your 2014 Schedule(s) C (Form 1040), line 28 and line 30, for activity of processing a farm commodity .... **2.** _____

3. Add lines 1 and 2. Is this amount less than $300,000 ($150,000 if married filing separately)? If yes, stop here. You do not have an excess farm loss in 2014. If no, continue to line 4 .... **3.** _____

4. Subtract $300,000 ($150,000 if married filing separately) from line 3 .... **4.** _____

5. Enter the amount from your 2014 Schedule(s) F (Form 1040), line 9 .... **5.** _____

6. Enter the amount from your 2014 Schedule(s) C (Form 1040), line 7 .... **6.** _____

7. Combine line 5 and line 6 .... **7.** _____

8. Is line 7 greater than or equal to line 4? If yes, stop here. You do not have an excess farm loss in 2014. If no, continue to line 9.

9. Enter your net gain/loss from the sale of farming business property reported on Form 4797 .... **9.** _____

10. Enter your net gain/loss from the sale of farming business property reported on Form 8949 .... **10.** _____

11. Combine line 9 and line 10. If zero or less, enter -0- .... **11.** _____

12. Add line 7 and line 11. Is this greater than or equal to line 4? If yes, stop here. You do not have an excess farm loss in 2014. If no, continue to line 13 .... **12.** _____

13. Enter the amount from your 2013 Schedule(s) F (Form 1040), line 34 .... **13.** _____

14. Enter the amount from your 2013 Schedule(s) C (Form 1040), line 31 .... **14.** _____

15. Enter your combined net gain/loss from the sale of farming business property reported on your 2013 Form 4797 and Form 8949. If zero or less, enter -0- .... **15.** _____

16. Enter the amount from your 2012 Schedule(s) F (Form 1040), line 34 .... **16.** _____

17. Enter the amount from your 2012 Schedule(s) C (Form 1040), line 31 .... **17.** _____

18. Enter your combined net gain/loss from the sale of farming business property reported on your 2012 Form 4797 and Form 8949. If zero or less, enter -0- .... **18.** _____

19. Enter the amount from your 2011 Schedule(s) F (Form 1040), line 34 .... **19.** _____

20. Enter the amount from your 2011 Schedule(s) C (Form 1040), line 31 .... **20.** _____

(Continued on next page)

Excess Farm Loss Worksheet 2 (Continued)

21. Enter your combined net gain/loss from the sale of farming business property reported on your 2011 Form 4797 and Form 8949. If zero or less, enter -0- . . . . **21.** _____

22. Enter the amount from your 2010 Schedule(s) F (Form 1040), line 36 . . . . **22.** _____

23. Enter the amount from your 2010 Schedule(s) C (Form 1040), line 31 . . . . **23.** _____

24. Enter your combined net gain/loss from the sale of farming business property reported on your 2010 Form 4797 and Schedule D (Form 1040). If zero or less, enter -0- . . . . **24.** _____

25. Enter the amount from your 2009 Schedule(s) F (Form 1040), line 36 . . . . **25.** _____

26. Enter the amount from your 2009 Schedule(s) C (Form 1040), line 31 . . . . **26.** _____

27. Enter your combined net gain/loss from the sale of farming business property reported on your 2009 Form 4797 and Schedule D (Form 1040). If zero or less, enter -0- . . . . **27.** _____

28. Combine lines 13 through 27. If zero or less, enter -0- . . . . **28.** _____

29. Enter the greater of line 28 or $300,000 ($150,000 if married filing separately) . . . . **29.** _____

30. Add lines 12 and 29 . . . . **30.** _____

31. **Excess farm loss.** Subtract line 3 from line 30. If zero or less, you have an excess farm loss that reduces the amount of loss you can deduct this year. If you have more than one farming business with an overall loss this year, allocate the excess farm loss amount on a *pro rata* basis among those farming businesses . . . . **31.** _____

Excess Farm Loss Worksheet 3—Schedule F (Form 1040) farming businesses and Schedule E (Form 1040) partnership or S corporation income or loss from farming businesses

Keep for Your Records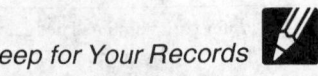

CAUTION: In determining if you have an excess farm loss, do not take into account any deductions for losses arising by reason of fire, storm, or other casualty, or by reason of disease or drought, involving your farming businesses.

Note. When instructed in the worksheet below to enter an amount from line 30, 31, or 32 of Schedule E, include only the amount on that line that relates to farming businesses.

1. Enter the amount from your 2014 Schedule(s) F (Form 1040), line 33 . . . . .   **1.** _____

2. Enter the amount from your 2014 Schedule(s) E (Form 1040), line 31, for interest in a partnership or S corporation involved in farming businesses . . . .   **2.** _____

3. Add lines 1 and 2. Is this amount less than $300,000 ($150,000 if married filing separately)? If yes, stop here. You do not have an excess farm loss in 2014. If no, continue to line 4 . . . .   **3.** _____

4. Subtract $300,000 ($150,000 if married filing separately) from line 3 . . . .   **4.** _____

5. Enter the amount from your 2014 Schedule(s) F (Form 1040), line 9 . . . . . .   **5.** _____

6. Enter the amount from your 2014 Schedule(s) E (Form 1040), line 30 . . . . .   **6.** _____

7. Combine line 5 and line 6 . . . .   **7.** _____

8. Is line 7 greater than or equal to line 4? If yes, stop here. You do not have an excess farm loss in 2014. If no, continue to line 9.

9. Enter your net gain/loss from the sale of farming business property reported on Form 4797 . . . .   **9.** _____

10. Enter your net gain/loss from the sale of farming business property reported on Form 8949 . . . .   **10.** _____

11. Combine line 9 and line 10. If zero or less, enter -0- . . . .   **11.** _____

12. Add line 7 and line 11. Is this greater than or equal to line 4? If yes, stop here. You do not have an excess farm loss in 2014. If no, continue to line 13 . . . .   **12.** _____

13. Enter the amount from your 2013 Schedule(s) F (Form 1040), line 34 . . . .   **13.** _____

14. Enter the amount from your 2013 Schedule(s) E (Form 1040), line 32 . . . .   **14.** _____

15. Enter your combined net gain/loss from the sale of farming business property reported on your 2013 Form 4797 and Form 8949. If zero or less, enter -0- . . . .   **15.** _____

16. Enter the amount from your 2012 Schedule(s) F (Form 1040), line 34 . . . .   **16.** _____

17. Enter the amount from your 2012 Schedule(s) E (Form 1040), line 32 . . . .   **17.** _____

18. Enter your combined net gain/loss from the sale of farming business property reported on your 2012 Form 4797 and Form 8949. If zero or less, enter -0- . . . .   **18.** _____

19. Enter the amount from your 2011 Schedule(s) F (Form 1040), line 34 . . . .   **19.** _____

20. Enter the amount from your 2011 Schedule(s) E (Form 1040), line 32 . . . .   **20.** _____

(Continued on next page)

Excess Farm Loss Worksheet 3 (Continued)

21. Enter your combined net gain/loss from the sale of farming business property reported on your 2011 Form 4797 and Form 8949. If zero or less, enter -0- . . . . 21. _____

22. Enter the amount from your 2010 Schedule(s) F (Form 1040), line 36 . . . . 22. _____

23. Enter the amount from your 2010 Schedule(s) E (Form 1040), line 32 . . . . 23. _____

24. Enter your combined net gain/loss from the sale of farming business property reported on your 2010 Form 4797 and Schedule D (Form 1040). If zero or less, enter -0- . . . . 24. _____

25. Enter the amount from your 2009 Schedule(s) F (Form 1040), line 36 . . . . 25. _____

26. Enter the amount from your 2009 Schedule(s) E (Form 1040), line 32 . . . . 26. _____

27. Enter your combined net gain/loss from the sale of farming business property reported on your 2009 Form 4797 and Schedule D (Form 1040). If zero or less, enter -0- . . . . 27. _____

28. Combine lines 13 through 27. If zero or less, enter -0- . . . . 28. _____

29. Enter the greater of line 28 or $300,000 ($150,000 if married filing separately) . . . . 29. _____

30. Add lines 12 and 29 . . . . 30. _____

31. **Excess farm loss.** Subtract line 3 from line 30. If zero or less, you have an excess farm loss that reduces the amount of loss you can deduct this year. If you have more than one farming business with an overall loss this year, allocate the excess farm loss amount on a *pro rata* basis among those farming businesses . . . . 31. _____

Excess Farm Loss Worksheet 4—Schedule F (Form 1040) farming businesses, Schedule C (Form 1040) activity of processing a farm commodity, Schedule E (Form 1040) partnership or S corporation income or loss from farming businesses, and Form 4835 rental income or loss

Keep for Your Records

CAUTION: In determining if you have an excess farm loss, do not take into account any deductions for losses arising by reason of fire, storm, or other casualty, or by reason of disease or drought, involving your farming businesses.

Note. When instructed in the worksheet below to enter an amount from line 30, 31, or 32 of Schedule E, include only the amount on that line that relates to farming businesses.

1. Enter the amount from your 2014 Schedule(s) F (Form 1040), line 33 . . . .   1. _____

2. Enter the total amount from your 2014 Schedule(s) C (Form 1040), line 28 and line 30, for activity of processing a farm commodity . . . .   2. _____

3. Enter the amount from your 2014 Schedule(s) E (Form 1040), line 31, for interest in a partnership or S corporation involved in farming businesses . . . .   3. _____

4. Enter the amount from your 2014 Form 4835, line 31 . . . .   4. _____

5. Add lines 1, 2, 3, and 4. Is this amount less than $300,000 ($150,000 if married filing separately)? If yes, stop here. You do not have an excess farm loss in 2014. If no, continue to line 6 . . . .   5. _____

6. Subtract $300,000 ($150,000 if married filing separately) from line 5 . . . .   6. _____

7. Enter the amount from your 2014 Schedule(s) F (Form 1040), line 9 . . . .   7. _____

8. Enter the amount from your 2014 Schedule(s) C (Form 1040), line 7 . . . .   8. _____

9. Enter the amount from your 2014 Schedule(s) E (Form 1040), line 30 . . . .   9. _____

10. Enter the amount from your 2014 Form 4835, line 7 . . . .   10. _____

11. Combine lines 7, 8, 9, and 10 . . . .   11. _____

12. Is line 11 greater than or equal to line 6? If yes, stop here. You do not have an excess farm loss in 2014. If no, continue to line 13.

13. Enter your net gain/loss from the sale of farming business property reported on Form 4797 . . . .   13. _____

14. Enter your net gain/loss from the sale of farming business property reported on Form 8949 . . . .   14. _____

15. Combine line 13 and line 14. If zero or less, enter -0- . . . .   15. _____

16. Add lines 11 and 15. Is this greater than or equal to line 6? If yes, stop here. You do not have an excess farm loss in 2014. If no, continue to line 17 . . . .   16. _____

TIP: Lines 17 through 43 help you calculate the threshold amount discussed in the instructions. The threshold amount is the greater of $300,000 ($150,000 if married filing separately) or your total net profit or loss from farming businesses for the last five years (2009-2013), including for each of those years any net gain from the sale of property used in your farming businesses.

17. Enter the amount from your 2013 Schedule(s) F (Form 1040), line 34 . . . .   17. _____

18. Enter the amount from your 2013 Schedule(s) C (Form 1040), line 31 . . . .   18. _____

19. Enter the amount from your 2013 Schedule(s) E (Form 1040), line 32 . . . .   19. _____

20. Enter the amount from your 2013 Form 4835, line 32 . . . .   20. _____

21. Enter your combined net gain/loss from the sale of farming business property reported on your 2013 Form 4797 and Form 8949. If zero or less, enter -0- . . . .   21. _____

22. Enter the amount from your 2012 Schedule(s) F (Form 1040), line 34 . . . .   22. _____

23. Enter the amount from your 2012 Schedule(s) C (Form 1040), line 31 . . . .   23. _____

24. Enter the amount from your 2012 Schedule(s) E (Form 1040), line 32 . . . .   24. _____

25. Enter the amount from your 2012 Form 4835, line 32 . . . .   25. _____

26. Enter your combined net gain/loss from the sale of farming business property reported on your 2012 Form 4797 and Form 8949. If zero or less, enter -0- . . . .   26. _____

27. Enter the amount from your 2011 Schedule(s) F (Form 1040), line 34 . . . .   27. _____

28. Enter the amount from your 2011 Schedule(s) C (Form 1040), line 31 . . . .   28. _____

(Continued on next page)

F-18

Excess Farm Loss Worksheet 4 (Continued)

29. Enter the amount from your 2011 Schedule(s) E (Form 1040), line 32 .... **29.** _____

30. Enter the amount from your 2011 Form 4835, line 32 .... **30.** _____

31. Enter your combined net gain/loss from the sale of farming business property reported on your 2011 Form 4797 and Form 8949. If zero or less, enter -0- .... **31.** _____

32. Enter the amount from your 2010 Schedule(s) F (Form 1040), line 36 .... **32.** _____

33. Enter the amount from your 2010 Schedule(s) C (Form 1040), line 31 .... **33.** _____

34. Enter the amount from your 2010 Schedule(s) E (Form 1040), line 32 .... **34.** _____

35. Enter the amount from your 2010 Form 4835, line 32 .... **35.** _____

36. Enter your combined net gain/loss from the sale of farming business property reported on your 2010 Form 4797 and Schedule D (Form 1040). If zero or less, enter -0- .... **36.** _____

37. Enter the amount from your 2009 Schedule(s) F (Form 1040), line 36 .... **37.** _____

38. Enter the amount from your 2009 Schedule(s) C (Form 1040), line 31 .... **38.** _____

39. Enter the amount from your 2009 Schedule(s) E (Form 1040), line 32 .... **39.** _____

40. Enter the amount from your 2009 Form 4835, line 32 .... **40.** _____

41. Enter your combined net gain/loss from the sale of farming business property reported on your 2009 Form 4797 and Schedule D (Form 1040). If zero or less, enter -0- .... **41.** _____

42. Combine lines 17 through 41. If zero or less, enter -0- .... **42.** _____

43. Enter the greater of line 42 or $300,000 ($150,000 if married filing separately) .... **43.** _____

44. Add lines 16 and 43 .... **44.** _____

45. **Excess farm loss.** Subtract line 5 from line 44. If zero or less, you have an excess farm loss that reduces the amount of loss you can deduct this year. If you have more than one farming business with an overall loss this year, allocate the excess farm loss amount on a *pro rata* basis among those farming businesses .... **45.** _____

Excess Farm Loss Worksheet 5—Form 4835 for farm rental income or loss from farming business

CAUTION: In determining if you have an excess farm loss, do not take into account any deductions for losses arising by reason of fire, storm, or other casualty, or by reason of disease or drought, involving your farming business.

1. Enter the amount from your 2014 Form 4835, line 31. Is this amount less than $300,000 ($150,000 if married filing separately)? If yes, stop here. You do not have an excess farm loss in 2014. If no, continue to line 2 . . . . 1._____

2. Subtract $300,000 ($150,000 if married filing separately) from line 1 . . . . 2._____

3. Enter the amount from your 2014 Form 4835, line 7 . . . . 3._____

4. Is line 3 greater than or equal to line 2? If yes, stop here. You do not have an excess farm loss in 2014. If no, continue to line 5.

5. Enter your net gain/loss from the sale of farming business property reported on Form 4797 . . . . 5._____

6. Enter your net gain/loss from the sale of farming business property reported on Form 8949 . . . . 6._____

7. Combine line 5 and line 6. If zero or less, enter -0- . . . . 7._____

8. Add line 3 and line 7. Is this greater than or equal to line 2? If yes, stop here. You do not have an excess farm loss in 2014. If no, continue to line 9 . . . . 8._____

9. Enter the amount from your 2013 Form 4835, line 32 . . . . 9._____

10. Enter your combined net gain/loss from the sale of farming business property reported on your 2013 Form 4797 and Form 8949. If zero or less, enter -0- . . . . 10._____

11. Enter the amount from your 2012 Form 4835, line 32 . . . . 11._____

12. Enter your combined net gain/loss from the sale of farming business property reported on your 2012 Form 4797 and Form 8949. If zero or less, enter -0- . . . . 12._____

13. Enter the amount from your 2011 Form 4835, line 32 . . . . 13._____

14. Enter your combined net gain/loss from the sale of farming business property reported on your 2011 Form 4797 and Form 8949. If zero or less, enter -0- . . . . 14._____

15. Enter the amount from your 2010 Form 4835, line 32 . . . . 15._____

16. Enter your combined net gain/loss from the sale of farming business property reported on your 2010 Form 4797 and Schedule D (Form 1040). If zero or less, enter -0- . . . . 16._____

17. Enter the amount from your 2009 Form 4835, line 32 . . . . 17._____

18. Enter your combined net gain/loss from the sale of farming business property reported on your 2009 Form 4797 and Schedule D (Form 1040). If zero or less, enter -0- . . . . 18._____

19. Combine lines 9 through 18. If zero or less, enter -0- . . . . 19._____

20. Enter the greater of line 19 or $300,000 ($150,000 if married filing separately) . . . . 20._____

21. Add lines 8 and 20 . . . . 21._____

22. **Excess farm loss.** Subtract line 1 from line 21. If zero or less, you have an excess farm loss that reduces the amount of loss you can deduct this year. If you have more than one farming business with an overall loss this year, allocate the excess farm loss amount on a *pro rata* basis among those farming businesses . . . . 22._____

Department of the Treasury
Internal Revenue Service

2014 Instructions for Schedule H (Form 1040) Household Employment Taxes

Household Employers

Here is a list of forms you need to complete:

- Schedule H for figuring your household employment taxes.
- Form W-2, Wage and Tax Statement, for reporting wages paid to your employees.
- Form W-3, Transmittal of Wage and Tax Statements, for sending Copy A of Form(s) W-2 to the Social Security Administration (SSA).

For more information, see *What Forms Must You File?* in Pub. 926, Household Employer's Tax Guide.

No household employees in 2014? If you did not have any household employees in 2014, you do not have to file Schedule H for 2014.

We have been asked:

What do I do after I fill in Schedule H? If you must file a 2014 tax return, enter the taxes from Schedule H on the "Household employment taxes" line of your Form 1040, 1040NR, 1040-SS, or 1041. You do this because these taxes are added to your income taxes.

How do I file Schedule H? File Schedule H with your Form 1040, 1040NR, 1040-SS, or 1041. If you are not filing a 2014 tax return, file Schedule H by itself.

Do I make a separate payment? No. You pay both income and employment taxes to the United States Treasury when you file Schedule H with your return.

When do I pay? Most filers must pay by April 15, 2015.

How many copies of Form W-3 do I send to the SSA? Send one copy of Form W-3 with Copy A of Form(s) W-2 to the SSA, and keep one copy of Form W-3 for your records. Instructions for filing Forms W-2 and Form W-3 electronically are available at *www.socialsecurity.gov/employer*.

Important Dates!

By	You must
February 2, 2015	Give your employee Form W-2.
March 2, 2015 (March 31, 2015 if you file electronically)	Send Copy A of Form(s) W-2 with Form W-3 to the SSA. Visit *www.socialsecurity.gov/employer* for details.
April 15, 2015	File Schedule H and pay your household employment taxes with your 2014 tax return.

Section references are to the Internal Revenue Code unless otherwise noted.

Contents

Future Developments

For the latest information about developments related to Schedule H and its instructions, such as legislation enacted after they were published, go to *www.irs.gov/scheduleh*.

What's New

Changes to tax rates and wage threshold. The social security tax rate is 6.2% each for the employee and employer, unchanged from 2013. The social security wage base limit is $117,000.

The Medicare tax rate is 1.45% each for the employee and employer, unchanged from 2013. There is no wage base limit for Medicare tax. Social security and Medicare taxes apply to the wages of household workers you pay $1,900 or more in cash or an equivalent form of compensation in 2014.

For information about the rates and wage threshold that will apply in 2015, see Pub. 926 (released in December 2014).

Credit reduction state. A state that has not repaid money it borrowed from the federal government to pay unemployment benefits is a "credit reduction state." The Department of Labor determines these states. If an employer pays wages that are subject to the unemployment tax laws of a credit reduction state, that employer must pay additional federal unemployment tax.

For 2014, there are credit reduction states. If you paid wages that were subject to the unemployment compensation laws of a credit reduction state, your credit against federal unemployment tax will be reduced based on the credit reduction rate (for example, .012, .015, or .017) for that credit reduction state.

Reminders

Additional Medicare Tax withholding. In addition to withholding Medicare tax at 1.45%, you must withhold a 0.9% Additional Medicare Tax from wages you pay to an employee in excess of $200,000 in a calendar year. You are required to begin withholding Additional Medicare Tax in the pay period in which you pay wages in excess of $200,000 to an employee and continue to withhold it each pay period until the end of the calendar year. Additional Medicare Tax is only imposed on the employee. There is no employer share of Additional Medicare Tax. All wages that are subject to Medicare tax are subject to Additional Medicare Tax withholding if paid in excess of the $200,000 withholding threshold.

For more information on Additional Medicare Tax, visit IRS.gov and enter "Additional Medicare Tax" in the search box.

Outsourcing payroll duties. Employers are responsible to ensure that tax returns are filed and deposits and payments are made, even if the employer contracts with a third party to perform these acts. The employer remains responsible if the third party fails to perform any required action. If you choose to outsource any of your payroll and related tax duties (that is, withholding, reporting, and paying over social security, Medicare, FUTA, and income taxes) to a third-party payer, such as a payroll service provider or reporting agent, visit IRS.gov and enter "outsourcing payroll duties" in the search box for helpful information on this topic.

Paid preparers are required to sign Schedule H. Your paid preparer must sign Schedule H in Part IV **unless** you are attaching Schedule H to Form 1040, 1040NR, 1040-SS, or Form 1041. A paid preparer must sign Schedule H and provide the information requested in the *Paid Preparer Use Only* section only if the preparer was paid to prepare Schedule H and is not your employee. The preparer must give you a copy of the return in addition to the copy to be filed with the IRS.

If you are required to file a 2014 Form W-2 for any household employee, you must also send Form W-3 with Copy A of Form(s) W-2 to the SSA. You are encouraged to file your Forms W-2 and W-3 electronically. Visit the SSA's Employer W-2 Filing Instructions & Information website at *www.socialsecurity.gov/employer* to learn about electronic filing.

Who Needs To File Schedule H?

You must file Schedule H if you answer "Yes" to any of the questions on lines A, B, or C of Schedule H.

Did you have a household employee? If you hired someone to do household work and you could control what work he or she did and how he or she did it, you had a household employee. This is true even if you gave the employee freedom of action. What matters is that you had the right to control the details of how the work was done.

Example. You paid Betty Oak to babysit your child and do light housework 4 days a week in your home. Betty followed your specific instructions about household and child care duties. You provided the household equipment and supplies Betty needed to do her work. Betty is your household employee.

Household work is work done in or around your home. Some examples of workers who do household work are:

Babysitters	Drivers	Nannies
Caretakers	Health aides	Private nurses
Cleaning people	Housekeepers	Yard workers

If a worker is your employee, it does not matter whether the work is full or part-time or that you hired the worker through an agency or from a list provided by an agency or association. Also, it does not matter if the wages paid are for work done hourly, daily, weekly, or by the job.

If you are a home care service recipient receiving home care services through a program administered by a federal, State, or local government agency, and the person who provides your care is your household employee, you can ask the IRS to authorize an agent under section 3504 to report, file, and pay all federal employment taxes, including FUTA taxes, on your behalf. See Form 2678, Employer/Payer Appointment of Agent, for more information.

Note. If a government agency or third party agent reports and pays the employment taxes on wages paid to your household employee on your behalf, you do not need to file Schedule H to report those taxes.

Workers who are not your employees. Workers you get from an agency are not your employees if the agency is responsible for who does the work and how it is done. Self-employed workers are also not your employees. A worker is self-employed if only he or she can control how the work is done. A self-employed worker usually provides his or her own tools and offers services to the general public in an independent business.

Example. You made an agreement with Paul Brown to care for your lawn. Paul runs a lawn care business and offers his services to the general public. He hires his own helpers, instructs them how to do their jobs, and provides his own tools and supplies. Neither Paul nor his helpers are your employees.

For more information, see Pub. 926.

Who Needs To File Form W-2 and Form W-3?

You must file Form W-2 for each household employee to whom you paid $1,900 or more of cash wages in 2014 that are subject to social security and Medicare taxes. To find out if the wages are subject to these taxes, see the instructions for Schedule H, lines 1, 3, and 5. Even if the wages are not subject to these taxes, if you withheld federal income tax from the wages of any household employee, you must file Form W-2 for that employee.

If you file one or more Forms W-2, you must also file Form W-3.

Do You Have an Employer Identification Number (EIN)?

If you have household employees, you will need an EIN to file Schedule H. If you do not have an EIN, see Form SS-4, Application for Employer Identification Number. Do not use a social security number in place of an EIN. The Instructions for Form SS-4 explain how you can get an EIN immediately over the internet, in 4 business days by fax, or in about 4 weeks if you apply by mail. See *How To Get Forms and Publications* for details on how to get forms and publications including Form SS-4. To get an EIN over the internet, visit IRS.gov and enter "EIN" in the search box.

Can Your Employee Legally Work in the United States?

It is unlawful to employ a person who cannot legally work in the United States. When you hire a household employee to work for you on a regular basis, you and the employee must each complete part of the U.S. Citizenship and Immigration Services (USCIS) Form I-9, Employment Eligibility Verification. You must verify that the employee is either a U.S. citizen or a person who can legally work in the United States and you must keep Form I-9 for your records. You can get the form and the USCIS Handbook for Employers by calling 1-800-870-3676, or by visiting the USCIS website at *www.uscis.gov*.

What About State Employment Taxes?

If you employed a household employee in 2014, you probably have to pay contributions to your state unemployment fund for 2014. To find out if you do, contact your state unemployment tax agency. For a list of state unemployment tax agencies, visit the U.S. Department of Labor's website at *www.workforcesecurity.doleta.gov/unemploy/agencies.asp*. You should also find out if you need to pay or collect other state employment taxes or carry workers' compensation insurance.

When and Where To File

Schedule H

If you file Form 1040, 1040NR, 1040-SS, or 1041 for 2014, remember to attach Schedule H to it. Mail your return, by April 15, 2015, to the address shown in your tax return instructions.

Exceptions. If you get an extension of time to file your return, file it with Schedule H by the extended due date. If you are a fiscal year filer, file your return and Schedule H by the due date of your fiscal year return, including extensions.

Note. If you are a calendar year taxpayer and have no household employees for 2014, you do not have to file Schedule H for 2014.

If you are not required to file a 2014 tax return (for example, because your income is below the amount that requires you to file), you must file Schedule H by itself by April 15, 2015. Complete Schedule H and put it in an envelope with your check or money order. Do not send cash. See the list of filing addresses in these instructions. Mail your completed Schedule H and payment to the address listed for the place where you live. Make your check or money order payable to the "United States Treasury" for the total household employment taxes due. Enter your name, address, social security number, daytime phone number, and "2014 Schedule H" on your check or money order. Household employers that are tax-exempt, such as churches, may also file Schedule H by itself.

Form W-2 and Form W-3

By February 2, 2015, you must give Copies B, C, and 2 of Form W-2 to each employee. You will meet this requirement if the form is properly addressed, mailed, and postmarked no later than February 2, 2015.

By March 2, 2015 (March 31, 2015, if you file Forms W-2 and W-3 electronically), send Copy A of all Forms W-2 with Form W-3 to the SSA. Mail Copy A of all Forms W-2 with Form W-3 to:

Social Security Administration
Data Operations Center
Wilkes-Barre, PA 18769-0001

For certified mail, the ZIP code is 18769-0002. If you use a carrier other than the U.S. Postal Service, add "ATTN: W-2 Process, 1150 E. Mountain Dr." to the address and change the ZIP code to "18702-7997."

If you file Forms W-2 and W-3 electronically, do not mail the paper Forms W-2 and W-3 to the Social Security Administration.

For more information on filing Forms W-2 and W-3 electronically, visit the SSA's Employer W-2 Filing Instructions & Information website at *www.socialsecurity.gov/employer*.

Note. Check with your state, city, or local tax department to find out if you must file Copy 1 of Form W-2.

Penalties. You may have to pay a penalty if you do not give Forms W-2 to your employees or file Copy A of the forms with the SSA by the due dates. You may also have to pay a penalty if you do not show your employee's social security number on Form W-2 or do not provide correct information on the form.

How To Fill In Schedule H, Form W-2, and Form W-3

Schedule H

If you were notified that your household employee received payments from a state disability plan, see State Disability Payments, *later.*

Social security number. Enter your social security number. Form 1041 filers, do not enter a number in this space. But be sure to enter your EIN in the space provided.

Employer identification number (EIN). An EIN is a nine-digit number assigned by the IRS. The digits are arranged as follows: 00-0000000. Enter your EIN in the space provided. If you do not have an EIN, see *Do You Have an Employer Identification Number (EIN),* earlier. If you applied for an EIN but have not received it, enter "Applied For" and the date you applied. Do not use your social security number as an EIN.

Line A. To figure the total cash wages you paid in 2014 to each household employee, do not include amounts paid to any of the following individuals.

• Your spouse.
• Your child who was under age 21.
• Your parent. (See *Exception for parents* below.)
• Your employee who was under age 18 at any time during 2014. If the employee was not a student, see *Exception for employees under age 18* below.

Exception for parents. Include the cash wages you paid your parent for work in or around your home if both 1 and 2 below apply.

1. Your child who lived with you was under age 18 or had a physical or mental condition that required the personal care of an adult for at least 4 continuous weeks during the calendar quarter in which services were performed. A calendar quarter is January through March, April through June, July through September, or October through December.

2. You were divorced and not remarried, a widow or widower, or married to and living with a person whose physical or mental condition prevented him or her from caring for the child during that 4-week period.

Exception for employees under age 18. Include the cash wages you paid to a person who was under age 18 and not a student if providing household services was his or her principal occupation.

Cash wages. Cash wages include wages paid by check, money order, etc. Cash wages do not include the value of food, lodging, clothing, or other noncash items you give a household employee.

Transportation (commuting) benefits. For 2014, you can generally give your employee transportation benefits such as $130 per month for combined commuter highway vehicle transportation and transit passes; $250 per month for qualified parking; or for a calendar year, $20 multiplied by the number of qualified bicycle commuting months during that year for qualified bicycle commuting reimbursement of expenses incurred during the year, without the benefits counting as cash. However, the value of benefits over the specified amounts a month is included as wages. See *Transportation (Commuting) Benefits* in Pub. 15-B, Employer's Tax Guide to Fringe Benefits, for more information.

Part I. Social Security, Medicare, and Federal Income Taxes

Social security and Medicare taxes fund retirement, survivor, disability, and health benefits for workers and their families. You and your employees generally pay these taxes in equal amounts.

You are not required to withhold federal income tax from wages you pay a household employee. You should withhold federal income tax only if your household employee asks you to withhold it and you agree. The employee must give you a completed Form W-4, Employee's Withholding Allowance Certificate.

For 2014, the social security tax rate is 6.2% each for you and your employee. The Medicare tax rate is 1.45% each. The limit on wages subject to social security tax is $117,000. There is no limit on wages subject to the Medicare tax. If you did not deduct the employee's share from his or her wages, you must pay the employee's share and your share (a total of 12.4% for social security and 2.9% for Medicare tax) of tax. See *Form W-2 and Form W-3* in these instructions for more information.

In addition to withholding Medicare tax at 1.45%, you must withhold a 0.9% Additional Medicare Tax from wages you pay to an employee in excess of $200,000 in a calendar year. You are required to begin withholding Additional Medicare Tax in the pay period in which you pay wages in excess of $200,000 to an employee and continue to withhold it each pay period until the end of the calendar year. Additional Medicare Tax is only imposed on the employee. There is no employer share of Additional Medicare Tax. All wages that are subject to Medicare tax are subject to Additional Medicare Tax withholding if paid in excess of the $200,000 withholding threshold.

For more information on Additional Medicare Tax, visit IRS.gov and enter "Additional Medicare Tax" in the search box.

$1,900 test. If you pay a household employee $1,900 or more in cash wages during 2014, you must report and pay social security and Medicare taxes on all the wages. The test applies to cash wages paid in 2014 regardless of when the wages were earned. See Pub. 926 for more information. Or, visit the SSA's website at *www.socialsecurity.gov/pubs/10021.html*.

Line 1. Enter on line 1 the total of cash wages (see *Cash wages* earlier) paid in 2014 to each household employee who meets the $1,900 test, explained earlier.

 If you paid any household employee cash wages of more than $117,000 in 2014, include on line 1 only the first $117,000 of that employee's cash wages.

Line 2. Multiply the amount on line 1 by 12.4% (.124) and enter the result on line 2.

Line 3. Enter on line 3 the total of cash wages (see *Cash wages* earlier) paid in 2014 to each employee who meets the $1,900 test. There is no limit on wages subject to the Medicare tax.

Line 4. Multiply the amount on line 3 by 2.9% (.029) and enter the result on line 4.

Line 5. Enter on line 5 the total cash wages (see *Cash wages* earlier) paid to each employee in 2014 that exceeded $200,000.

Line 6. Multiply the amount on line 5 by 0.9% (.009) and enter the result on line 6.

Line 7. Enter on line 7 any federal income tax you withheld from the wages you paid to your household employees in 2014. See Pub. 926 and Pub. 15 (Circular E), Employer's Tax Guide, for information on withholding federal income taxes.

Line 8. Add lines 2, 4, 6, and 7 and enter the result on line 8.

Line 9. Review the cash wages you paid to all your household employees for each calendar quarter of 2013 and 2014. Is the total for any quarter in 2013 or 2014 $1,000 or more?

Yes. Complete Schedule H, Part II.

No. Follow the instructions in the chart below.

If you file Form...	Then enter the amount from Schedule H, line 8, on...
1040	line 60a
1040NR	line 59a
1040-SS	Part I, line 4
1041	Schedule G, line 6

If you do not file any of the above forms, complete Schedule H, Part IV and follow the instructions under *When and Where To File*.

Part II. Federal Unemployment (FUTA) Tax

FUTA tax, with state unemployment systems, provides for payments of unemployment compensation to workers who have lost their jobs. Most employers pay both a federal and state unemployment tax.

The FUTA tax rate is 6.0% (.060). But see *Credit for contributions paid to state* below. Do not deduct the FUTA tax from your employee's wages. You must pay it from your own funds.

Credit for contributions paid to state. You may be able to take a credit of up to 5.4% against the FUTA tax, resulting in a net FUTA tax rate of 0.6% (.006). But to do so, you must pay all the required contributions for 2014 to your state unemployment fund by April 15, 2015. Fiscal year filers must pay all required contributions for 2014 by the due date of their federal income tax returns (not including extensions).

Contributions are payments that a state requires you, as an employer, to make to its unemployment fund for the payment of unemployment benefits. However, contributions do not include:

- Any payments deducted or deductible from your employees' pay;
- Penalties, interest, or special administrative taxes; or
- Voluntary contributions you paid to get a lower state experience rate. See the instructions for line 17 for more information.

If you paid contributions to any credit reduction state, see the instructions for line 23.

Lines 10 through 12. Answer the questions on lines 10 through 12 to see if you should complete Section A or Section B of Part II.

Fiscal year filers. If you paid all state unemployment contributions for 2014 by the due date of your return (not including extensions), check the "Yes" box on line 11. Check the "No" box if you did not pay all of your state contributions by the due date of your return.

Line 13. Enter the two-letter abbreviation of the name of the state (or the District of Columbia, Puerto Rico, or the U.S. Virgin Islands) to which you paid unemployment contributions.

Line 14. Enter the total of *contributions* (defined earlier) you paid to your state unemployment fund for 2014. If you did not have to make contributions because your state gave you a zero percent experience rate, enter "0% rate" on line 14.

Line 15. Enter the total of cash wages (see *Cash wages* earlier) you paid in 2014 to each household employee, including employees paid less than $1,000. However, do not include cash wages paid in 2014 to any of the following individuals.

- Your spouse.
- Your child who was under age 21.
- Your parent.

If you paid any household employee more than $7,000 in 2014, include on line 15 only the first $7,000 of that employee's cash wages.

Credit for 2014. The credit you can take for any state unemployment fund contributions for 2014 that you pay after April 15, 2015, is limited to 90% of the credit that would have been allowable if the contributions were paid on or before April 15, 2015.

 Use Worksheet A in Pub. 926 to figure the credit for late contributions if you paid any state contributions after the due date for filing Form 1040.

Line 16. Multiply the wages on line 15 by .6% (.006). Enter the result on line 16.

 *Complete lines 17 through 24 **only** if you checked a "No" box on lines 10, 11, or 12.*

Line 17. Complete all columns that apply. If you do not, you will not get a credit. If you need more space, attach a statement using the same format as line 17. Your state will provide the experience rate. If you do not know your rate, contact your state unemployment tax agency.

You must complete columns (a), (b), and (h), even if you were not given an experience rate. If you were given an experience rate of 5.4% or higher, you must also complete columns

(c) and (d). If you were given a rate of less than 5.4%, you must complete all columns.

If you were given a rate for only part of the year, or the rate changed during the year, you must complete a separate line for each rate period.

Column (b). Enter the taxable wages on which you must pay taxes to the unemployment fund of the state shown in column (a). If your experience rate is zero percent, enter the amount of wages you would have had to pay taxes on if that rate had not been granted.

Column (h). Enter the total *contributions* (defined earlier) you paid to the state unemployment fund for 2014 by April 15, 2015. Fiscal year filers, enter the total contributions you paid to the state unemployment fund for 2014 by the due date of your return (not including extensions). If you are claiming excess credits as payments of state unemployment contributions, attach a copy of the letter from your state.

Line 18. Add the amounts in columns (g) and (h) separately and enter the totals in the spaces provided.

Line 19. Add the amounts shown on line 18 and enter the total on line 19.

Line 20. Enter the total cash wages subject to FUTA tax. See the line 15 instructions for details.

Line 21. Multiply the wages on line 20 by 6.0% (.060). Enter the result on line 21.

Line 22. Multiply the wages on line 20 by 5.4% (.054). Enter the result on line 22.

Line 23. Complete the *Worksheet for Household Employers in a Credit Reduction State—Line 23* in these instructions **only** if you are a household employer in any of the credit reduction states. A state is a credit reduction state if the amount in the "Reduction Rate" column for the state in the worksheet is greater than zero.

State Names and Postal Abbreviations

State	Postal Abbreviation	State	Postal Abbreviation
Alabama	AL	Nebraska	NE
Alaska	AK	Nevada	NV
Arizona	AZ	New Hampshire	NH
Arkansas	AR	New Jersey	NJ
California	CA	New Mexico	NM
Colorado	CO	New York	NY
Connecticut	CT	North Carolina	NC
Delaware	DE	North Dakota	ND
District of Columbia	DC	Ohio	OH
Florida	FL	Oklahoma	OK
Georgia	GA	Oregon	OR
Hawaii	HI	Pennsylvania	PA
Idaho	ID	Rhode Island	RI
Illinois	IL	South Carolina	SC
Indiana	IN	South Dakota	SD
Iowa	IA	Tennessee	TN
Kansas	KS	Texas	TX
Kentucky	KY	Utah	UT
Louisiana	LA	Vermont	VT
Maine	ME	Virginia	VA
Maryland	MD	Washington	WA
Massachusetts	MA	West Virginia	WV
Michigan	MI	Wisconsin	WI
Minnesota	MN	Wyoming	WY
Mississippi	MS	Puerto Rico	PR
Missouri	MO	U.S. Virgin Islands	VI
Montana	MT		

1. Enter the **smaller** of the amount from Schedule H, line 19 or line 22 1

2. Enter the total taxable FUTA wages from Schedule H, line 20 2

3. Place an "X" in the box of **EVERY** state in which you had to pay state unemployment tax this year. If all of the states you check have a credit reduction rate of zero, do not enter an amount on line 23. For each state with a credit reduction rate greater than zero, enter the FUTA taxable wages, multiply by the reduction rate, and then enter the credit reduction amount. Do not include in the *FUTA Taxable Wages* box wages that were excluded from state unemployment tax. If any states do not apply to you, leave them blank.

Postal Abbreviation	FUTA Taxable Wages	Reduction Rate	Credit Reduction	Postal Abbreviation	FUTA Taxable Wages	Reduction Rate	Credit Reduction
AK		x .000		NC		x .012	
AL		x .000		ND		x .000	
AR		x .000		NE		x .000	
AZ		x .000		NH		x .000	
CA		x .012		NJ		x .000	
CO		x .000		NM		x .000	
CT		x .017		NV		x .000	
DC		x .000		NY		x .012	
DE		x .000		OH		x .012	
FL		x .000		OK		x .000	
GA		x .000		OR		x .000	
HI		x .000		PA		x .000	
IA		x .000		RI		x .000	
ID		x .000		SC		x .000	
IL		x .000		SD		x .000	
IN		x .015		TN		x .000	
KS		x .000		TX		x .000	
KY		x .012		UT		x .000	
LA		x .000		VA		x .000	
MA		x .000		VT		x .000	
MD		x .000		WA		x .000	
ME		x .000		WI		x .000	
MI		x .000		WV		x .000	
MN		x .000		WY		x .000	
MO		x .000		PR		x .000	
MS		x .000		VI		x .012	
MT		x .000					

4. **Total Credit Reduction.** Add all amounts shown in the *Credit Reduction* boxes. Enter the total here. 4

5. Subtract line 4 of this worksheet from line 1 of this worksheet and enter the result here **and** on Schedule H, line 23. 5

Part III. Total Household Employment Taxes

Line 25. Enter the amount from line 8. If there is no entry on line 8, enter -0-.

Line 26. Add the amounts on lines 16 and 25. If you were required to complete *Section B* of Part II, add the amounts on lines 24 and 25 and enter the total on line 26.

Line 27. Follow the instructions in the chart.

If you file Form. . .	Then do not complete Part IV but enter the amount from Schedule H, line 26, on . . .
1040	line 60a
1040NR	line 59a
1040-SS	Part I, line 4
1041	Schedule G, line 6

If you do not file any of the above forms, complete Schedule H, Part IV and follow the instructions under *When and Where To File.*

Paid Preparers

Paid preparer use only. You must complete this part if you were paid to prepare Schedule H, and are not an employee of the filing entity, and are not attaching Schedule H to Form 1040, 1040NR, 1040-SS, or Form 1041. You **must** sign in the space provided and give the filer a copy of the return in addition to the copy to be filed with the IRS.

Form W-2 and Form W-3

If you file one or more Forms W-2, you must also file Form W-3.

You must report both cash and noncash wages in box 1, as well as tips and other compensation. The completed Forms W-2 and W-3 in the example (in these instructions) show how the entries are made. For detailed information on preparing these forms, see the General Instructions for Forms W-2 and W-3.

Employee's portion of taxes paid by employer. If you paid all of your employee's share of social security and Medicare taxes, without deducting the amounts from the employee's pay, the employee's wages are increased by the amount of that tax for income tax withholding purposes. Follow steps 1 through 3 below. (See the example in these instructions.)

   1. Enter the amounts you paid on your employee's behalf in boxes 4 and 6 (do not include your share of these taxes).

   2. Add the amounts in boxes 3, 4, and 6. (However, if box 5 is greater than box 3, then add the amounts in boxes 4, 5, and 6.)

   3. Enter the total in box 1.

 On Form W-3, put an "X" in the "Hshld. emp." box located in box b, Kind of Payer.

For information on filing Forms W-2 and W-3 electronically, visit the SSA's Employer W-2 Filing Instructions & Information website at *www.socialsecurity.gov/employer*.

You Should Also Know

Estimated Tax Penalty

You may need to increase the federal income tax withheld from your pay, pension, annuity, etc., or make estimated tax payments to avoid an estimated tax penalty based on your household employment taxes shown on Schedule H, line 26. You may increase your federal income tax withheld by giving your employer a new Form W-4, or by giving the payor of your pension a new Form W-4P, Withholding Certificate for Pension or Annuity Payments. Make estimated tax payments by filing Form 1040-ES, Estimated Tax for Individuals. For more information, see Pub. 505, Tax Withholding and Estimated Tax.

 Estimated tax payments must be made as the tax liability is incurred: by April 15, 2014, June 16, 2014, September 15, 2014, and January 15, 2015. If you file your Form 1040 by February 2, 2015, and pay the rest of the tax that you owe with the form, you do not need to make the payment due on January 15, 2015.

Exception. You will not be penalized for failure to make estimated tax payments if both 1 and 2 below apply for the year.

   1. You will not have federal income tax withheld from wages, pensions, or any other payments you receive.

   2. Your income taxes, excluding your household employment taxes, would not be enough to require payment of estimated taxes.

What Records To Keep

You must keep copies of Schedule H and related Forms W-2, W-3, and W-4 for at least 4 years after the due date for filing Schedule H or the date the taxes were paid, whichever is later. If you have to file Form W-2, also keep a record of each employee's name and social security number. Each payday, you should record and keep the dates and amounts of:
- Cash and noncash wage payments,
- Any employee social security tax withheld,
- Any employee Medicare tax withheld, and
- Any federal income tax withheld.

What Is the Earned Income Credit (EIC)?

The EIC is a refundable tax credit for certain workers.

Which employees must I notify about the EIC? You must notify your household employee about the EIC if you agreed to withhold federal income tax from the employee's wages but did not do so because the income tax withholding tables showed that no tax should be withheld.

Note. You are encouraged to notify each employee whose wages for 2014 were less than $46,997 ($52,427 if married filing jointly) that he or she may be eligible for the EIC for 2014.

How and when must I notify my employees? You must give the employee one of the following items.
- The official IRS Form W-2, which has the required information about the EIC on the back of Copy B.
- A substitute Form W-2 with the same EIC information on the back of the employee's copy that is on Copy B of the official IRS Form W-2.
- Notice 797, Possible Federal Tax Refund Due to the Earned Income Credit (EIC).
- Your written statement with the same wording as Notice 797.

If you are not required to give the employee a Form W-2, you must provide the notification by February 9, 2015.

If the notification is not given on Form W-2 in a timely manner, you must hand the notice directly to the employee or send it by First-Class Mail to the employee's last known address.

How do my employees claim the EIC? Eligible employees claim the EIC on their 2014 tax returns.

Rules for Business Employers

Do not use Schedule H if you chose to report employment taxes for your household employees along with your other employees on Form 941, Employer's QUARTERLY Federal Tax Return; Form 943, Employer's Annual Federal Tax Return for Agricultural Employees; or Form 944, Employer's ANNUAL Federal Tax Return. If you report this way, be sure to include your household employees' wages on your Form 940, Employer's Annual Federal Unemployment (FUTA) Tax Return.

State Disability Payments

Certain state disability plan payments to household employees are treated as wages subject to social security and Medicare taxes. If your employee received payments from a plan that withheld the employee's share of social security and Medicare taxes, include the payments on lines 1 and 3 of Schedule H and complete the rest of Part I through line 7. Add lines 2, 4, 6, and 7. From that total, subtract the amount of these taxes withheld by the state. Enter the result on line 8. Also, enter "disability" and the amount subtracted on the dotted line next to line 8. See the notice issued by the state for more details.

How To Correct Schedule H

If you discover an error on a Schedule H that you previously filed with Form 1040, Form 1040NR, or Form 1040-SS, file Form 1040X, Amended U.S. Individual Income Tax Return, and attach a corrected Schedule H. If you discover an error on a Schedule H that you previously filed with Form 1041, file an "Amended" Form 1041 and attach a corrected Schedule H.

If you discover an error on a Schedule H that you filed as a stand-alone return, file another stand-alone Schedule H with the corrected information. In the top margin of your corrected Schedule H write (in red ink if possible) "CORRECTED" followed by the date you discovered the error.

If you owe tax, pay in full with your Form 1040X, Form 1041, or stand-alone Schedule H. If you overpaid tax on a previously filed Schedule H, then depending on whether you adjust or claim a refund, you must certify that you repaid or reimbursed the employee's share of social security and Medicare taxes, or that you have obtained consents from your employees to file a claim for refund for the employee tax. See Pub. 926 for complete instructions.

How To Get Forms and Publications

To get the IRS forms and publications mentioned in these instructions (including Notice 797), visit *www.irs.gov/formspubs* or call 1-800-TAX-FORM (1-800-829-3676).

Completed Examples of Schedule H, Form W-2, and Form W-3

On February 12, 2014, Susan Green hired Helen Maple to clean her house every Wednesday. Susan did not have a household employee in 2013 and had no household employees other than Helen during 2014.

Susan paid Helen $50 every Wednesday for her day's work. Susan decided not to withhold Helen's share of the social security and Medicare taxes from the wages she paid Helen. Instead, she will pay Helen's share of these taxes from her own funds. Susan did not withhold federal income tax because Helen did not give her a Form W-4 to request withholding and no withholding is otherwise required.

Helen was employed by Susan for the rest of the year (a total of 46 weeks). The following is some of the information Susan will need to complete Schedule H, Form W-2, and Form W-3.

Helen's total cash wages	$2,300.00
	($50 x 46 weeks)
Helen's share of the:	
Social security tax	$142.60
	($2,300 x 6.2% (.062))
Medicare tax	$33.35
	($2,300 x 1.45% (.0145))
Helen's total cash wages each quarter:	
1st quarter	$350.00 ($50 x 7 weeks)
2nd quarter	$650.00 ($50 x 13 weeks)
3rd quarter	$650.00 ($50 x 13 weeks)
4th quarter	$650.00 ($50 x 13 weeks)
Amount included in box 1 of Form W-2 and Form W-3:	
Cash wages	$2,300.00
Helen's share of social security tax paid by Susan	142.60
Helen's share of Medicare tax paid by Susan	33.35
Total	$2,475.95

Because Susan paid less than $1,000 per quarter to household employees during 2013 (no employees) and 2014 (see above), she is not liable for FUTA tax.

 See Pub. 926 for an example showing how to complete Forms W-2 and W-3 if the employer withheld social security and Medicare taxes from the employee's wages.

SCHEDULE H (Form 1040)	**Household Employment Taxes**	OMB No. 1545-1971

SCHEDULE H (Form 1040)

Department of the Treasury
Internal Revenue Service (99)

Household Employment Taxes

(For Social Security, Medicare, Withheld Income, and Federal Unemployment (FUTA) Taxes)

► **Attach to Form 1040, 1040NR, 1040-SS, or 1041.**

► **Information about Schedule H and its separate instructions is at** *www.irs.gov/scheduleh.*

OMB No. 1545-1971

2014

Attachment
Sequence No. **44**

Name of employer	Social security number
	001-11-1111
	Employer identification number
Susan Green	0 0 1 2 3 4 5 6 7

Calendar year taxpayers having no household employees in 2014 do not have to complete this form for 2014.

A Did you pay **any one** household employee cash wages of $1,900 or more in 2014? (If any household employee was your spouse, your child under age 21, your parent, or anyone under age 18, see the line A instructions before you answer this question.)

☑ **Yes.** Skip lines B and C and go to line 1.

☐ **No.** Go to line B.

〰〰〰〰〰〰〰〰〰〰〰〰〰〰〰〰〰〰〰〰〰〰〰〰〰〰〰〰〰〰〰

Part I Social Security, Medicare, and Federal Income Taxes

1	Total cash wages subject to social security tax	**1**	2,300 00	
2	Social security tax. Multiply line 1 by 12.4% (.124)	**2**	285	20
3	Total cash wages subject to Medicare tax	**3**	2,300 00	
4	Medicare tax. Multiply line 3 by 2.9% (.029)	**4**	66	70
5	Total cash wages subject to Additional Medicare Tax withholding	**5**		
6	Additional Medicare Tax withholding. Multiply line 5 by 0.9% (.009)	**6**		
7	Federal income tax withheld, if any	**7**		
8	**Total social security, Medicare, and federal income taxes.** Add lines 2, 4, 6, and 7	**8**	351	90

9 Did you pay **total** cash wages of $1,000 or more in **any** calendar **quarter** of 2013 or 2014 to **all** household employees?
(**Do not** count cash wages paid in 2013 or 2014 to your spouse, your child under age 21, or your parent.)

☑ **No. Stop.** Include the amount from line 8 above on Form 1040, line 60a. If you are not required to file Form 1040, see the line 9 instructions.

〰〰〰〰〰〰〰〰〰〰〰〰〰〰〰〰〰〰〰〰〰〰〰〰〰〰〰〰〰〰〰

Note: *Although not shown, Susan also enters on Form W-2 the required state or local income tax information in boxes 15 through 20.*

Visit the SSA website at ***www.socialsecurity.gov/employer*** *to file Copy A of Form W-2 electronically.*

22222 Void ☐	a Employee's social security number: 000-00-4567	For Official Use Only ▶ OMB No. 1545-0008
b Employer identification number (EIN): 00-1234567	1 Wages, tips, other compensation: 2475.95	2 Federal income tax withheld
c Employer's name, address, and ZIP code: Susan Green, 16 Gray Street, Anyplace, CA 92665	3 Social security wages: 2300.00	4 Social security tax withheld: 142.60
	5 Medicare wages and tips: 2300.00	6 Medicare tax withheld: 33.35
	7 Social security tips	8 Allocated tips
d Control number	9	10 Dependent care benefits
e Employee's first name and initial: Helen R. Last name: Maple Suff.	11 Nonqualified plans	12a See instructions for box 12
19 Pine Avenue, Anycity, CA 92666	13 Statutory employee ☐ Retirement plan ☐ Third-party sick pay ☐	12b
	14 Other	12c
f Employee's address and ZIP code		12d

15 State	Employer's state ID number	16 State wages, tips, etc.	17 State income tax	18 Local wages, tips, etc.	19 Local income tax	20 Locality name

Form **W-2** **Wage and Tax Statement** **2014**

Department of the Treasury—Internal Revenue Service

For Privacy Act and Paperwork Reduction Act Notice, see the separate instructions.

Copy A For Social Security Administration — Send this entire page with Form W-3 to the Social Security Administration; photocopies are **not** acceptable.

Cat. No. 10134D

33333	a Control number	For Official Use Only ▶ OMB No. 1545-0008
b Kind of Payer (Check one): 941 ☒ Military ☐ 943 ☐ 944 ☐ CT-1 ☐ Hshld. emp. ☒ Medicare govt. emp. ☐	Kind of Employer (Check one): None apply ☒ 501c non-govt. ☐ State/local non-501c ☐ State/local 501c ☐ Federal govt. ☐	Third-party sick pay (Check if applicable) ☐
c Total number of Forms W-2 d Establishment number	1 Wages, tips, other compensation: 2475.95	2 Federal income tax withheld
e Employer identification number (EIN): 00-1234567	3 Social security wages: 2300.00	4 Social security tax withheld: 142.60
f Employer's name: Susan Green, 16 Gray Street, Anyplace, CA 92665	5 Medicare wages and tips: 2300.00	6 Medicare tax withheld: 33.35
	7 Social security tips	8 Allocated tips
	9	10 Dependent care benefits
g Employer's address and ZIP code	11 Nonqualified plans	12a Deferred compensation
h Other EIN used this year	13 For third-party sick pay use only	12b
15 State Employer's state ID number	14 Income tax withheld by payer of third-party sick pay	
16 State wages, tips, etc. 17 State income tax	18 Local wages, tips, etc.	19 Local income tax
Employer's contact person	Employer's telephone number: (123) 456-7890	For Official Use Only
Employer's fax number	Employer's email address	

Under penalties of perjury, I declare that I have examined this return and accompanying documents and, to the best of my knowledge and belief, they are true, correct, and complete.

Signature ▶   Title ▶   Date ▶ 1/29/15

Form **W-3** **Transmittal of Wage and Tax Statements** **2014**

Department of the Treasury
Internal Revenue Service

Note: When you fill in Forms W-2 and W-3, please—

- Type entries using black ink.
- Enter all money amounts without the dollar sign and comma, but with the decimal point (for example, 2475.95 **not** $2,475.95).
- Do not round money amounts—show the cents portion.

Privacy Act and Paperwork Reduction Act Notice

We ask for the information on this form to carry out the Internal Revenue laws of the United States. You are required to give us the information. We need it to ensure that you are complying with these laws and to allow us to figure and collect the right amount of tax. If you do not provide the information we ask for, or provide false or fraudulent information, you may be subject to penalties.

You are not required to provide the information requested on a form that is subject to the Paperwork Reduction Act unless the form displays a valid OMB control number. Books or records relating to a form or instructions must be retained as long as their contents may become material in the administration of any Internal Revenue law.

Subtitle C, Employment Taxes, of the Internal Revenue Code imposes employment taxes on wages and provides for income tax withholding. This form is used to determine the amount of the taxes that you owe. Section 6011 requires you to provide the requested information if the tax is applicable to you. Section 6109 requires you to provide your identification number.

Generally, tax returns and return information are confidential, as required by section 6103. However, section 6103 allows or requires the IRS to disclose or give the information shown on your tax return to others as described in the Code. For example, we may disclose your tax information to the Department of Justice for civil and criminal litigation, and to cities, states, the District of Columbia, and U.S. commonwealths and possessions to administer their tax laws. We may also disclose this information to other countries under a tax treaty, to federal and state agencies to enforce federal nontax criminal laws, or to federal law enforcement and intelligence agencies to combat terrorism.

The time needed to complete and file this form will vary depending on individual circumstances. The estimated burden for individual taxpayers filing this form is approved under OMB control number 1545-0074 and is included in the estimates shown in the instructions for their individual income tax return.

The estimated burden for all other taxpayers who file this form is shown below.
Recordkeeping, 1 hr., 38 min.
Learning about the law or the form, 39 min.
Preparing the form, 1 hr.
Copying, assembling, and sending the form to the IRS, 34 min.

If you have comments concerning the accuracy of these time estimates or suggestions for making this form simpler, we would be happy to hear from you. You can send us comments from *www.irs.gov/formspubs*. Click on *More Information* and then click on *Give us feedback.* Or you can send your comments to Internal Revenue Service, Tax Forms and Publications Division, 1111 Constitution Ave. NW, IR-6526, Washington, DC 20224. Do not send Schedule H (Form 1040) to this address. Instead, see *When and Where To File* earlier.

Do You Have To File Form 1040, 1040NR, 1040-SS, or Form 1041?

Yes — Attach Schedule H to that form and mail to the address in your tax return instructions.

No — Mail your completed Schedule H and payment to the Department of the Treasury, Internal Revenue Service, for the place where you live. No street address is needed. See *When and Where To File* for the information to enter on your payment.

IF you live in...	THEN use this address...
Florida, Louisiana, Mississippi, Texas	Austin, TX 73301-0002
Alaska, Arkansas, Arizona, California, Colorado, Hawaii, Idaho, Illinois, Indiana, Iowa, Kansas, Michigan, Minnesota, Montana, Nebraska, Nevada, New Mexico, North Dakota, Ohio, Oklahoma, Oregon, South Dakota, Utah, Washington, Wisconsin, Wyoming	Fresno, CA 93888-0002
Alabama, Connecticut, Delaware, District of Columbia, Georgia, Kentucky, Maine, Maryland, Massachusetts, Missouri, New Hampshire, New Jersey, New York, North Carolina, Pennsylvania, Rhode Island, South Carolina, Tennessee, Vermont, Virginia, West Virginia	Kansas City, MO 64999-0002
APO, FPO, American Samoa, the Commonwealth of the Northern Mariana Islands, nonpermanent residents of Guam or the U.S. Virgin Islands*, Puerto Rico, dual-status aliens, a foreign country	Austin, TX 73301-0215
* Permanent residents of Guam should use: Department of Revenue and Taxation, Government of Guam, P.O. Box 23607, GMF, GU 96921; permanent residents of the U.S. Virgin Islands should use: USVI Bureau of Internal Revenue, 6115 Estate Smith Bay, St. Thomas, VI 00802.	

2014 Instructions for Schedule J

Income Averaging for Farmers and Fishermen

Use Schedule J (Form 1040) to elect to figure your 2014 income tax by averaging, over the previous 3 years (base years), all or part of your 2014 taxable income from your trade or business of farming or fishing. This election may give you a lower tax if your 2014 income from farming or fishing is high and your taxable income for one or more of the 3 prior years was low.

In order to qualify for this election, you are not required to have been in the business of farming or fishing during any of the base years.

You may elect to average farming or fishing income even if your filing status was not the same in the election year and the base years.

This election does not apply when figuring your alternative minimum tax on Form 6251. Also, you do not have to recompute, because of this election, the tax liability of any minor child who was required to use your tax rates in the prior years.

Section references are to the Internal Revenue Code unless otherwise noted.

Future Developments

For the latest information about developments related to Schedule J (Form 1040) and its instructions, such as legislation enacted after they were published, go to *www.irs.gov/schedulej*.

General Instructions

Prior Year Tax Returns

You may need copies of your original or amended income tax returns for 2011, 2012, and 2013 to figure your tax on Schedule J.

If you need copies of your tax returns, use Form 4506. There is a fee for each return requested. See Form 4506 for the fee amount. If your main home, principal place of business, or tax records are located in a federally declared disaster area, this fee will be waived. If you want a free transcript of your tax return or account, use Form 4506-T. See your Form 1040 instructions to find out how to get these forms.

Keep a copy of your 2014 income tax return to use for income averaging in 2015, 2016, or 2017.

Definitions

Farming business. A farming business is the trade or business of cultivating land or raising or harvesting any agricultural or horticultural commodity. This includes:

1. Operating a nursery or sod farm;

2. Raising or harvesting of trees bearing fruits, nuts, or other crops;

3. Raising ornamental trees (but not evergreen trees that are more than 6 years old when severed from the roots);

4. Raising, shearing, feeding, caring for, training, and managing animals; and

5. Leasing land to a tenant engaged in a farming business, but only if the lease payments are (a) based on a share of the tenant's production (not a fixed amount), and (b) determined under a written agreement entered into before the tenant begins significant activities on the land.

A farming business does not include:
- Contract harvesting of an agricultural or horticultural commodity grown or raised by someone else, or
- Merely buying or reselling plants or animals grown or raised by someone else.

Fishing business. A fishing business is the trade or business of fishing in which the fish harvested, either in whole or in part, are intended to enter commerce or enter commerce through sale, barter, or trade. This includes:

1. The catching, taking, or harvesting of fish;

2. The attempted catching, taking, or harvesting of fish;

3. Any other activity which can reasonably be expected to result in the catching, taking, or harvesting of fish;

4. Any operations at sea in support of, or in preparation for, any activity described in (1) through (3) above;

5. Leasing a fishing vessel, but only if the lease payments are (a) based on a share of the catch (or a share of the proceeds from the sale of the catch) from the lessee's use of the vessel in a fishing business (not a fixed payment), and (b) determined under a written lease entered into before the lessee begins any significant fishing activities resulting in the catch; and

6. Compensation as a crew member on a vessel engaged in a fishing business, but only if the compensation is based on a share of the catch (or a share of the proceeds from the sale of the catch).

The word fish means finfish, mollusks, crustaceans, and all other forms of marine animal and plant life other than marine mammals and birds.

A fishing business does not include any scientific research activity conducted by a scientific research vessel.

Settlement from Exxon Valdez litigation. You will be treated as engaged in a fishing business with respect to any qualified settlement income you received if either of the following applies.

1. You were a plaintiff in the civil action *In re Exxon Valdez,* No.

89-095-CV (HRH) (Consolidated) (D. Alaska); or

2. All of the following apply.

a. You were a beneficiary of a plaintiff described in (1) above,

b. You acquired the right to receive qualified settlement income from that plaintiff, and

c. You were the spouse or an immediate relative of that plaintiff.

Qualified settlement income is any taxable interest and punitive damage awards you received (whether as lump sums or periodic payments) in connection with the Exxon Valdez civil action described above. Qualified settlement income includes all such awards, whether received before or after the judgment and whether related to a settlement or a judgment.

Additional Information

See Pub. 225 and Regulations section 1.1301-1 for more information.

Specific Instructions

Line 2a

Elected Farm Income

To figure your elected farm income, first figure your taxable income from farming or fishing. This includes all income, gains, losses, and deductions attributable to your farming or fishing business. If you conduct both farming and fishing businesses, you must figure your elected farm income by combining income, gains, losses, and deductions attributable to your farming and fishing businesses.

Elected farm income also includes any gain or loss from the sale or other disposition of property regularly used in your farming or fishing business for a substantial period of time. However, if such gain or loss is realized after cessation of the farming or fishing business, the gain or loss is treated as attributable to a farming or fishing business only if the property is sold within a reasonable time after cessation of the farming or fishing business. A sale or other disposition within 1 year of the cessation is considered to be within a reasonable time.

Elected farm income does not include income, gain, or loss from the sale or other disposition of land or from the sale of development rights, grazing rights, and other similar rights.

You should find your income, gains, losses, and deductions from farming or fishing reported on different tax forms, such as:

• 2014 Form 1040, line 7, or Form 1040NR, line 8, income from wages and other compensation you received (a) as a shareholder in an S corporation engaged in a farming or fishing business or (b) as a crew member on a vessel engaged in a fishing business (but see *Fishing business*, earlier);

• 2014 Form 1040, line 21, or Form 1040NR, line 21, income from Exxon Valdez litigation;

• 2014 Form 1040, line 27, or Form 1040NR, line 27, deductible part of self-employment tax, but only to the extent that deduction is attributable to your farming or fishing business;

• 2014 Form 1040, line 43, or Form 1040NR, line 41, CCF reduction, except to the extent that any earnings (without regard to the carryback of any net operating or net capital loss) from the operation of agreement vessels in the fisheries of the United States or in the foreign or domestic commerce of the United States are not attributable to your fishing business;

• Schedule C or C-EZ;
• Schedule D;
• Schedule E, Part II;
• Schedule F;
• Form 4797;
• Form 4835;
• Form 8903, domestic production activities deduction, but only to the extent that deduction is attributable to your farming or fishing business; and
• Form 8949.

Your elected farm income is the amount of your taxable income from farming or fishing that you elect to include on line 2a.

 You do not have to include all of your taxable income from farming or fishing on line 2a. It may be to your advantage to include less than the entire amount, depending on how the amount you include on line 2a affects your tax bracket for the current and prior 3 tax years.

If you received certain subsidies in 2014, your elected farm income cannot include excess farm losses. See the Instructions for Schedule F (Form 1040).

Your elected farm income cannot exceed your taxable income.

Lines 2b and 2c

Complete lines 2b and 2c if the amount of your elected farm income on line 2a includes net capital gain. Net capital gain is the excess, if any, of net long-term capital gain over net short-term capital loss.

Line 2b. Enter on line 2b the portion of your elected farm income on line 2a treated as a net capital gain. The amount you enter on line 2b cannot exceed the **smaller** of your total net capital gain or the net capital gain attributable to your farming or fishing business.

Line 2c. Enter on line 2c the **smaller** of line 2b or the unrecaptured section 1250 gain attributable to your farming or fishing business, if any.

Line 4

Figure the tax on the amount on line 3 using:

• The 2014 Tax Table, Tax Computation Worksheet, or Qualified Dividends and Capital Gain Tax Worksheet from the 2014 Instructions for Form 1040 or Form 1040NR;
• The 2014 Foreign Earned Income Tax Worksheet from the 2014 Instructions for Form 1040; or
• The Schedule D Tax Worksheet in the 2014 Instructions for Schedule D.

Enter the tax on line 4.

Line 5

If you used Schedule J to figure your tax for:

• 2013 (that is, you entered the amount from the 2013 Schedule J, line 23, on line 44 of your 2013 Form 1040, on line 42 of your 2013 Form 1040NR, or on Form 1040X for 2013), enter on line 5 the amount from your 2013 Schedule J, line 11.
• 2012 but not 2013, enter on line 5 the amount from your 2012 Schedule J, line 15.
• 2011 but not 2012 or 2013, enter on line 5 the amount from your 2011 Schedule J, line 3.

If you figured your tax for 2011, 2012, and 2013 without using Schedule J, enter on line 5 the taxable income from your 2011 tax return (or as previously adjusted by the IRS, or corrected on an amended return). But if that amount is zero or less, complete the 2011 Taxable Income Worksheet to figure the amount to enter on line 5.

If you did not file a tax return for 2011, use the amount you would have reported as your taxable income had you been required to file a tax return. Be sure to keep all your records for 2011 for at least 3 years after April 15, 2015 (or the date you file your 2014 tax return, if later).

Instructions for 2011 Taxable Income Worksheet

Line 2. Any net capital loss deduction on your 2011 Schedule D, line 21, is not allowed for income averaging purposes to the extent it did not reduce your capital loss carryover to 2012. This could happen if the taxable income before subtracting exemptions—shown on your 2011 Form 1040, line 41, or your 2011 Form 1040NR, line 39 (or as previously adjusted) was less than zero. Enter on line 2 the amount by which your 2011 capital loss carryover to 2012 (the sum of your short- and long-term capital loss carryovers) exceeds the excess of the loss on your 2011 Schedule D, line 16,

over the loss on your 2011 Schedule D, line 21. If you had any Net Operating Loss (NOL) carrybacks to 2011, be sure you refigured your 2011 capital loss carryover to 2012.

Line 3. If you had an NOL for 2011, enter the amount of that NOL from line 25 of the 2011 Form 1045, Schedule A, you filed with Form 1045 or Form 1040X. If you did not have an NOL for 2011, enter the portion, if any, of the NOL carryovers and carrybacks to 2011 that were not used in 2011 and were carried to years after 2011.

Example. John Farmington, who is single, did not use income averaging for 2011, 2012, or 2013. For 2014, John has $18,000 of elected farm income on Schedule J, line 2a. The taxable income before subtracting exemptions on his 2011 Form 1040, line 41, is $4,550. A deduction for exemptions of $3,700 is shown on line 42, and line 43, taxable income, is $850. However, John had a $20,950 NOL for 2012, $9,000 of which was remaining to carry to 2011 after the NOL was carried back to 2010. To complete line 1 of the 2011 Taxable Income Worksheet, John combines the $9,000 NOL deduction with the $850 from his 2011 Form 1040, line 43. The result is a negative $8,150, John's 2011 taxable income, which he enters as a positive amount on line 1 of the 2011 Taxable Income Worksheet.

When John filed his 2011 tax return, he had a $3,000 net capital loss deduction on Schedule D, line 21 (which was also entered on Form 1040, line 13), a $7,000 loss on Schedule D, line 16, and a $4,000 capital loss carryover to 2012. However, when John carried back the 2012 NOL ($9,000 of which was carried to 2011), he refigured his 2011 capital loss carryover to 2012 as $7,000. John adds the $3,000 from Schedule D, line 21, and the $7,000 capital loss carryover. He subtracts from the $10,000 result the $7,000 loss on his Schedule D, line 16, and enters $3,000 on line 2 of the worksheet.

John had $850 of taxable income in 2011 that reduced the 2012 NOL carryback. The $3,700 exemption deduction and $3,000 net capital loss deduction also reduced the amount of the 2012 NOL carryback. As a result, only $1,450 ($9,000 - $850 - $3,700 - $3,000 = $1,450) was available to carry to 2013 and later years, as shown on line 10 of his 2012 Form 1045, Schedule B. John enters the $1,450 on line 3 of the worksheet, and $4,450 ($1,450 plus the $3,000 line 2 amount) on line 4. He then subtracts the $4,450 from the $8,150 on line 1 and enters the result, $3,700, on line 5 of the worksheet. He enters a negative $3,700 on Schedule J, line 5. He combines that amount with the $6,000 on Schedule J, line 6, and enters $2,300 on Schedule J, line 7.

2011 Taxable Income Worksheet—Line 5

Keep for Your Records

Complete this worksheet if you **did not** use Schedule J to figure your tax for 2012 and 2013 **and** your 2011 taxable income was zero or less. See the instructions above before completing this worksheet for line 5.

1. Figure the taxable income from your 2011 tax return (or as previously adjusted) without limiting it to zero. If you had an NOL for 2011, **do not** include any NOL carryovers or carrybacks to 2011. Enter the result as a positive amount .... 1. _____

2. If there is a loss on your 2011 Schedule D, line 21, add that loss (as a positive amount) and your 2011 capital loss carryover to 2012. Subtract from that sum the amount of the loss on your 2011 Schedule D, line 16, and enter the result .... 2. _____

3. If you had an NOL for 2011, enter it as a positive amount. Otherwise, enter as a positive amount the portion, if any, of the NOL carryovers and carrybacks to 2011 that were not used in 2011 and were carried to years after 2011 .... 3. _____

4. Add lines 2 and 3 .... 4. _____

5. Subtract line 4 from line 1. Enter the result as a **negative** amount on Schedule J, line 5 .... 5. _____

Line 8

If line 7 is zero, enter -0- on line 8. Otherwise, figure the tax on the amount on line 7 using:
- The 2011 Tax Rate Schedules below,
- The 2011 Qualified Dividends and Capital Gain Tax Worksheet, later,
- The 2011 Schedule D Tax Worksheet in the 2011 Schedule D instructions (but use the 2011 Tax Rate Schedules below when figuring the tax on lines 34 and 36 of the Schedule D Tax Worksheet), or
- The 2011 Foreign Earned Income Tax Worksheet, later.

If your elected farm income includes net capital gain, you must use the 2011 Schedule D Tax Worksheet to figure the tax on the amount on line 7. However, if you filed Form 2555 or 2555-EZ for 2011, you must first complete the 2011 Foreign Earned Income Tax Worksheet, and then use the 2011 Schedule D Tax Worksheet to figure the tax on the amount on line 3 of the Foreign Earned Income Tax Worksheet.

When completing the Schedule D Tax Worksheet, you must allocate 1/3 of the amount on line 2b (and 1/3 of the amount on line 2c, if any) to 2011. If for 2011 you had a capital loss that resulted in a capital loss carryover to 2012, do not reduce the elected farm income allocated to 2011 by any part of the carryover.

2011 Tax Rate Schedules—Line 8

Schedule X—Use if your **2011** filing status was **Single** or you checked filing status box 1 or 2 on Form 1040NR

If Schedule J, line 7, is: Over—	But not over—	Enter on Schedule J, line 8		of the amount over—
$0	$8,500	....	10%	$0
8,500	34,500	$850.00 +	15%	8,500
34,500	83,600	4,750.00 +	25%	34,500
83,600	174,400	17,025.00 +	28%	83,600
174,400	379,150	42,449.00 +	33%	174,400
379,150	....	110,016.50 +	35%	379,150

Schedule Y-2—Use if your **2011** filing status was **Married filing separately** or you checked filing status box 3, 4, or 5 on Form 1040NR

If Schedule J, line 7, is: Over—	But not over—	Enter on Schedule J, line 8		of the amount over—
$0	$8,500	....	10%	$0
8,500	34,500	$850.00 +	15%	8,500
34,500	69,675	4,750.00 +	25%	34,500
69,675	106,150	13,543.75 +	28%	69,675
106,150	189,575	23,756.75 +	33%	106,150
189,575	....	51,287.00 +	35%	189,575

Schedule Y-1—Use if your **2011** filing status was **Married filing jointly** or **Qualifying widow(er)** or you checked filing status box 6 on Form 1040NR

If Schedule J, line 7, is: Over—	But not over—	Enter on Schedule J, line 8		of the amount over—
$0	$17,000	....	10%	$0
17,000	69,000	$1,700.00 +	15%	17,000
69,000	139,350	9,500.00 +	25%	69,000
139,350	212,300	27,087.50 +	28%	139,350
212,300	379,150	47,513.50 +	33%	212,300
379,150	....	102,574.00 +	35%	379,150

Schedule Z—Use if your **2011** filing status was **Head of household**

If Schedule J, line 7, is: Over—	But not over—	Enter on Schedule J, line 8		of the amount over—
$0	$12,150	....	10%	$0
12,150	46,250	$1,215.00 +	15%	12,150
46,250	119,400	6,330.00 +	25%	46,250
119,400	193,350	24,617.50 +	28%	119,400
193,350	379,150	45,323.50 +	33%	193,350
379,150	....	106,637.50 +	35%	379,150

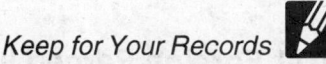

Use this worksheet **only** if both of the following apply.

- Your elected farm income on your 2014 Schedule J, line 2a, does not include any net capital gain.

- You **(a)** entered qualified dividends on your 2011 Form 1040, line 9b (or your 2011 Form 1040A, line 9b, or 2011 Form 1040NR, line 10b); **(b)** entered capital gain distributions directly on your 2011 Form 1040, line 13 (or your 2011 Form 1040A, line 10, or 2011 Form 1040NR, line 14) and were not required to file Schedule D; or **(c)** filed Schedule D in 2011 and you answered "Yes" on lines 17 and 20 of that Schedule D.

1.	Amount from your 2014 Schedule J, line 7. If for 2011 you filed Form 2555 or 2555-EZ, enter the amount from line 3 of the 2011 Foreign Earned Income Tax Worksheet	1.	_____
2.	Amount from your 2011 Form 1040, line 9b* (or your 2011 Form 1040A, line 9b, or 2011 Form 1040NR, line 10b)	2.	_____
3.	Did you file Schedule D in 2011?*		
	☐ **Yes.** Enter the **smaller** of line 15 or 16 of your 2011 Schedule D, but do not enter less than -0-		
	☐ **No.** Enter the amount from your 2011 Form 1040, line 13 (or your 2011 Form 1040A, line 10, or 2011 Form 1040NR, line 14)	3.	_____
4.	Add lines 2 and 3	4.	_____
5.	Amount, if any, from your 2011 Form 4952, line 4g	5.	_____
6.	Subtract line 5 from line 4. If zero or less, enter -0-	6.	_____
7.	Subtract line 6 from line 1. If zero or less, enter -0-	7.	_____
8.	Enter one of the of the following three amounts depending on your filing status:		
	• $34,500 if single or married filing separately, or if you checked filing status box 1, 2, 3, 4 or 5 on Form 1040NR;		
	• $69,000 if married filing jointly or qualifying widow(er) or if you checked filing status box 6 on Form 1040NR;		
	• $46,250 if head of household.	8.	_____
9.	Enter the smaller of line 1 or line 8	9.	_____
10.	Enter the smaller of line 7 or line 9	10.	_____
11.	Subtract line 10 from line 9. This amount is taxed at 0%	11.	_____
12.	Enter the smaller of line 1 or line 6	12.	_____
13.	Enter the amount from line 11	13.	_____
14.	Subtract line 13 from line 12	14.	_____
15.	Multiply line 14 by 15% (.15)	15.	_____
16.	Figure the tax on the amount on line 7. Use the 2011 Tax Rate Schedules	16.	_____
17.	Add lines 15 and 16	17.	_____
18.	Figure the tax on the amount on line 1. Use the 2011 Tax Rate Schedules	18.	_____
19.	**Tax.** Enter the **smaller** of line 17 or line 18 here and on your 2014 Schedule J, line 8. If for 2011 you filed Form 2555 or 2555-EZ, do not enter this amount on Schedule J, line 8. Instead, enter it on line 4 of the 2011 Foreign Earned Income Tax Worksheet	19.	_____

If for 2011 you filed Form 2555 or 2555-EZ, see the footnote in the 2011 Foreign Earned Income Tax Worksheet before completing this line.

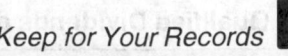

Use this worksheet if you claimed the foreign earned income exclusion or housing exclusion on your 2011 Form 1040 using Form 2555 or 2555-EZ. However, if Schedule J, line 7, is zero or less do not complete this worksheet.

1. Enter the amount from your 2014 Schedule J, line 7 .... **1.** _____

2. Enter the amount from your (and your spouse's, if filing jointly) 2011 Form 2555, lines 45 and 50, or Form 2555-EZ, line 18 .... **2.** _____

3. Add lines 1 and 2 .... **3.** _____

4. **Tax on the amount on line 3.** Use the 2011 Tax Rate Schedules, the 2011 Qualified Dividends and Capital Gain Tax Worksheet,* or the 2011 Schedule D Tax Worksheet in the 2011 Schedule D instructions,* whichever applies. .... **4.** _____

5. **Tax on the amount on line 2.** Use the 2011 Tax Rate Schedules. .... **5.** _____

6. Subtract line 5 from line 4. Enter the result. If zero or less, enter -0-. Also include this amount on your 2014 Schedule J, line 8 .... **6.** _____

Enter the amount from line 3 above on line 1 of the 2011 Qualified Dividends and Capital Gain Tax Worksheet or the 2011 Schedule D Tax Worksheet if you use either of those worksheets to figure the tax on line 4 above. Complete the rest of that worksheet through line 6 (line 10 if you use the Schedule D Tax Worksheet). Next, you must determine if you had a capital gain excess. To find out if you had a capital gain excess, subtract the amount from your 2014 Schedule J, line 7, from line 6 of your 2011 Qualified Dividends and Capital Gain Tax Worksheet (line 10 of your 2011 Schedule D Tax Worksheet). If the result is more than zero, that amount is your capital gain excess.

If you did not have a capital gain excess, complete the rest of either of those worksheets according to the worksheet's instructions. Then complete lines 5 and 6 above.

If you had a capital gain excess, complete a second 2011 Qualified Dividends and Capital Gain Tax Worksheet or 2011 Schedule D Tax Worksheet (whichever applies) as instructed above but in its entirety and with the following additional modifications. Then complete lines 5 and 6 above. These modifications are to be made only for purposes of filling out the 2011 Foreign Earned Income Tax Worksheet above.

1. Reduce (but not below zero) the amount you would otherwise enter on line 3 of your 2011 Qualified Dividends and Capital Gain Tax Worksheet or line 9 of your 2011 Schedule D Tax Worksheet by your capital gain excess.

2. Reduce (but not below zero) the amount you would otherwise enter on line 2 of your 2011 Qualified Dividends and Capital Gain Tax Worksheet or line 6 of your 2011 Schedule D Tax Worksheet by any of your capital gain excess not used in (1) above.

3. Reduce (but not below zero) the amount on your 2011 Schedule D (Form 1040), line 18, by your capital gain excess.

4. Include your capital gain excess as a loss on line 16 of your 2011 Unrecaptured Section 1250 Gain Worksheet in the 2011 Instructions for Schedule D (Form 1040).

Line 9

If you used Schedule J to figure your tax for:

- 2013 (that is, you entered the amount from the 2013 Schedule J, line 23, on line 44 of your 2013 Form 1040, on line 42 of 2013 Form 1040NR, or on Form 1040X for 2013), enter on line 9 the amount from your 2013 Schedule J, line 15.

- 2012 but not 2013, enter on line 9 the amount from your 2012 Schedule J, line 3.

If you figured your tax for both 2012 and 2013 without using Schedule J, enter on line 9 the taxable income from your 2012 tax return (or as previously adjusted by the IRS or corrected on an amended return). But if that amount is zero or less, complete the worksheet below to figure the amount to enter on line 9.

If you did not file a tax return for 2012, use the amount you would have reported as your taxable income had you been required to file a tax return. Be sure to keep all your records for 2012 until at least 3 years after April 15, 2015 (or the date you file your 2014 tax return, if later).

Instructions for 2012 Taxable Income Worksheet

Line 2. Any net capital loss deduction on your 2012 Schedule D, line 21, is not allowed for income averaging purposes to the extent it did not reduce your capi-

tal loss carryover to 2013. This could happen if the taxable income before subtracting exemptions—shown on your 2012 Form 1040, line 41, or your 2012 Form 1040NR, line 39 (or as previously adjusted)—was less than zero. Enter on line 2 the amount by which your 2012 capital loss carryover to 2013 (the sum of your short- and long-term capital loss carryovers) exceeds the excess of the loss on your 2012 Schedule D, line 16, over the loss on your 2012 Schedule D, line 21. If you had any NOL carrybacks to 2012, be sure you refigured your 2012 capital loss carryover to 2013.

Line 3. If you had an NOL for 2012, enter the amount of that NOL from line 25 of the 2012 Form 1045, Schedule A, you filed with Form 1045 or Form 1040X. If you did not have an NOL for 2012, enter the portion, if any, of the NOL carryovers and carrybacks to 2012 that were not used in 2012 and were carried to years after 2012.

Example. John Farmington did not use income averaging for 2011, 2012, or 2013. The taxable income before subtracting exemptions on his 2012 Form 1040, line 41, is a negative $29,900. A deduction for exemptions of $3,800 is shown on line 42, and line 43, taxable income, is limited to zero. John subtracts from the $29,900 loss the $3,800 deduction for exemptions. The result is a negative $33,700, John's 2012 taxable income, which he enters as a positive amount on line 1 of the 2012 Taxable Income Worksheet.

When John filed his 2012 tax return, he had a $3,000 net capital loss deduction on Schedule D, line 21 (which was also entered on Form 1040, line 13), and a $7,000 loss on Schedule D, line 16 (as adjusted). He also had a $7,000 capital loss carryover to 2013. John adds the $3,000 from Schedule D, line 21, and the $7,000 capital loss carryover. He subtracts from the $10,000 result the $7,000 loss on his Schedule D, line 16, and enters $3,000 on line 2 of the worksheet.

John enters $20,950 on line 3 of the worksheet, the 2012 NOL from his 2012 Form 1045, Schedule A, line 25. Of the $33,700 negative taxable income, the $3,800 deduction for exemptions, the $3,000 capital loss deduction, and his $5,950 standard deduction were not allowed in figuring the NOL. John had a $20,950 loss on his 2012 Schedule F, the only other item on his 2012 tax return.

John enters $23,950 (the $3,000 line 2 amount plus the $20,950 line 3 amount) on line 4 and $9,750 (the $33,700 line 1 amount minus the $23,950 line 4 amount) on line 5. He enters $9,750 as a negative amount on Schedule J, line 9. He enters $6,000 on Schedule J, line 10, and a negative $3,750 on Schedule J, line 11. If he uses Schedule J to figure his tax for 2015, he will enter the negative $3,750 amount on his 2015 Schedule J as his 2012 taxable income for income averaging purposes.

2012 Taxable Income Worksheet—Line 9

Keep for Your Records

Complete this worksheet if you **did not** use Schedule J to figure your tax for 2013 and your 2012 taxable income was zero or less. See the instructions above before completing this worksheet.

1. Figure the taxable income from your 2012 tax return (or as previously adjusted) without limiting it to zero. If you had an NOL for 2012, **do not** include any NOL carryovers or carrybacks to 2012. Enter the result as a positive amount .... **1.** _____

2. If there is a loss on your 2012 Schedule D, line 21, add that loss (as a positive amount) and your 2012 capital loss carryover to 2013. Subtract from that sum the amount of the loss on your 2012 Schedule D, line 16, and enter the result .... **2.** _____

3. If you had an NOL for 2012, enter it as a positive amount. Otherwise, enter as a positive amount the portion, if any, of the NOL carryovers and carrybacks to 2012 that were not used in 2012 and were carried to years after 2012 .... **3.** _____

4. Add lines 2 and 3 .... **4.** _____

5. Subtract line 4 from line 1. Enter the result as a **negative** amount on Schedule J, line 9 .... **5.** _____

Line 12

If line 11 is zero or less, enter -0- on line 12. Otherwise, figure the tax on the amount on line 11 using:
- The 2012 Tax Rate Schedules below,
- The 2012 Qualified Dividends and Capital Gain Tax Worksheet, later,
- The 2012 Schedule D Tax Worksheet in the 2012 Schedule D instructions (but use the 2012 Tax Rate Schedules below when figuring the tax on the Schedule D Tax Worksheet, lines 34 and 36), or
- The 2012 Foreign Earned Income Tax Worksheet, later.

If your elected farm income includes net capital gain, you must use the 2012 Schedule D Tax Worksheet to figure the tax on the amount on line 11. However, if you filed Form 2555 or 2555-EZ for 2012, you must first complete the 2012 Foreign Earned Income Tax Worksheet, and then use the 2012 Schedule D Tax Worksheet to figure the tax on the amount on line 3 of the Foreign Earned Income Tax Worksheet.

When completing the Schedule D Tax Worksheet, you must allocate 1/3 of the amount on line 2b (and 1/3 of the amount on line 2c, if any) to 2012. If for 2012 you had a capital loss that resulted in a capital loss carryover to 2013, do not reduce the elected farm income allocated to 2012 by any part of the carryover.

2012 Tax Rate Schedules—Line 12

Schedule X—Use if your **2012** filing status was **Single** or you checked filing status box 1 or 2 on Form 1040NR

If Schedule J, line 11, is: Over—	But not over—	Enter on Schedule J, line 12			of the amount over—
$0	$8,700	....	10%		$0
8,700	35,350	$870.00 +	15%		8,700
35,350	85,650	4,867.50 +	25%		35,350
85,650	178,650	17,442.50 +	28%		85,650
178,650	388,350	43,482.50 +	33%		178,650
388,350	....	112,683.50 +	35%		388,350

Schedule Y-2—Use if your **2012** filing status was **Married filing separately** or you checked filing status box 3, 4, or 5 on Form 1040NR

If Schedule J, line 11, is: Over—	But not over—	Enter on Schedule J, line 12			of the amount over—
$0	$8,700	....	10%		$0
8,700	35,350	$870.00 +	15%		8,700
35,350	71,350	4,867.50 +	25%		35,350
71,350	108,725	13,867.50 +	28%		71,350
108,725	194,175	24,332.50 +	33%		108,725
194,175	....	52,531.00 +	35%		194,175

Schedule Y-1—Use if your **2012** filing status was **Married filing jointly** or **Qualifying widow(er)** or you checked filing status box 6 on Form 1040NR

If Schedule J, line 11, is: Over—	But not over—	Enter on Schedule J, line 12			of the amount over—
$0	$17,400	....	10%		$0
17,400	70,700	$1,740.00 +	15%		17,400
70,700	142,700	9,735.00 +	25%		70,700
142,700	217,450	27,735.00 +	28%		142,700
217,450	388,350	48,665.00 +	33%		217,450
388,350	....	105,062.00 +	35%		388,350

Schedule Z—Use if your **2012** filing status was **Head of household**

If Schedule J, line 11, is: Over—	But not over—	Enter on Schedule J, line 12			of the amount over—
$0	$12,400	....	10%		$0
12,400	47,350	$1,240.00 +	15%		12,400
47,350	122,300	6,482.50 +	25%		47,350
122,300	198,050	25,220.00 +	28%		122,300
198,050	388,350	46,430.00 +	33%		198,050
388,350	....	109,229.00 +	35%		388,350

Use this worksheet **only** if both of the following apply.

- Your elected farm income on your 2014 Schedule J, line 2a, does not include any net capital gain.

- You **(a)** entered qualified dividends on your 2012 Form 1040, line 9b (or your 2012 Form 1040A, line 9b, or 2012 Form 1040NR, line 10b); **(b)** entered capital gain distributions directly on your 2012 Form 1040, line 13 (or your 2012 Form 1040A, line 10, or 2012 Form 1040NR, line 14) and were not required to file Schedule D; or **(c)** filed Schedule D in 2012 and you answered "Yes" on lines 17 and 20 of that Schedule D.

---

1. Amount from your 2014 Schedule J, line 11. If for 2012 you filed Form 2555 or 2555-EZ, enter the amount from line 3 of the 2012 Foreign Earned Income Tax Worksheet . . . . **1.** _____

2. Amount from your 2012 Form 1040, line 9b* (or your 2012 Form 1040A, line 9b, or 2012 Form 1040NR, line 10b) . . . . **2.** _____

3. Did you file Schedule D in 2012?*

   ☐ **Yes.** Enter the **smaller** of line 15 or 16 of your 2012 Schedule D, but do not enter less than -0-

   ☐ **No.** Enter the amount from your 2012 Form 1040, line 13 (or your 2012 Form 1040A, line 10, or 2012 Form 1040NR, line 14) . . **3.** _____

4. Add lines 2 and 3 . . . . **4.** _____

5. Amount, if any, from your 2012 Form 4952, line 4g . . . . **5.** _____

6. Subtract line 5 from line 4. If zero or less, enter -0- . . . . **6.** _____

7. Subtract line 6 from line 1. If zero or less, enter -0- . . . . **7.** _____

8. Enter one of the following three amounts depending on your filing status:

   - $35,350 if single or married filing separately, or if you checked filing status box 1, 2, 3, 4, or 5 on Form 1040NR;

   - $70,700 if married filing jointly or qualifying widow(er) or if you checked filing status box 6 on Form 1040NR;

   - $47,350 if head of household.
   . . . . **8.** _____

9. Enter the smaller of line 1 or line 8 . . . . **9.** _____

10. Enter the smaller of line 7 or line 9 . . . . **10.** _____

11. Subtract line 10 from line 9. This amount is taxed at 0% . . . . **11.** _____

12. Enter the smaller of line 1 or line 6 . . . . **12.** _____

13. Enter the amount from line 11 . . . . **13.** _____

14. Subtract line 13 from line 12 . . . . **14.** _____

15. Multiply line 14 by 15% (.15) . . . . **15.** _____

16. Figure the tax on the amount on line 7. Use the 2012 Tax Rate Schedules . . . . **16.** _____

17. Add lines 15 and 16 . . . . **17.** _____

18. Figure the tax on the amount on line 1. Use the 2012 Tax Rate Schedules . . . . **18.** _____

19. **Tax.** Enter the **smaller** of line 17 or line 18 here and on your 2014 Schedule J, line 12. If for 2012 you filed Form 2555 or 2555-EZ, do not enter this amount on Schedule J, line 12. Instead, enter it on line 4 of the 2012 Foreign Earned Income Tax Worksheet . . . . **19.** _____

If for 2012 you filed Form 2555 or 2555-EZ, see the footnote in the 2012 Foreign Earned Income Tax Worksheet before completing this line.

Use this worksheet if you claimed the foreign earned income exclusion or housing exclusion on your 2012 Form 1040 using Form 2555 or 2555-EZ. However, if Schedule J, line 11, is zero or less do not complete this worksheet.

1. Enter the amount from your 2014 Schedule J, line 11	**1.** _____
2. Enter the amount from your (and your spouse's, if filing jointly) 2012 Form 2555, lines 45 and 50, or Form 2555-EZ, line 18	**2.** _____
3. Add lines 1 and 2	**3.** _____
4. Tax on the amount on line 3. Use the 2012 Tax Rate Schedules, the 2012 Qualified Dividends and Capital Gain Tax Worksheet,* or the 2012 Schedule D Tax Worksheet in the 2012 Schedule D instructions,* whichever applies.	**4.** _____
5. Tax on the amount on line 2. Use the 2012 Tax Rate Schedules.	**5.** _____
6. Subtract line 5 from line 4. Enter the result. If zero or less, enter -0-. Also include this amount on your 2014 Schedule J, line 12	**6.** _____

*Enter the amount from line 3 above on line 1 of the 2012 Qualified Dividends and Capital Gain Tax Worksheet or the 2012 Schedule D Tax Worksheet if you use either of those worksheets to figure the tax on line 4 above. Complete the rest of that worksheet through line 6 (line 10 if you use the Schedule D Tax Worksheet). Next, you must determine if you had a capital gain excess. To find out if you had a capital gain excess, subtract the amount from your 2014 Schedule J, line 11, from line 6 of your 2012 Qualified Dividends and Capital Gain Tax Worksheet (line 10 of your 2012 Schedule D Tax Worksheet). If the result is more than zero, that amount is your capital gain excess.

If you did not have a capital gain excess, complete the rest of either of those worksheets according to the worksheet's instructions. Then complete lines 5 and 6 above.

If you had a capital gain excess, complete a second 2012 Qualified Dividends and Capital Gain Tax Worksheet or 2012 Schedule D Tax Worksheet (whichever applies) as instructed above but in its entirety and with the following additional modifications. Then complete lines 5 and 6 above. These modifications are to be made only for purposes of filling out the 2012 Foreign Earned Income Tax Worksheet above.

1. Reduce (but not below zero) the amount you would otherwise enter on line 3 of your 2012 Qualified Dividends and Capital Gain Tax Worksheet or line 9 of your 2012 Schedule D Tax Worksheet by your capital gain excess.

2. Reduce (but not below zero) the amount you would otherwise enter on line 2 of your 2012 Qualified Dividends and Capital Gain Tax Worksheet or line 6 of your 2012 Schedule D Tax Worksheet by any of your capital gain excess not used in (1) above.

3. Reduce (but not below zero) the amount on your 2012 Schedule D (Form 1040), line 18, by your capital gain excess.

4. Include your capital gain excess as a loss on line 16 of your 2012 Unrecaptured Section 1250 Gain Worksheet in the 2012 Instructions for Schedule D (Form 1040).

Line 13

If you used Schedule J to figure your tax for 2013 (that is, you entered the amount from the 2013 Schedule J, line 23, on line 44 of your 2013 Form 1040, on line 42 of your 2013 Form 1040NR, or on Form 1040X for 2013), enter on line 13 the amount from your 2013 Schedule J, line 3.

If you did not use Schedule J to figure your tax for 2013, enter on line 13 the taxable income from your 2013 tax return (or as previously adjusted by the IRS or corrected on an amended return). But if that amount is zero or less, complete the worksheet below to figure the amount to enter on line 13.

If you did not file a tax return for 2013, use the amount you would have reported as your taxable income had you been required to file a tax return. Be sure to keep all your records for 2013 until at least 3 years after April 15, 2015 (or the date you file your 2014 tax return, if later).

Instructions for 2013 Taxable Income Worksheet

Line 2. Any net capital loss deduction on your 2013 Schedule D, line 21, is not allowed for income averaging purposes to the extent it did not reduce your capital loss carryover to 2014. This could happen if the taxable income before subtracting exemptions—shown on your 2013 Form 1040, line 41, or your 2013 Form 1040NR, line 39 (or as previously adjusted)—was less than zero. Enter on line 2 the amount by which your 2013 capital loss carryover to 2014 (the sum of your short- and long-term capital loss carryovers) exceeds the excess of the loss on your 2013 Schedule D, line 16, over the loss on your 2013 Schedule D, line 21.

Line 3. If you had an NOL for 2013, enter the amount of that NOL from line 25 of the 2013 Form 1045, Schedule A, you filed with Form 1045 or Form 1040X. If you did not have an NOL for 2013, enter the portion, if any, of the NOL carryovers and carrybacks to 2013 that were not used in 2013 and were carried to years after 2013.

Example. John Farmington did not use income averaging for 2011, 2012, or 2013. The taxable income before subtracting exemptions on his 2013 Form 1040, line 41, is a negative $1,000. This amount includes an NOL deduction on his 2013 Form 1040, line 21, of $1,450. The $1,450 is the portion of the 2012 NOL that was remaining from 2011 to be carried to 2013. See the examples, earlier. A deduction for exemptions of $3,900 is shown on Form 1040, line 42, and line 43, taxable income, is limited to zero. John does not have an NOL for 2013. John subtracts from the $1,000 negative amount on Form 1040, line 41, the $3,900 deduction for exemptions. The result is a negative $4,900, John's 2013 taxable income, which he enters as a positive amount on line 1 of the 2013 Taxable Income Worksheet.

When John filed his 2013 tax return, he had a $3,000 net capital loss deduction on Schedule D, line 21 (which was also entered on Form 1040, line 13), a $7,000 loss on Schedule D, line 16, and a $5,000 capital loss carryover to 2014 (his 2013 capital loss carryover to 2014 was $5,000, not $4,000, because the amount on his Form 1040, line 41, was a negative $1,000). John adds the $3,000 from Schedule D, line 21, and the $5,000 carryover. He subtracts from the $8,000 result the $7,000 loss on his Schedule D, line 16, and enters $1,000 on line 2 of the worksheet.

John enters -0- on line 3 of the worksheet because he does not have an NOL for 2013 and did not have an NOL carryover from 2013 available to carry to 2014 and later years. The NOL deduction for 2013 of $1,450 was reduced to zero because it did not exceed his modified taxable income of $3,450. Modified taxable income is figured by adding back the $3,000 net capital loss deduction and the $3,900 exemption deduction to negative taxable income (figured without regard to the NOL deduction) of $3,450. John enters $1,000 on line 4 and $3,900 on line 5. He enters $3,900 as a negative amount on Schedule J, line 13. He enters $6,000 on Schedule J, line 14, and $2,100 on Schedule J, line 15. If he uses Schedule J to figure his tax for 2015, he will enter $2,100 on his 2015 Schedule J as his 2013 taxable income for income averaging purposes.

2013 Taxable Income Worksheet—Line 13

Keep for Your Records

Complete this worksheet if your 2013 taxable income was zero or less. See the instructions above before completing this worksheet.

1. Figure the taxable income from your 2013 tax return (or as previously adjusted) without limiting it to zero. If you had an NOL for 2013, **do not** include any NOL carryovers or carrybacks to 2013. Enter the result as a positive amount .... 1. _____

2. If there is a loss on your 2013 Schedule D, line 21, add that loss (as a positive amount) and your 2013 capital loss carryover to 2014. Subtract from that sum the amount of the loss on your 2013 Schedule D, line 16, and enter the result .... 2. _____

3. If you had an NOL for 2013, enter it as a positive amount. Otherwise, enter as a positive amount the portion, if any, of the NOL carryovers and carrybacks to 2013 that were not used in 2013 and were carried to years after 2013 .... 3. _____

4. Add lines 2 and 3 .... 4. _____

5. Subtract line 4 from line 1. Enter the result as a **negative** amount on Schedule J, line 13 .... 5. _____

Line 16

If line 15 is zero or less, enter -0- on line 16. Otherwise, figure the tax on the amount on line 15 using:

- The 2013 Tax Rate Schedules below,
- The 2013 Qualified Dividends and Capital Gain Tax Worksheet, later,
- The 2013 Schedule D Tax Worksheet in the 2013 Schedule D instructions (but use the 2013 Tax Rate Schedules when figuring the tax on the Schedule D Tax Worksheet, lines 42 and 44), or
- The 2013 Foreign Earned Income Tax Worksheet, later.

If your elected farm income includes net capital gain, you must use the 2013 Schedule D Tax Worksheet to figure the tax on the amount on line 15. However, if you filed Form 2555 or 2555-EZ for 2013, you must first complete the 2013 Foreign Earned Income Tax Worksheet, and then use the 2013 Schedule D Tax Worksheet to figure the tax on the amount on line 3 of the Foreign Earned Income Tax Worksheet.

When completing the Schedule D Tax Worksheet, you must allocate 1/3 of the amount on line 2b (and 1/3 of the amount on line 2c, if any) to 2013. If for 2013 you had a capital loss that resulted in a capital loss carryover to 2014, do not reduce the elected farm income allocated to 2013 by any part of the carryover.

2013 Tax Rate Schedules—Line 16

Schedule X—Use if your 2013 filing status was Single or you checked filing status box 1 or 2 on Form 1040NR				
If Schedule J, line 15, is: Over—	But not over—	Enter on Schedule J, line 16		of the amount over—
$0	$8,925	.... 10%		$0
8,925	36,250	$892.50 +	15%	8,925
36,250	87,850	4,991.25 +	25%	36,250
87,850	183,250	17,891.25 +	28%	87,850
183,250	398,350	44,603.25 +	33%	183,250
398,350	400,000	115,586.25 +	35%	398,350
400,000	....	116,163.75 +	39.6%	400,000

Schedule Y-2—Use if your 2013 filing status was Married filing separately or you checked filing status box 3, 4, or 5 on Form 1040NR				
If Schedule J, line 15, is: Over—	But not over—	Enter on Schedule J, line 16		of the amount over—
$0	$8,925	.... 10%		$0
8,925	36,250	$892.50 +	15%	8,925
36,250	73,200	4,991.25 +	25%	36,250
73,200	111,525	14,228.75 +	28%	73,200
111,525	199,175	24,959.75 +	33%	111,525
199,175	225,000	53,884.25 +	35%	199,175
225,000	....	62,923.00 +	39.6%	225,000

Schedule Y-1—Use if your 2013 filing status was Married filing jointly or Qualifying widow(er) or you checked filing status box 6 on Form 1040NR				
If Schedule J, line 15, is: Over—	But not over—	Enter on Schedule J, line 16		of the amount over—
$0	$17,850	.... 10%		$0
17,850	72,500	$1,785.00 +	15%	17,850
72,500	146,400	9,982.50 +	25%	72,500
146,400	223,050	28,457.50 +	28%	146,400
223,050	398,350	49,919.50 +	33%	223,050
398,350	450,000	107,768.50 +	35%	398,350
450,000	....	125,846.00 +	39.6%	450,000

Schedule Z—Use if your 2013 filing status was Head of household				
If Schedule J, line 15, is: Over—	But not over—	Enter on Schedule J, line 16		of the amount over—
$0	$12,750	.... 10%		$0
12,750	48,600	$1,275.00 +	15%	12,750
48,600	125,450	6,652.50 +	25%	48,600
125,450	203,150	25,865.00 +	28%	125,450
203,150	398,350	47,621.00 +	33%	203,150
398,350	425,000	112,037.00 +	35%	398,350
425,000	....	121,364.50 +	39.6%	425,000

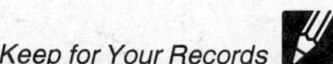
Use this worksheet **only** if both of the following apply.
- Your elected farm income on your 2014 Schedule J, line 2a, does not include any net capital gain.
- You **(a)** entered qualified dividends on your 2013 Form 1040, line 9b (or your 2013 Form 1040A, line 9b, or 2013 Form 1040NR, line 10b); **(b)** entered capital gain distributions directly on your 2013 Form 1040, line 13 (or your 2013 Form 1040A, line 10, or 2013 Form 1040NR, line 14) and were not required to file Schedule D; or **(c)** filed Schedule D in 2013 and you answered "Yes" on lines 17 and 20 of that Schedule D.

1. Amount from your 2014 Schedule J, line 15. If for 2013 you filed Form 2555 or 2555-EZ, enter the amount from line 3 of the 2013 Foreign Earned Income Tax Worksheet . . . . **1.** _____

2. Amount from your 2013 Form 1040, line 9b* (or your 2013 Form 1040A, line 9b, or 2013 Form 1040NR, line 10b) . . . . . **2.** _____

3. Did you file Schedule D in 2013?*
   ☐ **Yes.** Enter the **smaller** of line 15 or 16 of your 2013 Schedule D, but do not enter less than -0-   **3.** _____
   ☐ **No.** Enter the amount from your 2013 Form 1040, line 13 (or your 2013 Form 1040A, line 10, or 2013 Form 1040NR, line 14)

4. Add lines 2 and 3 . . . . **4.** _____

5. Amount, if any, from your 2013 Form 4952, line 4g . . . . **5.** _____

6. Subtract line 5 from line 4. If zero or less, enter -0- . . . . **6.** _____

7. Subtract line 6 from line 1. If zero or less, enter -0- . . . . **7.** _____

8. Enter one of the following three amounts depending on your filing status:
   - $36,250 if single or married filing separately, or if you checked filing status box 1, 2, 3, 4, or 5 on Form 1040NR;
   - $72,500 if married filing jointly or qualifying widow(er) or if you checked filing status box 6 on Form 1040NR;
   - $48,600 if head of household.   . . . . **8.** _____

9. Enter the smaller of line 1 or line 8 . . . . **9.** _____

10. Enter the smaller of line 7 or line 9 . . . . **10.** _____

11. Subtract line 10 from line 9. This amount is taxed at 0% . . . . **11.** _____

12. Enter the smaller of line 1 or line 6 . . . . **12.** _____

13. Enter the amount from line 11 . . . . **13.** _____

14. Subtract line 13 from line 12 . . . . **14.** _____

15. Enter:
    $400,000 if single,
    $225,000 if married filing separately,
    $450,000 if married filing jointly or qualifying widow(er),
    $425,000 if head of household.   . . . . **15.** _____

16. Enter the smaller of line 1 or line 15 . . . . **16.** _____

17. Add lines 7 and 11 . . . . **17.** _____

18. Subtract line 17 from line 16. If zero or less, enter -0- . . . . **18.** _____

19. Enter the smaller of line 14 or line 18 . . . . **19.** _____

20. Multiply line 19 by 15% (.15) . . . . **20.** _____

21. Add lines 11 and 19 . . . . **21.** _____

22. Subtract line 21 from 12 . . . . **22.** _____

23. Multiply line 22 by 20% (.20) . . . . **23.** _____

24. Figure the tax on the amount on line 7. Use the 2013 Tax Rate Schedules . . . . **24.** _____

25. Add lines 20, 23, and 24 . . . . **25.** _____

26. Figure the tax on the amount on line 1. Use the 2013 Tax Rate Schedules . . . . **26.** _____

27. **Tax.** Enter the **smaller** of line 25 or line 26 here and on your 2014 Schedule J, line 16. If for 2013 you filed Form 2555 or 2555-EZ, do not enter this amount on Schedule J, line 16. Instead, enter it on line 4 of the 2013 Foreign Earned Income Tax Worksheet . . . . **27.** _____

If for 2013 you filed Form 2555 or 2555-EZ, see the footnote in the 2013 Foreign Earned Income Tax Worksheet before completing this line.

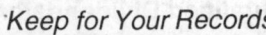

Use this worksheet if you claimed the foreign earned income exclusion or housing exclusion on your 2013 Form 1040 using Form 2555 or 2555-EZ. However, if Schedule J, line 15, is zero or less, do not complete this worksheet.

1. Enter the amount from your 2014 Schedule J, line 15 .... **1.** _____

2. Enter the amount from your (and your spouse's, if filing jointly) 2013 Form 2555, lines 45 and 50, or Form 2555-EZ, line 18 .... **2.** _____

3. Add lines 1 and 2 .... **3.** _____

4. **Tax on the amount on line 3.** Use the 2013 Tax Rate Schedules, the 2013 Qualified Dividends and Capital Gain Tax Worksheet,* or the 2013 Schedule D Tax Worksheet in the 2013 Schedule D instructions,* whichever applies. .... **4.** _____

5. **Tax on the amount on line 2.** Use the 2013 Tax Rate Schedules. .... **5.** _____

6. Subtract line 5 from line 4. Enter the result. If zero or less, enter -0-. Also include this amount on your 2014 Schedule J, line 16 .... **6.** _____

Enter the amount from line 3 above on line 1 of the 2013 Qualified Dividends and Capital Gain Tax Worksheet or the 2013 Schedule D Tax Worksheet if you use either of those worksheets to figure the tax on line 4 above. Complete the rest of that worksheet through line 6 (line 10 if you use the Schedule D Tax Worksheet). Next, you must determine if you had a capital gain excess. To find out if you had a capital gain excess, subtract the amount from your 2014 Schedule J, line 15, from line 6 of your 2013 Qualified Dividends and Capital Gain Tax Worksheet (line 10 of your 2013 Schedule D Tax Worksheet). If the result is more than zero, that amount is your capital gain excess.

If you did not have a capital gain excess, complete the rest of either of those worksheets according to the worksheet's instructions. Then complete lines 5 and 6 above.

If you had a capital gain excess, complete a second 2013 Qualified Dividends and Capital Gain Tax Worksheet or 2013 Schedule D Tax Worksheet (whichever applies) as instructed above but in its entirety and with the following additional modifications. Then complete lines 5 and 6 above. These modifications are to be made only for purposes of filling out the 2013 Foreign Earned Income Tax Worksheet above.

1. Reduce (but not below zero) the amount you would otherwise enter on line 3 of your 2013 Qualified Dividends and Capital Gain Tax Worksheet or line 9 of your 2013 Schedule D Tax Worksheet by your capital gain excess.

2. Reduce (but not below zero) the amount you would otherwise enter on line 2 of your 2013 Qualified Dividends and Capital Gain Tax Worksheet or line 6 of your 2013 Schedule D Tax Worksheet by any of your capital gain excess not used in (1) above.

3. Reduce (but not below zero) the amount on your 2013 Schedule D (Form 1040), line 18, by your capital gain excess.

4. Include your capital gain excess as a loss on line 16 of your 2013 Unrecaptured Section 1250 Gain Worksheet in the 2013 Instructions for Schedule D (Form 1040).

Lines 19, 20, and 21

For reporting purposes, the "tax" line of your tax return may include amounts that are not tax imposed by section 1 of the Internal Revenue Code. For example, your "tax" line may, in addition to the tax imposed by section 1, include amounts from Forms 8814 or 4972; alternative minimum tax if you filed Form 1040A; or amounts from the recapture of an education credit. Do not include these other tax amounts on lines 19 through 21.

If you amended your return or the IRS made changes to it, make sure you enter the corrected amount.

2014 Instructions for Schedule R (Form 1040A or 1040)

Credit for the Elderly or the Disabled

Use Schedule R (Form 1040A or 1040) to figure the credit for the elderly or the disabled.

Future Developments. For the latest information about developments related to Schedule R (Form 1040A or 1040) and its instructions, such as legislation enacted after they were published, go to *www.irs.gov/scheduler*.

Additional information. See Pub. 524 for more details.

Who Can Take the Credit

The credit is based on your filing status, age, and income. If you are married and filing a joint return, it is also based on your spouse's age and income. You may be able to take this credit if either of the following applies.

1. You were age 65 or older at the end of 2014, or

2. You were under age 65 at the end of 2014 and you meet all of the following.

a. You were permanently and totally disabled on the date you retired. If you retired before 1977, you must have been permanently and totally disabled on January 1, 1976, or January 1, 1977.

b. You received taxable disability income for 2014.

c. On January 1, 2014, you had not reached mandatory retirement age (the age when your employer's retirement program would have required you to retire).

For the definition of permanent and total disability, see *What Is Permanent and Total Disability*, later. Also, see the instructions for *Part II. Statement of Permanent and Total Disability*.

Age 65

You are considered age 65 on the day before your 65th birthday. As a result, if you were born on January 1, 1950, you are considered to be age 65 at the end of 2014.

Married Persons Filing Separate Returns

If your filing status is married filing separately and you lived with your spouse at any time during 2014, you cannot take the credit.

Nonresident Aliens

If you were a nonresident alien at any time during 2014, you may be able to take the credit only if your filing status is married filing jointly.

Income Limits

See *Income Limits for the Credit for the Elderly or the Disabled*, later.

Want the IRS To Figure Your Credit?

If you can take the credit and you want us to figure it for you, check the box in Part I of Schedule R (Form 1040A or 1040) for your filing status and age. Fill in Part II and lines 11 and 13 of Part III if they apply to you. If you file Form 1040A, enter "CFE" in the space to the left of Form 1040A, line 32. If you file Form 1040, check box **c** on Form 1040, line 54, and enter "CFE" on the line next to that box. Attach Schedule R (Form 1040A or 1040) to your return.

What Is Permanent and Total Disability?

A person is permanently and totally disabled if both 1 and 2 below apply.

1. He or she cannot engage in any substantial gainful activity because of a physical or mental condition.

2. A qualified physician determines that the condition has lasted or can be expected to last continuously for at least a year or can lead to death.

Examples 1 and 2, next, show situations in which the individuals are considered engaged in a substantial gainful activity. Example 3 shows a person who might not be considered engaged in a substantial gainful activity. In each example, the person was under age 65 at the end of the year.

Income Limits for the Credit for the Elderly or the Disabled

IF you are . . .	THEN you generally cannot take the credit if:	
	The amount on Form 1040A, line 22, or Form 1040, line 38, is . . .	Or you received . . .
Single, head of household, or qualifying widow(er) with dependent child	$17,500 or more	$5,000 or more of nontaxable social security or other nontaxable pensions, annuities, or disability income
Married filing jointly and only one spouse is eligible for the credit	$20,000 or more	$5,000 or more of nontaxable social security or other nontaxable pensions, annuities, or disability income
Married filing jointly and both spouses are eligible for the credit	$25,000 or more	$7,500 or more of nontaxable social security or other nontaxable pensions, annuities, or disability income
Married filing separately and you lived apart from your spouse for all of 2014	$12,500 or more	$3,750 or more of nontaxable social security or other nontaxable pensions, annuities, or disability income

Example 1. Sue retired on disability as a sales clerk. She now works as a full-time babysitter earning minimum wage. Although she does different work, Sue babysits on ordinary terms for the minimum wage. She cannot take the credit because she is engaged in a substantial gainful activity.

Example 2. Mary, the president of XYZ Corporation, retired on disability because of her terminal illness. On her doctor's advice, she works part time as a manager and is paid more than the minimum wage. Her employer sets her days and hours. Although Mary's illness is terminal and she works part time, the work is done at her employer's convenience. Mary is considered engaged in a substantial gainful activity and cannot take the credit.

Example 3. John, who retired on disability, took a job with a former employer on a trial basis. The purpose of the job was to see if John could do the work. The trial period lasted for some time during which John was paid at a rate equal to the minimum wage. But because of John's disability, he was given only light duties of a nonproductive, make-work nature. Unless the activity is both substantial and gainful, John is not engaged in a substantial gainful activity. The activity was gainful because John was paid at a rate at or above the minimum wage. However, the activity was not substantial because the duties were of a nonproductive, make-work nature. More facts are needed to determine if John is able to engage in a substantial gainful activity.

Disability Income

Generally, disability income is the total amount you were paid under your employer's accident and health plan or pension plan that is included in your income as wages or payments instead of wages for the time you were absent from work because of permanent and total disability. However, any payment you received from a plan that does not provide for disability retirement is not disability income.

In figuring the credit, disability income does not include any amount you received from your employer's pension plan after you have reached mandatory retirement age.

For more details on disability income, see Pub. 525.

Part II. Statement of Permanent and Total Disability

If you checked box 2, 4, 5, 6, or 9 in Part I and you did not file a physician's statement for 1983 or an earlier year, or you filed or got a statement for tax years after 1983 and your physician signed on line A of the statement, you must have your physician complete a statement certifying that:
* You were permanently and totally disabled on the date you retired, or
* If you retired before 1977, you were permanently and totally disabled on January 1, 1976, or January 1, 1977.

You do not have to file this statement with your tax return. But you must keep it for your records. You can use the physician's statement later in these instructions for this purpose. Your physician should show on the statement if the disability has lasted or can be expected to last continuously for at least a year, or if there is no reasonable probability that the disabled condition will ever improve. If you file a joint return and you checked box 5 in Part I, you and your spouse must each get a statement.

If you filed a physician's statement for 1983 or an earlier year, or you filed or got a statement for tax years after 1983 and your physician signed on line B of the statement, you do not have to get another statement for 2014. But you must check the box on line 2 in Part II to certify all three of the following.

1. You filed or got a physician's statement in an earlier year.

2. You were permanently and totally disabled during 2014.

3. You were unable to engage in any substantial gainful activity during 2014 because of your physical or mental condition.

If you checked box 4, 5, or 6 in Part I, enter in the space above the box on line 2 in Part II the first name(s) of the spouse(s) for whom the box is checked.

If the Department of Veterans Affairs (VA) certifies that you are permanently and totally disabled, you can use VA Form 21-0172 instead of the physician's statement. VA Form 21-0172 must be signed by a person authorized by the VA to do so. You can get this form from your local VA regional office.

Part III. Figure Your Credit

Line 11

If you checked box 2, 4, 5, 6, or 9 in Part I, use the following chart to complete line 11.

IF you checked . . .	THEN enter on line 11 . . .
Box 6	The total of $5,000 plus the disability income you reported on Form 1040A or 1040 for the spouse who was under age 65.
Box 2, 4, or 9	The total amount of disability income you reported on Form 1040A or 1040.
Box 5	The total amount of disability income you reported on Form 1040A or 1040 for both you and your spouse.

Example 1. Bill, age 63, retired on permanent and total disability in 2014. He received $4,000 of taxable disability income that he reports on Form 1040, line 7. He is filing jointly with his wife who was age 67 in 2014, and he checked box 6 in Part I. On line 11, Bill enters $9,000 ($5,000 plus the $4,000 of disability income he reports on Form 1040, line 7).

Example 2. John checked box 2 in Part I and enters $5,000 on line 10. He received $3,000 of taxable disability income, which he enters on line 11. John also enters $3,000 on line 12 (the smaller of line 10 or line 11). The largest amount he can use to figure the credit is $3,000.

Lines 13a Through 18

The amount on which you figure your credit can be reduced if you received certain types of nontaxable pensions, annuities, or disability income. The amount can also be reduced if your adjusted gross income is over a certain amount, depending on which box you checked in Part I.

Line 13a. Enter any social security benefits (before deduction of Medicare premiums) you (and your spouse if filing jointly) received for 2014 that are not taxable. Also, enter any tier 1 railroad retirement benefits treated as social security that are not taxable.

If any of your social security or equivalent railroad retirement benefits are taxable, the amount to enter on this line is generally the difference between the amounts entered on Form 1040A, line 14a and line 14b, or Form 1040, line 20a and line 20b.

 If your social security or equivalent railroad retirement benefits are reduced because of workers' compensation benefits, treat the workers' compensation benefits as social security benefits when completing Schedule R (Form 1040A or 1040), line 13a.

Line 13b. Enter the total of the following types of income that you (and your spouse if filing jointly) received for 2014.
- Veterans' pensions (but not military disability pensions).
- Any other pension, annuity, or disability benefit that is excluded from income under any provision of federal law other than the Internal Revenue Code. Do not include amounts that are treated as a return of your cost of a pension or annuity.

Do not include on line 13b any pension, annuity, or similar allowance for personal injuries or sickness resulting from active service in the armed forces of any country, or in the National Oceanic and Atmospheric Administration or the Public Health Service. Also, do not include a disability annuity payable under section 808 of the Foreign Service Act of 1980.

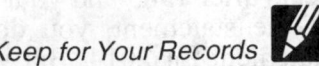
Use this worksheet to figure your credit limit.

1. Enter the amount from Form 1040A, line 30; or Form 1040, line 47 .... **1.** _____
2. Enter the amount from Form 1040A, line 31; or Form 1040, lines 48 and 49 .... **2.** _____
3. Subtract line 2 from line 1. Enter this amount on Schedule R (Form 1040A or 1040), line 21. But if zero or less, **STOP**, you cannot take this credit .... **3.** _____

Instructions for Physician's Statement

Taxpayer

If you retired after 1976, enter the date you retired in the space provided on the statement below.

Physician

A person is permanently and totally disabled if both of the following apply.

1. He or she cannot engage in any substantial gainful activity because of a physical or mental condition.

2. A physician determines that the disability has lasted or can be expected to last continuously for at least a year or can lead to death.

Physician's Statement

 Keep for Your Records

I certify that _____

Name of disabled person

was permanently and totally disabled on January 1, 1976, or January 1, 1977, or was permanently and totally

disabled on the date he or she retired. If retired after 1976, enter the date retired. ▶ _____

Physician: Sign your name on either line A or B below.

A The disability has lasted or can be expected to
last continuously for at least a year .... _____

Physician's signature	Date

B There is no reasonable probability that the
disabled condition will ever improve .... _____

Physician's signature	Date

Physician's name	Physician's address

![Department of the Treasury logo](IRS logo) **Department of the Treasury**
Internal Revenue Service

2014 Instructions for Schedule SE (Form 1040)

Self-Employment Tax

Use Schedule SE (Form 1040) to figure the tax due on net earnings from self-employment. The Social Security Administration uses the information from Schedule SE to figure your benefits under the social security program. This tax applies no matter how old you are and even if you are already getting social security or Medicare benefits.

Additional information. See Pub. 225 or Pub. 334.

Section references are to the Internal Revenue Code unless otherwise noted.

Future Developments

For the latest information about developments related to Schedule SE (Form 1040) and its instructions, such as legislation enacted after they were published, go to *www.irs.gov/schedulese*.

What's New

Maximum income subject to social security tax. For 2014, the maximum amount of self-employment income subject to social security tax is $117,000.

General Instructions

Who Must File Schedule SE

You must file Schedule SE if:
- The amount on line 4 of Short Schedule SE or line 4c of Long Schedule SE is $400 or more, **or**
- You had church employee income of $108.28 or more. See *Employees of Churches and Church Organizations*. However, see the Exception, next.

Exception. Self-employment income from earnings as a minister, member of a religious order, or Christian Science practitioner, **is not** church employee income. However, see *Ministers, Members of Religious Orders, and Christian Science Practitioners* for information on how to report these earnings.

 Even if you had a loss or a small amount of income from self-employment, it may be to your benefit to file Schedule SE and use either "optional method" in Part II of Long Schedule SE (discussed later).

Who Must Pay Self-Employment (SE) Tax

Self-Employed Persons

You must pay SE tax if you had net earnings of $400 or more as a self-employed person. If you are in business (farm or nonfarm) for yourself, you are self-employed.

You must also pay SE tax on your share of certain partnership income and your guaranteed payments. See *Partnership Income or Loss*, later.

Employees of Churches and Church Organizations

If you had church employee income of $108.28 or more, you must pay SE tax. Church employee income is wages you received as an employee (other than as a minister, a member of a religious order, or a Christian Science practitioner) of a church or qualified church-controlled organization that has a certificate in effect electing an exemption from employer social security and Medicare taxes.

Ministers, Members of Religious Orders, and Christian Science Practitioners

In most cases, you must pay SE tax on salaries and other income for services you performed as a minister, a member of a religious order who has not taken a vow of poverty, or a Christian Science practitioner. But if you filed Form 4361 and received IRS approval, you will be exempt from paying SE tax on those net earnings. If you had no other income subject to SE tax, enter "Exempt—Form 4361" on Form 1040, line 57, or Form 1040NR, line 55. However, if you had other earnings of $400 or more subject to SE tax, see line A at the top of Long Schedule SE.

 If you have ever filed Form 2031 to elect social security coverage on your earnings as a minister, you cannot revoke that election.

If you must pay SE tax, include this income on either Short or Long Schedule SE, line 2. But do not report it on Long Schedule SE, line 5a; it is not considered church employee income. Also, include on line 2:
- The rental value of a home or an allowance for a home furnished to you (including payments for utilities), and
- The value of meals and lodging provided to you, your spouse, and your dependents for your employer's convenience.

However, do not include on line 2:
- Retirement benefits you received from a church plan after retirement, or
- The rental value of a home or an allowance for a home furnished to you (including payments for utilities) after retirement.

If you were a duly ordained minister who was an employee of a church and you must pay SE tax, the unreimbursed business expenses that you incurred as a church employee are allowed only as an itemized deduction for income tax purposes. However, when figuring SE tax, subtract on line 2 the allowable expenses from your self-employment earnings and attach an explanation.

If you were a U.S. citizen or resident alien serving outside the United States as a minister or member of a religious order and you must pay SE tax, you cannot reduce your net earnings by the foreign earned income exclusion or the foreign housing exclusion or deduction.

See Pub. 517 for details.

Oct 30, 2014

Members of Certain Religious Sects

If you have conscientious objections to social security insurance because of your membership in and belief in the teachings of a religious sect recognized as being in existence at all times since December 31, 1950, and which has provided a reasonable level of living for its dependent members, you are exempt from SE tax if you received IRS approval by filing Form 4029. In this case, do not file Schedule SE. Instead, enter "Exempt—Form 4029" on Form 1040, line 57, or Form 1040NR, line 55. See Pub. 517 for details.

U.S. Citizens Employed by Foreign Governments or International Organizations

You must pay SE tax on income you earned as a U.S. citizen employed by a foreign government (or, in certain cases, by a wholly owned instrumentality of a foreign government or an international organization under the International Organizations Immunities Act) for services performed in the United States, Puerto Rico, Guam, American Samoa, the Commonwealth of the Northern Mariana Islands, or the U.S. Virgin Islands. Report income from this employment on either Short or Long Schedule SE, line 2. If you performed services elsewhere as an employee of a foreign government or an international organization, those earnings are exempt from SE tax.

Exception—Dual citizens. A person with dual U.S.-foreign citizenship is generally considered to be a U.S. citizen for social security purposes. However, if you are a U.S. citizen and also a citizen of a country with which the United States has a bilateral social security agreement, other than Canada or Italy, your work for the government of that foreign country is always exempt from U.S. social security taxes. For further information about these agreements, see the exception shown in the next section.

U.S. Citizens or Resident Aliens Living Outside the United States

If you are a self-employed U.S. citizen or resident alien living outside the United States, in most cases you must pay SE tax. You cannot reduce your foreign earnings from self-employment by your foreign earned income exclusion.

Exception. The United States has social security agreements with many countries to eliminate dual taxes under two social security systems. Under these agreements, you must generally pay social security and Medicare taxes to only the country you live in.

The United States now has social security agreements with the following countries: Australia, Austria, Belgium, Canada, Chile, Czech Republic, Denmark, Finland, France, Germany, Greece, Ireland, Italy, Japan, Luxembourg, the Netherlands, Norway, Poland, Portugal, South Korea, Spain, Slovak Republic, Sweden, Switzerland, and the United Kingdom.

If you have questions about international social security agreements, or to see if any additional agreements have been entered into, you can visit the Social Security Administration's (SSA's) International Programs website at *www.socialsecurity.gov/international*. The website also provides contact information for questions about benefits and the agreements.

If your self-employment income is exempt from SE tax, you should get a statement from the appropriate agency of the foreign country verifying that your self-employment income is subject to social security coverage in that country. If the foreign country will not issue the statement, contact the SSA Office of International Programs. Do not complete Schedule SE. Instead, attach a copy of the statement to Form 1040 and enter "Exempt, see attached statement" on Form 1040, line 57.

Nonresident Alien

If you are a self-employed nonresident alien living in the United States, you must pay SE tax if an international social security agreement in effect determines that you are covered under the U.S. social security system. See *Exception* under *U.S. Citizens or Resident Aliens Living Outside the United States*, earlier, for information about international social security agreements. If your self-employment income is subject to SE tax, complete Schedule SE and file it with your Form 1040NR.

Chapter 11 Bankruptcy Cases

While you are a debtor in a chapter 11 bankruptcy case, your net profit or loss from self-employment (for example, from Schedule C or Schedule F) will not be included in your Form 1040 income. Instead, it will be included on the income tax return (Form 1041) of the bankruptcy estate. However, you (not the bankruptcy estate) are responsible for paying SE tax on your net earnings from self-employment.

Enter on the dotted line to the left of Schedule SE, line 3, "Chap. 11 bankruptcy income" and the amount of your net profit or (loss). Combine that amount with the total of lines 1a, 1b, and 2 (if any) and enter the result on line 3.

For other reporting requirements, see *Chapter 11 Bankruptcy Cases* in the Instructions for Form 1040.

More Than One Business

If you had two or more businesses subject to self-employment tax, your net earnings from self-employment are the combined net earnings from all of your businesses. If you had a loss in one business, it reduces the income from another. Figure the combined SE tax on one Schedule SE.

Joint Returns

Show the name of the spouse with self-employment income on Schedule SE. If both spouses have self-employment income, each must file a separate Schedule SE. However, if one spouse qualifies to use Short Schedule SE (front of form) and the other must use Long Schedule SE (back of form), both can use the same form. One spouse should complete the front and the other the back.

Include the total profits or losses from all businesses on Form 1040. Enter the combined SE tax on Form 1040, line 57.

Community Income

If any of the income from a business (including farming) is community income, then the income and deductions are reported as follows.

• If only one spouse participates in the business, all of the income from that business is the self-employment earnings of the spouse who carried on the business.

- If both spouses participate, the income and deductions are allocated to the spouses based on their distributive shares.
- If either or both spouses are partners in a partnership, see *Partnership Income or Loss*, later.
- If both spouses elected to treat the business as a qualifying joint venture, see *Qualified Joint Ventures*, later.

Married filing separately. If you and your spouse had community income and file separate returns, attach Schedule SE to the return of each spouse with self-employment earnings under the rules described earlier. Also attach Schedule(s) C, C-EZ, or F (showing the spouse's share of community income and expenses) to the return of each spouse.

Spouse who carried on the business. If you are the only spouse who carried on the business, you must include on Schedule SE, line 3, the net profit or (loss) reported on the other spouse's Schedule C, C-EZ, or F (except in those cases described later under *Income and Losses Not Included in Net Earnings From Self-Employment*). Enter on the dotted line to the left of Schedule SE, line 3, "Community income taxed to spouse" and the amount of any net profit or (loss) allocated to your spouse as community income. Combine that amount with the total of lines 1a, 1b, and 2. Enter the result on line 3.

Spouse who did not carry on the business. If you are not the spouse who carried on the business and you had no other income subject to SE tax, enter "Exempt community income" on Form 1040, line 57, or Form 1040NR, line 55. Do not file Schedule SE.

But if you have $400 or more of other earnings subject to SE tax, you must file Schedule SE. Include on Schedule SE, line 1a or 2, the net profit or (loss) from Schedule(s) C, C-EZ, or F allocated to you as community income. On the dotted line to the left of Schedule SE, line 3, enter "Exempt community income" and the allocated amount. Figure the amount to enter on line 3 as follows.

- If the allocated amount is a net profit, subtract it from the total of lines 1a, 1b, and 2.

- If the allocated amount is a loss, treat it as a positive amount and add it to the total of lines 1a, 1b, and 2.

 Community income included on Schedule(s) C, C-EZ, or F must be divided for income tax purposes based on the community property laws of your state. See Pub. 555 for more information.

Qualified Joint Ventures

If you and your spouse materially participate as the only members of a jointly owned and operated business, and you file a joint return for the tax year, you can make a joint election to be taxed as a qualified joint venture instead of a partnership. For information on what it means to materially participate, see *Material participation* in the Instructions for Schedule C.

To make this election, you must divide all items of income, gain, loss, deduction, and credit attributable to the business between you and your spouse in accordance with your respective interests in the venture. Each of you must file a separate Schedule C, C-EZ, or F. On each line of your separate Schedule C, C-EZ, or F, you must enter your share of the applicable income, deduction, or loss. Each of you also must file a separate Schedule SE to pay SE tax, as applicable.

For more information on qualified joint ventures, go to IRS.gov and enter "qualified joint venture" in the search box.

Rental real estate business. If you and your spouse make the election to be taxed as a qualified joint venture for your rental real estate business, the income generally is not subject to SE tax. To indicate that election, be sure to check the "QJV" box in Part I, line 2, of each Schedule E that the rental property is listed on. Do not file Schedule SE unless you have other income subject to SE tax. For an exception to this income not being subject to SE tax, see item 3 under *Other Income and Losses Included in Net Earnings From Self-Employment*, later.

If the election is made for a farm rental business to be taxed as a qualified joint venture, the income from which is not subject to self-employment tax, file two Forms 4835, Farm Rental Income and Expenses.

Fiscal Year Filers

If your tax year is a fiscal year, use the tax rate and annual earnings limit that apply at the time the fiscal year begins. Do not prorate the tax or annual earnings limit for a fiscal year that overlaps the date of a change in the tax or annual earnings limit.

Line Instructions

Read the flowchart on page 1 of Schedule SE to see if you can use Section A—Short Schedule SE, or if you must use Section B—Long Schedule SE. For either section, you will need to figure your net earnings from self-employment. To find out what is included as net earnings from self-employment, see *Net Earnings From Self-Employment*, later.

 *Enter all negative amounts in parentheses.*

You Have Only Church Employee Income Subject to SE Tax

If your only income subject to SE tax is church employee income (described earlier under *Employees of Churches and Church Organizations*), skip lines 1 through 4b. Enter -0- on line 4c and go to line 5a.

Exception. Income from services you perform as a minister, a member of a religious order, or a Christian Science practitioner is **not** church employee income.

Line 1b (Short or Long Schedule SE)

If you were receiving social security retirement or social security disability benefits at the time you received your Conservation Reserve Program (CRP) payment(s), enter the amount of your taxable CRP payment(s) on line 1b. These payments are included on Schedule F, line 4b, or listed on Schedule K-1 (Form 1065), box 20, code Z.

Line 4 (Short Schedule SE)

If line 4 is less than $400 and you have an amount on line 1b, combine lines 1a and 2.

• If the total of lines 1a and 2 is $434 or more, file Schedule SE (completed through line 4) with your tax return. Enter -0- on Form 1040, line 57, or Form 1040NR, line 55.

• If the total of lines 1a and 2 is less than $434, **do not** file Schedule SE unless you choose to use an optional method for figuring your SE tax.

Lines 4a Through 4c (Long Schedule SE)

If both lines 4a and 4c are less than $400 and you have an amount on line 1b, combine lines 1a and 2.

• If the total of lines 1a and 2 is $434 or more, file Schedule SE (completed through line 4c) with your tax return. Enter -0- on Form 1040, line 57,* or Form 1040NR, line 55.*

• If the total of lines 1a and 2 is less than $434, **do not** file Schedule SE unless you choose to use an optional method to figure your SE tax.

If you also have church employee income (described earlier under Employees of Churches and Church Organizations), also complete lines 5a and 5b. Complete the rest of Schedule SE, as appropriate.

Additional Medicare Tax

A 0.9% Additional Medicare Tax may apply to you if the total amount from line 4 (Short Schedule SE) or line 6 (Long Schedule SE) of all your Schedules SE exceeds one of the following threshold amounts (based on your filing status).

• Married filing jointly—$250,000
• Married filing separately—$125,000
• Single, Head of household, or Qualifying widow(er)—$200,000

If you have both wages and self-employment income, the threshold amount for applying the Additional Medicare Tax on the self-employment income is reduced (but not below zero) by the amount of wages subject to Additional Medicare Tax.

Use Form 8959, Additional Medicare Tax, to figure this tax. For more information, see the Instructions for Form 8959, or visit IRS.gov and enter "Additional Medicare Tax" in the search box.

Net Earnings From Self-Employment

In most cases, net earnings include your net profit from a farm or nonfarm business.

Partnership Income or Loss

If you were a general or limited partner in a partnership, include on line 1a or line 2, whichever applies, the amount of net earnings from self-employment from Schedule K-1 (Form 1065), box 14, code A, and Schedule K-1 (Form 1065-B), box 9, code J1. General partners should reduce this amount by certain expenses before entering it on Schedule SE. See your Schedule K-1 instructions. If you reduce the amount you enter on Schedule SE, you must attach an explanation. Limited partners should include only guaranteed payments for services actually rendered to or on behalf of the partnership.

If a partner died and the partnership continued, include in self-employment income the deceased's distributive share of the partnership's ordinary income or loss through the end of the month in which he or she died. See section 1402(f).

If you were married and both you and your spouse were partners in a partnership, each of you must report your net earnings from self-employment from the partnership. Each of you must file a separate Schedule SE and report the partnership income or loss on Schedule E (Form 1040), Part II, for income tax purposes. If only one of you was a partner in a partnership, the spouse who was the partner must report his or her net earnings from self-employment from the partnership.

Community income. Your own distributive share of partnership income is included in figuring your net earnings from self-employment. Unlike the division of that income between spouses for figuring income tax, no part of your share can be included in figuring your spouse's net earnings from self-employment.

Share Farming

You are considered self-employed if you produce crops or livestock on someone else's land for a share of the crops or livestock produced (or a share of the proceeds from the sale of them). This applies even if you paid another person (an agent) to do the actual work or management for you. Report your net earnings for income tax purposes on Schedule F (Form 1040) and for SE tax purposes on Schedule SE. See Pub. 225 for details.

Other Income and Losses Included in Net Earnings From Self-Employment

1. Rental income from a farm if, as landlord, you materially participated in the production or management of the production of farm products on this land. This income is farm earnings. To determine whether you materially participated in farm management or production, do not consider the activities of any agent who acted for you. The material participation tests for landlords are explained in Pub. 225.

2. Cash or a payment-in-kind from the Department of Agriculture for participating in a land diversion program.

3. Payments for the use of rooms or other space when you also provided substantial services for the convenience of your tenants. Examples are hotel rooms, boarding houses, tourist camps or homes, trailer parks, parking lots, warehouses, and storage garages. See Pub. 334 for more information.

4. Income from the retail sale of newspapers and magazines if you were age 18 or older and kept the profits.

5. Income you receive as a direct seller. Newspaper carriers or distributors of any age are direct sellers if certain conditions apply. See Pub. 334 for details.

6. Amounts received by current or former self-employed insurance agents and salespersons that are:

a. Paid after retirement but figured as a percentage of commissions received from the paying company before retirement,

b. Renewal commissions, or

c. Deferred commissions paid after retirement for sales made before retirement.

However, certain termination payments received by former insurance salespersons are not included in net earnings from self-employment (as explained in item 10 under *Income and Losses Not Included in Net Earnings From Self-Employment*).

7. Income of certain crew members of fishing vessels with crews of normally fewer than 10 people. See Pub. 334 for details.

8. Fees as a state or local government employee if you were paid only on a fee basis and the job was not covered under a federal-state social security coverage agreement.

9. Interest received in the course of any trade or business, such as interest on notes or accounts receivable.

10. Fees and other payments received by you for services as a director of a corporation.

11. Recapture amounts under sections 179 and 280F that you included in gross income because the business use of the property dropped to 50% or less. Do not include amounts you recaptured on the disposition of property. See Form 4797.

12. Generally, fees you received as a professional fiduciary. This may also apply to fees paid to you as a nonprofessional fiduciary if the fees relate to active participation in the operation of the estate's business, or the management of an estate that required extensive management activities over a long period of time.

13. Gain or loss from section 1256 contracts or related property by an options or commodities dealer in the normal course of dealing in or trading section 1256 contracts.

Income and Losses Not Included in Net Earnings From Self-Employment

1. Salaries, fees, and other income subject to social security or Medicare tax that you received for performing services as an employee, including services performed as an employee under the railroad retirement system. This includes services performed as a public official (except as a fee basis government employee as explained in item 8 under *Other Income and Losses Included in Net Earnings From Self-Employment*, earlier).

2. Fees received for services performed as a notary public. If you had no other income subject to SE tax, enter "Exempt—Notary" on Form 1040, line 57. Do not file Schedule SE. However, if you had other earnings of $400 or more subject to SE tax, enter "Exempt—Notary" and the amount of your net profit as a notary public from Schedule C or Schedule C-EZ on the dotted line to the left of Schedule SE, line 3. Subtract that amount from the total of lines 1a, 1b, and 2, and enter the result on line 3.

3. Income you received as a retired partner under a written partnership plan that provides for lifelong periodic retirement payments if you had no other interest in the partnership and did not perform services for it during the year.

4. Income from real estate rentals if you did not receive the income in the course of a trade or business as a real estate dealer. Report this income on Schedule E.

5. Income from farm rentals (including rentals paid in crop shares) if, as landlord, you did not materially participate in the production or management of the production of farm products on the land. See Pub. 225 for details. Report this income on Form 4835. Use two Forms 4835 if you and your spouse made an election to be taxed as a qualified joint venture.

6. Payments you receive from the Conservation Reserve Program if you are receiving social security benefits for retirement or disability. Deduct these payments on line 1b of Schedule SE.

7. Dividends on shares of stock and interest on bonds, notes, or other evidence of indebtedness issued with interest coupons or in registered form by any corporation (including those issued by a government or its political subdivision), if you did not receive the income in the course of your trade or business as a dealer in stocks or securities.

8. Gain or loss from:

a. The sale or exchange of a capital asset;

b. The sale, exchange, involuntary conversion, or other disposition of property unless the property is stock in trade or other property that would be includible in inventory, or held primarily for sale to customers in the ordinary course of the business; or

c. Certain transactions in timber, coal, or domestic iron ore.

9. Net operating losses from other years.

10. Termination payments you received as a former insurance salesperson if all of the following conditions are met.

a. The payment was received from an insurance company because of services you performed as an insurance salesperson for the company.

b. The payment was received after termination of your agreement to perform services for the company.

c. You did not perform any services for the company after termination and before the end of the year in which you received the payment.

d. You entered into a covenant not to compete against the company for at least a 1-year period beginning on the date of termination.

e. The amount of the payment depended primarily on policies sold by or credited to your account during the last year of the agreement, or the extent to which those policies remain in force for some period after termination, or both.

f. The amount of the payment did not depend to any extent on length of service or overall earnings from services performed for the company (regardless of whether eligibility for the payment depended on length of service).

Statutory Employee Income

If you were a statutory employee, do not include the net profit or (loss) from Schedule C, line 31 (or the net profit from Schedule C-EZ, line 3), on Short or Long Schedule SE, line 2. But if you file Long Schedule SE, be sure to include statutory employee social security wages and tips from Form W-2 on line 8a.

Optional Methods

How the Optional Methods Can Help You

Social security coverage. The optional methods may give you credit toward your social security coverage even though you have a loss or a small amount of income from self-employment.

Earned income credit (EIC). Using the optional methods may qualify you to claim the EIC or give you a larger credit if your net earnings from self-employment (determined without using the optional methods) are less than $4,800. Figure the EIC with and without using the optional methods to see if the optional methods will benefit you.

Additional child tax credit. Using the optional methods may qualify you to claim the additional child tax credit or give you a larger credit if your net earnings from self-employment (determined without using the optional methods) are less than $4,800. Figure the additional child tax credit with and without using the optional methods to see if the optional methods will benefit you.

Child and dependent care credit. The optional methods may help you qualify for this credit or give you a larger credit if your net earnings from self-employment (determined without using the optional methods) are less than $4,800. Figure this credit with and without using the optional methods to see if the optional methods will benefit you.

Self-employed health insurance deduction. The optional methods of computing net earnings from self-employment may be used to figure your self-employed health insurance deduction.

 Using the optional methods may give you the benefits described above, but they may also increase your SE tax.

Changing Your Method

You can change the method used to figure your net earnings from self employment after you file your return. That is, you can change from the regular to the optional method or from the optional to the regular method. To do this, file Form 1040X.

Farm Optional Method

You may use this method to figure your net earnings from farm self-employment if your gross farm income was $7,200 or less or your net farm profits were less than $5,198. Net farm profits are:

• The total of the amounts from Schedule F (Form 1040), line 34, and Schedule K-1 (Form 1065), box 14, code A, minus

• The amount you would have entered on Schedule SE, line 1b, had you not used the optional method.

There is no limit on how many years you can use this method.

Under this method, report in Part II, line 15, two-thirds of your gross farm income, up to $4,800, as your net earnings. This method can increase or decrease your net earnings from farm self-employment even if the farming business had a loss.

For a farm partnership, figure your share of gross income based on the partnership agreement. With guaranteed payments, your share of the partnership's gross income is your guaranteed payments plus your share of the gross income after it is reduced by all guaranteed payments made by the partnership. If you were a limited partner, include only guaranteed payments for services you actually rendered to or on behalf of the partnership.

Nonfarm Optional Method

You may be able to use this method to figure your net earnings from nonfarm self-employment if your net nonfarm profits were less than $5,198 and also less than 72.189% of your gross nonfarm income. Net nonfarm profits are the total of the amounts from:

• Schedule C (Form 1040), line 31,

• Schedule C-EZ (Form 1040), line 3,

• Schedule K-1 (Form 1065), box 14, code A (from other than farm partnerships), and

• Schedule K-1 (Form 1065-B), box 9, code J1.

To use this method, you also must be regularly self-employed. You meet this requirement if your actual net earnings from self-employment were $400 or more in 2 of the 3 years before the year you use the nonfarm optional method. The net earnings of $400 or more could be from either farm or nonfarm earnings or both. The net earnings include your distributive share of partnership income or loss subject to SE tax.

You can use the nonfarm optional method to figure your earnings from self employment for only 5 years. The 5 years do not have to be consecutive.

Under this method, report in Part II, line 17, two-thirds of your gross nonfarm income, up to the amount on line 16, as your net earnings. But you cannot report less than your actual net earnings from nonfarm self-employment.

Figure your share of gross income from a nonfarm partnership in the same manner as a farm partnership. See *Farm Optional Method* for details.

Using Both Optional Methods

If you can use both methods, you can report less than your total actual net earnings from farm and nonfarm self-employment, but you cannot report less than your actual net earnings from nonfarm self-employment alone.

If you use both methods to figure net earnings, you cannot report more than $4,800 of net earnings from self-employment.

2014 Instructions for Schedule 8812

Child Tax Credit

Use Part I of Schedule 8812 to document that any child for whom you entered an ITIN on Form 1040, line 6c; Form 1040A, line 6c; or Form 1040NR, line 7c; and for whom you also checked the box in column 4 of that line, is a resident of the United States because the child meets the substantial presence test and is not otherwise treated as a nonresident alien.

Use Parts II–IV of Schedule 8812 to figure the additional child tax credit. The additional child tax credit may give you a refund even if you do not owe any tax.

Section references are to the Internal Revenue Code unless otherwise noted.

Future Developments

For the latest information about developments related to Schedule 8812 and its instructions, such as legislation enacted after they were published, go to *www.irs.gov/schedule8812*.

General Instructions

Who Should Use Part I

You only need to complete Part I if you are claiming the child tax credit for a child identified by an IRS individual taxpayer identification number (ITIN). When completing Part I, only answer the questions with regard to children identified by an ITIN; you do not need to complete Part I of Schedule 8812 for any child that is identified by a social security number (SSN) or an IRS adoption taxpayer identification number (ATIN).

If all the children for whom you checked the box in column 4 of line 6c on your Form 1040 or Form 1040A or column 4 of line 7c on your Form 1040NR are identified by an SSN or an ATIN, you do not need to complete Part I of Schedule 8812.

Who Should Use Parts II–IV

Parts II–IV are unrelated to Part I. Parts II–IV help you figure your additional child tax credit. Generally, you should only complete Parts II–IV if you are instructed to do so after completing the Child Tax Credit Worksheet in your tax return instructions or Pub. 972.

If all your children are identified by an SSN or an ATIN and you are not claiming the additional child tax credit, you do not need to complete any part of Schedule 8812.

Substantial Presence Test (Part I)

In general, to be a qualifying child for purposes of the child tax credit and additional child tax credit, the child must be a citizen, national, or resident of the United States. Use Part I of Schedule 8812 to document that any child for whom an IRS Individual Taxpayer Identification Number (ITIN) was entered on Form 1040, line 6c; Form 1040A, line 6c; or Form 1040NR, line 7c; and for whom the box in column 4 of that line was also checked, meets the substantial presence test and is not otherwise treated as a nonresident alien.

Note. A child who is a lawful permanent resident of the United States is eligible to obtain a social security number (SSN). Use an SSN to identify the child even if you obtained an ITIN for the child before the child became a lawful permanent resident.

To meet the substantial presence test, a child identified with an ITIN generally must be physically present in the United States on at least:

1. 31 days during 2014, and

2. 183 days during the 3-year period that includes 2014, 2013, and 2012, counting:

   a. All the days your child was present in 2014, and

   b. 1/3 of the days your child was present in 2013, and

   c. 1/6 of the days your child was present in 2012.

Not all days that your dependent is physically present in the United States count as days of presence for the substantial presence test. See *Days of Presence in the United States in Pub. 519.*

A child who is present in the United States for less than one-half of 2014 also must not have a closer connection to a foreign country. See Pub. 519 for more information. Also, see the chart, *Is Your Dependent (Identified by an ITIN) Considered a Resident of the United States Under the Substantial Presence Test*, later.

Additional Child Tax Credit (Parts II–IV)

If any of your dependents is a qualifying child for purposes of the child tax credit (whether identified by an ITIN or not), you may qualify for the additional child tax credit. Before completing Parts II–IV of Schedule 8812, complete the Child Tax Credit Worksheet that applies to you. See the instructions for Form 1040, line 52; Form 1040A, line 35; or Form 1040NR, line 49. If you meet the condition given in the TIP at the end of the Child Tax Credit Worksheet, complete Parts II–IV of this schedule to figure the amount of any additional child tax credit you can claim.

Effect of Credit on Welfare Benefits

Any refund you receive as a result of taking the additional child tax credit cannot be counted as income when determining if you or anyone else is eligible for benefits or assistance, or how much you or anyone else can receive, under any federal program or under any state or local program financed in whole or in part with federal funds. These programs include Temporary Assistance for Needy Families (TANF), Medicaid, Supplemental Security Income (SSI), and Supplemental

Oct 01, 2014 Cat. No. 59790P

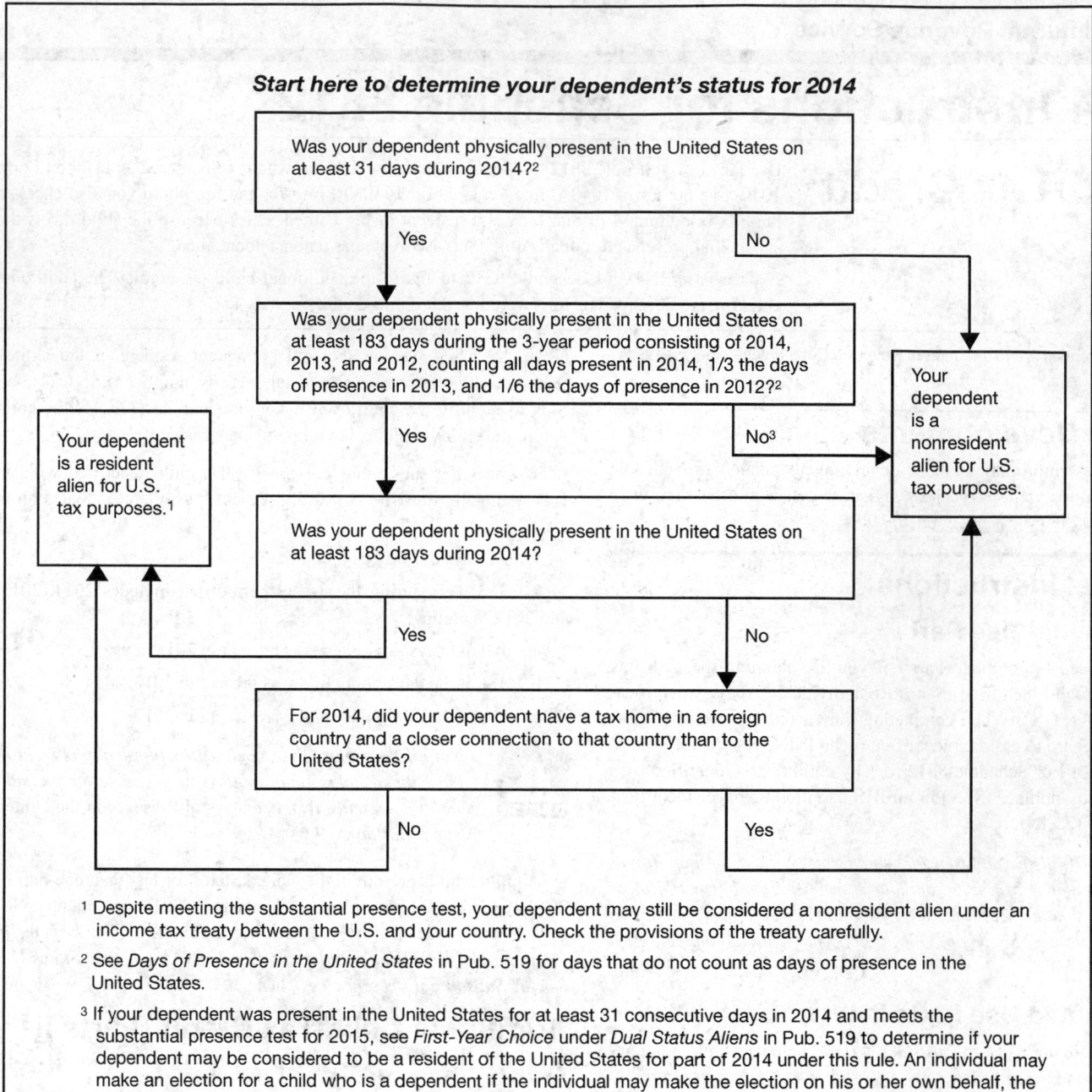

Start here to determine your dependent's status for 2014

Was your dependent physically present in the United States on at least 31 days during 2014?[2]

Yes → | No →

Was your dependent physically present in the United States on at least 183 days during the 3-year period consisting of 2014, 2013, and 2012, counting all days present in 2014, 1/3 the days of presence in 2013, and 1/6 the days of presence in 2012?[2]

Yes ↓ | No[3] →

Your dependent is a resident alien for U.S. tax purposes.[1]

Was your dependent physically present in the United States on at least 183 days during 2014?

Yes | No

Your dependent is a nonresident alien for U.S. tax purposes.

For 2014, did your dependent have a tax home in a foreign country and a closer connection to that country than to the United States?

No | Yes

[1] Despite meeting the substantial presence test, your dependent may still be considered a nonresident alien under an income tax treaty between the U.S. and your country. Check the provisions of the treaty carefully.

[2] See *Days of Presence in the United States* in Pub. 519 for days that do not count as days of presence in the United States.

[3] If your dependent was present in the United States for at least 31 consecutive days in 2014 and meets the substantial presence test for 2015, see *First-Year Choice* under *Dual Status Aliens* in Pub. 519 to determine if your dependent may be considered to be a resident of the United States for part of 2014 under this rule. An individual may make an election for a child who is a dependent if the individual may make the election on his or her own behalf, the child qualifies to make the election, and the child is not required to file a United States income tax return for the year for which the election is effective.

Nutrition Assistance Program (food stamps). In addition, when determining eligibility, the refund cannot be counted as a resource for at least 12 months after you receive it. Check with your local benefits coordinator to find out if your refund will affect your benefits.

Specific Instructions

Part I

Lines A through D. If you identified any of your dependents using an ITIN on your Form 1040, line 6c; Form 1040A, line 6c; or Form 1040NR, line 7c; and you also checked the box in column (4) of that line for that dependent, you must determine if that dependent meets the substantial presence test and is not otherwise treated as a nonresident alien. Complete Line A for the first dependent listed on your Form 1040, line 6c; Form 1040A, line 6c; or Form 1040NR, line 7c, who has an ITIN and that you indicated qualified for the child tax credit by checking the box in column (4). Use a separate line for each additional child identified by an ITIN for whom you checked the box in column (4).

Do not complete a line in Part I for a child if:

• You identified that child with an SSN or ATIN on the tax return, or

• You did not check the box in column 4 of line 6c on your Form 1040 or Form 1040A, or line 7c of your Form 1040NR.

If you only check "No" on any line in Part I, your child tax credit or additional child tax credit may be reduced or eliminated.

Child otherwise treated as a nonresident alien. Even if your child meets the substantial presence test, your child may still be treated as a nonresident alien due to a tax treaty or because the child has a closer connection to another country. See Pub. 519 for more details.

If you must complete Part I for a child and that child meets the substantial presence test, but is still treated as a nonresident alien, check the "No" box for that child.

Special circumstances. Even if your child does not meet the substantial presence test, your child may meet an exception or be treated as a resident of the United States in certain circumstances. If your child does not meet the substantial presence test, but one of the following special circumstances applies, check both the "Yes" and "No" boxes for that child.

- First-year election. If your child was present in the United States for at least 31 consecutive days in 2014 and meets the substantial presence test for 2015, your child may be considered a resident of the United States for part of 2014 if you make a valid election. See *First-Year Choice* under *Dual Status Aliens* in Pub. 519.

- Child adopted by U.S. citizen or national. A child legally adopted by you or lawfully placed with you for legal adoption is not required to meet the substantial presence test if you are a citizen or national of the United States, and, for your entire tax year, the child has the same main home as you and is a member of your household.

More than four children. If you must complete Part I for more than four children, check the box following Line D. Use page 1 of another Schedule 8812 and reletter Lines A–D in Part I as E–H. Complete the additional Part I of Schedule 8812 and attach it to your Schedule 8812.

Parts II through IV

Line 4a — Earned Income Chart. Use the chart, later, to determine the amount to enter on line 4a.

Line 4b — Nontaxable Combat Pay. Enter on line 4b the total amount of nontaxable combat pay that you, and your spouse if filing jointly, received in 2014. This amount should be shown in Form W-2, box 12, with code Q.

Line 7 — Additional Medicare Tax and Tier 1 RRTA Tax. Use the Line 7 Worksheet to figure the amount to enter on line 7 if your

Earned Income Chart — Line 4a

IF you...	AND you...	THEN enter on line 4a...
have net earnings from self-employment	use either optional method to figure those net earnings,	the amount figured using the *1040 and 1040NR Filers — Earned Income Worksheet* in Pub. 972 (even if you are also taking the EIC).
are taking the EIC on Form 1040, line 66a, or Form 1040A, line 42a,	completed Worksheet B of the EIC instructions in your Form 1040 instructions,	your earned income from Worksheet B, line 4b, plus all of your nontaxable combat pay if you did not elect to include it in earned income for the EIC. If you were a member of the clergy, subtract (a) the rental value of a home or the nontaxable portion of an allowance for a home furnished to you (including payments for utilities), and (b) the value of meals and lodging provided to you, your spouse, and your dependents for your employer's convenience.
	did not complete Worksheet B or filed Form 1040A,	your earned income from Step 5 of the EIC instructions in your tax return instructions, plus all of your nontaxable combat pay if you did not elect to include it in earned income for the EIC.
are not taking the EIC	were self-employed, or you are filing Schedule SE because you were a member of the clergy or you had church employee income, or you are filing Schedule C or C-EZ as a statutory employee,	the amount figured using the *1040 and 1040NR Filers — Earned Income Worksheet* in Pub. 972.
	are not self-employed or filing Schedule SE, C, or C-EZ for the above reasons,	your earned income figured as follows: Line 7 of Form 1040 or Form 1040A, or line 8 of Form 1040NR. **Subtract**, if included on line 7 (line 8 for Form 1040NR), any: • Taxable scholarship or fellowship grant not reported on a Form W-2. • Amount received for work performed while an inmate in a penal institution (put "PRI" and the amount subtracted in the space next to line 7 of Form 1040 or 1040A (line 8 for Form 1040NR)). • Amount received as a pension or annuity from a nonqualified deferred compensation plan or a nongovernmental section 457 plan (put "DFC" and the amount subtracted in the space next to line 7 of Form 1040 or Form 1040A (line 8 for Form 1040NR)). This amount may be shown in box 11 of your Form W-2. If you received such an amount but box 11 is blank, contact your employer for the amount received as a pension or annuity. • Amount from Form 2555, line 43, or Form 2555-EZ, line 18. • Medicaid waiver payment you excluded from income (see instructions for Form 1040, line 21, and Pub. 525 for information about these payments). **Add** all your nontaxable combat pay from Form(s) W-2, box 12, with code Q. Earned Income =

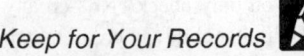
If your employer withheld or you paid Additional Medicare Tax or Tier 1 RRTA taxes, use this worksheet to figure the amount to enter on line 7.	

Social security tax, Medicare tax, and Additional Medicare Tax on Wages.

1. Enter the social security tax withheld (Form(s) W-2, box 4)	**1.**	
2. Enter the Medicare tax withheld (Form(s) W-2, box 6). Box 6 includes any Additional Medicare Tax withheld	**2.**	
3. Enter any amount from Form 8959, line 7	**3.**	
4. Add lines 1, 2, and 3	**4.**	
5. Enter the Additional Medicare Tax withheld (Form 8959, line 22)	**5.**	
6. Subtract line 5 from line 4	**6.**	

Additional Medicare Tax on Self-Employment Income.

7. Enter one-half of the Additional Medicare Tax, if any, on self-employment income (one-half of Form 8959, line 13)	**7.**	

Tier 1 RRTA taxes as an employee of a railroad (enter amounts on lines 8, 9, 10, and 11) **or employee representative** (enter amounts on lines 12, 13, 14, and 15). Do not include amounts in Form W-2, box 14 that are identified as Additional Medicare Tax or Tier 2 tax. Do not include amounts shown on Form CT-2 on line 3 for Additional Medicare Tax or line 4 for Tier 2 tax.

8. Enter the Tier 1 tax (Form(s) W-2, box 14)	**8.**	
9. Enter the Medicare Tax (Form(s) W-2, box 14)	**9.**	
10. Enter the Additional Medicare Tax, if any, on RRTA compensation as an employee (Form 8959, line 17). Do not use the same amount from Form 8959, line 17 for both this line 10 and line 14	**10.**	
11. Add lines 8, 9, and 10	**11.**	
12. Enter one-half of Tier 1 tax (one-half of Forms CT-2, line 1 for all 4 quarters of 2014)	**12.**	
13. Enter one-half of Tier 1 Medicare tax (one-half of Forms CT-2, line 2 for all 4 quarters of 2014)	**13.**	
14. Enter one-half of the Additional Medicare Tax, if any, on RRTA compensation as an employee representative (one-half of Form 8959, line 17). Do not use the same amount from Form 8959, line 17 for both this line 14 and line 10	**14.**	
15. Add lines 12, 13, and 14	**15.**	

Line 7 Amount

16. Add lines 6, 7, 11, and 15. Enter here and on Schedule 8812, line 7	**16.**	

employer withheld or you paid Additional Medicare Tax or tier 1 RRTA tax.

Line 10 — 1040A Filers. If you, or your spouse if filing jointly, had more than one employer for 2014 and total wages of over $117,000,

figure any excess social security and tier 1 RRTA taxes withheld. See Pub. 505. Include any excess on Schedule 8812, line 10.

Form **1040A**	Department of the Treasury—Internal Revenue Service **U.S. Individual Income Tax Return** (99)	**2014**	IRS Use Only—Do not write or staple in this space.

OMB No. 1545-0074

Your first name and initial	Last name		Your social security number
If a joint return, spouse's first name and initial	Last name		Spouse's social security number

Home address (number and street). If you have a P.O. box, see instructions. Apt. no.

▲ Make sure the SSN(s) above and on line 6c are correct.

City, town or post office, state, and ZIP code. If you have a foreign address, also complete spaces below (see instructions).

Presidential Election Campaign
Check here if you, or your spouse if filing jointly, want $3 to go to this fund. Checking a box below will not change your tax or refund. ☐ You ☐ Spouse

Foreign country name	Foreign province/state/county	Foreign postal code

Filing status
Check only one box.

1 ☐ Single
2 ☐ Married filing jointly (even if only one had income)
3 ☐ Married filing separately. Enter spouse's SSN above and full name here. ▶
4 ☐ Head of household (with qualifying person). (See instructions.) If the qualifying person is a child but not your dependent, enter this child's name here. ▶
5 ☐ Qualifying widow(er) with dependent child (see instructions)

Exemptions

6a ☐ **Yourself.** If someone can claim you as a dependent, **do not** check box 6a.
b ☐ **Spouse**

If more than six dependents, see instructions.

c Dependents:

(1) First name Last name	(2) Dependent's social security number	(3) Dependent's relationship to you	(4) ✓ if child under age 17 qualifying for child tax credit (see instructions)
			☐
			☐
			☐
			☐
			☐
			☐

Boxes checked on 6a and 6b

No. of children on 6c who:
• lived with you
• did not live with you due to divorce or separation (see instructions)

Dependents on 6c not entered above

Add numbers on lines above ▶

d Total number of exemptions claimed.

Income

Attach Form(s) W-2 here. Also attach Form(s) 1099-R if tax was withheld.

If you did not get a W-2, see instructions.

7	Wages, salaries, tips, etc. Attach Form(s) W-2.	7
8a	**Taxable** interest. Attach Schedule B if required.	8a
b	**Tax-exempt** interest. **Do not** include on line 8a. 8b	
9a	Ordinary dividends. Attach Schedule B if required.	9a
b	Qualified dividends (see instructions). 9b	
10	Capital gain distributions (see instructions).	10
11a	IRA distributions. 11a	11b Taxable amount (see instructions). 11b
12a	Pensions and annuities. 12a	12b Taxable amount (see instructions). 12b
13	Unemployment compensation and Alaska Permanent Fund dividends.	13
14a	Social security benefits. 14a	14b Taxable amount (see instructions). 14b
15	Add lines 7 through 14b (far right column). This is your **total income.** ▶	15

Adjusted gross income

16	Educator expenses (see instructions). 16	
17	IRA deduction (see instructions). 17	
18	Student loan interest deduction (see instructions). 18	
19	Tuition and fees. Attach Form 8917. 19	
20	Add lines 16 through 19. These are your **total adjustments.**	20
21	Subtract line 20 from line 15. This is your **adjusted gross income.** ▶	21

For Disclosure, Privacy Act, and Paperwork Reduction Act Notice, see separate instructions. Cat. No. 11327A Form **1040A** (2014)

Tax, credits, and payments	22	Enter the amount from line 21 (adjusted gross income).		22	
	23a	Check if: ☐ **You** were born before January 2, 1950, ☐ Blind ☐ **Spouse** was born before January 2, 1950, ☐ Blind } Total boxes checked ▶ 23a			
	b	If you are married filing separately and your spouse itemizes deductions, check here ▶ 23b ☐			

Standard Deduction for—

- People who check any box on line 23a or 23b **or** who can be claimed as a dependent, see instructions.
- All others:

Single or Married filing separately, $6,200

Married filing jointly or Qualifying widow(er), $12,400

Head of household, $9,100

	24	Enter your **standard deduction**.		24	
	25	Subtract line 24 from line 22. If line 24 is more than line 22, enter -0-.		25	
	26	**Exemptions.** Multiply $3,950 by the number on line 6d.		26	
	27	Subtract line 26 from line 25. If line 26 is more than line 25, enter -0-. This is your **taxable income.**	▶	27	
	28	**Tax,** including any alternative minimum tax (see instructions).	28		
	29	Excess advance premium tax credit repayment. Attach Form 8962.	29		
	30	Add lines 28 and 29.		30	
	31	Credit for child and dependent care expenses. Attach Form 2441.	31		
	32	Credit for the elderly or the disabled. Attach Schedule R.	32		
	33	Education credits from Form 8863, line 19.	33		
	34	Retirement savings contributions credit. Attach Form 8880.	34		
	35	Child tax credit. Attach Schedule 8812, if required.	35		
	36	Add lines 31 through 35. These are your **total credits.**		36	
	37	Subtract line 36 from line 30. If line 36 is more than line 30, enter -0-.		37	
	38	Health care: individual responsibility (see instructions). Full-year coverage ☐		38	
	39	Add line 37 and line 38. This is your **total tax.**		39	
	40	Federal income tax withheld from Forms W-2 and 1099.	40		
	41	2014 estimated tax payments and amount applied from 2013 return.	41		
	42a	**Earned income credit (EIC).**	42a		
	b	Nontaxable combat pay election. 42b			
	43	Additional child tax credit. Attach Schedule 8812.	43		
	44	American opportunity credit from Form 8863, line 8.	44		
	45	Net premium tax credit. Attach Form 8962.	45		
	46	Add lines 40, 41, 42a, 43, 44, and 45. These are your **total payments.** ▶		46	

If you have a qualifying child, attach Schedule EIC.

Refund	47	If line 46 is more than line 39, subtract line 39 from line 46. This is the amount you **overpaid.**		47	
	48a	Amount of line 47 you want **refunded to you.** If Form 8888 is attached, check here ▶ ☐ 48a			

Direct deposit? See instructions and fill in 48b, 48c, and 48d or Form 8888.

	▶ b	Routing number ☐☐☐☐☐☐☐☐☐ ▶ c Type: ☐ Checking ☐ Savings			
	▶ d	Account number ☐☐☐☐☐☐☐☐☐☐☐☐☐☐☐☐☐			
	49	Amount of line 47 you want **applied to your 2015 estimated tax.**	49		

Amount you owe	50	**Amount you owe.** Subtract line 46 from line 39. For details on how to pay, see instructions. ▶		50	
	51	Estimated tax penalty (see instructions).	51		

Third party designee	Do you want to allow another person to discuss this return with the IRS (see instructions)? ☐ **Yes.** Complete the following. ☐ **No**

Designee's name ▶　　　　Phone no. ▶　　　　Personal identification number (PIN) ▶ ☐☐☐☐☐

Sign here

Joint return? See instructions. Keep a copy for your records.

Under penalties of perjury, I declare that I have examined this return and accompanying schedules and statements, and to the best of my knowledge and belief, they are true, correct, and accurately list all amounts and sources of income I received during the tax year. Declaration of preparer (other than the taxpayer) is based on all information of which the preparer has any knowledge.

Your signature	Date	Your occupation	Daytime phone number
Spouse's signature. If a joint return, **both** must sign.	Date	Spouse's occupation	If the IRS sent you an Identity Protection PIN, enter it here (see inst.) ☐☐☐☐☐☐

Paid preparer use only	Print/type preparer's name	Preparer's signature	Date	Check ▶ ☐ if self-employed	PTIN
	Firm's name ▶			Firm's EIN ▶	
	Firm's address ▶			Phone no.	

1040A

INSTRUCTIONS 2014

 makes doing your taxes faster and easier.

 is the fast, safe, and free way to prepare and e-file your taxes. See *www.irs.gov/freefile*.

Get a faster refund, reduce errors, and save paper. For more information on **IRS** *e-file* and Free File, see *Options for e-filing your returns* in these instructions or click on **IRS** *e-file* at IRS.gov.

2014 Tax Changes

See *What's New* in these instructions.

FUTURE DEVELOPMENTS

For the latest information about developments related to Form 1040A and its instructions, such as legislation enacted after they were published, go to *www.irs.gov/form1040a*.

Department of the Treasury **Internal Revenue Service** IRS.gov

Table of Contents

**Department
of the
Treasury**

**Internal
Revenue
Service**

The Taxpayer Advocate Service Is Here To Help You

What is the Taxpayer Advocate Service?
The Taxpayer Advocate Service (TAS) is an *independent* organization within the Internal Revenue Service (IRS) that helps taxpayers and protects taxpayer rights. Our job is to ensure that every taxpayer is treated fairly and that you know and understand your rights under the *Taxpayer Bill of Rights*.

What can the Taxpayer Advocate Service do for you?
We can help you resolve problems that you can't resolve with the IRS. And our service is free. If you qualify for our assistance, your advocate will be with you at every turn and do everything possible. TAS can help you if:

- Your problem is causing financial difficulty for you, your family, or your business.
- You face (or your business is facing) an immediate threat of adverse action.
- You've tried repeatedly to contact the IRS but no one has responded, or the IRS hasn't responded by the date promised.

How can you reach us?
We have offices in *every state, the District of Columbia, and Puerto Rico*. Your local advocate's number is at *TaxpayerAdvocate.irs.gov*, at *irs.gov/advocate*, and in your local directory. You can also call us at 1-877-777-4778.

How can you learn about your taxpayer rights?
The Taxpayer Bill of Rights describes ten basic rights that all taxpayers have when dealing with the IRS. Our Tax Toolkit at *TaxpayerAdvocate.irs.gov* can help you understand *what these rights mean to you* and how they apply. These are *your* rights. Know them. Use them.

How else does the Taxpayer Advocate Service help taxpayers?
TAS works to resolve large-scale problems that affect many taxpayers. If you know of one of these broad issues, please report it to us at *www.irs.gov/sams*.

Low Income Taxpayer Clinics Help Taxpayers

Low Income Taxpayer Clinics (LITCs) are independent from the IRS. Some serve individuals whose income is below a certain level and who need to resolve a tax problem. These clinics provide professional representation before the IRS or in court on audits, appeals, tax collection disputes, and other issues for free or for a small fee. Some clinics provide information about taxpayer rights and responsibilities in many different languages for individuals who speak English as a second language. For more information, and to find a clinic near you, read the LITC page on *www.irs.gov/litc* or IRS *Publication 4134, Low Income Taxpayer Clinic List*. You can also get this publication at your local IRS office or by calling 1-800-829-3676.

Suggestions for Improving the IRS

Taxpayer Advocacy Panel

Have a suggestion for improving the IRS and do not know who to contact? The Taxpayer Advocacy Panel (TAP) is a diverse group of citizen volunteers who listen to taxpayers, identify taxpayers' issues, and make suggestions for improving IRS service and customer satisfaction. The panel is demographically and geographically diverse, with at least one member from each state, the District of Columbia, and Puerto Rico. Contact TAP at *www.improveirs.org* or 1-888-912-1227 (toll-free).

Options for *e-filing* your returns—safely, quickly, and easily.

Why do 80% of Americans file their taxes electronically?

- *Security*—The IRS uses the latest encryption technology to safeguard your information.
- *Flexible Payments*—File early; pay by April 15.
- *Greater Accuracy*—Fewer errors mean faster processing.
- *Quick Receipt*—Get an acknowledgment that your return was received and accepted.
- *Go Green*—Reduce the amount of paper used.
- *It's Free*—through Free File.
- *Faster Refunds*—Get your refund faster by *e-filing* using direct deposit.

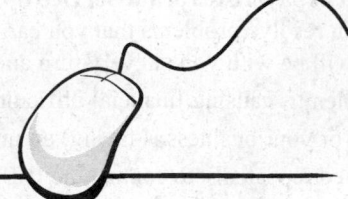

IRS *e-file:* It's Safe. It's Easy. It's Time.

Joining the more than 120 million Americans who already are using *e-file* is easy. Just ask your paid or volunteer tax preparer, use commercial software, or use Free File. IRS *e-file* is the safest, most secure way to transmit your tax return to the IRS. Since 1990, the IRS has processed more than 1 billion *e-filed* tax returns safely and securely. There's no paper return to be lost or stolen.

Most tax return preparers are now required to use IRS *e-file*. If you are asked if you want to *e-file*, just give it a try. IRS *e-file* is now the norm, not the exception. Most states also use electronic filing.

Free *e-file* Help Available Nationwide

Volunteers are available in communities nationwide providing free tax assistance to low to moderate income (generally under $53,000 in adjusted gross income) and elderly taxpayers (age 60 and older). At selected sites, taxpayers can input and electronically file their own tax return with the assistance of an IRS-certified volunteer.

See *How To Get Tax Help* near the end of these instructions for additional information or visit IRS.gov (Keyword: VITA) for a VITA/TCE site near you!

Do Your Taxes for Free

If your adjusted gross income was $60,000 or less in 2014, you can use free tax software to prepare and *e-file* your tax return. Earned more? Use Free File Fillable Forms.

Free File. This public-private partnership, between the IRS and tax software providers, makes approximately 15 brand name commercial software products and *e-file* available for free. Seventy percent of the nation's taxpayers are eligible.

Just visit *www.irs.gov/freefile* for details. Free File combines all the benefits of *e-file* and easy-to-use software at no cost. Guided questions will help ensure you get all the tax credits and deductions you are due. It's fast, safe, and free.

You can review each of the 15 software provider's criteria for free usage or use an online tool to find which free software products match your situation. Some software providers offer state tax return preparation for free. Free File is available in English and Spanish.

Free File Fillable Forms. The IRS offers electronic versions of IRS paper forms that also can be *e-filed* for free. Free File Fillable Forms is best for people experienced in preparing their own tax returns. There are no income limitations. Free File Fillable Forms does basic math calculations. It supports only federal tax forms.

IRS.gov is the gateway to all electronic services offered by the IRS, as well as the spot to download forms at *www.irs.gov/formspubs*.

Make your tax payments electronically—it's easy.

You can make electronic payments online, by phone, or from a mobile device. Paying electronically is safe and secure. The IRS uses the latest encryption technology and does not store banking information. When you use any of the IRS electronic payment options, it puts you in control of paying your tax bill and gives you peace of mind. You determine the payment date, and you will receive an immediate confirmation from the IRS. It's easy, secure, and much quicker than mailing in a check or money order. Go to *www.irs.gov/payments* to see all your electronic payment options.

What's New

For information about any additional changes to the 2014 tax law or any other developments affecting Form 1040A or its instructions, go to *www.irs.gov/form1040a*.

Health care: individual responsibility. You must either:

- Indicate on line 38 that you, your spouse (if filing jointly), and your dependents had health care coverage throughout 2014,
- Claim an exemption from the health care coverage requirement for some or all of 2014 and attach Form 8965, or
- Make a shared responsibility payment if, for any month in 2014, you, your spouse (if filing jointly), or your dependents did not have coverage and do not qualify for a coverage exemption.

See the instructions for line 38 and Form 8965 for more information.

Premium tax credit. You may be eligible to claim the premium tax credit if you, your spouse, or a dependent enrolled in health insurance through the Health Insurance Marketplace. See the instructions for line 45 and Form 8962 for more information.

Advance payments of the premium tax credit. Advance payments of the premium tax credit may have been made to the health insurer to help pay for the insurance coverage of you, your spouse, or your dependent. If advance payments of the premium tax credit were made, you must file a 2014 tax return and Form 8962. If you enrolled someone who is not claimed as a dependent on your tax return or for more information, see the instructions for Form 8962.

Form 1095-A. If you, your spouse, or a dependent enrolled in health insurance through the Marketplace, you should have received Form(s) 1095-A. If you receive Form(s) 1095-A for 2014, save it, it will help you figure your premium tax credit. If you did not receive a Form 1095-A, contact the Marketplace.

Medicaid waiver payments. If you received certain payments under a Medicaid waiver program for caring for someone who lives in your home with you, you may be able to exclude these payments from your income.

If you reported these payments on your return for 2013 or an earlier year, see *http://www.irs.gov/Individuals/Certain-Medicaid-Waiver-Payments-May-Be-Excludable-From-Income*. You may want to file Form 1040X to amend that prior year return.

Pell grants and other scholarships or fellowships. Choosing to include otherwise tax-free scholarships or fellowships in your income can increase an education credit and lower your total tax or increase your refund. See the instructions for line 44, the instructions for Form 8863, and Pub. 970 for more information.

Personal exemption amount increased for certain taxpayers. Your personal exemption is increased to $3,950.

Mailing your return. If you live in Missouri and need to make a payment with your paper return, you will need to mail it to a different address this year. See *Where do I file?* at the end of these instructions.

Direct deposit. To combat fraud and identity theft, the number of refunds that can be directly deposited to a single financial account or prepaid debit card is now limited to three a year. After this limit is exceeded, paper checks will be sent instead.

Direct Pay. The best way to pay your taxes is with IRS Direct Pay. It's the safe, easy, and free way to pay from your checking or savings account in one online session. Just click on "Pay Your Tax Bill" on IRS.gov.

Filing Requirements

These rules apply to all U.S. citizens, regardless of where they live, and resident aliens.

 Have you tried IRS *e-file?* It's the fastest way to get your refund and it's free if you are eligible. Visit IRS.gov for details.

Do You Have To File?

Use Chart A, B, or C to see if you must file a return.

 Even if you do not otherwise have to file a return, you should file one to get a refund of any federal income tax withheld. You should also file if you are eligible for any of the following credits.

- *Earned income credit.*
- *Additional child tax credit.*
- *American opportunity credit.*
- *Credit for federal tax on fuels (must file Form 1040).*
- *Premium tax credit.*

See Pub. 501 for details. Also see Pub. 501 if you do not have to file but received a Form 1099-B (or substitute statement).

Premium tax credit. If advance payments of the premium tax credit were made for you, your spouse, or a dependent who enrolled in coverage through the Health Insurance Marketplace, you must file a 2014 return and attach Form 8962.

Exception for certain children under age 19 or full-time students. If certain conditions apply, you can elect to include on your return the income of a child who was under age 19 at the end of 2014 or was a full-time student under age 24 at the end of 2014. To do so, use Form 1040 and Form 8814. If you make this election, your child does not have to file a return. For details, use TeleTax topic 553 or see Form 8814.

A child born on January 1, 1991, is considered to be age 24 at the end of 2014. Do not use Form 8814 for such a child.

Resident aliens. These rules also apply if you were a resident alien. Also, you may qualify for certain tax treaty benefits. See Pub. 519 for details.

Nonresident aliens and dual-status aliens. These rules also apply if you were a nonresident alien or dual-status alien and both of the following apply.

• You were married to a U.S. citizen or resident alien at the end of 2014.

• You elected to be taxed as a resident alien.

See Pub. 519 for details.

 Specific rules apply to determine if you are a resident alien, nonresident alien, or dual-status alien. Most nonresident aliens and dual-status aliens have different filing requirements and may have to file Form 1040NR or Form 1040NR-EZ. Pub. 519 discusses these requirements and other information to help aliens comply with U.S. tax law.

When and Where Should You File?

File Form 1040A by **April 15, 2015**. If you file after this date, you may have to pay interest and penalties. See *Interest and Penalties*, later.

If you were serving in, or in support of, the U.S. Armed Forces in a designated combat zone or contingency operation, you may be able to file later. See Pub. 3 for details.

Filing instructions and addresses are at the end of these instructions.

What If You Cannot File on Time?

You can get an automatic 6-month extension if, no later than the date your return is due, you file Form 4868. For details, see Form 4868.

 An automatic 6-month extension to file does not extend the time to pay your tax. If you do not pay your tax by the original due date of your return, you will owe interest on the unpaid tax and may owe penalties. See Form 4868.

If you are a U.S. citizen or resident alien, you may qualify for an automatic extension of time to file without filing Form 4868. You qualify if, on the due date of your return, you meet one of the following conditions.

• You live outside the United States and Puerto Rico and your main place of business or post of duty is outside the United States and Puerto Rico.

• You are in military or naval service on duty outside the United States and Puerto Rico.

This extension gives you an extra 2 months to file and pay the tax, but interest will be charged from the original due date of the return on any unpaid tax. You must include a statement showing that you meet the requirements. If you are still unable to file your return by the end of the 2-month period, you can get an additional 4 months if, no later than June 15, 2015, you file Form 4868. This 4-month extension of time to file does not extend the time to pay your tax. See Form 4868.

Private Delivery Services

If you *e-file* your return, there is no need to mail it. See the *e-file* page, earlier, or IRS.gov for more information. However, if you choose to mail it, you can use certain private delivery services designated by the IRS to meet the "timely mailing as timely filing/paying" rule for tax returns and payments. These private delivery services include only the following.

• United Parcel Service (UPS): UPS Next Day Air, UPS Next Day Air Saver, UPS 2nd Day Air, UPS 2nd Day Air A.M., UPS Worldwide Express Plus, and UPS Worldwide Express.

• Federal Express (FedEx): FedEx Priority Overnight, FedEx Standard Overnight, FedEx 2Day, FedEx International Priority, and FedEx International First.

For more information, go to IRS.gov and enter "private delivery service" in the search box. The search results will direct you to the IRS mailing address to use if you are using a private delivery service. You will also find any updates to the list of designated private delivery services. The private delivery service can tell you how to get written proof of the mailing date.

Chart A—For Most People

IF your filing status is . . .	AND at the end of 2014 you were* . . .	THEN file a return if your gross income** was at least . . .
Single (see the instructions for line 1)	under 65 65 or older	$10,150 11,700
Married filing jointly*** (see the instructions for line 2)	under 65 (both spouses) 65 or older (one spouse) 65 or older (both spouses)	$20,300 21,500 22,700
Married filing separately (see the instructions for line 3)	any age	$3,950
Head of household (see the instructions for line 4)	under 65 65 or older	$13,050 14,600
Qualifying widow(er) with dependent child (see the instructions for line 5)	under 65 65 or older	$16,350 17,550

* *If you were born on January 1, 1950, you are considered to be age 65 at the end of 2014. (If your spouse died in 2014 or if you are preparing a return for someone who died in 2014, see Pub. 501.)*

** **Gross income** *means all income you received in the form of money, goods, property, and services that is not exempt from tax, including any income from sources outside the United States or from the sale of your main home (even if you can exclude part or all of it).* **Do not** *include any social security benefits unless (a) you are married filing a separate return and you lived with your spouse at any time in 2014 or (b) one-half of your social security benefits plus your other gross income and any tax-exempt interest is more than $25,000 ($32,000 if married filing jointly). If (a) or (b) applies, see the instructions for lines 14a and 14b to figure the taxable part of social security benefits you must include in gross income.*

*** *If you did not live with your spouse at the end of 2014 (or on the date your spouse died) and your gross income was at least $3,950, you must file a return regardless of your age.*

Chart B—For Children and Other Dependents

See the instructions for line 6c to find out if someone can claim you as a dependent.

If your parent (or someone else) can claim you as a dependent, use this chart to see if you must file a return.

In this chart, **unearned income** includes taxable interest, ordinary dividends, and capital gain distributions. It also includes unemployment compensation, taxable social security benefits, pensions, annuities, and distributions of unearned income from a trust. **Earned income** includes salaries, wages, tips, professional fees, and taxable scholarship and fellowship grants. **Gross income** is the total of your unearned and earned income.

Single dependents. Were you **either** age 65 or older **or** blind?

☐   **No.** You must file a return if **any** of the following apply.

- Your **unearned income** was over $1,000.
- Your **earned income** was over $6,200.
- Your **gross income** was more than the **larger** of—
  - $1,000, or
  - Your earned income (up to $5,850) plus $350.

☐   **Yes.** You must file a return if **any** of the following apply.

- Your unearned income was over $2,550 ($4,100 if 65 or older **and** blind).
- Your earned income was over $7,750 ($9,300 if 65 or older **and** blind).
- Your gross income was more than the **larger** of—
  - $2,550 ($4,100 if 65 or older **and** blind), or
  - Your earned income (up to $5,850) plus $1,900 ($3,450 if 65 or older **and** blind).

Married dependents. Were you **either** age 65 or older **or** blind?

☐   **No.** You must file a return if **any** of the following apply.

- Your unearned income was over $1,000.
- Your earned income was over $6,200.
- Your gross income was at least $5 and your spouse files a separate return and itemizes deductions.
- Your gross income was more than the **larger** of—
  - $1,000, or
  - Your earned income (up to $5,850) plus $350.

☐   **Yes.** You must file a return if **any** of the following apply.

- Your unearned income was over $2,200 ($3,400 if 65 or older **and** blind).
- Your earned income was over $7,400 ($8,600 if 65 or older **and** blind).
- Your gross income was at least $5 and your spouse files a separate return and itemizes deductions.
- Your gross income was more than the **larger** of—
  - $2,200 ($3,400 if 65 or older **and** blind), or
  - Your earned income (up to $5,850) plus $1,550 ($2,750 if 65 or older **and** blind).

Chart C—Other Situations When You Must File

You must file a return for 2014 if you owe tax from the recapture of an education credit or the alternative minimum tax. See the instructions for line 28. You must also file a return for 2014 if advance payments of the premium tax credit were made for you, your spouse, or a dependent who enrolled in coverage through the Health Insurance Marketplace. You should have received Form(s) 1095-A showing the amount of the advance payments, if any.

You must file a return using Form 1040 if **any** of the following apply for 2014.

- You owe any special taxes, such as social security and Medicare tax on tips you did not report to your employer or on wages you received from an employer who did not withhold these taxes.
- You owe write-in taxes, including uncollected social security and Medicare or RRTA tax on tips you reported to your employer or on your group-term life insurance, or additional tax on a health savings account.
- You had net earnings from self-employment of at least $400.
- You had wages of $108.28 or more from a church or qualified church-controlled organization that is exempt from employer social security and Medicare taxes.
- You owe additional tax on a qualified plan, including an individual retirement arrangement (IRA), or other tax-favored account. But if you are filing a return only because you owe this tax, you can file **Form 5329** by itself.
- You owe household employment taxes. But if you are filing a return only because you owe this tax, you can file **Schedule H (Form 1040)** by itself.
- You owe any recapture taxes, including repayment of the first-time homebuyer credit.
- You (or your spouse, if filing jointly) received HSA, Archer MSA, or Medicare Advantage MSA distributions.

Would It Help You To Itemize Deductions on Form 1040?

You may be able to reduce your tax by itemizing deductions on Schedule A (Form 1040). Itemized deductions include amounts you paid for state and local income or sales taxes, real estate taxes, personal property taxes, and mortgage interest. You may also include gifts to charity and part of the amount you paid for medical and dental expenses. You would usually benefit by itemizing if—

Your filing status is:	AND	Your itemized deductions are more than:
Single		
• Under 65		• $6,200
• 65 or older **or** blind		• 7,750
• 65 or older **and** blind		• 9,300
Married filing jointly		
• Under 65 (both spouses)		• $12,400
• 65 or older **or** blind (one spouse)		• 13,600
• 65 or older **or** blind (both spouses)		• 14,800
• 65 or older **and** blind (one spouse)		• 14,800
• 65 or older **or** blind (one spouse) and 65 or older **and** blind (other spouse)		• 16,000
• 65 or older **and** blind (both spouses)		• 17,200
Married filing separately*		
• Your spouse itemizes deductions		• $0
• Under 65		• 6,200
• 65 or older **or** blind		• 7,400
• 65 or older **and** blind		• 8,600
Head of household		
• Under 65		• $9,100
• 65 or older **or** blind		• 10,650
• 65 or older **and** blind		• 12,200
Qualifying widow(er) with dependent child		
• Under 65		• $12,400
• 65 or older **or** blind		• 13,600
• 65 or older **and** blind		• 14,800

* If you can take an exemption for your spouse, complete the Standard Deduction Worksheet for the amount that applies to you.

If someone can claim you as a dependent, it would benefit you to itemize if your itemized deductions total more than your standard deduction figured on the Standard Deduction Worksheet.

Where To Report Certain Items From 2014 Forms W-2, 1097, 1098, and 1099

IRS e-file IRS *e-file* takes the guesswork out of preparing your return. You may also be eligible to use Free File to file your federal income tax return. Visit *www.irs.gov/efile* for details.

If any **federal income tax withheld** is shown on these forms, include the tax withheld on Form 1040A, line 40.

Form	Item and Box in Which It Should Appear	Where To Report
W-2	Wages, tips, other compensation (box 1)	Form 1040A, line 7
	Allocated tips (box 8)	See *Wages, Salaries, Tips, etc.*
	Dependent care benefits (box 10)	Form 2441, Part III
	Adoption benefits (box 12, code T)	Must file Form 1040
	Employer contributions to an Archer MSA (box 12, code R)	Must file Form 1040
	Employer contributions to a health savings account (box 12, code W)	Must file Form 1040 if required to file Form 8889 (see instructions for Form 8889)
	Uncollected social security and Medicare or RRTA tax (box 12, Code A, B, M, or N)	Must file Form 1040
W-2G	Gambling winnings (box 1)	Must file Form 1040
1097-BTC	Bond tax credit	Must file Form 1040 to take
1098	Mortgage interest (box 1) Points (box 2)	Must file Form 1040 to deduct
	Refund of overpaid interest (box 3)	See the instructions on Form 1098
	Mortgage insurance premiums (box 4)	Must file Form 1040 to deduct
1098-C	Contributions of motor vehicles, boats, and airplanes	Must file Form 1040 to deduct
1098-E	Student loan interest (box 1)	See the instructions for Form 1040A, line 18
1098-MA	Home mortgage payments (box 3)	Must file Form 1040 to deduct
1098-T	Qualified tuition and related expenses (box 1)	See the instructions for Form 1040A, line 19, or line 33, but first see the instructions on Form 1098-T
1099-A	Acquisition or abandonment of secured property	See Pub. 4681
1099-B	Broker and barter exchange transactions	Must file Form 1040
1099-C	Canceled debt (box 2)	Generally must file Form 1040 (see Pub. 4681)
1099-DIV	Total ordinary dividends (box 1a)	Form 1040A, line 9a
	Qualified dividends (box 1b)	See the instructions for Form 1040A, line 9b
	Total capital gain distributions (box 2a)	See the instructions for Form 1040A, line 10
	Amount reported in box 2b, 2c, or 2d	Must file Form 1040
	Nondividend distributions (box 3)	Must file Form 1040 if required to report as capital gains (see the instructions on Form 1099-DIV)
	Investment expenses (box 5)	Must file Form 1040 to deduct
	Foreign tax paid (box 6)	Must file Form 1040 to deduct or take a credit for the tax
1099-G	Unemployment compensation (box 1)	See the instructions for Form 1040A, line 13
	State or local income tax refund (box 2)	See the instructions under *Refunds of State or Local Income Taxes*, later
	Amount reported in box 5, 6, 7, or 9	Must file Form 1040
1099-INT	Interest income (box 1)	See the instructions on Form 1099-INT and the instructions for Form 1040A, line 8a
	Early withdrawal penalty (box 2)	Must file Form 1040 to deduct
	Interest on U.S. savings bonds and Treasury obligations (box 3)	See the instructions for Form 1040A, line 8a
	Investment expenses (box 5)	Must file Form 1040 to deduct
	Foreign tax paid (box 6)	Must file Form 1040 to deduct or take a credit for the tax
	Tax-exempt interest (box 8)	Form 1040A, line 8b
	Specified private activity bond interest (box 9)	Must file Form 1040
	Market discount (box 10)	See instructions on Form 1099-INT and Pub. 550
	Bond premium (box 11)	See instructions on Form 1099-INT and Pub. 550
1099-K	Payment card and third party network transactions	Must file Form 1040
1099-LTC	Long-term care and accelerated death benefits	Must file Form 1040 if required to file Form 8853 (see the instructions for Form 8853)
1099-MISC	Miscellaneous income	Must file Form 1040

Form	Item and Box in Which It Should Appear	Where To Report
1099-OID	Original issue discount (box 1)	See the instructions on Form 1099-OID
	Other periodic interest (box 2)	See the instructions on Form 1099-OID
	Early withdrawal penalty (box 3)	Must file Form 1040 to deduct
	Market discount (box 5)	See the instructions on Form 1099-OID and Pub. 550
	Acquisition premium (box 6)	See the instructions on Form 1099-OID and Pub. 550
	Original issue discount on U.S. Treasury obligations (box 8)	See the instructions on Form 1099-OID
	Investment expenses (box 9)	Must file Form 1040 to deduct
1099-PATR	Patronage dividends and other distributions from a cooperative (boxes 1, 2, 3, and 5)	Must file Form 1040 if taxable (see the instructions on Form 1099-PATR)
	Domestic production activities deduction (box 6)	Must file Form 1040 to deduct
	Amount reported in box 7, 8, 9, or 10	Must file Form 1040
1099-Q	Qualified education program payments	Must file Form 1040
1099-R	Distributions from IRAs*	See the instructions for Form 1040A, lines 11a and 11b
	Distributions from pensions, annuities, etc.	See the instructions for Form 1040A, lines 12a and 12b
	Capital gain (box 3)	See the instructions on Form 1099-R
	Disability income with code 3 in box 7	See the instructions for Form 1040A, line 7
1099-S	Gross proceeds from real estate transactions (box 2)	Must file Form 1040 if required to report the sale (see Pub. 523)
	Buyer's part of real estate tax (box 5)	Must file Form 1040
1099-SA	Distributions from HSAs and MSAs**	Must file Form 1040
SSA-1099	Social security benefits	See the instructions for lines 14a and 14b
RRB-1099	Railroad retirement benefits	See the instructions for lines 14a and 14b

*This includes distributions from Roth, SEP, and SIMPLE IRAs.
**This includes distributions from Archer and Medicare Advantage MSAs.

Who Can Use Form 1040A?

You can use Form 1040A if all six of the following apply.

1. You only had income from the following sources:
    a. Wages, salaries, tips.
    b. Interest and ordinary dividends.
    c. Capital gain distributions.
    d. Taxable scholarship and fellowship grants.
    e. Pensions, annuities, and IRAs.
    f. Unemployment compensation.
    g. Alaska Permanent Fund dividends.
    h. Taxable social security and railroad retirement benefits.
2. The only adjustments to income you can claim are:
    a. Educator expenses.
    b. IRA deduction.
    c. Student loan interest deduction.
    d. Tuition and fees deduction.
3. You do not itemize deductions.

4. Your taxable income (line 27) is less than $100,000.
5. The only tax credits you can claim are:
    a. Credit for child and dependent care expenses.
    b. Credit for the elderly or the disabled.
    c. Education credits.
    d. Retirement savings contributions credit.
    e. Child tax credit.
    f. Earned income credit.
    g. Additional child tax credit.
    h. Premium tax credit.
6. You did not have an alternative minimum tax adjustment on stock you acquired from the exercise of an incentive stock option (see Pub. 525).

You can also use Form 1040A if you received dependent care benefits or if you owe tax from the recapture of an education credit or the alternative minimum tax.

When Must You Use Form 1040?

Check *Where To Report Certain Items From 2013 Forms W-2, 1097, 1098, and 1099* to see if you must use Form 1040. You must also use Form 1040 if any of the following apply.

1. You received any of the following types of income:

a. Income from self-employment (business or farm income).

b. Certain tips you did not report to your employer. See the instructions for Form 1040A, line 7.

c. Income received as a partner in a partnership, shareholder in an S corporation, or a beneficiary of an estate or trust.

d. Dividends on insurance policies if they exceed the total of all net premiums you paid for the contract.

2. You can exclude any of the following types of income:

a. Foreign earned income you received as a U.S. citizen or resident alien.

b. Certain income received from sources in Puerto Rico if you were a bona fide resident of Puerto Rico.

c. Certain income received from sources in American Samoa if you were a bona fide resident of American Samoa for all of 2014.

3. You have an alternative minimum tax adjustment on stock you acquired from the exercise of an incentive stock option (see Pub. 525).

4. You received a distribution from a foreign trust.

5. You owe the excise tax on insider stock compensation from an expatriated corporation.

6. You owe household employment taxes. See Schedule H (Form 1040) and its instructions to find out if you owe these taxes.

7. You are claiming the adoption credit or received employer-provided adoption benefits. See Form 8839 for details.

8. You are an employee and your employer did not withhold social security and Medicare tax. See Form 8919 for details.

9. You had a qualified health savings account funding distribution from your IRA.

10. You are a debtor in a bankruptcy case filed after October 16, 2005.

11. You must repay the first-time homebuyer credit. See Form 5405 for details.

12. You had foreign financial assets in 2014, and you must file Form 8938. See Form 8938 and its instructions.

13. You owe Additional Medicare Tax or had Additional Medicare Tax withheld and must file Form 8959. See Form 8959 and its instructions.

14. You owe Net Investment Income Tax and must file Form 8960. See Form 8960 and its instructions.

15. You have adjusted gross income of more than $152,525 and must reduce the dollar amount of your exemptions. See the instructions for Form 1040.

16. You received a Form W-2 that incorrectly includes in box 1 amounts that are payments under a Medicaid waiver program, and you cannot get a corrected W-2, or you received a Form 1099-MISC that incorrectly reported these payments to the IRS.

Need more information or forms? Visit IRS.gov.

Line Instructions for Form 1040A

Section references are to the Internal Revenue Code unless otherwise noted.

Name and Address

Print or type the information in the spaces provided. If you are married filing a separate return, enter your spouse's name on line 3 instead of below your name.

 TIP *If you filed a joint return for 2013 and you are filing a joint return for 2014 with the same spouse, be sure to enter your names and SSNs in the same order as on your 2013 return.*

Name change

If you changed your name because of marriage, divorce, etc., be sure to report the change to your local Social Security Administration (SSA) office before filing your return. This prevents delays in processing your return and issuing refunds. It also safeguards your future social security benefits.

Address change

If you plan to move after filing your return, use Form 8822 to notify the IRS of your new address.

P.O. box

Enter your box number only if your post office does not deliver mail to your home.

Foreign address

If you have a foreign address, enter the city name on the appropriate line. Do not enter any other information on that line, but also complete the spaces below that line. Do not abbreviate the country name. Follow the country's practice for entering the postal code and the name of the province, county, or state.

Death of a taxpayer

See *Death of a taxpayer* under *General Information*, later.

Social Security Number (SSN)

An incorrect or missing SSN can increase your tax, reduce your refund, or delay your refund. To apply for an SSN, fill in Form SS-5 and return it, along with the appropriate evidence documents, to the Social Security Administration (SSA). You can get Form SS-5 online at *www.socialsecurity.gov*, from your local SSA office, or by calling the SSA at 1-800-772-1213. It usually takes about 2 weeks to get an SSN once the SSA has all the evidence and information it needs.

Check that both the name and SSN on your Forms 1040A, W-2, and 1099 agree with your social security card. If they do not, certain deductions and credits on your Form 1040A may be reduced or disallowed and you may not receive credit for your social security earnings. If your Form W-2 shows an incorrect SSN or name, notify your employer or the form-issuing agent as soon as possible to make sure your earnings are credited to your social security record. If the name or SSN on your social security card is incorrect, call the SSA.

IRS Individual Taxpayer Identification Numbers (ITINs) for aliens

If you are a nonresident or resident alien and you do not have and are not eligible to get an SSN, you must apply for an ITIN. For details on how to do so, see Form W-7 and its instructions. It takes 6 to 10 weeks to get an ITIN.

If you already have an ITIN, enter it wherever your SSN is requested on your tax return.

Note. An ITIN is for tax use only. It does not entitle you to social security benefits or change your employment or immigration status under U.S. law.

Nonresident alien spouse

If your spouse is a nonresident alien, he or she must have either an SSN or an ITIN if:
- You file a joint return,
- You file a separate return and claim an exemption for your spouse, or
- Your spouse is filing a separate return.

Presidential Election Campaign Fund

This fund helps pay for Presidential election campaigns. The fund reduces candidates' dependence on large contributions from individuals and groups and places candidates on an equal financial footing in the general election. The fund also helps pay for pediatric medical research. If you want $3 to go to this fund, check the box. If you are filing a joint return, your spouse can also have $3 go to the fund. If you check a box, your tax or refund will not change.

Filing Status

Check only the filing status that applies to you. The ones that will usually give you the lowest tax are listed last.

- Married filing separately.
- Single.
- Head of household.
- Married filing jointly.
- Qualifying widow(er) with dependent child.

Same-sex marriage. For federal tax purposes, individuals of the same sex are considered married if they were lawfully married in a state (or foreign country) whose laws authorize the marriage of two individuals of the same sex, even if the state (or foreign country) in which they now live does not recognize same-sex marriage. The term "spouse" includes an individual married to a person of the same sex if the couple is lawfully married under state (or foreign) law. However, individuals who have entered into a registered domestic partnership, civil union, or other similar relationship that is not considered a marriage under state (or foreign) law are not considered married for federal tax purposes. For more details, see Pub. 501.

 More than one filing status can apply to you. You can choose the one that will give you the lowest tax.

Line 1

Single

You can check the box on line 1 if any of the following was true on December 31, 2014.

- You were never married.
- You were legally separated according to your state law under a decree of divorce or separate maintenance. But if, at the end of 2014, your divorce was not final (an interlocutory decree), you are considered married and cannot check the box on line 1.
- You were widowed before January 1, 2014, and did not remarry before the end of 2014. But, if you have a dependent child, you may be able to use the qualifying widow(er) filing status. See the instructions for line 5.

Line 2

Married Filing Jointly

You can check the box on line 2 if any of the following apply.

- You were married at the end of 2014, even if you did not live with your spouse at the end of 2014.
- Your spouse died in 2014 and you did not remarry in 2014.
- You were married at the end of 2014, and your spouse died in 2015 before filing a 2014 return.

A married couple filing jointly report their combined income and deduct their combined allowable expenses on one return. They can file a joint return even if only one had income or if they did not live together all year. However, both persons must sign the return. Once you file a joint return, you cannot choose to file separate returns for that year after the due date of the return.

Joint and several tax liability. If you file a joint return, both you and your spouse are generally responsible for the tax and any interest or penalties due on the return. This means that if one spouse does not pay the tax due, the other may have to. Or, if one spouse does not report the correct tax, both spouses may be responsible for any additional taxes assessed by the IRS. You may want to file separately if:

- You believe your spouse is not reporting all of his or her income, or
- You do not want to be responsible for any taxes due if your spouse does not have enough tax withheld or does not pay enough estimated tax.

See the instructions for line 3. Also see *Innocent spouse relief* under *General Information*, later.

Nonresident aliens and dual-status aliens. Generally, a married couple cannot file a joint return if either spouse is a nonresident alien at any time during the year. However, if you were a nonresident alien or a dual-status alien and were married to a U.S. citizen or resident alien at the end of 2014, you can elect to be treated as a resident alien and file a joint return. See Pub. 519 for details.

Line 3

Married Filing Separately

If you are married and file a separate return, you generally report only your own income, exemptions, deductions, and credits. Generally, you are responsible only for the tax on your own income. Different rules apply to people in community property states; see Pub. 555.

However, you will usually pay more tax than if you use another filing status for which you qualify. Also, if you file a separate return, you cannot take the student loan interest deduction, the tuition and fees deduction, the education credits, or the earned income credit. You also cannot take the standard deduction if your spouse itemizes deductions.

Be sure to enter your spouse's SSN or ITIN on Form 1040A. If your spouse does not have and is not required to have an SSN or ITIN, enter "NRA."

 You may be able to file as head of household if you had a child living with you and you lived apart from your spouse during the last 6 months of 2014. See Married persons who live apart, *later.*

Line 4

Head of Household

This filing status is for unmarried individuals who provide a home for certain other persons. You are considered unmarried for this purpose if any of the following applies.

- You were legally separated according to your state law under a decree of divorce or separate maintenance at the end of 2014. But, if at the end of 2014, your divorce was not final (an interlocutory decree), you are considered married.

Need more information or forms? Visit IRS.gov.

• You are married but lived apart from your spouse for the last 6 months of 2014 and you meet the other rules under *Married persons who live apart*, later.

• You are married to a nonresident alien at any time during the year and you do not choose to treat him or her as a resident alien.

Check the box on line 4 only if you are unmarried (or considered unmarried) and either *Test 1* or *Test 2* applies.

Test 1. You paid over half the cost of keeping up a home that was the main home for all of 2014 of your parent whom you can claim as a dependent on line 6c, except under a multiple support agreement (see the line 6c instructions). Your parent did not have to live with you.

Test 2. You paid over half the cost of keeping up a home in which you lived and in which one of the following also lived for more than half of the year (if half or less, see *Exception to time lived with you*).

1. Any person whom you can claim as a dependent on line 6c. But do not include:

a. Your child whom you claim as your dependent because of the rule for *Children of divorced or separated parents* in the line 6c instructions,

b. Any person who is your dependent only because he or she lived with you for all of 2014, or

c. Any person you claimed as a dependent under a multiple support agreement. See the line 6c instructions.

2. Your unmarried qualifying child who is not your dependent.

3. Your married qualifying child who is not your dependent only because you can be claimed as a dependent on line 6c of someone else's 2014 return.

4. Your qualifying child who, even though you are the custodial parent, is not your dependent because of the rule for *Children of divorced or separated parents* in the line 6c instructions.

If the child is not claimed as your dependent on line 6c, enter the child's name on line 4. If you do not enter the name, it will take us longer to process your return.

Qualifying child. To find out if someone is your qualifying child, see Step 1 of the line 6c instructions.

Dependent. To find out if someone is your dependent, see the instructions for line 6c.

Exception to time lived with you. Temporary absences by you or the other person for special circumstances, such as school, vacation, business, medical care, military service, or detention in a juvenile facility, count as time lived in the home. Also see *Kidnapped child* in the line 6c instructions, if applicable.

If the person for whom you kept up a home was born or died in 2014, you still may be able to file as head of household. If the person is your qualifying child, the child must have lived with you for more than half the part of the year he or she was alive. If the person is anyone else, see Pub. 501.

Keeping up a home. To find out what is included in the cost of keeping up a home, see Pub. 501.

If you used payments you received under Temporary Assistance for Needy Families (TANF) or other public assistance programs to pay part of the cost of keeping up your home, you cannot count them as money you paid. However, you must include them in the total cost of keeping up your home to figure if you paid over half the cost.

Married persons who live apart. Even if you were not divorced or legally separated at the end of 2014, you are considered unmarried if all of the following apply.

• You lived apart from your spouse for the last 6 months of 2014. Temporary absences for special circumstances, such as for business, medical care, school, or military service, count as time lived in the home.

• You file a separate return from your spouse.

• You paid over half the cost of keeping up your home for 2014.

• Your home was the main home of your child, stepchild, or foster child for more than half of 2014 (if half or less, see *Exception to time lived with you*, earlier).

• You can claim this child as your dependent or could claim the child except that the child's other parent can claim him or her under the rule for *Children of divorced or separated parents* in the line 6c instructions.

Adopted child. An adopted child is always treated as your own child. An adopted child includes a child lawfully placed with you for legal adoption.

Foster child. A foster child is any child placed with you by an authorized placement agency or by judgment, decree, or other order of any court of competent jurisdiction.

Line 5

Qualifying Widow(er) With Dependent Child

You can check the box on line 5 and use joint return tax rates for 2014 if all of the following apply.

1. Your spouse died in 2012 or 2013 and you did not remarry before the end of 2014.

2. You have a child or stepchild you can claim as a dependent on line 6c. This does not include a foster child.

3. This child lived in your home for all of 2014. If the child did not live with you for the required time, see *Exception to time lived with you*, later.

4. You paid over half the cost of keeping up your home.

5. You could have filed a joint return with your spouse the year he or she died, even if you did not actually do so.

If your spouse died in 2014, you cannot file as qualifying widow(er) with dependent child. Instead, see the instructions for line 2.

Adopted child. An adopted child is always treated as your own child. An adopted child includes a child lawfully placed with you for legal adoption.

Dependent. To find out if someone is your dependent, see the instructions for line 6c.

Exception to time lived with you. Temporary absences by you or the child for special circumstances, such as school, vacation, business, medical care, military service, or detention in a juvenile facility, count as time lived in the home. Also see *Kidnapped child* in the line 6c instructions, if applicable.

A child is considered to have lived with you for all of 2014 if the child was born or died in 2014 and your home was the child's home for the entire time he or she was alive.

Keeping up a home. To find out what is included in the cost of keeping up a home, see Pub. 501.

If you used payments you received under Temporary Assistance for Needy Families (TANF) or other public assistance programs to pay part of the cost of keeping up your home, you cannot count them as money you paid. However, you must include them in the total cost of keeping up your home to figure if you paid over half the cost.

Exemptions

You can deduct $3,950 on line 26 for each exemption you can take.

Line 6b

Spouse

Check the box on line 6b if either of the following applies.

1. Your filing status is married filing jointly and your spouse cannot be claimed as a dependent on another person's return.

2. You were married at the end of 2014, your filing status is married filing separately or head of household, and both of the following apply.

   a. Your spouse had no income and is not filing a return.

   b. Your spouse cannot be claimed as a dependent on another person's return.

If your filing status is head of household and you check the box on line 6b, enter the name of your spouse on the line next to line 6b. Also, enter your spouse's social security number in the space provided at the top of your return. If you became divorced or legally separated during 2014, you cannot take an exemption for your former spouse.

Death of your spouse. If your spouse died in 2014 and you did not remarry by the end of 2014, check the box on line 6b if you could have taken an exemption for your spouse on the date of death. For other filing instructions, see *Death of a taxpayer* under *General Instructions*, later.

Line 6c—Dependents

Dependents and Qualifying Child for Child Tax Credit

Follow the steps below to find out if a person qualifies as your dependent, qualifies you to take the child tax credit, or both. If you have more than six dependents, include a statement showing the information required in columns (1) through (4).

Step 1 Do You Have a Qualifying Child?

A qualifying child is a child who is your...

Son, daughter, stepchild, foster child, brother, sister, stepbrother, stepsister, half brother, half sister, or a descendant of any of them (for example, your grandchild, niece, or nephew),

was ...

Under age 19 at the end of 2014 and younger than you (or your spouse, if filing jointly)

or

Under age 24 at the end of 2014, a _student_ (defined later), and younger than you (or your spouse, if filing jointly)

or

Any age and permanently and totally disabled (defined later)

Who did not provide over half of his or her own support for 2014 (see Pub. 501)

Who is not filing a joint return for 2014 or is filing a joint return for 2014 only to claim a refund of withheld income tax or estimated tax paid (see Pub. 501 for details and examples)

Who lived with you for more than half of 2014. If the child did not live with you for the required time, see _Exception to time lived with you_, later.

 _If the child meets the conditions to be a qualifying child of any other person (other than your spouse if filing jointly) for 2014, see_ Qualifying child of more than one person, _later._

1. Do you have a child who meets the conditions to be your qualifying child?

☐ **Yes.** Go to Step 2. ☐ **No.** Go to Step 4.

Step 2 Is Your Qualifying Child Your Dependent?

1. Was the child a U.S. citizen, U.S. national, U.S. resident alien, or a resident of Canada or Mexico? (See Pub. 519 for the definition of a U.S. national or U.S. resident alien. If the child was adopted, see _Exception to citizen test_, later.)

☐ **Yes.** Continue  ☐ **No.** You cannot claim this child as a dependent.

2. Was the child married?

☐ **Yes.** See _Married person_, later. ☐ **No.** Continue ⬎

3. Could you, or your spouse if filing jointly, be claimed as a dependent on someone else's 2014 tax return? See Steps 1, 2, and 4.

☐ **Yes.** (STOP) You cannot claim any dependents. Go to Form 1040A, line 7. ☐ **No.** You can claim this child as a dependent. Complete Form 1040A, line 6c, columns (1) through (3) for this child. Then, go to Step 3.

Step 3 Does Your Qualifying Child Qualify You for the Child Tax Credit?

1. Was the child under age 17 at the end of 2014?

☐ **Yes.** Continue  ☐ **No.** (STOP) This child is not a qualifying child for the child tax credit.

2. Was the child a U.S. citizen, U.S. national, or U.S. resident alien? (See Pub. 519 for the definition of a U.S. national or U.S. resident alien. If the child was adopted, see _Exception to citizen test_, later.)

☐ **Yes.** This child is a qualifying child for the child tax credit. Check the box on Form 1040A, line 6c, column (4). ☐ **No.** (STOP) This child is not a qualifying child for the child tax credit.

Step 4 — Is Your Qualifying Relative Your Dependent?

A qualifying relative is a person who is your...

Son, daughter, stepchild, foster child, or a descendant of any of them (for example, your grandchild)

or

Brother, sister, half brother, half sister, or a son or daughter of any of them (for example, your niece or nephew)

or

Father, mother, or an ancestor or sibling of either of them (for example, your grandmother, grandfather, aunt, or uncle)

or

Stepbrother, stepsister, stepfather, stepmother, son-in-law, daughter-in-law, father-in-law, mother-in-law, brother-in-law, or sister-in-law

or

Any other person (other than your spouse) who lived with you all year as a member of your household if your relationship did not violate local law. If the person did not live with you for the required time, see *Exception to time lived with you*, later

who was not...

A qualifying child (see Step 1) of any taxpayer for 2014. For this purpose, a person is not a taxpayer if he or she is not required to file a U.S. income tax return **and** either does not file such a return or files only to get a refund of withheld income tax or estimated tax paid. See Pub. 501 for details and examples

who...

Had gross income of less than $3,950 in 2014. If the person was permanently and totally disabled, see *Exception to gross income test*, later

For whom you provided...

Over half of his or her support in 2014. But see *Children of divorced or separated parents*, *Multiple support agreements*, and *Kidnapped child*, later.

1. Does any person meet the conditions to be your qualifying relative?

   ☐ **Yes.** Continue

   ☐ **No.** (STOP) Go to Form 1040A, line 7.

2. Was your qualifying relative a U.S. citizen, U.S. national, U.S. resident alien, or a resident of Canada or Mexico? (See Pub. 519 for the definition of a U.S. national or U.S. resident alien. If your qualifying relative was adopted, see *Exception to citizen test*, later.)

   ☐ **Yes.** Continue

   ☐ **No.** (STOP) You cannot claim this person as a dependent.

3. Was your qualifying relative married?

   ☐ **Yes.** See *Married person*, later.

   ☐ **No.** Continue

4. Could you, or your spouse if filing jointly, be claimed as a dependent on someone else's 2014 tax return? See Steps 1, 2, and 4.

   ☐ **Yes.** (STOP) You cannot claim any dependents. Go to Form 1040A, line 7.

   ☐ **No.** You can claim this person as a dependent. Complete Form 1040A, line 6c, columns (1) through (3). Do not check the box on Form 1040A, line 6c, column (4).

Definitions and Special Rules

Adopted child. An adopted child is always treated as your own child. An adopted child includes a child lawfully placed with you for legal adoption.

Adoption taxpayer identification numbers (ATINs). If you have a dependent who was placed with you for legal adoption and you do not know his or her SSN, you must get an ATIN for the dependent from the IRS. See Form W-7A for details. If the dependant is not a U.S. citizen or resident alien, apply for an ITIN instead, using Form W-7.

Children of divorced or separated parents. A child will be treated as the qualifying child or qualifying relative of his or her

Need more information or forms? Visit IRS.gov.

noncustodial parent (defined later) if all of the following conditions apply.

1. The parents are divorced, legally separated, separated under a written separation agreement, or lived apart at all times during the last 6 months of 2014 (whether or not they are or were married).

2. The child received over half of his or her support for 2014 from the parents (and the rules on *Multiple support agreements*, later, do not apply). Support of a child received from a parent's spouse is treated as provided by the parent.

3. The child is in custody of one or both of the parents for more than half of 2014.

4. Either of the following applies.

a. The custodial parent signs Form 8332 or a substantially similar statement that he or she will not claim the child as a dependent for 2014, and the noncustodial parent includes a copy of the form or statement with his or her return. If the divorce decree or separation agreement went into effect after 1984 and before 2009, the noncustodial parent may be able to attach certain pages from the decree or agreement instead of Form 8332. See *Post-1984 and pre-2009 decree or agreement* and *Post-2008 decree or agreement*, later.

b. A pre-1985 decree of divorce or separate maintenance or written separation agreement between the parents provides that the noncustodial parent can claim the child as a dependent, and the noncustodial parent provides at least $600 for support of the child during 2014.

If conditions (1) through (4) apply, only the noncustodial parent can claim the child for purposes of the dependency exemption (line 6c) and the child tax credits (lines 35 and 43). However, this special rule does not apply to head of household filing status, the credit for child and dependent care expenses, the exclusion for dependent care benefits, or the earned income credit. See Pub. 501 for details.

Custodial and noncustodial parents. The custodial parent is the parent with whom the child lived for the greater number of nights in 2014. The noncustodial parent is the other parent. If the child was with each parent for an equal number of nights, the custodial parent is the parent with the higher adjusted gross income. See Pub. 501 for an exception for a parent who works at night, rules for a child who is emancipated under state law, and other details.

Post-1984 and pre-2009 decree or agreement. The decree or agreement must state all three of the following.

1. The noncustodial parent can claim the child as a dependent without regard to any condition, such as payment of support.

2. The other parent will not claim the child as a dependent.

3. The years for which the claim is released.

The noncustodial parent must include all of the following pages from the decree or agreement.
• Cover page (include the other parent's SSN on that page).
• The pages that include all the information identified in (1) through (3) above.
• Signature page with the other parent's signature and date of agreement.

 You must include the required information even if you filed it with your return in an earlier year.

Post-2008 decree or agreement. If the divorce decree or separation agreement went into effect after 2008, the noncustodial parent cannot include pages from the decree or agreement instead of Form 8332. The custodial parent must sign either Form 8332 or a substantially similar statement the only purpose of which is to release the custodial parent's claim to an exemption for a child, and the noncustodial parent must include a copy with his or her return. The form or statement must release the custodial parent's claim to the child without any conditions. For example, the release must not depend on the noncustodial parent paying support.

Release of exemption revoked. A custodial parent who has revoked his or her previous release of a claim to exemption for a child must include a copy of the revocation with his or her return. For details, see Form 8332.

Exception to citizen test. If you are a U.S. citizen or U.S. national and your adopted child lived with you all year as a member of your household, that child meets the requirement to be a U.S. citizen in Step 2, question 1; Step 3, question 2; and Step 4, question 2.

Exception to gross income test. If your relative (including a person who lived with you all year as a member of your household) is permanently and totally disabled (defined later), certain income for services performed at a sheltered workshop may be excluded for this test. For details, see Pub. 501.

Exception to time lived with you. Temporary absences by you or the other person for special circumstances, such as school, vacation, business, medical care, military service, or detention in a juvenile facility, count as time the person lived with you. Also see *Children of divorced or separated parents*, earlier, or *Kidnapped child*.

A person is considered to have lived with you for all of 2014 if the person was born or died in 2014 and your home was this person's home for the entire time he or she was alive in 2014.

If the person meets all other requirements to be your qualifying child but was born or died in 2014, the person is considered to have lived with you for more than half of 2014 if your home was this person's home for more than half the time he or she was alive in 2014.

Foster child. A foster child is any child placed with you by an authorized placement agency or by judgment, decree, or other order of any court of competent jurisdiction.

Kidnapped child. If your child is presumed by law enforcement authorities to have been kidnapped by someone who is not a family member, you may be able to take the child into account in determining your eligibility for head of household or qualifying widow(er) filing status, the dependency exemption, the child tax credit, and the earned income credit (EIC). For details, see Pub. 501 (Pub. 596 for the EIC).

Married person. If the person is married and files a joint return, you cannot claim that person as your dependent. However, if the person is married but does not file a joint return or files a joint return only to claim a refund of withheld income tax or estimated tax paid, you may be able to claim him or her as a dependent. (See Pub. 501 for details and examples.) In that case, go to Step 2, question 3 (for a qualifying child) or Step 4, question 4 (for a qualifying relative).

Multiple support agreements. If no one person contributed over half of the support of your relative (or a person who lived with you all year as a member of your household) but you and another person(s) provided more than half of your relative's support, special rules may apply that would treat you as having provided over half of the support. For details, see Pub. 501.

Permanently and totally disabled. A person is permanently and totally disabled if, at any time in 2014, the person cannot engage in any substantial gainful activity because of a physical or mental condition and a doctor has determined that this condition has lasted or can be expected to last continuously for at least a year or can be expected to lead to death.

Qualifying child of more than one person. Even if a child meets the conditions to be the qualifying child of more than one person, only one person can claim the child as a qualifying child for all of the following tax benefits, unless the special rule for *Children of divorced or separated parents*, described earlier, applies.

1. Dependency exemption (line 6c).
2. Child tax credits (lines 35 and 43).
3. Head of household filing status (line 4).
4. Credit for child and dependent care expenses (line 31).
5. Exclusion for dependent care benefits (Form 2441, Part III).
6. Earned income credit (lines 42a and 42b).

No other person can take any of the six tax benefits listed above unless he or she has a different qualifying child. If you and any other person can claim the child as a qualifying child, the following rules apply.

• If only one of the persons is the child's parent, the child is treated as the qualifying child of the parent.

• If the parents file a joint return together and can claim the child as a qualifying child, the child is treated as the qualifying child of the parents.

• If the parents do not file a joint return together but both parents claim the child as a qualifying child, the IRS will treat the child as the qualifying child of the parent with whom the child lived for the longer period of time in 2014. If the child lived with each parent for the same amount of time, the IRS will treat the child as the qualifying child of the parent who had the higher adjusted gross income (AGI) for 2014.

• If no parent can claim the child as a qualifying child, the child is treated as the qualifying child of the person who had the highest AGI for 2014.

• If a parent can claim the child as a qualifying child but no parent does so claim the child, the child is treated as the qualifying child of the person who had the highest AGI for 2014, but only if that person's AGI is higher than the highest AGI of any parent of the child who can claim the child.

Example. Your daughter meets the conditions to be a qualifying child for both you and your mother. Your daughter does not meet the conditions to be a qualifying child of any other person, including her other parent. Under the rules just described, you can claim your daughter as a qualifying child for all of the six tax benefits listed earlier for which you otherwise qualify. Your mother cannot claim any of those six tax benefits unless she has a different qualifying child. However, if your mother's AGI is higher than yours and you do not claim your daughter as a qualifying child, your daughter is the qualifying child of your mother.

For more details and examples, see Pub. 501.

If you will be claiming the child as a qualifying child, go to Step 2. Otherwise, stop; you cannot claim any benefits based on this child.

Social security number. You must enter each dependent's social security number (SSN). Be sure the name and SSN entered agree with the dependent's social security card. Otherwise, at the time we process your return, we may disallow the exemption claimed for the dependent and reduce or disallow any other tax benefits (such as the child tax credit) based on that dependent. If the name or SSN on the dependent's social security card is not correct, or you need to get an SSN for your dependent, contact the Social Security Administration. See *Social Security Number (SSN)*, earlier. If your dependent will not have a number by the date your return is due, see *What If You Cannot File on Time?* earlier.

If your dependent child was born and died in 2014 and you do not have an SSN for the child, enter "Died" in column (2) and include a copy of the child's birth certificate, death certificate, or hospital records. The document must show the child was born alive.

Student. A student is a child who during any part of 5 calendar months of 2014 was enrolled as a full-time student at a school, or took a full-time, on-farm training course given by a school or a state, county, or local government agency. A school includes a technical, trade, or mechanical school. It does not include an on-the-job training course, correspondence school, or school offering courses only through the Internet.

Need more information or forms? Visit IRS.gov.

Income

Generally, you must report all income except income that is exempt from tax by law. For details, see the following instructions, especially the instructions for lines 7 through 14b. Also see Pub. 525.

Foreign-Source Income

You must report unearned income, such as interest, dividends, and pensions, from sources outside the United States unless exempt by law or a tax treaty. You must also report earned income, such as wages and tips, from sources outside the United States.

If you worked abroad, you may be able to exclude part or all of your foreign earned income if you file Form 1040. For details, see Pub. 54 and Form 2555 or 2555-EZ.

Foreign retirement plans. If you were a beneficiary of a foreign retirement plan, you may have to report the undistributed income earned in your plan. However, if you were the beneficiary of a Canadian registered retirement plan, see Revenue Procedure 2014-55, 2014-44 I.R.B. 753, available at *www.irs.gov//irb/2014-44_IRB/ar10.html*, to find out if you can elect to defer tax on the undistributed income. If you elect to defer tax, you must file Form 1040.

Report distributions from foreign pension plans on lines 12a and 12b.

Foreign accounts and trusts. You must complete Part III of Schedule B if you:
* Had a foreign account, or
* Received a distribution from, or were a grantor of, or a transferor to, a foreign trust.

Note. If you had foreign financial assets in 2014, you may have to file Form 8938. If you must file Form 8938, you cannot file Form 1040A. You must file Form 1040. See Form 8938 and its instructions.

Rounding Off to Whole Dollars

You can round off cents to whole dollars on your return and schedules. If you do round to whole dollars, you must round all amounts. To round, drop amounts under 50 cents and increase amounts from 50 to 99 cents to the next dollar. For example, $1.39 becomes $1 and $2.50 becomes $3.

If you have to add two or more amounts to figure the amount to enter on a line, include cents when adding the amounts and round off only the total.

Example. You received two Forms W-2, one showing wages of $5,009.55 and one showing wages of $8,760.73. On Form 1040A, line 7, you would enter $13,770 ($5,009.55 + $8,760.73 = $13,770.28).

Refunds of State or Local Income Taxes

If you received a refund, credit, or offset of state or local income taxes in 2014, you may receive a Form 1099-G.

For the year the tax was paid to the state or other taxing authority, did you itemize deductions?

☐ **No.**   None of your refund is taxable.

☐ **Yes.**   You may have to report part or all of the refund as income on Form 1040 for 2014. See Pub. 525 for details.

Community Property States

Community property states are Arizona, California, Idaho, Louisiana, Nevada, New Mexico, Texas, Washington, and Wisconsin. If you and your spouse lived in a community property state, you must usually follow state law to determine what is community income and what is separate income. For details, see Form 8958 and Pub. 555.

Nevada, Washington, and California domestic partners. A registered domestic partner in Nevada, Washington, or California generally must report half the combined community income of the individual and his or her domestic partner. See Form 8958 and see Pub 555.

Line 7

Wages, Salaries, Tips, etc.

Enter the total of your wages, salaries, tips, etc. If a joint return, also include your spouse's income. For most people, the amount to enter on this line should be shown in box 1 of their Form(s) W-2. But the following types of income must also be included in the total on line 7.

* All wages received as a household employee for which you did not receive a Form W-2 because your employer paid you less than $1,900 in 2014. Also, enter "HSH" and the amount not reported on a Form W-2 in the space to the left of line 7.
* Tip income you did not report to your employer. But you must use Form 1040 and Form 4137 if you received tips of $20 or more in any month and did not report the full amount to your employer, or your Form(s) W-2 shows allocated tips that you must report as income. You must report the allocated tips shown on your Form(s) W-2 unless you can prove that you received less. Allocated tips should be shown in box 8 of your Form(s) W-2. They are not included as income in box 1. See Pub. 531 for more details.
* Dependent care benefits, which should be shown in box 10 of your Form(s) W-2. But first complete Form 2441 to see if you can exclude part or all of the benefits.
* Scholarship and fellowship grants not reported on Form W-2. Also, enter "SCH" and the amount in the space to the left of line 7. However, if you were a degree candidate, include on line 7 only the amounts you used for expenses other than tuition and course-related expenses. For example, amounts used for room, board, and travel must be reported on line 7.
* Disability pensions shown on Form 1099-R if you have not reached the minimum retirement age set by your employer. But see *Insurance premiums for retired public safety officers*, in the instructions for lines 12a and 12b. Disability pensions received after you reach minimum retirement age and other payments shown on Form 1099-R (other than payments from an

IRA*) are reported on lines 12a and 12b of Form 1040A. Payments from an IRA are reported on lines 11a and 11b.

This includes a Roth, SEP, or SIMPLE IRA.

Missing or Incorrect Form W-2?

Your employer is required to provide or send Form W-2 to you no later than February 2, 2015. If you do not receive it by early February, use TeleTax topic 154 to find out what to do. Even if you do not get a Form W-2, you must still report your earnings on line 7. If you lose your Form W-2 or it is incorrect, ask your employer for a new one.

Line 8a

Taxable Interest

Each payer should send you a Form 1099-INT or Form 1099-OID. Enter your total taxable interest income on line 8a. But you must fill in and attach Schedule B if the total is over $1,500 or any of the other conditions listed at the beginning of the Schedule B instructions apply to you.

Interest credited in 2014 on deposits that you could not withdraw because of the bankruptcy or insolvency of the financial institution may not have to be included in your 2014 income. For details, see Pub. 550.

 If you get a 2014 Form 1099-INT for U.S. savings bond interest that includes amounts you reported before 2014, see Pub. 550.

Line 8b

Tax-Exempt Interest

If you received any tax-exempt interest, such as from municipal bonds, each payer should send you a Form 1099-INT. Your tax-exempt interest should be shown in box 8 of Form 1099-INT. Enter the total on line 8b. Also include on line 8b any exempt-interest dividends from a mutual fund or other regulated investment company. This amount should be shown in box 10 of Form 1099-DIV.

Do not include interest earned on your IRA, health savings account, Archer or Medicare Advantage MSA, or Coverdell education savings account.

If you received tax-exempt interest from private activity bonds issued after August 7, 1986, you must use Form 1040.

Line 9a

Ordinary Dividends

Each payer should send you a Form 1099-DIV. Enter your total ordinary dividends on line 9a. This amount should be shown in box 1a of Form(s) 1099-DIV.

You must fill in and attach Schedule B if the total is over $1,500 or you received, as a nominee, ordinary dividends that actually belong to someone else.

You must use Form 1040 if you received nondividend distributions (box 3 of Form 1099-DIV) required to be reported as capital gains.

For details, see Pub. 550.

Line 9b

Qualified Dividends

Enter your total qualified dividends on line 9b. Qualified dividends are also included in the ordinary dividend total required to be shown on line 9a. Qualified dividends are eligible for a lower tax rate than other ordinary income. Generally, these dividends are shown in box 1b of Form(s) 1099-DIV. See Pub. 550 for the definition of qualified dividends if you received dividends not reported on Form 1099-DIV.

Exception. Some dividends may be reported as qualified dividends in box 1b of Form 1099-DIV but are not qualified dividends. These include:

- Dividends you received as a nominee. See the Schedule B instructions.
- Dividends you received on any share of stock that you held for less than 61 days during the 121-day period that began 60 days before the ex-dividend date. The ex-dividend date is the first date following the declaration of a dividend on which the purchaser of a stock is not entitled to receive the next dividend payment. When counting the number of days you held the stock, include the day you disposed of the stock but not the day you acquired it. See the examples that follow. Also, when counting the number of days you held the stock, you cannot count certain days during which your risk of loss was diminished. See Pub. 550 for more details.
- Dividends attributable to periods totaling more than 366 days that you received on any share of preferred stock held for less than 91 days during the 181-day period that began 90 days before the ex-dividend date. When counting the number of days you held the stock, you cannot count certain days during which your risk of loss was diminished. See Pub. 550 for more details. Preferred dividends attributable to periods totaling less than 367 days are subject to the 61-day holding period rule just described.
- Dividends on any share of stock to the extent that you are under an obligation (including a short sale) to make related payments with respect to positions in substantially similar or related property.
- Payments in lieu of dividends, but only if you know or have reason to know that the payments are not qualified dividends.

Example 1. You bought 5,000 shares of XYZ Corp. common stock on July 8, 2014. XYZ Corp. paid a cash dividend of 10 cents per share. The ex-dividend date was July 16, 2014. Your Form 1099-DIV from XYZ Corp. shows $500 in box 1a (ordinary dividends) and in box 1b (qualified dividends). However, you sold the 5,000 shares on August 11, 2014. You held your shares of XYZ Corp. for only 34 days of the 121-day period (from July 9, 2014, through August 11, 2014). The 121-day period began on May 17, 2014, (60 days before the ex-dividend date) and ended on September 14, 2014. You have no qualified dividends from XYZ Corp. because you held the XYZ stock for less than 61 days.

Example 2. The facts are the same as in Example 1 except that you bought the stock on July 15, 2014 (the day before the ex-dividend date), and you sold the stock on September 16, 2014. You held the stock for 63 days (from July 15, 2014, through September 16, 2014). The $500 of qualified dividends shown in box 1b of your Form 1099-DIV are all qualified dividends because you held the stock for 61 days of the 121-day period (from July 16, 2014, through September 14, 2014).

Example 3. You bought 10,000 shares of ABC Mutual Fund common stock on July 8, 2014. ABC Mutual Fund paid a cash dividend of 10 cents a share. The ex-dividend date was July 16, 2014. The ABC Mutual Fund advises you that the portion of the dividend eligible to be treated as qualified dividends equals 2 cents per share. Your Form 1099-DIV from ABC Mutual Fund shows total ordinary dividends of $1,000, and qualified dividends of $200. However, you sold the 10,000 shares on August 11, 2014. You have no qualified dividends from ABC Mutual Fund because you held the ABC Mutual Fund stock for less than 61 days.

 Be sure you use the Qualified Dividends and Capital Gain Tax Worksheet to figure your tax.

Line 10

Capital Gain Distributions

Each payer should send you a Form 1099-DIV. Do any of the Forms 1099-DIV or substitute statements you, or your spouse if filing a joint return, received have an amount in box 2b (unrecaptured section 1250 gain), box 2c (section 1202 gain), or box 2d (collectibles (28%) gain)?

☐ **Yes.** You **must** use Form 1040.

☐ **No.** You can use Form 1040A. Enter your total capital gain distributions (from box 2a of Form(s) 1099-DIV) on line 10. Also, be sure you use the Qualified Dividends and Capital Gain Tax Worksheet to figure your tax.

If you received capital gain distributions as a nominee (that is, they were paid to you but actually belong to someone else), report on line 10 only the amount that belongs to you. Include a statement showing the full amount you received and the amount you received as a nominee. See the Schedule B instructions for filing requirements for Forms 1099-DIV and 1096.

Lines 11a and 11b

IRA Distributions

You should receive a Form 1099-R showing the total amount of any distribution from your IRA before income tax and other deductions were withheld. This amount should be shown in box 1 of Form 1099-R. Unless otherwise noted in the line 11a and 11b instructions, an IRA includes a traditional IRA, Roth IRA, simplified employee pension (SEP) IRA, and a savings incentive match plan for employees (SIMPLE) IRA. Except as provided below, leave line 11a blank and enter the total distribution (from Form 1099-R, box 1) on line 11b.

Exception 1. Enter the total distribution on line 11a if you rolled over part or all of the distribution from one:

• IRA to another IRA of the same type (for example, from one traditional IRA to another traditional IRA),
• SEP or SIMPLE IRA to a traditional IRA, or
• IRA to a qualified plan other than an IRA.

Also, enter "Rollover" next to line 11b. If the total distribution was rolled over in a qualified rollover, enter -0- on line 11b. If the total distribution was not rolled over in a qualified rollover, enter the part not rolled over on line 11b unless *Exception 2* applies to the part not rolled over. Generally, a qualified rollover must be made within 60 days after the day you received the distribution. For more details on rollovers, see Pub. 590-A and Pub. 590-B.

If you rolled over the distribution into a qualified plan other than an IRA or you made the rollover in 2014, include a statement explaining what you did.

Exception 2. If any of the following apply, enter the total distribution on line 11a and see Form 8606 and its instructions to figure the amount to enter on line 11b.

1. You received a distribution from an IRA (other than a Roth IRA) and you made nondeductible contributions to any of your traditional or SEP IRAs for 2014 or an earlier year. If you made nondeductible contributions to these IRAs for 2014, also see Pub. 590-A and Pub. 590-B.

2. You received a distribution from a Roth IRA. But if either (a) or (b) below applies, enter -0- on line 11b; you do not have to see Form 8606 or its instructions.

a. Distribution code T is shown in box 7 of Form 1099-R and you made a contribution (including a conversion) to a Roth IRA for 2009 or an earlier year.

b. Distribution code Q is shown in box 7 of Form 1099-R.

3. You converted part or all of a traditional, SEP, or SIMPLE IRA to a Roth IRA in 2014.

4. You had a 2013 or 2014 IRA contribution returned to you, with the related earnings or less any loss, by the due date (including extensions) of your tax return for that year.

5. You made excess contributions to your IRA for an earlier year and had them returned to you in 2014.

6. You recharacterized part or all of a contribution to a Roth IRA as a traditional IRA contribution, or vice versa.

Exception 3. If the distribution is a qualified charitable distribution (QCD), enter the total distribution on line 11a. If the total amount distributed is a QCD, enter -0- on line 11b. If only part of the distribution is a QCD, enter the part that is not a QCD on line 11b unless *Exception 2* applies to that part. Enter "QCD" next to line 11b.

A QCD is a distribution made directly by the trustee of your IRA (other than an ongoing SEP or SIMPLE IRA) to an organization eligible to receive tax-deductible contributions (with certain exceptions). You must have been at least age 70½ when the distribution was made.

Generally, your total QCDs for the year cannot be more than $100,000. (On a joint return, your spouse can also have a QCD of up to $100,000.) The amount of the QCD is limited to the amount that would otherwise be included in your income. If your IRA includes nondeductible contributions, the distribution is first considered to be paid out of otherwise taxable income. See Pub. 590-A for details.

 You cannot claim a charitable contribution deduction for any QCD not included in your income.

Exception 4. If the distribution is a health savings account (HSA) funding distribution (HFD), you must file Form 1040. See *Exception 4* in the instructions for Form 1040, lines 15a and 15b. An HFD is a distribution made directly by the trustee of your IRA (other than an ongoing SEP or SIMPLE IRA) to your HSA.

More than one exception applies. If more than one exception applies, include a statement showing the amount of each exception, instead of making an entry next to line 11b. For example: "Line 11b--$1,000 Rollover and $500 Distribution." But you do not need to attach a statement if only *Exception 2* and one other exception apply.

More than one distribution. If you (or your spouse if filing jointly) received more than one distribution, figure the taxable amount of each distribution and enter the total of the taxable amounts on line 11b. Enter the total amount of those distributions on line 11a.

 You may have to pay an additional tax if (a) you received an early distribution from your IRA and the total was not rolled over or (b) you were born before July 1, 1943, and received less than the minimum required distribution from your traditional, SEP, and SIMPLE IRAs. If you do owe this tax, you must use Form 1040.

More information. For more information about IRAs, see Pub. 590-A and Pub. 590-B.

Lines 12a and 12b

Pensions and Annuities

You should receive a Form 1099-R showing the total amount of your pension and annuity payments before income tax or other deductions were withheld. This amount should be shown in box 1 of Form 1099-R. Pension and annuity payments include distributions from 401(k), 403(b), and governmental 457(b) plans. Rollovers and lump-sum distributions are explained later. Do not include the following payments on lines 12a and 12b. Instead, report them on line 7.
- Disability pensions received before you reach the minimum retirement age set by your employer.
- Corrective distributions (including any earnings) of excess salary deferrals or excess contributions to retirement plans. The plan must advise you of the year(s) the distributions are includible in income.

 Attach Form(s) 1099-R to Form 1040A if any federal income tax was withheld.

Fully taxable pensions and annuities. Your payments are fully taxable if (a) you did not contribute to the cost (see *Cost,*

later) of your pension or annuity, or (b) you got back your entire cost tax free before 2014. But see *Insurance premiums for retired public safety officers,* later. If your pension or annuity is fully taxable, enter the total pension or annuity payments (from Form(s) 1099-R, box 1) on line 12b; do not make an entry on line 12a.

Fully taxable pensions and annuities also include military retirement pay shown on Form 1099-R. For details on military disability pensions, see Pub. 525. If you received a Form RRB-1099-R, see Pub. 575 to find out how to report your benefits.

Partially taxable pensions and annuities. Enter the total pension or annuity payments (from Form 1099-R, box 1) on line 12a. If your Form 1099-R does not show the taxable amount, you must use the General Rule explained in Pub. 939 to figure the taxable part to enter on line 12b. But if your annuity starting date (defined later) was after July 1, 1986, see *Simplified Method,* later, to find out if you must use that method to figure the taxable part.

You can ask the IRS to figure the taxable part for you for a $1,000 fee. For details, see Pub. 939.

If your Form 1099-R shows a taxable amount, you can report that amount on line 12b. But you may be able to report a lower taxable amount by using the General Rule or the Simplified Method or if the exclusion for retired public safety officers, discussed next, applies.

Insurance premiums for retired public safety officers. If you are an eligible retired public safety officer (law enforcement officer, firefighter, chaplain, or member of a rescue squad or ambulance crew), you can elect to exclude from income distributions made from your eligible retirement plan that are used to pay the premiums for coverage by an accident or health plan or a long-term care insurance contract. You can do this only if you retired because of disability or because you reached normal retirement age. The premiums can be for coverage for you, your spouse, or dependents. The distribution must be from a plan maintained by the employer from which you retired as a public safety officer. Also, the distribution must be made directly from the plan to the provider of the accident or health plan or long-term care insurance contract. You can exclude from income the smaller of the amount of the premiums or $3,000. You can only make this election for amounts that would otherwise be included in your income.

An eligible retirement plan is a governmental plan that is:
- a qualified trust,
- a section 403(a) plan,
- a section 403(b) plan, or
- a section 457(b) plan.

If you make this election, reduce the otherwise taxable amount of your pension or annuity by the amount excluded. The amount shown in box 2a of Form 1099-R does not reflect the exclusion. Report your total distributions on line 12a and the taxable amount on line 12b. Enter "PSO" next to line 12b.

If you are retired on disability and reporting your disability pension on line 7, include only the taxable amount on that line and enter "PSO" and the amount excluded in the space to the left of line 7.

Simplified Method. You must use the Simplified Method if either of the following applies.

1. Your annuity starting date was after July 1, 1986, and you used this method last year to figure the taxable part.

2. Your annuity starting date was after November 18, 1996, and both of the following apply.

a. The payments are from a qualified employee plan, a qualified employee annuity, or a tax-sheltered annuity.

b. On your annuity starting date, either you were under age 75 or the number of years of guaranteed payments was fewer than 5. See Pub. 575 for the definition of guaranteed payments.

If you must use the Simplified Method, complete the Simplified Method Worksheet in these instructions to figure the taxable part of your pension or annuity. For more details on the Simplified Method, see Pub. 575 or Pub. 721 for U.S. Civil Service retirement benefits.

 If you received U.S. Civil Service retirement benefits and you chose the alternative annuity option, see Pub. 721 to figure the taxable part of your annuity. Do not use the Simplified Method Worksheet in these instructions.

Annuity starting date. Your annuity starting date is the later of the first day of the first period for which you received a payment or the date the plan's obligations became fixed.

Age (or combined ages) at annuity starting date. If you are the retiree, use your age on the annuity starting date. If you are the survivor of a retiree, use the retiree's age on his or her annuity starting date. But if your annuity starting date was after 1997 and the payments are for your life and that of your beneficiary, use your combined ages on the annuity starting date.

If you are the beneficiary of an employee who died, see Pub. 575. If there is more than one beneficiary, see Pub. 575 or Pub. 721 to figure each beneficiary's taxable amount.

Cost. Your cost is generally your net investment in the plan as of the annuity starting date. It does not include pre-tax contributions. Your net investment should be shown in box 9b of Form 1099-R for the first year you received payments from the plan.

Rollovers. Generally, a qualified rollover is a tax-free distribution of cash or other assets from one retirement plan that is contributed to another plan within 60 days of receiving the distribution. However, a qualified rollover to a Roth IRA or a designated Roth account is generally not a tax-free distribution. Use lines 12a and 12b to report a qualified rollover, including a direct rollover, from one qualified employer's plan to another or to an IRA or SEP.

Enter on line 12a the distribution from Form 1099-R, box 1. From this amount, subtract any contributions (usually shown in box 5) that were taxable to you when made. From that result, subtract the amount of the qualified rollover. Enter the remaining amount on line 12b. If the remaining amount is zero and you have no other distribution to report on line 12b, enter zero on line 12b. Also, enter "Rollover" next to line 12b.

See Pub. 575 for more details on rollovers, including special rules that apply to rollovers from designated Roth accounts, partial rollovers of property, and distributions under qualified domestic relations orders.

Lump-sum distributions. If you received a lump-sum distribution from a profit-sharing or retirement plan, your Form 1099-R should have the "Total distribution" box in box 2b checked. You must use Form 1040 if you owe additional tax because you received an early distribution from a qualified retirement plan and the total amount was not rolled over in a qualified rollover. See Pub. 575 to find out if you owe this tax.

Enter the total distribution on line 12a and the taxable part on line 12b. For details, see Pub. 575.

 You may be able to pay less tax on the distribution if you were born before January 2, 1936, or you are the beneficiary of a deceased employee who was born before January 2, 1936. But you must use Form 1040 to do so. For details, see Form 4972.

Line 13

Unemployment Compensation and Alaska Permanent Fund Dividends

Unemployment compensation. You should receive a Form 1099-G showing in box 1 the total unemployment compensation paid to you in 2014. Report this amount on line 13. However, if you made contributions to a governmental unemployment compensation program or to a governmental paid family leave program, reduce the amount you report on line 13 by those contributions.

If you received an overpayment of unemployment compensation in 2014 and you repaid any of it in 2014, subtract the amount you repaid from the total amount you received. Enter the result on line 13. Also, enter "Repaid" and the amount you repaid in the space to the left of line 13. If, in 2014, you repaid unemployment compensation that you included in gross income in an earlier year, you can deduct the amount repaid. But you must use Form 1040 to do so. See Pub. 525 for details.

Alaska Permanent Fund dividends. Include the dividends in the total on line 13.

Lines 14a and 14b

Social Security Benefits

You should receive a Form SSA-1099 showing in box 3 the total social security benefits paid to you. Box 4 will show the amount of any benefits you repaid in 2014. If you received railroad retirement benefits treated as social security, you should receive a Form RRB-1099.

Use the Social Security Benefits Worksheet in these instructions to see if any of your benefits are taxable.

Exception. Do not use the Social Security Benefits Worksheet if any of the following applies.

Simplified Method Worksheet—Lines 12a and 12b

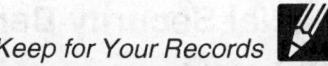

Keep for Your Records

Before you begin: ✓ If you are the beneficiary of a deceased employee or former employee who died **before** August 21, 1996, include any death benefit exclusion that you are entitled to (up to $5,000) in the amount entered on line 2 below.

More than one pension or annuity. If you had more than one partially taxable pension or annuity, figure the taxable part of each separately. Enter the total of the taxable parts on Form 1040A, line 12b. Enter the total pension or annuity payments received in 2014 on Form 1040A, line 12a.

1. Enter the total pension or annuity payments from Form 1099-R, box 1. Also, enter this amount on Form 1040A, line 12a . . . . 1. _____

2. Enter your cost in the plan at the annuity starting date . . . . 2. _____

   Note. If you completed this worksheet last year, skip line 3 and enter the amount from line 4 of last year's worksheet on line 4 below (even if the amount of your pension or annuity has changed). Otherwise, go to line 3.

3. Enter the appropriate number from **Table 1** below. **But** if your annuity starting date was **after** 1997 **and** the payments are for your life and that of your beneficiary, enter the appropriate number from **Table 2** below . . . . 3. _____

4. Divide line 2 by the number on line 3 . . . . 4. _____

5. Multiply line 4 by the number of months for which this year's payments were made. If your annuity starting date was **before** 1987, skip lines 6 and 7 and enter this amount on line 8. Otherwise, go to line 6 . . . . 5. _____

6. Enter the amount, if any, recovered tax free in years after 1986. If you completed this worksheet last year, enter the amount from line 10 of last year's worksheet . . . . 6. _____

7. Subtract line 6 from line 2 . . . . 7. _____

8. Enter the **smaller** of line 5 or line 7 . . . . 8. _____

9. **Taxable amount.** Subtract line 8 from line 1. Enter the result, but not less than zero. Also, enter this amount on Form 1040A, line 12b. If your Form 1099-R shows a larger amount, use the amount on this line instead of the amount from Form 1099-R. If you are a retired public safety officer, see *Insurance premiums for retired public safety officers* before entering an amount on line 12b . . . . 9. _____

10. Was your annuity starting date before 1987?

    ☐ Yes. (STOP) Do not complete the rest of this worksheet.

    ☐ No. Add lines 6 and 8. This is the **amount you have recovered tax free** through 2014. You will need this number if you need to fill out this worksheet next year . . . . 10. _____

11. **Balance of cost to be recovered.** Subtract line 10 from line 2. If zero, you will not have to complete this worksheet next year. The payment you receive next year will generally be fully taxable . . . . 11. _____

Table 1 for Line 3 Above

IF the age at annuity starting date was . . .	AND your annuity starting date was—	
	before November 19, 1996, enter on line 3 . . .	after November 18, 1996, enter on line 3 . . .
55 or under	300	360
56–60	260	310
61–65	240	260
66–70	170	210
71 or older	120	160

Table 2 for Line 3 Above

IF the combined ages at annuity starting date were . . .	THEN enter on line 3 . . .
110 or under	410
111–120	360
121–130	310
131–140	260
141 or older	210

• You made contributions to a traditional IRA for 2014 and you or your spouse were covered by a retirement plan at work. Instead, use the worksheets in Pub. 590-A to see if any of your social security benefits are taxable and to figure your IRA deduction.

• You repaid any benefits in 2014 and your total repayments (box 4) were more than your total benefits for 2014 (box 3). None of your benefits are taxable for 2014. Also, you may be able to take an itemized deduction or a credit for part of the excess repayments if they were for benefits you included in gross income in an earlier year. But you must use Form 1040 to do so. For more details, see Pub. 915.

• You file Form 8815. Instead, use the worksheet in Pub. 915.

 Benefits for earlier year received in 2014? *If any of your benefits are taxable for 2014, **and** they include a lump-sum benefit payment that was for an earlier year, you may be able to reduce the taxable amount. See Lump-Sum Election in Pub. 915 for details.*

Need more information or forms? Visit IRS.gov.

Social Security Benefits Worksheet—Lines 14a and 14b

Keep for Your Records

Before you begin: ✓ Complete Form 1040A, lines 16 and 17, if they apply to you.

✓ If you are married filing separately and you lived apart from your spouse for all of 2014, enter "D" to the right of the word "benefits" on line 14a. If you do not, you may get a math error notice from the IRS.

✓ Be sure you have read the **Exception** in the line 14a and 14b instructions to see if you can use this worksheet instead of a publication to find out if any of your benefits are taxable.

1. Enter the total amount from **box 5** of **all** your **Forms SSA-1099** and **Forms RRB-1099**. Also, enter this amount on Form 1040A, line 14a .... 1. _____

2. Enter one-half of line 1 .... 2. _____

3. Enter the total of the amounts from Form 1040A, lines 7, 8a, 9a, 10, 11b, 12b, and 13 .... 3. _____

4. Enter the amount, if any, from Form 1040A, line 8b .... 4. _____

5. Add lines 2, 3, and 4 .... 5. _____

6. Enter the total of the amounts from Form 1040A, lines 16 and 17 .... 6. _____

7. Is the amount on line 6 less than the amount on line 5?

☐ **No.** **STOP** None of your social security benefits are taxable. Enter -0- on Form 1040A, line 14b.

☐ **Yes.** Subtract line 6 from line 5 .... 7. _____

8. If you are:
   - Married filing jointly, enter $32,000.
   - Single, head of household, qualifying widow(er), or married filing separately and you **lived apart** from your spouse for all of 2014, enter $25,000.
   - Married filing separately and you lived with your spouse at any time in 2014, skip lines 8 through 15; multiply line 7 by 85% (.85) and enter the result on line 16. Then go to line 17.

   .... 8. _____

9. Is the amount on line 8 less than the amount on line 7?

☐ **No.** **STOP** None of your social security benefits are taxable. Enter -0- on Form 1040A, line 14b. If you are married filing separately and you **lived apart** from your spouse for all of 2014, be sure you entered "D" to the right of the word "benefits" on line 14a.

☐ **Yes.** Subtract line 8 from line 7 .... 9. _____

10. Enter: $12,000 if married filing jointly; $9,000 if single, head of household, qualifying widow(er), or married filing separately and you **lived apart** from your spouse for all of 2014 .... 10. _____

11. Subtract line 10 from line 9. If zero or less, enter -0- .... 11. _____

12. Enter the **smaller** of line 9 or line 10 .... 12. _____

13. Enter one-half of line 12 .... 13. _____

14. Enter the **smaller** of line 2 or line 13 .... 14. _____

15. Multiply line 11 by 85% (.85). If line 11 is zero, enter -0- .... 15. _____

16. Add lines 14 and 15 .... 16. _____

17. Multiply line 1 by 85% (.85) .... 17. _____

18. **Taxable social security benefits.** Enter the **smaller** of line 16 or line 17. Also enter this amount on Form 1040A, line 14b .... 18. _____

TIP *If any of your benefits are taxable for 2014 **and** they include a lump-sum benefit payment that was for an earlier year, you may be able to reduce the taxable amount. See Lump-Sum Election in Pub. 915 for details.*

Need more information or forms? Visit IRS.gov.   -28-

Adjusted Gross Income

Line 16

Educator Expenses

If you were an eligible educator in 2014, you can deduct on line 16 up to $250 of qualified expenses you paid in 2014. If you and your spouse are filing jointly and both of you were eligible educators, the maximum deduction is $500. However, neither spouse can deduct more than $250 of his or her qualified expenses on line 16. You may be able to deduct expenses that are more than the $250 (or $500) limit on Schedule A, line 21, but you must use Form 1040. An eligible educator is a kindergarten through grade 12 teacher, instructor, counselor, principal, or aide who worked in a school for at least 900 hours during a school year.

Qualified expenses include ordinary and necessary expenses paid in connection with books, supplies, equipment (including computer equipment, software, and services), and other materials used in the classroom. An ordinary expense is one that is common and accepted in your educational field. A necessary expense is one that is helpful and appropriate for your profession as an educator. An expense does not have to be required to be considered necessary.

Qualified expenses do not include expenses for home schooling or for nonathletic supplies for courses in health or physical education.

You must reduce your qualified expenses by the following amounts.

* Excludable U.S. series EE and I savings bond interest from Form 8815.
* Nontaxable qualified tuition program earnings or distributions.
* Any nontaxable distribution of Coverdell education savings account earnings.
* Any reimbursements you received for these expenses that were not reported to you in box 1 of your Form W-2.

For more details, use Teletax topic 458 or see Pub. 529.

Line 17

IRA Deduction

 If you made any nondeductible contributions to a traditional individual retirement arrangement (IRA) for 2014, you must report them on Form 8606.

If you made contributions to a traditional IRA for 2014, you may be able to take an IRA deduction. But you, or your spouse if filing a joint return, must have had earned income to do so. If you were a member of the U.S. Armed Forces, earned income includes any nontaxable combat pay you received. A statement should be sent to you by June 1, 2015, that shows all contributions to your traditional IRA for 2014.

Use the IRA Deduction Worksheet in these instructions to figure the amount, if any, of your IRA deduction. But read the following 11-item list before you fill in the worksheet.

1. If you were age 70½ or older at the end of 2014, you cannot deduct any contributions made to your traditional IRA for 2014 or treat them as nondeductible contributions.

2. You cannot deduct contributions to a Roth IRA. But you may be able to take the retirement savings contributions credit (saver's credit). See the instructions for line 34.

3. If you are filing a joint return and you or your spouse made contributions to both a traditional IRA and a Roth IRA for 2014, do not use the IRA Deduction Worksheet in these instructions. Instead, see Pub. 590-A to figure the amount, if any, of your IRA deduction.

4. You cannot deduct elective deferrals to a 401(k) plan, 403(b) plan, section 457 plan, SIMPLE plan, or the federal Thrift Savings Plan. These amounts are not included as income in box 1 of your Form W-2. But you may be able to take the retirement savings contributions credit. See the instructions for line 34.

5. If you made contributions to your IRA in 2014 that you deducted for 2013, do not include them in the worksheet.

6. If you received income from a nonqualified deferred compensation plan or nongovernmental section 457 plan that is included in box 1 of your Form W-2, do not include that income on line 8 of the worksheet. The income should be shown in (a) box 11 of your Form W-2 or (b) box 12 of your Form W-2 with code Z. If it is not, contact your employer for the amount of the income.

7. You must file a joint return to deduct contributions to your spouse's IRA. Enter the total IRA deduction for you and your spouse on line 17.

8. Do not include qualified rollover contributions in figuring your deduction. Instead, see the instructions for lines 11a and 11b.

9. Do not include trustees' fees that were billed separately and paid by you for your IRA. You may be able to deduct those fees as an itemized deduction. But you must use Form 1040 to do so.

10. Do not include any repayments of qualified reservist distributions. You cannot deduct them. For information on how to report these repayments, see *Qualified reservist repayments* in Pub. 590-A.

11. If the total of your IRA deduction on line 17 plus any nondeductible contribution to your traditional IRAs shown on Form 8606 is less than your total traditional IRA contributions for 2014, see Pub. 590-A for special rules.

 By April 1 of the year after the year in which you reach age 70½, you must start taking minimum required distributions from your traditional IRA. If you do not, you may have to pay a 50% additional tax on the amount that should have been distributed. For details, including how to figure the minimum required distribution, see Pub. 590-B.

Need more information or forms? Visit IRS.gov.

IRA Deduction Worksheet—Line 17

Keep for Your Records

 If you were age 70½ or older at the end of 2014, you cannot deduct any contributions made to your traditional IRA or treat them as nondeductible contributions. **Do not** *complete this worksheet for anyone age 70½ or older at the end of 2014. If you are married filing jointly and only one spouse was under age 70½ at the end of 2014, complete this worksheet only for that spouse.*

Before you begin:	✓ Be sure you have read the 11-item list in the instructions for this line. You may not be able to use this worksheet.
	✓ If you are married filing separately and you lived apart from your spouse for all of 2014, enter "D" in the space to the left of line 17. If you do not, you may get a math error notice from the IRS.

		Your IRA	**Spouse's IRA**
1a.	Were you covered by a retirement plan (see *Were you covered by a retirement plan?*)?	**1a.** ☐ Yes ☐ No	
b.	If married filing jointly, was your spouse covered by a retirement plan?		**1b.** ☐ Yes ☐ No

Next. If you checked "No" on line 1a (and "No" on line 1b if married filing jointly), skip lines 2 through 6, enter the applicable amount below on line 7a (and line 7b if applicable), and go to line 8.
- $5,500, if under age 50 at the end of 2014.
- $6,500, if age 50 or older but under age 70½ at the end of 2014.

Otherwise, go to line 2.

2. Enter the amount shown below that applies to you.

- Single, head of household, or married filing separately and you **lived apart** from your spouse for all of 2014, enter $70,000
- Qualifying widow(er), enter $116,000
- Married filing jointly, enter $116,000 in both columns. But if you checked "No" on either line 1a or 1b, enter $191,000 for the person who was not covered by a plan
- Married filing separately and you lived with your spouse at any time in 2014, enter $10,000

2a. _____ **2b.** _____

3. Enter the amount from Form 1040A, line 15 . . . . **3.** _____

4. Enter the amount, if any, from Form 1040A, line 16 . . . . . . **4.** _____

5. Subtract line 4 from line 3. If married filing jointly, enter the result in both columns . . . . **5a.** _____ **5b.** _____

6. Is the amount on line 5 less than the amount on line 2?

☐ **No.** (STOP) None of your IRA contributions are deductible. For details on nondeductible IRA contributions, see Form 8606.

☐ **Yes.** Subtract line 5 from line 2 in each column. Follow the instruction below that applies to you.

- If single, head of household, or married filing separately, and the result is $10,000 or more, enter the applicable amount below on line 7 for that column and go to line 8.
  - **i.** $5,500, if under age 50 at the end of 2014.
  - **ii.** $6,500, if age 50 or older but under age 70½ at the end of 2014.

If the result is less than $10,000, go to line 7.

- If married filing jointly or qualifying widow(er), and the result is $20,000 or more ($10,000 or more in the column for the IRA of a person who was not covered by a retirement plan), enter the applicable amount below on line 7 for that column and go to line 8.
  - **i.** $5,500, if under age 50 at the end of 2014.
  - **ii.** $6,500, if age 50 or older but under age 70½ at the end of 2014.

Otherwise, go to line 7.

6a. _____ **6b.** _____

IRA Deduction Worksheet— *(continued)*

		Your IRA	Spouse's IRA
7.	Multiply lines 6a and 6b by the percentage below that applies to you. If the result is not a multiple of $10, increase it to the next multiple of $10 (for example, increase $490.30 to $500). If the result is $200 or more, enter the result. But if it is less than $200, enter $200.		
	• Single, head of household, or married filing separately, multiply by 55% (.55) (or by 65% (.65) in the column for the IRA of a person who is age 50 or older at the end of 2014)		
	• Married filing jointly or qualifying widow(er), multiply by 27.5% (.275) (or by 32.5% (.325) in the column for the IRA of a person who is age 50 or older at the end of 2014). But if you checked "No" on either line 1a or 1b, then in the column for the IRA of the person who was not covered by a retirement plan, multiply by 55% (.55) (or by 65% (.65) if age 50 or older at the end of 2014)	7a. _____	7b. _____
8.	Enter the amount from Form 1040A, line 7. Include any nontaxable combat pay. This amount should be reported in box 12 of Form W-2 with code Q . . . . **8.** _____		

 If married filing jointly and line 8 is less than $11,000 ($12,000 if one spouse is age 50 or older at the end of 2014; $13,000 if both spouses are age 50 or older at the end of 2014), **stop here** *and see Pub. 590-A to figure your IRA deduction.*

9.	Enter traditional IRA contributions made, or that will be made by April 15, 2015, for 2014 to your IRA on line 9a and to your spouse's IRA on line 9b	9a. _____	9b. _____
10.	On line 10a, enter the **smallest** of line 7a, 8, or 9a. On line 10b, enter the smallest of line 7b, 8, or 9b. This is the most you can deduct. Add the amounts on lines 10a and 10b and enter the total on Form 1040A, line 17. Or, if you want, you can deduct a smaller amount and treat the rest as a nondeductible contribution (see Form 8606)	10a. _____	10b. _____

You must use Form 1040 if you owe tax on any excess contributions made to an IRA or any excess accumulations in an IRA. For details, see Pub. 590-A.

Were you covered by a retirement plan? If you were covered by a retirement plan (401(k), SIMPLE, etc.) at work, your IRA deduction may be reduced or eliminated. But you can still make contributions to an IRA even if you cannot deduct them. In any case, the income earned on your IRA contributions is not taxed until it is paid to you. The "Retirement plan" box in box 13 of your Form W-2 should be checked if you were covered by a plan at work even if you were not vested in the plan.

If you were covered by a retirement plan and you file Form 8815, see Pub. 590-A to figure the amount, if any, of your IRA deduction.

Married persons filing separately. If you were not covered by a retirement plan but your spouse was, you are considered covered by a plan unless you lived apart from your spouse for all of 2014.

TIP *You may be able to take the retirement savings contributions credit. See the line 34 instructions.*

Line 18

Student Loan Interest Deduction

You can take this deduction only if all of the following apply.
• You paid interest in 2014 on a qualified student loan (defined later).
• Your filing status is any status except married filing separately.
• Your modified adjusted gross income (AGI) is less than: $80,000 if single, head of household, or qualifying widow(er); $160,000 if married filing jointly. Use lines 2 through 4 of the Student Loan Interest Deduction Worksheet to figure your modified AGI.
• You, or your spouse if filing jointly, are not claimed as a dependent on someone's (such as your parent's) 2014 tax return.

Need more information or forms? Visit IRS.gov.

Student Loan Interest Deduction Worksheet—Line 18

Keep for Your Records

Before you begin: ✓ See the instructions for line 18.

1.	Enter the total interest you paid in 2014 on qualified student loans (see the instructions for line 18). **Do not** enter more than $2,500	1. _____
2.	Enter the amount from Form 1040A, line 15	2. _____
3.	Enter the total of the amounts from Form 1040A, lines 16 and 17	3. _____
4.	Subtract line 3 from line 2	4. _____
5.	Enter the amount shown below for your filing status. • Single, head of household, or qualifying widow(er)—$65,000 • Married filing jointly—$130,000	5. _____
6.	Is the amount on line 4 more than the amount on line 5? ☐ **No.** Skip lines 6 and 7, enter -0- on line 8, and go to line 9. ☐ **Yes.** Subtract line 5 from line 4	6. _____
7.	Divide line 6 by $15,000 ($30,000 if married filing jointly). Enter the result as a decimal (rounded to at least three places). If the result is 1.000 or more, enter 1.000	7. _____
8.	Multiply line 1 by line 7	8. _____
9.	**Student loan interest deduction.** Subtract line 8 from line 1. Enter the result here and on Form 1040A, line 18	9. _____

Use the Student Loan Interest Deduction Worksheet to figure your student loan interest deduction.

Qualified student loan. A qualified student loan is any loan you took out to pay the qualified higher education expenses for any of the following individuals who was an eligible student.

1. Yourself or your spouse.

2. Any person who was your dependent when the loan was taken out.

3. Any person you could have claimed as a dependent for the year the loan was taken out except that:

a. The person filed a joint return,

b. The person had gross income that was equal to or more than the exemption amount for that year ($3,950 for 2014), or

c. You, or your spouse if filing jointly, could be claimed as a dependent on someone else's return.

However, a loan is not a qualified student loan if (a) any of the proceeds were used for other purposes, or (b) the loan was from either a related person or a person who borrowed the proceeds under a qualified employer plan or a contract purchased under such a plan. For details, see Pub. 970.

Qualified higher education expenses. Qualified higher education expenses generally include tuition, fees, room and board, and related expenses such as books and supplies. The expenses must be for education in a degree, certificate, or similar program at an eligible educational institution. An eligible educational institution includes most colleges, universities, and certain vocational schools. For details, see Pub 970.

Line 19
Tuition and Fees

If you paid qualified tuition and fees for yourself, your spouse, or your dependent(s), you may be able to take this deduction. See Form 8917.

You may be able to take a credit for your educational expenses instead of a deduction. See the instructions for lines 33 and 44 for details.

Tax, Credits, and Payments
Line 23a

If you were born before January 2, 1950, or were blind at the end of 2014, check the appropriate boxes on line 23a. If you were married and checked the box on Form 1040A, line 6b, and your spouse was born before January 2, 1950, or was blind at the end of 2014, also check the appropriate boxes for your spouse. Be sure to enter the total number of boxes checked. Do not check any box(es) for your spouse if your filing status is head of household.

Death of spouse in 2014. If your spouse was born before January 2, 1950, but died in 2014 before reaching age 65, do not check the box that says "Spouse was born before January 2, 1950."

A person is considered to reach age 65 on the day before his or her 65th birthday.

Example. Your spouse was born on February 14, 1949, and died on February 13, 2014. Your spouse is considered age 65 at the time of death. Check the appropriate box for your spouse on line 23a. However, if your spouse died on February 12,

2014, your spouse is not considered age 65. Do not check the box.

Death of taxpayer in 2014. If you are preparing a return for someone who died in 2014, see Pub. 501 before completing line 23a.

Blindness. If you were not totally blind as of December 31, 2014, you must get a statement certified by your eye doctor (ophthalmologist or optometrist) that:

- You cannot see better than 20/200 in your better eye with glasses or contact lenses, or
- Your field of vision is 20 degrees or less.

If your eye condition is not likely to improve beyond the conditions listed above, you can get a statement certified by your eye doctor (ophthalmologist or optometrist) to this effect instead.

You must keep the statement for your records.

Line 23b

If your filing status is married filing separately (box 3 is checked) and your spouse itemizes deductions on Form 1040, check the box on line 23b. You cannot take the standard deduction even if you were born before January 2, 1950, or were blind. Enter -0- on line 24 and go to line 25.

 In most cases, your federal income tax will be less if you take the larger of any itemized deductions you may have or the standard deduction. To itemize deductions, you must file Form 1040.

Line 24

Standard Deduction

Most people can find their standard deduction by looking at the amounts listed under "All others" to the left of line 24.

Exception 1–dependent. If you, or your spouse if filing jointly, can be claimed as a dependent on someone else's 2014 return, use the Standard Deduction Worksheet for Dependents to figure your standard deduction.

Exception 2–box on line 23a checked. If you checked any box on line 23a, figure your standard deduction using the Standard Deduction Chart for People Who Were Born Before January 2, 1950, or Were Blind.

Exception 3–box on line 23b checked. If you checked the box on line 23b, your standard deduction is zero, even if your were born before January 2, 1950, or were blind.

Standard Deduction Worksheet for Dependents—Line 24

Keep for Your Records

Use this worksheet **only** if someone can claim you, or your spouse if filing jointly, as a dependent.

1. Is your **earned income*** more than $650? ☐ **Yes.** Add $350 to your earned income. Enter the total ☐ **No.** Enter $1,000	1. _____
2. Enter the amount shown below for your filing status. • Single or married filing separately—$6,200 • Married filing jointly or qualifying widow(er)—$12,400 • Head of household—$9,100	2. _____
3. **Standard deduction.**	
a. Enter the **smaller** of line 1 or line 2. If born after January 1, 1950, and not blind, **stop here** and enter this amount on Form 1040A, line 24. Otherwise, go to line 3b	3a. _____
b. If born before January 2, 1950, or blind, multiply the number on Form 1040A, line 23a, by $1,200 ($1,550 if single or head of household)	3b. _____
c. Add lines 3a and 3b. Enter the total here and on Form 1040A, line 24	3c. _____

***Earned income** includes wages, salaries, tips, professional fees, and other compensation received for personal services you performed. It also includes any taxable scholarship or fellowship grant. Generally, your earned income is the total of the amount you reported on Form 1040A, line 7.*

Need more information or forms? Visit IRS.gov.

Standard Deduction Chart for People Who Were Born Before January 2, 1950, or Were Blind—Line 24

Do not use this chart if someone can claim you, or your spouse if filing jointly, as a dependent. Instead, use the Standard Deduction Worksheet for Dependents.

Enter the number from the box on
Form 1040A, line 23a .... ▶ [   ]

⚠ CAUTION Do not use the number of exemptions from line 6d.

IF your filing status is . . .	AND the number in the box above is . . .	THEN your standard deduction is . . .
Single	1	$7,750
	2	9,300
Married filing jointly or Qualifying widow(er)	1	$13,600
	2	14,800
	3	16,000
	4	17,200
Married filing separately	1	$7,400
	2	8,600
	3	9,800
	4	11,000
Head of household	1	$10,650
	2	12,200

Line 26

Exemptions

You usually can deduct $3,950 on line 26 for each exemption you can take. But if your filing status is married filing separately, and the amount on line 21 is over $152,525, your exemption amount may be reduced. You must file Form 1040 instead of Form 1040A.

Line 28

Tax

Do you want the IRS to figure your tax for you?

☐ **Yes.** See chapter 30 of Pub. 17 for details, including who is eligible and what to do. If you have paid too much, we will send you a refund. If you did not pay enough, we will send you a bill.

☐ **No.** Use the Tax Table to figure your tax unless you are required to use Form 8615 (see *Form 8615*, later) or the Qualified Dividends and Capital Gain Tax Worksheet in these instructions. Also include in the total on line 28 any of the following taxes.

Tax from recapture of education credits. You may owe this tax if (a) you claimed an education credit in an earlier year, and (b) either tax-free educational assistance or a refund of qualified expenses was received in 2014 for the student. See the Instructions for Form 8863 for more details. If you owe this tax, enter the amount and "ECR" to the left of the entry space for line 28.

Alternative minimum tax. If both 1 and 2 next apply to you, use the Alternative Minimum Tax Worksheet in these instructions to see if you owe this tax and, if you do, the amount to include on line 28.

1. The amount on Form 1040A, line 26, is: $27,650 or more if single or married filing jointly; $31,600 if a qualifying widow(er); or $15,800 or more if head of household or married filing separately.

2. The amount on Form 1040A, line 22, is more than: $52,800 if single or head of household; $82,100 if married filing jointly or qualifying widow(er); $41,050 if married filing separately.

If filing for a child who must use Form 8615 to figure the tax (see below), and the amount on Form 1040A, line 22, is more than the total of $7,250 plus the amount on Form 1040A, line 7, do not file this form. Instead, file Form 1040 for the child. Use Form 6251 to see if the child owes this tax.

Alternative Minimum Tax Worksheet—Line 28

Keep for Your Records

Before you begin: ✓ Figure the amount you would enter on Form 1040A, line 30, if you do not owe this tax.

1. Enter the amount from Form 1040A, line 22 .... 1. _____

2. Enter the amount shown below for your filing status
   - Single or head of household—$52,800
   - Married filing jointly or qualifying widow(er)—$82,100
   - Married filing separately—$41,050
   } .... 2. _____

3. Subtract line 2 from line 1. If zero or less, **stop here;** you do not owe this tax .... 3. _____

4. Enter the amount shown below for your filing status.
   - Single or head of household—$117,300
   - Married filing jointly or qualifying widow(er)—$156,500
   - Married filing separately—$78,250
   } .... 4. _____

5. Subtract line 4 from line 1. If zero or less, enter -0- here and on line 6, and go to line 7 .... 5. _____

6. Multiply line 5 by 25% (.25) .... 6. _____

7. Add lines 3 and 6 .... 7. _____

8. If line 7 is $182,500 or less ($91,250 or less if married filing separately), multiply line 7 by 26% (.26). Otherwise, multiply line 7 by 28% (.28) and subtract $3,650 ($1,825 if married filing separately) from the result .... 8. _____

9. Did you use the **Qualified Dividends and Capital Gain Tax Worksheet** to figure the tax on the amount on Form 1040A, line 27?
   - ☐ **No.** Skip lines 9 through 19; enter the amount from line 8 on line 20 and go to line 21.
   - ☐ **Yes.** Enter the amount from line 4 of that worksheet .... 9. _____

10. Enter the **smaller** of line 7 or line 9 .... 10. _____

11. Subtract line 10 from line 7 .... 11. _____

12. If line 11 is $182,500 or less ($91,250 or less if married filing separately), multiply line 11 by 26% (.26). Otherwise, multiply line 11 by 28% (.28) and subtract $3,650 ($1,825 if married filing separately) from the result .... 12. _____

13. Enter the amount shown below for your filing status:
    - Single or married filing separately— $36,900
    - Married filing jointly or Qualifying widow(er)— $73,800
    - Head of household—$49,400
    } .... 13. _____

14. Enter the amount from line 5 of the **Qualified Dividends and Capital Gain Tax Worksheet** ...... 14. _____

15. Subtract line 14 from line 13. If zero or less, enter -0- .... 15. _____

16. Enter the **smaller** of line 10 or line 15 .... 16. _____

17. Subtract line 16 from line 10 .... 17. _____

18. Multiply line 17 by 15% (.15) .... 18. _____

19. Add lines 12 and 18 .... 19. _____

20. Enter the **smaller** of line 8 or line 19 .... 20. _____

21. Enter the amount you would enter on Form 1040A, line 30, if you do not owe this tax .... 21. _____

22. **Alternative minimum tax.** Is the amount on line 20 more than the amount on line 21?
    - ☐ **No.** You do not owe this tax.
    - ☐ **Yes.** Subtract line 21 from line 20. Also include this amount in the total on Form 1040A, line 28. Enter "AMT" and show the amount in the space to the left of line 28 .... 22. _____

Need more information or forms? Visit IRS.gov.

Before you begin: ✓ Be sure you do not have to file Form 1040 (see the Instructions for Form 1040A, line 10).

1. Enter the amount from Form 1040A, line 27	1. _____
2. Enter the amount from Form 1040A, line 9b	2. _____
3. Enter the amount from Form 1040A, line 10	3. _____
4. Add lines 2 and 3	4. _____
5. Subtract line 4 from line 1. If zero or less, enter -0-	5. _____
6. Enter the **smaller** of:	
• The amount on line 1, or	
• $36,900 if single or married filing separately, $73,800 if married filing jointly or qualifying widow(er), or $49,400 if head of household.	6. _____
7. Enter the smaller of line 5 or line 6	7. _____
8. Subtract line 7 from line 6. This amount is taxed at 0%	8. _____
9. Enter the smaller of line 1 or line 4	9. _____
10. Enter the amount from line 8	10. _____
11. Subtract line 10 from line 9	11. _____
12. Multiply line 11 by 15% (.15)	12. _____
13. Use the Tax Table to figure the tax on the amount on line 5. Enter the tax here	13. _____
14. Add lines 12 and 13	14. _____
15. Use the Tax Table to figure the tax on the amount on line 1. Enter the tax here	15. _____
16. **Tax on all taxable income.** Enter the **smaller** of line 14 or line 15 here and on Form 1040A, line 28	16. _____

Form 8615

Form 8615 generally must be used to figure the tax for any child who had more than $2,000 of unearned income, such as taxable interest, ordinary dividends, or capital gain distributions, and who either:

1. Was under age 18 at the end of 2014,

2. Was age 18 at the end of 2014 and did not have earned income that was more than half of the child's support, or

3. Was a full-time student at least age 19 but under age 24 at the end of 2014 and did not have earned income that was more than half of the child's support.

But if the child files a joint return for 2014 or if neither of the child's parents was alive at the end of 2014, do not use Form 8615 to figure the child's tax.

A child born on January 1, 1997, is considered to be age 18 at the end of 2014; a child born on January 1, 1996, is considered to be age 19 at the end of 2014; a child born on January 1, 1991, is considered to be age 24 at the end of 2014.

Qualified Dividends and Capital Gain Tax Worksheet

If you received qualified dividends or capital gain distributions, use the Qualified Dividends and Capital Gain Tax Worksheet to figure your tax.

Line 29

Excess Advance Premium Tax Credit Repayment

The premium tax credit helps pay premiums for health insurance purchased from the Health Insurance Marketplace. If advance payments of this credit were made for coverage for you, your spouse, or your dependent, complete Form 8962. If the advance payments were more than the premium tax credit you can claim, enter the amount, if any, from Form 8962, line 29.

If you enrolled someone who is not claimed as a dependent on your return or for more information, see the instructions for Form 8962.

Line 31

Credit for Child and Dependent Care Expenses

You may be able to take this credit if you paid someone to care for any of the following persons.

1. Your qualifying child under age 13 whom you claim as your dependent.

2. Your disabled spouse or any other disabled person who could not care for himself or herself.

3. Your child whom you could not claim as a dependent because of the rules for *Children of divorced or separated parents* in the instructions for line 6c.

For details, use TeleTax topic 602 or see Form 2441.

Line 32

Credit for the Elderly or the Disabled

You may be able to take this credit if by the end of 2014 (a) you were age 65 or older, or (b) you retired on permanent and total disability and you had taxable disability income. But you cannot take the credit if:

1. The amount on Form 1040A, line 22, is $17,500 or more ($20,000 or more if married filing jointly and only one spouse is eligible for the credit; $25,000 or more if married filing jointly and both spouses are eligible; $12,500 or more if married filing separately and you lived apart from your spouse all year), or

2. You received one or more of the following benefits totaling $5,000 or more ($7,500 or more if married filing jointly and both spouses are eligible for the credit; $3,750 or more if married filing separately and you lived apart from your spouse all year).

a. Nontaxable part of social security benefits.

b. Nontaxable part of tier 1 railroad retirement benefits treated as social security.

c. Nontaxable veterans' pensions (excluding military disability pensions).

d. Any other nontaxable pensions, annuities, or disability income excluded from income under any provision of law other than the Internal Revenue Code.

For this purpose, do not include amounts treated as a return of your cost of a pension or annuity. Also, do not include a disability annuity payable under section 808 of the Foreign Service Act of 1980 or any pension, annuity, or similar allowance for personal injuries or sickness resulting from active service in the armed forces of any country, the National Oceanic and Atmospheric Administration, or the Public Health Service.

You must include Schedule R with your return to claim this credit.

See Schedule R and its instructions for details.

Credit figured by the IRS. If you can take this credit and you want us to figure it for you, see the Instructions for Schedule R.

Line 33

Education Credits

If you (or your dependent) paid qualified expenses in 2014 for yourself, your spouse, or your dependent to enroll in or attend an eligible educational institution, you may be able to take an education credit. See Form 8863 for details. However, you cannot take an education credit if any of the following applies.

• You, or your spouse if filing jointly, are claimed as a dependent on someone else's (such as your parent's) 2014 tax return.

• Your filing status is married filing separately.

• The amount on Form 1040A, line 22, is $90,000 or more ($180,000 or more if married filing jointly).

• You are taking a deduction for tuition and fees on Form 1040A, line 19, for the same student.

• You, or your spouse, were a nonresident alien for any part of 2014 unless your filing status is married filing jointly.

To find out which education benefits you qualify for, go to *www.irs.gov/uac/Am-I-Eligible-to-Claim-an-Education-Credit%3F*.

You must include Form 8863 with your return to claim this credit.

See Form 8863 and its instructions for details.

Line 34

Retirement Savings Contributions Credit (Saver's Credit)

You may be able to take this credit if you, or your spouse if filing jointly, made (a) contributions, other than rollover contributions, to a traditional or Roth IRA; (b) elective deferrals to a 401(k) or 403(b) plan (including designated Roth contributions), or to a governmental 457, SEP, or SIMPLE plan; (c) voluntary employee contributions to a qualified retirement plan (including the federal Thrift Savings Plan); or (d) contributions to a 501(c)(18)(D) plan.

However, you cannot take the credit if either of the following applies.

1. The amount on Form 1040A, line 22, is more than $30,000 ($45,000 if head of household; $60,000 if married filing jointly).

2. The person(s) who made the qualified contribution or elective deferral (a) was born after January 1, 1997, (b) is claimed as a dependent on someone else's 2014 tax return, or (c) was a student (defined next).

You were a student if during any part of 5 calendar months of 2014 you:

• Were enrolled as a full-time student at a school, or

• Took a full-time, on-farm training course given by a school or a state, county, or local government agency.

A school includes a technical, trade, or mechanical school. It does not include an on-the-job training course, correspondence school, or school offering courses only through the Internet.

You must include Form 8880 with your return to claim this credit.

For more details, use TeleTax topic 610 or see Form 8880.

Need more information or forms? Visit IRS.gov.

2014 Child Tax Credit Worksheet—Line 35

1. To be a qualifying child for the child tax credit, the child must be your dependent, **under age 17** at the end of 2014, and meet all the conditions in Steps 1 through 3 in the instructions for line 6c. Make sure you check the box on Form 1040A, line 6c, column (4), for each qualifying child.
2. If you do not have a qualifying child, you cannot claim the child tax credit.
3. If your qualifying child has an ITIN instead of an SSN, file Schedule 8812.

Part 1

1. Number of qualifying children: _____ × $1,000. Enter the result. **1** _____

2. Enter the amount from Form 1040A, line 22. **2** _____

3. Enter the amount shown below for your filing status.

   • Married filing jointly — $110,000

   • Single, head of household, or qualifying widow(er) — $75,000

   • Married filing separately — $55,000

   3 _____

4. Is the amount on line 2 more than the amount on line 3?

   ☐ **No.** Leave line 4 blank. Enter -0- on line 5, and go to line 6.

   ☐ **Yes.** Subtract line 3 from line 2.
   If the result is not a multiple of $1,000, increase it to the next multiple of $1,000. For example, increase $425 to $1,000, increase $1,025 to $2,000, etc.

   4 _____

5. Multiply the amount on line 4 by 5% (.05). Enter the result. **5** _____

6. Is the amount on line 1 more than the amount on line 5?

   ☐ **No.** (STOP)
   You cannot take the child tax credit on Form 1040A, line 35. You also cannot take the additional child tax credit on Form 1040A, line 43. Complete the rest of your Form 1040A.

   ☐ **Yes.** Subtract line 5 from line 1. Enter the result. *Go to Part 2.*

   6 _____

Need more information or forms? Visit IRS.gov.

2014 Child Tax Credit Worksheet—Line 35 *(Continued)*

Keep for Your Records

Part 2		
	7. Enter the amount from Form 1040A, line 30.	**7**

8. Add the amounts from Form 1040A:

Line 31 _____

Line 32 + _____

Line 33 + _____

Line 34 + _____   Enter the total.   **8**

9. Are the amounts on lines 7 and 8 the same?

☐ **Yes.** (STOP) You cannot take this credit because there is no tax to reduce. However, you may be able to take the **additional child tax credit.** See the **TIP** below.

☐ **No.** Subtract line 8 from line 7.   **9**

10. Is the amount on line 6 more than the amount on line 9?

☐ **Yes.** Enter the amount from line 9. Also, you may be able to take the **additional child tax credit.** See the **TIP** below.

☐ **No.** Enter the amount from line 6.

This is your child tax credit.   **10**

Enter this amount on Form 1040A, line 35.

TIP You may be able to take the **additional child tax credit** on Form 1040A, line 43, if you answered "Yes" on line 9 **or** line 10 above.

• First, complete your Form 1040A through lines 42a and 42b.

• Then, use Schedule 8812 to figure any additional child tax credit.

1040A

Line 38

Health Care: Individual Responsibility

Beginning in 2014, individuals must have health care coverage, qualify for a health coverage exemption, or make a shared responsibility payment with their tax return.

If you had qualifying health care coverage (called minimum essential coverage) for every month of 2014 for yourself, your spouse (if filing jointly), and anyone you could or did claim as a dependent, check the box on this line and leave the entry space blank.

Otherwise, do not check the box on this line. See the instructions for Form 8965.

If you can be claimed as a dependent, do not check the box on this line. Leave the entry space blank. You do not need to attach Form 8965 or see its instructions.

Minimum essential coverage. Most health care coverage that people have is minimum essential coverage.

Minimum essential coverage includes:
• Health care coverage provided by your employer,
• Health insurance coverage you buy through the Health Insurance Marketplace,
• Many types of government-sponsored health coverage including Medicare, most Medicaid coverage, and most health care coverage provided to veterans and active duty service members, and

Need more information or forms? Visit IRS.gov.

• Certain types of coverage you buy directly from an insurance company.

See the instructions for Form 8965 for more information on what qualifies as minimum essential coverage.

Premium tax credit. If you, your spouse, or a dependent enrolled in health insurance through the Marketplace, you may be able to claim the premium tax credit. See the instructions for line 45 and Form 8962.

Line 40

Federal Income Tax Withheld

Add the amounts shown as federal income tax withheld on your Forms W-2 and 1099-R. Enter the total on line 40. The amount withheld should be shown in box 2 of Form W-2, and in box 4 of Form 1099-R. Attach Form(s) 1099-R to the front of your return if federal income tax was withheld.

If you received a 2014 Form 1099 showing federal income tax withheld on dividends, taxable or tax-exempt interest income, unemployment compensation, social security benefits, or railroad retirement benefits, include the amount withheld in the total on line 40. This should be shown in box 4 of Form 1099, box 6 of Form SSA-1099, or box 10 of Form RRB-1099. If federal income tax was withheld from your Alaska Permanent Fund dividends, include the tax withheld in the total on line 40.

Line 41

2014 Estimated Tax Payments

Enter any estimated federal income tax payments you made for 2014. Include any overpayment that you applied to your 2014 estimated tax from:

• Your 2013 return, or
• An amended return (Form 1040X).

If you and your spouse paid joint estimated tax but are now filing separate income tax returns, you can divide the amount paid in any way you choose as long as you both agree. If you cannot agree, you must divide the payments in proportion to each spouse's individual tax as shown on your separate returns for 2014. For an example of how to do this, see Pub. 505. You may want to attach an explanation of how you and your spouse divided the payments. Be sure to show both social security numbers (SSNs) in the space provided on the separate returns. If you or your spouse paid separate estimated tax but you are now filing a joint return, add the amounts you each paid. Follow these instructions even if your spouse died in 2014 or in 2015 before filing a 2014 return.

Divorced Taxpayers If you got divorced in 2014 and you made joint estimated tax payments with your former spouse, enter your former spouse's SSN in the space provided on the front of Form 1040A. If you were divorced and remarried in 2014, enter your present spouse's SSN in the space provided on the front of Form 1040A. Also, in the blank space to the left of line 41, enter your former spouse's SSN, followed by "DIV."

Name Change If you changed your name because of marriage, divorce, etc., and you made estimated tax payments using your former name, attach a statement to the front of Form 1040A. On the statement, explain all the payments you and your spouse made in 2014 and the name(s) and SSN(s) under which you made them.

Lines 42a and 42b—Earned Income Credit (EIC)

What is the EIC?

The EIC is a credit for certain people who work. The credit may give you a refund even if you do not owe any tax or did not have any tax withheld.

To Take the EIC:

- Follow the steps below.
- Complete the Earned Income Credit (EIC) Worksheet in these instructions or let the IRS figure the credit for you.
- If you have a qualifying child, complete and attach Schedule EIC.

For help in determining if you are eligible for the EIC, go to *www.irs.gov/eitc* and click on "EITC Assistant." This service is available in English and Spanish.

 If you take the EIC even though you are not eligible and it is determined that your error is due to reckless or intentional disregard of the EIC rules, you will not be allowed to take the credit for 2 years even if you are otherwise eligible to do so. If you fraudulently take the EIC, you will not be allowed to take the credit for 10 years. See Form 8862, who must file, *later. You may also have to pay penalties.*

Step 1   All Filers

1. If, in 2014:
   - 3 or more children lived with you, is the amount on Form 1040A, line 22, less than $46,997 ($52,427 if married filing jointly)?
   - 2 children lived with you, is the amount on Form 1040A, line 22, less than $43,756 ($49,186 if married filing jointly)?
   - 1 child lived with you, is the amount on Form 1040A, line 22, less than $38,511 ($43,941 if married filing jointly)?
   - No children lived with you, is the amount on Form 1040A, line 22, less than $14,590 ($20,020 if married filing jointly)?

   ☐ **Yes.** Continue ⬎   ☐ **No.**

   You cannot take the credit.

2. Do you, and your spouse if filing a joint return, have a social security number that allows you to work and is valid for EIC purposes (explained later under *Definitions and Special Rules*)?

   ☐ **Yes.** Continue ⬎   ☐ **No.**

   You cannot take the credit. Enter "No" to the left of the entry space for line 42a.

3. Is your filing status married filing separately?

   ☐ **Yes.** (STOP)   ☐ **No.** Continue ⬎

   You cannot take the credit.

4. Were you or your spouse a nonresident alien for any part of 2014?

   ☐ **Yes.** See *Nonresident aliens*, later, under *Definitions and Special Rules*.   ☐ **No.** Go to Step 2.

Step 2   Investment Income

1. Add the amounts from Form 1040A:

Line 8a		_____
Line 8b	+	_____
Line 9a	+	_____
Line 10	+	_____
Investment Income	**=**	_____

2. Is your investment income more than $3,350?

   ☐ **Yes.** (STOP)   ☐ **No.** Go to Step 3.

   You cannot take the credit.

Step 3   Qualifying Child

A qualifying child for the EIC is a child who is your...

Son, daughter, stepchild, foster child, brother, sister, stepbrother, stepsister, half brother, half sister, or a descendant of any of them (for example, your grandchild, niece, or nephew),

was ...

Under age 19 at the end of 2014 and younger than you (or your spouse, if filing jointly)

or

Under age 24 at the end of 2014, a student (defined later), and younger than you (or your spouse, if filing jointly)

or

Any age and permanently and totally disabled (defined later)

Who is not filing a joint return for 2014 or is filing a joint return for 2014 only to claim a refund of withheld income tax or estimated tax paid (see Pub. 596 for examples)

Need more information or forms? Visit IRS.gov.

AND

Who lived with you in the United States for more than half of 2014.
If the child did not live with you for the required time, see *Exception to time lived with you*, later.

> ⚠ **CAUTION** *If the child meets the conditions to be a qualifying child of any other person (other than your spouse if filing a joint return) for 2014, see Qualifying child of more than one person, later. If the child was married, see Married child, later.*

1. Do you have at least one child who meets the conditions to be your qualifying child?

☐ **Yes.** The child must have a valid social security number (SSN) as defined later, unless the child was born and died in 2014. If at least one qualifying child has a valid SSN (or was born or died in 2014), go to question 2. Otherwise, you cannot take the credit.

☐ **No.** Skip questions 2 and 3; go to Step 4.

2. Are you filing a joint return for 2014?

☐ **Yes.** Skip question 3 and Step 4; go to Step 5.

☐ **No.** Continue ↘

3. Could you be a qualifying child of another person for 2014? (Check "No" if the other person is not required to file, and is not filing, a 2014 tax return or is filing a 2014 return only to claim a refund of withheld income tax or estimated tax paid (see Pub. 596 for examples).)

☐ **Yes.** 🛑 You cannot take the credit. Enter "No" to the left of the entry space for line 42a.

☐ **No.** Skip Step 4; go to Step 5.

Step 4 Filers Without a Qualifying Child

1. Is the amount on Form 1040A, line 22, less than $14,590 ($20,020 if married filing jointly)?

☐ **Yes.** Continue ↘

☐ **No.** 🛑 You cannot take the credit.

2. Were you, or your spouse if filing a joint return, at least age 25 but under age 65 at the end of 2014? (Check "Yes" if you or your spouse if filing a joint return, were born after December 31, 1949, and before January 2, 1990.) If your spouse died in 2014 (or if you are preparing a return for someone who died in 2014), see Pub. 596 before you answer.

☐ **Yes.** Continue ↘

☐ **No.** 🛑 You cannot take the credit.

3. Was your main home, and your spouse's if filing a joint return, in the United States for more than half of 2014? Members of the military stationed outside the United States, see *Members of the military*, later, before you answer.

☐ **Yes.** Continue ↘

☐ **No.** 🛑 You cannot take the credit. Enter "No" to the left of the entry space for line 42a.

4. Are you filing a joint return for 2014?

☐ **Yes.** Skip questions 5 and 6; go to Step 5.

☐ **No.** Continue ↘

5. Could you be a qualifying child of another person for 2014? (Check "No" if the other person is not required to file, and is not filing, a 2014 tax return or is filing a 2014 return only to claim a refund of withheld income tax or estimated tax paid (see Pub. 596 for examples).)

☐ **Yes.** 🛑 Yes. You cannot take the credit. Enter "No" to the left of the entry space for line 42a.

☐ **No.** Continue ↘

6. Can you be claimed as a dependent on someone else's 2014 tax return?

☐ **Yes.** 🛑 You cannot take the credit.

☐ **No.** Go to Step 5.

Step 5 Earned Income

1. Complete the following worksheet.
Earned Income Worksheet

1.	Enter the amount from Form 1040A, line 7	1. _____
2.	Enter any amount included on Form 1040A, line 7, that is a taxable scholarship or fellowship grant not reported on a Form W-2	2. _____
3.	Enter any amount included on Form 1040A, line 7, that you received for work performed while an inmate in a penal institution. (Enter "PRI" and the same amount on the dotted line next to Form 1040A, line 7	3. _____
4.	Enter any amount included on Form 1040A, line 7, that you received as a pension or annuity from a nonqualified deferred compensation plan or a nongovernmental section 457 plan. (Enter "DFC" and the same amount on the dotted line next to Form 1040A, line 7). This amount may be shown in box 11 of Form W-2. If you received such an amount but box 11 is blank, contact your employer for the amount received	4. _____
5.	Add lines 2, 3, and 4	5. _____
6.	Subtract line 5 from line 1	6. _____
7.	Enter all your nontaxable combat pay if you elect to include it in earned income. Also enter this amount on Form 1040A, line 42b. See *Combat pay, nontaxable* later	7. _____

> **CAUTION** *Electing to include nontaxable combat pay may increase or decrease your EIC. Figure the credit with and without your nontaxable combat pay before making the election.*

8.	Add lines 6 and 7. **This is your earned income**	8. _____

2. If you have:
- 3 or more qualifying children, is your earned income less than $46,997 ($52,427 if married filing jointly)?
- 2 qualifying children, is your earned income less than $43,756 ($49,186 if married filing jointly)?
- 1 qualifying child, is your earned income less than $38,511 ($43,941 if married filing jointly)?
- No qualifying children, is your earned income less than $14,590 ($20,020 if married filing jointly)?

☐ **Yes.** Go to Step 6.   ☐ **No.** (STOP)

You cannot take the credit.

Step 6 How To Figure the Credit

1. Do you want the IRS to figure the credit for you?

☐ **Yes.** See *Credit figured by the IRS* later.   ☐ **No.** Go to the *Earned Income Credit Worksheet.*

Definitions and Special Rules

Adopted child. An adopted child is always treated as your own child. An adopted child includes a child lawfully placed with you for legal adoption.

Combat pay, nontaxable. If you were a member of the U.S. Armed Forces who served in a combat zone, certain pay is excluded from your income. See *Combat Zone Exclusion* in Pub. 3. You can elect to include this pay in your earned income when figuring the EIC. The amount of your nontaxable combat pay should be shown in box 12 of Form(s) W-2 with code Q. If you are filing a joint return and both you and your spouse received nontaxable combat pay, you can each make your own election. In other words, if one of you makes the election, the other one can also make it but does not have to.

Credit figured by the IRS. To have the IRS figure your EIC:

1. Enter "EIC" to the left of the entry space for Form 1040A, line 42a.

2. Be sure you enter the nontaxable combat pay you elect to include in earned income on Form 1040A, line 42b. See *Combat Pay, nontaxable*, earlier.

3. If you have a qualifying child, complete and attach Schedule EIC. If your EIC for a year after 1996 was reduced or disallowed, see *Form 8862, who must file* later.

Exception to time lived with you. Temporary absences by you or the child for special circumstances, such as school, vacation, business, medical care, military service, or detention in a juvenile facility, count as time the child lived with you. Also see *Kidnapped child* in the instructions for line 6c and *Members of the military*, later. A child is considered to have lived with you for more than half of 2014 if the child was born or died in 2014 and your home was this child's home for more than half the time he or she was alive in 2014.

Form 8862, who must file. You must file Form 8862 if your EIC for a year after 1996 was reduced or disallowed for any reason other than a math or clerical error. But do not file Form 8862 if either of the following applies.

- You filed Form 8862 for another year, the EIC was allowed for that year, and your EIC has not been reduced or disallowed again for any reason other than a math or clerical error.
- You are taking the EIC without a qualifying child and the only reason your EIC was reduced or disallowed in the other year was because it was determined that a child listed on Schedule EIC was not your qualifying child.

Also, do not file Form 8862 or take the credit for the:
- 2 years after the most recent tax year for which there was a final determination that your EIC claim was due to reckless or intentional disregard of the EIC rules, or
- 10 years after the most recent tax year for which there was a final determination that your EIC claim was due to fraud.

Foster child. A foster child is any child placed with you by an authorized placement agency or by judgment, decree, or other order of any court of competent jurisdiction. For more details on authorized placement agencies, see Pub. 596.

   Need more information or forms? Visit IRS.gov.

Married child. A child who was married at the end of 2014 is a qualifying child only if (a) you can claim him or her as your dependent on Form 1040A, line 6c, or (b) you could have claimed him or her as your dependent except for the special rule under *Children of divorced or separated parents* in the instructions for line 6c.

Members of the military. If you were on extended active duty outside the United States, your main home is considered to be in the United States during that duty period. Extended active duty is military duty ordered for an indefinite period or for a period of more than 90 days. Once you begin serving extended active duty, you are considered to be on extended active duty even if you do not serve more than 90 days.

Nonresident aliens. If your filing status is married filing jointly, go to Step 2. Otherwise, stop; you cannot take the EIC. Enter "No" to the left of the entry space for line 42a.

Permanently and totally disabled. A person is permanently and totally disabled if, at any time in 2014, the person could not engage in any substantial gainful activity because of a physical or mental condition and a doctor has determined that this condition (a) has lasted or can be expected to last continuously for at least a year, or (b) can be expected to lead to death.

Qualifying child of more than one person. Even if a child meets the conditions to be the qualifying child of more than one person, only one person can claim the child as a qualifying child for all of the following tax benefits, unless the special rule for *Children of divorced or separated parents* in the instructions for line 6c applies.

1. Dependency exemption (line 6c).
2. Child tax credits (lines 35 and 43).
3. Head of household filing status (line 4).
4. Credit for child and dependent care expenses (line 31).
5. Exclusion for dependent care benefits (Form 2441, Part III).
6. Earned income credit (lines 42a and 42b).

No other person can take any of the six tax benefits just listed unless he or she has a different qualifying child. If you and any other person can claim the child as a qualifying child, the following rules apply.

• If only one of the persons is the child's parent, the child is treated as the qualifying child of the parent.

• If the parents do not file a joint return together but both parents claim the child as a qualifying child, the IRS will treat the child as the qualifying child of the parent with whom the child lived for the longer period of time in 2014. If the child lived with each parent for the same amount of time, the IRS will treat the child as the qualifying child of the parent who had the higher adjusted gross income (AGI) for 2014.

• If no parent can claim the child as a qualifying child, the child is treated as the qualifying child of the person who had the highest AGI for 2014.

• If a parent can claim the child as a qualifying child but no parent does so claim the child, the child is treated as the qualifying child of the person who had the highest AGI for 2014, but only if that person's AGI is higher than the highest AGI of any parent of the child who can claim the child.

Example. Your daughter meets the conditions to be a qualifying child for both you and your mother. Your daughter does not meet the conditions to be the qualifying child of any other person, including her other parent. Under the rules just described, you can claim your daughter as a qualifying child for all of the six tax benefits previously listed for which you otherwise qualify. Your mother cannot claim any of those six tax benefits unless she has a different qualifying child. However, if your mother's AGI is higher than yours and you do not claim your daughter as a qualifying child, your daughter is the qualifying child of your mother.

For more details and examples, see Pub. 596.

If you will not be taking the EIC with a qualifying child, enter "No" to the left of the entry space for line 42a. Otherwise, go to Step 3, question 1.

Social security number (SSN). For the EIC, a valid SSN is a number issued by the Social Security Administration unless "Not Valid for Employment" is printed on the social security card and the number was issued solely to allow the recipient of the SSN to apply for or receive a federally funded benefit. However, if "Valid for Work Only With DHS Authorization" is printed on your social security card, your SSN is valid for EIC purposes only as long as the DHS authorization is still valid.

To find out how to get an SSN, see *Social Security Number (SSN)*, near the beginning of these instructions. If you will not have an SSN by the date your return is due, see *What If You Cannot File on Time*.

Student. A student is a child who during any part of 5 calendar months of 2014 was enrolled as a full-time student at a school, or took a full-time, on-farm training course given by a school or a state, county, or local government agency. A school includes a technical, trade, or mechanical school. It does not include an on-the-job training course, correspondence school, or school offering courses only through the Internet.

Welfare benefits, effect of credit on. Any refund you receive as a result of taking the EIC cannot be counted as income when determining if you or anyone else is eligible for benefits or assistance, or how much you or anyone else can receive, under any federal program or under any state or local program financed in whole or in part with federal funds. These programs include Temporary Assistance for Needy Families (TANF), Medicaid, Supplemental Security Income (SSI), and Supplemental Nutrition Assistance Program (food stamps). In addition, when determining eligibility, the refund cannot be counted as a resource for at least 12 months after you receive it. Check with your local benefit coordinator to find out if your refund will affect your benefits.

Earned Income Credit (EIC) Worksheet—Lines 42a and 42b

Keep for Your Records

Part 1

All Filers

1. Enter your earned income from Step 5.

   | 1 | |

---

2. Look up the amount on line 1 in the EIC Table to find the credit. Be sure you use the correct column for your filing status and the number of children you have. Enter the credit here.

   | 2 | |

   If line 2 is zero, **STOP** You cannot take the credit. Enter "No" to the left of the entry space for line 42a.

3. Enter the amount from Form 1040A, line 22.

   | 3 | |

4. Are the amounts on lines 3 and 1 the same?

   ☐ **Yes.** Skip line 5; enter the amount from line 2 on line 6.

   ☐ **No.** Go to line 5.

Part 2

Filers Who Answered "No" on Line 4

5. If you have:
   - No qualifying children, is the amount on line 3 less than $8,150 ($13,550 if married filing jointly)?
   - 1 or more qualifying children, is the amount on line 3 less than $17,850 ($23,300 if married filing jointly)?

   ☐ **Yes.** Leave line 5 blank; enter the amount from line 2 on line 6.

   ☐ **No.** Look up the amount on line 3 in the EIC Table to find the credit. Be sure you use the correct column for your filing status and the number of children you have. Enter the credit here.

   | 5 | |

   Look at the amounts on lines 5 and 2.
   Then, enter the smaller amount on line 6.

Part 3

Your Earned Income Credit

6. This is your earned income credit.

   | 6 | |

   Enter this amount on Form 1040A, line 42a.

Reminder—

✓ If you have a qualifying child, complete and attach Schedule EIC.

⚠ **CAUTION** *If your EIC for a year after 1996 was reduced or disallowed, see Form 8862, who must file, earlier, to find out if you must file Form 8862 to take the credit for 2014.*

Need more information or forms? Visit IRS.gov.

2014 Earned Income Credit (EIC) Table
Caution. This is **not** a tax table.

1. To find your credit, read down the "At least - But less than" columns and find the line that includes the amount you were told to look up from your EIC Worksheet.

2. Then, go to the column that includes your filing status and the number of qualifying children you have. Enter the credit from that column on your EIC Worksheet.

Example. If your filing status is single, you have one qualifying child, and the amount you are looking up from your EIC Worksheet is $2,455, you would enter $842.

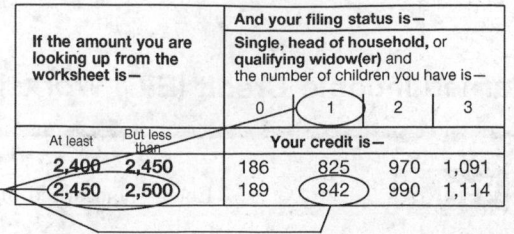

If the amount you are looking up from the worksheet is—		And your filing status is—			
		Single, head of household, or qualifying widow(er) and the number of children you have is—			
At least	But less than	0	1	2	3
		Your credit is—			
2,400	2,450	186	825	970	1,091
2,450	2,500	189	842	990	1,114

If the amount you are looking up from the worksheet is—		And your filing status is—							
		Single, head of household, or qualifying widow(er) and the number of children you have is—				Married filing jointly and the number of children you have is–			
At least	But less than	0	1	2	3	0	1	2	3
		Your credit is—				Your credit is—			
$1	$50	$2	$9	$10	$11	$2	$9	$10	$11
50	100	6	26	30	34	6	26	30	34
100	150	10	43	50	56	10	43	50	56
150	200	13	60	70	79	13	60	70	79
200	250	17	77	90	101	17	77	90	101
250	300	21	94	110	124	21	94	110	124
300	350	25	111	130	146	25	111	130	146
350	400	29	128	150	169	29	128	150	169
400	450	33	145	170	191	33	145	170	191
450	500	36	162	190	214	36	162	190	214
500	550	40	179	210	236	40	179	210	236
550	600	44	196	230	259	44	196	230	259
600	650	48	213	250	281	48	213	250	281
650	700	52	230	270	304	52	230	270	304
700	750	55	247	290	326	55	247	290	326
750	800	59	264	310	349	59	264	310	349
800	850	63	281	330	371	63	281	330	371
850	900	67	298	350	394	67	298	350	394
900	950	71	315	370	416	71	315	370	416
950	1,000	75	332	390	439	75	332	390	439
1,000	1,050	78	349	410	461	78	349	410	461
1,050	1,100	82	366	430	484	82	366	430	484
1,100	1,150	86	383	450	506	86	383	450	506
1,150	1,200	90	400	470	529	90	400	470	529
1,200	1,250	94	417	490	551	94	417	490	551
1,250	1,300	98	434	510	574	98	434	510	574
1,300	1,350	101	451	530	596	101	451	530	596
1,350	1,400	105	468	550	619	105	468	550	619
1,400	1,450	109	485	570	641	109	485	570	641
1,450	1,500	113	502	590	664	113	502	590	664
1,500	1,550	117	519	610	686	117	519	610	686
1,550	1,600	120	536	630	709	120	536	630	709
1,600	1,650	124	553	650	731	124	553	650	731
1,650	1,700	128	570	670	754	128	570	670	754
1,700	1,750	132	587	690	776	132	587	690	776
1,750	1,800	136	604	710	799	136	604	710	799
1,800	1,850	140	621	730	821	140	621	730	821
1,850	1,900	143	638	750	844	143	638	750	844
1,900	1,950	147	655	770	866	147	655	770	866
1,950	2,000	151	672	790	889	151	672	790	889
2,000	2,050	155	689	810	911	155	689	810	911
2,050	2,100	159	706	830	934	159	706	830	934
2,100	2,150	163	723	850	956	163	723	850	956
2,150	2,200	166	740	870	979	166	740	870	979
2,200	2,250	170	757	890	1,001	170	757	890	1,001
2,250	2,300	174	774	910	1,024	174	774	910	1,024
2,300	2,350	178	791	930	1,046	178	791	930	1,046
2,350	2,400	182	808	950	1,069	182	808	950	1,069
2,400	2,450	186	825	970	1,091	186	825	970	1,091
2,450	2,500	189	842	990	1,114	189	842	990	1,114
2,500	2,550	193	859	1,010	1,136	193	859	1,010	1,136
2,550	2,600	197	876	1,030	1,159	197	876	1,030	1,159
2,600	2,650	201	893	1,050	1,181	201	893	1,050	1,181
2,650	2,700	205	910	1,070	1,204	205	910	1,070	1,204
2,700	2,750	208	927	1,090	1,226	208	927	1,090	1,226
2,750	2,800	212	944	1,110	1,249	212	944	1,110	1,249

If the amount you are looking up from the worksheet is—		And your filing status is—							
		Single, head of household, or qualifying widow(er) and the number of children you have is–				Married filing jointly and the number of children you have is–			
At least	But less than	0	1	2	3	0	1	2	3
		Your credit is—				Your credit is—			
2,800	2,850	216	961	1,130	1,271	216	961	1,130	1,271
2,850	2,900	220	978	1,150	1,294	220	978	1,150	1,294
2,900	2,950	224	995	1,170	1,316	224	995	1,170	1,316
2,950	3,000	228	1,012	1,190	1,339	228	1,012	1,190	1,339
3,000	3,050	231	1,029	1,210	1,361	231	1,029	1,210	1,361
3,050	3,100	235	1,046	1,230	1,384	235	1,046	1,230	1,384
3,100	3,150	239	1,063	1,250	1,406	239	1,063	1,250	1,406
3,150	3,200	243	1,080	1,270	1,429	243	1,080	1,270	1,429
3,200	3,250	247	1,097	1,290	1,451	247	1,097	1,290	1,451
3,250	3,300	251	1,114	1,310	1,474	251	1,114	1,310	1,474
3,300	3,350	254	1,131	1,330	1,496	254	1,131	1,330	1,496
3,350	3,400	258	1,148	1,350	1,519	258	1,148	1,350	1,519
3,400	3,450	262	1,165	1,370	1,541	262	1,165	1,370	1,541
3,450	3,500	266	1,182	1,390	1,564	266	1,182	1,390	1,564
3,500	3,550	270	1,199	1,410	1,586	270	1,199	1,410	1,586
3,550	3,600	273	1,216	1,430	1,609	273	1,216	1,430	1,609
3,600	3,650	277	1,233	1,450	1,631	277	1,233	1,450	1,631
3,650	3,700	281	1,250	1,470	1,654	281	1,250	1,470	1,654
3,700	3,750	285	1,267	1,490	1,676	285	1,267	1,490	1,676
3,750	3,800	289	1,284	1,510	1,699	289	1,284	1,510	1,699
3,800	3,850	293	1,301	1,530	1,721	293	1,301	1,530	1,721
3,850	3,900	296	1,318	1,550	1,744	296	1,318	1,550	1,744
3,900	3,950	300	1,335	1,570	1,766	300	1,335	1,570	1,766
3,950	4,000	304	1,352	1,590	1,789	304	1,352	1,590	1,789
4,000	4,050	308	1,369	1,610	1,811	308	1,369	1,610	1,811
4,050	4,100	312	1,386	1,630	1,834	312	1,386	1,630	1,834
4,100	4,150	316	1,403	1,650	1,856	316	1,403	1,650	1,856
4,150	4,200	319	1,420	1,670	1,879	319	1,420	1,670	1,879
4,200	4,250	323	1,437	1,690	1,901	323	1,437	1,690	1,901
4,250	4,300	327	1,454	1,710	1,924	327	1,454	1,710	1,924
4,300	4,350	331	1,471	1,730	1,946	331	1,471	1,730	1,946
4,350	4,400	335	1,488	1,750	1,969	335	1,488	1,750	1,969
4,400	4,450	339	1,505	1,770	1,991	339	1,505	1,770	1,991
4,450	4,500	342	1,522	1,790	2,014	342	1,522	1,790	2,014
4,500	4,550	346	1,539	1,810	2,036	346	1,539	1,810	2,036
4,550	4,600	350	1,556	1,830	2,059	350	1,556	1,830	2,059
4,600	4,650	354	1,573	1,850	2,081	354	1,573	1,850	2,081
4,650	4,700	358	1,590	1,870	2,104	358	1,590	1,870	2,104
4,700	4,750	361	1,607	1,890	2,126	361	1,607	1,890	2,126
4,750	4,800	365	1,624	1,910	2,149	365	1,624	1,910	2,149
4,800	4,850	369	1,641	1,930	2,171	369	1,641	1,930	2,171
4,850	4,900	373	1,658	1,950	2,194	373	1,658	1,950	2,194
4,900	4,950	377	1,675	1,970	2,216	377	1,675	1,970	2,216
4,950	5,000	381	1,692	1,990	2,239	381	1,692	1,990	2,239
5,000	5,050	384	1,709	2,010	2,261	384	1,709	2,010	2,261
5,050	5,100	388	1,726	2,030	2,284	388	1,726	2,030	2,284
5,100	5,150	392	1,743	2,050	2,306	392	1,743	2,050	2,306
5,150	5,200	396	1,760	2,070	2,329	396	1,760	2,070	2,329
5,200	5,250	400	1,777	2,090	2,351	400	1,777	2,090	2,351
5,250	5,300	404	1,794	2,110	2,374	404	1,794	2,110	2,374
5,300	5,350	407	1,811	2,130	2,396	407	1,811	2,130	2,396
5,350	5,400	411	1,828	2,150	2,419	411	1,828	2,150	2,419
5,400	5,450	415	1,845	2,170	2,441	415	1,845	2,170	2,441
5,450	5,500	419	1,862	2,190	2,464	419	1,862	2,190	2,464
5,500	5,550	423	1,879	2,210	2,486	423	1,879	2,210	2,486
5,550	5,600	426	1,896	2,230	2,509	426	1,896	2,230	2,509

(Continued)

Need more information or forms? Visit IRS.gov.

Earned Income Credit (EIC) Table - Continued

(**Caution.** This is **not** a tax table.)

At least	But less than	Single, HoH, or qualifying widow(er) — 0	1	2	3	Married filing jointly — 0	1	2	3
5,600	5,650	430	1,913	2,250	2,531	430	1,913	2,250	2,531
5,650	5,700	434	1,930	2,270	2,554	434	1,930	2,270	2,554
5,700	5,750	438	1,947	2,290	2,576	438	1,947	2,290	2,576
5,750	5,800	442	1,964	2,310	2,599	442	1,964	2,310	2,599
5,800	5,850	446	1,981	2,330	2,621	446	1,981	2,330	2,621
5,850	5,900	449	1,998	2,350	2,644	449	1,998	2,350	2,644
5,900	5,950	453	2,015	2,370	2,666	453	2,015	2,370	2,666
5,950	6,000	457	2,032	2,390	2,689	457	2,032	2,390	2,689
6,000	6,050	461	2,049	2,410	2,711	461	2,049	2,410	2,711
6,050	6,100	465	2,066	2,430	2,734	465	2,066	2,430	2,734
6,100	6,150	469	2,083	2,450	2,756	469	2,083	2,450	2,756
6,150	6,200	472	2,100	2,470	2,779	472	2,100	2,470	2,779
6,200	6,250	476	2,117	2,490	2,801	476	2,117	2,490	2,801
6,250	6,300	480	2,134	2,510	2,824	480	2,134	2,510	2,824
6,300	6,350	484	2,151	2,530	2,846	484	2,151	2,530	2,846
6,350	6,400	488	2,168	2,550	2,869	488	2,168	2,550	2,869
6,400	6,450	492	2,185	2,570	2,891	492	2,185	2,570	2,891
6,450	6,500	496	2,202	2,590	2,914	496	2,202	2,590	2,914
6,500	6,550	496	2,219	2,610	2,936	496	2,219	2,610	2,936
6,550	6,600	496	2,236	2,630	2,959	496	2,236	2,630	2,959
6,600	6,650	496	2,253	2,650	2,981	496	2,253	2,650	2,981
6,650	6,700	496	2,270	2,670	3,004	496	2,270	2,670	3,004
6,700	6,750	496	2,287	2,690	3,026	496	2,287	2,690	3,026
6,750	6,800	496	2,304	2,710	3,049	496	2,304	2,710	3,049
6,800	6,850	496	2,321	2,730	3,071	496	2,321	2,730	3,071
6,850	6,900	496	2,338	2,750	3,094	496	2,338	2,750	3,094
6,900	6,950	496	2,355	2,770	3,116	496	2,355	2,770	3,116
6,950	7,000	496	2,372	2,790	3,139	496	2,372	2,790	3,139
7,000	7,050	496	2,389	2,810	3,161	496	2,389	2,810	3,161
7,050	7,100	496	2,406	2,830	3,184	496	2,406	2,830	3,184
7,100	7,150	496	2,423	2,850	3,206	496	2,423	2,850	3,206
7,150	7,200	496	2,440	2,870	3,229	496	2,440	2,870	3,229
7,200	7,250	496	2,457	2,890	3,251	496	2,457	2,890	3,251
7,250	7,300	496	2,474	2,910	3,274	496	2,474	2,910	3,274
7,300	7,350	496	2,491	2,930	3,296	496	2,491	2,930	3,296
7,350	7,400	496	2,508	2,950	3,319	496	2,508	2,950	3,319
7,400	7,450	496	2,525	2,970	3,341	496	2,525	2,970	3,341
7,450	7,500	496	2,542	2,990	3,364	496	2,542	2,990	3,364
7,500	7,550	496	2,559	3,010	3,386	496	2,559	3,010	3,386
7,550	7,600	496	2,576	3,030	3,409	496	2,576	3,030	3,409
7,600	7,650	496	2,593	3,050	3,431	496	2,593	3,050	3,431
7,650	7,700	496	2,610	3,070	3,454	496	2,610	3,070	3,454
7,700	7,750	496	2,627	3,090	3,476	496	2,627	3,090	3,476
7,750	7,800	496	2,644	3,110	3,499	496	2,644	3,110	3,499
7,800	7,850	496	2,661	3,130	3,521	496	2,661	3,130	3,521
7,850	7,900	496	2,678	3,150	3,544	496	2,678	3,150	3,544
7,900	7,950	496	2,695	3,170	3,566	496	2,695	3,170	3,566
7,950	8,000	496	2,712	3,190	3,589	496	2,712	3,190	3,589
8,000	8,050	496	2,729	3,210	3,611	496	2,729	3,210	3,611
8,050	8,100	496	2,746	3,230	3,634	496	2,746	3,230	3,634
8,100	8,150	496	2,763	3,250	3,656	496	2,763	3,250	3,656
8,150	8,200	491	2,780	3,270	3,679	496	2,780	3,270	3,679
8,200	8,250	487	2,797	3,290	3,701	496	2,797	3,290	3,701
8,250	8,300	483	2,814	3,310	3,724	496	2,814	3,310	3,724
8,300	8,350	479	2,831	3,330	3,746	496	2,831	3,330	3,746
8,350	8,400	475	2,848	3,350	3,769	496	2,848	3,350	3,769
8,400	8,450	472	2,865	3,370	3,791	496	2,865	3,370	3,791
8,450	8,500	468	2,882	3,390	3,814	496	2,882	3,390	3,814
8,500	8,550	464	2,899	3,410	3,836	496	2,899	3,410	3,836
8,550	8,600	460	2,916	3,430	3,859	496	2,916	3,430	3,859
8,600	8,650	456	2,933	3,450	3,881	496	2,933	3,450	3,881
8,650	8,700	452	2,950	3,470	3,904	496	2,950	3,470	3,904
8,700	8,750	449	2,967	3,490	3,926	496	2,967	3,490	3,926
8,750	8,800	445	2,984	3,510	3,949	496	2,984	3,510	3,949
8,800	8,850	441	3,001	3,530	3,971	496	3,001	3,530	3,971
8,850	8,900	437	3,018	3,550	3,994	496	3,018	3,550	3,994
8,900	8,950	433	3,035	3,570	4,016	496	3,035	3,570	4,016
8,950	9,000	430	3,052	3,590	4,039	496	3,052	3,590	4,039
9,000	9,050	426	3,069	3,610	4,061	496	3,069	3,610	4,061
9,050	9,100	422	3,086	3,630	4,084	496	3,086	3,630	4,084
9,100	9,150	418	3,103	3,650	4,106	496	3,103	3,650	4,106
9,150	9,200	414	3,120	3,670	4,129	496	3,120	3,670	4,129
9,200	9,250	410	3,137	3,690	4,151	496	3,137	3,690	4,151
9,250	9,300	407	3,154	3,710	4,174	496	3,154	3,710	4,174
9,300	9,350	403	3,171	3,730	4,196	496	3,171	3,730	4,196
9,350	9,400	399	3,188	3,750	4,219	496	3,188	3,750	4,219
9,400	9,450	395	3,205	3,770	4,241	496	3,205	3,770	4,241
9,450	9,500	391	3,222	3,790	4,264	496	3,222	3,790	4,264
9,500	9,550	387	3,239	3,810	4,286	496	3,239	3,810	4,286
9,550	9,600	384	3,256	3,830	4,309	496	3,256	3,830	4,309
9,600	9,650	380	3,273	3,850	4,331	496	3,273	3,850	4,331
9,650	9,700	376	3,290	3,870	4,354	496	3,290	3,870	4,354
9,700	9,750	372	3,305	3,890	4,376	496	3,305	3,890	4,376
9,750	9,800	368	3,305	3,910	4,399	496	3,305	3,910	4,399
9,800	9,850	365	3,305	3,930	4,421	496	3,305	3,930	4,421
9,850	9,900	361	3,305	3,950	4,444	496	3,305	3,950	4,444
9,900	9,950	357	3,305	3,970	4,466	496	3,305	3,970	4,466
9,950	10,000	353	3,305	3,990	4,489	496	3,305	3,990	4,489
10,000	10,050	349	3,305	4,010	4,511	496	3,305	4,010	4,511
10,050	10,100	345	3,305	4,030	4,534	496	3,305	4,030	4,534
10,100	10,150	342	3,305	4,050	4,556	496	3,305	4,050	4,556
10,150	10,200	338	3,305	4,070	4,579	496	3,305	4,070	4,579
10,200	10,250	334	3,305	4,090	4,601	496	3,305	4,090	4,601
10,250	10,300	330	3,305	4,110	4,624	496	3,305	4,110	4,624
10,300	10,350	326	3,305	4,130	4,646	496	3,305	4,130	4,646
10,350	10,400	322	3,305	4,150	4,669	496	3,305	4,150	4,669
10,400	10,450	319	3,305	4,170	4,691	496	3,305	4,170	4,691
10,450	10,500	315	3,305	4,190	4,714	496	3,305	4,190	4,714
10,500	10,550	311	3,305	4,210	4,736	496	3,305	4,210	4,736
10,550	10,600	307	3,305	4,230	4,759	496	3,305	4,230	4,759
10,600	10,650	303	3,305	4,250	4,781	496	3,305	4,250	4,781
10,650	10,700	299	3,305	4,270	4,804	496	3,305	4,270	4,804
10,700	10,750	296	3,305	4,290	4,826	496	3,305	4,290	4,826
10,750	10,800	292	3,305	4,310	4,849	496	3,305	4,310	4,849
10,800	10,850	288	3,305	4,330	4,871	496	3,305	4,330	4,871
10,850	10,900	284	3,305	4,350	4,894	496	3,305	4,350	4,894
10,900	10,950	280	3,305	4,370	4,916	496	3,305	4,370	4,916
10,950	11,000	277	3,305	4,390	4,939	496	3,305	4,390	4,939
11,000	11,050	273	3,305	4,410	4,961	496	3,305	4,410	4,961
11,050	11,100	269	3,305	4,430	4,984	496	3,305	4,430	4,984
11,100	11,150	265	3,305	4,450	5,006	496	3,305	4,450	5,006
11,150	11,200	261	3,305	4,470	5,029	496	3,305	4,470	5,029
11,200	11,250	257	3,305	4,490	5,051	496	3,305	4,490	5,051
11,250	11,300	254	3,305	4,510	5,074	496	3,305	4,510	5,074
11,300	11,350	250	3,305	4,530	5,096	496	3,305	4,530	5,096
11,350	11,400	246	3,305	4,550	5,119	496	3,305	4,550	5,119
11,400	11,450	242	3,305	4,570	5,141	496	3,305	4,570	5,141
11,450	11,500	238	3,305	4,590	5,164	496	3,305	4,590	5,164
11,500	11,550	234	3,305	4,610	5,186	496	3,305	4,610	5,186
11,550	11,600	231	3,305	4,630	5,209	496	3,305	4,630	5,209
11,600	11,650	227	3,305	4,650	5,231	496	3,305	4,650	5,231
11,650	11,700	223	3,305	4,670	5,254	496	3,305	4,670	5,254
11,700	11,750	219	3,305	4,690	5,276	496	3,305	4,690	5,276
11,750	11,800	215	3,305	4,710	5,299	496	3,305	4,710	5,299
11,800	11,850	212	3,305	4,730	5,321	496	3,305	4,730	5,321
11,850	11,900	208	3,305	4,750	5,344	496	3,305	4,750	5,344
11,900	11,950	204	3,305	4,770	5,366	496	3,305	4,770	5,366
11,950	12,000	200	3,305	4,790	5,389	496	3,305	4,790	5,389
12,000	12,050	196	3,305	4,810	5,411	496	3,305	4,810	5,411
12,050	12,100	192	3,305	4,830	5,434	496	3,305	4,830	5,434
12,100	12,150	189	3,305	4,850	5,456	496	3,305	4,850	5,456
12,150	12,200	185	3,305	4,870	5,479	496	3,305	4,870	5,479
12,200	12,250	181	3,305	4,890	5,501	496	3,305	4,890	5,501
12,250	12,300	177	3,305	4,910	5,524	496	3,305	4,910	5,524
12,300	12,350	173	3,305	4,930	5,546	496	3,305	4,930	5,546
12,350	12,400	169	3,305	4,950	5,569	496	3,305	4,950	5,569
12,400	12,450	166	3,305	4,970	5,591	496	3,305	4,970	5,591
12,450	12,500	162	3,305	4,990	5,614	496	3,305	4,990	5,614
12,500	12,550	158	3,305	5,010	5,636	496	3,305	5,010	5,636
12,550	12,600	154	3,305	5,030	5,659	496	3,305	5,030	5,659
12,600	12,650	150	3,305	5,050	5,681	496	3,305	5,050	5,681
12,650	12,700	146	3,305	5,070	5,704	496	3,305	5,070	5,704
12,700	12,750	143	3,305	5,090	5,726	496	3,305	5,090	5,726
12,750	12,800	139	3,305	5,110	5,749	496	3,305	5,110	5,749

(Continued)

If the amount you are looking up from the worksheet is—		Single, head of household, or qualifying widow(er) and the number of children you have is—				Married filing jointly and the number of children you have is—			
At least	But less than	0	1	2	3	0	1	2	3
		Your credit is—				Your credit is—			
12,800	12,850	135	3,305	5,130	5,771	496	3,305	5,130	5,771
12,850	12,900	131	3,305	5,150	5,794	496	3,305	5,150	5,794
12,900	12,950	127	3,305	5,170	5,816	496	3,305	5,170	5,816
12,950	13,000	124	3,305	5,190	5,839	496	3,305	5,190	5,839
13,000	13,050	120	3,305	5,210	5,861	496	3,305	5,210	5,861
13,050	13,100	116	3,305	5,230	5,884	496	3,305	5,230	5,884
13,100	13,150	112	3,305	5,250	5,906	496	3,305	5,250	5,906
13,150	13,200	108	3,305	5,270	5,929	496	3,305	5,270	5,929
13,200	13,250	104	3,305	5,290	5,951	496	3,305	5,290	5,951
13,250	13,300	101	3,305	5,310	5,974	496	3,305	5,310	5,974
13,300	13,350	97	3,305	5,330	5,996	496	3,305	5,330	5,996
13,350	13,400	93	3,305	5,350	6,019	496	3,305	5,350	6,019
13,400	13,450	89	3,305	5,370	6,041	496	3,305	5,370	6,041
13,450	13,500	85	3,305	5,390	6,064	496	3,305	5,390	6,064
13,500	13,550	81	3,305	5,410	6,086	496	3,305	5,410	6,086
13,550	13,600	78	3,305	5,430	6,109	493	3,305	5,430	6,109
13,600	13,650	74	3,305	5,450	6,131	489	3,305	5,450	6,131
13,650	13,700	70	3,305	5,460	6,143	485	3,305	5,460	6,143
13,700	13,750	66	3,305	5,460	6,143	482	3,305	5,460	6,143
13,750	13,800	62	3,305	5,460	6,143	478	3,305	5,460	6,143
13,800	13,850	59	3,305	5,460	6,143	474	3,305	5,460	6,143
13,850	13,900	55	3,305	5,460	6,143	470	3,305	5,460	6,143
13,900	13,950	51	3,305	5,460	6,143	466	3,305	5,460	6,143
13,950	14,000	47	3,305	5,460	6,143	462	3,305	5,460	6,143
14,000	14,050	43	3,305	5,460	6,143	459	3,305	5,460	6,143
14,050	14,100	39	3,305	5,460	6,143	455	3,305	5,460	6,143
14,100	14,150	36	3,305	5,460	6,143	451	3,305	5,460	6,143
14,150	14,200	32	3,305	5,460	6,143	447	3,305	5,460	6,143
14,200	14,250	28	3,305	5,460	6,143	443	3,305	5,460	6,143
14,250	14,300	24	3,305	5,460	6,143	439	3,305	5,460	6,143
14,300	14,350	20	3,305	5,460	6,143	436	3,305	5,460	6,143
14,350	14,400	16	3,305	5,460	6,143	432	3,305	5,460	6,143
14,400	14,450	13	3,305	5,460	6,143	428	3,305	5,460	6,143
14,450	14,500	9	3,305	5,460	6,143	424	3,305	5,460	6,143
14,500	14,550	5	3,305	5,460	6,143	420	3,305	5,460	6,143
14,550	14,600	*	3,305	5,460	6,143	417	3,305	5,460	6,143
14,600	14,650	0	3,305	5,460	6,143	413	3,305	5,460	6,143
14,650	14,700	0	3,305	5,460	6,143	409	3,305	5,460	6,143
14,700	14,750	0	3,305	5,460	6,143	405	3,305	5,460	6,143
14,750	14,800	0	3,305	5,460	6,143	401	3,305	5,460	6,143
14,800	14,850	0	3,305	5,460	6,143	397	3,305	5,460	6,143
14,850	14,900	0	3,305	5,460	6,143	394	3,305	5,460	6,143
14,900	14,950	0	3,305	5,460	6,143	390	3,305	5,460	6,143
14,950	15,000	0	3,305	5,460	6,143	386	3,305	5,460	6,143
15,000	15,050	0	3,305	5,460	6,143	382	3,305	5,460	6,143
15,050	15,100	0	3,305	5,460	6,143	378	3,305	5,460	6,143
15,100	15,150	0	3,305	5,460	6,143	374	3,305	5,460	6,143
15,150	15,200	0	3,305	5,460	6,143	371	3,305	5,460	6,143
15,200	15,250	0	3,305	5,460	6,143	367	3,305	5,460	6,143
15,250	15,300	0	3,305	5,460	6,143	363	3,305	5,460	6,143
15,300	15,350	0	3,305	5,460	6,143	359	3,305	5,460	6,143
15,350	15,400	0	3,305	5,460	6,143	355	3,305	5,460	6,143
15,400	15,450	0	3,305	5,460	6,143	352	3,305	5,460	6,143
15,450	15,500	0	3,305	5,460	6,143	348	3,305	5,460	6,143
15,500	15,550	0	3,305	5,460	6,143	344	3,305	5,460	6,143
15,550	15,600	0	3,305	5,460	6,143	340	3,305	5,460	6,143
15,600	15,650	0	3,305	5,460	6,143	336	3,305	5,460	6,143
15,650	15,700	0	3,305	5,460	6,143	332	3,305	5,460	6,143
15,700	15,750	0	3,305	5,460	6,143	329	3,305	5,460	6,143
15,750	15,800	0	3,305	5,460	6,143	325	3,305	5,460	6,143
15,800	15,850	0	3,305	5,460	6,143	321	3,305	5,460	6,143
15,850	15,900	0	3,305	5,460	6,143	317	3,305	5,460	6,143
15,900	15,950	0	3,305	5,460	6,143	313	3,305	5,460	6,143
15,950	16,000	0	3,305	5,460	6,143	309	3,305	5,460	6,143

If the amount you are looking up from the worksheet is—		Single, head of household, or qualifying widow(er) and the number of children you have is—				Married filing jointly and the number of children you have is—			
At least	But less than	0	1	2	3	0	1	2	3
		Your credit is—				Your credit is—			
16,000	16,050	0	3,305	5,460	6,143	306	3,305	5,460	6,143
16,050	16,100	0	3,305	5,460	6,143	302	3,305	5,460	6,143
16,100	16,150	0	3,305	5,460	6,143	298	3,305	5,460	6,143
16,150	16,200	0	3,305	5,460	6,143	294	3,305	5,460	6,143
16,200	16,250	0	3,305	5,460	6,143	290	3,305	5,460	6,143
16,250	16,300	0	3,305	5,460	6,143	286	3,305	5,460	6,143
16,300	16,350	0	3,305	5,460	6,143	283	3,305	5,460	6,143
16,350	16,400	0	3,305	5,460	6,143	279	3,305	5,460	6,143
16,400	16,450	0	3,305	5,460	6,143	275	3,305	5,460	6,143
16,450	16,500	0	3,305	5,460	6,143	271	3,305	5,460	6,143
16,500	16,550	0	3,305	5,460	6,143	267	3,305	5,460	6,143
16,550	16,600	0	3,305	5,460	6,143	264	3,305	5,460	6,143
16,600	16,650	0	3,305	5,460	6,143	260	3,305	5,460	6,143
16,650	16,700	0	3,305	5,460	6,143	256	3,305	5,460	6,143
16,700	16,750	0	3,305	5,460	6,143	252	3,305	5,460	6,143
16,750	16,800	0	3,305	5,460	6,143	248	3,305	5,460	6,143
16,800	16,850	0	3,305	5,460	6,143	244	3,305	5,460	6,143
16,850	16,900	0	3,305	5,460	6,143	241	3,305	5,460	6,143
16,900	16,950	0	3,305	5,460	6,143	237	3,305	5,460	6,143
16,950	17,000	0	3,305	5,460	6,143	233	3,305	5,460	6,143
17,000	17,050	0	3,305	5,460	6,143	229	3,305	5,460	6,143
17,050	17,100	0	3,305	5,460	6,143	225	3,305	5,460	6,143
17,100	17,150	0	3,305	5,460	6,143	221	3,305	5,460	6,143
17,150	17,200	0	3,305	5,460	6,143	218	3,305	5,460	6,143
17,200	17,250	0	3,305	5,460	6,143	214	3,305	5,460	6,143
17,250	17,300	0	3,305	5,460	6,143	210	3,305	5,460	6,143
17,300	17,350	0	3,305	5,460	6,143	206	3,305	5,460	6,143
17,350	17,400	0	3,305	5,460	6,143	202	3,305	5,460	6,143
17,400	17,450	0	3,305	5,460	6,143	199	3,305	5,460	6,143
17,450	17,500	0	3,305	5,460	6,143	195	3,305	5,460	6,143
17,500	17,550	0	3,305	5,460	6,143	191	3,305	5,460	6,143
17,550	17,600	0	3,305	5,460	6,143	187	3,305	5,460	6,143
17,600	17,650	0	3,305	5,460	6,143	183	3,305	5,460	6,143
17,650	17,700	0	3,305	5,460	6,143	179	3,305	5,460	6,143
17,700	17,750	0	3,305	5,460	6,143	176	3,305	5,460	6,143
17,750	17,800	0	3,305	5,460	6,143	172	3,305	5,460	6,143
17,800	17,850	0	3,305	5,460	6,143	168	3,305	5,460	6,143
17,850	17,900	0	3,298	5,451	6,133	164	3,305	5,460	6,143
17,900	17,950	0	3,290	5,440	6,122	160	3,305	5,460	6,143
17,950	18,000	0	3,282	5,429	6,112	156	3,305	5,460	6,143
18,000	18,050	0	3,274	5,419	6,101	153	3,305	5,460	6,143
18,050	18,100	0	3,266	5,408	6,091	149	3,305	5,460	6,143
18,100	18,150	0	3,258	5,398	6,080	145	3,305	5,460	6,143
18,150	18,200	0	3,250	5,387	6,070	141	3,305	5,460	6,143
18,200	18,250	0	3,242	5,377	6,059	137	3,305	5,460	6,143
18,250	18,300	0	3,234	5,366	6,049	133	3,305	5,460	6,143
18,300	18,350	0	3,226	5,356	6,038	130	3,305	5,460	6,143
18,350	18,400	0	3,218	5,345	6,028	126	3,305	5,460	6,143
18,400	18,450	0	3,210	5,335	6,017	122	3,305	5,460	6,143
18,450	18,500	0	3,202	5,324	6,007	118	3,305	5,460	6,143
18,500	18,550	0	3,194	5,314	5,996	114	3,305	5,460	6,143
18,550	18,600	0	3,186	5,303	5,986	111	3,305	5,460	6,143
18,600	18,650	0	3,178	5,293	5,975	107	3,305	5,460	6,143
18,650	18,700	0	3,170	5,282	5,965	103	3,305	5,460	6,143
18,700	18,750	0	3,162	5,272	5,954	99	3,305	5,460	6,143
18,750	18,800	0	3,154	5,261	5,943	95	3,305	5,460	6,143
18,800	18,850	0	3,146	5,250	5,933	91	3,305	5,460	6,143
18,850	18,900	0	3,138	5,240	5,922	88	3,305	5,460	6,143
18,900	18,950	0	3,130	5,229	5,912	84	3,305	5,460	6,143
18,950	19,000	0	3,122	5,219	5,901	80	3,305	5,460	6,143
19,000	19,050	0	3,114	5,208	5,891	76	3,305	5,460	6,143
19,050	19,100	0	3,106	5,198	5,880	72	3,305	5,460	6,143
19,100	19,150	0	3,098	5,187	5,870	68	3,305	5,460	6,143
19,150	19,200	0	3,090	5,177	5,859	65	3,305	5,460	6,143

* If the amount you are looking up from the worksheet is at least $14,550 but less than $14,590, and you have no qualifying children, your credit is $2. If the amount you are looking up from the worksheet is $14,590 or more, and you have no qualifying children, you cannot take the credit.

(Continued)

Need more information or forms? Visit IRS.gov.

Earned Income Credit (EIC) Table - *Continued*   (**Caution.** This is **not** a tax table.)

At least	But less than	Single, head of household, or qualifying widow(er) — 0	1	2	3	Married filing jointly — 0	1	2	3
19,200	19,250	0	3,082	5,166	5,849	61	3,305	5,460	6,143
19,250	19,300	0	3,074	5,156	5,838	57	3,305	5,460	6,143
19,300	19,350	0	3,066	5,145	5,828	53	3,305	5,460	6,143
19,350	19,400	0	3,058	5,135	5,817	49	3,305	5,460	6,143
19,400	19,450	0	3,050	5,124	5,807	46	3,305	5,460	6,143
19,450	19,500	0	3,042	5,114	5,796	42	3,305	5,460	6,143
19,500	19,550	0	3,034	5,103	5,786	38	3,305	5,460	6,143
19,550	19,600	0	3,026	5,093	5,775	34	3,305	5,460	6,143
19,600	19,650	0	3,018	5,082	5,764	30	3,305	5,460	6,143
19,650	19,700	0	3,010	5,071	5,754	26	3,305	5,460	6,143
19,700	19,750	0	3,002	5,061	5,743	23	3,305	5,460	6,143
19,750	19,800	0	2,994	5,050	5,733	19	3,305	5,460	6,143
19,800	19,850	0	2,986	5,040	5,722	15	3,305	5,460	6,143
19,850	19,900	0	2,978	5,029	5,712	11	3,305	5,460	6,143
19,900	19,950	0	2,970	5,019	5,701	7	3,305	5,460	6,143
19,950	20,000	0	2,962	5,008	5,691	3	3,305	5,460	6,143
20,000	20,050	0	2,954	4,998	5,680	*	3,305	5,460	6,143
20,050	20,100	0	2,946	4,987	5,670	0	3,305	5,460	6,143
20,100	20,150	0	2,938	4,977	5,659	0	3,305	5,460	6,143
20,150	20,200	0	2,930	4,966	5,649	0	3,305	5,460	6,143
20,200	20,250	0	2,922	4,956	5,638	0	3,305	5,460	6,143
20,250	20,300	0	2,914	4,945	5,628	0	3,305	5,460	6,143
20,300	20,350	0	2,906	4,935	5,617	0	3,305	5,460	6,143
20,350	20,400	0	2,898	4,924	5,607	0	3,305	5,460	6,143
20,400	20,450	0	2,890	4,913	5,596	0	3,305	5,460	6,143
20,450	20,500	0	2,882	4,903	5,585	0	3,305	5,460	6,143
20,500	20,550	0	2,874	4,892	5,575	0	3,305	5,460	6,143
20,550	20,600	0	2,866	4,882	5,564	0	3,305	5,460	6,143
20,600	20,650	0	2,858	4,871	5,554	0	3,305	5,460	6,143
20,650	20,700	0	2,850	4,861	5,543	0	3,305	5,460	6,143
20,700	20,750	0	2,842	4,850	5,533	0	3,305	5,460	6,143
20,750	20,800	0	2,834	4,840	5,522	0	3,305	5,460	6,143
20,800	20,850	0	2,826	4,829	5,512	0	3,305	5,460	6,143
20,850	20,900	0	2,818	4,819	5,501	0	3,305	5,460	6,143
20,900	20,950	0	2,810	4,808	5,491	0	3,305	5,460	6,143
20,950	21,000	0	2,802	4,798	5,480	0	3,305	5,460	6,143
21,000	21,050	0	2,794	4,787	5,470	0	3,305	5,460	6,143
21,050	21,100	0	2,786	4,777	5,459	0	3,305	5,460	6,143
21,100	21,150	0	2,778	4,766	5,449	0	3,305	5,460	6,143
21,150	21,200	0	2,770	4,756	5,438	0	3,305	5,460	6,143
21,200	21,250	0	2,762	4,745	5,428	0	3,305	5,460	6,143
21,250	21,300	0	2,754	4,734	5,417	0	3,305	5,460	6,143
21,300	21,350	0	2,746	4,724	5,406	0	3,305	5,460	6,143
21,350	21,400	0	2,738	4,713	5,396	0	3,305	5,460	6,143
21,400	21,450	0	2,730	4,703	5,385	0	3,305	5,460	6,143
21,450	21,500	0	2,722	4,692	5,375	0	3,305	5,460	6,143
21,500	21,550	0	2,714	4,682	5,364	0	3,305	5,460	6,143
21,550	21,600	0	2,706	4,671	5,354	0	3,305	5,460	6,143
21,600	21,650	0	2,698	4,661	5,343	0	3,305	5,460	6,143
21,650	21,700	0	2,690	4,650	5,333	0	3,305	5,460	6,143
21,700	21,750	0	2,682	4,640	5,322	0	3,305	5,460	6,143
21,750	21,800	0	2,674	4,629	5,312	0	3,305	5,460	6,143
21,800	21,850	0	2,666	4,619	5,301	0	3,305	5,460	6,143
21,850	21,900	0	2,658	4,608	5,291	0	3,305	5,460	6,143
21,900	21,950	0	2,650	4,598	5,280	0	3,305	5,460	6,143
21,950	22,000	0	2,642	4,587	5,270	0	3,305	5,460	6,143
22,000	22,050	0	2,634	4,577	5,259	0	3,305	5,460	6,143
22,050	22,100	0	2,626	4,566	5,249	0	3,305	5,460	6,143
22,100	22,150	0	2,618	4,555	5,238	0	3,305	5,460	6,143
22,150	22,200	0	2,610	4,545	5,227	0	3,305	5,460	6,143
22,200	22,250	0	2,602	4,534	5,217	0	3,305	5,460	6,143
22,250	22,300	0	2,594	4,524	5,206	0	3,305	5,460	6,143
22,300	22,350	0	2,586	4,513	5,196	0	3,305	5,460	6,143
22,350	22,400	0	2,579	4,503	5,185	0	3,305	5,460	6,143
22,400	22,450	0	2,571	4,492	5,175	0	3,305	5,460	6,143
22,450	22,500	0	2,563	4,482	5,164	0	3,305	5,460	6,143
22,500	22,550	0	2,555	4,471	5,154	0	3,305	5,460	6,143
22,550	22,600	0	2,547	4,461	5,143	0	3,305	5,460	6,143
22,600	22,650	0	2,539	4,450	5,133	0	3,305	5,460	6,143
22,650	22,700	0	2,531	4,440	5,122	0	3,305	5,460	6,143
22,700	22,750	0	2,523	4,429	5,112	0	3,305	5,460	6,143
22,750	22,800	0	2,515	4,419	5,101	0	3,305	5,460	6,143
22,800	22,850	0	2,507	4,408	5,091	0	3,305	5,460	6,143
22,850	22,900	0	2,499	4,398	5,080	0	3,305	5,460	6,143
22,900	22,950	0	2,491	4,387	5,069	0	3,305	5,460	6,143
22,950	23,000	0	2,483	4,376	5,059	0	3,305	5,460	6,143
23,000	23,050	0	2,475	4,366	5,048	0	3,305	5,460	6,143
23,050	23,100	0	2,467	4,355	5,038	0	3,305	5,460	6,143
23,100	23,150	0	2,459	4,345	5,027	0	3,305	5,460	6,143
23,150	23,200	0	2,451	4,334	5,017	0	3,305	5,460	6,143
23,200	23,250	0	2,443	4,324	5,006	0	3,305	5,460	6,143
23,250	23,300	0	2,435	4,313	4,996	0	3,305	5,460	6,143
23,300	23,350	0	2,427	4,303	4,985	0	3,294	5,446	6,129
23,350	23,400	0	2,419	4,292	4,975	0	3,286	5,436	6,118
23,400	23,450	0	2,411	4,282	4,964	0	3,278	5,425	6,108
23,450	23,500	0	2,403	4,271	4,954	0	3,270	5,415	6,097
23,500	23,550	0	2,395	4,261	4,943	0	3,262	5,404	6,087
23,550	23,600	0	2,387	4,250	4,933	0	3,254	5,394	6,076
23,600	23,650	0	2,379	4,240	4,922	0	3,246	5,383	6,066
23,650	23,700	0	2,371	4,229	4,912	0	3,238	5,373	6,055
23,700	23,750	0	2,363	4,219	4,901	0	3,230	5,362	6,045
23,750	23,800	0	2,355	4,208	4,890	0	3,223	5,352	6,034
23,800	23,850	0	2,347	4,197	4,880	0	3,215	5,341	6,024
23,850	23,900	0	2,339	4,187	4,869	0	3,207	5,330	6,013
23,900	23,950	0	2,331	4,176	4,859	0	3,199	5,320	6,002
23,950	24,000	0	2,323	4,166	4,848	0	3,191	5,309	5,992
24,000	24,050	0	2,315	4,155	4,838	0	3,183	5,299	5,981
24,050	24,100	0	2,307	4,145	4,827	0	3,175	5,288	5,971
24,100	24,150	0	2,299	4,134	4,817	0	3,167	5,278	5,960
24,150	24,200	0	2,291	4,124	4,806	0	3,159	5,267	5,950
24,200	24,250	0	2,283	4,113	4,796	0	3,151	5,257	5,939
24,250	24,300	0	2,275	4,103	4,785	0	3,143	5,246	5,929
24,300	24,350	0	2,267	4,092	4,775	0	3,135	5,236	5,918
24,350	24,400	0	2,259	4,082	4,764	0	3,127	5,225	5,908
24,400	24,450	0	2,251	4,071	4,754	0	3,119	5,215	5,897
24,450	24,500	0	2,243	4,061	4,743	0	3,111	5,204	5,887
24,500	24,550	0	2,235	4,050	4,733	0	3,103	5,194	5,876
24,550	24,600	0	2,227	4,040	4,722	0	3,095	5,183	5,866
24,600	24,650	0	2,219	4,029	4,711	0	3,087	5,173	5,855
24,650	24,700	0	2,211	4,018	4,701	0	3,079	5,162	5,845
24,700	24,750	0	2,203	4,008	4,690	0	3,071	5,151	5,834
24,750	24,800	0	2,195	3,997	4,680	0	3,063	5,141	5,823
24,800	24,850	0	2,187	3,987	4,669	0	3,055	5,130	5,813
24,850	24,900	0	2,179	3,976	4,659	0	3,047	5,120	5,802
24,900	24,950	0	2,171	3,966	4,648	0	3,039	5,109	5,792
24,950	25,000	0	2,163	3,955	4,638	0	3,031	5,099	5,781
25,000	25,050	0	2,155	3,945	4,627	0	3,023	5,088	5,771
25,050	25,100	0	2,147	3,934	4,617	0	3,015	5,078	5,760
25,100	25,150	0	2,139	3,924	4,606	0	3,007	5,067	5,750
25,150	25,200	0	2,131	3,913	4,596	0	2,999	5,057	5,739
25,200	25,250	0	2,123	3,903	4,585	0	2,991	5,046	5,729
25,250	25,300	0	2,115	3,892	4,575	0	2,983	5,036	5,718
25,300	25,350	0	2,107	3,882	4,564	0	2,975	5,025	5,708
25,350	25,400	0	2,099	3,871	4,554	0	2,967	5,015	5,697
25,400	25,450	0	2,091	3,860	4,543	0	2,959	5,004	5,687
25,450	25,500	0	2,083	3,850	4,532	0	2,951	4,994	5,676
25,500	25,550	0	2,075	3,839	4,522	0	2,943	4,983	5,665
25,550	25,600	0	2,067	3,829	4,511	0	2,935	4,972	5,655

* If the amount you are looking up from the worksheet is at least $20,000 but less than $20,020, and you have no qualifying children, your credit is $1. If the amount you are looking up from the worksheet is $20,020 or more, and you have no qualifying children, you cannot take the credit.

(Continued)

Earned Income Credit (EIC) Table - Continued

(Caution. This is not a tax table.)

If the amount you are looking up from the worksheet is— At least	But less than	Single, head of household, or qualifying widow(er) and the number of children you have is— 0	1	2	3	Married filing jointly and the number of children you have is— 0	1	2	3
		Your credit is—				Your credit is—			
25,600	25,650	0	2,059	3,818	4,501	0	2,927	4,962	5,644
25,650	25,700	0	2,051	3,808	4,490	0	2,919	4,951	5,634
25,700	25,750	0	2,043	3,797	4,480	0	2,911	4,941	5,623
25,750	25,800	0	2,035	3,787	4,469	0	2,903	4,930	5,613
25,800	25,850	0	2,027	3,776	4,459	0	2,895	4,920	5,602
25,850	25,900	0	2,019	3,766	4,448	0	2,887	4,909	5,592
25,900	25,950	0	2,011	3,755	4,438	0	2,879	4,899	5,581
25,950	26,000	0	2,003	3,745	4,427	0	2,871	4,888	5,571
26,000	26,050	0	1,995	3,734	4,417	0	2,863	4,878	5,560
26,050	26,100	0	1,987	3,724	4,406	0	2,855	4,867	5,550
26,100	26,150	0	1,979	3,713	4,396	0	2,847	4,857	5,539
26,150	26,200	0	1,971	3,703	4,385	0	2,839	4,846	5,529
26,200	26,250	0	1,963	3,692	4,375	0	2,831	4,836	5,518
26,250	26,300	0	1,955	3,681	4,364	0	2,823	4,825	5,508
26,300	26,350	0	1,947	3,671	4,353	0	2,815	4,815	5,497
26,350	26,400	0	1,939	3,660	4,343	0	2,807	4,804	5,486
26,400	26,450	0	1,931	3,650	4,332	0	2,799	4,793	5,476
26,450	26,500	0	1,923	3,639	4,322	0	2,791	4,783	5,465
26,500	26,550	0	1,915	3,629	4,311	0	2,783	4,772	5,455
26,550	26,600	0	1,907	3,618	4,301	0	2,775	4,762	5,444
26,600	26,650	0	1,899	3,608	4,290	0	2,767	4,751	5,434
26,650	26,700	0	1,891	3,597	4,280	0	2,759	4,741	5,423
26,700	26,750	0	1,883	3,587	4,269	0	2,751	4,730	5,413
26,750	26,800	0	1,875	3,576	4,259	0	2,743	4,720	5,402
26,800	26,850	0	1,867	3,566	4,248	0	2,735	4,709	5,392
26,850	26,900	0	1,859	3,555	4,238	0	2,727	4,699	5,381
26,900	26,950	0	1,851	3,545	4,227	0	2,719	4,688	5,371
26,950	27,000	0	1,843	3,534	4,217	0	2,711	4,678	5,360
27,000	27,050	0	1,835	3,524	4,206	0	2,703	4,667	5,350
27,050	27,100	0	1,827	3,513	4,196	0	2,695	4,657	5,339
27,100	27,150	0	1,819	3,502	4,185	0	2,687	4,646	5,329
27,150	27,200	0	1,811	3,492	4,174	0	2,679	4,636	5,318
27,200	27,250	0	1,803	3,481	4,164	0	2,671	4,625	5,307
27,250	27,300	0	1,795	3,471	4,153	0	2,663	4,614	5,297
27,300	27,350	0	1,787	3,460	4,143	0	2,655	4,604	5,286
27,350	27,400	0	1,780	3,450	4,132	0	2,647	4,593	5,276
27,400	27,450	0	1,772	3,439	4,122	0	2,639	4,583	5,265
27,450	27,500	0	1,764	3,429	4,111	0	2,631	4,572	5,255
27,500	27,550	0	1,756	3,418	4,101	0	2,623	4,562	5,244
27,550	27,600	0	1,748	3,408	4,090	0	2,615	4,551	5,234
27,600	27,650	0	1,740	3,397	4,080	0	2,607	4,541	5,223
27,650	27,700	0	1,732	3,387	4,069	0	2,599	4,530	5,213
27,700	27,750	0	1,724	3,376	4,059	0	2,591	4,520	5,202
27,750	27,800	0	1,716	3,366	4,048	0	2,583	4,509	5,192
27,800	27,850	0	1,708	3,355	4,038	0	2,575	4,499	5,181
27,850	27,900	0	1,700	3,345	4,027	0	2,567	4,488	5,171
27,900	27,950	0	1,692	3,334	4,016	0	2,559	4,478	5,160
27,950	28,000	0	1,684	3,323	4,006	0	2,551	4,467	5,150
28,000	28,050	0	1,676	3,313	3,995	0	2,543	4,456	5,139
28,050	28,100	0	1,668	3,302	3,985	0	2,535	4,446	5,128
28,100	28,150	0	1,660	3,292	3,974	0	2,527	4,435	5,118
28,150	28,200	0	1,652	3,281	3,964	0	2,519	4,425	5,107
28,200	28,250	0	1,644	3,271	3,953	0	2,511	4,414	5,097
28,250	28,300	0	1,636	3,260	3,943	0	2,503	4,404	5,086
28,300	28,350	0	1,628	3,250	3,932	0	2,495	4,393	5,076
28,350	28,400	0	1,620	3,239	3,922	0	2,487	4,383	5,065
28,400	28,450	0	1,612	3,229	3,911	0	2,479	4,372	5,055
28,450	28,500	0	1,604	3,218	3,901	0	2,471	4,362	5,044
28,500	28,550	0	1,596	3,208	3,890	0	2,463	4,351	5,034
28,550	28,600	0	1,588	3,197	3,880	0	2,455	4,341	5,023
28,600	28,650	0	1,580	3,187	3,869	0	2,447	4,330	5,013
28,650	28,700	0	1,572	3,176	3,859	0	2,439	4,320	5,002
28,700	28,750	0	1,564	3,166	3,848	0	2,431	4,309	4,992
28,750	28,800	0	1,556	3,155	3,837	0	2,424	4,299	4,981
28,800	28,850	0	1,548	3,144	3,827	0	2,416	4,288	4,971
28,850	28,900	0	1,540	3,134	3,816	0	2,408	4,277	4,960
28,900	28,950	0	1,532	3,123	3,806	0	2,400	4,267	4,949
28,950	29,000	0	1,524	3,113	3,795	0	2,392	4,256	4,939
29,000	29,050	0	1,516	3,102	3,785	0	2,384	4,246	4,928
29,050	29,100	0	1,508	3,092	3,774	0	2,376	4,235	4,918
29,100	29,150	0	1,500	3,081	3,764	0	2,368	4,225	4,907
29,150	29,200	0	1,492	3,071	3,753	0	2,360	4,214	4,897

If the amount you are looking up from the worksheet is— At least	But less than	Single, head of household, or qualifying widow(er) and the number of children you have is— 0	1	2	3	Married filing jointly and the number of children you have is— 0	1	2	3
		Your credit is—				Your credit is—			
29,200	29,250	0	1,484	3,060	3,743	0	2,352	4,204	4,886
29,250	29,300	0	1,476	3,050	3,732	0	2,344	4,193	4,876
29,300	29,350	0	1,468	3,039	3,722	0	2,336	4,183	4,865
29,350	29,400	0	1,460	3,029	3,711	0	2,328	4,172	4,855
29,400	29,450	0	1,452	3,018	3,701	0	2,320	4,162	4,844
29,450	29,500	0	1,444	3,008	3,690	0	2,312	4,151	4,834
29,500	29,550	0	1,436	2,997	3,680	0	2,304	4,141	4,823
29,550	29,600	0	1,428	2,987	3,669	0	2,296	4,130	4,813
29,600	29,650	0	1,420	2,976	3,658	0	2,288	4,120	4,802
29,650	29,700	0	1,412	2,965	3,648	0	2,280	4,109	4,792
29,700	29,750	0	1,404	2,955	3,637	0	2,272	4,098	4,781
29,750	29,800	0	1,396	2,944	3,627	0	2,264	4,088	4,770
29,800	29,850	0	1,388	2,934	3,616	0	2,256	4,077	4,760
29,850	29,900	0	1,380	2,923	3,606	0	2,248	4,067	4,749
29,900	29,950	0	1,372	2,913	3,595	0	2,240	4,056	4,739
29,950	30,000	0	1,364	2,902	3,585	0	2,232	4,046	4,728
30,000	30,050	0	1,356	2,892	3,574	0	2,224	4,035	4,718
30,050	30,100	0	1,348	2,881	3,564	0	2,216	4,025	4,707
30,100	30,150	0	1,340	2,871	3,553	0	2,208	4,014	4,697
30,150	30,200	0	1,332	2,860	3,543	0	2,200	4,004	4,686
30,200	30,250	0	1,324	2,850	3,532	0	2,192	3,993	4,676
30,250	30,300	0	1,316	2,839	3,522	0	2,184	3,983	4,665
30,300	30,350	0	1,308	2,829	3,511	0	2,176	3,972	4,655
30,350	30,400	0	1,300	2,818	3,501	0	2,168	3,962	4,644
30,400	30,450	0	1,292	2,807	3,490	0	2,160	3,951	4,634
30,450	30,500	0	1,284	2,797	3,479	0	2,152	3,941	4,623
30,500	30,550	0	1,276	2,786	3,469	0	2,144	3,930	4,612
30,550	30,600	0	1,268	2,776	3,458	0	2,136	3,919	4,602
30,600	30,650	0	1,260	2,765	3,448	0	2,128	3,909	4,591
30,650	30,700	0	1,252	2,755	3,437	0	2,120	3,898	4,581
30,700	30,750	0	1,244	2,744	3,427	0	2,112	3,888	4,570
30,750	30,800	0	1,236	2,734	3,416	0	2,104	3,877	4,560
30,800	30,850	0	1,228	2,723	3,406	0	2,096	3,867	4,549
30,850	30,900	0	1,220	2,713	3,395	0	2,088	3,856	4,539
30,900	30,950	0	1,212	2,702	3,385	0	2,080	3,846	4,528
30,950	31,000	0	1,204	2,692	3,374	0	2,072	3,835	4,518
31,000	31,050	0	1,196	2,681	3,364	0	2,064	3,825	4,507
31,050	31,100	0	1,188	2,671	3,353	0	2,056	3,814	4,497
31,100	31,150	0	1,180	2,660	3,343	0	2,048	3,804	4,486
31,150	31,200	0	1,172	2,650	3,332	0	2,040	3,793	4,476
31,200	31,250	0	1,164	2,639	3,322	0	2,032	3,783	4,465
31,250	31,300	0	1,156	2,628	3,311	0	2,024	3,772	4,455
31,300	31,350	0	1,148	2,618	3,300	0	2,016	3,762	4,444
31,350	31,400	0	1,140	2,607	3,290	0	2,008	3,751	4,433
31,400	31,450	0	1,132	2,597	3,279	0	2,000	3,740	4,423
31,450	31,500	0	1,124	2,586	3,269	0	1,992	3,730	4,412
31,500	31,550	0	1,116	2,576	3,258	0	1,984	3,719	4,402
31,550	31,600	0	1,108	2,565	3,248	0	1,976	3,709	4,391
31,600	31,650	0	1,100	2,555	3,237	0	1,968	3,698	4,381
31,650	31,700	0	1,092	2,544	3,227	0	1,960	3,688	4,370
31,700	31,750	0	1,084	2,534	3,216	0	1,952	3,677	4,360
31,750	31,800	0	1,076	2,523	3,206	0	1,944	3,667	4,349
31,800	31,850	0	1,068	2,513	3,195	0	1,936	3,656	4,339
31,850	31,900	0	1,060	2,502	3,185	0	1,928	3,646	4,328
31,900	31,950	0	1,052	2,492	3,174	0	1,920	3,635	4,318
31,950	32,000	0	1,044	2,481	3,164	0	1,912	3,625	4,307
32,000	32,050	0	1,036	2,471	3,153	0	1,904	3,614	4,297
32,050	32,100	0	1,028	2,460	3,143	0	1,896	3,604	4,286
32,100	32,150	0	1,020	2,449	3,132	0	1,888	3,593	4,276
32,150	32,200	0	1,012	2,439	3,121	0	1,880	3,583	4,265
32,200	32,250	0	1,004	2,428	3,111	0	1,872	3,572	4,254
32,250	32,300	0	996	2,418	3,100	0	1,864	3,561	4,244
32,300	32,350	0	988	2,407	3,090	0	1,856	3,551	4,233
32,350	32,400	0	981	2,397	3,079	0	1,848	3,540	4,223
32,400	32,450	0	973	2,386	3,069	0	1,840	3,530	4,212
32,450	32,500	0	965	2,376	3,058	0	1,832	3,519	4,202
32,500	32,550	0	957	2,365	3,048	0	1,824	3,509	4,191
32,550	32,600	0	949	2,355	3,037	0	1,816	3,498	4,181
32,600	32,650	0	941	2,344	3,027	0	1,808	3,488	4,170
32,650	32,700	0	933	2,334	3,016	0	1,800	3,477	4,160
32,700	32,750	0	925	2,323	3,006	0	1,792	3,467	4,149
32,750	32,800	0	917	2,313	2,995	0	1,784	3,456	4,139

(Continued)

Need more information or forms? Visit IRS.gov.

Earned Income Credit (EIC) Table - Continued

(Caution. This is not a tax table.)

If the amount you are looking up from the worksheet is–		Single, head of household, or qualifying widow(er) and the number of children you have is–				Married filing jointly and the number of children you have is–			
At least	But less than	0	1	2	3	0	1	2	3
		Your credit is–				Your credit is–			
32,800	32,850	0	909	2,302	2,985	0	1,776	3,446	4,128
32,850	32,900	0	901	2,292	2,974	0	1,768	3,435	4,118
32,900	32,950	0	893	2,281	2,963	0	1,760	3,425	4,107
32,950	33,000	0	885	2,270	2,953	0	1,752	3,414	4,097
33,000	33,050	0	877	2,260	2,942	0	1,744	3,403	4,086
33,050	33,100	0	869	2,249	2,932	0	1,736	3,393	4,075
33,100	33,150	0	861	2,239	2,921	0	1,728	3,382	4,065
33,150	33,200	0	853	2,228	2,911	0	1,720	3,372	4,054
33,200	33,250	0	845	2,218	2,900	0	1,712	3,361	4,044
33,250	33,300	0	837	2,207	2,890	0	1,704	3,351	4,033
33,300	33,350	0	829	2,197	2,879	0	1,696	3,340	4,023
33,350	33,400	0	821	2,186	2,869	0	1,688	3,330	4,012
33,400	33,450	0	813	2,176	2,858	0	1,680	3,319	4,002
33,450	33,500	0	805	2,165	2,848	0	1,672	3,309	3,991
33,500	33,550	0	797	2,155	2,837	0	1,664	3,298	3,981
33,550	33,600	0	789	2,144	2,827	0	1,656	3,288	3,970
33,600	33,650	0	781	2,134	2,816	0	1,648	3,277	3,960
33,650	33,700	0	773	2,123	2,806	0	1,640	3,267	3,949
33,700	33,750	0	765	2,113	2,795	0	1,632	3,256	3,939
33,750	33,800	0	757	2,102	2,784	0	1,625	3,246	3,928
33,800	33,850	0	749	2,091	2,774	0	1,617	3,235	3,918
33,850	33,900	0	741	2,081	2,763	0	1,609	3,224	3,907
33,900	33,950	0	733	2,070	2,753	0	1,601	3,214	3,896
33,950	34,000	0	725	2,060	2,742	0	1,593	3,203	3,886
34,000	34,050	0	717	2,049	2,732	0	1,585	3,193	3,875
34,050	34,100	0	709	2,039	2,721	0	1,577	3,182	3,865
34,100	34,150	0	701	2,028	2,711	0	1,569	3,172	3,854
34,150	34,200	0	693	2,018	2,700	0	1,561	3,161	3,844
34,200	34,250	0	685	2,007	2,690	0	1,553	3,151	3,833
34,250	34,300	0	677	1,997	2,679	0	1,545	3,140	3,823
34,300	34,350	0	669	1,986	2,669	0	1,537	3,130	3,812
34,350	34,400	0	661	1,976	2,658	0	1,529	3,119	3,802
34,400	34,450	0	653	1,965	2,648	0	1,521	3,109	3,791
34,450	34,500	0	645	1,955	2,637	0	1,513	3,098	3,781
34,500	34,550	0	637	1,944	2,627	0	1,505	3,088	3,770
34,550	34,600	0	629	1,934	2,616	0	1,497	3,077	3,760
34,600	34,650	0	621	1,923	2,605	0	1,489	3,067	3,749
34,650	34,700	0	613	1,912	2,595	0	1,481	3,056	3,739
34,700	34,750	0	605	1,902	2,584	0	1,473	3,045	3,728
34,750	34,800	0	597	1,891	2,574	0	1,465	3,035	3,717
34,800	34,850	0	589	1,881	2,563	0	1,457	3,024	3,707
34,850	34,900	0	581	1,870	2,553	0	1,449	3,014	3,696
34,900	34,950	0	573	1,860	2,542	0	1,441	3,003	3,686
34,950	35,000	0	565	1,849	2,532	0	1,433	2,993	3,675
35,000	35,050	0	557	1,839	2,521	0	1,425	2,982	3,665
35,050	35,100	0	549	1,828	2,511	0	1,417	2,972	3,654
35,100	35,150	0	541	1,818	2,500	0	1,409	2,961	3,644
35,150	35,200	0	533	1,807	2,490	0	1,401	2,951	3,633
35,200	35,250	0	525	1,797	2,479	0	1,393	2,940	3,623
35,250	35,300	0	517	1,786	2,469	0	1,385	2,930	3,612
35,300	35,350	0	509	1,776	2,458	0	1,377	2,919	3,602
35,350	35,400	0	501	1,765	2,448	0	1,369	2,909	3,591
35,400	35,450	0	493	1,754	2,437	0	1,361	2,898	3,581
35,450	35,500	0	485	1,744	2,426	0	1,353	2,888	3,570
35,500	35,550	0	477	1,733	2,416	0	1,345	2,877	3,559
35,550	35,600	0	469	1,723	2,405	0	1,337	2,866	3,549
35,600	35,650	0	461	1,712	2,395	0	1,329	2,856	3,538
35,650	35,700	0	453	1,702	2,384	0	1,321	2,845	3,528
35,700	35,750	0	445	1,691	2,374	0	1,313	2,835	3,517
35,750	35,800	0	437	1,681	2,363	0	1,305	2,824	3,507
35,800	35,850	0	429	1,670	2,353	0	1,297	2,814	3,496
35,850	35,900	0	421	1,660	2,342	0	1,289	2,803	3,486
35,900	35,950	0	413	1,649	2,332	0	1,281	2,793	3,475
35,950	36,000	0	405	1,639	2,321	0	1,273	2,782	3,465

If the amount you are looking up from the worksheet is–		Single, head of household, or qualifying widow(er) and the number of children you have is–				Married filing jointly and the number of children you have is–			
At least	But less than	0	1	2	3	0	1	2	3
		Your credit is–				Your credit is–			
36,000	36,050	0	397	1,628	2,311	0	1,265	2,772	3,454
36,050	36,100	0	389	1,618	2,300	0	1,257	2,761	3,444
36,100	36,150	0	381	1,607	2,290	0	1,249	2,751	3,433
36,150	36,200	0	373	1,597	2,279	0	1,241	2,740	3,423
36,200	36,250	0	365	1,586	2,269	0	1,233	2,730	3,412
36,250	36,300	0	357	1,575	2,258	0	1,225	2,719	3,402
36,300	36,350	0	349	1,565	2,247	0	1,217	2,709	3,391
36,350	36,400	0	341	1,554	2,237	0	1,209	2,698	3,380
36,400	36,450	0	333	1,544	2,226	0	1,201	2,687	3,370
36,450	36,500	0	325	1,533	2,216	0	1,193	2,677	3,359
36,500	36,550	0	317	1,523	2,205	0	1,185	2,666	3,349
36,550	36,600	0	309	1,512	2,195	0	1,177	2,656	3,338
36,600	36,650	0	301	1,502	2,184	0	1,169	2,645	3,328
36,650	36,700	0	293	1,491	2,174	0	1,161	2,635	3,317
36,700	36,750	0	285	1,481	2,163	0	1,153	2,624	3,307
36,750	36,800	0	277	1,470	2,153	0	1,145	2,614	3,296
36,800	36,850	0	269	1,460	2,142	0	1,137	2,603	3,286
36,850	36,900	0	261	1,449	2,132	0	1,129	2,593	3,275
36,900	36,950	0	253	1,439	2,121	0	1,121	2,582	3,265
36,950	37,000	0	245	1,428	2,111	0	1,113	2,572	3,254
37,000	37,050	0	237	1,418	2,100	0	1,105	2,561	3,244
37,050	37,100	0	229	1,407	2,090	0	1,097	2,551	3,233
37,100	37,150	0	221	1,396	2,079	0	1,089	2,540	3,223
37,150	37,200	0	213	1,386	2,068	0	1,081	2,530	3,212
37,200	37,250	0	205	1,375	2,058	0	1,073	2,519	3,201
37,250	37,300	0	197	1,365	2,047	0	1,065	2,508	3,191
37,300	37,350	0	189	1,354	2,037	0	1,057	2,498	3,180
37,350	37,400	0	182	1,344	2,026	0	1,049	2,487	3,170
37,400	37,450	0	174	1,333	2,016	0	1,041	2,477	3,159
37,450	37,500	0	166	1,323	2,005	0	1,033	2,466	3,149
37,500	37,550	0	158	1,312	1,995	0	1,025	2,456	3,138
37,550	37,600	0	150	1,302	1,984	0	1,017	2,445	3,128
37,600	37,650	0	142	1,291	1,974	0	1,009	2,435	3,117
37,650	37,700	0	134	1,281	1,963	0	1,001	2,424	3,107
37,700	37,750	0	126	1,270	1,953	0	993	2,414	3,096
37,750	37,800	0	118	1,260	1,942	0	985	2,403	3,086
37,800	37,850	0	110	1,249	1,932	0	977	2,393	3,075
37,850	37,900	0	102	1,239	1,921	0	969	2,382	3,065
37,900	37,950	0	94	1,228	1,910	0	961	2,372	3,054
37,950	38,000	0	86	1,217	1,900	0	953	2,361	3,044
38,000	38,050	0	78	1,207	1,889	0	945	2,350	3,033
38,050	38,100	0	70	1,196	1,879	0	937	2,340	3,022
38,100	38,150	0	62	1,186	1,868	0	929	2,329	3,012
38,150	38,200	0	54	1,175	1,858	0	921	2,319	3,001
38,200	38,250	0	46	1,165	1,847	0	913	2,308	2,991
38,250	38,300	0	38	1,154	1,837	0	905	2,298	2,980
38,300	38,350	0	30	1,144	1,826	0	897	2,287	2,970
38,350	38,400	0	22	1,133	1,816	0	889	2,277	2,959
38,400	38,450	0	14	1,123	1,805	0	881	2,266	2,949
38,450	38,500	0	6	1,112	1,795	0	873	2,256	2,938
38,500	38,550	0	*	1,102	1,784	0	865	2,245	2,928
38,550	38,600	0	0	1,091	1,774	0	857	2,235	2,917
38,600	38,650	0	0	1,081	1,763	0	849	2,224	2,907
38,650	38,700	0	0	1,070	1,753	0	841	2,214	2,896
38,700	38,750	0	0	1,060	1,742	0	833	2,203	2,886
38,750	38,800	0	0	1,049	1,731	0	826	2,193	2,875
38,800	38,850	0	0	1,038	1,721	0	818	2,182	2,865
38,850	38,900	0	0	1,028	1,710	0	810	2,171	2,854
38,900	38,950	0	0	1,017	1,700	0	802	2,161	2,843
38,950	39,000	0	0	1,007	1,689	0	794	2,150	2,833
39,000	39,050	0	0	996	1,679	0	786	2,140	2,822
39,050	39,100	0	0	986	1,668	0	778	2,129	2,812
39,100	39,150	0	0	975	1,658	0	770	2,119	2,801
39,150	39,200	0	0	965	1,647	0	762	2,108	2,791

* If the amount you are looking up from the worksheet is at least $38,500 but less than $38,511, and you have one qualifying child, your credit is $1.
  If the amount you are looking up from the worksheet is $38,511 or more, and you have one qualifying child, you cannot take the credit.

(Continued)

Earned Income Credit (EIC) Table - *Continued*

(Caution. This is **not** a tax table.)

If the amount you are looking up from the worksheet is–		Single, head of household, or qualifying widow(er) and the number of children you have is–				Married filing jointly and the number of children you have is–			
At least	But less than	0	1	2	3	0	1	2	3
		Your credit is–				Your credit is–			
39,200	39,250	0	0	954	1,637	0	754	2,098	2,780
39,250	39,300	0	0	944	1,626	0	746	2,087	2,770
39,300	39,350	0	0	933	1,616	0	738	2,077	2,759
39,350	39,400	0	0	923	1,605	0	730	2,066	2,749
39,400	39,450	0	0	912	1,595	0	722	2,056	2,738
39,450	39,500	0	0	902	1,584	0	714	2,045	2,728
39,500	39,550	0	0	891	1,574	0	706	2,035	2,717
39,550	39,600	0	0	881	1,563	0	698	2,024	2,707
39,600	39,650	0	0	870	1,552	0	690	2,014	2,696
39,650	39,700	0	0	859	1,542	0	682	2,003	2,686
39,700	39,750	0	0	849	1,531	0	674	1,992	2,675
39,750	39,800	0	0	838	1,521	0	666	1,982	2,664
39,800	39,850	0	0	828	1,510	0	658	1,971	2,654
39,850	39,900	0	0	817	1,500	0	650	1,961	2,643
39,900	39,950	0	0	807	1,489	0	642	1,950	2,633
39,950	40,000	0	0	796	1,479	0	634	1,940	2,622
40,000	40,050	0	0	786	1,468	0	626	1,929	2,612
40,050	40,100	0	0	775	1,458	0	618	1,919	2,601
40,100	40,150	0	0	765	1,447	0	610	1,908	2,591
40,150	40,200	0	0	754	1,437	0	602	1,898	2,580
40,200	40,250	0	0	744	1,426	0	594	1,887	2,570
40,250	40,300	0	0	733	1,416	0	586	1,877	2,559
40,300	40,350	0	0	723	1,405	0	578	1,866	2,549
40,350	40,400	0	0	712	1,395	0	570	1,856	2,538
40,400	40,450	0	0	701	1,384	0	562	1,845	2,528
40,450	40,500	0	0	691	1,373	0	554	1,835	2,517
40,500	40,550	0	0	680	1,363	0	546	1,824	2,506
40,550	40,600	0	0	670	1,352	0	538	1,813	2,496
40,600	40,650	0	0	659	1,342	0	530	1,803	2,485
40,650	40,700	0	0	649	1,331	0	522	1,792	2,475
40,700	40,750	0	0	638	1,321	0	514	1,782	2,464
40,750	40,800	0	0	628	1,310	0	506	1,771	2,454
40,800	40,850	0	0	617	1,300	0	498	1,761	2,443
40,850	40,900	0	0	607	1,289	0	490	1,750	2,433
40,900	40,950	0	0	596	1,279	0	482	1,740	2,422
40,950	41,000	0	0	586	1,268	0	474	1,729	2,412
41,000	41,050	0	0	575	1,258	0	466	1,719	2,401
41,050	41,100	0	0	565	1,247	0	458	1,708	2,391
41,100	41,150	0	0	554	1,237	0	450	1,698	2,380
41,150	41,200	0	0	544	1,226	0	442	1,687	2,370
41,200	41,250	0	0	533	1,216	0	434	1,677	2,359
41,250	41,300	0	0	522	1,205	0	426	1,666	2,349
41,300	41,350	0	0	512	1,194	0	418	1,656	2,338
41,350	41,400	0	0	501	1,184	0	410	1,645	2,327
41,400	41,450	0	0	491	1,173	0	402	1,634	2,317
41,450	41,500	0	0	480	1,163	0	394	1,624	2,306
41,500	41,550	0	0	470	1,152	0	386	1,613	2,296
41,550	41,600	0	0	459	1,142	0	378	1,603	2,285
41,600	41,650	0	0	449	1,131	0	370	1,592	2,275
41,650	41,700	0	0	438	1,121	0	362	1,582	2,264
41,700	41,750	0	0	428	1,110	0	354	1,571	2,254
41,750	41,800	0	0	417	1,100	0	346	1,561	2,243
41,800	41,850	0	0	407	1,089	0	338	1,550	2,233
41,850	41,900	0	0	396	1,079	0	330	1,540	2,222
41,900	41,950	0	0	386	1,068	0	322	1,529	2,212
41,950	42,000	0	0	375	1,058	0	314	1,519	2,201
42,000	42,050	0	0	365	1,047	0	306	1,508	2,191
42,050	42,100	0	0	354	1,037	0	298	1,498	2,180
42,100	42,150	0	0	343	1,026	0	290	1,487	2,170
42,150	42,200	0	0	333	1,015	0	282	1,477	2,159
42,200	42,250	0	0	322	1,005	0	274	1,466	2,148
42,250	42,300	0	0	312	994	0	266	1,455	2,138
42,300	42,350	0	0	301	984	0	258	1,445	2,127
42,350	42,400	0	0	291	973	0	250	1,434	2,117

If the amount you are looking up from the worksheet is–		Single, head of household, or qualifying widow(er) and the number of children you have is–				Married filing jointly and the number of children you have is–			
At least	But less than	0	1	2	3	0	1	2	3
		Your credit is–				Your credit is–			
42,400	42,450	0	0	280	963	0	242	1,424	2,106
42,450	42,500	0	0	270	952	0	234	1,413	2,096
42,500	42,550	0	0	259	942	0	226	1,403	2,085
42,550	42,600	0	0	249	931	0	218	1,392	2,075
42,600	42,650	0	0	238	921	0	210	1,382	2,064
42,650	42,700	0	0	228	910	0	202	1,371	2,054
42,700	42,750	0	0	217	900	0	194	1,361	2,043
42,750	42,800	0	0	207	889	0	186	1,350	2,033
42,800	42,850	0	0	196	879	0	178	1,340	2,022
42,850	42,900	0	0	186	868	0	170	1,329	2,012
42,900	42,950	0	0	175	857	0	162	1,319	2,001
42,950	43,000	0	0	164	847	0	154	1,308	1,991
43,000	43,050	0	0	154	836	0	146	1,297	1,980
43,050	43,100	0	0	143	826	0	138	1,287	1,969
43,100	43,150	0	0	133	815	0	130	1,276	1,959
43,150	43,200	0	0	122	805	0	122	1,266	1,948
43,200	43,250	0	0	112	794	0	114	1,255	1,938
43,250	43,300	0	0	101	784	0	106	1,245	1,927
43,300	43,350	0	0	91	773	0	98	1,234	1,917
43,350	43,400	0	0	80	763	0	90	1,224	1,906
43,400	43,450	0	0	70	752	0	82	1,213	1,896
43,450	43,500	0	0	59	742	0	74	1,203	1,885
43,500	43,550	0	0	49	731	0	66	1,192	1,875
43,550	43,600	0	0	38	721	0	58	1,182	1,864
43,600	43,650	0	0	28	710	0	50	1,171	1,854
43,650	43,700	0	0	17	700	0	42	1,161	1,843
43,700	43,750	0	0	7	689	0	34	1,150	1,833
43,750	43,800	0	0	*	678	0	27	1,140	1,822
43,800	43,850	0	0	0	668	0	19	1,129	1,812
43,850	43,900	0	0	0	657	0	11	1,118	1,801
43,900	43,950	0	0	0	647	0	**	1,108	1,790
43,950	44,000	0	0	0	636	0	0	1,097	1,780
44,000	44,050	0	0	0	626	0	0	1,087	1,769
44,050	44,100	0	0	0	615	0	0	1,076	1,759
44,100	44,150	0	0	0	605	0	0	1,066	1,748
44,150	44,200	0	0	0	594	0	0	1,055	1,738
44,200	44,250	0	0	0	584	0	0	1,045	1,727
44,250	44,300	0	0	0	573	0	0	1,034	1,717
44,300	44,350	0	0	0	563	0	0	1,024	1,706
44,350	44,400	0	0	0	552	0	0	1,013	1,696
44,400	44,450	0	0	0	542	0	0	1,003	1,685
44,450	44,500	0	0	0	531	0	0	992	1,675
44,500	44,550	0	0	0	521	0	0	982	1,664
44,550	44,600	0	0	0	510	0	0	971	1,654
44,600	44,650	0	0	0	499	0	0	961	1,643
44,650	44,700	0	0	0	489	0	0	950	1,633
44,700	44,750	0	0	0	478	0	0	939	1,622
44,750	44,800	0	0	0	468	0	0	929	1,611
44,800	44,850	0	0	0	457	0	0	918	1,601
44,850	44,900	0	0	0	447	0	0	908	1,590
44,900	44,950	0	0	0	436	0	0	897	1,580
44,950	45,000	0	0	0	426	0	0	887	1,569
45,000	45,050	0	0	0	415	0	0	876	1,559
45,050	45,100	0	0	0	405	0	0	866	1,548
45,100	45,150	0	0	0	394	0	0	855	1,538
45,150	45,200	0	0	0	384	0	0	845	1,527
45,200	45,250	0	0	0	373	0	0	834	1,517
45,250	45,300	0	0	0	363	0	0	824	1,506
45,300	45,350	0	0	0	352	0	0	813	1,496
45,350	45,400	0	0	0	342	0	0	803	1,485
45,400	45,450	0	0	0	331	0	0	792	1,475
45,450	45,500	0	0	0	320	0	0	782	1,464
45,500	45,550	0	0	0	310	0	0	771	1,453
45,550	45,600	0	0	0	299	0	0	760	1,443

* If the amount you are looking up from the worksheet is at least $43,750 but less than $43,756, and you have two qualifying children, your credit is $1.
If the amount you are looking up from the worksheet is $43,756 or more, and you have two qualifying children, you cannot take the credit.

** If the amount you are looking up from the worksheet is at least $43,900 but less than $43,941, and you have one qualifying child, your credit is $3.
If the amount you are looking up from the worksheet is $43,941 or more, and you have one qualifying child, you cannot take the credit.

(Continued)

Need more information or forms? Visit IRS.gov.

Earned Income Credit (EIC) Table - Continued

(Caution. This is **not** a tax table.)

At least	But less than	Single, head of household, or qualifying widow(er) 0	1	2	3	Married filing jointly 0	1	2	3
45,600	45,650	0	0	0	289	0	0	750	1,432
45,650	45,700	0	0	0	278	0	0	739	1,422
45,700	45,750	0	0	0	268	0	0	729	1,411
45,750	45,800	0	0	0	257	0	0	718	1,401
45,800	45,850	0	0	0	247	0	0	708	1,390
45,850	45,900	0	0	0	236	0	0	697	1,380
45,900	45,950	0	0	0	226	0	0	687	1,369
45,950	46,000	0	0	0	215	0	0	676	1,359
46,000	46,050	0	0	0	205	0	0	666	1,348
46,050	46,100	0	0	0	194	0	0	655	1,338
46,100	46,150	0	0	0	184	0	0	645	1,327
46,150	46,200	0	0	0	173	0	0	634	1,317
46,200	46,250	0	0	0	163	0	0	624	1,306
46,250	46,300	0	0	0	152	0	0	613	1,296
46,300	46,350	0	0	0	141	0	0	603	1,285
46,350	46,400	0	0	0	131	0	0	592	1,274
46,400	46,450	0	0	0	120	0	0	581	1,264
46,450	46,500	0	0	0	110	0	0	571	1,253
46,500	46,550	0	0	0	99	0	0	560	1,243
46,550	46,600	0	0	0	89	0	0	550	1,232
46,600	46,650	0	0	0	78	0	0	539	1,222
46,650	46,700	0	0	0	68	0	0	529	1,211
46,700	46,750	0	0	0	57	0	0	518	1,201
46,750	46,800	0	0	0	47	0	0	508	1,190
46,800	46,850	0	0	0	36	0	0	497	1,180
46,850	46,900	0	0	0	26	0	0	487	1,169
46,900	46,950	0	0	0	15	0	0	476	1,159
46,950	47,000	0	0	0	*	0	0	466	1,148
47,000	47,050	0	0	0	0	0	0	455	1,138
47,050	47,100	0	0	0	0	0	0	445	1,127
47,100	47,150	0	0	0	0	0	0	434	1,117
47,150	47,200	0	0	0	0	0	0	424	1,106
47,200	47,250	0	0	0	0	0	0	413	1,095
47,250	47,300	0	0	0	0	0	0	402	1,085
47,300	47,350	0	0	0	0	0	0	392	1,074
47,350	47,400	0	0	0	0	0	0	381	1,064
47,400	47,450	0	0	0	0	0	0	371	1,053
47,450	47,500	0	0	0	0	0	0	360	1,043
47,500	47,550	0	0	0	0	0	0	350	1,032
47,550	47,600	0	0	0	0	0	0	339	1,022
47,600	47,650	0	0	0	0	0	0	329	1,011
47,650	47,700	0	0	0	0	0	0	318	1,001
47,700	47,750	0	0	0	0	0	0	308	990
47,750	47,800	0	0	0	0	0	0	297	980
47,800	47,850	0	0	0	0	0	0	287	969
47,850	47,900	0	0	0	0	0	0	276	959
47,900	47,950	0	0	0	0	0	0	266	948
47,950	48,000	0	0	0	0	0	0	255	938
48,000	48,050	0	0	0	0	0	0	244	927
48,050	48,100	0	0	0	0	0	0	234	916
48,100	48,150	0	0	0	0	0	0	223	906
48,150	48,200	0	0	0	0	0	0	213	895
48,200	48,250	0	0	0	0	0	0	202	885
48,250	48,300	0	0	0	0	0	0	192	874
48,300	48,350	0	0	0	0	0	0	181	864
48,350	48,400	0	0	0	0	0	0	171	853
48,400	48,450	0	0	0	0	0	0	160	843
48,450	48,500	0	0	0	0	0	0	150	832
48,500	48,550	0	0	0	0	0	0	139	822
48,550	48,600	0	0	0	0	0	0	129	811
48,600	48,650	0	0	0	0	0	0	118	801
48,650	48,700	0	0	0	0	0	0	108	790
48,700	48,750	0	0	0	0	0	0	97	780
48,750	48,800	0	0	0	0	0	0	87	769

At least	But less than	Single, head of household, or qualifying widow(er) 0	1	2	3	Married filing jointly 0	1	2	3
48,800	48,850	0	0	0	0	0	0	76	759
48,850	48,900	0	0	0	0	0	0	65	748
48,900	48,950	0	0	0	0	0	0	55	737
48,950	49,000	0	0	0	0	0	0	44	727
49,000	49,050	0	0	0	0	0	0	34	716
49,050	49,100	0	0	0	0	0	0	23	706
49,100	49,150	0	0	0	0	0	0	13	695
49,150	49,200	0	0	0	0	0	0	**	685
49,200	49,250	0	0	0	0	0	0	0	674
49,250	49,300	0	0	0	0	0	0	0	664
49,300	49,350	0	0	0	0	0	0	0	653
49,350	49,400	0	0	0	0	0	0	0	643
49,400	49,450	0	0	0	0	0	0	0	632
49,450	49,500	0	0	0	0	0	0	0	622
49,500	49,550	0	0	0	0	0	0	0	611
49,550	49,600	0	0	0	0	0	0	0	601
49,600	49,650	0	0	0	0	0	0	0	590
49,650	49,700	0	0	0	0	0	0	0	580
49,700	49,750	0	0	0	0	0	0	0	569
49,750	49,800	0	0	0	0	0	0	0	558
49,800	49,850	0	0	0	0	0	0	0	548
49,850	49,900	0	0	0	0	0	0	0	537
49,900	49,950	0	0	0	0	0	0	0	527
49,950	50,000	0	0	0	0	0	0	0	516
50,000	50,050	0	0	0	0	0	0	0	506
50,050	50,100	0	0	0	0	0	0	0	495
50,100	50,150	0	0	0	0	0	0	0	485
50,150	50,200	0	0	0	0	0	0	0	474
50,200	50,250	0	0	0	0	0	0	0	464
50,250	50,300	0	0	0	0	0	0	0	453
50,300	50,350	0	0	0	0	0	0	0	443
50,350	50,400	0	0	0	0	0	0	0	432
50,400	50,450	0	0	0	0	0	0	0	422
50,450	50,500	0	0	0	0	0	0	0	411
50,500	50,550	0	0	0	0	0	0	0	400
50,550	50,600	0	0	0	0	0	0	0	390
50,600	50,650	0	0	0	0	0	0	0	379
50,650	50,700	0	0	0	0	0	0	0	369
50,700	50,750	0	0	0	0	0	0	0	358
50,750	50,800	0	0	0	0	0	0	0	348
50,800	50,850	0	0	0	0	0	0	0	337
50,850	50,900	0	0	0	0	0	0	0	327
50,900	50,950	0	0	0	0	0	0	0	316
50,950	51,000	0	0	0	0	0	0	0	306
51,000	51,050	0	0	0	0	0	0	0	295
51,050	51,100	0	0	0	0	0	0	0	285
51,100	51,150	0	0	0	0	0	0	0	274
51,150	51,200	0	0	0	0	0	0	0	264
51,200	51,250	0	0	0	0	0	0	0	253
51,250	51,300	0	0	0	0	0	0	0	243
51,300	51,350	0	0	0	0	0	0	0	232
51,350	51,400	0	0	0	0	0	0	0	221
51,400	51,450	0	0	0	0	0	0	0	211
51,450	51,500	0	0	0	0	0	0	0	200
51,500	51,550	0	0	0	0	0	0	0	190
51,550	51,600	0	0	0	0	0	0	0	179
51,600	51,650	0	0	0	0	0	0	0	169
51,650	51,700	0	0	0	0	0	0	0	158
51,700	51,750	0	0	0	0	0	0	0	148
51,750	51,800	0	0	0	0	0	0	0	137
51,800	51,850	0	0	0	0	0	0	0	127
51,850	51,900	0	0	0	0	0	0	0	116
51,900	51,950	0	0	0	0	0	0	0	106
51,950	52,000	0	0	0	0	0	0	0	95

* If the amount you are looking up from the worksheet is at least $46,950 but less than $46,998, and you have three qualifying children, your credit is $5.
If the amount you are looking up from the worksheet is $43,998 or more, and you have three qualifying children, you cannot take the credit.

** If the amount you are looking up from the worksheet is at least $49,150 but less than $49,186, and you have two qualifying children, your credit is $4.
If the amount you are looking up from the worksheet is $48,186 or more, and you have two qualifying children, you cannot take the credit.

(Continued)

If the amount you are looking up from the worksheet is—		And your filing status is—								If the amount you are looking up from the worksheet is—		And your filing status is—							
		Single, head of household, or **qualifying widow(er)** and the number of children you have is—				Married filing jointly and the number of children you have is—						Single, head of household, or **qualifying widow(er)** and the number of children you have is—				Married filing jointly and the number of children you have is—			
		0	1	2	3	0	1	2	3			0	1	2	3	0	1	2	3
At least	But less than	Your credit is—				Your credit is—				At least	But less than	Your credit is—				Your credit is—			
52,000	52,050	0	0	0	0	0	0	0	85	52,400	52,427	0	0	0	0	0	0	0	3
52,050	52,100	0	0	0	0	0	0	0	74										
52,100	52,150	0	0	0	0	0	0	0	64										
52,150	52,200	0	0	0	0	0	0	0	53										
52,200	52,250	0	0	0	0	0	0	0	42										
52,250	52,300	0	0	0	0	0	0	0	32										
52,300	52,350	0	0	0	0	0	0	0	21										
52,350	52,400	0	0	0	0	0	0	0	11										

Need more information or forms? Visit IRS.gov.

Line 43

Additional Child Tax Credit

What Is the Additional Child Tax Credit?

This credit is for certain people who have at least one qualifying child for the child tax credit (as defined in Steps 1, 2, and 3 of the instructions for line 6c). The additional child tax credit may give you a refund even if you do not owe any tax or did not have any tax withheld.

Two Steps To Take the Additional Child Tax Credit!	
Step 1.	Be sure you figured the amount, if any, of your child tax credit. See the instructions for line 35.
Step 2.	Read the TIP at the end of your Child Tax Credit Worksheet. Use Schedule 8812 to see if you can take the additional child tax credit, but only if you meet the condition given in that TIP.

Line 44

American Opportunity Credit

If you meet the requirements to claim an education credit (see the instructions for line 33), enter on this line the amount, if any, from Form 8863, line 8. You may be able to increase an education credit and reduce your total tax or increase your tax refund if the student chooses to include all or part of a Pell grant or certain other scholarships or fellowships in income. See Pub. 970 and the instructions for Form 8863 for more information.

Line 45

Net Premium Tax Credit

You may be eligible to claim the premium tax credit if you, your spouse, or a dependent enrolled in health insurance through the Health Insurance Marketplace. The premium tax credit helps pay for this health insurance. Complete Form 8962 to determine the amount of your premium tax credit, if any. Enter the amount, if any from Form 8962, line 26. See Pub. 974 and the instructions for Form 8962 for more information.

Line 46

Amount paid with Request for Extension to File

If you got an automatic extension of time to file Form 1040A by filing Form 4868 or by making a payment, enter the amount you paid with Form 4868. If you paid by debit or credit card, do not include on line 46 the convenience fee you were charged. To the left of the entry space for line 46, enter "Form 4868" and show the amount paid.

 If you pay your taxes by credit or debit card, you may be able to deduct the related credit or debit card convenience fees on your 2015 return, but you must file Form 1040 to do so.

Excess social security and tier 1 railroad retirement (RRTA) tax withheld. If you, or your spouse if filing a joint return, had more than one employer for 2014 and total wages of more than $117,000, too much social security or tier 1 RRTA tax may have been withheld. For more details, including how to figure the amount to include on line 46, see Pub. 505. Include the excess in the total on line 46. Write "Excess SST" and show the excess amount to the left of the line.

Refund

Line 47

Amount Overpaid

If line 47 is under $1, we will send a refund only on written request.

 If the amount you overpaid is large, you may want to decrease the amount of income tax withheld from your pay by filing a new Form W-4. See Income tax withholding and estimated tax payments for 2015 *under* General Information, *later.*

Refund offset. If you owe past due federal tax, state income tax, state unemployment compensation debts, child support, spousal support, or certain federal nontax debts, such as student loans, all or part of the overpayment on line 47 may be used (offset) to pay the past-due amount. Offsets for federal taxes are made by the IRS. All other offsets are made by the Treasury Department's Bureau of the Fiscal Service. For federal tax offsets, you will receive a notice from the IRS. For all other offsets, you will receive a notice from the Fiscal Service. To find out if you may have an offset or if you have any questions about it, contact the agency to which you owe the debt.

Injured spouse. If you file a joint return and your spouse has not paid past-due federal tax, state income tax, state unemployment compensation debts, child support, spousal support, or a federal nontax debt, such as a student loan, part or all of the overpayment on line 47 may be used (offset) to pay the past-due amount. But your part of the overpayment may be refunded to you if certain conditions apply and you complete Form 8379. For details, use TeleTax topic 203 or see Form 8379.

Lines 48a Through 48d

Amount Refunded to You

If you want to check the status of your refund, just use the IRS2Go phone app or go to IRS.gov and click on *Where's My Refund?* See *Refund Information*, later. Information about your return will generally be available within 24 hours after the IRS

Need more information or forms? Visit IRS.gov.

receives your e-filed return, or 4 weeks after you mail your paper return. If you filed Form 8379 with your return, wait 14 weeks (11 weeks if you filed electronically). Have your 2014 tax return handy so you can enter your social security number, your filing status, and the exact whole dollar amount of your refund.

Where's My Refund? will provide an actual personalized refund date as soon as the IRS processes your tax return and approves your refund.

Effect of refund on benefits. Any refund you receive cannot be counted as income when determining if you or anyone else is eligible for benefits or assistance, or how much you or anyone else can receive, under any federal program or under any state or local program financed in whole or in part with federal funds. These programs include Temporary Assistance for Needy Families (TANF), Medicaid, Supplemental Security Income (SSI), and Supplemental Nutrition Assistance Program (food stamps). In addition, when determining eligibility, the refund cannot be counted as a resource for at least 12 months after you receive it. Check with your local benefit coordinator to find out if your refund will affect your benefits.

DIRECT▸DEPOSIT
Simple. Safe. Secure.

Fast Refunds! Choose direct deposit—a fast, simple, safe, secure way to have your refund deposited automatically to your checking or savings account, including an individual retirement arrangement (IRA). See the information about IRAs, later.

If you want us to directly deposit the amount shown on line 48a to your checking or savings account, including an IRA, at a bank or other financial institution (such as a mutual fund, brokerage firm, or credit union) in the United States:

- Complete lines 48b through 48d if you want your refund deposited to only one account, or
- Check the box on line 48a and attach Form 8888 if you want to split the direct deposit of your refund into more than one account or use all or part of your refund to buy paper series I savings bonds.

If you do not want your refund directly deposited to your account, do not check the box on line 48a. Draw a line through the boxes on lines 48b and 48d. We will send you a check instead.

Do not request a deposit of any part of your refund to an account that is not in your name. Do not allow your tax preparer to deposit any part of your refund into his or her account. The number of direct deposits to a single account or prepaid debit card is limited to three refunds a year. After this limit is exceeded, paper checks will be sent instead. Learn more at IRS.gov.

Why Use Direct Deposit?

- You get your refund faster by direct deposit than you do by check.

- Payment is more secure. There is no check that can get lost or stolen.
- It is more convenient. You do not have to make a trip to the bank to deposit your check.
- It saves tax dollars. It costs the government less to refund by direct deposit.

 If you file a joint return and check the box on line 48a and attach Form 8888 or fill in lines 48b through 48d, your spouse may get at least part of the refund.

IRA. You can have your refund directly deposited to a traditional IRA, Roth IRA, or SEP-IRA, but not a SIMPLE IRA. You must establish the IRA at a bank or other financial institution before you request direct deposit. Make sure your direct deposit will be accepted. You must also notify the trustee or custodian of your account of the year to which the deposit is to be applied (unless the trustee or custodian will not accept a deposit for 2014). If you do not, the trustee or custodian can assume the deposit is for the year during which you are filing the return. For example, if you file your 2014 return during 2015 and do not notify the trustee or custodian in advance, the trustee or custodian can assume the deposit to your IRA is for 2015. If you designate your deposit to be for 2014, you must verify that the deposit was actually made to the account by the due date of the return (without regard to extensions). If the deposit is not made by that date, the deposit is not an IRA contribution for 2014. In that case, you must file an amended 2014 return and reduce any IRA deduction and any retirement savings contributions credit you claimed.

 You and your spouse, if filing jointly, each may be able to contribute up to $5,500 ($6,500 if age 50 or older at the end of 2014) to a traditional IRA or Roth IRA for 2014, and the limits may be lower depending on your income. For more information on IRA contributions, see Pub. 590-A. If the limits on IRA contributions change for 2015, Pub. 590-A will have the new 2015 limits. You may owe a penalty if your contributions exceed these limits.

 For more information on IRAs, see Pub. 590-A and Pub. 590-B.

TreasuryDirect®. You can request a deposit of your refund (or part of it) to a TreasuryDirect® online account to buy U.S. Treasury marketable securities and savings bonds. For more information, go to *www.treasurydirect.gov.*

Form 8888. You can have your refund directly deposited into more than one account or use it to buy up to $5,000 in paper series I savings bonds. You do not need a TreasuryDirect® account to do this. For more information, see the Form 8888 instructions.

Line 48a. You cannot file Form 8888 to split your refund into more than one account or buy paper series I savings bonds if Form 8379 is filed with your return.

Line 48b. The routing number must be nine digits. The first two digits must be 01 through 12 or 21 through 32. On the sample check below, the routing number is 250250025. Henry and Naomi Brown would use that routing number unless their financial institution instructed them to use a different routing number for direct deposits.

Ask your financial institution for the correct routing number to enter on line 48b if:
- The routing number on a deposit slip is different from the routing number on your checks,
- Your deposit is to a savings account that does not allow you to write checks, or
- Your checks state they are payable through a financial institution different from the one at which you have your checking account.

Line 48c. Check the appropriate box for the type of account. Do not check more than one box. If the deposit is to an account such as an IRA, health savings account, brokerage account, or other similar account, ask your financial institution whether you should check the "Checking" or "Savings" box. You must check the correct box to ensure your deposit is accepted. For a TreasuryDirect® online account, check the "Savings" box.

Sample Check—Lines 48b Through 48d

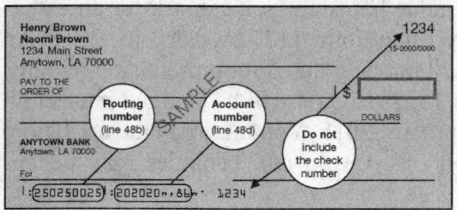

 The routing and account numbers may be in different places on your check.

Line 48d. The account number can be up to 17 characters (both numbers and letters). Include hyphens but omit spaces and special symbols. Enter the number from left to right and leave any unused boxes blank. On the sample check below, the account number is 20202086. Do not include the check number.

If the direct deposit to your account(s) is different from the amount you expected, you will receive an explanation in the mail about 2 weeks after your refund is deposited.

Reasons Your Direct Deposit Request May Be Rejected

If any of the following apply, your direct deposit request will be rejected and a check will be sent instead.
- Any numbers or letters on lines 48b through 48d are crossed out or whited out.
- Your financial institution(s) may not allow a joint refund to be deposited to an individual account. The IRS is not responsible if a financial institution rejects a direct deposit.
- You file your 2014 return after December 31, 2015.
- Three direct deposits of tax refunds have already been made to your account or prepaid debit card.
- The name on your account does not match the name on the tax refund.

 *The IRS is not responsible for a lost refund if you enter the wrong account information. Check with your financial institution to get the **correct** routing and account numbers and to make sure your direct deposit will be accepted.*

Line 49

Amount Applied to Your 2015 Estimated Tax

Enter on line 49 the amount, if any, of the overpayment on line 47 you want applied to your 2015 estimated tax. We will apply this amount to your account unless you include a statement requesting us to apply it to your spouse's account. Include your spouse's social security number in the statement.

 This election to apply part or all of the amount overpaid to your 2015 estimated tax cannot be changed later.

Amount You Owe

 IRS *e-file* offers two electronic payment options. With Electronic Funds Withdrawal, you can pay your current year balance due and also make up to four estimated tax payments. If you file early, you can schedule your payment for withdrawal from your account on a future date, up to and including the due date of the return. Or you can pay using a debit or credit card. Visit *www.irs.gov/e-pay* for details on both options.

Line 50

Amount You Owe

TIP *To save interest and penalties, pay your taxes in full by April 15, 2015. You do not have to pay if line 50 is under $1.*

Include any estimated tax penalty from line 51 in the amount you enter on line 50.

You can pay online, by phone, or by check or money order. Do not include any estimated tax payment for 2015 in this payment. Instead, make the estimated tax payment separately.

Bad check or payment. The penalty for writing a bad check to the IRS is $25 or 2% of the check, whichever is more. However, if the amount of the check is less than $25, the penalty equals the amount of the check. This penalty also applies to other forms of payment if the IRS does not receive the funds. Use TeleTax topic 206.

Pay online. Paying online is convenient and secure and helps make sure we get your payments on time. You can pay using either of the following electronic payment methods.
- Direct transfer from your bank account. Go to IRS.gov. Click on "Pay Your Tax Bill" and then "Direct Pay."
- Debit or credit card.

To pay your taxes online or for more information, go to *www.irs.gov/payments*. Also see the *e-file* information under *Amount You Owe*, earlier, for information about the Electronic

Need more information or forms? Visit IRS.gov.

Funds Withdrawal payment option offered when e-filing your return.

Pay by phone. Paying by phone is another safe and secure method of paying electronically. Use one of the following methods.
• Direct transfer using Electronic Federal Tax Payment System (EFTPS).
• Debit or credit card.

Direct transfer. To use EFTPS, you must be enrolled. You can enroll online or have an enrollment form mailed to you. To make a payment using EFTPS, call 1-800-555-4477 (English) or 1-800-244-4829 (Español). People who are deaf, hard of hearing, or have a speech disability and who have access to TTY/TDD equipment can call 1-800-733-4829. For more information about EFTPS, go to *www.irs.gov/payments*.

Debit or credit card. To pay using a debit or credit card, you can call one of the following service providers. There is a convenience fee charged by these providers that varies by provider, card type, and payment amount.

WorldPay US, Inc.
1-844-PAY-TAX-8™
(1-844-729-8298)
www.payUSAtax.com

Official Payments Corporation
1-888-UPAY-TAX™
(1-888-872-9829)
www.officialpayments.com

Link2Gov Corporation
1-888-PAY-1040™
(1-888-729-1040)
www.PAY1040.com

For the latest details on how to pay by phone, go to *www.irs.gov/payments*.

Pay by check or money order. Make your check or money order payable to "United States Treasury" for the full amount due. Do not send cash. Do not attach the payment to your return. Write "2014 Form 1040A" and your name, address, daytime phone number, and social security number (SSN) on your payment. If you are filing a joint return, enter the SSN shown first on your tax return.

To help us process your payment, enter the amount on the right side of the check like this: $ XXX.XX. Do not use dashes or lines (for example, do not enter "$ XXX–" or "$ XXX$^{xx}/_{100}$").

Then, complete Form 1040-V following the instructions on that form and enclose it in the envelope with your tax return and payment.

 You may need to (a) increase the amount of income tax withheld from your pay by filing a new Form W-4, (b) increase the tax withheld from other income by filing Form W-4P or W-4V, or (c) make estimated tax payments for 2015. See Income tax withholding and estimated tax payments for 2015 *under General Information, later.*

What If You Cannot Pay?

If you cannot pay the full amount shown on line 50 when you file, you can ask for:
• An installment agreement, or
• An extension of time to pay.

Installment agreement. Under an installment agreement, you can pay all or part of the tax you owe in monthly installments. However, even if your request to pay in installments is granted, you will be charged interest and may be charged a late payment penalty on the tax not paid by April 15, 2015. You must also pay a fee. To limit the interest and penalty charges, pay as much of the tax as possible when you file. But before requesting an installment agreement, you should consider other less costly alternatives, such as a bank loan or credit card payment.

To ask for an installment agreement, you can apply online or use Form 9465. To apply online, go to IRS.gov and click on "Tools" and then "Online Payment Agreement."

Extension of time to pay. If paying the tax when it is due would cause you an undue hardship, you can ask for an extension of time to pay by filing Form 1127 by April 15, 2015. An extension generally will not be granted for more than 6 months. If you pay after April 15, 2015, you will be charged interest on the tax not paid by April 15, 2015. You must pay the tax before the extension runs out. If you do not, penalties may be imposed.

Line 51

Estimated Tax Penalty

You may owe this penalty if:
• Line 50 is at least $1,000 and it is more than 10% of the tax shown on your return, or
• You did not pay enough estimated tax by any of the due dates. This is true even if you are due a refund.

For most people, the "tax shown on your return" is the amount on your 2014 Form 1040A, line 39, minus the total of any amounts shown on lines 38, 42a, 43, 44, and 45.

Exception. You will not owe the penalty if your 2013 tax return was for a tax year of 12 full months and either of the following applies.

1. You had no tax shown on your 2013 return and you were a U.S. citizen or resident for all of 2013.

2. The total of lines 40, 41, and any excess social security and tier 1 RRTA tax included on line 46 on your 2014 return is at least 100% of the tax shown on your 2013 return (110% of that amount if you are not a farmer or fisherman and your adjusted gross income (AGI) shown on your 2013 return was more than $150,000 (more than $75,000 if married filing separately for 2014)). Your estimated tax payments for 2014 must have been made on time and for the required amount.

For most people, the "tax shown on your 2013 return" is the amount on your 2013 Form 1040A, line 35, minus the total of any amounts shown on lines 38a, 39, and 40.

Figuring the penalty. If the *Exception* just described does not apply and you choose to figure the penalty yourself, use Form 2210.

Enter any penalty on line 51. Add the penalty to any tax due and enter the total on line 50. However, if you have an overpayment on line 47, subtract the penalty from the amount you would otherwise enter on line 48a or 49. Lines 48a, 49, and 51 must equal line 47.

If the penalty is more than the overpayment on line 47, enter -0- on lines 48a and 49. Then subtract line 47 from line 51 and enter the result on line 50.

Do not file Form 2210 with your return unless Form 2210 indicates that you must do so. Instead, keep it for your records.

 Because Form 2210 is complicated, you can leave line 51 blank and the IRS will figure the penalty and send you a bill. We will not charge you interest on the penalty if you pay by the date specified on the bill. If your income varied during the year, the annualized income installment method may reduce the amount of your penalty. But you must file Form 2210 because the IRS cannot figure your penalty under this method. See the Instructions for Form 2210 for other situations in which you may be able to lower your penalty by filing Form 2210.

Third Party Designee

If you want to allow your preparer, a friend, family member, or any other person you choose to discuss your 2014 tax return with the IRS, check the "Yes" box in the "Third party designee" area of your return. Also, enter the designee's name, phone number, and any five digits the designee chooses as his or her personal identification number (PIN).

If you check the "Yes" box, you, and your spouse if filing a joint return, are authorizing the IRS to call the designee to answer any questions that may arise during the processing of your return. You are also authorizing the designee to:

- Give the IRS any information that is missing from your return,
- Call the IRS for information about the processing of your return or the status of your refund or payment(s),
- Receive copies of notices or transcripts related to your return, upon request, and
- Respond to certain IRS notices about math errors, offsets, and return preparation.

You are not authorizing the designee to receive any refund check, bind you to anything (including any additional tax liability), or otherwise represent you before the IRS. If you want to expand the designee's authorization, see Pub. 947.

The authorization will automatically end no later than the due date (without regard to extensions) for filing your 2015 tax return. This is April 18, 2016, for most people.

Sign Your Return

Form 1040A is not considered a valid return unless you sign it. If you are filing a joint return, your spouse must also sign. If your spouse cannot sign the return, see Pub. 501. Be sure to date your return and enter your occupation(s). If you have someone prepare your return, you are still responsible for the correctness of the return. If your return is signed by a representative for you, you must have a power of attorney attached that specifically authorizes the representative to sign your return. To do this, you can use Form 2848. If you are filing a joint return as a surviving spouse, see *Death of a taxpayer*, later.

Court-appointed conservator, guardian, or other fiduciary. If you are a court-appointed conservator, guardian, or other fiduciary for a mentally or physically incompetent individual who has to file Form 1040A, sign your name for the individual and file Form 56.

Child's return. If your child cannot sign the return, either parent can sign the child's name in the space provided. Then, enter "By (your signature), parent for minor child."

Daytime phone number. Providing your daytime phone number may help speed the processing of your return. We may have questions about items on your return, such as the earned income credit, or the credit for child and dependent care expenses. If you answer our questions over the phone, we may be able to continue processing your return without mailing you a letter. If you are filing a joint return, you can enter either your or your spouse's daytime phone number.

IRS e-file **Electronic Return Signatures!**

To file your return electronically, you must sign the return electronically using a personal identification number (PIN). If you are filing online using software, you must use a Self-Select PIN. If you are filing electronically using a tax practitioner, you can use a Self-Select PIN or a Practitioner PIN.

Self-Select PIN. The Self-Select PIN method allows you to create your own PIN. If you are married filing jointly, you and your spouse will each need to create a PIN and enter these PINs as your electronic signatures.

A PIN is any combination of five digits you choose except five zeros. If you use a PIN, there is nothing to sign and nothing to mail—not even your Forms W-2.

To verify your identity, you will be prompted to enter your adjusted gross income (AGI) from your originally filed 2013 federal income tax return, if applicable. Do not use your AGI from an amended return (Form 1040X) or a math error correction made by IRS. AGI is the amount shown on your 2013 Form 1040, line 38; Form 1040A, line 22; or Form 1040EZ, line 4. If you do not have your 2013 income tax return, call the IRS at 1-800-908-9946 to get a free transcript of your return or visit IRS.gov and click on "Get Transcript of Your Tax Records" under "Tools." (If you filed electronically last year, you may use your prior year PIN to verify your identity instead of your prior year AGI. The prior year PIN is the five digit PIN you used to electronically sign your 2013 return.) You will also be prompted to enter your date of birth (DOB).

Need more information or forms? Visit IRS.gov.

You cannot use the Self-Select PIN method if you are a first-time filer under age 16 at the end of 2014.

 If you cannot locate your prior year AGI or prior year PIN use the Electronic Filing PIN Request. This can be found at IRS.gov. Click on "Request an Electronic Filing PIN." Or you can call 1-866-704-7388.

Practitioner PIN. The Practitioner PIN method allows you to authorize your tax practitioner to enter or generate your PIN. The practitioner can provide you with details.

Form 8453. You must send in a paper Form 8453 if you have to attach certain forms or other documents that cannot be electronically filed. For details, see Form 8453.

Identity Protection PIN. For 2014, if you received an Identity Protection Personal Identification Number (IP PIN) from the IRS, enter it in the IP PIN spaces provided below your daytime phone number. You must correctly enter all six numbers of your IP PIN. If you did not receive an IP PIN, leave these spaces blank.

 New IP PINs are issued every year. Enter the latest IP PIN you received. IP PINs for 2014 tax returns generally were sent in December 2014.

If you are filing a joint return and both taxpayers receive an IP PIN, only the taxpayer whose social security number (SSN) appears first on the tax return should enter his or her IP PIN. However, if you are filing electronically, both taxpayers must enter their IP PINs.

If you need more information or answers to frequently asked questions on how to use the IP PIN, go to *www.irs.gov/ Individuals/Understanding-Your-CP01A-Notice*. If you received an IP PIN but misplaced it, call 1-800-908-4490.

Paid preparer must sign your return. Generally, anyone you pay to prepare your return must sign it and include their Preparer Tax Identification Number (PTIN) in the space provided. The preparer must give you a copy of the return for your records. Someone who prepares your return but does not charge you should not sign your return.

Assemble Your Return

Assemble any schedules and forms behind Form 1040A in order of the "Attachment Sequence No." shown in the upper right corner of the schedule or form. If you have supporting statements, arrange them in the same order as the schedules or forms they support and attach them last. Do not attach correspondence or other items unless required to do so. Attach a copy of your Form(s) W-2 to the front of Form 1040A. If you received a Form W-2c (a corrected Form W-2), attach a copy of your original Form(s) W-2 and any Form(s) W-2c.

 If you received a 2014 Form 1099-R showing federal income tax withheld, also attach the form to the front of Form 1040A.

2014 Tax Table

Example. Mr. and Mrs. Reynolds are filing a joint return. Their taxable income on Form 1040A, line 27, is $25,300. First, they find the $25,300-25,350 taxable income line. Next, they find the column for married filing jointly and read down the column. The amount shown where the taxable income line and filing status column meet is $2,891. This is the tax amount they should enter on Form 1040A, line 28.

Sample Table

At Least	But Less Than	Single	Married filing jointly*	Married filing separately	Head of a household
			Your tax is—		
25,200	25,250	3,330	2,876	3,330	3,136
25,250	25,300	3,338	2,884	3,338	3,144
25,300	25,350	3,345	2,891	3,345	3,151
25,350	25,400	3,353	2,899	3,353	3,159

If line 27 (taxable income) is— At least	But less than	Single	Married filing jointly *	Married filing separately	Head of a household
			Your tax is—		
0	5	0	0	0	0
5	15	1	1	1	1
15	25	2	2	2	2
25	50	4	4	4	4
50	75	6	6	6	6
75	100	9	9	9	9
100	125	11	11	11	11
125	150	14	14	14	14
150	175	16	16	16	16
175	200	19	19	19	19
200	225	21	21	21	21
225	250	24	24	24	24
250	275	26	26	26	26
275	300	29	29	29	29
300	325	31	31	31	31
325	350	34	34	34	34
350	375	36	36	36	36
375	400	39	39	39	39
400	425	41	41	41	41
425	450	44	44	44	44
450	475	46	46	46	46
475	500	49	49	49	49
500	525	51	51	51	51
525	550	54	54	54	54
550	575	56	56	56	56
575	600	59	59	59	59
600	625	61	61	61	61
625	650	64	64	64	64
650	675	66	66	66	66
675	700	69	69	69	69
700	725	71	71	71	71
725	750	74	74	74	74
750	775	76	76	76	76
775	800	79	79	79	79
800	825	81	81	81	81
825	850	84	84	84	84
850	875	86	86	86	86
875	900	89	89	89	89
900	925	91	91	91	91
925	950	94	94	94	94
950	975	96	96	96	96
975	1,000	99	99	99	99

1,000

If line 27 (taxable income) is— At least	But less than	Single	Married filing jointly *	Married filing separately	Head of a household
			Your tax is—		
1,000	1,025	101	101	101	101
1,025	1,050	104	104	104	104
1,050	1,075	106	106	106	106
1,075	1,100	109	109	109	109
1,100	1,125	111	111	111	111
1,125	1,150	114	114	114	114
1,150	1,175	116	116	116	116
1,175	1,200	119	119	119	119
1,200	1,225	121	121	121	121
1,225	1,250	124	124	124	124
1,250	1,275	126	126	126	126
1,275	1,300	129	129	129	129
1,300	1,325	131	131	131	131
1,325	1,350	134	134	134	134
1,350	1,375	136	136	136	136
1,375	1,400	139	139	139	139
1,400	1,425	141	141	141	141
1,425	1,450	144	144	144	144
1,450	1,475	146	146	146	146
1,475	1,500	149	149	149	149
1,500	1,525	151	151	151	151
1,525	1,550	154	154	154	154
1,550	1,575	156	156	156	156
1,575	1,600	159	159	159	159
1,600	1,625	161	161	161	161
1,625	1,650	164	164	164	164
1,650	1,675	166	166	166	166
1,675	1,700	169	169	169	169
1,700	1,725	171	171	171	171
1,725	1,750	174	174	174	174
1,750	1,775	176	176	176	176
1,775	1,800	179	179	179	179
1,800	1,825	181	181	181	181
1,825	1,850	184	184	184	184
1,850	1,875	186	186	186	186
1,875	1,900	189	189	189	189
1,900	1,925	191	191	191	191
1,925	1,950	194	194	194	194
1,950	1,975	196	196	196	196
1,975	2,000	199	199	199	199

2,000

If line 27 (taxable income) is— At least	But less than	Single	Married filing jointly *	Married filing separately	Head of a household
			Your tax is—		
2,000	2,025	201	201	201	201
2,025	2,050	204	204	204	204
2,050	2,075	206	206	206	206
2,075	2,100	209	209	209	209
2,100	2,125	211	211	211	211
2,125	2,150	214	214	214	214
2,150	2,175	216	216	216	216
2,175	2,200	219	219	219	219
2,200	2,225	221	221	221	221
2,225	2,250	224	224	224	224
2,250	2,275	226	226	226	226
2,275	2,300	229	229	229	229
2,300	2,325	231	231	231	231
2,325	2,350	234	234	234	234
2,350	2,375	236	236	236	236
2,375	2,400	239	239	239	239
2,400	2,425	241	241	241	241
2,425	2,450	244	244	244	244
2,450	2,475	246	246	246	246
2,475	2,500	249	249	249	249
2,500	2,525	251	251	251	251
2,525	2,550	254	254	254	254
2,550	2,575	256	256	256	256
2,575	2,600	259	259	259	259
2,600	2,625	261	261	261	261
2,625	2,650	264	264	264	264
2,650	2,675	266	266	266	266
2,675	2,700	269	269	269	269
2,700	2,725	271	271	271	271
2,725	2,750	274	274	274	274
2,750	2,775	276	276	276	276
2,775	2,800	279	279	279	279
2,800	2,825	281	281	281	281
2,825	2,850	284	284	284	284
2,850	2,875	286	286	286	286
2,875	2,900	289	289	289	289
2,900	2,925	291	291	291	291
2,925	2,950	294	294	294	294
2,950	2,975	296	296	296	296
2,975	3,000	299	299	299	299

(Continued)

* This column must also be used by a qualifying widow(er).

Need more information or forms? Visit IRS.gov.

If line 27 (taxable income) is—		And you are—			
At least	But less than	Single	Married filing jointly *	Married filing separately	Head of a house-hold
		Your tax is—			

3,000

At least	But less than	Single	Married filing jointly *	Married filing separately	Head of a household
3,000	3,050	303	303	303	303
3,050	3,100	308	308	308	308
3,100	3,150	313	313	313	313
3,150	3,200	318	318	318	318
3,200	3,250	323	323	323	323
3,250	3,300	328	328	328	328
3,300	3,350	333	333	333	333
3,350	3,400	338	338	338	338
3,400	3,450	343	343	343	343
3,450	3,500	348	348	348	348
3,500	3,550	353	353	353	353
3,550	3,600	358	358	358	358
3,600	3,650	363	363	363	363
3,650	3,700	368	368	368	368
3,700	3,750	373	373	373	373
3,750	3,800	378	378	378	378
3,800	3,850	383	383	383	383
3,850	3,900	388	388	388	388
3,900	3,950	393	393	393	393
3,950	4,000	398	398	398	398

4,000

At least	But less than	Single	Married filing jointly *	Married filing separately	Head of a household
4,000	4,050	403	403	403	403
4,050	4,100	408	408	408	408
4,100	4,150	413	413	413	413
4,150	4,200	418	418	418	418
4,200	4,250	423	423	423	423
4,250	4,300	428	428	428	428
4,300	4,350	433	433	433	433
4,350	4,400	438	438	438	438
4,400	4,450	443	443	443	443
4,450	4,500	448	448	448	448
4,500	4,550	453	453	453	453
4,550	4,600	458	458	458	458
4,600	4,650	463	463	463	463
4,650	4,700	468	468	468	468
4,700	4,750	473	473	473	473
4,750	4,800	478	478	478	478
4,800	4,850	483	483	483	483
4,850	4,900	488	488	488	488
4,900	4,950	493	493	493	493
4,950	5,000	498	498	498	498

5,000

At least	But less than	Single	Married filing jointly *	Married filing separately	Head of a household
5,000	5,050	503	503	503	503
5,050	5,100	508	508	508	508
5,100	5,150	513	513	513	513
5,150	5,200	518	518	518	518
5,200	5,250	523	523	523	523
5,250	5,300	528	528	528	528
5,300	5,350	533	533	533	533
5,350	5,400	538	538	538	538
5,400	5,450	543	543	543	543
5,450	5,500	548	548	548	548
5,500	5,550	553	553	553	553
5,550	5,600	558	558	558	558
5,600	5,650	563	563	563	563
5,650	5,700	568	568	568	568
5,700	5,750	573	573	573	573
5,750	5,800	578	578	578	578
5,800	5,850	583	583	583	583
5,850	5,900	588	588	588	588
5,900	5,950	593	593	593	593
5,950	6,000	598	598	598	598

If line 27 (taxable income) is—		And you are—			
At least	But less than	Single	Married filing jointly *	Married filing separately	Head of a house-hold
		Your tax is—			

6,000

At least	But less than	Single	Married filing jointly *	Married filing separately	Head of a household
6,000	6,050	603	603	603	603
6,050	6,100	608	608	608	608
6,100	6,150	613	613	613	613
6,150	6,200	618	618	618	618
6,200	6,250	623	623	623	623
6,250	6,300	628	628	628	628
6,300	6,350	633	633	633	633
6,350	6,400	638	638	638	638
6,400	6,450	643	643	643	643
6,450	6,500	648	648	648	648
6,500	6,550	653	653	653	653
6,550	6,600	658	658	658	658
6,600	6,650	663	663	663	663
6,650	6,700	668	668	668	668
6,700	6,750	673	673	673	673
6,750	6,800	678	678	678	678
6,800	6,850	683	683	683	683
6,850	6,900	688	688	688	688
6,900	6,950	693	693	693	693
6,950	7,000	698	698	698	698

7,000

At least	But less than	Single	Married filing jointly *	Married filing separately	Head of a household
7,000	7,050	703	703	703	703
7,050	7,100	708	708	708	708
7,100	7,150	713	713	713	713
7,150	7,200	718	718	718	718
7,200	7,250	723	723	723	723
7,250	7,300	728	728	728	728
7,300	7,350	733	733	733	733
7,350	7,400	738	738	738	738
7,400	7,450	743	743	743	743
7,450	7,500	748	748	748	748
7,500	7,550	753	753	753	753
7,550	7,600	758	758	758	758
7,600	7,650	763	763	763	763
7,650	7,700	768	768	768	768
7,700	7,750	773	773	773	773
7,750	7,800	778	778	778	778
7,800	7,850	783	783	783	783
7,850	7,900	788	788	788	788
7,900	7,950	793	793	793	793
7,950	8,000	798	798	798	798

8,000

At least	But less than	Single	Married filing jointly *	Married filing separately	Head of a household
8,000	8,050	803	803	803	803
8,050	8,100	808	808	808	808
8,100	8,150	813	813	813	813
8,150	8,200	818	818	818	818
8,200	8,250	823	823	823	823
8,250	8,300	828	828	828	828
8,300	8,350	833	833	833	833
8,350	8,400	838	838	838	838
8,400	8,450	843	843	843	843
8,450	8,500	848	848	848	848
8,500	8,550	853	853	853	853
8,550	8,600	858	858	858	858
8,600	8,650	863	863	863	863
8,650	8,700	868	868	868	868
8,700	8,750	873	873	873	873
8,750	8,800	878	878	878	878
8,800	8,850	883	883	883	883
8,850	8,900	888	888	888	888
8,900	8,950	893	893	893	893
8,950	9,000	898	898	898	898

If line 27 (taxable income) is—		And you are—			
At least	But less than	Single	Married filing jointly *	Married filing separately	Head of a house-hold
		Your tax is—			

9,000

At least	But less than	Single	Married filing jointly *	Married filing separately	Head of a household
9,000	9,050	903	903	903	903
9,050	9,100	908	908	908	908
9,100	9,150	915	913	915	913
9,150	9,200	923	918	923	918
9,200	9,250	930	923	930	923
9,250	9,300	938	928	938	928
9,300	9,350	945	933	945	933
9,350	9,400	953	938	953	938
9,400	9,450	960	943	960	943
9,450	9,500	968	948	968	948
9,500	9,550	975	953	975	953
9,550	9,600	983	958	983	958
9,600	9,650	990	963	990	963
9,650	9,700	998	968	998	968
9,700	9,750	1,005	973	1,005	973
9,750	9,800	1,013	978	1,013	978
9,800	9,850	1,020	983	1,020	983
9,850	9,900	1,028	988	1,028	988
9,900	9,950	1,035	993	1,035	993
9,950	10,000	1,043	998	1,043	998

10,000

At least	But less than	Single	Married filing jointly *	Married filing separately	Head of a household
10,000	10,050	1,050	1,003	1,050	1,003
10,050	10,100	1,058	1,008	1,058	1,008
10,100	10,150	1,065	1,013	1,065	1,013
10,150	10,200	1,073	1,018	1,073	1,018
10,200	10,250	1,080	1,023	1,080	1,023
10,250	10,300	1,088	1,028	1,088	1,028
10,300	10,350	1,095	1,033	1,095	1,033
10,350	10,400	1,103	1,038	1,103	1,038
10,400	10,450	1,110	1,043	1,110	1,043
10,450	10,500	1,118	1,048	1,118	1,048
10,500	10,550	1,125	1,053	1,125	1,053
10,550	10,600	1,133	1,058	1,133	1,058
10,600	10,650	1,140	1,063	1,140	1,063
10,650	10,700	1,148	1,068	1,148	1,068
10,700	10,750	1,155	1,073	1,155	1,073
10,750	10,800	1,163	1,078	1,163	1,078
10,800	10,850	1,170	1,083	1,170	1,083
10,850	10,900	1,178	1,088	1,178	1,088
10,900	10,950	1,185	1,093	1,185	1,093
10,950	11,000	1,193	1,098	1,193	1,098

11,000

At least	But less than	Single	Married filing jointly *	Married filing separately	Head of a household
11,000	11,050	1,200	1,103	1,200	1,103
11,050	11,100	1,208	1,108	1,208	1,108
11,100	11,150	1,215	1,113	1,215	1,113
11,150	11,200	1,223	1,118	1,223	1,118
11,200	11,250	1,230	1,123	1,230	1,123
11,250	11,300	1,238	1,128	1,238	1,128
11,300	11,350	1,245	1,133	1,245	1,133
11,350	11,400	1,253	1,138	1,253	1,138
11,400	11,450	1,260	1,143	1,260	1,143
11,450	11,500	1,268	1,148	1,268	1,148
11,500	11,550	1,275	1,153	1,275	1,153
11,550	11,600	1,283	1,158	1,283	1,158
11,600	11,650	1,290	1,163	1,290	1,163
11,650	11,700	1,298	1,168	1,298	1,168
11,700	11,750	1,305	1,173	1,305	1,173
11,750	11,800	1,313	1,178	1,313	1,178
11,800	11,850	1,320	1,183	1,320	1,183
11,850	11,900	1,328	1,188	1,328	1,188
11,900	11,950	1,335	1,193	1,335	1,193
11,950	12,000	1,343	1,198	1,343	1,198

(Continued)

* This column must also be used by a qualifying widow(er).

If line 27 (taxable income) is—		And you are—			
At least	But less than	Single	Married filing jointly *	Married filing separately	Head of a house-hold
		Your tax is—			

12,000

At least	But less than	Single	Married filing jointly *	Married filing separately	Head of a household
12,000	12,050	1,350	1,203	1,350	1,203
12,050	12,100	1,358	1,208	1,358	1,208
12,100	12,150	1,365	1,213	1,365	1,213
12,150	12,200	1,373	1,218	1,373	1,218
12,200	12,250	1,380	1,223	1,380	1,223
12,250	12,300	1,388	1,228	1,388	1,228
12,300	12,350	1,395	1,233	1,395	1,233
12,350	12,400	1,403	1,238	1,403	1,238
12,400	12,450	1,410	1,243	1,410	1,243
12,450	12,500	1,418	1,248	1,418	1,248
12,500	12,550	1,425	1,253	1,425	1,253
12,550	12,600	1,433	1,258	1,433	1,258
12,600	12,650	1,440	1,263	1,440	1,263
12,650	12,700	1,448	1,268	1,448	1,268
12,700	12,750	1,455	1,273	1,455	1,273
12,750	12,800	1,463	1,278	1,463	1,278
12,800	12,850	1,470	1,283	1,470	1,283
12,850	12,900	1,478	1,288	1,478	1,288
12,900	12,950	1,485	1,293	1,485	1,293
12,950	13,000	1,493	1,298	1,493	1,299

13,000

At least	But less than	Single	Married filing jointly *	Married filing separately	Head of a household
13,000	13,050	1,500	1,303	1,500	1,306
13,050	13,100	1,508	1,308	1,508	1,314
13,100	13,150	1,515	1,313	1,515	1,321
13,150	13,200	1,523	1,318	1,523	1,329
13,200	13,250	1,530	1,323	1,530	1,336
13,250	13,300	1,538	1,328	1,538	1,344
13,300	13,350	1,545	1,333	1,545	1,351
13,350	13,400	1,553	1,338	1,553	1,359
13,400	13,450	1,560	1,343	1,560	1,366
13,450	13,500	1,568	1,348	1,568	1,374
13,500	13,550	1,575	1,353	1,575	1,381
13,550	13,600	1,583	1,358	1,583	1,389
13,600	13,650	1,590	1,363	1,590	1,396
13,650	13,700	1,598	1,368	1,598	1,404
13,700	13,750	1,605	1,373	1,605	1,411
13,750	13,800	1,613	1,378	1,613	1,419
13,800	13,850	1,620	1,383	1,620	1,426
13,850	13,900	1,628	1,388	1,628	1,434
13,900	13,950	1,635	1,393	1,635	1,441
13,950	14,000	1,643	1,398	1,643	1,449

14,000

At least	But less than	Single	Married filing jointly *	Married filing separately	Head of a household
14,000	14,050	1,650	1,403	1,650	1,456
14,050	14,100	1,658	1,408	1,658	1,464
14,100	14,150	1,665	1,413	1,665	1,471
14,150	14,200	1,673	1,418	1,673	1,479
14,200	14,250	1,680	1,423	1,680	1,486
14,250	14,300	1,688	1,428	1,688	1,494
14,300	14,350	1,695	1,433	1,695	1,501
14,350	14,400	1,703	1,438	1,703	1,509
14,400	14,450	1,710	1,443	1,710	1,516
14,450	14,500	1,718	1,448	1,718	1,524
14,500	14,550	1,725	1,453	1,725	1,531
14,550	14,600	1,733	1,458	1,733	1,539
14,600	14,650	1,740	1,463	1,740	1,546
14,650	14,700	1,748	1,468	1,748	1,554
14,700	14,750	1,755	1,473	1,755	1,561
14,750	14,800	1,763	1,478	1,763	1,569
14,800	14,850	1,770	1,483	1,770	1,576
14,850	14,900	1,778	1,488	1,778	1,584
14,900	14,950	1,785	1,493	1,785	1,591
14,950	15,000	1,793	1,498	1,793	1,599

15,000

At least	But less than	Single	Married filing jointly *	Married filing separately	Head of a household
15,000	15,050	1,800	1,503	1,800	1,606
15,050	15,100	1,808	1,508	1,808	1,614
15,100	15,150	1,815	1,513	1,815	1,621
15,150	15,200	1,823	1,518	1,823	1,629
15,200	15,250	1,830	1,523	1,830	1,636
15,250	15,300	1,838	1,528	1,838	1,644
15,300	15,350	1,845	1,533	1,845	1,651
15,350	15,400	1,853	1,538	1,853	1,659
15,400	15,450	1,860	1,543	1,860	1,666
15,450	15,500	1,868	1,548	1,868	1,674
15,500	15,550	1,875	1,553	1,875	1,681
15,550	15,600	1,883	1,558	1,883	1,689
15,600	15,650	1,890	1,563	1,890	1,696
15,650	15,700	1,898	1,568	1,898	1,704
15,700	15,750	1,905	1,573	1,905	1,711
15,750	15,800	1,913	1,578	1,913	1,719
15,800	15,850	1,920	1,583	1,920	1,726
15,850	15,900	1,928	1,588	1,928	1,734
15,900	15,950	1,935	1,593	1,935	1,741
15,950	16,000	1,943	1,598	1,943	1,749

16,000

At least	But less than	Single	Married filing jointly *	Married filing separately	Head of a household
16,000	16,050	1,950	1,603	1,950	1,756
16,050	16,100	1,958	1,608	1,958	1,764
16,100	16,150	1,965	1,613	1,965	1,771
16,150	16,200	1,973	1,618	1,973	1,779
16,200	16,250	1,980	1,623	1,980	1,786
16,250	16,300	1,988	1,628	1,988	1,794
16,300	16,350	1,995	1,633	1,995	1,801
16,350	16,400	2,003	1,638	2,003	1,809
16,400	16,450	2,010	1,643	2,010	1,816
16,450	16,500	2,018	1,648	2,018	1,824
16,500	16,550	2,025	1,653	2,025	1,831
16,550	16,600	2,033	1,658	2,033	1,839
16,600	16,650	2,040	1,663	2,040	1,846
16,650	16,700	2,048	1,668	2,048	1,854
16,700	16,750	2,055	1,673	2,055	1,861
16,750	16,800	2,063	1,678	2,063	1,869
16,800	16,850	2,070	1,683	2,070	1,876
16,850	16,900	2,078	1,688	2,078	1,884
16,900	16,950	2,085	1,693	2,085	1,891
16,950	17,000	2,093	1,698	2,093	1,899

17,000

At least	But less than	Single	Married filing jointly *	Married filing separately	Head of a household
17,000	17,050	2,100	1,703	2,100	1,906
17,050	17,100	2,108	1,708	2,108	1,914
17,100	17,150	2,115	1,713	2,115	1,921
17,150	17,200	2,123	1,718	2,123	1,929
17,200	17,250	2,130	1,723	2,130	1,936
17,250	17,300	2,138	1,728	2,138	1,944
17,300	17,350	2,145	1,733	2,145	1,951
17,350	17,400	2,153	1,738	2,153	1,959
17,400	17,450	2,160	1,743	2,160	1,966
17,450	17,500	2,168	1,748	2,168	1,974
17,500	17,550	2,175	1,753	2,175	1,981
17,550	17,600	2,183	1,758	2,183	1,989
17,600	17,650	2,190	1,763	2,190	1,996
17,650	17,700	2,198	1,768	2,198	2,004
17,700	17,750	2,205	1,773	2,205	2,011
17,750	17,800	2,213	1,778	2,213	2,019
17,800	17,850	2,220	1,783	2,220	2,026
17,850	17,900	2,228	1,788	2,228	2,034
17,900	17,950	2,235	1,793	2,235	2,041
17,950	18,000	2,243	1,798	2,243	2,049

18,000

At least	But less than	Single	Married filing jointly *	Married filing separately	Head of a household
18,000	18,050	2,250	1,803	2,250	2,056
18,050	18,100	2,258	1,808	2,258	2,064
18,100	18,150	2,265	1,813	2,265	2,071
18,150	18,200	2,273	1,819	2,273	2,079
18,200	18,250	2,280	1,826	2,280	2,086
18,250	18,300	2,288	1,834	2,288	2,094
18,300	18,350	2,295	1,841	2,295	2,101
18,350	18,400	2,303	1,849	2,303	2,109
18,400	18,450	2,310	1,856	2,310	2,116
18,450	18,500	2,318	1,864	2,318	2,124
18,500	18,550	2,325	1,871	2,325	2,131
18,550	18,600	2,333	1,879	2,333	2,139
18,600	18,650	2,340	1,886	2,340	2,146
18,650	18,700	2,348	1,894	2,348	2,154
18,700	18,750	2,355	1,901	2,355	2,161
18,750	18,800	2,363	1,909	2,363	2,169
18,800	18,850	2,370	1,916	2,370	2,176
18,850	18,900	2,378	1,924	2,378	2,184
18,900	18,950	2,385	1,931	2,385	2,191
18,950	19,000	2,393	1,939	2,393	2,199

19,000

At least	But less than	Single	Married filing jointly *	Married filing separately	Head of a household
19,000	19,050	2,400	1,946	2,400	2,206
19,050	19,100	2,408	1,954	2,408	2,214
19,100	19,150	2,415	1,961	2,415	2,221
19,150	19,200	2,423	1,969	2,423	2,229
19,200	19,250	2,430	1,976	2,430	2,236
19,250	19,300	2,438	1,984	2,438	2,244
19,300	19,350	2,445	1,991	2,445	2,251
19,350	19,400	2,453	1,999	2,453	2,259
19,400	19,450	2,460	2,006	2,460	2,266
19,450	19,500	2,468	2,014	2,468	2,274
19,500	19,550	2,475	2,021	2,475	2,281
19,550	19,600	2,483	2,029	2,483	2,289
19,600	19,650	2,490	2,036	2,490	2,296
19,650	19,700	2,498	2,044	2,498	2,304
19,700	19,750	2,505	2,051	2,505	2,311
19,750	19,800	2,513	2,059	2,513	2,319
19,800	19,850	2,520	2,066	2,520	2,326
19,850	19,900	2,528	2,074	2,528	2,334
19,900	19,950	2,535	2,081	2,535	2,341
19,950	20,000	2,543	2,089	2,543	2,349

20,000

At least	But less than	Single	Married filing jointly *	Married filing separately	Head of a household
20,000	20,050	2,550	2,096	2,550	2,356
20,050	20,100	2,558	2,104	2,558	2,364
20,100	20,150	2,565	2,111	2,565	2,371
20,150	20,200	2,573	2,119	2,573	2,379
20,200	20,250	2,580	2,126	2,580	2,386
20,250	20,300	2,588	2,134	2,588	2,394
20,300	20,350	2,595	2,141	2,595	2,401
20,350	20,400	2,603	2,149	2,603	2,409
20,400	20,450	2,610	2,156	2,610	2,416
20,450	20,500	2,618	2,164	2,618	2,424
20,500	20,550	2,625	2,171	2,625	2,431
20,550	20,600	2,633	2,179	2,633	2,439
20,600	20,650	2,640	2,186	2,640	2,446
20,650	20,700	2,648	2,194	2,648	2,454
20,700	20,750	2,655	2,201	2,655	2,461
20,750	20,800	2,663	2,209	2,663	2,469
20,800	20,850	2,670	2,216	2,670	2,476
20,850	20,900	2,678	2,224	2,678	2,484
20,900	20,950	2,685	2,231	2,685	2,491
20,950	21,000	2,693	2,239	2,693	2,499

(Continued)

* This column must also be used by a qualifying widow(er).

Need more information or forms? Visit IRS.gov.

If line 27 (taxable income) is—		And you are—			
At least	But less than	Single	Married filing jointly *	Married filing separately	Head of a household
		Your tax is—			

21,000

At least	But less than	Single	Married filing jointly *	Married filing separately	Head of a household
21,000	21,050	2,700	2,246	2,700	2,506
21,050	21,100	2,708	2,254	2,708	2,514
21,100	21,150	2,715	2,261	2,715	2,521
21,150	21,200	2,723	2,269	2,723	2,529
21,200	21,250	2,730	2,276	2,730	2,536
21,250	21,300	2,738	2,284	2,738	2,544
21,300	21,350	2,745	2,291	2,745	2,551
21,350	21,400	2,753	2,299	2,753	2,559
21,400	21,450	2,760	2,306	2,760	2,566
21,450	21,500	2,768	2,314	2,768	2,574
21,500	21,550	2,775	2,321	2,775	2,581
21,550	21,600	2,783	2,329	2,783	2,589
21,600	21,650	2,790	2,336	2,790	2,596
21,650	21,700	2,798	2,344	2,798	2,604
21,700	21,750	2,805	2,351	2,805	2,611
21,750	21,800	2,813	2,359	2,813	2,619
21,800	21,850	2,820	2,366	2,820	2,626
21,850	21,900	2,828	2,374	2,828	2,634
21,900	21,950	2,835	2,381	2,835	2,641
21,950	22,000	2,843	2,389	2,843	2,649

22,000

At least	But less than	Single	Married filing jointly *	Married filing separately	Head of a household
22,000	22,050	2,850	2,396	2,850	2,656
22,050	22,100	2,858	2,404	2,858	2,664
22,100	22,150	2,865	2,411	2,865	2,671
22,150	22,200	2,873	2,419	2,873	2,679
22,200	22,250	2,880	2,426	2,880	2,686
22,250	22,300	2,888	2,434	2,888	2,694
22,300	22,350	2,895	2,441	2,895	2,701
22,350	22,400	2,903	2,449	2,903	2,709
22,400	22,450	2,910	2,456	2,910	2,716
22,450	22,500	2,918	2,464	2,918	2,724
22,500	22,550	2,925	2,471	2,925	2,731
22,550	22,600	2,933	2,479	2,933	2,739
22,600	22,650	2,940	2,486	2,940	2,746
22,650	22,700	2,948	2,494	2,948	2,754
22,700	22,750	2,955	2,501	2,955	2,761
22,750	22,800	2,963	2,509	2,963	2,769
22,800	22,850	2,970	2,516	2,970	2,776
22,850	22,900	2,978	2,524	2,978	2,784
22,900	22,950	2,985	2,531	2,985	2,791
22,950	23,000	2,993	2,539	2,993	2,799

23,000

At least	But less than	Single	Married filing jointly *	Married filing separately	Head of a household
23,000	23,050	3,000	2,546	3,000	2,806
23,050	23,100	3,008	2,554	3,008	2,814
23,100	23,150	3,015	2,561	3,015	2,821
23,150	23,200	3,023	2,569	3,023	2,829
23,200	23,250	3,030	2,576	3,030	2,836
23,250	23,300	3,038	2,584	3,038	2,844
23,300	23,350	3,045	2,591	3,045	2,851
23,350	23,400	3,053	2,599	3,053	2,859
23,400	23,450	3,060	2,606	3,060	2,866
23,450	23,500	3,068	2,614	3,068	2,874
23,500	23,550	3,075	2,621	3,075	2,881
23,550	23,600	3,083	2,629	3,083	2,889
23,600	23,650	3,090	2,636	3,090	2,896
23,650	23,700	3,098	2,644	3,098	2,904
23,700	23,750	3,105	2,651	3,105	2,911
23,750	23,800	3,113	2,659	3,113	2,919
23,800	23,850	3,120	2,666	3,120	2,926
23,850	23,900	3,128	2,674	3,128	2,934
23,900	23,950	3,135	2,681	3,135	2,941
23,950	24,000	3,143	2,689	3,143	2,949

24,000

At least	But less than	Single	Married filing jointly *	Married filing separately	Head of a household
24,000	24,050	3,150	2,696	3,150	2,956
24,050	24,100	3,158	2,704	3,158	2,964
24,100	24,150	3,165	2,711	3,165	2,971
24,150	24,200	3,173	2,719	3,173	2,979
24,200	24,250	3,180	2,726	3,180	2,986
24,250	24,300	3,188	2,734	3,188	2,994
24,300	24,350	3,195	2,741	3,195	3,001
24,350	24,400	3,203	2,749	3,203	3,009
24,400	24,450	3,210	2,756	3,210	3,016
24,450	24,500	3,218	2,764	3,218	3,024
24,500	24,550	3,225	2,771	3,225	3,031
24,550	24,600	3,233	2,779	3,233	3,039
24,600	24,650	3,240	2,786	3,240	3,046
24,650	24,700	3,248	2,794	3,248	3,054
24,700	24,750	3,255	2,801	3,255	3,061
24,750	24,800	3,263	2,809	3,263	3,069
24,800	24,850	3,270	2,816	3,270	3,076
24,850	24,900	3,278	2,824	3,278	3,084
24,900	24,950	3,285	2,831	3,285	3,091
24,950	25,000	3,293	2,839	3,293	3,099

25,000

At least	But less than	Single	Married filing jointly *	Married filing separately	Head of a household
25,000	25,050	3,300	2,846	3,300	3,106
25,050	25,100	3,308	2,854	3,308	3,114
25,100	25,150	3,315	2,861	3,315	3,121
25,150	25,200	3,323	2,869	3,323	3,129
25,200	25,250	3,330	2,876	3,330	3,136
25,250	25,300	3,338	2,884	3,338	3,144
25,300	25,350	3,345	2,891	3,345	3,151
25,350	25,400	3,353	2,899	3,353	3,159
25,400	25,450	3,360	2,906	3,360	3,166
25,450	25,500	3,368	2,914	3,368	3,174
25,500	25,550	3,375	2,921	3,375	3,181
25,550	25,600	3,383	2,929	3,383	3,189
25,600	25,650	3,390	2,936	3,390	3,196
25,650	25,700	3,398	2,944	3,398	3,204
25,700	25,750	3,405	2,951	3,405	3,211
25,750	25,800	3,413	2,959	3,413	3,219
25,800	25,850	3,420	2,966	3,420	3,226
25,850	25,900	3,428	2,974	3,428	3,234
25,900	25,950	3,435	2,981	3,435	3,241
25,950	26,000	3,443	2,989	3,443	3,249

26,000

At least	But less than	Single	Married filing jointly *	Married filing separately	Head of a household
26,000	26,050	3,450	2,996	3,450	3,256
26,050	26,100	3,458	3,004	3,458	3,264
26,100	26,150	3,465	3,011	3,465	3,271
26,150	26,200	3,473	3,019	3,473	3,279
26,200	26,250	3,480	3,026	3,480	3,286
26,250	26,300	3,488	3,034	3,488	3,294
26,300	26,350	3,495	3,041	3,495	3,301
26,350	26,400	3,503	3,049	3,503	3,309
26,400	26,450	3,510	3,056	3,510	3,316
26,450	26,500	3,518	3,064	3,518	3,324
26,500	26,550	3,525	3,071	3,525	3,331
26,550	26,600	3,533	3,079	3,533	3,339
26,600	26,650	3,540	3,086	3,540	3,346
26,650	26,700	3,548	3,094	3,548	3,354
26,700	26,750	3,555	3,101	3,555	3,361
26,750	26,800	3,563	3,109	3,563	3,369
26,800	26,850	3,570	3,116	3,570	3,376
26,850	26,900	3,578	3,124	3,578	3,384
26,900	26,950	3,585	3,131	3,585	3,391
26,950	27,000	3,593	3,139	3,593	3,399

27,000

At least	But less than	Single	Married filing jointly *	Married filing separately	Head of a household
27,000	27,050	3,600	3,146	3,600	3,406
27,050	27,100	3,608	3,154	3,608	3,414
27,100	27,150	3,615	3,161	3,615	3,421
27,150	27,200	3,623	3,169	3,623	3,429
27,200	27,250	3,630	3,176	3,630	3,436
27,250	27,300	3,638	3,184	3,638	3,444
27,300	27,350	3,645	3,191	3,645	3,451
27,350	27,400	3,653	3,199	3,653	3,459
27,400	27,450	3,660	3,206	3,660	3,466
27,450	27,500	3,668	3,214	3,668	3,474
27,500	27,550	3,675	3,221	3,675	3,481
27,550	27,600	3,683	3,229	3,683	3,489
27,600	27,650	3,690	3,236	3,690	3,496
27,650	27,700	3,698	3,244	3,698	3,504
27,700	27,750	3,705	3,251	3,705	3,511
27,750	27,800	3,713	3,259	3,713	3,519
27,800	27,850	3,720	3,266	3,720	3,526
27,850	27,900	3,728	3,274	3,728	3,534
27,900	27,950	3,735	3,281	3,735	3,541
27,950	28,000	3,743	3,289	3,743	3,549

28,000

At least	But less than	Single	Married filing jointly *	Married filing separately	Head of a household
28,000	28,050	3,750	3,296	3,750	3,556
28,050	28,100	3,758	3,304	3,758	3,564
28,100	28,150	3,765	3,311	3,765	3,571
28,150	28,200	3,773	3,319	3,773	3,579
28,200	28,250	3,780	3,326	3,780	3,586
28,250	28,300	3,788	3,334	3,788	3,594
28,300	28,350	3,795	3,341	3,795	3,601
28,350	28,400	3,803	3,349	3,803	3,609
28,400	28,450	3,810	3,356	3,810	3,616
28,450	28,500	3,818	3,364	3,818	3,624
28,500	28,550	3,825	3,371	3,825	3,631
28,550	28,600	3,833	3,379	3,833	3,639
28,600	28,650	3,840	3,386	3,840	3,646
28,650	28,700	3,848	3,394	3,848	3,654
28,700	28,750	3,855	3,401	3,855	3,661
28,750	28,800	3,863	3,409	3,863	3,669
28,800	28,850	3,870	3,416	3,870	3,676
28,850	28,900	3,878	3,424	3,878	3,684
28,900	28,950	3,885	3,431	3,885	3,691
28,950	29,000	3,893	3,439	3,893	3,699

29,000

At least	But less than	Single	Married filing jointly *	Married filing separately	Head of a household
29,000	29,050	3,900	3,446	3,900	3,706
29,050	29,100	3,908	3,454	3,908	3,714
29,100	29,150	3,915	3,461	3,915	3,721
29,150	29,200	3,923	3,469	3,923	3,729
29,200	29,250	3,930	3,476	3,930	3,736
29,250	29,300	3,938	3,484	3,938	3,744
29,300	29,350	3,945	3,491	3,945	3,751
29,350	29,400	3,953	3,499	3,953	3,759
29,400	29,450	3,960	3,506	3,960	3,766
29,450	29,500	3,968	3,514	3,968	3,774
29,500	29,550	3,975	3,521	3,975	3,781
29,550	29,600	3,983	3,529	3,983	3,789
29,600	29,650	3,990	3,536	3,990	3,796
29,650	29,700	3,998	3,544	3,998	3,804
29,700	29,750	4,005	3,551	4,005	3,811
29,750	29,800	4,013	3,559	4,013	3,819
29,800	29,850	4,020	3,566	4,020	3,826
29,850	29,900	4,028	3,574	4,028	3,834
29,900	29,950	4,035	3,581	4,035	3,841
29,950	30,000	4,043	3,589	4,043	3,849

(Continued)

* This column must also be used by a qualifying widow(er).

Need more information or forms? Visit IRS.gov.

If line 27 (taxable income) is—		And you are—			
At least	But less than	Single	Married filing jointly *	Married filing separately	Head of a household
		Your tax is—			

30,000

At least	But less than	Single	Married filing jointly *	Married filing separately	Head of a household
30,000	30,050	4,050	3,596	4,050	3,856
30,050	30,100	4,058	3,604	4,058	3,864
30,100	30,150	4,065	3,611	4,065	3,871
30,150	30,200	4,073	3,619	4,073	3,879
30,200	30,250	4,080	3,626	4,080	3,886
30,250	30,300	4,088	3,634	4,088	3,894
30,300	30,350	4,095	3,641	4,095	3,901
30,350	30,400	4,103	3,649	4,103	3,909
30,400	30,450	4,110	3,656	4,110	3,916
30,450	30,500	4,118	3,664	4,118	3,924
30,500	30,550	4,125	3,671	4,125	3,931
30,550	30,600	4,133	3,679	4,133	3,939
30,600	30,650	4,140	3,686	4,140	3,946
30,650	30,700	4,148	3,694	4,148	3,954
30,700	30,750	4,155	3,701	4,155	3,961
30,750	30,800	4,163	3,709	4,163	3,969
30,800	30,850	4,170	3,716	4,170	3,976
30,850	30,900	4,178	3,724	4,178	3,984
30,900	30,950	4,185	3,731	4,185	3,991
30,950	31,000	4,193	3,739	4,193	3,999

31,000

At least	But less than	Single	Married filing jointly *	Married filing separately	Head of a household
31,000	31,050	4,200	3,746	4,200	4,006
31,050	31,100	4,208	3,754	4,208	4,014
31,100	31,150	4,215	3,761	4,215	4,021
31,150	31,200	4,223	3,769	4,223	4,029
31,200	31,250	4,230	3,776	4,230	4,036
31,250	31,300	4,238	3,784	4,238	4,044
31,300	31,350	4,245	3,791	4,245	4,051
31,350	31,400	4,253	3,799	4,253	4,059
31,400	31,450	4,260	3,806	4,260	4,066
31,450	31,500	4,268	3,814	4,268	4,074
31,500	31,550	4,275	3,821	4,275	4,081
31,550	31,600	4,283	3,829	4,283	4,089
31,600	31,650	4,290	3,836	4,290	4,096
31,650	31,700	4,298	3,844	4,298	4,104
31,700	31,750	4,305	3,851	4,305	4,111
31,750	31,800	4,313	3,859	4,313	4,119
31,800	31,850	4,320	3,866	4,320	4,126
31,850	31,900	4,328	3,874	4,328	4,134
31,900	31,950	4,335	3,881	4,335	4,141
31,950	32,000	4,343	3,889	4,343	4,149

32,000

At least	But less than	Single	Married filing jointly *	Married filing separately	Head of a household
32,000	32,050	4,350	3,896	4,350	4,156
32,050	32,100	4,358	3,904	4,358	4,164
32,100	32,150	4,365	3,911	4,365	4,171
32,150	32,200	4,373	3,919	4,373	4,179
32,200	32,250	4,380	3,926	4,380	4,186
32,250	32,300	4,388	3,934	4,388	4,194
32,300	32,350	4,395	3,941	4,395	4,201
32,350	32,400	4,403	3,949	4,403	4,209
32,400	32,450	4,410	3,956	4,410	4,216
32,450	32,500	4,418	3,964	4,418	4,224
32,500	32,550	4,425	3,971	4,425	4,231
32,550	32,600	4,433	3,979	4,433	4,239
32,600	32,650	4,440	3,986	4,440	4,246
32,650	32,700	4,448	3,994	4,448	4,254
32,700	32,750	4,455	4,001	4,455	4,261
32,750	32,800	4,463	4,009	4,463	4,269
32,800	32,850	4,470	4,016	4,470	4,276
32,850	32,900	4,478	4,024	4,478	4,284
32,900	32,950	4,485	4,031	4,485	4,291
32,950	33,000	4,493	4,039	4,493	4,299

33,000

At least	But less than	Single	Married filing jointly *	Married filing separately	Head of a household
33,000	33,050	4,500	4,046	4,500	4,306
33,050	33,100	4,508	4,054	4,508	4,314
33,100	33,150	4,515	4,061	4,515	4,321
33,150	33,200	4,523	4,069	4,523	4,329
33,200	33,250	4,530	4,076	4,530	4,336
33,250	33,300	4,538	4,084	4,538	4,344
33,300	33,350	4,545	4,091	4,545	4,351
33,350	33,400	4,553	4,099	4,553	4,359
33,400	33,450	4,560	4,106	4,560	4,366
33,450	33,500	4,568	4,114	4,568	4,374
33,500	33,550	4,575	4,121	4,575	4,381
33,550	33,600	4,583	4,129	4,583	4,389
33,600	33,650	4,590	4,136	4,590	4,396
33,650	33,700	4,598	4,144	4,598	4,404
33,700	33,750	4,605	4,151	4,605	4,411
33,750	33,800	4,613	4,159	4,613	4,419
33,800	33,850	4,620	4,166	4,620	4,426
33,850	33,900	4,628	4,174	4,628	4,434
33,900	33,950	4,635	4,181	4,635	4,441
33,950	34,000	4,643	4,189	4,643	4,449

34,000

At least	But less than	Single	Married filing jointly *	Married filing separately	Head of a household
34,000	34,050	4,650	4,196	4,650	4,456
34,050	34,100	4,658	4,204	4,658	4,464
34,100	34,150	4,665	4,211	4,665	4,471
34,150	34,200	4,673	4,219	4,673	4,479
34,200	34,250	4,680	4,226	4,680	4,486
34,250	34,300	4,688	4,234	4,688	4,494
34,300	34,350	4,695	4,241	4,695	4,501
34,350	34,400	4,703	4,249	4,703	4,509
34,400	34,450	4,710	4,256	4,710	4,516
34,450	34,500	4,718	4,264	4,718	4,524
34,500	34,550	4,725	4,271	4,725	4,531
34,550	34,600	4,733	4,279	4,733	4,539
34,600	34,650	4,740	4,286	4,740	4,546
34,650	34,700	4,748	4,294	4,748	4,554
34,700	34,750	4,755	4,301	4,755	4,561
34,750	34,800	4,763	4,309	4,763	4,569
34,800	34,850	4,770	4,316	4,770	4,576
34,850	34,900	4,778	4,324	4,778	4,584
34,900	34,950	4,785	4,331	4,785	4,591
34,950	35,000	4,793	4,339	4,793	4,599

35,000

At least	But less than	Single	Married filing jointly *	Married filing separately	Head of a household
35,000	35,050	4,800	4,346	4,800	4,606
35,050	35,100	4,808	4,354	4,808	4,614
35,100	35,150	4,815	4,361	4,815	4,621
35,150	35,200	4,823	4,369	4,823	4,629
35,200	35,250	4,830	4,376	4,830	4,636
35,250	35,300	4,838	4,384	4,838	4,644
35,300	35,350	4,845	4,391	4,845	4,651
35,350	35,400	4,853	4,399	4,853	4,659
35,400	35,450	4,860	4,406	4,860	4,666
35,450	35,500	4,868	4,414	4,868	4,674
35,500	35,550	4,875	4,421	4,875	4,681
35,550	35,600	4,883	4,429	4,883	4,689
35,600	35,650	4,890	4,436	4,890	4,696
35,650	35,700	4,898	4,444	4,898	4,704
35,700	35,750	4,905	4,451	4,905	4,711
35,750	35,800	4,913	4,459	4,913	4,719
35,800	35,850	4,920	4,466	4,920	4,726
35,850	35,900	4,928	4,474	4,928	4,734
35,900	35,950	4,935	4,481	4,935	4,741
35,950	36,000	4,943	4,489	4,943	4,749

36,000

At least	But less than	Single	Married filing jointly *	Married filing separately	Head of a household
36,000	36,050	4,950	4,496	4,950	4,756
36,050	36,100	4,958	4,504	4,958	4,764
36,100	36,150	4,965	4,511	4,965	4,771
36,150	36,200	4,973	4,519	4,973	4,779
36,200	36,250	4,980	4,526	4,980	4,786
36,250	36,300	4,988	4,534	4,988	4,794
36,300	36,350	4,995	4,541	4,995	4,801
36,350	36,400	5,003	4,549	5,003	4,809
36,400	36,450	5,010	4,556	5,010	4,816
36,450	36,500	5,018	4,564	5,018	4,824
36,500	36,550	5,025	4,571	5,025	4,831
36,550	36,600	5,033	4,579	5,033	4,839
36,600	36,650	5,040	4,586	5,040	4,846
36,650	36,700	5,048	4,594	5,048	4,854
36,700	36,750	5,055	4,601	5,055	4,861
36,750	36,800	5,063	4,609	5,063	4,869
36,800	36,850	5,070	4,616	5,070	4,876
36,850	36,900	5,078	4,624	5,078	4,884
36,900	36,950	5,088	4,631	5,088	4,891
36,950	37,000	5,100	4,639	5,100	4,899

37,000

At least	But less than	Single	Married filing jointly *	Married filing separately	Head of a household
37,000	37,050	5,113	4,646	5,113	4,906
37,050	37,100	5,125	4,654	5,125	4,914
37,100	37,150	5,138	4,661	5,138	4,921
37,150	37,200	5,150	4,669	5,150	4,929
37,200	37,250	5,163	4,676	5,163	4,936
37,250	37,300	5,175	4,684	5,175	4,944
37,300	37,350	5,188	4,691	5,188	4,951
37,350	37,400	5,200	4,699	5,200	4,959
37,400	37,450	5,213	4,706	5,213	4,966
37,450	37,500	5,225	4,714	5,225	4,974
37,500	37,550	5,238	4,721	5,238	4,981
37,550	37,600	5,250	4,729	5,250	4,989
37,600	37,650	5,263	4,736	5,263	4,996
37,650	37,700	5,275	4,744	5,275	5,004
37,700	37,750	5,288	4,751	5,288	5,011
37,750	37,800	5,300	4,759	5,300	5,019
37,800	37,850	5,313	4,766	5,313	5,026
37,850	37,900	5,325	4,774	5,325	5,034
37,900	37,950	5,338	4,781	5,338	5,041
37,950	38,000	5,350	4,789	5,350	5,049

38,000

At least	But less than	Single	Married filing jointly *	Married filing separately	Head of a household
38,000	38,050	5,363	4,796	5,363	5,056
38,050	38,100	5,375	4,804	5,375	5,064
38,100	38,150	5,388	4,811	5,388	5,071
38,150	38,200	5,400	4,819	5,400	5,079
38,200	38,250	5,413	4,826	5,413	5,086
38,250	38,300	5,425	4,834	5,425	5,094
38,300	38,350	5,438	4,841	5,438	5,101
38,350	38,400	5,450	4,849	5,450	5,109
38,400	38,450	5,463	4,856	5,463	5,116
38,450	38,500	5,475	4,864	5,475	5,124
38,500	38,550	5,488	4,871	5,488	5,131
38,550	38,600	5,500	4,879	5,500	5,139
38,600	38,650	5,513	4,886	5,513	5,146
38,650	38,700	5,525	4,894	5,525	5,154
38,700	38,750	5,538	4,901	5,538	5,161
38,750	38,800	5,550	4,909	5,550	5,169
38,800	38,850	5,563	4,916	5,563	5,176
38,850	38,900	5,575	4,924	5,575	5,184
38,900	38,950	5,588	4,931	5,588	5,191
38,950	39,000	5,600	4,939	5,600	5,199

(Continued)

* This column must also be used by a qualifying widow(er).

Need more information or forms? Visit IRS.gov.

39,000

If line 27 (taxable income) is—		And you are—			
At least	But less than	Single	Married filing jointly *	Married filing separately	Head of a household
		Your tax is—			
39,000	39,050	5,613	4,946	5,613	5,206
39,050	39,100	5,625	4,954	5,625	5,214
39,100	39,150	5,638	4,961	5,638	5,221
39,150	39,200	5,650	4,969	5,650	5,229
39,200	39,250	5,663	4,976	5,663	5,236
39,250	39,300	5,675	4,984	5,675	5,244
39,300	39,350	5,688	4,991	5,688	5,251
39,350	39,400	5,700	4,999	5,700	5,259
39,400	39,450	5,713	5,006	5,713	5,266
39,450	39,500	5,725	5,014	5,725	5,274
39,500	39,550	5,738	5,021	5,738	5,281
39,550	39,600	5,750	5,029	5,750	5,289
39,600	39,650	5,763	5,036	5,763	5,296
39,650	39,700	5,775	5,044	5,775	5,304
39,700	39,750	5,788	5,051	5,788	5,311
39,750	39,800	5,800	5,059	5,800	5,319
39,800	39,850	5,813	5,066	5,813	5,326
39,850	39,900	5,825	5,074	5,825	5,334
39,900	39,950	5,838	5,081	5,838	5,341
39,950	40,000	5,850	5,089	5,850	5,349

40,000

At least	But less than	Single	Married filing jointly *	Married filing separately	Head of a household
40,000	40,050	5,863	5,096	5,863	5,356
40,050	40,100	5,875	5,104	5,875	5,364
40,100	40,150	5,888	5,111	5,888	5,371
40,150	40,200	5,900	5,119	5,900	5,379
40,200	40,250	5,913	5,126	5,913	5,386
40,250	40,300	5,925	5,134	5,925	5,394
40,300	40,350	5,938	5,141	5,938	5,401
40,350	40,400	5,950	5,149	5,950	5,409
40,400	40,450	5,963	5,156	5,963	5,416
40,450	40,500	5,975	5,164	5,975	5,424
40,500	40,550	5,988	5,171	5,988	5,431
40,550	40,600	6,000	5,179	6,000	5,439
40,600	40,650	6,013	5,186	6,013	5,446
40,650	40,700	6,025	5,194	6,025	5,454
40,700	40,750	6,038	5,201	6,038	5,461
40,750	40,800	6,050	5,209	6,050	5,469
40,800	40,850	6,063	5,216	6,063	5,476
40,850	40,900	6,075	5,224	6,075	5,484
40,900	40,950	6,088	5,231	6,088	5,491
40,950	41,000	6,100	5,239	6,100	5,499

41,000

At least	But less than	Single	Married filing jointly *	Married filing separately	Head of a household
41,000	41,050	6,113	5,246	6,113	5,506
41,050	41,100	6,125	5,254	6,125	5,514
41,100	41,150	6,138	5,261	6,138	5,521
41,150	41,200	6,150	5,269	6,150	5,529
41,200	41,250	6,163	5,276	6,163	5,536
41,250	41,300	6,175	5,284	6,175	5,544
41,300	41,350	6,188	5,291	6,188	5,551
41,350	41,400	6,200	5,299	6,200	5,559
41,400	41,450	6,213	5,306	6,213	5,566
41,450	41,500	6,225	5,314	6,225	5,574
41,500	41,550	6,238	5,321	6,238	5,581
41,550	41,600	6,250	5,329	6,250	5,589
41,600	41,650	6,263	5,336	6,263	5,596
41,650	41,700	6,275	5,344	6,275	5,604
41,700	41,750	6,288	5,351	6,288	5,611
41,750	41,800	6,300	5,359	6,300	5,619
41,800	41,850	6,313	5,366	6,313	5,626
41,850	41,900	6,325	5,374	6,325	5,634
41,900	41,950	6,338	5,381	6,338	5,641
41,950	42,000	6,350	5,389	6,350	5,649

42,000

At least	But less than	Single	Married filing jointly *	Married filing separately	Head of a household
42,000	42,050	6,363	5,396	6,363	5,656
42,050	42,100	6,375	5,404	6,375	5,664
42,100	42,150	6,388	5,411	6,388	5,671
42,150	42,200	6,400	5,419	6,400	5,679
42,200	42,250	6,413	5,426	6,413	5,686
42,250	42,300	6,425	5,434	6,425	5,694
42,300	42,350	6,438	5,441	6,438	5,701
42,350	42,400	6,450	5,449	6,450	5,709
42,400	42,450	6,463	5,456	6,463	5,716
42,450	42,500	6,475	5,464	6,475	5,724
42,500	42,550	6,488	5,471	6,488	5,731
42,550	42,600	6,500	5,479	6,500	5,739
42,600	42,650	6,513	5,486	6,513	5,746
42,650	42,700	6,525	5,494	6,525	5,754
42,700	42,750	6,538	5,501	6,538	5,761
42,750	42,800	6,550	5,509	6,550	5,769
42,800	42,850	6,563	5,516	6,563	5,776
42,850	42,900	6,575	5,524	6,575	5,784
42,900	42,950	6,588	5,531	6,588	5,791
42,950	43,000	6,600	5,539	6,600	5,799

43,000

At least	But less than	Single	Married filing jointly *	Married filing separately	Head of a household
43,000	43,050	6,613	5,546	6,613	5,806
43,050	43,100	6,625	5,554	6,625	5,814
43,100	43,150	6,638	5,561	6,638	5,821
43,150	43,200	6,650	5,569	6,650	5,829
43,200	43,250	6,663	5,576	6,663	5,836
43,250	43,300	6,675	5,584	6,675	5,844
43,300	43,350	6,688	5,591	6,688	5,851
43,350	43,400	6,700	5,599	6,700	5,859
43,400	43,450	6,713	5,606	6,713	5,866
43,450	43,500	6,725	5,614	6,725	5,874
43,500	43,550	6,738	5,621	6,738	5,881
43,550	43,600	6,750	5,629	6,750	5,889
43,600	43,650	6,763	5,636	6,763	5,896
43,650	43,700	6,775	5,644	6,775	5,904
43,700	43,750	6,788	5,651	6,788	5,911
43,750	43,800	6,800	5,659	6,800	5,919
43,800	43,850	6,813	5,666	6,813	5,926
43,850	43,900	6,825	5,674	6,825	5,934
43,900	43,950	6,838	5,681	6,838	5,941
43,950	44,000	6,850	5,689	6,850	5,949

44,000

At least	But less than	Single	Married filing jointly *	Married filing separately	Head of a household
44,000	44,050	6,863	5,696	6,863	5,956
44,050	44,100	6,875	5,704	6,875	5,964
44,100	44,150	6,888	5,711	6,888	5,971
44,150	44,200	6,900	5,719	6,900	5,979
44,200	44,250	6,913	5,726	6,913	5,986
44,250	44,300	6,925	5,734	6,925	5,994
44,300	44,350	6,938	5,741	6,938	6,001
44,350	44,400	6,950	5,749	6,950	6,009
44,400	44,450	6,963	5,756	6,963	6,016
44,450	44,500	6,975	5,764	6,975	6,024
44,500	44,550	6,988	5,771	6,988	6,031
44,550	44,600	7,000	5,779	7,000	6,039
44,600	44,650	7,013	5,786	7,013	6,046
44,650	44,700	7,025	5,794	7,025	6,054
44,700	44,750	7,038	5,801	7,038	6,061
44,750	44,800	7,050	5,809	7,050	6,069
44,800	44,850	7,063	5,816	7,063	6,076
44,850	44,900	7,075	5,824	7,075	6,084
44,900	44,950	7,088	5,831	7,088	6,091
44,950	45,000	7,100	5,839	7,100	6,099

45,000

At least	But less than	Single	Married filing jointly *	Married filing separately	Head of a household
45,000	45,050	7,113	5,846	7,113	6,106
45,050	45,100	7,125	5,854	7,125	6,114
45,100	45,150	7,138	5,861	7,138	6,121
45,150	45,200	7,150	5,869	7,150	6,129
45,200	45,250	7,163	5,876	7,163	6,136
45,250	45,300	7,175	5,884	7,175	6,144
45,300	45,350	7,188	5,891	7,188	6,151
45,350	45,400	7,200	5,899	7,200	6,159
45,400	45,450	7,213	5,906	7,213	6,166
45,450	45,500	7,225	5,914	7,225	6,174
45,500	45,550	7,238	5,921	7,238	6,181
45,550	45,600	7,250	5,929	7,250	6,189
45,600	45,650	7,263	5,936	7,263	6,196
45,650	45,700	7,275	5,944	7,275	6,204
45,700	45,750	7,288	5,951	7,288	6,211
45,750	45,800	7,300	5,959	7,300	6,219
45,800	45,850	7,313	5,966	7,313	6,226
45,850	45,900	7,325	5,974	7,325	6,234
45,900	45,950	7,338	5,981	7,338	6,241
45,950	46,000	7,350	5,989	7,350	6,249

46,000

At least	But less than	Single	Married filing jointly *	Married filing separately	Head of a household
46,000	46,050	7,363	5,996	7,363	6,256
46,050	46,100	7,375	6,004	7,375	6,264
46,100	46,150	7,388	6,011	7,388	6,271
46,150	46,200	7,400	6,019	7,400	6,279
46,200	46,250	7,413	6,026	7,413	6,286
46,250	46,300	7,425	6,034	7,425	6,294
46,300	46,350	7,438	6,041	7,438	6,301
46,350	46,400	7,450	6,049	7,450	6,309
46,400	46,450	7,463	6,056	7,463	6,316
46,450	46,500	7,475	6,064	7,475	6,324
46,500	46,550	7,488	6,071	7,488	6,331
46,550	46,600	7,500	6,079	7,500	6,339
46,600	46,650	7,513	6,086	7,513	6,346
46,650	46,700	7,525	6,094	7,525	6,354
46,700	46,750	7,538	6,101	7,538	6,361
46,750	46,800	7,550	6,109	7,550	6,369
46,800	46,850	7,563	6,116	7,563	6,376
46,850	46,900	7,575	6,124	7,575	6,384
46,900	46,950	7,588	6,131	7,588	6,391
46,950	47,000	7,600	6,139	7,600	6,399

47,000

At least	But less than	Single	Married filing jointly *	Married filing separately	Head of a household
47,000	47,050	7,613	6,146	7,613	6,406
47,050	47,100	7,625	6,154	7,625	6,414
47,100	47,150	7,638	6,161	7,638	6,421
47,150	47,200	7,650	6,169	7,650	6,429
47,200	47,250	7,663	6,176	7,663	6,436
47,250	47,300	7,675	6,184	7,675	6,444
47,300	47,350	7,688	6,191	7,688	6,451
47,350	47,400	7,700	6,199	7,700	6,459
47,400	47,450	7,713	6,206	7,713	6,466
47,450	47,500	7,725	6,214	7,725	6,474
47,500	47,550	7,738	6,221	7,738	6,481
47,550	47,600	7,750	6,229	7,750	6,489
47,600	47,650	7,763	6,236	7,763	6,496
47,650	47,700	7,775	6,244	7,775	6,504
47,700	47,750	7,788	6,251	7,788	6,511
47,750	47,800	7,800	6,259	7,800	6,519
47,800	47,850	7,813	6,266	7,813	6,526
47,850	47,900	7,825	6,274	7,825	6,534
47,900	47,950	7,838	6,281	7,838	6,541
47,950	48,000	7,850	6,289	7,850	6,549

* This column must also be used by a qualifying widow(er).

(Continued)

If line 27 (taxable income) is—		And you are—			
At least	But less than	Single	Married filing jointly *	Married filing separately	Head of a household
		Your tax is—			

48,000

At least	But less than	Single	Married filing jointly *	Married filing separately	Head of a household
48,000	48,050	7,863	6,296	7,863	6,556
48,050	48,100	7,875	6,304	7,875	6,564
48,100	48,150	7,888	6,311	7,888	6,571
48,150	48,200	7,900	6,319	7,900	6,579
48,200	48,250	7,913	6,326	7,913	6,586
48,250	48,300	7,925	6,334	7,925	6,594
48,300	48,350	7,938	6,341	7,938	6,601
48,350	48,400	7,950	6,349	7,950	6,609
48,400	48,450	7,963	6,356	7,963	6,616
48,450	48,500	7,975	6,364	7,975	6,624
48,500	48,550	7,988	6,371	7,988	6,631
48,550	48,600	8,000	6,379	8,000	6,639
48,600	48,650	8,013	6,386	8,013	6,646
48,650	48,700	8,025	6,394	8,025	6,654
48,700	48,750	8,038	6,401	8,038	6,661
48,750	48,800	8,050	6,409	8,050	6,669
48,800	48,850	8,063	6,416	8,063	6,676
48,850	48,900	8,075	6,424	8,075	6,684
48,900	48,950	8,088	6,431	8,088	6,691
48,950	49,000	8,100	6,439	8,100	6,699

49,000

At least	But less than	Single	Married filing jointly *	Married filing separately	Head of a household
49,000	49,050	8,113	6,446	8,113	6,706
49,050	49,100	8,125	6,454	8,125	6,714
49,100	49,150	8,138	6,461	8,138	6,721
49,150	49,200	8,150	6,469	8,150	6,729
49,200	49,250	8,163	6,476	8,163	6,736
49,250	49,300	8,175	6,484	8,175	6,744
49,300	49,350	8,188	6,491	8,188	6,751
49,350	49,400	8,200	6,499	8,200	6,759
49,400	49,450	8,213	6,506	8,213	6,769
49,450	49,500	8,225	6,514	8,225	6,781
49,500	49,550	8,238	6,521	8,238	6,794
49,550	49,600	8,250	6,529	8,250	6,806
49,600	49,650	8,263	6,536	8,263	6,819
49,650	49,700	8,275	6,544	8,275	6,831
49,700	49,750	8,288	6,551	8,288	6,844
49,750	49,800	8,300	6,559	8,300	6,856
49,800	49,850	8,313	6,566	8,313	6,869
49,850	49,900	8,325	6,574	8,325	6,881
49,900	49,950	8,338	6,581	8,338	6,894
49,950	50,000	8,350	6,589	8,350	6,906

50,000

At least	But less than	Single	Married filing jointly *	Married filing separately	Head of a household
50,000	50,050	8,363	6,596	8,363	6,919
50,050	50,100	8,375	6,604	8,375	6,931
50,100	50,150	8,388	6,611	8,388	6,944
50,150	50,200	8,400	6,619	8,400	6,956
50,200	50,250	8,413	6,626	8,413	6,969
50,250	50,300	8,425	6,634	8,425	6,981
50,300	50,350	8,438	6,641	8,438	6,994
50,350	50,400	8,450	6,649	8,450	7,006
50,400	50,450	8,463	6,656	8,463	7,019
50,450	50,500	8,475	6,664	8,475	7,031
50,500	50,550	8,488	6,671	8,488	7,044
50,550	50,600	8,500	6,679	8,500	7,056
50,600	50,650	8,513	6,686	8,513	7,069
50,650	50,700	8,525	6,694	8,525	7,081
50,700	50,750	8,538	6,701	8,538	7,094
50,750	50,800	8,550	6,709	8,550	7,106
50,800	50,850	8,563	6,716	8,563	7,119
50,850	50,900	8,575	6,724	8,575	7,131
50,900	50,950	8,588	6,731	8,588	7,144
50,950	51,000	8,600	6,739	8,600	7,156

51,000

At least	But less than	Single	Married filing jointly *	Married filing separately	Head of a household
51,000	51,050	8,613	6,746	8,613	7,169
51,050	51,100	8,625	6,754	8,625	7,181
51,100	51,150	8,638	6,761	8,638	7,194
51,150	51,200	8,650	6,769	8,650	7,206
51,200	51,250	8,663	6,776	8,663	7,219
51,250	51,300	8,675	6,784	8,675	7,231
51,300	51,350	8,688	6,791	8,688	7,244
51,350	51,400	8,700	6,799	8,700	7,256
51,400	51,450	8,713	6,806	8,713	7,269
51,450	51,500	8,725	6,814	8,725	7,281
51,500	51,550	8,738	6,821	8,738	7,294
51,550	51,600	8,750	6,829	8,750	7,306
51,600	51,650	8,763	6,836	8,763	7,319
51,650	51,700	8,775	6,844	8,775	7,331
51,700	51,750	8,788	6,851	8,788	7,344
51,750	51,800	8,800	6,859	8,800	7,356
51,800	51,850	8,813	6,866	8,813	7,369
51,850	51,900	8,825	6,874	8,825	7,381
51,900	51,950	8,838	6,881	8,838	7,394
51,950	52,000	8,850	6,889	8,850	7,406

52,000

At least	But less than	Single	Married filing jointly *	Married filing separately	Head of a household
52,000	52,050	8,863	6,896	8,863	7,419
52,050	52,100	8,875	6,904	8,875	7,431
52,100	52,150	8,888	6,911	8,888	7,444
52,150	52,200	8,900	6,919	8,900	7,456
52,200	52,250	8,913	6,926	8,913	7,469
52,250	52,300	8,925	6,934	8,925	7,481
52,300	52,350	8,938	6,941	8,938	7,494
52,350	52,400	8,950	6,949	8,950	7,506
52,400	52,450	8,963	6,956	8,963	7,519
52,450	52,500	8,975	6,964	8,975	7,531
52,500	52,550	8,988	6,971	8,988	7,544
52,550	52,600	9,000	6,979	9,000	7,556
52,600	52,650	9,013	6,986	9,013	7,569
52,650	52,700	9,025	6,994	9,025	7,581
52,700	52,750	9,038	7,001	9,038	7,594
52,750	52,800	9,050	7,009	9,050	7,606
52,800	52,850	9,063	7,016	9,063	7,619
52,850	52,900	9,075	7,024	9,075	7,631
52,900	52,950	9,088	7,031	9,088	7,644
52,950	53,000	9,100	7,039	9,100	7,656

53,000

At least	But less than	Single	Married filing jointly *	Married filing separately	Head of a household
53,000	53,050	9,113	7,046	9,113	7,669
53,050	53,100	9,125	7,054	9,125	7,681
53,100	53,150	9,138	7,061	9,138	7,694
53,150	53,200	9,150	7,069	9,150	7,706
53,200	53,250	9,163	7,076	9,163	7,719
53,250	53,300	9,175	7,084	9,175	7,731
53,300	53,350	9,188	7,091	9,188	7,744
53,350	53,400	9,200	7,099	9,200	7,756
53,400	53,450	9,213	7,106	9,213	7,769
53,450	53,500	9,225	7,114	9,225	7,781
53,500	53,550	9,238	7,121	9,238	7,794
53,550	53,600	9,250	7,129	9,250	7,806
53,600	53,650	9,263	7,136	9,263	7,819
53,650	53,700	9,275	7,144	9,275	7,831
53,700	53,750	9,288	7,151	9,288	7,844
53,750	53,800	9,300	7,159	9,300	7,856
53,800	53,850	9,313	7,166	9,313	7,869
53,850	53,900	9,325	7,174	9,325	7,881
53,900	53,950	9,338	7,181	9,338	7,894
53,950	54,000	9,350	7,189	9,350	7,906

54,000

At least	But less than	Single	Married filing jointly *	Married filing separately	Head of a household
54,000	54,050	9,363	7,196	9,363	7,919
54,050	54,100	9,375	7,204	9,375	7,931
54,100	54,150	9,388	7,211	9,388	7,944
54,150	54,200	9,400	7,219	9,400	7,956
54,200	54,250	9,413	7,226	9,413	7,969
54,250	54,300	9,425	7,234	9,425	7,981
54,300	54,350	9,438	7,241	9,438	7,994
54,350	54,400	9,450	7,249	9,450	8,006
54,400	54,450	9,463	7,256	9,463	8,019
54,450	54,500	9,475	7,264	9,475	8,031
54,500	54,550	9,488	7,271	9,488	8,044
54,550	54,600	9,500	7,279	9,500	8,056
54,600	54,650	9,513	7,286	9,513	8,069
54,650	54,700	9,525	7,294	9,525	8,081
54,700	54,750	9,538	7,301	9,538	8,094
54,750	54,800	9,550	7,309	9,550	8,106
54,800	54,850	9,563	7,316	9,563	8,119
54,850	54,900	9,575	7,324	9,575	8,131
54,900	54,950	9,588	7,331	9,588	8,144
54,950	55,000	9,600	7,339	9,600	8,156

55,000

At least	But less than	Single	Married filing jointly *	Married filing separately	Head of a household
55,000	55,050	9,613	7,346	9,613	8,169
55,050	55,100	9,625	7,354	9,625	8,181
55,100	55,150	9,638	7,361	9,638	8,194
55,150	55,200	9,650	7,369	9,650	8,206
55,200	55,250	9,663	7,376	9,663	8,219
55,250	55,300	9,675	7,384	9,675	8,231
55,300	55,350	9,688	7,391	9,688	8,244
55,350	55,400	9,700	7,399	9,700	8,256
55,400	55,450	9,713	7,406	9,713	8,269
55,450	55,500	9,725	7,414	9,725	8,281
55,500	55,550	9,738	7,421	9,738	8,294
55,550	55,600	9,750	7,429	9,750	8,306
55,600	55,650	9,763	7,436	9,763	8,319
55,650	55,700	9,775	7,444	9,775	8,331
55,700	55,750	9,788	7,451	9,788	8,344
55,750	55,800	9,800	7,459	9,800	8,356
55,800	55,850	9,813	7,466	9,813	8,369
55,850	55,900	9,825	7,474	9,825	8,381
55,900	55,950	9,838	7,481	9,838	8,394
55,950	56,000	9,850	7,489	9,850	8,406

56,000

At least	But less than	Single	Married filing jointly *	Married filing separately	Head of a household
56,000	56,050	9,863	7,496	9,863	8,419
56,050	56,100	9,875	7,504	9,875	8,431
56,100	56,150	9,888	7,511	9,888	8,444
56,150	56,200	9,900	7,519	9,900	8,456
56,200	56,250	9,913	7,526	9,913	8,469
56,250	56,300	9,925	7,534	9,925	8,481
56,300	56,350	9,938	7,541	9,938	8,494
56,350	56,400	9,950	7,549	9,950	8,506
56,400	56,450	9,963	7,556	9,963	8,519
56,450	56,500	9,975	7,564	9,975	8,531
56,500	56,550	9,988	7,571	9,988	8,544
56,550	56,600	10,000	7,579	10,000	8,556
56,600	56,650	10,013	7,586	10,013	8,569
56,650	56,700	10,025	7,594	10,025	8,581
56,700	56,750	10,038	7,601	10,038	8,594
56,750	56,800	10,050	7,609	10,050	8,606
56,800	56,850	10,063	7,616	10,063	8,619
56,850	56,900	10,075	7,624	10,075	8,631
56,900	56,950	10,088	7,631	10,088	8,644
56,950	57,000	10,100	7,639	10,100	8,656

(Continued)

* This column must also be used by a qualifying widow(er).

Need more information or forms? Visit IRS.gov.

If line 27 (taxable income) is—		And you are—			
At least	But less than	Single	Married filing jointly *	Married filing separately	Head of a household
		Your tax is—			

57,000

At least	But less than	Single	Married filing jointly *	Married filing separately	Head of a household
57,000	57,050	10,113	7,646	10,113	8,669
57,050	57,100	10,125	7,654	10,125	8,681
57,100	57,150	10,138	7,661	10,138	8,694
57,150	57,200	10,150	7,669	10,150	8,706
57,200	57,250	10,163	7,676	10,163	8,719
57,250	57,300	10,175	7,684	10,175	8,731
57,300	57,350	10,188	7,691	10,188	8,744
57,350	57,400	10,200	7,699	10,200	8,756
57,400	57,450	10,213	7,706	10,213	8,769
57,450	57,500	10,225	7,714	10,225	8,781
57,500	57,550	10,238	7,721	10,238	8,794
57,550	57,600	10,250	7,729	10,250	8,806
57,600	57,650	10,263	7,736	10,263	8,819
57,650	57,700	10,275	7,744	10,275	8,831
57,700	57,750	10,288	7,751	10,288	8,844
57,750	57,800	10,300	7,759	10,300	8,856
57,800	57,850	10,313	7,766	10,313	8,869
57,850	57,900	10,325	7,774	10,325	8,881
57,900	57,950	10,338	7,781	10,338	8,894
57,950	58,000	10,350	7,789	10,350	8,906

58,000

At least	But less than	Single	Married filing jointly *	Married filing separately	Head of a household
58,000	58,050	10,363	7,796	10,363	8,919
58,050	58,100	10,375	7,804	10,375	8,931
58,100	58,150	10,388	7,811	10,388	8,944
58,150	58,200	10,400	7,819	10,400	8,956
58,200	58,250	10,413	7,826	10,413	8,969
58,250	58,300	10,425	7,834	10,425	8,981
58,300	58,350	10,438	7,841	10,438	8,994
58,350	58,400	10,450	7,849	10,450	9,006
58,400	58,450	10,463	7,856	10,463	9,019
58,450	58,500	10,475	7,864	10,475	9,031
58,500	58,550	10,488	7,871	10,488	9,044
58,550	58,600	10,500	7,879	10,500	9,056
58,600	58,650	10,513	7,886	10,513	9,069
58,650	58,700	10,525	7,894	10,525	9,081
58,700	58,750	10,538	7,901	10,538	9,094
58,750	58,800	10,550	7,909	10,550	9,106
58,800	58,850	10,563	7,916	10,563	9,119
58,850	58,900	10,575	7,924	10,575	9,131
58,900	58,950	10,588	7,931	10,588	9,144
58,950	59,000	10,600	7,939	10,600	9,156

59,000

At least	But less than	Single	Married filing jointly *	Married filing separately	Head of a household
59,000	59,050	10,613	7,946	10,613	9,169
59,050	59,100	10,625	7,954	10,625	9,181
59,100	59,150	10,638	7,961	10,638	9,194
59,150	59,200	10,650	7,969	10,650	9,206
59,200	59,250	10,663	7,976	10,663	9,219
59,250	59,300	10,675	7,984	10,675	9,231
59,300	59,350	10,688	7,991	10,688	9,244
59,350	59,400	10,700	7,999	10,700	9,256
59,400	59,450	10,713	8,006	10,713	9,269
59,450	59,500	10,725	8,014	10,725	9,281
59,500	59,550	10,738	8,021	10,738	9,294
59,550	59,600	10,750	8,029	10,750	9,306
59,600	59,650	10,763	8,036	10,763	9,319
59,650	59,700	10,775	8,044	10,775	9,331
59,700	59,750	10,788	8,051	10,788	9,344
59,750	59,800	10,800	8,059	10,800	9,356
59,800	59,850	10,813	8,066	10,813	9,369
59,850	59,900	10,825	8,074	10,825	9,381
59,900	59,950	10,838	8,081	10,838	9,394
59,950	60,000	10,850	8,089	10,850	9,406

60,000

At least	But less than	Single	Married filing jointly *	Married filing separately	Head of a household
60,000	60,050	10,863	8,096	10,863	9,419
60,050	60,100	10,875	8,104	10,875	9,431
60,100	60,150	10,888	8,111	10,888	9,444
60,150	60,200	10,900	8,119	10,900	9,456
60,200	60,250	10,913	8,126	10,913	9,469
60,250	60,300	10,925	8,134	10,925	9,481
60,300	60,350	10,938	8,141	10,938	9,494
60,350	60,400	10,950	8,149	10,950	9,506
60,400	60,450	10,963	8,156	10,963	9,519
60,450	60,500	10,975	8,164	10,975	9,531
60,500	60,550	10,988	8,171	10,988	9,544
60,550	60,600	11,000	8,179	11,000	9,556
60,600	60,650	11,013	8,186	11,013	9,569
60,650	60,700	11,025	8,194	11,025	9,581
60,700	60,750	11,038	8,201	11,038	9,594
60,750	60,800	11,050	8,209	11,050	9,606
60,800	60,850	11,063	8,216	11,063	9,619
60,850	60,900	11,075	8,224	11,075	9,631
60,900	60,950	11,088	8,231	11,088	9,644
60,950	61,000	11,100	8,239	11,100	9,656

61,000

At least	But less than	Single	Married filing jointly *	Married filing separately	Head of a household
61,000	61,050	11,113	8,246	11,113	9,669
61,050	61,100	11,125	8,254	11,125	9,681
61,100	61,150	11,138	8,261	11,138	9,694
61,150	61,200	11,150	8,269	11,150	9,706
61,200	61,250	11,163	8,276	11,163	9,719
61,250	61,300	11,175	8,284	11,175	9,731
61,300	61,350	11,188	8,291	11,188	9,744
61,350	61,400	11,200	8,299	11,200	9,756
61,400	61,450	11,213	8,306	11,213	9,769
61,450	61,500	11,225	8,314	11,225	9,781
61,500	61,550	11,238	8,321	11,238	9,794
61,550	61,600	11,250	8,329	11,250	9,806
61,600	61,650	11,263	8,336	11,263	9,819
61,650	61,700	11,275	8,344	11,275	9,831
61,700	61,750	11,288	8,351	11,288	9,844
61,750	61,800	11,300	8,359	11,300	9,856
61,800	61,850	11,313	8,366	11,313	9,869
61,850	61,900	11,325	8,374	11,325	9,881
61,900	61,950	11,338	8,381	11,338	9,894
61,950	62,000	11,350	8,389	11,350	9,906

62,000

At least	But less than	Single	Married filing jointly *	Married filing separately	Head of a household
62,000	62,050	11,363	8,396	11,363	9,919
62,050	62,100	11,375	8,404	11,375	9,931
62,100	62,150	11,388	8,411	11,388	9,944
62,150	62,200	11,400	8,419	11,400	9,956
62,200	62,250	11,413	8,426	11,413	9,969
62,250	62,300	11,425	8,434	11,425	9,981
62,300	62,350	11,438	8,441	11,438	9,994
62,350	62,400	11,450	8,449	11,450	10,006
62,400	62,450	11,463	8,456	11,463	10,019
62,450	62,500	11,475	8,464	11,475	10,031
62,500	62,550	11,488	8,471	11,488	10,044
62,550	62,600	11,500	8,479	11,500	10,056
62,600	62,650	11,513	8,486	11,513	10,069
62,650	62,700	11,525	8,494	11,525	10,081
62,700	62,750	11,538	8,501	11,538	10,094
62,750	62,800	11,550	8,509	11,550	10,106
62,800	62,850	11,563	8,516	11,563	10,119
62,850	62,900	11,575	8,524	11,575	10,131
62,900	62,950	11,588	8,531	11,588	10,144
62,950	63,000	11,600	8,539	11,600	10,156

63,000

At least	But less than	Single	Married filing jointly *	Married filing separately	Head of a household
63,000	63,050	11,613	8,546	11,613	10,169
63,050	63,100	11,625	8,554	11,625	10,181
63,100	63,150	11,638	8,561	11,638	10,194
63,150	63,200	11,650	8,569	11,650	10,206
63,200	63,250	11,663	8,576	11,663	10,219
63,250	63,300	11,675	8,584	11,675	10,231
63,300	63,350	11,688	8,591	11,688	10,244
63,350	63,400	11,700	8,599	11,700	10,256
63,400	63,450	11,713	8,606	11,713	10,269
63,450	63,500	11,725	8,614	11,725	10,281
63,500	63,550	11,738	8,621	11,738	10,294
63,550	63,600	11,750	8,629	11,750	10,306
63,600	63,650	11,763	8,636	11,763	10,319
63,650	63,700	11,775	8,644	11,775	10,331
63,700	63,750	11,788	8,651	11,788	10,344
63,750	63,800	11,800	8,659	11,800	10,356
63,800	63,850	11,813	8,666	11,813	10,369
63,850	63,900	11,825	8,674	11,825	10,381
63,900	63,950	11,838	8,681	11,838	10,394
63,950	64,000	11,850	8,689	11,850	10,406

64,000

At least	But less than	Single	Married filing jointly *	Married filing separately	Head of a household
64,000	64,050	11,863	8,696	11,863	10,419
64,050	64,100	11,875	8,704	11,875	10,431
64,100	64,150	11,888	8,711	11,888	10,444
64,150	64,200	11,900	8,719	11,900	10,456
64,200	64,250	11,913	8,726	11,913	10,469
64,250	64,300	11,925	8,734	11,925	10,481
64,300	64,350	11,938	8,741	11,938	10,494
64,350	64,400	11,950	8,749	11,950	10,506
64,400	64,450	11,963	8,756	11,963	10,519
64,450	64,500	11,975	8,764	11,975	10,531
64,500	64,550	11,988	8,771	11,988	10,544
64,550	64,600	12,000	8,779	12,000	10,556
64,600	64,650	12,013	8,786	12,013	10,569
64,650	64,700	12,025	8,794	12,025	10,581
64,700	64,750	12,038	8,801	12,038	10,594
64,750	64,800	12,050	8,809	12,050	10,606
64,800	64,850	12,063	8,816	12,063	10,619
64,850	64,900	12,075	8,824	12,075	10,631
64,900	64,950	12,088	8,831	12,088	10,644
64,950	65,000	12,100	8,839	12,100	10,656

65,000

At least	But less than	Single	Married filing jointly *	Married filing separately	Head of a household
65,000	65,050	12,113	8,846	12,113	10,669
65,050	65,100	12,125	8,854	12,125	10,681
65,100	65,150	12,138	8,861	12,138	10,694
65,150	65,200	12,150	8,869	12,150	10,706
65,200	65,250	12,163	8,876	12,163	10,719
65,250	65,300	12,175	8,884	12,175	10,731
65,300	65,350	12,188	8,891	12,188	10,744
65,350	65,400	12,200	8,899	12,200	10,756
65,400	65,450	12,213	8,906	12,213	10,769
65,450	65,500	12,225	8,914	12,225	10,781
65,500	65,550	12,238	8,921	12,238	10,794
65,550	65,600	12,250	8,929	12,250	10,806
65,600	65,650	12,263	8,936	12,263	10,819
65,650	65,700	12,275	8,944	12,275	10,831
65,700	65,750	12,288	8,951	12,288	10,844
65,750	65,800	12,300	8,959	12,300	10,856
65,800	65,850	12,313	8,966	12,313	10,869
65,850	65,900	12,325	8,974	12,325	10,881
65,900	65,950	12,338	8,981	12,338	10,894
65,950	66,000	12,350	8,989	12,350	10,906

(Continued)

* This column must also be used by a qualifying widow(er).

Need more information or forms? Visit IRS.gov.

66,000

At least	But less than	Single	Married filing jointly *	Married filing separately	Head of a household
66,000	66,050	12,363	8,996	12,363	10,919
66,050	66,100	12,375	9,004	12,375	10,931
66,100	66,150	12,388	9,011	12,388	10,944
66,150	66,200	12,400	9,019	12,400	10,956
66,200	66,250	12,413	9,026	12,413	10,969
66,250	66,300	12,425	9,034	12,425	10,981
66,300	66,350	12,438	9,041	12,438	10,994
66,350	66,400	12,450	9,049	12,450	11,006
66,400	66,450	12,463	9,056	12,463	11,019
66,450	66,500	12,475	9,064	12,475	11,031
66,500	66,550	12,488	9,071	12,488	11,044
66,550	66,600	12,500	9,079	12,500	11,056
66,600	66,650	12,513	9,086	12,513	11,069
66,650	66,700	12,525	9,094	12,525	11,081
66,700	66,750	12,538	9,101	12,538	11,094
66,750	66,800	12,550	9,109	12,550	11,106
66,800	66,850	12,563	9,116	12,563	11,119
66,850	66,900	12,575	9,124	12,575	11,131
66,900	66,950	12,588	9,131	12,588	11,144
66,950	67,000	12,600	9,139	12,600	11,156

67,000

At least	But less than	Single	Married filing jointly *	Married filing separately	Head of a household
67,000	67,050	12,613	9,146	12,613	11,169
67,050	67,100	12,625	9,154	12,625	11,181
67,100	67,150	12,638	9,161	12,638	11,194
67,150	67,200	12,650	9,169	12,650	11,206
67,200	67,250	12,663	9,176	12,663	11,219
67,250	67,300	12,675	9,184	12,675	11,231
67,300	67,350	12,688	9,191	12,688	11,244
67,350	67,400	12,700	9,199	12,700	11,256
67,400	67,450	12,713	9,206	12,713	11,269
67,450	67,500	12,725	9,214	12,725	11,281
67,500	67,550	12,738	9,221	12,738	11,294
67,550	67,600	12,750	9,229	12,750	11,306
67,600	67,650	12,763	9,236	12,763	11,319
67,650	67,700	12,775	9,244	12,775	11,331
67,700	67,750	12,788	9,251	12,788	11,344
67,750	67,800	12,800	9,259	12,800	11,356
67,800	67,850	12,813	9,266	12,813	11,369
67,850	67,900	12,825	9,274	12,825	11,381
67,900	67,950	12,838	9,281	12,838	11,394
67,950	68,000	12,850	9,289	12,850	11,406

68,000

At least	But less than	Single	Married filing jointly *	Married filing separately	Head of a household
68,000	68,050	12,863	9,296	12,863	11,419
68,050	68,100	12,875	9,304	12,875	11,431
68,100	68,150	12,888	9,311	12,888	11,444
68,150	68,200	12,900	9,319	12,900	11,456
68,200	68,250	12,913	9,326	12,913	11,469
68,250	68,300	12,925	9,334	12,925	11,481
68,300	68,350	12,938	9,341	12,938	11,494
68,350	68,400	12,950	9,349	12,950	11,506
68,400	68,450	12,963	9,356	12,963	11,519
68,450	68,500	12,975	9,364	12,975	11,531
68,500	68,550	12,988	9,371	12,988	11,544
68,550	68,600	13,000	9,379	13,000	11,556
68,600	68,650	13,013	9,386	13,013	11,569
68,650	68,700	13,025	9,394	13,025	11,581
68,700	68,750	13,038	9,401	13,038	11,594
68,750	68,800	13,050	9,409	13,050	11,606
68,800	68,850	13,063	9,416	13,063	11,619
68,850	68,900	13,075	9,424	13,075	11,631
68,900	68,950	13,088	9,431	13,088	11,644
68,950	69,000	13,100	9,439	13,100	11,656

69,000

At least	But less than	Single	Married filing jointly *	Married filing separately	Head of a household
69,000	69,050	13,113	9,446	13,113	11,669
69,050	69,100	13,125	9,454	13,125	11,681
69,100	69,150	13,138	9,461	13,138	11,694
69,150	69,200	13,150	9,469	13,150	11,706
69,200	69,250	13,163	9,476	13,163	11,719
69,250	69,300	13,175	9,484	13,175	11,731
69,300	69,350	13,188	9,491	13,188	11,744
69,350	69,400	13,200	9,499	13,200	11,756
69,400	69,450	13,213	9,506	13,213	11,769
69,450	69,500	13,225	9,514	13,225	11,781
69,500	69,550	13,238	9,521	13,238	11,794
69,550	69,600	13,250	9,529	13,250	11,806
69,600	69,650	13,263	9,536	13,263	11,819
69,650	69,700	13,275	9,544	13,275	11,831
69,700	69,750	13,288	9,551	13,288	11,844
69,750	69,800	13,300	9,559	13,300	11,856
69,800	69,850	13,313	9,566	13,313	11,869
69,850	69,900	13,325	9,574	13,325	11,881
69,900	69,950	13,338	9,581	13,338	11,894
69,950	70,000	13,350	9,589	13,350	11,906

70,000

At least	But less than	Single	Married filing jointly *	Married filing separately	Head of a household
70,000	70,050	13,363	9,596	13,363	11,919
70,050	70,100	13,375	9,604	13,375	11,931
70,100	70,150	13,388	9,611	13,388	11,944
70,150	70,200	13,400	9,619	13,400	11,956
70,200	70,250	13,413	9,626	13,413	11,969
70,250	70,300	13,425	9,634	13,425	11,981
70,300	70,350	13,438	9,641	13,438	11,994
70,350	70,400	13,450	9,649	13,450	12,006
70,400	70,450	13,463	9,656	13,463	12,019
70,450	70,500	13,475	9,664	13,475	12,031
70,500	70,550	13,488	9,671	13,488	12,044
70,550	70,600	13,500	9,679	13,500	12,056
70,600	70,650	13,513	9,686	13,513	12,069
70,650	70,700	13,525	9,694	13,525	12,081
70,700	70,750	13,538	9,701	13,538	12,094
70,750	70,800	13,550	9,709	13,550	12,106
70,800	70,850	13,563	9,716	13,563	12,119
70,850	70,900	13,575	9,724	13,575	12,131
70,900	70,950	13,588	9,731	13,588	12,144
70,950	71,000	13,600	9,739	13,600	12,156

71,000

At least	But less than	Single	Married filing jointly *	Married filing separately	Head of a household
71,000	71,050	13,613	9,746	13,613	12,169
71,050	71,100	13,625	9,754	13,625	12,181
71,100	71,150	13,638	9,761	13,638	12,194
71,150	71,200	13,650	9,769	13,650	12,206
71,200	71,250	13,663	9,776	13,663	12,219
71,250	71,300	13,675	9,784	13,675	12,231
71,300	71,350	13,688	9,791	13,688	12,244
71,350	71,400	13,700	9,799	13,700	12,256
71,400	71,450	13,713	9,806	13,713	12,269
71,450	71,500	13,725	9,814	13,725	12,281
71,500	71,550	13,738	9,821	13,738	12,294
71,550	71,600	13,750	9,829	13,750	12,306
71,600	71,650	13,763	9,836	13,763	12,319
71,650	71,700	13,775	9,844	13,775	12,331
71,700	71,750	13,788	9,851	13,788	12,344
71,750	71,800	13,800	9,859	13,800	12,356
71,800	71,850	13,813	9,866	13,813	12,369
71,850	71,900	13,825	9,874	13,825	12,381
71,900	71,950	13,838	9,881	13,838	12,394
71,950	72,000	13,850	9,889	13,850	12,406

72,000

At least	But less than	Single	Married filing jointly *	Married filing separately	Head of a household
72,000	72,050	13,863	9,896	13,863	12,419
72,050	72,100	13,875	9,904	13,875	12,431
72,100	72,150	13,888	9,911	13,888	12,444
72,150	72,200	13,900	9,919	13,900	12,456
72,200	72,250	13,913	9,926	13,913	12,469
72,250	72,300	13,925	9,934	13,925	12,481
72,300	72,350	13,938	9,941	13,938	12,494
72,350	72,400	13,950	9,949	13,950	12,506
72,400	72,450	13,963	9,956	13,963	12,519
72,450	72,500	13,975	9,964	13,975	12,531
72,500	72,550	13,988	9,971	13,988	12,544
72,550	72,600	14,000	9,979	14,000	12,556
72,600	72,650	14,013	9,986	14,013	12,569
72,650	72,700	14,025	9,994	14,025	12,581
72,700	72,750	14,038	10,001	14,038	12,594
72,750	72,800	14,050	10,009	14,050	12,606
72,800	72,850	14,063	10,016	14,063	12,619
72,850	72,900	14,075	10,024	14,075	12,631
72,900	72,950	14,088	10,031	14,088	12,644
72,950	73,000	14,100	10,039	14,100	12,656

73,000

At least	But less than	Single	Married filing jointly *	Married filing separately	Head of a household
73,000	73,050	14,113	10,046	14,113	12,669
73,050	73,100	14,125	10,054	14,125	12,681
73,100	73,150	14,138	10,061	14,138	12,694
73,150	73,200	14,150	10,069	14,150	12,706
73,200	73,250	14,163	10,076	14,163	12,719
73,250	73,300	14,175	10,084	14,175	12,731
73,300	73,350	14,188	10,091	14,188	12,744
73,350	73,400	14,200	10,099	14,200	12,756
73,400	73,450	14,213	10,106	14,213	12,769
73,450	73,500	14,225	10,114	14,225	12,781
73,500	73,550	14,238	10,121	14,238	12,794
73,550	73,600	14,250	10,129	14,250	12,806
73,600	73,650	14,263	10,136	14,263	12,819
73,650	73,700	14,275	10,144	14,275	12,831
73,700	73,750	14,288	10,151	14,288	12,844
73,750	73,800	14,300	10,159	14,300	12,856
73,800	73,850	14,313	10,169	14,313	12,869
73,850	73,900	14,325	10,181	14,325	12,881
73,900	73,950	14,338	10,194	14,338	12,894
73,950	74,000	14,350	10,206	14,350	12,906

74,000

At least	But less than	Single	Married filing jointly *	Married filing separately	Head of a household
74,000	74,050	14,363	10,219	14,363	12,919
74,050	74,100	14,375	10,231	14,375	12,931
74,100	74,150	14,388	10,244	14,388	12,944
74,150	74,200	14,400	10,256	14,400	12,956
74,200	74,250	14,413	10,269	14,413	12,969
74,250	74,300	14,425	10,281	14,425	12,981
74,300	74,350	14,438	10,294	14,438	12,994
74,350	74,400	14,450	10,306	14,450	13,006
74,400	74,450	14,463	10,319	14,463	13,019
74,450	74,500	14,475	10,331	14,477	13,031
74,500	74,550	14,488	10,344	14,491	13,044
74,550	74,600	14,500	10,356	14,505	13,056
74,600	74,650	14,513	10,369	14,519	13,069
74,650	74,700	14,525	10,381	14,533	13,081
74,700	74,750	14,538	10,394	14,547	13,094
74,750	74,800	14,550	10,406	14,561	13,106
74,800	74,850	14,563	10,419	14,575	13,119
74,850	74,900	14,575	10,431	14,589	13,131
74,900	74,950	14,588	10,444	14,603	13,144
74,950	75,000	14,600	10,456	14,617	13,156

(Continued)

* This column must also be used by a qualifying widow(er).

Need more information or forms? Visit IRS.gov.

75,000

At least	But less than	Single	Married filing jointly *	Married filing separately	Head of a household
75,000	75,050	14,613	10,469	14,631	13,169
75,050	75,100	14,625	10,481	14,645	13,181
75,100	75,150	14,638	10,494	14,659	13,194
75,150	75,200	14,650	10,506	14,673	13,206
75,200	75,250	14,663	10,519	14,687	13,219
75,250	75,300	14,675	10,531	14,701	13,231
75,300	75,350	14,688	10,544	14,715	13,244
75,350	75,400	14,700	10,556	14,729	13,256
75,400	75,450	14,713	10,569	14,743	13,269
75,450	75,500	14,725	10,581	14,757	13,281
75,500	75,550	14,738	10,594	14,771	13,294
75,550	75,600	14,750	10,606	14,785	13,306
75,600	75,650	14,763	10,619	14,799	13,319
75,650	75,700	14,775	10,631	14,813	13,331
75,700	75,750	14,788	10,644	14,827	13,344
75,750	75,800	14,800	10,656	14,841	13,356
75,800	75,850	14,813	10,669	14,855	13,369
75,850	75,900	14,825	10,681	14,869	13,381
75,900	75,950	14,838	10,694	14,883	13,394
75,950	76,000	14,850	10,706	14,897	13,406

76,000

At least	But less than	Single	Married filing jointly *	Married filing separately	Head of a household
76,000	76,050	14,863	10,719	14,911	13,419
76,050	76,100	14,875	10,731	14,925	13,431
76,100	76,150	14,888	10,744	14,939	13,444
76,150	76,200	14,900	10,756	14,953	13,456
76,200	76,250	14,913	10,769	14,967	13,469
76,250	76,300	14,925	10,781	14,981	13,481
76,300	76,350	14,938	10,794	14,995	13,494
76,350	76,400	14,950	10,806	15,009	13,506
76,400	76,450	14,963	10,819	15,023	13,519
76,450	76,500	14,975	10,831	15,037	13,531
76,500	76,550	14,988	10,844	15,051	13,544
76,550	76,600	15,000	10,856	15,065	13,556
76,600	76,650	15,013	10,869	15,079	13,569
76,650	76,700	15,025	10,881	15,093	13,581
76,700	76,750	15,038	10,894	15,107	13,594
76,750	76,800	15,050	10,906	15,121	13,606
76,800	76,850	15,063	10,919	15,135	13,619
76,850	76,900	15,075	10,931	15,149	13,631
76,900	76,950	15,088	10,944	15,163	13,644
76,950	77,000	15,100	10,956	15,177	13,656

77,000

At least	But less than	Single	Married filing jointly *	Married filing separately	Head of a household
77,000	77,050	15,113	10,969	15,191	13,669
77,050	77,100	15,125	10,981	15,205	13,681
77,100	77,150	15,138	10,994	15,219	13,694
77,150	77,200	15,150	11,006	15,233	13,706
77,200	77,250	15,163	11,019	15,247	13,719
77,250	77,300	15,175	11,031	15,261	13,731
77,300	77,350	15,188	11,044	15,275	13,744
77,350	77,400	15,200	11,056	15,289	13,756
77,400	77,450	15,213	11,069	15,303	13,769
77,450	77,500	15,225	11,081	15,317	13,781
77,500	77,550	15,238	11,094	15,331	13,794
77,550	77,600	15,250	11,106	15,345	13,806
77,600	77,650	15,263	11,119	15,359	13,819
77,650	77,700	15,275	11,131	15,373	13,831
77,700	77,750	15,288	11,144	15,387	13,844
77,750	77,800	15,300	11,156	15,401	13,856
77,800	77,850	15,313	11,169	15,415	13,869
77,850	77,900	15,325	11,181	15,429	13,881
77,900	77,950	15,338	11,194	15,443	13,894
77,950	78,000	15,350	11,206	15,457	13,906

78,000

At least	But less than	Single	Married filing jointly *	Married filing separately	Head of a household
78,000	78,050	15,363	11,219	15,471	13,919
78,050	78,100	15,375	11,231	15,485	13,931
78,100	78,150	15,388	11,244	15,499	13,944
78,150	78,200	15,400	11,256	15,513	13,956
78,200	78,250	15,413	11,269	15,527	13,969
78,250	78,300	15,425	11,281	15,541	13,981
78,300	78,350	15,438	11,294	15,555	13,994
78,350	78,400	15,450	11,306	15,569	14,006
78,400	78,450	15,463	11,319	15,583	14,019
78,450	78,500	15,475	11,331	15,597	14,031
78,500	78,550	15,488	11,344	15,611	14,044
78,550	78,600	15,500	11,356	15,625	14,056
78,600	78,650	15,513	11,369	15,639	14,069
78,650	78,700	15,525	11,381	15,653	14,081
78,700	78,750	15,538	11,394	15,667	14,094
78,750	78,800	15,550	11,406	15,681	14,106
78,800	78,850	15,563	11,419	15,695	14,119
78,850	78,900	15,575	11,431	15,709	14,131
78,900	78,950	15,588	11,444	15,723	14,144
78,950	79,000	15,600	11,456	15,737	14,156

79,000

At least	But less than	Single	Married filing jointly *	Married filing separately	Head of a household
79,000	79,050	15,613	11,469	15,751	14,169
79,050	79,100	15,625	11,481	15,765	14,181
79,100	79,150	15,638	11,494	15,779	14,194
79,150	79,200	15,650	11,506	15,793	14,206
79,200	79,250	15,663	11,519	15,807	14,219
79,250	79,300	15,675	11,531	15,821	14,231
79,300	79,350	15,688	11,544	15,835	14,244
79,350	79,400	15,700	11,556	15,849	14,256
79,400	79,450	15,713	11,569	15,863	14,269
79,450	79,500	15,725	11,581	15,877	14,281
79,500	79,550	15,738	11,594	15,891	14,294
79,550	79,600	15,750	11,606	15,905	14,306
79,600	79,650	15,763	11,619	15,919	14,319
79,650	79,700	15,775	11,631	15,933	14,331
79,700	79,750	15,788	11,644	15,947	14,344
79,750	79,800	15,800	11,656	15,961	14,356
79,800	79,850	15,813	11,669	15,975	14,369
79,850	79,900	15,825	11,681	15,989	14,381
79,900	79,950	15,838	11,694	16,003	14,394
79,950	80,000	15,850	11,706	16,017	14,406

80,000

At least	But less than	Single	Married filing jointly *	Married filing separately	Head of a household
80,000	80,050	15,863	11,719	16,031	14,419
80,050	80,100	15,875	11,731	16,045	14,431
80,100	80,150	15,888	11,744	16,059	14,444
80,150	80,200	15,900	11,756	16,073	14,456
80,200	80,250	15,913	11,769	16,087	14,469
80,250	80,300	15,925	11,781	16,101	14,481
80,300	80,350	15,938	11,794	16,115	14,494
80,350	80,400	15,950	11,806	16,129	14,506
80,400	80,450	15,963	11,819	16,143	14,519
80,450	80,500	15,975	11,831	16,157	14,531
80,500	80,550	15,988	11,844	16,171	14,544
80,550	80,600	16,000	11,856	16,185	14,556
80,600	80,650	16,013	11,869	16,199	14,569
80,650	80,700	16,025	11,881	16,213	14,581
80,700	80,750	16,038	11,894	16,227	14,594
80,750	80,800	16,050	11,906	16,241	14,606
80,800	80,850	16,063	11,919	16,255	14,619
80,850	80,900	16,075	11,931	16,269	14,631
80,900	80,950	16,088	11,944	16,283	14,644
80,950	81,000	16,100	11,956	16,297	14,656

81,000

At least	But less than	Single	Married filing jointly *	Married filing separately	Head of a household
81,000	81,050	16,113	11,969	16,311	14,669
81,050	81,100	16,125	11,981	16,325	14,681
81,100	81,150	16,138	11,994	16,339	14,694
81,150	81,200	16,150	12,006	16,353	14,706
81,200	81,250	16,163	12,019	16,367	14,719
81,250	81,300	16,175	12,031	16,381	14,731
81,300	81,350	16,188	12,044	16,395	14,744
81,350	81,400	16,200	12,056	16,409	14,756
81,400	81,450	16,213	12,069	16,423	14,769
81,450	81,500	16,225	12,081	16,437	14,781
81,500	81,550	16,238	12,094	16,451	14,794
81,550	81,600	16,250	12,106	16,465	14,806
81,600	81,650	16,263	12,119	16,479	14,819
81,650	81,700	16,275	12,131	16,493	14,831
81,700	81,750	16,288	12,144	16,507	14,844
81,750	81,800	16,300	12,156	16,521	14,856
81,800	81,850	16,313	12,169	16,535	14,869
81,850	81,900	16,325	12,181	16,549	14,881
81,900	81,950	16,338	12,194	16,563	14,894
81,950	82,000	16,350	12,206	16,577	14,906

82,000

At least	But less than	Single	Married filing jointly *	Married filing separately	Head of a household
82,000	82,050	16,363	12,219	16,591	14,919
82,050	82,100	16,375	12,231	16,605	14,931
82,100	82,150	16,388	12,244	16,619	14,944
82,150	82,200	16,400	12,256	16,633	14,956
82,200	82,250	16,413	12,269	16,647	14,969
82,250	82,300	16,425	12,281	16,661	14,981
82,300	82,350	16,438	12,294	16,675	14,994
82,350	82,400	16,450	12,306	16,689	15,006
82,400	82,450	16,463	12,319	16,703	15,019
82,450	82,500	16,475	12,331	16,717	15,031
82,500	82,550	16,488	12,344	16,731	15,044
82,550	82,600	16,500	12,356	16,745	15,056
82,600	82,650	16,513	12,369	16,759	15,069
82,650	82,700	16,525	12,381	16,773	15,081
82,700	82,750	16,538	12,394	16,787	15,094
82,750	82,800	16,550	12,406	16,801	15,106
82,800	82,850	16,563	12,419	16,815	15,119
82,850	82,900	16,575	12,431	16,829	15,131
82,900	82,950	16,588	12,444	16,843	15,144
82,950	83,000	16,600	12,456	16,857	15,156

83,000

At least	But less than	Single	Married filing jointly *	Married filing separately	Head of a household
83,000	83,050	16,613	12,469	16,871	15,169
83,050	83,100	16,625	12,481	16,885	15,181
83,100	83,150	16,638	12,494	16,899	15,194
83,150	83,200	16,650	12,506	16,913	15,206
83,200	83,250	16,663	12,519	16,927	15,219
83,250	83,300	16,675	12,531	16,941	15,231
83,300	83,350	16,688	12,544	16,955	15,244
83,350	83,400	16,700	12,556	16,969	15,256
83,400	83,450	16,713	12,569	16,983	15,269
83,450	83,500	16,725	12,581	16,997	15,281
83,500	83,550	16,738	12,594	17,011	15,294
83,550	83,600	16,750	12,606	17,025	15,306
83,600	83,650	16,763	12,619	17,039	15,319
83,650	83,700	16,775	12,631	17,053	15,331
83,700	83,750	16,788	12,644	17,067	15,344
83,750	83,800	16,800	12,656	17,081	15,356
83,800	83,850	16,813	12,669	17,095	15,369
83,850	83,900	16,825	12,681	17,109	15,381
83,900	83,950	16,838	12,694	17,123	15,394
83,950	84,000	16,850	12,706	17,137	15,406

(Continued)

* This column must also be used by a qualifying widow(er).

If line 27 (taxable income) is— At least	But less than	And you are— Single	Married filing jointly *	Married filing separately	Head of a household
			Your tax is—		

84,000

At least	But less than	Single	Married filing jointly *	Married filing separately	Head of a household
84,000	84,050	16,863	12,719	17,151	15,419
84,050	84,100	16,875	12,731	17,165	15,431
84,100	84,150	16,888	12,744	17,179	15,444
84,150	84,200	16,900	12,756	17,193	15,456
84,200	84,250	16,913	12,769	17,207	15,469
84,250	84,300	16,925	12,781	17,221	15,481
84,300	84,350	16,938	12,794	17,235	15,494
84,350	84,400	16,950	12,806	17,249	15,506
84,400	84,450	16,963	12,819	17,263	15,519
84,450	84,500	16,975	12,831	17,277	15,531
84,500	84,550	16,988	12,844	17,291	15,544
84,550	84,600	17,000	12,856	17,305	15,556
84,600	84,650	17,013	12,869	17,319	15,569
84,650	84,700	17,025	12,881	17,333	15,581
84,700	84,750	17,038	12,894	17,347	15,594
84,750	84,800	17,050	12,906	17,361	15,606
84,800	84,850	17,063	12,919	17,375	15,619
84,850	84,900	17,075	12,931	17,389	15,631
84,900	84,950	17,088	12,944	17,403	15,644
84,950	85,000	17,100	12,956	17,417	15,656

85,000

At least	But less than	Single	Married filing jointly *	Married filing separately	Head of a household
85,000	85,050	17,113	12,969	17,431	15,669
85,050	85,100	17,125	12,981	17,445	15,681
85,100	85,150	17,138	12,994	17,459	15,694
85,150	85,200	17,150	13,006	17,473	15,706
85,200	85,250	17,163	13,019	17,487	15,719
85,250	85,300	17,175	13,031	17,501	15,731
85,300	85,350	17,188	13,044	17,515	15,744
85,350	85,400	17,200	13,056	17,529	15,756
85,400	85,450	17,213	13,069	17,543	15,769
85,450	85,500	17,225	13,081	17,557	15,781
85,500	85,550	17,238	13,094	17,571	15,794
85,550	85,600	17,250	13,106	17,585	15,806
85,600	85,650	17,263	13,119	17,599	15,819
85,650	85,700	17,275	13,131	17,613	15,831
85,700	85,750	17,288	13,144	17,627	15,844
85,750	85,800	17,300	13,156	17,641	15,856
85,800	85,850	17,313	13,169	17,655	15,869
85,850	85,900	17,325	13,181	17,669	15,881
85,900	85,950	17,338	13,194	17,683	15,894
85,950	86,000	17,350	13,206	17,697	15,906

86,000

At least	But less than	Single	Married filing jointly *	Married filing separately	Head of a household
86,000	86,050	17,363	13,219	17,711	15,919
86,050	86,100	17,375	13,231	17,725	15,931
86,100	86,150	17,388	13,244	17,739	15,944
86,150	86,200	17,400	13,256	17,753	15,956
86,200	86,250	17,413	13,269	17,767	15,969
86,250	86,300	17,425	13,281	17,781	15,981
86,300	86,350	17,438	13,294	17,795	15,994
86,350	86,400	17,450	13,306	17,809	16,006
86,400	86,450	17,463	13,319	17,823	16,019
86,450	86,500	17,475	13,331	17,837	16,031
86,500	86,550	17,488	13,344	17,851	16,044
86,550	86,600	17,500	13,356	17,865	16,056
86,600	86,650	17,513	13,369	17,879	16,069
86,650	86,700	17,525	13,381	17,893	16,081
86,700	86,750	17,538	13,394	17,907	16,094
86,750	86,800	17,550	13,406	17,921	16,106
86,800	86,850	17,563	13,419	17,935	16,119
86,850	86,900	17,575	13,431	17,949	16,131
86,900	86,950	17,588	13,444	17,963	16,144
86,950	87,000	17,600	13,456	17,977	16,156

87,000

At least	But less than	Single	Married filing jointly *	Married filing separately	Head of a household
87,000	87,050	17,613	13,469	17,991	16,169
87,050	87,100	17,625	13,481	18,005	16,181
87,100	87,150	17,638	13,494	18,019	16,194
87,150	87,200	17,650	13,506	18,033	16,206
87,200	87,250	17,663	13,519	18,047	16,219
87,250	87,300	17,675	13,531	18,061	16,231
87,300	87,350	17,688	13,544	18,075	16,244
87,350	87,400	17,700	13,556	18,089	16,256
87,400	87,450	17,713	13,569	18,103	16,269
87,450	87,500	17,725	13,581	18,117	16,281
87,500	87,550	17,738	13,594	18,131	16,294
87,550	87,600	17,750	13,606	18,145	16,306
87,600	87,650	17,763	13,619	18,159	16,319
87,650	87,700	17,775	13,631	18,173	16,331
87,700	87,750	17,788	13,644	18,187	16,344
87,750	87,800	17,800	13,656	18,201	16,356
87,800	87,850	17,813	13,669	18,215	16,369
87,850	87,900	17,825	13,681	18,229	16,381
87,900	87,950	17,838	13,694	18,243	16,394
87,950	88,000	17,850	13,706	18,257	16,406

88,000

At least	But less than	Single	Married filing jointly *	Married filing separately	Head of a household
88,000	88,050	17,863	13,719	18,271	16,419
88,050	88,100	17,875	13,731	18,285	16,431
88,100	88,150	17,888	13,744	18,299	16,444
88,150	88,200	17,900	13,756	18,313	16,456
88,200	88,250	17,913	13,769	18,327	16,469
88,250	88,300	17,925	13,781	18,341	16,481
88,300	88,350	17,938	13,794	18,355	16,494
88,350	88,400	17,950	13,806	18,369	16,506
88,400	88,450	17,963	13,819	18,383	16,519
88,450	88,500	17,975	13,831	18,397	16,531
88,500	88,550	17,988	13,844	18,411	16,544
88,550	88,600	18,000	13,856	18,425	16,556
88,600	88,650	18,013	13,869	18,439	16,569
88,650	88,700	18,025	13,881	18,453	16,581
88,700	88,750	18,038	13,894	18,467	16,594
88,750	88,800	18,050	13,906	18,481	16,606
88,800	88,850	18,063	13,919	18,495	16,619
88,850	88,900	18,075	13,931	18,509	16,631
88,900	88,950	18,088	13,944	18,523	16,644
88,950	89,000	18,100	13,956	18,537	16,656

89,000

At least	But less than	Single	Married filing jointly *	Married filing separately	Head of a household
89,000	89,050	18,113	13,969	18,551	16,669
89,050	89,100	18,125	13,981	18,565	16,681
89,100	89,150	18,138	13,994	18,579	16,694
89,150	89,200	18,150	14,006	18,593	16,706
89,200	89,250	18,163	14,019	18,607	16,719
89,250	89,300	18,175	14,031	18,621	16,731
89,300	89,350	18,188	14,044	18,635	16,744
89,350	89,400	18,201	14,056	18,649	16,756
89,400	89,450	18,215	14,069	18,663	16,769
89,450	89,500	18,229	14,081	18,677	16,781
89,500	89,550	18,243	14,094	18,691	16,794
89,550	89,600	18,257	14,106	18,705	16,806
89,600	89,650	18,271	14,119	18,719	16,819
89,650	89,700	18,285	14,131	18,733	16,831
89,700	89,750	18,299	14,144	18,747	16,844
89,750	89,800	18,313	14,156	18,761	16,856
89,800	89,850	18,327	14,169	18,775	16,869
89,850	89,900	18,341	14,181	18,789	16,881
89,900	89,950	18,355	14,194	18,803	16,894
89,950	90,000	18,369	14,206	18,817	16,906

90,000

At least	But less than	Single	Married filing jointly *	Married filing separately	Head of a household
90,000	90,050	18,383	14,219	18,831	16,919
90,050	90,100	18,397	14,231	18,845	16,931
90,100	90,150	18,411	14,244	18,859	16,944
90,150	90,200	18,425	14,256	18,873	16,956
90,200	90,250	18,439	14,269	18,887	16,969
90,250	90,300	18,453	14,281	18,901	16,981
90,300	90,350	18,467	14,294	18,915	16,994
90,350	90,400	18,481	14,306	18,929	17,006
90,400	90,450	18,495	14,319	18,943	17,019
90,450	90,500	18,509	14,331	18,957	17,031
90,500	90,550	18,523	14,344	18,971	17,044
90,550	90,600	18,537	14,356	18,985	17,056
90,600	90,650	18,551	14,369	18,999	17,069
90,650	90,700	18,565	14,381	19,013	17,081
90,700	90,750	18,579	14,394	19,027	17,094
90,750	90,800	18,593	14,406	19,041	17,106
90,800	90,850	18,607	14,419	19,055	17,119
90,850	90,900	18,621	14,431	19,069	17,131
90,900	90,950	18,635	14,444	19,083	17,144
90,950	91,000	18,649	14,456	19,097	17,156

91,000

At least	But less than	Single	Married filing jointly *	Married filing separately	Head of a household
91,000	91,050	18,663	14,469	19,111	17,169
91,050	91,100	18,677	14,481	19,125	17,181
91,100	91,150	18,691	14,494	19,139	17,194
91,150	91,200	18,705	14,506	19,153	17,206
91,200	91,250	18,719	14,519	19,167	17,219
91,250	91,300	18,733	14,531	19,181	17,231
91,300	91,350	18,747	14,544	19,195	17,244
91,350	91,400	18,761	14,556	19,209	17,256
91,400	91,450	18,775	14,569	19,223	17,269
91,450	91,500	18,789	14,581	19,237	17,281
91,500	91,550	18,803	14,594	19,251	17,294
91,550	91,600	18,817	14,606	19,265	17,306
91,600	91,650	18,831	14,619	19,279	17,319
91,650	91,700	18,845	14,631	19,293	17,331
91,700	91,750	18,859	14,644	19,307	17,344
91,750	91,800	18,873	14,656	19,321	17,356
91,800	91,850	18,887	14,669	19,335	17,369
91,850	91,900	18,901	14,681	19,349	17,381
91,900	91,950	18,915	14,694	19,363	17,394
91,950	92,000	18,929	14,706	19,377	17,406

92,000

At least	But less than	Single	Married filing jointly *	Married filing separately	Head of a household
92,000	92,050	18,943	14,719	19,391	17,419
92,050	92,100	18,957	14,731	19,405	17,431
92,100	92,150	18,971	14,744	19,419	17,444
92,150	92,200	18,985	14,756	19,433	17,456
92,200	92,250	18,999	14,769	19,447	17,469
92,250	92,300	19,013	14,781	19,461	17,481
92,300	92,350	19,027	14,794	19,475	17,494
92,350	92,400	19,041	14,806	19,489	17,506
92,400	92,450	19,055	14,819	19,503	17,519
92,450	92,500	19,069	14,831	19,517	17,531
92,500	92,550	19,083	14,844	19,531	17,544
92,550	92,600	19,097	14,856	19,545	17,556
92,600	92,650	19,111	14,869	19,559	17,569
92,650	92,700	19,125	14,881	19,573	17,581
92,700	92,750	19,139	14,894	19,587	17,594
92,750	92,800	19,153	14,906	19,601	17,606
92,800	92,850	19,167	14,919	19,615	17,619
92,850	92,900	19,181	14,931	19,629	17,631
92,900	92,950	19,195	14,944	19,643	17,644
92,950	93,000	19,209	14,956	19,657	17,656

* This column must also be used by a qualifying widow(er).

(Continued)

Need more information or forms? Visit IRS.gov.

If line 27 (taxable income) is—		And you are—			
At least	But less than	Single	Married filing jointly *	Married filing separately	Head of a household
		Your tax is—			

93,000

At least	But less than	Single	Married filing jointly *	Married filing separately	Head of a household
93,000	93,050	19,223	14,969	19,671	17,669
93,050	93,100	19,237	14,981	19,685	17,681
93,100	93,150	19,251	14,994	19,699	17,694
93,150	93,200	19,265	15,006	19,713	17,706
93,200	93,250	19,279	15,019	19,727	17,719
93,250	93,300	19,293	15,031	19,741	17,731
93,300	93,350	19,307	15,044	19,755	17,744
93,350	93,400	19,321	15,056	19,769	17,756
93,400	93,450	19,335	15,069	19,783	17,769
93,450	93,500	19,349	15,081	19,797	17,781
93,500	93,550	19,363	15,094	19,811	17,794
93,550	93,600	19,377	15,106	19,825	17,806
93,600	93,650	19,391	15,119	19,839	17,819
93,650	93,700	19,405	15,131	19,853	17,831
93,700	93,750	19,419	15,144	19,867	17,844
93,750	93,800	19,433	15,156	19,881	17,856
93,800	93,850	19,447	15,169	19,895	17,869
93,850	93,900	19,461	15,181	19,909	17,881
93,900	93,950	19,475	15,194	19,923	17,894
93,950	94,000	19,489	15,206	19,937	17,906

94,000

At least	But less than	Single	Married filing jointly *	Married filing separately	Head of a household
94,000	94,050	19,503	15,219	19,951	17,919
94,050	94,100	19,517	15,231	19,965	17,931
94,100	94,150	19,531	15,244	19,979	17,944
94,150	94,200	19,545	15,256	19,993	17,956
94,200	94,250	19,559	15,269	20,007	17,969
94,250	94,300	19,573	15,281	20,021	17,981
94,300	94,350	19,587	15,294	20,035	17,994
94,350	94,400	19,601	15,306	20,049	18,006
94,400	94,450	19,615	15,319	20,063	18,019
94,450	94,500	19,629	15,331	20,077	18,031
94,500	94,550	19,643	15,344	20,091	18,044
94,550	94,600	19,657	15,356	20,105	18,056
94,600	94,650	19,671	15,369	20,119	18,069
94,650	94,700	19,685	15,381	20,133	18,081
94,700	94,750	19,699	15,394	20,147	18,094
94,750	94,800	19,713	15,406	20,161	18,106
94,800	94,850	19,727	15,419	20,175	18,119
94,850	94,900	19,741	15,431	20,189	18,131
94,900	94,950	19,755	15,444	20,203	18,144
94,950	95,000	19,769	15,456	20,217	18,156

95,000

At least	But less than	Single	Married filing jointly *	Married filing separately	Head of a household
95,000	95,050	19,783	15,469	20,231	18,169
95,050	95,100	19,797	15,481	20,245	18,181
95,100	95,150	19,811	15,494	20,259	18,194
95,150	95,200	19,825	15,506	20,273	18,206
95,200	95,250	19,839	15,519	20,287	18,219
95,250	95,300	19,853	15,531	20,301	18,231
95,300	95,350	19,867	15,544	20,315	18,244
95,350	95,400	19,881	15,556	20,329	18,256
95,400	95,450	19,895	15,569	20,343	18,269
95,450	95,500	19,909	15,581	20,357	18,281
95,500	95,550	19,923	15,594	20,371	18,294
95,550	95,600	19,937	15,606	20,385	18,306
95,600	95,650	19,951	15,619	20,399	18,319
95,650	95,700	19,965	15,631	20,413	18,331
95,700	95,750	19,979	15,644	20,427	18,344
95,750	95,800	19,993	15,656	20,441	18,356
95,800	95,850	20,007	15,669	20,455	18,369
95,850	95,900	20,021	15,681	20,469	18,381
95,900	95,950	20,035	15,694	20,483	18,394
95,950	96,000	20,049	15,706	20,497	18,406

96,000

At least	But less than	Single	Married filing jointly *	Married filing separately	Head of a household
96,000	96,050	20,063	15,719	20,511	18,419
96,050	96,100	20,077	15,731	20,525	18,431
96,100	96,150	20,091	15,744	20,539	18,444
96,150	96,200	20,105	15,756	20,553	18,456
96,200	96,250	20,119	15,769	20,567	18,469
96,250	96,300	20,133	15,781	20,581	18,481
96,300	96,350	20,147	15,794	20,595	18,494
96,350	96,400	20,161	15,806	20,609	18,506
96,400	96,450	20,175	15,819	20,623	18,519
96,450	96,500	20,189	15,831	20,637	18,531
96,500	96,550	20,203	15,844	20,651	18,544
96,550	96,600	20,217	15,856	20,665	18,556
96,600	96,650	20,231	15,869	20,679	18,569
96,650	96,700	20,245	15,881	20,693	18,581
96,700	96,750	20,259	15,894	20,707	18,594
96,750	96,800	20,273	15,906	20,721	18,606
96,800	96,850	20,287	15,919	20,735	18,619
96,850	96,900	20,301	15,931	20,749	18,631
96,900	96,950	20,315	15,944	20,763	18,644
96,950	97,000	20,329	15,956	20,777	18,656

97,000

At least	But less than	Single	Married filing jointly *	Married filing separately	Head of a household
97,000	97,050	20,343	15,969	20,791	18,669
97,050	97,100	20,357	15,981	20,805	18,681
97,100	97,150	20,371	15,994	20,819	18,694
97,150	97,200	20,385	16,006	20,833	18,706
97,200	97,250	20,399	16,019	20,847	18,719
97,250	97,300	20,413	16,031	20,861	18,731
97,300	97,350	20,427	16,044	20,875	18,744
97,350	97,400	20,441	16,056	20,889	18,756
97,400	97,450	20,455	16,069	20,903	18,769
97,450	97,500	20,469	16,081	20,917	18,781
97,500	97,550	20,483	16,094	20,931	18,794
97,550	97,600	20,497	16,106	20,945	18,806
97,600	97,650	20,511	16,119	20,959	18,819
97,650	97,700	20,525	16,131	20,973	18,831
97,700	97,750	20,539	16,144	20,987	18,844
97,750	97,800	20,553	16,156	21,001	18,856
97,800	97,850	20,567	16,169	21,015	18,869
97,850	97,900	20,581	16,181	21,029	18,881
97,900	97,950	20,595	16,194	21,043	18,894
97,950	98,000	20,609	16,206	21,057	18,906

98,000

At least	But less than	Single	Married filing jointly *	Married filing separately	Head of a household
98,000	98,050	20,623	16,219	21,071	18,919
98,050	98,100	20,637	16,231	21,085	18,931
98,100	98,150	20,651	16,244	21,099	18,944
98,150	98,200	20,665	16,256	21,113	18,956
98,200	98,250	20,679	16,269	21,127	18,969
98,250	98,300	20,693	16,281	21,141	18,981
98,300	98,350	20,707	16,294	21,155	18,994
98,350	98,400	20,721	16,306	21,169	19,006
98,400	98,450	20,735	16,319	21,183	19,019
98,450	98,500	20,749	16,331	21,197	19,031
98,500	98,550	20,763	16,344	21,211	19,044
98,550	98,600	20,777	16,356	21,225	19,056
98,600	98,650	20,791	16,369	21,239	19,069
98,650	98,700	20,805	16,381	21,253	19,081
98,700	98,750	20,819	16,394	21,267	19,094
98,750	98,800	20,833	16,406	21,281	19,106
98,800	98,850	20,847	16,419	21,295	19,119
98,850	98,900	20,861	16,431	21,309	19,131
98,900	98,950	20,875	16,444	21,323	19,144
98,950	99,000	20,889	16,456	21,337	19,156

99,000

At least	But less than	Single	Married filing jointly *	Married filing separately	Head of a household
99,000	99,050	20,903	16,469	21,351	19,169
99,050	99,100	20,917	16,481	21,365	19,181
99,100	99,150	20,931	16,494	21,379	19,194
99,150	99,200	20,945	16,506	21,393	19,206
99,200	99,250	20,959	16,519	21,407	19,219
99,250	99,300	20,973	16,531	21,421	19,231
99,300	99,350	20,987	16,544	21,435	19,244
99,350	99,400	21,001	16,556	21,449	19,256
99,400	99,450	21,015	16,569	21,463	19,269
99,450	99,500	21,029	16,581	21,477	19,281
99,500	99,550	21,043	16,594	21,491	19,294
99,550	99,600	21,057	16,606	21,505	19,306
99,600	99,650	21,071	16,619	21,519	19,319
99,650	99,700	21,085	16,631	21,533	19,331
99,700	99,750	21,099	16,644	21,547	19,344
99,750	99,800	21,113	16,656	21,561	19,356
99,800	99,850	21,127	16,669	21,575	19,369
99,850	99,900	21,141	16,681	21,589	19,381
99,900	99,950	21,155	16,694	21,603	19,394
99,950	100,000	21,169	16,706	21,617	19,406

$100,000 or over use Form 1040

* This column must also be used by a qualifying widow(er).

General Information

The IRS Mission. Provide America's taxpayers top-quality service by helping them understand and meet their tax responsibilities and enforce the law with integrity and fairness to all.

How to avoid common mistakes. Mistakes can delay your refund or result in notices being sent to you. One of the best ways to file an accurate return is to use IRS *e-file*. Tax software does the math for you and will help you avoid mistakes. Combining *e-file* with direct deposit is the fastest way to get your refund.

- Make sure you entered the correct name and social security number (SSN) for each dependent you claim on line 6c. Check that each dependent's name and SSN agrees with his or her social security card. For each child under age 17 who is a qualifying child for the child tax credit, make sure you checked the box in line 6c, column (4).

- Check your math, especially for the earned income credit (EIC), child tax credit, taxable social security benefits, deduction for exemptions, taxable income, federal income tax withheld, total tax, and refund or amount you owe.

- Be sure you used the correct method to figure your tax. See the instructions for line 28.

- Be sure to enter your SSN in the space provided on page 1 of Form 1040A. If you are married filing a joint or separate return, also enter your spouse's SSN. Be sure to enter your SSN in the space next to your name. Check that your name and SSN agree with your social security card.

- Make sure your name and address are correct. Enter your (and your spouse's) name in the same order as shown on your last return.

- If you live in an apartment, be sure to include your apartment number in your address.

- See the instructions for line 24 to be sure you entered the correct amount for the standard deduction.

- If you are taking the EIC, be sure you used the correct column of the EIC Table for your filing status and the number of children you have.

- Remember to sign and date Form 1040A and enter your occupation(s).

- Attach your Form(s) W-2 and any other required forms and schedules. Put all forms and schedules in the proper order. See *Assemble Your Return*, earlier.

- If you owe tax and are paying by check or money order, be sure to include all the required information on your payment. See the instructions for line 50 for details.

- Do not file more than one original return for the same year, even if you have not gotten your refund or have not heard from the IRS since you filed. Filing more than one original return for the same year, or sending in more than one copy of the same return (unless we ask you to do so), could delay your refund.

Innocent spouse relief. Generally, both you and your spouse are each responsible for paying the full amount of tax, interest, and penalties on your joint return. However, you may qualify for relief from liability for tax on a joint return if (a) there is an understatement of tax because your spouse omitted income or claimed false deductions or credits, (b) you are divorced, separated, or no longer living with your spouse, or (c) given all the facts and circumstances, it would not be fair to hold you liable for the tax. You may also qualify for relief if you were a married resident of a community property state, but did not file a joint return and are now liable for an unpaid or understated tax. File Form 8857 to request relief. In some cases, Form 8857 may need to be filed within 2 years of the date on which the IRS first attempted to collect the tax from you. Do not file Form 8857 with your Form 1040A. For more information, see Pub. 971 and Form 8857 or you can call the Innocent Spouse office toll-free at 1-855-851-2009.

Income tax withholding and estimated tax payments for 2015. If the amount you owe or the amount you overpaid is large, you may want to file a new Form W-4 with your employer to change the amount of income tax withheld from your 2015 pay. For details on how to complete Form W-4, see Pub. 505. If you have pension or annuity income, use Form W-4P. If you receive certain government payments (such as unemployment compensation or social security benefits) you can have tax withheld from those payments by giving the payer Form W-4V.

 You can use the IRS Withholding Calculator *at www.irs.gov/Individuals/IRS-Withholding-Calculator, instead of Pub. 505 or the worksheets included with Form W-4 or W-4P, to determine whether you need to have your withholding increased or decreased.*

In general, you do not have to make estimated tax payments if you expect that your 2015 tax return will show a tax refund, or a tax balance due of less than $1,000. If your total estimated tax for 2015 is $1,000 or more, see Form 1040-ES and Pub. 505 for a worksheet you can use to see if you have to make estimated tax payments. See Pub. 505 for more details.

Secure your tax records from identity theft. Identity theft occurs when someone uses your personal information such as your name, social security number (SSN), or other identifying information, without your permission, to commit fraud or other crimes. An identity thief may use your SSN to get a job or may file a tax return using your SSN to receive a refund.

To reduce your risk:
- Protect your SSN,
- Ensure your employer is protecting your SSN, and
- Be careful when choosing a tax preparer.

If your tax records are affected by identity theft and you receive a notice from the IRS, respond right away to the name and phone number printed on the IRS notice or letter. For more information, see Pub. 4535.

If your SSN has been lost or stolen or you suspect you are a victim of tax-related identity theft, visit *www.irs.gov/identitytheft* to learn what steps you should take.

Victims of identity theft who are experiencing economic harm or a systemic problem, or are seeking help in resolving tax problems that have not been resolved through normal channels, may be eligible for Taxpayer Advocate Service (TAS) assistance. You can reach TAS by calling the National Taxpayer Advocate helpline at 1-877-777-4778. People who are deaf, hard of hearing, or have a speech disability and who have access to TTY/TDD equipment can call 1-800-829-4059. Deaf or hard-of-hearing individuals can also contact the IRS through relay services such as the Federal Relay Service available at *www.gsa.gov/fedrelay*.

Protect yourself from suspicious emails or phishing schemes. Phishing is the creation and use of email and websites designed to mimic legitimate business emails and websites. The most common form is the act of sending an email to a user falsely claiming to be an established legitimate enterprise in an attempt to scam the user into surrendering private information that will be used for identity theft.

The IRS does not initiate contacts with taxpayers via emails. Also, the IRS does not request detailed personal information through email or ask taxpayers for the PIN numbers, passwords, or similar secret access information for their credit card, bank, or other financial accounts.

If you receive an unsolicited email claiming to be from the IRS, forward this message to *phishing@irs.gov*. You may also report misuse of the IRS name, logo, forms, or other IRS property to the Treasury Inspector General for Tax Administration toll-free at 1-800-366-4484. People who are deaf, hard of hearing, or have a speech disability and who have access to TTY/TDD equipment can call 1-800-877-8339. You can forward suspicious emails to the Federal Trade Commission at *spam@uce.gov* or contact them at *www.ftc.gov/idtheft* or 1-877-IDTHEFT (1-877-438-4338). People who are deaf, hard of hearing, or have a speech disability and who have access to TTY/TDD equipment can call 1-866-653-4261.

Visit IRS.gov and enter "identity theft" in the search box to learn more about identity theft and how to reduce your risk.

How do you make a gift to reduce debt held by the public? If you wish to do so, make a check payable to "Bureau of the Fiscal Service." You can send it to: Bureau of the Fiscal Service, Attn: Dept. G, P.O. Box 2188, Parkersburg, WV 26106-2188. Or you can enclose the check with your income tax return when you file. In the memo section of the check, make a note that it is a gift to reduce the debt held by the public. Do not add your gift to any tax you may owe. See the instructions for line 50 for details on how to pay any tax you owe. Go to *www.publicdebt.treas.gov/index1.htm* for information on how to make this type of gift online.

 If you itemize your deductions for 2015, you may be able to deduct this gift.

How long should records be kept? Keep a copy of your tax return, worksheets you used, and records of all items appearing on it (such as Forms W-2 and 1099) until the statute of limitations runs out for that return. Usually, this is 3 years from the date the return was due or filed or 2 years from the date the tax was paid, whichever is later. You should keep some records longer. For example, keep property records as long as they are needed to figure the basis of the original or replacement property. For more details, see chapter 1 of Pub. 17.

How do you amend your tax return information? File Form 1040X to change a return you already filed. Generally, Form 1040X must be filed within 3 years after the date the original return was filed or within 2 years after the date the tax was paid, whichever is later. But you may have more time to file Form 1040X if you live in a federally declared disaster area or you are physically or mentally unable to manage your financial affairs. See Pub. 556 for details.

Use the *Where's My Amended Return* application on IRS.gov to track the status of your amended return. It can take up to 3 weeks from the date you mailed it to show up in our system.

Need a copy of your tax return? Tax return transcripts are free and generally are used to validate income and tax filing status for mortgage applications, student and small business loan applications, and during tax preparation. To get a free transcript:
- Visit IRS.gov and click on "Get Transcript of Your Tax Records" under "Tools,"
- Use Form 4506-T or 4506T-EZ, or
- Call us at 1-800-908-9946.

If you need a copy of your actual tax return, use Form 4506. There is a fee for each return requested. See Form 4506 for the current fee. If your main home, principal place of business, or tax records are located in a federally declared disaster area, this fee will be waived.

Death of a taxpayer. If a taxpayer died before filing a return for 2014, the taxpayer's spouse or personal representative may have to file and sign a return for that taxpayer. A personal representative can be an executor, administrator, or anyone who is in charge of the deceased taxpayer's property. If the deceased taxpayer did not have to file a return but had tax withheld, a return must be filed to get a refund. The person who files the return must enter "Deceased," the deceased taxpayer's name, and the date of death across the top of the return. If this information is not provided, it may delay the processing of the return.

If your spouse died in 2014 and you did not remarry in 2014, or if your spouse died in 2015 before filing a return for 2014, you can file a joint return. A joint return should show your spouse's 2014 income before death and your income for all of 2014. Enter "Filing as surviving spouse" in the area where you sign the return. If someone else is the personal representative, he or she must also sign.

The surviving spouse or personal representative should promptly notify all payers of income, including financial institutions, of the taxpayer's death. This will ensure the proper reporting of income earned by the taxpayer's estate or heirs. A deceased taxpayer's social security number should not be used for tax years after the year of death, except for estate tax return purposes.

Claiming a refund for a deceased taxpayer. If you are filing a joint return as a surviving spouse, you only need to file the tax return to claim the refund. If you are a court-appointed representative, file the return and include a copy of the certificate that shows your appointment. All other filers requesting the deceased taxpayer's refund must file the return and attach Form 1310.

For more details, use TeleTax topic 356 or see Pub. 559.

Past due returns. If you or someone you know needs to file past due tax returns, use TeleTax topic 153 or go to *www.irs.gov/individuals* for help in filing those returns. Send the return to the address that applies to you in the latest Form 1040A instructions. For example, if you are filing a 2011 return in 2015, use the address at the end of these instructions. However, if you got an IRS notice, mail the return to the address in the notice.

How To Get Tax Help

Do you need help with a tax issue or preparing your tax return, or do you need a free publication or form?

Preparing and filing your tax return. Find free options to prepare and file your return on IRS.gov or in your local community if you qualify.

* Go to IRS.gov and click on the Filing tab to see your options.
* Enter "Free File" in the search box to use brand name software to prepare and *e-file* your federal tax return for free.
* Enter "VITA" in the search box, download the free IRS2Go app, or call 1-800-906-9887 to find the nearest Volunteer Income Tax Assistance or Tax Counseling for the Elderly (TCE) location for free tax preparation.
* Enter "TCE" in the search box, download the free IRS2Go app, or call 1-888-227-7669 to find the nearest Tax Counseling for the Elderly location for free tax preparation.

The Volunteer Income Tax Assistance (VITA) program offers free tax help to people who generally make $53,000 or less, persons with disabilities, the elderly, and limited-English-speaking taxpayers who need help preparing their own tax returns. The Tax Counseling for the Elderly (TCE) program offers free tax help for all taxpayers, particularly those who are 60 years of age and older. TCE volunteers specialize in answering questions about pensions and retirement-related issues unique to seniors.

Getting answers to your tax law questions. IRS.gov and IRS2Go are ready when you are—24 hours a day, 7 days a week.

* Enter "ITA" in the search box on IRS.gov for the Interactive Tax Assistant, a tool that will ask you questions on a number of tax law topics and provide answers. You can print the entire interview and the final response.

* Enter "Tax Map" or "Tax Trails" in the search box for detailed information by tax topic.
* Enter "Pub 17" in the search box to get Pub. 17, Your Federal Income Tax for Individuals, which features details on tax-saving opportunities, 2014 tax changes, and thousands of interactive links to help you find answers to your questions.
* Call TeleTax at 1-800-829-4477 for recorded information on a variety of tax topics. See *What Is TeleTax*, later, for a list of the topics covered.
* Access tax law information in your electronic filing software.
* Go to IRS.gov and click on the Help & Resources tab for more information.

Tax forms and publications. You can download or print all of the forms and publications you may need on *www.irs.gov/formspubs*. Otherwise, you can:

* Go to *www.irs.gov/orderforms* to place an order and have forms mailed to you.
* Call 1-800-829-3676 to order current-year forms, instructions, publications, and prior-year forms and instructions (limited to 5 years).

You should receive your order within 10 business days.

Where to file your tax return.

* Remember, there are many ways to file your return electronically. It's safe, quick and easy. See *Preparing and filing your tax return*, earlier, for more information.
* See *Where Do You File?* at the end of these instructions to determine where to mail your completed paper tax return.

Getting a transcript or copy of a return.

* Go to IRS.gov and click on "Get Transcript of Your Tax Records" under "Tools."
* Download the free IRS2Go app to your smart phone and use it to order transcripts of your tax returns or tax account.
* Call the transcript toll-free line at 1-800-908-9946.
* Mail Form 4506-T or Form 4506T-EZ (both available on IRS.gov).

Using online tools to help prepare your return. Go to IRS.gov and click on the Tools bar to use these and other self-service options.

* The *Earned Income Tax Credit Assistant* determines if you are eligible for the EIC.
* The *First Time Homebuyer Credit Account Look-up* tool provides information on your repayments and account balance.
* The *Alternative Minimum Tax (AMT) Assistant* determines whether you may be subject to AMT.
* The *Online EIN Application* helps you get an Employer Identification Number.
* The *IRS Withholding Calculator* estimates the amount you should have withheld from your paycheck for federal income tax purposes.
* The *Electronic Filing PIN Request* helps to verify your identity when you do not have your prior year AGI or prior year self-selected PIN available.

Understanding identity theft issues.

* Go to *www.irs.gov/uac/Identity-Protection* for information and videos.

- See *Secure your tax records from identity theft* under *General Information*, earlier.

Checking on the status of a refund.
- Go to *www.irs.gov/refunds*.
- Download the free IRS2Go app to your smart phone and use it to check your refund status.
- Call the automated refund hotline at 1-800-829-1954. See *Refund Information*, later.

Making a tax payment. You can make electronic payments online, by phone, or from a mobile device. Paying electronically is safe and secure. The IRS uses the latest encryption technology and does not store banking information. It's easy and secure and much quicker than mailing in a check or money order. Go to IRS.gov and click on the Payments tab or the "Pay Your Tax Bill" icon to make a payment using the following options.
- *Direct Pay* (only if you have a checking or savings account).
- Debit or credit card.
- Electronic Federal Tax Payment System.
- Check or money order.

What if I can't pay now? Click on the Payments tab or the "Pay Your Tax Bill" icon on IRS.gov to find more information about these additional options.
- An *online payment agreement* determines if you are eligible to apply for an installment agreement if you cannot pay your taxes in full today. With the needed information, you can complete the application in about 30 minutes, and get immediate approval.
- An offer in compromise allows you to settle your tax debt for less than the full amount you owe. Use the *Offer in Compromise Pre-Qualifier* to confirm your eligibility.

Checking the status of an amended return.
- Go to IRS.gov and click on the Tools tab and then *Where's My Amended Return?*

Understanding an IRS notice or letter.
- Enter "Understanding your notice" in the search box on IRS.gov to find additional information about your IRS notice or letter.

Visiting the IRS. Locate the nearest Taxpayer Assistance Center using the Office Locator tool on IRS.gov. Enter "office locator" in the search box. Or choose the "Contact Us" option on the IRS2Go app and search Local Offices. Before you visit, use the Locator tool to check hours and services available.

Watching IRS videos. The IRS Video portal *www.irsvideos.gov* contains video and audio presentations on topics of interest to individuals, small businesses, and tax professionals. You'll find video clips of tax topics, archived versions of live panel discussions and Webinars, and audio archives of tax practitioner phone forums.

Getting tax information in other languages. For taxpayers whose native language is not English, we have the following resources available.
- Taxpayers can find information on IRS.gov in the following languages.
  - *Spanish*.
  - *Chinese*.
  - *Vietnamese*.
  - *Korean*.
  - *Russian*.
- The IRS Taxpayer Assistance Centers provide over-the-phone interpreter service in over 170 languages, and the service is available free to taxpayers.

Interest and Penalties

You do not have to figure the amount of any interest or penalties you may owe. Because figuring these amounts can be complicated, we will do it for you if you want. We will send you a bill for any amount due.

If you include interest or penalties (other than the estimated tax penalty) with your payment, identify and enter the amount in the bottom margin of Form 1040A, page 2. Do not include interest or penalties (other than the estimated tax penalty) in the amount you owe on line 50.

Interest

We will charge you interest on taxes not paid by their due date, even if an extension of time to file is granted. We will also charge you interest on penalties imposed for failure to file, negligence, fraud, substantial valuation misstatements, substantial understatements of tax, and reportable transaction understatements. Interest is charged on the penalty from the due date of the return (including extensions).

Penalties

Late filing. If you do not file your return by the due date (including extensions), the penalty is usually 5% of the amount due for each month or part of a month your return is late, unless you have a reasonable explanation. If you do, include it with your return. The penalty can be as much as 25% of the tax due. The penalty is 15% per month, up to a maximum of 75%, if the failure to file is fraudulent. If your return is more than 60 days late, the minimum penalty will be $135 (adjusted for inflation) or the amount of any tax you owe, whichever is smaller.

Late payment of tax. If you pay your taxes late, the penalty is usually ½ of 1% of the unpaid amount for each month or part of a month the tax is not paid. The penalty can be as much as 25% of the unpaid amount. It applies to any unpaid tax on the return. This penalty is in addition to interest charges on late payments.

Frivolous return. In addition to any other penalties, the law imposes a penalty of $5,000 for filing a frivolous return. A frivolous return is one that does not contain information needed to figure the correct tax or shows a substantially incorrect tax because you take a frivolous position or desire to delay or interfere with the tax laws. This includes altering or striking out the preprinted language above the space where you sign. For a list of positions identified as frivolous, see Notice 2010-33, 2010-17 I.R.B. 609, available at *www.irs.gov/irb/2010-17_IRB/ar13.html*.

Other. Other penalties can be imposed for negligence, substantial understatement of tax, reportable transaction understatements, filing an erroneous refund claim, and fraud.

Criminal penalties may be imposed for willful failure to file, tax evasion, or making a false statement, or identity theft. See Pub. 17 for details on some of these penalties.

Taxpayer Bill of Rights

All taxpayers have fundamental rights they should be aware of when dealing with the IRS. The Taxpayer Bill of Rights, which the IRS adopted in June of 2014, takes existing rights in the tax code and groups them into the following 10 broad categories, making them easier to understand. Explore your rights and our obligations to protect them.

The right to be informed. Taxpayers have the right to know what they need to do to comply with the tax laws. They are entitled to clear explanations of the laws and IRS procedures in all tax forms, instructions, publications, notices, and correspondence. They have the right to be informed of IRS decisions about their tax accounts and to receive clear explanations of the outcomes.

The right to quality service. Taxpayers have the right to receive prompt, courteous, and professional assistance in their dealings with the IRS, to be spoken to in a way they can easily understand, to receive clear and easily understandable communications from the IRS, and to speak to a supervisor about inadequate service.

The right to pay no more than the correct amount of tax. Taxpayers have the right to pay only the amount of tax legally due, including interest and penalties, and to have the IRS apply all tax payments properly.

The right to challenge the IRS's position and be heard. Taxpayers have the right to raise objections and provide additional documentation in response to formal IRS actions or proposed actions, to expect that the IRS will consider their timely objections and documentation promptly and fairly, and to receive a response if the IRS does not agree with their position.

The right to appeal an IRS decision in an independent forum. Taxpayers are entitled to a fair and impartial administrative appeal of most IRS decisions, including many penalties, and have the right to receive a written response regarding the Office of Appeals' decision. Taxpayers generally have the right to take their cases to court.

The right to finality. Taxpayers have the right to know the maximum amount of time they have to challenge the IRS's position as well as the maximum amount of time the IRS has to audit a particular tax year or collect a tax debt. Taxpayers have the right to know when the IRS has finished an audit.

The right to privacy. Taxpayers have the right to expect that any IRS inquiry, examination, or enforcement action will comply with the law and be no more intrusive than necessary, and will respect all due process rights, including search and seizure protections and will provide, where applicable, a collection due process hearing.

The right to confidentiality. Taxpayers have the right to expect that any information they provide to the IRS will not be disclosed unless authorized by the taxpayer or by law. Taxpayers have the right to expect appropriate action will be taken against employees, return preparers, and others who wrongfully use or disclose taxpayer return information.

The right to retain representation. Taxpayers have the right to retain an authorized representative of their choice to represent them in their dealings with the IRS. Taxpayers have the right to seek assistance from a _Low Income Taxpayer Clinic_ if they cannot afford representation.

The right to a fair and just tax system. Taxpayers have the right to expect the tax system to consider facts and circumstances that might affect their underlying liabilities, ability to pay, or ability to provide information timely. Taxpayers have the right to receive assistance from the _Taxpayer Advocate Service_ if they are experiencing financial difficulty or if the IRS has not resolved their tax issues properly and timely through its normal channels.

Learn more at _www.irs.gov/taxpayerrights_.

Refund Information

 where's my refund? Visit IRS.gov and click on *Where's My Refund?* 24 hours a day, 7 days a week. Information about your return will generally be available within 24 hours after the IRS receives your e-filed return or 4 weeks after you mail a paper return. But if you filed Form 8379 with your return, allow 14 weeks (11 weeks if you filed electronically) before checking your refund status.

 To use *Where's My Refund?* have a copy of your tax return handy. You will need to enter the following information from your return:

* Your social security number (or individual taxpayer identification number),
* Your filing status, and
* The exact whole dollar amount of your refund.

Where's My Refund? will provide an actual personalized refund date as soon as the IRS processes your tax return and approves your refund.

TIP *Updates to refund status are made once a day—usually at night.*

 If you do not have Internet access, many services are available by phone:

* You can check the status of your refund on the free IRS2Go phone app.
* You can call 1-800-829-1954 24 hours a day, 7 days a week, for automated refund information. Our phone and walk-in assistors can research the status of your refund only if it's been 21 days or more since you filed electronically or more than 6 weeks since you mailed your paper return.

Do not send in a copy of your return unless asked to do so.

To get a refund, you generally must file your return within 3 years from the date the return was due (including extensions).

Where's My Refund? does not track refunds that are claimed on an amended tax return.

Refund information also is available in Spanish at *www.irs.gov/Spanish* and 1-800-829-1954.

What Is TeleTax?

Recorded Tax Information

Recorded tax information is available 24 hours a day, 7 days a week. Select the number of the topic you want to hear. Then, call 1-800-829-4477. Have paper and pencil handy to take notes.

Topics by Internet

TeleTax topics are also available through the IRS website at *www.irs.gov/taxtopics*.

TeleTax Topics

All topics are available in Spanish.

Topic No.	Subject
	IRS Help Available
101	IRS services—Volunteer tax assistance, outreach programs, and identity theft
102	Tax assistance for individuals with disabilities
103	Tax help for small businesses and the self-employed
104	Taxpayer Advocate Service—Your voice at the IRS
105	Armed Forces tax information
107	Tax relief in disaster situations
	IRS Procedures
151	Your appeal rights
152	Refund information

Topic No.	Subject
153	What to do if you haven't filed your tax return
154	Form W-2 and Form 1099-R (What to do if incorrect or not received)
155	Forms and publications—How to order
156	Copy or transcript of your tax return—How to get one
157	Change your address—How to notify the IRS
158	Ensuring proper credit of payments
159	Prior year(s) Form W-2 (How to get a copy)
161	Returning an erroneous refund—Paper check or direct deposit
	Collection
201	The balance due collection process
202	Tax payment options

Topic No.	Subject
203	Refund offsets for unpaid child support, certain federal and state debts, and unemployment compensation debts
204	Offers in compromise
205	Innocent spouse relief (Including separation of liability and equitable relief)
206	Dishonored payments
	Alternative Filing Methods
253	Substitute tax forms
254	How to choose a tax return preparer
255	Self-select PIN signature method
	General Information
301	When, how, and where to file
303	Checklist of common errors when preparing your tax return
304	Extensions of time to file your tax return

TeleTax Topics
(Continued)

Topic No.	Subject
305	Recordkeeping
306	Penalty for underpayment of estimated tax
307	Backup withholding
308	Amended returns
309	Roth IRA contributions
310	Coverdell education savings accounts
311	Power of attorney information
312	Disclosure authorizations
313	Qualified tuition programs (QTPs)

Which Forms to File

Topic No.	Subject
352	Which form—1040, 1040A, or 1040EZ?
356	Decedents

Types of Income

Topic No.	Subject
401	Wages and salaries
403	Interest received
404	Dividends
407	Business income
409	Capital gains and losses
410	Pensions and annuities
411	Pensions—The general rule and the simplified method
412	Lump-sum distributions
413	Rollovers from retirement plans
414	Rental income and expenses
415	Renting residential and vacation property
416	Farming and fishing income
417	Earnings for clergy
418	Unemployment compensation
419	Gambling income and losses
420	Bartering income
421	Scholarships, fellowship grants, and other grants
423	Social security and equivalent railroad retirement benefits
424	401(k) plans
425	Passive activities—Losses and credits
427	Stock options
429	Traders in securities (information for Form 1040 filers)
430	Receipt of stock in a demutualization
431	Canceled debt—Is it taxable or not?
432	Form 1099-A (Acquisition or Abandonment of Secured Property) and Form 1099-C (Cancellation of Debt)

Adjustments to Income

Topic No.	Subject
451	Individual retirement arrangements (IRAs)
452	Alimony paid
453	Bad debt deduction
455	Moving expenses
456	Student loan interest deduction
457	Tuition and fees deduction
458	Educator expense deduction

Itemized Deductions

Topic No.	Subject
501	Should I itemize?
502	Medical and dental expenses
503	Deductible taxes
504	Home mortgage points
505	Interest expense
506	Charitable contributions
508	Miscellaneous expenses
509	Business use of home
510	Business use of car
511	Business travel expenses
512	Business entertainment expenses
513	Educational expenses
514	Employee business expenses
515	Casualty, disaster, and theft losses (including federally declared disaster areas)

Tax Computation

Topic No.	Subject
551	Standard deduction
552	Tax and credits figured by the IRS
553	Tax on a child's investment income (Kiddie tax)
554	Self-employment tax
556	Alternative minimum tax
557	Additional tax on early distributions from traditional and Roth IRAs
558	Additional tax on early distributions from retirement plan, other than IRAs
559	Net Investment Income Tax
560	Additional Medicare Tax
561	Individual shared responsibility provision

Tax Credits

Topic No.	Subject
601	Earned income credit
602	Child and dependent care credit
607	Adoption credit and adoption assistance programs
608	Excess social security and RRTA tax withheld
610	Retirement savings contributions credit
611	Repayment of the first-time homebuyer credit
612	The premium tax credit

IRS Notices

Topic No.	Subject
651	Notices—What to do
652	Notice of underreported income—CP 2000
653	IRS notices and bills, penalties, and interest charges

Basis of Assets, Depreciation, and Sale of Assets

Topic No.	Subject
701	Sale of your home
703	Basis of assets
704	Depreciation
705	Installment sales

Employer Tax Information

Topic No.	Subject
751	Social security and Medicare withholding rates
752	Forms W-2 and W-3—Where, when, and how to file
753	Form W-4—Employee's Withholding Allowance Certificate
755	Employer identification number (EIN)—How to apply
756	Employment taxes for household employees
757	Forms 941 and 944—Deposit requirements
758	Form 941—Employer's Quarterly Federal Tax Return and Form 944—Employer's Annual Federal Tax Return
759	Form 940—Employer's Annual Federal Unemployment (FUTA) Tax Return—Filing and deposit requirements
760	Reporting and deposit requirements for agricultural employers
761	Tips—Withholding and reporting
762	Independent contractor vs. employee
763	The Affordable Care Act

Electronic Media Filers—1099 Series and Related Information Returns

Topic No.	Subject
801	Who must file information returns electronically
802	Applications, form, and information
803	Waivers and extensions
804	Test files and combined federal and state filing
805	Electronic filing of information returns

Tax Information for U.S. Resident Aliens and Citizens Living Abroad

Topic No.	Subject
851	Resident and nonresident aliens
856	Foreign tax credit
857	Individual taxpayer identification number (ITIN)
858	Alien tax clearance

Tax Information for Residents of Puerto Rico

Topic No.	Subject
901	Is a person with income from Puerto Rico required to file a U.S. federal income tax return?
902	Credits and deductions for taxpayers with Puerto Rican source income exempt from U.S. tax
903	Federal employment tax in Puerto Rico
904	Tax assistance for residents of Puerto Rico

Topic numbers are effective January 1, 2015.

Disclosure, Privacy Act, and Paperwork Reduction Act Notice

The IRS Restructuring and Reform Act of 1998, the Privacy Act of 1974, and the Paperwork Reduction Act of 1980 require that when we ask you for information we must first tell you our legal right to ask for the information, why we are asking for it, and how it will be used. We must also tell you what could happen if we do not receive it and whether your response is voluntary, required to obtain a benefit, or mandatory under the law.

This notice applies to all papers you file with us, including this tax return. It also applies to any questions we need to ask you so we can complete, correct, or process your return; figure your tax; and collect tax, interest, or penalties.

Our legal right to ask for information is Internal Revenue Code sections 6001, 6011, and 6012(a), and their regulations. They say that you must file a return or statement with us for any tax you are liable for. Your response is mandatory under these sections. Code section 6109 requires you to provide your identifying number on the return. This is so we know who you are, and can process your return and other papers. You must fill in all parts of the tax form that apply to you. But, you do not have to check the boxes for the Presidential Election Campaign Fund or for the third-party designee. You also do not have to provide your daytime phone number.

You are not required to provide the information requested on a form that is subject to the Paperwork Reduction Act unless the form displays a valid OMB control number. Books or records relating to a form or its instructions must be retained as long as their contents may become material in the administration of any Internal Revenue law.

We ask for tax return information to carry out the tax laws of the United States. We need it to figure and collect the right amount of tax.

If you do not file a return, do not provide the information we ask for, or provide fraudulent information, you may be charged penalties and be subject to criminal prosecution. We may also have to disallow the exemptions, exclusions, credits, deductions, or adjustments shown on your tax return. This could make the tax higher or delay any refund. Interest may also be charged.

Generally, tax returns and return information are confidential, as stated in Code section 6103. However, Code section 6103 allows or requires the Internal Revenue Service to disclose or give the information shown on your tax return to others as described in the Code. For example, we may disclose your tax information to the Department of Justice to enforce the tax laws, both civil and criminal, and to cities, states, the District of Columbia, and U.S. commonwealths or possessions to carry out their tax laws. We may disclose your tax information to the Department of Treasury and contractors for tax administration purposes; and to other persons as necessary to obtain information needed to determine the amount of or to collect the tax you owe. We may disclose your tax information to the Comptroller General of the United States to permit the Comptroller General to review the Internal Revenue Service. We may disclose your tax information to committees of Congress; federal, state, and local child support agencies; and to other federal agencies for the purposes of determining entitlement for benefits or the eligibility for and the repayment of loans. We may also disclose this information to other countries under a tax treaty, to federal and state agencies to enforce federal nontax criminal laws, or to federal law enforcement and intelligence agencies to combat terrorism.

Please keep this notice with your records. It may help you if we ask you for other information. If you have any questions about the rules for filing and giving information, please call or visit any Internal Revenue Service office.

We welcome comments on forms. We try to create forms and instructions that can be easily understood. Often this is difficult to do because our tax laws are very complex. For some people with income mostly from wages, filling in the forms is easy. For others who have businesses, pensions, stocks, rental income, or other investments, it is more difficult.

If you have suggestions for making these forms simpler, we would be happy to hear from you. You can send us comments from *www.irs.gov/formspubs*. Click on "More Information" and then on "Give us feedback." Or you can send your comments to Internal Revenue Service, Tax Forms and Publications Division, 1111 Constitution Ave. NW, IR-6526, Washington, DC 20224. Do not send your return to this address. Instead, see the addresses at the end of these instructions.

Although we cannot respond individually to each comment received, we do appreciate your feedback and will consider your comments as we revise our tax forms and instructions.

Estimates of Taxpayer Burden

The table below shows burden estimates based upon current statutory requirements as of November 2014 for taxpayers filing a 2014 Form 1040, 1040A, or 1040EZ tax return. Time spent and out-of-pocket costs are presented separately. Time burden is broken out by taxpayer activity, with record keeping representing the largest component. Out-of-pocket costs include any expenses incurred by taxpayers to prepare and submit their tax returns. Examples include tax return preparation and submission fees, postage and photocopying costs, and tax preparation software costs. While these estimates do not include burden associated with post-filing activities, IRS operational data indicate that electronically prepared and filed returns have fewer arithmetic errors, implying lower post-filing burden.

Reported time and cost burdens are national averages and do not necessarily reflect a "typical" case. Most taxpayers experience lower than average burden, with taxpayer burden varying considerably by taxpayer type. For instance, the estimated average time burden for all taxpayers filing a Form 1040, 1040A, or 1040EZ is 13 hours, with an average cost of $200 per return. This average includes all associated forms and schedules, across all preparation methods and taxpayer activities. The average burden for taxpayers filing Form 1040 is about 16 hours and $260; the average burden for taxpayers filing Form 1040A is about 8 hours and $80; and the average for Form 1040EZ filers is about 5 hours and $40.

Within each of these estimates there is significant variation in taxpayer activity. For example, non-business taxpayers are expected to have an average burden of about 8 hours and $110, while business taxpayers are expected to have an average burden of about 24 hours and $410. Similarly, tax preparation fees and other out-of-pocket costs vary extensively depending on the tax situation of the taxpayer, the type of software or professional preparer used, and the geographic location.

If you have comments concerning the time and cost estimates below, you can contact us at either one of the addresses shown under *We welcome comments on forms*.

Estimated Average Taxpayer Burden for Individuals by Activity

Primary Form Filed or Type of Taxpayer	Percentage of Returns	Average Time Burden (Hours)					Average Cost (Dollars)**
		Total Time*	Record Keeping	Tax Planning	Form Completion and Submission	All Other	
All taxpayers	100	13	6	2	4	1	$200
Primary forms filed							
1040	69	16	8	2	5	1	260
1040A	19	8	2	1	3	1	80
1040EZ	12	5	1	***	2	1	40
Type of taxpayer							
Nonbusiness****	68	8	3	1	3	1	110
Business****	32	24	13	3	6	2	410

*Detail may not add to total time due to rounding.

**Dollars rounded to the nearest $10.

***Rounds to less than one hour.

****You are considered a "business" filer if you file one or more of the following with Form 1040: Schedule C, C-EZ, E, or F or Form 2106 or 2106-EZ. You are considered a "nonbusiness" filer if you did not file any of those schedules or forms with Form 1040 or if you file Form 1040A or 1040EZ.

Order Form for Forms and Publications

 You can view and download the tax forms and publications you need at www.irs.gov/formspubs. You can also place an order for forms at www.irs.gov/formspubs to avoid having to complete and mail the order form.

The most frequently ordered forms and publications are listed on the order form. You will receive two copies of each form, one copy of the instructions, and one copy of each publication you order. To help reduce waste, please order only the items you need to prepare your return.

How To Use the Order Form

Circle the items you need on the order form below. Use the blank spaces to order items not listed. If you need more space, attach a separate sheet of paper.

Print or type your name and address accurately in the space provided on the order form to ensure delivery of your order. Enclose the order form in an envelope and mail it to the IRS address shown next. You should receive your order within 10 business days after we receive your request.

Do not send your tax return to the address shown on this page. Instead, see the addresses at the end of these instructions.

Mail Your Order Form To:

Internal Revenue Service
1201 N. Mitsubishi Motorway
Bloomington, IL 61705-6613

▲ *Cut here* ▲

Save Money and Time by Going Online!
Download or order these and other forms and publications at www.irs.gov/formspubs

Order Form

Please print.

Name

Postal mailing address ___ Apt./Suite/Room

City ___ State ___ ZIP code

Foreign country ___ International postal code

Daytime phone number
( )

Circle the forms and publications you need. The instructions for any form you order will be included.

Use the **blank spaces** to order items not listed.

Use your QR Reader app on your smartphone to scan this code and get connected to the IRS Forms and Publications homepage.

1040	Schedule F (1040)	1040-V	4868	8959	Pub. 505	Pub. 551	Pub. 946
Schedule A (1040)	Schedule H (1040)	1040X	5405	8960	Pub. 523	Pub. 554	Pub. 970
Schedule B (1040A or 1040)	Schedule J (1040)	2106	6251	8962	Pub. 525	Pub. 575	Pub. 972
Schedule C (1040)	Schedule R (1040A or 1040)	2441	8283	8965	Pub. 526	Pub. 583	Pub. 4681
Schedule C-EZ (1040)	Schedule SE (1040)	3903	8606	Pub. 1	Pub. 527	Pub. 587	
Schedule D (1040)	Schedule 8812 (1040A or 1040)	4506	8822	Pub. 334	Pub. 529	Pub. 590-A	
Form 8949	1040A	4506-T	8829	Pub. 463	Pub. 535	Pub. 590-B	
Schedule E (1040)	1040EZ	4562	8863	Pub. 501	Pub. 547	Pub. 596	
Schedule EIC (1040A or 1040)	1040-ES (2015)	4684	8917	Pub. 502	Pub. 550	Pub. 915	

Major Categories of Federal Income and Outlays for Fiscal Year 2013

Income and Outlays. These pie charts show the relative sizes of the major categories of federal income and outlays for fiscal year 2013.

Income

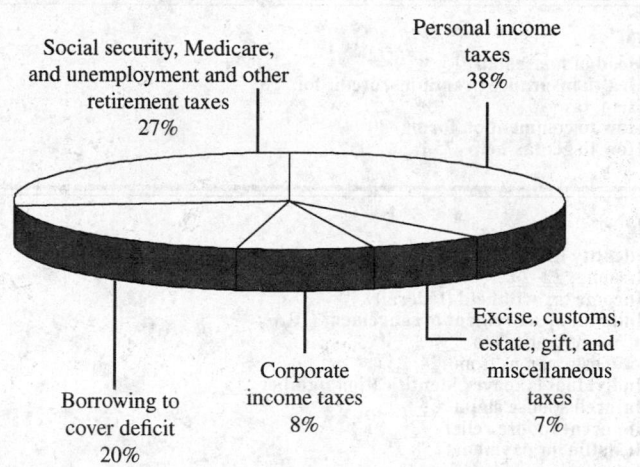

Social security, Medicare, and unemployment and other retirement taxes 27%

Personal income taxes 38%

Borrowing to cover deficit 20%

Corporate income taxes 8%

Excise, customs, estate, gift, and miscellaneous taxes 7%

Outlays

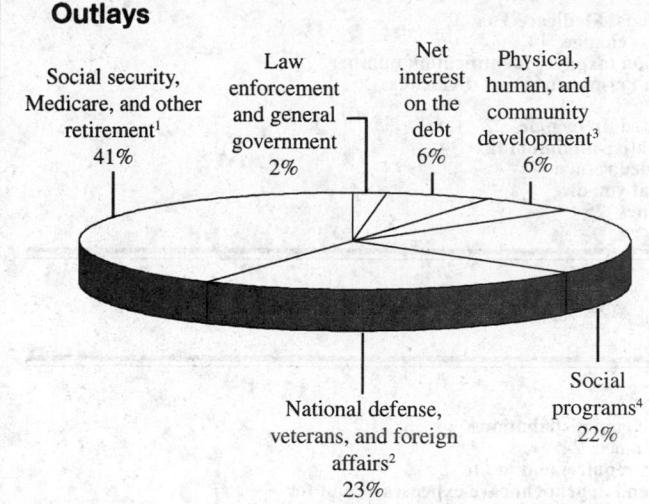

Social security, Medicare, and other retirement[1] 41%

Law enforcement and general government 2%

Net interest on the debt 6%

Physical, human, and community development[3] 6%

National defense, veterans, and foreign affairs[2] 23%

Social programs[4] 22%

On or before the first Monday in February of each year the President is required by law to submit to the Congress a budget proposal for the fiscal year that begins the following October. The budget plan sets forth the President's proposed receipts, spending, and the surplus or deficit for the Federal Government. The plan includes recommendations for new legislation as well as recommendations to change, eliminate, and add programs. After receipt of the President's proposal, the Congress reviews the proposal and makes changes. It first passes a budget resolution setting its own targets for receipts, outlays, and surplus or deficit. Next, individual spending and revenue bills that are consistent with the goals of the budget resolution are enacted.

In fiscal year 2013 (which began on October 1, 2012, and ended on September 30, 2013), Federal income was $2.775 trillion and outlays were $3.455 trillion, leaving a deficit of $680 billion.

Footnotes for Certain Federal Outlays

1. **Social security, Medicare, and other retirement:** These programs provide income support for the retired and disabled and medical care for the elderly.

2. **National defense, veterans, and foreign affairs:** About 18% of outlays were to equip, modernize, and pay our armed forces and to fund national defense activities; 4% were for veterans benefits and services; and about 1% were for international activities, including military and economic assistance to foreign countries and the maintenance of United States embassies abroad.

3. **Physical, human, and community development:** These outlays were for agriculture; natural resources; environment; transportation; aid for elementary and secondary education and direct assistance to college students; job training; deposit insurance, commerce and housing credit, and community development; and space, energy, and general science programs.

4. **Social programs:** About 15% of total outlays were for Medicaid, food stamps, temporary assistance for needy families, supplemental security income, and related programs; and the remaining outlays were for health research and public health programs, unemployment compensation, assisted housing, and social services.

Note. The percentages shown here exclude undistributed offsetting receipts, which were $93 billion in fiscal year 2013. In the budget, these receipts are offset against spending in figuring the outlay totals shown above. These receipts are for the U.S. Government's share of its employee retirement programs, rents and royalties on the Outer Continental Shelf, and proceeds from the sale of assets.

Index to Instructions

Where Do You File? Mail your return to the address shown below that applies to you. If you want to use a private delivery service, see *Private Delivery Services* under *Filing Requirements*, earlier.

 Envelopes without enough postage will be returned to you by the post office. Your envelope may need additional postage if it contains more than five pages or is oversized (for example, it is over $\frac{1}{4}$" thick). Also, include your complete return address.

IF you live in...	THEN use this address if you:	
	Are requesting a refund or are not enclosing a check or money order...	Are enclosing a check or money order...
Florida, Louisiana, Mississippi, Texas	Department of the Treasury Internal Revenue Service Austin, TX 73301-0015	Internal Revenue Service P.O. Box 1214 Charlotte, NC 28201-1214
Alaska, Arizona, California, Colorado, Hawaii, Idaho, Nevada, New Mexico, Oregon, Utah, Washington, Wyoming	Department of the Treasury Internal Revenue Service Fresno, CA 93888-0015	Internal Revenue Service P.O. Box 7704 San Francisco, CA 94120-7704
Arkansas, Illinois, Indiana, Iowa, Kansas, Michigan, Minnesota, Montana, Nebraska, North Dakota, Ohio, Oklahoma, South Dakota, Wisconsin	Department of the Treasury Internal Revenue Service Fresno, CA 93888-0015	Internal Revenue Service P.O. Box 802501 Cincinnati, OH 45280-2501
Alabama, Georgia, Kentucky, New Jersey, North Carolina, South Carolina, Tennessee, Virginia,	Department of the Treasury Internal Revenue Service Kansas City, MO 64999-0015	Internal Revenue Service P.O. Box 931000 Louisville, KY 40293-1000
Connecticut, Delaware, District of Columbia, Maine, Maryland, Massachusetts, Missouri, New Hampshire, New York, Pennsylvania, Rhode Island, Vermont, West Virginia	Department of the Treasury Internal Revenue Service Kansas City, MO 64999-0015	Internal Revenue Service P.O. Box 37008 Hartford, CT 06176-7008
A foreign country, America Samoa, or Puerto Rico (or are excluding income under Internal Revenue Code 933), or uses an APO or FPO address, or files Form 2555, 2555-EZ, or 4563, or is a dual-status alien or nonpermanent resident of Guam or the Virgin Islands.	Department of the Treasury Internal Revenue Service Austin, TX 73301-0215	Internal Revenue Service P.O. Box 1303 Charlotte, NC 28201-1303

*If you live in American Samoa, Puerto Rico, Guam, the U.S. Virgin Islands, or the Northern Mariana Islands, see Pub. 570.

SCHEDULE B
(Form 1040A or 1040)

Department of the Treasury
Internal Revenue Service (99)

Interest and Ordinary Dividends

▶ Attach to Form 1040A or 1040.
▶ Information about Schedule B and its instructions is at *www.irs.gov/scheduleb*.

OMB No. 1545-0074

2014

Attachment
Sequence No. **08**

Name(s) shown on return

Your social security number

				Amount
Part I **Interest** (See instructions on back and the instructions for Form 1040A, or Form 1040, line 8a.) **Note.** If you received a Form 1099-INT, Form 1099-OID, or substitute statement from a brokerage firm, list the firm's name as the payer and enter the total interest shown on that form.	**1**	List name of payer. If any interest is from a seller-financed mortgage and the buyer used the property as a personal residence, see instructions on back and list this interest first. Also, show that buyer's social security number and address ▶	**1**	
	2	Add the amounts on line 1	**2**	
	3	Excludable interest on series EE and I U.S. savings bonds issued after 1989. Attach Form 8815	**3**	
	4	Subtract line 3 from line 2. Enter the result here and on Form 1040A, or Form 1040, line 8a ▶	**4**	

Note. If line 4 is over $1,500, you must complete Part III.

				Amount
Part II **Ordinary Dividends** (See instructions on back and the instructions for Form 1040A, or Form 1040, line 9a.) **Note.** If you received a Form 1099-DIV or substitute statement from a brokerage firm, list the firm's name as the payer and enter the ordinary dividends shown on that form.	**5**	List name of payer ▶	**5**	
	6	Add the amounts on line 5. Enter the total here and on Form 1040A, or Form 1040, line 9a ▶	**6**	

Note. If line 6 is over $1,500, you must complete Part III.

			Yes	No
Part III **Foreign Accounts and Trusts** (See instructions on back.)	You must complete this part if you **(a)** had over $1,500 of taxable interest or ordinary dividends; **(b)** had a foreign account; or **(c)** received a distribution from, or were a grantor of, or a transferor to, a foreign trust.			
	7a	At any time during 2014, did you have a financial interest in or signature authority over a financial account (such as a bank account, securities account, or brokerage account) located in a foreign country? See instructions		
		If "Yes," are you required to file FinCEN Form 114, Report of Foreign Bank and Financial Accounts (FBAR), to report that financial interest or signature authority? See FinCEN Form 114 and its instructions for filing requirements and exceptions to those requirements		
	b	If you are required to file FinCEN Form 114, enter the name of the foreign country where the financial account is located ▶		
	8	During 2014, did you receive a distribution from, or were you the grantor of, or transferor to, a foreign trust? If "Yes," you may have to file Form 3520. See instructions on back		

For Paperwork Reduction Act Notice, see your tax return instructions.   Cat. No. 17146N   Schedule B (Form 1040A or 1040) 2014

General Instructions

Section references are to the Internal Revenue Code unless otherwise noted.

Future Developments

For the latest information about developments related to Schedule B (Form 1040A or 1040) and its instructions, such as legislation enacted after they were published, go to *www.irs.gov/scheduleb*.

Purpose of Form

Use Schedule B if any of the following applies.

• You had over $1,500 of taxable interest or ordinary dividends.

• You received interest from a seller-financed mortgage and the buyer used the property as a personal residence.

• You have accrued interest from a bond.

• You are reporting original issue discount (OID) in an amount less than the amount shown on Form 1099-OID.

• You are reducing your interest income on a bond by the amount of amortizable bond premium.

• You are claiming the exclusion of interest from series EE or I U.S. savings bonds issued after 1989.

• You received interest or ordinary dividends as a nominee.

• You had a financial interest in, or signature authority over, a financial account in a foreign country or you received a distribution from, or were a grantor of, or transferor to, a foreign trust. Part III of the schedule has questions about foreign accounts and trusts.

Specific Instructions

You can list more than one payer on each entry space for lines 1 and 5, but be sure to clearly show the amount paid next to the payer's name. Add the separate amounts paid by the payers listed on an entry space and enter the total in the "Amount" column. If you still need more space, attach separate statements that are the same size as the printed schedule. Use the same format as lines 1 and 5, but show your totals on Schedule B. Be sure to put your name and social security number (SSN) on the statements and attach them at the end of your return.

Part I. Interest

Line 1. Report on line 1 all of your taxable interest. Taxable interest should be shown on your Forms 1099-INT, Forms 1099-OID, or substitute statements. Include interest from series EE, H, HH, and I U.S. savings bonds. List each payer's name and show the amount. Do not report on this line any tax-exempt interest from box 8 or box 9 of Form 1099-INT. Instead, report the amount from box 8 on line 8b of Form 1040A or 1040. If an amount is shown in box 9 of Form 1099-INT, you generally must report it on line 12 of Form 6251. See the Instructions for Form 6251 for more details.

Seller-financed mortgages. If you sold your home or other property and the buyer used the property as a personal residence, list first any interest the buyer paid you on a mortgage or other form of seller financing. Be sure to show the buyer's name, address, and SSN. You must also let the buyer know your SSN. If you do not show the buyer's name, address, and SSN, or let the buyer know your SSN, you may have to pay a $50 penalty.

Nominees. If you received a Form 1099-INT that includes interest you received as a nominee (that is, in your name, but the interest actually belongs to someone else), report the total on line 1. Do this even if you later distributed some or all of this income to others. Under your last entry on line 1, put a subtotal of all interest listed on line 1. Below this subtotal, enter "Nominee Distribution" and show the total interest you received as a nominee. Subtract this amount from the subtotal and enter the result on line 2.

If you received interest as a nominee, you must give the actual owner a Form 1099-INT unless the owner is your spouse. You must also file a Form 1096 and a Form 1099-INT with the IRS. For more details, see the General Instructions for Certain Information Returns and the Instructions for Forms 1099-INT and 1099-OID.

Accrued interest. When you buy bonds between interest payment dates and pay accrued interest to the seller, this interest is taxable to the seller. If you received a Form 1099 for interest as a purchaser of a bond with accrued interest, follow the rules earlier under *Nominees* to see how to report the accrued interest. But identify the amount to be subtracted as "Accrued Interest."

Original issue discount (OID). If you are reporting OID in an amount less than the amount shown on Form 1099-OID, follow the rules earlier under *Nominees* to see how to report the OID. But identify the amount to be subtracted as "OID Adjustment."

Amortizable bond premium. If you are reducing your interest income on a bond by the amount of amortizable bond premium, follow the rules earlier under *Nominees* to see how to report the interest. But identify the amount to be subtracted as "ABP Adjustment."

Line 3. If, during 2014, you cashed series EE or I U.S. savings bonds issued after 1989 and you paid qualified higher education expenses for yourself, your spouse, or your dependents, you may be able to exclude part or all of the interest on those bonds. See Form 8815 for details.

Part II. Ordinary Dividends

You may have to file Form 5471 if, in 2014, you were an officer or director of a foreign corporation. You may also have to file Form 5471 if, in 2014, you owned 10% or more of the total (a) value of a foreign corporation's stock, or (b) combined voting power of all classes of a foreign corporation's stock with voting rights. For details, see Form 5471 and its instructions.

Line 5. Report on line 5 all of your ordinary dividends. This amount should be shown in box 1a of your Forms 1099-DIV or substitute statements. List each payer's name and show the amount.

Nominees. If you received a Form 1099-DIV that includes ordinary dividends you received as a nominee (that is, in your name, but the ordinary dividends actually belong to someone else), report the total on line 5. Do this even if you later distributed some or all of this income to others. Under your last entry on line 5, put a subtotal of all ordinary dividends listed on line 5. Below this subtotal, enter "Nominee Distribution" and show the total ordinary dividends you received as a nominee. Subtract this amount from the subtotal and enter the result on line 6.

If you received dividends as a nominee, you must give the actual owner a Form 1099-DIV unless the owner is your spouse. You must also file a Form 1096 and a Form 1099-DIV with the IRS. For more details, see the General Instructions for Certain Information Returns and the Instructions for Form 1099-DIV.

Part III. Foreign Accounts and Trusts

Regardless of whether you are required to file FinCEN Form 114 (FBAR), you may be required to file Form 8938, Statement of Specified Foreign Financial Assets, with your income tax return. Failure to file Form 8938 may result in penalties and extension of the statute of limitations. See www.irs.gov/form8938 for more information.

Line 7a–Question 1. Check the "Yes" box if at any time during 2014 you had a financial interest in or signature authority over a financial account located in a foreign country. See the definitions that follow. Check the "Yes" box even if you are not required to file FinCEN Form 114, Report of Foreign Bank and Financial Accounts (FBAR).

Financial account. A financial account includes, but is not limited to, a securities, brokerage, savings, demand, checking, deposit, time deposit, or other account maintained with a financial institution (or other person performing the services of a financial institution). A financial account also includes a commodity futures or options account, an insurance policy with a cash value (such as a whole life insurance policy), an annuity policy with a cash value, and shares in a mutual fund or similar pooled fund (that is, a fund that is available to the general public with a regular net asset value determination and regular redemptions).

Financial account located in a foreign country. A financial account is located in a foreign country if the account is physically located outside of the United States. For example, an account maintained with a branch of a United States bank that is physically located outside of the United States is a foreign financial account. An account maintained with a branch of a foreign bank that is physically located in the United States is not a foreign financial account.

Signature authority. Signature authority is the authority of an individual (alone or in conjunction with another individual) to control the disposition of assets held in a foreign financial account by direct communication (whether in writing or otherwise) to the bank or other financial institution that maintains the financial account. See the FinCEN Form 114 instructions for exceptions. Do not consider the exceptions relating to signature authority in answering Question 1 on line 7a.

Other definitions. For definitions of "financial interest," "United States," and other relevant terms, see the instructions for FinCEN Form 114.

Line 7a–Question 2. See FinCEN Form 114 and its instructions to determine whether you must file the form. Check the "Yes" box if you are required to file the form; check the "No" box if you are not required to file the form.

If you checked the "Yes" box to Question 2 on line 7a, FinCEN Form 114 must be electronically filed with the Financial Crimes Enforcement Network (FinCEN) at the following website: *http://bsaefiling. fincen.treas.gov/main.html*. Do not attach FinCEN Form 114 to your tax return. To be considered timely, FinCEN Form 114 **must be received** by June 30, 2015.

If you are required to file FinCEN Form 114 but do not properly do so, you may have to pay a civil penalty up to $10,000. A person who willfully fails to report an account or provide account identifying information may be subject to a civil penalty equal to the greater of $100,000 or 50 percent of the balance in the account at the time of the violation. Willful violations may also be subject to criminal penalties.

Line 7b. If you are required to file FinCEN Form 114, enter the name of the foreign country or countries in the space provided on line 7b. Attach a separate statement if you need more space.

Line 8. If you received a distribution from a foreign trust, you must provide additional information. For this purpose, a loan of cash or marketable securities generally is considered to be a distribution. See Form 3520 for details.

If you were the grantor of, or transferor to, a foreign trust that existed during 2014, you may have to file Form 3520.

Do not attach Form 3520 to Form 1040. Instead, file it at the address shown in its instructions.

If you were treated as the owner of a foreign trust under the grantor trust rules, you are also responsible for ensuring that the foreign trust files Form 3520-A. Form 3520-A is due on March 16, 2015, for a calendar year trust. See the instructions for Form 3520-A for more details.

SCHEDULE EIC
(Form 1040A or 1040)

Department of the Treasury
Internal Revenue Service (99)

Earned Income Credit
Qualifying Child Information

▶ Complete and attach to Form 1040A or 1040 only if you have a qualifying child.

▶ Information about Schedule EIC (Form 1040A or 1040) and its instructions is at *www.irs.gov/scheduleeic*.

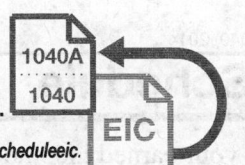

OMB No. 1545-0074

2014

Attachment
Sequence No. **43**

Name(s) shown on return

Your social security number

Before you begin:
- See the instructions for Form 1040A, lines 42a and 42b, or Form 1040, lines 66a and 66b, to make sure that **(a)** you can take the EIC, and **(b)** you have a qualifying child.
- Be sure the child's name on line 1 and social security number (SSN) on line 2 agree with the child's social security card. Otherwise, at the time we process your return, we may reduce or disallow your EIC. If the name or SSN on the child's social security card is not correct, call the Social Security Administration at 1-800-772-1213.

CAUTION

- *If you take the EIC even though you are not eligible, you may not be allowed to take the credit for up to 10 years. See the instructions for details.*
- *It will take us longer to process your return and issue your refund if you do not fill in all lines that apply for each qualifying child.*

Qualifying Child Information

	Child 1		**Child 2**		**Child 3**	
1 Child's name If you have more than three qualifying children, you have to list only three to get the maximum credit.	First name	Last name	First name	Last name	First name	Last name
2 Child's SSN The child must have an SSN as defined in the instructions for Form 1040A, lines 42a and 42b, or Form 1040, lines 66a and 66b, unless the child was born and died in 2014. If your child was born and died in 2014 and did not have an SSN, enter "Died" on this line and attach a copy of the child's birth certificate, death certificate, or hospital medical records.						
3 Child's year of birth	Year _ _ _ _ *If born after 1995 and the child is younger than you (or your spouse, if filing jointly), skip lines 4a and 4b; go to line 5.*		Year _ _ _ _ *If born after 1995 and the child is younger than you (or your spouse, if filing jointly), skip lines 4a and 4b; go to line 5.*		Year _ _ _ _ *If born after 1995 and the child is younger than you (or your spouse, if filing jointly), skip lines 4a and 4b; go to line 5.*	
4 a Was the child under age 24 at the end of 2014, a student, and younger than you (or your spouse, if filing jointly)?	☐ **Yes.** *Go to line 5.*	☐ **No.** *Go to line 4b.*	☐ **Yes.** *Go to line 5.*	☐ **No.** *Go to line 4b.*	☐ **Yes.** *Go to line 5.*	☐ **No.** *Go to line 4b.*
b Was the child permanently and totally disabled during any part of 2014?	☐ **Yes.** *Go to line 5.*	☐ **No.** The child is not a qualifying child.	☐ **Yes.** *Go to line 5.*	☐ **No.** The child is not a qualifying child.	☐ **Yes.** *Go to line 5.*	☐ **No.** The child is not a qualifying child.
5 Child's relationship to you (for example, son, daughter, grandchild, niece, nephew, foster child, etc.)						
6 Number of months child lived with you in the United States during 2014 • If the child lived with you for more than half of 2014 but less than 7 months, enter "7." • If the child was born or died in 2014 and your home was the child's home for more than half the time he or she was alive during 2014, enter "12."	___ months *Do not enter more than 12 months.*		___ months *Do not enter more than 12 months.*		___ months *Do not enter more than 12 months.*	

For Paperwork Reduction Act Notice, see your tax return instructions.

Cat. No. 13339M

Schedule EIC (Form 1040A or 1040) 2014

Purpose of Schedule

After you have figured your earned income credit (EIC), use Schedule EIC to give the IRS information about your qualifying child(ren).

To figure the amount of your credit or to have the IRS figure it for you, see the instructions for Form 1040A, lines 42a and 42b, or Form 1040, lines 66a and 66b.

Taking the EIC when not eligible. If you take the EIC even though you are not eligible and it is determined that your error is due to reckless or intentional disregard of the EIC rules, you will not be allowed to take the credit for 2 years even if you are otherwise eligible to do so. If you fraudulently take the EIC, you will not be allowed to take the credit for 10 years. You may also have to pay penalties.

Future developments. For the latest information about developments related to Schedule EIC (Form 1040A or 1040) and its instructions, such as legislation enacted after they were published, go to *www.irs.gov/scheduleeic*.

 You may also be able to take the additional child tax credit if your child was your dependent and under age 17 at the end of 2014. For more details, see the instructions for line 43 of Form 1040A or line 67 of Form 1040.

Qualifying Child

A qualifying child for the EIC is a child who is your . . .

Son, daughter, stepchild, foster child, brother, sister, stepbrother, stepsister, half brother, half sister, or a descendant of any of them (for example, your grandchild, niece, or nephew)

was. . .

Under age 19 at the end of 2014 and younger than you (or your spouse, if filing jointly)
or
Under age 24 at the end of 2014, a student, and younger than you (or your spouse, if filing jointly)
or
Any age and permanently and totally disabled

Who is not filing a joint return for 2014
or is filing a joint return for 2014 only to claim
a refund of withheld income tax or estimated tax paid

Who lived with you in the United States for more than half of 2014. If the child did not live with you for the required time, see *Exception to time lived with you* in the instructions for Form 1040A, lines 42a and 42b, or Form 1040, lines 66a and 66b.

 *If the child was married or meets the conditions to be a qualifying child of another person (other than your spouse if filing a joint return), special rules apply. For details, see* Married child *or* Qualifying child of more than one person *in the instructions for Form 1040A, lines 42a and 42b, or Form 1040, lines 66a and 66b.*

Schedule R (Form 1040A or 1040) Department of the Treasury Internal Revenue Service (99)	**Credit for the Elderly or the Disabled** ► Complete and attach to Form 1040A or 1040. ► **Information about Schedule R and its separate instructions is at** ***www.irs.gov/scheduler.***	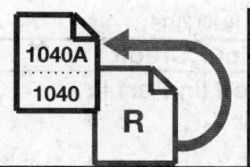	OMB No. 1545-0074 20**14** Attachment Sequence No. **16**

Name(s) shown on Form 1040A or 1040 | Your social security number

You may be able to take this credit and reduce your tax if by the end of 2014:

- You were age 65 or older **or** • You were under age 65, you retired on **permanent and total** disability, and you received taxable disability income.

But you must also meet other tests. See instructions.

TIP In most cases, the IRS can figure the credit for you. See instructions.

Part I — Check the Box for Your Filing Status and Age

If your filing status is:	And by the end of 2014:	Check only one box:
Single, Head of household, or Qualifying widow(er)	**1** You were 65 or older . . . . **1** ☐ **2** You were under 65 and you retired on permanent and total disability . . **2** ☐	
Married filing jointly	**3** Both spouses were 65 or older . . . . **3** ☐ **4** Both spouses were under 65, but only one spouse retired on permanent and total disability . . . . **4** ☐ **5** Both spouses were under 65, and both retired on permanent and total disability . . . . **5** ☐ **6** One spouse was 65 or older, and the other spouse was under 65 and retired on permanent and total disability . . . . **6** ☐ **7** One spouse was 65 or older, and the other spouse was under 65 and **not** retired on permanent and total disability . . . . **7** ☐	
Married filing separately	**8** You were 65 or older and you lived apart from your spouse for all of 2014 . **8** ☐ **9** You were under 65, you retired on permanent and total disability, and you lived apart from your spouse for all of 2014 . . . . **9** ☐	

Did you check box 1, 3, 7, or 8? ── **Yes** ──► Skip Part II and complete Part III on the back.

── **No** ──► Complete Parts II and III.

Part II — Statement of Permanent and Total Disability (Complete **only** if you checked box 2, 4, 5, 6, or 9 above.)

If: 1 You filed a physician's statement for this disability for 1983 or an earlier year, or you filed or got a statement for tax years after 1983 and your physician signed line B on the statement, **and**

2 Due to your continued disabled condition, you were unable to engage in any substantial gainful activity in 2014, check this box . . . . ► ☐

- If you checked this box, you do not have to get another statement for 2014.

- If you **did not** check this box, have your physician complete the statement in the instructions. You **must** keep the statement for your records.

For Paperwork Reduction Act Notice, see your tax return instructions. | Cat. No. 11359K | Schedule R (Form 1040A or 1040) 2014

Part III	Figure Your Credit

10   If you checked (in Part I):   **Enter:**

     Box 1, 2, 4, or 7 . . . . $5,000

     Box 3, 5, or 6 . . . . $7,500   } **10**

     Box 8 or 9 . . . . $3,750

Did you check box 2, 4, 5, 6, or 9 in Part I?	→ Yes ——→	You **must** complete line 11.
	→ No ——→	Enter the amount from line 10 on line 12 and go to line 13.

11   If you checked (in Part I):

    • Box 6, add $5,000 to the taxable disability income of the spouse who was under age 65. Enter the total.

    • Box 2, 4, or 9, enter your taxable disability income.   } **11**

    • Box 5, add your taxable disability income to your spouse's taxable disability income. Enter the total.

(TIP)   For more details on what to include on line 11, see *Figure Your Credit* in the instructions.

12   If you completed line 11, enter the **smaller** of line 10 or line 11. **All others,** enter the amount from line 10   . . . . **12**

13   Enter the following pensions, annuities, or disability income that you (and your spouse if filing jointly) received in 2014.

   a   Nontaxable part of social security benefits and nontaxable part of railroad retirement benefits treated as social security (see instructions). **13a**

   b   Nontaxable veterans' pensions and any other pension, annuity, or disability benefit that is excluded from income under any other provision of law (see instructions). **13b**

   c   Add lines 13a and 13b. (Even though these income items are not taxable, they **must** be included here to figure your credit.) If you did not receive any of the types of nontaxable income listed on line 13a or 13b, enter -0- on line 13c **13c**

14   Enter the amount from Form 1040A, line 22, or Form 1040, line 38 . . . . . **14**

15   If you checked (in Part I):   **Enter:**

     Box 1 or 2 . . . . $7,500

     Box 3, 4, 5, 6, or 7 . . . $10,000   **15**

     Box 8 or 9 . . . . $5,000

16   Subtract line 15 from line 14. If zero or less, enter -0- **16**

17   Enter one-half of line 16 . . . . **17**

18   Add lines 13c and 17 . . . . **18**

19   Subtract line 18 from line 12. If zero or less, **stop;** you **cannot** take the credit. Otherwise, go to line 20 . . . . **19**

20   Multiply line 19 by 15% (.15). **20**

21   Tax liability limit. Enter the amount from the Credit Limit Worksheet in the instructions . **21**

22   **Credit for the elderly or the disabled.** Enter the **smaller** of line 20 or line 21. Also enter this amount on Form 1040A, line 32, or include on Form 1040, line 54 (check box **c** and enter "Sch R" on the line next to that box) **22**

**Department of the Treasury
Internal Revenue Service**

2014 Instructions for Schedule R (Form 1040A or 1040)

Credit for the Elderly or the Disabled

Use Schedule R (Form 1040A or 1040) to figure the credit for the elderly or the disabled.

Future Developments. For the latest information about developments related to Schedule R (Form 1040A or 1040) and its instructions, such as legislation enacted after they were published, go to *www.irs.gov/scheduler*.

Additional information. See Pub. 524 for more details.

Who Can Take the Credit

The credit is based on your filing status, age, and income. If you are married and filing a joint return, it is also based on your spouse's age and income. You may be able to take this credit if either of the following applies.

1. You were age 65 or older at the end of 2014, or

2. You were under age 65 at the end of 2014 and you meet all of the following.

a. You were permanently and totally disabled on the date you retired. If you retired before 1977, you must have been permanently and totally disabled on January 1, 1976, or January 1, 1977.

b. You received taxable disability income for 2014.

c. On January 1, 2014, you had not reached mandatory retirement age (the age when your employer's retirement program would have required you to retire).

For the definition of permanent and total disability, see *What Is Permanent and Total Disability*, later. Also, see the instructions for *Part II. Statement of Permanent and Total Disability*.

Age 65

You are considered age 65 on the day before your 65th birthday. As a result, if you were born on January 1, 1950, you are considered to be age 65 at the end of 2014.

Married Persons Filing Separate Returns

If your filing status is married filing separately and you lived with your spouse at any time during 2014, you cannot take the credit.

Nonresident Aliens

If you were a nonresident alien at any time during 2014, you may be able to take the credit only if your filing status is married filing jointly.

Income Limits

See *Income Limits for the Credit for the Elderly or the Disabled*, later.

Want the IRS To Figure Your Credit?

If you can take the credit and you want us to figure it for you, check the box in Part I of Schedule R (Form 1040A or 1040) for your filing status and age. Fill in Part II and lines 11 and 13 of Part III if they apply to you. If you file Form 1040A, enter "CFE" in the space to the left of Form 1040A, line 32. If you file Form 1040, check box **c** on Form 1040, line 54, and enter "CFE" on the line next to that box. Attach Schedule R (Form 1040A or 1040) to your return.

What Is Permanent and Total Disability?

A person is permanently and totally disabled if both 1 and 2 below apply.

1. He or she cannot engage in any substantial gainful activity because of a physical or mental condition.

2. A qualified physician determines that the condition has lasted or can be expected to last continuously for at least a year or can lead to death.

Examples 1 and 2, next, show situations in which the individuals are considered engaged in a substantial gainful activity. Example 3 shows a person who might not be considered engaged in a substantial gainful activity. In each example, the person was under age 65 at the end of the year.

Income Limits for the Credit for the Elderly or the Disabled

| IF you are . . . | THEN you generally cannot take the credit if: | |
	The amount on Form 1040A, line 22, or Form 1040, line 38, is . . .	Or you received . . .
Single, head of household, or qualifying widow(er) with dependent child	$17,500 or more	$5,000 or more of nontaxable social security or other nontaxable pensions, annuities, or disability income
Married filing jointly and only one spouse is eligible for the credit	$20,000 or more	$5,000 or more of nontaxable social security or other nontaxable pensions, annuities, or disability income
Married filing jointly and both spouses are eligible for the credit	$25,000 or more	$7,500 or more of nontaxable social security or other nontaxable pensions, annuities, or disability income
Married filing separately and you lived apart from your spouse for all of 2014	$12,500 or more	$3,750 or more of nontaxable social security or other nontaxable pensions, annuities, or disability income

Example 1. Sue retired on disability as a sales clerk. She now works as a full-time babysitter earning minimum wage. Although she does different work, Sue babysits on ordinary terms for the minimum wage. She cannot take the credit because she is engaged in a substantial gainful activity.

Example 2. Mary, the president of XYZ Corporation, retired on disability because of her terminal illness. On her doctor's advice, she works part time as a manager and is paid more than the minimum wage. Her employer sets her days and hours. Although Mary's illness is terminal and she works part time, the work is done at her employer's convenience. Mary is considered engaged in a substantial gainful activity and cannot take the credit.

Example 3. John, who retired on disability, took a job with a former employer on a trial basis. The purpose of the job was to see if John could do the work. The trial period lasted for some time during which John was paid at a rate equal to the minimum wage. But because of John's disability, he was given only light duties of a nonproductive, make-work nature. Unless the activity is both substantial and gainful, John is not engaged in a substantial gainful activity. The activity was gainful because John was paid at a rate at or above the minimum wage. However, the activity was not substantial because the duties were of a nonproductive, make-work nature. More facts are needed to determine if John is able to engage in a substantial gainful activity.

Disability Income

Generally, disability income is the total amount you were paid under your employer's accident and health plan or pension plan that is included in your income as wages or payments instead of wages for the time you were absent from work because of permanent and total disability. However, any payment you re-ceived from a plan that does not provide for disability retirement is not disability income.

In figuring the credit, disability income does not include any amount you received from your employer's pension plan after you have reached mandatory retirement age.

For more details on disability income, see Pub. 525.

Part II. Statement of Permanent and Total Disability

If you checked box 2, 4, 5, 6, or 9 in Part I and you did not file a physician's statement for 1983 or an earlier year, or you filed or got a statement for tax years after 1983 and your physician signed on line A of the statement, you must have your physician complete a statement certifying that:
- You were permanently and totally disabled on the date you retired, or
- If you retired before 1977, you were permanently and totally disabled on January 1, 1976, or January 1, 1977.

You do not have to file this statement with your tax return. But you must keep it for your records. You can use the physician's statement later in these instructions for this purpose. Your physician should show on the statement if the disability has lasted or can be expected to last continuously for at least a year, or if there is no reasonable probability that the disabled condition will ever improve. If you file a joint return and you checked box 5 in Part I, you and your spouse must each get a statement.

If you filed a physician's statement for 1983 or an earlier year, or you filed or got a statement for tax years after 1983 and your physician signed on line B of the statement, you do not have to get another statement for 2014. But you must check the box on line 2 in Part II to certify all three of the following.

1. You filed or got a physician's statement in an earlier year.

2. You were permanently and totally disabled during 2014.

3. You were unable to engage in any substantial gainful activity during 2014 because of your physical or mental condition.

If you checked box 4, 5, or 6 in Part I, enter in the space above the box on line 2 in Part II the first name(s) of the spouse(s) for whom the box is checked.

If the Department of Veterans Affairs (VA) certifies that you are permanently and totally disabled, you can use VA Form 21-0172 instead of the physician's statement. VA Form 21-0172 must be signed by a person authorized by the VA to do so. You can get this form from your local VA regional office.

Part III. Figure Your Credit

Line 11

If you checked box 2, 4, 5, 6, or 9 in Part I, use the following chart to complete line 11.

IF you checked . . .	THEN enter on line 11 . . .
Box 6	The total of $5,000 plus the disability income you reported on Form 1040A or 1040 for the spouse who was under age 65.
Box 2, 4, or 9	The total amount of disability income you reported on Form 1040A or 1040.
Box 5	The total amount of disability income you reported on Form 1040A or 1040 for both you and your spouse.

Example 1. Bill, age 63, retired on permanent and total disability in 2014. He received $4,000 of taxable disability income that he reports on Form 1040, line 7. He is filing jointly with his wife who was age 67 in 2014, and he checked box 6 in Part I. On line 11, Bill enters $9,000 ($5,000 plus the $4,000 of disability income he reports on Form 1040, line 7).

Example 2. John checked box 2 in Part I and enters $5,000 on line 10. He received $3,000 of taxable disability income, which he enters on line 11. John also enters $3,000 on line 12 (the smaller of line 10 or line 11). The largest amount he can use to figure the credit is $3,000.

Lines 13a Through 18

The amount on which you figure your credit can be reduced if you received certain types of nontaxable pensions, annuities, or disability income. The amount can also be reduced if your adjusted gross income is over a certain amount, depending on which box you checked in Part I.

Line 13a. Enter any social security benefits (before deduction of Medicare premiums) you (and your spouse if filing jointly) received for 2014 that are not taxable. Also, enter any tier 1 railroad retirement benefits treated as social security that are not taxable.

If any of your social security or equivalent railroad retirement benefits are taxable, the amount to enter on this line is generally the difference between the amounts entered on Form 1040A, line 14a and line 14b, or Form 1040, line 20a and line 20b.

 If your social security or equivalent railroad retirement benefits are reduced because of workers' compensation benefits, treat the workers' compensation benefits as social security benefits when completing Schedule R (Form 1040A or 1040), line 13a.

Line 13b. Enter the total of the following types of income that you (and your spouse if filing jointly) received for 2014.
- Veterans' pensions (but not military disability pensions).
- Any other pension, annuity, or disability benefit that is excluded from income under any provision of federal law other than the Internal Revenue Code. Do not include amounts that are treated as a return of your cost of a pension or annuity.

Do not include on line 13b any pension, annuity, or similar allowance for personal injuries or sickness resulting from active service in the armed forces of any country, or in the National Oceanic and Atmospheric Administration or the Public Health Service. Also, do not include a disability annuity payable under section 808 of the Foreign Service Act of 1980.

Credit Limit Worksheet—Line 21

 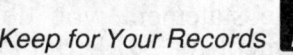

Use this worksheet to figure your credit limit.

1. Enter the amount from Form 1040A, line 30; or Form 1040, line 47 .... **1.** _____

2. Enter the amount from Form 1040A, line 31; or Form 1040, lines 48 and 49 .... **2.** _____

3. Subtract line 2 from line 1. Enter this amount on Schedule R (Form 1040A or 1040), line 21. But if zero or less, **STOP**, you cannot take this credit .... **3.** _____

Instructions for Physician's Statement

Taxpayer

If you retired after 1976, enter the date you retired in the space provided on the statement below.

Physician

A person is permanently and totally disabled if both of the following apply.

  1. He or she cannot engage in any substantial gainful activity because of a physical or mental condition.

  2. A physician determines that the disability has lasted or can be expected to last continuously for at least a year or can lead to death.

Physician's Statement

I certify that _____

Name of disabled person

was permanently and totally disabled on January 1, 1976, or January 1, 1977, or was permanently and totally disabled on the date he or she retired. If retired after 1976, enter the date retired. ▶

_____

Physician: Sign your name on either line A or B below.

A The disability has lasted or can be expected to last continuously for at least a year .... _____

                              Physician's signature   Date

B There is no reasonable probability that the disabled condition will ever improve .... _____

                              Physician's signature   Date

Physician's name   Physician's address

SCHEDULE 8812 (Form 1040A or 1040) Department of the Treasury Internal Revenue Service (99)	**Child Tax Credit** ► Attach to Form 1040, Form 1040A, or Form 1040NR. ► Information about Schedule 8812 and its separate instructions is at www.irs.gov/schedule8812.	OMB No. 1545-0074 20**14** Attachment Sequence No. 47

Name(s) shown on return | Your social security number

Part I   **Filers Who Have Certain Child Dependent(s) with an ITIN (Individual Taxpayer Identification Number)**

 Complete this part only for each dependent who has an ITIN and for whom you are claiming the child tax credit.
If your dependent is not a qualifying child for the credit, you cannot include that dependent in the calculation of this credit.

Answer the following questions for each dependent listed on Form 1040, line 6c; Form 1040A, line 6c; or Form 1040NR, line 7c, who has an ITIN (Individual Taxpayer Identification Number) and that you indicated is a qualifying child for the child tax credit by checking column (4) for that dependent.

A   For the first dependent identified with an ITIN and listed as a qualifying child for the child tax credit, did this child meet the substantial presence test? See separate instructions.

    ☐ Yes   ☐ No

B   For the second dependent identified with an ITIN and listed as a qualifying child for the child tax credit, did this child meet the substantial presence test? See separate instructions.

    ☐ Yes   ☐ No

C   For the third dependent identified with an ITIN and listed as a qualifying child for the child tax credit, did this child meet the substantial presence test? See separate instructions.

    ☐ Yes   ☐ No

D   For the fourth dependent identified with an ITIN and listed as a qualifying child for the child tax credit, did this child meet the substantial presence test? See separate instructions.

    ☐ Yes   ☐ No

Note. If you have more than four dependents identified with an ITIN and listed as a qualifying child for the child tax credit, see the instructions and check here . . . . ► ☐

Part II   **Additional Child Tax Credit Filers**

1   **1040 filers:**   Enter the amount from line 6 of your Child Tax Credit Worksheet (see the Instructions for Form 1040, line 52).

    1040A filers: Enter the amount from line 6 of your Child Tax Credit Worksheet (see the Instructions for Form 1040A, line 35).

    1040NR filers: Enter the amount from line 6 of your Child Tax Credit Worksheet (see the Instructions for Form 1040NR, line 49).

    If you used Pub. 972, enter the amount from line 8 of the Child Tax Credit Worksheet in the publication.   **1**

2   Enter the amount from Form 1040, line 52; Form 1040A, line 35; or Form 1040NR, line 49 . . . . .   **2**

3   Subtract line 2 from line 1. If zero, **stop;** you cannot take this credit **3**

4a   Earned income (see separate instructions) **4a**

  b   Nontaxable combat pay (see separate instructions) **4b**

5   Is the amount on line 4a more than $3,000?

    ☐ **No.**   Leave line 5 blank and enter -0- on line 6.

    ☐ **Yes.**   Subtract $3,000 from the amount on line 4a. Enter the result . . .   **5**

6   Multiply the amount on line 5 by 15% (.15) and enter the result **6**

    Next. Do you have three or more qualifying children?

    ☐ **No.**   If line 6 is zero, stop; you cannot take this credit. Otherwise, skip Part III and enter the **smaller** of line 3 or line 6 on line 13.

    ☐ **Yes.**   If line 6 is equal to or more than line 3, skip Part III and enter the amount from line 3 on line 13. Otherwise, go to line 7.

For Paperwork Reduction Act Notice, see your tax return instructions.   Cat. No. 59761M   Schedule 8812 (Form 1040A or 1040) 2014

Part III   Certain Filers Who Have Three or More Qualifying Children

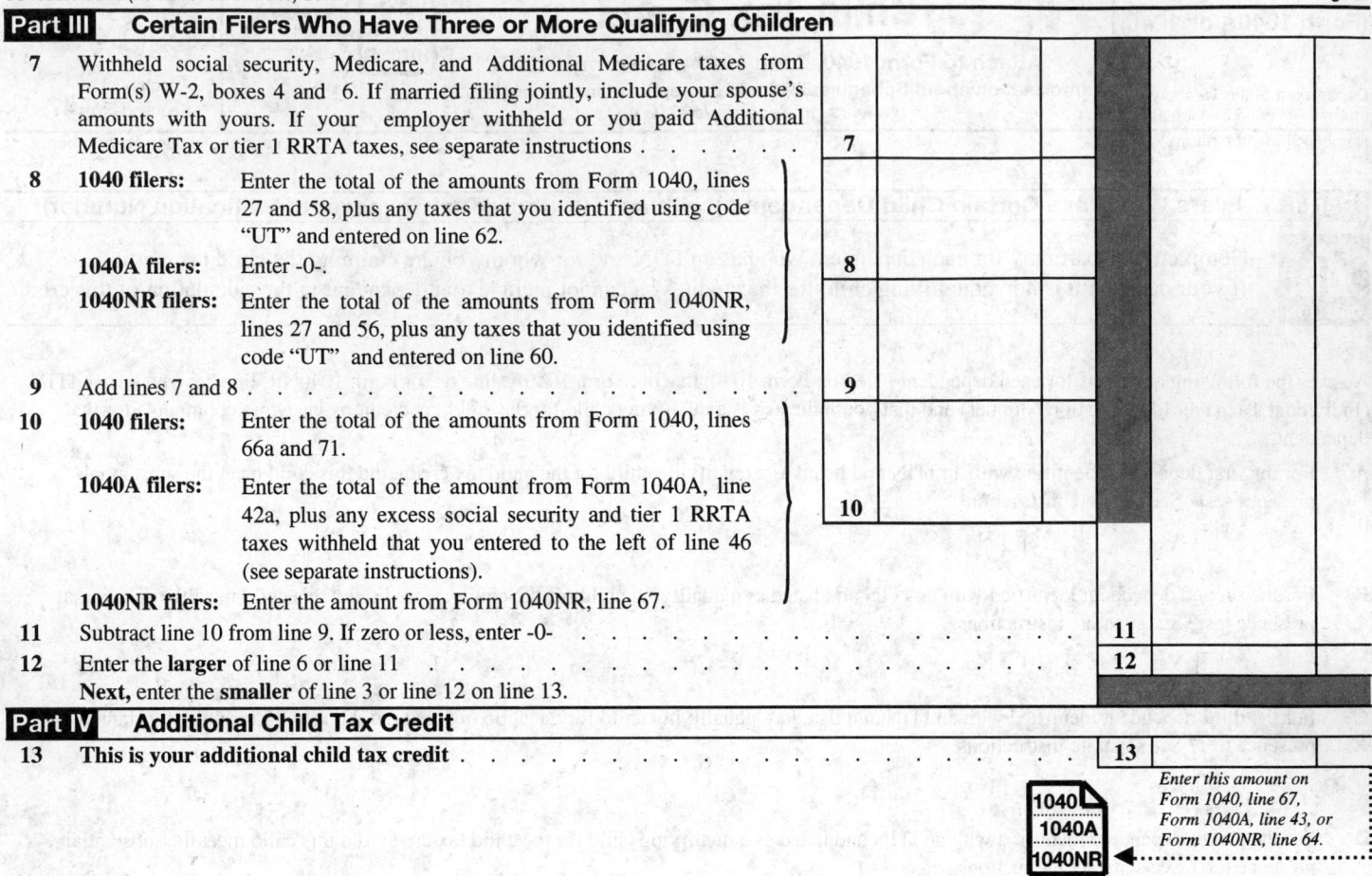

7 Withheld social security, Medicare, and Additional Medicare taxes from Form(s) W-2, boxes 4 and 6. If married filing jointly, include your spouse's amounts with yours. If your employer withheld or you paid Additional Medicare Tax or tier 1 RRTA taxes, see separate instructions	**7**
8 **1040 filers:** Enter the total of the amounts from Form 1040, lines 27 and 58, plus any taxes that you identified using code "UT" and entered on line 62.	
1040A filers: Enter -0-.	**8**
1040NR filers: Enter the total of the amounts from Form 1040NR, lines 27 and 56, plus any taxes that you identified using code "UT" and entered on line 60.	
9 Add lines 7 and 8	**9**
10 **1040 filers:** Enter the total of the amounts from Form 1040, lines 66a and 71.	
1040A filers: Enter the total of the amount from Form 1040A, line 42a, plus any excess social security and tier 1 RRTA taxes withheld that you entered to the left of line 46 (see separate instructions).	**10**
1040NR filers: Enter the amount from Form 1040NR, line 67.	
11 Subtract line 10 from line 9. If zero or less, enter -0-	**11**
12 Enter the **larger** of line 6 or line 11	**12**
Next, enter the **smaller** of line 3 or line 12 on line 13.	

Part IV   Additional Child Tax Credit

13 **This is your additional child tax credit**	**13**

1040
1040A
1040NR ◄

Enter this amount on Form 1040, line 67, Form 1040A, line 43, or Form 1040NR, line 64.

2014 Instructions for Schedule 8812

Child Tax Credit

Use Part I of Schedule 8812 to document that any child for whom you entered an ITIN on Form 1040, line 6c; Form 1040A, line 6c; or Form 1040NR, line 7c; and for whom you also checked the box in column 4 of that line, is a resident of the United States because the child meets the substantial presence test and is not otherwise treated as a nonresident alien.

Use Parts II–IV of Schedule 8812 to figure the additional child tax credit. The additional child tax credit may give you a refund even if you do not owe any tax.

Section references are to the Internal Revenue Code unless otherwise noted.

Future Developments

For the latest information about developments related to Schedule 8812 and its instructions, such as legislation enacted after they were published, go to *www.irs.gov/schedule8812*.

General Instructions

Who Should Use Part I

You only need to complete Part I if you are claiming the child tax credit for a child identified by an IRS individual taxpayer identification number (ITIN). When completing Part I, only answer the questions with regard to children identified by an ITIN; you do not need to complete Part I of Schedule 8812 for any child that is identified by a social security number (SSN) or an IRS adoption taxpayer identification number (ATIN).

If all the children for whom you checked the box in column 4 of line 6c on your Form 1040 or Form 1040A or column 4 of line 7c on your Form 1040NR are identified by an SSN or an ATIN, you do not need to complete Part I of Schedule 8812.

Who Should Use Parts II–IV

Parts II–IV are unrelated to Part I. Parts II–IV help you figure your additional child tax credit. Generally, you should only complete Parts II–IV if you are instructed to do so after completing the Child Tax Credit Worksheet in your tax return instructions or Pub. 972.

If all your children are identified by an SSN or an ATIN and you are not claiming the additional child tax credit, you do not need to complete any part of Schedule 8812.

Substantial Presence Test (Part I)

In general, to be a qualifying child for purposes of the child tax credit and additional child tax credit, the child must be a citizen, national, or resident of the United States. Use Part I of Schedule 8812 to document that any child for whom an IRS Individual Taxpayer Identification Number (ITIN) was entered on Form 1040, line 6c; Form 1040A, line 6c; or Form 1040NR, line 7c; and for whom the box in column 4 of that line was also checked, meets the substantial presence test and is not otherwise treated as a nonresident alien.

Note. A child who is a lawful permanent resident of the United States is eligible to obtain a social security number (SSN). Use an SSN to identify the child even if you obtained an ITIN for the child before the child became a lawful permanent resident.

To meet the substantial presence test, a child identified with an ITIN generally must be physically present in the United States on at least:

1. 31 days during 2014, and

2. 183 days during the 3-year period that includes 2014, 2013, and 2012, counting:

   a. All the days your child was present in 2014, and

   b. 1/3 of the days your child was present in 2013, and

   c. 1/6 of the days your child was present in 2012.

Not all days that your dependent is physically present in the United States count as days of presence for the substantial presence test. See Days of Presence in the United States *in Pub. 519.*

A child who is present in the United States for less than one-half of 2014 also must not have a closer connection to a foreign country. See Pub. 519 for more information. Also, see the chart, *Is Your Dependent (Identified by an ITIN) Considered a Resident of the United States Under the Substantial Presence Test*, later.

Additional Child Tax Credit (Parts II–IV)

If any of your dependents is a qualifying child for purposes of the child tax credit (whether identified by an ITIN or not), you may qualify for the additional child tax credit. Before completing Parts II–IV of Schedule 8812, complete the Child Tax Credit Worksheet that applies to you. See the instructions for Form 1040, line 52; Form 1040A, line 35; or Form 1040NR, line 49. If you meet the condition given in the TIP at the end of the Child Tax Credit Worksheet, complete Parts II–IV of this schedule to figure the amount of any additional child tax credit you can claim.

Effect of Credit on Welfare Benefits

Any refund you receive as a result of taking the additional child tax credit cannot be counted as income when determining if you or anyone else is eligible for benefits or assistance, or how much you or anyone else can receive, under any federal program or under any state or local program financed in whole or in part with federal funds. These programs include Temporary Assistance for Needy Families (TANF), Medicaid, Supplemental Security Income (SSI), and Supplemental

Oct 01, 2014

Cat. No. 59790P

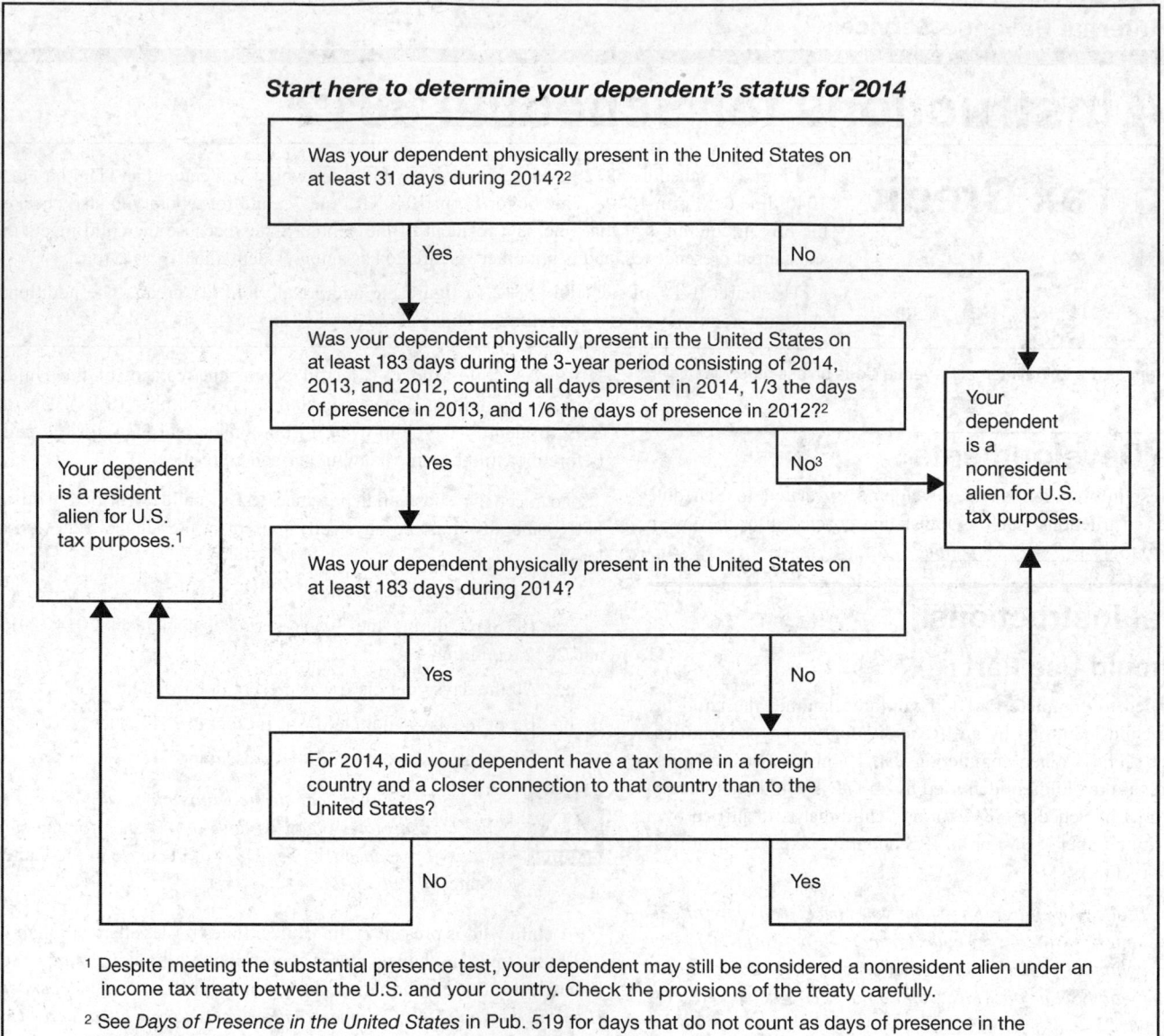

Start here to determine your dependent's status for 2014

Was your dependent physically present in the United States on at least 31 days during 2014?[2]

— Yes → Was your dependent physically present in the United States on at least 183 days during the 3-year period consisting of 2014, 2013, and 2012, counting all days present in 2014, 1/3 the days of presence in 2013, and 1/6 the days of presence in 2012?[2]

— No → Your dependent is a nonresident alien for U.S. tax purposes.

Was your dependent physically present in the United States on at least 183 days during the 3-year period... — Yes → Was your dependent physically present in the United States on at least 183 days during 2014?

— No[3] → Your dependent is a nonresident alien for U.S. tax purposes.

Was your dependent physically present in the United States on at least 183 days during 2014? — Yes → Your dependent is a resident alien for U.S. tax purposes.[1]

— No → For 2014, did your dependent have a tax home in a foreign country and a closer connection to that country than to the United States?

For 2014, did your dependent have a tax home... — No → Your dependent is a resident alien for U.S. tax purposes.[1]

— Yes → Your dependent is a nonresident alien for U.S. tax purposes.

[1] Despite meeting the substantial presence test, your dependent may still be considered a nonresident alien under an income tax treaty between the U.S. and your country. Check the provisions of the treaty carefully.

[2] See *Days of Presence in the United States* in Pub. 519 for days that do not count as days of presence in the United States.

[3] If your dependent was present in the United States for at least 31 consecutive days in 2014 and meets the substantial presence test for 2015, see *First-Year Choice* under *Dual Status Aliens* in Pub. 519 to determine if your dependent may be considered to be a resident of the United States for part of 2014 under this rule. An individual may make an election for a child who is a dependent if the individual may make the election on his or her own behalf, the child qualifies to make the election, and the child is not required to file a United States income tax return for the year for which the election is effective.

Nutrition Assistance Program (food stamps). In addition, when determining eligibility, the refund cannot be counted as a resource for at least 12 months after you receive it. Check with your local benefits coordinator to find out if your refund will affect your benefits.

Specific Instructions

Part I

Lines A through D. If you identified any of your dependents using an ITIN on your Form 1040, line 6c; Form 1040A, line 6c; or Form 1040NR, line 7c; and you also checked the box in column (4) of that line for that dependent, you must determine if that dependent meets the substantial presence test and is not otherwise treated as a nonresident alien. Complete Line A for the first dependent listed on your Form 1040, line 6c; Form 1040A, line 6c; or Form 1040NR, line 7c, who has an ITIN and that you indicated qualified for the child tax credit by checking the box in column (4). Use a separate line for each additional child identified by an ITIN for whom you checked the box in column (4).

Do not complete a line in Part I for a child if:

• You identified that child with an SSN or ATIN on the tax return, or

• You did not check the box in column 4 of line 6c on your Form 1040 or Form 1040A, or line 7c of your Form 1040NR.

If you only check "No" on any line in Part I, your child tax credit or additional child tax credit may be reduced or eliminated.

Child otherwise treated as a nonresident alien. Even if your child meets the substantial presence test, your child may still be treated as a nonresident alien due to a tax treaty or because the child has a closer connection to another country. See Pub. 519 for more details.

If you must complete Part I for a child and that child meets the substantial presence test, but is still treated as a nonresident alien, check the "No" box for that child.

Special circumstances. Even if your child does not meet the substantial presence test, your child may meet an exception or be treated as a resident of the United States in certain circumstances. If your child does not meet the substantial presence test, but one of the following special circumstances applies, check both the "Yes" and "No" boxes for that child.

- First-year election. If your child was present in the United States for at least 31 consecutive days in 2014 and meets the substantial presence test for 2015, your child may be considered a resident of the United States for part of 2014 if you make a valid election. See *First-Year Choice* under *Dual Status Aliens* in Pub. 519.

- Child adopted by U.S. citizen or national. A child legally adopted by you or lawfully placed with you for legal adoption is not required to meet the substantial presence test if you are a citizen or national of the United States, and, for your entire tax year, the child has the same main home as you and is a member of your household.

More than four children. If you must complete Part I for more than four children, check the box following Line D. Use page 1 of another Schedule 8812 and reletter Lines A–D in Part I as E–H. Complete the additional Part I of Schedule 8812 and attach it to your Schedule 8812.

Parts II through IV

Line 4a — Earned Income Chart. Use the chart, later, to determine the amount to enter on line 4a.

Line 4b — Nontaxable Combat Pay. Enter on line 4b the total amount of nontaxable combat pay that you, and your spouse if filing jointly, received in 2014. This amount should be shown in Form W-2, box 12, with code Q.

Line 7 — Additional Medicare Tax and Tier 1 RRTA Tax. Use the Line 7 Worksheet to figure the amount to enter on line 7 if your

Earned Income Chart — Line 4a

IF you...	AND you...	THEN enter on line 4a...
have net earnings from self-employment	use either optional method to figure those net earnings,	the amount figured using the *1040 and 1040NR Filers — Earned Income Worksheet* in Pub. 972 (even if you are also taking the EIC).
are taking the EIC on Form 1040, line 66a, or Form 1040A, line 42a,	completed Worksheet B of the EIC instructions in your Form 1040 instructions,	your earned income from Worksheet B, line 4b, plus all of your nontaxable combat pay if you did not elect to include it in earned income for the EIC. If you were a member of the clergy, subtract (a) the rental value of a home or the nontaxable portion of an allowance for a home furnished to you (including payments for utilities), and (b) the value of meals and lodging provided to you, your spouse, and your dependents for your employer's convenience.
	did not complete Worksheet B or filed Form 1040A,	your earned income from Step 5 of the EIC instructions in your tax return instructions, plus all of your nontaxable combat pay if you did not elect to include it in earned income for the EIC.
are not taking the EIC	were self-employed, or you are filing Schedule SE because you were a member of the clergy or you had church employee income, or you are filing Schedule C or C-EZ as a statutory employee,	the amount figured using the *1040 and 1040NR Filers — Earned Income Worksheet* in Pub. 972.
	are not self-employed or filing Schedule SE, C, or C-EZ for the above reasons,	your earned income figured as follows: Line 7 of Form 1040 or Form 1040A, or line 8 of Form 1040NR. **Subtract**, if included on line 7 (line 8 for Form 1040NR), any: • Taxable scholarship or fellowship grant not reported on a Form W-2. • Amount received for work performed while an inmate in a penal institution (put "PRI" and the amount subtracted in the space next to line 7 of Form 1040 or 1040A (line 8 for Form 1040NR)). • Amount received as a pension or annuity from a nonqualified deferred compensation plan or a nongovernmental section 457 plan (put "DFC" and the amount subtracted in the space next to line 7 of Form 1040 or Form 1040A (line 8 for Form 1040NR)). This amount may be shown in box 11 of your Form W-2. If you received such an amount but box 11 is blank, contact your employer for the amount received as a pension or annuity. • Amount from Form 2555, line 43, or Form 2555-EZ, line 18. • Medicaid waiver payment you excluded from income (see instructions for Form 1040, line 21, and Pub. 525 for information about these payments). **Add** all your nontaxable combat pay from Form(s) W-2, box 12, with code Q. Earned Income =

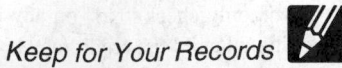

If your employer withheld or you paid Additional Medicare Tax or Tier 1 RRTA taxes, use this worksheet to figure the amount to enter on line 7.		

Social security tax, Medicare tax, and Additional Medicare Tax on Wages.

1. Enter the social security tax withheld (Form(s) W-2, box 4) .... **1.** _____

2. Enter the Medicare tax withheld (Form(s) W-2, box 6). Box 6 includes any Additional Medicare Tax withheld .... **2.** _____

3. Enter any amount from Form 8959, line 7 .... **3.** _____

4. Add lines 1, 2, and 3 .... **4.** _____

5. Enter the Additional Medicare Tax withheld (Form 8959, line 22) .... **5.** _____

6. Subtract line 5 from line 4 .... **6.** _____

Additional Medicare Tax on Self-Employment Income.

7. Enter one-half of the Additional Medicare Tax, if any, on self-employment income (one-half of Form 8959, line 13) .... **7.** _____

Tier 1 RRTA taxes as an employee of a railroad (enter amounts on lines 8, 9, 10, and 11) **or employee representative** (enter amounts on lines 12, 13, 14, and 15). Do not include amounts in Form W-2, box 14 that are identified as Additional Medicare Tax or Tier 2 tax. Do not include amounts shown on Form CT-2 on line 3 for Additional Medicare Tax or line 4 for Tier 2 tax.

8. Enter the Tier 1 tax (Form(s) W-2, box 14) .... **8.** _____

9. Enter the Medicare Tax (Form(s) W-2, box 14) .... **9.** _____

10. Enter the Additional Medicare Tax, if any, on RRTA compensation as an employee (Form 8959, line 17). Do not use the same amount from Form 8959, line 17 for both this line 10 and line 14 .... **10.** _____

11. Add lines 8, 9, and 10 .... **11.** _____

12. Enter one-half of Tier 1 tax (one-half of Forms CT-2, line 1 for all 4 quarters of 2014) .... **12.** _____

13. Enter one-half of Tier 1 Medicare tax (one-half of Forms CT-2, line 2 for all 4 quarters of 2014) .... **13.** _____

14. Enter one-half of the Additional Medicare Tax, if any, on RRTA compensation as an employee representative (one-half of Form 8959, line 17). Do not use the same amount from Form 8959, line 17 for both this line 14 and line 10 .... **14.** _____

15. Add lines 12, 13, and 14 .... **15.** _____

Line 7 Amount

16. Add lines 6, 7, 11, and 15. Enter here and on Schedule 8812, line 7 .... **16.** _____

employer withheld or you paid Additional Medicare Tax or tier 1 RRTA tax.

Line 10 — 1040A Filers. If you, or your spouse if filing jointly, had more than one employer for 2014 and total wages of over $117,000,

figure any excess social security and tier 1 RRTA taxes withheld. See Pub. 505. Include any excess on Schedule 8812, line 10.

Form **1040EZ**

Department of the Treasury—Internal Revenue Service

Income Tax Return for Single and Joint Filers With No Dependents (99) **2014**

OMB No. 1545-0074

Your first name and initial | Last name

Your social security number

If a joint return, spouse's first name and initial | Last name

Spouse's social security number

Home address (number and street). If you have a P.O. box, see instructions. | Apt. no.

▲ Make sure the SSN(s) above are correct.

City, town or post office, state, and ZIP code. If you have a foreign address, also complete spaces below (see instructions).

Presidential Election Campaign
Check here if you, or your spouse if filing jointly, want $3 to go to this fund. Checking a box below will not change your tax or refund. ☐ You ☐ Spouse

Foreign country name | Foreign province/state/county | Foreign postal code

Income

Attach Form(s) W-2 here.

Enclose, but do not attach, any payment.

1. Wages, salaries, and tips. This should be shown in box 1 of your Form(s) W-2. Attach your Form(s) W-2. ... **1**

2. Taxable interest. If the total is over $1,500, you cannot use Form 1040EZ. ... **2**

3. Unemployment compensation and Alaska Permanent Fund dividends (see instructions). ... **3**

4. Add lines 1, 2, and 3. This is your **adjusted gross income.** ... **4**

5. If someone can claim you (or your spouse if a joint return) as a dependent, check the applicable box(es) below and enter the amount from the worksheet on back.

   ☐ You ☐ Spouse

   If no one can claim you (or your spouse if a joint return), enter $10,150 if **single**; $20,300 if **married filing jointly.** See back for explanation. ... **5**

6. Subtract line 5 from line 4. If line 5 is larger than line 4, enter -0-. This is your **taxable income.** ▶ **6**

Payments, Credits, and Tax

7. Federal income tax withheld from Form(s) W-2 and 1099. ... **7**

8a. Earned Income credit (EIC) (see instructions) ... **8a**

   b. Nontaxable combat pay election. **8b**

9. Add lines 7 and 8a. These are your **total payments and credits.** ▶ **9**

10. **Tax.** Use the amount on **line 6 above** to find your tax in the tax table in the instructions. Then, enter the tax from the table on this line. ... **10**

11. Health care: individual responsibility (see instructions) Full-year coverage ☐ **11**

12. Add lines 10 and 11. This is your **total tax.** ... **12**

Refund

Have it directly deposited! See instructions and fill in 13b, 13c, and 13d, or Form 8888.

13a. If line 9 is larger than line 12, subtract line 12 from line 9. This is your **refund.** If Form 8888 is attached, check here ▶ ☐ ... **13a**

   ▶ b. Routing number | ▶ c Type: ☐ Checking ☐ Savings

   ▶ d. Account number

Amount You Owe

14. If line 12 is larger than line 9, subtract line 9 from line 12. This is the **amount you owe.** For details on how to pay, see instructions. ▶ **14**

Third Party Designee

Do you want to allow another person to discuss this return with the IRS (see instructions)? ☐ **Yes.** Complete below. ☐ **No**

Designee's name ▶ | Phone no. ▶ | Personal identification number (PIN) ▶

Sign Here

Joint return? See instructions.

Keep a copy for your records.

Under penalties of perjury, I declare that I have examined this return and, to the best of my knowledge and belief, it is true, correct, and accurately lists all amounts and sources of income I received during the tax year. Declaration of preparer (other than the taxpayer) is based on all information of which the preparer has any knowledge.

Your signature | Date | Your occupation | Daytime phone number

Spouse's signature. If a joint return, **both** must sign. | Date | Spouse's occupation | If the IRS sent you an Identity Protection PIN, enter it here (see inst.)

Paid Preparer Use Only

Print/Type preparer's name | Preparer's signature | Date | Check ☐ if self-employed | PTIN

Firm's name ▶ | Firm's EIN ▶

Firm's address ▶ | Phone no.

For Disclosure, Privacy Act, and Paperwork Reduction Act Notice, see instructions. Cat. No. 11329W Form **1040EZ** (2014)

Use this form if

- Your filing status is single or married filing jointly. If you are not sure about your filing status, see instructions.
- You (and your spouse if married filing jointly) were under age 65 and not blind at the end of 2014. If you were born on January 1, 1950, you are considered to be age 65 at the end of 2014.
- You do not claim any dependents. For information on dependents, see Pub. 501.
- Your taxable income (line 6) is less than $100,000.
- You do not claim any adjustments to income. For information on adjustments to income, use the TeleTax topics listed under *Adjustments to Income* at *www.irs.gov/taxtopics* (see instructions).
- The only tax credit you can claim is the earned income credit (EIC). The credit may give you a refund even if you do not owe any tax. You do not need a qualifying child to claim the EIC. For information on credits, use the TeleTax topics listed under *Tax Credits* at *www.irs.gov/taxtopics* (see instructions). If you received a Form 1098-T or paid higher education expenses, you may be eligible for a tax credit or deduction that you must claim on Form 1040A or Form 1040. For more information on tax benefits for education, see Pub. 970. If you can claim the premium tax credit or you received any advance payment of the premium tax credit in 2014, you must use Form 1040A or Form 1040.
- You had only wages, salaries, tips, taxable scholarship or fellowship grants, unemployment compensation, or Alaska Permanent Fund dividends, and your taxable interest was not over $1,500. But if you earned tips, including allocated tips, that are not included in box 5 and box 7 of your Form W-2, you may not be able to use Form 1040EZ (see instructions). If you are planning to use Form 1040EZ for a child who received Alaska Permanent Fund dividends, see instructions.

Filling in your return

If you received a scholarship or fellowship grant or tax-exempt interest income, such as on municipal bonds, see the instructions before filling in the form. Also, see the instructions if you received a Form 1099-INT showing federal income tax withheld or if federal income tax was withheld from your unemployment compensation or Alaska Permanent Fund dividends.

For tips on how to avoid common mistakes, see instructions.

Remember, you must report all wages, salaries, and tips even if you do not get a Form W-2 from your employer. You must also report all your taxable interest, including interest from banks, savings and loans, credit unions, etc., even if you do not get a Form 1099-INT.

Worksheet for Line 5 — Dependents Who Checked One or Both Boxes

Use this worksheet to figure the amount to enter on line 5 if someone can claim you (or your spouse if married filing jointly) as a dependent, even if that person chooses not to do so. To find out if someone can claim you as a dependent, see Pub. 501.

A. Amount, if any, from line 1 on front . . . . . .   + _____ 350.00 Enter total ▶   A. _____

B. Minimum standard deduction . . . .   B. _____ 1,000

C. Enter the **larger** of line A or line B here . . . .   C. _____

D. Maximum standard deduction. If **single,** enter $6,200; if **married filing jointly,** enter $12,400 .   D. _____

E. Enter the **smaller** of line C or line D here. This is your standard deduction . . . .   E. _____

F. Exemption amount.
  - If single, enter -0-.
  - If married filing jointly and —
    —both you and your spouse can be claimed as dependents, enter -0-.
    —only one of you can be claimed as a dependent, enter $3,950.   F. _____

G. Add lines E and F. Enter the total here and on line 5 on the front . . . .   G. _____

(keep a copy for your records)

If you did not check any boxes on line 5, enter on line 5 the amount shown below that applies to you.
- Single, enter $10,150. This is the total of your standard deduction ($6,200) and your exemption ($3,950).
- Married filing jointly, enter $20,300. This is the total of your standard deduction ($12,400), your exemption ($3,950), and your spouse's exemption ($3,950).

Mailing Return

Mail your return by **April 15, 2015.** Mail it to the address shown on the last page of the instructions.

1040EZ

INSTRUCTIONS 2014

 makes doing your taxes faster and easier.

 is the fast, safe, and free way to prepare and *e-file* your taxes.
See *www.irs.gov/freefile*.

Get a faster refund, reduce errors, and save paper. For more information on **IRS** *e-file* and Free File, see Options for *e-filing* your returns in these instructions or click on **IRS** *e-file* at IRS.gov.

2014 TAX CHANGES

See *What's New* in these instructions.

FUTURE DEVELOPMENTS

For the latest information about developments related to Form 1040EZ and its instructions, such as legislation enacted after they were published, go to *www.irs.gov/form1040ez*.

Department of the Treasury **Internal Revenue Service** IRS.gov

Dec 17, 2014 Cat. No. 12063Z

Table of Contents

Department of the Treasury

Internal Revenue Service

Introduction

About These Instructions

We have designed the instructions to make it as simple and clear as possible to file your tax return. We did this by arranging the instructions for Form 1040EZ preparation in the most helpful order.

- "Section 2—Filing Requirements" helps you decide if you even have to file.
- "Section 3—Line Instructions for Form 1040EZ" follows the main sections of the form, starting with "Top of the Form" and ending with "Signing Your Return." Cut-outs from the form connect the instructions visually to the form.
- "Section 4—After You Have Finished" gives you a checklist for completing a return. It also gives you information about filing the return.
- "Section 6—How To Get Tax Help" has topics such as how to get tax help, forms, instructions, and publications. It also gives you other useful information, such as how to check the status of a refund.

Helpful Hints

Future Developments. For the latest information about developments related to Form 1040EZ and its instructions, such as legislation enacted after they were published, go to *www.irs.gov/form1040ez*.

Filing status. We want you to use the proper filing status as you go through the instructions and tables. You can use Form 1040EZ to file as "Single" or "Married filing jointly."

If you qualify for another filing status, such as "Head of household" or "Qualifying widow(er) with dependent child," you may be able to lower your taxes by using Form 1040A or 1040 instead. See Pub. 501, Exemptions, Standard Deduction, and Filing Information, for more information.

Icons. We use icons throughout the booklet to draw your attention to special information. Here are some key icons:

 **IRS e-file.** This alerts you to many online benefits, particularly electronic tax filing, available to you at IRS.gov.

 Tip. This lets you know about possible tax benefits, helpful actions to take, or sources for additional information.

 Caution. This tells you about special rules, possible consequences to actions, and areas where you need to take special care to make correct entries.

Writing in information. Sometimes we will ask you to make an entry "in the space to the left of line . . ." The following example (using line 1) will help you make the proper entry:

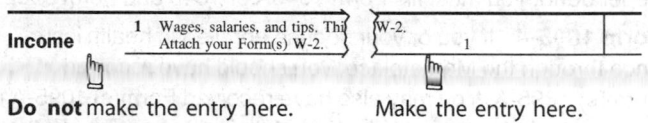

Do **not** make the entry here.   Make the entry here.

Section 1—Before You Begin

Even if you can use Form 1040EZ, it may benefit you to use Form 1040A or 1040 instead. See *Should You Use Another Form* in Section 2, later.

What's New

Health care: individual responsibility. You must either:

- Indicate on line 11 that you, your spouse (if filing jointly), and any individual you could claim as a dependent had health care coverage throughout 2014,
- Claim a coverage exemption from the health care coverage requirement for some or all of 2014 and attach Form 8965, or
- Make a shared responsibility payment if, for any month in 2014, you, your spouse (if filing jointly), or any individual you could claim as a dependent did not have coverage and do not qualify for a coverage exemption.

See the instructions for line 11 and Form 8965 for more information.

Earned income credit (EIC). You may be able to take the EIC if you earned less than $14,590 ($20,020 if married filing jointly).

See *Lines 8a and 8b, Earned Income Credit (EIC)* in Section 3, later.

Medicare waiver payments. If you received certain payments under a Medicaid waiver program for caring for someone who lives in your home with you, you may be able to exclude these payments from your income.

If you reported these payments on your return for 2013 or an earlier year, see *http://www.irs.gov/Individuals/Certain-Medicaid-Waiver-Payments-May-Be-Excludable-From-Income*. You may want to file Form 1040X to amend that prior year return.

Mailing your return. If you live in Missouri and need to make a payment with your paper return, you will need to mail it to a different address this year. See *Where Do You File?* at the end of these instructions.

Direct Deposit. To combat fraud and identity theft, the number of refunds that can be directly deposited to a single financial account or prepaid debit card is now limited to three a year. After this limit is exceeded, paper checks will be sent instead.

Direct pay. The best way to pay your taxes is with IRS Direct Pay. It's the safe, easy, and free way to pay from your checking or savings account in one online session. Just click on "Pay Your Tax Bill" on IRS.gov.

You May Benefit From Filing Form 1040A or 1040 in 2014

Due to the following tax law changes for 2014, you may benefit from filing Form 1040A or 1040, even if you normally file Form 1040EZ. See the instructions for Form 1040A or 1040, as applicable.

Premium tax credit. You may be eligible to claim the premium tax credit if you or your spouse enrolled in health insurance through the Health Insurance Marketplace, but you must use Form 1040A or 1040 to do so. You may also be eligible to claim the premium tax credit for any dependent you claim on Form 1040A or 1040 who enrolled in health insurance through the Health Insurance Marketplace.

Advance payments of the premium tax credit. Advance payments of the premium tax credit may have been made to the health insurer to help pay for the insurance coverage for you or your spouse. If advance payments of the premium tax credit were made, you must file a 2014 Form 1040A or 1040 and Form 8962. If you enrolled another individual in insurance coverage, advance payments of the premium tax credit were made for that individual, and no one else is claiming the personal exemption for that individual (for example, by claiming the individual as a dependent), you must file Form 1040A or 1040 and Form 8962.

Form 1095-A. If you or your spouse enrolled in health insurance through the Marketplace, you should have received Form(s) 1095-A. You may also have received Form(s) 1095-A if you enrolled another individual in health insurance through the Marketplace. If you received Form(s) 1095-A for 2014 for yourself, your spouse, or an individual you plan to claim as a dependent, file Form 1040A or 1040. Save any Form 1095-A you receive. It will help you figure your premium tax credit. If you received a Form 1095-A for an individual you do not claim as a dependent, you should provide a copy to the taxpayer who is claiming the personal exemption for that individual (for example, by claiming the individual as a dependent). If you did not receive a Form 1095-A, contact the Marketplace.

Earned income credit (EIC) if children lived with you. The maximum adjusted gross income (AGI) you can have and still claim the EIC has increased. You may be able to claim the credit if your AGI is less than the amount below that applies to you. The maximum investment income you can have and still claim the credit is $3,350.

You may be able to claim a larger EIC using Form 1040A or 1040 if:
- Three or more children lived with you and you earned less than $46,997 ($52,427 if married filing jointly),
- Two children lived with you and you earned less than $43,756 ($49,186 if married filing jointly), or
- One child lived with you and you earned less than $38,511 ($43,941 if married filing jointly).

Death of a Taxpayer

If a taxpayer died before filing a return for 2014, the taxpayer's spouse or personal representative may have to file and sign a return for that taxpayer. A personal representative can be an executor, administrator, or anyone who is in charge of the deceased taxpayer's property. If the deceased taxpayer did not have to file a return but had tax withheld, a return must be filed to get a refund. The person who files the return must enter "Deceased," the deceased taxpayer's name, and the date of death across the top of the return. If this information is not provided, it may delay the processing of the return.

You can file a joint return even if your spouse died in 2014 as long as you did not remarry in 2014. You can also file a joint return even if your spouse died in 2015 before filing a return for 2014. A joint return should show your spouse's 2014 income before death and your income for all of 2014. Enter "Filing as surviving spouse" in the area where you sign the return. If someone else is the personal representative, he or she also must sign.

The surviving spouse or personal representative should promptly notify all payers of income, including financial institutions, of the taxpayer's death. This will ensure the proper reporting of income earned by the taxpayer's estate or heirs. A deceased taxpayer's social security number should not be used for tax years after the year of death, except for estate tax return purposes.

Claiming a refund for a deceased taxpayer. If you are filing a joint return as a surviving spouse, you only need to file the tax return to claim the refund. If you are a court-appointed representative, file the return and include a copy of the certificate that shows your appointment. All other filers requesting the deceased taxpayer's refund must file the return and attach Form 1310.

For more details, use TeleTax topic 356 or see Pub. 559.

Foreign Financial Assets

If you had foreign financial assets in 2014, you may have to file Form 8938 with your return. If you have to file Form 8938, you must use Form 1040. You cannot use Form 1040EZ. For more information about foreign financial assets and the requirements for filing Form 8938, see the Instructions for Form 8938.

Parent of a Kidnapped Child

If your child is presumed by law enforcement authorities to have been kidnapped by someone who is not a family member, you may be able to take the child into account in determining your eligibility for the head of household or qualifying widow(er) filing status, the dependency exemption, the child tax credit, and the earned income credit (EIC). But you have to file Form 1040A or 1040 to claim these benefits. For details, see Pub. 501 (Pub. 596 for the EIC).

Section 2—Filing Requirements

These rules apply to all U.S. citizens, regardless of where they live, and resident aliens.

 Have you tried IRS *e-file*? It's the fastest way to get your refund and it's free if you are eligible. Visit IRS.gov for details.

Do You Have To File?

Were you (or your spouse if filing a joint return) age 65 or older at the end of 2014? If you were born on January 1, 1950, you are considered to be age 65 at the end of 2014.

☐ **Yes.** Use Pub. 501 to see if you must file a return. If so, use Form 1040A or 1040.

☐ **No.** Use the Filing Requirement Charts, later in this Section 2, to see if you must file a return. See the *Tip* next if you have earned income.

 Even if you do not have to file a return, you should file one to get a refund of any federal income tax withheld. You also should file if you are eligible for the earned income credit.

Death of taxpayer in 2014. If you are preparing a return for someone who died in 2014, use the Filing Requirement Charts, later in this section, only if the person died at least 2 days before his or her 65th birthday. Otherwise, use Pub. 501 to see if you must file a return.

Exception for certain children under age 19 or full-time students. If certain conditions apply, you can elect to include on your return the income of a child who was under age 19 at the end of 2014 or was a full-time student under age 24 at the end of 2014. To do so, use Forms 1040 and 8814. If you make this election, your child does not have to file a return. For details, use TeleTax topic 553 or see Form 8814.

A child born on January 1, 1991, is considered to be age 24 at the end of 2014. Do not use Form 8814 for such a child.

Resident aliens. These rules also apply if you were a resident alien. Also, you may qualify for certain tax treaty benefits. See Pub. 519 for details.

Nonresident aliens and dual-status aliens. These rules also apply if you were a nonresident alien or a dual-status alien and both of the following apply.

- You were married to a U.S. citizen or resident alien at the end of 2014.
- You elected to be taxed as a resident alien.

See Pub. 519 for details.

 Specific rules apply to determine if you are a resident alien, nonresident alien, or dual-status alien. Most nonresident aliens and dual-status aliens have different filing requirements and may have to file Form 1040NR or 1040NR-EZ. Pub. 519 discusses these requirements and other information to help aliens comply with U.S. tax law.

When Should You File?

File Form 1040EZ by **April 15, 2015**. If you file after this date, you may have to pay interest and penalties. See *What if You Cannot File on Time?* in Section 4, later, for information on how to get more time to file. There is also information about interest and penalties.

If you were serving in, or in support of, the U.S. Armed Forces in a designated combat zone or contingency operation, you may be able to file later. See Pub. 3 for details.

Checklist for Using Form 1040EZ

You can use Form 1040EZ if **all** the items in the following checklist apply.

☐ Your filing status is single or married filing jointly. If you were a nonresident alien at any time in 2014, see *Nonresident aliens* below.

☐ You do not claim any dependents.

☐ You do not claim any adjustments to income. See the TeleTax topics for *Adjustments to Income* at *www.irs.gov/taxtopics*.

☐ If you claim a tax credit, you claim only the earned income credit. See the TeleTax topics for *Tax Credits* at *www.irs.gov/taxtopics*.

☐ You (and your spouse if filing a joint return) were under age 65 and not blind at the end of 2014. If you were born on January 1, 1950, you are considered to be age 65 at the end of 2014 and cannot use Form 1040EZ.

☐ Your taxable income (line 6 of Form 1040EZ) is less than $100,000.

☐ You had only wages, salaries, tips, taxable scholarship or fellowship grants, unemployment compensation, or Alaska Permanent Fund dividends, and your taxable interest was not over $1,500.

☐ If you earned tips, they are included in boxes 5 and 7 of your Form W-2.

☐ You do not owe any household employment taxes on wages you paid to a household employee. To find out who owes these taxes, use TeleTax topic 756.

☐ You are not a debtor in a chapter 11 bankruptcy case filed after October 16, 2005.

☐ Advance payments of the premium tax credit were not made for you, your spouse, or any individual you enrolled in coverage for whom no one else is claiming the personal exemption.

If you do not meet all of the requirements, you must use Form 1040A or 1040. Use TeleTax topic 352 to find out which form to use.

Nonresident aliens. If you were a nonresident alien at any time in 2014, your filing status must be married filing jointly to use Form 1040EZ. If your filing status is not married filing jointly, you may have to use Form 1040NR or 1040NR-EZ. Specific rules apply to determine if you were a nonresident or resident alien. See Pub. 519 for details, including the rules for students and scholars who are aliens.

Should You Use Another Form?

Even if you can use Form 1040EZ, it may benefit you to use Form 1040A or 1040 instead. For example, you can claim the head of household filing status (which usually results in a lower tax than single) only on Form 1040A or 1040. You can claim the retirement savings contributions credit (saver's credit) only on Form 1040A or 1040. For more information on the retirement savings contributions credit, use TeleTax topic 610.

Premium tax credit. If you or your spouse enrolled in health insurance through the Health Insurance Marketplace you may be eligible for a premium tax credit. You must file Form 1040A or 1040 to claim the premium tax credit. You may also be eligible to claim the premium tax credit for any dependent you claim on Form 1040A or 1040 who enrolled in health insurance through the Health Insurance Marketplace. For more information on the premium tax credit, see Pub. 974.

Tax benefits for education. If you paid higher education expenses, you may be eligible for a tax credit or deduction. You may be eligible to claim a credit (and receive a refund) even if you owe no income tax. You must file Form 1040A or 1040 to claim these tax benefits. For more information on tax benefits for education, see Pub. 970.

Itemized deductions. You can itemize deductions only on Form 1040. You will benefit by itemizing if your itemized deductions total more than your standard deduction. For 2014, the standard deduction is $6,200 for most single people and $12,400 for most married people filing a joint return. Use Tele-Tax topic 501. But if someone can claim you (or your spouse if married) as a dependent, your standard deduction is the amount on line E of the Worksheet for Line 5 on the back of Form 1040EZ.

What Filing Status Can You Use?

Single. Use this filing status if any of the following was true on December 31, 2014.
- You were never married.
- You were legally separated, according to your state law, under a decree of divorce or separate maintenance. But if your divorce was not final (an interlocutory decree), you are considered married and cannot use the single filing status.
- You were widowed before January 1, 2014, and did not remarry in 2014.

Married filing jointly. Use this filing status if any of the following apply.
- You were married at the end of 2014, even if you did not live with your spouse at the end of 2014.
- Your spouse died in 2014, and you did not remarry in 2014.
- You were married at the end of 2014, and your spouse died in 2015 before filing a 2014 return.

If you and your spouse file jointly, report your combined income and deduct your combined allowable expenses on one return. You can file a joint return even if only one of you had income or if you did not live together all year. However, both of you must sign the return. Once you file a joint return, you cannot choose to file separate returns for that year after the due date of the return.

Same-sex marriage. For federal tax purposes, individuals of the same sex are considered married if they were lawfully married in a state (or foreign country) whose laws authorize the marriage of two individuals of the same sex, even if the state (or foreign country) in which they now live does not recognize same-sex marriage. The term "spouse" includes an individual married to a person of the same sex if the couple is lawfully married under state (or foreign) law. However, individuals who have entered into a registered domestic partnership, civil union, or other similar relationship that is not considered a marriage under state (or foreign) law are not considered married for federal tax purposes. For more details, see Pub. 501.

Joint and several tax liability. If you file a joint return, both you and your spouse are generally responsible for the tax and interest or penalties due on the return. This means that if one spouse does not pay the tax due, the other may have to. Or, if one spouse does not report the correct tax, both spouses may be responsible for any additional taxes assessed by the IRS. You may want to file separately if:
- You believe your spouse is not reporting all of his or her income, or
- You do not want to be responsible for any taxes due if your spouse does not have enough tax withheld or does not pay enough estimated tax.

If you want to file separately, you must use Form 1040A or 1040. You cannot use Form 1040EZ. See _Innocent spouse relief_ in Section 5, later.

Filing Requirement Charts

 Chart A and B users—if you have to file a return, you may be able to file Form 1040EZ. See <u>Checklist for Using Form 1040EZ</u>, earlier.

Chart A—For Most People

IF your filing status is . . .	AND your gross income* was at least . . .	THEN . . .
Single	$10,150	File a return
Married filing jointly**	$20,300	File a return

__Gross income__ means all income you received in the form of money, goods, property, and services that is not exempt from tax, including any income from sources outside the United States or from the sale of your main home (even if you can exclude part or all of it).

**If you did not live with your spouse at the end of 2014 (or on the date your spouse died) and your gross income was at least $3,950, you must file a return.*

Chart B—For Children and Other Dependents

If your parent (or someone else) can claim you as a dependent, use this chart.

To find out if your parent (or someone else) can claim you as a dependent, see Pub. 501.

File a return if any of the following apply.

- Your **unearned income**[1] was over $1,000.
- Your **earned income**[2] was over $6,200.
- Your **gross income**[3] was more than the **larger** of—
  - $1,000, or
  - Your earned income (up to $5,850) plus $350.

---

[1] **Unearned income** includes taxable interest, ordinary dividends, and capital gain distributions. It also includes unemployment compensation, taxable social security benefits, pensions, annuities, and distributions of unearned income from a trust.

[2] **Earned income** includes salaries, wages, tips, professional fees, and taxable scholarship or fellowship grants.

[3] **Gross income** is the total of your unearned and earned income.

Chart C—Other Situations When You Must File

You must file a return using Form 1040A or 1040 if **any** of the following apply for 2014.
- You owe tax from the recapture of an education credit (see **Form 8863**).
- You claim a credit for excess social security or tier 1 RRTA tax withheld.
- You claim a credit for the retirement savings contributions credit (saver's credit) (see **Form 8880**).
- You claim a premium tax credit (see **Form 8962**).
- Advance payments of the premium tax credit were made for you, your spouse, or any individual you enrolled in coverage for whom no one else is claiming the personal exemption. You should have received Form(s) 1095-A showing the amount of the advance payments, if any.

You must file a return using Form 1040 if **any** of the following apply for 2014.
- You owe any special taxes, such as social security and Medicare tax on tips you did not report to your employer or on wages you received from an employer who did not withhold these taxes.
- You owe write-in taxes, including uncollected social security and Medicare or RRTA tax on tips you reported to your employer or on group-term life insurance.
- You had net earnings from self-employment of at least $400.
- You had wages of $108.28 or more from a church or qualified church-controlled organization that is exempt from employer social security and Medicare taxes.
- You owe any recapture taxes, other than from the recapture of an education credit, including repayment of the first-time homebuyer credit (see **Form 5405**).
- You owe additional tax on a qualified plan, including an individual retirement arrangement (IRA), or other tax-favored account. But if you are filing a return only because you owe this tax, you can file **Form 5329** by itself.
- You owe household employment taxes. But if you are filing a return only because you owe this tax, you can file **Schedule H (Form 1040)** by itself.
- You (or your spouse if filing jointly) received Archer MSA, Medicare Advantage MSA, or health savings account distributions.
- You received a Form W-2 that incorrectly includes in box 1 amounts that are payments under a Medicaid waiver program, and you cannot get a corrected W-2, or you received a Form 1099-MISC that incorrectly reported these payments to the IRS.

Instructions for Form 1040EZ

Where To Report Certain Items From 2014 Forms W-2, 1097, 1098, and 1099

e-file IRS *e-file* takes the guesswork out of preparing your return. You may also be eligible to use Free File to file your federal income tax return. Visit *www.irs.gov/efile* or see *Options for e-filing your returns*, later, for details.

Part 1	Items That Can Be Reported on Form 1040EZ	If any federal income tax withheld is shown on the forms in Part 1, include the tax withheld on Form 1040EZ, line 7.
Form	**Item and Box in Which It Should Appear**	**Where To Report on Form 1040EZ**
W-2	Wages, tips, other compensation (box 1)	Line 1
	Allocated tips (box 8)	See the instructions for Form 1040EZ, line 1
1099-G	Unemployment compensation (box 1)	Line 3
1099-INT	Interest income (box 1)	See the instructions on Form 1099-INT and the instructions for Form 1040EZ, line 2
	Interest on U.S. savings bonds and Treasury obligations (box 3)	See the instructions for Form 1040EZ, line 2
	Tax-exempt interest (box 8)	See the instructions for Form 1040EZ, line 2
1099-OID	Original issue discount (box 1)	See the instructions on Form 1099-OID
	Other periodic interest (box 2)	See the instructions on Form 1099-OID
SSA-1099	Social security benefits	See the instructions for Form 1040EZ, line 6
RRB-1099	Railroad retirement benefits	See the instructions for Form 1040EZ, line 6
Part 2	**Items That May Require Filing Another Form**	
Form	**Item and Box in Which it Should Appear**	**Other Form**
W-2	Dependent care benefits (box 10)	Must file Form 1040A or 1040
	Adoption benefits (box 12, code T)	Must file Form 1040
	Employer contributions to a health savings account (box 12, code W)	Must file Form 1040 if required to file Form 8889 (see the instructions for Form 8889)
	Amount reported in box 12, code R or Z	Must file Form 1040
	Uncollected social security and Medicare or RRTA tax (box 12, Code A, B, M, or N)	Must file Form 1040
W-2G	Gambling winnings (box 1)	Must file Form 1040
1097-BTC	Bond tax credit	Must file Form 1040
1098-E	Student loan interest (box 1)	Must file Form 1040A or 1040 to deduct
1098-T	Qualified tuition and related expenses (box 1)	Must file Form 1040A or 1040 to claim, but first see the instructions on Form 1098-T
1099-C	Canceled debt (box 2)	Generally must file Form 1040 (see Pub. 4681)
1099-DIV	Dividends and distributions	Must file Form 1040A or 1040
1099-INT	Early withdrawal penalty (box 2)	Must file Form 1040 to deduct
	Interest on U.S. savings bonds and Treasury obligations (box 3)	See the instructions on Form 1099-INT
	Foreign tax paid (box 6)	Must file Form 1040 to deduct or take a credit for the tax
1099-LTC	Long-term care and accelerated death benefits	Must file Form 1040 if required to file Form 8853 (see the instructions for Form 8853)
1099-MISC	Miscellaneous income	Must file Form 1040
1099-OID	Early withdrawal penalty (box 3)	Must file Form 1040 to deduct
1099-Q	Qualified education program payments	Must file Form 1040
1099-R	Distributions from pensions, annuities, IRAs, etc.	Must file Form 1040A or 1040
1099-SA	Distributions from HSAs and MSAs*	Must file Form 1040

This includes distributions from Archer and Medicare Advantage MSAs.

Section 3—Line Instructions for Form 1040EZ

 IRS *e-file* takes the guesswork out of preparing your return. You also may be eligible to use Free File to file your federal income tax return. Visit *www.irs.gov/efile* for details.

Top of the Form

Your first name and initial	Last name		Your social security number
If a joint return, spouse's first name and initial	Last name		Spouse's social security number
Home address (number and street). If you have a P.O. box, see instructions.		Apt. no.	▲ Make sure the SSN(s) above are correct.
City, town or post office, state, and ZIP code. If you have a foreign address, also complete spaces below (see instructions).			**Presidential Election Campaign** Check here if you, or your spouse if filing jointly, want $3 to go to this fund. Checking a box below will not change your tax or refund. ☐ You ☐ Spouse
Foreign country name	Foreign province/state/county	Foreign postal code	

(A) at Name and Address section; (B) at Your social security number; (C) at Presidential Election Campaign.

 ## A · Name and Address

Print or type the information in the spaces provided.

 TIP *If you filed a joint return for 2013 and you are filing a joint return for 2014 with the same spouse, be sure to enter your names and SSNs in the same order as on your 2013 return.*

Name change. If you changed your name because of marriage, divorce, or for any other reason, be sure to report the change to the Social Security Administration (SSA) before filing your return. This prevents delays in processing your return and issuing refunds. It also safeguards your future social security benefits.

Address change. If you plan to move after filing your return, use Form 8822 to notify the IRS of your new address.

P.O. box. Enter your P.O. box number only if your post office does not deliver mail to your home.

Foreign address. If you have a foreign address, enter the city name on the appropriate line (do not enter any other information on that line), then also complete the spaces below that line. Do not abbreviate the country name. Follow the country's practice for entering the postal code and the name of the province, county, or state.

 ## B · Social Security Number (SSN)

An incorrect or missing SSN can increase your tax, reduce your refund, or delay your refund. To apply for an SSN, fill in Form SS-5 and return it, along with the appropriate evidence documents, to the Social Security Administration (SSA). You can get Form SS-5 online at *www.socialsecurity.gov*, from your local SSA office, or by calling the SSA at 1-800-772-1213. It usually

takes about 2 weeks to get an SSN once the SSA has all the evidence and information it needs.

Check that both the name and SSN on your Forms 1040EZ, W-2, and 1099 agree with your social security card. If they do not, your exemption(s) and any earned income credit may be disallowed, your refund may be delayed, and you may not receive credit for your social security earnings. If your Form W-2 shows an incorrect name or SSN, notify your employer or the form-issuing agent as soon as possible to make sure your earnings are credited to your social security record. If the name or SSN on your social security card is incorrect, call the SSA.

IRS individual taxpayer identification numbers (ITINs) for aliens. If you are a nonresident or resident alien and you do not have and are not eligible to get an SSN, you must apply for an ITIN. For details on how to do so, see Form W-7 and its instructions. It takes 6 to 10 weeks to get an ITIN.

If you already have an ITIN, enter it wherever your SSN is requested on your tax return.

Note. An ITIN is for tax use only. It does not entitle you to social security benefits or change your employment or immigration status under U.S. law.

Nonresident alien spouse. If your spouse is a nonresident alien, you cannot use Form 1040EZ unless he or she has either an SSN or an ITIN.

C · Presidential Election Campaign Fund

This fund helps pay for Presidential election campaigns. The fund reduces candidates' dependence on large contributions from individuals and groups and places candidates on an equal financial footing in the general election. The fund also helps pay for pediatric medical research. If you want $3 to go to this fund, check the box. If you are filing a joint return, your spouse also

Income	①	1	Wages, salaries, and tips. This should be shown in box 1 of your Form(s) W-2. Attach your Form(s) W-2.		1	
Attach Form(s) W-2 here.		2	Taxable interest. If the total is over $1,500, you cannot use Form 1040EZ.	②	2	
Enclose, but do not attach, any payment.		3	Unemployment compensation and Alaska Permanent Fund ③ ends (see instructions).		3	
		4	Add lines 1, 2, and 3. This is your **adjusted gross income.**		4	
		5	If someone can claim you (or your spouse if a joint return) as a dependent, check the applicable box(es) below and enter the amount from the worksheet on back. ☐ **You** ☐ **Spouse**			
			If no one can claim you (or your spouse if a joint return), enter $10,150 if **single;** $20,300 if **married filing jointly.** See back for explanation.		5	
		6	Subtract line 5 from line 4. If line 5 is larger than line 4, enter -0-. This is your **taxable income.**	⑥	▶ 6	

can have $3 go to the fund. If you check a box, your tax or refund will not change.

Income (Lines 1–6)

Rounding Off to Whole Dollars

You can round off cents to whole dollars on your return. If you do round to whole dollars, you must round all amounts. To round, drop amounts under 50 cents and increase amounts from 50 to 99 cents to the next dollar. For example, $1.39 becomes $1 and $2.50 becomes $3.

If you have to add two or more amounts to figure the amount to enter on a line, include cents when adding the amounts and round off only the total.

Example. You received two Forms W-2, one showing wages of $5,009.55 and one showing wages of $8,760.73. On Form 1040EZ, line 1, you would enter $13,770 ($5,009.55 + $8,760.73 = $13,770.28).

Refunds of State or Local Income Taxes

If you received a refund, credit, or offset of state or local income taxes in 2014, you may receive a Form 1099-G.

For the year the tax was paid to the state or other taxing authority, did you file Form 1040EZ or 1040A?

☐ **Yes.**   None of your refund is taxable.

☐ **No.**   You may have to report part or all of the refund as income on Form 1040 for 2014. For more information, see the Instructions for Form 1040 or Pub. 525.

Social Security Benefits

If you received social security or equivalent railroad retirement benefits, you should receive a Form SSA-1099 or Form RRB-1099. These forms will show the total benefits paid to you in 2014 and the amount of any benefits you repaid in 2014. Use the Worksheet To See if Any of Your Social Security Benefits Are Taxable, later in this Section 3. If any of your benefits are taxable, you must use Form 1040A or 1040. For more details, see Pub. 915.

Nevada, Washington, and California domestic partners

A registered domestic partner in Nevada, Washington, or California generally must report half the combined community income of the individual and his or her domestic partner. See Form 8958 and Pub. 555. If you file Form 8958, you must use Form 1040.

Line 1, Wages, Salaries, and Tips

Enter the total of your wages, salaries, and tips. If you are filing a joint return, also include your spouse's wages, salaries, and tips. For most people, the amount to enter on this line should be shown on their Form(s) W-2 in box 1. But you must include all of your wages, salaries, and tips in the total on line 1, even if they are not shown on your Form(s) W-2. For example, the following types of income must be included in the total on line 1.

- Wages received as a household employee for which you did not receive a Form W-2 because your employer paid you less than $1,900 in 2014. Also, enter "HSH" and the amount not reported on a Form W-2 in the space to the left of line 1.
- Tip income you did not report to your employer. But you must use Form 1040 and Form 4137 if (a) you received tips of $20 or more in any month and did not report the full amount to your employer, or (b) your Form(s) W-2 shows allocated tips that you must report as income. You must report the allocated tips shown on your Form(s) W-2 unless you can prove that you received less. Allocated tips should be shown on your Form(s) W-2 in box 8. They are not included as income in box 1. See Pub. 531 for more details.
- Scholarship and fellowship grants not reported on a Form W-2. Also, enter "SCH" and the amount in the space to the left of line 1. However, if you were a degree candidate, include on line 1 only the amounts you used for expenses other than tuition and course-related expenses. For example, amounts used for room, board, and travel must be reported on line 1. For more information on taxable scholarships and grants, see Pub. 970.

Worksheet To See if Any of Your Social Security Benefits Are Taxable

Keep for Your Records

Before you begin: ✓ If you are filing a joint return, be sure to include any amounts your spouse received when entering amounts on lines 1, 3, and 4 below.

1. Enter the amount from **box 5** of **all** your **Forms SSA-1099** and **Forms RRB-1099** . . . . **1.** _____

2. Is the amount on line 1 more than zero?

   ☐ **No.** (STOP) None of your social security benefits are taxable.

   ☐ **Yes.** Enter one-half of line 1 . . . . **2.** _____

3. Enter your total wages, salaries, tips, etc., from Form(s) W-2. Also, include any taxable unemployment compensation and Alaska Permanent Fund dividends you received (see the instructions for Form 1040EZ, line 3, later) . . . . **3.** _____

4. Enter your total interest income, including any tax-exempt interest . . . . **4.** _____

5. Add lines 2, 3, and 4 . . . . **5.** _____

6. If you are:
   • Single, enter $25,000
   • Married filing jointly, enter $32,000 } . . . . **6.** _____

7. Is the amount on line 6 less than the amount on line 5?

   ☐ **No.** None of your social security or railroad retirement benefits are taxable this year. You can use Form 1040EZ. **Do not** list your benefits as income.

   ☐ **Yes.** (STOP) Some of your benefits are taxable this year. You **must** use Form 1040A or 1040.

You must use Form 1040A or 1040 if you received dependent care benefits for 2014. You must use Form 1040 if you received employer-provided adoption benefits for 2014.

Missing or incorrect Form W-2? Your employer is required to provide or send Form W-2 to you no later than February 2, 2015. If you do not receive it by early February, use TeleTax topic 154 to find out what to do. Even if you do not get a Form W-2, you still must report your earnings on line 1. If you lose your Form W-2 or it is incorrect, ask your employer for a new one.

---

(2) Line 2, Taxable Interest

If you received interest payments, you should receive a Form 1099-INT or Form 1099-OID from each payer. Report all of your taxable interest income on line 2 even if you did not receive a Form 1099-INT or 1099-OID. If you are filing a joint return, also include any taxable interest received by your spouse.

Include interest received on amounts deposited with banks, savings and loan associations, credit unions, or similar organizations. If interest was credited in 2014 on deposits that you could not withdraw because of the bankruptcy or insolvency of the financial institution, you may be able to exclude part or all of that interest from your 2014 income. But you must use Form 1040A or 1040 to do so. See Pub. 550 for details.

For more information on interest received, use Tele-Tax topic 403.

You should also include taxable interest on bonds and other securities. If you cashed U.S. series EE or I savings bonds in 2014 that were issued after 1989 and you paid certain higher education expenses during the year, you may be able to exclude from income part or all of the interest on those bonds. But you must use Form 8815 and Form 1040A or 1040 to do so.

You must use Form 1040A or 1040 if you received taxable interest of more than $1,500. You also must use Form 1040A or 1040 if any of the following apply.

- You received interest as a nominee (that is, in your name but the interest income actually belongs to someone else).
- You received a 2014 Form 1099-INT for U.S. savings bond interest that includes amounts you reported before 2014.
- You owned or had authority over one or more foreign financial accounts (such as bank accounts) with a combined value over $10,000 at any time during 2014.

Tax-Exempt Interest

If you received tax-exempt interest, such as interest on municipal bonds, each payer should send you a Form 1099-INT. Your tax-exempt interest should be shown in box 8 of Form 1099-INT. Enter "TEI" and the amount in the space to the left of line 2. Do not include tax-exempt interest in the total on line 2.

Payments, Credits, and Tax	7	Federal income tax withheld from Form(s) W-2 and 109		7	
	8a	**Earned income credit (EIC)** (see instructions)		8a	
	b	Nontaxable combat pay election	8b		
	9	Add lines 7 and 8a. These are your **total payments and credits.**	▶	9	
	10	**Tax.** Use the amount on **line 6 above** to find your tax in the tax table in the instructions. Then, enter the tax from the table on this line.		10	
	11	Health care: individual responsibility (see instructions) Full-year cov ☐		11	
	12	Add lines 10 and 11. This is your **total tax.**		12	

Line 3, Unemployment Compensation and Alaska Permanent Fund Dividends

Unemployment compensation. You should receive a Form 1099-G showing in box 1 the total unemployment compensation paid to you in 2014. Report this amount on line 3. If you are filing a joint return, also report on line 3 any unemployment compensation received by your spouse. If you made contributions to a governmental unemployment compensation program or a governmental paid family leave program, reduce the amount you report on line 3 by those contributions.

If you received an overpayment of unemployment compensation in 2014 and you repaid any of it in 2014, subtract the amount you repaid from the total amount you received. Enter the result on line 3. However, if the result is zero or less, enter -0- on line 3. Also, enter "Repaid" and the amount you repaid in the space to the left of line 3. If, in 2014, you repaid unemployment compensation that you included in gross income in an earlier year, you can deduct the amount repaid; but you must use Form 1040 to do so. See Pub. 525 for details.

Alaska Permanent Fund dividends. If you received Alaska Permanent Fund dividends, include them in the total on line 3. If you are filing a joint return, also report on line 3 any Alaska Permanent Fund dividends received by your spouse. You cannot use Form 1040EZ if you (or your spouse) received any other kind of dividends.

If a child's interest and Alaska Permanent Fund dividends total more than $2,000, he or she may be required to file Form 8615 and Form 1040A or 1040 instead of Form 1040EZ. The child's parent may, however, be able to include the child's income on the parent's return. If so, the child need not file a return, but the parent must file Form 8814 and Form 1040. For more information, see *Exception for certain children under age 19 or full-time students* in Section 2, earlier, and Pub. 929.

Line 6, Taxable Income

Your taxable income and filing status will determine the amount of tax you enter on line 10.

Figuring taxable income incorrectly is one of the most common errors on Form 1040EZ. So please take extra care when subtracting line 5 from line 4.

If you received Forms SSA-1099 or RRB-1099 (showing amounts treated as social security) use the <u>Worksheet To See if</u>

<u>Any of Your Social Security Benefits Are Taxable</u>, earlier in this Section 3, to determine if you can file Form 1040EZ.

Payments, Credits, and Tax (Lines 7–11)

Line 7, Federal Income Tax Withheld

Enter the total amount of federal income tax withheld. This should be shown on your 2014 Form(s) W-2 in box 2.

If you received 2014 Form(s) 1099-INT, 1099-G, or 1099-OID showing federal income tax withheld, include the tax withheld in the total on line 7. This should be shown in box 4 of these forms.

Lines 8a and 8b, Earned Income Credit (EIC)

What Is the EIC?

The EIC is a credit for certain people who work. The credit may give you a refund even if you do not owe any tax or did not have any tax withheld.

Note. If you have a qualifying child (defined in Step 1, later), you may be able to take the credit, but you must use Schedule EIC and Form 1040A or 1040 to do so. For details, see Pub. 596.

To Take the EIC:

- Follow Steps 1 through 3 next.
- Complete the *Earned Income Credit (EIC) Worksheet—Lines 8a and 8b,* later, or let the IRS figure the credit for you.

TIP *For help in determining if you are eligible for the EIC, go to www.irs.gov/eitc and use the "EITC Assistant." This service is available in English and Spanish.*

CAUTION *If you take the EIC even though you are not eligible and it is determined that your error is due to reckless or intentional disregard of the EIC rules, you will not be allowed to take the credit for 2 years even if you are otherwise eligible to do so. If you fraudulently take the EIC, you will not be allowed to take the credit for 10 years. See Form 8862, who must file under Definitions and Special Rules, later. You also may have to pay penalties.*

Step 1   All Filers

1. Is the amount on Form 1040EZ, line 4, less than $14,590 ($20,020 if married filing jointly)?

    ☐ **Yes.** Go to question 2.   ☐ **No.** (STOP)

    You cannot take the credit.

2. Do you, and your spouse if filing a joint return, have a social security number that allows you to work and is valid for EIC purposes (explained later in *Social security number (SSN)* under *Definitions and Special Rules*)?

    ☐ **Yes.** Go to question 3.   ☐ **No.** (STOP)

    You cannot take the credit. Enter "No" in the space to the left of line 8a.

3. Did you have $3,350 or less of taxable and tax-exempt interest?

    ☐ **Yes.** Go to question 4.   ☐ **No.** (STOP)

    You cannot take the credit.

4. Were you, or your spouse if filing a joint return, at least age 25 but under age 65 at the end of 2014? (Check "Yes" if you, or your spouse if filing a joint return, were born after December 31, 1949, and before January 2, 1990) If your spouse died in 2014 (or if you are preparing a return for someone who died in 2014), see Pub. 596 before you answer.

    ☐ **Yes.** Go to question 5.   ☐ **No.** (STOP)

    You cannot take the credit.

5. Was your main home, and your spouse's if filing a joint return, in the United States for more than half of 2014? Members of the military stationed outside the United States, see *Members of the military* under *Definitions and Special Rules*, later, before you answer.

    ☐ **Yes.** Go to question 6.   ☐ **No.** (STOP)

    You cannot take the credit. Enter "No" in the space to the left of line 8a.

6. Are you filing a joint return for 2014?

    ☐ **Yes.** Skip questions 7 and 8; go to Step 2.   ☐ **No.** Go to question 7.

7. Look at the qualifying child conditions next. Could you be a qualifying child of another person in 2014? (Check "No" if the other person is not required to file, and is not filing, a 2014 return or is filing a 2014 return only as a <u>claim for</u>

refund (defined under *Definitions and Special Rules*, later.))

    ☐ **Yes.** (STOP)   ☐ **No.** Go to question 8.

    You cannot take the credit. Enter "No" in the space to the left of line 8a.

A **qualifying child** for the EIC is a child who is your...

Son, daughter, stepchild, foster child, brother, sister, stepbrother, stepsister, half brother, half sister, or a descendant of any of them (for example, your grandchild, niece, or nephew).

AND

was...

Under age 19 at the end of 2014 and younger than you (or your spouse if filing jointly)

or

Under age 24 at the end of 2014, a <u>student</u> (defined later), and younger than you (or your spouse if filing jointly)

or

Any age and <u>permanently and totally disabled</u> (defined later)

AND

Who is not filing a joint return for 2014 or is filing a joint return for 2014 only as a <u>claim for refund</u> (defined later)

AND

Who lived with you in the United States for more than half of 2014. If the child did not live with you for the required time, see *Exception to time lived with you* under *Definitions and Special Rules*, later.

⚠️ *Special rules apply if the child was married or also meets the conditions to be a qualifying child of another person (other than your spouse if filing a joint return). For details, use TeleTax topic 601 or see Pub. 596.*

---

8. Can you be claimed as a dependent on someone else's 2014 tax return?

    ☐ **Yes.** (STOP)   ☐ **No.** Go to Step 2.

    You cannot take the credit.

Step 2

1. Complete the following worksheet to figure your earned income:

Earned Income Worksheet

1. Enter the amount from Form 1040EZ, line 1 . . . . _____
2. Enter any amount included on Form 1040EZ, line 1, that is a taxable scholarship or fellowship grant not reported on Form W-2 . . . . _____
3. Enter any amount included on Form 1040EZ, line 1, that you received for work performed while an inmate in a penal institution. (Enter "PRI" and the same amount on the dotted line next to Form 1040EZ, line 1) . . . . _____
4. Enter any amount included on Form 1040EZ, line 1, that you received as a pension or annuity from a nonqualified deferred compensation plan or a nongovernmental section 457 plan. (Enter "DFC" and the same amount on the dotted line next to Form 1040EZ, line 1). This amount may be shown in box 11 of Form W-2. If you received such an amount but box 11 is blank, contact your employer for the amount received . . . . _____
5. Add lines 2, 3, and 4 . . . . _____
6. Subtract line 5 from line 1 . . . . . . _____
7. Enter all your nontaxable combat pay if you elect to include it in earned income. Also enter this amount on Form 1040EZ, line 8b. See *Combat pay, nontaxable*, under *Definitions and Special Rules*, later . . . . _____

   ⚠️ **CAUTION** *Electing to include nontaxable combat pay may increase or decrease your EIC. Figure the credit with and without your nontaxable combat pay before making the election.*

8. Add lines 6 and 7. **This is your earned income** . . . . _____

2. Is your earned income less than $14,590 ($20,020 if married filing jointly)?

   ☐ **Yes.** Go to Step 3.   ☐ **No.** 🛑
   You cannot take the credit.

Step 3 **How To Figure the Credit**

1. Do you want the IRS to figure the credit for you?

   ☐ **Yes.** See *Credit figured by the IRS* under *Definitions and Special Rules,* later.   ☐ **No.** Go to the *Earned Income Credit (EIC) Worksheet—Lines 8a and 8b*.

Definitions and Special Rules

(listed in alphabetical order)

Claim for refund. A claim for refund is a return filed only to get a refund of withheld income tax or estimated tax paid. A return is not a claim for refund if you claim the earned income credit or any other similar refundable credit.

Combat pay, nontaxable. If you were a member of the U.S. Armed Forces who served in a combat zone, certain pay is excluded from your income. See *Combat Zone Exclusion* in Pub. 3. You can elect to include this pay in your earned income when figuring the EIC. The amount of your nontaxable combat pay should be shown in box 12 of Form(s) W-2 with code Q. If you are filing a joint return and both you and your spouse received nontaxable combat pay, you can each make your own election. In other words, if one of you makes the election, the other one can also make it but does not have to.

Credit figured by the IRS. To have the IRS figure your EIC:

1. Enter "EIC" in the space to the left of line 8a on Form 1040EZ.

2. Be sure you enter the nontaxable combat pay you elect to include in earned income on Form 1040EZ, line 8b. See *Combat pay, nontaxable*, earlier.

3. If your EIC for a year after 1996 was reduced or disallowed, see *Form 8862, who must file*, later.

Exception to time lived with you. Temporary absences by you or the child for special circumstances, such as school, vacation, business, medical care, military service, or detention in a juvenile facility, count as time lived with you. A child is considered to have lived with you for more than half of 2014 if the child was born or died in 2014 and your home was this child's home for more than half the time he or she was alive in 2014. Special rules apply to members of the military (see *Members of the military*, later) or if the child was kidnapped (see Pub. 596).

Form 8862, who must file. You must file Form 8862 if your EIC for a year after 1996 was reduced or disallowed for any reason other than a math or clerical error. But do not file Form 8862 if either of the following applies.

1. You filed Form 8862 for another year, the EIC was allowed for that year, and your EIC has not been reduced or disallowed again for any reason other than a math or clerical error.

2. The only reason your EIC was reduced or disallowed in the earlier year was because it was determined that a child listed on Schedule EIC was not your qualifying child.

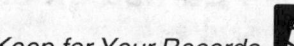

Earned Income Credit (EIC) Worksheet—Lines 8a and 8b

Keep for Your Records

1. Enter your earned income from Step 2, earlier . . . . 1. _____

2. Look up the amount on line 1 above in the EIC Table, later, to find the credit. Be sure you use the correct column for your filing status (single or married filing jointly).

   Enter the credit here . . . . 2. _____

   STOP If line 2 is zero, You cannot take the credit. Enter "No" in the space to the left of line 8a.

3. Enter the amount from Form 1040EZ, line 4 . . . . 3. _____

4. Are the amounts on lines 3 and 1 the same?

   ☐ **Yes.** Skip line 5; enter the amount from line 2 on line 6.

   ☐ **No.** Go to line 5.

5. Is the amount on line 3 less than $8,150 ($13,550 if married filing jointly)?

   ☐ **Yes.** Leave line 5 blank; enter the amount from line 2 on line 6.

   ☐ **No.** Look up the amount on line 3 in the EIC Table, later, to find the credit. Be sure you use the correct column for your filing status (single or married filing jointly).

   Enter the credit here . . . . 5. _____

   Look at the amounts on lines 5 and 2. Then, enter the **smaller** amount on line 6.

6. **Earned income credit.** Enter this amount on Form 1040EZ, **line 8a** . . . . 6. _____

⚠ **CAUTION** *If your EIC for a year after 1996 was reduced or disallowed, see* Form 8862, who must file *under* Definitions and Special Rules, *later, to find out if you must file Form 8862 to take the credit for 2014.*

Also, do not file Form 8862 or take the credit for:
- 2 years after the most recent tax year for which there was a final determination that your EIC claim was due to reckless or intentional disregard of the EIC rules, or
- 10 years after the most recent tax year for which there was a final determination that your EIC claim was due to fraud.

Members of the military. If you were on extended active duty outside the United States, your main home is considered to be in the United States during that duty period. Extended active duty is military duty ordered for an indefinite period or for a period of more than 90 days. Once you begin serving extended active duty, you are considered to be on extended active duty even if you do not serve more than 90 days.

Permanently and totally disabled. A person is permanently and totally disabled if, at any time in 2014, the person could not engage in any substantial gainful activity because of a physical or mental condition and a doctor has determined that this condition has lasted or can be expected to last continuously for at least a year or can be expected to lead to death.

Social security number (SSN). For the EIC, a valid SSN is a number issued by the Social Security Administration unless "Not Valid for Employment" is printed on the social security card and the number was issued solely to allow the recipient of the SSN to apply for or receive a federally funded benefit. However, if "Valid for Work Only with DHS Authorization" is printed on your social security card, your SSN is valid for EIC purposes only as long as the DHS authorization is still valid.

To find out how to get an SSN, see *Social Security Number (SSN),* earlier, at the beginning of this Section 3. If you will not have an SSN by the date your return is due, see *What If You Cannot File on Time?* in Section 4, later.

Student. For purposes of this credit, a student is a child who during any part of 5 calendar months of 2014 was enrolled as a full-time student at a school, or took a full-time, on-farm training course given by a school or a state, county, or local government agency. A school includes a technical, trade, or mechanical school. It does not include an on-the-job training course, correspondence school, or a school offering courses only through the Internet.

Welfare benefits, effect of credit on. Any refund you receive as a result of taking the EIC cannot be counted as income when determining if you or anyone else is eligible for benefits or assistance, or how much you or anyone else can receive, under any federal program or under any state or local program financed in whole or in part with federal funds. These programs include Temporary Assistance for Needy Families (TANF), Medicaid, Supplemental Security Income (SSI), and Supplemental Nutrition Assistance Program (food stamps). In addition, when determining eligibility, the refund cannot be counted as a resource for at least 12 months after you receive it. Check with your local benefits coordinator to find out if your refund will affect your benefits.

Instructions for Form 1040EZ

2014 Earned Income Credit (EIC) Table

 CAUTION This is not a tax table.

Follow the two steps below to find your credit.

Step 1. Read down the "At least—But less than" columns and find the line that includes the amount you were told to look up from your EIC Worksheet, earlier.

Step 2. Then, read across the column for your filing status (Single or Married filing jointly). Enter the credit from that column on your EIC Worksheet.

At least	But less than	Single	Married filing jointly
$1	$50	2	2
50	100	6	6
100	150	10	10
150	200	13	13
200	250	17	17
250	300	21	21
300	350	25	25
350	400	29	29
400	450	33	33
450	500	36	36
500	550	40	40
550	600	44	44
600	650	48	48
650	700	52	52
700	750	55	55
750	800	59	59
800	850	63	63
850	900	67	67
900	950	71	71
950	1,000	75	75
1,000	1,050	78	78
1,050	1,100	82	82
1,100	1,150	86	86
1,150	1,200	90	90
1,200	1,250	94	94
1,250	1,300	98	98
1,300	1,350	101	101
1,350	1,400	105	105
1,400	1,450	109	109
1,450	1,500	113	113
1,500	1,550	117	117
1,550	1,600	120	120
1,600	1,650	124	124
1,650	1,700	128	128
1,700	1,750	132	132
1,750	1,800	136	136
1,800	1,850	140	140
1,850	1,900	143	143
1,900	1,950	147	147
1,950	2,000	151	151
2,000	2,050	155	155
2,050	2,100	159	159
2,100	2,150	163	163
2,150	2,200	166	166
2,200	2,250	170	170
2,250	2,300	174	174
2,300	2,350	178	178
2,350	2,400	182	182
2,400	2,450	186	186
2,450	2,500	189	189
2,500	2,550	193	193
2,550	2,600	197	197
2,600	2,650	201	201
2,650	2,700	205	205
2,700	2,750	208	208
2,750	2,800	212	212
2,800	2,850	216	216
2,850	2,900	220	220
2,900	2,950	224	224
2,950	3,000	228	228

At least	But less than	Single	Married filing jointly
3,000	3,050	231	231
3,050	3,100	235	235
3,100	3,150	239	239
3,150	3,200	243	243
3,200	3,250	247	247
3,250	3,300	251	251
3,300	3,350	254	254
3,350	3,400	258	258
3,400	3,450	262	262
3,450	3,500	266	266
3,500	3,550	270	270
3,550	3,600	273	273
3,600	3,650	277	277
3,650	3,700	281	281
3,700	3,750	285	285
3,750	3,800	289	289
3,800	3,850	293	293
3,850	3,900	296	296
3,900	3,950	300	300
3,950	4,000	304	304
4,000	4,050	308	308
4,050	4,100	312	312
4,100	4,150	316	316
4,150	4,200	319	319
4,200	4,250	323	323
4,250	4,300	327	327
4,300	4,350	331	331
4,350	4,400	335	335
4,400	4,450	339	339
4,450	4,500	342	342
4,500	4,550	346	346
4,550	4,600	350	350
4,600	4,650	354	354
4,650	4,700	358	358
4,700	4,750	361	361
4,750	4,800	365	365
4,800	4,850	369	369
4,850	4,900	373	373
4,900	4,950	377	377
4,950	5,000	381	381
5,000	5,050	384	384
5,050	5,100	388	388
5,100	5,150	392	392
5,150	5,200	396	396
5,200	5,250	400	400
5,250	5,300	404	404
5,300	5,350	407	407
5,350	5,400	411	411
5,400	5,450	415	415
5,450	5,500	419	419
5,500	5,550	423	423
5,550	5,600	426	426
5,600	5,650	430	430
5,650	5,700	434	434
5,700	5,750	438	438
5,750	5,800	442	442
5,800	5,850	446	446
5,850	5,900	449	449
5,900	5,950	453	453
5,950	6,000	457	457

At least	But less than	Single	Married filing jointly
6,000	6,050	461	461
6,050	6,100	465	465
6,100	6,150	469	469
6,150	6,200	472	472
6,200	6,250	476	476
6,250	6,300	480	480
6,300	6,350	484	484
6,350	6,400	488	488
6,400	6,450	492	492
6,450	6,500	496	496
6,500	6,550	496	496
6,550	6,600	496	496
6,600	6,650	496	496
6,650	6,700	496	496
6,700	6,750	496	496
6,750	6,800	496	496
6,800	6,850	496	496
6,850	6,900	496	496
6,900	6,950	496	496
6,950	7,000	496	496
7,000	7,050	496	496
7,050	7,100	496	496
7,100	7,150	496	496
7,150	7,200	496	496
7,200	7,250	496	496
7,250	7,300	496	496
7,300	7,350	496	496
7,350	7,400	496	496
7,400	7,450	496	496
7,450	7,500	496	496
7,500	7,550	496	496
7,550	7,600	496	496
7,600	7,650	496	496
7,650	7,700	496	496
7,700	7,750	496	496
7,750	7,800	496	496
7,800	7,850	496	496
7,850	7,900	496	496
7,900	7,950	496	496
7,950	8,000	496	496
8,000	8,050	496	496
8,050	8,100	496	496
8,100	8,150	496	496
8,150	8,200	491	496
8,200	8,250	487	496
8,250	8,300	483	496
8,300	8,350	479	496
8,350	8,400	475	496
8,400	8,450	472	496
8,450	8,500	468	496
8,500	8,550	464	496
8,550	8,600	460	496
8,600	8,650	456	496
8,650	8,700	452	496
8,700	8,750	449	496
8,750	8,800	445	496
8,800	8,850	441	496
8,850	8,900	437	496
8,900	8,950	433	496
8,950	9,000	430	496

At least	But less than	Single	Married filing jointly
9,000	9,050	426	496
9,050	9,100	422	496
9,100	9,150	418	496
9,150	9,200	414	496
9,200	9,250	410	496
9,250	9,300	407	496
9,300	9,350	403	496
9,350	9,400	399	496
9,400	9,450	395	496
9,450	9,500	391	496
9,500	9,550	387	496
9,550	9,600	384	496
9,600	9,650	380	496
9,650	9,700	376	496
9,700	9,750	372	496
9,750	9,800	368	496
9,800	9,850	365	496
9,850	9,900	361	496
9,900	9,950	357	496
9,950	10,000	353	496
10,000	10,050	349	496
10,050	10,100	345	496
10,100	10,150	342	496
10,150	10,200	338	496
10,200	10,250	334	496
10,250	10,300	330	496
10,300	10,350	326	496
10,350	10,400	322	496
10,400	10,450	319	496
10,450	10,500	315	496
10,500	10,550	311	496
10,550	10,600	307	496
10,600	10,650	303	496
10,650	10,700	299	496
10,700	10,750	296	496
10,750	10,800	292	496
10,800	10,850	288	496
10,850	10,900	284	496
10,900	10,950	280	496
10,950	11,000	277	496
11,000	11,050	273	496
11,050	11,100	269	496
11,100	11,150	265	496
11,150	11,200	261	496
11,200	11,250	257	496
11,250	11,300	254	496
11,300	11,350	250	496
11,350	11,400	246	496
11,400	11,450	242	496
11,450	11,500	238	496
11,500	11,550	234	496
11,550	11,600	231	496
11,600	11,650	227	496
11,650	11,700	223	496
11,700	11,750	219	496
11,750	11,800	215	496
11,800	11,850	212	496
11,850	11,900	208	496
11,900	11,950	204	496
11,950	12,000	200	496

(Continued)

Instructions for Form 1040EZ

Earned Income Credit (EIC) Table - *Continued* (**Caution.** This is **not** a tax table.)

If the amount you are looking up from the worksheet is—		And your filing status is—		If the amount you are looking up from the worksheet is—		And your filing status is—		If the amount you are looking up from the worksheet is—		And your filing status is—		If the amount you are looking up from the worksheet is—		And your filing status is—	
At least	But less than	Single	Married filing jointly	At least	But less than	Single	Married filing jointly	At least	But less than	Single	Married filing jointly	At least	But less than	Single	Married filing jointly
		Your credit is—				Your credit is—				Your credit is—				Your credit is—	
12,000	12,050	196	496	14,500	14,550	5	420	17,000	17,050	0	229	19,500	19,550	0	38
12,050	12,100	192	496	14,550	14,600	*	417	17,050	17,100	0	225	19,550	19,600	0	34
12,100	12,150	189	496	14,600	14,650	0	413	17,100	17,150	0	221	19,600	19,650	0	30
12,150	12,200	185	496	14,650	14,700	0	409	17,150	17,200	0	218	19,650	19,700	0	26
12,200	12,250	181	496	14,700	14,750	0	405	17,200	17,250	0	214	19,700	19,750	0	23
12,250	12,300	177	496	14,750	14,800	0	401	17,250	17,300	0	210	19,750	19,800	0	19
12,300	12,350	173	496	14,800	14,850	0	397	17,300	17,350	0	206	19,800	19,850	0	15
12,350	12,400	169	496	14,850	14,900	0	394	17,350	17,400	0	202	19,850	19,900	0	11
12,400	12,450	166	496	14,900	14,950	0	390	17,400	17,450	0	199	19,900	19,950	0	7
12,450	12,500	162	496	14,950	15,000	0	386	17,450	17,500	0	195	19,950	20,000	0	3
12,500	12,550	158	496	15,000	15,050	0	382	17,500	17,550	0	191	20,000	20,020	0	**
12,550	12,600	154	496	15,050	15,100	0	378	17,550	17,600	0	187				
12,600	12,650	150	496	15,100	15,150	0	374	17,600	17,650	0	183				
12,650	12,700	146	496	15,150	15,200	0	371	17,650	17,700	0	179				
12,700	12,750	143	496	15,200	15,250	0	367	17,700	17,750	0	176				
12,750	12,800	139	496	15,250	15,300	0	363	17,750	17,800	0	172				
12,800	12,850	135	496	15,300	15,350	0	359	17,800	17,850	0	168				
12,850	12,900	131	496	15,350	15,400	0	355	17,850	17,900	0	164				
12,900	12,950	127	496	15,400	15,450	0	352	17,900	17,950	0	160				
12,950	13,000	124	496	15,450	15,500	0	348	17,950	18,000	0	156				
13,000	13,050	120	496	15,500	15,550	0	344	18,000	18,050	0	153				
13,050	13,100	116	496	15,550	15,600	0	340	18,050	18,100	0	149				
13,100	13,150	112	496	15,600	15,650	0	336	18,100	18,150	0	145				
13,150	13,200	108	496	15,650	15,700	0	332	18,150	18,200	0	141				
13,200	13,250	104	496	15,700	15,750	0	329	18,200	18,250	0	137				
13,250	13,300	101	496	15,750	15,800	0	325	18,250	18,300	0	133				
13,300	13,350	97	496	15,800	15,850	0	321	18,300	18,350	0	130				
13,350	13,400	93	496	15,850	15,900	0	317	18,350	18,400	0	126				
13,400	13,450	89	496	15,900	15,950	0	313	18,400	18,450	0	122				
13,450	13,500	85	496	15,950	16,000	0	309	18,450	18,500	0	118				
13,500	13,550	81	496	16,000	16,050	0	306	18,500	18,550	0	114				
13,550	13,600	78	493	16,050	16,100	0	302	18,550	18,600	0	111				
13,600	13,650	74	489	16,100	16,150	0	298	18,600	18,650	0	107				
13,650	13,700	70	485	16,150	16,200	0	294	18,650	18,700	0	103				
13,700	13,750	66	482	16,200	16,250	0	290	18,700	18,750	0	99				
13,750	13,800	62	478	16,250	16,300	0	286	18,750	18,800	0	95				
13,800	13,850	59	474	16,300	16,350	0	283	18,800	18,850	0	91				
13,850	13,900	55	470	16,350	16,400	0	279	18,850	18,900	0	88				
13,900	13,950	51	466	16,400	16,450	0	275	18,900	18,950	0	84				
13,950	14,000	47	462	16,450	16,500	0	271	18,950	19,000	0	80				
14,000	14,050	43	459	16,500	16,550	0	267	19,000	19,050	0	76				
14,050	14,100	39	455	16,550	16,600	0	264	19,050	19,100	0	72				
14,100	14,150	36	451	16,600	16,650	0	260	19,100	19,150	0	68				
14,150	14,200	32	447	16,650	16,700	0	256	19,150	19,200	0	65				
14,200	14,250	28	443	16,700	16,750	0	252	19,200	19,250	0	61				
14,250	14,300	24	439	16,750	16,800	0	248	19,250	19,300	0	57				
14,300	14,350	20	436	16,800	16,850	0	244	19,300	19,350	0	53				
14,350	14,400	16	432	16,850	16,900	0	241	19,350	19,400	0	49				
14,400	14,450	13	428	16,900	16,950	0	237	19,400	19,450	0	46				
14,450	14,500	9	424	16,950	17,000	0	233	19,450	19,500	0	42				

* If the amount you are looking up from the worksheet is at least $14,550 but less than $14,590, your credit is $2. If the amount you are looking up from the worksheet is $14,590 or more, you cannot take the credit.

** If the amount you are looking up from the worksheet is at least $20,000 but less than $20,020, your credit is $1. If the amount you are looking up from the worksheet is $20,020 or more, you cannot take the credit.

Line 9

Add lines 7 and 8a. Enter the total on line 9.

Amount paid with request for extension of time to file. If you requested an automatic extension of time to file Form 1040EZ using Form 4868, include on line 9 any amount paid with that form. Also include any amount you paid by electronic funds withdrawal, credit or debit card, or the Electronic Federal Tax Payment System (EFTPS) to get an extension. If you paid by credit or debit card, do not include on line 9 the convenience fee you were charged. To the left of line 9, enter "Form 4868" and show the amount paid.

 If you pay your taxes by credit or debit card, you may be able to deduct the related credit or debit card convenience fees on your 2015 tax return, but you must file Form 1040 to do so.

 Line 10, Tax

Do you want the IRS to figure your tax for you?

☐ **Yes.** See chapter 30 of Pub. 17 for details, including who is eligible and what to do. If you have paid too much, we will send you a refund. If you did not pay enough, we will send you a bill.

☐ **No.** Use the Tax Table later in these instructions.

Refund

If line 13a is under $1, we will send the refund only on written request.

If you want to check the status of your refund, see *Refund Information* in Section 6, later. Information about your return will generally be available within 24 hours after the IRS receives your e-filed return, or 4 weeks after you mail your paper return. If you filed Form 8379 with your return, wait 14 weeks (11 weeks if you filed electronically).

 If your refund is large, you may want to decrease the amount of income tax withheld from your pay by filing a new Form W-4. See Income tax withholding and estimated tax payments for 2015 *in Section 5, later.*

Effect of refund on benefits. Any refund you receive cannot be counted as income when determining if you or anyone else is eligible for benefits or assistance, or how much you or anyone else can receive, under any federal program or under any state or local program financed in whole or in part with federal funds. These programs include Temporary Assistance for Needy Families (TANF), Medicaid, Supplemental Security Income (SSI), and Supplemental Nutrition Assistance Program (food stamps). In addition, when determining eligibility, the refund cannot be counted as a resource for at least 12 months after you receive it. Check with your local benefit coordinator to find out if your refund will affect your benefits.

Refund Offset

If you owe past-due federal tax, state income tax, state unemployment compensation debts, child support, spousal support, or certain federal nontax debts, such as student loans, all or part of the refund on line 13a may be used (offset) to pay the past-due amount. Offsets for federal taxes are made by the IRS. All other offsets are made by the Treasury Department's Bureau of the Fiscal Service. For federal tax offsets, you will receive a notice from the IRS. For all other offsets, you will receive a notice from the Fiscal Service. To find out if you may have an offset or if you have a question about it, contact the agency to which you owe the debt.

Injured spouse. If you file a joint return and your spouse has not paid past-due federal tax, state income tax, state unemployment compensation debts, child support, spousal support, or a federal nontax debt, such as a student loan, part or all of the refund on line 13a may be used (offset) to pay the past-due amount. But your part of the refund may be refunded to you if certain conditions apply and you complete Form 8379. For details, use TeleTax topic 203 or see Form 8379.

 Line 11, Health Care: Individual Responsibility

Beginning in 2014, individuals must have health care coverage, qualify for a health coverage exemption, or make a shared responsibility payment with their tax return.

If you had qualifying health care coverage (called minimum essential coverage) for every month of 2014 for yourself, your spouse (if filing jointly), and anyone you could claim as a dependent, check the box on this line and leave the entry space blank. Otherwise, do not check the box on this line. See the instructions for Form 8965. To find out if you can claim someone as a dependent, see Pub. 501.

If you can be claimed as a dependent, do not check the box on this line. Leave the entry space blank. You do not need to attach Form 8965 or see its instructions.

Minimum essential coverage. Most health care coverage that people have is minimum essential coverage. Minimum essential coverage includes:
- Health coverage provided by your employer,
- Health insurance coverage you buy through the Health Insurance Marketplace,
- Many types of government-sponsored health coverage including Medicare, most Medicaid coverage, and most health care coverage provided to veterans and active duty service members, and
- Certain types of health care coverage you buy directly from an insurance company.

See the instructions for Form 8965 for more information on what qualifies as minimum essential coverage.

Premium tax credit. You may be eligible to claim the premium tax credit if you or your spouse enrolled in health insurance through the Health Insurance Marketplace, but you must use Form 1040A or 1040 to do so. You may also be eligible to claim the premium tax credit for any dependent you claim on Form 1040A or 1040 who enrolled in health insurance through the Health Insurance Marketplace.

Lines 13a Through 13d

DIRECT DEPOSIT
Simple. Safe. Secure.

Fast refunds! Choose direct deposit—a fast, simple, safe, secure way to have your refund deposited automatically into your checking or savings account, including an individual retirement arrangement (IRA). For more information about IRAs, see *IRA*, later.

If you want us to directly deposit the amount shown on line 13a to your checking or savings account, including an IRA, at a bank or other financial institution (such as a mutual fund, brokerage firm, or credit union) in the United States:

- Complete lines 13b through 13d (if you want your refund deposited to only one account), or
- Check the box on line 13a and attach Form 8888 if you want to split the direct deposit of your refund into more than one account or use all or part of your refund to buy paper series I savings bonds.

If you do not want your refund directly deposited to your account, do not check the box on line 13a. Draw a line through the boxes on lines 13b and 13d. We will send you a check instead.

Do not request a deposit of your refund to an account that is not in your name, such as your tax preparer's account. Do not allow your tax preparer to deposit any part of your refund into his or her account. The number of direct deposits to a single account or prepaid debit card is limited to three refunds a year. After this limit is exceeded, paper checks will be sent instead. Learn more at IRS.gov.

Why Use Direct Deposit?

- It is faster. You get your refund faster by direct deposit than you do by check.
- It is more secure. There is no check that can get lost or stolen.
- It is more convenient. You do not have to make a trip to the bank to deposit your check.
- It saves tax dollars. It costs the government less to refund by direct deposit.

 If you file a joint return and check the box on line 13a and attach Form 8888 or fill in lines 13b through 13d, your spouse may get at least part of the refund.

IRA. You can have your refund (or part of it) directly deposited to a traditional IRA, Roth IRA, or SEP-IRA, but not a SIMPLE IRA. You must establish the IRA at a bank or other financial institution before you request direct deposit. Make sure your direct deposit will be accepted. You must also notify the trustee or custodian of your account of the year to which the deposit is to be applied (unless the trustee or custodian will not accept a deposit for 2014). If you do not, the trustee or custodian can assume the deposit is for the year during which you are filing the return. For example, if you file your 2014 return during 2015 and do not notify the trustee or custodian in advance, the trustee or custodian can assume the deposit to your IRA is for 2015. If you designate your deposit to be for 2014, you must verify that the deposit was actually made to the account by the due date of the return (without regard to extensions). If the deposit is not made by that date, the deposit is not an IRA contribution for 2014. If you make a contribution to a traditional IRA for 2014, you may be able to take an IRA deduction, but you must file Form 1040A or 1040 to do so.

 You and your spouse each may be able to contribute up to $5,500 ($6,500 if age 50 or older at the end of 2014) to a traditional IRA or Roth IRA for 2014. You may owe a penalty if your contributions exceed these limits and the limits may be lower depending on your income. For more information on IRA contributions, see Pub. 590-A. If the limits on IRA contributions change for 2015, Pub. 590-A will have the new 2015 limits.

For more information on IRAs, see Pub. 590-A and Pub. 590-B.

TreasuryDirect®. You can request a deposit of your refund (or part of it) to a TreasuryDirect® online account to buy U.S. Treasury marketable securities and savings bonds. For more information, go to *www.treasurydirect.gov.*

Form 8888. You can have your refund directly deposited into more than one account or use it to buy up to $5,000 in paper series I savings bonds. You do not need a TreasuryDirect® account to do this. For more information, see the Form 8888 instructions.

Line 13a

You cannot file Form 8888 to split your refund into more than one account or buy paper series I savings bonds if Form 8379 is filed with your return.

Line 13b

The routing number must be nine digits. The first two digits must be 01 through 12 or 21 through 32. On the sample check later, the routing number is 250250025. Henry and Naomi Maple would use that routing number unless their financial institution instructed them to use a different routing number for direct deposits.

Ask your financial institution for the correct routing number to enter on line 13b if:

- The routing number on a deposit slip is different from the routing number on your checks,
- Your deposit is to a savings account that does not allow you to write checks, or
- Your checks state they are payable through a financial institution different from the one at which you have your checking account.

Line 13c

Check the appropriate box for the type of account. Do not check more than one box. If the deposit is to an account such as an IRA, health savings account, brokerage account, or other similar account, ask your financial institution whether you should check the "Checking" or "Savings" box. You must check the correct box to ensure your deposit is accepted. For a TreasuryDirect® online account, check the "Savings" box.

Line 13d

The account number can be up to 17 characters (both numbers and letters). Include hyphens but omit spaces and special symbols. Enter the number from left to right and leave any unused boxes blank. On the sample check below, the account number is 20202086. Do not include the check number.

If the direct deposit to your account(s) is different from the amount you expected, you will receive an explanation in the mail about 2 weeks after your refund is deposited.

Sample Check—Lines 13b Through 13d

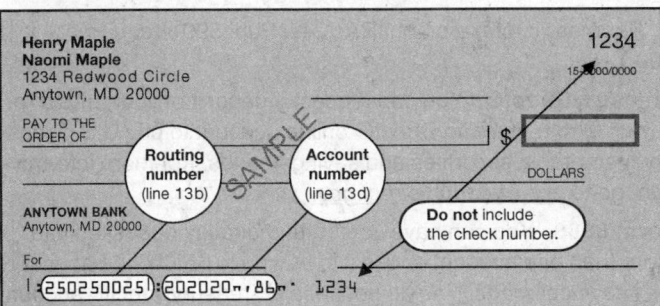

 *The routing and account numbers may be in different places on your check.*

Reasons Your Direct Deposit Request May Be Rejected

If any of the following apply, your direct deposit request will be rejected and a check will be sent instead.

- Any numbers or letters on lines 13b through 13d are crossed out or whited out.
- Your financial institution(s) may not allow a joint refund to be deposited to an individual account. The IRS is not responsible if a financial institution rejects a direct deposit.
- You file your 2014 return after December 31, 2015.
- Three direct deposits of tax refunds have already been made to your account or prepaid debit card.
- The name on your account does not match the name on the tax refund.

 The IRS is not responsible for a lost refund if you enter the wrong account information. Check with your financial institution to get the correct routing and account numbers and to make sure your direct deposit will be accepted.

Amount You Owe

 IRS *e-file* offers two electronic payment options. With Electronic Funds Withdrawal, you can pay your current year balance due and also make up to four estimated tax payments. If you file early, you can schedule your payment for withdrawal from your account on a future date, up to and including the due date of the return. Or you can pay using a debit or credit card. Visit *www.irs.gov/payments* for details on both options.

Line 14, Amount You Owe

TIP *To save interest and penalties, pay your taxes in full by April 15, 2015. You do not have to pay if line 14 is under $1.*

Include any estimated penalty for not paying enough tax during the year (explained later) in the amount you enter on line 14. You can pay online, by phone, or by check or money order. Do not include any estimated tax payments (for 2014 or 2015) in this payment. Instead, make the estimated tax payment separately.

Bad check or payment. The penalty for writing a bad check to the IRS is $25 or 2% of the check, whichever is more. However, if the amount of the check is less than $25, the penalty equals the amount of the check. This penalty also applies to other forms of payment if the IRS does not receive the funds. Use TeleTax topic 206.

Pay Online

Paying online is convenient and secure and helps make sure we get your payments on time. You can pay using either of the following electronic payment methods.

- Direct transfer from your bank account. Go to IRS.gov, click on "Pay Your Tax Bill" and "Direct Pay."
- Debit or credit card.

To pay your taxes online or for more information, go to *www.irs.gov/payments*. Also see the *e-file* information under *Amount You Owe*, earlier, for more information about the Electronic Funds Withdrawal payment option offered when e-filing your return.

Pay by Phone

Paying by phone is another safe and secure method of paying electronically. Use one of the following methods.

- Direct transfer using Electronic Federal Tax Payment System (EFTPS).
- Debit or credit card.

Direct transfer. To use EFTPS, you must be enrolled. You can enroll online or have an enrollment form mailed to you. To make a payment using EFTPS, call 1-800-555-4477 (English) or 1-800-244-4829 (Spanish). People who are deaf, hard of hearing, or have a speech disability and who have access to TTY/TDD equipment can call 1-800-733-4829. For more information about EFTPS, go to *www.irs.gov/payments*.

Debit or credit card. To pay using a debit or credit card, you can call one of the following service providers. There is a convenience fee charged by these providers that varies by provider, card type, and payment amount.

WorldPay US, Inc.
1-844-PAY-TAX-8™ (1-844-729-8298)
www.payUSAtax.com

Official Payments Corporation
1-888-UPAY-TAX™ (1-888-872-9829)
www.officialpayments.com

Link2Gov Corporation
1-888-PAY-1040™ (1-888-729-1040)
www.PAY1040.com

For the latest details on how to pay by phone, go to *www.irs.gov/payments*.

Pay by Check or Money Order

Make your check or money order payable to "United States Treasury" for the full amount due. Do not attach the payment to your return. Do not send cash. Write "2014 Form 1040EZ" and your name, address, daytime phone number, and social security number (SSN) on your payment. If you are filing a joint return, enter the SSN shown first on your return.

To help us process your payment, enter the amount on the right side of the check like this: $ XXX.XX. Do not use dashes or lines (for example, do not enter "$XXX–" or "$XXX ˣˣ/₁₀₀").

Then, complete Form 1040-V following the instructions on that form and enclose it in the envelope with your tax return and payment.

 You may need to (a) increase the amount of income tax withheld from your pay by filing a new Form W-4, (b) increase the tax withheld from other income by filing Form W-4V, or (c) make estimated tax payments for 2015. See Income tax withholding and estimated tax payments for 2015 *in Section 5, later.*

What if You Cannot Pay?

If you cannot pay the full amount shown on line 14 when you file, you can ask for:
- An installment agreement, or
- An extension of time to pay.

Installment agreement. Under an installment agreement, you can pay all or part of the tax you owe in monthly installments. However, even if your request to pay in installments is granted, you will be charged interest and may be charged a late payment penalty on the tax not paid by April 15, 2015. You also must pay a fee. To limit the interest and penalty charges, pay as much of the tax as possible when you file. But before requesting an installment agreement, you should consider other less costly alternatives, such as a bank loan or credit card payment.

To ask for an installment agreement, you can apply online or use Form 9465. To apply online, go to IRS.gov and click on "Tools" and then "Online Payment Agreement."

Extension of time to pay. If paying the tax when it is due would cause you an undue hardship, you can ask for an extension of time to pay by filing Form 1127 by April 15, 2015. You will still be charged interest on the tax not paid by April 15, 2015. An extension generally will not be granted for more than 6 months. You must pay the tax before the extension runs out. If you do not, penalties may be imposed.

Penalty for Not Paying Enough Tax During the Year

You may have to pay a penalty if line 14 is at least $1,000 and it is more than 10% of the tax shown on your return. The "tax shown on your return" is the amount on line 10 minus the amount on line 8a. You may choose to have the IRS figure the penalty for you. If you owe a penalty, the IRS will send you a bill. However, if you want to figure the penalty yourself on Form 2210, you must file Form 1040A or 1040 to do so.

The penalty may be waived under certain conditions. See Pub. 505 for details.

Exceptions to the penalty. You will not owe the penalty if your 2013 tax return was for a tax year of 12 full months and either of the following applies.

1. You had no tax shown on your 2013 return and you were a U.S. citizen or resident for all of 2013, or

2. Line 7 on your 2014 return is at least as much as the tax shown on your 2013 return.

Third Party Designee

If you want to allow your preparer, a friend, a family member, or any other person you choose to discuss your 2014 tax return with the IRS, check the "Yes" box in the "Third Party Designee" area of your return. Also, enter the designee's name, phone number, and any five digits the designee chooses as his or her personal identification number (PIN).

If you check the "Yes" box, you, and your spouse if filing a joint return, are authorizing the IRS to call the designee to answer any questions that may arise during the processing of your return. You also are authorizing the designee to:
- Give the IRS any information that is missing from your return,
- Call the IRS for information about the processing of your return or the status of your refund or payment(s),
- Receive copies of notices or transcripts related to your return, upon request, and
- Respond to certain IRS notices about math errors, offsets, and return preparation.

You are not authorizing the designee to receive any refund check, bind you to anything (including any additional tax liability), or otherwise represent you before the IRS.

The authorization will automatically end no later than the due date (without regard to extensions) for filing your 2015 tax return. This is April 18, 2016, for most people.

Signing Your Return

Form 1040EZ is not considered a valid return unless you sign it. If you are filing a joint return, your spouse also must sign. If your spouse cannot sign the return, see Pub. 501. Be sure to date your return and enter your occupation(s). If you have someone prepare your return, you are still responsible for the correctness of the return. If your return is signed for you by a representative, you must have a power of attorney attached that specifically authorizes the representative to sign your return. To do this, you can use Form 2848. If you are filing a joint return as a surviving spouse, see *Death of a Taxpayer* in Section 1, earlier.

Court-Appointed Conservator, Guardian, or Other Fiduciary. If you are a court-appointed conservator, guardian, or other fiduciary for a mentally or physically incompetent individual who has to file Form 1040EZ, sign your name for the individual. You should also file Form 56, Notice Concerning Fiduciary Relationship, when you first begin those duties for the individual.

Child's return. If your child cannot sign the return, either parent can sign the child's name in the space provided. Then, add "By (your signature), parent for minor child."

Daytime phone number. Providing your daytime phone number may help speed the processing of your return. We may have questions about items on your return, such as the earned income credit. If you answer our questions over the phone, we may be able to continue processing your return without mailing you a letter. If you are filing a joint return, you can enter either your or your spouse's daytime phone number.

Identity protection PIN. For 2014, if you received an IRS notice providing you with an Identity Protection Personal Identification Number (IP PIN), enter it in the IP PIN spaces provided below your daytime phone number. You must correctly enter all six numbers of your IP PIN. If you did not receive a notice containing an IP PIN, leave these spaces blank.

 New IP PINs are issued every year. Enter the latest IP PIN you received. IP PINs for 2014 tax returns generally were sent in December 2014.

If you are filing a joint return and both taxpayers receive an IP PIN, only the taxpayer whose social security number (SSN) appears first on the tax return should enter his or her IP PIN. However, if you are filing electronically, both taxpayers must enter their IP PINs.

If you need more information or answers to frequently asked questions on how to use the IP PIN, go to *www.irs.gov/Individuals/Understanding-Your-CP01A-Notice*. If you received an IP PIN but misplaced it, call 1-800-908-4490.

Paid preparer must sign your return. Generally, anyone you pay to prepare your return must sign it and include their preparer tax identification number (PTIN) in the space provided. The preparer must give you a copy of the return for your records. Someone who prepares your return but does not charge you should not sign your return.

 **Electronic return signatures!** To file your return electronically, you must sign the return electronically using a personal identification number (PIN). If you are filing online using software, you must use a Self-Select PIN. If you are filing electronically using a tax practitioner, you can use a Self-Select PIN or a Practitioner PIN.

Self-Select PIN. The Self-Select PIN method allows you to create your own PIN. If you are filing a joint return, both you and your spouse must create a separate PIN to enter as an electronic signature.

A PIN is any combination of five digits you choose except five zeros. If you use a PIN, there is nothing to sign and nothing to mail—not even your Forms W-2.

To verify your identity, you will be prompted to enter your adjusted gross income (AGI) from your originally filed 2013 federal income tax return, if applicable. Do not use your AGI from an amended return (Form 1040X) or a math error correction made by the IRS. AGI is the amount shown on your 2013 Form 1040, line 38; Form 1040A, line 22; or Form 1040EZ, line 4. If you do not have your 2013 income tax return, call the IRS at 1-800-908-9946 to get a free transcript of your return or visit IRS.gov and click on "Get Transcript of Your Tax Records" under "Tools." (If you filed electronically last year, you may use your prior year PIN to verify your identity instead of your prior year AGI. The prior year PIN is the five digit PIN you used to electronically sign your 2013 return.) You also will be prompted to enter your date of birth (DOB).

 You cannot use the Self-Select PIN method if you are a first-time filer under age 16 at the end of 2014.

 If you cannot locate your prior year AGI or prior year PIN, use the Electronic Filing PIN Request. This can be found at IRS.gov. Click on "Request an Electronic Filing PIN." Or you can call 1-866-704-7388.

Practitioner PIN. The Practitioner PIN method allows you to authorize your tax practitioner to enter or generate your PIN. The practitioner can provide you with details.

Form 8453. You must send in a paper Form 8453 if you are attaching or filing Form 2848 (for an electronic return signed by an agent).

Section 4—After You Have Finished

Return Checklist

This checklist can help you file a correct return. Mistakes can delay your refund or result in notices being sent to you. One of the best ways to file an accurate return is to use IRS *e-file*. Tax software does the math for you and will help you avoid mistakes. Combining *e-file* with direct deposit is the fastest way to get your refund.

Did you:

☐ Enter the correct social security number for you and your spouse, if married, in the space provided on Form 1040EZ? Check that your name and SSN agree with your social security card.

☐ Use the amount from line 6, and the proper filing status, to find your tax in the Tax Table? Be sure you entered the correct tax on line 10.

☐ Go through the three steps in the instructions for lines 8a and 8b, if you thought you could take the EIC? If you could take the EIC, did you take special care to use the proper filing status column in the EIC Table?

☐ Check your math, especially when figuring your taxable income, federal income tax withheld, earned income credit, total payments, and your refund or amount you owe?

☐ Check one or both boxes on line 5 if you (or your spouse) can be claimed as a dependent on someone's (such as your parents') 2014 return? Did you check the box even if that person chooses not to claim you (or your spouse)? Did you leave the boxes blank if no one can claim you (or your spouse) as a dependent?

☐ Enter an amount on line 5? If you checked any of the boxes, did you use the worksheet on the back of Form 1040EZ to figure the amount to enter? If you did not check any of the boxes, did you enter $10,150 if single; $20,300 if married filing jointly?

☐ Sign and date Form 1040EZ and enter your occupation(s)?

☐ Include your apartment number in your address if you live in an apartment?

☐ Attach your Form(s) W-2 to the left margin of Form 1040EZ?

☐ Include all the required information on your payment if you owe tax and are paying by check or money order? See the instructions for line 14 in Section 3, earlier.

☐ File only one original return for the same year, even if you have not gotten your refund or have not heard from the IRS since you filed? Filing more than one original return for the same year or sending in more than one copy of the same return (unless we ask you to do so) could delay your refund.

Filing the Return

Due Date

File Form 1040EZ by **April 15, 2015**. If you file after this date, you may have to pay interest and penalties, discussed later in this Section 4.

If you were serving in, or in support of, the U.S. Armed Forces in a designated combat zone or a contingency operation, you may be able to file later. See Pub. 3 for details.

What if You Cannot File on Time?

You can get an automatic 6-month extension to file your return if, no later than the date your return is due, you file Form 4868. For details, see Form 4868.

 An automatic 6-month extension to file does not extend the time to pay your tax. If you do not pay your tax by the original due date of your return, you will owe interest on the unpaid tax and may owe penalties. See Form 4868.

If you make a payment with your extension request, see the instructions for line 9 in Section 3, earlier.

What if You File or Pay Late?

We can charge you interest and penalties on the amount you owe.

Interest. We will charge you interest on taxes not paid by their due date, even if an extension of time to file is granted. We will also charge you interest on penalties imposed for failure to file, negligence, fraud, substantial valuation misstatements, substantial understatements of tax, and reportable transaction understatements. Interest is charged on the penalty from the due date of the return (including extensions).

Penalties

Late filing. If you do not file your return by the due date (including extensions), the penalty is usually 5% of the amount due for each month or part of a month your return is late, unless you have a reasonable explanation. If you do, include it with your return. The penalty can be as much as 25% of the tax due. The penalty is 15% per month, up to a maximum of 75%, if the failure to file is fraudulent. If your return is more than 60 days late, the minimum penalty could be as much as the amount of any tax you owe.

Late payment of tax. If you pay your taxes late, the penalty is usually ½ of 1% of the unpaid amount for each month or part of a month the tax is not paid. The penalty can be as much as 25% of the unpaid amount. It applies to any unpaid tax on the return. This penalty is in addition to interest charges on late payments.

Frivolous return. In addition to any other penalties, there is a penalty of $5,000 for filing a frivolous return. A frivolous return is one that does not contain information needed to figure the correct tax or shows a substantially incorrect tax because you take a frivolous position or desire to delay or interfere with the tax laws. This includes altering or striking out the preprinted language above the space where you sign. For a list of positions identified as frivolous, see Notice 2010-33, which is on page 609 of Internal Revenue Bulletin 2010-17 at *www.irs.gov/pub/irs-irbs/irb10-17.pdf*.

Are there other penalties? Yes. There are penalties for negligence, substantial understatement of tax, reportable transaction understatements, filing an erroneous refund claim, and fraud. Criminal penalties may be imposed for willful failure to file, tax evasion, making a false statement, or identity theft. See Pub. 17 for details.

Where Do You File?

See the last page of these instructions.

Private delivery services. If you *e-file* your return, there is no need to mail it. See the *e-file* page earlier, or IRS.gov for more information. However, if you choose to mail it, you can use only the following IRS-designated private delivery services to meet the "timely mailing as timely filing/paying" rule for tax returns and payments.

- United Parcel Service (UPS): UPS Next Day Air, UPS Next Day Air Saver, UPS 2nd Day Air, UPS 2nd Day Air A.M., UPS Worldwide Express Plus, and UPS Worldwide Express.
- Federal Express (FedEx): FedEx Priority Overnight, FedEx Standard Overnight, FedEx 2Day, FedEx International Priority, and FedEx International First.

For more information, go to IRS.gov and enter "private delivery service" in the search box. The search results will direct you to the IRS mailing address to use if you are using a private delivery service. You will also find any updates to the list of designated private delivery services. The private delivery service can tell you how to get written proof of the mailing date.

Section 5—General Information

The IRS Mission. Provide America's taxpayers top-quality service by helping them understand and meet their tax responsibilities and enforce the law with integrity and fairness to all.

Income tax withholding and estimated tax payments for 2015. If the amount you owe or your refund is large, you may want to file a new Form W-4 with your employer to change the amount of income tax withheld from your 2015 pay. For details on how to complete Form W-4, see Pub. 505. If you receive certain government payments (such as unemployment compensation or social security benefits), you can have tax withheld from those payments by giving the payer Form W-4V.

You can use the IRS Withholding Calculator *at www.irs.gov/Individuals/IRS-Withholding-Calculator, instead of Pub. 505 or the worksheets included with Form W-4 or W-4P, to determine whether you need to have your withholding increased or decreased.*

In general, you do not have to make estimated tax payments if you expect that your 2015 tax return will show a tax refund or a tax balance due of less than $1,000. See Pub. 505 for more details.

Secure your records from identity theft. Identity theft occurs when someone uses your personal information, such as your name, social security number (SSN), or other identifying information, without your permission, to commit fraud or other crimes. An identity thief may use your SSN to get a job or may file a tax return using your SSN to receive a refund.

To reduce your risk:
- Protect your SSN,
- Ensure your employer is protecting your SSN, and
- Be careful when choosing a tax preparer.

If your tax records are affected by identity theft and you receive a notice from the IRS, respond right away to the name and phone number printed on the IRS notice or letter. For more information, see Pub. 4535.

If your tax records are not currently affected by identity theft but you think you are at risk due to a lost or stolen purse or wallet, questionable credit card activity or credit report, etc., visit *www.irs.gov/identitytheft* to learn what steps you should take.

Victims of identity theft who are experiencing economic harm or a systemic problem, or are seeking help in resolving tax problems that have not been resolved through normal channels, may be eligible for Taxpayer Advocate Service (TAS) assistance. You can reach TAS by calling the National Taxpayer Advocate Helpline at 1-877-777-4778. People who are deaf, hard of hearing, or have a speech disability and who have access to TTY/TDD equipment can call 1-800-829-4059. Deaf or hard of hearing individuals can also contact the IRS through relay services such as the Federal Relay Service available at *www.gsa.gov/fedrelay*.

Protect yourself from suspicious emails or phishing schemes. Phishing is the creation and use of email and websites designed to mimic legitimate business emails and websites. The most common form is sending an email to a user falsely claiming to be an established legitimate enterprise in an attempt to scam the user into surrendering private information that will be used for identity theft.

The IRS does not initiate contacts with taxpayers via emails. Also, the IRS does not request detailed personal information through email or ask taxpayers for the PIN numbers, passwords, or similar secret access information for their credit card, bank, or other financial accounts.

If you receive an unsolicited email claiming to be from the IRS, forward the message to *phishing@irs.gov.* You may also report misuse of the IRS name, logo, forms, or other IRS property to the Treasury Inspector General for Tax Administration toll-free at 1-800-366-4484. People who are deaf, hard of hearing, or

---

have a speech disability and who have access to TTY/TDD equipment can call 1-800-877-8339.

You can forward suspicious emails to the Federal Trade Commission at *spam@uce.gov* or contact them at *www.ftc.gov/idtheft* or 1-877-IDTHEFT (1-877-438-4338). People who are deaf, hard of hearing, or have a speech disability and who have access to TTY/TDD equipment can call 1-866-653-4261.

Visit IRS.gov and enter "identity theft" in the search box to learn more about identity theft and how to reduce your risk.

How long should you keep your tax return? Keep a copy of your tax return, worksheets you used, and records of all items appearing on it (such as Forms W-2 and 1099) until the statute of limitations runs out for that return. Usually, this is 3 years from the date the return was due or filed or 2 years from the date the tax was paid, whichever is later. You should keep some records longer. For more details, see chapter 1 of Pub. 17.

How do you amend your tax return? File Form 1040X to change a return you already filed. Generally, Form 1040X must be filed within 3 years after the date the original return was filed or within 2 years after the date the tax was paid, whichever is later. But you may have more time to file Form 1040X if you live in a federally declared disaster area or you are physically or mentally unable to manage your financial affairs. See Pub. 556 for details.

Use the "Where's My Amended Return" application on IRS.gov to track the status of your amended return. It can take up to 3 weeks from the date you mailed it to show up in our system.

How do you get a copy of your tax return information? Tax return transcripts are free and are generally used to validate income and tax filing status for mortgage applications, student and small business loan applications, and during tax preparation. To get a free transcript:
- Visit IRS.gov and click on "Get Transcript of Your Tax Records" under "Tools,"
- Use Form 4506-T or 4506T-EZ, or
- Call us at 1-800-908-9946.

If you need a copy of your actual tax return, use Form 4506. There is a fee for each return requested. See Form 4506 for the current fee. If your main home, principal place of business, or tax records are located in a federally declared disaster area, this fee will be waived.

Past due returns. If you or someone you know needs to file past due tax returns, use TeleTax topic 153 or visit *www.irs.gov/individuals* for help in filing those returns. Send the returns to the address that applies to you in the latest Form 1040EZ instructions. For example, if you are filing a 2011 return in 2015, use the address at the end of these instructions. However, if you got an IRS notice, mail the return to the address in the notice.

Innocent spouse relief. Generally, both you and your spouse are each responsible for paying the full amount of tax, interest, and penalties on your joint return. However, you may qualify for relief from liability for tax on a joint return if (a) there is an understatement of tax because your spouse omitted income or claimed false deductions or credits, (b) you are divorced, separated, or no longer living with your spouse, or (c) given all the facts and circumstances, it would not be fair to hold you liable for the tax. File Form 8857 to request relief. In some cases, Form 8857 may need to be filed within 2 years of the date on which the IRS first attempted to collect the tax from you. Do not file Form 8857 with your Form 1040EZ. For more information, see Pub. 971 and Form 8857 or you can call the Innocent Spouse office toll-free at 1-855-851-2009.

How do you make a gift to reduce debt held by the public? If you wish to do so, make a check payable to "Bureau of the Fiscal Service." You can send it to:

> Bureau of the Fiscal Service
> Attn Dept G
> P.O. Box 2188
> Parkersburg, WV 26106-2188

Or you can enclose the check with your income tax return when you file. In the memo section of the check, note that it is a gift to reduce the debt held by the public. Do not add your gift to any tax you may owe. See the instructions for line 14 for details on how to pay any tax you owe.

Go to *www.publicdebt.treas.gov/index1.htm* for information on how to make this gift online.

 You may be able to deduct this gift on your 2015 tax return.

The Taxpayer Advocate Service Is Here To Help You

What is the Taxpayer Advocate Service?

The Taxpayer Advocate Service (TAS) is an *independent* organization within the Internal Revenue Service (IRS) that helps taxpayers and protects taxpayer rights. Our job is to ensure that every taxpayer is treated fairly and that you know and understand your rights under the *Taxpayer Bill of Rights*.

What can the Taxpayer Advocate Service do for you?

We can help you resolve problems that you can't resolve with the IRS. And our service is free. If you qualify for our assistance, your advocate will be with you at every turn and do everything possible. TAS can help you if:
- Your problem is causing financial difficulty for you, your family, or your business.
- You face (or your business is facing) an immediate threat of adverse action.
- You've tried repeatedly to contact the IRS but no one has responded, or the IRS hasn't responded by the date promised.

How can you reach us?

We have offices in *every state, the District of Columbia, and Puerto Rico*. Your local advocate's number is at

TaxpayerAdvocate.irs.gov, at *www.irs.gov/advocate*, and in your local directory. You can also call us toll-free at 1-877-777-4778.

How can you learn about your taxpayer rights?

The Taxpayer Bill of Rights describes ten basic rights that all tax-payers have when dealing with the IRS. Our Tax Toolkit at *TaxpayerAdvocate.irs.gov* can help you understand *what these rights mean to you* and how they apply. These are *your* rights. Know them. Use them.

How else does the Taxpayer Advocate Service help taxpayers?

TAS works to resolve large-scale problems that affect many tax-payers. If you know of one of these broad issues, please report it to us at *www.irs.gov/sams*.

Low Income Taxpayer Clinics Help Taxpayers

Low Income Taxpayer Clinics (LITCs) are independent from the IRS. Some serve individuals whose income is below a certain level and who need to resolve a tax problem. These clinics pro-vide professional representation before the IRS or in court on au-dits, appeals, tax collection disputes, and other issues for free or for a small fee. Some clinics provide information about taxpayer rights and responsibilities in many different languages for indi-viduals who speak English as a second language. For more in-formation, and to find a clinic near you, read the LITC page on *www.irs.gov/litc* or Pub. 4134, Low Income Taxpayer Clinic List. You can get this publication at your local IRS office or by calling 1-800-829-3676.

Suggestions for Improving the IRS Taxpayer Advocacy Panel

Have a suggestion for improving the IRS and do not know who to contact? The Taxpayer Advocacy Panel (TAP) is a diverse group of citizen volunteers who listen to taxpayers, identify tax-payers' issues, and make suggestions for improving IRS service and customer satisfaction. The panel is demographically and geographically diverse, with at least one member from each state, the District of Columbia, and Puerto Rico. Contact TAP at *www.improveirs.org* or 1-888-912-1227 (toll-free).

Section 6—How To Get Tax Help

Do you need help with a tax issue or preparing your tax return, or do you need a free publication or form?

Preparing and filing your tax return. Find free options to pre-pare and file your return on IRS.gov or in your local community if you qualify.
- Go to IRS.gov and click on the Filing tab to see your options.
- Enter "Free File" in the search box to use brand name soft-ware to prepare and e-file your federal tax return for free.
- Enter "VITA" in the search box, download the free IRS2Go app, or call 1-800-906- 9887 to find the nearest Volunteer In-come Tax Assistance or Tax Counseling for the Elderly (TCE) location for free tax preparation.
- Enter "TCE" in the search box, download the free IRS2Go app, or call 1-888-227- 7669 to find the nearest Tax Coun-seling for the Elderly location for free tax preparation.

The Volunteer Income Tax Assistance (VITA) program offers free tax help to people who generally make $53,000 or less, per-sons with disabilities, the elderly, and limited- English-speaking taxpayers who need help preparing their own tax returns. The Tax Counseling for the Elderly (TCE) program offers free tax help for all taxpayers, particularly those who are 60 years of age and older. TCE volunteers specialize in answering questions about pensions and retirement-related issues unique to seniors.

Getting answers to your tax law questions. *IRS.gov* and IRS2Go are ready when you are—24 hours a day, 7 days a week.
- Enter "ITA" in the search box on *IRS.gov* for the Interactive Tax Assistant, a tool that will ask you questions on a number of tax law topics and provide answers. You can print the en-tire interview and the final response.

- Enter "Tax Map" or "Tax Trails" in the search box for detailed information by tax topic.
- Enter "Pub 17" in the search box to get Pub. 17, Your Feder-al Income Tax for Individuals, which features details on tax-saving opportunities, 2014 tax changes, and thousands of interactive links to help you find answers to your ques-tions.
- Call TeleTax: 1-800-829-4477 for recorded information on a variety of tax topics. See *Recorded Tax Help (TeleTax)*, lat-er, for a list of the topics covered.
- Access tax law information in your electronic filing software.
- Go to *IRS.gov* and click on the Help & Resources tab for more information.

Tax forms and publications. You can download or print all of the forms and publications you may need on *IRS.gov/ formspubs*. Otherwise, you can:
- Go to *IRS.gov/formspubs* to place an order and have forms mailed to you.
- Call 1-800-829-3676 to order current-year forms, instruc-tions, publications, and prior-year forms and instructions (limited to 5 years).

You should receive your order within 10 business days.

Where to file your tax return.
- Remember, there are many ways to file your return electron-ically. It's safe, quick and easy. See *Preparing and filing your tax return*, above, for more information.
- See *Where Do You File?* at the end of these instructions to determine where to mail your completed paper tax return.

Getting a transcript or copy of a return.
- Go to *IRS.gov* and click on "Get Transcript of Your Tax Re-cords" under "Tools."

- Download the free IRS2Go app to your smart phone and use it to order transcripts of your tax returns or tax account.
- Call the transcript toll-free line: 1-800-908-9946.
- Mail Form 4506-T or Form 4506T-EZ (both available on IRS.gov).

Using online tools to help prepare your return. Go to *IRS.gov* and click on the Tools bar to use these and other self-service options.
- The *Earned Income Tax Credit Assistant* determines if you're eligible for the EIC.
- The *IRS Withholding Calculator* estimates the amount you should have withheld from your paycheck for federal income tax purposes.
- The *Electronic Filing PIN Request* helps to verify your identity when you do not have your prior year AGI or prior self-selected PIN available.

Understanding identity theft issues.
- Go to *irs.gov/uac/Identity-Protection* for information and videos.
- See *Secure your records from identity theft* under *General Information*, earlier.

Checking on the status of a refund.
- Go to *IRS.gov/refunds*.
- Download the free IRS2Go app to your smart phone and use it to check your refund status.
- Call the automated refund hotline: 1-800-829-1954. See *Refund Information*, later.

Making a tax payment. You can make electronic payments online, by phone, or from a mobile device. Paying electronically is safe and secure. The IRS uses the latest encryption technology and does not store banking information. It's easy and secure and much quicker than mailing in a check or money order. Go to *IRS.gov* and click on the Payments tab or the "Pay Your Tax Bill" icon to make a payment using the following options.
- *Direct Pay* (only if you have a checking or savings account).
- Debit or credit card.
- Electronic Federal Tax Payment System.
- Check or money order.

What if I can't pay now? Click on the Payments tab or the "Pay Your Tax Bill" icon on IRS.gov to find more information about these additional options.
- An *online payment agreement* determines if you are eligible to apply for an installment agreement if you cannot pay your taxes in full today. With the needed information, you can complete the application in about 30 minutes, and get immediate approval.
- An offer in compromise allows you to settle your tax debt for less than the full amount you owe. Use the *Offer in Compromise Pre-Qualifier* to confirm your eligibility.

Checking the status of an amended return.
- Go to IRS.gov and click on the Tools tab and then *Where's My Amended Return?*

Understanding an IRS notice or letter.
- Enter "Understanding your notice" in the search box on IRS.gov to find additional information about your IRS notice or letter.

Visiting the IRS. Locate the nearest Taxpayer Assistance Center using the Office Locator tool on *IRS.gov*. Enter "office locator" in the search box. Or choose the "Contact Us" option on the IRS2Go app and search Local Offices. Before you visit, use the Locator tool to check hours and services available.

Watching IRS videos. The IRS Video portal contains video and audio presentations on topics of interest to individuals, small businesses, and tax professionals. You'll find video clips of tax topics, archived versions of live panel discussions and Webinars, and audio archives of tax practitioner phone forums.

Getting tax information in other languages. For taxpayers whose native language is not English, we have the following resources available.
- Spanish – *www.irs.gov/Spanish*
- Chinese – *www.irs.gov/Chinese*
- Korean – *www.irs.gov/Korean*
- Vietnamese – *www.irs.gov/Vietnamese*
- Russian – *www.irs.gov/Russian*
- Over-the-phone interpreter service - The IRS Taxpayer Assistance Centers provide telephone interpreter service in over 170 languages, and the service is available free to taxpayers.

Online ordering of tax forms and publications. To order tax forms and publications delivered by mail, go to *www.irs.gov/formspubs* and click on "Order Forms & Pubs." For current year tax forms and publications, click on "Forms and Publications by Mail."

Refund Information

Information about your return will generally be available within 24 hours after the IRS receives your e-filed return, or 4 weeks after you mail a paper return. But if you filed Form 8379 with your return, allow 14 weeks (11 weeks if you filed electronically) before checking your refund status.

 Visit IRS.gov and click on *Where's My Refund?* 24 hours a day, 7 days a week.

To use *Where's My Refund?* have a copy of your tax return handy. You will need to enter the following information from your return:
- Your social security number (or individual taxpayer identification number),
- Your filing status, and
- The exact whole dollar amount of your refund.

Instructions for Form 1040EZ

Where's My Refund? will provide an actual personalized refund date as soon as the IRS processes your tax return and approves your refund.

Where's My Refund? does not track refunds that are claimed on an amended tax return.

 Updates to refund status are made no more than once a day—usually at night.

You can also check the status of your refund on the free IRS2Go phone app.

 If you do not have Internet access, many services are available by phone. Call 1-800-829-1954 24 hours a day, 7 days a week, for automated refund information.

Note. Our phone and walk-in assistors can research the status of your refund only if it's been 21 days or more since you filed

electronically or more than 6 weeks since you mailed your paper return.

Do not send in a copy of your return unless asked to do so.

To get a refund, you generally must file your return within 3 years from the date the return was due (including extensions).

Refund information also is available in Spanish at *www.irs.gov/Spanish* and the phone number listed above.

Recorded Tax Help (TeleTax)

TeleTax is a wide-ranging directory of recorded tax information that is available anytime. A complete list of topics is available online at *www.irs.gov/taxtopics* and in the instructions for Form 1040A and 1040. Select the number of the topic you want to hear. Then call **1-800-829-4477.** Be ready to take notes.

Taxpayer Bill of Rights

All taxpayers have fundamental rights they should be aware of when dealing with the IRS. The Taxpayer Bill of Rights, which the IRS adopted in June of 2014, takes existing rights in the tax code and groups them into the following 10 broad categories, making them easier to understand. Explore your rights and our obligations to protect them.

The right to be informed. Taxpayers have the right to know what they need to do to comply with the tax laws. They are entitled to clear explanations of the laws and IRS procedures in all tax forms, instructions, publications, notices, and correspondence. They have the right to be informed of IRS decisions about their tax accounts and to receive clear explanations of the outcomes.

The right to quality service. Taxpayers have the right to receive prompt, courteous, and professional assistance in their dealings with the IRS, to be spoken to in a way they can easily understand, to receive clear and easily understandable communications from the IRS, and to speak to a supervisor about inadequate service.

The right to pay no more than the correct amount of tax. Taxpayers have the right to pay only the amount of tax legally due, including interest and penalties, and to have the IRS apply all tax payments properly.

The right to challenge the IRS's position and be heard. Taxpayers have the right to raise objections and provide additional documentation in response to formal IRS actions or proposed actions, to expect that the IRS will consider their timely objections and documentation promptly and fairly, and to receive a response if the IRS does not agree with their position.

The right to appeal an IRS decision in an independent forum. Taxpayers are entitled to a fair and impartial administrative appeal of most IRS decisions, including many penalties, and have the right to receive a written response regarding the Office of Appeals' decision. Taxpayers generally have the right to take their cases to court.

The right to finality. Taxpayers have the right to know the maximum amount of time they have to challenge the IRS's position as well as the maximum amount of time the IRS has to audit a particular tax year or collect a tax debt. Taxpayers have the right to know when the IRS has finished an audit.

The right to privacy. Taxpayers have the right to expect that any IRS inquiry, examination, or enforcement action will comply with the law and be no more intrusive than necessary, and will respect all due process rights, including search and seizure protections and will provide, where applicable, a collection due process hearing.

The right to confidentiality. Taxpayers have the right to expect that any information they provide to the IRS will not be disclosed unless authorized by the taxpayer or by law. Taxpayers have the right to expect appropriate action will be taken against employees, return preparers, and others who wrongfully use or disclose taxpayer return information.

The right to retain representation. Taxpayers have the right to retain an authorized representative of their choice to represent them in their dealings with the IRS. Taxpayers have the right to seek assistance from a *Low Income Taxpayer Clinic* if they cannot afford representation.

The right to a fair and just tax system. Taxpayers have the right to expect the tax system to consider facts and circumstances that might affect their underlying liabilities, ability to pay, or ability to provide information timely. Taxpayers have the right to receive assistance from the *Taxpayer Advocate Service* if they are experiencing financial difficulty or if the IRS has not resolved their tax issues properly and timely through its normal channels.

Learn more at *www.irs.gov/taxpayerrights*.

Instructions for Form 1040EZ

2014 Tax Table

Example. Mr. Brown is single. His **taxable income** on line 6 of Form 1040EZ is $26,250. He follows two easy steps to figure his tax: **1.** He finds the $26,250-26,300 taxable income line. **2.** He finds the Single filing status column and reads down the column. The **tax** amount shown where the taxable income line and the filing status line meet is $3,488. He enters this amount on line 10 of Form 1040EZ.

At least	But less than	Single	Married filing jointly
		Your tax is—	
26,200	26,250	3,480	3,026
26,250	26,300	3,488	3,034
26,300	26,350	3,495	3,041
26,350	26,400	3,503	3,049

If Form 1040EZ, line 6, is— At least	But less than	And you are— Single	Married filing jointly
		Your tax is—	
0	5	0	0
5	15	1	1
15	25	2	2
25	50	4	4
50	75	6	6
75	100	9	9
100	125	11	11
125	150	14	14
150	175	16	16
175	200	19	19
200	225	21	21
225	250	24	24
250	275	26	26
275	300	29	29
300	325	31	31
325	350	34	34
350	375	36	36
375	400	39	39
400	425	41	41
425	450	44	44
450	475	46	46
475	500	49	49
500	525	51	51
525	550	54	54
550	575	56	56
575	600	59	59
600	625	61	61
625	650	64	64
650	675	66	66
675	700	69	69
700	725	71	71
725	750	74	74
750	775	76	76
775	800	79	79
800	825	81	81
825	850	84	84
850	875	86	86
875	900	89	89
900	925	91	91
925	950	94	94
950	975	96	96
975	1,000	99	99

1,000

At least	But less than	Single	Married filing jointly
1,000	1,025	101	101
1,025	1,050	104	104
1,050	1,075	106	106
1,075	1,100	109	109
1,100	1,125	111	111
1,125	1,150	114	114
1,150	1,175	116	116
1,175	1,200	119	119
1,200	1,225	121	121
1,225	1,250	124	124
1,250	1,275	126	126
1,275	1,300	129	129
1,300	1,325	131	131
1,325	1,350	134	134
1,350	1,375	136	136
1,375	1,400	139	139
1,400	1,425	141	141
1,425	1,450	144	144
1,450	1,475	146	146
1,475	1,500	149	149
1,500	1,525	151	151
1,525	1,550	154	154
1,550	1,575	156	156
1,575	1,600	159	159
1,600	1,625	161	161
1,625	1,650	164	164
1,650	1,675	166	166
1,675	1,700	169	169
1,700	1,725	171	171
1,725	1,750	174	174
1,750	1,775	176	176
1,775	1,800	179	179
1,800	1,825	181	181
1,825	1,850	184	184
1,850	1,875	186	186
1,875	1,900	189	189
1,900	1,925	191	191
1,925	1,950	194	194
1,950	1,975	196	196
1,975	2,000	199	199

2,000

At least	But less than	Single	Married filing jointly
2,000	2,025	201	201
2,025	2,050	204	204
2,050	2,075	206	206
2,075	2,100	209	209
2,100	2,125	211	211
2,125	2,150	214	214
2,150	2,175	216	216
2,175	2,200	219	219
2,200	2,225	221	221
2,225	2,250	224	224
2,250	2,275	226	226
2,275	2,300	229	229
2,300	2,325	231	231
2,325	2,350	234	234
2,350	2,375	236	236
2,375	2,400	239	239
2,400	2,425	241	241
2,425	2,450	244	244
2,450	2,475	246	246
2,475	2,500	249	249
2,500	2,525	251	251
2,525	2,550	254	254
2,550	2,575	256	256
2,575	2,600	259	259
2,600	2,625	261	261
2,625	2,650	264	264
2,650	2,675	266	266
2,675	2,700	269	269
2,700	2,725	271	271
2,725	2,750	274	274
2,750	2,775	276	276
2,775	2,800	279	279
2,800	2,825	281	281
2,825	2,850	284	284
2,850	2,875	286	286
2,875	2,900	289	289
2,900	2,925	291	291
2,925	2,950	294	294
2,950	2,975	296	296
2,975	3,000	299	299

3,000

At least	But less than	Single	Married filing jointly
3,000	3,050	303	303
3,050	3,100	308	308
3,100	3,150	313	313
3,150	3,200	318	318
3,200	3,250	323	323
3,250	3,300	328	328
3,300	3,350	333	333
3,350	3,400	338	338
3,400	3,450	343	343
3,450	3,500	348	348
3,500	3,550	353	353
3,550	3,600	358	358
3,600	3,650	363	363
3,650	3,700	368	368
3,700	3,750	373	373
3,750	3,800	378	378
3,800	3,850	383	383
3,850	3,900	388	388
3,900	3,950	393	393
3,950	4,000	398	398

4,000

At least	But less than	Single	Married filing jointly
4,000	4,050	403	403
4,050	4,100	408	408
4,100	4,150	413	413
4,150	4,200	418	418
4,200	4,250	423	423
4,250	4,300	428	428
4,300	4,350	433	433
4,350	4,400	438	438
4,400	4,450	443	443
4,450	4,500	448	448
4,500	4,550	453	453
4,550	4,600	458	458
4,600	4,650	463	463
4,650	4,700	468	468
4,700	4,750	473	473
4,750	4,800	478	478
4,800	4,850	483	483
4,850	4,900	488	488
4,900	4,950	493	493
4,950	5,000	498	498

(Continued)

If Form 1040EZ, line 6, is— At least	But less than	And you are— Single	Married filing jointly
		Your tax is—	

5,000

At least	But less than	Single	Married filing jointly
5,000	5,050	503	503
5,050	5,100	508	508
5,100	5,150	513	513
5,150	5,200	518	518
5,200	5,250	523	523
5,250	5,300	528	528
5,300	5,350	533	533
5,350	5,400	538	538
5,400	5,450	543	543
5,450	5,500	548	548
5,500	5,550	553	553
5,550	5,600	558	558
5,600	5,650	563	563
5,650	5,700	568	568
5,700	5,750	573	573
5,750	5,800	578	578
5,800	5,850	583	583
5,850	5,900	588	588
5,900	5,950	593	593
5,950	6,000	598	598

6,000

At least	But less than	Single	Married filing jointly
6,000	6,050	603	603
6,050	6,100	608	608
6,100	6,150	613	613
6,150	6,200	618	618
6,200	6,250	623	623
6,250	6,300	628	628
6,300	6,350	633	633
6,350	6,400	638	638
6,400	6,450	643	643
6,450	6,500	648	648
6,500	6,550	653	653
6,550	6,600	658	658
6,600	6,650	663	663
6,650	6,700	668	668
6,700	6,750	673	673
6,750	6,800	678	678
6,800	6,850	683	683
6,850	6,900	688	688
6,900	6,950	693	693
6,950	7,000	698	698

7,000

At least	But less than	Single	Married filing jointly
7,000	7,050	703	703
7,050	7,100	708	708
7,100	7,150	713	713
7,150	7,200	718	718
7,200	7,250	723	723
7,250	7,300	728	728
7,300	7,350	733	733
7,350	7,400	738	738
7,400	7,450	743	743
7,450	7,500	748	748
7,500	7,550	753	753
7,550	7,600	758	758
7,600	7,650	763	763
7,650	7,700	768	768
7,700	7,750	773	773
7,750	7,800	778	778
7,800	7,850	783	783
7,850	7,900	788	788
7,900	7,950	793	793
7,950	8,000	798	798

8,000

At least	But less than	Single	Married filing jointly
8,000	8,050	803	803
8,050	8,100	808	808
8,100	8,150	813	813
8,150	8,200	818	818
8,200	8,250	823	823
8,250	8,300	828	828
8,300	8,350	833	833
8,350	8,400	838	838
8,400	8,450	843	843
8,450	8,500	848	848
8,500	8,550	853	853
8,550	8,600	858	858
8,600	8,650	863	863
8,650	8,700	868	868
8,700	8,750	873	873
8,750	8,800	878	878
8,800	8,850	883	883
8,850	8,900	888	888
8,900	8,950	893	893
8,950	9,000	898	898

9,000

At least	But less than	Single	Married filing jointly
9,000	9,050	903	903
9,050	9,100	908	908
9,100	9,150	915	913
9,150	9,200	923	918
9,200	9,250	930	923
9,250	9,300	938	928
9,300	9,350	945	933
9,350	9,400	953	938
9,400	9,450	960	943
9,450	9,500	968	948
9,500	9,550	975	953
9,550	9,600	983	958
9,600	9,650	990	963
9,650	9,700	998	968
9,700	9,750	1,005	973
9,750	9,800	1,013	978
9,800	9,850	1,020	983
9,850	9,900	1,028	988
9,900	9,950	1,035	993
9,950	10,000	1,043	998

10,000

At least	But less than	Single	Married filing jointly
10,000	10,050	1,050	1,003
10,050	10,100	1,058	1,008
10,100	10,150	1,065	1,013
10,150	10,200	1,073	1,018
10,200	10,250	1,080	1,023
10,250	10,300	1,088	1,028
10,300	10,350	1,095	1,033
10,350	10,400	1,103	1,038
10,400	10,450	1,110	1,043
10,450	10,500	1,118	1,048
10,500	10,550	1,125	1,053
10,550	10,600	1,133	1,058
10,600	10,650	1,140	1,063
10,650	10,700	1,148	1,068
10,700	10,750	1,155	1,073
10,750	10,800	1,163	1,078
10,800	10,850	1,170	1,083
10,850	10,900	1,178	1,088
10,900	10,950	1,185	1,093
10,950	11,000	1,193	1,098

11,000

At least	But less than	Single	Married filing jointly
11,000	11,050	1,200	1,103
11,050	11,100	1,208	1,108
11,100	11,150	1,215	1,113
11,150	11,200	1,223	1,118
11,200	11,250	1,230	1,123
11,250	11,300	1,238	1,128
11,300	11,350	1,245	1,133
11,350	11,400	1,253	1,138
11,400	11,450	1,260	1,143
11,450	11,500	1,268	1,148
11,500	11,550	1,275	1,153
11,550	11,600	1,283	1,158
11,600	11,650	1,290	1,163
11,650	11,700	1,298	1,168
11,700	11,750	1,305	1,173
11,750	11,800	1,313	1,178
11,800	11,850	1,320	1,183
11,850	11,900	1,328	1,188
11,900	11,950	1,335	1,193
11,950	12,000	1,343	1,198

12,000

At least	But less than	Single	Married filing jointly
12,000	12,050	1,350	1,203
12,050	12,100	1,358	1,208
12,100	12,150	1,365	1,213
12,150	12,200	1,373	1,218
12,200	12,250	1,380	1,223
12,250	12,300	1,388	1,228
12,300	12,350	1,395	1,233
12,350	12,400	1,403	1,238
12,400	12,450	1,410	1,243
12,450	12,500	1,418	1,248
12,500	12,550	1,425	1,253
12,550	12,600	1,433	1,258
12,600	12,650	1,440	1,263
12,650	12,700	1,448	1,268
12,700	12,750	1,455	1,273
12,750	12,800	1,463	1,278
12,800	12,850	1,470	1,283
12,850	12,900	1,478	1,288
12,900	12,950	1,485	1,293
12,950	13,000	1,493	1,298

13,000

At least	But less than	Single	Married filing jointly
13,000	13,050	1,500	1,303
13,050	13,100	1,508	1,308
13,100	13,150	1,515	1,313
13,150	13,200	1,523	1,318
13,200	13,250	1,530	1,323
13,250	13,300	1,538	1,328
13,300	13,350	1,545	1,333
13,350	13,400	1,553	1,338
13,400	13,450	1,560	1,343
13,450	13,500	1,568	1,348
13,500	13,550	1,575	1,353
13,550	13,600	1,583	1,358
13,600	13,650	1,590	1,363
13,650	13,700	1,598	1,368
13,700	13,750	1,605	1,373
13,750	13,800	1,613	1,378
13,800	13,850	1,620	1,383
13,850	13,900	1,628	1,388
13,900	13,950	1,635	1,393
13,950	14,000	1,643	1,398

14,000

At least	But less than	Single	Married filing jointly
14,000	14,050	1,650	1,403
14,050	14,100	1,658	1,408
14,100	14,150	1,665	1,413
14,150	14,200	1,673	1,418
14,200	14,250	1,680	1,423
14,250	14,300	1,688	1,428
14,300	14,350	1,695	1,433
14,350	14,400	1,703	1,438
14,400	14,450	1,710	1,443
14,450	14,500	1,718	1,448
14,500	14,550	1,725	1,453
14,550	14,600	1,733	1,458
14,600	14,650	1,740	1,463
14,650	14,700	1,748	1,468
14,700	14,750	1,755	1,473
14,750	14,800	1,763	1,478
14,800	14,850	1,770	1,483
14,850	14,900	1,778	1,488
14,900	14,950	1,785	1,493
14,950	15,000	1,793	1,498

15,000

At least	But less than	Single	Married filing jointly
15,000	15,050	1,800	1,503
15,050	15,100	1,808	1,508
15,100	15,150	1,815	1,513
15,150	15,200	1,823	1,518
15,200	15,250	1,830	1,523
15,250	15,300	1,838	1,528
15,300	15,350	1,845	1,533
15,350	15,400	1,853	1,538
15,400	15,450	1,860	1,543
15,450	15,500	1,868	1,548
15,500	15,550	1,875	1,553
15,550	15,600	1,883	1,558
15,600	15,650	1,890	1,563
15,650	15,700	1,898	1,568
15,700	15,750	1,905	1,573
15,750	15,800	1,913	1,578
15,800	15,850	1,920	1,583
15,850	15,900	1,928	1,588
15,900	15,950	1,935	1,593
15,950	16,000	1,943	1,598

16,000

At least	But less than	Single	Married filing jointly
16,000	16,050	1,950	1,603
16,050	16,100	1,958	1,608
16,100	16,150	1,965	1,613
16,150	16,200	1,973	1,618
16,200	16,250	1,980	1,623
16,250	16,300	1,988	1,628
16,300	16,350	1,995	1,633
16,350	16,400	2,003	1,638
16,400	16,450	2,010	1,643
16,450	16,500	2,018	1,648
16,500	16,550	2,025	1,653
16,550	16,600	2,033	1,658
16,600	16,650	2,040	1,663
16,650	16,700	2,048	1,668
16,700	16,750	2,055	1,673
16,750	16,800	2,063	1,678
16,800	16,850	2,070	1,683
16,850	16,900	2,078	1,688
16,900	16,950	2,085	1,693
16,950	17,000	2,093	1,698

(Continued)

Instructions for Form 1040EZ

If Form 1040EZ, line 6, is—		And you are—	
At least	But less than	Single	Married filing jointly
		Your tax is—	

17,000

At least	But less than	Single	Married filing jointly
17,000	17,050	2,100	1,703
17,050	17,100	2,108	1,708
17,100	17,150	2,115	1,713
17,150	17,200	2,123	1,718
17,200	17,250	2,130	1,723
17,250	17,300	2,138	1,728
17,300	17,350	2,145	1,733
17,350	17,400	2,153	1,738
17,400	17,450	2,160	1,743
17,450	17,500	2,168	1,748
17,500	17,550	2,175	1,753
17,550	17,600	2,183	1,758
17,600	17,650	2,190	1,763
17,650	17,700	2,198	1,768
17,700	17,750	2,205	1,773
17,750	17,800	2,213	1,778
17,800	17,850	2,220	1,783
17,850	17,900	2,228	1,788
17,900	17,950	2,235	1,793
17,950	18,000	2,243	1,798

18,000

At least	But less than	Single	Married filing jointly
18,000	18,050	2,250	1,803
18,050	18,100	2,258	1,808
18,100	18,150	2,265	1,813
18,150	18,200	2,273	1,819
18,200	18,250	2,280	1,826
18,250	18,300	2,288	1,834
18,300	18,350	2,295	1,841
18,350	18,400	2,303	1,849
18,400	18,450	2,310	1,856
18,450	18,500	2,318	1,864
18,500	18,550	2,325	1,871
18,550	18,600	2,333	1,879
18,600	18,650	2,340	1,886
18,650	18,700	2,348	1,894
18,700	18,750	2,355	1,901
18,750	18,800	2,363	1,909
18,800	18,850	2,370	1,916
18,850	18,900	2,378	1,924
18,900	18,950	2,385	1,931
18,950	19,000	2,393	1,939

19,000

At least	But less than	Single	Married filing jointly
19,000	19,050	2,400	1,946
19,050	19,100	2,408	1,954
19,100	19,150	2,415	1,961
19,150	19,200	2,423	1,969
19,200	19,250	2,430	1,976
19,250	19,300	2,438	1,984
19,300	19,350	2,445	1,991
19,350	19,400	2,453	1,999
19,400	19,450	2,460	2,006
19,450	19,500	2,468	2,014
19,500	19,550	2,475	2,021
19,550	19,600	2,483	2,029
19,600	19,650	2,490	2,036
19,650	19,700	2,498	2,044
19,700	19,750	2,505	2,051
19,750	19,800	2,513	2,059
19,800	19,850	2,520	2,066
19,850	19,900	2,528	2,074
19,900	19,950	2,535	2,081
19,950	20,000	2,543	2,089

20,000

At least	But less than	Single	Married filing jointly
20,000	20,050	2,550	2,096
20,050	20,100	2,558	2,104
20,100	20,150	2,565	2,111
20,150	20,200	2,573	2,119
20,200	20,250	2,580	2,126
20,250	20,300	2,588	2,134
20,300	20,350	2,595	2,141
20,350	20,400	2,603	2,149
20,400	20,450	2,610	2,156
20,450	20,500	2,618	2,164
20,500	20,550	2,625	2,171
20,550	20,600	2,633	2,179
20,600	20,650	2,640	2,186
20,650	20,700	2,648	2,194
20,700	20,750	2,655	2,201
20,750	20,800	2,663	2,209
20,800	20,850	2,670	2,216
20,850	20,900	2,678	2,224
20,900	20,950	2,685	2,231
20,950	21,000	2,693	2,239

21,000

At least	But less than	Single	Married filing jointly
21,000	21,050	2,700	2,246
21,050	21,100	2,708	2,254
21,100	21,150	2,715	2,261
21,150	21,200	2,723	2,269
21,200	21,250	2,730	2,276
21,250	21,300	2,738	2,284
21,300	21,350	2,745	2,291
21,350	21,400	2,753	2,299
21,400	21,450	2,760	2,306
21,450	21,500	2,768	2,314
21,500	21,550	2,775	2,321
21,550	21,600	2,783	2,329
21,600	21,650	2,790	2,336
21,650	21,700	2,798	2,344
21,700	21,750	2,805	2,351
21,750	21,800	2,813	2,359
21,800	21,850	2,820	2,366
21,850	21,900	2,828	2,374
21,900	21,950	2,835	2,381
21,950	22,000	2,843	2,389

22,000

At least	But less than	Single	Married filing jointly
22,000	22,050	2,850	2,396
22,050	22,100	2,858	2,404
22,100	22,150	2,865	2,411
22,150	22,200	2,873	2,419
22,200	22,250	2,880	2,426
22,250	22,300	2,888	2,434
22,300	22,350	2,895	2,441
22,350	22,400	2,903	2,449
22,400	22,450	2,910	2,456
22,450	22,500	2,918	2,464
22,500	22,550	2,925	2,471
22,550	22,600	2,933	2,479
22,600	22,650	2,940	2,486
22,650	22,700	2,948	2,494
22,700	22,750	2,955	2,501
22,750	22,800	2,963	2,509
22,800	22,850	2,970	2,516
22,850	22,900	2,978	2,524
22,900	22,950	2,985	2,531
22,950	23,000	2,993	2,539

23,000

At least	But less than	Single	Married filing jointly
23,000	23,050	3,000	2,546
23,050	23,100	3,008	2,554
23,100	23,150	3,015	2,561
23,150	23,200	3,023	2,569
23,200	23,250	3,030	2,576
23,250	23,300	3,038	2,584
23,300	23,350	3,045	2,591
23,350	23,400	3,053	2,599
23,400	23,450	3,060	2,606
23,450	23,500	3,068	2,614
23,500	23,550	3,075	2,621
23,550	23,600	3,083	2,629
23,600	23,650	3,090	2,636
23,650	23,700	3,098	2,644
23,700	23,750	3,105	2,651
23,750	23,800	3,113	2,659
23,800	23,850	3,120	2,666
23,850	23,900	3,128	2,674
23,900	23,950	3,135	2,681
23,950	24,000	3,143	2,689

24,000

At least	But less than	Single	Married filing jointly
24,000	24,050	3,150	2,696
24,050	24,100	3,158	2,704
24,100	24,150	3,165	2,711
24,150	24,200	3,173	2,719
24,200	24,250	3,180	2,726
24,250	24,300	3,188	2,734
24,300	24,350	3,195	2,741
24,350	24,400	3,203	2,749
24,400	24,450	3,210	2,756
24,450	24,500	3,218	2,764
24,500	24,550	3,225	2,771
24,550	24,600	3,233	2,779
24,600	24,650	3,240	2,786
24,650	24,700	3,248	2,794
24,700	24,750	3,255	2,801
24,750	24,800	3,263	2,809
24,800	24,850	3,270	2,816
24,850	24,900	3,278	2,824
24,900	24,950	3,285	2,831
24,950	25,000	3,293	2,839

25,000

At least	But less than	Single	Married filing jointly
25,000	25,050	3,300	2,846
25,050	25,100	3,308	2,854
25,100	25,150	3,315	2,861
25,150	25,200	3,323	2,869
25,200	25,250	3,330	2,876
25,250	25,300	3,338	2,884
25,300	25,350	3,345	2,891
25,350	25,400	3,353	2,899
25,400	25,450	3,360	2,906
25,450	25,500	3,368	2,914
25,500	25,550	3,375	2,921
25,550	25,600	3,383	2,929
25,600	25,650	3,390	2,936
25,650	25,700	3,398	2,944
25,700	25,750	3,405	2,951
25,750	25,800	3,413	2,959
25,800	25,850	3,420	2,966
25,850	25,900	3,428	2,974
25,900	25,950	3,435	2,981
25,950	26,000	3,443	2,989

26,000

At least	But less than	Single	Married filing jointly
26,000	26,050	3,450	2,996
26,050	26,100	3,458	3,004
26,100	26,150	3,465	3,011
26,150	26,200	3,473	3,019
26,200	26,250	3,480	3,026
26,250	26,300	3,488	3,034
26,300	26,350	3,495	3,041
26,350	26,400	3,503	3,049
26,400	26,450	3,510	3,056
26,450	26,500	3,518	3,064
26,500	26,550	3,525	3,071
26,550	26,600	3,533	3,079
26,600	26,650	3,540	3,086
26,650	26,700	3,548	3,094
26,700	26,750	3,555	3,101
26,750	26,800	3,563	3,109
26,800	26,850	3,570	3,116
26,850	26,900	3,578	3,124
26,900	26,950	3,585	3,131
26,950	27,000	3,593	3,139

27,000

At least	But less than	Single	Married filing jointly
27,000	27,050	3,600	3,146
27,050	27,100	3,608	3,154
27,100	27,150	3,615	3,161
27,150	27,200	3,623	3,169
27,200	27,250	3,630	3,176
27,250	27,300	3,638	3,184
27,300	27,350	3,645	3,191
27,350	27,400	3,653	3,199
27,400	27,450	3,660	3,206
27,450	27,500	3,668	3,214
27,500	27,550	3,675	3,221
27,550	27,600	3,683	3,229
27,600	27,650	3,690	3,236
27,650	27,700	3,698	3,244
27,700	27,750	3,705	3,251
27,750	27,800	3,713	3,259
27,800	27,850	3,720	3,266
27,850	27,900	3,728	3,274
27,900	27,950	3,735	3,281
27,950	28,000	3,743	3,289

28,000

At least	But less than	Single	Married filing jointly
28,000	28,050	3,750	3,296
28,050	28,100	3,758	3,304
28,100	28,150	3,765	3,311
28,150	28,200	3,773	3,319
28,200	28,250	3,780	3,326
28,250	28,300	3,788	3,334
28,300	28,350	3,795	3,341
28,350	28,400	3,803	3,349
28,400	28,450	3,810	3,356
28,450	28,500	3,818	3,364
28,500	28,550	3,825	3,371
28,550	28,600	3,833	3,379
28,600	28,650	3,840	3,386
28,650	28,700	3,848	3,394
28,700	28,750	3,855	3,401
28,750	28,800	3,863	3,409
28,800	28,850	3,870	3,416
28,850	28,900	3,878	3,424
28,900	28,950	3,885	3,431
28,950	29,000	3,893	3,439

(Continued)

If Form 1040EZ, line 6, is–		And you are–	
At least	But less than	Single	Married filing jointly
		Your tax is–	

29,000

At least	But less than	Single	Married filing jointly
29,000	29,050	3,900	3,446
29,050	29,100	3,908	3,454
29,100	29,150	3,915	3,461
29,150	29,200	3,923	3,469
29,200	29,250	3,930	3,476
29,250	29,300	3,938	3,484
29,300	29,350	3,945	3,491
29,350	29,400	3,953	3,499
29,400	29,450	3,960	3,506
29,450	29,500	3,968	3,514
29,500	29,550	3,975	3,521
29,550	29,600	3,983	3,529
29,600	29,650	3,990	3,536
29,650	29,700	3,998	3,544
29,700	29,750	4,005	3,551
29,750	29,800	4,013	3,559
29,800	29,850	4,020	3,566
29,850	29,900	4,028	3,574
29,900	29,950	4,035	3,581
29,950	30,000	4,043	3,589

30,000

At least	But less than	Single	Married filing jointly
30,000	30,050	4,050	3,596
30,050	30,100	4,058	3,604
30,100	30,150	4,065	3,611
30,150	30,200	4,073	3,619
30,200	30,250	4,080	3,626
30,250	30,300	4,088	3,634
30,300	30,350	4,095	3,641
30,350	30,400	4,103	3,649
30,400	30,450	4,110	3,656
30,450	30,500	4,118	3,664
30,500	30,550	4,125	3,671
30,550	30,600	4,133	3,679
30,600	30,650	4,140	3,686
30,650	30,700	4,148	3,694
30,700	30,750	4,155	3,701
30,750	30,800	4,163	3,709
30,800	30,850	4,170	3,716
30,850	30,900	4,178	3,724
30,900	30,950	4,185	3,731
30,950	31,000	4,193	3,739

31,000

At least	But less than	Single	Married filing jointly
31,000	31,050	4,200	3,746
31,050	31,100	4,208	3,754
31,100	31,150	4,215	3,761
31,150	31,200	4,223	3,769
31,200	31,250	4,230	3,776
31,250	31,300	4,238	3,784
31,300	31,350	4,245	3,791
31,350	31,400	4,253	3,799
31,400	31,450	4,260	3,806
31,450	31,500	4,268	3,814
31,500	31,550	4,275	3,821
31,550	31,600	4,283	3,829
31,600	31,650	4,290	3,836
31,650	31,700	4,298	3,844
31,700	31,750	4,305	3,851
31,750	31,800	4,313	3,859
31,800	31,850	4,320	3,866
31,850	31,900	4,328	3,874
31,900	31,950	4,335	3,881
31,950	32,000	4,343	3,889

32,000

At least	But less than	Single	Married filing jointly
32,000	32,050	4,350	3,896
32,050	32,100	4,358	3,904
32,100	32,150	4,365	3,911
32,150	32,200	4,373	3,919
32,200	32,250	4,380	3,926
32,250	32,300	4,388	3,934
32,300	32,350	4,395	3,941
32,350	32,400	4,403	3,949
32,400	32,450	4,410	3,956
32,450	32,500	4,418	3,964
32,500	32,550	4,425	3,971
32,550	32,600	4,433	3,979
32,600	32,650	4,440	3,986
32,650	32,700	4,448	3,994
32,700	32,750	4,455	4,001
32,750	32,800	4,463	4,009
32,800	32,850	4,470	4,016
32,850	32,900	4,478	4,024
32,900	32,950	4,485	4,031
32,950	33,000	4,493	4,039

33,000

At least	But less than	Single	Married filing jointly
33,000	33,050	4,500	4,046
33,050	33,100	4,508	4,054
33,100	33,150	4,515	4,061
33,150	33,200	4,523	4,069
33,200	33,250	4,530	4,076
33,250	33,300	4,538	4,084
33,300	33,350	4,545	4,091
33,350	33,400	4,553	4,099
33,400	33,450	4,560	4,106
33,450	33,500	4,568	4,114
33,500	33,550	4,575	4,121
33,550	33,600	4,583	4,129
33,600	33,650	4,590	4,136
33,650	33,700	4,598	4,144
33,700	33,750	4,605	4,151
33,750	33,800	4,613	4,159
33,800	33,850	4,620	4,166
33,850	33,900	4,628	4,174
33,900	33,950	4,635	4,181
33,950	34,000	4,643	4,189

34,000

At least	But less than	Single	Married filing jointly
34,000	34,050	4,650	4,196
34,050	34,100	4,658	4,204
34,100	34,150	4,665	4,211
34,150	34,200	4,673	4,219
34,200	34,250	4,680	4,226
34,250	34,300	4,688	4,234
34,300	34,350	4,695	4,241
34,350	34,400	4,703	4,249
34,400	34,450	4,710	4,256
34,450	34,500	4,718	4,264
34,500	34,550	4,725	4,271
34,550	34,600	4,733	4,279
34,600	34,650	4,740	4,286
34,650	34,700	4,748	4,294
34,700	34,750	4,755	4,301
34,750	34,800	4,763	4,309
34,800	34,850	4,770	4,316
34,850	34,900	4,778	4,324
34,900	34,950	4,785	4,331
34,950	35,000	4,793	4,339

35,000

At least	But less than	Single	Married filing jointly
35,000	35,050	4,800	4,346
35,050	35,100	4,808	4,354
35,100	35,150	4,815	4,361
35,150	35,200	4,823	4,369
35,200	35,250	4,830	4,376
35,250	35,300	4,838	4,384
35,300	35,350	4,845	4,391
35,350	35,400	4,853	4,399
35,400	35,450	4,860	4,406
35,450	35,500	4,868	4,414
35,500	35,550	4,875	4,421
35,550	35,600	4,883	4,429
35,600	35,650	4,890	4,436
35,650	35,700	4,898	4,444
35,700	35,750	4,905	4,451
35,750	35,800	4,913	4,459
35,800	35,850	4,920	4,466
35,850	35,900	4,928	4,474
35,900	35,950	4,935	4,481
35,950	36,000	4,943	4,489

36,000

At least	But less than	Single	Married filing jointly
36,000	36,050	4,950	4,496
36,050	36,100	4,958	4,504
36,100	36,150	4,965	4,511
36,150	36,200	4,973	4,519
36,200	36,250	4,980	4,526
36,250	36,300	4,988	4,534
36,300	36,350	4,995	4,541
36,350	36,400	5,003	4,549
36,400	36,450	5,010	4,556
36,450	36,500	5,018	4,564
36,500	36,550	5,025	4,571
36,550	36,600	5,033	4,579
36,600	36,650	5,040	4,586
36,650	36,700	5,048	4,594
36,700	36,750	5,055	4,601
36,750	36,800	5,063	4,609
36,800	36,850	5,070	4,616
36,850	36,900	5,078	4,624
36,900	36,950	5,088	4,631
36,950	37,000	5,100	4,639

37,000

At least	But less than	Single	Married filing jointly
37,000	37,050	5,113	4,646
37,050	37,100	5,125	4,654
37,100	37,150	5,138	4,661
37,150	37,200	5,150	4,669
37,200	37,250	5,163	4,676
37,250	37,300	5,175	4,684
37,300	37,350	5,188	4,691
37,350	37,400	5,200	4,699
37,400	37,450	5,213	4,706
37,450	37,500	5,225	4,714
37,500	37,550	5,238	4,721
37,550	37,600	5,250	4,729
37,600	37,650	5,263	4,736
37,650	37,700	5,275	4,744
37,700	37,750	5,288	4,751
37,750	37,800	5,300	4,759
37,800	37,850	5,313	4,766
37,850	37,900	5,325	4,774
37,900	37,950	5,338	4,781
37,950	38,000	5,350	4,789

38,000

At least	But less than	Single	Married filing jointly
38,000	38,050	5,363	4,796
38,050	38,100	5,375	4,804
38,100	38,150	5,388	4,811
38,150	38,200	5,400	4,819
38,200	38,250	5,413	4,826
38,250	38,300	5,425	4,834
38,300	38,350	5,438	4,841
38,350	38,400	5,450	4,849
38,400	38,450	5,463	4,856
38,450	38,500	5,475	4,864
38,500	38,550	5,488	4,871
38,550	38,600	5,500	4,879
38,600	38,650	5,513	4,886
38,650	38,700	5,525	4,894
38,700	38,750	5,538	4,901
38,750	38,800	5,550	4,909
38,800	38,850	5,563	4,916
38,850	38,900	5,575	4,924
38,900	38,950	5,588	4,931
38,950	39,000	5,600	4,939

39,000

At least	But less than	Single	Married filing jointly
39,000	39,050	5,613	4,946
39,050	39,100	5,625	4,954
39,100	39,150	5,638	4,961
39,150	39,200	5,650	4,969
39,200	39,250	5,663	4,976
39,250	39,300	5,675	4,984
39,300	39,350	5,688	4,991
39,350	39,400	5,700	4,999
39,400	39,450	5,713	5,006
39,450	39,500	5,725	5,014
39,500	39,550	5,738	5,021
39,550	39,600	5,750	5,029
39,600	39,650	5,763	5,036
39,650	39,700	5,775	5,044
39,700	39,750	5,788	5,051
39,750	39,800	5,800	5,059
39,800	39,850	5,813	5,066
39,850	39,900	5,825	5,074
39,900	39,950	5,838	5,081
39,950	40,000	5,850	5,089

40,000

At least	But less than	Single	Married filing jointly
40,000	40,050	5,863	5,096
40,050	40,100	5,875	5,104
40,100	40,150	5,888	5,111
40,150	40,200	5,900	5,119
40,200	40,250	5,913	5,126
40,250	40,300	5,925	5,134
40,300	40,350	5,938	5,141
40,350	40,400	5,950	5,149
40,400	40,450	5,963	5,156
40,450	40,500	5,975	5,164
40,500	40,550	5,988	5,171
40,550	40,600	6,000	5,179
40,600	40,650	6,013	5,186
40,650	40,700	6,025	5,194
40,700	40,750	6,038	5,201
40,750	40,800	6,050	5,209
40,800	40,850	6,063	5,216
40,850	40,900	6,075	5,224
40,900	40,950	6,088	5,231
40,950	41,000	6,100	5,239

(Continued)

If Form 1040EZ, line 6, is–		And you are–		If Form 1040EZ, line 6, is–		And you are–		If Form 1040EZ, line 6, is–		And you are–		If Form 1040EZ, line 6, is–		And you are–	
At least	But less than	Single	Married filing jointly	At least	But less than	Single	Married filing jointly	At least	But less than	Single	Married filing jointly	At least	But less than	Single	Married filing jointly
		Your tax is–				Your tax is–				Your tax is–				Your tax is–	

41,000 / 44,000 / 47,000 / 50,000

At least	But less than	Single	Married	At least	But less than	Single	Married	At least	But less than	Single	Married	At least	But less than	Single	Married
41,000	41,050	6,113	5,246	44,000	44,050	6,863	5,696	47,000	47,050	7,613	6,146	50,000	50,050	8,363	6,596
41,050	41,100	6,125	5,254	44,050	44,100	6,875	5,704	47,050	47,100	7,625	6,154	50,050	50,100	8,375	6,604
41,100	41,150	6,138	5,261	44,100	44,150	6,888	5,711	47,100	47,150	7,638	6,161	50,100	50,150	8,388	6,611
41,150	41,200	6,150	5,269	44,150	44,200	6,900	5,719	47,150	47,200	7,650	6,169	50,150	50,200	8,400	6,619
41,200	41,250	6,163	5,276	44,200	44,250	6,913	5,726	47,200	47,250	7,663	6,176	50,200	50,250	8,413	6,626
41,250	41,300	6,175	5,284	44,250	44,300	6,925	5,734	47,250	47,300	7,675	6,184	50,250	50,300	8,425	6,634
41,300	41,350	6,188	5,291	44,300	44,350	6,938	5,741	47,300	47,350	7,688	6,191	50,300	50,350	8,438	6,641
41,350	41,400	6,200	5,299	44,350	44,400	6,950	5,749	47,350	47,400	7,700	6,199	50,350	50,400	8,450	6,649
41,400	41,450	6,213	5,306	44,400	44,450	6,963	5,756	47,400	47,450	7,713	6,206	50,400	50,450	8,463	6,656
41,450	41,500	6,225	5,314	44,450	44,500	6,975	5,764	47,450	47,500	7,725	6,214	50,450	50,500	8,475	6,664
41,500	41,550	6,238	5,321	44,500	44,550	6,988	5,771	47,500	47,550	7,738	6,221	50,500	50,550	8,488	6,671
41,550	41,600	6,250	5,329	44,550	44,600	7,000	5,779	47,550	47,600	7,750	6,229	50,550	50,600	8,500	6,679
41,600	41,650	6,263	5,336	44,600	44,650	7,013	5,786	47,600	47,650	7,763	6,236	50,600	50,650	8,513	6,686
41,650	41,700	6,275	5,344	44,650	44,700	7,025	5,794	47,650	47,700	7,775	6,244	50,650	50,700	8,525	6,694
41,700	41,750	6,288	5,351	44,700	44,750	7,038	5,801	47,700	47,750	7,788	6,251	50,700	50,750	8,538	6,701
41,750	41,800	6,300	5,359	44,750	44,800	7,050	5,809	47,750	47,800	7,800	6,259	50,750	50,800	8,550	6,709
41,800	41,850	6,313	5,366	44,800	44,850	7,063	5,816	47,800	47,850	7,813	6,266	50,800	50,850	8,563	6,716
41,850	41,900	6,325	5,374	44,850	44,900	7,075	5,824	47,850	47,900	7,825	6,274	50,850	50,900	8,575	6,724
41,900	41,950	6,338	5,381	44,900	44,950	7,088	5,831	47,900	47,950	7,838	6,281	50,900	50,950	8,588	6,731
41,950	42,000	6,350	5,389	44,950	45,000	7,100	5,839	47,950	48,000	7,850	6,289	50,950	51,000	8,600	6,739

42,000 / 45,000 / 48,000 / 51,000

At least	But less than	Single	Married	At least	But less than	Single	Married	At least	But less than	Single	Married	At least	But less than	Single	Married
42,000	42,050	6,363	5,396	45,000	45,050	7,113	5,846	48,000	48,050	7,863	6,296	51,000	51,050	8,613	6,746
42,050	42,100	6,375	5,404	45,050	45,100	7,125	5,854	48,050	48,100	7,875	6,304	51,050	51,100	8,625	6,754
42,100	42,150	6,388	5,411	45,100	45,150	7,138	5,861	48,100	48,150	7,888	6,311	51,100	51,150	8,638	6,761
42,150	42,200	6,400	5,419	45,150	45,200	7,150	5,869	48,150	48,200	7,900	6,319	51,150	51,200	8,650	6,769
42,200	42,250	6,413	5,426	45,200	45,250	7,163	5,876	48,200	48,250	7,913	6,326	51,200	51,250	8,663	6,776
42,250	42,300	6,425	5,434	45,250	45,300	7,175	5,884	48,250	48,300	7,925	6,334	51,250	51,300	8,675	6,784
42,300	42,350	6,438	5,441	45,300	45,350	7,188	5,891	48,300	48,350	7,938	6,341	51,300	51,350	8,688	6,791
42,350	42,400	6,450	5,449	45,350	45,400	7,200	5,899	48,350	48,400	7,950	6,349	51,350	51,400	8,700	6,799
42,400	42,450	6,463	5,456	45,400	45,450	7,213	5,906	48,400	48,450	7,963	6,356	51,400	51,450	8,713	6,806
42,450	42,500	6,475	5,464	45,450	45,500	7,225	5,914	48,450	48,500	7,975	6,364	51,450	51,500	8,725	6,814
42,500	42,550	6,488	5,471	45,500	45,550	7,238	5,921	48,500	48,550	7,988	6,371	51,500	51,550	8,738	6,821
42,550	42,600	6,500	5,479	45,550	45,600	7,250	5,929	48,550	48,600	8,000	6,379	51,550	51,600	8,750	6,829
42,600	42,650	6,513	5,486	45,600	45,650	7,263	5,936	48,600	48,650	8,013	6,386	51,600	51,650	8,763	6,836
42,650	42,700	6,525	5,494	45,650	45,700	7,275	5,944	48,650	48,700	8,025	6,394	51,650	51,700	8,775	6,844
42,700	42,750	6,538	5,501	45,700	45,750	7,288	5,951	48,700	48,750	8,038	6,401	51,700	51,750	8,788	6,851
42,750	42,800	6,550	5,509	45,750	45,800	7,300	5,959	48,750	48,800	8,050	6,409	51,750	51,800	8,800	6,859
42,800	42,850	6,563	5,516	45,800	45,850	7,313	5,966	48,800	48,850	8,063	6,416	51,800	51,850	8,813	6,866
42,850	42,900	6,575	5,524	45,850	45,900	7,325	5,974	48,850	48,900	8,075	6,424	51,850	51,900	8,825	6,874
42,900	42,950	6,588	5,531	45,900	45,950	7,338	5,981	48,900	48,950	8,088	6,431	51,900	51,950	8,838	6,881
42,950	43,000	6,600	5,539	45,950	46,000	7,350	5,989	48,950	49,000	8,100	6,439	51,950	52,000	8,850	6,889

43,000 / 46,000 / 49,000 / 52,000

At least	But less than	Single	Married	At least	But less than	Single	Married	At least	But less than	Single	Married	At least	But less than	Single	Married
43,000	43,050	6,613	5,546	46,000	46,050	7,363	5,996	49,000	49,050	8,113	6,446	52,000	52,050	8,863	6,896
43,050	43,100	6,625	5,554	46,050	46,100	7,375	6,004	49,050	49,100	8,125	6,454	52,050	52,100	8,875	6,904
43,100	43,150	6,638	5,561	46,100	46,150	7,388	6,011	49,100	49,150	8,138	6,461	52,100	52,150	8,888	6,911
43,150	43,200	6,650	5,569	46,150	46,200	7,400	6,019	49,150	49,200	8,150	6,469	52,150	52,200	8,900	6,919
43,200	43,250	6,663	5,576	46,200	46,250	7,413	6,026	49,200	49,250	8,163	6,476	52,200	52,250	8,913	6,926
43,250	43,300	6,675	5,584	46,250	46,300	7,425	6,034	49,250	49,300	8,175	6,484	52,250	52,300	8,925	6,934
43,300	43,350	6,688	5,591	46,300	46,350	7,438	6,041	49,300	49,350	8,188	6,491	52,300	52,350	8,938	6,941
43,350	43,400	6,700	5,599	46,350	46,400	7,450	6,049	49,350	49,400	8,200	6,499	52,350	52,400	8,950	6,949
43,400	43,450	6,713	5,606	46,400	46,450	7,463	6,056	49,400	49,450	8,213	6,506	52,400	52,450	8,963	6,956
43,450	43,500	6,725	5,614	46,450	46,500	7,475	6,064	49,450	49,500	8,225	6,514	52,450	52,500	8,975	6,964
43,500	43,550	6,738	5,621	46,500	46,550	7,488	6,071	49,500	49,550	8,238	6,521	52,500	52,550	8,988	6,971
43,550	43,600	6,750	5,629	46,550	46,600	7,500	6,079	49,550	49,600	8,250	6,529	52,550	52,600	9,000	6,979
43,600	43,650	6,763	5,636	46,600	46,650	7,513	6,086	49,600	49,650	8,263	6,536	52,600	52,650	9,013	6,986
43,650	43,700	6,775	5,644	46,650	46,700	7,525	6,094	49,650	49,700	8,275	6,544	52,650	52,700	9,025	6,994
43,700	43,750	6,788	5,651	46,700	46,750	7,538	6,101	49,700	49,750	8,288	6,551	52,700	52,750	9,038	7,001
43,750	43,800	6,800	5,659	46,750	46,800	7,550	6,109	49,750	49,800	8,300	6,559	52,750	52,800	9,050	7,009
43,800	43,850	6,813	5,666	46,800	46,850	7,563	6,116	49,800	49,850	8,313	6,566	52,800	52,850	9,063	7,016
43,850	43,900	6,825	5,674	46,850	46,900	7,575	6,124	49,850	49,900	8,325	6,574	52,850	52,900	9,075	7,024
43,900	43,950	6,838	5,681	46,900	46,950	7,588	6,131	49,900	49,950	8,338	6,581	52,900	52,950	9,088	7,031
43,950	44,000	6,850	5,689	46,950	47,000	7,600	6,139	49,950	50,000	8,350	6,589	52,950	53,000	9,100	7,039

(Continued)

53,000

If Form 1040EZ, line 6, is– At least	But less than	Single	Married filing jointly
		Your tax is–	
53,000	53,050	9,113	7,046
53,050	53,100	9,125	7,054
53,100	53,150	9,138	7,061
53,150	53,200	9,150	7,069
53,200	53,250	9,163	7,076
53,250	53,300	9,175	7,084
53,300	53,350	9,188	7,091
53,350	53,400	9,200	7,099
53,400	53,450	9,213	7,106
53,450	53,500	9,225	7,114
53,500	53,550	9,238	7,121
53,550	53,600	9,250	7,129
53,600	53,650	9,263	7,136
53,650	53,700	9,275	7,144
53,700	53,750	9,288	7,151
53,750	53,800	9,300	7,159
53,800	53,850	9,313	7,166
53,850	53,900	9,325	7,174
53,900	53,950	9,338	7,181
53,950	54,000	9,350	7,189

54,000

At least	But less than	Single	Married filing jointly
54,000	54,050	9,363	7,196
54,050	54,100	9,375	7,204
54,100	54,150	9,388	7,211
54,150	54,200	9,400	7,219
54,200	54,250	9,413	7,226
54,250	54,300	9,425	7,234
54,300	54,350	9,438	7,241
54,350	54,400	9,450	7,249
54,400	54,450	9,463	7,256
54,450	54,500	9,475	7,264
54,500	54,550	9,488	7,271
54,550	54,600	9,500	7,279
54,600	54,650	9,513	7,286
54,650	54,700	9,525	7,294
54,700	54,750	9,538	7,301
54,750	54,800	9,550	7,309
54,800	54,850	9,563	7,316
54,850	54,900	9,575	7,324
54,900	54,950	9,588	7,331
54,950	55,000	9,600	7,339

55,000

At least	But less than	Single	Married filing jointly
55,000	55,050	9,613	7,346
55,050	55,100	9,625	7,354
55,100	55,150	9,638	7,361
55,150	55,200	9,650	7,369
55,200	55,250	9,663	7,376
55,250	55,300	9,675	7,384
55,300	55,350	9,688	7,391
55,350	55,400	9,700	7,399
55,400	55,450	9,713	7,406
55,450	55,500	9,725	7,414
55,500	55,550	9,738	7,421
55,550	55,600	9,750	7,429
55,600	55,650	9,763	7,436
55,650	55,700	9,775	7,444
55,700	55,750	9,788	7,451
55,750	55,800	9,800	7,459
55,800	55,850	9,813	7,466
55,850	55,900	9,825	7,474
55,900	55,950	9,838	7,481
55,950	56,000	9,850	7,489

56,000

If Form 1040EZ, line 6, is– At least	But less than	Single	Married filing jointly
		Your tax is–	
56,000	56,050	9,863	7,496
56,050	56,100	9,875	7,504
56,100	56,150	9,888	7,511
56,150	56,200	9,900	7,519
56,200	56,250	9,913	7,526
56,250	56,300	9,925	7,534
56,300	56,350	9,938	7,541
56,350	56,400	9,950	7,549
56,400	56,450	9,963	7,556
56,450	56,500	9,975	7,564
56,500	56,550	9,988	7,571
56,550	56,600	10,000	7,579
56,600	56,650	10,013	7,586
56,650	56,700	10,025	7,594
56,700	56,750	10,038	7,601
56,750	56,800	10,050	7,609
56,800	56,850	10,063	7,616
56,850	56,900	10,075	7,624
56,900	56,950	10,088	7,631
56,950	57,000	10,100	7,639

57,000

At least	But less than	Single	Married filing jointly
57,000	57,050	10,113	7,646
57,050	57,100	10,125	7,654
57,100	57,150	10,138	7,661
57,150	57,200	10,150	7,669
57,200	57,250	10,163	7,676
57,250	57,300	10,175	7,684
57,300	57,350	10,188	7,691
57,350	57,400	10,200	7,699
57,400	57,450	10,213	7,706
57,450	57,500	10,225	7,714
57,500	57,550	10,238	7,721
57,550	57,600	10,250	7,729
57,600	57,650	10,263	7,736
57,650	57,700	10,275	7,744
57,700	57,750	10,288	7,751
57,750	57,800	10,300	7,759
57,800	57,850	10,313	7,766
57,850	57,900	10,325	7,774
57,900	57,950	10,338	7,781
57,950	58,000	10,350	7,789

58,000

At least	But less than	Single	Married filing jointly
58,000	58,050	10,363	7,796
58,050	58,100	10,375	7,804
58,100	58,150	10,388	7,811
58,150	58,200	10,400	7,819
58,200	58,250	10,413	7,826
58,250	58,300	10,425	7,834
58,300	58,350	10,438	7,841
58,350	58,400	10,450	7,849
58,400	58,450	10,463	7,856
58,450	58,500	10,475	7,864
58,500	58,550	10,488	7,871
58,550	58,600	10,500	7,879
58,600	58,650	10,513	7,886
58,650	58,700	10,525	7,894
58,700	58,750	10,538	7,901
58,750	58,800	10,550	7,909
58,800	58,850	10,563	7,916
58,850	58,900	10,575	7,924
58,900	58,950	10,588	7,931
58,950	59,000	10,600	7,939

59,000

If Form 1040EZ, line 6, is– At least	But less than	Single	Married filing jointly
		Your tax is–	
59,000	59,050	10,613	7,946
59,050	59,100	10,625	7,954
59,100	59,150	10,638	7,961
59,150	59,200	10,650	7,969
59,200	59,250	10,663	7,976
59,250	59,300	10,675	7,984
59,300	59,350	10,688	7,991
59,350	59,400	10,700	7,999
59,400	59,450	10,713	8,006
59,450	59,500	10,725	8,014
59,500	59,550	10,738	8,021
59,550	59,600	10,750	8,029
59,600	59,650	10,763	8,036
59,650	59,700	10,775	8,044
59,700	59,750	10,788	8,051
59,750	59,800	10,800	8,059
59,800	59,850	10,813	8,066
59,850	59,900	10,825	8,074
59,900	59,950	10,838	8,081
59,950	60,000	10,850	8,089

60,000

At least	But less than	Single	Married filing jointly
60,000	60,050	10,863	8,096
60,050	60,100	10,875	8,104
60,100	60,150	10,888	8,111
60,150	60,200	10,900	8,119
60,200	60,250	10,913	8,126
60,250	60,300	10,925	8,134
60,300	60,350	10,938	8,141
60,350	60,400	10,950	8,149
60,400	60,450	10,963	8,156
60,450	60,500	10,975	8,164
60,500	60,550	10,988	8,171
60,550	60,600	11,000	8,179
60,600	60,650	11,013	8,186
60,650	60,700	11,025	8,194
60,700	60,750	11,038	8,201
60,750	60,800	11,050	8,209
60,800	60,850	11,063	8,216
60,850	60,900	11,075	8,224
60,900	60,950	11,088	8,231
60,950	61,000	11,100	8,239

61,000

At least	But less than	Single	Married filing jointly
61,000	61,050	11,113	8,246
61,050	61,100	11,125	8,254
61,100	61,150	11,138	8,261
61,150	61,200	11,150	8,269
61,200	61,250	11,163	8,276
61,250	61,300	11,175	8,284
61,300	61,350	11,188	8,291
61,350	61,400	11,200	8,299
61,400	61,450	11,213	8,306
61,450	61,500	11,225	8,314
61,500	61,550	11,238	8,321
61,550	61,600	11,250	8,329
61,600	61,650	11,263	8,336
61,650	61,700	11,275	8,344
61,700	61,750	11,288	8,351
61,750	61,800	11,300	8,359
61,800	61,850	11,313	8,366
61,850	61,900	11,325	8,374
61,900	61,950	11,338	8,381
61,950	62,000	11,350	8,389

62,000

If Form 1040EZ, line 6, is– At least	But less than	Single	Married filing jointly
		Your tax is–	
62,000	62,050	11,363	8,396
62,050	62,100	11,375	8,404
62,100	62,150	11,388	8,411
62,150	62,200	11,400	8,419
62,200	62,250	11,413	8,426
62,250	62,300	11,425	8,434
62,300	62,350	11,438	8,441
62,350	62,400	11,450	8,449
62,400	62,450	11,463	8,456
62,450	62,500	11,475	8,464
62,500	62,550	11,488	8,471
62,550	62,600	11,500	8,479
62,600	62,650	11,513	8,486
62,650	62,700	11,525	8,494
62,700	62,750	11,538	8,501
62,750	62,800	11,550	8,509
62,800	62,850	11,563	8,516
62,850	62,900	11,575	8,524
62,900	62,950	11,588	8,531
62,950	63,000	11,600	8,539

63,000

At least	But less than	Single	Married filing jointly
63,000	63,050	11,613	8,546
63,050	63,100	11,625	8,554
63,100	63,150	11,638	8,561
63,150	63,200	11,650	8,569
63,200	63,250	11,663	8,576
63,250	63,300	11,675	8,584
63,300	63,350	11,688	8,591
63,350	63,400	11,700	8,599
63,400	63,450	11,713	8,606
63,450	63,500	11,725	8,614
63,500	63,550	11,738	8,621
63,550	63,600	11,750	8,629
63,600	63,650	11,763	8,636
63,650	63,700	11,775	8,644
63,700	63,750	11,788	8,651
63,750	63,800	11,800	8,659
63,800	63,850	11,813	8,666
63,850	63,900	11,825	8,674
63,900	63,950	11,838	8,681
63,950	64,000	11,850	8,689

64,000

At least	But less than	Single	Married filing jointly
64,000	64,050	11,863	8,696
64,050	64,100	11,875	8,704
64,100	64,150	11,888	8,711
64,150	64,200	11,900	8,719
64,200	64,250	11,913	8,726
64,250	64,300	11,925	8,734
64,300	64,350	11,938	8,741
64,350	64,400	11,950	8,749
64,400	64,450	11,963	8,756
64,450	64,500	11,975	8,764
64,500	64,550	11,988	8,771
64,550	64,600	12,000	8,779
64,600	64,650	12,013	8,786
64,650	64,700	12,025	8,794
64,700	64,750	12,038	8,801
64,750	64,800	12,050	8,809
64,800	64,850	12,063	8,816
64,850	64,900	12,075	8,824
64,900	64,950	12,088	8,831
64,950	65,000	12,100	8,839

(Continued)

Instructions for Form 1040EZ

65,000

At least	But less than	Single	Married filing jointly
65,000	65,050	12,113	8,846
65,050	65,100	12,125	8,854
65,100	65,150	12,138	8,861
65,150	65,200	12,150	8,869
65,200	65,250	12,163	8,876
65,250	65,300	12,175	8,884
65,300	65,350	12,188	8,891
65,350	65,400	12,200	8,899
65,400	65,450	12,213	8,906
65,450	65,500	12,225	8,914
65,500	65,550	12,238	8,921
65,550	65,600	12,250	8,929
65,600	65,650	12,263	8,936
65,650	65,700	12,275	8,944
65,700	65,750	12,288	8,951
65,750	65,800	12,300	8,959
65,800	65,850	12,313	8,966
65,850	65,900	12,325	8,974
65,900	65,950	12,338	8,981
65,950	66,000	12,350	8,989

66,000

At least	But less than	Single	Married filing jointly
66,000	66,050	12,363	8,996
66,050	66,100	12,375	9,004
66,100	66,150	12,388	9,011
66,150	66,200	12,400	9,019
66,200	66,250	12,413	9,026
66,250	66,300	12,425	9,034
66,300	66,350	12,438	9,041
66,350	66,400	12,450	9,049
66,400	66,450	12,463	9,056
66,450	66,500	12,475	9,064
66,500	66,550	12,488	9,071
66,550	66,600	12,500	9,079
66,600	66,650	12,513	9,086
66,650	66,700	12,525	9,094
66,700	66,750	12,538	9,101
66,750	66,800	12,550	9,109
66,800	66,850	12,563	9,116
66,850	66,900	12,575	9,124
66,900	66,950	12,588	9,131
66,950	67,000	12,600	9,139

67,000

At least	But less than	Single	Married filing jointly
67,000	67,050	12,613	9,146
67,050	67,100	12,625	9,154
67,100	67,150	12,638	9,161
67,150	67,200	12,650	9,169
67,200	67,250	12,663	9,176
67,250	67,300	12,675	9,184
67,300	67,350	12,688	9,191
67,350	67,400	12,700	9,199
67,400	67,450	12,713	9,206
67,450	67,500	12,725	9,214
67,500	67,550	12,738	9,221
67,550	67,600	12,750	9,229
67,600	67,650	12,763	9,236
67,650	67,700	12,775	9,244
67,700	67,750	12,788	9,251
67,750	67,800	12,800	9,259
67,800	67,850	12,813	9,266
67,850	67,900	12,825	9,274
67,900	67,950	12,838	9,281
67,950	68,000	12,850	9,289

68,000

At least	But less than	Single	Married filing jointly
68,000	68,050	12,863	9,296
68,050	68,100	12,875	9,304
68,100	68,150	12,888	9,311
68,150	68,200	12,900	9,319
68,200	68,250	12,913	9,326
68,250	68,300	12,925	9,334
68,300	68,350	12,938	9,341
68,350	68,400	12,950	9,349
68,400	68,450	12,963	9,356
68,450	68,500	12,975	9,364
68,500	68,550	12,988	9,371
68,550	68,600	13,000	9,379
68,600	68,650	13,013	9,386
68,650	68,700	13,025	9,394
68,700	68,750	13,038	9,401
68,750	68,800	13,050	9,409
68,800	68,850	13,063	9,416
68,850	68,900	13,075	9,424
68,900	68,950	13,088	9,431
68,950	69,000	13,100	9,439

69,000

At least	But less than	Single	Married filing jointly
69,000	69,050	13,113	9,446
69,050	69,100	13,125	9,454
69,100	69,150	13,138	9,461
69,150	69,200	13,150	9,469
69,200	69,250	13,163	9,476
69,250	69,300	13,175	9,484
69,300	69,350	13,188	9,491
69,350	69,400	13,200	9,499
69,400	69,450	13,213	9,506
69,450	69,500	13,225	9,514
69,500	69,550	13,238	9,521
69,550	69,600	13,250	9,529
69,600	69,650	13,263	9,536
69,650	69,700	13,275	9,544
69,700	69,750	13,288	9,551
69,750	69,800	13,300	9,559
69,800	69,850	13,313	9,566
69,850	69,900	13,325	9,574
69,900	69,950	13,338	9,581
69,950	70,000	13,350	9,589

70,000

At least	But less than	Single	Married filing jointly
70,000	70,050	13,363	9,596
70,050	70,100	13,375	9,604
70,100	70,150	13,388	9,611
70,150	70,200	13,400	9,619
70,200	70,250	13,413	9,626
70,250	70,300	13,425	9,634
70,300	70,350	13,438	9,641
70,350	70,400	13,450	9,649
70,400	70,450	13,463	9,656
70,450	70,500	13,475	9,664
70,500	70,550	13,488	9,671
70,550	70,600	13,500	9,679
70,600	70,650	13,513	9,686
70,650	70,700	13,525	9,694
70,700	70,750	13,538	9,701
70,750	70,800	13,550	9,709
70,800	70,850	13,563	9,716
70,850	70,900	13,575	9,724
70,900	70,950	13,588	9,731
70,950	71,000	13,600	9,739

71,000

At least	But less than	Single	Married filing jointly
71,000	71,050	13,613	9,746
71,050	71,100	13,625	9,754
71,100	71,150	13,638	9,761
71,150	71,200	13,650	9,769
71,200	71,250	13,663	9,776
71,250	71,300	13,675	9,784
71,300	71,350	13,688	9,791
71,350	71,400	13,700	9,799
71,400	71,450	13,713	9,806
71,450	71,500	13,725	9,814
71,500	71,550	13,738	9,821
71,550	71,600	13,750	9,829
71,600	71,650	13,763	9,836
71,650	71,700	13,775	9,844
71,700	71,750	13,788	9,851
71,750	71,800	13,800	9,859
71,800	71,850	13,813	9,866
71,850	71,900	13,825	9,874
71,900	71,950	13,838	9,881
71,950	72,000	13,850	9,889

72,000

At least	But less than	Single	Married filing jointly
72,000	72,050	13,863	9,896
72,050	72,100	13,875	9,904
72,100	72,150	13,888	9,911
72,150	72,200	13,900	9,919
72,200	72,250	13,913	9,926
72,250	72,300	13,925	9,934
72,300	72,350	13,938	9,941
72,350	72,400	13,950	9,949
72,400	72,450	13,963	9,956
72,450	72,500	13,975	9,964
72,500	72,550	13,988	9,971
72,550	72,600	14,000	9,979
72,600	72,650	14,013	9,986
72,650	72,700	14,025	9,994
72,700	72,750	14,038	10,001
72,750	72,800	14,050	10,009
72,800	72,850	14,063	10,016
72,850	72,900	14,075	10,024
72,900	72,950	14,088	10,031
72,950	73,000	14,100	10,039

73,000

At least	But less than	Single	Married filing jointly
73,000	73,050	14,113	10,046
73,050	73,100	14,125	10,054
73,100	73,150	14,138	10,061
73,150	73,200	14,150	10,069
73,200	73,250	14,163	10,076
73,250	73,300	14,175	10,084
73,300	73,350	14,188	10,091
73,350	73,400	14,200	10,099
73,400	73,450	14,213	10,106
73,450	73,500	14,225	10,114
73,500	73,550	14,238	10,121
73,550	73,600	14,250	10,129
73,600	73,650	14,263	10,136
73,650	73,700	14,275	10,144
73,700	73,750	14,288	10,151
73,750	73,800	14,300	10,159
73,800	73,850	14,313	10,169
73,850	73,900	14,325	10,181
73,900	73,950	14,338	10,194
73,950	74,000	14,350	10,206

74,000

At least	But less than	Single	Married filing jointly
74,000	74,050	14,363	10,219
74,050	74,100	14,375	10,231
74,100	74,150	14,388	10,244
74,150	74,200	14,400	10,256
74,200	74,250	14,413	10,269
74,250	74,300	14,425	10,281
74,300	74,350	14,438	10,294
74,350	74,400	14,450	10,306
74,400	74,450	14,463	10,319
74,450	74,500	14,475	10,331
74,500	74,550	14,488	10,344
74,550	74,600	14,500	10,356
74,600	74,650	14,513	10,369
74,650	74,700	14,525	10,381
74,700	74,750	14,538	10,394
74,750	74,800	14,550	10,406
74,800	74,850	14,563	10,419
74,850	74,900	14,575	10,431
74,900	74,950	14,588	10,444
74,950	75,000	14,600	10,456

75,000

At least	But less than	Single	Married filing jointly
75,000	75,050	14,613	10,469
75,050	75,100	14,625	10,481
75,100	75,150	14,638	10,494
75,150	75,200	14,650	10,506
75,200	75,250	14,663	10,519
75,250	75,300	14,675	10,531
75,300	75,350	14,688	10,544
75,350	75,400	14,700	10,556
75,400	75,450	14,713	10,569
75,450	75,500	14,725	10,581
75,500	75,550	14,738	10,594
75,550	75,600	14,750	10,606
75,600	75,650	14,763	10,619
75,650	75,700	14,775	10,631
75,700	75,750	14,788	10,644
75,750	75,800	14,800	10,656
75,800	75,850	14,813	10,669
75,850	75,900	14,825	10,681
75,900	75,950	14,838	10,694
75,950	76,000	14,850	10,706

76,000

At least	But less than	Single	Married filing jointly
76,000	76,050	14,863	10,719
76,050	76,100	14,875	10,731
76,100	76,150	14,888	10,744
76,150	76,200	14,900	10,756
76,200	76,250	14,913	10,769
76,250	76,300	14,925	10,781
76,300	76,350	14,938	10,794
76,350	76,400	14,950	10,806
76,400	76,450	14,963	10,819
76,450	76,500	14,975	10,831
76,500	76,550	14,988	10,844
76,550	76,600	15,000	10,856
76,600	76,650	15,013	10,869
76,650	76,700	15,025	10,881
76,700	76,750	15,038	10,894
76,750	76,800	15,050	10,906
76,800	76,850	15,063	10,919
76,850	76,900	15,075	10,931
76,900	76,950	15,088	10,944
76,950	77,000	15,100	10,956

(Continued)

77,000

At least	But less than	Single	Married filing jointly
77,000	77,050	15,113	10,969
77,050	77,100	15,125	10,981
77,100	77,150	15,138	10,994
77,150	77,200	15,150	11,006
77,200	77,250	15,163	11,019
77,250	77,300	15,175	11,031
77,300	77,350	15,188	11,044
77,350	77,400	15,200	11,056
77,400	77,450	15,213	11,069
77,450	77,500	15,225	11,081
77,500	77,550	15,238	11,094
77,550	77,600	15,250	11,106
77,600	77,650	15,263	11,119
77,650	77,700	15,275	11,131
77,700	77,750	15,288	11,144
77,750	77,800	15,300	11,156
77,800	77,850	15,313	11,169
77,850	77,900	15,325	11,181
77,900	77,950	15,338	11,194
77,950	78,000	15,350	11,206

78,000

At least	But less than	Single	Married filing jointly
78,000	78,050	15,363	11,219
78,050	78,100	15,375	11,231
78,100	78,150	15,388	11,244
78,150	78,200	15,400	11,256
78,200	78,250	15,413	11,269
78,250	78,300	15,425	11,281
78,300	78,350	15,438	11,294
78,350	78,400	15,450	11,306
78,400	78,450	15,463	11,319
78,450	78,500	15,475	11,331
78,500	78,550	15,488	11,344
78,550	78,600	15,500	11,356
78,600	78,650	15,513	11,369
78,650	78,700	15,525	11,381
78,700	78,750	15,538	11,394
78,750	78,800	15,550	11,406
78,800	78,850	15,563	11,419
78,850	78,900	15,575	11,431
78,900	78,950	15,588	11,444
78,950	79,000	15,600	11,456

79,000

At least	But less than	Single	Married filing jointly
79,000	79,050	15,613	11,469
79,050	79,100	15,625	11,481
79,100	79,150	15,638	11,494
79,150	79,200	15,650	11,506
79,200	79,250	15,663	11,519
79,250	79,300	15,675	11,531
79,300	79,350	15,688	11,544
79,350	79,400	15,700	11,556
79,400	79,450	15,713	11,569
79,450	79,500	15,725	11,581
79,500	79,550	15,738	11,594
79,550	79,600	15,750	11,606
79,600	79,650	15,763	11,619
79,650	79,700	15,775	11,631
79,700	79,750	15,788	11,644
79,750	79,800	15,800	11,656
79,800	79,850	15,813	11,669
79,850	79,900	15,825	11,681
79,900	79,950	15,838	11,694
79,950	80,000	15,850	11,706

80,000

At least	But less than	Single	Married filing jointly
80,000	80,050	15,863	11,719
80,050	80,100	15,875	11,731
80,100	80,150	15,888	11,744
80,150	80,200	15,900	11,756
80,200	80,250	15,913	11,769
80,250	80,300	15,925	11,781
80,300	80,350	15,938	11,794
80,350	80,400	15,950	11,806
80,400	80,450	15,963	11,819
80,450	80,500	15,975	11,831
80,500	80,550	15,988	11,844
80,550	80,600	16,000	11,856
80,600	80,650	16,013	11,869
80,650	80,700	16,025	11,881
80,700	80,750	16,038	11,894
80,750	80,800	16,050	11,906
80,800	80,850	16,063	11,919
80,850	80,900	16,075	11,931
80,900	80,950	16,088	11,944
80,950	81,000	16,100	11,956

81,000

At least	But less than	Single	Married filing jointly
81,000	81,050	16,113	11,969
81,050	81,100	16,125	11,981
81,100	81,150	16,138	11,994
81,150	81,200	16,150	12,006
81,200	81,250	16,163	12,019
81,250	81,300	16,175	12,031
81,300	81,350	16,188	12,044
81,350	81,400	16,200	12,056
81,400	81,450	16,213	12,069
81,450	81,500	16,225	12,081
81,500	81,550	16,238	12,094
81,550	81,600	16,250	12,106
81,600	81,650	16,263	12,119
81,650	81,700	16,275	12,131
81,700	81,750	16,288	12,144
81,750	81,800	16,300	12,156
81,800	81,850	16,313	12,169
81,850	81,900	16,325	12,181
81,900	81,950	16,338	12,194
81,950	82,000	16,350	12,206

82,000

At least	But less than	Single	Married filing jointly
82,000	82,050	16,363	12,219
82,050	82,100	16,375	12,231
82,100	82,150	16,388	12,244
82,150	82,200	16,400	12,256
82,200	82,250	16,413	12,269
82,250	82,300	16,425	12,281
82,300	82,350	16,438	12,294
82,350	82,400	16,450	12,306
82,400	82,450	16,463	12,319
82,450	82,500	16,475	12,331
82,500	82,550	16,488	12,344
82,550	82,600	16,500	12,356
82,600	82,650	16,513	12,369
82,650	82,700	16,525	12,381
82,700	82,750	16,538	12,394
82,750	82,800	16,550	12,406
82,800	82,850	16,563	12,419
82,850	82,900	16,575	12,431
82,900	82,950	16,588	12,444
82,950	83,000	16,600	12,456

83,000

At least	But less than	Single	Married filing jointly
83,000	83,050	16,613	12,469
83,050	83,100	16,625	12,481
83,100	83,150	16,638	12,494
83,150	83,200	16,650	12,506
83,200	83,250	16,663	12,519
83,250	83,300	16,675	12,531
83,300	83,350	16,688	12,544
83,350	83,400	16,700	12,556
83,400	83,450	16,713	12,569
83,450	83,500	16,725	12,581
83,500	83,550	16,738	12,594
83,550	83,600	16,750	12,606
83,600	83,650	16,763	12,619
83,650	83,700	16,775	12,631
83,700	83,750	16,788	12,644
83,750	83,800	16,800	12,656
83,800	83,850	16,813	12,669
83,850	83,900	16,825	12,681
83,900	83,950	16,838	12,694
83,950	84,000	16,850	12,706

84,000

At least	But less than	Single	Married filing jointly
84,000	84,050	16,863	12,719
84,050	84,100	16,875	12,731
84,100	84,150	16,888	12,744
84,150	84,200	16,900	12,756
84,200	84,250	16,913	12,769
84,250	84,300	16,925	12,781
84,300	84,350	16,938	12,794
84,350	84,400	16,950	12,806
84,400	84,450	16,963	12,819
84,450	84,500	16,975	12,831
84,500	84,550	16,988	12,844
84,550	84,600	17,000	12,856
84,600	84,650	17,013	12,869
84,650	84,700	17,025	12,881
84,700	84,750	17,038	12,894
84,750	84,800	17,050	12,906
84,800	84,850	17,063	12,919
84,850	84,900	17,075	12,931
84,900	84,950	17,088	12,944
84,950	85,000	17,100	12,956

85,000

At least	But less than	Single	Married filing jointly
85,000	85,050	17,113	12,969
85,050	85,100	17,125	12,981
85,100	85,150	17,138	12,994
85,150	85,200	17,150	13,006
85,200	85,250	17,163	13,019
85,250	85,300	17,175	13,031
85,300	85,350	17,188	13,044
85,350	85,400	17,200	13,056
85,400	85,450	17,213	13,069
85,450	85,500	17,225	13,081
85,500	85,550	17,238	13,094
85,550	85,600	17,250	13,106
85,600	85,650	17,263	13,119
85,650	85,700	17,275	13,131
85,700	85,750	17,288	13,144
85,750	85,800	17,300	13,156
85,800	85,850	17,313	13,169
85,850	85,900	17,325	13,181
85,900	85,950	17,338	13,194
85,950	86,000	17,350	13,206

86,000

At least	But less than	Single	Married filing jointly
86,000	86,050	17,363	13,219
86,050	86,100	17,375	13,231
86,100	86,150	17,388	13,244
86,150	86,200	17,400	13,256
86,200	86,250	17,413	13,269
86,250	86,300	17,425	13,281
86,300	86,350	17,438	13,294
86,350	86,400	17,450	13,306
86,400	86,450	17,463	13,319
86,450	86,500	17,475	13,331
86,500	86,550	17,488	13,344
86,550	86,600	17,500	13,356
86,600	86,650	17,513	13,369
86,650	86,700	17,525	13,381
86,700	86,750	17,538	13,394
86,750	86,800	17,550	13,406
86,800	86,850	17,563	13,419
86,850	86,900	17,575	13,431
86,900	86,950	17,588	13,444
86,950	87,000	17,600	13,456

87,000

At least	But less than	Single	Married filing jointly
87,000	87,050	17,613	13,469
87,050	87,100	17,625	13,481
87,100	87,150	17,638	13,494
87,150	87,200	17,650	13,506
87,200	87,250	17,663	13,519
87,250	87,300	17,675	13,531
87,300	87,350	17,688	13,544
87,350	87,400	17,700	13,556
87,400	87,450	17,713	13,569
87,450	87,500	17,725	13,581
87,500	87,550	17,738	13,594
87,550	87,600	17,750	13,606
87,600	87,650	17,763	13,619
87,650	87,700	17,775	13,631
87,700	87,750	17,788	13,644
87,750	87,800	17,800	13,656
87,800	87,850	17,813	13,669
87,850	87,900	17,825	13,681
87,900	87,950	17,838	13,694
87,950	88,000	17,850	13,706

88,000

At least	But less than	Single	Married filing jointly
88,000	88,050	17,863	13,719
88,050	88,100	17,875	13,731
88,100	88,150	17,888	13,744
88,150	88,200	17,900	13,756
88,200	88,250	17,913	13,769
88,250	88,300	17,925	13,781
88,300	88,350	17,938	13,794
88,350	88,400	17,950	13,806
88,400	88,450	17,963	13,819
88,450	88,500	17,975	13,831
88,500	88,550	17,988	13,844
88,550	88,600	18,000	13,856
88,600	88,650	18,013	13,869
88,650	88,700	18,025	13,881
88,700	88,750	18,038	13,894
88,750	88,800	18,050	13,906
88,800	88,850	18,063	13,919
88,850	88,900	18,075	13,931
88,900	88,950	18,088	13,944
88,950	89,000	18,100	13,956

(Continued)

Instructions for Form 1040EZ

If Form 1040EZ, line 6, is—		And you are—	
At least	But less than	Single	Married filing jointly
		Your tax is—	

89,000

At least	But less than	Single	Married filing jointly
89,000	89,050	18,113	13,969
89,050	89,100	18,125	13,981
89,100	89,150	18,138	13,994
89,150	89,200	18,150	14,006
89,200	89,250	18,163	14,019
89,250	89,300	18,175	14,031
89,300	89,350	18,188	14,044
89,350	89,400	18,201	14,056
89,400	89,450	18,215	14,069
89,450	89,500	18,229	14,081
89,500	89,550	18,243	14,094
89,550	89,600	18,257	14,106
89,600	89,650	18,271	14,119
89,650	89,700	18,285	14,131
89,700	89,750	18,299	14,144
89,750	89,800	18,313	14,156
89,800	89,850	18,327	14,169
89,850	89,900	18,341	14,181
89,900	89,950	18,355	14,194
89,950	90,000	18,369	14,206

90,000

At least	But less than	Single	Married filing jointly
90,000	90,050	18,383	14,219
90,050	90,100	18,397	14,231
90,100	90,150	18,411	14,244
90,150	90,200	18,425	14,256
90,200	90,250	18,439	14,269
90,250	90,300	18,453	14,281
90,300	90,350	18,467	14,294
90,350	90,400	18,481	14,306
90,400	90,450	18,495	14,319
90,450	90,500	18,509	14,331
90,500	90,550	18,523	14,344
90,550	90,600	18,537	14,356
90,600	90,650	18,551	14,369
90,650	90,700	18,565	14,381
90,700	90,750	18,579	14,394
90,750	90,800	18,593	14,406
90,800	90,850	18,607	14,419
90,850	90,900	18,621	14,431
90,900	90,950	18,635	14,444
90,950	91,000	18,649	14,456

91,000

At least	But less than	Single	Married filing jointly
91,000	91,050	18,663	14,469
91,050	91,100	18,677	14,481
91,100	91,150	18,691	14,494
91,150	91,200	18,705	14,506
91,200	91,250	18,719	14,519
91,250	91,300	18,733	14,531
91,300	91,350	18,747	14,544
91,350	91,400	18,761	14,556
91,400	91,450	18,775	14,569
91,450	91,500	18,789	14,581
91,500	91,550	18,803	14,594
91,550	91,600	18,817	14,606
91,600	91,650	18,831	14,619
91,650	91,700	18,845	14,631
91,700	91,750	18,859	14,644
91,750	91,800	18,873	14,656
91,800	91,850	18,887	14,669
91,850	91,900	18,901	14,681
91,900	91,950	18,915	14,694
91,950	92,000	18,929	14,706

92,000

At least	But less than	Single	Married filing jointly
92,000	92,050	18,943	14,719
92,050	92,100	18,957	14,731
92,100	92,150	18,971	14,744
92,150	92,200	18,985	14,756
92,200	92,250	18,999	14,769
92,250	92,300	19,013	14,781
92,300	92,350	19,027	14,794
92,350	92,400	19,041	14,806
92,400	92,450	19,055	14,819
92,450	92,500	19,069	14,831
92,500	92,550	19,083	14,844
92,550	92,600	19,097	14,856
92,600	92,650	19,111	14,869
92,650	92,700	19,125	14,881
92,700	92,750	19,139	14,894
92,750	92,800	19,153	14,906
92,800	92,850	19,167	14,919
92,850	92,900	19,181	14,931
92,900	92,950	19,195	14,944
92,950	93,000	19,209	14,956

93,000

At least	But less than	Single	Married filing jointly
93,000	93,050	19,223	14,969
93,050	93,100	19,237	14,981
93,100	93,150	19,251	14,994
93,150	93,200	19,265	15,006
93,200	93,250	19,279	15,019
93,250	93,300	19,293	15,031
93,300	93,350	19,307	15,044
93,350	93,400	19,321	15,056
93,400	93,450	19,335	15,069
93,450	93,500	19,349	15,081
93,500	93,550	19,363	15,094
93,550	93,600	19,377	15,106
93,600	93,650	19,391	15,119
93,650	93,700	19,405	15,131
93,700	93,750	19,419	15,144
93,750	93,800	19,433	15,156
93,800	93,850	19,447	15,169
93,850	93,900	19,461	15,181
93,900	93,950	19,475	15,194
93,950	94,000	19,489	15,206

94,000

At least	But less than	Single	Married filing jointly
94,000	94,050	19,503	15,219
94,050	94,100	19,517	15,231
94,100	94,150	19,531	15,244
94,150	94,200	19,545	15,256
94,200	94,250	19,559	15,269
94,250	94,300	19,573	15,281
94,300	94,350	19,587	15,294
94,350	94,400	19,601	15,306
94,400	94,450	19,615	15,319
94,450	94,500	19,629	15,331
94,500	94,550	19,643	15,344
94,550	94,600	19,657	15,356
94,600	94,650	19,671	15,369
94,650	94,700	19,685	15,381
94,700	94,750	19,699	15,394
94,750	94,800	19,713	15,406
94,800	94,850	19,727	15,419
94,850	94,900	19,741	15,431
94,900	94,950	19,755	15,444
94,950	95,000	19,769	15,456

95,000

At least	But less than	Single	Married filing jointly
95,000	95,050	19,783	15,469
95,050	95,100	19,797	15,481
95,100	95,150	19,811	15,494
95,150	95,200	19,825	15,506
95,200	95,250	19,839	15,519
95,250	95,300	19,853	15,531
95,300	95,350	19,867	15,544
95,350	95,400	19,881	15,556
95,400	95,450	19,895	15,569
95,450	95,500	19,909	15,581
95,500	95,550	19,923	15,594
95,550	95,600	19,937	15,606
95,600	95,650	19,951	15,619
95,650	95,700	19,965	15,631
95,700	95,750	19,979	15,644
95,750	95,800	19,993	15,656
95,800	95,850	20,007	15,669
95,850	95,900	20,021	15,681
95,900	95,950	20,035	15,694
95,950	96,000	20,049	15,706

96,000

At least	But less than	Single	Married filing jointly
96,000	96,050	20,063	15,719
96,050	96,100	20,077	15,731
96,100	96,150	20,091	15,744
96,150	96,200	20,105	15,756
96,200	96,250	20,119	15,769
96,250	96,300	20,133	15,781
96,300	96,350	20,147	15,794
96,350	96,400	20,161	15,806
96,400	96,450	20,175	15,819
96,450	96,500	20,189	15,831
96,500	96,550	20,203	15,844
96,550	96,600	20,217	15,856
96,600	96,650	20,231	15,869
96,650	96,700	20,245	15,881
96,700	96,750	20,259	15,894
96,750	96,800	20,273	15,906
96,800	96,850	20,287	15,919
96,850	96,900	20,301	15,931
96,900	96,950	20,315	15,944
96,950	97,000	20,329	15,956

97,000

At least	But less than	Single	Married filing jointly
97,000	97,050	20,343	15,969
97,050	97,100	20,357	15,981
97,100	97,150	20,371	15,994
97,150	97,200	20,385	16,006
97,200	97,250	20,399	16,019
97,250	97,300	20,413	16,031
97,300	97,350	20,427	16,044
97,350	97,400	20,441	16,056
97,400	97,450	20,455	16,069
97,450	97,500	20,469	16,081
97,500	97,550	20,483	16,094
97,550	97,600	20,497	16,106
97,600	97,650	20,511	16,119
97,650	97,700	20,525	16,131
97,700	97,750	20,539	16,144
97,750	97,800	20,553	16,156
97,800	97,850	20,567	16,169
97,850	97,900	20,581	16,181
97,900	97,950	20,595	16,194
97,950	98,000	20,609	16,206

98,000

At least	But less than	Single	Married filing jointly
98,000	98,050	20,623	16,219
98,050	98,100	20,637	16,231
98,100	98,150	20,651	16,244
98,150	98,200	20,665	16,256
98,200	98,250	20,679	16,269
98,250	98,300	20,693	16,281
98,300	98,350	20,707	16,294
98,350	98,400	20,721	16,306
98,400	98,450	20,735	16,319
98,450	98,500	20,749	16,331
98,500	98,550	20,763	16,344
98,550	98,600	20,777	16,356
98,600	98,650	20,791	16,369
98,650	98,700	20,805	16,381
98,700	98,750	20,819	16,394
98,750	98,800	20,833	16,406
98,800	98,850	20,847	16,419
98,850	98,900	20,861	16,431
98,900	98,950	20,875	16,444
98,950	99,000	20,889	16,456

99,000

At least	But less than	Single	Married filing jointly
99,000	99,050	20,903	16,469
99,050	99,100	20,917	16,481
99,100	99,150	20,931	16,494
99,150	99,200	20,945	16,506
99,200	99,250	20,959	16,519
99,250	99,300	20,973	16,531
99,300	99,350	20,987	16,544
99,350	99,400	21,001	16,556
99,400	99,450	21,015	16,569
99,450	99,500	21,029	16,581
99,500	99,550	21,043	16,594
99,550	99,600	21,057	16,606
99,600	99,650	21,071	16,619
99,650	99,700	21,085	16,631
99,700	99,750	21,099	16,644
99,750	99,800	21,113	16,656
99,800	99,850	21,127	16,669
99,850	99,900	21,141	16,681
99,900	99,950	21,155	16,694
99,950	100,000	21,169	16,706

$100,000
or over —
use
Form 1040

Disclosure, Privacy Act, and Paperwork Reduction Act Notice

The IRS Restructuring and Reform Act of 1998, the Privacy Act of 1974, and the Paperwork Reduction Act of 1980 require that when we ask you for information we must first tell you our legal right to ask for the information, why we are asking for it, and how it will be used. We must also tell you what could happen if we do not receive it and whether your response is voluntary, required to obtain a benefit, or mandatory under the law.

This notice applies to all papers you file with us, including this tax return. It also applies to any questions we need to ask you so we can complete, correct, or process your return; figure your tax; and collect tax, interest, or penalties.

Our legal right to ask for information is Internal Revenue Code sections 6001, 6011, and 6012(a), and their regulations. They say that you must file a return or statement with us for any tax you are liable for. Your response is mandatory under these sections. Code section 6109 requires you to provide your identifying number on the return. This is so we know who you are, and can process your return and other papers. You must fill in all parts of the tax form that apply to you. But you do not have to check the boxes for the Presidential Election Campaign Fund or for the third-party designee. You also do not have to provide your day-time phone number.

You are not required to provide the information requested on a form that is subject to the Paperwork Reduction Act unless the form displays a valid OMB control number. Books or records relating to a form or its instructions must be retained as long as their contents may become material in the administration of any Internal Revenue law.

We ask for tax return information to carry out the tax laws of the United States. We need it to figure and collect the right amount of tax.

If you do not file a return, do not provide the information we ask for, or provide fraudulent information, you may be charged penalties and be subject to criminal prosecution. We may also have to disallow the exemptions, exclusions, credits, deductions, or adjustments shown on the tax return. This could make the tax higher or delay any refund. Interest may also be charged.

Generally, tax returns and return information are confidential, as stated in Code section 6103. However, Code section 6103 allows or requires the Internal Revenue Service to disclose or give the information shown on your tax return to others as described in the Code. For example, we may disclose your tax information to the Department of Justice to enforce the tax laws, both civil and criminal, and to cities, states, the District of Columbia, and U.S. commonwealths and possessions to carry out their tax laws. We may disclose your tax information to the Department of Treasury and contractors for tax administration purposes; and to other persons as necessary to obtain information needed to determine the amount of or to collect the tax you owe. We may disclose your tax information to the Comptroller General of the United States to permit the Comptroller General to review the Internal Revenue Service. We may disclose your tax information to committees of Congress; federal, state, and local child support agencies; and to other federal agencies for the purposes of determining entitlement for benefits or the eligibility for and the repayment of loans. We may also disclose this information to other countries under a tax treaty, to federal and state agencies to enforce federal nontax criminal laws, or to federal law enforcement and intelligence agencies to combat terrorism.

Please keep this notice with your records. It may help you if we ask you for other information. If you have questions about the rules for filing and giving information, please call or visit any Internal Revenue Service office.

We welcome comments on forms. We try to create forms and instructions that can be easily understood. Often this is difficult to do because our tax laws are very complex. For some people with income mostly from wages, filling in the forms is easy. For others who have businesses, pensions, stocks, rental income, or other investments, it is more difficult.

If you have suggestions for making these forms simpler, we would be happy to hear from you. You can send us comments from *www.irs.gov/formspubs*. Click on "More Information" and then on "Give us feedback." Or you can send your comments to Internal Revenue Service, Tax Forms and Publications Division, 1111 Constitution Ave. NW, IR-6526, Washington, DC 20224. Do not send your return to this address. Instead, see the addresses at the end of these instructions.

Although we cannot respond individually to each comment received, we do appreciate your feedback and will consider your comments as we revise our tax forms and instructions.

Estimates of Taxpayer Burden

The table, later, shows burden estimates based upon current statutory requirements as of November 2014, for taxpayers filing a 2014 Form 1040EZ tax return. Time spent and out-of-pocket costs are presented separately. Time burden is broken out by taxpayer activity, with recordkeeping representing the largest component. Out-of-pocket costs include any expenses incurred by taxpayers to prepare and submit their tax returns. Examples include tax return preparation and submission fees, postage and photocopying costs, and tax preparation software costs. While these estimates do not include burden associated with post-filing activities, IRS operational data indicate that electronically prepared and filed returns have fewer arithmetic errors, implying lower post-filing burden.

Tax preparation fees and other out-of-pocket costs vary extensively depending on the tax situation of the taxpayer, the type of software or professional preparer used, and the geographic location. Reported time and cost burdens are national averages and do not necessarily reflect a "typical" case. Most taxpayers experience lower than average burden, with taxpayer burden varying considerably by taxpayer type. The average for Form 1040EZ filers is about 5 hours and $40.

If you have comments concerning the time and cost estimates that follow, you can contact us at either one of the addresses shown under *We welcome comments on forms*, earlier.

Estimated Average Taxpayer Burden for Individuals by Activity

Primary Form Filed	Percentage of Returns	Average Time Burden (Hours)					Average Cost (Dollars)
		Total Time	Record Keeping	Tax Planning	Form Completion and Submission	All Other	
1040EZ	12	5	1	*	2	1	$40

* Rounds to less than 1 hour.

Detail may not add to total time due to rounding. Dollars rounded to the nearest $10.

Major Categories of Federal Income and Outlays for Fiscal Year 2013

Income and Outlays. These pie charts show the relative sizes of the major categories of federal income and outlays for fiscal year 2013.

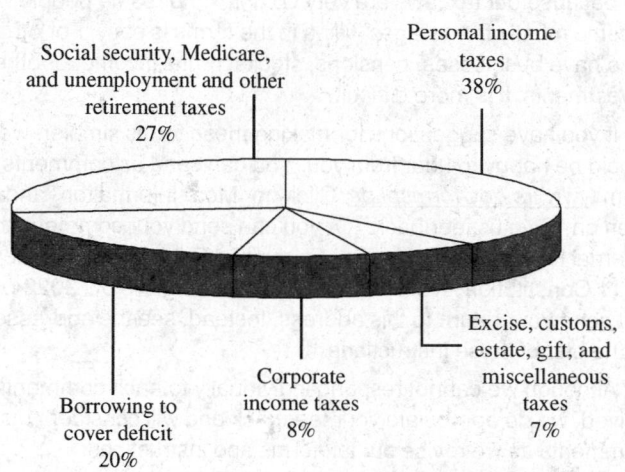

Income

- Social security, Medicare, and unemployment and other retirement taxes 27%
- Personal income taxes 38%
- Borrowing to cover deficit 20%
- Corporate income taxes 8%
- Excise, customs, estate, gift, and miscellaneous taxes 7%

Outlays

- Social security, Medicare, and other retirement[1] 41%
- Law enforcement and general government 2%
- Net interest on the debt 6%
- Physical, human, and community development[3] 6%
- National defense, veterans, and foreign affairs[2] 23%
- Social programs[4] 22%

On or before the first Monday in February of each year the President is required by law to submit to the Congress a budget proposal for the fiscal year that begins the following October. The budget plan sets forth the President's proposed receipts, spending, and the surplus or deficit for the Federal Government. The plan includes recommendations for new legislation as well as recommendations to change, eliminate, and add programs. After receipt of the President's proposal, the Congress reviews the proposal and makes changes. It first passes a budget resolution setting its own targets for receipts, outlays, and surplus or deficit. Next, individual spending and revenue bills that are consistent with the goals of the budget resolution are enacted.

In fiscal year 2013 (which began on October 1, 2012, and ended on September 30, 2013), Federal income was $2.775 trillion and outlays were $3.455 trillion, leaving a deficit of $680 billion.

Footnotes for Certain Federal Outlays

1. **Social security, Medicare, and other retirement:** These programs provide income support for the retired and disabled and medical care for the elderly.

2. **National defense, veterans, and foreign affairs:** About 18% of Federal outlays were to equip, modernize, and pay our armed forces and to fund national defense activities; 4% were for veterans' benefits and services; and about 1% were for international activities, including military and economic assistance to foreign countries and the maintenance of United States embassies abroad.

3. **Physical, human, and community development:** These outlays were for agriculture; natural resources; environment; transportation; aid for elementary and secondary education and direct assistance to college students; job training; deposit insurance, commerce and housing credit, and community development; and space, energy, and general science programs.

4. **Social programs:** About 15% of total outlays were for Medicaid, food stamps, temporary assistance for needy families, supplemental security income, and related programs; and the remaining outlays were for health research and public health programs, unemployment compensation, assisted housing, and social services.

Note. The percentage calculations in this section and the dollar chart for outlays exclude undistributed offsetting receipts, which were $93 billion in 2013. In the budget, these receipts are offset against spending in the calculation of the outlay total. These receipts are for the U.S. Government's share of its employee retirement programs, rents and royalties on the Outer Continental Shelf, and proceeds from the sale of assets.

Options for *e-filing* your returns—safely, quickly, and easily.

Why do 80% of Americans file their taxes electronically?

- *Security*—The IRS uses the latest encryption technology to safeguard your information.
- *Flexible Payments*—File early; pay by April 15.
- *Greater Accuracy*—Fewer errors mean faster processing.
- *Quick Receipt*—Get an acknowledgment that your return was received and accepted.
- *Go Green*—Reduce the amount of paper used.
- *It's Free*—through Free File.
- *Faster Refunds*—Get your refund faster by *e-filing* using direct deposit.

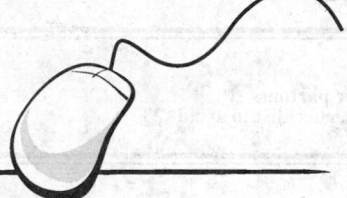

IRS *e-file:* It's Safe. It's Easy. It's Time.

Joining the more than 120 million Americans who already are using *e-file* is easy. Just ask your paid or volunteer tax preparer, use commercial software, or use Free File. IRS *e-file* is the safest, most secure way to transmit your tax return to the IRS. Since 1990, the IRS has processed more than 1 billion *e-filed* tax returns safely and securely. There's no paper return to be lost or stolen.

Most tax return preparers are now required to use IRS *e-file*. If you are asked if you want to *e-file*, just give it a try. IRS *e-file* is now the norm, not the exception. Most states also use electronic filing.

Free *e-file* Help Available Nationwide

Volunteers are available in communities nationwide providing free tax assistance to low to moderate income (generally under $53,000 in adjusted gross income) and elderly taxpayers (age 60 and older). At selected sites, taxpayers can input and electronically file their own tax return with the assistance of an IRS-certified volunteer.

See *How To Get Tax Help* near the end of these instructions for additional information or visit IRS.gov (Keyword: VITA) for a VITA/TCE site near you!

Do Your Taxes for Free

If your adjusted gross income was $60,000 or less in 2014, you can use free tax software to prepare and *e-file* your tax return. Earned more? Use Free File Fillable Forms.

Free File. This public-private partnership, between the IRS and tax software providers, makes approximately 15 brand name commercial software products and *e-file* available for free. Seventy percent of the nation's taxpayers are eligible.

Just visit *www.irs.gov/freefile* for details. Free File combines all the benefits of *e-file* and easy-to-use software at no cost. Guided questions will help ensure you get all the tax credits and deductions you are due. It's fast, safe, and free.

You can review each of the 15 software provider's criteria for free usage or use an online tool to find which free software products match your situation. Some software providers offer state tax return preparation for free. Free File is available in English and Spanish.

Free File Fillable Forms. The IRS offers electronic versions of IRS paper forms that also can be *e-filed* for free. Free File Fillable Forms is best for people experienced in preparing their own tax returns. There are no income limitations. Free File Fillable Forms does basic math calculations. It supports only federal tax forms.

IRS.gov is the gateway to all electronic services offered by the IRS, as well as the spot to download forms at *www.irs.gov/formspubs*.

Make your tax payments electronically—it's easy.

You can make electronic payments online, by phone, or from a mobile device. Paying electronically is safe and secure. The IRS uses the latest encryption technology and does not store banking information. When you use any of the IRS electronic payment options, it puts you in control of paying your tax bill and gives you peace of mind. You determine the payment date, and you will receive an immediate confirmation from the IRS. It's easy, secure, and much quicker than mailing in a check or money order. Go to *www.irs.gov/payments* to see all your electronic payment options.

Instructions for Form 1040EZ

Index to Instructions

Where Do You File?

 Mail your return to the address shown below that applies to you. If you want to use a private delivery service, see *Private delivery services* in Section 4, earlier. Envelopes without enough postage will be returned to you by the post office. Also, include your complete return address.

IF you live in...	THEN use this address if you:	
	Are requesting a refund or are not enclosing a check or money order...	Are enclosing a check or money order...
Florida, Louisiana, Mississippi, Texas	Department of the Treasury Internal Revenue Service Austin, TX 73301-0014	Internal Revenue Service P.O. Box 1214 Charlotte, NC 28201-1214
Alaska, Arizona, California, Colorado, Hawaii, Idaho, Nevada, New Mexico, Oregon, Utah, Washington, Wyoming	Department of the Treasury Internal Revenue Service Fresno, CA 93888-0014	Internal Revenue Service P.O. Box 7704 San Francisco, CA 94120-7704
Arkansas, Illinois, Indiana, Iowa, Kansas, Michigan, Minnesota, Montana, Nebraska, North Dakota, Ohio, Oklahoma, South Dakota, Wisconsin	Department of the Treasury Internal Revenue Service Fresno, CA 93888-0014	Internal Revenue Service P.O. Box 802501 Cincinnati, OH 45280-2501
Alabama, Georgia, Kentucky, New Jersey, North Carolina, South Carolina, Tennessee, Virginia	Department of the Treasury Internal Revenue Service Kansas City, MO 64999-0014	Internal Revenue Service P.O. Box 931000 Louisville, KY 40293-1000
Connecticut, Delaware, District of Columbia, Maine, Maryland, Massachusetts, Missouri, New Hampshire, New York, Pennsylvania, Rhode Island, Vermont, West Virginia	Department of the Treasury Internal Revenue Service Kansas City, MO 64999-0014	Internal Revenue Service P.O. Box 37008 Hartford, CT 06176-7008
A foreign country, U.S. possession or territory*, or use an APO or FPO address, or file Form 2555, 2555-EZ, or 4563, or are a dual-status alien.	Department of the Treasury Internal Revenue Service Austin, TX 73301-0215	Internal Revenue Service P.O. Box 1303 Charlotte, NC 28201-1303

* If you live in American Samoa, Puerto Rico, Guam, the U.S. Virgin Islands, or the Northern Mariana Islands, see Pub. 570.

2014 Form 1040-V  Department of the Treasury
Internal Revenue Service

What Is Form 1040-V

It is a statement you send with your check or money order for any balance due on the "Amount you owe" line of your 2014 Form 1040, Form 1040A, or Form 1040EZ.

 *You can also pay your taxes online or by phone either by a direct transfer from your bank account or by credit or debit card. Paying online or by phone is convenient and secure and helps make sure we get your payments on time. For more information, go to www.irs.gov/e-pay.*

How To Fill In Form 1040-V

Line 1. Enter your social security number (SSN). If you are filing a joint return, enter the SSN shown first on your return.

Line 2. If you are filing a joint return, enter the SSN shown second on your return.

Line 3. Enter the amount you are paying by check or money order.

Line 4. Enter your name(s) and address exactly as shown on your return. Please print clearly.

How To Prepare Your Payment

• Make your check or money order payable to "**United States Treasury.**" Do not send cash.

• Make sure your name and address appear on your check or money order.

• Enter your daytime phone number and your SSN on your check or money order. If you are filing a joint return, enter the SSN shown first on your return. Also enter "2014 Form 1040," "2014 Form 1040A," or "2014 Form 1040EZ," whichever is appropriate.

• To help us process your payment, enter the amount on the right side of your check like this: $ XXX.XX. Do not use dashes or lines (for example, do not enter "$ XXX—" or "$ XXX ˣˣ/₁₀₀").

How To Send In Your 2014 Tax Return, Payment, and Form 1040-V

• Detach Form 1040-V along the dotted line.

• Do not staple or otherwise attach your payment or Form 1040-V to your return or to each other. Instead, just put them loose in the envelope.

• Mail your 2014 tax return, payment, and Form 1040-V to the address shown on the back that applies to you.

Cat. No. 20975C

Form **1040-V** (2014)

▼ **Detach Here and Mail With Your Payment and Return** ▼

Form **1040-V**

Department of the Treasury
Internal Revenue Service (99)

Payment Voucher

▶ **Do not staple or attach this voucher to your payment or return.**

OMB No. 1545-0074

2014

1 Your social security number (SSN)	**2** If a joint return, SSN shown second on your return	**3 Amount you are paying by check or money order.** Make your check or money order payable to "**United States Treasury**"	Dollars	Cents
4 Your first name and initial		Last name		
If a joint return, spouse's first name and initial		Last name		
Home address (number and street)	Apt. no.	City, town or post office, state, and ZIP code (If a foreign address, also complete spaces below.)		
Foreign country name		Foreign province/state/county		Foreign postal code

Print or type (vertical label at left of form)

For Paperwork Reduction Act Notice, see your tax return instructions.

Cat. No. 20975C

IF you live in. . .	THEN use this address to send in your payment . . .
Florida, Louisiana, Mississippi, Texas	Internal Revenue Service P.O. Box 1214 Charlotte, NC 28201-1214
Alaska, Arizona, California, Colorado, Hawaii, Idaho, Nevada, New Mexico, Oregon, Utah, Washington, Wyoming	Internal Revenue Service P.O. Box 7704 San Francisco, CA 94120-7704
Arkansas, Illinois, Indiana, Iowa, Kansas, Michigan, Minnesota, Montana, Nebraska, North Dakota, Ohio, Oklahoma, South Dakota, Wisconsin	Internal Revenue Service P.O. Box 802501 Cincinnati, OH 45280-2501
Alabama, Georgia, Kentucky, New Jersey, North Carolina, South Carolina, Tennessee, Virginia	Internal Revenue Service P.O. Box 931000 Louisville, KY 40293-1000
Connecticut, Delaware, District of Columbia, Maine, Maryland, Massachusetts, Missouri, New Hampshire, New York, Pennsylvania, Rhode Island, Vermont, West Virginia	Internal Revenue Service P.O. Box 37008 Hartford, CT 06176-7008
A foreign country, American Samoa, or Puerto Rico (or are excluding income under Internal Revenue Code 933), or use an APO or FPO address, or file Form 2555, 2555-EZ, or 4563, or are a dual-status alien or nonpermanent resident of Guam or the U.S. Virgin Islands.	Internal Revenue Service P.O. Box 1303 Charlotte, NC 28201-1303

Form **1040X**
(Rev. December 2014)

Department of the Treasury—Internal Revenue Service

Amended U.S. Individual Income Tax Return

▶ Information about Form 1040X and its separate instructions is at *www.irs.gov/form1040x*.

OMB No. 1545-0074

This return is for calendar year ☐ 2014 ☐ 2013 ☐ 2012 ☐ 2011
Other year. Enter one: calendar year   **or** fiscal year (month and year ended):

Your first name and initial	Last name	Your social security number

If a joint return, spouse's first name and initial	Last name	Spouse's social security number

Current home address (number and street). If you have a P.O. box, see instructions.	Apt. no.	Your phone number

City, town or post office, state, and ZIP code. If you have a foreign address, also complete spaces below (see instructions).

Foreign country name	Foreign province/state/county	Foreign postal code

Amended return filing status. You **must** check one box even if you are not changing your filing status. *Caution. In general, you cannot change your filing status from joint to separate returns after the due date.*

☐ Single
☐ Qualifying widow(er)
☐ Married filing jointly
☐ Married filing separately
☐ Head of household (If the qualifying person is a child but not your dependent, see instructions.)

Full-year coverage.
If all members of your household have full-year minimal essential health care coverage, check "Yes." Otherwise, check "No." (See instructions.)
☐ Yes ☐ No

Use Part III on the back to explain any changes

			A. Original amount or as previously adjusted (see instructions)	B. Net change— amount of increase or (decrease)— explain in Part III	C. Correct amount
Income and Deductions					
1	Adjusted gross income. If net operating loss (NOL) carryback is included, check here . . . . ▶ ☐	1			
2	Itemized deductions or standard deduction	2			
3	Subtract line 2 from line 1	3			
4	Exemptions. **If changing, complete Part I on page 2 and enter the amount from line 29**	4			
5	Taxable income. Subtract line 4 from line 3	5			
Tax Liability					
6	Tax. Enter method(s) used to figure tax (see instructions):	6			
7	Credits. If general business credit carryback is included, check here . . . . ▶ ☐	7			
8	Subtract line 7 from line 6. If the result is zero or less, enter -0- . . .	8			
9	Health care: individual responsibility (see instructions)	9			
10	Other taxes	10			
11	Total tax. Add lines 8, 9, and 10	11			
Payments					
12	Federal income tax withheld and excess social security and tier 1 RRTA tax withheld (**if changing**, see instructions)	12			
13	Estimated tax payments, including amount applied from prior year's return	13			
14	Earned income credit (EIC)	14			
15	Refundable credits from: ☐ Schedule 8812 Form(s) ☐ 2439 ☐ 4136 ☐ 5405 ☐ 8801 ☐ 8812 (2011) ☐ 8839 ☐ 8863 ☐ 8885 ☐ 8962 or ☐ other (specify):	15			
16	Total amount paid with request for extension of time to file, tax paid with original return, and additional tax paid after return was filed	16			
17	Total payments. Add lines 12 through 16	17			
Refund or Amount You Owe (*Note. Allow up to 16 weeks for Form 1040X to be processed.*)					
18	Overpayment, if any, as shown on original return or as previously adjusted by the IRS	18			
19	Subtract line 18 from line 17 (If less than zero, see instructions)	19			
20	**Amount you owe.** If line 11, column C, is more than line 19, enter the difference	20			
21	If line 11, column C, is less than line 19, enter the difference. This is the amount **overpaid** on this return	21			
22	Amount of line 21 you want **refunded to you**	22			
23	Amount of line 21 you want **applied to your** (enter year): estimated tax .	23			

Complete and sign this form on Page 2.

For Paperwork Reduction Act Notice, see instructions.
Cat. No. 11360L
Form **1040X** (Rev. 12-2014)

Part I   **Exemptions**

Complete this part **only** if you are increasing or decreasing the number of exemptions (personal and dependents) claimed on line 6d of the return you are amending.

	See *Form 1040 or Form 1040A instructions and Form 1040X instructions.*		**A. Original number** of exemptions or amount reported or as previously adjusted	**B. Net change**	**C. Correct number or amount**
24	Yourself and spouse. *Caution.* If someone can claim you as a dependent, you cannot claim an exemption for yourself	24			
25	Your dependent children who lived with you	25			
26	Your dependent children who did not live with you due to divorce or separation	26			
27	Other dependents	27			
28	Total number of exemptions. Add lines 24 through 27	28			
29	Multiply the number of exemptions claimed on line 28 by the exemption amount shown in the instructions for line 29 for the year you are amending. Enter the result here and on line 4 on page 1 of this form. .	29			

30   List **ALL** dependents (children and others) claimed on this amended return. If more than 4 dependents, see instructions.

(a) First name Last name	**(b)** Dependent's social security number	**(c)** Dependent's relationship to you	**(d)** Check box if qualifying child for child tax credit (see instructions)
			☐
			☐
			☐
			☐

Part II   **Presidential Election Campaign Fund**

Checking below will not increase your tax or reduce your refund.

☐   Check here if you did not previously want $3 to go to the fund, but now do.

☐   Check here if this is a joint return and your spouse did not previously want $3 to go to the fund, but now does.

Part III   **Explanation of changes.** In the space provided below, tell us why you are filing Form 1040X.

▶ Attach any supporting documents and new or changed forms and schedules.

Sign Here

Remember to keep a copy of this form for your records.

Under penalties of perjury, I declare that I have filed an original return and that I have examined this amended return, including accompanying schedules and statements, and to the best of my knowledge and belief, this amended return is true, correct, and complete. Declaration of preparer (other than taxpayer) is based on all information about which the preparer has any knowledge.

▶

Your signature Date	Spouse's signature. If a joint return, **both** must sign. Date

Paid Preparer Use Only

▶

Preparer's signature	Date	Firm's name (or yours if self-employed)
Print/type preparer's name		Firm's address and ZIP code
PTIN	☐ Check if self-employed	Phone number EIN

Form **1041**

Department of the Treasury—Internal Revenue Service

U.S. Income Tax Return for Estates and Trusts

2014

OMB No. 1545-0092

▶ Information about Form 1041 and its separate instructions is at *www.irs.gov/form1041.*

A Check all that apply:

☐ Decedent's estate
☐ Simple trust
☐ Complex trust
☐ Qualified disability trust
☐ ESBT (S portion only)
☐ Grantor type trust
☐ Bankruptcy estate-Ch. 7
☐ Bankruptcy estate-Ch. 11
☐ Pooled income fund

For calendar year 2014 or fiscal year beginning , 2014, and ending , 20

Name of estate or trust (If a grantor type trust, see the instructions.)

Name and title of fiduciary

Number, street, and room or suite no. (If a P.O. box, see the instructions.)

City or town, state or province, country, and ZIP or foreign postal code

C Employer identification number

D Date entity created

E Nonexempt charitable and split-interest trusts, check applicable box(es), see instructions.

☐ Described in sec. 4947(a)(1). Check here if not a private foundation . . ▶ ☐

☐ Described in sec. 4947(a)(2)

B Number of Schedules K-1 attached (see instructions) ▶

F Check applicable boxes:
☐ Initial return ☐ Final return ☐ Amended return ☐ Net operating loss carryback
☐ Change in trust's name ☐ Change in fiduciary ☐ Change in fiduciary's name ☐ Change in fiduciary's address

G Check here if the estate or filing trust made a section 645 election . . . . . . ▶ ☐ Trust TIN ▶

Income

1	Interest income	**1**
2a	Total ordinary dividends	**2a**
b	Qualified dividends allocable to: **(1)** Beneficiaries _____ **(2)** Estate or trust _____	
3	Business income or (loss). Attach Schedule C or C-EZ (Form 1040) . . .	**3**
4	Capital gain or (loss). Attach Schedule D (Form 1041)	**4**
5	Rents, royalties, partnerships, other estates and trusts, etc. Attach Schedule E (Form 1040) .	**5**
6	Farm income or (loss). Attach Schedule F (Form 1040)	**6**
7	Ordinary gain or (loss). Attach Form 4797	**7**
8	Other income. List type and amount _____	**8**
9	**Total income.** Combine lines 1, 2a, and 3 through 8 . . . . . . ▶	**9**

Deductions

10	Interest. Check if Form 4952 is attached ▶ ☐	**10**
11	Taxes	**11**
12	Fiduciary fees	**12**
13	Charitable deduction (from Schedule A, line 7)	**13**
14	Attorney, accountant, and return preparer fees	**14**
15a	Other deductions **not** subject to the 2% floor (attach schedule) . . .	**15a**
b	Net operating loss deduction (see instructions)	**15b**
c	Allowable miscellaneous itemized deductions subject to the 2% floor . . .	**15c**
16	Add lines 10 through 15c . . . . ▶	**16**
17	Adjusted total income or (loss). Subtract line 16 from line 9 . . . **17**	
18	Income distribution deduction (from Schedule B, line 15). Attach Schedules K-1 (Form 1041)	**18**
19	Estate tax deduction including certain generation-skipping taxes (attach computation) . . .	**19**
20	Exemption	**20**
21	Add lines 18 through 20 . . . . . . ▶	**21**
22	Taxable income. Subtract line 21 from line 17. If a loss, see instructions	**22**
23	**Total tax** (from Schedule G, line 7)	**23**

Tax and Payments

24	**Payments: a** 2014 estimated tax payments and amount applied from 2013 return	**24a**
b	Estimated tax payments allocated to beneficiaries (from Form 1041-T) . . .	**24b**
c	Subtract line 24b from line 24a	**24c**
d	Tax paid with Form 7004 (see instructions)	**24d**
e	Federal income tax withheld. If any is from Form(s) 1099, check ▶ ☐ . . .	**24e**
	Other payments: **f** Form 2439 _____ ; **g** Form 4136 _____ ; Total ▶	**24h**
25	**Total payments.** Add lines 24c through 24e, and 24h . . . . . . ▶	**25**
26	Estimated tax penalty (see instructions)	**26**
27	**Tax due.** If line 25 is smaller than the total of lines 23 and 26, enter amount owed . . .	**27**
28	**Overpayment.** If line 25 is larger than the total of lines 23 and 26, enter amount overpaid . .	**28**
29	Amount of line 28 to be: **a Credited to 2015 estimated tax** ▶ _____ ; **b Refunded** ▶	**29**

Sign Here

Under penalties of perjury, I declare that I have examined this return, including accompanying schedules and statements, and to the best of my knowledge and belief, it is true, correct, and complete. Declaration of preparer (other than taxpayer) is based on all information of which preparer has any knowledge.

▶

▶ Signature of fiduciary or officer representing fiduciary | Date | EIN of fiduciary if a financial institution

May the IRS discuss this return with the preparer shown below (see instr.)? ☐ Yes ☐ No

Paid Preparer Use Only

Print/Type preparer's name	Preparer's signature	Date	Check ☐ if self-employed	PTIN

Firm's name ▶ | Firm's EIN ▶

Firm's address ▶ | Phone no.

For Paperwork Reduction Act Notice, see the separate instructions. | Cat. No. 11370H | Form **1041** (2014)

Schedule A	Charitable Deduction. Do not complete for a simple trust or a pooled income fund.			
1	Amounts paid or permanently set aside for charitable purposes from gross income (see instructions)	1		
2	Tax-exempt income allocable to charitable contributions (see instructions)	2		
3	Subtract line 2 from line 1	3		
4	Capital gains for the tax year allocated to corpus and paid or permanently set aside for charitable purposes	4		
5	Add lines 3 and 4	5		
6	Section 1202 exclusion allocable to capital gains paid or permanently set aside for charitable purposes (see instructions)	6		
7	**Charitable deduction.** Subtract line 6 from line 5. Enter here and on page 1, line 13	7		

Schedule B	Income Distribution Deduction			
1	Adjusted total income (see instructions)	1		
2	Adjusted tax-exempt interest	2		
3	Total net gain from Schedule D (Form 1041), line 19, column (1) (see instructions)	3		
4	Enter amount from Schedule A, line 4 (minus any allocable section 1202 exclusion)	4		
5	Capital gains for the tax year included on Schedule A, line 1 (see instructions)	5		
6	Enter any gain from page 1, line 4, as a negative number. If page 1, line 4, is a loss, enter the loss as a positive number	6		
7	**Distributable net income.** Combine lines 1 through 6. If zero or less, enter -0-	7		
8	If a complex trust, enter accounting income for the tax year as determined under the governing instrument and applicable local law	8		
9	Income required to be distributed currently	9		
10	Other amounts paid, credited, or otherwise required to be distributed	10		
11	Total distributions. Add lines 9 and 10. If greater than line 8, see instructions	11		
12	Enter the amount of tax-exempt income included on line 11	12		
13	Tentative income distribution deduction. Subtract line 12 from line 11	13		
14	Tentative income distribution deduction. Subtract line 2 from line 7. If zero or less, enter -0-	14		
15	**Income distribution deduction.** Enter the smaller of line 13 or line 14 here and on page 1, line 18	15		

Schedule G	Tax Computation (see instructions)			
1	**Tax: a** Tax on taxable income (see instructions)	1a		
	b Tax on lump-sum distributions. Attach Form 4972	1b		
	c Alternative minimum tax (from Schedule I (Form 1041), line 56)	1c		
	d Total. Add lines 1a through 1c	1d		
2a	Foreign tax credit. Attach Form 1116	2a		
b	General business credit. Attach Form 3800	2b		
c	Credit for prior year minimum tax. Attach Form 8801	2c		
d	Bond credits. Attach Form 8912	2d		
e	**Total credits.** Add lines 2a through 2d	2e		
3	Subtract line 2e from line 1d. If zero or less, enter -0-	3		
4	Net investment income tax from Form 8960, line 21	4		
5	Recapture taxes. Check if from: ☐ Form 4255　☐ Form 8611	5		
6	Household employment taxes. Attach Schedule H (Form 1040)	6		
7	**Total tax.** Add lines 3 through 6. Enter here and on page 1, line 23	7		

	Other Information	Yes	No
1	Did the estate or trust receive tax-exempt income? If "Yes," attach a computation of the allocation of expenses. Enter the amount of tax-exempt interest income and exempt-interest dividends ▶ $		
2	Did the estate or trust receive all or any part of the earnings (salary, wages, and other compensation) of any individual by reason of a contract assignment or similar arrangement?		
3	At any time during calendar year 2014, did the estate or trust have an interest in or a signature or other authority over a bank, securities, or other financial account in a foreign country?		
	See the instructions for exceptions and filing requirements for FinCEN Form 114. If "Yes," enter the name of the foreign country ▶		
4	During the tax year, did the estate or trust receive a distribution from, or was it the grantor of, or transferor to, a foreign trust? If "Yes," the estate or trust may have to file Form 3520. See instructions		
5	Did the estate or trust receive, or pay, any qualified residence interest on seller-provided financing? If "Yes," see the instructions for required attachment		
6	If this is an estate or a complex trust making the section 663(b) election, check here (see instructions) ▶ ☐		
7	To make a section 643(e)(3) election, attach Schedule D (Form 1041), and check here (see instructions) ▶ ☐		
8	If the decedent's estate has been open for more than 2 years, attach an explanation for the delay in closing the estate, and check here ▶ ☐		
9	Are any present or future trust beneficiaries skip persons? See instructions		

2014

Department of the Treasury
Internal Revenue Service

Instructions for Form 1041 and Schedules A, B, G, J, and K-1

U.S. Income Tax Return for Estates and Trusts

Section references are to the Internal Revenue Code unless otherwise noted.

Future Developments

For the latest information about developments related to Form 1041 and Schedules A, B, G, J, K-1 and its instructions, such as legislation enacted after they were published, go to *www.irs.gov/form1041*.

What's New

Form 1041 E-filing. For tax year 2014, Form 1041 must be e-Filed using Form 8453-FE, U.S. Estate or Trust Declaration for an IRS e-File Return.

Note: Form 8453-F, U.S. Estate or Trust Income Tax Declaration and Signature for Electronic Filing, is obsolete.

For Form 1041 e-File signature authorizations, see Form 8879-F, IRS *e-file* Signature Authorization for Form 1041, and its instructions.

 Beginning January 1, 2015, Form 8879-F can only be associated with a single Form 1041. Form 8879-F can no longer be used with multiple Forms 1041.

For more information about e-filing returns through MeF, see Publication 4164, Modernization e-File (MeF) Guide for Software Developers and Transmitters.

Capital gains and qualified dividends. For tax year 2014, the 20% maximum capital gains rate applies to estates and trusts with income above $12,150. The 0% and 15% rates continue to apply to certain threshold amounts. The 0% rate applies to amounts up to $2,500. The 15% rate applies to amounts over $2,500 and up to $12,150.

Bankruptcy estate filing threshold. For tax year 2014, the requirement to file a return for a bankruptcy estate applies only if gross income is at least $10,150.

Qualified disability trust. For tax year 2014, a qualified disability trust can claim an exemption of up to $3,950. A trust with modified adjusted gross income above $254,200 loses part of the exemption deduction. See the instructions for *Line 20—Exemption*, later, for more details.

Section 67(e) regulations. For 2014, the proposed regulations for section 67(e) clarify which costs, such as investment advisory and bundled fiduciary fees, incurred by estates and nongrantor trusts are and are not exempt from the 2% floor for miscellaneous itemized deductions. Notice 2011-37 (available at *www.irs.gov/irb/2011-20_IRB/ar08.html*) extends the existing interim guidance under the proposed regulations for section 67(e) providing that taxpayers will not determine the portion of a bundled fiduciary fee that is subject to the 2% floor.

Note. The final regulations under section 67(e) have been issued (available at *www.irs.gov/irb/2014-22_IRB/ar05.html*, amended at *www.irs.gov/irb/2014–32_IRB/ar06.html*). The effective date of the regulations has been amended to apply to tax years beginning on or after January 1, 2015.

Reminders

● Review a copy of the will or trust instrument, including any amendments or codicils, before preparing an estate's or trust's return.
● We encourage you to use Form 1041-V, Payment Voucher, to accompany your payment of a balance of tax due on Form 1041, particularly if your payment is made by check or money order.

Net investment income tax. This tax applies to certain investment income of estates and trusts. Use Form 8960 and its instructions to figure your net investment income tax. See *Net Investment Income Tax*, later, for more information.

Item A. Type of Entity. On page 1 of Form 1041, Item A, taxpayers should select more than one box, when appropriate, to reflect the type of entity.

Item F. Net operating loss (NOL) carryback. A *Net operating loss carryback* check box was added in Item F of the heading. If an amended return is filed for an NOL carryback, check the box. See *Amended Return*, later, for complete information.

Item G. Section 645 election. If the estate has made a section 645 election the executor must check Item G and provide the taxpayer identification number (TIN) of the electing trust with the highest total asset value in the box provided.

The executor must also attach a statement to Form 1041 providing the following information for each electing trust (including the electing trust provided in Item G): (a) the name of the electing trust, (b) the TIN of the electing trust, and (c) the name and address of the trustee of the electing trust.

Net operating loss deduction (NOLD). Line 15b was revised to report net operating loss deductions. Prior to tax year 2013, NOLDs were reported on line 15a.

Note. Miscellaneous itemized deductions subject to the 2% floor are reported on line 15c.

Specified domestic entity. The IRS anticipates issuing regulations that will require a domestic entity to file Form 8938 if the entity is formed or availed of to hold specified foreign financial assets and the value of those assets exceeds the appropriate reporting threshold. Until the IRS issues such regulations, only individuals must file Form 8938.

Photographs of Missing Children

The Internal Revenue Service is a proud partner with the National Center for Missing and Exploited Children. Photographs of missing children selected by the Center may appear in instructions on pages that would otherwise be blank. You can help bring these children home by looking at the photographs and calling

1-800-THE-LOST (1-800-843-5678) if you recognize a child.

Unresolved Tax Issues

If you have attempted to deal with an IRS problem unsuccessfully, you should contact the Taxpayer Advocate Service (TAS). The Taxpayer Advocate independently represents the estate's or trust's interests and concerns within the IRS by protecting its rights and resolving problems that have not been fixed through normal channels.

While Taxpayer Advocates cannot change the tax law or make a technical tax decision, they can clear up problems that resulted from previous contacts and ensure that the estate's or trust's case is given a complete and impartial review.

The estate's or trust's assigned personal advocate will listen to its point of view and will work with the estate or trust to address its concerns. The estate or trust can expect the advocate to provide:
• An impartial and independent look at your problem,
• Timely acknowledgment,
• The name and phone number of the individual assigned to its case,
• Updates on progress,
• Timeframes for action,
• Speedy resolution, and
• Courteous service.

When contacting the Taxpayer Advocate, you should provide the following information:
• The estate's or trust's name, address, and employer identification number (EIN).
• The name and telephone number of an authorized contact person and the hours he or she can be reached.
• The type of tax return and year(s) involved.
• A detailed description of the problem.
• Previous attempts to solve the problem and the office that had been contacted.
• A description of the hardship the estate or trust is facing and supporting documentation (if applicable).

You can contact a Taxpayer Advocate as follows:
• Call the Taxpayer Advocate's toll-free number: 1-877-777-4778.
• Call, write, or fax the Taxpayer Advocate office in its area (see Pub. 1546, Taxpayer Advocate Service, Your Voice At The IRS, for addresses and phone numbers).
• TTY/TDD help is available by calling 1-800-829-4059.

• Visit the website at *www.irs.gov/advocate*.

How To Get Forms and Publications

 Internet. You can access the IRS website 24 hours a day, 7 days a week, at *IRS.gov* to:
• Download forms, including talking tax forms, instructions, and publications;
• Order IRS products;
• Use the online Internal Revenue Code, regulations, and other official guidance;
• Research your tax questions;
• Search publications by topic or keyword;
• Apply for an Employer Identification Number (EIN); and
• Sign up to receive local and national tax news by email.

 Phone. You can order forms and publications by calling 1-800-TAX-FORM (1-800-829-3676). If you have access to TTY/TDD equipment, you can call 1-800-829-4059 to ask tax questions or order forms and publications. The TTY/TDD telephone number is for people who are deaf, hard of hearing, or have a speech disability. These individuals can also contact the IRS through relay services such as the Federal Relay Service available at *www.gsa.gov/fedrelay*.

 Walk-in. You can also get most forms and publications at your local IRS office.

General Instructions

Purpose of Form

The fiduciary of a domestic decedent's estate, trust, or bankruptcy estate uses Form 1041 to report:
• The income, deductions, gains, losses, etc. of the estate or trust;
• The income that is either accumulated or held for future distribution or distributed currently to the beneficiaries;
• Any income tax liability of the estate or trust;
• Employment taxes on wages paid to household employees; and
• Net Investment Income Tax. See Schedule G, line 4, and the Instructions for Form 8960.

2014 Instructions for Form 1041

Income Taxation of Trusts and Decedents' Estates

A trust or a decedent's estate is a separate legal entity for federal tax purposes. A decedent's estate comes into existence at the time of death of an individual. A trust may be created during an individual's life (*inter vivos*) or at the time of his or her death under a will (testamentary). If the trust instrument contains certain provisions, then the person creating the trust (the grantor) is treated as the owner of the trust's assets. Such a trust is a grantor type trust. See *Grantor Type Trusts*, later, under *Special Reporting Instructions*.

A trust or decedent's estate figures its gross income in much the same manner as an individual. Most deductions and credits allowed to individuals are also allowed to estates and trusts. However, there is one major distinction. A trust or decedent's estate is allowed an income distribution deduction for distributions to beneficiaries. To figure this deduction, the fiduciary must complete Schedule B. The income distribution deduction determines the amount of any distributions taxed to the beneficiaries.

For this reason, a trust or decedent's estate sometimes is referred to as a "pass-through" entity. The beneficiary, and not the trust or decedent's estate, pays income tax on his or her distributive share of income. Schedule K-1 (Form 1041) is used to notify the beneficiaries of the amounts to be included on their income tax returns.

Before preparing Form 1041, the fiduciary must figure the accounting income of the estate or trust under the will or trust instrument and applicable local law to determine the amount, if any, of income that is required to be distributed, because the income distribution deduction is based, in part, on that amount.

Abusive Trust Arrangements

Certain trust arrangements claim to reduce or eliminate federal taxes in ways that are not permitted under the law. Abusive trust arrangements typically are promoted by the promise of tax benefits with no meaningful change in the taxpayer's control over or benefit from the taxpayer's income or assets. The promised benefits may include reduction or elimination of income subject to tax; deductions for personal expenses paid by the trust; depreciation deductions of an owner's personal residence and furnishings; a stepped-up basis for property transferred to the trust; the reduction or elimination of self-employment taxes; and the reduction or elimination of gift and estate taxes. These promised benefits are inconsistent with the tax rules applicable to trust arrangements.

Abusive trust arrangements often use trusts to hide the true ownership of assets and income or to disguise the substance of transactions. These arrangements frequently involve more than one trust, each holding different assets of the taxpayer (for example, the taxpayer's business, business equipment, home, automobile, etc.). Some trusts may hold interests in other trusts, purport to involve charities, or are foreign trusts. Funds may flow from one trust to another trust by way of rental agreements, fees for services, purchase agreements, and distributions.

Some of the abusive trust arrangements that have been identified include unincorporated business trusts (or organizations), equipment or service trusts, family residence trusts, charitable trusts, and final trusts. In each of these trusts, the original owner of the assets nominally subject to the trust effectively retains the authority to cause financial benefits of the trust to be directly or indirectly returned or made available to the owner. For example, the trustee may be the promoter, a relative, or a friend of the owner who simply carries out the directions of the owner whether or not permitted by the terms of the trust.

When trusts are used for legitimate business, family, or estate planning purposes, either the trust, the beneficiary, or the transferor of assets to the trust will pay the tax on income generated by the trust property. Trusts cannot be used to transform a taxpayer's personal, living, or educational expenses into deductible items, and cannot seek to avoid tax liability by ignoring either the true ownership of income and assets or the true substance of transactions. Therefore, the tax results promised by the promoters of abusive trust arrangements are not allowable under the law, and the participants in and promoters of these arrangements may be subject to civil or criminal penalties in appropriate cases.

For more details, including the legal principles that control the proper tax treatment of these abusive trust arrangements, see Notice 97-24, 1997-1 C.B. 409.

For additional information about abusive tax arrangements, visit the IRS website at IRS.gov and type "Abusive Trusts" in the search box.

Definitions

Beneficiary. A beneficiary includes an heir, a legatee, or a devisee.

Decedent's estate. The decedent's estate is an entity that is formed at the time of an individual's death and generally is charged with gathering the decedent's assets, paying the decedent's debts and expenses, and distributing the remaining assets. Generally, the estate consists of all the property, real or personal, tangible or intangible, wherever situated, that the decedent owned an interest in at death.

Distributable net income (DNI). The income distribution deduction allowable to estates and trusts for amounts paid, credited, or required to be distributed to beneficiaries is limited to DNI. This amount, which is figured on Schedule B, line 7, is also used to determine how much of an amount paid, credited, or required to be distributed to a beneficiary will be includible in his or her gross income.

Income in respect of a decedent. When completing Form 1041, you must take into account any items that are income in respect of a decedent (IRD).

In general, IRD is income that a decedent was entitled to receive but that was not properly includible in the decedent's final income tax return under the decedent's method of accounting.

IRD includes:
- All accrued income of a decedent who reported his or her income on the cash method of accounting,
- Income accrued solely because of the decedent's death in the case of a decedent who reported his or her income on the accrual method of accounting, and
- Income to which the decedent had a contingent claim at the time of his or her death.

Some examples of IRD for a decedent who kept his or her books on the cash method are:
- Deferred salary payments that are payable to the decedent's estate,
- Uncollected interest on U.S. savings bonds,
- Proceeds from the completed sale of farm produce, and
- The portion of a lump-sum distribution to the beneficiary of a decedent's IRA that equals the balance

in the IRA at the time of the owner's death. This includes unrealized appreciation and income accrued to that date, less the aggregate amount of the owner's nondeductible contributions to the IRA. Such amounts are included in the beneficiary's gross income in the tax year that the distribution is received.

The IRD has the same character it would have had if the decedent had lived and received such amount.

Deductions and credits in respect of a decedent. The following deductions and credits, when paid by the decedent's estate, are allowed on Form 1041 even though they were not allowable on the decedent's final income tax return.
- Business expenses deductible under section 162.
- Interest deductible under section 163.
- Taxes deductible under section 164.
- Investment expenses described in section 212 (in excess of 2% of adjusted gross income (AGI)).
- Percentage depletion allowed under section 611.
- Foreign tax credit.

For more information on IRD, see section 691 and Pub. 559, Survivors, Executors, and Administrators.

Income required to be distributed currently. Income required to be distributed currently is income that is required under the terms of the governing instrument and applicable local law to be distributed in the year it is received. The fiduciary must be under a duty to distribute the income currently, even if the actual distribution is not made until after the close of the trust's tax year. See Regulations section 1.651(a)-2.

Fiduciary. A fiduciary is a trustee of a trust, or an executor, executrix, administrator, administratrix, personal representative, or person in possession of property of a decedent's estate.

Note. Any reference in these instructions to "you" means the fiduciary of the estate or trust.

Trust. A trust is an arrangement created either by a will or by an *inter vivos* declaration by which trustees take title to property for the purpose of protecting or conserving it for the beneficiaries under the ordinary rules applied in chancery or probate courts.

Revocable living trust. A revocable living trust is an arrangement created by a written agreement or declaration during the life of an individual and can be changed or ended at any time during the individual's life. A revocable living trust is generally created to manage and distribute property. Many people use this type of trust instead of (or in addition to) a will.

Because this type of trust is revocable, it is treated as a grantor type trust for tax purposes. See *Grantor Type Trusts* under *Special Reporting Instructions*, later, for special filing instructions that apply to grantor trusts.

 TIP *Be sure to read* Optional Filing Methods for Certain Grantor Type Trusts. *Generally, most people that have revocable living trusts will be able to use Optional Method 1. This method is the easiest and least burdensome way to meet your obligations.*

Who Must File

Decedent's Estate

The fiduciary (or one of the joint fiduciaries) must file Form 1041 for a domestic estate that has:

1. Gross income for the tax year of $600 or more, or

2. A beneficiary who is a nonresident alien.

An estate is a domestic estate if it is not a foreign estate. A foreign estate is one the income of which is from sources outside the United States that is not effectively connected with the conduct of a U.S. trade or business and is not includible in gross income. If you are the fiduciary of a foreign estate, file Form 1040NR, U.S. Nonresident Alien Income Tax Return, instead of Form 1041.

Trust

The fiduciary (or one of the joint fiduciaries) must file Form 1041 for a domestic trust taxable under section 641 that has:

1. Any taxable income for the tax year,

2. Gross income of $600 or more (regardless of taxable income), or

3. A beneficiary who is a nonresident alien.

Two or more trusts are treated as one trust if the trusts have substantially the same grantor(s) and substantially the same primary beneficiary(ies) and a principal purpose of such trusts is avoidance of tax. This provision applies only to that portion of the trust that is attributable to contributions to corpus made after March 1, 1984.

A trust is a domestic trust if:
- A U.S. court is able to exercise primary supervision over the administration of the trust (court test), and
- One or more U.S. persons have the authority to control all substantial decisions of the trust (control test).

See Regulations section 301.7701-7 for more information on the court and control tests.

Also treated as a domestic trust is a trust (other than a trust treated as wholly owned by the grantor) that:
- Was in existence on August 20, 1996,
- Was treated as a domestic trust on August 19, 1996, and
- Elected to continue to be treated as a domestic trust.

A trust that is not a domestic trust is treated as a foreign trust. If you are the trustee of a foreign trust, file Form 1040NR instead of Form 1041. Also, a foreign trust with a U.S. owner generally must file Form 3520-A, Annual Information Return of Foreign Trust With a U.S. Owner.

If a domestic trust becomes a foreign trust, it is treated under section 684 as having transferred all of its assets to a foreign trust, except to the extent a grantor or another person is treated as the owner of the trust when the trust becomes a foreign trust.

Grantor Type Trusts

If all or any portion of a trust is a grantor type trust, then that trust or portion of a trust must follow the special reporting requirements discussed later, under *Special Reporting Instructions*. See *Grantor Type Trust* under *Specific Instructions* for more details on what makes a trust a grantor type trust.

Note. A trust may be part grantor trust and part "other" type of trust, for example, simple or complex, or electing small business trust (ESBT).

Qualified subchapter S trusts (QSSTs). QSSTs must follow the special reporting requirements for these trusts discussed later, under *Special Reporting Instructions*.

Special Rule for Certain Revocable Trusts

Section 645 provides that if both the executor (if any) of an estate (the related estate) and the trustee of a qualified revocable trust (QRT) elect the treatment in section 645, the trust must be treated and taxed as part of the related estate during the election period. This election may be made by a QRT even if no executor is appointed for the related estate.

In general, Form 8855, Election To Treat a Qualified Revocable Trust as Part of an Estate, must be filed by the due date for Form 1041 for the first tax year of the related estate. This applies even if the combined related estate and electing trust do not have sufficient income to be required to file Form 1041. However, if the estate is granted an extension of time to file Form 1041 for its first tax year, the due date for Form 8855 is the extended due date.

Once made, the election is irrevocable.

Qualified revocable trusts. In general, a QRT is any trust (or part of a trust) that, on the day the decedent died, was treated as owned by the decedent because the decedent held the power to revoke the trust as described in section 676. An electing trust is a QRT for which a section 645 election has been made.

Election period. The election period is the period of time during which an electing trust is treated as part of its related estate.

The election period begins on the date of the decedent's death and terminates on the earlier of:
• The day on which the electing trust and related estate, if any, distribute all of their assets, or
• The day before the applicable date. To determine the applicable date, first determine whether a Form 706, United States Estate (and Generation-Skipping Transfer) Tax Return, is required to be filed as a result of the decedent's death. If no Form 706 is required to be filed, the applicable date is 2 years after the date of the decedent's death. If Form 706 is required, the applicable date is the later of 2 years after the date of the decedent's death or 6 months after the final determination of liability for estate tax. For additional information, see Regulations section 1.645-1(f).

Taxpayer identification number (TIN). All QRTs must obtain a new TIN following the death of the decedent whether or not a section 645 election is made. (Use Form W-9, Request for Taxpayer Identification Number and Certification, to notify payers of the new TIN.)

An electing trust that continues after the termination of the election period

does not need to obtain a new TIN following the termination unless:
• An executor was appointed and agreed to the election after the electing trust made a valid section 645 election, and the electing trust filed a return as an estate under the trust's TIN, or
• No executor was appointed and the QRT was the filing trust (as explained later).

A related estate that continues after the termination of the election period does not need to obtain a new TIN.

For more information about TINs, including trusts with multiple owners, see Regulations sections 1.645-1 and 301.6109-1(a).

General procedures for completing Form 1041 during the election period.

If there is an executor. The following rules apply to filing Form 1041 while the election is in effect.
• The executor of the related estate is responsible for filing Form 1041 for the estate and all electing trusts. The return is filed under the name and TIN of the related estate. Be sure to check the Decedent's estate box at the top of Form 1041 and Item G if the estate has made a section 645 election. The executor continues to file Form 1041 during the election period even if the estate distributes all of its assets before the end of the election period.
• The Form 1041 includes all items of income, deduction, and credit for the estate and all electing trusts.
• For Item G, the executor must provide the TIN of the electing trust with the highest total asset value.
• The executor must attach a statement to Form 1041 providing the following information for each electing trust (including the electing trust provided in Item G): (a) the name of the electing trust, (b) the TIN of the electing trust, and (c) the name and address of the trustee of the electing trust.
• The related estate and the electing trust are treated as separate shares for purposes of computing DNI and applying distribution provisions. Also, each of those shares can contain two or more separate shares. For more information, see *Separate share rule*, later, and Regulations section 1.645-1(e)(2)(iii).
• The executor is responsible for insuring that the estate's share of the combined tax obligation is paid.

For additional information, including treatment of transfers between shares

and charitable contribution deductions, see Regulations section 1.645-1(e).

If there is no executor. If no executor has been appointed for the related estate, the trustee of the electing trust files Form 1041 as if it was an estate. File using the TIN that the QRT obtained after the death of the decedent. The trustee can choose a fiscal year as the trust's tax year during the election period. Be sure to check the Decedent's estate box at the top of Form 1041 and Item G if the filing trust has made a section 645 election. For Item G, the filing trustee must provide the TIN of the electing trust with the highest total asset value. The electing trust is entitled to a single $600 personal exemption on returns filed for the election period.

If there is more than one electing trust, the trusts must appoint one trustee as the filing trustee. Form 1041 is filed under the name and TIN of the filing trustee's trust. A statement providing the same information about the electing trusts (except the filing trust) that is listed under, *If there is an executor*, above must be attached to these Forms 1041. All electing trusts must choose the same tax year.

If there is more than one electing trust, the filing trustee is responsible for ensuring that the filing trust's share of the combined tax liability is paid.

For additional information on filing requirements when there is no executor, including application of the separate share rule, see Regulations section 1.645-1(e). For information on the requirements when an executor is appointed after an election is made and the executor does not agree to the election, see below.

Responsibilities of the trustee when there is an executor (or there is no executor and the trustee is not the filing trustee). When there is an executor (or there is no executor and the trustee is not the filing trustee), the trustee of an electing trust is responsible for the following during the election period.
• To timely provide the executor with all the trust information necessary to allow the executor to file a complete, accurate, and timely Form 1041.
• To ensure that the electing trust's share of the combined tax liability is paid.

The trustee does not file a Form 1041 during the election period (except for a final return if the trust terminates during the election period as explained later).

Procedure for completing Form 1041 for the year in which the election terminates.

If there is an executor. If there is an executor, the Form 1041 filed under the name and TIN of the related estate for the tax year in which the election terminates includes (a) the items of income, deduction, and credit for the related estate for its entire tax year, and (b) the income, deductions, and credits for the electing trust for the period that ends with the last day of the election period. If the estate will not continue after the close of the tax year, indicate that this Form 1041 is a final return.

At the end of the last day of the election period, the combined entity is deemed to distribute the share comprising the electing trust to a new trust. All items of income, including net capital gains, that are attributable to the share comprising the electing trust are included in the calculation of DNI of the electing trust and treated as distributed. The distribution rules of sections 661 and 662 apply to this deemed distribution. The combined entity is entitled to an income distribution deduction for this deemed distribution, and the "new" trust must include its share of the distribution in its income. See Regulations sections 1.645-1(e)(2)(iii) and 1.645-1(h) for more information.

If the electing trust continues in existence after the termination of the election period, the trustee must file Form 1041 under the name and TIN of the trust, using the calendar year as its accounting period, if it is otherwise required to file.

If there is no executor. If there is no executor, the following rules apply to filing Form 1041 for the tax year in which the election period ends.
• The tax year of the electing trust closes on the last day of the election period, and the Form 1041 filed for that tax year includes all items of income, deduction, and credit for the electing trust for the period beginning with the first day of the tax year and ending with the last day of the election period.
• The deemed distribution rules discussed above apply.
• Check the box to indicate that this Form 1041 is a final return.
• If the filing trust continues after the termination of the election period, the trustee must obtain a new TIN. If the trust meets the filing requirements, the trustee must file a Form 1041 under the new TIN for the period beginning with the day after the close of the election

period and, in general, ending December 31 of that year.

Responsibilities of the trustee when there is an executor (or there is no executor and the trustee is not the filing trustee). In addition to the requirements listed above under this same heading, the trustee is responsible for the following.
• If the trust will not continue after the close of the election period, the trustee must file a Form 1041 under the name and TIN of the trust. Complete the entity information and items *A, C, D,* and *F.* Indicate in item *F* that this is a final return. Do not report any items of income, deduction, or credit.
• If the trust will continue after the close of the election period, the trustee must file a Form 1041 for the trust for the tax year beginning the day after the close of the election period and, in general, ending December 31 of that year. Use the TIN obtained after the decedent's death. Follow the general rules for completing the return.

Special filing instructions.

When the election is not made by the due date of the QRT's Form 1041. If the section 645 election has not been made by the time the QRT's first income tax return would be due for the tax year beginning with the decedent's death, but the trustee and executor (if any) have decided to make a section 645 election, then the QRT is not required to file a Form 1041 for the short tax year beginning with the decedent's death and ending on December 31 of that year. However, if a valid election is not subsequently made, the QRT may be subject to penalties and interest for failure to file and failure to pay.

If the QRT files a Form 1041 for this short period, and a valid section 645 election is subsequently made, then the trustee must file an amended Form 1041 for the electing trust, excluding all items of income, deduction, and credit of the electing trust. These amounts are then included on the first Form 1041 filed by the executor for the related estate (or the filing trustee for the electing trust filing as an estate).

Later appointed executor. If an executor for the related estate is not appointed until after the trustee has made a valid section 645 election, the executor must agree to the trustee's election and they must file a revised Form 8855 within 90 days of the appointment of the executor. If the executor does not agree to the election,

the election terminates as of the date of appointment of the executor.

If the executor agrees to the election, the trustee must amend any Form 1041 filed under the name and TIN of the electing trust for the period beginning with the decedent's death. The amended returns are still filed under the name and TIN of the electing trust, and they must include the items of income, deduction, and credit for the related estate for the periods covered by the returns. Also, attach a statement to the amended Forms 1041 identifying the name and TIN of the related estate, and the name and address of the executor. Check the Final return box on the amended return for the tax year that ends with the appointment of the executor. Except for this amended return, all returns filed for the combined entity after the appointment of the executor must be filed under the name and TIN of the related estate.

If the election terminates as the result of a later appointed executor, the executor of the related estate must file Forms 1041 under the name and TIN of the related estate for all tax years of the related estate beginning with the decedent's death. The electing trust's election period and tax year terminate the day before the appointment of the executor. The trustee is not required to amend any of the returns filed by the electing trust for the period prior to the appointment of the executor. The trust must file a final Form 1041 following the instructions above for completing Form 1041 in the year in which the election terminates and there is no executor.

Termination of the trust during the election period. If an electing trust terminates during the election period, the trustee of that trust must file a final Form 1041 by completing the entity information (using the trust's EIN), checking the Final return box, and signing and dating the form. Do not report items of income, deduction, and credit. These items are reported on the related estate's return.

Alaska Native Settlement Trusts

The trustee of an Alaska Native Settlement Trust may elect the special tax treatment for the trust and its beneficiaries provided for in section 646. The election must be made by the due date (including extensions) for filing the trust's tax return for its first tax year ending after June 7, 2001. Do not use Form 1041. Use Form 1041-N, U.S. Income Tax Return for Electing Alaska

Native Settlement Trusts, to make the election. Additionally, Form 1041-N is the trust's income tax return and satisfies the section 6039H information reporting requirement for the trust.

Bankruptcy Estate

The bankruptcy trustee or debtor-in-possession must file Form 1041 for the estate of an individual involved in bankruptcy proceedings under chapter 7 or 11 of title 11 of the United States Code if the estate has gross income for the tax year of $10,150 or more. See *Bankruptcy Estates*, later, for details.

Charitable Remainder Trusts

A section 664 charitable remainder trust (CRT) does not file Form 1041. Instead, a CRT files Form 5227, Split-Interest Trust Information Return. If the CRT has any unrelated business taxable income, it also must file Form 4720, Return of Certain Excise Taxes Under Chapters 41 and 42 of the Internal Revenue Code.

Common Trust Funds

Do not file Form 1041 for a common trust fund maintained by a bank. Instead, the fund may use Form 1065, U.S. Return of Partnership Income, for its return. For more details, see section 584 and Regulations section 1.6032-1.

Electing Small Business Trusts

Electing small business trusts file Form 1041. However, see *Electing Small Business Trusts (ESBTs)*, later, for a discussion of the special reporting requirements for these trusts.

Pooled Income Funds

Pooled income funds file Form 1041. See *Pooled Income Funds*, later, for the special reporting requirements for these trusts. Additionally, pooled income funds must file Form 5227, Split-Interest Trust Information Return.

Qualified Funeral Trusts

Trustees of pre-need funeral trusts who elect treatment under section 685 file Form 1041-QFT, U.S. Income Tax Return for Qualified Funeral Trusts. All other pre-need funeral trusts, see *Grantor Type Trusts*, later, for Form 1041 reporting requirements.

Qualified Settlement Funds

The trustee of a designated or qualified settlement fund (QSF) generally must file Form 1120-SF, U.S. Income Tax Return for Settlement Funds, instead of Form 1041.

Special election. If a QSF has only one transferor, the transferor may elect to treat the QSF as a grantor type trust.

To make the grantor trust election, the transferor must attach an election statement to a timely filed Form 1041, including extensions, that the administrator files for the QSF for the tax year in which the settlement fund is established. If Form 1041 is not filed because *Optional Method 1* or *2* (described later) was chosen, attach the election statement to a timely filed income tax return, including extensions, of the transferor for the tax year in which the settlement fund is established.

Election statement. The election statement may be made separately or, if filed with Form 1041, on the attachment described under *Grantor Type Trusts*, later. At the top of the election statement, write "Section 1.468B-1(k) Election" and include the transferor's:
• Name,
• Address,
• TIN, and
• A statement that he or she will treat the qualified settlement fund as a grantor type trust.

Widely Held Fixed Investment Trust (WHFITs)

Trustees and middlemen of WHFITs do not file Form 1041. Instead, they report all items of gross income and proceeds on the appropriate Form 1099. For the definition of a WHFIT, see Regulations section 1.671-5(b)(22). A tax information statement that includes the information given to the IRS on Forms 1099, as well as additional information identified in Regulations section 1.671-5(e) must be given to trust interest holders. See the General Instructions for Certain Information Returns for more information.

Electronic Filing

 Applications to become an IRS e-file provider must be submitted online. The IRS no longer accepts paper applications on Form 8633, Application to Participate in the IRS e-file Program.

Qualified fiduciaries or transmitters may be able to file Form 1041 and related schedules electronically. To become an *e-file* provider complete the following steps:

1. Create an IRS *e-Services account.*

2. Submit your *e-file provider application* online.

3. Pass a *suitability check.*

The online application process takes 4-6 weeks to complete.

Note. Existing *e-file* providers must now use *e*-Services to make account updates.

Help is available at IRS.gov or through the e-Help Desk at 1-866-255-0654 (512-416-7750 for international calls), Monday through Friday, 6:30 a.m.- 6:00 p.m. (Central time). *Frequently asked questions* under "Help," and *On-line Tutorials* are available to answer questions or to guide users through the application process.

If you file Form 1041 electronically, you may sign the return electronically by using a personal identification number (PIN). See Form 8879-F, IRS *e-file* Signature Authorization for Form 1041, for details.

 Beginning January 1, 2015, Form 8879-F can only be associated with a single Form 1041. Form 8879-F can no longer be used with multiple Forms 1041.

 For tax year 2014, Form 1041 must be e-Filed using Form 8453-FE, U.S. Estate or Trust Declaration for an IRS e-file return. Form 8453-F, U.S. Estate or Trust Income Tax Declaration and Signature for Electronic Filing, is obsolete.

For more information about e-filing returns through MeF, see Publication 4164, Modernized e-File (MeF) Guide for Software Developers and Transmitters.

If Form 1041 is *e-filed* and there is a balance due, the fiduciary may authorize an electronic funds withdrawal with the return.

Private Delivery Services

You can use certain private delivery services designated by the IRS to meet the "timely mailing as timely filing/paying" rule for tax returns and payments. These private delivery services include only the following.
• Federal Express (FedEx): FedEx Priority Overnight, FedEx Standard Overnight, FedEx 2Day, FedEx International Priority, and FedEx International First.
• United Parcel Service (UPS): UPS Next Day Air, UPS Next Day Air Saver, UPS 2nd Day Air, UPS 2nd Day Air A.M., UPS Worldwide Express Plus, and UPS Worldwide Express.

Where To File

For all estates and trusts, including charitable and split-interest trusts (other than Charitable Remainder Trusts).

IF you are located in ...	THEN use this address if you:	
	Are not enclosing a check or money order ...	Are enclosing a check or money order ...
Connecticut, Delaware, District of Columbia, Florida, Georgia, Illinois, Indiana, Kentucky, Maine, Maryland, Massachusetts, Michigan, New Hampshire, New Jersey, New York, North Carolina, Ohio, Pennsylvania, Rhode Island, South Carolina, Tennessee, Vermont, Virginia, West Virginia, Wisconsin	Department of the Treasury Internal Revenue Service Cincinnati, Ohio 45999-0048	Department of the Treasury Internal Revenue Service Cincinnati, Ohio 45999-0148
Alabama, Alaska, Arizona, Arkansas, California, Colorado, Hawaii, Idaho, Iowa, Kansas, Louisiana, Minnesota, Mississippi, Missouri, Montana, Nebraska, Nevada, New Mexico, North Dakota, Oklahoma, Oregon, South Dakota, Texas, Utah, Washington, Wyoming	Department of the Treasury Internal Revenue Service Ogden, Utah 84201-0048	Department of the Treasury Internal Revenue Service Ogden, Utah 84201-0148
A foreign country or United States possession	Internal Revenue Service P.O. Box 409101 Ogden, Utah 84409	Internal Revenue Service P.O. Box 409101 Ogden, Utah 84409

For the IRS mailing address to use if you are using a private delivery service, go to IRS.gov and enter "private delivery service" in the search box.

The private delivery service can tell you how to get written proof of the mailing date.

 Private delivery services cannot deliver items to P.O. boxes. You must use the U.S. Postal Service to mail any item to an IRS P.O. box address.

When To File

For calendar year estates and trusts, file Form 1041 and Schedule(s) K-1 on or before April 15, 2015. For fiscal year estates and trusts, file Form 1041 by the 15th day of the 4th month following the close of the tax year. For example, an estate that has a tax year that ends on June 30, 2015, must file Form 1041 by October 15, 2015. If the due date falls on a Saturday, Sunday, or legal holiday, file on the next business day.

Extension of Time To File

If more time is needed to file the estate or trust return, use Form 7004, Application for Automatic Extension of Time To File Certain Business Income Tax, Information, and Other Returns, to apply for an automatic 5 month extension of time to file.

Period Covered

File the 2014 return for calendar year 2014 and fiscal years beginning in 2014 and ending in 2015. If the return is for a fiscal year or a short tax year (less than 12 months), fill in the tax year space at the top of the form.

The 2014 Form 1041 may also be used for a tax year beginning in 2015 if:

1. The estate or trust has a tax year of less than 12 months that begins and ends in 2015, and

2. The 2015 Form 1041 is not available by the time the estate or trust is required to file its tax return. However, the estate or trust must show its 2015 tax year on the 2014 Form 1041 and incorporate any tax law changes that are effective for tax years beginning after December 31, 2014.

Who Must Sign

Fiduciary

The fiduciary, or an authorized representative, must sign Form 1041. If there are joint fiduciaries, only one is required to sign the return.

A financial institution that submitted estimated tax payments for trusts for which it is the trustee must enter its EIN in the space provided for the EIN of the fiduciary. Do not enter the EIN of the trust. For this purpose, a financial institution is one that maintains a Treasury Tax and Loan (TT&L) account. If you are an attorney or other individual functioning in a fiduciary capacity, leave this space blank. Do not enter your individual social security number (SSN).

Paid Preparer

Generally, anyone who is paid to prepare a tax return must sign the return and fill in the other blanks in the "Paid Preparer Use Only" area of the return.

The person required to sign the return must:
- Complete the required preparer information,
- Sign it in the space provided for the preparer's signature (a facsimile signature is acceptable), and
- Give you a copy of the return for your records.

If you, as fiduciary, fill in Form 1041, leave the "Paid Preparer Use Only" space blank.

If someone prepares this return and does not charge you, that person should not sign the return.

Paid Preparer Authorization

If the fiduciary wants to allow the IRS to discuss the estate's or trust's 2014 tax return with the paid preparer who signed it, check the "Yes," box in the signature area of the return. This authorization applies only to the individual whose signature appears in the *Paid Preparer Use Only* area of the estate's or trust's return. It does not apply to the firm, if any, shown in that section.

If the "Yes," box is checked, the fiduciary is authorizing the IRS to call the paid preparer to answer any questions that may arise during the processing of the estate's or trust's return. The fiduciary is also authorizing the paid preparer to:

• Give the IRS any information that is missing from the estate's or trust's return,

• Call the IRS for information about the processing of the estate's or trust's return or the status of its refund or payment(s), and

• Respond to certain IRS notices that the fiduciary has shared with the preparer about math errors, offsets, and return preparation. The notices will not be sent to the preparer.

The fiduciary is not authorizing the paid preparer to receive any refund check, bind the estate or trust to anything (including any additional tax liability), or otherwise represent the estate or trust before the IRS.

The authorization will automatically end no later than the due date (without regard to extensions) for filing the estate's or trust's 2015 tax return. If the fiduciary wants to expand the paid preparer's authorization or revoke the authorization before it ends, see Pub. 947, Practice Before the IRS and Power of Attorney.

Accounting Methods

Figure taxable income using the method of accounting regularly used in keeping the estate's or trust's books and records. Generally, permissible methods include the cash method, the accrual method, or any other method authorized by the Internal Revenue Code. In all cases, the method used must clearly reflect income.

Generally, the estate or trust may change its accounting method (for income as a whole or for any material item) only by getting consent on Form 3115, Application for Change in Accounting Method. For more information, see Pub. 538, Accounting Periods and Methods.

Accounting Periods

For a decedent's estate, the moment of death determines the end of the decedent's tax year and the beginning of the estate's tax year. As executor or administrator, you choose the estate's tax period when you file its first income tax return. The estate's first tax year may be any period of 12 months or less that ends on the last day of a month. If you select the last day of any month other than December, you are adopting a fiscal tax year.

To change the accounting period of an estate, use Form 1128, Application To Adopt, Change, or Retain a Tax Year.

Generally, a trust must adopt a calendar year. The following trusts are exempt from this requirement:

• A trust that is exempt from tax under section 501(a);

• A charitable trust described in section 4947(a)(1); and

• A trust that is treated as wholly owned by a grantor under the rules of sections 671 through 679.

Rounding Off to Whole Dollars

You may round off cents to whole dollars on the estate's or trust's return and schedules. If you do round to whole dollars, you must round all amounts. To round, drop amounts under 50 cents and increase amounts from 50 to 99 cents to the next dollar. For example, $1.39 becomes $1 and $2.50 becomes $3.

If you have to add two or more amounts to figure the amount to enter on a line, include cents when adding the amounts and round off only the total.

Estimated Tax

Generally, an estate or trust must pay estimated income tax for 2015 if it expects to owe, after subtracting any withholding and credits, at least $1,000 in tax, and it expects the withholding and credits to be less than the smaller of:

1. 90% of the tax shown on the 2015 tax return, or

2. 100% of the tax shown on the 2014 tax return (110% of that amount if the estate's or trust's adjusted gross income on that return is more than $150,000, and less than ⅔ of gross income for 2014 or 2015 is from farming or fishing).

However, if a return was not filed for 2014 or that return did not cover a full 12 months, item 2 does not apply.

For this purpose, include household employment taxes in the tax shown on the tax return, but only if either of the following is true:

• The estate or trust will have federal income tax withheld for 2015 (see the instructions for line 24e), or

• The estate or trust would be required to make estimated tax payments for 2015 even if it did not include household employment taxes when figuring estimated tax.

Exceptions

Estimated tax payments are not required from:

1. An estate of a domestic decedent or a domestic trust that had no tax liability for the full 12-month 2014 tax year;

2. A decedent's estate for any tax year ending before the date that is 2 years after the decedent's death; or

3. A trust that was treated as owned by the decedent if the trust will receive the residue of the decedent's estate under the will (or if no will is admitted to probate, the trust primarily responsible for paying debts, taxes, and expenses of administration) for any tax year ending before the date that is 2 years after the decedent's death.

For more information, see Form 1041-ES, Estimated Income Tax for Estates and Trusts.

Electronic Deposits

A financial institution that has been designated as an authorized federal tax depository, and acts as a fiduciary for at least 200 taxable trusts that are required to pay estimated tax, is required to deposit the estimated tax payments electronically using the Electronic Federal Tax Payment System (EFTPS).

A fiduciary that is not required to make electronic deposits of estimated tax on behalf of a trust or an estate may voluntarily participate in EFTPS. To enroll in or get more information about EFTPS, visit the EFTPS website at www.eftps.gov or call 1-800-555-4477. Also, see Pub. 966, Electronic Federal Tax Payment System: A Guide to Getting Started.

Depositing on time. For a deposit using EFTPS to be on time, the deposit must be submitted by 8:00 p.m. Eastern time the day before the due date of the deposit.

Section 643(g) Election

Fiduciaries of trusts that pay estimated tax may elect under section 643(g) to have any portion of their estimated tax payments allocated to any of the beneficiaries.

The fiduciary of a decedent's estate may make a section 643(g) election only for the final year of the estate.

Make the election by filing Form 1041-T, Allocation of Estimated Tax Payments to Beneficiaries, by the 65th day after the close of the estate's or trust's tax year. Then, include that amount on Schedule K-1 (Form 1041), box 13, code A, for any beneficiaries for whom it was elected.

If Form 1041-T was timely filed, the payments are treated as paid or credited to the beneficiary on the last day of the tax year and must be included as an other amount paid, credited, or required to be distributed on Form 1041, Schedule B, line 10. See the instructions for Schedule B, line 10, later.

Failure to make a timely election will result in the estimated tax payments not being transferred to the beneficiary(ies) even if you entered the amount on Schedule K-1.

See the instructions for line 24b for more details.

Interest and Penalties

Interest

Interest is charged on taxes not paid by the due date, even if an extension of time to file is granted.

Interest is also charged on penalties imposed for failure to file, negligence, fraud, substantial valuation misstatements, substantial understatements of tax, and reportable transaction understatements. Interest is charged on the penalty from the due date of the return (including extensions). The interest charge is figured at a rate determined under section 6621.

Late Filing of Return

The law provides a penalty of 5% of the tax due for each month, or part of a month, for which a return is not filed up to a maximum of 25% of the tax due (15% for each month, or part of a month, up to a maximum of 75% if the failure to file is fraudulent). If the return is more than 60 days late, the minimum penalty is the smaller of $135 or the tax due.

The penalty will not be imposed if you can show that the failure to file on time was due to reasonable cause. If you receive a notice about penalty and interest after you file this return, send us an explanation and we will determine if you meet reasonable-cause criteria. Do **not** attach an explanation when you file Form 1041.

Late Payment of Tax

Generally, the penalty for not paying tax when due is ½ of 1% of the unpaid amount for each month or part of a month it remains unpaid. The maximum penalty is 25% of the unpaid amount. The penalty applies to any unpaid tax on

the return. Any penalty is in addition to interest charges on late payments.

 If you include interest on either of these penalties with your payment, identify and enter these amounts in the bottom margin of Form 1041, page 1. Do not include the interest or penalty amount in the balance of tax due on line 27.

Failure To Provide Information Timely

You must provide Schedule K-1 (Form 1041), on or before the day you are required to file Form 1041, to each beneficiary who receives a distribution of property or an allocation of an item of the estate.

For each failure to provide Schedule K-1 to a beneficiary when due and each failure to include on Schedule K-1 all the information required to be shown (or the inclusion of incorrect information), a $100 penalty may be imposed with regard to each Schedule K-1 for which a failure occurs. The maximum penalty is $1.5 million for all such failures during a calendar year. If the requirement to report information is intentionally disregarded, each $100 penalty is increased to $250 or, if greater, 10% of the aggregate amount of items required to be reported, and the $1.5 million maximum does not apply.

The penalty will not be imposed if the fiduciary can show that not providing information timely was due to reasonable cause and not due to willful neglect.

Underpaid Estimated Tax

If the fiduciary underpaid estimated tax, use Form 2210, Underpayment of Estimated Tax by Individuals, Estates, and Trusts, to figure any penalty. Enter the amount of any penalty on Form 1041, line 26.

Trust Fund Recovery Penalty

This penalty may apply if certain excise, income, social security, and Medicare taxes that must be collected or withheld are not collected or withheld, or these taxes are not paid. These taxes are generally reported on Forms 720, 941, 943, 944, or 945. The trust fund recovery penalty may be imposed on all persons who are determined by the IRS to have been responsible for collecting, accounting for, or paying over these taxes, and who acted willfully in not doing so. The penalty is equal to the unpaid trust fund tax. See the Instructions for Form 720, Pub. 15 (Circular E), Employer's Tax Guide, or

Pub. 51 (Circular A), Agricultural Employer's Tax Guide, for more details, including the definition of responsible persons.

Other Penalties

Other penalties can be imposed for negligence, substantial understatement of tax, and fraud. See Pub. 17, Your Federal Income Tax, for details on these penalties.

Other Forms That May Be Required

Form W-2, Wage and Tax Statement, and Form W-3, Transmittal of Wage and Tax Statements.

Form 56, Notice Concerning Fiduciary Relationship. You must notify the IRS of the creation or termination of a fiduciary relationship. You may use Form 56 to provide this notice to the IRS.

Form 706, United States Estate (and Generation-Skipping Transfer) Tax Return, or Form 706-NA, United States Estate (and Generation-Skipping Transfer) Tax Return, Estate of nonresident not a citizen of the United States.

Form 706-GS(D), Generation-Skipping Transfer Tax Return for Distributions.

Form 706-GS(D-1), Notification of Distribution From a Generation-Skipping Trust.

Form 706-GS(T), Generation-Skipping Transfer Tax Return for Terminations.

Form 709, United States Gift (and Generation-Skipping Transfer) Tax Return.

Form 720, Quarterly Federal Excise Tax Return. Use Form 720 to report environmental excise taxes, communications and air transportation taxes, fuel taxes, luxury tax on passenger vehicles, manufacturers' taxes, ship passenger tax, and certain other excise taxes.

Caution. See *Trust Fund Recovery Penalty* earlier.

Form 926, Return by a U.S. Transferor of Property to a Foreign Corporation. Use this form to report certain information required under section 6038B.

Form 940, Employer's Annual Federal Unemployment (FUTA) Tax Return. The estate or trust may be liable for FUTA tax and may have to file Form

940 if it paid wages of $1,500 or more in any calendar quarter during the calendar year (or the preceding calendar year) or one or more employees worked for the estate or trust for some part of a day in any 20 different weeks during the calendar year (or the preceding calendar year).

Form 941, Employer's QUARTERLY Federal Tax Return. Employers must file this form quarterly to report income tax withheld on wages and employer and employee social security and Medicare taxes. Certain small employers must file Form 944, Employer's ANNUAL Federal Tax Return, instead of Form 941. For more information, see the Instructions for Form 944. Agricultural employers must file Form 943, Employer's Annual Federal Tax Return for Agricultural Employees, instead of Form 941, to report income tax withheld and employer and employee social security and Medicare taxes on farmworkers.

Caution. See *Trust Fund Recovery Penalty* earlier.

Form 945, Annual Return of Withheld Federal Income Tax. Use this form to report income tax withheld from nonpayroll payments, including pensions, annuities, IRAs, gambling winnings, and backup withholding.

Caution. See *Trust Fund Recovery Penalty* earlier.

Form 1040, U.S. Individual Income Tax Return.

Form 1040NR, U.S. Nonresident Alien Income Tax Return.

Form 1041-A, U.S. Information Return Trust Accumulation of Charitable Amounts.

Form 1042, Annual Withholding Tax Return for U.S. Source Income of Foreign Persons, and Form 1042-S, Foreign Person's U.S. Source Income Subject to Withholding. Use these forms to report and transmit withheld tax on payments or distributions made to nonresident alien individuals, foreign partnerships, or foreign corporations to the extent such payments or distributions constitute gross income from sources within the United States that is not effectively connected with a U.S. trade or business. For more information, see sections 1441 and 1442, and Pub. 515, Withholding of Tax on Nonresident Aliens and Foreign Entities.

Forms 1099-A, B, INT, LTC, MISC, OID, Q, R, S, and SA. You may have to file these information returns to report acquisitions or abandonments of secured property; proceeds from broker and barter exchange transactions; interest payments; payments of long-term care and accelerated death benefits; miscellaneous income payments; original issue discount; distributions from Coverdell ESAs; distributions from pensions, annuities, retirement or profit-sharing plans, IRAs (including SEPs, SIMPLEs, Roth IRAs, Roth Conversions, and IRA recharacterizations), insurance contracts, etc.; proceeds from real estate transactions; and distributions from an HSA, Archer MSA, or Medicare Advantage MSA.

Also, use certain of these returns to report amounts received as a nominee on behalf of another person, except amounts reported to beneficiaries on Schedule K-1 (Form 1041).

Form 8275, Disclosure Statement. File Form 8275 to disclose items or positions, except those contrary to a regulation, that are not otherwise adequately disclosed on a tax return. The disclosure is made to avoid parts of the accuracy-related penalty imposed for disregard of rules or substantial understatement of tax. Form 8275 is also used for disclosures relating to preparer penalties for understatements due to unrealistic positions or disregard of rules.

Form 8275-R, Regulation Disclosure Statement, is used to disclose any item on a tax return for which a position has been taken that is contrary to Treasury regulations.

Form 8288, U.S. Withholding Tax Return for Dispositions by Foreign Persons of U.S. Real Property Interests, and Form 8288-A, Statement of Withholding on Dispositions by Foreign Persons of U.S. Real Property Interests. Use these forms to report and transmit withheld tax on the sale of U.S. real property by a foreign person. Also, use these forms to report and transmit tax withheld from amounts distributed to a foreign beneficiary from a "U.S. real property interest account" that a domestic estate or trust is required to establish under Regulations section 1.1445-5(c)(1)(iii).

Form 8300, Report of Cash Payments Over $10,000 Received in a Trade or Business. Generally, this form is used to report the receipt of more than $10,000 in cash or foreign currency in one transaction (or a series of related transactions).

Form 8855, Election To Treat a Qualified Revocable Trust as Part of an Estate. This election allows a qualified revocable trust to be treated and taxed (for income tax purposes) as part of its related estate during the election period.

Form 8865, Return of U.S. Persons With Respect to Certain Foreign Partnerships. The estate or trust may have to file Form 8865 if it:

1. Controlled a foreign partnership (that is, owned more than a 50% direct or indirect interest in a foreign partnership);

2. Owned at least a 10% direct or indirect interest in a foreign partnership while U.S. persons controlled that partnership;

3. Had an acquisition, disposition, or change in proportional interest in a foreign partnership that:

a. Increased its direct interest to at least 10%;

b. Reduced its direct interest of at least 10% to less than 10%; or

c. Changed its direct interest by at least a 10% interest.

4. Contributed property to a foreign partnership in exchange for a partnership interest if:

a. Immediately after the contribution, the estate or trust owned, directly or indirectly, at least a 10% interest in the foreign partnership or

b. The fair market value (FMV) of the property the estate or trust contributed to the foreign partnership, for a partnership interest, when added to other contributions of property made to the foreign partnership during the preceding 12-month period, exceeds $100,000.

Also, the estate or trust may have to file Form 8865 to report certain dispositions by a foreign partnership of property it previously contributed to that foreign partnership if it was a partner at the time of the disposition.

For more details, including penalties for failing to file Form 8865, see Form 8865 and its separate instructions.

Form 8886, Reportable Transaction Disclosure Statement. Use Form 8886 to disclose information for each reportable transaction in which the trust participated, directly or indirectly. Form 8886 must be filed for each tax year that the federal income tax liability of the estate or trust is affected by its participation in the transaction. The estate or trust may have to pay a penalty if it has a requirement to file

Form 8886 but you fail to file it. The following are reportable transactions.
- Any transaction that is the same as or substantially similar to tax avoidance transactions identified by the IRS as listed transactions.
- Any transaction offered under conditions of confidentiality and for which the estate or trust paid a minimum fee (confidential transaction).
- Any transaction for which the estate or trust or a related party has contractual protection against disallowance of the tax benefits (transaction with contractual protection).
- Any transaction resulting in a loss of at least $2 million in any single year or $4 million in any combination of years ($50,000 in any single year if the loss is generated by a section 988 transaction) (loss transactions).
- Any transaction substantially similar to one of the types of transactions identified by the IRS as a transaction of interest.

See the Instructions for Form 8886 for more details and exceptions.

Form 8918, Material Advisor Disclosure Statement. Material advisors who provide material aid, assistance, or advice on organizing, managing, promoting, selling, implementing, insuring, or carrying out any reportable transaction, and who directly or indirectly receive or expect to receive a minimum fee, must use Form 8918 to disclose any reportable transaction under Regulations section 301.6111-3. For more information, see Form 8918 and its instructions.

Form 8939, Allocation of Increase in Basis for Property Acquired From a Decedent. This form is used to allocate any additional basis when an executor makes the special section 1022 election for property acquired from a decedent who died in 2010.

Form 8960, Net Investment Income Tax—Individuals, Estates, and Trusts.

Additional Information

The following publications may assist you in preparing Form 1041:
- Pub. 550, Investment Income and Expenses,
- Pub. 559, Survivors, Executors, and Administrators,
- Pub. 590-A, Contributions to Individual Retirement Arrangements (IRAs),
- Pub. 590-B, Distributions from Individual Retirement Arrangements (IRAs), and

- Pub 4895, Tax Treatment of Property Acquired From a Decedent Dying in 2010.

Assembly and Attachments

Assemble any schedules, forms, and attachments behind Form 1041 in the following order:

1. Schedule I (Form 1041);
2. Schedule D (Form 1041);
3. Form 4952;
4. Schedule H (Form 1040);
5. Form 3800;
6. Form 4136;
7. Form 8855;
8. Form 8960;
9. All other schedules and forms; and
10. All attachments.

Attachments

If you need more space on the forms or schedules, attach separate sheets. Use the same size and format as on the printed forms. But show the totals on the printed forms.

Attach these separate sheets after all the schedules and forms. Enter the estate's or trust's EIN on each sheet.

Do not file a copy of the decedent's will or the trust instrument unless the IRS requests it.

Special Reporting Instructions

Grantor type trusts, the S portion of electing small business trusts (ESBTs), and bankruptcy estates all have reporting requirements that are significantly different than other Subchapter J trusts and decedent's estates. Additionally, grantor type trusts have optional filing methods available. Pooled income funds have many similar reporting requirements that other Subchapter J trusts (other than grantor type trusts and electing small business trusts) have but there are some very important differences. These reporting differences and optional filing methods are discussed below by entity.

Grantor Type Trusts

A trust is a grantor trust if the grantor retains certain powers or ownership benefits. This can also apply to only a portion of a trust. See *Grantor Type Trust*, later, for details on what makes a trust a grantor trust.

In general, a grantor trust is ignored for income tax purposes and all of the income, deductions, etc., are treated as belonging directly to the grantor. This also applies to any portion of a trust that is treated as a grantor trust.

Note. If only a portion of the trust is a grantor type trust, indicate both grantor trust *and* the other type of trust, for example, simple or complex trust, as the type of entities checked in Section A on page 1 of Form 1041.

 The following instructions apply only to grantor type trusts that are not using an optional filing method.

How to report. If the entire trust is a grantor trust, fill in only the entity information of Form 1041. Do not show any dollar amounts on the form itself; show dollar amounts only on an attachment to the form. Do not use Schedule K-1 (Form 1041) as the attachment.

If only part of the trust is a grantor type trust, the portion of the income, deductions, etc., that is allocable to the non-grantor part of the trust is reported on Form 1041, under normal reporting rules. The amounts that are allocable directly to the grantor are shown only on an attachment to the form. Do not use Schedule K-1 (Form 1041) as the attachment. However, Schedule K-1 is used to reflect any income distributed from the portion of the trust that is not taxable directly to the grantor or owner.

The fiduciary must give the grantor (owner) of the trust a copy of the attachment.

Attachment. On the attachment, show:
- The name, identifying number, and address of the person(s) to whom the income is taxable;
- The income of the trust that is taxable to the grantor or another person under sections 671 through 678. Report the income in the same detail as it would be reported on the grantor's return had it been received directly by the grantor; and
- Any deductions or credits that apply to this income. Report these deductions and credits in the same detail as they would be reported on the grantor's return had they been received directly by the grantor.

The income taxable to the grantor or another person under sections 671 through 678 and the deductions and credits that apply to that income must be reported by that person on their own income tax return.

Example. The John Doe Trust is a grantor type trust. During the year, the trust sold 100 shares of ABC stock for $1,010 in which it had a basis of $10 and 200 shares of XYZ stock for $10 in which it had a $1,020 basis.

The trust does not report these transactions on Form 1041. Instead, a schedule is attached to the Form 1041 showing each stock transaction separately and in the same detail as John Doe (grantor and owner) will need to report these transactions on his Form 8949, Sales and Other Dispositions of Capital Assets and Schedule D (Form 1040). The trust does not net the capital gains and losses, nor does it issue John Doe a Schedule K-1 (Form 1041) showing a $10 long-term capital loss.

QSSTs. Income allocated to S corporation stock held by the trust is treated as owned by the income beneficiary of the portion of the trust that owns the stock. Report this income following the rules discussed above for grantor type trusts. A QSST cannot elect any of the optional filing methods discussed below.

However, the trust, and not the income beneficiary, is treated as the owner of the S corporation stock for figuring and attributing the tax results of a disposition of the stock. For example, if the disposition is a sale, the QSST election ends as to the stock sold and any gain or loss recognized on the sale will be that of the trust. For more information on QSSTs, see Regulations section 1.1361-1(j).

Optional Filing Methods for Certain Grantor Type Trusts

Generally, if a trust is treated as owned by one grantor or other person, the trustee may choose *Optional Method 1* or *Optional Method 2* as the trust's method of reporting instead of filing Form 1041. A husband and wife will be treated as one grantor for purposes of these two optional methods if:
• All of the trust is treated as owned by the husband and wife, and
• The husband and wife file their income tax return jointly for that tax year.

Generally, if a trust is treated as owned by two or more grantors or other persons, the trustee may choose *Optional Method 3* as the trust's method of reporting instead of filing Form 1041.

Once you choose the trust's filing method, you must follow the rules under *Changing filing methods* if you want to change to another method.

Exceptions. The following trusts cannot report using the optional filing methods.
• A common trust fund (as defined in section 584(a)).
• A foreign trust or a trust that has any of its assets located outside the United States.
• A qualified subchapter S trust (as defined in section 1361(d)(3)).
• A trust all of which is treated as owned by one grantor or one other person whose tax year is other than a calendar year.
• A trust all of which is treated as owned by one or more grantors or other persons, one of which is not a U.S. person.
• A trust all of which is treated as owned by one or more grantors or other persons if at least one grantor or other person is an exempt recipient for information reporting purposes, unless at least one grantor or other person is not an exempt recipient and the trustee reports without treating any of the grantors or other persons as exempt recipients.

Optional Method 1. For a trust treated as owned by one grantor or by one other person, the trustee must give all payers of income during the tax year the name and TIN of the grantor or other person treated as the owner of the trust and the address of the trust. This method may be used only if the owner of the trust provides the trustee with a signed Form W-9, Request for Taxpayer Identification Number and Certification. In addition, unless the grantor or other person treated as owner of the trust is the trustee or a co-trustee of the trust, the trustee must give the grantor or other person treated as owner of the trust a statement that:
• Shows all items of income, deduction, and credit of the trust;
• Identifies the payer of each item of income;
• Explains how the grantor or other person treated as owner of the trust takes those items into account when figuring the grantor's or other person's taxable income or tax; and
• Informs the grantor or other person treated as the owner of the trust that those items must be included when figuring taxable income and credits on his or her income tax return.

 Grantor trusts that have not applied for an EIN and are going to file under Optional Method 1 do not need an EIN for the trust as long as they continue to report under that method.

Optional Method 2. For a trust treated as owned by one grantor or by one other person, the trustee must give all payers of income during the tax year the name, address, and TIN of the trust. The trustee also must file with the IRS the appropriate Forms 1099 to report the income or gross proceeds paid to the trust during the tax year that shows the trust as the payer and the grantor, or other person treated as owner, as the payee. The trustee must report each type of income in the aggregate and each item of gross proceeds separately. The due date for any Forms 1099 required to be filed with the IRS by a trustee under this method is March 2, 2015 (March 31, 2015, if filed electronically).

In addition, unless the grantor, or other person treated as owner of the trust, is the trustee or a co-trustee of the trust, the trustee must give the grantor or other person treated as owner of the trust a statement that:
• Shows all items of income, deduction, and credit of the trust;
• Explains how the grantor or other person treated as owner of the trust takes those items into account when figuring the grantor's or other person's taxable income or tax; and
• Informs the grantor or other person treated as the owner of the trust that those items must be included when figuring taxable income and credits on his or her income tax return. This statement satisfies the requirement to give the recipient copies of the Forms 1099 filed by the trustee.

Optional Method 3. For a trust treated as owned by two or more grantors or other persons, the trustee must give all payers of income during the tax year the name, address, and TIN of the trust. The trustee also must file with the IRS the appropriate Forms 1099 to report the income or gross proceeds paid to the trust by all payers during the tax year attributable to the part of the trust treated as owned by each grantor, or other person, showing the trust as the payer and each grantor, or other person treated as owner of the trust, as the payee. The trustee must report each type of income in the aggregate and each item of gross proceeds separately. The due date for any Forms 1099 required to be filed with the IRS by a trustee under this method is March 2, 2015 (March 31, 2015, if filed electronically).

In addition, the trustee must give each grantor or other person treated as owner of the trust a statement that:
• Shows all items of income, deduction, and credit of the trust attributable to the part of the trust treated as owned by the grantor or other person;
• Explains how the grantor or other person treated as owner of the trust takes those items into account when figuring the grantor's or other person's taxable income or tax; and
• Informs the grantor or other person treated as the owner of the trust that those items must be included when figuring taxable income and credits on his or her income tax return. This statement satisfies the requirement to give the recipient copies of the Forms 1099 filed by the trustee.

Changing filing methods. A trustee who previously had filed Form 1041 can change to one of the optional methods by filing a final Form 1041 for the tax year that immediately precedes the first tax year for which the trustee elects to report under one of the optional methods. On the front of the final Form 1041, the trustee must write "Pursuant to section 1.671-4(g), this is the final Form 1041 for this grantor trust," and check the Final return box in item F.

For more details on changing reporting methods, including changes from one optional method to another, see Regulations section 1.671-4(g).

Backup withholding. The following grantor trusts are treated as payors for purposes of backup withholding.

1. A trust established after 1995, all of which is owned by two or more grantors (treating spouses filing a joint return as one grantor).

2. A trust with 10 or more grantors established after 1983 but before 1996.

The trustee must withhold a certain percentage of reportable payments made to any grantor who is subject to backup withholding.

For more information, see section 3406 and its regulations.

Pooled Income Funds

If you are filing for a pooled income fund, attach a statement to support the following:
• The calculation of the yearly rate of return,
• The computation of the deduction for distributions to the beneficiaries, and

• The computation of any charitable deduction.
See section 642 and the regulations thereunder for more information.

You do not have to complete Schedules A or B of Form 1041.

Also, you must file Form 5227, Split-Interest Trust Information Return, for the pooled income fund. However, if all amounts were transferred in trust before May 27, 1969, or if an amount was transferred to the trust after May 26, 1969, for which no deduction was allowed under any of the sections listed under section 4947(a)(2), then Form 5227 does not have to be filed.

Note. Form 1041-A is no longer filed by pooled income funds.

Electing Small Business Trusts (ESBTs)

Special rules apply when figuring the tax on the S portion of an ESBT. The S portion of an ESBT is the portion of the trust that consists of stock in one or more S corporations and is not treated as a grantor type trust. The tax on the S portion:
• Must be figured separately from the tax on the remainder of the ESBT (if any) and attached to the return,
• Is entered to the left of the Schedule G, line 7, entry space preceded by "Sec. 641(c)," and
• Is included in the total tax on Schedule G, line 7.

The tax on the remainder (non-S portion) of the ESBT is figured in the normal manner on Form 1041.

Tax computation attachment. Attach to the return the tax computation for the S portion of the ESBT.

To compute the tax on the S portion:
• Treat that portion of the ESBT as if it were a separate trust;
• Include only the income, losses, deductions, and credits allocated to the ESBT as an S corporation shareholder and gain or loss from the disposition of S corporation stock;
• Aggregate items of income, losses, deductions, and credits allocated to the ESBT as an S corporation shareholder if the S portion of the ESBT has stock in more than one S corporation;
• Deduct state and local income taxes and administrative expenses directly related to the S portion or allocated to the S portion if the allocation is reasonable in light of all the circumstances;

• Deduct interest expense paid or accrued on indebtedness incurred to acquire stock in an S corporation;
• Do not claim a deduction for capital losses in excess of capital gains;
• Do not claim an income distribution deduction or an exemption amount;
• Do not claim an exemption amount in figuring the AMT; and
• Do not use the tax rate schedule to figure the tax. The tax is 39.6% of the S portion's taxable income except in figuring the maximum tax on qualified dividends and capital gains.

For additional information, see Regulations section 1.641(c)-1.

Other information. When figuring the tax and DNI on the remaining (non-S) portion of the trust, disregard the S corporation items.

Do not apportion to the beneficiaries any of the S corporation items.

If the ESBT consists entirely of stock in one or more S corporations, do not make any entries on lines 1–22 of page 1. Instead:
• Complete the entity portion;
• Follow the instructions above for figuring the tax on the S corporation items;
• Carry the tax from line 7 of Schedule G to line 23 on page 1; and
• Complete the rest of the return.

The grantor portion (if any) of an ESBT will follow the rules discussed under *Grantor Type Trusts*, earlier.

Bankruptcy Estates

The bankruptcy estate that is created when an individual debtor files a petition under either chapter 7 or 11 of title 11 of the U.S. Code is treated as a separate taxable entity. The bankruptcy estate is administered by a trustee or a debtor-in-possession. If the case is later dismissed by the bankruptcy court, the individual debtor is treated as if the bankruptcy petition had never been filed.

A separate taxable entity is not created if a partnership or corporation files a petition under any chapter of title 11 of the U.S. Code.

For additional information about bankruptcy estates, see Pub. 908, Bankruptcy Tax Guide.

Who Must File

Every trustee (or debtor-in-possession) for an individual's bankruptcy estate under chapter 7 or 11 of title 11 of the U.S. Code must file a return if the bankruptcy estate has gross income of

$10,150 or more for tax years beginning in 2014.

Failure to do so may result in an estimated Request for Administrative Expenses being filed by the IRS in the bankruptcy proceeding or a motion to compel filing of the return.

 The filing of a tax return for the bankruptcy estate does not relieve the individual debtor(s) of his, her, or their individual tax obligations.

EIN

Every bankruptcy estate of an individual required to file a return must have its own EIN. The SSN of the individual debtor cannot be used as the EIN for the bankruptcy estate.

Accounting Period

A bankruptcy estate is allowed to have a fiscal year. However, this period cannot be longer than 12 months.

When To File

File Form 1041 on or before the 15th day of the 4th month following the close of the tax year. Use Form 7004 to apply for an automatic 6-month extension of time to file.

Disclosure of Return Information

Under section 6103(e)(5), tax returns of individual debtors who have filed for bankruptcy under chapters 7 or 11 of title 11 are, upon written request, open to inspection by or disclosure to the trustee.

The returns subject to disclosure to the trustee are those for the year the bankruptcy begins and prior years. Use Form 4506, Request for Copy of Tax Return, to request copies of the individual debtor's tax returns.

If the bankruptcy case was not voluntary, disclosure cannot be made before the bankruptcy court has entered an order for relief, unless the court rules that the disclosure is needed for determining whether relief should be ordered.

Transfer of Tax Attributes From the Individual Debtor to the Bankruptcy Estate

The bankruptcy estate succeeds to the following tax attributes of the individual debtor:

1. Net operating loss (NOL)

carryovers;

2. Charitable contribution carryovers;

3. Recovery of tax benefit items;

4. Credit carryovers;

5. Capital loss carryovers;

6. Basis, holding period, and character of assets;

7. Method of accounting;

8. Unused passive activity losses;

9. Unused passive activity credits; and

10. Unused section 465 losses.

Income, Deductions, and Credits

Under section 1398(c), the taxable income of the bankruptcy estate generally is figured in the same manner as that of an individual. The gross income of the bankruptcy estate includes any income included in property of the estate as defined in U.S. Code, title 11, sections 541 and 1115.

Under section 1115 of title 11, property of the bankruptcy estate includes (a) earnings from services performed by the debtor after the beginning of the case (both wages and self-employment income) and before the case is closed, dismissed, or converted to a case under a different chapter and (b) property described in section 541 of title 11 and income earned therefrom that the debtor acquires after the beginning of the case and before the case is closed, dismissed, or converted. If section 1115 of title 11 applies, the bankruptcy estate's gross income includes, as described above, (a) the debtor's earnings from services performed after the beginning of the case and (b) the income from property acquired after the beginning of the case.

The income from property owned by the debtor when the case began is also included in the bankruptcy estate's gross income. However, if this property is exempted from the bankruptcy estate or is abandoned by the trustee or debtor-in-possession, the income from the property is not included in the bankruptcy estate's gross income. Also included in income is gain from the sale of the bankruptcy estate's property. To figure gain, the trustee or debtor-in-possession must determine the correct basis of the property.

To determine whether any amount paid or incurred by the bankruptcy estate is allowable as a deduction or

credit, or is treated as wages for employment tax purposes, treat the amount as if it were paid or incurred by the individual debtor in the same trade or business or other activity the debtor engaged in before the bankruptcy proceedings began.

Administrative expenses. The bankruptcy estate is allowed a deduction for any administrative expense allowed under section 503 of title 11 of the U.S. Code, and any fee or charge assessed under chapter 123 of title 28 of the U.S. Code, to the extent not disallowed under an Internal Revenue Code provision (for example, section 263, 265, or 275).

Administrative expense loss. When figuring an NOL, nonbusiness deductions (including administrative expenses) are limited under section 172(d)(4) to the bankruptcy estate's nonbusiness income. The excess nonbusiness deductions are an administrative expense loss that may be carried back to each of the 3 preceding tax years and forward to each of the 7 succeeding tax years of the bankruptcy estate. The amount of an administrative expense loss that may be carried to any tax year is determined after the NOL deductions allowed for that year. An administrative expense loss is allowed only to the bankruptcy estate and cannot be carried to any tax year of the individual debtor.

Carryback of NOLs and credits. If the bankruptcy estate itself incurs an NOL (apart from losses carried forward to the estate from the individual debtor), it can carry back its NOLs not only to previous tax years of the bankruptcy estate, but also to tax years of the individual debtor prior to the year in which the bankruptcy proceedings began. Excess credits, such as the foreign tax credit, also may be carried back to pre-bankruptcy years of the individual debtor.

Exemption. A bankruptcy estate is allowed a personal exemption of $3,950, for tax year 2014.

Note. The personal exemption is subject to phaseout. See the Instructions for Form 1040, Line 42, regarding the personal exemption phaseout for a taxpayer using the married filing separately status.

Standard deduction. A bankruptcy estate that does not itemize deductions is allowed a standard deduction of $6,200, for tax year 2014.

Discharge of indebtedness. In a title 11 case, gross income does not include amounts that normally would be included in gross income resulting from the discharge of indebtedness. However, any amounts excluded from gross income must be applied to reduce certain tax attributes in a certain order. Attach Form 982, Reduction of Tax Attributes Due to Discharge of Indebtedness (and Section 1082 Basis Adjustment), to show the reduction of tax attributes.

Tax Rate Schedule

Figure the tax for the bankruptcy estate using the tax rate schedule below. Enter the tax on Form 1040, line 44.

If taxable income is:			
Over—	But not over—	The tax is:	Of the amount over—
$0	$9,075	10%	$0
9,075	36,900	$907.50 + 15%	9,075
36,900	74,425	5,081.25 + 25%	36,900
74,425	113,425	14,462.50 + 28%	74,425
113,425	202,550	25,382.50 + 33%	113,425
202,550	228,800	54,793.75 + 35%	202,550
228,800	......	63,981.25 + 39.6%	228,800

Prompt Determination of Tax Liability

To request a prompt determination of the tax liability of the bankruptcy estate, the trustee or debtor-in-possession must file a written request for the determination with the IRS. The request must be submitted in duplicate and executed under penalties of perjury. The request must include a statement indicating that it is a request for prompt determination of tax liability and: (a) the return type, and all the tax periods for which prompt determination is sought; (b) the name and location of the office where the return was filed; (c) the debtor's name; (d) the debtor's SSN, TIN, or EIN; (e) the type of bankruptcy estate; (f) the bankruptcy case number; and (g) the court where the bankruptcy is pending. Send the request to the Centralized Insolvency Operation, P.O. Box 7346, Philadelphia, PA 19101-7346 (marked "Request for Prompt Determination").

The IRS will notify the trustee or debtor-in-possession within 60 days from receipt of the request if the return filed by the trustee or debtor-in-possession has been selected for examination or has been accepted as filed. If the return is selected for examination, it will be examined as soon as possible. The IRS will notify the trustee or debtor-in-possession of any tax due within 180 days from receipt of the request or within any additional time permitted by the bankruptcy court.

See Rev. Proc. 2006-24, 2006-22 I.R.B. 943, available at *www.irs.gov/irb/2006-22_IRB/ar12.html*, modified by Announcement 2011–77, available at *www.irs.gov/irb/2011-51_IRB/ar13.*

Special Filing Instructions for Bankruptcy Estates

Use Form 1041 only as a transmittal for Form 1040. In the top margin of Form 1040 write "Attachment to Form 1041. DO NOT DETACH." Attach Form 1040 to Form 1041. Complete only the identification area at the top of Form 1041. Enter the name of the individual debtor in the following format: "John Q. Public Bankruptcy Estate." Beneath, enter the name of the trustee in the following format: "Avery Snow, Trustee." In item D, enter the date the petition was filed or the date of conversion to a chapter 7 or 11 case.

Enter on Form 1041, line 23, the total tax from line 63 of Form 1040. Complete lines 24 through 29 of Form 1041, and sign and date it.

In a chapter 11 case filed after October 16, 2005, the bankruptcy estate's gross income may be affected by section 1115 of title 11 of the U.S. Code. See *Income, Deductions, and Credits* earlier. The debtor may receive a Form W-2, 1099-INT, 1099-DIV, or 1099-MISC or other information return reporting wages or other income to the debtor for the entire year, even though some or all of this income is includible in the bankruptcy estate's gross income under section 1115 of title 11 of the U.S. Code. If this happens, the income reported to the debtor on the Form W-2 or 1099, or other information return (and the withheld income tax shown on these forms) must be reasonably allocated between the debtor and the bankruptcy estate. The debtor-in-possession (or the chapter 11 trustee, if one was appointed) must attach a schedule that shows (a) all the income reported on the Form W-2, Form 1099, or other information return, (b) the portion of this income includible in the bankruptcy estate's gross income, and (c) all the withheld income tax, if any, and the portion of withheld tax reasonably allocated to the bankruptcy estate. Also, the debtor-in-possesion (or the chapter 11 trustee, if one was appointed) must attach a copy of the Form W-2, if any, issued to the debtor for the tax year if the Form W-2 reports wages to the debtor and some or all of the wages are includible in the bankruptcy estate's gross income because of section 1115 of title 11 of the U.S. Code. For more details, including acceptable allocation methods, see Notice 2006-83, 2006-40 I.R.B. 596, available at *www.irs.gov/irb/2006-40_IRB/ar12.html*.

Specific Instructions

Name of Estate or Trust

Copy the exact name of the estate or trust from the Form SS-4, Application for Employer Identification Number, that you used to apply for the EIN. If the name of the trust was changed during the tax year for which you are filing, enter the trust's new name and check the *Change in trust's name* box in item F.

If a grantor type trust (discussed later), write the name, identification number, and address of the grantor(s) or other owner(s) in parentheses after the name of the trust.

Name and Title of Fiduciary

Enter the name and title of the fiduciary. If the name entered is different than the name on the prior year's return, see *Change in Fiduciary's Name* and *Change in Fiduciary*, later.

Address

Include the suite, room, or other unit number after the street address. If the post office does not deliver mail to the street address and the fiduciary has a P.O. box, show the box number instead.

If you want a third party (such as an accountant or an attorney) to receive mail for the estate or trust, enter on the street address line "C/O" followed by the third party's name and street address or P.O. box.

If the estate or trust has had a change of address (including a change to an "in care of" name and address) and did not file Form 8822-B, Change of Address or Responsible Party — Business, check the *Change in fiduciary's address* box in item F.

If the estate or trust has a change of mailing address (including a new "in care of" name and address) or responsible party after filing its return, file Form 8822-B to notify the IRS of the change.

A. Type of Entity

Check the appropriate box(es) that describes the entity for which you are filing the return.

In some cases, more than one box is checked. Check **all** boxes that apply to your trust. For example, if only a portion of a trust is a grantor type trust or if only a portion of an electing small business trust is the S portion, then more than one box is checked.

Note. Determination of entity status is made on an annual basis.

 There are special reporting requirements for grantor type trusts, pooled income funds, electing small business trusts, and bankruptcy estates. See Special Reporting Instructions, *earlier.*

Decedent's Estate

An estate of a deceased person is a taxable entity separate from the decedent. It generally continues to exist until the final distribution of the assets of the estate is made to the heirs and other beneficiaries. The income earned from the property of the estate during the period of administration or settlement must be accounted for and reported by the estate.

Simple Trust

A trust may qualify as a simple trust if:

1. The trust instrument requires that all income must be distributed currently;

2. The trust instrument does not provide that any amounts are to be paid, permanently set aside, or used for charitable purposes; and

3. The trust does not distribute amounts allocated to the corpus of the trust.

Complex Trust

A complex trust is any trust that does not qualify as a simple trust as explained above.

Qualified Disability Trust

A qualified disability trust is any nongrantor trust:

1. Described in 42 U.S.C. 1396p(c)(2)(B)(iv) and established solely for the benefit of an individual under 65 years of age who is disabled, and

2. All the beneficiaries of which are determined by the Commissioner of Social Security to have been disabled

for some part of the tax year within the meaning of 42 U.S.C. 1382c(a)(3).

A trust will not fail to meet item 2 above just because the trust's corpus may revert to a person who is not disabled after the trust ceases to have any disabled beneficiaries.

ESBT (S Portion Only)

The S portion of an ESBT is the portion of the trust that consists of S corporation stock and that is not treated as owned by the grantor or another person. See *Electing Small Business Trusts (ESBTs)*, earlier, for more information about an ESBT.

Grantor Type Trust

A grantor type trust is a legal trust under applicable state law that is not recognized as a separate taxable entity for income tax purposes because the grantor or other substantial owners have not relinquished complete dominion and control over the trust.

Generally, for transfers made in trust after March 1, 1986, the grantor is treated as the owner of any portion of a trust in which he or she has a reversionary interest in either the income or corpus therefrom, if, as of the inception of that portion of the trust, the value of the reversionary interest is more than 5% of the value of that portion. Also, the grantor is treated as holding any power or interest that was held by either the grantor's spouse at the time that the power or interest was created or who became the grantor's spouse after the creation of that power or interest. See *Grantor Type Trusts*, earlier, for more information.

Pre-need funeral trusts. The purchasers of pre-need funeral services are the grantors and the owners of pre-need funeral trusts established under state laws. See Rev. Rul. 87-127, 1987-2 C.B. 156. However, the trustees of pre-need funeral trusts can elect to file the return and pay the tax for qualified funeral trusts. For more information, see Form 1041-QFT, U.S. Income Tax Return for Qualified Funeral Trusts.

Nonqualified deferred compensation plans. Taxpayers may adopt and maintain grantor trusts in connection with nonqualified deferred compensation plans (sometimes referred to as "rabbi trusts"). Rev. Proc. 92-64, 1992-2 C.B. 422, provides a "model grantor trust" for use in rabbi trust arrangements. The procedure also provides guidance for requesting rulings on the plans that use these trusts.

QSSTs. The beneficiary of a qualified subchapter S trust is treated as the substantial owner of that portion of the trust which consists of stock in an S corporation for which an election under section 1361(d)(2) has been made. See *QSSTs*, earlier.

Bankruptcy Estate

A chapter 7 or 11 bankruptcy estate is a separate and distinct taxable entity from the individual debtor for federal income tax purposes. See *Bankruptcy Estates*, earlier.

For more information, see section 1398 and Pub. 908, Bankruptcy Tax Guide.

Pooled Income Fund

A pooled income fund is a split-interest trust with a remainder interest for a public charity and a life income interest retained by the donor or for another person. The property is held in a pool with other pooled income fund property and does not include any tax-exempt securities. The income for a retained life interest is figured using the yearly rate of return earned by the trust. See section 642(c) and the related regulations for more information.

B. Number of Schedules K-1 Attached

Every trust or decedent's estate claiming an income distribution deduction on page 1, line 18, must enter the number of Schedules K-1 (Form 1041) that are attached to Form 1041.

C. Employer Identification Number

Every estate or trust that is required to file Form 1041 must have an EIN. An EIN may be applied for:
• Online by clicking on the EIN link at *www.irs.gov/businesses/small*. The EIN is issued immediately once the application information is validated.
• By mailing or faxing Form SS-4, Application for Employer Identification Number.

If the estate or trust has not received its EIN by the time the return is due, write "Applied for" and the date you applied in the space for the EIN. For more details, see Pub. 583, Starting a Business and Keeping Records.

D. Date Entity Created

Enter the date the trust was created, or, if a decedent's estate, the date of the decedent's death.

E. Nonexempt Charitable and Split-Interest Trusts

Section 4947(a)(1) Trust

Check this box if the trust is a nonexempt charitable trust within the meaning of section 4947(a)(1).

A nonexempt charitable trust is a trust:
• That is not exempt from tax under section 501(a);
• In which all of the unexpired interests are devoted to one or more charitable purposes described in section 170(c)(2)(B); and
• For which a deduction was allowed under section 170 (for individual taxpayers) or similar Code section for personal holding companies, foreign personal holding companies, or estates or trusts (including a deduction for estate or gift tax purposes).

Nonexempt charitable trust treated as a private foundation. If a nonexempt charitable trust is treated as though it were a private foundation under section 509, then the fiduciary must file Form 990-PF, Return of Private Foundation, in addition to Form 1041.

If a nonexempt charitable trust is treated as though it were a private foundation, and it has no taxable income under Subtitle A, it may check the box on Form 990-PF, Part VII-A, line 15 and enter the tax-exempt interest received or accrued during the year on that line, instead of filing Form 1041 to meet its section 6012 filing requirement for that tax year.

Excise taxes. If a nonexempt charitable trust is treated as a private foundation, then it is subject to the same excise taxes under chapters 41 and 42 that a private foundation is subject to. If the nonexempt charitable trust is liable for any of these taxes (except the section 4940 tax), then it reports these taxes on Form 4720, Return of Certain Excise Taxes Under Chapters 41 and 42 of the Internal Revenue Code. Taxes paid by the trust on Form 4720 or on Form 990-PF (the section 4940 tax) cannot be taken as a deduction on Form 1041.

Not a Private Foundation

Check this box if the nonexempt charitable trust (section 4947(a)(1)) is not treated as a private foundation under section 509. For more information, see Regulations section 53.4947-1.

Other returns that must be filed. If a nonexempt charitable trust is not treated

as though it were a private foundation, the fiduciary must file Form 990, Return of Organization Exempt From Income Tax, or Form 990-EZ, Short Form Return of Organization Exempt From Income Tax, in addition to Form 1041, if the trust meets the filing requirements for either of those forms.

If a nonexempt charitable trust is not treated as though it were a private foundation, and it has no taxable income under Subtitle A, it may answer "Yes" on Form 990, Part V, line 12a and enter the tax-exempt interest received or accrued during the year on Form 990, Part V, line 12b instead of filing Form 1041 to meet its section 6012 filing requirement for that tax year (or if Form 990-EZ is filed instead of Form 990, you may check the box on Form 990-EZ, line 43 and enter the tax-exempt interest received or accrued during the year on that line).

Section 4947(a)(2) Trust

Check this box if the trust is a split-interest trust described in section 4947(a)(2).

A split-interest trust is a trust that:
• Is not exempt from tax under section 501(a);
• Has some unexpired interests that are devoted to purposes other than religious, charitable, or similar purposes described in section 170(c)(2)(B); and
• Has amounts transferred in trust after May 26, 1969, for which a deduction was allowed under section 170 (for individual taxpayers) or similar Code sections for personal holding companies, foreign personal holding companies, or estates or trusts (including a deduction for estate or gift tax purposes).

Other returns that must be filed. The fiduciary of a split-interest trust must file Form 5227. However, see the Instructions for Form 5227 for the exception that applies to split-interest trusts other than section 664 charitable remainder trusts.

F. Initial Return, Amended Return, etc.

Amended Return

If you are filing an amended Form 1041:
• Check the "Amended return" box in Item F,
• Complete the entire return,
• Correct the appropriate lines with the new information, and
• Refigure the estate's or trust's tax liability.

Note. If you are amending the return for an NOL carryback, also check the "Net operating loss carryback" box in Item F.

If the total tax on line 23 is larger on the amended return than on the original return, you generally should pay the difference with the amended return. However, you should adjust this amount if there is any increase or decrease in the total payments shown on line 25.

Attach a sheet that explains the reason for the amendments and identifies the lines and amounts being changed on the amended return.

Amended Schedule H (Form 1040). If you discover an error on a Schedule H that you previously filed with Form 1041, file an "Amended" Form 1041 and attach a corrected Schedule H.

In the top margin of your corrected Schedule H, write "Amended," (using red ink, if possible) and the date you discovered the error. Also, on an attachment explain the reason for your correction. If you owe tax, pay the tax in full with your amended Form 1041. If you overpaid tax on a previously filed Schedule H, depending on whether you choose the adjustment or claim for refund process to correct the error, you must either repay or reimburse the employee's share of social security and Medicare tax or get the employee's consent to the filing of a refund claim for their share. See Pub. 926, Household Employer's Tax Guide, for more information.

Amended Schedule K-1 (Form 1041). If the amended return results in a change to income, or a change in distribution of any income or other information provided to a beneficiary, an amended Schedule K-1 (Form 1041) must also be filed with the amended Form 1041 and given to each beneficiary. Check the "Amended K-1" box at the top of the amended Schedule K-1.

Final Return

Check this box if this is a final return because the estate or trust has terminated. Also, check the "Final K-1" box at the top of Schedule K-1.

If, on the final return, there are excess deductions, an unused capital loss carryover, or an NOL carryover, see the instructions for Schedule K-1, box 11, later.

Change in Trust's Name

If the name of the trust has changed from the name shown on the prior year's return (or Form SS-4 if this is the first return being filed), be sure to check this box.

Change in Fiduciary

If a different fiduciary enters his or her name on the line for *Name and title of fiduciary* than was shown on the prior year's return (or Form SS-4 if this is the first return being filed) and you did not file a Form 8822-B, be sure to check this box. If there is a change in the fiduciary whose address is used as the mailing address for the estate or trust after the return is filed, use Form 8822-B to notify the IRS.

Change in Fiduciary's Name

If the fiduciary changed his or her name from the name that he or she entered on the prior year's return (or Form SS-4 if this is the first return being filed), be sure to check this box.

Change in Fiduciary's Address

If the same fiduciary who filed the prior year's return (or Form SS-4 if this is the first return being filed) files the current year's return and changed the address on the return (including a change to an "in care of" name and address), and did not report the change on Form 8822-B, check this box.

If the address shown on Form 1041 changes after you file the form (including a change to an "in care of" name and address), file Form 8822-B to notify the IRS of the change.

G. Section 645 Election

If a section 645 election was made by filing Form 8855, check the box in item G. See *Special Rule for Certain Revocable Trusts* under *Who Must File* and Form 8855 for more information about this election.

Income

Special Rule for Blind Trust

If you are reporting income from a qualified blind trust (under the Ethics in Government Act of 1978), do not identify the payer of any income to the trust but complete the rest of the return as provided in the instructions. Also write "Blind Trust" at the top of page 1.

Extraterritorial Income Exclusion

The extraterritorial income exclusion is not allowed for transactions after 2006. However, income from certain long-term sales and leases may still qualify for the exclusion. For details and to figure the amount of the exclusion, see Form 8873, Extraterritorial Income Exclusion, and its separate instructions. The estate or trust must report the extraterritorial income exclusion on line 15a of Form 1041, page 1.

Although the extraterritorial income exclusion is entered on line 15a, it is an exclusion from income and should be treated as tax-exempt income when completing other parts of the return.

Line 1—Interest Income

Report the estate's or trust's share of all taxable interest income that was received during the tax year. Examples of taxable interest include interest from:
• Accounts (including certificates of deposit and money market accounts) with banks, credit unions, and thrift institutions;
• Notes, loans, and mortgages;
• U.S. Treasury bills, notes, and bonds;
• U.S. savings bonds;
• Original issue discount; and
• Income received as a regular interest holder of a real estate mortgage investment conduit (REMIC).

For taxable bonds acquired after 1987, amortizable bond premium is treated as an offset to the interest income instead of as a separate interest deduction. See Pub. 550.

For the year of the decedent's death, Forms 1099-INT issued in the decedent's name may include interest income earned after the date of death that should be reported on the income tax return of the decedent's estate. When preparing the decedent's final income tax return, report on Schedule B (Form 1040A or 1040), line 1 the total interest shown on Form 1099-INT. Under the last entry on line 1, subtotal all the interest reported on line 1. Below the subtotal, write "Form 1041" and the name and address shown on Form 1041 for the decedent's estate. Also, show the part of the interest reported on Form 1041 and subtract it from the subtotal.

Line 2a—Total Ordinary Dividends

Report the estate's or trust's share of all ordinary dividends received during the tax year.

For the year of the decedent's death, Forms 1099-DIV issued in the decedent's name may include dividends earned after the date of death that should be reported on the income tax return of the decedent's estate. When preparing the decedent's final income tax return, report on Schedule B (Form 1040A or 1040), line 5 the ordinary dividends shown on Form 1099-DIV. Under the last entry on line 5, subtotal all the dividends reported on line 5. Below the subtotal, write "Form 1041" and the name and address shown on Form 1041 for the decedent's estate. Also, show the part of the ordinary dividends reported on Form 1041 and subtract it from the subtotal.

 Report capital gain distributions on Schedule D (Form 1041), Line 13.

Line 2b—Qualified Dividends

Enter the beneficiary's allocable share of qualified dividends on line 2b(1) and enter the estate's or trust's allocable share on line 2b(2).

If the estate or trust received qualified dividends that were derived from IRD, you must reduce the amount on line 2b(2) by the portion of the estate tax deduction claimed on Form 1041, page 1, line 19, that is attributable to those qualified dividends. Do not reduce the amounts on line 2b by any other allocable expenses.

Note. The beneficiary's share (as figured above) may differ from the amount entered on line 2b of Schedule K-1 (Form 1041).

Qualified dividends. Qualified dividends are eligible for a lower tax rate than other ordinary income. Generally, these dividends are reported to the estate or trust in box 1b of Form(s) 1099-DIV. See Pub. 550 for the definition of qualified dividends if the estate or trust received dividends not reported on Form 1099-DIV.

Exception. Some dividends may be reported to the estate or trust as in box 1b of Form 1099-DIV but are not qualified dividends. These include:
• Dividends received on any share of stock that the estate or trust held for less than 61 days during the 121-day period that began 60 days before the ex-dividend date. The ex-dividend date is the first date following the declaration of a dividend on which the purchaser of a stock is not entitled to receive the next dividend payment. When counting the number of days the stock was held, include the day the estate or trust disposed of the stock but not the day it acquired the stock. However, you cannot count certain days during which the estate's or trust's risk of loss was diminished. See Pub. 550 for more details.

- Dividends attributable to periods totaling more than 366 days that the estate or trust received on any share of preferred stock held for less than 91 days during the 181-day period that began 90 days before the ex-dividend date. When counting the number of days the stock was held, include the day the estate or trust disposed of the stock but not the day it acquired the stock. However, you cannot count certain days during which the estate's or trust's risk of loss was diminished. See Pub. 550 for more details. Preferred dividends attributable to periods totaling less than 367 days are subject to the 61-day holding period rule above.
- Dividends on any share of stock to the extent that the estate or trust is under an obligation (including a short sale) to make related payments with respect to positions in substantially similar or related property.
- Payments in lieu of dividends, but only if you know or have reason to know that the payments are not qualified dividends.

 If you have an entry on line 2b(2), be sure you use Schedule D (Form 1041), the Schedule D Tax Worksheet, or the Qualified Dividends Tax Worksheet, whichever applies, to figure the estate's or trust's tax. Figuring the estate's or trust's tax liability in this manner will usually result in a lower tax.

Line 3—Business Income or (Loss)

If the estate operated a business, report the income and expenses on Schedule C (Form 1040), Profit or Loss From Business (or Schedule C-EZ (Form 1040), Net Profit From Business). Enter the net profit or (loss) from Schedule C (or Schedule C-EZ) on line 3.

Line 4—Capital Gain or (Loss)

Enter the gain from Schedule D (Form 1041), Part III, line 19, column (3) or the loss from Part IV, line 20.

 Do not substitute Schedule D (Form 1040) for Schedule D (Form 1041).

Line 5—Rents, Royalties, Partnerships, Other Estates and Trusts, etc.

Use Schedule E (Form 1040), Supplemental Income and Loss, to report the estate's or trust's share of income or (losses) from rents, royalties, partnerships, S corporations, other estates and trusts, and REMICs. Also use Schedule E (Form 1040) to report farm rental income and expenses based on crops or livestock produced by a tenant. Enter the net profit or (loss) from Schedule E on line 5. See the Instructions for Schedule E (Form 1040) for reporting requirements.

If the estate or trust received a Schedule K-1 from a partnership, S corporation, or other flow-through entity, use the corresponding lines on Form 1041 to report the interest, dividends, capital gains, etc., from the flow-through entity.

Line 6—Farm Income or (Loss)

If the estate or trust operated a farm, use Schedule F (Form 1040), Profit or Loss From Farming, to report farm income and expenses. Enter the net profit or (loss) from Schedule F on line 6.

 *If an estate or trust has farm rental income and expenses based on crops or livestock produced by a tenant, report the income and expenses on Schedule E (Form 1040). Do **not** use Form 4835, Farm Rental Income and Expenses, or Schedule F (Form 1040) to report such income and expenses and do **not** include the net profit or (loss) from such income and expenses on line 6.*

Line 7—Ordinary Gain or (Loss)

Enter from line 17, Form 4797, Sales of Business Property, the ordinary gain or loss from the sale or exchange of property other than capital assets and also from involuntary conversions (other than casualty or theft).

Line 8—Other Income

Enter other items of income not included on lines 1, 2a, and 3 through 7. List the type and amount on an attached schedule if the estate or trust has more than one item.

Items to be reported on line 8 include:
- Unpaid compensation received by the decedent's estate that is IRD, and
- Any part of a total distribution shown on Form 1099-R, Distributions From Pensions, Annuities, Retirement or Profit-Sharing Plans, IRAs, Insurance Contracts, etc., that is treated as ordinary income. For more information, see Form 4972, Tax on Lump-Sum Distributions, and its instructions.

Deductions
Depreciation, Depletion, and Amortization

A trust or decedent's estate is allowed a deduction for depreciation, depletion, and amortization only to the extent the deductions are not apportioned to the beneficiaries. An estate or trust is not allowed to make an election under section 179 to expense depreciable business assets.

The estate's or trust's share of depreciation, depletion, and amortization is generally reported on the appropriate lines of Schedule C (or C-EZ), E, or F (Form 1040), the net income or loss from which is shown on lines 3, 5, or 6 of Form 1041. If the deduction is not related to a specific business or activity, then report it on line 15a.

Depreciation. For a decedent's estate, the depreciation deduction is apportioned between the estate and the heirs, legatees, and devisees on the basis of the estate's income allocable to each.

For a trust, the depreciation deduction is apportioned between the income beneficiaries and the trust on the basis of the trust income allocable to each, unless the governing instrument (or local law) requires or permits the trustee to maintain a depreciation reserve. If the trustee is required to maintain a reserve, the deduction is first allocated to the trust, up to the amount of the reserve. Any excess is allocated among the income beneficiaries and the trust in the same manner as the trust's accounting income. See Regulations section 1.167(h)-1(b).

Depletion. For mineral or timber property held by a decedent's estate, the depletion deduction is apportioned between the estate and the heirs, legatees, and devisees on the basis of the estate's income from such property allocable to each.

For mineral or timber property held in trust, the depletion deduction is apportioned between the income beneficiaries and the trust based on the trust income from such property allocable to each, unless the governing instrument (or local law) requires or permits the trustee to maintain a reserve for depletion. If the trustee is required to maintain a reserve, the deduction is first allocated to the trust, up to the amount of the reserve. Any excess is allocated among the beneficiaries and the trust in the same manner as the trust's accounting income. See Regulations section 1.611-1(c)(4).

Amortization. The deduction for amortization is apportioned between an estate or trust and its beneficiaries under the same principles used to apportion the deductions for depreciation and depletion.

The deduction for the amortization of reforestation expenditures under section 194 is allowed only to an estate.

Allocable share from a pass-through entity. Depreciation, depletion, and amortization received from a pass-through entity on a Schedule K-1 is apportioned and reported in the same manner as discussed above. A section 179 expense received from a pass-through entity on a Schedule K-1 is not deductible by the estate or trust.

Allocation of Deductions for Tax-Exempt Income

Generally, no deduction that would otherwise be allowable is allowed for any expense (whether for business or for the production of income) that is allocable to tax-exempt income. Examples of tax-exempt income include:
- Certain death benefits (section 101),
- Interest on state or local bonds (section 103),
- Compensation for injuries or sickness (section 104), and
- Income from discharge of indebtedness in a title 11 case (section 108).

Exception. State income taxes and business expenses that are allocable to tax-exempt interest are deductible.

Expenses that are directly allocable to tax-exempt income are allocated only to tax-exempt income. A reasonable proportion of expenses indirectly allocable to both tax-exempt income and other income must be allocated to each class of income.

Deductions That May Be Allowable for Estate Tax Purposes

Administration expenses and casualty and theft losses deductible on Form 706 may be deducted, to the extent otherwise deductible for income tax purposes, on Form 1041 if the fiduciary files a statement waiving the right to deduct the expenses and losses on Form 706. The statement must be filed before the expiration of the statutory period of limitations for the tax year the deduction is claimed. See Pub. 559 for more information.

Accrued Expenses

Generally, an accrual basis taxpayer can deduct accrued expenses in the tax year that: (a) all events have occurred that determine the liability; and (b) the amount of the liability can be figured with reasonable accuracy. However, all the events that establish liability are treated as occurring only when economic performance takes place. There are exceptions for recurring items. See section 461(h).

Limitations on Deductions

At-Risk Loss Limitations

Generally, the amount the estate or trust has "at-risk" limits the loss it can deduct for any tax year. Use Form 6198, At-Risk Limitations, to figure the deductible loss for the year and file it with Form 1041. For more information, see Pub. 925, Passive Activity and At-Risk Rules.

Passive Activity Loss and Credit Limitations

In general. Section 469 and the regulations thereunder generally limit losses from passive activities to the amount of income derived from all passive activities. Similarly, credits from passive activities are generally limited to the tax attributable to such activities. These limitations are first applied at the estate or trust level.

Generally, an activity is a passive activity if it involves the conduct of any trade or business, and the taxpayer does not materially participate in the activity. Passive activities do not include working interests in oil and gas properties. See section 469(c)(3).

Note. Material participation standards for estates and trusts have not been established by regulations.

For a grantor trust, material participation is determined at the grantor level.

If the estate or trust distributes an interest in a passive activity, the basis of the property immediately before the distribution is increased by the passive activity losses allocable to the interest, and such losses cannot be deducted. See section 469(j)(12).

 Losses from passive activities are first subject to the at-risk rules. When the losses are deductible under the at-risk rules, the passive activity rules then apply.

Rental activities. Generally, rental activities are passive activities, whether or not the taxpayer materially participates. However, certain taxpayers who materially participate in real property trades or businesses are not subject to the passive activity limitations on losses from rental real estate activities in which they materially participate. For more details, see section 469(c)(7).

For tax years of an estate ending less than 2 years after the decedent's date of death, up to $25,000 of deductions and deduction equivalents of credits from rental real estate activities in which the decedent actively participated are allowed. Any excess losses or credits are suspended for the year and carried forward.

Portfolio income. Portfolio income is not treated as income from a passive activity, and passive losses and credits generally may not be applied to offset it. Portfolio income generally includes interest, dividends, royalties, and income from annuities. Portfolio income of an estate or trust must be accounted for separately.

Forms to file. See Form 8582, Passive Activity Loss Limitations, to figure the amount of losses allowed from passive activities. See Form 8582-CR, Passive Activity Credit Limitations, to figure the amount of credit allowed for the current year.

Transactions Between Related Taxpayers

Under section 267, a trust that uses the accrual method of accounting may only deduct business expenses and interest owed to a related party in the year the payment is included in the income of the related party. For this purpose, a related party includes:

1. A grantor and a fiduciary of any trust;

2. A fiduciary of a trust and a fiduciary of another trust, if the same person is a grantor of both trusts;

3. A fiduciary of a trust and a beneficiary of such trust;

4. A fiduciary of a trust and a beneficiary of another trust, if the same person is a grantor of both trusts;

5. A fiduciary of a trust and a corporation more than 50% in value of the outstanding stock of which is owned, directly or indirectly, by or for the trust or by or for a person who is a grantor of the trust; and

6. An executor of an estate and a beneficiary of that estate, except for a sale or exchange to satisfy a pecuniary

bequest (that is, a bequest of a sum of money).

Line 10—Interest

Enter the amount of interest (subject to limitations) paid or incurred by the estate or trust on amounts borrowed by the estate or trust, or on debt acquired by the estate or trust (for example, outstanding obligations from the decedent) that is not claimed elsewhere on the return.

If the proceeds of a loan were used for more than one purpose (for example, to purchase a portfolio investment and to acquire an interest in a passive activity), the fiduciary must make an interest allocation according to the rules in Temporary Regulations section 1.163-8T.

Do not include interest paid on indebtedness incurred or continued to purchase or carry obligations on which the interest is wholly exempt from income tax.

Personal interest is not deductible. Examples of personal interest include interest paid on:
• Revolving charge accounts used to purchase personal use property;
• Personal notes for money borrowed from a bank, credit union, or other person;
• Installment loans on personal use property; and
• Underpayments of federal, state, or local income taxes.

Interest that is paid or incurred on indebtedness allocable to a trade or business (including a rental activity) should be deducted on the appropriate line of Schedule C (or C-EZ), E, or F (Form 1040), the net income or loss from which is shown on line 3, 5, or 6 of Form 1041.

Types of interest to include on line 10 are:

1. Any investment interest (subject to limitations—see below);

2. Any qualified residence interest (see later); and

3. Any interest payable under section 6601 on any unpaid portion of the estate tax attributable to the value of a reversionary or remainder interest in property for the period during which an extension of time for payment of such tax is in effect.

Investment interest. Generally, investment interest is interest (including amortizable bond premium on taxable bonds acquired after October 22, 1986,

but before January 1, 1988) that is paid or incurred on indebtedness that is properly allocable to property held for investment. Investment interest does not include any qualified residence interest, or interest that is taken into account under section 469 in figuring income or loss from a passive activity.

Generally, net investment income is the excess of investment income over investment expenses. Investment expenses are those expenses (other than interest) allowable after application of the 2% floor on miscellaneous itemized deductions.

The amount of the investment interest deduction may be limited. Use Form 4952, Investment Interest Expense Deduction, to figure the allowable investment interest deduction.

If you must complete Form 4952, check the box on line 10 of Form 1041 and attach Form 4952. Then, add the deductible investment interest to the other types of deductible interest and enter the total on line 10.

Qualified residence interest. Interest paid or incurred by an estate or trust on indebtedness secured by a qualified residence of a beneficiary of an estate or trust is treated as qualified residence interest if the residence would be a qualified residence (that is, the principal residence or the secondary residence selected by the beneficiary) if owned by the beneficiary. The beneficiary must have a present interest in the estate or trust or an interest in the residuary of the estate or trust. See Pub. 936, Home Mortgage Interest Deduction, for an explanation of the general rules for deducting home mortgage interest.

See section 163(h)(3) for a definition of qualified residence interest and for limitations on indebtedness.

Qualified mortgage insurance premiums. Enter (on the worksheet later) the qualified mortgage insurance premiums paid under a mortgage insurance contract issued after December 31, 2006, in connection with qualified residence acquisition debt that was secured by a principal or secondary residence. See *Prepaid mortgage insurance* below if the estate or trust paid any premiums allocable after 2014. If at least one other person was liable for and paid the premiums in connection with the loan, and the premiums were reported on Form 1098, Mortgage Interest Statement, include the estate's or trust's share of the 2014 premiums on the worksheet later.

Qualified mortgage insurance is mortgage insurance provided by the Department of Veterans Affairs, the Federal Housing Administration, or the Rural Housing Service, and private mortgage insurance (as defined in section 2 of the Homeowners Protection Act of 1998 as in effect on December 20, 2006).

Mortgage insurance provided by the Department of Veterans Affairs and the Rural Housing Service is commonly known as a funding fee and guarantee fee, respectively. These fees can be deducted fully in 2014 if the mortgage insurance contract was issued in 2014. Contact the mortgage insurance issuer to determine the deductible amount if it is not included in box 4 of Form 1098.

Prepaid mortgage insurance. If the estate or trust paid mortgage insurance premiums allocable to periods after 2014, such premiums must be allocated over the shorter of:
• The stated term of the mortgage, or
• 84 months, beginning with the month the insurance was obtained.

The premiums are treated as paid in the year to which they are allocated. If the mortgage is satisfied before its term, no deduction is allowed for the unamortized balance. See Pub. 936 for details. These allocation rules do not apply to qualified mortgage insurance provided by the Department of Veterans Affairs or the Rural Housing Service.

Limit on the amount that is deductible. The estate or trust cannot deduct mortgage insurance premiums if the estate's or trust's AGI is more than $109,000. If the estate's or trust's AGI is more than $100,000, its deduction is limited and you must use the worksheet later to figure the deduction. See *How to figure AGI for estates and trusts*, later, for information on figuring AGI.

Line 11—Taxes

Enter any deductible taxes paid or incurred during the tax year that are not deductible elsewhere on Form 1041. Deductible taxes include the following:
• State and local income taxes. You can deduct state and local income taxes unless you elect to deduct state and local general sales taxes. You cannot deduct both.
• State and local general sales taxes. You can elect to deduct state and local general sales taxes instead of state and local income taxes. Generally, you can elect to deduct the actual state and local general sales taxes (including compensating use taxes) you paid in 2014 if the tax rate was the same as the

Qualified Mortgage Insurance Premiums Deduction Worksheet

1. Enter the total premiums the estate or trust paid in 2014 for qualified mortgage insurance for a contract issued after December 31, 2006 . . . . **1.** _____

2. Enter the estate's or trust's AGI . . . . **2.** _____

3. Enter $100,000 . . . . **3.** _____

4. Is the amount on line 2 more than the amount on line 3?

   No.   The deduction is not limited. Include the amount from line 1 above on Form 1041, line 10. **Do not** complete the rest of this worksheet.

   Yes.   Subtract line 3 from line 2. If the result is not a multiple of $1,000, increase it to the next multiple of $1,000. For example, increase $425 to $1,000, increase $2,025 to $3,000, etc. . . . . **4.** _____

5. Divide line 4 by $10,000. Enter the result as a decimal. If the result is 1.0 or more, enter 1.0 . . . . **5.** . _____

6. Multiply line 1 by line 5 . . . . **6.** _____

7. **Qualified mortgage insurance premiums deduction.** Subtract line 6 from line 1. Enter the result here and include the amount on Form 1041, line 10 . . . . **7.** _____

---

general sales tax rate. However, sales taxes on food, clothing, medical supplies, and motor vehicles are deductible as a general sales tax even if the tax rate was less than the general sales tax rate. Sales taxes on motor vehicles are also deductible as a general sales tax if the tax rate was more than the general sales tax rate, but the tax is deductible only up to the amount of tax that would have been imposed at the general sales tax rate. Motor vehicles include cars, motorcycles, motor homes, recreational vehicles, sport utility vehicles, trucks, vans, and off-road vehicles. Also include any state and local general sales taxes paid for a leased motor vehicle.

Do not include sales taxes paid on items used in a trade or business. An estate or trust **cannot** use the Optional Sales Tax Tables for individuals in the Instructions for Schedule A (Form 1040), Itemized Deductions, to figure its deduction.

- State, local, and foreign real property taxes.
- State and local personal property taxes.
- Foreign or U.S. possession income taxes. You may want to take a credit for the tax instead of a deduction. See the instructions for Schedule G, line 2a, later, for more details.
- The generation-skipping transfer (GST) tax imposed on income distributions.

Do not deduct:
- Federal income taxes;
- Estate, inheritance, legacy, succession, and gift taxes; or

- Federal duties and excise taxes.

Line 12—Fiduciary Fees

Enter the deductible fees paid or incurred to the fiduciary for administering the estate or trust during the tax year.

 Fiduciary fees deducted on Form 706 cannot be deducted on Form 1041.

Line 15a—Other Deductions Not Subject to the 2% Floor

Attach your own statement, listing by type and amount all allowable deductions that are not deductible elsewhere on Form 1041.

Do not include any losses on worthless bonds and similar obligations and nonbusiness bad debts. Report these losses as applicable on Form 8949, Sales and Other Dispositions of Capital Assets.

Do not deduct medical or funeral expenses on Form 1041. Medical expenses of the decedent paid by the estate may be deductible on the decedent's income tax return for the year incurred. See section 213(c). Funeral expenses are deductible only on Form 706.

The following are examples of deductions that are reported on line 15a.

Bond premium(s). For taxable bonds acquired before October 23, 1986, if the fiduciary elected to amortize the premium, report the amortization on this line. If you made the election to amortize the premium, the basis in the taxable

bond must be reduced by the amount of amortization.

For tax-exempt bonds, you cannot deduct the premium that is amortized. Although the premium cannot be deducted, you must amortize the premium and reduce the estate's or trust's basis in the tax-exempt bond by the amount of premium amortized.

For more information, see section 171 and Pub. 550.

If you claim a bond premium deduction for the estate or trust, figure the deduction on a separate sheet and attach it to Form 1041.

Casualty and theft losses. Use Form 4684, Casualties and Thefts, to figure any deductible casualty and theft losses.

Domestic production activities deduction. The estate or trust may be able to deduct up to 9% of its share of qualified production activities income (QPAI) from the following activities.

1. Construction performed in the United States.

2. Engineering or architectural services performed in the United States for construction projects in the United States.

3. Any lease, rental, license, sale, exchange, or other disposition of:

   a. Tangible personal property, computer software, and sound recordings that the estate or trust manufactured, produced, grew, or extracted in whole or in significant part within the United States;

   b. Any qualified film the estate or trust produced; or

c. Electricity, natural gas, or potable water the estate or trust produced in the United States.
In certain cases, the United States includes the Commonwealth of Puerto Rico.

The deduction does not apply to income derived from:
• The sale of food and beverages the estate or trust prepared at a retail establishment;
• Property the estate or trust leased, licensed, or rented for use by any related person; or
• The transmission or distribution of electricity, natural gas, or potable water.

The deduction cannot exceed 9% of modified AGI or 50% of certain Form W-2 wages. QPAI, as well as Form W-2 wages, must be apportioned between the trust or estate and its beneficiaries. For more details, see Form 8903, Domestic Production Activities Deduction, and its separate instructions.

Special rule for oil-related QPAI. If the estate or trust has oil-related QPAI, the domestic production activities deduction is reduced by 3% of the smallest of:
• Oil-related QPAI,
• QPAI, or
• Modified AGI.
See Form 8903 for details.

Estate's or trust's share of amortization, depreciation, and depletion not claimed elsewhere. If you cannot deduct the estate's or trust's apportioned share of amortization, depreciation, and depletion as rent or royalty expenses on Schedule E (Form 1040), or as business or farm expenses on Schedule C, C-EZ, or F (Form 1040), itemize the estate's or trust's apportioned share of the deductions on an attached sheet and include them on line 15a.

Note. Do not report the beneficiary's apportioned share of depreciation, depletion, and amortization on line 15a. Report the beneficiary's apportioned share of deductions on Schedule K-1 (Form 1041), box 9.

Itemize each beneficiary's apportioned share of the deductions and report them in the appropriate box of Schedule K-1 (Form 1041).

Line 15b—Net Operating Loss Deduction

An estate or trust is allowed a net operating loss deduction (NOLD) under section 172.

If you claim a NOLD for the estate or trust, figure the deduction on a separate sheet and attach it to the return.

Line 15c—Allowable Miscellaneous Itemized Deductions Subject to the 2% Floor

Miscellaneous itemized deductions are deductible only to the extent that the aggregate amount of such deductions exceeds 2% of AGI.

Among the miscellaneous itemized deductions that must be included on line 15c are expenses for the production or collection of income under section 212, such as investment advisory fees, subscriptions to investment advisory publications, and the cost of safe deposit boxes.

Miscellaneous itemized deductions do not include deductions for:
• Interest under section 163,
• Taxes under section 164,
• The amortization of bond premium under section 171,
• Estate taxes attributable to IRD under section 691(c), or
• Expenses paid or incurred in connection with the administration of the estate or trust that would not have been incurred if the property were not held in the estate or trust.

For other exceptions, see section 67(b).

How to figure AGI for estates and trusts. You figure AGI by subtracting the following from total income on line 9 of page 1:

1. The administration costs of the estate or trust (the total of lines 12, 14, and 15a to the extent they are costs incurred in the administration of the estate or trust) that would not have been incurred if the property were not held by the estate or trust;

2. The income distribution deduction (line 18);

3. The amount of the exemption (line 20);

4. The domestic production activities deduction claimed on line 15a; and

5. The NOLD claimed on line 15b.

For those estates and trusts whose income distribution deduction is limited to the actual distribution, and not the DNI (that is, the income distribution is less than the DNI), when computing the AGI, use the amount of the actual distribution.

For those estates and trusts whose income distribution deduction is limited to the DNI (that is, the actual distribution exceeds the DNI), the DNI must be figured taking into account the allowable miscellaneous itemized deductions (AMID) after application of the 2% floor. In this situation there are two unknown amounts: (a) the AMID and (b) the DNI.

Computing line 15c. To compute line 15c, use the equation below:

AMID = Total miscellaneous itemized deductions − (.02(AGI))

The following example illustrates how algebraic equations can be used to solve for these unknown amounts.

Example. The Malcolm Smith Trust, a complex trust, earned $20,000 of dividend income, $20,000 of capital gains, and a fully deductible $5,000 loss from XYZ partnership (chargeable to corpus) in 2014. The trust instrument provides that capital gains are added to corpus. Fifty percent of the fiduciary fees are allocated to income and 50% to corpus. The trust claimed a $2,000 deduction on line 12 of Form 1041. The trust incurred $1,500 of miscellaneous itemized deductions (chargeable to income), which are subject to the 2% floor. There are no other deductions. The trustee made a discretionary distribution of the accounting income of $17,500 to the trust's sole beneficiary.

Because the actual distribution can reasonably be expected to exceed the DNI, the trust must figure the DNI, taking into account the allowable miscellaneous itemized deductions, to determine the amount to enter on line 15c.

The trust also claims an exemption of $100 on line 20.

Using the facts in this example:

AMID = 1,500 − (.02(AGI))

In all situations, use the following equation to compute the AGI:

AGI = (line 9) − (the total of lines 12, 14, and 15a to the extent they are costs incurred in the administration of the estate or trust that would not have been incurred if the property were not held by the estate or trust) − (line 15b) − (line 18) − (line 20).

Note. There are no other deductions claimed by the trust on line 15a that are deductible in arriving at AGI.

Figuring AGI in this example, we get:

AGI = 35,000 − 2,000 − DNI − 100

Since the value of line 18 is not known because it is limited to the DNI, you are left with the following:

AGI = 32,900 – DNI

Substitute the value of AGI in the equation:

AMID = 1,500 – (.02(32,900 – DNI))

The equation cannot be solved until the value of DNI is known. The DNI can be expressed in terms of the AMID. To do this, compute the DNI using the known values. In this example, the DNI is equal to the total income of the trust (less any capital gains allocated to corpus or plus any capital loss from line 4); less total deductions from line 16 (excluding any miscellaneous itemized deductions); less the AMID.

Thus, DNI = (line 9) – (line 19, column (2) of Schedule D (Form 1041)) – (line 16) – (AMID)

Substitute the known values:

DNI = 35,000 – 20,000 – 2,000 – AMID

DNI = 13,000 – AMID

Substitute the value of DNI in the equation to solve for AMID:

AMID = 1,500 – (.02(32,900 – (13,000 – AMID)))

AMID = 1,500 – (.02(32,900 – 13,000 + AMID))

AMID = 1,500 – (658 – 260 + .02AMID)

AMID = 1,102 – .02AMID

1.02AMID = 1,102

AMID = 1,080

DNI = 11,920 (i.e., 13,000 – 1,080)

AGI = 20,980 (i.e., 32,900 – 11,920)

Note. The income distribution deduction is equal to the smaller of the distribution ($17,500) or the DNI ($11,920).

Enter the value of AMID on line 15b (the DNI should equal line 7 of Schedule B) and complete the rest of Form 1041 according to the instructions.

If the 2% floor is more than the deductions subject to the 2% floor, no deductions are allowed.

Line 18—Income Distribution Deduction

If the estate or trust was required to distribute income currently or if it paid, credited, or was required to distribute any other amounts to beneficiaries during the tax year, complete Schedule B to determine the estate's or trust's income distribution deduction. However, if you are filing for a pooled

income fund, do not complete Schedule B. Instead, attach a statement to support the computation of the income distribution deduction. For more information, see *Pooled Income Funds*, earlier.

If the estate or trust claims an income distribution deduction, complete and attach:
• Part I (through line 26) and Part II of Schedule I (Form 1041) to refigure the deduction on a minimum tax basis, and
• Schedule K-1 (Form 1041) for each beneficiary to which a distribution was made or required to be made.

Cemetery perpetual care fund. On line 18, deduct the amount, not more than $5 per gravesite, paid for maintenance of cemetery property. To the right of the entry space for line 18, enter the number of gravesites. Also write "Section 642(i) trust" in parentheses after the trust's name at the top of Form 1041. You do not have to complete Schedules B of Form 1041 and K-1 (Form 1041).

Do not enter less than zero on line 18.

Line 19—Estate Tax Deduction (Including Certain Generation-Skipping Transfer Taxes)

If the estate or trust includes IRD in its gross income, and such amount was included in the decedent's gross estate for estate tax purposes, the estate or trust is allowed to deduct in the same tax year that the income is included that portion of the estate tax imposed on the decedent's estate that is attributable to the inclusion of the IRD in the decedent's estate. For an example of the computation, see Regulations section 1.691(c)-1 and Pub. 559.

If any amount properly paid, credited, or required to be distributed by an estate or trust to a beneficiary consists of IRD received by the estate or trust, do not include such amounts in determining the estate tax deduction for the estate or trust. Figure the deduction on a separate sheet. Attach the sheet to your return.

⚠️ **CAUTION** *If you claim a deduction for estate tax attributable to qualified dividends or capital gains, you may have to adjust the amount on Form 1041, page 1, line 2b(2), or Schedule D (Form 1041), line 22.*

Also, a deduction is allowed for the GST tax imposed as a result of a

taxable termination or a direct skip occurring as a result of the death of the transferor. See section 691(c)(3). Enter the estate's or trust's share of these deductions on line 19.

Line 20—Exemption

Decedents' estates. A decedent's estate is allowed a $600 exemption.

Trusts required to distribute all income currently. A trust whose governing instrument requires that all income be distributed currently is allowed a $300 exemption, even if it distributed amounts other than income during the tax year.

Qualified disability trusts. A qualified disability trust is allowed a $3,950 exemption if the trust's modified AGI is less than or equal to $254,200. If its modified AGI exceeds $254,200, complete the worksheet, later, to figure the amount of the trust's exemption. To figure modified AGI, follow the instructions for figuring AGI for line 15c earlier, except use zero as the amount of the trust's exemption when figuring AGI.

A qualified disability trust is any trust:

1. Described in 42 U.S.C. 1396p(c)(2)(B)(iv) and established solely for the benefit of an individual under 65 years of age who is disabled, and

2. All of the beneficiaries of which are determined by the Commissioner of Social Security to have been disabled for some part of the tax year within the meaning of 42 U.S.C. 1382c(a)(3).

A trust will not fail to meet item 2 above just because the trust's corpus may revert to a person who is not disabled after the trust ceases to have any disabled beneficiaries.

All other trusts. A trust not described above is allowed a $100 exemption.

Tax and Payments

Line 22—Taxable Income

Minimum taxable income. Line 22 cannot be less than the larger of:
• The inversion gain of the estate or trust, as figured under section 7874, if the estate or trust is an expatriated entity or a partner in an expatriated entity, or
• The sum of the excess inclusions of the estate or trust from Schedule Q (Form 1066), Quarterly Notice to Residual Interest Holder of REMIC Taxable Income or Net Loss Allocation, line 2c.

Note: *If the trust's modified AGI* is less than or equal to $254,200, enter $3,950 on Form 1041, line 20. Otherwise, complete the worksheet below to figure the trust's exemption.*

1. Maximum exemption	**1.**	$3,950
2. Enter the trust's modified AGI*	**2.**	
3. Threshold amount	**3.**	$254,200
4. Subtract line 3 from line 2	**4.**	

Note: *If line 4 is more than $122,500, enter -0- on line 8 below.* **Do not** *complete lines 5 through 7.*

5. Divide line 4 by $2,500. If the result is not a whole number, increase it to the next higher whole number (for example, increase 0.0004 to 1)	**5.**	
6. Multiply line 5 by 2% (.02) and enter the result as a decimal	**6.**	
7. Multiply line 1 by line 6	**7.**	
8. **Exemption.** Subtract line 7 from line 1. Enter the result here and on Form 1041, line 20	**8.**	

*Figure the trust's modified AGI in the same manner as AGI is figured in the line 15c instructions earlier, **except** *use zero when figuring the amount of the trust's exemption.*

Net operating loss (NOL). If line 22 (figured without regard to the minimum taxable income rule stated above) is a loss, the estate or trust may have an NOL. Do not include the deductions claimed on lines 13, 18, and 20 when figuring the amount of the NOL.

Generally, an NOL may be carried back to the prior 2 tax years and forward for up to 20 years. The 2-year carryback period does not apply to the portion of an NOL attributable to an eligible loss; a farming loss; a qualified disaster, GO Zone, or disaster recovery assistance loss; or a specified liability loss. An estate or trust may also elect to carry an NOL forward only, instead of first carrying it back. For more information, see the Instructions for Form 1045, Application for Tentative Refund.

Complete Schedule A of Form 1045 to figure the amount of the NOL that is available for carryback or carryover. Use Form 1045 or file an amended return to apply for a refund based on an NOL carryback. For more details, see Pub. 536, Net Operating Losses (NOLs) for Individuals, Estates, and Trusts.

On the termination of the estate or trust, any unused NOL carryover that would be allowable to the estate or trust in a later tax year, but for the termination, is allowed to the beneficiaries succeeding to the property of the estate or trust. See the instructions for Schedule K-1 (Form 1041), box 11, codes D and E, later.

Excess deductions on termination. If the estate or trust has for its final year deductions (excluding the charitable deduction and exemption) in excess of

its gross income, the excess is allowed as an itemized deduction to the beneficiaries succeeding to the property of the estate or trust.

In general, an unused NOL carryover that is allowed to beneficiaries (as explained above) cannot also be treated as an excess deduction. However, if the final year of the estate or trust is also the last year of the NOL carryover period, the NOL carryover not absorbed in that tax year by the estate or trust is included as an excess deduction. See the instructions for Schedule K-1 (Form 1041), box 11, code A, later.

Line 24a—2014 Estimated Tax Payments and Amount Applied From 2013 Return

Enter the amount of any estimated tax payment you made with Form 1041-ES for 2014 plus the amount of any overpayment from the 2013 return that was applied to the 2014 estimated tax.

If the estate or trust is the beneficiary of another trust and received a payment of estimated tax that was credited to the trust (as reflected on the Schedule K-1 issued to the trust), then report this amount separately with the notation "section 643(g)" in the space next to line 24a and include this amount in the amount entered on line 24a.

 Do not include on Form 1041 estimated tax paid by an individual before death. Instead, include those payments on the decedent's final income tax return.

Line 24b—Estimated Tax Payments Allocated to Beneficiaries

The trustee (or executor, for the final year of the estate) may elect under section 643(g) to have any portion of its estimated tax treated as a payment of estimated tax made by a beneficiary or beneficiaries. The election is made on Form 1041-T, Allocation of Estimated Tax Payments to Beneficiaries, which must be filed by the 65th day after the close of the trust's tax year. Form 1041-T shows the amounts to be allocated to each beneficiary. This amount is reported on the beneficiary's Schedule K-1 (Form 1041), box 13, code A.

Attach Form 1041-T to your return only if you have not yet filed it; however, attaching Form 1041-T to Form 1041 does not extend the due date for filing Form 1041-T. If you have already filed Form 1041-T, do not attach a copy to your return.

 Failure to file Form 1041-T by the due date (March 6, 2015, for calendar year estates and trusts) will result in an invalid election. An invalid election will require the filing of amended Schedules K-1 for each beneficiary who was allocated a payment of estimated tax.

Line 24d—Tax Paid With Form 7004

If you filed Form 7004 to request an extension of time to file Form 1041, enter the amount that you paid with the extension request.

Line 24e—Federal Income Tax Withheld

Use line 24e to claim a credit for any federal income tax withheld (and not repaid) by: (a) an employer on wages and salaries of a decedent received by the decedent's estate; (b) a payer of certain gambling winnings (for example, state lottery winnings); or (c) a payer of distributions from pensions, annuities, retirement or profit-sharing plans, IRAs, insurance contracts, etc., received by a decedent's estate or trust. Attach a copy of Form W-2, Form W-2G, or Form 1099-R to the front of the return.

 Except for backup withholding (as explained below), withheld income tax cannot be passed through to beneficiaries on either Schedule K-1 or Form 1041-T.

Backup withholding. If the estate or trust received a 2014 Form 1099 showing federal income tax withheld (that is, backup withholding) on interest income, dividends, or other income, check the box and include the amount withheld on income retained by the estate or trust in the total for line 24e.

Report on Schedule K-1 (Form 1041), box 13, code B, any credit for backup withholding on income distributed to the beneficiary.

Line 24f—Credit for Tax Paid on Undistributed Capital Gains

Attach Copy B of Form 2439, Notice to Shareholder of Undistributed Long-Term Capital Gains.

Line 24g—Credit for Federal Tax on Fuels

Enter any credit for federal excise taxes paid on fuels that are ultimately used for nontaxable purposes (for example, an off-highway business use). Attach Form 4136, Credit for Federal Tax Paid on Fuels. See Pub. 510, Excise Taxes, for more information.

Line 26—Estimated Tax Penalty

If line 27 is at least $1,000 and more than 10% of the tax shown on Form 1041, or the estate or trust underpaid its 2014 estimated tax liability for any payment period, it may owe a penalty. See Form 2210 to determine whether the estate or trust owes a penalty and to figure the amount of the penalty.

Note. The penalty may be waived under certain conditions. See Pub. 505, Tax Withholding and Estimated Tax, for details.

Line 27—Tax Due

You must pay the tax in full when the return is filed. You may pay by EFTPS. For more information about EFTPS, see *Electronic Deposits*, earlier. Also, you may pay by check or money order or by credit or debit card.

To pay by check or money order. If you pay by check or money order:
- Make it payable to "United States Treasury",
- Make sure the name of the estate or trust appears on the payment,
- Write the estate's or trust's EIN and "2014 Form 1041" on the payment,
- Consider completing the 2014 Form 1041-V, and
- Enclose, but do not attach, the payment (and Form 1041-V, if completed) with Form 1041.

To pay by credit or debit card. For information on paying your taxes electronically, including by credit or debit card, go to *www.irs.gov/e-pay.*

Line 29a—Credited to 2015 Estimated Tax

Enter the amount from line 28 that you want applied to the estate's or trust's 2015 estimated tax.

Schedule A—Charitable Deduction

General Instructions

Generally, any part of the gross income of an estate or trust (other than a simple trust) that, under the terms of the will or governing instrument, is paid (or treated as paid) during the tax year for a charitable purpose specified in section 170(c) is allowed as a deduction to the estate or trust. It is not necessary that the charitable organization be created or organized in the United States.

A pooled income fund or a section 4947(a)(1) nonexempt charitable trust treated as a private foundation must attach a separate sheet to Form 1041 instead of using Schedule A of Form 1041 to figure the charitable deduction.

Additional return to be filed by trusts. Trusts, other than split-interest trusts or nonexempt charitable trusts, that claim a charitable deduction also file Form 1041-A unless the trust is required to distribute currently to the beneficiaries all the income for the year determined under section 643(b) and related regulations.

Pooled income funds and charitable lead trusts also file Form 5227. See Form 5227 for information about any exceptions.

Election to treat contributions as paid in the prior tax year. The fiduciary of an estate or trust may elect to treat as paid during the tax year any amount of gross income received during that tax year or any prior tax year that was paid in the next tax year for a charitable purpose.

For example, if a calendar year estate or trust makes a qualified charitable contribution on February 7, 2015, from income earned in 2014 or prior, then the fiduciary can elect to treat the contribution as paid in 2014.

To make the election, the fiduciary must file a statement with Form 1041 for the tax year in which the contribution is treated as paid. This statement must include:

1. The name and address of the fiduciary;

2. The name of the estate or trust;

3. An indication that the fiduciary is making an election under section 642(c)(1) for contributions treated as paid during such tax year;

4. The name and address of each organization to which any such contribution is paid; and

5. The amount of each contribution and date of actual payment or, if applicable, the total amount of contributions paid to each organization during the next tax year, to be treated as paid in the prior tax year.

The election must be filed by the due date (including extensions) for Form 1041 for the next tax year. If the original return was filed on time, you may make the election on an amended return filed no later than 6 months after the due date of the return (excluding extensions). Write "Filed pursuant to section 301.9100-2" at the top of the amended return and file it at the same address you used for your original return.

For more information about the charitable deduction, see section 642(c) and related regulations.

Specific Instructions

Line 1—Amounts Paid or Permanently Set Aside for Charitable Purposes From Gross Income

Enter amounts that were paid for a charitable purpose out of the estate's or trust's gross income, including any capital gains that are attributable to income under the governing instrument or local law. Include amounts paid during the tax year from gross income received in a prior tax year, but only if no deduction was allowed for any prior tax year for these amounts.

Estates, and certain trusts, may claim a deduction for amounts permanently set aside for a charitable purpose from gross income. Such amounts must be permanently set aside during the tax year to be used exclusively for religious, charitable, scientific, literary, or educational purposes, or for the prevention of cruelty to children or animals, or for the establishment, acquisition, maintenance, or operation of a public cemetery not operated for profit.

For a trust to qualify, the trust may not be a simple trust, and the set aside amounts must be required by the terms of a trust instrument that was created on or before October 9, 1969.

Further, the trust instrument must provide for an irrevocable remainder interest to be transferred to or for the use of an organization described in section 170(c); or the trust must have been created by a grantor who was at all times after October 9, 1969, under a mental disability to change the terms of the trust.

Also, certain testamentary trusts that were established by a will that was executed on or before October 9, 1969, may qualify. See Regulations section 1.642(c)-2(b).

Do not include any capital gains for the tax year allocated to corpus and paid or permanently set aside for charitable purposes. Instead, enter these amounts on line 4.

Line 2—Tax-Exempt Income Allocable to Charitable Contributions

Any estate or trust that pays or sets aside any part of its income for a charitable purpose must reduce the deduction by the portion allocable to any tax-exempt income. If the governing instrument specifically provides as to the source from which amounts are paid, permanently set aside, or to be used for charitable purposes, the specific provisions control. In all other cases, determine the amount of tax-exempt income allocable to charitable contributions by multiplying line 1 by a fraction, the numerator of

which is the total tax-exempt income of the estate or trust, and the denominator of which is the gross income of the estate or trust. Do not include in the denominator any losses allocated to corpus.

Line 4—Capital Gains for the Tax Year Allocated to Corpus and Paid or Permanently Set Aside for Charitable Purposes

Enter the total of all capital gains for the tax year that are:
• Allocated to corpus, and
• Paid or permanently set aside for charitable purposes.

Line 6—Section 1202 Exclusion Allocable to Capital Gains Paid or Permanently Set Aside for Charitable Purposes

If the exclusion of gain from the sale or exchange of qualified small business (QSB) stock was claimed, enter the part of the gain included on Schedule A, lines 1 and 4, that was excluded under section 1202.

Schedule B—Income Distribution Deduction

General Instructions

If the estate or trust was required to distribute income currently or if it paid, credited, or was required to distribute any other amounts to beneficiaries during the tax year, complete Schedule B to determine the estate's or trust's income distribution deduction.

Note. Use Schedule I (Form 1041) to compute the DNI and income distribution deduction on a minimum tax basis.

Pooled income funds. Do not complete Schedule B for these funds. Instead, attach a separate statement to support the computation of the income distribution deduction. See *Pooled Income Funds*, earlier, for more information.

Separate share rule. If a single trust or an estate has more than one beneficiary, and if different beneficiaries have substantially separate and independent shares, their shares are treated as separate trusts or estates for the sole purpose of determining the DNI allocable to the respective beneficiaries.

If the separate share rule applies, figure the DNI allocable to each beneficiary on a separate sheet and

attach the sheet to this return. Any deduction or loss that is applicable solely to one separate share of the trust or estate is not available to any other share of the same trust or estate.

For more information, see section 663(c) and related regulations.

Withholding of tax on foreign persons. The fiduciary may be liable for withholding tax on distributions to beneficiaries who are foreign persons. For more information, see Pub. 515, Withholding of Tax on Nonresident Aliens and Foreign Entities, and Forms 1042 and 1042-S.

Specific Instructions

Line 1—Adjusted Total Income

Generally, enter on line 1, Schedule B, the amount from line 17 on page 1 of Form 1041. However, if both line 4 and line 17 on page 1 of Form 1041 are losses, enter on line 1, Schedule B, the smaller of those losses. If line 4 is zero or a gain and line 17 is a loss, enter zero on line 1, Schedule B.

If you are filing for a simple trust, subtract from adjusted total income any extraordinary dividends or taxable stock dividends included on page 1, line 2, and determined under the governing instrument and applicable local law to be allocable to corpus.

Line 2—Adjusted Tax-Exempt Interest

To figure the adjusted tax-exempt interest:

Step 1. Add tax-exempt interest income on line 2 of Schedule A, any expenses allowable under section 212 allocable to tax-exempt interest, and any interest expense allocable to tax-exempt interest.

Step 2. Subtract the Step 1 total from the amount of tax-exempt interest (including exempt-interest dividends) received.

Section 212 expenses that are directly allocable to tax-exempt interest are allocated only to tax-exempt interest. A reasonable proportion of section 212 expenses that are indirectly allocable to both tax-exempt interest and other income must be allocated to each class of income.

Figure the interest expense allocable to tax-exempt interest according to the guidelines in Rev. Proc. 72-18, 1972-1 C.B. 740.

See Regulations sections 1.643(a)-5 and 1.265-1 for more information.

Line 3

Include all capital gains, whether or not distributed, that are attributable to income under the governing instrument or local law. For example, if the trustee distributed 50% of the current year's capital gains to the income beneficiaries (and reflects this amount in column (1), line 19 of Schedule D (Form 1041)), but under the governing instrument all capital gains are attributable to income, then include 100% of the capital gains on line 3. If the amount on Schedule D (Form 1041), line 19, column (1), is a net loss, enter zero.

If the exclusion of gain from the sale or exchange of QSB stock was claimed, do not reduce the gain on line 3 by any amount excluded under section 1202.

Line 5

In figuring the amount of long-term and short-term capital gain for the tax year included on Schedule A, line 1, the specific provisions of the governing instrument control if the instrument specifically provides as to the source from which amounts are paid, permanently set aside, or to be used for charitable purposes.

In all other cases, determine the amount to enter by multiplying line 1 of Schedule A by a fraction, the numerator of which is the amount of net capital gains that are included in the accounting income of the estate or trust (that is, not allocated to corpus) and are distributed to charities, and the denominator of which is all items of income (including the amount of such net capital gains) included in the DNI.

Reduce the amount on line 5 by any allocable section 1202 exclusion.

Line 8—Accounting Income

If you are filing for a decedent's estate or a simple trust, skip this line. If you are filing for a complex trust, enter the income for the tax year determined under the terms of the governing instrument and applicable local law. Do not include extraordinary dividends or taxable stock dividends determined under the governing instrument and applicable local law to be allocable to corpus.

Lines 9 and 10

Do not include any:
- Amount that was deducted on the prior year's return that was required to be distributed in the prior year;
- Amount that is paid or permanently set aside for charitable purposes or otherwise qualifying for the charitable deduction; or
- Amount that is properly paid or credited as a gift or bequest of a specific amount of money or specific property.

Note. An amount that can be paid or credited only from income is not considered a gift or bequest. Also, to qualify as a gift or bequest, the amount must be paid in three or fewer installments.

Line 9—Income Required To Be Distributed Currently

Line 9 is to be completed by all simple trusts as well as complex trusts and decedent's estates that are required to distribute income currently, whether it is distributed or not. The determination of whether trust income is required to be distributed currently depends on the terms of the governing instrument and the applicable local law.

The line 9 distributions are referred to as first tier distributions and are deductible by the estate or trust to the extent of the DNI. The beneficiary includes such amounts in his or her income to the extent of his or her proportionate share of the DNI.

Line 10—Other Amounts Paid, Credited, or Otherwise Required To Be Distributed

Line 10 is to be completed only by a decedent's estate or complex trust. These distributions consist of any other amounts paid, credited, or required to be distributed and are referred to as second tier distributions. Such amounts include annuities to the extent not paid out of income, mandatory and discretionary distributions of corpus, and distributions of property in kind.

If Form 1041-T was timely filed to elect to treat estimated tax payments as made by a beneficiary, the payments are treated as paid or credited to the beneficiary on the last day of the tax year and must be included on line 10.

Unless a section 643(e)(3) election is made, the value of all noncash property actually paid, credited, or required to be

distributed to any beneficiaries is the smaller of:

1. The estate's or trust's adjusted basis in the property immediately before distribution, plus any gain or minus any loss recognized by the estate or trust on the distribution (basis of beneficiary), or

2. The FMV of such property.

If a section 643(e)(3) election is made by the fiduciary, then the amount entered on line 10 will be the FMV of the property.

A fiduciary of a complex trust or a decedent's estate may elect to treat any amount paid or credited to a beneficiary within 65 days following the close of the tax year as being paid or credited on the last day of that tax year. To make this election, see the instructions for Question 6, later.

The beneficiary includes the amounts on line 10 in his or her income only to the extent of his or her proportionate share of the DNI.

Complex trusts. If the second tier distributions exceed the DNI allocable to the second tier, the trust may have an accumulation distribution. See the line 11 instructions below.

Line 11—Total Distributions

If line 11 is more than line 8, and you are filing for a complex trust that has previously accumulated income, see the instructions for Schedule J, later, to see if you must complete Schedule J (Form 1041).

Line 12—Adjustment for Tax-Exempt Income

In figuring the income distribution deduction, the estate or trust is not allowed a deduction for any item of the DNI that is not included in the gross income of the estate or trust. Thus, for purposes of figuring the allowable income distribution deduction, the DNI (line 7) is figured without regard to any tax-exempt interest.

If tax-exempt interest is the only tax-exempt income included in the total distributions (line 11), and the DNI (line 7) is less than or equal to line 11, then enter on line 12 the amount from line 2.

If tax-exempt interest is the only tax-exempt income included in the total distributions (line 11), and the DNI is more than line 11 (that is, the estate or trust made a distribution that is less than the DNI), then figure the adjustment by multiplying line 2 by a fraction, the numerator of which is the total distributions (line 11), and the denominator of which is the DNI (line 7). Enter the result on line 12.

If line 11 includes tax-exempt income other than tax-exempt interest, figure line 12 by subtracting the total of the following from tax-exempt income included on line 11:

1. The charitable contribution deduction allocable to such tax-exempt income, and

2. Expenses allocable to tax-exempt income.

Expenses that are directly allocable to tax-exempt income are allocated only to tax-exempt income. A reasonable proportion of expenses indirectly allocable to both tax-exempt income and other income must be allocated to each class of income.

Schedule G—Tax Computation

Line 1a

2014 tax rate schedule. For tax years beginning in 2014, figure the tax using the Tax Rate Schedule below and enter the tax on line 1a. However, see the Instructions for Schedule D (Form 1041) and the *Qualified Dividends Tax Worksheet* later.

2014 Tax Rate Schedule			
If taxable income is:			
Over—	But not over—	Its tax is:	Of the amount over—
$0	$2,500	15%	$0
2,500	5,800	$375 + 25%	2,500
5,800	8,900	1,200.00 + 28%	5,800
8,900	12,150	2,068.00 + 33%	8,900
12,150	-----	3,140.50 + 39.6%	12,150

Schedule D (Form 1041) and Schedule D Tax Worksheet. Use Part V of Schedule D (Form 1041) or the *Schedule D Tax Worksheet*, whichever is applicable, to figure the estate's or trust's tax if the estate or trust files Schedule D (Form 1041) and has:
- A net capital gain and any taxable income, or
- Qualified dividends on line 2b(2) of Form 1041 and any taxable income.

Qualified Dividends Tax Worksheet. If you do not have to complete Part I or

Part II of Schedule D and the estate or trust has an amount entered on line 2b(2) of Form 1041 and any taxable income (line 22), then figure the estate's or trust's tax using the worksheet, later, and enter the tax on line 1a.

Note. You must reduce the amount you enter on line 2b(2) of Form 1041 by the portion of the section 691(c) deduction claimed on line 19 of Form 1041 if the estate or trust received qualified dividends that were IRD.

Line 1c—AMT. Attach Schedule I (Form 1041) if:
- The estate or trust must complete Schedule B.
- The estate or trust claims a credit on line 2b, 2c, or 2d of Schedule G.
- The estate's or trust's share of alternative minimum taxable income (line 29 of Schedule I (Form 1041)) exceeds $23,500.
Enter the amount from line 56 of Schedule I (Form 1041) on line 1c.

Line 2a—Foreign Tax Credit

Attach Form 1116, Foreign Tax Credit (Individual, Estate, or Trust), if you elect to claim credit for income or profits taxes paid or accrued to a foreign country or a U.S. possession. The estate or trust may claim credit for that part of the foreign taxes not allocable to the beneficiaries (including charitable beneficiaries). Enter the estate's or trust's share of the credit on line 2a. See Pub. 514, Foreign Tax Credit for Individuals, for details.

Line 2b—General Business Credit

 Do not include any amounts that are allocated to a beneficiary. Credits that are allocated between the estate or trust and the beneficiaries are listed in the instructions for Schedule K-1, box 13, later. Generally, these credits are apportioned on the basis of the income allocable to the estate or trust and the beneficiaries.

Enter on line 2b the estate's or trust's total general business credit allowed for the current year from Form 3800. The estate or trust must file Form 3800 to claim any of the general business credits. Generally, if the estate's or trust's only source of a credit is from a pass-through entity and the beneficiary is not entitled to an allocable share of a credit, you are not required to complete the source form for that credit. However, certain credits have limitations and special computations that may require

you to complete the source form. See the Instructions for Form 3800 for more information.

Line 2c—Credit for Prior Year Minimum Tax

An estate or trust that paid AMT in a previous year may be eligible for a minimum tax credit in 2014. See Form 8801, Credit for Prior Year Minimum Tax—Individuals, Estates, and Trusts.

Line 2d—Bond Credits

Complete and attach Form 8912, Credit to Holders of Tax Credit Bonds, if the estate or trust claims a credit for holding a tax credit bond. Also, be sure to include the credit in interest income.

Line 2e—Total Credits

To claim a credit allowable to the estate or trust other than the credits entered on lines 2a through 2d, include the allowable credit in the total for line 2e. Complete and attach the appropriate form and write the form number and amount of the allowable credit on the dotted line to the left of the entry space.

Line 4—Net Investment Income Tax

Enter the amount of net investment income tax calculated and attach Form 8960. See the Instructions for Form 8960 to calculate the tax and *Net Investment Income Tax*, later, for more information.

Line 5—Recapture Taxes

Recapture of investment credit. If the estate or trust disposed of investment credit property or changed its use before the end of the recapture period, see Form 4255, Recapture of Investment Credit, to figure the recapture tax allocable to the estate or trust. Include the tax on line 5 and write "ICR" on the dotted line to the left of the entry space.

Recapture of low-income housing credit. If the estate or trust disposed of property (or there was a reduction in the qualified basis of the property) on which the low-income housing credit was claimed, see Form 8611, Recapture of Low-Income Housing Credit, to figure any recapture tax allocable to the estate or trust. Include the tax on line 5 and write "LIHCR" on the dotted line to the left of the entry space.

Recapture of qualified electric vehicle credit. If the estate or trust claimed the qualified electric vehicle credit in a prior tax year for a vehicle that ceased to qualify for the credit, part or all of the

Qualified Dividends Tax Worksheet—Schedule G, line 1a

Caution: *Do not* use this worksheet if the estate or trust must complete Schedule D (Form 1041).

1.	Enter the amount from Form 1041, line 22	**1.**	_____
2.	Enter the amount from Form 1041, line 2b(2) .... **2.** _____		
3.	If you are claiming investment interest expense on Form 4952, enter the amount from line 4g; otherwise enter -0- .... **3.** _____		
4.	Subtract line 3 from line 2. If zero or less, enter -0-	**4.**	_____
5.	Subtract line 4 from line 1. If zero or less, enter -0-	**5.**	_____
6.	Enter the **smaller** of the amount on line 1 or $2,500	**6.**	_____
7.	Enter the **smaller** of the amount on line 5 or line 6	**7.**	_____
8.	Subtract line 7 from line 6. If zero or less, enter -0-. This amount is taxed at 0%	**8.**	_____
9.	Enter the **smaller** of line 1 or line 4	**9.**	_____
10.	Subtract line 8 from line 4	**10.**	_____
11.	Enter the **smaller** of line 1 or $12,150	**11.**	_____
12.	Add lines 5 and 8	**12.**	_____
13.	Subtract line 12 from line 11. If zero or less, enter -0-	**13.**	_____
14.	Enter the **smaller** of line 10 or line 13	**14.**	_____
15.	Multiply line 14 by 15% (.15)	**15.**	_____
16.	Enter the amount from line 9	**16.**	_____
17.	Add lines 8 and 14	**17.**	_____
18.	Subtract line 17 from line 16. If zero or less, enter -0-	**18.**	_____
19.	Multiply line 18 by 20% (.20)	**19.**	_____
20.	Figure the tax on the amount on line 5. Use the 2014 Tax Rate Schedule	**20.**	_____
21.	Add lines 15, 19 and 20	**21.**	_____
22.	Figure the tax on the amount on line 1. Use the 2014 Tax Rate Schedule	**22.**	_____
23.	**Tax on all taxable income.** Enter the **smaller** of line 21 or line 22 here and on Sch. G, line 1a	**23.**	_____

credit may have to be recaptured. See Regulations section 1.30-1(b) for details. If the estate or trust owes any recapture tax, include it on line 5 and write "QEVCR" on the dotted line to the left of the entry space.

Recapture of the Indian employment credit. Generally, if the estate or trust terminates a qualified employee less than 1 year after the date of initial employment, any Indian employment credit allowed for a prior tax year by reason of wages paid or incurred to that employee must be recaptured. See Form 8845 for details. If the estate or trust owes any recapture tax, include it on line 5 and write "IECR" on the dotted line to the left of the entry space.

Recapture of the new markets credit. If the estate or trust owes any new markets recapture tax, include it on line 5 and write "NMCR" on the dotted line to the left of the entry space. For

more information, including how to figure the recapture amount, see section 45D(g).

Recapture of the credit for employer-provided child care facilities. If the facility ceased to operate as a qualified child care facility or there was a change in ownership, part or all of the credit may have to be recaptured. See Form 8882 for details. If the estate or trust owes any recapture tax, include it on line 5 and write "ECCFR" on the dotted line to the left of the entry space.

Recapture of the alternative motor vehicle credit. See section 30B(h)(8) for details. Include the tax on line 5 and write "AMVCR" on the dotted line to the left of the entry space.

Recapture of the alternative fuel vehicle refueling property credit. See section 30C(e)(5) for details. Include the tax on line 5 and write "ARPCR" on the dotted line to the left of the entry space.

Line 6—Household Employment Taxes

If any of the following apply, get Schedule H (Form 1040), Household Employment Taxes, and its instructions, to see if the estate or trust owes these taxes.

1. The estate or trust paid any one household employee cash wages of $1,900 or more in 2014. Cash wages include wages paid by checks, money orders, etc. When figuring the amount of cash wages paid, combine cash wages paid by the estate or trust with cash wages paid to the household employee in the same calendar year by the household of the decedent or beneficiary for whom the administrator, executor, or trustee of the estate or trust is acting.

2. The estate or trust withheld federal income tax during 2014 at the request of any household employee.

3. The estate or trust paid total cash wages of $1,000 or more in any calendar quarter of 2013 or 2014 to household employees.

Note. See *Amended Schedule H (Form 1040)* under *F. Initial Return, Amended Return, etc.*, earlier for information on filing an amended Schedule H (Form 1040) for a Form 1041.

Line 7—Total Tax

Tax on ESBTs. Attach the tax computation to the return. To the left of the line 7 entry space, write "Sec. 641(c)" and the amount of tax on the S corporation items. Include this amount in the total tax on line 7.

See *Electing Small Business Trusts (ESBTs)*, earlier, for the special tax computation rules that apply to the portion of an ESBT consisting of stock in one or more S corporations.

Interest on deferred tax attributable to installment sales of certain time-shares and residential lots and certain nondealer real property installment obligations. If an obligation arising from the disposition of real property to which section 453(l) or 453A applies is outstanding at the close of the year, the estate or trust must include the interest due under section 453(l)(3)(B) or 453A(c), whichever is applicable, in the amount to be entered on line 7 of Schedule G, Form 1041, with the notation "Section 453(l) interest" or "Section 453A(c) interest," whichever is applicable. Attach a schedule showing the computation.

Form 4970, Tax on Accumulation Distribution of Trusts. Include on this line any tax due on an accumulation distribution from a trust. To the left of the entry space, write "From Form 4970" and the amount of the tax.

Form 8697, Interest Computation Under the Look-Back Method for Completed Long-Term Contracts. Include the interest due under the look-back method of section 460(b)(2). To the left of the entry space, write "From Form 8697" and the amount of interest due.

Form 8866, Interest Computation Under the Look-Back Method for Property Depreciated Under the Income Forecast Method. Include the interest due under the look-back method of section 167(g)(2). To the left of the entry space, write "From Form 8866" and the amount of interest due.

Interest on deferral of gain from certain constructive ownership transac- tions. Include the interest due under section 1260(b) on any deferral of gain from certain constructive ownership transactions. To the left of the entry space, write "1260(b)" and the amount of interest due.

Form 5329, Additional Taxes on Qualified Plans (Including IRAs) and Other Tax-Favored Accounts. If the estate or trust fails to receive the minimum distribution under section 4974, use Form 5329 to pay the excise tax. To the left of the entry space, write "From Form 5329" and the amount of the tax.

Net Investment Income Tax

For taxable years beginning after December 31, 2012, certain estates and trusts may be subject to the Net Investment Income Tax (NIIT). Estates and trusts use Form 8960 to report their Net Investment Income (NII) and calculate the tax. The amount of NIIT payable by the estate or trust is reported on Form 1041, Schedule G, line 4.

The NIIT is imposed on estates and trusts to the extent that they have undistributed net investment income and adjusted gross income (AGI) exceeding $12,150. See instructions to line 15c for the calculation of an estate or trust's AGI. The following types of estates and trusts may owe the NIIT in addition to their regular income tax liability:
- Decedent's estates,
- Simple and complex trusts,
- Electing small business trusts (ESBTs),
- Pooled income funds, and
- Bankruptcy estates.

However, in the case of bankruptcy estates, the adjusted gross income threshold is $125,000.

Calculation of Net Investment Income. In general, an estate or trust's NII is calculated in the same way as an individual. However, there are special rules for the calculation of NII in the case of an ESBT. See instructions to Form 8960 and Regulations section 1.1411-3(e) for information on the calculation (and Regulations section 1.1411-3(c)(1) for information on the ESBT calculation).

Distributions on Net Investment Income. The NIIT is imposed on estates and trusts to the extent it has undistributed net investment income. In order to arrive at the estate or trust's undistributed net investment income, the estate or trust's NII is reduced for (1) distributions of NII to beneficiaries, and (2) NII allocable to charities when the estate or trust is allowed a deduction under section 642(c). Instructions for Form 8960, line 18, provide more information on the calculation of undistributed net investment income.

NII allocable to the deduction under section 642(c). An estate, trust, or pooled income fund's NII is reduced by the amount of NII allocable to the charitable deduction allowed under section 642(c). In the case of an estate, trust, or pooled income fund that has NII and non-NII income in a year when a section 642(c) deduction is claimed, the amount of the NII deduction allocable to the section 642(c) deduction will be less than the amount reported on Form 1041, Schedule A, line 7 (or on the separate calculation in the case of a pooled income fund).

Beneficiary reporting. In general, the amount of the income distribution deduction (from Form 1041, Schedule B, line 15) that reduces the estate or trust's NII will be the amount of NII that will be taxable to the beneficiaries on their Schedules K-1(Form 1041).

The Schedule K-1 has a code H in box 14 to report the amount of net investment income distributed to the beneficiary. The amount reported in code H represents an adjustment (either positive or negative) that the beneficiary must use in completing its Form 8960 (if necessary). In the case where the trust's income distribution deduction allowed in calculating undistributed net investment income is less than the amount on Schedule B, line 15, then code H will show a negative number that is the difference between the two amounts. In the case of an estate or trust that issues more than one Schedule K-1 for a year, the sum of the amounts reported in code H on all of the Schedules K-1 will be the difference between Schedule B, line 15, and the amount deducted on Form 8960, line 18b, for amounts of NII distributed to a beneficiary.

 The beneficiary's NII will equal all taxable amounts reported on the Schedule K-1, adjusted by the amount reported in box 14, code H.

 The only instance where code H will be a positive number is when:
- *The estate or trust owns directly, or indirectly, an (a) interest in a section 1291 fund, or (b) interest in a controlled foreign corporation or qualified electing*

fund and no election under Regulations section 1.1411–10(g) has been made with respect to that interest, and
- The distribution from one of the entities described above is (a) net investment income to the estate or trust, but not included in its taxable income, and (b) the distributions from the estate or trust to the beneficiary(s) in the year exceed the amount of the income distribution deduction allowed for regular tax purposes (from Schedule B, line 15).

Special rules. In the final year of an estate or trust, deductions in excess of income may be reported to the beneficiary on Schedule K-1, box 11. These deductions may also be deductible by the beneficiary for NIIT purposes. In this situation, the terminating estate or trust should provide the beneficiary information regarding whether the amounts reported in box 11, codes A through D, include any amounts that are deductible for NIIT purposes. See Regulations section 1.1411-4(g)(4).

Other Information

Question 1
If the estate or trust received tax-exempt income, figure the allocation of expenses between tax-exempt and taxable income on a separate sheet and attach it to the return. Enter only the deductible amounts on the return. Do not figure the allocation on the return itself. For more information, see the instructions for *Allocation of Deductions for Tax-Exempt Income*, earlier.

Report the amount of tax-exempt interest income received or accrued in the space provided below Question 1.

Also, include any exempt-interest dividends the estate or trust received as a shareholder in a mutual fund or other regulated investment company.

Question 2
All salaries, wages, and other compensation for personal services must be included on the return of the person who earned the income, even if the income was irrevocably assigned to a trust by a contract assignment or similar arrangement.

The grantor or person creating the trust is considered the owner if he or she keeps "beneficial enjoyment" of or substantial control over the trust property. The trust's income, deductions, and credits are allocable to the owner.

If you checked "Yes" for Question 2, see *Special Reporting Instructions*, earlier.

Question 3
Check the "Yes" box and enter the name of the foreign country if either 1 or 2 below applies.

1. The estate or trust owns more than 50% of the stock in any corporation that owns one or more foreign bank accounts.

2. At any time during the year the estate or trust had an interest in or signature or other authority over a bank, securities, or other financial account in a foreign country.

Exception. Check "No" if either of the following applies to the estate or trust:
- The combined value of the accounts was $10,000 or less during the whole year, or
- The accounts were with a U.S. military banking facility operated by a U.S. financial institution.

If you checked "Yes" for Question 3, electronically file FinCEN Form 114, Report of Foreign Bank and Financial Accounts (FBAR) by June 30, 2015, with the Department of the Treasury using the FinCEN's BSA E-Filing Sytem. Because FinCEN Form 114 is not a tax form, do not file it with Form 1041.

See *www.fincen.gov* for more information.

 If you are required to file FinCEN Form 114 but do not, you may have to pay a penalty of up to $10,000 (or more in some cases).

Question 4
The estate or trust may be required to file Form 3520, Annual Return To Report Transactions With Foreign Trusts and Receipt of Certain Foreign Gifts, if:
- It directly or indirectly transferred property or money to a foreign trust. For this purpose, any U.S. person who created a foreign trust is considered a transferor;
- It is treated as the owner of any part of the assets of a foreign trust under the grantor trust rules; or
- It received a distribution from a foreign trust.

 An owner of a foreign trust must ensure that the trust files an annual information return on Form 3520-A, Annual Information Return of Foreign Trust With a U.S. Owner.

Question 5
An estate or trust claiming an interest deduction for qualified residence interest (as defined in section 163(h)(3)) on seller-provided financing must include on an attachment to the 2014 Form 1041 the name, address, and TIN of the person to whom the interest was paid or accrued (that is, the seller).

If the estate or trust received or accrued such interest, it must provide identical information on the person liable for such interest (that is, the buyer). This information does not need to be reported if it duplicates information already reported on Form 1098.

Question 6
To make the section 663(b) election to treat any amount paid or credited to a beneficiary within 65 days following the close of the tax year as being paid or credited on the last day of that tax year, check the box. This election can be made by the fiduciary of a complex trust or the executor of a decedent's estate. For the election to be valid, you must file Form 1041 by the due date (including extensions). Once made, the election is irrevocable.

Question 7
To make the section 643(e)(3) election to recognize gain on property distributed in kind, check the box and see the Instructions for Schedule D (Form 1041).

Question 9
Generally, a beneficiary is a skip person if the beneficiary is in a generation that is two or more generations below the generation of the transferor to the trust.

To determine if a beneficiary that is a trust is a skip person, and for exceptions to the general rules, see the definition of a skip person in the instructions for Schedule R of Form 706.

Schedule J (Form 1041) — Accumulation Distribution for Certain Complex Trusts

General Instructions
Use Schedule J (Form 1041) to report an accumulation distribution for a domestic complex trust that was:
- Previously treated at any time as a foreign trust (unless an exception is provided in future regulations), or
- Created before March 1, 1984, unless that trust would not be aggregated with other trusts under the

rules of section 643(f) if that section applied to the trust.

An accumulation distribution is the excess of amounts properly paid, credited, or required to be distributed (other than income required to be distributed currently) over the DNI of the trust reduced by income required to be distributed currently. To have an accumulation distribution, the distribution must exceed the accounting income of the trust.

Specific Instructions

Part I—Accumulation Distribution in 2014

Line 1—Distribution Under Section 661(a)(2)

Enter the amount from Form 1041, Schedule B, line 10, for 2014. This is the amount properly paid, credited, or required to be distributed other than the amount of income for the current tax year required to be distributed currently.

Line 2—DNI

Enter the amount from Form 1041, Schedule B, line 7, for 2014. This is the amount of DNI for the current tax year determined under section 643(a).

Line 3—Distribution Under Section 661(a)(1)

Enter the amount from Form 1041, Schedule B, line 9, for 2014. This is the amount of income for the current tax year required to be distributed currently.

Line 5—Accumulation Distribution

If line 11 of Form 1041, Schedule B, is more than line 8 of Form 1041, Schedule B, complete the rest of Schedule J and file it with Form 1041, unless the trust has no previously accumulated income.

Generally, amounts accumulated before a beneficiary reaches age 21 may be excluded by the beneficiary. See sections 665 and 667(c) for exceptions relating to multiple trusts. The trustee reports to the IRS the total amount of the accumulation distribution before any reduction for income accumulated before the beneficiary reaches age 21. If the multiple trust rules do not apply, the beneficiary claims the exclusion when filing Form 4970, as you may not be aware that the beneficiary may be a beneficiary of other trusts with other trustees.

For examples of accumulation distributions that include payments from one trust to another trust, and amounts distributed for a dependent's support, see Regulations section 1.665(b)-1A(b).

Part II—Ordinary Income Accumulation Distribution

Enter the applicable year at the top of each column for each throwback year.

Line 6—DNI for Earlier Years

Enter the applicable amounts as follows:

Throwback year(s)	Amount from line
1969–1977	Form 1041, Schedule C, line 5
1978–1979	Form 1041, line 61
1980	Form 1041, line 60
1981–1982	Form 1041, line 58
1983–1996	Form 1041, Schedule B, line 9
1997–2013	Form 1041, Schedule B, line 7

For information about throwback years, see the instructions for line 13. For purposes of line 6, in figuring the DNI of the trust for a throwback year, subtract any estate tax deduction for IRD if the income is includible in figuring the DNI of the trust for that year.

Line 7—Distributions Made During Earlier Years

Enter the applicable amounts as follows:

Throwback year(s)	Amount from line
1969–1977	Form 1041, Schedule C, line 8
1978	Form 1041, line 64
1979	Form 1041, line 65
1980	Form 1041, line 64
1981–1982	Form 1041, line 62
1983–1996	Form 1041, Schedule B, line 13
1997–2013	Form 1041, Schedule B, line 11

Line 11—Prior Accumulation Distribution Thrown Back to Any Throwback Year

Enter the amount of prior accumulation distributions thrown back to the throwback years. Do not enter distributions excluded under section 663(a)(1) for gifts, bequests, etc.

Line 13—Throwback Years

Allocate the amount on line 5 that is an accumulation distribution to the earliest applicable year first, but do not allocate more than the amount on line 12 for any throwback year. An accumulation

distribution is thrown back first to the earliest preceding tax year in which there is undistributed net income (UNI). Then, it is thrown back beginning with the next earliest year to any remaining preceding tax years of the trust. The portion of the accumulation distribution allocated to the earliest preceding tax year is the amount of the UNI for that year. The portion of the accumulation distribution allocated to any remaining preceding tax year is the amount by which the accumulation distribution is larger than the total of the UNI for all earlier preceding tax years.

A tax year of a trust during which the trust was a simple trust for the entire year is not a preceding tax year unless (a) during that year the trust received outside income, or (b) the trustee did not distribute all of the trust's income that was required to be distributed currently for that year. In this case, UNI for that year must not be more than the greater of the outside income or income not distributed during that year.

The term "outside income" means amounts that are included in the DNI of the trust for that year but that are not "income" of the trust as defined in Regulations section 1.643(b)-1. Some examples of outside income are: (a) income taxable to the trust under section 691; (b) unrealized accounts receivable that were assigned to the trust; and (c) distributions from another trust that include the DNI or UNI of the other trust.

Line 16—Tax-Exempt Interest Included on Line 13

For each throwback year, divide line 15 by line 6 and multiply the result by the following:

Throwback year(s)	Amount from line
1969–1977	Form 1041, Schedule C, line 2(a)
1978–1979	Form 1041, line 58(a)
1980	Form 1041, line 57(a)
1981–1982	Form 1041, line 55(a)
1983–2013	Form 1041, Schedule B, line 2

Part III—Taxes Imposed on Undistributed Net Income

For the regular tax computation, if there is a capital gain, complete lines 18 through 25 for each throwback year. If the trustee elected the alternative tax on capital gains, complete lines 26 through 31 instead of lines 18 through 25 for each applicable year. If there is no capital gain for any year, or there is a capital loss for every year, enter on line 9 the amount of the tax for each year identified in the instruction for line 18 and do not complete Part III. If the trust received an accumulation distribution from another trust, see Regulations section 1.665(b)-1A.

Note. The alternative tax on capital gains was repealed for tax years beginning after December 31, 1978. The maximum rate on net capital gain for 1981, 1987, and 1991 through 2013 is not an alternative tax for this purpose.

Line 18—Regular Tax

Enter the applicable amounts as follows:

Throwback year(s)	Amount from line
1969–1976 . . .	Form 1041, page 1, line 24
1977	Form 1041, page 1, line 26
1978–1979 . . .	Form 1041, line 27
1980–1984 . . .	Form 1041, line 26c
1985–1986 . . .	Form 1041, line 25c
1987	Form 1041, line 22c
1988–2013 . . .	Form 1041, Schedule G, line 1a

Line 19—Trust's Share of Net Short-Term Gain

For each throwback year, enter the smaller of the capital gain from the two lines indicated. If there is a capital loss or a zero on either or both of the two lines indicated, enter zero on line 19.

Throwback year(s)	Amount from line
1969–1970 . . .	Schedule D, line 10, column 2, or Schedule D, line 12, column 2
1971–1978 . . .	Schedule D, line 14, column 2, or Schedule D, line 16, column 2
1979	Schedule D, line 18, column (b), or Schedule D, line 20, column (b)
1980–1981 . . .	Schedule D, line 14, column (b), or Schedule D, line 16, column (b)
1982	Schedule D, line 16, column (b), or Schedule D, line 18, column (b)
1983–1996 . . .	Schedule D, line 15, column (b), or Schedule D, line 17, column (b)
1997–2002 . . .	Schedule D, line 14, column (2), or Schedule D, line 16, column (2)
2003	Schedule D, line 14a, column (2), or Schedule D, line 16a, column (2)
2004–2012 . . .	Schedule D, line 13, column (2), or Schedule D, line 15, column (2)
2013 . . .	Schedule D, line 17, column (2), or Schedule D, line 19, column (2)

Line 20—Trust's Share of Net Long-Term Gain

Enter the applicable amounts as follows:

Throwback year(s)	Amount from line
1969–1970	50% of Schedule D, line 13(e)
1971–1977	50% of Schedule D, line 17(e)
1978	Schedule D, line 17(e), or line 31, whichever is applicable, less Form 1041, line 23
1979	Schedule D, line 25 or line 27, whichever is applicable, less Form 1041, line 23
1980–1981	Schedule D, line 21, less Schedule D, line 22
1982	Schedule D, line 23, less Schedule D, line 24
1983–1986	Schedule D, line 22, less Schedule D, line 23
1987–1996	Schedule D, the smaller of any gain on line 16 or line 17, column (b)
1997–2001	Schedule D, the smaller of any gain on line 15c or line 16, column (2)
2002	Schedule D, the smaller of any gain on line 15a or line 16, column (2)
2003	Schedule D, the smaller of any gain on line 15a or line 16a, column (2)
2004–2012	Schedule D, the smaller of any gain on line 14a or line 15, column (2)
2013	Schedule D, the smaller of any gain on line 18a or line 19, column (2)

Line 22—Taxable Income

Enter the applicable amounts as follows:

Throwback year(s)	Amount from line
1969–1976	Form 1041, page 1, line 23
1977	Form 1041, page 1, line 25
1978–1979	Form 1041, line 26
1980–1984	Form 1041, line 25
1985–1986	Form 1041, line 24
1987	Form 1041, line 21
1988–1996	Form 1041, line 22
1997	Form 1041, line 23
1998–2013	Form 1041, line 22

Line 26—Tax on Income Other Than Long-Term Capital Gain

Enter the applicable amounts as follows:

Throwback year(s)	Amount from line
1969	Schedule D, line 20
1970	Schedule D, line 19
1971	Schedule D, line 50
1972–1975	Schedule D, line 48
1976–1978	Schedule D, line 27

Line 27—Trust's Share of Net Short-Term Gain

If there is a loss on any of the following lines, enter zero on line 27 for the applicable throwback year. Otherwise, enter the applicable amounts as follows:

Throwback year(s)	Amount from line
1969–1970	Schedule D, line 10, column 2
1971–1978	Schedule D, line 14, column 2

Line 28—Trust's Share of Taxable Income Less Section 1202 Deduction

Enter the applicable amounts as follows:

Throwback year(s)	Amount from line
1969	Schedule D, line 19
1970	Schedule D, line 18
1971	Schedule D, line 38
1972–1975	Schedule D, line 39
1976–1978	Schedule D, line 21

Part IV—Allocation to Beneficiary

Complete Part IV for each beneficiary. If the accumulation distribution is allocated to more than one beneficiary, attach an additional copy of Schedule J with Part IV completed for each additional beneficiary. Give each beneficiary a copy of his or her respective Part IV information. If more than 5 throwback years are involved, use another Schedule J, completing Parts II and III for each additional throwback year.

If the beneficiary is a nonresident alien individual or a foreign corporation, see section 667(e) about retaining the character of the amounts distributed to determine the amount of the U.S. withholding tax.

The beneficiary uses Form 4970 to figure the tax on the distribution. The beneficiary also uses Form 4970 for the section 667(b)(6) tax adjustment if an accumulation distribution is subject to estate or generation-skipping transfer tax. This is because the trustee may not be the estate or generation-skipping transfer tax return filer.

Schedule K-1 (Form 1041)— Beneficiary's Share of Income, Deductions, Credits, etc.

General Instructions

Use Schedule K-1 (Form 1041) to report the beneficiary's share of income, deductions, and credits from a trust or a decedent's estate.

 Grantor type trusts do not use Schedule K-1 (Form 1041) to report the income, deductions, or credits of the grantor (or other person treated as owner). See Grantor Type Trusts, earlier.

Who Must File

The fiduciary (or one of the joint fiduciaries) must file Schedule K-1. A copy of each beneficiary's Schedule K-1 is attached to the Form 1041 filed with the IRS, and each beneficiary is given a copy of his or her respective Schedule K-1. One copy of each Schedule K-1 must be retained for the fiduciary's records.

Beneficiary's Identifying Number

As a payer of income, you are required to request and provide a proper identifying number for each recipient of income. Enter the beneficiary's number on the respective Schedule K-1 when you file Form 1041. Individuals and business recipients are responsible for giving you their TINs upon request. You may use Form W-9 to request the beneficiary's identifying number.

Penalty. You may be charged a $100 penalty for each failure to provide a required TIN, unless reasonable cause is established for not providing it. Explain any reasonable cause in a signed affidavit and attach it to this return.

Truncating recipient's identification number on beneficiary's statement.

The estate or trust can truncate a beneficiary's identifying number on the Schedule K-1 the estate or trust sends to the beneficiary. Truncation is not allowed on the Schedule K-1 the estate or trust files with the IRS. Also, the estate or trust may not truncate its own identification number on any form.

To truncate, where allowed, replace the first five digits of the nine-digit number with asterisks (*) or Xs (for example, a SSN xxx-xx-xxxx would appear as ***-**-xxxx or XXX-XX-xxxx).

For more information, see Regulations section 301.6109-4.

Substitute Forms

You do not need IRS approval to use a substitute Schedule K-1 if it is an exact copy of the IRS schedule. The boxes must use the same numbers and titles and must be in the same order and format as on the comparable IRS Schedule K-1. The substitute schedule must include the OMB number and the 6-digit form ID code in the upper right-hand corner of the schedule.

You must provide each beneficiary with the Instructions for Beneficiary Filing Form 1040 or other prepared specific instructions for each item reported on the beneficiary's Schedule K-1.

Inclusion of Amounts in Beneficiaries' Income

Simple trust. The beneficiary of a simple trust must include in his or her gross income the amount of the income required to be distributed currently, whether or not distributed, or if the income required to be distributed currently to all beneficiaries exceeds the DNI, his or her proportionate share of the DNI. The determination of whether trust income is required to be distributed currently depends on the terms of the trust instrument and applicable local law. See Regulations section 1.652(c)-4 for a comprehensive example.

Estates and complex trusts. The beneficiary of a decedent's estate or complex trust must include in his or her gross income the sum of:

1. The amount of the income required to be distributed currently, or if the income required to be distributed currently to all beneficiaries exceeds the DNI (figured without taking into account the charitable deduction), his or her proportionate share of the DNI (as so figured), and

2. All other amounts properly paid, credited, or required to be distributed, or if the sum of the income required to be distributed currently and other amounts properly paid, credited, or required to be distributed to all beneficiaries exceeds the DNI, his or her proportionate share of the excess of DNI over the income required to be distributed currently.

See Regulations section 1.662(c)-4 for a comprehensive example.

For complex trusts that have more than one beneficiary, and if different beneficiaries have substantially separate and independent shares, their shares are treated as separate trusts for the sole purpose of determining the amount of DNI allocable to the respective beneficiaries. A similar rule applies to treat substantially separate and independent shares of different beneficiaries of an estate as separate estates. For examples of the application of the separate share rule, see the regulations under section 663(c).

Gifts and bequests. Do not include in the beneficiary's income any gifts or bequests of a specific sum of money or of specific property under the terms of the governing instrument that are paid or credited in three installments or less.

Amounts that can be paid or credited only from income of the estate or trust do not qualify as a gift or bequest of a specific sum of money.

Past years. Do not include in the beneficiary's income any amounts deducted on Form 1041 for an earlier year that were credited or required to be distributed in that earlier year.

Character of income. The beneficiary's income is considered to have the same proportion of each class of items entering into the computation of DNI that the total of each class has to the DNI (for example, half dividends and half interest if the income of the estate or trust is half dividends and half interest).

Allocation of deductions. Generally, items of deduction that enter into the computation of DNI are allocated among the items of income to the extent such allocation is not inconsistent with the rules set out in section 469 and its regulations, relating to passive activity loss limitations, in the following order.

First, all deductions directly attributable to a specific class of income are deducted from that income. For example, rental expenses, to the extent allowable, are deducted from rental income.

Second, deductions that are not directly attributable to a specific class of income generally may be allocated to any class of income, as long as a reasonable portion is allocated to any tax-exempt income. Deductions considered not directly attributable to a specific class of income under this rule include fiduciary fees, safe deposit box rental charges, and state income and personal property taxes. The charitable deduction, however, must be ratably apportioned among each class of income included in DNI.

Finally, any excess deductions that are directly attributable to a class of income may be allocated to another class of income. However, in no case can excess deductions from a passive activity be allocated to income from a nonpassive activity, or to portfolio income earned by the estate or trust. Excess deductions attributable to tax-exempt income cannot offset any other class of income.

In no case can deductions be allocated to an item of income that is not included in the computation of DNI, or attributable to corpus.

You cannot show any negative amounts for any class of income shown in boxes 1 through 8 of Schedule K-1. However, for the final year of the estate or trust, certain deductions or losses can be passed through to the beneficiary(ies). See the instructions for box 11 for more information on these deductions and losses. Also, the beneficiary's share of depreciation and depletion is apportioned separately. These deductions may be allocated to the beneficiary(ies) in amounts greater than his or her income. See *Depreciation, Depletion, and Amortization*, earlier, and Rev. Rul. 74-530, 1974-2 C.B. 188.

Beneficiary's Tax Year

The beneficiary's income from the estate or trust must be included in the beneficiary's tax year during which the tax year of the estate or trust ends. See Pub. 559 for more information, including the effect of the death of a beneficiary during the tax year of the estate or trust.

General Reporting Information

If the return is for a fiscal year or a short tax year, fill in the tax year space at the top of each Schedule K-1. On each Schedule K-1, enter the information about the estate or trust and the beneficiary in Parts I and II (items A through H). In Part III, enter the beneficiary's share of each item of income, deduction, credit, and any other information the beneficiary needs to file his or her income tax return.

Codes. In box 9 and boxes 11 through 14, identify each item by entering a code in the column to the left of the entry space for the dollar amount. These codes are identified in these instructions and on the back of the Schedule K-1.

Attached statements. Enter an asterisk (*) after the code, if any, in the column to the left of the dollar amount entry space for each item for which you have attached a statement providing additional information. For those informational items that cannot be reported as a single dollar amount, enter the code and asterisk in the left-hand column and enter "STMT" in the entry space to the right to indicate that the information is provided on an attached statement. More than one attached statement can be placed on the same sheet of paper and should be identified in alphanumeric order by box number followed by the letter code (if any). For example: "Box 9, Code A—Depreciation" (followed by the information the beneficiary needs).

Too few entry spaces on Schedule K-1? If the estate or trust has more coded items than the number of spaces in box 9 or boxes 11 through 14, do not enter a code or dollar amount in the last entry space of the box. In the last entry space, enter an asterisk in the left column and enter "STMT" in the entry space to the right. Report the additional items on an attached statement and provide the box number, code, description, and dollar amount or information for each additional item. For example: "Box 13, Code H—Biofuel Producer Credit, $500.00."

Specific Instructions

Part I. Information About the Estate or Trust

On each Schedule K-1, enter the name, address, and identifying number of the estate or trust. Also, enter the name and address of the fiduciary.

Item D

If the fiduciary of a trust or decedent's estate filed Form 1041-T, you must check this box and enter the date it was filed.

Item E

If this is the final year of the estate or trust, you must check this box.

Note. If this is the final K-1 for the beneficiary, check the "Final K-1" box at the top of Schedule K-1.

Part II. Information About the Beneficiary

Complete a Schedule K-1 for each beneficiary. On each Schedule K-1, enter the beneficiary's name, address, and identifying number.

Item H

Check the foreign beneficiary box if the beneficiary is a nonresident alien individual, a foreign corporation, or a foreign estate or trust. Otherwise, check the domestic beneficiary box.

Part III. Beneficiary's Share of Current Year Income, Deductions, Credits, and Other Items

Box 1—Interest

Enter the beneficiary's share of the taxable interest income minus allocable deductions.

Box 2a—Total Ordinary Dividends

Enter the beneficiary's share of ordinary dividends minus allocable deductions.

Box 2b—Total Qualified Dividends

Enter the beneficiary's share of qualified dividends minus allocable deductions.

Box 3—Net Short-Term Capital Gain

Enter the beneficiary's share of the net short-term capital gain from Schedule D (Form 1041), line 17, column (1), minus allocable deductions. Do not enter a loss in box 3. If, for the final year of the estate or trust, there is a capital loss carryover, enter in box 11, code B, the beneficiary's share of short-term capital loss carryover. However, if the beneficiary is a corporation, enter in box 11, code B, the beneficiary's share of all short- and long-term capital loss carryovers as a single item. See section 642(h) and related regulations for more information.

Boxes 4a through 4c—Net Long-Term Capital Gain

Enter the beneficiary's share of the net long-term capital gain from Schedule D (Form 1041), lines 18a through 18c, column (1), minus allocable deductions.

Do not enter a loss in boxes 4a through 4c. If, for the final year of the estate or trust, there is a capital loss carryover, enter in box 11, code C, the beneficiary's share of the long-term capital loss carryover. (If the beneficiary is a corporation, see the instructions for box 3.) See section 642(h) and related regulations for more information.

Gains or losses from the complete or partial disposition of a rental, rental real estate, or trade or business activity that is a passive activity must be shown on an attachment to Schedule K-1.

Box 5—Other Portfolio and Nonbusiness Income

Enter the beneficiary's share of annuities, royalties, or any other income, minus allocable deductions (other than directly apportionable deductions), that is not subject to any passive activity loss limitation rules at the beneficiary level. Use boxes 6 through 8 to report income items subject to the passive activity rules at the beneficiary's level.

Boxes 6 through 8—Ordinary Business Income, Rental Real Estate, and Other Rental Income

Enter the beneficiary's share of trade or business, rental real estate, and other rental income, minus allocable deductions (other than directly apportionable deductions). To assist the beneficiary in figuring any applicable passive activity loss limitations, also attach a separate schedule showing the beneficiary's share of income derived from each trade or business, rental real estate, and other rental activity.

Box 9—Directly Apportioned Deductions

 The limitations on passive activity losses and credits under section 469 apply to estates and trusts. Estates and trusts that distribute income to beneficiaries are allowed to apportion depreciation, depletion, and amortization deductions to the beneficiaries. These deductions are referred to as "directly apportionable deductions."

Rules for treating a beneficiary's income and directly apportionable deductions from an estate or trust and other rules for applying the passive loss and credit limitations to beneficiaries of estates and trusts have not yet been issued.

Any directly apportionable deduction, such as depreciation, is treated by the beneficiary as having been incurred in the same activity as incurred by the estate or trust. However, the character of such deduction may be determined as if the beneficiary incurred the deduction directly.

To assist the beneficiary in figuring any applicable passive activity loss limitations, also attach a separate schedule showing the beneficiary's share of directly apportionable

deductions derived from each trade or business, rental real estate, and other rental activity.

Enter the beneficiary's share of directly apportioned deductions using codes A through C.

Depreciation (code A). Enter the beneficiary's share of the depreciation deductions directly apportioned to each activity reported in boxes 5 through 8. See the instructions under *Deductions*, earlier, for a discussion of how the depreciation deduction is apportioned between the beneficiaries and the estate or trust. Report any AMT adjustment or tax preference item attributable to depreciation separately in box 12, using code G.

Note. An estate or trust cannot make an election under section 179 to expense certain depreciable business assets.

Depletion (code B). Enter the beneficiary's share of the depletion deduction under section 611 directly apportioned to each activity reported in boxes 5 through 8. See *Depreciation, Depletion, and Amortization*, earlier, for a discussion of how the depletion deduction is apportioned between the beneficiaries and the estate or trust. Report any tax preference item attributable to depletion separately in box 12, using code H.

Amortization (code C). Itemize the beneficiary's share of the amortization deductions directly apportioned to each activity reported in boxes 5 through 8. Apportion the amortization deductions between the estate or trust and the beneficiaries in the same way that the depreciation and depletion deductions are divided. Report any AMT adjustment attributable to amortization separately in box 12, using code I.

Box 10—Estate Tax Deduction (Including Certain Generation-Skipping Transfer Taxes)

If the distribution deduction consists of any IRD, and the estate or trust was allowed a deduction under section 691(c) for the estate tax paid attributable to such income (see the line 19 instructions), then the beneficiary is allowed an estate tax deduction in proportion to his or her share of the distribution that consists of such income. For an example of the computation, see Regulations section 1.691(c)-2. Figure the computation on a

separate sheet and attach it to the return.

Box 11, Code A—Excess Deductions on Termination

If this is the final return of the estate or trust, and there are excess deductions on termination (see the instructions for line 22), enter the beneficiary's share of the excess deductions in box 11, using code A. Figure the deductions on a separate sheet and attach it to the return.

Excess deductions on termination occur only during the last tax year of the trust or decedent's estate when the total deductions (excluding the charitable deduction and exemption) are greater than the gross income during that tax year.

Generally, a deduction based on an NOL carryover is not available to a beneficiary as an excess deduction. However, if the last tax year of the estate or trust is also the last year in which an NOL carryover may be taken (see section 172(b)), the NOL carryover is considered an excess deduction on the termination of the estate or trust to the extent it is not absorbed by the estate or trust during its final tax year. For more information, see Regulations section 1.642(h)-4 for a discussion of the allocation of the carryover among the beneficiaries.

Only the beneficiary of an estate or trust that succeeds to its property is allowed to deduct that entity's excess deductions on termination. A beneficiary who does not have enough income in that year to absorb the entire deduction may not carry the balance over to any succeeding year. An individual beneficiary must be able to itemize deductions in order to claim the excess deductions in determining taxable income.

Box 11, Codes B and C—Unused Capital Loss Carryover

Upon termination of the trust or decedent's estate, the beneficiary succeeding to the property is allowed as a deduction any unused capital loss carryover under section 1212. If the estate or trust incurs capital losses in the final year, use the *Capital Loss Carryover Worksheet* in the Instructions for Schedule D (Form 1041) to figure the amount of capital loss carryover to be allocated to the beneficiary.

Box 11, Codes D and E—NOL Carryover

Upon termination of a trust or decedent's estate, a beneficiary succeeding to its property is allowed to deduct any unused NOL (and any ATNOL) carryover for regular and AMT purposes if the carryover would be allowable to the estate or trust in a later tax year but for the termination. Enter in box 11, using codes D and E, the unused carryover amounts.

Box 12—AMT Items

Adjustment for minimum tax purposes (code A). Enter the beneficiary's share of the adjustment for minimum tax purposes.

To figure the adjustment, subtract the beneficiary's share of the *income distribution deduction* figured on Schedule B, line 15, from the beneficiary's share of the *income distribution deduction on a minimum tax basis* figured on Schedule I (Form 1041), line 44. The difference is the beneficiary's share of the adjustment for minimum tax purposes.

Note. Schedule B, line 15 equals the sum of all Schedules K-1, boxes 1, 2a, 3, 4a, 5, 6, 7, and 8.

AMT adjustment attributable to qualified dividends, net short-term capital gains, or net long-term capital gains (codes B through D). If any part of the amount reported in box 12, code A, is attributable to qualified dividends (code B), net short-term capital gain (code C), or net long-term capital gain (code D), enter that part using the applicable code.

AMT adjustment attributable to unrecaptured section 1250 gain or 28% rate gain (codes E and F). Enter the beneficiary's distributive share of any AMT adjustments to the unrecaptured section 1250 gain (code E) or 28% rate gain (code F), whichever is applicable, in box 12.

Accelerated depreciation, depletion, and amortization (codes G through I). Enter any adjustments or tax preference items attributable to depreciation, depletion, or amortization that were directly apportioned to the beneficiary. For property placed in service before 1987, report separately the accelerated depreciation of real and leased personal property.

Exclusion items (code J). Enter the beneficiary's share of the adjustment for minimum tax purposes from Schedule K-1, box 12, code A, that is attributable to exclusion items (Schedule I (Form 1041), lines 2 through 6 and 8).

Box 13—Credits and Credit Recapture

Enter each beneficiary's share of the credits and credit recapture using the applicable codes. Listed below are the credits that can be allocated to the beneficiary(ies). Attach a statement if additional information must be provided to the beneficiary as explained below.

- Credit for estimated taxes (code A)—Payment of estimated tax to be credited to the beneficiary (section 643(g)).

 See the instructions for line 24b before you make an entry to allocate any estimated tax payments to a beneficiary. If the fiduciary does not make a valid election, then the IRS will disallow the estimated tax payment that is reported on Schedule K-1 and claimed on the beneficiary's return.

- Credit for backup withholding (code B).

 Income tax withheld on wages cannot be distributed to the beneficiary.

- The low-income housing credit (code C). Attach a statement that shows the beneficiary's share of the amount, if any, entered on line 6 of Form 8586, Low-Income Housing Credit, with instructions to report that amount on Form 8586, line 4 or Form 3800, Part III, line 1d, if the beneficiary's only source for the credit is a pass-through entity. Also, show the beneficiary's share of the amount, if any, entered on line 13 of Form 8586 with instructions to report that amount on Form 8586, line 11 or Form 3800, Part III, line 4d, if the beneficiary's only source for the credit is a pass-through entity.
- Rehabilitation credit and energy credit (code D). Attach a statement that shows the beneficiary's apportioned share of basis, expenditures, and other information that is necessary for the beneficiary to complete Form 3468, Investment Credit, for the rehabilitation credit and the energy credit. See the Instructions for Form 3468 for more information.
- Other qualifying investment credit (code E). Attach a statement that shows the beneficiary's apportioned share of qualified investment and other

information that is necessary for the beneficiary to complete Form 3468 for the qualifying advanced coal project credit, qualifying gasification project credit, and qualifying advanced energy project credit. See the Instructions for Form 3468 for more information.

- Work opportunity credit (code F).
- Credit for small employer health insurance premiums (code G).
- Biofuel producer credit (code H).
- Credit for increasing research activities (code I).
- Renewable electricity, refined coal, and Indian coal production credit (code J). Attach a statement that shows the amount of the credit the beneficiary must report on line 9 and line 29 of Form 8835, in case the beneficiary is required to file that form in addition to Form 3800.
- Empowerment zone employment credit (code K).
- Indian employment credit (code L).
- Orphan drug credit (code M).
- Credit for employer provided child care and facilities (code N).
- Biodiesel and renewable diesel fuels credit (code O). If the credit includes the small agri-biodiesel credit, attach a statement that shows the beneficiary's share of the small agri-biodiesel credit, the number of gallons claimed for the small agri-biodiesel credit, and the estate's or trust's productive capacity for agri-biodiesel.
- Nonconventional source fuel credit (code P).
- Credit to holders of tax credit bonds (code Q).
- Agricultural chemicals security credit (code R).
- Energy efficient appliance credit (code S).
- Credit for employer differential wage payments (code T).
- Recapture of credits (code U). On an attached statement to Schedule K-1, provide any information the beneficiary will need to report recapture of credits.

Box 14—Other Information

Enter the dollar amounts and applicable codes for the items listed under Other Information.

Foreign taxes (code B). Enter the beneficiary's allocable share of taxes paid or accrued to a foreign country. Attach a statement reporting the beneficiary's share of foreign tax (paid or accrued) and income by category including interest, dividends, rents and royalties, and other income. See Form 1116 and Pub. 514 for more information.

Domestic production activities information. The estate or trust allocates QPAI (whether positive or negative) and Form W-2 wages based on the relative proportion of the estate's or trust's DNI that is distributed or required to be distributed to the beneficiary. If the estate or trust has no DNI for the tax year, QPAI and Form W-2 wages are allocated entirely to the estate or trust.

Qualified production activities income (code C). Enter the beneficiary's share, if any, of the estate's or trust's QPAI from all activities. The QPAI will be less than zero if the cost of goods sold and deductions allocated and apportioned to domestic production gross receipts (DPGR) is more than the estate's or trust's DPGR. If any of the QPAI is oil-related QPAI, attach a statement that shows the amount of oil-related QPAI. See Form 8903, Domestic Production Activities Deduction, and its instructions for more details.

Form W-2 wages (code D). Use code D to report the beneficiary's share, if any, of Form W-2 wages. Do not enter more than 9% of the beneficiary's share, if any, of the estate's or trust's QPAI. See Form 8903 and its instructions for more details.

Foreign trading gross receipts (code G). Enter the beneficiary's share, if any, of foreign trading gross receipts. See Form 8873, Extraterritorial Income Exclusion, for more information.

Net investment income tax (code H). Use code H to identify the amount of the beneficiary's adjustment for section 1411 net investment income or deductions. See the Instructions for Form 8960. An attachment may be provided with the K-1 informing the beneficiary of the detailed items to be reported on Form 1040. See *Net Investment Income Tax*, earlier, for more information on these amounts.

Other information (code I). List on a separate sheet the tax information the beneficiary will need to complete his or her return that is not entered elsewhere on Schedule K-1.

For example, if the estate or trust participates in a transaction that must be disclosed on Form 8886 (see earlier), both the estate or trust and its beneficiaries may be required to file Form 8886. The estate or trust must determine if any of its beneficiaries are required to disclose the transaction and provide those beneficiaries with information they will need to file Form 8886. This determination is based on the category(ies) under which a transaction qualified for disclosure. See the Instructions for Form 8886 for details.

In addition, if the beneficiary is a "covered person" in connection with a foreign tax credit splitter arrangement under section 909, attach a statement that identifies the arrangement including the foreign taxes paid or accrued.

Paperwork Reduction Act Notice. We ask for the information on this form to carry out the Internal Revenue laws of the United States. You are required to give us the information. We need it to ensure that you are complying with these laws and to allow us to figure and collect the right amount of tax.

You are not required to provide the information requested on a form that is subject to the Paperwork Reduction Act unless the form displays a valid OMB control number. Books or records relating to a form or its instructions must be retained as long as their contents may become material in the administration of any Internal Revenue law. Generally, tax returns and return information are confidential, as required by Code section 6103.

The time needed to complete and file this form and related schedules will vary depending on individual circumstances. The estimated average times are:

	Form 1041	Schedule D	Schedule I	Schedule J	Schedule K-1	Form 1041-V
Recordkeeping	38 hr., 58 min.	26 hr., 33 min.	17 hr., 42 min.	11 hr., 00 min.	6 hr., 27 min.	43 min.
Learning about the law or the form	16 hr., 11 min.	4 hr., 5 min.	4 hr., 22 min.	1 hr., 27 min.	35 min.	- - - -
Preparing the form	30 hr., 34 min.	5 hr., 37 min.	4 hr., 51 min.	2 hr., 37 min.	43 min.	- - - -
Copying, assembling, and sending the form to the IRS	3 hr., 45 min.	51 min.	- - - -	16 min.	- - - -	- - - -

If you have comments concerning the accuracy of these time estimates or suggestions for making this form and related schedules simpler, we would be happy to hear from you. You can send your comments to Internal Revenue Service, Tax Forms and Publications Division,1111 Constitution Ave. NW, IR-6526, Washington, DC 20224. Do not send the tax form to this address. Instead, see *Where To File*, earlier.

Index

SCHEDULE D
(Form 1041)

Department of the Treasury
Internal Revenue Service

Capital Gains and Losses

▶ Attach to Form 1041, Form 5227, or Form 990-T.
▶ Use Form 8949 to list your transactions for lines 1b, 2, 3, 8b, 9 and 10.
▶ Information about Schedule D and its separate instructions is at *www.irs.gov/form1041*.

OMB No. 1545-0092

2014

Name of estate or trust	Employer identification number

Note: *Form 5227 filers need to complete **only** Parts I and II.*

Part I — Short-Term Capital Gains and Losses—Assets Held One Year or Less

See instructions for how to figure the amounts to enter on the lines below.

This form may be easier to complete if you round off cents to whole dollars.

	(d) Proceeds (sales price)	(e) Cost (or other basis)	(g) Adjustments to gain or loss from Form(s) 8949, Part I, line 2, column (g)	(h) Gain or (loss) Subtract column (e) from column (d) and combine the result with column (g)
1a Totals for all short-term transactions reported on Form 1099-B for which basis was reported to the IRS and for which you have no adjustments (see instructions). However, if you choose to report all these transactions on Form 8949, leave this line blank and go to line 1b .				
1b Totals for all transactions reported on Form(s) 8949 with **Box A** checked				
2 Totals for all transactions reported on Form(s) 8949 with **Box B** checked				
3 Totals for all transactions reported on Form(s) 8949 with **Box C** checked				

4	Short-term capital gain or (loss) from Forms 4684, 6252, 6781, and 8824	4
5	Net short-term gain or (loss) from partnerships, S corporations, and other estates or trusts . . .	5
6	Short-term capital loss carryover. Enter the amount, if any, from line 9 of the 2013 Capital Loss Carryover Worksheet	6 ( )
7	Net short-term capital gain or (loss). Combine lines 1a through 6 in column (h). Enter here and on line 17, column (3) on the back . . . . ▶	7

Part II — Long-Term Capital Gains and Losses—Assets Held More Than One Year

See instructions for how to figure the amounts to enter on the lines below.

This form may be easier to complete if you round off cents to whole dollars.

	(d) Proceeds (sales price)	(e) Cost (or other basis)	(g) Adjustments to gain or loss from Form(s) 8949, Part II, line 2, column (g)	(h) Gain or (loss) Subtract column (e) from column (d) and combine the result with column (g)
8a Totals for all long-term transactions reported on Form 1099-B for which basis was reported to the IRS and for which you have no adjustments (see instructions). However, if you choose to report all these transactions on Form 8949, leave this line blank and go to line 8b .				
8b Totals for all transactions reported on Form(s) 8949 with **Box D** checked				
9 Totals for all transactions reported on Form(s) 8949 with **Box E** checked				
10 Totals for all transactions reported on Form(s) 8949 with **Box F** checked				

11	Long-term capital gain or (loss) from Forms 2439, 4684, 6252, 6781, and 8824	11
12	Net long-term gain or (loss) from partnerships, S corporations, and other estates or trusts . . .	12
13	Capital gain distributions	13
14	Gain from Form 4797, Part I	14
15	Long-term capital loss carryover. Enter the amount, if any, from line 14 of the 2013 Capital Loss Carryover Worksheet	15 ( )
16	**Net long-term capital gain or (loss).** Combine lines 8a through 15 in column (h). Enter here and on line 18a, column (3) on the back . . . . ▶	16

For Paperwork Reduction Act Notice, see the Instructions for Form 1041.　　　　Cat. No. 11376V　　　　Schedule D (Form 1041) 2014

Part III	Summary of Parts I and II Caution: *Read the instructions **before** completing this part.*		**(1)** Beneficiaries' (see instr.)	**(2)** Estate's or trust's	**(3)** Total
17	Net short-term gain or (loss)	**17**			
18	Net long-term gain or (loss):				
a	Total for year	**18a**			
b	Unrecaptured section 1250 gain (see line 18 of the wrksht.) .	**18b**			
c	28% rate gain	**18c**			
19	**Total net gain or (loss).** Combine lines 17 and 18a . . ▶	**19**			

Note: *If line 19, column (3), is a net gain, enter the gain on Form 1041, line 4 (or Form 990-T, Part I, line 4a). If lines 18a and 19, column (2), are net gains, go to Part V, and **do not** complete Part IV. If line 19, column (3), is a net loss, complete Part IV and the **Capital Loss Carryover Worksheet,** as necessary.*

Part IV	Capital Loss Limitation

20   Enter here and enter as a (loss) on Form 1041, line 4 (or Form 990-T, Part I, line 4c, if a trust), the **smaller** of:

     a   The loss on line 19, column (3)   **or**   **b** $3,000   . . . .   **20** (   )

Note: *If the loss on line 19, column (3), is more than $3,000, **or** if Form 1041, page 1, line 22 (or Form 990-T, line 34), is a loss, complete the **Capital Loss Carryover Worksheet** in the instructions to figure your capital loss carryover.*

Part V	Tax Computation Using Maximum Capital Gains Rates

Form 1041 filers. Complete this part **only** if both lines 18a and 19 in column (2) are gains, or an amount is entered in Part I or Part II and there is an entry on Form 1041, line 2b(2), **and** Form 1041, line 22, is more than zero.

Caution: *Skip this part and complete the **Schedule D Tax Worksheet** in the instructions if:*

- *Either line 18b, col. (2) or line 18c, col. (2) is more than zero, or*
- *Both Form 1041, line 2b(1), and Form 4952, line 4g are more than zero.*

Form 990-T trusts. Complete this part **only** if both lines 18a and 19 are gains, or qualified dividends are included in income in Part I of Form 990-T, **and** Form 990-T, line 34, is more than zero. Skip this part and complete the **Schedule D Tax Worksheet** in the instructions if either line 18b, col. (2) or line 18c, col. (2) is more than zero.

21	Enter taxable income from Form 1041, line 22 (or Form 990-T, line 34) . .	**21**		
22	Enter the **smaller** of line 18a or 19 in column (2) but not less than zero	**22**		
23	Enter the estate's or trust's qualified dividends from Form 1041, line 2b(2) (or enter the qualified dividends included in income in Part I of Form 990-T) . . .	**23**		
24	Add lines 22 and 23	**24**		
25	If the estate or trust is filing Form 4952, enter the amount from line 4g; otherwise, enter -0- . . ▶	**25**		
26	Subtract line 25 from line 24. If zero or less, enter -0-		**26**	
27	Subtract line 26 from line 21. If zero or less, enter -0-		**27**	
28	Enter the **smaller** of the amount on line 21 or $2,500		**28**	
29	Enter the **smaller** of the amount on line 27 or line 28		**29**	
30	Subtract line 29 from line 28. If zero or less, enter -0-. This amount is taxed at 0% . . . . . ▶		**30**	
31	Enter the **smaller** of line 21 or line 26		**31**	
32	Subtract line 30 from line 26		**32**	
33	Enter the **smaller** of line 21 or $12,150		**33**	
34	Add lines 27 and 30		**34**	
35	Subtract line 34 from line 33. If zero or less, enter -0-		**35**	
36	Enter the **smaller** of line 32 or line 35		**36**	
37	Multiply line 36 by 15% . . . . ▶		**37**	
38	Enter the amount from line 31		**38**	
39	Add lines 30 and 36		**39**	
40	Subtract line 39 from line 38. If zero or less, enter -0-		**40**	
41	Multiply line 40 by 20% . . . . ▶		**41**	
42	Figure the tax on the amount on line 27. Use the 2014 Tax Rate Schedule for Estates and Trusts (see the Schedule G instructions in the instructions for Form 1041) . .	**42**		
43	Add lines 37, 41, and 42		**43**	
44	Figure the tax on the amount on line 21. Use the 2014 Tax Rate Schedule for Estates and Trusts (see the Schedule G instructions in the instructions for Form 1041) . .	**44**		
45	**Tax on all taxable income.** Enter the **smaller** of line 43 or line 44 here and on Form 1041, Schedule G, line 1a (or Form 990-T, line 36) . . . . ▶		**45**	

2014

Department of the Treasury
Internal Revenue Service

Instructions for Schedule D (Form 1041)

Capital Gains and Losses

Section references are to the Internal Revenue Code unless otherwise noted.

Future Developments

For the latest information about developments related to Schedule D and its instructions, such as legislation enacted after they were published, go to *www.irs.gov/form1041*.

What's New

 Form 1041 E-filing. *For tax year 2014, Form 1041 must be e-Filed using Form 8453-FE, U.S. Estate or Trust Declaration for an IRS e-File Return. If the 2014 Form 1041 is e-filed, then any Schedule D (Form 1041) and Form 8949 that are part of the return must also be e-filed.*

Note. Form 8453-F, U.S. Estate or Trust Income Tax Declaration and Signature for Electronic Filing, is obsolete.

Capital gains and qualified dividends. For tax year 2014, the 20% maximum capital gain rate applies to estates and trusts with income above $12,150. The 0% and 15% rates continue to apply to certain threshold amounts. The 0% rate applies up to $2,500. The 15% rate applies to amounts over $2,500 and up to $12,150.

Section 1202 exclusion. Line 2 of the 28% Rate Gain Worksheet was revised to reflect the 75% exclusion of gain on QSB stock acquired during certain periods of 2009, and held for more than 5 years when sold in 2014.

Form 1099-B. Form 1099-B has been redesigned so that the information is reported in boxes that are numbered to match the corresponding line and column on Form 8949. A new box has also been added at the top of Form 1099-B to tell you which box to check when completing Form 8949. These changes will make it easier for you to complete Form 8949.

A Form 1099-B (or substitute statement) for transactions involving certain types of debt instruments acquired after 2013 will have more detailed information than a Form 1099-B (or substitute statement) for transactions involving debt instruments acquired before 2014. This is also true for a Form 1099-B (or substitute statement) for options granted or acquired after 2013 or securities futures contracts entered into after 2013. This additional information will help you complete Form 8949 and Schedule D.

General Instructions

Any reference in these instructions to "you" means the fiduciary of the estate or trust.

Purpose of Schedule

These instructions explain how to complete Schedule D (Form 1041). Complete Form 8949 before you complete line 1b, 2, 3, 8b, 9, or 10 of Schedule D.

Use Schedule D to report the following.
* The overall capital gains and losses from transactions reported on Form 8949.
* Certain transactions that the estate or trust does not have to report on Form 8949.
* Gain from Part I of Form 4797, Sales of Business Property.
* Capital gain or loss from Form 4684, Casualties and Thefts.
* Capital gain from Form 6252, Installment Sale Income.
* Capital gain or loss from Form 6781, Gains and Losses From Section 1256 Contracts and Straddles.
* Capital gain or loss from Form 8824, Like-Kind Exchanges.
* Undistributed long-term capital gains from Form 2439.
* Capital gain or loss from partnerships, S corporations, or other estates or trusts.

For more information, see Pub. 544, Sales and Other Dispositions of Assets, and the Instructions for Form 8949.

Other Forms You May Have To File

Use Form 8949 to report the sale or exchange of a capital asset (defined later) not reported on another form or schedule. See Lines 1a and 8a, later, for more information about when Form 8949 is needed and when it is not.

Use Form 4797 to report the following.
1. The sale or exchange of:
   a. Property used in a trade or business;
   b. Depreciable and amortizable property;
   c. Oil, gas, geothermal, or other mineral property; and
   d. Section 126 property.
2. The involuntary conversion (other than from casualty or theft) of property used in a trade or business and capital assets held for business or profit.
3. The disposition of noncapital assets other than inventory or property held primarily for sale to customers in the ordinary course of a trade or business.
4. Ordinary loss on the sale, exchange, or worthlessness of small business investment company (section 1242) stock.
5. Ordinary loss on the sale, exchange, or worthlessness of small business (section 1244) stock.

Use Form 4684, to report involuntary conversions of property due to casualty or theft.

Use Form 6781 to report gains and losses from section 1256 contracts and straddles.

Use Form 8824 if the estate or trust made one or more *like-kind* exchanges. A like-kind exchange occurs when the estate or trust exchanges business or investment property for property of a like kind.

Special Rules for Determining Basis of Estate and Trust Property

Basis of trust property. Generally, the basis of property acquired by gift is the same as its basis in the hands of the donor. However, if the FMV of the property at the time it was transferred to the trust is less than the transferor's

Cat. No. 11378R

basis, then the FMV is used to determine any loss upon disposition.

If the property was transferred to the trust after 1976, and a gift tax was paid under Chapter 12, then increase the donor's basis as follows:

Multiply the amount of the gift tax paid by a fraction, the numerator of which is the net appreciation in value of the gift (defined below), and the denominator of which is the amount of the gift. For this purpose, the net appreciation in value of the gift is the amount by which the FMV of the gift exceeds the donor's adjusted basis.

Basis of decedent's estate property. Generally, the basis of property acquired by a decedent's estate is the FMV of the property at the date of the decedent's death, or the alternate valuation date if the executor elected to use an alternate valuation under section 2032.

See Pub. 551 and the Instructions for Form 706 for a discussion of the valuation of qualified real property under section 2032A.

Basis of property acquired from a decedent who died in 2010. See Pub. 4895, Tax Treatment of Property Acquired From a Decedent Dying in 2010, for details about determining the basis of property acquired from a decedent who died in 2010.

Basis of assets held on January 1, 2001, where an election to recognize gain was made. If you elected on behalf of an estate or trust to recognize gain on an asset held on January 1, 2001, the basis in the asset is its closing market price or FMV, whichever applies, on the date of the deemed sale and reacquisition, whether the deemed sale resulted in a gain or an unallowed loss.

Carryover basis. Carryover basis determined under repealed section 1023 applies to property acquired from a decedent who died after December 31, 1976, and before November 7, 1978, only if the executor made a timely filed election on Form 5970-A, Election of Carryover Basis.

Capital Asset

Each item of property held by the estate or trust (whether or not connected with a trade or business) is a capital asset, *except* the following:
- Stock in trade, inventory or property held primarily for sale to customers.
- Depreciable or real property used in a trade or business, even if it is fully depreciated.

- Copyrights; literary, musical, or artistic compositions; letters or memoranda; or similar property eligible for copyright protection that the trust received from someone whose personal efforts created them or for whom they were created in a way (such as by gift) that entitled the trust to the basis of the previous owner. In the case of letters, memoranda, or similar property, such property may also be prepared or produced for the trust.

Note. Under section 1221(b)(3), the trust can elect to treat musical compositions and copyrights in musical works as capital assets if it acquired the assets under circumstances entitling it to the basis of the person who created the property or for whom it was prepared or produced.

- Accounts or notes receivable acquired in the ordinary course of a trade or business for services rendered or from the sale of inventoriable assets or property held primarily for sale to customers.
- Certain U.S. Government publications not purchased at the public sale price.
- Certain "commodities derivative financial instruments" held by a dealer (see section 1221(a)(6)).
- Certain hedging transactions entered into in the normal course of a trade or business (see section 1221(a)(7)).
- Supplies regularly used in a trade or business.

You may find additional helpful information in the following publications.
- Pub. 544, Sales and Other Dispositions of Assets.
- Pub. 551, Basis of Assets.

Short-Term or Long-Term

Separate the capital gains and losses according to how long the estate or trust held or owned the property. The holding period for short-term capital gains and losses is 1 year or less. The holding period for long-term capital gains and losses is more than 1 year. Property acquired from a decedent is treated as held for more than 1 year.

Note. Long-term treatment may not apply to property acquired from a decedent who died in 2010 where the estate elected the use of carryover basis if the property was held less than 1 year. See Pub. 4895 for details.

To figure the length of the period the estate or trust held property, begin counting on the day after the estate or trust acquired the property and include the day it was disposed. Use the trade dates for the dates of acquisition and

sale of stocks and bonds traded on an exchange or over-the-counter market.

Section 643(e)(3) Election

For in-kind noncash property distributions, a fiduciary may elect to have the estate or trust recognize gain or loss in the same manner as if the distributed property had been sold to the beneficiary at its fair market value (FMV). The distribution deduction is the property's FMV. This election applies to all distributions made by the estate or trust during the tax year. Once the election is made, it may only be revoked with IRS consent.

Note. Section 267 does not allow a trust or a decedent's estate to claim a deduction for any loss on property to which a section 643(e)(3) election applies. In addition, when a trust or a decedent's estate distributes depreciable property, section 1239 applies to deny capital gains treatment for any gain on property to which a section 643(e)(3) election applies.

Related Persons

A trust cannot deduct a loss from the sale or exchange of property directly or indirectly between any of the following:
- A grantor and a fiduciary of a trust,
- A fiduciary and a fiduciary or beneficiary of another trust created by the same grantor,
- A fiduciary and a beneficiary of the same trust,
- A trust fiduciary and a corporation of which more than 50% in value of the outstanding stock is owned directly or indirectly by or for the trust or by or for the grantor of the trust, or
- An executor of an estate and a beneficiary of that estate, except when the sale or exchange is to satisfy a pecuniary bequest (that is, a bequest of a sum of money).

Items for Special Treatment

- Bonds and other debt instruments. See Pub. 550, Investment Income and Expenses.
- Gain on the disposition of a market discount bond. The gain is recharacterized as interest income to the extent of accrued market discount as of the date of disposition. See sections 1276 through 1278 and Pub. 550 for more information on market discount. See the Instructions for Form 8949 for detailed information about how to report the disposition of a market discount bond.
- Gain or loss recognized on the disposition of a contingent payment debt instrument subject to the

noncontingent bond method. The gain is treated as interest income rather than as capital gain. In certain situations, all or a portion of a loss recognized on the disposition of a contingent payment debt instrument subject to the noncontingent bond method may be treated as an ordinary loss rather than as a capital loss. See Regulations section 1.1275-4(b) and Pub. 550 for more information on contingent payment debt instruments subject to the noncontingent bond method.

- A nonbusiness bad debt must be treated as a short-term capital loss and can be deducted only in the year the debt becomes totally worthless. See Pub. 550 for details.
- Wash sales of stock or securities (including contracts or options to acquire or sell stock or securities) (section 1091).
- Gain or loss on options to buy or sell. See Pub. 550.
- Certain real estate subdivided for sale that may be considered a capital asset (section 1237).
- Gain on disposition of stock in an interest charge domestic international sales corporation (DISC) (section 995(c)).
- Gain on the sale or exchange of stock in certain foreign corporations (section 1248).
- Sales of stock received under a qualified public utility dividend reinvestment plan. See Pub. 550 for details.
- Transfer of appreciated property to a political organization (section 84).
- Amounts received by shareholders in corporate liquidations. See Pub. 550.
- Cash received in lieu of fractional shares of stock as a result of a stock split or stock dividend. See Pub. 550.
- Load charges to acquire stock in a regulated investment company (including a mutual fund), which may not be taken into account in determining gain or loss on certain dispositions of the stock if reinvestment rights were exercised. See Pub. 550.
- The sale or exchange of S corporation stock or an interest in a trust held for more than 1 year, which may result in collectibles gain (28% rate gain). See the instructions for line 18c.
- The sale or other disposition of a partnership interest may result in ordinary income, collectibles gain, or unrecaptured section 1250 gain.
- Gain or loss on the disposition of securities futures contracts. See Pub. 550.
- Gains from certain constructive ownership transactions. Gain in excess

of the gain the estate or trust would have recognized if the estate or trust held a financial asset directly during the term of a derivative contract must be treated as ordinary income. See section 1260 for details.
- If qualified dividends include extraordinary dividends, any loss on the sale or exchange of the stock is a long-term capital loss to the extent of the extraordinary dividends. An extraordinary dividend is a dividend that is at least 10% (5% in the case of preferred stock) of the basis in the stock.
- Certain virtual currencies. See Notice 2014-21, 2014-16 I.R.B 938.
- NAV method for certain money market funds. Report capital gain or loss determined under the net asset value (NAV) method with respect to shares in a floating-NAV money market fund on Form 8949, Part I, with box C checked. Enter the name of each fund followed by "(NAV)" in column (a). Enter the net gain or loss in column (h). Leave all other columns blank. See the Instructions for Form 8949.

Constructive Sales Treatment for Certain Appreciated Positions

Generally, the estate or trust must recognize gain (but not loss) on the date it enters into a constructive sale of any appreciated position in stock, a partnership interest, or certain debt instruments as if the position were disposed of at FMV on that date.

The estate or trust is treated as making a constructive sale of an appreciated position when it (or a related person, in some cases) does one of the following:
- Enters into a short sale of the same or substantially identical property (that is, a "short sale against the box"),
- Enters into an offsetting notional principal contract relating to the same or substantially identical property,
- Enters into a futures or forward contract to deliver the same or substantially identical property, or
- Acquires the same or substantially identical property (if the appreciated position is a short sale, offsetting notional principal contract, or a futures or forward contract).

Exception. Generally, constructive sale treatment does not apply if:
- The estate or trust closed the transaction before the end of the 30th day after the end of the year in which it was entered into,

- The estate or trust held the appreciated position to which the transaction relates throughout the 60-day period starting on the date the transaction was closed, and
- At no time during that 60-day period was the estate's or trust's risk of loss reduced by holding certain other positions.

For details and other exceptions to these rules, see Pub. 550.

Exclusion of Gain on Qualified Small Business (QSB) Stock (Section 1202)

Section 1202 provides for an exclusion of 50% of the eligible gain on the sale or exchange of QSB stock. This exclusion can be up to 60% for certain empowerment zone business stock. The exclusion can also be increased to 75% on the sale or exchange of QSB stock acquired after February 17, 2009. The section 1202 exclusion applies only to QSB stock held for more than 5 years.

To be QSB stock, the stock must meet all of the following tests:

1. It must be stock in a C corporation (that is, not S corporation stock).

2. It must have been originally issued after August 10, 1993.

3. As of the date the stock was issued, the corporation was a QSB. A QSB is a domestic C corporation with total gross assets of $50 million or less (a) at all times after August 9, 1993, and before the stock was issued, and (b) immediately after the stock was issued. Gross assets include those of any predecessor of the corporation. All corporations that are members of the same parent-subsidiary controlled group are treated as one corporation.

4. The estate or trust acquired the stock at its original issue (either directly or through an underwriter), either in exchange for money or other property or as pay for services (other than as an underwriter) to the corporation. In certain cases, the estate or trust may meet the test if it acquired the stock from another person who met this test (such as by gift or inheritance) or through a conversion or exchange of QSB stock the estate or trust held.

5. During substantially all the time the estate or trust held the stock:

a. The corporation was a C corporation,

b. At least 80% of the value of the corporation's assets was used in the active conduct of one or more qualified businesses (defined below), and

   c. The corporation was not a foreign corporation, DISC, former DISC, corporation that has made (or that has a subsidiary that has made) a section 936 election, regulated investment company, real estate investment trust, REMIC, FASIT, or cooperative.

Note. A specialized small business investment company (SSBIC) is treated as having met test 5b above.

Qualified business. A qualified business is any business other than the following:

* One involving services performed in the fields of health, law, engineering, architecture, accounting, actuarial science, performing arts, consulting, athletics, financial services, or brokerage services;
* One whose principal asset is the reputation or skill of one or more employees;
* Any banking, insurance, financing, leasing, investing, or similar business;
* Any farming business (including the raising or harvesting of trees);
* Any business involving the production of products for which percentage depletion can be claimed; or
* Any business of operating a hotel, motel, restaurant, or similar business.

   For more details about limits and additional requirements that may apply, see Pub. 550 or section 1202.

Holding period of stock acquired after February 17, 2009. When determining whether the exclusion is limited to 50% or 75% of the gain from the stock, the acquisition date is considered to be the first day the stock is held (determined after applying the holding period rules in section 1223).

Empowerment zone business stock. Generally, the estate or trust can exclude up to 60% of its gain on certain QSB stock if it meets the following additional requirements.

   1. The stock sold or exchanged was stock in a corporation that qualified as an empowerment zone business during substantially all of the time the estate or trust held the stock.

   2. The estate or trust acquired the stock after December 21, 2000, and before February 18, 2009.

   Requirement 1 will still be met if the corporation ceased to qualify after the 5-year period that began on the date the estate or trust acquired the stock. However, the gain that qualifies for the

60% exclusion cannot be more than the gain the estate or trust would have had if it had sold the stock on the date the corporation ceased to qualify.

   See section 1397C for more details.

Stock acquired after February 17, 2009. The estate or trust can exclude up to 75% of the gain if it acquired the stock after February 17, 2009.

Pass-through entities. If the estate or trust held an interest in a pass-through entity (a partnership, S corporation, mutual fund, or other regulated investment company) that sold QSB stock, the estate or trust generally must have held the interest on the date the pass-through entity acquired the QSB stock and at all times thereafter until the stock was sold to qualify for the exclusion.

   How to report. Report the sale or exchange of QSB stock on Form 8949, Part II, with the appropriate box checked, as it would be reported if the exclusion was not taken. Then enter "Q" in column (f) and enter the amount of the excluded gain as a negative number in column (g). Put it in parentheses to show it is negative. Complete all remaining columns. See the Instructions for Form 8949, columns (f), (g), and (h). On line 2 of the *28% Rate Gain Worksheet*, include an amount equal to the 50% exclusion (⅔ of the exclusion if a 60% exclusion was claimed; ⅓ of the exclusion if a 75% exclusion was claimed). Also, see the Instructions for Schedule I (Form 1041), line 9, for information on the amount of the exclusion to include on Schedule I (Form 1041).

   Gain from Form 1099-DIV. If the estate or trust received a Form 1099-DIV, Dividends and Distributions, with a gain in box 2c, part or all of that gain (which is also included in box 2a) may be eligible for the section 1202 exclusion. In column (a) of Form 8949, Part II, enter the name of the corporation whose stock was sold. In column (f), enter "Q" and in column (g) enter the amount of the excluded gain as a negative number. See the Instructions for Form 8949, columns (f), (g), and (h). Also, include the amount of the 50% exclusion as a gain on line 2 of the *28% Rate Gain Worksheet* (include ⅔ of the exclusion if a 60% exclusion was claimed; ⅓ of the exclusion if a 75% exclusion was claimed).

   Gain from Form 2439. If the estate or trust received a Form 2439, Notice to Shareholder of Undistributed

Long-Term Capital Gains, with a gain in box 1c, part or all of that gain (which is also included in box 1a) may be eligible for the section 1202 exclusion. In column (a) of Form 8949, Part II, enter the name of the corporation whose stock was sold. In column (f), enter "Q" and in column (g) enter the amount of the excluded gain as a negative number. See the Instructions for Form 8949, columns (f), (g), and (h). Also, include the amount of the 50% exclusion as a gain on line 2 of the *28% Rate Gain Worksheet* (include ⅔ of the exclusion if a 60% exclusion was claimed; ⅓ of the exclusion if a 75% exclusion was claimed).

   Gain from an installment sale of QSB stock. If all payments are not received in the year of sale, a sale of QSB stock that is not traded on an established securities market generally is treated as an installment sale and is reported on Form 6252. Part or all of any gain from the sale that is reported on Form 6252 for the current year may be eligible for the section 1202 exclusion. In column (a) of Form 8949, Part II, enter the name of the corporation whose stock was sold. In column (f), enter "Q" and in column (g) enter the amount of the allowable exclusion as a negative number. See the Instructions for Form 8949, columns (f), (g), and (h). Also, include the amount of the 50% exclusion as a gain on line 2 of the *28% Rate Gain Worksheet* (include ⅔ of the exclusion if a 60% exclusion was claimed; ⅓ of the exclusion if a 75% exclusion was claimed).

   Alternative minimum tax. You must enter 7% of the estate's or trust's allowable exclusion for the year on line 9 of Schedule I (Form 1041).

Rollover of gain from QSB stock. If the estate or trust held QSB stock (as defined earlier) for more than 6 months, it may elect to postpone gain if it purchased other QSB stock during the 60-day period that began on the date of the sale.

   The estate or trust must recognize gain to the extent the sale proceeds exceed the cost of the replacement stock. Reduce the basis of the replacement stock by any postponed gain.

   The estate or trust must make the election no later than the due date (including extensions) for filing Form 1041 for the tax year in which the stock was sold. If the original Form 1041 was filed on time, the election may be made on an amended return filed no later than

6 months after the due date of the original return (excluding extensions). Write "Filed pursuant to section 301.9100-2" at the top of the amended return, and file it at the same address used for the original Form 1041.

How to report. To make the election, report the sale on Part I or Part II of Form 8949 (depending on how long the estate or trust owned the stock), as it would be reported if the election was not made. Then enter "R" in column (f) and the amount of the postponed gain from the section 1045 rollover as a negative number in column (g). Complete all remaining columns. See the Instructions for Form 8949, columns (f), (g), and (h).

Rollover of gain from empowerment zone assets. If the estate or trust sold a qualified empowerment zone asset that the estate or trust held for more than 1 year, it may be able to elect to postpone part or all of the gain that it would otherwise include in income. If the election is made, the gain on the sale generally is recognized only to the extent, if any, that the amount realized on the sale exceeds the cost of qualified empowerment zone assets (replacement property) the estate or trust purchased during the 60-day period beginning on the date of the sale.

See sections 1397B and 1397C for the definition of empowerment zone and enterprise zone business and for details regarding the rules that apply to this election.

How to report. Report the sale on Part II of Form 8949 as the estate or trust otherwise would if it were not making the election. Enter "R" in column (f). Enter the amount of the postponed gain as a negative number in column (g). Put it in parentheses to show it is negative. See the instructions for Form 8949, columns (f), (g), and (h). Complete all remaining columns.

Exclusion of gain from DC Zone assets or qualified community assets. If the estate or trust sold or exchanged a District of Columbia Enterprise Zone asset or a qualified community asset that it held for more than 5 years, it may be able to exclude the amount of qualified capital gain that it would otherwise include in income. The exclusion of gain from DC Zone assets applies to an interest in, or property of, certain businesses operating in the District of Columbia. See section 1400B for more details on this exclusion. The exclusion of gain from qualified community assets applies to an interest

in, or property of, certain renewal community businesses. See section 1400F for more details on this exclusion.

How to report. Report the sale or exchange of a "DC Zone asset" or "qualified community asset" on Form 8949, Part II, with the appropriate box checked, as it would be reported if the exclusion was not taken. Enter "X" in column (f) and the amount of the allowable exclusion as a negative number in column (g). Put the amount in column (g) in parentheses to show it is negative. Complete all remaining columns. See the Instructions for Form 8949, columns (f), (g), and (h).

Specific Instructions

 The instructions below assume the estate or trust is a cash basis calendar year taxpayer.

Rounding Off Whole Dollars

You can round off cents to whole dollars on your Schedule D (Form 1041). If you do round to whole dollars, you must round all amounts. To round, drop amounts under 50 cents and increase amounts from 50 to 99 cents to the next dollar. For example, $1.39 becomes $1 and $2.50 becomes $3.

If you have to add two or more amounts to figure the amount to enter on a line, include cents when adding the amounts and round off only the total.

Lines 1a and 8a—Transactions Not Reported on Form 8949

The estate or trust can report on line 1a (for short-term transactions) or line 8a (for long-term transactions) the aggregate totals from any transactions (except sales of collectibles) for which:
• The estate or trust received a Form 1099-B (or substitute statement) that shows basis was reported to the IRS and does not show any adjustments in box 1g, and
• The estate or trust does not need to make any adjustments to the basis or type of gain or loss (short term or long term) reported on Form 1099-B (or substitute statement), or to its gain or loss.

See *How To Complete Form 8949, Columns (f) and (g),* in the Form 8949 instructions for details about possible adjustments to your gain or loss.

If the estate or trust chooses to report these transactions on lines 1a and 8a, do not report them on Form 8949. You

do not need to attach a statement to explain the entries on lines 1a and 8a.

Figure gain or loss on each line. First, subtract the cost or other basis in column (e) from the proceeds (sales price) in column (d). Enter the gain or loss in column (h). Enter negative amounts in parentheses.

Example 1 – basis reported to the IRS. The estate or trust received a Form 1099-B reporting the sale of stock held for 3 years. It shows proceeds (in box 1d) of $6,000 and cost or other basis (in box 1e) of $2,000. Box 3 is checked, meaning that basis was reported to the IRS. The estate or trust does not need to make any adjustments to the amounts reported on Form 1099-B or enter any codes. This was the estate or trust's only 2014 transaction. Instead of reporting this transaction on Form 8949, the estate or trust can enter $6,000 on Schedule D, line 8a, column (d), $2,000 in column (e), and $4,000 ($6,000 – $2,000) in column (h).

If you had a second transaction that was the same except that the proceeds were $5,000 and the basis was $3,000, combine the two transactions. Enter $11,000 ($6,000 + $5,000) on Schedule D, line 8a, column (d); $5,000 ($2,000 + $3,000) in column (e); and $6,000 ($11,000 – $5,000) in column (h).

Example 2 – basis not reported to the IRS. The estate or trust received a Form 1099-B showing proceeds (in box 1d) of $6,000 and cost or other basis (in box 1e) of $2,000. Box 3 is not checked, meaning that basis was not reported to the IRS. Do not report this transaction on line 1a or line 8a. Instead, report the transaction on Form 8949. Complete all necessary pages of Form 8949 before completing line 1b, 2, 3, 8b, 9, or 10 of Schedule D (Form 1041).

Example 3 – adjustment. The estate or trust received a Form 1099-B showing proceeds (in box 1d) of $6,000 and cost or other basis (in box 1e) of $2,000. Box 3 is checked, meaning that basis was reported to the IRS. However, the basis shown in box 1e is incorrect. Do not report this transaction on line 1a or line 8a. Instead, report the transaction on Form 8949. See the instructions for Form 8949, columns (f), (g), and (h). Complete all necessary pages of Form 8949 before completing line 1b, 2, 3, 8b, 9, or 10 of Schedule D (Form 1041).

Lines 1b, 2, 3, 8b, 9, and 10, Column (h)—Transactions Reported on Form 8949

Figure gain or loss on each line. First, subtract the cost or other basis in column (e) from the proceeds (sales price) in column (d). Then combine the result with any adjustments in column (g). Enter the gain or loss in column (h). Enter negative amounts in parentheses.

Example 1 – gain. Column (d) is $6,000 and column (e) is $2,000. Enter $4,000 in column (h).

Example 2 – loss. Column (d) is $6,000 and column (e) is $8,000. Enter ($2,000) in column (h).

Example 3 – adjustment. Column (d) is $6,000, column (e) is $2,000, and column (g) is ($1,000). Enter $3,000 ($6,000 – $2,000 – $1,000) in column (h).

Lines 4 and 11

Undistributed capital gains. Include on line 11, column (h), the amount from box 1a of Form 2439. This amount represents the estate's or trust's share of undistributed long-term capital gains from a regulated investment company (mutual fund) or real estate investment trust.

If there is an amount in box 1b of Form 2439, include that amount on line 11 of the *Unrecaptured Section 1250 Gain Worksheet*, later, if you are required to complete line 18b, column (2) of the schedule. If there is an amount in box 1c of Form 2439, see *Exclusion of Gain on Qualified Small Business (QSB) Stock (Section 1202)*, earlier. If there is an amount in box 1d of Form 2439, include that amount on line 4 of the *28% Rate Gain Worksheet.*

Enter on Form 1041, line 24f , the tax paid as reported in box 2 of Form 2439. Increase the basis of the stock by the excess of the amount included in income over the amount of the credit for tax paid. See Pub. 550 for more details.

Installment sales. If the estate or trust sold property (other than publicly traded stocks or securities) at a gain during the tax year and will receive a payment in a later tax year, you generally report the sale on the installment method and file Form 6252, unless you elect not to do so.

Also, use Form 6252 to report any payment received in 2014 from a sale made in an earlier tax year that was reported on the installment method.

To elect out of the installment method, report the full amount of the gain on Form 8949 on a timely filed return (including extensions) for the year of the sale. If the original return was filed timely, the election may be made on an amended return filed no later than 6 months after the due date of the original return (*excluding* extensions). Write "Filed pursuant to section 301.9100-2" at the top of the amended return, and file it at the same address as the original Form 1041.

Exchange of "like-kind" property. Generally, no gain or loss is recognized when property held for productive use in a trade or business or for investment is exchanged solely for property of a like kind to be held either for productive use in a trade or business or for investment. However, if a trust exchanges like-kind property with a related person (see *Related Persons*, earlier) and within 2 years of the last transfer that was part of the exchange, the related person disposes of the property, or the trust disposes of the property received in exchange from the related person, then the original exchange will not qualify for nonrecognition. See section 1031(f) for exceptions.

Complete and attach Form 8824 to Form 1041 for each exchange.

Line 13—Capital Gain Distributions

Enter as a long-term capital gain on line 13, column (h), the total capital gain distributions paid during the year, regardless of how long the estate or trust held its investment. This amount is reported in box 2a of Form 1099-DIV. If there is an amount in box 2b, include that amount on line 11 of the *Unrecaptured Section 1250 Gain Worksheet*, later, if the worksheet is required. If there is an amount in box 2c, see *Exclusion of Gain on Qualified Small Business (QSB) Stock (Section 1202)*, earlier. If there is an amount in box 2d of Form 1099-DIV, include the amount on line 4 of the *28% Rate Gain Worksheet.*

Line 17, Column (1)—Beneficiaries' Net Short-Term Capital Gain or Loss

Enter the amount of net short-term capital gain or loss allocable to the beneficiary or beneficiaries. Include only those short-term capital losses that are taken into account in determining the amount of gain from the sale or exchange of capital assets that is paid, credited, or required to be distributed to any beneficiary during the tax year. See

Regulations section 1.643(a)-3 for more information about allocation of capital gains and losses.

If the losses from the sale or exchange of capital assets are more than the gains, the net loss must be allocated to the estate or trust and not to the beneficiaries.

Line 17, Column (2)—Estate's or Trust's Net Short-Term Capital Gain or Loss

Enter the amount of the net short-term capital gain or loss allocable to the estate or trust. Include any capital gain paid or permanently set aside for a charitable purpose specified in section 642(c).

Line 17, Column (3)—Total

Enter the total of the amounts entered in columns (1) and (2). The amount in column (3) should be the same as the amount on line 7.

Line 18a—Net Long-Term Capital Gain or Loss

Allocate the net long-term capital gain or loss on line 18a in the same manner as the net short-term capital gain or loss on line 17. However, do not take the section 1202 exclusion on gain from the sale or exchange of qualified small business stock into account when figuring net long-term capital gain or loss allocable to the beneficiaries.

Line 18b—Unrecaptured Section 1250 Gain

Complete the *Unrecaptured Section 1250 Gain Worksheet*, later, if any of the following apply.

• During the tax year, the estate or trust sold or otherwise disposed of section 1250 property (generally, real property that was depreciated) held more than 1 year.

• The estate or trust received installment payments during the tax year for section 1250 property held more than 1 year and is reporting gain on the installment method.

• The estate or trust received a Schedule K-1 from an estate or trust, partnership, or S corporation that reports "unrecaptured section 1250 gain" for the tax year.

• The estate or trust received a Form 1099-DIV or Form 2439 from a real estate investment trust or regulated investment company (including a mutual fund) that reports "unrecaptured section 1250 gain" for the tax year.

• The estate or trust reported a long-term capital gain from the sale or

Unrecaptured Section 1250 Gain Worksheet—Line 18b

Keep for Your Records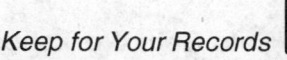

> **If the estate or trust is not reporting a gain on Form 4797, line 7, skip lines 1 through 9 and go to line 10.**

1. If the estate or trust has a section 1250 property in Part III of Form 4797 for which you made an entry in Part I of Form 4797 (but not on Form 6252), enter the **smaller** of line 22 or line 24 of Form 4797 for that property. If the estate or trust did not have any such property, go to line 4. If it had more than one such property, see instructions .... **1.** _____

2. Enter the amount from Form 4797, line 26g, for the property for which you made an entry on line 1 .... **2.** _____

3. Subtract line 2 from line 1 .... **3.** _____

4. Enter the total unrecaptured section 1250 gain included on line 26 or line 37 of Form(s) 6252 from installment sales of trade or business property held more than 1 year (see instructions) .... **4.** _____

5. Enter the total of any amounts reported to the estate or trust on a Schedule K-1 from a partnership or an S corporation as "unrecaptured section 1250 gain" .... **5.** _____

6. Add lines 3 through 5 .... **6.** _____

7. Enter the **smaller** of line 6 or the gain from Form 4797, line 7 .... **7.** _____

8. Enter the amount, if any, from Form 4797, line 8 .... **8.** _____

9. Subtract line 8 from line 7. If zero or less, enter -0- .... **9.** _____

10. Enter the amount of any gain from the sale or exchange of an interest in a partnership attributable to unrecaptured section 1250 gain (see instructions) .... **10.** _____

11. Enter the total of any amounts reported to the estate or trust on a Schedule K-1, Form 1099-DIV, or Form 2439 as "unrecaptured section 1250 gain" from an estate, trust, real estate investment trust, or mutual fund (or other regulated investment company) .... **11.** _____

12. Enter the total of any unrecaptured section 1250 gain from sales (including installment sales) or other dispositions of section 1250 property held more than 1 year for which you did not make an entry in Part I of Form 4797 for the year of sale (see instructions) .... **12.** _____

13. Add lines 9 through 12 .... **13.** _____

14. If the estate or trust had any section 1202 gain or collectibles gain or (loss), enter the total of lines 1 through 4 of the *28% Rate Gain Worksheet.* Otherwise, enter -0- .... **14.** _____

15. Enter the (loss), if any, from Schedule D, line 7. If Schedule D, line 7, is zero or a gain, enter -0- .... **15.** (_____)

16. Enter the estate's or trust's long-term capital loss carryovers from Schedule D, line 15, and from Schedule K-1 (Form 1041), box 11, code C, from another estate or trust .... **16.** (_____)

17. Combine lines 14 through 16. If the result is a (loss), enter it as a positive amount. If the result is zero or a gain, enter -0- .... **17.** _____

18. **Unrecaptured section 1250 gain.** Subtract line 17 from line 13. If zero or less, enter -0-. Enter the result here and in the appropriate columns of Schedule D, line 18b .... **18.** _____

---

exchange of an interest in a partnership that owned section 1250 property.

Instructions for the Unrecaptured Section 1250 Gain Worksheet

Lines 1 through 3. If the estate or trust had more than one property, complete lines 1 through 3 for each property on a separate worksheet. Next, enter the total amount for all properties on line 3, then go to line 4.

Line 4. To figure the amount to enter on line 4, follow the steps below for each installment sale of trade or business property held more than 1 year.

Step 1. Figure the smaller of (a) the depreciation allowed or allowable or (b) the total gain for the sale. This is the smaller of line 22 or line 24 of the 2014 Form 4797 (or the comparable lines of Form 4797 for the year of sale) for that property.

Step 2. Reduce the amount figured in step 1 by any section 1250 ordinary income recapture for the sale. This is the amount from line 26g of the 2014 Form 4797 (or the comparable line of Form 4797 for the year of sale) for that property. The result is the total unrecaptured section 1250 gain that must be allocated to the installment payments received from the sale.

Step 3. Generally, the amount of section 1231 gain on each installment payment is treated as unrecaptured section 1250 gain until the total unrecaptured section 1250 gain figured in step 2 has been used in full. Figure the amount of gain treated as unrecaptured section 1250 gain for installment payments received during the tax year as the smaller of (a) the amount from line 26 or line 37 of the 2014 Form 6252, whichever applies, or (b) the amount of unrecaptured section 1250 gain remaining to be reported. This amount is generally the total

unrecaptured section 1250 gain for the sale reduced by all gain reported in prior years (excluding section 1250 ordinary income recapture). However, if you chose not to treat all of the gain from payments received after May 6, 1997, and before August 24, 1999, as unrecaptured section 1250 gain, use only the amount you chose to treat as unrecaptured section 1250 gain for those payments to reduce the total unrecaptured section 1250 gain remaining to be reported for the sale. Include this amount on line 4.

Line 10. Include on line 10 the estate's or trust's share of the partnership's unrecaptured section 1250 gain that would result if the partnership had transferred all of its section 1250 property in a fully taxable transaction immediately before the estate or trust sold or exchanged its interest in that partnership. If the estate or trust recognized less than all of the realized gain, the partnership will be treated as

1. Enter the total of all collectibles gain or (loss) from items reported on Form 8949, Part II . . . .   **1.** _____

2. Enter as a positive number the total of:

    - Any section 1202 exclusion you reported in column (g) of Form 8949, Part II, with code "Q" in column (f), for which you excluded 50% of the gain;

    - ⅔ of any section 1202 exclusion you reported in column (g) of Form 8949, Part II, with code "Q" in column (f), for which you excluded 60% of the gain; and   . . . .   **2.** _____

    - ⅓ of any section 1202 exclusion you reported in column (g) of Form 8949, Part II, with code "Q" in column (f), for which you excluded 75% of the gain.

3. Enter the total of all collectibles gain or (loss) from Form 4684, line 4 (but only if Form 4684, line 15 is more than zero); Form 6252; Form 6781, Part II; and Form 8824 . . . .   **3.** _____

4. Enter the total of any collectibles gain reported to the estate or trust on:

    - Form 1099-DIV, box 2d;

    - Form 2439, box 1d; and   . . . .   **4.** _____

    - Schedule K-1 from a partnership, S corporation, estate, or trust.

5. Enter the estate's or trust's long-term capital loss carryovers from Schedule D, line 15, and from box 11, code C of Schedule K-1 (Form 1041) from another estate or trust . . . .   **5.** (_____)

6. If Schedule D, line 7 is a (loss), enter that (loss) here. Otherwise, enter -0- . . . .   **6.** (_____)

7. Combine lines 1 through 6. If zero or less, enter -0-. If more than zero, also enter this amount in the appropriate columns of Schedule D, line 18c . . . .   **7.** _____

---

having transferred only a proportionate amount of each section 1250 property.

Line 12. An example of an amount reported on line 12 as an "other disposition" includes unrecaptured section 1250 gain from the sale of a vacation home previously used as a rental property that was converted to personal use before the sale. To figure the amount to enter on line 12, follow the applicable instructions below.

Installment sales. To figure the amount to include on line 12, follow the steps below for each installment sale of property held more than 1 year for which you did not make an entry in Part I of Form 4797 for the year of sale.

Step 1. Figure the smaller of (a) the depreciation allowed or allowable or (b) the total gain for the sale. This is the smaller of line 22 or line 24 of the 2014 Form 4797 (or comparable lines of Form 4797 for the year of sale) for that property.

Step 2. Reduce the amount figured in step 1 by any section 1250 ordinary income recapture for the sale. This is the amount from line 26g of the 2014 Form 4797 (or the comparable line of Form 4797 for the year of sale) for that property. The result is the total unrecaptured section 1250 gain that must be allocated to the installment payments received from the sale.

Step 3. Generally, the amount of capital gain on each installment payment is treated as unrecaptured section 1250 gain until the total unrecaptured section 1250 gain figured in step 2 has been used in full. Figure the amount of gain treated as unrecaptured section 1250 gain for installment payments received during the tax year as the smaller of (a) the amount from line 26 or line 37 of the 2014 Form 6252, whichever applies, or (b) the amount of unrecaptured section 1250 gain remaining to be reported. This amount is generally the total unrecaptured section 1250 gain for the sale reduced by all gain reported in prior years (excluding section 1250 ordinary income recapture). However, if you chose not to treat all of the gain from payments received after May 6, 1997, and before August 24, 1999, as unrecaptured section 1250 gain, use only the amount you chose to treat as unrecaptured section 1250 gain for those payments to reduce the total unrecaptured section 1250 gain remaining to be reported for the sale. Include this amount on line 12.

Other sales or dispositions of section 1250 property. For each sale of property held more than 1 year (for which an entry was not made in Part I of Form 4797), figure the smaller of (a) the depreciation allowed or allowable or (b) the total gain for the sale. This amount is the smaller of line 22 or line 24 of Form

4797 for that property. Then, reduce that amount by any section 1250 ordinary income recapture for the sale. This is the amount from line 26g of Form 4797 for that property. The result is the total unrecaptured section 1250 gain for the sale. Include this amount on line 12.

Line 18c—28% Rate Gain

Complete the *28% Rate Gain Worksheet,* earlier, if lines 18a and 19 of column (3) are both greater than zero and at least one of the following applies:

- The estate or trust reported in Part II of Form 8949 a section 1202 exclusion from the eligible gain on qualified small business stock (as discussed earlier), or

- The estate or trust reported in Part II of Form 8949 a collectibles gain or loss.

A collectibles gain or loss is any long-term gain or deductible long-term loss from the sale or exchange of a collectible that is a capital asset.

Collectibles include works of art, rugs, antiques, metals (such as gold, silver, and platinum bullion), gems, stamps, coins, alcoholic beverages, and certain other tangible property.

Also include gain (but not loss) from the sale or exchange of an interest in a partnership, S corporation, or trust held for more than 1 year that is attributable to the unrealized appreciation of collectibles. For details, see Regulations section 1.1(h)-1. Attach the statement required under Regulations section 1.1(h)-1(e) to Schedule D.

Capital Loss Carryover Worksheet

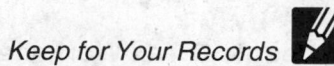 *Keep for Your Records*

Use this worksheet to figure the estate's or trust's capital loss carryovers from 2014 to 2015 if Schedule D, line 20 is a loss and (a) the loss on Schedule D, line 19, col. (3) is more than $3,000 or (b) Form 1041, page 1, line 22 is a loss.

1. Enter taxable income or (loss) from Form 1041, line 22 .... 1. _____

2. Enter the loss from line 20 of Schedule D as a positive amount .... 2. _____

3. Enter amount from Form 1041, line 20 .... 3. _____

4. Adjusted taxable income. Combine lines 1, 2, and 3. If zero or less, enter -0- .... 4. _____

5. Enter the **smaller** of line 2 or line 4 .... 5. _____

   Note: *If line 7 of Schedule D is a loss, go to line 6; otherwise, enter -0- on line 6 and go to line 10.*

6. Enter loss from Schedule D, line 7 as a positive amount .... 6. _____

7. Enter gain, if any, from Schedule D, line 16. If that line is blank or shows a loss, enter -0- .... 7. _____

8. Add lines 5 and 7 .... 8. _____

9. **Short-term capital loss carryover to 2015.** Subtract line 8 from line 6. If zero or less, enter -0-. If this is the final return of the estate or trust, also enter on Schedule K-1 (Form 1041), box 11, using code B .... 9. _____

   Note: *If line 16 of Schedule D is a loss, go to line 10; otherwise, skip lines 10 through 14.*

10. Enter loss from Schedule D, line 16, as a positive amount .... 10. _____

11. Enter gain, if any, from Schedule D, line 7. If that line is blank or shows a loss, enter -0- .... 11. _____

12. Subtract line 6 from line 5. If zero or less, enter -0- .... 12. _____

13. Add lines 11 and 12 .... 13. _____

14. **Long-term capital loss carryover to 2015.** Subtract line 13 from line 10. If zero or less, enter -0-. If this is the final return of the estate or trust, also enter on Schedule K-1 (Form 1041), box 11, using code C .... 14. _____

Part IV—Capital Loss Limitation

If the sum of all capital losses is more than the sum of all capital gains, the capital losses are allowed as a deduction, but only to the extent of the smaller of the net loss or $3,000.

For any year (including the final year) in which capital losses exceed capital gains, the estate or trust may have a capital loss carryover. Use the *Capital Loss Carryover Worksheet*, earlier, to figure any capital loss carryover. A capital loss carryover may be carried forward indefinitely. Capital losses keep their character as either short-term or long-term when carried over to the following year.

Part V—Tax Computation Using Maximum Capital Gains Rates

Line 26

If the estate or trust received qualified dividends or capital gains as income in respect of a decedent and a section 691(c) deduction was claimed, you must reduce the amount on Form 1041, page 1, line 2b(2), or Schedule D, line 22, (line 7 of the Schedule D Tax Worksheet, if applicable) by the portion of the section 691(c) deduction claimed on Form 1041, page 1, line 19, that is attributable to the estate's or trust's portion of qualified dividends or capital gains.

Line 45

If the tax using the maximum capital gains rates is less than the regular tax, enter the amount from line 45 on line 1a of Schedule G, Form 1041.

Schedule D Tax Worksheet

If you completed the *Schedule D Tax Worksheet* instead of Part V of Schedule D, be sure to enter the amount from line 44 of the worksheet on line 1a of Schedule G, Form 1041.

Schedule D Tax Worksheet

Complete this worksheet only if:
- On Schedule D, line 18b, column (2), **or** line 18c, column (2), is more than zero, **or**
- Both line 2b(1) of Form 1041 **and** line 4g of Form 4952 are more than zero.

Exception: Do not use this worksheet to figure the estate's or trust's tax if line 18a, column (2), or line 19, column (2), of Schedule D or Form 1041, line 22 is zero or less; instead, see the Instructions for Form 1041, Schedule G, line 1a.

1. Enter the estate's or trust's taxable income from Form 1041, line 22	1. _____
2. Enter qualified dividends, if any, from Form 1041, line 2b(2) . . . . 2. _____	
3. Enter the amount from Form 4952, line 4g . . . . 3. _____	
4. Enter the amount from Form 4952, line 4e* . . . . 4. _____	
5. Subtract line 4 from line 3. If zero or less, enter -0- . . . . 5. _____	
6. Subtract line 5 from line 2. If zero or less, enter -0- . . . . 6. _____	
7. Enter the **smaller** of line 18a, col. (2) or line 19, col. (2) from Sch. D . . . . 7. _____	
8. Enter the **smaller** of line 3 or line 4 . . . . 8. _____	
9. Subtract line 8 from line 7. If zero or less, enter -0- . . . . 9. _____	
10. Add lines 6 and 9	10. _____
11. Add lines 18b, column (2) and 18c, column (2) from Schedule D	11. _____
12. Enter the **smaller** of line 9 or line 11	12. _____
13. Subtract line 12 from line 10.	13. _____
14. Subtract line 13 from line 1. If zero or less, enter -0-.	14. _____
15. Enter the **smaller** of line 1 or $2,500 . . . . 15. _____	
16. Enter the **smaller** of line 14 or line 15 . . . . 16. _____	
17. Subtract line 10 from line 1. If zero or less, enter -0- . . . . 17. _____	
18. Enter the **larger** of line 16 or line 17 . . . . ▶ 18. _____	
19. Subtract line 16 from line 15. This amount is taxed at 0% . . . . ▶ 19. _____	
If lines 1 and 15 are the same, skip lines 20 through 40 and go to line 41. Otherwise, go to line 20.	
20. Enter the **smaller** of line 1 or line 13	20. _____
21. Enter the amount from line 19 (if line 19 is blank, enter -0-)	21. _____
22. Subtract line 21 from line 20. If zero or less, enter -0- . . . . ▶ 22. _____	
23. Enter the **smaller** of line 1 or $12,150 . . . . 23. _____	
24. Add lines 18 and 19 . . . . 24. _____	
25. Subtract line 24 from line 23. If zero or less, enter -0- . . . . 25. _____	
26. Enter the **smaller** of line 22 or line 25 . . . . ▶ 26. _____	
27. Multiply line 26 by 15%	27. _____
28. Reserved . . . . 28. ▓▓▓▓▓	
29. Add lines 19 and 26 . . . . 29. _____	
If lines 1 and 29 are the same, skip lines 30 through 40 and go to line 41. Otherwise, go to line 30	
30. Subtract line 29 from line 20. If zero or less, enter -0- . . . . ▶ 30. _____	
31. Multiply line 30 by 20%	31. _____
32. Enter the **smaller** of line 9 (above) or line 18b, col. (2) (from Schedule D) . . . . 32. _____	
33. Add lines 10 and 18 . . . . 33. _____	
34. Enter the amount from line 1 above . . . . 34. _____	
35. Subtract line 34 from line 33. If zero or less, enter -0- . . . . 35. _____	
36. Subtract line 35 from line 32. If zero or less, enter -0- . . . . ▶ 36. _____	
37. Multiply line 36 by 25% (.25)	37. _____
If Schedule D, line 18c, column (2) is zero or blank, skip lines 38 through 40 and go to line 41. Otherwise, go to line 38.	
38. Add lines 18, 19, 26, 30, and 36 . . . . 38. _____	
39. Subtract line 38 from line 1 . . . . 39. _____	
40. Multiply line 39 by 28% (.28)	40. _____
41. Figure the tax on the amount on line 18. Use the 2014 Tax Rate Schedule in the Instructions for Form 1041	41. _____
42. Add lines 27, 31, 37, 40 and 41	42. _____
43. Figure the tax on the amount on line 1. Use the 2014 Tax Rate Schedule in the Instructions for Form 1041	43. _____
44. **Tax on all taxable income (including capital gains and qualified dividends).** Enter the **smaller** of line 42 or line 43 here **and** on Form 1041, Schedule G, line 1a	44. _____

*If applicable, enter instead the smaller amount entered on the dotted line next to line 4e of Form 4952.

SCHEDULE I (Form 1041)

Alternative Minimum Tax—Estates and Trusts

OMB No. 1545-0092

2014

Department of the Treasury
Internal Revenue Service

▶ Attach to Form 1041.
▶ Information about Schedule I (Form 1041) and its separate instructions is at *www.irs.gov/form1041.*

Name of estate or trust	Employer identification number

Part I — Estate's or Trust's Share of Alternative Minimum Taxable Income

1	Adjusted total income or (loss) (from Form 1041, line 17)	1	
2	Interest	2	
3	Taxes	3	
4	Miscellaneous itemized deductions (from Form 1041, line 15c)	4	
5	Refund of taxes	5	( )
6	Depletion (difference between regular tax and AMT)	6	
7	Net operating loss deduction. Enter as a positive amount	7	
8	Interest from specified private activity bonds exempt from the regular tax	8	
9	Qualified small business stock (see instructions)	9	
10	Exercise of incentive stock options (excess of AMT income over regular tax income)	10	
11	Other estates and trusts (amount from Schedule K-1 (Form 1041), box 12, code A)	11	
12	Electing large partnerships (amount from Schedule K-1 (Form 1065-B), box 6)	12	
13	Disposition of property (difference between AMT and regular tax gain or loss)	13	
14	Depreciation on assets placed in service after 1986 (difference between regular tax and AMT)	14	
15	Passive activities (difference between AMT and regular tax income or loss)	15	
16	Loss limitations (difference between AMT and regular tax income or loss)	16	
17	Circulation costs (difference between regular tax and AMT)	17	
18	Long-term contracts (difference between AMT and regular tax income)	18	
19	Mining costs (difference between regular tax and AMT)	19	
20	Research and experimental costs (difference between regular tax and AMT)	20	
21	Income from certain installment sales before January 1, 1987	21	( )
22	Intangible drilling costs preference	22	
23	Other adjustments, including income-based related adjustments	23	
24	Alternative tax net operating loss deduction (See the instructions for the limitation that applies.)	24	( )
25	Adjusted alternative minimum taxable income. Combine lines 1 through 24	25	

Note: *Complete Part II below before going to line 26.*

26	Income distribution deduction from Part II, line 44	26	
27	Estate tax deduction (from Form 1041, line 19)	27	
28	Add lines 26 and 27	28	
29	Estate's or trust's share of alternative minimum taxable income. Subtract line 28 from line 25	29	

If line 29 is:

• $23,500 or less, stop here and enter -0- on Form 1041, Schedule G, line 1c. The estate or trust is not liable for the alternative minimum tax.

• Over $23,500, but less than $172,250, go to line 45.

• $172,250 or more, enter the amount from line 29 on line 51 and go to line 52.

Part II — Income Distribution Deduction on a Minimum Tax Basis

30	Adjusted alternative minimum taxable income (see instructions)	30	
31	Adjusted tax-exempt interest (other than amounts included on line 8)	31	
32	Total net gain from Schedule D (Form 1041), line 19, column (1). If a loss, enter -0-	32	
33	Capital gains for the tax year allocated to corpus and paid or permanently set aside for charitable purposes (from Form 1041, Schedule A, line 4)	33	
34	Capital gains paid or permanently set aside for charitable purposes from gross income (see instructions)	34	
35	Capital gains computed on a minimum tax basis included on line 25	35	( )
36	Capital losses computed on a minimum tax basis included on line 25. Enter as a positive amount	36	
37	Distributable net alternative minimum taxable income (DNAMTI). Combine lines 30 through 36. If zero or less, enter -0-	37	
38	Income required to be distributed currently (from Form 1041, Schedule B, line 9)	38	
39	Other amounts paid, credited, or otherwise required to be distributed (from Form 1041, Schedule B, line 10)	39	
40	Total distributions. Add lines 38 and 39	40	
41	Tax-exempt income included on line 40 (other than amounts included on line 8)	41	
42	Tentative income distribution deduction on a minimum tax basis. Subtract line 41 from line 40	42	

For Paperwork Reduction Act Notice, see the Instructions for Form 1041.   Cat. No. 51517Q   Schedule I (Form 1041) (2014)

Part II	Income Distribution Deduction on a Minimum Tax Basis *(continued)*				
43	Tentative income distribution deduction on a minimum tax basis. Subtract line 31 from line 37. If zero or less, enter -0-		**43**		
44	**Income distribution deduction on a minimum tax basis.** Enter the smaller of line 42 or line 43. Enter here and on line 26		**44**		

Part III	Alternative Minimum Tax				
45	Exemption amount		**45**	$23,500	00
46	Enter the amount from line 29	**46**			
47	Phase-out of exemption amount	**47**	$78,250	00	
48	Subtract line 47 from line 46. If zero or less, enter -0-	**48**			
49	Multiply line 48 by 25% (.25)		**49**		
50	Subtract line 49 from line 45. If zero or less, enter -0-		**50**		
51	Subtract line 50 from line 46		**51**		
52	Go to Part IV of Schedule I to figure line 52 if the estate or trust has qualified dividends or has a gain on lines 18a and 19 of column (2) of Schedule D (Form 1041) (as refigured for the AMT, if necessary). Otherwise, if line 51 is— • $182,500 or less, multiply line 51 by 26% (.26). • Over $182,500, multiply line 51 by 28% (.28) and subtract $3,650 from the result		**52**		
53	Alternative minimum foreign tax credit (see instructions)		**53**		
54	Tentative minimum tax. Subtract line 53 from line 52		**54**		
55	Enter the tax from Form 1041, Schedule G, line 1a (minus any foreign tax credit from Schedule G, line 2a)		**55**		
56	**Alternative minimum tax.** Subtract line 55 from line 54. If zero or less, enter -0-. Enter here and on Form 1041, Schedule G, line 1c		**56**		

Part IV	Line 52 Computation Using Maximum Capital Gains Rates				
	Caution: *If you did not complete Part V of Schedule D (Form 1041), the Schedule D Tax Worksheet, or the Qualified Dividends Tax Worksheet in the Instructions for Form 1041, see the instructions before completing this part.*				
57	Enter the amount from line 51		**57**		
58	Enter the amount from Schedule D (Form 1041), line 26, line 13 of the Schedule D Tax Worksheet, or line 4 of the Qualified Dividends Tax Worksheet in the Instructions for Form 1041, whichever applies (as refigured for the AMT, if necessary)	**58**			
59	Enter the amount from Schedule D (Form 1041), line 18b, column (2) (as refigured for the AMT, if necessary). If you did not complete Schedule D for the regular tax or the AMT, enter -0-	**59**			
60	If you did not complete a Schedule D Tax Worksheet for the regular tax or the AMT, enter the amount from line 58. Otherwise, add lines 58 and 59 and enter the **smaller** of that result or the amount from line 10 of the Schedule D Tax Worksheet (as refigured for the AMT, if necessary) . .	**60**			
61	Enter the **smaller** of line 57 or line 60		**61**		
62	Subtract line 61 from line 57		**62**		
63	If line 62 is $182,500 or less, multiply line 62 by 26% (.26). Otherwise, multiply line 62 by 28% (.28) and subtract $3,650 from the result . . . . ▶		**63**		
64	Maximum amount subject to the 0% rate	**64**	$2,500	00	
65	Enter the amount from line 27 of Schedule D (Form 1041), line 14 of the Schedule D Tax Worksheet, or line 5 of the Qualified Dividends Tax Worksheet in the Instructions for Form 1041, whichever applies (as figured for the regular tax). If you did not complete Schedule D or either worksheet for the regular tax, enter the amount from Form 1041, line 22; if zero or less, enter -0-	**65**			
66	Subtract line 65 from line 64. If zero or less, enter -0-	**66**			
67	Enter the **smaller** of line 57 or line 58	**67**			
68	Enter the **smaller** of line 66 or line 67. This amount is taxed at 0% . .	**68**			
69	Subtract line 68 from line 67	**69**			

Part IV	Line 52 Computation Using Maximum Capital Gains Rates *(continued)*					

70	Maximum amount subject to rates below 20%	**70**	$12,150	00		
71	Enter the amount from line 66	**71**				
72	Enter the amount from line 27 of Schedule D (Form 1041), line 18 of the Schedule D Tax Worksheet, or line 5 of the Qualified Dividends Tax Worksheet, whichever applies (as figured for the regular tax). If you did not complete Schedule D or either worksheet for the regular tax, enter the amount from Form 1041, line 22; if zero or less, enter -0- ▶	**72**				
73	Add line 71 and line 72	**73**				
74	Subtract line 73 from line 70. If zero or less, enter -0-	**74**				
75	Enter the **smaller** of line 69 or 74	**75**				
76	Multiply line 75 by 15% (.15) . . . . ▶				**76**	
77	Add lines 68 and 75	**77**				
	If lines 77 and 57 are the same, skip lines 78 through 82 and go to line 83. Otherwise, go to line 78.					
78	Subtract line 77 from line 67	**78**				
79	Multiply line 78 by 20% (.20) . . . . ▶				**79**	
	If line 59 is zero or blank, skip lines 80 through 82 and go to line 83. Otherwise, go to line 80.					
80	Add lines 62, 77, and 78	**80**				
81	Subtract line 80 from line 57	**81**				
82	Multiply line 81 by 25% (.25) . . . . ▶				**82**	
83	Add lines 63, 76, 79, and 82				**83**	
84	If line 57 is $182,500 or less, multiply line 57 by 26% (.26). Otherwise, multiply line 57 by 28% (.28) and subtract $3,650 from the result				**84**	
85	Enter the **smaller** of line 83 or line 84 here and on line 52				**85**	

2014

Department of the Treasury
Internal Revenue Service

Instructions for Schedule I (Form 1041)

Alternative Minimum Tax—Estates and Trusts

Section references are to the Internal Revenue Code unless otherwise noted.

Future Developments

For the latest information about developments related to Schedule I and its instructions, such as legislation enacted after they were published, go to www.irs.gov/form1041.

What's New

AMT tax brackets. The threshold for the 28% AMT tax bracket increased to amounts over $182,500.

AMT exemption amount and phase-out. The AMT exemption amount increased to $23,500. The exemption amount begins to be phased-out at amounts over $78,250 and is completely phased-out at $172,250.

Capital gains and qualified dividends. For tax year 2014, the 20% maximum capital gains rate applies to estates and trusts with income above $12,150. The 0% and 15% rates continue to apply to certain threshold amounts. The 0% rate applies to amounts up to $2,500. The 15% rate applies to amounts over $2,500 and up to $12,150.

General Instructions

Purpose of Schedule

Use Schedule I (Form 1041) to figure:
- The estate's or trust's alternative minimum taxable income;
- The income distribution deduction on a minimum tax basis; and
- The estate's or trust's alternative minimum tax (AMT).

Who Must Complete Schedule I (Form 1041)

- Complete Parts I and II if the estate or trust is required to complete Form 1041, Schedule B, Income Distribution Deduction.
- Complete Schedule I if the estate's or trust's share of alternative minimum taxable income (Part I, line 29) exceeds $23,500.

- Complete Schedule I if the estate or trust claims any general business credit and line 6 of Part I or line 3 of Part III of Form 3800, General Business Credit, is more than zero.

Recordkeeping

Schedule I contains adjustments and tax preference items that are treated differently for regular tax and AMT purposes. If you, as fiduciary for the estate or trust, completed a form to figure an item for regular tax purposes, you may have to complete it a second time for AMT purposes. Generally, the difference between the amounts on the two forms is the AMT adjustment or tax preference item to enter on Schedule I. Except for Form 1116, Foreign Tax Credit (Individual, Estate, or Trust), any additional form completed for AMT purposes does not have to be filed with Form 1041.

For regular tax purposes, some deductions and credits may result in carrybacks or carryforwards to other tax years. Examples are investment interest expense, a net operating loss deduction (NOLD), a capital loss, and the foreign tax credit. Because these items may be refigured for the AMT, the carryback or carryforward amount may be different for regular and AMT purposes. Therefore, you should keep records of these different carryforward and carryback amounts for the AMT and regular tax. The AMT carryforward will be important in completing Schedule I for 2015.

Credit for Prior Year Minimum Tax

Estates and trusts that paid AMT in 2013, or had a minimum tax credit carryforward from the 2013 Form 8801, Credit for Prior Year Minimum Tax—Individuals, Estates, and Trusts, may be eligible for a minimum tax credit in 2014. See Form 8801.

Partners and Shareholders

An estate or trust that is a partner in a partnership or a shareholder in an S corporation must take into account its share of items of income and deductions that enter into the

computation of its adjustments and tax preference items.

Allocation of Deductions to Beneficiaries

The distributable net alternative minimum taxable income (DNAMTI) of the estate or trust does not include amounts of depreciation, depletion, and amortization that are allocated to the beneficiaries, just as the distributable net income of the estate or trust does not include these items for regular tax purposes.

Report separately in box 12 of Schedule K-1 (Form 1041), Beneficiary's Share of Income, Deductions, Credits, etc., any adjustments or tax preference items attributable to accelerated depreciation (code G), depletion (code H), and amortization (code I) that were allocated to the beneficiaries.

Optional Write-Off for Certain Expenditures

There is no AMT adjustment for the following items if the estate or trust elects to deduct them ratably over the period of time shown for the regular tax.
- Circulation expenditures—3 years (section 173).
- Research and experimental expenditures—10 years (section 174(a)).
- Intangible drilling costs—60 months (section 263(c)).
- Mining exploration and development costs—10 years (sections 616(a) and 617(a)).

The election must be made in the year the expenditure was made and may be revoked only with IRS consent. See section 59(e) and Regulations section 1.59-1 for more details.

Specific Instructions

Part I—Estate's or Trust's Share of Alternative Minimum Taxable Income

Line 2—Interest

In determining the alternative minimum taxable income, qualified residence interest (other than qualified housing interest defined in section 56(e)) is not allowed.

If you completed Form 4952, Investment Interest Expense Deduction, for regular tax purposes, you may have an adjustment on this line. Refigure your investment interest expense on a separate AMT Form 4952 as follows.

Step 1. On line 1 of the AMT Form 4952, follow the instructions for that line, but also include the following amounts.
• Any qualified residence interest (other than qualified housing interest) that was paid or accrued on a loan or part of a loan that is allocable to property held for investment as defined in section 163(d)(5) (for example, interest on a home equity loan whose proceeds were invested in stocks or bonds).
• Any interest that would have been deductible if interest on specified private activity bonds had been included in income. See the instructions for line 8 for the definition of specified private activity bonds.

Step 2. On line 2, enter the AMT disallowed investment interest expense from 2013.

Step 3. When completing Part II of the AMT Form 4952, refigure gross income from property held for investment, any net gain from the disposition of property held for investment, net capital gain from the disposition of property held for investment, and any investment expenses, taking into account all AMT adjustments and tax preference items that apply. Include any interest income and investment expenses from private activity bonds issued after August 7, 1986.

When completing line 4g of the AMT Form 4952, enter the smaller of:
• The amount from line 4g of the regular tax Form 4952, or
• The total of lines 4b and 4e of the AMT Form 4952.

Step 4. Complete Part III.

Enter on Schedule I, line 2 the difference between line 8 of the AMT Form 4952 and line 8 of the regular tax Form 4952. If the AMT deduction is greater, enter the difference as a negative amount.

Line 3—Taxes

Enter any state, local, or foreign real property taxes; state or local personal property taxes; state and local general sales taxes; and any state, local, or foreign income taxes that were included on Form 1041, page 1, line 11.

Line 5—Refund of Taxes

Enter any refunds received in 2014 of taxes described for line 3 above and included in income.

Line 6—Depletion

Refigure the depletion deduction for AMT purposes by using only the income and deductions allowed for the AMT when refiguring the limit based on taxable income from the property under section 613(a) and the limit based on taxable income, with certain adjustments, under section 613A(d)(1). Also, the depletion deduction for mines, wells, and other natural deposits under section 611 is limited to the property's adjusted basis at the end of the year, as refigured for the AMT, unless the estate or trust is an independent producer or royalty owner claiming percentage depletion for oil and gas wells. Figure this limit separately for each property. When refiguring the property's adjusted basis, take into account any AMT adjustments made this year or in previous years that affect basis (other than the current year's depletion).

Enter on line 6 the difference between the regular tax and AMT deduction. If the AMT deduction is more than the regular tax deduction, enter the difference as a negative amount.

Line 7—Net Operating Loss Deduction

Enter any NOLD from line 15b of page 1 of the Form 1041 as a positive amount.

Line 8—Interest From Specified Private Activity Bonds Exempt From the Regular Tax

Enter the interest earned from specified private activity bonds reduced (but not below zero) by any deduction that would have been allowable if the interest were includible in gross income for regular tax purposes. Each payer of this type of interest should send a Form 1099-INT, Interest Income, to the estate or trust showing the amount of this interest in box 9. Generally, specified private activity bonds are any qualified bonds (as defined in section 141) issued after August 7, 1986, and before 2009 or after 2010, the interest on which is not includible in gross income for the regular tax. See section 57(a)(5) for more information.

Do not include interest on qualified Gulf Opportunity Zone bonds described in section 1400N(a) or qualified Midwestern disaster area bonds.

Exempt-interest dividends paid by a regulated investment company are treated as interest from specified private activity bonds to the extent the dividends are attributable to interest on the bonds received by the company, minus an allocable share of the expenses paid or incurred by the company in earning the interest. This amount should also be reported to the estate or trust on Form 1099-DIV in box 11.

Line 9—Qualified Small Business Stock

If the estate or trust claimed the exclusion under section 1202 for gain on qualified small business stock held more than 5 years, multiply the excluded gain (as shown on Form 8949 in column (g)) by 7% (.07). Enter the result on line 9 as a positive amount.

Line 10—Exercise of Incentive Stock Options

For regular tax purposes, no income is recognized when an incentive stock option (as defined in section 422(b)) is exercised. However, this rule does not apply for AMT purposes. Instead, the estate or trust must generally include on line 10 the excess, if any, of:

1. The fair market value (FMV) of the stock acquired through exercise of the option (determined without regard to any lapse restriction) when its rights in the acquired stock first become transferable or when these rights are no longer subject to a substantial risk of forfeiture, over

2. The amount paid for the stock, including any amount paid for the option used to acquire the stock.

 Even if the estate's or trust's rights in the stock are not transferable and are subject to a substantial risk of forfeiture, you may elect to include in AMT income the excess of the stock's FMV (determined without regard to any lapse restriction) over the exercise price upon the transfer to the estate or trust of the stock acquired through exercise of the option. See section 83(b) for more details. The

election must be made no later than 30 days after the date of transfer.

If the estate or trust acquired stock by exercising an option and it disposed of that stock in the same year, the tax treatment under the regular tax and the AMT is the same, and no adjustment is required.

Increase the AMT basis of any stock acquired through the exercise of an incentive stock option by the amount of the adjustment.

Note. If a Form 3921, Exercise of an Incentive Stock Option Under Section 422(b), was received, it may help you figure the adjustment.

Line 11—Other Estates and Trusts

If the estate or trust is the beneficiary of another estate or trust, enter the adjustment for minimum tax purposes from box 12, code A, Schedule K-1 (Form 1041).

Line 12—Electing Large Partnerships

If the estate or trust is a partner in an electing large partnership, enter on line 12 the amount from Schedule K-1 (Form 1065-B), Partner's Share of Income (Loss) From an Electing Large Partnership, box 6. Take into account any amount from Schedule K-1 (Form 1065-B), box 5, when figuring the amount to enter on line 15.

Line 13—Disposition of Property

Use this line to report any AMT adjustment related to the disposition of property resulting from refiguring:

1. Gain or loss from the sale, exchange, or involuntary conversion of property reported on Form 4797, Sales of Business Property;

2. Casualty gain or loss to business or income-producing property reported on Form 4684, Casualties and Thefts;

3. Ordinary income from the disposition of property not taken into account in 1 or 2 above or on any other line on Schedule I, such as a disqualifying disposition of stock acquired in a prior year by exercising an incentive stock option; and

4. Capital gain or loss (including any carryover that is different for the AMT) reported on Form 8949, Sales and Other Dispositions of Capital Assets, or Schedule D (Form 1041), Capital Gains and Losses.

 The $3,000 capital loss limitation for the regular tax applies separately for the AMT.

First, figure any ordinary income adjustment related to 3 above. Then, refigure Form 4684, Form 4797, Form 8949, and Schedule D (Form 1041) for the AMT, if applicable, by taking into account any adjustments you made this year or in previous years that affect the estate's or trust's basis or otherwise result in a different amount for AMT. If the estate or trust has a capital loss after refiguring Schedule D for the AMT, apply the $3,000 capital loss limitation separately to the AMT loss. For each of the four items listed above, figure the difference between the amount included in taxable income for the regular tax and the amount included in income for the AMT. Treat the difference as a negative amount if (a) both the AMT and regular tax amounts are zero or more and the AMT amount is less than the regular tax amount or (b) the AMT amount is a loss, and the regular tax amount is a smaller loss, or zero or more.

Enter on line 13 the combined adjustments for the four items earlier.

Line 14—Depreciation on Assets Placed in Service After 1900

This section describes when depreciation must be refigured for the AMT and how to figure the amount to enter on line 14.

Do not include on this line any depreciation adjustment from:
- An activity for which the estate or trust is not at risk or income or loss from a partnership or an S corporation if the basis limitations under section 704(d) or 1366(d) apply. Take this adjustment into account on line 16;
- A tax shelter farm activity. Take this adjustment into account on line 23; or
- A passive activity. Take this adjustment into account on line 15.

What depreciation must be refigured for the AMT? Generally, you must refigure depreciation for the AMT, including depreciation allocable to inventory costs, for:
- Property placed in service after 1998 that is depreciated for the regular tax using the 200% declining balance method (generally 3-, 5-, 7-, or 10-year property under the modified accelerated cost recovery system (MACRS)),
- Section 1250 property placed in service after 1998 that is not depreciated for the regular tax using the straight line method, and

- Tangible property placed in service after 1986 and before 1999. If the transitional election was made under section 203(a)(1)(B) of the Tax Reform Act of 1986, this rule applies to property placed in service after July 31, 1986.

What depreciation is not refigured for the AMT? Do not refigure depreciation for the AMT for the following items.
- Residential rental property placed in service after 1998.
- Nonresidential real property with a class life of 27.5 years or more placed in service after 1998 that is depreciated for the regular tax using the straight line method.
- Other section 1250 property placed in service after 1998 that is depreciated for the regular tax using the straight line method.
- Property (other than section 1250 property) placed in service after 1998 that is depreciated for the regular tax using the 150% declining balance method or the straight line method.
- Property for which you elected to use the alternative depreciation system (ADS) of section 168(g) for the regular tax.
- Qualified property that is or was eligible for the special depreciation allowance if the depreciable basis of the property for the AMT is the same as for the regular tax. This applies to any special depreciation allowance, including those for qualified disaster assistance property, qualified reuse and recycling property, qualified cellulosic biofuel plant property, qualified New York Liberty Zone property, qualified Gulf Opportunity Zone property, and Kansas disaster area qualified recovery assistance property. The special allowance is deductible for the AMT, and there also is no adjustment required for any depreciation figured on the remaining basis of the qualified property if the depreciable basis of the property for the AMT is the same as for the regular tax. Property for which an election is in effect to not have the special allowance apply is not qualified property.
- Motion picture films, videotapes, or sound recordings.
- Property depreciated under the unit-of-production method or any other method not expressed in a term of years.
- Qualified Indian reservation property.
- A natural gas gathering line placed in service after April 11, 2005.

How is depreciation refigured for the AMT? See methods below.

Property placed in service before 1999. Refigure depreciation for the AMT using ADS with the same convention used for the regular tax. See the table below for the method and recovery period to use.

Property Placed in Service Before 1999	
IF the property is...	**THEN use the...**
Section 1250 property.	Straight line method over 40 years.
Tangible property (other than section 1250 property) depreciated using straight line for the regular tax.	Straight line method over the property's AMT class life.
Any other tangible property.	150% declining balance method, switching to straight line the first tax year it gives a larger deduction, over the property's AMT class life.

Property placed in service after 1998. Use the same convention and recovery period used for the regular tax. For property other than section 1250 property, use the 150% declining balance method, switching to straight line the first tax year it gives a larger deduction. For section 1250 property, use the straight line method.

How is the AMT class life determined? The class life used for the AMT is not necessarily the same as the recovery period used for the regular tax. The class lives for the AMT are listed in Rev. Proc. 87-56, 1987-2 C.B. 674, and in Pub. 946, How To Depreciate Property. Use 12 years for any tangible personal property not assigned a class life.

 See Pub. 946 for optional tables that can be used to figure AMT depreciation. Rev. Proc. 89-15, 1989-1 C.B. 816, has special rules for short tax years and for property disposed of before the end of the recovery period.

How is the line 14 adjustment figured? Subtract the AMT deduction for depreciation from the regular tax deduction and enter the result. If the AMT deduction is more than the regular tax deduction, enter the difference as a negative amount.

In addition to the AMT adjustment to your deduction for depreciation, you must also adjust the amount of depreciation that was capitalized, if any, to account for the difference between the rules for the regular tax and the AMT. Include on this line the current year adjustment to taxable income, if any, resulting from the difference.

Line 15—Passive Activities

 Do not enter again elsewhere on this schedule any AMT adjustment or tax preference item included on this line.

For AMT purposes, the rules described in section 469 apply, except that in applying the limitations, minimum tax rules apply.

Refigure passive activity gains and losses on an AMT basis. Refigure a passive activity gain or loss by taking into account all AMT adjustments or tax preference items that pertain to that activity.

You may complete a second Form 8582, Passive Activity Loss Limitations, to determine the passive activity losses allowed for AMT purposes, but do not send this AMT Form 8582 to the IRS.

Enter the difference between the loss reported for regular tax purposes and the AMT loss, if any.

 The amount of any passive activity loss that is not deductible (and is therefore carried forward) for AMT purposes is likely to differ from the amount (if any) that is carried forward for regular tax purposes. Therefore, it is essential that you retain adequate records for both AMT and regular tax purposes.

Publicly traded partnerships (PTPs). If the estate or trust had a loss from a PTP, refigure the loss using any AMT adjustments, tax preference items, and any AMT prior year unallowed loss.

Line 16—Loss Limitations

 If the loss is from a passive activity, use line 15 instead. If the loss is from a tax shelter farm activity (that is not passive), use line 23.

Refigure your allowable losses for AMT purposes from activities for which you are not at risk and basis limitations applicable to interests in partnerships and stock in S corporations by taking into account your AMT adjustments and tax preference items. See sections 59(h), 465, 704(d), and 1366(d).

Enter the difference between the loss reported for regular tax purposes and the AMT loss. If the AMT loss is more than the loss reported for regular tax purposes, enter the adjustment as a negative amount.

Line 17—Circulation Costs

 Do not make this adjustment for expenditures for which you elected the optional 3-year write-off period for regular tax purposes.

Circulation expenditures deducted under section 173(a) for regular tax purposes must be amortized for AMT purposes over 3 years beginning with the year the expenditures were paid or incurred.

Enter the difference between the regular tax and AMT deduction. If the AMT deduction is greater, enter the difference as a negative amount.

If the estate or trust had a loss on property for which circulation expenditures have not been fully amortized for the AMT, the AMT deduction is the smaller of (a) the amount of the loss allowable for the expenditures had they remained capitalized or (b) the remaining expenditures to be amortized for the AMT.

Line 18—Long-Term Contracts

For AMT purposes, the percentage of completion method of accounting described in section 460(b) generally must be used. However, this rule does not apply to any home construction contract (as defined in section 460(e)(6)).

Note. Contracts described in section 460(e)(1)(B) are subject to the simplified method of cost allocation of section 460(b)(4).

Enter the difference between the AMT and regular tax income. If the AMT income is smaller, enter the difference as a negative amount.

Line 19—Mining Costs

 Do not make this adjustment for costs for which you elected the optional 10-year write-off period under section 59(e) for regular tax purposes.

Expenditures for the development or exploration of a mine or certain other mineral deposits (other than an oil, gas, or geothermal well) deducted under sections 616(a) and 617(a) for regular tax purposes must be amortized for AMT purposes over 10 years beginning with the year the expenditures were paid or incurred.

Enter the difference between the amount allowed for AMT purposes and the amount allowed for regular tax purposes. If the amount allowed for AMT purposes exceeds the amount deducted for regular tax purposes, enter the difference as a negative amount.

If the estate or trust had a loss on property for which mining expenditures have not been fully amortized for the AMT, the AMT deduction is the smaller of (a) the amount of the loss allowable for the expenditures had they remained capitalized or (b) the remaining expenditures to be amortized for the AMT.

Line 20—Research and Experimental Costs

 Do not make this adjustment for costs paid or incurred in connection with an activity in which the estate or trust materially participated under the passive activity rules or for costs for which you elected the optional 10-year write-off for research and experimental expenditures under section 59(e) for regular tax purposes.

Research and experimental expenditures deducted under section 174(a) for regular tax purposes generally must be amortized for AMT purposes over 10 years beginning with the year the expenditures were paid or incurred.

Enter the difference between the amount allowed for AMT purposes and the amount allowed for regular tax purposes. If the amount for AMT purposes exceeds the amount allowed for regular tax purposes, enter the difference as a negative amount.

If the estate or trust had a loss on property for which research and experimental costs have not been fully amortized for the AMT, the AMT deduction is the smaller of (a) the loss allowable for the costs had they remained capitalized or (b) the remaining costs to be amortized for the AMT.

Line 21—Income From Certain Installment Sales Before January 1, 1987

The installment method does not apply for AMT purposes to any nondealer disposition of property that occurred after August 16, 1986, but before the first day of your tax year that began in 1987, if an installment obligation to which the proportionate disallowance rule applied arose from the disposition.

Enter on line 21 the amount of installment sale income that was reported for regular tax purposes.

Line 22—Intangible Drilling Costs Preference (IDCs)

 Do not make this adjustment for costs for which you elected the optional 60-month write-off under section 59(e) for regular tax purposes.

IDCs from oil, gas, and geothermal wells are a preference to the extent that the excess IDCs exceed 65% of the net income from the wells. Figure the preference for all oil and gas properties separately from the preference for all geothermal properties.

Figure excess IDCs as follows:

1. Determine the amount of the estate's or trust's IDCs allowed for the regular tax under section 263(c), but do not include any section 263(c) deduction for nonproductive wells, then

2. Subtract the amount that would have been allowed had you amortized these IDCs over a 120-month period starting with the month the well was placed in production.

 Cost depletion can be substituted for the amount allowed using amortization over 120 months.

Net income. Determine net income by reducing the gross income that the estate or trust received or accrued during the tax year from all oil, gas, and geothermal wells by the deductions allocable to those wells (reduced by the excess IDCs). When refiguring net income, use only income and deductions allowed for the AMT.

Exception. The preference for IDCs from oil and gas wells does not apply to taxpayers who are independent producers (that is, not integrated oil companies as defined in section 291(b)(4)). However, this benefit may be limited. First, figure the IDC preference as if this exception did not apply. For purposes of this exception, complete and combine lines 1 through 23, including the IDC preference. If the amount of the IDC preference exceeds 40% of the total of lines 1 through 23, enter the excess on line 22 (the benefit of this exception is limited). Otherwise, do not enter an amount on line 22 (the estate's or trust's benefit from this exception is not limited).

Line 23—Other Adjustments

Enter on line 23 the total of any other adjustments that apply including the following.

• **Depreciation figured using pre-1987 rules.** For AMT purposes, use the straight line method to figure depreciation on real property. Use a recovery period of 19 years for 19-year real property and 15 years for low-income housing. Enter the excess of depreciation claimed for regular tax purposes over depreciation refigured using the straight line method. Figure this amount separately for each property and include on line 23 only positive amounts.

For leased personal property other than recovery property, enter the amount by which the regular tax depreciation using the pre-1987 rules exceeds the depreciation allowable using the straight line method. For leased 10-year recovery property and leased 15-year public utility property, enter the amount by which the depreciation deduction determined for regular tax purposes is more than the deduction allowable using the straight line method with a half-year convention, no salvage value, and a recovery period of 15 years (22 years for 15-year public utility property). Figure this amount separately for each property and include on line 23 only positive amounts.

• **Patron's adjustment.** Distributions the estate or trust received from a cooperative may be includible in income. Unless the distributions are nontaxable, include on line 23 the total AMT patronage dividend adjustment reported to the estate or trust from the cooperative.

• **Amortization of pollution control facilities.** The amortization deduction under section 169 must be refigured for the AMT. For facilities placed in service after 1986 and before 1999, figure the amortization deduction for the AMT using the ADS described in section 168(g). For facilities placed in service after 1998, figure the AMT deduction under MACRS using the straight line method. Enter the difference between the regular tax and AMT deduction. If the AMT amount is greater, enter the difference as a negative amount.

• **Tax shelter farm activities.** Figure this adjustment only if the tax shelter farm activity (as defined in section 58(a)(2)) is not a passive activity. If the activity is passive, include it with any other passive activities on line 15.

Refigure all gains and losses reported for the regular tax from tax shelter farm activities by taking into account any AMT adjustments and preferences. Determine tax shelter farm activity gain or loss for the AMT using the same rules used for the regular tax with the following modifications. No refigured loss is allowed, except to the extent an estate or trust is insolvent (see section 58(c)(1)). A refigured loss may not be used in the current tax year to offset gains from other tax shelter farm activities. Instead, any refigured loss must be suspended and carried forward indefinitely until (a) the estate or trust has a gain in a subsequent tax year from the same activity or (b) the activity is disposed of.

The AMT amount of any tax shelter farm activity loss that is not deductible and is carried forward is likely to differ from the regular tax amount. Keep adequate records for both the AMT and regular tax.

Enter the difference between the amount that would be reported for the activity on Schedule E (Form 1040), Supplemental Income and Loss, or Schedule F (Form 1040), Profit or Loss From Farming, for the AMT and the regular tax amount. If (a) the AMT loss is more than the regular tax loss, (b) the AMT gain is less than the regular tax gain, or (c) there is an AMT loss and a regular tax gain, then enter the adjustment as a negative amount.

Enter any adjustment for amounts reported on Form 8949, Schedule D (Form 1041), Form 4684, or Form 4797 for the activity on line 13 instead of line 23.

- **Biofuel producer credit and biodiesel and renewable diesel fuels credit.** If the adjusted total income (Form 1041, line 17) includes the amount of the biofuel producer credit or biodiesel and renewable diesel fuels credit, include that amount as a negative amount on line 23.

- **Related adjustments.** AMT adjustments and tax preference items may affect deductions that are based on an income limit other than adjusted gross income (AGI) or modified AGI (for example, farm conservation expenses). Refigure these deductions using the income limit as modified for the AMT. Include the difference between the regular tax and AMT deduction on line 23. If the AMT deduction is more than the regular tax deduction, include the difference as a negative amount.

 Do not make an adjustment on line 23 for an item you refigured on another line of Schedule I (for example, line 6).

Line 24—Alternative Tax Net Operating Loss Deduction

The ATNOLD is the sum of the alternative tax net operating loss (ATNOL) carryovers and carrybacks to the tax year, subject to the limitation explained below.

The net operating loss (NOL) under section 172(c) is modified for alternative tax purposes by (a) taking into account the adjustments made under sections 56 and 58 and (b) reducing the NOL by any item of tax preference under section 57. For an estate or trust that held a residual interest in a real estate mortgage investment conduit (REMIC), figure the ATNOLD without regard to any excess inclusion.

If this estate or trust is the beneficiary of another estate or trust that terminated in 2014, include any ATNOL carryover that was reported in box 11, code E of Schedule K-1 (Form 1041).

The estate's or trust's ATNOLD may be limited. To figure the ATNOLD limitation, first figure alternative minimum taxable income (AMTI) without regard to the ATNOLD and any domestic production activities deduction. For this purpose, figure a tentative amount for line 6 of Schedule I (Form 1041) by treating line 24 as if it were zero. Then, figure a tentative total by combining lines 1–23 of Schedule I (Form 1041) using the line 6 tentative amount. Add any domestic production activities deduction to this tentative total. The ATNOLD limitation is 90% of the result.

However, the 90% limit does not apply to an ATNOL that is attributable to qualified disaster losses (as defined in section 172(j)), qualified Gulf Opportunity Zone losses as defined in section 1400N(k)(2), qualified recovery assistance losses (as defined in Pub. 4492-A, Information for Taxpayers Affected by the May 4, 2007, Kansas Storms and Tornadoes), qualified disaster recovery assistance losses (as defined in Pub. 4492-B, Information for Affected Taxpayers in the Midwestern Disaster Areas) or a 2008 or 2009 loss that you elected to carryback more than 2 years under section 172(b)(1)(H). If an ATNOL that is carried back or carried forward to a tax year is attributable to any of those losses, the ATNOLD for the tax year is limited to the sum of:

1. The smaller of:

a. The sum of the ATNOL carrybacks and carryforwards to the tax year attributable to NOLs other than the losses described in 2a below, or

b. 90% of AMTI for the tax year (figured without regard to the ATNOLD and any domestic production activities deduction, as discussed earlier), plus

2. The smaller of:

a. The sum of the ATNOL carrybacks and carryforwards to the tax year attributable to qualified disaster losses, qualified Gulf Opportunity Zone losses, qualified recovery assistance losses, qualified disaster recovery assistance losses, and any 2008 or 2009 loss that you elected to carry back more than 2 years under section 172(b) (1)(H), or

b. 100% of AMTI for the tax year (figured without regard to the ATNOLD and any domestic production activities deduction, as discussed earlier) reduced by the amount determined under 1, above.

Enter on line 24 the smaller of the ATNOLD or the ATNOLD limitation.

Any ATNOL not used may be carried back 2 years or forward up to 20 years. In some cases, the carryback period is longer than 2 years; for details, see Pub. 536, Net Operating Losses (NOLs) for Individuals, Estates, and Trusts.

The treatment of ATNOLs does not affect your regular tax NOL.

 If you elected under section 172(b)(3) to forego the carryback period for regular tax purposes, the election will also apply for the AMT.

Line 29—Estate's or Trust's Share of Alternative Minimum Taxable Income

For an estate or trust that held a residual interest in a REMIC, line 29 may not be less than the estate's or trust's share of the amount on Schedule E (Form 1040), line 38, column (c). If that amount is larger than the amount you would otherwise enter on line 29, enter that amount instead and write "Sch. Q" on the dotted line next to line 29.

Part II—Income Distribution Deduction on a Minimum Tax Basis

Line 30—Adjusted Alternative Minimum Taxable Income

Generally, enter on line 30, Schedule I, the amount from line 25, Schedule I. However, if Form 1041, page 1, line 4 and line 25 are losses, enter on line 30 the smaller of those losses. If Form 1041, line 4 is zero or a gain and line 25 is a loss, enter zero on line 30.

Line 31—Adjusted Tax-Exempt Interest

To figure the adjusted tax-exempt interest (including exempt-interest dividends received as a shareholder in a mutual fund or other regulated investment company), subtract the total of any:

1. Tax-exempt interest from Form 1041, Schedule A, line 2 figured for AMT purposes, and

2. Section 212 expenses allowable for AMT purposes allocable to tax-exempt interest, from the amount of tax-exempt interest received.

Do not subtract any deductions reported on lines 2 through 4, Schedule I (Form 1041).

Section 212 expenses that are directly allocable to tax-exempt interest are allocated only to tax-exempt interest. A reasonable proportion of section 212 expenses that are indirectly allocable to both tax-exempt interest and other income must be allocated to each class of income.

Line 33

Reduce the amount on line 33 by any allocable section 1202 exclusion (as refigured for AMT purposes).

Line 34

Enter any capital gains that were paid or permanently set aside for charitable purposes from the current year's income included on line 1 of Form 1041, Schedule A. Reduce the amount on line 34 by any allocable section 1202 exclusion (as refigured for AMT purposes).

Lines 35 and 36

Capital gains and losses must take into account any basis adjustments from line 13, Part I of Form 1041 (Schedule I).

Line 41—Adjustment for Tax-Exempt Income

In figuring the income distribution deduction on a minimum tax basis, the estate or trust is not allowed a deduction for any item of DNAMTI (line 37) that is not included in the gross income of the estate or trust figured on an AMT basis. Thus, for purposes of figuring the allowable income distribution deduction on a minimum tax basis, the DNAMTI is figured without regard to any tax-exempt interest (except for amounts from line 8).

If tax-exempt interest is the only tax-exempt income included in the total distributions (line 40), and the DNAMTI (line 37) is less than or equal to line 40, then enter on line 41 the amount from line 31.

If tax-exempt interest is the only tax-exempt income included in the total distributions (line 40), and the DNAMTI is more than line 40 (that is, the estate or trust made a distribution that is less than the DNAMTI), then figure the adjustment by multiplying line 31 by a fraction, the numerator of which is the total distributions (line 40), and the denominator of which is the DNAMTI (line 37). Enter the result on line 41.

If line 40 includes tax-exempt income other than tax-exempt interest (except for amounts from line 8), figure line 41 by subtracting the total expenses allocable to tax-exempt income that are allowable for AMT purposes from tax-exempt income included on line 40.

Expenses that are directly allocable to tax-exempt income are allocated only to tax-exempt income. A reasonable proportion of expenses indirectly allocable to both tax-exempt income and other income must be allocated to each class of income.

Line 44—Income Distribution Deduction on a Minimum Tax Basis

Allocate the income distribution deduction figured on a minimum tax basis among the beneficiaries in the same manner as income was allocated for regular tax purposes. You need the allocated income distribution deduction figured on a minimum tax basis to figure the beneficiary's adjustment for minimum tax purposes, as explained under *Box 12—Alternative minimum tax (AMT) items* in the Schedule K-1 instruction section of the Instructions for Form 1041 and Schedules A, B, G, J, and K-1.

Part III—Alternative Minimum Tax Computation

Line 53—Alternative Minimum Foreign Tax Credit

 To see if you need to figure the estate's or trust's AMT foreign tax credit, fill in line 55 of Schedule I as instructed. If the amount on line 55 is greater than or equal to the amount on line 52, the estate or trust does not owe the AMT. Enter zero on line 56 and see Who Must Complete *earlier to find out if you must file Schedule I with Form 1041. However, even if the estate or trust does not owe AMT, you may need to complete line 53 to see if you have an AMT foreign tax credit carryback or carryforward to other tax years.*

To figure the AMT foreign tax credit, follow the steps discussed below.

Step 1. Complete and attach a separate AMT Form 1116, with the notation at the top "Alt Min Tax" for each separate limitation category specified at the top of Form 1116.

Note. When applying the separate limitation categories, use the applicable AMT rate instead of the regular tax rate to determine if any income is "high-taxed."

Step 2. If you (on behalf of the estate or trust) previously made or are making the *Simplified limitation election* (as discussed later), skip Part I and enter on the AMT Form 1116, line 17, the same amount you entered on that line for the regular tax. If you did not complete Form 1116 for the regular tax and you previously made or are making the simplified limitation election (on behalf of the estate or trust), complete Part I and lines 15 through 17 of the AMT Form 1116 using regular tax amounts.

If the election does not apply, complete Part I, using only income and deductions allowed for the AMT that are attributable to sources outside the United States. If the estate or trust has any foreign source qualified dividends or foreign source capital gains or losses, use the instructions under *Step 3* to determine whether you must make adjustments to those amounts before you include the amounts on line 1a or line 5 of the AMT Form 1116.

Step 3. Follow the instructions below, if applicable, to determine the amount of foreign source qualified dividends and foreign source capital gains and losses to include on line 1a and line 5 of the AMT Form 1116.

Foreign qualified dividends. You must adjust the estate's or trust's foreign source qualified dividends before you include those amounts on line 1a of the AMT Form 1116 if:
- Line 62 of Schedule I (Form 1041) is greater than zero,
- Line 83 of Schedule I (Form 1041) is smaller than line 84, and
- The exception for foreign qualified dividends below does not apply.

But, you do not need to make any adjustments if:
- The estate or trust qualifies for the adjustment exception under *Qualified Dividends Tax Worksheet (Estates and Trusts)* or *Schedule D Filers* in the Instructions for Form 1116 and
- Line 62 of Schedule I (Form 1041) is not more than $182,500.

Note. Use the estate's or trust's capital gains and losses as refigured for the AMT to determine whether your total amounts are less than the $20,000 threshold under the adjustment exception.

To adjust foreign source qualified dividends, multiply the estate's or trust's foreign source qualified dividends in each separate category by 0.5357 if the foreign source qualified dividends are taxed at a rate of 15%. Include the results on line 1a of the AMT Form 1116.

If they are taxed at a rate of 20%, multiply your foreign source qualified dividends in each separate category by 0.7143. Include the results on line 1a of the AMT Form 1116.

You adjust the estate's or trust's foreign source qualified dividends taxed at the 0% rate by **not** including them on line 1a of Form 1116. Amounts taxed at the 0% rate are on line 8 of the Qualified Dividends Tax Worksheet in the Instructions for Form 1041, line 30 of Schedule D (Form 1041), or line 19 of the Schedule D Tax Worksheet in the Instructions for Schedule D (Form 1041).

 Do not adjust the amount of any foreign source qualified dividends you elected to include on line 4g of the AMT Form 4952.

Foreign capital gains or losses. If any capital gain or loss from U.S. or foreign sources is different for the AMT, use the refigured amounts to complete this step.

To figure the adjustment for the estate's or trust's foreign source capital gains or losses, you must first determine whether you can use *Worksheet A* or *Worksheet B* in the Instructions for Form 1116. Otherwise, you must use the instructions for *Capital Gains and Losses* in Pub. 514, Foreign Tax Credit for Individuals, to figure the adjustments you must make to the estate's or trust's foreign source capital gains and losses.

Use Worksheet A if the estate or trust has foreign source capital gains or losses in no more than two separate categories, and any of the following apply.
- You were not required to make adjustments to the estate's or trust's foreign source qualified dividends under the rules described earlier (or if the estate or trust had foreign source qualified dividends, you would not have been required to make those adjustments).
- Schedule D (Form 1041), line 18a, column (2) or line 19, column (2), as refigured for the AMT if necessary, is zero or a loss.
- On the AMT Schedule D Tax Worksheet for Form 1041, a) line 17 is zero, b) line 9 is zero, or c) line 42 is equal to or greater than line 43.
- On the AMT Part V of Schedule D (Form 1041), a) line 22 of that AMT Part V minus the amount on Form 4952, line 4e, that you elected to include on Form 4952, line 4g, is zero or less, b) line 27 of that AMT Part V of Schedule D (Form 1041) is zero, or c) line 43 of that AMT Part V is equal to or greater than line 44.

Use Worksheet B if you:
- Cannot use Worksheet A,
- Have foreign source capital gains and losses in no more than two separate categories,
- Did not have any item of unrecaptured section 1250 gain or any item of 28% rate gain or loss for either regular tax or AMT, and
- Did not have any capital gains taxed at a rate of 0% or 20%.

Instructions for Worksheets A and B. When you complete Worksheet A or B, use foreign source capital gains and losses as refigured for the AMT, if necessary, and do not use any foreign source capital gains that you elected to include on line 4g of the AMT Form 4952. If you must complete a Schedule D (Form 1041) for the AMT, use line 19 of that AMT Schedule D (Form 1041) to complete line 3 of Worksheet A or line 4 of the Line 2 Worksheet for Worksheet B. Use

0.5357 instead of 0.3788 to complete lines 11, 13, and 15 of Worksheet B and to complete lines 8, 11, and 17 of the Line 15 Worksheet for Worksheet B.

If the estate or trust does not qualify to use Worksheet A or Worksheet B, use the instructions for *Capital Gains and Losses* in Pub. 514 to determine the adjustments you make.

Step 4. Complete Part II and lines 9 through 14 of the AMT Form 1116. Use the estate's or trust's AMT foreign tax credit carryover, if any, on line 10.

Step 5. If the simplified limitation election does not apply, complete lines 15 through 17 of the AMT Form 1116.

Step 6. If you did not complete Part IV of Schedule I (Form 1041), enter the amount from Schedule I (Form 1041), line 29 on line 18 of the AMT Form 1116 and go to Step 7 later.

If you completed Part IV of Schedule I (Form 1041), complete an AMT Worksheet for Line 18 in the Instructions for Form 1116 to figure the amount to enter on Form 1116, line 18, if:
- Line 62 of Schedule I (Form 1041) is greater than zero, and
- Line 83 of Schedule I (Form 1041) is smaller than line 84.

But you do not need to complete the Worksheet for Line 18 if:
- The estate or trust qualifies for the adjustment exception discussed in the Instructions for Form 1116 and
- Line 62 of Schedule I (Form 1041) is not more than $182,500.

Note. Use the estate's and trust's capital gains and losses as refigured for the AMT to determine if its total amounts are less than the $20,000 threshold under the adjustment exception.

If you do not have to complete an AMT Worksheet for Line 18, enter the amount from line 29 of Schedule I on line 18 of the AMT Form 1116.

Instructions for completing an AMT Worksheet for Line 18. To complete an AMT Worksheet for Line 18 in the Instructions for Form 1116, follow these instructions.

1. Enter the amount from Schedule I (Form 1041), line 29 on line 1 of the worksheet.

2. Skip lines 2 and 3 of the worksheet.

3. Enter the amount from Schedule I (Form 1041), line 81 on line 4 of the worksheet.

4. Multiply line 4 of the worksheet by 0.1071 (instead of 0.3687) and enter the results on line 5 of the worksheet.

5. Enter the amount from Schedule I (Form 1041), line 78 on line 6 of the worksheet.

6. Multiply line 6 of the worksheet by 0.2857 (instead of 0.4949) and enter the result on line 7 of the worksheet.

7. Enter the amount from Schedule I (Form 1041), line 75 on line 8 of the worksheet.

8. Multiply line 8 of the worksheet by 0.4643 (instead of 0.6212). Enter the result on line 9 of the worksheet.

9. Enter the amount from Schedule I, line 68, on line 10 of the worksheet.

10. Complete lines 11 and 12 of the worksheet as instructed on the worksheet.

Step 7. Enter the amount from Schedule I (Form 1041), line 52 on the AMT Form 1116, line 20. Complete lines 19, 21, and 22 of the AMT Form 1116.

Step 8. Complete Part IV of the first AMT Form 1116 only.

Enter on line 53 of Schedule I the amount from line 30 of the first AMT Form 1116.

Attach to the estate's or trust's return all AMT Forms 1116 you used to figure your AMT foreign tax credit.

AMT foreign tax credit carryback and carryforward. If the AMT foreign tax credit is limited, any unused amount can be carried back or forward under section 904(c). The election to forego the carryback period for regular tax purposes also applies for the AMT.

Simplified limitation election. The estate or trust may elect to use a simplified section 904 limitation to figure its AMT foreign tax credit. To do so, use the estate's or trust's regular tax income for Form 1116, Part I, instead of refiguring the estate's or trust's foreign source income for the AMT, as described in Step 2 in the instructions for line 53, earlier. The estate or trust must make the election for the first tax year after 1997 for which it claims an AMT foreign tax credit. If it does not make the election for that year, it may not make it for a later year. Once made, the election applies to all later tax years and may be revoked only with IRS consent.

Part IV—Line 52 Computation Using Maximum Capital Gains Rates

Lines 58, 59, and 60

If you used Schedule D (Form 1041), the Schedule D Tax Worksheet in the Instructions for Schedule D (Form 1041), or the Qualified Dividends Tax Worksheet in the Instructions for Form 1041, you generally may enter the amounts as instructed on Schedule I, lines 58, 59, and 60. But do not use those amounts if any of the following apply.

1. The gain or loss from any transaction reported on Form 8949 or Schedule D (Form 1041) is different for the AMT (for example, because the AMT basis was different due to depreciation adjustments or an incentive stock option adjustment or the AMT capital loss carryover from 2013 was different).

2. You did not complete Part V of Schedule D (Form 1041), the Schedule D Tax Worksheet in the Instructions for Schedule D (Form 1041), or the Qualified Dividends Tax Worksheet in the Instructions for Form 1041 because Form 1041, line 22, was zero or less.

3. The estate or trust received a Schedule K-1 (Form 1041) that shows an amount in box 12 with code B, C, D, E, or F. If this applies, see *If the estate or trust is a beneficiary of another estate or trust*, later.

If 1 above applies, complete an AMT Form 8949. Next, if 1 or 3 applies, complete Parts I through IV of an AMT Schedule D (Form 1041) by refiguring the amounts of your gains and losses for the AMT. Then, if 1, 2, or 3 applies, complete the following lines of the applicable schedule or worksheet:

• Lines 22 through 26 of an AMT Schedule D (Form 1041),
• Lines 2 through 13 of an AMT Schedule D Tax Worksheet in the Instructions for Schedule D (Form 1041), or
• Lines 2 through 4 of a Qualified Dividends Tax Worksheet in the Instructions for Form 1041.

If you were required to complete an AMT Form 4952, use it to figure the amount to enter on line 25 of the AMT Schedule D (Form 1041), lines 3 and 4 of the AMT Schedule D Tax Worksheet in the Instructions for Schedule D (Form 1041), and line 3 of the Qualified Dividends Tax Worksheet. Use amounts from the AMT Schedule D (Form 1041), AMT Schedule D Tax Worksheet in the Instructions for Schedule D (Form 1041) or Qualified Dividends Tax Worksheet in the Instructions for Form 1041 to complete Schedule I (Form 1041), lines 58, 59, and 60. Keep the AMT Form 8949, AMT Schedule D (Form 1041) and applicable AMT worksheet for your records, but do not attach any of them to Form 1041.

 Do not decrease the estate's or trust's section 1202 exclusion by the amount, if any, included on line 9 of Schedule I (Form 1041).

If the estate or trust is a beneficiary of another estate or trust. If the estate or trust received a Schedule K-1 (Form 1041) from another estate or trust that shows an amount in box 12 with code B, C, D, E, or F, follow the instructions in the table below.

IF the code in box 12 is...	THEN include that amount in the total on...
B	line 2 of an AMT Qualified Dividends Tax Worksheet in the Instructions for Form 1041; line 23 of an AMT Schedule D (Form 1041); or line 2 of an AMT Schedule D Tax Worksheet in the Instructions for Schedule D (Form 1041), whichever applies.
C	line 5, column (h), of an AMT Schedule D (Form 1041).
D	line 12, column (h), of an AMT Schedule D (Form 1041).
E	line 11 of an AMT Unrecaptured Section 1250 Gain Worksheet in the Instructions for Schedule D (Form 1041).
F	line 4 of an AMT 28% Rate Gain Worksheet in the Instructions for Schedule D (Form 1041).

SCHEDULE J (Form 1041)	Accumulation Distribution for Certain Complex Trusts	OMB No. 1545-0092
Department of the Treasury Internal Revenue Service	► Attach to Form 1041. ► Information about Schedule J (Form 1041) and its separate instructions is at *www.irs.gov/form1041*.	2014

Name of trust — Employer identification number

Part I — Accumulation Distribution in 2014

Note: *See the Form 4970 instructions for certain income that minors may exclude and special rules for multiple trusts.*

1	Other amounts paid, credited, or otherwise required to be distributed for 2014 (from Form 1041, Schedule B, line 10)	1
2	Distributable net income for 2014 (from Form 1041, Schedule B, line 7)	2
3	Income required to be distributed currently for 2014 (from Form 1041, Schedule B, line 9)	3
4	Subtract line 3 from line 2. If zero or less, enter -0-	4
5	Accumulation distribution for 2014. Subtract line 4 from line 1	5

Part II — Ordinary Income Accumulation Distribution (Enter the applicable throwback years below.)

		Throwback year ending -----------	Throwback year ending -----------	Throwback year ending -----------	Throwback year ending -----------	Throwback year ending -----------
	Note: *If the distribution is thrown back to more than 5 years (starting with the earliest applicable tax year beginning after 1968), attach additional schedules. (If the trust was a simple trust, see Regulations section 1.665(e)-1A(b).)*					
6	Distributable net income (see the instructions)					
7	Distributions (see the instructions)					
8	Subtract line 7 from line 6 .					
9	Enter amount from page 2, line 25 or line 31, as applicable					
10	Undistributed net income Subtract line 9 from line 8 .					
11	Enter amount of prior accumulation distributions thrown back to any of these years					
12	Subtract line 11 from line 10 .					
13	Allocate the amount on line 5 to the earliest applicable year first. Do not allocate an amount greater than line 12 for the same year (see the instructions)					
14	Divide line 13 by line 10 and multiply result by amount on line 9					
15	Add lines 13 and 14 . . .					
16	Tax-exempt interest included on line 13 (see the instructions)					
17	Subtract line 16 from line 15 .					

For Paperwork Reduction Act Notice, see the Instructions for Form 1041. Cat. No. 11382Z Schedule J (Form 1041) 2014

Part III   Taxes Imposed on Undistributed Net Income (Enter the applicable throwback years below.) (See the instructions.)

Note: *If more than 5 throwback years are involved, attach additional schedules. If the trust received an accumulation distribution from another trust, see Regulations section 1.665(d)-1A.*

If the trust elected the alternative tax on capital gains (repealed for tax years beginning after 1978), **skip** lines 18 through 25 and **complete** lines 26 through 31.		Throwback year ending ---------------	Throwback year ending ---------------	Throwback year ending ---------------	Throwback year ending ---------------	Throwback year ending ---------------
18	Regular tax	**18**					
19	Trust's share of net short-term gain	**19**					
20	Trust's share of net long-term gain	**20**					
21	Add lines 19 and 20 . . .	**21**					
22	Taxable income	**22**					
23	Enter percent. Divide line 21 by line 22, but do not enter more than 100%	**23**	%	%	%	%	%
24	Multiply line 18 by the percentage on line 23 . . .	**24**					
25	Tax on undistributed net income. Subtract line 24 from line 18. Enter here and on page 1, line 9	**25**					

Do not complete lines 26 through 31 unless the trust elected the alternative tax on long-term capital gain.

26	Tax on income other than long-term capital gain . . .	**26**					
27	Trust's share of net short-term gain	**27**					
28	Trust's share of taxable income less section 1202 deduction	**28**					
29	Enter percent. Divide line 27 by line 28, but do not enter more than 100%	**29**	%	%	%	%	%
30	Multiply line 26 by the percentage on line 29 . . .	**30**					
31	Tax on undistributed net income. Subtract line 30 from line 26. Enter here and on page 1, line 9	**31**					

Part IV   Allocation to Beneficiary

Note: *Be sure to complete Form 4970, Tax on Accumulation Distribution of Trusts.*

Beneficiary's name

Identifying number

Beneficiary's address (number and street including apartment number or P.O. box)

City, state, and ZIP code

			(a) This beneficiary's share of line 13	(b) This beneficiary's share of line 14	(c) This beneficiary's share of line 16
32	Throwback year -----------	**32**			
33	Throwback year -----------	**33**			
34	Throwback year -----------	**34**			
35	Throwback year -----------	**35**			
36	Throwback year -----------	**36**			
37	Total. Add lines 32 through 36. Enter here and on the appropriate lines of Form 4970	**37**			

☐ Final K-1   ☐ Amended K-1   OMB No. 1545-0092

Schedule K-1
(Form 1041)
Department of the Treasury
Internal Revenue Service

2014

For calendar year 2014,
or tax year beginning _____ , 2014,
and ending _____ , 20 _____

Beneficiary's Share of Income, Deductions, Credits, etc.

▶ See back of form and instructions.

Part I	**Information About the Estate or Trust**

A Estate's or trust's employer identification number

B Estate's or trust's name

C Fiduciary's name, address, city, state, and ZIP code

D ☐ Check if Form 1041-T was filed and enter the date it was filed
_____

E ☐ Check if this is the final Form 1041 for the estate or trust

Part II	**Information About the Beneficiary**

F Beneficiary's identifying number

G Beneficiary's name, address, city, state, and ZIP code

H ☐ Domestic beneficiary   ☐ Foreign beneficiary

Part III	**Beneficiary's Share of Current Year Income, Deductions, Credits, and Other Items**

1	Interest income	**11**	Final year deductions
2a	Ordinary dividends		
2b	Qualified dividends		
3	Net short-term capital gain		
4a	Net long-term capital gain		
4b	28% rate gain	**12**	Alternative minimum tax adjustment
4c	Unrecaptured section 1250 gain		
5	Other portfolio and nonbusiness income		
6	Ordinary business income		
7	Net rental real estate income		
8	Other rental income	**13**	Credits and credit recapture
9	Directly apportioned deductions		
		14	Other information
10	Estate tax deduction		

*See attached statement for additional information.

Note. A statement must be attached showing the beneficiary's share of income and directly apportioned deductions from each business, rental real estate, and other rental activity.

For IRS Use Only

This list identifies the codes used on Schedule K-1 for beneficiaries and provides summarized reporting information for beneficiaries who file Form 1040. For detailed reporting and filing information, see the Instructions for Schedule K-1 (Form 1041) for a Beneficiary Filing Form 1040 and the instructions for your income tax return.

	Report on
1. Interest income	Form 1040, line 8a
2a. Ordinary dividends	Form 1040, line 9a
2b. Qualified dividends	Form 1040, line 9b
3. Net short-term capital gain	Schedule D, line 5
4a. Net long-term capital gain	Schedule D, line 12
4b. 28% rate gain	28% Rate Gain Worksheet, line 4 (Schedule D Instructions)
4c. Unrecaptured section 1250 gain	Unrecaptured Section 1250 Gain Worksheet, line 11 (Schedule D Instructions)
5. Other portfolio and nonbusiness income	Schedule E, line 33, column (f)
6. Ordinary business income	Schedule E, line 33, column (d) or (f)
7. Net rental real estate income	Schedule E, line 33, column (d) or (f)
8. Other rental income	Schedule E, line 33, column (d) or (f)
9. Directly apportioned deductions	
Code	
A Depreciation	Form 8582 or Schedule E, line 33, column (c) or (e)
B Depletion	Form 8582 or Schedule E, line 33, column (c) or (e)
C Amortization	Form 8582 or Schedule E, line 33, column (c) or (e)
10. Estate tax deduction	Schedule A, line 28
11. Final year deductions	
A Excess deductions	Schedule A, line 23
B Short-term capital loss carryover	Schedule D, line 5
C Long-term capital loss carryover	Schedule D, line 12; line 5 of the wksht. for Sch. D, line 18; and line 16 of the wksht. for Sch. D, line 19
D Net operating loss carryover — regular tax	Form 1040, line 21
E Net operating loss carryover — minimum tax	Form 6251, line 11

12. Alternative minimum tax (AMT) items

A Adjustment for minimum tax purposes	Form 6251, line 15
B AMT adjustment attributable to qualified dividends	
C AMT adjustment attributable to net short-term capital gain	
D AMT adjustment attributable to net long-term capital gain	
E AMT adjustment attributable to unrecaptured section 1250 gain	See the beneficiary's instructions and the Instructions for Form 6251
F AMT adjustment attributable to 28% rate gain	
G Accelerated depreciation	
H Depletion	
I Amortization	
J Exclusion items	2015 Form 8801

13. Credits and credit recapture

Code	*Report on*
A Credit for estimated taxes	Form 1040, line 65
B Credit for backup withholding	Form 1040, line 64
C Low-income housing credit	
D Rehabilitation credit and energy credit	
E Other qualifying investment credit	
F Work opportunity credit	
G Credit for small employer health insurance premiums	
H Biofuel producer credit	
I Credit for increasing research activities	
J Renewable electricity, refined coal, and Indian coal production credit	
K Empowerment zone employment credit	
L Indian employment credit	
M Orphan drug credit	See the beneficiary's instructions
N Credit for employer-provided child care and facilities	
O Biodiesel and renewable diesel fuels credit	
P Nonconventional source fuel credit	
Q Credit to holders of tax credit bonds	
R Agricultural chemicals security credit	
S Energy efficient appliance credit	
T Credit for employer differential wage payments	
U Recapture of credits	

14. Other information

A Tax-exempt interest	Form 1040, line 8b
B Foreign taxes	Form 1040, line 48 or Sch. A, line 8
C Qualified production activities income	Form 8903, line 7, col. (b) (also see the beneficiary's instructions)
D Form W-2 wages	Form 8903, line 17
E Net investment income	Form 4952, line 4a
F Gross farm and fishing income	Schedule E, line 42
G Foreign trading gross receipts (IRC 942(a))	See the Instructions for Form 8873
H Adjustment for section 1411 net investment income or deductions	Form 8960, line 7 (also see the beneficiary's instructions)
I Other information	See the beneficiary's instructions

Note. If you are a beneficiary who does not file a Form 1040, see instructions for the type of income tax return you are filing.

2014

Department of the Treasury
Internal Revenue Service

Instructions for Schedule K-1 (Form 1041) for a Beneficiary Filing Form 1040

Note. The fiduciary's instructions for completing Schedule K-1 are in the Instructions for Form 1041.

Section references are to the Internal Revenue Code unless otherwise noted.

Future Developments

For the latest information about developments related to Schedule K-1 (Form 1041) and its instructions, such as legislation enacted after they were published, go to *www.irs.gov/form1041*.

What's New

Beneficiary's identification number. For your protection, Schedule K-1 may show only the last four digits of your identifying number (social security number (SSN), etc.). However, the estate or trust has reported your complete identifying number to the IRS.

Reminders

Net investment income tax. This tax applies to certain investment income of individuals, estates, and trusts. Use Form 8960, Net Investment Income Tax—Individuals, Estates, and Trusts, and its instructions to figure your net investment income tax.

Backup withholding. If Schedule K-1 shows backup withholding in box 13, code B, attach a copy to your return.

General Instructions

Purpose of Form

Use Schedule K-1 to report a beneficiary's share of the estate's or trust's income, credits, deductions, etc. on your Form 1040, U.S. Individual Income Tax Return. Keep it for your records. Do not file it with your tax return, unless backup withholding was reported in box 13, code B.

Inconsistent Treatment of Items

Generally, you must report items shown on your Schedule K-1 (including attached schedules) the same way that the estate or trust treated the items on its return.

If the treatment of an item on your original or amended return is inconsistent with the estate's or trust's treatment (or if the estate or trust was required to but has not filed a return), you must file Form

8082, Notice of Inconsistent Treatment or Administrative Adjustment Request (AAR), with your original or amended return to identify and explain any inconsistency (or to note that an estate or trust return has not been filed).

If you are required to file Form 8082 but fail to do so, you may be subject to the accuracy-related penalty. This penalty is in addition to any tax that results from making your amount or treatment of the item consistent with that shown on the estate's or trust's return. Any deficiency that results from making the amounts consistent may be assessed immediately.

Errors

If you believe the fiduciary has made an error on your Schedule K-1, notify the fiduciary and ask for an amended or a corrected Schedule K-1. Do not change any items on your copy. Be sure that the fiduciary sends a copy of the amended Schedule K-1 to the IRS. If you are unable to reach an agreement with the fiduciary regarding the inconsistency, you must file Form 8082.

Beneficiaries of Generation-Skipping Trusts

If you received Form 706-GS(D-1), Notification of Distribution From a Generation-Skipping Trust, and paid a generation-skipping transfer (GST) tax on Form 706-GS(D), Generation-Skipping Transfer Tax Return for Distributions, you can deduct the GST tax paid on income distributions on Schedule A (Form 1040), line 8. To figure the deduction, see the Instructions for Form 706-GS(D).

Specific Instructions

Part I—Information About the Estate or Trust

Item E

If the Item E box is checked, this is the final year of the estate or trust.

Note. If the "Final K-1" box at the top of Schedule K-1 is checked, this is the final return for the beneficiary.

Part III—Beneficiary's Share of Current Year Income, Deductions, Credits, and Other Items

The amounts shown in boxes 1 through 14 reflect your share of income, loss, deductions, credits, etc., from an estate or trust. For Form 1040 filers, page 2 of Schedule K-1 provides summarized reporting information. The summarized reporting information reflects references to forms in use for calendar year 2014.

Note. If you are not an individual, report the amounts in each box as instructed on your tax return.

Codes. In box 9 and boxes 11 through 14, the fiduciary will identify each item by entering a code in the column to the left of the dollar amount entry space. These codes are identified on page 2 of Schedule K-1.

Attached statements. The fiduciary will enter an asterisk (*) after the code, if any, in the column to the left of the dollar amount entry space for each item for which it has attached a statement providing additional information. For those informational items that cannot be reported as a single dollar amount, the estate or trust will enter an asterisk in the left column and write "STMT" in the dollar amount entry space to indicate the information is provided on an attached statement.

Box 1—Interest

This box reports the beneficiary's share of the taxable interest income. This amount is reported on line 8a of Form 1040 and Schedule B, Part I, line 1, if applicable.

Box 2a—Ordinary Dividends

This box reports the beneficiary's share of ordinary dividends. This amount is reported on line 9a of Form 1040 and Schedule B, Part II, line 5, if applicable.

Cat. No. 11374Z

Box 2b—Qualified Dividends

This box reports the beneficiary's share of qualified dividends. This amount is reported on line 9b of Form 1040.

Boxes 3 and 4a—Net Short-Term and Net Long-Term Capital Gain

Net short-term capital gains are reported on line 5 of Schedule D (Form 1040) and net long-term capital gains are reported on line 12 of Schedule D (Form 1040).

If there is an attachment to this Schedule K-1 reporting a disposition of a passive activity, see the Instructions for Form 8582, Passive Activity Loss Limitations, for information on the treatment of a disposition of an interest in a passive activity.

Boxes 4b and 4c—28% Rate Gain and Unrecaptured Section 1250 Gain

A 28% rate gain is reported on line 4 of the 28% Rate Gain Worksheet—Line 18 in the Schedule D (Form 1040) instructions.

An unrecaptured section 1250 gain is reported on line 11 of the Unrecaptured Section 1250 Gain Worksheet—Line 19 in the Schedule D (Form 1040) instructions.

Box 5—Other Portfolio and Nonbusiness Income

The amount reported in this box is your distributive share of royalties, annuities, and other income that is not subject to the passive activity rules. It also includes income in respect of a decedent (IRD), which is not included in boxes 1, 2a, 3, 4a, 6, 7, or 8.

Boxes 6 through 8—Ordinary Business Income, Net Rental Real Estate Income, and Other Rental Income

The fiduciary will provide you with a separate schedule showing your distributive share of income from each trade or business, net rental real estate, or other rental activity.

Any losses reported in boxes 6 through 8 may be subject to the passive loss limitations of section 469, which generally limits deducting passive losses only from passive activity income. The rules for applying these limitations to beneficiaries have not yet been issued. For more details, see Pub. 925, Passive Activity and At-Risk Rules.

Box 9—Directly Apportioned Deductions

The fiduciary must attach a statement showing depreciation, depletion, and amortization directly apportioned to you, if any, for each activity reported in boxes 5 through 8.

Box 10—Estate Tax Deduction (Including Certain Generation-Skipping Transfer Taxes)

If an estate or trust distributes income in respect of a decedent (IRD) to a beneficiary, the beneficiary is entitled to deduct the portion of the estate tax imposed on the decedent's estate which is attributable to the IRD distributed to the beneficiary. You may claim this amount on line 28 of Schedule A (Form 1040) as a miscellaneous itemized deduction *not* subject to the 2% floor. For an example on how this amount was computed, see Regulations section 1.691(c)-2 and Pub. 559, Survivors, Executors, and Administrators.

Box 11, Code A—Excess Deductions on Termination

If this is the final return of the estate or trust, and there are excess deductions on termination, you may deduct the beneficiary's share of the excess deductions on line 23 of Schedule A (Form 1040) as a miscellaneous itemized deduction subject to the 2% floor.

Excess deductions on termination occur only during the last tax year of the trust or decedent's estate when the total deductions (excluding the charitable deduction and exemption) are greater than the gross income during that tax year. Only the beneficiary of an estate or trust that succeeds to its property is allowed to deduct that entity's excess deductions on termination. A beneficiary who does not have enough income in that year to absorb the entire deduction may not carry the balance over to any succeeding year.

Box 11, Codes B and C—Unused Capital Loss Carryover

Upon termination of the trust or decedent's estate, the beneficiary succeeding to the property is allowed to deduct any unused capital loss carryover under section 1212.

A short-term capital loss carryover, reported as code B, is reported on Schedule D (Form 1040), line 5.

A long-term capital loss carryover, reported as code C, is reported, as appropriate, on Schedule D (Form 1040),

line 12; line 5 of the 28% Rate Gain Worksheet for Schedule D, line 18; and line 16 of the Unrecaptured Section 1250 Gain Worksheet for Schedule D, line 19.

Box 11, Codes D and E—NOL Carryover

Upon termination of a trust or decedent's estate, a beneficiary succeeding to its property is allowed to deduct any unused net operating loss (NOL) if the carryover would be allowable to the trust or estate in a later tax year but for the termination. The deduction for regular tax purposes, reported as code D, is reported on Form 1040, line 21.

A deduction for an Alternative Tax NOL (ATNOL) carryover for Alternative Minimum Tax (AMT) purposes, reported as code E, is reported on Form 6251, line 11.

Box 12—Alternative Minimum Tax Items

The information reported in box 12, codes A through I is used to prepare your Form 6251, Alternative Minimum Tax—Individuals. Code A, Adjustment for minimum tax purposes, is the total amount reported on Form 6251, line 15. Codes B through F represent the portion, if any, of the amount included in code A.

Codes B through F. If you have an amount in box 12 with code B, C, D, E, or F, see the instructions for lines 37, 38, and 39 of Form 6251.

Codes G through I. Include the amount with any of these codes on the applicable line of Form 6251.

Code J. Exclusion items. If you pay alternative minimum tax in 2014, the amount in box 12, code J will help you figure any minimum tax credit for 2015. See the 2015 Form 8801, Credit for Prior Year Minimum Tax—Individuals, Estates, and Trusts, for more information.

Box 13—Credits and Credit Recapture

Codes A through T list all the credits that may be allocated to you as a beneficiary.

Generally, you must file the source credit form along with Form 3800, General Business Credit, to claim the general business credits listed on Schedule K-1 (Form 1041), codes C through T. However, if your only source for the credits listed on Form 3800, Part III is from pass-through entities, you may not be required to complete the source credit form. Instead, you may be able to report the credit directly on Form 3800. See below for the instructions for specific credits.

Code A. Credit for estimated taxes. The beneficiary treats this amount as a payment of estimated tax. To figure any underpayment and penalty on Form 2210, Underpayment of Estimated Tax by Individuals, Estates, and Trusts, treat the amount entered in box 13, code A, as an estimated tax payment made on January 15, 2015.

Note. Form 1041-T, Allocation of Estimated Tax Payments to Beneficiaries, must be timely filed by the fiduciary for the beneficiary to get the credit for an estimated tax payment.

Code B. Credit for backup withholding. Include this amount on line 64 of your Form 1040 and attach a copy of Schedule K-1 (Form 1041) to your return.

Code C. Low-income housing credit. The fiduciary will provide you with a statement showing the amount to report on lines 4 and 11 of Form 8586, Low-Income Housing Credit. If your only source for the credit is a pass-through entity, such as an estate or trust, you can report the amounts from lines 4 and 11 of Form 8586 directly on Form 3800, Part III, lines 1d and 4d, respectively.

Code D. Rehabilitation credit and energy credit. The fiduciary must give you a statement that shows the information you will need and where to enter it on Form 3468, Investment Credit, so that you can figure the amount of any rehabilitation credit and energy credit that you may claim.

Code E. Other qualifying investment credit. This code is used to report the qualified investment for figuring the qualifying advanced coal project credit, the qualifying gasification project credit, and the qualifying advanced energy project credit. The fiduciary must provide you with a statement that shows the information you will need and where to report it on Form 3468 so that you can figure the amount of the previously listed credits that you may claim.

Code H. Biofuel producer credit. See the Instructions for Form 6478, Biofuel Producer Credit, for more information. If your only source for the credit is a pass-through entity, such as an estate or trust, you can report the amount on Form 3800, Part III, line 4c.

Code J. Renewable electricity, refined coal, and Indian coal production credit. Complete Form 8835, Renewable Electricity, Refined Coal, and Indian Coal Production Credit, to figure the amount of your credit. The fiduciary must provide you with a statement showing the amount of credit to report on line 9 in Part I, and how much to report on line 29 in Part II of Form 8835. If your only source for the credit is a pass-through entity and the credit is reported only on line 9 in Part I of Form 8835, you can enter that amount directly on Form 3800, Part III, line 1f. Otherwise, complete Form 8835 as directed.

Code O. Biodiesel and renewable diesel fuels credit. If this credit includes the small agri-biodiesel producer credit, the fiduciary will provide additional information on an attached statement. If no statement is attached, report this amount on line 9 of Form 8864, Biodiesel and Renewable Diesel Fuels Credit. If a statement is attached, see the Instructions for Form 8864, line 11.

Code S. Energy efficient appliance credit. The energy efficient appliance credit is not available for qualified energy efficient appliances manufactured after December 31, 2013. However, a fiscal year trust or estate can report an energy efficient appliance credit on Schedule K-1 for tax year 2014.

Code U. Recapture of credits. If you are required to recapture any credits, the fiduciary will provide a statement with the information you need to figure your credit recapture.

Box 14—Other Information

Code C. Qualified production activities income. If any of the income is oil-related qualified production activities income, the fiduciary must give you a statement that shows the amount. Enter the oil-related amount on Form 8903, line 7, col. (a). Enter the amount from all activities on Form 8903, line 7, col. (b).

Code F. Gross farming and fishing income. The amount of farming and fishing income is included in box 6. This income is separately stated to help determine if you are subject to a penalty for underpayment of estimated tax. Report the amount of gross farming and fishing income on Schedule E (Form 1040), Supplemental Income and Loss, line 42.

Code H. Net investment income tax. This amount is the beneficiary's adjustment for section 1411 net investment income or deductions. Enter this amount on Line 7 of Form 8960, as applicable. See the Instructions for Form 8960.

Code I. Other information. If this code is used, the fiduciary will provide you with any additional information you may need to file your return that is not shown elsewhere on this Schedule K-1.

If you receive a statement regarding the splitting of foreign tax credits from the income to which it relates, section 909 may prevent you from deducting the foreign tax credit until the related foreign income is taken into account. See Form 1116, Foreign Tax Credit (Individuals, Estate, or Trust), and Pub. 514, Foreign Tax Credit for Individuals, for more information.

Form 1045

Department of the Treasury Internal Revenue Service

Application for Tentative Refund

▶ Separate instructions and additional information are available at *irs.gov/form1045*.
▶ Do not attach to your income tax return. Mail in a separate envelope.
▶ For use by individuals, estates, or trusts.

OMB No. 1545-0098

2014

Type or print

Name(s) shown on return	Social security or employer identification number
Number, street, and apt. or suite no. If a P.O. box, see instructions.	Spouse's social security number (SSN)
City, town or post office, state, and ZIP code. If a foreign address, also complete spaces below (see instructions).	Daytime phone number
Foreign country name	Foreign province/county	Foreign postal code

1 This application is filed to carry back:

a Net operating loss (NOL) (Sch. A, line 25, page 2) $	**b** Unused general business credit $	**c** Net section 1256 contracts loss $

2a For the calendar year 2014, or other tax year

beginning , 2014, and ending , 20

b Date tax return was filed

3 If this application is for an unused credit created by another carryback, enter year of first carryback ▶

4 If you filed a joint return (or separate return) for some, but not all, of the tax years involved in figuring the carryback, list the years and specify whether joint (J) or separate (S) return for each ▶

5 If SSN for carryback year is different from above, enter **a** SSN ▶ and **b** Year(s) ▶

6 If you changed your accounting period, give date permission to change was granted ▶

7 Have you filed a petition in Tax Court for the year(s) to which the carryback is to be applied? . . . . . ☐ Yes ☐ No

8 Is any part of the decrease in tax due to a loss or credit resulting from a reportable transaction required to be disclosed on Form 8886, Reportable Transaction Disclosure Statement? . . . . ☐ Yes ☐ No

9 If you are carrying back an NOL or net section 1256 contracts loss, did this cause the release of foreign tax credits or the release of other credits due to the release of the foreign tax credit (see instructions)? . . . ☐ Yes ☐ No

Computation of Decrease in Tax
(see instructions)

Note: *If 1a and 1c are blank, skip lines 10 through 15.*

		_____ preceding tax year ended ▶		_____ preceding tax year ended ▶		_____ preceding tax year ended ▶	
		Before carryback	After carryback	Before carryback	After carryback	Before carryback	After carryback
10	NOL deduction after carryback (see instructions)						
11	Adjusted gross income						
12	Deductions (see instructions) . . .						
13	Subtract line 12 from line 11 . . .						
14	Exemptions (see instructions) . . .						
15	Taxable income. Line 13 minus line 14						
16	Income tax. See instructions and attach an explanation						
17	Alternative minimum tax						
18	Add lines 16 and 17						
19	General business credit (see instructions)						
20	Other credits. Identify						
21	Total credits. Add lines 19 and 20 .						
22	Subtract line 21 from line 18 . . .						
23	Self-employment tax						
24	Other taxes						
25	Total tax. Add lines 22 through 24 .						
26	Enter the amount from the "After carryback" column on line 25 for each year						
27	Decrease in tax. Line 25 minus line 26						
28	Overpayment of tax due to a claim of right adjustment under section 1341(b)(1) (attach computation) . . .						

Sign Here

Keep a copy of this application for your records.

Under penalties of perjury, I declare that I have examined this application and accompanying schedules and statements, and to the best of my knowledge and belief, they are true, correct, and complete.

▶ Your signature / Date

▶ Spouse's signature. If Form 1045 is filed jointly, **both** must sign. / Date

Paid Preparer Use Only

Print/Type preparer's name	Preparer's signature	Date	Check ☐ if self-employed	PTIN
Firm's name ▶			Firm's EIN ▶	
Firm's address ▶			Phone no.	

For Disclosure, Privacy Act, and Paperwork Reduction Act Notice, see instructions.

Cat. No. 10670A

Form **1045** (2014)

Schedule A—NOL (see instructions)

1	Enter the amount from your 2014 Form 1040, line 41, or Form 1040NR, line 39. Estates and trusts, enter taxable income increased by the total of the charitable deduction, income distribution deduction, and exemption amount	**1**	
2	Nonbusiness capital losses before limitation. Enter as a positive number	**2**	
3	Nonbusiness capital gains (without regard to any section 1202 exclusion)	**3**	
4	If line 2 is more than line 3, enter the difference. Otherwise, enter -0-	**4**	
5	If line 3 is more than line 2, enter the difference. Otherwise, enter -0-	**5**	
6	Nonbusiness deductions (see instructions)	**6**	
7	Nonbusiness income other than capital gains (see instructions)	**7**	
8	Add lines 5 and 7	**8**	
9	If line 6 is more than line 8, enter the difference. Otherwise, enter -0-	**9**	
10	If line 8 is more than line 6, enter the difference. Otherwise, enter -0-. **But do not enter more than line 5**	**10**	
11	Business capital losses before limitation. Enter as a positive number	**11**	
12	Business capital gains (without regard to any section 1202 exclusion)	**12**	
13	Add lines 10 and 12	**13**	
14	Subtract line 13 from line 11. If zero or less, enter -0-	**14**	
15	Add lines 4 and 14	**15**	
16	Enter the loss, if any, from line 16 of your 2014 Schedule D (Form 1040). (Estates and trusts, enter the loss, if any, from line 19, column (3), of Schedule D (Form 1041).) Enter as a positive number. If you do not have a loss on that line (and do not have a section 1202 exclusion), skip lines 16 through 21 and enter on line 22 the amount from line 15	**16**	
17	Section 1202 exclusion. Enter as a positive number	**17**	
18	Subtract line 17 from line 16. If zero or less, enter -0-	**18**	
19	Enter the loss, if any, from line 21 of your 2014 Schedule D (Form 1040). (Estates and trusts, enter the loss, if any, from line 20 of Schedule D (Form 1041).) Enter as a positive number	**19**	
20	If line 18 is more than line 19, enter the difference. Otherwise, enter -0-	**20**	
21	If line 19 is more than line 18, enter the difference. Otherwise, enter -0-	**21**	
22	Subtract line 20 from line 15. If zero or less, enter -0-	**22**	
23	Domestic production activities deduction from your 2014 Form 1040, line 35, or Form 1040NR, line 34 (or included on Form 1041, line 15a)	**23**	
24	NOL deduction for losses from other years. Enter as a positive number	**24**	
25	**NOL.** Combine lines 1, 9, 17, and 21 through 24. If the result is less than zero, enter it here and on page 1, line 1a. If the result is zero or more, you **do not** have an NOL	**25**	

Schedule B—NOL Carryover (see instructions)

Complete one column before going to the next column. Start with the earliest carryback year.	_____ preceding tax year ended ▶		_____ preceding tax year ended ▶		_____ preceding tax year ended ▶	
1 NOL deduction (see instructions). Enter as a positive number						
2 Taxable income before 2014 NOL carryback (see instructions). Estates and trusts, increase this amount by the sum of the charitable deduction and income distribution deduction . . .						
3 Net capital loss deduction (see instructions)						
4 Section 1202 exclusion. Enter as a positive number						
5 Domestic production activities deduction						
6 Adjustment to adjusted gross income (see instructions)						
7 Adjustment to itemized deductions (see instructions)						
8 Individuals, enter deduction for exemptions (minus any amount on Form 8914, line 6, for 2006 and 2009; line 2 for 2005 and 2008). Estates and trusts, enter exemption amount .						
9 Modified taxable income. Combine lines 2 through 8. If zero or less, enter -0-						
10 NOL carryover (see instructions) . .						
Adjustment to Itemized Deductions (Individuals Only) Complete lines 11 through 38 for the carryback year(s) for which you itemized deductions **only** if line 3, 4, or 5 above is more than zero.						
11 Adjusted gross income before 2014 NOL carryback						
12 Add lines 3 through 6 above . . .						
13 Modified adjusted gross income. Add lines 11 and 12						
14 Medical expenses from Sch. A (Form 1040), line 4 (or as previously adjusted)						
15 Medical expenses from Sch. A (Form 1040), line 1 (or as previously adjusted)						
16 Multiply line 13 by percentage from Sch. A (Form 1040), line 3						
17 Subtract line 16 from line 15. If zero or less, enter -0-						
18 Subtract line 17 from line 14						
19 Mortgage insurance premiums from Sch. A (Form 1040), line 13 (or as previously adjusted)						
20 Refigured mortgage insurance premiums (see instructions)						
21 Subtract line 20 from line 19						

Schedule B—NOL Carryover *(Continued)*

Complete one column before going to the next column. Start with the earliest carryback year.	____ preceding tax year ended ▶		____ preceding tax year ended ▶		____ preceding tax year ended ▶	
22 Modified adjusted gross income from line 13 on page 3 of the form . . .						
23 Enter as a positive number any NOL carryback from a year before 2014 that was deducted to figure line 11 on page 3 of the form						
24 Add lines 22 and 23						
25 Charitable contributions from Sch. A (Form 1040), line 19 (line 18 for 2004 through 2006), or Sch. A (Form 1040NR), line 5 (line 7 for 2004 through 2010), or as previously adjusted						
26 Refigured charitable contributions (see instructions)						
27 Subtract line 26 from line 25 . . .						
28 Casualty and theft losses from Form 4684, line 18 (line 23 for 2008; line 21 for 2009; line 20 for 2005, 2006, and 2010)						
29 Casualty and theft losses from Form 4684, line 16 (line 21 for 2008; line 18 for 2005, 2006, and 2010; line 19 for 2009)						
30 Multiply line 22 by 10% (.10) . . .						
31 Subtract line 30 from line 29. If zero or less, enter -0-						
32 Subtract line 31 from line 28 . . .						
33 Miscellaneous itemized deductions from Sch. A (Form 1040), line 27 (line 26 for 2004 through 2006), or Sch. A (Form 1040NR), line 13 (line 15 for 2004 through 2010), or as previously adjusted						
34 Miscellaneous itemized deductions from Sch. A (Form 1040), line 24 (line 23 for 2004 through 2006), or Sch. A (Form 1040NR), line 10 (line 12 for 2004 through 2010), or as previously adjusted						
35 Multiply line 22 by 2% (.02)						
36 Subtract line 35 from line 34. If zero or less, enter -0-						
37 Subtract line 36 from line 33 . . .						
38 Complete the worksheet in the instructions if line 22 is **more than** the applicable amount shown in the instructions. Otherwise, combine lines 18, 21, 27, 32, and 37; enter the result here and on line 7 (page 3)						

Form **1045** (2014)

Form **1065**	**U.S. Return of Partnership Income**	OMB No. 1545-0123
Department of the Treasury Internal Revenue Service	For calendar year 2014, or tax year beginning _____ , 2014, ending _____ , 20____ . ▶ Information about Form 1065 and its separate instructions is at *www.irs.gov/form1065*.	**2014**

A Principal business activity		Name of partnership	D **Employer identification number**
B Principal product or service	**Type or Print**	Number, street, and room or suite no. If a P.O. box, see the instructions.	E Date business started
C Business code number		City or town, state or province, country, and ZIP or foreign postal code	F Total assets (see the instructions) $

G Check applicable boxes: **(1)** ☐ Initial return **(2)** ☐ Final return **(3)** ☐ Name change **(4)** ☐ Address change **(5)** ☐ Amended return
(6) ☐ Technical termination - also check (1) or (2)

H Check accounting method: **(1)** ☐ Cash **(2)** ☐ Accrual **(3)** ☐ Other (specify) ▶ _____

I Number of Schedules K-1. Attach one for each person who was a partner at any time during the tax year ▶ _____

J Check if Schedules C and M-3 are attached . . . . ☐

Caution. *Include **only** trade or business income and expenses on lines 1a through 22 below. See the instructions for more information.*

Income

1a	Gross receipts or sales	1a	
b	Returns and allowances	1b	
c	Balance. Subtract line 1b from line 1a	1c	
2	Cost of goods sold (attach Form 1125-A)	2	
3	Gross profit. Subtract line 2 from line 1c	3	
4	Ordinary income (loss) from other partnerships, estates, and trusts (attach statement) .	4	
5	Net farm profit (loss) (attach Schedule F (Form 1040))	5	
6	Net gain (loss) from Form 4797, Part II, line 17 (attach Form 4797)	6	
7	Other income (loss) (attach statement)	7	
8	**Total income (loss). Combine lines 3 through 7**	8	

Deductions *(see the instructions for limitations)*

9	Salaries and wages (other than to partners) (less employment credits)	9	
10	Guaranteed payments to partners	10	
11	Repairs and maintenance	11	
12	Bad debts	12	
13	Rent	13	
14	Taxes and licenses	14	
15	Interest	15	
16a	Depreciation (if required, attach Form 4562)	16a	
b	Less depreciation reported on Form 1125-A and elsewhere on return	16b		16c	
17	Depletion **(Do not deduct oil and gas depletion.)**	17	
18	Retirement plans, etc.	18	
19	Employee benefit programs	19	
20	Other deductions (attach statement)	20	
21	**Total deductions.** Add the amounts shown in the far right column for lines 9 through 20 .	21	
22	**Ordinary business income (loss).** Subtract line 21 from line 8	22	

Sign Here

Under penalties of perjury, I declare that I have examined this return, including accompanying schedules and statements, and to the best of my knowledge and belief, it is true, correct, and complete. Declaration of preparer (other than general partner or limited liability company member manager) is based on all information of which preparer has any knowledge.

▶ _____ ▶ _____
Signature of general partner or limited liability company member manager   Date

May the IRS discuss this return with the preparer shown below (see instructions)? ☐ **Yes** ☐ **No**

Paid Preparer Use Only

Print/Type preparer's name	Preparer's signature	Date	Check ☐ if self-employed	PTIN
Firm's name ▶			Firm's EIN ▶	
Firm's address ▶			Phone no.	

For Paperwork Reduction Act Notice, see separate instructions.   Cat. No. 11390Z   Form **1065** (2014)

Schedule B	Other Information		

		Yes	No
1	What type of entity is filing this return? Check the applicable box:		

a ☐ Domestic general partnership   **b** ☐ Domestic limited partnership
c ☐ Domestic limited liability company   **d** ☐ Domestic limited liability partnership
e ☐ Foreign partnership   **f** ☐ Other ▶

2 At any time during the tax year, was any partner in the partnership a disregarded entity, a partnership (including an entity treated as a partnership), a trust, an S corporation, an estate (other than an estate of a deceased partner), or a nominee or similar person?

3 At the end of the tax year:

a Did any foreign or domestic corporation, partnership (including any entity treated as a partnership), trust, or tax-exempt organization, or any foreign government own, directly or indirectly, an interest of 50% or more in the profit, loss, or capital of the partnership? For rules of constructive ownership, see instructions. If "Yes," attach Schedule B-1, Information on Partners Owning 50% or More of the Partnership

b Did any individual or estate own, directly or indirectly, an interest of 50% or more in the profit, loss, or capital of the partnership? For rules of constructive ownership, see instructions. If "Yes," attach Schedule B-1, Information on Partners Owning 50% or More of the Partnership

4 At the end of the tax year, did the partnership:

a Own directly 20% or more, or own, directly or indirectly, 50% or more of the total voting power of all classes of stock entitled to vote of any foreign or domestic corporation? For rules of constructive ownership, see instructions. If "Yes," complete (i) through (iv) below

(i) Name of Corporation	(ii) Employer Identification Number (if any)	(iii) Country of Incorporation	(iv) Percentage Owned in Voting Stock

b Own directly an interest of 20% or more, or own, directly or indirectly, an interest of 50% or more in the profit, loss, or capital in any foreign or domestic partnership (including an entity treated as a partnership) or in the beneficial interest of a trust? For rules of constructive ownership, see instructions. If "Yes," complete (i) through (v) below .

(i) Name of Entity	(ii) Employer Identification Number (if any)	(iii) Type of Entity	(iv) Country of Organization	(v) Maximum Percentage Owned in Profit, Loss, or Capital

		Yes	No
5	Did the partnership file Form 8893, Election of Partnership Level Tax Treatment, or an election statement under section 6231(a)(1)(B)(ii) for partnership-level tax treatment, that is in effect for this tax year? See Form 8893 for more details		

6 Does the partnership satisfy **all four** of the following conditions?

a The partnership's total receipts for the tax year were less than $250,000.

b The partnership's total assets at the end of the tax year were less than $1 million.

c Schedules K-1 are filed with the return and furnished to the partners on or before the due date (including extensions) for the partnership return.

d The partnership is not filing and is not required to file Schedule M-3
If "Yes," the partnership is not required to complete Schedules L, M-1, and M-2; Item F on page 1 of Form 1065; or Item L on Schedule K-1.

7 Is this partnership a publicly traded partnership as defined in section 469(k)(2)?

8 During the tax year, did the partnership have any debt that was cancelled, was forgiven, or had the terms modified so as to reduce the principal amount of the debt?

9 Has this partnership filed, or is it required to file, Form 8918, Material Advisor Disclosure Statement, to provide information on any reportable transaction?

10 At any time during calendar year 2014, did the partnership have an interest in or a signature or other authority over a financial account in a foreign country (such as a bank account, securities account, or other financial account)? See the instructions for exceptions and filing requirements for FinCEN Form 114, Report of Foreign Bank and Financial Accounts (FBAR). If "Yes," enter the name of the foreign country. ▶

Schedule B	Other Information *(continued)*		

		Yes	No
11	At any time during the tax year, did the partnership receive a distribution from, or was it the grantor of, or transferor to, a foreign trust? If "Yes," the partnership may have to file Form 3520, Annual Return To Report Transactions With Foreign Trusts and Receipt of Certain Foreign Gifts. See instructions		
12a	Is the partnership making, or had it previously made (and not revoked), a section 754 election? . . . . See instructions for details regarding a section 754 election.		
b	Did the partnership make for this tax year an optional basis adjustment under section 743(b) or 734(b)? If "Yes," attach a statement showing the computation and allocation of the basis adjustment. See instructions		
c	Is the partnership required to adjust the basis of partnership assets under section 743(b) or 734(b) because of a substantial built-in loss (as defined under section 743(d)) or substantial basis reduction (as defined under section 734(d))? If "Yes," attach a statement showing the computation and allocation of the basis adjustment. See instructions		
13	Check this box if, during the current or prior tax year, the partnership distributed any property received in a like-kind exchange or contributed such property to another entity (other than disregarded entities wholly owned by the partnership throughout the tax year) . . . . ▶ ☐		
14	At any time during the tax year, did the partnership distribute to any partner a tenancy-in-common or other undivided interest in partnership property?		
15	If the partnership is required to file Form 8858, Information Return of U.S. Persons With Respect To Foreign Disregarded Entities, enter the number of Forms 8858 attached. See instructions ▶		
16	Does the partnership have any foreign partners? If "Yes," enter the number of Forms 8805, Foreign Partner's Information Statement of Section 1446 Withholding Tax, filed for this partnership. ▶		
17	Enter the number of Forms 8865, Return of U.S. Persons With Respect to Certain Foreign Partnerships, attached to this return. ▶		
18a	Did you make any payments in 2014 that would require you to file Form(s) 1099? See instructions		
b	If "Yes," did you or will you file required Form(s) 1099?		
19	Enter the number of Form(s) 5471, Information Return of U.S. Persons With Respect To Certain Foreign Corporations, attached to this return. ▶		
20	Enter the number of partners that are foreign governments under section 892. ▶		

Designation of Tax Matters Partner (see instructions)

Enter below the general partner or member-manager designated as the tax matters partner (TMP) for the tax year of this return:

Name of designated TMP ▶		Identifying number of TMP ▶	
If the TMP is an entity, name of TMP representative ▶		Phone number of TMP ▶	
Address of designated TMP ▶			

Schedule K		Partners' Distributive Share Items		Total amount
Income (Loss)	**1**	Ordinary business income (loss) (page 1, line 22)	**1**	
	2	Net rental real estate income (loss) (attach Form 8825)	**2**	
	3a	Other gross rental income (loss) 3a		
	b	Expenses from other rental activities (attach statement) 3b		
	c	Other net rental income (loss). Subtract line 3b from line 3a	**3c**	
	4	Guaranteed payments	**4**	
	5	Interest income	**5**	
	6	Dividends: **a** Ordinary dividends	**6a**	
		b Qualified dividends 6b		
	7	Royalties	**7**	
	8	Net short-term capital gain (loss) (attach Schedule D (Form 1065))	**8**	
	9a	Net long-term capital gain (loss) (attach Schedule D (Form 1065))	**9a**	
	b	Collectibles (28%) gain (loss) 9b		
	c	Unrecaptured section 1250 gain (attach statement) . . 9c		
	10	Net section 1231 gain (loss) (attach Form 4797)	**10**	
	11	Other income (loss) (see instructions) Type ▶	**11**	
Deductions	**12**	Section 179 deduction (attach Form 4562)	**12**	
	13a	Contributions	**13a**	
	b	Investment interest expense	**13b**	
	c	Section 59(e)(2) expenditures: **(1)** Type ▶_____ **(2)** Amount ▶	**13c(2)**	
	d	Other deductions (see instructions) Type ▶	**13d**	
Self-Employment	**14a**	Net earnings (loss) from self-employment	**14a**	
	b	Gross farming or fishing income	**14b**	
	c	Gross nonfarm income	**14c**	
Credits	**15a**	Low-income housing credit (section 42(j)(5))	**15a**	
	b	Low-income housing credit (other)	**15b**	
	c	Qualified rehabilitation expenditures (rental real estate) (attach Form 3468, if applicable)	**15c**	
	d	Other rental real estate credits (see instructions) Type ▶_____	**15d**	
	e	Other rental credits (see instructions) Type ▶_____	**15e**	
	f	Other credits (see instructions) Type ▶_____	**15f**	
Foreign Transactions	**16a**	Name of country or U.S. possession ▶_____		
	b	Gross income from all sources	**16b**	
	c	Gross income sourced at partner level	**16c**	
		Foreign gross income sourced at partnership level		
	d	Passive category ▶_____ **e** General category ▶_____ **f** Other ▶	**16f**	
		Deductions allocated and apportioned at partner level		
	g	Interest expense ▶_____ **h** Other . . . . ▶	**16h**	
		Deductions allocated and apportioned at partnership level to foreign source income		
	i	Passive category ▶_____ **j** General category ▶_____ **k** Other ▶	**16k**	
	l	Total foreign taxes (check one): ▶ Paid ☐ Accrued ☐	**16l**	
	m	Reduction in taxes available for credit (attach statement)	**16m**	
	n	Other foreign tax information (attach statement)		
Alternative Minimum Tax (AMT) Items	**17a**	Post-1986 depreciation adjustment	**17a**	
	b	Adjusted gain or loss	**17b**	
	c	Depletion (other than oil and gas)	**17c**	
	d	Oil, gas, and geothermal properties—gross income	**17d**	
	e	Oil, gas, and geothermal properties—deductions	**17e**	
	f	Other AMT items (attach statement)	**17f**	
Other Information	**18a**	Tax-exempt interest income	**18a**	
	b	Other tax-exempt income	**18b**	
	c	Nondeductible expenses	**18c**	
	19a	Distributions of cash and marketable securities	**19a**	
	b	Distributions of other property	**19b**	
	20a	Investment income	**20a**	
	b	Investment expenses	**20b**	
	c	Other items and amounts (attach statement)		

Analysis of Net Income (Loss)

1	Net income (loss). Combine Schedule K, lines 1 through 11. From the result, subtract the sum of Schedule K, lines 12 through 13d, and 16l	**1**

2	Analysis by partner type:	(i) Corporate	(ii) Individual (active)	(iii) Individual (passive)	(iv) Partnership	(v) Exempt Organization	(vi) Nominee/Other
a	General partners						
b	Limited partners						

Schedule L　　Balance Sheets per Books

	Assets	Beginning of tax year (a)	(b)	End of tax year (c)	(d)
1	Cash				
2a	Trade notes and accounts receivable . . .				
b	Less allowance for bad debts				
3	Inventories				
4	U.S. government obligations				
5	Tax-exempt securities				
6	Other current assets (attach statement) . .				
7a	Loans to partners (or persons related to partners)				
b	Mortgage and real estate loans . . .				
8	Other investments (attach statement) . . .				
9a	Buildings and other depreciable assets . .				
b	Less accumulated depreciation				
10a	Depletable assets				
b	Less accumulated depletion				
11	Land (net of any amortization)				
12a	Intangible assets (amortizable only) . . .				
b	Less accumulated amortization				
13	Other assets (attach statement)				
14	Total assets				
	Liabilities and Capital				
15	Accounts payable				
16	Mortgages, notes, bonds payable in less than 1 year				
17	Other current liabilities (attach statement) .				
18	All nonrecourse loans				
19a	Loans from partners (or persons related to partners)				
b	Mortgages, notes, bonds payable in 1 year or more				
20	Other liabilities (attach statement)				
21	Partners' capital accounts				
22	Total liabilities and capital				

Schedule M-1　　Reconciliation of Income (Loss) per Books With Income (Loss) per Return

Note. The partnership may be required to file Schedule M-3 (see instructions).

1	Net income (loss) per books		6	Income recorded on books this year not included on Schedule K, lines 1 through 11 (itemize):	
2	Income included on Schedule K, lines 1, 2, 3c, 5, 6a, 7, 8, 9a, 10, and 11, not recorded on books this year (itemize):		a	Tax-exempt interest $ _____	
3	Guaranteed payments (other than health insurance)		7	Deductions included on Schedule K, lines 1 through 13d, and 16l, not charged against book income this year (itemize):	
4	Expenses recorded on books this year not included on Schedule K, lines 1 through 13d, and 16l (itemize):		a	Depreciation $ _____	
a	Depreciation $ _____		8	Add lines 6 and 7	
b	Travel and entertainment $ _____		9	Income (loss) (Analysis of Net Income (Loss), line 1). Subtract line 8 from line 5 .	
5	Add lines 1 through 4				

Schedule M-2　　Analysis of Partners' Capital Accounts

1	Balance at beginning of year . . .		6	Distributions: **a** Cash	
2	Capital contributed: **a** Cash . . .			**b** Property	
	b Property . . .		7	Other decreases (itemize): _____	
3	Net income (loss) per books				
4	Other increases (itemize): _____		8	Add lines 6 and 7	
5	Add lines 1 through 4		9	Balance at end of year. Subtract line 8 from line 5	

SCHEDULE B-1
(Form 1065)

(Rev. December 2011)
Department of the Treasury
Internal Revenue Service

Information on Partners Owning 50% or More of the Partnership

▶ Attach to Form 1065. See instructions on back.

OMB No. 1545-0099

Name of partnership

Employer identification number (EIN)

Part I   **Entities Owning 50% or More of the Partnership** (Form 1065, Schedule B, Question 3a)

Complete columns (i) through (v) below for any foreign or domestic corporation, partnership (including any entity treated as a partnership), trust, tax-exempt organization, or any foreign government that owns, directly or indirectly, an interest of 50% or more in the profit, loss, or capital of the partnership (see instructions).

(i) Name of Entity	(ii) Employer Identification Number (if any)	(iii) Type of Entity	(iv) Country of Organization	(v) Maximum Percentage Owned in Profit, Loss, or Capital

---

Part II   **Individuals or Estates Owning 50% or More of the Partnership** (Form 1065, Schedule B, Question 3b)

Complete columns (i) through (iv) below for any individual or estate that owns, directly or indirectly, an interest of 50% or more in the profit, loss, or capital of the partnership (see instructions).

(i) Name of Individual or Estate	(ii) Identifying Number (if any)	(iii) Country of Citizenship (see instructions)	(iv) Maximum Percentage Owned in Profit, Loss, or Capital

---

For Paperwork Reduction Act Notice, see the Instructions for Form 1065.   Cat. No. 49842K   Schedule B-1 (Form 1065) (Rev. 12-2011)

General Instructions

Section references are to the Internal Revenue Code unless otherwise noted.

Purpose of Form

Use Schedule B-1 (Form 1065) to provide the information applicable to certain entities, individuals, and estates that own, directly or indirectly, an interest of 50% or more in the profit, loss, or capital of the partnership.

Who Must File

Schedule B-1 (Form 1065) must be filed by all partnerships that answer "Yes" to question 3a or question 3b on Schedule B of Form 1065. Attach Schedule B-1 to Form 1065.

Specific Instructions

Part I

Complete Part I if the partnership answered "Yes" to Form 1065, Schedule B, question 3a. List each corporation, partnership, trust, tax-exempt organization, or foreign government owning, directly or indirectly, an interest of 50% or more in the profit, loss, or capital of the partnership at the end of the tax year. Enter the name, EIN, type of entity (corporation, partnership, trust, tax-exempt organization, or foreign government), country of organization, and the maximum percentage interests owned, directly or indirectly, in the profit, loss, or capital of the partnership. For an affiliated group filing a consolidated tax return, list the parent corporation rather than the subsidiary members. List the entity owner of a disregarded entity rather than the disregarded entity. If the owner of a disregarded entity is an individual rather than an entity, list the individual in Part II. In the case of a tax-exempt organization, enter "tax-exempt organization" in column (iii).

Example 1. Corporation A owns, directly, an interest of 50% in the profit, loss, or capital of Partnership B. Corporation A also owns, directly, an interest of 15% in the profit, loss, or capital of Partnership C. Partnership B owns, directly, an

interest of 70% in the profit, loss, or capital of Partnership C. Therefore, Corporation A owns, directly or indirectly, an interest of 50% in the profit, loss, or capital of Partnership C (15% directly and 35% indirectly through Partnership B). On Partnership C's Form 1065, it must answer "Yes" to question 3a of Schedule B. Partnership C must also complete Part I of Schedule B-1. In Part I, Partnership C must identify Corporation A, which includes entering "50%" in column (v) (its maximum percentage owned). It also must identify Partnership B, and enter "70%" in column (v).

Part II

Complete Part II if the partnership answered "Yes" to Form 1065, Schedule B, question 3b. List each individual or estate owning, directly or indirectly, an interest of 50% or more in the profit, loss, or capital of the partnership at the end of the tax year. Enter the name, social security or employer identification number, country of citizenship (for an estate, the citizenship of the decedent), and the maximum percentage interests owned, directly or indirectly, in the profit, loss, or capital of the partnership.

Example 2. A owns, directly, 50% of the profit, loss, or capital of Partnership X. B, the daughter of A, does not own, directly, any interest in X and does not own, indirectly, any interest in X through any entity (corporation, partnership, trust, or estate). Because family attribution rules apply only when an individual (in this example, B) owns a direct interest in the partnership or an indirect interest through another entity, A's interest in Partnership X is not attributable to B. On Partnership X's Form 1065, it must answer "Yes" to question 3b of Schedule B. Partnership X must also complete Part II of Schedule B-1. In Part II, Partnership X must identify A, which includes entering "50%" in column (iv). Partnership X will **not** identify B in Part II.

Additional Information for Schedule M-3 Filers

▶ Attach to Form 1065. See separate instructions.

▶ Information about Schedule C (Form 1065) and its instructions is at *www.irs.gov/form1065*.

OMB No. 1545-0123

Name of partnership

Employer identification number

		Yes	No
1	At any time during the tax year, were there any transfers between the partnership and its partners subject to the disclosure requirements of Regulations section 1.707-8?		
2	Does any amount reported on Schedule M-3, Part II, lines 7 or 8, column (d), reflect allocations to this partnership from another partnership of income, gain, loss, deduction, or credit that are disproportionate to this partnership's share of capital in that partnership or its ratio for sharing other items of that partnership?		
3	At any time during the tax year, did the partnership sell, exchange, or transfer any interest in an intangible asset to a related person as defined in sections 267(b) and 707(b)(1)?		
4	At any time during the tax year, did the partnership acquire any interest in an intangible asset from a related person as defined in sections 267(b) and 707(b)(1)?		
5	At any time during the tax year, did the partnership make any change in accounting principle for financial accounting purposes? See instructions for a definition of change in accounting principle		
6	At any time during the tax year, did the partnership make any change in a method of accounting for U.S. income tax purposes?		

For Paperwork Reduction Act Notice, see the Instructions for Form 1065.   Cat. No. 49945S   Schedule C (Form 1065) (Rev. 12-2014)

Instructions for Schedule C (Form 1065)

(Rev. December 2014)

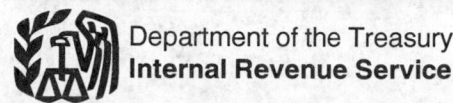

Department of the Treasury
Internal Revenue Service

Additional Information for Schedule M-3 Filers

Section references are to the Internal Revenue Code unless otherwise noted.

General Instructions

Future Developments

For the latest information about developments related to Schedule C (Form 1065) and its instructions, such as legislation enacted after they were published, go to *www.irs.gov/form1065*.

What's New

Some filers of Form 1065, U.S. Return of Partnership Income, that file Schedule M-3 (Form 1065), Net Income (Loss) Reconciliation for Certain Partnerships, with tax years ending on December 31, 2014 or later are not required to file Schedule C (Form 1065). See *Who Must File*, later.

Purpose of Form

Use Schedule C (Form 1065) to provide answers to additional questions for some filers of Schedule M-3 (Form 1065), Net Income (Loss) Reconciliation for Certain Partnerships.

Who Must File

Generally, filers of Form 1065, U.S. Return of Partnership Income, that file Schedule M-3 (Form 1065), Net Income (Loss) Reconciliation for Certain Partnerships, must complete and file Schedule C (Form 1065) and attach it to their return. However, for tax years ending on December 31, 2014 or later, partnerships that (a) are required to file Schedule M-3 and have less than $50 million in total assets at the end of the tax year or (b) are not required to file Schedule M-3 and voluntarily file Schedule M-3, are not required to file Schedule C (Form 1065). For more information, visit IRS.gov and enter "Schedule M-3 for Large Business International (LBI)" in the Search box. Also see the Instructions for Schedule M-3 (Form 1065) for more information.

Specific Instructions

Question 1. For certain transfers that are presumed to be sales, the partnership or the partners must comply with the disclosure requirements in Regulations section 1.707-8. Generally, disclosure is required when:

1. Certain transfers to a partner are made within two years of a transfer of property by the partner to the partnership;

2. Certain debt is incurred by a partner within two years of the earlier of:
- A written agreement to transfer or
- A transfer of the property that secures the debt, if the debt, nevertheless, is treated as a qualified liability; or

3. Transfers from a partnership to a partner occur which are the equivalent to those listed in 1 or 2 above.

The disclosure must be made on the transferor partner's return using Form 8275, Disclosure Statement, or on an attached statement providing the same information. When more than one partner transfers property to a partnership under a plan, the disclosure may be made by the partnership rather than by each partner.

Question 2. Answer "Yes" if this partnership is a partner in another partnership and has received special allocations of income, gain, loss, deduction, or credit from that partnership. For more information on special allocations, see *Special Allocations,* in the Instructions for Form 1065.

Example. P, a partnership, joins with B, an individual, in forming the PB partnership. P and B each contribute $50,000 cash to PB partnership. Profits and losses are split 50/50, with the exception of depreciation, which is allocated 99% to P and 1% to B. P answers "Yes" to question 2 because its 99% allocation of depreciation deductions from PB partnership is disproportionate to its ratio of sharing other items from PB partnership.

Question 5. The term "change in accounting principle" means a change from one generally accepted accounting principle to another generally accepted accounting principle as described in "Statement of Financial Accounting Standards No. 154–Accounting Changes and Error Corrections."

For purposes of this question, answer "Yes" if such a change in accounting principle occurred during the tax year and such change resulted in, or is expected to result in, an effect on the amount of income reported for financial statement purposes.

Question 6. File Form 3115, Application for Change in Accounting Method, to request a change in a method of accounting. See the Instructions for Form 3115 for information on requesting a change in accounting method.

SCHEDULE D
(Form 1065)

Department of the Treasury
Internal Revenue Service

Capital Gains and Losses

▶ Attach to Form 1065 or Form 8865.
▶ Use Form 8949 to list your transactions for lines 1b, 2, 3, 8b, 9, and 10.
▶ Information about Schedule D (Form 1065) and its separate instructions is at *www.irs.gov/form1065*.

OMB No. 1545-0123

2014

Name of partnership

Employer identification number

Part I — Short-Term Capital Gains and Losses—Assets Held One Year or Less

See instructions for how to figure the amounts to enter on the lines below.

This form may be easier to complete if you round off cents to whole dollars.

	(d) Proceeds (sales price)	(e) Cost (or other basis)	(g) Adjustments to gain or loss from Form(s) 8949, Part I, line 2, column (g)	(h) Gain or (loss) Subtract column (e) from column (d) and combine the result with column (g)
1a Totals for all short-term transactions reported on Form 1099-B for which basis was reported to the IRS and for which you have no adjustments (see instructions). However, if you choose to report all these transactions on Form 8949, leave this line blank and go to line 1b .				
1b Totals for all transactions reported on Form(s) 8949 with **Box A** checked				
2 Totals for all transactions reported on Form(s) 8949 with **Box B** checked				
3 Totals for all transactions reported on Form(s) 8949 with **Box C** checked				

4 Short-term capital gain from installment sales from Form 6252, line 26 or 37	**4**	
5 Short-term capital gain or (loss) from like-kind exchanges from Form 8824	**5**	
6 Partnership's share of net short-term capital gain (loss), including specially allocated short-term capital gains (losses), from other partnerships, estates, and trusts	**6**	
7 **Net short-term capital gain or (loss).** Combine lines 1a through 6 in column (h). Enter here and on Form 1065, Schedule K, line 8 or 11; or Form 8865, Schedule K, line 8 or 11 . . .	**7**	

Part II — Long-Term Capital Gains and Losses—Assets Held More Than One Year

See instructions for how to figure the amounts to enter on the lines below.

This form may be easier to complete if you round off cents to whole dollars.

	(d) Proceeds (sales price)	(e) Cost (or other basis)	(g) Adjustments to gain or loss from Form(s) 8949, Part II, line 2, column (g)	(h) Gain or (loss) Subtract column (e) from column (d) and combine the result with column (g)
8a Totals for all long-term transactions reported on Form 1099-B for which basis was reported to the IRS and for which you have no adjustments (see instructions). However, if you choose to report all these transactions on Form 8949, leave this line blank and go to line 8b .				
8b Totals for all transactions reported on Form(s) 8949 with **Box D** checked				
9 Totals for all transactions reported on Form(s) 8949 with **Box E** checked				
10 Totals for all transactions reported on Form(s) 8949 with **Box F** checked				

11 Long-term capital gain from installment sales from Form 6252, line 26 or 37	**11**	
12 Long-term capital gain or (loss) from like-kind exchanges from Form 8824	**12**	
13 Partnership's share of net long-term capital gain (loss), including specially allocated long-term capital gains (losses), from other partnerships, estates, and trusts	**13**	
14 Capital gain distributions (see instructions)	**14**	
15 **Net long-term capital gain or (loss).** Combine lines 8a through 14 in column (h). Enter here and on Form 1065, Schedule K, line 9a or 11; or Form 8865, Schedule K, line 9a or 11	**15**	

For Paperwork Reduction Act Notice, see the Instructions for Form 1065.   Cat. No. 11393G   Schedule D (Form 1065) 2014

☐ Final K-1   ☐ Amended K-1   OMB No. 1545-0123

Schedule K-1
(Form 1065)

2014

Department of the Treasury
Internal Revenue Service

For calendar year 2014, or tax
year beginning _____, 2014
ending _____, 20 _____

Partner's Share of Income, Deductions, Credits, etc. ▶ See back of form and separate instructions.

Part III	Partner's Share of Current Year Income, Deductions, Credits, and Other Items

1	Ordinary business income (loss)	15	Credits
2	Net rental real estate income (loss)		
3	Other net rental income (loss)	16	Foreign transactions
4	Guaranteed payments		
5	Interest income		
6a	Ordinary dividends		
6b	Qualified dividends		
7	Royalties		
8	Net short-term capital gain (loss)		
9a	Net long-term capital gain (loss)	17	Alternative minimum tax (AMT) items
9b	Collectibles (28%) gain (loss)		
9c	Unrecaptured section 1250 gain		
10	Net section 1231 gain (loss)	18	Tax-exempt income and nondeductible expenses
11	Other income (loss)		
		19	Distributions
12	Section 179 deduction		
13	Other deductions		
		20	Other information
14	Self-employment earnings (loss)		

Part I   Information About the Partnership

A Partnership's employer identification number

B Partnership's name, address, city, state, and ZIP code

C IRS Center where partnership filed return

D ☐ Check if this is a publicly traded partnership (PTP)

Part II   Information About the Partner

E Partner's identifying number

F Partner's name, address, city, state, and ZIP code

G ☐ General partner or LLC member-manager   ☐ Limited partner or other LLC member

H ☐ Domestic partner   ☐ Foreign partner

I1 What type of entity is this partner? _____

I2 If this partner is a retirement plan (IRA/SEP/Keogh/etc.), check here . . . . ☐

J Partner's share of profit, loss, and capital (see instructions):

	Beginning	Ending
Profit	%	%
Loss	%	%
Capital	%	%

K Partner's share of liabilities at year end:

Nonrecourse . . . . $ _____
Qualified nonrecourse financing $ _____
Recourse . . . . $ _____

L Partner's capital account analysis:

Beginning capital account . . . $ _____
Capital contributed during the year $ _____
Current year increase (decrease) . $ _____
Withdrawals & distributions . . $ (_____)
Ending capital account . . . . $ _____

☐ Tax basis   ☐ GAAP   ☐ Section 704(b) book
☐ Other (explain)

M Did the partner contribute property with a built-in gain or loss?
☐ Yes   ☐ No
If "Yes," attach statement (see instructions)

*See attached statement for additional information.

For IRS Use Only

For Paperwork Reduction Act Notice, see Instructions for Form 1065.   IRS.gov/form1065   Cat. No. 11394R   Schedule K-1 (Form 1065) 2014

This list identifies the codes used on Schedule K-1 for all partners and provides summarized reporting information for partners who file Form 1040. For detailed reporting and filing information, see the separate Partner's Instructions for Schedule K-1 and the instructions for your income tax return.

1. **Ordinary business income (loss).** Determine whether the income (loss) is passive or nonpassive and enter on your return as follows.

	Report on
Passive loss	See the Partner's Instructions
Passive income	Schedule E, line 28, column (g)
Nonpassive loss	Schedule E, line 28, column (h)
Nonpassive income	Schedule E, line 28, column (j)

2. **Net rental real estate income (loss)**   See the Partner's Instructions
3. **Other net rental income (loss)**

Net income	Schedule E, line 28, column (g)
Net loss	See the Partner's Instructions

4. **Guaranteed payments**   Schedule E, line 28, column (j)
5. **Interest income**   Form 1040, line 8a
6a. **Ordinary dividends**   Form 1040, line 9a
6b. **Qualified dividends**   Form 1040, line 9b
7. **Royalties**   Schedule E, line 4
8. **Net short-term capital gain (loss)**   Schedule D, line 5
9a. **Net long-term capital gain (loss)**   Schedule D, line 12
9b. **Collectibles (28%) gain (loss)**   28% Rate Gain Worksheet, line 4 (Schedule D instructions)
9c. **Unrecaptured section 1250 gain**   See the Partner's Instructions
10. **Net section 1231 gain (loss)**   See the Partner's Instructions
11. **Other income (loss)**

Code		
A	Other portfolio income (loss)	See the Partner's Instructions
B	Involuntary conversions	See the Partner's Instructions
C	Sec. 1256 contracts & straddles	Form 6781, line 1
D	Mining exploration costs recapture	See Pub. 535
E	Cancellation of debt	Form 1040, line 21 or Form 982
F	Other income (loss)	See the Partner's Instructions

12. **Section 179 deduction**   See the Partner's Instructions
13. **Other deductions**

A	Cash contributions (50%)	
B	Cash contributions (30%)	
C	Noncash contributions (50%)	
D	Noncash contributions (30%)	See the Partner's Instructions
E	Capital gain property to a 50% organization (30%)	
F	Capital gain property (20%)	
G	Contributions (100%)	
H	Investment interest expense	Form 4952, line 1
I	Deductions—royalty income	Schedule E, line 19
J	Section 59(e)(2) expenditures	See the Partner's Instructions
K	Deductions—portfolio (2% floor)	Schedule A, line 23
L	Deductions—portfolio (other)	Schedule A, line 28
M	Amounts paid for medical insurance	Schedule A, line 1 or Form 1040, line 29
N	Educational assistance benefits	See the Partner's Instructions
O	Dependent care benefits	Form 2441, line 12
P	Preproductive period expenses	See the Partner's Instructions
Q	Commercial revitalization deduction from rental real estate activities	See Form 8582 instructions
R	Pensions and IRAs	See the Partner's Instructions
S	Reforestation expense deduction	See the Partner's Instructions
T	Domestic production activities information	See Form 8903 instructions
U	Qualified production activities income	Form 8903, line 7b
V	Employer's Form W-2 wages	Form 8903, line 17
W	Other deductions	See the Partner's Instructions

14. **Self-employment earnings (loss)**

Note. *If you have a section 179 deduction or any partner-level deductions, see the Partner's Instructions before completing Schedule SE.*

A	Net earnings (loss) from self-employment	Schedule SE, Section A or B
B	Gross farming or fishing income	See the Partner's Instructions
C	Gross non-farm income	See the Partner's Instructions

15. **Credits**

A	Low-income housing credit (section 42(j)(5)) from pre-2008 buildings	
B	Low-income housing credit (other) from pre-2008 buildings	
C	Low-income housing credit (section 42(j)(5)) from post-2007 buildings	See the Partner's Instructions
D	Low-income housing credit (other) from post-2007 buildings	
E	Qualified rehabilitation expenditures (rental real estate)	
F	Other rental real estate credits	
G	Other rental credits	
H	Undistributed capital gains credit	Form 1040, line 73; check box a
I	Biofuel producer credit	
J	Work opportunity credit	See the Partner's Instructions
K	Disabled access credit	

Code		Report on
L	Empowerment zone employment credit	
M	Credit for increasing research activities	
N	Credit for employer social security and Medicare taxes	See the Partner's Instructions
O	Backup withholding	
P	Other credits	

16. **Foreign transactions**

A	Name of country or U.S. possession	
B	Gross income from all sources	Form 1116, Part I
C	Gross income sourced at partner level	

Foreign gross income sourced at partnership level

D	Passive category	
E	General category	Form 1116, Part I
F	Other	

Deductions allocated and apportioned at partner level

G	Interest expense	Form 1116, Part I
H	Other	Form 1116, Part I

Deductions allocated and apportioned at partnership level to foreign source income

I	Passive category	
J	General category	Form 1116, Part I
K	Other	

Other information

L	Total foreign taxes paid	Form 1116, Part II
M	Total foreign taxes accrued	Form 1116, Part II
N	Reduction in taxes available for credit	Form 1116, line 12
O	Foreign trading gross receipts	Form 8873
P	Extraterritorial income exclusion	Form 8873
Q	Other foreign transactions	See the Partner's Instructions

17. **Alternative minimum tax (AMT) items**

A	Post-1986 depreciation adjustment	
B	Adjusted gain or loss	See the Partner's
C	Depletion (other than oil & gas)	Instructions and
D	Oil, gas, & geothermal—gross income	the Instructions for
E	Oil, gas, & geothermal—deductions	Form 6251
F	Other AMT items	

18. **Tax-exempt income and nondeductible expenses**

A	Tax-exempt interest income	Form 1040, line 8b
B	Other tax-exempt income	See the Partner's Instructions
C	Nondeductible expenses	See the Partner's Instructions

19. **Distributions**

A	Cash and marketable securities	
B	Distribution subject to section 737	See the Partner's Instructions
C	Other property	

20. **Other information**

A	Investment income	Form 4952, line 4a
B	Investment expenses	Form 4952, line 5
C	Fuel tax credit information	Form 4136
D	Qualified rehabilitation expenditures (other than rental real estate)	See the Partner's Instructions
E	Basis of energy property	See the Partner's Instructions
F	Recapture of low-income housing credit (section 42(j)(5))	Form 8611, line 8
G	Recapture of low-income housing credit (other)	Form 8611, line 8
H	Recapture of investment credit	See Form 4255
I	Recapture of other credits	See the Partner's Instructions
J	Look-back interest—completed long-term contracts	See Form 8697
K	Look-back interest—income forecast method	See Form 8866
L	Dispositions of property with section 179 deductions	
M	Recapture of section 179 deduction	
N	Interest expense for corporate partners	
O	Section 453(l)(3) information	
P	Section 453A(c) information	
Q	Section 1260(b) information	
R	Interest allocable to production expenditures	See the Partner's
S	CCF nonqualified withdrawals	Instructions
T	Depletion information—oil and gas	
U	Reserved	
V	Unrelated business taxable income	
W	Precontribution gain (loss)	
X	Section 108(i) information	
Y	Net investment income	
Z	Other information	

2014

Partner's Instructions for Schedule K-1 (Form 1065)

Partner's Share of Income, Deductions, Credits, etc. (For Partner's Use Only)

Department of the Treasury
Internal Revenue Service

Section references are to the Internal Revenue Code unless otherwise noted.

Future Developments

For the latest information about developments related to Schedule K-1 (Form 1065) and the Partner's Instructions for Schedule K-1 (Form 1065), such as legislation enacted after they were published, go to *www.irs.gov/form1065*.

General Instructions

Purpose of Schedule K-1

The partnership uses Schedule K-1 to report your share of the partnership's income, deductions, credits, etc. Keep it for your records. Do not file it with your tax return unless you are specifically required to do so. (See the instructions for *Code O. Backup withholding*, later.) The partnership files a copy of Schedule K-1 (Form 1065) with the IRS.

For your protection, Schedule K-1 may show only the last four digits of your identifying number (social security number (SSN), etc.). However, the partnership has reported your complete identifying number to the IRS.

Although the partnership generally is not subject to income tax, you may be liable for tax on your share of the partnership income, whether or not distributed. Include your share on your tax return if a return is required. Use these instructions to help you report the items shown on Schedule K-1 on your tax return.

The amount of loss and deduction you may claim on your tax return may be less than the amount reported on Schedule K-1. It is the partner's responsibility to consider and apply any applicable limitations. See *Limitations on Losses, Deductions, and Credits*, later, for more information.

Inconsistent Treatment of Items

Generally, you must report partnership items shown on your Schedule K-1 (and any attached statements) the same way that the partnership treated the items on its return. This rule does not apply if your partnership is within the "small partnership exception" and does not elect to have the tax treatment of partnership items determined at the partnership level.

If the treatment on your original or amended return is inconsistent with the partnership's treatment, or if the partnership was required to but has not filed a return, you must file Form 8082, Notice of Inconsistent Treatment or Administrative Adjustment Request (AAR), with your original or amended return to identify and explain any inconsistency (or to note that a partnership return has not been filed).

If you are required to file Form 8082 but do not do so, you may be subject to the accuracy-related penalty. This penalty is in addition to any tax that results from making your amount or treatment of the item consistent with that shown on the partnership's return. Any deficiency that results from making the amounts consistent may be assessed immediately.

Errors

If you believe the partnership has made an error on your Schedule K-1, notify the partnership and ask for a corrected Schedule K-1. Do not change any items on your copy of Schedule K-1. Be sure that the partnership sends a copy of the corrected Schedule K-1 to the IRS. If you are a partner in a partnership that does not meet the small partnership exception and you report any partnership item on your return in a manner different from the way the partnership reported it, you must file Form 8082.

Sale or Exchange of Partnership Interest

Generally, a partner who sells or exchanges a partnership interest in a section 751(a) exchange must notify the partnership, in writing, within 30 days of the exchange (or, if earlier, by January 15 of the calendar year following the calendar year in which the exchange occurred). A "section 751(a) exchange" is any sale or exchange of a partnership interest in which any money or other property received by the partner in exchange for that partner's interest is attributable to unrealized receivables (as defined in section 751(c)) or inventory items (as defined in section 751(d)).

The written notice to the partnership must include the names and addresses of both parties to the exchange, the identifying numbers of the transferor and (if known) of the transferee, and the exchange date.

An exception to this rule is made for sales or exchanges of publicly traded partnership interests for which a broker is required to file

Form 1099-B, Proceeds From Broker and Barter Exchange Transactions.

If a partner is required to notify the partnership of a section 751(a) exchange but fails to do so, the penalty is $100 for each such failure. However, no penalty will be imposed if the partner can show that the failure was due to reasonable cause and not willful neglect.

Note. Gain or loss from the disposition of your partnership interest is generally net investment income under section 1411 and may be subject to the net investment income tax. See Form 8960, Net Investment Income Tax—Individuals, Estates, and Trusts, and its instructions for information about how to report and figure the tax due.

Nominee Reporting

Any person who holds, directly or indirectly, an interest in a partnership as a nominee for another person must furnish a written statement to the partnership by the last day of the month following the end of the partnership's tax year. This statement must include the name, address, and identifying number of the nominee and such other person, description of the partnership interest held as nominee for that person, and other information required by Temporary Regulations section 1.6031(c)-1T. A nominee that fails to furnish this statement must furnish to the person for whom the nominee holds the partnership interest a copy of Schedule K-1 and related information within 30 days of receiving it from the partnership.

A nominee who fails to furnish all the information required by Temporary Regulations section 1.6031(c)-1T when due, or who furnishes incorrect information, is subject to a $100 penalty for each failure. The maximum penalty is $1,500,000 for all such failures during a calendar year. If the nominee intentionally disregards the requirement to report correct information, each $100 penalty increases to $250 or, if greater, 10% of the aggregate amount of items required to be reported, and the $1,500,000 maximum does not apply.

International Boycotts

Every partnership that had operations in, or related to, a boycotting country, company, or a national of a boycotting country must file Form 5713, International Boycott Report.

If the partnership cooperated with an international boycott, it must give you a copy

Cat. No. 11396N

of its Form 5713. You must file your own Form 5713 to report the partnership's activities and any other boycott operations that you may have. You may lose certain tax benefits if the partnership participated in, or cooperated with, an international boycott. See Form 5713 and its instructions for more information.

Definitions

General Partner

A general partner is a partner who is personally liable for partnership debts.

Limited Partner

A limited partner is a partner in a partnership formed under a state limited partnership law, whose personal liability for partnership debts is limited to the amount of money or other property that the partner contributed or is required to contribute to the partnership. Some members of other entities, such as domestic or foreign business trusts or limited liability companies that are classified as partnerships, may be treated as limited partners for certain purposes.

Nonrecourse Loans

Nonrecourse loans are those liabilities of the partnership for which no partner or related person bears the economic risk of loss.

Elections

Generally, the partnership decides how to figure taxable income from its operations. However, certain elections are made by you separately on your income tax return and not by the partnership. These elections are made under the following code sections.
- Section 59(e) (deduction of certain qualified expenditures ratably over the period of time specified in that section). For details, see the instructions for code J in box 13.
- Section 108(b)(5) (election related to reduction of tax attributes due to exclusion from gross income of discharge of indebtedness).
- Section 263A(d) (preproductive expenses). See the instructions for code P in box 13.
- Section 617 (deduction and recapture of certain mining exploration expenditures).
- Section 901 (foreign tax credit).

Additional Information

For more information on the treatment of partnership income, deductions, credits, etc., see Pub. 535, Business Expenses.

To get forms and publications, see the instructions for your tax return or visit the IRS website at *IRS.gov*.

Limitations on Losses, Deductions, and Credits

There are potential limitations on partnership losses that you can deduct on your return. These limitations and the order in which you must apply them are as follows: the basis rules, the at-risk limitations, and the passive

---

Worksheet for Adjusting the Basis of a Partner's Interest in the Partnership
Keep for Your Records

1. Your adjusted basis at the end of the prior year. Do not enter less than zero. Enter -0- if this is your first tax year . . . . 1._____

   Increases:

2. Money and your adjusted basis in property contributed to the partnership less the associated liabilities (but not less than zero) . . . . 2._____

3. Your increased share of or assumption of partnership liabilities. (Subtract your share of liabilities shown in item K of your 2013 Schedule K-1 from your share of liabilities shown in item K of your 2014 Schedule K-1 and add the amount of any partnership liabilities you assumed during the tax year (but not less than zero)) . . . . 3._____

4. Your share of the partnership's income or gain (including tax-exempt income) reduced by any amount included in interest income with respect to the credit to holders of clean renewable energy bonds . . . . 4._____

5. Any gain recognized this year on contributions of property. Do not include gain from transfer of liabilities . . . . 5._____

6. Your share of the excess of the deductions for depletion (other than oil and gas depletion) over the basis of the property subject to depletion . . . . 6._____

   Decreases:

7. Withdrawals and distributions of money and the adjusted basis of property distributed to you from the partnership. Do not include the amount of property distributions included in the partner's income (taxable income) . . . . 7._____

   Caution: A distribution may be taxable if the amount exceeds your adjusted basis of your partnership interest immediately before the distribution.

8. Your decreased share of partnership liabilities and any decrease in your individual liabilities because they were assumed by the partnership. (Subtract your share of liabilities shown in item K of your 2014 Schedule K-1 from your share of liabilities shown in item K of your 2013 Schedule K-1 and add the amount of your individual liabilities that the partnership assumed during the tax year (but not less than zero)) . . . . 8._____

9. Your share of the partnership's nondeductible expenses that are not capital expenditures . . . . 9._____

10. Your share of the partnership's losses and deductions (including capital losses). However, include your share of the partnership's section 179 expense deduction for this year even if you cannot deduct all of it because of limitations . . . . . . 10._____

11. The amount of your deduction for depletion of any partnership oil and gas property, not to exceed your allocable share of the adjusted basis of that property . . . . 11._____

12. Your adjusted basis in the partnership at the end of this tax year. (Add lines 1 through 6 and subtract lines 7 through 11 from the total. If zero or less, enter -0-.) . . . . 12._____

Caution: The deduction for your share of the partnership's losses and deductions is limited to your adjusted basis in your partnership interest. If you entered zero on line 12 and the amount figured for line 12 was less than zero, a portion of your share of the partnership losses and deductions may not be deductible. (See *Basis Rules*, earlier, for more information.)

---

activity limitations. These limitations are discussed below.

Other limitations may apply to specific deductions (for example, the section 179 expense deduction). Generally, specific limitations apply before the basis, at-risk, and passive loss limitations.

Basis Rules

Generally, you may not claim your share of a partnership loss (including a capital loss) to the extent that it is greater than the adjusted basis of your partnership interest at the end of the partnership's tax year. Any losses and deductions not allowed this year because of the basis limit can be carried forward indefinitely and deducted in a later year subject to the basis limit for that year.

The partnership is not responsible for keeping the information needed to figure the basis of your partnership interest. Although the partnership does provide an analysis of the changes to your capital account in item L of Schedule K-1, that information is based on the partnership's books and records and cannot be used to figure your basis.

You can figure the adjusted basis of your partnership interest by adding items that

increase your basis and then subtracting items that decrease your basis.

Use the worksheet above to figure the basis of your interest in the partnership.

For more details on the basis rules, see Pub. 541, Partnerships.

At-Risk Limitations

Generally, if you have (a) a loss or other deduction from any activity carried on as a trade or business or for the production of income by the partnership and (b) amounts in the activity for which you are not at risk, you will have to complete Form 6198, At-Risk Limitations, to figure your allowable loss.

The at-risk rules generally limit the amount of loss and other deductions that you can claim to the amount you could actually lose in the activity. These losses and deductions include a loss on the disposition of assets and the section 179 expense deduction. However, if you acquired your partnership interest before 1987, the at-risk rules do not apply to losses from an activity of holding real property placed in service before 1987 by the partnership. The activity of holding mineral property does not qualify for this exception. The partnership should identify on a statement attached to Schedule K-1 any losses that are not subject to the at-risk limitations.

Generally, you are not at risk for amounts such as the following.
• Nonrecourse loans used to finance the activity, to acquire property used in the activity, or to acquire your interest in the activity, that are not secured by your own property (other than the property used in the activity). See the instructions for item K, later, for the exception for qualified nonrecourse financing secured by real property.
• Cash, property, or borrowed amounts used in the activity (or contributed to the activity, or used to acquire your interest in the activity) that are protected against loss by a guarantee, stop-loss agreement, or other similar arrangement (excluding casualty insurance and insurance against tort liability).
• Amounts borrowed for use in the activity from a person who has an interest in the activity, other than as a creditor, or who is related, under section 465(b)(3), to a person (other than you) having such an interest.

You should get a separate statement of income, expenses, etc., for each activity from the partnership.

Passive Activity Limitations

Section 469 provides rules that limit the deduction of certain losses and credits. These rules apply to partners who:
• Are individuals, estates, trusts, closely held C corporations, or personal service corporations and
• Have a passive activity loss or credit for the tax year.

Generally, passive activities include the following.
1. Trade or business activities in which you did not materially participate and
2. Activities that meet the definition of rental activities under Temporary Regulations section 1.469-1T(e)(3) and Regulations section 1.469-1(e)(3).

Passive activities do not include:
1. Trade or business activities in which you materially participated.
2. Rental real estate activities in which you materially participated if you were a **real estate professional** for the tax year. You were a real estate professional only if you met both of the following conditions.
    a. More than half of the personal services you performed in trades or businesses were performed in real property trades or businesses in which you materially participated and
    b. You performed more than 750 hours of services in real property trades or businesses in which you materially participated.

Note. For a closely held C corporation (defined in section 465(a)(1)(B)), the above

conditions are treated as met if more than 50% of the corporation's gross receipts were from real property trades or businesses in which the corporation materially participated.

For purposes of this rule, each interest in rental real estate is a separate activity, unless you elect to treat all interests in rental real estate as one activity. For details on making this election, see the Instructions for Schedule E (Form 1040) Supplemental Income and Loss.

If you are married filing jointly, either you or your spouse must separately meet both (a and b) of the above conditions, without taking into account services performed by the other spouse.

A real property trade or business is any real property development, redevelopment, construction, reconstruction, acquisition, conversion, rental, operation, management, leasing, or brokerage trade or business. Services you performed as an employee are not treated as performed in a real property trade or business unless you owned more than 5% of the stock (or more than 5% of the capital or profits interest) in the employer.
3. Working interests in oil or gas wells if you were a general partner.
4. The rental of a dwelling unit any partner used for personal purposes during the year for more than the greater of 14 days or 10% of the number of days that the residence was rented at fair rental value.
5. Activities of trading personal property for the account of owners of interests in the activities.

If you are an individual, an estate, or a trust, and you have a passive activity loss or credit, use Form 8582, Passive Activity Loss Limitations, to figure your allowable passive losses and Form 8582-CR, Passive Activity Credit Limitations, to figure your allowable passive credits. For a corporation, use Form 8810, Corporate Passive Activity Loss and Credit Limitations. See the instructions for these forms for details.

If the partnership had more than one activity, it will attach a statement to your Schedule K-1 that identifies each activity (trade or business activity, rental real estate activity, rental activity other than rental real estate, etc.) and specifies the income (loss), deductions, and credits from each activity.

Material participation. You must determine if you materially participated (a) in each trade or business activity held through the partnership and (b) if you were a real estate professional (defined earlier), in each rental real estate activity held through the partnership. All determinations of material participation are based on your participation during the partnership's tax year.

Material participation standards for partners who are individuals are listed below. Special rules apply to certain retired or disabled farmers and to the surviving spouses of farmers. See the Instructions for Form 8582 for details.

Corporations should refer to the Instructions for Form 8810 for the material participation standards that apply to them.

Individuals (other than limited partners). If you are an individual (either a general partner or a limited partner who owned a general partnership interest at all times during the tax year), you materially participated in an activity only if one or more of the following apply.
1. You participated in the activity for more than 500 hours during the tax year.
2. Your participation in the activity for the tax year constituted substantially all the participation in the activity of all individuals (including individuals who are not owners of interests in the activity).
3. You participated in the activity for more than 100 hours during the tax year, and your participation in the activity for the tax year was not less than the participation in the activity of any other individual (including individuals who were not owners of interests in the activity) for the tax year.
4. The activity was a significant participation activity for the tax year, and you participated in all significant participation activities (including activities outside the partnership) during the year for more than 500 hours. A significant participation activity is any trade or business activity in which you participated for more than 100 hours during the year and in which you did not materially participate under any of the material participation tests (other than this test).
5. You materially participated in the activity for any 5 tax years (whether or not consecutive) during the 10 tax years that immediately precede the tax year.
6. The activity was a personal service activity and you materially participated in the activity for any 3 tax years (whether or not consecutive) preceding the tax year. A personal service activity involves the performance of personal services in the fields of health, law, engineering, architecture, accounting, actuarial science, performing arts, consulting, or any other trade or business in which capital is not a material income-producing factor.
7. Based on all the facts and circumstances, you participated in the activity on a regular, continuous, and substantial basis during the tax year.

Limited partners. If you are a limited partner, you do not materially participate in an activity unless you meet one of the tests in paragraphs 1, 5, or 6, above.

Work counted toward material participation. Generally, any work that you or your spouse does in connection with an activity held through a partnership (where you own your partnership interest at the time the work is done) is counted toward material participation. However, work in connection with the activity is not counted toward material participation if either of the following applies.

1. The work is not the type of work that owners of the activity would usually do and one of the principal purposes of the work that you or your spouse does is to avoid the passive loss or credit limitations.

2. You do the work in your capacity as an investor and you are not directly involved in the day-to-day operations of the activity. Examples of work done as an investor that would not count toward material participation include:

a. Studying and reviewing financial statements or reports on operations of the activity,

b. Preparing or compiling summaries or analyses of the finances or operations of the activity for your own use, and

c. Monitoring the finances or operations of the activity in a non-managerial capacity.

Effect of determination. Income (loss), deductions, and credits from an activity are nonpassive if you determine that:
• You materially participated in a trade or business activity of the partnership or
• You were a real estate professional (defined earlier) in a rental real estate activity of the partnership.

If you determine that you did not materially participate in a trade or business activity of the partnership or if you have income (loss), deductions, or credits from a rental activity of the partnership (other than a rental real estate activity in which you materially participated as a real estate professional), the amounts from that activity are passive. Report passive income (losses), deductions, and credits as follows.

1. If you have an overall gain (the excess of income over deductions and losses, including any prior year unallowed loss) from a passive activity, report the income, deductions, and losses from the activity as indicated in these instructions.

2. If you have an overall loss (the excess of deductions and losses, including any prior year unallowed loss, over income) or credits from a passive activity, report the income, deductions, losses, and credits from all passive activities using the Instructions for Form 8582 or Form 8582-CR (or Form 8810), to see if your deductions, losses, and credits are limited under the passive activity rules.

Publicly traded partnerships. The passive activity limitations are applied separately for items (other than the low-income housing credit and the rehabilitation credit) from each publicly traded partnership (PTP). Thus, a net passive loss from a PTP may not be deducted from other passive income. Instead, a passive loss from a PTP is suspended and carried forward to be applied against passive income from the same PTP in later years. If the partner's entire interest in the PTP is completely disposed of, any unused losses are allowed in full in the year of disposition.

If you have an overall gain from a PTP, the net gain is nonpassive income. In addition, the nonpassive income is included in investment income to figure your investment interest expense deduction.

Do not report passive income, gains, or losses from a PTP on Form 8582. Instead, use the following rules to figure and report on the proper form or schedule your income, gains, and losses from passive activities that you held through each PTP you owned during the tax year.

1. Combine any current year income, gains and losses, and any prior year unallowed losses to see if you have an overall gain or loss from the PTP. Include only the same types of income and losses you would include in your net income or loss from a non-PTP passive activity. See Pub. 925, Passive Activity and At-Risk Rules, for more details.

2. If you have an overall gain, the net gain portion (total gain minus total losses) is nonpassive income. On the form or schedule you normally use, report the net gain portion as nonpassive income and the remaining income and the total losses as passive income and loss. To the left of the entry space, enter "From PTP." It is important to identify the nonpassive income because the nonpassive portion is included in modified adjusted gross income for purposes of figuring on Form 8582 the "special allowance" for active participation in a non-PTP rental real estate activity. In addition, the nonpassive income is included in investment income when figuring your investment interest expense deduction on Form 4952, Investment Interest Expense Deduction.

Example. If you have Schedule E (Form 1040) income of $8,000, and a Form 4797, Sales of Business Property, prior year unallowed loss of $3,500 from the passive activities of a particular PTP, you have a $4,500 overall gain ($8,000 – $3,500). On Schedule E (Form 1040), line 28, report the $4,500 net gain as nonpassive income in column (j). In column (g), report the remaining Schedule E (Form 1040) gain of $3,500 ($8,000 – $4,500). On the appropriate line of Form 4797, report the prior year unallowed loss of $3,500. Be sure to enter "From PTP" to the left of each entry space.

3. If you have an overall loss (but did not dispose of your entire interest in the PTP to an unrelated person in a fully taxable transaction during the year), the losses are allowed to the extent of the income, and the excess loss is carried forward to use in a future year when you have income to offset it. Report as a passive loss on the schedule or form you normally use the portion of the loss equal to the income. Report the income as passive income on the form or schedule you normally use.

Example. You have a Schedule E (Form 1040) loss of $12,000 (current year losses plus prior year unallowed losses) and a Form

4797 gain of $7,200. Report the $7,200 gain on the appropriate line of Form 4797. On Schedule E (Form 1040), line 28, report $7,200 of the losses as a passive loss in column (f). Carry forward to 2015 the unallowed loss of $4,800 ($12,000 – $7,200).

If you have unallowed losses from more than one activity of the PTP or from the same activity of the PTP that must be reported on different forms, you must allocate the unallowed losses on a *pro rata* basis to figure the amount allowed from each activity or on each form.

TIP *To allocate and keep a record of the unallowed losses, use Worksheets 5, 6, and 7 of Form 8582. List each activity of the PTP in Worksheet 5. Enter the overall loss from each activity in column (a). Complete column (b) of Worksheet 5 according to its instructions. Multiply the total unallowed loss from the PTP by each ratio in column (b) and enter the result in column (c) of Worksheet 5. Then, complete Worksheet 6 if all the loss from the same activity is to be reported on one form or schedule. Use Worksheet 7 instead of Worksheet 6 if you have more than one loss to be reported on different forms or schedules for the same activity. Enter the net loss plus any prior year unallowed losses in column (a) of Worksheet 6 (or Worksheet 7 if applicable). The losses in column (c) of Worksheet 6 (column (e) of Worksheet 7) are the allowed losses to report on the forms or schedules. Report both these losses and any income from the PTP on the forms and schedules you normally use.*

4. If you have an overall loss and you disposed of your entire interest in the PTP to an unrelated person in a fully taxable transaction during the year, your losses (including prior year unallowed losses) allocable to the activity for the year are not limited by the passive loss rules. A fully taxable transaction is one in which you recognize all your realized gain or loss. Report the income and losses on the forms and schedules you normally use.

Note. For rules on the disposition of an entire interest reported using the installment method, see the Instructions for Form 8582.

Special allowance for a rental real estate activity. If you actively participated in a rental real estate activity, you may be able to deduct up to $25,000 of the loss from the activity from nonpassive income. This "special allowance" is an exception to the general rule disallowing losses in excess of income from passive activities. The special allowance is not available if you were married, file a separate return for the year, and did not live apart from your spouse at all times during the year.

Only individuals, qualifying estates, and qualifying revocable trusts that made a section 645 election can actively participate in a rental real estate activity. Estates (other than qualifying estates), trusts (other than qualifying revocable trusts that made a section 645 election), and corporations cannot actively participate. Limited partners cannot actively participate unless future regulations provide an exception.

You are not considered to actively participate in a rental real estate activity if, at any time during the tax year, your interest (including your spouse's interest) in the activity was less than 10% (by value) of all interests in the activity.

Active participation is a less stringent requirement than material participation. You may be treated as actively participating if you participated, for example, in making management decisions or arranging for others to provide services (such as repairs) in a significant and bona fide sense. Management decisions that can count as active participation include approving new tenants, deciding rental terms, approving capital or repair expenditures, and other similar decisions.

An estate is a qualifying estate if the decedent would have satisfied the active participation requirement for the activity for the tax year the decedent died. A qualifying estate is treated as actively participating for tax years ending less than 2 years after the date of the decedent's death.

Modified adjusted gross income limitation. The maximum special allowance that single individuals and married individuals filing a joint return can qualify for is $25,000. The maximum is $12,500 for married individuals who file separate returns and who lived apart at all times during the year. The maximum special allowance for which an estate can qualify is $25,000 reduced by the special allowance for which the surviving spouse qualifies.

If your modified adjusted gross income (defined below) is $100,000 or less ($50,000 or less if married filing separately), your loss is deductible up to the maximum special allowance referred to in the preceding paragraph. If your modified adjusted gross income is more than $100,000 (more than $50,000 if married filing separately), the special allowance is limited to 50% of the difference between $150,000 ($75,000 if married filing separately) and your modified adjusted gross income. When modified adjusted gross income is $150,000 or more ($75,000 or more if married filing separately), there is no special allowance.

Modified adjusted gross income is your adjusted gross income figured without taking into account the following amounts, if applicable:
- Any passive activity loss.
- Any rental real estate loss allowed under section 469(c)(7) to real estate professionals (defined earlier).
- Any overall loss from a publicly traded partnership.
- Any taxable social security or equivalent railroad retirement benefits.
- Any deductible contributions to an IRA or certain other qualified retirement plans under section 219.

- The domestic production activities deduction.
- The student loan interest deduction.
- The tuition and fees deduction.
- The deductible part of self-employment taxes.
- The exclusion from income of interest from Series EE or I U.S. Savings Bonds used to pay higher education expenses.
- The exclusion of amounts received under an employer's adoption assistance program.

Commercial revitalization deduction. The special $25,000 allowance for the commercial revitalization deduction from rental real estate activities is not subject to the active participation rules or modified adjusted gross income limits discussed earlier. See the instructions for box 13, code Q, for more information.

Special rules for certain other activities. If you have net income (loss), deductions, or credits from any activity to which special rules apply, the partnership will identify the activity and all amounts relating to it on Schedule K-1 or on an attached statement.

If you have net income subject to recharacterization under Temporary Regulations section 1.469-2T(f) and Regulations section 1.469-2(f), report such amounts according to the Instructions for Form 8582 (or Form 8810).

If you have net income (loss), deductions, or credits from any of the following activities, treat such amounts as nonpassive and report them as indicated in these instructions.

1. Working interests in oil and gas wells if you are a general partner.

2. The rental of a dwelling unit any partner used for personal purposes during the year for more than the greater of 14 days or 10% of the number of days that the residence was rented at fair rental value.

3. Trading personal property for the account of owners of interests in the activity.

Self-charged interest. The partnership will report any "self-charged" interest income or expense that resulted from loans between you and the partnership (or between the partnership and another partnership or S corporation if both entities have the same owners with the same proportional ownership interest in each entity). If there was more than one activity, the partnership will provide a statement allocating the interest income or expense with respect to each activity. The self-charged interest rules do not apply to your partnership interest if the partnership made an election under Regulations section 1.469-7(g) to avoid the application of these rules. See the Instructions for Form 8582 for details.

Specific Instructions

Part I. Information About the Partnership

Item D

If the box in item D is checked, you are a partner in a publicly traded partnership and must follow the rules discussed, earlier, under *Publicly traded partnerships.*

Part II. Information About the Partner

Item E

For your protection, this form may show only the last four digits of your social security number (SSN), individual taxpayer identification number (ITIN), or employer identification number (EIN). However, the partnership has reported your complete identification number to the IRS.

Item J

Generally, the amounts reported in item J are based on the partnership agreement. If your interest commenced after the beginning of the partnership's tax year, the partnership will have entered, in the *Beginning* column, the percentages that existed for you immediately after admission. If your interest terminated before the end of the partnership's tax year, the partnership will have entered, in the *Ending* column, the percentages that existed immediately before termination.

The ending percentage share shown on the *Capital* line is the portion of the capital you would receive if the partnership was liquidated at the end of its tax year by the distribution of undivided interests in the partnership's assets and liabilities. If your capital account is negative or zero, the partnership will have entered zero on this line.

Item K

Item K should show your share of the partnership's nonrecourse liabilities, partnership-level qualified nonrecourse financing, and other recourse liabilities as of the end of the partnership's tax year. If you terminated your interest in the partnership during the tax year, item K should show the share that existed immediately before the total disposition. A partner's "recourse liability" is any partnership liability for which a partner is personally liable.

Use the total of the three amounts for computing the adjusted basis of your partnership interest.

Generally, you may use only the amounts shown next to "Qualified nonrecourse financing" and "Recourse" to figure your amount at risk. Do not include any amounts that are not at risk if such amounts are included in either of these categories.

If your partnership is engaged in two or more different types of activities subject to the at-risk provisions, or a combination of at-risk activities and any other activity, the partnership should give you a statement showing your share of nonrecourse liabilities, partnership-level qualified nonrecourse financing, and other recourse liabilities for each activity.

Qualified nonrecourse financing secured by real property used in an activity of holding real property that is subject to the at-risk rules is treated as an amount at risk. Qualified nonrecourse financing generally includes financing for which no one is personally liable for repayment that is borrowed for use in an activity of holding real property and that is loaned or guaranteed by a federal, state, or local government or borrowed from a "qualified" person.

Qualified persons include any persons actively and regularly engaged in the business of lending money, such as a bank or savings and loan association. Qualified persons generally do not include related parties (unless the nonrecourse financing is commercially reasonable and on substantially the same terms as loans involving unrelated persons), the seller of the property, or a person who receives a fee for the partnership's investment in the real property.

See Pub. 925 for more information on qualified nonrecourse financing.

Both the partnership and you must meet the qualified nonrecourse rules on this debt before you can include the amount shown next to "Qualified nonrecourse financing" in your at-risk computation.

See _Limitations on Losses, Deductions, and Credits_, earlier, for more information on the at-risk limitations.

Item M

If you have contributed property with a built-in gain or loss during the tax year, the partnership will check the "Yes" box. Also, the partnership will attach a statement showing the property contributed, the date of the contribution, and the amount of any built-in gain or loss. A built-in gain or loss is the difference between the fair market value of the property and your adjusted basis in the property at the time it was contributed to the partnership. If you contributed more than 10 properties on a single date during the tax year, the statement may instead show the number of properties contributed on that date, the total amount of built-in gain, and the total amount of built-in loss.

The partnership is providing this for your information. Contributions of property with a built-in gain or loss could affect a partner's tax liability (in matters concerning precontribution gain or loss, and distributions subject to section 737), and may also affect how the partnership allocated certain items on your Schedule K-1. For information on precontribution gain or loss, see the instructions for box 20, Code W. For information on distributions subject to section 737 see the instructions for box 19, Code B.

Part III. Partner's Share of Current Year Income, Deductions, Credits, and Other Items

The amounts shown in boxes 1 through 20 reflect your share of income, loss, deductions, credits, etc., from partnership business or rental activities without reference to limitations on losses or adjustments that may be required of you because of:

1. The adjusted basis of your partnership interest,

2. The amount for which you are at risk,

3. The passive activity limitations, or

4. Any other limitations that must be taken into account at the partner level in figuring taxable income (for example, the section 179 expense limitation).

For information on these provisions, see _Limitations on Losses, Deductions, and Credits_, earlier.

If you are an individual and the passive activity rules do not apply to the amounts shown on your Schedule K-1, take the amounts shown and enter them on the lines on your tax return as indicated in the summarized reporting information shown on page 2 of the Schedule K-1. If the passive activity rules do apply, report the amounts shown as indicated in these instructions.

If you are not an individual, report the amounts in each box as instructed on your tax return.

The line numbers in the summarized reporting information on page 2 of Schedule K-1 are references to forms in use for calendar year 2014. If you file your tax return on a calendar year basis, but your partnership files a return for a fiscal year, report the amounts on your tax return for the year in which the partnership's fiscal year ends. For example, if the partnership's tax year ends in February 2015, report the amounts on your 2015 tax return.

If you have losses, deductions, or credits from a prior year that were not deductible or usable because of certain limitations, such as the basis rules or the at-risk limitations, take them into account in determining your net income, loss, or credits for this year. However, except for passive activity losses and credits, do not combine the prior-year amounts with any amounts shown on this Schedule K-1 to get a net figure to report on any supporting schedules, statements, or forms attached to your return. Instead, report the amounts on the attached schedule, statement, or form on a year-by-year basis.

If the partnership reports a section 743(b) adjustment to partnership items, report these adjustments as separate items on Form 1040 in accordance with the reporting instructions for the partnership item being adjusted. A section 743(b) adjustment increases or decreases your share of income, deduction, gain, or loss for a

partnership item. For example, if the partnership reports a section 743(b) adjustment to depreciation for property used in its trade or business, report the adjustment on line 28 of Schedule E (Form 1040) in accordance with the instructions for box 1 of Schedule K-1.

 If you have amounts other than those shown on Schedule K-1 to report on Schedule E (Form 1040), enter each item separately on line 28 of Schedule E (Form 1040).

Codes. In box 11 and boxes 13 through 20, the partnership will identify each item by entering a code in the column to the left of the dollar amount entry space. These codes are identified on page 2 of Schedule K-1 and in these instructions.

Attached statements. The partnership will enter an asterisk (*) after the code, if any, in the column to the left of the dollar amount entry space for each item for which it has attached a statement providing additional information. For those informational items that cannot be reported as a single dollar amount, the partnership will enter an asterisk in the left column and enter "STMT" in the dollar amount entry space to indicate the information is provided on an attached statement.

Income (Loss)

Box 1. Ordinary Business Income (Loss)

The amount reported in box 1 is your share of the ordinary income (loss) from trade or business activities of the partnership. Generally, where you report this amount on Form 1040 depends on whether the amount is from an activity that is a passive activity to you. If you are an individual partner filing a 2014 Form 1040, find your situation below and report your box 1 income (loss) as instructed, after applying the basis and at-risk limitations on losses. If the partnership had more than one trade or business activity, it will attach a statement identifying the income or loss from each activity.

1. Report box 1 income (loss) from partnership trade or business activities in which you materially participated on Schedule E (Form 1040), line 28, column (h) or (j).

2. Report box 1 income (loss) from partnership trade or business activities in which you did not materially participate, as follows.

a. If income is reported in box 1, report the income on Schedule E (Form 1040), line 28, column (g). However, if the box in item D is checked, report the income following the rules for _Publicly traded partnerships_, earlier.

b. If a loss is reported in box 1, follow the Instructions for Form 8582 to figure how much of the loss can be reported on Schedule E (Form 1040), line 28, column (f).

However, if the box in item D is checked, report the loss following the rules for *Publicly traded partnerships*, earlier.

Box 2. Net Rental Real Estate Income (Loss)

Generally, the income (loss) reported in box 2 is a passive activity amount for all partners. However, the income (loss) in box 2 is not from a passive activity if you were a real estate professional (defined earlier) and you materially participated in the activity. If the partnership had more than one rental real estate activity, it will attach a statement identifying the income or loss from each activity.

If you are filing a 2014 Form 1040, use the following instructions to determine where to report a box 2 amount.

1.   If you have a loss from a passive activity in box 2 and you meet all the following conditions, report the loss on Schedule E (Form 1040), line 28, column (f).

a.   You actively participated in the partnership rental real estate activities. See *Special allowance for a rental real estate activity*, earlier.

b.   Rental real estate activities with active participation were your only passive activities.

c.   You have no prior year unallowed losses from these activities.

d.   Your total loss from the rental real estate activities was not more than $25,000 (not more than $12,500 if married filing separately and you lived apart from your spouse all year).

e.   If you are a married person filing separately, you lived apart from your spouse all year.

f.   You have no current or prior year unallowed credits from a passive activity.

g.   Your modified adjusted gross income was not more than $100,000 (not more than $50,000 if married filing separately and you lived apart from your spouse all year).

h.   Your interest in the rental real estate activity was not held as a limited partner.

2.   If you have a loss from a passive activity in box 2 and you do not meet all the conditions in 1, above, follow the Instructions for Form 8582 to figure how much of the loss you can report on Schedule E (Form 1040), line 28, column (f). However, if the box in item D is checked, report the loss following the rules for *Publicly traded partnerships*, earlier.

3.   If you were a real estate professional and you materially participated in the activity, report box 2 income (loss) on Schedule E (Form 1040), line 28, column (h) or (j).

4.   If you have income from a passive activity in box 2, report the income on Schedule E (Form 1040), line 28, column (g). However, if the box in item D is checked, report the income following the rules for *Publicly traded partnerships*, earlier.

Box 3. Other Net Rental Income (Loss)

The amount in box 3 is a passive activity amount for all partners. If the partnership had more than one rental activity, it will attach a statement identifying the income or loss from each activity. Report the income or loss as follows.

1.   If box 3 is a loss, follow the Instructions for Form 8582 to figure how much of the loss can be reported on Schedule E (Form 1040), line 28, column (f). However, if the box in item D is checked, report the loss following the rules for *Publicly traded partnerships*, earlier.

2.   If income is reported in box 3, report the income on Schedule E (Form 1040), line 28, column (g). However, if the box in item D is checked, report the income following the rules for *Publicly traded partnerships*, earlier.

Box 4. Guaranteed Payments

Generally, amounts on this line are not passive income, and you should report them on Schedule E (Form 1040), line 28, column (j) (for example, guaranteed payments for personal services).

Portfolio Income

Portfolio income or loss (shown in boxes 5 through 9b and in box 11, code A) is not subject to the passive activity limitations. Portfolio income includes income (not derived in the ordinary course of a trade or business) from interest, ordinary dividends, annuities or royalties, and gain or loss on the sale of property that produces such income or is held for investment.

Box 5. Interest Income

Report interest income on line 8a of Form 1040. If the amount of interest income included in box 5 includes interest from the credit for holders of clean renewable energy bonds, the partnership will attach a statement to Schedule K-1 showing your share of interest income from these credits. Because the basis of your interest in the partnership has been increased by your share of the interest income from these credits, you must reduce your basis by the same amount. See line 4 of the *Worksheet for Adjusting the Basis of a Partner's Interest in the Partnership*, earlier.

Box 6a. Ordinary Dividends

Report ordinary dividends on line 9a of Form 1040.

Box 6b. Qualified Dividends

Report any qualified dividends on line 9b of Form 1040.

Note.   Qualified dividends are excluded from investment income, but you may elect to include part or all of these amounts in investment income. See the instructions for line 4g of Form 4952, Investment Interest Expense Deduction, for important information on making this election.

 If you have any foreign source qualified dividends, see the instructions for box 16, later.

Note.   In the case of a corporate partner, the partnership will attach a statement to the Schedule K-1 explaining what part of the dividends included in boxes 6a and 6b is eligible for the "dividends received by corporations deduction" under section 243(a), (b), or (c).

Box 7. Royalties

Report royalties on Schedule E (Form 1040), line 4.

Box 8. Net Short-Term Capital Gain (Loss)

Report the net short-term capital gain (loss) on Schedule D (Form 1040), line 5.

Box 9a. Net Long-Term Capital Gain (Loss)

Report the net long-term capital gain (loss) on Schedule D (Form 1040), line 12.

 If you have any foreign source net long-term capital gain (loss), see the instructions for box 16, later.

Box 9b. Collectibles (28%) Gain (Loss)

Report collectibles gain or loss on line 4 of the *28% Rate Gain Worksheet—Line 18* in the Instructions for Schedule D (Form 1040).

 If you have any foreign source collectibles (28%) gain (loss), see the instructions for box 16, later.

Box 9c. Unrecaptured Section 1250 Gain

There are three types of unrecaptured section 1250 gain. Report your share of this unrecaptured gain on the *Unrecaptured Section 1250 Gain Worksheet—Line 19* in the Instructions for Schedule D (Form 1040) as follows.

• Report unrecaptured section 1250 gain from the sale or exchange of the partnership's business assets on line 5.
• Report unrecaptured section 1250 gain from the sale or exchange of an interest in a partnership on line 10.
• Report unrecaptured section 1250 gain from an estate, trust, regulated investment company (RIC), or real estate investment trust (REIT) on line 11.

If the partnership reports only unrecaptured section 1250 gain from the sale or exchange of its business assets, it will enter a dollar amount in box 9c. If it reports the other two types of unrecaptured gain, it will provide an attached statement that shows the amount for each type of unrecaptured section 1250 gain.

 If you have any foreign source unrecaptured section 1250 gain, see the instructions for box 16, later.

Box 10. Net Section 1231 Gain (Loss)

The amount in box 10 is generally passive if it is from a:
- Rental activity or
- Trade or business activity in which you did not materially participate.

However, an amount from a rental real estate activity is not from a passive activity if you were a real estate professional (defined earlier) and you materially participated in the activity.

If the amount is either **(a)** a loss that is not from a passive activity or **(b)** a gain, report it on line 2, column (g), of Form 4797, Sales of Business Property. Do not complete columns (b) through (f) on line 2 of Form 4797. Instead, enter "From Schedule K-1 (Form 1065)" across these columns.

If the amount is a loss from a passive activity, see *Passive Loss Limitations* in the Instructions for Form 4797. Report the loss following the Instructions for Form 8582 to figure how much of the loss is allowed on Form 4797. However, if the box in item D is checked, report the loss following the rules for *Publicly traded partnerships*, earlier. If the partnership had net section 1231 gain (loss) from more than one activity, it will attach a statement that will identify the section 1231 gain (loss) from each activity.

 If you have any foreign source net section 1231 gain (loss), see the instructions for box 16, later.

Box 11. Other Income (Loss)

Code A. Other portfolio income (loss). The partnership will report portfolio income other than interest, ordinary dividend, royalty, and capital gain (loss) income, and attach a statement to tell you what kind of portfolio income is reported.

If the partnership held a residual interest in a real estate mortgage investment conduit (REMIC), it will report on the statement your share of REMIC taxable income (net loss) that you report on Schedule E (Form 1040), line 38, column (d). The statement will also report your share of any "excess inclusion" that you report on Schedule E (Form 1040), line 38, column (c), and your share of section 212 expenses that you report on Schedule E (Form 1040), line 38, column (e). If you itemize your deductions on Schedule A (Form 1040), you may also deduct these section 212 expenses as a miscellaneous deduction subject to the 2% limit on Schedule A (Form 1040), line 23.

Code B. Involuntary conversions. This is your net gain (loss) from involuntary conversions due to casualty or theft. The partnership will give you a statement that shows the amounts to be reported on Form 4684, Casualties and Thefts, line 34, columns (b)(i), (b)(ii), and (c).

If there was a gain (loss) from a casualty or theft to property not used in a trade or business or for income-producing purposes,

the partnership will provide you with the information you need to complete Form 4684.

Code C. Section 1256 contracts and straddles. The partnership will report any net gain or loss from section 1256 contracts. Report this amount on Form 6781, Gains and Losses From Section 1256 Contracts and Straddles.

Code D. Mining exploration costs recapture. The partnership will give you a statement that shows the information needed to recapture certain mining exploration costs (section 617). See Pub. 535 for details.

Code E. Cancellation of debt. Generally, this cancellation of debt (COD) amount is included in your gross income (Form 1040, line 21). Under section 108(b)(5), you may elect to apply any portion of the COD amount excluded from gross income to the reduction of the basis of depreciable property. See Form 982 for more details.

Code F. Other income (loss). Amounts with code F are other items of income, gain, or loss not included in boxes 1 through 10 or reported in box 11 using codes A through E. The partnership should give you a description and the amount of your share for each of these items.

Report loss items that are passive activity amounts to you following the Instructions for Form 8582. However, if the box in item D is checked, report the loss following the rules for *Publicly traded partnerships*, earlier.

Code F items may include the following.
- Gain or loss attributable to the sale or exchange of qualified preferred stock of the Federal National Mortgage Association (Fannie Mae) and the Federal Home Loan Mortgage Corporation (Freddie Mac). The partnership will report on an attached statement the amount of gain or loss attributable to the sale or exchange of the qualified preferred stock, the date the stock was acquired by the partnership, and the date the stock was sold or exchanged by the partnership. If the partner is **not** a financial institution, report the gain or loss on line 5 or line 12 of Schedule D (Form 1040) in accordance with the Instructions for Schedule D and Instructions for Form 8949. If a partner is a financial institution referred to in section 582(c)(2) or a depositary institution holding company (as defined in section 3(w)(1) of the Federal Deposit Insurance Act), report the gain or loss in accordance with the Instructions for Form 4797 and Rev. Proc. 2008-64, 2008-47 I.R.B. 1195.
- Partnership gains from the disposition of farm recapture property (see the instructions for line 27 of Form 4797) and other items to which section 1252 applies.
- Income from recoveries of tax benefit items. A tax benefit item is an amount you deducted in a prior tax year that reduced your income tax. Report this amount on line 21 of Form 1040 to the extent it reduced your tax in the prior tax year.
- Gambling gains and losses.

1. If the partnership was not engaged in the trade or business of gambling, (a) report gambling winnings on Form 1040, line 21, and (b) deduct gambling losses to the extent of winnings on Schedule A (Form 1040), line 28.

2. If the partnership was engaged in the trade or business of gambling, (a) report gambling winnings on line 28 of Schedule E (Form 1040) and (b) deduct gambling losses (to the extent of winnings) on line 28 of Schedule E (Form 1040), column (h).

- Gain (loss) from the disposition of an interest in oil, gas, geothermal, or other mineral properties. The partnership will attach a statement that provides a description of the property, your share of the amount realized from the disposition, your share of the partnership's adjusted basis in the property (for other than oil or gas properties), and your share of the total intangible drilling costs, development costs, and mining exploration costs (section 59(e) expenditures) passed through for the property. You must figure your gain or loss from the disposition by increasing your share of the adjusted basis by the intangible drilling costs, development costs, or mine exploration costs for the property that you capitalized (that is, costs that you did not elect to deduct under section 59(e)). Report a loss in Part I of Form 4797. Report a gain in Part III of Form 4797 in accordance with the instructions for line 28. See Regulations section 1.1254-5 for details.
- Any income, gain, or loss to the partnership under section 751(b) (certain distributions treated as sales or exchanges). Report this amount on Form 4797, line 10.
- Specially allocated ordinary gain (loss). Report this amount on Form 4797, line 10.
- Net short-term capital gain (loss) and net long-term capital gain (loss) from Schedule D (Form 1065) that is not portfolio income. An example is gain or loss from the disposition of nondepreciable personal property used in a trade or business activity of the partnership. Report total net short-term gain (loss) on Schedule D (Form 1040), line 5. Report the total net long-term gain (loss) on Schedule D (Form 1040), line 12.
- Current year section 108(i) cancellation of debt (COD) income. The partnership will provide your share of the deferred COD income amount that you must include in income in the current tax year under section 108(i)(1) or section 108(i)(5)(D)(i) or (ii).
- Gain from the sale or exchange of qualified small business (QSB) stock (as defined in the Instructions for Schedule D (Form 1065)) that is eligible for a section 1202 exclusion. The partnership should also give you **(a)** the name of the corporation that issued the QSB stock, **(b)** your share of the partnership's adjusted basis and sales price of the QSB stock, and **(c)** the dates the QSB stock was bought and sold. Corporate partners are not eligible for the section 1202 exclusion. The following additional limitations apply at the partner level.

1. You must have held an interest in the partnership when the partnership acquired

the QSB stock and at all times thereafter until the partnership disposed of the QSB stock.

2. Your share of the eligible section 1202 gain cannot exceed the amount that would have been allocated to you based on your interest in the partnership at the time the QSB stock was acquired.

See the Instructions for Schedule D (Form 1040) and the Instructions for Form 8949 for details on how to report the gain and the amount of the allowable exclusion.

• Gain eligible for section 1045 rollover.

Replacement stock purchased by the partnership. The partnership should give you (a) the name of the corporation that issued the qualified small business (QSB) stock, (b) your share of the partnership's adjusted basis and sales price of the QSB stock, (c) the dates the QSB stock was bought and sold, (d) your share of gain from the sale of the QSB stock, and (e) your share of the gain that was deferred by the partnership under section 1045. Corporate partners are not eligible for the section 1045 rollover. To qualify for the section 1045 rollover:

1. You must have held an interest in the partnership during the entire period in which the partnership held the QSB stock (more than 6 months prior to the sale) and

2. Your share of the gain eligible for the section 1045 rollover cannot exceed the amount that would have been allocated to you based on your interest in the partnership at the time the QSB stock was acquired.

See the Instructions for Schedule D (Form 1040) and the Instructions for Form 8949 for details on how to report the gain and the amount of the allowable postponed gain.

Opting out of partnership election. You can opt out of the partnership's section 1045 election and either (1) recognize the gain or (2) elect to purchase different replacement QSB stock, either directly or through ownership of a different partnership that acquired replacement QSB stock. You satisfy the requirement to purchase replacement QSB stock if you own an interest in a partnership that purchases QSB stock during the 60-day period. You also must notify the partnership, in writing, if you opt out of the partnership's section 1045 election. If you recognize gain, you must notify the partnership, in writing, of the amount of the gain that you are recognizing.

Replacement stock not purchased by the partnership. The partnership should give you (a) the name of the corporation that issued the qualified small business (QSB) stock, (b) your share of the partnership's adjusted basis and sales price of the QSB stock, (c) the dates the QSB stock was bought and sold, and (d) your share of gain from the sale of the QSB stock. Corporate partners are not eligible for the section 1045 rollover. To qualify for the section 1045 rollover:

1. You must have held an interest in the partnership during the entire period in which the partnership held the QSB stock,

2. Your share of the gain eligible for the section 1045 rollover cannot exceed the amount that would have been allocated to you based on your interest in the partnership at the time the QSB stock was acquired, and

3. You must purchase other QSB stock (as defined in the Instructions for Schedule D (Form 1040)) during the 60-day period that began on the date the QSB stock was sold by the partnership.

See the Instructions for Schedule D (Form 1040) and the Instructions for Form 8949 for details on how to report the gain and the amount of the allowable postponed gain.

Making the section 1045 election. You make a section 1045 election on a timely filed return for the tax year during which the partnership's tax year ends. See the Instructions for Form 8949 and the Instructions for Schedule D (Form 1040) for more information. Attach to your Schedule D (Form 1040) a statement that includes the following information for each amount of gain that you do not recognize under section 1045.

• The name of the corporation that issued the QSB stock.

• The name and EIN of the selling partnership.

• The dates the QSB stock was purchased and sold.

• The amount of gain that is not recognized under section 1045.

• If a partner purchases QSB stock, the name of the corporation that issued the replacement QSB stock, the date the stock was purchased, and the cost of the stock.

• If a partner treats the partner's interest in QSB stock that is purchased by a purchasing partnership as the partner's replacement QSB stock, the name and EIN of the purchasing partnership, the name of the corporation that issued the replacement QSB stock, the partner's share of the cost of the QSB stock that was purchased by the partnership, the computation of the partner's adjustment to basis with respect to that QSB stock, and the date the stock was purchased by the partnership.

Distribution of replacement qualified small business (QSB) stock to a partner that reduces another partner's interest in replacement QSB stock. You must recognize gain upon a distribution of replacement QSB stock to another partner that reduces your share of the replacement QSB stock held by a partnership. The amount of gain that you must recognize is based on the amount of gain that you would recognize upon a sale of the distributed replacement QSB stock for its fair market value on the date of the distribution, but not to exceed the amount you previously deferred under section 1045 with respect to the distributed replacement QSB stock. If the partnership distributed your share of

replacement QSB stock to another partner, the partnership should give you (a) the name of the corporation that issued the replacement QSB stock, (b) the date the replacement QSB stock was distributed to another partner or partners, and (c) your share of the partnership's adjusted basis and fair market value of the replacement QSB stock on such date.

For more information see Regulations section 1.1045-1.

Deductions

Box 12. Section 179 Deduction

Use this amount, along with the total cost of section 179 property placed in service during the year from other sources, to complete Part I of Form 4562, Depreciation and Amortization. The partnership will report on an attached statement your allowable share of the cost of any qualified enterprise zone, qualified section 179 disaster assistance, or qualified real property it placed in service during the tax year. Report the amount from line 12 of Form 4562 allocable to a passive activity using the Instructions for Form 8582. If the amount is not a passive activity deduction, report it on Schedule E (Form 1040), line 28, column (i). However, if the box in item D is checked, report this amount following the rules for *Publicly traded partnerships*, earlier.

Box 13. Other Deductions

Contributions. Codes A through G. The partnership will give you a statement that shows charitable contributions subject to the 100%, 50%, 30%, and 20% adjusted gross income limitations. For more details, see Pub. 526, Charitable Contributions, and the Instructions for Schedule A (Form 1040). If your contributions are subject to more than one of the AGI limitations, see *Worksheet 2. Applying the Deduction Limits* in Pub. 526.

Charitable contribution deductions are not taken into account in figuring your passive activity loss for the year. Do not include them on Form 8582.

Code A. Cash contributions (50%). Report this amount, subject to the 50% AGI limitation, on line 16 of Schedule A (Form 1040).

Code B. Cash contributions (30%). Report this amount, subject to the 30% AGI limitation, on line 16 of Schedule A (Form 1040).

Code C. Noncash contributions (50%). If property other than cash is contributed, and if the claimed deduction for one item or group of similar items of property exceeds $5,000, the partnership must give you a copy of Form 8283, Noncash Charitable Contributions, to attach to your tax return. Do not deduct the amount shown on Form 8283. It is the partnership's contribution. Instead, deduct the amount identified by code C, box 13, subject to the 50% AGI limitation, on line 17 of Schedule A (Form 1040).

If the partnership provides you with information that the contribution was property other than cash and does not give you a Form 8283, see the Instructions for Form 8283 for filing requirements. Do not file Form 8283 unless the total claimed deduction for all contributed items of property exceeds $500.

Food inventory contributions. The partnership will report on an attached statement your share of qualified food inventory contributions. The food inventory contribution is not included in the amount reported in box 13 using code C. The partnership will also report your share of the partnership's net income from the business activities that made the food inventory contribution(s). Your deduction for food inventory contributions cannot exceed 10% of your aggregate net income for the tax year from the business activities from which the food inventory contribution was made (including your share of net income from partnership or S corporation businesses that made food inventory contributions). Report the deduction, subject to the 50% AGI limitation, on line 17 of Schedule A (Form 1040).

Code D. Noncash contributions (30%). Report this amount, subject to the 30% AGI limitation, on line 17 of Schedule A (Form 1040).

Code E. Capital gain property to a 50% organization (30%). Report this amount, subject to the 30% AGI limitation, on line 17 of Schedule A (Form 1040). See *Special 30% Limit for Capital Gain Property* in Pub. 526.

Code F. Capital gain property (20%). Report this amount, subject to the 20% AGI limitation, on line 17 of Schedule A (Form 1040).

Code G. Contributions (100%). The partnership will report your share of qualified conservation contributions of property used in agriculture or livestock production. This contribution is not included in the amount reported in box 13 using code C. If you are a farmer or rancher, you qualify for a 100% AGI limitation for this contribution. Otherwise, your deduction for this contribution is subject to a 50% AGI limitation. Report this deduction on line 17 of Schedule A (Form 1040). See Pub. 526 for more information on qualified conservation contributions.

Code H. Investment interest expense. Include this amount on Form 4952, line 1. If the partnership has investment income or other investment expenses, it will report your share of these items in box 20 using codes A and B. Include investment income and expenses from other sources to figure how much of your total investment interest is deductible. You will also need this information to figure your investment interest expense deduction.

If the partnership paid or accrued interest on debts properly allocable to investment property, the amount of interest you are allowed to deduct may be limited.

For more information on the special provisions that apply to investment interest expense, see Form 4952 and Pub. 550, Investment Income and Expenses.

Code I. Deductions—royalty income. Include deductions allocable to royalties on Schedule E (Form 1040), line 19. For this type of expense, enter "From Schedule K-1 (Form 1065)."

These deductions are not taken into account in figuring your passive activity loss for the year. Do not enter them on Form 8582.

Code J. Section 59(e)(2) expenditures. On an attached statement, the partnership will show the type and the amount of qualified expenditures for which you may make a section 59(e) election. The statement will also identify the property for which the expenditures were paid or incurred. If there is more than one type of expenditure, the amount of each type will also be listed.

If you deduct these expenditures in full in the current year, they are treated as adjustments or tax preference items for purposes of alternative minimum tax. However, you may elect to amortize these expenditures over the number of years in the applicable period rather than deduct the full amount in the current year. If you make this election, these items are not treated as adjustments or tax preference items.

Under the election, you can deduct circulation expenditures ratably over a 3-year period. Research and experimental expenditures and mining exploration and development costs can be amortized over a 10-year period. Intangible drilling and development costs can be amortized over a 60-month period. The amortization period begins with the month in which such costs were paid or incurred.

Make the election on Form 4562. If you make the election, report the current year amortization of section 59(e) expenditures from Part VI of Form 4562 on line 28 of Schedule E (Form 1040). If you do not make the election, report the section 59(e)(2) expenditures on line 28 of Schedule E (Form 1040) and figure the resulting adjustment or tax preference item (see Form 6251, Alternative Minimum Tax—Individuals). Whether you deduct the expenditures or elect to amortize them, report the amount on a separate line in column (h) of line 28 if you materially participated in the partnership activity. If you did not materially participate, follow the Instructions for Form 8582 to figure how much of the deduction can be reported in column (f).

Code K. Deductions—portfolio (2% floor). Amounts entered with code K are deductions that are clearly and directly allocable to portfolio income (other than investment interest expense and section 212 expenses from a REMIC). Generally, you should report these amounts on Schedule A (Form 1040), line 23. See the Instructions for

Schedule A (Form 1040), lines 23 and 28, for details.

These deductions are not taken into account in figuring your passive activity loss for the year. Do not enter them on Form 8582.

Code L. Deductions—portfolio (other). Generally, you should report these amounts on Schedule A (Form 1040), line 28. See the Instructions for Schedule A, lines 23 and 28, for details. These deductions are not taken into account in figuring your passive activity loss for the year. Do not enter them on Form 8582.

Code M. Amounts paid for medical insurance. Any amounts paid during the tax year for insurance that constitutes medical care for you, your spouse, your dependents, and your children under age 27 who are not dependents. On line 29 of Form 1040, you may be allowed to deduct such amounts, even if you do not itemize deductions. If you do itemize deductions, enter on line 1 of Schedule A (Form 1040) any amounts not deducted on line 29 of Form 1040.

Code N. Educational assistance benefits. Deduct your educational assistance benefits on a separate line of Schedule E (Form 1040), line 28, up to the $5,250 limitation. If your benefits exceed $5,250, you may be able to use the excess amount on Form 8863 to figure the education credits.

Code O. Dependent care benefits. The partnership will report the dependent care benefits you received. You must use Form 2441, Part III, to figure the amount, if any, of the benefits you may exclude from your income.

Code P. Preproductive period expenses. You may be able to deduct these expenses currently or you may need to capitalize them under section 263A. See Pub. 225, Farmer's Tax Guide, and Regulations section 1.263A-4 for details.

Code Q. Commercial revitalization deduction from rental real estate activities. Follow the Instructions for Form 8582 to figure how much of the deduction can be reported on Schedule E (Form 1040), line 28, column (f).

Code R. Pensions and IRAs. Payments made on your behalf to an IRA, qualified plan, simplified employee pension (SEP), or a SIMPLE IRA plan. See Form 1040 instructions for line 32 to figure your IRA deduction. Enter payments made to a qualified plan, SEP, or SIMPLE IRA plan on Form 1040, line 28. If the payments to a qualified plan were to a defined benefit plan, the partnership should give you a statement showing the amount of the benefit accrued for the current tax year.

Code S. Reforestation expense deduction. The partnership will provide a statement that describes the qualified timber property for these reforestation expenses. The expense deduction is limited to $10,000 ($5,000 if married filing separately) for each qualified timber property, including your share of the partnership's expense and any reforestation expenses you separately paid or incurred during the tax year.

If you did not materially participate in the activity, use Form 8582 to figure the amount to report on Schedule E (Form 1040), line 28. If you materially participated in the reforestation activity, report the deduction on line 28, column (h), of Schedule E (Form 1040).

Code T. Domestic production activities information. The partnership will provide you with a statement with information that you must use to figure the domestic production activities deduction. Use Form 8903, Domestic Production Activities Deduction, to figure this deduction. See the Instructions for Form 8903 for details.

Code U. Qualified production activities income (QPAI). Report the QPAI reported to you by the partnership (in box 13 of Schedule K-1) in the applicable column of Form 8903, line 7.

Code V. Employer's Form W-2 wages. Report the portion of Form W-2 wages reported to you by the partnership (in box 13 of Schedule K-1) on line 17 of Form 8903.

Code W. Other deductions. Amounts with this code may include:
• Itemized deductions that Form 1040 filers report on Schedule A (Form 1040).
• Soil and water conservation expenditures and endangered species recovery expenditures. See section 175 for limitations on the amount you are allowed to deduct.
• Expenditures for the removal of architectural and transportation barriers to the elderly and disabled that the partnership elected to treat as a current expense. The deductions are limited by section 190(c) to $15,000 per year from all sources.
• Interest expense allocated to debt-financed distributions. The manner in which you report such interest expense depends on your use of the distributed debt proceeds. If the proceeds were used in a trade or business activity, report the interest on line 28 of Schedule E (Form 1040). In column (a) enter the name of the partnership and "interest expense." If you materially participated in the trade or business activity, enter the interest expense in column (h). If you did not materially participate in the activity, follow the Instructions for Form 8582 to figure the interest expense you can report in column (f). See the definition of *material participation*, earlier. If the proceeds were used in an investment activity, report the interest on Form 4952. If the proceeds are used for personal purposes, the interest is generally not deductible.
• Interest paid or accrued on debt properly allocable to your share of a working interest in any oil or gas property (if your liability is not limited). If you did not materially participate in the oil or gas activity, this interest is investment interest reportable as described earlier, under *Code H. Investment interest expense*; otherwise, it is trade or business interest. If you did not materially participate in the oil or gas activity, this

interest is investment interest expense and should be reported on Form 4952. If you materially participated in the activity, report the interest on line 28 of Schedule E (Form 1040). On a separate line, enter "interest expense" and the name of the partnership in column (a) and the amount in column (h).
• Contributions to a capital construction fund (CCF). The deduction for a CCF investment is not taken on Schedule E (Form 1040). Instead, you subtract the deduction from the amount that would normally be entered as taxable income on line 43 (Form 1040). In the margin to the left of line 43, enter "CCF" and the amount of the deduction.
• Penalty on early withdrawal of savings. Report this amount on Form 1040, line 30.
• Film and television production expenses. The partnership will provide a statement that describes the film or television production generating these expenses. Generally, if the aggregate cost of the production exceeds $15 million, you are not entitled to the deduction. The limitation is $20 million for productions in certain areas (see section 181 for details). If you did not materially participate in the activity, use Form 8582 to determine the amount that can be reported on Schedule E (Form 1040), line 28, column (f). If you materially participated in the production activity, report the deduction on Schedule E (Form 1040), line 28, column (h).
• Current year section 108(i) original issue discount (OID) deduction. The partnership will provide your share of the partnership's OID deduction deferred under section 108(i)(2)(A)(i) that is allowable as a deduction in the current tax year under section 108(i)(2)(A)(ii) or section 108(i)(5)(D)(i) or (ii).

The partnership will give you a description and the amount of your share for each of these items.

Box 14. Self-Employment Earnings (Loss)

If you and your spouse are both partners, each of you must complete and file your own Schedule SE (Form 1040), Self-Employment Tax, to report your partnership net earnings (loss) from self-employment.

Code A. Net earnings (loss) from self-employment. If you are a general partner, reduce this amount before entering it on Schedule SE (Form 1040) by any section 179 expense deduction claimed, unreimbursed partnership expenses claimed, and depletion claimed on oil and gas properties. Do not reduce net earnings from self-employment by any separately stated deduction for health insurance expenses.

If the amount on this line is a loss, enter only the deductible amount on Schedule SE (Form 1040). See *Limitations on Losses, Deductions, and Credits*, earlier.

If your partnership is an options dealer or a commodities dealer, see section 1402(i).

If your partnership is an investment club, see Rev. Rul. 75-525, 1975-2 C.B. 350.

Code B. Gross farming or fishing income. If you are an individual partner, enter the amount from this line, as an item of information, on Schedule E (Form 1040), line 42. Also use this amount to figure net earnings from self-employment under the farm optional method on Schedule SE (Form 1040), Section B, Part II.

Code C. Gross nonfarm income. If you are an individual partner, use this amount to figure net earnings from self-employment under the nonfarm optional method on Schedule SE (Form 1040), Section B, Part II.

Box 15. Credits

If you have credits that are passive activity credits to you, you must complete Form 8582-CR (or Form 8810 for corporations) in addition to the credit forms identified below. See *Passive Activity Limitations*, earlier, and the Instructions for Form 8582-CR (or Form 8810) for details.

 Generally, you are not required to complete the source credit form or attach it to Form 3800 if you are a taxpayer that is not a partnership or S corporation, and your only source for a credit listed in Form 3800, Part III, is from a partnership, S corporation, estate, trust, or cooperative. (Instead, you can report this credit directly on Form 3800, Part III, and enter the EIN of the partnership in column (b) of Part III.) The following exceptions apply:
• *You are claiming the investment credit (Form 3468) or the biodiesel and renewable diesel fuels credit (Form 8864) in Part III with box A or B checked.*
• *The taxpayer is an estate or trust and the source credit can be allocated to beneficiaries. For more details, see the Instructions for Form 1041, U.S. Income Tax Return for Estates and Trusts, Schedule K-1, box 13.*
• *The taxpayer is a cooperative and the source credit can or must be allocated to patrons. For more details, see the Instructions for Form 1120-C, U.S. Income Tax Return for Cooperative Associations, Schedule J, line 5c.*

Codes A, B, C, and D. Low-income housing credit. If section 42(j)(5) applies, the partnership will report your share of the low-income housing credit using code A or code C, depending on the date the building was placed in service. If section 42(j)(5) does not apply, your share of the credit will be reported using code B or code D, depending on the date the building was placed in service. Any allowable low-income housing credit reported using code A or code B is reported on line 4 of Form 8586, Low-Income Housing Credit, or line 1d of Form 3800 (see TIP, earlier). Any allowable low-income housing credit reported using code C or code D is reported on line 11 of Form 8586 or line 4d of Form 3800.

Keep a separate record of the low-income housing credit from each separate source so that you can correctly figure any recapture of low-income housing credit that may result from the disposition of all or part of your partnership interest. For more information on recapture, see the Instructions for Form 8611, Recapture of Low-Income Housing Credit.

Code E. Qualified rehabilitation expenditures (rental real estate). The partnership will report your share of the qualified rehabilitation expenditures and other information you need to complete Form 3468 related to rental real estate activities using code E. Your share of qualified rehabilitation expenditures from property not related to rental real estate activities will be reported in box 20 using code D. See the Instructions for Form 3468 for details. If the partnership is reporting expenditures from more than one activity, the attached statement will separately identify the expenditures from each activity.

Combine the expenditures (for Form 3468 reporting) from box 15, code E and box 20, code D. The expenditures related to rental real estate activities (box 15, code E) are reported on Schedule K-1 separately from other qualified rehabilitation expenditures (box 20, code D) because they are subject to different passive activity limitation rules. See the Instructions for Form 8582-CR for details.

Code F. Other rental real estate credits. The partnership will identify the type of credit and any other information you need to figure these credits from rental real estate activities (other than the low-income housing credit and qualified rehabilitation expenditures). These credits may be limited by the passive activity limitations. If the credits are from more than one activity, the partnership will identify the credits from each activity on an attached statement. See *Passive Activity Limitations*, earlier, and the Instructions for Form 8582-CR for details.

Code G. Other rental credits. The partnership will identify the type of credit and any other information you need to figure these rental credits. These credits may be limited by the passive activity limitations. If the credits are from more than one activity, the partnership will identify the credits from each activity on an attached statement. See *Passive Activity Limitations*, earlier, and the Instructions for Form 8582-CR for details.

Code H. Undistributed capital gains credit. Code H represents taxes paid on undistributed capital gains by a regulated investment company or real estate investment trust. Report these taxes on line 73 of Form 1040, check box "a" for Form 2439, and enter "Form 1065."

Code I. Biofuel producer credit. Report this amount on line 3 of Form 6478, Biofuel Producer Credit, or line 4c of Form 3800, Part III (see TIP, earlier).

Code J. Work opportunity credit. Report this amount on line 3 of Form 5884, Work Opportunity Credit, or line 4b of Form 3800, Part III (see TIP, earlier).

Code K. Disabled access credit. Report this amount on line 7 of Form 8826, Disabled Access Credit, or line 1e of Form 3800, Part III (see TIP, earlier).

Code L. Empowerment zone employment credit. Report this amount on line 3 of Form 8844, Empowerment Zone Employment Credit, or line 3 of Form 3800, Part III (see TIP, earlier).

Code M. Credit for increasing research activities. Report this amount on line 37 of Form 6765, Credit for Increasing Research Activities, or line 1c of Form 3800, Part III (see TIP, earlier).

Code N. Credit for employer social security and Medicare taxes. Report this amount on line 5 of Form 8846, Credit for Employer Social Security and Medicare Taxes Paid on Certain Employee Tips, or line 4f of Form 3800, Part III (see TIP, earlier).

Code O. Backup withholding. This is your share of the credit for backup withholding on dividends, interest income, and other types of income. Include this amount in the total you enter on Form 1040, line 64 and attach a copy of the Schedule K-1 to your tax return. Instead of attaching a copy of the Schedule K-1 to the tax return, you can include a statement with the return that provides the partnership's name, address, EIN, and backup withholding amount.

Code P. Other credits. On a statement attached to Schedule K-1, the partnership will identify the type of credit and any other information you need to figure credits other than those reported with codes A through O. Most credits identified by code P will be reported on Form 3800 (see TIP, earlier).

Credits that may be reported with code P include the following:
- New markets credit (Form 8874).
- Nonconventional source fuel credit (Form 8907).
- Qualified railroad track maintenance credit (Form 8900).
- Unused investment credit from the qualifying advanced coal project credit, qualifying gasification project credit, or qualifying advanced energy project credit allocated from cooperatives (Form 3468, line 9).
- Unused investment credit from the rehabilitation credit or energy credit allocated from cooperatives (Form 3468, line 13).
- Renewable electricity, refined coal, and Indian coal production credit. The partnership will provide a statement showing separately the amount of credit from Part I and Part II of Form 8835.
- Indian employment credit (Form 8845).
- Orphan drug credit (Form 8820).
- Credit for small employer pension plan startup costs (Form 8881).
- Credit for employer-provided childcare facilities and services (Form 8882).
- Biodiesel and renewable diesel fuels credit. If this credit includes the small agri-biodiesel producer credit, the

partnership will provide additional information on an attached statement. If no statement is attached, report this amount on line 9 of Form 8864. If a statement is attached, see the instructions for Form 8864, line 9.
- Low sulfur diesel fuel production credit (Form 8896).
- General credits from an electing large partnership. Report these credits on Form 3800, Part III, line 1bb.
- Distilled spirits credit (Form 8906).
- Energy efficient home credit (Form 8908).
- Energy efficient appliance credit (Form 8909).
- Alternative motor vehicle credit (Form 8910).
- Alternative fuel vehicle refueling property credit (Form 8911).
- Clean renewable energy bond credit. Report this amount on Form 8912.
- **New** clean renewable energy bond credit. Report this amount on Form 8912.
- Qualified energy conservation bond credit. Report this amount on Form 8912.
- Qualified zone academy bond credit. Report this amount on Form 8912.
- Qualified school construction bond credit. Report this amount on Form 8912.
- Build America bond credit. Report this amount on Form 8912.
- Mine rescue team training credit (Form 8923).
- Agricultural chemicals security credit (Form 8931).
- Credit for employer differential wage payments (Form 8932).
- Carbon dioxide sequestration credit (Form 8933).
- Qualified plug-in electric drive motor vehicle credit (Form 8936).
- Credit for small employer health insurance premiums (Form 8941).

Box 16. Foreign Transactions

Codes A through N. Use the information identified by codes A through N, code Q, and any attached statements to figure your foreign tax credit.

 Taxpayers filing Form 1116—If you have any qualified dividends, capital gains (including any capital gain distributions), capital losses, collectibles gain, collectibles losses, unrecaptured section 1250 gain, net section 1231 gain, or net section 1231 losses, you may have to make certain adjustments to those amounts before taking them into account on Form 1116.

For details, see Form 1116, Foreign Tax Credit, and its instructions; Form 1118, Foreign Tax Credit—Corporations, and its instructions; and Pub. 514, Foreign Tax Credit for Individuals.

Codes O and P. Extraterritorial income exclusion.

1. *Partnership did not claim the exclusion.* If the partnership reports your share of foreign trading gross receipts (code O) and the extraterritorial income exclusion (code P), the partnership was not entitled to claim the exclusion because it did not meet the foreign economic process requirements. You may still qualify for your share of this exclusion if the partnership's foreign trading gross receipts for the tax year were $5 million or less. To qualify for this exclusion, your foreign trading gross receipts from all sources for the tax year also must have been $5 million or less. If you qualify for the exclusion, report the exclusion amount in accordance with the instructions for *Income (Loss)*, earlier, for box 1, 2, or 3, whichever applies. See Form 8873, Extraterritorial Income Exclusion, for details.

2. *Partnership claimed the exclusion.* If the partnership reports your share of foreign trading gross receipts but not the amount of the extraterritorial income exclusion, the partnership met the foreign economic process requirements and claimed the exclusion when figuring your share of partnership income. You also may need to know the amount of your share of foreign trading gross receipts from this partnership to determine if you met the $5 million or less exception discussed above for purposes of qualifying for an extraterritorial income exclusion from other sources.

Note. Upon request, the partnership should furnish you a copy of the partnership's Form 8873 if there is a reduction for international boycott operations, illegal bribes, kickbacks, etc.

Code Q. Other foreign transactions. On a statement attached to Schedule K-1, the partnership will report any other information on foreign transactions that you may need using code Q.

The partnership will attach a statement that separately identifies any arrangement, along with the taxes paid or accrued in connection with the arrangement, in which the partnership participates that would qualify as a splitter arrangement under section 909 if one or more partners are covered persons regarding an entity that took into account related income from the arrangement. The statement will also indicate whether the partnership has taken into account any related income from any such splitter arrangement. See section 909 and the related regulations for rules regarding splitter arrangements.

Box 17. Alternative Minimum Tax (AMT) Items

Use the information reported in box 17 (as well as your adjustments and tax preference items from other sources) to prepare your Form 6251, Alternative Minimum Tax—Individuals; Form 4626, Alternative Minimum Tax—Corporations; or Schedule I (Form 1041), Alternative Minimum Tax—Estates and Trusts.

Note. A partner that is a corporation subject to alternative minimum tax must notify the partnership of its status.

Code A. This amount is your share of the partnership's post-1986 depreciation adjustment. If you are an individual partner, report this amount on line 18 of Form 6251.

Code B. This amount is your share of the partnership's adjusted gain or loss. If you are an individual partner, report this amount on line 17 of Form 6251.

Code C. This amount is your share of the partnership's depletion adjustment. If you are an individual partner, report this amount on line 9 of Form 6251.

Codes D and E. Oil, gas, & geothermal properties—gross income and deductions. The amounts reported on these lines include only the gross income (code D) from, and deductions (code E) allocable to, oil, gas, and geothermal properties included in box 1 of Schedule K-1. The partnership should have attached a statement that shows any income from or deductions allocable to such properties that are included in boxes 2 through 13, 18, and 20 of Schedule K-1. Use the amounts reported and the amounts on the attached statement to help you figure the net amount to enter on line 26 of Form 6251.

Code F. Other AMT items. Enter the information on the statement attached by the partnership on the applicable lines of Form 6251, Form 4626, or Schedule I (Form 1041).

Box 18. Tax-Exempt Income and Nondeductible Expenses

Code A. Tax-exempt interest income. Report on your return, as an item of information, your share of the tax-exempt interest received or accrued by the partnership during the year. Individual partners include this amount on Form 1040, line 8b. Increase the adjusted basis of your interest in the partnership by this amount.

Code B. Other tax-exempt income. Increase the adjusted basis of your interest in the partnership by the amount shown, but do not include it in income on your tax return.

Note. The partnership will attach a statement for the amount included under code B that is exempt by reason of section 892 and describe the nature of the income.

Code C. Nondeductible expenses. The nondeductible expenses paid or incurred by the partnership are not deductible on your tax return. Decrease the adjusted basis of your interest in the partnership by this amount.

Box 19. Distributions

Code A. Cash and marketable securities. Code A shows the distributions the

partnership made to you of cash and certain marketable securities. The marketable securities are included at their fair market value (FMV) on the date of distribution (minus your share of the partnership's gain on the securities distributed to you). If the amount shown as code A exceeds the adjusted basis of your partnership interest immediately before the distribution, the excess is treated as gain from the sale or exchange of your partnership interest. Generally, this gain is treated as gain from the sale of a capital asset and should be reported on Form 8949 and the Schedule D for your return. However, if you receive cash or property in exchange for any part of a partnership interest, the amount of the distribution attributable to your share of the partnership's unrealized receivable or inventory items results in ordinary income (see Regulations section 1.751-1(a) and *Sale or Exchange of Partnership Interest*, earlier). For details, see Pub. 541.

The partnership will separately identify both of the following.
• The FMV of the marketable securities when distributed (minus your share of the gain on the securities distributed to you).
• The partnership's adjusted basis of those securities immediately before the distribution.

Decrease the adjusted basis of your interest in the partnership (but not below zero) by the amount of cash distributed to you and the partnership's adjusted basis of the distributed securities. Advances or drawings of money or property against your share are treated as current distributions made on the last day of the partnership's tax year.

Your basis in the distributed marketable securities (other than in liquidation of your interest) is the smaller of:
• The partnership's adjusted basis in the securities immediately before the distribution increased by any gain recognized on the distribution of the securities or
• The adjusted basis of your partnership interest reduced by any cash distributed in the same transaction and increased by any gain recognized on the distribution of the securities.

If you received the securities in liquidation of your partnership interest, your basis in the marketable securities is equal to the adjusted basis of your partnership interest reduced by any cash distributed in the same transaction and increased by any gain recognized on the distribution of the securities.

Code B. Distribution subject to section 737. If a partner contributed section 704(c) built-in gain property within the last 7 years and the partnership made a distribution of property to that partner **other than** the previously contributed built-in gain property, the partner may be required to recognize gain under section 737. This gain is in addition to any gain recognized under section 731 on the distribution.

When this occurs, the partnership will enter code B in box 19 of the contributing partner's Schedule K-1 and attach a statement that provides the information the partner needs to figure the recognized gain under section 737. The partnership is required to provide the following information.
• The fair market value (FMV) of the distributed property (other than money).
• The amount of money received in the distribution.
• The net precontribution gain of the partner.

Using the information from the attached statement, complete the worksheet below to figure your recognized gain under section 737.

Computation of Section 737 Gain

1. Enter the FMV of the distributed property (other than money) . . . . $ ___
2. Enter your adjusted basis in the partnership immediately before the distribution. See *Basis Rules*, earlier . . . ___
3. Enter the amount of money received in the distribution . ___
4. Subtract line 3 from line 2. If zero or less, enter -0- . . . . ___
5. Subtract line 4 from line 1 . . ___
6. Enter your net precontribution gain . . . . ___
7. **Section 737 gain.** Enter the lesser of the amount on line 5 or line 6 . . . . ___

The type of gain (section 1231 gain, capital gain) generated is determined by the type of gain you would have recognized if you sold the property rather than contributing it to the partnership. Accordingly, report the amount from line 7, above, on Form 4797 or Form 8949 and the Schedule D of your tax return.

Code C. Other property. Code C shows the partnership's adjusted basis of property other than money immediately before the property was distributed to you. In addition, the partnership should report the adjusted basis and FMV of each property distributed. Decrease the adjusted basis of your interest in the partnership by the amount of your basis in the distributed property. Your basis in the distributed property (other than in liquidation of your interest) is the smaller of:
• The partnership's adjusted basis immediately before the distribution or
• The adjusted basis of your partnership interest reduced by any cash distributed in the same transaction.

If you received the property in liquidation of your interest, your basis in the distributed property is equal to the adjusted basis of your partnership interest reduced by any cash distributed in the same transaction.

If you receive cash or property in exchange for any part of a partnership interest, the amount of the distribution attributable to your share of the partnership's unrealized receivable or inventory items results in ordinary income (see Regulations section 1.751-1(a) and *Sale or Exchange of Partnership Interest*, earlier).

Box 20. Other Information

Code A. Investment income. Report this amount on line 4a of Form 4952.

Code B. Investment expenses. Report this amount on line 5 of Form 4952.

Code C. Fuel tax credit information. The partnership will report the number of gallons of each fuel sold or used during the tax year for a nontaxable use qualifying for the credit for taxes paid on fuels, type of use, and the applicable credit per gallon. Use this information to complete Form 4136, Credit for Federal Tax Paid on Fuels.

Code D. Qualified rehabilitation expenditures (other than rental real estate). The partnership will report your share of qualified rehabilitation expenditures and other information you need to complete Form 3468 for property not related to rental real estate activities in box 20 using code D. Your share of qualified rehabilitation expenditures related to rental real estate activities is reported in box 15 using code E. See the Instructions for Form 3468 for details. If the partnership is reporting expenditures from more than one activity, the attached statement will separately identify the expenditures from each activity.

Combine the expenditures (for Form 3468 reporting) from box 15, code E and box 20, code D. The expenditures related to rental real estate activities (box 15, code E) are reported on Schedule K-1 separately from other qualified rehabilitation expenditures (box 20, code D) because they are subject to different passive activity limitation rules. See the Instructions for Form 8582-CR for details.

Code E. Basis of energy property. If the partnership provides an attached statement for code E, use the information on the statement to complete lines 12a-d, 12f, 12g, 12i, 12j, 12l, 12m, 12o, and 12q-s of Form 3468.

Codes F and G. Recapture of low-income housing credit. A section 42(j)(5) partnership will report recapture of a low-income housing credit with code F. All other partnerships will report recapture of a low-income housing credit with code G. Keep a separate record of recapture from each of these sources so that you will be able to correctly figure any recapture of low-income housing credit that may result from the disposition of all or part of your partnership interest. For details, see Form 8611.

Code H. Recapture of investment credit. The partnership will provide any information you need to figure your recapture tax on Form 4255, Recapture of Investment Credit. See the Form 3468 on which you took the original credit for other information you need to complete Form 4255.

You may also need Form 4255 if you disposed of more than one-third of your interest in a partnership.

Code I. Recapture of other credits. On a statement attached to Schedule K-1, the partnership will report any information you need to figure the recapture of the new markets credit (see Form 8874 and Form 8874-B, Notice of Recapture Event for New Markets Credit); qualified plug-in electric and electric vehicle credit (see Form 8834); Indian employment credit (see section 45A(d)); any credit for employer-provided childcare facilities and services (see Form 8882); alternative motor vehicle credit (see section 30B(h)(8)); alternative fuel vehicle refueling property credit (see section 30C(e)(5)); or the new qualified plug-in electric drive motor vehicles credit (see section 30D(f)(5)).

Code J. Look-back interest—completed long-term contracts. The partnership will report any information you need to figure the interest due or to be refunded under the look-back method of section 460(b)(2) on certain long-term contracts. Use Form 8697, Interest Computation Under the Look-Back Method for Completed Long-Term Contracts, to report any such interest.

Code K. Look-back interest—income forecast method. The partnership will report any information you need to figure the interest due or to be refunded under the look-back method of section 167(g)(2) for certain property placed in service after September 13, 1995, and depreciated under the income forecast method. Use Form 8866, Interest Computation Under the Look-Back Method for Property Depreciated Under the Income Forecast Method, to report any such interest.

Code L. Dispositions of property with section 179 deductions. The partnership will report your share of gain or loss on the sale, exchange, or other disposition of property for which a section 179 expense deduction was passed through to partners with code L. If the partnership passed through a section 179 expense deduction for the property, you must report the gain or loss and any recapture of the section 179 expense deduction for the property on your income tax return (see the Instructions for Form 4797 for details). The partnership will provide all the following information.

1. Description of the property.
2. Date the property was acquired and placed in service.
3. Date of the sale or other disposition of the property.
4. Your share of the gross sales price or amount realized.
5. Your share of the cost or other basis plus the expense of sale.
6. Your share of the depreciation allowed or allowable.
7. Your share of the section 179 expense deduction (if any) passed through

for the property and the partnership's tax year(s) in which the amount was passed through. To figure the amount of depreciation allowed or allowable for Form 4797, line 22, add to the amount from item 6, above, the amount of your share of the section 179 expense deduction, reduced by any unused carryover of the deduction for this property. This amount may be different than the amount of section 179 expense you deducted for the property if your interest in the partnership has changed.

8. If the disposition is due to a casualty or theft, a statement providing the information you need to complete Form 4684.

9. If the sale was an installment sale made during the partnership's tax year, any information you need to complete Form 6252, Installment Sale Income. The partnership will separately report your share of all payments received for the property in future tax years. See the Form 6252 instructions for details.

Code M. Recapture of section 179 deduction. The partnership will report your share of any recapture of section 179 expense deduction if business use of any property for which the section 179 expense deduction was passed through to partners dropped to 50% or less. If this occurs, the partnership must provide the following information.

1. Your share of the depreciation allowed or allowable (not including the section 179 expense deduction).

2. Your share of the section 179 expense deduction (if any) passed through for the property and the partnership's tax year(s) in which the amount was passed through. Reduce this amount by the portion, if any, of your unused (carryover) section 179 expense deduction for this property.

Code N. Interest expense for corporate partners. The partnership will report each corporate partner's share of the partnership's interest expense. This amount is reported elsewhere on Schedule K-1 and the total amount is reported here for information only. Your share of interest income is reported in box 5 and your share of the partnership's liabilities is reported in Part II, item K. A corporate partner's share of interest income, interest expense, and partnership liabilities are treated as income, expense, and liabilities of the corporation for purposes of the limitation on the deduction for interest under section 163(j).

Code O. Section 453(l)(3) information. The partnership will report any information you need to figure the interest due under section 453(l)(3) with respect to the disposition of certain timeshares and residential lots on the installment method. If you are an individual, report the interest on Form 1040, line 62. Check box c and enter "453(l)(3)" and the amount of the interest in the space to the left of line 62.

Code P. Section 453A(c) information. The partnership will report any information

you need to figure the interest due under section 453A(c) with respect to certain installment sales. If you are an individual, report the interest on Form 1040, line 62. Check box c and enter "453A(c)" and the amount of the interest in the space to the left of line 62. See the Form 6252 instructions for more information. Also see section 453A(c) for details on how to figure the interest.

Code Q. Section 1260(b) information. The partnership will report any information you need to figure the interest due under section 1260(b). If the partnership had gain from certain constructive ownership transactions, your tax liability must be increased by the interest charge on any deferral of gain recognition under section 1260(b). Report the interest on Form 1040, line 62. Enter "1260(b)" and the amount of the interest in the space to the left of line 62. See section 1260(b) for details, including how to figure the interest.

Code R. Interest allocable to production expenditures. The partnership will report any information you need relating to interest you are required to capitalize under section 263A for production expenditures. See Regulations sections 1.263A-8 through 1.263A-15 for details.

Code S. CCF nonqualified withdrawals. The partnership will report your share of nonqualified withdrawals from a capital construction fund (CCF). These withdrawals are taxed separately from your other gross income at the highest marginal ordinary income or capital gains tax rate. Attach a statement to your federal income tax return to show your computation of both the tax and interest for a nonqualified withdrawal. Include the tax and interest on Form 1040, line 62. In the space to the left of line 62, enter the amount of tax and interest and "CCF."

Code T. Depletion information—oil and gas. This is your share of gross income from the property, share of production for the tax year, etc., needed to figure your depletion deduction for oil and gas wells. The partnership should also allocate to you a share of the adjusted basis of each partnership oil or gas property. See Pub. 535 for details on how to figure your depletion deduction.

Code U. Reserved.

Code V. Unrelated business taxable income. The partnership will report any information you need to figure unrelated business taxable income under section 512(a)(1) (but excluding any modifications required by paragraphs (8) through (15) of section 512(b)) for a partner that is a tax-exempt organization.

Note. A partner is required to notify the partnership of its tax-exempt status.

Code W. Precontribution gain (loss). If the partnership distributed any property with precontribution gain or loss to any partner **other than** the contributing partner, and the date of the distribution was within 7 years of

the date the property was contributed to the partnership, the contributing partner must recognize a gain or loss under section 704(c)(1)(B). If the partnership made such a distribution during its tax year, it will enter code W in box 20 of the contributing partner's Schedule K-1 and attach a statement providing the amount of the partner's precontribution gain (loss) and identifying the character of the gain or loss (for example, capital gain (loss) or section 1231 gain (loss)). Report the precontribution gain or loss on Form 8949/Schedule D or Form 4797 in accordance with the information provided by the partnership.

Code X. Section 108(i) information. If the partnership made a section 108(i) election or allocates any section 108(i) items to its partners, it will provide a statement identifying your share of the following:
• The deferred section 108(i) cancellation of debt (COD) income that has not been included in income in the current or prior tax years,
• The partnership's original issue discount (OID) deduction deferred under section 108(i)(2)(A)(i) that has not been deducted in the current or prior tax years,
• The deferred section 752 amount that is treated as a distribution of money under section 752 in the current tax year, and
• The deferred section 752 amount remaining as of the end of the current tax year.

Code Y. Net investment income. The partnership may use this code Y to report information you may need to determine your net investment income tax under section 1411, including information regarding income from controlled foreign corporations (CFCs) and passive foreign investment companies (PFICs) the stock of which is owned by the partnership. Any information that is not provided elsewhere on Schedule K-1 (or an attachment to Schedule K-1) is provided using code Y. For CFCs and PFICs that you treat as qualified electing funds (QEFs), the information that is relevant to you will depend on whether you, the partnership, or a lower-tier entity has made an election under Regulations section 1.1411-10(g) with respect to the CFC or QEF. For example, if the partnership made an election under Regulations section 1.1411–10(g) for a CFC the stock of which is owned by the partnership, and the relevant income and deduction items derived from that CFC are reported elsewhere on the Schedule K-1, then you will not need the information provided in code Y to complete your Form 8960.

If you are an individual who is a U.S. citizen or resident, or a domestic trust or estate, follow the Instructions for Form 8960 to figure and report your net investment income and adjusted gross income or modified adjusted gross income. Corporate partners are not subject to the net investment income tax. See Regulations sections 1.1411-1 through -10 for details.

Code Z. Other information. The partnership will report:

1. Any information a publicly traded partnership needs to determine whether it meets the 90% qualifying income test of section 7704(c)(2).

Note. A partner is required to notify the partnership of its status as a publicly traded partnership.

2. Any information you need to complete a disclosure statement for reportable transactions in which the partnership participates. If the partnership participates in a transaction that must be disclosed on Form 8886, Reportable Transaction Disclosure Statement, both you and the partnership may be required to file Form 8886 for the transaction. The determination of whether you are required to disclose a transaction of the partnership is based on the category(s) under which the transaction qualifies for disclosure and is determined by you and the partnership. You may have to pay a penalty if you are required to file Form 8886 and do not do so. See the Instructions for Form 8886 for details.

3. Interest and additional tax on compensation deferred under a section 409A nonqualified deferred compensation plan that does not meet the requirements of section 409A. See section 409A(a)(1)(B) to figure the interest and additional tax on this income. Report this interest and tax on line 62 of Form 1040. This income is included in the amount in box 4, Guaranteed Payments.

4. Inversion gain. The partnership will provide a statement showing the amounts of each type of income or gain that is included in inversion gain. The partnership has included inversion gain in income elsewhere on Schedule K-1. Inversion gain is also reported under code Z because your taxable income and alternative minimum taxable income cannot be less than the inversion gain. Also, your inversion gain (a) is not taken into account in figuring the net operating loss (NOL) for the tax year or the NOL that can be carried over to each tax year, (b) may limit your credits, and (c) is treated as income from sources within the U.S. for the foreign tax credit. See section 7874 for details.

5. Qualifying advanced coal project property. Use the amounts the partnership provides you to figure the amounts to report on Form 3468, lines 5a through 5c.

6. Qualifying gasification project property. Use the amounts the partnership provides you to figure the amounts to report on Form 3468, lines 6a and 6b.

7. Qualifying advanced energy project property. Use the amount the partnership provides you to figure the amount to report on Form 3468, line 7.

8. The information needed to complete Schedule P (Form 1120-F), List of Foreign Partner Interests in Partnerships. When required, the partnership will make this report on an attached statement to partners that are a corporation (identified as a foreign partner under Regulations section 1.1446-1(c)(3)) or partners that are a partnership (domestic or foreign) if the reporting partnership knows, or has reason to know, that one or more of the partners is a foreign corporation. If the partnership allocates effectively connected income to the partner, the statement will contain the information needed to complete lines 1 through 10, 13, 14, 15b, 17a, 17b, and 18 of Schedule P (Form 1120-F). If the partnership does not allocate effectively connected income to the partner, the statement will contain the information needed to complete lines 13, 14, and 18 of Schedule P (Form 1120-F).

9. Conservation reserve program payments. Individuals who received social security retirement or disability benefits, and are partners in farm partnerships that receive conservation reserve program payments, do not pay self-employment tax on their portion of the payments. The partnership will report your portion of the conservation reserve program payments in box 20 using code Z. See Schedule SE (Form 1040) for information on excluding the payment from your calculation of self-employment tax.

10. Acceleration of AMT credit (corporations only). If a corporate partner has made an election to accelerate the AMT credit in lieu of bonus depreciation, it is required to notify the partnership in writing of this election. See Rev. Proc. 2009-16, 2009-6 I.R.B. 449 and Rev. Proc. 2009-33, 2009-29 I.R.B. 150 for more information about the written notification that the electing corporate partner must provide the partnership. The partnership is required to recompute the electing corporate partner's share of depreciation on any eligible qualified property or extension property to eliminate bonus depreciation and use the straight line depreciation method for such property. The partnership will attach a statement to Schedule K-1 that lists each partnership item that includes bonus depreciation and shows the electing corporate partner's adjustment for each item that results from the recomputed depreciation and elimination of the bonus depreciation. The partner must adjust the amount shown on Schedule K-1 for these partnership items by the amount of the corresponding adjustment. See section 168(k)(4) for more information.

11. Any information you may need to comply with the limitation on excess farm losses of certain taxpayers under section 461(j).

12. Any other information you may need to file your return not shown elsewhere on Schedule K-1.

The partnership should give you a description and the amount of your share for each of these items.

SCHEDULE M-3 (Form 1065) Department of the Treasury Internal Revenue Service	**Net Income (Loss) Reconciliation for Certain Partnerships** ▶ Attach to Form 1065 or Form 1065-B. ▶ Information about Schedule M-3 (Form 1065) and its instructions is at *www.irs.gov/form1065.*	OMB No. 1545-0123 20**14**

Name of partnership	Employer identification number

This Schedule M-3 is being filed because (check all that apply):

A ☐ The amount of the partnership's total assets at the end of the tax year is equal to $10 million or more.

B ☐ The amount of the partnership's adjusted total assets for the tax year is equal to $10 million or more. If box B is checked, enter the amount of adjusted total assets for the tax year _____ .

C ☐ The amount of total receipts for the tax year is equal to $35 million or more. If box C is checked, enter the total receipts for the tax year _____ .

D ☐ An entity that is a reportable entity partner with respect to the partnership owns or is deemed to own an interest of 50 percent or more in the partnership's capital, profit, or loss, on any day during the tax year of the partnership.

Name of Reportable Entity Partner	Identifying Number	Maximum Percentage Owned or Deemed Owned

E ☐ Voluntary Filer.

Part I	**Financial Information and Net Income (Loss) Reconciliation**

1a Did the partnership file SEC Form 10-K for its income statement period ending with or within this tax year?
  ☐ **Yes.** Skip lines 1b and 1c and complete lines 2 through 11 with respect to that SEC Form 10-K.
  ☐ **No.** Go to line 1b. See instructions if multiple non-tax-basis income statements are prepared.
b Did the partnership prepare a certified audited non-tax-basis income statement for that period?
  ☐ **Yes.** Skip line 1c and complete lines 2 through 11 with respect to that income statement.
  ☐ **No.** Go to line 1c.
c Did the partnership prepare a non-tax-basis income statement for that period?
  ☐ **Yes.** Complete lines 2 through 11 with respect to that income statement.
  ☐ **No.** Skip lines 2 through 3b and enter the partnership's net income (loss) per its books and records on line 4a.

2 Enter the income statement period: Beginning ____/____/____ Ending ____/____/____

3a Has the partnership's income statement been restated for the income statement period on line 2?
  ☐ **Yes.** (If "Yes," attach a statement and the amount of each item restated.)
  ☐ **No.**
b Has the partnership's income statement been restated for any of the five income statement periods immediately preceding the period on line 2?
  ☐ **Yes.** (If "Yes," attach a statement and the amount of each item restated.)
  ☐ **No.**

4a	Worldwide consolidated net income (loss) from income statement source identified in Part I, line 1	**4a**	
b	Indicate accounting standard used for line 4a (see instructions): **1** ☐ GAAP **2** ☐ IFRS **3** ☐ 704(b) **4** ☐ Tax-basis **5** ☐ Other: (Specify) ▶ _____		
5a	Net income from nonincludible foreign entities (attach statement)	**5a**	( )
b	Net loss from nonincludible foreign entities (attach statement and enter as a positive amount) . . .	**5b**	
6a	Net income from nonincludible U.S. entities (attach statement)	**6a**	( )
b	Net loss from nonincludible U.S. entities (attach statement and enter as a positive amount)	**6b**	
7a	Net income (loss) of other foreign disregarded entities (attach statement)	**7a**	
b	Net income (loss) of other U.S. disregarded entities (attach statement)	**7b**	
8	Adjustment to eliminations of transactions between includible entities and nonincludible entities (attach statement)	**8**	
9	Adjustment to reconcile income statement period to tax year (attach statement)	**9**	
10	Other adjustments to reconcile to amount on line 11 (attach statement)	**10**	
11	**Net income (loss) per income statement of the partnership.** Combine lines 4a through 10 . .	**11**	

Note. Part I, line 11, must equal Part II, line 26, column (a) or Schedule M-1, line 1 (see instructions).

12 Enter the total amount (not just the partnership's share) of the assets and liabilities of all entities included or removed on the following lines:

		Total Assets	Total Liabilities
a	Included on Part I, line 4		
b	Removed on Part I, line 5		
c	Removed on Part I, line 6		
d	Included on Part I, line 7		

Name of partnership

Employer identification number

| **Part II** | **Reconciliation of Net Income (Loss) per Income Statement of Partnership With Income (Loss) per Return** |

Income (Loss) Items	(a) Income (Loss) per Income Statement	(b) Temporary Difference	(c) Permanent Difference	(d) Income (Loss) per Tax Return
(Attach statements for lines 1 through 10)				
1 Income (loss) from equity method foreign corporations				
2 Gross foreign dividends not previously taxed . . .				
3 Subpart F, QEF, and similar income inclusions . .				
4 Gross foreign distributions previously taxed . . .				
5 Income (loss) from equity method U.S. corporations				
6 U.S. dividends				
7 Income (loss) from U.S. partnerships				
8 Income (loss) from foreign partnerships				
9 Income (loss) from other pass-through entities . .				
10 Items relating to reportable transactions				
11 Interest income (see instructions)				
12 Total accrual to cash adjustment				
13 Hedging transactions				
14 Mark-to-market income (loss)				
15 Cost of goods sold (see instructions)	( )			( )
16 Sale versus lease (for sellers and/or lessors) . .				
17 Section 481(a) adjustments				
18 Unearned/deferred revenue				
19 Income recognition from long-term contracts . . .				
20 Original issue discount and other imputed interest .				
21a Income statement gain/loss on sale, exchange, abandonment, worthlessness, or other disposition of assets other than inventory and pass-through entities .				
b Gross capital gains from Schedule D, excluding amounts from pass-through entities				
c Gross capital losses from Schedule D, excluding amounts from pass-through entities, abandonment losses, and worthless stock losses				
d Net gain/loss reported on Form 4797, line 17, excluding amounts from pass-through entities, abandonment losses, and worthless stock losses .				
e Abandonment losses				
f Worthless stock losses (attach statement)				
g Other gain/loss on disposition of assets other than inventory				
22 Other income (loss) items with differences (attach statement)				
23 **Total income (loss) items.** Combine lines 1 through 22				
24 **Total expense/deduction items.** (from Part III, line 31) (see instructions)				
25 Other items with no differences				
26 **Reconciliation totals.** Combine lines 23 through 25				

Note. Line 26, column (a), must equal Part I, line 11, and column (d) must equal Form 1065, Analysis of Net Income (Loss), line 1.

Name of partnership

Employer identification number

| Part III | Reconciliation of Net Income (Loss) per Income Statement of Partnership With Income (Loss) per Return—Expense/Deduction Items |

Expense/Deduction Items	(a) Expense per Income Statement	(b) Temporary Difference	(c) Permanent Difference	(d) Deduction per Tax Return
1 State and local current income tax expense . . .				
2 State and local deferred income tax expense . . .				
3 Foreign current income tax expense (other than foreign withholding taxes)				
4 Foreign deferred income tax expense				
5 Equity-based compensation				
6 Meals and entertainment				
7 Fines and penalties				
8 Judgments, damages, awards, and similar costs . .				
9 Guaranteed payments				
10 Pension and profit-sharing				
11 Other post-retirement benefits				
12 Deferred compensation				
13 Charitable contribution of cash and tangible property				
14 Charitable contribution of intangible property . . .				
15 Organizational expenses as per Regulations section 1.709-2(a)				
16 Syndication expenses as per Regulations section 1.709-2(b)				
17 Current year acquisition/reorganization investment banking fees				
18 Current year acquisition/reorganization legal and accounting fees				
19 Amortization/impairment of goodwill				
20 Amortization of acquisition, reorganization, and start-up costs				
21 Other amortization or impairment write-offs . . .				
22 Reserved				
23a Depletion—Oil & Gas				
b Depletion—Other than Oil & Gas				
24 Intangible drilling & development costs				
25 Depreciation				
26 Bad debt expense				
27 Interest expense (see instructions)				
28 Purchase versus lease (for purchasers and/ or lessees)				
29 Research and development costs				
30 Other expense/deduction items with differences (attach statement)				
31 **Total expense/deduction items.** Combine lines 1 through 30. Enter here and on Part II, line 24, reporting positive amounts as negative and negative amounts as positive				

2014

Department of the Treasury
Internal Revenue Service

Instructions for Schedule M-3 (Form 1065)

Net Income (Loss) Reconciliation for Certain Partnerships

Section references are to the Internal Revenue Code unless otherwise noted.

Future Developments

For the latest information about developments related to Schedule M-3 (Form 1065) and its instructions, such as legislation enacted after they were published, go to *www.irs.gov/form1065*.

What's New

For tax years ending December 31, 2014, and later:
- Form 1065 and Form 1065-B filers that (a) are required to file Schedule M-3 (Form 1065) and have less than $50 million total assets at the end of the tax year or (b) are not required to file Schedule M-3 (Form 1065) and voluntarily file Schedule M-3 (Form 1065), must either complete Schedule M-3 (Form 1065) entirely or complete Schedule M-3 (Form 1065) through Part I and complete Form 1065, Schedule M-1 instead of completing Parts II and III of Schedule M-3 (Form 1065). These filers are not required to file Schedule C (Form 1065) nor Form 8916-A. If these filers choose to complete Form 1065, Schedule M-1 instead of completing Parts II and III of Schedule M-3 (Form 1065), line 1 of Form 1065, Schedule M-1 must equal line 11 of Part I of Schedule M-3 (Form 1065).
- Any filer that completes Parts II and III of Schedule M-3 (Form 1065) must complete all columns, without exception.

General Instructions

Applicable schedule and instructions. Use the 2014 Schedule M-3 (Form 1065) with these instructions for tax years ending December 31, 2014, through December 30, 2015. For previous tax years, see the applicable Schedule M-3 (Form 1065) and instructions. (For example, use the 2013 Schedule M-3 (Form 1065) with the 2013 instructions for tax years ending December 31, 2013, through December 30, 2014.)

Forms 1065 and 1065-B. Schedule M-3 (Form 1065) is filed with Forms 1065, U.S. Return of Partnership Income, and 1065-B, U.S. Return of Income for Electing Large Partnerships. Line references to these returns are the same unless otherwise noted.

Purpose of Schedule

Schedule M-3, Part I, asks certain questions about the partnership's financial statements and reconciles financial statement net income (loss) for the consolidated financial statement group to income (loss) per the income statement for the partnership.

Schedule M-3, Parts II and III, reconcile financial statement net income (loss) for the partnership (per Schedule M-3, Part I, line 11) to line 1 of the *Analysis of Net Income (Loss)* found on Form 1065 and Form 1065-B.

Where To File

If the partnership is required to file (or voluntarily files) Schedule M-3 (Form 1065), the partnership **must** file Form 1065 or Form 1065-B and all attachments and schedules, including Schedule M-3 (Form 1065), at the following address.

Department of the Treasury
Internal Revenue Service Center
Ogden, UT 84201-0011

Who Must File

Any entity that files Form 1065 or Form 1065-B must file Schedule M-3 (Form 1065), if any of the following is true:

1. The amount of total assets at the end of the tax year reported on Schedule L, line 14, column (d), is equal to $10 million or more.

2. The amount of adjusted total assets for the tax year is equal to $10 million or more. See *Total Assets and Adjusted Total Assets*, below.

3. The amount of total receipts for the tax year is equal to $35 million or more. Total receipts is defined in the instructions for *Codes for Principal Business Activity and Principal Product or Service* in the Instructions for Form 1065 or Instructions for Form 1065-B.

4. An entity that is a reportable entity partner with respect to the partnership (as defined under these instructions) owns or is deemed to own, directly or indirectly, an interest of 50% or more in the partnership's capital, profit, or loss, on any day during the tax year of the partnership.

A common trust fund or foreign partnership must file Schedule M-3 if it meets any of the tests discussed above.

Note. All references to a U.S. partnership in these instructions refer to any entity required to file Schedule M-3 (Form 1065), where appropriate.

Partnerships not required to file Schedule M-3 may voluntarily file Schedule M-3.

Completing Schedule M-3 (Form 1065)

Form 1065 and Form 1065-B filers that are required to file Schedule M-3 (Form 1065) and have at least $50 million total assets at the end of the tax year must complete Schedule M-3 (Form 1065) entirely.

Form 1065 and Form 1065-B filers that (a) are required to file Schedule M-3 (Form 1065) and have less than $50 million total assets at the end of the tax year or (b) are not required to file Schedule M-3 (Form 1065) and voluntarily file Schedule M-3 (Form 1065) must either (i) complete Schedule M-3 (Form 1065) entirely or (ii) complete Schedule M-3 (Form 1065) through Part I and complete Form 1065, Schedule M-1 instead of completing Parts II and III of Schedule M-3 (Form 1065). If the filer chooses to complete Form 1065, Schedule M-1 instead of completing Parts II and III of Schedule M-3 (Form 1065), line 1 of Form 1065, Schedule M-1 must equal line 11 of Part I of Schedule M-3 (Form 1065).

For any part of Schedule M-3 (Form 1065) that is completed, all columns must be completed, all applicable questions must be answered, all numerical data requested must be provided, any statement required to support a line item must be attached and provide the information required for that line item. Any partnership required to file Schedule M-3 must check all boxes above Part I that apply for the reason(s) for which the Schedule M-3 is required to be filed. A partnership not required to file Schedule M-3, but that is doing so voluntarily, should check box E above Part I.

Note. For tax years ending before December 31, 2014, there were different completion rules. See the applicable

Cat. No. 38800Y

Schedule M-3 (Form 1065) and its instructions.

Total Assets and Adjusted Total Assets

The partnership should figure its adjusted total assets using the *Adjusted Total Assets Worksheet*, below.

For purposes of determining for Schedule M-3 whether the partnership's adjusted total assets (under these instructions) equal $10 million or more, the partnership's total assets at the end of the tax year must be determined on an overall accrual method of accounting unless both of the following apply: (a) the tax return of the partnership is prepared using an overall cash method of accounting, and (b) the partnership does not prepare financial statements using, and is not included in financial statements prepared on, an accrual basis.

See the instructions for Schedule M-3, Part I, line 1, regarding non-tax-basis income statements and related non-tax-basis balance sheets to be used in the preparation of Schedule M-3 and the related non-tax-basis balance sheets to be used in the preparation of Schedule L.

In the case of a partnership year ending because of a section 708 termination (sale or exchange within a 12-month period of 50% or more of the partnership interest in income and capital), the total assets of the partnership at the end of the year for determining the requirement to file Schedule M-3 are determined immediately before the section 708 termination and any actual or deemed contribution or distribution of the partnership assets under the provisions of section 708.

Example 1.

1. U.S. partnership A, a limited liability company (LLC), owns 60% of the income and capital of U.S. partnership B, also an LLC. For its 2014 tax year ending December 31, 2014, A prepares non-tax-basis GAAP (generally accepted accounting principles) consolidated financial statements with B that report total assets at the end of the year of $12 million. For 2014, A files Form 1065 and reports on its non-tax-basis unconsolidated GAAP Schedule L total assets at the end of the year of $7 million. The $7 million total includes $3 million for its investment in B under the equity method of accounting. The amount of total liabilities at the end of 2014 reported to A's partners on Schedules K-1 is $5 million. A made distributions of $1 million during 2014 reflected on Schedule M-2, line 6. The amount of A's adjusted total assets is $8 million for the 2014 tax year. A has total

receipts for the 2014 tax year of $15 million. A has no reportable entity partners (as defined under *Reportable Entity Partner Reporting Responsibilities,* later). A is not required to file Schedule M-3 under any of the four tests discussed earlier. A may voluntarily file Schedule M-3 for the 2014 tax year. If A does not file Schedule M-3, it must complete Schedule M-1. If A files Schedule M-3, it must either: (i) complete Schedule M-3 entirely; or (ii) complete Schedule M-3 through Part I and complete Schedule M-1 instead of completing Parts II and III of Schedule M-3.

2. Same facts as in Example 1.1 except that A has total receipts for 2014 of $40 million. A must file Schedule M-3 for 2014 and either: (i) complete Schedule M-3 entirely; or (ii) complete Schedule M-3 through Part I and complete Schedule M-1 instead of completing Parts II and III of Schedule M-3.

3. R, a U.S. partnership, files Form 1065 for the tax year ending December 31, 2014. R has total assets at the end of 2014 reported on Schedule L, line 14, column (d), of $7.5 million. The aggregate amount of total liabilities at the end of 2014 reported to R's partners on Schedules K-1 is $5 million. R made distributions of $3 million during 2014 reflected on Schedule M-2, line 6. R did not report a loss for 2014 on Schedule M-2, line 3. R did not report adjustments to capital on Schedule M-2, lines 4 or 7. R has adjusted total assets for 2014 in the tentative amount of $10.5 million, the sum of $7.5 million plus $3 million (the amount of distributions that must be added back to determine adjusted total assets for 2014), an amount that is not less than the total liabilities at the end of 2014 reported to R's partners on Schedules K-1. Because R has adjusted total assets of $10 million or more for its tax year ending December 31, 2014, R must file Schedule M-3 for 2014 and either: (i) complete Schedule M-3 entirely; or (ii) complete Schedule M-3 through Part I and complete Schedule M-1 instead of completing Parts II and III of Schedule M-3.

4. Same facts as in Example 1.3 except that the amount of total liabilities at the end of 2014 reported to R's partners on Schedules K-1 is $11 million. R made distributions of $1.5 million during 2014 as reflected on Schedule M-2, line 6. R has adjusted total assets for 2014 equal to $11 million, the greater of the tentative amount of $9 million, the sum of $7.5 million plus $1.5 million (the amount of distributions that must be added back to determine adjusted total assets for 2014), or $11 million (the amount of the total liabilities at the end of 2014 reported to R's partners on Schedules K-1). Because R has adjusted total assets of $10 million or

more for its tax year ending December 31, 2014, R must file Schedule M-3 for 2014 and either: (i) complete Schedule M-3 entirely; or (ii) complete Schedule M-3 through Part I and complete Schedule M-1 instead of completing Parts II and III of Schedule M-3.

5. S, a U.S. partnership, files Form 1065 for the tax year ending December 31, 2014. S has total assets at the end of 2014 reported on Schedule L, line 14, column (d), of $7.5 million. The amount of total liabilities at the end of 2014 reported to S's partners on Schedules K-1 is $5 million. S made no distributions during 2014 reflected on Schedule M-2, line 6. S reported a loss of ($3 million) for 2014 on Schedule M-2, line 3. S did not report adjustments to capital on Schedule M-2, lines 4 or 7. S has adjusted total assets for 2014 in the tentative amount of $10.5 million, the sum of $7.5 million plus $3 million (the amount of the loss stated as a positive amount that must be added back to determine adjusted total assets for 2014). This tentative amount is compared to the total liabilities at the end of 2014 as reported to S's partners on Schedules K-1, and the greater of the two amounts is considered the adjusted total assets. Because S has adjusted total assets of $10 million or more for its tax year ending December 31, 2014, S must file Schedule M-3 for 2014 and either: (i) complete Schedule M-3 entirely; or (ii) complete Schedule M-3 through Part I and complete Schedule M-1 instead of completing Parts II and III of Schedule M-3.

6. T, a U.S. partnership, files Form 1065 for the tax year ending December 31, 2014. T has total assets at the end of 2014 reported on Schedule L, line 14, column (d), of $7.5 million. The amount of total liabilities at the end of 2014 reported to T's partners on Schedules K-1 is $5 million. T made no distributions during 2014 reflected on Schedule M-2, line 6. T did not report a loss for 2014 on Schedule M-2, line 3. T did not report adjustments to capital on Schedule M-2, line 7, but did report a negative adjustment of ($3 million) on Schedule M-2, line 4. T has adjusted total assets for 2014 in the tentative amount of $10.5 million, the sum of $7.5 million plus $3 million (the amount of the negative adjustment stated as a positive amount that must be added back to determine adjusted total assets for 2014), an amount that is not less than the total liabilities at the end of 2014 reported to T's partners on Schedules K-1. Because T has adjusted total assets of $10 million or more for its tax year ending December 31, 2014, T must file Schedule M-3 for 2014 and either: (i) complete Schedule M-3 entirely; or (ii) complete Schedule M-3 through Part I and complete Schedule M-1 instead of

Adjusted Total Assets Worksheet

1. Enter total assets at the end of the tax year on Schedule L, line 14, column (d)	1. _____
2. Enter capital distributions on Schedule M-2, lines 6a and 6b (shown as a positive amount)	2. _____
3. Enter any loss reported on Schedule M-2, line 3 (shown as a positive amount)	3. _____
4. Enter the amount of any positive adjustment on Schedule M-2, line 7	4. _____
5. Enter the amount of any negative adjustment on Schedule M-2, line 4 (shown as a positive amount)	5. _____
6. Add lines 1 through 5	6. _____
7. Enter combined total liabilities (recourse and nonrecourse) on all Schedules K-1 (Form 1065), Part II, Item K, or Schedules K-1 (Form 1065-B)	7. _____
8. Adjusted Total Assets. Enter the greater of line 6 or line 7	8. _____

Note: For line 2 above, if the partnership reflects partner capital account changes resulting from the sale of a partnership interest on Schedule M-2 as matching contributions and distributions (on lines 2a and 2b and on lines 6a and 6b, respectively), reduce the amounts shown on lines 6a and 6b by such matching amounts.

completing Parts II and III of Schedule M-3.

7. Z has $50 million in total assets at the end of its 2014 tax year ending December 31, 2014, and files Form 1065. Z must file Schedule M-3 and complete it entirely.

Reportable Entity Partner Reporting Responsibilities

For the purposes of these instructions, a reportable entity partner with respect to a partnership filing Form 1065 or Form 1065-B is an entity that:
- Owns or is deemed to own, directly or indirectly, under these instructions, a 50% or greater interest in the income, loss, or capital of the partnership on any day of the tax year, and
- Was required to file Schedule M-3 on its most recently filed U.S. federal income tax return or return of income filed prior to that day.

For the purposes of these instructions, the following rules apply.

1. The parent corporation of a consolidated tax group is deemed to own all corporate and partnership interests owned or deemed to be owned under these instructions by any member of the tax consolidated group.

2. The owner of a disregarded entity is deemed to own all corporate and partnership interests owned or deemed to be owned under these instructions by the disregarded entity.

3. The owner of 50% or more of a corporation by vote on any day of the corporation tax year is deemed to own all corporate and partnership interests owned or deemed to be owned under these

instructions by the corporation during the corporation tax year.

4. The owner of 50% or more of partnership income, loss, or capital on any day of the partnership tax year is deemed to own all corporate and partnership interests owned or deemed to be owned under these instructions by the partnership during the partnership tax year.

5. The beneficial owner of 50% or more of the beneficial interest of a trust or nominee arrangement on any day of the trust or nominee arrangement tax year is deemed to own all corporate and partnership interests owned or deemed to be owned under these instructions by the trust or nominee arrangement.

A reportable entity partner with respect to a partnership (as defined above) must report the following to the partnership within 30 days of first becoming a reportable entity partner and, after first reporting to the partnership under these instructions, thereafter within 30 days of the date of any change in the interest it owns or is deemed to own, directly or indirectly, under these instructions, in the partnership.

1. Name.
2. Mailing address.
3. Employer identification number (EIN), if applicable.
4. Entity or organization type.
5. State or country in which it is organized.
6. Date on which it first became a reportable entity partner.
7. Date with respect to which it is reporting a change in its ownership interest in the partnership, if applicable.

8. The interest in the partnership it owns or is deemed to own in the partnership, directly or indirectly (as defined under these instructions) as of the date with respect to which it is reporting.

9. Any change in that interest as of the date with respect to which it is reporting.

The reportable entity partner must retain copies of required reports it makes to partnerships under these instructions. Each partnership must retain copies of the required reports it receives under these instructions from reportable entity partners.

For more information, see *Item D. Reportable Entity Partner*, below.

Example 2.

1. P, a U.S. corporation, is the parent of a financial consolidation group with 50 domestic subsidiaries, DS1 through DS50, and 50 foreign subsidiaries, FS1 through FS50, all 100% owned on September 16, 2014. On September 15, 2014, P filed a consolidated tax return on Form 1120 and was required to file Schedule M-3 for the tax year ending December 31, 2013. On September 16, 2014, DS1, DS2, DS3, FS1, and FS2 each acquire a 10% partnership interest in partnership K, which files Form 1065 for the tax year ending December 31, 2014. P is deemed to own, directly or indirectly, under these instructions, all corporate and partnership interests of DS1, DS2, and DS3, as the parent of the tax consolidation group, and therefore is deemed to own 30% of K on September 16, 2014. P is deemed to own, directly or indirectly, under these instructions all corporate and partnership interests of FS1 and FS2 as the owner of 50% or more of each corporation by vote and therefore is deemed to own 20% of K on September 16, 2014. P is therefore deemed to own 50% of K on September 16, 2014. P owns or is deemed to own, directly or indirectly, under these instructions 50% or more of K on September 16, 2014, and was required to file Schedule M-3 on its most recently filed U.S. income tax return filed before that date. Therefore, P is a reportable entity partner of K as of September 16, 2014. On October 5, 2014, P reports to K, as it is required to do, that P is a reportable entity partner as of September 16, 2014, deemed to own under these instructions a 50% interest in K. K is therefore required to file Schedule M-3 when it files its Form 1065 for its tax year ending December 31, 2014.

2. Throughout 2014, A, a limited liability company (LLC) filing Form 1065 for calendar year 2014, owns, as its only asset, 50% of each of B, C, D, and E, each also an LLC filing Form 1065 for calendar year 2014. A is owned by individuals and S corporations not required to file

Schedule M-3 for 2013, 2014, or 2015. B, C, D, and E are owned by A and by individuals and S corporations not required to file Schedule M-3 for 2013, 2014, or 2015. For the partnership tax years ending December 31, 2014, each of B, C, D, and E has no year-end liabilities, $3 million in total assets and $6 million in adjusted total assets (the difference equal to the distributions by each in 2014), and 2014 total receipts of $20 million. As of December 31, 2014, no owner, direct or indirect, of B, C, D, or E was required to file Schedule M-3 on its most recently filed U.S. income tax return or return of income. Neither B, C, D, or E is required to file Schedule M-3 for 2014. For the partnership tax year ending December 31, 2014, A has no year-end liabilities, $6 million in total assets and $12 million in adjusted total assets (the difference equal to the distributions in 2014), and 2014 total receipts of $6 million. As of December 31, 2014, no owner, direct or indirect, of A was required to file Schedule M-3 on its most recently filed U.S. income tax return. A must file Schedule M-3 when it files its Form 1065 for 2014 because A has adjusted total assets of $10 million or more.

3. Same ownership facts as in Example 2.2 continued to calendar year 2015. On March 3, 2015, A files its Form 1065 with Schedule M-3 for the partnership tax year ended December 31, 2014. As of March 4, 2015, A becomes a reportable entity partner with respect to any partnership in which it owns or is deemed to own, directly or indirectly, under these instructions a 50% or greater interest in the income, loss, or capital of the partnership. A owns 50% of each of B, C, D, and E and is therefore a reportable entity partner with respect to each as of March 4, 2015, the day after it filed its 2014 Form 1065 with a required Schedule M-3. On March 20, 2015, A reports to B, C, D, and E, as it is required to do within 30 days of March 4, that it is a reportable entity partner owning a 50% interest. Each of B, C, D, and E is required to file Schedule M-3 for 2015 because each has a reportable entity partner. A will determine if it must file Schedule M-3 for 2015 based on its separate facts for 2015.

4. Same ownership facts as in Example 2.2 for calendar year 2014 except that A is owned 50% by corporation Z that was first required to file Schedule M-3 for its corporate tax year ended December 31, 2013, and that filed its Form 1120 with Schedule M-3 for 2013 on September 15, 2014. As of September 16, 2014, Z was a reportable entity partner with respect to A and, through A, with respect to B, C, D, and E. On October 5, 2014, Z reports to A, B, C, D, and E, as it is required to do within 30 days of September 16, that Z is a reportable entity partner directly owning (with respect to A) or deemed to own indirectly (with respect to B, C, D, and E) a 50% interest. Therefore, because Z was a reportable entity partner for 2014, each of A, B, C, D, and E is required to file Schedule M-3 for 2014, regardless of whether they would otherwise be required to file Schedule M-3 for that year.

Other Form 1065 Schedules Affected by Schedule M-3 Requirements

Schedule L

If a non-tax-basis income statement and related non-tax-basis balance sheet are prepared for any purpose for a period ending with or within the tax year, Schedule L must be prepared showing non-tax-basis amounts. See the discussion in the instructions for Schedule M-3, Part I, line 1, of non-tax-basis income statements and related non-tax-basis balance sheets prepared for any purpose and the impact on the selection of the income statement used for Schedule M-3 and the related non-tax-basis balance sheet amounts that must be used for Schedule L.

Total assets at the end of the tax year shown on Schedule L, line 14, column (d), must equal the total assets of the partnership as of the last day of the tax year, and must be the same total assets reported by the partnership in the non-tax-basis financial statements, if any, used for Schedule M-3. If the partnership prepares non-tax-basis financial statements, Schedule L must report the non-tax-basis financial statement total assets. If the partnership does not prepare non-tax-basis financial statements, Schedule L must be based on the partnership's books and records. The Schedule L balance sheet can show tax-basis balance sheet amounts if the partnership is allowed to use books and records for Schedule M-3 and the partnership's books and records reflect only tax-basis amounts.

Generally, total assets at the beginning of the year (Schedule L, line 14, column (b)) must equal total assets at the close of the prior year (Schedule L, line 14, column (d)). For each Schedule L balance sheet item reported for which there is a difference between the current opening balance sheet amount and the prior closing balance sheet amount, attach a statement that reports the balance sheet item, the prior closing amount, the current opening amount, and a short explanation of the change. Such reasons for these differences include technical terminations and mergers.

For purposes of measuring total assets at the end of the year, the partnership's assets may not be netted or reduced by partnership liabilities. In addition, total assets may not be reported as a negative amount. If Schedule L is prepared on a non-tax-basis method, an investment in another partnership may be shown as appropriate under the partnership's non-tax-basis method of accounting, including, if required by the partnership's reporting methodology, the equity method of accounting for investments. If Schedule L is prepared on a tax-basis method, an investment by the partnership in another partnership must be shown as an asset and measured by the partnership's adjusted basis in its partnership interest. Any liabilities contributing to such adjusted basis must be shown on Schedule L as partnership liabilities.

Example 3. A, a limited liability company (LLC), files Form 1065 for calendar year 2014. B, a general partnership, also files Form 1065 for calendar year 2014. A is a general partner in B. A's capital account in B at the close of 2014 is negative $4 million. This reflects A's 2014 contribution to B's capital of $2 million reduced by A's share of 2014 losses passing through to it from B, $6 million. A's adjusted basis in B at December 31, 2014, is $16 million, its $4 million negative tax capital account in B plus its $20 million share of B's liabilities under section 752. A prepares only tax-basis income statements and balance sheets. On its Schedule L, A reports as an asset the adjusted basis of its investment in B, $16 million. A also reports its $20 million share of B's liabilities in the liabilities section of Schedule L. A does not report its $4 million negative capital account in B on Schedule L.

Example 4. Same facts as in Example 3, except that B is an LLC and A is a member of B. None of B's liabilities are recourse with respect to A. A is not obligated to restore any deficit capital account in B. A prepares non-tax-basis income statements and balance sheets under an accounting method that requires the use of the equity method of accounting to account for its investment in B. On its non-tax-basis books and records, A initially reports $2 million as its investment in B, the amount of A's capital contribution. A then reduces its $2 million investment in B by its share of B's allocable losses. Because A's allocable share of B's losses is $6 million, A's investment in B under the equity method is reduced to $0. Because A is not liable to repay any of B's liabilities and is not obligated to restore any deficit with respect to its capital account in B, A does not report any of B's liabilities on A's Schedule L balance sheet.

Entity Considerations for Schedule M-3

For purposes of Schedule M-3, references to the classification of an entity (for example, as a corporation, a partnership, or a trust) are references to the treatment of the entity for U.S. income tax purposes. An entity that generally is disregarded as separate from its owner for U.S. income tax purposes (disregarded entity) must not be separately reported on Schedule M-3 except, if required, on Part I, line 7a or 7b. On Schedule M-3, Parts II and III, any item of income, gain, loss, deduction, or credit of a disregarded entity must be reported as an item of its owner. In particular, the income or loss of a disregarded entity must not be reported on Part II, lines 7, 8, or 9 as from a separate partnership or other pass-through. The financial statement income or loss of a disregarded entity is included on Part I, line 7a or 7b, only if its financial statement income or loss is included on Part I, line 11, but not on Part I, line 4a.

Specific Instructions

Item D. Reportable Entity Partner

On Schedule M-3, page 1, if the partnership has any reportable entity partners for the year, check Item D. A partnership must report the name, EIN if applicable, and maximum percentage of actual or deemed ownership of each reportable entity partner if there are one or two reportable entity partners for the tax year of the partnership, or, if there are more than two reportable entity partners for the tax year of the partnership, of the two reportable entity partners with the largest maximum percentage of actual or deemed ownership for the tax year of the partnership. The maximum percentage of actual or deemed ownership for a reportable entity partner for a tax year of the partnership is the maximum percentage interest owned or deemed owned under these instructions by the reportable entity partner in the partnership's capital, profit, or loss on any day during the tax year of the partnership.

The reportable entity partner must retain copies of required reports it makes to partnerships under these instructions. Each partnership must retain copies of the required reports it received under these instructions from reportable entity partners. See *Reportable Entity Partner Reporting Responsibilities*, above.

Part I. Financial Information and Net Income (Loss) Reconciliation

Line 1. Questions Regarding the Type of Income Statement Prepared

For lines 1 through 11, use only the financial statements of the U.S. partnership filing Form 1065 or Form 1065-B. If the U.S. partnership filing Form 1065 or Form 1065-B is controlled by another entity, the U.S. partnership must use for its Schedule M-3, Part I, its own financial statements and not the financial statements of the controlling entity.

Non-Tax-Basis Financial Statements and Tax-Basis Financial Statements

A tax-basis income statement is allowed for Schedule M-3 and a tax-basis balance sheet for Schedule L only if no non-tax-basis income statement and no non-tax-basis balance sheet were prepared for any purpose and the books and records of the partnership reflect only tax-basis amounts. The partnership is deemed to have non-tax-basis income statements and the related non-tax-basis balance sheets for the current tax year for purposes of Schedule M-3 and Schedule L if such non-tax-basis financial statements were prepared for and presented to management, creditors, members or partners, government regulators, or any other third parties for a period ending with or within the tax year.

If a Form 10-K is filed with the Securities and Exchange Commission (SEC) for the period ending with or within the tax year, the partnership must check "Yes" for line 1a and use that income statement for Schedule M-3. If Form 10-K is not filed and a non-tax-basis income statement is prepared that is a certified non-tax-basis income statement for the period ending with or within the tax year, the partnership must check "Yes" for line 1b and use that income statement for Schedule M-3. If Form 10-K is not filed and no certified non-tax-basis income statement is prepared but an unaudited non-tax-basis income statement is prepared for the period ending with or within the tax year, the partnership must check "Yes" for line 1c and use that income statement for Schedule M-3.

Order of priority in accounting standards. If no Form 10-K is filed and two or more non-tax-basis income statements are both certified non-tax-basis income statements for the period, the income

statement prepared according to the following order of priority in accounting standards must be used.

 1. U.S. Generally Accepted Accounting Principles (GAAP).

 2. International Financial Reporting Standards (IFRS).

 3. Any other International Accounting Standards (IAS).

 4. Any regulatory accrual accounting.

 5. Any other accrual accounting standard.

 6. Section 704(b) book accounting.

 7. Any other fair market value reporting standard.

 8. Any cash basis standard.

If no non-tax-basis income statement is certified and two or more non-tax-basis income statements are prepared, the income statement prepared according to the first listed of the accounting standards above must be used.

If no non-tax-basis financial statements are prepared for the U.S. partnership filing Schedule M-3, the U.S. partnership must check "No" on questions 1a, 1b, and 1c, skip lines 2 through 3b, and enter the net income (loss) per the books and records of the U.S. partnership on line 4a.

Consolidated Financial Statements

If a partnership filing a Schedule M-3 **(a)** is included in the non-tax-basis consolidated financial statements of a group (consolidated financial statement group) with an entity parent filing a U.S tax return and Schedule M-3, **(b)** has its income (loss) included and removed by the entity parent on that entity parent's Schedule M-3, Part I, and **(c)** does not have a separate non-tax-basis financial statement (certified or otherwise) of its own, the partnership must answer questions 1a, 1b, and 1c as appropriate for its own tax return and must report on its own Schedule M-3, as appropriate, the amount for the partnership's net income (loss) that is equal to the amount included and removed in the entity parent's Schedule M-3, Part I. However, if in the circumstances described immediately above, the partnership does have separate non-tax-basis financial statements (certified or otherwise) of its own, independent of the amount of the partnership's net income included in the consolidated financial statements with the entity parent, the partnership must answer questions 1a, 1b, and 1c, as appropriate, for its own tax return, based on its own separate non-tax-basis income statement, and must report on line 4a the net income (loss) amounts shown on its separate income statement.

Lines 2 and 3. Questions Regarding Income Statement Period and Restatements

Enter the beginning and ending dates on line 2 for the partnership's annual income statement period ending with or within the current tax year.

The questions on lines 3a and 3b, regarding income statement restatements, refer to the worldwide consolidated income statement issued by the partnership filing Form 1065 or Form 1065-B and used to prepare Schedule M-3. Answer "Yes" on lines 3a and/or 3b if the partnership's annual income statement has been restated for any reason. Attach a short statement of the reasons for the restatement in net income for each annual income statement period that is restated, including the original amount and restated amount of each annual statement period's net income. The attached statement is not required to report restatements on an entity-by-entity basis.

Line 4. Worldwide Consolidated Net Income (Loss) per Income Statement

Report on line 4a the worldwide consolidated net income (loss) per the income statement (or books and records, if applicable) of the partnership.

In completing Schedule M-3, the partnership must use financial statement amounts from the financial statement type checked "Yes" on line 1, or from its books and records if line 1c is checked "No." If line 1a is checked "Yes," report on line 4a the net income amount reported in the income statement presented to the SEC on the partnership's Form 10-K.

If a partnership prepares non-tax-basis financial statements, the amount on line 4a must equal the financial statement net income (loss) for the income statement period ending with or within the tax year as indicated on line 2.

If the partnership prepares non-tax-basis financial statements and the income statement period differs from the partnership's tax year, the income statement period indicated on line 2 applies for purposes of lines 4a through 8.

If the partnership does not prepare non-tax-basis financial statements and has checked "No" on line 1c, enter the net income (loss) per the books and records of the partnership on line 4a.

Check the appropriate box on line 4b to indicate which of the following accounting standards was used for line 4a:

1. U.S. Generally Accepted Accounting Principles (GAAP).

2. International Financial Reporting Standards (IFRS).

3. Section 704(b).

4. Tax-basis.

5. Other (specify).

Report on lines 5a through 10, as instructed below, all adjustment amounts required to adjust worldwide net income (loss) reported on line 4a (whether from financial statements or books and records) to net income (loss) of the partnership that must be reported on line 11. Report on line 12a the worldwide consolidated total assets and total liabilities amounts for the partnership using the same financial statements (or books and records) used for the worldwide consolidated income (loss) amount reported on line 4a.

Line 5. Net Income (Loss) of Nonincludible Foreign Entities

Remove the financial statement net income (line 5a) or loss (line 5b) of each foreign entity that is included on line 4a and is not the partnership (nonincludible foreign entity). In addition, on line 8, adjust for consolidation eliminations and correct for minority interest and intercompany dividends between any nonincludible foreign entity and the partnership filing Form 1065 or Form 1065-B. Do not remove in Part I the financial statement net income (loss) of any nonincludible foreign entity accounted for on line 4a using the equity method.

Attach a supporting statement that provides the name, EIN (if applicable), and net income (loss) included on line 4a that is removed on this line 5 for each separate nonincludible foreign entity. Also state the total assets and total liabilities for each such separate nonincludible foreign entity and include those assets and liabilities amounts in the total assets and total liabilities reported on Part I, line 12b. The amounts of income (loss) detailed on the supporting statement should be reported for each separate nonincludible foreign entity without regard to the effect of consolidation or elimination entries. If there are consolidation or elimination entries relating to nonincludible foreign entities whose income (loss) is reported on the attached statement that are not reportable on line 8, the net amounts of all such consolidation and elimination entries must be reported on a separate line on the attached statement, so that the separate financial accounting income (loss) of each nonincludible foreign entity remains separately stated.

For example, if the net income (after consolidation and elimination entries) of a nonincludible foreign sub-consolidated group is being reported on line 5a, the attached supporting statement should report the income (loss) of each separate nonincludible foreign legal entity from each such entity's own financial accounting net income statement or books and records, and any consolidation or elimination entries (for intercompany dividends, minority interests, etc.) not reportable on line 8 should be reported on the attached supporting statement as a net amount on a line separate and apart from lines that report each nonincludible foreign entity's separate net income (loss).

Line 6. Net Income (Loss) of Nonincludible U.S. Entities

Remove the financial statement net income (line 6a) or loss (line 6b) of each U.S. entity that is included on line 4a and is not an includible entity in the partnership return (nonincludible U.S. entity). In addition, on line 8, adjust for consolidation eliminations and correct for minority interest and intercompany dividends between any nonincludible U.S. entity and any includible entity. Do not remove in Part I the financial statement net income (loss) of any nonincludible U.S. entity accounted for on line 4a using the equity method.

Attach a supporting statement that provides the name, EIN (if applicable), and net income (loss) included on line 4a that is removed on line 6 for each separate nonincludible U.S. entity. Also state the total assets and total liabilities for each such separate nonincludible U.S. entity and include those assets and liabilities amounts in the total assets and total liabilities reported on Part I, line 12c. The amounts of income (loss) detailed on the supporting statement should be reported for each separate nonincludible U.S. entity without regard to the effect of consolidation or elimination entries. If there are consolidation or elimination entries relating to nonincludible U.S. entities whose income (loss) is reported on the attached statement that are not reportable on line 8, the net amounts of all such consolidation and elimination entries must be reported on a separate line on the attached statement, so that the separate financial accounting income (loss) of each nonincludible U.S. entity remains separately stated.

For example, if the net income (after consolidation and elimination entries) of a nonincludible U.S. sub-consolidated group is being reported on line 6a, the attached supporting statement should report the income (loss) of each separate nonincludible U.S. legal entity from each such entity's own financial accounting net income statement or books and records, and any consolidation or elimination entries (for intercompany dividends, minority interests, etc.) not reportable on line 8 should be reported on the attached supporting statement as a net amount on a line separate and apart from lines that report each nonincludible U.S. entity's separate net income (loss).

Lines 7a and 7b. Net Income (Loss) of Other Foreign Disregarded Entities and Net Income (Loss) of Other U.S. Disregarded Entities

Include on line 7a or 7b the financial net income or (loss) of each disregarded entity in the U.S. tax return that is not included in the consolidated financial group, and therefore not included in the income reported on line 4a, but that is included on line 11. Include on line 7a the financial income or (loss) of any foreign disregarded entity that is not included in the income reported on line 4a but that is included on line 11 (other foreign disregarded entities). Include on line 7b the financial income or (loss) of any U.S. disregarded entity that is not included in the income reported on line 4a but that is included on line 11 (other U.S. disregarded entities). In addition, on line 8, adjust for consolidation eliminations and correct for minority interest and intercompany dividends for any other disregarded entity.

Attach a supporting statement that provides the name, EIN, and net income (loss) per the financial statement or books and records included on line 7a or 7b for each separate foreign or U.S. disregarded entity. Also state the total assets and total liabilities for each such separate included entity and include those assets and liabilities amounts in the total assets and total liabilities reported on Part I, line 12d. The amounts of income (loss) detailed on the supporting statement should be reported for each separate other disregarded entity without regard to the effect of consolidation or elimination entries solely between or among the entities listed. If there are consolidation or elimination entries relating to such separate other disregarded entities whose income (loss) is reported on the attached statement that are not reportable on line 8, the net amounts of all such consolidation and elimination entries must be reported on a separate line on the attached statement, so that the separate financial accounting income (loss) of each separate other disregarded entity remains separately stated.

For example, if the net income (after consolidation and elimination entries) of a sub-consolidated group of other foreign disregarded entities is being reported on line 7a, the attached supporting statement should report the income (loss) of each separate other foreign disregarded entity from each disregarded entity's own financial accounting net income statement or books and records, and any consolidation or elimination entries (for intercompany dividends, minority interests, etc.) not reportable on line 8 should be reported on the attached supporting statement as a net amount on a line separate and apart from lines that report each other foreign disregarded entity's separate net income (loss).

Line 8. Adjustment to Eliminations of Transactions Between Includible Entities and Nonincludible Entities

Adjustments on line 8 to reverse certain financial accounting consolidation or elimination entries are necessary to ensure that transactions between includible entities and nonincludible U.S. or foreign entities are not eliminated, in order to report the correct total amount on line 11. Also, additional consolidation entries and elimination entries may be necessary on line 8 related to transactions between includible entities that are in the consolidated financial statement group and other includible entities that are not in the consolidated financial statement group but that are reported on line 7a or 7b in order to report the correct total amount on line 11.

Include on line 8 the total of the following: **(a)** amounts of any adjustments to consolidation entries and elimination entries that are contained in the amount reported on line 4a, required as a result of removing amounts on line 5 or 6; and **(b)** amounts of any additional consolidation entries and elimination entries that are required as a result of including amounts on line 7a or 7b. This is necessary in order that the consolidation entries and intercompany elimination entries included in the amount reported on line 11 are only those applicable to the financial net income (loss) of includible entities for the financial statement period. For example, adjustments must be reported on line 8 to remove minority interest and to reverse the elimination of intercompany dividends included on line 4a that relate to the net income of entities removed on line 5 or 6 because the income to which the consolidation or elimination entries relate has been removed. Also, for example, consolidation or elimination entries must be reported on line 8 to eliminate any intercompany dividends between entities whose income is included on line 7a or 7b and other entities included in the U.S. income tax return.

If an entity owner of an interest in another entity **(a)** accounts for the interest in the other entity in the owner's separate general ledger on the equity method, and **(b)** fully consolidates the other entity in the owner's consolidated financial statements, but that entity is not includible in the owner's Form 1065 or Form 1065-B, then, as part of reversing all consolidation and elimination entries for the nonincludible entity, the owner must reverse on line 8 the elimination of the equity income inclusion from the other entity. If the owner does not account for the other entity on the equity method on its own general ledger, it will not have eliminated the equity income for consolidated financial statement purposes, and therefore will have no elimination of equity income to reverse.

The attached supporting statement for line 8 must identify the type (for example, minority interest, intercompany dividends, etc.) and amount of consolidation or elimination entries reported, as well as the names of the entities to which they pertain. It is not necessary, but it is permitted, to report on line 8 intercompany eliminations that net to zero, such as intercompany interest income and expense.

Line 9. Adjustment to Reconcile Income Statement Period to Tax Year

Include on line 9 any adjustments necessary to the income (loss) of the partnership to reconcile differences between the partnership's income statement period reported on line 2 and the partnership's tax year. Attach a statement describing the adjustment.

Line 10. Other Adjustments To Reconcile to Amount on Line 11

Include on line 10 any other adjustments to reconcile net income (loss) on line 4a through line 9, with net income (loss) of the partnership reported on line 11.

For any adjustment reported on line 10, attach a supporting statement with an explanation of each net adjustment included on line 10.

Line 11. Net Income (Loss) per Income Statement of the Partnership

Report on line 11 the net income (loss) per the income statement (or books and records, if applicable) of the partnership. Amounts reported in column (a) of Parts II and III (see later) must be reported on the same accounting method as is used to report the amount of net income (loss) per income statement of the partnership on line 11.

Do not, in any event, report on line 11 the net income of entities other than the partnership filing Form 1065 or Form 1065-B for the tax year. For example, it is not permissible to remove the income of nonincludible entities on lines 5 and/or 6, above, then to add back such income on lines 7 through 10, such that the amount reported on line 11 includes the net income of entities not includible in the U.S. income tax return. A principal purpose of

Schedule M-3 is to report on line 11 only the financial accounting net income of only the partnership (including any other includible entities) filing Form 1065 or Form 1065-B.

Whether or not the partnership prepares financial statements, line 11 must include all items that impact the net income (loss) of the partnership even if they are not recorded in the profit and loss accounts in the partnership's general ledger, including, for example, all post-closing adjusting entries (including workpaper adjustments) and dividend income or other income received from nonincludible entities. If the partnership prepares unconsolidated financial statements using the same accounting method used to determine worldwide consolidated net income (loss) for Part I, line 4, and if it uses the equity method for investments, the amount reported on Part I, line 11, will equal the amount of the unconsolidated net income (loss) reported on the unconsolidated financial statements. See examples 5.3, 5.4, and 5.5.

Example 5.

1. U.S. partnership P owns 60% of corporation DS1 which is fully consolidated in P's financial statements. P does not account for DS1 in P's separate general ledger on the equity method. DS1 has net income of $100 (before minority interests) and pays dividends of $50, of which P receives $30. The dividend is eliminated in the consolidated financial statements. In its financial statements, P consolidates DS1 and includes $60 of net income ($100 less the minority interest of $40) on line 4a.

P must remove the $100 net income of DS1 on line 6a. P must reverse on line 8 the elimination of the $40 minority interest net income of DS1. In addition, P reverses its elimination of the $30 intercompany dividend in its financial statements on line 8. The net result is that P includes the $30 dividend from DS1 on line 11 and on Part II, line 6, column (a). P's dividend income included on the tax return from DS1 must be reported on Part II, line 6, column (d).

2. U.S. partnership C owns 60% of the capital and profits interests in U.S. LLC N. C does not account for N in C's separate general ledger on the equity method. N has net income of $100 (before minority interests) and makes no distributions during the tax year. C treats N as a corporation for financial statement purposes and as a partnership for U.S. income tax purposes. In its financial statements, C consolidates N and includes $60 of net income ($100 less the minority interest of $40) on line 4a.

C must remove the $100 net income of N on line 6a. C must reverse on line 8 the

elimination of the $40 minority interest net income of N. The result is that C includes no income for N either on line 11 or on Part II, line 7, column (a). C's taxable income from N must be reported by C on Part II, line 7, column (d).

3. U.S. partnership P owns 60% of corporation DS1, which is fully consolidated in P's financial statements. P accounts for DS1 in P's separate general ledger on the equity method. DS1 has net income of $100 (before minority interests) and pays dividends of $50, of which P receives $30. The dividend reduces P's investment in DS1 for equity method reporting on P's separate general ledger where P includes its 60% equity share of DS1 income, which is $60. In its financial statements, P eliminates the DS1 equity method income of $60 and consolidates DS1, including $60 of net income ($100 less the minority interest of $40) on line 4a.

P must remove the $100 net income of DS1 on line 6a. P must reverse on line 8 the elimination of the $40 minority interest net income of DS1 and the elimination of the $60 of DS1 equity income. The net result is that P includes the $60 of equity method income from DS1 on line 11 and on Part II, line 5, column (a). P's dividend income on the tax return from its investment in DS1 must be reported on Part II, line 6, column (d).

4. U.S. partnership C owns 60% of the capital and profits interests in U.S. LLC N. C accounts for N in C's separate general ledger on the equity method. N has net income of $100 (before minority interests) and makes no distributions during the tax year. C treats N as a corporation for financial statement purposes and as a partnership for U.S. income tax purposes. For equity method reporting on C's separate general ledger, C includes its 60% equity share of N income, which is $60. In its financial statements, C eliminates the $60 of N equity method income and consolidates N, including $60 of net income ($100 less the minority interest of $40) on line 4a.

C must remove the $100 net income of N on line 6a. C must reverse on line 8 the elimination of the $40 minority interest net income of N and the elimination of the $60 of N equity method income. The result is that C includes the $60 of equity method income for N on line 11 and on Part II, line 7, column (a). C's taxable income from N must be reported by C on Part II, line 7, column (d).

5. U.S. partnership C owns 60% of the capital and profits interests in U.S. LLC N. C accounts for N in C's separate general ledger on the equity method. N has net income of $100 (before minority interests) and pays a $50 cash distribution, of which C receives $30. The distribution reduces

C's investment in N for equity method reporting on C's separate general ledger. C treats N as a corporation for financial statement purposes and as a partnership for U.S. income tax purposes. For equity method reporting on C's separate general ledger, C includes its 60% equity share of N income, which is $60. In its financial statements, C eliminates the $60 of N equity method income and consolidates N and includes $60 of net income ($100 less the minority interest of $40) on line 4a.

C must remove the $100 net income of N on line 6a. C must reverse on line 8 the elimination of the $40 minority interest net income of N and the elimination of the $60 of N equity method income. The result is that C includes the $60 of equity method income for N on line 11 and on Part II, line 7, column (a). C's taxable income from N must be reported by C on Part II, line 7, column (d).

6. U.S. partnership P owns 100% of the stock of U.S. LLC Q, a disregarded entity. Q is included in P's federal income tax return, even though Q is not included in P's consolidated financial statements on either a consolidated basis or on the equity method. Q has current year net income of $100 after taking into account its $40 interest payment to P. P has net income of $1,040 after recognition of the interest income from Q. Because Q is a disregarded entity, 100% of the net income of both P and Q must be reported on P's Form 1065 or Form 1065-B and the intercompany interest income and expense must be removed by consolidation elimination entries.

P must report its financial statement net income of $1,040 on line 4a and reports Q's net income of $100 on line 7b as a U.S. disregarded entity not included on line 4a, but included on line 11. Then, in order to reflect the full consolidation of the financial accounting net income of P and Q at line 11, the following consolidation and elimination entry is reported on line 8: offsetting entries to remove the $40 of interest income received from Q included by P on line 4a, and to remove the $40 of interest expense of Q included in line 7b for a net change of zero. The result is that line 11 reports $1,140: $1,040 from line 4a, and $100 from line 7. Stated another way, line 11 includes the entire $1,000 net income of P, measured before recognition of the intercompany interest income from Q and the consolidation of Q operations, plus the entire $140 net income of Q, measured before interest expense to P. P is not required to include on the attached supporting statement for line 8 the offsetting adjustment to the intercompany elimination of interest income and interest expense (though it is permitted to do so).

Line 12. Total Assets and Liabilities of Entities Included or Removed on Part I, Lines 4, 5, 6, and 7

Line 12 must be completed by all partnerships that file Schedule M-3. Report on lines 12a, 12b, 12c, and 12d the total amounts (not just the partnership's share) of assets and liabilities of entities included or removed on Part I, lines 4, 5, 6, and 7. All assets and liabilities reported on Part I, lines 12a through 12d must be reported as positive amounts. On line 12a, enter the worldwide consolidated total assets and total liabilities of all of the entities included in completing Part I, line 4. On line 12b, enter the total assets and total liabilities of the entities removed in completing Part I, line 5. On line 12c, enter the total assets and total liabilities of the entities removed in completing Part I, line 6. On line 12d, enter the total assets and total liabilities of the entities included in completing Part I, line 7.

Parts II and III

General Reporting Information

A schedule or statement may be attached to any line even if none is required.

For each line item in Parts II and III, report in column (a) the amount of net income (loss) included on Part I, line 11, and report in column (d) the amount included on line 1 of the *Analysis of Net Income (Loss)* found on Form 1065 and Form 1065-B.

Note. Part II, line 26, column (a) must equal Part I, line 11, and column (d) must equal line 1 of the*Analysis of Net Income (Loss)* found on Form 1065 and Form 1065-B. Thus, column (d) on Part II and Part III must include certain of the separately stated items on Schedule K.

For any item of income, gain, loss, expense, or deduction for which there is a difference between columns (a) and (d), the portion of the difference that is temporary must be entered in column (b) and the portion of the difference that is permanent must be entered in column (c).

If financial statements are prepared by the partnership under generally accepted accounting principles (GAAP), differences that are treated as temporary under GAAP must be reported in column (b) and differences that are permanent (that is, not temporary) for GAAP must be reported in column (c). Generally, under GAAP, a temporary difference affects (creates, increases, or decreases) a deferred tax asset or liability.

If the partnership does not prepare financial statements, or the financial statements are not prepared under GAAP,

report in column (b) any difference that the partnership believes will reverse in a future tax year (that is, have an opposite effect on taxable income in a future tax year (or years) due to the difference in timing of recognition for financial accounting and U.S. income tax purposes) or is the reversal of such a difference that arose in a prior tax year. Report in column (c) any difference that the partnership believes will not reverse in a future tax year (and is not the reversal of such a difference that arose in a prior tax year).

If the partnership is unable to determine whether a difference between column (a) and column (d) for an item will reverse in a future tax year or is the reversal of a difference that arose in a prior tax year, report the difference for that item in column (c).

Example 6. At the end of Partnership A's first tax year, December 31, 2014, it was not required to file Schedule M-3 for any reason.

A may elect to file Schedule M-3 instead of completing Schedule M-1.

If A elects to file Schedule M-3, it must either (i) complete Schedule M-3 entirely or (ii) complete Schedule M-3 through Part I and complete Schedule M-1 instead of completing Parts II and III of Schedule M-3.

If A elects to complete Schedule M-3 entirely, it must complete all columns of Parts II and III.

If A completes Schedule M-3 through Part I and completes Schedule M-1 instead of completing Parts II and III of Schedule M-3, line 11 of Part I of Schedule M-3 must equal line 1 of Schedule M-1.

Reporting Requirements for Parts II and III

General Reporting Requirements

If an amount is attributable to a reportable transaction described in Regulations section 1.6011-4(b), the amount must be reported in columns (a), (b), (c), and (d), as applicable, of Part II, line 10, Items relating to reportable transactions, regardless of whether the amount would otherwise be reported on Schedule M-3, Part II or Part III. Thus, if a taxpayer files Form 8886, Reportable Transaction Disclosure Statement, the amounts attributable to that reportable transaction must be reported on Part II, line 10.

A partnership is required to report in column (a) of Parts II and III the amount of any item specifically listed on Schedule M-3 that is in any manner included in the partnership's current year financial statement net income (loss) or in an income or expense account maintained

in the partnership's books and records, even if there is no difference between that amount and the amount included in net income (loss) for tax purposes unless **(a)** otherwise instructed in these instructions or **(b)** the amount is attributable to a reportable transaction described in Regulations section 1.6011-4(b) and is therefore reported on Part II, line 10. For example, with the exception of interest income reflected on a Schedule K-1 received by the partnership as a result of the partnership's investment in a partnership or other pass-through entity, all interest income included on Part I, line 11, whether from unconsolidated affiliated entities, third parties, banks, or other entities, whether from foreign or domestic sources, whether taxable or exempt from tax, and whether classified as some other type of income for U.S. income tax purposes (such as dividends), must be included on Part II, line 11, column (a). Likewise, all fines and penalties included on Part I, line 11, paid to a government or other authority for the violation of any law for which fines or penalties are assessed must be included on Part III, line 7, column (a), regardless of the government authority that imposed the fines or penalties, regardless of whether the fines or penalties are civil or criminal, regardless of the classification, nomenclature, or terminology attached to the fines or penalties by the imposing authority in its actions or documents.

If a partnership would be required to report in column (a) of Parts II and III the amount of any item specifically listed on Schedule M-3 in accordance with the preceding paragraph, except that the partnership has capitalized the item of income or expense and reports the amount in its financial statement balance sheet or in asset and liability accounts maintained in the partnership's books and records, the partnership must report the proper tax treatment of the item in columns (b), (c), and (d), as applicable.

Furthermore, in applying the two preceding paragraphs, a partnership is required to report in column (a) of Parts II and III the amount of any item specifically listed on Schedule M-3 that is included in the partnership's financial statements or exists in the partnership's books and records, regardless of the nomenclature associated with that item in the financial statements or books and records. Accurate completion of Schedule M-3 requires reporting amounts according to the substantive nature of the specific line items included in Schedule M-3 and consistent reporting of all transactions of like substantive nature that occurred during the tax year. For example, all expense amounts that are included in the financial statements or exist in the books and records that represent some form of "Bad debt expense" must be reported on Part III, line 26, in column (a), regardless of whether the amounts are recorded or stated under different nomenclature in the financial statements or the books and records such as: "Provision for doubtful accounts"; "Expense for uncollectible notes receivable"; or "Impairment of trade accounts receivable." Likewise, as stated in the preceding paragraph, all fines and penalties must be included on Part III, line 7, column (a), regardless of the terminology or nomenclature attached to them by the partnership in its books and records or financial statements.

With limited exceptions, Part II includes lines for specific items of income, gain, or loss (income items). (See lines 1 through 21.) If an income item is described on lines 1 through 21, report the amount of the item on the applicable line, regardless of whether there is a difference for the item. If there is a difference for the income item, or only a portion of the income item has a difference and a portion of the item does not have a difference, and the item is not described on lines 1 through 21, report and describe the entire amount of the item on line 22.

With limited exceptions, Part III includes lines for specific items of expense or deduction (expense items). (See lines 1 through 29.) If an expense item is described on lines 1 through 29, report the amount of the item on the applicable line, regardless of whether there is a difference for the item. If there is a difference for the expense item, or only a portion of the expense item has a difference and a portion of the item does not have a difference and the item is not described on lines 1 through 29, report and describe the entire amount of the item on line 30.

If there is no difference between the financial accounting amount and the amount reported for tax purposes of an entire item of income, loss, expense, or deduction and the item is not described or included on Part II, lines 1 through 22, or Part III, lines 1 through 30, report the entire amount of the item in column (a) and (d) of Part II, line 25.

Separately stated and adequately disclosed. Each difference reported in Parts II and III must be separately stated and adequately disclosed. In general, a difference is adequately disclosed if the difference is labeled in a manner that clearly identifies the item or transaction from which the difference arises. For further guidance about adequate disclosure, see Regulations section 1.6662-4(f). If a specific item of income, gain, loss, expense, or deduction is

described on Part II, lines 7 through 21, or Part III, lines 1 through 29, and the line does not indicate to "attach schedule" or "attach details," and the specific instructions for the line do not call for an attachment of a schedule or explanation, then the item is considered separately stated and adequately disclosed if the item is reported on the applicable line and the amount(s) of the item(s) are reported in the applicable columns of the applicable line. See the instructions for Part II, lines 1 through 9, for specific additional information required to be provided for these particular lines.

Except as otherwise provided, differences for the same item must be combined or netted together and reported as one amount on the applicable line of Schedule M-3. However, differences for separate items must not be combined or netted together. Each item (and corresponding amount attributable to that item) must be separately stated and adequately disclosed on the applicable line of Schedule M-3 or any statement required to be attached, even if the amounts are below a certain dollar amount.

Required statements for Part II, line 22 and Part III, line 30. A separate statement must be attached to Schedule M-3 (Form 1065) that includes a detailed description of each item and adjustment entered on Part II, line 22, and Part III, line 30.

The description for each amount entered in column (a) must be readily identifiable to the name of the account in the financial statements or books and records of the taxpayer, under which the amount in column (a) was recorded in the accounting records. Also, the description for each amount entered in column (a) must include detailed information supporting each adjustment reported in columns (b) and (c), including how the adjustment is identified in the accounting records. The entire description is considered the tax description for the amount reported in column (d) for each item reported on Part II, line 22, or Part III, line 30.

Each description should adequately describe all four columns of Part II, line 22, or Part III, line 30. If additional information is required to provide an acceptable description, provide a supporting statement.

Example 7. Partnership B prepares GAAP financial statements. In prior years, B acquired intellectual property (IP) and goodwill. The IP is amortizable for both U.S. income tax and financial statement purposes. In the current year, B's annual amortization expense for IP is $9,000 for U.S. income tax purposes and $6,000 for financial statement purposes. The

goodwill is not amortizable for U.S. income tax purposes and is subject to impairment for financial statement purposes. In the current year, B records an impairment charge on the goodwill of $5,000. B must report the amortization attributable to the IP on Part III, line 21, and report $6,000 in column (a), a temporary difference of $3,000 in column (b), and $9,000 in column (d). B must report the goodwill impairment on Part III, line 19, and report $5,000 in column (a), a permanent difference of ($5,000) in column (c), and $0 in column (d).

Example 8. Partnership C is a calendar year partnership that files and entirely completes Schedule M-3 for its 2014 tax year. C placed in service 10 depreciable fixed assets in a previous tax year. C's total depreciation expense for its 2014 tax year for five of the assets is $50,000 for income statement purposes and $70,000 for U.S. income tax purposes. C's total annual depreciation expense for its 2014 tax year for the other five assets is $40,000 for income statement purposes and $30,000 for U.S. income tax purposes. C treats the differences between financial statement and U.S. income tax depreciation expense as giving rise to temporary differences that will reverse in future years. C must combine all of its depreciation adjustments. Accordingly, C must report on Part III, line 25, for its 2014 tax year income statement depreciation expense of $90,000 in column (a), a temporary difference of $10,000 in column (b), and U.S. income tax depreciation expense of $100,000 in column (d).

Example 9. Partnership D is a calendar year partnership that files and entirely completes Schedule M-3 for its 2014 tax year. On December 31, 2014, D establishes three reserve accounts in the amount of $100,000 for each account. One reserve account is an allowance for accounts receivable that are estimated to be uncollectible. The second reserve is an estimate of coupons outstanding that may have to be paid. The third reserve is an estimate of future warranty expenses. In its financial statements, D treats the three reserve accounts as giving rise to temporary differences that will reverse in future years. The three reserves are expenses in D's 2014 financial statements but are not deductions for U.S. income tax purposes in 2014. D must not combine the Schedule M-3 differences for the three reserve accounts. D must report the amounts attributable to the allowance for uncollectible accounts receivable on Part III, line 26, Bad debt expense, and must separately state and adequately disclose the amounts attributable to each of the other two reserves, coupons outstanding and warranty costs, on a required, attached statement that supports the amounts on Part III, line 30. D must also provide a description for each reserve that meets the requirements for Part III, line 30, discussed earlier under *Required statements for Part II, line 22, and Part III, line 30*. In this example, an acceptable description for warranty costs would be: Future Warranty Expense Reserve.

Note. There is no need to add the title of the reserve account to the description if the account name for the amount in column (a) is already part of the adjustment description.

Example 10. Partnership E is a calendar year partnership that files and entirely completes Schedule M-3 for its 2014 tax year. On January 2, 2014, E establishes an allowance for uncollectible accounts receivable (bad debt reserve) of $100,000. During 2014, E increased the reserve by $250,000 for additional accounts receivable that may become uncollectible. Additionally, during 2014, E decreases the reserve by $75,000 for accounts receivable that were discharged in bankruptcy during 2014. The balance in the reserve account on December 31, 2014, is $275,000. The $100,000 amount to establish the reserve account and the $250,000 to increase the reserve account are expenses on E's 2014 financial statements but are not deductible for U.S. income tax purposes in 2014. However, the $75,000 decrease to the reserve is deductible for U.S. income tax purposes in 2014. In its financial statements, E treats the reserve account as giving rise to a temporary difference that will reverse in future tax years. E must report on Part III, line 26, Bad debt expense, for its 2014 tax year income statement bad debt expense of $350,000 in column (a), a temporary difference of ($275,000) in column (b), and U.S. income tax bad debt expense of $75,000 in column (d).

Example 11. Partnership F is a calendar year partnership that files and entirely completes Schedule M-3 for its 2014 tax year. During 2014, F incurs $200 of meals and entertainment expenses that F deducts in computing net income per the income statement. $50 of the $200 is subject to the 50% limitation under section 274(n). In its financial statements, F treats the limitation on deductions for meals and entertainment as a permanent difference. Because meals and entertainment expenses are specifically described on Part III, line 6, Meals and entertainment, F must report all of its meals and entertainment expenses on this line, regardless of whether there is a difference. Accordingly, F must report $200 in column (a), $25 in column (c), and $175 in column (d). F must not report the $150 of meals and entertainment expenses that are deducted in F's financial statement net income and are

fully deductible for U.S. income tax purposes on Part II, line 25, Other items with no differences, nor the $50 subject to the limitation under section 274(n) on Part III, line 6.

Part II. Reconciliation of Net Income (Loss) per Income Statement of Partnership With Income (Loss) per Return

Lines 1 Through 9. Additional Information for Each Entity

For any item reported on lines 1 or 3 through 5, attach a supporting statement that provides the name of the entity for which the item is reported, the entity's EIN (if applicable), the type of entity (corporation, partnership, etc.), and the item amounts for columns (a) through (d). See the instructions for lines 2 and 6 through 9 for the specific information required for those particular lines.

Line 1. Income (Loss) From Equity Method Foreign Corporations

Report on line 1, column (a), the financial income (loss) included on Part I, line 11, for any foreign corporation accounted for on the equity method and remove such amount in column (b) or (c), as applicable. Report the amount of dividends received and other taxable amounts received or includible from foreign corporations on lines 2 through 4, as applicable.

Line 2. Gross Foreign Dividends Not Previously Taxed

Except as otherwise provided in this paragraph, report on line 2, column (d), the amount (before any withholding tax) of any foreign dividends included on line 1 of the *Analysis of Net Income (Loss)* found on Form 1065 and Form 1065-B, and report on line 2, column (a), the amount of dividends from any foreign corporation included on Part I, line 11. Do not report on line 2 any amounts that must be reported on line 3 or dividends that were previously taxed and must be reported on line 4. (See the instructions below for lines 3 and 4.) Report withholding taxes on Part III, line 30, Other expense/deduction items with differences, or line 25, Other items with no differences, as applicable.

For any dividends reported on line 2 that are received on a class of voting stock of which the partnership directly or indirectly owned 10% or more of the outstanding shares of that class at any time during the tax year, report on an attached supporting statement for line 2: **(a)** the name of the dividend payer, **(b)** the

payer's EIN (if applicable), **(c)** the class of voting stock on which the dividend was paid, **(d)** the percentage of the class directly or indirectly owned, and **(e)** the amounts for columns (a) through (d).

Line 3. Subpart F, QEF, and Similar Income Inclusions

Report on line 3, column (d), the amount included in taxable income under section 951 (relating to Subpart F), gains or other income inclusions resulting from elections under sections 1291(d)(2) and 1298(b)(1), and any amount included in taxable income pursuant to section 1293 (relating to qualified electing funds). The amount of Subpart F income corresponds to the total of the amounts reported by the partnership on line 6, Schedule I, of all Forms 5471, Information Return of U.S. Persons With Respect To Certain Foreign Corporations. The amount of qualified electing fund income corresponds to the total of the amounts reported by the partnership on Part III, line 8a, of all Forms 8621, Information Return by a Shareholder of a Passive Foreign Investment Company or Qualified Electing Fund.

Also include on line 3 passive foreign investment company mark-to-market gains and losses under section 1296. Do not report such gains and losses on line 14.

Line 4. Gross Foreign Distributions Previously Taxed

Report on line 4, column (a), any distributions received from foreign corporations that were included on Part I, line 11, and that were previously taxed for U.S. income tax purposes. For example, include in column (a) amounts that are excluded from taxable income under sections 959 and 1293(c). Remove such amounts in column (b) or (c), as applicable. Report the full amount of the distribution before any withholding tax. Report withholding taxes on Part III, line 30, Other expense/deduction items with differences, or line 25, Other items with no differences, as applicable. Since previously taxed foreign distributions are not currently taxable, line 4, column (d), is shaded. (Also, see instructions above for line 2.)

Line 5. Income (Loss) From Equity Method U.S. Corporations

Report on line 5, column (a), the financial income (loss) included on Part I, line 11, for any U.S. corporation accounted for on the equity method and remove such amount in column (b) or (c), as applicable. Report on line 6 the amount of dividends received from any U.S. corporations.

Line 6. U.S. Dividends

Report on line 6, column (a), the amount of dividends included on Part I, line 11, that were received from any U.S. corporation. Report on line 6, column (d), the amount of any U.S. dividends included in taxable income on line 1 of the *Analysis of Net Income (Loss)* found on Form 1065 and Form 1065-B.

For any dividends reported on line 6 that are received on classes of voting stock in which the partnership directly or indirectly owned 10% or more of the outstanding shares of that class at any time during the tax year, report on an attached supporting statement for line 6: (1) the name of the dividend payer, (2) the payer's EIN (if applicable), (3) the class of voting stock on which the dividend was paid, (4) the percentage of the class directly or indirectly owned, and (5) the amounts for columns (a) through (d).

Line 7. Income (Loss) From U.S. Partnerships and Line 8. Income (Loss) From Foreign Partnerships

For any interest owned by the partnership that is treated as an investment in a partnership for U.S. income tax purposes (other than an interest in a disregarded entity), report amounts on line 7 or 8, as described below:

1. In column (a), the sum of the partnership's distributive share of income or loss from a U.S. or foreign partnership that is included on Part I, line 11;

2. In column (b) or (c), as applicable, the sum of all differences, if any, attributable to the partnership's distributive share of income or loss from a U.S. or foreign partnership; and

3. In column (d), the sum of all amounts of income, gain, loss, or deduction attributable to the partnership's distributive share of income or loss from a U.S. or foreign partnership (that is, the sum of all amounts reportable on the partnership's Schedule(s) K-1 received from the partnership (if applicable)), without regard to any limitations computed at the partner level (for example, limitations on utilization of charitable contributions, capital losses, and interest expense).

For each partnership reported on line 7 or 8, attach a supporting statement that provides the name, EIN (if applicable), end of year profit-sharing percentage (if applicable), end of year loss-sharing percentage (if applicable), and the amount reported in column (a), (b), (c), or (d) of lines 7 or 8, as applicable.

Example 12. U.S. partnership H is a calendar year partnership that files and entirely completes Schedule M-3 for its 2014 tax year. H has an investment in a U.S. partnership USP. H prepares financial statements in accordance with GAAP. For its 2014 tax year, H's financial statement net income includes $10,000 of income attributable to its share of USP's net income. H's Schedule K-1 from USP reports $5,000 of ordinary income, $7,000 of long-term capital gains, $4,000 of charitable contributions, and $200 of section 179 expense. H must report on line 7 $10,000 in column (a), a permanent difference of ($2,200) in column (c), and $7,800 in column (d).

Line 9. Income (Loss) From Other Pass-Through Entities

For any interest in a pass-through entity (other than an interest in a partnership reportable on line 7 or 8, as applicable) owned by the U.S. partnership (other than an interest in a disregarded entity), report the following on line 9:

1. In column (a), the sum of the partnership's distributive share of income or loss from the pass-through entity that is included on Part I, line 11;

2. In column (b) or (c), as applicable, the sum of all differences, if any, attributable to the pass-through entity; and

3. In column (d), the sum of all taxable amounts of income, gain, loss, or deduction reportable on the partnership's Schedule(s) K-1 received from the pass-through entity (if applicable).

For each pass-through entity reported on line 9, attach a supporting statement that provides that entity's name, EIN (if applicable), the partnership's end of year profit-sharing percentage (if applicable), the partnership's end of year loss-sharing percentage (if applicable), and the amounts reported by the partnership in column (a), (b), (c), or (d), of line 9, as applicable.

Line 10. Items Relating to Reportable Transactions

Any amounts attributable to any reportable transactions (as described in Regulations section 1.6011-4) must be included on line 10 regardless of whether the difference, or differences, would otherwise be reported elsewhere in Part II or Part III. Thus, if a taxpayer files Form 8886 for any reportable transaction described in Regulations section 1.6011-4, the amounts attributable to that reportable transaction must be reported on line 10. In addition, all income and expense amounts attributable to a reportable transaction must be reported on line 10, columns (a) and (d), even if there is no difference between the financial statement amounts and the tax return amounts.

Each difference attributable to a reportable transaction must be separately stated and adequately disclosed. A partnership will be considered to have separately stated and adequately disclosed a reportable transaction on line 10 if the partnership sequentially numbers each Form 8886 and lists by statement number (shown on line A of Form 8886) on the supporting statement for line 10 each sequentially numbered reportable transaction and the amounts required for line 10, columns (a) through (d).

Instead of satisfying the requirements of the preceding paragraph, a partnership will be considered to have separately stated and adequately disclosed a reportable transaction if the partnership attaches a supporting statement that provides the following for each reportable transaction:

1. A description of the reportable transaction disclosed on Form 8886 for which amounts are reported on line 10;

2. The name and reportable transaction or tax shelter registration number, if applicable, as reported on lines 1a and 1c, respectively, of Form 8886; and

3. The type of reportable transaction (that is, listed transaction, confidential transaction, transaction with contractual protection, etc.) as reported on line 2 of Form 8886.

If a transaction is a listed transaction described in Regulations section 1.6011-4(b)(2), the description also must include the published guidance number shown on line 3 of Form 8886. In addition, if the reportable transaction involves an investment in the transaction through another entity such as a partnership, the description must include the name and EIN (if applicable) of that entity as reported on line 5 of Form 8886.

Example 13. Partnership J is a calendar year partnership that files and entirely completes Schedule M-3 for its 2014 tax year. J incurred seven different abandonment losses during its 2014 tax year. One loss of $12 million results from a reportable transaction described in Regulations section 1.6011-4(b)(5), another loss of $5 million results from a reportable transaction described in Regulations section 1.6011-4(b)(4), and the remaining five abandonment losses are not reportable transactions. J discloses the reportable transactions giving rise to the $12 million and $5 million losses on separate Forms 8886 and sequentially numbers them X1 and X2, respectively. J must separately state and adequately disclose the $12 million and $5 million losses on line 10. The $12 million loss and the $5 million loss will be adequately disclosed if J attaches a supporting statement for line 10 that lists each of the sequentially numbered forms, Form 8886-X1 and Form 8886-X2, and with respect to each reportable transaction reports the appropriate amounts required for line 10, columns (a) through (d). Alternatively, J's disclosures will be adequate if the description provided for each loss on the supporting statement includes the names and reportable transaction or tax shelter registration numbers, if any, disclosed on the applicable Form 8886, identifies the type of reportable transaction for the loss, and reports the appropriate amounts required for line 10, columns (a) through (d). J must report the losses attributable to the other five abandonment losses on line 21e, regardless of whether a difference exists for any or all of those abandonment losses.

Example 14. Partnership K is a calendar year partnership that files and entirely completes Schedule M-3 for its 2014 tax year. K enters into a transaction with contractual protection that is a reportable transaction described in Regulations section 1.6011-4(b)(4). This reportable transaction is the only reportable transaction for K's 2014 tax year and results in a $7 million capital loss for both financial accounting purposes and U.S. income tax purposes. Although the transaction does not result in a difference, K is required to report on line 10 the following amounts: ($7 million) in column (a), zero in columns (b) and (c), and ($7 million) in column (d). The transaction will be adequately disclosed if K attaches a supporting statement for line 10 that (a) sequentially numbers the Form 8886 and refers to the sequentially numbered Form 8886-X1 and (b) reports the applicable amounts required for line 10, columns (a) through (d). Alternatively, the transaction will be adequately disclosed if the supporting statement for line 10 includes a description of the transaction, the name and reportable transaction number, if any, and the type of reportable transaction disclosed on Form 8886.

Line 11. Interest Income

Attach Form 8916-A, Supplemental Attachment to Schedule M-3. Complete Part II and enter the amounts shown on line 6, columns (a) through (d), on Schedule M-3, line 11, columns (a) through (d), as applicable.

Note. For tax years ending December 31, 2014, or later, any separate entity that (a) is required to file a Schedule M-3 and has less than $50 million in total assets at the end of the tax year or (b) is not required to file a Schedule M-3 and voluntarily files a Schedule M-3, is not required to file Form 8916-A but may voluntarily do so.

Report on line 11, column (a), the total amount of interest income included on

Part I, line 11, and report on line 11, column (d), the total amount of interest income included on line 1 of the *Analysis of Net Income (Loss)* found on Form 1065 and Form 1065-B that is not required to be reported elsewhere on Schedule M-3. In columns (b) or (c), as applicable, adjust for any amounts treated for U.S. income tax purposes as interest income that are treated as some other form of income for financial accounting purposes, or vice versa. For example, adjustments to interest income resulting from adjustments made in accordance with instructions for line 16, Sale versus lease, should be made in columns (b) and (c) of line 11.

Do not report on line 11 amounts reported in accordance with instructions for lines 7, 8, 9, 10, and 20.

Line 12. Total Accrual to Cash Adjustment

This line is completed by a partnership that prepares financial statements (or books and records, if permitted) using an overall accrual method of accounting and uses an overall cash method of accounting for U.S. income tax purposes (or vice versa). With the exception of amounts required to be reported on line 10, the partnership must report on line 12 a single amount net of all adjustments attributable solely to the use of the different overall methods of accounting (for example, adjustments related to accounts receivable, accounts payable, compensation, accrued liabilities, etc.), regardless of whether a separate line on Schedule M-3 corresponds to an item within the accrual to cash reconciliation. Differences not attributable to the use of the different overall methods of accounting must be reported on the appropriate lines of Schedule M-3 (for example, a depreciation difference must be reported on Part III, line 25).

Example 15. Partnership L is a calendar year partnership that files and entirely completes Schedule M-3 for its 2014 tax year. L prepares financial statements in accordance with GAAP using an overall accrual method of accounting. L uses an overall cash method of accounting for U.S. income tax purposes. L's financial statements for the year ending December 31, 2014, report accounts receivable of $35,000, an allowance for bad debts of $10,000, and accounts payable of $17,000 related to current year acquisition and reorganization legal and accounting fees. In addition, for L's year ending December 31, 2014, L reported financial statement depreciation expense of $15,000 and depreciation for U.S. income tax purposes of $25,000. For L's 2014 tax year using an overall cash method of accounting, L does not recognize the $35,000 of revenue attributable to the accounts receivable,

cannot deduct the $10,000 allowance for bad debt, and cannot deduct the $17,000 of accounts payable. In its financial statements, L treats both the difference in overall accounting methods used for financial statement and U.S. income tax purposes and the difference in depreciation expense as temporary differences. L must combine all adjustments attributable to the differences related to the overall accounting methods on line 12. As a result, L must report on line 12 $8,000 in column (a) ($35,000 – $10,000 – $17,000), ($8,000) in column (b), and zero in column (d). L must not report the accrual to cash adjustment attributable to the legal and accounting fees on Part III, line 18, Current year acquisition/reorganization legal and accounting fees. Because the difference in depreciation expense does not relate to the use of the cash or accrual method of accounting, L must report the depreciation difference on Part III, line 25, Depreciation, and report $15,000 in column (a), $10,000 in column (b), and $25,000 in column (d).

Line 13. Hedging Transactions

Report on line 13, column (a), the net gain or loss from hedging transactions on Part I, line 11. Report in column (d) the amount of taxable income from hedging transactions as defined in section 1221(b)(2). Use columns (b) and (c) to report all differences caused by treating hedging transactions differently for financial accounting purposes and for U.S. income tax purposes. For example, if a portion of a hedge is considered ineffective under GAAP but still is a valid hedge under section 1221(b)(2), the difference must be reported on line 13. The hedge of a capital asset, which is not a valid hedge for U.S. income tax purposes but may be considered a hedge for GAAP purposes, must also be reported here.

Report hedging gains and losses computed under the mark-to-market method of accounting on line 13 and not on line 14.

Report any gain or loss from inventory hedging transactions on line 13 and not on line 15.

Line 14. Mark-to-Market Income (Loss)

Report on line 14 any amount representing the mark-to-market income or loss for any securities held by a dealer in securities, a dealer in commodities having made a valid election under section 475(e), or a trader in securities or commodities having made a valid election under section 475(f). "Securities" for these purposes are securities described in section 475(c)(2) and commodities described in section 475(e)(2). "Securities" do not include any items specifically excluded from sections 475(c)

(2) and 475(e)(2), such as certain contracts to which section 1256(a) applies.

Report hedging gains and losses computed under the mark-to-market method of accounting on line 13, Hedging transactions, and not on line 14.

Traders in securities or commodities. For a trader in securities or commodities that made a valid election under section 475(f) to use the mark-to-market method to account for securities or commodities held in connection with a trading business that files Form 4797, Sales of Business Property, any Schedule M-3 entries required as a result of marking to market these securities or commodities are reported as follows: (a) mark-to-market gains and losses from Form 4797, line 10, are included on Schedule M-3, Part II, line 14; (b) any other Schedule M-3 entries required based on other results (non-mark-to-market gains and losses) included in the total reported on Form 4797, line 17, should be reported on Schedule M-3, Part II, line 21d, unless the instructions for Schedule M-3 require the amounts to be reported on another line.

Line 15. Cost of Goods Sold

Report on line 15 any amounts deducted as part of cost of goods sold during the tax year, regardless of whether the amounts would otherwise be reported elsewhere in Part II or Part III. However, do not report the items mentioned in the next paragraph on line 15. Examples of amounts that must be included on line 15 are amounts attributable to inventory valuation, such as amounts attributable to cost-flow assumptions, additional costs required to be capitalized (including depreciation) such as section 263A costs, inventory shrinkage accruals, inventory obsolescence reserves, and lower of cost or market (LCM) write-downs.

Note. The entries in columns (a) and (d) are negative amounts.

Do not report the following on line 15 or on Form 8916-A:
- Amounts reportable on line 10;
- Any gain or loss from inventory hedging transactions reportable on line 13;
- Amounts reportable on line 16;
- Amounts reportable on line 19;
- Mark-to-market income or (loss) associated with the inventories of dealers in securities under section 475 reportable on line 14;
- Section 481(a) adjustments related to cost of goods sold or inventory valuation reportable on line 17;
- Fines and penalties reportable on Part III, line 7;
- Judgments, damages, awards, and similar costs, reportable on Part III, line 8; and

- Amounts included on Part III, line 28, Purchase versus lease.

Important. Complete and attach Form 8916-A, Part I, for each item listed on line 15 in columns (a) through (d).

Note. For tax years ending December 31, 2014, or later, any separate entity that (a) is required to file a Schedule M-3 and has less than $50 million in total assets at the end of the tax year or (b) is not required to file a Schedule M-3 and voluntarily files a Schedule M-3, is not required to file Form 8916-A but may voluntarily do so.

Example 16. Partnership C is a calendar year partnership that files and entirely completes Schedule M-3 for its 2014 tax year. C placed in service 10 depreciable fixed assets in a previous tax year. C's total depreciation expense for its 2014 tax year for five of the assets is $50,000 for financial accounting purposes and $70,000 for U.S. income tax purposes. C's total annual depreciation expense for its 2014 tax year for the other five assets is $40,000 for financial accounting purposes and $30,000 for U.S. income tax purposes. In addition, C incurs $200 of meals and entertainment expenses that C deducts in computing net income for financial accounting purposes. All $200 of the meals and entertainment expenses is subject to the 50% limitation under section 274(n). In its financial statements, C treats the $50,000 depreciation and $100 of the meals and entertainment as other costs in computing cost of goods sold. C must include on Form 8916-A and on line 15, in column (a), the $50,000 of depreciation and $100 of meals and entertainment. C must also include a temporary difference of $20,000 in column (b), a permanent difference of ($50) in column (c), and $70,050 in column (d) ($70,000 depreciation and $50 meals). In addition, C must report on Part III, line 25, for its 2014 tax year income statement, depreciation expense of $40,000 in column (a), a temporary difference of ($10,000) in column (b), and $30,000 in column (d); and on Part III, line 6, meals and entertainment expense of $100 in column (a), a permanent difference of ($50) in column (c), and $50 in column (d). All other cost of goods sold items would be added to the amounts included on line 15, detailed in this example, and reported on Form 8916-A and on line 15 in the appropriate columns.

Line 16. Sale Versus Lease (for Sellers and/or Lessors)

Note. Also see the instructions at Part III, line 28, Purchase Versus Lease (for Purchasers and/or Lessees), later.

Asset transfer transactions with periodic payments characterized for financial accounting purposes as either a sale or a

lease may, under some circumstances, be characterized as the opposite for tax purposes. If the transaction is treated as a lease, the seller/lessor reports the periodic payments as gross rental income and also reports depreciation expense or deduction. If the transaction is treated as a sale, the seller/lessor reports gross profit (sale price less cost of goods sold) from the sale of assets and reports the periodic payments as payments of principal and interest income.

On line 16, column (a), report the gross profit or gross rental income for financial accounting purposes for all sale or lease transactions that must be given the opposite characterization for tax purposes. On line 16, column (d), report the gross profit or gross rental income for federal income tax purposes. Interest income amounts for such transactions must be reported on line 11, in column (a) or (d), as applicable. Depreciation expense for such transactions must be reported on Part III, line 25, in column (a) or (d), as applicable. Use columns (b) and (c) of lines 11 and 16, and Part III, line 25, as applicable, to report the differences between columns (a) and (d).

Example 17. M is a calendar year partnership that files and entirely completes Schedule M-3 for its 2014 tax year. M sells and leases property to customers. For financial accounting purposes, M accounts for each transaction as a sale. For U.S. income tax purposes, each of M's transactions must be treated as a lease. In its financial statements, M treats the difference in the financial accounting and the U.S. income tax treatment of these transactions as temporary. During 2014, M reports in its financial statements $1,000 of sales and $700 of cost of goods sold with respect to 2014 lease transactions. M receives periodic payments of $500 in 2014 with respect to these 2014 transactions and similar transactions from prior years and treats $400 as principal and $100 as interest income. For financial accounting purposes, M reports gross profit of $300 ($1,000 – $700) and interest income of $100 from these transactions. For U.S. income tax purposes, M reports $500 of gross rental income (the periodic payments) and (based on other facts) $200 of depreciation deduction on the property. On its 2014 Schedule M-3, M must report on line 11 $100 in column (a), ($100) in column (b), and zero in column (d). In addition, M must report on line 16 $300 of gross profit in column (a), $200 in column (b), and $500 of gross rental income in column (d). Lastly, M must report on Part III, line 25, $200 in columns (b) and (d).

Line 17. Section 481(a) Adjustments

With the exception of a section 481(a) adjustment that is required to be reported on Part I, line 10, for reportable transactions, any difference between an income or expense item attributable to an authorized (or unauthorized) change in method of accounting made for U.S. income tax purposes that results in a section 481(a) adjustment must be reported on line 17, regardless of whether a separate line for that income or expense item exists in Part II or Part III.

Example 18. Partnership N is a calendar year partnership that files and entirely completes Schedule M-3 for its 2014 tax year. N was depreciating certain fixed assets over an erroneous recovery period and, effective for its 2014 tax year, N receives IRS consent to change its method of accounting for the depreciable fixed assets and begins using the proper recovery period. The change in method of accounting results in a positive section 481(a) adjustment of $100,000 that is required to be spread over four tax years, beginning with the 2014 tax year. In its financial statements, N treats the section 481(a) adjustment as a temporary difference. N must report on line 17 $25,000 in columns (b) and (d) for its 2014 tax year and each of the subsequent three tax years (unless N is otherwise required to recognize the remainder of the 481(a) adjustment earlier). N must not report the section 481(a) adjustment on Part III, line 25.

Line 18. Unearned/Deferred Revenue

Report on line 18, column (a), amounts of revenues included on Part I, line 11, that were deferred from a prior financial accounting year. Report on line 18, column (d), amounts of revenues recognizable for U.S. income tax purposes in the current tax year that are recognized for financial accounting purposes in a different year. Also report on line 18, column (d), any amount of revenues reported on line 18, column (a), that are recognizable for U.S. income tax purposes in the current tax year. Use columns (b) and (c) of line 18, as applicable, to report differences between columns (a) and (d).

Line 18 must not be used to report income recognized from long-term contracts. Instead, use line 19.

Line 19. Income Recognition From Long-Term Contracts

Report on line 19 the amount of net income or loss for financial statement purposes (or books and records, if applicable) or U.S. income tax purposes for any contract accounted for under a long-term contract method of accounting.

Line 20. Original Issue Discount and Other Imputed Interest

Report on line 20 any amounts of original issue discount (OID) and other imputed interest. The term "original issue discount and other imputed interest" includes, but is not limited to:

1. The excess of a debt instrument's stated redemption price at maturity over its issue price, as determined under section 1273;

2. Amounts that are imputed interest on a deferred sales contract under section 483;

3. Amounts treated as interest or OID under the stripped bond rules under section 1286; and

4. Amounts treated as OID under the below-market interest rate rules under section 7872.

Line 21a. Income Statement Gain/Loss on Sale, Exchange, Abandonment, Worthlessness, or Other Disposition of Assets Other Than Inventory and Pass-Through Entities

Report on line 21a, column (a), all gains and losses on the disposition of assets except for **(a)** gains and losses on the disposition of inventory, and **(b)** gains and losses allocated to the partnership from a pass-through entity (for example, on Schedule K-1) that are included in the net income (loss) of the partnership reported on Part I, line 11. Reverse the amount reported in column (a) in column (b) or (c), as applicable. The corresponding gains and losses for U.S. income tax purposes are reported on lines 21b through 21g, as applicable.

Line 21b. Gross Capital Gains From Schedule D, Excluding Amounts From Pass-Through Entities

Report on line 21b gross capital gains reported on Schedule D, Capital Gains and Losses, excluding capital gains from pass-through entities, which must be reported on lines 7, 8, or 9, as applicable.

Line 21c. Gross Capital Losses From Schedule D, Excluding Amounts From Pass-Through Entities, Abandonment Losses, and Worthless Stock Losses

Report on line 21c gross capital losses reported on Schedule D, excluding capital losses from **(a)** pass-through entities, which must be reported on lines 7, 8, or 9, as applicable; **(b)** abandonment losses, which must be reported on line 21e; and **(c)** worthless stock losses, which must be reported on line 21f.

Line 21d. Net Gain/Loss Reported on Form 4797, Line 17, Excluding Amounts From Pass-Through Entities, Abandonment Losses, and Worthless Stock Losses

Report on line 21d the net gain or loss reported on line 17 of Form 4797, excluding amounts from **(a)** pass-through entities, which must be reported on lines 7, 8, or 9, as applicable; **(b)** abandonment losses, which must be reported on line 21e; and **(c)** worthless stock losses, which must be reported on line 21f.

Note. Traders in securities or commodities that have made a valid election under section 475(f) to use the mark-to-market method to account for securities or commodities, see the instructions for Part II, line 14, above.

Line 21e. Abandonment Losses

Report on line 21e any abandonment losses, regardless of whether the loss is characterized as an ordinary loss or a capital loss.

Line 21f. Worthless Stock Losses

Report on line 21f any worthless stock loss, regardless of whether the loss is characterized as an ordinary loss or a capital loss. Attach a statement that separately states and adequately discloses each transaction that gives rise to a worthless stock loss and the amount of each loss.

Line 21g. Other Gain/Loss on Disposition of Assets Other Than Inventory

Report on line 21g any gains or losses from the sale or exchange of property other than inventory that are not reported on lines 21b through 21f.

Line 22. Other Income (Loss) Items With Differences

Separately state and adequately disclose on line 22 all items of income (loss) with differences that are not otherwise listed on lines 1 through 21. Attach a statement that describes and itemizes the type of income (loss) and the amount of each item and provides a description that states the income (loss) name for book purposes for the amount recorded in column (a) and describes the adjustment being recorded in column (b) or (c). The entire description completes the tax description for the amount included in column (d) for each item separately stated on this line.

The attached statement should have five columns. The first column has the description for the next four columns. The second column is column (a), income (loss) per income statement. The third column is column (b), temporary difference. The fourth column is column (c), permanent difference. The fifth column is column (d), income (loss) per tax return. Every item listed on the attached statement for line 22 must always have columns (a) + (b) + (c) = (d). Each item with amounts in columns (a), (b), (c), and (d) will be totaled and included as one line on line 22.

If any "comprehensive income" as defined by Statement of Financial Accounting Standards (SFAS) No. 130 is reported on this line, describe the item(s) in detail. Examples of sufficiently detailed descriptions include "Foreign currency translation adjustments - comprehensive income" and "Gains and losses on available-for-sale securities - comprehensive income."

Line 23. Total Income (Loss) Items

Combine lines 1 through 22 and enter the total on line 23.

Note. Line 15, Cost of goods sold, columns (a) and (d), are negative amounts that will affect the totals entered on line 23.

Line 24. Total Expense/ Deduction Items

Report on line 24, columns (a) through (d), as applicable, the negative of the amounts reported on Part III, line 31, columns (a) through (d). For example, if Part III, line 31, column (a), reflects an amount of $1 million, then report on line 24, column (a), ($1 million). Similarly, if Part III, line 31, column (b), reflects an amount of ($50,000), then report on line 24, column (b), $50,000.

Line 25. Other Items With No Differences

If there is no difference between the financial accounting amount and the taxable amount of an entire item of income, gain, loss, expense, or deduction and the item is not described or included on lines 1 through 22, or Part III, lines 1 through 30, report the entire amount of the item in columns (a) and (d) of line 25. If a portion of an item of income, loss, expense, or deduction has a difference and a portion of the item does not have a difference, do not report any portion of the item on line 25. Instead, report the entire amount of the item (that is, both the portion with a difference and the portion without a difference) on the applicable line of lines 1 through 22, or Part III, lines 1 through 30. See *Example 11*, above.

Part III. Reconciliation of Net Income (Loss) per Income Statement of Partnership With Income (Loss) per Return — Expense/Deduction Items

Note. Expense amounts that reduce financial income must be reported on Part III, column (a), as positive amounts. Deduction amounts that reduce taxable income must be reported on Part III, column (d), as positive amounts. Amounts reported on Part II, line 24, must be the negative of the amounts reported on Part III, line 31.

Lines 1 Through 4. Income Tax Expense

If the partnership does not distinguish between current and deferred income tax expense in its financial statements (or its books and records, if applicable), report income tax expense as current income tax expense using lines 1 and 3, as applicable.

Line 5. Equity-Based Compensation

Report on line 5 any amounts for equity-based compensation or consideration that are reflected as expense for financial accounting purposes (column (a)) or deducted in the U.S. income tax return (column (d)) other than amounts reportable elsewhere on Schedule M-3, Parts II and III. Examples of amounts reportable on line 5 include expense/deduction items attributable to options to acquire capital interest units, profits interest units, and other rights to acquire partnership equity, regardless of whether such payments are made to employees or non-employees, or as payment for property or compensation for services.

Line 6. Meals and Entertainment

Report on line 6, column (a), any amounts paid or accrued by the partnership during the tax year for meals, beverages, and entertainment that are accounted for in financial accounting income, regardless of the classification, nomenclature, or terminology used for such amounts, and regardless of how or where such amounts are classified in the partnership's financial income statement or the income and expense accounts maintained in the partnership's books and records. Report only amounts not otherwise reportable elsewhere on Schedule M-3, Parts II and III (for example, Part II, line 15).

Line 7. Fines and Penalties

Report on line 7 any fines or similar penalties paid to a government or other authority for the violation of any law for which fines or penalties are assessed. All fines and penalties expensed in financial accounting income (paid or accrued) must be included on line 7, column (a), regardless of the government or other authority that imposed the fines or penalties, regardless of whether the fines and penalties are civil or criminal, regardless of the classification, nomenclature, or terminology used for the fines or penalties by the imposing authority in its actions or documents, and regardless of how or where the fines or penalties are classified in the partnership's financial income statement or the income and expense accounts maintained in the partnership's books and records. Also report on line 7, column (a), the reversal of any overaccrual of any amount described in this paragraph. See sections 162(f) and 162(g) for additional guidance.

Report on line 7, column (d), any such amounts described in the preceding paragraph that are includible in taxable income, regardless of the financial accounting period in which such amounts were or are included in financial accounting net income. Complete columns (b) and (c), as appropriate.

Do not report on line 7 amounts required to be reported in accordance with instructions for line 8.

Do not report on line 7 amounts recovered from insurers or any other indemnitors for any fines and penalties described above.

Line 8. Judgments, Damages, Awards, and Similar Costs

Report on line 8, column (a), the amount of any estimated or actual judgments, damages, awards, settlements, and similar costs, however named or classified, included in financial accounting income, regardless of whether the amount deducted was attributable to an estimate of future anticipated payments or actual payments. Also report on line 8, column (a), the reversal of any overaccrual of any amount described in this paragraph.

Report on line 8, column (d), any such amounts described in the preceding paragraph that are includible in taxable income, regardless of the financial accounting period in which such amounts were or are included in financial accounting net income. Complete columns (b) and (c), as appropriate.

Do not report on line 8 amounts required to be reported in accordance with instructions for line 7.

Do not report on line 8 amounts recovered from insurers or any other indemnitors for any judgments, damages, awards, or similar costs described above.

Line 9. Guaranteed Payments

Include on line 9, column (a), the amount of guaranteed payments expense that is included on Part I, line 11. Report in column (d) the net amount of guaranteed payments deduction. The net amount of the deduction reported in column (d) is the amount reported as a deduction on Form 1065, page 1, line 10, or on Form 1065-B, page 1, line 13, reduced by the amount reported as income on Form 1065, Schedule K, line 4 or Form 1065-B, Schedule K, line 7. The net amount of the guaranteed payments reported in column (d) will be zero if no guaranteed payments are capitalized and all are deducted on Form 1065, page 1, line 10, or Form 1065-B, page 1, line 13, or a negative amount (reported in parentheses), if any of the guaranteed payments are capitalized by the partnership. Generally, if guaranteed payments expense is recognized for financial accounting purposes, the amount reported in column (c) as a permanent difference will be the negative of the guaranteed payment income reported on Form 1065, Schedule K, line 4 or Form 1065-B, Schedule K, line 7. If no guaranteed payment expense is recognized for financial accounting purposes, the amount reported in column (c) as a permanent difference generally will be zero. Any amount of guaranteed payments capitalized for tax purposes on Form 1065 or Form 1065-B, page 1, but not capitalized for financial accounting purposes, generally will be reported as a negative temporary difference amount in column (b).

Example 19.

1. AZ is a calendar year partnership that files and entirely completes Schedule M-3 for its 2014 tax year. AZ has total income in 2014 of $5,000 for both financial accounting and tax accounting purposes before taking into account guaranteed payments expense or deductions. Partner A is paid a deductible guaranteed payment of $3,000 for services rendered to the partnership during the tax year. Partner Z is paid a $1,000 guaranteed payment, which is capitalized to land for tax accounting. Both guaranteed payments, in the total amount of $4,000, are treated as expenses in arriving at net financial accounting income. There are no other expenses or deductions for financial accounting or tax accounting purposes. The amount shown on Part I, line 11, Net income (loss) per income statement of the partnership, is $1,000 ($5,000 – $3,000 – $1,000 = $1,000). The amount shown on line 9,

column (a), is $4,000, the amount of guaranteed payments expenses for financial accounting purposes. The amount shown on line 9, column (d), is ($1,000), the net amount deducted after taking into consideration the $4,000 of total guaranteed payments allocated to the partners as income on Schedule K, netted against $3,000 deducted on Form 1065, page 1, line 10. The amount reported on line 9, column (b), is a temporary difference of ($1,000), the negative of the amount of guaranteed payments capitalized for Form 1065, page 1. The amount reported on line 9, column (c), is a permanent difference of ($4,000), equal to the guaranteed payment income shown on Form 1065, Schedule K, line 4 or Form 1065-B, Schedule K, line 7, expressed as a negative amount. Part II, line 23, reports $5,000 in column (a), 0 in column (b), 0 in column (c), and $5,000 in column (d). Part II, line 24, reports ($4,000) in column (a), $1,000 in column (b), $4,000 in column (c), and $1,000 in column (d). Part II, line 26, reports $1,000 in column (a), $1,000 in column (b), $4,000 in column (c), and $6,000 in column (d).

2. Same facts as in Example 19.1, except that no guaranteed payments expense is recognized for financial accounting purposes. The amount shown on Part I, line 11, is $5,000. On line 9, AZ reports 0 in column (a), ($1,000) in column (b), 0 in column (c), and ($1,000) in column (d). Part II, line 23, reports 0 in column (a), $1,000 in column (b), 0 in column (c), and $1,000 in column (d). On Part II, line 25, AZ reports $5,000 in column (a), $1,000 in column (b), 0 in column (c), and $6,000 in column (d).

Line 10. Pension and Profit-Sharing

Report on line 10 any amounts attributable to the partnership's pension plans, profit-sharing plans, and any other retirement plans.

Line 11. Other Post-Retirement Benefits

Report on line 11 any amounts attributable to other post-retirement benefits not otherwise includible on line 10 (for example, retiree health and life insurance coverage, dental coverage, etc.).

Line 12. Deferred Compensation

Report on line 12, column (a), any compensation expense included in the net income (loss) amount reported on Part I, line 11, that is not deductible for U.S. income tax purposes in the current tax year and that was not reported elsewhere on Schedule M-3, column (a). Report on line 12, column (d), any compensation deductible in the current tax year that was

not included in the net income (loss) amount reported on Part I, line 11, for the current tax year and that is not reportable elsewhere on Schedule M-3, including any compensation deductions deferred in a prior tax year. For example, report originations and reversals of deferred compensation subject to section 409A on line 12.

Line 14. Charitable Contribution of Intangible Property

Report on line 14 any charitable contribution of intangible property, for example, contributions of:
- Intellectual property, patents (including any amounts of additional contributions allowable by virtue of income earned by donees subsequent to the year of donation), copyrights, trademarks;
- Securities (including stocks and their derivatives, stock options, and bonds);
- Conservation easements (including scenic easements or air rights);
- Railroad rights of way;
- Mineral rights; and
- Other intangible property.

Line 15. Organizational Expenses as per Regulations section 1.709-2(a)

Include on line 15, column (a), organizational expenses as defined in Regulations section 1.709-2(a). Include on line 15, column (d), the amount of organizational expense deducted per section 709(b).

Line 16. Syndication Expenses as per Regulations section 1.709-2(b)

Include on line 16 syndication expenses as defined in Regulations section 1.709-2(b).

Line 17. Current Year Acquisition/Reorganization Investment Banking Fees

Report on line 17 any investment banking fees paid or incurred in connection with a taxable or tax-free acquisition of property (for example, ownership interests or assets) or a tax-free reorganization not otherwise reportable on Schedule M-3 (for example, line 15 or 16). Report on this line any investment banking fees paid or incurred at any stage of the acquisition or reorganization process including, for example, fees paid or incurred to evaluate whether to investigate an acquisition, fees to conduct an actual investigation, and fees to consummate the acquisition or reorganization.

Line 18. Current Year Acquisition/Reorganization Legal and Accounting Fees

Report on line 18 any legal and accounting fees paid or incurred in connection with a taxable or tax-free acquisition of property (for example, ownership interests or assets) or a tax-free reorganization not otherwise reportable on Schedule M-3 (for example, line 15 or 16). Report on this line any legal and accounting fees paid or incurred at any stage of the acquisition or reorganization process including, for example, fees paid or incurred to evaluate whether to investigate an acquisition, fees to conduct an actual investigation, and fees to consummate the acquisition or reorganization.

Line 19. Amortization/Impairment of Goodwill

Report on line 19 amortization of goodwill or amounts attributable to the impairment of goodwill.

Line 20. Amortization of Acquisition, Reorganization, and Start-Up Costs

Report on line 20 amortization of acquisition, reorganization, and start-up costs. For purposes of columns (b), (c), and (d), include amounts amortizable under section 167 or 195.

Line 21. Other Amortization or Impairment Write-Offs

Report on line 21 any amortization or impairment write-offs not otherwise includible on Schedule M-3.

Line 22. Reserved

When using this line to figure amounts on other tax forms or worksheets, this line should be considered to be zero.

Line 23a. Depletion—Oil & Gas

Form 1065 filers report on line 23a, column (a), any oil and gas depletion included on Part I, line 11.

Note. Form 1065-B filers report oil and gas depletion on line 23b.

Line 23b. Depletion—Other than Oil & Gas

Report on line 23b any depletion expense/deduction other than oil and gas that is not required to be reported elsewhere on Schedule M-3 (for example, on Part II, lines 7, 8, 9, or 15).

Additionally, Form 1065-B filers also report oil and gas depletion on line 23b.

Line 24. Intangible Drilling and Development Costs (IDC)

Intangible Drilling and Development Costs (IDC) are costs of developing oil, gas, or geothermal wells. Report on line 24, column (a), the total amount of intangible drilling and development costs (or such equivalent costs as classified in the partnership's financial statements) included on Part I, line 11, and report on line 24, column (d), the total amount of IDC paid or incurred during the current tax year under section 263(c) and Regulations section 1.612-4.

Line 25. Depreciation

Report on line 25 any depreciation expense/deduction that is not required to be reported elsewhere on Schedule M-3 (for example, on Part II, lines 7, 8, 9, or 15).

Line 26. Bad Debt Expense

Report on line 26, column (a), any amounts attributable to an allowance for uncollectible accounts receivable or actual write-offs of accounts receivable included on Part I, line 11. Report in column (d) the amount of bad debt expense deductible for federal income tax purposes under section 166.

Line 27. Interest Expense

Attach Form 8916-A. Complete Part III and enter the amounts shown on line 5, columns (a) through (d), on Schedule M-3, line 27, columns (a) through (d), as applicable.

Note. For tax years ending December 31, 2014, or later, any separate entity that (a) is required to file a Schedule M-3 and has less than $50 million in total assets at the end of the tax year or (b) is not required to file a Schedule M-3 and voluntarily files a Schedule M-3, is not required to file Form 8916-A but may voluntarily do so.

Report on line 27, column (a), the total amount of interest expense included on Part I, line 11, and report on line 27, column (d), the total amount of interest deduction included on line 1 of the *Analysis of Net Income (Loss)* found on Form 1065 and Form 1065-B that is not reported elsewhere on Schedule M-3. In columns (b) or (c), as applicable, adjust for any amounts treated for U.S. income tax purposes as interest deduction that are treated as some other form of expense for financial accounting purposes, or vice versa. For example, adjustments to interest expense/deduction resulting from adjustments made in accordance with instructions for line 28 should be made in columns (b) and (c), as applicable, of line 27.

Do not report on Form 8916-A and on line 27 amounts reported in accordance

with instructions for (a) Part II, lines 7, 8 and 9, Income (loss) from U.S. partnerships, foreign partnerships and other pass-through entities, and (b) Part II, line 10, Items relating to reportable transactions.

Line 28. Purchase Versus Lease (for Purchasers and/or Lessees)

Note. Also see the instructions for Part II, line 16, for sellers and/or lessors.

Asset transfer transactions with periodic payments characterized for financial accounting purposes as either a purchase or a lease may, under some circumstances, be characterized as the opposite for tax purposes.

If a transaction is treated as a lease, the purchaser/lessee reports the periodic payments as gross rental expense. If the transaction is treated as a purchase, the purchaser/lessee reports the periodic payments as payments of principal and interest and also reports depreciation expense or deduction with respect to the purchased asset.

Report in column (a) gross rent expense for a transaction treated as a lease for financial accounting purposes but as a sale for U.S. income tax purposes. Report in column (d) gross rental deductions for a transaction treated as a lease for U.S. income tax purposes but as a purchase for financial accounting purposes. Report interest expense or deduction amounts for such transactions on line 27, in column (a) or (d), as applicable. Report depreciation expense or deductions for such transactions on line 25, in column (a) or (d), as applicable. Use columns (b) and (c) of lines 25, 27, and 28, as applicable, to report the differences between columns (a) and (d) for such recharacterized transactions.

Example 20. X is a calendar year U.S. partnership that files and entirely completes Schedule M-3 for its 2014 tax year. X acquired property in a transaction that, for financial accounting purposes, X treats as a lease. Because of its terms, the transaction is treated for U.S. income tax purposes as a purchase, and X must treat the periodic payments it makes partially as a payment of principal and partially as a payment of interest. In its financial statements, X treats the difference between the financial accounting and U.S. income tax treatment of this transaction as a temporary difference. During 2014, X reports in its financial statements $1,000 of gross rental expense that, for U.S. income tax purposes, is recharacterized as a $700 payment of principal and a $300 payment of interest, accompanied by a depreciation deduction of $1,200 (based on other facts). On its 2014 Schedule M-3, X must report the following on line 28:

column (a), $1,000, its financial accounting gross rental expense; column (b), ($1,000); and column (d), zero. On line 27, X reports zero in column (a) and $300 in columns (b) and (d) for the interest deduction. On line 25, X reports zero in column (a) and $1,200 in columns (b) and (d) for the depreciation deduction.

Line 29. Research and Development Costs

Report in column (a) the amount of expenses included in net income reported on Part I, line 11, that are related to research and development expense. Report in column (d) the amount of deductions included on page 1 of the return and/or separately reported on Schedule K of the return, that are recognized and reported as section 174 research and experimental expenditures consistent with the partnership's adopted method of accounting for such expenditures. In column (c), as applicable, include any adjustments for any amounts treated for U.S. income tax purposes as research or experimental expenditures that are treated as some other form of expense for financial accounting purposes, or vice versa. Report any difference in timing recognition in column (b). For example, if the partnership's financial accounting method does not specify otherwise, column (b) adjustments include adjustments for timing differences between financial and tax accounting for deferral and amortization of research expenditures, section 59(e) election, reduction of section 174 expenditures under section 280C or section 482, costs attributable to obtaining a patent, research in social sciences, and cost elements for property of a character subject to depreciation.

Section 174 provides two methods for treating research and experimental expenditures paid or incurred by a taxpayer in connection with the taxpayer's trade or business. These expenditures may be treated as expenses not chargeable to capital account and deducted in the year in which they are paid or incurred, or they may be deferred and amortized. The method for treatment of research and experimental expenditures is adopted at the partnership level.

Example 21.

1. Partnership X is a calendar year taxpayer that files and entirely completes Schedule M-3 for its 2014 tax year. During 2014, X incurred $100,000 of research and development costs that X recognized as an expense in its financial statements. Also, X incurred $20,000 in attorney fees in obtaining a patent application that X capitalized and amortized in its financial statements. X recognized $2,000 of amortization deduction. In compliance with its adopted method of accounting under section 174, X deducts research and experimental expenditures for U.S. income tax purposes. Accordingly, X must report $100,000 in column (a), $20,000 in column (b), and $120,000 in column (d). X must also report $2,000 in column (a), ($2,000) in column (b), and $0 in column (d) on Part III, line 21.

2. Assume the same facts as example 21.1 except X elected to capitalize and amortize its research and expenditures over 60 months with respect to all its research programs for U.S. tax purposes. X first realized benefits from such expenditures on August 1. Accordingly, X must report $100,000 in column (a), a temporary difference of ($90,000) [i.e., $100,000 – $10,000] in column (b), and $10,000 [i.e., $120,000/60 months, times 5 months] in column (d).

3. Partnership X is a calendar year taxpayer that files and entirely completes Schedule M-3 for its 2014 tax year. X adopted the current expense method for research and experimental expenditures for U.S. income tax purposes. During 2014, X incurred $50,000 of research and development costs that X recognized as an expense in its financial statements. Also, X undertook to develop a new machine for its business. X expended $30,000 on the project of which $10,000 represents actual costs of material, labor and component cost to construct the machine, and $20,000 represents research costs not attributable to the machine itself. X capitalized all costs of $30,000 related to the machine and recognized $6,000 of depreciation expense in its financial statements. X's depreciation expense on the $10,000 of costs related to the machine itself was $2,000 for U.S. income tax purposes. Accordingly, X must report $50,000 in column (a), $20,000 (research costs which are not attributable to the machine itself) in column (b), and $70,000 in column (d). X must also report $6,000 in column (a), ($4,000) in column (b) and $2,000 in column (c) on Part III, line 25.

4. Partnership X is a calendar year taxpayer that files and entirely completes Schedule M-3 for its 2014 tax year. During 2014, X incurred $10,000 of research and development costs related to social sciences that it recognized as an expense in its financial statements. X adopted the current expense method for research and experimental expenditures for U.S. income tax purposes. Because such costs are not allowable costs under section 174, X must report $10,000 in column (a), permanent difference ($10,000) in column (c) and $0 in column (d). If such costs are otherwise deductible for U.S. income tax purposes, X must report this item of expense on Part III, line 30.

5. Partnership X is a calendar year taxpayer that files and entirely completes Schedule M-3 for its 2014 tax year. During 2014, X paid $75,000 to acquire or in-license intangible assets under a collaborative arrangement with another company that X recognized as a research and development expense in its financial statements. X adopted the current expense method for research and experimental expenditures for U.S. income tax purposes. Because payments made to acquire rights to a product or technology are excluded costs from the definition of research and experimental expenditures, X must report $75,000 in column (a), ($75,000) in column (c) and $0 in column (d). X must report any amortization otherwise allowable related to the payments on Part III, line 21.

Line 30. Other Expense/ Deduction Items With Differences

Separately state and adequately disclose on line 30 all items of expense/deduction that are not otherwise listed on lines 1 through 29.

Attach a statement that describes and itemizes the type of expense/deduction and the amount of each item, and provides a description that states the expense/deduction name for book purposes for the amount recorded in column (a) and describes the adjustment being recorded in column (b) or (c). The entire description completes the tax description for the amount included in column (d) for each item separately stated on this line.

The statement of details attached to the return for line 30 must separately state and adequately disclose the nature and amount of the expense related to each reserve and/or contingent liability. The appropriate level of disclosure depends upon each taxpayer's operational activity and the nature of its accounting records. For example, if a partnership's net income amount reported in the income statement includes anticipated expenses for a discontinued operation as a single amount, and its general ledger or other books, records, and workpapers provide details for the anticipated expenses under more explanatory and defined categories such as employee termination costs, lease cancellation costs, loss on sale of equipment, etc., a supporting statement that lists those categories of expenses and their details will satisfy the requirement to separately state and adequately disclose. In order to separately state and adequately disclose the employee termination costs, it is not required that an anticipated termination cost amount be listed for each employee, or that each asset (or category of asset) be listed along with the anticipated loss on disposition.

The attached statement should have five columns. The first column has the description for the next four columns; the second column is column (a), *expense per income statement*; the third column is column (b), *temporary difference*; the fourth column is column (c), *permanent difference*; and the fifth column is column (d), *deduction per tax return*. Every item listed on the attached statement for line 30 must always have columns (a) + (b) + (c) = (d). Each item with amounts in columns (a), (b), (c), and (d) will be totaled and included as one line on line 30 of the face of the schedule.

Comprehensive income. If any "comprehensive income" as defined by SFAS No. 130 is reported on this line, describe the item(s) in detail as, for example, "Foreign currency translation adjustments – comprehensive income" and "Gains and losses on available-for-sale securities – comprehensive income."

Reserves and contingent liabilities. Report on line 30 amounts related to the change in each reserve or contingent liability that is not required to be reported elsewhere on Schedule M-3. Report on line 30, column (a), expenses included in net income reported on Part I, line 11, that are related to reserves and contingent liabilities. Report on line 30, column (d), amounts related to liabilities for reserves and contingent liabilities that are deductible in the current tax year for U.S. income tax purposes. Examples of items that must be reported on line 30 include warranty reserves, restructuring reserves, reserves for discontinued operations, and reserves for acquisitions and dispositions. Only report on line 30 items that are not required to be reported elsewhere on Schedule M-3, Parts II and III. For example, the expense for a reserve for inventory obsolescence must be reported on Part II, line 15.

Example 22. Partnership Q is a calendar year partnership that files and entirely completes Schedule M-3 for its 2014 tax year. On July 1 of each year, Q has a fixed liability for its annual insurance premiums that provides a 12-month coverage period beginning July 1 through June 30. In addition, Q historically prepays 12 months of advertising expense on July 1. On July 1, 2014, Q prepays its insurance premium of $500,000 and advertising expenses of $800,000. For financial accounting purposes, Q capitalizes and amortizes the prepaid insurance and advertising over 12 months. For U.S. income tax purposes, Q deducts the insurance premium when paid and amortizes the advertising over the 12-month period. In its financial statements, Q treats the differences attributable to the financial statement treatment and U.S. income tax treatment of the prepaid insurance and advertising as temporary differences.

Q also has a Legal reserve where $300,000 was expensed for financial accounting purposes and a ($100,000) temporary difference was calculated to arrive at the income tax deduction of $200,000. The statement attached to Q's return for Part III, line 30, must be separately stated and adequately disclosed as follows:

Description	Column (a) Expense per Income Statement	Column (b) Temporary Difference	Column (c) Permanent Difference	Column (d) Deduction per Tax Return
Prepaid Insurance premium expenses not capitalized	$250,000	$250,000	-0-	$500,000
Legal Expense Reserve	300,000	(100,000)	-0-	200,000
Total Line 30	$550,000	$150,000	-0-	$700,000

Line 31. Total Expense/ Deduction Items

Enter on Part II, line 24, columns (a) through (d), as applicable, positive amounts from line 31 as negative (in parentheses) and negative amounts as positive. For example, if line 31, column (a), reflects an amount of $1 million, then report on Part II, line 24, column (a), ($1 million). Similarly, if line 31, column (b), reflects an amount of ($50,000), then report on Part II, line 24, column (b), $50,000.

Form **1116**

Department of the Treasury
Internal Revenue Service (99)

Foreign Tax Credit

(Individual, Estate, or Trust)

▶ Attach to Form 1040, 1040NR, 1041, or 990-T.
▶ Information about Form 1116 and its separate instructions is at *www.irs.gov/form1116*.

OMB No. 1545-0121

2014

Attachment
Sequence No. **19**

Name | Identifying number as shown on page 1 of your tax return

Use a separate Form 1116 for each category of income listed below. See **Categories of Income** in the instructions. Check only one box on each Form 1116. Report all amounts in U.S. dollars except where specified in Part II below.

a ☐ Passive category income
b ☐ General category income
c ☐ Section 901(j) income
d ☐ Certain income re-sourced by treaty
e ☐ Lump-sum distributions

f Resident of (name of country) ▶

Note: *If you paid taxes to only one foreign country or U.S. possession, use column A in Part I and line A in Part II. If you paid taxes to **more than one** foreign country or U.S. possession, use a separate column and line for each country or possession.*

Part I — Taxable Income or Loss From Sources Outside the United States (for Category Checked Above)

		Foreign Country or U.S. Possession			Total (Add cols. A, B, and C.)
		A	B	C	
g	Enter the name of the foreign country or U.S. possession ▶				
1a	Gross income from sources within country shown above and of the type checked above (see instructions):				
	----------------- -----------------				**1a**
b	Check if line 1a is compensation for personal services as an employee, your total compensation from all sources is $250,000 or more, and you used an alternative basis to determine its source (see instructions) . . ▶ ☐				
Deductions and losses (*Caution: See instructions*):					
2	Expenses **definitely related** to the income on line 1a (attach statement)				
3	Pro rata share of other deductions **not definitely related:**				
a	Certain itemized deductions or standard deduction (see instructions)				
b	Other deductions (attach statement)				
c	Add lines 3a and 3b				
d	Gross foreign source income (see instructions) .				
e	Gross income from all sources (see instructions) .				
f	Divide line 3d by line 3e (see instructions) . . .				
g	Multiply line 3c by line 3f				
4	Pro rata share of interest expense (see instructions):				
a	Home mortgage interest (use the Worksheet for Home Mortgage Interest in the instructions) . .				
b	Other interest expense				
5	Losses from foreign sources				
6	Add lines 2, 3g, 4a, 4b, and 5				**6**
7	Subtract line 6 from line 1a. Enter the result here and on line 15, page 2 . . . . ▶				**7**

Part II — Foreign Taxes Paid or Accrued (see instructions)

Country	Credit is claimed for taxes (you must check one)		Foreign taxes paid or accrued								
	(h) ☐ Paid		In foreign currency				In U.S. dollars				
	(i) ☐ Accrued		Taxes withheld at source on:			(n) Other foreign taxes paid or accrued	Taxes withheld at source on:			(r) Other foreign taxes paid or accrued	(s) Total foreign taxes paid or accrued (add cols. (o) through (r))
	(j) Date paid or accrued	(k) Dividends	(l) Rents and royalties	(m) Interest			(o) Dividends	(p) Rents and royalties	(q) Interest		
A											
B											
C											

8 Add lines A through C, column (s). Enter the total here and on line 9, page 2 . . . . ▶ | **8**

For Paperwork Reduction Act Notice, see instructions.

Cat. No. 11440U

Form **1116** (2014)

Part III Figuring the Credit

9 Enter the amount from line 8. These are your total foreign taxes paid or accrued for the category of income checked above Part I . . | **9** |

10 Carryback or carryover (attach detailed computation) . . . . | **10** |

11 Add lines 9 and 10 . . . . | **11** |

12 Reduction in foreign taxes (see instructions) . . . . . . | **12** | (|) |

13 Taxes reclassified under high tax kickout (see instructions) . . | **13** |

14 Combine lines 11, 12, and 13. This is the total amount of foreign taxes available for credit . . . | **14** |

15 Enter the amount from line 7. This is your taxable income or (loss) from sources outside the United States (before adjustments) for the category of income checked above Part I (see instructions) . . . . . | **15** |

16 Adjustments to line 15 (see instructions) . . . . | **16** |

17 Combine the amounts on lines 15 and 16. This is your net foreign source taxable income. (If the result is zero or less, you have no foreign tax credit for the category of income you checked above Part I. Skip lines 18 through 22. However, if you are filing more than one Form 1116, you must complete line 20.) . . . . . . | **17** |

18 **Individuals:** Enter the amount from Form 1040, line 41, or Form 1040NR, line 39. **Estates and trusts:** Enter your taxable income without the deduction for your exemption . . . . | **18** |

Caution: *If you figured your tax using the lower rates on qualified dividends or capital gains, see instructions.*

19 Divide line 17 by line 18. If line 17 is more than line 18, enter "1" . . . . | **19** |

20 **Individuals:** Enter the amounts from Form 1040, lines 44 and 46. If you are a nonresident alien, enter the amounts from Form 1040NR, lines 42 and 44. **Estates and trusts:** Enter the amount from Form 1041, Schedule G, line 1a, or the total of Form 990-T, lines 36 and 37 . . . . | **20** |

Caution: *If you are completing line 20 for separate category e (lump-sum distributions), see instructions.*

21 Multiply line 20 by line 19 (maximum amount of credit) . . . . | **21** |

22 Enter the **smaller** of line 14 or line 21. If this is the only Form 1116 you are filing, skip lines 23 through 27 and enter this amount on line 28. Otherwise, complete the appropriate line in Part IV (see instructions) . . . . ▶ | **22** |

Part IV Summary of Credits From Separate Parts III (see instructions)

23 Credit for taxes on passive category income . . . . . . | **23** |

24 Credit for taxes on general category income . . . . . . | **24** |

25 Credit for taxes on certain income re-sourced by treaty . . . . | **25** |

26 Credit for taxes on lump-sum distributions . . . . | **26** |

27 Add lines 23 through 26 . . . . | **27** |

28 Enter the **smaller** of line 20 or line 27 . . . . | **28** |

29 Reduction of credit for international boycott operations. See instructions for line 12 . . . . . | **29** |

30 Subtract line 29 from line 28. This is your **foreign tax credit.** Enter here and on Form 1040, line 48; Form 1040NR, line 46; Form 1041, Schedule G, line 2a; or Form 990-T, line 40a . . . . . . ▶ | **30** |

Form 1120

Department of the Treasury
Internal Revenue Service

U.S. Corporation Income Tax Return

For calendar year 2014 or tax year beginning _____ , 2014, ending _____ , 20 ____

▶ Information about Form 1120 and its separate instructions is at *www.irs.gov/form1120*.

OMB No. 1545-0123

2014

A Check if:
1a Consolidated return (attach Form 851) ☐
b Life/nonlife consolidated return . ☐
2 Personal holding co. (attach Sch. PH) . ☐
3 Personal service corp. (see instructions) . ☐
4 Schedule M-3 attached ☐

TYPE OR PRINT

Name

Number, street, and room or suite no. If a P.O. box, see instructions.

City or town, state, or province, country and ZIP or foreign postal code

B Employer identification number

C Date incorporated

D Total assets (see instructions)
$

E Check if: **(1)** ☐ Initial return **(2)** ☐ Final return **(3)** ☐ Name change **(4)** ☐ Address change

Income

1a	Gross receipts or sales	1a
b	Returns and allowances	1b
c	Balance. Subtract line 1b from line 1a	1c
2	Cost of goods sold (attach Form 1125-A)	2
3	Gross profit. Subtract line 2 from line 1c	3
4	Dividends (Schedule C, line 19)	4
5	Interest	5
6	Gross rents	6
7	Gross royalties	7
8	Capital gain net income (attach Schedule D (Form 1120))	8
9	Net gain or (loss) from Form 4797, Part II, line 17 (attach Form 4797)	9
10	Other income (see instructions—attach statement)	10
11	**Total income.** Add lines 3 through 10 ▶	11

Deductions (See instructions for limitations on deductions.)

12	Compensation of officers (see instructions—attach Form 1125-E) ▶	12
13	Salaries and wages (less employment credits)	13
14	Repairs and maintenance	14
15	Bad debts	15
16	Rents	16
17	Taxes and licenses	17
18	Interest	18
19	Charitable contributions	19
20	Depreciation from Form 4562 not claimed on Form 1125-A or elsewhere on return (attach Form 4562)	20
21	Depletion	21
22	Advertising	22
23	Pension, profit-sharing, etc., plans	23
24	Employee benefit programs	24
25	Domestic production activities deduction (attach Form 8903)	25
26	Other deductions (attach statement)	26
27	**Total deductions.** Add lines 12 through 26 ▶	27
28	Taxable income before net operating loss deduction and special deductions. Subtract line 27 from line 11.	28
29a	Net operating loss deduction (see instructions)	29a
b	Special deductions (Schedule C, line 20)	29b
c	Add lines 29a and 29b	29c

Tax, Refundable Credits, and Payments

30	**Taxable income.** Subtract line 29c from line 28 (see instructions)	30
31	Total tax (Schedule J, Part I, line 11)	31
32	Total payments and refundable credits (Schedule J, Part II, line 21)	32
33	Estimated tax penalty (see instructions). Check if Form 2220 is attached ▶ ☐	33
34	**Amount owed.** If line 32 is smaller than the total of lines 31 and 33, enter amount owed	34
35	**Overpayment.** If line 32 is larger than the total of lines 31 and 33, enter amount overpaid	35
36	Enter amount from line 35 you want: **Credited to 2015 estimated tax** ▶ ____ Refunded ▶	36

Sign Here

Under penalties of perjury, I declare that I have examined this return, including accompanying schedules and statements, and to the best of my knowledge and belief, it is true, correct, and complete. Declaration of preparer (other than taxpayer) is based on all information of which preparer has any knowledge.

▶ _____ _____ ▶ _____
Signature of officer   Date   Title

May the IRS discuss this return with the preparer shown below (see instructions)? ☐ Yes ☐ No

Paid Preparer Use Only

Print/Type preparer's name	Preparer's signature	Date	Check ☐ if self-employed	PTIN

Firm's name ▶

Firm's address ▶

Firm's EIN ▶

Phone no.

For Paperwork Reduction Act Notice, see separate instructions.

Cat. No. 11450Q

Form **1120** (2014)

Schedule C	Dividends and Special Deductions (see instructions)	(a) Dividends received	(b) %	(c) Special deductions (a) × (b)
1	Dividends from less-than-20%-owned domestic corporations (other than debt-financed stock)		70	
2	Dividends from 20%-or-more-owned domestic corporations (other than debt-financed stock)		80	
3	Dividends on debt-financed stock of domestic and foreign corporations		see instructions	
4	Dividends on certain preferred stock of less-than-20%-owned public utilities . . .		42	
5	Dividends on certain preferred stock of 20%-or-more-owned public utilities		48	
6	Dividends from less-than-20%-owned foreign corporations and certain FSCs . . .		70	
7	Dividends from 20%-or-more-owned foreign corporations and certain FSCs . . .		80	
8	Dividends from wholly owned foreign subsidiaries		100	
9	**Total.** Add lines 1 through 8. See instructions for limitation			
10	Dividends from domestic corporations received by a small business investment company operating under the Small Business Investment Act of 1958		100	
11	Dividends from affiliated group members		100	
12	Dividends from certain FSCs		100	
13	Dividends from foreign corporations not included on lines 3, 6, 7, 8, 11, or 12 . . .			
14	Income from controlled foreign corporations under subpart F (attach Form(s) 5471) .			
15	Foreign dividend gross-up			
16	IC-DISC and former DISC dividends not included on lines 1, 2, or 3			
17	Other dividends			
18	Deduction for dividends paid on certain preferred stock of public utilities			
19	**Total dividends.** Add lines 1 through 17. Enter here and on page 1, line 4 . . . ▶			
20	**Total special deductions.** Add lines 9, 10, 11, 12, and 18. Enter here and on page 1, line 29b . . . . ▶			

Schedule J	Tax Computation and Payment (see instructions)				

Part I–Tax Computation

1	Check if the corporation is a member of a controlled group (attach Schedule O (Form 1120)) ▶ ☐				
2	Income tax. Check if a qualified personal service corporation (see instructions) ▶ ☐		2		
3	Alternative minimum tax (attach Form 4626)		3		
4	Add lines 2 and 3		4		
5a	Foreign tax credit (attach Form 1118)	5a			
b	Credit from Form 8834 (see instructions)	5b			
c	General business credit (attach Form 3800)	5c			
d	Credit for prior year minimum tax (attach Form 8827)	5d			
e	Bond credits from Form 8912	5e			
6	**Total credits.** Add lines 5a through 5e		6		
7	Subtract line 6 from line 4		7		
8	Personal holding company tax (attach Schedule PH (Form 1120))		8		
9a	Recapture of investment credit (attach Form 4255)	9a			
b	Recapture of low-income housing credit (attach Form 8611)	9b			
c	Interest due under the look-back method—completed long-term contracts (attach Form 8697)	9c			
d	Interest due under the look-back method—income forecast method (attach Form 8866)	9d			
e	Alternative tax on qualifying shipping activities (attach Form 8902)	9e			
f	Other (see instructions—attach statement)	9f			
10	**Total.** Add lines 9a through 9f		10		
11	**Total tax.** Add lines 7, 8, and 10. Enter here and on page 1, line 31		11		

Part II–Payments and Refundable Credits

12	2013 overpayment credited to 2014		12		
13	2014 estimated tax payments		13		
14	2014 refund applied for on Form 4466		14	(	)
15	Combine lines 12, 13, and 14		15		
16	Tax deposited with Form 7004		16		
17	Withholding (see instructions)		17		
18	**Total payments.** Add lines 15, 16, and 17		18		
19	Refundable credits from:				
a	Form 2439	19a			
b	Form 4136	19b			
c	Form 8827, line 8c	19c			
d	Other (attach statement—see instructions)	19d			
20	**Total credits.** Add lines 19a through 19d		20		
21	**Total payments and credits.** Add lines 18 and 20. Enter here and on page 1, line 32		21		

Schedule K	Other Information (see instructions)			

		Yes	No
1	Check accounting method: **a** ☐ Cash　**b** ☐ Accrual　**c** ☐ Other (specify) ▶ _____		
2	See the instructions and enter the:		
a	Business activity code no. ▶ _____		
b	Business activity ▶ _____		
c	Product or service ▶ _____		
3	Is the corporation a subsidiary in an affiliated group or a parent-subsidiary controlled group?		
	If "Yes," enter name and EIN of the parent corporation ▶ _____		
4	At the end of the tax year:		
a	Did any foreign or domestic corporation, partnership (including any entity treated as a partnership), trust, or tax-exempt organization own directly 20% or more, or own, directly or indirectly, 50% or more of the total voting power of all classes of the corporation's stock entitled to vote? If "Yes," complete Part I of Schedule G (Form 1120) (attach Schedule G) .		
b	Did any individual or estate own directly 20% or more, or own, directly or indirectly, 50% or more of the total voting power of all classes of the corporation's stock entitled to vote? If "Yes," complete Part II of Schedule G (Form 1120) (attach Schedule G) .		

Form **1120** (2014)

Schedule K	**Other Information** *continued* (see instructions)			Yes	No

5 At the end of the tax year, did the corporation:

a Own directly 20% or more, or own, directly or indirectly, 50% or more of the total voting power of all classes of stock entitled to vote of any foreign or domestic corporation not included on **Form 851,** Affiliations Schedule? For rules of constructive ownership, see instructions. If "Yes," complete (i) through (iv) below.

(i) Name of Corporation	**(ii)** Employer Identification Number (if any)	**(iii)** Country of Incorporation	**(iv)** Percentage Owned in Voting Stock

b Own directly an interest of 20% or more, or own, directly or indirectly, an interest of 50% or more in any foreign or domestic partnership (including an entity treated as a partnership) or in the beneficial interest of a trust? For rules of constructive ownership, see instructions. If "Yes," complete (i) through (iv) below.

(i) Name of Entity	**(ii)** Employer Identification Number (if any)	**(iii)** Country of Organization	**(iv)** Maximum Percentage Owned in Profit, Loss, or Capital

6 During this tax year, did the corporation pay dividends (other than stock dividends and distributions in exchange for stock) in excess of the corporation's current and accumulated earnings and profits? (See sections 301 and 316.) . . . .

If "Yes," file **Form 5452,** Corporate Report of Nondividend Distributions.

If this is a consolidated return, answer here for the parent corporation and on Form 851 for each subsidiary.

7 At any time during the tax year, did one foreign person own, directly or indirectly, at least 25% of **(a)** the total voting power of all classes of the corporation's stock entitled to vote or **(b)** the total value of all classes of the corporation's stock? . . . .

For rules of attribution, see section 318. If "Yes," enter:

(i) Percentage owned ▶ _____ and **(ii)** Owner's country ▶ _____

(c) The corporation may have to file **Form 5472,** Information Return of a 25% Foreign-Owned U.S. Corporation or a Foreign Corporation Engaged in a U.S. Trade or Business. Enter the number of Forms 5472 attached ▶ _____

8 Check this box if the corporation issued publicly offered debt instruments with original issue discount . . . . . . ▶ ☐

If checked, the corporation may have to file **Form 8281,** Information Return for Publicly Offered Original Issue Discount Instruments.

9 Enter the amount of tax-exempt interest received or accrued during the tax year ▶ $ _____

10 Enter the number of shareholders at the end of the tax year (if 100 or fewer) ▶ _____

11 If the corporation has an NOL for the tax year and is electing to forego the carryback period, check here . . . . . ▶ ☐

If the corporation is filing a consolidated return, the statement required by Regulations section 1.1502-21(b)(3) must be attached or the election will not be valid.

12 Enter the available NOL carryover from prior tax years (do not reduce it by any deduction on line 29a.) ▶ $ _____

13 Are the corporation's total receipts (page 1, line 1a, plus lines 4 through 10) for the tax year **and** its total assets at the end of the tax year less than $250,000? . . . .

If "Yes," the corporation is not required to complete Schedules L, M-1, and M-2. Instead, enter the total amount of cash distributions and the book value of property distributions (other than cash) made during the tax year ▶ $ _____

14 Is the corporation required to file Schedule UTP (Form 1120), Uncertain Tax Position Statement (see instructions)? . . . .

If "Yes," complete and attach Schedule UTP.

15a Did the corporation make any payments in 2014 that would require it to file Form(s) 1099? . . . .

b If "Yes," did or will the corporation file required Forms 1099? . . . .

16 During this tax year, did the corporation have an 80% or more change in ownership, including a change due to redemption of its own stock?

17 During or subsequent to this tax year, but before the filing of this return, did the corporation dispose of more than 65% (by value) of its assets in a taxable, non-taxable, or tax deferred transaction? . . . .

18 Did the corporation receive assets in a section 351 transfer in which any of the transferred assets had a fair market basis or fair market value of more than $1 million? . . . .

Schedule L	Balance Sheets per Books	Beginning of tax year		End of tax year	
	Assets	(a)	(b)	(c)	(d)
1	Cash				
2a	Trade notes and accounts receivable				
b	Less allowance for bad debts	( )		( )	
3	Inventories				
4	U.S. government obligations				
5	Tax-exempt securities (see instructions)				
6	Other current assets (attach statement)				
7	Loans to shareholders				
8	Mortgage and real estate loans				
9	Other investments (attach statement)				
10a	Buildings and other depreciable assets				
b	Less accumulated depreciation	( )		( )	
11a	Depletable assets				
b	Less accumulated depletion	( )		( )	
12	Land (net of any amortization)				
13a	Intangible assets (amortizable only)				
b	Less accumulated amortization	( )		( )	
14	Other assets (attach statement)				
15	Total assets				
	Liabilities and Shareholders' Equity				
16	Accounts payable				
17	Mortgages, notes, bonds payable in less than 1 year				
18	Other current liabilities (attach statement)				
19	Loans from shareholders				
20	Mortgages, notes, bonds payable in 1 year or more				
21	Other liabilities (attach statement)				
22	Capital stock: a Preferred stock				
	b Common stock				
23	Additional paid-in capital				
24	Retained earnings—Appropriated (attach statement)				
25	Retained earnings—Unappropriated				
26	Adjustments to shareholders' equity (attach statement)				
27	Less cost of treasury stock		( )		( )
28	Total liabilities and shareholders' equity				

Schedule M-1	**Reconciliation of Income (Loss) per Books With Income per Return**

Note: The corporation may be required to file Schedule M-3 (see instructions).

1	Net income (loss) per books		7	Income recorded on books this year not included on this return (itemize):	
2	Federal income tax per books				
3	Excess of capital losses over capital gains			Tax-exempt interest $ _____	
4	Income subject to tax not recorded on books this year (itemize): _____				
	_____		8	Deductions on this return not charged against book income this year (itemize):	
5	Expenses recorded on books this year not deducted on this return (itemize):		a	Depreciation . . $ _____	
a	Depreciation . . . . $ _____		b	Charitable contributions $ _____	
b	Charitable contributions . $ _____				
c	Travel and entertainment . $ _____				
	_____		9	Add lines 7 and 8	
6	Add lines 1 through 5		10	Income (page 1, line 28)—line 6 less line 9	

Schedule M-2	**Analysis of Unappropriated Retained Earnings per Books (Line 25, Schedule L)**

1	Balance at beginning of year		5	Distributions: a Cash	
2	Net income (loss) per books			b Stock	
3	Other increases (itemize): _____			c Property	
	_____		6	Other decreases (itemize): _____	
	_____		7	Add lines 5 and 6	
4	Add lines 1, 2, and 3		8	Balance at end of year (line 4 less line 7)	

2014

Instructions for Form 1120

U.S. Corporation Income Tax Return

Department of the Treasury
Internal Revenue Service

Section references are to the Internal Revenue Code unless otherwise noted.

Future Developments

For the latest information about developments related to Form 1120 and its instructions, such as legislation enacted after they were published, go to *www.irs.gov/form1120*.

What's New

Information reporting requirements for health insurance offers and coverage. Under the Affordable Care Act, employers that offer (or fail to offer) and others that provide minimum essential coverage to individuals are required under sections 6055 and 6056 to provide certain information to the IRS and to the individuals. The information is required for calendar years beginning after December 31, 2014, but may voluntarily be filed with the IRS and provided to individuals for 2014. For more information, see the final regulations under sections 6055 and 6056. Also, for information related to the Affordable Care Act, visit *www.irs.gov/ ACA*.

Deduction and capitalization of expenditures related to tangible property. Final regulations under sections 162(a) and 263(a) provide guidance for taxpayers that acquire, produce or improve tangible property. The final regulations clarify and expand the standards of previous regulations under sections 162(a) and 263(a). The regulations generally apply to tax years beginning after 2013. However, certain provisions may retroactively be applied to tax years beginning after 2011. See TD 9636, 2013-43 I. R. B. 331, at *www.irs.gov/irb/2013-43*.

Schedule M-3. For tax years ending December 31, 2014, and later, Form 1120 filers that (a) are required to file Schedule M-3 (Form 1120) and have less than $50 million total assets at the end of the tax year or (b) are not required to file Schedule M-3 (Form 1120) and voluntarily file Schedule M-3 (Form 1120), must either complete Schedule M-3 (Form 1120) entirely or complete Form 1120, Schedule M-1, instead of completing Parts II and III of Schedule M-3 (Form 1120). These filers are not required to file Schedule B (Form 1120) nor Form 8916-A, Supplemental Attachment to Schedule M-3. If these filers choose to complete Form 1120, Schedule M-1, instead of completing Parts II and III of Schedule M-3 (Form 1120), line 1 of Form 1120, Schedule M-1, must equal line 11 of Part I of Schedule M-3 (Form 1120). See Schedule M-3 (Form 1120) and Schedule M-1. Reconciliation of Income (Loss) per Books With Income per Return, later in the instructions.

Online payment agreement. The corporation may be able to apply for an installment agreement online if it has a balance due when the corporation's return is filed. See the instructions for line 34.

Photographs of Missing Children

The Internal Revenue Service is a proud partner with the National Center for Missing and Exploited Children. Photographs of missing children selected by the Center may appear in instructions on pages that would otherwise be blank. You can help bring these children home by looking at the photographs and calling 1-800-THE-LOST (1-800-843-5678) if you recognize a child.

Unresolved Tax Issues

The Taxpayer Advocate Service (TAS) is your voice at the IRS. Its job is to ensure that every taxpayer is treated fairly and that you know and understand your rights. TAS offers free help to guide you through the often-confusing process of resolving tax problems that you haven't been able to solve on your own. Remember, the worst thing you can do is nothing at all.

As a taxpayer, the corporation has rights that the IRS must abide by in its dealings with the corporation. The TAS tax toolkit at *www.taxpayeradvocate.irs.gov/* can help the corporation understand these rights.

TAS can help the corporation if:
- A problem is causing financial difficulty for the business.
- The business is facing an immediate threat of adverse action.
- The corporation has tried repeatedly to contact the IRS but no one has responded, or the IRS hasn't responded by the date promised.

TAS have offices in every state, the District of Columbia, and Puerto Rico. Local advocates' numbers are in their local directories and at *www.irs.gov/ Advocate/Local-Taxpayer-Advocate*. The corporation can also call TAS at 1-877-777-4778.

TAS also handles large-scale or systemic problems that affect many taxpayers. If the corporation knows of one of these broad issues, please report it to us through the Systemic Advocacy

Cat. No. 11455T

Management System at www.irs.gov/sams.

For more information, go to www.irs.gov/advocate.

Direct Deposit of Refund

To request a direct deposit of the corporation's income tax refund into an account at a U.S. bank or other financial institution, attach Form 8050, Direct Deposit of Corporate Tax Refund. See the instructions for line 36.

How To Make a Contribution To Reduce Debt Held by the Public

To help reduce debt held by the public, make a check payable to "Bureau of the Public Debt." Send it to: Bureau of the Public Debt, Department G, P.O. Box 2188, Parkersburg, WV 26106-2188. Or, enclose a check with the income tax return.

Do not add the contributions to any tax the corporation may owe. Contributions to reduce debt held by the public are deductible subject to the rules and limitations for charitable contributions.

How To Get Forms and Publications

Internet. You can access the IRS website 24 hours a day, 7 days a week, at IRS.gov to:
- Download forms, instructions, and publications;
- Order IRS products online;
- Research your tax questions online;
- Search publications online by topic or keyword;
- View Internal Revenue Bulletins (IRBs) published in recent years; and
- Sign up to receive local and national tax news by email.

Tax forms and publications. The corporation can download or print all of the forms and publications it may need on www.irs.gov/formspubs. Otherwise the corporation can:
- Go to www.irs.gov/orderforms to place an order and have forms mailed to it, or
- Call 1-800-829-3676 to order current year forms, instructions, publications and prior year forms and instructions (limited to 5 years).
The corporation should receive its order within 10 business days.

General Instructions

Purpose of Form

Use Form 1120, U.S. Corporation Income Tax Return, to report the income, gains, losses, deductions, credits, and to figure the income tax liability of a corporation.

Who Must File

Unless exempt under section 501, all domestic corporations (including corporations in bankruptcy) must file an income tax return whether or not they have taxable income. Domestic corporations must file Form 1120, unless they are required, or elect to file a special return. See *Special Returns for Certain Organizations,* below.

Entities electing to be taxed as corporations. A domestic entity electing to be classified as an association taxable as a corporation must file Form 1120, unless it is required to, or elects to file a special return listed under *Special Returns for Certain Organizations,* below. The entity must also file Form 8832, Entity Classification Election, and attach a copy of Form 8832 to Form 1120 (or the applicable return) for the year of the election. For more information, see Form 8832 and its instructions.

Limited liability companies (LLC). If an entity with more than one owner was formed as an LLC under state law, it generally is treated as a partnership for federal income tax purposes and files Form 1065, U.S. Return of Partnership Income. Generally, a single-member LLC is disregarded as an entity separate from its owner and reports its income and deductions on its owner's federal income tax return. The LLC can file a Form 1120 only if it has filed Form 8832 to elect to be treated as an association taxable as a corporation. For more information about LLCs, see Pub. 3402, Taxation of Limited Liability Companies.

Corporations engaged in farming. A corporation (other than a corporation that is a subchapter T cooperative) that engages in farming should use Form 1120 to report the income (loss) from such activities. Enter the income and deductions of the corporation according to the instructions for lines 1 through 10 and 12 through 29.

Ownership interest in a Financial Asset Securitization Investment Trust (FASIT). Special rules apply to a FASIT in existence on October 22, 2004, to the extent that regular interests issued by the FASIT before October 22, 2004, continue to remain outstanding in accordance with their original terms.

If a corporation holds an ownership interest in a FASIT to which these special rules apply, it must report all items of income, gain, deductions, losses, and credits on the corporation's income tax return (except as provided in section 860H). Show a breakdown of the items on an attached statement. For more information, see sections 860H and 860L (repealed with certain exceptions).

Special Returns for Certain Organizations

Instead of filing Form 1120, certain organizations, as shown below, file special returns.

If the organization is a: ▼	File Form ▼
Exempt organization with unrelated trade or business income	990-T
Religious or apostolic organization exempt under section 501(d)	1065
Entity formed as a limited liability company under state law and treated as a partnership for federal income tax purposes	1065
Subchapter T cooperative association (including a farmers' cooperative)	1120-C
Entity that elects to be treated as a real estate mortgage investment conduit (REMIC) under section 860D	1066
Interest charge domestic international sales corporation (section 992)	1120-IC-DISC
Foreign corporation (other than life and property and casualty insurance company filing Form 1120-L or Form 1120-PC)	1120-F
Foreign sales corporation (section 922)	1120-FSC
Condominium management, residential real estate management, or timeshare association that elects to be treated as a homeowners association under section 528	1120-H
Life insurance company (section 801)	1120-L
Fund set up to pay for nuclear decommissioning costs (section 468A)	1120-ND
Property and casualty insurance company (section 831)	1120-PC
Political organization (section 527)	1120-POL
Real estate investment trust (section 856)	1120-REIT

Regulated investment company (section 851)	1120-RIC
S corporation (section 1361)	1120S
Settlement fund (section 468B)	1120-SF

Electronic Filing

Corporations can generally electronically file (e-file) Form 1120, related forms, schedules, and attachments, Form 7004 (automatic extension of time to file) and Forms 940, 941, and 944 (employment tax returns). If there is a balance due, the corporation can authorize an electronic funds withdrawal while e-filing. Form 1099 and other information returns can also be electronically filed. The option to e-file does not, however, apply to certain returns.

Certain corporations with total assets of $10 million or more that file at least 250 returns a year are required to e-file Form 1120. See Regulations section 301.6011-5. However, these corporations can request a waiver of the electronic filing requirements. See Notice 2010-13, 2010-4 I.R.B. 327.

For more information, visit www.irs.gov/Filing. Click on the "Self-Employed & Small Businesses" and "Corporations" links.

When To File

Generally, a corporation must file its income tax return by the 15th day of the 3rd month after the end of its tax year. A new corporation filing a short-period return must generally file by the 15th day of the 3rd month after the short period ends. A corporation that has dissolved must generally file by the 15th day of the 3rd month after the date it dissolved.

If the due date falls on a Saturday, Sunday, or legal holiday, the corporation can file on the next business day.

Private Delivery Services

Corporations can use certain private delivery services designated by the IRS to meet the "timely mailing as timely filing" rule for tax returns. These private delivery services include only the following.

- Federal Express (FedEx): FedEx Priority Overnight, FedEx Standard Overnight, FedEx 2Day, FedEx International Priority, and FedEx International First.
- United Parcel Service (UPS): UPS Next Day Air, UPS Next Day Air Saver, UPS 2nd Day Air, UPS 2nd Day Air A.M., UPS Worldwide Express Plus, and UPS Worldwide Express.

The private delivery service can tell you how to get written proof of the mailing date.

For the IRS mailing address to use if you are using a private delivery service, go to IRS.gov and enter "private delivery services" in the search box.

 Private delivery services cannot deliver items to P.O. boxes. You must use the U.S. Postal Service to mail any item to an IRS P.O. box address.

Extension of Time To File

File Form 7004, Application for Automatic Extension of Time To File Certain Business Income Tax, Information, and Other Returns, to request a 6-month extension of time to file. Generally, the corporation must file Form 7004 by the regular due date of the return. See the Instructions for Form 7004.

Who Must Sign

The return must be signed and dated by:
- The president, vice president, treasurer, assistant treasurer, chief accounting officer; or

- Any other corporate officer (such as tax officer) authorized to sign.

If a return is filed on behalf of a corporation by a receiver, trustee, or assignee, the fiduciary must sign the return, instead of the corporate officer. Returns and forms signed by a receiver or trustee in bankruptcy on behalf of a corporation must be accompanied by a copy of the order or instructions of the court authorizing signing of the return or form.

If an employee of the corporation completes Form 1120, the paid preparer space should remain blank. Anyone who prepares Form 1120 but does not charge the corporation should not complete that section. Generally, anyone who is paid to prepare the return must sign it and fill in the "Paid Preparer Use Only" area.

The paid preparer must complete the required preparer information and:
- Sign the return in the space provided for the preparer's signature.
- Give a copy of the return to the taxpayer.

Note. A paid preparer may sign original or amended returns by rubber stamp,

Where To File

File the corporation's return at the applicable IRS address listed below.

If the corporation's principal business, office, or agency is located in:	And the total assets at the end of the tax year are:	Use the following address:
Connecticut, Delaware, District of Columbia, Florida, Georgia, Illinois, Indiana, Kentucky, Maine, Maryland, Massachusetts, Michigan, New Hampshire, New Jersey, New York, North Carolina, Ohio, Pennsylvania, Rhode Island, South Carolina, Tennessee, Vermont, Virginia, West Virginia, Wisconsin	Less than $10 million and Schedule M-3 is not filed	Department of the Treasury Internal Revenue Service Center Cincinnati, OH 45999-0012
	$10 million or more or less than $10 million and Schedule M-3 is filed	Department of the Treasury Internal Revenue Service Center Ogden, UT 84201-0012
Alabama, Alaska, Arizona, Arkansas, California, Colorado, Hawaii, Idaho, Iowa, Kansas, Louisiana, Minnesota, Mississippi, Missouri, Montana, Nebraska, Nevada, New Mexico, North Dakota, Oklahoma, Oregon, South Dakota, Texas, Utah, Washington, Wyoming	Any amount	Department of the Treasury Internal Revenue Service Center Ogden, UT 84201-0012
A foreign country or U.S. possession	Any amount	Internal Revenue Service Center P.O. Box 409101 Ogden, UT 84409

A group of corporations with members located in more than one service center area will often keep all the books and records at the principal office of the managing corporation. In this case, the tax returns of the corporations may be filed with the service center for the area in which the principal office of the managing corporation is located.

mechanical device, or computer software program.

Paid Preparer Authorization

If the corporation wants to allow the IRS to discuss its 2014 tax return with the paid preparer who signed it, check the "Yes" box in the signature area of the return. This authorization applies only to the individual whose signature appears in the "Paid Preparer Use Only" section of the return. It does not apply to the firm, if any, shown in that section.

If the "Yes" box is checked, the corporation is authorizing the IRS to call the paid preparer to answer any questions that may arise during the processing of its return. The corporation is also authorizing the paid preparer to:
• Give the IRS any information that is missing from the return,
• Call the IRS for information about the processing of the return or the status of any related refund or payment(s), and
• Respond to certain IRS notices about math errors, offsets, and return preparation.

The corporation is not authorizing the paid preparer to receive any refund check, bind the corporation to anything (including any additional tax liability), or otherwise represent the corporation before the IRS.

The authorization will automatically end no later than the due date (excluding extensions) for filing the corporation's 2015 tax return. If the corporation wants to expand the paid preparer's authorization or revoke the authorization before it ends, see Pub. 947, Practice Before the IRS and Power of Attorney.

Assembling the Return

To ensure that the corporation's tax return is correctly processed, attach all schedules and other forms after page 5 of Form 1120 in the following order.

1. Schedule N (Form 1120).

2. Schedule D (Form 1120).

3. Schedule O (Form 1120).

4. Form 4626.

5. Form 8050.

6. Form 1125-A.

7. Form 4136.

8. Form 8941.

9. Form 3800.

10. Additional schedules in alphabetical order.

11. Additional forms in numerical order.

12. Supporting statements and attachments.

Complete every applicable entry space on Form 1120. Do not enter "See Attached" or "Available Upon Request" instead of completing the entry spaces. If more space is needed on the forms or schedules, attach separate sheets using the same size and format as the printed forms.

If there are supporting statements and attachments, arrange them in the same order as the schedules or forms they support and attach them last. Show the totals on the printed forms. Enter the corporation's name and EIN on each supporting statement or attachment.

Tax Payments

Generally, the corporation must pay any tax due in full no later than the 15th day of the 3rd month after the end of the tax year. See the instructions for line 34.

Electronic Deposit Requirement

Corporations must use electronic funds transfer to make all federal tax deposits (such as deposits of employment, excise, and corporate income tax). Generally, electronic funds transfers are made using the Electronic Federal Tax Payment System (EFTPS). However, if the corporation does not want to use EFTPS, it can arrange for its tax professional, financial institution, payroll service, or other trusted third party to make deposits on its behalf. Also, it may arrange for its financial institution to submit a same-day payment (discussed below) on its behalf. EFTPS is a free service provided by the Department of the Treasury. Services provided by a tax professional, financial institution, payroll service, or other third party may have a fee.

To get more information about EFTPS or to enroll in EFTPS, visit _www.eftps.gov,_ or call 1-800-555-4477 (TTY/TDD 1-800-733-4829).

Depositing on time. For any deposit made by EFTPS to be on time, the corporation must submit the deposit by 8 p.m. Eastern time the day before the date the deposit is due. If the corporation uses a third party to make deposits on its behalf, they may have different cutoff times.

Same-day wire payment option. If the corporation fails to submit a deposit transaction on EFTPS by 8 p.m. Eastern time the day before the date a deposit is due, it can still make its deposit on time by using the Federal Tax Collection Service (FTCS). To use the same-day wire payment method, the corporation will need to make arrangements with its financial institution ahead of time regarding availability, deadlines, and costs. Financial institutions may charge a fee for payments made this way. To learn more about the information the corporation will need to provide to its financial institution to make a same-day wire payment, visit the IRS website at _www.irs.gov/e-pay_ and click on "Same-Day Wire Federal Tax Payments."

Estimated Tax Payments

Generally, the following rules apply to the corporation's payments of estimated tax.
• The corporation must make installment payments of estimated tax if it expects its total tax for the year (less applicable credits) to be $500 or more.
• The installments are due by the 15th day of the 4th, 6th, 9th, and 12th months of the tax year. If any date falls on a Saturday, Sunday, or legal holiday, the installment is due on the next regular business day.
• The corporation must use electronic funds transfer to make installment payments of estimated tax.
• Use Form 1120-W, Estimated Tax for Corporations, as a worksheet to compute estimated tax. See the Instructions for Form 1120-W.
• Penalties may apply if the corporation does not make required estimated tax payment deposits. See _Estimated tax penalty,_ below.
• If the corporation overpaid estimated tax, it may be able to get a quick refund by filing Form 4466, Corporation Application for Quick Refund of Overpayment of Estimated Tax. See the instructions for Schedule J, Part II, line 14, later.

Estimated tax penalty. A corporation that does not make estimated tax payments when due may be subject to an underpayment penalty for the period of underpayment. Generally, a corporation is subject to the penalty if its tax liability is $500 or more and it did not timely pay at least the smaller of:
• Its tax liability for the current year, or
• Its prior year's tax.

Use Form 2220, Underpayment of Estimated Tax by Corporations, to see if the corporation owes a penalty and to figure the amount of the penalty. If Form 2220 is completed, enter the penalty on line 33. See the instructions for line 33.

Interest and Penalties

 If the corporation receives a notice about penalties after it files its return, send the IRS an explanation and we will determine if the corporation meets reasonable-cause criteria. **Do not** attach an explanation when the corporation's return is filed.

Interest. Interest is charged on taxes paid late even if an extension of time to file is granted. Interest is also charged on penalties imposed for failure to file, negligence, fraud, substantial valuation misstatements, substantial understatements of tax, and reportable transaction understatements from the due date (including extensions) to the date of payment. The interest charge is figured at a rate determined under section 6621.

Late filing of return. A corporation that does not file its tax return by the due date, including extensions, may be penalized 5% of the unpaid tax for each month or part of a month the return is late, up to a maximum of 25% of the unpaid tax. The minimum penalty for a return that is over 60 days late is the smaller of the tax due or $135. The penalty will not be imposed if the corporation can show that the failure to file on time was due to reasonable cause. See *Caution*, above.

Late payment of tax. A corporation that does not pay the tax when due generally may be penalized ½ of 1% of the unpaid tax for each month or part of a month the tax is not paid, up to a maximum of 25% of the unpaid tax. See *Caution*, above.

Trust fund recovery penalty. This penalty may apply if certain excise, income, social security, and Medicare taxes that must be collected or withheld are not collected or withheld, or these taxes are not paid. These taxes are generally reported on:
• Form 720, Quarterly Federal Excise Tax Return;
• Form 941, Employer's QUARTERLY Federal Tax Return;
• Form 943, Employer's Annual Federal Tax Return for Agricultural Employees;
• Form 944, Employer's ANNUAL Federal Tax Return; or
• Form 945, Annual Return of Withheld Federal Income Tax.

The trust fund recovery penalty may be imposed on all persons who are determined by the IRS to have been responsible for collecting, accounting for, and paying over these taxes, and who acted willfully in not doing so. The penalty is equal to the full amount of the unpaid trust fund tax. See the Instructions for Form 720, Pub. 15 (Circular E), Employer's Tax Guide, or Pub. 51 (Circular A), Agricultural Employer's Tax Guide, for details, including the definition of responsible persons.

Other penalties. Other penalties can be imposed for negligence, substantial understatement of tax, reportable transaction understatements, and fraud. See sections 6662, 6662A, and 6663.

Accounting Methods

Figure taxable income using the method of accounting regularly used in keeping the corporation's books and records. In all cases, the method used must clearly show taxable income. Permissible methods include cash, accrual, or any other method authorized by the Internal Revenue Code.

Generally, the following rules apply. For more information, see Pub. 538, Accounting Periods and Methods.
• A corporation (other than a qualified personal service corporation) must use the accrual method of accounting if its average annual gross receipts exceed $5 million. However, see *Nonaccrual experience method for service providers*, in the instructions for line 1a.

• Unless it is a qualifying taxpayer or a qualifying small business taxpayer, a corporation must use the accrual method for sales and purchases of inventory items. See the instructions for Form 1125-A.
• A corporation engaged in farming must use the accrual method. For exceptions, see section 447.
• Special rules apply to long-term contracts. See section 460.
• Dealers in securities must use the mark-to-market accounting method. Dealers in commodities and traders in securities and commodities can elect to use the mark-to-market accounting method. See section 475.

Change in accounting method. Generally, the corporation must get IRS consent to change the method of accounting used to report taxable income (for income as a whole or for the treatment of any material item). To do so, the corporation generally must file Form 3115, Application for Change in Accounting Method. For more information, see the Instructions for Form 3115, and Pub. 538.

There are some instances when the corporation can obtain automatic consent from the IRS to change to certain accounting methods. See Rev. Proc. 2011-14, 2011-4 I.R.B. 330, as modified and clarified by Rev. Proc. 2014-16, 2014-9 I.R.B. 606; Rev. Proc. 2014-17, 2014-12 I.R.B. 661; and Rev. Proc. 2014-54, 2014-41 I.R.B. 675, or any successor.

Section 481(a) adjustment. If the corporation's taxable income for the current tax year is figured under a method of accounting different from the method used in the preceding tax year, the corporation may have to make an adjustment under section 481(a) to prevent amounts of income or expense from being duplicated or omitted. The section 481(a) adjustment period is generally 1 year for a net negative adjustment and 4 years for a net positive adjustment. However, in some cases, a corporation can elect to modify the section 481(a) adjustment period. The corporation must complete the appropriate lines of Form 3115 to make an election. See the instructions for Form 3115. If the net section 481(a) adjustment is positive, report it on line 10 as other income. If the net section 481(a) adjustment is negative, report it on line 26 as a deduction.

Accounting Period

A corporation must figure its taxable income on the basis of a tax year. A tax year is the annual accounting period a corporation uses to keep its records and report its income and expenses. Generally, corporations can use a calendar year or a fiscal year. Personal service corporations, however, must use a calendar year unless they meet one of the exceptions, discussed later under *Personal Service Corporation.*

Change of tax year. Generally, a corporation, including a personal service corporation, must get the consent of the IRS before changing its tax year by filing Form 1128, Application To Adopt, Change, or Retain a Tax Year. However, exceptions may apply. See the Instructions for Form 1128 and Pub. 538 for more information.

Rounding Off to Whole Dollars

The corporation can round off cents to whole dollars on its return and schedules. If the corporation does round to whole dollars, it must round all amounts. To round, drop amounts under 50 cents and increase amounts from 50 to 99 cents to the next dollar. For example, $1.39 becomes $1 and $2.50 becomes $3.

If two or more amounts must be added to figure the amount to enter on a line, include cents when adding the amounts and round off only the total.

Recordkeeping

Keep the corporation's records for as long as they may be needed for the administration of any provision of the Internal Revenue Code. Usually, records that support an item of income, deduction, or credit on the return must be kept for 3 years from the date the return is due or filed, whichever is later. Keep records that verify the corporation's basis in property for as long as they are needed to figure the basis of the original or replacement property.

The corporation should keep copies of all filed returns. They help in preparing future and amended returns and in the calculation of earnings and profits.

Other Forms and Statements That May Be Required

Amended return. Use Form 1120X, Amended U.S. Corporation Income Tax

Return, to correct a previously filed Form 1120.

Reportable transaction disclosure statement. Disclose information for each reportable transaction in which the corporation participated. Form 8886, Reportable Transaction Disclosure Statement, must be filed for each tax year that the federal income tax liability of the corporation is affected by its participation in the transaction. The following are reportable transactions.

1. Any listed transaction, which is a transaction that is the same as or substantially similar to one of the types of transactions that the IRS has determined to be a tax avoidance transaction and identified by notice, regulation, or other published guidance as a listed transaction.

2. Any transaction offered under conditions of confidentiality for which the corporation (or a related party) paid an advisor a fee of at least $250,000.

3. Certain transactions for which the corporation (or a related party) has contractual protection against disallowance of the tax benefits.

4. Certain transactions resulting in a loss of at least $10 million in any single year or $20 million in any combination of years.

5. Any transaction identified by the IRS by notice, regulation, or other published guidance as a "transaction of interest."

For more information, see Regulations section 1.6011-4. Also see the Instructions for Form 8886.

Penalties. The corporation may have to pay a penalty if it is required to disclose a reportable transaction under section 6011 and fails to properly complete and file Form 8886. Penalties may also apply under section 6707A if the corporation fails to file Form 8886 with its corporate return, fails to provide a copy of Form 8886 to the Office of Tax Shelter Analysis (OTSA), or files a form that fails to include all the information required (or includes incorrect information). Other penalties, such as an accuracy-related penalty under section 6662A, may also apply. See the Instructions for Form 8886 for details on these and other penalties.

Reportable transactions by material advisors. Material advisors to any reportable transaction must disclose certain information about the reportable transaction by filing Form 8918, Material Advisor Disclosure Statement, with the IRS. For details, see the Instructions for Form 8918.

Transfers to a corporation controlled by the transferor. Every significant transferor (as defined in Regulations section 1.351-3(d)) that receives stock of a corporation in exchange for property in a nonrecognition event must include the statement required by Regulations section 1.351-3(a) on or with the transferor's tax return for the tax year of the exchange. The transferee corporation must include the statement required by Regulations section 1.351-3(b) on or with its return for the tax year of the exchange, unless all the required information is included in any statement(s) provided by a significant transferor that is attached to the same return for the same section 351 exchange. If the transferor or transferee corporation is a controlled foreign corporation, each U.S. shareholder (within the meaning of section 951(b)) must include the required statement on or with its return.

Distributions under section 355. Every corporation that makes a distribution of stock or securities of a controlled corporation, as described in section 355 (or so much of section 356 as it relates to section 355), must include the statement required by Regulations section 1.355-5(a) on or with its return for the year of the distribution. A significant distributee (as defined in Regulations section 1.355-5(c)) that receives stock or securities of a controlled corporation must include the statement required by Regulations section 1.355-5(b) on or with its return for the year of receipt. If the distributing or distributee corporation is a controlled foreign corporation, each U.S. shareholder (within the meaning of section 951(b)) must include the statement on or with its return.

Dual consolidated losses. If a domestic corporation incurs a dual consolidated loss (as defined in Regulations section 1.1503-2(c)(5)), the corporation (or consolidated group) may need to attach an elective relief agreement and/or an annual certification as provided in Regulations section 1.1503-2(g)(2).

Election to reduce basis under section 362(e)(2)(C). If property is transferred to a corporation subject to section 362(e)(2), the transferor and the acquiring corporation may elect, under section 362(e)(2)(C), to reduce the transferor's basis in the stock received instead of reducing the acquiring corporation's basis in the property transferred. Once made, the election is irrevocable. For more information see section 362(e)(2) and Regulations section 1.362-4. If an election is made, a statement must be filed in accordance with Regulations section 1.362-4(d)(3).

Annual information statement for elections under section 108(i). If the corporation made an election in 2009 or 2010 to defer income from cancellation of debt (COD) in connection with the reacquisition of an applicable debt instrument, the corporation must attach a statement to its return beginning with the tax year following the tax year for which the corporation made the election, and ending the first tax year all income deferred has been included in income. The statement must be labeled "Section 108(i) Information Statement" and must clearly identify, for each applicable debt instrument to which an election under section 108(i) applies, the following.

1. Any deferred COD income that is included in income in the current tax year.

2. Any deferred COD income that has been accelerated because of an event described in section 108(i)(5)(D) and must be included in income in the current tax year. Include a description and the date of the acceleration event.

3. Any deferred COD income that has not been included in income in the current or prior tax years.

4. Any deferred OID deduction allowed as a deduction in the current tax year.

5. Any deferred OID deduction that is allowed as a deduction in the current tax year because of an accelerated event described in section 108(i)(5)(D).

6. Any deferred OID deduction that has not been deducted in the current or prior tax years.

In addition, the corporation must annually include a copy of the election statement it filed to make the election to defer the income.

For more information regarding the annual information statement, see Rev. Proc. 2009-37, 2009-36 I.R.B. 309. For more information on deferring COD income, see the instructions for line 10.

Other forms and statements. See Pub. 542, Corporations, for a list of other forms and statements a corporation may need to file in addition to the forms and statements discussed throughout these instructions.

Specific Instructions

Period Covered

File the 2014 return for calendar year 2014 and fiscal years that begin in 2014 and end in 2015. For a fiscal or short tax year return, fill in the tax year space at the top of the form.

The 2014 Form 1120 can also be used if:
• The corporation has a tax year of less than 12 months that begins and ends in 2015, and
• The 2015 Form 1120 is not available at the time the corporation is required to file its return.

The corporation must show its 2015 tax year on the 2014 Form 1120 and take into account any tax law changes that are effective for tax years beginning after December 31, 2014.

Name and Address

Enter the corporation's true name (as set forth in the charter or other legal document creating it), address, and EIN on the appropriate lines. Enter the address of the corporation's principal office or place of business. Include the suite, room, or other unit number after the street address. If the post office does not deliver mail to the street address and the corporation has a P.O. box, show the box number instead.

Note. Do not use the address of the registered agent for the state in which the corporation is incorporated. For example, if a business is incorporated in Delaware or Nevada and the corporation's principal office is located in Little Rock, AR, the corporation should enter the Little Rock address.

If the corporation receives its mail in care of a third party (such as an accountant or an attorney), enter on the street address line "C/O" followed by the third party's name and street address or P.O. box.

If the corporation has a foreign address, include the city or town, state or province, country, and foreign postal code. Do not abbreviate the country name. Follow the country's practice for entering the name of the state or province and postal code.

Item A. Identifying Information

Consolidated Return

Corporations filing a consolidated return must check Item A, box 1a, and attach Form 851, Affiliations Schedule, and other supporting statements to the return. Also, for the first year a subsidiary corporation is being included in a consolidated return, attach Form 1122, Authorization and Consent of Subsidiary Corporation To Be Included in a Consolidated Income Tax Return, to the parent's consolidated return. Attach a separate Form 1122 for each new subsidiary being included in the consolidated return.

File supporting statements for each corporation included in the consolidated return. Do not use Form 1120 as a supporting statement. On the supporting statement, use columns to show the following, both before and after adjustments.

1. Items of gross income and deductions.

2. A computation of taxable income.

3. Balance sheets as of the beginning and end of the tax year.

4. A reconciliation of income per books with income per return.

5. A reconciliation of retained earnings.

Enter on Form 1120 the totals for each item of income, gain, loss, expense, or deduction, net of eliminating entries for intercompany transactions between corporations within the consolidated group. Attach consolidated balance sheets and a reconciliation of consolidated retained earnings.

 The corporation does not have to provide the information requested in (3), (4), and (5), above, if its total receipts (line 1a plus lines 4 through 10 on page 1 of the return) and its total assets at the end of the tax year (Schedule L, line 15(d)) are less than $250,000. See Schedule K, question 13.

For more information on consolidated returns, see the regulations under section 1502.

Life-Nonlife Consolidated Return

If Item A, box 1a, is checked and the corporation is the common parent of a consolidated group that includes a life-nonlife insurance company, also check box 1b. See Regulations section 1.1502-47(s) for the filing requirements of a life-nonlife consolidated return.

Personal Holding Company

A personal holding company must check Item A, box 2 and attach Schedule PH (Form 1120), U.S. Personal Holding Company (PHC) Tax. See the Instructions for Schedule PH (Form 1120) for details.

Personal Service Corporation

If the corporation is a personal service corporation, check Item A, box 3. A personal service corporation is a corporation whose principal activity for the testing period is the performance of personal services. The testing period for a tax year is generally the prior tax year unless the corporation has just been formed. Personal services include any activity performed in the fields of accounting, actuarial science, architecture, consulting, engineering, health, law, and the performing arts. The services must be substantially performed by employee-owners.

A personal service corporation must use a calendar tax year unless:
• It elects to use a 52-53-week tax year that ends with reference to the calendar year or tax year elected under section 444;
• It can establish a business purpose for a different tax year and obtains the

approval of the IRS (see the Instructions for Form 1128 and Pub. 538); or
• It elects under section 444 to have a tax year other than a calendar year. To make the election, use Form 8716, Election To Have a Tax Year Other Than a Required Tax Year.

If a corporation makes the section 444 election, its deduction for certain amounts paid to employee-owners may be limited. See Schedule H (Form 1120), Section 280H Limitations for a Personal Service Corporation (PSC), to figure the maximum deduction.

If a section 444 election is terminated and the termination results in a short tax year, type or print at the top of the first page of Form 1120 for the short tax year "SECTION 444 ELECTION TERMINATED."

Schedule M-3 (Form 1120)

A corporation with total assets (non-consolidated or consolidated for all corporations included within a tax consolidation group) of $10 million or more on the last day of the tax year must file Schedule M-3 (Form 1120), Net Income (Loss) Reconciliation for Corporations With Total Assets of $10 Million or More, instead of Schedule M-1. A corporation filing Form 1120 that is not required to file Schedule M-3 may voluntarily file Schedule M-3 instead of Schedule M-1.

For tax years ending December 31, 2014, and later, corporations that (a) are required to file Schedule M-3 (Form 1120) and have less than $50 million total assets at the end of the tax year, or (b) are not required to file Schedule M-3 (Form 1120) and voluntarily file Schedule M-3 (Form 1120), must either (i) complete Schedule M-3 (Form 1120) entirely or (ii) complete Schedule M-3 (Form 1120) through Part I, and complete Form 1120, Schedule M-1, instead of completing Parts II and III of Schedule M-3 (Form 1120). If the corporation chooses to complete Schedule M-1 instead of completing Parts II and III of Schedule M-3, line 1 of Schedule M-1 must equal line 11 of Part I of Schedule M-3. See the Instructions for Schedule M-3 (Form 1120) for more details. Also, see the instructions for Schedule M-1, later.

If you are filing Schedule M-3, check Item A, box 4, to indicate that Schedule M-3 is attached.

Item B. Employer Identification Number (EIN)

Enter the corporation's EIN. If the corporation does not have an EIN, it must apply for one. An EIN can be applied for:

- Online—Click on the Employer ID Numbers link at *www.irs.gov/businesses*. The EIN is issued immediately once the application information is validated.
- By faxing or mailing Form SS-4, Application for Employer Identification Number.

 Corporations located in the United States or U.S. possessions can use the online application. Foreign corporations should call 1-267-941-1099 for more information on obtaining an EIN.

EIN applied for, but not received. If the corporation has not received its EIN by the time the return is due, enter "Applied For" and the date the corporation applied in the space for the EIN. However, if the corporation is filing its return electronically, an EIN is required at the time the return is filed. An exception applies to subsidiaries of corporations whose returns are filed with the parent's electronically filed consolidated Form 1120. These subsidiaries should enter "Applied For" in the space for the EIN on their returns. The subsidiaries' returns are identified under the parent corporation's EIN.

For more information, see the Instructions for Form SS-4.

Item D. Total Assets

Enter the corporation's total assets (as determined by the accounting method regularly used in keeping the corporation's books and records) at the end of the tax year. If there are no assets at the end of the tax year, enter -0-.

If the corporation is required to complete Schedule L, enter on page 1, Item D. Total assets from Schedule L, line 15, column (d). If filing a consolidated return, report total consolidated assets for all corporations joining in the return.

Item E. Initial Return, Final Return, Name Change, or Address Change

- If this is the corporation's first return, check the "Initial return" box.
- If this is the corporation's final return and it will no longer exist, check the "Final return" box.
- If the corporation changed its name since it last filed a return, check the "Name change" box. Generally, a corporation also must have amended its articles of incorporation and filed the amendment with the state in which it was incorporated.
- If the corporation has changed its address since it last filed a return (including a change to an "in care of" address), check the "Address change" box.

Note. If a change in address or responsible party occurs after the return is filed, use Form 8822-B, Change of Address or Responsible Party— Business, to notify the IRS. See the instructions for Form 8822-B for details.

Income

Except as otherwise provided in the Internal Revenue Code, gross income includes all income from whatever source derived.

Exception for income from qualifying shipping activities. Gross income does not include income from qualifying shipping activities if the corporation makes an election under section 1354 to be taxed on its notional shipping income (as defined in section 1353) at the highest corporate tax rate (35%). If the election is made, the corporation generally may not claim any loss, deduction, or credit with respect to qualifying shipping activities. A corporation making this election also may elect to defer gain on the disposition of a qualifying vessel.

Use Form 8902, Alternative Tax on Qualifying Shipping Activities, to figure the tax. Include the alternative tax on Schedule J, line 9e.

Line 1. Gross Receipts or Sales

Line 1a. Gross receipts or sales. Enter on line 1a gross receipts or sales from all business operations, except for amounts that must be reported on lines 4 through 10.

Special rules apply to certain income, as discussed below.

Advance payments. In general, advance payments are reported in the year of receipt. For exceptions to this general rule for corporations that use the accrual method of accounting, see the following.
- To report income from long-term contracts, see section 460.
- For special rules for reporting certain advance payments for goods and long-term contracts, see Regulations section 1.451-5.
- For rules that allow a limited deferral of advance payments beyond the current tax year, see Rev. Proc. 2004-34, 2004-22 I.R.B. 991. For rules for the deferral of advance payments from the sale of certain gift cards, see Rev. Proc. 2011-18, 2011-5 I.R.B. 443, as modified and clarified by Rev. Proc. 2013-29, 2013-33 I.R.B. 141.
- For information on adopting or changing to a permissible method for reporting advance payments for services and certain goods by an accrual method corporation, see the Instructions for Form 3115.

Installment sales. Generally, the installment method cannot be used for dealer dispositions of property. A "dealer disposition" is any disposition of: (a) personal property by a person who regularly sells or otherwise disposes of personal property of the same type on the installment plan or (b) real property held for sale to customers in the ordinary course of the taxpayer's trade or business.

The restrictions on using the installment method do not apply to the following.
- Dispositions of property used or produced in the trade or business of farming.
- Certain dispositions of timeshares and residential lots reported under the installment method for which the corporation elects to pay interest under section 453(l)(3).

Enter on line 1a (and carry to line 3), the gross profit on collections from these installment sales. Attach a statement showing the following information for the current and the 3 preceding years: (a) gross sales, (b) cost of goods sold, (c) gross profits, (d) percentage of gross profits to gross sales, (e) amount collected, and (f) gross profit on the amount collected.

For sales of timeshares and residential lots reported under the installment method, if the corporation elects to pay interest under section 453(l)(3), the corporation's income tax is increased by the interest payable under section 453(l)(3). Report this addition to the tax on Schedule J, Part I, line 9f.

Nonaccrual experience method for service providers. Accrual method corporations are not required to accrue certain amounts to be received from the performance of services that, on the basis of their experience, will not be collected, if:
- The services are in the fields of health, law, engineering, architecture, accounting, actuarial science, performing arts, or consulting, or
- The corporation's average annual gross receipts have not exceeded $5 million for any prior 3-tax-year period. For more details, see Regulations sections 1.448-2(a)(2) and 1.448-1T(f)(2).

This provision does not apply to any amount if interest is required to be paid on the amount or if there is any penalty for failure to timely pay the amount. See Regulations section 1.448-2 for information on the nonaccrual experience method, including information on safe harbor methods. See Rev. Proc. 2011-46, 2011-42 I.R.B. 518, for information on a book safe harbor method of accounting for corporations that use the nonaccrual experience method of accounting. Also,

Instructions for Form 1120

see Rev. Proc. 2011-46, for procedures to obtain automatic consent to change to this method or make certain changes within this method.

Corporations that qualify to use the nonaccrual experience method should attach a statement showing total gross receipts, the amount not accrued as a result of the application of section 448(d)(5), and the net amount accrued. Enter the net amount on line 1a.

Line 1b. Returns and allowances. Enter cash and credit refunds the corporation made to customers for returned merchandise, rebates, and other allowances made on gross receipts or sales.

Line 2. Cost of Goods Sold

Complete and attach Form 1125-A, Cost of Goods Sold, if applicable. Enter on Form 1120, line 2, the amount from Form 1125-A, line 8. See Form 1125-A and its instructions.

Line 4. Dividends

See the instructions for Schedule C, later. Then, complete Schedule C and enter on line 4 the amount from Schedule C, line 19.

Line 5. Interest

Enter taxable interest on U.S. obligations and on loans, notes, mortgages, bonds, bank deposits, corporate bonds, tax refunds, etc. Do not offset interest expense against interest income. Special rules apply to interest income from certain below-market-rate loans. See section 7872 for details.

Note. Report tax-exempt interest income on Schedule K, item 9. Also, if required, include the same amount on Schedule M-1, line 7, or Schedule M-3 (Form 1120), Part II, line 13, if applicable.

Line 6. Gross Rents

Enter the gross amount received for the rental of property. Deduct expenses such as repairs, interest, taxes, and depreciation on the proper lines for deductions. A rental activity held by a closely held corporation or a personal service corporation may be subject to the passive activity loss rules. See *Passive activity limitations*, later.

Line 10. Other Income

Enter any other taxable income not reported on lines 1 through 9. List the type and amount of income on an attached statement. If the corporation has only one item of other income, describe it in parentheses on line 10.

Examples of other income to report on line 10 include the following.

• Recoveries of bad debts deducted in prior years under the specific charge-off method.
• The amount included in income from Form 6478, Biofuel Producer Credit.
• The amount included in income from Form 8864, Biodiesel and Renewable Diesel Fuels Credit.
• Refunds of taxes deducted in prior years to the extent they reduced the amount of tax imposed. See section 111 and the related regulations. Do not offset current year taxes against tax refunds.
• Ordinary income from trade or business activities of a partnership (from Schedule K-1 (Form 1065 or 1065-B)). Do not offset ordinary losses against ordinary income. Instead, include the losses on line 26. Show the partnership's name, address, and EIN on a separate statement attached to this return. If the amount entered is from more than one partnership, identify the amount from each partnership.
• Any LIFO recapture amount under section 1363(d). The corporation may have to include a LIFO recapture amount in income if it:

1. Used the LIFO inventory method for its last tax year before the first tax year for which it elected to become an S corporation or

2. Transferred LIFO inventory assets to an S corporation in a nonrecognition transaction in which those assets were transferred basis property.

The LIFO recapture amount is the amount by which the C corporation's inventory under the FIFO method exceeds the inventory amount under the LIFO method at the close of the corporation's last tax year as a C corporation (or for the year of the transfer, if (2) above applies). Also see the instructions for Schedule J, Part I, line 11.
• Any net positive section 481(a) adjustment.
• Part or all of the proceeds received from certain corporate-owned life insurance contracts issued after August 17, 2006. Corporations that own one or more employer-owned life insurance contracts issued after this date must file Form 8925, Report of Employer-Owned Life Insurance Contracts. See section 101(j) for details.
• Income from cancellation of debt (COD) from the repurchase of a debt instrument for less than its adjusted issue price.
• Any COD income deferred from 2009 or 2010 that is includible in income in 2014. See section 108(i), Regulations section 1.108(i)-1, and Rev. Proc. 2009-37. If the corporation is a direct or indirect partner in a partnership, other special rules apply. See Regulations section 1.108(i)-2.
• The corporation's share of the following income from Form 8621, Information Return by a Shareholder of a Passive Foreign Investment Company or Qualified Electing Fund.

1. Ordinary earnings of a qualified electing fund.

2. Gain or loss from marking passive foreign investment company (PFIC) stock to market.

3. Gain or loss from sale or other disposition of Section 1296 stock.

4. Excess distributions from a section 1291 fund.

See Form 8621 and the Instructions for Form 8621 for details.

Deductions

Limitations on Deductions

Uniform capitalization rules. The uniform capitalization rules of section 263A require corporations to capitalize, or include in inventory, certain costs. Corporations subject to the section 263A uniform capitalization rules are required to capitalize:

1. Direct costs, and

2. An allocable part of most indirect costs (including taxes) that (a) benefit the assets produced or acquired for resale, or (b) are incurred because of the performance of production or resale activities.

The costs required to be capitalized under section 263A are not deductible until the property (to which the costs relate) is sold, used, or otherwise disposed of by the corporation. You recover these costs through depreciation, amortization, or cost of goods sold.

For more details, including exceptions to the uniform capitalization rules, see Pub. 538. Also see Regulations sections 1.263A-1 through 1.263A-3. See Regulations section 1.263A-4 for rules for property produced in a farming business.

Transactions between related taxpayers. Generally, an accrual basis taxpayer can only deduct business expenses and interest owed to a related party in the year the payment is included in the income of the related party. See sections 163(e)(3), 163(j), and 267 for limitations on deductions for unpaid interest and expenses.

Corporations use Form 8926, Disqualified Corporate Interest Expense Disallowed Under Section 163(j) and Related Information, to figure the amount of any corporate interest expense disallowed by section 163(j).

Section 291 limitations. Corporations may be required to adjust deductions for depletion of iron ore and coal, intangible drilling and exploration and development costs, certain deductions for financial institutions, and the amortizable basis of pollution control facilities. See section 291 to determine the amount of the adjustment.

Election to deduct business start-up and organizational costs. A corporation can elect to deduct up to $5,000 of business start-up and up to $5,000 of organizational costs paid or incurred after October 22, 2004. Any remaining costs must be amortized ratably over an 180-month period. The $5,000 deduction is reduced (but not below zero) by the amount the total costs exceed $50,000. If the total costs are $55,000 or more, the deduction is reduced to zero.

Time for making an election. The corporation generally elects to deduct start-up or organizational costs by claiming the deduction on its income tax return filed by the due date (including extensions) for the tax year in which the active trade or business begins. However, for start-up or organizational costs paid or incurred before September 9, 2008, the corporation may be required to attach a statement to its return to elect to deduct such costs.

If the corporation timely filed its return for the year without making an election, it can still make an election by filing an amended return within 6 months of the due date of the return (excluding extensions). Clearly indicate the election on the amended return and write "Filed pursuant to section 301.9100-2" at the top of the amended return. File the amended return at the same address the corporation filed its original return. The election applies when figuring taxable income for the current tax year and all subsequent years.

The corporation can choose to forgo the elections above by affirmatively electing to capitalize its start-up or organizational costs on its income tax return filed by the due date (including extensions) for the tax year in which the active trade or business begins.

Note. The election to either amortize or capitalize start-up costs is irrevocable and applies to all start-up costs that are related to the trade or business.

Report the deductible amount of start-up and organizational costs and any amortization on line 26. For amortization that begins during the current tax year, complete and attach Form 4562, Depreciation and Amortization.

For more details on business start-up and organizational costs, see the Instructions for Form 4562. Also see Pub. 535, Business Expenses.

Passive activity limitations. Limitations on passive activity losses and credits under section 469 apply to personal

service corporations (defined earlier) and closely held corporations (defined later).

Generally, the two kinds of passive activities are:
• Trade or business activities in which the corporation did not materially participate for the tax year; and
• Rental activities, regardless of its participation.
For exceptions, see Form 8810, Corporate Passive Activity Loss and Credit Limitations.

Corporations subject to the passive activity limitations must complete Form 8810 to compute their allowable passive activity loss and credit. Before completing Form 8810, see Temporary Regulations section 1.163-8T, which provides rules for allocating interest expense among activities. If a passive activity is also subject to the earnings stripping rules of section 163(j), the at-risk rules of section 465, or the tax-exempt use loss rules of section 470, those rules apply before the passive loss rules.

For more information, see section 469, the related regulations, and Pub. 925, Passive Activity and At-Risk Rules.

Closely held corporations. A corporation is a closely held corporation if:
• At any time during the last half of the tax year more than 50% in value of its outstanding stock is directly or indirectly owned by or for not more than five individuals, and
• The corporation is not a personal service corporation.

Certain organizations are treated as individuals for purposes of this test. See section 542(a)(2). For rules for determining stock ownership, see section 544 (as modified by section 465(a)(3)).

Reducing certain expenses for which credits are allowable. If the corporation claims certain credits, it may need to reduce the otherwise allowable deductions for expenses used to figure the credit. This applies to credits such as the following.
• Work opportunity credit (Form 5884).
• Credit for increasing research activities (Form 6765).
• Orphan drug credit (Form 8820).
• Disabled access credit (Form 8826).
• Empowerment zone employment credit (Form 8844).
• Indian employment credit (Form 8845).
• Credit for employer social security and Medicare taxes paid on certain employee tips (Form 8846).
• Credit for small employer pension plan start-up costs (Form 8881).
• Credit for employer-provided childcare facilities and services (Form 8882).
• Low sulfur diesel fuel production credit (Form 8896).

• Mine rescue team training credit (Form 8923).
• Credit for employer differential wage payments (Form 8932).
• Credit for small employer health insurance premiums (Form 8941).

If the corporation has any of these credits, figure the current year credit before figuring the deduction for expenses on which the credit is based. If the corporation capitalized any costs on which it figured the credit, it may need to reduce the amount capitalized by the credit attributable to these costs.

See the instructions for the form used to figure the applicable credit for more details.

Limitations on deductions related to property leased to tax-exempt entities. If a corporation leases property to a governmental or other tax-exempt entity, the corporation cannot claim deductions related to the property to the extent that they exceed the corporation's income from the lease payments. This disallowed tax-exempt use loss can be carried over to the next tax year and treated as a deduction with respect to the property for that tax year. See section 470(d) for exceptions.

Limitation on tax benefits for remuneration under the Patient Protection and Affordable Care Act. The $1 million compensation limit is reduced to $500,000 for remuneration for services provided by individuals for or on behalf of certain health insurance providers in taxable years beginning after December 31, 2009. The $500,000 limitation applies to remuneration that is deductible in the taxable year during which the services were performed and remuneration for services during the year that is deductible in a future taxable year (called "deferred deduction remuneration"). The $500,000 limitation is reduced by any amounts disallowed as excess parachute payments. See section 162(m)(6) for definitions and other special rules. Also see Notice 2011-2, 2011-2 I.R.B. 260, for additional guidance.

Line 12. Compensation of Officers

Enter deductible officers' compensation on line 12. Do not include compensation deductible elsewhere on the return, such as amounts included in cost of goods sold, elective contributions to a section 401(k) cash or deferred arrangement, or amounts contributed under a salary reduction SEP agreement or a SIMPLE IRA plan.

If the corporation's total receipts (line 1a, plus lines 4 through 10) are $500,000 or more, complete Form 1125-E, Compensation of Officers. Enter on Form 1120, line 12, the amount from Form 1125-E, line 4.

Line 13. Salaries and Wages

Enter the total salaries and wages paid for the tax year. Do not include salaries and wages deductible elsewhere on the return, such as amounts included in officers' compensation, cost of goods sold, elective contributions to a section 401(k) cash or deferred arrangement, or amounts contributed under a salary reduction SEP agreement or a SIMPLE IRA plan.

If the corporation claims a credit for any wages paid or incurred, it may need to reduce its deduction for officer's compensation and salaries and wages. See *Reducing certain expenses for which credits are allowable*, earlier.

If the corporation provided taxable fringe benefits to its employees, such as personal use of a car, do not deduct as wages the amount allocated for depreciation and other expenses claimed on lines 20 and 26.

Line 14. Repairs and Maintenance

Enter the cost of repairs and maintenance not claimed elsewhere on the return, such as labor and supplies, that do not add to the value of the property or appreciably prolong its life. See Regulations section 1.162-4. The corporation may elect to capitalize certain repair and maintenance costs consistent with its books and records. See Regulations section 1.263(a)-3 for information on how to make the election.

New buildings, machinery, or permanent improvements that increase the value of the property are not deductible. They must be depreciated or amortized. However, amounts paid for routine maintenance on property, including buildings, may be deductible. See Regulations section 1.263(a)-3(i).

Line 15. Bad Debts

Enter the total debts that became worthless in whole or in part during the tax year. A small bank or thrift institution using the reserve method of section 585 should attach a statement showing how it figured the current year's provision. A corporation that uses the cash method of accounting cannot claim a bad debt deduction unless the amount was previously included in income.

Line 16. Rents

If the corporation rented or leased a vehicle, enter the total annual rent or lease expense paid or incurred during the year. Also complete Part V of Form 4562. If the corporation leased a vehicle for a term of 30 days or more, the deduction for vehicle lease expense may have to be reduced by

an amount includible in income called the inclusion amount. The corporation may have an inclusion amount if:

The lease term began:	And the vehicle's FMV on the first day of the lease exceeded:
Cars (excluding trucks and vans)	
After 12/31/13 but before 1/1/15	$18,500
After 12/31/12 but before 1/1/14	$19,000
After 12/31/07 but before 1/1/13	$18,500
Trucks and Vans	
After 12/31/09 but before 1/1/15	$19,000
After 12/31/08 but before 1/1/10	$18,500
After 12/31/07 but before 1/1/09	$19,000

See Pub. 463, Travel, Entertainment, Gift and Car Expenses, for instructions on figuring the inclusion amount. The inclusion amount for lease terms beginning in 2015 will be published in the Internal Revenue Bulletin in early 2015.

Line 17. Taxes and Licenses

Enter taxes paid or accrued during the tax year, but do not include the following.
- Federal income taxes.
- Foreign or U.S. possession income taxes if a foreign tax credit is claimed.
- Taxes not imposed on the corporation.
- Taxes, including state or local sales taxes, that are paid or incurred in connection with an acquisition or disposition of property (these taxes must be treated as a part of the cost of the acquired property or, in the case of a disposition, as a reduction in the amount realized on the disposition).
- Taxes assessed against local benefits that increase the value of the property assessed (such as for paving, etc.).
- Taxes deducted elsewhere on the return, such as those reflected in cost of goods sold.

See section 164(d) for information on apportionment of taxes on real property between seller and purchaser.

Line 18. Interest

Note. Do not offset interest income against interest expense.

The corporation must make an interest allocation if the proceeds of a loan were

used for more than one purpose (for example, to purchase a portfolio investment and to acquire an interest in a passive activity). See Temporary Regulations section 1.163-8T for the interest allocation rules.

Mutual savings banks, building and loan associations, and cooperative banks can deduct the amounts paid or credited to the accounts of depositors as dividends, interest, or earnings. See section 591.

Do not deduct the following interest.
- Interest on indebtedness incurred or continued to purchase or carry obligations if the interest is wholly exempt from income tax. See section 265(b) for special rules and exceptions for financial institutions. Also see section 265(b)(7) for a de minimis exception for financial institutions for certain tax-exempt bonds issued in 2009 and 2010.
- For cash basis taxpayers, prepaid interest allocable to years following the current tax year. For example, a cash basis calendar year taxpayer who in 2014 prepaid interest allocable to any period after 2014 can deduct only the amount allocable to 2014.
- Interest and carrying charges on straddles. Generally, these amounts must be capitalized. See section 263(g).
- Interest on debt allocable to the production of designated property by a corporation for its own use or for sale. The corporation must capitalize this interest. Also capitalize any interest on debt allocable to an asset used to produce the property. See section 263A(f) and Regulations sections 1.263A-8 through 1.263A-15 for definitions and more information.
- Interest paid or incurred on any portion of an underpayment of tax that is attributable to an understatement arising from an undisclosed listed transaction or an undisclosed reportable avoidance transaction (other than a listed transaction) entered into in tax years beginning after October 22, 2004.

Special rules apply to:
- Disqualified interest on certain indebtedness under section 163(j). See Form 8926, and the related instructions.
- Interest on which no tax is imposed (see section 163(j)). A corporation that owns an interest in a partnership, directly or indirectly, must treat its distributive share of the partnership liabilities, interest income, and interest expense as liabilities, income, and expenses of the corporation for purposes of applying the earnings stripping rules. For more details, see section 163(j)(8).
- Forgone interest on certain below-market-rate loans (see section 7872).

- Original issue discount (OID) on certain high-yield discount obligations. See section 163(e)(5) to determine the amount of the deduction for original issue discount that is deferred and the amount that is disallowed on a high-yield discount obligation. The rules under section 163(e)(5) do not apply to certain high-yield discount obligations issued after August 31, 2008 and before January 1, 2011. See section 163(e)(5)(F). Also see Notice 2010-11, 2010-4 I.R.B. 326.
- Interest which is allocable to unborrowed policy cash values of life insurance, endowment, or annuity contracts issued after June 8, 1997. See section 264(f). Attach a statement showing the computation of the deduction.
- Section 108(i) OID deduction. If the corporation issued a debt instrument with OID that is subject to section 108(i)(2) because of an election to defer the income from the cancellation of debt (COD), the interest deduction for this OID is deferred until the COD is includible in income. The accrued OID is allowed as a deduction ratably over the 5-year period that the income from COD is includible in income. The deduction is limited to the amount of COD subject to the section 108(i) election. In addition, a deferred COD deduction may be allowed as a deduction in the current year because of an accelerated event. See section 108(i)(5)(D).

Line 19. Charitable Contributions

Enter contributions or gifts actually paid within the tax year to or for the use of charitable and governmental organizations described in section 170(c) and any unused contributions carried over from prior years. Special rules and limits apply to contributions to organizations conducting lobbying activities. See section 170(f)(9).

Corporations reporting taxable income on the accrual method can elect to treat as paid during the tax year any contributions paid by the 15th day of the 3rd month after the end of the tax year if the contributions were authorized by the board of directors during the tax year. Attach a declaration to the return stating that the resolution authorizing the contributions was adopted by the board of directors during the tax year. The declaration must include the date the resolution was adopted. See Regulations section 1.170A-11.

Limitation on deduction. The total amount claimed cannot be more than 10% of taxable income (line 30) computed without regard to the following.
- Any deduction for contributions.
- The special deductions on line 29b.
- The limitation under section 249 on the deduction for bond premium.

- The domestic production activities deduction under section 199.
- Any net operating loss (NOL) carryback to the tax year under section 172.
- Any capital loss carryback to the tax year under section 1212(a)(1).

Suspension of 10% limitation for farmers and ranchers. A corporation that is a qualified farmer or rancher (as defined in section 170(b)(1)(E)) that does not have publicly traded stock, can deduct contributions of qualified conservation property without regard to the general 10% limit. The total amount of the contribution claimed for the qualified conservation property cannot exceed 100% of the excess of the corporation's taxable income (as computed above substituting "100%" for "10%") over all other allowable charitable contributions. Any excess qualified conservation contributions can be carried over to the next 15 years, subject to the 100% limitation. See section 170(b)(2)(B).

Carryover. Charitable contributions over the 10% limitation cannot be deducted for the tax year but can be carried over to the next 5 tax years.

Special rules apply if the corporation has an NOL carryover to the tax year. In figuring the charitable contributions deduction for the current tax year, the 10% limit is applied using the taxable income after taking into account any deduction for the NOL.

To figure the amount of any remaining NOL carryover to later years, taxable income must be modified (see section 172(b)). To the extent that contributions are used to reduce taxable income for this purpose and increase an NOL carryover, a contributions carryover is not allowed. See section 170(d)(2)(B).

Cash contributions. For contributions of cash, check, or other monetary gifts (regardless of the amount), the corporation must maintain a bank record, or a receipt, letter, or other written communication from the donee organization indicating the name of the organization, the date of the contribution, and the amount of the contribution.

Contributions of $250 or more. A corporation can deduct a contribution of $250 or more only if it gets a written acknowledgment from the donee organization that shows the amount of cash contributed, describes any property contributed (but not its value), and, either gives a description and a good faith estimate of the value of any goods or services provided in return for the contribution or states that no goods or services were provided in return for the contribution. The acknowledgment must be obtained by the due date (including extensions) of the corporation's return, or,

if earlier, the date the return is filed. Do not attach the acknowledgment to the tax return, but keep it with the corporation's records.

Contributions of property other than cash. If a corporation (other than a closely held or personal service corporation) contributes property other than cash and claims over a $500 deduction for the property, it must attach a statement to the return describing the kind of property contributed and the method used to determine its fair market value (FMV). Closely held corporations and personal service corporations must complete Form 8283, Noncash Charitable Contributions, and attach it to their returns. All other corporations generally must complete and attach Form 8283 to their returns for contributions of property (other than money) if the total claimed deduction for all property contributed was more than $5,000. Special rules apply to the contribution of certain property. See the Instructions for Form 8283.

Qualified conservation contributions. Special rules apply to qualified conservation contributions, including contributions of certain easements on buildings located in a registered historic district. See section 170(h) and Pub. 526, Charitable Contributions.

Other special rules. The corporation must reduce its deduction for contributions of certain capital gain property. See sections 170(e)(1) and 170(e)(5).

A larger deduction is allowed for certain contributions including:
- Inventory and other property to certain organizations for use in the care of the ill, needy, or infants (see section 170(e)(3)), including qualified contributions of "apparently wholesome food" made before January 1, 2015 (see section 170(e)(3)(C)); and
- Scientific equipment used for research to institutions of higher learning or to certain scientific research organizations (other than by personal holding companies and service organizations). See section 170(e)(4).

For more information on charitable contributions, including substantiation and recordkeeping requirements, see section 170 and the related regulations and Pub. 526. For other special rules that apply to corporations, see Pub. 542.

Line 20. Depreciation

Include on line 20 depreciation and the cost of certain property that the corporation elected to expense under section 179 from Form 4562, include amounts not claimed on Form 1125-A or elsewhere on the return. See Form 4562 and the Instructions for Form 4562.

Line 21. Depletion

See sections 613 and 613A for percentage depletion rates applicable to natural deposits. Also see section 291 for the limitation on the depletion deduction for iron ore and coal (including lignite).

Attach Form T (Timber), Forest Activities Schedule, if a deduction for depletion of timber is taken.

Foreign intangible drilling costs and foreign exploration and development costs must either be added to the corporation's basis for cost depletion purposes or be deducted ratably over a 10-year period. See sections 263(i), 616, and 617 for details.

See Pub. 535 for more information on depletion.

Line 23. Pension, Profit-Sharing, etc., Plans

Enter the deduction for contributions to qualified pension, profit-sharing, or other funded deferred compensation plans. Employers who maintain such a plan generally must file one of the forms listed below unless exempt from filing under regulations or other applicable guidance, even if the plan is not a qualified plan under the Internal Revenue Code. The filing requirement applies even if the corporation does not claim a deduction for the current tax year. There are penalties for failure to file these forms on time and for overstating the pension plan deduction. See sections 6652(e) and 6662(f). Also see the instructions for the applicable form.

Form 5500, Annual Return/Report of Employee Benefit Plan.

Form 5500-SF, Short Form Annual Return/Report of Small Employee Benefit Plan, instead of Form 5500, generally if under 100 participants at the beginning of the plan year.

Note. Form 5500 and Form 5500-SF must be filed electronically under the computerized ERISA Filing Acceptance System (EFAST2). For more information, see the EFAST2 website at _www.efast.dol.gov._

Form 5500-EZ, Annual Return of One-Participant (Owners and Their Spouses) Retirement Plan. File this form for a plan that only covers the owner (or the owner and his or her spouse) but only if the owner (or the owner and his or her spouse) owns the entire business.

Line 24. Employee Benefit Programs

Enter contributions to employee benefit programs not claimed elsewhere on the return (for example, insurance, health and welfare programs, etc.) that are not an incidental part of a pension, profit-sharing, etc., plan included on line 23.

Line 26. Other Deductions

Attach a statement, listing by type and amount, all allowable deductions that are not deductible elsewhere on Form 1120. Enter the total on line 26.

Examples of other deductions include the following. See Pub. 535 for details on other deductions that may apply to corporations.
- Amortization. See Part VI of Form 4562.
- Certain production costs of qualified film or television productions commencing before January 1, 2015, that the corporation elects to deduct. See section 181 and the related regulations.
- Certain business start-up and organizational costs (discussed earlier, under _Limitations on Deductions_).
- Reforestation costs. The corporation can elect to deduct up to $10,000 of qualifying reforestation expenses for each qualified timber property. The corporation can elect to amortize over 84 months any amount not deducted. See Pub. 535.
- Insurance premiums.
- Legal and professional fees.
- Supplies used and consumed in the business.
- Travel, meals, and entertainment expenses. Special rules apply (discussed below).
- Utilities.
- Ordinary losses from trade or business activities of a partnership (from Schedule K-1 (Form 1065 or 1065-B)). Do not offset ordinary income against ordinary losses. Instead, include the income on line 10. Show the partnership's name, address, and EIN on a separate statement attached to this return. If the amount is from more than one partnership, identify the amount from each partnership.
- Any extraterritorial income exclusion (from Form 8873).
- Any negative net section 481(a) adjustment. See _Section 481(a) adjustment_, earlier.
- Deduction for certain energy efficient commercial building property placed in service before January 1, 2015. See section 179D. Also see Notice 2006-52, 2006-26 I.R.B. 1175, as amplified and clarified by Notice 2008-40, 2008-14 I.R.B. 725, and as modified by Notice 2012-26, 2012-17 I.R.B. 847.
- Dividends paid in cash on stock held by an employee stock ownership plan. However, a deduction can only be taken for the dividends above if, according to the plan, the dividends are:

1. Paid in cash directly to the plan participants or beneficiaries;

2. Paid to the plan, which distributes them in cash to the plan participants or their beneficiaries no later than 90 days after the end of the plan year in which the dividends are paid;

3. At the election of such participants or their beneficiaries (a) payable as provided under (1) or (2) above, or (b) paid to the plan and reinvested in qualifying employer securities; or

4. Used to make payments on a loan described in section 404(a)(9).

See section 404(k) for more details and the limitation on certain dividends.

Do not deduct the following.
- Fines or penalties paid to a government for violating any law.
- Any amount that is allocable to a class of exempt income. See section 265(b) for exceptions.
- Lobbying expenses. However, see exceptions (discussed below).

Travel, meals, and entertainment. Subject to limitations and restrictions discussed below, a corporation can deduct ordinary and necessary travel, meals, and entertainment expenses paid or incurred in its trade or business. Also, special rules apply to deductions for gifts, skybox rentals, luxury water travel, convention expenses, and entertainment tickets. See section 274 and Pub. 463 for details.

Travel. The corporation cannot deduct travel expenses of any individual accompanying a corporate officer or employee, including a spouse or dependent of the officer or employee, unless:
- That individual is an employee of the corporation, and
- His or her travel is for a bona fide business purpose and would otherwise be deductible by that individual.

Meals and entertainment. Generally, the corporation can deduct only 50% of the amount otherwise allowable for meals and entertainment expenses paid or incurred in its trade or business. In addition (subject to exceptions under section 274(k)(2)):
- Meals must not be lavish or extravagant;
- A bona fide business discussion must occur during, immediately before, or immediately after the meal; and
- An employee of the corporation must be present at the meal.

See section 274(n)(3) for a special rule that applies to expenses for meals consumed by individuals subject to the hours of service limits of the Department of Transportation.

Membership dues. The corporation can deduct amounts paid or incurred for membership dues in civic or public service organizations, professional organizations (such as bar and medical associations), business leagues, trade associations, chambers of commerce, boards of trade, and real estate boards. However, no deduction is allowed if a principal purpose of the organization is to entertain, or provide entertainment facilities for, members or their guests. In addition, corporations cannot deduct membership dues in any club organized for business, pleasure, recreation, or other social purpose. This includes country clubs, golf and athletic clubs, airline and hotel clubs, and clubs operated to provide meals under conditions favorable to business discussion.

Entertainment facilities. The corporation cannot deduct an expense paid or incurred for a facility (such as a yacht or hunting lodge) used for an activity usually considered entertainment, amusement, or recreation.

Amounts treated as compensation. Generally, the corporation may be able to deduct otherwise nondeductible entertainment, amusement, or recreation expenses if the amounts are treated as compensation to the recipient and reported on Form W-2 for an employee or on Form 1099-MISC for an independent contractor.

However, if the recipient is an officer, director, beneficial owner (directly or indirectly), or other "specified individual" (as defined in section 274(e)(2)(B) and Regulations section 1.274-9(b)), special rules apply. See section 274(e)(2) and Regulations sections 1.274-9 and 1.274-10.

Lobbying expenses. Generally, lobbying expenses are not deductible. These expenses include:
- Amounts paid or incurred in connection with influencing federal or state legislation (but not local legislation) or
- Amounts paid or incurred in connection with any communication with certain federal executive branch officials in an attempt to influence the official actions or positions of the officials. See Regulations section 1.162-29 for the definition of "influencing legislation."

Dues and other similar amounts paid to certain tax-exempt organizations may not be deductible. See section 162(e)(3). If certain in-house lobbying expenditures do not exceed $2,000, they are deductible.

Line 28. Taxable Income Before NOL Deduction and Special Deductions

At-risk rules. Generally, special at-risk rules under section 465 apply to closely held corporations (see *Passive activity limitations,* earlier) engaged in any activity as a trade or business or for the production of income. These corporations

may have to adjust the amount on line 28. (See below.)

The at-risk rules do not apply to:
- Holding real property placed in service by the taxpayer before 1987;
- Equipment leasing under sections 465(c)(4), (5), and (6); or
- Any qualifying business of a qualified corporation under section 465(c)(7).

However, the at-risk rules do apply to the holding of mineral property.

If the at-risk rules apply, adjust the amount on this line for any section 465(d) losses. These losses are limited to the amount for which the corporation is at risk for each separate activity at the close of the tax year. If the corporation is involved in one or more activities, any of which incurs a loss for the year, report the losses for each activity separately. Attach Form 6198, At-Risk Limitations, showing the amount at risk and gross income and deductions for the activities with the losses.

If the corporation sells or otherwise disposes of an asset or its interest (either total or partial) in an activity to which the at-risk rules apply, determine the net profit or loss from the activity by combining the gain or loss on the sale or disposition with the profit or loss from the activity. If the corporation has a net loss, it may be limited because of the at-risk rules.

Treat any loss from an activity not allowed for the tax year as a deduction allocable to the activity in the next tax year.

Line 29a. Net Operating Loss Deduction

A corporation can use the NOL incurred in one tax year to reduce its taxable income in another tax year. Enter on line 29a the total NOL carryovers from other tax years, but do not enter more than the corporation's taxable income (after special deductions). Attach a statement showing the computation of the NOL deduction. Complete item 12 on Schedule K.

The following special rules apply.
- A personal service corporation may not carry back or forward an NOL to or from any tax year to which an election under section 444 to have a tax year other than a required tax year applies.
- A corporate equity reduction interest loss may not be carried back to a tax year preceding the year of the equity reduction transaction (see section 172(b)(1)(E)).
- If an ownership change (described in section 382(g)) occurs, the amount of the taxable income of a loss corporation that may be offset by the pre-change NOL carryovers may be limited. See section 382 and the related regulations. A loss corporation must include the information statement as provided in Regulations

section 1.382-11(a), with its income tax return for each tax year that it is a loss corporation in which an ownership shift, equity structures shift, or other transaction described in Temporary Regulations section 1.382-2T(a)(2)(i) occur. If the corporation makes the closing-of-the-books election, see Regulations section 1.382-6(b).

The limitations under section 382 do not apply to certain ownership changes after February 17, 2009, made pursuant to a restructuring plan under the Emergency Economic Stabilization Act of 2008. See section 382(n).

For guidance in applying section 382 to loss corporations whose instruments were acquired by Treasury under certain programs under the Emergency Economic Stabilization Act of 2008, see Notice 2010-2, 2010-2 I.R.B. 251.
- If a corporation acquires control of another corporation (or acquires its assets in a reorganization), the amount of pre-acquisition losses that may offset recognized built-in gain may be limited (see section 384).
- If a corporation elects the alternative tax on qualifying shipping activities under section 1354, no deduction is allowed for an NOL attributable to the qualifying shipping activities to the extent that the loss is carried forward from a tax year preceding the first tax year for which the alternative tax election was made. See section 1358(b)(2).
- If a corporation has a loss attributable to a disaster, special rules apply. See the Instructions for Form 1139.

For more details on the NOL deduction, see section 172 and the Instructions for Form 1139.

Line 29b. Special Deductions

See the instructions for Schedule C.

Line 30. Taxable Income

Minimum taxable income. The corporation's taxable income cannot be less than the largest of the following amounts.
- The inversion gain of the corporation for the tax year, if the corporation is an expatriated entity or a partner in an expatriated entity. See section 7874(a).
- The sum of the corporation's excess inclusions from its residual interest in a REMIC from Schedules Q (Form 1066), line 2c, and the corporation's taxable income determined solely with respect to its ownership and high-yield interests in FASITs. See sections 860E(a) and 860J (repealed).

Net operating loss (NOL). If line 30 (figured without regard to the items listed above under minimum taxable income), is zero or less, the corporation may have an

NOL that can be carried back or forward as a deduction to other tax years.

Generally, a corporation first carries back an NOL 2 tax years. However, the corporation can elect to waive the carryback period and instead carry the NOL forward to future tax years. See the instructions for Schedule K, item 11 below.

Special rules and exceptions to the 2-year carryback period apply to certain NOLs. See the Instructions for Form 1139 for details on these special rules and other elections that may be available.

Merchant Marine capital construction fund. To take a deduction for amounts contributed to a capital construction fund (CCF), reduce the amount that would otherwise be entered on line 30 by the amount of the deduction. On the dotted line next to the entry space, enter "CCF" and the amount of the deduction. For more information, see section 7518.

Line 33. Estimated Tax Penalty

Generally, the corporation does not have to file Form 2220 because the IRS can figure the penalty amount, if any, and bill the corporation. However, even if the corporation does not owe the penalty, it must complete and attach Form 2220 if:
• The annualized income or adjusted method is used, or
• The corporation is a large corporation (as defined in the Instructions for Form 2220) computing its first required installment based on the prior year's tax.

If Form 2220 is attached, check the box on line 33, and enter any penalty on this line.

Line 34. Amount Owed

If the corporation cannot pay the full amount of tax owed, it can apply for an installment agreement online. The corporation can apply for an installment agreement online if:
• It cannot pay the full amount shown on line 34,
• The total amount owed is $25,000 or less, and
• The corporation can pay the liability in full in 24 months.
To apply using the Online Payment Agreement Application, go to irs.gov., click on "Tools." Then click on "Online Payment Agreement."

Under an installment agreement, the corporation can pay what it owes in monthly installments. There are certain conditions that must be met to enter into and maintain an installment agreement, such as paying the liability within 24 months and making all required deposits and timely filing tax returns during the length of the agreement.

If the installment agreement is accepted, the corporation will be charged

a fee and it will be subject to penalties and interest on the amount of tax not paid by the due date of the return.

Line 36

Enter the amount of any overpayment that should be refunded or applied to next year's estimated tax.

Note. This election to apply some or all of the overpayment amount to the corporation's 2015 estimated tax cannot be changed at a later date.

Direct deposit of refund. If the corporation wants its refund directly deposited into its checking or savings account at any U.S. bank or other financial institution instead of having a check sent to the corporation, complete Form 8050, Direct Deposit of Corporate Tax Refund, and attach it to the corporation's tax return.

Schedule C. Dividends and Special Deductions

For purposes of the 20% ownership test on lines 1 through 7, the percentage of stock owned by the corporation is based on voting power and value of the stock. Preferred stock described in section 1504(a)(4) is not taken into account.

Consolidated returns. Corporations filing a consolidated return should see Regulations sections 1.1502-13, 1.1502-26, and 1.1502-27 before completing Schedule C.

Corporations filing a consolidated return must not report as dividends on Schedule C any amounts received from corporations within the tax consolidation group. Such dividends are eliminated in consolidation rather than offset by the dividends-received deduction.

Line 1, Column (a)

Enter dividends (except those received on debt-financed stock acquired after July 18, 1984—see section 246A) that are:
• Received from less-than-20%-owned domestic corporations subject to income tax, and
• Qualified for the 70% deduction under section 243(a)(1).

Also include on line 1 the following.
• Taxable distributions from an IC-DISC or former DISC that are designated as eligible for the 70% deduction and certain dividends of Federal Home Loan Banks. See section 246(a)(2).
• Dividends (except those received on debt-financed stock acquired after July 18, 1984) from a regulated investment company (RIC). The amount of dividends eligible for the dividends-received deduction under section 243 is limited by section 854(b). The corporation should receive a notice from the RIC specifying

the amount of dividends that qualify for the deduction.

Report so-called dividends or earnings received from mutual savings banks, etc., as interest. Do not treat them as dividends.

Line 2, Column (a)

Enter on line 2:
• Dividends (except those received on debt-financed stock acquired after July 18, 1984) that are received from 20%-or-more-owned domestic corporations subject to income tax and that are subject to the 80% deduction under section 243(c), and
• Taxable distributions from an IC-DISC or former DISC that are considered eligible for the 80% deduction.

Line 3, Column (a)

Enter the following.
• Dividends received on debt-financed stock acquired after July 18, 1984, from domestic and foreign corporations subject to income tax that would otherwise be subject to the dividends-received deduction under section 243(a)(1), 243(c), or 245(a). Generally, debt-financed stock is stock that the corporation acquired by incurring a debt (for example, it borrowed money to buy the stock).
• Dividends received from a RIC on debt-financed stock. The amount of dividends eligible for the dividends-received deduction is limited by section 854(b). The corporation should receive a notice from the RIC specifying the amount of dividends that qualify for the deduction.

Line 3, Columns (b) and (c)

Dividends received on debt-financed stock acquired after July 18, 1984, are not entitled to the full 70% or 80% dividends-received deduction. The 70% or 80% deduction is reduced by a percentage that is related to the amount of debt incurred to acquire the stock. See section 246A. Also see section 245(a) before making this computation for an additional limitation that applies to dividends received from foreign corporations. Attach a statement to Form 1120 showing how the amount on line 3, column (c), was figured.

Line 4, Column (a)

Enter dividends received on preferred stock of a less-than-20%-owned public utility that is subject to income tax and is allowed the deduction provided in section 247 for dividends paid.

Line 5, Column (a)

Enter dividends received on preferred stock of a 20%-or-more-owned public utility that is subject to income tax and is allowed the deduction provided in section 247 for dividends paid.

Worksheet for Schedule C, line 9 — *Keep for Your Records*

1. Refigure line 28, page 1, Form 1120, without any domestic production activities deduction, any adjustment under section 1059, and without any capital loss carryback to the tax year under section 1212(a)(1) . . . . . . 1. _____

2. Complete lines 10, 11, and 12, column (c), and enter the total here . . . . 2. _____

3. Subtract line 2 from line 1 . . . . 3. _____

4. Multiply line 3 by 80% . . . . 4. _____

5. Add lines 2, 5, 7, and 8, column (c), and the part of the deduction on line 3, column (c), that is attributable to dividends from 20%-or-more-owned corporations . . . . 5. _____

6. Enter the smaller of line 4 or 5. If line 5 is greater than line 4, stop here; enter the amount from line 6 on line 9, column (c), and do not complete the rest of this worksheet . . . . 6. _____

7. Enter the total amount of dividends from 20%-or-more-owned corporations that are included on lines 2, 3, 5, 7, and 8, column (a) . . . . 7. _____

8. Subtract line 7 from line 3 . . . . 8. _____

9. Multiply line 8 by 70% . . . . 9. _____

10. Subtract line 5 from line 9, column (c) . . . . 10. _____

11. Enter the smaller of line 9 or line 10 . . . . 11. _____

12. **Dividends-received deduction after limitation** (sec. 246(b)). Add lines 6 and 11. Enter the result here and on line 9, column (c) . . . . . . 12. _____

Line 6, Column (a)

Enter the U.S.-source portion of dividends that:
* Are received from less-than-20%-owned foreign corporations, and
* Qualify for the 70% deduction under section 245(a). To qualify for the 70% deduction, the corporation must own at least 10% of the stock of the foreign corporation by vote and value.

Also include dividends received from a less-than-20%-owned FSC that:
* Are attributable to income treated as effectively connected with the conduct of a trade or business within the United States (excluding foreign trade income), and
* Qualify for the 70% deduction under section 245(c)(1)(B).

Line 7, Column (a)

Enter the U.S.-source portion of dividends that:
* Are received from 20%-or-more-owned foreign corporations, and
* Qualify for the 80% deduction under section 245(a).

Also include dividends received from 20%-or-more-owned FSC that:

* Are attributable to income treated as effectively connected with the conduct of a trade or business within the United States (excluding foreign trade income), and
* Qualify for the 80% deduction under section 245(c)(1)(B).

Line 8, Column (a)

Enter dividends received from wholly owned foreign subsidiaries that are eligible for the 100% deduction under section 245(b).

In general, the deduction under section 245(b) applies to dividends paid out of the earnings and profits of a foreign corporation for a tax year during which:
* All of its outstanding stock is directly or indirectly owned by the domestic corporation receiving the dividends, and
* All of its gross income from all sources is effectively connected with the conduct of a trade or business within the United States.

Line 9, Column (c)

Generally, line 9, column (c), cannot exceed the amount from the worksheet below. However, in a year in which an NOL occurs, this limitation does not apply even if the loss is created by the dividends-received deduction. See sections 172(d) and 246(b).

Line 10, Columns (a) and (c)

Small business investment companies operating under the Small Business Investment Act of 1958 (see 15 U.S.C. 661 and following) must enter dividends that are received from domestic corporations subject to income tax even though a deduction is allowed for the entire amount of those dividends. To claim the 100% deduction on line 10, column (c), the company must file with its return a statement that it was a federal licensee under the Small Business Investment Act

of 1958 at the time it received the dividends.

Line 11, Columns (a) and (c)

Enter only dividends that qualify under section 243(b) for the 100% dividends-received deduction described in section 243(a)(3). Corporations taking this deduction are subject to the provisions of section 1561.

The 100% deduction does not apply to affiliated group members that are joining in the filing of a consolidated return.

Line 12, Column (a)

Enter dividends from FSCs that are attributable to foreign trade income and that are eligible for the 100% deduction provided in section 245(c)(1)(A).

Line 13, Column (a)

Enter foreign dividends not reportable on lines 3, 6, 7, 8, 11, or 12 of column (a). Include on line 13 the corporation's share of distributions from a section 1291 fund from Form 8621, to the extent that the amounts are taxed as dividends under section 301. See Form 8621 and the Instructions for Form 8621.

Line 14, Column (a)

Include income constructively received from CFCs under subpart F. This amount should equal the total subpart F income reported on Schedule I of Form 5471, Information Return of U.S. Persons With Respect To Certain Foreign Corporations.

Line 15, Column (a)

Include gross-up for taxes deemed paid under sections 902 and 960.

Line 16, Column (a)

Enter taxable distributions from an IC-DISC or former DISC that are designated as not eligible for a dividends-received deduction.

No deduction is allowed under section 243 for a dividend from an IC-DISC or former DISC (as defined in section 992(a)) to the extent the dividend:
* Is paid out of the corporation's accumulated IC-DISC income or previously taxed income, or
* Is a deemed distribution under section 995(b)(1).

Line 17, Column (a)

Include the following.

1. Dividends (other than capital gain distributions reported on Schedule D (Form 1120) and exempt-interest dividends) that are received from RICs and that are not subject to the 70% deduction.

2. Dividends from tax-exempt organizations.

3. Dividends (other than capital gain distributions) received from a REIT that,

Instructions for Form 1120

for the tax year of the trust in which the dividends are paid, qualifies under sections 856 through 860.

4. Dividends not eligible for a dividends-received deduction, which include the following.

a. Dividends received on any share of stock held for less than 46 days during the 91-day period beginning 45 days before the ex-dividend date. When counting the number of days the corporation held the stock, you cannot count certain days during which the corporation's risk of loss was diminished. See section 246(c)(4) and Regulations section 1.246-5 for more details.

b. Dividends attributable to periods totaling more than 366 days that the corporation received on any share of preferred stock held for less than 91 days during the 181-day period that began 90 days before the ex-dividend date. When counting the number of days the corporation held the stock, you cannot count certain days during which the corporation's risk of loss was diminished. See section 246(c)(4) and Regulations section 1.246-5 for more details. Preferred dividends attributable to periods totaling less than 367 days are subject to the 46-day holding period rule, above.

c. Dividends on any share of stock to the extent the corporation is under an obligation (including a short sale) to make related payments with respect to positions in substantially similar or related property.

5. Any other taxable dividend income not properly reported elsewhere on Schedule C.

If patronage dividends or per-unit retain allocations are included on line 17, identify the total of these amounts in a statement attached to Form 1120.

Line 18, Column (c)

Section 247 allows public utilities a deduction of 40% of the smaller of (a) dividends paid on their preferred stock during the tax year, or (b) taxable income computed without regard to this deduction. In a year in which an NOL occurs, compute the deduction without regard to section 247(a)(1)(B). See section 172(d).

Schedule J.
Tax Computation and Payment

Part I—Tax Computation

Line 1

If the corporation is a member of a controlled group, check the box on line 1. Complete and attach Schedule O (Form 1120), Consent Plan and Apportionment Schedule for a Controlled Group. Component members of a controlled group must use Schedule O to report the apportionment of taxable income, income tax, and certain tax benefits between the members of the group. See Schedule O and the Instructions for Schedule O for more information.

Line 2

If the corporation is a member of a controlled group and is filing Schedule O (Form 1120), enter the corporation's tax from Part III of Schedule O. Most corporations that are not members of a controlled group and not filing a consolidated return figure their tax by using the Tax Rate Schedule below. Qualified personal service corporations should see instructions below.

Tax Rate Schedule

If taxable income (line 30, Form 1120) on page 1 is:

Over—	But not over—	Tax is:	Of the amount over—
$0	$50,000	15%	$0
50,000	75,000	$ 7,500 + 25%	50,000
75,000	100,000	13,750 + 34%	75,000
100,000	335,000	22,250 + 39%	100,000
335,000	10,000,000	113,900 + 34%	335,000
10,000,000	15,000,000	3,400,000 + 35%	10,000,000
15,000,000	18,333,333	5,150,000 + 38%	15,000,000
18,333,333	—	35%	0

Qualified personal service corporation. A qualified personal service corporation is taxed at a flat rate of 35% on taxable income. If the corporation is a qualified personal service corporation, check the box on line 2 even if the corporation has no tax liability.

A corporation is a qualified personal service corporation if it meets both of the following tests.

1. Substantially all of the corporation's activities involve the performance of services in the fields of health, law, engineering, architecture, accounting, actuarial science, performing arts, or consulting.

2. At least 95% of the corporation's stock, by value, is directly or indirectly owned by

a. Employees performing the services,

b. Retired employees who had performed the services listed above,

c. Any estate of an employee or retiree described above, or

d. Any person who acquired the stock of the corporation as a result of the death of an employee or retiree (but only for the 2-year period beginning on the date of the employee's or retiree's death).

Mutual savings bank conducting life insurance business. The tax under section 594 consists of the sum of (a), a partial tax computed on Form 1120 on the taxable income of the bank, determined without regard to income or deductions allocable to the life insurance department, and (b), a partial tax on the taxable income computed on Form 1120-L of the life insurance department. Enter the combined tax on line 2. Attach Form 1120-L as a schedule (and identify it as such), together with the annual statements and schedules required to be filed with Form 1120-L. See Regulations section 1.6012-2(c)(1)(ii).

Exception for insurance companies filing their Federal income tax returns electronically. If an insurance company files its income tax return electronically, it should not include the annual statements and schedules required to be filed with Form 1120-L. However, such statements must be available at all times for inspection by the IRS and retained for so long as such statements may be material in the administration of any internal revenue law.

Deferred tax under section 1291. If the corporation was a shareholder in a PFIC and received an excess distribution or disposed of its investment in the PFIC during the year, it must include the increase in taxes due under section 1291(c)(2) (from Form 8621) in the total for line 2. On the dotted line next to line 2, enter "Section 1291" and the amount.

Do not include on line 2 any interest due under section 1291(c)(3). Instead, include the amount of interest owed on Schedule J, line 9f.

For more information on reporting the deferred tax and interest, see the Instructions for Form 8621.

Additional tax under section 197(f). A corporation that elects to recognize gain and pay tax on the sale of a section 197 intangible under the related person exception to the anti-churning rules should include any additional tax due in the total for line 2. On the dotted line next to line 2, enter "Section 197" and the amount. See section 197(f)(9)(B)(ii).

Line 3

 A corporation that is not a small corporation exempt from the AMT may be required to file Form 4626, Alternative Minimum Tax—Corporations, if it claims certain credits, even though it does not owe any AMT. See the Instructions for Form 4626 for details.

Unless the corporation is treated as a small corporation exempt from the AMT, it may owe the AMT if it has any of the adjustments and tax preference items listed on Form 4626. The corporation must file Form 4626 if its taxable income (or loss) before the NOL deduction, combined with these adjustments and tax preference items is more than the smaller of $40,000 or the corporation's allowable exemption amount (from Form 4626). For this purpose, taxable income does not include the NOL deduction.

See Form 4626 for definitions and details on how to figure the tax.

Line 5

Line 5a. To find out when a corporation can take the credit for payment of income tax to a foreign country or U.S. possession, see Form 1118, Foreign Tax Credit — Corporations.

Line 5b. Enter any qualified electric vehicle passive activity credits from prior years allowed for the current tax year from Form 8834, Qualified Electric Vehicle Credit, line 7. Attach Form 8834. Include on line 5b any credits from Form 5735, American Samoa Economic Development Credit. See the Instructions for Form 5735. Attach Form 5735.

Line 5c. Enter on line 5c the allowable credit from Form 3800, Part II, line 38.

The corporation is required to file Form 3800, General Business Credit, to claim any of the business credits. See the Instructions for Form 3800 for exceptions. For a list of allowable credits, see Form 3800. Also, see the applicable credit form and its instructions.

Line 5d. To figure the minimum tax credit and any carryforward of that credit, complete and attach Form 8827, Credit for Prior Year Minimum Tax—Corporations.

Line 5e. Enter the allowable credits from Form 8912, Credit to Holders of Tax Credit Bonds, line 12.

Line 8

A corporation is taxed as a personal holding company under section 542 if:
• At least 60% of its adjusted ordinary gross income for the tax year is personal holding company income, and
• At any time during the last half of the tax year more than 50% in value of its outstanding stock is directly or indirectly owned by five or fewer individuals.

See Schedule PH (Form 1120) for definitions and details on how to figure the tax.

Line 9

Include any of the following taxes and interest.

Line 9a. Recapture of investment credit. If the corporation disposed of investment credit property or changed its use before the end of its useful life or recovery period, or is required to recapture a qualifying therapeutic discovery project grant, enter the increase in tax from Form 4255, Recapture of Investment Credit.

Line 9b. Recapture of low-income housing credit. If the corporation disposed of property (or there was a reduction in the qualified basis of the property) for which it took the low-income housing credit, and the corporation did not follow the procedures that would have prevented recapture of the credit, it may owe a tax. See Form 8611, Recapture of Low-Income Housing Credit.

Line 9c. Interest due under the look-back method-completed long-term contracts. If the corporation used the look-back method under section 460(b)(2) for certain long-term contracts, use Form 8697, Interest Computation Under the Look-Back Method for Completed Long-Term Contracts, to figure the interest the corporation may have to include. See the Instructions for Form 8697.

Line 9d. Interest due under the look-back method-income forecast method. If the corporation used the look-back method for property depreciated under the income forecast method, use Form 8866, Interest Computation Under the Look-Back Method for Property Depreciated Under the Income Forecast Method, to figure any interest due or to be refunded. See the Instructions for Form 8866.

Line 9e. Alternative tax on qualifying shipping activities. Enter any alternative tax on qualifying shipping activities from Form 8902.

Line 9f. Other. Include on line 9f additional taxes and interest such as the following. Attach a statement showing the computation of each item included in the total for line 9f and identify the applicable Code section and the type of tax or interest.
• Recapture of Indian employment credit. Generally, if an employer terminates the employment of a qualified employee less than 1 year after the date of initial employment, any Indian employment credit allowed for a prior tax year because of wages paid or incurred to that employee must be recaptured. For details, see Form 8845 and section 45A.
• Recapture of new markets credit (see Form 8874, New Markets Credit, and

Form 8874-B, Notice of Recapture Event for New Markets Credit).
• Recapture of employer-provided childcare facilities and services credit (see Form 8882).
• Tax and interest on a nonqualified withdrawal from a capital construction fund (section 7518(g)).
• Interest on deferred tax attributable to (a) installment sales of certain timeshares and residential lots (section 453(l)(3)) and (b) certain nondealer installment obligations (section 453A(c)).
• Interest due on deferred gain (section 1260(b)).
• Interest due under section 1291(c)(3). See Form 8621 and the Instructions for Form 8621.

Line 11

Include any deferred tax on the termination of a section 1294 election applicable to shareholders in a qualified electing fund in the amount entered on line 11.

Subtract the following amounts from the total for line 11.
• Deferred tax on the corporation's share of undistributed earnings of a qualified electing fund. See the Instructions for Form 8621.
• Deferred LIFO recapture tax (section 1363(d)). This tax is the part of the LIFO recapture tax that will be deferred and paid with Form 1120S in the future. To figure the deferred tax, first figure the total LIFO recapture tax. Follow the steps below to figure the total LIFO recapture tax and the deferred amount. Also see, *Line 10, Other Income,* earlier.

Step 1. Figure the tax on the corporation's income including the LIFO recapture amount. Complete Schedule J through line 10.

Step 2. Using a separate worksheet, complete Schedule J again, but do not include the LIFO recapture amount in the corporation's taxable income.

Step 3. Compare the tax in Step 2 to the tax in Step 1. The difference between the two is the LIFO recapture tax.

Step 4. Multiply the amount figured in Step 3 by 75%. The result is the deferred LIFO recapture tax.

How to report. Attach a statement showing the computation of each item included in, or subtracted from, the total for line 11. On the dotted line next to line 11, specify (a) the applicable Code section, (b) the type of tax, and (c) enter the amount of tax. For example, if the corporation is deferring a $100 LIFO recapture tax, subtract this amount from the total on line 11, then enter "Section

1363-Deferred Tax-$100" on the dotted line next to line 11.

Part II–Payments and Refundable Credits

Line 13. Enter any estimated tax payments the corporation made for the tax year.

Beneficiaries of trusts. If the corporation is the beneficiary of a trust, and the trust makes a section 643(g) election to credit its estimated tax payments to its beneficiaries, include the corporation's share of the payment in the total for line 13. Enter "T" and the amount on the dotted line next to the entry space.

Special estimated tax payments for certain life insurance companies. If the corporation is required to make or apply special estimated tax payments (SETP) under section 847 in addition to its regular estimated tax payments, enter on line 13, the corporation's total estimated tax payments. On the dotted line next to line 13, enter "Form 8816" and the amount. Attach a statement showing your computation of estimated tax payments. See Form 8816, Special Loss Discount Account and Special Estimated Tax Payments for Insurance Companies.

Line 14. If the corporation overpaid estimated tax, it may be able to get a quick refund by filing Form 4466. The overpayment must be at least 10% of the corporation's expected income tax liability and at least $500. File Form 4466 after the end of the corporation's tax year, and no later than the 15th day of the third month after the end of the tax year. Form 4466 must be filed before the corporation files its tax return.

Line 17. If the corporation had federal income tax withheld from any payments it received because, for example, it failed to give the payer its correct EIN or was otherwise subjected to back-up withholding, include the amount withheld in the total for line 17.

Line 19. Refundable Credits

Line 19a. Credit from Form 2439. Enter any credit from Form 2439, Notice to Shareholder of Undistributed Long-Term Capital Gains, for the corporation's share of the tax paid by a regulated investment company (RIC) or a real estate investment trust (REIT) on undistributed long-term capital gains included in the corporation's income. Attach Form 2439.

Line 19b. Credit for federal tax on fuels. Enter the total income tax credit claimed on Form 4136, Credit for Federal Tax Paid on Fuels. Attach Form 4136.

Line 19c. Refundable credits from Form 8827. If the corporation elected to claim certain unused minimum tax credits instead of claiming any additional first-year special depreciation allowance for eligible property, see the instructions for Form 8827. Enter on line 19c the amounts from Form 8827, line 8c.

Line 19d. Other. Include on line 19d any other refundable credit the corporation is claiming, including the following. Attach a statement listing the type of credit and the amount of the credit.
• Credit for tax on ozone-depleting chemicals. See section 4682(g)(2).
• Credit under section 960(b). If an increase in the limitation under section 960(b) exceeds the total tax on Schedule J, line 11, for the tax year, the amount of the excess is deemed an overpayment of tax for the tax year. See section 960(b) for more information regarding the circumstances under which such an excess arises.

Schedule K. Other Information

Complete all items that apply to the corporation.

Question 2

See the list of Principal Business Activity Codes later in the instructions. Using the list of codes and activities, determine from which activity the corporation derives the highest percentage of its total receipts. Enter on lines 2a, 2b, and 2c the principal business activity code number, the corporation's business activity, and a description of the principal product or service of the corporation.

Question 3

Check the "Yes" box for question 3 if:
• The corporation is a subsidiary in an affiliated group (defined below), but is not filing a consolidated return for the tax year with that group, or
• The corporation is a subsidiary in a parent-subsidiary controlled group. For a definition of a parent-subsidiary controlled group, see the Instructions for Schedule O (Form 1120).

Any corporation that meets either of the requirements above should check the "Yes" box. This applies even if the corporation is a subsidiary member of one group and the parent corporation of another.

Note. If the corporation is an "excluded member" of a controlled group (see definition in the Instructions for Schedule O (Form 1120)), it is still considered a member of a controlled group for this purpose.

Affiliated group. An affiliated group is one or more chains of includible corporations (section 1504(a)) connected through stock ownership with a common parent corporation. The common parent must be an includible corporation and the following requirements must be met.

1. The common parent must own directly stock that represents at least 80% of the total voting power and at least 80% of the total value of the stock of at least one of the other includible corporations.

2. Stock that represents at least 80% of the total voting power and at least 80% of the total value of the stock of each of the other corporations (except for the common parent) must be owned directly by one or more of the other includible corporations.

For this purpose, the term "stock" generally does not include any stock that (a) is nonvoting, (b) is nonconvertible, (c) is limited and preferred as to dividends and does not participate significantly in corporate growth, and (d) has redemption and liquidation rights that do not exceed the issue price of the stock (except for a reasonable redemption or liquidation premium). See section 1504(a)(4).

Question 4. Constructive Ownership of the Corporation

For purposes of question 4, the constructive ownership rules of section 267(c) (excluding section 267(c)(3)) apply to ownership of interests in corporate stock and ownership of interests in profit, loss, or capital of a partnership. If the corporation checked "Yes" to question 4a or 4b, complete and attach Schedule G (Form 1120), Information on Certain Persons Owning the Corporation's Voting Stock.

Question 5. Constructive Ownership of Other Entities

For purposes of determining the corporation's constructive ownership of other entities, the constructive ownership rules of section 267(c) (excluding section 267(c)(3)) apply to ownership of interests in partnerships and trusts as well as corporate stock. Generally, if an entity (a corporation, partnership, or trust) is owned, directly or indirectly, by or for another entity (corporation, partnership, estate, or trust), the owned entity is considered to be owned proportionately by or for the owners (shareholders, partners, or beneficiaries) of the owning entity.

Question 5a

List each foreign or domestic corporation not included on Form 851, Affiliations Schedule, in which the corporation, at the end of the tax year, owned directly 20% or more, or owned, directly or indirectly, 50% or more of the total voting power of all classes of stock entitled to vote. Indicate the name of the corporation, EIN (if any), country of incorporation, and the percentage interest owned, directly or indirectly, in the total voting power. List the parent corporation of an affiliated group of corporations filing a consolidated tax return rather than the subsidiary members except for subsidiary members in which an interest is owned, directly or indirectly, independent of the interest owned, directly or indirectly, in the parent corporation. List a corporation owned through a disregarded entity rather than the disregarded entity.

Question 5b

List each foreign or domestic partnership in which the corporation, at the end of the tax year, owned directly an interest of 20% or more, or owned, directly or indirectly, an interest of 50% or more in the profit, loss, or capital of the partnership. List each trust in which the corporation, at the end of the tax year, owned directly an interest of 20% or more, or owned, directly or indirectly, an interest of 50% or more in the trust beneficial interest. Indicate the name, EIN (if any), country of organization, and the maximum percentage interest owned, directly or indirectly, in the profit, loss, or capital of the partnership at the end of the partnership tax year, or, for a trust, the percentage interest owned in the trust beneficial interest. List a partnership or trust owned through a disregarded entity rather than the disregarded entity.

Maximum percentage owned in partnership profit, loss, or capital. For the purposes of question 5b, the term "maximum percentage owned" means the highest percentage of interest in a partnership's profit, loss, or capital as of the end of the partnership's tax year, as determined under the partnership agreement, when taking into account the constructive ownership rules earlier. If the partnership agreement does not express the partner's share of profit, loss, and capital as fixed percentages, use a reasonable method in arriving at the percentage items for the purposes of completing question 5b. Such method must be consistent with the partnership agreement. The method used to compute a percentage share of profit, loss, and capital must be applied consistently from year to year. Maintain records to support the determination of the share of profits, losses, and share of capital.

Example. Corporation A owns, directly, a 50% interest in the profit, loss, or capital of Partnership B. Corporation A also owns, directly, a 15% interest in the profit, loss, or capital of Partnership C and owns, directly, 15% of the voting stock of Corporation D. Partnership B owns, directly, a 70% interest in the profit, loss, or capital of Partnership C and owns, directly, 70% of the voting stock of

Corporation D. Corporation A owns, indirectly, through Partnership B, a 35% interest (50% of 70%) in the profit, loss, or capital of Partnership C and owns, indirectly, 35% of the voting stock of Corporation D. Corporation A owns, directly or indirectly, a 50% interest in the profit, loss, or capital of Partnership C (15% directly and 35% indirectly), and owns, directly or indirectly, 50% of the voting stock of Corporation D (15% directly and 35% indirectly).

Corporation A reports in its answer to question 5a that it owns, directly or indirectly, 50% of the voting stock of Corporation D. Corporation A reports in its answer to question 5b that it owns, directly, an interest of 50% in the profit, loss, or capital of Partnership B and owns, directly or indirectly, 50% of the profit, loss, or capital of Partnership C.

Question 7

Check the "Yes" box if one foreign person owned at least 25% of (a) the total voting power of all classes of stock of the corporation entitled to vote, or (b) the total value of all classes of stock of the corporation.

The constructive ownership rules of section 318 apply in determining if a corporation is foreign owned. See section 6038A(c)(5) and the related regulations.

Enter on line 7a the percentage owned by the foreign person specified in question 7. On line 7b, enter the name of the owner's country.

Note. If there is more than one 25%-or-more foreign owner, complete lines 7a and 7b for the foreign person with the highest percentage of ownership.

Foreign person. The term "foreign person" means:
• An individual who is not a citizen or resident of the United States;
• An individual who is a citizen or resident of a U.S. possession who is not otherwise a citizen or resident of the United States;
• Any partnership, association, company, or corporation that is not created or organized in the United States;
• Any foreign estate or trust within the meaning of section 7701(a)(31); or
• A foreign government (or one of its agencies or instrumentalities) to the extent that it is engaged in the conduct of a commercial activity as described in section 892.

However, the term "foreign person" does not include any foreign person who consents to the filing of a joint U.S. income tax return.

Owner's country. For individuals, the term "owner's country" means the country of residence. For all others, it is the

country where incorporated, organized, created, or administered.

Requirement to file Form 5472. If the corporation checked "Yes," it may have to file Form 5472, Information Return of a 25% Foreign-Owned U.S. Corporation or a Foreign Corporation Engaged in a U.S. Trade or Business. Generally, a 25% foreign-owned corporation that had a reportable transaction with a foreign or domestic related party during the tax year must file Form 5472. See the Instructions for Form 5472, for filing instructions and penalties for failure to file.

Item 9

Show any tax-exempt interest received or accrued. Include any exempt-interest dividends received as a shareholder in a mutual fund or other RIC. Also, if required, include the same amount on Schedule M-1, line 7 (or Schedule M-3, Part II, line 13, if applicable).

Item 11

If the corporation has an NOL, it generally can elect to waive the entire carryback period for the NOL and instead carry the NOL forward to future tax years. To do so, check the box on line 11 and file the tax return by its due date, including extensions. Do not attach the statement described in Temporary Regulations section 301.9100-12T. Once made, the election is irrevocable.

If the corporation timely filed its return for the loss year without making the election, it can make the election on an amended return filed within 6 months of the due date of the loss year return (excluding extensions). Attach the election to the amended return and write "Filed pursuant to section 301.9100-2" on the election statement. See the Instructions for Form 1139.

Corporations filing a consolidated return that elect to waive the entire carryback period for the group must also attach the statement required by Regulations section 1.1502-21(b)(3) or the election will not be valid.

Item 12

Enter the amount of the NOL carryover to the tax year from prior years, even if some of the loss is used to offset income on this return. The amount to enter is the total of all NOLs generated in prior years but not used to offset income (either as a carryback or carryover) to a tax year prior to 2014. Do not reduce the amount by any NOL deduction reported on line 29a.

Question 14

A corporation that files Form 1120 must file Schedule UTP (Form 1120), Uncertain Tax Position Statement, with its 2014 income tax return if:

- For 2014, the corporation's total assets equal or exceed $10 million;
- The corporation or a related party issued audited financial statements reporting all or a portion of the corporation's operations for all or a portion of the corporation's tax year; and
- The corporation has one or more tax positions that must be reported on Schedule UTP.

Attach Schedule UTP to the corporation's income tax return. Do not file it separately. A taxpayer that files a protective Form 1120 must also file Schedule UTP if it satisfies the requirements set forth, above.

For details, see the Instructions for Schedule UTP.

Schedule L. Balance Sheets per Books

The balance sheets should agree with the corporation's books and records.

Corporations with total receipts (page 1, line 1a plus lines 4 through 10) and total assets at the end of the tax year less than $250,000 are not required to complete Schedules L, M-1, and M-2 if the "Yes" box on Schedule K, question 13, is checked.

Corporations with total assets non-consolidated (or consolidated for all corporations included within the tax consolidation group) of $10 million or more on the last day of the tax year must file Schedule M-3 (Form 1120) instead of Schedule M-1. However, see the instructions for Schedule M-1, below. See the separate Instructions for Schedule M-3 (Form 1120) for provisions that also affect Schedule L.

If filing a consolidated return, report total consolidated assets, liabilities, and shareholder's equity for all corporations joining in the return. See *Consolidated Return*, earlier.

Line 1

Include certificates of deposit as cash on this line.

Line 5

Include on this line:
- State and local government obligations, the interest on which is excludable from gross income under section 103(a), and
- Stock in a mutual fund or other RIC that distributed exempt-interest dividends during the tax year of the corporation.

Line 26

Some examples of adjustments to report on this line include:
- Unrealized gains and losses on securities held "available for sale."
- Foreign currency translation adjustments.
- The excess of additional pension liability over unrecognized prior service cost.
- Guarantees of employee stock (ESOP) debt.
- Compensation related to employee stock award plans.

If the total adjustment to be entered on line 26 is a negative amount, enter the amount in parentheses.

Schedule M-1. Reconciliation of Income (Loss) per Books With Income per Return

In completing Schedule M-1, the following apply.
- Corporations with total receipts (page 1, line 1a plus lines 4 through 10) and total assets at the end of the tax year less than $250,000 are not required to complete Schedules L, M-1, and M-2 if the "Yes" box on Schedule K, question 13, is checked.
- Corporations with total assets non-consolidated (or consolidated for all corporations included within the tax consolidation group) of $10 million or more on the last day of the tax year must file Schedule M-3 (Form 1120) instead of Schedule M-1.
- A corporation filing Form 1120 that is not required to file Schedule M-3 may voluntarily file Schedule M-3 instead of Schedule M-1. See the Instructions for

Schedule M-3 (Form 1120) for more information.
- For tax years ending December 31, 2014, and later, corporations that (a) are required to file Schedule M-3 (Form 1120) and have less than $50 million total assets at the end of the tax year, or (b) are not required to file Schedule M-3 (Form 1120) and voluntarily file Schedule M-3 (Form 1120), must either (i) complete Schedule M-3 (Form 1120) entirely or (ii) complete Schedule M-3 (Form 1120) through Part I, and complete Form 1120, Schedule M-1 instead of completing Parts II and III of Schedule M-3 (Form 1120). If the corporation chooses to complete Schedule M-1 instead of completing Parts II and III of Schedule M-3, line 1 of Schedule M-1 must equal line 11 of Part I of Schedule M-3. See the Instructions for Schedule M-3 (Form 1120) for more information.

Line 5c

Include any of the following.
- Meal and entertainment expenses not deductible under section 274(n).
- Expenses for the use of an entertainment facility.
- The part of business gifts over $25.
- Expenses of an individual over $2,000, which are allocable to conventions on cruise ships.
- Employee achievement awards over $400.
- The cost of entertainment tickets over face value (also subject to 50% limit under section 274(n)).
- The cost of skyboxes over the face value of nonluxury box seat tickets.
- The part of luxury water travel expenses not deductible under section 274(m).
- Expenses for travel as a form of education.
- Other nondeductible travel and entertainment expenses.

For more information, see Pub. 535.

Line 7

Report any tax exempt interest received or accrued, including any exempt-interest dividends received as a shareholder in a mutual fund or other RIC. Also report this same amount on Schedule K, item 9.

Paperwork Reduction Act Notice. We ask for the information on these forms to carry out the Internal Revenue laws of the United States. You are required to give us the information. We need it to ensure that you are complying with these laws and to allow us to figure and collect the right amount of tax.

You are not required to provide the information requested on a form that is subject to the Paperwork Reduction Act unless the form displays a valid OMB control number. Books or records relating to a form or its instructions must be retained as long as their contents may become material in the administration of any Internal Revenue law. Generally, tax returns and return information are confidential, as required by section 6103.

The time needed to complete and file the following forms will vary depending on individual circumstances. The estimated average times are:

Form	Recordkeeping	Learning about the law or the form	Preparing the form	Copying, assembling, and sending the form to the IRS
1120	65 hr., 31 min.	41 hr., 16 min.	71 hr., 8 min.	7 hr., 46 min.
Sch. B (1120)	3 hr., 6 min.	1 hr.	1 hr., 5 min.	- - - - -
Sch. D (1120)	9 hr., 5 min.	3 hr., 55 min.	6 hr., 5 min.	32 min.
Sch. G (1120)	2 hr., 37 min.	30 min.	34 min.	- - - - -
Sch. H (1120)	5 hr., 58 min.	35 min.	43 min.	- - - - -
Sch. M-3 (1120)	79 hr., 52 min.	3 hr., 40 min.	5 hr., 8 min.	- - - - -
Sch. N (1120)	3 hr., 21 min.	1 hr., 30 min.	4 hr., 24 min.	48 min.
Sch. O (1120)	13 hr., 23 min.	2 hr., 5 min.	2 hr., 23 min.	- - - - -
Sch. PH (1120)	12 hr., 54 min.	4 hr., 18 min.	6 hr., 34 min.	32 min.
Sch. UTP (1120)	2 hr., 48 min.	36 min.	34 min.	- - - - -

If you have comments concerning the accuracy of these time estimates or suggestions for making these forms simpler, we would be happy to hear from you. You can send us comments from *www.irs.gov/formspubs/*. Click on "More Information" and then on "Give us feedback." Or you can send your comments to: Internal Revenue Service, Tax Forms and Publications Division, 1111 Constitution Ave. NW, IR-6526, Washington, DC 20224. Do not send the tax form to this address. Instead, see *Where To File*, earlier.

Principal Business Activity Codes

This list of principal business activities and their associated codes is designed to classify an enterprise by the type of activity in which it is engaged to facilitate the administration of the Internal Revenue Code. These principal business activity codes are based on the North American Industry Classification System.

Using the list of activities and codes below, determine from which activity the company derives the largest percentage of its "total receipts." Total receipts is defined as the sum of gross receipts or sales (page 1, line 1a) plus all other income (page 1, lines 4 through 10). If the company purchases raw materials and supplies them to a subcontractor to produce the finished product, but retains title to the product, the company is considered a manufacturer and must use one of the manufacturing codes (311110-339900).

Once the principal business activity is determined, entries must be made on Form 1120, Schedule K, lines 2a, 2b, and 2c. On line 2a, enter the six digit code selected from the list below. On line 2b, enter the company's business activity. On line 2c, enter a brief description of the principal product or service of the company.

Agriculture, Forestry, Fishing and Hunting

Crop Production

111100	Oilseed & Grain Farming
111210	Vegetable & Melon Farming (including potatoes & yams)
111300	Fruit & Tree Nut Farming
111400	Greenhouse, Nursery, & Floriculture Production
111900	Other Crop Farming (including tobacco, cotton, sugarcane, hay, peanut, sugar beet & all other crop farming)

Animal Production

112111	Beef Cattle Ranching & Farming
112112	Cattle Feedlots
112120	Dairy Cattle & Milk Production
112210	Hog & Pig Farming
112300	Poultry & Egg Production
112400	Sheep & Goat Farming
112510	Aquaculture (including shellfish & finfish farms & hatcheries)
112900	Other Animal Production

Forestry and Logging

113110	Timber Tract Operations
113210	Forest Nurseries & Gathering of Forest Products
113310	Logging

Fishing, Hunting and Trapping

114110	Fishing
114210	Hunting & Trapping

Support Activities for Agriculture and Forestry

115110	Support Activities for Crop Production (including cotton ginning, soil preparation, planting, & cultivating)
115210	Support Activities for Animal Production
115310	Support Activities For Forestry

Mining

211110	Oil & Gas Extraction
212110	Coal Mining
212200	Metal Ore Mining
212310	Stone Mining & Quarrying
212320	Sand, Gravel, Clay, & Ceramic & Refractory Minerals Mining & Quarrying
212390	Other Nonmetallic Mineral Mining & Quarrying
213110	Support Activities for Mining

Utilities

221100	Electric Power Generation, Transmission & Distribution
221210	Natural Gas Distribution
221300	Water, Sewage & Other Systems
221500	Combination Gas & Electric

Construction

Construction of Buildings

236110	Residential Building Construction
236200	Nonresidential Building Construction

Heavy and Civil Engineering Construction

237100	Utility System Construction
237210	Land Subdivision
237310	Highway, Street, & Bridge Construction
237990	Other Heavy & Civil Engineering Construction

Specialty Trade Contractors

238100	Foundation, Structure, & Building Exterior Contractors (including framing carpentry, masonry, glass, roofing, & siding)
238210	Electrical Contractors
238220	Plumbing, Heating, & Air-Conditioning Contractors
238290	Other Building Equipment Contractors
238300	Building Finishing Contractors (including drywall, insulation, painting, wallcovering, flooring, tile, & finish carpentry)
238900	Other Specialty Trade Contractors (including site preparation)

Manufacturing

Food Manufacturing

311110	Animal Food Mfg
311200	Grain & Oilseed Milling
311300	Sugar & Confectionery Product Mfg
311400	Fruit & Vegetable Preserving & Specialty Food Mfg
311500	Dairy Product Mfg
311610	Animal Slaughtering and Processing
311710	Seafood Product Preparation & Packaging
311800	Bakeries, Tortilla & Dry Pasta Mfg
311900	Other Food Mfg (including coffee, tea, flavorings & seasonings)

Beverage and Tobacco Product Manufacturing

312110	Soft Drink & Ice Mfg
312120	Breweries
312130	Wineries
312140	Distilleries
312200	Tobacco Manufacturing

Textile Mills and Textile Product Mills

313000	Textile Mills
314000	Textile Product Mills

Apparel Manufacturing

315100	Apparel Knitting Mills
315210	Cut & Sew Apparel Contractors
315220	Men's & Boys' Cut & Sew Apparel Mfg
315240	Women's, Girls' and Infants' Cut & Sew Apparel Mfg
315280	Other Cut & Sew Apparel Mfg
315990	Apparel Accessories & Other Apparel Mfg

Leather and Allied Product Manufacturing

316110	Leather & Hide Tanning & Finishing
316210	Footwear Mfg (including rubber & plastics)
316990	Other Leather & Allied Product Mfg

Wood Product Manufacturing

321110	Sawmills & Wood Preservation
321210	Veneer, Plywood, & Engineered Wood Product Mfg
321900	Other Wood Product Mfg

Paper Manufacturing

322100	Pulp, Paper, & Paperboard Mills
322200	Converted Paper Product Mfg

Printing and Related Support Activities

323100	Printing & Related Support Activities

Petroleum and Coal Products Manufacturing

324110	Petroleum Refineries (including integrated)
324120	Asphalt Paving, Roofing, & Saturated Materials Mfg
324190	Other Petroleum & Coal Products Mfg

Chemical Manufacturing

325100	Basic Chemical Mfg
325200	Resin, Synthetic Rubber, & Artificial & Synthetic Fibers & Filaments Mfg
325300	Pesticide, Fertilizer, & Other Agricultural Chemical Mfg
325410	Pharmaceutical & Medicine Mfg
325500	Paint, Coating, & Adhesive Mfg
325600	Soap, Cleaning Compound, & Toilet Preparation Mfg
325900	Other Chemical Product & Preparation Mfg

Plastics and Rubber Products Manufacturing

326100	Plastics Product Mfg
326200	Rubber Product Mfg

Nonmetallic Mineral Product Manufacturing

327100	Clay Product & Refractory Mfg
327210	Glass & Glass Product Mfg
327300	Cement & Concrete Product Mfg
327400	Lime & Gypsum Product Mfg
327900	Other Nonmetallic Mineral Product Mfg

Primary Metal Manufacturing

331110	Iron & Steel Mills & Ferroalloy Mfg
331200	Steel Product Mfg from Purchased Steel
331310	Alumina & Aluminum Production & Processing
331400	Nonferrous Metal (except Aluminum) Production & Processing
331500	Foundries

Fabricated Metal Product Manufacturing

332110	Forging & Stamping
332210	Cutlery & Handtool Mfg
332300	Architectural & Structural Metals Mfg
332400	Boiler, Tank, & Shipping Container Mfg
332510	Hardware Mfg
332610	Spring & Wire Product Mfg
332700	Machine Shops; Turned Product; & Screw, Nut, & Bolt Mfg
332810	Coating, Engraving, Heat Treating, & Allied Activities
332900	Other Fabricated Metal Product Mfg

Machinery Manufacturing

333100	Agriculture, Construction, & Mining Machinery Mfg
333200	Industrial Machinery Mfg
333310	Commercial & Service Industry Machinery Mfg
333410	Ventilation, Heating, Air-Conditioning, & Commercial Refrigeration Equipment Mfg
333510	Metalworking Machinery Mfg
333610	Engine, Turbine & Power Transmission Equipment Mfg
333900	Other General Purpose Machinery Mfg

Computer and Electronic Product Manufacturing

334110	Computer & Peripheral Equipment Mfg
334200	Communications Equipment Mfg
334310	Audio & Video Equipment Mfg
334410	Semiconductor & Other Electronic Component Mfg
334500	Navigational, Measuring, Electromedical, & Control Instruments Mfg
334610	Manufacturing & Reproducing Magnetic & Optical Media

Electrical Equipment, Appliance, and Component Manufacturing

335100	Electric Lighting Equipment Mfg
335200	Household Appliance Mfg
335310	Electrical Equipment Mfg
335900	Other Electrical Equipment & Component Mfg

Transportation Equipment Manufacturing

336100	Motor Vehicle Mfg
336210	Motor Vehicle Body & Trailer Mfg
336300	Motor Vehicle Parts Mfg
336410	Aerospace Product & Parts Mfg
336510	Railroad Rolling Stock Mfg
336610	Ship & Boat Building
336990	Other Transportation Equipment Mfg

Furniture and Related Product Manufacturing

337000	Furniture & Related Product Manufacturing

Miscellaneous Manufacturing

339110	Medical Equipment & Supplies Mfg
339900	Other Miscellaneous Manufacturing

Wholesale Trade

Merchant Wholesalers, Durable Goods

423100	Motor Vehicle & Motor Vehicle Parts & Supplies
423200	Furniture & Home Furnishings
423300	Lumber & Other Construction Materials
423400	Professional & Commercial Equipment & Supplies
423500	Metal & Mineral (except Petroleum)
423600	Household Appliances and Electrical & Electronic Goods
423700	Hardware, & Plumbing & Heating Equipment & Supplies
423800	Machinery, Equipment, & Supplies
423910	Sporting & Recreational Goods & Supplies
423920	Toy & Hobby Goods & Supplies
423930	Recyclable Materials
423940	Jewelry, Watch, Precious Stone, & Precious Metals
423990	Other Miscellaneous Durable Goods

Merchant Wholesalers, Nondurable Goods

424100	Paper & Paper Products
424210	Drugs & Druggists' Sundries
424300	Apparel, Piece Goods, & Notions
424400	Grocery & Related Products
424500	Farm Product Raw Materials
424600	Chemical & Allied Products
424700	Petroleum & Petroleum Products
424800	Beer, Wine, & Distilled Alcoholic Beverages
424910	Farm Supplies
424920	Book, Periodical, & Newspapers
424930	Flower, Nursery Stock, & Florists' Supplies
424940	Tobacco & Tobacco Products
424950	Paint, Varnish, & Supplies
424990	Other Miscellaneous Nondurable Goods

Wholesale Electronic Markets and Agents and Brokers

425110	Business to Business Electronic Markets
425120	Wholesale Trade Agents & Brokers

Retail Trade

Motor Vehicle and Parts Dealers

441110	New Car Dealers
441120	Used Car Dealers
441210	Recreational Vehicle Dealers
441222	Boat Dealers
441228	Motorcycle, ATV and All Other Motor Vehicle Dealers
441300	Automotive Parts, Accessories, & Tire Stores

Furniture and Home Furnishings Stores

442110	Furniture Stores
442210	Floor Covering Stores
442291	Window Treatment Stores
442299	All Other Home Furnishings Stores

Electronics and Appliance Stores

443141	Household Appliance Stores
443142	Electronics Stores (including Audio, Video, Computer, and Camera Stores)

Building Material and Garden Equipment and Supplies Dealers
444110 Home Centers
444120 Paint & Wallpaper Stores
444130 Hardware Stores
444190 Other Building Material Dealers
444200 Lawn & Garden Equipment & Supplies Stores

Food and Beverage Stores
445110 Supermarkets and Other Grocery (except Convenience) Stores
445120 Convenience Stores
445210 Meat Markets
445220 Fish & Seafood Markets
445230 Fruit & Vegetable Markets
445291 Baked Goods Stores
445292 Confectionery & Nut Stores
445299 All Other Specialty Food Stores
445310 Beer, Wine, & Liquor Stores

Health and Personal Care Stores
446110 Pharmacies & Drug Stores
446120 Cosmetics, Beauty Supplies, & Perfume Stores
446130 Optical Goods Stores
446190 Other Health & Personal Care Stores

Gasoline Stations
447100 Gasoline Stations (including convenience stores with gas)

Clothing and Clothing Accessories Stores
448110 Men's Clothing Stores
448120 Women's Clothing Stores
448130 Children's & Infants' Clothing Stores
448140 Family Clothing Stores
448150 Clothing Accessories Stores
448190 Other Clothing Stores
448210 Shoe Stores
448310 Jewelry Stores
448320 Luggage & Leather Goods Stores

Sporting Goods, Hobby, Book, and Music Stores
451110 Sporting Goods Stores
451120 Hobby, Toy, & Game Stores
451130 Sewing, Needlework, & Piece Goods Stores
451140 Musical Instrument & Supplies Stores
451211 Book Stores
451212 News Dealers & Newsstands

General Merchandise Stores
452110 Department Stores
452900 Other General Merchandise Stores

Miscellaneous Store Retailers
453110 Florists
453210 Office Supplies & Stationery Stores
453220 Gift, Novelty, & Souvenir Stores
453310 Used Merchandise Stores
453910 Pet & Pet Supplies Stores
453920 Art Dealers
453930 Manufactured (Mobile) Home Dealers
453990 All Other Miscellaneous Store Retailers (including tobacco, candle, & trophy shops)

Nonstore Retailers
454110 Electronic Shopping & Mail-Order Houses
454210 Vending Machine Operators
454310 Fuel Dealers (including Heating Oil and Liquefied Petroleum)
454390 Other Direct Selling Establishments (including door-to-door retailing, frozen food plan providers, party plan merchandisers, & coffee-break service providers)

Transportation and Warehousing

Air, Rail, and Water Transportation
481000 Air Transportation
482110 Rail Transportation
483000 Water Transportation

Truck Transportation
484110 General Freight Trucking, Local

484120 General Freight Trucking, Long-distance
484200 Specialized Freight Trucking

Transit and Ground Passenger Transportation
485110 Urban Transit Systems
485210 Interurban & Rural Bus Transportation
485310 Taxi Service
485320 Limousine Service
485410 School & Employee Bus Transportation
485510 Charter Bus Industry
485990 Other Transit & Ground Passenger Transportation

Pipeline Transportation
486000 Pipeline Transportation

Scenic & Sightseeing Transportation
487000 Scenic & Sightseeing Transportation

Support Activities for Transportation
488100 Support Activities for Air Transportation
488210 Support Activities for Rail Transportation
488300 Support Activities for Water Transportation
488410 Motor Vehicle Towing
488490 Other Support Activities for Road Transportation
488510 Freight Transportation Arrangement
488990 Other Support Activities for Transportation

Couriers and Messengers
492110 Couriers
492210 Local Messengers & Local Delivery

Warehousing and Storage
493100 Warehousing & Storage (except lessors of miniwarehouses & self-storage units)

Information

Publishing Industries (except Internet)
511110 Newspaper Publishers
511120 Periodical Publishers
511130 Book Publishers
511140 Directory & Mailing List Publishers
511190 Other Publishers
511210 Software Publishers

Motion Picture and Sound Recording Industries
512100 Motion Picture & Video Industries (except video rental)
512200 Sound Recording Industries

Broadcasting (except Internet)
515100 Radio & Television Broadcasting
515210 Cable & Other Subscription Programming

Telecommunications
517000 Telecommunications (including paging, cellular, satellite, cable & other program distribution, resellers, other telecommunications, & Internet service providers)

Data Processing Services
518210 Data Processing, Hosting, & Related Services

Other Information Services
519100 Other Information Services (including news syndicates, libraries, Internet publishing & broadcasting)

Finance and Insurance

Depository Credit Intermediation
522110 Commercial Banking
522120 Savings Institutions
522130 Credit Unions
522190 Other Depository Credit Intermediation

Nondepository Credit Intermediation
522210 Credit Card Issuing
522220 Sales Financing
522291 Consumer Lending
522292 Real Estate Credit (including mortgage bankers & originators)
522293 International Trade Financing
522294 Secondary Market Financing
522298 All Other Nondepository Credit Intermediation

Activities Related to Credit Intermediation
522300 Activities Related to Credit Intermediation (including loan brokers, check clearing, & money transmitting)

Securities, Commodity Contracts, and Other Financial Investments and Related Activities
523110 Investment Banking & Securities Dealing
523120 Securities Brokerage
523130 Commodity Contracts Dealing
523140 Commodity Contracts Brokerage
523210 Securities & Commodity Exchanges
523900 Other Financial Investment Activities (including portfolio management & investment advice)

Insurance Carriers and Related Activities
524140 Direct Life, Health, & Medical Insurance & Reinsurance Carriers
524150 Direct Insurance & Reinsurance (except Life, Health & Medical) Carriers
524210 Insurance Agencies & Brokerages
524290 Other Insurance Related Activities (including third-party administration of insurance and pension funds)

Funds, Trusts, and Other Financial Vehicles
525100 Insurance & Employee Benefit Funds
525910 Open-End Investment Funds (Form 1120-RIC)
525920 Trusts, Estates, & Agency Accounts
525990 Other Financial Vehicles (including mortgage REITs & closed-end investment funds)

"Offices of Bank Holding Companies" and "Offices of Other Holding Companies" are located under **Management of Companies (Holding Companies)**, later.

Real Estate and Rental and Leasing

Real Estate
531110 Lessors of Residential Buildings & Dwellings (including equity REITs)
531120 Lessors of Nonresidential Buildings (except Miniwarehouses) (including equity REITs)
531130 Lessors of Miniwarehouses & Self-Storage Units (including equity REITs)
531190 Lessors of Other Real Estate Property (including equity REITs)
531210 Offices of Real Estate Agents & Brokers
531310 Real Estate Property Managers
531320 Offices of Real Estate Appraisers
531390 Other Activities Related to Real Estate

Rental and Leasing Services
532100 Automotive Equipment Rental & Leasing
532210 Consumer Electronics & Appliances Rental
532220 Formal Wear & Costume Rental
532230 Video Tape & Disc Rental
532290 Other Consumer Goods Rental
532310 General Rental Centers
532400 Commercial & Industrial Machinery & Equipment Rental & Leasing

Lessors of Nonfinancial Intangible Assets (except copyrighted works)
533110 Lessors of Nonfinancial Intangible Assets (except copyrighted works)

Professional, Scientific, and Technical Services

Legal Services
541110 Offices of Lawyers
541190 Other Legal Services

Accounting, Tax Preparation, Bookkeeping, and Payroll Services
541211 Offices of Certified Public Accountants

541213 Tax Preparation Services
541214 Payroll Services
541219 Other Accounting Services

Architectural, Engineering, and Related Services
541310 Architectural Services
541320 Landscape Architecture Services
541330 Engineering Services
541340 Drafting Services
541350 Building Inspection Services
541360 Geophysical Surveying & Mapping Services
541370 Surveying & Mapping (except Geophysical) Services
541380 Testing Laboratories

Specialized Design Services
541400 Specialized Design Services (including interior, industrial, graphic, & fashion design)

Computer Systems Design and Related Services
541511 Custom Computer Programming Services
541512 Computer Systems Design Services
541513 Computer Facilities Management Services
541519 Other Computer Related Services

Other Professional, Scientific, and Technical Services
541600 Management, Scientific, & Technical Consulting Services
541700 Scientific Research & Development Services
541800 Advertising & Related Services
541910 Marketing Research & Public Opinion Polling
541920 Photographic Services
541930 Translation & Interpretation Services
541940 Veterinary Services
541990 All Other Professional, Scientific, & Technical Services

Management of Companies (Holding Companies)
551111 Offices of Bank Holding Companies
551112 Offices of Other Holding Companies

Administrative and Support and Waste Management and Remediation Services

Administrative and Support Services
561110 Office Administrative Services
561210 Facilities Support Services
561300 Employment Services
561410 Document Preparation Services
561420 Telephone Call Centers
561430 Business Service Centers (including private mail centers & copy shops)
561440 Collection Agencies
561450 Credit Bureaus
561490 Other Business Support Services (including repossession services, court reporting, & stenotype services)
561500 Travel Arrangement & Reservation Services
561600 Investigation & Security Services
561710 Exterminating & Pest Control Services
561720 Janitorial Services
561730 Landscaping Services
561740 Carpet & Upholstery Cleaning Services
561790 Other Services to Buildings & Dwellings
561900 Other Support Services (including packaging & labeling services, & convention & trade show organizers)

Waste Management and Remediation Services
562000 Waste Management & Remediation Services

Educational Services
611000 Educational Services (including schools, colleges, & universities)

Principal Business Activity Codes *(Continued)*

Health Care and Social Assistance

Offices of Physicians and Dentists

621111 Offices of Physicians (except mental health specialists)
621112 Offices of Physicians, Mental Health Specialists
621210 Offices of Dentists

Offices of Other Health Practitioners

621310 Offices of Chiropractors
621320 Offices of Optometrists
621330 Offices of Mental Health Practitioners (except Physicians)
621340 Offices of Physical, Occupational & Speech Therapists, & Audiologists
621391 Offices of Podiatrists
621399 Offices of All Other Miscellaneous Health Practitioners

Outpatient Care Centers

621410 Family Planning Centers
621420 Outpatient Mental Health & Substance Abuse Centers
621491 HMO Medical Centers
621492 Kidney Dialysis Centers
621493 Freestanding Ambulatory Surgical & Emergency Centers
621498 All Other Outpatient Care Centers

Medical and Diagnostic Laboratories

621510 Medical & Diagnostic Laboratories

Home Health Care Services

621610 Home Health Care Services

Other Ambulatory Health Care Services

621900 Other Ambulatory Health Care Services (including ambulance services & blood & organ banks)

Hospitals

622000 Hospitals

Nursing and Residential Care Facilities

623000 Nursing & Residential Care Facilities

Social Assistance

624100 Individual & Family Services
624200 Community Food & Housing, & Emergency & Other Relief Services
624310 Vocational Rehabilitation Services
624410 Child Day Care Services

Arts, Entertainment, and Recreation

Performing Arts, Spectator Sports, and Related Industries

711100 Performing Arts Companies
711210 Spectator Sports (including sports clubs & racetracks)
711300 Promoters of Performing Arts, Sports, & Similar Events
711410 Agents & Managers for Artists, Athletes, Entertainers, & Other Public Figures
711510 Independent Artists, Writers, & Performers

Museums, Historical Sites, and Similar Institutions

712100 Museums, Historical Sites, & Similar Institutions

Amusement, Gambling, and Recreation Industries

713100 Amusement Parks & Arcades
713200 Gambling Industries
713900 Other Amusement & Recreation Industries (including golf courses, skiing facilities, marinas, fitness centers, & bowling centers)

Accommodation and Food Services

Accommodation

721110 Hotels (except Casino Hotels) & Motels
721120 Casino Hotels
721191 Bed & Breakfast Inns
721199 All Other Traveler Accommodation
721210 RV (Recreational Vehicle) Parks & Recreational Camps
721310 Rooming & Boarding Houses

Food Services and Drinking Places

722300 Special Food Services (including food service contractors & caterers)
722410 Drinking Places (Alcoholic Beverages)
722511 Full-Service Restaurants
722513 Limited-Service Restaurants
722514 Cafeterias and Buffets
722515 Snack and Non-alcoholic Beverage Bars

Other Services

Repair and Maintenance

811110 Automotive Mechanical & Electrical Repair & Maintenance
811120 Automotive Body, Paint, Interior, & Glass Repair
811190 Other Automotive Repair & Maintenance (including oil change & lubrication shops & car washes)
811210 Electronic & Precision Equipment Repair & Maintenance
811310 Commercial & Industrial Machinery & Equipment (except Automotive & Electronic) Repair & Maintenance
811410 Home & Garden Equipment & Appliance Repair & Maintenance
811420 Reupholstery & Furniture Repair
811430 Footwear & Leather Goods Repair
811490 Other Personal & Household Goods Repair & Maintenance

Personal and Laundry Services

812111 Barber Shops
812112 Beauty Salons
812113 Nail Salons
812190 Other Personal Care Services (including diet & weight reducing centers)
812210 Funeral Homes & Funeral Services
812220 Cemeteries & Crematories
812310 Coin-Operated Laundries & Drycleaners
812320 Drycleaning & Laundry Services (except Coin-Operated)
812330 Linen & Uniform Supply
812910 Pet Care (except Veterinary) Services
812920 Photofinishing
812930 Parking Lots & Garages
812990 All Other Personal Services

Religious, Grantmaking, Civic, Professional, and Similar Organizations

813000 Religious, Grantmaking, Civic, Professional, & Similar Organizations (including condominium and homeowners associations)

Index

SCHEDULE B
(Form 1120)
(Rev. December 2014)
Department of the Treasury
Internal Revenue Service

Additional Information for Schedule M-3 Filers

▶ Attach to Form 1120.
▶ See instructions on page 2.

OMB No. 1545-0123

Name | Employer identification number (EIN)

		Yes	No
1	Does any amount reported on Schedule M-3 (Form 1120), Part II, lines 9 or 10, column (d), reflect allocations to this corporation from a partnership of income, gain, loss, deduction, or credit that are disproportionate to this corporation's capital contribution to the partnership or its ratio for sharing other items of the partnership? . . .		
2	At any time during the tax year, did the corporation sell, exchange, or transfer any interest in an intangible asset to a related person as defined in section 267(b)?		
3	At any time during the tax year, did the corporation acquire any interest in an intangible asset from a related person as defined in section 267(b)?		
4a	During the tax year, did the corporation enter into a cost-sharing arrangement with any related foreign party on whose behalf the corporation did not file Form 5471, Information Return of U.S. Persons With Respect To Certain Foreign Corporations?		
b	At any time during the tax year, was the corporation a participant in a cost-sharing arrangement with any related foreign party on whose behalf the corporation did not file Form 5471?		
5	At any time during the tax year, did the corporation make any change in accounting principle for financial accounting purposes? See instructions for the definition of change in accounting principle		
6	At any time during the tax year, did the corporation make any change in a method of accounting for U.S. income tax purposes?		
7	At any time during the tax year, did the corporation own any voluntary employees' beneficiary association (VEBA) trusts that were used to hold funds designated for employee benefits?		
8	At any time during the tax year, did the corporation use an allocation method for indirect costs capitalized to self-constructed assets that varied from its financial method of accounting?		
9	At any time during the tax year, did the corporation treat for tax purposes indirect costs, as defined in Regulations sections 1.263A-1(e)(3)(ii)(F), (G), and (H), as mixed-service costs, as defined in Regulations section 1.263A-1(e)(4)(ii)(C)?		
10	Did the corporation, under section 118 or 362(c) and the related regulations, take a return filing position characterizing any amount as a contribution to the capital of the corporation during the tax year by any non-shareholders? Amounts so characterized may include, without limitation, incentives, inducements, money, and property		

For Paperwork Reduction Act Notice, see the Instructions for Form 1120.   Cat. No. 49737Q   Schedule B (Form 1120) (Rev. 12-2014)

General Instructions

Section references are to the Internal Revenue Code unless otherwise noted.

Future Developments

For the latest information about developments related to Schedule B (Form 1120) and its instructions, such as legislation enacted after they were published, go to *www.irs.gov/form1120*.

What's New

Some filers of Form 1120, U.S. Corporation Income Tax Return, that file Schedule M-3 (Form 1120), Net Income (Loss) Reconciliation for Corporations With Total Assets of $10 Million or More, with tax years ending December 31, 2014, or later, are not required to file Schedule B (Form 1120). See *Who Must File,* later.

Purpose of Form

Use Schedule B (Form 1120) to provide answers to additional questions for filers of Schedule M-3 (Form 1120).

Who Must File

Generally, filers of Form 1120 that file Schedule M-3 (Form 1120), must complete and file Schedule B (Form 1120). However, for tax years ending December 31, 2014, or later, filers that (a) are required to file Schedule M-3 and have less than $50 million in total assets at the end of the tax year or (b) are not required to file Schedule M-3 and voluntarily file Schedule M-3, are not required to file Schedule B (Form 1120). See the Instructions for Schedule M-3 (Form 1120) for more information.

In the case of a consolidated group, a parent corporation files one Schedule B for the entire group.

Specific Instructions

Question 1. Partnership Allocations

Answer "Yes" if this corporation is a partner in a partnership and has received special allocations of income, gain, loss, deduction, or credit from such partnership.

Example. P, a corporation, joins with B, an individual, in forming the PB Partnership. P and B each contribute $50,000 in cash to PB Partnership. Profits and losses are allocated equally, with the exception of depreciation, which is allocated 99% to P and 1% to B.

P answers "Yes" to question 1 because its 99% allocation of depreciation deductions from PB Partnership is disproportionate to its ratio of sharing other items of income, gain, loss, deduction, or credit from PB partnership.

Question 5. Changes in Accounting Principle

The term "change in accounting principle," means a change from one generally accepted accounting principle to another generally accepted accounting principle as described in Statement of Financial Accounting Standards (SFAS) No. 154—Accounting Changes and Error Corrections.

Answer "Yes" if a change in accounting principle occurred during the tax year that affected (or is expected to affect) the amount of income reported for financial statement purposes.

 *If the corporation has audited financial statements, any changes in accounting principle should be identified in footnotes to those statements.*

Question 6. Change in Method of Accounting

Corporations are generally required to file Form 3115, Application for Change in Accounting Method, or a statement in lieu thereof, to request a change in a method of accounting. See the Instructions for Form 3115 for information on requesting a change in accounting method.

Question 7. Voluntary Employees' Beneficiary Association Trusts

Employers that establish and fund welfare benefit plans on behalf of their employees do so through a tax-exempt trust that is referred to as a voluntary employees' beneficiary association (VEBA). See section 501(c)(9) and Regulations sections 1.501(c)(9)-1 through 1.501(c)(9)-8 for details.

Answer "Yes" if the corporation owned any VEBA trusts that were used to hold funds designated for employee benefits.

Question 8. Indirect Costs

Section 446(a) and Regulation section 1.446-1(a)(1) generally provide that taxable income shall be computed under the method of accounting on the basis of which the corporation regularly computes its income in keeping its books. An exception applies if book income does not clearly reflect income.

Answer "Yes" if the corporation, during the tax year, used an allocation method for indirect costs capitalized to self-constructed assets that varied from its financial statement method of accounting. Otherwise, answer "No." Also answer "No" if the corporation used the same method of allocating indirect costs to self-constructed assets, but capitalized a different amount due to differences in the amount of costs which are includible in the computation of income for the tax year.

Question 9. Mixed Service Costs

Answer "Yes" if the corporation, during the tax year, treated purchasing, handling, and storage, as discussed in Regulations sections 1.263A-3(c)(1) through (5), and as defined in Regulations section 1.263A-1(e)(3)(ii)(F), (G), and (H), as mixed-service costs as defined in Regulations section 1.263A-1(e)(4)(ii)(C). Otherwise, answer "No."

SCHEDULE D (Form 1120)	Capital Gains and Losses	OMB No. 1545-0123
Department of the Treasury Internal Revenue Service	▶ Attach to Form 1120, 1120-C, 1120-F, 1120-FSC, 1120-H, 1120-IC-DISC, 1120-L, 1120-ND, 1120-PC, 1120-POL, 1120-REIT, 1120-RIC, 1120-SF, or certain Forms 990-T. ▶ Information about Schedule D (Form 1120) and its separate instructions is at www.irs.gov/form1120.	2014

Name	Employer identification number

Part I — Short-Term Capital Gains and Losses—Assets Held One Year or Less

See instructions for how to figure the amounts to enter on the lines below. This form may be easier to complete if you round off cents to whole dollars.	(d) Proceeds (sales price)	(e) Cost (or other basis)	(g) Adjustments to gain or loss from Form(s) 8949, Part I, line 2, column (g)	(h) Gain or (loss) Subtract column (e) from column (d) and combine the result with column (g)
1a Totals for all short-term transactions reported on Form 1099-B for which basis was reported to the IRS and for which you have no adjustments (see instructions). However, if you choose to report all these transactions on Form 8949, leave this line blank and go to line 1b				
1b Totals for all transactions reported on Form(s) 8949 with **Box A** checked				
2 Totals for all transactions reported on Form(s) 8949 with **Box B** checked				
3 Totals for all transactions reported on Form(s) 8949 with **Box C** checked				

4 Short-term capital gain from installment sales from Form 6252, line 26 or 37	**4**	
5 Short-term capital gain or (loss) from like-kind exchanges from Form 8824	**5**	
6 Unused capital loss carryover (attach computation)	**6** ( )	
7 Net short-term capital gain or (loss). Combine lines 1a through 6 in column h.	**7**	

Part II — Long-Term Capital Gains and Losses—Assets Held More Than One Year

See instructions for how to figure the amounts to enter on the lines below. This form may be easier to complete if you round off cents to whole dollars.	(d) Proceeds (sales price)	(e) Cost (or other basis)	(g) Adjustments to gain or loss from Form(s) 8949, Part II, line 2, column (g)	(h) Gain or (loss) Subtract column (e) from column (d) and combine the result with column (g)
8a Totals for all long-term transactions reported on Form 1099-B for which basis was reported to the IRS and for which you have no adjustments (see instructions). However, if you choose to report all these transactions on Form 8949, leave this line blank and go to line 8b				
8b Totals for all transactions reported on Form(s) 8949 with **Box D** checked				
9 Totals for all transactions reported on Form(s) 8949 with **Box E** checked				
10 Totals for all transactions reported on Form(s) 8949 with **Box F** checked				

11 Enter gain from Form 4797, line 7 or 9	**11**	
12 Long-term capital gain from installment sales from Form 6252, line 26 or 37	**12**	
13 Long-term capital gain or (loss) from like-kind exchanges from Form 8824	**13**	
14 Capital gain distributions (see instructions)	**14**	
15 Net long-term capital gain or (loss). Combine lines 8a through 14 in column h	**15**	

Part III — Summary of Parts I and II

16 Enter excess of net short-term capital gain (line 7) over net long-term capital loss (line 15)	**16**	
17 Net capital gain. Enter excess of net long-term capital gain (line 15) over net short-term capital loss (line 7)	**17**	
18 Add lines 16 and 17. Enter here and on Form 1120, page 1, line 8, or the proper line on other returns . .	**18**	

Note. If losses exceed gains, see **Capital losses** in the instructions.

For Paperwork Reduction Act Notice, see the Instructions for Form 1120.　　　　Cat. No. 11460M　　　　Schedule D (Form 1120) (2014)

2014

Instructions for Schedule D (Form 1120)

Capital Gains and Losses

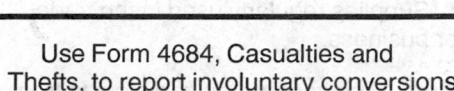

Department of the Treasury
Internal Revenue Service

Section references are to the Internal Revenue Code unless otherwise noted.

Future Developments

For the latest information about developments to Schedule D (Form 1120) and its instructions, such as legislation enacted after they were published, go to *www.irs.gov/form1120*.

What's New

Form 1099-B. Form 1099-B has been redesigned so that the information is reported in boxes that are numbered to match the corresponding line and column on Form 8949. Also, a new box was added at the top of Form 1099-B to indicate which box to check when completing Form 8949. These changes will make it easier to complete Form 8949.

A Form 1099-B (or substitute statement) for transactions involving certain types of debt instruments acquired after 2013 will have more detailed information than a Form 1099-B (or substitute statement) for transactions involving debt instruments acquired before 2014. This is also true for a Form 1099-B (or substitute statement) for options granted or acquired after 2013 or securities futures contracts entered into after 2013. This additional information will help complete Form 8949 and Schedule D.

General Instructions

Purpose of Schedule

Use Schedule D to:
- Figure the overall gain or loss from transactions reported on Form 8949;
- Report certain transactions the corporation does not have to report on Form 8949; and
- Report capital gain distributions not reported directly on Form 1120, line 8 (or effectively connected capital gain distributions not reported directly on Form 1120-F, 1120-C, 1120-H, or all other related forms).

Who Must File

Complete and attach Schedule D (Form 1120) to Form 1120, 1120-C, 1120-F, 1120-FSC, 1120-H, 1120-IC-DISC, 1120-L, 1120-ND, 1120-PC, 1120-POL, 1120-REIT, 1120-RIC, 1120-SF, or certain Forms 990-T.

Other Forms the Corporation May Have To File

Use Form 8949 to report:
- Sales or exchanges of capital assets (defined later) not reported on another form or schedule;
- Nonbusiness bad debts;
- Undistributed long-term capital gains from Form 2439; and
- The corporation's share of gain or loss from a partnership, S corporation, estate, or trust.

Complete all applicable lines of Form 8949 before completing lines 1b, 2, 3, 8b, 9, or 10 of Schedule D (Form 1120). See the instructions for Form 8949 for special provisions and exceptions to completing Form 8949 for certain corporations. Also, see *Lines 1a and 8a,* later, for more information about when to use Form 8949.

Use Form 4797, Sales of Business Property, to report the following.
- The sale or exchange of:
  1. Property used in a trade or business;
  2. Depreciable and amortizable property;
  3. Oil, gas, geothermal, or other mineral property; and
  4. Section 126 property.
- The involuntary conversion (other than from casualty or theft) of property and capital assets held for business or profit.
- The disposition of noncapital assets other than inventory or property held primarily for sale to customers in the ordinary course of the corporation's trade or business.
- The section 291 adjustment to section 1250 property.

Use Form 4684, Casualties and Thefts, to report involuntary conversions of property due to casualty or theft.

Use Form 6781, Gains and Losses From Section 1256 Contracts and Straddles, to report gains and losses from section 1256 contracts and straddles.

Use Form 8824, Like-Kind Exchanges, if the corporation made one or more "like-kind" exchanges. A like-kind exchange occurs when the corporation exchanges business or investment property for property of a like kind. For exchanges of capital assets, include the gain or (loss) from Form 8824, if any, on Schedule D (Form 1120), line 5 or line 13, as applicable.

Additional information. For more information, see Pub. 544, Sales and Other Dispositions of Assets, and Pub. 550, Investment Income and Expenses (Including Capital Gains and Losses).

Capital Assets

Each item of property the corporation held (whether or not connected with its trade or business) is a capital asset except the following. See section 1221(a).
- Stock in trade or other property included in inventory or held mainly for sale to customers. However, see the *Note* below.
- Accounts or notes receivable acquired in the ordinary course of the trade or business for services rendered or from the sale of stock in trade or other property included in inventory or held mainly for sale to customers.
- Depreciable or real property used in the trade or business, even if it is fully depreciated.
- Certain copyrights; literary, musical, or artistic compositions; letters or memoranda; or similar property. However, see the *Note* below.
- U.S. Government publications, including the Congressional Record, that the corporation received from the Government, other than by purchase at the normal sales price, or that the corporation got from another taxpayer who had received it in a similar way, if

Cat. No. 26358T

the corporation's basis is determined by reference to the previous owner's basis.
• Certain commodities derivative financial instruments held by a dealer in connection with its dealer activities.
• Certain identified hedging transactions entered into in the normal course of the trade or business.
• Supplies regularly used in the trade or business.

Note. The corporation can elect to treat as capital assets certain musical compositions or copyrights it sold or exchanged. See section 1221(b)(3) and Pub. 550 for details.

Capital Losses

For a corporation, capital losses are allowed in the current tax year only to the extent of capital gains. A net capital loss is carried back 3 years and forward up to 5 years as a short-term capital loss. Carry back a capital loss to the extent it does not increase or produce a net operating loss in the tax year to which it is carried. Foreign expropriation capital losses cannot be carried back, but are carried forward up to 10 years. A net capital loss of a regulated investment company (RIC) incurred in tax years beginning before December 23, 2010, is carried forward up to 8 years. There is no limit on the number of tax years a RIC is allowed to carryover a net capital loss incurred in tax years beginning after December 22, 2010.

Items for Special Treatment
Note. For more information, see Pub. 544.

Special rules for determining basis. In general, the basis of property is its cost. See section 1012 and the related regulations. Special rules for determining basis are provided in sections in subchapters C, K, O, and P of the Code. These rules may apply to the:
• Receipt of certain distributions with respect to stock (section 301 or 1059),
• Liquidation of another corporation (section 334),
• Transfer to another corporation (section 358),
• Transfer from a shareholder or reorganization (section 362),
• Bequest (section 1014),
• Contribution or gift (section 1015),
• Tax-free exchange (section 1031),
• Involuntary conversion (section 1033),
• Certain asset acquisitions (section 1060), or
• Wash sale of stock (section 1091).

Attach an explanation if the corporation uses a basis other than actual cost of the property. See the instructions for Form 8949, column (e).

A RIC or REIT's basis in an asset it held on January 1, 2001, for which it made an election to recognize any gain under section 311 of the Taxpayer Relief Act of 1997, is the asset's closing market price or FMV, whichever applies, on the date of the deemed sale and reacquisition, whether the deemed sale resulted in a gain or unallowed loss.

See section 852(f) for the treatment of certain load charges incurred in acquiring stock in a RIC with a reinvestment right.

Gain from installment sales. If the corporation sold property at a gain and it will receive a payment in a tax year after the year of sale, it generally must report the sale on the installment method unless it elects not to. However, the installment method may not be used to report sales of stock or securities traded on an established securities market.

Use Form 6252, Installment Sale Income, to report the sale on the installment method. Also use Form 6252 to report any payment received during the tax year from a sale made in an earlier year that was reported on the installment method. Enter gain from the installment sales on Schedule D, line 4 or line 12, as applicable. See the instructions for Form 6252.

To elect out of the installment method, report the full amount of the gain on Form 8949 for the year of the sale on a return filed by the due date (including extensions). If the original return was filed on time without making the election, the corporation may make the election on an amended return filed no later than 6 months after the original due date (excluding extensions). Write "Filed pursuant to section 301.9100-2" at the top of the amended return.

Gain on distributions of appreciated property. Generally, gain (but not loss) is recognized on a nonliquidating distribution of appreciated property to the extent that the property's fair market value (FMV) exceeds its adjusted basis. See section 311.

Rollover of gain from empowerment zone assets. If the corporation sold a qualified empowerment zone asset held for more than 1 year, it may be able to elect to postpone part or all of the gain that it would otherwise include in income. See section 1397B(b)(1) for the definition of a qualified empowerment zone asset. If the corporation makes the

election, the gain on the sale generally is recognized only to the extent, if any, that the amount realized on the sale exceeds the cost of qualified empowerment zone assets (replacement property) the corporation purchased during the 60-day period beginning on the date of the sale. For more information, see section 1397B.

How to report. Report the sale on Part II of Form 8949 as the corporation otherwise would if it were not making the election. Enter "R" in column (f). Enter the amount of the postponed gain as a negative number in column (g). Put it in parentheses to show it is negative. See the instructions for Form 8949, columns (f), (g), and (h). Complete all remaining columns.

Exclusion of gain from DC Zone assets. If the corporation sold or exchanged a qualified District of Columbia Enterprise Zone (DC Zone) asset acquired after 1997 and before 2012, and held for more than 5 years, it may exclude any qualified capital gain that the corporation would otherwise include in income. The exclusion applies to an interest in, or property of, certain businesses operating in the District of Columbia.

DC Zone asset. A DC Zone asset is any of the following.
• DC Zone business stock.
• DC Zone partnership interest.
• DC Zone business property.

Qualified capital gain. Qualified capital gain is any gain recognized on the sale or exchange of a DC Zone asset, but does not include any of the following.
• Gain treated as ordinary income under section 1245.
• Section 1250 gain figured as if section 1250 applied to all depreciation rather than the additional depreciation.
• Gain attributable to real property, or an intangible asset, that is not an integral part of a DC Zone business.
• Gain from a related-party transaction. See *Sales and Exchanges Between Related Persons* in chapter 2 of Pub. 544.

See section 1400B for more details on DC Zone assets and special rules.

How to report. Report the sale or exchange on Form 8949, Part II, as the corporation otherwise would without regard to the exclusion (with the appropriate box checked). Enter "X" in column (f). Enter the amount of the exclusion as a negative number (in parentheses) in column (g). Complete all remaining columns. See the Instructions for Form 8949 for details.

Exclusion of gain from qualified community assets. If the corporation sold or exchanged a qualified community asset acquired after 2001 and before 2010, and held for more than 5 years, it may be able to exclude any qualified capital gain that the corporation would otherwise include in income. The exclusion applies to an interest in, or property of, certain renewal community businesses.

Qualified community asset. A qualified community asset is any of the following.
- Qualified community stock.
- Qualified community partnership interest.
- Qualified community business property.

Qualified capital gain. Qualified capital gain is any gain recognized on the sale or exchange of a qualified community asset, but does not include any of the following.
- Gain treated as ordinary income under section 1245.
- Section 1250 gain figured as if section 1250 applied to all depreciation rather than the additional depreciation.
- Gain attributable to real property, or an intangible asset, that is not an integral part of a qualified community business.
- Gain from a related-party transaction. See *Sales and Exchanges Between Related Persons* in chapter 2 of Pub. 544.

See section 1400F for more details on qualified community assets and special rules.

How to report. Report the sale or exchange on Form 8949, Part II, as the corporation otherwise would without regard to the exclusion (with the appropriate box checked). Enter "X" in column (f) and enter the amount of the excluded gain as a negative number (in parentheses) in column (g). Complete all remaining columns. See the Instructions for Form 8949.

Gain on the constructive sale of certain appreciated financial positions. Generally, if the corporation holds an appreciated financial position in stock or certain other interests, it may have to recognize gain (but not loss) if it enters into a constructive sale (such as a "short sale against the box"). See Pub. 550.

Gain from certain constructive ownership transactions. Gain in excess of the underlying net long-term capital gain the corporation would have recognized if it had held a financial asset directly during the term of a derivative contract must be treated as ordinary income. See section 1260. If any portion of the constructive ownership transaction was open in any prior year, the corporation may have to pay interest. See section 1260(b) for details, including how to figure the interest. Include the interest as an additional tax on Form 1120, Schedule J, line 9f (or the applicable line for other income tax returns).

Rollover of publicly traded securities gain into specialized small business investment companies (SSBICs). If the corporation sold publicly traded securities, it may elect under section 1044(a) to postpone all or part of the gain on that sale if it bought common stock or a partnership interest in an SSBIC during the 60-day period that began on the date of the sale. An SSBIC is any partnership or corporation licensed by the Small Business Administration under section 301(d) of the Small Business Investment Act of 1958. The corporation must recognize gain to the extent the sale proceeds exceed the cost (not taken into account previously) of its SSBIC stock or partnership interest purchased during the 60-day period that began on the date of the sale. The gain a corporation may postpone each tax year is limited to the smaller of (a) $1 million, reduced by the gain previously excluded under section 1044(a) or (b) $250,000. Reduce the basis of the SSBIC stock or partnership interest by any postponed gain.

Attach a statement showing (a) how the postponed gain was figured, (b) the name of the SSBIC stock in which the common stock or partnership interest was purchased, (c) the date of purchase, and (d) the new basis in that SSBIC stock or partnership interest. For more details, see section 1044 and Regulations section 1.1044(a)-1.

The corporation must make the election no later than the due date (including extensions) for filing its tax return for the year in which it sold the securities or partnership interest. If the original return was filed on time without making the election, the corporation may make the election on an amended return filed no later than 6 months after the original due date (excluding extensions). Write "Filed pursuant to section 301.9100-2" at the top of the amended return.

How to report. To make the election to postpone gain, report the sale on Form 8949, Part I or II (depending on how long the corporation owned the stock), as the corporation would if it were not making the election. Enter "R" in column (f). Enter the amount of the postponed gain as a negative number (in parentheses) in column (g). Complete all remaining columns.

Gain on disposition of market discount bonds. In general, if the corporation realizes a capital gain upon the disposition of a market discount bond, the gain is recharacterized as interest income to the extent of accrued market discount as of the date of disposition. See sections 1276 through 1278 and Pub. 550 for more information on market discount. See the Instructions for Form 8949 for detailed information about how to report the disposition of a market discount bond.

Gains on certain insurance property. Form 1120-L filers with gains on property held on December 31, 1958, and certain substituted property acquired after 1958, should see section 818(c).

Gains and losses from passive activities. A closely held or personal service corporation that has a gain or loss that relates to a passive activity (section 469) may be required to complete Form 8810, Corporate Passive Activity Loss and Credit Limitations, before completing Form 8949 and Schedule D. An applicable loss may be limited under the passive activity rules. See Form 8810 and the Instructions for Form 8810.

Gains and losses of foreign corporations from the disposition of investment in U.S. real property. Foreign corporations must report gains and losses from the disposition of U.S. real property interests. See section 897.

Gain or loss on distribution of property in complete liquidation. Generally, gain or loss is recognized on property distributed in a complete liquidation. Treat the property as if it had been sold at its FMV. An exception to this rule applies for liquidations of certain subsidiaries. See sections 336 and 337 for more information and other exceptions to the general rules.

Gain or loss on certain asset transfers to a tax-exempt entity. A taxable corporation that transfers all or substantially all of its assets to a tax-exempt entity or converts from a taxable corporation to a tax-exempt entity in a transaction other than a liquidation generally must recognize gain or loss as if it had sold the assets transferred at their FMV. For details and exceptions, see Regulations section 1.337(d)-4.

Gain or loss on an option to buy or sell property. See sections 1032 and 1234 for the rules that apply to a purchaser or grantor of an option or a securities futures contract (as defined in section 1234B). See Pub. 550 for details.

Gain or loss from a short sale of property. Report the gain or loss to the extent that the property used to close the short sale is considered a capital asset in the hands of the taxpayer. Report any short sale on Form 8949 in the year the sale closes.

If a short sale closed in 2014 but you did not get a 2014 Form 1099-B (or substitute statement) for it because you entered into it before 2011, report it on Form 8949 in Part I with box C checked or Part II with box F checked (whichever applies). In column (a), enter (for example) "100 sh. XYZ Co. —2010 short sale closed." Fill in the other columns according to their instructions. Report the short sale the same way if you received a 2014 Form 1099-B (or substitute statement) that does not show the proceeds (sales price).

Gain or loss on certain short-term federal, state, and municipal obligations (other than tax-exempt organizations). These obligations are treated as capital assets in determining gain or loss. On any gain realized, a portion is treated as ordinary income and any remaining balance as a short-term capital gain. See section 1271.

Contingent payment debt instruments. Any gain recognized on the sale, exchange, or retirement of a contingent payment debt instrument subject to the noncontingent bond method is treated as interest income rather than as capital gain. In certain situations, all or a portion of a loss recognized on the sale, exchange, or retirement of a contingent payment debt instrument subject to the noncontingent bond method may be treated as an ordinary loss rather than as a capital loss. See Regulations section 1.1275-4(b) and Pub. 550 for more information on contingent payment debt instruments subject to the noncontingent bond method.

At-risk limitations (section 465). If the corporation sold or exchanged a capital asset used in an activity to which the at-risk rules apply, combine the gain or loss on the sale or exchange with the profit or loss from the activity. If the result is a net loss, complete Form 6198, At-Risk Limitations. Report any gain from the capital asset on Form 8949, Schedule D, and Form 6198.

Loss from a sale or exchange between the corporation and a related person. Except for distributions in complete liquidation of a corporation, no loss is allowed from the sale or exchange of property between the corporation and certain related persons. See section 267.

Loss from a wash sale. The corporation cannot deduct a loss from a wash sale of stock or securities (including contracts or options to acquire or sell stock or securities) unless the corporation is a dealer in stock or securities and the loss was sustained in a transaction made in the ordinary course of the corporation's trade or business. A wash sale occurs if the corporation acquires (by purchase or exchange), or has a contract or option to acquire, substantially identical stock or securities within 30 days before or after the date of the sale or exchange. See section 1091.

Report the transaction as the corporation otherwise would, on Form 8949, Part I or Part II (depending on how long the corporation owned the stock or securities). Check the appropriate box. Enter "W" in column (f). Enter the nondeductible loss as a positive number in column (g). Complete all remaining columns. See the Instructions for Form 8949.

Loss from securities that are capital assets that become worthless during the year. Except for securities held by a bank, treat the loss as a capital loss as of the last day of the tax year. See section 582 for the rules on the treatment of securities held by a bank.

Losses limited after an ownership change or acquisition. If the corporation has undergone an "ownership change" as defined in section 382(g), section 383 may limit the amount of capital gains that may be offset by prechange capital losses. In addition, section 382(h) may in some cases limit capital losses recognized after an ownership change when the loss accrued before the ownership change. Also, if a corporation acquires control of another corporation (or acquires its assets in a reorganization), section 384 may limit the amount of recognized built-in capital gains that may be offset by preacquisition capital losses.

Loss from the sale or exchange of capital assets of an insurance company taxable under section 831. Capital losses of a casualty insurance company are deductible to the extent that the assets were sold to meet abnormal insurance losses or to provide for the payment of dividend and similar distributions to policyholders. See section 834(c)(6).

Gains and losses from partnerships, estates, or trusts. Report the corporation's share of capital gains and losses from investments in partnerships, estates, or trusts on the appropriate Part of Form 8949. Report a net short-term capital gain (loss) on Part I, with box C checked. Report a net long-term capital gain (loss) on Part II, with box F checked. See the Instructions for Form 8949.

Undistributed long-term gains from a regulated investment company (RIC) or real estate investment trust (REIT). Report the corporation's share of long-term gains from Form 2439, Notice to Shareholder of Undistributed Long-Term Capital Gains, on Form 8949, Part II (with box F checked). Enter "From Form 2439" in column (a). Enter the gain in column (h). Leave all other columns blank. See the Instructions for Form 8949.

Amounts from Form 2438. Enter any net short-term capital gain from line 4 of Form 2438, Undistributed Capital Gains Tax Return, on Form 8949, Part I, with box C checked. Identify the gain as "Net short-term capital gain from Form 2438 line 4" in column (a). Enter the amount of the gain in column (h). Leave all other columns blank.

Enter the amount from line 12 of Form 2438, on Form 8949, Part II, with box F checked. Identify the gain as "Undistributed capital gains not designated (from Form 2438)" in column (a). Enter the amount of the gain in column (h). Leave all other columns blank.

NAV method for certain money market funds. Report capital gain or loss determined under the net asset value (NAV) method with respect to shares in a floating-NAV money market fund on Form 8949, Part I, with box C checked. Enter the name of each fund followed by "(NAV)" in column (a). Enter the net gain or loss in column (h). Leave all other columns blank. See the Instructions for Form 8949.

Specific Instructions

In Part I, report the sale, exchange, or distribution of capital assets held 1 year or less. In Part II, report the sale, exchange, or distribution of capital assets held more than 1 year.

Lines 1a and 8a – Transactions not reported on Form 8949. The corporation can report on line 1a (for short-term transactions) or line 8a (for long-term transactions) the aggregate totals from any transactions (other than sales of collectibles) for which:

• The corporation received a Form 1099-B (or substitute statement) that shows basis was reported to the IRS and does not show any adjustments in box 1g; and

• The corporation does not need to make any adjustments to the basis or type of gain or loss (short term or long term) reported on Form 1099-B (or substitute statement), or to its gain or loss.

See *How To Complete Form 8949, Columns (f) and (g)*, in the Instructions for Form 8949 for details about possible adjustments to the corporation's gain or loss.

If the corporation chooses to report these transactions on lines 1a and 8a, do not report them on Form 8949. Also, the corporation does not need to attach a statement to explain the entries on lines 1a and 8a.

Figure gain or loss on each line. First, subtract the cost or other basis in column (e) from the proceeds (sales price) in column (d). Enter the gain or loss in column (h). Enter negative amounts in parentheses.

Example 1 – basis reported to the IRS. The corporation received a Form 1099-B reporting the sale of stock held for 3 years, showing proceeds (in box 1d) of $6,000 and cost or other basis (in box 1e) of $2,000. Box 3 is checked, meaning that basis was reported to the IRS. The corporation does not need to make any adjustments to the amounts reported on Form 1099-B or enter any codes. This was the corporation's only 2014 transaction. Instead of reporting this transaction on Form 8949, the corporation can enter $6,000 on Schedule D, line 8a, column (d), $2,000 in column (e), and $4,000 ($6,000 - $2,000) in column (h).

If you had a second transaction that was the same except that the proceeds were $5,000 and the basis was $3,000, combine the two transactions. Enter $11,000 ($6,000 + $5,000) on Schedule D, line 8a, column (d); $5,000 ($2,000 + $3,000) in column (e); and $6,000 ($11,000 - $5,000) in column (h).

Example 2 – basis not reported to IRS. The corporation received a Form 1099-B showing proceeds (in box 1d) of $6,000 and cost or other basis (in box 1e) of $2,000. Box 3 is not checked, meaning that basis was not reported to the IRS. Do not report this transaction on line 1a or line 8a. Instead, report the transaction on Form 8949. Complete all necessary pages of Form 8949 before completing lines 1b, 2, 3, 8b, 9, or 10 of Schedule D.

Example 3 – adjustment. The corporation received a Form 1099-B showing proceeds (in box 1d) of $6,000 and cost or other basis (in box 1e) of $2,000. Box 3 is checked, meaning that basis was reported to the IRS. However, the basis shown in box 1e is incorrect. Do not report this transaction on line 1a or line 8a. Instead, report the transaction on Form 8949. See the instructions for Form 8949, columns (f), (g), and (h). Complete all necessary pages of Form 8949 before completing lines 1b, 2, 3, 8b, 9, or 10 of Schedule D.

Lines 1b, 2, 3, 8b, 9, and 10 – Transactions reported on Form 8949. Complete Form 8949 before completing Schedule D, lines 1b, 2, 3, 8b, 9, and 10. Enter on Schedule D, lines 1b, 2, and 3, respectively, the short-term totals from all Forms 8949, Part I, line 2, with box A, B, or C, respectively, checked. Enter on Schedule D, lines 8b, 9, and 10, respectively, the long-term totals from all Forms 8949, Part II, line 2, with box D, E, or F, respectively, checked.

Line 6. Enter any unused capital loss carryover. Attach a statement showing how the carryover was computed.

Line 14. Enter the total capital gain distributions paid by a RIC or REIT during the year, regardless of how long the corporation owned stock in the RIC or REIT.

Also enter any amount received from a RIC or REIT that qualifies as a distribution in complete liquidation under section 332(b) and is designated by the RIC or REIT as a capital gain distribution. See section 332(c).

SCHEDULE G
(Form 1120)
(Rev. December 2011)
Department of the Treasury
Internal Revenue Service

Information on Certain Persons Owning the Corporation's Voting Stock

▶ Attach to Form 1120.
▶ See instructions on page 2.

OMB No. 1545-0123

Name

Employer identification number (EIN)

Part I **Certain Entities Owning the Corporation's Voting Stock.** (Form 1120, Schedule K, Question 4a). Complete columns (i) through (v) below for any foreign or domestic corporation, partnership (including any entity treated as a partnership), trust, or tax-exempt organization that owns directly 20% or more, or owns, directly or indirectly, 50% or more of the total voting power of all classes of the corporation's stock entitled to vote (see instructions).

(i) Name of Entity	(ii) Employer Identification Number (if any)	(iii) Type of Entity	(iv) Country of Organization	(v) Percentage Owned in Voting Stock

---

Part II **Certain Individuals and Estates Owning the Corporation's Voting Stock.** (Form 1120, Schedule K, Question 4b). Complete columns (i) through (iv) below for any individual or estate that owns directly 20% or more, or owns, directly or indirectly, 50% or more of the total voting power of all classes of the corporation's stock entitled to vote (see instructions).

(i) Name of Individual or Estate	(ii) Identifying Number (if any)	(iii) Country of Citizenship (see instructions)	(iv) Percentage Owned in Voting Stock

---

For Paperwork Reduction Act Notice, see the Instructions for Form 1120.

Cat. No. 52684S

Schedule G (Form 1120) (Rev. 12-2011)

General Instructions

Purpose of Form

Use Schedule G (Form 1120) to provide information applicable to certain entities, individuals, and estates that own, directly, 20% or more, or own, directly or indirectly, 50% or more, of the total voting power of all classes of the corporation's stock entitled to vote.

Who Must File

Every corporation that answers "Yes" to Form 1120, Schedule K, Questions 4a or 4b, must file Schedule G to provide the additional information requested for certain entities, individuals, and estates owning the corporation's voting stock.

Constructive Ownership of the Corporation

For purposes of Schedule G (Form 1120), the constructive ownership rules of section 267(c) (excluding section 267(c)(3)) apply to ownership of interests in corporate stock and ownership of interests in the profit, loss, or capital of a partnership. An interest in the corporation owned directly or indirectly by or for another entity (corporation, partnership, estate, or trust) is considered to be owned proportionately by the owners (shareholders, partners, or beneficiaries) of the owning entity. Also, under section 267(c), an individual is considered to own an interest owned directly or indirectly by or for his or her family. The family of an individual includes only that individual's spouse, brothers, sisters, ancestors, and lineal descendants.

An interest will be attributed from an individual under the family attribution rules only if the person to whom the interest is attributed owns a direct or an indirect interest in the corporation under section 267(c)(1) or (5). However, for purposes of these instructions, an individual will not be considered to own, under section 267(c)(2), an interest in the corporation owned, directly or indirectly, by a family member unless the individual also owns an interest in the corporation either directly or indirectly through a corporation, partnership or trust.

Example 1. Corporation A owns, directly, a 50% interest in the profit, loss, or capital of Partnership B. Corporation A also owns, directly, a 15% interest in the profit, loss, or capital of Partnership C and owns, directly, 15% of the voting stock of Corporation D. Partnership B owns, directly, a 70% interest in the profit, loss, or capital of Partnership C and owns, directly, 70% of the voting stock of Corporation D. Corporation A owns, indirectly, through Partnership B, a 35% interest (50% of 70%) in the profit, loss, or capital of Partnership C and owns, indirectly, 35% of the voting stock of Corporation D. Corporation A owns, directly or indirectly, a 50% interest in the profit, loss, or capital of Partnership C (15% directly and 35% indirectly), and owns, directly or indirectly, 50% of the voting stock of Corporation D (15% directly and 35% indirectly).

Corporation D reports in Part I that its voting stock is owned, directly or indirectly, 50% by Corporation A and is owned, directly, 70% by Partnership B.

Example 2. A owns, directly, 50% of the voting stock of Corporation X. B, the daughter of A, does not own, directly, any interest in Corporation X and does not own, indirectly, any interest in Corporation X through any entity (corporation, partnership, trust, or estate). Therefore, the family attribution rules do not apply and, for the purposes of Part II, the 50% interest of A in Corporation X is not attributed to B.

Example 3. A owns, directly, 50% of the voting stock of Corporation X. B, the daughter of A, does not own, directly, any interest in X but does own, indirectly, 10% of the voting stock of Corporation X through Trust T of which she is the sole beneficiary. No other family member of A or B owns, directly, any interest in Corporation X nor does any own, indirectly, any interest in Corporation X through any entity. Neither A nor B owns any other interest in Corporation X through any entity.

For the purposes of Part II, the 50% interest of A in the voting stock of Corporation X is attributed to B and the 10% interest of B in the voting stock of Corporation X is attributed to A. A owns, directly or indirectly, 60% of the voting stock of Corporation X, 50% directly and 10% indirectly through B. B owns, directly or indirectly, 60% of the voting stock of Corporation X (50% indirectly through A and 10% indirectly through Trust T).

Specific Instructions

Part I

Complete Part I if the corporation answered "Yes" to Form 1120, Schedule K, Question 4a. List each foreign or domestic corporation, partnership, trust, or tax-exempt organization that owns, at the end of the tax year, directly 20% or more, or owns, directly or indirectly, 50% or more of the total voting power of all classes of the corporation's stock entitled to vote. Indicate the name of the entity, employer identification number (if any), type of entity (corporation, partnership, trust, or tax-exempt organization), country of organization, and the percentage owned, directly or indirectly, of the voting stock of the corporation.

For an affiliated group filing a consolidated tax return, list the parent corporation rather than the subsidiary members. List the entity owner of a disregarded entity rather than the disregarded entity. If the owner of a disregarded entity is an individual rather than an entity, list the individual in Part II.

Part II

Complete Part II if the corporation answered "Yes" to Form 1120, Schedule K, Question 4b. List each individual or estate that owns, at the end of the tax year, directly 20% or more, or owns, directly or indirectly, 50% or more, of the total voting power of all classes of the corporation's stock entitled to vote. Indicate the name of the individual or estate, taxpayer identification number (if any), country of citizenship (for an estate, the citizenship of the decedent), and the percentage owned, directly or indirectly, of the voting stock of the corporation.

SCHEDULE H
(Form 1120)
(Rev. December 2011)
Department of the Treasury
Internal Revenue Service

Section 280H Limitations for a Personal Service Corporation (PSC)

▶ **Attach to PSC's income tax return if Part II is completed.**

OMB No. 1545-0123

Name | Employer identification number

Note: *A newly organized PSC is considered to have met the section 280H distribution requirements for the first year of its existence and does not have to complete Schedule H. If, during the tax year, an existing corporation becomes a PSC and makes a section 444 election, the corporation is treated as if it were a PSC for the 3 preceding tax years. See Temporary Regulations section 1.280H-1T(e).*

Part I	Minimum Distribution Requirement (see instructions)			
1	Enter applicable amounts from preceding tax year	1		
2	Divide number of months in deferral period of preceding tax year by number of months in preceding tax year. Enter the result as a percentage	2		%
3	**Amount figured under preceding year test.** Multiply line 1 by the percentage on line 2	3		
4	Enter applicable amounts from the deferral period of the applicable election year	4		
	If line 4 is less than line 3, go to line 5. Otherwise, **stop here.** The PSC has met the minimum distribution requirement. **Do not** attach Schedule H to the PSC's income tax return. Keep Schedule H with the PSC's tax records.			
5	Enter applicable amounts from the:			
a	1st tax year before applicable election year	5a		
b	2nd tax year before applicable election year	5b		
c	3rd tax year before applicable election year	5c		
6	**Total.** Add lines 5a through 5c	6		
7	Enter adjusted taxable income for the:			
a	1st tax year before applicable election year	7a		
b	2nd tax year before applicable election year	7b		
c	3rd tax year before applicable election year 1	7c		
8	**Total.** Add lines 7a through 7c	8		
9	Divide line 6 by line 8	9		%
10	Enter the percentage from line 9 or 66%, whichever is smaller	10		%
11	Enter adjusted taxable income for the deferral period of the applicable election year	11		
12	**Amount figured under 3-year average test.** Multiply line 11 by line 10	12		
13	**Minimum distribution requirement.** Enter the smaller of line 3 or line 12	13		
	• If line 13 is **equal to or less** than line 4, **stop here.** The PSC has met the minimum distribution requirement. **Do not** complete Part II and **do not** attach Schedule H to the PSC's income tax return. Keep Schedule H with the PSC's tax records.			
	• If line 13 is **more than** line 4, the PSC's deduction for applicable amounts is limited under section 280H. Complete Part II to figure the maximum amount the PSC can deduct.			
Part II	**Maximum Deductible Amount** (see instructions)			
14	Enter amount from line 4	14		
15	Enter number of months in deferral period of applicable election year	15		
16	Divide line 14 by line 15	16		
17	**Nondeferral period.** Subtract the number of months in the deferral period from the number of months in the applicable tax year. Enter the result	17		
18	Multiply line 16 by line 17	18		
19	**Maximum deductible amount.** Add lines 14 and 18. The PSC's deduction for applicable amounts paid or incurred to employee-owners is limited to this amount. **Attach Schedule H to the PSC's income tax return.** Any amount not allowed because of the section 280H(d) limitation is treated as paid or incurred in the PSC's succeeding tax year	19		

For Paperwork Reduction Act Notice, see the Instructions for Form 1120.   Cat. No. 14491P   Schedule H (Form 1120) (Rev. 12-2011)

General Instructions

Section references are to the Internal Revenue Code unless otherwise noted.

Purpose of Schedule

A personal service corporation (PSC) (as defined in section 441(i)(2)) may elect under section 444 to have a tax year other than a calendar year. A PSC that makes the election is subject to the minimum distribution requirement of section 280H for the year the election is made and for each tax year the election remains in effect. If the PSC does not meet the requirement, its deduction for amounts paid or incurred to employee-owners (see *Applicable amount* below) is limited.

Use Part I of Schedule H to determine if the PSC meets the minimum distribution requirement of section 280H(c) for the tax year. Use Part II to figure the limits on deductions under section 280H(d) if the requirement is not met.

Who Must File

A PSC that has elected under section 444 to have a tax year other than a calendar year must complete Schedule H. If the PSC does not meet the minimum distribution requirement of section 280H for the tax year, it must file Schedule H with its Form 1120. If it does meet the requirement, it does not need to attach the completed Schedule H to its tax return, but it should keep it with its tax records.

Definitions

Applicable election year. An applicable election year is any tax year in which a section 444 election is in effect.

Applicable amount. An applicable amount is any amount otherwise deductible by a PSC in a tax year that is includible (directly or indirectly) in the gross income of a taxpayer who is an employee-owner at any time during that year. See the instructions for line 1 for an example of how to figure a PSC's applicable amounts.

Exception. Dividends paid by the corporation and gain on the sale or exchange of property between the owner-employee and the corporation are not applicable amounts.

An amount is indirectly includible in the gross income of an employee-owner if the amount is includible in the gross income of certain related parties. For details and examples, see Temporary Regulations sections 1.280H-1T(b)(4)(ii) and 1.280H-1T(b)(4)(iii).

Employee-owner. An employee-owner is a person who, on any day of the PSC's tax years:

• Is an employee of the PSC or who performs services for or on behalf of the PSC (including an independent contractor) and

• Owns any outstanding stock of the PSC.

Deferral period. The deferral period is the number of months between the last day of the elected tax year and the last day of the required tax year.

Example. The PSC elects a tax year that ends on September 30. Since the required tax year for a PSC is the calendar year, the deferral period is 3 months (the number of months between September 30 and December 31).

Nondeferral period. The nondeferral period is the part of the tax year that occurs after the part of the year that constitutes the deferral period.

Adjusted taxable income. Adjusted taxable income is taxable income determined without regard to:

• Applicable amounts and

• Any NOL carryover to the extent the carryover is attributable to applicable amounts.

Adjusted taxable income for the deferral period of an applicable election year is the adjusted taxable income that would result if the PSC filed an income tax return for the deferral period under its normal method of accounting. Reasonable estimates are acceptable.

For more information, see Temporary Regulations section 1.280H-1T(c)(3)(iii).

Specific Instructions

Part I

Complete Part I to see if the PSC meets the minimum distribution requirement of section 280H(c). The PSC meets the requirement if, during the deferral period of the tax year, the applicable amounts paid or incurred for all employee-owners are equal to or greater than the smaller of:

• The amount determined under the preceding year test or

• The amount determined under the 3-year average test.

Complete lines 1 through 4 to determine if the preceding year test applies to the PSC. If it does not, complete the rest of Part I to see if the 3-year average test applies.

Line 1. Enter the applicable amount that was paid or incurred in the preceding tax year to any employee-owner of the PSC and that was otherwise deductible by the PSC on its preceding income tax return.

Example. PEK, an accrual basis personal service corporation with a tax year ending September 30, made a section 444 election for its tax year beginning October 1, 2010. On October 1, 2010, S, an employee of PEK, owned no stock of PEK; however, on March 31, 2011, S acquired 10 of the 200 outstanding shares of PEK stock. During the period October 1, 2010 to March 31, 2011, S earned $40,000 of compensation as an employee of PEK. During the period April 1, 2011, to September 30, 2011, S earned $60,000 of compensation as an employee-owner of PEK. The entire $100,000 compensation paid to S during PEK's tax year ending September 30, 2011, was otherwise deductible by PEK and includible in S's gross income. For its 2011 tax year, it is an applicable amount for PEK from the preceding tax year.

See Temporary Regulations section 1.280H-1T(c) for more information, including examples of the computation of the preceding-year test and the 3-year average test.

Part II

Complete Part II to figure the maximum deduction under section 280H(d) for applicable amounts if the PSC did not meet the minimum distribution requirement figured in Part I.

Net Income (Loss) Reconciliation for Corporations With Total Assets of $10 Million or More

► Attach to Form 1120 or 1120-C. ► Information about Schedule M-3 (Form 1120) and its separate instructions is available at *www.irs.gov/form1120*.

OMB No. 1545-0123

2014

Name of corporation (common parent, if consolidated return)	Employer identification number

Check applicable box(es): (1) ☐ Non-consolidated return (2) ☐ Consolidated return (Form 1120 only)

(3) ☐ Mixed 1120/L/PC group (4) ☐ Dormant subsidiaries schedule attached

Part I Financial Information and Net Income (Loss) Reconciliation (see instructions)

1a Did the corporation file SEC Form 10-K for its income statement period ending with or within this tax year?
  ☐ **Yes.** Skip lines 1b and 1c and complete lines 2a through 11 with respect to that SEC Form 10-K.
  ☐ **No.** Go to line 1b. See instructions if multiple non-tax-basis income statements are prepared.
b Did the corporation prepare a certified audited non-tax-basis income statement for that period?
  ☐ **Yes.** Skip line 1c and complete lines 2a through 11 with respect to that income statement.
  ☐ **No.** Go to line 1c.
c Did the corporation prepare a non-tax-basis income statement for that period?
  ☐ **Yes.** Complete lines 2a through 11 with respect to that income statement.
  ☐ **No.** Skip lines 2a through 3c and enter the corporation's net income (loss) per its books and records on line 4a.
2a Enter the income statement period: Beginning MM/DD/YYYY Ending MM/DD/YYYY
b Has the corporation's income statement been restated for the income statement period on line 2a?
  ☐ **Yes.** (If "Yes," attach an explanation and the amount of each item restated.)
  ☐ **No.**
c Has the corporation's income statement been restated for any of the five income statement periods immediately preceding the period on line 2a?
  ☐ **Yes.** (If "Yes," attach an explanation and the amount of each item restated.)
  ☐ **No.**
3a Is any of the corporation's voting common stock publicly traded?
  ☐ **Yes.**
  ☐ **No.** If "No," go to line 4a.
b Enter the symbol of the corporation's primary U.S. publicly traded voting common stock . . . .
c Enter the nine-digit CUSIP number of the corporation's primary publicly traded voting common stock . . . .

4a Worldwide consolidated net income (loss) from income statement source identified in Part I, line 1 .	**4a**	
b Indicate accounting standard used for line 4a (see instructions): (1)☐ GAAP (2) ☐ IFRS (3) ☐ Statutory (4) ☐ Tax-basis (5) ☐ Other (specify) _____		
5a Net income from nonincludible foreign entities (attach statement)	**5a**	( )
b Net loss from nonincludible foreign entities (attach statement and enter as a positive amount)	**5b**	
6a Net income from nonincludible U.S. entities (attach statement)	**6a**	( )
b Net loss from nonincludible U.S. entities (attach statement and enter as a positive amount)	**6b**	
7a Net income (loss) of other includible foreign disregarded entities (attach statement)	**7a**	
b Net income (loss) of other includible U.S. disregarded entities (attach statement)	**7b**	
c Net income (loss) of other includible entities (attach statement)	**7c**	
8 Adjustment to eliminations of transactions between includible entities and nonincludible entities (attach statement)	**8**	
9 Adjustment to reconcile income statement period to tax year (attach statement)	**9**	
10a Intercompany dividend adjustments to reconcile to line 11 (attach statement)	**10a**	
b Other statutory accounting adjustments to reconcile to line 11 (attach statement)	**10b**	
c Other adjustments to reconcile to amount on line 11 (attach statement)	**10c**	
11 **Net income (loss) per income statement of includible corporations.** Combine lines 4 through 10 .	**11**	

Note. Part I, line 11, must equal Part II, line 30, column (a) or Schedule M-1, line 1 (see instructions).

12 Enter the total amount (not just the corporation's share) of the assets and liabilities of all entities included or removed on the following lines.

	Total Assets	Total Liabilities
a Included on Part I, line 4 . . . . ►		
b Removed on Part I, line 5 . . . . ►		
c Removed on Part I, line 6 . . . . ►		
d Included on Part I, line 7 . . . . ►		

Name of corporation (common parent, if consolidated return)	Employer identification number

Check applicable box(es): **(1)** ☐ Consolidated group **(2)** ☐ Parent corp **(3)** ☐ Consolidated eliminations **(4)** ☐ Subsidiary corp **(5)** ☐ Mixed 1120/L/PC group

Check if a sub-consolidated: **(6)** ☐ 1120 group **(7)** ☐ 1120 eliminations

Name of subsidiary (if consolidated return)	Employer identification number

Part II Reconciliation of Net Income (Loss) per Income Statement of Includible Corporations With Taxable Income per Return (see instructions)

Income (Loss) Items (Attach statements for lines 1 through 12)	(a) Income (Loss) per Income Statement	(b) Temporary Difference	(c) Permanent Difference	(d) Income (Loss) per Tax Return
1 Income (loss) from equity method foreign corporations				
2 Gross foreign dividends not previously taxed				
3 Subpart F, QEF, and similar income inclusions				
4 Section 78 gross-up				
5 Gross foreign distributions previously taxed				
6 Income (loss) from equity method U.S. corporations				
7 U.S. dividends not eliminated in tax consolidation				
8 Minority interest for includible corporations				
9 Income (loss) from U.S. partnerships				
10 Income (loss) from foreign partnerships				
11 Income (loss) from other pass-through entities				
12 Items relating to reportable transactions				
13 Interest income (see instructions)				
14 Total accrual to cash adjustment				
15 Hedging transactions				
16 Mark-to-market income (loss)				
17 Cost of goods sold (see instructions)	( )			( )
18 Sale versus lease (for sellers and/or lessors)				
19 Section 481(a) adjustments				
20 Unearned/deferred revenue				
21 Income recognition from long-term contracts				
22 Original issue discount and other imputed interest				
23a Income statement gain/loss on sale, exchange, abandonment, worthlessness, or other disposition of assets other than inventory and pass-through entities				
b Gross capital gains from Schedule D, excluding amounts from pass-through entities				
c Gross capital losses from Schedule D, excluding amounts from pass-through entities, abandonment losses, and worthless stock losses				
d Net gain/loss reported on Form 4797, line 17, excluding amounts from pass-through entities, abandonment losses, and worthless stock losses				
e Abandonment losses				
f Worthless stock losses (attach statement)				
g Other gain/loss on disposition of assets other than inventory				
24 Capital loss limitation and carryforward used				
25 Other income (loss) items with differences (attach statement)				
26 **Total income (loss) items.** Combine lines 1 through 25				
27 **Total expense/deduction items** (from Part III, line 38)				
28 Other items with no differences				
29a Mixed groups, see instructions. All others, combine lines 26 through 28				
b PC insurance subgroup reconciliation totals				
c Life insurance subgroup reconciliation totals				
30 **Reconciliation totals.** Combine lines 29a through 29c				

Note. Line 30, column (a), must equal Part I, line 11, and column (d) must equal Form 1120, page 1, line 28.

Name of corporation (common parent, if consolidated return)	Employer identification number

Check applicable box(es): **(1)** ☐ Consolidated group   **(2)** ☐ Parent corp   **(3)** ☐ Consolidated eliminations   **(4)** ☐ Subsidiary corp   **(5)** ☐ Mixed 1120/L/PC group

Check if a sub-consolidated: **(6)** ☐ 1120 group   **(7)** ☐ 1120 eliminations

Name of subsidiary (if consolidated return)	Employer identification number

Part III   Reconciliation of Net Income (Loss) per Income Statement of Includible Corporations With Taxable Income per Return—Expense/Deduction Items (see instructions)

Expense/Deduction Items	(a) Expense per Income Statement	(b) Temporary Difference	(c) Permanent Difference	(d) Deduction per Tax Return
1 U.S. current income tax expense				
2 U.S. deferred income tax expense				
3 State and local current income tax expense				
4 State and local deferred income tax expense				
5 Foreign current income tax expense (other than foreign withholding taxes)				
6 Foreign deferred income tax expense				
7 Foreign withholding taxes				
8 Interest expense (see instructions)				
9 Stock option expense				
10 Other equity-based compensation				
11 Meals and entertainment				
12 Fines and penalties				
13 Judgments, damages, awards, and similar costs				
14 Parachute payments				
15 Compensation with section 162(m) limitation				
16 Pension and profit-sharing				
17 Other post-retirement benefits				
18 Deferred compensation				
19 Charitable contribution of cash and tangible property				
20 Charitable contribution of intangible property				
21 Charitable contribution limitation/carryforward				
22 Domestic production activities deduction				
23 Current year acquisition or reorganization investment banking fees				
24 Current year acquisition or reorganization legal and accounting fees				
25 Current year acquisition/reorganization other costs				
26 Amortization/impairment of goodwill				
27 Amortization of acquisition, reorganization, and start-up costs				
28 Other amortization or impairment write-offs				
29 Reserved				
30 Depletion				
31 Depreciation				
32 Bad debt expense				
33 Corporate owned life insurance premiums				
34 Purchase versus lease (for purchasers and/or lessees)				
35 Research and development costs				
36 Section 118 exclusion (attach statement)				
37 Other expense/deduction items with differences (attach statement)				
38 **Total expense/deduction items.** Combine lines 1 through 37. Enter here and on Part II, line 27, reporting positive amounts as negative and negative amounts as positive				

Instructions for Schedule M-3 (Form 1120)

Net Income (Loss) Reconciliation for Corporations With Total Assets of $10 Million or More

Section references are to the Internal Revenue Code unless otherwise noted.

Future Developments

For the latest information about developments related to Schedule M-3 (Form 1120) and its instructions, such as legislation enacted after they were published, go to www.irs.gov/form1120.

What's New

For tax years ending December 31, 2014, and later:

• Form 1120 and Form 1120-C filers that (a) are required to file Schedule M-3 (Form 1120) and have less than $50 million total assets at the end of the tax year, or (b) are not required to file Schedule M-3 (Form 1120) and voluntarily file Schedule M-3 (Form 1120), must either (i) complete Schedule M-3 (Form 1120) entirely or (ii) complete Schedule M-3 (Form 1120) through Part I, and complete Schedule M-1 of Form 1120 (or Form 1120-C, if applicable) instead of completing Parts II and III of Schedule M-3 (Form 1120). These filers are not required to file Schedule B (Form 1120) nor Form 8916-A. If these filers choose to complete Schedule M-1 instead of completing Parts II and III of Schedule M-3, line 1 of the applicable M-1 must equal line 11 of Part I of Schedule M-3.

• In the case of an 1120 mixed group, Parts II and III of Schedule M-3 (Form 1120) must be completed for all members of the mixed group whether Schedule M-3 (Form 1120) is required or voluntarily filed.

• Any filer that completes Parts II and III of Schedule M-3 (Form 1120), must complete all columns, without exception.

See *Completing Schedule M-3*, later.

General Instructions

Applicable schedules and instructions. Use the 2014 Schedule M-3 (Form 1120) and the 2014 Instructions for Schedule M-3 (Form 1120) for tax years ending December 31, 2014,

through December 31, 2015. For previous tax years, use the applicable Schedule M-3 (Form 1120) and instructions. For example, for tax years ending after December 31, 2013, and before December 31, 2014, see the 2013 Schedule M-3 (Form 1120) and the 2013 instructions for Schedule M-3 (Form 1120).

Purpose of Schedule

Schedule M-3, Part I, asks certain questions about the corporation's financial statements and reconciles financial statement net income (loss) for the corporation (or consolidated financial statement group, if applicable), as reported on Part I, line 4a, to net income (loss) of the corporation for U.S. taxable income purposes, as reported on Part I, line 11.

Schedule M-3, Parts II and III, reconcile financial statement net income (loss) for the U.S. corporation (or consolidated tax group, if applicable), as reported on Schedule M-3, Part I, line 11, to taxable income on Form 1120, page 1, line 28.

Where To File

If the corporation is required to file (or voluntarily files) Schedule M-3 (Form 1120), the corporation **must** file Form 1120 (or Form 1120-C, if applicable) and all attachments and schedules, including Schedule M-3 (Form 1120) at the following address.

Department of the Treasury
Internal Revenue Service Center
Ogden, UT 84201-0012

Who Must File

Generally the following apply.

• A domestic corporation or group of corporations required to file Form 1120, U.S. Corporation Income Tax Return, that reports on Form 1120, Schedule L, Balance Sheets per Books, total assets at the end of the corporation's tax year that equal or exceed $10 million must file Schedule M-3 instead of Schedule M-1, Reconciliation of Income

(Loss) per Books With Income per Return.

• A corporation filing a non-consolidated Form 1120 that reports on Schedule L total assets that equal or exceed $10 million must complete and file Schedule M-3 and must check box (1) Non-consolidated return, at the top of page 1 of Schedule M-3.

• Any U.S. consolidated tax group consisting of a U.S. parent corporation and additional includible corporations listed on Form 851, Affiliations Schedule, required to file Form 1120, that reports on Schedule L total consolidated assets at the end of the tax year that equal or exceed $10 million must file Schedule M-3 and must check box (2) Consolidated return (Form 1120 only), or box (3) Mixed 1120/L/PC group, as applicable, at the top of page 1 of Schedule M-3.

• Cooperatives filing Form 1120-C, U.S. Income Tax Return for Cooperative Associations, that report total assets at tax year end that equal or exceed $10 million must file Schedule M-3 (Form 1120).

• A corporation filing Form 1120 (or Form 1120-C) that is not required to file Schedule M-3 may voluntarily file Schedule M-3.

• If a corporation was required to file Schedule M-3 for the preceding tax year, but reports on Form 1120, page 1, Item D, and on Form 1120, Schedule L, total consolidated assets at the end of the current tax year of less than $10 million, the corporation is not required to file Schedule M-3 for the current tax year.

See *Completing Schedule M-3*, later.

In the case of a U.S. consolidated tax group, total assets at the end of the tax year must be determined based on the total year-end assets of all includible corporations listed on Form 851, net of eliminations for intercompany transactions and balances between the includible corporations. In addition, for purposes of determining whether the corporation (or U.S. consolidated tax group) has total assets at the end of the current tax year of $10 million or more, the corporation's total consolidated assets must be determined on an overall accrual method of accounting unless both of the following apply: (a) the tax returns of all includible corporations in the U.S. consolidated tax group are prepared using an overall cash method of accounting, and (b) no includible corporation in the U.S. consolidated tax group prepares or is included in financial statements prepared on an accrual basis.

Special Filing Requirements for Certain Groups

Mixed groups. If the parent corporation of a U.S. consolidated tax group files Form 1120 and files and completes Schedule M-3, Parts II and III, Schedule M-3, Parts II and III, must be completed for each member of the group. However, if the parent corporation of a U.S. consolidated tax group files Form 1120 and any member of the group files Form 1120-PC, U.S. Property and Casualty Insurance Company Income Tax Return, or Form 1120-L, U.S. Life Insurance Company Income Tax Return, that member must complete Parts II and III of Schedule M-3 (Form 1120-PC) or Schedule M-3 (Form 1120-L), respectively, and the group must comply with the mixed group consolidated Schedule M-3 instructions under *Schedule M-3 Consolidation for Mixed Groups (1120/L/PC)*, later. A mixed group must also file Form 8916, Reconciliation of Schedule M-3 Taxable Income with Tax Return Taxable Income for Mixed Groups and, if applicable, Form 8916-A, Supplemental Attachment to Schedule M-3.

If the parent company of a U.S. consolidated tax group files Form 1120 and any member of the group files Form 1120-PC or Form 1120-L and the consolidated Schedule L reported in the return includes the assets of all of the companies (the insurance companies as well as the non-insurance companies), in order to determine if the group meets the $10 million threshold test for the requirement to file Schedule M-3, use the amount of total assets reported on Schedule L of the consolidated return. If the parent company of a U.S. consolidated tax group files Form 1120 and any member of the group files Form 1120-PC or Form 1120-L and the consolidated Schedule L reported in the return does not include the assets of one or more of the insurance companies in the U.S. consolidated tax group, in order to

determine if the group meets the $10 million threshold test, use the sum of the amount of total assets reported on the consolidated Schedule L plus the amounts of all assets reported on Forms 1120-PC and 1120-L that are included in the consolidated return but not included on the consolidated Schedule L.

Other entities. There is a unique separate Schedule M-3 for taxpayers required to file Form 1065, U.S. Return of Partnership Income; Form 1120S, U.S. Income Tax Return for an S Corporation; Form 1120-F, U.S. Income Tax Return of a Foreign Corporation; and for Forms 1120-PC or 1120-L. For more information, see the instructions for the applicable Schedule M-3.

For insurance companies included in the consolidated U.S. income tax return, see the instructions for Part I, lines 10 and 11, and Part II, line 7, for guidance on Schedule M-3 reporting of intercompany dividends and statutory accounting adjustments.

No Schedule M-3 is required for taxpayers filing Form 1120-REIT, U.S. Income Tax Return for Real Estate Investment Trusts; Form 1120-RIC, U.S. Income Tax Return for Regulated Investment Companies; Form 1120-H, U.S. Income Tax Return for Homeowners Associations; and Form 1120-SF, U.S. Income Tax Return for Settlement Funds.

Completing Schedule M-3

A corporation (or any member of a U.S. consolidated tax group) required to file Schedule M-3 and has at least $50 million total assets at the end of the tax year must complete the schedule in its entirety. In particular, a corporation filing a nonconsolidated return that has at least $50 million total assets at the end of the tax year must complete Parts I, II, and III. Such a corporation does not check any of the checkboxes at the top of Parts II and III. In the case of a U.S. consolidated tax group, Part I must be completed once, on the consolidated Schedule M-3, by the parent corporation. Parts II and III must be completed by the parent corporation, each includible corporation, and a consolidating eliminations entity.

Form 1120 and Form 1120-C filers that (a) are required to file Schedule M-3 (Form 1120) and have less than $50 million total assets at the end of the tax year, or (b) are not required to file Schedule M-3 (Form 1120) and voluntarily file Schedule M-3 (Form 1120), must either (i) complete

Schedule M-3 (Form 1120) entirely or (ii) complete Schedule M-3 (Form 1120) through Part I, and complete Schedule M-1 of Form 1120 (or Form 1120-C, if applicable) instead of completing Parts II and III of Schedule M-3 (Form 1120). If the filer chooses to complete Schedule M-1 instead of completing Parts II and III of Schedule M-3, line 1 of the applicable M-1 must equal line 11 of Part I of Schedule M-3.

Note. In the case of an 1120 mixed group, Parts II and III of Schedule M-3 (Form 1120) must be completed for all members of the mixed group whether Schedule M-3 (Form 1120) is required or voluntarily filed.

For any part of Schedule M-3 (Form 1120) that is completed, all applicable questions must be answered on Part I, all columns must be completed on Parts II and III, and all numerical data required by Schedule M-3 must be provided. Any statement required to support a line item on Schedule M-3 must be attached at the time Schedule M-3 is filed and must provide the information required for that line item.

All detailed statements for Part II and Part III of Schedule M-3 must be attached for each separate entity included in the consolidated Part II and Part III, including those for the parent company and the eliminations entity, if applicable. It is not required that the same supporting detailed information be presented for Part II and Part III of the consolidated Schedule M-3.

Example 1.

1. U.S. corporation A owns U.S. subsidiary B and foreign subsidiary F. For its 2014 tax year, A prepares consolidated financial statements with B and F that report total assets of $12 million. A files a consolidated U.S. income tax return with B and reports total consolidated assets on Schedule L of $8 million. A's U.S. consolidated tax group is not required to file Schedule M-3 for the 2014 tax year.

2. U.S. corporation C owns U.S. subsidiary D. For its 2014 tax year, C prepares consolidated financial statements with D, but C and D file separate U.S. income tax returns. The consolidated accrual basis financial statements for C and D report total assets at the end of the tax year of $12 million after intercompany eliminations. C reports separate company total year-end assets on its Schedule L of $7 million. D reports separate company total year-end assets on its Schedule L

of $6 million. Neither C nor D is required to file Schedule M-3 for the 2014 tax year.

3. Foreign corporation A owns 100 percent of both U.S. corporation B and U.S. corporation C. C owns 100 percent of U.S. corporation D. For its 2014 tax year, A prepares a consolidated worldwide financial statement for the ABCD consolidated group. The ABCD consolidated financial statement reports total year-end assets of $65 million. A is not required to file a U.S. income tax return. B files a separate U.S. income tax return and reports separate company total year-end assets on its Schedule L of $52 million. C files a consolidated U.S. income tax return with D and, after eliminating intercompany transactions between C and D, reports consolidated total year-end assets on Schedule L of $8 million. B is required to file Schedule M-3 because its total year-end assets reported on Schedule L exceed $50 million. The CD U.S. consolidated tax group is not required to file Schedule M-3 because its total year-end assets do not exceed $10 million.

Example 2. At the end of Corporation A's tax year ending December 31, 2014, A's total assets were less than $10 million. A is not required to file Schedule M-3 for any reason. A may elect to file Schedule M-3 instead of completing Schedule M-1 of Form 1120. If A elects to file Schedule M-3, A must either (i) complete Schedule M-3 entirely, or (ii) complete Schedule M-3 through Part I and complete Schedule M-1 instead of completing Parts II and III of Schedule M-3. If A elects to complete Schedule M-3 entirely, A must complete all columns of Parts II and III.

Certain Allocations, Limitations, and Carryovers

If an item attributable to an includible corporation is not shared by or allocated to the appropriate member of the group but is retained in the parent corporation's financial statements (or books and records, if applicable), then the item must be reported by the parent corporation in its separate Schedule M-3. For example, if the parent of a U.S. consolidated tax group prepares financial statements that include all members of the U.S. consolidated tax group and the parent does not allocate the group's income tax expense as reflected in the financial statements among the members of the

group but retains it in the parent corporation, the parent corporation must report on its separate Schedule M-3 the U.S. consolidated tax group's income tax expense as reflected in the financial statements.

Any adjustments made at the consolidated group level that are not attributable to any specific member of the U.S. consolidated tax group (for example, disallowance of net capital losses, contribution deduction carryovers, and limitation of contribution deductions) must not be reported on the separate consolidating parent or subsidiary Schedules M-3 but rather on the consolidated Schedule M-3 and on the consolidating Schedule M-3 for consolidation eliminations (or on Form 8916 in the case of a mixed group).

If an includible corporation has: (1) no activity for the tax year (for example, because the corporation is dormant or inactive); (2) no amount for the corporation to include in Part I, line 11; and (3) no amounts to report on Part II and Part III of Schedule M-3 for the tax year; the parent corporation of the U.S. consolidated tax group may attach to the consolidated Schedule M-3 a statement that provides the name and EIN of the includible corporation in lieu of filing a blank Part II and Part III of Schedule M-3 for such entity. On Part I, check box (4), Dormant subsidiaries schedule attached.

Other Form 1120 Schedules Affected by Schedule M-3 Requirements

Schedule B

Generally, a corporation or group of corporations that files a Form 1120 and is required to file Schedule M-3, must also file Schedule B (Form 1120), Additional Information for Schedule M-3 Filers. In the case of a consolidated group, a parent corporation files one Schedule B (Form 1120) for the entire consolidated group.

For tax years ending December 31, 2014, and later, certain corporations or groups of corporations filing Form 1120 that (a) are required to file Schedule M-3 and have less than $50 million in total assets at the end of the tax year or (b) are not required to file Schedule M-3 and voluntarily file Schedule M-3, are not required to file Schedule B (Form 1120).

Schedule L

If a non-tax-basis income statement and related non-tax-basis balance sheet is prepared for any purpose for a period ending with or within the tax year, Schedule L must be prepared showing non-tax-basis amounts. See the instructions for Part I, line 1, for the discussion of non-tax-basis income statements and related non-tax-basis balance sheets prepared for any purpose and the impact on the selection of the income statement used for Schedule M-3 and the related non-tax-basis balance sheet amounts that must be used for Schedule L.

Total assets shown on Schedule L, line 15, column (d) (or, in the case of some consolidated mixed groups with a Form 1120 parent and an insurance subsidiary, the assets reported on Form 1120, page 1, Item D), must equal the total assets of the corporation (or, in the case of a U.S. consolidated tax group, the total assets of all members of the group listed on Form 851) as of the last day of the tax year, and must be the same total assets reported by the corporation (or by each member of the U.S. consolidated tax group) in the non-tax-basis financial statements, if any, used for Schedule M-3. If the corporation prepares non-tax-basis financial statements, Schedule L must equal the sum of the financial statement total assets for each corporation listed on Form 851 and included in the consolidated U.S. income tax return (includible corporation) net of eliminations for intercompany transactions between includible corporations. If the corporation does not prepare non-tax-basis financial statements, Schedule L must be based on the corporation's books and records. The Schedule L balance sheet can show tax-basis balance sheet amounts if the corporation is allowed to use books and records for Schedule M-3 and the corporation's books and records reflect only tax-basis amounts.

Generally, total assets at the beginning of the year (Schedule L, line 15, column (b)) must equal total assets at the close of the prior year (Schedule L, line 15, column (d)). For each Schedule L balance sheet item reported for which there is a difference between the current opening balance sheet amount and the prior closing balance sheet amount, attach a statement that reports the balance sheet item, the prior closing amount, the current opening amount, and a short explanation of the change. Such reasons for these differences include mergers and acquisitions.

For purposes of measuring total assets at the end of the year, the corporation's assets may not be netted or reduced by the corporation's liabilities. In addition, total assets may not be reported as a negative amount. If Schedule L is prepared on a non-tax-basis method, an investment in a partnership may be shown as appropriate under the corporation's non-tax-basis method of accounting, including, if required by the corporation's reporting methodology, the equity method of accounting for investments. If Schedule L is prepared on a tax-basis, an investment by the corporation in a partnership must be shown as an asset and measured by the corporation's adjusted basis in its partnership interest. Any liabilities contributing to such adjusted basis must be shown on Schedule L as corporate liabilities.

Schedule M-2

The amount shown on Schedule M-2, line 2, Net income (loss) per books, must equal the amount shown on Schedule M-3, Part I, line 11. Schedule M-2 must reflect activity only of corporations included in the consolidated U.S. income tax return.

Consolidated Return (Form 1120, Page 1)

Report on Form 1120, page 1, each item of income, gain, loss, expense, or deduction net of elimination entries for intercompany transactions between includible corporations. The corporation must not report as dividends on Form 1120, Schedule C, any amounts received from an includible corporation. In general, dividends received from an includible corporation must be eliminated in consolidation rather than offset by the dividends-received deduction.

Entity Considerations for Schedule M-3

For purposes of Schedule M-3, references to the classification of an entity (for example, as a corporation, a partnership, or a trust) are references to the treatment of the entity for U.S. income tax purposes. An entity that generally is disregarded as separate from its owner for U.S. income tax purposes (disregarded entity) must not be separately reported on Schedule M-3 except, if required, on Part I, line 7a or 7b. On Schedule M-3, Parts II and III, any item of income, gain, loss,

deduction, or credit of a disregarded entity must be reported as an item of its owner. In particular, the income or loss of a disregarded entity must not be reported on Part II, lines 9, 10, or 11, as from a separate partnership or other pass-through entity. The financial statement income or loss of a disregarded entity is included on Part I, line 7a or 7b, only if its financial statement income or loss is included on Part I, line 11, but not on Part I, line 4a.

Reportable Entity Partner Reporting Responsibilities

A reportable entity partner with respect to a partnership filing Form 1065 is an entity that:
• Owns or is deemed to own, directly or indirectly, under these instructions a 50 percent or greater interest in the income, loss or capital of the partnership on any day of the tax year; and
• Was required to file Schedule M-3 with its most recently filed U.S. income tax return or return of income filed prior to that day.

For the purposes of these instructions, the following rules apply.

1. The parent corporation of a consolidated tax group is deemed to own all corporate and partnership interests owned or deemed to be owned under these instructions by any member of the tax consolidated group.

2. The owner of a disregarded entity is deemed to own all corporate and partnership interests owned or deemed to be owned under these instructions by the disregarded entity.

3. The owner of 50 percent or more of a corporation by vote on any day of its tax year is deemed to own all corporate and partnership interests owned or deemed to be owned under these instructions by the corporation during its tax year.

4. The owner of 50 percent or more of partnership income, loss, or capital on any day of the partnership tax year is deemed to own all corporate and partnership interests owned or deemed to be owned under these instructions by the partnership during the partnership tax year.

5. The beneficial owner of 50 percent or more of the beneficial interest of a trust or nominee arrangement on any day of the trust or nominee arrangement tax year is deemed to own all corporate and partnership interests owned or deemed to be owned under

these instructions by the trust or nominee arrangement.

A reportable entity partner with respect to a partnership (as defined above) must report the following to the partnership within 30 days of first becoming a reportable entity partner and, after first reporting to the partnership under these instructions, thereafter within 30 days of the date of any change in the interest it owns or is deemed to own, directly or indirectly, under these instructions, in the partnership.

1. Name.

2. Mailing address.

3. Taxpayer identification number (TIN or EIN), if applicable.

4. Entity or organization type.

5. State or country in which it is organized.

6. Date on which it first became a reportable entity partner.

7. Date with respect to which it is reporting a change in its ownership interest in the partnership, if applicable.

8. The interest in the partnership it owns or is deemed to own in the partnership, directly or indirectly (as defined under these instructions) as of the date with respect to which it is reporting.

9. Any change in that interest as of the date with respect to which it is reporting.

The reportable entity partner must retain copies of required reports it makes to partnerships under these instructions. Each partnership must retain copies of the required reports it receives under these instructions from reportable entity partners.

Example 3.

1. A, an LLC filing a Form 1065 for 2014, is owned 50 percent by U.S. corporation Z. A owns 50 percent of B, C, D, and E, which are also LLCs filing a Form 1065 for calendar year 2014. Z was first required to file Schedule M-3 (Form 1120) for its corporate tax year ended December 31, 2013, and filed its Form 1120 with Schedule M-3 for 2013 on September 15, 2014. As of September 16, 2014, Z was a reportable entity partner with respect to A and, through A, with respect to B, C, D, and E. On October 5, 2014, Z reports to A, B, C, D, and E, as it is required to do within 30 days of September 16, that Z is a reportable entity partner directly owning (with respect to A) or deemed to own indirectly (with respect to B, C, D,

and E) a 50 percent interest. Therefore, because Z was a reportable entity partner for 2014, each of A, B, C, D, and E is required to file Schedule M-3 (Form 1065) for 2014, regardless of whether they would otherwise be required to file Schedule M-3 for that year.

2. P, a U.S. corporation, is the parent of a financial consolidation group with 50 domestic subsidiaries DS1 through DS50 and 50 foreign subsidiaries FS1 through FS50, all 100 percent owned on September 16, 2014. On September 15, 2014, P filed a consolidated tax return on Form 1120 and was required to file Schedule M-3 for the tax year ending December 31, 2013. On September 16, 2014, DS1, DS2, DS3, FS1, and FS2 each acquires a 10 percent partnership interest in partnership K which files Form 1065 for the tax year ending December 31, 2014. P is deemed to own, directly or indirectly (under these instructions) all corporate and partnership interests of DS1, DS2, DS3, as the parent of the tax consolidation group and therefore is deemed to own 30 percent of K on September 16, 2014. P is deemed to own, directly or indirectly, (under these instructions) all corporate and partnership interests of FS1 and FS2 as the owner of 50 percent or more of each corporation by vote and therefore is deemed to own 20 percent of K on September 16, 2014. P is therefore deemed to own 50 percent of K on September 16, 2014. Since P owns or is deemed to own, directly or indirectly, (under these instructions) 50 percent or more of K on September 16, 2014, and was required to file Schedule M-3 on its most recently filed U.S. income tax return filed prior to that date, P is a reportable entity partner of K as of September 16, 2014. On October 5, 2014, P reports to K, as it is required to do, that P is a reportable entity partner as of September 16, 2014, deemed to own (under these instructions) a 50 percent interest in K. K is therefore required to file Schedule M-3 when it files its Form 1065 for its tax year ending December 31, 2014.

Consolidated Schedule M-3 Versus Consolidating Schedules M-3 for Form 1120 Groups

A consolidated tax return group with a parent corporation that files a Form 1120 is a mixed group if any member is a life insurance company (files using Form 1120-L) or a property and casualty insurance company (files using Form 1120-PC). See *Schedule M-3 Consolidation for Mixed Groups (1120/L/PC)*, below.

A U.S. consolidated tax group must file a consolidated Schedule M-3. Parts I, II, and III of the consolidated Schedule M-3 must reflect the activity of the entire U.S. consolidated tax group. The parent corporation also must complete Parts II and III of a separate Schedule M-3 to reflect the parent's own activity. In addition, Parts II and III of a separate Schedule M-3 must be completed by each includible corporation to reflect the activity of that includible corporation. Lastly, it generally will be necessary to complete Parts II and III of a separate Schedule M-3 for consolidation eliminations.

If a U.S. consolidated tax group that is not a mixed group consists of four includible corporations (the parent and three subsidiaries) all filing Form 1120, the U.S. consolidated tax group must complete six Schedules M-3 as follows:
• One consolidated Schedule M-3 with Parts I, II, and III completed to reflect the activity of the entire U.S. consolidated tax group.
• Parts II and III of a separate Schedule M-3 for each of the four includible corporations to reflect the activity of each includible corporation.
• Parts II and III of a separate Schedule M-3 to eliminate intercompany transactions between includible corporations and to include limitations on deductions (charitable contribution limitations and capital loss limitations) and carryover amounts (charitable contribution carryovers and capital loss carryovers).
See *Completing Schedule M-3* and *Certain Allocations, Limitations, and Carryovers*, earlier.

Note. Complete only one Schedule M-3, Part I, for each consolidated group. A subsidiary of a consolidated group does not complete Schedule M-3, Part I. Enter on Schedule M-3, Part I, the name and EIN of the common parent of the consolidated group. Indicate on Schedule M-3, Parts II and III, on the line after the common parent's name and EIN, whether the Schedule M-3, Parts II and III, is for the: (1) consolidated group; (2) parent corporation; (3) consolidation eliminations; or (4) subsidiary corporation, by checking the appropriate box. If Schedule M-3, Parts II and III, are for a subsidiary in a consolidated return, also enter the name and EIN of the subsidiary.

Schedule M-3 Consolidation for Mixed Groups (1120/L/PC)

Special Schedule M-3 consolidation rules apply to a mixed group, that is, a consolidated tax group that includes: (a) both a corporation that is an insurance company and a corporation that is not an insurance company; or (b) both a life insurance company and a property and casualty insurance company; or (c) a life insurance company, a property and casualty insurance company, and a corporation that is not an insurance company.

Mixed group consolidation for Schedule M-3, Parts II and III, requires (a) subgroup sub-consolidation of the 1120 subgroup, the 1120-PC subgroup, and the 1120-L subgroup, each with its own sub-consolidated Schedule M-3, Parts II and III, and (b) consolidation of the subgroup sub-consolidation totals on a consolidated Schedule M-3, Part II that ties to a consolidated Schedule M-3, Part I, and a consolidated Form 8916.

In addition to one Schedule M-3, Part II, and one Schedule M-3, Part III, for each corporation in the three subgroup sub-consolidations, there will be generally a total of six additional Schedule M-3, Parts II, and six additional Schedule M-3, Parts III, for the subgroup sub-consolidations. Specifically, there must be one Part II and one Part III for each subgroup's sub-consolidated amounts and one Part II and one Part III for each subgroup's sub-consolidation eliminations amounts.

At the mixed group consolidated level, there must be a consolidated Schedule M-3, Part II, and, if applicable, a Part II for consolidation eliminations not includible in the subgroup eliminations. At the consolidated level, there must also be a consolidated Schedule M-3, Part I, and a consolidated Form 8916. For a mixed group, there is no Schedule M-3, Part III, at the consolidated level.

The corporation must check the applicable mixed group checkboxes on all Schedules M-3, Parts I, II, and III, as discussed below.

Subgroup Sub-Consolidation: 1120 Subgroup, 1120-PC Subgroup, and 1120-L Subgroup

A subgroup Schedule M-3, Parts II and III, sub-consolidation must be prepared with all necessary eliminations within the subgroup for each of the three possible subgroups that are in fact present: one subgroup for those corporations reporting on Form 1120; one subgroup for those corporations reporting on Form 1120-PC; and one subgroup for those reporting on Form 1120-L. The parent corporation is included in the subgroup that corresponds to the form on which it reports and the entire consolidated group files. For example, in the case of a Form 1120 parent and Form 1120 consolidated group, the parent is included in the Form 1120 subgroup sub-consolidation. Each subgroup uses its own Schedule M-3 (Forms 1120, 1120-PC, or 1120-L), Parts II and III, for each corporation within the subgroup and for the subgroup sub-consolidation and the subgroup eliminations.

The three subgroup sub-consolidation taxable income calculations on Schedule M-3 must follow the separate return requirements of the regulation under Section 1502 and all other applicable regulations taking into account the amounts separately reported on Form 8916. Capital loss limitation and carryforward used and charitable deduction limitation and carryforward used are not taken into account in the determination of the three subgroup sub-consolidated taxable incomes on Schedule M-3, but are reflected on Form 8916 and in the calculation of the life/non-life loss limitation and carryforward used. See *Life/Non-Life Loss Limitation and Carryforward Used Calculations*, later.

The reconciliation totals for book, temporary difference, permanent difference, and taxable income for each subgroup are reported on Forms 1120, 1120-PC, or 1120-L, as applicable, Schedule M-3, Part II, line 29a, columns (a), (b), (c), and (d), and equal the sum of the line amounts on Part II, lines 26 through 28. For a mixed group, Schedule M-3, Part II, lines 29b, 29c, and 30 are blank on the Forms 1120, 1120-PC, or 1120-L, as applicable, for the separate corporations (parent and subsidiary) and for the three subgroup sub-consolidations.

Note. A sub-consolidation is required for every subgroup, even if the subgroup consists of only one corporation. In addition, Form 8916-A, if applicable, is required at the sub-consolidated level and the sub-consolidated elimination level.

Reconciliation of Mixed Group Subgroup Sub-Consolidation Amounts to Schedule M-3, Part I, line 11, and to Tax Return Taxable Income

At the consolidated level, use the Schedule M-3 (Forms 1120, 1120-PC, or 1120-L), Parts I and II, that matches the form on which the parent corporation reports and the entire consolidated group files. For a mixed group, the consolidated Schedule M-3, Part II, lines 29a, 29b, and 29c, report the applicable amounts from the three subgroup sub-consolidation Part II, line 29a, amounts. (If a consolidated level Part II for consolidation eliminations not includible in the subgroup eliminations is applicable, the applicable amounts must be adjusted by the applicable elimination amounts.) The consolidated Schedule M-3, Part II, line 30, amounts are the sum of the applicable amounts on the consolidated Part II, lines 29a, 29b, and 29c. For a mixed group, the consolidated Part II, lines 1 through 28, are blank and no consolidated Part III is required to be completed.

For mixed groups, the consolidated Part II, line 30, column (a), must equal Part I, line 11, with appropriate adjustments for statutory accounting requirements reflected on Part I, lines 10a and 10b. The consolidated taxable income indicated on Part II, line 30, column (d), must equal the amount shown on Form 8916, line 1. Form 8916, line 8, must equal taxable income reported on the tax return.

Completion of Mixed Group Checkboxes for Schedule M-3, Part II and Part III

Note. The following discussion of checkboxes will assume that the 1120 subgroup includes the corporate parent of the mixed group.

Forms 1120, 1120-PC, and 1120-L, Schedule M-3, Parts II and III, each have a checkbox (5) at the top indicating a mixed group. Checkbox (5) and one or more other applicable checkboxes must be checked.

For example, an 1120 parent corporation included in the 1120 subgroup must check Schedule M-3 (Form 1120), Parts II and III, box (2) Parent corporation, and box (5) Mixed 1120/L/PC group. An 1120 subsidiary corporation within the 1120 subgroup

must check Schedule M-3 (Form 1120), Parts II and III, box (4) Subsidiary corporation, and box (5) Mixed 1120/L/PC group. An 1120-PC subsidiary corporation within the 1120-PC subgroup must check Schedule M-3 (Form 1120-PC), Parts II and III, box (4) Subsidiary corporation, and box (5) Mixed 1120/L/PC group. An 1120-L subsidiary corporation within the 1120-L subgroup must check Schedule M-3 (Form 1120-L), Parts II and III, box (4) Subsidiary corporation, and box (5) Mixed 1120/L/PC group.

The 1120 subgroup sub-consolidation Schedule M-3 (Form 1120), Parts II and III, must be indicated by checking box (5) Mixed 1120/L/PC group, and box (6) 1120 group for the sub-consolidation, and by checking box (5) Mixed 1120/L/PC group, and box (7) 1120 eliminations for the eliminations. The 1120-PC subgroup sub-consolidation Form 1120-PC, Schedule M-3, Parts II and III, must be indicated by checking box (5) Mixed 1120/L/PC group, and box (6) 1120-PC group for the sub-consolidation, and by checking box (5) Mixed 1120/L/PC group, and box (7) 1120-PC eliminations for the eliminations. The 1120-L subgroup sub-consolidation Schedule M-3 (Form 1120-L), Parts II and III, must be indicated by checking box (5) Mixed 1120/L/PC group, and box (6) 1120-L group for the sub-consolidation, and by checking box (5) Mixed 1120/L/PC group, and box (7) 1120-L eliminations for the eliminations.

A mixed group with a Form 1120 parent corporation completes a consolidated level Schedule M-3 (Form 1120), Parts I and II, and a consolidated Form 8916. The mixed group consolidated Schedule M-3, Part II, must be indicated by checking box (1) Consolidated group, and box (5) Mixed 1120/L/PC group. (If a consolidated level Part II for consolidation eliminations not includible in the subgroup eliminations is applicable, that Part II must be indicated by checking box (3) Consolidated eliminations, and box (5) Mixed 1120/L/PC group.)

Life/Non-Life Loss Limitation and Carryforward Used Calculations

The applicable life/non-life loss limitation and all carryforward used calculations are made using the amounts determined for taxable income in the three subgroup sub-consolidations and other applicable amounts separately reported on Form

8910. The calculated life/non-life loss limitation or carryforward used amounts, if any, are not entered on Schedule M-3. The calculated amounts, if any, are entered on Form 8916.

Specific Instructions for Part I

Part I. Financial Information and Net Income (Loss) Reconciliation

When To Complete Part I

Part I must be completed for any tax year for which the corporation files Schedule M-3. Check either box (1) Non-consolidated return, (2) Consolidated return (Form 1120 only), or (3) Mixed 1120/L/PC group, as applicable. In addition, check box (4), Dormant subsidiaries schedule attached, if applicable.

Line 1. Questions Regarding the Type of Income Statement Prepared

For Part I, lines 1 through 12, use only the financial statements of the U.S. corporation filing the U.S. income tax return (the consolidated financial statements for the U.S. parent corporation of a U.S. consolidated tax group). If the U.S. corporation filing a U.S. income tax return (or the U.S. parent corporation of a U.S. consolidated tax group) prepares its own financial statements but is controlled by another corporation (U.S. or foreign) that prepares financial statements that include the U.S. corporation, the U.S. corporation (or the U.S. parent corporation of a U.S. consolidated tax group) must use for its Schedule M-3, Part I, its own financial statements and not the financial statements of the controlling corporation.

If a non-publicly traded U.S. parent corporation of a U.S. consolidated tax group prepares financial statements and that group includes a publicly traded subsidiary that files financial statements with the Securities and Exchange Commission (SEC), the consolidated financial statements of the parent corporation are the appropriate financial statements for purposes of completing Part I. Do not use any separate company financial statements that might be prepared for publicly traded subsidiaries.

Non-Tax-Basis Financial Statements and Tax-Basis Financial Statements

A tax-basis income statement is allowed for Schedule M-3, and a tax-basis balance sheet for Schedule L, only if no non-tax-basis income statement and no non-tax-basis balance sheet were prepared for any purpose and the books and records of the corporation reflect only tax-basis amounts. The corporation is deemed to have non-tax-basis income statements and the related non-tax-basis balance sheets for the current tax year for purposes of Schedule M-3 and Schedule L if such non-tax-basis financial statements were prepared for and presented to management, creditors, shareholders, government regulators, or any other third parties for a period ending with or within the tax year.

If a Form 10-K is filed with the SEC for the period ending with or within the tax year, the corporation must check "Yes" for Part I, line 1a, and use that income statement for Schedule M-3. If Form 10-K is not filed and a non-tax-basis income statement is prepared that is a certified non-tax-basis income statement for the period ending with or within the tax year, the corporation must check "Yes" for Part I, line 1b, and use that income statement for Schedule M-3. If Form 10-K is not filed and no certified non-tax-basis income statement is prepared but an unaudited non-tax-basis income statement is prepared for the period ending with or within the tax year, the corporation must check "Yes" for Part I, line 1c, and use that income statement for Schedule M-3.

Order of priority in accounting standards. If no Form 10-K is filed and two or more non-tax-basis income statements are both certified non-tax-basis income statements for the period, the income statement prepared according to the following order of priority in accounting standards shall be used.

1. U.S. Generally Accepted Accounting Principles (GAAP).

2. International Financial Reporting Standards (IFRS).

3. Any other International Accounting Standards (IAS).

4. Statutory accounting for insurance companies.

5. Other regulatory accrual accounting.

6. Any other accrual accounting standard.

7. Any fair market value standard.

8. Any cash basis standard.

If no non-tax-basis income statement is certified and two or more non-tax-basis income statements are prepared, the income statement prepared according to the first listed of the accounting standards listed above shall be used.

If no non-tax-basis financial statements are prepared for a U.S. corporation (or, in the case of a U.S. consolidated tax group, for the U.S. parent corporation's consolidated group) filing Schedule M-3 (Form 1120), the U.S. corporation (or the U.S. parent corporation of a U.S. consolidated tax group) must check "No" on questions 1a, 1b, and 1c, skip Part I, lines 2a through 3c, and enter the net income (loss) per the books and records of the U.S. corporation (or U.S. consolidated tax group) on Part I, line 4a.

If no non-tax-basis financial statements are prepared for a U.S. corporation (or, in the case of a U.S. consolidated tax group, for the U.S. parent corporation's consolidated group) filing Schedule M-3 (Form 1120), and the U.S. corporation is owned by a foreign corporation that prepares financial statements that includes the U.S. corporation (or the U.S. parent corporation's consolidated group), the U.S. corporation (or the U.S. parent corporation of the U.S. consolidated tax group) must enter "No" on questions 1a, 1b, and 1c, skip Part I, lines 2a through 3c, and enter the net income (loss) per the books and records of the U.S. corporation (or U.S. consolidated tax group) on Part I, line 4a.

Line 2. Questions Regarding Income Statement Period and Restatements

Enter the beginning and ending dates on line 2a for the corporation's annual income statement period ending with or within the current tax year.

The questions on Part I, lines 2b and 2c, regarding income statement restatements refer to the worldwide consolidated income statement issued by the corporation filing the U.S. income tax return (the consolidated financial statements for the U.S. parent corporation of a U.S. consolidated tax group) and used to prepare Schedule M-3. Answer "Yes" on lines 2b and/or 2c if the corporation's annual income statement has been restated for any reason. Attach a short explanation of the reasons for the restatement in net income for each annual income statement period that is restated, including the original amount and restated amount of each annual statement period's net income. The attached statement is not required to report restatements on an entity-by-entity basis.

Line 3. Questions Regarding Publicly Traded Voting Common Stock

The primary U.S. publicly traded voting common stock class is the most widely held or most heavily traded within the U.S. as determined by the corporation. If the corporation has more than one class of publicly traded voting common stock, attach a list of the classes of publicly traded voting common stock and the trading symbol and the nine-digit CUSIP number of each class.

Line 4a. Worldwide Consolidated Net Income (Loss) per Income Statement

Report on Part I, line 4a, the worldwide consolidated net income (loss) per the income statement (or books and records, if applicable) of the corporation. A corporation filing a non-consolidated Form 1120 for itself must report its worldwide income on Part I, line 4a.

In completing Schedule M-3, the corporation must use financial statement amounts from the financial statement type checked "Yes" on Part I, line 1, or from its books and records if Part I, line 1c is checked "No." If Part I, line 1a, is checked "Yes," report on Part I, line 4a, the net income amount reported in the income statement presented to the SEC on the corporation's Form 10-K (the Form 10-K for the security identified on Part I, line 3b, if applicable).

If a corporation prepares non-tax-basis financial statements, the amount on line 4a must equal the financial statement net income (loss) for the income statement period ending with or within the tax year as indicated on Part I, line 2a.

If the corporation prepares non-tax-basis financial statements and the income statement period differs from the corporation's tax year, the income statement period indicated on Part I, line 2a, applies for purposes of Part I, lines 4a through 8.

If the corporation does not prepare non-tax-basis financial statements and has checked "No" on Part I, line 1c, enter the net income (loss) per the books and records of the U.S. corporation or the U.S. consolidated tax group on Part I, line 4a.

Indicate on Part I, line 4b, which of the following accounting standards were used for line 4a.

1. U.S. Generally Accepted Accounting Principles (GAAP).

2. International Financial Reporting Standards (IFRS).

3. Statutory.

4. Tax Basis.

5. Other (Specify).

Report on Part I, lines 5a through 10, as instructed below, all adjustment amounts required to adjust worldwide net income (loss) reported on this Part I, line 4a (whether from financial statements or books and records), to net income (loss) of includible corporations that must be reported on Part I, line 11.

Report on line 12a the worldwide consolidated total assets and total liabilities amounts for the corporation using the same financial statements (or books and records) used for the worldwide consolidated income (loss) amount reported on Part I, line 4a.

If a U.S. corporation: (a) has net income (loss) included on Part I, line 4a, and removed on Part I, line 6a or 6b, on another U.S. corporation's Schedule M-3; (b) files its own Form 1120 (separate or consolidated); (c) does not have a separate non-tax-basis financial statement (certified or otherwise) of its own; and (d) reports on Schedule L of its own Form 1120 total consolidated assets that equal or exceed $10 million at the end of the corporation's tax year, the corporation must answer questions 1a, 1b, and 1c of Part I as appropriate for its own Form 1120 and must report on Part I, line 4a, the amount for the corporation's net income (loss) that is removed on Part I, line 6a or 6b, of the other corporation's Schedule M-3. However, if in the circumstances described immediately above, the corporation does have separate non-tax-basis financial statements (certified or otherwise) of its own, independent of the amount of the corporation's net income included in Part I, line 4a, of the other U.S. corporation, the corporation must answer questions 1a, 1b, and 1c of Part I, as appropriate, for its own Form 1120,

based on its own separate income statement, and must report on Part I, line 4a, the net income amounts shown on its separate income statement.

If line 4a includes net income (loss) for a corporation that files Form 1120-PC or Form 1120-L, see the instructions for Part I, line 10, for adjustments that may be necessary to reconcile financial statement income to statutory income.

Line 5. Net Income (Loss) of Nonincludible Foreign Entities

Remove the financial net income (line 5a) or loss (line 5b) of each foreign entity that is included on line 4a and is not an includible corporation in the U.S. consolidated tax group (nonincludible foreign entity). In addition, on Part I, line 8, adjust for consolidation eliminations and correct for minority interest and intercompany dividends between any nonincludible foreign entity and any includible corporation. Do not remove in Part I the financial net income (loss) of any nonincludible foreign entity accounted for on line 4a using the equity method.

Attach a supporting statement that provides the name, EIN (if applicable), and net income (loss) included on line 4a that is removed on this line 5 for each separate nonincludible foreign entity. Also state the total assets and total liabilities for each such separate nonincludible foreign entity and include those assets and liabilities amounts in the total assets and total liabilities reported on Part I, line 12b. The amounts of income (loss) detailed on the supporting statement should be reported for each separate nonincludible foreign entity without regard to the effect of consolidation or elimination entries. If there are consolidation or elimination entries relating to nonincludible foreign entities whose income (loss) is reported on the attached statement that are not reportable on Part I, line 8, the net amounts of all such consolidation and elimination entries must be reported on a separate line on the attached statement, so that the separate financial accounting income (loss) of each nonincludible foreign entity remains separately stated.

For example, if the net income (after consolidation and elimination entries) of a nonincludible foreign sub-consolidated group is being reported on line 5a, the attached supporting statement should report the income (loss) of each separate noninclarible foreign legal entity from each such entity's own financial accounting net income statement or books and records, and any consolidation or elimination entries (for intercompany dividends, minority interests, etc.) not reportable on Part I, line 8, should be reported on the attached supporting statement as a net amount on a line separate and apart from lines that report each noninclarible foreign entity's separate net income (loss).

Line 6. Net Income (Loss) of Noninclarible U.S. Entities

Remove the financial net income (line 6a) or loss (line 6b) of each U.S. entity that is included on line 4a and is not an includible corporation in the U.S. consolidated tax group (noninclarible U.S. entity). In addition, on Part I, line 8, adjust for consolidation eliminations and correct for minority interest and intercompany dividends between any noninclarible U.S. entity and any includible corporation. Do not remove in Part I the financial net income (loss) of any noninclarible U.S. entity accounted for on line 4a using the equity method.

Attach a supporting statement that provides the name, EIN, and net income (loss) included on line 4a that is removed on this line 6 for each separate noninclarible U.S. entity. Also, state the total assets and total liabilities for each such separate noninclarible U.S. entity and include those assets and liabilities amounts in the total assets and total liabilities reported on Part I, line 12c. The amounts of income (loss) detailed on the supporting statement should be reported for each separate noninclarible U.S. entity without regard to the effect of consolidation or elimination entries. If there are consolidation or elimination entries relating to noninclarible U.S. entities whose income (loss) is reported on the attached statement that are not reportable on Part I, line 8, the net amounts of all such consolidation and elimination entries must be reported on a separate line on the attached statement, so that the separate financial accounting income (loss) of each noninclarible U.S. entity remains separately stated. For example, if the net income (after consolidation and elimination entries) of a noninclarible U.S. sub-consolidated group is being reported on line 6a, the attached supporting statement should report the income (loss) of each separate noninclarible U.S. legal entity from each such entity's own financial accounting

net income statement or books and records, and any consolidation or elimination entries (for intercompany dividends, minority interests, etc.) not reportable on Part I, line 8, should be reported on the attached supporting statement as a net amount on a line separate and apart from lines that report each noninclarible U.S. entity's separate net income (loss).

Line 7. Net Income (Loss) of Other Includible Foreign Disregarded Entities, Other Includible U.S. Disregarded Entities, and Other Includible Entities

Include on line 7a, 7b, or 7c, the financial net income or (loss) of each foreign or U.S. disregarded entity or other includible entity that is not included in the consolidated financial group and therefore not included in the income reported on Part I, line 4a. Include on line 7a or 7b financial income of any disregarded entity that is not included in the income reported on Part I, line 4a, but is included in Part I, line 11 (other disregarded entities). Include on line 7c the financial income of any entity not a disregarded entity that is not included in the income reported on line 4a, but is included on line 11 (other includible entities). In addition, on Part I, line 8, adjust for consolidation eliminations and correct for minority interest and intercompany dividends for any other disregarded entity or other includible entities.

Attach a supporting statement that provides the name, EIN, and net income (loss) per the financial statement or books and records on lines 7a, 7b, and 7c, for each separate other U.S. disregarded entity or other includible entity. Also, state the total assets and total liabilities for each such separate included entity and include those asset and liability amounts in the total assets and total liabilities reported on Part I, line 12d. The amounts of income (loss) detailed on the supporting statement should be reported for each separate other disregarded entity or other includible entity without regard to the effect of consolidation or elimination entries solely between or among the entities listed. If there are consolidation or elimination entries relating to such disregarded entity or other includible entities whose income (loss) is reported on the attached statement that are not reportable on Part I, line 8, the net amounts of all such consolidation and elimination entries must be reported on

a separate line on the attached statement, so that the separate financial accounting income (loss) of each other disregarded entity or other includible entity remains separately stated. For example, if the net income (after consolidation and elimination entries) of a sub-consolidated group of other U.S. disregarded entities is being reported on line 7b, the attached supporting statement should report the income (loss) of each separate other U.S. disregarded entity from each entity's own financial accounting net income statement or books and records, and any consolidation or elimination entries (for intercompany dividends, minority interests, etc.) not reportable on Part I, line 8, should be reported on the attached supporting statement as a net amount on a line separate and apart from lines that report each other includible corporation's or entity's separate net income (loss).

Line 8. Adjustment to Eliminations of Transactions Between Includible Entities and Noninclarible Entities

Adjustments on Part I, line 8, to reverse certain financial accounting consolidation or elimination entries are necessary to ensure that transactions between includible entities and noninclarible U.S. or foreign entities are not eliminated, in order to report the correct total amount on Part I, line 11. Also, additional consolidation entries and elimination entries may be necessary on Part I, line 8, related to transactions between includible entities that are in the consolidated financial group and other disregarded entities and other includible entities that are not in the consolidated financial group but that are reported on Part I, line 7a, 7b, or 7c, in order to report the correct total amount on Part I, line 11.

Include on Part I, line 8, the total of the following: (a) amounts of any adjustments to consolidation entries and elimination entries that are contained in the amount reported on Part I, line 4a, required as a result of removing amounts on Part I, line 5 or 6; and (b) amounts of any additional consolidation entries and elimination entries that are required as a result of including amounts on Part I, line 7a, 7b, or 7c. This is necessary in order that the consolidation entries and intercompany elimination entries included in the amount reported on Part I, line 11, are only those applicable to the financial net income (loss) of includible entities for the financial statement period. For example, adjustments must be reported on line 8 to remove minority interest and to reverse the elimination of intercompany dividends included on Part I, line 4a, that relate to the net income of entities removed on Part I, line 5 or 6, because the income to which the consolidation or elimination entries relate has been removed. Also, for example, consolidation or elimination entries must be reported on line 8 to reflect any minority interest ownership in the net income of other disregarded entities or other includible entities reported on Part I, line 7a, 7b, or 7c; and to eliminate any intercompany dividends between entities whose income is included on Part I, line 7a, 7b, or 7c, and other entities included in the consolidated U.S. income tax return. See Examples 3, 4, and 5 in the instructions for line 11.

If a corporate owner of an interest in another entity: (a) accounts for the interest in entity in the owner corporation's separate general ledger on the equity method, and (b) fully consolidates entity in the owner corporation's consolidated financial statements, but entity is not includible in the owner corporation's consolidated U.S. income tax return, then, as part of reversing all consolidation and elimination entries for the nonincludible entity, the corporate owner must reverse on Schedule M-3, Part I, line 8, the elimination of the equity income inclusion from entity. If the owner corporation does not account for entity on the equity method on its own general ledger, it will not have eliminated the equity income for consolidated financial statement purposes, and therefore will have no elimination of equity income to reverse.

The attached supporting statement for Part I, line 8, must identify the type (for example, minority interest, intercompany dividends, etc.) and amount of consolidation or elimination entries reported, as well as the names of the entities to which they pertain. It is not necessary, but it is permitted, to report intercompany eliminations that net to zero on Part I, line 8, such as intercompany interest income and expense.

Line 9. Adjustment To Reconcile Income Statement Period To Tax Year

Include on line 9 any adjustments necessary to the income (loss) of includible corporations to reconcile differences between the corporation's

income statement period reported on line 2a and the corporation's tax year. Attach a statement describing the adjustment.

Statutory accounting for an insurance company subsidiary acquired or merged may require the use of a financial statement period for income reported on Part I, line 11, that differs from the period reported on Part I, line 4a or line 7. Report on Part I, line 10b, adjustments to income because of such differences in accounting period.

Line 10a. Intercompany Dividend Adjustments To Reconcile to Line 11, Line 10b. Other Statutory Accounting Adjustments To Reconcile to Line 11, and Line 10c. Other Adjustments To Reconcile to Amount on Line 11

Include on lines 10a, 10b, and 10c, any other adjustments to reconcile net income (loss) on Part I, line 4a, through Part I, line 9, with net income (loss) on Part I, line 11. Include on line 10a the amount of any intercompany dividend adjustment required by statutory accounting. Include on line 10b the amount of any other required statutory accounting adjustment. Include on line 10c the amount of any other adjustment not required by statutory accounting.

Normally, all intercompany dividends will have been eliminated or excluded from the financial accounting consolidated net income (loss) reported on Part I, line 4a. However, an insurance company may be required to include certain intercompany dividends on Part I, line 11, so that the amount reported on Part I, line 11, agrees with statutory accounting net income (Annual Statement). If the net income (loss) of a corporation that files Form 1120-PC or Form 1120-L is included on Part I, line 4a or line 7, and is computed on a basis other than statutory accounting, include on line 10a the adjustments necessary such that Part I, line 11, includes intercompany dividends in the net income (loss) for such corporation to the extent required by statutory accounting principles. (For insurance companies included in the consolidated U.S. income tax return, see instructions for Part I, line 11, and Part II, line 7.)

Statutory accounting for an insurance company subsidiary acquired or merged may require the use of a financial statement period for income reported on Part I, line 11, that differs from the

period reported on Part I, line 4a or line 7. Report on Part I, line 10b, adjustments to income because of such differences in accounting period.

For any adjustments reported on Part I, lines 10a, 10b, and 10c, attach a supporting statement that provides, for each corporation to which an adjustment relates: the name and EIN of the corporation; the amount of net income included in Part I before any adjustments on line 10; the amount of net income included on Part I, line 11; the amount of the net adjustment that is attributable to intercompany dividend adjustments required to be reported by statutory accounting and included on Part I, line 10a; the amount of the net adjustment attributable to other statutory accounting requirements and included on Part I, line 10b; and the amount of the remainder of the net adjustment not required because of statutory accounting and included on Part I, line 10c. If any net adjustment is included for the corporation on Part I, lines 10b or 10c, attach a supplemental supporting statement identifying the line (10b or 10c), the type, and the amount of each adjustment included in the net adjustment.

Line 11. Net Income (Loss) per Income Statement of Includible Corporations

Report on line 11 the net income (loss) per the income statement (or books and records, if applicable) of the corporation. In the case of a U.S. consolidated tax group, report the consolidated income statement net income (loss) of all corporations listed on Form 851 and included in the consolidated U.S. income tax return for the tax year. Amounts reported in column (a) of Parts II and III (see instructions later) must be reported on the same accounting method used to report the amount of net income (loss) per income statement of includible corporations on Part I, line 11, which for insurance companies is statutory accounting. If an insurance company is included in a consolidated Form 1120, the amount of net income reported on Part I, Line 11, will include the statutory accounting net income for the insurance corporation and the GAAP net income for the non-insurance corporations included in the U.S. consolidated tax group. (For insurance companies included in the consolidated U.S. income tax return, see the instructions for Part I, line 10, and Part II, line 7.)

Instructions for Schedule M-3 (Form 1120)

Do not, in any event, report on this line 11 the net income of entities not listed on Form 851 and not included in the consolidated U.S. income tax return for the tax year. For example, it is not permissible to remove the income of nonincludible entities on lines 5 and/or 6, discussed earlier; then to add back such income on lines 7 through 10, such that the amount reported at line 11 includes the net income of entities not includible in the consolidated U.S. income tax return. A principal purpose of Schedule M-3 is to report on this Part I, line 11, only the financial accounting net income of only the corporations included in the consolidated U.S. income tax return.

Whether or not the corporation prepares financial statements, Part I, line 11, must include all items that impact the net income (loss) of the corporation even if they are not recorded in the profit and loss accounts in the corporation's general ledger, including, for example, all post-closing adjusting entries (including workpaper adjustments) and dividend income or other income received from nonincludible corporations.

Example 4.

1. U.S. corporation P is publicly traded and files Form 10-K with the SEC. P owns 80% or more of the stock of 75 U.S. corporations, DS1 through DS75, between 51% and 79% of the stock of 25 U.S. corporations DS76 through DS100, and 100% of the stock of 50 foreign subsidiaries FS1 through FS50. P eliminates all dividend income from DS1 through DS100 and FS1 through FS50 in financial statement consolidation entries. Furthermore, P eliminates the minority interest ownership, if any, of DS1 through DS100 in financial statement consolidation entries. P's SEC Form 10-K includes P, DS1 through DS100 and FS1 through FS50 on a fully consolidated basis. P files a consolidated U.S. income tax return with DS1 through DS75.

P must check "Yes" on Part I, line 1a. On Part I, line 4a, P must report the consolidated net income from the SEC Form 10-K for the consolidated financial statement group of P, DS1 through DS100, and FS1 through FS50. P must remove the net income (loss) of FS1 through FS50 on Part I, line 5a or 5b, as applicable. P must remove the net income (loss) before minority interests of DS76 through DS100 on Part I, line 6a or 6b, as applicable. P must reverse on Part I, line 8:

a. The elimination of dividends received by P and DS1 through DS75 from DS76 through DS100 and FS1 through FS50; and

b. The recognition of minority interests' share of the net income (loss) of DS76 through DS100. (Note: The minority interests' share, if any, of the income of DS1 through DS75 must be reported in Part II, line 8, Minority interest for includible corporations.)

P reports on Part I, line 11, the consolidated financial statement net income (loss) attributable to the includible corporations. Intercompany transactions between the includible corporations that had been eliminated in the net income amount on line 4a remain eliminated in the net income amount on line 11. Transactions between the includible corporations and the nonincludible entities that are eliminated in the net income amount on line 4a are included in the net income amount on line 11 since the elimination of those transactions was reversed on line 8.

2. Foreign corporation F owns 100% of the stock of U.S. corporation P. P owns 100% of the stock of DS1, 60% of the stock of DS2, and 100% of the stock of FS1. F prepares certified audited financial statements. P does not prepare any financial statements. P files a consolidated U.S. income tax return with DS1.

P must not complete Schedule M-3, Part I, with reference to the financial statements of its foreign parent F. P must check "No" on Part I, lines 1a, 1b, and 1c, skip lines 2a through 3c of Part I, and enter worldwide net income (loss) per the books and records of the includible corporations (P and DS1) on Part I, line 4a. P must enter any necessary adjustments on lines 5a through 10 in order for Part I, line 11, to report the net income (loss) of includible corporations P and DS1, net of eliminations for transactions between P and DS1.

Example 5.

1. U.S. corporation P owns 60% of corporation DS1 which is fully consolidated in P's financial statements. P does not account for DS1 in P's separate general ledger on the equity method. DS1 has net income of $100 (before minority interests) and pays dividends of $50, of which P receives $30. The dividend is eliminated in the consolidated financial statements. In its financial statements, P consolidates DS1 and includes $60 of net income

($100 less the minority interest of $40) on Part I, line 4a.

P must remove the $100 net income of DS1 on Part I, line 6a. P must reverse on Part I, line 8, the elimination of the $40 minority interest net income of DS1. In addition, P reverses its elimination of the $30 intercompany dividend in its financial statements on Part I, line 8. The net result is that P includes the $30 dividend from DS1 at Part I, line 11, and on Part II, line 7, column (a). P's dividend income included on the tax return from DS1 must be reported on Part II, line 7, column (d).

2. U.S. corporation C owns 60% of the capital and profits interests in U.S. LLC N. C does not account for N in C's separate general ledger on the equity method. N has net income of $100 (before minority interests) and makes no distributions during the tax year. C treats N as a corporation for financial statement purposes; and as a partnership for U.S. income tax purposes. In its financial statements, C consolidates N and includes $60 of net income ($100 less the minority interest of $40) on Part I, line 4a.

C must remove the $100 net income of N on Part I, line 6a. C must reverse on Part I, line 8, the elimination of the $40 minority interest net income of N. The result is that C includes no income for N either on Part I, line 11, or on Part II, line 9, column (a). C's taxable income from N must be reported by C on Part II, line 9, column (d).

3. U.S. corporation P owns 60% of corporation DS1, which is fully consolidated in P's financial statements. P accounts for DS1 in P's separate general ledger on the equity method. DS1 has net income of $100 (before minority interests) and pays dividends of $50, of which P receives $30. The dividend reduces P's investment in DS1 for equity method reporting on P's separate general ledger where P includes its 60% equity share of DS1 income, which is $60. In its financial statements, P eliminates the DS1 equity method income of $60 and consolidates DS1, including $60 of net income ($100 less the minority interest of $40) on Part I, line 4a.

P must remove the $100 net income of DS1 on Part I, line 6a. P must reverse on Part I, line 8, the elimination of the $40 minority interest net income of DS1 and the elimination of the $60 of DS1 equity income. The net result is that P includes the $60 of equity method income from DS1 at Part I, line 11, and on Part II, line 6, column (a). P's dividend income included on the tax return from its investment in DS1 must be reported on Part II, line 7, column (d).

4. U.S. corporation C owns 60% of the capital and profits interests in U.S. LLC N. C accounts for N in C's separate general ledger on the equity method. N has net income of $100 (before minority interests) and makes no distributions during the tax year. C treats N as a corporation for financial statement purposes and as a partnership for U.S. income tax purposes. For equity method reporting on C's separate general ledger, C includes its 60% equity share of N income, which is $60. In its financial statements, C eliminates the $60 of N equity method income and consolidates N, including $60 of net income ($100 less the minority interest of $40) on Part I, line 4a.

C must remove the $100 net income of N on Part I, line 6a. C must reverse on Part I, line 8, the elimination of the $40 minority interest net income of N and the elimination of the $60 of N equity method income. The result is that C includes the $60 of equity method income for N on Part I, line 11, and on Part II, line 9, column (a). C's taxable income from N must be reported by C on Part II, line 9, column (d).

5. U.S. corporation C owns 60% of the capital and profits interests in U.S. LLC N. C accounts for N in C's separate general ledger on the equity method. N has net income of $100 (before minority interests) and pays a $50 cash distribution, of which C receives $30. The distribution reduces C's investment in N for equity method reporting on C's separate general ledger. C treats N as a corporation for financial statement purposes and as a partnership for U.S. income tax purposes. For equity method reporting on C's separate general ledger, C includes its 60% equity share of N income, which is $60. In its financial statements, C eliminates the $60 of N equity method income and consolidates N and includes $60 of net income ($100 less the minority interest of $40) on Part I, line 4a.

C must remove the $100 net income of N on Part I, line 6a. C must reverse on Part I, line 8, the elimination of the $40 minority interest net income of N and the elimination of the $60 of N equity method income. The result is that C includes the $60 of equity method income for N on Part I, line 11, and on Part II, line 9, column (a). C's taxable income from N must be reported by C on Part II, line 9, column (d).

Example 6. U.S. corporation P owns 80% of the stock of corporation DS1. DS1 is included in P's consolidated income tax return, even though DS1 is not included in P's consolidated financial statements on either a consolidated basis or on the equity method. DS1 has current year net income of $100 after taking into account its $40 interest payment to P. P has net income of $1,040 after recognition of the interest income from DS1. Because DS1 is an includible corporation, 100% of the net income of both P and DS1 must be reported on Form 1120, page 1, of the PDS consolidated U.S. income tax return, and the intercompany interest income and expense must be removed by consolidation elimination entries.

P must report its financial statement net income of $1,040 on Part I, line 4a, and reports DS1's net income of $100 on Part I, line 7c. Then, in order to reflect the full consolidation of the financial accounting net income of P and DS1 at Part I, line 11, the following consolidation and elimination entries are reported on Part I, line 8: (a) offsetting entries to remove the $40 of interest income received from DS1 included by P on line 4a, and to remove the $40 of interest expense of DS1 included in line 7c for a net change of zero; and (b) an entry to reflect the $20 minority interest in the net income of DS1 (DS1 net income of $100 times 20% minority interest). The result is that Part I, line 11, reports $1,120: $1,040 from line 4a, $100 from line 7c, and ($20) from line 8. Stated another way, Part I, line 11, includes the entire $1,000 net income of P, measured before recognition of the intercompany interest income from DS1 and the consolidation of DS1 operations, plus the entire $140 net income of DS1, measured before interest expense to P, less the minority interest ownership of $20 in DS1's separate net income ($100). The consolidated U.S. income tax group is required to include on the attached supporting statement for Part I, line 8, the details of the adjustment to the minority interest in the net income of DS1, but is not required to report the offsetting adjustment to the intercompany elimination of interest income and interest expense (though it is permitted to do so).

Line 12. Total Assets and Liabilities of Entities Included or Removed on Part I, Lines 4, 5, 6, and 7

Line 12 must be completed by all corporations that file Schedule M-3. Report on lines 12a, 12b, 12c, and 12d, the total amount (not just the corporation's share) of assets and liabilities of entities included or removed on Part I, lines 4, 5, 6, and 7. All assets and liabilities reported for Schedule M-3, Part I, lines 12a, 12b, 12c, and 12d, must be entered as positive amounts.

On line 12a, enter the worldwide consolidated total assets and total liabilities of all of the entities included in completing Part I, line 4a. On line 12b, enter the total assets and total liabilities of the entities removed in completing Part I, line 5. On line 12c, enter the total assets and total liabilities removed in completing Part I, line 6. On line 12d, enter total assets and total liabilities included in completing Part I, line 7.

Specific Instructions for Parts II and III

For consolidated U.S. income tax returns, attach supporting statements for each includible corporation. See the instructions for consolidated returns in the Instructions for Form 1120.

General Format of Parts II and III

Check the applicable box(es) at the top of pages 2 and 3 of Schedule M-3 to indicate whether the Schedule M-3 is for the:

1. Consolidated group;
2. Parent corporation;
3. Consolidated eliminations;
4. Subsidiary corporation; or
5. Mixed 1120/L/PC group.

Also check the applicable box to indicate whether the Schedule M-3 is for a sub-consolidated: (6) 1120 group; or (7) 1120 eliminations. See *Consolidated Schedule M-3 Versus Consolidating Schedules M-3 for Form 1120 Groups* and *Schedule M-3 Consolidation for Mixed Groups (1120/L/PC)*, earlier.

For each line item in Parts II and III, report in column (a) the amount of net income (loss) included in Part I, line 11, and report in column (d) the amount included in taxable income on Form 1120, page 1, line 28.

Instructions for Schedule M-3 (Form 1120)

For any item of income, gain, loss, expense, or deduction for which there is a difference between columns (a) and (d), the portion of the difference that is temporary must be entered in column (b) and the portion of the difference that is permanent must be entered in column (c).

Note. A statement or explanation may be attached to any line item even if none is required.

If financial statements are prepared by the corporation in accordance with generally accepted accounting principles (GAAP), differences that are treated as temporary for GAAP must be reported in column (b) and differences that are permanent (that is, not temporary for GAAP) must be reported in column (c). Generally, pursuant to GAAP, a temporary difference affects (creates, increases, or decreases) a deferred tax asset or liability.

If the corporation does not prepare financial statements, or the financial statements are not prepared in accordance with GAAP, report in column (b) any difference that the corporation believes will reverse in a future tax year (that is, have an opposite effect on taxable income in a future tax year (or years) due to the difference in timing of recognition for financial accounting and U.S. income tax purposes) or is the reversal of such a difference that arose in a prior tax year. Report in column (c) any difference that the corporation believes will not reverse in a future tax year (and is not the reversal of such a difference that arose in a prior tax year).

If the corporation is unable to determine whether a difference between column (a) and column (d) for an item will reverse in a future tax year or is the reversal of a difference that arose in a prior tax year, report the difference for that item in column (c).

Example 7. Corporation B is a U.S. publicly traded corporation that files a consolidated U.S. income tax return and prepares consolidated GAAP financial statements. In prior years, B acquired intellectual property (IP) and goodwill through several corporate acquisitions. The IP is amortizable for both U.S. income tax and financial statement purposes. In the current year, B's annual amortization expense for IP is $9,000 for U.S. income tax purposes and $6,000 for financial statement purposes. In its financial statements, B treats the difference in IP amortization as a temporary difference. The goodwill is

not amortizable for U.S. income tax purposes and is subject to impairment for financial statement purposes. In the current year, B records an impairment charge on the goodwill of $5,000. In its financial statements, B treats the goodwill impairment as a permanent difference. B must report the amortization attributable to the IP on Part III, line 28, and report $6,000 in column (a), a temporary difference of $3,000 in column (b), and $9,000 in column (d). B must report the goodwill impairment on Part III, line 26, and report $5,000 in column (a), a permanent difference of ($5,000) in column (c), and $0 in column (d).

Reporting Requirements for Parts II and III

Except for mixed group consolidation, the number of Parts II must equal the number of Parts III filed by the corporation. Mixed groups should see *Schedule M-3 Consolidation for Mixed Groups (1120/L/PC),* earlier.

General Reporting Requirements

If an amount is attributable to a reportable transaction described in Regulations section 1.6011-4(b), the amount must be reported in columns (a), (b), (c), and (d), as applicable, of Part II, line 12, regardless of whether the amount would otherwise be reported on Part II or Part III of Schedule M-3. Thus, if a taxpayer files Form 8886, Reportable Transaction Disclosure Statement, the amounts attributable to that reportable transaction must be entered on Part II, line 12.

A corporation is required to report in column (a) of Parts II and III the amount of any item specifically listed on Schedule M-3 that is in any manner included in the corporation's current year financial statement net income (loss) or in an income or expense account maintained in the corporation's books and records, even if there is no difference between that amount and the amount included in taxable income unless (a) otherwise provided in these instructions or (b) the amount is attributable to a reportable transaction described in Regulations section 1.6011-4(b) and is therefore reported on Part II, line 12. For example, with the exception of interest income reflected on a Schedule K-1 received by a corporation as a result of the corporation's investment in a partnership or other pass-through entity, all interest income, included on Part I,

line 11, whether from unconsolidated affiliated companies, third parties, banks, or other entities, whether from foreign or domestic sources, whether taxable or exempt from tax, and whether classified as some other type of income for U.S. income tax purposes (such as dividends), must be included on Part II, line 13, column (a). Likewise, all fines and penalties included in Part I, line 11, paid to a government or other authority for the violation of any law for which fines or penalties are assessed must be included on Part III, line 12, column (a), regardless of the government authority that imposed the fines or penalties, regardless of whether the fines or penalties are civil or criminal, regardless of the classification, nomenclature, or terminology attached to the fines or penalties by the imposing authority in its actions or documents.

If a corporation would be required to report in column (a) of Parts II and III the amount of any item specifically listed on Schedule M-3 in accordance with the preceding paragraph, except that the corporation has capitalized the item of income or expense and reports the amount in its financial statement balance sheet or in asset and liability accounts maintained in the corporation's books and records, the corporation must report the proper tax treatment of the item in columns (b), (c), and (d), as applicable.

Furthermore, in applying the two preceding paragraphs, a corporation is required to report in column (a) of Parts II and III the amount of any item specifically listed on Schedule M-3 that is included in the corporation's financial statements or exists in the corporation's books and records, regardless of the nomenclature associated with that item in the financial statements or books and records. Accurate completion of Schedule M-3 requires reporting amounts according to the substantive nature of the specific line items included in Schedule M-3 and consistent reporting of all transactions of like substantive nature that occurred during the tax year. For example, all expense amounts that are included in the financial statements or exist in the books and records that represent some form of "Bad debt expense," must be reported on Part III, line 32, in column (a), regardless of whether the amounts are recorded or stated under different nomenclature in the financial statements or the books and records such as: "Provision for doubtful accounts;" "Expense for uncollectible notes receivable;" or "Impairment of trade accounts receivable." Likewise, as stated in the preceding paragraph, all fines and penalties must be included on Part III, line 12, column (a), regardless of the terminology or nomenclature attached to them by the corporation in its books and records or financial statements.

With limited exceptions, Part II includes lines for specific items of income, gain, or loss (income items). (See Part II, lines 1 through 24.) If an income item is described in Part II, lines 1 through 24, report the amount of the item on the applicable line, regardless of whether there is a difference for the item. If there is a difference for the income item, or only a portion of the income item has a difference and a portion of the item does not have a difference, and the item is not described in Part II, lines 1 through 24, report and describe the entire amount of the item on Part II, line 25.

With limited exceptions, Part III includes lines for specific items of expense or deduction (expense items). (See Part III, lines 1 through 36.) If an expense item is described on Part III, lines 1 through 36, report the amount of the item on the applicable line, regardless of whether there is a difference for the item. If there is a difference for the expense item, or only a portion of the expense item has a difference and a portion of the item does not have a difference and the item is not described in Part III, lines 1 through 36, report and describe the entire amount of the item on Part III, line 37.

If there is no difference between the financial accounting amount and the taxable amount of an entire item of income, loss, expense, or deduction and the item is not described or included in Part II, lines 1 through 25, or Part III, lines 1 through 37, report the entire amount of the item in columns (a) and (d) of Part II, line 28.

Special instructions for Part II, lines 25 and 28, and Part III, line 37. Whether a given income (loss) item is reported on Part II, line 25, or on Part II, line 28, or a given expense/deduction item on Part III, line 37, or on Part II, line 28, is determined separately by each member of the U.S. consolidated tax group and not at the U.S. consolidated tax group level. For example, U.S. corporation P has two subsidiaries, A and B, that are included in P's consolidated financial statements and in P's consolidated U.S. income tax return. For financial statement purposes, P, A, and B recognize real

estate tax expense when accrued. For U.S. income tax purposes, P and A recognize such expense consistent with the method used for financial statement purposes, whereas B recognizes such deduction based on a method different from that used for financial statement purposes. P and A must report this expense/deduction in column (a) and (d) on Part II, line 28. B must report the following on Part III, line 37: in column (a), B's expense recognized in the financial statements when accrued; in column (d), B's real estate tax expense recognized for U.S. income tax purposes; and in column (b) or (c), as applicable, the difference between B's real estate tax expense in its financial statements and its real estate tax deduction recognized for U.S. taxable income purposes.

Separately stated and adequately disclosed. Each difference reported in Parts II and III must be separately stated and adequately disclosed. In general, a difference is adequately disclosed if the difference is labeled in a manner that clearly identifies the item or transaction from which the difference arises. See Regulations section 1.6662-4(f). If a specific item of income, gain, loss, expense, or deduction is described on Part II, lines 9 through 24, or Part III, lines 1 through 37, and the line does not indicate to "attach statement" and the specific instructions for the line do not call for an attachment of a statement, then the item is considered separately stated and adequately disclosed if the item is entered on the applicable line and the amount(s) of the item(s) are entered in the applicable columns of the applicable line. See the instructions for Part II, lines 1 through 8, for specific additional information required to be provided for these particular lines.

Note. A statement or explanation may be attached to any line even if none is required.

Except as otherwise provided, differences for the same item must be combined or netted together and reported as one amount on the applicable line of Schedule M-3. However, differences for separate items must not be combined or netted together. Each item (and corresponding amount attributable to that item) must be separately stated and adequately disclosed on the applicable line of Schedule M-3, or any statement required to be attached, even if the amounts are below a certain dollar amount.

Required statements for Part II, line 25, and Part III, line 37. A separate statement must be attached to Schedule M-3 (Form 1120) that includes a detailed description of each item and adjustment entered on Part II, line 25, and Part III, line 37.

The description for each amount entered in column (a) must be readily identifiable to the name of the account in the financial statements or books and records of the taxpayer, under which the amount in column (a) was recorded in the accounting records. Also, the description for each amount entered in column (a) must include detailed information supporting each adjustment reported in columns (b) and (c), including how the adjustment is identified in the accounting records. The entire description is considered the tax description for the amount reported in column (d) for each item reported on Part II, line 25, or Part III, line 37.

Each description should adequately describe all four columns of Part II, line 25, or Part III, line 37. If additional information is required to provide an acceptable description, provide a supporting statement.

Example 8. Corporation C is a calendar year taxpayer that placed in service ten depreciable fixed assets in a previous tax year. C files and entirely completes Schedule M-3 for its 2014 tax year. C's total depreciation expense for its 2014 tax year for five of the assets is $50,000 for income statement purposes and $70,000 for U.S. income tax purposes. C's total annual depreciation expense for its 2014 tax year for the other five assets is $40,000 for income statement purposes and $30,000 for U.S. income tax purposes. In its financial statements, C treats the differences between financial statement and U.S. income tax depreciation expense as giving rise to temporary differences that will reverse in future years. C must combine all of its depreciation adjustments. Accordingly, C must report on Part III, line 31, for its 2014 tax year income statement depreciation expense of $90,000 in column (a), a temporary difference of $10,000 in column (b), and U.S. income tax depreciation expense of $100,000 in column (d).

Example 9. Corporation D is a calendar year taxpayer that files and entirely completes Schedule M-3 for its 2014 tax year. On December 31, 2014, D establishes three reserve accounts in the amount of $100,000 for each account. One reserve account is an allowance for accounts receivable that are estimated to be uncollectible. The second reserve is an estimate of coupons outstanding that may have to be paid. The third reserve is an estimate of future warranty expenses. In its financial statements, D treats the three reserve accounts as giving rise to temporary differences that will reverse in future years. The three reserves are expenses in D's 2014 financial statements but are not deductions for U.S. income tax purposes in 2014. D must not combine the Schedule M-3 differences for the three reserve accounts. D must report the amounts attributable to the allowance for uncollectible accounts receivable on Part III, line 32, Bad debt expense, and must separately state and adequately disclose the amounts attributable to each of the other two reserves, coupons outstanding and warranty costs, on a required, attached statement that supports the amounts at Part III, line 37. D must also provide a description for each reserve that meets the requirements for Part III, line 37, discussed earlier under *Required statements for Part II, line 25, and Part III, line 37.* In this example, an acceptable description would be "Coupon Issue Reserves — Rewards Expense" and "Future Warranty Expense Reserve."

Note. There is no need to add the title of the reserve account to the description if the account name for the amount in column (a) is already part of the adjustment description.

Example 10. Corporation E is a calendar year taxpayer that files and entirely completes Schedule M-3 for its 2014 tax year. On January 2, 2014, E establishes an allowance for uncollectible accounts receivable (bad debt reserve) of $100,000. During 2014, E increased the reserve by $250,000 for additional accounts receivable that may become uncollectible. Additionally, during 2014, E decreases the reserve by $75,000 for accounts receivable that were discharged in bankruptcy during 2014. The balance in the reserve account on December 31, 2014, is $275,000. The $100,000 amount to establish the reserve account and the $250,000 to increase the reserve account are expenses on E's 2014 financial statements but are not deductible for U.S. income tax purposes in 2014. However, the $75,000 decrease to the reserve is deductible for U.S. income tax purposes in 2014. In its financial statements, E treats the

reserve account as giving rise to a temporary difference that will reverse in future tax years. E must report on Part III, line 32, for its 2014 tax year income statement bad debt expense of $350,000 in column (a), a temporary difference of ($275,000) in column (b), and U.S. income tax bad debt expense of $75,000 in column (d).

Example 11. Corporation F is a calendar year taxpayer that files and entirely completes Schedule M-3 for its 2014 tax year. During 2014, F incurs $200 of meals and entertainment expenses that F deducts in computing net income per the income statement. $50 of the $200 is subject to the 50% limitation under section 274(n). In its financial statements, F treats the limitation on deductions for meals and entertainment as a permanent difference. Because meals and entertainment expenses are specifically described in Part III, line 11, F must report all of its meals and entertainment expenses on this line, regardless of whether there is a difference. Accordingly, F must report $200 in column (a), $25 in column (c), and $175 in column (d). F must not report the $150 of meals and entertainment expenses that are deducted in F's financial statement net income and are fully deductible for U.S. income tax purposes on Part II, line 28, Other items with no differences, nor the $50 subject to the limitation under section 274(n) on Part III, line 11.

Part II. Reconciliation of Net Income (Loss) per Income Statement of Includible Corporations With Taxable Income per Return

Attach supporting statements for Parts II, lines 1 through 12. For any item reported on lines 1, 3 through 6, or 8, include in the supporting statement the name of the entity for which the item is reported, the entity's EIN (if applicable), the type of entity (corporation, partnership, etc.), and the item amounts for columns (a) through (d). See the instructions for Part II, lines 2, 7, and 9 through 12, for the specific information required for those particular lines.

Line 1. Income (Loss) From Equity Method Foreign Corporations

Report on line 1, column (a), the financial income (loss) included in Part I,

line 11, for any foreign corporation accounted for on the equity method and remove such amount in column (b) or (c), as applicable. Report the amount of dividends received and other taxable amounts received or includible from foreign corporations on Part II, lines 2 through 5, as applicable.

Line 2. Gross Foreign Dividends Not Previously Taxed

Except as otherwise provided in this paragraph, report on line 2, column (d), the amount (before any withholding tax) of any foreign dividends included in current year taxable income on Form 1120, page 1, line 28, and report on line 2, column (a), the amount of dividends from any foreign corporation included in Part I, line 11. Do not report on line 2 any amounts that must be reported on Part II, line 3 or 4, or dividends that were previously taxed and must be reported on Part II, line 5. (See the instructions below for Part II, lines 3, 4, and 5.)

For any dividends reported on Part II, line 2, that are received on a class of voting stock of which the corporation directly or indirectly owned 10% or more of the outstanding shares of that class at any time during the tax year, report on an attached supporting statement: (1) the name of the dividend payer, (2) the payer's EIN (if applicable), (3) the class of voting stock on which the dividend was paid, (4) the percentage of the class directly or indirectly owned, and (5) the amounts for columns (a) through (d).

Line 3. Subpart F, QEF, and Similar Income Inclusions

Report on line 3, column (d), the amount included in taxable income under section 951, relating to Subpart F, gains or other income inclusions resulting from elections under sections 1291(d)(2) and 1298(b)(1), and any amount included in taxable income pursuant to section 1293, relating to a qualified electing fund (QEF). The amount of Subpart F income corresponds to the total of the amounts reported by the corporation on Schedule I, line 6, of all Forms 5471, Information Return of U.S. Persons With Respect To Certain Foreign Corporations. The amount of QEF income corresponds to the total of the amounts of income from a QEF reported by the corporation on all Forms 8621, Information Return by a Shareholder of a Passive Foreign Investment Company or Qualified

Electing Fund. See Form 8621 and the Instructions for Form 8621.

Also include on line 3 passive foreign investment company (PFIC) mark-to-market gains and losses under section 1296. Do not report such gains and losses on Part II, line 16.

Line 4. Section 78 Gross-Up

Report on line 4, column (d), the amount of any section 78 gross-up not included in column (d) of Part II, lines 9, 10, and 11, Income (loss) from U.S. partnerships, foreign partnerships, and other pass-through entities. The section 78 gross-up amount on this line 4 must correspond to the total section 78 gross-up amounts reported by the corporation on all Forms 1118, Foreign Tax Credit—Corporations, excluding the amounts reported in column (d) of Part II, lines 9, 10, and 11.

Line 5. Gross Foreign Distributions Previously Taxed

Report on line 5, column (a), any distributions received from foreign corporations that were included in Part I, line 11, and that were previously taxed for U.S. income tax purposes. For example, include in column (a) amounts that are excluded from taxable income under sections 959 and 1293(c). Remove such amount in column (b) or (c), as applicable. Report the full amount of the distribution before any withholding tax. Since previously taxed foreign distributions are not currently taxable, line 5, column (d), is shaded. (Also, see the instructions for Part II, line 2.)

Line 6. Income (Loss) From Equity Method U.S. Corporations

Report on line 6, column (a), the financial income (loss) included in Part I, line 11, for any U.S. corporation accounted for on the equity method and remove such amount in column (b) or (c), as applicable. Report on Part II, line 7, dividends received from any U.S. corporation accounted for on the equity method.

Line 7. U.S. Dividends Not Eliminated in Tax Consolidation

Report on line 7, column (a), the amount of dividends included in Part I, line 11, that were received from any U.S. corporation. Report on line 7, column (d), the amount of any U.S. dividends included in taxable income on Form 1120, page 1, line 28.

Usually, the amounts included on line 7, columns (a) and (d) include only dividends received from U.S. corporations that are not included in the U.S. consolidated tax group because intercompany dividends (dividends received from includible corporations listed on Form 851) are eliminated or excluded for financial accounting purposes and eliminated for the calculation of U.S. taxable income. In the case of an insurance company included in the consolidated U.S. income tax return required to report intercompany dividends as part of statutory accounting net income, include such intercompany dividends on Part II, line 7, column (a), and the taxable amount of those dividends on Part II, line 7, column (d). (For insurance companies included in the consolidated U.S. income tax return, see the instructions for Part I, lines 10 and 11.)

For any intercompany dividends (dividends received from includible corporations listed on Form 851) included on Part II, line 7, report on an attached supporting statement: (1) the name of the dividend payer, (2) the payer's EIN, (3) the class of stock or security on which the dividends were paid, (4) the amount of any net adjustment included on Part I, line 10a, for such dividends, and (5) the item amounts for columns (a) through (d).

For any dividends included on Part II, line 7, that are not intercompany dividends (dividends received from includible corporations listed on Form 851) that are received on classes of voting stock in which the corporation directly or indirectly owned 10% or more of the outstanding shares of that class at any time during the tax year, report on an attached supporting statement for Part II, line 7: (1) the name of the dividend payer, (2) the payer's EIN (if applicable), (3) the class of voting stock on which the dividend was paid, (4) the percentage of the class directly or indirectly owned, and (5) the item amounts for columns (a) through (d).

Line 8. Minority Interest for Includible Corporations

Report on line 8, column (a), the minority interest included in the financial income (loss) on Part I, line 11, for any member of the U.S. consolidated tax group that is less than 100% owned.

Example 12. Corporation G is a calendar year taxpayer that files and entirely completes Schedule M-3 for its 2014 tax year. G owns 90% of the stock of U.S. corporation DS1. G files a consolidated U.S. income tax return with DS1 as the GDS1 U.S.

consolidated group. G prepares certified GAAP financial statements for the consolidated financial statement group consisting of G and DS1. G has no net income of its own, and G does not report its equity interest in the income of DS1 on its separate financial statements. DS1 has financial statement net income (before minority interests) and taxable income of $1,000 ($2,500 of revenue less $1,500 cost of goods sold).

On the consolidated Schedule M-3, Part I, line 4, Worldwide consolidated net income (loss) per income statement, and on line 11, Net income (loss) per income statement of includible corporations, the U.S. consolidated tax group GDS1 must report $900 of financial statement net income ($1,000 net income less $100 minority interest).

The GDS1 group must prepare one consolidated Schedule M-3, Parts II and III, and three additional Schedules M-3, Parts II and III: one for G, one for DS1, and one for consolidation eliminations.

On the Schedule M-3, Parts II and III, for DS1, $1,000 is reported on Part II, line 28 and line 30, in both columns (a) and (d). On G's Schedule M-3, Parts II and III, zero is reported on Part II, line 30, in both columns (a) and (d). On the consolidation eliminations Schedule M-3, Parts II and III, on Part II, line 8 and line 30, the minority interest elimination for the U.S. consolidated tax group is reported as ($100) in column (a), $100 in column (c), and $0 in column (d).

On the Schedule M-3, Parts II and III, for the U.S. consolidated tax group, on Part II, line 8, Minority interest for includible corporations, ($100) is reported in column (a), $100 in column (c), and $0 in column (d). On Part II, line 28, the U.S. consolidated tax group reports $1,000 in both columns (a) and (d). As a result, financial statement net income on Part II, line 30, column (a), will total $900, net permanent differences on Part II, line 30, column (c), will total $100, and taxable income on line 30, column (d), will total $1,000.

Line 9. Income (Loss) From U.S. Partnerships and Line 10. Income (Loss) From Foreign Partnerships

For any interest owned by the corporation or a member of the U.S. consolidated tax group that is treated as an investment in a partnership for U.S. income tax purposes (other than an interest in a disregarded entity), report

Instructions for Schedule M-3 (Form 1120)

amounts on Part II, line 9 or 10, as described below:

1. In column (a) the sum of the corporation's distributive share of income or loss from a U.S. or foreign partnership that is included in Part I, line 11;

2. In column (b) or (c), as applicable, except for amounts described in item 4, below, the sum of all differences, if any, attributable to the corporation's distributive share of income or loss from a U.S. or foreign partnership; and

3. In column (d), except for amounts described in item 4, below, the sum of all amounts of income, gain, loss, or deduction attributable to the corporation's distributive share of income or loss from a U.S. or foreign partnership (that is, the sum of all amounts reportable on the corporation's Schedule(s) K-1 received from the partnership (if applicable)), without regard to any limitations computed at the partner level (for example, limitations on utilization of charitable contributions, capital losses, and interest expense).

4. Do not report on Part II, line 9 or 10, as applicable, any portion of a corporation's domestic production activities deduction under section 199 even if some or all of the corporation's deduction is attributable to a partnership interest held by the corporation. A corporation must report this deduction only on Part III, line 22.

For each partnership reported on line 9 or 10, attach a supporting statement that provides the name, EIN (if applicable), end of year profit-sharing percentage (if applicable), end of year loss-sharing percentage (if applicable), and the amount reported in column (a), (b), (c), or (d) of lines 9 or 10, as applicable.

Example 13. U.S. corporation H is a calendar year taxpayer that files and entirely completes Schedule M-3 for its 2014 tax year. H has an investment in a U.S. partnership USP. H prepares financial statements in accordance with GAAP. In its financial statements, H treats the difference between financial statement net income and taxable income from its investment in USP as a permanent difference. For its 2014 tax year, H's financial statement net income includes $10,000 of income attributable to its share of USP's net income. H's Schedule K-1 from USP reports $5,000 of ordinary income, $7,000 of long-term capital gains, $4,000 of charitable

contributions, and $200 of section 179 expense. H must report on Part II, line 9, $10,000 in column (a), a permanent difference of ($2,200) in column (c), and $7,800 in column (d).

Example 14. Same facts as *Example 13*, except that corporation H's charitable contribution deduction is wholly attributable to its partnership interest in USP and is limited to $90 pursuant to section 170(b)(2) due to other investment losses incurred by H. In its financial statements, H treated this limitation as a temporary difference. H must not report the charitable contribution limitation of $3,910 ($4,000 -$90) on Part II, line 9. H must report the limitation on Part III, line 21, and report the disallowed charitable contributions of ($3,910) in columns (b) and (d).

Line 11. Income (Loss) From Other Pass-Through Entities

For any interest in a pass-through entity (other than an interest in a partnership reportable on Part II, line 9 or 10, as applicable) owned by a member of the U.S. consolidated tax group (other than an interest in a disregarded entity), report the following on line 11:

1. In column (a) the sum of the corporation's distributive share of income or loss from the pass-through entity that is included in Part I, line 11;

2. In column (b) or (c), as applicable, except for amounts described in item 4, below, the sum of all differences, if any, attributable to the pass-through entity; and

3. In column (d), except for amounts described in item 4, below, the sum of all taxable amounts of income, gain, loss, or deduction reportable on the corporation's Schedule(s) K-1 received from the pass-through entity (if applicable).

4. Do not report on Part II, line 11, any portion of a corporation's domestic production activities deduction even if some or all of the corporation's deduction is attributable to an interest in a pass-through entity held by the corporation. A corporation must report this deduction only on Part III, line 22.

For each pass-through entity reported on line 11, attach a supporting statement that provides that entity's name, EIN (if applicable), the corporation's end of year profit-sharing percentage (if applicable), the corporation's end of year loss-sharing percentage (if applicable), and the amounts reported by the corporation in

column (a), (b), (c), or (d) of line 11, as applicable.

Line 12. Items Relating to Reportable Transactions

Any amounts attributable to any reportable transactions (as described in Regulations section 1.6011-4) must be included on Part II, line 12, regardless of whether the difference, or differences, would otherwise be reported elsewhere in Part II or Part III. Thus, if a taxpayer files Form 8886 for any reportable transaction described in Regulations section 1.6011-4, the amounts attributable to that reportable transaction must be reported on Part II, line 12. In addition, all income and expense amounts attributable to a reportable transaction must be reported on Part II, line 12, columns (a) and (d) even if there is no difference between the financial amounts and the taxable amounts.

Each difference attributable to a reportable transaction must be separately stated and adequately disclosed. A corporation will be considered to have separately stated and adequately disclosed a reportable transaction on line 12 if the corporation sequentially numbers each Form 8886 and lists by identifying number on the supporting statement for Part II, line 12, each sequentially numbered reportable transaction and the amounts required for Part II, line 12, columns (a) through (d).

In lieu of the requirements of the preceding paragraph, a corporation will be considered to have separately stated and adequately disclosed a reportable transaction if the corporation attaches a supporting statement that provides the following for each reportable transaction:

1. A description of the reportable transaction disclosed on Form 8886 for which amounts are reported on Part II, line 12;

2. The name and tax shelter registration number, if applicable, as reported on lines 1a and 1c, respectively, of Form 8886; and

3. The type of reportable transaction (that is, listed transaction, confidential transaction, transaction with contractual protection, etc.) as reported on line 2 of Form 8886.

If a transaction is a listed transaction described in Regulations section 1.6011-4(b)(2), the description also must include the description provided on line 3 of Form 8886. In addition, if the reportable transaction involves an investment in the transaction through another entity such as a partnership, the description must include the name and EIN (if applicable) of that entity as reported on line 5 of Form 8886.

Example 15. Corporation J is a calendar year taxpayer that files and entirely completes Schedule M-3 for its 2014 tax year. J incurred seven different abandonment losses during its 2014 tax year. One loss of $12 million results from a reportable transaction described in Regulations section 1.6011-4(b)(5), another loss of $5 million results from a reportable transaction described in Regulations section 1.6011-4(b)(4), and the remaining five abandonment losses are not reportable transactions. J discloses the reportable transactions giving rise to the $12 million and $5 million losses on separate Forms 8886 and sequentially numbers them X1 and X2, respectively. J must separately state and adequately disclose the $12 million and $5 million losses on Part II, line 12. The $12 million loss and the $5 million loss will be adequately disclosed if J attaches a supporting statement for line 12 that lists each of the sequentially numbered forms, Form 8886-X1 and Form 8886-X2, and with respect to each reportable transaction reports the appropriate amounts required for Part II, line 12, columns (a) through (d). Alternatively, J's disclosures will be adequate if the description provided for each loss on the supporting statement includes the names and tax shelter registration numbers, if any, disclosed on the applicable Form 8886, identifies the type of reportable transaction for the loss, and reports the appropriate amounts required for Part II, line 12, columns (a) through (d). J must report the losses attributable to the other five abandonment losses on Part II, line 23e, regardless of whether a difference exists for any or all of those abandonment losses.

Example 16. Corporation K is a calendar year taxpayer that files and entirely completes Schedule M-3 for its 2014 tax year. K enters into a transaction with contractual protection that is a reportable transaction described in Regulations section 1.6011-4(b)(4). This reportable transaction is the only reportable transaction for K's 2014 tax year and results in a $7 million capital loss for both financial accounting purposes and U.S. income tax purposes. Although the transaction does not result in a difference, K is required to report on Part II, line 12, the following amounts:

($7 million) in column (a), zero in columns (b) and (c), and ($7 million) in column (d). The transaction will be adequately disclosed if K attaches a supporting statement for line 12 that (a) sequentially numbers the Form 8886 and refers to the sequentially-numbered Form 8886-X1 and (b) reports the applicable amounts required for line 12, columns (a) through (d). Alternatively, the transaction will be adequately disclosed if the supporting statement for line 12 includes a description of the transaction, the name and tax shelter registration number, if any, and the type of reportable transaction disclosed on Form 8886.

Line 13. Interest Income

Report on Part II, line 13, column (a), the total amount of interest income included on Part I, line 11, and report on Part II, line 13, column (d), the total amount of interest income included on Form 1120, page 1, line 28, that is not required to be reported elsewhere on Schedule M-3. In columns (b) or (c), as applicable, adjust for any amounts treated for U.S. income tax purposes as interest income that are treated as some other form of income for financial accounting purposes, or vice versa. For example, adjustments to interest income resulting from adjustments made in accordance with the instructions for Part II, line 18, should be made in columns (b) and (c) of this line 13.

Complete Part II of Form 8916-A. Enter the amounts from line 6, columns (a) through (d) of Form 8916-A, on Schedule M-3, Part II, line 13, columns (a) through (d), as applicable. Attach Form 8916-A.

Do not report on this line 13 or include on Form 8916-A amounts reported in accordance with the instructions for Part II, lines 9, 10, 11, 12, and 22.

Note. For tax years ending December 31, 2014, or later, any corporation that files Form 1120 (or Form 1120-C) that (a) is required to file Schedule M-3 (Form 1120) and has less than $50 million in total assets at the end of the tax year, or (b) is not required to file Schedule M-3 and voluntarily files Schedule M-3, is not required to file Form 8916-A, but may voluntarily do so.

Line 14. Total Accrual to Cash Adjustment

This line is completed by a corporation that prepares financial statements (or books and records, if permitted) using

an overall accrual method of accounting and uses an overall cash method of accounting for U.S. income tax purposes (or vice versa). With the exception of amounts required to be reported on Part II, line 12, the corporation must report on Part II, line 14, a single amount net of all adjustments attributable solely to the use of the different overall methods of accounting (for example, adjustments related to accounts receivable, accounts payable, compensation, accrued liabilities, etc.), regardless of whether a separate line on Schedule M-3 corresponds to an item within the accrual to cash reconciliation. Differences not attributable to the use of the different overall methods of accounting must be reported on the appropriate lines of Schedule M-3 (for example, a depreciation difference must be reported on Part III, line 31).

Example 17. Corporation L is a calendar year taxpayer that files and entirely completes Schedule M-3 for its 2014 tax year. L prepares financial statements in accordance with GAAP using an overall accrual method of accounting. L uses an overall cash method of accounting for U.S. income tax purposes. L's financial statements for the year ending December 31, 2014, report accounts receivable of $35,000, an allowance for bad debts of $10,000, and accounts payable of $17,000 related to current year acquisition and reorganization legal and accounting fees. In addition, for L's year ending December 31, 2014, L reported financial statement depreciation expense of $15,000 and depreciation for U.S. income tax purposes of $25,000. For L's 2014 tax year using an overall cash method of accounting, L does not recognize the $35,000 of revenue attributable to the accounts receivable, cannot deduct the $10,000 allowance for bad debt, and cannot deduct the $17,000 of accounts payable. In its financial statements, L treats both the difference in overall accounting methods used for financial statement and U.S. income tax purposes and the difference in depreciation expense as temporary differences. L must combine all adjustments attributable to the differences related to the overall accounting methods on Part II, line 14. As a result, L must report on Part II, line 14, $8,000 in column (a) ($35,000 -$10,000 - $17,000), ($8,000) in column (b), and zero in column (d). L must not report the accrual to cash adjustment attributable to the legal and accounting fees on Part III, line 24,

Instructions for Schedule M-3 (Form 1120)

Current year acquisition or reorganization legal and accounting fees. Because the difference in depreciation expense does not relate to the use of the cash or accrual method of accounting, L must report the depreciation difference on Part III, line 31, Depreciation, and report $15,000 in column (a), $10,000 in column (b), and $25,000 in column (d).

Line 15. Hedging Transactions

Report on line 15, column (a), the net gain or loss from hedging transactions included on Part I, line 11. Report in column (d) the amount of taxable income from hedging transactions as defined in section 1221(b)(2). Use columns (b) and (c) to report all differences caused by treating hedging transactions differently for financial accounting purposes and for U.S. income tax purposes. For example, if a portion of a hedge is considered ineffective under GAAP but still is a valid hedge under section 1221(b)(2), the difference must be reported on line 15. The hedge of a capital asset, which is not a valid hedge for U.S. income tax purposes but may be considered a hedge for GAAP purposes, must also be reported here.

Report hedging gains and losses computed under the mark-to-market method of accounting on line 15 and not on Part II, line 16.

Report any gain or loss from inventory hedging transactions on line 15 and not on Part II, line 17.

Line 16. Mark-to-Market Income (Loss)

Report on line 16 any amount representing the mark-to-market income or loss for any securities held by a dealer in securities, a dealer in commodities having made a valid election under section 475(e), or a trader in securities or commodities having made a valid election under section 475(f). "Securities" for these purposes are securities described in section 475(c)(2) and commodities described in section 475(e)(2). "Securities" do not include any items specifically excluded from sections 475(c)(2) and 475(e)(2), such as certain contracts to which section 1256(a) applies.

Report hedging gains and losses computed under the mark-to-market method of accounting on Part II, line 15, Hedging transactions, and not on line 16.

Traders in securities and commodities. For a trader in securities or commodities that made a valid election under section 475(f) to use the mark-to-market method to account for securities or commodities held in connection with a trading business that files Form 4797, any Schedule M-3 entries required as a result of marking to market these securities or commodities are reported as follows: (a) mark-to-market gains and losses from Form 4797, line 10, are included on Part II, line 16, of Schedule M-3 (Form 1120); (b) any other Schedule M-3 entries required based on other results (non mark-to-market gains and losses) included in the total reported on Form 4797, line 17, should be reported on Part II, line 23d, of Schedule M-3 (Form 1120), unless the instructions for Schedule M-3 require the amounts to be reported on another line.

Line 17. Cost of Goods Sold

Report on line 17 any amounts deducted as part of cost of goods sold during the tax year, regardless of whether the amounts would otherwise be reported elsewhere in Part II or Part III.

Examples of amounts that must be included as cost of goods sold items are amounts attributable to inventory valuation, such as amounts attributable to cost-flow assumptions, additional costs required to be capitalized (including depreciation) such as section 263A costs, inventory shrinkage accruals, inventory obsolescence reserves, and lower of cost or market (LCM) write-downs.

Complete Part I of Form 8916-A. Enter the amounts from line 8, columns (a) through (d) of Form 8916-A, on Schedule M-3, Part II, line 17, columns (a) through (d), as applicable. Attach Form 8916-A, if applicable.

Note. The entries in columns (a) and (d) of Schedule M-3, line 17, are negative amounts.

Do not report the following on this line 17 or on Form 8916-A:
- Amounts reportable on Part II, line 12;
- Any gain or loss from inventory hedging transactions reportable on Part II, line 15;
- Amounts reportable on Part II, line 18;
- Amounts reportable on Part II, line 21;
- Mark-to-market income or (loss) associated with the inventories of dealers in securities under section 475, reportable on Part II, line 16;

- Section 481(a) adjustments related to cost of goods sold or inventory valuation, reportable on Part II, line 19;
- Fines and penalties reportable on Part III, line 12;
- Judgments, damages, awards, and similar costs, reportable on Part III, line 13; and
- Amounts included on Part III, line 34.

Note. For tax years ending December 31, 2014, or later, any corporation that files Form 1120 (or Form 1120-C) that (a) is required to file Schedule M-3 (Form 1120) and has less than $50 million in total assets at the end of the tax year, or (b) is not required to file Schedule M-3 and voluntarily files Schedule M-3, is not required to file Form 8916-A, but may voluntarily do so.

Example 18. Corporation C is a calendar year taxpayer that placed in service ten depreciable fixed assets in a prior tax year. C is required to file and entirely complete Schedule M-3 for its 2014 tax year. C's total depreciation expense for its 2014 tax year for five of the assets is $50,000 for financial accounting purposes and $70,000 for U.S. income tax purposes. C's total annual depreciation expense for its 2014 tax year for the other five assets is $40,000 for financial accounting purposes and $30,000 for U.S. income tax purposes. In addition, C incurs $200 of meals and entertainment expenses that C deducts in computing net income for financial accounting purposes. All $200 of the meals and entertainment expenses is subject to the 50% limitation under section 274(n). In its financial statements, C treats the $50,000 depreciation and $100 of the meals and entertainment as other costs in computing cost of goods sold. C must include on Form 8916-A and on Schedule M-3, Part II, line 17, in column (a), the $50,000 of depreciation and $100 of meals and entertainment. C must also include a temporary difference of $20,000 in column (b), a permanent difference of ($50) in column (c), and $70,050 in column (d) ($70,000 depreciation and $50 meals and entertainment expenses). In addition, C must report on Part III, line 31, for its 2014 tax year income statement, depreciation expense of $40,000 in column (a), a temporary difference of ($10,000) in column (b) and $30,000 in column (d); and on Part III, line 11, meals and entertainment expense of $100 in column (a), a permanent difference of ($50) in column (c), and $50 in column (d). All other cost of goods sold items would be added to the amounts included on Part II, line 17, detailed in this example and reported on Form 8916-A and on Part II, line 17, in the appropriate columns.

Line 18. Sale Versus Lease (for Sellers and/or Lessors)

Note. Also see the instructions at Part III, line 34, Purchase Versus Lease (for Purchasers and/or Lessees).

Asset transfer transactions with periodic payments characterized for financial accounting purposes as either a sale or a lease may, under some circumstances, be characterized as the opposite for tax purposes. If the transaction is treated as a lease, the seller/lessor reports the periodic payments as gross rental income and also reports depreciation expense. If the transaction is treated as a sale, the seller/lessor computes gain from the sale of assets and reports the periodic payments as payments of principal and interest income.

On Part II, line 18, column (a), report the gross profit or gross rental income for financial accounting purposes for all sale or lease transactions that must be given the opposite characterization for U.S. income tax purposes. On Part II, line 18, column (d), report the gross profit or gross rental income for federal income tax purposes. Interest income amounts for such transactions must be reported on Part II, line 13, in column (a) or (d), as applicable. Depreciation expense for such transactions must be reported on Part III, line 31, in column (a) or (d), as applicable. Use columns (b) and (c) of Part II, lines 13 and 18, and Part III, line 31, as applicable to report the differences between column (a) and (d).

Example 19. Corporation M sells and leases property to customers. M is a calendar year taxpayer that files and entirely completes Schedule M-3 for its 2014 tax year. For financial accounting purposes, M accounts for each transaction as a sale. For U.S. income tax purposes, each of M's transactions must be treated as a lease. In its financial statements, M treats the difference in the financial accounting and the U.S. income tax treatment of these transactions as temporary. During 2014, M reports in its financial statements $1,000 of sales and $700 of cost of goods sold with respect to 2014 lease transactions. M receives periodic payments of $500 in 2014 with respect to these 2014 transactions and similar transactions from prior years and treats $400 as principal and $100 as interest

income. For financial accounting purposes, M reports gross profit of $300 ($1,000 -$700) and interest income of $100 from these transactions. For U.S. income tax purposes, M reports $500 of gross rental income (the periodic payments) and (based on other facts) $200 of depreciation deduction on the property. On its 2014 Schedule M-3, M must report on Part II, line 13, $100 in column (a), ($100) in column (b), and zero in column (d). In addition, M must report on Part II, line 18, $300 of gross profit in column (a), $200 in column (b), and $500 of gross rental income in column (d). Lastly, M must report on Part III, line 31, $200 in column (b) and (d).

Line 19. Section 481(a) Adjustments

With the exception of a section 481(a) adjustment that is required to be reported on Part II, line 12, for reportable transactions, any difference between an income or expense item attributable to an authorized (or unauthorized) change in method of accounting made for U.S. income tax purposes that results in a section 481(a) adjustment must be reported on Part II, line 19, regardless of whether a separate line for that income or expense item exists in Part II or Part III.

Example 20. Corporation N is a calendar year taxpayer that files and entirely completes Schedule M-3 for its 2014 tax year. N was depreciating certain fixed assets over an erroneous recovery period and, effective for its 2014 tax year, N receives IRS consent to change its method of accounting for the depreciable fixed assets and begins using the proper recovery period. The change in method of accounting results in a positive section 481(a) adjustment of $100,000 that is required to be spread over four tax years, beginning with the 2014 tax year. In its financial statements, N treats the section 481(a) adjustment as a temporary difference. N must report on Part II, line 19, $25,000 in columns (b) and (d) for its 2014 tax year and each of the subsequent three tax years (unless N is otherwise required to recognize the remainder of the 481(a) adjustment earlier). N must not report the section 481(a) adjustment on Part III, line 31.

Line 20. Unearned/Deferred Revenue

Report on line 20, column (a), amounts of revenues included in Part I, line 11, that were deferred from a prior financial accounting year. Report on line 20,

column (d), amounts of revenues recognizable for U.S. income tax purposes in the current tax year that are recognized for financial accounting purposes in a different year. Also, report on line 20, column (d), any amount of revenues reported on line 20, column (a), that are recognizable for U.S. income tax purposes in the current tax year. Use columns (b) and (c) of line 20, as applicable, to report the differences between column (a) and (d).

Line 20 must not be used to report income recognized from long-term contracts. Instead, use line 21.

Line 21. Income Recognition From Long-Term Contracts

Report on line 21 the amount of net income or loss for financial statement purposes (or books and records, if applicable) or U.S. income tax purposes for any contract accounted for under a long-term contract method of accounting.

Line 22. Original Issue Discount and Other Imputed Interest

Report on line 22 any amounts of original issue discount (OID) and other imputed interest. The term "original issue discount and other imputed interest" includes, but is not limited to:

1. The excess of a debt instrument's stated redemption price at maturity over its issue price, as determined under section 1273;

2. Amounts that are imputed interest on a deferred sales contract under section 483;

3. Amounts treated as interest or OID under the stripped bond rules under section 1286; and

4. Amounts treated as OID under the below-market interest rate rules under section 7872.

Line 23a. Income Statement Gain/Loss on Sale, Exchange, Abandonment, Worthlessness, or Other Disposition of Assets Other Than Inventory and Pass-Through Entities

Report on line 23a, column (a), all gains and losses on the disposition of assets except for (a) gains and losses on the disposition of inventory, and (b) gains and losses allocated to the corporation from a pass-through entity (for example, on Schedule K-1) that are included in the net income (loss) of includible corporations reported on Part I, line 11. Reverse the amount reported in column (a) in column (b) or (c), as applicable.

The corresponding gains and losses for U.S. income tax purposes are reported on Part II, lines 23b through 23g, as applicable.

Line 23b. Gross Capital Gains From Schedule D, Excluding Amounts From Pass-Through Entities

Report on line 23b gross capital gains reported on Schedule D (Form 1120), Capital Gains and Losses, excluding capital gains from pass-through entities, which must be reported on Part II, lines 9, 10, or 11, as applicable.

Line 23c. Gross Capital Losses From Schedule D, Excluding Amounts From Pass-Through Entities, Abandonment Losses, and Worthless Stock Losses

Report on line 23c gross capital losses reported on Schedule D (Form 1120), excluding capital losses from (a) pass-through entities, which must be reported on Part II, lines 9, 10, or 11, as applicable; (b) abandonment losses, which must be reported on Part II, line 23e; and (c) worthless stock losses, which must be reported on Part II, line 23f. Do not report on line 23c capital losses carried over from a prior tax year and utilized in the current tax year. See the instructions for Part II, line 24, regarding the reporting requirements for capital loss carryovers utilized in the current tax year.

Line 23d. Net Gain/Loss Reported on Form 4797, Line 17, Excluding Amounts From Pass-Through Entities, Abandonment Losses, and Worthless Stock Losses

Report on line 23d the net gain or loss reported on line 17 of Form 4797, Sales of Business Property, excluding amounts from (a) pass-through entities, which must be reported on Part II, lines 9, 10, or 11, as applicable; (b) abandonment losses, which must be reported on Part II, line 23e; and (c) worthless stock losses, which must be reported on Part II, line 23f.

Note. Traders in securities or commodities that have made a valid election under section 475(f) to use the mark-to-market method to account for securities or commodities, see the instructions for Part II, line 16, earlier.

Line 23e. Abandonment Losses

Report on line 23e any abandonment losses, regardless of whether the loss is

characterized as an ordinary loss or a capital loss.

Line 23f. Worthless Stock Losses

Report on line 23f any worthless stock loss, regardless of whether the loss is characterized as an ordinary loss or a capital loss. Attach a statement that separately states and adequately discloses each event that gives rise to a worthless stock loss and the amount of each loss.

Line 23g. Other Gain/Loss on Disposition of Assets Other Than Inventory

Report on line 23g any gains or losses from the sale or exchange of property other than inventory that are not reported on lines 23b through 23f.

Line 24. Capital Loss Limitation and Carryforward Used

Report as a positive amount on line 24, columns (b) or (c), as applicable, and (d) the excess of the net capital losses over the net capital gains reported on Schedule D (Form 1120) by the corporation. For a U.S. consolidated tax group, the Schedule M-3 adjustment for the amount of the consolidated net capital loss that is disallowed should not be made on the separate consolidating Schedules M-3 of the includible corporations, but on the separate Schedule M-3 for consolidated eliminations (or on Form 8916 in the case of a mixed group) as described under *Completing Schedule M-3* and *Certain Allocations, Limitations, and Carryovers*, earlier.

If the corporation utilizes a capital loss carryforward on Schedule D in the current tax year, report the carryforward utilized as a negative amount on Part II, line 24, columns (b) or (c), as applicable, and column (d). For a U.S. consolidated tax group, the Schedule M-3 adjustment for the amount of the consolidated capital loss carryforward should not be made on the separate consolidating Schedules M-3 of the includible corporations, but on the separate Schedule M-3 for consolidation eliminations (or on Form 8916 in the case of a mixed group) as described under *Completing Schedule M-3* and *Certain Allocations, Limitations, and Carryovers*, earlier.

Line 25. Other Income (Loss) Items With Differences

Separately state and adequately disclose on Part II, line 25, all items of income (loss) with differences that are

not otherwise listed on Part II, lines 1 through 24. Attach a statement that itemizes the type of income (loss) and the amount of each item and provides a description that states the income (loss) name for book purposes for the amount recorded in column (a) and describes the adjustment being recorded in column (b) or (c). The entire description completes the tax description for the amount included in column (d) for each item separately stated on this line.

The attached statement should have five columns. The first column has the description for the next four columns. The second column is column (a) income (loss) per income statement, the third column is column (b) temporary difference, the fourth column is column (c) permanent difference, and the fifth column is column (d) income (loss) per tax return. Every item listed on the attached statement for line 25 must always have columns (a) + (b) + (c) = (d). Each item with amounts in columns (a), (b), (c), and (d) will be totaled and included as one line on Part II, line 25.

If any "comprehensive income" as defined by Statement of Financial Accounting Standards (SFAS) No. 130 is reported on this line, describe the item(s) in detail. Examples of sufficiently detailed descriptions include "foreign currency translation adjustments — comprehensive income" and "gains and losses on available-for-sale securities — comprehensive income."

Whether an item of income (loss) is reported on line 25, or is reported on Part II, line 28, is determined separately by each member of the U.S. consolidated tax group and not at the U.S. consolidated tax group level.

Example 21. U.S. corporation P has two subsidiaries, corporations A and B, that are included in P's consolidated financial statements and in P's consolidated U.S. income tax return. For financial statement purposes, P, A, and B recognize revenue from the sale of inventory upon delivery to the customer. For U.S. income tax purposes, P and A recognize such revenue consistent with the method used for financial statement purposes, whereas B recognizes such revenue based upon customer acceptance. P and A must report this revenue in column (a) and (d) on Part II, line 28. B must report the following on Part II, line 25: in column (a), B's revenue recognized in the financial statements based upon delivery to the customer; in column (d), B's revenue recognized for U.S. income tax purposes based upon customer acceptance; and in column (b) or (c), as applicable, the difference between B's revenue recognized in its financial statements and in its U.S. taxable income.

Note. In this example, the first column of the attached statement for Part II, line 25, discussed earlier, must include an adequate description, such as, "Inventory Sales Revenue recognized upon acceptance, not delivery."

Line 26. Total Income (Loss) Items

Combine lines 1 through 25 and enter the total on line 26.

Note. Line 17, Cost of goods sold, columns (a) and (d), if applicable, are negative amounts which will affect the totals entered on line 26.

Line 27. Total Expense/ Deduction Items

Report on Part II, line 27, columns (a) through (d), as applicable, the negative of the amounts reported on Part III, line 38, columns (a) through (d), as applicable. Report positive amounts as negative and negative amounts as positive. For example, if Part III, line 38, column (a), reflects an amount of $1 million, then report on Part II, line 27, column (a), ($1 million). Similarly, if Part III, line 38, column (b), reflects an amount of ($50,000), then report on Part II, line 27, column (b), $50,000.

Line 28. Other Items With No Differences

If there is no difference between the financial accounting amount and the taxable amount of an entire item of income, gain, loss, expense, or deduction and the item is not described or included in Part II, lines 1 through 25, or Part III, lines 1 through 37, report the entire amount of the item in columns (a) and (d) of line 28. If a portion of an item of income, loss, expense, or deduction has a difference and a portion of the item does not have a difference, do not report any portion of the item on line 28. Instead, report the entire amount of the item (that is, both the portion with a difference and the portion without a difference) on the applicable line of Part II, lines 1 through 25, or Part III, lines 1 through 37. See *Example 11*, earlier.

Line 29a. 1120 Subgroup Reconciliation Totals

For filers other than a mixed group, combine lines 26 through 28 and skip lines 29b and 29c. On the sub-consolidated Schedule M-3 for a mixed group, combine lines 26 through 28 and skip lines 29b and 29c. For the consolidated Schedule M-3 of a mixed group, complete only lines 29a through 29c and line 30 of Part II. No Part III is required to be completed for the consolidated Schedule M-3 of a mixed group.

Line 29b. PC Insurance Subgroup Reconciliation Totals

Line 29b is only used by mixed groups. See *Schedule M-3 Consolidation for Mixed Groups (1120/L/PC)*, earlier.

Line 29c. Life Insurance Subgroup Reconciliation Totals

Line 29c is only used by mixed groups. See *Schedule M-3 Consolidation for Mixed Groups (1120/L/PC)*, earlier.

Line 30. Reconciliation Totals

Mixed groups see *Schedule M-3 Consolidation for Mixed Groups (1120/L/PC)*, earlier.

Part III. Reconciliation of Net Income (Loss) per Income Statement of Includible Corporations With Taxable Income per Return—Expense/ Deduction Items

Note. Expense amounts that reduce financial accounting income must be reported on Part III, column (a), as positive amounts. Deduction amounts that reduce taxable income must be reported on Part III, column (d), as positive amounts. Amounts reported on Part II, line 27, must be the negative of the amounts reported on Part III, line 38.

Lines 1 Through 6. Income Tax Expense

If the corporation does not distinguish between current and deferred income tax expense in its financial statements (or its books and records, if applicable), report income tax expense as current income tax expense using lines 1, 3, and 5, as applicable.

A U.S. consolidated tax group must complete lines 1 through 6 in accordance with the allocation of tax expense among the members of the U.S. consolidated tax group in the financial statements (or its books and records, if applicable). If the current and deferred U.S., state, and foreign income tax expense for the U.S. consolidated tax group (income tax expense) is allocated among the members of the U.S. consolidated tax group in the group's financial statements (or its books and records, if applicable), then each member must report its allocated income tax expense on Part III, lines 1 through 6, of that member's separate Schedule M-3. However, if the income tax expense is not shared or allocated among members of the U.S. consolidated tax group but is retained in the parent corporation's financial statements (or books and records, if applicable), then amounts are reported only on Part III, lines 1 through 6, of the parent's separate Schedule M-3.

Line 7. Foreign Withholding Taxes

Report on line 7, column (a), the amount of foreign withholding taxes included in financial accounting net income on Part I, line 11. If the corporation is deducting foreign tax, use column (b) or (c), as applicable, to correct for any difference between foreign withholding tax included in financial accounting net income and the amount of foreign withholding taxes being deducted in the return. If the corporation is crediting foreign withholding taxes against the U.S. income tax liability, use column (b) or (c), as applicable, to negate the amount reported in column (a).

Line 8. Interest Expense

Report on Part III, line 8, column (a), the total amount of interest expense included on Part I, line 11, and report on Part III, line 8, column (d), the total amount of interest deduction included on Form 1120, page 1, line 28, that is not required to be reported elsewhere on Schedule M-3. In columns (b) or (c), as applicable, include any adjustments for any amounts treated for U.S. income tax purposes as interest deduction that are treated as some other form of expense for financial accounting purposes, or vice versa. For example, adjustments to interest expense/ deduction resulting from adjustments made in accordance with the instructions for Part III, line 34, Purchase versus lease (for purchasers and/or lessees), should be made in columns (b) and (c), as applicable, on this line 8.

Complete Part III of Form 8916-A. Enter the amounts from line 5, columns (a) through (d), Form 8916-A, on Schedule M-3, Part III, line 8, columns (a) through (d), as applicable. Attach Form 8916-A.

Do not report on Form 8916-A and this line 8 amounts reported in accordance with the instructions for Part II, lines 9, 10, 11, and 12.

Note. For tax years ending December 31, 2014, or later, any corporation that files Form 1120 (or Form 1120-C) that (a) is required to file Schedule M-3 (Form 1120) and has less than $50 million in total assets at the end of the tax year, or (b) is not required to file Schedule M-3 and voluntarily files Schedule M-3, is not required to file Form 8916-A, but may voluntarily do so.

Line 9. Stock Option Expense

Report on line 9, column (a), amounts expensed on Part I, line 11, net income per the income statement, that are attributable to all stock options. Report on line 9, column (d), deduction amounts attributable to all stock options.

Line 10. Other Equity-Based Compensation

Report on line 10 any amounts for equity-based compensation or consideration that are reflected as expense for financial accounting purposes (column (a)) or deducted in the U.S. income tax return (column (d)) other than amounts reportable elsewhere on Schedule M-3, Parts II and III (for example, on Part III, line 9, for stock options expense). Examples of amounts reportable on line 10 include payments attributable to employee stock purchase plans (ESPPs), phantom stock options, phantom stock units, stock warrants, stock appreciation rights, and restricted stock, regardless of whether such payments are made to employees or non-employees, or as payment for property or compensation for services.

Line 11. Meals and Entertainment

Report on line 11, column (a), any amounts paid or accrued by the corporation during the tax year for meals, beverages, and entertainment that are accounted for in financial accounting income, regardless of the classification, nomenclature, or terminology used for such amounts, and regardless of how or where such amounts are classified in the corporation's financial income statement or the income and expense accounts maintained in the corporation's books and records. Report only amounts not otherwise reportable elsewhere on Schedule M-3, Parts II and III (for example, Part II, line 17).

Line 12. Fines and Penalties

Report on line 12 any fines or similar penalties paid to a government or other authority for the violation of any law for which fines or penalties are assessed. All fines and penalties expensed in financial accounting income (paid or accrued) must be included on this line 12, column (a), regardless of the government or other authority that imposed the fines or penalties, regardless of whether the fines and penalties are civil or criminal, regardless of the classification, nomenclature, or terminology used for the fines or penalties by the imposing authority in its actions or documents, and regardless of how or where the fines or penalties are classified in the corporation's financial income statement or the income and expense accounts maintained in the corporation's books and records. Also report on line 12, column (a), the reversal of any overaccrual of any amount described in this paragraph. See section 162(f) for additional guidance.

Report on line 12, column (d), any such amounts as described in the preceding paragraph that are includible in taxable income, regardless of the financial accounting period in which such amounts were or are included in financial accounting net income. Complete columns (b) and (c) as appropriate.

Do not report on line 12 amounts required to be reported in accordance with instructions for Part III, line 13.

Do not report on line 12 amounts recovered from insurers or any other indemnitors for any fines and penalties described above.

Line 13. Judgments, Damages, Awards, and Similar Costs

Report on line 13, column (a), the amount of any estimated or actual judgments, damages, awards, settlements, and similar costs, however named or classified, included in financial accounting income, regardless of whether the amount deducted was attributable to an estimate of future anticipated payments or actual payments. Also report on line 13, column (a), the reversal of any overaccrual of any amount described in this paragraph.

Report on line 13, column (d), any such amounts as are described in the preceding paragraph that are includible in taxable income, regardless of the financial accounting period in which such amounts were or are included in financial accounting net income. Complete columns (b) and (c) as appropriate.

Do not report on line 13, amounts required to be reported in accordance with instructions for Part III, line 12.

Do not report on line 13, amounts recovered from insurers or any other indemnitors for any judgments, damages, awards, or similar costs described above.

Line 14. Parachute Payments

Report on line 14, column (a), the total expense included in financial accounting net income on Part I, line 11, that is subject to section 280G. Report in column (b) or (c), as applicable, the amount of nondeductible parachute payments pursuant to section 280G, and report in column (d) the deductible amount of compensation after any excess parachute payment limitations under section 280G. If a payment is subject to limitation under both sections 162(m) and 280G, report the total payment on this line 14.

Line 15. Compensation With Section 162(m) Limitation

Report on line 15, column (a), the total amount of non-performance-based current compensation expense for the corporate officers to whom section 162(m) applies. Report in column (b) or (c) as applicable, the nondeductible amount of current compensation in excess of $1 million ($500,000 if the corporation receives or has received financial assistance under the Treasury Troubled Asset Relief Program (TARP)). Report the deductible compensation in column (d). If a payment is subject to limitation under both sections 162(m) and 280G, report the total payment on Part III, line 14, Parachute payments. See Regulations section 1.162-27(g) for the interaction between sections 162(m) and 280G.

Line 16. Pension and Profit-Sharing

Report on line 16 any amounts attributable to the corporation's pension plans, profit-sharing plans, and any other retirement plans.

Line 17. Other Post-Retirement Benefits

Report on line 17 any amounts attributable to other post-retirement benefits not otherwise includible on Part III, line 16 (for example, retiree health and life insurance coverage, dental coverage, etc.).

Line 18. Deferred Compensation

Report on line 18, column (a), any compensation expense included in the net income (loss) amount reported in Part I, line 11, that is not deductible for U.S. income tax purposes in the current tax year and that was not reported elsewhere on Schedule M-3, column (a). Report on line 18, column (d), any compensation deductible in the current tax year that was not included in the net income (loss) amount reported in Part I, line 11, for the current tax year and that is not reportable elsewhere on Schedule M-3. For example, report originations and reversals of deferred compensation subject to section 409A on line 18.

Line 20. Charitable Contribution of Intangible Property

Report on line 20 any charitable contribution of intangible property, for example, contributions of:
- Intellectual property, patents (including any amounts of additional contributions allowable by virtue of income earned by donees subsequent to the year of donation), copyrights, trademarks;
- Securities (including stocks and their derivatives, stock options, and bonds);
- Conservation easements (including scenic easements or air rights);
- Railroad rights of way;
- Mineral rights; and
- Other intangible property.

Line 21. Charitable Contribution Limitation/ Carryforward

Report as a negative amount on line 21, columns (b), (c), and (d), as applicable, the excess of charitable contributions made during the tax year over the amount of the charitable contribution limitation amount.

If the corporation utilizes a contribution carryforward in the current tax year, report the carryforward utilized as a positive amount on columns (b), (c), and (d), as applicable.

When a consolidated income tax return is being filed, Schedule M-3 adjustments for the amount of charitable contributions in excess of the limitation, or for charitable contribution carryforward utilized, should not be made on the separate consolidating Schedules M-3 of the includible corporations, but on the separate consolidating Schedule M-3 for

consolidation eliminations (or on Form 8916 in the case of a mixed group). See *Completing Schedule M-3* and *Certain Allocations, Limitations, and Carryovers,* earlier.

Line 22. Domestic Production Activities Deduction

Report on line 22, column (d), the corporation's domestic production activities deduction under section 199 that is reported on Form 1120, page 1, line 25. Complete columns (b) and (c) as appropriate. Do not report any portion of the corporation's domestic production activities deduction on any other line of Schedule M-3.

Line 23. Current Year Acquisition or Reorganization Investment Banking Fees

Report on line 23 any investment banking fees paid or incurred in connection with a taxable or tax-free acquisition of property (for example, stock or assets) or a tax-free reorganization. Report on this line any investment banking fees incurred at any stage of the acquisition or reorganization process including, for example, fees paid or incurred to evaluate whether to investigate an acquisition, fees to conduct an actual investigation, and fees to consummate the acquisition. Also include on this line investment banking fees incurred in connection with the liquidation of a subsidiary, a spin-off of a subsidiary, or an initial public stock offering.

Line 24. Current Year Acquisition or Reorganization Legal and Accounting Fees

Report on line 24 any legal and accounting fees paid or incurred in connection with a taxable or tax-free acquisition of property (for example, stock or assets) or tax-free reorganization. Report on this line any legal and accounting fees incurred at any stage of the acquisition or reorganization process including, for example, fees paid or incurred to evaluate whether to investigate an acquisition, fees to conduct an actual investigation, and fees to consummate the acquisition. Also include on this line legal and accounting fees incurred in connection with the liquidation of a subsidiary, a spin-off of a subsidiary, or an initial public stock offering.

Line 25. Current Year Acquisition/Reorganization Other Costs

Report on line 25 any other fees paid or incurred in connection with a taxable or tax-free acquisition of property (for example, stock or assets) or a tax-free reorganization not otherwise reportable on Schedule M-3 (for example, Part III, line 23 or 24). Report on this line any fees paid or incurred at any stage of the acquisition or reorganization process including, for example, fees paid or incurred to evaluate whether to investigate an acquisition, fees to conduct an actual investigation, and fees to consummate the acquisition. Also include on this line other acquisition/reorganization costs incurred in connection with the liquidation of a subsidiary, a spin-off of a subsidiary, or an initial public stock offering.

Line 26. Amortization/ Impairment of Goodwill

Report on line 26 amortization of goodwill or amounts attributable to the impairment of goodwill.

Line 27. Amortization of Acquisition, Reorganization, and Start-Up Costs

Report on line 27 amortization of acquisition, reorganization, and start-up costs. For purposes of column (b), (c), and (d), include amounts amortizable under section 167, 195, or 248.

Line 28. Other Amortization or Impairment Write-Offs

Report on line 28 any amortization or impairment write-offs not otherwise includible on Schedule M-3.

Line 29. Reserved

When using this line to figure amounts on other tax forms or worksheets, this line should be considered to be zero.

Line 31. Depreciation

Report on line 31 any depreciation expense that is not required to be reported elsewhere on Schedule M-3 (for example, on Part II, line 9, 10, 11, or 17).

Line 32. Bad Debt Expense

Report on line 32, column (a), any amounts attributable to an allowance for uncollectible accounts receivable or actual write-offs of accounts receivable included on Part I, line 11. Report in column (d) the amount of bad debt expense deductible for federal income tax purposes under section 166.

Line 33. Corporate Owned Life Insurance Premiums

Report on line 33 all amounts of insurance premiums attributable to any life insurance policy if the corporation is directly or indirectly a beneficiary under the policy or if the policy has a cash value. Report in column (d) the amount of the premiums that are deductible for federal income tax purposes.

Line 34. Purchase Versus Lease (for Purchasers and/or Lessees)

Note. Also see the instructions for sellers and/or lessors in the instructions for Part II, line 18.

Asset transfer transactions with periodic payments characterized for financial accounting purposes as either a purchase or a lease may, under some circumstances, be characterized as the opposite for tax purposes.

If a transaction is treated as a lease, the purchaser/lessee reports the periodic payments as gross rental expense. If the transaction is treated as a purchase, the purchaser/lessee reports the periodic payments as payments of principal and interest and also reports depreciation expense or deduction with respect to the purchased asset.

Report in column (a), gross rent expense for a transaction treated as a lease for financial accounting purposes but as a sale for U.S. income tax purposes. Report in column (d), gross rental deductions for a transaction treated as a lease for U.S. income tax purposes but as a purchase for financial accounting purposes. Report interest expense for such transactions on Part III, line 8, column (a) or (d), as applicable. Report depreciation expense or deductions for such transactions on Part III, line 31, column (a) or (d), as applicable. Use columns (b) and (c) of Part III, lines 8, 31, and 34, as applicable, to report the differences between column (a) and (d) for such recharacterized transactions.

Example 22. U.S. corporation X acquired property in a transaction that, for financial accounting purposes, X treats as a lease. X is a calendar year taxpayer that files and entirely completes Schedule M-3 for its 2014 tax year. Because of its terms, the transaction is treated for U.S. income tax purposes as a purchase and X must treat the periodic payments it makes partially as payment of principal and partially as payment of interest. In its financial statements, X treats the difference between the financial accounting and U.S. income tax treatment of this transaction as a temporary difference. During 2014, X reports in its financial statements $1,000 of gross rental expense that, for U.S. income tax purposes, is recharacterized as a $700 payment of principal and a $300 payment of interest, accompanied by a depreciation deduction of $1,200 (based on other facts). On its 2014 Schedule M-3, X must report the following on Part III, line 34: column (a) $1,000, its financial accounting gross rental expense; column (b), ($1,000); and column (d), zero. On Part III, line 8, X reports zero in column (a) and $300 in columns (b) and (d) for the interest deduction. On Part III, line 31, X reports zero in column (a) and $1,200 in columns (b) and (d) for the depreciation deduction.

Line 35. Research and Development Costs

Report in column (a) the amount of expenses included in net income reported on Part I, line 11, that are related to research and development expense. Report in column (d) the amount of deductions included in Form 1120, page 1, line 27, that are recognized and reported as Section 174 research and experimental expenditures consistent with the corporation's adopted method of accounting for such expenditures. In column (c), as applicable, include any adjustments for any amounts treated for U.S. income tax purposes as research or experimental expenditures that are treated as some other form of expense for financial accounting purposes, or vice versa. Report any difference in timing recognition in column (b). For example, if the taxpayer's financial accounting method does not specify otherwise, column (b) adjustments include adjustments for timing differences between financial and tax accounting for: (1) deferral and amortization of research expenditures, (2) a section 59(e) election, (3) reduction of section 174 expenditures under section 280C or section 482, (4) costs attributable to obtaining a patent, (5) research in social sciences, and (6) cost elements for property of a character subject to depreciation.

Section 174 provides two methods for the treatment of research and experimental expenditures paid or incurred by a taxpayer in connection with the taxpayer's trade or business. These expenditures may be treated as expenses not chargeable to a capital account and deducted in the year in which they are paid or incurred, or they may be deferred and amortized. Since the method for treatment of research and experimental expenditures is adopted at the subsidiary level, the expense/deduction item is determined separately by each member of a U.S. consolidated tax group and not at the U.S. consolidated tax group level. For example, U.S. Corporation P has two subsidiaries, A and B, which are included in P's consolidated financial statements and in P's consolidated U.S. income tax return. For financial purposes, P, A, and B recognize research and development cost as an expense when accrued. For U.S. income tax purposes, P and A recognize such costs consistent with the method used for financial purposes, whereas B capitalizes and amortizes such costs. P and A must report these expenses in columns (a) and (d). B must report its expense recognized in the financial statements when accrued in column (a); in column (d), B's research and development expenditures recognized for U.S. income tax purposes; and in columns (b) and (c), as applicable, the difference between B's research and development costs in its financial statements and its research and experimental expenditures for U.S. taxable income purposes.

Example 23. Corporation X is a calendar year taxpayer that files and entirely completes Schedule M-3 for its 2014 tax year. During 2014, X incurred $100,000 of research and development costs that X recognized as an expense in its financial statements. Also, X incurred $20,000 in attorney fees in obtaining a patent application that X capitalized and amortized in its financial statements. X recognized a $2,000 amortization deduction. In compliance with its adopted method of accounting under section 174, X deducts research and experimental expenditures for U.S. income tax purposes. Accordingly, X must report $100,000 in column (a), $20,000 in column (b), and $120,000 in column (d). X must also report $2,000 in column (a), ($2,000) in column (b), and $0 in column (d) on Part III, line 28, Other amortization or impairment write-offs.

Example 24. Assume the same facts as *Example 23*, except Corporation X makes an annual election under section 59(e) to deduct $80,000 of its $120,000 of research and experimental expenditures over a

10-year period. Accordingly, X must report $100,000 in column (a), a temporary difference of ($52,000) ($20,000 less ($80,000/10 years X 9 years)) in column (b), and $48,000 in column (d). X must also report $2000 in column (a), ($2000) in column (b), and $0 in column (d) on Part III, line 28, Other amortization or impairment write-offs.

Example 25. Assume the same facts as *Example 23*, except Corporation X elected to capitalize and amortize its research and expenditures over 60 months with respect to all its research programs for U.S. tax purposes. X first realized benefits from such expenditures on August 1. Accordingly, X must report $100,000 in column (a), a temporary difference of ($90,000) ($20,000 less ($120,000/60 months X 55 months)) in column (b), and $10,000 in column (d).

Example 26. Corporation X is a calendar year taxpayer that files and entirely completes Schedule M-3 for its 2014 tax year. X adopted the current expense method to research and experimental expenditures for U.S. income tax purposes. During 2014, X incurred $50,000 of research and development costs that X recognized as an expense in its financial statements. Also, X undertook to develop a new machine for its business. X expended $30,000 on the project of which $10,000 represents actual costs of material, labor, and component cost to construct the machine, and $20,000 represents research costs not attributable to the machine itself. X capitalized $30,000 of costs related to the machine and recognized $6,000 of depreciation expense in its financial statements. X's depreciation expense on the $10,000 of costs related to the machine itself was $2,000 for U.S. income tax purposes. Accordingly, X must report $50,000 in column (a), $20,000 (research costs which are not attributable to the machine itself) in column (b), and $70,000 in column (d). X must also report $6,000 in column (a), ($4,000) in column (b), and $2,000 in column (d) on Part III, line 31, Depreciation.

Example 27. Corporation X is a calendar year taxpayer that files and entirely completes Schedule M-3 for its 2014 tax year. During 2014, X incurred $10,000 of research and development costs related to social sciences that it recognized as an expense in its financial statements. X adopted the current expense method to research and experimental expenditures for U.S.

income tax purposes. Because such costs are not allowable costs under section 174, X must report $10,000 in column (a), permanent difference ($10,000) in column (c), and $0 in column (d). If such costs are otherwise deductible for U.S. income tax purposes, X must report this item of expense on Part III, line 37, Other expense/deduction items with differences.

Example 28. Corporation X is a calendar year taxpayer that files and entirely completes Schedule M-3 for its 2014 tax year. During 2014, X paid $75,000 to acquire or in-license intangible assets under a collaborative arrangement with another company that X recognized as a research and development expense in its financial statements. X adopted the current expense method to research and experimental expenditures for U.S. income tax purposes. Because payments made to acquire rights to a product or technology are excluded costs from the definition of research and experimental expenditures, X must report $75,000 in column (a), ($75,000) in column (c), and $0 in column (d). X must report any amortization otherwise allowable related to the payments on Part III, line 28, Other amortization or impairment write-offs.

Line 36. Section 118 exclusion

Report on line 36 any inducements received in the current year and treated as contributions to the capital of a corporation by a non-shareholder. Report in column (a) any income amount as a negative number and any expense amount as a positive number.

Corporations must identify on an accompanying statement referencing line 36 the fair market value of land or other property (including cash) provided to the corporation by any non-shareholder, including a governmental unit or civic group, as an inducement, or for any other purpose. Include inducements for the corporation to locate its business in a particular state, municipality, community, or locality for the purpose of enabling the corporation to expand its existing operating facilities, including corporate headquarters, distribution center(s), or factory(ies) ("inducements").

On the accompanying statement also identify any inducements that include refundable or transferable tax credits, including transferable credits that were sold.

The statement must separately state, adequately disclose, and identify all of the dollar amounts summarized by this line. An accompanying statement is required even if there are no dollar amounts reported on line 36.

Line 37. Other Expense/ Deduction Items With Differences

Separately state and adequately disclose on Part III, line 37, all items of expense/deduction that are not otherwise listed on Part III, lines 1 through 36.

Attach a statement that describes and itemizes the type of expense/ deduction and the amount of each item, and provides a description that states the expense/deduction name for book purposes for the amount recorded in column (a) and describes the adjustment being recorded in column (b) or (c). The entire description completes the tax description for the amount included in column (d) for each item separately stated on this line.

The statement attached to the Schedule M-3 for line 37 must separately state and adequately disclose the nature and amount of the expense related to each reserve and/or contingent liability. The appropriate level of disclosure depends upon each taxpayer's operational activity and the nature of its accounting records. For example, if a corporation's net income amount reported in the income statement includes anticipated expenses for a discontinued operation as a single amount, and its general ledger or other books, records, and workpapers provide details for the anticipated expenses under more explanatory and defined categories such as employee termination costs, lease cancellation costs, loss on sale of equipment, etc., a supporting statement that lists those categories of expenses and their details will satisfy the requirement to separately state and adequately disclose. In order to separately state and adequately disclose the employee termination costs, it is not required that an anticipated termination cost amount be listed for each employee, or that each asset (or category of asset) be listed along with the anticipated loss on disposition.

The attached statement should have five columns. The first column has the description for the next four columns. The second column is column (a) expense per income statement, the third column is column (b) temporary difference, the fourth column is column (c) permanent difference, and the fifth column is column (d) deduction per tax return. Every item listed on the attached statement for line 37 must always have columns (a) + (b) + (c) = (d). Each item with amounts in columns (a), (b), (c), and (d) will be totaled and included as one line on Part III, line 37.

Comprehensive income. If any "comprehensive income" as defined by SFAS No. 130 is reported on this line, describe the item(s) in detail as, for example, "Foreign currency translation adjustments—comprehensive income" and "Gains and losses on available-for-sale securities—comprehensive income."

Reserves and contingent liabilities. Report on line 37 amounts related to the change in each reserve or contingent liability that is not required to be reported elsewhere on Schedule M-3. For example: (1) amounts relating to changes in reserves for litigation must be reported on Part III, line 13, Judgments, damages, awards, and similar costs; and (2) amounts relating to changes in reserves for uncollectible accounts receivable must be reported

on Part III, line 32, Bad debt expense. See Example 9.

Report on line 37 the amortization of various items of prepaid expense, such as prepaid subscriptions and license fees, prepaid insurance, etc.

Report on line 37, column (a), expenses included in net income reported on Part I, line 11, that are related to reserves and contingent liabilities. Report on line 37, column (d), amounts related to liabilities for reserves and contingent liabilities that are deductible in the current tax year for U.S. income tax purposes. Examples of reserves that are allowed for book purposes, but not for tax purposes, include warranty reserves, restructuring reserves, reserves for discontinued operations, and reserves for acquisitions and dispositions. Only report on line 37 items that are not required to be reported elsewhere on Schedule M-3, Parts II and III.

Example 29. Corporation Q is a calendar year taxpayer that files and entirely completes Schedule M-3 for its 2014 tax year. On July 1 of each year, Q has a fixed liability for its annual insurance premiums on its home office building that provides a 12-month

coverage period beginning July 1 through June 30. In addition, Q historically prepays 12 months of advertising expense on July 1. On July 1, 2014, Q prepays its insurance premium of $500,000 and advertising expenses of $800,000. For statutory accounting purposes, Q capitalizes and amortizes the prepaid insurance and advertising over 12 months. For U.S. income tax purposes, Q deducts the insurance premium when paid and amortizes the advertising over the 12-month period. In its annual statement, Q treats the difference attributable to the annual statement treatment and U.S. income tax treatment of the prepaid insurance as a temporary difference. As there is no difference between the book and tax treatment of advertising expense, it should be included on Part II, line 28, Other items with no differences.

Q also has a Legal reserve where $300,000 was expensed for financial accounting purposes and a ($100,000) temporary difference was calculated to arrive at the income tax deduction of $200,000. The statement attached to Q's return for Part III, line 37 must be separately stated and adequately disclosed as follows:

Line 37—Example 29
Statement Concerning Other Expense/Deduction Items With Differences

Description	Column (a) Expense per Income Statement	Column (b) Temporary Difference	Column (c) Permanent Difference	Column (d) Deduction per Tax Return
Prepaid insurance premium expensed not capitalized	$250,000	$250,000	-0-	$500,000
Legal expense reserve	$300,000	($100,000)	-0-	$200,000
Total line 37	**$550,000**	**$150,000**	-0-	**$700,000**

Line 38. Total Expense/Deduction Items

Report on Part II, line 27, columns (a) through (d), as applicable, the negative of the amounts reported on Part III, line 38, columns (a) through (d), as applicable. Report positive amounts as negative and negative amounts as positive. For example, if Part III, line 38, column (a), reflects an amount of $1 million, then report on Part II, line 27, column (a), ($1 million). Similarly, if Part III, line 38, column (b), reflects an amount of ($50,000), then report on Part II, line 27, column (b), $50,000.

Index

SCHEDULE N
(Form 1120)

Department of the Treasury
Internal Revenue Service

Foreign Operations of U.S. Corporations

▶ Attach to Form 1120, 1120-C, 1120-IC-DISC, 1120-L, 1120-PC, 1120-REIT, 1120-RIC, or 1120S.
▶ Information about Schedule N (Form 1120) and its instructions is available at *www.irs.gov/form1120.*

OMB No. 1545-0123

2014

Name | Employer identification number (EIN)

Foreign Operations Information

		Yes	No
1a	During the tax year, did the corporation own (directly or indirectly) any foreign entity that was disregarded as an entity separate from its owner under Regulations sections 301.7701-2 and 301.7701-3 (see instructions)?		
	If "Yes," you are generally required to attach **Form 8858,** Information Return of U.S. Persons With Respect to Foreign Disregarded Entities, for each foreign disregarded entity (see instructions).		
b	Enter the number of Forms 8858 attached to the tax return . . . . ▶ _____		
2	Enter the number of **Forms 8865**, Return of U.S. Persons With Respect to Certain Foreign Partnerships, attached to the corporation's income tax return . . . . ▶ _____		
3	Excluding any partnership for which a Form 8865 is attached to the tax return, did the corporation own at least a 10% interest, directly or indirectly, in any other foreign partnership (including an entity treated as a foreign partnership under Regulations section 301.7701-2 or 301.7701-3)?		
	If "Yes," see instructions for required statement.		
4a	Was the corporation a U.S. shareholder of any controlled foreign corporation (CFC)? (See sections 951 and 957.) . .		
	If "Yes," attach **Form 5471**, Information Return of U.S. Persons With Respect to Certain Foreign Corporations, for each CFC.		
b	Enter the number of Forms 5471 attached to the tax return . . . . ▶ _____		
5	During the tax year, did the corporation receive a distribution from, or was it the grantor of, or transferor to, a foreign trust?		
	If "Yes," the corporation may have to file **Form 3520**, Annual Return To Report Transactions With Foreign Trusts and Receipt of Certain Foreign Gifts.		
6a	At any time during the 2014 calendar year, did the corporation have an interest in or a signature or other authority over a financial account (such as a bank account, securities account, or other financial account) in a foreign country?		
	See the instructions for exceptions and filing requirements for **FinCEN Form 114**, Report of Foreign Bank and Financial Accounts (FBAR).		
b	If "Yes," enter the name of the foreign country . . . . . . ▶ _____		
7a	Is the corporation claiming the extraterritorial income exclusion?		
	If "Yes," attach a separate **Form 8873**, Extraterritorial Income Exclusion, for **each** transaction or group of transactions.		
b	Enter the number of Forms 8873 attached to the tax return . . . . ▶ _____		
c	Enter the total of the amounts from line 52 (extraterritorial income exclusion (net of disallowed deductions)) of **all** Forms 8873 attached to the tax return . . . . ▶ $		

Instructions

Section references are to the Internal Revenue Code unless otherwise noted.

Who Must File

Corporations that, at any time during the tax year, had assets in or operated a business in a foreign country or a U.S. possession may have to file Schedule N. If the corporation answers "Yes" to any of the questions above, attach Schedule N and the applicable forms and schedules to the corporation's income tax return.

Question 1a

Check the "Yes" box if the corporation is the "tax owner" (defined below) of a foreign disregarded entity (FDE) or it is required to file Form 5471 or Form 8865 with respect to a CFC or a CFP that is the tax owner of an FDE.

Tax owner of an FDE. The tax owner of an FDE is the person that is treated as owning the assets and liabilities of the FDE for purposes of U.S. income tax law.

A corporation that is the tax owner of an FDE is generally required to attach Form 8858 to its return. However, if the **Exception** below applies, the corporation should attach a statement (described below) in lieu of Form 8858.

Exception. In certain cases where a corporation owns an FDE indirectly or constructively through a foreign entity, the corporation may not be required to attach Form 8858. See **Who Must File** in the Instructions for Form 8858.

Statement in lieu of Form 8858. This statement must list the name, country under whose laws the entity was organized, and EIN (if any) of each applicable FDE.

Question 3

If the corporation owned at least a 10% interest, directly or indirectly, in any foreign partnership (other than any partnership for which a Form 8865 is attached to the tax return), attach a statement listing the following information for each foreign partnership. For this purpose, a foreign partnership includes an entity treated as a foreign partnership under Regulations section 301.7701-2 or 301.7701-3.

1. Name and EIN (if any) of the foreign partnership.

2. Identify which, if any, of the following forms the foreign partnership filed for its tax year ending with or within the corporation's tax year: Form 1042, 1065 or 1065-B, or 8804.

3. Name of the tax matters partner (if any).

4. Beginning and ending dates of the foreign partnership's tax year.

Question 5

The corporation may be required to file Form 3520 if:

• It directly or indirectly transferred money or property to a foreign trust (for this purpose, any U.S. person who created a foreign trust is considered a transferor),

• It is treated as the owner of any part of the assets of a foreign trust under the grantor trust rules, or

• It received a distribution from a foreign trust.

For more information, see the Instructions for Form 3520.

Note. An owner of a foreign trust must ensure that the trust files an annual information return on **Form 3520-A**, Annual Information Return of Foreign Trust With a U.S. Owner. For details, see Form 3520-A.

Question 6

Check the "Yes" box if either **1** or **2** below applies to the corporation. Otherwise, check the "No" box.

1. At any time during the 2014 calendar year, the corporation had a financial interest in or signature or other authority over a bank, securities, or other financial account in a foreign country (see FinCEN Form 114, Report of Foreign Bank and Financial Accounts (FBAR)) **and:**

• The combined value of the accounts was more than $10,000 at any time during the calendar year and

• The account was **not** with a U.S. military banking facility operated by a U.S. financial institution.

2. The corporation owns more than 50% of the stock in any corporation that would answer "Yes" to item **1** above.

If "Yes" is checked for this question:

• Enter the name of the foreign country or countries (attach a statement if more space is needed) and

• Electronically file FinCEN Form 114, on or before June 30, 2015, with the Department of the Treasury using the FinCEN's BSA e-Filing System. Because FinCEN Form 114 is not a tax form, do not file it with your return.

SCHEDULE O
(Form 1120)
(Rev. December 2012)
Department of the Treasury
Internal Revenue Service

Consent Plan and Apportionment Schedule
for a Controlled Group

▶ Attach to Form 1120, 1120-C, 1120-F, 1120-FSC, 1120-L, 1120-PC, 1120-REIT, or 1120-RIC.
▶ Information about Schedule O (Form 1120) and its instructions is available at *www.irs.gov/form1120.*

OMB No. 1545-0123

Name

Employer identification number

Part I	Apportionment Plan Information

1 Type of controlled group:
a ☐ Parent-subsidiary group
b ☐ Brother-sister group
c ☐ Combined group
d ☐ Life insurance companies only

2 This corporation has been a member of this group:
a ☐ For the entire year.
b ☐ From _____, 20 _____, until _____, 20 _____ .

3 This corporation consents and represents to:
a ☐ Adopt an apportionment plan. All the other members of this group are adopting an apportionment plan effective for the current tax year which ends on _____, 20 _____, and for all succeeding tax years.
b ☐ Amend the current apportionment plan. All the other members of this group are currently amending a previously adopted plan, which was in effect for the tax year ending _____, 20 _____, and for all succeeding tax years.
c ☐ Terminate the current apportionment plan and not adopt a new plan. All the other members of this group are not adopting an apportionment plan.
d ☐ Terminate the current apportionment plan and adopt a new plan. All the other members of this group are adopting an apportionment plan effective for the current tax year which ends on _____, 20 _____, and for all succeeding tax years.

4 If you checked box 3c or 3d above, check the applicable box below to indicate if the termination of the current apportionment plan was:
a ☐ Elected by the component members of the group.
b ☐ Required for the component members of the group.

5 If you did not check a box on line 3 above, check the applicable box below concerning the status of the group's apportionment plan (see instructions).
a ☐ No apportionment plan is in effect and none is being adopted.
b ☐ An apportionment plan is already in effect. It was adopted for the tax year ending _____, 20 _____, and for all succeeding tax years.

6 If all the members of this group are adopting a plan or amending the current plan for a tax year after the due date (including extensions) of the tax return for this corporation, is there at least one year remaining on the statute of limitations from the date this corporation filed its amended return for such tax year for assessing any resulting deficiency? See instructions.
a ☐ Yes.
  (i) ☐ The statute of limitations for this year will expire on _____, 20 _____ .
  (ii) ☐ On _____, 20 _____, this corporation entered into an agreement with the Internal Revenue Service to extend the statute of limitations for purposes of assessment until _____, 20 _____ .
b ☐ No. The members may not adopt or amend an apportionment plan.

7 Required information and elections for component members. Check the applicable box(es) (see instructions).
a ☐ The corporation will determine its tax liability by applying the maximum tax rate imposed by section 11 to the entire amount of its taxable income.
b ☐ The corporation and the other members of the group elect the FIFO method (rather than defaulting to the proportionate method) for allocating the additional taxes for the group imposed by section 11(b)(1).
c ☐ The corporation has a short tax year that does not include December 31.

For Paperwork Reduction Act Notice, see Instructions for Form 1120.   Cat. No. 48100N   Schedule O (Form 1120) (Rev. 12-2012)

Part II Taxable Income Apportionment (See instructions)

Caution: Each total in Part II, column (g) for each component member must equal taxable income from Form 1120, page 1, line 30 or the comparable line of such member's tax return.

(a) Group member's name and employer identification number	(b) Tax year end (Yr-Mo)	Taxable Income Amount Allocated to Each Bracket					(g) Total (add columns (c) through (f))
		(c) 15%	(d) 25%	(e) 34%	(f) 35%		
1							
2							
3							
4							
5							
6							
7							
8							
9							
10							
Total							

Part III Income Tax Apportionment (See instructions)

Income Tax Apportionment

(a) Group member's name	(b) 15%	(c) 25%	(d) 34%	(e) 35%	(f) 5%	(g) 3%	(h) Total income tax (combine lines (b) through (g))
1							
2							
3							
4							
5							
6							
7							
8							
9							
10							
Total							

Part IV   Other Apportionments (See instructions)

Other Apportionments

(a) Group member's name	(b) Accumulated earnings credit	(c) AMT exemption amount	(d) Phaseout of AMT exemption amount	(e) Penalty for failure to pay estimated tax	(f) Other
1					
2					
3					
4					
5					
6					
7					
8					
9					
10					
Total					

Instructions for Schedule O (Form 1120)

(Rev. December 2012)

Department of the Treasury
Internal Revenue Service

Consent Plan and Apportionment Schedule for a Controlled Group

Section references are to the Internal Revenue Code unless otherwise noted.

Future Developments

For the latest information about developments related to Schedule O (Form 1120) and its instructions, such as legislation enacted after they were published, go to *www.irs.gov/ form1120*.

General Instructions

Purpose of Schedule

A corporation that is a component member (defined below) of a controlled group must use Schedule O to report the apportionment of taxable income, income tax, and certain tax benefits between all component members of the group. These members will be subject to limitations on the use of certain tax benefits for their applicable tax year. See *Apportionment of Tax Benefit Items*.

Also use Schedule O to indicate that the member filing this return consents to and represents that all the other component members of the controlled group:
- Are adopting an apportionment plan, effective for the current tax year;
- Are amending the existing apportionment plan;
- Are terminating the existing apportionment plan and not adopting a new plan;
- Are terminating the existing apportionment plan and adopting a new plan;
- Have no apportionment plan in effect and are not adopting an apportionment plan; or
- Already have an apportionment plan in effect.

Who Must File

A corporation must file Schedule O with its income tax return, amended return, or claim for refund for each tax year that the corporation is a component member of a controlled group, even if (1) no apportionment plan is in effect, or (2) the amounts apportioned have not changed from the previous tax year. See *Definitions and Special Rules,* below.

Consolidated groups. If any of the component members of a controlled group are also members of a consolidated group, then the common parent of that consolidated group must file, as part of its consolidated income tax return, one Schedule O on behalf of the members of that consolidated group. No subsidiary of that consolidated group should file Schedule O on its own behalf. The Schedule O should contain the required consolidated information for all members of the consolidated group. See *Identifying Information*.

Exception. If all of the members of a parent-subsidiary controlled group that are required to file a U.S. tax return join in filing the same consolidated tax return, then the parent of that group does not have to file Schedule O on behalf of the group.

Completing and Filing Schedule O

In completing Schedule O, the following apply.
- The filing of Schedule O by a component member provides the required information as to the status of the group's apportionment plan. Such information must indicate, when applicable, whether all the component members of the controlled group are adopting, amending, or terminating an apportionment plan.
- If all such members complete the required written agreement setting forth the terms of the adopted or amended apportionment plan (or an agreement to terminate a previously adopted plan), then each member of that group may rely on this agreement as the member's basis for representing on its Schedule O that the other component members of the group have also consented to

adopting, amending, or terminating the apportionment plan.
- The agreement must be signed by a person authorized to sign on behalf of each component member of the controlled group and retained. No member should attach this agreement (or a copy of it) to their federal income tax returns. Each component member must keep, as part of its records, either the original or a copy of the signed agreement. The agreement must contain the group's apportionment methodology (for example, percentages) for each tax benefit item that is apportioned.

Definitions and Special Rules

Types of Controlled Groups

Parent-subsidiary group. A parent-subsidiary group is one or more chains of corporations connected through stock ownership with a common parent corporation if:
- Stock possessing at least 80% of the total combined voting power of all classes of stock entitled to vote or at least 80% of the total value of shares of all classes of stock of each of the corporations, except the common parent corporation, is directly or indirectly owned by one or more of the other corporations; and
- The common parent corporation directly or indirectly owns stock possessing at least 80% of the total combined voting power of all classes of stock entitled to vote or at least 80% of the total value of shares of all classes of stock of at least one of the other corporations, excluding, in computing such voting power or value, stock owned directly by such other corporations.

For purposes of determining whether a corporation is a member of a parent-subsidiary controlled group of corporations within the meaning of section 1563(a)(1), stock owned by a corporation means:
- Stock owned directly by the corporation, and

- Stock constructively owned by that corporation under sections 1563(e)(1), (2), and (3).

Brother-sister group. A brother-sister group generally is two or more corporations where the same five or fewer persons who are individuals, estates, or trusts directly or indirectly own stock possessing:
- At least 80% of the total combined voting power of all classes of stock entitled to vote or at least 80% of the total value of shares of all classes of the stock of each corporation (the 80% test), and
- More than 50% of the total combined voting power of all classes of stock entitled to vote or more than 50% of the total value of shares of all classes of stock of each corporation, taking into account the stock ownership of each such person only to the extent such stock ownership is identical with respect to each such corporation (the 50% test).

Brother-sister group for purposes of certain tax attributes. For purposes of allocating the following, a brother-sister group is defined using only the 50% test above:
- The taxable income brackets,
- The additional taxes,
- The alternative minimum tax (AMT) exemption amount,
- The reduction of the AMT exemption amount, and
- The accumulated earnings credit.

For purposes of determining whether a corporation is a member of a brother-sister controlled group of corporations within the meaning of section 1563(a)(2), stock owned by a person who is an individual, estate, or trust includes:
- Stock owned directly by such person, and
- Stock constructively owned under section 1563(e).

Combined group. A combined controlled group is three or more corporations each of which is a member of either a parent-subsidiary group or a brother-sister group, and at least one of which is both the common parent of a parent-subsidiary group and also a member of a brother-sister group.

Life insurance companies only group. Two or more life insurance companies subject to tax under section 801 which are members of any parent-subsidiary, brother-sister, or combined controlled group will be treated as a controlled group of corporations separate from any other type of controlled group to which these corporations would otherwise belong if they were not life insurance companies. The life insurance companies that make up a life insurance controlled group do not have to be in a direct ownership relationship with each other.

Example. Life insurance companies Corporation X and Corporation Z make up a life insurance company only group, where Corporation X, a life insurance company, owns all the stock of Corporation Y, a non-life insurance company, and Corporation Y, a non-life insurance company owns all the stock of Corporation Z, a life insurance company.

Exception for life-nonlife consolidated group. The rule above does not apply to any life insurance company that is a member (whether eligible or ineligible to join in filing a consolidated return) of a life-nonlife affiliated group for which a section 1504(c)(2) election is in effect. Instead, an eligible life insurance company will be treated as a member of a life-nonlife consolidated group, and an ineligible life insurance company will be treated as a member of a life-nonlife controlled group (deemed to constitute a parent-subsidiary controlled group).

Component Member

A corporation qualifies as a component member of a controlled group of corporations, for a tax year, if the corporation:
- Is not a member of the controlled group on the applicable December 31 testing date (defined below), but is treated as an additional member (defined below); or
- Is a member of the controlled group on the applicable December 31 testing date and is not treated as an excluded member (defined below).

In general, in determining if a member of a controlled group is a component member of that group, the applicable tax year of that corporation must be tested to determine if it was a member of the controlled group for at least one-half of the number of days in its testing period. Also, in order to determine the applicable tax year of the member being tested, the group's testing date must be determined. See *Testing date* and *Testing period*.

Note. If a controlled group has an apportionment plan in effect and some of the members of that controlled group join in filing a consolidated return, then the members of that consolidated group are treated, together, as if they were a single member of the controlled group. If a controlled group does not have an apportionment plan in effect and any of the members of that group join in filing a consolidated return, then each member of that consolidated group will be treated as a separate member of the controlled group.

Additional member. A member of a controlled group is treated as an additional member if the corporation:
- Was a member of the controlled group at any time during a calendar year,
- Was not a member of the controlled group on that testing date,
- Was a member of the controlled group for at least one-half the number of days of its testing period, and
- Is not an excluded member (defined next).

Any member of a controlled group that is treated as an additional member is also treated as a component member of that group.

Excluded member. A corporation is treated as an excluded member of a controlled group of corporations on the December 31 testing date for its tax year that includes that December 31 testing date, if the corporation is:
- A member of such group for less than one-half the number of days in its testing period,
- Exempt from tax under section 501(a) (except a corporation which is subject to tax on its unrelated business taxable income under section 511) or 521 for such year,
- A foreign corporation not subject to tax under section 882(a) for such tax year,
- A life insurance company subject to tax under section 801 other than either a life insurance company which is a member of a life insurance controlled group or a life insurance company which is a member (whether

eligible or ineligible) of a life-nonlife affiliated group for which a section 1504(c)(2) election is in effect,
• Not a franchised corporation as defined in section 1563(f)(4), or
• An S corporation, as defined in section 1361.

Any member of a controlled group that is treated as an excluded member is not a component member, but is a member of the group. However, no tax benefit items should be apportioned to an excluded member. And, an excluded member's taxable income is not taken into account in determining the additional taxes liability imposed by section 11(b)(1). Also, an excluded member's alternative minimum taxable income (AMTI) is not taken into account in determining the phase-out of the AMT exemption amount. If an excluded member of the group owns a controlling interest in a corporation that meets the entity status requirements for being a component member, that corporation is a component member of the group.

Example. Domestic corporation P owns all of the stock of domestic corporation S. Domestic corporation S owns all of the stock of foreign corporation F. Foreign corporation F owns all of the stock of domestic corporation X. Corporations P, S, and X are component members of a controlled group.

Exception. A corporation that (1) was included in a controlled group at any time during its tax year, (2) was not included in that controlled group on the group's December 31 testing date, and (3) was not included in the controlled group for at least one-half the number of days of its testing period, is not treated as a component member, additional member, or excluded member.

Example. For years prior to 2012, Corporation X has been a component member of controlled group XYZ. Corporations X, Y, and Z do not file consolidated tax returns. Corporation X is on a calendar tax year. On February 28, 2012, Corporation X was sold to an unrelated party that is not a member of any consolidated group. Corporation X remained in existence throughout its entire 2012 calendar year. For the period from January 1, 2012, through February 28, 2012, Corporation X is a member of that controlled group which includes Corporations Y and Z and which has a testing date of December 31, 2012. However, Corporation X is not a component member, additional member, or excluded member of that group for that testing period. Corporations Y and Z therefore are not required to include any information about Corporation X in their respective 2012 Schedules O, filed with their 2012 income tax returns. Further, Corporation X does not have to file Schedule O with its 2012 income tax return, for the controlled group that includes Corporations Y and Z.

Testing date. The testing date is the date for determining whether amounts of certain tax benefits otherwise available to a corporation will be limited in their use with regard to a particular tax year of a component member of a controlled group. Each member of the group uses a December 31 date, when possible, as its testing date, whether such member uses a calendar, or fiscal, tax year. When a member of a controlled group qualifies as a component member of that group on a particular December 31 date, it will be required to limit its use of certain specified tax benefits with regard to a tax year that includes a December 31 date. Each member of the group uses the December 31 date included within that member's tax year as its testing date, whether such member uses a calendar, or fiscal, tax year. However, if a component member of a controlled group has a short tax year that does not include a December 31 date, then the last day of that short tax year will be the testing date for that member. See *Special allocation rules for a short tax year, later.* Each member of a controlled group will apply those limitations to that tax year that is governed by the applicable December 31 testing date applied to that group.

Testing period. The testing period is the time period for determining whether a particular member of a controlled group qualifies either as a component member, or as an excluded member. The testing period begins on the first day of that member's tax year and ends on the day before its testing date. However, for a component member having a short tax year not including a December 31 date, the last day of its short tax year is deemed to function as the December 31 testing date for that member only. For a member on a full fiscal tax year, the portion of its tax year beginning on the December 31 testing date and ending on the last day of its tax year is not taken into account for determining its status either as a component member or as an excluded member. In determining how many days comprise a member's testing period, the group takes into account the day that the member is sold, but does not take into account either the day that such member is acquired, or the member's December 31 testing date.

Overlapping Groups

If a corporation is a component member of more than one controlled group of corporations with respect to any tax year, that corporation will be treated as a component member of only one controlled group. The determination as to the group of which such corporation is a component member shall be made under regulations prescribed by the Secretary.

Excluded Stock

To be a member of a controlled group, a corporation cannot be connected through stock ownership based on "excluded stock." Excluded stock includes:
• Nonvoting stock which is limited and preferred as to dividends,
• Treasury stock, and
• Stock which is treated as excluded stock under section 1563(c)(2)(A) for a parent-subsidiary controlled group or section 1563(c)(2)(B) for a brother-sister controlled group.

Apportionment Plan

An apportionment plan is an agreement between the component members of a controlled group of corporations for apportioning certain corporate tax benefits among the members of that group, such as the apportioning of bracketed income amounts entitled to different tax rates. By contrast, a tax sharing agreement is an agreement entered into between members of an affiliated group of corporations which have joined in the filing of a consolidated tax return. Such an agreement generally provides that the members of the affiliated group will compensate each other for certain tax benefits incurred by members separately and shared by all members on the consolidated tax return.

An apportionment plan becomes effective for a controlled group when it is adopted by all the component members of that group for their tax years which are subject to the same December 31 testing date. Once the members of a controlled group adopt an apportionment plan, it remains in effect until it is terminated.

Amending or terminating an apportionment plan.

An apportionment plan is amended when the same component members (for example, when no component members have left or joined the group during their testing periods governed by the applicable December 31 testing date) make any different apportionment of the specified tax-benefit items among themselves.

An apportionment plan is terminated when each component member of the controlled group consents or is deemed to consent to the termination of that plan. Each such member is deemed to have consented to the termination of the plan for a tax year if:
• The controlled group ceased to remain in existence (within the meaning of section 1563) as of the testing date for that calendar year,
• A corporation that was a component member of the group on the testing date in the preceding tax year is not a component member on the testing date in the current tax year, or
• A corporation that was not a component member of the group on the testing date in the preceding tax year is a component member on the testing date in the current tax year.

Exception. If the members of a consolidated return group are treated as if they are one component member, then changes as to the members which belong to that consolidated group (as long as that consolidated group remains in existence within the meaning of Regulations section 1.1502-75(d)) will not serve to terminate the group's apportionment plan.

Apportionment of Tax Benefit Items

Apportionment plan in effect.

If the component members of a controlled group have an apportionment plan in effect, they must apportion the specified tax-benefit items, such as the tax bracket amounts, according to the terms of that plan. The component members of a group are not required to apportion equally any tax-benefit item among each of them. Nor is any component member required to adopt the same percentage of apportionment for each tax-benefit item. A group therefore may apportion all, some, or none of the amount of any these tax-benefit items to a component member. However, except for a member with a short tax year that does not include a December 31 testing date, the total amount of a tax-benefit item apportioned to all the component members of the group cannot be more than the total amount of a tax item that would be allowed to a corporation that is not subject to the limitations imposed on the members of a controlled group. See *Special allocation rules for a short tax year,* below.

No apportionment plan in effect.

If no apportionment plan is adopted or in effect, the component members of a controlled group must divide the amount of any tax-benefit item equally among themselves (without regard to whether any members are also members of a consolidated return group).

Example. The Controlled Group ABCDE consists of Corporations A, B, C, D, and E. Corporations B, C, D, and E file a consolidated return. However, since the controlled group does not have an apportionment plan in effect, each member of the consolidated group is treated as a separate member of the controlled group. Therefore, corporations A, B, C, D, and E are required to allocate one-fifth of the tax-bracketed income amounts between them in the following manner:
• $10,000 (one-fifth of $50,000) on Part II, column (c),
• $5,000 (one-fifth of $25,000) on Part II, column (d), and
• $1,985,000 (one-fifth of $9,925,000) on Part II, column (e).

Special allocation rules for a short tax year.

Special apportionment rules apply to the tax bracket amount and the accumulated earnings credit, if a component member has a short tax year that does not include a December 31 date. A corporation's tax year will end before the last day of its annual tax year and will have a short tax year if:
• The corporation is sold to a consolidated group, or
• The corporation is merged or liquidated, including a deemed liquidation resulting from a section 338 election.

Example. For years prior to 2012, Corporation X has been a member of controlled group XYZ and has a calendar tax year. On May 31, 2012, Corporation X is liquidated. Corporation X has a short tax year that begins on January 1, 2012, and ends on May 31, 2012. Corporation X therefore applies the special allocation rule to the tax bracket amount and the accumulated earnings credit.

Determining the amount to be apportioned. A short-year member cannot use the group's apportionment method for determining the amount of a tax-benefit item to be apportioned to it for its short tax year, even though that method has been adopted by the group under its existing apportionment plan. Rather, the short-year member must divide the full amount of the tax-benefit item by the number of component members in the controlled group as of the last day of that member's short tax year. That amount is the amount of that tax-benefit item to be allocated to that member (and only to that member). The remaining component members will, in accordance with the terms of their apportionment plan, apportion a full amount of each specified tax-benefit item between those corporations which are the component members of the group as of the ensuing December 31 testing date.

Calculation of the additional taxes. A component member with a short tax year determines its liability for additional taxes imposed by section 11(b)(1) solely for its own taxable income. The remaining component members will determine their additional taxes based on their own combined income.

AMT calculation. If a component member has a short tax year, whether or not that tax year includes a December 31 testing date, see the annualization rule of section 443(d) for calculating the member's AMT.

See section 1561 and the related regulations for additional details regarding apportionment plans and a listing of some of the tax-benefit items.

Exceptions. This special apportionment rule does not apply if a component member has a short tax year that includes the December 31 testing date in its short tax year. For example, Corporation Y is a fiscal year taxpayer with a tax year ending on September 30. On January 31, 2012, Corporation Y is liquidated. Corporation Y's tax year beginning on October 1, 2011, and ending on January 31, 2012, is not a short tax year within the meaning of section 1561(b). Thus, the normal apportionment rules apply.

This special allocation rule also does not apply if a member of a controlled group has a short tax year and is a member of a consolidated group. Instead, such corporation's income for the short tax year is included in the consolidated return filed by the consolidated group for that corporation's tax year.

Component Member's Liability for its Additional Taxes

To determine a component member's liability for its additional taxes imposed by section 11(b)(1), each of the component members of a controlled group, for their tax years that are subject to the same December 31 testing date, must:
• Combine their taxable incomes from such tax years,
• Determine the amount of the additional taxes imposed by section 11(b)(1) by applying the appropriate tax rate (see *Determining the amount of additional taxes,* later) to the amount of such combined taxable income, and
• Apportion that amount among those members by applying the proportionate method (defined later), unless all of those members instead elect to apply the FIFO method (defined later).

Combined taxable income. All the component members of a controlled group, to which any part of a tax bracket was apportioned, must combine their taxable incomes for their tax years that are subject to the same December 31 testing date. Each corporation that is a component member of a controlled group must include its income for its entire tax year (their tax years that are subject to the same December 31 testing date) in the calculation of the combined taxable income, even if it was not a member of the group for each day of that tax year.

In determining the additional taxes, only the positive taxable incomes of those component members of a controlled group, to which any part of a tax bracket amount were apportioned, are combined for purposes of determining the liability of those members. If a component member incurs a loss for the tax year, the member is treated as having zero taxable income for purposes of determining the controlled group's combined taxable income.

Example. A controlled group includes Corporations X, Y, and Z. For the current calendar tax year, Corporation X has taxable income of $80,000, Corporation Y has taxable income of $70,000, and Corporation Z incurred a loss of ($60,000). Under the XYZ apportionment plan, Corporation Z was apportioned $1 of the $50,000 amount under the 15% tax bracket and Corporations X and Y were equally apportioned the remaining amount. The combined taxable income of the XYZ controlled group is $150,000 ($80,000 + $70,000). Thus, the XYZ group is liable for the additional taxes. Corporation Z's loss is not taken into account in determining the combined taxable income of the controlled group.

Note. If a component member has subsequent positive adjustments to its taxable income (for example, the result of an IRS audit), for a tax year (the adjustment year), all the members of the controlled group for their tax years that share the same testing date as that adjustment year, must redetermine the amount of any additional taxes imposed by section 11(b)(1) and pay those additional

taxes. These corporations have this responsibility even if none of the corporations that were component members of the group in the adjustment year remain as component members of the group.

Determining the amount of additional taxes. After the component members of a controlled group have determined their combined taxable income, those members must determine if they are liable for any additional taxes imposed by section 11(b)(1) in the following manner.
• If that combined taxable income exceeds $100,000, but is not greater than $335,000, the total amount of the liability for additional tax of such members is the lesser amount of 5% of such excess or $11,750 (the 5% additional tax).
• If that combined taxable income exceeds $335,000, but is not greater than $15,000,000, the total amount of the liability for the 5% additional tax of such members will be reflected in its aggregate income tax liability. No allocation is necessary and no such allocation needs to be reported in Part III of Schedule O.
• If that combined taxable income exceeds $15,000,000, but is not greater than $18,333,333, the total amount for that additional tax liability is the lesser of 3% of such excess, or $100,000 (the 3% additional tax). Thus, a controlled group with a combined taxable income that exceeds $15,000,000 will be liable for not only the 3% additional tax, but also the full amount of the 5% additional tax, or $11,750.
• A controlled group with a combined taxable income that exceeds $18,333,333 will be liable for the full amount of the additional taxes, or $111,750. That amount will be reflected in the group's aggregate income tax liability and is not required to be separately reported in Part III of Schedule O. The additional taxes will not require any apportionment among the component members of the group.

 See the tax rate schedule in the Instructions for Form 1120, U.S. Corporation Income Tax Return, which effectively incorporates both of the additional taxes imposed by section 11(b)(1) by imposing a 39% tax on taxable income over $100,000, but not over $335,000, and also imposing a 38%

tax on taxable income over $15,000,000, but not over $18,333,333.

Apportioning the additional taxes. The additional taxes imposed by section 11(b)(1) must be apportioned among the component members in the same manner as the applicable tax bracket amount is apportioned. The component members are required to use the proportionate method unless all component members affirmatively elect to adopt the FIFO method by checking the box on line 7b. See the instructions for line 7.

The proportionate method. Under the proportionate method, the additional taxes are allocated to each component member to which a tax bracket amount was apportioned, in the same proportion as the portion of the tax-benefit from that tax bracket which was allocated bears to the total tax-benefit amount provided to all members from the use of that tax bracket. These tax-benefits are attributable to the tax savings that the members of the group realized from having tax bracket amounts taxed at a lower rate instead of the higher tax rates to which income of the group would otherwise be subject.

The steps for applying the proportionate method are as follows:

Step 1. The regular tax (not including the additional taxes imposed by section 11(b)(1)) owed by a component member under a particular tax bracket is divided by the total tax owed by all component members under that tax bracket.

The maximum amount of tax that a corporation owes under the 15% tax bracket is $7,500. The maximum amount of tax that a corporation owes under the 25% tax bracket is $6,250. The maximum amount of tax that a corporation owes under the 34% tax bracket is $3,374,500.

Step 2. The percentage calculated under step 1 is multiplied by the total tax-benefit amount received by all the members of the group from their use of this tax bracket. This computed amount equals the portion of the group's tax-benefit amount received by a particular member from using its portion of this tax bracket.

Step 3. The amount determined under step 2 is divided by the total tax-benefit amount, received by all the component members of the group from using all the tax brackets to which any component member's income was subject.

Step 4. The percentage calculated under step 3 is multiplied by the amount of the group's additional taxes. The amount determined under this step 4 equals the amount of the additional taxes apportioned to such component member for that tax bracket.

Step 5. If a component member is liable for regular tax (not including the additional taxes imposed by section 11(b)(1)) under more than one tax bracket, that member must calculate the amount of additional taxes with respect to each tax bracket to be apportioned to that member.

Accordingly, steps 1 through 4 must be applied for each tax bracket applicable to that member. The sum of all the amounts of additional taxes apportioned to a component member from each tax bracket, to which that member is subject, is the total amount of the additional taxes apportioned to that member.

The FIFO method. Under a first-in-first-out (FIFO) method for allocating the additional taxes among the component members of the controlled group, the first dollars of additional taxes imposed by section 11(b)(1) owed by the component members of a controlled group are to be allocated proportionately to those members availing themselves of the lowest tax bracket (the first tax bracket), up to the amount of the tax-benefit received by those members from having availed themselves of that tax-bracket amount. Any remaining amount of unallocated additional taxes is then allocated proportionately among the component members which avail themselves of the next higher tax bracket, and so on, until the entire amount of the additional taxes has been fully apportioned among the component members. For example, the first $9,500 of additional tax liability of a controlled group is apportioned entirely to the component members that availed themselves of the benefit of the 15% tax bracket.

Allocation of AMT Exemption Amount and the Reduction of the AMT Exemption Amount

In determining the AMT liability of a corporation, the amount of AMTI to which the AMT rate is applied is reduced by the $40,000 AMT exemption amount. For a controlled group of corporations, the AMT exemption amount must be apportioned among the component members of the group. That amount must be divided equally among the component members for those tax years, which are subject to the same December 31 testing date, except where all those members have adopted an apportionment plan providing for an unequal apportionment of the AMT exemption amount. If so, the component members of the group will apportion the AMT exemption amount according to the terms of that apportionment plan.

The $40,000 AMT exemption amount shall be reduced, but not below zero, as the amount of AMTI increases. For a controlled group of corporations, to compute the amount of this reduction to the AMT exemption amount, the AMTI of all component members must be combined in order to compute the amount of that reduction. This exemption amount completely phases out when a controlled group's combined AMTI is at least $310,000. This reduction to the AMT exemption amount will effectively be allocated to each of the component members to which the exemption amount was apportioned and will effectively be apportioned to the component members in the same manner as is the exemption amount.

Only the positive AMTI of those component members of a controlled group are combined for purposes of determining those members' reduction of the AMT exemption amount.

Report the AMT exemption amount and the phaseout of the exemption amount in Part IV, columns (c) and (d), respectively.

Specific Instructions

Identifying Information

Component member filing Schedule O. On page 1, enter the name and employer identification number (EIN) of the component member filing this Schedule O.

In Part II, column (a), line 1, enter the component member's name and EIN. In column (b), enter the member's tax year ending date (Yr-Mo). In Parts III and IV, column (a), line 1, enter only the name of the component member.

Other component members of the controlled group. For Parts II, III, and IV, column (a), lines 2 through 10, and Part II, column (b), enter the corresponding information for each of the other component members of the controlled group, in the same manner as the member filing this Schedule O. If more space is needed, attach additional sheets.

Consolidated groups. If several component members are also members of a single consolidated group, then with respect to those members, in Parts II, III, and IV, column (a), and Part II, column (b), enter only the information of the common parent of the consolidated group.

 If any component members of the controlled group are also members of a consolidated group, the parent of such consolidated group should file only one Schedule O on behalf of all such members of the controlled group. Such form must contain the required information for each such member. See Regulations section 1.1561-3(a)(2).

Part I. Apportionment Plan Information

Line 1. Type of controlled group. A component member of a controlled group must check the applicable box to indicate the type of group. For more information, see *Types of Controlled Groups*, earlier.

For a brother-sister controlled group, check box 1b whether that group is a brother-sister group for purposes of applying only the 50% test, or for purposes of applying both the 80% and 50% test.

Line 2. Member status. If a corporation was not a component member of the group for each day of its tax year, check box 2b and provide the required information. If the taxable year of this corporation does not include a December 31 date, a special apportionment rule applies. See *Special allocation rules for a short tax year*, earlier.

Line 3. Consent and represent. If all the component members consent to adopt an apportionment plan, check box 3a. By checking box 3a, this corporation is consenting to the adoption of an apportionment plan and is also representing that the other component members of the group are also consenting to the adoption of that plan. See *Completing and Filing Schedule O*, earlier.

If all the component members consent to amend an apportionment plan, check box 3b. By checking box 3b this corporation is consenting to the amendment of an apportionment plan and is also representing that the other component members of the group are consenting to the amendment of that plan. However, to amend a plan both of the following conditions must be satisfied.
• The controlled group already has an apportionment plan in effect, and
• There has been no change in the component-member composition of the group from the previous taxable year.

If the component members of a group are either adopting a new apportionment plan or amending an existing apportionment plan that involves prior tax years of those component members, at least one year must remain on each of the statutes of limitations for assessing a tax deficiency against all of the component members of the group for such prior tax years. See the instructions, below.

If the apportionment plan for the component members of a controlled group is terminated:
• Check box 3c, if the remaining component members choose not to adopt (or are not able to adopt) a new apportionment plan; or
• Check box 3d, if the remaining component members choose to adopt a new apportionment plan.

With regard to box 3c, the remaining component members will not be able to adopt a new apportionment plan if, for example, such component members have left the group.

Example. For years prior to 2012, Corporation X has been a member of controlled group XYZ and has a calendar tax year. Corporations X, Y, and Z are component members of a controlled group and each has a calendar tax year. On August 31, 2012, X is sold to an unrelated party. Even though X will not be a member of the group on its December 31, 2012, testing date, it is treated as an additional member of the group on that date. Consequently, for 2012 the XYZ controlled group must apportion the tax-benefit items according to the terms of its apportionment plan. Therefore, X, Y, and Z would each check box 3c on its 2012 Schedule O.

If box 3c or 3d is checked, complete Parts II, III, and IV under either of the following circumstances.
• If a corporation which is joining or leaving the group still qualifies as a component member for its tax year, complete Parts II, III, and IV according to the terms of any applicable apportionment plan.
• If a corporation which is joining or leaving the group will not qualify as a component member for its tax year then, following the corporation's name in column (a), enter the notation "(E)" for excluded member. In Part II, column (b), enter the ending date of the tax year (Yr-Mo) and enter "0" in the remaining columns, as applicable. The remaining component members of the group will apportion the various tax items according to terms of any newly adopted apportionment plan, in the event a new apportionment plan is adopted by those remaining members.

Note. Do not check more than one box on line 3. If a corporation does not adopt an apportionment plan, amend a previous apportionment plan, or terminate an existing apportionment plan, skip line 3 and go to line 5.

Line 4. Reason for termination of existing apportionment plan. Check box 4a if all the component members of a controlled group of corporations are consenting to terminate the apportionment plan. Check box 4b if:

- The controlled group has ceased to remain in existence within the meaning of section 1563,
- A corporation that was a component member of the group on the testing date for the preceding tax year is no longer a component member in the current tax year, or
- A corporation that was not a component member of the group on the testing date for the preceding tax year is a component member for the current tax year.

Line 5. Status of apportionment plan. Check the applicable box to indicate the status of any apportionment plan of the controlled group.

- Check box 5a, if the controlled group does not have an apportionment plan in effect and is not adopting one.
- Check box 5b, if the controlled group already has an apportionment plan in effect and is not amending or terminating this plan.

If box 5a is checked, then the component members must share all tax-benefits equally and tax-benefit information is to be reported in Parts II, III, and IV.

Line 6. Statute of limitations. An apportionment plan may not be adopted or amended for a tax year of a component member unless there is at least one year remaining in the statutory period (including any extensions) for assessing a deficiency against the corporation for that tax year, but only where the tax liability for such tax year of that corporation would be increased by adopting such plan.

If there is less than one year remaining in the statutory period, the corporation must have entered into an agreement with the IRS extending the statutory period for the limited purpose of assessing any deficiency against that corporation for a tax year affected by the adoption or the amendment of an apportionment plan. See Regulations section 1.1561-3(c) (2).

Line 7. Required information and elections for component members. The component members of a controlled group must determine their additional taxes liability, as imposed by section 11(b)(1), for their tax years that are subject to the same December 31 testing date by combining their taxable incomes for such tax years and then apportioning the additional taxes among such component members in the same manner that the tax brackets were so allocated. See *Component Member's Liability for its Additional Taxes*, earlier.

If a corporation does not know the combined taxable income of the other component members of its group (for example, because those other component members have adopted substantially different tax years), it can avoid underpayment of tax by applying the maximum tax rate of 35% to the entire amount of its taxable income. If the corporation later determines its tax liability is less, it may file a claim for refund of overpayment.

Line 7a. A corporation choosing to compute its tax liability by applying the maximum 35% rate to the entire amount of its taxable income should check box 7a. Further, a corporation checking box 7a does not have to provide taxable income or tax apportionment information with respect to the other component members of the group. Instead, only provide the identifying information (for example, name, EIN, and ending date of the tax year) for these other members. Enter zero in the other columns for these members.

Line 7b. The controlled group may elect to apportion their additional taxes liability under the FIFO method, rather than the proportionate method. To make this election, each component member of the group must check box 7b. If the members do not check box 7b, they will be required to apportion their additional taxes liability using the proportionate method of allocation. See *The proportionate method* and *The FIFO method*, earlier.

Line 7c. If a component member of a controlled group of corporations has a short tax year that does not include a December 31 date, check

box 7c. If a corporation checks box 7c, it does not have to provide taxable income or tax apportionment information with regard to the other component members of the group. Instead, only provide the identifying information (for example, name, EIN, and ending date of the tax year) for these other members. See *Special allocation rules for a short tax year*, earlier.

Part II. Taxable Income Apportionment

Enter each component member's share of the taxable income used from each tax bracket, as is applicable. The component members of a controlled group, collectively, are entitled to one $50,000, one $25,000, and one $9,925,000 taxable income bracket amount (in that order) for columns (c), (d), and (e).

Note. If a corporation has a loss, enter zero in columns (c) through (g).

Column (c). Enter the lesser of the corporation's taxable income (as shown on Form 1120, or on the applicable corporation's income tax return) or the corporation's computed share of the $50,000 bracket.

Column (d). Enter the lesser of the corporation's taxable income (as shown on Form 1120, or on the applicable corporation's income tax return) minus the amount entered for this corporation in column (c), or the corporation's computed share of the $25,000 bracket.

Column (e). Enter the lesser of the corporation's taxable income (as shown on Form 1120, or on the applicable corporation's income tax return) minus the amounts entered for this corporation in columns (c) and (d), or the corporation's computed share of the $9,925,000 bracket.

Column (f). Enter the corporation's taxable income (from Form 1120 or the applicable corporation's income tax return) minus the amounts entered for this corporation in columns (c) through (e).

Column (g). Enter the total allocated taxable income amounts of each component member (add columns (c) through (f)). Each total in Part II, column (g), for each component member must equal taxable income from such component member's income tax return.

Part III. Income Tax Apportionment

Column (b). Multiply the taxable income amount in Part II, column (c) by 15% (0.15) and enter the result here.

Column (c). Multiply the taxable income amount in Part II, column (d) by 25% (0.25) and enter the result here.

Column (d). Multiply the taxable income amount in Part II, column (e) by 34% (0.34) and enter the result here.

Column (e). Multiply the taxable income amount in Part II, column (f) by 35% (0.35) and enter the result here.

Column (f) and (g). A corporation's share of any additional taxes liability imposed by section 11(b)(1) is determined as explained in *Determining the amount of additional taxes*, earlier.

Column (h). Enter here the total apportioned income tax for each component member. Combine all the amounts of apportioned tax of each such member, as shown in columns (b) through (g).

Part IV. Other Apportionments

Brother-sister controlled group. For purposes of apportioning the amounts included in columns (b) through (d), determine the component members of a brother-sister controlled group, using only the 50% test as provided in section 1563(a)(2). For purposes of apportioning the amounts included in column (e) and, except as provided elsewhere in the Internal Revenue Code, in column (f), determine the component members of a brother-sister controlled group using both the 50% and 80% tests as provided in section 1563(f)(5). See *Brother-sister group*, earlier.

Column (a). If a corporation qualifies as a component member of a brother-sister controlled group, solely because it satisfies only the 50% ownership affiliation test, insert the notation "(50)" after that corporation's name. If a corporation is a component member of that group because it satisfies both the 50% and 80% ownership affiliation tests, no notation is necessary.

Column (b). The component members of a controlled group may allocate the $250,000 accumulated earnings credit unequally if they adopt an apportionment plan or have an apportionment plan in effect.

Note. If any component member of a controlled group is the type of service corporation described in section 535(c)(2)(B), the amount to be apportioned among the component members is $150,000 (rather than $250,000).

Column (c). The component members of a controlled group may allocate the $40,000 AMT exemption amount unequally if they adopt an apportionment plan or have an apportionment plan in effect.

Column (d). The component members of a controlled group must apportion the reduction to the AMT exemption amount to the same corporations, and in the same proportions, as the AMT exemption amount was apportioned in Column (c). If the combined AMTI of the members of the group is at least $310,000, the corporation is not required to complete columns (c) and (d) of Part IV, since the exemption amount is fully phased out at $310,000. See *Allocation of AMT Exemption Amount and the Reduction of the AMT Exemption Amount*, earlier.

Column (e). For purposes of determining whether the component members of a controlled group are subject to a penalty for failure to pay the correct amount of estimated tax under section 6655(g), those component members of a controlled group must combine their taxable incomes for their tax years that were subject to the same December 31 testing date. If that amount is at least $1 million for any tax year during the testing period (as defined in section 6655(g)(2)(B)(i)), those members must then divide that $1 million amount equally unless they have an apportionment plan in effect.

Column (f). Enter each component member's share of any other tax-benefit items not included in columns (b) through (e). Provide the applicable Internal Revenue Code section followed by the amount apportioned to that member.

Note. Do not include on Schedule O an apportionment among the component members of any deduction for certain depreciable property for which a section 179 expense election has been made. Report this apportionment as required under section 179. See Regulations section 1.179-2(b)(7).

SCHEDULE PH
(Form 1120)

(Rev. December 2013)

Department of the Treasury
Internal Revenue Service

U.S. Personal Holding Company (PHC) Tax

► Attach to tax return.
► Information about Schedule PH (Form 1120) and its separate instructions is at *www.irs.gov/form1120.*

OMB No. 1545-0123

Name | Employer identification number

Part I — Undistributed Personal Holding Company Income (see instructions)

Additions

1	Taxable income before net operating loss deduction and special deductions. Enter amount from Form 1120, line 28	1
2	Contributions deducted in figuring line 1. Enter amount from Form 1120, line 19	2
3	Excess expenses and depreciation under section 545(b)(6). Enter amount from Part V, line 2	3
4	Total. Add lines 1 through 3	4

Deductions

5	Federal and foreign income, war profits, and excess profits taxes not deducted in figuring line 1 (attach schedule)		5
6	Contributions deductible under section 545(b)(2). See instructions for limitation		6
7	Net operating loss for the preceding tax year deductible under section 545(b)(4)		7
8a	Net capital gain from Schedule D (Form 1120), line 17	8a	
b	**Less:** Income tax on this net capital gain (see section 545(b)(5)) (attach computation)	8b	8c
9	Deduction for dividends paid (other than dividends paid after the end of the tax year). Enter amount from Part VI, line 5		9
10	Total. Add lines 5 through 9		10
11	Subtract line 10 from line 4		11
12	Dividends paid after the end of the tax year (other than deficiency dividends defined in section 547(d)), but not more than the smaller of line 11 or 20% of Part VI, line 1		12
13	**Undistributed PHC income.** Subtract line 12 from line 11		13

Note: *If the information in Part II and Part IV is not submitted with the return, the limitation period for assessment and collection of the PHC tax is any time within 6 years after the return is filed. See section 6501(f).*

Part II — Personal Holding Company Income (see instructions)

14	Dividends			14
15a	Interest	15a		
b	**Less:** Amounts excluded (attach schedule)	15b		15c
16	Royalties (other than mineral, oil, gas, or copyright royalties)			16
17	Annuities			17
18a	Rents	18a		
b	**Less:** Adjustments to rents (attach schedule)	18b		18c
19a	Mineral, oil, and gas royalties	19a		
b	**Less:** Adjustments to mineral, oil, and gas royalties (attach schedule)	19b		19c
20	Copyright royalties			20
21	Produced film rents			21
22	Compensation received for use of corporation property by 25% or more shareholder			22
23	Amounts received under personal service contracts and from their sale			23
24	Amounts includible in taxable income from estates and trusts			24
25	**PHC income.** Add lines 14 through 24			25

Part III — Tax on Undistributed Personal Holding Company Income (see instructions)

26	**PHC tax.** Multiply the amount on line 13 by 20%. Enter the result here and on Schedule J (Form 1120), line 8, or on the proper line of the appropriate tax return	26

For Paperwork Reduction Act Notice, see the Instructions for Form 1120.　　　Cat. No. 11465P　　　Schedule PH (Form 1120) (Rev. 12-2013)

Part IV — Stock Ownership Requirement Under Section 542(a)(2)

Enter the names and addresses of the individuals who together owned, directly or indirectly, at any time during the last half of the tax year, more than 50% in value of the outstanding stock of the corporation.

(a) Name	(b) Address	Highest percentage of shares owned during last half of tax year	
		(c) Preferred	(d) Common
1			
		%	%
		%	%
		%	%
		%	%
		%	%
2 Add the amounts in columns (c) and (d) and enter the totals here ▶		%	%

Part V — Excess of Expenses and Depreciation Over Income From Property Not Allowable Under Section 545(b)(6) (see instructions for Part I, line 3)

(a) Description of property	(b) Date acquired	(c) Cost or other basis	(d) Depreciation deduction	(e) Repairs, insurance, and other expenses (section 162) (attach schedule)	(f) Total of columns (d) and (e)	(g) Income from rent or other compensation	(h) Excess (col. (f) less col. (g))
1							

2   Total excess of expenses and depreciation over rent or other compensation. Add the amounts in column (h). Enter the total here and on Part I, line 3 . . . .

Note: *Attach a statement showing the names and addresses of persons from whom rent or other compensation was received for the use of, or the right to use, each property.*

Part VI — Deduction for Dividends Paid Under Sections 561 and 562

1	Taxable dividends paid. Do not include dividends considered as paid in the preceding tax year under section 563 or deficiency dividends as defined in section 547	1	
2	Consent dividends. Attach Forms 972 and 973	2	
3	Taxable distributions. Add lines 1 and 2	3	
4	Dividend carryover from first and second preceding tax years. Attach computation	4	
5	**Deduction for dividends paid.** Add lines 3 and 4. Enter the total here and on Part I, line 9 . .	5	

Instructions for Schedule PH (Form 1120)

(Rev. December 2013)

Department of the Treasury
Internal Revenue Service

U.S. Personal Holding Company (PHC) Tax

Section references are to the Internal Revenue Code unless otherwise noted.

Future Developments

For the latest information about developments related to Schedule PH (Form 1120) and its instructions, such as legislation enacted after they were published, go to *www.irs.gov/ form1120*.

What's New

For tax years beginning in 2013, the tax on undistributed personal holding company income has increased to 20%.

General Instructions

Purpose of Schedule

Use Schedule PH to figure the personal holding company (PHC) tax.

Who Must File

A corporation that is a PHC must file Schedule PH by attaching it to its income tax return.

Personal Holding Company

Generally, a corporation is a PHC if it meets both of the following requirements.

1. **PHC income test.** At least 60% of the corporation's adjusted ordinary gross income for the tax year is PHC income. See the instructions for Part II and the *Worksheet for Figuring Ordinary Gross Income, Adjusted Ordinary Gross Income, and the PHC Income Test* (Worksheet), later. Also, see *Specific Instructions* below.

2. **Stock ownership requirement.** At any time during the last half of the tax year, more than 50% in value of the corporation's outstanding stock is directly or indirectly owned by five or fewer individuals.

For purposes of this requirement, the following organizations are considered individuals.

- A qualified pension, profit-sharing, or stock bonus plan described in section 401(a).
- A trust described in section 501(c)(17) that provides for the payment of supplemental unemployment compensation under certain conditions.
- A private foundation described in section 509(a).
- A part of a trust permanently set aside or exclusively used for the purpose described in section 642(c).

Exceptions. The term "personal holding company" does not include the following corporations, even if the two requirements above are met.
- Tax-exempt corporations.
- Banks, domestic building and loan associations, and certain lending or finance companies.
- Life insurance and surety companies.
- Certain small business investment companies operating under the Small Business Investment Act of 1958.
- Corporations under the jurisdiction of the court in a title 11 or similar case.
- Foreign corporations.

At-risk, passive activities, and earnings stripping rules. A corporation that has an activity subject to the at-risk or passive activity rules or interest expense subject to the earnings stripping rules (or both) may have deductions and losses suspended or limited under these rules. As a result, do not use deductions and losses limited or suspended in any of the PHC computations. Treat any prior year deductions and losses allowed under the at-risk, passive activity, and earnings stripping rules as current year deductions and losses.

Specific Instructions

Important: To determine if a corporation is a PHC, follow the steps below to complete Schedule PH and the Worksheet, later.

1. Complete Part I. Then, complete lines 1 through 5 of the Worksheet.

2. Complete Part II and then line 6 of the Worksheet.

3. Generally, if line 6 of the Worksheet is 60% or more and the stock ownership requirement (Part IV) is met, the corporation must file Schedule PH and pay the PHC tax. However, see *Exceptions* above.

4. If the corporation determines that it must file Schedule PH and pay the PHC tax, it must complete Part III, line 26, to figure the amount of the PHC tax.

Part I. Undistributed Personal Holding Company Income

Additions

Line 1. Taxable income before net operating loss deduction and special deductions. Enter the amount from Form 1120, line 28. If the income on line 28 was figured using section 443(b) (placing the income on an annual basis), refigure it without using that section.

Line 3. Excess expenses and depreciation. If the corporation earned rent or other compensation for the use of, or right to use, property and that rent or compensation was less than the total allowable expenses and depreciation, complete Part V in most cases and enter the excess on line 3. However, if the corporation can establish that it meets all three of the requirements listed below, it can attach a statement instead of completing Part V. The statement must include:
- A list of the deductions, with the complete facts, circumstances, and arguments supporting them, and
- The information required by Regulations section 1.545-2(h)(2).

To qualify, the corporation must establish that:

Cat. No. 10826K

- The rent or other compensation it received was the highest obtainable (if none was received, it must show that none was obtainable),
- The property was held in the course of a business carried on for profit, and
- There was a reasonable expectation that the property's operation would result in a profit, or that the property was necessary to conduct the business.

Deductions

Line 5. Federal and foreign income, war profits, and excess profits taxes not deducted in figuring line 1. The corporation can deduct:
- Federal income taxes accrued during the tax year, and
- Income, war profits, and excess profits taxes accrued (or deemed paid) during the tax year to foreign countries and U.S. possessions.*

The corporation cannot deduct:
- The accumulated earnings tax under section 531, or
- The PHC tax under section 541.

*The foreign tax credit is not allowed against PHC tax. But, as described above, the corporation can take a deduction for taxes paid to foreign countries and U.S. possessions even if a credit was claimed when figuring the corporation's income tax.

Attach a schedule showing the type of tax, the tax year, and the amount. For more information, see section 545(b)(1).

Line 6. Contributions. Figure the deduction using the limitations under sections 170(b)(1)(A), (B), (D), and (E), but without sections 170(b)(2) and (d)(1). When figuring the limitations under section 170(b)(1), use taxable income figured with the adjustments (other than the 10% limitation) provided in sections 170(b)(2) and (d)(1) and without any expenses and depreciation disallowed under section 545(b)(6).

Line 7. Net operating loss. Instead of the net operating loss deduction provided in section 172, a deduction is allowed for the net operating loss (as defined in section 172(c)) for the preceding tax year figured without the special dividends-received deductions for corporations.

Line 10. Total. Include in the total for line 10 any deduction for amounts used or irrevocably set aside to pay or retire qualified indebtedness under section 545(c) (as in effect before November 5, 1990). See Regulations section 1.545-3. Enter the amount and "Section 545(c)" on the dotted line next to line 10.

Line 12. Dividends paid after the end of the tax year. The corporation can elect to treat dividends (other than deficiency dividends) paid after the end of the year and before the 16th day of the 3rd month following the end of the tax year as paid during the tax year. Enter these dividends on line 12 but not in Part VI.

Part II. Personal Holding Company Income

Note. The term "ordinary gross income" (used below) means line 3 of the Worksheet. The term "adjusted ordinary gross income" means line 5 of the Worksheet.

A corporation may be subject to the PHC tax if at least 60% of its adjusted ordinary gross income for the tax year is PHC income. Use Part II to figure the amount of the corporation's PHC income. Then, complete line 6 of the Worksheet to determine if the corporation is a PHC.

Line 15b. Amounts excluded. Enter the total of interest excluded on line 15b. The following interest can be excluded from PHC income.

1. Interest constituting rent.

2. Interest on amounts set aside in a reserve fund under section 511 or 607 of the Merchant Marine Act of 1936.

3. Interest received by a broker or dealer (within the meaning of section 3(a)(4) or (5) of the Securities Exchange Act of 1934) in connection with:

a. Any securities or money market instruments held as property described in section 1221(a)(1),

b. Margin accounts, or

c. Any financing for a customer secured by securities or money market instruments.

4. Interest from line 4d of the Worksheet.

See sections 543(a)(1) and 543(b)(2)(C) for more information.

Line 18. Rents. Rents can be excluded from PHC income if both of the following tests are met.

Test 1. The adjusted income from rents (line 18c) is at least 50% of adjusted ordinary gross income.

Test 2. The sum of taxable distributions (Part VI, line 3) and the deduction for dividends paid after the end of the tax year (Part I, line 12) is at least equal to:

1. The excess, if any, of PHC income, over

2. 10% of ordinary gross income.

For this purpose, PHC income includes copyright royalties and adjusted income from mineral, oil, and gas royalties, but does not include the amounts from lines 18c and 22.

If both of the above tests are met, rents can be excluded from PHC income. Do not complete lines 18a through 18c.

If the rents cannot be excluded, enter rents (as defined in section 543(b)(3)) on line 18a. Enter the amount from line 4a of the Worksheet on line 18b and complete line 18c.

See section 543(a)(2) for more information.

Line 19. Mineral, oil, and gas royalties. Mineral, oil, and gas royalties can be excluded from PHC income if all three of the tests below are met.

Test 1. The adjusted income from mineral, oil, and gas royalties (line 19c) is at least 50% of adjusted ordinary gross income.

Test 2. PHC income is not more than 10% of ordinary gross income.

For this purpose, PHC income includes copyright royalties and the adjusted income from rents, but does not include line 19c.

Test 3. The deductions allowable under section 162 (other than compensation for personal services rendered by a shareholder and deductions specifically allowable under other sections) are at least 15% of adjusted ordinary gross income.

If all of the above tests are met, mineral, oil, and gas royalties can be excluded from PHC income. Do not complete lines 19a through 19c.

If mineral, oil, and gas royalties are not excluded, enter the total mineral, oil, and gas royalties (including production payments and overriding royalties) on line 19a. Enter the amount from line 4b of the Worksheet on line 19b and complete line 19c.

Line 20. Copyright royalties. Note. For royalties received in connection with the licensing of computer software, see below.

Copyright royalties can be excluded from PHC income if all three of the tests below are met.

Test 1. Income from copyright royalties is at least 50% of ordinary gross income. For this purpose, copyright royalties do not include royalties received for the use of, or right to use, copyrights or interests in copyrights on works created in whole or in part by any shareholder.

Test 2. PHC income is not more than 10% of ordinary gross income.

For this purpose, PHC income includes:
• The adjusted income from rents (line 18c);
• The adjusted income from mineral, oil, and gas royalties (line 19c); and
• Copyright royalties received for the use of, or right to use, copyrights on works created in whole or in part by any shareholder owning more than 10% of the corporation's stock.

PHC income does not include:
• Copyright royalties (other than as stated above), or
• Dividends from any corporation that meets Test 1 above and Test 3 below, and in which the corporation owns at least 50% (by vote and value) of the stock.

Test 3. Total allowable deductions allowable under section 162 (other than compensation for personal services rendered by a shareholder,

deductions for royalties paid or accrued, and deductions specifically allowable under other sections) are at least 25% of the excess of:

1. Ordinary gross income, over

2. The sum of royalties paid or accrued and depreciation for copyright royalties.

Royalties received in connection with the licensing of computer software. Royalties received in connection with the licensing of computer software can be excluded from PHC income if all four of the tests below are met.

Test 1. The corporation is engaged in the active business of developing, manufacturing, or producing computer software.

Test 2. The royalties are at least 50% of ordinary gross income.

Test 3. Total allowable deductions under sections 162, 174, and 195 that are allocable to the computer software business are at least 25% of ordinary gross income (or, the average of the deductions for the 5 tax years ending with the current tax year is at least 25% of the average ordinary gross income for that period).

Test 4. The sum of taxable distributions (Part VI, line 3) and the deduction for dividends paid after the end of the tax year (Part I, line 12) is at least equal to the excess, if any, of:

1. PHC income (as defined in section 543(d)(5)(B)), over

2. 10% of ordinary gross income.

See section 543(d) for more information.

Line 21. Produced film rents. Produced film rents can be excluded from PHC income if the rents constitute at least 50% of ordinary gross income. See section 543(a)(5)

for the definition of produced film rents.

Line 22. Compensation received for the use of corporation property by a 25% or more shareholder. This line applies only to a corporation with other PHC income in excess of 10% of ordinary gross income. For purposes of this limitation, other PHC income is defined in section 543(a)(6)(C).

Enter on line 22 amounts received as compensation for the use of, or right to use, tangible property of the corporation by or for an individual, who at any time during the tax year directly or indirectly owned at least 25% in value of the corporation's outstanding stock.

Line 23. Amounts received under personal service contracts and from their sale. This line applies only if the individual who has performed, is to perform, or may be designated to perform such services owned at any time during the tax year 25% or more in value of the corporation's outstanding stock.

Enter amounts received under a contract that requires the corporation to furnish personal services if any person other than the corporation has the right to designate the individual who is to perform the services (or if the individual who is to perform the services is designated in the contract). Also include amounts received from the sale or other disposition of such a contract.

Line 26. PHC tax. The tax rate on undistributed personal holding company income for tax years beginning in 2013 is 20%.

Multiply the amount on Part I, line 13, by 20%. Enter the result here and on Schedule J (Form 1120), line 8, or on the proper line of the appropriate tax return.

Worksheet for Figuring Ordinary Gross Income, Adjusted Ordinary Gross Income, and the PHC Income Test

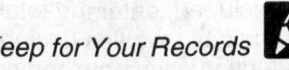 *Keep for Your Records*

Before you begin: (see instructions below)		
1. Gross income. Insurance companies, other than life insurance companies, see section 543(c)	**1**	_____
2. **Less:** Gains from the sale or disposition of capital assets and section 1231(b) property	**2** (	_____)
3. **Ordinary gross income.** Combine lines 1 and 2.	**3**	_____
4. Adjustments:		
a Deductions allocable to rents	**4a** _____	
b Deductions allocable to certain royalties and working interests in oil and gas wells	**4b** _____	
c Deductions allocable to compensation described in section 543(b)(3)(D)	**4c** _____	
d Certain excluded interest income under section 543(b)(2)(C)	**4d** _____	
e Total adjustments. Add lines 4a through 4d.	**4e**	_____
5. **Adjusted ordinary gross income.** Subtract line 4e from line 3	**5**	_____
6. Complete Part II of Schedule PH. Divide Part II, line 25, by line 5 above. Enter the result as a percentage	**6**	_____ %

Important: *If line 6 is **less than 60%**, the corporation is not a PHC. Do not file Schedule PH.*

*Generally, if line 6 is **60% or more** and the stock ownership requirement of section 542(a) is met, the corporation is a PHC. Complete Parts III and IV. For details and exceptions, see **Who Must File** and **Personal Holding Company**, earlier.*

Worksheet Instructions

Line 1. Gross income. Enter gross income as defined in section 61 and the related regulations.

Line 4. Adjustments. Ordinary gross income on line 3 must be adjusted as described below. Each type of income (rents, royalties, income from working interests in oil and gas wells, and certain excluded rents) is separately adjusted by the deductions allocable to it. Enter the allocable deductions on lines 4a, 4b, and 4c to the extent of the gross income (for example, enter deductions allocable to royalties on line 4b, but do not enter more than the gross income from royalties).

Also, in figuring adjusted ordinary gross income, certain interest income is excluded (see the instructions for line 4d below).

Line 4a. Deductions allocable to rents. Enter deductions (listed below) allocable to rents (as defined in section 543(b)(3)).
- Depreciation and amortization of property (other than certain tangible personal property not customarily retained by any lessee for more than 3 years).
- Property taxes.
- Interest.
- Rent.

Line 4b. Deductions allocable to certain royalties and working interests in oil and gas wells. Enter deductions (listed below) allocable to mineral, oil, and gas royalties (including production payments and overriding royalties) and to gross income from a working interest in an oil or gas well.
- Depreciation and amortization.
- Depletion.
- Property and severance taxes.
- Interest.
- Rent.

Line 4c. Deductions allocable to compensation. Compensation for the use of, or right to use, tangible personal property manufactured or produced by the corporation does not count as rents if the corporation is engaged in substantial manufacturing or production of the same type of property during the tax year. Enter deductions (listed below) allocable to this type of compensation.
- Depreciation and amortization of property (other than certain tangible personal property).
- Property taxes.
- Interest.
- Rent.

Line 4d. Certain excluded interest income. Include:
- Interest on a direct obligation of the United States held for sale by a dealer who is making a primary market for these obligations, and
- Interest on condemnation awards, judgments, and tax refunds.

SCHEDULE UTP (Form 1120)	Uncertain Tax Position Statement	OMB No. 1545-0123
Department of the Treasury Internal Revenue Service	► File with Form 1120, 1120-F, 1120-L, or 1120-PC. ► Information about Schedule UTP (Form 1120) and its separate instructions is at *www.irs.gov/scheduleutp*.	2014

Name of entity as shown on page 1 of tax return	EIN of entity

This Part I, Schedule UTP (Form 1120) is page _____ of _____ Part I pages.

Part I   **Uncertain Tax Positions for the Current Tax Year.** See instructions for how to complete columns (a) through (g). Enter, in Part III, a description for each uncertain tax position (UTP).

Check this box if the corporation was unable to obtain information from related parties sufficient to determine whether a tax position is a UTP (see instructions) ► ☐

(a) UTP No.	(b) Primary IRC Sections (e.g., "61", "108", "263A", etc.) / Primary IRC Subsections (e.g. (f)(2)(A)(ii))			(c) Timing Codes (check if Permanent, Temporary, or both)		(d) Pass-Through Entity EIN	(e) Major Tax Position	(f) Ranking of Tax Position	(g) Reserved for Future Use
C				P	T				
	( )( )( )( )	( )( )( )( )	( )( )( )( )			-	☐		
C				P	T				
	( )( )( )	( )( )( )( )	( )( )( )( )			-	☐		
C				P	T				
	( )( )( )	( )( )( )( )	( )( )( )( )			-	☐		
C				P	T				
	( )( )( )( )	( )( )( )( )	( )( )( )( )			-	☐		
C				P	T				
	( )( )( )( )	( )( )( )( )	( )( )( )( )			-	☐		
C				P	T				
	( )( )( )( )	( )( )( )( )	( )( )( )( )				☐		
C				P	T				
	( )( )( )( )	( )( )( )( )	( )( )( )( )			-	☐		
C				P	T				
	( )( )( )( )	( )( )( )( )	( )( )( )( )			-	☐		
C				P	T				
	( )( )( )( )	( )( )( )( )	( )( )( )( )			-	☐		
C				P	T				
	( )( )( )( )	( )( )( )( )	( )( )( )( )			-	☐		
C				P	T				
	( )( )( )( )	( )( )( )( )	( )( )( )( )			-	☐		
C				P	T				
	( )( )( )( )	( )( )( )( )	( )( )( )( )			-	☐		
C				P	T				
	( )( )( )( )	( )( )( )( )	( )( )( )( )			-	☐		
C				P	T				
	( )( )( )( )	( )( )( )( )	( )( )( )( )			-	☐		
C				P	T				
	( )( )( )( )	( )( )( )( )	( )( )( )( )			-	☐		
C				P	T				
	( )( )( )( )	( )( )( )( )	( )( )( )( )			-	☐		
C				P	T				
	( )( )( )( )	( )( )( )( )	( )( )( )( )			-	☐		
C				P	T				
	( )( )( )( )	( )( )( )( )	( )( )( )( )			-	☐		
C				P	T				
	( )( )( )( )	( )( )( )( )	( )( )( )( )			-	☐		
C				P	T				
	( )( )( )( )	( )( )( )( )	( )( )( )( )			-	☐		
C				P	T				
	( )( )( )	( )( )( )	( )( )( )( )			-	☐		
C				P	T				
	( )( )( )	( )( )( )( )	( )( )( )( )				☐		

For Paperwork Reduction Act Notice, see the Instructions for Form 1120.   Cat. No. 54658Q   Schedule UTP (Form 1120) 2014

Name of entity as shown on page 1 of tax return	EIN of entity

This Part II, Schedule UTP (Form 1120) is page _____ of _____ Part II pages.

Part II — Uncertain Tax Positions for Prior Tax Years.

See instructions for how to complete columns (a) through (h). Enter, in Part III, a description for each uncertain tax position (UTP).

Check this box if the corporation was unable to obtain information from related parties sufficient to determine whether a tax position is a UTP (see instructions) ▶ ☐

(a) UTP No.	(b) Primary IRC Sections (e.g., "61", "108", "263A", etc.) / Primary IRC Subsections (e.g. (f)(2)(A)(ii))			(c) Timing Codes (check if Permanent, Temporary, or both)		(d) Pass-Through Entity EIN	(e) Major Tax Position	(f) Ranking of Tax Position	(g) Reserved for Future Use	(h) Year of Tax Position
P	( )( )( )(	)( )( )( )(	)( )( )( )( )	P	T	-	☐			
P	( )( )( )(	)( )( )( )(	)( )( )( )( )	P	T	-	☐			
P	( )( )( )(	)( )( )( )(	)( )( )( )( )	P	T	-	☐			
P	( )( )( )(	)( )( )( )(	)( )( )( )( )	P	T	-	☐			
P	( )( )( )(	)( )( )( )(	)( )( )( )( )	P	T	-	☐			
P	( )( )( )(	)( )( )( )(	)( )( )( )( )	P	T	-	☐			
P	( )( )( )(	)( )( )( )(	)( )( )( )( )	P	T	-	☐			
P	( )( )( )(	)( )( )( )(	)( )( )( )( )	P	T	-	☐			
P	( )( )( )(	)( )( )( )(	)( )( )( )( )	P	T	-	☐			
P	( )( )( )(	)( )( )( )(	)( )( )( )( )	P	T	-	☐			
P	( )( )( )(	)( )( )( )(	)( )( )( )( )	P	T	-	☐			
P	( )( )( )(	)( )( )( )(	)( )( )( )( )	P	T	-	☐			
P	( )( )( )(	)( )( )( )(	)( )( )( )( )	P	T	-	☐			
P	( )( )( )(	)( )( )( )(	)( )( )( )( )	P	T	-	☐			
P	( )( )( )(	)( )( )( )(	)( )( )( )( )	P	T	-	☐			
P	( )( )( )(	)( )( )( )(	)( )( )( )( )	P	T	-	☐			
P	( )( )( )(	)( )( )( )(	)( )( )( )( )	P	T	-	☐			
P	( )( )( )(	)( )( )( )(	)( )( )( )( )	P	T	-	☐			
P	( )( )( )(	)( )( )( )(	)( )( )( )( )	P	T	-	☐			
P	( )( )( )(	)( )( )( )(	)( )( )( )( )	P	T	-	☐			
P	( )( )( )(	)( )( )( )(	)( )( )( )( )	P	T	-	☐			
P	( )( )( )(	)( )( )( )(	)( )( )( )( )	P	T	-	☐			

Name of entity as shown on page 1 of tax return	EIN of entity

This Part III, Schedule UTP (Form 1120) is page _____ of _____ Part III pages.

Part III	**Concise Descriptions of UTPs.** Indicate the corresponding UTP number from Part I, column (a) (e.g. C1) or Part II column (a) (e.g. P2). Use as many Part III pages as necessary (see instructions).

UTP No.	Concise Description of Uncertain Tax Position

2014
Instructions for Schedule UTP (Form 1120)

Uncertain Tax Position Statement

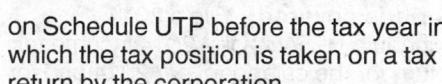
Department of the Treasury
Internal Revenue Service

Section references are to the Internal Revenue Code unless otherwise noted.

Future Developments

For the latest information about developments related to Schedule UTP (Form 1120) and its instructions, such as legislation enacted after they were published, go to *www.irs.gov/scheduleutp*.

What's New

For tax years beginning in 2014, and later, the asset threshold for reporting uncertain tax positions on Schedule UTP (Form 1120) has decreased from assets that equal or exceed $50 million to assets that equal or exceed $10 million.

General Instructions

Purpose of Schedule

Schedule UTP asks for information about tax positions that affect the U.S. federal income tax liabilities of certain corporations that issue or are included in audited financial statements and have assets that equal or exceed $10 million.

Reporting Uncertain Tax Positions on Schedule UTP

Tax positions to be reported. Schedule UTP requires the reporting of each U.S. federal income tax position taken by an applicable corporation on its U.S. federal income tax return for which two conditions are satisfied.

1. The corporation has taken a tax position on its U.S. federal income tax return for the current tax year or for a prior tax year.

2. Either the corporation or a related party has recorded a reserve with respect to that tax position for U.S. federal income tax in audited financial statements, or the corporation or related party did not record a reserve for that tax position because the corporation expects to litigate the position.

A tax position for which a reserve was recorded (or for which no reserve was recorded because of an expectation to litigate) must be reported regardless of whether the audited financial statements are prepared based on U.S. generally accepted accounting principles (GAAP), International Financial Reporting Standards (IFRS), or other country-specific accounting standards, including a modified version of any of the above (for example, modified GAAP).

If the corporation reconsiders whether a reserve is required for a tax position and eliminates the reserve in an interim audited financial statement issued before the tax position is taken in a return, the corporation need not report the tax position to which the reserve relates on Schedule UTP.

A tax position is based on the unit of account used to prepare the audited financial statements in which the reserve is recorded (or in which no reserve was recorded because of an expectation to litigate). A tax position taken on a tax return is a tax position that would result in an adjustment to a line item on that tax return if the position is not sustained. If multiple tax positions affect a single line item on a tax return, report each tax position separately on Schedule UTP. See *Tax position taken on a tax return,* later.

Reporting current year and prior year tax positions. Tax positions taken by the corporation on the current year's tax return are reported in Part I. Tax positions taken by the corporation on a prior year's tax return are reported on Part II. A corporation is not required to report a tax position it has taken in a prior tax year if the corporation reported that tax position on a Schedule UTP filed with a prior year tax return. If a transaction results in tax positions taken on more than one tax return, the tax positions must be reported in Part I of the Schedule UTP attached to each tax return in which a tax position is taken regardless of whether the transaction or a tax position resulting from the transaction was disclosed in a Schedule UTP filed with a prior year's tax return. See Example 7 and Example 8. Do not report a tax position

on Schedule UTP before the tax year in which the tax position is taken on a tax return by the corporation.

If, after a subsidiary member leaves a consolidated group, the subsidiary, or a related party of the subsidiary, records a reserve in an audited financial statement with respect to one of the subsidiary's tax positions in its former group's prior return, the subsidiary should report the tax position on Part II of the Schedule UTP filed with its current tax return, if it files a separate return. If the subsidiary is included in the return of another consolidated group that is required to file Schedule UTP, the common parent of that consolidated group should report the tax position on Part II of the Schedule UTP filed with its current tax return.

Concise description of tax position. A corporation that reports a tax position in either Part I or Part II is required to provide a concise description of each tax position in Part III. See Examples 12 and 13.

Consistency with financial statement reporting. The analysis of whether a reserve has been recorded for the purpose of completing Schedule UTP is determined by reference to those reserve decisions made by the corporation or a related party for audited financial statement purposes. If the corporation or a related party determined that, under applicable accounting standards, either no reserve was required for a tax position taken on a tax return because the amount was immaterial for audited financial statement purposes, or that a tax position was sufficiently certain so that no reserve was required, then the corporation need not report the tax position on Schedule UTP. For a corporation subject to FIN 48, a tax position is considered "sufficiently certain so that no reserve was required," and therefore need not be reported on Schedule UTP, if the position is "highly certain" within the meaning of FIN 48.

Transition rule. A corporation is not required to report on Schedule UTP a tax position taken in a tax year beginning before January 1, 2010, even if a reserve is recorded with respect to that tax position in audited financial statements issued in 2010 or later. See Example 9. In addition, a corporation is not required to report accruals of interest on a tax reserve recorded with respect to a tax position taken on a pre-2010 tax return.

Periods covered. File a 2014 Schedule UTP with the 2014 income tax return for the calendar year 2014 and for a fiscal year that begins in 2014.

Who Must File

A corporation must file Schedule UTP with its 2014 income tax return if:

1. The corporation files Form 1120, U.S. Corporation Income Tax Return; Form 1120-F, U.S. Income Tax Return of a Foreign Corporation; Form 1120-L, U.S. Life Insurance Company Income Tax Return; or Form 1120-PC, U.S. Property and Casualty Insurance Company Income Tax Return;

2. The corporation has assets that equal or exceed $10 million;

3. The corporation or a related party issued audited financial statements reporting all or a portion of the corporation's operations for all or a portion of the corporation's tax year; and

4. The corporation has one or more tax positions that must be reported on Schedule UTP.

Do not file a blank Schedule UTP if there are no tax positions to be reported.

Attach Schedule UTP to the corporation's income tax return. Do not file it separately. A taxpayer that files a protective Form 1120, 1120-F, 1120-L, or 1120-PC must also file Schedule UTP if it satisfies the four requirements set forth above.

A corporation required to file Schedule UTP also must check "Yes" to Form 1120, Schedule K, Question 14; Form 1120-F, Additional Information, Question AA; Form 1120-L, Schedule M, Question 15; or Form 1120-PC, Schedule I, Question 13.

Five-year phase-in period. Corporations meeting all other Schedule UTP filing requirements must file a Schedule UTP if total assets equal or exceed the applicable asset threshold for the tax year, as follows:

Tax Year	Assets Threshold
2010, 2011	$100 million
2012, 2013	$50 million
2014 and after	$10 million

Computation of assets that equal or exceed $10 million. For the following corporate income tax returns:

Forms 1120, 1120-L, and 1120-PC. A corporation's assets equal or exceed $10 million if the amount reported on page 1, item D of Form 1120, or the higher of the beginning or end of year total assets reported on Schedule L of Form 1120-L or Form 1120-PC, is at least $10 million.

Form 1120-F. The assets of a corporation filing a Form 1120-F equal or exceed $10 million if the higher of the beginning or end of year total worldwide assets of the corporation reported on Form 1120-F, Schedule L, Line 17, would be at least $10 million if the corporation were to prepare a Schedule L on a worldwide basis.

Affiliated groups. An affiliated group of corporations filing a consolidated return will file one Schedule UTP for the affiliated group. The affiliated group need not identify the member of the group to which the tax position relates or which member recorded the reserve for the tax position. Any affiliate that files its U.S. federal income tax return separately and satisfies the requirements set forth above must file a Schedule UTP with its return setting forth its own tax positions.

Definitions and Special Rules

Note. All examples in these instructions assume the calendar year is the reporting year both for U.S. federal income tax and financial statement purposes and the independent auditor's opinion on the audited financial statements is issued before the filing of the tax return.

Audited financial statements. Audited financial statements mean financial statements on which an independent auditor has expressed an opinion, whether qualified, unqualified, disclaimed, or adverse, under GAAP, IFRS, or another country-specific accounting standard, including a modified version of any of the above (for example, modified GAAP). Compiled or reviewed financial statements are not audited financial statements.

Record a reserve. A corporation or a related party records a reserve for a U.S. federal income tax position when a reserve for U.S. federal income tax, interest, or penalties with respect to that position is recorded in audited financial statements of the corporation or a related party. A reserve is recorded when an uncertain tax position or a FIN 48 liability is stated anywhere in a corporation's or related party's financial statements, including footnotes and any other disclosures, and may be indicated by any of several types of accounting journal entries. Some of the types of entries that, entered alone or in tandem, indicate the recording of a reserve are: (1) an increase in a current or non-current liability for income taxes, interest or penalties payable, or a reduction of a current or non-current receivable for income taxes and/or interest with respect to the tax position; or (2) a reduction in a deferred tax asset or an increase in a deferred tax liability with respect to the tax position.

The initial recording of a reserve will trigger reporting of a tax position taken on a return. However, subsequent reserve increases or decreases with respect to the tax position will not.

If a corporation is included in multiple audited financial statements, the corporation must report a tax position on Schedule UTP if a reserve for that position was recorded in any of those audited financial statements.

Example 1. General rule regarding recording a reserve. A corporation recorded a reserve in its 2012 audited financial statements relating to a tax position taken on its tax return for the 2012 tax year. The corporation filed its 2012 tax return on September 15, 2013. The corporation reported the 2012 tax position on Part I of Schedule UTP and filed Schedule UTP with its 2012 tax return. If the corporation increases its reserve with respect to the tax position taken on its 2012 tax return in its 2014 audited financial statements, the corporation is not required to report the 2012 tax position again on its 2014 tax return as a result of the reserve increase in 2014.

Example 2. Reporting reserves in subsequent years. A corporation claimed a deduction in 2012 and determined under applicable accounting standards that it could recognize the full benefit of the position. In 2014 the IRS began an examination of the 2012 tax return and decided to examine whether the deduction was proper. The corporation subsequently reevaluated the tax position and recorded a reserve for that position in 2014. The corporation has taken a tax position in its 2012 tax return and recorded a reserve with respect to that tax position. The corporation must report the tax position on Schedule UTP filed with its 2014 tax return even if the IRS identifies the tax position for examination prior to the recording of the reserve.

Related party. A related party is any entity that has a relationship to the corporation that is described in sections 267(b), 318(a), or 707(b), or any entity that is included in consolidated audited financial statements in which the corporation is also included.

Example 3. Related party general rule. Corporation A is a corporation filing Form 1120 that has $160 million of assets. Corporation B is a foreign corporation not doing business in the United States and is a related party to Corporation A. Corporations A and B issue their own audited financial statements. Corporation A takes a tax position on its tax return. If Corporation B records a reserve with respect to that tax position in its own audited financial statements, even though Corporation A does not, then that tax position must be reported by Corporation A on its Schedule UTP.

Example 4. Reserve recorded in consolidated financial statements. Corporation C files a tax return and has assets of $100 million. Corporations C and D issue consolidated audited financial statements, but they do not file a consolidated tax return. Corporation C takes a tax position for which a reserve was recorded in the consolidated financial statements of Corporations C and D. The tax position taken by Corporation C on its tax return must be reported on its Schedule UTP because a reserve was recorded for its tax position in consolidated financial statements in which Corporation C was included.

Reserve not recorded based on expectation to litigate. A corporation must report on Schedule UTP a tax position taken on its return for which no reserve for income tax was recorded if the tax position is one which the corporation or a related party determines the probability of settling with the IRS to be less than 50% and, under applicable accounting standards, no reserve was recorded in the audited financial statements because the corporation intends to litigate the tax position and has determined that it is more likely than not to prevail on the merits in the litigation.

Example 5. Reserve not recorded after a change in circumstances based on expectation to litigate. A corporation takes a tax position on its 2012 tax return for which no reserve is recorded because the corporation determines the tax position is correct. Circumstances change, and in 2014 the corporation determines that the tax position is uncertain, but does not record a reserve because of its expectation to litigate the position. That is, the corporation or a related party determines the probability of settling with the IRS to be less than 50% and, under applicable accounting standards, no reserve was recorded because the corporation intends to litigate the tax position and has determined that it is more likely than not to prevail on the merits in the litigation. The corporation must report that position on Part II of the Schedule UTP filed with the 2014 tax return either if it records a reserve or if it does not record a reserve because it expects to litigate, even if that decision to record or not record occurs because of a change in circumstances in a later year.

Tax position taken on a tax return. A tax position taken on a tax return means a tax position that would result in an adjustment to a line item on any schedule or form attached to the tax return (or would be included in a section 481(a) adjustment) if the position is not sustained. If multiple tax positions affect a single line item on a tax return, each tax position is a separate tax position taken on a tax return. For example, a tax position that is reported on a line item on Form 5471 is a tax position taken on a return, even though an adjustment to that line item might not result in the payment of any additional tax.

A single decision about how to report an item of income, gain, loss, deduction, or credit may affect line items in multiple years' returns. If so, that decision can result in a tax position taken on each affected year's return. For example, a decision to amortize an expense rather than currently deduct that expense, or a decision to currently deduct rather than amortize an expense, affects line items on each year's return in which the tax position is taken during the period of amortization. Whether these tax positions taken on a return are reported on Schedule UTP for a particular tax year, and when they are reported, depends on whether and when a reserve is recorded. See Example 7 and Example 8.

Note. Although the use of an NOL or a credit carryforward is a tax position taken on a tax return, do not report the use of the NOL or credit carryforward if the corporation has previously reported the tax position that created or added to the NOL or credit carryforward on Schedule UTP. See Example 10.

Unit of account. A unit of account is the level of detail used in analyzing a tax position, taking into account both the level at which the taxpayer prepares and supports the tax return and the level at which the taxpayer anticipates addressing the issue with the IRS. The unit of account used by a GAAP or modified GAAP taxpayer for reporting a tax position on Schedule UTP must be the same unit of account used by the taxpayer for GAAP or modified GAAP.

In the case of audited financial statements prepared under accounting standards other than GAAP or modified GAAP, a corporation that issues audited financial statements with a unit of account that is based upon the entire tax year may not use that unit of account for Schedule UTP. The corporation must instead identify a unit of account based on similar principles applicable to GAAP or modified GAAP taxpayers, or use any other level of detail that is consistently applied if that identification is reasonably expected to apprise the IRS of the identity and nature of the issue underlying the tax position taken on the tax return.

Example 6. Unit of account. Corporation A and Corporation B each have two individual research projects and each anticipates claiming a research and development credit arising out of their projects. Corporation A chooses each individual research project as the unit of account for GAAP financial reporting purposes, since the corporation accumulates information for the tax return about the projects at the project level and expects the IRS to address the issues during an examination of each project separately. Corporation B determines that the appropriate unit of account for GAAP financial reporting purposes is the functional expenditures, based on the amount of its expenditures, the anticipated credits to be claimed, its previous experience, and the advice of its tax advisors. Based on the unit of account used for financial reporting purposes, Corporation A must use each project as its unit of account for Schedule UTP reporting, and Corporation B must use functional expenditures as its unit of account for

Schedule UTP reporting, regarding the research and development credit.

Ranking Tax Positions by Size

The corporation must rank by size each tax position listed in Part I. The size of a tax position, however, need not be reported anywhere on Schedule UTP. See the instructions for Part I, column (f), regarding coding to be used to rank the corporation's tax positions.

Size. The size of each tax position is determined on an annual basis and is the amount of U.S. federal income tax reserve recorded for that position. If a reserve is recorded for multiple tax positions, then a reasonable allocation of that reserve among the tax positions to which it relates must be made in determining the size of each tax position.

If an amount of interest or penalties relating to a tax position is not separately identified in the books and records as associated with that position, then that amount of interest and penalties is not included in the size of a tax position used to rank that position or compute whether the position is a major tax position.

Expectation to litigate. Do not determine a size for positions listed because of an expectation to litigate. See the instructions for Parts I and II, column (f), regarding ranking of these positions.

Affiliated groups. The determination of the size of a tax position taken in a tax return by an affiliated group filing a consolidated return is to be determined at the affiliated group level for all members of the affiliated group.

Coordination with Other Reporting Requirements

A complete and accurate disclosure of a tax position on the appropriate year's Schedule UTP will be treated as if the corporation filed a Form 8275, Disclosure Statement, or Form 8275-R, Regulation Disclosure Statement, regarding the tax position. A separate Form 8275 or Form 8275-R need not be filed to avoid certain accuracy-related penalties with respect to that tax position.

Comprehensive Examples

Example 7. Multiple year positions. A corporation incurred an expenditure in 2011 and claimed the entire amount as a deduction on its 2011 return. During the course of reviewing its tax positions for purposes of establishing reserves for U.S. federal income taxes for its 2011 audited financial statements, the corporation determines it is uncertain whether the expenditure should instead be amortized over 5 years and records a reserve with respect to the position taken in 2011. The corporation did not record a reserve for any of the positions taken in tax years 2012 through 2015. The corporation has taken a tax position in each of the 5 tax years because, on each year's tax return, there would be an adjustment to a line item on that return if the position taken in that year's return is not sustained. The tax position taken in the 2011 tax year must be reported on Part I of Schedule UTP filed with the 2011 tax return. None of the 2012 to 2015 tax positions must be reported on Schedule UTP because the corporation did not record a reserve with respect to any of those tax positions.

Example 8. Multiple year positions. A corporation incurred an expenditure in 2011 and takes the position that the expenditure may be amortized over 5 years beginning on its 2011 tax return. During the course of reviewing its tax positions for purposes of establishing reserves for U.S. federal income taxes for its 2011 audited financial statements, the corporation determines it is uncertain whether any deduction or amortization of this expenditure is allowable. In the 2011 audited financial statements, the corporation recorded a reserve with respect to the amortization deduction to be claimed in each tax year. The corporation has taken a tax position in each of the 5 tax years because on each year's tax return there would be an adjustment to a line item on that return if the position taken in that year is not sustained. The corporation must report the 2011 tax position on Part I of Schedule UTP for the 2011 tax year. In addition, the tax position to be taken in each of the 2012 to 2015 tax years must be reported on Part I of the Schedule UTP filed with the tax return for the respective tax year in which the tax position was taken. The result would be the same if, instead of recording the reserve in 2011 for all of the tax positions taken in each of the 5 years, the corporation records a reserve in each year that specifically relates to the tax position taken on the return for that year.

Example 9. Transition rule. The facts are the same as in Example 8, except that the corporation incurred the expenditure and recorded the reserve in 2009. The corporation has taken a tax position in each of the 5 tax years (2009 through 2013) because on each year's tax return there would be an adjustment to a line item on that return if the position taken in that year is not sustained. However, the corporation was not required to report the tax position taken in the 2009 tax year because it was taken in a tax year beginning before January 1, 2010. The tax position taken in each of the 2010 to 2013 tax years must be reported on Part I of the Schedule UTP filed with the tax return for the respective tax year in which the position was taken.

Example 10. Creation and use of net operating loss (NOL). A corporation incurred a $50 expenditure in 2013 and claimed the entire amount as a deduction on its 2013 tax return. The deduction increases the corporation's NOL carryforward from $100 to $150. The corporation uses the entire $150 NOL carryforward on its 2014 tax return. Claiming the $50 deduction in 2013 is a tax position taken in the 2013 tax year because the position would result in an adjustment to a line item on the 2013 tax return if the position is not sustained. The deduction in 2014 of the NOL carried forward from 2013 is a tax position taken on the 2014 tax return, because the position would result in an adjustment to a line item on the 2014 tax return if the position is not sustained. The corporation recorded a reserve with respect to its 2013 tax position, in its 2013 audited financial statements. Because the corporation recorded a reserve with respect to the tax position taken in 2013, it reported the 2013 tax position on the Schedule UTP filed with its 2013 tax return. Because it reported the tax position in its 2013 tax return, the corporation should not report the 2014 tax position on the Schedule UTP filed with its tax return for the 2014 tax year.

Example 11. Corporate merger. On June 30, 2014, MergerCo merges into AcquiringCo, in a transaction in which AcquiringCo survives. MergerCo's tax year ends on that date. After the merger, AcquiringCo records a reserve with respect to a tax position that is taken on MergerCo's final return in its audited financial statements. That tax position must be reported on Part I of the Schedule UTP filed with MergerCo's 2014 tax return even though the reserve was recorded by AcquiringCo. AcquiringCo should not report the tax position on the Schedule UTP filed with its 2014 tax return because MergerCo's final return is a prior year tax return on which the tax position was reported.

Specific Instructions

Part I. Uncertain Tax Positions For the Current Tax Year

When to Complete Part I

Complete Part I to report tax positions taken by the corporation on its 2014 tax return.

Information from Related Parties

Check the box at the top of Part I if the corporation was unable to obtain sufficient information from one or more related parties and was therefore unable to determine whether a tax position taken on its current year's tax return is required to be reported in Part I of this schedule.

Column (a). UTP No.

Enter a number in column (a) for each tax position reported. The UTP numbers on Part I, column (a), include a preprinted "C" prefix to indicate that they are positions for the current tax year. A corresponding UTP number with the letter "C" prefix will be used on Part III for reporting the concise description of the tax position. Begin with the number 1, do not skip any whole numbers, do not enter extraneous characters, and do not duplicate any numbers (e.g., C1, C2, C3, where the letters "C" are preprinted on the Schedule and the numbers are entered).

Column (b). Primary IRC Sections

Provide the primary IRC sections (up to three) relating to the tax position. Enter one primary IRC Section in each box (e.g., "61", "108", "263A", etc.). Do not include descriptive references or any other text such as "IRC", "Section", or "IRC Sec". Beneath each Primary IRC Section, you may enter the applicable IRC Subsections (e.g., (f)(2)(A)(ii)), using the preprinted parentheses. If there are more than four subsection components, list only the first four.

Column (c). Timing Codes

Check "T" for temporary differences, "P" for permanent differences, or check both "T" and "P" for a tax position that creates both a temporary and permanent difference. Categorization as a temporary difference, permanent difference, or both must be consistent with the accounting standards used to prepare the audited financial statements.

Column (d). Pass-Through Entity EIN

If the tax position taken by the corporation relates to a tax position of a pass-through entity, enter the EIN of the pass-through entity to which the tax position relates. For example, if the corporation is a partner in a partnership and the tax position involves the partner's distributive share of an item of income, gain, loss, deduction, or credit of the partnership, enter the EIN of the partnership. A pass-through entity is any entity listed in section 1(h)(10). If the tax position is not related to a tax position of a pass-through entity, leave this blank. Enter "F" if the pass-through entity is a foreign entity that does not have an EIN.

Column (e). Major Tax Position

Check this box if the relative size of the tax position is greater than or equal to 0.10 (10%). The relative size of a tax position is the amount computed by dividing the size of that position by the sum of all of the sizes for all of the tax positions listed on Parts I and II. Disregard expectation to litigate positions for column (e) purposes. Round amounts using rules similar to the rules in the Instructions for Form 1120 for rounding dollar amounts.

Column (f). Ranking of Tax Position

Enter a letter and a ranking number for each tax position. Use the letter T for transfer pricing positions and the letter G for all other tax positions.

Rank all tax positions in Parts I and II together, regardless of type. Starting with the largest size, assign the number 1 to the largest, the number 2 to the next largest, and so on, in order. This number is the ranking number for the tax position. Expectation to litigate positions may be assigned any ranking number.

For example, the corporation has 1 transfer pricing tax position and 2 other tax positions. The transfer pricing position is the largest and one of the other tax positions is the expectation to litigate position. The expectation to litigate position is assigned a rank of 2. Enter T1 for the transfer pricing position, G2 for the expectation to litigate position, and G3 for the second other tax position.

Part II. Uncertain Tax Positions For Prior Tax Years

When to Complete Part II

Complete Part II to report tax positions taken by the corporation in a prior tax year that have not been reported on a Schedule UTP filed with a prior year's tax return. Do not report a tax position taken in a tax year beginning before January 1, 2010. See *Transition rule* under *Reporting Uncertain Tax Positions on Schedule UTP,* earlier.

Information from Related Parties

Check the box at the top of Part II if the corporation was unable to obtain sufficient information from one or more related parties and was therefore unable to determine whether a tax position taken on its prior year's tax return is required to be reported in Part II of this schedule.

Column (a). UTP No.

Continue the numeric sequence based on the last UTP number entered on Part I. For example, if the last UTP listed on Part I is 3, enter 4 for the first UTP listed on Part II. The UTP numbers on Part II, column (a), include a preprinted "P" prefix to indicate that they are positions for prior tax years. A corresponding UTP number with a letter "P" prefix will be used on Part III for reporting the concise description of the tax position. Do not skip any whole numbers, do not enter extraneous characters, and do not duplicate any numbers (e.g., P4, P5, P6, where the letters "P" are preprinted on the Schedule and the numbers are entered).

Column (b). Primary IRC Sections

See the instructions for Part I, column (b).

Column (c). Timing Codes

See the instructions for Part I, column (c).

Column (d). Pass-Through Entity EIN

See the instructions for Part I, column (d).

Column (e). Major Tax Position

See the instructions for Part I, column (e).

Column (f). Ranking of Tax Position

See the instructions for Part I, column (f).

Column (h). Year of Tax Position

List the prior tax year in which the tax position was taken and the last month of that tax year, using a six-digit number. For example, enter 201112 for tax years ending December 31, 2011, and 201208 for tax years ending August 2012.

Part III. Concise Description of UTPs

When to Complete Part III

Part III must be completed for every tax position listed in Part I or Part II. Enter the corresponding UTP number from Part I, column (a) (e.g., C1, C2, C3) or Part II, column (a) (e.g., P4, P5, P6), related to the description.

Concise description. Provide a concise description of the tax position, including a description of the relevant facts affecting the tax treatment of the position and information that reasonably can be expected to apprise the IRS of the identity of the tax position and the nature of the issue. In most cases, the description should not exceed a few sentences. Stating that a concise description is "Available upon Request" is not an adequate description.

A concise description should not include an assessment of the hazards of a tax position or an analysis of the support for or against the tax position.

Examples of Concise Descriptions for Hypothetical Fact Patterns

The following examples set out a description of hypothetical facts and the uncertainties about a tax position that would be reportable on Schedule UTP. Following each set of hypothetical facts, which would not be disclosed on the schedule, is an example of a sufficient concise description that would be reported in Part III to disclose that hypothetical case.

Example 12. Allocation of costs between uncompleted and completed acquisitions.

Facts. The corporation investigated and negotiated several potential business acquisitions during the tax year. One of the transactions was completed during the tax year, but all other negotiations failed and the other potential transactions were abandoned during the tax year. The corporation deducted costs of investigating and partially negotiating potential business acquisitions that were not completed and capitalized costs allocable to one business acquisition that was completed. The corporation established a reserve for financial accounting purposes in recognition of the possibility that the amount of costs allocated to the uncompleted acquisition attempts was excessive.

Sample concise description. The corporation incurred costs of completing one business acquisition and also incurred costs investigating and partially negotiating potential business acquisitions that were not completed. The costs were allocated between the completed and uncompleted acquisitions. The issue is whether the allocation of costs between uncompleted acquisitions and the completed acquisition is appropriate.

Example 13. Recharacterization of distribution as a sale.

Facts. The corporation is a member of Venture LLC, which is treated as a U.S. partnership for tax purposes. During the tax year, Venture LLC raised funds through (i) admitting a new member for a cash contribution and (ii) borrowing funds from a financial institution, using a loan partially guaranteed by the corporation. Also during the tax year, Venture LLC made a cash distribution to the corporation that caused its membership interest in Venture LLC to be reduced from 25% to 2%. The corporation has taken the position that the cash distribution is properly characterized as a nontaxable distribution that does not exceed its basis in its Venture LLC interest, but has established a reserve for financial accounting purposes, recognizing that the transaction might be recharacterized as a taxable sale of a portion of its Venture LLC interest under section 707(a)(2).

Sample concise description. The corporation is a member of Venture LLC, which is treated as a U.S. partnership for tax purposes. The corporation received a cash distribution during the year from Venture LLC. The issue is the potential application of section 707(a)(2) to recharacterize the distribution as a sale of a portion of the corporation's Venture LLC interest.

Form **1120S**	**U.S. Income Tax Return for an S Corporation**	OMB No. 1545-0123

Department of the Treasury
Internal Revenue Service

► Do not file this form unless the corporation has filed or is attaching Form 2553 to elect to be an S corporation.
► Information about Form 1120S and its separate instructions is at *www.irs.gov/form1120s*.

2014

For calendar year 2014 or tax year beginning _____ , 2014, ending _____ , 20____

A S election effective date		D Employer identification number
B Business activity code number (see instructions)	TYPE OR PRINT — Name / Number, street, and room or suite no. If a P.O. box, see instructions. / City or town, state or province, country, and ZIP or foreign postal code	E Date incorporated
		F Total assets (see instructions) $
C Check if Sch. M-3 attached ☐		

G Is the corporation electing to be an S corporation beginning with this tax year? ☐ Yes ☐ No If "Yes," attach Form 2553 if not already filed

H Check if: **(1)** ☐ Final return **(2)** ☐ Name change **(3)** ☐ Address change **(4)** ☐ Amended return **(5)** ☐ S election termination or revocation

I Enter the number of shareholders who were shareholders during any part of the tax year . . . . ▶

Caution. Include **only** trade or business income and expenses on lines 1a through 21. See the instructions for more information.

Income

1a	Gross receipts or sales	1a	
b	Returns and allowances	1b	
c	Balance. Subtract line 1b from line 1a	1c	
2	Cost of goods sold (attach Form 1125-A)	2	
3	Gross profit. Subtract line 2 from line 1c	3	
4	Net gain (loss) from Form 4797, line 17 (attach Form 4797)	4	
5	Other income (loss) (see instructions—attach statement)	5	
6	**Total income (loss).** Add lines 3 through 5 . . . . ▶	6	

Deductions (see instructions for limitations)

7	Compensation of officers (see instructions—attach Form 1125-E)	7	
8	Salaries and wages (less employment credits)	8	
9	Repairs and maintenance	9	
10	Bad debts	10	
11	Rents	11	
12	Taxes and licenses	12	
13	Interest	13	
14	Depreciation not claimed on Form 1125-A or elsewhere on return (attach Form 4562) . . .	14	
15	Depletion (**Do not deduct oil and gas depletion.**)	15	
16	Advertising	16	
17	Pension, profit-sharing, etc., plans	17	
18	Employee benefit programs	18	
19	Other deductions (attach statement)	19	
20	**Total deductions.** Add lines 7 through 19 . . . . ▶	20	
21	**Ordinary business income (loss).** Subtract line 20 from line 6	21	

Tax and Payments

22a	Excess net passive income or LIFO recapture tax (see instructions)	22a		
b	Tax from Schedule D (Form 1120S)	22b		
c	Add lines 22a and 22b (see instructions for additional taxes)		22c	
23a	2014 estimated tax payments and 2013 overpayment credited to 2014	23a		
b	Tax deposited with Form 7004	23b		
c	Credit for federal tax paid on fuels (attach Form 4136) . .	23c		
d	Add lines 23a through 23c		23d	
24	Estimated tax penalty (see instructions). Check if Form 2220 is attached . . . . ▶ ☐		24	
25	**Amount owed.** If line 23d is smaller than the total of lines 22c and 24, enter amount owed		25	
26	**Overpayment.** If line 23d is larger than the total of lines 22c and 24, enter amount overpaid . .		26	
27	Enter amount from line 26 **Credited to 2015 estimated tax** ▶ ____ **Refunded** ▶		27	

Sign Here

Under penalties of perjury, I declare that I have examined this return, including accompanying schedules and statements, and to the best of my knowledge and belief, it is true, correct, and complete. Declaration of preparer (other than taxpayer) is based on all information of which preparer has any knowledge.

▶ _____ Signature of officer   Date   ▶ _____ Title

May the IRS discuss this return with the preparer shown below (see instructions)? ☐ Yes ☐ No

Paid Preparer Use Only

Print/Type preparer's name	Preparer's signature	Date	Check ☐ if self-employed	PTIN
Firm's name ▶			Firm's EIN ▶	
Firm's address ▶			Phone no.	

For Paperwork Reduction Act Notice, see separate instructions.   Cat. No. 11510H   Form **1120S** (2014)

Schedule B	Other Information (see instructions)		Yes	No

1 Check accounting method: **a** ☐ Cash　　**b** ☐ Accrual

　　　　　　　　　　　　　　c ☐ Other (specify) ▶ _____

2 See the instructions and enter the:

　a Business activity ▶ _____　**b** Product or service ▶ _____

3 At any time during the tax year, was any shareholder of the corporation a disregarded entity, a trust, an estate, or a nominee or similar person? If "Yes," attach Schedule B-1, Information on Certain Shareholders of an S Corporation .　.

4 At the end of the tax year, did the corporation:

　a Own directly 20% or more, or own, directly or indirectly, 50% or more of the total stock issued and outstanding of any foreign or domestic corporation? For rules of constructive ownership, see instructions. If "Yes," complete (i) through (v) below . . . .

(i) Name of Corporation	(ii) Employer Identification Number (if any)	(iii) Country of Incorporation	(iv) Percentage of Stock Owned	(v) If Percentage in (iv) is 100%, Enter the Date (if any) a Qualified Subchapter S Subsidiary Election Was Made

　b Own directly an interest of 20% or more, or own, directly or indirectly, an interest of 50% or more in the profit, loss, or capital in any foreign or domestic partnership (including an entity treated as a partnership) or in the beneficial interest of a trust? For rules of constructive ownership, see instructions. If "Yes," complete (i) through (v) below . . . .

(i) Name of Entity	(ii) Employer Identification Number (if any)	(iii) Type of Entity	(iv) Country of Organization	(v) Maximum Percentage Owned in Profit, Loss, or Capital

5 a At the end of the tax year, did the corporation have any outstanding shares of restricted stock? . . . .

　　If "Yes," complete lines (i) and (ii) below.

　　(i)　Total shares of restricted stock . . . . ▶ _____

　　(ii)　Total shares of non-restricted stock . . . . ▶ _____

　b At the end of the tax year, did the corporation have any outstanding stock options, warrants, or similar instruments? .

　　If "Yes," complete lines (i) and (ii) below.

　　(i)　Total shares of stock outstanding at the end of the tax year　▶ _____

　　(ii)　Total shares of stock outstanding if all instruments were executed ▶ _____

6 Has this corporation filed, or is it required to file, **Form 8918**, Material Advisor Disclosure Statement, to provide information on any reportable transaction? .　.　.　.　.　.　.　.　.　.　.　.　.　.　.　.　.　.　.

7 Check this box if the corporation issued publicly offered debt instruments with original issue discount . . . . ▶ ☐

　　If checked, the corporation may have to file **Form 8281**, Information Return for Publicly Offered Original Issue Discount Instruments.

8 If the corporation: **(a)** was a C corporation before it elected to be an S corporation **or** the corporation acquired an asset with a basis determined by reference to the basis of the asset (or the basis of any other property) in the hands of a C corporation **and (b)** has net unrealized built-in gain in excess of the net recognized built-in gain from prior years, enter the net unrealized built-in gain reduced by net recognized built-in gain from prior years (see instructions) .　.　.　.　.　.　.　.　.　.　.　.　.　.　▶ $ _____

9 Enter the accumulated earnings and profits of the corporation at the end of the tax year.　　$ _____

10 Does the corporation satisfy **both** of the following conditions?

　a The corporation's total receipts (see instructions) for the tax year were less than $250,000 .　.　.　.　.　.　.

　b The corporation's total assets at the end of the tax year were less than $250,000　.　.　.　.　.　.　.　.

　　If "Yes," the corporation is not required to complete Schedules L and M-1.

11 During the tax year, did the corporation have any non-shareholder debt that was canceled, was forgiven, or had the terms modified so as to reduce the principal amount of the debt? .　.　.　.　.　.　.　.　.　.　.　.　.

　　If "Yes," enter the amount of principal reduction　$ _____

12 During the tax year, was a qualified subchapter S subsidiary election terminated or revoked? If "Yes," see instructions .

13a Did the corporation make any payments in 2014 that would require it to file Form(s) 1099? .　.　.　.　.　.　.

　　b If "Yes," did the corporation file or will it file required Forms 1099? .　.　.　.　.　.　.　.　.　.　.

Schedule K		Shareholders' Pro Rata Share Items		Total amount	
Income (Loss)	**1**	Ordinary business income (loss) (page 1, line 21)	**1**		
	2	Net rental real estate income (loss) (attach Form 8825)	**2**		
	3a	Other gross rental income (loss) **3a**			
	b	Expenses from other rental activities (attach statement) . . **3b**			
	c	Other net rental income (loss). Subtract line 3b from line 3a	**3c**		
	4	Interest income	**4**		
	5	Dividends: **a** Ordinary dividends	**5a**		
		b Qualified dividends **5b**			
	6	Royalties	**6**		
	7	Net short-term capital gain (loss) (attach Schedule D (Form 1120S))	**7**		
	8a	Net long-term capital gain (loss) (attach Schedule D (Form 1120S))	**8a**		
	b	Collectibles (28%) gain (loss) **8b**			
	c	Unrecaptured section 1250 gain (attach statement) . . . **8c**			
	9	Net section 1231 gain (loss) (attach Form 4797)	**9**		
	10	Other income (loss) (see instructions) . . . Type ▶	**10**		
Deductions	**11**	Section 179 deduction (attach Form 4562)	**11**		
	12a	Charitable contributions	**12a**		
	b	Investment interest expense	**12b**		
	c	Section 59(e)(2) expenditures **(1)** Type ▶ _____ **(2)** Amount ▶	**12c(2)**		
	d	Other deductions (see instructions) . . . Type ▶	**12d**		
Credits	**13a**	Low-income housing credit (section 42(j)(5))	**13a**		
	b	Low-income housing credit (other)	**13b**		
	c	Qualified rehabilitation expenditures (rental real estate) (attach Form 3468, if applicable) . .	**13c**		
	d	Other rental real estate credits (see instructions) Type ▶ _____	**13d**		
	e	Other rental credits (see instructions) . . . Type ▶ _____	**13e**		
	f	Biofuel producer credit (attach Form 6478)	**13f**		
	g	Other credits (see instructions) . . . . . Type ▶	**13g**		
Foreign Transactions	**14a**	Name of country or U.S. possession ▶ _____			
	b	Gross income from all sources	**14b**		
	c	Gross income sourced at shareholder level	**14c**		
		Foreign gross income sourced at corporate level			
	d	Passive category	**14d**		
	e	General category	**14e**		
	f	Other (attach statement)	**14f**		
		Deductions allocated and apportioned at shareholder level			
	g	Interest expense	**14g**		
	h	Other	**14h**		
		Deductions allocated and apportioned at corporate level to foreign source income			
	i	Passive category	**14i**		
	j	General category	**14j**		
	k	Other (attach statement)	**14k**		
		Other information			
	l	Total foreign taxes (check one): ▶ ☐ Paid ☐ Accrued	**14l**		
	m	Reduction in taxes available for credit (attach statement)	**14m**		
	n	Other foreign tax information (attach statement)			
Alternative Minimum Tax (AMT) Items	**15a**	Post-1986 depreciation adjustment	**15a**		
	b	Adjusted gain or loss	**15b**		
	c	Depletion (other than oil and gas)	**15c**		
	d	Oil, gas, and geothermal properties—gross income	**15d**		
	e	Oil, gas, and geothermal properties—deductions	**15e**		
	f	Other AMT items (attach statement)	**15f**		
Items Affecting Shareholder Basis	**16a**	Tax-exempt interest income	**16a**		
	b	Other tax-exempt income	**16b**		
	c	Nondeductible expenses	**16c**		
	d	Distributions (attach statement if required) (see instructions)	**16d**		
	e	Repayment of loans from shareholders	**16e**		

Schedule K		Shareholders' Pro Rata Share Items (continued)		Total amount	

	17a	Investment income	17a		
Other Information	b	Investment expenses	17b		
	c	Dividend distributions paid from accumulated earnings and profits	17c		
	d	Other items and amounts (attach statement)			
Recon-ciliation	18	**Income/loss reconciliation.** Combine the amounts on lines 1 through 10 in the far right column. From the result, subtract the sum of the amounts on lines 11 through 12d and 14l	18		

Schedule L	Balance Sheets per Books	Beginning of tax year		End of tax year	
	Assets	(a)	(b)	(c)	(d)
1	Cash				
2a	Trade notes and accounts receivable . . .				
b	Less allowance for bad debts	( )		( )	
3	Inventories				
4	U.S. government obligations				
5	Tax-exempt securities (see instructions) . .				
6	Other current assets (attach statement) . . .				
7	Loans to shareholders				
8	Mortgage and real estate loans				
9	Other investments (attach statement) . . .				
10a	Buildings and other depreciable assets . . .				
b	Less accumulated depreciation	( )		( )	
11a	Depletable assets				
b	Less accumulated depletion	( )		( )	
12	Land (net of any amortization)				
13a	Intangible assets (amortizable only)				
b	Less accumulated amortization	( )		( )	
14	Other assets (attach statement)				
15	Total assets				
	Liabilities and Shareholders' Equity				
16	Accounts payable				
17	Mortgages, notes, bonds payable in less than 1 year				
18	Other current liabilities (attach statement) . .				
19	Loans from shareholders				
20	Mortgages, notes, bonds payable in 1 year or more				
21	Other liabilities (attach statement)				
22	Capital stock				
23	Additional paid-in capital				
24	Retained earnings				
25	Adjustments to shareholders' equity (attach statement)				
26	Less cost of treasury stock		( )		( )
27	Total liabilities and shareholders' equity . .				

Schedule M-1	Reconciliation of Income (Loss) per Books With Income (Loss) per Return

Note. The corporation may be required to file Schedule M-3 (see instructions)

1	Net income (loss) per books		**5**	Income recorded on books this year not included on Schedule K, lines 1 through 10 (itemize):	
2	Income included on Schedule K, lines 1, 2, 3c, 4, 5a, 6, 7, 8a, 9, and 10, not recorded on books this year (itemize)		**a**	Tax-exempt interest $	
3	Expenses recorded on books this year not included on Schedule K, lines 1 through 12 and 14l (itemize):		**6**	Deductions included on Schedule K, lines 1 through 12 and 14l, not charged against book income this year (itemize):	
a	Depreciation $		**a**	Depreciation $	
b	Travel and entertainment $				
			7	Add lines 5 and 6	
4	Add lines 1 through 3		**8**	Income (loss) (Schedule K, line 18). Line 4 less line 7	

Schedule M-2	Analysis of Accumulated Adjustments Account, Other Adjustments Account, and Shareholders' Undistributed Taxable Income Previously Taxed (see instructions)

		(a) Accumulated adjustments account	(b) Other adjustments account	(c) Shareholders' undistributed taxable income previously taxed
1	Balance at beginning of tax year			
2	Ordinary income from page 1, line 21 . . .			
3	Other additions			
4	Loss from page 1, line 21	( )		
5	Other reductions	( )	( )	
6	Combine lines 1 through 5			
7	Distributions other than dividend distributions			
8	Balance at end of tax year. Subtract line 7 from line 6			

Form **1120S** (2014)

SCHEDULE B-1
(Form 1120S)

(December 2013)
Department of the Treasury
Internal Revenue Service

Information on Certain Shareholders of an S Corporation

▶ Attach to Form 1120S.
▶ Information about Schedule B-1 (Form 1120S) and
its instructions is at *www.irs.gov/form1120s.*

OMB No. 1545-0130

Name of corporation	Employer identification number

Information on Any Shareholder That Was a Disregarded Entity, a Trust, an Estate, or a Nominee or Similar Person at Any Time During the Tax Year (Form 1120S, Schedule B, Question 3)

(a) Name of Shareholder of Record—Disregarded Entity, Trust, Estate, Nominee or Similar Person	(b) Social Security Number (SSN) or Employer Identification Number (EIN) (if any) of Shareholder of Record	(c) Type of Shareholder of Record	(d) Name and SSN or EIN (if any) of Individual or Entity Responsible for Reporting Shareholder's Income, Deductions, Credits, etc., From Schedule K-1

For Paperwork Reduction Act Notice, see the Instructions for Form 1120S.   Cat. No. 60837X   Schedule B-1 (Form 1120S) (12-2013)

General Instructions

Section references are to the Internal Revenue Code unless otherwise noted.

Future Developments

For the latest information about developments related to Schedule B-1 (Form 1120S) and its instructions, such as legislation enacted after they were published, go to *www.irs.gov/form1120s*.

Purpose of Form

Use Schedule B-1 (Form 1120S) to provide the information applicable to any shareholder in the S corporation that was a disregarded entity, a trust, an estate, or a nominee or similar person at any time during the tax year.

If the shareholder was a disregarded entity, provide the information even if the name, address, and social security number (SSN) or employer identification number (EIN) (if any) of the owner of the disregarded entity was entered on Schedule K-1 (Form 1120S), Shareholder's Share of Income, Deductions, Credit, etc. If the shareholder was a nominee, guardian, custodian, or agent, provide the information even if the name, address, and SSN or EIN (if any) of the person for whom the stock was held was entered on Schedule K-1 (Form 1120S).

Who Must File

Schedule B-1 (Form 1120S) must be filed by all S corporations that answer "Yes" to Form 1120S, Schedule B, question 3. Attach Schedule B-1 to Form 1120S.

Specific Instructions

Column (a)

Enter the name of the shareholder (owner) of record in column (a). For example:

• If a disregarded entity (for example, a single member limited liability company (LLC) that did not elect to be taxed as a corporation for federal income tax purposes) is the shareholder (owner) of record, enter the name of the disregarded entity.

• If a nominee or similar person (for example, a guardian, custodian, or agent) is the shareholder (owner) of record, enter the name of the nominee or similar person.

Column (c)

Enter the type of shareholder (owner) of record. For example, the shareholder (owner) of record may be a disregarded entity, trust, estate, nominee, guardian, custodian, agent, or similar person.

Column (d)

Enter the name and SSN or EIN (if any) of the individual or entity responsible for reporting shareholder's income, deductions, credits, etc., from Schedule K-1 (Form 1120S). For example:

1. If a disregarded entity is the shareholder (owner) of record, the owner of the disregarded entity must be eligible to be an S corporation shareholder. Enter the name and SSN or EIN (if any) of the owner. For example, if a single member LLC owns stock in the corporation, and the LLC is treated as a disregarded entity for federal income tax purposes, enter the member's name and SSN or EIN (if any). An LLC that elects to be treated as a corporation for federal income tax purposes is not eligible to be an S corporation shareholder.

2. If a trust is the shareholder (owner) of record, the information entered in column (d) is dependent on the type of trust.

   a. If the trust is a grantor trust, the grantor must be an individual. Enter the name and SSN of the grantor.

   b. If the trust is a qualified subchapter S trust (QSST), there can only be one beneficiary, who must be an individual. Enter the name and SSN of the individual beneficiary.

   c. If the trust is an electing small business trust (ESBT), enter the information you entered under columns (a) and (b). Do not enter any beneficiary information.

3. If an estate is the shareholder (owner) of record, enter the information you entered under columns (a) and (b). Do not enter any beneficiary information.

SCHEDULE M-3 (Form 1120S) Department of the Treasury Internal Revenue Service	**Net Income (Loss) Reconciliation for S Corporations With Total Assets of \$10 Million or More** ▶ Attach to Form 1120S. ▶ Information about Sch. M-3 (Form 1120S) and its separate instructions is at *www.irs.gov/form1120s*.	OMB No. 1545-0123 2014

Name of corporation	Employer identification number

Part I — Financial Information and Net Income (Loss) Reconciliation (see instructions)

1a Did the corporation prepare a certified audited non-tax-basis income statement for the period ending with or within this tax year? (See instructions if multiple non-tax-basis income statements are prepared.)

☐ **Yes.** Skip line 1b and complete lines 2 through 11 with respect to that income statement.

☐ **No.** Go to line 1b.

b Did the corporation prepare a non-tax-basis income statement for that period?

☐ **Yes.** Complete lines 2 through 11 with respect to that income statement.

☐ **No.** Skip lines 2 through 3b and enter the corporation's net income (loss) per its books and records on line 4a.

2 Enter the income statement period: Beginning _____ / _____ / _____ Ending _____ / _____ / _____

3a Has the corporation's income statement been restated for the income statement period on line 2?

☐ **Yes.** (If "Yes," attach an explanation and the amount of each item restated.)

☐ **No.**

b Has the corporation's income statement been restated for any of the five income statement periods immediately preceding the period on line 2?

☐ **Yes.** (If "Yes," attach an explanation and the amount of each item restated.)

☐ **No.**

4a	Worldwide consolidated net income (loss) from income statement source identified in Part I, line 1 .	**4a**	
b	Indicate accounting standard used for line 4a (see instructions): (1) ☐ GAAP (2) ☐ IFRS (3) ☐ Tax-basis (4) ☐ Other (specify) _____		
5a	Net income from nonincludible foreign entities (attach statement)	**5a**	( )
b	Net loss from nonincludible foreign entities (attach statement and enter as a positive amount) . . .	**5b**	
6a	Net income from nonincludible U.S. entities (attach statement)	**6a**	( )
b	Net loss from nonincludible U.S. entities (attach statement and enter as a positive amount)	**6b**	
7a	Net income (loss) of other foreign disregarded entities (attach statement)	**7a**	
b	Net income (loss) of other U.S. disregarded entities (except qualified subchapter S subsidiaries) (attach statement)	**7b**	
c	Net income (loss) of other qualified subchapter S subsidiaries (QSubs) (attach statement)	**7c**	
8	Adjustment to eliminations of transactions between includible entities and nonincludible entities (attach statement)	**8**	
9	Adjustment to reconcile income statement period to tax year (attach statement)	**9**	
10	Other adjustments to reconcile to amount on line 11 (attach statement)	**10**	
11	**Net income (loss) per income statement of the corporation.** Combine lines 4 through 10 . . .	**11**	

Note. Part I, line 11, must equal Part II, line 26, column (a) or Schedule M-1, line 1 (see instructions).

12 Enter the total amount (not just the corporation's share) of the assets and liabilities of all entities included or removed on the following lines:

		Total Assets	Total Liabilities
a	Included on Part I, line 4		
b	Removed on Part I, line 5		
c	Removed on Part I, line 6		
d	Included on Part I, line 7		

For Paperwork Reduction Act Notice, see the Instructions for Form 1120S. Cat. No. 39666W Schedule M-3 (Form 1120S) 2014

Name of corporation	Employer identification number

Part II   Reconciliation of Net Income (Loss) per Income Statement of the Corporation With Total Income (Loss) per Return (see instructions)

	Income (Loss) Items (Attach statements for lines 1 through 10)	(a) Income (Loss) per Income Statement	(b) Temporary Difference	(c) Permanent Difference	(d) Income (Loss) per Tax Return
1	Income (loss) from equity method foreign corporations				
2	Gross foreign dividends not previously taxed				
3	Subpart F, QEF, and similar income inclusions				
4	Gross foreign distributions previously taxed				
5	Income (loss) from equity method U.S. corporations				
6	U.S. dividends not eliminated in tax consolidation				
7	Income (loss) from U.S. partnerships				
8	Income (loss) from foreign partnerships				
9	Income (loss) from other pass-through entities				
10	Items relating to reportable transactions				
11	Interest income (see instructions)				
12	Total accrual to cash adjustment				
13	Hedging transactions				
14	Mark-to-market income (loss)				
15	Cost of goods sold (see instructions)	( )			( )
16	Sale versus lease (for sellers and/or lessors)				
17	Section 481(a) adjustments				
18	Unearned/deferred revenue				
19	Income recognition from long-term contracts				
20	Original issue discount and other imputed interest				
21a	Income statement gain/loss on sale, exchange, abandonment, worthlessness, or other disposition of assets other than inventory and pass-through entities				
b	Gross capital gains from Schedule D, excluding amounts from pass-through entities				
c	Gross capital losses from Schedule D, excluding amounts from pass-through entities, abandonment losses, and worthless stock losses				
d	Net gain/loss reported on Form 4797, line 17, excluding amounts from pass-through entities, abandonment losses, and worthless stock losses				
e	Abandonment losses				
f	Worthless stock losses (attach statement)				
g	Other gain/loss on disposition of assets other than inventory				
22	Other income (loss) items with differences (attach statement)				
23	**Total income (loss) items.** Combine lines 1 through 22				
24	**Total expense/deduction items** (from Part III, line 32)				
25	Other items with no differences				
26	**Reconciliation totals.** Combine lines 23 through 25				

Note. Line 26, column (a), must equal Part I, line 11, and column (d) must equal Form 1120S, Schedule K, line 18.

Name of corporation	Employer identification number

Part III — Reconciliation of Net Income (Loss) per Income Statement of the Corporation With Total Income (Loss) per Return—Expense/Deduction Items (see instructions)

	Expense/Deduction Items	(a) Expense per Income Statement	(b) Temporary Difference	(c) Permanent Difference	(d) Deduction per Tax Return
1	U.S. current income tax expense				
2	U.S. deferred income tax expense				
3	State and local current income tax expense				
4	State and local deferred income tax expense				
5	Foreign current income tax expense (other than foreign withholding taxes)				
6	Foreign deferred income tax expense				
7	Equity-based compensation				
8	Meals and entertainment				
9	Fines and penalties				
10	Judgments, damages, awards, and similar costs				
11	Pension and profit-sharing				
12	Other post-retirement benefits				
13	Deferred compensation				
14	Charitable contribution of cash and tangible property				
15	Charitable contribution of intangible property				
16	Current year acquisition or reorganization investment banking fees				
17	Current year acquisition or reorganization legal and accounting fees				
18	Current year acquisition/reorganization other costs				
19	Amortization/impairment of goodwill				
20	Amortization of acquisition, reorganization, and start-up costs				
21	Other amortization or impairment write-offs				
22	Reserved				
23a	Depletion—Oil & Gas				
b	Depletion—Other than Oil & Gas				
24	Depreciation				
25	Bad debt expense				
26	Interest expense (see instructions)				
27	Corporate owned life insurance premiums				
28	Purchase versus lease (for purchasers and/or lessees)				
29	Research and development costs				
30	Section 118 exclusion (attach statement)				
31	Other expense/deduction items with differences (attach statement)				
32	**Total expense/deduction items.** Combine lines 1 through 31. Enter here and on Part II, line 24, reporting positive amounts as negative and negative amounts as positive				

2014

Department of the Treasury
Internal Revenue Service

Instructions for Schedule M-3 (Form 1120S)

Net Income (Loss) Reconciliation for S Corporations With Total Assets of $10 Million or More

Section references are to the Internal Revenue Code unless otherwise noted.

Future Developments

For the latest information about developments related to Schedule M-3 (Form 1120S) and its instructions, such as legislation enacted after they were published, go to *www.irs.gov/form1120s*.

What's New

For tax years ending December 31, 2014, and later:

- A corporation that (a) is required to file Schedule M-3 (Form 1120S) and has less than $50 million total assets at the end of the tax year or (b) is not required to file Schedule M-3 (Form 1120S) and voluntarily files Schedule M-3 (Form 1120S), must either complete Schedule M-3 (Form 1120S) entirely or complete Schedule M-3 (Form 1120S) through Part I and complete Form 1120S, Schedule M-1 instead of completing Parts II and III of Schedule M-3 (Form 1120S). These filers are not required to file Form 8916-A. If these filers choose to complete Form 1120S, Schedule M-1 instead of completing Parts II and III of Schedule M-3 (Form 1120S), line 1 of Form 1120S, Schedule M-1 must equal line 11 of Part I of Schedule M-3 (Form 1120S).
- Any filer that completes Parts II and III of Schedule M-3 (Form 1120S) must complete all columns, without exception.

General Instructions

Applicable schedule and instructions. Use the 2014 Schedule M-3 (Form 1120S) with these instructions for tax years ending December 31, 2014, through December 30, 2015. For previous tax years, see the applicable Schedule M-3 (Form 1120S) and instructions. (For example, use the 2013 Schedule M-3 (Form 1120S) with the 2013 instructions for tax years ending December 31, 2013, through December 30, 2014.)

Purpose of Schedule

Schedule M-3, Part I, asks certain questions about the corporation's financial statements and reconciles financial statement worldwide net income (loss) for the corporation (or consolidated financial statement group, if applicable), as reported on Part I, line 4a, to income (loss) per the income statement of the corporation for U.S. income tax purposes, as reported on Part I, line 11.

Schedule M-3, Parts II and III, reconcile financial statement net income (loss) for the U.S. tax return (per Schedule M-3, Part I, line 11) to total income (loss) on Form 1120S, Schedule K, line 18.

Where To File

If the corporation is required to file (or voluntarily files) Schedule M-3 (Form 1120S), the corporation **must** file Form 1120S and all attachments, schedules, including Schedule M-3 (Form 1120S), and statements at the following address.

> Department of the Treasury
> Internal Revenue Service Center
> Ogden, UT 84201-0013

Who Must File

Any corporation required to file Form 1120S, U.S. Income Tax Return for an S Corporation, that reports on Schedule L of Form 1120S total assets at the end of the corporation's tax year that equal or exceed $10 million must file Schedule M-3 (Form 1120S). A corporation or group of corporations that completes Parts II and III of Schedule M-3, is not required to complete Form 1120S, Schedule M-1, Reconciliation of Income (Loss) per Books With Income (Loss) per Return.

A U.S. corporation filing Form 1120S that is not required to file Schedule M-3 may voluntarily file Schedule M-3 instead of Schedule M-1.

Any corporation filing Schedule M-3 must check the box on Form 1120S, item C, indicating that Schedule M-3 is attached (whether required or voluntary).

Example 1.

1. U.S. corporation A owns U.S. subsidiary B and foreign subsidiary F. For its 2014 tax year, A prepares consolidated financial statements with B and F that report total assets of $12 million. A files a U.S. income tax return with B (a corporation that has made a qualified subchapter S subsidiary election) and reports total assets on Schedule L of $8 million. A's U.S. tax group is not required to file Schedule M-3 for the 2014 tax year. A may voluntarily file Schedule M-3 for the 2014 tax year. If A does not file Schedule M-3, it must file Schedule M-1. If A files Schedule M-3, it must either: (i) complete Schedule M-3 entirely; or (ii) complete Schedule M-3 through Part I and complete Schedule M-1 instead of completing Parts II and III of Schedule M-3.

2. U.S. corporation C owns U.S. subsidiary D. For its 2014 tax year, C prepares consolidated financial statements with D, but C and D file separate U.S. income tax returns. The consolidated accrual basis financial statements for C and D report total assets at the end of the tax year of $12 million after intercompany eliminations. C reports separate company total year-end assets on its Schedule L of $7 million. D reports separate company total year-end assets on its Schedule L of $6 million. Neither C nor D is required to file Schedule M-3 for the 2014 tax year. C or D may voluntarily file Schedule M-3 for the 2014 tax year. If C or D does not file Schedule M-3, it must file Schedule M-1. If C or D files Schedule M-3, it must either: (i) complete Schedule M-3 entirely; or (ii) complete Schedule M-3 through Part I and complete Schedule M-1 instead of completing Parts II and III of Schedule M-3.

Completing Schedule M-3 (Form 1120S)

A corporation that is required to file Schedule M-3 (Form 1120S) and has at least $50 million total assets at the end of the tax year must complete Schedule M-3 (Form 1120S) entirely.

A corporation that (a) is required to file Schedule M-3 (Form 1120S) and has less than $50 million total assets at the end of the tax year or (b) is not required to file Schedule M-3 (Form 1120S) and voluntarily files Schedule M-3 (Form 1120S) must either (i) complete Schedule M-3 (Form 1065) entirely or (ii) complete Schedule M-3 (Form 1120S) through Part I and complete Form 1120S, Schedule M-1 instead of completing Parts II and III of Schedule M-3 (Form 1120S). If the corporation chooses to complete Form 1120S, Schedule M-1 instead of completing Parts II and III of Schedule M-3 (Form 1120S), line 1 of Form 1120S, Schedule M-1 must equal line 11 of Part I of Schedule M-3 (Form 1120S).

For any part of Schedule M-3 (Form 1120S) that is completed, all columns must be completed, all applicable questions must be answered, all numerical data requested must be provided, any statement required to support a line item must be attached and provide the information required for that line item.

Any corporation filing Schedule M-3 must check the box on Form 1120S, item C, indicating that Schedule M-3 is attached (whether required or voluntary).

Note. For tax years ending before December 31, 2014, there were different completion rules. See the applicable Schedule M-3 (Form 1120S) and its instructions.

Other Issues Affecting Schedule M-3 Filing Requirements

If a corporation was required to file Schedule M-3 for the preceding tax year, but reports on Form 1120S, Schedule L, total assets at the end of the current tax year of less than $10 million, the corporation is not required to file Schedule M-3 for the current tax year.

For purposes of determining whether the corporation has total assets at the end of the current tax year of $10 million or more, the corporation's total assets

must be determined on an overall accrual method of accounting unless both of the following apply: (a) the tax return of the corporation is prepared using an overall cash method of accounting, and (b) no includible entity in the U.S. tax return prepares or is included in financial statements prepared on an accrual basis.

Note. See the instructions for Part I, line 1, for a discussion of non-tax-basis income statements and related non-tax-basis balance sheets to be used in the preparation of Schedule M-3 and of Form 1120S, Schedule L.

Other Form 1120S Schedules Affected by Schedule M-3 Requirements

Schedule L

If a non-tax-basis income statement and related non-tax-basis balance sheet is prepared for any purpose for a period ending with or within the tax year, Schedule L must be prepared showing non-tax-basis amounts. See the instructions for Part I, line 1, for a discussion of non-tax-basis income statements and related non-tax-basis balance sheets prepared for any purpose and the impact on the selection of the income statement used for Schedule M-3 and the related non-tax-basis balance sheet amounts that must be used for Schedule L.

Total assets shown on Schedule L, line 15, column (d), must equal the total assets of the corporation as of the last day of the tax year, and must be the same total assets reported by the corporation in the non-tax-basis financial statements, if any, used for Schedule M-3. If the corporation does not prepare non-tax-basis financial statements, Schedule L must be based on the corporation's books and records. The Schedule L balance sheet can show tax-basis balance sheet amounts if the corporation is allowed to use books and records for Schedule M-3 and the corporation's books and records reflect only tax-basis amounts.

Generally, total assets at the beginning of the year (Schedule L, line 15, column (b)) must equal total assets at the close of the prior year (Schedule L, line 15, column (d)). For each Schedule L balance sheet item reported for which there is a difference between the current opening balance sheet amount and the prior closing balance sheet amount, attach a

statement that reports the balance sheet item, the prior closing amount, the current opening amount, and a short explanation of the difference. In particular, indicate if the differences occurred because of acquisitions or mergers.

For purposes of measuring total assets at the end of the year, the corporation's assets may not be netted or reduced by the corporation's liabilities. In addition, total assets may not be reported as a negative amount. If Schedule L is prepared on a non-tax-basis method, an investment in a partnership may be shown as appropriate under the corporation's non-tax-basis method of accounting, including, if required by the corporation's reporting methodology, the equity method of accounting for investments. If Schedule L is prepared on a tax-basis method, an investment by the corporation in a partnership must be shown as an asset and measured by the corporation's adjusted basis in its partnership interest. Any liabilities contributing to such adjusted basis must be shown on Schedule L as corporate liabilities. In any event, any investments or other assets reported on Schedule L can never be reported as negative amounts.

Schedule M-1

A corporation that completes Parts II and III of Schedule M-3 is not required to complete Form 1120S, Schedule M-1.

Entity Considerations for Schedule M-3

For purposes of Schedule M-3, references to the classification of an entity (for example, as a corporation, a partnership, or a trust) are references to the treatment of the entity for U.S. income tax purposes. An entity that generally is disregarded as separate from its owner for U.S. income tax purposes (disregarded entity) must not be separately reported on Schedule M-3 except, if required, on Part I, line 7a, 7b, or 7c. On Schedule M-3, Parts II and III, any item of income, gain, loss, deduction, or credit of a disregarded entity must be reported as an item of its owner. In particular, the income or loss of a disregarded entity must not be reported on Part II, lines 7, 8, or 9 as from a separate partnership or other pass-through. The financial statement income or loss of a disregarded entity other than a qualified subchapter S subsidiary (QSub) is included on Part I, line 7b, if and only if its financial statement income or loss is included on Part I, line 11, but not on Part I, line 4a. The financial statement income or loss of a QSub is included on Part I, line 7c, if and only if its financial statement income or loss is included on Part I, line 11, but not on Part I, line 4a.

Qualified Subchapter S Subsidiaries (QSubs). Because a QSub is a disregarded entity, for purposes of Schedule M-3, Schedule L, and the tax return in general, the subsidiary is deemed to have liquidated into the parent S corporation. As such, all QSubs are treated as divisions of the S corporation parent and they must not be separately reported on Schedule M-3 except, if required, on Part I, line 7c.

Reportable Entity Partner Reporting Responsibilities

A reportable entity partner to a partnership filing Form 1065, U.S. Return of Partnership Income, is an entity that:
- Owns or is deemed to own, directly or indirectly, under these instructions, a 50% or greater interest in the income, loss, or capital of the partnership on any day of the tax year, and
- Was required to file Schedule M-3 on its most recently filed U.S. federal income tax return or return of income filed prior to that day.

For the purposes of these instructions:

1. The parent corporation of a consolidated tax group is deemed to own all corporate and partnership interests owned or deemed to be owned under these instructions by any member of the tax consolidated group;

2. The owner of a disregarded entity is deemed to own all corporate and partnership interests owned or deemed to be owned under these instructions by the disregarded entity;

3. The owner of 50% or more of a corporation by vote on any day of the corporation tax year is deemed to own all corporate and partnership interests owned or deemed to be owned under these instructions by the corporation during the corporation tax year;

4. The owner of 50% or more of partnership income, loss, or capital on any day of the partnership tax year is deemed to own all corporate and partnership interests owned or deemed to be owned under these instructions by the partnership during the partnership tax year; and

5. The beneficial owner of 50% or more of the beneficial interest of a trust

or nominee arrangement on any day of the trust or nominee arrangement tax year is deemed to own all corporate and partnership interests owned or deemed to be owned under these instructions by the trust or nominee arrangement.

A reportable entity partner to a partnership (as defined above) must report the following to the partnership within 30 days of first becoming a reportable entity partner and, after first reporting to the partnership under these instructions, after that within 30 days of the date of any change in the interest it owns or is deemed to own, directly or indirectly, under these instructions, in the partnership.

1. Name.

2. Mailing address.

3. Taxpayer identification number (TIN or EIN), if applicable.

4. Entity or organization type.

5. State or country in which it is organized.

6. Date on which it first became a reportable entity partner.

7. Date for which it is reporting a change in its ownership interest in the partnership, if applicable.

8. The interest in the partnership it owns or is deemed to own in the partnership, directly or indirectly (as defined under these instructions) as of the date for which it is reporting.

9. Any change in that interest as of the date for which it is reporting.

The reportable entity partner must retain copies of required reports it makes to partnerships under these instructions. Each partnership must retain copies of the required reports it receives under these instructions from reportable entity partners.

Example 2. A, a limited liability company (LLC) filing a Form 1065 for 2014, is owned 50% by U.S. corporation Z which files Form 1120S. A owns 50% of each of B, C, D, and E, each also an LLC filing a Form 1065 for calendar year 2014. Z was first required to file Schedule M-3 (Form 1120S) for its corporate tax year ended December 31, 2013, and filed its Form 1120S with Schedule M-3 for 2013 on September 15, 2014. As of September 16, 2014, Z was a reportable entity partner regarding A and, through A, regarding B, C, D, and E. On October 5, 2014, Z reports to A, B, C, D, and E, as it is required to do within 30 days of September 16, that Z is a reportable entity partner directly owning (regarding

A) or deemed to own indirectly (regarding B, C, D, and E) a 50% interest. So, because Z was a reportable entity partner for 2014, each of A, B, C, D, and E is required to file Schedule M-3 (Form 1065) for 2014, regardless of whether they would otherwise be required to file Schedule M-3 for that year.

Specific Instructions for Part I

Part I. Financial Information and Net Income (Loss) Reconciliation

Line 1. Questions Regarding the Type of Income Statement Prepared

For Part I, lines 1 through 12, use only the financial statements of the U.S. corporation filing the U.S. income tax return.

Non-Tax-Basis Financial Statements and Tax-Basis Financial Statements

A tax-basis income statement is allowed for Schedule M-3 and a tax-basis balance sheet for Schedule L only if no non-tax-basis income statement and no non-tax-basis balance sheet was prepared for any purpose and the books and records of the corporation reflect only tax-basis amounts. The corporation is deemed to have non-tax-basis income statements and the related non-tax-basis balance sheets for the current tax year for purposes of Schedule M-3 and Schedule L if such non-tax-basis financial statements were prepared for and presented to management, creditors, shareholders, government regulators, or any other third parties for a period ending with or within the tax year.

If a non-tax-basis income statement is prepared that is a certified non-tax-basis income statement for the period ending with or within the tax year, the corporation must check "Yes" for Part I, line 1a, and use that income statement for Schedule M-3. If no certified non-tax-basis income statement is prepared but an unaudited non-tax-basis income statement is prepared for the period ending with or within the tax year, the corporation must check "Yes" for Part I, line 1b, and use that income statement for Schedule M-3.

Order of priority in accounting standards. If two or more non-tax-basis income statements are both certified non-tax-basis income statements for the period, the income statement prepared according to the following order of priority in accounting standards must be used.

1. U.S. Generally Accepted Accounting Principles (GAAP).

2. International Financial Reporting Standards (IFRS).

3. Any other International Accounting Standards (IAS).

4. Other regulatory accrual accounting.

5. Any other accrual accounting standard.

6. Any fair market value standard.

7. Any cash basis standard.

If no non-tax-basis income statement is certified and two or more non-tax-basis income statements are prepared, the income statement prepared according to the first listed of the accounting standards listed above must be used.

If no non-tax-basis financial statements are prepared for a U.S. corporation filing Schedule M-3 (Form 1120S), the U.S. corporation must check "No" on questions 1a and 1b, skip Part I, lines 2, 3a, and 3b, and enter the net income (loss) per the books and records of the U.S. corporation on Part I, line 4a.

Lines 2 and 3. Questions Regarding Income Statement Period and Restatements

Enter the beginning and ending dates on line 2 for the corporation's annual income statement period ending with or within the current tax year.

The questions on Part I, lines 3a and 3b, regarding income statement restatements refer to the worldwide consolidated income statement issued by the corporation filing the U.S. income tax return and used to prepare Schedule M-3. Answer "Yes" on lines 3a and/or 3b if the corporation's annual income statement has been restated for any reason. Attach a short explanation of the reasons for the restatement in net income for each annual income statement period that is restated, including the original amount and restated amount of each annual statement period's net income.

Line 4. Worldwide Consolidated Net Income (Loss) per Income Statement

Report on Part I, line 4a, the worldwide consolidated net income (loss) per the income statement (or books and records, if applicable) of the corporation.

In completing Schedule M-3, the corporation must use financial statement amounts from the financial statement type checked "Yes" on Part I, line 1, or from its books and records if Part I, line 1b, is checked "No."

If a corporation prepares non-tax-basis financial statements, the amount on line 4a must equal the financial statement net income (loss) for the income statement period ending with or within the tax year as indicated on Part I, line 2.

If the corporation prepares non-tax-basis financial statements and the income statement period differs from the corporation's tax year, the income statement period indicated on Part I, line 2, applies for purposes of Part I, lines 4 through 8.

If the corporation does not prepare non-tax-basis financial statements and has checked "No" on Part I, line 1b, enter the net income (loss) per the books and records of the U.S. corporation on Part I, line 4a.

Indicate on Part I, line 4b, which of the following accounting standards were used for line 4a:

1. U.S. Generally Accepted Accounting Principles (GAAP).

2. International Financial Reporting Standards (IFRS).

3. Tax basis.

4. Other (Specify).

Report on Part I, lines 5a through 10, as instructed below, all adjustment amounts required to adjust worldwide net income (loss) reported on this Part I, line 4a (whether from financial statements or books and records), to net income (loss) of the corporation that must be reported on Part I, line 11. Report on line 12a the worldwide consolidated total assets and total liabilities amounts for the corporation using the same financial statements (or book and records) used for the worldwide consolidated income (loss) amount reported on line 4a.

Line 5. Net Income (Loss) of Nonincludible Foreign Entities

Remove the financial net income (line 5a) or loss (line 5b) of each foreign entity that is included on line 4a and is not an includible entity in the U.S. tax return (nonincludible foreign entity). In addition, on Part I, line 8, adjust for consolidation eliminations and correct for minority interest and intercompany dividends between any nonincludible foreign entity and the entity filing Form 1120S. Do not remove in Part I the financial net income (loss) of any nonincludible foreign entity accounted for on line 4a using the equity method.

Attach a supporting statement that provides the name, EIN (if applicable), and net income (loss) included on line 4a that is removed on this line 5 for each separate nonincludible foreign entity. Also state the total assets and total liabilities for each such separate nonincludible foreign entity and include those assets and liabilities amounts in the total assets and total liabilities reported on Part I, line 12b. The amounts of income (loss) detailed on the supporting statement should be reported for each separate nonincludible foreign entity without regard to the effect of consolidation or elimination entries. If there are consolidation or elimination entries relating to nonincludible foreign entities whose income (loss) is reported on the attached statement that are not reportable on Part I, line 8, the net amounts of all such consolidation and elimination entries must be reported on a separate line on the attached statement, so that the separate financial accounting income (loss) of each nonincludible foreign entity remains separately stated.

For example, if the net income (after consolidation and elimination entries) of a nonincludible foreign sub-consolidated group is being reported on line 5a, the attached supporting statement should report the income (loss) of each separate nonincludible foreign legal entity from each such entity's own financial accounting net income statement or books and records, and any consolidation or elimination entries (for intercompany dividends, minority interests, etc.) not reportable on Part I, line 8, should be reported on the attached supporting statement as a net amount on a line separate and apart from lines that report each nonincludible foreign entity's separate net income (loss).

Line 6. Net Income (Loss) of Nonincludible U.S. Entities

Remove the financial net income (line 6a) or loss (line 6b) of each U.S. entity that is included on line 4a and is not an includible entity in the U.S. tax return (nonincludible U.S. entity). In addition, on Part I, line 8, adjust for consolidation eliminations and correct for minority interest and intercompany dividends between any nonincludible U.S. entity and any includible entity. Do not remove in Part I the financial net income (loss) of any nonincludible U.S. entity accounted for on line 4a using the equity method.

Attach a supporting statement that provides the name, EIN, and net income (loss) included on line 4a that is removed on this line 6 for each separate nonincludible U.S. entity. Also state the total assets and total liabilities for each such separate nonincludible U.S. entity and include those assets and liabilities amounts in the total assets and total liabilities reported on Part I, line 12c. The amounts of income (loss) detailed on the supporting statement should be reported for each separate nonincludible U.S. entity without regard to the effect of consolidation or elimination entries. If there are consolidation or elimination entries relating to nonincludible U.S. entities whose income (loss) is reported on the attached statement that are not reportable on Part I, line 8, the net amounts of all such consolidation and elimination entries must be reported on a separate line on the attached statement, so that the separate financial accounting income (loss) of each nonincludible U.S. entity remains separately stated. For example, if the net income (after consolidation and elimination entries) of a nonincludible U.S. sub-consolidated group is being reported on line 6a, the attached supporting statement should report the income (loss) of each separate nonincludible U.S. legal entity from each such entity's own financial accounting net income statement or books and records, and any consolidation or elimination entries (for intercompany dividends, minority interests, etc.) not reportable on Part I, line 8, should be reported on the attached supporting statement as a net amount on a line separate and apart from lines that report each nonincludible U.S. entity's separate net income (loss).

Lines 7a, 7b, and 7c. Net Income (Loss) of Other Foreign Disregarded Entities, Net Income (Loss) of Other Disregarded Entities (Except Qualified Subchapter S Subsidiaries), and Net Income (Loss) of Other Qualified Subchapter S Subsidiaries (QSubs)

Include on line 7a the financial income of any foreign disregarded entity that is not included on Part I, line 4a, but is included in Part I, line 11 (other foreign disregarded entities). Include on line 7b or 7c the financial net income or (loss) of each disregarded entity in the U.S. tax return that is not included in the consolidated financial group and therefore not included in the income reported on Part I, line 4a. Include on line 7b the financial income of any U.S. disregarded entity that is not a qualified subchapter S subsidiary (QSub) or a foreign disregarded entity and that is not included in the income reported on Part I, line 4a, but is included in Part I, line 11 (other disregarded entities). Include on line 7c the financial income of any QSub that is not included in the income reported on line 4a, but is included on line 11 (other QSub). In addition, on Part I, line 8, adjust for consolidation eliminations and correct for minority interest and intercompany dividends for any other disregarded entity or other QSub.

Attach a supporting statement that provides the name, EIN, and net income (loss) per the financial statement or books and records on this line 7 for each separate other disregarded entity or other QSub. Also state the total assets and total liabilities for each such separate included entity and include those assets and liabilities amounts in the total assets and total liabilities reported on Part I, line 12d. The amounts of income (loss) detailed on the supporting statement should be reported for each separate other disregarded entity or other QSub without regard to the effect of consolidation or elimination entries solely between or among the entities listed. If there are consolidation or elimination entries relating to such other disregarded entities or other QSub whose income (loss) is reported on the attached statement that are not reportable on Part I, line 8, the net amounts of all such consolidation and elimination entries must be reported on a separate line on the attached statement, so that the separate financial accounting income (loss) of each other disregarded entity or other QSub remains separately stated. For example, if the net income (after consolidation and elimination entries) of a sub-consolidated group of other disregarded entities is being reported on line 7b, the attached supporting statement should report the income (loss) of each separate other disregarded entity from each entity's own financial accounting net income statement or books and records, and any consolidation or elimination entries (for intercompany dividends, minority interests, etc.) not reportable on Part I, line 8, should be reported on the attached supporting statement as a net amount on a line separate and apart from lines that report each other disregarded entity's separate net income (loss).

Line 8. Adjustment to Eliminations of Transactions Between Includible Entities and Nonincludible Entities

Adjustments on Part I, line 8, to reverse certain financial accounting consolidation or elimination entries are necessary to ensure that transactions between includible entities and nonincludible U.S. or foreign entities are not eliminated, in order to report the correct total amount on Part I, line 11. Also, additional consolidation entries and elimination entries may be necessary on Part I, line 8, related to transactions between includible entities that are in the consolidated financial group and other disregarded entities and QSubs that are not in the consolidated financial group but that are reported on Part I, line 7a, 7b, or 7c, in order to report the correct total amount on Part I, line 11.

Include on Part I, line 8, the total of the following: (a) amounts of any adjustments to consolidation entries and elimination entries that are contained in the amount reported on Part I, line 4a, required as a result of removing amounts on Part I, line 5 or 6; and (b) amounts of any additional consolidation entries and elimination entries that are required as a result of including amounts on Part I, line 7a, 7b, or 7c. This is necessary in order that the consolidation entries and intercompany elimination entries included in the amount reported on Part I, line 11, are only those applicable to the financial net income (loss) of includible entities for the financial statement period. For example, adjustments must be reported on line 8 to remove minority interest and to reverse the elimination of intercompany dividends included on Part I, line 4a, that relate to the net income of entities removed on Part I, line 5 or 6, because the income to which the consolidation or elimination entries relate has been removed. Also, for example, consolidation or elimination entries must be reported on line 8 to eliminate any intercompany dividends between entities whose income is included on Part I, line 7a, 7b, or 7c, and other entities included in the U.S. income tax return. See *Example 3A*, *3B*, and *4* in the instructions for line 11.

If a corporate owner of an interest in another entity: (a) accounts for the interest in entity in the owner corporation's separate general ledger on the equity method, and (b) fully consolidates entity in the owner corporation's consolidated financial statements, but entity is not includible in the owner corporation's U.S. income tax return, then, as part of reversing all consolidation and elimination entries for the nonincludible entity, the corporate owner must reverse on Schedule M-3, Part I, line 8, the elimination of the equity income inclusion from entity. If the owner corporation does not account for entity on the equity method on its own general ledger, it will not have eliminated the equity income for consolidated financial statement purposes, so it will have no elimination of equity income to reverse.

The attached supporting statement for Part I, line 8, must identify the type (for example, minority interest, intercompany dividends, etc.) and amount of consolidation or elimination entries reported, as well as the names of the entities to which they pertain. It is not necessary, but it is permitted, to report intercompany eliminations that net to zero on Part I, line 8, such as intercompany interest income and expense.

Line 9. Adjustment To Reconcile Income Statement Period to Tax Year

Include on line 9 any adjustments necessary to the income (loss) of includible entities to reconcile differences between the corporation's income statement period reported on line 2 and the corporation's tax year. Attach a statement describing the adjustment.

Line 10. Other Adjustments To Reconcile to Amount on Line 11

Include on line 10 any other adjustments to reconcile net income (loss) on Part I, line 4a, through Part I, line 9, with net income (loss) on Part I, line 11.

For any adjustments reported on Part I, line 10, attach a supporting statement with an explanation of each net adjustment included on line 10.

Line 11. Net Income (Loss) per Income Statement of the Corporation

Report on line 11 the net income (loss) per the income statement (or books and records, if applicable) of the corporation. Amounts reported in column (a) of Parts II and III (see later) must be reported on the same accounting method used to report the amount of net income (loss) per income statement of the corporation on Part I, line 11.

Do not, in any event, report on this line 11 the net income of entities not included in the U.S. income tax return for the tax year. For example, it is not permissible to remove the income of nonincludible entities on lines 5 and/or 6, above, then to add back such income on lines 7 through 10, such that the amount reported on line 11 includes the net income of entities not includible in the U.S. income tax return. A principal purpose of Schedule M-3 is to report on this Part I, line 11, only the financial accounting net income of only the entities included in the U.S. income tax return.

Whether or not the corporation prepares financial statements, Part I, line 11, must include all items that impact the net income (loss) of the corporation even if they are not recorded in the profit and loss accounts in the corporation's general ledger, including, for example, all post-closing adjusting entries (including workpaper adjustments) and dividend income or other income received from nonincludible entities. If the corporation prepares unconsolidated financial statements using the same accounting method used to determine worldwide consolidated net income (loss) for Part I, line 4a, and if it uses the equity method for investments, the amount reported on Part I, line 11, will equal the amount of the unconsolidated net income (loss) reported on the unconsolidated financial statements. See *Example 3B.3* and *3B.4*.

Example 3A. U.S. corporation P files a Form 1120S U.S. tax return and prepares certified audited income statements for GAAP. P owns 100% of the stock of U.S. corporations DS1 through DS75, between 51% and 99% of the stock of U.S. corporations DS76 through DS100, and 100% of the stock of foreign entities FS1 through FS50. P eliminates all dividend income from DS1 through DS100 and FS1 through FS50 in financial statement consolidation entries. Furthermore, P eliminates the minority interest ownership, if any, of DS76 through DS100 in financial statement consolidation entries.

P must check "Yes" on Part I, line 1a. On Part I, line 4a, P must report the consolidated net income for the consolidated financial statement group of P, DS1 through DS100, and FS1 through FS50. P must remove the net income (loss) of FS1 through FS50 on Part I, lines 5a or 5b, as applicable, and remove on Part I, lines 6a or 6b, as applicable, any net income (loss) from DS1 through DS75 where a QSub election has not been made by P. P must remove the net income (loss) before minority interests of DS76 through DS100 on Part I, lines 6a or 6b, as applicable. P must reverse on Part I, line 8, the elimination of any transactions between the includible entity (P and any QSubs) and the nonincludible entities (DS1 through DS75 with no QSub election, DS76 through DS100 and FS1 through FS50), including dividends received from non-QSub DS1 through DS75, DS76 through DS100, and FS1 through FS50 and the minority interest's share of the net income (loss) of DS76 through DS100.

P reports on Part I, line 11, the consolidated financial statement net income (loss) attributable to the corporation and QSubs. Intercompany transactions between the corporation and the QSubs that had been eliminated in the net income amount on line 4a remain eliminated in the net income amount on line 11. Transactions between the corporation and the nonincludible entities that are eliminated in the net income amount on line 4a are included in the net income amount on line 11 since the elimination of those transactions were reversed on line 8.

Example 3B.

1. U.S. corporation P owns 60% of corporation DS1 which is fully consolidated in P's financial statements. P does not account for DS1 in P's separate general ledger on the equity

　　Instructions for Schedule M-3 (Form 1120S) (2014)

method. DS1 has net income of $100 (before minority interests) and pays dividends of $50, of which P receives $30. The dividend is eliminated in the consolidated financial statements. In its financial statements, P consolidates DS1 and includes $60 of net income ($100 less the minority interest of $40) on Part I, line 4a.

P must remove the $100 net income of DS1 on Part I, line 6a. P must reverse on Part I, line 8, the elimination of the $40 minority interest net income of DS1. In addition, P reverses its elimination of the $30 intercompany dividend in its financial statements on Part I, line 8. The net result is that P includes the $30 dividend from DS1 at Part I, line 11, and on Part II, line 6, column (a). P's dividend income included on the tax return from DS1 must be reported on Part II, line 6, column (d).

2. U.S. corporation C owns 60% of the capital and profits interests in U.S. LLC N. C does not account for N in C's separate general ledger on the equity method. N has net income of $100 (before minority interests) and makes no distributions during the tax year. C treats N as a corporation for financial statement purposes and as a partnership for U.S. income tax purposes. In its financial statements, C consolidates N and includes $60 of net income ($100 less the minority interest of $40) on Part I, line 4a.

C must remove the $100 net income of N on Part I, line 6a. C must reverse on Part I, line 8, the elimination of the $40 minority interest net income of N. The result is that C includes no income for N either on Part I, line 11, or on Part II, line 7, column (a). C's taxable income from N must be reported by C on Part II, line 7, column (d).

3. U.S. corporation P owns 60% of corporation DS1, which is fully consolidated in P's financial statements. P accounts for DS1 in P's separate general ledger on the equity method. DS1 has net income of $100 (before minority interests) and pays dividends of $50, of which P receives $30. The dividend reduces P's investment in DS1 for equity method reporting on P's separate general ledger where P includes its 60% equity share of DS1 income, which is $60. In its financial statements, P eliminates the DS1 equity method income of $60 and consolidates DS1, including $60 of net income ($100 less the minority interest of $40) on Part I, line 4a.

P must remove the $100 net income of DS1 on Part I, line 6a. P must reverse

on Part I, line 8, the elimination of the $40 minority interest net income of DS1 and the elimination of the $60 of DS1 equity income. The net result is that P includes the $60 of equity method income from DS1 at Part I, line 11, and on Part II, line 5, column (a). P's dividend income included on the tax return from its investment in DS1 must be reported on Part II, line 6, column (d).

4. U.S. corporation C owns 60% of the capital and profits interests in U.S. LLC N. C accounts for N in C's separate general ledger on the equity method. N has net income of $100 (before minority interests) and makes no distributions during the tax year. C treats N as a corporation for financial statement purposes and as a partnership for U.S. income tax purposes. For equity method reporting on C's separate general ledger, C includes its 60% equity share of N income, which is $60. In its financial statements, C eliminates the $60 of N net income ($100 less the minority interest of $40) on Part I, line 4a.

C must remove the $100 net income of N on Part I, line 6a. C must reverse on Part I, line 8, the elimination of the $40 minority interest net income of N and the elimination of the $60 of N equity method income. The result is that C includes the $60 of equity method income for N on Part I, line 11, and on Part II, line 7, column (a). C's taxable income from N must be reported by C on Part II, line 7, column (d).

Example 4. U.S. corporation P owns 100% of the stock of QSub corporation DS1. DS1 is included in P's federal income tax return, even though DS1 is not included in P's consolidated financial statements on either a consolidated basis or on the equity method. DS1 has current year net income of $100 after taking into account its $40 interest payment to P. P has net income of $1,040 after recognition of the interest income from DS1. Because DS1 is a QSub, 100% of the net income of both P and DS1 must be reported on Form 1120S of P's U.S. income tax return, and the intercompany interest income and expense must be removed by consolidation elimination entries.

P must report its financial statement net income of $1,040 on Part I, line 4a, and reports DS1's net income of $100 on Part I, line 7c. Then, in order to reflect the full consolidation of the financial accounting net income of P and DS1 at Part I, line 11, the following consolidation and elimination entries are reported on Part I, line 8: offsetting

entries to remove the $40 of interest income received from DS1 included by P on line 4a, and to remove the $40 of interest expense of DS1 included in line 7c for a net change of zero. The result is that Part I, line 11, reports $1,140: $1,040 from line 4a, and $100 from line 7c. Stated another way, Part I, line 11, includes the entire $1,000 net income of P, measured before recognition of the intercompany interest income from DS1 and the consolidation of DS1 operations, plus the entire $140 net income of DS1, measured before interest expense to P. P's U.S. income tax group is not required to include on the attached supporting statement for Part I, line 8, the offsetting adjustment to the intercompany elimination of interest income and interest expense (though it is permitted to do so).

Line 12. Total Assets and Liabilities of Entities Included or Removed on Part I, Lines 4, 5, 6, and 7

Line 12 must be completed by all corporations that file Schedule M-3. Report on lines 12a, 12b, 12c, and 12d the total amount (not just the corporation's share) of assets and liabilities of entities included or removed on Part I, lines 4, 5, 6, and 7. All assets and liabilities reported on lines 12a through 12d must be reported as positive amounts.

On line 12a, enter the worldwide consolidated total assets and total liabilities of all of the entities included in computing Part I, line 4a. On line 12b, enter the total assets and total liabilities of the entities removed in completing Part I, line 5. On line 12c, enter the total assets and total liabilities removed in completing Part I, line 6. On line 12d, enter total assets and total liabilities included in completing Part I, line 7.

Specific Instructions for Parts II and III

General Reporting information

A schedule or statement may be attached to any line even if none is required.

For each line item in Parts II and III, report in column (a) the amount of net income (loss) included in Part I, line 11, and report in column (d) the amount included in total income (loss) on Form 1120S, Schedule K, line 18.

Note. Part II, line 26, column (a) must equal Part I, line 11, and column (d) must equal the amount on Form 1120S, Schedule K, line 18.

For any item of income, gain, loss, expense, or deduction for which there is a difference between columns (a) and (d), the portion of the difference that is temporary must be entered in column (b) and the portion of the difference that is permanent must be entered in column (c).

If financial statements are prepared by the corporation under with generally accepted accounting principles (GAAP), differences that are treated as temporary under GAAP must be reported in column (b) and differences that are permanent (that is, not temporary) for GAAP must be reported in column (c). Generally, under to GAAP, a temporary difference affects (creates, increases, or decreases) a deferred tax asset or liability.

If the corporation does not prepare financial statements, or the financial statements are not prepared under GAAP, report in column (b) any difference that the corporation believes will reverse in a future tax year (that is, have an opposite effect on total income (loss) in a future tax year (or years) due to the difference in timing of recognition for financial accounting and U.S. income tax purposes) or is the reversal of such a difference that arose in a prior tax year. Report in column (c) any difference that the corporation believes will not reverse in a future tax year (and is not the reversal of such a difference that arose in a prior tax year).

If the corporation is unable to determine whether a difference between column (a) and column (d) for an item will reverse in a future tax year or is the reversal of a difference that arose in a prior tax year, report the difference for that item in column (c).

Example 5. At the end of Corporation A's first tax year, December 31, 2014, it was not required to file Schedule M-3 for any reason.

A may elect to file Schedule M-3 instead of completing Schedule M-1.

If A elects to file schedule M-3, it must either (i) complete Schedule M-3 entirely or (ii) complete Schedule M-3 through Part I and complete Schedule M-1 instead of completing Parts II and III of Schedule M-3.

If A elects to complete Schedule M-3 entirely, it must complete all columns of Parts II and III.

If A completes Schedule M-3 through Part I and completes Schedule M-1 instead of completing Parts II and III of

Schedule M-3, line 11 of Part I of Schedule M-3 must equal line 1 of Schedule M-1.

Example 6. Corporation B is a U.S. corporation that files a U.S. tax return and prepares GAAP financial statements. In prior years, B acquired intellectual property (IP) and goodwill. The IP is amortizable for both U.S. income tax and financial statement purposes. In the current year, B's annual amortization expense for IP is $9,000 for U.S. income tax purposes and $6,000 for financial statement purposes. In its financial statements, B treats the difference in IP amortization as a temporary difference. The goodwill is not amortizable for U.S. income tax purposes and is subject to impairment for financial statement purposes. In the current year, B records an impairment charge on the goodwill of $5,000. In its financial statements, B treats the goodwill impairment as a permanent difference. B must report the amortization attributable to the IP on Part III, line 21, and report $6,000 in column (a), a temporary difference of $3,000 in column (b), and $9,000 in column (d). B must report the goodwill impairment on Part III, line 19, and report $5,000 in column (a), a permanent difference of ($5,000) in column (c), and $0 in column (d).

Reporting Requirements for Parts II and III

General Reporting Requirements

If an amount is attributable to a reportable transaction described in Regulations section 1.6011-4(b), the amount must be reported in columns (a), (b), (c), and (d), as applicable, of Part II, line 10, regardless of whether the amount would otherwise be reported on Schedule M, Part II or Part III. So, if a taxpayer is required to file Form 8886, Reportable Transaction Disclosure Statement, the amounts attributable to that reportable transaction must be reported on Part II, line 10.

A corporation is required to report in column (a) of Parts II and III the amount of any item specifically listed on Schedule M-3 that is in any manner included in the corporation's current year financial statement net income (loss) or in an income or expense account maintained in the corporation's books and records, even if there is no difference between that amount and the amount included in total income (loss) unless **(a)** otherwise provided in these

instructions or **(b)** the amount is attributable to a reportable transaction described in Regulations section 1.6011-4(b) so it is reported on Part II, line 10. For example, with the exception of interest income reflected on a Schedule K-1 received by a corporation as a result of the corporation's investment in a partnership or other pass-through entity, all interest income included on Part I, line 11, whether from affiliated companies, third parties, banks, or other entities, whether from foreign or domestic sources, whether taxable or exempt from tax, and whether classified as some other type of income for U.S. income tax purposes (such as dividends), must be included on Part II, line 11, column (a). Likewise, all fines and penalties included in Part I, line 11, paid to a government or other authority for the violation of any law for which fines or penalties are assessed must be included on Part III, line 9, column (a), regardless of the government authority that imposed the fines or penalties, regardless of whether the fines or penalties are civil or criminal, regardless of the classification, nomenclature, or terminology attached to the fines or penalties by the imposing authority in its actions or documents.

If a corporation would be required to report in column (a) of Parts II and III the amount of any item specifically listed on Schedule M-3 in accordance with the preceding paragraph, except that the corporation has capitalized the item of income or expense and reports the amount in its financial statement balance sheet or in asset and liability accounts maintained in the corporation's books and records, the corporation must report the proper tax treatment of the item in columns (b), (c), and (d), as applicable.

Furthermore, in applying the two preceding paragraphs, a corporation is required to report in column (a) of Parts II and III the amount of any item specifically listed on Schedule M-3 that is included in the corporation's financial statements or exists in the corporation's books and records, regardless of the nomenclature associated with that item in the financial statements or books and records. Accurate completion of Schedule M-3 requires reporting amounts according to the substantive nature of the specific line items included in Schedule M-3 and consistent reporting of all transactions of like substantive nature that occurred during the tax year. For example, all expense amounts that are included in the financial statements or exist in the books and records that represent some form of "Bad debt expense," must be reported on Part III, line 25, in column (a), regardless of whether the amounts are recorded or stated under different nomenclature in the financial statements or the books and records such as: "Provision for doubtful accounts"; "Expense for uncollectible notes receivable"; or "Impairment of trade accounts receivable." Likewise, as stated in the preceding paragraph, all fines and penalties must be included on Part III, line 9, column (a), regardless of the terminology or nomenclature attached to them by the corporation in its books and records or financial statements.

With limited exceptions, Part II includes lines for specific items of income, gain, or loss (income items). (See Part II, lines 1 through 21.) If an income item is described in Part II, lines 1 through 21, report the amount of the item on the applicable line, regardless of whether there is a difference for the item. If there is a difference for the income item, or only a portion of the income item has a difference and a portion of the item does not have a difference, and the item is not described in Part II, lines 1 through 21, report and describe the entire amount of the item on Part II, line 22.

With limited exceptions, Part III includes lines for specific items of expense or deduction (expense items). (See Part III, lines 1 through 28.) If an expense item is described on Part III, lines 1 through 28, report the amount of the item on the applicable line, regardless of whether there is a difference for the item. If there is a difference for the expense item, or only a portion of the expense item has a difference and a portion of the item does not have a difference and the item is not described in Part III, lines 1 through 28, report and describe the entire amount of the item on Part III, line 31.

If there is no difference between the financial accounting amount and the taxable amount of an entire item of income, loss, expense, or deduction and the item is not described or included in Part II, lines 1 through 21, or Part III, lines 1 through 28, report the entire amount of the item in columns (a) and (d) of Part II, line 25.

Separately stated and adequately disclosed. Each difference reported in Parts II and III must be separately stated and adequately disclosed. In general, a difference is adequately disclosed if the difference is labeled in a manner that clearly identifies the item or transaction from which the difference arises. For further guidance about adequate disclosure, see Regulations section 1.6662-4(f). If a specific item of income, gain, loss, expense, or deduction is described on Part II, lines 7 through 21, or Part III, lines 1 through 28, and the line does not indicate to "attach statement," and the specific instructions for the line do not call for an attachment of a statement, then the item is considered separately stated and adequately disclosed if the item is reported on the applicable line and the amount(s) of the item(s) are reported in the applicable columns of the applicable line. See the instructions for Part II, lines 1 through 6, for specific additional information required to be provided for these particular lines.

Except as otherwise provided, differences for the same item must be combined or netted together and reported as one amount on the applicable line of Schedule M-3. However, differences for separate items must not be combined or netted together. Each item (and corresponding amount attributable to that item) must be separately stated and adequately disclosed on the applicable line of Schedule M-3, or any statement required to be attached, even if the amounts are below a certain dollar amount.

Required statements for Part II, line 22, and Part III, line 31. A separate statement must be attached to Schedule M-3 (Form 1120S) that includes a detailed description of each item and adjustment entered on Part II, line 22, and Part III, line 31.

The description for each amount entered in column (a) must be readily identifiable to the name of the account in the financial statements or books and records of the taxpayer, under which the amount in column (a) was recorded in the accounting records. Also, the description for each amount entered in column (a) must include detailed information supporting each adjustment reported in columns (b) and (c), including how the adjustment is identified in the accounting records. The entire description is considered the tax description for the amount reported in column (d) for each item reported on Part II, line 22, or Part III, line 31.

Each description should adequately describe all four columns of Part II, line 22, or Part III, line 31. If additional information is required to provide an acceptable description, provide a supporting statement.

Example 7. Corporation C is a calendar year taxpayer that files and entirely completes Schedule M-3 for its 2014 tax year. C placed in service 10 depreciable fixed assets in a previous year. C's total depreciation expense for its 2014 tax year for five of the assets is $50,000 for income statement purposes and $70,000 for U.S. income tax purposes. C's total annual depreciation expense for its 2014 tax year for the other five assets is $40,000 for income statement purposes and $30,000 for U.S. income tax purposes. In its financial statements, C treats the differences between financial statement and U.S. income tax depreciation expense as giving rise to temporary differences that will reverse in future years. C must combine all of its depreciation adjustments. Accordingly, C must report on Part III, line 24, for its 2014 tax year income statement depreciation expense of $90,000 in column (a), a temporary difference of $10,000 in column (b), and U.S. income tax depreciation expense of $100,000 in column (d).

Example 8. Corporation D is a calendar year taxpayer that files and entirely completes Schedule M-3 for its 2014 tax year. On December 31, 2014, D establishes three reserve accounts in the amount of $100,000 for each account. One reserve account is an allowance for accounts receivable that are estimated to be uncollectible. The second reserve is an estimate of coupons outstanding that may have to be paid. The third reserve is an estimate of future warranty expenses. In its financial statements, D treats the three reserve accounts as giving rise to temporary differences that will reverse in future years. The three reserves are expenses in D's 2014 financial statements but are not deductions for U.S. income tax purposes in 2014. D must not combine the Schedule M-3 differences for the three reserve accounts. D must report the amounts attributable to the allowance for uncollectible accounts receivable on Part III, line 25, and must separately state and adequately disclose the amounts attributable to each of the other two reserves, coupons outstanding and warranty costs, on a required, attached statement that supports the amounts at Part III, line 31.

D must also provide a description for each reserve that meets the requirements for Part III, line 31, discussed earlier under _Required statements for Part II, line 22, and Part III, line 31_. In this example, an acceptable description would be "Coupon Issue Reserves - Rewards Expense" and "Future Warranty Expense Reserve."

Note. There is no need to add the title of the reserve account to the description if the account name for the amount in column (a) is already part of the adjustment description.

Example 9. Corporation E is a calendar year taxpayer that files and entirely completes Schedule M-3 for its 2014 tax year. On January 2, 2014, E establishes an allowance for uncollectible accounts receivable (bad debt reserve) of $100,000. During 2014, E increased the reserve by $250,000 for additional accounts receivable that may become uncollectible. Additionally, during 2014 E decreases the reserve by $75,000 for accounts receivable that were discharged in bankruptcy during 2014. The balance in the reserve account on December 31, 2014, is $275,000. The $100,000 amount to establish the reserve account and the $250,000 to increase the reserve account are expenses on E's 2014 financial statements but are not deductible for U.S. income tax purposes in 2014. However, the $75,000 decrease to the reserve is deductible for U.S. income tax purposes in 2014. In its financial statements, E treats the reserve account as giving rise to a temporary difference that will reverse in future tax years. E must report on Part III, line 25, for its 2014 tax year income statement bad debt expense of $350,000 in column (a), a temporary difference of ($275,000) in column (b), and U.S. income tax bad debt expense of $75,000 in column (d).

Example 10. Corporation F is a calendar year taxpayer that files and entirely completes Schedule M-3 for its 2014 tax year. During 2014, F incurs $200 of meals and entertainment expenses that F deducts in computing net income per the income statement. $50 of the $200 is subject to the 50% limitation under section 274(n). In its financial statements, F treats the limitation on deductions for meals and entertainment as a permanent difference. Because meals and entertainment expenses are specifically described in Part III, line 8, F must report all of its meals and entertainment expenses on this line, regardless of whether there is a difference. Accordingly, F must report $200 in

column (a), $25 in column (c), and $175 in column (d). F must not report the $150 of meals and entertainment expenses that are deducted in F's financial statement net income and are fully deductible for U.S. income tax purposes on Part II, line 25, and the $50 subject to the limitation under section 274(n) on Part III, line 8.

Part II. Reconciliation of Net Income (Loss) per Income Statement of the Corporation With Total Income (Loss) per Return

Lines 1 Through 9. Additional Information for Each Entity

For any item reported on Part II, lines 1, and 3 through 5, attach a supporting statement that provides the name of the entity for which the item is reported, the entity's EIN (if applicable), the type of entity (corporation, partnership, etc.), and the item amounts for columns (a) through (d). See the instructions for Part II, lines 2 and 6 through 9, for the specific information required for those particular lines.

Line 1. Income (Loss) From Equity Method Foreign Corporations

Report on line 1, column (a), the financial income (loss) included in Part I, line 11, for any foreign corporation accounted for on the equity method and remove such amount in column (b) or (c), as applicable. Report the amount of dividends received and other taxable amounts received or includible from foreign corporations on Part II, lines 2 through 4, as applicable.

Line 2. Gross Foreign Dividends Not Previously Taxed

Except as otherwise provided in this paragraph, report on line 2, column (d), the amount (before any withholding tax) of any foreign dividends included in current year total income (loss) on Form 1120S, Schedule K, line 18, and report on line 2, column (a), the amount of dividends from any foreign corporation included in Part I, line 11. Do not report on line 2 any amounts that must be reported on Part II, line 3, or dividends that were previously taxed and must be reported on Part II, line 4. (See the instructions below for Part II, lines 3 and 4.) Report withholding taxes on Part III, line 31, or Part II, line 25, as applicable.

For any dividends reported on Part II, line 2, that are received on a class of voting stock of which the corporation directly or indirectly owned 10% or more of the outstanding shares of that class at any time during the tax year, report on an attached supporting statement: (1) the name of the dividend payer, (2) the payer's EIN (if applicable), (3) the class of voting stock on which the dividend was paid, (4) the percentage of the class directly or indirectly owned, and (5) the amounts for columns (a) through (d).

Line 3. Subpart F, QEF, and Similar Income Inclusions

Report on line 3, column (d), the amount included in income under section 951 (relating to Subpart F), gains or other income inclusions resulting from elections under sections 1291(d)(2) and 1298(b)(1), and any amount included in income pursuant to section 1293 (relating to qualified electing funds (QEF)). The amount of Subpart F income corresponds to the total of the amounts reported by the corporation on line 6, Schedule I, of all Forms 5471, Information Return of U.S. Persons With Respect To Certain Foreign Corporations. The amount of QEF income corresponds to the total of the amounts reported by the corporation on all Forms 8621, Information Return by a Shareholder of a Passive Foreign Investment Company or Qualified Electing Fund. See Form 8621 and the Instructions for Form 8621.

Also include on line 3 passive foreign investment company (PFIC) mark-to-market gains and losses under section 1296. Do not report such gains and losses on Part II, line 14.

Line 4. Gross Foreign Distributions Previously Taxed

Report on line 4, column (a), any distributions received from foreign corporations that were included in Part I, line 11, and that were previously taxed for U.S. income tax purposes. For example, include in column (a) amounts that are excluded from income under sections 959 and 1293(c). Remove such amount in column (b) or (c), as applicable. Report the full amount of the distribution before any withholding tax. Report withholding taxes on Part III, line 31, or Part II, line 25, as applicable. Since previously taxed foreign distributions are not currently taxable, line 4, column (d) is shaded. (Also, see instructions above for Part II, line 2.)

Line 5. Income (Loss) From Equity Method U.S. Corporations

Report on line 5, column (a), the financial income (loss) included in Part I, line 11, for any U.S. corporation accounted for on the equity method and remove such amount in column (b) or (c), as applicable. Report on Part II, line 6, dividends received from any U.S. corporation accounted for on the equity method.

Line 6. U.S. Dividends Not Eliminated in Tax Consolidation

Report on line 6, column (a), the amount of dividends included in Part I, line 11, that were received from any U.S. corporation. Report on line 6, column (d), the amount of any U.S. dividends included in total income (loss) on Form 1120S, Schedule K, line 18.

For any dividends included on Part II, line 6, that are received on classes of voting stock in which the corporation directly or indirectly owned 10% or more of the outstanding shares of that class at any time during the tax year, report on an attached supporting statement for Part II, line 6: (1) the name of the dividend payer, (2) the payer's EIN (if applicable), (3) the class of voting stock on which the dividend was paid, (4) the percentage of the class directly or indirectly owned, and (5) the item amounts for columns (a) through (d).

Line 7. Income (Loss) From U.S. Partnerships and Line 8. Income (Loss) From Foreign Partnerships

For any interest owned by the corporation that is treated as an investment in a partnership for U.S. income tax purposes (other than an interest in a disregarded entity), report amounts on Part II, line 7 or 8, as described below.

1. In column (a), the sum of the corporation's distributive share of income or loss from a U.S. or foreign partnership that is included in Part I, line 11.

2. In column (b) or (c), as applicable, the sum of all differences, if any, attributable to the corporation's distributive share of income or loss from a U.S. or foreign partnership.

3. In column (d), the sum of all amounts of income, gain, loss, or deduction attributable to the corporation's distributive share of income or loss from a U.S. or foreign partnership (that is, the sum of all amounts reportable on the corporation's Schedule(s) K-1 received from the partnership (if applicable)), without regard to any limitations computed at the partner level.

For each partnership reported on line 7 or 8, attach a supporting statement that provides the name, EIN (if applicable), end of year profit-sharing percentage (if applicable), end of year loss-sharing percentage (if applicable), and the amount reported in column (a), (b), (c), or (d) of lines 7 or 8, as applicable.

Example 11. U.S. corporation H is a calendar year taxpayer that files and entirely completes Schedule M-3 for its 2014 tax year. H has an investment in a U.S. partnership USP. H prepares financial statements in accordance with GAAP. In its financial statements, H treats the difference between financial statement net income and taxable income from its investment in USP as a permanent difference. For its 2014 tax year, H's financial statement net income includes $10,000 of income attributable to its share of USP's net income. H's Schedule K-1 from USP reports $5,000 of ordinary income, $7,000 of long-term capital gains, $4,000 of charitable contributions, and $200 of section 179 expense. H must report on Part II, line 7, $10,000 in column (a), a permanent difference of ($2,200) in column (c), and $7,800 in column (d).

Line 9. Income (Loss) From Other Pass-Through Entities

For any interest in a pass-through entity (other than an interest in a partnership reportable on Part II, line 7 or 8, as applicable) owned by the corporation (other than an interest in a disregarded entity), report the following on line 9:

1. In column (a), the sum of the corporation's distributive share of income or loss from the pass-through entity that is included in Part I, line 11;

2. In column (b) or (c), as applicable, the sum of all differences, if any, attributable to the pass-through entity; and

3. In column (d), the sum of all taxable amounts of income, gain, loss, or deduction reportable on the corporation's Schedules K-1 received from the pass-through entity (if applicable).

For each pass-through entity reported on line 9, attach a supporting statement that provides that entity's name, EIN (if applicable), the corporation's end of year profit-sharing percentage (if applicable), the corporation's end of year loss-sharing percentage (if applicable), and the amounts reported by the corporation in column (a), (b), (c), or (d) of line 9, as applicable.

Line 10. Items Relating to Reportable Transactions

Any amounts attributable to any reportable transactions (as described in Regulations section 1.6011-4(b)) must be included on Part II, line 10, regardless of whether the difference, or differences, would otherwise be reported elsewhere in Part II or Part III. So, if a taxpayer is required to file Form 8886 for any reportable transaction described in Regulations section 1.6011-4(b), the amounts attributable to that reportable transaction must be reported on Part II, line 10. In addition, all income and expense amounts attributable to a reportable transaction must be reported on Part II, line 10, columns (a) and (d), even if there is no difference between the financial amounts and the taxable amounts.

Each difference attributable to a reportable transaction must be separately stated and adequately disclosed. A corporation will be considered to have separately stated and adequately disclosed a reportable transaction on line 10 if the corporation sequentially numbers each Form 8886 and lists by identifying number on the supporting statement for Part II, line 10, each sequentially numbered reportable transaction and the amounts required for Part II, line 10, columns (a) through (d).

In lieu of the requirements of the preceding paragraph, a corporation will be considered to have separately stated and adequately disclosed a reportable transaction if the corporation attaches a supporting statement that provides the following for each reportable transaction:

1. A description of the reportable transaction disclosed on Form 8886 for which amounts are reported on Part II, line 10;

2. The name and reportable transaction or tax shelter registration number, if applicable, as reported on lines 1a and 1c, respectively, of Form 8886; and

3. The type of reportable transaction (that is, listed transaction, confidential transaction, transaction with contractual protection, etc.) as reported on line 2 of Form 8886.

If a transaction is a listed transaction described in Regulations section 1.6011-4(b)(2), the description also must include the description provided on line 3 of Form 8886. In addition, if the reportable transaction involves an investment in the transaction through another entity such as a partnership, the description must include the name and EIN (if applicable) of that entity as reported on line 5 of Form 8886.

Example 12. Corporation J is a calendar year taxpayer that files and entirely completes Schedule M-3 for its 2014 tax year. J incurred seven different abandonment losses during its 2014 tax year. One loss of $12 million results from a reportable transaction described in Regulations section 1.6011-4(b)(5), another loss of $5 million results from a reportable transaction described in Regulations section 1.6011-4(b)(4), and the remaining five abandonment losses are not reportable transactions. J discloses the reportable transactions giving rise to the $12 million and $5 million losses on separate Forms 8886 and sequentially numbers them X1 and X2, respectively. J must separately state and adequately disclose the $12 million and $5 million losses on Part II, line 10. The $12 million loss and the $5 million loss will be adequately disclosed if J attaches a supporting statement for line 10 that lists each of the sequentially numbered forms, Form 8886-X1 and Form 8886-X2, and for each reportable transaction reports the appropriate amounts required for Part II, line 10, columns (a) through (d). Alternatively, J's disclosures will be adequate if the description provided for each loss on the supporting statement includes the names and reportable transaction or tax shelter registration numbers, if any, disclosed on the applicable Form 8886, identifies the type of reportable transaction for the loss, and reports the appropriate amounts required for Part II, line 10, columns (a) through (d). J must report the losses attributable to the other five abandonment losses on Part II, line 21e, regardless of whether a difference exists for any or all of those abandonment losses.

Example 13. Corporation K is a calendar year taxpayer that files and entirely completes Schedule M-3 for its 2014 tax year. K enters into a transaction with contractual protection that is a reportable transaction described in Regulations section 1.6011-4(b)(4). This reportable transaction is the only reportable transaction for K's 2014 tax year and results in a $7 million capital loss for both financial accounting purposes and U.S. income tax purposes. Although the transaction does not result in a difference, K is required to report on Part II, line 10, the following amounts: ($7 million) in column (a), zero in columns (b) and (c), and ($7 million) in column (d). The transaction will be adequately disclosed if K attaches a supporting statement for line 10 that (a) sequentially numbers the Form 8886 and refers to the sequentially-numbered Form 8886-X1 and (b) reports the applicable amounts required for line 10, columns (a) through (d). Alternatively, the transaction will be adequately disclosed if the supporting statement for line 10 includes a description of the transaction, the name and tax shelter registration number, if any, and the type of reportable transaction disclosed on Form 8886.

Line 11. Interest Income

Attach Form 8916-A, Supplemental Attachment to Schedule M-3. Complete Part II and enter the amounts shown on line 6, columns (a) through (d), on Schedule M-3, line 11, columns (a) through (d), as applicable.

Note. For tax years ending December 31, 2014, or later, any corporation filing Form 1120S that (a) is required to file a Schedule M-3 and has less than $50 million in total assets at the end of the tax year or (b) is not required to file a Schedule M-3 and voluntarily files a Schedule M-3, is not required to file Form 8916-A but may voluntarily do so.

Report on Part II, line 11, column (a), the total amount of interest income included on Part I, line 11, and report on Part II, line 11, column (d), the total amount of interest income included on Form 1120S, Schedule K, line 18, that is not required to be reported elsewhere on Schedule M-3. In columns (b) or (c), as applicable, adjust for any amounts treated for U.S. income tax purposes as interest income that are treated as some other form of income for financial accounting purposes, or vice versa. For example, adjustments to interest income resulting from adjustments made in accordance with the instructions for Part II, line 16, should be made in columns (b) and (c) of this line 11.

Do not report on this line 11 or include on Form 8916-A amounts reported in accordance with instructions for Part II, lines 7, 8, 9, 10, and 20.

Line 12. Total Accrual to Cash Adjustment

This line is completed by a corporation that prepares financial statements (or books and records, if permitted) using an overall accrual method of accounting and uses an overall cash method of accounting for U.S. income tax purposes (or vice versa). With the exception of amounts required to be reported on Part II, line 10, the corporation must report on Part II, line 12, a single amount net of all adjustments attributable solely to the use of the different overall methods of accounting (for example, adjustments related to accounts receivable, accounts payable, compensation, accrued liabilities, etc.), regardless of whether a separate line on Schedule M-3 corresponds to an item within the accrual to cash reconciliation. Differences not attributable to the use of the different overall methods of accounting must be reported on the appropriate lines of Schedule M-3 (for example, a depreciation difference must be reported on Part III, line 24).

Example 14. Corporation L is a calendar year taxpayer that files and entirely completes Schedule M-3 for its 2014 tax year. L prepares financial statements in accordance with GAAP using an overall accrual method of accounting. L uses an overall cash method of accounting for U.S. income tax purposes. L's financial statements for the year ending December 31, 2014, report accounts receivable of $35,000, an allowance for bad debts of $10,000, and accounts payable of $17,000 related to current year acquisition and reorganization legal and accounting fees. In addition, for L's year ending December 31, 2014, L reported financial statement depreciation expense of $15,000 and depreciation for U.S. income tax purposes of $25,000. For L's 2014 tax year using an overall cash method of accounting, L does not recognize the $35,000 of revenue attributable to the accounts receivable, cannot deduct the $10,000 allowance for bad debt, and cannot deduct the $17,000 of accounts payable. In its financial statements, L treats both the difference in overall accounting methods used for financial statement and U.S. income tax purposes and the difference in depreciation expense as temporary differences. L must combine all adjustments attributable to the differences related to the overall accounting methods on Part II, line 12. As a result, L must report on Part II,

line 12, $8,000 in column (a) ($35,000 –
$10,000 – $17,000), ($8,000) in column
(b), and zero in column (d). L must not
report the accrual to cash adjustment
attributable to the legal and accounting
fees on Part III, line 17. Because the
difference in depreciation expense does
not relate to the use of the cash or
accrual method of accounting, L must
report the depreciation difference on
Part III, line 24, and report $15,000 in
column (a), $10,000 in column (b), and
$25,000 in column (d).

Line 13. Hedging Transactions

Report on line 13, column (a), the net
gain or loss from hedging transactions
included on Part I, line 11. Report in
column (d) the amount of income (loss)
from hedging transactions as defined in
section 1221(b)(2). Use columns (b)
and (c) to report all differences caused
by treating hedging transactions
differently for financial accounting
purposes and for U.S. income tax
purposes. For example, if a portion of a
hedge is considered ineffective under
GAAP but still is a valid hedge under
section 1221(b)(2), the difference must
be reported on line 13. The hedge of a
capital asset, which is not a valid hedge
for U.S. income tax purposes but may
be considered a hedge for GAAP
purposes, must also be reported here.

Report hedging gains and losses
computed under the mark-to-market
method of accounting on line 13 and not
on Part II, line 14.

Report any gain or loss from
inventory hedging transactions on
line 13 and not on Part II, line 15.

Line 14. Mark-to-Market Income (Loss)

Report on line 14 any amount
representing the mark-to-market income
or loss for any securities held by a
dealer in securities, a dealer in
commodities having made a valid
election under section 475(e), or a
trader in securities or commodities
having made a valid election under
section 475(f). "Securities" for these
purposes are securities described in
section 475(c)(2) and "commodities" are
described in section 475(e)(2).
"Securities" do not include any items
specifically excluded from sections
475(c)(2) and 475(e)(2), such as certain
contracts to which section 1256(a)
applies.

Report hedging gains and losses
computed under the mark-to-market
method of accounting on Part II, line 13,
and not on line 14.

Traders in securities and commodities. For a trader in securities or
commodities that made a valid election
under section 475(f) to use the
mark-to-market method to account for
securities or commodities held in
connection with a trading business that
files Form 4797, Sales of Business
Property, any Schedule M-3 entries
required as a result of marking to market
these securities or commodities are
reported as follows: (a) mark-to-market
gains and losses from Form 4797,
line 10, are included on Schedule M-3
(Form 1120S), Part II, line 14; (b) any
other Schedule M-3 entries required
based on other results (non
mark-to-market gains and losses)
included in the total reported on Form
4797, line 17, should be reported on
Schedule M-3 (Form 1120S), Part II,
line 21d, unless the instructions for
Schedule M-3 require the amounts to be
reported on another line.

Line 15. Cost of Goods Sold

Report on line 15 any amounts
deducted as part of cost of goods sold
during the tax year, regardless of
whether the amounts would otherwise
be reported elsewhere in Part II or Part
III.

Examples of amounts that must be
included as cost of goods sold items are
amounts attributable to inventory
valuation, such as amounts attributable
to cost-flow assumptions, additional
costs required to be capitalized
(including depreciation) such as section
263A costs, inventory shrinkage
accruals, inventory obsolescence
reserves, and lower of cost or market
(LCM) write-downs.

Complete Part I of Form 8916-A.
Enter the amounts from line 8, columns
(a) through (d) of Form 8916-A, on
Schedule M-3, Part II, line 15, columns
(a) through (d), as applicable. Attach
Form 8916-A.

Note. The entries in columns (a) and
(d) of Schedule M-3, line 15, are
negative amounts.

Do not report the following on line 15
or on Form 8916-A.
• Amounts reportable on Part II, line 10.
• Any gain or loss from inventory
hedging transactions reportable on Part
II, line 13.
• Amounts reportable on Part II, line 16.
• Amounts reportable on Part II, line 19.
• Mark-to-market income or (loss)
associated with the inventories of
dealers in securities under section 475
reportable on Part II, line 14.

• Section 481(a) adjustments related to
cost of goods sold or inventory valuation
reportable on Part II, line 17.
• Fines and penalties reportable on
Part III, line 9.
• Judgments, damages, awards, and
similar costs, reportable on Part III,
line 10.
• Amounts included on Part III, line 28.

Example 15. Corporation C is a
calendar year taxpayer that files and
entirely completes Schedule M-3 for its
2014 tax year. C placed in service 10
depreciable fixed assets in a previous
tax year. C's total depreciation expense
for its 2014 tax year for five of the assets
is $50,000 for financial accounting
purposes and $70,000 for U.S. income
tax purposes. C's total annual
depreciation expense for its 2014 tax
year for the other five assets is $40,000
for financial accounting purposes and
$30,000 for U.S. income tax purposes.
In addition, C incurs $200 of meals and
entertainment expenses that C deducts
in computing net income for financial
accounting purposes. All $200 of the
meals and entertainment expenses is
subject to the 50% limitation under
section 274(n). In its financial
statements, C treats the $50,000
depreciation and $100 of the meals and
entertainment as other costs in
computing cost of goods sold. C must
include on Form 8916-A and on
Schedule M-3, Part II, line 15, in column
(a), the $50,000 of depreciation and
$100 of meals and entertainment. C
must also include a temporary
difference of $20,000 in column (b), a
permanent difference of ($50) in column
(c), and $70,050 in column (d) ($70,000
depreciation and $50 meals and
entertainment expenses). In addition, C
must report on Part III, line 24, for its
2014 tax year income statement,
depreciation expense of $40,000 in
column (a), a temporary difference of
($10,000) in column (b), and $30,000 in
column (d); and on Part III, line 8, meals
and entertainment expense of $100 in
column (a), a permanent difference of
($50) in column (c), and $50 in column
(d). All other cost of goods sold items
would be added to the amounts
included on Part II, line 15, detailed in
this example and reported on Form
8916-A and on Part II, line 15, in the
appropriate columns.

Note. For tax years ending December
31, 2014, or later, any corporation filing
Form 1120S that (a) is required to file a
Schedule M-3 and has less than $50
million in total assets at the end of the
tax year or (b) is not required to file a

Schedule M-3 and voluntarily files a Schedule M-3, is not required to file Form 8916-A but may voluntarily do so.

Line 16. Sale Versus Lease (for Sellers and/or Lessors)

Note. Also see the instructions at Part III, line 28.

Asset transfer transactions with periodic payments characterized for financial accounting purposes as either a sale or a lease may, under some circumstances, be characterized as the opposite for tax purposes. If the transaction is treated as a lease, the seller/lessor reports the periodic payments as gross rental income and also reports depreciation expense or deduction. If the transaction is treated as a sale, the seller/lessor reports gross profit (sale price less cost of goods sold) from the sale of assets and reports the periodic payments as payments of principal and interest income.

On Part II, line 16, column (a), report the gross profit or gross rental income for financial accounting purposes for all sale or lease transactions that must be given the opposite characterization for U.S. income tax purposes. On Part II, line 16, column (d), report the gross profit or gross rental income for federal income tax purposes. Interest income amounts for such transactions must be reported on Part II, line 11, in column (a) or (d), as applicable. Depreciation expense for such transactions must be reported on Part III, line 24, in column (a) or (d), as applicable. Use columns (b) and (c) of Part II, lines 11 and 16, and Part III, line 24, as applicable to report the differences between column (a) and (d).

Example 16. Corporation M is a calendar year taxpayer that files and entirely completes Schedule M-3 for its 2014 tax year. M sells and leases property to customers. For financial accounting purposes, M accounts for each transaction as a sale. For U.S. income tax purposes, each of M's transactions must be treated as a lease. In its financial statements, M treats the difference in the financial accounting and the U.S. income tax treatment of these transactions as temporary. During 2014, M reports in its financial statements $1,000 of sales and $700 of cost of goods sold regarding 2014 lease transactions. M receives periodic payments of $500 in 2014 for these 2014 transactions and similar transactions from prior years and treats $400 as principal and $100 as interest income. For financial accounting purposes, M reports gross profit of $300

($1,000 − $700) and interest income of $100 from these transactions. For U.S. income tax purposes, M reports $500 of gross rental income (the periodic payments) and (based on other facts) $200 of depreciation deduction on the property. On its 2014 Schedule M-3, M must report on Part II, line 11, $100 in column (a), ($100) in column (b), and zero in column (d). In addition, M must report on Part II, line 16, $300 of gross profit in column (a), $200 in column (b), and $500 of gross rental income in column (d). Lastly, M must report on Part III, line 24, $200 in column (b) and (d).

Line 17. Section 481(a) Adjustments

With the exception of a section 481(a) adjustment that is required to be reported on Part II, line 10, for reportable transactions, any difference between an income or expense item attributable to an authorized (or unauthorized) change in method of accounting made for U.S. income tax purposes that results in a section 481(a) adjustment must be reported on Part II, line 17, regardless of whether a separate line for that income or expense item exists in Part II or Part III.

Example 17. Corporation N is a calendar year taxpayer that files and entirely completes Schedule M-3 for its 2014 tax year. N was depreciating certain fixed assets over an erroneous recovery period and, effective for its 2014 tax year, N receives IRS consent to change its method of accounting for the depreciable fixed assets and begins using the proper recovery period. The change in method of accounting results in a positive section 481(a) adjustment of $100,000 that is required to be spread over four tax years, beginning with the 2014 tax year. In its financial statements, N treats the section 481(a) adjustment as a temporary difference. N must report on Part II, line 17, $25,000 in columns (b) and (d) for its 2014 tax year and each of the subsequent three tax years (unless N is otherwise required to recognize the remainder of the 481(a) adjustment earlier). N must not report the section 481(a) adjustment on Part III, line 24.

Line 18. Unearned/Deferred Revenue

Report on line 18, column (a), amounts of revenues included in Part I, line 11, that were deferred from a prior financial accounting year. Report on line 18, column (d), amounts of revenues recognizable for U.S. income tax

purposes in the current tax year that are recognized for financial accounting purposes in a different year. Also report on line 18, column (d), any amount of revenues reported on line 18, column (a), that are recognizable for U.S. income tax purposes in the current tax year. Use columns (b) and (c) of line 18, as applicable, to report the differences between columns (a) and (d).

Line 18 must not be used to report income recognized from long-term contracts. Instead, use line 19.

Line 19. Income Recognition From Long-Term Contracts

Report on line 19 the amount of net income or loss for financial statement purposes (or books and records, if applicable) or U.S. income tax purposes for any contract accounted for under a long-term contract method of accounting.

Line 20. Original Issue Discount and Other Imputed Interest

Report on line 20 any amounts of original issue discount (OID) and other imputed interest. The term "original issue discount and other imputed interest" includes, but is not limited to:

1. The excess of a debt instrument's stated redemption price at maturity over its issue price, as determined under section 1273;

2. Amounts that are imputed interest on a deferred sales contract under section 483;

3. Amounts treated as interest or OID under the stripped bond rules under section 1286; and

4. Amounts treated as OID under the below-market interest rate rules under section 7872.

Line 21a. Income Statement Gain/Loss on Sale, Exchange, Abandonment, Worthlessness, or Other Disposition of Assets Other Than Inventory and Pass-Through Entities

Report on line 21a, column (a), all gains and losses on the disposition of assets except for (a) gains and losses on the disposition of inventory, and (b) gains and losses allocated to the corporation from a pass-through entity (for example, on Schedule K-1) that are included in the net income (loss) of the corporation reported on Part I, line 11. Reverse the amount reported in column (a) in column (b) or (c), as applicable. The corresponding gains and losses for U.S. income tax purposes are reported on

Part II, lines 21b through 21g, as applicable.

Line 21b. Gross Capital Gains From Schedule D, Excluding Amounts From Pass-Through Entities

Report on line 21b gross capital gains reported on Schedule D (Form 1120S), Capital Gains and Losses and Built-in Gains, or Form 8949, Sales and Other Dispositions of Capital Assets, excluding capital gains from pass-through entities, which must be reported on Part II, lines 7, 8, or 9, as applicable.

Line 21c. Gross Capital Losses From Schedule D, Excluding Amounts From Pass-Through Entities, Abandonment Losses, and Worthless Stock Losses

Report on line 21c gross capital losses reported on Schedule D (Form 1120S) or Form 8949, excluding capital losses from (a) pass-through entities, which must be reported on Part II, lines 7, 8, or 9, as applicable; (b) abandonment losses, which must be reported on Part II, line 21e; and (c) worthless stock losses, which must be reported on Part II, line 21f.

Line 21d. Net Gain/Loss Reported on Form 4797, Line 17, Excluding Amounts From Pass-Through Entities, Abandonment Losses, and Worthless Stock Losses

Report on line 21d the net gain or loss reported on line 17 of Form 4797, excluding amounts from (a) pass-through entities, which must be reported on Part II, lines 7, 8, or 9, as applicable; (b) abandonment losses, which must be reported on Part II, line 21e; and (c) worthless stock losses, which must be reported on Part II, line 21f. The amount reported on line 21d is the amount that would have been carried to line 17 of Form 4797 in the case of a corporation that is not an S corporation.

Note. Traders in securities or commodities that have made a valid election under section 475(f) to use the mark-to-market method to account for securities or commodities, see the instructions for Part II, line 14, earlier.

Line 21e. Abandonment Losses

Report on line 21e any abandonment losses, regardless of whether the loss is characterized as an ordinary loss or a capital loss.

Line 21f. Worthless Stock Losses

Report on line 21f any worthless stock loss, regardless of whether the loss is characterized as an ordinary loss or a capital loss. Attach a statement that separately states and adequately discloses each transaction that gives rise to a worthless stock loss and the amount of each loss.

Line 21g. Other Gain/Loss on Disposition of Assets Other Than Inventory

Report on line 21g any gains or losses from the sale or exchange of property other than inventory that are not reported on lines 21b through 21f.

Line 22. Other Income (Loss) Items With Differences

Separately state and adequately disclose on Part II, line 22, all items of income (loss) with differences that are not otherwise listed on Part II, lines 1 through 21. Attach a statement that itemizes the type of income (loss) and the amount of each item and provides a description that states the income (loss) name for book purposes for the amount recorded in column (a) and describes the adjustment being recorded in column (b) or (c). The entire description completes the tax description for the amount included in column (d) for each item separately stated on this line.

The attached statement should have five columns. The first column has the description for the next four columns. The second column is column (a) income (loss) per income statement, third column is column (b) temporary difference, the fourth column is column (c) permanent difference, and the fifth column is column (d) income (loss) per tax return. Every item listed on the attached statement for line 22 must always have columns (a) + (b) + (c) = (d). Each item with amounts in columns (a), (b), (c), and (d) will be totaled and included as one line on line 22.

If any "comprehensive income" as defined by Statement of Financial Accounting Standards (SFAS) No. 130 is reported on this line, describe the item(s) in detail. Examples of sufficiently detailed descriptions include "Foreign currency translation adjustments—comprehensive income" and "Gains and losses on available-for-sale securities—comprehensive income."

Line 23. Total Income (Loss) Items

Combine lines 1 through 22 and enter the total on line 23.

Note. Line 15, Cost of goods sold, columns (a) and (d), are negative amounts which will affect the totals entered on line 23.

Line 24. Total Expense/ Deduction Items

Report on Part II, line 24, columns (a) through (d), as applicable, the negative of the amounts reported on Part III, line 32, columns (a) through (d). For example, if Part III, line 32, column (a), reflects an amount of $1 million, then report on Part II, line 24, column (a), ($1 million). Similarly, if Part III, line 32, column (b), reflects an amount of ($50,000), then report on Part II, line 24, column (b), $50,000.

Line 25. Other Items With No Differences

If there is no difference between the financial accounting amount and the taxable amount of an entire item of income, gain, loss, expense, or deduction and the item is not described or included in Part II, lines 1 through 22, or Part III, lines 1 through 31, report the entire amount of the item in columns (a) and (d) of line 25. If a portion of an item of income, loss, expense, or deduction has a difference and a portion of the item does not have a difference, do not report any portion of the item on line 25. Instead, report the entire amount of the item (that is, both the portion with a difference and the portion without a difference) on the applicable line of Part II, lines 1 through 22, or Part III, lines 1 through 31. See *Example 10*, earlier.

Part III. Reconciliation of Net Income (Loss) per Income Statement of the Corporation With Total Income (Loss) per Return—Expense/ Deduction Items

Note. Expense amounts that reduce financial accounting income must be reported on Part III, column (a), as positive amounts. Deduction amounts that reduce taxable income must be reported on Part III, column (d), as positive amounts. Amounts reported on Part II, line 24, must be the negative of the amounts reported on Part III, line 32.

Lines 1 Through 6. Income Tax Expense

If the corporation does not distinguish between current and deferred income tax expense in its financial statements (or its books and records, if applicable), report income tax expense as current income tax expense using lines 1, 3, and 5, as applicable.

Line 7. Equity-Based Compensation

Report on line 7 any amounts for equity-based compensation or consideration that are reflected as expense for financial accounting purposes (column (a)) or deducted in the U.S. income tax return (column (d)) other than amounts reportable elsewhere on Schedule M-3, Parts II and III. Examples of amounts reportable on line 7 include payments attributable to stock options (including incentive stock options and nonqualified stock options), employee stock purchase plans (ESPPs), phantom stock options, phantom stock units, stock warrants, stock appreciation rights, and restricted stock, regardless of whether such payments are made to employees or non-employees, or as payment for property or compensation for services.

Line 8. Meals and Entertainment

Report on line 8, column (a), any amounts paid or accrued by the corporation during the tax year for meals, beverages, and entertainment that are accounted for in financial accounting income, regardless of the classification, nomenclature, or terminology used for such amounts, and regardless of how or where such amounts are classified in the corporation's financial income statement or the income and expense accounts maintained in the corporation's books and records. Report only amounts not otherwise reportable elsewhere on Schedule M-3, Parts II and III (for example, Part II, line 15).

Line 9. Fines and Penalties

Report on line 9 any fines or similar penalties paid to a government or other authority for the violation of any law for which fines or penalties are assessed. All fines and penalties expensed in financial accounting income (paid or accrued) must be included on this line 9, column (a), regardless of the government or other authority that imposed the fines or penalties, regardless of whether the fines and penalties are civil or criminal, regardless of the classification, nomenclature, or terminology used for the fines or penalties by the imposing authority in its actions or documents, and regardless of how or where the fines or penalties are classified in the corporation's financial income statement or the income and expense accounts maintained in the corporation's books and records. Also report on line 9, column (a), the reversal of any overaccrual of any amount described in this paragraph. See section 162(f) for additional guidance.

Report on line 9, column (d), any such amounts as described in the preceding paragraph that are includible in taxable income, regardless of the financial accounting period in which such amounts were or are included in financial accounting net income. Complete columns (b) and (c) as appropriate.

Do not report on this Part III, line 9, amounts required to be reported in accordance with instructions for Part III, line 10.

Do not report on this Part III, line 9, amounts recovered from insurers or any other indemnitors for any fines and penalties described above.

Line 10. Judgments, Damages, Awards, and Similar Costs

Report on line 10, column (a), the amount of any estimated or actual judgments, damages, awards, settlements, and similar costs, however named or classified, included in financial accounting income, regardless of whether the amount deducted was attributable to an estimate of future anticipated payments or actual payments. Also report on line 10, column (a), the reversal of any overaccrual of any amount described in this paragraph.

Report on line 10, column (d), any such amounts as are described in the preceding paragraph that are includible in taxable income, regardless of the financial accounting period in which such amounts were or are included in financial accounting net income. Complete columns (b) and (c) as appropriate.

Do not report on this Part III, line 10, amounts required to be reported in accordance with instructions for Part III, line 9.

Do not report on this Part III, line 10, amounts recovered from insurers or any other indemnitors for any judgments, damages, awards, or similar costs described above.

Line 11. Pension and Profit-Sharing

Report on line 11 any amounts attributable to the corporation's pension plans, profit-sharing plans, and any other retirement plans.

Line 12. Other Post-Retirement Benefits

Report on line 12 any amounts attributable to other post-retirement benefits not otherwise includible on Part III, line 11 (for example, retiree health and life insurance coverage, dental coverage, etc.).

Line 13. Deferred Compensation

Report on line 13, column (a), any compensation expense included in the net income (loss) amount reported in Part I, line 11, that is not deductible for U.S. income tax purposes in the current tax year and that was not reported elsewhere on Schedule M-3, column (a). Report on line 13, column (d), any compensation deductible in the current tax year that was not included in the net income (loss) amount reported in Part I, line 11, for the current tax year and that is not reportable elsewhere on Schedule M-3. For example, report originations and reversals of deferred compensation subject to section 409A on line 13.

Line 15. Charitable Contribution of Intangible Property

Report on line 15 any charitable contribution of intangible property, for example, contributions of:
- Intellectual property, patents (including any amounts of additional contributions allowable by virtue of income earned by donees subsequent to the year of donation), copyrights, trademarks;
- Securities (including stocks and their derivatives, stock options, and bonds);
- Conservation easements (including scenic easements or air rights);
- Railroad rights of way;
- Mineral rights; and
- Other intangible property.

Line 16. Current Year Acquisition or Reorganization Investment Banking Fees

Report on line 16 any investment banking fees paid or incurred in connection with a taxable or tax-free acquisition of property (for example, stock or assets) or a tax-free reorganization. Report on this line any

Investment banking fees incurred at any stage of the acquisition or reorganization process including, for example, fees paid or incurred to evaluate whether to investigate an acquisition, fees to conduct an actual investigation, and fees to consummate the acquisition. Also include on this line 16 investment banking fees incurred in connection with the liquidation of a subsidiary, a spin-off of a subsidiary, or an initial public stock offering.

Line 17. Current Year Acquisition or Reorganization Legal and Accounting Fees

Report on line 17 any legal and accounting fees paid or incurred in connection with a taxable or tax-free acquisition of property (for example, stock or assets) or tax-free reorganization. Report on this line any legal and accounting fees incurred at any stage of the acquisition or reorganization process including, for example, fees paid or incurred to evaluate whether to investigate an acquisition, fees to conduct an actual investigation, and fees to consummate the acquisition. Also include on this line legal and accounting fees incurred in connection with the liquidation of a subsidiary, a spin-off of a subsidiary, or an initial public stock offering.

Line 18. Current Year Acquisition/Reorganization Other Costs

Report on line 18 any other fees paid or incurred in connection with a taxable or tax-free acquisition of property (for example, stock or assets) or a tax-free reorganization not otherwise reportable on Schedule M-3 (for example, Part III, line 16 or 17). Report on this line any fees paid or incurred at any stage of the acquisition or reorganization process including, for example, fees paid or incurred to evaluate whether to investigate an acquisition, fees to conduct an actual investigation, and fees to consummate the acquisition. Also include on this line other acquisition/reorganization costs incurred in connection with the liquidation of a subsidiary, a spin-off of a subsidiary, or an initial public stock offering.

Line 19. Amortization/Impairment of Goodwill

Report on line 19 amortization of goodwill or amounts attributable to the impairment of goodwill.

Line 20. Amortization of Acquisition, Reorganization, and Start-Up Costs

Report on line 20 amortization of acquisition, reorganization, and start-up costs. For purposes of columns (b), (c), and (d), include amounts amortizable under section 167, 195, or 248.

Line 21. Other Amortization or Impairment Write-Offs

Report on line 21 any amortization or impairment write-offs not otherwise includible on Schedule M-3.

Line 22.

When using this line to figure amounts on other tax forms or worksheets, this line should be considered to be zero.

Line 23a. Depletion—Oil & Gas

Report on line 23a, column (a), any oil and gas depletion included on Part I, line 11.

Line 23b. Depletion—Other than Oil & Gas

Report on line 23b any depletion expense/deduction other than oil and gas that is not required to be reported elsewhere on Schedule M-3 (for example, on Part II, line 7, 8, 9, or 15).

Line 24. Depreciation

Report on line 24 any depreciation expense that is not required to be reported elsewhere on Schedule M-3 (for example, on Part II, line 7, 8, 9, or 15).

Line 25. Bad Debt Expense

Report on line 25, column (a), any amounts attributable to an allowance for uncollectible accounts receivable or actual write-offs of accounts receivable included on Part I, line 11. Report in column (d) the amount of bad debt expense deductible for federal income tax purposes under section 166.

Line 26. Interest Expense

Attach Form 8916-A. Complete Part III and enter the amounts shown on line 5, columns (a) through (d), on Schedule M-3, line 27, columns (a) through (d), as applicable.

Note. For tax years ending December 31, 2014, or later, any corporation filing Form 1120S that (a) is required to file a Schedule M-3 and has less than $50 million in total assets at the end of the tax year or (b) is not required to file a Schedule M-3 and voluntarily files a Schedule M-3, is not required to file Form 8916-A but may voluntarily do so.

Report on Part III, line 26, column (a), the total amount of interest expense included on Part I, line 11, and report on Part III, line 26, column (d), the total amount of interest deduction included on Form 1120S, Schedule K, line 18, that is not required to be reported elsewhere on Schedule M-3. In columns (b) or (c), as applicable, include any adjustments for any amounts treated for U.S. income tax purposes as interest deduction that are treated as some other form of expense for financial accounting purposes, or vice versa. For example, adjustments to interest expense/deduction resulting from adjustments made in accordance with the instructions for Part III, line 28, should be made in columns (b) and (c), as applicable, of this line 26.

Do not report on Form 8916-A and on line 26 amounts reported in accordance with the instructions for Part II, lines 7, 8, 9, and 10.

Line 27. Corporate Owned Life Insurance Premiums

Report on line 27 all amounts of insurance premiums attributable to any life insurance policy if the corporation is directly or indirectly a beneficiary under the policy or if the policy has a cash value. Report in column (d) the amount of the premiums that are deductible for federal income tax purposes.

Line 28. Purchase Versus Lease (for Purchasers and/or Lessees)

Note. Also see the instructions for sellers and/or lessors in the instructions for Part II, line 16.

Asset transfer transactions with periodic payments characterized for financial accounting purposes as either a purchase or a lease may, under some circumstances, be characterized as the opposite for tax purposes.

If a transaction is treated as a lease, the purchaser/lessee reports the periodic payments as gross rental expense. If the transaction is treated as a purchase, the purchaser/lessee reports the periodic payments as payments of principal and interest and also reports depreciation expense or deduction regarding the purchased asset.

Report in column (a) gross rent expense for a transaction treated as a lease for financial accounting purposes but as a sale for U.S. income tax purposes. Report in column (d), gross rental deductions for a transaction treated as a lease for U.S. income tax purposes but as a purchase for financial accounting purposes. Report interest expense for such transactions on Part III, line 26, in column (a) or (d), as applicable. Report depreciation expense or deductions for such transactions on Part III, line 24, in column (a) or (d), as applicable. Use columns (b) and (c) of Part III, lines 24, 26, and 28, as applicable, to report the differences between column (a) and (d) for such recharacterized transactions.

Example 18. U.S. Corporation X is a calendar-year taxpayer that files and entirely completes Schedule M-3 for its 2014 tax year. X acquired property in a transaction that, for financial accounting purposes, X treats as a lease. Because of its terms, the transaction is treated for U.S. income tax purposes as a purchase and X must treat the periodic payments it makes partially as payment of principal and partially as payment of interest. In its financial statements, X treats the difference between the financial accounting and U.S. income tax treatment of this transaction as a temporary difference. During 2014, X reports in its financial statements $1,000 of gross rental expense that, for U.S. income tax purposes, is recharacterized as a $700 payment of principal and a $300 payment of interest, accompanied by a depreciation deduction of $1,200 (based on other facts). On its 2014 Schedule M-3, X must report the following on Part III, line 28: column (a), $1,000, its financial accounting gross rental expense; column (b), ($1,000); and column (d), zero. On Part III, line 26, X reports zero in column (a) and $300 in columns (b) and (d) for the interest deduction. On Part III, line 24, X reports zero in column (a) and $1,200 in columns (b) and (d) for the depreciation deduction.

Line 29. Research and Development Costs

Report in column (a) the amount of expenses included in net income reported on Part I, line 11, that are related to research and development expense. Report in column (d) the amount of deductions included in Form 1120S, line 21, and/or separately reported on Form 1120S, Schedule K, that are recognized and reported as Section 174 research and experimental expenditures consistent with the corporation's adopted method of accounting for such expenditures. In column (c), as applicable, include any adjustments for any amounts treated for U.S. income tax purposes as research or experimental expenditures that are

treated as some other form of expense for financial accounting purposes, or vice versa. Report any difference in timing recognition in column (b). For example, if the taxpayer's financial accounting method does not specify otherwise, column (b) adjustments include adjustments for timing differences between financial and tax accounting for: (1) deferral and amortization of research expenditures, (2) reduction of section 174 expenditures under section 280C or section 482, (3) costs attributable to obtaining a patent, (4) research in social sciences, and (5) cost elements for property of a character subject to depreciation.

Section 174 provides two methods for the treatment of research and experimental expenditures paid or incurred by a taxpayer in connection with the taxpayer's trade or business. These expenditures may be treated as expenses not chargeable to a capital account and deducted in the year in which they are paid or incurred, or they may be deferred and amortized.

Example 19. Corporation X is a calendar year taxpayer that files and entirely completes Schedule M-3 for its 2014 tax year. During 2014, X incurred $100,000 of research and development costs that X recognized as an expense in its financial statements. Also, X incurred $20,000 in attorney fees in obtaining a patent application that X capitalized and amortized in its financial statements. X recognized a $2,000 amortization deduction. In compliance with its adopted method of accounting under section 174, X deducts research and experimental expenditures for U.S. income tax purposes. Accordingly, X must report $100,000 in column (a), $20,000 in column (b), and $120,000 in column (d). X must also report $2,000 in column (a), ($2,000) in column (b), and $0 in column (d) on Part III, line 21.

Example 20. Assume the same facts as *Example 19* except Corporation X elected to capitalize and amortize its research and expenditures over 60 months for all its research programs for U.S. tax purposes. X first realized benefits from such expenditures on August 1. Accordingly, X must report $100,000 in column (a), a temporary difference of ($90,000) ($20,000 less ($120,000/60 months X 55 months)) in column (b), and $10,000 in column (d).

Example 21. Corporation X is a calendar year taxpayer that files and entirely completes Schedule M-3 for its 2014 tax year. X adopted the current

expense method for research and experimental expenditures for U.S. income tax purposes. During 2014, X incurred $50,000 of research and development costs that X recognized as an expense in its financial statements. Also, X undertook to develop a new machine for its business. X expended $30,000 on the project of which $10,000 represents actual costs of material, labor, and component cost to construct the machine, and $20,000 represents research costs not attributable to the machine itself. X capitalized all costs of $30,000 related to the machine and recognized $6,000 of depreciation expense in its financial statements. X's depreciation expense on the $10,000 of costs related to the machine itself was $2,000 for U.S. income tax purposes. Accordingly, X must report $50,000 in column (a), $20,000 (research costs which are not attributable to the machine itself) in column (b), and $70,000 in column (d). X must also report $6,000 in column (a), ($4,000) in column (b), and $2,000 in column (d) on Part III, line 24.

Example 22. Corporation X is a calendar year taxpayer that files and entirely completes Schedule M-3 for its 2014 tax year. During 2014, X incurred $10,000 of research and development costs related to social sciences that it recognized as an expense in its financial statements. X adopted the current expense method for research and experimental expenditures for U.S. income tax purposes. Because such costs are not allowable costs under section 174, X must report $10,000 in column (a), permanent difference ($10,000) in column (c), and $0 in column (d). If such costs are otherwise deductible for U.S. income tax purposes, X must report this item of expense on Part III, line 31.

Example 23. Corporation X is a calendar year taxpayer that files and entirely completes Schedule M-3 for its 2014 tax year. During 2014, X paid $75,000 to acquire or in-license intangible assets under a collaborative arrangement with another company that X recognized as a research and development expense in its financial statements. X adopted the current expense method for research and experimental expenditures for U.S. income tax purposes. Because payments made to acquire rights to a product or technology are excluded costs from the definition of research and experimental expenditures, X must report $75,000 in column (a), ($75,000) in column (c), and $0 in column (d). X must report any amortization otherwise allowable related to the payments on Part III, line 21.

Line 30. Section 118 Exclusion

Report on line 30 any inducements received in the current year and treated as contributions to the capital of a corporation by a non-shareholder. Report in column (a) any income amount as a negative number and any expense amount as a positive number.

Corporations must identify on an accompanying statement referencing line 30 the fair market value of land or other property (including cash) provided to the corporation by any non-shareholder, including a governmental unit or civic group, as an inducement, or for any other purpose. Include inducements for the corporation to locate its business in a particular state, municipality, community, or locality for the purpose of enabling the corporation to expand its existing operating facilities, including corporate headquarters, distribution center(s), or factory(ies) ("inducements").

On the accompanying statement also identify any inducements that include refundable or transferable tax credits, including transferable credits that were sold.

The statement must separately state, adequately disclose, and identify all of the dollar amounts summarized by this line. An accompanying statement is required even if there are no dollar amounts reported on line 30.

Line 31. Other Expense/ Deduction Items With Differences

Separately state and adequately disclose on Part III, line 31, all items of expense/deduction that are not otherwise listed on Part III, lines 1 through 30.

Attach a statement that describes and itemizes the type of expense/ deduction and the amount of each item, and provides a description that states the expense/deduction name for book purposes for the amount recorded in column (a) and describes the adjustment being recorded in column (b) or (c). The entire description completes the tax description for the amount included in column (d) for each item separately stated on this line.

The statement of details attached to the Schedule M-3 for line 31 must

separately state and adequately disclose the nature and amount of the expense related to each reserve and/or contingent liability. The appropriate level of disclosure depends upon each taxpayer's operational activity and the nature of its accounting records. For example, if a corporation's net income amount reported in the income statement includes anticipated expenses for a discontinued operation as a single amount, and its general ledger or other books, records, and work papers provide details for the anticipated expenses under more explanatory and defined categories, such as employee termination costs, lease cancellation costs, loss on sale of equipment, etc., a supporting statement that lists those categories of expenses and their details will satisfy the requirement to separately state and adequately disclose. In order to separately state and adequately disclose the employee termination costs, it is not required that an anticipated termination cost amount be listed for each employee, or that each asset (or category of asset) be listed along with the anticipated loss on disposition.

The attached statement should have five columns. The first column has the description for the next four columns. The second column is column (a) expense per income statement, the third column is column (b) temporary difference, the fourth column is column (c) permanent difference, and the fifth column is column (d) deduction per tax return. Every item listed on the attached statement for line 31 must always have columns (a) + (b) + (c) = (d). Each item with amounts in columns (a), (b), (c), and (d) will be totaled and included as one line on line 31.

Comprehensive income. If any "comprehensive income" as defined by SFAS No. 130 is reported on this line, describe the item(s) in detail as, for example, "Foreign currency translation adjustments—comprehensive income" and "Gains and losses on available-for-sale securities—comprehensive income."

Reserves and contingent liabilities. Report on line 31 amounts related to the change in each reserve or contingent liability that is not required to be reported elsewhere on Schedule M-3. For example: (1) amounts relating to changes in reserves for litigation must be reported on Part III, line 10; and (2) amounts relating to changes in reserves for uncollectible accounts receivable

must be reported on Part III, line 25. See *Example 8*, *Example 9*, and *Example 24*.

Report on line 31, the amortization of various items of prepaid expense, such as prepaid subscriptions and license fees, prepaid insurance, etc.

Report on line 31, column (a), expenses included in net income reported on Part I, line 11, that are related to reserves and contingent liabilities. Report on line 31, column (d), amounts related to liabilities for reserves and contingent liabilities that are deductible in the current tax year for U.S. income tax purposes. Examples of reserves that are allowed for book purposes, but not for tax purposes, include warranty reserves, restructuring reserves, reserves for discontinued operations, and reserves for acquisitions and dispositions. Only report on line 31 items that are not required to be reported elsewhere on Schedule M-3, Parts II and III.

Example 24. Corporation Q is a calendar year taxpayer that files and entirely completes Schedule M-3 for its 2014 tax year. On July 1 of each year, Q has a fixed liability for its annual insurance premiums on its home office building that provides a 12-month coverage period beginning July 1 through June 30. In addition, Q historically prepays 12 months of advertising expense on July 1. On July 1, 2014, Q prepays its insurance premium of $500,000 and advertising expenses of $800,000. For financial accounting purposes, Q capitalizes and amortizes the prepaid insurance and advertising over 12 months. For U.S. income tax purposes, Q deducts the insurance premium when paid and amortizes the advertising over the 12-month period. In its financial statements, Q treats the differences attributable to the financial statement treatment and U.S. income tax treatment of the prepaid insurance and advertising as temporary differences.

Q also has a legal expense reserve where $300,000 was expensed for financial accounting purposes and a ($100,000) temporary difference was calculated to arrive at the income tax deduction of $200,000. The statement attached to Q's return for Part III, line 31, must be separately stated and adequately disclosed as shown below.

Line 31—Example 24
Statement Concerning Other Expense/Deduction Items With Differences

Description	Column (a) Expense per Income Statement	Column (b) Temporary Difference	Column (c) Permanent Difference	Column (d) Deduction per Tax Return
Prepaid insurance premium expensed not capitalized	$250,000	$250,000	-0-	$500,000
Legal expense reserve	$300,000	($100,000)	-0-	$200,000
Total line 31	**$550,000**	**$150,000**	**-0-**	**$700,000**

Line 32. Total Expense/Deduction Items

Report on Part II, line 24, columns (a) though (d), as applicable, the negative of the amounts reported on Part III, line 32, columns (a) through (d), as applicable. Report positive amounts as negative and negative amounts as positive. For example, if Part III, line 32, column (a), reflects an amount of $1 million, then report on Part II, line 24, column (a), ($1 million). Similarly, if Part III, line 32, column (b), reflects an amount of ($50,000), then report on Part II, line 24, column (b), $50,000.

671113

Schedule K-1
(Form 1120S)
Department of the Treasury
Internal Revenue Service

2014

For calendar year 2014, or tax
year beginning _____, 2014
ending _____, 20_____

Shareholder's Share of Income, Deductions,
Credits, etc.
► See back of form and separate instructions.

Part I	Information About the Corporation

A Corporation's employer identification number

B Corporation's name, address, city, state, and ZIP code

C IRS Center where corporation filed return

Part II	Information About the Shareholder

D Shareholder's identifying number

E Shareholder's name, address, city, state, and ZIP code

F Shareholder's percentage of stock
ownership for tax year . . . . _____ %

For IRS Use Only

Part III	Shareholder's Share of Current Year Income, Deductions, Credits, and Other Items

1	Ordinary business income (loss)	13	Credits
2	Net rental real estate income (loss)		
3	Other net rental income (loss)		
4	Interest income		
5a	Ordinary dividends		
5b	Qualified dividends	14	Foreign transactions
6	Royalties		
7	Net short-term capital gain (loss)		
8a	Net long-term capital gain (loss)		
8b	Collectibles (28%) gain (loss)		
8c	Unrecaptured section 1250 gain		
9	Net section 1231 gain (loss)		
10	Other income (loss)	15	Alternative minimum tax (AMT) items
11	Section 179 deduction	16	Items affecting shareholder basis
12	Other deductions		
		17	Other information

* See attached statement for additional information.

This list identifies the codes used on Schedule K-1 for all shareholders and provides summarized reporting information for shareholders who file Form 1040. For detailed reporting and filing information, see the separate Shareholder's Instructions for Schedule K-1 and the instructions for your income tax return.

1. Ordinary business income (loss). Determine whether the income (loss) is passive or nonpassive and enter on your return as follows:

	Report on
Passive loss	See the Shareholder's Instructions
Passive income	Schedule E, line 28, column (g)
Nonpassive loss	Schedule E, line 28, column (h)
Nonpassive income	Schedule E, line 28, column (j)

2. Net rental real estate income (loss)   See the Shareholder's Instructions

3. Other net rental income (loss)

Net income	Schedule E, line 28, column (g)
Net loss	See the Shareholder's Instructions

4. Interest income	Form 1040, line 8a
5a. Ordinary dividends	Form 1040, line 9a
5b. Qualified dividends	Form 1040, line 9b
6. Royalties	Schedule E, line 4
7. Net short-term capital gain (loss)	Schedule D, line 5
8a. Net long-term capital gain (loss)	Schedule D, line 12
8b. Collectibles (28%) gain (loss)	28% Rate Gain Worksheet, line 4 (Schedule D instructions)
8c. Unrecaptured section 1250 gain	See the Shareholder's Instructions
9. Net section 1231 gain (loss)	See the Shareholder's Instructions

10. Other income (loss)

Code
A	Other portfolio income (loss)	See the Shareholder's Instructions
B	Involuntary conversions	See the Shareholder's Instructions
C	Sec. 1256 contracts & straddles	Form 6781, line 1
D	Mining exploration costs recapture	See Pub. 535
E	Other income (loss)	See the Shareholder's Instructions

11. Section 179 deduction   See the Shareholder's Instructions

12. Other deductions
A	Cash contributions (50%)	
B	Cash contributions (30%)	
C	Noncash contributions (50%)	
D	Noncash contributions (30%)	See the Shareholder's Instructions
E	Capital gain property to a 50% organization (30%)	
F	Capital gain property (20%)	
G	Contributions (100%)	
H	Investment interest expense	Form 4952, line 1
I	Deductions—royalty income	Schedule E, line 19
J	Section 59(e)(2) expenditures	See the Shareholder's Instructions
K	Deductions—portfolio (2% floor)	Schedule A, line 23
L	Deductions—portfolio (other)	Schedule A, line 28
M	Preproductive period expenses	See the Shareholder's Instructions
N	Commercial revitalization deduction from rental real estate activities	See Form 8582 instructions
O	Reforestation expense deduction	See the Shareholder's Instructions
P	Domestic production activities information	See Form 8903 instructions
Q	Qualified production activities income	Form 8903, line 7b
R	Employer's Form W-2 wages	Form 8903, line 17
S	Other deductions	See the Shareholder's Instructions

13. Credits
A	Low-income housing credit (section 42(j)(5)) from pre-2008 buildings	
B	Low-income housing credit (other) from pre-2008 buildings	
C	Low-income housing credit (section 42(j)(5)) from post-2007 buildings	See the Shareholder's Instructions
D	Low-income housing credit (other) from post-2007 buildings	
E	Qualified rehabilitation expenditures (rental real estate)	
F	Other rental real estate credits	
G	Other rental credits	
H	Undistributed capital gains credit	Form 1040, line 73, box a
I	Biofuel producer credit	
J	Work opportunity credit	
K	Disabled access credit	See the Shareholder's Instructions
L	Empowerment zone employment credit	
M	Credit for increasing research activities	

Code		Report on
N	Credit for employer social security and Medicare taxes	
O	Backup withholding	See the Shareholder's Instructions
P	Other credits	

14. Foreign transactions
A	Name of country or U.S. possession	
B	Gross income from all sources	Form 1116, Part I
C	Gross income sourced at shareholder level	

Foreign gross income sourced at corporate level
D	Passive category	
E	General category	Form 1116, Part I
F	Other	

Deductions allocated and apportioned at shareholder level
G	Interest expense	Form 1116, Part I
H	Other	Form 1116, Part I

Deductions allocated and apportioned at corporate level to foreign source income
I	Passive category	
J	General category	Form 1116, Part I
K	Other	

Other information
L	Total foreign taxes paid	Form 1116, Part II
M	Total foreign taxes accrued	Form 1116, Part II
N	Reduction in taxes available for credit	Form 1116, line 12
O	Foreign trading gross receipts	Form 8873
P	Extraterritorial income exclusion	Form 8873
Q	Other foreign transactions	See the Shareholder's Instructions

15. Alternative minimum tax (AMT) items
A	Post-1986 depreciation adjustment	
B	Adjusted gain or loss	See the
C	Depletion (other than oil & gas)	Shareholder's
D	Oil, gas, & geothermal—gross income	Instructions and the Instructions for
E	Oil, gas, & geothermal—deductions	Form 6251
F	Other AMT items	

16. Items affecting shareholder basis
A	Tax-exempt interest income	Form 1040, line 8b
B	Other tax-exempt income	
C	Nondeductible expenses	See the Shareholder's
D	Distributions	Instructions
E	Repayment of loans from shareholders	

17. Other information
A	Investment income	Form 4952, line 4a
B	Investment expenses	Form 4952, line 5
C	Qualified rehabilitation expenditures (other than rental real estate)	See the Shareholder's Instructions
D	Basis of energy property	See the Shareholder's Instructions
E	Recapture of low-income housing credit (section 42(j)(5))	Form 8611, line 8
F	Recapture of low-income housing credit (other)	Form 8611, line 8
G	Recapture of investment credit	See Form 4255
H	Recapture of other credits	See the Shareholder's Instructions
I	Look-back interest—completed long-term contracts	See Form 8697
J	Look-back interest—income forecast method	See Form 8866
K	Dispositions of property with section 179 deductions	
L	Recapture of section 179 deduction	
M	Section 453(l)(3) information	
N	Section 453A(c) information	
O	Section 1260(b) information	
P	Interest allocable to production expenditures	See the Shareholder's Instructions
Q	CCF nonqualified withdrawals	
R	Depletion information—oil and gas	
S	Reserved	
T	Section 108(i) information	
U	Net investment income	
V	Other information	

Shareholder's Instructions for Schedule K-1 (Form 1120S)

Shareholder's Share of Income, Deductions, Credits, etc.
(For Shareholder's Use Only)

Section references are to the Internal Revenue Code unless otherwise noted.

Future Developments

For the latest information about developments related to Schedule K-1 (Form 1120S) and its instructions, such as legislation enacted after they were published, go to www.irs.gov/form1120s.

General Instructions

Purpose of Schedule K-1

The corporation uses Schedule K-1 to report your share of the corporation's income (reduced by any tax the corporation paid on the income), deductions, credits, etc. Keep it for your records. Do not file it with your tax return unless backup withholding is reported in box 13 using code O. (See the instructions for Code O. Backup withholding, later.) The corporation files a copy of Schedule K-1 with the IRS.

For your protection, Schedule K-1 may show only the last four digits of your identifying number (social security number (SSN), etc.). However, the corporation has reported your complete identifying number to the IRS.

You may be liable for tax on your share of the corporation's income, whether or not distributed. Include your share on your tax return if a return is required. Use these instructions to help you report the items shown on Schedule K-1 on your tax return.

Your share of S corporation income is not self-employment income and it is not subject to self-employment tax.

The amount of loss and deduction you may claim on your tax return may be less than the amount reported on Schedule K-1. It is the shareholder's

responsibility to consider and apply any applicable limitations. See Limitations on Losses, Deductions, and Credits, later, for more information.

Schedule K-1 does not show actual dividend distributions the corporation made to you. The corporation must report such amounts totaling $10 or more for the calendar year on Form 1099-DIV, Dividends and Distributions.

Inconsistent Treatment of Items

Generally, you must report corporate items shown on your Schedule K-1 (and any attached statements) the same way that the corporation treated the items on its return.

If the treatment on your original or amended return is inconsistent with the corporation's treatment, or if the corporation has not filed a return, file Form 8082, Notice of Inconsistent Treatment or Administrative Adjustment Request (AAR), with your original or amended return to identify and explain any inconsistency (or to note that a corporate return has not been filed).

If you are required to file Form 8082 but do not do so, you may be subject to the accuracy-related penalty. This penalty is in addition to any tax that results from making your amount or treatment of the item consistent with that shown on the corporation's return. Any deficiency that results from making the amounts consistent may be assessed immediately.

Errors

If you believe the corporation has made an error on your Schedule K-1, notify the corporation and ask for a corrected Schedule K-1. Do not change any items on your copy of Schedule K-1. Be sure that the

corporation sends a copy of the corrected Schedule K-1 to the IRS. If you are unable to reach agreement with the corporation regarding the inconsistency, file Form 8082.

Sale of S Corporation Stock

Gain or loss from the disposition of your S corporation stock is generally net investment income under section 1411 and may be subject to the net investment income tax. See Form 8960, Net Investment Income Tax—Individuals, Estates, and Trusts, and its instructions for information about how to figure and report the tax.

International Boycotts

Every corporation that had operations in, or related to, a boycotting country, company, or a national of a boycotting country must file Form 5713, International Boycott Report.

If the corporation cooperated with an international boycott, it must give you a copy of its Form 5713. You must file your own Form 5713 to report the corporation's activities and any other boycott operations that you may have. You may lose certain tax benefits if the corporation participated in, or cooperated with, an international boycott. See Form 5713 and its instructions for details.

Elections

Generally, the corporation decides how to figure taxable income from its operations. However, certain elections are made by you separately on your income tax return and not by the corporation. These elections are made under the following code sections.
• Section 59(e) (deduction of certain qualified expenditures ratably over the period of time specified in that

section). For details, see the instructions for code J in box 12.

- Section 263A(d) (preproductive expenses). See the instructions for code M in box 12.
- Section 617 (deduction and recapture of certain mining exploration expenditures).
- Section 901 (foreign tax credit).

Additional Information

For more information on the treatment of S corporation income, deductions, credits, etc., see Pub. 535, Business Expenses; Pub. 550, Investment Income and Expenses; and Pub. 925, Passive Activity and At-Risk Rules.

To get forms and publications, see the instructions for your tax return or visit the IRS website at IRS.gov.

Limitations on Losses, Deductions, and Credits

There are potential limitations on corporate losses that you can deduct on your return. These limitations and the order in which you must apply them are as follows: the basis rules, the at-risk limitations, and the passive activity limitations. These limitations are discussed below.

Other limitations may apply to specific deductions (for example, the section 179 expense deduction). Generally, specific limitations apply before the basis, at-risk, and passive loss limitations.

Basis Rules

Generally, the deduction for your share of aggregate losses and deductions reported on Schedule K-1 is limited to the basis of your stock (determined with regard to distributions received during the tax year) and loans from you to the corporation. For details and exceptions, see section 1366(d). The basis of your stock is generally figured at the end of the corporation's tax year. Any losses and deductions not allowed this year because of the basis limit can be carried forward indefinitely and deducted in a later year subject to the basis limit for that year.

You are responsible for keeping the information needed to figure the basis of your stock in the corporation. Schedule K-1 provides information to help you figure your stock basis at the end of each corporate tax year. The

basis of your stock (generally, its cost) is adjusted as follows and, except as noted, in the order listed. In addition, basis may be adjusted under other provisions of the Internal Revenue Code. You can generally use the Worksheet for Figuring a Shareholder's Stock Basis to figure your aggregate stock basis.

1. Basis is increased by (a) all income (including tax-exempt income) reported on Schedule K-1 and (b) the excess of the deduction for depletion (other than oil and gas depletion) over the basis of the property subject to depletion.

 You must report on your return (if you are required to file one) any amount required to be included in gross income for it to increase your basis.

 Basis is not increased by income from discharge of your indebtedness in the S corporation (nor by any amount included in income with respect to clean renewable energy or (for bonds issued before October 4, 2008) qualified zone academy bonds).

2. Basis is decreased by (a) property distributions (including cash) made by the corporation reported on Schedule K-1, box 16, code D, minus (b) the amount of such distributions in excess of the basis in your stock.

3. Basis is decreased by (a) nondeductible expenses and (b) the depletion deduction for any oil and gas property held by the corporation, but only to the extent your share of the property's adjusted basis exceeds that deduction.

4. Basis is decreased by all deductible losses and deductions reported on Schedule K-1 adjusted, if the corporation made a charitable contribution of property, by subtracting your share of the property's fair market value and adding your share of the property's adjusted basis.

You may elect to decrease your basis under (4) prior to decreasing your basis under (3). If you make this election, any amount described under (3) that exceeds the basis of your stock and debt owed to you by the corporation is treated as an amount described under (3) for the following tax year.

To make the election, attach a statement to your timely filed original or amended return that states you agree to the carryover rule of Regulations section 1.1367-1(g) and the name of the S corporation to which the rule applies. Once made, the election applies to the year for which it is made and all future tax years for that S corporation, unless the IRS agrees to revoke your election.

The basis of each share of stock is increased or decreased (but not below zero) based on its *pro rata* share of the above adjustments. If the total decreases in basis attributable to a share exceed that share's basis, the excess reduces (but not below zero) the remaining bases of all other shares of stock in proportion to the remaining basis of each of those shares.

Basis of loans. The basis of your loans to the corporation is generally the balance the corporation owes you, adjusted for any reductions and restorations of loan basis (see the instructions for box 16, code E). Any amounts described in (3) and (4), earlier, not used to offset amounts in (1), earlier, or reduce your stock basis, are used to reduce your loan basis (to the extent of such basis prior to such reduction).

 When determining your basis in loans to the corporation, remember that:
- *Distributions do not reduce loan basis, and*
- *Loans that a shareholder guarantees or co-signs are not part of a shareholder's loan basis.*

See section 1367 and its regulations for more details.

Worksheet instructions. For lines 6 and 7, do not enter more than the aggregate sum of the preceding lines. Any excess of the amounts that would otherwise be entered on lines 6 and 7 without regard to this limit over the amounts actually entered on those lines is a reduction to your basis, if any, in loans you made to the corporation (to the extent of such basis). Any portion of the excess not used to reduce your basis in stock and loans is not deductible in the current year and is carried over to next year and subject to that year's

At-Risk Limitations

Generally, if you have (a) a loss or other deduction from any activity carried on as a trade or business or for the production of income by the corporation, and (b) amounts in the activity for which you are not at risk, you will have to complete Form 6198, At-Risk Limitations, to figure your allowable loss.

The at-risk rules generally limit the amount of loss and other deductions that you can claim to the amount you could actually lose in the activity. These losses and deductions include a loss on the disposition of assets and the section 179 expense deduction. However, if you acquired your stock before 1987, the at-risk rules do not apply to losses from an activity of holding real property placed in service before 1987 by the corporation. The activity of holding mineral property does not qualify for this exception. The corporation should identify on a statement attached to Schedule K-1 any losses that are not subject to the at-risk limitations.

Generally, you are not at risk for amounts such as the following.
• The basis of your stock in the corporation or the basis of your loans to the corporation if the cash or other property used to purchase the stock or make the loans was from a source (a) covered by nonrecourse indebtedness (except for certain qualified nonrecourse financing, as defined in section 465(b)(6)); (b) protected against loss by a guarantee, stop-loss agreement, or other similar arrangement; or (c) that is covered by indebtedness from a person who has an interest in the activity or from a person related to a person (except you) having such an interest, other than a creditor.
• Any cash or property contributed to a corporate activity, or your interest in the corporate activity, that is (a) covered by nonrecourse indebtedness (except for certain qualified nonrecourse financing, as defined in section 465(b)(6)); (b) protected against loss by a guarantee, stop-loss agreement, or other similar arrangement; or (c) that is covered by indebtedness from a person who has an interest in the activity or from a person related to a person (except

you) having such an interest, other than a creditor.

Any loss from a section 465 activity not allowed for this tax year will be treated as a deduction allocable to the activity in the next tax year.

You should get a separate statement of income, expenses, etc., for each activity from the corporation.

Passive Activity Limitations

Section 469 provides rules that limit the deduction of certain losses and credits. These rules apply to shareholders who:
• Are individuals, estates, or trusts; and
• Have a passive activity loss or credit for the tax year.

Generally, passive activities include:

1. Trade or business activities in which you did not materially participate, and

2. Activities that meet the definition of rental activities under Temporary Regulations section 1.469-1T(e)(3) and Regulations section 1.469-1(e)(3).

Passive activities do not include the following.

1. Trade or business activities in which you materially participated.

2. Rental real estate activities in which you materially participated if you were a real estate professional for the tax year. You were a **real estate**

Worksheet for Figuring a Shareholder's Stock Basis *Keep for Your Records*

1. Your stock basis at the beginning of the year .... 1._____

   Increases:

2. Money and your adjusted basis in property contributed to the corporation .... 2._____

3. Your share of the corporation's income (including tax-exempt income) reduced by any amount included in income with respect to clean renewable energy or (for bonds issued before October 4, 2008) qualified zone academy bonds .... 3._____

4. Other increases to basis, including your share of the excess of the deductions for depletion (other than oil and gas depletion) over the basis of the property subject to depletion .... 4._____

   Decreases:

5. Distributions of money and the fair market value of property (excluding dividend distributions reportable on Form 1099-DIV and distributions in excess of basis (the sum of lines 1 through 4)) .... 5. (_____)

6. Enter (a) your share of the corporation's nondeductible expenses and the depletion deduction for any oil and gas property held by the corporation (but only to the extent your share of the property's adjusted basis exceeds the depletion deduction); **or (b)** if the election under Regulations section 1.1367-1(g) applies, your share of the corporation's deductions and losses (include your entire share of the section 179 expense deduction even if your allowable section 179 expense deduction is smaller) adjusted, if the corporation made a charitable contribution of property as described in (4) under *Basis Rules* .... 6. (_____)

7. If the election under Regulations section 1.1367-1(g) applies, enter the amount from 6(a) above. Otherwise, enter the amount from 6(b) .... 7. (_____)

8. Enter the smaller of (a) the excess, as of the beginning of the tax year, of the amount you are owed for loans you made to the corporation over your basis in those loans; **or (b)** the sum of lines 1 through 7. This amount increases your loan basis .... 8. (_____)

9. Your stock basis in the corporation at the end of the year. Combine lines 1 through 8 .... 9._____

---

professional only if you met both of the following conditions.

a. More than half of the personal services you performed in trades or businesses were performed in real property trades or businesses in which you materially participated.

b. You performed more than 750 hours of services in real property trades or businesses in which you materially participated.

For purposes of this rule, each interest in rental real estate is a separate activity, unless you elect to treat all interests in rental real estate as one activity. For details on making this election, see the Instructions for Schedule E (Form 1040), Supplemental Income and Loss.

If you are married filing jointly, either you or your spouse must separately meet both (a) and (b) of the above conditions, without taking into account services performed by the other spouse.

A real property trade or business is any real property development, redevelopment, construction, reconstruction, acquisition, conversion, rental, operation, management, leasing, or brokerage trade or business. Services you performed as an employee are not treated as performed in a real property trade or business unless you owned more than 5% of the stock (or more than 5% of the capital or profits interest) in the employer.

3. The rental of a dwelling unit any shareholder used for personal purposes during the year for more than the greater of 14 days or 10% of the number of days that the residence was rented at fair rental value.

4. Activities of trading personal property for the account of owners of interests in the activities.

If you have a passive activity loss or credit, use Form 8582, Passive Activity Loss Limitations, to figure your allowable passive losses and Form 8582-CR, Passive Activity Credit Limitations, to figure your allowable passive credits. See the instructions for these forms for details.

If the corporation had more than one activity, it will attach a statement to your Schedule K-1 that identifies each activity (trade or business activity, rental real estate activity,

rental activity other than rental real estate, etc.) and specifies the income (loss), deductions, and credits from each activity.

Material participation. You must determine if you materially participated (a) in each trade or business activity held through the corporation and (b) if you were a real estate professional (defined earlier), in each rental real estate activity held through the corporation. All determinations of material participation are based on your participation during the corporation's tax year.

Material participation standards for shareholders who are individuals are listed below. Special rules apply to certain retired or disabled farmers and to the surviving spouses of farmers. See the Instructions for Form 8582 for details.

Individuals. If you are an individual, you materially participated in an activity only if one or more of the following apply.

1. You participated in the activity for more than 500 hours during the tax year.

2. Your participation in the activity for the tax year constituted substantially all the participation in the activity of all individuals (including individuals who are not owners of interests in the activity).

3. You participated in the activity for more than 100 hours during the tax year, and your participation in the activity for the tax year was not less than the participation in the activity of any other individual (including individuals who were not owners of interests in the activity) for the tax year.

4. The activity was a significant participation activity for the tax year, and you participated in all significant participation activities (including activities outside the corporation) during the year for more than 500 hours. A significant participation activity is any trade or business activity in which you participated for more than 100 hours during the year and in which you did not materially participate under any of the material participation tests (other than this test).

5. You materially participated in the activity for any 5 tax years

(whether or not consecutive) during the 10 tax years that immediately precede the tax year.

6. The activity was a personal service activity and you materially participated in the activity for any 3 tax years (whether or not consecutive) preceding the tax year. A personal service activity involves the performance of personal services in the fields of health, law, engineering, architecture, accounting, actuarial science, performing arts, consulting, or any other trade or business in which capital is not a material income-producing factor.

7. Based on all the facts and circumstances, you participated in the activity on a regular, continuous, and substantial basis during the tax year.

Work counted toward material participation. Generally, any work that you or your spouse does in connection with an activity held through an S corporation (where you own your stock at the time the work is done) is counted toward material participation. However, work in connection with the activity is not counted toward material participation if either of the following applies.

1. The work is not the type of work that owners of the activity would usually do and one of the principal purposes of the work that you or your spouse does is to avoid the passive loss or credit limitations.

2. You do the work in your capacity as an investor and you are not directly involved in the day-to-day operations of the activity. Examples of work done as an investor that would not count toward material participation include:

a. Studying and reviewing financial statements or reports on operations of the activity,

b. Preparing or compiling summaries or analyses of the finances or operations of the activity for your own use, and

c. Monitoring the finances or operations of the activity in a nonmanagerial capacity.

Effect of determination. Income (loss), deductions, and credits from an activity are nonpassive if you determine that:

- You materially participated in a trade or business activity of the corporation, or
- You were a real estate professional (defined earlier) in a rental real estate activity of the corporation.

If you determine that you did not materially participate in a trade or business activity of the corporation or if you have income (loss), deductions, or credits from a rental activity of the corporation (other than a rental real estate activity in which you materially participated as a real estate professional), the amounts from that activity are passive. Report passive income (losses), deductions, and credits as follows.

1. If you have an overall gain (the excess of income over deductions and losses, including any prior year unallowed loss) from a passive activity, report the income, deductions, and losses from the activity as indicated in these instructions.

2. If you have an overall loss (the excess of deductions and losses, including any prior year unallowed loss, over income) or credits from a passive activity, report the income, deductions, losses, and credits from all passive activities using the Instructions for Form 8582 or Form 8582-CR, to see if your deductions, losses, and credits are limited under the passive activity rules.

Special allowance for a rental real estate activity. If you actively participated in a rental real estate activity, you may be able to deduct up to $25,000 of the loss (or credit equivalent to a $25,000 deduction) from the activity from nonpassive income. This "special allowance" is an exception to the general rule disallowing losses in excess of income from passive activities. The special allowance is not available if you were married, file a separate return for the year, and did not live apart from your spouse at all times during the year.

Only individuals can actively participate in a rental real estate activity. However, a decedent's estate (including a qualified revocable trust for which a section 645 election has been made) is treated as actively participating for its tax years ending less than 2 years after the decedent's death, if the decedent would have satisfied the active participation requirement for the activity for the tax year the decedent died.

You are not considered to actively participate in a rental real estate activity if, at any time during the tax year, your interest (including your spouse's interest) in the activity was less than 10% (by value) of all interests in the activity.

Active participation is a less stringent requirement than material participation. You may be treated as actively participating if you participated, for example, in making management decisions or arranging for others to provide services (such as repairs) in a significant and bona fide sense. Management decisions that can count as active participation include approving new tenants, deciding rental terms, approving capital or repair expenditures, and other similar decisions.

Modified adjusted gross income limitation. The maximum special allowance that single individuals and married individuals filing a joint return can qualify for is $25,000. The maximum is $12,500 for married individuals who file separate returns and who lived apart at all times during the year. The maximum special allowance for which an estate can qualify is $25,000 reduced by the special allowance for which the surviving spouse qualifies.

If your modified adjusted gross income (defined below) is $100,000 or less ($50,000 or less if married filing separately), your loss is deductible up to the maximum special allowance referred to in the preceding paragraph. If your modified adjusted gross income is more than $100,000 (more than $50,000 if married filing separately), the special allowance is limited to 50% of the difference between $150,000 ($75,000 if married filing separately) and your modified adjusted gross income. When modified adjusted gross income is $150,000 or more ($75,000 or more if married filing separately), there is no special allowance.

Modified adjusted gross income is your adjusted gross income figured without taking into account the following amounts, if applicable.
- Any passive activity loss.

- Any rental real estate loss allowed under section 469(c)(7) to real estate professionals (defined earlier).
- Any overall loss from a publicly traded partnership.
- Any taxable social security or equivalent railroad retirement benefits.
- Any deductible contributions to an IRA or certain other qualified retirement plans under section 219.
- The domestic production activities deduction.
- The student loan interest deduction.
- The tuition and fees deduction.
- The deductible part of self-employment taxes.
- The exclusion from income of interest from Series EE or I U.S. Savings Bonds used to pay higher education expenses.
- The exclusion of amounts received under an employer's adoption assistance program.

Commercial revitalization deduction. The special $25,000 allowance for the commercial revitalization deduction from rental real estate activities is not subject to the active participation rules or modified adjusted gross income limits discussed above. See the instructions for box 12, code N for more information.

Special rules for certain other activities. If you have net income (loss), deductions, or credits from any activity to which special rules apply, the corporation will identify the activity and all amounts relating to it on Schedule K-1 or on an attached statement.

If you have net income subject to recharacterization under Temporary Regulations section 1.469-2T(f) and Regulations section 1.469-2(f), report such amounts according to the Instructions for Form 8582.

If you have net income (loss), deductions, or credits from either of the following activities, treat such amounts as nonpassive and report them as indicated in these instructions.

1. The rental of a dwelling unit any shareholder used for personal purposes during the year for more than the greater of 14 days or 10% of the number of days that the residence was rented at fair rental value.

2. Trading personal property for the account of owners of interests in the activity.

Self-charged interest. The corporation will report any "self-charged" interest income or expense that resulted from loans between you and the corporation (or between the corporation and another S corporation or partnership if both entities have the same owners with the same proportional interest in each entity). If there was more than one activity, the corporation will provide a statement allocating the interest income or expense with respect to each activity. The self-charged interest rules do not apply to your interest in the S corporation if the corporation made an election under Regulations section 1.469-7(g) to avoid the application of these rules. See the Instructions for Form 8582 for details.

Specific Instructions

Part III. Shareholder's Share of Current Year Income, Deductions, Credits, and Other Items

The amounts shown in boxes 1 through 17 reflect your share of income, loss, deductions, credits, etc., from corporate business or rental activities without reference to limitations on losses, credits, or other items that may have to be adjusted because of:

1. The adjusted basis of your stock and debt in the corporation,

2. The at-risk limitations,

3. The passive activity limitations, or

4. Any other limitations that must be taken into account at the shareholder level in figuring taxable income (for example, the section 179 expense limitation).

For information on these provisions, see _Limitations on Losses, Deductions, and Credits,_ earlier.

If you are an individual, and the above limitations do not apply to the amounts shown on your Schedule K-1, take the amounts shown and report them on the lines of your tax return as indicated in the summarized reporting information

shown on page 2 of the Schedule K-1. If any of the above limitations apply, adjust the amounts on Schedule K-1 before you report them on your return.

When applicable, the passive activity limitations on losses are applied after the limitations on losses for a shareholder's basis in stock and debt and the shareholder's at-risk amount.

The line numbers in the summarized reporting information on page 2 of Schedule K-1 are references to forms in use for calendar year 2014. If you file your tax return on a calendar year basis, but the corporation files a return for a fiscal year, report the amounts on your tax return for the year in which the corporation's fiscal year ends. For example, if the corporation's tax year ends in February 2015, report the amounts on your 2015 tax return.

If you have losses, deductions, or credits from a prior year that were not deductible or usable because of certain limitations, such as the basis rules or the at-risk limitations, take them into account in determining your income, loss, or credits for this year. However, except for passive activity losses and credits, do not combine the prior year amounts with any amounts shown on this Schedule K-1 to get a net figure to report on your return. Instead, report the amounts on your return on a year-by-year basis.

 If you have amounts other than those shown on Schedule K-1 to report on Schedule E (Form 1040), enter each item separately on Schedule E (Form 1040), line 28.

Codes. In box 10 and boxes 12 through 17, the corporation will identify each item by entering a code in the column to the left of the dollar amount entry space. These codes are identified on page 2 of Schedule K-1 and in these instructions.

Attached statements. The corporation will enter an asterisk (*) after the code, if any, in the column to the left of the dollar amount entry space for each item for which it has attached a statement providing additional information. For those informational items that cannot be reported as a single dollar amount, the corporation will enter an asterisk in

the left column and enter "STMT" in the dollar amount entry space to indicate the information is provided on an attached statement.

Income (Loss)

Box 1. Ordinary Business Income (Loss)

The amount reported in box 1 is your share of the ordinary income (loss) from trade or business activities of the corporation. Generally, where you report this amount on Form 1040 depends on whether the amount is from an activity that is a passive activity to you. If you are an individual shareholder filing a 2014 Form 1040, find your situation below and report your box 1 income (loss) as instructed after applying the basis and at-risk limitations on losses. If the corporation had more than one trade or business activity, it will attach a statement identifying the income or loss from each activity.

1. Report box 1 income (loss) from corporate trade or business activities in which you materially participated on Schedule E (Form 1040), line 28, column (h) or (j).

2. Report box 1 income (loss) from corporate trade or business activities in which you did not materially participate, as follows.

a. If income is reported in box 1, report the income on Schedule E (Form 1040), line 28, column (g).

b. If a loss is reported in box 1, follow the Instructions for Form 8582 to figure how much of the loss can be reported on Schedule E (Form 1040), line 28, column (f).

Box 2. Net Rental Real Estate Income (Loss)

Generally, the income (loss) reported in box 2 is a passive activity amount for all shareholders. However, the income (loss) in box 2 is not from a passive activity if you were a real estate professional (defined earlier) and you materially participated in the activity. If the corporation had more than one rental real estate activity, it will attach a statement identifying the income or loss from each activity.

If you are filing a 2014 Form 1040, use the following instructions to determine where to report a box 2 amount.

1. If you have a loss from a passive activity in box 2 and you meet all the following conditions, report the loss on Schedule E (Form 1040), line 28, column (f).

a. You actively participated in the corporate rental real estate activities. See *Special allowance for a rental real estate activity*, earlier.

b. Rental real estate activities with active participation were your only passive activities.

c. You have no prior year unallowed losses from these activities.

d. Your total loss from the rental real estate activities was not more than $25,000 (not more than $12,500 if married filing separately and you lived apart from your spouse all year).

e. If you are a married person filing separately, you lived apart from your spouse all year.

f. You have no current or prior year unallowed credits from a passive activity.

g. Your modified adjusted gross income was not more than $100,000 (not more than $50,000 if married filing separately and you lived apart from your spouse all year).

2. If you have a loss from a passive activity in box 2 and you do not meet all the conditions in (1) above, follow the Instructions for Form 8582 to figure how much of the loss you can report on Schedule E (Form 1040), line 28, column (f).

3. If you were a real estate professional and you materially participated in the activity, report box 2 income (loss) on Schedule E (Form 1040), line 28, column (h) or (j).

4. If you have income from a passive activity in box 2, report the income on Schedule E (Form 1040), line 28, column (g).

Box 3. Other Net Rental Income (Loss)

The amount in box 3 is a passive activity amount for all shareholders. If the corporation had more than one rental activity, it will attach a statement identifying the income or loss from each activity. Report the income or loss as follows.

1. If box 3 is a loss, follow the Instructions for Form 8582 to figure how much of the loss can be reported

on Schedule E (Form 1040), line 28, column (f).

2. If income is reported in box 3, report the income on Schedule E (Form 1040), line 28, column (g).

Portfolio Income

Portfolio income or loss (shown in boxes 4 through 8b and in box 10, code A) is not subject to the passive activity limitations. Portfolio income includes income (not derived in the ordinary course of a trade or business) from interest, ordinary dividends, annuities, or royalties, and gain or loss on the sale of property that produces such income or is held for investment.

Box 4. Interest Income

Report interest income on Form 1040, line 8a.

Box 5a. Ordinary Dividends

Report ordinary dividends on Form 1040, line 9a.

Box 5b. Qualified Dividends

Report any qualified dividends on Form 1040, line 9b.

Note. Qualified dividends are excluded from investment income, but you may elect to include part or all of these amounts in investment income. See the instructions for line 4g of Form 4952, Investment Interest Expense Deduction, for important information on making this election.

 If you have any foreign source qualified dividends, see the instructions for box 14, later.

Box 6. Royalties

Report royalties on Schedule E (Form 1040), line 4.

Box 7. Net Short-Term Capital Gain (Loss)

Report the net short-term capital gain (loss) on Schedule D (Form 1040), line 5.

Box 8a. Net Long-Term Capital Gain (Loss)

Report the net long-term capital gain (loss) on Schedule D (Form 1040), line 12.

 If you have any foreign source net long-term capital gain (loss), see the instructions for box 14, later.

Box 8b. Collectibles (28%) Gain (Loss)

Report collectibles gain or loss on line 4 of the 28% Rate Gain Worksheet—Line 18 in the Instructions for Schedule D (Form 1040).

Box 8c. Unrecaptured Section 1250 Gain

There are three types of unrecaptured section 1250 gain. Report your share of this unrecaptured gain on the Unrecaptured Section 1250 Gain Worksheet—Line 19 in the Instructions for Schedule D (Form 1040) as follows.

• Report unrecaptured section 1250 gain from the sale or exchange of the corporation's business assets on line 5.

• Report unrecaptured section 1250 gain from the sale or exchange of an interest in a partnership on line 10.

• Report unrecaptured section 1250 gain from an estate, trust, regulated investment company (RIC), or real estate investment trust (REIT) on line 11.

If the corporation reports only unrecaptured section 1250 gain from the sale or exchange of its business assets, it will enter a dollar amount in box 8c. If it reports the other two types of unrecaptured gain, it will provide an attached statement that shows the amount for each type of unrecaptured section 1250 gain.

 If you have any foreign source unrecaptured section 1250 gain, see the instructions for box 14, later.

Box 9. Net Section 1231 Gain (Loss)

The amount in box 9 is generally passive if it is from a:
• Rental activity, or
• Trade or business activity in which you did not materially participate.

However, an amount from a rental real estate activity is not from a passive activity if you were a real estate professional (defined earlier) and you materially participated in the activity.

If the amount is either (a) a loss that is not from a passive activity or (b) a gain, report it on Form 4797, line 2, column (g). Do not complete columns (b) through (f) on line 2 of Form 4797,

Sales of Business Property. Instead, enter "From Schedule K-1 (Form 1120S)" across these columns.

If the amount is a loss from a passive activity, see *Passive Loss Limitations* in the Instructions for Form 4797. Report the loss following the Instructions for Form 8582 to figure how much of the loss is allowed on Form 4797. If the corporation had net section 1231 gain (loss) from more than one activity, it will attach a statement that will identify the section 1231 gain (loss) from each activity.

 If you have any foreign source net section 1231 gain (loss), see the instructions for box 14, later.

Box 10. Other Income (Loss)

Code A. Other portfolio income (loss). The corporation will report portfolio income other than interest, ordinary dividend, royalty, and capital gain (loss) income, and attach a statement to tell you what kind of portfolio income is reported.

If the corporation held a residual interest in a real estate mortgage investment conduit (REMIC), it will report on the statement your share of REMIC taxable income (net loss) that you report on Schedule E (Form 1040), line 38, column (d). The statement will also report your share of any "excess inclusion" that you report on Schedule E (Form 1040), line 38, column (c), and your share of section 212 expenses that you report on Schedule E (Form 1040), line 38, column (e). If you itemize your deductions on Schedule A (Form 1040), you may also deduct these section 212 expenses as a miscellaneous deduction subject to the 2% limit on Schedule A (Form 1040), line 23.

Code B. Involuntary conversions. This is your net loss from involuntary conversions due to casualty or theft. The corporation will give you a statement that shows the amounts to be reported on Form 4684, Casualties and Thefts, line 34, columns (b)(i), (b)(ii), and (c).

If there was a gain (loss) from a casualty or theft to property not used in a trade or business or for income-producing purposes, the corporation will provide you with the information you need to complete Form 4684.

Code C. Section 1256 contracts and straddles. The corporation will report any net gain or loss from section 1256 contracts. Report this amount on Form 6781, Gains and Losses From Section 1256 Contracts and Straddles.

Code D. Mining exploration costs recapture. The corporation will give you a statement that shows the information needed to recapture certain mining exploration costs (section 617). See Pub. 535 for details.

Code E. Other income (loss). Amounts with code E are other items of income, gain, or loss not included in boxes 1 through 9 or in box 10 using codes A through D. The corporation should give you a description and the amount of your share for each of these items.

Report loss items that are passive activity amounts to you following the Instructions for Form 8582.

Code E items may include the following.
- Income from recoveries of tax benefit items. A tax benefit item is an amount you deducted in a prior tax year that reduced your income tax. Report this amount on Form 1040, line 21, to the extent it reduced your tax in the prior year.
- Gambling gains and losses.

1. If the corporation was not engaged in the trade or business of gambling, (a) report gambling winnings on Form 1040, line 21, and (b) deduct gambling losses to the extent of winnings on Schedule A (Form 1040), line 28.

2. If the corporation was engaged in the trade or business of gambling, (a) report gambling winnings on Schedule E (Form 1040), line 28, and (b) deduct gambling losses (to the extent of winnings) on Schedule E (Form 1040), line 28, column (h).

- Gain (loss) from the disposition of an interest in oil, gas, geothermal, or other mineral properties. The corporation will attach a statement that provides a description of the property, your share of the amount realized from the disposition, your share of the corporation's adjusted basis in the property (for other than oil or gas properties), and your share of the total intangible drilling costs, development costs, and mining exploration costs (section 59(e) expenditures) passed through for the property. You must figure your gain or loss from the disposition by increasing your share of the adjusted basis by the intangible drilling costs, development costs, or mine exploration costs for the property that you capitalized (that is, costs that you did not elect to deduct under section 59(e)). Report a loss in Part I of Form 4797. Report a gain in Part III of Form 4797 in accordance with the instructions for line 28. See Regulations section 1.1254-4 for details.

- Net short-term capital gain (loss) and net long-term capital gain (loss) from Schedule D (Form 1120S) that is not portfolio income. An example is gain or loss from the disposition of nondepreciable personal property used in a trade or business activity of the corporation. Report total net short-term gain (loss) on Schedule D (Form 1040), line 5. Report the total net long-term gain (loss) on Schedule D (Form 1040), line 12.

- Current year section 108(i) cancellation of debt income. The corporation will provide your share of the deferred amount that you must include in income in the current tax year under section 108(i)(1) or section 108(i)(5)(D)(i) or (ii).

- Gain from the sale or exchange of qualified small business (QSB) stock (as defined in the Instructions for Schedule D (Form 1040)) eligible for the section 1202 exclusion. The corporation should also give you (a) the name of the corporation that issued the QSB stock, (b) your share of the corporation's adjusted basis and sales price of the QSB stock, and (c) the dates the QSB stock was bought and sold. The following additional limitations apply at the shareholder level.

1. You must have held an interest in the corporation when the corporation acquired the QSB stock and at all times thereafter until the corporation disposed of the QSB stock.

2. Your share of the eligible section 1202 gain cannot exceed the amount that would have been allocated to you based on your

Interest in the corporation at the time the QSB stock was acquired.

See Form 8949, Sales and Other Dispositions of Capital Assets, Schedule D (Form 1040), and the related instructions for details on how to report the gain and the amount of the allowable exclusion.

• Gain eligible for section 1045 rollover (replacement stock purchased by the corporation). The corporation should also give you (a) the name of the corporation that issued the qualified small business (QSB) stock, (b) your share of the corporation's adjusted basis and sales price of the QSB stock, and (c) the dates the QSB stock was bought and sold. To qualify for the section 1045 rollover:

1. You must have held an interest in the corporation during the entire period in which the corporation held the QSB stock (more than 6 months prior to the sale), and

2. Your share of the gain eligible for the section 1045 rollover cannot exceed the amount that would have been allocated to you based on your interest in the corporation at the time the QSB stock was acquired.

See Form 8949, Schedule D (Form 1040), and the related instructions for details on how to report the gain and the amount of the allowable postponed gain.

• Gain eligible for section 1045 rollover (replacement stock not purchased by the corporation). The corporation should also give you (a) the name of the corporation that issued the qualified small business (QSB) stock, (b) your share of the corporation's adjusted basis and sales price of the QSB stock, and (c) the dates the QSB stock was bought and sold. To qualify for the section 1045 rollover:

1. You must have held an interest in the corporation during the entire period in which the corporation held the QSB stock (more than 6 months prior to the sale),

2. Your share of the gain eligible for the section 1045 rollover cannot exceed the amount that would have been allocated to you based on your interest in the corporation at the time the QSB stock was acquired, and

3. You must purchase other QSB stock (as defined in the Instructions

for Schedule D (Form 1040)) during the 60-day period that began on the date the QSB stock was sold by the corporation.

See Form 8949, Schedule D (Form 1040), and the related instructions for details on how to report the gain and the amount of the allowable postponed gain.

Deductions

Box 11. Section 179 Deduction

Use this amount, along with the total cost of section 179 property placed in service during the year from other sources, to complete Part I of Form 4562, Depreciation and Amortization. The corporation will report on an attached statement your share of the cost of any qualified enterprise zone property, qualified section 179 disaster assistance property, or qualified real property it placed in service during its tax year. Report the amount from line 12 of Form 4562 allocable to a passive activity using the Instructions for Form 8582. If the amount is not a passive activity deduction, report it on Schedule E (Form 1040), line 28, column (i).

Box 12. Other Deductions

Contributions. Codes A through G. The corporation will give you a statement that shows charitable contributions subject to the 100%, 50%, 30%, and 20% adjusted gross income limitations.

If the corporation made a property contribution, it will report on an attached statement your share of both the fair market value and adjusted basis of the property. Use these amounts to adjust your stock basis. If the corporation made a qualified conservation contribution, it will report the fair market value of the underlying property before and after the donation, the type of legal interest contributed, and a description of the conservation purpose furthered by the donation. If the corporation made a contribution of real property located in a registered historic district, it will report any information you will need to take a deduction.

For more details, see Pub. 526, Charitable Contributions, and the Instructions for Schedule A (Form 1040). If your contributions are subject

to more than one of the AGI limitations, see Pub. 526.

Charitable contribution deductions are not taken into account in figuring your passive activity loss for the year. Do not enter them on Form 8582.

Code A. Cash contributions (50%). Report this amount, subject to the 50% AGI limitation, on Schedule A (Form 1040), line 16.

Code B. Cash contributions (30%). Report this amount, subject to the 30% AGI limitation, on Schedule A (Form 1040), line 16.

Code C. Noncash contributions (50%). If property other than cash is contributed, and if the claimed deduction for one item or group of similar items of property exceeds $5,000, the corporation must give you a copy of Form 8283, Noncash Charitable Contributions, to attach to your tax return. Do not deduct the amount shown on Form 8283. It is the corporation's contribution. Instead, deduct the amount identified by code C, box 12, subject to the 50% AGI limitation, on Schedule A (Form 1040), line 17.

If the corporation provides you with information that the contribution was property other than cash and does not give you a Form 8283, see the Instructions for Form 8283 for filing requirements. Do not file Form 8283 unless the total claimed deduction for all contributed items of property exceeds $500.

Food inventory contributions. The corporation will report on an attached statement your share of qualified food inventory contributions. The food inventory contribution is not included in the amount reported in box 12 using code C. The corporation will also report your share of the corporation's net income from the business activities that made the food inventory contribution(s). Your deduction for food inventory contributions cannot exceed 10% of your aggregate net income for the tax year from the business activities from which the food inventory contribution was made (including your share of net income from partnership or S corporation businesses that made food inventory contributions). Report the deduction, subject to the 50% AGI limitation, on Schedule A (Form 1040), line 17.

Code D. Noncash contributions (30%). Report this amount, subject to the 30% AGI limitation, on Schedule A (Form 1040), line 17.

Code E. Capital gain property to a 50% organization (30%). Report this amount, subject to the 30% AGI limitation, on Schedule A (Form 1040), line 17. See *Special 30% Limit for Capital Gain Property* in Pub. 526.

Code F. Capital gain property (20%). Report this amount, subject to the 20% AGI limitation, on Schedule A (Form 1040), line 17.

Code G. Contributions (100%). The corporation will report your share of qualified conservation contributions of property used in agriculture or livestock production. This contribution is not included in the amount reported in box 12 using code C. If you are a farmer or rancher, you qualify for a 100% AGI limitation for this contribution. Otherwise, your deduction for this contribution is subject to a 50% AGI limitation. Report this deduction on Schedule A (Form 1040), line 17. See Pub. 526 for more information on qualified conservation contributions.

Code H. Investment interest expense. Report this amount on Form 4952, line 1.

If the corporation has investment income or other investment expense, it will report your share of these items in box 17 using codes A and B. Include investment income and expenses from other sources to figure how much of your total investment interest is deductible.

For more information on the special provisions that apply to investment interest expense, see Form 4952 and Pub. 550.

Code I. Deductions—royalty income. Report deductions allocable to royalties on Schedule E (Form 1040), line 19. For this type of expense, enter "From Schedule K-1 (Form 1120S)."

These deductions are not taken into account in figuring your passive activity loss for the year. Do not enter them on Form 8582.

Code J. Section 59(e)(2) expenditures. The corporation will show on an attached statement the type and the amount of qualified expenditures for which you may make a section 59(e) election. The statement will also

identify the property for which the expenditures were paid or incurred. If there is more than one type of expenditure, the amount of each type will also be listed.

If you deduct these expenditures in full in the current year, they are treated as adjustments or tax preference items for purposes of alternative minimum tax. However, you may elect to amortize these expenditures over the number of years in the applicable period rather than deduct the full amount in the current year. If you make this election, these items are not treated as adjustments or tax preference items.

Under the election, you can deduct circulation expenditures ratably over a 3-year period. Research and experimental expenditures and mining exploration and development costs can be amortized over a 10-year period. Intangible drilling and development costs can be amortized over a 60-month period. The amortization periods begin with the month in which such costs were paid or incurred.

Make the election on Form 4562. If you make the election, report the current year amortization of section 59(e) expenditures from Part VI of Form 4562 on Schedule E (Form 1040), line 28. If you do not make the election, report the section 59(e)(2) expenditures on Schedule E (Form 1040), line 28, and figure the resulting adjustment or tax preference item (see Form 6251, Alternative Minimum Tax—Individuals). Whether you deduct the expenditures or elect to amortize them, report the amount on a separate line in column (h) of line 28 if you materially participated in the activity. If you did not materially participate, follow the Instructions for Form 8582 to figure how much of the deduction can be reported in column (f).

Code K. Deductions—portfolio (2% floor). Amounts entered with code K are deductions that are clearly and directly allocable to portfolio income (other than investment interest expense and section 212 expenses from a REMIC). Generally, you should report these amounts on Schedule A (Form 1040), line 23. See the instructions for Schedule A (Form 1040), lines 23 and 28, for details.

These deductions are not taken into account in figuring your passive activity loss for the year. Do not enter them on Form 8582.

Code L. Deductions—portfolio (other). Generally, you should report these amounts on Schedule A (Form 1040), line 28. See the instructions for Schedule A (Form 1040), lines 23 and 28, for details.

These deductions are not taken into account in figuring your passive activity loss for the year. Do not enter them on Form 8582.

Code M. Preproductive period expenses. You may be able to deduct these expenses currently or you may need to capitalize them under section 263A. See Pub. 225, Farmer's Tax Guide, and Regulations section 1.263A-4 for details.

Code N. Commercial revitalization deduction from rental real estate activities. Follow the Instructions for Form 8582 to figure how much of the deduction can be reported on Schedule E (Form 1040), line 28, column (f).

Code O. Reforestation expense deduction. The corporation will provide a statement that describes the qualified timber property for these reforestation expenses. The expense deduction is limited to $10,000 ($5,000 if married filing separately) for each qualified timber property, including your share of the corporation's expense and any reforestation expenses you separately paid or incurred during the tax year.

If you did not materially participate in the activity, use Form 8582 to figure the amount to report on Schedule E (Form 1040), line 28, column (f). If you materially participated in the reforestation activity, report the deduction on Schedule E (Form 1040), line 28, column (h).

Code P. Domestic production activities information. The corporation will provide you with a statement with information that you must use to figure the domestic production activities deduction. Use Form 8903, Domestic Production Activities Deduction, to figure this deduction. For details, see the Instructions for Form 8903.

Code Q. Qualified production activities income (QPAI). Report the QPAI reported to you by the corporation (in box 12 of Schedule K-1) in the applicable column of Form 8903, line 7.

Code R. Employer's Form W-2 wages. Report the portion of Form W-2 wages reported to you by the corporation (in box 12 of Schedule K-1) on Form 8903, line 17.

Code S. Other deductions. Amounts with this code may include the following.

- Itemized deductions that Form 1040 filers report on Schedule A (Form 1040).
- Soil and water conservation expenditures and endangered species recovery expenditures. See section 175 for limitations on the amount you are allowed to deduct.
- Expenditures for the removal of architectural and transportation barriers to the elderly and disabled that the corporation elected to treat as a current expense. The deductions are limited by section 190(c) to $15,000 per year from all sources.
- Interest expense allocated to debt-financed distributions. The manner in which you report such interest expense depends on your use of the distributed debt proceeds. If the proceeds were used in a trade or business activity, report the interest on Schedule E (Form 1040), line 28. In column (a) enter the name of the corporation and "interest expense." If you materially participated in the trade or business activity, enter the interest expense in column (h). If you did not materially participate in the activity, follow the Instructions for Form 8582 to figure the interest expense you can report in column (f). Material participation is defined earlier under *Passive Activity Limitations*. If the proceeds were used in an investment activity, report the interest on Form 4952. If the proceeds are used for personal purposes, the interest is generally not deductible.
- Contributions to a capital construction fund (CCF). The deduction for a CCF investment is not taken on Schedule E (Form 1040). Instead, you subtract the deduction from the amount that would normally be entered as taxable income on Form 1040, line 43. In the margin to the left of line 43, enter "CCF" and the amount of the deduction.

- Penalty on early withdrawal of savings. Report this amount on Form 1040, line 30.
- Film and television production expenses. The corporation will provide a statement that describes the film or television production generating these expenses. Generally, if the aggregate cost of the production exceeds $15 million, you are not entitled to the deduction. The limitation is $20 million for productions in certain areas (see section 181 for details). If you did not materially participate in the activity, use Form 8582 to determine the amount that can be reported on Schedule E (Form 1040), line 28, column (f). If you materially participated in the production activity, report the deduction on Schedule E (Form 1040), line 28, column (h).
- Current year section 108(i) original issue discount (OID) deduction. The corporation will provide your share of the corporation's OID deduction deferred under section 108(i)(2)(A)(i) that is allowable as a deduction in the current tax year under section 108(i)(2)(A)(ii) or section 108(i)(5)(D)(i) or (ii).

The corporation will give you a description and the amount of your share for each of these items.

Box 13. Credits

If you have credits that are passive activity credits to you, you must complete Form 8582-CR in addition to the credit forms identified below. See *Passive Activity Limitations*, earlier, and the Instructions for Form 8582-CR for details.

 In general, shareholders whose only sources for a credit listed on Form 3800, General Business Credit, Part III, are partnerships, S corporations, estates, trusts, and cooperatives, are not required to complete the applicable credit form or attach it to their return. Instead, they can report the credit amounts reported to them by these pass-through entities directly on Form 3800, Part III, and enter the EIN of the entity in column (b) of Part III. However, when applicable, all shareholders must complete and attach the following credit forms to their return.

- *Form 3468, Investment Credit (Form 3800, Part III, line 1a).*

- *Form 8864, Biodiesel and Renewable Diesel Fuels Credit (Form 3800, Part III, line 1l).*

See the Instructions for Form 3800 for more details.

Codes A, B, C, and D. Low-income housing credit. If section 42(j)(5) applies, the corporation will report your share of the low-income housing credit using code A or code C, depending on the date the building was placed in service. If section 42(j)(5) does not apply, your share of the credit will be reported using code B or code D, depending on the date the building was placed in service. Any allowable low-income housing credit reported using code A or code B is reported on line 4 of Form 8586, Low-Income Housing Credit, or Form 3800, Part III, line 1d (see *TIP*, earlier). Any allowable low-income housing credit reported using code C or code D is reported on Form 8586, line 11, or Form 3800, Part III, line 4d (see *TIP*, earlier).

Keep a separate record of the low-income housing credit from each separate source so that you can correctly figure any recapture of low-income housing credit that may result from the disposition of all or part of your stock in the corporation. For more information on recapture, see the instructions for Form 8611, Recapture of Low-Income Housing Credit.

Code E. Qualified rehabilitation expenditures (rental real estate). The corporation will report your share of the qualified rehabilitation expenditures and other information you need to complete Form 3468 related to rental real estate activities using code E. Your share of qualified rehabilitation expenditures from property not related to rental real estate activities will be reported in box 17 using code C. See the Instructions for Form 3468 for details. If the corporation is reporting expenditures from more than one activity, an attached statement will separately identify the expenditures from each activity.

Combine the expenditures (for Form 3468 reporting) from box 13, code E, and from box 17, code C. The expenditures related to rental real estate activities (box 13, code E) are reported on Schedule K-1 separately from other qualified rehabilitation expenditures (box 17, code C) because they are subject to different passive activity limitation rules. See the Instructions for Form 8582-CR for details.

Code F. Other rental real estate credits. The corporation will identify the type of credit and any other information you need to figure these credits from rental real estate activities (other than the low-income housing credit and qualified rehabilitation expenditures). These credits may be limited by the passive activity limitations. If the credits are from more than one activity, the corporation will identify the credits from each activity on an attached statement. See *Passive Activity Limitations*, earlier, and the Instructions for Form 8582-CR for details.

Code G. Other rental credits. The corporation will identify the type of credit and any other information you need to figure these rental credits. These credits may be limited by the passive activity limitations. If the credits are from more than one activity, the corporation will identify the credits from each activity on an attached statement. See *Passive Activity Limitations*, earlier, and the Instructions for Form 8582-CR for details.

Code H. Undistributed capital gains credit. Code H represents taxes paid on undistributed capital gains by a regulated investment company or real estate investment trust. Report these taxes on Form 1040, line 73, check box "a" for Form 2439, and enter "Form 1120S" to the right of line 73. Reduce the basis of your stock by this tax.

Code I. Biofuel producer credit. Report this amount on line 3 of Form 6478, Biofuel Producer Credit, or Form 3800, Part III, line 4c (see *TIP*, earlier).

Code J. Work opportunity credit. Report this amount on line 3 of Form 5884, Work Opportunity Credit, or Form 3800, Part III, line 4b (see *TIP*, earlier).

Code K. Disabled access credit. Report this amount on line 7 of Form 8826, Disabled Access Credit, or Form 3800, Part III, line 1e (see *TIP*, earlier).

Code L. Empowerment zone employment credit. Report this amount on line 3 of Form 8844, Empowerment Zone Employment Credit, or Form 3800, Part III, line 3 (see *TIP*, earlier).

Code M. Credit for increasing research activities. Report this amount on line 37 of Form 6765, Credit for Increasing Research Activities, or Form 3800, Part III, line 1c (see *TIP*, earlier).

Code N. Credit for employer social security and Medicare taxes. Report this amount on line 5 of Form 8846, Credit for Employer Social Security and Medicare Taxes Paid on Certain Employee Tips, or Form 3800, Part III, line 4f (see *TIP*, earlier).

Code O. Backup withholding. This is your share of the credit for backup withholding on dividends, interest income, and other types of income. Include this amount in the total you enter on Form 1040, line 64, and attach a copy of your Schedule K-1 to your tax return. Instead of attaching a copy of your Schedule K-1 to your tax return, you can include a statement with your return that provides the corporation's name, address, EIN, and backup withholding amount.

Code P. Other credits. On a statement attached to Schedule K-1, the corporation will identify the type of credit and any other information you need to figure credits other than those reported with codes A through O. Most credits identified by code P will be reported on Form 3800, Part III (see *TIP*, earlier).

Credits that may be reported with code P include the following.
* Unused investment credit from the qualifying advanced coal project credit, qualifying gasification project credit, or qualifying advanced energy project credit allocated from cooperatives (Form 3468, line 9).
* Unused investment credit from the rehabilitation credit or energy credit allocated from cooperatives (Form 3468, line 13).
* Orphan drug credit (Form 8820).
* Renewable electricity, refined coal, and Indian coal production credit. The corporation will provide a statement showing separately the amount of credit from Part I and Part II of Form 8835.
* Indian employment credit (Form 8845).

* Biodiesel and renewable diesel fuels credit. If this credit includes the small agri-biodiesel producer credit, the corporation will provide additional information on an attached statement. If no statement is attached, report this amount on Form 8864, line 9. If a statement is attached, see the instructions for Form 8864, line 9.
* New markets credit (Form 8874).
* Credit for small employer pension plan startup costs (Form 8881).
* Credit for employer-provided childcare facilities and services (Form 8882).
* Low sulfur diesel fuel production credit (Form 8896).
* Qualified railroad track maintenance credit (Form 8900).
* Distilled spirits credit (Form 8906).
* Nonconventional source fuel credit (Form 8907).
* Energy efficient home credit (Form 8908).
* Energy efficient appliance credit (Form 8909).
* Alternative motor vehicle credit (Form 8910).
* Alternative fuel vehicle refueling property credit (Form 8911).
* Qualified zone academy bond credit. Report this amount on Form 8912.
* Clean renewable energy bond credit. Report this amount on Form 8912.
* New clean renewable energy bond credit. Report this amount on Form 8912.
* Qualified energy conservation bond credit. Report this amount on Form 8912.
* Build America bond credit. Report this amount on Form 8912.
* Qualified school construction bond credit. Report this amount on Form 8912.
* Mine rescue team training credit (Form 8923).
* Credit for employer differential wage payments (Form 8932).
* Carbon dioxide sequestration credit (Form 8933).
* Qualified plug-in electric drive motor vehicle credit (Form 8936).
* Credit for small employer health insurance premiums (Form 8941).
* General credits from an electing large partnership. Report these credits on Form 3800, Part III, line 1bb.

Box 14. Foreign Transactions

Codes A through N. Use the information identified by codes A through N, code Q, and any attached statements to figure your foreign tax credit.

 If you have any qualified dividends, capital gains (including any capital gain distributions), capital losses, net section 1231 gains, or net section 1231 losses, you may have to make certain adjustments to those amounts before taking them into account on line 1a, line 5, or line 18 of Form 1116, Foreign Tax Credit.

For details, see Form 1116 and its separate instructions and Pub. 514, Foreign Tax Credit for Individuals.

Codes O and P. Extraterritorial income exclusion.

1. *Corporation did not claim the exclusion.* If the corporation reports your share of foreign trading gross receipts (code O) and the extraterritorial income exclusion (code P), the corporation was not entitled to claim the exclusion because it did not meet the foreign economic process requirements. You may still qualify for your share of this exclusion if the corporation's foreign trading gross receipts for the tax year were $5 million or less. To qualify for this exclusion, your foreign trading gross receipts from all sources for the tax year also must have been $5 million or less. If you qualify for the exclusion, report the exclusion amount in accordance with the instructions for box 1, 2, or 3, whichever applies. See Form 8873, Extraterritorial Income Exclusion, for details.

2. *Corporation claimed the exclusion.* If the corporation reports your share of foreign trading gross receipts but not the amount of the extraterritorial income exclusion, the corporation met the foreign economic process requirements and claimed the exclusion when figuring your share of corporate income. You also may need to know your share of foreign trading gross receipts from this corporation to determine if you met the $5 million or less exception discussed above for purposes of qualifying for an extraterritorial income exclusion from other sources.

Note. Upon request, the corporation should furnish you a copy of the corporation's Form 8873 if there is a reduction for international boycott operations, illegal bribes, kickbacks, etc.

Code Q. Other foreign transactions. On a statement attached to Schedule K-1, the corporation will report any other information on foreign transactions that you may need using code Q.

Box 15. Alternative Minimum Tax (AMT) Items

Use the information reported in box 15 (as well as your adjustments and tax preference items from other sources) to prepare your Form 6251, Alternative Minimum Tax—Individuals, or Schedule I (Form 1041), Alternative Minimum Tax—Estates and Trusts.

Code A. This amount is your share of the corporation's post-1986 depreciation adjustment. If you are an individual shareholder, report this amount on Form 6251, line 18.

Code B. This amount is your share of the corporation's adjusted gain or loss. If you are an individual shareholder, report this amount on Form 6251, line 17.

Code C. This amount is your share of the corporation's depletion adjustment. If you are an individual shareholder, report this amount on Form 6251, line 9.

Codes D and E. Oil, gas, & geothermal properties—gross income and deductions. The amounts reported on these lines include only the gross income (code D) from, and deductions (code E) allocable to, oil, gas, and geothermal properties included in box 1 of Schedule K-1. The corporation should have attached a statement that shows any income from or deductions allocable to such properties that are included in boxes 2 through 12, 16, and 17 of Schedule K-1. Use the amounts reported here and any other reported amounts to help you figure the net amount to enter on Form 6251, line 26.

Code F. Other AMT items. Report the information on the statement attached by the corporation on the applicable lines of Form 6251 or Schedule I (Form 1041).

Box 16. Items Affecting Shareholder Basis

Code A. Tax-exempt interest income. Report on your return, as an item of information, your share of the tax-exempt interest received or accrued by the corporation during the year. Individual shareholders include this amount on Form 1040, line 8b. Generally, you must increase the basis of your stock by this amount.

Code B. Other tax-exempt income. Generally, you must increase the basis of your stock by the amount shown, but do not include it in income on your tax return.

Code C. Nondeductible expenses. The nondeductible expenses paid or incurred by the corporation are not deductible on your tax return. Generally, you must decrease the basis of your stock by this amount.

Code D. Property distributions. Reduce the basis of your stock (as explained earlier) by distributions, not reported on Form 1099-DIV, of property or money. This amount will include any amounts included in income with respect to new clean renewable energy, qualified energy conservation, qualified school construction, build America, or (for bonds issued after October 3, 2008) qualified zone academy bonds. If these distributions exceed the basis of your stock, the excess is treated as capital gain from the sale or exchange of property and is reported on Form 8949 and Schedule D (Form 1040).

Code E. Repayment of loans from shareholders. If these payments are made on a loan with a reduced basis, the repayments must be allocated in part to a return of your basis in the loan and in part to the receipt of income. See Regulations section 1.1367-2 for information on reduction in basis of a loan and restoration in basis of a loan with a reduced basis. See Rev. Rul. 64-162, 1964-1 (Part 1) C.B. 304, and Rev. Rul. 68-537, 1968-2 C.B. 372, for details.

Box 17. Other Information

Code A. Investment income. Report this amount on Form 4952, line 4a.

Code B. Investment expenses. Report this amount on Form 4952, line 5.

Code C. Qualified rehabilitation expenditures (other than rental real estate). The corporation will report your share of qualified rehabilitation expenditures and other information you need to complete Form 3468 for property not related to rental real estate activities in box 17 using code C. Your share of qualified rehabilitation expenditures related to rental real estate activities is reported in box 13 using code E. See the Instructions for Form 3468 for details. If the corporation is reporting expenditures from more than one activity, the attached statement will separately identify the expenditures from each activity.

Combine the expenditures (for Form 3468 reporting) from box 13, code E and from box 17, code C. The expenditures related to rental real estate activities (box 13, code E) are reported on Schedule K-1 separately from other qualified rehabilitation expenditures (box 17, code C) because they are subject to different passive activity limitation rules. See the Instructions for Form 8582-CR for details.

Code D. Basis of energy property. If the corporation provides an attached statement for code D, use the information on the statement to complete lines 12a–12d, 12f, 12g, 12i, 12j, 12l, 12m, 12o, and 12q–12s of Form 3468.

Codes E and F. Recapture of low-income housing credit. The corporation will identify by code E your share of any recapture of a low-income housing credit from its investment in partnerships to which the provisions of section 42(j)(5) apply. All other recapture of low-income housing credits will be identified by code F.

Keep a separate record of each type of recapture so that you will be able to correctly figure any credit recapture that may result from the disposition of all or part of your corporate stock. For details, see Form 8611.

Code G. Recapture of investment credit. The corporation will provide any information you need to figure your recapture tax on Form 4255,

Recapture of Investment Credit. See the Form 3468 on which you took the original credit for other information you need to complete Form 4255.

You may also need Form 4255 if your proportionate stock interest in the corporation is reduced by more than one-third after you were allocated part of an investment credit.

Code H. Recapture of other credits. On a statement attached to Schedule K-1, the corporation will report any information you need to figure the recapture of other credits including the new markets credit, qualified plug-in electric vehicle credit, Indian employment credit, credit for employer-provided childcare facilities and services, alternative motor vehicle credit, alternative fuel vehicle refueling property credit, and qualified plug-in electric drive motor vehicle credit.

Code I. Look-back interest—completed long-term contracts. The corporation will report any information you need to figure the interest due or to be refunded under the look-back method of section 460(b)(2) on certain long-term contracts. Use Form 8697, Interest Computation Under the Look-Back Method for Completed Long-Term Contracts, to report any such interest.

Code J. Look-back interest—income forecast method. The corporation will report any information you need to figure the interest due or to be refunded under the look-back method of section 167(g)(2) for certain property placed in service after September 13, 1995, and depreciated under the income forecast method. Use Form 8866, Interest Computation Under the Look-Back Method for Property Depreciated Under the Income Forecast Method, to report any such interest.

Code K. Dispositions of property with section 179 deductions. The corporation will report your share of gain or loss on the sale, exchange, or other disposition of property for which a section 179 expense deduction was passed through to shareholders with code K. If the corporation passed through a section 179 expense deduction for the property, you must report the gain or loss, if any, and any recapture of the section 179 expense deduction for the property on your

income tax return (see the Instructions for Form 4797 for details). The corporation will provide all the following information.

1. Description of the property.

2. Date the property was acquired and placed in service.

3. Date of the sale or other disposition of the property.

4. Your share of the gross sales price or amount realized.

5. Your share of the cost or other basis plus the expense of sale.

6. Your share of the depreciation allowed or allowable.

7. Your share of the section 179 expense deduction (if any) passed through for the property and the corporation's tax year(s) in which the amount was passed through.

To figure the depreciation allowed or allowable for Form 4797, line 22, add to the amount from item (6) above the amount of your share of the section 179 expense deduction, reduced by any unused carryover of the deduction for this property. This amount may be different than the amount of section 179 expense you deducted for the property if your interest in the corporation has changed.

8. If the disposition is due to a casualty or theft, any information you need to complete Form 4684.

9. If the sale was an installment sale made during the corporation's tax year, any information you need to complete Form 6252, Installment Sale Income. The corporation will separately report your share of all payments received for the property in the following tax years. See the Form 6252 instructions for details.

Code L. Recapture of section 179 deduction. The corporation will report your share of any recapture of section 179 expense deduction if business use of any property for which the section 179 expense deduction was passed through to shareholders dropped to 50% or less before the end of the recapture period. If this occurs, the corporation must provide the following information.

1. Your share of the depreciation allowed or allowable (not including the section 179 expense deduction).

2. Your share of the section 179 expense deduction (if any) passed through for the property and the corporation's tax year(s) in which the amount was passed through. Reduce this amount by the portion, if any, of your unused (carryover) section 179 expense deduction for this property.

Code M. Section 453(l)(3) information. The corporation will report any information you need to figure the interest due under section 453(l)(3) with respect to the disposition of certain timeshares and residential lots on the installment method. Report the interest on Form 1040, line 62. Check box "c" and enter "453(l)(3)" and the amount of the interest in the space next to that box. See section 453(l)(3) for details on how to figure the interest.

Code N. Section 453A(c) information. The corporation will report any information you need to figure the interest due under section 453A(c) with respect to certain installment sales. Report the interest on Form 1040, line 62. Check box "c" and enter "453A(c)" and the amount of the interest in the space next to that box. See section 453A(c) for details on how to figure the interest.

Code O. Section 1260(b) information. The corporation will report any information you need to figure the interest due under section 1260(b). If the corporation had gain from certain constructive ownership transactions, your tax liability must be increased by the interest charge on any deferral of gain recognition under section 1260(b). Report the interest on Form 1040, line 62. Enter "1260(b)" and the amount of the interest in the space to the left of line 62. See section 1260(b) for details on how to figure the interest.

Code P. Interest allocable to production expenditures. The corporation will report any information you need relating to interest you are required to capitalize under section 263A for production expenditures. See Regulations sections 1.263A-8 through 1.263A-15 for details.

Code Q. CCF nonqualified withdrawals. The corporation will report your share of nonqualified withdrawals from a capital construction fund (CCF). These withdrawals are taxed separately from your other gross income at the highest marginal ordinary income or capital gains tax rate. Attach a statement to your federal income tax return to show your computation of both the tax and interest for a nonqualified withdrawal. Include the tax and interest on Form 1040, line 62. In the space to the left of line 62, enter the amount of tax and interest and "CCF."

Code R. Depletion information—oil and gas. This is your share of gross income from the property, share of production for the tax year, etc., needed to figure your depletion deduction for oil and gas wells. The corporation should also allocate to you a proportionate share of the adjusted basis of each corporate oil or gas property. See Pub. 535 for details on how to figure your depletion deduction.

Reduce the basis of your stock by the amount of this deduction up to the extent of your adjusted basis in the property.

Code S. Reserved.

Code T. Section 108(i) information. If the corporation made a section 108(i) election, it will provide all the information you will need to determine your share of the following.
- Deferred cancellation of debt income.
- Deferred original issue discount deduction.

Code U. Net investment income. The corporation may use code U to report information you may need to determine your net investment income tax under section 1411, including information regarding income from controlled foreign corporations (CFCs) and passive foreign investment companies (PFICs) the stock of which is owned by the corporation. Any information not provided elsewhere on Schedule K-1 (or an attachment to Schedule K-1) is provided using code U. For CFCs and PFICs that you treat as qualified electing funds (QEFs), the information that is relevant to you will depend on whether you, the corporation, or a subsidiary pass-through entity has made an election under Regulations section 1.1411-10(g) with respect to the CFC or QEF. For example, if the corporation made an election under Regulations section 1.1411-10(g) for a CFC the stock of which is owned by the corporation, and the relevant income and deduction items derived from that CFC are reported elsewhere on Schedule K-1, you will not need the information provided using code U to complete your Form 8960, Net Investment Income Tax—Individuals, Estates, and Trusts.

Follow the Instructions for Form 8960 to figure and report your net investment income and adjusted gross income or modified adjusted gross income. See Regulations sections 1.1411-1 through 1.1411-10 for more details.

Code V. Other information. The corporation will use code V to report the following to shareholders.

1. Any information you need to complete a disclosure statement for reportable transactions in which the corporation participates. If the corporation participates in a transaction that must be disclosed on Form 8886, Reportable Transaction Disclosure Statement, both you and the corporation may be required to file Form 8886 for the transaction. The determination of whether you are required to disclose a transaction of the corporation is based on the category(ies) under which the transaction qualifies for disclosure and is determined by you and the corporation. You may have to pay a penalty if you are required to file Form 8886 and do not do so. See the Instructions for Form 8886 for details.

2. Gross farming and fishing income. If you are an individual shareholder, report this income, as an item of information, on Schedule E (Form 1040), Part V, line 42. Do not report this income elsewhere on Form 1040.

For a shareholder that is an estate or trust, report this income to the beneficiaries, as an item of information, on Schedule K-1 (Form 1041). Do not report it elsewhere on Form 1041.

3. Excess farm loss limitation. If the corporation has deductions attributable to a farming activity, it will provide a statement showing the aggregate gross income or gain and the aggregate deductions from the farming activity that you need to figure any excess farm loss limitation. It will also provide information on any applicable subsidy it receives that would trigger the excess farm loss

limitation. See section 461(j) and Pub. 225 for details.

4. The amount included in gross income with respect to qualified zone academy bonds issued before October 4, 2008. Income with respect to these qualified zone academy bonds cannot be used to increase your stock basis. Because this amount is already included in income elsewhere on Schedule K-1, you must reduce your stock basis by this amount. See line 3 of the Worksheet for Figuring a Shareholder's Stock Basis.

5. The amount included in gross income with respect to clean renewable energy bonds. Income with respect to clean renewable energy bonds cannot be used to increase your stock basis. Because this amount is already included in income elsewhere on Schedule K-1, you must reduce your stock basis by this

amount. See line 3 of the Worksheet for Figuring a Shareholder's Stock Basis.

6. Qualified investment in qualifying advanced coal project property. Use the amounts the corporation provides you to figure the amounts to report on Form 3468, lines 5a, 5b, and 5c.

7. Qualified investment in qualifying gasification property. Use the amounts the corporation provides you to figure the amounts to report on Form 3468, lines 6a and 6b.

8. Qualified investment in qualifying advanced energy project credit property. Use the amounts the corporation provides you to figure the amount to report on Form 3468, line 7.

9. Inversion gain. The corporation will provide a statement showing the amounts of each type of income or gain that is included in inversion gain.

The corporation has included inversion gain in income elsewhere on Schedule K-1. Inversion gain is also reported under code V because your taxable income and alternative minimum taxable income cannot be less than the inversion gain. Also, your inversion gain (a) is not taken into account in figuring the net operating loss (NOL) for the tax year or the NOL that can be carried over to each tax year, (b) may limit your credits, and (c) is treated as income from sources within the United States for the foreign tax credit. See section 7874 for details.

10. Any other information you may need to file your return not shown elsewhere on Schedule K-1.

The corporation should give you a description and the amount of your share for each of these items.

Form **1120-W**	**Estimated Tax for Corporations**	OMB No. 1545-0975
(WORKSHEET)	For calendar year 2015, or tax year beginning _____ , 2015, and ending _____ , 20 _____	**20**15
Department of the Treasury Internal Revenue Service	▶ Information about Form 1120-W and its separate instructions is at *www.irs.gov/form1120*. (Keep for the corporation's records—Do *not* send to the Internal Revenue Service.)	

Estimated Tax Computation

1	Taxable income expected for the tax year	**1**	
	Qualified personal service corporations (defined in the instructions), skip lines 2 through 13 and go to line 14. Members of a controlled group, see instructions.		
2	Enter the **smaller** of line 1 or $50,000	**2**	
3	Multiply line 2 by 15%	**3**	
4	Subtract line 2 from line 1	**4**	
5	Enter the **smaller** of line 4 or $25,000	**5**	
6	Multiply line 5 by 25%	**6**	
7	Subtract line 5 from line 4	**7**	
8	Enter the **smaller** of line 7 or $9,925,000	**8**	
9	Multiply line 8 by 34%	**9**	
10	Subtract line 8 from line 7	**10**	
11	Multiply line 10 by 35%	**11**	
12	If line 1 is greater than $100,000, enter the **smaller** of (a) 5% of the excess over $100,000 or (b) $11,750. Otherwise, enter -0-	**12**	
13	If line 1 is greater than $15 million, enter the **smaller** of (a) 3% of the excess over $15 million or (b) $100,000. Otherwise, enter -0-	**13**	
14	Add lines 3, 6, 9, and 11 through 13. (Qualified personal service corporations, multiply line 1 by 35%.) .	**14**	
15	Alternative minimum tax (see instructions)	**15**	
16	**Total.** Add lines 14 and 15	**16**	
17	Tax credits (see instructions)	**17**	
18	Subtract line 17 from line 16	**18**	
19	Other taxes (see instructions)	**19**	
20	**Total tax.** Add lines 18 and 19	**20**	
21	Credit for federal tax paid on fuels and other refundable credits (see instructions)	**21**	
22	Subtract line 21 from line 20. **Note:** *If the result is less than $500, the corporation is not required to make estimated tax payments*	**22**	
23a	Enter the tax shown on the corporation's 2014 tax return (see instructions). **Caution:** *If the tax is zero or the tax year was for less than 12 months, skip this line and enter the amount from line 22 on line 23b* .	**23a**	
b	Enter the **smaller** of line 22 or line 23a. If the corporation is required to skip line 23a, enter the amount from line 22	**23b**	

		(a)	(b)	(c)	(d)
24	**Installment due dates** (see instructions) · · · · · ▶ **24**				
25	**Required installments.** Enter 25% of line 23b in columns (a) through (d). If the corporation uses the annualized income installment method or adjusted seasonal installment method or is a "large corporation," see the instructions for the amount to enter **25**				

For Paperwork Reduction Act Notice, see instructions.   Cat. No. 11525G   Form **1120-W** (2015)

Schedule A   Adjusted Seasonal Installment Method and Annualized Income Installment Method
(see instructions)

Part I   Adjusted Seasonal Installment Method

(Use this method only if the base period percentage for any 6 consecutive months is at least 70%.)

			(a)	(b)	(c)	(d)
			First 3 months	First 5 months	First 8 months	First 11 months
1	Enter taxable income for the following periods:					
a	Tax year beginning in 2012.	**1a**				
b	Tax year beginning in 2013.	**1b**				
c	Tax year beginning in 2014.	**1c**				
2	Enter taxable income for each period for the tax year beginning in 2015 (see instructions for the treatment of extraordinary items).	**2**				
			First 4 months	First 6 months	First 9 months	Entire year
3	Enter taxable income for the following periods:					
a	Tax year beginning in 2012.	**3a**				
b	Tax year beginning in 2013.	**3b**				
c	Tax year beginning in 2014.	**3c**				
4	Divide the amount in each column on line 1a by the amount in column (d) on line 3a.	**4**				
5	Divide the amount in each column on line 1b by the amount in column (d) on line 3b.	**5**				
6	Divide the amount in each column on line 1c by the amount in column (d) on line 3c.	**6**				
7	Add lines 4 through 6.	**7**				
8	Divide line 7 by 3.0.	**8**				
9a	Divide line 2 by line 8.	**9a**				
b	Extraordinary items (see instructions).	**9b**				
c	Add lines 9a and 9b.	**9c**				
10	Figure the tax on the amount on line 9c by following the same steps used to figure the tax on page 1, line 14.	**10**				
11a	Divide the amount in columns (a) through (c) on line 3a by the amount in column (d) on line 3a.	**11a**				
b	Divide the amount in columns (a) through (c) on line 3b by the amount in column (d) on line 3b.	**11b**				
c	Divide the amount in columns (a) through (c) on line 3c by the amount in column (d) on line 3c.	**11c**				
12	Add lines 11a through 11c.	**12**				
13	Divide line 12 by 3.0.	**13**				
14	Multiply the amount in columns (a) through (c) of line 10 by the amount in the corresponding column of line 13. In column (d), enter the amount from line 10, column (d).	**14**				
15	Enter any alternative minimum tax for each payment period (see instructions).	**15**				
16	Enter any other taxes for each payment period (see instructions).	**16**				
17	Add lines 14 through 16.	**17**				
18	For each period, enter the same type of credits as allowed on page 1, lines 17 and 21 (see instructions).	**18**				
19	Subtract line 18 from line 17. If zero or less, enter -0-.	**19**				

Part II	Annualized Income Installment Method		(a)	(b)	(c)	(d)
			First ___ months	First ___ months	First ___ months	First ___ months
20	Annualization periods (see instructions).	20				
21	Enter taxable income for each annualization period (see instructions for the treatment of extraordinary items).	21				
22	Annualization amounts (see instructions).	22				
23a	Annualized taxable income. Multiply line 21 by line 22.	23a				
b	Extraordinary items (see instructions).	23b				
c	Add lines 23a and 23b.	23c				
24	Figure the tax on the amount in each column on line 23c by following the same steps used to figure the tax on page 1, line 14.	24				
25	Enter any alternative minimum tax for each annualization period (see instructions).	25				
26	Enter any other taxes for each annualization period (see instructions).	26				
27	Total tax. Add lines 24 through 26.	27				
28	For each annualization period, enter the same type of credits as allowed on page 1, lines 17 and 21 (see instructions).	28				
29	Total tax after credits. Subtract line 28 from line 27. If zero or less, enter -0-.	29				
30	Applicable percentage.	30	25%	50%	75%	100%
31	Multiply line 29 by line 30.	31				

Part III	Required Installments					
Note: Complete lines 32 through 38 of one column before completing the next column.			1st installment	2nd installment	3rd installment	4th installment
32	If only Part I or Part II is completed, enter the amount in each column from line 19 **or** line 31. If both parts are completed, enter the **smaller** of the amounts in each column from line 19 or line 31.	32				
33	Add the amounts in all preceding columns of line 38 (see instructions).	33	▓▓▓			
34	**Adjusted seasonal or annualized income installments.** Subtract line 33 from line 32. If zero or less, enter -0-.	34				
35	Enter 25% of page 1, line 23b in each column. (**Note:** "Large corporations," see the instructions for page 1, line 25 for the amount to enter.)	35				
36	Subtract line 38 of the preceding column from line 37 of the preceding column.	36	▓▓▓			
37	Add lines 35 and 36.	37				
38	**Required installments.** Enter the **smaller** of line 34 or line 37 here and on page 1, line 25 (see instructions).	38				

Form **1120-W** (2015)

2015
Instructions for Form 1120-W

Department of the Treasury
Internal Revenue Service

Section references are to the Internal Revenue Code unless otherwise noted.

Future Developments

For the latest information about developments affecting Form 1120-W and its instructions, such as legislation enacted after they were published, go to *www.irs.gov/form1120.*

General Instructions

Who Must Make Estimated Tax Payments

- Corporations generally must make estimated tax payments if they expect their estimated tax (income tax less credits) to be $500 or more.
- S corporations must make estimated tax payments for certain taxes. S corporations should see the Instructions for Form 1120S, U.S. Income Tax Return for an S Corporation, to figure their estimated tax payments.
- Tax-exempt corporations, tax-exempt trusts, and domestic private foundations must make estimated tax payments for certain taxes. These entities should see the instructions for their tax return, to figure the amount of their estimated tax payments.

When To Make Estimated Tax Payments

The installments generally are due by the 15th day of the 4th, 6th, 9th, and 12th months of the tax year. If any due date falls on a Saturday, Sunday, or legal holiday, the installment is due on the next regular business day.

Underpayment of Estimated Tax

A corporation that does not make estimated tax payments when due may be subject to an underpayment penalty for the period of underpayment. Use Form 2220, Underpayment of Estimated Tax by Corporations, to see if the corporation owes a penalty and to figure the amount of the penalty. See Form 2220 and the Instructions for Form 2220.

Overpayment of Estimated Tax

A corporation that has overpaid its estimated tax may apply for a quick refund if the overpayment is at least 10% of its expected income tax liability and at least $500. To apply, file Form 4466, Corporation Application for Quick Refund of Overpayment of Estimated Tax, after the end of the tax year and before the corporation files its income tax return. Form 4466 may not be filed later than the 15th day of the 3rd month after the end of the tax year.

Methods of Tax Payment

Some corporations (described below) are required to electronically deposit all depository taxes, including estimated tax payments.

Electronic Deposit Requirement

Corporations must use electronic funds transfer to make all federal tax deposits (such as deposits of employment, excise, and corporate income tax). This includes installment payments of estimated tax. Generally, electronic funds transfer is made using the Electronic Federal Tax Payment System (EFTPS). However, if the corporation does not want to use EFTPS, it can arrange for its tax professional, financial institution, payroll service, or other trusted third party to make deposits on its behalf. Also, it may arrange for its financial institution to initiate a same-day tax wire payment (discussed below) on its behalf. EFTPS is a free service provided by the Department of the Treasury. Services provided by a tax professional, financial institution, payroll service, or other third party may have a fee.

To get more information about EFTPS or to enroll in EFTPS, visit *www.eftps.gov* or call 1-800-555-4477.

Depositing on time. For deposits made by EFTPS to be on time, the corporation must submit the deposit by 8 p.m. Eastern time the day before the date the deposit is due. If the corporation uses a third party to make deposits on its behalf, they may have different cutoff times.

Same-day wire payment option. If the corporation fails to submit a deposit transaction on EFTPS by 8 p.m. Eastern time the day before the date a deposit is due, it can still make the deposit on time by using the Federal Tax Collection Service (FTCS). Before using the same-day wire payment option, the corporation will need to make arrangements with its financial institution ahead of time. Please check with the financial institution regarding availability, deadlines, and costs. To learn more about the information the corporation will need to provide its financial institution to make a same-day wire payment, visit *www.irs.gov/e-pay* and click on *Same-Day Wire Federal Tax Payments.*

Foreign corporations. If a foreign corporation maintains an office or place of business in the United States, it must use electronic funds transfer (as discussed above) to make installment payments of estimated tax.

If the foreign corporation does not maintain an office or place of business in the United States, it may pay the estimated tax by EFTPS if it has a U.S. bank account. The foreign corporation may also arrange for its financial institution to submit a same-day payment on its behalf or can arrange for either a qualified intermediary, tax professional, payroll service, or other trusted third party to make a deposit on its behalf using a master account.

In addition, the foreign corporation has the option to pay the estimated tax due by check or money order, payable to the "United States Treasury." To ensure proper crediting, enter the foreign corporation's EIN, "Form 1120-F (or 1120-FSC, if applicable) estimated tax payment," and the tax period to which the payment applies on the check or money order. The payments must be sent to the Internal Revenue Service Center, P.O. Box 409101, Ogden, UT 84409.

Refiguring Estimated Tax

If, after the corporation figures and deposits estimated tax, it finds that its tax liability for the year will be more or less than originally estimated, it may have to refigure its required installments. If earlier installments were underpaid, the corporation may owe a penalty.

An immediate catchup payment should be made to reduce the amount of any penalty resulting from the underpayment of any earlier installments, whether caused by a change in estimate, failure to make a deposit, or a mistake.

Specific Instructions

 All line references on Form 1120-W are references to Form 1120, U.S. Corporation Income Tax Return. All other entities must determine their estimated tax liability by using the applicable line from their income tax return and the maximum rate that is in effect for their applicable tax year.

Line 1. Qualified Personal Service Corporations

A qualified personal service corporation is taxed at a flat rate of 35% on taxable income. A corporation is a qualified personal service corporation if it meets both of the following tests.
• Substantially all of the corporation's activities involve the performance of services in the fields of health, law, engineering, architecture, accounting, actuarial science, performing arts, or consulting.
• At least 95% of the corporation's stock, by value, is owned, directly or indirectly, by employees performing the services listed above, retired employees who had performed such services, any estate of an employee or retiree described above, or any person who acquired the stock of the corporation as a result of the death of an employee or retiree (but only for the 2-year period beginning on the date of the employee's or retiree's death).

Lines 2, 5, and 8. Members of a Controlled Group

Members of a controlled group, complete lines 2, 5, and 8 as follows:
• Enter on line 2 the smaller of the amount on line 1, or the member's share of the $50,000 amount.
• Enter on line 5 the smaller of the amount on line 4, or the member's share of the $25,000 amount.
• Enter on line 8 the smaller of the amount on line 7, or the member's share of the $9,925,000 amount.

Equal apportionment plan. If no apportionment plan is adopted, members of a controlled group must divide the amount in each taxable income bracket equally among themselves. For example, Controlled Group AB consists of Corporation A and Corporation B. They do not elect an apportionment plan. Therefore, each corporation is entitled to:
• $25,000 (one-half of $50,000) on line 2,
• $12,500 (one-half of $25,000) on line 5, and
• $4,962,500 (one-half of $9,925,000) on line 8.

Unequal apportionment plan. Members of a controlled group can elect an unequal apportionment plan and divide the taxable income brackets as they want. There is no need for consistency among taxable income brackets. Any member may be entitled to all, some, or none of the taxable income bracket. However, the total amount for all members cannot be more than the total amount in each taxable income bracket.

Line 12. Additional 5% Tax

Members of a controlled group are treated as one group to figure the applicability of the additional 5% tax and the additional 3% tax. If an additional tax applies, each member will pay that tax based on the part of the amount used in each taxable income bracket to reduce that member's tax. See section 1561(a). Each member of the group must enter on line 12 its share of the smaller of (a) 5% of the taxable income in excess of $100,000 or (b) $11,750.

Line 13. Additional 3% Tax

If the additional 3% tax applies, each member of the controlled group must enter on line 13 its share of the smaller of (a) 3% of the taxable income in excess of $15 million or (b) $100,000. See the instructions for line 12 above.

Line 15. Alternative Minimum Tax (AMT)

Note. Skip this line if the corporation is treated as a "small corporation" exempt from the AMT under section 55(e).

AMT is generally the excess of tentative minimum tax (TMT) for the tax year over the regular tax for the tax year. A limited amount of the foreign tax credit, as refigured for the AMT, is allowed in computing the TMT. Use the 2014 Form 4626 and the 2014 Instructions for Form 4626 as a guide.

Line 17. Tax Credits

For information on tax credits the corporation can take, see the 2014 Instructions for Form 1120, Schedule J, lines 5a through 5e, or the instructions for the applicable lines and schedule of other income tax returns.

Line 19. Other Taxes

For information on other taxes the corporation may owe, see the 2014 Instructions for Form 1120, Schedule J, line 9, or the instructions for the applicable line and schedule of other income tax returns.

Line 21. Credit for Federal Tax Paid on Fuels and Other Refundable Credits

See Form 4136, Credit for Federal Tax Paid on Fuels, to find out if the corporation qualifies to take this credit. Also include on line 21 any other refundable credit, including any credit the corporation is claiming under section 4682(g)(2) for tax on ozone-depleting chemicals. For information on other refundable credits, see the Instructions for Form 1120, Schedule J, line 19, or the instructions for the applicable line or schedule of other income tax returns.

Line 23a. 2014 Tax

Figure the corporation's 2014 tax in the same way that line 22 of this worksheet was figured, using the taxes and credits from the 2014 income tax return. Large corporations, see the instructions for line 25 below.

If a return was not filed for the 2014 tax year showing a liability for at least some amount of tax or the 2014 tax year was for less than 12 months, do not complete line 23a. Instead, skip line 23a and enter the amount from line 22 on line 23b.

Line 24. Installment Due Dates

Calendar-year taxpayers: Enter 4-15-2015, 6-15-2015, 9-15-2015, and 12-15-2015, respectively, in columns (a) through (d).

Fiscal-year taxpayers: Enter the 15th day of the 4th, 6th, 9th, and 12th months of your tax year in columns (a) through (d). If the due date falls on a Saturday, Sunday, or legal holiday, enter the next business day.

Line 25. Required Installments

Payments of estimated tax should reflect any 2014 overpayment that the corporation chose to credit against its 2015 tax. The overpayment is credited against unpaid required installments in the order in which the installments are required to be paid.

If the corporation uses the annualized income installment method and/or the adjusted seasonal installment method, or is a "large corporation," see the instructions below.

Annualized income installment method and/or adjusted seasonal installment method. If the corporation's income is expected to vary during the year because, for example, it operates its business on a seasonal basis, it may be able to lower the amount of one or more required installments by using the annualized income installment method and/or the adjusted seasonal installment method. For example, a ski shop, which receives most of its income during the winter months, may be able to benefit from using one or both of these methods in figuring one or more of its required installments.

To use one or both of these methods, complete Schedule A. If Schedule A is used for any payment date, it must be used for all payment due dates. To get the amount of each required installment, Schedule A automatically selects the smallest of (a) the annualized income installment (if applicable), (b) the adjusted seasonal installment (if applicable), or (c) the regular installment under section 6655(d)(1) (increased by any recapture of a reduction in a required installment under section 6655(e)(1)(B)).

Large corporations. A large corporation is a corporation that had, or whose predecessor had, taxable income of $1 million or more for any of the 3 tax years immediately preceding the 2015 tax year, or if less, the number of years the corporation has been in existence. For this purpose, taxable income is modified to exclude net operating loss and capital loss carrybacks or carryovers. Members of a controlled group, as defined in section 1563, must divide the $1 million amount among themselves according to rules similar to those in section 1561.

Large corporations figure the amount to enter on line 25 as follows. If Schedule A is used, also follow these instructions to figure the amounts to enter on Schedule A, Part III, line 35.
- If line 22 is smaller than line 23a: Enter 25% of line 22 in columns (a) through (d) of line 25.
- If line 23a is smaller than line 22: Enter 25% of line 23a in column (a) of line 25. In column (b), determine the amount to enter as follows:
  1. Subtract line 23a from line 22,
  2. Add the result to the amount on line 22, and
  3. Multiply the result in 2 above by 25% and enter the result in column (b). Enter 25% of line 22 in columns (c) and (d).

Schedule A

If only the adjusted seasonal installment method (Part I) is used, complete Parts I and III of Schedule A. If only the annualized income installment method (Part II) is used, complete Parts II and III. If both methods are used, complete all three parts. Enter in each column on page 1, Part I, line 25, the amounts from the corresponding column of line 38. If Schedule A is used for any payment date, it must be used for all payment dates.

 Do not figure any required installment until after the end of the month preceding the due date for that installment.

Extraordinary items. Generally, under the annualized income installment method, extraordinary items must be taken into account after annualizing the taxable income for the annualization period. Similar rules apply in determining taxable

income under the adjusted seasonal installment method. An extraordinary item includes:
- Any item identified in Regulations section 1.1502-76(b)(2)(ii)(C)(1), (2), (3), (4), (7), and (8);
- A net operating loss carryover;
- A section 481(a) adjustment; and
- Net gain or loss from the disposition of 25% or more of the fair market value of the corporation's business assets during the tax year.

These extraordinary items must be accounted for in the appropriate annualization period. However, a net operating loss deduction and a section 481(a) adjustment (unless the corporation makes the alternative choice under Regulations section 1.6655-2(f)(ii)(C)) are treated as extraordinary items occurring on the first day of the tax year in which the item is taken into account in determining taxable income.

De minimis rule. Extraordinary items identified above that are less than $1,000,000 (other than a net operating loss carryover or a section 481(a) adjustment) may be annualized using the general rules of Regulations section 1.6655-2(f), or if the corporation chooses, may be taken into account after annualizing the taxable income for the annualization period.

For more information regarding extraordinary items, see Regulations section 1.6655-2(f)(ii) and the examples in Regulations section 1.6655-2(f)(vii). Also see Regulations section 1.6655-3(d)(3).

Part I. Adjusted Seasonal Installment Method

Complete this part only if the corporation's base period percentage for any 6 consecutive months of the tax year equals or exceeds 70% (.70). Figure the base period percentage using the 6-month period in which the corporation normally receives the largest part of its taxable income. The base period percentage for any period of 6 consecutive months is the average of the three percentages figured by dividing the taxable income for the corresponding 6-consecutive-month period in each of the 3 preceding tax years by the taxable income for each of their respective tax years.

Example. An amusement park with a calendar year as its tax year receives the largest part of its taxable income during the 6-month period from May through October. To compute its base period percentage for this 6-month period in 2015, the amusement park figures its taxable income for each May–October period in 2012, 2013, and 2014. It then divides the taxable income for each May–October period by the total taxable income for that particular tax year. The resulting percentages are 69% (.69) for May–October 2012, 74% (.74) for May–October 2013, and 67% (.67) for May–October 2014. Because the average of 69%, 74%, and 67% is 70%, the base period percentage for May through October 2015 is 70%. Therefore, the amusement park qualifies for the adjusted seasonal installment method.

Line 2

If the corporation has certain extraordinary items, special rules apply. Do not include on line 2 the de minimis extraordinary items that the corporation chooses to include on line 9b. See *Extraordinary items* above.

Line 9b

If the corporation has extraordinary items of $1,000,000 or more, a net operating loss deduction, or a section 481(a) adjustment, special rules apply. Include these amounts on line 9b for the appropriate period. Also include on line 9b the de minimis items that the corporation chooses to exclude from line 2. See *Extraordinary items* above.

Line 10

Figure the tax on the amount on line 9c by following the same steps used to figure the tax on Form 1120-W, page 1, line 14.

Line 15. Alternative Minimum Tax

The corporation may owe AMT unless it will be a "small corporation" exempt from the AMT under section 55(e) for its 2015 tax year. To figure the AMT, use the 2014 Form 4626 and its instructions as a guide. Figure alternative minimum taxable income (AMTI) using income and deductions for the months shown in the column headings above line 1. Divide the AMTI by the amounts on line 8 before subtracting the exemption amount. Multiply that result by 20% and subtract any AMT foreign tax credit plus the amount on line 10 to arrive at the AMT. For columns (a) through (c), multiply the AMT by the amount shown on line 13.

Line 16. Other Taxes

For the same taxes used to figure page 1, Part I, line 19, figure the amounts for the months shown in the column headings above line 1.

Line 18. Credits

Enter the credits to which the corporation is entitled for the months shown in the column headings above line 1.

Part II. Annualized Income Installment Method

Line 20. Annualization Periods

Enter in the space on line 20, columns (a) through (d), respectively, the annualization periods that the corporation is using, based on the options listed below. For example, if the corporation elects Option 1, enter on line 20 the annualization periods 2, 4, 7, and 10, in columns (a) through (d), respectively.

 Use Option 1 or Option 2 only if the corporation elected to use one of these options by filing Form 8842, Election To Use Different Annualization Periods for Corporate Estimated Tax, on or before the due date of the first required installment payment. Once made, the election is irrevocable for the particular tax year.

	1st Installment	2nd Installment	3rd Installment	4th Installment
Standard option	3	3	6	9
Option 1	2	4	7	10
Option 2	3	5	8	11

Line 21. Taxable Income

If a corporation has income includible under section 951(a) (controlled foreign corporation income), special rules apply.

Amounts includible in income under section 951(a) generally must be taken into account in figuring the amount of any annualized income installment as the income is earned. The amounts are figured in a manner similar to the way in which partnership income inclusions are taken into account in figuring a partner's annualized income installments as provided in Regulations section 1.6654-2(d)(2).

Safe harbor election. Corporations may be able to make a prior year safe harbor election. Under the election, an eligible corporation is treated as having received ratably during the tax

year items of income under section 951(a) equal to 115% (100% for a noncontrolling shareholder) of the amounts shown on the corporation's return for the first preceding tax year (the second preceding tax year for the first and second required installments).

For more information, see section 6655(e)(4)(B) and Regulations section 1.6655-2(f)(3)(v)(B)(2).

Extraordinary items. If the corporation has extraordinary items, special rules apply. Do not include on line 21 the de minimis extraordinary items that the corporation chooses to include on line 23b. See *Extraordinary items* earlier.

Line 22. Annualization Amounts

Enter the annualization amounts for the option used on line 20. For example, if the corporation elects Option 1, enter on line 22 the annualization amounts 6, 3, 1.71429, and 1.2, in columns (a) through (d), respectively.

	1st Installment	2nd Installment	3rd Installment	4th Installment
Standard option	4	4	2	1.33333
Option 1	6	3	1.71429	1.2
Option 2	4	2.4	1.5	1.09091

Line 23b

If the corporation has certain extraordinary items of $1,000,000 or more, a net operating loss deduction, or a section 481(a) adjustment, special rules apply. Include these amounts on line 23b. Also include on line 23b the de minimis extraordinary items that the corporation chooses to exclude from line 21. See *Extraordinary items* earlier.

Line 24

Figure the tax on the amount in each column on line 23c by following the same steps used to figure the tax on Form 1120-W, page 1, line 14.

Line 25. Alternative Minimum Tax

The corporation may owe AMT unless it will be a "small corporation" exempt from the AMT under section 55(e) for its 2015 tax year. To figure the AMT, use the 2014 Form 4626 and its instructions as a guide. Figure AMTI using income and deductions for the annualization period entered in each column on line 20. Multiply the AMTI by the annualization amounts on line 22 before subtracting the exemption amount. Multiply that result by 20% and subtract any AMT foreign tax credit plus the amount on line 24 to arrive at the AMT.

Line 26. Other Taxes

For the same taxes used to figure line 19 of Form 1120-W, figure the amounts for the months shown on line 20.

Line 28. Credits

Enter the credits to which the corporation is entitled for the months shown in each column on line 20. Do not annualize any credit. However, when figuring the credits, annualize any item of income or deduction used to figure the credit.

Part III. Required Installments

Line 33

Before completing line 33 in columns (b) through (d), complete lines 34 through 38 in each of the preceding columns. For example, complete lines 34 through 38 in column (a) before completing line 33 in column (b).

Line 35

"Large corporations," see the instructions for page 1, line 25, for the amount to enter.

Line 38. Required Installments

For each installment, enter the smaller of line 34 or line 37 on line 38. Also enter the result on page 1, Part I, line 25.

Paperwork Reduction Act Notice. Your use of this form is optional. It is provided to aid the corporation in determining its tax liability.

You are not required to provide the information requested on a form that is subject to the Paperwork Reduction Act unless the form displays a valid OMB control number. Books or records relating to a form or its instructions must be retained as long as their contents may become material in the administration of any Internal Revenue law. Generally, tax returns and return information are confidential, as required by section 6103.

The time needed to complete this form will vary depending on individual circumstances. The estimated average time is:

Form	Recordkeeping	Learning about the law or the form	Preparing the form & sending
1120-W	10 hr., 45 min.	1 hr., 35 min.	1 hr., 50 min.
1120-W, Sch. A (Pt.I)	24 hr., 37 min.	1hr.	1hr., 26 min.
1120-W, Sch. A (Pt.II)	12 hr., 26 min.	35 min.	49 min.
1120-W, Sch. A (Pt.III)	6 hr., 13 min.	6 min.	12 min.

If you have comments concerning the accuracy of these time estimates or suggestions for making this form simpler, we would be happy to hear from you. You can send us comments from *www.irs.gov/formspubs.* Click on "More Information" and then "Give us feedback." You can also send your comments to the Internal Revenue Service, Tax Forms and Publications Division, 1111 Constitution Ave. NW, IR-6526, Washington, DC 20224. Do not send the tax form to this office. Instead, keep the form for your records.

Form **2106**	**Employee Business Expenses**	OMB No. 1545-0074
Department of the Treasury Internal Revenue Service (99)	▶ Attach to Form 1040 or Form 1040NR. ▶ Information about Form 2106 and its separate instructions is available at *www.irs.gov/form2106*.	**20 14** Attachment Sequence No. **129**

Your name	Occupation in which you incurred expenses	Social security number

Part I Employee Business Expenses and Reimbursements

Step 1 Enter Your Expenses

			Column A Other Than Meals and Entertainment		**Column B** Meals and Entertainment
1	Vehicle expense from line 22 or line 29. (Rural mail carriers: See instructions.)	**1**			
2	Parking fees, tolls, and transportation, including train, bus, etc., that **did not** involve overnight travel or commuting to and from work	**2**			
3	Travel expense while away from home overnight, including lodging, airplane, car rental, etc. **Do not** include meals and entertainment	**3**			
4	Business expenses not included on lines 1 through 3. **Do not** include meals and entertainment	**4**			
5	Meals and entertainment expenses (see instructions)	**5**			
6	**Total expenses.** In Column A, add lines 1 through 4 and enter the result. In Column B, enter the amount from line 5	**6**			

Note. *If you were not reimbursed for any expenses in Step 1, skip line 7 and enter the amount from line 6 on line 8.*

Step 2 Enter Reimbursements Received From Your Employer for Expenses Listed in Step 1

7	Enter reimbursements received from your employer that were not reported to you in box 1 of Form W-2. Include any reimbursements reported under code "L" in box 12 of your Form W-2 (see instructions).	**7**			

Step 3 Figure Expenses To Deduct on Schedule A (Form 1040 or Form 1040NR)

8	Subtract line 7 from line 6. If zero or less, enter -0-. However, if line 7 is greater than line 6 in Column A, report the excess as income on Form 1040, line 7 (or on Form 1040NR, line 8)	**8**			

Note. *If both columns of line 8 are zero, you cannot deduct employee business expenses. Stop here and attach Form 2106 to your return.*

9	In Column A, enter the amount from line 8. In Column B, multiply line 8 by 50% (.50). (Employees subject to Department of Transportation (DOT) hours of service limits: Multiply meal expenses incurred while away from home on business by 80% (.80) instead of 50%. For details, see instructions.)	**9**			
10	Add the amounts on line 9 of both columns and enter the total here. **Also, enter the total on Schedule A (Form 1040), line 21** (or on **Schedule A (Form 1040NR), line 7**). (Armed Forces reservists, qualified performing artists, fee-basis state or local government officials, and individuals with disabilities: See the instructions for special rules on where to enter the total.) ▶	**10**			

For Paperwork Reduction Act Notice, see your tax return instructions.   Cat. No. 11700N   Form **2106** (2014)

Part II   **Vehicle Expenses**

Section A—General Information (You must complete this section if you are claiming vehicle expenses.)

			(a) Vehicle 1	**(b)** Vehicle 2
11	Enter the date the vehicle was placed in service	11	/ /	/ /
12	Total miles the vehicle was driven during 2014	12	miles	miles
13	Business miles included on line 12	13	miles	miles
14	Percent of business use. Divide line 13 by line 12	14	%	%
15	Average daily roundtrip commuting distance	15	miles	miles
16	Commuting miles included on line 12	16	miles	miles
17	Other miles. Add lines 13 and 16 and subtract the total from line 12	17	miles	miles
18	Was your vehicle available for personal use during off-duty hours?		☐ Yes ☐ No	
19	Do you (or your spouse) have another vehicle available for personal use?		☐ Yes ☐ No	
20	Do you have evidence to support your deduction?		☐ Yes ☐ No	
21	If "Yes," is the evidence written?		☐ Yes ☐ No	

Section B—Standard Mileage Rate (See the instructions for Part II to find out whether to complete this section or Section C.)

22	Multiply line 13 by 56¢ (.56). Enter the result here and on line 1	22	

Section C—Actual Expenses

			(a) Vehicle 1	**(b)** Vehicle 2
23	Gasoline, oil, repairs, vehicle insurance, etc.	23		
24a	Vehicle rentals	24a		
b	Inclusion amount (see instructions)	24b		
c	Subtract line 24b from line 24a	24c		
25	Value of employer-provided vehicle (applies only if 100% of annual lease value was included on Form W-2—see instructions)	25		
26	Add lines 23, 24c, and 25.	26		
27	Multiply line 26 by the percentage on line 14	27		
28	Depreciation (see instructions)	28		
29	Add lines 27 and 28. Enter total here and on line 1	29		

Section D—Depreciation of Vehicles (Use this section only if you owned the vehicle and are completing Section C for the vehicle.)

			(a) Vehicle 1	**(b)** Vehicle 2
30	Enter cost or other basis (see instructions)	30		
31	Enter section 179 deduction (see instructions)	31		
32	Multiply line 30 by line 14 (see instructions if you claimed the section 179 deduction)	32		
33	Enter depreciation method and percentage (see instructions)	33		
34	Multiply line 32 by the percentage on line 33 (see instructions)	34		
35	Add lines 31 and 34	35		
36	Enter the applicable limit explained in the line 36 instructions	36		
37	Multiply line 36 by the percentage on line 14	37		
38	Enter the **smaller** of line 35 or line 37. If you skipped lines 36 and 37, enter the amount from line 35. Also enter this amount on line 28 above	38		

2014

**Department of the Treasury
Internal Revenue Service**

Instructions for Form 2106

Employee Business Expenses

Section references are to the Internal Revenue Code unless otherwise noted.

Future Developments

For the latest developments related to Form 2106 and its instructions, such as legislation enacted after they were published, go to *www.irs.gov/ form2106*.

What's New

Standard mileage rate. The 2014 rate for business use of your vehicle is 56 cents a mile.

Depreciation limits on vehicles. For 2014, the first-year limit on depreciation, special depreciation allowance, and section 179 deduction for most vehicles remains at $11,160 ($3,160 if you elect not to claim the special depreciation allowance). For

trucks and vans, the first-year limit is $11,460 ($3,460 if you elect not to claim the special depreciation allowance). For more details, see the discussion under *Section D – Depreciation of Vehicles*, later.

General Instructions

Purpose of Form

Use Form 2106 if you were an employee deducting ordinary and necessary expenses for your job. See the flowchart below to find out if you must file this form.

An ordinary expense is one that is common and accepted in your field of trade, business, or profession. A necessary expense is one that is helpful and appropriate for your business. An expense does not have

to be required to be considered necessary.

Form 2106-EZ. You can file Form 2106-EZ, Unreimbursed Employee Business Expenses, provided you were an employee deducting ordinary and necessary expenses for your job and you:

- Use the standard mileage rate (if claiming vehicle expense), and
- Were not reimbursed by your employer for any expense (amounts your employer included in box 1 of your Form W-2 are not considered reimbursements for this purpose).

Recordkeeping

You cannot deduct expenses for travel (including meals unless you used the standard meal allowance), entertainment, gifts, or use of a car or

Who Must File Form 2106

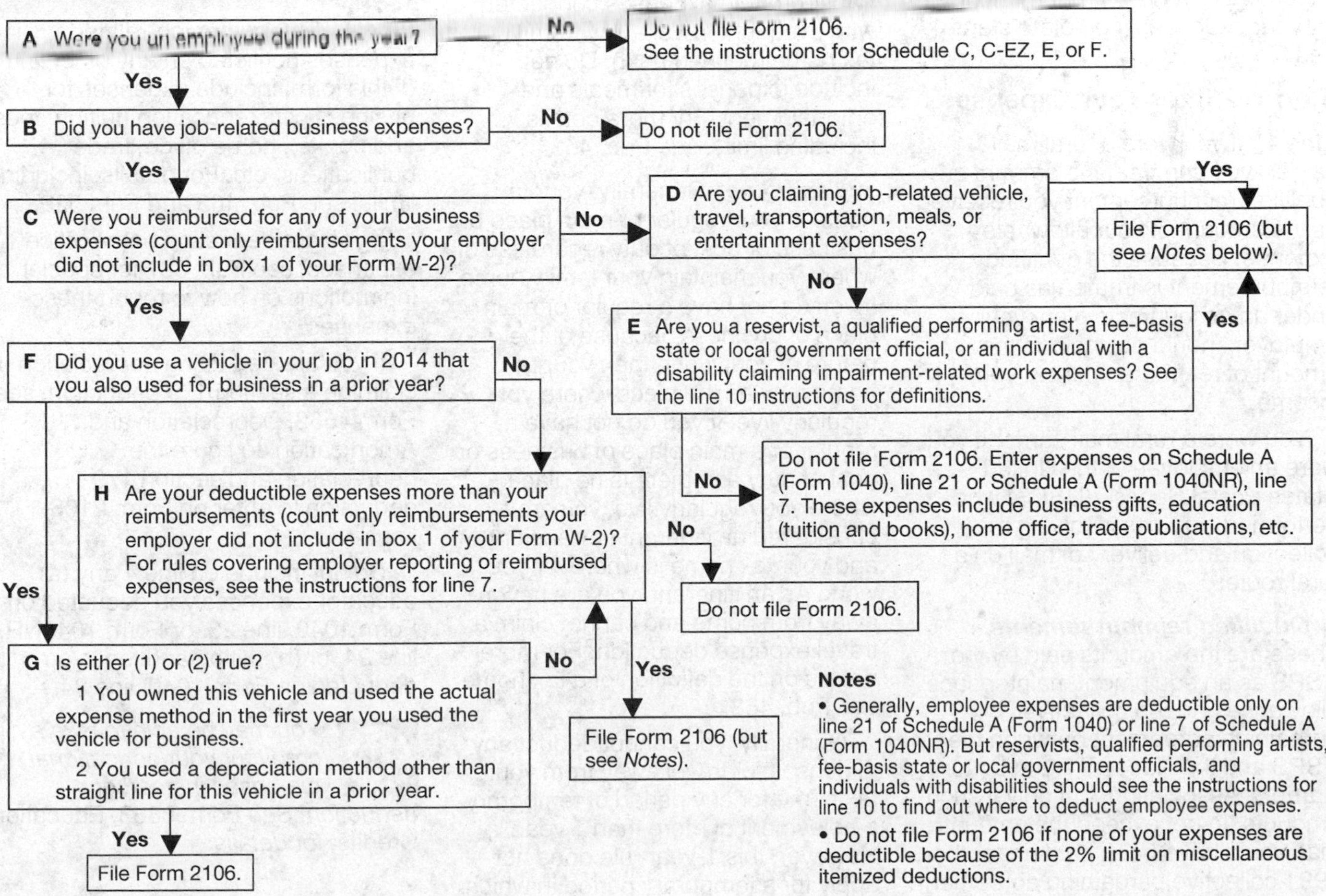

A Were you an employee during the year? — **No** → Do not file Form 2106. See the instructions for Schedule C, C-EZ, E, or F.

↓ **Yes**

B Did you have job-related business expenses? — **No** → Do not file Form 2106.

↓ **Yes**

C Were you reimbursed for any of your business expenses (count only reimbursements your employer did not include in box 1 of your Form W-2)? — **No** →

D Are you claiming job-related vehicle, travel, transportation, meals, or entertainment expenses? — **Yes** → File Form 2106 (but see *Notes* below).

↓ **Yes** (from C)

F Did you use a vehicle in your job in 2014 that you also used for business in a prior year? — **No** →

(from D) ↓ **No**

E Are you a reservist, a qualified performing artist, a fee-basis state or local government official, or an individual with a disability claiming impairment-related work expenses? See the line 10 instructions for definitions. — **Yes** → File Form 2106 (but see *Notes* below).

↓ **No** (from E)

H Are your deductible expenses more than your reimbursements (count only reimbursements your employer did not include in box 1 of your Form W-2)? For rules covering employer reporting of reimbursed expenses, see the instructions for line 7.

No → Do not file Form 2106. Enter expenses on Schedule A (Form 1040), line 21 or Schedule A (Form 1040NR), line 7. These expenses include business gifts, education (tuition and books), home office, trade publications, etc.

No → Do not file Form 2106.

Yes (from H) ↓

G Is either (1) or (2) true?

1 You owned this vehicle and used the actual expense method in the first year you used the vehicle for business.

2 You used a depreciation method other than straight line for this vehicle in a prior year.

— **No** → File Form 2106 (but see *Notes*).

↓ **Yes**

File Form 2106.

Notes

- Generally, employee expenses are deductible only on line 21 of Schedule A (Form 1040) or line 7 of Schedule A (Form 1040NR). But reservists, qualified performing artists, fee-basis state or local government officials, and individuals with disabilities should see the instructions for line 10 to find out where to deduct employee expenses.

- Do not file Form 2106 if none of your expenses are deductible because of the 2% limit on miscellaneous itemized deductions.

other listed property unless you keep records to prove the time, place, business purpose, business relationship (for entertainment and gifts), and amounts of these expenses. Generally, you must also have receipts for all lodging expenses (regardless of the amount) and any other expense of $75 or more.

Additional Information

For more details about employee business expenses, see:
• Pub. 463, Travel, Entertainment, Gift, and Car Expenses.
• Pub. 529, Miscellaneous Deductions.
• Pub. 587, Business Use of Your Home (Including Use by Daycare Providers).
• Pub. 946, How To Depreciate Property.

Specific Instructions

Part I—Employee Business Expenses and Reimbursements

Fill in all of Part I if you were reimbursed for employee business expenses. If you were not reimbursed for your expenses, complete steps 1 and 3 only.

Step 1—Enter Your Expenses

Line 1. If you were a rural mail carrier, you can treat the amount of qualified reimbursement you received as the amount of your allowable expense. Because the qualified reimbursement is treated as paid under an accountable plan, your employer should not include the amount of reimbursement in your income.

You were a rural mail carrier if you were an employee of the United States Postal Service (USPS) who performed services involving the collection and delivery of mail on a rural route.

Qualified reimbursements. These are the amounts paid by the USPS as an equipment maintenance allowance under a collective bargaining agreement between the USPS and the National Rural Letter Carriers' Association, but only if such amounts do not exceed the amount that would have been paid under the 1991 collective bargaining agreement

(adjusted for changes in the Consumer Price Index since 1991).

If you were a rural mail carrier and your vehicle expenses were:
• Less than or equal to your qualified reimbursements, do not file Form 2106 unless you have deductible expenses other than vehicle expenses. If you have deductible expenses other than vehicle expenses, skip line 1 and do not include any qualified reimbursements in column A on line 7.
• More than your qualified reimbursements, first complete Part II of Form 2106. Enter your total vehicle expenses from line 29 on line 1 and the amount of your qualified reimbursements in column A on line 7.

 If you are a rural mail carrier and received a qualified reimbursement, you cannot use the standard mileage rate.

Line 2. The expenses of commuting to and from work are not deductible. See the line 15 instructions for the definition of commuting.

Line 3. Enter lodging and transportation expenses connected with overnight travel away from your tax home (defined next). Do not include expenses for meals and entertainment. For more details, including limits, see Pub. 463.

Tax home. Generally, your tax home is your regular or main place of business or post of duty regardless of where you maintain your family home. If you do not have a regular or main place of business because of the nature of your work, then your tax home may be the place where you regularly live. If you do not have a regular or a main place of business or post of duty and there is no place where you regularly live, you are considered an itinerant (a transient) and your tax home is wherever you work. As an itinerant, you are never away from home and cannot claim a travel expense deduction. For more details on the definition of a tax home, see Pub. 463.

Generally, you cannot deduct any expenses for travel away from your tax home for any period of temporary employment of more than 1 year. However, this 1-year rule does not apply for a temporary period in which

you were a federal employee certified by the Attorney General (or his or her designee) as traveling in temporary duty status for the U.S. government to investigate or prosecute a federal crime (or to provide support services for the investigation or prosecution of a federal crime).

Incidental expenses. The term "incidental expenses" means fees and tips given to porters, baggage carriers, hotel staff, and staff on ships.

Incidental expenses do not include expenses for laundry, cleaning and pressing of clothing, lodging taxes, costs of telegrams or telephone calls, transportation between places of lodging or business and places where meals are taken, or the mailing cost of filing travel vouchers and paying employer-sponsored charge card billings.

You can use an optional method (instead of actual cost) for deducting incidental expenses only. The amount of the deduction is $5 a day. You can use this method only if you did not pay or incur any meal expenses. You cannot use this method on any day you use the standard meal allowance (defined in the instructions for line 5).

Line 4. Enter other job-related expenses not listed on any other line of this form. Include expenses for business gifts, education (tuition, fees, and books), home office, trade publications, etc. For details, including limits, see Pub. 463 and Pub. 529.

If you are deducting home office expenses, see Pub. 587 for special instructions on how to report these expenses.

If you are deducting depreciation or claiming a section 179 deduction, see Form 4562, Depreciation and Amortization, to figure the depreciation and section 179 deduction to enter on Form 2106, line 4.

Do not include on line 4 any (a) educator expenses you deducted on Form 1040, line 23, or Form 1040NR, line 24, or (b) tuition and fees you deducted on Form 1040, line 34.

 You may be able to take a credit for your educational expenses instead of a deduction. See Form 8863, Education Credits, for details.

Instructions for Form 2106 (2014)

Do not include expenses for meals and entertainment, taxes, or interest on line 4. Deductible taxes are entered on Schedule A (Form 1040), lines 5 through 9; or Schedule A (Form 1040NR), line 1. Employees cannot deduct car loan interest.

Note. If line 4 is your only entry, do not complete Form 2106 unless you are claiming:
• Performing-arts-related business expenses as a qualified performing artist,
• Expenses for performing your job as a fee-basis state or local government official, or
• Impairment-related work expenses as an individual with a disability.

See the line 10 instructions. If you are not required to file Form 2106, enter your expenses directly on Schedule A (Form 1040), line 21 (or Schedule A (Form 1040NR), line 7).

Line 5. Enter your allowable meals and entertainment expense. Include meals while away from your tax home overnight and other business meals and entertainment.

Standard meal allowance. Instead of actual cost, you may be able to claim the standard meal allowance for your daily meals and incidental expenses (M&IE) while away from your tax home overnight. Under this method, instead of keeping records of your actual meal expenses, you deduct a specified amount, depending on where you travel. However, you must still keep records to prove the time, place, and business purpose of your travel.

The standard meal allowance is the federal M&IE rate. For most small localities in the United States, this rate is $46 a day. Most major cities and many other localities in the United States qualify for higher rates. You can find the rates that applied during 2014 on the Internet at *www.gsa.gov/perdiem*. At the Per Diem Overview page select "2014" for the rates in effect for the period January 1, 2014–September 30, 2014. Select "Fiscal Year 2015" for the period October 1, 2014–December 31, 2014. However, you can apply the rates in effect before October 1, 2014, for expenses of all travel within the United States for 2014 instead of the updated rates. For the period October 1, 2014–December 31, 2014, you must

consistently use either the rates for the first 9 months of 2014 or the updated rates.

For locations outside the continental United States, the applicable rates are published each month. You can find these rates on the Internet at *www.state.gov/travel* and select the option for "Foreign Per Diem Rates."

See Pub. 463 for details on how to figure your deduction using the standard meal allowance, including special rules for partial days of travel and transportation workers.

Step 2—Enter Reimbursements Received From Your Employer for Expenses Listed in Step 1

Line 7. Enter reimbursements received from your employer (or third party) for expenses shown in Step 1 that were not reported to you in box 1 of your Form W-2. This includes reimbursements reported under code "L" in box 12 of Form W-2. Amounts reported under code "L" are reimbursements you received for business expenses that were not included as wages on Form W-2 because the expenses met specific IRS substantiation requirements.

Generally, when your employer pays for your expenses, the payments should not be included in box 1 of your Form W-2 if, within a reasonable period of time, you:
• Accounted to your employer for the expenses, and
• Were required to return, and did return, any payment not spent (or considered not spent) for business expenses.

If these payments were incorrectly included in box 1, ask your employer for a corrected Form W-2.

Accounting to your employer. This means that you gave your employer documentary evidence and an account book, diary, log, statement of expenses, trip sheets, or similar statement to verify the amount, time, place, and business purpose of each expense. You are also treated as having accounted for your expenses if either of the following applies.
• Your employer gave you a fixed travel allowance that is similar in form to the per diem allowance specified by the Federal Government and you

verified the time, place, and business purpose of the travel for that day.
• Your employer reimbursed you for vehicle expenses at the standard mileage rate or according to a flat rate or stated schedule, and you verified the date of each trip, mileage, and business purpose of the vehicle use.

See Pub. 463 for more details.

Allocating your reimbursement. If your employer paid you a single amount that covers meals and entertainment as well as other business expenses, you must allocate the reimbursement so that you know how much to enter in Column A and Column B of line 7. Use the following worksheet to figure this allocation.

Reimbursement Allocation Worksheet
(keep for your records)

1. Enter the total amount of reimbursements your employer gave you that were not reported to you in box 1 of Form W-2 . . . _____

2. Enter the total amount of your expenses for the periods covered by this reimbursement . . . . _____

3. Enter the part of the amount on line 2 that was your total expense for meals and entertainment . . . . _____

4. Divide line 3 by line 2. Enter the result as a decimal (rounded to three places) . . . . _____._

5. Multiply line 1 by line 4. Enter the result here and in Column B, line 7 . . . . _____

6. Subtract line 5 from line 1. Enter the result here and in Column A, line 7 . . . . _____

Step 3—Figure Expenses To Deduct on Schedule A (Form 1040 or Form 1040NR)

Line 9. Generally, you can deduct only 50% of your business meal and entertainment expenses, including meals incurred while away from home on business. However, if you were an employee subject to the DOT hours of service limits, that percentage is increased to 80% for business meals consumed during, or incident to, any period of duty for which those limits are in effect.

Employees subject to the DOT hours of service limits include certain air transportation employees, such as pilots, crew, dispatchers, mechanics, and control tower operators; interstate truck operators and interstate bus drivers; certain railroad employees, such as engineers, conductors, train crews, dispatchers, and control operations personnel; and certain merchant mariners.

Line 10. If you are one of the individuals discussed below, special rules apply to deducting your employee business expenses. Any part of the line 10 total that is not deducted according to the special rules should be entered on Schedule A (Form 1040), line 21 (or Schedule A (Form 1040NR), line 7).

Ministers. Before entering your total expenses on line 10, you must reduce them by the amount allocable to your tax-free allowance(s). See Pub. 517 for more information.

Armed Forces reservist (member of a reserve component). You are a member of a reserve component of the Armed Forces of the United States if you are in the Army, Navy, Marine Corps, Air Force, or Coast Guard Reserve; the Army National Guard of the United States; the Air National Guard of the United States; or the Reserve Corps of the Public Health Service.

If you qualify, complete Form 2106 and include the part of the line 10 amount attributable to the expenses for travel more than 100 miles away from home in connection with your performance of services as a member of the reserves on Form 1040, line 24, and attach Form 2106 to your return. The amount of expenses you can deduct on Form 1040, line 24, is limited to the regular federal per diem rate (for lodging, meals, and incidental expenses) and the standard mileage rate (for car expenses), plus any parking fees, ferry fees, and tolls. These reserve-related travel expenses are deductible whether or not you itemize deductions. See Pub. 463 for additional details on how to report these expenses.

Fee-basis state or local government official. You are a qualifying fee-basis official if you are

employed by a state or political subdivision of a state and are compensated, in whole or in part, on a fee basis.

If you qualify, include the part of the line 10 amount attributable to the expenses you incurred for services performed in that job in the total on Form 1040, line 24, and attach Form 2106 to your return. These employee business expenses are deductible whether or not you itemize deductions.

Qualified performing artist. You are a qualified performing artist if you:

1. Performed services in the performing arts as an employee for at least two employers during the tax year,

2. Received from at least two of those employers wages of $200 or more per employer,

3. Had allowable business expenses attributable to the performing arts of more than 10% of gross income from the performing arts, and

4. Had adjusted gross income of $16,000 or less before deducting expenses as a performing artist.

In addition, if you are married, you must file a joint return unless you lived apart from your spouse for all of 2014. If you file a joint return, you must figure requirements (1), (2), and (3) separately for both you and your spouse. However, requirement (4) applies to the combined adjusted gross income of both you and your spouse.

If you meet all the requirements for a qualified performing artist, include the part of the line 10 amount attributable to performing-arts-related expenses in the total on Form 1040, line 24 (or Form 1040NR, line 35), and attach Form 2106 to your return. Your performing-arts-related business expenses are deductible whether or not you itemize deductions.

Disabled employee with impairment-related work expenses. Impairment-related work expenses are the allowable expenses of an individual with physical or mental disabilities for attendant care at his or her place of employment. They also include other expenses in connection with the place of employment that enable the employee

to work. See Pub. 463 for more details.

If you qualify, enter the part of the line 10 amount attributable to impairment-related work expenses on Schedule A (Form 1040), line 28 (or Schedule A (Form 1040NR), line 14). These expenses are not subject to the 2% limit that applies to most other employee business expenses.

Part II—Vehicle Expenses

There are two methods for computing vehicle expenses—the standard mileage rate and the actual expense method. You can use the standard mileage rate for 2014 only if:

• You owned the vehicle and used the standard mileage rate for the first year you placed the vehicle in service, or

• You leased the vehicle and are using the standard mileage rate for the entire lease period (except the period, if any, before 1998).

You cannot use actual expenses for a leased vehicle if you previously used the standard mileage rate for that vehicle.

If you have the option of using either the standard mileage rate or actual expense method, you should figure your expenses both ways to find the method most beneficial to you. But when completing Form 2106, fill in only the sections that apply to the method you choose.

If you were a rural mail carrier and received an equipment maintenance allowance, see the line 1 instructions.

For more information on the standard mileage rate and actual expenses, see Pub. 463.

Section A—General Information

If you used two vehicles for business during the year, use a separate column in Sections A, C, and D for each vehicle. If you used more than two vehicles, complete and attach a second Form 2106, page 2.

Line 11. Date placed in service is generally the date you first start using your vehicle. However, if you first start using your vehicle for personal use and later convert it to business use, the vehicle is treated as placed in service on the date you started using it for business.

Instructions for Form 2106 (2014)

Line 12. Enter the total number of miles you drove each vehicle during 2014.

Change from personal to business use. If you converted your vehicle during the year from personal to business use (or vice versa) and you do not have mileage records for the time before the change to business use, enter the total number of miles driven after the change to business use.

Line 13. Do not include commuting miles on this line; commuting miles are not considered business miles. See the line 15 instructions below for the definition of commuting.

Line 14. Divide line 13 by line 12 to figure your business use percentage.

Change from personal to business use. If you entered on line 12 the total number of miles driven after the change to business use, multiply the percentage you figured by the number of months you drove the vehicle for business and divide the result by 12.

Line 15. Enter your average daily round trip commuting distance. If you went to more than one work location, figure the average.

Commuting. Generally, commuting is travel between your home and a work location. However, travel that meets any of the following conditions is not commuting.
• You have at least one regular work location away from your home and the travel is to a temporary work location in the same trade or business, regardless of the distance. Generally, a temporary work location is one where your employment is expected to last 1 year or less. See Pub. 463 for more details.
• The travel is to a temporary work location outside the metropolitan area where you live and normally work.
• Your home is your principal place of business under section 280A(c)(1)(A) (for purposes of deducting expenses for business use of your home) and the travel is to another work location in the same trade or business, regardless of whether that location is regular or temporary and regardless of distance.

Line 16. If you do not know the total actual miles you used your vehicle for commuting during the year, figure the amount to enter on line 16 by multiplying the number of days during the year that you used each vehicle for commuting by the average daily round trip commuting distance in miles. However, if you converted your vehicle during the year from personal to business use (or vice versa), enter your commuting miles only for the period you drove your vehicle for business.

Section B—Standard Mileage Rate

You may be able to use the standard mileage rate instead of actual expenses to figure the deductible costs of operating a passenger vehicle, including a van, sport utility vehicle (SUV), pickup, or panel truck.

If you want to use the standard mileage rate for a vehicle you own, you must do so in the first year you place your vehicle in service. In later years, you can deduct actual expenses instead, but you must use straight line depreciation.

If you lease your vehicle, you can use the standard mileage rate, but only if you use the rate for the entire lease period (except for the period, if any, before January 1, 1998).

If you use more than two vehicles, complete and attach a second Form 2106, page 2, providing the information requested in lines 11 through 22. Be sure to include the amount from line 22 of both pages in the total on Form 2106, line 1.

You can also deduct state and local personal property taxes. Enter these taxes on Schedule A (Form 1040), line 7. (Personal property taxes are not deductible on Form 1040NR.)

If you are claiming the standard mileage rate for mileage driven in more than one business activity, you must figure the deduction for each business on a separate form or schedule (for example, Form 2106 or Schedule C, C-EZ, E, or F).

Section C—Actual Expenses

Line 23. Enter your total annual expenses for gasoline, oil, repairs, insurance, tires, license plates, and similar items. Do not include state and local personal property taxes or interest expense you paid. Deduct state and local personal property taxes on Schedule A (Form 1040), line 7. Employees cannot deduct car loan interest.

Line 24a. If during 2014 you rented or leased instead of using your own vehicle, enter the cost of renting. Also, include on this line any temporary rentals, such as when your car was being repaired, except for amounts included on line 3.

Line 24b. If you leased a vehicle for a term of 30 days or more, you may have to reduce your deduction for vehicle lease payments by an amount called the inclusion amount. You may have an inclusion amount for a passenger automobile if:

Passenger Automobiles (Except Trucks and Vans)

The lease term began in:	And the vehicle's fair market value on the first day of the lease exceeded:
2014	$ 18,500
2013	19,000
2010, 2011, or 2012	18,500

If the lease term began before 2010, see Pub. 463 to find out if you have an inclusion amount.

You may have an inclusion amount for a truck or van if:

Trucks and Vans

The lease term began in:	And the vehicle's fair market value on the first day of the lease exceeded:
2010, 2011, 2012, 2013, or 2014	$ 19,000

See Pub. 463 to figure the inclusion amount.

Line 25. If during 2014 your employer provided a vehicle for your business use and included 100% of its annual lease value in box 1 of your Form W-2, enter this amount on line 25. If less than 100% of the annual lease value was included in box 1 of your Form W-2, skip line 25.

Line 28. If you completed Section D, enter the amount from line 38. If you used Form 4562 to figure your depreciation deduction, enter the total of the following amounts.
• Depreciation allocable to your vehicle(s) (from Form 4562, line 28).
• Any section 179 deduction allocable to your vehicle(s) (from Form 4562, line 29).

Section D—Depreciation of Vehicles

Depreciation is an amount you can deduct to recover the cost or other basis of your vehicle over a certain number of years. In some cases, you can elect to claim a special depreciation allowance or to expense, under section 179, part of the cost of your vehicle in the year of purchase. For details, see Pub. 463.

Vehicle trade-in. If you traded in one vehicle (the "old vehicle") for another vehicle (the "new vehicle") in 2014, there are two ways you can treat the transaction.

1. You can elect to treat the transaction as a tax-free disposition of the old vehicle and the purchase of the new vehicle. If you make this election, you treat the old vehicle as disposed of at the time of the trade-in. The depreciable basis of the new vehicle is the adjusted basis of the old vehicle (figured as if 100% of the vehicle's use had been for business purposes) plus any additional amount you paid for the new vehicle. You then figure your depreciation deduction for the new vehicle beginning with the date you placed it in service. You make this election by completing Form 2106, Part II, Section D.

2. If you do not make the election described in (1), you must figure depreciation separately for the remaining basis of the old vehicle and for any additional amount you paid for the new vehicle. You must apply two depreciation limits. The limit that applies to the remaining basis of the old vehicle generally is the amount that would have been allowed had you not traded the old vehicle. The limit that applies to the additional amount you paid for the new vehicle generally is the limit that applies for the tax year it was placed in service, reduced by the depreciation allowance for the remaining basis of the old vehicle. You must use Form 4562 to compute your depreciation deduction. You cannot use Form 2106, Part II, Section D.

If you elect to use the method described in (1), you must do so on a timely filed tax return (including extensions). Otherwise, you must use the method described in (2).

Line 30. Enter the vehicle's actual cost or other basis. Do not reduce your basis by any prior year's depreciation. However, you must reduce your basis by any deductible casualty loss, deduction for clean-fuel vehicle, gas guzzler tax, alternative motor vehicle credit, or qualified plug-in electric vehicle credit you claimed. Increase your basis by any sales tax paid (unless you deducted sales taxes in the year you purchased your vehicle) and any substantial improvements to your vehicle.

If you traded in your vehicle, your basis is the adjusted basis of the old vehicle (reduced by depreciation figured as if 100% of the vehicle's use had been for business purposes) plus any additional amount you pay for the new vehicle. See Pub. 463 for more information.

If you converted the vehicle from personal use to business use, your basis for depreciation is the smaller of the vehicle's adjusted basis or its fair market value on the date of conversion.

Line 31. Enter the amount of any section 179 deduction and, if applicable, any special depreciation allowance claimed for this year.

Section 179 deduction. If 2014 is the first year your vehicle was placed in service and the percentage on line 14 is more than 50%, you can elect to deduct as an expense a portion of the cost (subject to a yearly limit). To calculate this section 179 deduction, multiply the part of the cost of the vehicle that you choose to expense by the percentage on line 14. The total of your depreciation and section 179 deduction generally cannot be more than the percentage on line 14 multiplied by the applicable limit explained in the line 36 instructions. Your section 179 deduction for the year cannot be more than the income from your job and any other active trade or business on your Form 1040.

 If you are claiming a section 179 deduction on other property, or you placed more than $2,000,000 of section 179 property in service during the year, use Form 4562 to figure your section 179 deduction. Enter the amount of the section 179 deduction allocable to your vehicle (from Form 4562, line 12) on Form 2106, line 31.

Note. For section 179 purposes, the cost of the new vehicle does not include the adjusted basis of the vehicle you traded in.

Example.

Cost including taxes	$25,000
Adjusted basis of trade-in	– 3,000
Section 179 basis	$22,000
Limit on depreciation and section 179 deduction . . .	$11,160*

Smaller of:

Section 179 basis, or limit on depreciation	$11,160
Percentage on line 14 . . .	×.75
Section 179 deduction . . .	$8,370

* $3,160 if electing out of special depreciation allowance or not qualified property.

Limit for sport utility and certain other vehicles. For sport utility and certain other vehicles placed in service in 2014, the portion of the vehicle's cost taken into account in figuring your section 179 deduction is limited to $25,000. This rule applies to any 4-wheeled vehicle primarily designed or used to carry passengers over public streets, roads, or highways that is not subject to any of the passenger automobile limits explained in the line 36 instructions and is rated at no more than 14,000 pounds gross vehicle weight. However, the $25,000 limit does not apply to any vehicle:

• Designed to have a seating capacity of more than nine persons behind the driver's seat,

• Equipped with a cargo area of at least 6 feet in interior length that is an open area or is designed for use as an open area but is enclosed by a cap and is not readily accessible directly from the passenger compartment, or

• That has an integral enclosure, fully enclosing the driver compartment and load carrying device, does not have seating rearward of the driver's seat, and has no body section protruding more than 30 inches ahead of the leading edge of the windshield.

Special depreciation allowance. The special depreciation allowance applies only for the first year a new vehicle is placed in service. To qualify for the special depreciation allowance, the new vehicle must be qualified property (see Pub. 463, chapter 4, for more information). The special allowance is an additional first year depreciation deduction of 50%. Your total section 179 deduction, special depreciation allowance, and regular depreciation deduction cannot be more than $11,160 for cars and $11,460 for trucks and vans, multiplied by your business use percentage on line 14. See the line 36 instructions for depreciation limits. You cannot recover the amount by which your depreciation deduction exceeds the depreciation limits for the year placed in service until after the end of the recovery period for your vehicle.

Use the following worksheet to figure the amount of the special depreciation allowance.

Worksheet for the Special Depreciation Allowance
(keep for your records)

1. Enter the total amount from Form 2106, line 30 . . . . _____

2. Multiply line 1 by the percentage on Form 2106, line 14, and enter the result . . . . _____

3. Enter any section 179 deduction . . . . _____

4. Subtract line 3 from line 2 . . . . _____

5. Multiply the applicable limit explained in the line 36 instructions by the percentage on Form 2106, line 14, and enter the result . . . . _____

6. Subtract line 3 from line 5 . . . . _____

7. Enter the **smaller** of line 4 or line 6. Add the result to any section 179 deduction (line 3 above) and enter the total on Form 2106, line 31 . . . . _____

Election out. You can elect not to claim the special depreciation allowance for your vehicle. If you make this election, it applies to all property in the same class placed in service during the year.

To make the election, attach a statement to your timely filed return (including extensions) indicating that you are electing not to claim the special depreciation allowance and the class of property for which you are making the election.

More information. See Pub. 463, chapter 4, for more information on the special depreciation allowance.

Line 32. To figure the basis for depreciation, multiply line 30 by the percentage on line 14. From that result, subtract the total amount of any section 179 deduction and special depreciation allowance claimed this year (see line 31) or any section 179 deduction and special depreciation allowance claimed in any previous year for this vehicle.

Line 33. If you used the standard mileage rate in the first year the vehicle was placed in service and now elect to use the actual expense method, you must use the straight line method of depreciation for the vehicle's estimated useful life. Otherwise, use the following Depreciation Method and Percentage Chart to find the depreciation method and percentage to enter on line 33.

To use the chart, first find the date you placed the vehicle in service (line 11). Then, select the depreciation method and percentage from column (a), (b), or (c). For example, if you placed a car in service on July 1, 2014, and you use the method in column (a), enter "200 DB 20%" on line 33.

For vehicles placed in service before 2014, use the same method you used on last year's return unless a decline in your business use requires a change to the straight line method. For vehicles placed in service during 2014, select the depreciation method and percentage after reading the explanation for each column.

Column (a)—200% declining balance method. You can use column (a) only if the business use percentage on line 14 is more than 50%. Of the three depreciation methods, the 200% declining balance method may give you the largest depreciation deduction for the first 3 years (after considering the depreciation limit for your vehicle). See the depreciation limit tables, later.

Column (b)—150% declining balance method. You can use column (b) only if the business use percentage on line 14 is more than 50%. The 150% declining balance method may give you a smaller depreciation deduction than in column (a) for the first 3 years. However, you will not have a "depreciation adjustment" on this vehicle for the alternative minimum tax. This may result in a smaller tax liability if you must file Form 6251, Alternative Minimum Tax—Individuals.

Column (c)—straight line method. You must use column (c) if the business use percentage on line 14 is 50% or less. The method for these vehicles is the straight line method over 5 years. The use of this column is optional for these vehicles if the business use percentage on line 14 is more than 50%.

Note. If your vehicle was used more than 50% for business in the year it was placed in service and used 50% or less in a later year, part of the depreciation, section 179 deduction, and special depreciation allowance previously claimed may have to be added back to your income in the later year. Figure the amount to be included in income in Part IV of Form 4797, Sales of Business Property.

More information. For more information on depreciating your vehicle, see Pub. 463.

 If you placed other business property in service in the same year you placed your vehicle in service or you used your vehicle mainly within an Indian reservation, you may not be able to use the chart. See Pub. 946 to figure your depreciation.

Line 34. If you sold or exchanged your vehicle during the year, use the following instructions to figure the amount to enter on line 34.

If your vehicle was placed in service:

1. Before 2009, enter the result of multiplying line 32 by the percentage on line 33;

2. After 2008, from January 1 through September 30, enter the amount figured by multiplying the result in (1) by 50%; or

3. After 2008, from October 1 through December 31, enter the amount figured by multiplying the

Depreciation Method and Percentage Chart—Line 33

Date Placed in Service	(a)[1]	(b)[1]	(c)
Oct. 1 – Dec. 31, 2014	200 DB 5.0 %	150 DB 3.75%	SL 2.5%
Jan. 1 – Sept. 30, 2014	200 DB 20.0	150 DB 15.0	SL 10.0
Oct. 1 – Dec. 31, 2013	200 DB 38.0	150 DB 28.88	SL 20.0
Jan. 1 – Sept. 30, 2013	200 DB 32.0	150 DB 25.5	SL 20.0
Oct. 1 – Dec. 31, 2012	200 DB 22.8	150 DB 20.21	SL 20.0
Jan. 1 – Sept. 30, 2012	200 DB 19.2	150 DB 17.85	SL 20.0
Oct. 1 – Dec. 31, 2011	200 DB 13.68	150 DB 16.4	SL 20.0
Jan. 1 – Sept. 30, 2011	200 DB 11.52	150 DB 16.66	SL 20.0
Oct. 1 – Dec. 31, 2010	200 DB 10.94	150 DB 16.41	SL 20.0
Jan. 1 – Sept. 30, 2010	200 DB 11.52	150 DB 16.66	SL 20.0
Oct. 1 – Dec. 31, 2009	200 DB 9.58	150 DB 14.35	SL 17.5
Jan. 1 – Sept. 30, 2009	200 DB 5.76	150 DB 8.33	SL 10.0
Prior to 2009[2]			

[1]You can use this column only if the business use of your car is more than 50%.

[2]If your car was subject to the maximum limits for depreciation and you have unrecovered basis in the car, you can continue to claim depreciation. See Pub. 463 for more information.

result in (1) by the percentage shown below for the month you disposed of the vehicle.

Month of Disposal	Percentage
Jan., Feb., March	12.5%
April, May, June	37.5%
July, Aug., Sept.	62.5%
Oct., Nov., Dec.	87.5%

Line 36. Using the applicable chart for your type of vehicle, find the date you placed your vehicle in service. Then, enter on line 36 the corresponding amount from the "Limit" column. Before using the charts, please read the following definitions.

• A passenger automobile is a 4-wheeled vehicle manufactured primarily for use on public roads that is rated at 6,000 pounds unloaded gross vehicle weight or less. Certain vehicles, such as ambulances, hearses, and taxicabs, are not considered passenger automobiles and are not subject to the line 36 limits. See Pub. 463 for more details.

• A truck or van is a passenger automobile that is classified by the manufacturer as a truck or van, and that is rated at 6,000 pounds gross vehicle weight or less.

If your vehicle is not subject to any of the line 36 limits, skip lines 36 and 37, and enter the amount from line 35 on line 38.

Limits for Passenger Automobiles (Except Trucks and Vans)

Date Vehicle Was Placed in Service	Limit
Jan. 1 – Dec. 31, 2014 . .	$11,160*
Jan. 1 – Dec. 31, 2013 . .	5,100
Jan. 1 – Dec. 31, 2012 . .	3,050
Each succeeding year . .	1,875

* If you elect not to claim the special depreciation allowance for the vehicle or the vehicle is not qualified property, the limit is $3,160.

Limits for Trucks and Vans

Date Vehicle Was Placed in Service	Limit
Jan. 1 – Dec. 31, 2014 . .	$11,460*
Jan. 1 – Dec. 31, 2013 . .	5,500
Jan. 1 – Dec. 31, 2012 . .	3,350
Each succeeding year . .	1,975

* If you elect not to claim the special depreciation allowance for the vehicle or the vehicle is not qualified property, the limit is $3,460.

Paperwork Reduction Act Notice. For the Paperwork Reduction Act

Notice, see your tax return
instructions.

Form **2106-EZ**

Department of the Treasury
Internal Revenue Service (99)

Unreimbursed Employee Business Expenses

▶ **Attach to Form 1040 or Form 1040NR.**
▶ Information about Form 2106 and its separate instructions is available at *www.irs.gov/form2106*.

OMB No. 1545-0074

2014

Attachment
Sequence No. **129A**

Your name	Occupation in which you incurred expenses	Social security number

You Can Use This Form Only if All of the Following Apply.

• You are an employee deducting ordinary and necessary expenses attributable to your job. An ordinary expense is one that is common and accepted in your field of trade, business, or profession. A necessary expense is one that is helpful and appropriate for your business. An expense does not have to be required to be considered necessary.

• You **do not** get reimbursed by your employer for any expenses (amounts your employer included in box 1 of your Form W-2 are not considered reimbursements for this purpose).

• If you are claiming vehicle expense, you are using the standard mileage rate for 2014.

Caution: *You can use the standard mileage rate for 2014* **only if: (a)** *you owned the vehicle and used the standard mileage rate for the first year you placed the vehicle in service,* **or (b)** *you leased the vehicle and used the standard mileage rate for the portion of the lease period after 1997.*

Part I   Figure Your Expenses

1	Complete Part II. Multiply line 8a by 56¢ (.56). Enter the result here	**1**	
2	Parking fees, tolls, and transportation, including train, bus, etc., that **did not** involve overnight travel or commuting to and from work	**2**	
3	Travel expense while away from home overnight, including lodging, airplane, car rental, etc. **Do not** include meals and entertainment	**3**	
4	Business expenses not included on lines 1 through 3. **Do not** include meals and entertainment	**4**	
5	Meals and entertainment expenses: $\$$ _____ × 50% (.50). (Employees subject to Department of Transportation (DOT) hours of service limits: Multiply meal expenses incurred while away from home on business by 80% (.80) instead of 50%. For details, see instructions.)	**5**	
6	**Total expenses.** Add lines 1 through 5. Enter here and on **Schedule A (Form 1040), line 21** (or on **Schedule A (Form 1040NR), line 7**). (Armed Forces reservists, fee-basis state or local government officials, qualified performing artists, and individuals with disabilities: See the instructions for special rules on where to enter this amount.)	**6**	

Part II   Information on Your Vehicle. Complete this part **only** if you are claiming vehicle expense on line 1.

7   When did you place your vehicle in service for business use? (month, day, year) ▶ _____ / _____ / _____

8   Of the total number of miles you drove your vehicle during 2014, enter the number of miles you used your vehicle for:

a   Business _____   b   Commuting (see instructions) _____   c   Other _____

9   Was your vehicle available for personal use during off-duty hours? . . . . ☐ Yes ☐ No

10   Do you (or your spouse) have another vehicle available for personal use? . . . . ☐ Yes ☐ No

11a   Do you have evidence to support your deduction? . . . . ☐ Yes ☐ No

 b   If "Yes," is the evidence written? . . . . ☐ Yes ☐ No

For Paperwork Reduction Act Notice, see your tax return instructions.   Cat. No. 20604Q   Form **2106-EZ** (2014)

[This Page Left Intentionally Blank]

Instructions for Form 2106-EZ

Section references are to the Internal Revenue Code.

What's New

Standard mileage rate. The 2014 rate for business use of your vehicle is 56 cents a mile.

Purpose of Form

You can use Form 2106-EZ instead of Form 2106 to claim your unreimbursed employee business expenses if you meet all the requirements listed above Part I of the form.

Recordkeeping

You cannot deduct expenses for travel (including meals, unless you used the standard meal allowance) entertainment, gifts, or use of a car or other listed property, unless you keep records to prove the time, place, business purpose, business relationship (for entertainment and gifts), and amounts of these expenses. Generally, you must also have receipts for all lodging expenses (regardless of the amount) and any other expense of $75 or more.

Additional Information

For more details about employee business expenses, see:

Pub. 463, Travel, Entertainment, Gift, and Car Expenses

Pub. 529, Miscellaneous Deductions

Pub. 587, Business Use of Your Home (Including Use by Daycare Providers)

Pub. 946, How To Depreciate Property

Specific Instructions

Part I—Figure Your Expenses

Line 2. See the line 8b instructions for the definition of commuting.

Line 3. Enter lodging and transportation expenses connected with overnight travel away from your tax home (defined on this page). You generally cannot deduct expenses for travel away from your tax home for any period of temporary employment of more than 1 year. Do not include expenses for meals and entertainment on this line. For more details, including limits, see Pub. 463.

If you did not pay or incur meal expenses on a day you were traveling away from your tax home, you can use an optional method for deducting incidental expenses instead of keeping records of your actual incidental expenses. The amount of the deduction is $5 a day. The term "incidental expenses" means fees and tips given to porters, baggage carriers, hotel staff, and staff on ships. It does not include expenses for laundry, cleaning and pressing of clothing, lodging taxes, costs of telegrams or telephone calls, transportation between places of lodging or business and places where meals are taken, or the mailing cost of filing travel vouchers and paying employer-sponsored charge card billings. You cannot use this method on any day that you use the standard meal allowance (as explained in the instructions for line 5).

Tax home. Generally, your tax home is your regular or main place of business or post of duty regardless of where you maintain your family home. If you do not have a regular or main place of business because of the nature of your work, then your tax home may be the place where you regularly live. If you do not fit in either of these categories, you are considered an itinerant and your tax home is wherever you work. As an itinerant, you are never away from home and cannot claim a travel expense deduction. For more information about determining your tax home, see Pub. 463.

Line 4. Enter other job-related expenses not listed on any other line of this form. Include expenses for business gifts, education (tuition, fees, and books), home office, trade publications, etc. For details, including limits, see Pub. 463 and Pub. 529.

If you are deducting home office expenses, see Pub. 587 for special instructions on how to report these expenses.

If you are deducting depreciation or claiming a section 179 deduction, see Form 4562, Depreciation and Amortization, to figure the depreciation and section 179 deduction to enter on line 4.

Do not include on line 4 any (a) educator expenses you deducted on Form 1040, line 23, or Form 1040NR, line 24, or (b) any tuition and fees you deducted on Form 1040, line 34.

 **TIP** *You may be able to take a credit for your educational expenses instead of a deduction. See Form 8863, Education Credits, for details.*

Do not include expenses for meals and entertainment, taxes, or interest on line 4. Deductible taxes are entered on Schedule A (Form 1040), lines 5 through 9; Schedule A (Form 1040NR), line 1. Employees cannot deduct car loan interest.

Note. If line 4 is your only entry, do not complete Form 2106-EZ unless you are claiming:

• Expenses for performing your job as a fee-basis state or local government official,

• Performing-arts-related business expenses as a qualified performing artist, or

• Impairment-related work expenses as an individual with a disability.

See the line 6 instructions, below, for definitions. If you are not required to file Form 2106-EZ, enter your expenses directly on Schedule A (Form 1040), line 21 (or on Schedule A (Form 1040NR), line 7).

Line 5. Generally, you can deduct only 50% of your business meal and entertainment expenses, including meals incurred while away from home on business. If you were an employee subject to the DOT hours of service limits, that percentage is 80% for business meals consumed during, or incident to, any period of duty for which those limits are in effect.

Employees subject to the DOT hours of service limits include certain air transportation employees, such as pilots, crew, dispatchers, mechanics, and control tower operators; interstate truck operators and interstate bus drivers; certain railroad employees, such as engineers, conductors, train crews, dispatchers, and control operations personnel; and certain merchant mariners.

Instead of actual cost, you may be able to claim the standard meal allowance for your daily meals and incidental expenses (M&IE) while away from your tax home overnight. Under this method, instead of keeping records of your actual meal expenses, you deduct a specified amount, depending on where you travel. However, you must still keep records to prove the time, place, and business purpose of your travel.

The standard meal allowance is the federal M&IE rate. For most small localities in the United States, this rate is $46 a day. Most major cities and many other localities in the United States qualify for higher rates. You can find these rates at *www.gsa.gov/perdiem*.

For locations outside the continental United States, the applicable rates are published each month. You can find these rates at *www.state.gov/travel/* and select the option for "Foreign Per Diem Rates."

See Pub. 463 for details on how to figure your deduction using the standard meal allowance, including special rules for partial days of travel and for transportation workers.

Line 6. If you are one of the individuals discussed below, special rules apply to deducting your employee business expenses.

Ministers. Before entering your total expenses on line 6, you must reduce them by the amount allocable to your tax-free allowance(s). See Pub. 517 for more information.

Armed Forces reservist (member of a reserve component). You are a member of a reserve component of the Armed Forces of the United States if you are in the Army, Navy, Marine Corps, Air Force, or Coast Guard Reserve; the Army National Guard of the United States; the Air National Guard of the United States; or the Reserve Corps of the Public Health Service.

If you qualify, complete Form 2106-EZ and include the part of the line 6 amount attributable to the expenses for travel more than 100 miles away from home in connection with your performance of services as a member of the reserves on Form 1040, line 24, and attach Form 2106-EZ to your return. The amount of expenses you can deduct on Form 1040, line 24, is limited to the regular federal per diem rate (for lodging, meals, and incidental expenses) and the standard mileage rate (for car expenses), plus any parking fees, ferry fees, and tolls. These reserve-related travel expenses are deductible whether or not you itemize deductions. Enter the remaining expenses from line 6 on Schedule A (Form 1040), line 21. See Pub. 463 for more information.

Fee-basis state or local government official. You are a qualifying fee-basis official if you are employed by a state or political subdivision of a state and are compensated, in whole or part, on a fee basis.

If you qualify, include the part of the line 6 amount attributable to expenses you incurred for services performed in that job in the total on Form 1040, line 24, and attach Form 2106-EZ to your return. These employee business expenses are deductible whether or not you itemize deductions. Enter the remaining expenses from line 6 on Schedule A (Form 1040), line 21.

Qualified performing artist. You are a qualified performing artist if you:

1. Performed services in the performing arts as an employee for at least two employers during the tax year,

2. Received at least $200 each from any two of these employers,

3. Had allowable business expenses attributable to the performing arts of more than 10% of gross income from the performing arts, and

4. Had adjusted gross income of $16,000 or less before deducting expenses as a performing artist.

In addition, if you are married, you must file a joint return unless you lived apart from your spouse for all of 2014. If you file a joint return, you must figure requirements (1), (2), and (3) separately for both you and your spouse. However, requirement (4) applies to the combined adjusted gross income of both you and your spouse.

If you meet all of the above requirements, include the part of the line 6 amount attributable to performing-arts-related expenses in the total on Form 1040, line 24 (or on Form 1040NR, line 35), and attach Form 2106-EZ to your return. Your performing-arts-related business expenses are deductible whether or not you itemize deductions. Enter the remaining expenses from line 6 on Schedule A (Form 1040), line 21 (or on Schedule A (Form 1040NR), line 7).

Disabled employee with impairment-related work expenses. Impairment-related work expenses are the allowable expenses of an individual with physical or mental disabilities for attendant care at his or her place of employment. They also include other expenses in connection with the place of employment that enable the employee to work. See Pub. 463 for details.

If you qualify, enter the part of the line 6 amount attributable to impairment-related work expenses on Schedule A (Form 1040), line 28 (or on Schedule A (Form 1040NR), line 14). These expenses are not subject to the 2% limit that applies to most other employee business expenses. Enter the remaining expenses from line 6 on Schedule A (Form 1040), line 21 (or on Schedule A (Form 1040NR), line 7).

Part II—Information on Your Vehicle

If you claim vehicle expense, you must provide certain information on the use of your vehicle by completing Part II. Include an attachment listing the information requested in Part II for any additional vehicles you used for business during the year.

Line 7. The date placed in service is generally the date you first start using your vehicle. However, if you first start using your vehicle for personal use and later convert it to business use, the vehicle is treated as placed in service on the date you started using it for business.

Line 8a. Do not include commuting miles on this line; commuting miles are not considered business miles. See the definition of commuting under *Line 8b.*

Line 8b. If you do not know the total actual miles you used your vehicle for commuting during the year, figure the amount to enter on line 8b by multiplying the number of days during the year that you used your vehicle for commuting by the average daily roundtrip commuting distance in miles. However, if you converted your vehicle during the year from personal to business use (or vice versa), enter your commuting miles only for the period you drove your vehicle for business.

Generally, commuting is travel between your home and a work location. However, travel that meets any of the following conditions is not commuting.

• You have at least one regular work location away from your home and the travel is to a temporary work location in the same trade or business, regardless of the distance. Generally, a temporary work location is one where your employment is expected to last 1 year or less. See Pub. 463 for details.

• The travel is to a temporary work location outside the metropolitan area where you live and normally work.

• Your home is your principal place of business under section 280A(c)(1)(A) (for purposes of deducting expenses for business use of your home) and the travel is to another work location in the same trade or business, regardless of whether that location is regular or temporary and regardless of distance.

Form 2210

Department of the Treasury
Internal Revenue Service

Underpayment of Estimated Tax by Individuals, Estates, and Trusts

▶ Information about Form 2210 and its separate instructions is at *www.irs.gov/form2210*.
▶ **Attach to Form 1040, 1040A, 1040NR, 1040NR-EZ, or 1041.**

OMB No. 1545-0074

2014

Attachment
Sequence No. **06**

Name(s) shown on tax return

Identifying number

Do You Have To File Form 2210?

Complete lines 1 through 7 below. Is line 7 less than $1,000? → **Yes** → **Do not file Form 2210.** You do not owe a penalty.

↓ **No**

Complete lines 8 and 9 below. Is line 6 equal to or more than line 9? → **Yes** → You do not owe a penalty. **Do not file Form 2210** (but if box E in Part II applies, you must file page 1 of Form 2210).

↓ **No**

You may owe a penalty. Does any box in Part II below apply? → **Yes** → You **must** file Form 2210. Does box **B, C,** or **D** in Part II apply?

↓ **No** → **No** / **Yes** → You must figure your penalty.

Do not file Form 2210. You are not required to figure your penalty because the IRS will figure it and send you a bill for any unpaid amount. If you want to figure it, you may use Part III or Part IV as a worksheet and enter your penalty amount on your tax return, but **do not file Form 2210.**

You are **not** required to figure your penalty because the IRS will figure it and send you a bill for any unpaid amount. If you want to figure it, you may use Part III or Part IV as a worksheet and enter your penalty amount on your tax return, but **file only page 1 of Form 2210.**

Part I — Required Annual Payment

1	Enter your 2014 tax after credits from Form 1040, line 56 (see instructions if not filing Form 1040)	**1**	
2	Other taxes, including self-employment tax and, if applicable, Additional Medicare Tax and/or Net Investment Income Tax (see instructions)	**2**	
3	Refundable credits, including the premium tax credit (see instructions)	**0**	( )
4	Current year tax. Combine lines 1, 2, and 3. If less than $1,000, **stop;** you do not owe a penalty. **Do not** file Form 2210	**4**	
5	Multiply line 4 by 90% (.90) **5**		
6	Withholding taxes. **Do not** include estimated tax payments (see instructions)	**6**	
7	Subtract line 6 from line 4. If less than $1,000, **stop;** you do not owe a penalty. **Do not** file Form 2210	**7**	
8	Maximum required annual payment based on prior year's tax (see instructions)	**8**	
9	**Required annual payment.** Enter the **smaller** of line 5 or line 8	**9**	

Next: Is line 9 more than line 6?

☐ **No.** You **do not** owe a penalty. **Do not** file Form 2210 unless box **E** below applies.

☐ **Yes.** You may owe a penalty, but **do not** file Form 2210 unless one or more boxes in Part II below applies.

- If box **B, C,** or **D** applies, you must figure your penalty and file Form 2210.
- If box **A** or **E** applies (but not **B, C,** or **D**) file only page 1 of Form 2210. You are **not** required to figure your penalty; the IRS will figure it and send you a bill for any unpaid amount. If you want to figure your penalty, you may use Part III or IV as a worksheet and enter your penalty on your tax return, but **file only page 1 of Form 2210.**

Part II — Reasons for Filing. Check applicable boxes. If none apply, **do not** file Form 2210.

A ☐ You request a **waiver** (see instructions) of your entire penalty. You must check this box and file page 1 of Form 2210, but you are not required to figure your penalty.

B ☐ You request a **waiver** (see instructions) of part of your penalty. You must figure your penalty and waiver amount and file Form 2210.

C ☐ Your income varied during the year and your penalty is reduced or eliminated when figured using the **annualized income installment method.** You must figure the penalty using Schedule AI and file Form 2210.

D ☐ Your penalty is lower when figured by treating the federal income tax withheld from your income as paid on the dates it was actually withheld, instead of in equal amounts on the payment due dates. You must figure your penalty and file Form 2210.

E ☐ You filed or are filing a joint return for either 2013 or 2014, but not for both years, and line 8 above is smaller than line 5 above. You must file page 1 of Form 2210, but you are **not** required to figure your penalty (unless box **B, C,** or **D** applies).

For Paperwork Reduction Act Notice, see separate instructions. Cat. No. 11744P Form **2210** (2014)

Part III   Short Method

Can You Use the Short Method?	You can use the short method if:
	• You made no estimated tax payments (or your only payments were withheld federal income tax), **or**
	• You paid the same amount of estimated tax on each of the four payment due dates.

Must You Use the Regular Method?	You must use the regular method (Part IV) instead of the short method if:
	• You made any estimated tax payments late,
	• You checked box **C** or **D** in Part II, **or**
	• You are filing Form 1040NR or 1040NR-EZ and you did not receive wages as an employee subject to U.S. income tax withholding.

Note. *If any payment was made earlier than the due date, you can use the short method, but using it may cause you to pay a larger penalty than the regular method. If the payment was only a few days early, the difference is likely to be small.*

10	Enter the amount from Form 2210, line 9	**10**	
11	Enter the amount, if any, from Form 2210, line 6	**11**	
12	Enter the total amount, if any, of estimated tax payments you made .	**12**	
13	Add lines 11 and 12	**13**	
14	**Total underpayment for year.** Subtract line 13 from line 10. If zero or less, **stop;** you do not owe a penalty. **Do not file Form 2210 unless you checked box E in Part II**	**14**	
15	Multiply line 14 by .01995	**15**	

16	• If the amount on line 14 was paid **on or after** 4/15/15, enter -0-.
	 • If the amount on line 14 was paid **before** 4/15/15, make the following computation to find the amount to enter on line 16.
	
	     Amount on Number of days paid
	       line 14 × before 4/15/15 × .00008 . . . .
		16	

17	**Penalty.** Subtract line 16 from line 15. Enter the result here and on Form 1040, line 79; Form 1040A, line 51; Form 1040NR, line 76; Form 1040NR-EZ, line 26; or Form 1041, line 26. **Do not file Form 2210 unless you checked a box in Part II** . . . . ▶	**17**	

Part IV	**Regular Method** (See the instructions if you are filing Form 1040NR or 1040NR-EZ.)					

			Payment Due Dates			
Section A—Figure Your Underpayment			**(a)** 4/15/14	**(b)** 6/15/14	**(c)** 9/15/14	**(d)** 1/15/15
18	**Required installments.** If box C in Part II applies, enter the amounts from Schedule AI, line 25. Otherwise, enter 25% (.25) of line 9, Form 2210, in each column	**18**				
19	Estimated tax paid and tax withheld (see the instructions). For column (a) only, also enter the amount from line 19 on line 23. If line 19 is equal to or more than line 18 for all payment periods, stop here; you do not owe a penalty. **Do not file Form 2210 unless you checked a box in Part II**	**19**				
	Complete lines 20 through 26 of one column before going to line 20 of the next column.					
20	Enter the amount, if any, from line 26 in the previous column	**20**				
21	Add lines 19 and 20	**21**				
22	Add the amounts on lines 24 and 25 in the previous column	**22**				
23	Subtract line 22 from line 21. If zero or less, enter -0-. For column (a) only, enter the amount from line 19	**23**				
24	If line 23 is zero, subtract line 21 from line 22. Otherwise, enter -0-	**24**				
25	**Underpayment.** If line 18 is equal to or more than line 23, subtract line 23 from line 18. Then go to line 20 of the next column. Otherwise, go to line 26 ▶	**25**				
26	**Overpayment.** If line 23 is more than line 18, subtract line 18 from line 23. Then go to line 20 of the next column	**26**				

Section B—Figure the Penalty (Use the Worksheet for Form 2210, Part IV, Section B—Figure the Penalty in the instructions.)

27	**Penalty.** Enter the total penalty from line 14 of the Worksheet for Form 2210, Part IV, Section B—Figure the Penalty. Also include this amount on Form 1040, line 79; Form 1040A, line 51; Form 1040NR, line 76; Form 1040NR-EZ, line 26; or Form 1041, line 26. **Do not file Form 2210 unless you checked a box in Part II** ▶	**27**	

Schedule AI—Annualized Income Installment Method (See the instructions.)

Estates and trusts, **do not** use the period ending dates shown to the right. Instead, use the following: 2/28/14, 4/30/14, 7/31/14, and 11/30/14.

		(a) 1/1/14–3/31/14	**(b)** 1/1/14–5/31/14	**(c)** 1/1/14–8/31/14	**(d)** 1/1/14–12/31/14
Part I	**Annualized Income Installments**				
1	Enter your adjusted gross income for each period (see instructions). (Estates and trusts, enter your taxable income without your exemption for each period.)				
2	Annualization amounts. (Estates and trusts, see instructions)	4	2.4	1.5	1
3	Annualized income. Multiply line 1 by line 2				
4	If you itemize, enter itemized deductions for the period shown in each column. All others enter -0-, and skip to line 7. **Exception:** Estates and trusts, skip to line 9 and enter amount from line 3				
5	Annualization amounts	4	2.4	1.5	1
6	Multiply line 4 by line 5 (see instructions if line 3 is more than $152,525)				
7	In each column, enter the full amount of your standard deduction from Form 1040, line 40, or Form 1040A, line 24. (Form 1040NR or 1040NR-EZ filers, enter -0-. **Exception:** Indian students and business apprentices, see instructions.)				
8	Enter the **larger** of line 6 or line 7				
9	Subtract line 8 from line 3				
10	In each column, multiply $3,950 by the total number of exemptions claimed (see instructions if line 3 is more than $152,525). (Estates, trusts, and Form 1040NR or 1040NR-EZ filers, see instructions.)				
11	Subtract line 10 from line 9. If zero or less, enter -0-				
12	Figure your tax on the amount on line 11 (see instructions)				
13	Self-employment tax from line 34 (complete Part II below)				
14	Enter other taxes for each payment period including, if applicable, Additional Medicare Tax and/or Net Investment Income Tax (see instructions)				
15	Total tax. Add lines 12, 13, and 14				
16	For each period, enter the same type of credits as allowed on Form 2210, Part I, lines 1 and 3 (see instructions)				
17	Subtract line 16 from line 15. If zero or less, enter -0-				
18	Applicable percentage	22.5%	45%	67.5%	90%
19	Multiply line 17 by line 18				
	Complete lines 20–25 of one column before going to line 20 of the next column.				
20	Enter the total of the amounts in all previous columns of line 25				
21	Subtract line 20 from line 19. If zero or less, enter -0-				
22	Enter 25% (.25) of line 9 on page 1 of Form 2210 in each column				
23	Subtract line 25 of the previous column from line 24 of that column				
24	Add lines 22 and 23				
25	Enter the **smaller** of line 21 or line 24 here and on Form 2210, Part IV, line 18 ▶				
Part II	**Annualized Self-Employment Tax** (Form 1040 and Form 1040NR filers only)				
26	Net earnings from self-employment for the period (see instructions)				
27	Prorated social security tax limit	$29,250	$48,750	$78,000	$117,000
28	Enter actual wages for the period subject to social security tax or the 6.2% portion of the 7.65% railroad retirement (tier 1) tax. **Exception:** If you filed Form 4137 or Form 8919, see instructions				
29	Subtract line 28 from line 27. If zero or less, enter -0-				
30	Annualization amounts	0.496	0.2976	0.186	0.124
31	Multiply line 30 by the **smaller** of line 26 or line 29				
32	Annualization amounts	0.116	0.0696	0.0435	0.029
33	Multiply line 26 by line 32				
34	Add lines 31 and 33. Enter here and on line 13 above ▶				

2014

Department of the Treasury
Internal Revenue Service

Instructions for Form 2210

Underpayment of Estimated Tax by Individuals, Estates, and Trusts

Section references are to the Internal Revenue Code unless otherwise noted.

General Instructions

Future Developments

For the latest information about developments related to Form 2210 and its instructions, such as legislation enacted after they were published, go to *www.irs.gov/form2210*.

What's New

Personal exemption amount increased for certain taxpayers. For tax years beginning in 2014, the personal exemption amount is increased to $3,950. There is a phaseout of the exemption, the amount of which is determined by the taxpayer's filing status and adjusted gross income.

Limit on itemized deductions. For tax years beginning in 2014, itemized deductions for taxpayers with adjusted gross incomes above $152,525 may be reduced.

Health coverage tax credit. The health coverage tax credit claimed on Form 8885 expired at the end of 2013.

Premium Tax Credit. Beginning in 2014, you may be eligible to claim the premium tax credit (PTC). The PTC is a tax credit for certain people who enroll, or whose family member enrolls, in a qualified health plan offered through a Health Insurance Marketplace (also called an Exchange). The PTC provides financial assistance to pay the premiums by reducing the amount of tax you owe, giving you a refund, or increasing your refund amount.

Advance payment of the PTC may be made through the Marketplace directly to your insurance provider. If you received premium assistance through advance payments of the PTC in 2014, and the amount advanced exceeded the amount of PTC you can take, you could be subject to a penalty for underpaying your estimated tax. (For example, you completed Form 8962 and have additional income tax liability because too much was advanced to your insurance provider.) However, if you are otherwise current with your filing and payment obligations to the IRS, you are entitled to a waiver of the penalty. Generally, you are considered current with your filing and payment obligations if you filed all required tax returns and have paid or are paying your tax liabilities. See *Waiver of Penalty* below for specific instructions.

For more information about the PTC and advance payments of the PTC, see Form 8962 and Publication 974, Premium Tax Credit.

Reminders

Additional Medicare Tax. A 0.9% Additional Medicare Tax applies to Medicare wages, railroad retirement act (RRTA) compensation, and self-employment income over a threshold amount based on your filing status. See Form 8959, Additional Medicare Tax.

Net Investment Income Tax. You may be subject to Net Investment Income Tax (NIIT). NIIT is a 3.8% (.038) tax on the lesser of net investment income or the excess of your modified adjusted gross income over a threshold amount. See Form 8960, Net Investment Income Tax—Individuals, Estates, and Trusts.

Purpose of Form

Generally, use Form 2210 to see if you owe a penalty for underpaying your estimated tax and, if you do, to figure the amount of the penalty. Even if you are not required to file Form 2210, you can use it to figure your penalty if you wish to do so. In that case, enter the penalty on your return, but do not file Form 2210.

Who Must File Form 2210

Use the flowchart at the top of page 1 of Form 2210 to see if you must file this form.

 If box B, C, or D in Part II is checked, you must figure the penalty yourself and attach Form 2210 to your return.

The IRS Will Figure the Penalty for You

If you did not check box B, C, or D in Part II, you do not need to figure the penalty. The IRS will figure any penalty for underpayment of estimated tax and send you a bill. If you file your return by April 15, 2015, no interest will be charged on the penalty if you pay the penalty by the date shown on the bill.

If you want us to figure the penalty for you, complete your return as usual. Leave the penalty line on your return blank; do not file Form 2210.

Other Methods of Figuring the Penalty

We realize that there are different ways to figure the correct penalty. You do not have to use the method used on Form 2210 as long as you enter the correct penalty amount on the "Estimated tax penalty" line of your return.

However, if you are required to file Form 2210 because one or more of the boxes in Part II applies, you must complete certain lines and enter the penalty on the "Estimated tax penalty" line of your return.

• If you use the short method, complete Part I, check the box(es) that applies in Part II, and complete Part III. Enter the penalty on line 17 and on the "Estimated tax penalty" line on your tax return.

• If you use the regular method, complete Part I, check the box(es) that applies in Part II, complete Part IV, Section A, and the Penalty Worksheet, later. Enter the penalty on line 27 of the form, and on the "Estimated tax penalty" line on your tax return.

• If you use the annualized income installment method, complete Part I, check the box(es) that applies in Part II, complete Schedule AI, complete Part IV, Section A, and the Penalty Worksheet, later. Enter the penalty on line 27 of the form, and on the "Estimated tax penalty" line on your tax return.

Who Must Pay the Underpayment Penalty

In general, you may owe the penalty for 2014 if the total of your withholding and timely estimated tax payments did not equal at least the smaller of:

1. 90% of your 2014 tax, or

2. 100% of your 2013 tax. (Your 2013 tax return must cover a 12-month period.)

Special rules for certain individuals. Different percentages are used for farmers and fishermen, and certain higher income taxpayers.

Farmers and fishermen. If at least two-thirds of your gross income for 2013 or 2014 is from farming and fishing, substitute 66⅔% for 90% in (1) above. See *Farmers and fishermen*, later, to see if you qualify.

Higher income taxpayers. If your adjusted gross income (AGI) for 2013 was more than $150,000 ($75,000 if your 2014 filing status is married filing separately), substitute 110% for 100% in (2) above.

Penalty figured separately for each required payment. The penalty is figured separately for each installment due date. Therefore, you may owe the penalty for an earlier due date even if you paid enough tax later to make up the underpayment. This is true even if you are due a refund when you file your tax return. However, you may be able to reduce or eliminate the penalty by using the annualized income installment method. For details, see the Schedule AI instructions later.

Return. In these instructions, "return" refers to your original return. However, an amended return is considered the original return if it is filed by the due date (including extensions) of the original return. Also, a joint return that replaces previously filed separate returns is considered the original return.

Exceptions to the Penalty

You will not have to pay the penalty or file this form if either of the following applies.

• You had no tax liability for 2013, you were a U.S. citizen or resident alien for the entire year (or an estate of a domestic decedent or a domestic trust), and your 2013 tax return was (or would have been had you been required to file) for a full 12 months.

• The total tax shown on your 2014 return minus the amount of tax you paid through withholding is less than $1,000. To determine whether the total tax is less than $1,000, complete Part 1, lines 1 through 7.

Estates and trusts. No penalty applies to either of the following.

• A decedent's estate for any tax year ending before the date that is 2 years after the decedent's death.

• A trust that was treated as owned by the decedent if the trust will receive the residue of the decedent's estate under the will (or if no will is admitted to probate, the trust primarily responsible for paying debts, taxes, and expenses of administration) for any tax year ending before the date that is 2 years after the decedent's death.

Farmers and fishermen. If you meet both tests 1 and 2 below, you do not owe a penalty for underpaying estimated tax.

1. Your gross income from farming or fishing is at least two-thirds of your annual gross income from all sources for 2013 or 2014.

2. You filed Form 1040 or 1041 and paid the entire tax due by March 2, 2015.

See chapter 2 of Pub. 505, Tax Withholding and Estimated Tax, for the definition of gross income from farming and fishing.

If you meet test 1 but not test 2, use Form 2210-F, Underpayment of Estimated Tax by Farmers and Fishermen, to see if you owe a penalty. If you do not meet test 1, use Form 2210.

Waiver of Penalty

If you have an underpayment, all or part of the penalty for that underpayment will be waived if the IRS determines that:

• In 2014, you received excess advance payment of the PTC from a Marketplace and you are current with your filing and payment obligations;

• In 2013 or 2014, you retired after reaching age 62 or became disabled, and your underpayment was due to reasonable cause; or

• The underpayment was due to a casualty, disaster, or other unusual circumstance, and it would be inequitable to impose the penalty. For federally declared disaster areas, see *Federally declared disaster*, later.

To request any of the above waivers, do the following.

1. Check box A or box B in Part II.

a. If you checked box A, complete only page 1 of Form 2210 and attach it to your tax return (you are not required to figure the amount of penalty to be waived).

b. If you checked box B, complete Form 2210 through line 16 (or if you use the regular method, line 26 plus the Penalty Worksheet, later) without regard to the waiver. Enter the amount you want waived in parentheses on the dotted line next to line 17 (line 27 for the regular method). Subtract this amount from the total penalty you figured without regard to the waiver, and enter the result on line 17 (line 27 for the regular method).

2. Attach Form 2210 and a statement to your return explaining the reasons you were unable to meet the estimated tax requirements and the time period for which you are requesting a waiver.

3. If you are requesting a waiver because you received excess advance payment of the PTC from a Marketplace and you are current with your filing and payment obligations (generally meaning you have filed all required tax returns and have paid or are paying your tax liability), check box A and include a statement with your return providing: "Received excess advance payment of the PTC." You do not need to attach documentation from the Marketplace or explain the circumstances under which you received an excess advance payment.

4. If you are requesting a waiver due to retirement or disability, attach documentation that shows your retirement date (and your age on that date) or the date you became disabled.

5. If you are requesting a waiver due to a casualty, disaster (other than a federally declared disaster as discussed next), or other unusual circumstance, attach documentation such as copies of police and insurance company reports.

The IRS will review the information you provide and decide whether to grant your request for a waiver.

Federally declared disaster. Certain estimated tax payment deadlines for taxpayers who reside or have a business in a federally declared disaster area are postponed for a period during and after the disaster. During the processing of your tax return, the IRS automatically identifies taxpayers located in a covered disaster area (by county or parish) and applies the appropriate penalty relief. **Do not** file Form 2210 if your underpayment was due to a federally declared disaster. If you still owe a penalty after the automatic waiver is applied, the IRS will send you a bill.

An individual or a fiduciary for an estate or trust not in a covered disaster area but whose books, records, or tax professionals' offices are in a covered area is also entitled to relief. Also eligible are relief workers affiliated with a recognized government or charitable organization assisting in the relief activities in a covered disaster area. If you meet either of these eligibility requirements, you must call the IRS disaster hotline at 1-866-562-5227 and identify yourself as eligible for this relief.

Details on the applicable disaster postponement period can be found at IRS.gov. Enter "disaster relief" in the search box, then select "Tax Relief in Disaster Situations." Select the federally declared disaster that affected you.

Additional Information

See Pub. 505, Tax Withholding and Estimated Tax, chapter 4, for more details.

For guidance on figuring estimated taxes for trusts and certain estates, see Notice 87-32, 1987-1 C.B. 477.

Specific Instructions

Part I—Required Annual Payment

Complete lines 1 through 9 to figure your required annual payment.

If you file an amended return by the due date of your original return, use the amounts shown on your amended return to figure your underpayment. If you file an amended return after the due date, use the amounts shown on the original return.

Exception. If you and your spouse file a joint return after the due date to replace previously filed separate returns, use the amounts shown on the joint return to figure your underpayment.

Line 1

Enter the amount from Form 1040, line 56; Form 1040A, line 39; Form 1040NR, line 53; or Form 1040NR-EZ, line 15. For an estate or trust, enter the amount from Form 1041, Schedule G, line 3.

Line 2

Enter the total of the following amounts.

IF you file...	THEN include on line 2 the amounts on...
1040	Lines 57, 59 (additional tax on distributions only), 60a*, 60b, and if applicable, the Additional Medicare Tax and/or Net Investment Income Tax on line 62, and any write-ins on line 62 with the exception of: • Uncollected social security and Medicare tax or RRTA tax on tips or group-term life insurance (identified as "UT"), • Tax on excess golden parachute payments (identified as "EPP"), • Excise tax on insider stock compensation from an expatriated corporation (identified as "ISC"), • Look-back interest due under section 167(g) (identified as "From Form 8866") and under section 460(b) (identified as "From Form 8697"), and • Recapture of federal mortgage subsidy (identified as "FMSR").
1040NR	Lines 54, 55, 57 (additional tax on distributions only), 58, 59a*, 59b, and if applicable, Additional Medicare Tax and/or Net Investment Income Tax on line 60, and any write-ins on line 60 with the exception of: • Uncollected social security and Medicare tax or RRTA tax on tips or group-term life insurance (identified as "UT"), • Tax on excess golden parachute payments (identified as "EPP"), • Excise tax on insider stock compensation from an expatriated corporation (identified as "ISC"), • Look-back interest due under section 167(g) (identified as "From Form 8866"), and under section 460(b) (identified as "From Form 8697"), and • Recapture of federal mortgage subsidy (identified as "FMSR").
1041	Schedule G, lines 4, 5, 6*, and any write-ins on line 7 with the exception of: • Look-back interest due under section 167(g) (identified as "From Form 8866"), and • Look-back interest due under section 460(b) (identified as "From Form 8697").

* If you are a household employer, include your household employment taxes on line 2 only if you had federal income tax withheld from your income and would be required to make estimated tax payments even if the household employment taxes were not included.

If you file Form 1040NR-EZ or Form 1040A, you will not have an entry on line 2.

Line 3

Enter the total amount of the following refundable credits, if any, that you claim on your tax return.
• Earned income credit.
• Additional child tax credit.
• Refundable American opportunity credit (Form 8863, Line 8).
• Credit for federal tax paid on fuels.
• Premium tax credit (Form 8962).
• Credit determined under section 1341(a)(5)(B).

To figure the amount of the section 1341 credit, see *Repayments* in Pub. 525, Taxable and Nontaxable Income.

Line 6

Enter the taxes withheld from Form 1040, lines 64 and 71; Form 1040A, line 40, plus any excess social security and tier 1 railroad retirement tax (RRTA) included on line 46; Form 1040NR, lines 62a, 62b, 62c, 62d, and 67; or Form 1040NR-EZ, lines 18a and 18b. For an estate or trust, enter the amount from Form 1041, line 24e.

Form 8689 filers. Also enter on this line the amount(s) from Form 8689, lines 40 and 45 that you entered on line 74 of your 2014 Form 1040.

Line 8

To figure your 2013 tax, first add the amounts listed in (1) later, then subtract from that total amount the refundable credits listed in (2) later that are shown on your 2013 tax return. **(1) Add the amounts listed in the chart below based on which tax return you filed for 2013.**

IF you filed for 2013...	Add the following amounts shown on your 2013 tax return.
1040	Lines 55, 56, 58 (additional tax on distributions only), 59a*, 59b, and any write-ins on line 60 with the exception of: • Uncollected social security and Medicare tax or RRTA tax on tips or group-term life insurance (identified as "UT"), • Tax on excess golden parachute payments (identified as "EPP"), • Excise tax on insider stock compensation from an expatriated corporation (identified as "ISC"), • Look-back interest due under section 167(g) (identified as "From Form 8866"), and under section 460(b) (identified as "From Form 8697"), • Recapture of federal mortgage subsidy (identified as "FMSR"), and • Advance payments of the health coverage tax credit when not eligible (identified as "HCTC").
1040A	Line 35
1040NR	Lines 52, 53, 54, 56 (additional tax on distributions only), 57, 58a*, 58b, and any write-ins on line 59 with the exception of: • Uncollected social security and Medicare tax or RRTA tax on tips or group-term life insurance (identified as "UT"), • Tax on excess golden parachute payments (identified as "EPP"), • Excise tax on insider stock compensation from an expatriated corporation (identified as "ISC"), • Look-back interest due under section 167(g) (identified as "From Form 8866"), and under section 460(b) (identified as "From Form 8697"), • Recapture of federal mortgage subsidy (identified as "FMSR"), and • Advance payments of the health coverage tax credit when not eligible (identified as "HCTC").
1040NR-EZ	Line 15
1041	Schedule G, lines 4, 5, 6*, and any write-ins on line 7 with the exception of: • Look-back interest due under section 167(g) (identified as "From Form 8866"), and • Look-back interest due under section 460(b) (identified as "From Form 8697").

*If you are a household employer, include your household employment taxes on line 2 only if you had federal income tax withheld from your income and would be required to make estimated tax payments even if the household employment taxes were not included.

(2) Subtract refundable credits listed below:
Subtract the total of the following refundable credits, if any, that you claimed on your 2013 tax return:
• Your earned income credit.
• Additional child tax credit.
• Refundable part of the American opportunity credit (Form 8863, line 8).
• Credit for federal tax paid on fuels.
• Health coverage tax credit.
• Credit determined under section 1341(a)(5)(B).

Enter the 2013 tax you figured above unless the AGI on your 2013 return is more than $150,000 ($75,000 if married filing separately for 2014). If the AGI shown on your 2013 tax return is more than $150,000 ($75,000 if married filing separately), enter 110% of the amount of the tax computed earlier.

If you are filing a joint return for 2014, but you did not file a joint return for 2013, add your 2013 tax (as figured earlier) to your spouse's 2013 tax (as figured earlier) and enter the total on line 8.

If you filed a joint return for 2013 but you are not filing a joint return for 2014, see Pub. 505, chapter 4, *General Rule,* to figure your share of the 2013 tax to enter on line 8.

If you did not file a return for 2013 or your 2013 tax year was less than 12 months, do not complete line 8. Instead, enter the amount from line 5 on line 9. However, see *Exceptions to the Penalty,* earlier.

Part III—Short Method

If you can use the short method (see Form 2210, Part III, *Can You Use the Short Method?*), complete lines 10 through 14 to figure your total underpayment for the year, and lines 15 through 17 to figure the penalty.

In certain circumstances, the IRS will waive all or part of the underpayment penalty. See *Waiver of Penalty,* earlier.

Part IV—Regular Method

Use the regular method if you are not eligible to use the short method. See Form 2210, Part III, *Must You Use the Regular Method?*

If you checked box C in Part II, complete Schedule AI before Part IV.

Form 1040NR or 1040NR-EZ filers. If you are filing Form 1040NR or 1040NR-EZ and did not receive wages as an employee subject to U.S. income tax withholding, the instructions for completing Part IV are modified as follows.

1. Skip column (a).

2. On line 18, column (b), enter one-half of the amount on line 9 of Part I (unless you are using the annualized income installment method).

3. On line 19, column (b), enter the total tax payments made through June 16, 2014, for the 2014 tax year (June 15 was a Sunday, so payments made June 16 are treated as made on June 15). If you are treating federal income tax (and excess social security or tier 1 railroad retirement tax) as having been withheld evenly throughout the year, you are considered to have paid one-third of these amounts on each payment due date.

4. Skip all lines in column (b) that are shaded in column (a).

Section A—Figure Your Underpayment
Line 18

Enter on line 18, columns (a) through (d), the amount of your required installment for the due date shown in each column heading. For most taxpayers, this is one-fourth of the required annual payment shown in Part I, line 9. However, it may be to your benefit to figure your required installments by using the annualized income installment method. See the Schedule AI instructions later.

Line 19

Table 1—List your estimated tax payments for 2014.
Before completing line 19, enter in Table 1 the payments you made for 2014. Include the following payments.
• Any overpayment from your 2013 return applied to your 2014 estimated tax payments. Generally, treat the payment as made on April 15, 2014.

- Estimated tax payments you made for the 2014 tax year, plus any federal income tax and excess social security and tier 1 railroad retirement tax withheld.
- Any payment made on your balance due return for 2014. Use the date you filed (or will file) your return or April 15, 2015, whichever is earlier, as the payment date.

Table 1. Estimated Tax Payments

Date	Payment amount	Date	Payment amount

Entries on Form 2210. Enter on line 19 the following tax payments.
- Column (a)—payments you made by April 15, 2014.
- Column (b)—payments you made after April 15, 2014, through June 16, 2014 (June 15 was a Sunday, so payments made June 16 are treated as made on June 15) .
- Column (c)—payments you made after June 16, 2014, through September 15, 2014.
- Column (d)—payments you made after September 15, 2014, through January 15, 2015.

When figuring your payment dates and the amounts to enter on line 19 of each column, apply the following rules.
- For withheld federal income tax and excess social security or tier 1 railroad retirement tax (RRTA), you are considered to have paid one-fourth of these amounts on each payment due date unless you can show otherwise. You will find these amounts on Form 1040, lines 64 and 71; Form 1040A, line 40, plus any excess social security and tier 1 RRTA included on line 46; Form 1040NR, lines 62a, 62b, 62c, 62d, and 67; Form 1040NR-EZ, lines 18a and 18b; and Form 1041, line 24e.

 If you treat withholding as paid for estimated tax purposes when it was actually withheld, you must check box D in Part II and complete and attach Form 2210 to your return.

- Include all estimated tax payments you made for each period. Include any overpayment from your 2013 tax return you elected to apply to your 2014 estimated tax. If your 2013 return was fully paid by the due date, treat the overpayment as a payment made on April 15, 2014. If you mail your estimated tax payments, use the date of the U.S. postmark as the date of payment.
- If an overpayment is generated on your 2013 return from a payment made after the due date, treat the payment as made on the date of payment. For example, you paid $500 due on your 2013 return on July 1, 2014, and later amended the return and were due a $400 refund which you elected to have applied to your estimated taxes. The $400 overpayment would be treated as paid on July 1.
- If you file your return and pay the tax due by February 2, 2015, include on line 19, column (d), the amount of tax you pay with your tax return. In this case, you will not owe a penalty for the payment due on January 15, 2015.

Example 1. You filed your 2013 tax return on June 1, 2014, showing a $2,000 refund. You elected to have $1,000 of your 2013 overpayment applied to your 2014 estimated tax payments. In 2014, you had $4,000 of federal income tax withheld from wages. You also made $500 estimated tax payments on 9/15/14 and 1/15/15. On line 19, column (a), enter $2,000 ($1,000 withholding + $1,000 overpayment). In column (b) enter $1,000 (withholding), and in columns (c) and (d), enter $1,500 ($1,000 withholding + $500 estimated tax payment).

Line 25

If line 25 is zero for all payment periods, you do not owe a penalty. But if you checked box C or D in Part II, you must file Form 2210 with your return. If you checked box E, you must file page 1 of Form 2210 with your return.

In certain circumstances, the IRS will waive all or part of the underpayment penalty. See *Waiver of Penalty* earlier.

Section B—Figure the Penalty

Use the Penalty Worksheet, later, to figure your penalty for each period by applying the appropriate rate against each underpayment shown in Section A, line 25. The penalty is figured for the number of days that each underpayment remains unpaid.

Your payments are applied first to any underpayment balance on an earlier installment even if you designate a payment for a later period. See *Example 2*.

Use lines 3, 6, 9, and 12 of the Penalty Worksheet to show the number of days an underpayment remained unpaid. Use lines 4, 7, 10, and 13 to figure the actual penalty amount by applying the appropriate rate to an underpayment for the number of days it remained unpaid.

Example 2. You had a $500 underpayment remaining after your April 15 payment. The June 15 installment required a payment of $1,200. On June 10, you made a payment of $1,200 to cover the June 15 installment. However, $500 of this payment is applied first to the April 15 installment. The penalty for the April 15 installment is figured from April 15 to June 10 (56 days). The amount remaining to be applied to the June 15 installment is $700.

Total days per rate period. If an underpayment remained unpaid for an entire rate period, use the chart below to determine the number of days to enter in each column. The chart is organized in the same format as the Penalty Worksheet.

Table 2. Chart of Total Days

Rate Period	(a) 4/15/14	(b) 6/15/14	(c) 9/15/14	(d) 1/15/15
4/16/14-6/30/14	76	15	—	—
7/1/14-9/30/14	92	92	15	—
10/1/14-12/31/14	92	92	92	—
1/1/15-4/15/15	105	105	105	90

For example, if you have an underpayment on line 25, column (a), but Table 1 shows you have no payments until after December 31, 2014, you would enter "76" on line 3, column (a), of the Penalty Worksheet.

 If you make a payment during a rate period, see Table 4-1 (Pub. 505, chapter 4) for an easy way to figure the number of days the payment is late.

Worksheet for Form 2210, Part IV, Section B—Figure the Penalty

Line 1b. If more than one payment was applied to fully pay the underpayment amount in a column (line 1a), enter on line 1b the date and amount applied up to the underpayment amount. If a payment was more than the underpayment amount, enter the excess in the next column with the same date.

Example 3. Your required installment for each payment due date is $4,000. You made the following estimated tax payments.

Date	Payments
4/30/14	$2,000
6/15/14	$3,000
9/15/14	$4,000
1/15/15	$4,000

Line 1a, column (a), shows $4,000. You enter "4/30 $2,000" and "6/15 $2,000" on line 1b, column (a). The remaining $1,000 ($3,000 – $2,000) of the June 15 payment is entered on line 1b, column (b), "6/15 $1,000." Also enter "9/15 $3,000" on line 1b, column (b), because $3,000 of the $4,000 September payment must be used to fully pay the June underpayment. Continue in this manner until all your payments are used.

Line 3. If more than one payment was applied to an underpayment on line 1a, enter the number of days each payment was late.

Example 4. Using the same facts as *Example 3* above, enter "15" (number of days from 4/15 to 4/30) and "61" (number of days from 4/15 to 6/15) on line 3, column (a) (see illustration under *Example 5*).

Line 4. Make the computation requested on line 4 and enter the result. If more than one payment was required to fully satisfy an underpayment amount, make a separate computation for each payment. See *Example 5* and the example in chapter 4 of Pub. 505.

Example 5. Assume the same facts as in *Example 3*. On line 4, enter the penalty for each underpayment: "$2.47" ($2,000 × (15 ÷ 365) × .03) and "$10.03" ($2,000 × (61 ÷ 365) × .03). The entries are illustrated below.

	(a)	
2		**4/15/14**
3	Days: 15	Days: 61
4	$2.47	$10.03

Column (a) is fully paid in the first rate period; therefore, lines 6, 7, 9, 10, 12 and 13 for column (a) would be blank. Continue with the underpayment in columns (b), (c), and (d) in the same manner.

Note. If an underpayment balance remains for the remaining rate periods, calculate the penalty using the same steps as explained above, but use the dates and interest rates on lines 6 and 7 for rate period 2, lines 9 and 10 for rate period 3, and lines 12 and 13 for rate period 4.

Schedule AI—Annualized Income Installment Method

If your income varied during the year because, for example, you operated your business on a seasonal basis or had a large capital gain late in the year, you may be able to lower or eliminate the amount of one or more required installments by using the annualized income installment method. Use Schedule AI to figure the required installments to enter on Form 2210, Part IV, line 18.

 If you use Schedule AI for any payment due date, you must use it for all payment due dates.

To use the annualized income installment method to figure the penalty, you must do all of the following.

1. Complete Schedule AI, Part I (and Part II, if necessary). Enter the amounts from Schedule AI, Part I, line 25, columns (a) through (d), in the corresponding columns of Form 2210, Part IV, line 18.

2. Complete Part IV to figure the penalty. This includes completing the Penalty Worksheet in the instructions.

3. Check box C in Part II.

4. Attach Form 2210, Parts I, II, IV, and Schedule AI to your return.

Additional information. See Pub. 505, chapter 4, for more details about the annualized income installment method. Estates and trusts, see Notice 87-32.

Individuals filing Form 1040NR or 1040NR-EZ. If you are filing Form 1040NR or 1040NR-EZ and you did not receive wages as an employee subject to U.S. income tax withholding, follow these modified instructions for Schedule AI.

1. Skip column (a).

2. Beginning with column (b), enter on line 1 your income for the period that is effectively connected with a U.S. trade or business.

3. Increase the amount on line 17 by the amount determined by multiplying your income for the period that is not effectively connected with a U.S. trade or business by the following.
- In column (b), 72%.
- In column (c), 45%.
- In column (d), 30%.

However, if you can use a treaty rate lower than 30%, use the percentages determined by multiplying your treaty rate by 2.4, 1.5, and 1, respectively.

4. Enter on line 22, column (b), one-half of the amount from Form 2210, Part I, line 9. In columns (c) and (d), enter one-fourth of that amount.

5. Skip column (b) of lines 20 and 23.

Part I—Annualized Income Installments

To figure the amount of each required installment, Schedule AI selects the smaller of the annualized income installment or the regular installment (that has been increased by the amount saved by using the annualized income installment method in figuring any earlier installments).

Line 1

For each period (column), figure your total income minus your adjustments to income. Include your share of partnership or S corporation income or loss items for the period.

If you are self-employed, be sure to take into account the deductible part of your self-employment tax. For more information on how to figure this amount for each period, see Pub. 505, chapter 4.

Line 2

Estates and trusts do not use the amounts shown in columns (a) through (d). Instead, use 6, 3, 1.71429, and 1.09091, respectively, as the annualization amounts.

Worksheet for Form 2210, Part IV, Section B—Figure the Penalty

Keep for Your Records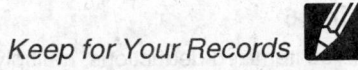

Complete Rate Period 1 of each column before going to the next column; then go to Rate Periods 2, 3, and 4 in the same manner. If multiple estimated tax payments are applied to the underpayment amount in a column of line 1a, you will need to make more than one computation for that column.

		Payment Due Dates			
		(a) 4/15/14	**(b)** 6/15/14	**(c)** 9/15/14	**(d)** 1/15/15
1a Enter your underpayment from Part IV, Section A, line 25	**1a**				
1b Date and amount of each payment applied to the underpayment in the same column. Do not enter more than the underpayment amount on line 1a for each column (see instructions). **Note.** Your payments are applied in the order made first to any underpayment balance in an earlier column until that underpayment is fully paid.	**1b**				
Rate Period 1: April 16, 2014—June 30, 2014					
2 Computation starting dates for this period	**2**	4/15/14	6/15/14		
3 Number of days **from** the date on line 2 to the date the amount on line 1a was paid **or** 6/30/14, whichever is earlier	**3**	Days:	Days:		
4 Underpayment on line 1a $\times$ $\dfrac{\text{Number of days on line 3}}{365}$ $\times$ .03	**4**	$	$		
Rate Period 2: July 1, 2014—September 30, 2014					
5 Computation starting dates for this period	**5**	6/30/14	6/30/14	9/15/14	
6 Number of days **from** the date on line 5 to the date the amount on line 1a was paid **or** 9/30/14, whichever is earlier	**6**	Days:	Days:	Days:	
7 Underpayment on line 1a $\times$ $\dfrac{\text{Number of days on line 6}}{365}$ $\times$ .03	**7**	$	$	$	
Rate Period 3: October 1, 2014—December 31, 2014					
8 Computation starting dates for this period	**8**	9/30/14	9/30/14	9/30/14	
9 Number of days **from** the date on line 8 to the date the amount on line 1a was paid **or** 12/31/14, whichever is earlier	**9**	Days:	Days:	Days:	
10 Underpayment on line 1a $\times$ $\dfrac{\text{Number of days on line 9}}{365}$ $\times$ .03	**10**	$	$	$	
Rate Period 4: January 1, 2015—April 15, 2015					
11 Computation starting dates for this period	**11**	12/31/14	12/31/14	12/31/14	1/15/15
12 Number of days **from** the date on line 11 to the date the amount on line 1a was paid **or** 4/15/15, whichever is earlier	**12**	Days:	Days:	Days:	Days:
13 Underpayment on line 1a $\times$ $\dfrac{\text{Number of days on line 12}}{365}$ $\times$ .03	**13**	$	$	$	$
14 Penalty. Add all amounts on lines 4, 7, 10, and 13 in all columns. Enter the total here and on line 27 of Part IV, Section B . . . . ▶	**14**	$			

Line 6

If you itemized deductions, multiply line 4 of each column by line 5 and enter the result on line 6. But if line 3 is more than the following amounts based on your filing status, use the Itemized Deductions Worksheet – Line 6 to figure the amount to enter on line 6.

- Married filing jointly or Qualifying widow(er) $305,050
- Head of household $279,650
- Single $254,200
- Married filing separately $152,525

Itemized Deductions Worksheet – Line 6

1. Enter line 4 of Schedule AI . . . . 1. _____
2. Enter the total amount included on line 1 above for medical and dental expenses, investment interest, casualty or theft losses, and gambling losses (after applying the same limits used in line 1) . . . . 2. _____
3. Subtract line 2 from line 1 . . . . 3. _____
4. Enter line 5 of Schedule AI . . . . 4. _____
5. Multiply line 1 by line 4 . . . . 5. _____

   Note. If line 3 is zero or less, your deduction is not limited. **Stop** *here and enter line 5 above on Schedule AI, line 6.*

6. Multiply line 3 by line 4 . . . . 6. _____
7. Multiply line 6 by 80% (.80) . . . . 7. _____
8. Enter line 3 of Schedule AI . . . . 8. _____
9. Enter the amount shown below for your filing status:

   - $305,050 if married filing jointly or qualifying widow(er),
   - $279,650 if head of household,
   - $254,200 if single, or
   - $152,525 if married filing separately . . . . 9. _____

10. Subtract line 9 from line 8 . . . . . . 10. _____

    Note. If line 10 is zero or less, your deduction is not limited. **Stop** *here and enter line 5 above on Schedule AI, line 6*

11. Multiply line 10 by 3% (.03) . . . . . . 11. _____
12. Enter the **smaller** of line 7 or line 11 . . . . 12. _____
13. **Total itemized deductions.** Subtract line 12 from line 5. Enter the result here and in the appropriate column of Schedule AI, line 6 . . . . 13. _____

Line 7

If you are a resident of India and a student or business apprentice, enter your standard deduction from Form 1040NR, line 38; or Form 1040NR-EZ, line 11.

Line 10

For each column, multiply $3,950 by your total exemptions. But if line 3 is more than the following amount based on your filing status, use the Deduction for Exemptions Worksheet – Line 10 to figure the amount to enter on line 10.

- Married filing jointly or Qualifying widow(er) $305,050
- Head of household $279,650
- Single $254,200
- Married filing separately $152,525

Deduction for Exemptions Worksheet – Line 10

1. Multiply $3,950 by the number of exemptions you plan to claim . . . . 1. _____
2. Enter line 3 of Schedule AI . . . . 2. _____
3. Enter the amount shown below for your filing status:

   - $305,050 if married filing jointly or qualifying widow(er),
   - $279,650 if head of household,
   - $254,200 if single, or
   - $152,525 if married filing separately . . . . 3. _____

4. Subtract line 3 from line 2 . . . . 4. _____
5. Is line 4 more than $122,500 (more than $61,250 if married filing separately)?

   ☐ **Yes. Stop** here. Enter -0- on lines 5 and 8. Do not complete the rest of this worksheet.

   ☐ **No.** Divide line 4 by $2,500 ($1,250 if married filing separately). If the result is not a whole number, increase it to the next highest whole number (for example, increase 0.0004 to 1) . . . . 5. _____

6. Multiply line 5 by 2% (.02). Enter the result as a decimal . . . . 6. _____
7. Multiply line 1 by line 6 . . . . 7. _____
8. **Deduction for exemptions.** Subtract line 7 from line 1. Enter the result here and in the appropriate column of Schedule AI, line 10 . . . . 8. _____

Estates, trusts, and Form 1040NR or 1040NR-EZ filers. Use the exemption amount shown on your return.

Line 12

To compute the tax, use the Tax Table, Tax Computation Worksheet, Qualified Dividends and Capital Gain Tax Worksheet, Schedule D Tax Worksheet, Foreign Earned Income Tax Worksheet, Schedule J, or Form 8615, as appropriate. See the instructions for your tax return for the applicable Tax Table or worksheet.

Note. Chapter 4 of Pub. 505 contains a Qualified Dividends and Capital Gain Tax Worksheet and a Foreign Earned Income Tax Worksheet designed for use with Schedule AI.

Line 14

Enter all of the other taxes you owed because of events that occurred during the months shown in the column headings. Include the same taxes used to figure Form 2210, Part I, line 2 (except self-employment tax), plus the tax from Form 4972, Tax on Lump-Sum Distributions; Form 8814, Parents' Election To Report Child's Interest and Dividends; and any alternative minimum tax (AMT).

To figure the AMT, Form 1040 filers use Form 6251, Alternative Minimum Tax—Individuals; Form 1040A filers use the Alternative Minimum Tax Worksheet in the Form 1040A instructions; and estates and trusts use Schedule I (Form 1041), Alternative Minimum Tax—Estates and Trusts. Figure alternative minimum taxable income based on your income and deductions during the periods shown in the column headings. Multiply this amount by the annualization amounts shown for each column on Schedule AI, line 2, before subtracting the AMT exemption.

Line 16

For each column, enter the credits you are entitled to because of events that occurred during the months shown in the column headings. These are the credits you used to arrive at the amounts on lines 1 and 3 of Part I, Required Annual Payment.

When figuring your credits, annualize any item of income or deduction used to figure each credit. For example, if your earned income (and AGI) for the first period (column (a)) is $8,000 and you qualify for the earned income credit (EIC), use your annualized earned income ($32,000) to figure your EIC for column (a).

Part II—Annualized Self-Employment Tax

If you had net earnings from self-employment during any period, complete Part II for that period to figure your annualized self-employment tax.

If you are married and filing a joint return and both you and your spouse had net earnings from self-employment, complete a separate Part II for each spouse. Enter on line 13 of Schedule AI, Part I, the combined amounts from line 34 of each spouse's Part II.

Any Additional Medicare Tax on self-employment income will be computed in Part I.

Line 26

Generally, to figure your net earnings from self-employment on line 26, multiply your net profit from all trades or businesses for each period by 92.35% (.9235).

However, if your Form W-2 showed church employee income or you deducted Conservation Reserve Program payments on your Schedule SE, use a separate Schedule SE as a worksheet to calculate net earnings from self-employment for each period. For this purpose, net earnings from self-employment is the amount on line 4 of the Short Schedule SE or line 6 of the Long Schedule SE.

Line 28

If you filed Form 4137 or Form 8919, use the following instructions to figure the additional amount to include in the appropriate columns of line 28.

- Form 4137: Include the actual unreported tips for the period subject to social security tax. This will be the amount on Form 4137, line 10, when the form is completed for a specific period.
- Form 8919: Include the actual wages for the period from which the social security tax was not withheld. This will be the amount on Form 8919, line 10, when the form is completed for a specific period.

Paperwork Reduction Act Notice. We ask for the information on this form to carry out the Internal Revenue laws of the United States. You are required to give us the information. We need it to ensure that you are complying with these laws and to allow us to figure and collect the right amount of tax.

You are not required to provide the information requested on a form that is subject to the Paperwork Reduction Act unless the form displays a valid OMB control number. Books or records relating to a form or its instructions must be retained as long as their contents may become material in the administration of any Internal Revenue law. Generally, tax returns and return information are confidential, as required by section 6103.

The time needed to complete and file this form will vary depending on individual circumstances. The estimated burden for individual taxpayers filing this form is approved under OMB control number 1545-0074 and is included in the estimates shown in the instructions for their individual income tax return. The estimated burden for all other taxpayers who file this form is shown below.

	Short Method	Regular Method
Recordkeeping	13 min.	13 min.
Learning about the law or the form	15 min.	34 min.
Preparing the form	35 min.	4 hr. 1 min.
Copying, assembling, and sending the form to the IRS	16 min.	41 min.

If you have comments concerning the accuracy of these time estimates or suggestions for making this form simpler, we would be happy to hear from you. See the instructions for the tax return with which this form is filed.

Form **2210-F**	**Underpayment of Estimated Tax by Farmers and Fishermen**	OMB No. 1545-0140
Department of the Treasury Internal Revenue Service	▶ Attach to Form 1040, Form 1040NR, or Form 1041. ▶ Information about Form 2210-F and its separate instructions is at *www.irs.gov/form2210f.*	**2014** Attachment Sequence No. **06A**

Name(s) shown on tax return	Identifying number

Generally, you do not need to file Form 2210-F. The IRS will figure any penalty you owe and send you a bill. File Form 2210-F **only** if one or both of the boxes in Part I apply to you. If you do not need to file Form 2210-F, you still can use it to figure your penalty. Enter the amount from line 16 on the penalty line of your return, but do not attach Form 2210-F.

Part I	**Reasons for Filing.** Check applicable boxes. If neither applies, **do not file Form 2210-F.**
A	☐ You request a **waiver**. In certain circumstances, the IRS will waive all or part of the penalty. See *Waiver of Penalty* in the instructions.
B	☐ You filed or are filing a joint return for either 2013 or 2014, but not for both years, and line 10 below is smaller than line 7 below.

Part II	**Figure Your Underpayment**		
1	Enter your 2014 tax after credits from Form 1040, line 56; Form 1040NR, line 53; or Form 1041, Schedule G, line 3	**1**	
2	Other taxes, including self-employment tax and, if applicable, Additional Medicare Tax and/or Net Investment Income Tax (see instructions)	**2**	
3	Add lines 1 and 2. If less than $1,000, you do not owe a penalty; **do not file Form 2210-F** . .	**3**	
4	Refundable credits you claimed on your tax return.		
a	Earned income credit (EIC)	**4a**	
b	Additional child tax credit	**4b**	
c	American opportunity credit (Form 8863, line 8)	**4c**	
d	Credit for federal tax paid on fuels	**4d**	
e	Premium tax credit	**4e**	
f	Credit determined under section 1341(a)(5)(B) (see instructions) .	**4f**	
5	Add lines 4a through 4f	**5**	
6	Current year tax. Subtract line 5 from line 3. If less than $1,000, you do not owe a penalty; do not file Form 2210-F	**6**	
7	Multiply line 6 by 66⅔% (.667)	**7**	
8	Withholding taxes. **Do not** include any estimated tax payments on this line (see instructions) .	**8**	
9	Subtract line 8 from line 6. If less than $1,000, you do not owe a penalty; **do not file Form 2210-F**	**9**	
10	Enter the tax shown on your 2013 tax return (see instructions if your 2014 filing status changed to or from married filing jointly)	**10**	
11	**Required annual payment.** Enter the **smaller** of line 7 or line 10	**11**	
	Note: *If line 8 is equal to or more than line 11, stop here; you do not owe the penalty.* **Do not file Form 2210-F** *unless you checked box B above.*		
12	Enter the estimated tax payments you made by January 15, 2015, and any federal income tax and excess social security or tier 1 railroad retirement tax withheld during 2014	**12**	
13	**Underpayment.** Subtract line 12 from line 11. If the result is zero or less, stop here; you do not owe the penalty. **Do not file Form 2210-F** unless you checked box **B** above	**13**	

Part III	**Figure the Penalty**		
14	Enter the date the amount on line 13 was paid or April 15, 2015, whichever is earlier	**14**	/ / 15
15	Number of days **from** January 15, 2015, **to** the date on line 14	**15**	
16	**Penalty.** Underpayment on line 13 × (Number of days on line 15 / 365) × .03 . . . . ▶	**16**	

- Form 1040 filers, enter the amount from line 16 on Form 1040, line 79.
- Form 1040NR filers, enter the amount from line 16 on Form 1040NR, line 76.
- Form 1041 filers, enter the amount from line 16 on Form 1041, line 26.

For Paperwork Reduction Act Notice, see separate instructions.	Cat. No. 11745A	Form **2210-F** (2014)

Section references are to the Internal Revenue Code unless otherwise noted.

General Instructions

Future Developments

For the latest information about developments related to Form 2210-F and its instructions, such as legislation enacted after they were published, go to *www.irs.gov/form2210f*.

What's New

Personal exemption amount increased for certain taxpayers. For tax years beginning in 2014, the personal exemption amount is increased to $3,950. There is a phaseout of the exemption, the amount of which is determined by the taxpayer's filing status and adjusted gross income.

Limit on itemized deductions. For tax years beginning in 2014, itemized deductions for taxpayers with adjusted gross incomes above $152,250 may be reduced.

Health coverage tax credit. The health coverage tax credit claimed on Form 8885 expired at the end of 2013.

Premium Tax Credit. Beginning in 2014, you may be eligible to claim the premium tax credit. The premium tax credit provides assistance for premiums for health insurance coverage enrolled in through a Health Insurance Marketplace (also called an Exchange). The credit may reduce the amount of tax you owe or increase your refund. For more information, see Form 8962 and Publication 974, Premium Tax Credit.

Reminders

Additional Medicare Tax. A 0.9% Additional Medicare Tax applies to Medicare wages, Railroad Retirement Tax Act (RRTA) compensation, and self-employment income over a threshold amount based on your filing status. See Form 8959, Additional Medicare Tax.

Net Investment Income Tax. You may be subject to Net Investment Income Tax (NIIT). NIIT is a 3.8% tax on the lesser of net investment income or the excess of your modified adjusted gross income over a threshold amount. See Form 8960, Net Investment Income Tax—Individuals, Estates, and Trusts.

Purpose of Form

If you are an individual, estate, or trust and at least two-thirds of your 2013 or 2014 gross income is from farming or fishing, use Form 2210-F to see if you owe a penalty for underpaying your estimated tax.

For a definition of gross income from farming and fishing and more details, see chapter 2 of Pub. 505, Tax Withholding and Estimated Tax.

Who Must File Form 2210-F

If you checked box A or B in Part I of Form 2210-F, you must figure the penalty yourself and attach the completed form to your return.

The IRS Will Figure the Penalty for You

If you did not check box A or B in Part I, you do not need to figure the penalty or file Form 2210-F. Complete your return as usual, leave the penalty line on your return blank, and do not attach Form 2210-F. If you owe the penalty, the IRS will send you a bill. Interest will not be charged on the penalty if you pay by the date specified on the bill.

Who Must Pay the Underpayment Penalty

You may owe the penalty for 2014 if you did not pay at least the smaller of:

1. Two-thirds of the tax shown on your 2014 return, or

2. 100% of the tax shown on your 2013 return (your 2013 tax return must cover a 12-month period).

Return. In these instructions, "return" refers to your original income tax return. However, an amended return is considered the original return if it is filed by the due date (including extensions) of the original return. Also, a joint return that replaces previously filed separate returns is considered the original return.

Exceptions to the Penalty

You will not have to pay the penalty or file this form if any of the following applies.

*   You file your return and pay the tax due by March 2, 2015. If you do not file your return and pay the tax due by March 2, 2015, you may be able to request a waiver of the underpayment penalty.
*   You had no tax liability for 2013, you were a U.S. citizen or resident alien for the entire year (or an estate of a domestic decedent or a domestic trust), and your 2013 return was (or would have been had you been required to file) for a full 12 months.
*   The total tax shown on your 2014 return minus the amount of tax you paid through withholding is less than $1,000. To determine whether the total tax is less than $1,000, complete lines 1 through 9.

Waiver of Penalty

If you have an underpayment on line 13, all or part of the penalty for that underpayment will be waived if the IRS determines that:

*   In 2013 or 2014, you retired after reaching age 62 or became disabled, and your underpayment was due to reasonable cause, or
*   The underpayment was due to a casualty, disaster, or other unusual circumstance, and it would be inequitable to impose the penalty. For federally declared disasters, see the separate information, later.

To request either of the above waivers, do the following.
*   Check box A in Part I.
*   Complete Form 2210-F through line 15 without regard to the waiver. Enter the amount you want waived in parentheses on the dotted line to the left of line 16. Subtract this amount from the

total penalty you figured without regard to the waiver, and enter the result on line 16.

- Attach Form 2210-F and a statement to your return explaining the reasons you were unable to meet the estimated tax requirements.

- If you are requesting a waiver due to retirement or disability, attach documentation that shows your retirement date (and your age on that date) or the date you became disabled.

- If you are requesting a waiver due to a casualty, disaster (other than a federally declared disaster as discussed later), or other unusual circumstance, attach documentation such as copies of police and insurance company reports.

The IRS will review the information you provide and will decide whether to grant your request for a waiver.

Federally declared disaster. Certain estimated tax payment deadlines for taxpayers who reside or have a business in a federally declared disaster area are postponed for a period during and after the disaster. During the processing of your tax return, the IRS automatically identifies taxpayers located in a covered disaster area (by county or parish) and applies the appropriate penalty relief. **Do not** file Form 2210-F if your underpayment was due to a federally declared disaster. If you still owe a penalty after the automatic waiver is applied, the IRS will send you a bill.

An individual or a fiduciary for an estate or trust not in a covered disaster area but whose books, records, or tax professionals' offices are in a covered area is also entitled to relief. Also eligible are relief workers affiliated with a recognized government or charitable organization assisting in the relief activities in a covered disaster area. If you meet either of these eligibility requirements, you must call the IRS disaster hotline at 1-866-562-5227 and identify yourself as eligible for this relief.

Details on the applicable disaster postponement period can be found at IRS.gov. Enter "disaster relief" in the search box, then select "Tax Relief in Disaster Situations." Select the federally declared disaster that affected you.

Specific Instructions

Complete lines 1 through 11 to figure your required annual payment.

If you file an amended return by the due date of your original return, use the amounts shown on your amended return to figure your underpayment. If you file an amended return after the due date, use the amounts shown on the original return.

Exception. If you and your spouse file a joint return after the due date to replace previously filed separate returns, use the amounts shown on the joint return to figure your underpayment.

Line 2

Enter the total of the following amounts.

IF you file...	THEN include on line 2 the amounts on...
1040	Lines 57, 59 (additional tax on distributions only), 60a*, 60b, and, if applicable, Additional Medicare Tax and/or Net Investment Income Tax on line 62, and any write-ins on line 62 with the exception of: • Uncollected social security and Medicare tax or RRTA tax on tips or on group-term life insurance (identified as "UT"), • Tax on excess golden parachute payments (identified as "EPP"), • Excise tax on insider stock compensation from an expatriated corporation (identified as "ISC"), • Look-back interest due under section 167(g) (identified as "From Form 8866"), • Look-back interest due under section 460(b) (identified as "From Form 8697"), and • Recapture of federal mortgage subsidy (identified as "FMSR").
1040NR	Lines 54, 55, 57 (additional tax on distributions only), 58, 59a*, 59b, and, if applicable, Additional Medicare Tax and/or Net Investment Income Tax on line 60, and any write-ins on line 60 with the exception of: • Uncollected social security and Medicare tax or RRTA tax on tips or on group-term life insurance (identified as "UT"), • Tax on excess golden parachute payments (identified as "EPP"), • Excise tax on insider stock compensation from an expatriated corporation (identified as "ISC"), • Look-back interest due under section 167(g) (identified as "From Form 8866"), • Look-back interest due under section 460(b) (identified as "From Form 8697"), and • Recapture of federal mortgage subsidy (identified as "FMSR").
1041	Schedule G, lines 4, 5, 6*, and any write-ins on line 7 with the exception of: • Look-back interest due under section 167(g) (identified as "From Form 8866"), and • Look-back interest due under section 460(b) (identified as "From Form 8697").

*If you are a household employer, include your household employment taxes on line 2 only if you had federal income tax withheld from your income and would be required to make estimated tax payments even if the household employment taxes were not included.

Line 4

To figure the amount of the section 1341 credit, see *Repayments* in Pub. 525, Taxable and Nontaxable Income.

Line 8

Enter the taxes withheld shown on Form 1040, lines 64 and 71; Form 1040NR, lines 62a, 62b, 62c, 62d, and 67; or Form 1041, line 24e.

Form 8689 filers. Also enter on this line the amount from Form 8689, lines 40 and 45, that you entered on line 74 of your 2014 Form 1040.

Line 10

Figure your 2013 tax using the taxes and credits shown on your 2013 tax return. Use the same type of taxes and credits as shown on lines 1, 2, and 4a through 4f.

If you are filing a joint return for 2014 but you did not file a joint return for 2013, add the tax shown on your 2013 return to the tax shown on your spouse's 2013 return and enter the total on line 10 (both taxes figured as explained earlier).

If you filed a joint return for 2013 but you are not filing a joint return for 2014, see Pub. 505, chapter 4, *General Rule,* to figure your share of the 2013 tax to enter on line 10.

If you did not file a return for 2013 or if your 2013 tax year was less than 12 months, do not complete line 10. Instead, enter the amount from line 7 on line 11. However, see *Exceptions to the Penalty*, earlier.

Paperwork Reduction Act Notice. We ask for the information on this form to carry out the Internal Revenue laws of the United States. You are required to give us the information. We need it to ensure that you are complying with these laws and to allow us to figure and collect the right amount of tax.

You are not required to provide the information requested on a form that is subject to the Paperwork Reduction Act unless the form displays a valid OMB control number. Books or records relating to a form or its instructions must be retained as long as their contents may become material in the administration of any Internal Revenue law. Generally, tax returns and return information are confidential, as required by section 6103.

The time needed to complete and file this form will vary depending on individual circumstances. The estimated burden for individual taxpayers filing this form is approved under OMB control number 1545-0074 and is included in the estimates shown in the instructions for their individual income tax return. The estimated burden for all other taxpayers who file this form is as follows.

Recordkeeping	39 min.
Learning about the law or the form	10 min.
Preparing the form	37 min.
Copying, assembling, and sending the form to the IRS	20 min.

If you have comments concerning the accuracy of these time estimates or suggestions for making this form simpler, we would be happy to hear from you. See the instructions for the tax return with which this form is filed.

Form **2220**	**Underpayment of Estimated Tax by Corporations**	OMB No. 1545-0123
Department of the Treasury Internal Revenue Service	▶ Attach to the corporation's tax return. ▶ Information about Form 2220 and its separate instructions is at *www.irs.gov/form2220*.	20**14**

Name	Employer identification number

Note: *Generally, the corporation is not required to file Form 2220 (see Part II below for exceptions) because the IRS will figure any penalty owed and bill the corporation. However, the corporation may still use Form 2220 to figure the penalty. If so, enter the amount from page 2, line 38 on the estimated tax penalty line of the corporation's income tax return, but* **do not** *attach Form 2220.*

Part I — Required Annual Payment

1	Total tax (see instructions)	**1**	
2a	Personal holding company tax (Schedule PH (Form 1120), line 26) included on line 1	**2a**	
b	Look-back interest included on line 1 under section 460(b)(2) for completed long-term contracts or section 167(g) for depreciation under the income forecast method . .	**2b**	
c	Credit for federal tax paid on fuels (see instructions)	**2c**	
d	**Total.** Add lines 2a through 2c	**2d**	
3	Subtract line 2d from line 1. If the result is less than $500, **do not** complete or file this form. The corporation does not owe the penalty	**3**	
4	Enter the tax shown on the corporation's 2013 income tax return (see instructions). **Caution:** *If the tax is zero or the tax year was for less than 12 months, skip this line and enter the amount from line 3 on line 5* . .	**4**	
5	**Required annual payment.** Enter the **smaller** of line 3 or line 4. If the corporation is required to skip line 4, enter the amount from line 3	**5**	

Part II — Reasons for Filing—Check the boxes below that apply. If any boxes are checked, the corporation **must** file Form 2220 even if it does not owe a penalty (see instructions).

6	☐	The corporation is using the adjusted seasonal installment method.
7	☐	The corporation is using the annualized income installment method.
8	☐	The corporation is a "large corporation" figuring its first required installment based on the prior year's tax.

Part III — Figuring the Underpayment

			(a)	(b)	(c)	(d)
9	**Installment due dates.** Enter in columns (a) through (d) the 15th day of the 4th (**Form 990-PF filers:** Use 5th month), 6th, 9th, and 12th months of the corporation's tax year	**9**				
10	**Required installments.** If the box on line 6 and/or line 7 above is checked, enter the amounts from Schedule A, line 38. If the box on line 8 (but not 6 or 7) is checked, see instructions for the amounts to enter. If none of these boxes are checked, enter 25% of line 5 above in each column	**10**				
11	Estimated tax paid or credited for each period (see instructions). For column (a) only, enter the amount from line 11 on line 15	**11**				
	Complete lines 12 through 18 of one column before going to the next column.					
12	Enter amount, if any, from line 18 of the preceding column	**12**				
13	Add lines 11 and 12	**13**				
14	Add amounts on lines 16 and 17 of the preceding column	**14**				
15	Subtract line 14 from line 13. If zero or less, enter -0-	**15**				
16	If the amount on line 15 is zero, subtract line 13 from line 14. Otherwise, enter -0-	**16**				
17	**Underpayment.** If line 15 is less than or equal to line 10, subtract line 15 from line 10. Then go to line 12 of the next column. Otherwise, go to line 18	**17**				
18	**Overpayment.** If line 10 is less than line 15, subtract line 10 from line 15. Then go to line 12 of the next column	**18**				

Go to Part IV on page 2 to figure the penalty. Do not go to Part IV if there are no entries on line 17—no penalty is owed.

For Paperwork Reduction Act Notice, see separate instructions.　　　　Cat. No. 11746L　　　　Form **2220** (2014)

Part IV　Figuring the Penalty

			(a)	(b)	(c)	(d)
19	Enter the date of payment or the 15th day of the 3rd month after the close of the tax year, whichever is earlier (see instructions). ***(Form 990-PF and Form 990-T filers:* Use 5th month instead of 3rd month.)**	**19**				
20	Number of days from due date of installment on line 9 to the date shown on line 19	**20**				
21	Number of days on line 20 after 4/15/2014 and before 7/1/2014	**21**				
22	Underpayment on line 17 × $\dfrac{\text{Number of days on line 21}}{365}$ × 3%	**22**	$	$	$	$
23	Number of days on line 20 after 6/30/2014 and before 10/1/2014	**23**				
24	Underpayment on line 17 × $\dfrac{\text{Number of days on line 23}}{365}$ × 3%	**24**	$	$	$	$
25	Number of days on line 20 after 9/30/2014 and before 1/1/2015	**25**				
26	Underpayment on line 17 × $\dfrac{\text{Number of days on line 25}}{365}$ × 3%	**26**	$	$	$	$
27	Number of days on line 20 after 12/31/2014 and before 4/1/2015	**27**				
28	Underpayment on line 17 × $\dfrac{\text{Number of days on line 27}}{365}$ × 3%	**28**	$	$	$	$
29	Number of days on line 20 after 3/31/2015 and before 7/1/2015	**29**				
30	Underpayment on line 17 × $\dfrac{\text{Number of days on line 29}}{365}$ × *%	**30**	$	$	$	$
31	Number of days on line 20 after 6/30/2015 and before 10/1/2015	**31**				
32	Underpayment on line 17 × $\dfrac{\text{Number of days on line 31}}{365}$ × *%	**32**	$	$	$	$
33	Number of days on line 20 after 9/30/2015 and before 1/1/2016	**33**				
34	Underpayment on line 17 × $\dfrac{\text{Number of days on line 33}}{365}$ × *%	**34**	$	$	$	$
35	Number of days on line 20 after 12/31/2015 and before 2/16/2016	**35**				
36	Underpayment on line 17 × $\dfrac{\text{Number of days on line 35}}{366}$ × *%	**36**	$	$	$	$
37	Add lines 22, 24, 26, 28, 30, 32, 34, and 36	**37**	$	$	$	$

38 **Penalty.** Add columns (a) through (d) of line 37. Enter the total here and on Form 1120, line 33; or the comparable line for other income tax returns . . . . **38** $

*Use the penalty interest rate for each calendar quarter, which the IRS will determine during the first month in the preceding quarter. These rates are published quarterly in an IRS News Release and in a revenue ruling in the Internal Revenue Bulletin. To obtain this information on the Internet, access the IRS website at ***www.irs.gov.*** You can also call 1-800-829-4933 to get interest rate information.

Schedule A   Adjusted Seasonal Installment Method and Annualized Income Installment Method
(see instructions)

Form 1120S filers: *For lines 1, 2, 3, and 21, below, "taxable income" refers to excess net passive income or the amount on which tax is imposed under section 1374(a), whichever applies.*

Part I	Adjusted Seasonal Installment Method (**Caution:** *Use this method only if the base period percentage for any 6 consecutive months is at least 70%. See instructions.*)

			(a)	(b)	(c)	(d)
			First 3 months	First 5 months	First 8 months	First 11 months
1	Enter taxable income for the following periods:					
a	Tax year beginning in 2011	1a				
b	Tax year beginning in 2012	1b				
c	Tax year beginning in 2013	1c				
2	Enter taxable income for each period for the tax year beginning in 2014 (see instructions for the treatment of extraordinary items) .	2				
3	Enter taxable income for the following periods:		First 4 months	First 6 months	First 9 months	Entire year
a	Tax year beginning in 2011.	3a				
b	Tax year beginning in 2012	3b				
c	Tax year beginning in 2013	3c				
4	Divide the amount in each column on line 1a by the amount in column (d) on line 3a	4				
5	Divide the amount in each column on line 1b by the amount in column (d) on line 3b	5				
6	Divide the amount in each column on line 1c by the amount in column (d) on line 3c	6				
7	Add lines 4 through 6	7				
8	Divide line 7 by 3.0	8				
9a	Divide line 2 by line 8	9a				
b	Extraordinary items (see instructions)	9b				
c	Add lines 9a and 9b .	9c				
10	Figure the tax on the amount on line 9c using the instructions for Form 1120, Schedule J, line 2 (or comparable line of corporation's return)	10				
11a	Divide the amount in columns (a) through (c) on line 3a by the amount in column (d) on line 3a	11a				
b	Divide the amount in columns (a) through (c) on line 3b by the amount in column (d) on line 3b	11b				
c	Divide the amount in columns (a) through (c) on line 3c by the amount in column (d) on line 3c	11c				
12	Add lines 11a through 11c	12				
13	Divide line 12 by 3.0	13				
14	Multiply the amount in columns (a) through (c) of line 10 by columns (a) through (c) of line 13. In column (d), enter the amount from line 10, column (d)	14				
15	Enter any alternative minimum tax for each payment period (see instructions)	15				
16	Enter any other taxes for each payment period (see instructions)	16				
17	Add lines 14 through 16	17				
18	For each period, enter the same type of credits as allowed on Form 2220, lines 1 and 2c (see instructions)	18				
19	Total tax after credits. Subtract line 18 from line 17. If zero or less, enter -0-	19				

Part II   Annualized Income Installment Method

			(a)	(b)	(c)	(d)
			First ___ months	First ___ months	First ___ months	First ___ months
20	Annualization periods (see instructions)	20				
21	Enter taxable income for each annualization period (see instructions for the treatment of extraordinary items) . . .	21				
22	Annualization amounts (see instructions)	22				
23a	Annualized taxable income. Multiply line 21 by line 22 . . .	23a				
b	Extraordinary items (see instructions)	23b				
c	Add lines 23a and 23b	23c				
24	Figure the tax on the amount on line 23c using the instructions for Form 1120, Schedule J, line 2 (or comparable line of corporation's return)	24				
25	Enter any alternative minimum tax for each payment period (see instructions)	25				
26	Enter any other taxes for each payment period (see instructions)	26				
27	Total tax. Add lines 24 through 26	27				
28	For each period, enter the same type of credits as allowed on Form 2220, lines 1 and 2c (see instructions)	28				
29	Total tax after credits. Subtract line 28 from line 27. If zero or less, enter -0-	29				
30	Applicable percentage	30	25%	50%	75%	100%
31	Multiply line 29 by line 30	31				

Part III   Required Installments

			1st installment	2nd installment	3rd installment	4th installment
	Note: *Complete lines 32 through 38 of one column before completing the next column.*					
32	If only Part I or Part II is completed, enter the amount in each column from line 19 or line 31. If both parts are completed, enter the **smaller** of the amounts in each column from line 19 or line 31 . .	32				
33	Add the amounts in all preceding columns of line 38 (see instructions)	33				
34	**Adjusted seasonal or annualized income installments.** Subtract line 33 from line 32. If zero or less, enter -0- . . .	34				
35	Enter 25% of line 5 on page 1 of Form 2220 in each column. **Note:** *"Large corporations," see the instructions for line 10 for the amounts to enter*	35				
36	Subtract line 38 of the preceding column from line 37 of the preceding column	36				
37	Add lines 35 and 36	37				
38	**Required installments.** Enter the **smaller** of line 34 or line 37 here and on page 1 of Form 2220, line 10 (see instructions) .	38				

Section references are to the Internal Revenue Code unless otherwise noted.

Future Developments

For the latest information about developments affecting Form 2220 and its instructions, such as legislation enacted after they were published, go to *www.irs.gov/form2220.*

General Instructions

Purpose of Form

Corporations (including S corporations), tax-exempt organizations subject to the unrelated business income tax, and private foundations use Form 2220 to determine:
- Whether they are subject to the penalty for underpayment of estimated tax and, if so,
- The amount of the underpayment penalty for the period that applies.

Who Must File

Generally, the corporation does not have to file this form with its income tax return because the IRS will figure the amount of any penalty and notify the corporation of any amount due. However, even if the corporation does not owe a penalty, complete and attach this form to the corporation's tax return if the Part I, line 3 amount Is $500 or more and any of the following apply.

1. The adjusted seasonal installment method is used.

2. The annualized income installment method is used.

3. The corporation is a large corporation (as defined in the instructions for Part II, line 8) figuring its first required installment based on the prior year's tax.

Who Must Pay the Underpayment Penalty

Generally, a corporation is subject to the penalty if it did not timely pay at least the smaller of:

1. The tax shown on its 2014 return, or

2. The tax shown on its 2013 return (if it filed a 2013 return showing at least some amount of tax and the return was for a full 12 months). However, a large corporation can base only its first required installment on the prior year's tax.

In these instructions, "return" generally refers to the corporation's original return. However, an amended return is considered the original return if the amended return is filed by the due date (including extensions) of the original return. Also, for purposes of determining a required installment, if an amended return is filed for the prior tax year, then "prior tax year" includes the amended return, but only if the amended return is filed before the applicable installment due date.

The penalty is figured separately for each installment due date. Therefore, the corporation may owe a penalty for an earlier due date even if it paid enough tax later to make up the underpayment. This is true even if the corporation is due a refund when its return is filed. However, the corporation may be able to reduce or eliminate the penalty by using the annualized income installment method or the adjusted seasonal installment method. See the instructions for Part II for details.

Exception to the Penalty

A corporation will not have to pay a penalty if the tax shown on the corporation's 2014 return (the Part I, line 3 amount) is less than $500.

How To Use Form 2220

- Complete lines 1 through 3 of Part I. If line 3 is $500 or more, complete the rest of Part I to determine the required annual payment and go to Part II.
- Check one or more boxes in Part II if the corporation uses the adjusted seasonal installment method, the annualized income installment method, or if the corporation is a large corporation.

If the corporation checked a box in Part II, attach Form 2220 to the income tax return. Be sure to check the box on Form 1120, page 1, line 33; or the comparable line of any other income tax return the corporation is required to file (for example, Form 1120-C, 1120-L, or 1120S).
- Complete Part III to determine the underpayment for any of the installment due dates
- If there is an underpayment on Part III, line 17 (column (a), (b), (c), or (d)), go to Part IV to figure the penalty.
- Complete Schedule A if the corporation uses the adjusted seasonal installment method and/or the annualized income installment method.

Specific Instructions

Part I. Required Annual Payment

Complete lines 1 through 5 to figure the corporation's required annual payment.

Line 1. Generally, enter the tax from Form 1120, line 31; or the applicable line for other income tax returns. However, if that amount includes any tax attributable to a sale described in section 338(a)(1), do not include that tax on line 1. Instead, write "Sec. 338 gain" and show the amount of tax in brackets on the dotted line next to line 1. This exclusion from the line 1 amount does not apply if a section 338(h)(10) election is made.

For information on how to figure the total tax for estimated tax purposes for other entities, see the following forms or their instructions.

• 990-PF	• 1120-FSC	• 1120-REIT
• 990-T	• 1120-L	• 1120-RIC
• 1120-C	• 1120-ND	• 1120S
• 1120-F	• 1120-PC	• 1120-SF

Line 2c. Enter the amount from Form 1120, Schedule J, Line 19b, or the applicable line for other income tax returns.

Line 4. All filers (other than S corporations). Figure the corporation's 2013 tax the same way the amount on line 3 of this form was determined, using the taxes and credits from its 2013 tax return. However, skip line 4 and enter on line 5 the amount from line 3 if either of the following applies.

• The corporation did not file a tax return for 2013 that showed a liability for at least some amount of tax.

• The corporation had a 2013 tax year of less than 12 months.

S corporations. Enter on line 4 the sum of:

1. The total of the investment credit recapture tax and the built-in gains tax shown on the return for the 2014 tax year and

2. Any excess net passive income tax shown on the S corporation's return for the 2013 tax year.

If the 2013 tax year was less than 12 months, skip line 4 and enter on line 5 the amount from line 3.

Part II. Reasons for Filing

Lines 6 and 7. Adjusted seasonal installment method and/or annualized income installment method. If the corporation's income varied during the year because, for example, it operated its business on a seasonal basis, it may be able to lower or eliminate the amount of one or more required installments by using the adjusted seasonal installment method and/or the annualized income installment method.

Example. A ski shop, which receives most of its income during the winter months, may benefit from using one or both of these methods to figure its required installments. The annualized income installment or adjusted seasonal installment may be less than the required installment under the regular method for one or more due dates. Using one or both of these methods may reduce or eliminate the penalty for those due dates.

Use Schedule A on pages 3 and 4 of Form 2220 to figure one or more required installments. If Schedule A is used for any payment due date, it must be used for all payment due dates. To arrive at the amount of each required installment, Schedule A automatically selects the smallest of:

• The adjusted seasonal installment (if applicable),

• The annualized income installment (if applicable), or

• The regular installment under section 6655(d)(1) (increased by any recapture of a reduction in a required installment under section 6655(e)(1)(B)).

Follow the steps below to determine which parts of the form have to be completed.

• If the corporation is using only the adjusted seasonal installment method, check the box in Part II, line 6, and complete Schedule A, Parts I and III.

• If the corporation is using only the annualized income installment method, check the box on Part II, line 7, and complete Schedule A, Parts II and III.

• If the corporation is using both methods, check the boxes in Part II, lines 6 and 7, and complete all three parts of Schedule A.

Line 8. Large corporations. A large corporation is a corporation (other than an S corporation) that had, or whose predecessor had, taxable income (defined below) of $1 million or more for any of the 3 tax years immediately preceding the 2014 tax year, or if less, the number of years the corporation has been in existence. See Regulations section 1.6655-4.

Taxable income, for this purpose, is modified to exclude net operating loss and capital loss carrybacks and carryovers. Members of a controlled group, as defined in section 1563, must divide the $1 million amount among themselves under rules similar to those in section 1561.

If the corporation is a large corporation, check the box on Part II, line 8, and, if applicable, check the box(es) on Part II, line 6 and/or line 7. Also, if applicable, complete Parts I, II, and III of Schedule A, as discussed below in the instructions for line 10.

Part III. Figuring the Underpayment

Line 9. The corporation is generally required to enter the 15th day of the 4th (Form 990-PF filers use the 5th month), 6th, 9th, and 12th months of its tax year.

Line 10. If multiple columns have the same due date, see the instructions for line 9.

Large corporations. Large corporations, follow the instructions below.

1. If the box on line 8 (but not line 6 or line 7) is checked and line 3 is smaller than line 4, enter 25% of line 3 in columns (a) through (d) of line 10.

2. If the box on line 8 (but not line 6 or line 7) is checked and line 4 is smaller than line 3, enter 25% of line 4 in column (a) of line 10. In column (b), figure the amount to enter as follows:

a. Subtract line 4 from line 3,

b. Add the result to the amount on line 3, and

c. Multiply the total in item b above by 25%, and enter the result in column (b).

In columns (c) and (d), enter 25% of line 3.

3. If the box on line 8 and the box on line 6 and/or line 7 are checked, follow the instructions in items 1 and 2 above by substituting Schedule A, line 35 for line 10 and complete the rest of Schedule A, Part III.

Line 11. Enter the estimated tax payments made by the corporation for its tax year as indicated below. Include any overpayment from the corporation's 2013 tax return that was credited to the corporation's 2014 estimated tax. If an installment is due on a Saturday, Sunday, or legal holiday, payments made on the next day that is not a Saturday, Sunday, or legal holiday are considered made on the due date to the extent the payment is applied against that required installment. If multiple columns have the same due date, see the instructions for line 9.

Column (a). Enter payments made by the date on line 9, column (a).

Columns (b), (c), and (d). Enter payments made by the date on line 9 for that column and after the date on line 9 of the preceding column.

Line 17. If any of the columns in line 17 shows an underpayment, complete Part IV to figure the penalty.

Part IV. Figuring the Penalty

Complete lines 19 through 38 to determine the amount of the penalty. The penalty is figured for the period of underpayment using the underpayment rate determined under section 6621. The period of underpayment runs from the installment due date to the earlier of the date the underpayment is actually paid or the 15th day of the third month after the close of the tax year. For information on obtaining the interest rate on underpayments, see the footnote on page 2 of Form 2220.

Line 19. A payment of estimated tax is applied against unpaid required installments in the order in which installments are required to be paid, regardless of the installment to which the payment pertains.

Example. A corporation with a calendar tax year underpaid the April 15 installment by $1,000. The June 15 installment requires a payment of $2,500. On June 10, the corporation deposits $2,500 to cover the June 15 installment. However, $1,000 of this payment is applied against the April 15 installment. The penalty for the April 15 installment is figured from April 15 to June 10 (56 days). The remaining $1,500 is applied to the June 15 installment.

If the corporation has made more than one payment for a required installment, attach a separate computation for each payment.

Schedule A

Extraordinary items. Generally, under the annualized income installment method, extraordinary items must be taken into account after annualizing the taxable income for the annualization period. Similar rules apply in determining taxable income under the adjusted seasonal installment method. An extraordinary item includes:
- Any item identified in Regulations section 1.1502-76(b)(2)(ii)(C)(1), (2),(3),(4), (7) and (8);
- A net operating loss carryover;
- A section 481(a) adjustment; and
- Net gain or loss from the disposition of 25% or more of the fair market value of the corporation's business assets during the tax year.

These extraordinary items must be accounted for, in the appropriate annualization period. However, a net operating loss deduction and a section 481(a) adjustment (unless the corporation makes the alternative choice under Regulations section 1.6655-2(f)(3)(ii)(C)) are treated as extraordinary items occurring on the first day of the tax year in which the item is taken into account in determining taxable income.

De minimis rule. Extraordinary items identified above that are less than $1,000,000 (other than a net operating loss carryover or a section 481(a) adjustment) may be annualized using the general rules of Regulations section 1.6655-2(f), or, if the corporation chooses, may be taken into account after annualizing the taxable income for the annualization period.

In Part II of Schedule A, make the appropriate adjustments to annualized taxable income before figuring the estimated tax for each reporting period. Similar adjustments must be made, if applicable, to Part I of Schedule A, if the adjusted

seasonal installment method applies. See the instructions for lines 2, 9b, 21, and 23b, below.

For more information regarding extraordinary items, see Regulations section 1.6655-2(f)(3)(ii) and the examples in Regulations section 1.6655-2(f)(3)(vii).

Part I. Adjusted Seasonal Installment Method

The corporation can use the adjusted seasonal installment method only if the corporation's base period percentage for any 6 consecutive months of the tax year is 70% or more. The base period percentage for any period of 6 consecutive months is the average of the 3 percentages figured by dividing the taxable income for the corresponding 6-consecutive-month period in each of the 3 preceding tax years by the total taxable income for each of the 3 preceding tax years, respectively. Figure the base period percentage using the 6-month period in which the corporation normally receives the largest part of its taxable income.

Example. An amusement park with a 2014 calendar tax year receives the largest part of its taxable income during the 6-month period from May through October. To compute its base period percentage for this 6-month period in 2014, the amusement park figures its taxable income for each May–October period in 2011, 2012, and 2013. It then divides the taxable income for each May–October period by the total taxable income for that particular tax year. The resulting percentages are: 69% (.69) for May–October 2011, 74% (.74) for May–October 2012, and 67% (.67) for May–October 2013. Because the average of 69%, 74%, and 67% is 70%, the base period percentage for May–October 2014 is 70%. Therefore, the amusement park qualifies for the adjusted seasonal installment method.

Line 2. If the corporation has certain extraordinary items, special rules apply. Do not include on line 2 the de minimis items that the corporation chooses to include on line 9b. See *Extraordinary items* earlier.

Line 9b. If the corporation has extraordinary items of $1,000,000 or more, a net operating loss deduction, or a section 481(a) adjustment, special rules apply. Include these amounts on line 9b for the appropriate period. Also include on line 9b the de minimis items that the corporation chooses to exclude from line 2. See *Extraordinary items* earlier.

Line 15. Compute the alternative minimum tax (AMT) on Form 4626, Alternative Minimum Tax-Corporations, if applicable. Figure alternative minimum taxable income (AMTI) based on the corporation's income and deductions for the months shown in the column headings directly above line 1. For each column, divide the AMTI by the amount shown on line 8 before subtracting the AMT exemption amount under section 55(d). Enter on line 15, column (d), the AMT determined for column (d). For columns (a) through (c) only, first multiply the AMT determined by the amounts shown in columns (a) through (c) of line 13 and then enter on line 15 the result for each column.

Line 16. Enter on line 16 any other taxes the corporation owed for the months shown in each column heading directly above line 1. Include the same taxes used to figure Part I, line 1 of Form 2220, but do not include the personal holding company tax and interest due under the look-back method of section 460(b)(2) for completed long-term contracts or section 167(g)(2) for property depreciated under the income forecast method.

Line 18. Enter the credits the corporation is entitled to for the months shown in each column heading above line 1. Enter the same type of credits that are allowed on Form 2220, page 1, lines 1 and 2c.

Part II. Annualized Income Installment Method

Line 20. Annualization periods. Enter on line 20, columns (a) through (d), respectively, the annualization periods for the option shown in the tables below. For example, if the corporation elected Option 1, enter on line 20 the annualization periods 2, 4, 7, and 10, in columns (a) through (d), respectively.

 Use Option 1 or Option 2 only if the corporation elected to do so by filing Form 8842, Election To Use Different Annualization Periods for Corporate Estimated Tax, by the due date of the first required installment payment. Once made, the election is irrevocable for the particular tax year.

Option 2 is not available to tax-exempt organizations and private foundations. For these entities, see the options shown in the table in the instructions for line 22.

Corporations

	1st Installment	2nd Installment	3rd Installment	4th Installment
Standard option	3	3	6	9
Option 1 . . .	2	4	7	10
Option 2 . . .	3	5	8	11

Tax-Exempt Organizations and Private Foundations

	1st Installment	2nd Installment	3rd Installment	4th Installment
Standard option	2	3	6	9
Option 1 . . .	2	4	7	10

Line 21. Enter on line 21 the taxable income (line 30, Form 1120; or the applicable line for other income tax returns) that the corporation received for the months entered for each annualization period in columns (a) through (d) on line 20.

If the corporation has extraordinary items, special rules apply. Do not include on line 21 the de minimis extraordinary items that the corporation chooses to include on line 23b. See *Extraordinary items* earlier.

Line 22. Annualization amounts. Enter on line 22, columns (a) through (d), respectively, the annualization amounts shown in the tables below for the option used for line 20 above. For example, if the corporation elected Option 1, enter on line 22 the annualization amounts 6, 3, 1.71429, and 1.2, in columns (a) through (d), respectively.

Corporations

	1st Installment	2nd Installment	3rd Installment	4th Installment
Standard option	4	4	2	1.33333
Option 1 . . .	6	3	1.71429	1.2
Option 2 . . .	4	2.4	1.5	1.09091

Tax-Exempt Organizations and Private Foundations

	1st Installment	2nd Installment	3rd Installment	4th Installment
Standard option	6	4	2	1.33333
Option 1 . . .	6	3	1.71429	1.2

Line 23b. If the corporation has certain extraordinary items of $1,000,000 or more, a net operating loss deduction, or a section 481(a) adjustment, special rules apply. Include these amounts on line 23b. Also include on line 23b the de minimis extraordinary items that the corporation chooses to exclude from line 21. See *Extraordinary items* earlier.

Line 25. Compute the alternative minimum tax (AMT) on Form 4626, if applicable. Figure alternative minimum taxable income (AMTI) based on the corporation's income and deductions for the annualization period entered in each column on line 20. Multiply AMTI by the annualization amounts (line 22) used to figure annualized taxable income before subtracting the AMT exemption amount under section 55(d). Enter on line 25 the result for each column.

Line 26. Enter any other taxes the corporation owed for the months shown in each column on line 20. Include the same taxes used to figure Part I, line 1 of Form 2220, but do not include the personal holding company tax and interest due under the look-back method of section 460(b)(2) for completed long-term contracts or section 167(g)(2) for property depreciated under the income forecast method.

Line 28. Enter the credits the corporation is entitled to for the months shown in each column on line 20. Do not annualize any credit. However, when figuring the credits, annualize any item of income or deduction used to figure the credit.

Part III. Required Installments

Line 33. Before completing line 33 in columns (b) through (d), complete lines 34 through 38 in each of the preceding columns. For example, complete lines 34 through 38 in column (a) before completing line 33 in column (b).

Line 35. Enter in each column of line 35, 25% of the amount from page 1, Part I, line 5. Large corporations, see the instructions for line 10 for the amounts to enter.

Line 38. For each installment, enter the smaller of line 34 or line 37 on line 38. Also enter the result on page 1, Part III, line 10.

Paperwork Reduction Act Notice. We ask for the information on this form to carry out the Internal Revenue laws of the United States. You are required to give us the information. We need it to ensure that you are complying with these laws and to allow us to figure and collect the right amount of tax.

You are not required to provide the information requested on a form that is subject to the Paperwork Reduction Act unless the form displays a valid OMB control number. Books or records relating to a form or its instructions must be retained as long as their contents can become material in the administration of any Internal Revenue law. Generally, tax returns and return information are confidential, as required by section 6103.

The time needed to complete and file this form will vary depending on individual circumstances. The estimated average time is:

Form	Recordkeeping	Learning about the law or the form	Preparing and sending the form to the IRS
2220	28 hr., 27 min.	1 hr., 53 min.	2 hr., 25 min.
2220, Schedule A, Part I	25 hr., 49 min.	— —	25 min.
2220, Schedule A, Part II	12 hr., 26 min.	— —	12 min.
2220, Schedule A, Part III	6 hr., 13 min.	— —	6 min.

If you have comments concerning the accuracy of these time estimates or suggestions for making this form simpler, we would be happy to hear from you. See the instructions for the tax return with which this form is filed.

Form **2441**	**Child and Dependent Care Expenses**		OMB No. 1545-0074
Department of the Treasury Internal Revenue Service (99)	▶ Attach to Form 1040, Form 1040A, or Form 1040NR. ▶ Information about Form 2441 and its separate instructions is at *www.irs.gov/form2441.*	1040 1040A 1040NR ◀ 2441	**2014** Attachment Sequence No. **21**

Name(s) shown on return   **Your social security number**

Part I — Persons or Organizations Who Provided the Care—You **must** complete this part.
(If you have more than two care providers, see the instructions.)

1	(a) Care provider's name	(b) Address (number, street, apt. no., city, state, and ZIP code)	(c) Identifying number (SSN or EIN)	(d) Amount paid (see instructions)

Did you receive **dependent care benefits?**
No ——▶ Complete only Part II below.
Yes ——▶ Complete Part III on the back next.

Caution. If the care was provided in your home, you may owe employment taxes. If you do, you cannot file Form 1040A. For details, see the instructions for Form 1040, line 60a, or Form 1040NR, line 59a.

Part II — Credit for Child and Dependent Care Expenses

2 Information about your **qualifying person(s)**. If you have more than two qualifying persons, see the instructions.

(a) Qualifying person's name		(b) Qualifying person's social security number	(c) **Qualified expenses** you incurred and paid in 2014 for the person listed in column (a)
First	Last		

3	Add the amounts in column (c) of line 2. **Do not** enter more than $3,000 for one qualifying person or $6,000 for two or more persons. If you completed Part III, enter the amount from line 31	**3**	
4	Enter your **earned income.** See instructions	**4**	
5	If married filing jointly, enter your spouse's earned income (if you or your spouse was a student or was disabled, see the instructions); **all others**, enter the amount from line 4	**5**	
6	Enter the **smallest** of line 3, 4, or 5	**6**	
7	Enter the amount from Form 1040, line 38; Form 1040A, line 22; or Form 1040NR, line 37 . . . . . **7**		
8	Enter on line 8 the decimal amount shown below that applies to the amount on line 7		

If line 7 is:

Over	But not over	Decimal amount is		Over	But not over	Decimal amount is
$0—15,000		.35		$29,000—31,000		.27
15,000—17,000		.34		31,000—33,000		.26
17,000—19,000		.33		33,000—35,000		.25
19,000—21,000		.32		35,000—37,000		.24
21,000—23,000		.31		37,000—39,000		.23
23,000—25,000		.30		39,000—41,000		.22
25,000—27,000		.29		41,000—43,000		.21
27,000—29,000		.28		43,000—No limit		.20

8 | X .

9	Multiply line 6 by the decimal amount on line 8. If you paid 2013 expenses in 2014, see the instructions	**9**	
10	Tax liability limit. Enter the amount from the Credit Limit Worksheet in the instructions. **10**		
11	**Credit for child and dependent care expenses.** Enter the **smaller** of line 9 or line 10 here and on Form 1040, line 49; Form 1040A, line 31; or Form 1040NR, line 47	**11**	

For Paperwork Reduction Act Notice, see your tax return instructions.   Cat. No. 11862M   Form **2441** (2014)

Part III	**Dependent Care Benefits**

12 Enter the total amount of **dependent care benefits** you received in 2014. Amounts you received as an employee should be shown in box 10 of your Form(s) W-2. **Do not** include amounts reported as wages in box 1 of Form(s) W-2. If you were self-employed or a partner, include amounts you received under a dependent care assistance program from your sole proprietorship or partnership **12**

13 Enter the amount, if any, you carried over from 2013 and used in 2014 during the grace period. See instructions **13**

14 Enter the amount, if any, you forfeited or carried forward to 2015. See instructions . . . **14** ( )

15 Combine lines 12 through 14. See instructions **15**

16 Enter the total amount of **qualified expenses** incurred in 2014 for the care of the **qualifying person(s)** . . . **16**

17 Enter the **smaller** of line 15 or 16 . . . . **17**

18 Enter your **earned income.** See instructions **18**

19 Enter the amount shown below that applies to you.
- If married filing jointly, enter your spouse's earned income (if you or your spouse was a student or was disabled, see the instructions for line 5). } . . . **19**
- If married filing separately, see instructions. }
- All others, enter the amount from line 18. }

20 Enter the **smallest** of line 17, 18, or 19 . . . . . **20**

21 Enter $5,000 ($2,500 if married filing separately **and** you were required to enter your spouse's earned income on line 19). **21**

22 Is any amount on line 12 from your sole proprietorship or partnership? (Form 1040A filers go to line 25.)

☐ **No.** Enter -0-.

☐ **Yes.** Enter the amount here **22**

23 Subtract line 22 from line 15 . . . . **23**

24 **Deductible benefits.** Enter the **smallest** of line 20, 21, or 22. Also, include this amount on the appropriate line(s) of your return. See instructions **24**

25 **Excluded benefits. Form 1040 and 1040NR filers:** If you checked "No" on line 22, enter the smaller of line 20 or 21. Otherwise, subtract line 24 from the smaller of line 20 or line 21. If zero or less, enter -0-. **Form 1040A filers:** Enter the **smaller** of line 20 or line 21 . . **25**

26 **Taxable benefits. Form 1040 and 1040NR filers:** Subtract line 25 from line 23. If zero or less, enter -0-. Also, include this amount on Form 1040, line 7, or Form 1040NR, line 8. On the dotted line next to Form 1040, line 7, or Form 1040NR, line 8, enter "DCB." **Form 1040A filers:** Subtract line 25 from line 15. Also, include this amount on Form 1040A, line 7. In the space to the left of line 7, enter "DCB". **26**

To claim the child and dependent care
credit, complete lines 27 through 31 below.

27 Enter $3,000 ($6,000 if two or more qualifying persons) **27**

28 **Form 1040 and 1040NR filers:** Add lines 24 and 25. **Form 1040A filers:** Enter the amount from line 25 . . . . **28**

29 Subtract line 28 from line 27. If zero or less, **stop.** You cannot take the credit. **Exception.** If you paid 2013 expenses in 2014, see the instructions for line 9 . . . . . **29**

30 Complete line 2 on the front of this form. **Do not** include in column (c) any benefits shown on line 28 above. Then, add the amounts in column (c) and enter the total here. . . . **30**

31 Enter the **smaller** of line 29 or 30. Also, enter this amount on line 3 on the front of this form and complete lines 4 through 11 . . . . **31**

Instructions for Form 2441
Child and Dependent Care Expenses

Future Developments

For the latest information about developments related to Form 2441 and its instructions, such as legislation enacted after they were published, go to *www.irs.gov/form2441*.

Purpose of Form

If you paid someone to care for your child or other qualifying person so you (and your spouse if filing jointly) could work or look for work in 2014, you may be able to take the credit for child and dependent care expenses. You (and your spouse if filing jointly) must have earned income to take the credit. But see *If You or Your Spouse Was a Student or Disabled*, later. If you can take the credit, use Form 2441 to figure the amount of your credit.

If you (or your spouse if filing jointly) received any dependent care benefits for 2014, you must use Form 2441 to figure the amount, if any, of the benefits you can exclude from your income on Form 1040, line 7; Form 1040A, line 7; or Form 1040NR, line 8. You must complete Part III of Form 2441 before you can figure the credit, if any, in Part II.

Additional information. See Pub. 503, Child and Dependent Care Expenses, for more details.

Definitions

Dependent Care Benefits

Dependent care benefits include:
- Amounts your employer paid directly to either you or your care provider for the care of your qualifying person(s) while you worked,
- The fair market value of care in a daycare facility provided or sponsored by your employer, and
- Pre-tax contributions you made under a dependent care flexible spending arrangement (FSA).

Your salary may have been reduced to pay for these benefits. If you received dependent care benefits as an employee, they should be shown in box 10 of your 2014 Form(s) W-2. Benefits you received as a partner should be shown in box 13 of your Schedule K-1 (Form 1065) with code O.

Qualifying Person(s)

A qualifying person is:

1. A qualifying child under age 13 whom you can claim as a dependent. If the child turned 13 during the year, the child is a qualifying person for the part of the year he or she was under age 13.

2. Your disabled spouse who was not physically or mentally able to care for himself or herself.

3. Any disabled person who was not physically or mentally able to care for himself or herself whom you can claim as a dependent or could claim as a dependent except:

    a. The disabled person had gross income of $3,950 or more,

    b. The disabled person filed a joint return, or

    c. You (or your spouse if filing jointly) could be claimed as a dependent on another taxpayer's 2014 return.

If you are divorced or separated, see *Special rule for children of divorced or separated parents*, below.

To find out who is a qualifying child and who is a dependent, see Pub. 501, Exemptions, Standard Deduction, and Filing Information.

 To be a qualifying person, the person must have lived with you for more than half of 2014.

Special rule for children of divorced or separated parents. Even if you cannot claim your child as a dependent, he or she is treated as your qualifying person if:
- The child was under age 13 or was not physically or mentally able to care for himself or herself, and
- You were the child's custodial parent. The custodial parent is the parent with whom the child lived for the greater number of nights in 2014. If the child was with each parent for an equal number of nights, the custodial parent is the parent with the higher adjusted gross income. For details and an exception for a parent who works at night, see Pub. 501.

The noncustodial parent cannot treat the child as a qualifying person even if that parent is entitled to claim the child as a dependent under the special rules for a child of divorced or separated parents.

Qualified Expenses

These include amounts paid for household services and care of the qualifying person while you worked or looked for work. Child support payments are not qualified expenses. Also, expenses reimbursed by a state social service agency are not qualified expenses unless you included the reimbursement in your income.

Generally, if you worked or actively looked for work during only part of the period in which you incurred the expenses, you must figure your expenses for each day. However, there are special rules for temporary absences or part-time work. See Pub. 503 for more details.

Household Services

These are services needed to care for the qualifying person as well as to run the home. They include, for example, the services of a cook, maid, babysitter, housekeeper, or cleaning person if the services were partly for the care of the qualifying person. Do not include services of a chauffeur or gardener.

You can also include your share of the employment taxes paid on wages for qualifying child and dependent care services.

Care of the Qualifying Person

Care includes the cost of services for the qualifying person's well-being and protection. It does not include the cost of food, lodging, education, clothing, or entertainment.

You can include the cost of care provided outside your home for your dependent under age 13 or any other qualifying person who regularly spends at least 8 hours a day in your home. If the care was provided by a dependent care center, the center must meet all applicable state and local regulations. A dependent care center is a place that provides care for more than six persons (other than persons who live there) and receives a fee, payment, or grant for providing services for any of those persons, even if the center is not run for profit.

You can include amounts paid for items other than the care of your child (such as food and schooling) only if the items are incidental to the care of the child and cannot be separated from the total cost. But do not include the cost of schooling for a child in kindergarten or above. You can include the cost of a day camp, even if it specializes in a particular activity, such as computers or soccer. But do not include any expenses for sending your child to an overnight camp, summer school, or a tutoring program.

Medical Expenses

Some disabled spouse and dependent care expenses can qualify as medical expenses if you itemize deductions on Schedule A (Form 1040). However, you cannot claim the same expense as both a dependent care expense and a medical expense. See Pub. 502, Medical and Dental Expenses, and Pub. 503 for details.

Who Can Take the Credit or Exclude Dependent Care Benefits?

You can take the credit or the exclusion if all five of the following apply.

1. Your filing status may be single, head of household, qualifying widow(er) with dependent child, or married filing jointly. If your filing status is married filing separately, see *Married Persons Filing Separately*, later.

2. The care was provided so you (and your spouse if filing jointly) could work or look for work. However, if you did not find a job and have no earned income for the year, you cannot take the credit or the exclusion. But if you or your spouse was a full-time student or disabled, see the instructions for lines 4 and 5, later.

3. The care must be for one or more qualifying persons.

4. The person who provided the care was not your spouse, the parent of your qualifying child, or a person whom you can claim as a dependent. If your child

provided the care, he or she must have been age 19 or older by the end of 2014, and he or she cannot be your dependent.

5. You report the required information about the care provider on line 1 and, if taking the credit, the information about the qualifying person on line 2.

Married Persons Filing Separately

Generally, married persons must file a joint return to claim the credit. If your filing status is married filing separately and all of the following apply, you are considered unmarried for purposes of claiming the credit on Form 2441.
• You lived apart from your spouse during the last 6 months of 2014.
• Your home was the qualifying person's main home for more than half of 2014.
• You paid more than half of the cost of keeping up that home for 2014.

If you meet all the requirements to be treated as unmarried and meet items 2 through 5 listed earlier, you can take the credit or the exclusion. If you do not meet all the requirements to be treated as unmarried, you cannot take the credit. However, you can take the exclusion if you meet items 2 through 5.

Example. Amy separated from her spouse in March. She is not separated under a decree of divorce or separate maintenance agreement and uses the married filing separate filing status. Amy maintains a home for herself and Sam, her disabled brother. Sam is permanently and totally disabled and unable to care for himself.

Because Sam earns $5,600 in interest income Amy cannot claim him as a dependent (his gross income is greater than the exemption amount, $3,950). And, because Amy is not able to claim Sam as a dependent and she is still married as of the end of the year, she cannot use the head of household filing status. Amy's filing status is married filing separately and Sam qualifies as a qualifying person for the child and dependent care credit.

Because of the following facts Amy is able to claim the credit for child and dependent care expenses even though Amy uses the married filing separate filing status:
• Amy did not live with her spouse for the last six months of the year.
• She has maintained a home for herself and Sam (a qualifying individual) since she separated from her spouse in March.
• She maintains her own household and provides more than half of the cost of maintaining that home for herself and Sam.
• Amy pays an adult daycare center to care for Sam to allow her to work.

Line Instructions

Line 1

Complete columns (a) through (d) for each person or organization that provided the care. You can use Form W-10, Dependent Care Provider's Identification and Certification, or any other source listed in its instructions to get the information from the care provider. If you do not give correct or complete information, your credit (and exclusion, if applicable) may be disallowed unless you can show you used due diligence in trying to get the required information.

If you have more than two care providers, attach a statement to your return with the required information. Be sure to put your name and social security number (SSN) on the statement. Also, enter "See Attached" right above the *Caution* under line 1.

If you did not have a qualifying person nor any care providers for 2014, and you are filing Form 2441 only to report taxable income in Part III, enter "none" on line 1, column (a).

Due Diligence

You can show a serious and earnest effort (due diligence) to get the information by keeping in your records a Form W-10 completed by the care provider. Or you may keep one of the other sources of information listed in the instructions for Form W-10. If the provider does not give you the information, complete the entries you can on line 1. For example, enter the provider's name and address. Enter "See Attached Statement" in the columns for which you do not have the information. Then, attach a statement to your return explaining that the provider did not give you the information you requested.

Columns (a) and (b)

Enter the care provider's name and address. If you were covered by your employer's dependent care plan and your employer furnished the care (either at your workplace or by hiring a care provider), enter your employer's name in column (a). Next, enter "See W-2" in column (b). Then, leave columns (c) and (d) blank. But if your employer paid a third party (not hired by your employer) on your behalf to provide the care, you must give information on the third party in columns (a) through (d).

Column (c)

If the care provider is an individual, enter his or her social security number (SSN). Otherwise, enter the provider's employer identification number (EIN). If the provider is a tax-exempt organization, enter "Tax-Exempt" in column (c).

U.S. citizens and resident aliens living abroad. If you are living abroad, your care provider may not have, and may not be required to get, a U.S. taxpayer identification number (for example, an SSN or EIN). If so, enter "LAFCP" (Living Abroad Foreign Care Provider) in the space for the care provider's taxpayer identification number.

Column (d)

Enter the total amount you actually paid in 2014 to the care provider. Also, include amounts your employer paid to a third party on your behalf. It does not matter when the expenses were incurred. Do not reduce this amount by any reimbursement you received.

Line 2

Complete columns (a) through (c) for each qualifying person. If you have more than two qualifying persons, attach a statement to your return with the required information. Be sure to put your name and social security number (SSN) on the statement. Also, enter "See Attached" on the dotted line next to line 3.

Column (b)

You must enter the qualifying person's SSN. Be sure the name and SSN entered agree with the person's social security card. Otherwise, at the time we process your return, we may reduce or disallow your credit. If the child was born and died in 2014 and did not have an SSN, enter "Died" in column (b) and attach a copy of the child's birth certificate, death certificate, or hospital medical records.

To find out how to get an SSN, see *Social Security Number (SSN)* in the Form 1040 or Form 1040A instructions, or *Identifying Number* in the Form 1040NR instructions. If the name or SSN on the person's social security card is not correct, call the Social Security Administration at 1-800-772-1213.

Column (c)

Enter the qualified expenses you incurred and paid in 2014 for the person listed in column (a). Prepaid expenses are treated as paid in the year the care is provided. Do not include in column (c) qualified expenses:
- You incurred in 2014 but did not pay until 2015. You may be able to use these expenses to increase your 2015 credit.
- You incurred in 2013 but did not pay until 2014. Instead, see the instructions for line 9.
- You prepaid in 2014 for care to be provided in 2015. These expenses can only be used to figure your 2015 credit.

 If you paid qualified expenses for the care of two or more qualifying persons, the applicable dollar limit is $6,000. This limit does not need to be divided equally. For example, if you paid and incurred $2,500 of qualified expenses for the care of one qualifying person and $3,500 for the care of another qualifying person, you can use the total, $6,000, to figure the credit.

To qualify for the credit, you must have one or more qualifying persons. You should show the expenses for each child in column (c) of line 2. However, it is possible a qualifying child could have no expenses and a second child could have expenses exceeding $3,000. You should list -0- for the one child and the actual amount for the second child. The $6,000 limit would still be used to compute your credit unless you have already excluded or deducted, in Part III, certain dependent care benefits paid to you (or on your behalf) by your employer.

Lines 4 and 5

If filing jointly, figure your and your spouse's earned income separately. Enter your earned income on line 4 and your spouse's earned income on line 5.

Earned income for figuring the credit includes the following amounts.

1. The amount shown on Form 1040, line 7; Form 1040A, line 7; or Form 1040NR, line 8; minus any amount:

a. Included for a scholarship or fellowship grant that was not reported to you on a Form W-2,

b. Also reported on Schedule SE (Form 1040) because you were a member of the clergy or you received $108.28 or more of church employee income,

c. Received for work performed while an inmate in a penal institution, or

d. Received as a pension or annuity from a nonqualified deferred compensation plan or a nongovernmental section 457(b) plan. This amount may be reported in box 11 of Form W-2. If you received such an amount but box 11 is blank, contact your employer for the amount received as a pension or annuity.

2. The amount shown on Schedule SE, line 3, minus any deduction you claim on Form 1040 or Form 1040NR, line 27.

If you use either optional method to figure self-employment tax, subtract any deduction you claim on Form 1040 or Form 1040NR, line 27, from the total of the amounts shown on Schedule SE, Section B, lines 3 and 4b.

If you received church employee income of $108.28 or more, subtract any deduction you claim on Form 1040 or Form 1040NR, line 27, from the total of the amounts shown on Schedule SE, Section B, lines 3, 4b, and 5a.

3. If you are filing Schedule C (Form 1040) or C-EZ (Form 1040) as a statutory employee, the amount shown on line 1 of the schedule.

4. Nontaxable combat pay, if you elect to include it in earned income. However, including this income will only give you a larger credit if your (or your spouse's) other earned income is less than the amount entered on line 3. To make the election, include all of your nontaxable combat pay in the amount you enter on line 4 (line 5 for your spouse if filing jointly).

If you are filing jointly and both you and your spouse received nontaxable combat pay, you can each make your own election. (In other words, if one of you makes the election, the other one can also make it but does not have to.) The amount of your nontaxable combat pay should be shown in box 12 of your Form(s) W-2 with code Q.

 You can choose to include your nontaxable combat pay in earned income when figuring your credit, even if you choose not to include it in earned income for the earned income credit (EIC) or the exclusion or deduction for child and dependent care benefits.

 You must reduce your earned income by any loss from self-employment.

Child support payments received by you are not included in your gross income and are not considered as earned income for figuring this credit.

If You or Your Spouse Was a Student or Disabled

Your spouse's earned income. Your spouse was a full-time student if he or she was enrolled as a full-time student at a school for some part of each of 5 calendar months during 2014. The months need not be consecutive. A school does not include an on-the-job training course, correspondence school, or a school offering courses only through the Internet. Your spouse was disabled if he or she was not physically or mentally capable of self-care. Figure your spouse's earned income on a monthly basis.

For each month or part of a month your spouse was a student or was disabled, he or she is considered to have worked and earned income. His or her earned income for each month is considered to be at least $250 ($500 if more than one qualifying person was cared for in 2014). Enter that amount on line 5. If your spouse also worked during that month, use the higher of $250 (or $500) or his or her actual earned income for that month.

For any month that your spouse was not a student or disabled, use your spouse's actual earned income if he or she worked during the month.

Your earned income. These rules for a spouse who was a student or disabled also apply to you if you were a student or disabled. For each month or part of a month you were a student or disabled, your earned income is considered to be at least $250 ($500 if more than one qualifying person was cared for in 2014). Enter that amount on line 4. If you also worked during that month, enter the higher of $250 (or $500) or your actual earned income for that month.

Both spouses were students or disabled. If, in the same month, both you and your spouse were either students or disabled, only one of you can be treated as having earned income in that month under these rules.

Special Situations

• If you are filing jointly, disregard community property laws.

• If your spouse died in 2014, see Pub. 503.

Line 9

Credit for Prior Year's Expenses

If you had qualified expenses for 2013 that you did not pay until 2014, you may be able to increase the amount of credit you can take in 2014. To figure the credit, see Worksheet A in Pub. 503. If you can take a credit for your 2013 expenses, enter the amount of the additional credit and "CPYE" (Credit for Prior Year Expenses) on the dotted line next to line 9. Add the credit to the amount on line 9 and replace the amount on line 9 with that total. Also, attach a statement to your tax return showing the name and taxpayer identification number of the person for whom you paid the prior year's expenses and how you figured the credit.

Line 10

Credit Limit Worksheet

Complete this worksheet to figure the amount to enter on line 10.

1. Enter the amount from Form 1040, line 47; Form 1040A, line 28; or Form 1040NR, line 45 . . . . **1.** _____
2. Enter the amount from Form 1040, line 48; or Form 1040NR, line 46; Form 1040A filers enter -0- . . . . . **2.** _____
3. Subtract line 2 from line 1. Also enter this amount on Form 2441, line 10. But if zero or less, **stop**; you cannot take the credit . . . . **3.** _____

Line 13

If you had an employer-provided dependent care plan, your employer may have permitted you to carry forward any unused amount from 2013 to use during a grace period in 2014. Enter on line 13 the amount you carried forward and used in 2014 during the grace period.

Line 14

If you had an employer-provided dependent care plan, enter on line 14 the total of the following amounts included on line 12.

● Any amount you forfeited. You forfeited an amount if you did not receive it because you did not incur the expense. Do not include amounts you expect to receive at a future date.

● Any amount you did not receive but are permitted by your employer to carry forward and use in the following year during a grace period.

Example. Under your employer's dependent care plan, you chose to have your employer set aside $5,000 to cover your 2013 dependent care expenses. The $5,000 is shown on your Form W-2, in box 10. In 2014, you incurred and were reimbursed for $4,950 of qualified expenses. You would enter $5,000 on line 12 and $50, the amount forfeited, on line 14. You would also enter $50 on line 14 if, instead of forfeiting the amount, your employer permitted you to carry the $50 forward to use during the grace period in 2015.

Line 15

Add the amounts on lines 12 and 13 and subtract from that total the amount on line 14. Enter the result on line 15.

Line 16

Enter the total of all qualified expenses incurred in 2014 for the care of your qualifying person(s). It does not matter when the expenses were paid.

Example. You received $2,000 in cash under your employer's dependent care plan for 2014. The $2,000 is shown on your Form W-2, in box 10. Only $900 of qualified expenses were incurred in 2014 for the care of your 5-year-old dependent child. You would enter $2,000 on line 12 and $900 on line 16.

Line 18

If filing jointly, figure your and your spouse's earned income separately. Enter your earned income on line 18 and your spouse's earned income on line 19. If your filing status is married filing separately or you or your spouse was a student or disabled, see the instructions for line 19.

Earned income for figuring the amount of dependent care benefits you are able to exclude or deduct from your income includes the following amounts.

1. The amount shown on Form 1040, line 7; Form 1040A, line 7; or Form 1040NR, line 8; minus any amount:

a. Included for a scholarship or fellowship grant that was not reported to you on a Form W-2,

b. Also reported on Schedule SE (Form 1040) because you were a member of the clergy or you received $108.28 or more of church employee income,

c. Received for work performed while an inmate in a penal institution, and

d. Received as a pension or annuity from a nonqualified deferred compensation plan or a nongovernmental section 457(b) plan. This amount may be reported in box 11 of Form W-2. If you received such an amount but box 11 is blank, contact your employer for the amount received as a pension or annuity.

2. The amount shown on Schedule SE, line 3, minus any deduction you claim on Form 1040 or Form 1040NR, line 27.

If you use either optional method to figure self-employment tax, subtract any deduction you claim on Form 1040 or Form 1040NR, line 27, from the total of the amounts shown on Schedule SE, Section B, lines 3 and 4b.

If you received church employee income of $108.28 or more, subtract any deduction you claim on Form 1040 or Form 1040NR, line 27, from the total of the amounts shown on Schedule SE, Section B, lines 3, 4b, and 5a.

3. If you are filing Schedule C (Form 1040) or C-EZ (Form 1040) as a statutory employee, the amount shown on line 1 of the schedule.

4. Nontaxable combat pay, if you elect to include it in earned income. However, including this income will only give you a larger exclusion or deduction if your (or your spouse's) other earned income is less than the amount entered on line 17. To make the election, include all of your nontaxable combat pay in the amount you enter on line 18 (line 19 for your spouse if filing jointly).

If you are filing jointly and both you and your spouse received nontaxable combat pay, you can each make your own election. (In other words, if one of you makes the election, the other one can also make it but does not have to.) The amount of your nontaxable combat pay should be shown in box 12 of your Form(s) W-2 with code Q.

 You can choose to include your nontaxable combat pay in earned income when figuring your exclusion or deduction, even if you choose not to include it in earned income for the earned income credit (EIC) or the credit for child and dependent care expenses.

 For purposes of line 18, earned income does not include any dependent care benefits shown on line 12.

You must reduce your earned income by any loss from self-employment.

Special Situations

- If you are filing jointly, disregard community property laws.
- If your spouse was a full-time student or disabled in 2014, see the instructions for lines 4 and 5, earlier.

Line 19

If your filing status is married filing separately, see *Married Persons Filing Separately*, earlier. Are you considered unmarried under that rule?

☐ **Yes.** Enter your earned income (from line 18) on line 19. On line 21, enter $5,000.

☐ **No.** Enter your spouse's earned income on line 19. If you or your spouse was a full-time student or disabled in 2014, see the instructions for lines 4 and 5. On line 21, enter $2,500.

Line 24

Include your deductible benefits in the total entered on Schedule C, line 14; Schedule E, line 19 or line 28; or Schedule F, line 15; whichever applies.

Lines 27 through 31

If you are reporting dependent care benefits in Part III of the form, you will need to complete lines 27 through 31 if you are also claiming the credit for child and dependent care expenses in Part II of the form.

Form **3800**	**General Business Credit**	OMB No. 1545-0895

Department of the Treasury
Internal Revenue Service (99)

▶ Information about Form 3800 and its separate instructions is at *www.irs.gov/form3800*.
▶ You must attach all pages of Form 3800, pages 1, 2, and 3, to your tax return.

2014
Attachment Sequence No. **22**

Name(s) shown on return

Identifying number

Part I — Current Year Credit for Credits Not Allowed Against Tentative Minimum Tax (TMT)
(See instructions and complete Part(s) III before Parts I and II)

1	General business credit from line 2 of all Parts III with box A checked	1	
2	Passive activity credits from line 2 of all Parts III with box B checked	2	
3	Enter the applicable passive activity credits allowed for 2014 (see instructions)	3	
4	Carryforward of general business credit to 2014. Enter the amount from line 2 of Part III with box C checked. See instructions for statement to attach	4	
5	Carryback of general business credit from 2015. Enter the amount from line 2 of Part III with box D checked (see instructions)	5	
6	Add lines 1, 3, 4, and 5	6	

Part II — Allowable Credit

7	Regular tax before credits: • Individuals. Enter the sum of the amounts from Form 1040, lines 44 and 46, or the sum of the amounts from Form 1040NR, lines 42 and 44 • Corporations. Enter the amount from Form 1120, Schedule J, Part I, line 2; or the applicable line of your return • Estates and trusts. Enter the sum of the amounts from Form 1041, Schedule G, lines 1a and 1b; or the amount from the applicable line of your return	7	
8	Alternative minimum tax: • Individuals. Enter the amount from Form 6251, line 35 • Corporations. Enter the amount from Form 4626, line 14 • Estates and trusts. Enter the amount from Schedule I (Form 1041), line 56	8	
9	Add lines 7 and 8	9	
10a	Foreign tax credit	10a	
b	Certain allowable credits (see instructions)	10b	
c	Add lines 10a and 10b	10c	
11	**Net income tax.** Subtract line 10c from line 9. If zero, skip lines 12 through 15 and enter -0- on line 16	11	
12	**Net regular tax.** Subtract line 10c from line 7. If zero or less, enter -0-	12	
13	Enter 25% (.25) of the excess, if any, of line 12 over $25,000 (see instructions)	13	
14	Tentative minimum tax: • Individuals. Enter the amount from Form 6251, line 33 • Corporations. Enter the amount from Form 4626, line 12 • Estates and trusts. Enter the amount from Schedule I (Form 1041), line 54	14	
15	Enter the greater of line 13 or line 14	15	
16	Subtract line 15 from line 11. If zero or less, enter -0-	16	
17	Enter the **smaller** of line 6 or line 16	17	
	C corporations: See the line 17 instructions if there has been an ownership change, acquisition, or reorganization.		

For Paperwork Reduction Act Notice, see separate instructions.

Cat. No. 12392F

Form **3800** (2014)

| **Part II** | **Allowable Credit** (Continued) |

Note. If you are not required to report any amounts on lines 22 or 24 below, skip lines 18 through 25 and enter -0- on line 26.

18	Multiply line 14 by 75% (.75) (see instructions)	18	
19	Enter the greater of line 13 or line 18	19	
20	Subtract line 19 from line 11. If zero or less, enter -0-	20	
21	Subtract line 17 from line 20. If zero or less, enter -0-	21	
22	Combine the amounts from line 3 of all Parts III with box A, C, or D checked	22	
23	Passive activity credit from line 3 of all Parts III with box B checked 23		
24	Enter the applicable passive activity credit allowed for 2014 (see instructions)	24	
25	Add lines 22 and 24	25	
26	Empowerment zone and renewal community employment credit allowed. Enter the smaller of line 21 or line 25	26	
27	Subtract line 13 from line 11. If zero or less, enter -0-	27	
28	Add lines 17 and 26	28	
29	Subtract line 28 from line 27. If zero or less, enter -0-	29	
30	Enter the general business credit from line 5 of all Parts III with box A checked	30	
31	Reserved	31	
32	Passive activity credits from line 5 of all Parts III with box B checked 32		
33	Enter the applicable passive activity credits allowed for 2014 (see instructions)	33	
34	Carryforward of business credit to 2014. Enter the amount from line 5 of Part III with box C checked and line 6 of Part III with box G checked. See instructions for statement to attach . .	34	
35	Carryback of business credit from 2015. Enter the amount from line 5 of Part III with box D checked (see instructions)	35	
36	Add lines 30, 33, 34, and 35	36	
37	Enter the **smaller** of line 29 or line 36	37	
38	**Credit allowed for the current year.** Add lines 28 and 37. Report the amount from line 38 (if smaller than the sum of Part I, line 6, and Part II, lines 25 and 36, see instructions) as indicated below or on the applicable line of your return: • Individuals. Form 1040, line 54, or Form 1040NR, line 51 . . . . • Corporations. Form 1120, Schedule J, Part I, line 5c . . . . • Estates and trusts. Form 1041, Schedule G, line 2b	38	

Name(s) shown on return	Identifying number

Part III   General Business Credits or Eligible Small Business Credits (see instructions)

Complete a separate Part III for each box checked below. (see instructions)

A ☐ General Business Credit From a Non-Passive Activity   E ▨ Reserved

B ☐ General Business Credit From a Passive Activity   F ▨ Reserved

C ☐ General Business Credit Carryforwards   G ☐ Eligible Small Business Credit Carryforwards

D ☐ General Business Credit Carrybacks   H ▨ Reserved

I   If you are filing more than one Part III with box A or B checked, complete and attach first an additional Part III combining amounts from all Parts III with box A or B checked. Check here if this is the consolidated Part III . . . . ▶ ☐

(a) Description of credit		(b) If claiming the credit from a pass-through entity, enter the EIN	(c) Enter the appropriate amount
Note. On any line where the credit is from more than one source, a separate Part III is needed for each pass-through entity.			
1a	Investment (Form 3468, Part II only) (attach Form 3468)	1a		
b	Reserved	1b ▨	▨	▨
c	Increasing research activities (Form 6765)	1c		
d	Low-income housing (Form 8586, Part I only)	1d		
e	Disabled access (Form 8826) (see instructions for limitation)	1e		
f	Renewable electricity, refined coal, and Indian coal production (Form 8835)	1f		
g	Indian employment (Form 8845)	1g		
h	Orphan drug (Form 8820)	1h		
i	New markets (Form 8874)	1i		
j	Small employer pension plan startup costs (Form 8881) (see instructions for limitation)	1j		
k	Employer-provided child care facilities and services (Form 8882) (see instructions for limitation)	1k		
l	Biodiesel and renewable diesel fuels (attach Form 8864)	1l		
m	Low sulfur diesel fuel production (Form 8896)	1m		
n	Distilled spirits (Form 8906)	1n		
o	Nonconventional source fuel (Form 8907)	1o		
p	Energy efficient home (Form 8908)	1p		
q	Energy efficient appliance (Form 8909)	1q		
r	Alternative motor vehicle (Form 8910)	1r		
s	Alternative fuel vehicle refueling property (Form 8911)	1s		
t	Reserved	1t ▨	▨	▨
u	Mine rescue team training (Form 8923)	1u		
v	Agricultural chemicals security (Form 8931) (see instructions for limitation) .	1v		
w	Employer differential wage payments (Form 8932)	1w		
x	Carbon dioxide sequestration (Form 8933)	1x		
y	Qualified plug-in electric drive motor vehicle (Form 8936)	1y		
z	Qualified plug-in electric vehicle (carryforward only)	1z		
aa	New hire retention (carryforward only)	1aa		
bb	General credits from an electing large partnership (Schedule K-1 (Form 1065-B))	1bb		
zz	Other	1zz		
2	Add lines 1a through 1zz and enter here and on the applicable line of Part I	2 ▨		
3	Enter the amount from Form 8844 here and on the applicable line of Part II .	3		
4a	Investment (Form 3468, Part III) (attach Form 3468)	4a		
b	Work opportunity (Form 5884)	4b		
c	Biofuel producer (Form 6478)	4c		
d	Low-income housing (Form 8586, Part II)	4d		
e	Renewable electricity, refined coal, and Indian coal production (Form 8835)	4e		
f	Employer social security and Medicare taxes paid on certain employee tips (Form 8846)	4f		
g	Qualified railroad track maintenance (Form 8900)	4g		
h	Small employer health insurance premiums (Form 8941)	4h		
i	Reserved	4i ▨	▨	▨
j	Reserved	4j ▨	▨	▨
z	Other	4z		
5	Add lines 4a through 4z and enter here and on the applicable line of Part II .	5 ▨		
6	Add lines 2, 3, and 5 and enter here and on the applicable line of Part II .	6 ▨		

2014
Instructions for Form 3800
General Business Credit

Department of the Treasury
Internal Revenue Service

Section references are to the Internal Revenue Code unless otherwise noted.

Future Developments

For the latest information about developments related to Form 3800 and its instructions, such as legislation enacted after they were published, go to *www.irs.gov/form3800*.

General Instructions

Partnerships and S corporations must always complete the source credit form. All other filers whose only source for a credit listed on Form 3800, Part III, is from a partnership, S corporation, estate, trust, or cooperative can report the credit directly on Form 3800. The following exceptions apply.

- *You are claiming the investment credit (Form 3468) or the biodiesel and renewable diesel fuels credit (Form 8864) in Part III with box A or B checked.*
- *The taxpayer is an estate or trust and the source credit must be allocated to beneficiaries. For more details, see the Instructions for Form 1041, U.S. Income Tax Return for Estates and Trusts, Schedule K-1, box 13.*
- *The taxpayer is a cooperative and the source credit can or must be allocated to patrons. For more details, see the Instructions for Form 1120-C, U.S. Income Tax Return for Cooperative Associations, Schedule J, line 5c.*

Who Must File

You must file Form 3800 to claim any of the general business credits.

Carryback and Carryforward of Unused Credit

The carryforward may have to be reduced in the event of any recapture event (change in ownership, change in use of property, etc.). If a section 1603 grant is received, the carryforward must be reduced to zero. For further information, see Form 4255, Recapture of Investment Credit.

If you cannot use part or all of your general business credit because of the tax liability limit (Part II, line 38, is less than the sum of Part I, line 6, and Part II, lines 25 and 36), carry the unused credit back one year. To carry back an unused credit, file

an amended return (Form 1040X, Amended U.S. Individual Income Tax Return, Form 1120X, Amended U.S. Corporation Income Tax Return, or other amended return) for the prior tax year or an application for tentative refund (Form 1045, Application for Tentative Refund, or Form 1139, Corporation Application for Tentative Refund). Generally, if you file an application for a tentative refund, it must be filed by the end of the tax year following the tax year in which the credit arose.

Note. No part of the unused credit for any year attributable to any credit can be carried back to any tax year before the first tax year for which that credit was first allowable. See *Credit Ordering Rule*, later, to determine which credits are allowed first.

If you have an unused credit after carrying it back 1 year, carry it forward to each of the 20 tax years after the year of the credit. Any qualified business credits (as defined in section 196(c)) that are unused after the last tax year of the 20-year carryforward period (or at the time an individual taxpayer dies or other taxpayer, such as a corporation or partnership, ceases to exist) may be taken as a deduction in the earlier of:

- The tax year following the last tax year of the 20-year carryforward period, or
- The tax year in which the individual taxpayer dies or other taxpayer ceases to exist.

Carryforward of the energy credit and the renewable electricity credit. The energy credit must be recaptured in full if a grant is paid under Public Law 111-5, section 1603, for investment in energy property that an energy credit was previously claimed or for investment in renewable energy property that an election was made to treat the property as energy property. Recapture is applicable to those amounts previously constituting the qualified basis for an energy credit, including progress expenditures, that are also the basis for the 1603 grant. Recapture is accomplished as follows:

1. Any portion of the energy credit related to that property that was used to offset tax in a prior tax year must be added to tax in the tax year the 1603 grant is received. Recaptured tax is calculated on Form 4255.

2. Any carryforward of the energy credit related to that property is reduced to

zero to recapture the unused portion of the credit.

See Form 4255 for any other recapture event (change in ownership or change in use of property, etc.).

Carryforward of certain Form 6478 credits. The alcohol mixture credit, the alcohol credit, and the small ethanol producer credit expired for fuels sold or used after 2011. The carryforward period for all unused alcohol mixture credits, alcohol credits, and small ethanol producer credits (for all tax years) ends at the end of the 3-tax-year period beginning with the tax year that includes the first day after the date the credit expired.

Example. Your tax year is a calendar year and you have unused alcohol mixture credits from 2007, 2008, and 2009 because of the tax liability limitation. Your 3-tax-year carryforward period begins with your 2012 tax year (includes the day January 1, 2012) and ends with your 2014 tax year. You cannot carry the unused credits to your 2015 tax year. Instead, the unused credits can be taken as a deduction under section 196 in your 2015 tax year.

Change in Filing or Marital Status

Your general business credit is limited to your tax liability. Therefore, if you filed a joint return in a carryback or carryforward year and your marital status or filing status has changed, you may need to figure your separate tax liability in that carryback or carryforward year. This would apply if:

- You filed as single in the credit year, but filed a joint return in the carryback or carryforward year;
- You filed a joint return in the credit year, but filed a joint return with a different spouse in the carryback or carryforward year; or
- You were married and filed a separate return in the credit year, but filed a joint return with the same or a different spouse in the carryback or carryforward year.

Determine your separate tax liability in the carryback or carryforward year as follows.

1. Figure your tax for the carryback or carryforward year as though you were married filing a separate return.

2. Figure your spouse's tax in that year as though he or she was married filing a separate return.

3. Add the amounts in steps (1) and (2).

4. Divide the amount in step (1) by the amount in step (3). The result should be rounded to at least three decimal places.

5. Multiply the decimal in step (4) by the total tax shown on your joint return for the carryback or carryforward year. The result is your separate tax liability and a carryback or carryforward credit is applied against this amount only.

Although your carryback or carryforward of the credit is limited to your separate tax liability, the amount of your refund resulting from the carryback or carryforward is further limited to your share of the joint overpayment. This is found by subtracting your separate tax liability (as determined above) from your contribution toward the payment.

Unless you have an agreement or clear evidence of each spouse's contribution toward the payment of the joint liability, your contribution includes the tax withheld on your wages and your share of the joint estimated tax or tax paid with the return. Your share of these payments is found by using the same formula used in determining your separate tax liability. Substitute the joint estimated tax, or tax paid with the return, for the tax in step (5). If the original return for the carryback year resulted in an overpayment, reduce your contribution by your share of the refund.

Attach a copy of the computation to your amended return or application for tentative refund.

Credit Ordering Rule

General business credits reported on Form 3800 are treated as used on a first-in, first-out basis by offsetting the earliest-earned credits first. Therefore, the order in which the credits are used in any tax year is:
- Carryforwards to that year, the earliest ones first;
- The general business credit earned in that year; and
- The carryback to that year.

If your general business credits exceed your tax liability limit, the credits are used in the following order and based on the order shown under *Order in which credits are used* next.

- Credits reported on line 2 of all Parts III with boxes A, B, C, and D checked.
- Credits reported on Part II, line 25.
- Non-ESBC credits reported on line 5 of all Parts III with boxes A, B, C, and D checked.
- ESBC credits reported on line 6 of all Parts III with box G checked.

Order in which credits are used. When relevant, the components of the general business credit reported on Form 3800

arising in a single tax year are used in the following order.

- Investment credit (in the following order—rehabilitation credit, energy credit, qualifying advanced coal project credit, qualifying gasification project credit, and qualifying advanced energy project credit) (Form 3468).
- Qualifying therapeutic discovery project credit (carryforward only).
- Work opportunity credit (Form 5884).
- Biofuel producer credit (Form 6478).
- Credit for increasing research activities (Form 6765).
- Low-income housing credit (Form 8586, Part I only).
- Disabled access credit (Form 8826).
- Renewable electricity, refined coal, and Indian coal production credit (Form 8835).
- Empowerment zone employment credit (Form 8844).
- Renewal community employment credit (carryforward only).
- Indian employment credit (Form 8845).
- Employer social security and Medicare taxes paid on certain employee tips (Form 8846).
- Orphan drug credit (Form 8820).
- New markets credit (Form 8874).
- Credit for small employer pension plan startup costs (Form 8881).
- Credit for employer-provided child care facilities and services (Form 8882).
- Qualified railroad track maintenance credit (Form 8900).
- Biodiesel and renewable diesel fuels credit (Form 8864).
- Low sulfur diesel fuel production credit (Form 8896).
- Distilled spirits credit (Form 8906).
- Nonconventional source fuel credit (Form 8907).
- Energy efficient home credit (Form 8908).
- Energy efficient appliance credit (Form 8909).
- Alternative motor vehicle credit (Form 8910).
- Alternative fuel vehicle refueling property credit (Form 8911).
- Mine rescue team training credit (Form 8923).
- Agricultural chemicals security credit (carryforward only).
- Credit for employer differential wage payments (Form 8932).
- Carbon dioxide sequestration credit (Form 8933).
- Qualified plug-in electric drive motor vehicle credit (Form 8936).
- Qualified plug-in electric vehicle credit (carryforward only).
- Credit for small employer health insurance premiums (Form 8941).
- New hire retention credit (carryforward only).

- General credits from an electing large partnership (Schedule K-1 (Form 1065-B)).

 Although these credits are aggregated on Form 3800, keep a separate record of each credit, including whether the credit was an eligible small business credit, to ensure proper accounting of the credits.

Specific Instructions

Complete and attach the appropriate credit forms used to figure your current year credit. See exceptions under *General Instructions*, earlier.

Assembling Form 3800. To ensure Form 3800 is correctly processed, assemble Form 3800 in the following order.

1. Page 1.
2. Page 2.
3. Part III with box I checked.
4. All Parts III with box A checked.
5. All Parts III with box B checked.
6. Part III with box C checked.
7. Part III with box D checked.
8. Part III with box G checked.

Part I. Current Year Credit for Credits Not Allowed Against Tentative Minimum Tax (TMT)

 Complete all Parts III before completing Part I and Part II. See Part III. General Business Credits or Eligible Small Business Credits for more information.

Line 3

Enter the applicable passive activity credit amount allowed from Form 8582-CR, Passive Activity Credit Limitations, or Form 8810, Corporate Passive Activity Loss and Credit Limitations. The passive activity credit amount allowed on Part I, line 3, only applies to the general business credits not allowed against TMT from Part I, line 2, plus any prior year unallowed passive activity credit from general business credits not allowed against TMT.

Passive activity. Generally, a passive activity is a trade or business in which you did not materially participate. Generally, rental activities are passive activities, whether or not you materially participated. See Form 8582-CR or Form 8810 for details.

Line 4

Enter the amount of all carryforwards to 2014 of unused credits that are reported from line 2 of Part III with box C checked.

Required statement. For each credit, attach a statement with the following information.

- Show the tax year the credit originated, the amount of the credit as reported on the original return, and the amount allowed for that year. Also state whether the total carryforward amount was changed from the originally reported amount and identify the type of credit(s) involved. If the revised carryforward amount relates to unused additional research credits, attach an additional statement detailing the changes to the originally reported Form 6765 information for all originating credit years applicable.
- For each carryback year, show the year and the amount of the credit allowed after you applied the carryback.
- For each carryforward year, show the year and the amount of the credit carryforward allowed for that year.

Note. Individuals claiming the research credit from a sole proprietorship or pass-through entity do not include any carryforward of that credit on Part I, line 4, before computing the limitation on Part III, line 1c. Include the carryforward when figuring the research credit limitation on line 1c of any Parts III with the applicable box A or B checked. Then include the allowable carryforward amount on Part I, line 4, and attach the statement required above.

Line 5

Use Part I, line 5, only when you amend your 2014 return to carry back unused credits from 2015. Enter the amount that is reported from line 2 of Part III with box D checked.

Note. Individuals claiming the research credit from a sole proprietorship or pass-through entity do not include any carryback of that credit on Part I, line 5, before computing the limitation on Part III, line 1c. Include the carryback when figuring the research credit limitation on line 1c of any Parts III with the applicable box A or B checked. Then include the allowable carryback amount on Part I, line 5. **See the instructions for Part I, line 4, for the required statement that must be attached to your tax return.**

Part II. Allowable Credit

Line 10b

Enter the total allowable credit, if any, from your tax return as follows.

Individuals. The amount from Form 1040, lines 49 through 54 (Form 1040-NR, lines 47 through 51). Do not include any general business credit claimed on Form 3800, any prior year minimum tax, or any credit claimed on Form 8912, Credit to Holders of Tax Credit Bonds.

Estates and trusts. Enter the total of any write-in credits from Form 1041, Schedule G, line 2e.

Corporations. Enter the amount from Form 1120, Schedule J, Part I, line 5b (or the applicable line of your return).

Line 13

See section 38(c)(6) for special rules that apply to married couples filing separate returns, controlled corporate groups, regulated investment companies, real estate investment trusts, estates, and trusts.

Line 17

C Corporations. If the corporation has undergone a post-1986 ownership change (as defined in section 382(g)), section 383 may limit the amount of tax that may be offset by pre-change general business credits. Also, if a corporation acquires control of another corporation (or acquires its assets in a reorganization), section 384 may limit the amount of tax attributable to recognized built-in gains that may be offset by pre-acquisition general business credits. If either of these limitations apply, attach a computation of the allowable general business credit, enter the amount on Part II, line 17, and write "Sec. 383" or "Sec. 384" in the margin next to your entry on Part II, line 17.

Line 18

Complete Part II, lines 18 through 26, if any of the following apply.

- An amount is entered for the empowerment zone employment credit on line 3 of Part(s) III with box A, B, C, or D checked;
- An amount is entered for the renewal community employment credit on line 3 of Part III with box C checked; or
- If you have prior year unallowed passive activity credit carryover for the empowerment zone or renewal community employment credit.

If any of the above apply, multiply Part II, line 14, by 75% (.75).

All others, skip Part II, lines 18 through 25, and enter zero on Part II, line 26.

Line 24

Enter the applicable passive activity credit amount for the empowerment zone and renewal community employment credit allowed from Form 8582-CR or Form 8810. The passive activity credit amount allowed on Part II, line 24, only applies to the empowerment zone and renewal community employment credit reported on Part III, line 3, plus any prior year unallowed passive activity empowerment zone and renewal community employment credit. See the instructions for the applicable form for details.

See the instructions for Part I, line 3, for the definition of a passive activity.

Line 33

Enter the applicable passive activity credit amount for general business credits allowed against TMT and eligible small business credits allowed from Form 8582-CR or Form 8810. See the instructions for the applicable form for details.

The passive activity credit amount allowed on Part II, line 33, only applies to the general business credits from Part II, line 32, plus any prior year unallowed passive activity credit from general business credits reported on Part III, line 4, and eligible small business credit.

See the instructions for Part I, line 3, for the definition of a passive activity.

Line 34

Enter the amount of all carryforwards to 2014 of unused credits that are reported from line 5 of Part III with box C checked and line 6 of Part III with box G checked.

Note. Individuals claiming the research credit from a sole proprietorship or pass-through entity do not include any carryforward of that credit on Part II, line 34, before computing the limitation on Part III, line 1c. Include the carryforward when figuring the research credit limitation on line 1c of any Parts III with the applicable box A or B checked. Then include the allowable carryforward amount on Part II, line 34. **See the instructions for Part I, line 4, for the required statement that must be attached to your tax return.**

Line 35

Use Part II, line 35, only when you amend your 2014 return to carry back unused credits from 2015. Enter the amount that is reported from line 5 of Part III with box D checked.

Note. Individuals claiming the research credit from a sole proprietorship or pass-through entity do not include any carryback of that credit on Part II, line 35, before computing the limitation on Part III, line 1c. Include the carryback when figuring the research credit limitation on line 1c of any Parts III with the applicable box A or B checked. Then include the allowable carryback amount on Part II, line 35. **See the instructions for Part I, line 4, for the required statement that must be attached to your tax return.**

Line 38

If Part II, line 38, is smaller than the sum of Part I, line 6, and Part II, lines 25 and 36, see *Carryback and Carryforward of Unused Credit*, earlier.

Part III. General Business Credits or Eligible Small Business Credits

Complete a separate Part III for each box checked. In addition, for each box A or B checked, if you have a credit from more than one source and one of the sources is a pass-through entity, including a cooperative (see *Column (b)*, later), a separate Part III is needed for each pass-through entity for which you received the same credit. As a result, one checkbox could have multiple Parts III if you receive a single credit from multiple pass-through entities.

 After you have completed all necessary Parts III, complete Part I, if necessary, then Part II.

Box A Through D and G

Check the box that identifies the credit being reported.

Box I

Check box I if you are reporting credits on more than one Part III with box A or B checked. You must use a Part III with box I checked to consolidate the amounts from all Parts III with box A or B checked. Consolidate the Parts III with box A or B checked by combining the amounts for each credit line on each Part III with box A or B checked; then, enter the total for each credit on the applicable line of the Part III with box I checked.

A consolidated Part III is needed if there is more than one Part III with box A or B checked. More than one box A or B means more than one individual letter box (for example, if there is more than one Parts III with box B checked, a consolidated Part III is needed to reflect the total of all the boxes B checked) or more than one combination of letters (for example, if there is a box A checked and a box B checked, a consolidated Part III is needed to reflect the total of boxes A and B).

Column (b)

If you are reporting a credit from a pass-through entity, you must enter that pass-through entity's employer identification number (EIN) under column (b) for that credit.

If you are reporting a credit reported to you on Form 1099-PATR, Taxable Distributions Received From Cooperatives, you must enter that cooperative's EIN under column (b) for that credit.

A separate Part III will be needed to report the EIN of the pass-through entity, including cooperatives, and the amount of credit from that entity, if a credit is received from more than one source and one of the sources is a pass-through entity, including a cooperative. Column (b) is only completed for any Part III with box A or B checked.

Limitation on Certain Credits

The aggregate amount from each credit form is usually reported on the appropriate line of Form 3800, Part III, for the applicable boxes A and B, to reflect self-generated credit sources and all pass-through entity sources. However, certain credits have limitations imposed. They include:

• Form 3468, Part III, line 12p – $4,000 limitation for qualified small wind energy property (reported on Part III, line 4a);
• Form 8826, line 8 – $5,000 limitation for the overall credit (reported on Part III, line 1e);
• Form 8881, line 5 – $500 limitation for the overall credit (reported on Part III, line 1j);
• Form 8882, line 7 – $150,000 limitation for the overall credit (reported on Part III, line 1k); and
• Form 8909, line 23. See the Form 8909 instructions for information on the limitation that applies (reported on Part III, line 1q).

In situations where there is a limitation on the credit amount, the limited amount allowed is allocated *pro rata* and anything above the limitation is lost.

Lines 1a and 4a

If you are a cooperative described in section 1381(a), you must allocate to your patrons the investment credit in excess of your tax liability limit. Allocate to your patrons the portion, if any, of the investment credit on Part I, line 6, or Part II, line 36, in excess of Part II, line 16 or line 29, respectively. While any excess is allocated to patrons, any credit recapture applies as if you as the cooperative had claimed the entire credit.

Note. Any carryforward of the qualifying therapeutic discovery project credit may be claimed on Part III, line 1a.

Line 1c

Research credit limitation. If you are an individual, the amount of the research credit that may be included on Part III, line 1c, is limited to the amount of tax attributable to your taxable income from the sole proprietorship or your interest in the pass-through entity (partnership, S corporation, estate, or trust) generating the credit. Figure the research credit limitation separately for each sole proprietorship or pass-through entity by using the following formula:

$$\text{Line 11} \times \frac{\text{Taxable income attributable to the sole proprietorship or your interest in the pass-through entity}}{\text{Your taxable income for the year}}$$

The sum of the fractions used for determining the limits cannot exceed one. The research credit used to determine the limitation is the sum of the current year credit (determined without regard to the limitation), any carryforwards of the credit not used in prior years, and any carryback of the credit from 2015. For information on how to compute your taxable income for the year, your taxable income attributable to the sole proprietorship, or your interest in the pass-through entity, see Regulations sections 1.41-7(c) and 1.53-3.

If in the current tax year you had no taxable income attributable to a particular business interest, you cannot claim any research credit this year related to that business.

If any of your research credit is not allowed to be used because of this limitation, see *Carryback and Carryforward of Unused Credit*, earlier.

Line 1e

When reporting the disabled access credit from Form 8826 on Part III, line 1e, do not enter more than $5,000 in column (c) of Parts III with box A or B checked, combined.

Line 1f

Cooperatives, estates, and trusts: enter the amount from Form 8835, Part I, line 12, and the applicable part of the amount from Form 8835, Part II, line 32. All others: enter the amount from Form 8835, Part I, line 10, and the applicable part of the amount from Form 8835, Part II, line 30. Do not enter an amount from Form 8835 that is included on Form 3800, Part III, line 4e.

Line 1j

When reporting the credit for small employer pension plan startup costs from Form 8881 on Part III, line 1j, do not enter more than $500 in column (c) of Parts III with box A or B checked, combined.

Line 1k

When reporting the credit for employer-provided childcare facilities and services from Form 8882 on Part III, line 1k, do not enter more than $150,000 in column (c) of Parts III with box A or B checked, combined.

Line 1v

Only the carryforward of the agricultural chemicals security credit from Form 8931 can be reported on Part III, line 1v.

Line 1z

Only the carryforward of the qualified plug-in electric vehicle credit claimed in Part I, Section B, of 2009 through 2012 Form 8834 can be reported on Part III, line 1z.

Line 1bb

Enter the total of the amounts shown in box 7 of the Schedules K-1 (Form 1065-B), Partner's Share of Income (Loss) From an Electing Large Partnership, you received from electing large partnerships (ELPs).

Line 1zz

Enter any carryforward to 2014 of any unused credit from:
- Form 3468 (for years prior to 2008 for the rehabilitation credit) (for tax years beginning before October 4, 2008, for the energy credit);
- Form 5884 for years prior to 2007;
- Form 6478 for years prior to 2005;
- Form 8846 for years prior to 2007; or
- Form 8900 for years prior to 2008.

Also use Part III, line 1zz, to enter any carryforward to 2014 of any unused credit from general business credits no longer covered on Form 3800 due to, and not limited to, expiration of a tax provision. The following list identifies these credits.
- Trans-Alaska pipeline liability fund credit.
- Credit for employers affected by Hurricane Katrina, Rita, or Wilma (Form 5884-A, Section A only).
- Hurricane Katrina housing credit (Form 5884-A, Section B only).
- Credit for affected Midwestern disaster area employers (Form 5884-A, Section A only).
- Employer housing credit (Form 5884-A, Section B only).
- Enhanced oil recovery credit (Form 8830).
- Credit for contributions to selected community development corporations (Form 8847).
- Welfare-to-work credit (Form 8861).
- New York Liberty Zone business employee credit (Form 8884).

Only Part III with box C checked is to be used with a Part III, line 1zz, credit entry under column (c). No EINs are required under column (b).

Note. If an amount is entered on Part III, line 1zz, see the instructions for Part I, line 4 for the statement to attach.

Line 3

Include any carryforward of the renewal community employment credit on Part III, line 3.

Line 4h

Credit for Small Employer Health Insurance Premiums (Form 8941):
- Tax-exempt eligible small employers, other than certain farmers' cooperatives, do not report the credit for small employer health insurance premiums on Part III, line 4h. Eligible tax-exempt small employers will report this credit on Form 990-T, Exempt Organization Business Income Tax Return.
- If your only source of credit listed on Part III, line 4h, is from pass-through entities, you are not required to complete or attach Form 8941. Instead, enter the credit directly on Part III, line 4h.
- Eligible small employers (other than tax-exempt eligible small employers) will enter the credit from Form 8941, line 16 or line 18.

See the Instructions for Form 8941 for more information.

Paperwork Reduction Act Notice. We ask for the information on this form to carry out the Internal Revenue laws of the United States. You are required to give us the information. We need it to ensure that you are complying with these laws and to allow us to figure and collect the right amount of tax.

You are not required to provide the information requested on a form that is subject to the Paperwork Reduction Act unless the form displays a valid OMB control number. Books or records relating to a form or its instructions must be retained as long as their contents may become material in the administration of any Internal Revenue law. Generally, tax returns and return information are confidential, as required by Internal Revenue Code section 6103.

The time needed to complete and file this form will vary depending on individual circumstances. The estimated burden for individual taxpayers filing this form is approved under OMB control number 1545-0074 and is included in the estimates shown in the instructions for their individual income tax return. The estimated burden for all other taxpayers who file this form is shown below.

Recordkeeping	30 hr., 51 min.
Learning about the law or the form	1 hr.
Preparing and sending the form to the IRS	1 hr., 32 min.

If you have comments concerning the accuracy of these time estimates or suggestions for making this form simpler, we would be happy to hear from you. See the instructions for the tax return with which this form is filed.

Form **4562**	**Depreciation and Amortization**	OMB No. 1545-0172
Department of the Treasury Internal Revenue Service (99)	**(Including Information on Listed Property)** ▶ Attach to your tax return. ▶ Information about Form 4562 and its separate instructions is at *www.irs.gov/form4562*.	**2014** Attachment Sequence No. **179**

Name(s) shown on return	Business or activity to which this form relates	Identifying number

Part I Election To Expense Certain Property Under Section 179
Note: *If you have any listed property, complete Part V before you complete Part I.*

1	Maximum amount (see instructions)	**1**	
2	Total cost of section 179 property placed in service (see instructions)	**2**	
3	Threshold cost of section 179 property before reduction in limitation (see instructions)	**3**	
4	Reduction in limitation. Subtract line 3 from line 2. If zero or less, enter -0-	**4**	
5	Dollar limitation for tax year. Subtract line 4 from line 1. If zero or less, enter -0-. If married filing separately, see instructions	**5**	

6	(a) Description of property	(b) Cost (business use only)	(c) Elected cost

7	Listed property. Enter the amount from line 29	**7**	
8	Total elected cost of section 179 property. Add amounts in column (c), lines 6 and 7	**8**	
9	Tentative deduction. Enter the **smaller** of line 5 or line 8	**9**	
10	Carryover of disallowed deduction from line 13 of your 2013 Form 4562	**10**	
11	Business income limitation. Enter the smaller of business income (not less than zero) or line 5 (see instructions)	**11**	
12	Section 179 expense deduction. Add lines 9 and 10, but do not enter more than line 11	**12**	
13	Carryover of disallowed deduction to 2015. Add lines 9 and 10, less line 12 ▶	**13**	

Note: *Do not use Part II or Part III below for listed property. Instead, use Part V.*

Part II Special Depreciation Allowance and Other Depreciation (Do not include listed property.) (See instructions.)

14	Special depreciation allowance for qualified property (other than listed property) placed in service during the tax year (see instructions)	**14**	
15	Property subject to section 168(f)(1) election	**15**	
16	Other depreciation (including ACRS)	**16**	

Part III MACRS Depreciation (Do not include listed property.) (See instructions.)

Section A

17	MACRS deductions for assets placed in service in tax years beginning before 2014	**17**	
18	If you are electing to group any assets placed in service during the tax year into one or more general asset accounts, check here . . . . ▶ ☐		

Section B—Assets Placed in Service During 2014 Tax Year Using the General Depreciation System

(a) Classification of property	(b) Month and year placed in service	(c) Basis for depreciation (business/investment use only—see instructions)	(d) Recovery period	(e) Convention	(f) Method	(g) Depreciation deduction
19a 3-year property						
b 5-year property						
c 7-year property						
d 10-year property						
e 15-year property						
f 20-year property						
g 25-year property			25 yrs.		S/L	
h Residential rental property			27.5 yrs.	MM	S/L	
			27.5 yrs.	MM	S/L	
i Nonresidential real property			39 yrs.	MM	S/L	
				MM	S/L	

Section C—Assets Placed in Service During 2014 Tax Year Using the Alternative Depreciation System

20a Class life					S/L	
b 12-year			12 yrs.		S/L	
c 40-year			40 yrs.	MM	S/L	

Part IV Summary (See instructions.)

21	Listed property. Enter amount from line 28	**21**	
22	**Total.** Add amounts from line 12, lines 14 through 17, lines 19 and 20 in column (g), and line 21. Enter here and on the appropriate lines of your return. Partnerships and S corporations—see instructions .	**22**	
23	For assets shown above and placed in service during the current year, enter the portion of the basis attributable to section 263A costs	**23**	

Part V **Listed Property** (Include automobiles, certain other vehicles, certain aircraft, certain computers, and property used for entertainment, recreation, or amusement.)

Note: *For any vehicle for which you are using the standard mileage rate or deducting lease expense, complete **only** 24a, 24b, columns (a) through (c) of Section A, all of Section B, and Section C if applicable.*

Section A—Depreciation and Other Information (Caution: *See the instructions for limits for passenger automobiles.*)

24a Do you have evidence to support the business/investment use claimed? ☐ Yes ☐ No   **24b** If "Yes," is the evidence written? ☐ Yes ☐ No

(a) Type of property (list vehicles first)	(b) Date placed in service	(c) Business/ investment use percentage	(d) Cost or other basis	(e) Basis for depreciation (business/investment use only)	(f) Recovery period	(g) Method/ Convention	(h) Depreciation deduction	(i) Elected section 179 cost
25 Special depreciation allowance for qualified listed property placed in service during the tax year and used more than 50% in a qualified business use (see instructions) .				**25**				
26 Property used more than 50% in a qualified business use:								
		%						
		%						
		%						
27 Property used 50% or less in a qualified business use:								
		%				S/L –		
		%				S/L –		
		%				S/L –		
28 Add amounts in column (h), lines 25 through 27. Enter here and on line 21, page 1 .						**28**		
29 Add amounts in column (i), line 26. Enter here and on line 7, page 1							**29**	

Section B—Information on Use of Vehicles

Complete this section for vehicles used by a sole proprietor, partner, or other "more than 5% owner," or related person. If you provided vehicles to your employees, first answer the questions in Section C to see if you meet an exception to completing this section for those vehicles.

	(a) Vehicle 1		(b) Vehicle 2		(c) Vehicle 3		(d) Vehicle 4		(e) Vehicle 5		(f) Vehicle 6	
30 Total business/investment miles driven during the year (**do not** include commuting miles) .												
31 Total commuting miles driven during the year												
32 Total other personal (noncommuting) miles driven												
33 Total miles driven during the year. Add lines 30 through 32												
34 Was the vehicle available for personal use during off-duty hours?	Yes	No	Yes	No	Yes	No	Yes	No	Yes	No	Yes	No
35 Was the vehicle used primarily by a more than 5% owner or related person? . .												
36 Is another vehicle available for personal use?												

Section C—Questions for Employers Who Provide Vehicles for Use by Their Employees

Answer these questions to determine if you meet an exception to completing Section B for vehicles used by employees who **are not** more than 5% owners or related persons (see instructions).

		Yes	No
37	Do you maintain a written policy statement that prohibits all personal use of vehicles, including commuting, by your employees?		
38	Do you maintain a written policy statement that prohibits personal use of vehicles, except commuting, by your employees? See the instructions for vehicles used by corporate officers, directors, or 1% or more owners . .		
39	Do you treat all use of vehicles by employees as personal use?		
40	Do you provide more than five vehicles to your employees, obtain information from your employees about the use of the vehicles, and retain the information received?		
41	Do you meet the requirements concerning qualified automobile demonstration use? (See instructions.) . . .		

Note: *If your answer to 37, 38, 39, 40, or 41 is "Yes," do not complete Section B for the covered vehicles.*

Part VI **Amortization**

(a) Description of costs	(b) Date amortization begins	(c) Amortizable amount	(d) Code section	(e) Amortization period or percentage	(f) Amortization for this year
42 Amortization of costs that begins during your 2014 tax year (see instructions):					
43 Amortization of costs that began before your 2014 tax year			**43**		
44 **Total.** Add amounts in column (f). See the instructions for where to report			**44**		

2014

Instructions for Form 4562

Depreciation and Amortization (Including Information on Listed Property)

Department of the Treasury
Internal Revenue Service

Section references are to the Internal Revenue Code unless otherwise noted.

Future Developments

For the latest information about developments related to Form 4562 and its instructions, such as legislation enacted after this form and instructions were published, go to *www.irs.gov/form4562*.

What's New

• For tax years beginning in 2014, the maximum section 179 expense deduction is $500,000 ($535,000 for enterprise zone property). This limit is reduced by the amount by which the cost of section 179 property placed in service during the tax year exceeds $2 million. See the instructions for Part I for more information.

• For tax years ending after December 31, 2013, a corporation can elect to claim pre-2006 unused minimum tax credits in lieu of the special depreciation allowance for round 4 extension property.

General Instructions

Purpose of Form

Use Form 4562 to:
• Claim your deduction for depreciation and amortization,
• Make the election under section 179 to expense certain property, and
• Provide information on the business/investment use of automobiles and other listed property.

Who Must File

Except as otherwise noted, complete and file Form 4562 if you are claiming any of the following.
• Depreciation for property placed in service during the 2014 tax year.
• A section 179 expense deduction (which may include a carryover from a previous year).
• Depreciation on any vehicle or other listed property (regardless of when it was placed in service).
• A deduction for any vehicle reported on a form other than Schedule C (Form 1040), Profit or Loss From Business, or Schedule C-EZ (Form 1040), Net Profit From Business.
• Any depreciation on a corporate income tax return (other than Form 1120S).
• Amortization of costs that begins during the 2014 tax year.

If you are an employee deducting job-related vehicle expenses using either the standard mileage rate or actual expenses, use Form 2106, Employee Business Expenses, or Form 2106-EZ, Unreimbursed Employee Business Expenses, for this purpose.

File a separate Form 4562 for each business or activity on your return for which Form 4562 is required. If you need more space, attach additional sheets. However, complete only one Part I in its entirety when computing your section 179 expense deduction. See the instructions for line 12, later.

Additional Information

For more information about depreciation and amortization (including information on listed property), see the following.
• Pub. 463, Travel, Entertainment, Gift, and Car Expenses.
• Pub. 534, Depreciating Property Placed in Service Before 1987.
• Pub. 535, Business Expenses.
• Pub. 551, Basis of Assets.
• Pub. 946, How To Depreciate Property.

Definitions

Depreciation

Depreciation is the annual deduction that allows you to recover the cost or other basis of your business or investment property over a certain number of years. Depreciation starts when you first use the property in your business or for the production of income. It ends when you either take the property out of service, deduct all your depreciable cost or basis, or no longer use the property in your business or for the production of income.

Generally, you can depreciate:
• Tangible property such as buildings, machinery, vehicles, furniture, and equipment; and
• Intangible property such as patents, copyrights, and computer software.

Exception. You cannot depreciate land.

Accelerated Cost Recovery System

The Accelerated Cost Recovery System (ACRS) applies to property first used before 1987. It is the name given for the tax rules that allow a taxpayer to recover through depreciation deductions the cost of property used in a trade or business or to produce income. These rules are mandatory and generally apply to tangible property placed in service after 1980 and before 1987. If you placed property in service during this period, you must continue to figure your depreciation under ACRS.

ACRS consists of accelerated depreciation methods and an alternate ACRS method that could have been elected. The alternate ACRS method used a recovery percentage based on a modified straight line method. See the instructions for line 16 for more information. For a complete discussion of ACRS, see Publication 534.

Modified Accelerated Cost Recovery System

The Modified Accelerated Cost Recovery System (MACRS) is the current method of accelerated asset depreciation required by the tax code. Under MACRS, all assets are divided into classes which dictate the number of years over which an asset's cost will be recovered. Each MACRS class has a predetermined schedule which determines the percentage of the asset's costs which is depreciated each year. For more information, see *Part III–MACRS Depreciation*, later. For a complete discussion of MACRS, see *chapter 4* of Publication 946.

Section 179 Property

Section 179 property is property that you acquire by purchase for use in the active conduct of your trade or business, and is one of the following.
- Tangible personal property, including cellular telephones and similar telecommunications equipment.
- Qualified section 179 real property. For more information, see *Special rules for qualified section 179 real property,* later.
- Other tangible property (except buildings and their structural components) used as:

   1. An integral part of manufacturing, production, or extraction or of furnishing transportation, communications, electricity, gas, water, or sewage disposal services;

   2. A research facility used in connection with any of the activities in (1) above; or

   3. A facility used in connection with any of the activities in (1) above for the bulk storage of fungible commodities.

- Single purpose agricultural (livestock) or horticultural structures.
- Storage facilities (except buildings and their structural components) used in connection with distributing petroleum or any primary product of petroleum.
- Off-the-shelf computer software placed in service before January 1, 2015.

   Section 179 property does not include the following.
- Property held for investment (section 212 property).
- Property used mainly outside the United States (except for property described in section 168(g)(4)).
- Property used mainly to furnish lodging or in connection with the furnishing of lodging (except as provided in section 50(b)(2)).
- Property used by a tax-exempt organization (other than a section 521 farmers' cooperative) unless the property is used mainly in a taxable unrelated trade or business.
- Property used by a governmental unit or foreign person or entity (except for property used under a lease with a term of less than 6 months).
- Air conditioning or heating units.

See the instructions for Part I and Pub. 946.

Special rules for qualified section 179 real property. You can elect to treat certain qualified real property placed in service during the tax year as section 179 property. See *Election for certain qualified section 179 real property* in Part I for information on how to make this election. If the election is made, the term "section 179 property" will include any qualified real property which is:
- Qualified leasehold improvement property as described in section 168(e)(6),
- Qualified restaurant property as described in section 168(e)(7), or
- Qualified retail improvement property as described in section 168(e)(8).

   This property is considered "qualified section 179 real property."

   The maximum section 179 expense deduction that may be expensed for qualified section 179 real property is $250,000 of the total cost of all section 179 property placed in service in 2014. A 2013 deduction attributable to qualified real property which is disallowed under the trade or business income limitation (see *Business Income Limit* in chapter 2 of Pub. 946) is carried over to 2014. The carryover amount from 2013 (or a portion of the amount) not deducted in 2014 is considered placed in service on the first day of the 2014 tax year. Thus, any such amounts that are not deducted in 2014, plus any 2014 disallowed section 179 expense deductions attributable to qualified section 179 real property, are treated as property placed in service on the first day of 2014 for purposes of computing depreciation (including the special depreciation allowance, if applicable). Any of these amounts will **not** be reported on line 13 of Form 4562. They will instead be reported on the appropriate line under Part II or Part III of Form 4562. For more information on qualified section 179 real property, see section 179(f) and Pub. 946. Also, see Notice 2013-59.

Amortization

Amortization is similar to the straight line method of depreciation in that an annual deduction is allowed to recover certain costs over a fixed time period. You can amortize such items

as the costs of starting a business, goodwill, and certain other intangibles. See the instructions for Part VI.

Listed Property

Listed property generally includes the following.
- Passenger automobiles weighing 6,000 pounds or less. See *Limits for passenger automobiles*, later.
- Any other property used for transportation if the nature of the property lends itself to personal use, such as motorcycles, pick-up trucks, sport utility vehicles, etc.
- Any property used for entertainment or recreational purposes (such as photographic, phonographic, communication, and video recording equipment).
- Computers or peripheral equipment.

Exceptions. Listed property does not include:

   1. Photographic, phonographic, communication, or video equipment used exclusively in a taxpayer's trade or business or at the taxpayer's regular business establishment;

   2. Any computer or peripheral equipment used exclusively at a regular business establishment and owned or leased by the person operating the establishment;

   3. An ambulance, hearse, or vehicle used for transporting persons or property for compensation or hire; or

   4. Any truck or van placed in service after July 6, 2003, that is a qualified nonpersonal use vehicle.

   For purposes of the exceptions above, a portion of the taxpayer's home is treated as a regular business establishment only if that portion meets the requirements for deducting expenses attributable to the business use of a home. However, for any property listed in (1) above, the regular business establishment of an employee is his or her employer's regular business establishment.

Commuting

Generally, commuting is defined as travel between your home and a work location. However, travel that meets any of the following conditions is not commuting.

• You have at least one regular work location away from your home and the travel is to a temporary work location in the same trade or business, regardless of the distance. Generally, a temporary work location is one where your employment is expected to last 1 year or less. See Pub. 463 for details.

• The travel is to a temporary work location outside the metropolitan area where you live and normally work.

• Your home is your principal place of business for purposes of deducting expenses for business use of your home and the travel is to another work location in the same trade or business, regardless of whether that location is regular or temporary and regardless of distance.

Alternative Minimum Tax (AMT)

Depreciation may be an adjustment for the AMT. However, no adjustment applies in several instances. See Form 4626, Alternative Minimum Tax—Corporations; Form 6251, Alternative Minimum Tax—Individuals; Schedule I (Form 1041), Alternative Minimum Tax—Estates and Trusts; and the related instructions.

Recordkeeping

Except for Part V (relating to listed property), the IRS does not require you to submit detailed information with your return on the depreciation of assets placed in service in previous tax years. However, the information needed to compute your depreciation deduction (basis, method, etc.) must be part of your permanent records.

 You may use the depreciation worksheet, later, to assist you in maintaining depreciation records. However, the worksheet is designed only for federal income tax purposes. You may need to keep additional records for accounting and state income tax purposes.

Specific Instructions

Part I. Election To Expense Certain Property Under Section 179

Note. An estate or trust cannot make this election.

You can elect to expense part or all of the cost of section 179 property (defined earlier) that you placed in service during the tax year and used predominantly (more than 50%) in your trade or business.

However, for taxpayers other than a corporation, this election does not apply to any section 179 property you purchased and leased to others unless:

• You manufactured or produced the property or

• The term of the lease is less than 50% of the property's class life and, for the first 12 months after the property is transferred to the lessee, the deductions related to the property allowed to you as trade or business expenses (except rents and reimbursed amounts) are more than 15% of the rental income from the property.

Election. You must make the election on Form 4562 filed with either:

• The original return you file for the tax year the property was placed in service (whether or not you file your return on time) or

• An amended return filed within the time prescribed by law for the applicable tax year. The election made on an amended return must specify the item of section 179 property to which the election applies and the part of the cost of each such item to be taken into account. The amended return must also include any resulting adjustments to taxable income.

Election for certain qualified section 179 real property. You can elect to expense certain qualified real property that you first placed in service as section 179 property for tax years beginning in 2014. If you elect to treat this property as section 179 property, you must elect the application of the special rules for qualified real property under section 179(f) in order for the term section 179 property to include qualified real property placed in service during the tax year.

To make the election, attach a separate statement to your original 2014 tax return, whether or not you file it timely, indicating that you are

"electing the application of section 179(f) of the Internal Revenue Code" for the tax year. Then, indicate on the statement your election to expense certain qualified real property under section 179 on your tax return. The election to expense must specify one or more of the three types of qualified real property (described under *Special rules for qualified section 179 real property*, earlier) to which the election applies, the cost of each such type, and the portion of cost of each such type to be taken into account. Report this information on line 6 of Form 4562. For more information on how to report your election, see the instructions for Line 6, later.

You can also make the election by attaching a separate statement (containing the same information discussed above) to an amended return for 2014 filed within the time prescribed by law. The amended return must also include any resulting adjustments to the tax year.

Revocation. The election (or any specification made in the election) can be revoked without obtaining IRS approval by filing an amended return. The amended return must be filed within the time prescribed by law for the applicable tax year. The amended return must include any resulting adjustments to taxable income or to the tax liability (for example, allowable depreciation in that tax year for the item of section 179 property which the revocation pertains). For more information and examples, see Regulations section 1.179-5(c)(3) and (c)(4). Once made, the revocation is irrevocable.

 If you elect to expense section 179 property, you must reduce the amount on which you figure your depreciation or amortization deduction (including any special depreciation allowance) by the section 179 expense deduction.

Line 1

Generally, the maximum section 179 expense deduction is $500,000 for section 179 property placed in service in 2014 during the tax year beginning in 2014.

Qualified real property that is elected to be treated as section 179 property is limited to $250,000 of the maximum section 179 deduction of $500,000 for 2014. For more

Worksheet 1. Worksheet for Lines 1, 2, and 3   *Keep for Your Records*

	Maximum section 179 limitation calculation.	
*1.	Total cost of qualified section 179 real property placed in service in 2014 during the tax year beginning in 2014 of the type(s) of property for which you are making the election	
2.	$250,000 of the maximum section 179 deduction limitation of $500,000 allowed for 2014 can be expensed for qualified section 179 real property	**$250,000**
3.	Enter the smaller of line 1 or line 2	
*4.	Enter total cost of section 179 property (except qualified section 179 real property) placed in service in 2014 during the tax year beginning in 2014	
5.	The maximum section 179 deduction limitation for 2014	**$500,000**
6.	If you have an enterprise zone business (see the instructions for *Line 1*, earlier), enter the smaller of $35,000 or the cost of the qualified section 179 property that is also qualified empowerment zone property	
7.	Add lines 5 and 6. Enter this amount here and on Form 4562, line 1	
	Maximum threshold cost of section 179 property before reduction in limitation calculation.	
8.	Add lines 1 and 4. Enter this amount here and on Form 4562, line 2	
9.	Base maximum threshold cost of section 179 property before reduction in limitation for 2014. Enter this amount on Form 4562, line 3.	**$2,000,000**
	Maximum elected cost for Form 4562, lines 6 and 7, column (c).	
10.	Add lines 3 and 4	
11.	Enter the smaller of line 7 or line 10. **The total amount you enter on Form 4562, lines 6 and 7, column (c), cannot exceed this amount**	

*For lines 1 and 4 of this worksheet include the total amount of eligible section 179 property or section 179 property, not just the amount for which you are making the election.

information, see *Special rules for qualified section 179 real property,* earlier.

 You can use Worksheet 1, *later, to assist you in determining the amount to write on line 1. You can also use the worksheet to figure the maximum qualified section 179 real property deduction allowed for 2014.*

For an enterprise zone business, the maximum deduction is increased by the smaller of:
• $35,000 or
• The cost of section 179 property that is also qualified empowerment zone property placed in service before January 1, 2015 (including such property placed in service or purchased by your spouse, even if you are filing a separate return).

Recapture rule. If any qualified section 179 disaster assistance property placed in service prior to

2014 in a federally declared disaster area where the disaster occurred after December 31, 2007, and before January 1, 2010, ceases to be used in the applicable federally declared disaster area in 2014, the benefit of the increased section 179 expense deduction must be reported as "other income" on your return. Similar rules apply if qualified Liberty Zone property ceases to be used in the Liberty Zone, if qualified section 179 GO Zone property ceases to be used in the GO Zone, if qualified section 179 Recovery Assistance property ceases to be used in the Recovery Assistance area, if qualified empowerment zone property ceases to be used in an empowerment zone by an enterprise zone business, or if qualified renewal property ceases to be used in a renewal community by a renewal community business in any year after you claim the increased section 179 expense deduction.

Line 2
Enter the total cost of all section 179 property (including the total cost of qualified real property that you elect to treat as section 179 property) you placed in service during the tax year. Also, include the cost of the following.
• Any listed property from Part V.
• Any property placed in service by your spouse, even if you are filing a separate return. This includes qualified section 179 real property your spouse made the election to treat as section 179 property for 2014.
• 50% of the cost of section 179 property that is also qualified empowerment zone property placed in service during the tax year.

Line 3
The amount of section 179 property for which you can make the election is limited to the maximum dollar amount on line 1. This amount is reduced if the cost of all section 179 property placed in service in 2014 is more than $2 million.

For a partnership (other than an electing large partnership), these limitations apply to the partnership and each partner. For an electing large partnership, the limitations apply only to the partnership. For an S corporation, these limitations apply to the S corporation and each shareholder. For a controlled group, all component members are treated as one taxpayer.

Line 5
If line 5 is zero, you cannot elect to expense any section 179 property. In this case, skip lines 6 through 11, enter zero on line 12, and enter the carryover of any disallowed deduction from 2013 (excluding carryover amounts attributable to qualified section 179 real property) on line 13.

See *Special rules for qualified section 179 real property,* earlier.

If you are married filing separately, you and your spouse must allocate the dollar limitation for the tax year. To do so, multiply the total limitation that you would otherwise enter on line 5 by 50%, unless you both elect a different allocation. If you both elect a different allocation, multiply the total limitation by the percentage elected. The sum of the percentages you and your spouse elect must equal 100%.

Do not enter on line 5 more than your share of the total dollar limitation.

Line 6

Do not include any listed property on line 6. Enter the elected section 179 cost of listed property in column (i) of line 26.

Column (a) — Description of property. Enter a brief description of the property you elect to expense (e.g., truck, office furniture, etc.). For all qualified section 179 real property, enter "qualified real property".

Column (b) — Cost (business use only). Enter the cost of the property. If you acquired the property through a trade-in, do not include any carryover basis of the property traded in. Include only the excess of the cost of the property over the value of the property traded in.

Column (c) — Elected cost. Enter the amount you elect to expense (including the combined cost of all qualified real property that you elected to treat as section 179 property). You do not have to expense the entire cost of the property. You can depreciate the amount you do not expense . See the line 19 and line 20 instructions.

To report your share of a section 179 expense deduction from a partnership or an S corporation, write "from Schedule K-1 (Form 1065)" or "from Schedule K-1 (Form 1120S)" across columns (a) and (b).

Line 7

Enter the amount that you elected to expense for listed property (defined earlier) on line 29 here. For more information, see *Part V–Listed Property*, later.

Line 10

The carryover of disallowed deduction from 2013 is the amount of section 179 property, if any, you elected to expense in previous years that was not allowed as a deduction because of the business income limitation. If you filed Form 4562 for 2013, enter the amount from line 13 of your 2013 Form 4562.

Line 11

The total cost you can deduct is limited to your taxable income from the active conduct of a trade or business during the year. You are considered to actively conduct a trade or business only if you meaningfully participate in its management or operations. A mere passive investor is not considered to actively conduct a trade or business.

Note. If you have to apply another Code section that has a limitation based on taxable income, see Pub. 946 for rules on how to apply the business income limitation for the section 179 expense deduction.

Individuals. Enter the smaller of line 5 or the total taxable income from any trade or business you actively conducted, computed without regard to any section 179 expense deduction, the deduction for one-half of self-employment taxes under section 164(f), or any net operating loss deduction. Also include all wages, salaries, tips, and other compensation you earned as an employee (from Form 1040, line 7). Do not reduce this amount by unreimbursed employee business expenses. If you are married filing a joint return, combine the total taxable incomes for you and your spouse.

Partnerships. Enter the smaller of line 5 or the partnership's total items of income and expense described in section 702(a) from any trade or business the partnership actively conducted (other than credits, tax-exempt income, the section 179 expense deduction, and guaranteed payments under section 707(c)).

S corporations. Enter the smaller of line 5 or the corporation's total items of income and expense described in section 1366(a) from any trade or business the corporation actively conducted (other than credits, tax-exempt income, the section 179 expense deduction, and the deduction for compensation paid to the corporation's shareholder-employees).

Corporations other than S corporations. Enter the smaller of line 5 or the corporation's taxable income before the section 179 expense deduction, net operating loss deduction, and special deductions (excluding items not derived from a trade or business actively conducted by the corporation).

Line 12

The limitations on lines 5 and 11 apply to the taxpayer, and not to each separate business or activity.

Therefore, if you have more than one business or activity, you may allocate your allowable section 179 expense deduction among them.

To do so, write "Summary" at the top of Part I of the separate Form 4562 you are completing for the total amounts from all businesses or activities. Do not complete the rest of that form. On line 12 of the Form 4562 you prepare for each separate business or activity, enter the amount allocated to the business or activity from the "Summary." No other entry is required in Part I of the separate Form 4562 prepared for each business or activity.

Part II. Special Depreciation Allowance and Other Depreciation

Line 14

For qualified property (defined below) placed in service during the tax year, you may be able to take an additional 50% special depreciation allowance. The special depreciation allowance applies only for the first year the property is placed in service. The allowance is an additional deduction you can take after any section 179 expense deduction and before you figure regular depreciation under the modified accelerated cost recovery system (MACRS).

Qualified property. You can take the special depreciation allowance for qualified second generation biofuel plant property, certain qualified property acquired after December 31, 2007, and placed in service before January 1, 2015, and qualified reuse and recycling property.

Qualified second generation biofuel plant property. Qualified second generation biofuel plant property is property used in the United States solely to produce second generation biofuel (as defined in section 40(b)(6)(E)).

The 50% special depreciation allowance applies to qualified second generation biofuel plant property. The property must also meet the following requirements.
• The original use of the property must begin with you after December 20, 2006.
• You must have acquired the property by purchase after December

20, 2006. If a binding contract to acquire the property existed before December 21, 2006, the property does not qualify.

• Qualified second generation biofuel plant property must be placed in service for use in your trade or business or for the production of income after January 2, 2013, and before January 1, 2015.

• For property you sold and leased back or for self-constructed property, special rules apply. See section 168(l)(4).

Certain qualified property acquired after December 31, 2007, and placed in service before January 1, 2015. Certain qualified property (defined below) acquired after December 31, 2007, is eligible for a 50% special depreciation allowance. If a binding contract to acquire the property existed before January 1, 2008, the property does not qualify.

Qualified property is:
• Tangible property depreciated under MACRS with a recovery period of 20 years or less.
• Water utility property (see 25-year property, later).
• Computer software defined in and depreciated under section 167(f)(1).
• Qualified leasehold improvement property.

Qualified property must also be placed in service before September 9, 2010, or after December 31, 2011, and before January 1, 2015 (or before September 9, 2010, or after December 31, 2012, and before January 1, 2016, for certain property with a long production period and for certain aircraft). The original use of the property must begin with you after December 31, 2007.

See Pub. 946 for more information.

Qualified reuse and recycling property. Certain qualified reuse and recycling property (defined below) placed in service after August 31, 2008, is eligible for a 50% special depreciation allowance.

Qualified reuse and recycling property includes any machinery and equipment (not including buildings or real estate), along with any appurtenance, that is used exclusively to collect, distribute, or recycle qualified reuse and recyclable materials. This includes software

necessary to operate such equipment. See section 168(m)(3) for more information.

Qualified reuse and recycling property must also meet all of the following tests.
• The property must be depreciated under MACRS.
• The property must have a useful life of at least 5 years.
• You must have acquired the property by purchase after August 31, 2008. If a binding contract to acquire the property existed before September 1, 2008, the property does not qualify.
• The property must be placed in service after August 31, 2008.
• The original use of the property must begin with you after August 31, 2008.
• For self-constructed property, special rules apply. See section 168(m)(2)(C).

Qualified reuse and recycling property does not include rolling stock or other equipment used to transport reuse and recyclable materials or any property to which section 168(g) or (k) applies.

Election to accelerate minimum tax credit in lieu of special depreciation allowance. An election to claim pre-2006 unused minimum tax credits in lieu of claiming the special depreciation allowance made by a corporation for either its first tax year ending after March 31, 2008, its first tax year ending after December 31, 2008, or its first tax year ending after December 31, 2010, continues to apply to round 3 extension property (as defined in section 168(k)(4)(J)), unless the corporation made an election not to apply the section 168(k)(4) election to round 3 extension property for its first tax year ending after December 31, 2012. For 2014, round 3 extension property generally is long production period property and noncommercial aircraft if acquired after March 31, 2008, and placed in service after December 31, 2013, but before January 1, 2015.

An election to claim pre-2006 unused minimum tax credits in lieu of claiming the special depreciation allowance made by a corporation for either its first tax year ending after March 31, 2008, its first tax year ending after December 31, 2008, its

first tax year ending after December 31, 2010, or for its first tax year ending after December 31, 2012, continues to apply to round 4 extension property (as defined in section 168(k)(4)(K)), unless the corporation makes an election not to apply the section 168(k)(4) election to round 4 extension property for its first year ending after December 31, 2013. If a corporation did not make a section 168(k)(4) election for either its first tax year ending after March 31, 2008, its first tax year ending after December 31, 2008, its first tax year ending after December 31, 2010, or its first tax year ending after December 31, 2012, the corporation may elect for its first tax year ending after December 31, 2013, to claim pre-2006 unused minimum tax credits in lieu of claiming the special depreciation allowance for only round 4 extension property.

If you make an election to accelerate this credit in lieu of claiming the special depreciation allowance for qualified property, you must **not** take the 50% special depreciation allowance for the property and **must** depreciate the basis in the property under MACRS using the straight line method. See *Lines 19a Through 19i*, later, for more information.

Once made, this election cannot be revoked without IRS consent.

For more information on making this election, see Form 8827, Credit for Prior Year Minimum Tax—Corporations; and related instructions.

 The IRS will release guidance concerning round 4 extension property. The guidance will be published in the Internal Revenue Bulletin.

Exceptions. Qualified property does not include:
• Listed property used 50% or less in a qualified business use (as defined in the instructions for lines 26 and 27);
• Any property required to be depreciated under the alternative depreciation system (ADS) (that is, not property for which you elected to use ADS);
• Property placed in service and disposed of in the same tax year;
• Property converted from business or income-producing use to personal use in the same tax year it is acquired;

- Property for which you elected not to claim any special depreciation allowance;
- Any qualified restaurant property (as defined in section 168(e)(7)) that is not qualified leasehold improvement property (as defined in sections 168(e)(6) and 168(k)(3)); or
- Any qualified retail improvement property (as defined in section 168(e)(8)) that is not qualified leasehold improvement property (as defined in sections 168(e)(6) and 168(k)(3)).

In addition, qualified second generation biofuel plant property does not include the following:
- Any tax-exempt bond financed property under section 103.
- Any property for which a deduction was taken under section 179C for certain qualified refinery property.
- Other bonus depreciation property to which section 168(k) applies.

See sections 168(k), 168(l), and 168(m) for additional information. Also, see Pub. 946.

How to figure the allowance. Figure the special depreciation allowance by multiplying the depreciable basis of the property by 50%.

To figure the depreciable basis, subtract from the business/investment portion of the cost or other basis of the property any credits and deductions allocable to the property. The following are examples of some credits and deductions that reduce the depreciable basis.
- Section 179 expense deduction.
- Deduction for removal of barriers to the disabled and the elderly.
- Disabled access credit.
- Enhanced oil recovery credit.
- Credit for employer-provided childcare facilities and services.
- Basis adjustment to investment credit property under section 50(c). For additional credits and deductions that affect the depreciable basis, see section 1016. Also, see Pub. 946.

Note. If you acquired qualified property through a like-kind exchange or involuntary conversion, the carryover basis and any excess basis of the acquired property is eligible for the special depreciation allowance. See Regulations section 1.168(k)-1(f)(5).

 If you take the 50% special depreciation allowance, you must reduce the amount on which you figure your regular depreciation or amortization deduction by the amount deducted. Also, you will not have any AMT adjustment for the property if the depreciable basis of the property for the AMT is the same as for the regular tax.

Election out. You can elect, for any class of property, to not deduct any special depreciation allowance for all such property in such class placed in service during the tax year.

To make an election, attach a statement to your timely filed return (including extensions) indicating the class of property for which you are making the election and that, for such class you are not to claim any special depreciation allowance.

The election must be made separately by each person owning qualified property (for example, by the partnership, by the S corporation, or by the common parent of a consolidated group).

If you timely filed your return without making an election, you can still make the election by filing an amended return within 6 months of the due date of the return (excluding extensions). Write "Filed pursuant to section 301.9100-2" on the amended return.

Once made, the election cannot be revoked without IRS consent.

Note. If you elect not to have any special depreciation allowance apply, the property may be subject to an AMT adjustment for depreciation.

Recapture. When you dispose of property for which you claimed a special depreciation allowance, any gain on the disposition is generally recaptured (included in income) as ordinary income up to the amount of the special depreciation allowance you deducted. If qualified GO Zone property (including specified GO Zone property) ceases to be qualified GO Zone property, if qualified Recovery Assistance property ceases to be qualified Recovery Assistance property, if qualified cellulosic biomass ethanol plant property ceases to be qualified cellulosic biomass ethanol plant property, if

qualified second generation biofuel plant property ceases to be qualified second generation biofuel plant property, or if qualified disaster assistance property ceases to be qualified disaster assistance property in any year after the year you claim the special depreciation allowance, the excess benefit you received from claiming the special depreciation allowance must be recaptured as ordinary income. For information on depreciation recapture, see Pub. 946. Also, see Notice 2008-25, 2008-9 I.R.B. 484, available at *www.irs.gov/ irb/2008-09_irb/ar10.html* for additional guidance on recapture of qualified GO Zone property.

Line 15

Report on this line depreciation for property that you elect to depreciate under the unit-of-production method or any other method not based on a term of years (other than the retirement-replacement-betterment method).

Attach a separate sheet showing:
- A description of the property and the depreciation method you elect that excludes the property from MACRS or the Accelerated Cost Recovery System (ACRS); and
- The depreciable basis (cost or other basis reduced, if applicable, by salvage value, any section 179 expense deduction, deduction for removal of barriers to the disabled and the elderly, disabled access credit, enhanced oil recovery credit, credit for employer-provided childcare facilities and services, any special depreciation allowance, and any other applicable deduction or credit).

For additional credits and deductions that may affect the depreciable basis, see section 1016. Also, see section 50(c) to determine the basis adjustment for investment credit property.

Line 16

Enter the total depreciation you are claiming for the following types of property (except listed property and property subject to a section 168(f)(1) election).
- ACRS property (pre-1987 rules). See Pub. 534.
- Property placed in service before 1981.

- Certain public utility property which does not meet certain normalization requirements.
- Certain property acquired from related persons.
- Property acquired in certain nonrecognition transactions.
- Certain sound recordings, movies, and videotapes.
- Property depreciated under the income forecast method. The use of the income forecast method is limited to motion picture films, videotapes, sound recordings, copyrights, books, and patents.

If you use the income forecast method for any property placed in service after September 13, 1995, you may owe interest or be entitled to a refund for the 3rd and 10th tax years beginning after the tax year the property was placed in service. For details, see Form 8866, Interest Computation Under the Look-Back Method for Property Depreciated Under the Income Forecast Method.

For property placed in service in the current tax year, you can either include certain participations and residuals in the adjusted basis of the property or deduct these amounts when paid. See section 167(g)(7). You cannot use this method to depreciate any amortizable section 197 intangible. For more details, see the instructions on section 197 intangibles, later.
- Intangible property, other than section 197 intangibles, including:

1. Computer software. Use the straight line method over 36 months. A longer period may apply to software leased under a lease agreement entered into after March 12, 2004, to a tax-exempt organization, governmental unit, or foreign person or entity (other than a partnership). See section 167(f)(1)(C).

 If you elect the section 179 expense deduction or take the special depreciation allowance for qualified computer software, you must reduce the amount on which you figure your regular depreciation deduction by the amount deducted.

2. Any right to receive tangible property or services under a contract or granted by a governmental unit (not acquired as part of a business).

3. Any interest in a patent or copyright not acquired as part of a business.

4. Residential mortgage servicing rights. Use the straight line method over 108 months.

5. Other intangible assets with a limited useful life that cannot be estimated with reasonable accuracy. Generally, use the straight line method over 15 years. See Regulations section 1.167(a)-3(b) for details and exceptions.

 Prior years' depreciation, plus current year's depreciation, can never exceed the depreciable basis of the property.

Part III. MACRS Depreciation

The term "Modified Accelerated Cost Recovery System" (MACRS) includes the General Depreciation System and the Alternative Depreciation System. Generally, MACRS is used to depreciate any tangible property placed in service after 1986. However, MACRS does not apply to films, videotapes, and sound recordings. For more details and exceptions, see Pub. 946.

Section A

Line 17

For tangible property placed in service in tax years beginning before 2014 and depreciated under MACRS, enter the deductions for the current year. To figure the deductions, see the instructions for line 19, column (g).

Line 18

To simplify the computation of MACRS depreciation, you can elect to group assets into one or more general asset accounts. The assets in each general asset account are depreciated as a single asset.

Each general asset account must include only assets that were placed in service during the same tax year and that have the same depreciation method, recovery period, and convention. However, an asset cannot be included in a general asset account if the asset is used both for personal purposes and business/investment purposes.

When an asset in an account is disposed of, the amount realized generally must be recognized as ordinary income. The unadjusted depreciable basis and depreciation reserve of the general asset account are not affected as a result of a disposition.

Special rules apply to passenger automobiles, assets generating foreign source income, assets converted to personal use, certain asset dispositions, and like-kind exchanges or involuntary conversions of property in a general asset account. For more details, see Regulations section 1.168(i)-1, (as in effect for tax years beginning on or after January 1, 2014).

To make the election, check the box on line 18. You must make the election on your return filed no later than the due date (including extensions) for the tax year in which the assets included in the general asset account were placed in service. Once made, the election is irrevocable and applies to the tax year for which the election is made and all later tax years.

For more information on depreciating property in a general asset account, see Pub. 946.

Section B

Property acquired in a like-kind exchange or involuntary conversion. Generally, you must depreciate the carryover basis of property you acquire in a like-kind exchange or involuntary conversion during the current tax year over the remaining recovery period of the property exchanged or involuntarily converted. Use the same depreciation method and convention that was used for the exchanged or involuntarily converted property. Treat any excess basis as newly placed in service property. Figure depreciation separately for the carryover basis and the excess basis, if any.

These rules apply only to acquired property with the same or a shorter recovery period or the same or a more accelerated depreciation method than the property exchanged or involuntarily converted. For additional rules, see Regulations section 1.168(i)-6(c) and Pub. 946.

Election out. Instead of using the above rules, you can elect, for depreciation purposes, to treat the adjusted basis of the exchanged property as if it was disposed of at the time of the exchange or involuntary conversion. Generally, treat the carryover basis and excess basis, if any, for the acquired property as if placed in service on the date you acquired it. The depreciable basis of the new property is the adjusted basis of the exchanged or involuntarily converted property plus any additional amount paid for it. See Regulations section 1.168(i)-6(i).

To make the election, figure the depreciation deduction for the new property in Part III. For listed property, use Part V. Attach a statement indicating "Election made under section 1.168(i)-6(i)" for each property involved in the exchange or involuntary conversion. The election must be made separately by each person acquiring replacement property (for example, by the partnership, by the S corporation, or by the common parent of a consolidated group). The election must be made on your timely filed return (including extensions). Once made, the election cannot be revoked without IRS consent.

 If you trade in a vehicle used for employee business use, complete Form 2106, Part II, Section D, instead of Form 4562, to "elect out" of Regulations section 1.168(i)-6. If you do not "elect out," you must use Form 4562 instead of Form 2106. See the Instructions for Form 2106.

Lines 19a Through 19i

Use lines 19a through 19i only for assets placed in service during the tax year beginning in 2014 and depreciated under the General Depreciation System (GDS), except for automobiles and other listed property (which are reported in Part V).

Column (a) — Classification of property. Sort the property you acquired and placed in service during the tax year beginning in 2014 according to its classification (3-year property, 5-year property, etc.) as shown in column (a) of lines 19a through 19i. The classifications for some property are shown below. For property not shown, see *Determining the classification*, later.

3-year property includes:
- A race horse that is more than 2 years old at the time it is placed in service before January 1, 2009.

Note. Any race horse placed in service after December 31, 2008, and before January 1, 2015, is treated as 3-year property (regardless of the age of the race horse).
- Any horse (other than a race horse) that is more than 12 years old at the time it is placed in service.
- Any qualified rent-to-own property (as defined in section 168(i)(14)).

5-year property includes:
- Automobiles.
- Light general purpose trucks.
- Typewriters, calculators, copiers, and duplicating equipment.
- Any semi-conductor manufacturing equipment.
- Any computer or peripheral equipment.
- Any section 1245 property used in connection with research and experimentation.
- Certain energy property specified in section 168(e)(3)(B)(vi).
- Appliances, carpets, furniture, etc., used in a rental real estate activity.

7-year property includes:
- Office furniture and equipment.
- Railroad track.
- Any motorsports entertainment complex (as defined in section 168(i)(15)) placed in service before January 1, 2015.
- Any natural gas gathering line (as defined in section 168(i)(17)) placed in service after April 11, 2005, the original use of which begins with you after April 11, 2005, and is not under self-construction or subject to a binding contract in existence before April 12, 2005. Also, no AMT adjustment is required.
- Any property that does not have a class life and is not otherwise classified.

10-year property includes:
- Vessels, barges, tugs, and similar water transportation equipment.
- Any single purpose agricultural or horticultural structure (see section 168(i)(13)).
- Any tree or vine bearing fruit or nuts.
- Any qualified smart electric meter property.
- Any qualified smart electric grid system property.

15-year property includes:
- Any municipal wastewater treatment plant.
- Any telephone distribution plant and comparable equipment used for 2-way exchange of voice and data communications.
- Any section 1250 property that is a retail motor fuels outlet (whether or not food or other convenience items are sold there).
- Any qualified leasehold improvement property placed in service before January 1, 2015.
- Any qualified restaurant property that is a building and placed in service before January 1, 2015.
- Any qualified restaurant property that is section 1250 property and an improvement to a building and placed in service before January 1, 2015.
- Any qualified retail improvement property (as defined in section 168(e)(8)) placed in service before January 1, 2015.
- Initial clearing and grading land improvements for gas utility property.
- Certain electric transmission property specified in section 168(e)(3)(E)(vii) placed in service after April 11, 2005, the original use of which begins with you after April 11, 2005, and is not under self-construction or subject to a binding contract in existence before April 12, 2005.

20-year property includes:
- Farm buildings (other than single purpose agricultural or horticultural structures).
- Municipal sewers not classified as 25-year property.
- Initial clearing and grading land improvements for electric utility transmission and distribution plants.

25-year property is water utility property, which is:
- Property that is an integral part of the gathering, treatment, or commercial distribution of water that, without regard to this classification, would be 20-year property.
- Municipal sewers. This classification does not apply to property placed in service under a binding contract in effect at all times since June 9, 1996.

Residential rental property is a building in which 80% or more of the total rent is from dwelling units.

Nonresidential real property is any real property that is neither residential rental property nor property with a class life of less than 27.5 years.

50-year property includes any improvements necessary to construct or improve a roadbed or right-of-way for railroad track that qualifies as a railroad grading or tunnel bore under section 168(e)(4).

There is no separate line to report 50-year property. Therefore, attach a statement showing the same information as required in columns (a) through (g). Include the deduction in the line 22 "Total" and write "See attachment" in the bottom margin of the form.

Determining the classification. If your depreciable property is not listed above, determine the classification as follows.

1. Find the property's class life. See the Table of Class Lives and Recovery Periods in Pub. 946.

2. Use the following table to find the classification in column (b) that corresponds to the class life of the property in column (a).

(a) Class life (in years) (See Pub. 946)	(b) Classification
4 or less	3-year property
More than 4 but less than 10	5-year property
10 or more but less than 16	7-year property
16 or more but less than 20	10-year property
20 or more but less than 25	15-year property
25 or more	20-year property

Column (b) — Month and year placed in service. For lines 19h and 19i, enter the month and year you placed the property in service. If you converted property held for personal use to use in a trade or business or for the production of income, treat the property as being placed in service on the conversion date.

Column (c) — Basis for depreciation (business/investment use only). To find the basis for depreciation, multiply the cost or other basis of the property by the percentage of business/investment use. From that result, subtract any credits and deductions allocable to the property. The following are examples of some credits and deductions that reduce the basis for depreciation.

- Section 179 expense deduction.
- Deduction under section 179C for certain qualified refinery property.
- Deduction under section 179D for certain energy efficient commercial building property.
- Deduction for removal of barriers to the disabled and the elderly.
- Disabled access credit.
- Enhanced oil recovery credit.
- Credit for alternative fuel vehicle refueling property.
- Credit for employer-provided childcare facilities and services.
- Any special depreciation allowance included on line 14.
- Any basis adjustment for investment credit property. See section 50(c).

For additional credits and deductions that affect the depreciable basis, see section 1016 and Pub. 946.

Column (d) — Recovery period. Determine the recovery period from the following table. See Pub. 946 for more information on the recovery period for MACRS property.

Recovery Period for Most Property

Classification	Recovery period
3-year property	3 yrs.
5-year property	5 yrs.
7-year property	7 yrs.
10-year property	10 yrs.
15-year property	15 yrs.
20-year property	20 yrs.
25-year property	25 yrs.
Residential rental property	27.5 yrs.
Nonresidential real property	39 yrs.
Railroad gradings and tunnel bores	50 yrs.

Indian reservation property. For qualified Indian reservation property placed in service before January 1, 2015, the following shorter recovery periods apply.

Recovery Period for Qualified Indian Reservation Property

Property class	Recovery period
3-year property	2 yrs.
5-year property	3 yrs.
7-year property	4 yrs.
10-year property	6 yrs.
15-year property	9 yrs.
20-year property	12 yrs.
Nonresidential real property	22 yrs.

For example, figure depreciation on 5-year property acquired during the tax year that is qualified Indian reservation property in the same manner as depreciation is figured for 3-year property that is not qualified Indian reservation property. Report the depreciation on line 19b, entering "3 yrs." as the recovery period in column (d). For more information, including the definition of qualified property, see Pub. 946.

Column (e) — Convention. The applicable convention determines the portion of the tax year for which depreciation is allowable during a year property is either placed in service or disposed of. There are three types of conventions. To select the correct convention, you must know the type of property and when you placed the property in service.

Half-year convention. This convention applies to all property reported on lines 19a through 19g, unless the mid-quarter convention applies. It does not apply to residential rental property, nonresidential real property, and railroad gradings and tunnel bores. It treats all property placed in service (or disposed of) during any tax year as placed in service (or disposed of) on the midpoint of that tax year. Enter "HY" in column (e).

Mid-quarter convention. If the total depreciable bases (before any special depreciation allowance) of MACRS property placed in service during the last 3 months of your tax year exceed 40% of the total depreciable bases of MACRS property placed in service during the entire tax year, the mid-quarter, instead of the half-year, convention generally applies.

In determining whether the mid-quarter convention applies, do not take into account the following.
- Property that is being depreciated under a method other than MACRS.
- Any residential rental property, nonresidential real property, or railroad gradings and tunnel bores.
- Property that is placed in service and disposed of within the same tax year.

The mid-quarter convention treats all property placed in service (or disposed of) during any quarter as placed in service (or disposed of) on the midpoint of that quarter. However, no depreciation is allowed under this convention for property that is placed in service and disposed of within the same tax year. Enter "MQ" in column (e).

Mid-month convention. This convention applies only to residential rental property (line 19h), nonresidential real property (line 19i), and railroad gradings and tunnel bores. It treats all property placed in service (or disposed of) during any month as placed in service (or disposed of) on the midpoint of that month. Enter "MM" in column (e).

Column (f) — Method Applicable depreciation methods are prescribed for each classification of property as follows. However, you can make an irrevocable election to use the straight line method for all property within a classification that is placed in service during the tax year. Enter "200 DB" for 200% declining balance, "150 DB" for 150% declining balance, or "S/L" for straight line.

Note. If you elected to accelerate pre-2006 unused minimum tax credit in lieu of special depreciation allowance for round 3 extension property or round 4 extension property (as discussed earlier), you must depreciate the basis in the property using the straight line method. Enter "S/L" in this column for the applicable property classification. If you are depreciating other property in the same classification as the property for which this election was made and using a different method, enter "Various" in this column.

- **3-, 5-, 7-, and 10-year property.** Generally, the applicable method is the 200% declining balance method, switching to the straight line method in the first tax year that the straight line rate exceeds the declining balance rate.

Note. The straight line method is the only applicable method for trees and vines bearing fruit or nuts. The 150% declining balance method is the only applicable method for any qualified smart electric meter or any qualified smart electric grid system property placed in service after October 3, 2008.

For 3-, 5-, 7-, or 10-year property eligible for the 200% declining balance method, you can make an irrevocable election to use the 150% declining balance method, switching to the straight line method in the first tax year that the straight line rate exceeds the declining balance rate. The election applies to all property within the classification for which it is made and that was placed in service during the tax year. You will not have an AMT adjustment for any property included under this election.

- **15- and 20-year property (not including qualified leasehold improvement property, qualified restaurant property, or qualified retail improvement property) and property used in a farming business.** The applicable method is the 150% declining balance method, switching to the straight line method in the first tax year that the straight line rate exceeds the declining balance rate.
- **Water utility property, residential rental property, nonresidential real property, qualified leasehold improvement property, qualified restaurant property, qualified retail improvement property, or any railroad grading or tunnel bore.** The only applicable method is the straight line method.

Column (g) — Depreciation deduction. To figure the depreciation deduction, you may use optional Tables A through E, which begin later. Multiply column (c) by the applicable rate from the appropriate table. See Pub. 946 for complete tables. If you disposed of the property during the current tax year, multiply the result by the applicable decimal amount from the tables in Step 3 later. Or, you may compute the deduction yourself by completing the following steps.

Step 1. Determine the depreciation rate as follows.
- If you are using the 200% or 150% declining balance method in column (f), divide the declining balance rate (use 2.00 for 200 DB or 1.50 for 150 DB) by the number of years in the recovery period in column (d). For example, for property depreciated using the 200 DB method over a recovery period of 5 years, divide 2.00 by 5 for a rate of 40%. You must switch to the straight line rate in the first year that the straight line rate exceeds the declining balance rate.
- If you are using the straight line method, divide 1.00 by the remaining number of years in the recovery period as of the beginning of the tax year (but not less than one). For example, if there are 6½ years remaining in the recovery period as of the beginning of the year, divide 1.00 by 6.5 for a rate of 15.38%.

Step 2. Multiply the percentage rate determined in Step 1 by the property's unrecovered basis (basis for depreciation (as defined in column (c)) reduced by all prior years' depreciation.

Step 3. For property placed in service or disposed of during the current tax year, multiply the result from Step 2 by the applicable decimal amount from the tables below (based on the convention shown in column (e)).

Half-year (HY) convention		0.5
Mid-quarter (MQ) convention		
Placed in service (or disposed of) during the:	Placed in service	Disposed of
1st quarter . . .	0.875	0.125
2nd quarter . . .	0.625	0.375
3rd quarter . . .	0.375	0.625
4th quarter . . .	0.125	0.875

Placed in service (or disposed of) during the:	Placed in service	Disposed of
1st month	0.9583	0.0417
2nd month	0.8750	0.1250
3rd month	0.7917	0.2083
4th month	0.7083	0.2917
5th month	0.6250	0.3750
6th month	0.5417	0.4583
7th month	0.4583	0.5417
8th month	0.3750	0.6250
9th month	0.2917	0.7083
10th month	0.2083	0.7917
11th month	0.1250	0.8750
12th month	0.0417	0.9583

Short tax years. See Pub. 946 for rules on how to compute the depreciation deduction for property placed in service in a short tax year.

Section C

Lines 20a Through 20c

Complete lines 20a through 20c for assets, other than automobiles and other listed property, placed in service only during the tax year beginning in 2014 and depreciated under the Alternative Depreciation System (ADS). Report on line 17 MACRS depreciation on assets placed in service in prior years.

Under ADS, use the applicable depreciation method, the applicable recovery period, and the applicable convention to compute depreciation.

The following types of property must be depreciated under ADS.
• Tangible property used predominantly outside the United States.
• Tax-exempt use property.
• Tax-exempt bond financed property.
• Imported property covered by an executive order of the President of the United States.
• Property used predominantly in a farming business and placed in service during any tax year in which you made an election under section 263A(d)(3) not to have the uniform capitalization rules of section 263A apply.

Instead of depreciating property under GDS (line 19), you can make an irrevocable election for any classification of property for any tax year to use ADS. For residential rental and nonresidential real property, you can make this election separately for each property. You make this election by completing line 20 of Form 4562.

Column (a) — Classification of property. Use the following rules to determine the classification of the property under ADS.

Under ADS, the depreciation deduction for most property is based on the property's class life. See section 168(g)(3) for special rules for determining the class life for certain property. See Pub. 946 for information on recovery periods for ADS and the Table of Class Lives and Recovery Periods.

Use line 20a for all property depreciated under ADS, except property that does not have a class life, residential rental and nonresidential real property, water utility property, and railroad gradings and tunnel bores. Use line 20b for property that does not have a class life. Use line 20c for residential rental and nonresidential real property.

Water utility property and railroad gradings and tunnel bores. These assets are 50-year property under ADS. There is no separate line to report 50-year property. Therefore, attach a statement showing the same information required in columns (a) through (g). Include the deduction in the line 22 "Total" and write "See attachment" in the bottom margin of the form.

Column (b) — Month and year placed in service. For 40-year property, enter the month and year placed in service or converted to use in a trade or business or for the production of income.

Column (c) — Basis for depreciation (business/investment use only). See the instructions for line 19, column (c).

Column (d) — Recovery period. On line 20a, enter the property's class life.

Column (e) — Convention. Under ADS, the applicable conventions are the same as those used under GDS. See the instructions for line 19, column (e).

Column (g) — Depreciation deduction. Figure the depreciation deduction in the same manner as under GDS, except use the straight line method over the ADS recovery period and use the applicable convention.

MACRS recapture. If you later dispose of property you depreciated using MACRS, any gain on the disposition is generally recaptured (included in income) as ordinary income up to the amount of the depreciation previously allowed or allowable for the property. Depreciation, for this purpose, includes any of the following deductions taken during the 2014 tax year.
• Any section 179 expense deduction claimed on the property,
• Any special depreciation allowance available for the property (unless you elected not to claim it),
• Any deduction under section 179B for capital costs incurred in complying with Environmental Protection Agency sulfur regulations, and
• Any deduction under section 179D for certain energy efficient commercial building property placed in service before January 1, 2015.

There is no recapture for residential rental and nonresidential real property, unless that property is qualified property for which you claimed a special depreciation allowance (discussed earlier). For more information on depreciation recapture, see Pub. 946.

Part IV. Summary

Line 22

A partnership (other than an electing large partnership) or S corporation does not include any section 179 expense deduction (line 12) on this line. Instead, any section 179 expense deduction is passed through separately to the partners and shareholders on the appropriate line of their Schedules K-1.

Line 23

If you are subject to the uniform capitalization rules of section 263A, enter the increase in basis from costs you must capitalize. For a detailed discussion of who is subject to these rules, which costs must be capitalized, and allocation of costs among activities, see Regulations section 1.263A-1.

Part V. Listed Property

If you claim the standard mileage rate, actual vehicle expenses (including depreciation), or depreciation on other listed property, you must provide the information requested in Part V, regardless of the tax year the property was placed in service. However, if you file Form 2106 or 2106-EZ, report this information on that form and not in Part V. Also, if you file Schedule C (Form 1040) or Schedule C-EZ (Form 1040) and are claiming the standard mileage rate or actual vehicle expenses (except depreciation), and you are not required to file Form 4562 for any other reason, report vehicle information in Part IV of Schedule C or in Part III of Schedule C-EZ and not on Form 4562.

Section A

 The section 179 expense deduction should be computed before calculating any special depreciation allowance and/or regular depreciation deduction. See the instructions for line 26, column (i).

Listed property used 50% or less in a qualified business use (as defined in the instructions for lines 26 and 27 below) does not qualify for the section 179 expense deduction or special depreciation allowance.

Line 25

If you placed in service certain qualified listed property during the tax year, you may be able to deduct an additional special depreciation allowance. This property includes certain qualified property acquired after December 31, 2007, and placed in service before January 1, 2015. See the instructions for line 14 for the definition of qualified property and how to figure the deduction. This special depreciation allowance is included in the overall limit on depreciation and section 179 expense deduction for passenger automobiles. See the tables for limitations on passenger vehicles and trucks and vans, later. Enter on line 25 your total special depreciation allowance for all qualified listed property.

Lines 26 and 27

Use line 26 to figure depreciation for property used more than 50% in a qualified business use. Use line 27 to figure the depreciation for property used 50% or less in a qualified business use. Also see *Limits for passenger automobiles*, later.

 If you acquired the property through a trade-in, special rules apply for determining the basis, recovery period, depreciation method, and convention. For more details, see Property acquired in a like-kind exchange or involuntary conversion, *earlier. Also, see Regulations section 1.168(i)-6(d)(3).*

Qualified business use. To determine whether to use line 26 or line 27 to report your listed property, you must first determine the percentage of qualified business use for each property. Generally, a qualified business use is any use in your trade or business. However, it does not include any of the following.
• Investment use.
• Leasing the property to a 5% owner or related person.
• The use of the property as compensation for services performed by a 5% owner or related person.
• The use of the property as compensation for services performed by any person (who is not a 5% owner or related person), unless an amount is included in that person's income for the use of the property and, if required, income tax was withheld on that amount.

Excluding these uses above from the numerator, determine your percentage of qualified business use similar to the method used to figure the business/investment use percentage in column (c). Your percentage of qualified business use may be smaller than the business/investment use percentage.

For more information, including the definition of a 5% owner and related person and exceptions, see Pub. 946.

Listed property recapture. If you used listed property more than 50% in a qualified business use in the year you placed the property in service, and used it 50% or less in a later year, you may have to include as income part of the depreciation deducted in prior years. Use Form 4797, Sales of Business Property, to figure the recapture amount.

Column (a) — Type of property. List on a property-by-property basis all your listed property in the following order.

1. Automobiles and other vehicles.

2. Other listed property (computers and peripheral equipment, etc.).

In column (a), list the make and model of automobiles, and give a general description of other listed property.

If you have more than five vehicles used 100% for business/investment purposes, you may group them by tax year. Otherwise, list each vehicle separately.

Column (b) — Date placed in service. Enter the date the property was placed in service. If property held for personal use is converted to business/investment use, treat the property as placed in service on the date of conversion.

Column (c) — Business/investment use percentage. Enter the percentage of business/investment use. For automobiles and other vehicles, determine this percentage by dividing the number of miles the vehicle is driven for trade or business purposes or for the production of income during the year (not to include any commuting mileage) by the total number of miles the vehicle is driven for all purposes. Treat vehicles used by employees as being used 100% for business/investment purposes if the value of personal use is included in the employees' gross income, or the employees reimburse the employer for the personal use.

Employers who report the amount of personal use of the vehicle in the employee's gross income, and withhold the appropriate taxes, should enter "100%" for the percentage of business/investment use. For more information, see Pub. 463.

For other listed property (such as computers or video equipment), allocate the use based on the most appropriate unit of time the property is actually used (rather than merely being available for use).

If during the tax year you convert property used solely for personal purposes to business/investment use (or vice versa), figure the percentage of business/investment use only for the number of months you use the property in your business or for the production of income. Multiply that percentage by the number of months you use the property in your business or for the production of income, and divide the result by 12.

Column (d) — Cost or other basis. Enter the property's actual cost (including sales tax) or other basis (unadjusted for prior years' depreciation). If you traded in old property, see *Property acquired in a like-kind exchange or involuntary conversion*, earlier.

For a vehicle, reduce your basis by any qualified electric vehicle credit you claimed for property placed in service before January 1, 2007, or by any alternative motor vehicle credit allowed.

If you converted the property from personal use to business/investment use, your basis for depreciation is the smaller of the property's adjusted basis or its fair market value on the date of conversion.

Column (e) — Basis for depreciation (business/investment use only). Multiply column (d) by the percentage in column (c). From that result, subtract any section 179 expense deduction, any special depreciation allowance, any credit for employer-provided childcare facilities and services, and half of any investment credit taken before 1986 (unless you claimed the reduced credit). For automobiles and other listed property placed in service after 1985 (i.e., transition property), reduce the depreciable basis by the entire investment credit.

Column (f) — Recovery period. Enter the recovery period. For property placed in service after 1986 and used more than 50% in a qualified business use, use the table in the instructions for line 19, column (d). For property placed in service after 1986 and used 50% or less in a qualified business use, depreciate the property using the straight line method over its ADS recovery period. The ADS recovery period is 5 years for automobiles and computers.

Column (g) — Method/convention. Enter the method and convention

used to figure your depreciation deduction. See the instructions for line 19, columns (e) and (f). Write "200 DB," "150 DB," or "S/L," for the depreciation method, and "HY," "MM," or "MQ," for half-year, mid-month, or mid-quarter conventions, respectively. For property placed in service before 1987, write "PRE" if you used the prescribed percentages under ACRS. If you elected an alternate percentage or if you are required to depreciate the property using the straight line method, enter "S/L."

Column (h) — Depreciation deduction. See *Limits for passenger automobiles*, later, before entering an amount in column (h).

For property used more than 50% in a qualified business use (line 26) and placed in service after 1986, figure column (h) by following the instructions for line 19, column (g). If placed in service before 1987, multiply column (e) by the applicable percentage given in Pub. 534 for ACRS property. If the recovery period for an automobile ended before your tax year beginning in 2014, enter your unrecovered basis, if any, in column (h).

For property used 50% or less in a qualified business use (line 27) and placed in service after 1986, figure column (h) by dividing the amount in column (e) by the amount in column (f). Use the same conventions as discussed in the instructions for line 19, column (e). The amount in column (h) cannot exceed the property's unrecovered basis. If the recovery period for an automobile ended before your tax year beginning in 2014, enter your unrecovered basis, if any, in column (h).

For property placed in service before 1987 that was disposed of during the year, enter zero.

Limits for passenger automobiles. The depreciation deduction, including section 179 expense deduction, for passenger automobiles is limited. For any passenger automobile (including an electric passenger automobile) you list on line 26 or line 27, the total of columns (h) and (i) on line 26 or 27 and column (h) on line 25 for that automobile cannot exceed the applicable limit shown in *Table 1, 2, 3, or 4*. If the business/investment use percentage in column (c) for the automobile is less than 100%, you

must reduce the applicable limit to an amount equal to the limit multiplied by that percentage. For example, for an automobile (other than a truck or van) placed in service in 2014 (for which you elect not to claim any special depreciation allowance) that is used 60% for business/investment, the limit is $1,896 ($3,160 x 60%).

For purposes of the limits for passenger automobiles, the following apply.
• Passenger automobiles are 4-wheeled vehicles manufactured primarily for use on public roads that are rated at 6,000 pounds unloaded gross vehicle weight or less (for a truck or van, gross vehicle weight is substituted for unloaded gross vehicle weight).
• Electric passenger automobiles are vehicles produced by an original equipment manufacturer and designed to run primarily on electricity, placed in service after August 5, 1997, and before January 1, 2007.

Exception. The following vehicles are not considered passenger automobiles.
• An ambulance, hearse, or combination ambulance-hearse used in your trade or business.
• A vehicle used in your trade or business of transporting persons or property for compensation or hire.
• Any truck or van placed in service after July 6, 2003, that is a qualified nonpersonal use vehicle. A truck or van is a qualified nonpersonal use vehicle only if it has been specially modified with the result that it is not likely to be used more than a de minimis amount for personal purposes. For example, a van that has only a front bench for seating, in which permanent shelving has been installed, that constantly carries merchandise or equipment, and that has been specially painted with advertising or the company's name, is a vehicle not likely to be used more than a de minimis amount for personal purposes.

Exception for leasehold property. The business use requirement and the limits for passenger automobiles generally do not apply to passenger automobiles leased or held by anyone regularly engaged in the business of leasing passenger automobiles.

-14-

For a detailed discussion on passenger automobiles, including leased automobiles, see Pub. 463.

Table 1—Limits for Passenger Automobiles Placed in Service Before 2004 (excluding electric passenger automobiles placed in service after August 5, 1997)

IF you placed your automobile in service:	THEN the limit on your depreciation and section 179 expense deduction is:
June 19 — Dec. 31, 1984	$6,000
Jan. 1 — Apr. 2, 1985	$6,200
Apr. 3, 1985 — Dec. 31, 1986	$4,800
Jan. 1, 1987 — Dec. 31, 1990	$1,475
Jan. 1, 1991 — Dec. 31, 1992	$1,575
Jan. 1, 1993 — Dec. 31, 1994	$1,675
Jan. 1, 1995 — Dec. 31, 2003	$1,775

Table 2—Limits for Electric Passenger Automobiles Placed in Service After August 5, 1997, and Before January 1, 2007

If you placed your electric automobile in service:	AND the number of tax years in which this automobile has been in service is:	THEN the limit on your depreciation and section 179 expense deduction is:
Aug. 6, 1997 — Dec. 31, 1998	4 or more . . .	$5,425
Jan. 1, 1999 — Dec. 31, 2002	4 or more . . .	$5,325
Jan. 1 — Dec. 31, 2003	4 or more . . .	$5,225
Jan. 1, 2004 — Dec. 31, 2005	4 or more . . .	$5,125
Jan. 1 — Dec. 31, 2006	4 or more . . .	$5,225

Table 3—Limits for Passenger Automobiles Placed in Service After 2003 (excluding trucks and vans placed in service after 2002 and electric passenger automobiles placed in service before January 1, 2007)

IF you placed your automobile in service:	AND the number of tax years in which this automobile has been in service is:	THEN the limit on your depreciation and section 179 expense deduction is:
Jan. 1, 2004–Dec. 31, 2005	4 or more . . .	$1,675
Jan. 1, 2006 — Dec. 31, 2011	4 or more . . .	$1,775
Jan. 1 — Dec. 31, 2012	3	$3,050
	4	$1,875
Jan. 1 — Dec. 31, 2013	2	$5,100
	3	$3,050
Jan. 1 — Dec. 31, 2014	1	$3,160*
	2	$5,100

* If you take the special depreciation allowance for qualified passenger automobiles placed in service in 2014, the limit is $11,160.

Table 4—Limits for Trucks and Vans Placed in Service After 2002

IF you placed your truck or van in service:	AND the number of tax years in which this truck or van has been in service is:	THEN the limit on your depreciation and section 179 expense deduction is:
Jan. 1, 2004 — Dec. 31, 2008	4 or more . . .	$1,875
Jan. 1 — Dec. 31, 2009	4 or more . . .	$1,775
Jan. 1, 2010 — Dec. 31, 2011	4 or more . . .	$1,875
Jan. 1 — Dec. 31, 2012	3	$3,150
	4	$1,875
Jan. 1 — Dec. 31, 2013	2	$5,400
	3	$3,250
Jan. 1 — Dec. 31, 2014	1	$3,460*
	2	$5,500

* If you take the special depreciation allowance for qualified trucks and vans placed in service in 2014, the limit is $11,460.

Column (i) — Elected section 179 cost. Enter the amount you elect to expense for section 179 property used more than 50% in a qualified business use (subject to the limits for passenger automobiles). Refer to the instructions for Part I to determine if the property qualifies under section 179.

You cannot elect to expense more than $25,000 of the cost of any sport utility vehicle (SUV) and certain other vehicles placed in service during the tax year. This rule applies to any 4-wheeled vehicle primarily designed or used to carry passengers over public streets, roads, or highways, that is rated at more than 6,000 pounds gross vehicle weight and not more than 14,000 pounds gross vehicle weight. However, the $25,000 limit does not apply to any vehicle:
• Designed to seat more than nine persons behind the driver's seat,
• Equipped with a cargo area (either open or enclosed by a cap) of at least six feet in interior length that is not readily accessible directly from the passenger compartment, or
• That has an integral enclosure fully enclosing the driver compartment and load carrying device, does not have seating rearward of the driver's seat, and has no body section protruding more than 30 inches ahead of the leading edge of the windshield.

Recapture of section 179 expense deduction. If you used listed property more than 50% in a qualified business use in the year you placed the property in service and used it 50% or less in a later year, you may have to recapture in the later year part of the section 179 expense deduction. Use Form 4797 to figure the recapture amount.

Section B

Except as noted below, you must complete lines 30 through 36 for each vehicle identified in Section A. Employees must provide their employers with the information requested on lines 30 through 36 for each automobile or vehicle provided for their use.

Exception. Employers are not required to complete lines 30 through 36 for vehicles used by employees who are not more than 5% owners or related persons and for which the question on line 37, 38, 39, 40, or 41 is answered "Yes."

Section C

Employers providing vehicles to their employees satisfy the employer's substantiation requirements under section 274(d) by maintaining a written policy statement that:
- Prohibits personal use including commuting or
- Prohibits personal use except for commuting.

An employee does not need to keep a separate set of records for any vehicle that satisfies these written policy statement rules.

For both written policy statements, there must be evidence that would enable the IRS to determine whether use of the vehicle meets the conditions stated below.

Line 37

A policy statement that prohibits personal use (including commuting) must meet all of the following conditions.
- The employer owns or leases the vehicle and provides it to one or more employees for use in the employer's trade or business.
- When the vehicle is not used in the employer's trade or business, it is kept on the employer's business premises, unless it is temporarily located elsewhere (e.g., for maintenance or because of a mechanical failure).
- No employee using the vehicle lives at the employer's business premises.
- No employee may use the vehicle for personal purposes, other than de minimis personal use (e.g., a stop for lunch between two business deliveries).
- Except for de minimis use, the employer reasonably believes that no employee uses the vehicle for any personal purpose.

Line 38

A policy statement that prohibits personal use (except for commuting) is not available if the commuting employee is an officer, director, or 1% or more owner. This policy must meet all of the following conditions.
- The employer owns or leases the vehicle and provides it to one or more employees for use in the employer's trade or business, and it is used in the employer's trade or business.

- For bona fide noncompensatory business reasons, the employer requires the employee to commute to and/or from work in the vehicle.
- The employer establishes a written policy under which the employee may not use the vehicle for personal purposes, other than commuting or de minimis personal use (e.g., a stop for a personal errand between a business delivery and the employee's home).
- Except for de minimis use, the employer reasonably believes that the employee does not use the vehicle for any personal purpose other than commuting.
- The employer accounts for the commuting use by including an appropriate amount in the employee's gross income.

Line 40

An employer that provides more than five vehicles to its employees who are not 5% owners or related persons need not complete Section B for such vehicles. Instead, the employer must obtain the information from its employees and retain the information received.

Line 41

An automobile meets the requirements for qualified demonstration use if the employer maintains a written policy statement that:
- Prohibits its use by individuals other than full-time automobile salespersons,
- Prohibits its use for personal vacation trips,
- Prohibits storage of personal possessions in the automobile, and
- Limits the total mileage outside the salesperson's normal working hours.

Part VI. Amortization

Each year you can deduct part of certain capital costs over a fixed period.

 If you amortize property, the part you amortize does not qualify for the section 179 expense deduction or for depreciation.

Attach any information the Code and regulations may require to make a valid election. See the applicable Code section, regulations, and Pub. 535 for more information.

Line 42

Complete line 42 only for those costs you amortize for which the amortization period begins during your tax year beginning in 2014.

Column (a) — Description of costs. Describe the costs you are amortizing. You can amortize the following.

Geological and geophysical expenditures (section 167(h)). You must amortize geological and geophysical expenses paid or incurred in connection with the exploration or development of oil and gas within the United States ratably over a 24-month period. For a major integrated oil company (as defined in section 167(h)(5)), the costs paid or incurred after December 19, 2007, must be amortized ratably over a 7-year period (a 5-year period for costs paid or incurred after May 17, 2006, and before December 20, 2007), beginning on the mid-point of the tax year in which the expenses were paid or incurred.

Pollution control facilities (section 169). You can elect to amortize the cost of a certified pollution control facility over a 60-month period (84 months for certain atmospheric pollution control facilities placed in service after April 11, 2005). See section 169 and the related regulations for details and information required in making the election. See Pub. 535 for more information.

 You can deduct a special depreciation allowance on a certified pollution control facility that is qualified property. However, you must reduce the amount on which you figure your amortization deduction by any special depreciation allowance allowed or allowable, whichever is greater.

Also, a corporation must reduce its amortizable basis of a pollution control facility by 20% before figuring the amortization deduction.

Bond premium (section 171). For individuals reporting amortization of bond premium for taxable bonds acquired before October 23, 1986, do not report the deduction here. See the instructions for Schedule A (Form 1040), line 28.

For taxpayers (other than corporations) claiming a deduction for amortization of bond premium for taxable bonds acquired after October 22, 1986, but before January 1, 1988, the deduction is treated as interest expense and is subject to the investment interest limitations. Use Form 4952, Investment Interest Expense Deduction, to compute the allowable deduction.

For taxable bonds acquired after 1987, you can elect to amortize the bond premium over the life of the bond. See section 171 and Regulations section 1.171-4 for more information. Individuals, also see Pub. 550, Investment Income and Expenses. A bond premium carryforward as of the end of a taxpayer's final accrual period is treated as a deduction. See Regulations section 1.171-2T. For an individual, do not report the deduction here. See the instructions for Schedule A (Form 1040), line 28.

Research and experimental expenditures (section 174). You can elect to either amortize your research and experimental costs, deduct them as current business expenses, or write them off over a 10-year period. If you elect to amortize these costs, deduct them in equal amounts over 60 months or more. For more information, see Pub. 535.

The cost of acquiring a lease (section 178). Amortize these costs over the term of the lease. For more information, see Pub. 535.

Qualified forestation and reforestation costs (section 194). You can elect to deduct a limited amount of qualifying reforestation costs paid or incurred during the tax year for each qualified timber property. You can elect to amortize the qualifying costs that are not deducted currently over an 84-month period. There is no limit on the amount of your amortization deduction for reforestation costs paid or incurred during the tax year.

If you are otherwise required to file Form T (Timber), Forest Activities Schedule, you can make the election to amortize qualifying reforestation costs by completing Part IV of the form. See the instructions for Form T (Timber) for more information.

See Pub. 535 for more information on amortizing reforestation costs.

Partnerships and S corporations, also see the instructions for line 44.

Optional write-off of certain tax preferences over the period specified in section 59(e). You can elect to amortize certain tax preference items over an optional period. If you make this election, there is no AMT adjustment for these expenditures. The applicable expenditures and the optional recovery periods are as follows:
- Circulation expenditures (section 173) — 3 years,
- Intangible drilling and development costs (section 263(c)) — 60 months, and
- Research and experimental expenditures (section 174(a)), mining exploration and development costs (sections 616(a) and 617(a)) — 10 years.

For information on making the election, see Regulations section 1.59-1. Also see Pub. 535.

Certain section 197 intangibles. The following costs must be amortized over 15 years (180 months) starting with the later of (a) the month the intangibles were acquired or (b) the month the trade or business or activity engaged in for the production of income begins:
- Goodwill;
- Going concern value;
- Workforce in place;
- Business books and records, operating systems, or any other information base;
- A patent, copyright, formula, process, design, pattern, know-how, format, or similar item;
- A customer-based intangible (e.g., composition of market or market share);
- A supplier-based intangible;
- A license, permit, or other right granted by a governmental unit;
- A covenant not to compete entered into in connection with the acquisition of a business; and
- A franchise, trademark, or trade name (including renewals).

A longer period may apply to section 197 intangibles leased under a lease agreement entered into after March 12, 2004, to a tax-exempt organization, governmental unit, or foreign person or entity (other than a partnership). See section 197(f)(10).

 A section 197 intangible is treated as depreciable property used in your trade or business. When you dispose of a section 197 intangible, any gain on the disposition, up to the amount of allowable amortization, is recaptured as ordinary income. If multiple section 197 intangibles are disposed of in a single transaction or a series of related transactions, calculate the recapture as if all of the section 197 intangibles were a single asset. This rule does not apply to section 197 intangibles disposed of for which the adjusted basis exceeds the fair market value.

For more details on section 197 intangibles, see Pub. 535.

Start-up and organizational costs. You can elect to amortize the following costs for setting up your business.
- Business start-up costs (section 195).
- Organizational costs for a corporation (section 248).
- Organizational costs for a partnership (section 709).

For business start-up and organizational costs paid or incurred after September 8, 2008, you can elect to deduct a limited amount of start-up or organizational costs for the year that your business begins. You are not required to attach a statement to make this election. Once made, the election is irrevocable. Any cost not deducted currently must be amortized ratably over a 180-month period. The amortization period starts with the month you begin business operations. See Regulations sections 1.195-1 and 1.248-1.

For business start-up and organizational costs paid or incurred after October 22, 2004, and before September 9, 2008, you can elect to deduct a limited amount of start-up and organizational costs for the year that your business begins. If the election is made, you must attach any statement required by Regulations sections 1.195-1(b) and 1.248-1(c), as in effect before September 9, 2008. Any costs not deducted currently can be amortized ratably over a 180-month period, beginning with the month you begin business.

Note. You can apply the provisions of Regulations sections 1.195-1 and

1.248-1 to all expenses paid or incurred after October 22, 2004, provided the period of limitations on assessment has not expired for the year of the election. Otherwise, for business start-up and organizational costs paid or incurred after October 22, 2004, and before September 9, 2008, the provisions under Regulations sections 1.195-1(b) and 1.248-1(c), as in effect before September 9, 2008, will apply.

For business start-up and organizational costs paid or incurred before October 23, 2004, you can elect an amortization period of 60 months or more.

Attach any statements required by the appropriate section and related regulations to Form 4562 by the due date, including extensions, of your return for the year in which the active trade or business begins. If you have both start-up and organizational costs, attach a separate statement for each type of cost. If you timely filed your return without making the election, you can still make the election on an amended return filed within 6 months of the due date, excluding extensions, of the return. Write "Filed pursuant to section 301.9100-2" on the amended return. See Pub. 535 for more details.

Creative property costs. These are costs paid or incurred to acquire and develop screenplays, scripts, story outlines, motion picture production rights to books and plays, and other similar properties for purposes of potential future film development, production, and exploitation. You may be able to amortize creative property costs for properties not set for production within 3 years of the first capitalized transaction. These costs are amortized ratably over a 15-year period under the rules of Rev. Proc. 2004-36, 2004-24 I.R.B. 1063.

Column (b) — Date amortization begins. Enter the date the amortization period begins under the applicable Code section.

Column (c) — Amortizable amount. Enter the total amount you are amortizing. See the applicable Code section for limits on the amortizable amount.

Column (d) — Code section. Enter the Code section under which you amortize the costs. For examples, see the Code sections referenced in the instructions for line 42, column (a), earlier.

Column (f) — Amortization for this year. Compute the amortization deduction by:

1. Dividing the amount in column (c) by the number of months over which the costs are to be amortized and multiplying the result by the number of months in the amortization period included in your tax year beginning in 2014 or

2. Multiplying the amount in column (c) by the percentage in column (e).

Line 43

If you are reporting the amortization of costs that began before your 2014 tax year and you are not required to file Form 4562 for any other reason, do not file Form 4562. Report the amortization directly on the "Other Deductions" or "Other Expenses" line of your return.

Line 44

Report the total amortization, including the allowable portion of forestation or reforestation amortization, on the applicable "Other Deductions" or "Other Expenses" line of your return. For more details, including limitations that apply, see Pub. 535. Partnerships (other than electing large partnerships) and S corporations, report the amortizable basis of any forestation or reforestation expenses for which amortization is elected and the year in which the amortization begins as a separately stated item on Schedules K and K-1 (Form 1065 or 1120S). See the instructions for Schedule K (Form 1065 or 1120S) for more details on how to report.

Paperwork Reduction Act Notice. We ask for the information on this form to carry out the Internal Revenue laws of the United States. You are required to give us the information. We need it to ensure that you are complying with these laws and to allow us to figure and collect the right amount of tax.

You are not required to provide the information requested on a form that is subject to the Paperwork Reduction Act unless the form displays a valid OMB control number. Books or records relating to a form or its instructions must be retained as long as their contents may become material in the administration of any Internal Revenue law. Generally, tax returns and return information are confidential, as required by section 6103.

The time needed to complete and file this form will vary depending on individual circumstances. The estimated burden for individual taxpayers filing this form is approved under OMB control number 1545-0074 and is included in the estimates shown in the instructions for their individual income tax return. The estimated burden for all other taxpayers who file this form is shown below.

Recordkeeping . . . . 30 hr., 22 min.
Learning about the law or the form. . . . . 4 hr., 16 min.
Preparing and sending the form to the IRS . . . . . 4 hr., 58 min.

If you have comments concerning the accuracy of these time estimates or suggestions for making this form simpler, we would be happy to hear from you. See the instructions for the tax return with which this form is filed.

Table A—General Depreciation System
Method: 200% declining balance switching to straight line
Convention: Half-year

Year	If the recovery period is:			
	3 years	5 years	7 years	10 years
1	33.33%	20.00%	14.29%	10.00%
2	44.45%	32.00%	24.49%	18.00%
3	14.81%	19.20%	17.49%	14.40%
4	7.41%	11.52%	12.49%	11.52%
5		11.52%	8.93%	9.22%
6		5.76%	8.92%	7.37%
7			8.93%	6.55%
8			4.46%	6.55%
9				6.56%
10				6.55%
11				3.28%

Table B—General and Alternative Depreciation System
Method: 150% declining balance switching to straight line
Convention: Half-year

Year	If the recovery period is:					
	5 years	7 years	10 years	12 years	15 years	20 years
1	15.00%	10.71%	7.50%	6.25%	5.00%	3.750%
2	25.50%	19.13%	13.88%	11.72%	9.50%	7.219%
3	17.85%	15.03%	11.79%	10.25%	8.55%	6.677%
4	16.66%	12.25%	10.02%	8.97%	7.70%	6.177%
5	16.66%	12.25%	8.74%	7.85%	6.93%	5.713%
6	8.33%	12.25%	8.74%	7.33%	6.23%	5.285%
7		12.25%	8.74%	7.33%	5.90%	4.888%
8		6.13%	8.74%	7.00%	5.90%	4.522%
9			8.74%	7.33%	5.91%	4.462%
10			8.74%	7.33%	5.90%	4.461%
11			4.37%	7.32%	5.91%	4.462%
12				7.33%	5.90%	4.461%
13				3.66%	5.91%	4.462%
14					5.90%	4.461%
15					5.91%	4.462%
16					2.95%	4.461%
17						4.462%
18						4.461%
19						4.462%
20						4.461%
21						2.231%

Table C—General Depreciation System

Method: Straight line
Convention: Mid-month
Recovery period: 27.5 years

Year	The month in the 1st recovery year the property is placed in service:											
	1	2	3	4	5	6	7	8	9	10	11	12
1	3.485%	3.182%	2.879%	2.576%	2.273%	1.970%	1.667%	1.364%	1.061%	0.758%	0.455%	0.152%
2–9	3.636%	3.636%	3.636%	3.636%	3.636%	3.636%	3.636%	3.636%	3.636%	3.636%	3.636%	3.636%
10,12,14,16,18, 20, 22, 24, 26	3.637%	3.637%	3.637%	3.637%	3.637%	3.637%	3.636%	3.636%	3.636%	3.636%	3.636%	3.636%
11,13,15,17,19, 21, 23, 25, 27	3.636%	3.636%	3.636%	3.636%	3.636%	3.636%	3.637%	3.637%	3.637%	3.637%	3.637%	3.637%
28	1.97%	2.273%	2.576%	2.879%	3.182%	3.485%	3.636%	3.636%	3.636%	3.636%	3.636%	3.636%

Table D—General Depreciation System

Method: Straight line
Convention: Mid-month
Recovery period: 31.5 years

Year	The month in the 1st recovery year the property is placed in service:											
	1	2	3	4	5	6	7	8	9	10	11	12
13,15,17,19, 21, 23, 25, 27, 29, 31	3.174%	3.175%	3.174%	3.175%	3.174%	3.175%	3.174%	3.175%	3.174%	3.175%	3.174%	3.175%
14,16,18, 20, 22, 24, 26, 28, 30	3.175%	3.174%	3.175%	3.174%	3.175%	3.174%	3.175%	3.174%	3.175%	3.174%	3.175%	3.174%
32	1.720%	1.984%	2.249%	2.513%	2.778%	3.042%	3.175%	3.174%	3.175%	3.174%	3.175%	3.174%

Table E—General Depreciation System

Method: Straight line
Convention: Mid-month
Recovery period: 39 years

Year	The month in the 1st recovery year the property is placed in service:											
	1	2	3	4	5	6	7	8	9	10	11	12
1	2.461%	2.247%	2.033%	1.819%	1.605%	1.391%	1.177%	0.963%	0.749%	0.535%	0.321%	0.107%
2–39	2.564%	2.564%	2.564%	2.564%	2.564%	2.564%	2.564%	2.564%	2.564%	2.564%	2.564%	2.564%
40	0.107%	0.321%	0.535%	0.749%	0.963%	1.177%	1.391%	1.605%	1.819%	2.033%	2.247%	2.461%

Depreciation Worksheet (Keep for your records.)

Description of Property	Date Placed in Service	Cost or Other Basis	Business/ Investment Use %	Section 179 Deduction and Special Allowance	Depreciation Prior Years	Basis for Depreciation	Method/ Convention	Recovery Period	Rate or Table %	Depreciation Deduction

Index

Form **4626**	**Alternative Minimum Tax—Corporations**	OMB No. 1545-0123
Department of the Treasury Internal Revenue Service	▶ Attach to the corporation's tax return. ▶ Information about Form 4626 and its separate instructions is at *www.irs.gov/form4626.*	2014

Name	Employer identification number

Note: *See the instructions to find out if the corporation is a small corporation exempt from the alternative minimum tax (AMT) under section 55(e).*

1 Taxable income or (loss) before net operating loss deduction . . . . | **1** |

2 **Adjustments and preferences:**

a Depreciation of post-1986 property . . . . | **2a** |
b Amortization of certified pollution control facilities. . . . . | **2b** |
c Amortization of mining exploration and development costs . . . . | **2c** |
d Amortization of circulation expenditures (personal holding companies only) . . . . . . | **2d** |
e Adjusted gain or loss . . . . | **2e** |
f Long-term contracts . . . . | **2f** |
g Merchant marine capital construction funds. . . . . | **2g** |
h Section 833(b) deduction (Blue Cross, Blue Shield, and similar type organizations only) . . . . | **2h** |
i Tax shelter farm activities (personal service corporations only) . . . . | **2i** |
j Passive activities (closely held corporations and personal service corporations only) . . . . . | **2j** |
k Loss limitations . . . . | **2k** |
l Depletion . . . . | **2l** |
m Tax-exempt interest income from specified private activity bonds . . . . | **2m** |
n Intangible drilling costs . . . . | **2n** |
o Other adjustments and preferences . . . . | **2o** |
3 Pre-adjustment alternative minimum taxable income (AMTI). Combine lines 1 through 2o. . . . . | **3** |

4 **Adjusted current earnings (ACE) adjustment:**

a ACE from line 10 of the ACE worksheet in the instructions . . . . | **4a** |
b Subtract line 3 from line 4a. If line 3 exceeds line 4a, enter the difference as a negative amount (see instructions) . . . . | **4b** |
c Multiply line 4b by 75% (.75). Enter the result as a positive amount . . . . . | **4c** |
d Enter the excess, if any, of the corporation's total increases in AMTI from prior year ACE adjustments over its total reductions in AMTI from prior year ACE adjustments (see instructions). **Note:** *You **must** enter an amount on line 4d (even if line 4b is positive).* | **4d** |
e ACE adjustment.
• If line 4b is zero or more, enter the amount from line 4c
• If line 4b is less than zero, enter the **smaller** of line 4c or line 4d as a negative amount | **4e** |
5 Combine lines 3 and 4e. If zero or less, stop here; the corporation does not owe any AMT . . . . | **5** |
6 Alternative tax net operating loss deduction (see instructions). . . . . | **6** |

7 **Alternative minimum taxable income.** Subtract line 6 from line 5. If the corporation held a residual interest in a REMIC, see instructions . . . . | **7** |

8 **Exemption phase-out** (if line 7 is $310,000 or more, skip lines 8a and 8b and enter -0- on line 8c):

a Subtract $150,000 from line 7 (if completing this line for a member of a controlled group, see instructions). If zero or less, enter -0- . . . . | **8a** |
b Multiply line 8a by 25% (.25). . . . . | **8b** |
c Exemption. Subtract line 8b from $40,000 (if completing this line for a member of a controlled group, see instructions). If zero or less, enter -0- . . . . | **8c** |
9 Subtract line 8c from line 7. If zero or less, enter -0- . . . . | **9** |
10 Multiply line 9 by 20% (.20) . . . . | **10** |
11 Alternative minimum tax foreign tax credit (AMTFTC) (see instructions) . . . . | **11** |
12 Tentative minimum tax. Subtract line 11 from line 10 . . . . | **12** |
13 Regular tax liability before applying all credits except the foreign tax credit . . . . | **13** |
14 **Alternative minimum tax.** Subtract line 13 from line 12. If zero or less, enter -0-. Enter here and on Form 1120, Schedule J, line 3, or the appropriate line of the corporation's income tax return . . . | **14** |

For Paperwork Reduction Act Notice, see separate instructions.   Cat. No. 12955I   Form **4626** (2014)

Department of the Treasury
Internal Revenue Service

Instructions for Form 4626

Alternative Minimum Tax—Corporations

Section references are to the Internal Revenue Code unless otherwise noted.

Future Developments

For the latest information about developments to Form 4626 and its instructions, such as legislation enacted after they were published, go to *www.irs.gov/form4626*.

General Instructions

Purpose of Form

Use Form 4626 to figure the alternative minimum tax (AMT) under section 55 for a corporation that is not exempt from the AMT.

Consolidated returns. For an affiliated group filing a consolidated return under the rules of section 1501, AMT must be figured on a consolidated basis.

Who Must File

Generally, file Form 4626 if any of the following apply.
• The corporation is not a "small corporation" exempt from the AMT (as explained below).
• The corporation's taxable income or (loss) before the net operating loss (NOL) deduction plus its adjustments and preferences total more than $40,000 or, if smaller, its allowable exemption amount.
• The corporation claims any general business credit, any qualified electric vehicle passive activity credit from prior years, or the credit for prior year minimum tax.

Exemption for Small Corporations

A corporation is treated as a small corporation exempt from the AMT for its current tax year:

1. The current year is the corporation's first tax year in existence (regardless of its gross receipts for the year), or

2. Both of the following apply.

a. It was treated as a small corporation exempt from the AMT for all prior tax years beginning after 1997.

b. Its average annual gross receipts for all 3-tax-year periods (or portions thereof during which the corporation was in existence) ending before its current tax year did not exceed $7.5 million ($5 million for the corporation's first 3-tax-year period. See section 55(e)).

The following rules apply when figuring gross receipts under 2b above.
• Gross receipts must be figured using the corporation's tax accounting method and include total sales (net of returns and allowances), amounts received for services, and income from investments and other sources. See Temporary Regulations section 1.448-1T(f)(2)(iv) for more details.
• Gross receipts include those of any predecessor of the corporation, including non-corporate entities.
• For a short tax year, gross receipts must be annualized by multiplying them by 12 and dividing the result by the number of months in the tax year.
• The gross receipts of all persons treated as a single employer under section 52(a), 52(b), 414(m), or 414(o) must be aggregated.

Loss of small corporation status. If the corporation qualified as a small corporation exempt from the AMT for its previous tax year, but does not meet the gross receipts test for its current tax year, it loses its AMT exemption status. Special rules apply in figuring AMT for the tax year beginning on the "change date." The change date is the first day of the corporation's tax year for which the corporation ceased to be a small corporation. Where this applies, complete Form 4626 taking into account the following modifications.
• The adjustments for depreciation and amortization of pollution control facilities apply only to property placed in service on or after the change date.
• The adjustment for mining exploration and development costs applies only to amounts paid or incurred on or after the change date.
• The adjustment for long-term contracts applies only to contracts entered into on or after the change date.
• When figuring the amount to enter on line 6, for any loss year beginning

before the change date, use the corporation's regular tax NOL for that year.
• Figure the limitation on line 4d only for prior tax years beginning on or after the change date.
• Enter zero on line 2c of the Adjusted Current Earnings (ACE) Worksheet. When completing line 5 of the ACE Worksheet, take into account only amounts from tax years beginning on or after the change date. Also, for line 8 of the ACE Worksheet, take into account only property placed in service on or after the change date.

Note. No additional modification in figuring AMT is required for exceptions related to any item acquired in a corporate acquisition under section 381 or to any substituted basis property, if any of the AMT adjustment modifications listed earlier applied to the item or property while it was held by the transferor.

 Once the corporation loses its small corporation status, it **CAUTION** *cannot qualify for any subsequent tax year.*

Credit for Prior Year Minimum Tax

A corporation may be able to take a minimum tax credit against the regular tax for AMT incurred in prior years. See Form 8827, Credit for Prior Year Minimum Tax—Corporations, for details.

Recordkeeping

Certain items of income, deductions, credits, etc., receive different tax treatment for the AMT than for the regular tax. Therefore, the corporation should keep adequate records to support items refigured for the AMT. Examples include:
• Tax forms used for regular tax purposes that are completed a second time to refigure items of income, deductions, etc., for the AMT;
• The computation of a carryback or carryforward to other tax years of certain deductions or credits (for example, net operating loss, capital

loss, and foreign tax credit) if the AMT amount is different from the regular tax amount;

• The computation of a carryforward of a passive loss or tax shelter farm activity loss if the AMT amount is different from the regular tax amount; and

• A "running balance" of the excess of the corporation's total increases in alternative minimum taxable income (AMTI) from prior year adjusted current earnings (ACE) adjustments over the total reductions in AMTI from prior year ACE adjustments (see the instructions for line 4d).

Short Period Return

If the corporation is filing for a period of less than 12 months, AMTI must be annualized and the tentative minimum tax prorated based on the number of months in the short period. Complete Form 4626 as follows.

1. Complete lines 1 through 6 in the normal manner. Subtract line 6 from line 5 to figure AMTI for the short period, but do not enter it on line 7.

2. Multiply AMTI for the short period by 12. Divide the result by the number of months in the short period. Enter this result on line 7 and write "Sec. 443(d)(1)" on the dotted line to the left of the entry space.

3. Complete lines 8 through 11.

4. Subtract line 11 from line 10. Multiply the result by the number of months in the short period and divide that result by 12. Enter the final result on line 12 and write "Sec. 443(d)(2)" on the dotted line to the left of the entry space.

5. Complete the rest of the form in the normal manner.

Allocating Differently Treated Items Between Certain Entities and Their Investors

For a regulated investment company, a real estate investment trust, or a common trust fund, see section 59(d) for details on allocating certain differently treated items between the entity and its investors.

Optional Write-Off for Certain Expenditures

There is no AMT adjustment for the following items if the corporation elects to deduct them ratably over the period of time shown for the regular tax.

• Circulation expenditures (personal holding companies only)—3 years.

• Mining exploration and development costs—10 years.

• Intangible drilling costs—60 months.

See section 59(e) for more details.

Specific Instructions

Line 1. Taxable Income or (Loss) Before Net Operating Loss Deduction

Enter the corporation's taxable income or (loss) before the NOL deduction, after the special deductions, and without regard to any excess inclusion (for example, if filing Form 1120, subtract line 29b from line 28 of that form).

Line 2. Adjustments and Preferences

 To avoid duplication, do not include any AMT adjustment or preference taken into account on line 2i, 2j, 2k, or 2o in the amounts to be entered on any other line of this form.

Line 2a. Depreciation of Post-1986 Property

What Adjustments Are Not Included As Depreciation Adjustments?

Do not make a depreciation adjustment on line 2a for:

• A tax shelter farm activity. Take this adjustment into account on line 2i.

• Passive activities. Take this adjustment into account on line 2j.

• An activity for which the corporation is not at risk, or income or loss from a partnership interest, or stock in an S corporation if the basis limitations apply. Take this adjustment into account on line 2k.

What Depreciation Must Be Refigured for the AMT?

Generally, the corporation must refigure depreciation for the AMT, including depreciation allocable to inventory costs, for the following.

• Property placed in service after 1998 depreciated for the regular tax using the 200% declining balance method (generally 3-, 5-, 7-, or 10-year property under the modified accelerated cost recovery system (MACRS)), except for qualified property eligible for the special depreciation allowance.

• Section 1250 property placed in service after 1998 that is not depreciated for the regular tax using the straight line method.

• Tangible property placed in service after 1986 and before 1999. (If the transitional election was made under section 203(a)(1)(B) of the Tax Reform Act of 1986, this rule applies to property placed in service after July 31, 1986.)

What Depreciation Is Not Refigured for the AMT?

Do not refigure depreciation for the AMT for the following.

• Residential rental property placed in service after 1998.

• Nonresidential real property with a class life of 27.5 years or more (generally, a building and its structural components) placed in service after 1998 that is depreciated for the regular tax using the straight line method.

• Other section 1250 property placed in service after 1998 that is depreciated for the regular tax using the straight line method.

• Property (other than section 1250 property) placed in service after 1998 that is depreciated for the regular tax using the 150% declining balance method or the straight line method.

• Property for which the corporation elected to use the alternative depreciation system (ADS) for the regular tax.

• Any qualified property eligible for a special depreciation allowance if the depreciable basis of the property for the AMT is the same as for the regular tax. In addition, no adjustment is required for any depreciation figured on the remaining basis of the qualified property. However, if an election is in effect to not have the special allowance apply, the corporation must refigure depreciation for the AMT.

• Any part of the cost of any property that the corporation elected to expense under section 179. The reduction to the depreciable basis of section 179 property by the amount of the section 179 expense deduction is the same for the regular tax and the AMT.

• Certain public utility property (if a normalization method of accounting is not used), motion picture films and video tape, sound recordings, and property that the corporation elects to exclude from MACRS by using a depreciation method that is not based on a term of years, such as the unit-of-production method.

• Any qualified Indian reservation property. See section 168(j)(3).

• Any natural gas gathering line (as defined in section 168(i)(17)) placed in service after April 11, 2005, the original use of which begins with the corporation

-2-

after April 11, 2005, and which is not under self-construction or subject to a binding contract in existence before April 12, 2005.

How Is Depreciation Refigured for the AMT?

Property placed in service after 1998. Use the same convention and recovery period used for the regular tax. Use the straight line method for section 1250 property. For property other than section 1250 property, use the 150% declining balance method, switching to the straight line method the first tax year it gives a larger deduction.

Property placed in service before 1999. Refigure depreciation for the AMT using ADS, with the same convention used for the regular tax. See the table below for the method and recovery period to use.

Property Placed in Service Before 1999

IF the property is . .	THEN use the. . . . .
Section 1250 property.	Straight line method over 40 years.
Tangible property (other than section 1250 property) depreciated using the straight line method for the regular tax.	Straight line method over the property's AMT class life.
Any other tangible property.	150% declining balance method, switching to the straight line method the first tax year it gives a larger deduction, over the property's AMT class life.

How is the AMT class life determined? For property placed in service before 1999, the class life used for the AMT is not necessarily the same as the recovery period used for the regular tax.

The class lives are listed in Rev. Proc. 87-56, 1987-2 C.B. 674, Rev. Proc. 88-22, 1988-1 C.B. 785, and in Pub. 946, How To Depreciate Property.

 See Pub. 946 for tables that can be used to figure AMT depreciation. Rev. Proc. 89-15, 1989-1 C.B. 816, and Pub. 946 have special rules for short tax years and for property disposed of before the end of the recovery period.

How Is the Line 2a Adjustment Figured?

Subtract the AMT deduction for depreciation from the regular tax deduction and enter the result on line 2a. If the AMT deduction is more than the regular tax deduction, enter the difference as a negative amount.

In addition to the AMT adjustment to the deduction for depreciation, also adjust the amount of depreciation that was capitalized, if any, to account for the difference between the rules for the regular tax and the AMT. Include on this line the current year adjustment to taxable income, if any, resulting from the difference.

Line 2b. Amortization of Certified Pollution Control Facilities

For facilities placed in service before 1999, figure the amortization deduction for the AMT using ADS (that is, the straight line method over the facility's class life). For facilities placed in service after 1998, figure the amortization deduction for the AMT under MACRS using the straight line method. Figure the AMT deduction using 100% of the asset's amortizable basis. Do not reduce the corporation's AMT basis by the 20% section 291 adjustment that applied for the regular tax.

Enter the difference between the AMT deduction and the regular tax deduction on line 2b. If the AMT deduction is more than the regular tax deduction, enter the difference as a negative amount.

Line 2c. Amortization of Mining Exploration and Development Costs

 Do not make this adjustment for costs for which the corporation elected the optional 10-year write-off for the regular tax.

For the AMT, the regular tax deductions under sections 616(a) and 617(a) are not allowed. Instead, capitalize these costs and amortize them ratably over a 10-year period beginning with the tax year in which the corporation paid or incurred them. The 10-year amortization applies to 100% of the mining development and exploration costs paid or incurred during the tax year. Do not reduce the corporation's AMT basis by the 30% section 291 adjustment that applied for the regular tax.

If the corporation had a loss on property for which mining exploration and development costs have not been fully amortized for the AMT, the AMT deduction is the smaller of (a) the loss allowable for the costs had they remained capitalized or (b) the remaining costs to be amortized for the AMT.

Subtract the AMT deduction from the regular tax deduction. Enter the result on line 2c. If the AMT deduction is more than the regular tax deduction, enter the difference as a negative amount.

Line 2d. Amortization of Circulation Expenditures

 Complete this line only if the corporation is a personal holding company. Do not make this adjustment for expenditures of a personal holding company for which the company elected the optional 3-year write-off for the regular tax.

For the regular tax, circulation expenditures may be deducted in full when paid or incurred. For the AMT, these expenditures must be capitalized and amortized over 3 years beginning with the tax year in which the expenditures were made.

If the corporation had a loss on property for which circulation expenditures have not been fully amortized for the AMT, the AMT deduction is the smaller of (a) the loss allowable for the expenditures had they remained capitalized or (b) the remaining expenditures to be amortized for the AMT.

Subtract the AMT deduction from the regular tax deduction. Enter the result on line 2d. If the AMT deduction is more than the regular tax deduction, enter the difference as a negative amount.

Line 2e. Adjusted Gain or Loss

If, during the tax year, the corporation disposed of property for which it is making (or previously made) any of the adjustments described on lines 2a through 2d above, refigure the property's adjusted basis for the AMT. Then refigure the gain or loss on the disposition.

The property's adjusted basis for the AMT is its cost minus all applicable depreciation or amortization deductions allowed for the AMT during the current tax year and previous tax years. Subtract this AMT basis from the sales price to get the AMT gain or loss.

Dispositions for which line 2i, 2j, and 2k adjustments are made. The corporation may also have gains or losses from lines 2i, 2j, and 2k that must be considered on line 2e. For example, if for the regular tax the corporation reports a loss from the disposition of an asset used in a passive activity, include the loss in the computations for line 2j to determine if any passive activity loss is limited for the AMT. Then, include the AMT passive activity loss allowed that relates to the disposition of the asset on line 2e in determining the corporation's AMT basis adjustment. It may be helpful to refigure the following for the AMT: Form 8810, Corporate Passive Activity Loss and Credit Limitations, and related worksheets, Schedule D (Form 1120), Capital Gains and Losses, Section B of Form 4684, Casualties and Thefts, or Form 4797, Sale of Business Property.

Enter on line 2e the difference between the regular tax gain or loss and the AMT gain or loss. Enter the difference as a negative amount if any of the following apply.
• The AMT gain is less than the regular tax gain.
• The AMT loss exceeds the regular tax loss.
• The corporation has an AMT loss and a regular tax gain.

Line 2f. Long-Term Contracts

For the AMT, the corporation generally must use the percentage-of-completion method described in section 460(b) to determine the taxable income from any long-term contract (defined in section 460(f)). However, this rule does not apply to any home construction contract (as defined in section 460(e)(6)).

For contracts excepted from the percentage-of-completion method for the regular tax by section 460(e)(1), determine the percentage of completion using the simplified procedures for allocating costs outlined in section 460(b)(3).

Subtract the regular tax income from the AMT income. Enter the difference on line 2f. If the AMT income is less than the regular tax income, enter the difference as a negative amount.

Line 2g. Merchant Marine Capital Construction Funds

Amounts deposited in these funds are not deductible for the AMT. Earnings on these funds must be included in gross income for the AMT. If the corporation deducted these amounts or excluded them from income for the regular tax, add them back on line 2g.

Line 2h. Section 833(b) Deduction

This deduction is not allowed for the AMT. If the corporation took this deduction for the regular tax, add it back on line 2h.

Line 2i. Tax Shelter Farm Activities

 Complete this line only if the corporation is a personal service corporation and it has a gain or loss from a tax shelter farm activity that is not a passive activity. If the tax shelter farm activity is a passive activity, include the gain or loss in the computations for line 2j.

Refigure all gains and losses reported for the regular tax from tax shelter farm activities by taking into account any AMT adjustments and preferences. Determine the AMT gain or loss using the rules for the regular tax with the following modifications.
• No loss is allowed except to the extent the personal service corporation is insolvent.
• Do not use a loss in the current tax year to offset gains from other tax shelter farm activities. Instead, suspend any loss and carry it forward indefinitely until the corporation has a gain in a subsequent tax year from that same tax shelter farm activity or it disposes of the activity.

 Keep adequate records for losses that are not deductible (and therefore carried forward) for both the AMT and regular tax.

Enter on line 2i the difference between the AMT gain or loss and the regular tax gain or loss. Enter the difference as a negative amount if the corporation had:
• An AMT loss and a regular tax gain,
• An AMT loss that exceeds the regular tax loss, or
• A regular tax gain that exceeds the AMT gain.

Line 2j. Passive Activities

 This adjustment applies only to closely held corporations and personal service corporations.

Refigure all passive activity gains and losses reported for the regular tax by taking into account the corporation's AMT adjustments and preferences and AMT prior year unallowed losses that apply to that activity.

Determine the corporation's AMT passive activity gain or loss using the same rules used for the regular tax. Generally, no loss is allowed. However, if the corporation is insolvent, special rules apply. See section 58(c).

Disallowed losses of a personal service corporation are suspended until the corporation has income from that (or any other) passive activity or until the passive activity is disposed of (that is, its passive losses cannot offset "net active income" (defined in section 469(e)(2)(B) or "portfolio income")). Disallowed losses of a closely held corporation that is not a personal service corporation are treated the same except that, in addition, they may be used to offset "net active income."

 Keep adequate records for losses that are not deductible (and therefore carried forward) for both the AMT and regular tax.

Enter on line 2j the difference between the AMT gain or loss and the regular tax gain or loss. Enter the difference as a negative amount if the corporation had:
• An AMT loss and a regular tax gain,
• An AMT loss that exceeds the regular tax loss, or
• A regular tax gain that exceeds the AMT gain.

Tax Shelter Farm Activities That Are Passive Activities

Refigure all gains and losses reported for the regular tax by taking into account the corporation's AMT adjustments and preferences and AMT prior year unallowed losses.

Use the same rules as outlined above for other passive activities, with the following modifications.
• AMT gains from tax shelter farm activities that are passive activities may be used to offset AMT losses from other passive activities.
• AMT losses from tax shelter farm activities that are passive activities may not be used to offset AMT gains from other passive activities. These losses must be suspended and carried forward indefinitely until the corporation has a gain in a subsequent year from that same activity or it disposes of the activity.

Line 2k. Loss Limitations

Refigure gains and losses reported for the regular tax from at-risk activities and the corporation's share of distributive items from partnerships by taking into account the corporation's AMT adjustments and preferences. If the corporation has recomputed losses that must be limited for the AMT by section 465 or section 704(d) or the corporation reported losses for the regular tax from at-risk activities or distributive shares of partnership losses that were limited by those sections, figure the difference between the loss limited for the AMT and the loss limited for the regular tax for each applicable at-risk activity or distributive share of partnership loss. "Loss limited" means the amount of loss that is not allowable for the year because of the limitations above.

Enter on line 2k the excess of the loss limited for the AMT over the loss limited for the regular tax. If the loss limited for the regular tax is more than the loss limited for the AMT, enter the difference as a negative amount.

Line 2l. Depletion

Refigure depletion using only income and deductions allowed for the AMT when refiguring the limit based on taxable income from the property under section 613(a) and the limit based on taxable income, with certain adjustments, under section 613A(d)(1). Also, the depletion deduction for mines, wells, and other natural deposits is limited to the property's adjusted basis at the end of the year, as refigured for the AMT, unless the corporation is an independent producer or royalty owner claiming percentage depletion for oil and gas wells. Figure this limit separately for each property. When refiguring the property's adjusted basis, take into account any AMT adjustments the corporation made this year or in previous years that affect basis (other than the current year's depletion). Do not include in the property's adjusted basis any unrecovered costs of depreciable tangible property used to exploit the deposits (for example, machinery, tools, pipes, etc.).

For iron ore and coal (including lignite), apply the section 291 adjustment before figuring this preference.

Enter on line 2l the difference between the regular tax and the AMT deduction. If the AMT deduction is more than the regular tax deduction, enter the difference as a negative amount.

Line 2m. Tax-Exempt Interest Income From Specified Private Activity Bonds

Enter on line 2m interest income from specified private activity bonds, reduced by any deduction that would have been allowable if the interest were includible in gross income for the regular tax.

Generally, a specified private activity bond is any private activity bond (as defined in section 141) issued after August 7, 1986, on which the interest is not includible in gross income for the regular tax. Specified private activity bonds do not include:
• Qualified 501(c)(3) bonds;
• Certain housing bonds issued after July 30, 2008; and
• Bonds issued in 2009 and 2010. See section 57(a)(5)(C) for more information and other exceptions.

Do not include interest on qualified Gulf Opportunity Zone bonds or qualified Midwestern disaster area bonds.

Line 2n. Intangible Drilling Costs

 Do not make this adjustment for costs for which the corporation elected the optional 60-month write-off for the regular tax.

Intangible drilling costs (IDCs) from oil, gas, and geothermal properties are a preference to the extent excess IDCs exceed 65% of the net income from the properties. Figure the preference for all geothermal deposits separately from the preference for all oil and gas properties that are not geothermal deposits.

Excess IDCs. Excess IDCs are the excess of:
• The amount of IDCs the corporation paid or incurred for oil, gas, or geothermal properties that it elected to expense for the regular tax (not including any IDCs paid or incurred for nonproductive wells) reduced by the section 291(b)(1) adjustment for integrated oil companies and increased by any IDCs allowed to be amortized under section 291(b)(2) over
• The amount that would have been allowed if the corporation had amortized that amount over a 120-month period starting with the month the well was placed in production or, alternatively, had elected any method that is permissible in determining cost depletion.

Net income from oil, gas, and geothermal properties. Net income is the gross income the corporation received or accrued from all oil, gas, and geothermal wells minus the deductions allocable to these properties (reduced by the excess IDCs). When refiguring net income, use only income and deductions allowed for the AMT.

Exception. The preference for IDCs from oil and gas wells does not apply to corporations that are independent producers (that is, not integrated oil companies as defined in section 291(b)(4)). However, this benefit may be limited. First, figure the IDC preference as if this exception did not apply. Then, for purposes of this exception, complete a second Form 4626 through line 5, including the IDC preference. If the amount of the IDC preference exceeds 40% of the amount figured for line 5, enter the excess on line 2n (the benefit of this exception is limited). If the amount of the IDC preference is equal to or less than 40% of the amount figured for line 5, do not include an amount on line 2n for oil and gas wells (the benefit of this exception is not limited).

Line 2o. Other Adjustments And Preferences

Enter the net amount of any other adjustments and preferences, including the following.

Income eligible for the American Samoa economic development credit. If this income was included in the corporation's taxable income for the regular tax, include this amount on line 2o as a negative amount.

Income from the biofuel producer, biodiesel, and renewable diesel fuels credits. If this income was included in the corporation's income for the regular tax, include this amount on line 2o as a negative amount.

Income as the beneficiary of an estate or trust. If the corporation is the beneficiary of an estate or trust, include on line 2o the AMT adjustment from Schedule K-1 (Form 1041), Part III, box 12.

Net AMT adjustment from an electing large partnership. If the corporation is a partner in an electing large partnership, include on line 2o the amount from Schedule K-1 (Form 1065-B), box 6. Also include on line 2o any amount from Schedule K-1 (Form 1065-B), box 5, unless the corporation is a closely held or personal service corporation. Closely held and personal service corporations should take any amount from box 5 into account when figuring the amount to enter on line 2j.

Patron's AMT adjustment. Distributions the corporation received from a cooperative may be includible in income. Unless the distributions are nontaxable, include on line 2o the total AMT patronage dividend adjustment reported to the corporation from the cooperative.

Cooperative's AMT adjustment. If the corporation is a cooperative, refigure the cooperative's deduction for patronage dividends by taking into account the cooperative's AMT adjustments and preferences. Subtract the cooperative's AMT deduction for patronage dividends from its regular tax deduction for patronage dividends and include the result on line 2o. If the AMT deduction is more than the regular tax deduction, include the result as a negative amount.

Domestic production activities deduction. For the AMT, figure the corporation's domestic production activities deduction under section 199 without taking into account any AMT adjustments and preferences. The section 199 deduction for the corporation's AMT is 9% of the smaller of (a) the qualified production activities income or (b) the alternative minimum taxable income (AMTI), determined without taking into account the section 199 deduction. Subtract the corporation's AMT section 199 deduction from its regular tax section 199 deduction and include the result on line 2o. If the AMT deduction is more than the regular tax deduction, include the result as a negative amount.

Installment sales. The installment method does not apply for the AMT to any nondealer disposition of property that occurred after August 16, 1986, but before the first day of the corporation's tax year that began in 1987, if an installment obligation to which the proportionate disallowance rule applied arose from the disposition. Include as a negative adjustment on line 2o the amount of installment sale income reported for the regular tax.

Accelerated depreciation of real property and certain leased personal property (pre-1987). Refigure depreciation for the AMT using the straight line method for real property for which accelerated depreciation was determined for the regular tax using pre-1987 rules. Use a recovery period of 19 years for 19-year real property and 15 years for low-income housing property. Figure the excess of the regular tax depreciation over the AMT depreciation separately for each property and include only positive adjustments on line 2o.

The adjustment for leased personal property only applies to personal holding companies. For leased personal

property other than recovery property, enter the excess of the depreciation claimed for the property for the regular tax using pre-1987 rules over the depreciation allowable for the AMT as refigured using the straight line method.

For leased 10-year recovery property and leased 15-year public utility property, enter the excess of the regular tax depreciation over the depreciation allowable using the straight line method with a half-year convention, no salvage value, and a recovery period of 15 years (22 years for 15-year public utility property).

Figure this amount separately for each property and include only positive adjustments on line 2o.

 This preference generally applies only to property placed in service after 1987, but depreciated using pre-1987 rules due to transition provisions of the Tax Reform Act of 1986.

Related adjustments. AMT adjustments and preferences may affect deductions that are based on an income limit (for example, charitable contributions). Refigure these deductions using the income limit as modified for the AMT. Include on line 2o an adjustment for the difference between the regular tax and AMT amounts for all such deductions. If the AMT deduction is more than the regular tax deduction, include the difference as a negative amount.

Line 4. Adjusted Current Earnings (ACE) Adjustment

 The ACE adjustment does not apply to a regulated investment company or a real estate investment trust. Also, for an affiliated group filing a consolidated return under the rules of section 1501, figure line 4b on a consolidated basis.

Line 4b. The following examples illustrate the manner in which line 3 is subtracted from line 4a to get the amount to enter on line 4b.

Example 1. Corporation A has line 4a ACE of $25,000. If Corporation A has line 3 pre-adjustment AMTI in the amounts shown below, its line 3 and line 4a amounts would be combined as follows to determine the amount to enter on line 4b.

Line 4a ACE	$25,000	$25,000	$25,000
Line 3 pre-adj. AMTI	10,000	30,000	(50,000)
Amount to enter on line 4b	$15,000	$(5,000)	$75,000

Example 2. Corporation B has line 4a ACE of $(25,000). If Corporation B has line 3 pre-adjustment AMTI in the amounts shown below, its line 3 and line 4a amounts would be combined as follows to determine the amount to enter on line 4b.

Line 4a ACE	$(25,000)	$(25,000)	$(25,000)
Line 3 pre-adj. AMTI	(10,000)	(30,000)	50,000
Amount to enter on line 4b	$(15,000)	$5,000	$(75,000)

Line 4d. A potential negative ACE adjustment (that is, a negative amount on line 4b multiplied by 75%) is allowed as a negative ACE adjustment on line 4e only if the corporation's total increases in AMTI from prior year ACE adjustments exceed its total reductions in AMTI from prior year ACE adjustments (line 4d). The purpose of line 4d is to provide a "running balance" of this limitation amount. As such, the corporation must keep adequate records (for example, a copy of Form 4626 completed at least through line 5) from year to year (even in years in which it does not owe any AMT).

Any potential negative ACE adjustment that is not allowed as a negative ACE adjustment in a tax year because of the line 4d limitation cannot be used to reduce a positive ACE adjustment in any other tax year. Combine lines 4d and 4e of the 2013 Form 4626 and enter the result on line 4d of the 2014 form, but do not enter less than zero.

Example. Corporation C, a calendar-year corporation, was incorporated January 1, 2010. Its ACE and pre-adjustment AMTI for 2010 through 2014 were as follows.

Year	ACE Line 4a	Pre-adjustment AMTI Line 3
2010	$700,000	$800,000
2011	900,000	600,000
2012	400,000	500,000
2013	(100,000)	300,000
2014	250,000	100,000

Corporation C subtracts its pre-adjustment AMTI from its ACE in each of the years and then multiplies the result by 75% to get the following potential ACE adjustments for 2010 through 2014.

Year	ACE minus pre-adjustment AMTI Line 4b	Potential ACE adjustment Line 4c
2010	$(100,000)	$ (75,000)
2011	300,000	225,000
2012	(100,000)	(75,000)
2013	(400,000)	(300,000)
2014	150,000	112,500

Under these facts, Corporation C has the following increases or reductions in AMTI for 2010 through 2014.

Year	Increase or (reduction) in AMTI from ACE adjustment Line 4e
2010	$0
2011	225,000
2012	(75,000)
2013	(150,000)
2014	112,500

In 2010, Corporation C was not allowed to reduce its AMTI by any part of the potential negative ACE adjustment because it had no increases in AMTI from prior year ACE adjustments.

In 2011, Corporation C had to increase its AMTI by the full amount of its potential ACE adjustment. It was not allowed to use any part of its 2010 unallowed potential negative ACE adjustment of $75,000 to reduce its 2011 positive ACE adjustment of $225,000.

In 2012, Corporation C was allowed to reduce its AMTI by the full amount of its potential negative ACE adjustment because that amount is less than its line 4d limit of $225,000.

In 2013, Corporation C was allowed to reduce its AMTI by only $150,000. Its potential negative ACE adjustment of $300,000 was limited to its 2011 increase in AMTI of $225,000 minus its 2012 reduction in AMTI of $75,000.

In 2014, Corporation C must increase its AMTI by the full amount of its potential ACE adjustment. It cannot use any part of its 2013 unallowed potential negative ACE adjustment of $150,000 to reduce its 2014 positive ACE adjustment of $112,500. Corporation C would complete the relevant portion of its 2014 Form 4626 as follows.

Line	Amount
4a	$250,000
4b	150,000
4c	112,500
4d	-0-
4e	112,500

Line 6. Alternative Tax Net Operating Loss Deduction (ATNOLD)

The ATNOLD is the sum of the alternative tax net operating loss (ATNOL) carrybacks and carryforwards to the tax year, subject to the limitation explained below. For a corporation that held a residual interest in a real estate mortgage investment conduit (REMIC), figure the ATNOLD without regard to any excess inclusion.

The ATNOL for a loss year is the excess of the deductions allowed in figuring AMTI (excluding the ATNOLD) over the income included in AMTI. This excess is figured with the modifications in section 172(d), taking into account the adjustments in sections 56 and 58 and preferences in section 57 (that is, the section 172(d) modifications must be separately figured for the ATNOL).

In applying the rules relating to the determination of the amount of carrybacks and carryforwards, use the modification to those rules described in section 56(d)(1)(B)(ii).

The ATNOLD is generally limited to 90% of AMTI determined without regard to the ATNOLD and any domestic production activities deduction under section 199. To figure AMTI without regard to the ATNOLD, use a second Form 4626 as a worksheet. Complete the second Form 4626 through line 5, but when figuring lines 2l and 2o, treat line 6 as if it were zero. The amount figured on line 5 of the second Form 4626 is the corporation's AMTI determined without regard to the ATNOLD. Add any domestic production activities deduction to this tentative total. The ATNOLD limitation is 90% of this amount.

However, if an ATNOL carried back or carried forward to the tax year is attributable to qualified disaster losses (as defined in section 172(j)), qualified Gulf Opportunity Zone losses (as defined in section 1400N(k)(2)), qualified recovery assistance losses (as defined in Pub. 4492-A, Information for Taxpayers Affected by the May 4, 2007 Kansas Storms and Tornadoes), qualified disaster recovery assistance losses (as defined in Pub. 4492-B, Information for Affected Taxpayers in the Midwestern Disaster Area), or an applicable 2008 or 2009 NOL for which the corporation elected a 3, 4, or 5-year carryback period (under section 172(b)(1)(H)), the ATNOLD for the tax year is limited to the sum of:

1. The smaller of:

a. The sum of the ATNOL carrybacks and carryforwards to the tax year attributable to net operating losses other than qualified disaster losses, qualified Gulf Opportunity Zone losses, qualified recovery assistance losses, qualified disaster recovery assistance losses, and applicable 2008 and 2009 NOLs for which the corporation made the election under section 172(b)(1)(H); or

b. 90% of AMTI for the tax year (figured without regard to the ATNOLD, as discussed earlier, and the domestic production activities deduction under section 199) plus

2. The smaller of:

a. The sum of the ATNOL carrybacks and carryforwards to the tax year attributable to qualified disaster losses, qualified Gulf Opportunity Zone losses, qualified recovery assistance losses, qualified disaster recovery assistance losses, and applicable 2008 and 2009 NOLs for which the corporation made the election under section 172(b)(1)(H); or

b. 100% of AMTI for the tax year (figured without regard to the ATNOLD, as discussed earlier, and the domestic production activities deduction under section 199) reduced by the amount determined under 1, above.

Enter on line 6 the smaller of the ATNOLD or the ATNOLD limitation. The ATNOL can be carried back or forward using the rules outlined in section 172(b), generally, a two-year carryback and a twenty-year carryforward. An election under section 172(b)(3) to forgo the carryback period for the regular tax also applies for the AMT.

The ATNOL carried back or forward may differ from the NOL (if any) that is carried back or forward for the regular tax. Keep adequate records for both the AMT and the regular tax.

Line 7. Alternative Minimum Taxable Income

For a corporation that held a residual interest in a REMIC and is not a thrift institution, line 7 may not be less than the total of the amounts shown on Schedule(s) Q (Form 1066), Quarterly Notice to Residual Interest Holder of REMIC Taxable Income or Net Loss Allocation, line 2c, for the periods included in the corporation's tax year. If the total of the line 2c amounts is larger than the amount the corporation would otherwise enter on line 7, enter that total and write "Sch. Q" on the dotted line next to line 7.

Line 8. Exemption Phase-Out Computation

 If alternative minimum taxable income entered on line 7 is $310,000 or more, skip lines 8a and 8b and enter - 0- on line 8c. You cannot take an exemption.

Line 8a. If this Form 4626 is for a member of a controlled group of corporations, subtract $150,000 from the combined AMTI of all members of the controlled group. Divide the result among the members of the group in the same manner as the $40,000 tentative exemption is divided among the members. Enter this member's share on line 8a. The tentative exemption must be divided equally among the members, unless all members consent to a different allocation. See section 1561 for details.

Line 8c. If this Form 4626 is for a member of a controlled group of corporations, reduce the member's share of the $40,000 tentative exemption by the amount entered on line 8b.

Line 10

Multiply line 9 by 20% (.20) and enter that amount on line 10.

Line 11. Alternative Minimum Tax Foreign Tax Credit (AMTFTC)

The AMTFTC is the foreign tax credit refigured as follows.

1. Complete a separate AMT Form 1118, Foreign Tax

Credit—Corporations, for each separate limitation category specified at the top of Form 1118. Include as a separate limitation category, dividends received from a corporation that qualifies for the American Samoa economic development credit, if the dividends-received deduction for those dividends is disallowed under the ACE rules.

In determining if any income is "high-taxed" in applying the separate limitation categories, use the AMT rate (20%) instead of the regular tax rate.

2. For each separate AMT Form 1118, if the corporation previously made or is making the simplified limitation election (discussed below), skip Schedule A and enter on Schedule B, Part II, line 7, the same amount you entered on that line for the regular tax. Otherwise, complete Schedule A using only income and deductions that are allowed for the AMT and attributable to sources outside the United States.

3. For each separate AMT Form 1118, complete Schedule B, Part II. Enter any AMTFTC carryover on Schedule B, Part II, line 5. Enter the AMTI from Form 4626, line 7, on Schedule B, Part II, line 8a. Enter the amount from Form 4626, line 10, on Schedule B, Part II, line 10. When completing Schedule B, treat as a tax paid to a foreign country 75% of any withholding or income tax paid to American Samoa on dividends received from a corporation that qualified for the American Samoa economic development credit (if the dividends-received deduction for those dividends is disallowed under the ACE rules).

4. For the AMT Form 1118, complete Schedule B, Part III, Summary of Separate Credits. The total foreign tax credit is the amount on line 6.

5. Enter on Form 4626, line 11, the smaller of:
• The amount on Form 4626, line 10, or
• The amount from the AMT Form 1118, Schedule B, Part III, line 6.

The corporation can use any reasonable method, consistently applied, to apportion the disallowed amount among the separate limitation categories (including the general limitation income category). Any AMT foreign tax credit for each separate limitation category that the corporation cannot claim (because of the limitation fraction) is treated as a credit carryback or carryforward for that limitation category under section 904(c). Because

these amounts may differ from the amounts that are carried back or forward for the regular tax, keep adequate records for both the AMT and regular tax. When carried back or forward, the credit is reported on Schedule B, Part II, line 5, of the carryover year's AMT Form 1118 for that separate limitation category.

Simplified Limitation Election

The corporation may elect to use a simplified section 904 limitation to figure its AMTFTC. The corporation must make the election for its first tax year beginning after 1997 for which it claims an AMTFTC. If it does not make the election for that tax year, it may not make the election for a later tax year. Once made, the election applies to all later tax years and may only be revoked with IRS consent.

If the corporation made the election for each of its AMT separate limitations, the corporation uses its separate limitation income or loss that it determined for the regular tax (instead of refiguring the separate limitation income or loss for the AMT, as described earlier).

Line 13

Enter the corporation's regular tax liability (as defined in section 26(b)) minus any foreign tax credit (for example, Form 1120, Schedule J, line 2, minus any foreign tax credit entered on Schedule J, line 5a), and minus any applicable American Samoa economic development credit from Form 5735 included on Schedule J, line 5b.

Do not include any:
• Tax on accumulation distribution of trusts from Form 4970,
• Recapture of investment credit (under section 49(b) or 50(a)) from Form 4255,
• Recapture of low-income housing credit (under section 42(j) or (k)) from Form 8611, or
• Recapture of any other credit.

Adjusted Current Earnings (ACE) Worksheet Instructions

Treatment of Certain Ownership Changes

If a corporation with a net unrealized built-in loss (within the meaning of section 382(h)) undergoes an ownership change (within the meaning of section 382(g) and Regulations section 1.56(g)-1(k)(2)), refigure the adjusted basis of each asset of the corporation (immediately after the ownership change). The new adjusted basis of each asset is its proportionate share (based on respective fair market values) of the fair market value of the corporation's assets (determined under section 382(h)) immediately before the ownership change.

To determine if the corporation has a net unrealized built-in loss immediately before an ownership change, use the aggregate adjusted basis of its assets used for figuring its ACE. Also, use these new adjusted bases for all future ACE calculations (such as depreciation and gain or loss on disposition of an asset).

Line 2. ACE Depreciation Adjustment

Line 2a. AMT depreciation. Generally, the amount entered on this line is the depreciation the corporation claimed for the regular tax (Form 4562, line 22), modified by the AMT depreciation adjustments reported on lines 2a and 2o of Form 4626.

Line 2b(1). Post-1993 property. For property placed in service after 1993, the ACE depreciation is the same as the AMT depreciation. Therefore, enter on line 2b(1) the same depreciation expense you included on line 2a of this worksheet for such property.

Line 2b(2). Post-1989, pre-1994 property. For property placed in service in a tax year that began after 1989 and before 1994, use the ADS depreciation described in section 168(g). However, for property (a) placed in service in a tax year that began after 1989 and (b) described in sections 168(f)(1) through (4), use the same depreciation claimed for the regular tax and enter it on line 2b(5).

Line 2b(3). Pre-1990 MACRS property. For MACRS property generally placed in service after 1986 and in a tax year that began before 1990, figure depreciation by using the property's AMT adjusted basis as of the close of the last tax year beginning before 1990 and by using the straight line method over the remainder of the recovery period for the property under ADS. In doing so, use the convention that would have applied to the property under section 168(d). For more information (including an example that illustrates the application of these rules), see Regulations section 1.56(g)-1(b)(2).

Line 2b(4). Pre-1990 original ACRS property. For ACRS property generally

placed in service in a tax year that began after 1980 and before 1987, figure depreciation by using the property's regular tax adjusted basis as of the close of the last tax year beginning before 1990 and by using the straight line method over the remainder of the recovery period for the property under ADS. In doing so, use the convention that would have applied to the property under section 168(d) (without regard to section 168(d)(3)). For more information (including an example that illustrates the application of these rules), see Regulations section 1.56(g)-1(b)(3).

Line 2b(5). Property described in sections 168(f)(1) through (4). For this property, use the regular tax depreciation, regardless of when the property was placed in service.

 Line 2b(5) takes priority over lines 2b(1), 2b(2), 2b(3), and 2b(4). For property that is described in sections 168(f)(1) through (4), use line 2b(5) instead of the line 2b(1), 2b(2), 2b(3), or 2b(4) that would otherwise apply.

Line 2b(6). Other property. Use the regular tax depreciation for (a) property placed in service before 1981 and (b) property placed in service after 1980, in a tax year that began before 1990, that is excluded from MACRS by section 168(f)(5)(A)(i) or original ACRS by section 168(e)(4), as in effect before the Tax Reform Act of 1986.

Line 2c. Total ACE depreciation. Subtract line 2b(7) from line 2a and enter the result on line 2c. If line 2b(7) exceeds line 2a, enter the difference as a negative amount.

Line 3. Inclusion in ACE of Items Included in Earnings and Profits (E&P)

In general, any income item that is not taken into account (see below) in determining the corporation's pre-adjustment AMTI but that is taken into account in determining its E&P must be included in ACE. Any such income item can be reduced by all items related to that income item and that would be deductible when figuring pre-adjustment AMTI if the income items to which they relate were included in the corporation's pre-adjustment AMTI for the tax year. Examples of these income items and the adjustments that relate to them include:
- Interest income from tax-exempt obligations excluded under section 103

minus any costs incurred in carrying these tax-exempt obligations and
- Proceeds of life insurance contracts excluded under section 101 minus the basis in the contract for purposes of ACE.

An income item is considered taken into account without regard to the timing of its inclusion in a corporation's pre-adjustment AMTI or its E&P. Only income items that are permanently excluded from pre-adjustment AMTI are included in ACE. An income item will not be considered taken into account merely because the proceeds from that item might eventually be reflected in the pre-adjustment AMTI of another taxpayer (for example, that of a shareholder) on the liquidation or disposal of a business.

Exceptions. Do not make an adjustment for the following.
- Any income from discharge of indebtedness excluded from gross income under section 108 (or the corresponding provision of prior law).
- Any extraterritorial income excluded from gross income under repealed section 114.
- For an insurance company taxed under section 831(b), any amount not included in gross investment income (as defined in section 834(b)).
- Any special subsidy payment for prescription drug plans excluded from gross income under section 139A.
- Any qualified shipping income excluded under section 1357.
- Tax-exempt interest on certain housing bonds issued after July 30, 2008, excluded under section 57(a)(5)(C)(iii).
- Tax-exempt interest on certain private activity bonds issued in 2009 and 2010. Special rules apply to refunding bonds. See section 56(g)(4)(B)(iv).

Line 3d. Include in ACE the income on life insurance contracts (as determined under section 7702(g)) for the tax year minus the part of any premium attributable to insurance coverage.

Line 3e. Do not include any adjustment related to the E&P effects of any charitable contribution.

Line 4. Disallowance of Items Not Deductible From E&P

Generally, no deduction is allowed when figuring ACE for items not taken into account (see below) in figuring E&P for the tax year. These amounts increase ACE if they are deductible in figuring pre-adjustment AMTI (that is, they would be positive adjustments).

However, there are exceptions. Do not add back:
• Any deduction allowable under section 243 or 245 for any dividend that qualifies for a 100% dividends-received deduction under section 243(a), 245(b), or 245(c);
• Any dividend received from a 20%-owned corporation (see section 243(c)(2)), but only if the dividend is from income of the paying corporation that is subject to federal income tax; and
• Any allowable domestic production activities deduction under section 199.

Special rules apply to:
• Dividends from certain possession corporations operating in American Samoa.
• Certain dividends received by certain cooperatives.

An item is considered taken into account without regard to the timing of its deductibility in figuring pre-adjustment AMTI or E&P. Therefore, only deduction items that are permanently disallowed in figuring E&P are disallowed in figuring ACE.

Items for which no adjustment is necessary. Generally, no deduction is allowed for an item in figuring ACE if the item is not deductible in figuring pre-adjustment AMTI (even if the item is deductible in figuring E&P). The only exceptions to this general rule are the related reductions to an income item described in the second sentence of the instructions for line 3 above. Deductions that are not allowed in figuring ACE include:
• Capital losses that exceed capital gains;
• Bribes, fines, and penalties disallowed under section 162;
• Charitable contributions that exceed the limitations of section 170;
• Meals and entertainment expenses that exceed the limitations of section 274;
• Federal taxes disallowed under section 275; and
• Golden parachute payments that exceed the limitation of section 280G.

Line 4e. Do not include any adjustment related to the E&P effects of any charitable contribution.

Line 5. Other Adjustments

Line 5a. Except as noted below, in figuring ACE, determine the deduction for intangible drilling costs under section 312(n)(2)(A).

Subtract the ACE expense (if any) from the AMT expense (used to figure line 2n of Form 4626) and enter the result on line 5a. If the ACE expense exceeds the AMT amount, enter the result as a negative amount.

Exception. The above rule does not apply to amounts paid or incurred for any oil or gas well by corporations that are independent producers (that is, not integrated oil companies as defined in section 291(b)(4)). If this exception applies, do not enter an amount on line 5a for oil and gas wells.

Line 5b. When figuring ACE, the current year deduction for circulation expenditures under section 173 does not apply. Therefore, treat circulation expenditures for ACE using the case law that existed before section 173 was enacted.

Subtract the ACE expense (if any) from the regular tax expense (for a personal holding company, from the AMT expense used to figure line 2d of Form 4626) and enter the result on line 5b. If the ACE expense exceeds the regular tax amount (for a personal holding company, the AMT amount), enter the result as a negative amount.

 Do not make this adjustment for expenditures for which the corporation elected the optional 3-year write-off under section 59(e) for the regular tax.

Line 5c. When figuring ACE, the amortization provisions of section 248 do not apply. Therefore, charge all organizational expenditures to a capital account and do not take them into account when figuring ACE until the corporation is sold or otherwise disposed of. Enter on line 5c all amortization deductions for organizational expenditures that were taken for the regular tax during the tax year.

Line 5d. The LIFO inventory adjustments provided in section 312(n)(4) apply in figuring ACE. See Regulations section 1.56(g)-1(f)(3).

Line 5e. For any installment sale in a tax year that began after 1989, a corporation generally cannot use the installment method to figure ACE. However, it may use the installment method for the applicable percentage (as determined under section 453A) of the gain from any installment sale to which section 453A(a)(1) applies.

Subtract the installment sale income reported for AMT from the ACE income from the sales and enter the result on line 5e. If the ACE income from the sales is less than the AMT amount, enter the difference as a negative amount.

Line 6. Disallowance of Loss on Exchange of Debt Pools

When figuring ACE, a corporation may not recognize any loss on the exchange of any pool of debt obligations for any other pool of debt obligations having substantially the same effective interest rates and maturities. Add back (that is, enter as a positive adjustment) on line 6 any such loss to the extent recognized for the regular tax.

Line 7. Acquisition Expenses of Life Insurance Companies for Qualified Foreign Contracts

For ACE, acquisition expenses of life insurance companies for qualified foreign contracts (as defined in section 807(e)(4) without regard to the treatment of reinsurance contract rules of section 848(e)(5)) must be capitalized and amortized by applying the treatment generally required under generally accepted accounting principles (and as if this rule applied to such contracts for all applicable tax years).

Subtract the ACE expense (if any) from the regular tax expense and enter the result on line 7. If the ACE expense is more than the regular tax expense, enter the result as a negative amount.

Line 8. Depletion

When figuring ACE, the allowance for depletion for any property placed in service in a tax year that began after 1989 generally must be determined under the cost depletion method.

Subtract the ACE expense (if any) from the AMT expense (used to figure line 2l of Form 4626) and enter the result on line 8 of the worksheet. If the ACE expense is more than the AMT amount, enter the result as a negative amount.

Exception. Independent oil and gas producers and royalty owners that figured their regular tax depletion deduction under section 613A(c) do not have an adjustment for ACE purposes.

Line 9. Basis Adjustments in Determining Gain or Loss From Sale or Exchange of Pre-1994 Property

If, during the tax year, the corporation disposed of property for which it is making (or previously made) any of the ACE adjustments, refigure the property's adjusted basis for ACE. Then refigure the property's gain or loss.

Enter the difference between the AMT gain or loss (used to figure line 2e of Form 4626) and the ACE gain or loss. Enter the difference as a negative amount if any of the following apply.
• The ACE gain is less than the AMT gain.
• The ACE loss is more than the AMT loss.
• The corporation had an ACE loss and an AMT gain.

Adjusted Current Earnings (ACE) Worksheet

Keep for Your Records

▶ See ACE Worksheet Instructions.

1	Pre-adjustment AMTI . Enter the amount from line 3 of Form 4626			**1**	
2	ACE depreciation adjustment:				
a	AMT depreciation		**2a**		
b	ACE depreciation:				
	(1) Post-1993 property	**2b(1)**			
	(2) Post-1989, pre-1994 property	**2b(2)**			
	(3) Pre-1990 MACRS property	**2b(3)**			
	(4) Pre-1990 original ACRS property	**2b(4)**			
	(5) Property described in sections 168(f)(1) through (4)	**2b(5)**			
	(6) Other property	**2b(6)**			
	(7) Total ACE depreciation. Add lines 2b(1) through 2b(6)	**2b(7)**			
c	ACE depreciation adjustment. Subtract line 2b(7) from line 2a			**2c**	
3	Inclusion in ACE of items included in earnings and profits (E&P):				
a	Tax-exempt interest income		**3a**		
b	Death benefits from life insurance contracts		**3b**		
c	All other distributions from life insurance contracts (including surrenders)		**3c**		
d	Inside buildup of undistributed income in life insurance contracts		**3d**		
e	Other items (see Regulations sections 1.56(g)-1(c)(6)(iii) through (ix) for a partial list)		**3e**		
f	Total increase to ACE from inclusion in ACE of items included in E&P. Add lines 3a through 3e			**3f**	
4	Disallowance of items not deductible from E&P:				
a	Certain dividends received		**4a**		
b	Dividends paid on certain preferred stock of public utilities that are deductible under section 247		**4b**		
c	Dividends paid to an ESOP that are deductible under section 404(k)		**4c**		
d	Nonpatronage dividends that are paid and deductible under section 1382(c)		**4d**		
e	Other items (see Regulations sections 1.56(g)-1(d)(3)(i) and (ii) for a partial list)		**4e**		
f	Total increase to ACE because of disallowance of items not deductible from E&P. Add lines 4a through 4e			**4f**	
5	Other adjustments based on rules for figuring E&P:				
a	Intangible drilling costs		**5a**		
b	Circulation expenditures		**5b**		
c	Organizational expenditures		**5c**		
d	LIFO inventory adjustments		**5d**		
e	Installment sales		**5e**		
f	Total other E&P adjustments. Combine lines 5a through 5e			**5f**	
6	Disallowance of loss on exchange of debt pools			**6**	
7	Acquisition expenses of life insurance companies for qualified foreign contracts			**7**	
8	Depletion			**8**	
9	Basis adjustments in determining gain or loss from sale or exchange of pre-1994 property			**9**	
10	**Adjusted current earnings.** Combine lines 1, 2c, 3f, 4f, and 5f through 9. Enter the result here and on line 4a of Form 4626			**10**	

Form **4684**

Department of the Treasury
Internal Revenue Service

Casualties and Thefts

▶ Information about Form 4684 and its separate instructions is at *www.irs.gov/form4684.*
▶ **Attach to your tax return.**
▶ **Use a separate Form 4684 for each casualty or theft.**

OMB No. 1545-0177

2014

Attachment
Sequence No. **26**

Name(s) shown on tax return | Identifying number

SECTION A—Personal Use Property (Use this section to report casualties and thefts of property **not** used in a trade or business or for income-producing purposes.)

1 Description of properties (show type, location, and date acquired for each property). Use a separate line for each property lost or damaged from the same casualty or theft.

Property **A** _____
Property **B** _____
Property **C** _____
Property **D** _____

		Properties			
		A	**B**	**C**	**D**
2 Cost or other basis of each property	**2**				
3 Insurance or other reimbursement (whether or not you filed a claim) (see instructions)	**3**				
Note: If line 2 is **more** than line 3, skip line 4.					
4 Gain from casualty or theft. If line 3 is **more** than line 2, enter the difference here and skip lines 5 through 9 for that column. See instructions if line 3 includes insurance or other reimbursement you did not claim, or you received payment for your loss in a later tax year	**4**				
5 Fair market value **before** casualty or theft	**5**				
6 Fair market value **after** casualty or theft	**6**				
7 Subtract line 6 from line 5	**7**				
8 Enter the **smaller** of line 2 or line 7	**8**				
9 Subtract line 3 from line 8. If zero or less, enter -0-	**9**				

10 Casualty or theft loss. Add the amounts on line 9 in columns A through D	**10**	
11 Enter the **smaller** of line 10 or $100	**11**	
12 Subtract line 11 from line 10	**12**	
Caution: Use only one Form 4684 for lines 13 through 18.		
13 Add the amounts on line 12 of all Forms 4684	**13**	
14 Add the amounts on line 4 of all Forms 4684	**14**	
15 • If line 14 is **more** than line 13, enter the difference here and on Schedule D. **Do not** complete the rest of this section (see instructions). • If line 14 is **less** than line 13, enter -0- here and go to line 16. • If line 14 is **equal** to line 13, enter -0- here. **Do not** complete the rest of this section.	**15**	
16 If line 14 is **less** than line 13, enter the difference	**16**	
17 Enter 10% of your adjusted gross income from Form 1040, line 38, or Form 1040NR, line 37. Estates and trusts, see instructions	**17**	
18 Subtract line 17 from line 16. If zero or less, enter -0-. Also enter the result on Schedule A (Form 1040), line 20, or Form 1040NR, Schedule A, line 6. Estates and trusts, enter the result on the "Other deductions" line of your tax return	**18**	

For Paperwork Reduction Act Notice, see instructions. | Cat. No. 12997O | Form **4684** (2014)

Name(s) shown on tax return. Do not enter name and identifying number if shown on other side.

Identifying number

SECTION B—Business and Income-Producing Property

Part I   **Casualty or Theft Gain or Loss** (Use a separate Part I for each casualty or theft.)

19 Description of properties (show type, location, and date acquired for each property). Use a separate line for each property lost or damaged from the same casualty or theft. **See instructions if claiming a loss due to a Ponzi-type investment scheme and Section C is not completed.**

Property **A** _____

Property **B** _____

Property **C** _____

Property **D** _____

		Properties			
		A	**B**	**C**	**D**
20 Cost or adjusted basis of each property	20				
21 Insurance or other reimbursement (whether or not you filed a claim). See the instructions for line 3	21				
Note: If line 20 is **more** than line 21, skip line 22.					
22 Gain from casualty or theft. If line 21 is **more** than line 20, enter the difference here and on line 29 or line 34, column (c), except as provided in the instructions for line 33. Also, skip lines 23 through 27 for that column. See the instructions for line 4 if line 21 includes insurance or other reimbursement you did not claim, or you received payment for your loss in a later tax year	22				
23 Fair market value **before** casualty or theft	23				
24 Fair market value **after** casualty or theft	24				
25 Subtract line 24 from line 23	25				
26 Enter the **smaller** of line 20 or line 25	26				
Note: If the property was totally destroyed by casualty or lost from theft, enter on line 26 the amount from line 20.					
27 Subtract line 21 from line 26. If zero or less, enter -0-	27				
28 Casualty or theft loss. Add the amounts on line 27. Enter the total here and on line 29 **or** line 34 (see instructions)			28		

Part II   **Summary of Gains and Losses** (from separate Parts I)

(a) Identify casualty or theft	(b) Losses from casualties or thefts		(c) Gains from casualties or thefts includible in income
	(i) Trade, business, rental or royalty property	(ii) Income-producing and employee property	

Casualty or Theft of Property Held One Year or Less

29		( )	( )	
		( )	( )	
30 Totals. Add the amounts on line 29	30	( )	( )	

31 Combine line 30, columns (b)(i) and (c). Enter the net gain or (loss) here and on Form 4797, line 14. If Form 4797 is not otherwise required, see instructions   **31**

32 Enter the amount from line 30, column (b)(ii) here. Individuals, enter the amount from income-producing property on Schedule A (Form 1040), line 28, or Form 1040NR, Schedule A, line 14, and enter the amount from property used as an employee on Schedule A (Form 1040), line 23, or Form 1040NR, Schedule A, line 9. Estates and trusts, partnerships, and S corporations, see instructions   **32**

Casualty or Theft of Property Held More Than One Year

33 Casualty or theft gains from Form 4797, line 32   **33**

34		( )	( )	
		( )	( )	

35 Total losses. Add amounts on line 34, columns (b)(i) and (b)(ii)   **35** (   ) (   )

36 Total gains. Add lines 33 and 34, column (c)   **36**

37 Add amounts on line 35, columns (b)(i) and (b)(ii)   **37**

38 If the loss on line 37 is **more** than the gain on line 36:

   a Combine line 35, column (b)(i) and line 36, and enter the net gain or (loss) here. Partnerships (except electing large partnerships) and S corporations, see the note below. All others, enter this amount on Form 4797, line 14. If Form 4797 is not otherwise required, see instructions   **38a**

   b Enter the amount from line 35, column (b)(ii) here. Individuals, enter the amount from income-producing property on Schedule A (Form 1040), line 28, or Form 1040NR, Schedule A, line 14, and enter the amount from property used as an employee on Schedule A (Form 1040), line 23, or Form 1040NR, Schedule A, line 9. Estates and trusts, enter on the "Other deductions" line of your tax return. Partnerships (except electing large partnerships) and S corporations, see the note below. Electing large partnerships, enter on Form 1065-B, Part II, line 11   **38b**

39 If the loss on line 37 is **less** than or **equal** to the gain on line 36, combine lines 36 and 37 and enter here. Partnerships (except electing large partnerships), see the note below. All others, enter this amount on Form 4797, line 3   **39**

Note: Partnerships, enter the amount from line 38a, 38b, or line 39 on Form 1065, Schedule K, line 11.
S corporations, enter the amount from line 38a or 38b on Form 1120S, Schedule K, line 10.

Name(s) shown on tax return | Identifying number

SECTION C—Theft Loss Deduction for Ponzi-Type Investment Scheme Using the Procedures in Revenue Procedure 2009-20 (Complete this section in lieu of Appendix A in Revenue Procedure 2009-20. See instructions.)

Part I Computation of Deduction

40	Initial investment	40
41	Subsequent investments (see instructions)	41
42	Income reported on your tax returns for tax years prior to the discovery year (see instructions)	42
43	Add lines 40, 41, and 42	43
44	Withdrawals for all years (see instructions)	44
45	Subtract line 44 from line 43. This is your total qualified investment	45
46	Enter .95 (95%) if you have no potential third-party recovery. Enter .75 (75%) if you have potential third-party recovery	46
47	Multiply line 46 by line 45	47
48	Actual recovery	48
49	Potential insurance/Securities Investor Protection Corporation (SIPC) recovery	49
50	Add lines 48 and 49. This is your total recovery	50
51	Subtract line 50 from line 47. This is your deductible theft loss. Include this amount on line 28 of Section B, Part I. Do not complete lines 19-27 for this loss. Then complete Section B, Part II	51

Part II Required Statements and Declarations (See instructions.)

- I am claiming a theft loss deduction pursuant to Revenue Procedure 2009-20 from a specified fraudulent arrangement conducted by the following individual or entity.

  Name of individual or entity _____

  Taxpayer identification number (if known) _____

  Address _____

- I have written documentation to support the amounts reported in Part I of this Section C.

- I am a qualified investor as defined in section 4.03 of Revenue Procedure 2009-20.

- If I have determined the amount of my theft loss deduction using .95 on line 46 above, I declare that I have not pursued and do not intend to pursue any potential third-party recovery, as that term is defined in section 4.10 of Revenue Procedure 2009-20.

- I agree to comply with the conditions and agreements set forth in Revenue Procedure 2009-20 and this Section C.

- If I have already filed a return or amended return that does not satisfy the conditions in section 6.02 of Revenue Procedure 2009-20, I agree to all adjustments or actions that are necessary to comply with those conditions. The tax year(s) for which I filed the return(s) or amended return(s) and the date(s) on which they were filed are as follows:

_____

_____

_____

2014

Department of the Treasury
Internal Revenue Service

Instructions for Form 4684

Casualties and Thefts

Section references are to the Internal Revenue Code unless otherwise noted.

General Instructions

Future Developments

For the latest information about developments related to Form 4684 and its instructions, such as legislation enacted after they were published, go to *www.irs.gov/ form4684*.

Purpose of Form

Use Form 4684 to report gains and losses from casualties and thefts. Attach Form 4684 to your tax return.

Losses You Can Deduct

You can deduct losses of property from fire, storm, shipwreck, or other casualty, or theft (for example, larceny, embezzlement, robbery, and Ponzi-type investment schemes). See Pub. 547, Casualties, Disasters, and Thefts, for more examples.

If your property is covered by insurance, you must file a timely insurance claim for reimbursement of your loss. Otherwise, you cannot deduct the loss as a casualty or theft loss. However, the part of the loss that is not covered by insurance is still deductible.

Related expenses. The related expenses you have due to a casualty or theft, such as expenses for the treatment of personal injuries or for the rental of a car, are not deductible as casualty or theft losses.

Costs for protection against future casualties are not deductible but should be capitalized as permanent improvements. An example would be the cost of a levee to stop flooding.

Losses You Cannot Deduct

- Money or property misplaced or lost may not be deducted as a theft loss.
- Breakage of china, glassware, furniture, and similar items under normal conditions.
- Progressive damage to property (buildings, clothes, trees, etc.) caused by termites, moths, other insects, or disease.
- A decline in market value of stock, caused by disclosure of accounting or other illegal misconduct by the officers or directors of the corporation that issues the stock, that was acquired on the open market for investment. You may be able to deduct it as a capital loss on Schedule D (Form 1040) if the stock is sold or exchanged or becomes completely worthless. See chapter 4 of Pub. 550, Investment Income and Expenses.

Note. Victims of fraudulent investment schemes can claim a theft loss deduction if certain conditions apply. See *Losses From Ponzi-Type Investment Schemes*, later, for more information.

Gain on Reimbursement

If the amount you receive in insurance or other reimbursement is more than the cost or other basis of the property, you have a gain. If you have a gain, you may have to pay tax on it, or you may be able to postpone the gain.

Do not report the gain on damaged, destroyed, or stolen property if you receive property that is similar or related to it in service or use. Your basis in the new property is the same as your basis in the old property.

Any tangible replacement property held for use in a trade or business is treated as similar or related in service or use to property held for use in a trade or business or for investment if:

- The property you are replacing was damaged or destroyed in a disaster, and
- The area in which the property was damaged or destroyed was declared by the President of the United States to warrant federal assistance because of that disaster.

Generally, you must recognize the gain if you receive unlike property or money as reimbursement. But you generally can choose to postpone all or part of the gain if, within 2 years of the end of the first tax year in which any part of the gain is realized, you purchase:

- Property similar or related in service or use to the damaged, destroyed, or stolen property, or
- A controlling interest (at least 80%) in a corporation owning such property.

The replacement period is 5 years, instead of 2 years, if the property was located in the Midwestern disaster areas (as defined in Pub. 4492-B, Information for Affected Taxpayers in the Midwestern Disaster Areas).(For details, see *Replacement Period* under *Figuring a Gain* in Pub. 547.)

To postpone all of the gain, the cost of the replacement property must be equal to or more than the reimbursement you received for your property. If the cost of the replacement property is less than the reimbursement received, you must recognize the gain to the extent the reimbursement exceeds the cost of the replacement property.

If the replacement property or stock is acquired from a related person, gain generally cannot be postponed by:

- Corporations (other than S corporations),
- Partnerships in which more than 50% of the capital or profits interest is owned by corporations (other than S corporations), or
- All other taxpayers, unless the aggregate realized gains on the involuntarily converted property are $100,000 or less for the tax year. This rule applies to partnerships and S corporations at both the entity and partner or shareholder level.

For details on how to postpone the gain, see *Postponement of Gain* under *Figuring a Gain* in Pub. 547.

If your main home was located in a disaster area and that home or any of its contents were damaged or destroyed due to the disaster, special rules apply. See *Gains Realized on Homes in Disaster Areas*, later.

When To Deduct a Loss

Deduct the part of your casualty or theft loss that is not reimbursable in the tax year the casualty occurred or the theft was discovered. However, a disaster loss and a loss from deposits in insolvent or bankrupt financial institutions may be treated differently. See *Disaster Losses* and *Special Treatment for Losses on Deposits in Insolvent or Bankrupt Financial Institutions*, later.

If you are not sure whether part of your casualty or theft loss will be reimbursed, do not deduct that part until the tax year when you become reasonably certain that it will not be reimbursed.

If you are reimbursed for a loss you deducted in an earlier year, include the reimbursement in your income in the year you received it, but only to the extent the deduction reduced your tax in an earlier year.

See *Lessee's loss* in Pub. 547 for special rules on when to deduct losses from casualties and thefts to leased property.

Disaster Losses

A disaster loss is a loss that occurred in an area determined by the President of the United States to warrant federal disaster assistance. It includes a major disaster or emergency declaration. A list of areas warranting public or individual assistance (or both) is available at the Federal Emergency Management Agency (FEMA) website at *www.fema.gov*.

If you have a casualty loss from a disaster that occurred in an area warranting public or individual assistance (or both), you can elect to deduct the loss in the tax year immediately before the tax year in which the disaster

Cat. No. 12998Z

occurred as long as the loss would otherwise be allowed as a deduction in the tax year it occurred.

This election must be made by filing your return or amended return for the earlier year, and claiming your disaster loss on it, by the later of:

• The due date for filing your original return (without extensions) for the tax year in which the disaster actually occurred, or
• The due date for filing your original return (including extensions) for the tax year immediately before the tax year in which the disaster actually occurred.

If you make this election, include a statement that you are making this election. The statement can be made on the return or on an attachment filed with the return.

You can revoke your election within 90 days after making it by returning to the IRS any refund or credit you received from the election. If you revoke your election before receiving a refund, you must repay the refund within 30 days after receiving it.

On line 1 of the Form 4684 on which you claim the disaster loss (or on an attachment), specify the date(s) of the disaster and the city, town, county or parish, and state in which the damaged or destroyed property was located.

To determine the amount to deduct for a disaster loss, you must take into account as reimbursements any benefits you received or which you have a reasonable possibility of receiving from federal or state programs to restore your property.

Home made unsafe by disaster. If your home was located in a disaster area and your state or local government ordered you to tear it down or move it because it was no longer safe to use as a home due to the disaster, the resulting loss in value is treated as a disaster loss. The order for you to tear down or move the home must have been issued within 120 days after the area was officially declared a disaster area.

For purposes of figuring the disaster loss, use the value of your home before you moved it or tore it down as its fair market value after the casualty.

Gains Realized on Homes in Disaster Areas

The following rules apply if your main home was located in an area declared by the President of the United States to warrant federal assistance as the result of a disaster, and the home or any of its contents were damaged or destroyed due to the disaster. These rules also apply to renters who receive insurance proceeds for damaged or destroyed property in a rented home that is their main home.

1. No gain is recognized on any insurance proceeds received for unscheduled personal property that was part of the contents of the home.

2. Any other insurance proceeds you receive for the home or its contents are treated as received for a single item of property, and any replacement property you purchase that is similar or related in service or use to the home or its contents is treated as similar or related in service or use to that single item of property. Therefore, you can choose to recognize gain only to the extent the insurance proceeds treated as received for that single item of property exceed the cost of the replacement property.

3. If you choose to postpone any gain from the receipt of insurance or other reimbursement for your main home or any of its contents, the period in which you must purchase replacement property is extended until 4 years after the end of the first tax year in which any part of the gain is realized. However, the 4-year period is extended to 5 years if your main home or any of its contents were located in the Midwestern disaster areas (as defined in Pub. 4492-B). (For details, see *Replacement Period* under *Figuring a Gain* in Pub. 547.)

For details on how to postpone gain, see *Postponement of Gain* under *Figuring a Gain* in Pub. 547.

Example. Your main home and its contents were completely destroyed in 2014 by a tornado in a federally declared disaster area. In 2014, you received insurance proceeds of $200,000 for the home, $25,000 for unscheduled personal property in your home, $5,000 for jewelry, and $10,000 for a stamp collection. The jewelry and stamp collection were kept in your home and were scheduled property on your insurance policy. No gain is recognized on the $25,000 you received for the unscheduled personal property. If you reinvest the remaining proceeds of $215,000 in a replacement home, any type of replacement contents (whether scheduled or unscheduled), or both, you can elect to postpone any gain on your home, jewelry, or stamp collection. If you reinvest less than $215,000, any gain is recognized only to the extent $215,000 exceeds the amount you reinvest in a replacement home, any type of replacement contents (whether scheduled or unscheduled), or both. To postpone gain, you must purchase the replacement property before 2019. Your basis in the replacement property equals its cost decreased by the amount of any postponed gain.

Special Treatment for Losses on Deposits in Insolvent or Bankrupt Financial Institutions

If you are an individual who incurred a loss from a deposit in a bank, credit union, or other financial institution because of the bankruptcy or insolvency of that institution and you can reasonably estimate your loss, you can elect to deduct the loss as:

• A casualty loss to personal use property on Form 4684, or
• An ordinary loss (miscellaneous itemized deduction) on Schedule A (Form 1040), Itemized Deductions, line 23, or Form 1040NR, Schedule A, Itemized Deductions, line 9. You cannot elect the ordinary loss deduction if any part of the deposits related to the loss is federally insured. The maximum amount you can claim is $20,000 ($10,000 if you are married filing separately). Your deduction is reduced by any expected state insurance proceeds and is subject to the 2%-of-adjusted-gross-income (AGI) limit.

If you elect to deduct the estimated loss as a casualty loss or as an ordinary loss, you cannot claim the same loss as a nonbusiness bad debt. If the estimated loss deducted is less than the actual loss, you can claim the difference as a nonbusiness bad debt for the year in which the final determination of the loss occurs. A nonbusiness bad debt is deducted on Schedule D (Form 1040), Capital Gains and Losses, as a short-term capital loss.

If you are a 1% or more owner or an officer of the financial institution, or are related to any such owner or officer, you cannot deduct the loss as a casualty loss or as an ordinary loss. See chapter 4 of Pub. 550 for the definition of "related."

If you elect to deduct the loss as a casualty loss or as an ordinary loss and you have more than one account in the same financial institution, you must include all your accounts. Once you make the election, you cannot change it without permission from the IRS. See Notice 89-28, 1989-1 C.B. 667, for more details.

To elect to deduct the loss as a casualty loss, complete Form 4684 as follows: On line 1, enter the name of the financial institution and "Insolvent Financial Institution." Skip lines 2 through 9. Enter the amount of the loss on line 10, and complete the rest of Section A.

If, in a later year, you recover an amount you deducted as a loss, you may have to include in your income the amount recovered for that year. For details, see *Recoveries* in Pub. 525, Taxable and Nontaxable Income.

Damage From Corrosive Drywall

Under a special procedure, you may be able to claim a casualty loss deduction for amounts you paid to repair damage to your home and household appliances that resulted from corrosive drywall. For details, see *Special Procedure for Damage From Corrosive Drywall* under *Casualty* in Pub. 547.

Specific Instructions

Which Sections To Complete

Use Section A to figure casualty or theft gains and losses for property that is not used in a trade or business or for income-producing purposes. Also use Section A to figure casualty or theft losses and gains related to the portion of your home used for business if you used the simplified method to determine your deductible expenses for business use of your home.

Casualty or theft losses of personal use property are deductible only to the extent that the amount of the loss from each separate casualty or theft is more than $100 and the total amount of all losses (as so reduced) during the year is more than 10% of your AGI (Form 1040, line 38, or Form 1040NR, line 37).

Use Section B to figure casualty or theft gains and losses for property that is used in a trade or business or for income-producing purposes.

If property is used partly in a trade or business and partly for personal purposes, such as a personal home with a rental unit, figure the personal part in Section A and the business part in Section B.

Use Section C to figure a theft loss deduction from a Ponzi-type investment scheme if you qualify to use Revenue Procedure 2009-20, as modified by Revenue Procedure 2011-58, and choose to follow the procedures in the guidance. Section C of Form 4684 replaces Appendix A in Revenue Procedure 2009-20. You do not need to complete Appendix A. See Losses From Ponzi-Type Investment Schemes, later.

Section A—Personal Use Property

Use a separate column for lines 2 through 9 to show each item lost or damaged from a single casualty or theft described on line 1. If more than four items were lost or damaged, use additional sheets following the format of lines 1 through 9.

Use a separate Form 4684 through line 12 for each casualty or theft involving property not used in a trade or business or for income-producing purposes.

Do not include any loss previously deducted on an estate tax return.

If you are liable for casualty or theft losses to property you lease from someone else, see Leased property under Figuring a Loss in Pub. 547.

Line 1

Describe the type of property (for example, furniture, jewelry, car, etc.).

If you claim a disaster loss (defined earlier), specify the date(s) of the disaster and the city, town, county or parish, and state in which the damaged or destroyed property was located. Include this information on line 1 or on an attached statement.

Line 2

Cost or other basis usually means original cost plus improvements. Subtract any postponed gain from the sale of a previous main home. Special rules apply to property received as a gift or inheritance. See Basis Other Than Cost in Pub. 551, Basis of Assets, for details. If you inherited the property from someone who died in 2010 and the executor of the decedent's estate made the election to file Form 8939, Allocation of Increase in Basis for Property Received From a Decedent, refer to the information provided by the executor or see Pub. 4895, Tax Treatment of Property Acquired From a Decedent Dying in 2010.

Line 3

Enter on this line the amount of insurance or other reimbursement you received or expect to receive for each property. Include your insurance coverage whether or not you are filing a claim for reimbursement. For example, your car worth $2,000 is totally destroyed in a collision. You are insured with a $500 deductible, but decide not to report it to your insurance company because you are afraid the insurance company will cancel your policy. In this case, enter $1,500 on this line.

If you expect to be reimbursed but have not yet received payment, you must still enter the expected reimbursement from the loss. If, in a later tax year, you determine with reasonable certainty that you will not be reimbursed for all or part of the loss, you can deduct for that year the amount of the loss that is not reimbursed.

Types of reimbursements. Insurance is the most common way to be reimbursed for a casualty or theft loss, but if.
• Part of a federal disaster loan is forgiven, the part you do not have to pay back is considered a reimbursement.
• The person who leases your property must make repairs or must repay you for any part of a loss, the repayment and the cost of the repairs are considered reimbursements.
• A court awards you damages for a casualty or theft loss, the amount you are able to collect, minus lawyers' fees and other necessary expenses, is a reimbursement.
• You accept repairs, restoration, or cleanup services provided by relief agencies, it is considered a reimbursement.
• A bonding company pays you for a theft loss, the payment is also considered a reimbursement.

Lump-sum reimbursement. If you have a casualty or theft loss of several assets at the same time and you receive a lump-sum reimbursement, you must divide the amount you receive among the assets according to the fair market value of each asset at the time of the loss.

Grants, gifts, and other payments. Grants and other payments you receive to help you after a casualty are considered reimbursements only if they must be used specifically to repair or replace your property. Such payments will reduce your casualty loss deduction. If there are no conditions on how you have to use the money you receive, it is not a reimbursement.

Use and occupancy insurance. If insurance reimburses you for your loss of business income, it does not reduce your casualty or theft loss. The reimbursement is income, and is taxed in the same manner as your business income.

Main home destroyed. If you have a gain because your main home was destroyed, you generally can exclude the gain from your income as if you had sold or exchanged your home. You may be able to exclude up to $250,000 of the gain (up to $500,000 if married filing jointly). To exclude a gain, you generally must have owned and lived in the property as your main home for at least 2 years during the 5-year period ending on the date it was destroyed. For information on this exclusion, see Pub. 523, Selling Your Home.

If you exclude the gain and the entire gain is excludable, do not report the casualty on Form 4684. If the gain is more than you can exclude, reduce the insurance or other reimbursement by the amount of the exclusion and enter the result on line 3. Attach a statement showing the full amount of insurance or other reimbursement and the amount of the exclusion. You may be able to postpone reporting the excess gain if you buy replacement property. See Gain on Reimbursement and Gains Realized on Homes in Disaster Areas, earlier.

Line 4

If you are entitled to an insurance payment or other reimbursement for any part of a casualty or theft loss but you choose not to file a claim for the loss, you cannot realize a gain from that payment or reimbursement. Therefore, figure the gain on line 4 by subtracting your cost or other basis in the property (line 2) only from the amount of reimbursement you actually received. Enter the result on line 4, but do not enter less than zero.

If you filed a claim for reimbursement but did not receive it until after the year of the casualty or theft, include the gain in your income in the year you received the reimbursement.

Lines 5 and 6

Fair market value (FMV) is the price at which the property would be sold between a willing buyer and a willing seller, each having knowledge of the relevant facts. The difference between the FMV immediately before the casualty or theft and the FMV immediately after represents the decrease in FMV because of the casualty or theft.

The FMV of property after a theft is zero if the property is not recovered.

FMV is generally determined by a competent appraisal. The appraiser's knowledge of sales of comparable property about the same time as the casualty or theft, knowledge of your property before and after the occurrence, and the methods of determining FMV are important elements in proving your loss.

The appraised value of property immediately after the casualty must be adjusted (increased) for the effects of any general market decline that may occur at the same time as the casualty or theft. For example, the value of all nearby property may become depressed because it is in an area where such occurrences are commonplace. This general decline in market value is not part of the property's decrease in FMV as a result of the casualty or theft.

Replacement cost or the cost of repairs is not necessarily FMV. However, you may be able to use the cost of repairs to the damaged property as evidence of loss in value if:
● The repairs are actually made,
● The repairs are necessary to restore the property to the condition it was in immediately before the casualty,
● The amount spent for repairs is not excessive,
● The repairs only correct the damage caused by the casualty, and
● The value of the property after the repairs is not, as a result of the repairs, more than the value of the property immediately before the casualty.

To figure a casualty loss to real estate not used in a trade, business, or for income-producing purposes, measure the decrease in value of the property as a whole. All improvements, such as buildings, trees, and shrubs, are considered together as one item. Figure the loss separately for other items. For example, figure the loss separately for each piece of furniture.

Line 15

If line 14 is more than line 13:
● Combine your short-term gains with your short-term losses and include the net short-term gain or (loss) on Schedule D (Form 1040), line 4. Estates and trusts include this amount on Schedule D (Form 1041), line 4.
● Combine your long-term gains with your long-term losses and include the net long-term gain or (loss) on Schedule D (Form 1040), line 11. Estates and trusts include this amount on Schedule D (Form 1041), line 11.

The holding period for long-term gains and losses is more than 1 year. For short-term gains and losses, it is 1 year or less. To figure the holding period, begin counting on the day after you received the property and include the day the casualty or theft occurred.

Generally, if you inherit property, you are considered to have held the property for longer than 1 year, regardless of how long you actually held it. If you inherited property from someone who died in 2010 and the executor made the election to file Form 8939, refer to the information provided by the executor or see Pub. 4895 to determine your holding period.

Line 17

Estates and trusts figure AGI in the same way as individuals, except that the costs of administration are allowed in figuring AGI.

Section B—Business and Income-Producing Property

Use a separate column of Part I, lines 20 through 27, to show each item lost or damaged from a single casualty or theft described on line 19. If more than four items were lost or damaged, use additional sheets following the format of Part I, lines 19 through 27.

Use a separate Form 4684, Section B, Part I, for each casualty or theft involving property used in a trade or business or for income-producing purposes. Use one Section B, Part II, to combine all Sections B, Part I.

For details on the treatment of casualties or thefts to business or income-producing property, including rules on the loss of inventory through casualty or theft, see *Figuring a Loss* in Pub. 547.

Home Used for Business or Rented Out

If you had a casualty or theft loss involving a home you used for business or rented out, your deductible loss may be limited. First, complete Form 4684, Section B, lines 19 through 26. If the loss involved a home used for a business for which you are filing Schedule C (Form 1040), Profit or Loss From Business, figure your deductible casualty or theft loss on Form 8829, Expenses for Business Use of Your Home (if you are using Form 8829). Enter on Form 4684, line 27, the deductible loss from Form 8829, line 34, and "See Form 8829" above line 27. For a home you rented out or used for a business for which you are not filing Schedule C (Form 1040), see section 280A(c)(5) to figure your deductible loss. Attach a statement showing your computation of the deductible loss, enter that amount on line 27 and "See attached statement" above line 27.

If you used the simplified method to determine your deductible expenses for business use of your home for 2014, figure the casualty or theft loss for the home office in Section A instead of on Form 8829 and Section B.

Property Used in a Passive Activity

A gain or loss from a casualty or theft of property used in a passive activity is not taken into account in determining the loss from a passive activity unless losses similar in cause and severity recur regularly in the activity. See Form 8582, Passive Activity Loss Limitations, and its instructions for details.

Losses From Ponzi-Type Investment Schemes

The IRS has issued the following guidance to assist taxpayers who are victims of losses from Ponzi-type investment schemes.
● Revenue Ruling 2009-9, 2009-14 I.R.B. 735 (available at *www.irs.gov/irb/ 2009-14_IRB/ar07.html*).
● Revenue Procedure 2009-20, 2009-14 I.R.B. 749 (available at *www.irs.gov/irb/ 2009-14_IRB/ar11.html*).
● Revenue Procedure 2011-58, 2011-50 I.R.B. 849 (available at *www.irs.gov/irb/ 2011-50_IRB/ar11.html*).

If you qualify to use Revenue Procedure 2009-20, as modified by Revenue Procedure 2011-58, and choose to follow the procedures in the guidance, first fill out Section C to determine the amount to enter on Section B, line 28. Skip lines 19 to 27. Section C of Form 4684 replaces Appendix A in Revenue Procedure 2009-20. You do not need to complete Appendix A.

For more information, see the instructions for Section C later and the above revenue ruling and revenue procedures.

If you choose not to use the procedures in Revenue Procedure 2009-20, you may claim your theft loss by filling out Section B, lines 19 to 39, as appropriate.

Section 179 Property of a Partnership or S Corporation

Partnerships (other than electing large partnerships) and S corporations that have a casualty or theft involving property for which the section 179 expense deduction was previously claimed and passed through to the partners or shareholders must not use Form 4684 to report the transaction. Instead, see the Instructions for Form 4797 for details on how to report it. Partners and S corporation shareholders who receive a Schedule K-1 reporting such a transaction should see the Instructions for Form 4797 for details on how to figure the amount to enter on Form 4684, line 20.

Line 19

If you are claiming a loss from a fraudulent investment arrangement and you are **not** filling out Section C, you must enter the name, Taxpayer Identification Number (if known), and address (if known) of the individual or entity that conducted the fraudulent arrangement. Complete the rest of Section B, Part I.

Line 20

Cost or adjusted basis usually means original cost plus improvements, minus depreciation allowed or allowable (including any section 179 expense deduction), amortization, depletion, etc. Special rules apply to property received as a gift or inheritance. See *Basis Other Than Cost* in

Pub. 551 for details. If you inherited the property from someone who died in 2010 and the executor of the decedent's estate made the election to file Form 8939, refer to the information provided by the executor or see Pub. 4895.

Line 21

See the instructions for line 3.

Line 22

See the instructions for line 4.

Lines 23 and 24

See the instructions for lines 5 and 6 for details on determining FMV.

Loss on each item figured separately. Unlike a casualty loss to personal use real estate, in which all improvements are considered one item, a casualty loss to business or income-producing property must be figured separately for each item. For example, if casualty damage occurs to both a building and to trees on the same piece of real estate, measure the loss separately for the building and for the trees.

Line 28

If the amount on line 28 includes losses on property held 1 year or less, and losses on property held for more than 1 year, you must allocate the amount between lines 29 and 34 according to how long you held each property. Enter on line 29 all gains and losses on property held 1 year or less. Enter on line 34 all gains and losses on property held more than 1 year, except as provided in the instructions for line 33.

If you are claiming a theft loss from a Ponzi-type investment scheme and are following the procedures in Revenue Procedure 2009-20, 2009-14 I.R.B. 749, enter on line 28 the amount from Section C, line 51. Do not complete Section B, lines 19 to 27 of Form 4684 for that loss. You must fill out Section B, Part II.

Part II, Column (a)

On lines 29 and 34, use a separate line to identify each casualty or theft. If you have more than two casualties or thefts, attach an additional sheet following the format of lines 29 and 34.

Example. Ishmael is claiming two casualty losses for his business property. One loss is due to a fire in July and the other loss is due to a hurricane in October. He fills out one Section B, Part I for the fire and another separate Section B, Part I for the hurricane. He held the property for one year or less. He fills out only one Section B, Part II, to summarize the two losses he is claiming. On line 29, he enters "Fire" on the first line and "Hurricane" on the second line.

 TIP *If you are claiming a theft loss from a Ponzi-type investment scheme, enter the name of the individual or entity that conducted the fraudulent arrangement.*

Part II, Column (b)(i)

Enter the part of line 28 from trade, business, rental, or royalty property (other than property you used in performing services as an employee).

Part II, Column (b)(ii)

Enter the part of line 28 from income-producing property and from property you used in performing services as an employee. Income-producing property is property held for investment, such as stocks, notes, bonds, gold, silver, vacant lots, and works of art.

Part II, Column (c)

On line 29, enter the part of line 22 that is from property held for one year or less.

On line 34, enter the part of line 22 that is from property held for more than one year.

Line 30

Include in the total any amounts from the additional sheet you attached because you had more than two casualties or thefts on line 29.

Line 31

If Form 4797, Sales of Business Property, is not otherwise required, enter the amount from this line on page 1 of your tax return, on the line identified as from Form 4797. Next to that line, enter "Form 4684."

Line 32

Estates and trusts, enter on the "Other deductions" line of your tax return. Partnerships (except electing large partnerships), enter on Form 1065, Schedule K, line 13d. Electing large partnerships, enter on Form 1065-B, Part II, line 11. S corporations, enter on Form 1120S, Schedule K, line 12d. Next to that line, enter "Form 4684."

Line 33

If you had a casualty or theft gain from certain trade, business, or income-producing property held more than 1 year, you may have to recapture part or all of the gain as ordinary income. See the instructions for Form 4797, Part III, for more information on the types of property subject to recapture. If recapture applies, complete Form 4797, Part III, and this line, instead of Form 4684, line 34.

Line 35

Include in the total any amounts from the additional sheet you attached because you had more than two casualties or thefts.

Line 38a

Taxpayers, other than partnerships and S corporations, if Form 4797 is not otherwise required, enter the amount from this line on page 1 of your tax return, on the line identified as from Form 4797. Next to that line, enter "Form 4684."

Section C—Theft Loss Deduction for Ponzi-Type Investment Scheme Using the Procedures in Revenue Procedure 2009-20

Fill out this section if you claim a theft loss deduction for a Ponzi-type investment scheme and you meet **both** of the following conditions.
• You qualify to use Revenue Procedure 2009-20, as modified by Revenue Procedure 2011-58.
• You choose to follow the procedures in the guidance.

If you meet both conditions, fill out Section C in lieu of Appendix A in Revenue Procedure 2009-20.

For more information about claiming a theft loss deduction from a Ponzi-type investment scheme, see the following guidance.
• Revenue Ruling 2009-9, 2009-14 I.R.B. 735 (available at *www.irs.gov/irb/ 2009-14_IRB/ar07.html*).
• Revenue Procedure 2009-20, 2009-14 I.R.B. 749 (available at *www.irs.gov/irb/ 2009-14_IRB/ar11.html*).
• Revenue Procedure 2011-58, 2011-50 I.R.B. 849 (available at *www.irs.gov/irb/ 2011-50_IRB/ar11.html*).

 !CAUTION *Do not fill out Section C if you do not qualify to use the procedures in Revenue Procedure 2009-20, as modified by Revenue Procedure 2011-58, or you do not choose to follow them. Instead, go to the instructions for Section B.*

Line 40

Enter the initial amount of cash or basis of property that you invested in the investment arrangement. Do not include any of the following on this line, line 41, or line 42:
• Amounts borrowed from the responsible group and invested in the specified fraudulent arrangement, to the extent the borrowed amounts were not repaid at the time the theft was discovered;
• Amounts such as fees that were paid to the responsible group and deducted for federal income tax purposes;
• Amounts reported to you (the qualified investor) as taxable income that were not included in gross income on the investor's federal income tax returns; or

- Cash or property that you (the qualified investor) invested in a fund or other entity (separate from you (the qualified investor) for federal income tax purposes) that invested in a specified fraudulent arrangement.

For definitions of responsible group, specified fraudulent arrangement, and qualified investor, see Section 4 of Revenue Procedure 2009-20.

Line 41

Enter the amounts of cash or the basis of property that you invested after you made the initial investment (including amounts reinvested).

Line 42

Enter the total amounts of net income (for example, interest and dividends minus expenses) from the specified fraudulent arrangement that, consistent with information received from that arrangement, you included in income for federal tax purposes for all tax years before the discovery year, including tax years for which a refund is barred by the statute of limitations.

Discovery year. The discovery year is the tax year when one of the following occurs:
- The indictment, information, or complaint described in section 4.02(1) or (2) of Revenue Procedure 2009-20 (as modified by Revenue Procedure 2011-58) is filed; or
- The complaint or similar document described in section 4.02(3) of Revenue Procedure 2009-20 (as modified by Revenue Procedure 2011-58) is filed, or the death of the lead figure occurs, whichever is later.

Line 44

Enter the total amount of cash or property that you withdrew from the investment arrangement in all years (whether designated as income or principal).

Line 45

This is the amount of your investment that is eligible for a deduction before any actual or potential recoveries are taken into account.

Line 46

Potential third-party recovery. This is the amount of all actual or potential claims for

recovery, as of the last day of the discovery year (defined earlier), that are **not** from potential insurance or Securities Investor Protection Corporation (SIPC) recovery, or a potential direct recovery.

Potential insurance/SIPC recovery. This is the total of all actual or potential claims for reimbursement that, as of the last day of the discovery year, are attributable to:
- Insurance policies in your name that protect you from this type of loss;
- Contractual arrangements, other than insurance, that guaranteed or otherwise protected against this type of loss; or
- Amounts payable from SIPC, as advances for customer claims under the Securities Investor Protection Act of 1970, or by a similar entity under a similar provision.

Potential direct recovery. This is the amount of all actual or potential claims for recovery, as of the last day of the discovery year (defined earlier), against the responsible individual or group.

Line 48

Enter the amounts you actually received as a reimbursement or recovery from any source. Do not include amounts that are potential direct recoveries (defined earlier) or potential third-party recoveries (defined earlier).

Line 49

Enter the amount of potential insurance/SIPC recovery (defined earlier).

Line 51

Enter the amount from line 51 on line 28 of Section B. Do not complete lines 19 to 27 for this loss. Then complete Section B, Part II.

 If you had other casualties or thefts, fill out a separate Section B, Part I, for them.

Part II

Read the statements and declarations in this part carefully. Enter the required information in the spaces provided. You are agreeing to these statements and declarations when you sign your tax return. The information that you enter in this part will be used to verify the fraudulent investment arrangement.

Paperwork Reduction Act Notice. We ask for the information on this form to carry out the Internal Revenue laws of the United States. You are required to give us the information. We need it to ensure that you are complying with these laws and to allow us to figure and collect the right amount of tax.

You are not required to provide the information requested on a form that is subject to the Paperwork Reduction Act unless the form displays a valid OMB control number. Books or records relating to a form or its instructions must be retained as long as their contents may become material in the administration of any Internal Revenue law. Generally, tax returns and return information are confidential, as required by section 6103.

The time needed to complete and file this form will vary depending on individual circumstances. The estimated burden for individual taxpayers filing this form is approved under OMB control number 1545-0074 and is included in the estimates shown in the instructions for their individual income tax return. The estimated burden for all other taxpayers who file this form is shown below.

Recordkeeping . . . . . 2 hrs., 37 min.

Learning about the law or the form . . . . . . 43 min.

Preparing the form . . . 1 hr., 34 min.

Copying, assembling, and sending the form to the IRS . . . . 48 min.

If you have comments concerning the accuracy of these time estimates or suggestions for making this form simpler, we would be happy to hear from you. See the instructions for the tax return with which this form is filed.

Form **4797**

Department of the Treasury
Internal Revenue Service

Sales of Business Property
(Also Involuntary Conversions and Recapture Amounts Under Sections 179 and 280F(b)(2))

► Attach to your tax return.

► Information about Form 4797 and its separate instructions is at *www.irs.gov/form4797.*

OMB No. 1545-0184

2014

Attachment
Sequence No. **27**

Name(s) shown on return | Identifying number

1 Enter the gross proceeds from sales or exchanges reported to you for 2014 on Form(s) 1099-B or 1099-S (or substitute statement) that you are including on line 2, 10, or 20 (see instructions) . . . . | **1**

Part I Sales or Exchanges of Property Used in a Trade or Business and Involuntary Conversions From Other Than Casualty or Theft—Most Property Held More Than 1 Year (see instructions)

2	(a) Description of property	(b) Date acquired (mo., day, yr.)	(c) Date sold (mo., day, yr.)	(d) Gross sales price	(e) Depreciation allowed or allowable since acquisition	(f) Cost or other basis, plus improvements and expense of sale	(g) Gain or (loss) Subtract (f) from the sum of (d) and (e)

3 Gain, if any, from Form 4684, line 39 . . . . | **3**

4 Section 1231 gain from installment sales from Form 6252, line 26 or 37 . . . . | **4**

5 Section 1231 gain or (loss) from like-kind exchanges from Form 8824 . . . . | **5**

6 Gain, if any, from line 32, from other than casualty or theft . . . . | **6**

7 Combine lines 2 through 6. Enter the gain or (loss) here and on the appropriate line as follows: . . . . | **7**

Partnerships (except electing large partnerships) and S corporations. Report the gain or (loss) following the instructions for Form 1065, Schedule K, line 10, or Form 1120S, Schedule K, line 9. Skip lines 8, 9, 11, and 12 below.

Individuals, partners, S corporation shareholders, and all others. If line 7 is zero or a loss, enter the amount from line 7 on line 11 below and skip lines 8 and 9. If line 7 is a gain and you did not have any prior year section 1231 losses, or they were recaptured in an earlier year, enter the gain from line 7 as a long-term capital gain on the Schedule D filed with your return and skip lines 8, 9, 11, and 12 below.

8 Nonrecaptured net section 1231 losses from prior years (see instructions) . . . . | **8**

9 Subtract line 8 from line 7. If zero or less, enter -0-. If line 9 is zero, enter the gain from line 7 on line 12 below. If line 9 is more than zero, enter the amount from line 8 on line 12 below and enter the gain from line 9 as a long-term capital gain on the Schedule D filed with your return (see instructions) . . . . | **9**

Part II Ordinary Gains and Losses (see instructions)

10 Ordinary gains and losses not included on lines 11 through 16 (include property held 1 year or less):

11 Loss, if any, from line 7 . . . . | **11** ( )

12 Gain, if any, from line 7 or amount from line 8, if applicable . . . . | **12**

13 Gain, if any, from line 31 . . . . | **13**

14 Net gain or (loss) from Form 4684, lines 31 and 38a . . . . | **14**

15 Ordinary gain from installment sales from Form 6252, line 25 or 36 . . . . | **15**

16 Ordinary gain or (loss) from like-kind exchanges from Form 8824 . . . . | **16**

17 Combine lines 10 through 16 . . . . | **17**

18 For all except individual returns, enter the amount from line 17 on the appropriate line of your return and skip lines a and b below. For individual returns, complete lines a and b below:

a If the loss on line 11 includes a loss from Form 4684, line 35, column (b)(ii), enter that part of the loss here. Enter the part of the loss from income-producing property on Schedule A (Form 1040), line 28, and the part of the loss from property used as an employee on Schedule A (Form 1040), line 23. Identify as from "Form 4797, line 18a." See instructions . . . | **18a**

b Redetermine the gain or (loss) on line 17 excluding the loss, if any, on line 18a. Enter here and on Form 1040, line 14 | **18b**

For Paperwork Reduction Act Notice, see separate instructions.

Cat. No. 13086I

Form **4797** (2014)

Part III Gain From Disposition of Property Under Sections 1245, 1250, 1252, 1254, and 1255 (see instructions)

19	(a) Description of section 1245, 1250, 1252, 1254, or 1255 property:	(b) Date acquired (mo., day, yr.)	(c) Date sold (mo., day, yr.)
A			
B			
C			
D			

These columns relate to the properties on lines 19A through 19D. ▶		Property A	Property B	Property C	Property D
20 Gross sales price (**Note:** See line 1 before completing.)	20				
21 Cost or other basis plus expense of sale	21				
22 Depreciation (or depletion) allowed or allowable	22				
23 Adjusted basis. Subtract line 22 from line 21	23				
24 Total gain. Subtract line 23 from line 20	24				
25 **If section 1245 property:**					
a Depreciation allowed or allowable from line 22	25a				
b Enter the **smaller** of line 24 or 25a	25b				
26 **If section 1250 property:** If straight line depreciation was used, enter -0- on line 26g, except for a corporation subject to section 291.					
a Additional depreciation after 1975 (see instructions)	26a				
b Applicable percentage multiplied by the **smaller** of line 24 or line 26a (see instructions)	26b				
c Subtract line 26a from line 24. If residential rental property **or** line 24 is not more than line 26a, skip lines 26d and 26e	26c				
d Additional depreciation after 1969 and before 1976	26d				
e Enter the **smaller** of line 26c or 26d	26e				
f Section 291 amount (corporations only)	26f				
g Add lines 26b, 26e, and 26f	26g				
27 **If section 1252 property:** Skip this section if you did not dispose of farmland or if this form is being completed for a partnership (other than an electing large partnership).					
a Soil, water, and land clearing expenses	27a				
b Line 27a multiplied by applicable percentage (see instructions)	27b				
c Enter the **smaller** of line 24 or 27b	27c				
28 **If section 1254 property:**					
a Intangible drilling and development costs, expenditures for development of mines and other natural deposits, mining exploration costs, and depletion (see instructions)	28a				
b Enter the **smaller** of line 24 or 28a	28b				
29 **If section 1255 property:**					
a Applicable percentage of payments excluded from income under section 126 (see instructions)	29a				
b Enter the **smaller** of line 24 or 29a (see instructions)	29b				

Summary of Part III Gains. Complete property columns A through D through line 29b before going to line 30.

30 Total gains for all properties. Add property columns A through D, line 24	30	
31 Add property columns A through D, lines 25b, 26g, 27c, 28b, and 29b. Enter here and on line 13	31	
32 Subtract line 31 from line 30. Enter the portion from casualty or theft on Form 4684, line 33. Enter the portion from other than casualty or theft on Form 4797, line 6	32	

Part IV Recapture Amounts Under Sections 179 and 280F(b)(2) When Business Use Drops to 50% or Less (see instructions)

			(a) Section 179	(b) Section 280F(b)(2)
33 Section 179 expense deduction or depreciation allowable in prior years	33			
34 Recomputed depreciation (see instructions)	34			
35 Recapture amount. Subtract line 34 from line 33. See the instructions for where to report	35			

2014

Department of the Treasury
Internal Revenue Service

Instructions for Form 4797

Sales of Business Property
(Also Involuntary Conversions and Recapture Amounts
Under Sections 179 and 280F(b)(2))

Section references are to the Internal Revenue Code unless otherwise noted.

Future Developments

For the latest information about developments related to Form 4797 and its instructions, such as legislation enacted after they were published, go to *www.irs.gov/form4797.*

General Instructions

Purpose of Form

Use Form 4797 to report:
* The sale or exchange of:
    1. Property used in your trade or business;
    2. Depreciable and amortizable property;
    3. Oil, gas, geothermal, or other mineral properties; and
    4. Section 126 property.

* The involuntary conversion (from other than casualty or theft) of property used in your trade or business and capital assets held in connection with a trade or business or a transaction entered into for profit.
* The disposition of noncapital assets (other than inventory or property held primarily for sale to customers in the ordinary course of your trade or business).
* The disposition of capital assets not reported on Schedule D.
* The gain or loss (including any related recapture) for partners and S corporation shareholders from certain section 179 property dispositions by partnerships (other than electing large partnerships) and S corporations.
* The computation of recapture amounts under sections 179 and 280F(b)(2) when the business use of section 179 or listed property decreases to 50% or less.
* Gains or losses treated as ordinary gains or losses, if you are a trader in securities or commodities and made a mark-to-market election under Internal Revenue Code section 475(f).

Other Forms You May Have To File

* Use Form 4684, Casualties and Thefts, to report involuntary conversions from casualties and thefts.
* Use Form 6252, Installment Sale Income, to report the sale of property under the installment method.
* Use Form 8824, Like-Kind Exchanges, to report exchanges of qualifying business or investment property for property of a like kind. For exchanges of property used in a trade or business (and other noncapital assets), enter the gain or (loss) from Form 8824, if any, on Form 4797, line 5 or line 16.
* If you sold property on which you claimed investment credit, see Form 4255, Recapture of Investment Credit, to find out if you must recapture some or all of the credit.
* Use Form 8949, Sales and Other Dispositions of Capital Assets, to report the sale or exchange of capital assets not reported on another form or schedule; gains from involuntary conversions (other than casualty or theft) of capital assets not held for business or profit; and nonbusiness bad debts.

Where To Make First Entry for Certain Items Reported on This Form

	(a) Type of property	(b) Held 1 year or less	(c) Held more than 1 year
1	**Depreciable trade or business property:**		
	a Sold or exchanged at a gain	Part II	Part III (1245, 1250)
	b Sold or exchanged at a loss	Part II	Part I
2	**Depreciable residential rental property:**		
	a Sold or exchanged at a gain	Part II	Part III (1250)
	b Sold or exchanged at a loss	Part II	Part I
3	**Farmland held less than 10 years upon which soil, water, or land clearing expenses were deducted:**		
	a Sold at a gain	Part II	Part III (1252)
	b Sold at a loss	Part II	Part I
4	**All other farmland**	Part II	Part I
5	**Disposition of cost-sharing payment property described in section 126**	Part II	Part III (1255)
6	**Cattle and horses used in a trade or business for draft, breeding, dairy, or sporting purposes:**	**Held less than 24 months**	**Held 24 months or more**
	a Sold at a gain	Part II	Part III (1245)
	b Sold at a loss	Part II	Part I
	c Raised cattle and horses sold at a gain	Part II	Part I
7	**Livestock other than cattle and horses used in a trade or business for draft, breeding, dairy, or sporting purposes:**	**Held less than 12 months**	**Held 12 months or more**
	a Sold at a gain	Part II	Part III (1245)
	b Sold at a loss	Part II	Part I
	c Raised livestock sold at a gain	Part II	Part I

Cat. No. 13087T

- Use the applicable Schedule D, Capital Gains and Losses, for the return you are filing to figure the overall gain or loss from transactions reported on Form 8949 and to report transactions you do not have to report on Form 8949. See the Instructions for Form 8949 and the instructions for the applicable Schedule D.

Additional Information. See Pub. 544, Sales and Other Dispositions of Assets. Also see Pub. 550, Investment Income and Expenses (Including Capital Gains and Losses).

Special Rules

At-Risk Rules

If you report a loss on an asset used in an activity for which you are not at risk, in whole or in part, see the Instructions for Form 6198, At-Risk Limitations. Also, see Pub. 925, Passive Activity and At-Risk Rules. Losses from passive activities are subject first to the at-risk rules and then to the passive activity rules.

Depreciable Property and Other Property Disposed of in the Same Transaction

If you disposed of both depreciable property and other property (for example, a building and land) in the same transaction and realized a gain, you must allocate the amount realized between the two types of property based on their respective fair market values (FMVs) to figure the part of the gain to be recaptured as ordinary income because of depreciation. The disposition of each type of property is reported separately in the appropriate part of Form 4797 (for example, for property held more than 1 year, report the sale of a building in Part III and land in Part I).

Disposition of Assets That Constitute a Trade or Business

If you sell a group of assets that make up a trade or business and the buyer's bases in the assets are determined wholly by the amount paid for the assets, both you and the buyer generally must allocate the total sales price to the assets transferred. File Form 8594, Asset Acquisition Statement, to report the sale. See Pub. 544 for more details on the sale of business assets.

Installment Sales

If you sold property at a gain and you will receive a payment in a tax year after the year of sale, you generally must report the sale on the installment method unless you elect not to do so.

Use Form 6252 to report the sale on the installment method. Also use Form 6252 to report any payment received during your 2014 tax year from a sale made in an earlier year that you reported on the installment method.

To elect out of the installment method, report the full amount of the gain on a timely filed return (including extensions). If you timely filed your tax return without making the election, you can still make the election by filing an amended return within 6 months of the due date of your return (excluding extensions). Write "Filed pursuant to section 301.9100-2" at the top of the amended return.

For a detailed discussion of installment sales, see Publication 537, Installment Sales.

Traders Who Made a Mark-To-Market Election

A trader in securities or commodities may elect under section 475(f) to use the mark-to-market method to account for securities or commodities held in connection with a trading business. Under this method of accounting, any security or commodity held at the end of the tax year is treated as sold (and reacquired) at its FMV on the last business day of that year.

Unless you are a new taxpayer, the election must be made by the due date (not including extensions) of the tax return for the year prior to the year for which the election becomes effective.

If you are a trader in securities or commodities with a mark-to-market election under section 475(f) in effect for the tax year, the following special rules apply.
- Gains and losses from all securities or commodities held in connection with your trading business (including those marked to market) are treated as ordinary income and losses, instead of capital gains and losses. As a result, the lower capital gain tax rates and the limitation on capital losses do not apply.
- The gain or loss from each security or commodity held in connection with your trading business (including those marked to market) is reported on Form 4797, line 10. See the instructions for line 10.
- The wash sale rule does not apply to securities or commodities held in connection with your trading business.

For details on the mark-to-market election and how to make it, see sections 475(e) and 475(f). Also see Pub. 550.

Sale of Home Used for Business

If you sold property that was your home and you used it for business or to produce rental income, you may need to use Form 4797 to report the sale of the business or rental part (or the sale of the entire property if used entirely for business or rental). If you use property partly as a home, and partly for business or to produce income, the treatment of any gain on the sale depends on whether the business or rental part of the property is part of your home or separate from it. For more details, see *Property Used Partly for Business or Rental* in Pub. 523, Selling Your Home.

Exclusion of gain on sale of home used for business. You may be able to exclude part or all of the gain figured on Form 4797 if the property sold was used for business or to produce rental income and was also owned and used as your principal residence during the 5-year period ending on the date of the sale. During that 5-year period, you must have owned and used the property as your personal residence for 2 or more years. However, the exclusion may not apply to the part of the gain that is allocated to any period after December 31, 2008, during which the property was not used as your principal residence.

If the property was held more than 1 year, complete Part III to figure the amount of the gain. Do not take the exclusion into account when figuring the gain on line 24. If line 22 includes depreciation for periods after May 6, 1997, you cannot exclude gain to the extent of that depreciation. On line 2 of Form 4797, write "Section 121 exclusion," and enter the amount of the exclusion as a (loss) in column (g).

If the property was held for 1 year or less, report the sale and the amount of the exclusion, if any, in a similar manner on line 10 of Form 4797.

For details and exceptions including how to figure gain on the sale of a home used for business and the amount of the exclusion, see section 121 and Pub. 523.

Involuntary Conversion of Property

You may not have to pay tax on a gain from an involuntary or compulsory conversion of property. See Pub. 544 for details.

Passive Loss Limitations

If you have an overall loss from passive activities and you report a loss on an asset used in a passive activity, use Form 8582, Passive Activity Loss Limitations, or Form 8810, Corporate Passive Activity Loss and Credit Limitations, as applicable, to see how much loss is allowed before entering it on Form 4797.

You cannot claim unused passive activity credits when you dispose of your interest in an activity. However, if you dispose of your entire interest in an activity, you may elect to increase the basis of the credit property by the original basis reduction of the property to the extent that the credit has not been allowed because of the passive activity rules. Make the election on Form 8582-CR, Passive Activity Credit Limitations, or Form 8810, as applicable. No basis adjustment may be elected on a partial disposition of your interest in an activity.

Recapture of Preproductive Expenses

If you elect not to use the uniform capitalization rules of section 263A, any plant that you produce is treated as section 1245 property. For dispositions of plants reportable on Form 4797, enter the recapture amount taxed as ordinary income on line 22 of Form 4797. See *Disposition of plants and animals* in chapter 9 of Pub. 225, Farmer's Tax Guide, for details.

Section 197(f)(9)(B)(ii) Election

If you made the election under section 197(f)(9)(B)(ii) to recognize gain on the disposition of a section 197 intangible and to pay a tax on that gain at the highest tax rate, include the additional tax on Form 1040, line 44 (or the appropriate line of other income tax returns). Check box c and enter "197" and the tax in the space next to that box. The additional tax is the amount that, when added to any other income tax on the gain, equals the gain multiplied by the highest tax rate.

Rollover of Gain From Sale of Empowerment Zone Assets

If you sold a qualified empowerment zone asset that you held for more than 1 year, you may be able to elect to postpone part or all of the gain that you would otherwise include on Form 4797, Part I. If you make the election, you generally recognize gain on the sale

only to the extent, if any, that the amount realized on the sale is more than the cost of qualified empowerment zone assets (replacement property) you purchased during the 60-day period beginning on the date of the sale. The following rules apply.

• No portion of the cost of the replacement property may be taken into account to the extent the cost is taken into account to exclude gain on a different empowerment zone asset.

• The replacement property must qualify as an empowerment zone asset with respect to the same empowerment zone as the asset sold.

• You must reduce the basis of the replacement property by the amount of postponed gain.

• This election does not apply to any gain (a) treated as ordinary income or (b) attributable to real property, or an intangible asset, that is not an integral part of an enterprise zone business.

• The District of Columbia enterprise zone is not treated as an empowerment zone for this purpose.

• The election is irrevocable without IRS consent.

See section 1397C for the definition of empowerment zone and enterprise zone business. You can find out if your business is located within an empowerment zone by using the EZ/RC Address Locator at *http://egis.hud.gov/ezrclocator/*.

Qualified empowerment zone assets are

1. Tangible property, if:

a. You acquired the property after December 21, 2000,

b. The original use of the property in the empowerment zone began with you, and

c. Substantially all of the use of the property, during substantially all of the time that you held it, was in your enterprise zone business; and

2. Stock in a domestic corporation or a capital or profits interest in a domestic partnership, if:

a. You acquired the stock or partnership interest after December 21, 2000, solely in exchange for cash, from the corporation at its original issue (directly or through an underwriter) or from the partnership;

b. The business was an enterprise zone business (or a new business being organized as an enterprise zone business) as of the time you acquired the stock or partnership interest; and

c. The business qualified as an enterprise zone business during substantially all of the time you held the stock or partnership interest.

See section 1397B for more details.

How to report. Report the entire gain realized from the sale as you otherwise would without regard to the election. On Form 4797, line 2, enter "Section 1397B Rollover" in column (a) and enter as a (loss) in column (g) the amount of gain included on Form 4797 that you are electing to postpone. If you are reporting the sale directly on Form 4797, line 2, use the line directly below the line on which you reported the sale.

Exclusion of Gain From Sale of DC Zone Assets

If you sold or exchanged a District of Columbia Enterprise Zone (DC Zone) asset that you acquired after 1997 and before 2012, and held for more than 5 years, you may be able to exclude the amount of "qualified capital gain." The qualified gain is, generally, any gain recognized in a trade or business that you would otherwise include on Form 4797, Part I. This exclusion also applies to an interest in, or property of, certain businesses operating in the District of Columbia.

DC Zone asset. A DC Zone asset is any of the following.
• DC Zone business stock.
• DC Zone partnership interest.
• DC Zone business property.

Qualified capital gain. The qualified capital gain is any gain recognized on the sale or exchange of a DC Zone asset that is a capital asset or property used in a trade or business. It does not include any of the following gain:
• Gain treated as ordinary income under section 1245;
• Gain treated as unrecaptured section 1250 gain. The section 1250 gain must be figured as if it applied to all depreciation rather than the additional depreciation;
• Gain attributable to real property, or an intangible asset, which is not an integral part of a DC Zone business; and
• Gain from a related-party transaction. See *Sales and Exchanges Between Related Persons* in chapter 2 of Pub. 544.

See section 1400B for more details on DC Zone assets and special rules.

How to report. Report the entire gain realized from the sale or exchange as you otherwise would without regard to the exclusion. To report the exclusion, enter "DC Zone Asset Exclusion" on Form 4797, line 2, column (a) and enter as a (loss) in column (g) the amount of the exclusion that offsets the gain reported in Part I, line 6.

 Any unrecaptured section 1250 gain is not qualified capital gain. Identify the amount of gain that is unrecaptured section 1250 gain and report it on the Schedule D for the return you are filing.

Exclusion of Gain From Qualified Community Assets

If you sold or exchanged a qualified community asset acquired after 2001 and before 2010 that you held for more than 5 years, you may be able to exclude the "qualified capital gain." The qualified gain is, generally, any gain recognized in a trade or business that you would otherwise include on Form 4797, Part I. This exclusion also applies to an interest in, or property of, certain renewal community businesses.

Qualified community asset. A qualified community asset is any of the following.
* Qualified community stock.
* Qualified community partnership interest.
* Qualified community business property.

Qualified capital gain. Qualified capital gain is any gain recognized on the sale or exchange of a qualified community asset that is a capital asset or property used in a trade or business. It does not include any of the following gains:
* Gain treated as ordinary income under section 1245;
* Section 1250 gain figured as if section 1250 applied to all depreciation rather than the additional depreciation;
* Gain attributable to real property, or an intangible asset, that is not an integral part of a qualified community business; and
* Gain from a related-party transaction. See *Sales and Exchanges Between Related Persons* in chapter 2 of Pub. 544.

See section 1400F for more details and special rules.

How to report. Report the entire gain realized from the sale or exchange as you otherwise would without regard to the exclusion. To report the exclusion, enter "Qualified Community Asset Exclusion" on Form 4797, line 2, column (a) and enter as a (loss) in column (g)

the amount of the exclusion that offsets the gain reported in Part I, line 6.

Specific Instructions

Note. To show losses, enclose figures in (parentheses).

If you disposed of property you acquired by inheritance from someone who died before or after 2010, enter "INHERITED" in column (b) instead of the date you acquired the property. Also report the sale or exchange that way if you inherited the property from someone who died in 2010 and the executor of the decedent's estate did not elect under section 1022 to file Form 8939.

Disposition by a Partnership or S Corporation of Section 179 Property

Partners and S corporation shareholders. If you received a Schedule K-1 from a partnership or S corporation reporting the sale, exchange, or other disposition of property for which a section 179 expense deduction was previously claimed and passed through to its partners or shareholders, you must report your share of the transaction on Form 4797, 4684, 6252, or 8824 (whether or not you were a partner or shareholder at the time the section 179 deduction was claimed).

Use the worksheet, later, to figure the amount to report on Form 4797, 4684, 6252, or 8824, and to figure any reduction in your carryforward of the unused section 179 expense deduction. The partnership or S corporation must provide the following information on Schedule K-1 for the transaction.
* Description of the property.
* Date the property was acquired and placed in service.
* Date of the sale or other disposition of the property.
* The partner's or shareholder's share of the gross sales price or amount realized. Enter this amount on line 1 of the worksheet.
* The partner's or shareholder's share of the cost or other basis plus the expense of sale. Enter this amount on line 2 of the worksheet.
* The partner's or shareholder's share of the depreciation allowed or allowable, but excluding the section 179 expense deduction. Enter this amount on line 3a of the worksheet.

* The partner's or shareholder's share of the section 179 expense deduction passed through for the property and the partnership's or S corporation's tax year(s) in which the amount was passed through. Enter on line 3b of the worksheet your share of the total amount of the section 179 expense deduction passed through for the property (even if you were not a partner or shareholder for the tax year in which it was passed through or you did not deduct all or part of the section 179 expense because of the dollar or taxable income limitations). The tax year(s) in which the amount was passed through are provided so you can determine the amount of unused carryover section 179 expense (if any) for the property to report on line 3c.
* If the disposition is due to a casualty or theft, a statement indicating so, and any additional information needed by the partner or shareholder to complete Form 4684.
* If the disposition was an installment sale made during the partnership's or S corporation's tax year reported using the installment method, any information needed by the partner or shareholder to complete Form 6252. The partnership or S corporation also must separately report the partner's or shareholder's share of all payments received for the property in the following tax years.
* If the disposition was a disposition of property given up in an exchange involving like-kind property made during the partnership's or S corporation's tax year, any information needed by the partner or shareholder to complete Form 8824.

If you have a carryforward of unused section 179 expense deduction that includes section 179 expense deduction previously passed through to you for the disposed asset, you must reduce your carryforward by your share of the section 179 expense deduction shown on Schedule K-1 (or the amount attributable to that property included in your carryforward amount).

Note. Partnerships (other than electing large partnerships) and S corporations do not report these transactions on Forms 4797, 4684, 6252, or 8824. Instead, they provide their partners and shareholders the information they need to report the transactions. See the instructions for Form 1065 or Form 1120S for details on the information that must be reported on Schedule K-1.

Line 1

Enter on line 1 the total gross proceeds from:

• Sales or exchanges of real estate reported to you for 2014 on Form(s) 1099-S (or substitute statement) that you are including on line 2, 10, or 20 and

• Sales of securities or commodities reported to you for 2014 on Forms 1099-B (or substitute statements) that you are including on line 10 because you are a trader with a mark-to-market election under section 475(f) in effect for the tax year. See _Traders Who Made a Mark-To-Market Election,_ earlier, and the Instructions for line 10, later.

Part I

Use Part I to report section 1231 transactions that are not required to be reported in Part III.

Section 1231 transactions. The following are section 1231 transactions.

• Sales or exchanges of real or depreciable property used in a trade or business and held for more than 1 year. To figure the holding period, begin counting on the day after you received the property and include the day you disposed of it.

• Cutting of timber that the taxpayer elects to treat as a sale or exchange under section 631(a).

• Disposal of timber with a retained economic interest that is treated as a sale, or an outright sale of timber, under section 631(b).

• Disposal of coal (including lignite) or domestic iron ore with a retained economic interest that is treated as a sale under section 631(c).

• Sales or exchanges of cattle and horses, regardless of age, used in a trade or business for draft, breeding, dairy, or sporting purposes and held for 24 months or more from acquisition date.

• Sales or exchanges of livestock other than cattle and horses, regardless of age, used in a trade or business for draft, breeding, dairy, or sporting purposes and held for 12 months or more from acquisition date.

Note. Livestock does not include poultry, chickens, turkeys, pigeons, geese, other birds, fish, frogs, reptiles, etc.

• Sales or exchanges of unharvested crops. See section 1231(b)(4).

• Involuntary conversions of trade or business property or capital assets held more than 1 year in connection with a trade or business or a transaction

entered into for profit. These conversions may result from (a) part or total destruction, (b) theft or seizure, or (c) requisition or condemnation (whether threatened or carried out). If any recognized losses were from involuntary conversions from fire, storm, shipwreck, or other casualty or from theft and the losses exceed the recognized gains from the conversions, do not include any gains or losses from such conversions when figuring your net section 1231 losses.

Transactions to which section 1231 does not apply. Section 1231 transactions do not include sales or exchanges of:

• Inventory or property held primarily for sale to customers;

• Copyrights, literary, musical, or artistic compositions, letters or memoranda, or similar property (a) created by your personal efforts, (b) prepared or produced for you (in the case of letters, memoranda, or similar property), or (c) received from someone who created them or for whom they were created, as mentioned in (a) or (b), in a way that entitled you to the basis of the previous owner (such as by gift); or

• U.S. Government publications, including the Congressional Record, that you received from the Government other than by purchase at the normal sales price or that you got from someone who had received it in a similar way, if your basis is determined by reference to the previous owner's basis.

Line 7

Partners and S corporation shareholders receive a Schedule K-1 (Form 1065 or Form 1120S), which includes amounts that must be reported on the Form 4797. Following the instructions for Schedule K-1, enter any amounts from your Schedule K-1 (Form 1120S), box 9, or Schedule K-1 (Form 1065), box 10, in Part I of Form 4797.

If the amount from line 7 is a gain and you do not have nonrecaptured section 1231 losses from prior years (see instructions for line 8), enter the gain from line 7 as a long-term capital gain on the Schedule D for the return you are filing.

Line 8

Your net section 1231 gain on line 7 is treated as ordinary income to the extent of your "nonrecaptured section 1231 losses." Your nonrecaptured section 1231 losses are your net section 1231 losses deducted during the 5 preceding tax years that have not yet been applied

against any net section 1231 gain to determine how much net section 1231 gain is treated as ordinary income under this rule.

Example. You had net section 1231 losses of $4,000 and $6,000 in 2009 and 2010, respectively, and net section 1231 gains of $3,000 and $2,000 in 2013 and 2014, respectively. The 2014 net section 1231 gain of $2,000 is entered on line 7 and the nonrecaptured net section 1231 losses of $7,000 ($10,000 net section 1231 losses minus the $3,000 that was applied against the 2014 net section 1231 gain) are entered on line 8. The entire $2,000 net section 1231 gain on line 7 is treated as ordinary income and is entered on line 12 of Form 4797. For recordkeeping purposes, the $4,000 loss from 2009 is all recaptured ($3,000 in 2013 and $1,000 in 2014), and you have $5,000 of section 1231 losses from 2010 left to recapture ($6,000 minus the $1,000 recaptured this year).

Figuring the Prior Year Losses

You had a net section 1231 loss if section 1231 losses exceeded section 1231 gains. Gains are included only to the extent taken into account in figuring gross income. Losses are included only to the extent taken into account in figuring taxable income except that the limitation on capital losses does not apply.

Line 9

For recordkeeping purposes, if line 9 is zero, the amount on line 7 is the amount of net section 1231 loss recaptured in 2014. If line 9 is more than zero, you have recaptured all of your net section 1231 losses from prior years.

Enter the gain from line 9 as a long-term capital gain on the Schedule D for the return you are filing.

Part II

If a transaction is not reportable in Part I or Part III and the property is not a capital asset reportable on Schedule D, report the transaction in Part II.

If you received ordinary income from a sale or other disposition of your interest in a partnership, see Pub. 541, Partnerships.

Line 10

Report other ordinary gains and losses, including gains and losses from property held 1 year or less, on this line.

Deduct the loss from a qualifying abandonment of business or investment

Worksheet for Partners and S Corporation Shareholders To Figure Gain or Loss on Dispositions of Property for Which a Section 179 Deduction Was Claimed

Keep for Your Records

Caution: See the *worksheet instructions* below before starting.

1. Gross sales price . . . . 1. _____
2. Cost or other basis . . . . 2. _____
3. a   Depreciation (excluding section 179 expense deduction) . . . . 3a. _____
    b   Section 179 expense deduction . . . . 3b. _____
    c   Unused carryover of section 179 expense deduction . . . . 3c. _____
    d   Subtract line 3c from line 3b . . . . 3d. _____
    e   Add lines 3a and 3d . . . . 3e. _____
4. **Adjusted basis.** Subtract line 3e from line 2 . . . . 4. _____
5. **Gain or loss.** Subtract line 4 from line 1 (see *Where To Report Amounts From Worksheet,* below) . . . . 5. _____

Worksheet Instructions

Caution: *For a disposition due to casualty or theft, skip lines 1 and 5 and enter the amount from line 4 on Form 4684, line 20, and complete the rest of Form 4684.*

Lines 1, 2, 3a, and 3b. Enter these amounts from Schedule K-1 (Form 1065 or 1120S).

Line 3c. If you were unable to claim all of the section 179 expense deduction previously passed through to you for the property (if any), enter the smaller of line 3b or the portion of your unused carryover of section 179 expense deduction attributable to the property. Make sure you reduce your carryover of disallowed section 179 expense deduction shown on Form 4562 by the amount on line 3c.

Where To Report Amounts From Worksheet

Generally, the information from the above worksheet is reported on the lines specified below for Form 4797, Part III. However, for a disposition under the installment method, complete the lines shown below for Form 6252. For dispositions of property given up in an exchange involving like-kind property, complete the lines shown below for Form 8824.

    If line 5 is a gain and the property was held more than 1 year, report the disposition as follows.
- Complete Form 4797, line 19, columns (a), (b), and (c); Form 6252, lines 1 through 4; or Form 8824, Parts I and II.
- Report the amount from line 1 above on Form 4797, line 20; Form 6252, line 5; or Form 8824, line 12 or 16.
- Report the amount from line 2 above on Form 4797, line 21; or Form 6252, line 8.
- Report the amount from line 3e above on Form 4797, line 22; or Form 6252, line 9.
- Report the amount from line 4 above on Form 4797, line 23; Form 6252, line 10; or Form 8824, line 13 or 18.
- Complete the rest of the applicable form.

    If line 5 is zero or a loss and the property was held more than 1 year, report the disposition as follows. Do not report a loss on Form 6252; instead, report the disposition on the lines shown for Form 4797.
- Complete Form 4797, line 2, columns (a), (b), and (c); or Form 8824, Parts I and II.
- Report the amount from line 1 above on Form 4797, line 2, column (d); or Form 8824, line 12 or 16.
- Report the amount from line 2 above on Form 4797, line 2, column (f).
- Report the amount from line 3e above on Form 4797, line 2, column (e).
- Report the amount from line 4 above on Form 8824, line 13 or 18.
- Complete the rest of the applicable form.

    If the property was held 1 year or less, report the gain or loss on the disposition as shown below. Do not report a loss on Form 6252; instead, report the disposition on the lines shown for Form 4797.
- Complete Form 4797, line 10, columns (a), (b), and (c); Form 6252, lines 1 through 4; or Form 8824, Parts I and II.
- Report the amount from line 1 above on Form 4797, line 10, column (d); Form 6252, line 5; or Form 8824, line 12 or 16.
- Report the amount from line 2 above on Form 4797, line 10, column (f); or Form 6252, line 8.
- Report the amount from line 3e above on Form 4797, line 10, column (e); or Form 6252, line 9.
- Report the amount from line 4 above on Form 6252, line 10; or Form 8824, line 13 or 18.
- Complete the rest of the applicable form.

property on line 10. See *Abandonments* in Pub. 544 for more information.

Gain or Loss From Certain Preferred Stock

Gain or loss recognized by any "applicable financial institution" from the sale or exchange of "any applicable

preferred stock" is ordinary income or loss. An applicable financial institution includes:
- A financial institution defined in section 582(c)(2), and
- A depository institution holding company defined in section 3(w)(1) of the Federal Deposit Insurance Act.

    Also, for this purpose, "applicable preferred stock" is preferred stock of Federal National Mortgage Association (Fannie Mae), or the Federal Home Loan Mortgage Corporation (Freddie Mac) that was:
- Held by the applicable financial institution on September 6, 2008, or

- Sold or exchanged by the applicable financial institution after December 31, 2007, and before September 7, 2008.

In the case of a sale or exchange of applicable preferred stock after September 6, 2008, by a taxpayer that held such preferred stock on September 6, 2008, these provisions apply only where the taxpayer was an applicable financial institution at all times during the period beginning on September 6, 2008, and ending on the date of the sale or exchange of the applicable preferred stock. Therefore, any Fannie Mae or Freddie Mac preferred stock held by a taxpayer that was not an applicable financial institution on September 6, 2008, is not applicable preferred stock (even if such taxpayer subsequently became an applicable financial institution).

For guidance on preferred stock held indirectly by applicable financial institutions through partnerships and subsidiaries, see Rev. Proc. 2008-64, 2008-47 I.R.B. 1195, available at _www.irs.gov/irb/2008–47_IRB/ ar12.html_.

Deferred Gain from Qualifying Electric Transmission Transaction

If you sold or exchanged qualifying electric transmission property before January 1, 2008 (before January 1, 2015, for a qualified electric utility), and elected under section 451(i) to defer the realized gain, the deferred gain is recognized ratably over the 8-year period that began with the tax year that includes the date of the disposition. Include the applicable portion of the deferred gain for the current tax year on line 10. Enter "Deferred gain under section 451(i)" in column (a) and 1/8 of the deferred gain in column (g). See section 451(i) for more details.

Securities or Commodities Held by a Trader Who Made a Mark-To-Market Election

Report on line 10 all gains and losses from sales and dispositions of securities or commodities held in connection with your trading business, including gains and losses from marking to market securities and commodities held at the end of the tax year (see _Traders Who Made a Mark-To-Market Election_, earlier. Attach to your tax return a statement, using the same format as line 10, showing the details of each transaction. Separately show and identify securities or commodities held

and marked to market at the end of the year. On line 10, enter "Trader—see attached" in column (a) and the totals from the statement in columns (d), (f), and (g). Also, see the instructions for line 1, earlier.

Small Business Investment Company Stock

Report on line 10 ordinary losses from the sale or exchange (including worthlessness) of stock in a small business investment company operating under the Small Business Investment Act of 1958. See section 1242.

Also attach a statement that includes the name and address of the small business investment company and, if applicable, the reason the stock is worthless and the approximate date it became worthless.

Section 1244 (Small Business) Stock

Individuals report ordinary losses from the sale or exchange (including worthlessness) of section 1244 (small business) stock on line 10.

To qualify as section 1244 stock, all six of the following requirements must be met.

1. You acquired the stock after June 30, 1958, upon original issuance of the shares from a domestic corporation (or the stock was acquired by a partnership in which you were a partner continuously from the date the stock was issued until the time of the loss).

2. If the stock was issued before November 7, 1978, it was issued under a written plan that met the requirements of Regulations section 1.1244(c)-1(f), and when that plan was adopted, the corporation was treated as a small business corporation under Regulations section 1.1244(c)-2(c).

3. If the stock was issued after November 6, 1978, the corporation was treated as a small business corporation at the time the stock was issued under Regulations section 1.1244(c)-2(b). To be treated as a small business corporation, the total amount of money and other property received by the corporation for its stock as a contribution to capital and paid-in surplus generally may not exceed $1 million.

4. The stock was issued for money or other property (excluding stock or securities).

5. The corporation, for its 5 most recent tax years ending before the date of the loss, derived more than 50% of its gross receipts from sources other than royalties, rents, dividends, interest, annuities, and gains from sales and exchanges of stocks or securities. If the corporation was in existence for at least 1 tax year but fewer than 5 tax years ending before the date of the loss, the 50% test applies for the tax years ending before that date. If the corporation was not in existence for at least 1 tax year ending before the date of the loss, the 50% test applies for the entire period ending before that date. The 50% test does not apply if the corporation's deductions (other than the net operating loss and dividends-received deductions) exceeded its gross income during the applicable period. But this exception to the 50% test applies only if the corporation was largely an operating company within the 5 most recent tax years ending before the date of the loss (or, if less, the entire period the corporation was in existence).

6. If the stock was issued before July 19, 1984, it must have been common stock.

The maximum amount that may be treated as an ordinary loss on Form 4797 is $50,000 ($100,000 if married filing jointly). Special rules may limit the amount of your ordinary loss if (a) you received section 1244 stock in exchange for property with a basis in excess of its FMV or (b) your stock basis increased because of contributions to capital or otherwise. See Pub. 550 for more details.

Attach a computation of the loss from the sale or exchange of section 1244 property. On line 10, enter "Losses on Section 1244 (Small Business Stock)," in column (a), and enter the allowable loss in column (g). Report on Schedule D losses in excess of the maximum amount that may be treated as an ordinary loss (and all gains) from the sale or exchange of section 1244 stock.

Keep adequate records to distinguish section 1244 stock from any other stock owned in the same corporation.

Line 18a

You must complete this line if there is a gain on Form 4797, line 3; a loss on Form 4797, line 11; and a loss on Form 4684, line 35, column (b)(ii). Enter on this line the smaller of the loss on Form 4797, line 11, or the loss on Form 4684, line 35, column (b)(ii). To figure which loss is smaller, treat both losses as positive numbers. Enter the part of the loss from income-producing property on Schedule A (Form 1040), line 28, and the part of the loss from property used as an employee on Schedule A (Form 1040), line 23.

Part III

 Partners and shareholders reporting a disposition of section 179 property which was separately reported to you on Schedule K-1 (Form 1065 or 1120S), see Partners and S corporation shareholders *at the beginning of the* Specific Instructions.

Generally, for property held 1 year or less, do not complete Part III; instead use Part II. For exceptions, see the chart *Where To Make First Entry for Certain Items Reported on This Form,* earlier.

Use Part III to figure recapture of depreciation and certain other items that must be reported as ordinary income on the disposition of property. Complete lines 19 through 24 to determine the gain on the disposition of the property. If you have more than four properties to report, use additional forms. For more details on depreciation recapture, see Pub. 544.

If the property was sold on the installment sale basis, see the Instructions for Form 6252 before completing Part III. Also, if you have both installment sales and noninstallment sales, you may want to use separate Forms 4797, Part III, for the installment sales and the noninstallment sales.

Note. If you sold or otherwise disposed of property for which you elected under section 179(f) to treat as an expense the costs of certain real property placed in service in tax years beginning in 2010, 2011, 2012, or 2013, special rules apply. See Notice 2013-59, 2013-40 I.R. B. 297, at *www.irs.gov/irb/2013-40_IRB/ar14.html.*

Line 20

The gross sales price includes money, the FMV of other property received, and any existing mortgage or other debt the buyer assumes or takes the property subject to. For casualty or theft gains, include insurance or other reimbursement you received or expect to receive for each item. Include on this line your insurance coverage, whether or not you are submitting a claim for reimbursement.

For section 1255 property disposed of in a sale, exchange, or involuntary conversion, enter the amount realized. For section 1255 property disposed of in any other way, enter the FMV.

Line 21

Reduce the cost or other basis of the property by the amount of any enhanced oil recovery credit or disabled access credit. However, do not adjust the cost or other basis for any of the items taken into account on line 22.

Line 22

Complete the following steps to figure the amount to enter on line 22.

Step 1. Add amounts such as the following.
• Deductions allowed or allowable for depreciation (including any special depreciation allowance (see the Form 4562 Instructions)), amortization, depletion, or preproductive expenses (see *Disposition of plants and animals* in chapter 9 of Pub. 225).
• The section 179 expense deduction.
• The commercial revitalization deduction, for buildings placed in service before 2010.
• The downward basis adjustment under section 50(c) (or the corresponding provision of prior law).
• The deduction for qualified clean-fuel vehicle property or refueling property.
• Deductions claimed under section 190, 193, or 1253(d)(2) or (3) (as in effect before the enactment of P.L. 103-66).
• The basis reduction for any qualified plug-in electric or qualified electric vehicle credit.
• The basis reduction for the employer-provided childcare facility credit.
• The deduction for qualified energy efficient commercial building property.
• The basis reduction for the alternative motor vehicle credit.
• The basis reduction for the alternative fuel vehicle refueling property credit.

Step 2. From the Step 1 total, subtract amounts such as the following.
• Any investment credit recapture amount if the basis of the property was reduced in the tax year the property was placed in service under section 50(c)(1) (or the corresponding provision of prior law). See section 50(c)(2) (or the corresponding provision of prior law).
• Any section 179 or 280F(b)(2) recapture amount included in gross income in a prior tax year because the business use of the property decreased to 50% or less.

• Any qualified clean-fuel vehicle property or refueling property deduction you were required to recapture.
• Any basis increase for qualified plug-in electric or qualified electric vehicle credit recapture.
• Any basis increase for recapture of the employer-provided childcare facility credit.
• Any basis increase for recapture of the alternative motor vehicle credit.
• Any basis increase for recapture of the alternative fuel vehicle refueling property credit.
• Any qualified disaster expense recapture.

For more information on amounts recaptured as depreciation allowed or allowable, see chapter 3 of Pub. 544.

You may have to include depreciation allowed or allowable on another asset (and refigure the basis amount for line 21) if you use its adjusted basis in determining the adjusted basis of the property described on line 19. An example is property acquired by a trade-in. See Regulations section 1.1245-2(a)(4). Also, see *Like-Kind Exchanges* under *Nontaxable Exchanges* in chapter 1 of Pub. 544.

Line 23

For section 1255 property, enter the adjusted basis of the section 126 property disposed of.

Line 25

Section 1245 property. Section 1245 property is property that is depreciable (or amortizable under section 185 (repealed), 197, or 1253(d)(2) or (3) (as in effect before the enactment of P.L. 103-66)) and is one of the following.
• Personal property.
• Elevators and escalators placed in service before 1987.
• Real property (other than property described under tangible real property below) adjusted for the following.

   1. Amortization of certified pollution control facilities.

   2. The section 179 expense deduction.

   3. Deduction for clean-fuel vehicles and certain refueling property.

   4. Deduction for capital costs incurred in complying with Environmental Protection Agency sulfur regulations.

   5. Deduction for certain qualified refinery property.

   6. Deduction for qualified energy efficient commercial building property.

7. Deduction for election to expense qualified advanced mine safety equipment property.

8. Amortization of railroad grading and tunnel bores if in effect before the repeal by the revenue Reconciliation Act of 1990. (Repealed by P.L. 99-514, Tax Reform Act of 1986, section 242(a).)

9. Certain expenditures for child care facilities if in effect before the repeal by P.L. 101-508, section 11801 (a)(13). (Repealed by P.L. 101-508, Omnibus Budget Reconciliation Act of 1990, section 11801(a)(13), except with regards to deductions made prior to November 5, 1990.)

10. Expenditures to remove architectural and transportation barriers to the handicapped and elderly.

11. Deduction for qualified tertiary injectant expenses.

12. Certain reforestation expenditures.

• Tangible real property (except buildings and their structural components) if it is used in any of the following ways.

1. As an integral part of manufacturing, production, or extraction or of furnishing transportation, communications, or certain public utility services.

2. As a research facility in these activities.

3. For the bulk storage of fungible commodities (including commodities in a liquid or gaseous state) used in these activities.

• A single purpose agricultural or horticultural structure (as defined in section 168(i)(13)).
• A storage facility (not including a building or its structural components) used in connection with the distribution of petroleum or any primary petroleum product.
• Any railroad grading or tunnel bore (as defined in section 168(e)(4)).

Exceptions and limits. Special rules apply to the following.
• Gifts.
• Transfers at death.
• Certain tax-free transactions.
• Certain like-kind exchanges, involuntary conversions, etc.
• Property distributed by a partnership to a partner.
• Transfers to tax-exempt organizations where the property will be used in an unrelated business.
• Timber property.

• Dispositions of amortizable section 197 intangibles.
For more information see section 1245(b). Also, see Pub. 544.

Line 26

Section 1250 property is depreciable real property (other than section 1245 property). Generally, section 1250 recapture applies if you used an accelerated depreciation method or you claimed any special depreciation allowance, or the commercial revitalization deduction.

 Section 1250 recapture does not apply to dispositions of the following MACRS property placed in service after 1986 (or after July 31, 1986, if elected). You are not required to calculate additional depreciation for these properties on line 26.
• *27.5-year (or 40-year, if elected) residential rental property (except for 27.5-year qualified New York Liberty Zone property acquired after September 10, 2001).*
• *22-, 31.5-, or 39-year (or 40-year, if elected) nonresidential real property (except for 39-year qualified New York Liberty Zone property acquired after September 10, 2001, and property for which you elected to claim a commercial revitalization deduction).*

ACRS property. Real property depreciable under ACRS (pre-1987 rules) is subject to recapture under section 1245, except for the following, which are treated as section 1250 property.
• 15-, 18-, or 19-year real property and low-income housing that is residential rental property.
• 15-, 18-, or 19-year real property and low-income housing that is used mostly outside the United States.
• 15-, 18-, or 19-year real property and low-income housing for which a straight line election was made.
• Low-income rental housing described in clause (i), (ii), (iii), or (iv) of section 1250(a)(1)(B). See the instructions for line 26b.

Exceptions and limits. See section 1250(d) for exceptions and limits involving the following.
• Gifts.
• Transfers at death.
• Certain tax-free transactions.
• Certain like-kind exchanges, involuntary conversions, etc.
• Property distributed by a partnership to a partner.

• Disposition of qualified low-income housing.
• Transfers of property to tax-exempt organizations if the property will be used in an unrelated business.
• Dispositions of property as a result of foreclosure proceedings.

Special rules. Special rules apply in the following cases.
• For additional depreciation attributable to rehabilitation expenditures, see section 1250(b)(4).
• If substantial improvements have been made, see section 1250(f).

Line 26a

Enter the additional depreciation for the period after 1975. Additional depreciation is the excess of actual depreciation (including any special depreciation allowance, or commercial revitalization deduction) over depreciation figured using the straight line method. For this purpose, do not reduce the basis under section 50(c)(1) (or the corresponding provision of prior law) to figure straight line depreciation. Also, if you claimed a commercial revitalization deduction, figure straightline depreciation using the property's applicable recovery period under section 168.

Line 26b

Generally, use 100% as the percentage for this line. However, for low-income rental housing described in clause (i), (ii), (iii), or (iv) of section 1250(a)(1)(B), see that section for the percentage to use.

Line 26d

Enter the additional depreciation after 1969 and before 1976. If straight line depreciation exceeds the actual depreciation for the period after 1975, reduce line 26d by the excess. Do not enter less than zero on line 26d.

Line 26f

The amount the corporation treats as ordinary income under section 291 is 20% of the excess, if any, of the amount that would be treated as ordinary income if such property were section 1245 property, over the amount treated as ordinary income under section 1250. If the corporation used the straight line method of depreciation, the ordinary income under section 291 is 20% of the amount figured under section 1245.

Line 27

Partnerships (other than electing large partnerships) skip this section. Partners must enter on the applicable lines of Part III amounts subject to section 1252 according to instructions from the partnership.

You may have ordinary income on the disposition of certain farmland held more than 1 year but less than 10 years.

See section 1252 to determine if there is ordinary income on the disposition of certain farmland for which deductions were allowed under sections 175 (soil and water conservation) and 182 (land clearing) ((as in effect on the day before the date of the enactment of the Tax Reform Act of 1986 on 10/22/1986).

Gain from disposition of certain farmland is subject to ordinary income rules under section 1252 before the application of section 1231 (Part I).

Enter 100% of line 27a on line 27b except as follows.
* 80% if the farmland was disposed of within the 6th year after it was acquired.
* 60% if disposed of within the 7th year.
* 40% if disposed of within the 8th year.
* 20% if disposed of within the 9th year.

Skip line 27 if you dispose of such farmland during the 10th or later year after you acquired it.

Line 28

If you had a gain on the disposition of oil, gas, or geothermal property placed in service before 1987, treat all or part of the gain as ordinary income. Include on line 22 of Form 4797 any depletion allowed (or allowable) in determining the adjusted basis of the property.

If you had a gain on the disposition of oil, gas, geothermal, or other mineral properties (section 1254 property) placed in service after 1986, you must recapture all expenses that were deducted as intangible drilling costs, depletion, mine exploration costs, and development costs under sections 263, 616, and 617.

Exception. Property placed in service after 1986 and acquired under a written contract entered into before September 26, 1985, and binding at all times thereafter is treated as placed in service before 1987.

Note. A corporation that is an integrated oil company completes line 28a by treating amounts amortized under section 291(b)(2) as deductions under section 263(c).

Line 28a

If the property was placed in service before 1987, enter the total expenses after 1975 that:
* Were deducted by the taxpayer or any other person as intangible drilling and development costs under section 263(c) (except previously expensed mining costs that were included in income upon reaching the producing state), and
* Would have been reflected in the adjusted basis of the property if they had not been deducted.

If the property was placed in service after 1986, enter the total expenses that:
* Were deducted under section 263, 616, or 617 by the taxpayer or any other person; and
* But for such deduction, would have been included in the basis of the property, plus
* The deduction under section 611 that reduced the adjusted basis of such property.

If you disposed of a portion of section 1254 property or an undivided interest in it, see section 1254(a)(2).

Line 29a

Use 100% if the property is disposed of less than 10 years after receipt of payments excluded from income. Use 100% minus 10% for each year, or part of a year, that the property was held over 10 years after receipt of the excluded payments. Use zero if 20 years or more.

Line 29b

If any part of the gain shown on line 24 is treated as ordinary income under sections 1231 through 1254 (for example, section 1252), enter the smaller of (a) line 24 reduced by the part of the gain treated as ordinary income under the other provision or (b) line 29a.

Part IV

Column (a)

If you took a section 179 expense deduction for property placed in service after 1986 (other than listed property, as defined in section 280F(d)(4)) and the business use of the property decreased to 50% or less this year, complete column (a) of lines 33 through 35 to figure the recapture amount.

Column (b)

If you have listed property that you placed in service in a prior year and the business use decreased to 50% or less this year, figure the amount to be recaptured under section 280F(b)(2). Complete column (b), lines 33 through 35. See Pub. 463, Travel, Entertainment, Gift, and Car Expenses, for more details on recapture of excess depreciation.

Note. If you have more than one property subject to the recapture rules, figure the recapture amounts separately for each property. Show these calculations on a separate statement and attach it to your tax return.

Line 33

In column (a), enter the section 179 expense deduction you claimed when the property was placed in service. In column (b), enter the depreciation allowable on the property in prior tax years (plus any section 179 expense deduction you claimed when the property was placed in service).

Line 34

In column (a), enter the depreciation that would have been allowable on the section 179 property from the year the property was placed in service through (and including) the current year. See Pub. 946, How To Depreciate Property.

In column (b), enter the depreciation that would have been allowable if the property had not been used more than 50% in a qualified business. Figure the depreciation from the year it was placed in service up to (but not including) the current year. See Pub. 463 and Pub. 946.

Line 35

Subtract line 34 from line 33 and enter the recapture amount as "other income" on the same form or schedule on which you took the deduction. For example, if you took the deduction on Schedule C (Form 1040), report the recapture amount as other income on Schedule C (Form 1040).

Note. If you filed Schedule C or F (Form 1040) and the property was used in both your trade or business and for the production of income, the portion of the recapture amount attributable to your trade or business is subject to self-employment tax. Allocate the amount on line 35 to the appropriate schedules.

Be sure to increase your basis in the property by the recapture amount.

Paperwork Reduction Act Notice. We ask for the information on this form to carry out the Internal Revenue laws of the United States. You are required to give us the information. We need it to ensure that you are complying with these laws and to allow us to figure and collect the right amount of tax.

You are not required to provide the information requested on a form that is subject to the Paperwork Reduction Act unless the form displays a valid OMB control number. Books or records relating to a form or its instructions must be retained as long as their contents may become material in the administration of any Internal Revenue law. Generally, tax returns and return information are confidential, as required by section 6103.

The time needed to complete and file this form will vary depending on individual circumstances. The estimated burden for individual taxpayers filing this form is approved under OMB control number 1545-0074 and is included in the estimates shown in the instructions for their individual income tax return. The estimated burden for all other taxpayers who file this form is shown below.

Recordkeeping	33 hr., 14min.
Learning about the law or the form	2 hr., 52min.
Preparing and sending the form to the IRS	3 hr., 33 min.

If you have comments concerning the accuracy of these time estimates or suggestions for making this form simpler, we would be happy to hear from you. See the instructions for the tax return with which this form is filed.

Form **4868**	**Application for Automatic Extension of Time** **To File U.S. Individual Income Tax Return**	OMB No. 1545-0074
Department of the Treasury Internal Revenue Service (99)	▶ Information about Form 4868 and its instructions is available at *www.irs.gov/form4868.*	2014

There are three ways to request an automatic extension of time to file a U.S. individual income tax return.

1. You can file Form 4868 and pay all or part of your estimated income tax due. See *How To Make a Payment,* on page 3.
2. You can file Form 4868 electronically by accessing IRS *e-file* using your home computer or by using a tax professional who uses *e-file.*
3. You can file a paper Form 4868.

 ### It's Convenient, Safe, and Secure

IRS *e-file* is the IRS's electronic filing program. You can get an automatic extension of time to file your tax return by filing Form 4868 electronically. You will receive an electronic acknowledgment once you complete the transaction. Keep it with your records. Do not mail in Form 4868 if you file electronically, unless you are making a payment with a check or money order (see page 3).

Complete Form 4868 to use as a worksheet. If you think you may owe tax when you file your return, you will need to estimate your total tax liability and subtract how much you have already paid (lines 4, 5, and 6 below).

Several companies offer free e-filing of Form 4868 through the Free File program. For more details, go to IRS.gov and click on *freefile.*

 ### Pay Electronically

You **do not** need to submit a paper Form 4868 if you file it with a payment using our electronic payment options. Your extension will be automatically processed when you pay part or all of your estimated income tax electronically. You can pay online or by phone (see page 3).

 ### *E-file* Using Your Personal Computer or Through a Tax Professional

Refer to your tax software package or tax preparer for ways to file electronically. Be sure to have a copy of your 2013 tax return—you will be asked to provide information from the return for taxpayer verification. If you wish to make a payment, you can pay by electronic funds withdrawal or send your check or money order to the address shown in the middle column under *Where To File a Paper Form 4868* (see page 4).

 ### File a Paper Form 4868

If you wish to file on paper instead of electronically, fill in the Form 4868 below and mail it to the address shown on page 4.

For information on using a private delivery service, see page 4.

Note. If you are a fiscal year taxpayer, you must file a paper Form 4868.

General Instructions

Purpose of Form

Use Form 4868 to apply for 6 more months (4 if "out of the country" (defined on page 2) and a U.S. citizen or resident) to file Form 1040, 1040A, 1040EZ, 1040NR, 1040NR-EZ, 1040-PR, or 1040-SS.

Gift and generation–skipping transfer (GST) tax return (Form 709). An extension of time to file your 2014 calendar year income tax return also extends the time to file Form 709 for 2014. However, it does not extend the time to pay any gift and GST tax you may owe for 2014. To make a payment of gift and GST tax, see Form 8892. If you do not pay the amount due by the regular due date for Form 709, you will owe interest and may also be charged penalties. If the donor died during 2014, see the instructions for Forms 709 and 8892.

Qualifying for the Extension

To get the extra time you must:

1. Properly estimate your 2014 tax liability using the information available to you,
2. Enter your total tax liability on line 4 of Form 4868, and
3. File Form 4868 by the regular due date of your return.

⚠ CAUTION *Although you are not required to make a payment of the tax you estimate as due, Form 4868 does not extend the time to pay taxes. If you do not pay the amount due by the regular due date, you will owe interest. You may also be charged penalties. For more details, see* Interest *and* Late Payment Penalty *on page 2. Any remittance you make with your application for extension will be treated as a payment of tax.*

You do not have to explain why you are asking for the extension. We will contact you only if your request is denied.

Do not file Form 4868 if you want the IRS to figure your tax or you are under a court order to file your return by the regular due date.

▼ DETACH HERE ▼

Form **4868**	**Application for Automatic Extension of Time** **To File U.S. Individual Income Tax Return**	OMB No. 1545-0074
Department of the Treasury Internal Revenue Service (99)	For calendar year 2014, or other tax year beginning _____ , 2014, ending _____ , 20 ___ .	2014

Part I Identification	**Part II** Individual Income Tax
1 Your name(s) (see instructions) Address (see instructions) City, town, or post office State ZIP Code **2** Your social security number **3** Spouse's social security number	**4** Estimate of total tax liability for 2014 . . $ _____ **5** Total 2014 payments . . . . . . _____ **6** **Balance due.** Subtract line 5 from line 4 (see instructions) . . . . _____ **7** Amount you are paying (see instructions) . . . . ▶ _____ **8** Check here if you are "out of the country" and a U.S. citizen or resident (see instructions) . . . . ▶ ☐ **9** Check here if you file Form 1040NR or 1040NR-EZ and did not receive wages as an employee subject to U.S. income tax withholding . . . . ▶ ☐

For Privacy Act and Paperwork Reduction Act Notice, see page 4.   Cat. No. 13141W   Form **4868** (2014)

When To File Form 4868

File Form 4868 by April 15, 2015. Fiscal year taxpayers, file Form 4868 by the original due date of the fiscal year return.

Taxpayers who are out of the country. If, on the regular due date of your return, you are out of the country and a U.S. citizen or resident, you are allowed 2 extra months to file your return and pay any amount due without requesting an extension. Interest will still be charged, however, on payments made after the regular due date, without regard to the extension. For a calendar year return, this is June 15, 2015. File this form and be sure to check the box on line 8 if you need an additional 4 months to file your return.

If you are out of the country and a U.S. citizen or resident, you may qualify for special tax treatment if you meet the *bona fide* residence or physical presence tests. If you do not expect to meet either of those tests by the due date of your return, request an extension to a date after you expect to meet the tests by filing Form 2350, Application for Extension of Time To File U.S. Income Tax Return.

You are out of the country if:

• You live outside the United States and Puerto Rico and your main place of work is outside the United States and Puerto Rico, or

• You are in military or naval service on duty outside the United States and Puerto Rico.

If you qualify as being out of the country, you will still be eligible for the extension even if you are physically present in the United States or Puerto Rico on the regular due date of the return.

For more information on extensions for taxpayers out of the country, see Pub. 54, Tax Guide for U.S. Citizens and Resident Aliens Abroad.

Form 1040NR or 1040NR-EZ filers. If you cannot file your return by the due date, you should file Form 4868. You must file Form 4868 by the regular due date of the return.

If you did not receive wages as an employee subject to U.S. income tax withholding, and your return is due June 15, 2015, check the box on line 9.

Total Time Allowed

Generally, we cannot extend the due date of your return for more than 6 months (October 15, 2015, for most calendar year taxpayers). However, there may be an exception if you are living out of the country. See Pub. 54 for more information.

Filing Your Tax Return

You can file your tax return any time before the extension expires. Do not attach a copy of Form 4868 to your return.

Interest

You will owe interest on any tax not paid by the regular due date of your return, even if you qualify for the 2-month extension because you were out of the country. The interest runs until you pay the tax. Even if you had a good reason for not paying on time, you will still owe interest.

Late Payment Penalty

The late payment penalty is usually ½ of 1% of any tax (other than estimated tax) not paid by April 15, 2015. It is charged for each month or part of a month the tax is unpaid. The maximum penalty is 25%.

The late payment penalty will not be charged if you can show reasonable cause for not paying on time. Attach a statement to your return fully explaining the reason. Do not attach the statement to Form 4868.

You are considered to have reasonable cause for the period covered by this automatic extension if at least 90% of your actual 2014 tax liability is paid before the regular due date of your return through withholding, estimated tax payments, or payments made with Form 4868.

Late Filing Penalty

A late filing penalty is usually charged if your return is filed after the due date (including extensions). The penalty is usually 5% of the amount due for each month or part of a month your return is late. The maximum penalty is 25%. If your return is more than 60 days late, the minimum penalty is $135 or the balance of the tax due on your return, whichever is smaller. You might not owe the penalty if you have a reasonable explanation for filing late. Attach a statement to your return fully explaining your reason for filing late. Do not attach the statement to Form 4868.

How To Claim Credit for Payment Made With This Form

When you file your 2014 return, include the amount of any payment you made with Form 4868 on the appropriate line of your tax return.

The instructions for the following line of your tax return will tell you how to report the payment.

• Form 1040, line 70.
• Form 1040A, line 46.
• Form 1040EZ, line 9.
• Form 1040NR, line 66.
• Form 1040NR-EZ, line 21.
• Form 1040-PR, line 11.
• Form 1040-SS, line 11.

If you and your spouse each filed a separate Form 4868 but later file a joint return for 2014, enter the total paid with both Forms 4868 on the appropriate line of your joint return.

If you and your spouse jointly file Form 4868 but later file separate returns for 2014, you can enter the total amount paid with Form 4868 on either of your separate returns. Or you and your spouse can divide the payment in any agreed amounts.

Specific Instructions

How To Complete Form 4868

Part I—Identification

Enter your name(s) and address. If you plan to file a joint return, include both spouses' names in the order in which they will appear on the return.

If you want correspondence regarding this extension to be sent to you at an address other than your own, enter that address. If you want the correspondence sent to an agent acting for you, include the agent's name (as well as your own) and the agent's address.

If you changed your name after you filed your last return because of marriage, divorce, etc., be sure to report this to the Social Security Administration before filing Form 4868. This prevents delays in processing your extension request.

If you changed your mailing address after you filed your last return, you should use Form 8822, Change of Address, to notify the IRS of the change. Showing a new address on Form 4868 will not update your record. You can get IRS forms by calling 1-800-TAX-FORM (1-800-829-3676). You can also download forms at IRS.gov.

If you plan to file a joint return, enter on line 2 the SSN that you will show first on your return. Enter on line 3 the other SSN to be shown on the joint return. If you are filing Form 1040NR as an estate or trust, enter your employer identification number (EIN) instead of an SSN on line 2. In the left margin, next to the EIN, write "estate" or "trust."

IRS individual taxpayer identification numbers (ITINs) for aliens. If you are a nonresident or resident alien and you do not have and are not eligible to get an SSN, you must apply for an ITIN. Although an ITIN is not required to file Form 4868, you will need one to file your income tax return. For details on how to apply for an ITIN, see Form W-7 and its instructions. If you already have an ITIN, enter it wherever an SSN is requested. If you do not have an ITIN, enter "ITIN TO BE REQUESTED" wherever an SSN is requested.

 An ITIN is for tax use only. It does not entitle you to social security benefits or change your employment or immigration status under U.S. law.

Part II—Individual Income Tax

Rounding off to whole dollars. You can round off cents to whole dollars on Form 4868. If you do round to whole dollars, you must round all amounts. To round, drop amounts under 50 cents and increase amounts from 50 to 99 cents to the next dollar. For example, $1.39 becomes $1 and $2.50 becomes $3. If you have to add two or more amounts to figure the amount to enter on a line, include cents when adding the amounts and round off only the total.

Line 4—Estimate of Total Tax Liability for 2014

Enter on line 4 the total tax liability you expect to report on your 2014:

- Form 1040, line 63.
- Form 1040A, line 39.
- Form 1040EZ, line 12.
- Form 1040NR, line 61.
- Form 1040NR-EZ, line 17.
- Form 1040-PR, line 6.
- Form 1040-SS, line 6.

  If you expect this amount to be zero, enter -0-.

 Make your estimate as accurate as you can with the information you have. If we later find that the estimate was not reasonable, the extension will be null and void.

Line 5—Estimate of Total Payments for 2014

Enter on line 5 the total payments you expect to report on your 2014:

- Form 1040, line 74 (excluding line 70).
- Form 1040A, line 46.
- Form 1040EZ, line 9.
- Form 1040NR, line 71 (excluding line 66).
- Form 1040NR-EZ, line 21.
- Form 1040-PR, line 11.
- Form 1040-SS, line 11.

 For Forms 1040A, 1040EZ, 1040NR-EZ, 1040-PR, and 1040-SS, do not include on line 5 the amount you are paying with this Form 4868.

Line 6—Balance Due

Subtract line 5 from line 4. If line 5 is more than line 4, enter -0-.

Line 7—Amount You Are Paying

If you find you cannot pay the amount shown on line 6, you can still get the extension. But you should pay as much as you can to limit the amount of interest you will owe. Also, you may be charged the late payment penalty on the unpaid tax from the regular due date of your return. See *Late Payment Penalty* on page 2.

Line 8—Out of the Country

If you are out of the country on the regular due date of your return, check the box on line 8. "Out of the country" is defined on page 2.

Line 9—Form 1040NR or 1040NR-EZ Filers

If you did not receive wages subject to U.S. income tax withholding, and your return is due June 15, 2015, check the box on line 9.

How To Make a Payment

Making Payments Electronically

You can pay online with a direct transfer from your bank account using Direct Pay, the Electronic Federal Tax Payment System, or by debit or credit card. You can also pay by phone using the Electronic Federal Tax Payment System or by debit or credit card. For more information, go to *www.irs.gov/payments*.

Confirmation number. You will receive a confirmation number when you pay online or by phone. Enter the confirmation number below and keep for your records.

Enter confirmation number here ▶ ------------------------------------

Note. **Do not** file a paper Form 4868 if you already submitted it electronically and are not mailing in a payment.

Pay by Check or Money Order

- When paying by check or money order with Form 4868, use the appropriate address in the middle column under *Where To File a Paper Form 4868* on page 4.
- Make your check or money order payable to the "United States Treasury." Do not send cash.
- Write your SSN, daytime phone number, and "2014 Form 4868" on your check or money order.
- Do not staple or attach your payment to Form 4868.

Note. If you e-file Form 4868 and mail a check or money order to the IRS for payment, use a completed paper Form 4868 as a voucher.

Where To File a Paper Form 4868

If you live in:

If you live in:	And you are making a payment, send Form 4868 with your payment to Internal Revenue Service:	And you are not making a payment, send Form 4868 to Department of the Treasury, Internal Revenue Service Center:
Alabama, Georgia, Kentucky, New Jersey, North Carolina, South Carolina, Tennessee, Virginia	P.O. Box 931300 Louisville, KY 40293-1300	Kansas City, MO 64999-0045
Connecticut, Delaware, District of Columbia, Maine, Maryland, Massachusetts, Missouri, New Hampshire, New York, Pennsylvania, Rhode Island, Vermont, West Virginia	P.O. Box 37009 Hartford, CT 06176-7009	Kansas City, MO 64999-0045
Florida, Louisiana, Mississippi, Texas	P.O. Box 1302 Charlotte, NC 28201-1302	Austin, TX 73301-0045
Alaska, Arizona, California, Colorado, Hawaii, Idaho, Nevada, New Mexico, Oregon, Utah, Washington, Wyoming	P.O. Box 7122 San Francisco, CA 94120-7122	Fresno, CA 93888-0045
Arkansas, Illinois, Indiana, Iowa, Kansas, Michigan, Minnesota, Montana, Nebraska, North Dakota, Ohio, Oklahoma, South Dakota, Wisconsin	P.O. Box 802503 Cincinnati, OH 45280-2503	Fresno, CA 93888-0045
A foreign country, American Samoa, or Puerto Rico, or are excluding income under Internal Revenue Code section 933, or use an APO or FPO address, or file Form 2555, 2555-EZ, or 4563, or are a dual-status alien, or are a nonpermanent resident of Guam or the U.S. Virgin Islands	P.O. Box 1302 Charlotte, NC 28201-1302 USA	Austin, TX 73301-0215 USA
All foreign estate and trust Form 1040NR filers	P.O. Box 1303 Charlotte, NC 28201-1303 USA	Cincinnati, OH 45999-0048 USA
All other Form 1040NR, 1040NR-EZ, 1040-PR, and 1040-SS filers	P.O. Box 1302 Charlotte, NC 28201-1302 USA	Austin, TX 73301-0045 USA

Private Delivery Services

You can use certain private delivery services designated by the IRS to meet the "timely mailing as timely filing/paying" rule for tax returns and payments. These private delivery services include only the following.

• Federal Express (FedEx): FedEx Priority Overnight, FedEx Standard Overnight, FedEx 2 Day, FedEx International Priority, and FedEx International First.

• United Parcel Service (UPS): UPS Next Day Air, UPS Next Day Air Saver, UPS 2nd Day Air, UPS 2nd Day Air A.M., UPS Worldwide Express Plus, and UPS Worldwide Express.

The private delivery service can tell you how to get written proof of the mailing date.

 Private delivery services cannot deliver items to P.O. boxes. You must use the U.S. Postal Service to mail any item to an IRS P.O. box address.

Privacy Act and Paperwork Reduction Act Notice. We ask for the information on this form to carry out the Internal Revenue laws of the United States. We need this information so that our records will reflect your intention to file your individual income tax return within 6 months after the regular due date. If you choose to apply for an automatic extension of time to file, you are required by Internal Revenue Code section 6081 to provide the information requested on this form. Under section 6109, you must disclose your social security number or individual taxpayer identification number. Routine uses of this information include giving it to the Department of Justice for civil and criminal litigation, and to cities, states, the District of Columbia, and U.S. commonwealths and possessions for use in administering their tax laws. We may also disclose this information to other countries under a tax treaty, to federal and state agencies to enforce federal nontax criminal laws, or to federal law enforcement and intelligence agencies to combat terrorism. If you fail to provide this information in a timely manner or provide incomplete or false information, you may be liable for penalties.

You are not required to provide the information requested on a form that is subject to the Paperwork Reduction Act unless the form displays a valid OMB control number. Books or records relating to a form or its instructions must be retained as long as their contents may become material in the administration of any Internal Revenue law. Generally, tax returns and return information are confidential, as required by Internal Revenue Code section 6103.

The average time and expenses required to complete and file this form will vary depending on individual circumstances. For the estimated averages, see the instructions for your income tax return.

If you have suggestions for making this form simpler, we would be happy to hear from you. See the instructions for your income tax return.

Form **4970**	**Tax on Accumulation Distribution of Trusts**	OMB No. 1545-0192
Department of the Treasury Internal Revenue Service	▶ Attach to beneficiary's tax return. ▶ Information about Form 4970 and its instructions is at *www.irs.gov/form4970*.	**2014** Attachment Sequence No. **178**

A Name(s) as shown on return	**B** Social security number

C Name and address of trust	**D** Employer identification number

E Type of trust (see instructions) ☐ Domestic ☐ Foreign   **F** Beneficiary's date of birth   **G** Enter the number of trusts from which you received accumulation distributions in this tax year . . . . . ▶

Part I — Average Income and Determination of Computation Years

1	Amount of current distribution that is considered distributed in earlier tax years (from Schedule J (Form 1041), line 37, column (a))	**1**	
2	Distributions of income accumulated before you were born or reached age 21	**2**	
3	Subtract line 2 from line 1	**3**	
4	Taxes imposed on the trust on amounts from line 3 (from Schedule J (Form 1041), line 37, column (b)) .	**4**	
5	Total (add lines 3 and 4)	**5**	
6	Tax-exempt interest included on line 5 (from Schedule J (Form 1041), line 37, column (c))	**6**	
7	Taxable part of line 5 (subtract line 6 from line 5)	**7**	
8	Number of trust's earlier tax years in which amounts on line 7 are considered distributed . . .	**8**	
9	Average annual amount considered distributed (divide line 3 by line 8) . . . **9**		
10	Multiply line 9 by 25% (.25) **10**		
11	Number of earlier tax years to be taken into account (see instructions)	**11**	
12	Average amount for recomputing tax (divide line 7 by line 11). Enter here and in each column on line 15	**12**	

13	Enter your taxable income before this distribution for the 5 immediately preceding tax years.	**(a) 2013**	**(b) 2012**	**(c) 2011**	**(d) 2010**	**(e) 2009**

Part II — Tax Attributable to the Accumulation Distribution

			(a)	**(b)**	**(c)**
14	Enter the amounts from line 13, eliminating the highest and lowest taxable income years	**14**			
15	Enter amount from line 12 in each column	**15**			
16	Recomputed taxable income (add lines 14 and 15)	**16**			
17	Income tax on amounts on line 16	**17**			
18	Income tax before credits on line 14 income	**18**			
19	Additional tax before credits (subtract line 18 from line 17) . . .	**19**			
20	Tax credit adjustment	**20**			
21	Subtract line 20 from line 19	**21**			
22	Alternative minimum tax adjustments	**22**			
23	Combine lines 21 and 22	**23**			
24	Add columns (a), (b), and (c), line 23	**24**		
25	Divide the line 24 amount by 3	**25**		
26	Multiply the amount on line 25 by the number of years on line 11	**26**		
27	Enter the amount from line 4	**27**		
28	Partial tax attributable to the accumulation distribution (subtract line 27 from line 26) (If zero or less, enter -0-)	**28**		

For Paperwork Reduction Act Notice, see back of form.   Cat. No. 13180V   Form **4970** (2014)

General Instructions

Section references are to the Internal Revenue Code unless otherwise noted.

Future Developments

For the latest information about developments related to Form 4970 and its instructions, such as legislation enacted after they were published, go to *www.irs.gov/form4970*.

Purpose of Form

A beneficiary of certain domestic trusts (see *Who Must File* below) uses Form 4970 to figure the partial tax on accumulation distributions under section 667. The fiduciary notifies the beneficiary of an "accumulation distribution" by completing Part IV of Schedule J (Form 1041).

If you received a distribution for this tax year from a trust that accumulated its income instead of distributing it each year (and the trust paid taxes on that income), you must complete Form 4970 to compute any additional tax liability. The trustee must give you a completed Part IV of Schedule J (Form 1041) so you can complete this form.

If you received accumulation distributions from more than one trust during the current tax year, prepare a separate Form 4970 for each trust from which you received an accumulation distribution. You can arrange the distributions in any order you want them considered to have been made.

Who Must File

Beneficiaries who received an accumulation distribution from certain domestic trusts that were created before March 1, 1984, must file Form 4970. For details, see section 665(c).

Foreign trust beneficiaries. If you received an accumulation distribution from a foreign trust, you must report the distribution and the partial tax on a 2014 Form 3520, Annual Return To Report Transactions With Foreign Trusts and Receipt of Certain Foreign Gifts.

Do not file Form 4970 for distributions from any foreign trusts, except to attach it as a worksheet to Form 3520 if those instructions direct you to.

Note: *If the accumulation distributions are from a domestic trust that used to be a foreign trust, see Rev. Rul. 91-6, 1991-1 C.B. 89.*

Definitions

Undistributed net income (UNI). Undistributed net income is the distributable net income (DNI) of the trust for any tax year less (1) the amount of income required to be distributed currently and any other amounts properly paid or credited or required to be distributed to beneficiaries in the tax year and (2) the taxes imposed on the trust attributable to such DNI.

Accumulation distribution. An accumulation distribution is the excess of amounts properly paid, credited, or required to be distributed (other than income required to be distributed currently) over the DNI of the trust reduced by income required to be distributed currently.

Generally, except for tax-exempt interest, the distribution loses its character upon distribution to the beneficiary. See section 667(d) for special rules for foreign trusts.

Specific Instructions

Item E—Type of trust. If you received an accumulation distribution from a foreign trust, see *Foreign trust beneficiaries* above. Do not file this form other than as an attachment to Form 3520.

Line 1. For a nonresident alien or foreign corporation, include only the part of the accumulation distribution that is attributable to U.S. sources or is effectively connected with a trade or business carried on in the United States.

Line 2. Enter any amount from line 1 that represents UNI of a domestic trust accumulated before you were born or reached age 21. However, if the multiple trust rule applies, see the instructions for line 4.

Line 4. Multiple trust rule. If you received accumulation distributions from two or more other trusts that were considered to have been made in any of the earlier tax years in which the current accumulation distribution is considered to have been made, do not include on line 4 the taxes attributable to the current accumulation distribution considered to have been distributed in the same earlier tax year(s).

For this special rule, only count as trusts those trusts for which the sum of this accumulation distribution and any earlier accumulation distributions from the trust, which are considered under section 666(a) to have been distributed in the same earlier tax year(s), is $1,000 or more.

Foreign trust. If the trust is a foreign trust, see section 665(d)(2).

Line 8. You can determine the number of years in which the UNI is deemed to have been distributed by counting the "throwback years" for which there are entries on lines 32 through 36 of Part IV of Schedule J (Form 1041). These throwback rules apply even if you would not have been entitled to receive a distribution in the earlier tax year if the distribution had actually been made then. There can be more than 5 "throwback years."

Line 11. From the number of years entered on line 8, subtract any year in which the distribution from column (a), Part IV of Schedule J (Form 1041) is less than the amount on line 10 of Form 4970. If the distribution for each throwback year is more than line 10, then enter the same number on line 11 as you entered on line 8.

Line 13. Enter your taxable incomes for years 2009-2013, even if less than 5 years of the trust had accumulated income after you became 21. Use the taxable income as reported by you or as changed by the IRS. Include in the taxable income amounts considered distributed in that year as a result of prior accumulation distributions, whether from the same or another trust, and whether made in an earlier year or the current year.

If your taxable income as adjusted is less than zero, enter zero.

Line 17. Figure the income tax (excluding any alternative minimum tax (AMT)) on the income on line 16 using the tax rates in effect for your particular earlier tax year shown in each of the three columns. Use the Tax Rate Schedules, etc., as applicable. You can get the Tax Rate Schedules and prior year forms from many IRS offices by calling 1-800-TAX-FORM (1-800-829-3676), or by downloading them at IRS.gov.

Line 18. Enter your income tax (excluding any AMT) as originally reported, corrected, or amended, before reduction for any credits for your particular earlier year shown in each of the three columns.

Line 20. Nonrefundable credits that are limited to tax liability, such as the general business credit, may be changed because of an accumulation distribution. If the total allowable credits for any of the 3 computation years increase, enter the increase on line 20. However, do not treat as an increase the part of the credit that was allowable as a carryback or carryforward credit in the current or any preceding year other than the computation year.

To refigure these credits, you must consider changes to the tax before credits for each of the 3 computation years due to previous accumulation distributions.

If the accumulation distribution is from a domestic trust that paid foreign income taxes, the limitation on the foreign tax credit under section 904 is applied separately to the accumulation distribution. If the distribution is from a foreign trust, see sections 667(d) and 904 (f)(4) for special rules.

Attach the proper form for any credit you refigure. The amount determined for items on this line is limited to tax law provisions in effect for those years involved.

Line 22. For each year entered in Part II, columns a-c, use and attach that year's Form 4626, Alternative Minimum Tax—Corporations, Form 6251, Alternative Minimum Tax—Individuals or Schedule I (Form 1041), Alternative Minimum Tax—Estates and Trusts to recompute the AMT for that year. Show any change in the AMT below the bottom margin of the appropriate form or schedule and enter the change on line 22.

Line 28. If estate taxes or generation-skipping transfer taxes apply to the accumulation distribution, reduce the partial tax proportionately for those taxes. See section 667(b)(6) for the computation.

Individuals. Include the amount from this line on Form 1040, line 60. Write "ADT" to the left of the line 60 entry space.

Trusts and decedents' estates. Include the amount on Form 1041, Schedule G, line 7. Write "From Form 4970" and the amount of the tax to the left of the line 7 entry space.

Other filers. Add the result to the total tax liability before the refundable credits on your income tax return for the year of the accumulation distribution. Attach this form to that return.

Paperwork Reduction Act Notice. We ask for the information on this form to carry out the Internal Revenue laws of the United States. You are required to give us the information. We need it to ensure that you are complying with these laws and to allow us to figure and collect the right amount of tax.

You are not required to provide the information requested on a form that is subject to the Paperwork Reduction Act unless the form displays a valid OMB control number. Books or records relating to a form or its instructions must be retained as long as their contents may become material in the administration of any Internal Revenue law. Generally, tax returns and return information are confidential, as required by section 6103.

The time needed to complete and file this form will vary depending on individual circumstances. The estimated burden for individual taxpayers filing this form is approved under OMB control number 1545-0074 and is included in the estimates shown in the instructions for their individual income tax return. The estimated burden for all other taxpayers who file this form is shown below.

Recordkeeping . . . . . 1 hr., 12 min.

Learning about the law or the form . . . . 15 min.

Preparing the form . . . . 1 hr., 25 min.

Copying, assembling, and sending the form to the IRS . . 20 min.

If you have comments concerning the accuracy of these time estimates or suggestions for making this form simpler, we would be happy to hear from you. See the instructions for the tax return with which this form is filed.

Form **5329**	**Additional Taxes on Qualified Plans (Including IRAs) and Other Tax-Favored Accounts**	OMB No. 1545-0074
Department of the Treasury Internal Revenue Service (99)	▶ Attach to Form 1040 or Form 1040NR. ▶ Information about Form 5329 and its separate instructions is at *www.irs.gov/form5329*.	**20**14 Attachment Sequence No. **29**

Name of individual subject to additional tax. If married filing jointly, see instructions.	**Your social security number**

Fill in Your Address Only If You Are Filing This Form by Itself and Not With Your Tax Return ▶

Home address (number and street), or P.O. box if mail is not delivered to your home	Apt. no.
City, town or post office, state, and ZIP code. If you have a foreign address, also complete the spaces below (see instructions).	If this is an amended return, check here ▶ ☐
Foreign country name	Foreign province/state/county	Foreign postal code

If you **only** owe the additional 10% tax on early distributions, you may be able to report this tax directly on Form 1040, line 59, or Form 1040NR, line 57, without filing Form 5329. See the instructions for Form 1040, line 59, or for Form 1040NR, line 57.

Part I   Additional Tax on Early Distributions

Complete this part if you took a taxable distribution before you reached age 59½ from a qualified retirement plan (including an IRA) or modified endowment contract (unless you are reporting this tax directly on Form 1040 or Form 1040NR—see above). You may also have to complete this part to indicate that you qualify for an exception to the additional tax on early distributions or for certain Roth IRA distributions (see instructions).

1	Early distributions included in income. For Roth IRA distributions, see instructions	**1**	
2	Early distributions included on line 1 that are not subject to the additional tax (see instructions). Enter the appropriate exception number from the instructions: _____	**2**	
3	Amount subject to additional tax. Subtract line 2 from line 1	**3**	
4	**Additional tax.** Enter 10% (.10) of line 3. Include this amount on Form 1040, line 59, or Form 1040NR, line 57	**4**	
	Caution: *If any part of the amount on line 3 was a distribution from a SIMPLE IRA, you may have to include 25% of that amount on line 4 instead of 10% (see instructions).*		

Part II   Additional Tax on Certain Distributions From Education Accounts

Complete this part if you included an amount in income, on Form 1040 or Form 1040NR, line 21, from a Coverdell education savings account (ESA) or a qualified tuition program (QTP).

5	Distributions included in income from Coverdell ESAs and QTPs	**5**	
6	Distributions included on line 5 that are not subject to the additional tax (see instructions)	**6**	
7	Amount subject to additional tax. Subtract line 6 from line 5	**7**	
8	**Additional tax.** Enter 10% (.10) of line 7. Include this amount on Form 1040, line 59, or Form 1040NR, line 57	**8**	

Part III   Additional Tax on Excess Contributions to Traditional IRAs

Complete this part if you contributed more to your traditional IRAs for 2014 than is allowable or you had an amount on line 17 of your 2013 Form 5329.

9	Enter your excess contributions from line 16 of your 2013 Form 5329 (see instructions). If zero, go to line 15		**9**	
10	If your traditional IRA contributions for 2014 are less than your maximum allowable contribution, see instructions. Otherwise, enter -0-	**10**		
11	2014 traditional IRA distributions included in income (see instructions)	**11**		
12	2014 distributions of prior year excess contributions (see instructions)	**12**		
13	Add lines 10, 11, and 12		**13**	
14	Prior year excess contributions. Subtract line 13 from line 9. If zero or less, enter -0-		**14**	
15	Excess contributions for 2014 (see instructions)		**15**	
16	Total excess contributions. Add lines 14 and 15		**16**	
17	**Additional tax.** Enter 6% (.06) of the **smaller** of line 16 **or** the value of your traditional IRAs on December 31, 2014 (including 2014 contributions made in 2015). Include this amount on Form 1040, line 59, or Form 1040NR, line 57		**17**	

Part IV   Additional Tax on Excess Contributions to Roth IRAs

Complete this part if you contributed more to your Roth IRAs for 2014 than is allowable or you had an amount on line 25 of your 2013 Form 5329.

18	Enter your excess contributions from line 24 of your 2013 Form 5329 (see instructions). If zero, go to line 23		**18**	
19	If your Roth IRA contributions for 2014 are less than your maximum allowable contribution, see instructions. Otherwise, enter -0-	**19**		
20	2014 distributions from your Roth IRAs (see instructions)	**20**		
21	Add lines 19 and 20		**21**	
22	Prior year excess contributions. Subtract line 21 from line 18. If zero or less, enter -0-		**22**	
23	Excess contributions for 2014 (see instructions)		**23**	
24	Total excess contributions. Add lines 22 and 23		**24**	
25	**Additional tax.** Enter 6% (.06) of the **smaller** of line 24 **or** the value of your Roth IRAs on December 31, 2014 (including 2014 contributions made in 2015). Include this amount on Form 1040, line 59, or Form 1040NR, line 57		**25**	

For Privacy Act and Paperwork Reduction Act Notice, see your tax return instructions.   Cat. No. 13329Q   Form **5329** (2014)

Part V	**Additional Tax on Excess Contributions to Coverdell ESAs**		
	Complete this part if the contributions to your Coverdell ESAs for 2014 were more than is allowable or you had an amount on line 33 of your 2013 Form 5329.		
26	Enter the excess contributions from line 32 of your 2013 Form 5329 (see instructions). If zero, go to line 31	**26**	
27	If the contributions to your Coverdell ESAs for 2014 were less than the maximum allowable contribution, see instructions. Otherwise, enter -0-	**27**	
28	2014 distributions from your Coverdell ESAs (see instructions) . . .	**28**	
29	Add lines 27 and 28	**29**	
30	Prior year excess contributions. Subtract line 29 from line 26. If zero or less, enter -0-	**30**	
31	Excess contributions for 2014 (see instructions)	**31**	
32	Total excess contributions. Add lines 30 and 31	**32**	
33	**Additional tax.** Enter 6% (.06) of the **smaller** of line 32 **or** the value of your Coverdell ESAs on December 31, 2014 (including 2014 contributions made in 2015). Include this amount on Form 1040, line 59, or Form 1040NR, line 57	**33**	

Part VI	**Additional Tax on Excess Contributions to Archer MSAs**		
	Complete this part if you or your employer contributed more to your Archer MSAs for 2014 than is allowable or you had an amount on line 41 of your 2013 Form 5329.		
34	Enter the excess contributions from line 40 of your 2013 Form 5329 (see instructions). If zero, go to line 39	**34**	
35	If the contributions to your Archer MSAs for 2014 are less than the maximum allowable contribution, see instructions. Otherwise, enter -0-	**35**	
36	2014 distributions from your Archer MSAs from Form 8853, line 8 . .	**36**	
37	Add lines 35 and 36	**37**	
38	Prior year excess contributions. Subtract line 37 from line 34. If zero or less, enter -0-	**38**	
39	Excess contributions for 2014 (see instructions)	**39**	
40	Total excess contributions. Add lines 38 and 39	**40**	
41	**Additional tax.** Enter 6% (.06) of the **smaller** of line 40 **or** the value of your Archer MSAs on December 31, 2014 (including 2014 contributions made in 2015). Include this amount on Form 1040, line 59, or Form 1040NR, line 57	**41**	

Part VII	**Additional Tax on Excess Contributions to Health Savings Accounts (HSAs)**		
	Complete this part if you, someone on your behalf, or your employer contributed more to your HSAs for 2014 than is allowable or you had an amount on line 49 of your 2013 Form 5329.		
42	Enter the excess contributions from line 48 of your 2013 Form 5329. If zero, go to line 47 . . .	**42**	
43	If the contributions to your HSAs for 2014 are less than the maximum allowable contribution, see instructions. Otherwise, enter -0- . . .	**43**	
44	2014 distributions from your HSAs from Form 8889, line 16	**44**	
45	Add lines 43 and 44	**45**	
46	Prior year excess contributions. Subtract line 45 from line 42. If zero or less, enter -0-	**46**	
47	Excess contributions for 2014 (see instructions)	**47**	
48	Total excess contributions. Add lines 46 and 47	**48**	
49	**Additional tax.** Enter 6% (.06) of the **smaller** of line 48 **or** the value of your HSAs on December 31, 2014 (including 2014 contributions made in 2015). Include this amount on Form 1040, line 59, or Form 1040NR, line 57	**49**	

Part VIII	**Additional Tax on Excess Accumulation in Qualified Retirement Plans (Including IRAs)**		
	Complete this part if you did not receive the minimum required distribution from your qualified retirement plan.		
50	Minimum required distribution for 2014 (see instructions)	**50**	
51	Amount actually distributed to you in 2014	**51**	
52	Subtract line 51 from line 50. If zero or less, enter -0-	**52**	
53	**Additional tax.** Enter 50% (.50) of line 52. Include this amount on Form 1040, line 59, or Form 1040NR, line 57	**53**	

Sign Here Only If You Are Filing This Form by Itself and Not With Your Tax Return

Under penalties of perjury, I declare that I have examined this form, including accompanying attachments, and to the best of my knowledge and belief, it is true, correct, and complete. Declaration of preparer (other than taxpayer) is based on all information of which preparer has any knowledge.

▶ _____   ▶ _____
Your signature   Date

Paid Preparer Use Only	Print/Type preparer's name	Preparer's signature	Date	Check ☐ if self-employed	PTIN
	Firm's name ▶			Firm's EIN ▶	
	Firm's address ▶			Phone no.	

Form **5329** (2014)

2014

Instructions for Form 5329

Additional Taxes on Qualified Plans (Including IRAs) and Other Tax-Favored Accounts

Department of the Treasury
Internal Revenue Service

Section references are to the Internal Revenue Code unless otherwise noted.

General Instructions

Future Developments

For the latest information about developments related to Form 5329 and its instructions, such as legislation enacted after they were published, go to *www.irs.gov/form5329*.

Purpose of Form

Use Form 5329 to report additional taxes on:
- IRAs,
- Other qualified retirement plans,
- Modified endowment contracts,
- Coverdell ESAs,
- QTPs,
- Archer MSAs, or
- HSAs.

Who Must File

You must file Form 5329 if any of the following apply.
- You received an early distribution from a Roth IRA, the amount on line 23 of Form 8606, Nondeductible IRAs, is more than zero, and you are required to enter an amount that is more than zero on Form 5329, line 1 (see *Distributions from Roth IRAs*, later).
- You received an early distribution subject to the tax on early distributions from a qualified retirement plan (other than a Roth IRA). However, if distribution code 1 is correctly shown in box 7 of all your Forms 1099-R, and you owe the additional tax on each Form 1099-R, you do not have to file Form 5329. Instead, see the instructions for Form 1040, line 59, or Form 1040NR, line 57, for how to report the 10% additional tax directly on that line.
- You received an early distribution subject to the tax on early distributions from a qualified retirement plan (other than a Roth IRA), you meet an exception to the tax on early distributions from the list shown later, and distribution code 1 is shown in box 7 of Form 1099-R.
- You received an early distribution subject to the tax on early distributions from a qualified retirement plan (other

than a Roth IRA), you meet an exception to the tax on early distributions from the list shown later, but box 7 of your Form 1099-R does not indicate an exception or the exception does not apply to the entire distribution.
- You received taxable distributions from Coverdell ESAs or QTPs.
- The contributions for 2014 to your traditional IRAs, Roth IRAs, Coverdell ESAs, Archer MSAs, or HSAs exceed your maximum contribution limit, or you had a tax due from an excess contribution on line 17, 25, 33, 41, or 49 of your 2013 Form 5329.
- You did not receive the minimum required distribution from your qualified retirement plan. This also includes trusts and estates that did not receive this amount.

 If you rolled over part or all of a distribution from a qualified retirement plan, the part rolled over is not subject to the 10% additional tax on early distributions. On the instructions for Form 1040, lines 15a and 15b or lines 16a and 16b; Form 1040A, lines 11a and 11b or 12a and 12b; or Form 1040NR, lines 16a and 16b or 17a and 17b, for how to report the rollover.

When and Where To File

File Form 5329 with your 2014 Form 1040 or Form 1040NR by the due date, including extensions, of your Form 1040 or Form 1040NR.

If you do not have to file a 2014 income tax return, complete and file Form 5329 by itself at the time and place you would be required to file Form 1040 or Form 1040NR. Be sure to include your address on page 1 of the form and your signature and the date on page 2 of the form. Enclose, but do not attach, a check or money order payable to "United States Treasury" for any taxes due. Write your SSN and "2014 Form 5329" on the check. For information on other payment options, including credit or debit card payments, see the instructions for Form 1040 or Form 1040NR, or go to IRS.gov.

Prior tax years. If you are filing Form 5329 for a prior year, you must use the

prior year's version of the form. If you do not have any other changes and have not previously filed a federal income tax return for the prior year, file the prior year's version of Form 5329 by itself (discussed earlier). If you have other changes, file Form 5329 for the prior year with Form 1040X, Amended U.S. Individual Income Tax Return.

Definitions

Qualified retirement plan. A qualified retirement plan includes:
- A qualified pension, profit-sharing, or stock bonus plan (including a 401(k) plan),
- A tax-sheltered annuity contract,
- A qualified annuity plan, and
- An IRA.

Note. Modified endowment contracts are not qualified retirement plans.

Traditional IRAs. For purposes of Form 5329, a traditional IRA is any IRA, including a simplified employee pension (SEP) IRA, other than a SIMPLE IRA or Roth IRA.

Early distribution. Generally, any distribution from your IRA, other qualified retirement plan, or modified endowment contract before you reach age 59½ is an early distribution.

Rollover. Generally, a rollover is a tax-free distribution of assets from one qualified retirement plan that is reinvested in another plan or the same plan. Generally, you must complete the rollover within 60 days of receiving the distribution. Any taxable amount not rolled over must be included in income and may be subject to the 10% additional tax on early distributions.

You can roll over (convert) amounts from a qualified retirement plan to a Roth IRA. Any amount rolled over to a Roth IRA is subject to the same rules for converting a traditional IRA to a Roth IRA. You must include in your gross income distributions from a qualified retirement plan that you would have had to include in income if you had not rolled them into a Roth IRA. Generally, the 10% additional tax on early distributions does not apply. For more information, see chapter 2 of Pub. 590-A.

Cat. No. 13330R

The IRS may waive the 60-day requirement if failing to waive it would be against equity or good conscience, such as situations where a casualty, disaster, or other events beyond your reasonable control prevented you from meeting the 60-day requirement. Also, the 60-day period may be extended if you had a frozen deposit. See *Time Limit for Making a Rollover Contribution* under *Can You Move Retirement Plan Assets?* in Pub. 590-A for details.

In-plan Roth rollover. If you are a participant in a 401(k), 403(b), or governmental 457(b) plan, your plan may permit you to roll over amounts from those plans to a designated Roth account within the same plan. The rollover of any untaxed amounts must be included in income. Generally, the 10% additional tax on early distributions does not apply. For more information, see *In-plan Roth rollovers* under *Rollovers* in Pub. 575.

Compensation. Compensation includes wages, salaries, tips, bonuses, and other pay you receive for services you perform. It also includes sales commissions, commissions on insurance premiums, and pay based on a percentage of profits. It includes net earnings from self-employment, but only for a trade or business in which your personal services are a material income-producing factor.

For IRAs, treat nontaxable combat pay and any differential wage payments, and all taxable alimony received under a decree of divorce or separate maintenance as compensation.

Compensation does not include any amounts received as a pension or annuity and does not include any amount received as deferred compensation.

Taxable compensation is your compensation that is included in gross income reduced by any deductions on Form 1040 or Form 1040NR, lines 27 and 28, but not by any loss from self-employment.

Additional Information

See the following publications for more information about the items in these instructions:
- Pub. 590-A, Contributions to Individual Retirement Arrangements (IRAs);
- Pub. 590-B, Distributions from Individual Retirement Arrangements (IRAs);
- Pub. 560, Retirement Plans for Small Business;

- Pub. 575, Pension and Annuity Income;
- Pub. 969, Health Savings Accounts and Other Tax-Favored Health Plans;
- Pub. 970, Tax Benefits for Education; and
- Pub. 721, Tax Guide to U.S. Civil Service Retirement Benefits.

Specific Instructions

Joint returns. If both you and your spouse are required to file Form 5329, complete a separate form for each of you. Include the combined tax on Form 1040, line 59.

Amended returns. If you are filing an amended 2014 Form 5329, check the box at the top of page 1 of the form. Do not use the 2014 Form 5329 to amend your return for any other year. For information about amending a Form 5329 for a prior year, see *Prior tax years*, earlier.

Part I—Additional Tax on Early Distributions

In general, if you receive an early distribution (including an involuntary cashout) from an IRA, other qualified retirement plan, or modified endowment contract, the part of the distribution included in income generally is subject to the 10% additional tax. But see *Distributions from a designated Roth account* below and *Distributions from Roth IRAs*, later.

The additional tax on early distributions does not apply to any of the following:
- A qualified HSA funding distribution from an IRA (other than a SEP or SIMPLE IRA). See *Qualified HSA funding distribution* under *Health Savings Accounts* in Pub. 969 for details.
- A distribution from a traditional or SIMPLE IRA that was converted to a Roth IRA.
- A rollover from a qualified retirement plan to a Roth IRA.
- An in-plan rollover to a designated Roth account.
- A distribution of certain excess IRA contributions (see the instructions for line 15, later, and the instructions for line 23, later).

Note. Any related IRA earnings withdrawn with excess IRA contributions are subject to the 10% additional tax on early distributions if you were under age 59½ at the time of the distribution.

- A distribution of excess deferrals. Excess deferrals include distributions of excess contributions from a qualified cash or deferred arrangement (section 401(k) plan), excess contributions from a tax-sheltered annuity (section 403(b) plan), excess contributions from a SEP IRA, and excess contributions from a SIMPLE IRA.
- A distribution of excess aggregate contributions to meet nondiscrimination requirements for employee contributions and matching employer contributions.
- A distribution from an eligible governmental section 457 deferred compensation plan to the extent the distribution is not attributable to an amount transferred from a qualified retirement plan.

See the instructions for line 2, later, for other distributions that are not subject to the additional tax.

Line 1

Enter the amount of early distributions included in income that you received from:
- A qualified retirement plan, including earnings on withdrawn excess contributions to your IRAs included in income in 2014, or
- A modified endowment contract entered into after June 20, 1988.

Certain prohibited transactions involving your IRA, such as borrowing from your IRA or pledging your IRA assets as security for a loan, are considered to be distributions and are generally subject to the additional tax on early distributions. See *Prohibited Transactions* under *What Acts Result in Penalties or Additional Taxes?* in Pub. 590-B for details.

Distributions from a designated Roth account. If you received an early distribution from your designated Roth account, include on line 1 the amount of the distribution that you must include in your income. You will find this amount in box 2a of your 2014 Form 1099-R. You may also need to include a recapture amount on line 1 if you have ever made an in-plan Roth rollover (discussed later).

 If you never made an in-plan Roth rollover, you need to include on line 1 of this form only the amount from box 2a of your 2014 Form 1099-R reporting the early distribution.

Instructions for Form 5329 (2014)

Recapture amount subject to the additional tax on early distributions. If you have ever made an in-plan Roth rollover and you received an early distribution for 2014, the recapture amount to include on line 1 is a portion of the amounts you rolled over.

The recapture amount that you must include on line 1 will not exceed the amount of your early distribution; and, for purposes of determining this recapture amount, you will allocate a rollover amount (or portion thereof) to an early distribution only once.

For more information about the recapture amount for early distributions from a designated Roth account, including how to calculate it, see *Tax on Early Distributions* under *Special Additional Taxes* in Pub. 575.

Distributions from Roth IRAs. If you received an early distribution from your Roth IRAs, include on line 1 the part of the distribution that you must include in your income. You will find this amount on line 25 of your 2014 Form 8606. You will also need to include on line 1 the following amounts.

- A qualified first-time homebuyer distribution from line 20 of your 2014 Form 8606. Also include this amount on line 2 and enter exception number 09.
- Recapture amounts attributable to any conversions or rollovers to your Roth IRAs in 2010 through 2014. See *Recapture amount subject to the additional tax on early distributions* next.

 If you did not have a qualified first-time homebuyer distribution in 2014, and you did not convert or roll over an amount to your Roth IRAs in 2010 through 2014, you only need to include the amount from line 25 of your 2014 Form 8606 on line 1 of this form.

Recapture amount subject to the additional tax on early distributions. If you converted or rolled over an amount to your Roth IRAs in 2010 through 2014 and you received an early distribution for 2014, the recapture amount you must include on line 1 is the amount, if any, of the early distribution allocated to the taxable portion of your 2010 through 2014 conversions or rollovers.

Generally, an early distribution is allocated to your Roth IRA contributions first, then to your conversions and rollovers on a first-in, first-out basis. For each conversion or rollover, you must first allocate the early distribution to the portion that was subject to tax in the

year of the conversion or rollover, and then to the portion that was not subject to tax. The recapture amount is the sum of the early distribution amounts that you allocate to these taxable portions of your conversions or rollovers.

The recapture amount that you must include on line 1 will not exceed the amount of your early distribution; and, for purposes of determining this recapture amount, you will allocate a contribution, conversion, or rollover amount (or portion thereof) to an early distribution only once.

For more information about the recapture amount for distributions from a Roth IRA, including how to calculate it, see *Ordering Rules for Distributions* under *Are Distributions Taxable?* in chapter 2 of Pub. 590-B. Also, see *Example* next, which illustrates a situation where a taxpayer must include a recapture amount on line 1.

Example. You converted $20,000 from a traditional IRA to a Roth IRA in 2010 and converted $10,000 in 2011. Your 2010 Form 8606 had $5,000 on line 17 and $15,000 on line 18 and your 2011 Form 8606 had $3,000 on line 17 and $7,000 on line 18. You made Roth IRA contributions of $2,000 for 2010 and 2011. You did not make any Roth IRA conversions or contributions for 2012 through 2014, or take any Roth IRA distributions before 2014.

On July 9, 2014, at age 53, you took a $33,000 distribution from your Roth IRA. Your 2014 Form 8606 shows $33,000 on line 19; $29,000 on line 23 ($33,000 minus $4,000 for your contributions on line 22) and $0 on line 25 ($29,000 minus your basis in conversions of $30,000).

First, $4,000 of the $33,000 is allocated to your 2014 Form 8606, line 22; then $15,000 to your 2010 Form 8606, line 18; $5,000 to your 2010 Form 8606, line 17; and $7,000 to your 2011 Form 8606, line 18. The remaining $2,000 is allocated to the $3,000 on your 2011 Form 8606, line 17. On line 1, enter $22,000 ($15,000 allocated to your 2010 Form 8606, line 18, plus the $7,000 that was allocated to your 2011 Form 8606, line 18).

If you take a Roth IRA distribution in 2015, the first $1,000 will be allocated to the $1,000 remaining from your 2011 Form 8606, line 17, and will not be subject to the additional tax on early distributions.

Additional information. For more details, see *Are Distributions Taxable?* in chapters 1 and 2 of Pub. 590-B.

Line 2

The additional tax on early distributions does not apply to the distributions described next. Enter on line 2 the amount that you can exclude. In the space provided, enter the applicable exception number (01–12). If more than one exception applies, enter 12.

No. Exception

01 Qualified retirement plan distributions (does not apply to IRAs) you receive after separation from service when the separation from service occurs in or after the year you reach age 55 (age 50 for qualified public safety employees).

02 Distributions made as part of a series of substantially equal periodic payments (made at least annually) for your life (or life expectancy) or the joint lives (or joint life expectancies) of you and your designated beneficiary (if from an employer plan, payments must begin after separation from service).

03 Distributions due to total and permanent disability. You are considered disabled if you can furnish proof that you cannot do any substantial gainful activity because of your physical or mental condition. A medical determination that your condition can be expected to result in death or to be of long, continued, and indefinite duration must be made.

04 Distributions due to death (does not apply to modified endowment contracts).

05 Qualified retirement plan distributions up to the amount you paid for unreimbursed medical expenses during the year **minus** 10% (or 7.5% if you or your spouse were born before January 2, 1950) of your adjusted gross income (AGI) for the year.

06 Qualified retirement plan distributions made to an alternate payee under a qualified domestic relations order (does not apply to IRAs).

07 IRA distributions made to certain unemployed individuals for health insurance premiums.

08 IRA distributions made for qualified higher education expenses.

09 IRA distributions made for the purchase of a first home, up to $10,000.

10 Qualified retirement plan distributions made due to an IRS levy.

11 Qualified distributions to reservists while serving on active duty for at least 180 days.

12 Other (see *Other* next). Also, enter this code if more than one exception applies.

Other. The following exceptions also apply.
• Distributions incorrectly indicated as early distributions by code 1, J, or S in box 7 of Form 1099-R. Include on line 2 the amount you received when you were age 59½ or older.
• Distributions from a section 457 plan, which are not from a rollover from a qualified retirement plan.
• Distributions from a plan maintained by an employer if:

1. You separated from service by March 1, 1986;

2. As of March 1, 1986, your entire interest was in pay status under a written election that provides a specific schedule for the distribution of your entire interest; and

3. The distribution is actually being made under the written election.

• Distributions that are dividends paid with respect to stock described in section 404(k).
• Distributions from annuity contracts to the extent that the distributions are allocable to the investment in the contract before August 14, 1982. For additional exceptions that apply to annuities, see *Tax on Early Distributions* under *Special Additional Taxes* in Pub. 575.

• Distributions that are phased retirement annuity payments made to federal employees. See Pub. 721 for more information on the phased retirement program.

Line 4

If any amount on line 3 was a distribution from a SIMPLE IRA received within 2 years from the date you first participated in the SIMPLE IRA plan, you must multiply that amount by 25% instead of 10%. These distributions are included in boxes 1 and 2a of Form 1099-R and are designated with code S in box 7.

Part II—Additional Tax on Certain Distributions From Education Accounts

Line 6

The additional tax does not apply to the distributions that are includible in income described next. Enter on line 6 the amount from line 5 that you can exclude.
• Distributions made due to the death or disability of the beneficiary.
• Distributions made on account of a tax-free scholarship, allowance, or payment described in section 25A(g)(2).
• Distributions made because of attendance by the beneficiary at a U.S. military academy. This exception applies only to the extent that the distribution does not exceed the costs of advanced education (as defined in title 10 of the U.S. Code) at the academy.
• Distributions included in income because you used the qualified education expenses to figure the American opportunity and lifetime learning credits.

Part III—Additional Tax on Excess Contributions to Traditional IRAs

If you contributed more for 2014 than is allowable or you had an amount on line 17 of your 2013 Form 5329, you may owe this tax. But you may be able

to avoid the tax on any 2014 excess contributions (see the instructions for line 15, later).

Line 9

Enter the amount from line 16 of your 2013 Form 5329 only if the amount on line 17 of your 2013 Form 5329 is more than zero.

Line 10

Enter the difference, if any, of your contribution limit for traditional IRAs less your contributions to traditional IRAs and Roth IRAs for 2014.

If you are not married filing jointly, your contribution limit for traditional IRAs is the smaller of your taxable compensation (defined earlier) or $5,500 ($6,500 if age 50 or older at the end of 2014). If you are married filing jointly, your contribution limit is generally $5,500 ($6,500 if age 50 or older at the end of 2014) and your spouse's contribution limit is $5,500 ($6,500 if age 50 or older at the end of 2014). But if the combined taxable compensation for you and your spouse is less than $11,000 ($12,000 if one spouse is 50 or older at the end of 2014; $13,000 if both spouses are 50 or older at the end of 2014), see *How Much Can Be Contributed?* in Pub. 590-A for special rules.

Also include on line 11a or 11b (line 11 for Form 1040NR) of the IRA Deduction Worksheet—Line 32 in the instructions for Form 1040 or Form 1040NR, the smaller of:
• Form 5329, line 10, or
• The excess, if any, of Form 5329, line 9, over the sum of Form 5329, lines 11 and 12 (which you will complete next).

Line 11

Enter on line 11 any withdrawals from your traditional IRAs that are included in your income. Do not include any withdrawn contributions reported on line 12.

Line 12

Enter on line 12 any amounts included on line 9 that are excess contributions to your traditional IRAs for 1976 through 2012 that you had returned to you in 2014 and any 2013 excess contributions that you had returned to you in 2014 after the due date (including extensions) of your 2013 income tax return if:

- You did not claim a deduction for the excess contributions,
- No traditional IRA deduction was allowable (without regard to the modified AGI limitation) for the excess contributions, and
- The total contributions to your traditional IRAs for the tax year for which the excess contributions were made were not more than the amounts shown in the following table.

Year(s)	Contribution limit	Contribution limit if age 50 or older at the end of the year
2013	$5,500	$6,500
2008 through 2012	$5,000	$6,000
2006 or 2007	$4,000	$5,000
2005	$4,000	$4,500
2002 through 2004	$3,000	$3,500
1997 through 2001	$2,000	—
before 1997	$2,250	—

If the excess contribution to your traditional IRA for the year included a rollover and the excess occurred because the information the plan was required to give you was incorrect, increase the contribution limit amount for the year shown in the table above by the amount of the excess that is due to the incorrect information.

If the total contributions for the year included employer contributions to a SEP, increase the contribution limit amount for the year shown in the table above by the smaller of the amount of the employer contributions or:

2013	$51,000
2012	$50,000
2009, 2010, or 2011	$49,000
2008	$46,000
2007	$45,000
2006	$44,000
2005	$42,000
2004	$41,000
2002 or 2003	$40,000
2001	$35,000
before 2001	$30,000

Line 15

Enter the excess of your contributions to traditional IRAs for 2014 (unless withdrawn—discussed next) over your contribution limit for traditional IRAs. See the instructions for line 10, earlier, to figure your contribution limit for traditional IRAs. Any amount you contribute for the year in which you reach age 70½ or for a later year is an excess contribution because your contribution limit is zero. Do not include rollovers in figuring your excess contributions.

You can withdraw some or all of your excess contributions for 2014 and they will be treated as not having been contributed if:

- You make the withdrawal by the due date, including extensions, of your 2014 tax return,
- You do not claim a traditional IRA deduction for the withdrawn contributions, and
- You withdraw any earnings on the withdrawn contributions and include the earnings in gross income (see the Instructions for Form 8606 for details). Also, if you had not reached age 59½ at the time of the withdrawal, include the earnings as an early distribution on line 1 of Form 5329 for the year in which you report the earnings.

If you timely filed your return without withdrawing the excess contributions, you can still make the withdrawal no later than 6 months after the due date of your tax return, excluding extensions. If you do, file an amended return with "Filed pursuant to section 301.9100-2" written at the top. Report any related earnings for 2014 on the amended return and include an explanation of the withdrawal. Make any other necessary changes on the amended return (for example, if you reported the contributions as excess contributions on

your original return, include an amended Form 5329 reflecting that the withdrawn contributions are no longer treated as having been contributed).

Part IV—Additional Tax on Excess Contributions to Roth IRAs

If you contributed more to your Roth IRA for 2014 than is allowable or you had an amount on line 25 of your 2013 Form 5329, you may owe this tax. But you may be able to avoid the tax on any 2014 excess contributions (see the instructions for line 23, later).

Line 18

Enter the amount from line 24 of your 2013 Form 5329 only if the amount on line 25 of your 2013 Form 5329 is more than zero.

Line 19

If you contributed less to your Roth IRAs for 2014 than your contribution limit for Roth IRAs, enter the difference. Your contribution limit for Roth IRAs is generally your contribution limit for traditional IRAs (see the instructions for line 10, earlier) reduced by the amount you contributed to traditional IRAs. But your contribution limit for Roth IRAs may be further reduced or eliminated if your modified AGI for Roth IRA purposes is over:

- $181,000 if married filing jointly or qualifying widow(er),
- $114,000 if single, head of household, or married filing separately and you did not live with your spouse at any time in 2014, or
- $0 if married filing separately and you lived with your spouse at any time in 2014.

See Can You Contribute to a Roth IRA? in Pub. 590-A for details.

Line 20

Generally, enter the amount from Form 8606, line 19, plus any qualified distributions. But if you withdrew the entire balance of all of your Roth IRAs, do not enter less than the amount on Form 5329, line 18 (see Example next).

Example. You contributed $1,000 to a Roth IRA in 2012, your only contribution to Roth IRAs. In 2014, you discovered you were not eligible to contribute to a Roth IRA in 2012. On September 9, 2014, you withdrew $800, the entire balance in the Roth IRA. You must file Form 5329 for 2012 and 2013 to pay the additional taxes for those years. When you complete Form 5329 for 2014, you enter $1,000 (not $800) on line 20, because you withdrew the entire balance.

Line 23

Enter the excess of your contributions to Roth IRAs for 2014 (unless withdrawn—discussed below) over your contribution limit for Roth IRAs. See the instructions for line 19, earlier, to figure your contribution limit for Roth IRAs.

Do not include rollovers in figuring your excess contributions.

You can withdraw some or all of your excess contributions for 2014 and they will be treated as not having been contributed if:
• You make the withdrawal by the due date, including extensions, of your 2014 tax return, and
• You withdraw any earnings on the withdrawn contributions and include the earnings in gross income (see the Instructions for Form 8606 for details). Also, if you had not reached age 59½ at the time of the withdrawal, include the earnings as an early distribution on line 1 of Form 5329 for the year in which you report the earnings.

Note. A Form 5329 is not required if the excess Roth IRA contributions are treated as not having been contributed and you do not have any earnings to report as early distributions on the form.

If you timely filed your return without withdrawing the excess contributions, you can still make the withdrawal no later than 6 months after the due date of your tax return, excluding extensions. If you do, file an amended return with "Filed pursuant to section 301.9100-2" written at the top. Report any related earnings for 2014 on the amended return and include an explanation of the withdrawal. Make any other necessary changes on the amended return (for example, if you reported the contributions as excess contributions on your original return, include an amended Form 5329 reflecting that the withdrawn contributions are no longer treated as having been contributed).

Part V—Additional Tax on Excess Contributions to Coverdell ESAs

If the contributions to your Coverdell ESAs for 2014 were more than is allowable or you had an amount on line 33 of your 2013 Form 5329, you may owe this tax. But you may be able to avoid the tax on any 2014 excess contributions (see the instructions for line 31, later).

Line 26

Enter the amount from line 32 of your 2013 Form 5329 only if the amount on line 33 of your 2013 Form 5329 is more than zero.

Line 27

Enter the excess, if any, of the maximum amount that can be contributed to your Coverdell ESAs for 2014 over the amount actually contributed for 2014. Your contribution limit is the smaller of $2,000 or the sum of the maximum amounts the contributor(s) to your Coverdell ESAs are allowed to contribute. The maximum contribution may be limited based on the contributor's modified AGI. See *Contributions* under chapter 7 in Pub. 970 for details.

Line 28

Enter your total distributions from Coverdell ESAs in 2014. Do not include rollovers or withdrawn excess contributions.

Line 31

Enter the excess of the contributions to your Coverdell ESAs for 2014 (unless withdrawn—discussed below) over your contribution limit for Coverdell ESAs. See the instructions for line 27 above to figure your contribution limit for Coverdell ESAs.

Do not include rollovers in figuring your excess contributions.

You can withdraw some or all of the excess contributions for 2014 and they will be treated as not having been contributed if:
• You make the withdrawal before June 1, 2015, and
• You also withdraw any income earned on the withdrawn contributions and include the earnings in gross income for the year in which the contribution was made.

If you filed your return without withdrawing the excess contributions, you can still make the withdrawal, but it must be made before June 1, 2015. If you do, file an amended return. Report any related earnings for 2014 on the amended return and include an explanation of the withdrawal. Make any other necessary changes on the amended return (for example, if you reported the contributions as excess contributions on your original return, include an amended Form 5329 reflecting that the withdrawn contributions are no longer treated as having been contributed).

Part VI—Additional Tax on Excess Contributions to Archer MSAs

If you or your employer contributed more to your Archer MSA for 2014 than is allowable or you had an amount on line 41 of your 2013 Form 5329, you may owe this tax. But you may be able to avoid the tax on any 2014 excess contributions (see the instructions for line 39 below).

Line 34

Enter the amount from line 40 of your 2013 Form 5329 only if the amount on line 41 of your 2013 Form 5329 is more than zero.

Line 35

If contributions to your Archer MSAs for 2014 were less than your contribution limit for Archer MSAs, enter the difference on line 35. Your contribution limit for Archer MSAs is the smaller of line 3 or line 4 of Form 8853, Archer MSAs and Long-Term Care Insurance Contracts.

Also include on your 2014 Form 8853, line 5, the smaller of:
• Form 5329, line 35, or
• The excess, if any, of Form 5329, line 34, over Form 5329, line 36.

Line 39

Enter the excess of your contributions to your Archer MSA for 2014 from Form 8853, line 2 (unless withdrawn—discussed next), over your contribution limit (the smaller of line 3 or line 4 of Form 8853). Also include on line 39 any excess contributions your employer made. See the Instructions for Form 8853 for details.

You can withdraw some or all of the excess contributions for 2014 and they will be treated as not having been contributed if:
• You make the withdrawal by the due date, including extensions, of your 2014 tax return, and
• You withdraw any income earned on the withdrawn contributions and include the earnings in gross income for the year in which you receive the withdrawn contributions and earnings.

Include the withdrawn contributions and related earnings on Form 8853, lines 6a and 6b.

If you timely filed your return without withdrawing the excess contributions, you can still make the withdrawal no later than 6 months after the due date of your tax return, excluding extensions. If you do, file an amended return with

"Filed pursuant to section 301.9100-2" written at the top. Report any related earnings for 2014 on the amended return and include an explanation of the withdrawal. Make any other necessary changes on the amended return (for example, if you reported the contributions as excess contributions on your original return, include an amended Form 5329 reflecting that the withdrawn contributions are no longer treated as having been contributed).

Part VII—Additional Tax on Excess Contributions to Health Savings Accounts (HSAs)

If you, someone on your behalf, or your employer contributed more to your HSAs for 2014 than is allowable or you had an amount on line 49 of your 2013 Form 5329, you may owe this tax. But you may be able to avoid the tax on any 2014 excess contributions (see the instructions for line 47 below).

Line 42

Enter the amount from line 48 of your 2013 Form 5329 only if the amount on line 49 of your 2013 Form 5329 is more than zero.

Line 43

If contributions to your HSAs for 2014 (line 2 of Form 8889, Health Savings Accounts (HSAs)) were less than your contribution limit for HSAs, enter the difference on line 43. Your contribution limit for HSAs is the amount on line 12 of Form 8889.

Also include on your 2014 Form 8889, line 13, the smaller of:
- Form 5329, line 43, or
- The excess, if any, of Form 5329, line 42, over Form 5329, line 44.

Line 47

Enter the excess of your contributions (including those made on your behalf) to your HSAs for 2014 from Form 8889, line 2 (unless withdrawn—discussed next), over your contribution limit (Form 8889, line 12). Also include on line 47 any excess contributions your employer made. See the Instructions for Form 8889 for details.

You can withdraw some or all of the excess contributions for 2014 and they will be treated as not having been contributed if:
- You make the withdrawal by the due date, including extensions, of your 2014 return, and
- You withdraw any income earned on the withdrawn contributions and include

the earnings in gross income for the year in which you receive the withdrawn contributions and earnings.

Include the withdrawn contributions and related earnings on Form 8889, lines 14a and 14b.

If you timely filed your return without withdrawing the excess contributions, you can still make the withdrawal no later than 6 months after the due date of your tax return, excluding extensions. If you do, file an amended return with "Filed pursuant to section 301.9100-2" written at the top. Report any related earnings for 2014 on the amended return and include an explanation of the withdrawal. Make any other necessary changes on the amended return (for example, if you reported the contributions as excess contributions on your original return, include an amended Form 5329 reflecting that the withdrawn contributions are no longer treated as having been contributed).

Part VIII—Additional Tax on Excess Accumulation in Qualified Retirement Plans (Including IRAs)

You owe this tax if you do not receive the required minimum distribution from your qualified retirement plan, including an IRA or an eligible section 457 deferred compensation plan. The additional tax is 50% of the excess accumulation, which is the difference between the amount that was required to be distributed and the amount that was actually distributed. The tax is due for the tax year that includes the last day by which the minimum required distribution must be taken.

Line 50

IRA (other than a Roth IRA). You must start receiving distributions from your IRA by April 1 of the year following the year in which you reach age 70½. At that time, you can receive your entire interest in the IRA or begin receiving periodic distributions. If you choose to receive periodic distributions, you must receive a minimum required distribution each year. You can figure the minimum required distribution by dividing the account balance of your IRAs (other than Roth IRAs) on December 31 of the year preceding the distribution by the applicable life expectancy. For applicable life expectancies, see *Figuring the Owner's Required Minimum Distribution* under *When Must You Withdraw Assets?* in Pub. 590-B.

If the trustee, custodian, or issuer of your IRA informs you of the minimum required distribution, you can use that amount.

If you have more than one IRA, you can take the minimum required distribution from any one or more of the IRAs (other than Roth IRAs).

For more details on the minimum distribution rules (including examples), see *When Must You Withdraw Assets?* in Pub. 590-B.

 A qualified charitable distribution will count towards your required minimum distribution. See Qualified charitable distributions *under* Are Distributions Taxable? *in chapter 1 of Pub. 590-B for more information.*

Trusts and estates. Include the amount of tax, if any, on Form 1041, Schedule G, line 7. Write "From Form 5329" and the amount of the tax to the left of the line 7 entry space.

Roth IRA. There are no minimum required distributions during the lifetime of the owner of a Roth IRA. Following the death of the Roth IRA owner, required distribution rules apply to the beneficiary. See *Must You Withdraw or Use Assets?* in Pub. 590-B for details.

Qualified retirement plans (other than IRAs) and eligible section 457 deferred compensation plans. In general, you must begin receiving distributions from your plan no later than April 1 following the later of (a) the year in which you reach age 70½ or (b) the year in which you retire.

Exception. If you owned more than 5% of the employer maintaining the plan, you must begin receiving distributions no later than April 1 of the year following the year in which you reach age 70½, regardless of when you retire.

Your plan administrator should figure the amount that must be distributed each year.

Waiver of tax. The IRS can waive part or all of this tax if you can show that any shortfall in the amount of distributions was due to reasonable error and you are taking reasonable steps to remedy the shortfall. If you believe you qualify for this relief, attach a statement of explanation and file Form 5329 as follows.

1. Complete lines 50 and 51 as instructed.

2. Enter "RC" and the amount you want waived in parentheses on the

dotted line next to line 52. Subtract this amount from the total shortfall you figured without regard to the waiver, and enter the result on line 52.

3. Complete line 53 as instructed. You must pay any tax due that is reported on line 53.

The IRS will review the information you provide and decide whether to grant your request for a waiver.

Privacy Act and Paperwork Reduction Act Notice. We ask for the information on this form to carry out the Internal Revenue laws of the United States. We need this information to ensure that you are complying with these laws and to allow us to figure and collect the right amount of tax. You are required to give us this information if you made certain contributions or received certain distributions from qualified plans, including IRAs, and other tax-favored accounts. Our legal right to ask for the information requested on this form is sections 6001, 6011, 6012(a), and 6109 and their regulations. If you do not provide this information, or you provide incomplete or false information, you may be subject to penalties.

You are not required to provide the information requested on a form that is subject to the Paperwork Reduction Act unless the form displays a valid OMB control number. Books or records relating to a form or its instructions must be retained as long as their contents may become material in the administration of any Internal Revenue law. Generally, tax returns and return information are confidential, as required by section 6103. However, we may give this information to the Department of Justice for civil and criminal litigation, and to cities, states, the District of Columbia, and U.S. commonwealths and possessions to carry out their tax laws. We may also disclose this information to other countries under a tax treaty, to federal and state agencies to enforce federal nontax criminal laws, or to federal law enforcement and intelligence agencies to combat terrorism.

The average time and expenses required to complete and file this form will vary depending on individual circumstances. For the estimated averages, see the instructions for your income tax return.

If you have suggestions for making this form simpler, we would be happy to hear from you. See the instructions for your income tax return.

Form **6251**	**Alternative Minimum Tax—Individuals**	OMB No. 1545-0074
Department of the Treasury Internal Revenue Service (99)	▶ Information about Form 6251 and its separate instructions is at *www.irs.gov/form6251*. ▶ Attach to Form 1040 or Form 1040NR.	**2014** Attachment Sequence No. **32**

Name(s) shown on Form 1040 or Form 1040NR | Your social security number

Part I Alternative Minimum Taxable Income (See instructions for how to complete each line.)

1	If filing Schedule A (Form 1040), enter the amount from Form 1040, line 41, and go to line 2. Otherwise, enter the amount from Form 1040, line 38, and go to line 7. (If less than zero, enter as a negative amount.)	1
2	Medical and dental. If you or your spouse was 65 or older, enter the **smaller** of Schedule A (Form 1040), line 4, **or** 2.5% (.025) of Form 1040, line 38. If zero or less, enter -0-	2
3	Taxes from Schedule A (Form 1040), line 9	3
4	Enter the home mortgage interest adjustment, if any, from line 6 of the worksheet in the instructions for this line	4
5	Miscellaneous deductions from Schedule A (Form 1040), line 27	5
6	If Form 1040, line 38, is $152,525 or less, enter -0-. Otherwise, see instructions	6 ( )
7	Tax refund from Form 1040, line 10 or line 21	7 ( )
8	Investment interest expense (difference between regular tax and AMT)	8
9	Depletion (difference between regular tax and AMT)	9
10	Net operating loss deduction from Form 1040, line 21. Enter as a positive amount	10
11	Alternative tax net operating loss deduction	11 ( )
12	Interest from specified private activity bonds exempt from the regular tax	12
13	Qualified small business stock (7% of gain excluded under section 1202)	13
14	Exercise of incentive stock options (excess of AMT income over regular tax income)	14
15	Estates and trusts (amount from Schedule K-1 (Form 1041), box 12, code A)	15
16	Electing large partnerships (amount from Schedule K-1 (Form 1065-B), box 6)	16
17	Disposition of property (difference between AMT and regular tax gain or loss)	17
18	Depreciation on assets placed in service after 1986 (difference between regular tax and AMT)	18
19	Passive activities (difference between AMT and regular tax income or loss)	19
20	Loss limitations (difference between AMT and regular tax income or loss)	20
21	Circulation costs (difference between regular tax and AMT)	21
22	Long-term contracts (difference between AMT and regular tax income)	22
23	Mining costs (difference between regular tax and AMT)	23
24	Research and experimental costs (difference between regular tax and AMT)	24
25	Income from certain installment sales before January 1, 1987	25 ( )
26	Intangible drilling costs preference	26
27	Other adjustments, including income-based related adjustments	27
28	**Alternative minimum taxable income.** Combine lines 1 through 27. (If married filing separately and line 28 is more than $242,450, see instructions.)	28

Part II Alternative Minimum Tax (AMT)

29	Exemption. (If you were under age 24 at the end of 2014, see instructions.)	

IF your filing status is . . .	AND line 28 is not over . . .	THEN enter on line 29 . . .	
Single or head of household	$117,300	$52,800	
Married filing jointly or qualifying widow(er)	156,500	82,100	}
Married filing separately	78,250	41,050	29

If line 28 is **over** the amount shown above for your filing status, see instructions.

30	Subtract line 29 from line 28. If more than zero, go to line 31. If zero or less, enter -0- here and on lines 31, 33, and 35, and go to line 34	30
31	• If you are filing Form 2555 or 2555-EZ, see instructions for the amount to enter. • If you reported capital gain distributions directly on Form 1040, line 13; you reported qualified dividends on Form 1040, line 9b; **or** you had a gain on both lines 15 and 16 of Schedule D (Form 1040) (as refigured for the AMT, if necessary), complete Part III on the back and enter the amount from line 64 here. • **All others:** If line 30 is $182,500 or less ($91,250 or less if married filing separately), multiply line 30 by 26% (.26). Otherwise, multiply line 30 by 28% (.28) and subtract $3,650 ($1,825 if married filing separately) from the result.	31
32	Alternative minimum tax foreign tax credit (see instructions)	32
33	Tentative minimum tax. Subtract line 32 from line 31	33
34	Add Form 1040, line 44 (minus any tax from Form 4972), and Form 1040, line 46. Subtract from the result any foreign tax credit from Form 1040, line 48. If you used Schedule J to figure your tax on Form 1040, line 44, refigure that tax without using Schedule J before completing this line (see instructions)	34
35	**AMT.** Subtract line 34 from line 33. If zero or less, enter -0-. Enter here and on Form 1040, line 45	35

For Paperwork Reduction Act Notice, see your tax return instructions. Cat. No. 13600G Form **6251** (2014)

Part III **Tax Computation Using Maximum Capital Gains Rates**

Complete Part III only if you are required to do so by line 31 or by the Foreign Earned Income Tax Worksheet in the instructions.

36	Enter the amount from Form 6251, line 30. If you are filing Form 2555 or 2555-EZ, enter the amount from line 3 of the worksheet in the instructions for line 31	**36**	
37	Enter the amount from line 6 of the Qualified Dividends and Capital Gain Tax Worksheet in the instructions for Form 1040, line 44, or the amount from line 13 of the Schedule D Tax Worksheet in the instructions for Schedule D (Form 1040), whichever applies (as refigured for the AMT, if necessary) (see instructions). If you are filing Form 2555 or 2555-EZ, see instructions for the amount to enter	**37**	
38	Enter the amount from Schedule D (Form 1040), line 19 (as refigured for the AMT, if necessary) (see instructions). If you are filing Form 2555 or 2555-EZ, see instructions for the amount to enter	**38**	
39	If you did not complete a Schedule D Tax Worksheet for the regular tax or the AMT, enter the amount from line 37. Otherwise, add lines 37 and 38, and enter the **smaller** of that result or the amount from line 10 of the Schedule D Tax Worksheet (as refigured for the AMT, if necessary). If you are filing Form 2555 or 2555-EZ, see instructions for the amount to enter	**39**	
40	Enter the **smaller** of line 36 or line 39	**40**	
41	Subtract line 40 from line 36	**41**	
42	If line 41 is $182,500 or less ($91,250 or less if married filing separately), multiply line 41 by 26% (.26). Otherwise, multiply line 41 by 28% (.28) and subtract $3,650 ($1,825 if married filing separately) from the result . . . ▶	**42**	
43	Enter: • $73,800 if married filing jointly or qualifying widow(er), • $36,900 if single or married filing separately, or • $49,400 if head of household.	**43**	
44	Enter the amount from line 7 of the Qualified Dividends and Capital Gain Tax Worksheet in the instructions for Form 1040, line 44, or the amount from line 14 of the Schedule D Tax Worksheet in the instructions for Schedule D (Form 1040), whichever applies (as figured for the regular tax). If you did not complete either worksheet for the regular tax, enter the amount from Form 1040, line 43; if zero or less, enter -0-. If you are filing Form 2555 or 2555-EZ, see instructions for the amount to enter	**44**	
45	Subtract line 44 from line 43. If zero or less, enter -0-	**45**	
46	Enter the **smaller** of line 36 or line 37	**46**	
47	Enter the **smaller** of line 45 or line 46. This amount is taxed at 0%	**47**	
48	Subtract line 47 from line 46	**48**	
49	Enter: • $406,750 if single • $228,800 if married filing separately • $457,600 if married filing jointly or qualifying widow(er) • $432,200 if head of household	**49**	
50	Enter the amount from line 45	**50**	
51	Enter the amount from line 7 of the Qualified Dividends and Capital Gain Tax Worksheet in the instructions for Form 1040, line 44, or the amount from line 19 of the Schedule D Tax Worksheet, whichever applies (as figured for the regular tax). If you did not complete either worksheet for the regular tax, enter the amount from Form 1040, line 43; if zero or less, enter -0-. If you are filing Form 2555 or Form 2555-EZ, see instructions for the amount to enter	**51**	
52	Add line 50 and line 51	**52**	
53	Subtract line 52 from line 49. If zero or less, enter -0-	**53**	
54	Enter the smaller of line 48 or line 53	**54**	
55	Multiply line 54 by 15% (.15) . . . . ▶	**55**	
56	Add lines 47 and 54	**56**	
	If lines 56 and 36 are the same, skip lines 57 through 61 and go to line 62. Otherwise, go to line 57.		
57	Subtract line 56 from line 46	**57**	
58	Multiply line 57 by 20% (.20) . . . . ▶	**58**	
	If line 38 is zero or blank, skip lines 59 through 61 and go to line 62. Otherwise, go to line 59.		
59	Add lines 41, 56, and 57	**59**	
60	Subtract line 59 from line 36	**60**	
61	Multiply line 60 by 25% (.25) . . . . ▶	**61**	
62	Add lines 42, 55, 58, and 61	**62**	
63	If line 36 is $182,500 or less ($91,250 or less if married filing separately), multiply line 36 by 26% (.26). Otherwise, multiply line 36 by 28% (.28) and subtract $3,650 ($1,825 if married filing separately) from the result	**63**	
64	Enter the **smaller** of line 62 or line 63 here and on line 31. If you are filing Form 2555 or 2555-EZ, do not enter this amount on line 31. Instead, enter it on line 4 of the worksheet in the instructions for line 31 . . .	**64**	

2014

Department of the Treasury
Internal Revenue Service

Instructions for Form 6251

Alternative Minimum Tax—Individuals

Section references are to the Internal Revenue Code unless otherwise noted.

General Instructions

Future Developments

For the latest information about developments related to Form 6251 and its instructions, such as legislation enacted after they were published, go to *www.irs.gov/form6251*.

What's New

Exemption amount. The exemption amount on Form 6251, line 29, has increased to $52,800 ($82,100 if married filing jointly or qualifying widow(er); $41,050 if married filing separately).

AMT tax brackets. For 2014, the 26% tax rate applies to the first $182,500 ($91,250 if married filing separately) of taxable excess (the amount on line 30). This change is reflected in lines 31, 42, and 63.

Limit on itemized deductions. You cannot deduct all of your itemized deductions for regular tax purposes if your adjusted gross income is more than:
- $152,525 if married filing separately,
- $254,200 if single,
- $279,650 if head of household, or
- $305,050 if married filing jointly or qualifying widow(er).

This limit does not apply for the AMT. See the instructions for line 6.

Who Must File

Attach Form 6251 to your return if any of the following statements is true.

1. Form 6251, line 31, is greater than line 34.

2. You claim any general business credit, and either line 6 (in Part I) or line 25 of Form 3800 is more than zero.

3. You claim the qualified electric vehicle credit, the personal use part of the alternative fuel vehicle refueling property credit, or the credit for prior year minimum tax.

4. The total of Form 6251, lines 8 through 27, is negative and line 31 would be greater than line 34 if you did not take into account lines 8 through 27.

Purpose of Form

Use Form 6251 to figure the amount, if any, of your alternative minimum tax (AMT). The AMT applies to taxpayers who have certain types of income that receive favorable treatment, or who qualify for certain deductions, under the tax law. These tax benefits can significantly reduce the regular tax of some taxpayers with higher economic incomes. The AMT sets a limit on the amount these benefits can be used to reduce total tax.

Also use Form 6251 to figure your tentative minimum tax (Form 6251, line 33). You may need to know that amount to figure the tax liability limit on the credits listed under *Who Must File*.

Recordkeeping

For the AMT, certain items of income, deductions, etc., receive different tax treatment than for the regular tax. Therefore, you need to refigure items for the AMT that you figured for the regular tax. In some cases, you may wish to do this by completing the applicable tax form a second time. If you do complete another form, do not attach it to your tax return, but keep it for your records. However, you may have to attach an AMT Form 1116, Foreign Tax Credit, to your return; see the instructions for line 32.

For the regular tax, some deductions and credits may result in carrybacks or carryforwards to other tax years. Examples are investment interest expense, a net operating loss, a capital loss, a passive activity loss, and the foreign tax credit. Because you may have to refigure these items for the AMT, the carryback or carryforward amount may be different for the AMT than for the regular tax. Your at-risk limits and basis amounts also may differ for the AMT. Therefore, you must keep records of these different amounts.

Partners and Shareholders

If you are a partner in a partnership or a shareholder in an S corporation, see Schedule K-1 and its instructions to figure your adjustments or preferences from the partnership or S corporation to include on Form 6251.

Nonresident Aliens

If you are a nonresident alien and you disposed of U.S. real property interests at a gain, you must make a special computation. Fill in Form 6251 through line 30. If your net gain from the disposition of U.S. real property interests and the amount on line 28 are both greater than the tentative amount you figured for line 30, replace the amount on line 30 with the smaller of that net gain or the amount on line 28. Also, enter "RPI" on the dotted line next to line 30. Otherwise, do not change line 30.

Credit for Prior Year Minimum Tax

See Form 8801, Credit for Prior Year Minimum Tax—Individuals, Estates, and Trusts, if you paid AMT for 2013 or you had a minimum tax credit carryforward on your 2013 Form 8801. If you pay AMT for 2014, you may be able to take a credit on Form 8801 for 2015.

Optional Write-Off for Certain Expenditures

There is no AMT adjustment for the following items if you elect for the regular tax to deduct them ratably over the period of time shown.
- Circulation expenditures—3 years (section 173).
- Research and experimental expenditures—10 years (section 174(a)).
- Mining exploration and development costs—10 years (sections 616(a) and 617(a)).
- Intangible drilling costs—60 months (section 263(c)).

For information on making the election, see section 59(e) and Regulations section 1.59-1. Also see Pub. 535, Business Expenses.

Specific Instructions

If you owe AMT, you may be able to lower your total tax (regular tax plus AMT) by claiming itemized deductions on Form 1040, even if your total itemized deductions are less than the standard deduction. This is because the standard

Cat. No. 64277P

deduction is not allowed for the AMT and, if you claim the standard deduction on Form 1040, you cannot claim itemized deductions for the AMT.

Part I—Alternative Minimum Taxable Income (AMTI)

 To avoid duplication, any adjustment or preference for line 5, 19, or 20 or for a tax shelter farm activity on line 27 must not be taken into account in figuring the amount to enter for any other adjustment or preference.

Line 1

If Form 1040, line 43, includes a write-in amount (such as a capital construction fund deduction for commercial fishermen), adjust line 1 by the write-in amount.

Form 1040NR. If you are filing Form 1040NR, enter the amount from Form 1040NR, line 39. If less than zero, enter as a negative amount.

Line 2—Medical Expenses

Do not complete line 2 unless you completed Schedule A (Form 1040), line 3, by multiplying Schedule A, line 2, by 7.5% (.075).

Line 3—Taxes

Enter the amount of all taxes from Schedule A (Form 1040), line 9, except any generation-skipping transfer taxes on income distributions.

Be sure to include any state and local general sales taxes from Schedule A, line 5.

Form 1040NR. If you are filing Form 1040NR, enter the amount of all taxes from Schedule A (Form 1040NR), line 1, except any generation-skipping transfer taxes on income distributions.

Line 4—Home Mortgage Interest Adjustment

Complete the Home Mortgage Interest Adjustment Worksheet to figure the amount to enter on this line. The definitions of certain terms used in the worksheet are as follows.

Eligible mortgage. An eligible mortgage is a mortgage whose proceeds were used to buy, build, or substantially improve your main home or a second home that is a qualified dwelling. A mortgage whose proceeds were used to refinance another mortgage is not an eligible mortgage.

Qualified dwelling. A qualified dwelling is any house, apartment, condominium, or mobile home not used on a transient basis.

Family. Family includes only your brothers and sisters (whether by whole or half blood), your spouse, your ancestors, and your lineal descendants.

Example. In 2014, Dave and Jennifer paid $10,000 in interest on a mortgage they took out to buy their home (an eligible mortgage). In May 2014, they refinanced that mortgage and paid $9,000 in interest through the rest of the year. The balance of the new mortgage is the same as the balance of the old mortgage. In July 2014, they obtained a home equity loan on their home and used the proceeds to buy a new car. They paid $5,000 in interest on the home equity loan in 2014. They enter the following amounts on the Home Mortgage Interest Adjustment Worksheet: $24,000 on line 1 ($10,000 plus $9,000 plus $5,000), $10,000 on line 2, $9,000 on line 3, $ -0- on line 4, $19,000 on line 5 ($10,000 plus $9,000), and $5,000 on line 6 ($24,000 minus $19,000).

Line 5—Miscellaneous Deductions

If you are filing Form 1040NR, enter the amount from Schedule A (Form 1040NR), line 13.

Line 6—Overall Limit on Itemized Deductions

If Form 1040, line 38, is over $254,200 ($279,650 if head of household; $305,050 if married filing jointly or qualifying widow(er); or $152,525 if married filing separately), enter the amount from line 9 of the Itemized Deductions Worksheet in the Instructions for Schedule A (Form 1040). Enter it as a negative amount.

If Form 1040, line 38, is not more than the amount listed above for your filing status, enter -0-.

Form 1040NR. Enter the amount from line 9 of the Itemized Deductions Worksheet in the instructions for Form 1040NR if you are filing Form 1040NR and line 37 of Form 1040NR is over the amount listed below for your filing status:
• $254,200 and you checked filing status box 1 or 2,

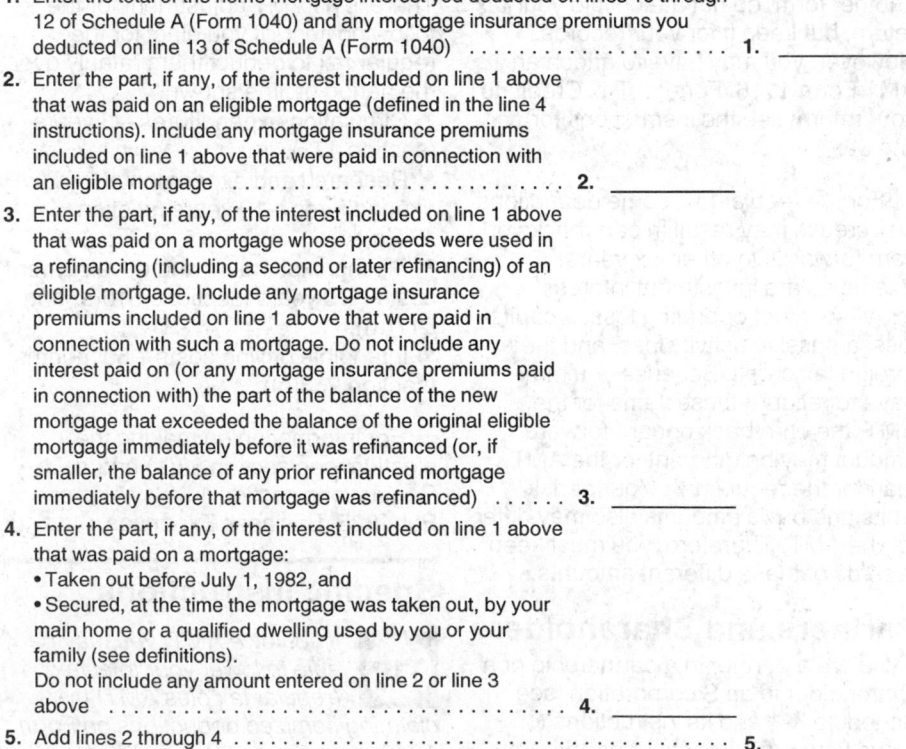

Home Mortgage Interest Adjustment Worksheet—Line 4   *Keep for Your Records*

1. Enter the total of the home mortgage interest you deducted on lines 10 through 12 of Schedule A (Form 1040) and any mortgage insurance premiums you deducted on line 13 of Schedule A (Form 1040) . . . . **1.** _____

2. Enter the part, if any, of the interest included on line 1 above that was paid on an eligible mortgage (defined in the line 4 instructions). Include any mortgage insurance premiums included on line 1 above that were paid in connection with an eligible mortgage . . . . **2.** _____

3. Enter the part, if any, of the interest included on line 1 above that was paid on a mortgage whose proceeds were used in a refinancing (including a second or later refinancing) of an eligible mortgage. Include any mortgage insurance premiums included on line 1 above that were paid in connection with such a mortgage. Do not include any interest paid on (or any mortgage insurance premiums paid in connection with) the part of the balance of the new mortgage that exceeded the balance of the original eligible mortgage immediately before it was refinanced (or, if smaller, the balance of any prior refinanced mortgage immediately before that mortgage was refinanced) . . . . . . **3.** _____

4. Enter the part, if any, of the interest included on line 1 above that was paid on a mortgage:
• Taken out before July 1, 1982, and
• Secured, at the time the mortgage was taken out, by your main home or a qualified dwelling used by you or your family (see definitions).
Do not include any amount entered on line 2 or line 3 above . . . . **4.** _____

5. Add lines 2 through 4 . . . . **5.** _____

6. Subtract line 5 from line 1 and enter the result on Form 6251, line 4 . . . . **6.** _____

- $152,525 and you checked filing status box 3, 4, or 5, or
- $305,050 and you checked filing status box 6.

Enter it as a negative amount.

If Form 1040NR, line 37, is not more than the amount just listed for your filing status, enter -0-.

Line 7—Refund of Taxes

Include any refund from Form 1040, line 10 (or Form 1040NR, line 11), that is attributable to state or local income taxes. Also include any refunds received in 2014 and included in income on Form 1040, line 21, that are attributable to state or local personal property taxes or general sales taxes, foreign income taxes, or state, local, or foreign real property taxes. Enter the total as a negative amount. If you include an amount from Form 1040, line 21, you must enter a description and the amount next to the entry space for line 7. For example, if you include a refund of real property taxes, enter "real property" and the amount next to the entry space.

Line 8—Investment Interest

If you filled out Form 4952, Investment Interest Expense Deduction, for your regular tax, you will need to fill out a second Form 4952 for the AMT as follows.

Step 1. Follow the Form 4952 instructions for line 1, but also include the following amounts when completing line 1.
- Any interest expense on Form 6251, line 4, that was paid or accrued on indebtedness attributable to property held for investment within the meaning of section 163(d)(5) (for example, interest on a home equity loan whose proceeds were invested in stocks or bonds).
- Any interest that would have been deductible if tax-exempt interest on private activity bonds were includible in gross income.

Step 2. Enter your AMT disallowed investment interest expense from 2013 on line 2. Complete line 3.

Step 3. When completing Part II, refigure the following amounts, taking into account all adjustments and preferences.
- Gross income from property held for investment.
- Net gain from the disposition of property held for investment.
- Net capital gain from the disposition of property held for investment.
- Investment expenses.

Include on line 4a any tax-exempt interest income from private activity bonds that must be included on Form 6251, line 12. If you have any investment expenses that would have been deductible if the interest on the bonds were includible in gross income for the regular tax, you can use them to reduce the amount on line 4a or include them on line 5.

On line 4g, enter the smaller of:

1. The amount from line 4g of your regular tax Form 4952, or

2. The total of lines 4b and 4e of this AMT Form 4952.

Step 4. Complete Part III.

Enter on Form 6251, line 8, the difference between line 8 of your AMT Form 4952 and line 8 of your regular tax Form 4952. If your AMT expense is greater, enter the difference as a negative amount.

Investment interest expense that is not an itemized deduction. If you did not itemize deductions and you had investment interest expense, do not enter an amount on Form 6251, line 8, unless you reported investment interest expense on Schedule E, Supplemental Income and Loss (Form 1040). If you did, follow the steps above for completing Form 4952. Allocate the investment interest expense allowed on line 8 of the AMT Form 4952 in the same way you did for the regular tax. Enter on Form 6251, line 8, the difference between the amount allowed on Schedule E for the regular tax and the amount allowed on Schedule E for the AMT.

Line 9—Depletion

Refigure your depletion deduction for the AMT. To do so, use only income and deductions allowed for the AMT when refiguring the limit based on taxable income from the property under section 613(a) and the limit based on taxable income, with certain adjustments, under section 613A(d)(1). Also, your depletion deduction for mines, wells, and other natural deposits under section 611 is limited to the property's adjusted basis at the end of the year, as refigured for the AMT, unless you are an independent producer or royalty owner claiming percentage depletion for oil and gas wells under section 613A(c). Figure this limit separately for each property. When refiguring the property's adjusted basis, take into account any AMT adjustments you made this year or in previous years

that affect basis (other than current year depletion).

Enter the difference between the regular tax and AMT deduction. If the AMT deduction is more than the regular tax deduction, enter the difference as a negative amount.

Line 10—Net Operating Loss Deduction

If you are filing Form 1040NR, enter your net operating loss deduction from Form 1040NR, line 21, as a positive amount.

Line 11—Alternative Tax Net Operating Loss Deduction (ATNOLD)

The ATNOLD is the sum of the alternative tax net operating loss (ATNOL) carrybacks and carryforwards to the tax year, subject to the limitation explained later. Figure your ATNOLD as follows.

Your ATNOL for a loss year is the excess of the deductions allowed for figuring AMTI (excluding the ATNOLD) over the income included in AMTI. Figure this excess with the modifications in section 172(d), taking into account your AMT adjustments and preferences (that is, the section 172(d) modifications must be separately figured for the ATNOL). For example, the limitation of nonbusiness deductions to the amount of nonbusiness income must be separately figured for the ATNOL, using only nonbusiness income and deductions that are included in AMTI.

Your ATNOLD may be limited. To figure the ATNOLD limitation, you must first figure your AMTI without regard to the ATNOLD and any domestic production activities deduction. To do this, first figure a tentative amount for line 9 by treating line 11 as if it were zero. Next, figure a tentative total of lines 1 through 27 using the tentative line 9 amount and treating line 11 as if it were zero. This is your AMTI figured without regard to the ATNOLD. Add any domestic production activities deduction to this tentative total. **Your ATNOLD is limited to 90% of the result.**

However, the 90% limit does not apply to an ATNOL that is attributable to qualified disaster losses (as defined in section 172(j)), qualified Gulf Opportunity Zone losses (as defined in section 1400N(k)(2)), qualified recovery assistance losses (as defined in Pub. 4492-A, Information for Taxpayers Affected by the May 4, 2007, Kansas

Storms and Tornadoes), qualified disaster recovery assistance losses (as defined in Pub. 4492-B, Information for Affected Taxpayers in the Midwestern Disaster Areas), or a 2008 or 2009 loss that you elected to carry back more than 2 years under section 172(b)(1)(H). Therefore, if an ATNOL that is carried back or carried forward to the tax year is attributable to any of those losses, the ATNOLD for the tax year is limited to the sum of:

1. The smaller of:

a. The sum of the ATNOL carrybacks and carryforwards to the tax year attributable to net operating losses other than those losses described in 2a below, or

b. 90% of AMTI for the tax year (figured without regard to the ATNOLD and any domestic production activities deduction, as discussed earlier), plus

2. The smaller of:

a. The sum of the ATNOL carrybacks and carryforwards to the tax year attributable to qualified disaster losses, qualified Gulf Opportunity Zone losses, qualified recovery assistance losses, qualified disaster recovery assistance losses, and any 2008 or 2009 loss that you elected to carry back more than 2 years under section 172(b)(1)(H), or

b. 100% of AMTI for the tax year (figured without regard to the ATNOLD and any domestic production activities deduction, as discussed earlier) reduced by the amount determined under (1).

Enter on line 11 the smaller of the ATNOLD or the ATNOLD limitation. Enter it as a negative amount.

Any ATNOL not used may be carried back 2 years or forward up to 20 years. In some cases, the carryback period is longer than 2 years; for details, see Pub. 536.

The treatment of ATNOLs does not affect your regular tax NOL. However, if you elected under section 172(b)(3) to forgo the carryback period for the regular tax, the election also applies for the AMT.

Line 12—Interest From Private Activity Bonds

Enter on line 12 interest income from "specified private activity bonds" reduced (but not below zero) by any deduction that would have been allowable if the interest were includible in gross income for the regular tax. Each payer of this type of interest should send you a Form 1099-INT showing the amount of this interest in box 9.

Generally, the term "specified private activity bond" means any private activity bond (as defined in section 141) the interest on which is not includible in gross income for the regular tax, if the bond was issued after August 7, 1986. But specified private activity bonds generally do not include any bonds issued in 2009 or 2010. See section 57(a)(5) for other exceptions and more details.

Do not include interest on qualified Gulf Opportunity Zone bonds or qualified Midwestern disaster area bonds.

Exempt-interest dividends paid by a mutual fund or other regulated investment company are treated as interest income on specified private activity bonds to the extent the dividends are attributable to interest on the bonds received by the company, minus an allocable share of the expenses paid or incurred by the company in earning the interest. This amount should be reported to you on Form 1099-DIV in box 11.

If you are filing Form 8814, Parents' Election To Report Child's Interest and Dividends, include on this line any tax-exempt interest income from line 1b of that form that is a preference item.

Line 13—Qualified Small Business Stock

If you claimed the exclusion under section 1202 for gain on qualified small business stock held more than 5 years, multiply the excluded gain (as shown on Form 8949 in column (g)) by 7% (.07). Enter the result on line 13 as a positive amount.

Line 14—Exercise of Incentive Stock Options

For the regular tax, no income is recognized when an incentive stock option (ISO), as defined in section 422(b), is exercised. However, this rule does not apply for the AMT. Instead, you generally must include on line 14 the excess, if any, of:

1. The fair market value of the stock acquired through exercise of the option (determined without regard to any lapse restriction) when your rights in the acquired stock first become transferable or when these rights are no longer subject to a substantial risk of forfeiture, over

2. The amount you paid for the stock, including any amount you paid for the ISO used to acquire the stock.

Even if your rights in the stock are not transferable and are subject to a substantial risk of forfeiture, you may elect to include in AMT income the excess of the stock's fair market value (determined without regard to any lapse restriction) over the exercise price upon the transfer to you of the stock acquired through exercise of the option. You must make the election by the 30th day after the date of the transfer. See Pub. 525, Taxable and Nontaxable Income, for more details.

If you acquired stock by exercising an ISO and you disposed of that stock in the same year, the tax treatment under the regular tax and the AMT is the same, and no adjustment is required.

Increase your AMT basis in any stock acquired through the exercise of an ISO by the amount of the adjustment. Keep adequate records for both the AMT and regular tax so that you can figure your adjustment. See the instructions for line 17.

Form 3921. If you received a Form 3921, it may help you figure your adjustment.

Example. You exercised an ISO to acquire 100 shares of stock in 2014. Your rights in the acquired stock first became transferable on the date you exercised the ISO and were not subject to a substantial risk of forfeiture. You did not pay anything for the ISO. You did not sell the acquired stock during 2014. You received a Form 3921 that shows $10 in box 3 (the exercise price you paid for each share), $25 in box 4 (the fair market value of each share on the exercise date), and 100 shares in box 5 (the number of shares you acquired). To figure your adjustment, multiply the amount in box 4, $25, by the 100 shares in box 5. The result is $2,500, the fair market value of all the shares. Then multiply the amount in box 3, $10, by the 100 shares in box 5. The result is $1,000, the amount you paid for all the shares. Your adjustment is $1,500 ($2,500 − $1,000). Enter it on Form 6251, line 14.

Line 16—Large Partnerships

If you were a partner in an electing large partnership, enter the amount from Schedule K-1 (Form 1065-B), box 6. Take into account any amount from box 5 on Form 6251, line 19.

Line 17—Disposition of Property

Your AMT gain or loss from the disposition of property may be different from your gain or loss for the regular tax.

This is because the property may have a different adjusted basis for the AMT. Use this line to report any AMT adjustment resulting from refiguring:

1. Gain or loss from the sale, exchange, or involuntary conversion of property reported on Form 4797, Sales of Business Property;

2. Casualty gain or loss to business or income-producing property reported on Form 4684, Casualties and Thefts;

3. Ordinary income from the disposition of property not already taken into account in (1) or (2) or on any other line on Form 6251, such as a disqualifying disposition of stock acquired in a prior year by exercising an incentive stock option; and

4. Capital gain or loss (including any carryover that is different for the AMT) reported on Form 8949, Sales and Other Dispositions of Capital Assets, or Schedule D (Form 1040), Capital Gains and Losses.

First figure any ordinary income adjustment related to (3) above. Then, refigure Form 4684, Form 4797, Form 8949, and Schedule D for the AMT, if applicable, by taking into account any adjustments you made this year or in previous years that affect your basis or otherwise result in a different amount for the AMT.

If you have a capital loss after refiguring Schedule D for the AMT, apply the $3,000 capital loss limitation separately to the AMT loss. Because the amount of your gains and losses may be different for the AMT, the amount of any capital loss carryover also may be different for the AMT. See the following example. To figure your AMT capital loss carryover, fill out an AMT Capital Loss Carryover Worksheet in the Schedule D instructions.

For each of the four items listed earlier, figure the difference between the amount included in taxable income for the regular tax and the amount included in income for the AMT. Include the difference as a negative amount on line 17 if (a) both the AMT and regular tax amounts are zero or more and the AMT amount is less than the regular tax amount or (b) the AMT amount is a loss, and the regular tax amount is a smaller loss or is zero or more.

Enter on line 17 the combined adjustments for the four items listed earlier.

Example. On March 13, 2013, Victor Ash, whose filing status is single, paid $20,000 to exercise an incentive

stock option (which was granted to him on January 3, 2012) to buy 200 shares of stock worth $200,000. The $180,000 difference between his cost and the value of the stock at the time he exercised the option is not taxable for the regular tax. His regular tax basis in the stock at the end of 2013 is $20,000. For the AMT, however, Ash must include the $180,000 as an adjustment on his 2013 Form 6251. His AMT basis in the stock at the end of 2013 is $200,000.

On January 18, 2014, Ash sold 100 of the shares for $75,000. Because Ash did not hold these shares more than 1 year, that sale is a disqualifying disposition. For the regular tax, Ash has ordinary income of $65,000 ($75,000 minus his $10,000 basis in the 100 shares). Ash has no capital gain or loss for the regular tax resulting from the sale. For the AMT, Ash has no ordinary income, but has a short-term capital loss of $25,000 ($75,000 minus his $100,000 AMT basis in the 100 shares).

On April 21, 2014, Ash sold the other 100 shares for $60,000. Because he held the shares for more than 1 year and more than 2 years had passed since the option was granted to him, the sale is not a disqualifying disposition. For the regular tax, Ash has a long-term capital gain of $50,000 ($60,000 minus his regular tax basis of $10,000). For the AMT, Ash has a long-term capital loss of $40,000 ($60,000 minus his AMT basis of $100,000).

Ash has no other sales of stock or other capital assets for 2014. Ash enters a total negative adjustment of $118,000 on line 17 of his 2014 Form 6251, figured as follows:
• Ash figures a negative adjustment of $65,000 for the difference between the $65,000 of regular tax ordinary income and the $0 of AMT ordinary income for the first sale.
• For the regular tax, Ash has $50,000 capital gain net income from the second sale. For the AMT, Ash has a $25,000 short-term capital loss from the first sale, and a $40,000 long-term capital loss from the second sale, resulting in a net capital loss of $65,000 for the AMT. However, only $3,000 of the $65,000 net capital loss is allowed for 2014 for the AMT. The difference between the regular tax gain of $50,000 and the $3,000 loss allowed for the AMT results in a $53,000 negative adjustment to include on line 17.

Ash has an AMT capital loss carryover from 2014 to 2015 of $62,000, of which $22,000 is short-term and

$40,000 is long-term. If he has no other Form 8949 or Schedule D transactions for 2015, his adjustment reported on his 2015 Form 6251 would be limited to ($3,000), the amount of his capital loss limitation for 2015.

Line 18—Post-1986 Depreciation

This section describes when depreciation must be refigured for the AMT and how to figure the amount to enter on line 18.

Do not use line 18 for depreciation related to the following.
• Employee business expenses claimed on line 21 of Schedule A (Form 1040) or line 7 of Schedule A (Form 1040NR). You should have already taken this adjustment into account on line 5 as part of your miscellaneous itemized deductions.
• Passive activities. Take this adjustment into account on line 19.
• An activity for which you are not at risk. Take this adjustment into account on line 20.
• Income or loss from a partnership or an S corporation if the basis limitations apply. Take this adjustment into account on line 20.
• A tax shelter farm activity. Take this adjustment into account on line 27.

What Depreciation Must Be Refigured for the AMT?

Generally, you must refigure depreciation for the AMT, including depreciation allocable to inventory costs, for:
• Property placed in service after 1998 that is depreciated for the regular tax using the 200% declining balance method (generally 3-, 5-, 7-, and 10-year property under the modified accelerated cost recovery system (MACRS), except for qualified property eligible for the special depreciation allowance (discussed later));
• Section 1250 property placed in service after 1998 that is not depreciated for the regular tax using the straight line method; and
• Tangible property placed in service after 1986 and before 1999. (If the transitional election was made under section 203(a)(1)(B) of the Tax Reform Act of 1986, this rule applies to property placed in service after July 31, 1986.)

What Depreciation Is Not Refigured for the AMT?

Do not refigure depreciation for the AMT for the following.

- Residential rental property placed in service after 1998.
- Nonresidential real property with a class life of 27.5 years or more placed in service after 1998 that is depreciated for the regular tax using the straight line method.
- Other section 1250 property placed in service after 1998 that is depreciated for the regular tax using the straight line method.
- Property (other than section 1250 property) placed in service after 1998 that is depreciated for the regular tax using the 150% declining balance method or the straight line method.
- Property for which you elected to use the alternative depreciation system (ADS) of section 168(g) for the regular tax.
- Qualified property that is or was eligible for a special depreciation allowance if the depreciable basis of the property is the same for the AMT and the regular tax. This applies to any special depreciation allowance, including those for disaster assistance property, reuse and recycling property, cellulosic biofuel plant property, second generation biofuel plant property, New York Liberty Zone property, Gulf Opportunity Zone property, and Kansas disaster area recovery assistance property. The special allowance is deductible for the AMT, and no adjustment is required for any depreciation figured on the remaining basis of the qualified property because the depreciable basis of the property is the same for the AMT and the regular tax. Property for which you elected to not have the special allowance apply is not qualified property.
- Any part of the cost of any property for which you elected to take a section 179 expense deduction. The reduction to the depreciable basis of section 179 property by the amount of the section 179 expense deduction is the same for the regular tax and the AMT.
- Motion picture films, videotapes, or sound recordings.
- Property depreciated under the unit-of-production method or any other method not expressed in a term of years.
- Indian reservation property that meets the requirements of section 168(j).
- Qualified revitalization expenditures for which you elected to claim the commercial revitalization deduction under section 1400I.
- A natural gas gathering line placed in service after April 11, 2005.

How Is Depreciation Refigured for the AMT?

Property placed in service before 1999. Refigure depreciation for the AMT using ADS, with the same convention used for the regular tax. See the following table for the method and recovery period to use.

Property Placed in Service Before 1999	
IF the property is...	THEN use the...
section 1250 property	straight line method over 40 years.
tangible property (other than section 1250 property) depreciated using straight line method for the regular tax	straight line method over the property's AMT class life.
any other tangible property	150% declining balance method, switching to straight line method the first tax year it gives a larger deduction, over the property's AMT class life.

Property placed in service after 1998. Use the same convention and recovery period used for the regular tax. For property other than section 1250 property, use the 150% declining balance method, switching to straight line the first tax year it gives a larger deduction. For section 1250 property, use the straight line method.

How Is the AMT Class Life Determined?

The class life used for the AMT is not necessarily the same as the recovery period used for the regular tax. The class lives for the AMT are listed in Rev. Proc. 87-56, 1987-2 C.B. 674, and in Pub. 946, How To Depreciate Property. Use 12 years for any tangible personal property not assigned a class life.

 See Pub. 946 for tables that can be used to figure AMT depreciation. Rev. Proc. 89-15, 1989-1 C.B. 816, has special rules for short years and for property disposed of before the end of the recovery period.

How Is the Adjustment Figured?

Subtract the AMT deduction for depreciation from the regular tax deduction and enter the result. If the AMT deduction is more than the regular tax deduction, enter the difference as a negative amount.

In addition to the AMT adjustment to your deduction for depreciation, also adjust the amount of depreciation that was capitalized, if any, to account for the difference between the rules for the regular tax and the AMT. Include on this line the current year adjustment to taxable income, if any, resulting from the difference.

Line 19—Passive Activities

Refigure your passive activity gains and losses for the AMT by taking into account all adjustments and preferences and any AMT prior year unallowed losses that apply to that activity. You may fill out a second Form 8582, Passive Activity Loss Limitations, and the other forms or schedules on which your passive activities are reported, to determine your passive activity loss allowed for the AMT, but do not file the second set of forms and schedules with your tax return.

Example. You are a partner in a partnership and the Schedule K-1 (Form 1065) you received shows the following.
- A passive activity loss of $4,125,
- A depreciation adjustment of $500 on post-1986 property, and
- An adjustment of $225 on the disposition of property.

Because the two adjustments above are from the passive activity and are not allowed for the AMT, you must first reduce the passive activity loss by those amounts. The result is a passive activity loss for the AMT of $3,400. You then enter this amount on the AMT Form 8582 and refigure the allowable passive activity loss for the AMT.

 The amount of any AMT passive activity loss that is not deductible and is carried forward is likely to differ from the regular tax amount, if any. Therefore, keep adequate records for both the AMT and regular tax.

Enter the difference between the amount that would be reported for the activity on Schedule C, C-EZ, E, or F or Form 4835, Farm Rental Income and Expenses, for the AMT and the regular tax amount. If (a) the AMT loss is more than the regular tax loss, (b) the AMT gain is less than the regular tax gain, or (c) you have an AMT loss and a regular tax gain, enter the adjustment as a negative amount.

Enter any adjustment for amounts reported on Form 8949, Schedule D,

Form 4684, or Form 4797 for the activity on line 17 instead of line 19. See the instructions for line 17.

Publicly Traded Partnership (PTP)

If you had a loss from a PTP, refigure the loss using any AMT adjustments and preferences and any AMT prior year unallowed loss.

Tax Shelter Passive Farm Activities

Refigure any gain or loss from a tax shelter passive farm activity taking into account all AMT adjustments and preferences and any AMT prior year unallowed losses. If the amount is a gain, include it on the AMT Form 8582. If the amount is a loss, do not include it on the AMT Form 8582. Carry the loss forward to 2015 to see if you have a gain or loss from tax shelter passive farm activities for 2015.

Insolvency

If at the end of the tax year your liabilities exceed the fair market value of your assets, increase your passive activity loss allowed by that excess (but not by more than your total loss). See section 58(c)(1).

Line 20—Loss Limitations

For passive activities, see the line 19 instructions instead. For tax shelter farm activities (that are not passive), see the line 27 instructions.

Refigure your gains and losses from activities for which you are not at risk and basis limitations applicable to partnerships and S corporations by taking into account all AMT adjustments and preferences that apply. See sections 59(h), 465, 704(d), and 1366(d).

Enter the difference between the amount that would be reported for the activity on Schedule C, C-EZ, E, or F or Form 4835 for the AMT and the regular tax amount. If (a) the AMT loss is more than the regular tax loss, (b) the AMT gain is less than the regular tax gain, or (c) you have an AMT loss and a regular tax gain, enter the adjustment as a negative amount.

The AMT amount of any gain or loss from activities for which you are not at risk is likely to differ from the regular tax amount. Your AMT basis in partnerships and S corporations is also likely to differ from your regular tax basis. Therefore, keep adequate records for both the AMT and regular tax.

Enter any adjustment for amounts reported on Form 8949, Schedule D, Form 4684, or Form 4797 for the activity on line 17 instead of line 20.

Line 21—Circulation Costs

 Do not make this adjustment for costs for which you elected the optional 3-year write-off for the regular tax.

Circulation costs (expenditures to establish, maintain, or increase the circulation of a newspaper, magazine, or other periodical) deducted in full for the regular tax in the year they were paid or incurred must be capitalized and amortized over 3 years for the AMT. Enter the difference between the regular tax and AMT deduction. If the AMT deduction is more than the regular tax deduction, enter the difference as a negative amount.

If you had a loss on property for which circulation costs have not been fully amortized for the AMT, your AMT deduction is the smaller of (a) the loss allowable for the costs had they remained capitalized or (b) the remaining costs to be amortized for the AMT.

Line 22—Long-Term Contracts

For the AMT, you generally must use the percentage-of-completion method described in section 460(b) to determine your income from any long-term contract (defined in section 460(f)). However, this rule does not apply to any home construction contract (as defined in section 460(e)(6)). For contracts excepted from the percentage-of-completion method for the regular tax by section 460(e)(1), use the simplified procedures for allocating costs outlined in section 460(b)(3) to determine the percentage of completion.

Enter the difference between the AMT and regular tax income. If the AMT income is smaller, enter the difference as a negative amount.

Note. If you are required to use the percentage-of-completion method for either the regular tax or the AMT, you may owe or be entitled to a refund of interest for the tax year the contract is completed or adjusted. For details, see Form 8697, Interest Computation Under the Look-Back Method for Completed Long-Term Contracts.

Line 23—Mining Costs

 Do not make this adjustment for costs for which you elected the optional 10-year write-off for the regular tax.

Mining exploration and development costs deducted in full for the regular tax in the tax year they were paid or incurred must be capitalized and amortized over 10 years for the AMT. Enter the difference between the regular tax and AMT deduction. If the AMT deduction is more than the regular tax deduction, enter the difference as a negative amount.

If you had a loss on property for which mining costs have not been fully amortized for the AMT, your AMT deduction is the smaller of (a) the loss allowable for the costs had they remained capitalized or (b) the remaining costs to be amortized for the AMT.

Line 24—Research and Experimental Costs

 Do not make this adjustment for costs paid or incurred in connection with an activity in which you materially participated under the passive activity rules or for costs for which you elected the optional 10-year write-off for the regular tax.

Research and experimental costs deducted in full for the regular tax in the tax year they were paid or incurred must be capitalized and amortized over 10 years for the AMT. Enter the difference between the regular tax and AMT deduction. If the AMT deduction is more than the regular tax deduction, enter the difference as a negative amount.

If you had a loss on property for which research and experimental costs have not been fully amortized for the AMT, your AMT deduction is the smaller of (a) the loss allowable for the costs had they remained capitalized or (b) the remaining costs to be amortized for the AMT.

Line 25—Installment Sales

The installment method does not apply for the AMT to any nondealer disposition of property after August 16, 1986, but before January 1, 1987, if an installment obligation to which the proportionate disallowance rule applied arose from the disposition. Enter the amount of installment sale income reported for the regular tax as a negative amount on line 25.

Line 26—Intangible Drilling Costs (IDCs)

 Do not make this adjustment for costs for which you elected the optional 60-month write-off for the regular tax.

IDCs from oil, gas, and geothermal wells are a preference to the extent that the excess IDCs are more than 65% of the net income from the wells. Figure the preference for all oil and gas properties separately from the preference for all geothermal properties.

Excess IDCs. Figure excess IDCs as follows.

Step 1. Determine the amount of your IDCs allowed for the regular tax under section 263(c), but do not include any section 263(c) deduction for nonproductive wells.

Step 2. Subtract from the amount determined in step 1 the amount that would have been allowed had you amortized these IDCs over a 120-month period starting with the month the well was placed in production. If you prefer not to use the 120-month period, you can elect to use any method that is permissible in determining cost depletion.

Net income. Determine net income by reducing the gross income that you received or accrued during the tax year from all oil, gas, and geothermal wells by the deductions allocable to those wells (reduced by the excess IDCs). When refiguring net income, use only income and deductions allowed for the AMT.

Exception. The preference for IDCs from oil and gas wells does not apply to taxpayers who are independent producers (that is, not integrated oil companies as defined in section 291(b)(4)). However, this benefit may be limited. First, figure the IDC preference as if this exception did not apply. Then, for purposes of this exception, complete Form 6251 through line 27, including the IDC preference and treating line 11 as if it were zero, and combine lines 1 through 27. If the amount of the IDC preference exceeds 40% of the total of lines 1 through 27 (figured as described in the preceding sentence), enter the excess on line 26 (your benefit from this exception is limited). Otherwise, do not enter an amount on line 26 (your benefit from this exception is not limited).

Line 27—Other Adjustments

Enter on line 27 the total of any other adjustments that apply to you, including the following.

Depreciation Figured Using Pre-1987 Rules

This preference generally applies only to property placed in service after 1987, but depreciated using pre-1987 rules due to transitional provisions of the Tax Reform Act of 1986.

For the AMT, you must use the straight line method to figure depreciation on real property for which accelerated depreciation was determined using pre-1987 rules. Use a recovery period of 19 years for 19-year real property and 15 years for low-income housing. For leased personal property other than recovery property, enter the amount by which your regular tax depreciation using the pre-1987 rules exceeds the depreciation allowable using the straight line method. For leased 10-year recovery property and leased 15-year public utility property, enter the amount by which your regular tax depreciation exceeds the depreciation allowable using the straight line method with a half-year convention, no salvage value, and a recovery period of 15 years (22 years for 15-year public utility property).

Figure the excess of the regular tax depreciation over the AMT depreciation separately for each property and include on line 27 only positive amounts.

Patron's Adjustment

Distributions you received from a cooperative may be includible in income. Unless the distributions are nontaxable, include on line 27 the total AMT patronage dividend adjustment reported to you by the cooperative, such as on Form 1099-PATR.

Pollution Control Facilities

The section 169 election to amortize the basis of a certified pollution control facility over a 60-month or 84-month period is not available for the AMT. For facilities placed in service before 1999, figure the AMT deduction using ADS. For facilities placed in service after 1998, figure the AMT deduction under MACRS using the straight line method. Enter the difference between the regular tax and AMT deduction. If the AMT deduction is more than the regular tax deduction, enter the difference as a negative amount.

Tax Shelter Farm Activities

Figure this adjustment only if you have a gain or loss from a tax shelter farm activity (as defined in section 58(a)(2)) that is not a passive activity. If the activity is passive, you must include it with your other passive activities on line 19.

Refigure all gains and losses you reported for the regular tax from tax shelter farm activities by taking into account any AMT adjustments and preferences. Determine your tax shelter farm activity gain or loss for the AMT using the same rules you used for the regular tax with the following modifications.
* No refigured loss is allowed, except to the extent you are insolvent (see section 58(c)(1)).
* Do not use a refigured loss in the current tax year to offset gains from other tax shelter farm activities. Instead, suspend any refigured loss and carry it forward indefinitely until (a) you have a gain in a subsequent tax year from that same activity or (b) you dispose of the activity.

Enter the difference between the amount that would be reported for the activity on Schedule E or F or Form 4835 for the AMT and the regular tax amount. If (a) the AMT loss is more than the regular tax loss, (b) the AMT gain is less than the regular tax gain, or (c) you have an AMT loss and a regular tax gain, enter the adjustment as a negative amount.

Enter any adjustment for amounts reported on Form 8949, Schedule D, Form 4684, or Form 4797 for the activity on line 17 instead of line 27.

Charitable Contributions of Certain Property

If you made a charitable contribution of property to which section 170(e) applies and you had a different basis for AMT purposes, you may have to make an adjustment. See section 170(e) for details.

Biofuel Producer Credit and Biodiesel and Renewable Diesel Fuels Credit

If your taxable income includes an amount from the biofuel producer credit on Form 6478 or the biodiesel and

Instructions for Form 6251 (2014)

renewable diesel fuels credit on Form 8864, include that amount as a negative amount on line 27.

Related Adjustments

If you have an entry on line 8 because you deducted investment interest allocable to an interest in a trade or business, or on line 9, 13, 14, or 16 through 26, or you have any amount included on line 27 from pre-1987 depreciation, patron's adjustment, pollution control facilities, or tax shelter farm activities, you may have to refigure any item of income or deduction based on a limit of income other than AGI or modified AGI.

Affected items include the following.
• Section 179 expense deduction (Form 4562, Depreciation and Amortization, line 12).
• Expenses for business or rental use of your home.
• Conservation expenses (Schedule F, line 12).
• Taxable IRA distributions (Form 1040, line 15b, or Form 1040NR, line 16b), if prior year IRA deductions

were different for the AMT and the regular tax.
• Self-employed health insurance deduction (Form 1040, line 29, or Form 1040NR, line 29).
• Self-employed SEP, SIMPLE, and qualified plans deduction (Form 1040, line 28, or Form 1040NR, line 28).
• IRA deduction (Form 1040, line 32, or Form 1040NR, line 32), affected by the earned income limitation of section 219(b)(1)(B).

Figure the difference between the AMT and regular tax amount for each item. Combine the amounts for all your related adjustments and include the total on line 27. Keep a copy of all computations for your records, including any AMT carryover and basis amounts.

 Do not include on line 27 any adjustment for an item you refigured on another line of this form (for example, line 9).

Example. On your Schedule C (Form 1040) you have a net profit of $9,000 before figuring your section 179 deduction. You do not report any other business income on your return. During

the year, you purchased an asset for $10,000 for which you elect to take the section 179 deduction. You also have an AMT depreciation adjustment of $700 for other assets depreciated on your Schedule C.

Your section 179 deduction for the regular tax is limited to your net profit (before any section 179 deduction) of $9,000. The $1,000 excess is a section 179 deduction carryforward for the regular tax.

For the AMT, your net profit is $9,700, and you are allowed a section 179 deduction of $9,700 for the AMT. You have a section 179 deduction carryforward of $300 for the AMT.

You include a $700 negative adjustment on line 27 because your section 179 deduction for the AMT is $700 greater than your allowable regular tax deduction. In the following year, when you use the $1,000 regular tax carryforward, you will have a $700 positive related adjustment for the AMT because your AMT carryforward is only $300.

Line 28—Alternative Minimum Taxable Income

If your filing status is married filing separately and line 28 is more than $242,450, you must include an additional amount on line 28. If line 28 is $406,650 or more, include an additional $41,050. Otherwise, include 25% of the excess of the amount on line 28 over $242,450. For example, if the amount on line 28 is $262,450, enter $267,450 instead—the additional $5,000 is 25% of $20,000 ($262,450 minus $242,450).

Special Rule for Holders of a Residual Interest in a REMIC

If you held a residual interest in a real estate mortgage investment conduit (REMIC) in 2014, the amount you enter on line 28 may not be less than the amount on Schedule E, line 38, column (c). If the amount in column (c) is larger than the amount you would otherwise enter on line 28, enter the amount from column (c) instead and enter "Sch. Q" on the dotted line next to line 28.

If your filing status is married filing separately, be sure to include the additional amount that must be added to line 28 (as explained above) before you compare line 28 with the amount on Schedule E, line 38, column (c).

Exemption Worksheet— Line 29

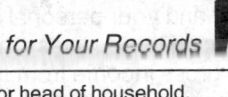 *Keep for Your Records*

Note. If Form 6251, line 28, is equal to or more than: $328,500 if single or head of household, $484,900 if married filing jointly or qualifying widow(er), or $242,450 if married filing separately, your exemption is zero. **Do not** complete this worksheet; instead, enter the amount from Form 6251, line 28, on line 30 and go to line 31.

1. Enter: $52,800 if single or head of household; $82,100 if married filing jointly or qualifying widow(er); $41,050 if married filing separately .... **1.** _____

2. Enter your alternative minimum taxable income (AMTI) from Form 6251, line 28 .... **2.** _____

3. Enter: $117,300 if single or head of household; $156,500 if married filing jointly or qualifying widow(er); $78,250 if married filing separately .... **3.** _____

4. Subtract line 3 from line 2. If zero or less, enter -0- .... **4.** _____

5. Multiply line 4 by 25% (.25) .... **5.** _____

6. Subtract line 5 from line 1. If zero or less, enter -0-. If any of the three conditions under *Certain Children Under Age 24* apply to you, complete lines 7 through 10. Otherwise, **stop here** and enter this amount on Form 6251, line 29, and go to Form 6251, line 30 .... ► **6.** _____

7. Minimum exemption amount for certain children under age 24 .... **7.** $7,250

8. Enter your **earned income,** if any (see instructions) .... **8.** _____

9. Add lines 7 and 8 .... **9.** _____

10. Enter the **smaller** of line 6 or line 9 here and on Form 6251, line 29, and go to Form 6251, line 30 .... ► **10.** _____

Part II—Alternative Minimum Tax

Line 29—Exemption Amount

If line 28 is more than the amount shown for your filing status in the middle column of the chart on line 29, see the Exemption Worksheet to figure the amount to enter on line 29.

Form 1040NR. If you are filing Form 1040NR, use the following chart to figure the amount to enter on line 29. However, if line 28 is more than the amount shown for your filing status in the middle column of the chart, use the Exemption Worksheet to figure the amount to enter on line 29.

IF you check filing status box...	AND line 28 is not over...	THEN enter on line 29...
1 or 2	$117,300	$52,800
3, 4, or 5	78,250	41,050
6	156,500	82,100

Certain Children Under Age 24

Your exemption amount is limited to the amount of your earned income plus $7,250 if condition 1, 2, or 3 below applies to you.

1. You were under age 18 at the end of 2014.

2. You were age 18 at the end of 2014 and did not have earned income that was more than half of your support.

3. You were a full-time student over age 18 and under age 24 at the end of 2014 and did not have earned income that was more than half of your support.

If condition 1, 2, or 3 applies to you, complete the Exemption Worksheet, including lines 7 through 10, to figure the amount to enter on Form 6251, line 29.

Exception. If you filed a joint return for 2014 **or** neither of your parents was alive at the end of 2014, do not complete lines 7 through 10 of the Exemption Worksheet. However, you still must complete lines 1 through 6 of the worksheet if Form 6251, line 28, is more than the amount shown for your filing status in the middle column of the chart on line 29 (or the chart earlier in the line 29 instructions if you file Form 1040NR).

Certain January 1 birthdays. If you were born on January 1, 1997, you are considered to be 18 at the end of 2014.

Your exemption amount is limited only if you did not have earned income that was more than half of your support.

If you were born on January 1, 1996, you are considered to be 19 at the end of 2014. Your exemption amount is limited only if you were a full-time student who did not have earned income that was more than half of your support.

If you were born on January 1, 1991, you are considered to be 24 at the end of 2014. Your exemption amount is not limited.

Line 8 of the worksheet. Earned income includes wages, tips, and other amounts received for personal services performed. If you are a sole proprietor or a partner in a trade or business in which both personal services and capital are material income-producing factors, earned income also includes a reasonable allowance for compensation for personal services, but not more than 30% of your share of the net profits from that trade or business (after subtracting the deduction for part of your self-employment tax). However, the 30% limit does not apply if there are no net profits from the trade or business. If capital is not an income-producing factor and your personal services produced the business income, all of your gross income from the trade or business is considered earned income.

Line 31

If you claimed the foreign earned income exclusion, housing exclusion, or housing deduction on Form 2555 or Form 2555-EZ, you must use the Foreign Earned Income Tax Worksheet in these instructions to figure the amount to enter on line 31.

Form 1040NR. If you are filing Form 1040NR and you reported capital gain distributions directly on Form 1040NR, line 14; you reported qualified dividends on Form 1040NR, line 10b; **or** you had a gain on both lines 15 and 16 of Schedule D (Form 1040) (as refigured for the AMT, if necessary), complete Part III of Form 6251 and enter the amount from line 64 on line 31. All other Form 1040NR filers, do not complete Part III. Instead, if Form 6251, line 30, is $182,500 or less ($91,250 or less if you checked filing status box 3, 4, or 5 on Form 1040NR), figure the amount to enter on line 31 by multiplying line 30 by 26% (.26). Otherwise, figure the amount to enter on line 31 by multiplying line 30 by 28% (.28) and subtracting $3,650 ($1,825 if you checked filing status box 3, 4, or 5) from the result.

Line 32—Alternative Minimum Tax Foreign Tax Credit (AMTFTC)

 To see if you need to figure your AMTFTC, fill in Form 6251, line 34, as instructed. (You will first need to figure your foreign tax credit for the regular tax and complete Form 1040, line 48, or Form 1040NR, line 46.) If the amount on line 34 is greater than or equal to the amount on line 31, you do not owe the AMT. Enter -0- on line 35 and see Who Must File, *earlier, to find out if you must attach Form 6251 to your return. However, even if you do not owe the AMT, you may need to complete line 32 to see if you have an AMTFTC carryback or carryforward to other tax years.*

If you made an election to claim the foreign tax credit on Form 1040 (or Form 1040NR) without filing Form 1116, your AMTFTC is the same as the foreign tax credit on Form 1040, line 48 (or Form 1040NR, line 46). Enter that amount on Form 6251, line 32. Otherwise, your AMTFTC is your foreign tax credit refigured as follows.

Step 1. Use a separate AMT Form 1116 for each separate category of income. Write "AMT" and specify the category of income in the top margin of each Form 1116.

When applying the separate categories of income, use the applicable AMT rate instead of the regular tax rate to determine if any income is "high-taxed."

Step 2. If you previously made or are making the simplified limitation election, skip Part I and enter on the AMT Form 1116, line 17, the same amount you entered on that line for the regular tax. If you did not complete Form 1116 for the regular tax and you previously made or are making the simplified limitation election, complete Part I and lines 15 through 17 of the AMT Form 1116 using regular tax amounts.

If the election does not apply, complete Part I using only income and deductions that are allowed for the AMT and attributable to sources outside the United States. If you have any foreign source qualified dividends or foreign source capital gains (including any foreign source capital gain distributions) or losses, use the instructions under *Step 3* to determine whether you must make adjustments to those amounts before you include the amounts on line 1a or line 5 of the AMT Form 1116.

Step 3. Follow the instructions below, if applicable, to determine the amount of foreign source qualified dividends, capital gain distributions, and other capital gains and losses to include on line 1a and line 5 of the AMT Form 1116.

Foreign qualified dividends. You must adjust your foreign source qualified dividends before you include those amounts on line 1a of the AMT Form 1116 if:
- Line 62 of Form 6251 is smaller than line 63, and
- Line 41 of Form 6251 is greater than zero.

But you do not need to make any adjustments if:
- You qualify for the adjustment exception under *Qualified Dividends and Capital Gain Tax Worksheet (Individuals)* or *Adjustments to foreign qualified dividends* under *Schedule D Filers* in the Form 1116 instructions, and
- Line 41 of Form 6251 is not more than $182,500 ($91,250 if married filing separately or if you checked filing status box 3, 4, or 5 on Form 1040NR).

Use your capital gains and losses as refigured for the AMT to determine whether your total amounts are less than the $20,000 threshold under the adjustment exception.

To adjust your foreign source qualified dividends, multiply your foreign source qualified dividends in each separate category by 0.5357 if the foreign source qualified dividends are taxed at a rate of 15%, and by 0.7143 if they are taxed at a rate of 20%. Include the results on line 1a of the applicable AMT Form 1116.

You adjust your foreign source qualified dividends taxed at the 0% rate by **not** including them on line 1a. Amounts taxed at the 0% rate are on line 11 of the Qualified Dividends and Capital Gain Tax Worksheet in the Form 1040 instructions, line 9 of the Qualified Dividends and Capital Gain Tax Worksheet in the Form 1040NR instructions, or line 20 of the Schedule D Tax Worksheet.

 Do not adjust the amount of any foreign source qualified dividends you elected to include on line 4g of AMT Form 4952.

Individuals with capital gain distributions only. If you have no capital gains or losses other than capital gain distributions from box 2a of Form(s) 1099-DIV or substitute statement(s), you must adjust your foreign source capital gain distributions if you are required to adjust your foreign source qualified dividends under the rules just described or you would be

required to adjust your foreign source qualified dividends if you had any.

To adjust your foreign source capital gain distributions, multiply your foreign source capital gain distributions in each separate category by 0.5357 if the foreign source capital gain distributions are taxed at a rate of 15%, and by 0.7143 if they are taxed at a rate of 20%. Include the results on line 1a of the applicable AMT Form 1116.

You adjust your foreign source capital gain distributions taxed at the 0% rate by **not** including them on line 1a. Amounts taxed at the 0% rate are on line 11 of the Qualified Dividends and Capital Gain Tax Worksheet in the Form 1040 instructions, line 9 of the Qualified Dividends and Capital Gain Tax Worksheet in the Form 1040NR instructions, or line 20 of the Schedule D Tax Worksheet.

 Do not adjust the amount of any foreign source capital gain distributions you elected to include on line 4g of AMT Form 4952.

Individuals with other capital gains or losses. If any capital gain or loss is different for the AMT, use amounts as refigured for the AMT to complete this step. Use Worksheet A in the instructions for Form 1116 to determine the adjustments you must make to your foreign source capital

---

Foreign Earned Income Tax Worksheet—Line 31   *Keep for Your Records*

Before you begin: ✓ If Form 6251, line 30, is zero, do not complete this worksheet.

1. Enter the amount from Form 6251, line 30 . . . . **1.** _____

2a. Enter the amount from your (and your spouse's if filing jointly) Form 2555, lines 45 and 50, or Form 2555-EZ, line 18 . . . . **2a.** _____

   b. Enter the total amount of any itemized deductions or exclusions you could not claim because they are related to excluded income . . . . **2b.** _____

   c. Subtract line 2b from line 2a. If zero or less, enter -0- . . . . **2c.** _____

3. Add lines 1 and 2c . . . . **3.** _____

4. **Tax on the amount on line 3.**

   • If you reported capital gain distributions directly on Form 1040, line 13; **or** you reported qualified dividends on Form 1040, line 9b; **or** you had a gain on both lines 15 and 16 of Schedule D (Form 1040) (as refigured for the AMT, if necessary), enter the amount from line 3 of this worksheet on Form 6251, line 36. Complete the rest of Part III of Form 6251. However, before completing Part III, see *Forms 2555 and 2555-EZ,* later, to see if you must complete Part III with certain modifications. Then enter the amount from Form 6251, line 64, here.

   • **All others:** If line 3 is $182,500 or less ($91,250 or less if married filing separately), multiply line 3 by 26% (.26). Otherwise, multiply line 3 by 28% (.28) and subtract $3,650 ($1,825 if married filing separately) from the result.   **4.** _____

5. **Tax on the amount on line 2c.** If line 2c is $182,500 or less ($91,250 or less if married filing separately), multiply line 2c by 26% (.26). Otherwise, multiply line 2c by 28% (.28) and subtract $3,650 ($1,825 if married filing separately) from the result . . . . **5.** _____

6. Subtract line 5 from line 4. Enter the result here and on Form 6251, line 31 . . . . **6.** _____

gains or losses (as refigured for the AMT) if you have foreign source capital gains or losses (as refigured for the AMT) in no more than two separate categories and any of the following apply.

- You are not required to make adjustments to your foreign source qualified dividends under the rules described earlier (or you would not be required to make those adjustments if you had foreign source qualified dividends).
- Line 15 or 16 of the AMT Schedule D (Form 1040) is zero or a loss.
- On the AMT Qualified Dividends and Capital Gain Tax Worksheet in the Form 1040 instructions, (a) line 3 of that worksheet minus the amount on Form 4952, line 4e, that you elected to include on Form 4952, line 4g, is zero or less, (b) line 7 of that worksheet is zero, or (c) line 25 of that worksheet is equal to or greater than line 26.
- On the AMT Qualified Dividends and Capital Gain Tax Worksheet in the Form 1040NR instructions, (a) line 3 of that worksheet is zero, (b) line 5 of that worksheet is zero, or (c) line 23 of that worksheet is equal to or greater than line 24.
- On the AMT Schedule D Tax Worksheet (Form 1040), (a) line 18 is zero, (b) line 9 is zero or less, or (c) line 43 is equal to or greater than line 44.

Use Worksheet B if you:
- Cannot use Worksheet A,
- Have foreign source capital gains and losses in no more than two separate categories,
- Did not have any item of unrecaptured section 1250 gain or 28% rate gain or loss for the AMT, and
- Do not have any capital gains taxed at a rate of 0% or 20%.

Instructions for Worksheets A and B. When you complete Worksheet A or Worksheet B, use foreign source capital gains and losses, as refigured for the AMT if necessary, and do not use any foreign source capital gains you elected to include on line 4g of AMT Form 4952. If you are required to complete a Schedule D for the AMT, use line 16 of that AMT Schedule D to complete line 3 of Worksheet A or line 4 of the Line 2 Worksheet for Worksheet B. Use 0.5357 instead of 0.3788 to complete lines 11, 13, and 15 of Worksheet B and to complete lines 8, 11, and 17 of the Line 15 Worksheet for Worksheet B.

If you do not qualify to use Worksheet A or Worksheet B, use the instructions for *Capital Gains and*

Losses in Pub. 514 to determine the adjustments you make.

Step 4. Complete Part II and lines 9 through 14 of the AMT Form 1116. Use your AMTFTC carryover, if any, on line 10.

Step 5. If the simplified limitation election does not apply, complete lines 15 through 17 of the AMT Form 1116.

Step 6. If you did not complete Part III of Form 6251, enter the amount from line 28 of Form 6251 on line 18 of the AMT Form 1116 and go to *Step 7*. If you completed Part III of Form 6251, you must complete, for the AMT, the Worksheet for Line 18 in the Form 1116 instructions to determine the amount to enter on line 18 of the AMT Form 1116 if:
- Line 62 of Form 6251 is smaller than line 63, and
- Line 41 of Form 6251 is greater than zero.

But you do not need to complete the Worksheet for Line 18 if:
- You qualify for the adjustment exception under *Qualified Dividends and Capital Gain Tax Worksheet (Individuals)* or *Adjustments to foreign qualified dividends* under *Schedule D Filers* in the Form 1116 instructions, and
- Line 41 of Form 6251 is not more than $182,500 ($91,250 if married filing separately or if you checked filing status box 3, 4, or 5 on Form 1040NR).

Note. Use your capital gains and losses as refigured for the AMT to determine whether your total amounts are less than the $20,000 threshold under the adjustment exception.

If you do not need to complete the Worksheet for Line 18, enter the amount from line 28 of Form 6251 on line 18 of the AMT Form 1116.

Instructions for AMT Worksheet for Line 18. Follow these steps to complete, for the AMT, the Worksheet for Line 18 in the Form 1116 instructions.

1. Enter the amount from Form 6251, line 28, on line 1 of the worksheet.

2. Skip lines 2 and 3 of the worksheet.

3. Enter the amount from Form 6251, line 60, on line 4 of the worksheet.

4. Multiply line 4 of the worksheet by 0.1071 (instead of 0.3687). Enter the result on line 5 of the worksheet.

5. Enter the amount from Form 6251, line 57, on line 6 of the worksheet.

6. Multiply line 6 of the worksheet by 0.2857 (instead of 0.4949). Enter the result on line 7 of the worksheet.

7. Enter the amount from Form 6251, line 54, on line 8 of the worksheet.

8. Multiply line 8 of the worksheet by 0.4643 (instead of 0.6212). Enter the result on line 9 of the worksheet.

9. Enter the amount from Form 6251, line 47, on line 10 of the worksheet.

10. Complete lines 11 and 12 of the worksheet as instructed on the worksheet.

Step 7. Enter the amount from Form 6251, line 31, on the AMT Form 1116, line 20. Complete lines 19, 21, and 22 of the AMT Form 1116.

Step 8. Complete Part IV of the first AMT Form 1116 only.

Enter on Form 6251, line 32, the amount from line 30 of the first AMT Form 1116.

Attach to your tax return, after Form 6251, all AMT Forms 1116 you used to figure your AMTFTC. But do not attach AMT Forms 1116 if your AMTFTC is the same as your regular tax foreign tax credit.

AMTFTC Carryback and Carryforward

If your AMTFTC is limited, the unused amount generally may be carried back or forward according to section 904(c). However, if you made the election to claim the foreign tax credit on Form 1040 (or Form 1040NR) without filing Form 1116, any unused AMTFTC cannot be carried back or forward. In addition, no unused AMTFTC from another year can be used in any year for which the election has been made.

Simplified Limitation Election

You may elect to use a simplified section 904 limitation to figure your AMTFTC. If you do, use your regular tax income for Form 1116, Part I, instead of refiguring your foreign source income for the AMT, as described earlier. You must make the election for the first tax year after 1997 for which you claim an AMTFTC. If you do not make the election for that year, you may not make it for a later year. Once made, the election applies to all later tax years and may be revoked only with IRS consent.

Line 34

If you used Schedule J, Income Averaging for Farmers and Fishermen, to figure your tax on Form 1040, line 44 (or Form 1040NR, line 42), you must refigure that tax (including any tax from Form 8814) without using Schedule J before completing this line. This is only for Form 6251; do not change the amount on Form 1040, line 44 (or Form 1040NR, line 42).

Form 1040NR. If you are filing Form 1040NR, add Form 1040NR, line 42 (minus any tax from Form 4972, Tax on Lump-Sum Distributions) and Form 1040NR, line 44. Subtract from the result any foreign tax credit from Form 1040NR, line 46. If you used Schedule J to figure your tax on Form 1040NR, line 42, refigure that tax without using Schedule J before completing Form 6251, line 34 (see preceding paragraph).

Line 35

If you are filing Form 1040NR, enter the amount from line 35 on Form 1040NR, line 43.

Part III—Tax Computation Using Maximum Capital Gains Rates

Lines 37, 38, and 39

You generally can fill out lines 37, 38, and 39 using the amounts from the Qualified Dividends and Capital Gain Tax Worksheet or the Schedule D Tax Worksheet, whichever applies, and Schedule D (Form 1040), if you completed Schedule D. But do not use those amounts if any of the following statements apply.

1. The gain or loss from any transaction reported on Form 8949 or Schedule D is different for the AMT (for example, because of a different basis for the AMT due to depreciation adjustments, an incentive stock option adjustment, or a different AMT capital loss carryover from 2013).

2. You did not complete either the Qualified Dividends and Capital Gain Tax Worksheet or the Schedule D Tax Worksheet because Form 1040, line 43 (or Form 1040NR, line 41), is zero.

3. You received a Schedule K-1 (Form 1041) that shows an amount in box 12 with code B, C, D, E, or F. If this applies, see *Beneficiaries of estates or trusts*. Then read the following instructions.

If (1) applies, complete an AMT Form 8949 or, if applicable, lines 1a and 8a of an AMT Schedule D, by refiguring, for example, your basis for the AMT. Next, if (1) or (3) applies, complete lines 1b through 20 of an AMT Schedule D. Then, if (1), (2), or (3) applies, complete lines 2 through 6 of an AMT Qualified Dividends and Capital Gain Tax Worksheet or lines 2 through 13 of an AMT Schedule D Tax Worksheet, whichever applies. (See line 20 of your AMT Schedule D, if you completed one, to determine which worksheet applies.) Complete line 5 of the AMT Qualified Dividends and Capital Gain Tax Worksheet or lines 3 and 4 of the AMT Schedule D Tax Worksheet, whichever applies, using your AMT Form 4952. Use amounts from Schedule D or the AMT Schedule D, whichever applies, and either the AMT Qualified Dividends and Capital Gain Tax Worksheet or the AMT Schedule D Tax Worksheet, whichever applies, to complete lines 37, 38, and 39 of Form 6251. Keep the AMT Form 8949, AMT Schedule D, and the applicable AMT worksheet for your records, but do not attach any of them to your tax return.

Note. Do not decrease your section 1202 exclusion by the amount, if any, on line 13.

Forms 2555 and 2555-EZ. If you are filing either of those forms and you have a capital gain excess, you must complete Part III of Form 6251 with certain modifications. To see if you have a capital gain excess, subtract Form 6251, line 30, from line 6 of your AMT Qualified Dividends and Capital Gain Tax Worksheet (or line 10 of your AMT Schedule D Tax Worksheet). If the result is greater than zero, that amount is your capital gain excess.

If you have capital gain excess, figure the amounts to enter on lines 37, 38, and 39 of Form 6251 using the following modifications (only for purposes of Part III of Form 6251).

1. Reduce the amount you would otherwise enter on line 3 of your AMT Qualified Dividends and Capital Gain Tax Worksheet or line 9 of your AMT Schedule D Tax Worksheet (but not below zero) by your capital gain excess.

2. Reduce the amount you would otherwise enter on line 2 of your AMT Qualified Dividends and Capital Gain Tax Worksheet or line 6 of your AMT Schedule D Tax Worksheet (but not below zero) by any of your capital gain excess not used in (1).

3. Reduce the amount on your AMT Schedule D (Form 1040), line 18, (but not below zero) by your capital gain excess.

4. Include your capital gain excess as a loss on line 16 of your AMT Unrecaptured Section 1250 Gain Worksheet in the Instructions for Schedule D (Form 1040).

Also see the instructions for line 44.

Beneficiaries of estates or trusts. If you received a Schedule K-1 (Form 1041) that shows an adjustment in box 12, follow the instructions in the following table.

IF the code in box 12 is...	THEN include that adjustment in figuring the amount on...
B	line 2 of an AMT Qualified Dividends and Capital Gain Tax Worksheet or an AMT Schedule D Tax Worksheet, whichever applies.
C	line 5 of an AMT Schedule D.
D	line 12 of an AMT Schedule D.
E	line 11 of an AMT Unrecaptured Section 1250 Gain Worksheet.
F	line 4 of an AMT 28% Rate Gain Worksheet.

Form 1040NR. If you are filing Form 1040NR, enter on Form 6251, line 37, the amount from line 4 of the Qualified Dividends and Capital Gain Tax Worksheet in the instructions for Form 1040NR, line 42, or the amount from line 13 of the Schedule D Tax Worksheet in the instructions for Schedule D (Form 1040), whichever applies (as refigured for the AMT, if necessary).

Line 42

If you are filing Form 1040NR and Form 6251, line 41, is $182,500 or less ($91,250 or less if you checked filing status box 3, 4, or 5), multiply line 41 by 26% (.26). Otherwise, multiply line 41 by 28% (.28) and subtract $3,650 ($1,825 if you checked filing status box 3, 4, or 5) from the result.

Line 43

If you are filing Form 1040NR, enter $36,900 ($73,800 if you checked filing status box 6).

Line 44

If you are filing Form 1040NR, enter on Form 6251, line 44, the amount from line 5 of the Qualified Dividends and Capital Gain Tax Worksheet in the instructions for Form 1040NR, line 42, or the amount from line 14 of the Schedule D Tax Worksheet in the instructions for Schedule D (Form 1040), whichever applies (as figured for the regular tax). If you did not complete either worksheet for the regular tax, enter the amount from Form 1040NR, line 41; if zero or less, enter -0-.

Forms 2555 and 2555-EZ. If you are filing either of these forms **and** you did not complete either the Qualified Dividends and Capital Gain Tax Worksheet or the Schedule D Tax Worksheet for the regular tax, enter the amount from line 3 of the Foreign Earned Income Tax Worksheet in the Form 1040 instructions (as figured for the regular tax).

Line 49

If you are filing Form 1040NR, enter on Form 6251, line 49, the amount from the list below that corresponds to your filing status.

- $406,750 if you checked filing status box 1 or 2,
- $228,800 if you checked filing status box 3, 4, or 5, or
- $457,600 if you checked filing status box 6.

Line 51

If you are filing Form 1040NR, enter on Form 6251, line 51, the amount from line 5 of the Qualified Dividends and Capital Gain Tax Worksheet in the instructions for Form 1040NR, line 42, or the amount from line 19 of the Schedule D Tax Worksheet in the instructions for Schedule D (Form 1040), whichever applies (as figured for the regular tax). If you did not complete either worksheet for the regular tax, enter the amount from Form 1040NR, line 41; if zero or less, enter -0-.

Forms 2555 and 2555-EZ. If you are filing either of these forms **and** you did not complete either the Qualified Dividends and Capital Gain Tax Worksheet or the Schedule D Tax Worksheet for the regular tax, enter the amount from Form 6251, line 44.

Line 63

If you are filing Form 1040NR and Form 6251, line 36, is $182,500 or less ($91,250 or less if you checked filing status box 3, 4, or 5), multiply line 36 by 26% (.26). Otherwise, multiply line 36 by 28% (.28) and subtract $3,650 ($1,825 if you checked filing status box 3, 4, or 5) from the result.

Form **6781**	**Gains and Losses From Section 1256 Contracts and Straddles**	OMB No. 1545-0644
Department of the Treasury Internal Revenue Service	▶ Information about Form 6781 and its instructions is at *www.irs.gov/form6781*. ▶ Attach to your tax return.	**2014** Attachment Sequence No. **82**

Name(s) shown on tax return	Identifying number

Check all applicable boxes (see instructions). **A** ☐ Mixed straddle election   **C** ☐ Mixed straddle account election
B ☐ Straddle-by-straddle identification election   **D** ☐ Net section 1256 contracts loss election

| **Part I** | **Section 1256 Contracts Marked to Market** |

(a) Identification of account	(b) (Loss)	(c) Gain	
1			

2 Add the amounts on line 1 in columns (b) and (c)	**2** ( )		
3 Net gain or (loss). Combine line 2, columns (b) and (c)	**3**		
4 Form 1099-B adjustments. See instructions and attach statement	**4**		
5 Combine lines 3 and 4	**5**		

Note: *If line 5 shows a net gain, skip line 6 and enter the gain on line 7. Partnerships and S corporations, see instructions.*

6 If you have a net section 1256 contracts loss and checked box D above, enter the amount of loss to be carried back. Enter the loss as a positive number. If you did not check box D, enter -0-	**6**	
7 Combine lines 5 and 6	**7**	
8 **Short-term capital gain or (loss).** Multiply line 7 by 40% (.40). Enter here and include on line 4 of Schedule D or on Form 8949 (see instructions)	**8**	
9 **Long-term capital gain or (loss).** Multiply line 7 by 60% (.60). Enter here and include on line 11 of Schedule D or on Form 8949 (see instructions)	**9**	

| **Part II** | **Gains and Losses From Straddles.** Attach a separate statement listing each straddle and its components. |

Section A—Losses From Straddles

(a) Description of property	(b) Date entered into or acquired	(c) Date closed out or sold	(d) Gross sales price	(e) Cost or other basis plus expense of sale	(f) Loss. If column (e) is more than (d), enter difference. Otherwise, enter -0-	(g) Unrecognized gain on offsetting positions	(h) Recognized loss. If column (f) is more than (g), enter difference. Otherwise, enter -0-
10							

11a Enter the short-term portion of losses from line 10, column (h), here and include on line 4 of Schedule D or on Form 8949 (see instructions)	**11a** (	)
b Enter the long-term portion of losses from line 10, column (h), here and include on line 11 of Schedule D or on Form 8949 (see instructions)	**11b** (	)

Section B—Gains From Straddles

(a) Description of property	(b) Date entered into or acquired	(c) Date closed out or sold	(d) Gross sales price	(e) Cost or other basis plus expense of sale	(f) Gain. If column (d) is more than (e), enter difference. Otherwise, enter -0-
12					

13a Enter the short-term portion of gains from line 12, column (f), here and include on line 4 of Schedule D or on Form 8949 (see instructions)	**13a**	
b Enter the long-term portion of gains from line 12, column (f), here and include on line 11 of Schedule D or on Form 8949 (see instructions)	**13b**	

| **Part III** | **Unrecognized Gains From Positions Held on Last Day of Tax Year.** Memo Entry Only (see instructions) |

(a) Description of property	(b) Date acquired	(c) Fair market value on last business day of tax year	(d) Cost or other basis as adjusted	(e) Unrecognized gain. If column (c) is more than (d), enter difference. Otherwise, enter -0-
14				

For Paperwork Reduction Act Notice, see instructions.   Cat. No. 13715G   Form **6781** (2014)

Future Developments

For the latest information about developments related to Form 6781 and its instructions, such as legislation enacted after they were published, go to *www.irs.gov/form6781*.

General Instructions

Section references are to the Internal Revenue Code unless otherwise noted.

Purpose of Form

Use Form 6781 to report:

• Any gain or loss on section 1256 contracts under the mark-to-market rules, and

• Gains and losses under section 1092 from straddle positions.

For details on section 1256 contracts and straddles, see Pub. 550, Investment Income and Expenses.

Section 1256 Contract

A section 1256 contract is any:

• Regulated futures contract,

• Foreign currency contract,

• Nonequity option,

• Dealer equity option, or

• Dealer securities futures contract.

For definitions of these terms and more details, see section 1256(g) and Pub. 550.

Note. A section 1256 contract does not include any interest rate swap, currency swap, basis swap, commodity swap, equity swap, equity index swap, credit default swap, interest rate cap, interest rate floor, or similar agreement.

Special rules apply to certain foreign currency contracts. See section 988 and Regulations sections 1.988-1(a)(7) and 1.988-3. If an election is made under section 988(a)(1)(B) or 988(c)(1)(D), attach to your return a list of the contracts covered by the election(s). On the attachment, show the net gain or loss reported from those contracts and identify where the gain or loss is reported on the return. If an election is made under section 988(a)(1)(B), report on Form 6781 the gains and losses from section 1256 contracts that are also section 988 transactions.

Options and commodities dealers must take any gain or loss from the trading of section 1256 contracts into account in figuring net earnings subject to self-employment tax. See section 1402(i).

Mark-to-Market Rules

Under these rules, each section 1256 contract held at year end is treated as if it were sold at fair market value (FMV) on the last business day of the tax year. The wash sale rules do not apply.

Gains or losses on section 1256 contracts open at the end of the year, or terminated during the year, are treated as 60% long term and 40% short term, regardless of how long the contracts were held.

Straddle

A straddle means offsetting positions with respect to personal property of a type that is actively traded.

Offsetting Positions

If there is a substantial decrease in risk of loss to a taxpayer holding a position because that taxpayer or a related party also holds one or more other positions, then those positions are offsetting and may be part of a straddle. However, if an identified straddle is properly established, other positions held by the taxpayer will not be treated as offsetting with respect to any position which is part of the identified straddle.

Box A. Mixed Straddle Election

Under section 1256(d), you can elect to have the mark-to-market rules not apply to section 1256 contracts that are part of a mixed straddle. A mixed straddle is any straddle in which at least one but not all of the positions is a section 1256 contract. On the day the first section 1256 contract forming part of the straddle is acquired, each position forming part of the straddle must be clearly identified as being part of such straddle. If you make this election, it will apply for all later years and cannot be revoked without IRS consent. If you are making or have previously made this election, check box A and report the section 1256 component in Part II instead of Part I.

Box B. Straddle-By-Straddle Identification Election

Make this election for mixed straddles according to Temporary Regulations section 1.1092(b)-3T(d) by clearly identifying each position by the earlier of (a) the close of the day the identified mixed straddle is established or (b) the time the position is disposed of. No straddle-by-straddle identification election may be made for any straddle for which a mixed straddle election was made or if one or more positions are includible in a mixed straddle account. If you are making or have previously made this election, check box B.

If you make this election, any positions you held on the day before the election are deemed sold for their fair market value at the close of the last business day before the day of the election. For elections made on or before August 18, 2014, take this gain or loss into account when computing taxable income for the year in which the election was made. For elections made after August 18, 2014, take this gain or loss into account in the year you would have reported the gain or loss if the identified mixed straddle had not been established. In addition, when the gain or loss that accrued prior to the time the identified mixed straddle was established is taken into account, it will have the same character it would have had if the identified mixed straddle had not been established. See Regulations section 1.1092(b)-6 for details.

Each year you hold positions subject to this election, you must mark to market your section 1256 contracts and determine, in accordance with Regulations sections 1.1092(b)-3T and 1.1092(b)-6, whether you have a net gain or loss. If the net gain or loss is attributable to a net non-section 1256 position, then the net gain or loss is treated as a short-term capital gain or loss. Enter it directly on Form 8949 and identify the election. If the net gain or loss is attributable to a section 1256 position, enter the gain or loss in Part I of Form 6781 and identify the election.

Box C. Mixed Straddle Account Election

Make this election according to Temporary Regulations section 1.1092(b)-4T(f) to establish one or more mixed straddle accounts for 2015 by the due date (without extensions) of your 2014 tax return. To make this election, check box C and attach to your return (or your request for an extension of time to file) the statement required by the regulations. Report the annual account net gain or loss from a mixed straddle account in Part II and identify the election. See Temporary Regulations section 1.1092(b)-4T(c)(4) for limits on the total annual account net gain or loss.

Note. If you did not make any of the above elections and you have a loss on the section 1256 component, use Part II to reduce the loss by any unrecognized gain on the non-section 1256 component before making an entry in Part I. You also must reduce the loss from any section 1256 component of a straddle that would be a mixed straddle if the positions had been properly identified as such.

Box D. Net Section 1256 Contracts Loss Election

If you have a net section 1256 contracts loss for 2014, you can elect to carry it back 3 years. Corporations, partnerships, estates, and trusts are not eligible to make this election. Your net section 1256 contracts loss is the smaller of:

• The **excess** of your losses from section 1256 contracts over the total of (a) your gains from section 1256 contracts plus (b) $3,000 ($1,500 if married filing separately), or

• The total you would figure as your short-term and long-term capital loss carryovers to 2015 if line 6 of Form 6781 were zero. Use a separate Schedule D (Form 1040) and Capital Loss Carryover Worksheet (in Pub. 550) to figure this amount.

The amount you can carry back to any prior year is limited to the smaller of:

• The gain, if any, that you would report on line 16 of Schedule D (Form 1040) for that carryback year if only gains and losses from section 1256 contracts were taken into account, or

• The gain, if any, reported on line 16 of Schedule D (Form 1040) for that carryback year.

The amounts just described are figured prior to any carryback from the loss year. Also, the carryback is allowed only to the extent it does not increase or produce a net operating loss for the carryback year. The loss is carried to the earliest year first.

Make the election by checking box D and entering the amount to be carried back on line 6. To carry your loss back, file Form 1045, Application for Tentative Refund, or an amended return. Attach an amended Form 6781 and an amended Schedule D (Form 1040) for the applicable years.

On the amended Forms 6781 for the years to which the loss is carried back, report the carryback on line 1 of that year's amended Form 6781. Enter "Net section 1256 contracts loss carried back from" and the tax year in column (a), and enter the amount of the loss carried back in column (b).

Specific Instructions

Part I

Line 1

Include on line 1 all gains and losses from section 1256 contracts open at the end of your tax year or closed out during the year. If you received a Form 1099-B, Proceeds From Broker and Barter Exchange Transactions, or substitute statement, include on line 1 the amount from box 11 of each form. In column (a), write "Form 1099-B" and the broker's name. List separately each transaction

for which you did not receive a Form 1099-B or substitute statement, or received a Form 1099-B that is not for your tax year.

If you are completing an amended 2014 Form 6781 to carry back a net section 1256 contracts loss from 2015 or a later year, report the carryback on line 1. Enter "Net section 1256 contracts loss carried back from" and the tax year in column (a), and enter the amount of the loss carried back to 2014 in column (b). See the instructions for box D for details.

Line 4

If the Form 1099-B you received includes a straddle or hedging transaction (as defined in section 1256(e)(2)), you may need to make certain adjustments listed next. Attach a statement listing each of these adjustments and enter the total(s) on line 4.

• The regulated futures part of a mixed straddle, if you made any of the mixed straddle elections.

• The amount of the loss, if you did not make any of the mixed straddle elections or the straddle was not identified as a mixed straddle and you had a loss on the regulated futures part that was less than the unrecognized gain on the nonregulated futures part. If the unrecognized gain is less than the loss, enter the unrecognized gain. Use Part I for a loss on the disposition of one or more positions that are part of a mixed straddle and that are non-section 1256 positions if no disposition of a non-section 1256 position in the straddle would be a long-term capital gain or loss, and the disposition of one or more section 1256 positions in the straddle would be a capital gain or loss.

• The regulated futures part of a hedging transaction. The gain or loss on a hedging transaction is treated as ordinary income or loss. See Pub. 550 for details.

Line 5

Partnerships enter the amount from line 5 on Form 1065, Schedule K, line 11. Electing large partnerships enter the amount from line 5 on Form 1065-B, Part II, line 5. S corporations enter the amount from line 5 on Form 1120S, Schedule K, line 10. Lines 6 through 9 in Part I of Form 6781 do not apply to partnerships or S corporations and are left blank.

Line 6

See the instructions for box D.

Line 8

Include this amount on Schedule D (Form 1040), line 4; or on Schedule D (Form 1041), line 4.

For other returns, enter it in Part I of a Form 8949 with Box B checked (if you received a Form 1099-B or substitute statement for every transaction included on line 1) or Box C checked (if you cannot check Box B). Enter "Form 6781, Part I" on line 1 in column (a). Enter the gain or (loss) in column (h). Leave all other columns blank

Line 9

Include this amount on Schedule D (Form 1040), line 11; or on Schedule D (Form 1041), line 11.

For other returns, enter it in Part II of a Form 8949 with Box E checked (if you received a Form 1099-B or substitute statement for every transaction included on line 1) or Box F checked (if you cannot check Box E). Enter "Form 6781, Part I" on line 1 in column (a). Enter the gain or (loss) in column (h). Leave all other columns blank.

Part II

Use Section A for losses from positions that are part of a straddle. Generally, a loss is allowed to the extent it exceeds the unrecognized gain on offsetting positions. The part of the loss not allowed is treated as if incurred in the following year and is allowed to the same extent. However, a loss from a position established in an identified straddle after October 21, 2004, is not allowed. Instead, the basis of each offsetting position in the identified straddle that has unrecognized gain is increased by the amount of the unallowed loss multiplied by the following fraction:

The unrecognized gain (if any) on the offsetting position

―――――――――――――――――――――――

The total unrecognized gain on all positions that offset the loss position in the identified straddle.

For more details, see Pub. 550, chapter 4.

Use Section B for gains from positions that are part of a straddle.

Do not include in Part II a disposition of any of the following.

• A position that is part of a hedging transaction.

• A loss position included in an identified straddle established before October 22, 2004, unless you disposed of all of the positions making up the straddle.

• A loss position included in an identified straddle established after October 21, 2004.

• A position that is part of a straddle if all of the positions of the straddle are section 1256 contracts.

Column (a)

Enter the property and delivery date, and indicate whether the property is a long or short position.

Column (d)

For positions closed out or sold, enter the closing price or sales price.

Column (e)

For positions closed out or sold, enter the cost or other basis plus commissions paid. Include nondeductible interest and carrying charges allocable to personal property that is part of a straddle. If any part of an unallowed loss from an offsetting position established in an identified straddle after October 21, 2004, increased your basis in the position, also include that amount. See Pub. 550 for details.

Line 10, Column (f)

Include in this column any loss not allowed in the prior year to the extent of the unrecognized gain.

Line 10, Column (g)

Enter the unrecognized gain on positions offsetting those in columns (a) through (f). Figure the amount to enter in this column by subtracting the cost or other basis of the offsetting position from the settlement price of that position as of the close of the last business day of your 2014 tax year.

Lines 11 and 13

Separate recognized gains and losses into short-term and long-term. Attach a separate statement for each. For information about holding periods for straddle positions, see Pub. 550 and Temporary Regulations section 1.1092(b)-2T.

Attach separate statements for (a) section 988 contracts that are part of a mixed straddle, and (b) any gain on the disposition or other termination of any position held as part of a conversion transaction (as defined in section 1258(c)). Identify the net gain or loss and report it on Form 4797, line 10.

Line 11a

Include this amount on Schedule D (Form 1040), line 4; or on Schedule D (Form 1041), line 4.

For other returns, enter it in Part I of a Form 8949 with Box C checked. Enter "Form 6781, Part II" on line 1 in column (a). Enter the (loss) as a negative number (in parentheses) in column (h). Leave all other columns blank.

Line 11b

Include this amount on Schedule D (Form 1040), line 11; or on Schedule D (Form 1041), line 11.

For other returns, enter it in Part II of a Form 8949 with Box F checked. Enter "Form 6781, Part II" on line 1 in column (a). Enter the (loss) as a negative number (in parentheses) in column (h). Leave all other columns blank.

Line 13a

Include this amount on Schedule D (Form 1040), line 4; or on Schedule D (Form 1041), line 4.

For other returns, enter it in Part I of a Form 8949 with Box C checked. Enter "Form 6781, Part II" on line 1 in column (a). Enter the gain in column (h). Leave all other columns blank.

Line 13b

Include this amount on Schedule D (Form 1040), line 11; or on Schedule D (Form 1041), line 11.

For other returns, enter it in Part II of a Form 8949 with Box F checked. Enter "Form 6781, Part II" on line 1 in column (a). Enter the gain in column (h). Leave all other columns blank.

Collectibles gain or (loss). A collectibles gain or (loss) is any long-term gain or deductible long-term loss from the sale or exchange of a collectible that is a capital asset. Collectibles include works of art, rugs, antiques, metals (such as gold, silver, and platinum bullion), gems, stamps, coins, alcoholic beverages, and certain other tangible property.

If any of the gain or loss you reported in Part II is a collectibles gain or (loss) and you are filing Form 1040 or Form 1041, follow the instructions below for the form you file.

Form 1040. If you checked "Yes" on line 17 of Schedule D (Form 1040), include the collectibles gain or (loss) from Part II on line 3 of the 28% Rate Gain Worksheet in the Instructions for Schedule D (Form 1040).

Form 1041. If you must complete the 28% Rate Gain Worksheet in the Instructions for Schedule D (Form 1041), include the collectibles gain or (loss) from Part II on line 3 of that worksheet.

Part III

Complete Part III by listing each position (whether or not part of a straddle) that you held at the end of the tax year (including any position you are treated as holding because it is held by a related party) if the FMV of the position at such time exceeds your cost or other basis as adjusted.

Do not include positions that are part of an identified straddle or hedging transaction, property that is stock in trade or inventory, or property subject to depreciation used in a trade or business.

Do not complete Part III if you do not have a recognized loss on any position (including regulated futures contracts).

Paperwork Reduction Act Notice. We ask for the information on this form to carry out the Internal Revenue laws of the United States. You are required to give us the information. We need it to ensure that you are complying with these laws and to allow us to figure and collect the right amount of tax.

You are not required to provide the information requested on a form that is subject to the Paperwork Reduction Act unless the form displays a valid OMB control number. Books or records relating to a form or its instructions must be retained as long as their contents may become material in the administration of any Internal Revenue law. Generally, tax returns and return information are confidential, as required by section 6103.

The time needed to complete and file this form will vary depending on individual circumstances. The estimated burden for individual taxpayers filing this form is approved under OMB control number 1545-0074 and is included in the estimates shown in the instructions for their individual income tax return. The estimated burden for all other taxpayers who file this form is shown below.

Recordkeeping . . . 10 hr., 31 min.

Learning about the law or the form . . . 1 hr., 57 min.

Preparing the form . . 3 hr., 9 min.

Copying, assembling, and sending the form to the IRS . . . . 16 min.

If you have comments concerning the accuracy of these time estimates or suggestions for making this form simpler, we would be happy to hear from you. See the instructions for the tax return with which this form is filed.

Form **8396**	**Mortgage Interest Credit**	OMB No. 1545-0074

Form **8396**

Department of the Treasury
Internal Revenue Service (99)

Mortgage Interest Credit

(For Holders of Qualified Mortgage Credit Certificates Issued by
State or Local Governmental Units or Agencies)

▶ Information about Form 8396 and its instructions is at *www.irs.gov/form8396*.
▶ **Attach to Form 1040 or 1040NR.**

OMB No. 1545-0074

2014

Attachment
Sequence No. **138**

Name(s) shown on your tax return

Your social security number

Enter the address of your main home to which the qualified mortgage certificate relates if it is different from the address shown on your tax return.

Name of Issuer of Mortgage Credit Certificate	Mortgage Credit Certificate Number	Issue Date

Before you begin Part I, figure the amounts of any of the following credits you are claiming: Credit for the elderly or the disabled, alternative motor vehicle credit, and qualified plug-in electric drive motor vehicle credit.

Part I — Current Year Mortgage Interest Credit

1	Interest paid on the certified indebtedness amount. If someone else (other than your spouse if filing jointly) also held an interest in the home, enter only your share of the interest paid	**1**	
2	Enter the certificate credit rate shown on your **mortgage credit certificate. Do not** enter the interest rate on your home mortgage	**2**	%
3	If line 2 is 20% or less, multiply line 1 by line 2. If line 2 is more than 20%, or you refinanced your mortgage and received a reissued certificate, see the instructions for the amount to enter .	**3**	
	You must reduce your deduction for home mortgage interest on Schedule A (Form 1040) by the amount on line 3.		
4	Enter any 2011 credit carryforward from line 16 of your 2013 Form 8396	**4**	
5	Enter any 2012 credit carryforward from line 14 of your 2013 Form 8396	**5**	
6	Enter any 2013 credit carryforward from line 17 of your 2013 Form 8396	**6**	
7	Add lines 3 through 6	**7**	
8	Limitation based on tax liability. Enter the amount from the Credit Limit Worksheet (see instructions)	**8**	
9	**Current year mortgage interest credit.** Enter the **smaller** of line 7 or line 8. Also include this amount in the total on Form 1040, line 54, or Form 1040NR, line 51. Check box **c** on that line and enter "8396" in the space next to that box	**9**	

Part II — Mortgage Interest Credit Carryforward to 2015. (Complete **only** if line 9 is less than line 7.)

10	Add lines 3 and 4	**10**	
11	Enter the amount from line 7	**11**	
12	Enter the **larger** of line 9 or line 10	**12**	
13	Subtract line 12 from line 11	**13**	
14	**2013 credit carryforward to 2015.** Enter the **smaller** of line 6 or line 13	**14**	
15	Subtract line 14 from line 13	**15**	
16	**2012 credit carryforward to 2015.** Enter the **smaller** of line 5 or line 15	**16**	
17	**2014 credit carryforward to 2015.** Subtract line 9 from line 3. If zero or less, enter -0-	**17**	

For Paperwork Reduction Act Notice, see your tax return instructions.   Cat. No. 62502X   Form **8396** (2014)

General Instructions

Future Developments

For the latest information about developments related to Form 8396 and its instructions, such as legislation enacted after they were published, go to *www.irs.gov/form8396*.

Purpose of Form

Use Form 8396 to figure the mortgage interest credit for 2014 and any credit carryforward to 2015.

Who Can Claim the Credit

You can claim the credit only if you were issued a qualified Mortgage Credit Certificate (MCC) by a state or local governmental unit or agency under a qualified mortgage credit certificate program.

 *Certificates issued by the Federal Housing Administration, Department of Veterans Affairs, and Farmers Home Administration, and Homestead Staff Exemption Certificates do not qualify for the credit.*

The home to which the certificate relates must be your main home and also must be located in the jurisdiction of the governmental unit that issued the certificate.

If the interest on the mortgage was paid to a related person, you cannot claim the credit.

Refinanced Mortgage

You can refinance your mortgage without losing this credit if your existing MCC is reissued and the reissued certificate meets all of the following conditions.

• It must be issued to the holder(s) of the existing certificate for the same property.

• It must entirely replace the existing certificate. The holder cannot retain any portion of the outstanding balance of the existing certificate.

• The certified indebtedness on the reissued certificate cannot exceed the outstanding balance shown on the existing certificate.

• The credit rate of the reissued certificate cannot exceed the credit rate of the existing certificate.

• The reissued certificate cannot result in a larger amount on line 3 than would otherwise have been allowable under the existing certificate for any tax year.

For each tax year, you must determine the amount of credit that you would have been allowed using your original MCC. To do this, multiply the interest that was scheduled to be paid on your original mortgage by the certificate rate on your original MCC. The result may limit your line 3 credit allowed when you have a reissued MCC, even if your new loan has a lower interest rate.

If the certificate credit rates are different in the year you refinanced, attach a statement showing separate calculations for lines 1, 2, and 3 for the applicable parts of the year when the original MCC and the reissued MCC were in effect. Combine the amounts from both calculations for line 3. Enter that total on line 3 of the form and enter "see attached" on the dotted line next to line 2.

For more details, see Regulations section 1.25-3(p).

Recapture of Credit

If you buy a home using an MCC and sell it within 9 years, you may have to recapture (repay) some of the credit. See Pub. 523, Selling Your Home, and Form 8828, Recapture of Federal Mortgage Subsidy.

Additional Information

See Pub. 530, Tax Information for Homeowners, for more details.

Specific Instructions

Part I—Current Year Mortgage Interest Credit

Line 1

Enter the interest you paid during the year on the loan amount (certified indebtedness amount) shown on your MCC. In most cases, this will be the amount in box 1 on Form 1098, Mortgage Interest Statement, or on a similar statement you received from your mortgage holder. If the loan amount on your MCC is less than your total mortgage loan, you must allocate the interest to determine the part that relates to the loan covered by the MCC. See Pub. 530 for an example of how to allocate the interest.

Line 2

The certificate credit rate cannot be less than 10% or more than 50%.

Line 3

If you refinanced, see *Refinanced Mortgage* on this page.

If the certificate credit rate shown on line 2 is more than 20%, multiply line 1 by line 2, but do not enter more than $2,000 on line 3. If you and someone else (other than your spouse if filing jointly) held an interest in the home, the $2,000 limit must be allocated to each owner in proportion to the interest held. See *Dividing the Credit* in Pub. 530 for an example of how to make the allocation.

Reduction of home mortgage interest deduction on Schedule A (Form 1040). If you itemize your deductions on Schedule A, you must reduce the amount of home mortgage interest you would otherwise deduct on Schedule A by the amount on Form 8396, line 3, and report the reduced amount on Schedule A. You must do this even if part of the amount on line 3 is carried forward to 2015.

Line 8—Credit Limit Worksheet
Keep for Your Records

1. Enter the amount from Form 1040, line 47, or Form 1040NR, line 45 . . . . **1.** _____

2. **Form 1040 filers:** Enter the amounts from Form 1040, lines 48 through 51; line 12 of the Line 11 Worksheet in Pub. 972*; Form 5695, line 30; Form 8910, line 15; Form 8936, line 23; and Schedule R (Form 1040A or 1040), line 22.

   Form 1040NR filers: Enter the amounts from Form 1040NR, lines 46 through 48; line 12 of the Line 11 Worksheet in Pub. 972*; Form 5695, line 30; Form 8910, line 15; and Form 8936, line 23. **2.** _____

3. Subtract line 2 from line 1. Enter this amount on Form 8396, line 8. If zero or less, enter -0- here and on Form 8396, lines 8 and 9, and go to Part II of Form 8396 . . . . **3.** _____

*If you are not claiming the child tax credit, you do not need Pub. 972.

Part II—Mortgage Interest Credit Carryforward to 2015

If the amount on line 9 is less than the amount on line 7, you may have an unused credit to carry forward to the next 3 tax years or until used, whichever comes first. The current year credit is used first and then the prior year credits, beginning with the earliest prior year.

If you have any unused credit to carry forward to 2015, keep a copy of this form to figure your credit for 2015.

 *If you are subject to the $2,000 credit limit because your certificate credit rate is more than 20%, no amount over the $2,000 limit (or your prorated share of the $2,000 if you must allocate the credit) may be carried forward for use in a later year.*

Form **8606**	**Nondeductible IRAs**	OMB No. 1545-0074
Department of the Treasury Internal Revenue Service (99)	▶ Information about Form 8606 and its separate instructions is at *www.irs.gov/form8606*. ▶ Attach to Form 1040, Form 1040A, or Form 1040NR.	**20****14** Attachment Sequence No. **48**

Name. If married, file a separate form for each spouse required to file Form 8606. See instructions. | **Your social security number**

Fill in Your Address Only If You Are Filing This Form by Itself and Not With Your Tax Return ▶

Home address (number and street, or P.O. box if mail is not delivered to your home) | Apt. no.

City, town or post office, state, and ZIP code. If you have a foreign address, also complete the spaces below.

Foreign country name | Foreign province/state/county | Foreign postal code

---

Part I — **Nondeductible Contributions to Traditional IRAs and Distributions From Traditional, SEP, and SIMPLE IRAs**

Complete this part only if one or more of the following apply.

- You made nondeductible contributions to a traditional IRA for 2014.
- You took distributions from a traditional, SEP, or SIMPLE IRA in 2014 **and** you made nondeductible contributions to a traditional IRA in 2014 or an earlier year. For this purpose, a distribution does not include a rollover, one-time distribution to fund an HSA, conversion, recharacterization, or return of certain contributions.
- You converted part, but not all, of your traditional, SEP, and SIMPLE IRAs to Roth IRAs in 2014 (excluding any portion you recharacterized) **and** you made nondeductible contributions to a traditional IRA in 2014 or an earlier year.

1	Enter your nondeductible contributions to traditional IRAs for 2014, including those made for 2014 from January 1, 2015, through April 15, 2015 (see instructions)	**1**
2	Enter your total basis in traditional IRAs (see instructions)	**2**
3	Add lines 1 and 2	**3**

In 2014, did you take a distribution from traditional, SEP, or SIMPLE IRAs, or make a Roth IRA conversion? —— **No** ——▶ Enter the amount from line 3 on line 14. Do not complete the rest of Part I.

—— **Yes** ——▶ Go to line 4.

4	Enter those contributions included on line 1 that were made from January 1, 2015, through April 15, 2015	**4**
5	Subtract line 4 from line 3	**5**
6	Enter the value of **all** your traditional, SEP, and SIMPLE IRAs as of December 31, 2014, plus any outstanding rollovers (see instructions) . .	**6**
7	Enter your distributions from traditional, SEP, and SIMPLE IRAs in 2014. **Do not** include rollovers, a one-time distribution to fund an HSA, conversions to a Roth IRA, certain returned contributions, or recharacterizations of traditional IRA contributions (see instructions) .	**7**
8	Enter the net amount you converted from traditional, SEP, and SIMPLE IRAs to Roth IRAs in 2014. **Do not** include amounts converted that you later recharacterized (see instructions). Also enter this amount on line 16 .	**8**
9	Add lines 6, 7, and 8	**9**
10	Divide line 5 by line 9. Enter the result as a decimal rounded to at least 3 places. If the result is 1.000 or more, enter "1.000"	**10** × .
11	Multiply line 8 by line 10. This is the nontaxable portion of the amount you converted to Roth IRAs. Also enter this amount on line 17 . . .	**11**
12	Multiply line 7 by line 10. This is the nontaxable portion of your distributions that you did not convert to a Roth IRA	**12**
13	Add lines 11 and 12. This is the nontaxable portion of all your distributions	**13**
14	Subtract line 13 from line 3. This is **your total basis in traditional IRAs for 2014 and earlier years**	**14**
15	**Taxable amount.** Subtract line 12 from line 7. If more than zero, also include this amount on Form 1040, line 15b; Form 1040A, line 11b; or Form 1040NR, line 16b	**15**

Note. You may be subject to an additional 10% tax on the amount on line 15 if you were under age 59½ at the time of the distribution (see instructions).

For Privacy Act and Paperwork Reduction Act Notice, see separate instructions. | Cat. No. 63966F | Form **8606** (2014)

Part II   2014 Conversions From Traditional, SEP, or SIMPLE IRAs to Roth IRAs

Complete this part if you converted part or all of your traditional, SEP, and SIMPLE IRAs to a Roth IRA in 2014 (excluding any portion you recharacterized).

16	If you completed Part I, enter the amount from line 8. Otherwise, enter the net amount you converted from traditional, SEP, and SIMPLE IRAs to Roth IRAs in 2014. **Do not** include amounts you later recharacterized back to traditional, SEP, or SIMPLE IRAs in 2014 or 2015 (see instructions)	16
17	If you completed Part I, enter the amount from line 11. Otherwise, enter your basis in the amount on line 16 (see instructions)	17
18	**Taxable amount.** Subtract line 17 from line 16. If more than zero, also include this amount on Form 1040, line 15b; Form 1040A, line 11b; or Form 1040NR, line 16b	18

Part III   Distributions From Roth IRAs

Complete this part only if you took a distribution from a Roth IRA in 2014. For this purpose, a distribution does not include a rollover, one-time distribution to fund an HSA, recharacterization, or return of certain contributions (see instructions).

19	Enter your total nonqualified distributions from Roth IRAs in 2014, including any qualified first-time homebuyer distributions (see instructions)	19
20	Qualified first-time homebuyer expenses (see instructions). **Do not** enter more than $10,000 . .	20
21	Subtract line 20 from line 19. If zero or less, enter -0-	21
22	Enter your basis in Roth IRA contributions (see instructions). If line 21 is zero, **stop here** . . .	22
23	Subtract line 22 from line 21. If zero or less, enter -0- and skip lines 24 and 25. If more than zero, you may be subject to an additional tax (see instructions)	23
24	Enter your basis in conversions from traditional, SEP, and SIMPLE IRAs and rollovers from qualified retirement plans to a Roth IRA (see instructions)	24
25	**Taxable amount.** Subtract line 24 from line 23. If more than zero, also include this amount on Form 1040, line 15b; Form 1040A, line 11b; or Form 1040NR, line 16b	25

Sign Here Only If You Are Filing This Form by Itself and Not With Your Tax Return

Under penalties of perjury, I declare that I have examined this form, including accompanying attachments, and to the best of my knowledge and belief, it is true, correct, and complete. Declaration of preparer (other than taxpayer) is based on all information of which preparer has any knowledge.

▶ _____ Your signature   ▶ _____ Date

Paid Preparer Use Only	Print/Type preparer's name	Preparer's signature	Date	Check ☐ if self-employed	PTIN
	Firm's name ▶			Firm's EIN ▶	
	Firm's address ▶			Phone no.	

Form **8606** (2014)

2014

Instructions for Form 8606

Nondeductible IRAs

Department of the Treasury
Internal Revenue Service

Section references are to the Internal Revenue Code unless otherwise noted.

General Instructions

Future Developments

For the latest information about developments related to Form 8606 and its instructions, such as legislation enacted after they were published, go to *www.irs.gov/form8606*.

What's New

Modified AGI limit for Roth IRA contributions increased. You can contribute to a Roth IRA for 2014 only if your 2014 modified adjusted gross income (AGI) for Roth IRA purposes is less than:
* $191,000 if married filing jointly or qualifying widow(er),
* $129,000 if single, head of household, or married filing separately and you did not live with your spouse at any time in 2014, or
* $10,000 if married filing separately and you lived with your spouse at any time in 2014.
See *Roth IRAs*, later.

Purpose of Form

Use Form 8606 to report:
* Nondeductible contributions you made to traditional IRAs;
* Distributions from traditional, SEP, or SIMPLE IRAs, if you have ever made nondeductible contributions to traditional IRAs;
* Conversions from traditional, SEP, or SIMPLE IRAs to Roth IRAs; and
* Distributions from Roth IRAs.

Additional information. For more details on IRAs, see Pub. 590-A, Contributions to Individual Retirement Arrangements (IRAs) and Pub. 590-B, Distributions from Individual Retirement Arrangements (IRAs).

 If you received distributions from a traditional, SEP, or SIMPLE IRA in 2014 and you have never made nondeductible contributions (including nontaxable amounts you rolled over from a qualified retirement plan) to traditional IRAs, do not report the distributions on Form 8606. Instead, see the instructions for Form 1040, lines 15a and 15b; Form 1040A, lines 11a and 11b; or Form 1040NR, lines 16a and 16b. Also, to find out if any of your contributions to traditional IRAs are deductible, see the instructions for Form 1040, line 32; Form 1040A, line 17; or Form 1040NR, line 32.

Who Must File

File Form 8606 if any of the following apply.
* You made nondeductible contributions to a traditional IRA for 2014, including a repayment of a qualified reservist distribution.
* You received distributions from a traditional, SEP, or SIMPLE IRA in 2014 and your basis in traditional IRAs is more than zero. For this purpose, a distribution does not include a rollover, qualified charitable distribution, one-time distribution to fund an HSA, conversion, recharacterization, or return of certain contributions.
* You converted an amount from a traditional, SEP, or SIMPLE IRA to a Roth IRA in 2014 (unless you recharacterized the entire conversion—see *Recharacterizations*, later).
* You received distributions from a Roth IRA in 2014 (other than a rollover, recharacterization, or return of certain contributions—see the instructions for Part III, later).
* You received a distribution from an inherited traditional IRA that has basis, you rolled over an inherited plan account to a Roth IRA, or you received a distribution from an inherited Roth IRA that was not a qualified distribution. You may need to file more than one Form 8606. See Pub. 590-A and Pub. 590-B for more information.

Note. If you recharacterized a 2014 Roth IRA contribution as a traditional IRA contribution, or vice versa, treat the contribution as having been made to the second IRA, not the first IRA. See *Recharacterizations*, later.

 You do not have to file Form 8606 solely to report regular contributions to Roth IRAs. But see What Records Must I Keep, *later.*

When and Where To File

File Form 8606 with your 2014 Form 1040, 1040A, or 1040NR by the due date, including extensions, of your return.

If you are not required to file an income tax return but are required to file Form 8606, sign Form 8606 and send it to the Internal Revenue Service at the same time and place you would otherwise file Form 1040, 1040A, or 1040NR. Be sure to include your address on page 1 of the form and your signature and the date on page 2 of the form.

Definitions

Deemed IRAs

A qualified employer plan (retirement plan) can maintain a separate account or annuity under the plan (a deemed IRA) to receive voluntary employee contributions. If in 2014 you had a deemed IRA, use the rules for either a traditional IRA or a Roth IRA depending on which type it was. See Pub. 590-A for more details.

Traditional IRAs

For purposes of Form 8606, a traditional IRA is an individual retirement account or an individual retirement annuity other than a SEP, SIMPLE, or Roth IRA.

Contributions. An overall contribution limit applies to traditional IRAs and Roth IRAs. See *Overall Contribution Limit for Traditional and Roth IRAs*, later. Contributions to a traditional IRA may be fully deductible, partially deductible, or completely nondeductible.

Basis. Your basis in traditional IRAs is the total of all your nondeductible contributions and nontaxable amounts included in rollovers made to traditional IRAs minus the total of all your nontaxable distributions, adjusted if necessary (see the instructions for line 2, later).

 Keep track of your basis to figure the nontaxable part of your future distributions.

SEP IRAs

A simplified employee pension (SEP) is an employer-sponsored plan under

Cat. No. 25399E

which an employer can make contributions to traditional IRAs for its employees. If you make contributions to that IRA (excluding employer contributions you make if you are self-employed), they are treated as contributions to a traditional IRA and may be deductible or nondeductible. SEP IRA distributions are reported in the same manner as traditional IRA distributions.

SIMPLE IRAs

A SIMPLE IRA plan is a tax-favored retirement plan that certain small employers (including self-employed individuals) can set up for the benefit of their employees. Your participation in your employer's SIMPLE IRA plan does not prevent you from making contributions to a traditional or Roth IRA.

Roth IRAs

A Roth IRA is similar to a traditional IRA, but has the following features.
- Contributions are never deductible.
- Contributions can be made after the owner reaches age 70½.
- No minimum distributions are required during the Roth IRA owner's lifetime.
- Qualified distributions are not includible in income.

Qualified distribution. Generally, a qualified distribution is any distribution from your Roth IRA that meets the following requirements.

1. It is made after the 5-year period beginning with the first year for which a contribution was made to a Roth IRA (including a conversion or, in the case of a qualified retirement plan, a rollover) set up for your benefit, and

2. The distribution is made:

a. On or after the date you reach age 59½,

b. After your death,

c. Due to your disability, or

d. For qualified first-time homebuyer expenses.

Contributions. You can contribute to a Roth IRA for 2014 only if your 2014 modified AGI for Roth IRA purposes is less than:
- $191,000 if married filing jointly or qualifying widow(er),
- $129,000 if single, head of household, or if married filing separately and you did not live with your spouse at any time in 2014, or

- $10,000 if married filing separately and you lived with your spouse at any time in 2014.

Use the Maximum Roth IRA Contribution Worksheet, later, to figure the maximum amount you can contribute to a Roth IRA for 2014. If you are married filing jointly, complete the worksheet separately for you and your spouse.

 If you contributed too much to your Roth IRA, see Recharacterizations, later.

Modified AGI for Roth IRA purposes. First, figure your AGI (Form 1040, line 38; Form 1040A, line 22; or Form 1040NR, line 37). Then, refigure it by:

1. Subtracting the following.

a. Roth IRA conversions included on Form 1040, line 15b; Form 1040A, line 11b; or Form 1040NR, line 16b.

b. Roth IRA rollovers from qualified retirement plans included on Form 1040, line 16b; Form 1040A, line 12b; or Form 1040NR, line 17b.

2. Adding the following.

a. IRA deduction from Form 1040, line 32; Form 1040A, line 17; or Form 1040NR, line 32.

b. Student loan interest deduction from Form 1040, line 33; Form 1040A, line 18; or Form 1040NR, line 33.

c. Tuition and fees deduction from Form 1040, line 34; or Form 1040A, line 19.

d. Domestic production activities deduction from Form 1040, line 35; or Form 1040NR, line 34.

e. Exclusion of interest from Form 8815, Exclusion of Interest From Series EE and I U.S. Savings Bonds Issued After 1989.

f. Exclusion of employer-provided adoption benefits from Form 8839, Qualified Adoption Expenses.

g. Foreign earned income exclusion from Form 2555, Foreign Earned Income, or Form 2555-EZ, Foreign Earned Income Exclusion.

h. Foreign housing exclusion or deduction from Form 2555.

 When figuring modified AGI for Roth IRA purposes, you may have to refigure items based on modified AGI, such as taxable social security benefits and passive activity losses allowed under the special allowance for rental real estate activities. See Can You Contribute to a Roth IRA? in Pub. 590-A for details.

Distributions. See the instructions for Part III, later.

Overall Contribution Limit for Traditional and Roth IRAs

If you are not married filing jointly, your limit on contributions to traditional and Roth IRAs is generally the smaller of $5,500 ($6,500 if age 50 or older at the end of 2014) or your taxable compensation (defined below).

If you are married filing jointly, your contribution limit is generally $5,500 ($6,500 if age 50 or older at the end of 2014) and your spouse's contribution limit is $5,500 ($6,500 if age 50 or older at the end of 2014) as well. But if the combined taxable compensation of both you and your spouse is less than $11,000 ($12,000 if one spouse is 50 or older at the end of 2014; $13,000 if both spouses are 50 or older at the end of 2014), see *Kay Bailey Hutchison Spousal IRA Limit* in Pub. 590-A for special rules.

This limit does not apply to employer contributions to a SEP or SIMPLE IRA.

Note. Rollovers, Roth IRA conversions, Roth IRA rollovers from qualified retirement plans and qualified reservist distributions do not affect your contribution limit.

 The amount you can contribute to a Roth IRA may also be limited by your modified AGI (see Contributions, earlier, and the Maximum Roth IRA Contribution Worksheet, later).

Taxable compensation. Taxable compensation includes the following.
- Wages, salaries, tips, etc. If you received a distribution from a nonqualified deferred compensation plan or nongovernmental section 457 plan that is included in Form W-2, box 1, or in Form 1099-MISC, box 7, do not include that distribution in taxable compensation. The distribution should be shown in (a) Form W-2, box 11, (b) Form W-2, box 12, with code Z, or (c) Form 1099-MISC, box 15b. If it is not, contact your employer for the amount of the distribution.
- Nontaxable combat pay if you were a member of the U.S. Armed Forces.
- Self-employment income. If you are self-employed (a sole proprietor or a partner), taxable compensation is your net earnings from your trade or business (provided your personal services are a material income-producing factor) reduced by your deduction for contributions made on your behalf to

retirement plans and the deductible part of your self-employment tax.

• Alimony and separate maintenance.

See *What Is Compensation?* under *Who Can Open a Traditional IRA?* in chapter 1 of Pub. 590-A for details.

Recharacterizations

Generally, you can recharacterize (correct) an IRA contribution, Roth IRA conversion, or a Roth IRA rollover from a qualified retirement plan by making a trustee-to-trustee transfer from one IRA to another type of IRA.
Trustee-to-trustee transfers are made directly between financial institutions or within the same financial institution. You generally must make the transfer by the due date of your return (including extensions) and reflect it on your return. However, if you timely filed your return without making the transfer, you can make the transfer within 6 months of the due date of your return, excluding extensions. If necessary, file an amended return reflecting the transfer (see *Amending Form 8606*, later). Write

"Filed pursuant to section 301.9100-2" on the amended return.

Reporting recharacterizations. Treat any recharacterized IRA contribution, Roth IRA conversion, or Roth IRA rollover from a qualified retirement plan as though the amount of the contribution, conversion, or rollover was originally contributed to the second IRA, not the first IRA. For the recharacterization, you must transfer the amount of the original contribution, conversion, or rollover plus any related earnings or less any related loss. In most cases, your IRA trustee or custodian figures the amount of the related earnings you must transfer. If you need to figure the related earnings, see *How Do You Recharacterize a Contribution?* in chapter 1 of Pub. 590-A. Treat any earnings or loss that occurred in the first IRA as having occurred in the second IRA. You cannot deduct any loss that occurred while the funds were in the first IRA. Also, you cannot take a deduction for a contribution to a traditional IRA if you later recharacterize the amount. The

following discussion explains how to report the four different types of recharacterizations, including the statement that you must attach to your return explaining the recharacterization.

1. You made a contribution to a traditional IRA and later recharacterized part or all of it in a trustee-to-trustee transfer to a Roth IRA. If you recharacterized only part of the contribution, report the nondeductible traditional IRA portion of the remaining contribution, if any, on Form 8606, Part I. If you recharacterized the entire contribution, do not report the contribution on Form 8606. In either case, attach a statement to your return explaining the recharacterization. If the recharacterization occurred in 2014, include the amount transferred from the traditional IRA on Form 1040, line 15a; Form 1040A, line 11a; or Form 1040NR, line 16a. If the recharacterization occurred in 2015, report the amount transferred only in the attached statement, and not on your 2014 or 2015 tax return.

Maximum Roth IRA Contribution Worksheet

Keep for Your Records

Caution: *If married filing jointly and the combined taxable compensation (defined earlier) for you and your spouse is less than $11,000 ($12,000 if one spouse is 50 or older at the end of 2014; $13,000 if both spouses are 50 or older at the end of 2014),* **do not** *use this worksheet. Instead, see Pub. 590-A for special rules.*

1. If married filing jointly, enter $5,500 ($6,500 if age 50 or older at the end of 2014). All others, enter the **smaller** of $5,500 ($6,500 if age 50 or older at the end of 2014) or your <u>taxable compensation</u> (defined earlier)	1. _____
2. Enter your total contributions to traditional IRAs for 2014	2. _____
3. Subtract line 2 from line 1	3. _____
4. Enter: $191,000 if married filing jointly or qualifying widow(er); $10,000 if married filing separately and you lived with your spouse at any time in 2014. All others, enter $129,000	4. _____
5. Enter your <u>modified AGI for Roth IRA purposes</u> (discussed earlier)	5. _____
6. Subtract line 5 from line 4. If zero or less, **stop here**; you may not contribute to a Roth IRA for 2014. See *Recharacterizations* above if you made Roth IRA contributions for 2014	6. _____
7. If line 4 above is $129,000, enter $15,000; otherwise, enter $10,000. If line 6 is more than or equal to line 7, skip lines 8 and 9 and enter the amount from line 3 on line 10	7. _____
8. Divide line 6 by line 7 and enter the result as a decimal (rounded to at least 3 places)	8. _____
9. Multiply line 1 by line 8. If the result is not a multiple of $10, increase it to the next multiple of $10 (for example, increase $490.30 to $500). Enter the result, but not less than $200	9. _____
10. **Maximum 2014 Roth IRA Contribution.** Enter the **smaller** of line 3 or line 9. See *Recharacterizations* above if you contributed more than this amount to Roth IRAs for 2014	10. _____

Example. You are single, covered by an employer retirement plan, and you contributed $4,000 to a new traditional IRA on May 27, 2014. On February 24, 2015, you determine that your 2014 modified AGI will limit your traditional IRA deduction to $1,000. The value of your traditional IRA on that date is $4,400. You decide to recharacterize $3,000 of the traditional IRA contribution as a Roth IRA contribution, and have $3,300 ($3,000 contribution plus $300 related earnings) transferred from your traditional IRA to a Roth IRA in a trustee-to-trustee transfer. You deduct the $1,000 traditional IRA contribution on Form 1040. You do not file Form 8606. You attach a statement to your return explaining the recharacterization. The statement indicates that you contributed $4,000 to a traditional IRA on May 27, 2014; recharacterized $3,000 of that contribution on February 24, 2015, by transferring $3,000 plus $300 of related earnings from your traditional IRA to a Roth IRA in a trustee-to-trustee transfer; and deducted the remaining traditional IRA contribution of $1,000 on Form 1040. You do not report the $3,300 distribution from your traditional IRA on your 2014 Form 1040 because the distribution occurred in 2015. You do not report the distribution on your 2015 Form 1040 because the recharacterization related to 2014 and was explained in an attachment to your 2014 return.

2. You made a contribution to a Roth IRA and later recharacterized part or all of it in a trustee-to-trustee transfer to a traditional IRA. Report the nondeductible traditional IRA portion of the recharacterized contribution, if any, on Form 8606, Part I. Do not report the Roth IRA contribution (whether or not you recharacterized all or part of it) on Form 8606. Attach a statement to your return explaining the recharacterization. If the recharacterization occurred in 2014, include the amount transferred from the Roth IRA on Form 1040, line 15a; Form 1040A, line 11a; or Form 1040NR, line 16a. If the recharacterization occurred in 2015, report the amount transferred only in the attached statement, and not on your 2014 or 2015 tax return.

Example. You are single, covered by an employer retirement plan, and you contributed $4,000 to a new Roth IRA on June 16, 2014. On December 29, 2014, you determine that your 2014 modified AGI will allow a full traditional

IRA deduction. You decide to recharacterize the Roth IRA contribution as a traditional IRA contribution and have $4,200, the balance in the Roth IRA account ($4,000 contribution plus $200 related earnings), transferred from your Roth IRA to a traditional IRA in a trustee-to-trustee transfer. You deduct the $4,000 traditional IRA contribution on Form 1040. You do not file Form 8606. You attach a statement to your return explaining the recharacterization. The statement indicates that you contributed $4,000 to a new Roth IRA on June 16, 2014; recharacterized that contribution on December 29, 2014, by transferring $4,200, the balance in the Roth IRA, to a traditional IRA in a trustee-to-trustee transfer; and deducted the traditional IRA contribution of $4,000 on Form 1040. You include the $4,200 distribution from your Roth IRA on your 2014 Form 1040, line 15a.

3. You converted an amount from a traditional, SEP, or SIMPLE IRA to a Roth IRA in 2014 and later recharacterized all or part of the amount in a trustee-to-trustee transfer to a traditional, SEP, or SIMPLE IRA. If you recharacterized only part of the amount converted, report the amount not recharacterized on Form 8606, Part II. If you recharacterized the entire amount converted, do not report the conversion on Form 8606. In either case, attach a statement to your return explaining the recharacterization and include the amount converted (whether or not recharacterized) in the total on Form 1040, line 15a; Form 1040A, line 11a; or Form 1040NR, line 16a. If the recharacterization occurred in 2014, also include the amount transferred out from the Roth IRA on that line. If the recharacterization occurred in 2015, report the amount transferred only in the attached statement, and not on your 2014 or 2015 tax return (a 2015 Form 1099-R should be sent to you by January 31, 2016, stating that you made a recharacterization of an amount converted in the prior year).

Example. You are married filing jointly and converted $20,000 from your traditional IRA to a new Roth IRA on May 20, 2014. On April 7, 2015, you decide to recharacterize the conversion. The value of the Roth IRA on that date is $19,000. You recharacterize the conversion by transferring that entire amount to a traditional IRA in a trustee-to-trustee transfer. You report $20,000 on Form 1040, line 15a. You do

not include the $19,000 on line 15a because it did not occur in 2014 (you also do not report that amount on your 2015 return because it does not apply to the 2015 tax year). You attach a statement to Form 1040 explaining that (a) you made a conversion of $20,000 from a traditional IRA on May 20, 2014, and (b) you recharacterized the entire amount, which was then valued at $19,000, back to a traditional IRA on April 7, 2015.

4. You rolled over an amount from a qualified retirement plan to a Roth IRA in 2014 and later recharacterized all or part of the amount in a trustee-to-trustee transfer to a traditional IRA. Do not report the rollover (whether or not you recharacterized all or part of it) or the recharacterization on Form 8606. Attach a statement to your return explaining the recharacterization and include the amount of the original rollover on Form 1040, line 16a; Form 1040A, line 12a; or Form 1040NR, line 17a. If the recharacterization occurred in 2014, also include the amount transferred from the Roth IRA on Form 1040, line 15a; Form 1040A, line 11a; or Form 1040NR, line 16a. If the recharacterization occurred in 2015, report the amount transferred from the Roth IRA only in the attached statement, and not on your 2014 or 2015 tax return (a 2015 Form 1099-R should be sent to you by January 31, 2016, stating that you made a recharacterization of an amount in the prior year).

Example. You are single and you rolled over $50,000 from your 401(k) plan to a new Roth IRA on July 20, 2014. On March 25, 2015, you decide to recharacterize the rollover. The value of the Roth IRA on that date is $49,000. You recharacterize the rollover by transferring that entire amount to a traditional IRA in a trustee-to-trustee transfer. You report $50,000 on Form 1040, line 16a. You do not include the $49,000 on line 15a because the transfer to the traditional IRA did not occur in 2014 (you also do not report that amount on your 2015 return because the recharacterization does not apply to the 2015 tax year). You do not file Form 8606. You attach a statement to Form 1040 explaining that (a) you made a rollover of $50,000 from a 401(k) plan to a Roth IRA on July 20, 2014, and (b) you recharacterized the entire amount, which was then valued at $49,000, to a traditional IRA on March 25, 2015.

Return of IRA Contributions

If, in 2014 or 2015, you made traditional IRA contributions or Roth IRA contributions for 2014 and you had those contributions returned to you with any related earnings (or minus any loss) by the due date (including extensions) of your 2014 tax return, the returned contributions are treated as if they were never contributed. Do not report the contribution or distribution on Form 8606 or take a deduction for the contribution. However, you must include the amount of the distribution of the returned contributions you made in 2014 and any related earnings on your 2014 Form 1040, line 15a; Form 1040A, line 11a; or Form 1040NR, line 16a. Also include the related earnings on your 2014 Form 1040, line 15b; Form 1040A, line 11b; or Form 1040NR, line 16b. Attach a statement explaining the distribution. You cannot deduct any loss that occurred (see Pub. 590-B for an exception if you withdrew the entire amount in all your traditional or Roth IRAs). Also, if you were under age 59½ at the time of a distribution with related earnings, you generally are subject to the additional 10% tax on early distributions (see Form 5329, Additional Taxes on Qualified Plans (Including IRAs) and Other Tax-Favored Accounts).

If you timely filed your 2014 tax return without withdrawing a contribution that you made in 2014, you can still have the contribution returned to you within 6 months of the due date of your 2014 tax return, excluding extensions. If you do, file an amended return with "Filed pursuant to section 301.9100-2" written at the top. Report any related earnings on the amended return and include an explanation of the withdrawn contribution. Make any other necessary changes on the amended return (for example, if you reported the contributions as excess contributions on your original return, include an amended Form 5329 reflecting that the withdrawn contributions are no longer treated as having been contributed).

In most cases, the related earnings that you must withdraw are figured by your IRA trustee or custodian. If you need to figure the related earnings on IRA contributions that were returned to you, see *Contributions Returned Before Due Date of Return* in chapter 1 of Pub. 590-A. If you made a contribution or distribution while the IRA held the returned contribution, see Pub. 590-A.

If you made a contribution for 2013 and you had it returned to you in 2014 as described above, do not report the distribution on your 2014 tax return. Instead, report it on your 2013 original or amended return in the manner described above.

Example. On May 28, 2014, you contributed $4,000 to your traditional IRA. The value of the IRA was $18,000 prior to the contribution. On December 29, 2014, when you are age 57 and the value of the IRA is $23,600, you realize you cannot make the entire contribution because your taxable compensation for the year will be only $3,000. You decide to have $1,000 of the contribution returned to you and withdraw $1,073 from your IRA ($1,000 contribution plus $73 earnings). You did not make any other withdrawals or contributions. You do not file Form 8606. You deduct the $3,000 remaining contribution on Form 1040. You include $1,073 on Form 1040, line 15a, and $73 on line 15b. You attach a statement to your tax return explaining the distribution. Because you properly removed the excess contribution with the related earnings by the due date of your tax return, you are not subject to the additional 6% tax on excess contributions, reported on Form 5329. However, because you were under age 59½ at the time of the distribution, the $73 of earnings is subject to the additional 10% tax on early distributions. You include $7.30 on Form 1040, line 59.

Return of Excess Traditional IRA Contributions

The return (distribution) in 2014 of excess traditional IRA contributions for years prior to 2014 is not taxable if all three of the following apply.

1. The distribution was made after the due date, including extensions, of your tax return for the year for which the contribution was made (if the distribution was made earlier, see *Return of IRA Contributions* above).

2. No deduction was allowable (without regard to the modified AGI limitation) or taken for the excess contributions.

3. The total contributions (excluding rollovers) to your traditional and SEP IRAs for the year for which the excess contributions were made did not exceed the amounts shown in the following table.

Year(s)	Contribution limit	Contribution limit if age 50 or older at the end of the year
2013	$5,500	$6,500
2008 through 2012	$5,000	$6,000
2006 or 2007	$4,000	$5,000
2005	$4,000	$4,500
2002 through 2004	$3,000	$3,500
1997 through 2001	$2,000	—
before 1997	$2,250	—

If the excess contribution to your traditional IRA for the year included a rollover and the excess occurred because the information the plan was required to give you was incorrect, increase the contribution limit amount for the year shown in the table above by the amount of the excess that is due to the incorrect information.

If the total contributions for the year included employer contributions to a SEP IRA, increase the contribution limit amount for the year shown in the table above by the smaller of the amount of the employer contributions or:

2013	$51,000
2012	$50,000
2009, 2010, or 2011	$49,000
2008	$46,000
2007	$45,000
2006	$44,000
2005	$42,000
2004	$41,000
2002 or 2003	$40,000
2001	$35,000
before 2001	$30,000

Include the total amount distributed on Form 1040, line 15a; Form 1040A, line 11a; or Form 1040NR, line 16a; and attach a statement to your return explaining the distribution. See *Example*, later.

If you meet these conditions and are otherwise required to file Form 8606:
• Do not take into account the amount of the withdrawn contributions in figuring line 2 (for 2014 or for any later year), and
• Do not include the amount of the withdrawn contributions on line 7.

Example. You are single, you retired in 2011, and you had no taxable compensation after 2011. However, you made traditional IRA contributions (that you did not deduct) of $3,000 in 2012 and $4,000 in 2013. In November 2014, a tax practitioner informed you that you had made excess contributions for those years because you had no taxable compensation. You withdrew the $7,000 and filed amended returns for 2012 and 2013 reflecting the additional 6% tax on excess contributions on Form 5329. You include the $7,000 distribution on your 2014 Form 1040, line 15a, enter -0- on line 15b, and attach a statement to your return explaining the distribution, including the fact that you filed amended returns for 2012 and 2013 and paid the additional 6% tax on the excess contributions for those years. The statement indicates that the distribution is not taxable because (a) it was made after the due dates of your 2012 and 2013 tax returns, including extensions, (b) your total IRA contributions for 2012 did not exceed $5,000 ($6,000 if age 50 or older at the end of 2012) and your total IRA contributions for 2013 did not exceed $5,500 ($6,500 if age 50 or older at the end of 2013), and (c) you did not take a deduction for the contributions, and no deduction was allowable because you did not have any taxable compensation for those years. The statement also indicates that the distribution reduced your excess contributions to -0-, as reflected on your 2014 Form 5329. Do not file Form 8606 for 2014. If you are required to file Form 8606 in a year after 2014, do not include the $7,000 you withdrew in 2014 on line 2.

Amending Form 8606

Generally, after you file your return, you can change a nondeductible contribution to a traditional IRA to a deductible contribution or vice versa if you make the change within the time limit for filing Form 1040X, Amended U.S. Individual Income Tax Return (see *When To File* in the Form 1040X Instructions). You also may be able to make a recharacterization (discussed earlier). If necessary, complete a new

Form 8606 showing the revised information and file it with Form 1040X.

Penalty for Not Filing

If you are required to file Form 8606 to report a nondeductible contribution to a traditional IRA for 2014, but do not do so, you must pay a $50 penalty, unless you can show reasonable cause.

Overstatement Penalty

If you overstate your nondeductible contributions, you must pay a $100 penalty, unless you can show reasonable cause.

What Records Must I Keep?

To verify the nontaxable part of distributions from your IRAs, including Roth IRAs, keep a copy of the following forms and records until all distributions are made.
• Page 1 of Forms 1040 (or Forms 1040A, 1040NR, or 1040-T) filed for each year you made a nondeductible contribution to a traditional IRA.
• Forms 8606 and any supporting statements, attachments, and worksheets for all applicable years.
• Forms 5498, IRA Contribution Information, or similar statements you received each year showing contributions you made to a traditional IRA or Roth IRA.
• Forms 5498 or similar statements you received showing the value of your traditional IRAs for each year you received a distribution.
• Forms 1099-R or W-2P you received for each year you received a distribution.

Note. Forms 1040-T and W-2P are forms that were used in prior years.

Specific Instructions

Name and social security number (SSN). If you file a joint return, enter only the name and SSN of the spouse whose information is being reported on Form 8606. If both you and your spouse are required to file Form 8606, file a separate Form 8606 for each of you.

Part I—Nondeductible Contributions to Traditional IRAs and Distributions From Traditional, SEP, and SIMPLE IRAs

Line 1

If you used the IRA Deduction Worksheet in the Form 1040, 1040NR, or 1040A instructions, subtract line 12 (line 10 for Form 1040A) of the worksheet (or the amount you chose to deduct on Form 1040 or Form 1040NR, line 32, or Form 1040A, line 17, if less) from the smaller of line 10 or line 11 (line 8 or line 9 for Form 1040A) of the worksheet. Enter the result on line 1 of Form 8606. You cannot deduct the amount included on line 1.

If you used the worksheet Figuring Your Reduced IRA Deduction for 2014 in Pub. 590-A, enter on line 1 of Form 8606 any nondeductible contributions from the appropriate lines of that worksheet.

If you did not have any deductible contributions, you can make nondeductible contributions up to your contribution limit (see *Overall Contribution Limit for Traditional and Roth IRAs*, earlier). Enter on line 1 of Form 8606 your nondeductible contributions.

Include on line 1 any repayment of a qualified reservist distribution.

Do not include on line 1 contributions that you had returned to you with the related earnings (or less any loss). See *Return of IRA Contributions*, earlier.

Line 2

Generally, if this is the first year you are required to file Form 8606, enter -0-. Otherwise, use the Total Basis Chart, later, to find the amount to enter on line 2.

However, you may need to enter an amount that is more than -0- (even if this is the first year you are required to file Form 8606) or increase or decrease the amount from the chart if your basis changed because of any of the following.
• You had a return of excess traditional IRA contributions (see *Return of Excess Traditional IRA Contributions*, earlier).
• Incident to divorce, you transferred or received part or all of a traditional IRA (see the last bulleted item under *Line 7*, later).
• You rolled over any nontaxable portion of your qualified retirement plan

Total Basis Chart

IF the last Form 8606 you filed was for . . .	THEN enter on line 2 . . .
A year after 2000 and before 2014	The amount from line 14 of that Form 8606
A year after 1992 and before 2001	The amount from line 12 of that Form 8606
A year after 1988 and before 1993	The amount from line 14 of that Form 8606
1988	The total of the amounts on lines 7 and 16 of that Form 8606
1987	The total of the amounts on lines 4 and 13 of that Form 8606

to a traditional or SEP IRA that was not previously reported on Form 8606, line 2. Include the nontaxable portion on line 2.

Line 4

If you made contributions to traditional IRAs for 2014 in 2014 and 2015 and you have both deductible and nondeductible contributions, you can choose to treat the contributions made in 2014 first as nondeductible contributions and then as deductible contributions, or vice versa.

Example. You made contributions for 2014 of $2,000 in May 2014 and $2,000 in January 2015, of which $3,000 are deductible and $1,000 are nondeductible. You choose $1,000 of your contribution in 2014 to be nondeductible. You enter the $1,000 on line 1, but not line 4, and it becomes part of your basis for 2014.

Although the contributions to traditional IRAs for 2014 that you made from January 1, 2015, through April 15, 2015, can be treated as nondeductible, they are not included in figuring the nontaxable part of any distributions you received in 2014.

Line 6

Enter the total value of all your traditional, SEP, and SIMPLE IRAs as of December 31, 2014, plus any outstanding rollovers. A statement should be sent to you by January 31, 2015, showing the value of each IRA on December 31, 2014. However, if you recharacterized any amounts originally contributed, converted, or rolled over from a qualified plan in 2014, enter on line 6 the total value, taking into account all recharacterizations of those amounts, including recharacterizations made after December 31, 2014.

For purposes of line 6, a rollover is a tax-free distribution from one traditional, SEP, or SIMPLE IRA that is contributed to another traditional, SEP, or SIMPLE

IRA. The rollover must be completed within 60 days after receiving the distribution from the first IRA. An outstanding rollover is generally the amount of any distribution received in 2014 after November 1, 2014, that was rolled over in 2015, but within the 60-day rollover period.

The IRS may waive the 60-day requirement if failing to waive it would be against equity or good conscience, such as situations where a casualty, disaster, or other events beyond your reasonable control prevented you from meeting the 60-day requirement. Also, the 60-day period will be extended for certain frozen deposits. See *Can You Move Retirement Plan Assets?* in chapter 1 of Pub. 590-A for details.

Note. Do not include a rollover from a traditional, SEP, or SIMPLE IRA to a qualified retirement plan even if it was an outstanding rollover.

Line 7

 If you received a distribution in 2014 from a traditional, SEP, or SIMPLE IRA, and you also made contributions for 2014 to a traditional IRA that may not be fully deductible because of the income limits, you must make a special computation before completing the rest of this form. For details, including how to complete Form 8606, see Are Distributions Taxable? *in chapter 1 of Pub. 590-B.*

Do not include any of the following on line 7.
- Distributions that you converted to a Roth IRA.
- Recharacterizations of traditional IRA contributions to Roth IRA contributions.
- Distributions you rolled over to another traditional, SEP, or SIMPLE IRA (whether or not the distribution is an outstanding rollover included on line 6).
- Distributions you rolled over to a qualified retirement plan.

- A one-time distribution to fund an HSA. For details, see Pub. 969, Health Savings Accounts and Other Tax-Favored Health Plans.
- Distributions that are treated as a return of contributions under *Return of IRA Contributions*, earlier.
- Qualified charitable distributions (QCDs). For details, see *Are Distributions Taxable?* in chapter 1 of Pub. 590-B.
- Distributions that are treated as a return of excess contributions under *Return of Excess Traditional IRA Contributions*, earlier.
- Distributions that are incident to divorce. The transfer of part or all of your traditional, SEP, or SIMPLE IRA to your spouse under a divorce or separation agreement is not taxable to you or your spouse. If this transfer results in a change in the basis of the traditional IRA of either spouse, both spouses must file Form 8606 and show the increase or decrease in the amount of basis on line 2. Attach a statement explaining this adjustment. Include in the statement the character of the amounts in the traditional IRA, such as the amount attributable to nondeductible contributions. Also, include the name and social security number of the other spouse.

Line 8

If, in 2014, you converted any amounts from traditional, SEP, or SIMPLE IRAs to a Roth IRA, enter on line 8 the net amount you converted. To figure that amount, subtract from the total amount converted in 2014 any portion that you recharacterized back to traditional, SEP, or SIMPLE IRAs in 2014 or 2015 (see *Recharacterizations*, earlier). Do not take into account related earnings that were transferred with the recharacterized amount or any loss that occurred while the amount was in the Roth IRA. See item (3) under *Reporting recharacterizations*, earlier, for details.

Line 15

If you were under age 59½ at the time you received distributions from your traditional, SEP, or SIMPLE IRA, there generally is an additional 10% tax on the portion of the distribution that is included in income (25% for a distribution from a SIMPLE IRA during the first 2 years of your participation in the plan). See the instructions for Form 1040, line 59, or the instructions for Form 1040NR, line 57.

Part II—2014 Conversions From Traditional, SEP, or SIMPLE IRAs to Roth IRAs

Complete Part II if you converted part or all of your traditional, SEP, or SIMPLE IRAs to a Roth IRA in 2014, excluding any portion you recharacterized. See item (3) under *Reporting recharacterizations*, earlier, for details.

Limit on number of conversions. If you converted an amount from a traditional, SEP, or SIMPLE IRA to a Roth IRA in 2014 and then recharacterized the amount back to a traditional, SEP, or SIMPLE IRA, you cannot reconvert that amount until the later of January 1, 2015, or 30 days after the recharacterization. See *Can You Move Retirement Plan Assets?* in chapter 1 of Pub. 590-A for details.

Line 16

If you did not complete line 8, see the instructions for that line. Then, enter on line 16 the amount you would have entered on line 8 had you completed it.

Line 17

If you did not complete line 11, enter on line 17 the amount from line 2 (or the amount you would have entered on line 2 if you had completed that line) plus any contributions included on line 1 that you made before the conversion.

Line 18

If your entry on line 18 is zero or less, do not include the result on Form 1040, line 15b; Form 1040A, line 11b; or Form 1040NR, line 16b. Include the full amount of the distribution on Form 1040, line 15a; Form 1040A, line 11a; or Form 1040NR, line 16a.

Part III—Distributions From Roth IRAs

Complete Part III to figure the taxable part, if any, of your 2014 Roth IRA distributions.

Line 19

Do not include on line 19 any of the following.
- Distributions that you rolled over, including distributions made in 2014 and rolled over after December 31, 2014 (outstanding rollovers).
- Recharacterizations.
- Distributions that are a return of contributions under *Return of IRA Contributions*, earlier.
- Distributions made on or after age 59½ if you made a contribution (including a conversion) for any year from 1998 through 2009.

- A one-time distribution to fund an HSA. For details, see Pub. 969.
- Qualified charitable distributions (QCDs). For details, see *Are Distributions Taxable?* in chapter 1 of Pub. 590-B.
- Distributions made upon death or due to disability if a contribution was made (including a conversion) for any year from 1998 through 2009.
- Distributions that are incident to divorce. The transfer of part or all of your Roth IRA to your spouse under a divorce or separation agreement is not taxable to you or your spouse.

If, after considering the items above, you do not have an amount to enter on line 19, do not complete Part III; your Roth IRA distribution(s) is not taxable. Instead, include your total Roth IRA distribution(s) on Form 1040, line 15a; Form 1040A, line 11a; or Form 1040NR, line 16a.

Line 20

If you had a qualified first-time homebuyer distribution from your Roth IRA and you made a contribution (including a conversion) to a Roth IRA for any year from 1998 through 2009, enter the amount of your qualified expenses on line 20, but do not enter more than $10,000. For details, see *Are Distributions Taxable?* in chapter 2 of Pub. 590-B.

Line 22

Figure the amount to enter on line 22 as follows.
- If you did not take a Roth IRA distribution before 2014 (other than an amount rolled over or recharacterized or a returned contribution), enter on line 22 the total of all your regular contributions to Roth IRAs for 1998 through 2014 (excluding rollovers from other Roth IRAs and any contributions that you had returned to you), adjusted for any recharacterizations.
- If you did take such a distribution before 2014, see the Basis in Regular Roth IRA Contributions Worksheet—Line 22, later, to figure the amount to enter.
- Increase the amount on line 22 by any amount rolled in from a designated Roth account that is treated as investment in the contract.
- Increase or decrease the amount on line 22 by any basis in regular contributions received or transferred incident to divorce. Also attach a statement similar to the one explained in the last bulleted item under *Line 7*, earlier.

- Increase the amount on line 22 by the amounts received as a military gratuity or SGLI payment that was rolled over to your Roth IRA.
- Increase the amount on line 22 by any amount received as qualified settlement income in connection with the Exxon Valdez litigation and rolled over to your Roth IRA.
- Increase the amount on line 22 by any "airline payments" you received as a result of your employment with an airline that you rolled over to your Roth IRA. However, do not include the amounts attributable to airline payments that you transferred from a Roth IRA to a traditional IRA because of the FAA Modernization and Reform Act of 2012.

Line 23

Generally, there is an additional 10% tax on 2014 distributions from a Roth IRA that are shown on line 23. The additional tax is figured on Form 5329, Part I. See the instructions for Form 5329, line 1, for details and exceptions.

Line 24

Figure the amount to enter on line 24 as follows.
- If you have never made a Roth IRA conversion or rolled over an amount from a qualified retirement plan to a Roth IRA, enter -0- on line 24.
- If you took a Roth IRA distribution (other than an amount rolled over or recharacterized or a returned contribution) before 2014 in excess of your basis in regular Roth IRA contributions, see the Basis in Roth IRA Conversions and Rollovers From Qualified Retirement Plans to Roth IRAs—Line 24 chart, later, to figure the amount to enter on line 24.
- If you did not take such a distribution before 2014, enter on line 24 the total of all your conversions to Roth IRAs (other than amounts recharacterized). These amounts are shown on line 14c of your 1998, 1999, and 2000 Forms 8606 and line 16 of your 2001 through 2014 Forms 8606. Also include on line 24 any amounts rolled over from a qualified retirement plan to a Roth IRA for 2008, 2009, and 2011 to 2014 reported on your Form 1040, Form 1040A, or Form 1040NR, and line 21 of your 2010 Form 8606.
- Increase or decrease the amount on line 24 by any basis in conversions to Roth IRAs and amounts rolled over from a qualified retirement plan to a Roth IRA received or transferred incident to divorce. Also attach a statement similar to the one explained in the last bulleted item under *Line 7*, earlier.

Instructions for Form 8606 (2014)

Privacy Act and Paperwork Reduction Act Notice. We ask for the information on this form to carry out the Internal Revenue laws of the United States. We need this information to ensure that you are complying with these laws and to allow us to figure and collect the right amount of tax. You are required to give us this information if you made certain contributions or received certain distributions from qualified plans, including IRAs and other tax-favored accounts. Our legal right to ask for the information requested on this form is sections 6001, 6011, 6012(a), and 6109 and their regulations. If you do not provide this information, or you provide incomplete or false information, you may be subject to penalties.

You are not required to provide the information requested on a form that is subject to the Paperwork Reduction Act unless the form displays a valid OMB control number. Books or records relating to a form or its instructions must be retained as long as their contents may become material in the administration of any Internal Revenue law. Generally, tax returns and return information are confidential, as required by section 6103. However, we may give the information to the Department of Justice for civil and criminal litigation, and to cities, states, the District of Columbia, and U.S. commonwealths and possessions to carry out their tax laws. We may also disclose this information to other countries under a tax treaty, to federal and state agencies to enforce federal nontax criminal laws, or to federal law enforcement and intelligence agencies to combat terrorism.

The average time and expenses required to complete and file this form will vary depending on individual circumstances. For the estimated averages, see the instructions for your income tax return.

If you have suggestions for making this form simpler, we would be happy to hear from you. See the instructions for your income tax return.

Basis in Regular Roth IRA Contributions
Worksheet—Line 22

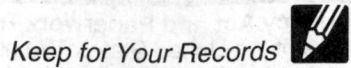

Keep for Your Records

Before you begin: You will need your Form 8606 for the most recent year prior to 2014 where you received a distribution.

Note. Do not complete this worksheet if you never received a distribution from your Roth IRAs prior to 2014.

1. Enter the most recent year prior to 2014 you reported distributions on Form 8606 (for example, 2 0 1 2) .... **1.** _ _ _ _

2. Enter your basis in Roth IRA contributions reported on Form 8606 for the year entered on line 1 (see Table 1 below) .... **2.** _____

3. Enter your Roth IRA distributions* reported on Form 8606 for the year entered on line 1 (see Table 2 below) .... **3.** _____

4. Subtract line 3 from line 2. Enter zero if the resulting amount is zero or less .... **4.** _____

5. Enter the total of all your regular contributions** to Roth IRAs after the year entered on line 1 .... **5.** _____

6. Add lines 4 and 5. Enter this amount on your 2014 Form 8606, line 22 .... **6.** _____

*Excluding rollovers, recharacterizations, and contributions that you had returned to you.

**Excluding rollovers, conversions, Roth IRA contributions that were recharacterized, and any contributions that you had returned to you.

Table 1 for Line 2 above

IF the year entered on Line 1 was	THEN enter on Line 2 the amount from the following line
2013, 2012, 2011, 2009, 2008, 2007, 2006, 2005, and 2004	Form 8606, Line 22
2010	Form 8606, Line 29
2003, 2002, 2001	Form 8606, Line 20
2000 and 1999	Form 8606, Line 18d
1998	Form 8606, Line 19c

Table 2 for Line 3 above

IF the year entered on Line 1 was	THEN enter on Line 3 the amount from the following line
2013, 2012, 2011, 2009, 2008, 2007, 2006, 2005, 2004, 2003, 2002, and 2001	Form 8606, line 19
2010	Form 8606, line 26
2000 and 1999	Form 8606, line 17
1998	Form 8606, line 18

Instructions for Form 8606 (2014)

Basis in Roth IRA Conversions and Rollovers From Qualified Retirement Plans to Roth IRAs—Line 24

IF the most recent year prior to 2014 in which you had a distribution[1] in excess of your basis in contributions was . . .	THEN enter on Form 8606, line 24, this amount	PLUS the sum of the amounts on the following lines . . . .
2013 (your 2013 Form 8606, line 22, was less than line 19 of that Form 8606)	The excess, if any, of your 2013 Form 8606, line 24, over line 23[2] of that Form 8606.	Line 16 of your 2014 Form 8606 and certain rollovers[3] reported on your 2014 tax return.
2012 (your 2012 Form 8606, line 22, was less than line 19 of that Form 8606)	The excess, if any, of your 2012 Form 8606, line 24, over line 23[2] of that Form 8606.	Line 16 of your 2013 and 2014 Forms 8606 and certain rollovers[3] reported on your 2013 and 2014 tax returns.
2011 (your 2011 Form 8606, line 22, was less than line 19 of that Form 8606)	The excess, if any, of your 2011 Form 8606, line 24, over line 23[2] of that Form 8606.	Line 16 of your 2012 through 2014 Forms 8606 and certain rollovers[3] reported on your 2012 through 2014 tax returns.
2010 (your 2010 Form 8606, line 29, was less than line 26 of that Form 8606)	The excess, if any, of your 2010 Form 8606, line 31, over line 30 of that Form 8606 (refigure line 30 without taking into account any amount entered on Form 8606, line 27).	Line 16 of your 2011 through 2014 Forms 8606 and certain rollovers[3] reported on your 2011 through 2014 tax returns, **OR** Line 16 of your 2011 through 2014 Forms 8606; lines 16 and 21 of your 2010 Form 8606[4] if you did not check the boxes on lines 19 or 24 of your 2010 Form 8606; and certain rollovers[3] reported on your 2011 through 2014 tax returns.
2009 (your 2009 Form 8606, line 22, was less than line 19 of that Form 8606)	The excess, if any, of your 2009 Form 8606, line 24, over line 23[2] of that Form 8606.	Line 16 of your 2010 through 2014 Forms 8606; line 21 of your 2010 Form 8606[4]; and certain rollovers[3] reported on your 2011 through 2014 tax returns.
2008 (your 2008 Form 8606, line 22, was less than line 19 of that Form 8606)	The excess, if any, of your 2008 Form 8606, line 24, over line 23[2] of that Form 8606.	Line 16 of your 2009 through 2014 Forms 8606; line 21 of your 2010 Form 8606[4]; and certain rollovers[3] reported on your 2009 and 2011 through 2014 tax returns.
2007 (your 2007 Form 8606, line 22, was less than line 19 of that Form 8606)	The excess, if any, of your 2007 Form 8606, line 24, over line 23[2] of that Form 8606.	Line 16 of your 2008 through 2014 Forms 8606; line 21 of your 2010 Form 8606[4]; and certain rollovers[3] reported on your 2008, 2009, and 2011 through 2014 tax returns.
2006 (your 2006 Form 8606, line 22, was less than line 19 of that Form 8606)	The excess, if any, of your 2006 Form 8606, line 24, over line 23[2] of that Form 8606.	Line 16 of your 2007 through 2014 Forms 8606; line 21 of your 2010 Form 8606[4]; and certain rollovers[3] reported on your 2008, 2009, and 2011 through 2014 tax returns.
2005 (your 2005 Form 8606, line 22, was less than line 19 of that Form 8606)	The excess, if any, of your 2005 Form 8606, line 24, over line 23[2] of that Form 8606.	Line 16 of your 2006 through 2014 Forms 8606; line 21 of your 2010 Form 8606[4]; and certain rollovers[3] reported on your 2008, 2009, and 2011 through 2014 tax returns.

1. Excluding rollovers, recharacterizations, and contributions that you had returned to you.

2. Refigure line 23 without taking into account any amount entered on Form 8606, line 20.

3. Amounts rolled over from qualified retirement plans to Roth IRAs from your Form 1040, line 16a; Form 1040A, line 12a; or Form 1040NR, line 17a.

4. Do not include any in-plan Roth rollovers entered on line 21.

Continued on next page.

Basis in Roth IRA Conversions and Rollovers From Qualified Retirement Plans to Roth IRAs—Line 24 (*continued*)

IF the most recent year prior to 2014 in which you had a distribution[1] in excess of your basis in contributions was . . .	THEN enter on Form 8606, line 24, this amount	PLUS the sum of the amounts on the following lines . . . .
2004 (your 2004 Form 8606, line 22, was less than line 19 of that Form 8606)	The excess, if any, of your 2004 Form 8606, line 24, over line 23[2] of that Form 8606.	Line 16 of your 2005 through 2014 Forms 8606; line 21 of your 2010 Form 8606[4]; and certain rollovers[3] reported on your 2008, 2009, and 2011 through 2014 tax returns.
2003 (you had an amount on your 2003 Form 8606, line 21)	The excess, if any, of your 2003 Form 8606, line 22, over line 21 of that Form 8606.	Line 16 of your 2004 through 2014 Forms 8606; line 21 of your 2010 Form 8606[4]; and certain rollovers[3] reported on your 2008, 2009, and 2011 through 2014 tax returns.
2002 (you had an amount on your 2002 Form 8606, line 21)	The excess, if any, of your 2002 Form 8606, line 22, over line 21 of that Form 8606.	Line 16 of your 2003 through 2014 Forms 8606; line 21 of your 2010 Form 8606[4]; and certain rollovers[3] reported on your 2008, 2009, and 2011 through 2014 tax returns.
2001 (you had an amount on your 2001 Form 8606, line 21)	The excess, if any, of your 2001 Form 8606, line 22, over line 21 of that Form 8606.	Line 16 of your 2002 through 2014 Forms 8606; line 21 of your 2010 Form 8606[4]; and certain rollovers[3] reported on your 2008, 2009, and 2011 through 2014 tax returns.
2000 (you had an amount on your 2000 Form 8606, line 19)	The excess, if any, of your 2000 Form 8606, line 25, over line 19 of that Form 8606.	Line 16 of your 2001 through 2014 Forms 8606; line 21 of your 2010 Form 8606[4]; and certain rollovers[3] reported on your 2008, 2009, and 2011 through 2014 tax returns.
1999 (you had an amount on your 1999 Form 8606, line 19)	The excess, if any, of your 1999 Form 8606, line 25, over line 19 of that Form 8606.	Line 14c of your 2000 Form 8606; Line 16 of your 2001 through 2014 Forms 8606; line 21 of your 2010 Form 8606[4]; and certain rollovers[3] reported on your 2008, 2009, and 2011 through 2014 tax returns.
1998 (you had an amount on your 1998 Form 8606, line 20)	The excess, if any, of your 1998 Form 8606, line 14c, over line 20 of that Form 8606.	Line 14c of your 1999 and 2000 Forms 8606; line 16 of your 2001 through 2014 Forms 8606; line 21 of your 2010 Form 8606[4]; and certain rollovers[3] reported on·your 2008, 2009, and 2011 through 2014 tax returns.
Did not have such a distribution in excess of your basis in contributions	The amount from your 2014 Form 8606, line 16	Line 14c of your 1998 through 2000 Forms 8606; line 16 of your 2001 through 2013 Forms 8606; line 21 of your 2010 Form 8606[4]; and certain rollovers[3] reported on your 2008, 2009, and 2011 through 2014 tax returns.

1. Excluding rollovers, recharacterizations, and contributions that you had returned to you.

2. Refigure line 23 without taking into account any amount entered on Form 8606, line 20.

3. Amounts rolled over from qualified retirement plans to Roth IRAs from your Form 1040, line 16a; Form 1040A, line 12a; or Form 1040NR, line 17a.

4. Do not include any in-plan Roth rollovers entered on line 21.

Form **8615**

Department of the Treasury
Internal Revenue Service (99)

Tax for Certain Children Who Have Unearned Income

► Attach only to the child's Form 1040, Form 1040A, or Form 1040NR.
► Information about Form 8615 and its separate instructions is at *www.irs.gov/form8615*.

OMB No. 1545-0074

2014

Attachment Sequence No. **33**

Child's name shown on return

Child's social security number

Before you begin: If the child, the parent, or any of the parent's other children for whom Form 8615 must be filed must use the Schedule D Tax Worksheet or has income from farming or fishing, see **Pub. 929**, Tax Rules for Children and Dependents. It explains how to figure the child's tax using the **Schedule D Tax Worksheet** or **Schedule J** (Form 1040).

A Parent's name (first, initial, and last). **Caution:** *See instructions before completing.*

B Parent's social security number

C Parent's filing status (check one):

☐ Single   ☐ Married filing jointly   ☐ Married filing separately   ☐ Head of household   ☐ Qualifying widow(er)

Part I — Child's Net Unearned Income

1	Enter the child's unearned income (see instructions)	1	
2	If the child **did not** itemize deductions on **Schedule A** (Form 1040 or Form 1040NR), enter $2,000. Otherwise, see instructions	2	
3	Subtract line 2 from line 1. If zero or less, **stop;** do not complete the rest of this form but **do** attach it to the child's return	3	
4	Enter the child's **taxable income** from Form 1040, line 43; Form 1040A, line 27; or Form 1040NR, line 41. If the child files Form 2555 or 2555-EZ, see the instructions	4	
5	Enter the **smaller** of line 3 or line 4. If zero, **stop;** do not complete the rest of this form but **do** attach it to the child's return	5	

Part II — Tentative Tax Based on the Tax Rate of the Parent

6	Enter the parent's **taxable income** from Form 1040, line 43; Form 1040A, line 27; Form 1040EZ, line 6; Form 1040NR, line 41; or Form 1040NR-EZ, line 14. If zero or less, enter -0-. If the parent files Form 2555 or 2555-EZ, see the instructions	6	
7	Enter the total, if any, from Forms 8615, line 5, of **all other** children of the parent named above. **Do not** include the amount from line 5 above	7	
8	Add lines 5, 6, and 7 (see instructions)	8	
9	Enter the tax on the amount on line 8 based on the **parent's** filing status above (see instructions). If the Qualified Dividends and Capital Gain Tax Worksheet, Schedule D Tax Worksheet, or Schedule J (Form 1040) is used to figure the tax, check here . . . . ► ☐	9	
10	Enter the parent's tax from Form 1040, line 44; Form 1040A, line 28, minus any alternative minimum tax; Form 1040EZ, line 10; Form 1040NR, line 42; or Form 1040NR-EZ, line 15. **Do not** include any tax from **Form 4972** or **8814** or any tax from recapture of an education credit. If the parent files Form 2555 or 2555-EZ, see the instructions. If the Qualified Dividends and Capital Gain Tax Worksheet, Schedule D Tax Worksheet, or Schedule J (Form 1040) was used to figure the tax, check here . . . . ► ☐	10	
11	Subtract line 10 from line 9 and enter the result. If line 7 is blank, also enter this amount on line 13 and go to **Part III**	11	
12a	Add lines 5 and 7 . . . . 12a		
b	Divide line 5 by line 12a. Enter the result as a decimal (rounded to at least three places) . . .	12b	× .
13	Multiply line 11 by line 12b	13	

Part III — Child's Tax—If lines 4 and 5 above are the same, enter -0- on line 15 and go to line 16.

14	Subtract line 5 from line 4 14		
15	Enter the tax on the amount on line 14 based on the **child's** filing status (see instructions). If the Qualified Dividends and Capital Gain Tax Worksheet, Schedule D Tax Worksheet, or Schedule J (Form 1040) is used to figure the tax, check here . . . . ► ☐	15	
16	Add lines 13 and 15	16	
17	Enter the tax on the amount on line 4 based on the **child's** filing status (see instructions). If the Qualified Dividends and Capital Gain Tax Worksheet, Schedule D Tax Worksheet, or Schedule J (Form 1040) is used to figure the tax, check here . . . . ► ☐	17	
18	Enter the **larger** of line 16 or line 17 here and on the **child's** Form 1040, line 44; Form 1040A, line 28; or Form 1040NR, line 42. If the child files Form 2555 or 2555-EZ, see the instructions . .	18	

2014

Instructions for Form 8615

Tax for Certain Children Who Have Unearned Income

Department of the Treasury
Internal Revenue Service

Future Developments

For the latest information about developments related to Form 8615 and its instructions, such as legislation enacted after they were published, go to *www.irs.gov/form8615*.

General Instructions

Purpose of Form

For children under age 18 and certain older children described below in *Who Must File*, unearned income over $2,000 is taxed at the parent's rate if the parent's rate is higher than the child's. If the child's unearned income is more than $2,000, use Form 8615 to figure the child's tax.

Unearned Income

For Form 8615, "unearned income" includes all taxable income other than earned income as defined later. Unearned income includes taxable interest, ordinary dividends, capital gains (including capital gain distributions), rents, royalties, etc. It also includes taxable social security benefits, pension and annuity income, taxable scholarship and fellowship grants not reported on Form W-2, unemployment compensation, alimony, and income (other than earned income) received as the beneficiary of a trust.

Who Must File

Form 8615 must be filed for any child who meets all of the following conditions.

1. The child had more than $2,000 of unearned income.

2. The child is required to file a tax return.

3. The child either:

a. Was under age 18 at the end of 2014,

b. Was age 18 at the end of 2014 and did not have earned income that was more than half of the child's support, or

c. Was a full-time student at least age 19 and under age 24 at the end of 2014 and did not have earned income that was more than half of the child's support.

(Earned income is defined later. Support is defined below.)

4. At least one of the child's parents was alive at the end of 2014.

5. The child does not file a joint return for 2014.

Support. Your child's support includes all amounts spent to provide the child with food, lodging, clothing, education, medical and dental care, recreation, transportation, and similar necessities. To figure your child's support, count support provided by you, your child, and others. However, a scholarship received by your child is not considered support if your child is a full-time student. For details, see Pub. 501, Exemptions, Standard Deduction, and Filing Information.

Certain January 1 birthdays. Use the following chart to determine whether certain children with January 1 birthdays meet condition 3 under *Who Must File*.

IF a child was born on...	THEN, at the end of 2014, the child is considered to be...
January 1, 1997	18*
January 1, 1996	19**
January 1, 1991	24***

*This child is not **under** age 18. The child meets condition 3 only if the child did not have earned income that was more than half of the child's support.

**This child meets condition 3 only if the child was a full-time student who did not have earned income that was more than half of the child's support.

***Do not use Form 8615 for this child.

 The parent may be able to elect to report the child's interest, ordinary dividends, and capital gain distributions on the parent's return. If the parent makes this election, the child will not have to file a return or Form 8615. However, the federal income tax on the child's income, including qualified dividends and capital gain distributions, may be higher if this election is made. For more details, see Form 8814, Parents' Election To Report Child's Interest and Dividends.

Additional Information

For more details, see Pub. 929, Tax Rules for Children and Dependents.

Incomplete Information for Parent or Other Children

If the parent's taxable income, filing status, or the net unearned income of the parent's other children is not known by the due date of the child's return, reasonable estimates can be used. Enter "Estimated" next to the appropriate line(s) of Form 8615. When the correct information is available, file Form 1040X, Amended U.S. Individual Income Tax Return.

Instead of using estimates, the child can get an automatic 6-month extension of time to file. For details, see Form 4868, Application for Automatic Extension of Time To File U.S. Individual Income Tax Return.

Amended Return

If the parent's income changes after the child's return is filed, the tax must be refigured using the adjusted amounts. The child's tax must also be refigured if there are changes to the net unearned income of other children for whom the parent is required to file a Form 8615. If the child's tax changes, file Form 1040X to correct the child's tax.

Alternative Minimum Tax

A child whose tax is figured on Form 8615 may owe the alternative minimum tax. For details, see Form 6251, Alternative Minimum Tax—Individuals, and its instructions.

Net Investment Income Tax

A child whose tax is figured on Form 8615 may be subject to the Net Investment Income Tax (NIIT). NIIT is a 3.8% tax on the lesser of net investment income or the excess of the child's modified adjusted gross income (MAGI) over the threshold amount. Use Form 8960, Net Investment Income Tax, to figure this tax. For more information on NIIT, go to *www.irs.gov* and enter "Net Investment Income Tax" in the search box.

Line Instructions

Lines A and B

If the child's parents were married to each other and filed a joint return, enter the name and social security number (SSN) of the parent who is listed first on the joint return.

If the parents were married but filed separate returns, enter the name and SSN of the parent who had the higher taxable income. If you do not know which parent had the higher taxable income, see Pub. 929.

If the parents were unmarried, treated as unmarried for federal income tax purposes, or separated by either a divorce or separate maintenance decree, enter the name and SSN of the parent with whom the child lived for most of the year (the custodial parent).

Exceptions. If the custodial parent remarried and filed a joint return with his or her new spouse, enter the name and SSN of the person listed first on the joint return, even if that person is not the child's parent. If the custodial parent and his or her new spouse filed separate returns, enter the name and SSN of the person with the higher taxable income, even if that person is not the child's parent.

If the parents were unmarried but lived together during the year with the child, enter the name and SSN of the parent who had the higher taxable income.

Line 1

If the child had no earned income (defined below), enter the child's adjusted gross income from Form 1040, line 38; Form 1040A, line 22; or Form 1040NR, line 37.

If the child had earned income, use the Child's Unearned Income Worksheet, later, to figure the amount to enter on line 1. But use Pub. 929 instead of the worksheet to figure the amount to enter on line 1 if the child:

- Files Form 2555 or 2555-EZ (relating to foreign earned income),
- Has a net loss from self-employment, or
- Claims a net operating loss deduction.

Earned income. Earned income includes wages, tips, and other payments received for personal services performed.

If the child is a sole proprietor or a partner in a trade or business in which both personal services and capital are material income-producing factors, earned income also includes a reasonable allowance for compensation for personal services, but not more than 30% of the child's share of the net profits from that trade or business (after subtracting the deduction for one-half of self-employment tax). However, the 30% limit does not apply if there are no net profits from the trade or business.

If capital is not an income-producing factor and the child's personal services produced the business income, all of the child's gross income from the trade or business is considered earned income. In that case, earned income is generally the total of the amounts reported on Form 1040, lines 7, 12, and 18; Form 1040A, line 7; or Form 1040NR, lines 8, 13, and 19.

Earned income also includes any taxable distribution from a qualified disability trust. A qualified disability trust is any nongrantor trust:

1. Described in 42 U.S.C. 1396p(c)(2)(B)(iv) and established solely for the benefit of an individual under 65 years of age who is disabled, and

2. All the beneficiaries of which are determined by the Commissioner of Social Security to have been disabled for some part of the tax year within the meaning of 42 U.S.C. 1382c(a)(3).

A trust will not fail to meet (2) above just because the trust's corpus may revert to a person who is not disabled after the trust ceases to have any disabled beneficiaries.

Child's Unearned Income Worksheet—Line 1
Keep for Your Records

1. Enter the amount from the child's Form 1040, line 22; Form 1040A, line 15; or Form 1040NR, line 23, whichever applies . . . . _____

2. Enter the child's **earned income** (defined earlier) plus the amount of any penalty on early withdrawal of savings from the child's Form 1040, line 30, or Form 1040NR, line 30, whichever applies . . . . _____

3. Subtract line 2 from line 1. Enter the result here and on Form 8615, line 1 . . . . _____

Line 2

If the child itemized deductions, enter the larger of:
- $2,000, or
- $1,000 plus the portion of the amount on Schedule A (Form 1040), line 29 (or Form 1040NR, Schedule A, line 15), that is directly connected with the production of the unearned income on Form 8615, line 1.

Line 4

If the child files Form 2555 or 2555-EZ (relating to foreign earned income), enter the amount from line 3 of the child's Foreign Earned Income Tax Worksheet (in the Form 1040 instructions), instead of the child's taxable income.

Line 6

If the parent filed a joint return, enter the taxable income shown on that return even if the parent's spouse is not the child's parent.

If the Foreign Earned Income Tax Worksheet (in the Form 1040 instructions) was used to figure the parent's tax, enter the amount from line 3 of that worksheet, instead of the parent's taxable income.

Line 8

Enter on this line the total of lines 5, 6, and 7. You must determine the amount of net capital gain and qualified dividends included on this line before completing line 9.

Net capital gain. Net capital gain is the smaller of the gain, if any, on Schedule D (Form 1040), line 15, or the gain, if any, on Schedule D, line 16. If Schedule D is not required, it is the amount on Form 1040, line 13; Form 1040A, line 10; or Form 1040NR, line 14.

Qualified dividends. Qualified dividends are those dividends reported on line 9b of Form 1040 or Form 1040A or line 10b of Form 1040NR.

Net capital gain and qualified dividends on line 8. If neither the child, nor the parent, nor any other child has net capital gain, the net capital gain on line 8 is zero. (The term "other child" means any other child whose Form 8615 uses the tax return information of the parent identified on Lines A and B of Form 8615.)

If neither the child, nor the parent, nor any other child has qualified dividends, the amount of qualified dividends on line 8 is zero.

If the child, parent, or any other child has net capital gain, figure the amount of net capital gain included on line 8 by adding together the net capital gain amounts included on lines 5, 6, and 7.

If the child, parent, or any other child has qualified dividends, figure the amount of qualified dividends included on line 8 by adding together the qualified dividend amounts included on lines 5, 6, and 7. Use the following discussions to find these amounts.

Net capital gain or qualified dividends on line 5. If the child has a net capital gain or qualified dividends, use the appropriate Line 5 Worksheet in these instructions to find the amount included on line 5. These worksheets are needed to adjust the child's net capital gain and qualified dividends by the appropriate allocated amount of the child's deductions.

Net capital gain or qualified dividends on line 6. If the parent has a net capital gain, its full amount is the net capital gain included on line 6. If the parent has qualified dividends, the full amount is the amount of qualified dividends included on line 6.

Net capital gain or qualified dividends on line 7. The net capital gain included on line 7 is the total of the amounts of net capital gain included on line 5 of the other children's Forms 8615. The qualified dividends included on line 7 is the total of the amounts of qualified dividends included on line 5 of the other children's Forms 8615. Find these amounts for each other child as explained under *Net capital gain or qualified dividends on line 5* discussed earlier. (Do not attach the other children's Forms 8615 to this child's return.)

2014 Line 5 Worksheet #1 *Keep for Your Records*

Use this worksheet only if line 2 of the child's Form 8615 is $2,000 and lines 3 and 5 are the same amount.

1.	Enter the child's qualified dividends	1. _____
2.	Enter the child's net capital gain	2. _____
3.	Enter the amount from the child's Form 8615, line 1	3. _____
4.	Divide line 1 by line 3. Enter the result as a decimal (rounded to at least three places). Do not enter more than 1.000	4. _____
5.	Divide line 2 by line 3. Enter the result as a decimal (rounded to at least three places). Do not enter more than 1.000	5. _____
6.	Multiply $2,000 by line 4	6. _____
7.	Multiply $2,000 by line 5	7. _____
8.	**Qualified dividends on Form 8615, line 5.** Subtract line 6 of this worksheet from line 1 (but do not enter less than zero or more than the amount on Form 8615, line 5)	8. _____
9.	**Net capital gain on Form 8615, line 5.** Subtract line 7 of this worksheet from line 2 (but do not enter less than zero or more than the excess of Form 8615, line 5, over line 8 of this worksheet)	9. _____

Use this worksheet only if line 2 of the child's Form 8615 is more than $2,000 and lines 3 and 5 of the child's Form 8615 are the same amount.

1.	Enter the child's qualified dividends	1. _____
2.	Enter the child's net capital gain	2. _____
3.	Add lines 1 and 2	3. _____
4.	Divide line 1 by line 3. Enter the result as a decimal (rounded to at least three places)	4. _____
5.	Enter the child's itemized deductions directly connected with the production of the child's qualified dividends or net capital gain	5. _____
6.	Multiply line 4 by line 5	6. _____
7.	Subtract line 6 from line 5	7. _____
8.	Subtract line 7 from line 2	8. _____
9.	Subtract line 6 from line 1	9. _____
10.	Enter the amount from the child's Form 8615, line 1	10. _____
11.	Divide line 1 by line 10. Enter the result as a decimal (rounded to at least three places). Do not enter more than 1.000	11. _____
12.	Divide line 2 by line 10. Enter the result as a decimal (rounded to at least three places). Do not enter more than 1.000 minus the amount on line 11	12. _____
13.	Multiply $1,000 by line 11	13. _____
14.	Multiply $1,000 by line 12	14. _____
15.	**Qualified dividends on Form 8615, line 5.** Subtract line 13 from line 9 (but do not enter less than zero or more than the amount on Form 8615, line 5)	15. _____
16.	**Net capital gain on Form 8615, line 5.** Subtract line 14 from line 8 (but do not enter less than zero or more than the excess of Form 8615, line 5, over line 15 of this worksheet)	16. _____

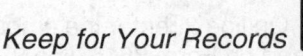
Use this worksheet only if the child's Form 8615, line 5, is less than line 3.

1.	Enter the child's qualified dividends	1. _____
2.	Enter the child's net capital gain	2. _____
3.	Add lines 1 and 2	3. _____
4.	Divide line 1 by line 3. Enter the result as a decimal (rounded to at least three places)	4. _____
5.	If the child itemized deductions, enter the child's itemized deductions directly connected with the production of the income on line 3	5. _____
6.	Multiply line 4 by line 5	6. _____
7.	Subtract line 6 from line 5	7. _____
8.	Subtract line 7 from line 2	8. _____
9.	Subtract line 6 from line 1	9. _____
10.	If the child can claim his or her own exemption, enter $3,950*. Otherwise, enter -0-	10. _____
11.	If the child itemized deductions, enter the child's itemized deductions not directly connected with the production of the income shown on line 3 of this worksheet. Otherwise, enter the child's standard deduction	11. _____
12.	Add lines 10 and 11	12. _____
13.	Enter the child's adjusted gross income (Form 1040, line 38; Form 1040A, line 22; or Form 1040NR, line 37)	13. _____
14.	Divide line 3 by line 13. Enter the result as a decimal (rounded to at least three places). Do not enter more than 1.000	14. _____
15.	Multiply line 12 by line 14	15. _____
16.	Multiply line 15 by line 4	16. _____
17.	Subtract line 16 from line 15	17. _____
18.	**Qualified dividends on Form 8615, line 5.** Subtract line 16 of this worksheet from line 9. Enter the result here (but do not enter less than zero or more than the amount on Form 8615, line 5)	18. _____
19.	**Net capital gain on Form 8615, line 5.** Subtract line 17 of this worksheet from line 8 (but do not enter less than zero or more than the excess of Form 8615, line 5, over line 18 of this worksheet)	19. _____

*If you enter more than $152,525 on line 13, see the Deduction for Exemptions Worksheet in the Form 1040, Form 1040A, or Form 1040NR instructions for the amount to enter on line 10.

Line 9

Figure the tax using the Tax Table, Tax Computation Worksheet, Qualified Dividends and Capital Gain Tax Worksheet, Schedule D Tax Worksheet, or Schedule J (Form 1040), whichever applies.

If line 8 includes any net capital gain or qualified dividends, use the Qualified Dividends and Capital Gain Tax Worksheet in the Form 1040, 1040A, or 1040NR instructions to figure the tax, unless you have to use the Schedule D Tax Worksheet or Schedule J (see below).

Schedule D Tax Worksheet. If the child, parent, or any other child has to file Schedule D and line 18 or 19 of any Schedule D is more than zero, use the Schedule D Tax Worksheet in the Instructions for Schedule D to figure the tax. See Pub. 929 for details on how to figure the line 9 tax using the Schedule D Tax Worksheet.

Schedule J (Form 1040). If any farming or fishing income (including certain amounts received in connection with the Exxon Valdez litigation) is included on line 8, the tax may be less if you use Schedule J. If Schedule J was used to figure the tax on the parent's return, see Pub. 929 for details on how to figure the tax.

Child files Form 2555 or 2555-EZ. If line 8 includes any net capital gain or qualified dividends and the child or any other child filing Form 8615 also files Form 2555 or 2555-EZ, see Pub. 929 for instructions on how to figure the line 9 tax.

Using the Qualified Dividends and Capital Gain Tax Worksheet for line 9 tax. If you use the Qualified Dividends and Capital Gain Tax Worksheet to figure the line 9 tax, complete that worksheet as follows.

1. On line 1, enter the amount from Form 8615, line 8.

2. On line 2, enter the amount of qualified dividends included on Form 8615, line 8. (See the instructions for line 8.)

3. On line 3, enter the amount of the net capital gain included on Form 8615, line 8. (See the instructions for line 8.)

4. Complete line 4 following the worksheet instructions.

5. If you are completing the worksheet in the Form 1040 instructions, enter on line 5 the total of the amounts, if any, on line 4g of all Forms 4952 filed by the child, parent, or any other child. Then complete line 6 following the worksheet instructions.

6. If the Foreign Earned Income Tax Worksheet was used to figure the parent's tax, go to step 7 below. Otherwise, skip steps 7, 8, and 9 of these instructions below, and go to step 10.

7. Determine whether there is a line 8 capital gain excess. To do this, subtract from line 1 of the worksheet the amount on line 2 of the parent's Foreign Earned Income Tax Worksheet. Subtract the result from line 6 of this Qualified Dividends and Capital Gain Tax Worksheet (line 4 of the worksheet in the Form 1040A or Form 1040NR instructions). If the result is more than zero, that amount is the line 8 capital gain excess. If the result is zero or less, there is no line 8 capital gain excess.

8. If there is no line 8 capital gain excess, skip step 9 below and go to step 10.

9. If there is a line 8 capital gain excess, complete a second Qualified Dividends and Capital Gain Tax Worksheet as instructed above and in step 10 below but in its entirety and with the following additional modifications.

a. Reduce the amount you would otherwise enter on line 3 (but not below zero) by the line 8 capital gain excess.

b. Reduce the amount you would otherwise enter on line 2 (but not below zero) by any of the line 8 capital gain excess not used in (a) earlier.

10. Complete lines 7 through 27 (lines 5 through 16 of the worksheet in the Form 1040A instructions or lines 5 through 25 in the Form 1040NR instructions) following the worksheet instructions. Use the parent's filing status to complete lines 8, 15, 24, and 26 (lines 6, 13, and 15 of the worksheet in the Form 1040A instructions or lines 6, 13, 22, and 24 of the worksheet in the Form 1040NR instructions).

Enter the amount from line 27 of the Qualified Dividends and Capital Gain Tax Worksheet (or line 16 of the worksheet in the Form 1040A instructions or line 25 of the worksheet in the Form 1040NR instructions) on Form 8615, line 9, and check the box on that line. Do not attach this worksheet to the child's return.

Line 10

If the parent filed a joint return, enter the tax shown on that return even if the parent's spouse is not the child's parent.

If the Foreign Earned Income Tax Worksheet (in the Form 1040 instructions) was used to figure the parent's

tax, enter the amount from line 4 of that worksheet, instead of the parent's tax from Form 1040, line 44.

Line 15

Figure the tax using the Tax Table, Tax Computation Worksheet, Qualified Dividends and Capital Gain Tax Worksheet, Schedule D Tax Worksheet, or Schedule J, whichever applies.

 If line 14 includes any net capital gain or qualified dividends, use the Qualified Dividends and Capital Gain Tax Worksheet to figure this tax. However, if the child has to file Schedule D and line 18 or line 19 of the child's Schedule D is more than zero, use the Schedule D Tax Worksheet to figure this tax instead. See Pub. 929 for details on how to figure the line 15 tax using the Schedule D Tax Worksheet.

Before using the Qualified Dividends and Capital Gain Tax Worksheet to figure the line 15 tax, you will need to know the amount of net capital gain and qualified dividends, if any, included on line 14.

Net capital gain and qualified dividends on line 14. If the child does not have any net capital gain or qualified dividends, line 14 does not include any net capital gain or qualified dividends.

If the child has net capital gain, the amount of net capital gain included on line 14 is the amount from line 2 of the child's completed Line 5 Worksheet minus the amount from the last line of that worksheet.

If the child has qualified dividends, the amount of qualified dividends included on line 14 is the amount from line 1 of the child's completed Line 5 Worksheet minus the amount from the next to the last line of that worksheet.

Child files Form 2555 or 2555-EZ. If line 14 includes any net capital gain or qualified dividends and the child files Form 2555 or 2555-EZ, see Pub. 929 for instructions on how to figure the line 15 tax.

Using the Qualified Dividends and Capital Gain Tax Worksheet for line 15 tax. If you use the Qualified Dividends and Capital Gain Tax Worksheet to figure the line 15 tax, complete that worksheet as follows.

1. On line 1, enter the amount from Form 8615, line 14.

2. On line 2, enter the amount of the qualified dividends included on Form 8615, line 14. (See *Net capital gain and qualified dividends on line 14*, earlier.)

3. On line 3, enter the amount of the net capital gain included on Form 8615, line 14. (See *Net capital gain and qualified dividends on line 14*, earlier.)

4. Complete line 4 following the worksheet instructions.

5. If you are completing the worksheet in the Form 1040 instructions, leave line 5 blank.

6. Complete lines 7 through 27 (lines 5 through 16 of the worksheet in the Form 1040A instructions or lines 5 through 25 of the worksheet in the Form 1040NR instructions) following the worksheet instructions. Use the child's filing status to complete lines 8, 15, 24, and 26 of the worksheet for Form 1040 (lines 6, 13, and 15 of the

worksheet for Form 1040A or lines 6, 13, 22, and 24 of the worksheet for Form 1040NR).

Enter the amount from line 27 of this Qualified Dividends and Capital Gain Tax Worksheet (line 16 of the worksheet in the Form 1040A instructions or line 25 of the worksheet in the Form 1040NR instructions) on line 15 of Form 8615 and check the box on that line. Do not attach this worksheet to the child's return.

Using Schedule J (Form 1040) for line 15 tax. If line 14 includes any farming or fishing income (including certain amounts received in connection with the Exxon Valdez litigation), the tax may be less if you use Schedule J. See Pub. 929 for details on how to figure the line 15 tax using Schedule J.

Line 17

Figure the tax using the Tax Table, Tax Computation Worksheet, Qualified Dividends and Capital Gain Tax Worksheet, Schedule D Tax Worksheet, or Schedule J, whichever applies.

If line 4 includes any qualified dividends or net capital gain, use the Qualified Dividends and Capital Gain Tax Worksheet to figure the tax unless the Schedule D Tax Worksheet has to be used instead.

If any farming or fishing income (including certain amounts received in connection with the Exxon Valdez litigation) is included on line 4, the tax may be less if you use Schedule J.

Child files Form 2555 or 2555-EZ. If line 4 includes any qualified dividends or net capital gain and the child files Form 2555 or 2555-EZ, see Pub. 929 for instructions on how to figure the line 17 tax.

Line 18

If the child files Form 2555 or 2555-EZ, do **not** enter the amount from Form 8615, line 18, on the child's Form 1040, line 44. Instead, enter the amount from Form 8615, line 18, on line 4 of the child's Foreign Earned Income Tax Worksheet (in the Form 1040 instructions). Then complete the rest of the Foreign Earned Income Tax Worksheet to figure the child's tax.

Form **8829**	**Expenses for Business Use of Your Home**	OMB No. 1545-0074
Department of the Treasury Internal Revenue Service (99)	▶ File only with Schedule C (Form 1040). Use a separate Form 8829 for each home you used for business during the year. ▶ Information about Form 8829 and its separate instructions is at *www.irs.gov/form8829*.	20**14** Attachment Sequence No. **176**

Name(s) of proprietor(s)   Your social security number

Part I   Part of Your Home Used for Business

1	Area used regularly and exclusively for business, regularly for daycare, or for storage of inventory or product samples (see instructions)	**1**	
2	Total area of home	**2**	
3	Divide line 1 by line 2. Enter the result as a percentage	**3**	%

For daycare facilities not used exclusively for business, go to line 4. All others, go to line 7.

4	Multiply days used for daycare during year by hours used per day	**4**	hr.
5	Total hours available for use during the year (365 days x 24 hours) (see instructions)	**5**	8,760 hr.
6	Divide line 4 by line 5. Enter the result as a decimal amount . . .	**6**	.
7	Business percentage. For daycare facilities not used exclusively for business, multiply line 6 by line 3 (enter the result as a percentage). All others, enter the amount from line 3 . . . . . ▶	**7**	%

Part II   Figure Your Allowable Deduction

		(a) Direct expenses	(b) Indirect expenses		
8	Enter the amount from Schedule C, line 29, **plus** any gain derived from the business use of your home, **minus** any loss from the trade or business not derived from the business use of your home (see instructions)			**8**	
	See instructions for columns (a) and (b) before completing lines 9–21.				
9	Casualty losses (see instructions). **9**				
10	Deductible mortgage interest (see instructions) **10**				
11	Real estate taxes (see instructions) **11**				
12	Add lines 9, 10, and 11 . . . . **12**				
13	Multiply line 12, column (b) by line 7		**13**		
14	Add line 12, column (a) and line 13			**14**	
15	Subtract line 14 from line 8. If zero or less, enter -0-			**15**	
16	Excess mortgage interest (see instructions) . **16**				
17	Insurance **17**				
18	Rent **18**				
19	Repairs and maintenance **19**				
20	Utilities **20**				
21	Other expenses (see instructions). **21**				
22	Add lines 16 through 21 . . . . **22**				
23	Multiply line 22, column (b) by line 7 . . . . **23**				
24	Carryover of prior year operating expenses (see instructions) . . **24**				
25	Add line 22, column (a), line 23, and line 24			**25**	
26	Allowable operating expenses. Enter the **smaller** of line 15 or line 25			**26**	
27	Limit on excess casualty losses and depreciation. Subtract line 26 from line 15			**27**	
28	Excess casualty losses (see instructions) **28**				
29	Depreciation of your home from line 41 below **29**				
30	Carryover of prior year excess casualty losses and depreciation (see instructions) **30**				
31	Add lines 28 through 30			**31**	
32	Allowable excess casualty losses and depreciation. Enter the **smaller** of line 27 or line 31 . .			**32**	
33	Add lines 14, 26, and 32			**33**	
34	Casualty loss portion, if any, from lines 14 and 32. Carry amount to **Form 4684** (see instructions)			**34**	
35	**Allowable expenses for business use of your home.** Subtract line 34 from line 33. Enter here and on Schedule C, line 30. If your home was used for more than one business, see instructions ▶			**35**	

Part III   Depreciation of Your Home

36	Enter the **smaller** of your home's adjusted basis or its fair market value (see instructions) . .	**36**	
37	Value of land included on line 36	**37**	
38	Basis of building. Subtract line 37 from line 36	**38**	
39	Business basis of building. Multiply line 38 by line 7	**39**	
40	Depreciation percentage (see instructions).	**40**	%
41	Depreciation allowable (see instructions). Multiply line 39 by line 40. Enter here and on line 29 above	**41**	

Part IV   Carryover of Unallowed Expenses to 2015

42	Operating expenses. Subtract line 26 from line 25. If less than zero, enter -0-	**42**	
43	Excess casualty losses and depreciation. Subtract line 32 from line 31. If less than zero, enter -0-	**43**	

For Paperwork Reduction Act Notice, see your tax return instructions.   Cat. No. 13232M   Form **8829** (2014)

Section references are to the Internal Revenue Code unless otherwise noted.

Future Developments

For the latest information about developments related to Form 8829 and its instructions, such as legislation enacted after they were published, go to *www.irs.gov/form8829*.

What's New

Simplified method used for 2013. If you used the simplified method for 2013 but are not using it for 2014, you can use any unallowed expenses from 2012 on your 2014 Form 8829. See the instructions for lines 24 and 30.

General Instructions

Purpose of Form

Use Form 8829 to figure the allowable expenses for business use of your home on Schedule C (Form 1040) and any carryover to 2015 of amounts not deductible in 2014.

You must meet specific requirements to deduct expenses for the business use of your home. Even if you meet these requirements, your deductible expenses may be limited. Part IV is used to figure any allowable carryover of expenses that are more than the limit. For details, see Pub. 587, Business Use of Your Home (Including Use by Daycare Providers).

Who cannot use Form 8829. Do not use Form 8829 in the following situations.
* You are claiming expenses for business use of your home as an employee or a partner, or you are claiming these expenses on Schedule F (Form 1040). Instead, complete the worksheet in Pub. 587.
* All of the expenses for business use of your home are properly allocable to inventory costs. Instead, figure these expenses in Schedule C, Part III.
* You have elected to use the simplified method for this home for 2014. If you had more than one home during the year that you used for business, you can use the simplified method for only one home. Use Form 8829 to claim expenses for business use of the other home. For more information about the simplified method, see the Instructions for Schedule C and Pub. 587.

Who Can Deduct Expenses for Business Use of a Home

Generally, you can deduct business expenses that apply to a part of your home only if that part is exclusively used on a regular basis:
* As your principal place of business for any of your trades or businesses,
* As a place of business used by your patients, clients, or customers to meet or deal with you in the normal course of your trade or business, or
* In connection with your trade or business if it is a separate structure that is not attached to your home.

As explained later, exceptions to this rule apply to space used on a regular basis for:
* Storage of inventory or product samples, and

* Certain daycare facilities.

Principal Place of Business

In determining whether the office in your home qualifies as your principal place of business, you must consider the following two items.
* The relative importance of the activities performed at each place where you conduct business, and
* The amount of time spent at each place where you conduct business.

Your home office will qualify as your principal place of business if you meet the following requirements.
* You use it exclusively and regularly for administrative or management activities of your trade or business.
* You have no other fixed location where you conduct substantial administrative or management activities of your trade or business.

Administrative or management activities. There are many activities that are administrative or managerial in nature. The following are a few examples.
* Billing customers, clients, or patients.
* Keeping books and records.
* Ordering supplies.
* Setting up appointments.
* Forwarding orders or writing reports.

Administrative or management activities performed at other locations. The following activities performed by you or others will not disqualify your home office from being your principal place of business.
* You have others conduct your administrative or management activities at locations other than your home. (For example, another company does your billing from its place of business.)
* You conduct administrative or management activities at places that are not fixed locations of your business, such as in a car or a hotel room.
* You occasionally conduct minimal administrative or management activities at a fixed location outside your home.
* You conduct substantial nonadministrative or nonmanagement business activities at a fixed location outside your home. (For example, you meet with or provide services to customers, clients, or patients at a fixed location of the business outside your home.)
* You have suitable space to conduct administrative or management activities outside your home, but choose to use your home office for those activities instead.

More information. For information on other ways to qualify to deduct business use of the home expenses, see Pub. 587.

Storage of Inventory or Product Samples

You can also deduct expenses that apply to space within your home used on a regular basis to store inventory or product samples from your trade or business of selling products at retail or wholesale. Your home must be the only fixed location of your trade or business.

Daycare Facilities

If you use space in your home on a regular basis in the trade or business of providing daycare, you may be able to deduct the business expenses even though you use the same space for nonbusiness purposes. To qualify for this exception, you must have applied for (and not have been rejected), been granted (and still have in effect), or be exempt from having a license, certification, registration, or approval as a daycare center or as a family or group daycare home under state law.

Expenses Related to Tax-Exempt Income

Generally, you cannot deduct expenses that are allocable to tax-exempt income. However, if you receive a tax-exempt parsonage allowance or a tax-exempt military housing allowance, your expenses for mortgage interest and real property taxes are deductible under the normal rules. No deduction is allowed for other expenses allocable to the tax-exempt allowance.

Specific Instructions

Part I

Lines 1 and 2

To determine the area on lines 1 and 2, you can use square feet or any other reasonable method if it accurately figures your business percentage on line 7.

Do not include on line 1 the area of your home you used to figure any expenses allocable to inventory costs. The business percentage of these expenses should have been taken into account in Schedule C, Part III.

Special Computation for Certain Daycare Facilities

If the part of your home used as a daycare facility includes areas used exclusively for business as well as other areas used only partly for business, you cannot figure your business percentage using Part I. Instead, follow these three steps:

1. Figure the business percentage of the part of your home used exclusively for business by dividing the area used exclusively for business by the total area of the home.

2. Figure the business percentage of the part of your home used only partly for business by following the same method used in Part I of the form, but enter on line 1 of your computation only the area of the home used partly for business.

3. Add the business percentages you figured in the first two steps and enter the result on line 7. Attach a statement with your computation and enter "See attached computation" directly above the percentage you entered on line 7.

Line 4

Enter the total number of hours the facility was used for daycare during the year.

Example. Your home is used Monday through Friday for 12 hours per day for 250 days during the year. It is also used on 50 Saturdays for 8 hours per day. Enter 3,400 hours on line 4 (3,000 hours for weekdays plus 400 hours for Saturdays).

Line 5

If you started or stopped using your home for daycare in 2014, you must prorate the number of hours based on the number of days the home was available for daycare. Cross out the preprinted entry on line 5. Multiply 24 hours by the number of days available and enter the result.

Part II

Line 8

If all the gross income from your trade or business is from the business use of your home, enter on line 8 the amount from Schedule(s) C, line 29, **plus** any gain derived from the business use of your home and shown on Form 8949 (and included on Schedule D (Form 1040)) or Form 4797, **minus** any loss shown on Form 8949 (and included in Schedule D) or Form 4797 that is allocable to the trade or business in which you use your home but is not allocable to the use of the home. If you file more than one Form 8829, include only the income earned and the deductions attributable to that income during the period you owned the home for which Part I was completed.

If some of the income is from a place of business other than your home, you must first determine the part of your gross income (Schedule C, line 7, and gains from Form 8949, Schedule D, and Form 4797) from the business use of your home. In making this determination, consider the amount of time you spend at each location as well as other facts. After determining the part of your gross income from the business use of your home, subtract from that amount the total expenses shown on Schedule C, line 28, plus any losses shown on Form 8949 (and included in Schedule D) or Form 4797 that are allocable to the trade or business in which you use your home but that are not allocable to the use of the home. Enter the result on Form 8829, line 8.

Columns (a) and (b)

Enter as direct or indirect expenses only expenses for the business use of your home (that is, expenses allowable only because your home is used for business). If you did not operate a business for the entire year, you can deduct only the expenses paid or incurred for the portion of the year you used your home for business. Other expenses not allocable to the business use of your home, such as salaries, supplies, and advertising, are deductible elsewhere on Schedule C and should not be entered on Form 8829.

Direct expenses benefit only the business part of your home. They include painting or repairs made to the specific area or rooms used for business. Enter 100% of your direct expenses on the appropriate line in column (a).

Indirect expenses are for keeping up and running your entire home. They benefit both the business and personal parts of your home. Generally, enter 100% of your indirect expenses on the appropriate line in column (b).

Exception. If the business percentage of an indirect expense is different from the percentage on line 7, enter only the business part of the expense on the appropriate line in column (a), and leave that line in column (b) blank. For example, your electric bill is $800 for lighting, cooking, laundry, and television. If you reasonably estimate $300 of your electric bill is for lighting and you use 10% of your home for business, enter $30 on line 20 in column (a). Do not make an entry on line 20 in column (b) for any part of your electric bill.

Lines 9, 10, and 11

Enter only the amounts that would be deductible whether or not you used your home for business (that is, amounts allowable as itemized deductions on Schedule A (Form 1040)).

Treat casualty losses as personal expenses for this step. Figure the amount to enter on line 9 by completing Form 4684, Section A. If you are filing Schedule A, enter 10% of your adjusted gross income excluding the gross income from business use of your home and the deductions attributable to that income when figuring the amount to enter on Form 4684, line 17. Include on Form 8829, line 9, the amount from Form 4684, line 18. See the instructions for line 28, later, to deduct part of the casualty losses not allowed because of the limits on Form 4684. Do not file or use this Form 4684 to figure the amount of casualty losses to deduct on Schedule A. Instead, complete a separate Form 4684 to deduct the personal portion of your casualty losses.

On line 10, include only the total of your mortgage interest and qualified mortgage insurance premiums that would be deductible on Schedule A and that qualifies as a direct or indirect expense. Mortgage interest on a separate structure you used in connection with your trade or business is a direct expense. Do not include mortgage interest on a loan that did not benefit your home (for example, a home equity loan used to pay off credit card bills, to buy a car, or to pay tuition costs).

Treat qualified mortgage insurance premiums as personal expenses for this step. Figure the amount to enter on line 10 by completing Schedule A, line 13, in accordance with the Instructions for Schedule A (Form 1040). However, when figuring your adjusted gross income (Form 1040, line 38) for this purpose, exclude the gross income from business use of your home and the deductions attributable to that income. Include on Form 8829, line 10, the amount from Schedule A, line 13. See the instructions for line 16, later, to deduct part of the qualified mortgage insurance premiums not allowed because of the adjusted gross income limit. Do not file or use that Schedule A to figure the amount to deduct on line 13 of that schedule. Instead, complete a separate Schedule A to deduct the personal portion of your qualified mortgage insurance premiums.

If you itemize your deductions, be sure to claim only the personal portion of your deductible mortgage interest, qualified mortgage insurance premiums, and real estate taxes on Schedule A. For example, if your business percentage on line 7 is 30%, you can claim 70% of your deductible mortgage interest, qualified mortgage insurance premiums, and real estate taxes on Schedule A.

Line 16

If the amount of home mortgage interest or qualified mortgage insurance premiums you deduct on Schedule A is limited, enter the part of the excess that qualifies as a direct or indirect expense. Do not include mortgage interest on a loan that did not benefit your home (explained earlier).

Line 18

If you rent rather than own your home, include the rent you paid on line 18, column (b).

If your housing is provided free of charge and the value of the housing is tax exempt, you cannot deduct the rental value of any portion of the housing.

Line 21

Include on this line any 2014 operating expenses not included on lines 9 through 20.

Line 24

Enter any amount from your 2013 Form 8829, line 42.

If you used the simplified method for 2013 but are not using it for 2014, enter the amount from line 6a of your 2013 Simplified Method Worksheet (or line 42 of your 2012 Form 8829).

Line 28

Multiply your casualty losses in excess of the amount on line 9 by the business percentage of those losses and enter the result.

Line 30

Enter any amount from your 2013 Form 8829, line 43.

If you used the simplified method for 2013 but are not using it for 2014, enter the amount from line 6b of your 2013 Simplified Method Worksheet (or line 43 of your 2012 Form 8829).

Line 34

Enter this amount on Form 4684, line 27, and enter "See Form 8829" above line 27.

Line 35

If your home was used in more than one business, allocate the amount shown on line 35 to each business using any method that is reasonable under the circumstances. For each business, enter on Schedule C, line 30, only the amount allocated to that business.

Part III

Lines 36 Through 38

Enter on line 36 the cost or other basis of your home (including land), or, if less, the fair market value of your home on the date you first used the home for business. Do not adjust this amount for depreciation claimed or changes in fair market value after the year you first used your home for business.

Enter on line 37 the cost or other basis of the land on which your home sits, or, if less, the fair market value of the land on the date you first used your home for business. Do not adjust this amount for changes in fair market value after the year you first used your home for business.

Attach your own statement showing the cost or other basis of additions and improvements, used at least partially for business, that were placed in service after you began to use your home for business. Do not include any amounts on lines 36 through 39 for these expenditures. Instead, see the instructions for line 41.

Line 40

IF you first used your home for business in the following month in 2014...	THEN enter the following percentage on line 40*...
January	2.461%
February	2.247%
March	2.033%
April	1.819%
May	1.605%
June	1.391%
July	1.177%
August	0.963%
September	0.749%
October	0.535%
November	0.321%
December	0.107%

*Exception. If the business part of your home is Indian reservation property that meets the requirements of section 168(j), see Pub. 946 to figure the depreciation.

IF you first used your home for business...	THEN the percentage to enter on line 40 is...
after May 12, 1993, and before 2014 (except as noted below),	2.564%.*
after May 12, 1993, and before 1994, and you either started construction or had a binding contract to buy or build that home before May 13, 1993,	the percentage given in Pub. 946.
after May 12, 1993, and you stopped using your home for business before the end of the year,	the percentage given in Pub. 946 as adjusted by the instructions under *Sale or Other Disposition Before the Recovery Period Ends* in that publication.
after 1986 and before May 13, 1993,	the percentage given in Pub. 946.
before 1987,	the percentage given in Pub. 534, *Depreciating Property Placed in Service Before 1987.*

*Exception. If the business part of your home is Indian reservation property that meets the requirements of section 168(j), see Pub. 946 to figure the depreciation.

Simplified method used for 2013. If you used the simplified method for 2013, use the preceding table to find the percentage to enter.

Example. You first used your home for business for 2013 and used the simplified method for that year. For 2014, you want to use Form 8829 instead. Enter 2.564%.

Line 41

If no additions and improvements were placed in service after you began using your home for business, multiply line 39 by the percentage on line 40. Enter the result on lines 41 and 29.

IF additions and improvements were placed in service...	THEN figure the depreciation allowed on these expenditures by multiplying the business part of their cost or other basis by...
during 2014 (but after you began using your home for business),	the percentage in the line 40 instructions for the month placed in service.
after May 12, 1993, and before 2014 (except as noted below),	2.564%.*
after May 12, 1993, and before 1994, and you either started construction or had a binding contract to buy or build that home before May 13, 1993,	the percentage given in Pub. 946.
after May 12, 1993, and you stopped using your home for business before the end of the year,	the percentage given in Pub. 946 as adjusted by the instructions under *Sale or Other Disposition Before the Recovery Period Ends* in that publication.
after 1986 and before May 13, 1993,	the percentage given in Pub. 946.
before 1987,	the percentage given in Pub. 534.

*Exception. If the business part of your home is Indian reservation property that meets the requirements of section 168(j), see Pub. 946 to figure the depreciation.

Attach a statement showing your computation and include the amount you figured in the total for line 41. Enter "See attached" below the entry space.

Complete and attach Form 4562, Depreciation and Amortization, only if:
- You first used your home for business in 2014, or
- You are depreciating additions and improvements placed in service in 2014.

If you first used your home for business in 2014, enter the amounts from Form 8829, lines 39 and 41, in columns (c) and (g) of line 19i, Form 4562. In column (b) of line 19i, enter the month and year you first used your home for business. Do not include the amount from Form 8829, line 41, on Schedule C, line 13.

If you are depreciating additions and improvements placed in service in 2014, enter in column (b) of line 19i on Form 4562 the month and year the additions or improvements were placed in service. Enter the business basis of the additions or improvements in column (c) and the depreciation allowable on the additions or improvements in column (g). Do not include the amount entered in column (g) on Schedule C, line 13.

Part IV

If your expenses are greater than the current year's limit, you can carry over the excess to 2015. The carryover will be subject to the deduction limit for that year, whether or not you live in the same home during that year.

Line 42

Figure the amount of operating expenses you can carry over to 2015 by subtracting line 26 from line 25. If the result is zero or less, you have no amount to carry over.

Line 43

Figure the amount of excess casualty losses and depreciation you can carry over to 2015 by subtracting line 32 from line 31. If the result is zero or less, you have no amount to carry over.

For Paperwork Reduction Act Notice, see Instructions for Form 1040.

Form **8839**

Department of the Treasury
Internal Revenue Service (99)

Qualified Adoption Expenses

▶ Attach to Form 1040 or 1040NR.
▶ **For information about Form 8839 and its separate instructions, see** *www.irs.gov/form8839.*

OMB No. 1545-0074

2014

Attachment
Sequence No. **38**

Name(s) shown on return

Your social security number

Part I — Information About Your Eligible Child or Children—You **must** complete this part. See instructions for details, including what to do if you need more space.

1	(a) Child's name — First / Last	(b) Child's year of birth	(c) born **before 1997** and disabled	(d) a child with special needs	(e) a foreign child	(f) Child's identifying number	(g) Check if adoption became final in 2014 or earlier
			Check if child was—				
Child 1			☐	☐	☐		☐
Child 2			☐	☐	☐		☐
Child 3			☐	☐	☐		☐

Caution. If the child was a foreign child, see **Special rules** in the instructions for line 1, column (e) before you complete Part II or Part III. If you received **employer-provided adoption benefits,** complete Part III on the back next.

Part II — Adoption Credit

			Child 1		Child 2		Child 3			
2	Maximum adoption credit per child	2	$13,190	00	$13,190	00	$13,190	00		
3	Did you file Form 8839 for a prior year for the same child? ☐ **No.** Enter -0-. ☐ **Yes.** See instructions for the amount to enter.	3								
4	Subtract line 3 from line 2	4								
5	**Qualified adoption expenses** (see instructions)	5								
	Caution. Your qualified adoption expenses may not be equal to the adoption expenses you paid in 2014.									
6	Enter the **smaller** of line 4 or line 5	6								
7	Enter modified adjusted gross income (see instructions)	7								
8	Is line 7 more than $197,880? ☐ **No.** Skip lines 8 and 9, and enter -0- on line 10. ☐ **Yes.** Subtract $197,880 from line 7	8								
9	Divide line 8 by $40,000. Enter the result as a decimal (rounded to at least three places). Do not enter more than 1.000	9	× .							
10	Multiply each amount on line 6 by line 9	10									
11	Subtract line 10 from line 6 .	11									
12	Add the amounts on line 11	12								
13	Credit carryforward, if any, from prior years. See your Adoption Credit Carryforward Worksheet in the 2013 Form 8839 instructions	13								
14	Add lines 12 and 13	14								
15	Enter the amount from line 5 of the Credit Limit Worksheet in the instructions	15								
16	**Adoption Credit.** Enter the smaller of line 14 or line 15 here and on Form 1040, line 54, or Form 1040NR, line 51. Check box **c** on that line and enter "**8839**" in the space next to box **c**. If line 15 is smaller than line 14, you may have a credit carryforward (see instructions)	16								

For Paperwork Reduction Act Notice, see your tax return instructions.

Cat. No. 22843L

Form **8839** (2014)

Part III	Employer-Provided Adoption Benefits		Child 1		Child 2		Child 3				
17	Maximum exclusion per child	17	$13,190	00	$13,190	00	$13,190	00			
18	Did you receive employer-provided adoption benefits for a prior year for the same child? ☐ **No.** Enter -0-. ☐ **Yes.** See instructions for the amount to enter.	18									
19	Subtract line 18 from line 17	19									
20	Employer-provided adoption benefits you received in 2014. This amount should be shown in box 12 of your 2014 Form(s) W-2 with code **T**	20									
21	Add the amounts on line 20								21		
22	Enter the **smaller** of line 19 or line 20. But if the child was a child with special needs and the adoption became final in 2014, enter the amount from line 19	22									
23	Enter modified adjusted gross income (from the worksheet in the instructions)	23									
24	Is line 23 more than $197,880? ☐ **No.** Skip lines 24 and 25, and enter -0- on line 26. ☐ **Yes.** Subtract $197,880 from line 23	24									
25	Divide line 24 by $40,000. Enter the result as a decimal (rounded to at least three places). Do not enter more than 1.000	25		×							
26	Multiply each amount on line 22 by line 25	26									
27	**Excluded benefits.** Subtract line 26 from line 22	27									
28	Add the amounts on line 27								28		
29	**Taxable benefits.** Is line 28 more than line 21? ☐ **No.** Subtract line 28 from line 21. Also, include this amount, if more than zero, on line 7 of Form 1040 or line 8 of Form 1040NR. On the dotted line next to line 7 of Form 1040 or line 8 of Form 1040NR, enter "AB." ☐ **Yes.** Subtract line 21 from line 28. Enter the result as a negative number. Reduce the total you would enter on line 7 of Form 1040 or line 8 of Form 1040NR by the amount on Form 8839, line 29. Enter the result on line 7 of Form 1040 or line 8 of Form 1040NR. Enter "SNE" on the dotted line next to the entry line.								29		

You may be able to claim the adoption credit in Part II on the front of this form if any of the following apply.

- You paid adoption expenses in 2013, those expenses were not fully reimbursed by your employer or otherwise, and the adoption was not final by the end of 2013.

- The total adoption expenses you paid in 2014 were not fully reimbursed by your employer or otherwise, and the adoption became final in 2014 or earlier.

- You adopted a child with special needs and the adoption became final in 2014.

Instructions for Form 8839

Qualified Adoption Expenses

Section references are to the Internal Revenue Code unless otherwise noted.

What's New

2014 maximum credit. The maximum credit and the exclusion for employer-provided benefits are both $13,190 per eligible child in 2014. This amount begins to phase out if you have modified adjusted gross income in excess of $197,880 and is completely phased out for modified adjusted gross income of $237,880 or more.

Future Developments

For the latest information about developments related to Form 8839 and its instructions, such as legislation enacted after they are published, go to _www.irs.gov/form8839_.

General Instructions

Purpose of Form

Use Form 8839 to figure your adoption credit and any employer-provided adoption benefits you can exclude from your income. You can claim both the exclusion and the credit for expenses of adopting an eligible child. For example, depending on the cost of the adoption, you may be able to exclude up to $13,190 from your income and also be able to claim a credit of up to $10,190. But, you cannot claim both a credit and exclusion for the same expenses. See _Qualified Adoption Expenses_ and _Employer-Provided Adoption Benefits_, later.

Adoption credit. Use Form 8839, Part II, to figure the adoption credit you can take on Form 1040, line 54 or Form 1040NR, line 51. Check box c on that line and enter "8839" in the space next to box c. You may be able to take this credit in 2014 if any of the following statements are true.

1. You paid qualified adoption expenses in connection with the adoption of an eligible U.S. child (including any expenses paid in connection with adopting an eligible U.S. child with special needs) in:

   a. 2013 and the adoption was not final at the end of 2013, or

   b. 2014 and the adoption became final in or before 2014.

2. You adopted an eligible U.S. child with special needs and the adoption became final in 2014. (In this case, you may be able to take the credit even if you did not pay any qualified adoption expenses.)

3. You paid qualified adoption expenses in connection with the adoption of an eligible foreign child in:

   a. 2014 or prior years and the adoption became final in 2014, or

   b. 2014 and the adoption became final before 2014. See _Column (e)_, later.

4. You have a carryforward of an adoption credit from 2013.

Income exclusion for employer-provided adoption benefits. Use Form 8839, Part III, to figure the employer-provided adoption benefits you can exclude from your income on Form 1040, line 7, or Form 1040NR, line 8. You may be able to exclude these benefits from income if your employer had a written qualified adoption assistance program (see _Employer-Provided Adoption Benefits_, later) and any of the following statements are true.

1. You received employer-provided adoption benefits in 2014. However, special rules apply for benefits received in connection with the adoption of an eligible foreign child. See _Column (e)_, later.

2. You adopted an eligible U.S. child with special needs and the adoption became final in 2014.

3. You received employer-provided adoption benefits in connection with the adoption of an eligible foreign child in:

   a. 2014 or prior years and the adoption became final in 2014, or

   b. 2014 and the adoption became final before 2014. See _Column (e)_, later.

For purposes of calculating the adoption credit in Part II, qualified adoption expenses (defined later) do not include expenses reimbursed by an employer under a written qualified adoption assistance program (see _Employer-Provided Adoption Benefits_, later). For this reason, you must complete Form 8839, Part III, before you can figure the credit, if any, in Part II. But see _Child with special needs_, later.

 You cannot exclude employer-provided adoption benefits if your employer is an S corporation in which you own more than 2% of the stock or stock with more than 2% of the voting power.

Income limit. The income limit on the adoption credit or exclusion is based on modified adjusted gross income (MAGI). For 2014, use the following table to see if the income limit will affect your credit or exclusion.

IF your MAGI is...	THEN the income limit...
$197,880 or less	will not affect your credit or exclusion.
Between $197,881 and $237,879	will reduce your credit or exclusion.
$237,880 or more	will eliminate your credit or exclusion.

Definitions

Eligible Child

An eligible child is:

• Any child under age 18. If the child turned 18 during the year, the child is an eligible child for the part of the year he or she was under age 18.

• Any disabled individual physically or mentally unable to take care of himself or herself.

 If you and another person (other than your spouse if filing jointly) adopted or tried to adopt an eligible U.S. child, see Line 2 _(or_ Line 17_, if applicable), later, before completing Part II (or Part III)._

Qualified Adoption Expenses

Qualified adoption expenses are reasonable and necessary expenses directly related to, and for the principal purpose of, the legal adoption of an eligible child.

Qualified adoption expenses include:
- Adoption fees,
- Attorney fees,
- Court costs,
- Travel expenses (including meals and lodging) while away from home, and
- Re-adoption expenses relating to the adoption of a foreign child.

Qualified adoption expenses do not include expenses:
- For which you received funds under any state, local, or federal program,
- That violate state or federal law,
- For carrying out a surrogate parenting arrangement,
- For the adoption of your spouse's child,
- Reimbursed by your employer or otherwise, or
- Allowed as a credit or deduction under any other provision of federal income tax law.

Employer-Provided Adoption Benefits

In most cases, employer-provided adoption benefits are amounts your employer paid directly to either you or a third party for qualified adoption expenses under a qualified adoption assistance program. But see *Child with special needs*, later.

A qualified adoption assistance program is a separate written plan set up by an employer to provide adoption assistance to its employees. For more details, see Pub. 15-B, Employer's Tax Guide to Fringe Benefits.

Employer-provided adoption benefits should be shown in box 12 of your Form(s) W-2 with code T. Your salary may have been reduced to pay these benefits. You may also be able to exclude amounts not shown in box 12 of your Form W-2 if all of the following apply.
- You adopted a child with special needs. See *Column (d)*, later, for the definition of a child with special needs.
- The adoption became final in 2014.
- Your employer had a written qualified adoption assistance program as described earlier.

The following examples help illustrate how qualified adoption expenses and employer-provided adoption benefits apply to the maximum adoption credit allowed.

Example 1. Madelyn paid $10,000 in qualified adoption expenses for the adoption of an eligible child. Under a qualified adoption assistance program, Madelyn's employer reimbursed her for $4,000 of those expenses. Madelyn may exclude the $4,000 reimbursement from her income. However, because of the employer reimbursement, $4,000 of her expenses no longer meet the definition of qualified adoption expenses. As a result, Madelyn's maximum adoption credit is limited to $6,000 ($10,000 - $4,000).

Example 2. Haylee paid $20,000 in qualified adoption expenses for the adoption of an eligible child, including $8,000 of legal fees. Under a qualified adoption assistance program, Haylee's employer reimbursed the $8,000 of legal fees. Haylee may exclude the $8,000 employer reimbursement from her income. However, because of the employer reimbursement, $8,000 of Haylee's expenses no longer meet the definition of qualified adoption expenses. As a result, Haylee's maximum adoption credit is limited to $12,000 ($20,000 - $8,000).

Example 3. The facts are the same as in *Example 2* except that instead of reimbursing Haylee for her legal fees, the employer directly paid the $8,000 to the law firm. The employer's payment of the legal fees produces the same result as the employer's reimbursement of the legal fees in *Example 2* ($8,000 exclusion and $12,000 credit).

Example 4. Paul paid $30,000 in qualified adoption expenses to adopt an eligible foreign child, and the adoption became final in 2014. Under a qualified adoption assistance program, Paul's employer reimbursed him for $13,190 of those expenses. Paul may exclude the $13,190 reimbursement from his income. The remaining $16,810 of expenses ($30,000 - $13,190) continue to be qualified adoption expenses that are eligible for the credit. However, Paul's credit is dollar-limited to $13,190. The remaining $3,620 ($30,000 - $13,190 - $13,190) may never be claimed as a credit or excluded from gross income.

Who Can Take the Adoption Credit or Exclude Employer-Provided Adoption Benefits?

You may be able to take the credit or exclusion if all three of the following statements are true.

1. Your filing status is single, head of household, qualifying widow(er), or married filing jointly. Generally, if you are married, you must file a joint return to take the credit or exclusion. However, if you are married and are not filing jointly, you may be able to take the credit or exclusion on your own return if you are considered unmarried because you are legally separated or living apart from your spouse and you meet certain other requirements. See *Married Persons Not Filing Jointly*, later.

2. Your modified adjusted gross income (MAGI) is less than $237,880 or you have a carryforward of an adoption credit from 2013. To figure your MAGI, see *Line 7* (for the credit) or *Line 23* (for the exclusion), later.

3. You report the required information about the eligible child in Part I.

Married Persons Not Filing Jointly

You may be able to take the credit or exclusion if all of the following apply.
- Statements (2) and (3) under *Who Can Take the Adoption Credit or Exclude Employer-Provided Adoption Benefits* are true.
- You lived apart from your spouse during the last 6 months of 2014.
- The eligible child lived in your home more than half of 2014.
- You provided over half the cost of keeping up your home.

Additionally, a person who is filing separately may claim an adoption credit carryforward from a prior year or years, provided that, if the person was married in the year in which the qualified adoption expenses first became allowable for the credit, the person filed a joint return for that year.

When To Take the Credit or Exclusion

When you can take the adoption credit or exclusion depends on whether the eligible child is a citizen or resident of the United States (including U.S. possessions) at the time the adoption effort began (domestic adoption).

Child who is a U.S. citizen or resident (U.S. child). If the eligible child is a U.S. citizen or resident, you can take the adoption credit or exclusion even if the adoption never became final. Take the credit or exclusion as shown in the following table.

Form 8839 (2014)

Domestic Adoption

IF you pay qualifying expenses in...	THEN take the credit in...
Any year before the year the adoption becomes final*	The year **after** the year of the payment.
The year the adoption becomes final	The year the adoption becomes final.
Any year after the year the adoption becomes final	The year of the payment.

IF your employer pays for qualifying expenses under an adoption assistance program in...	THEN take the exclusion in....
Any year	The year of the payment.

*In the case of a U.S. child, an adoption credit may be allowable for an attempted or unsuccessful adoption, as well as for an adoption that is not yet final. See the instructions for *Line 1* and *Line 5* for additional information.

Child with special needs. If you adopt a U.S. child with special needs, you may be able to exclude up to $13,190 and claim a credit for additional expenses up to $13,190 (minus any qualified adoption expenses claimed for the same child in a prior year). The exclusion may be available, even if you or your employer did not pay any qualified adoption expenses, provided the employer has a written qualified adoption assistance program. See *Column (d)*, later, for more information.

Foreign child. If the eligible child is a foreign child, you cannot take the adoption credit or exclusion unless the adoption becomes final. A child is a foreign child if he or she was not a citizen or resident of the United States (including U.S. possessions) at the time the adoption effort began. Take the credit or exclusion as shown in the following table.

Foreign Adoption

IF you pay qualifying expenses in...	THEN take the credit in...
Any year before the year the adoption becomes final	The year the adoption becomes final.
The year the adoption becomes final	The year the adoption becomes final.
Any year after the year the adoption becomes final	The year of the payment.

IF your employer pays for qualifying expenses under an adoption assistance program in...	THEN take the exclusion in....
Any year before the year the adoption becomes final	The year the adoption becomes final.
The year the adoption becomes final	The year the adoption becomes final.
Any year after the year the adoption becomes final	The year of the payment.

For more information, see *Column (e)* later. To find out when a foreign adoption is treated as final, see Rev. Proc. 2005-31, 2005-26 I.R.B. 1374, available at *www.irs.gov/irb/2005-26_IRB/*

ar14.html, and Rev. Proc. 2010-31, 2010-40 I.R.B. 413, available at *www.irs.gov/irb/2010-40_IRB/ar10.html*.

If your employer makes adoption assistance payments in a year before the adoption of a foreign child is final, you must include the payments in your income in the year of the payment. Then, on your return for the year the adoption becomes final, you can make an adjustment to take the exclusion.

 Your employer is not required to withhold income tax on payments for qualifying expenses under an adoption assistance program. If you must include the payments in income in the year paid because your adoption of a foreign child is not final, your withholding may not be enough to cover the tax on those payments. You may need to give your employer a new Form W-4 to adjust your withholding or make estimated tax payments to avoid a penalty for underpayment of estimated tax.

Specific Instructions
Part I—Information About Your Eligible Child or Children
Line 1

Complete all columns that apply to the eligible child you adopted or tried to adopt.

If you cannot give complete information about an eligible child you tried to adopt in 2013 because the adoption was either unsuccessful or was not final by the end of 2014, complete the entries that you can on line 1. Leave blank any entries you are unable to complete. For example, if you do not have an SSN or ATIN for your eligible child, leave column (f) blank.

 For examples of the type of records you may want to keep to substantiate your claim for the adoption credit, see Notice 2010-66, 2010-42 I.R.B. 437 available at www.irs.gov/irb/2010-42_IRB/ar09.html.

Attempted Adoptions of U.S. Children

In general, the dollar limitation requires you to combine the qualified adoption expenses you paid if you made more than one attempt to adopt one eligible U.S. child. When you combine the amounts you spent, complete only the "Child 1" line. Do not report the additional attempt(s) on the "Child 2" or "Child 3" line. Complete the "Child 2" or "Child 3" lines only if you adopted or tried to adopt two or three eligible children.

Example 1. You planned to adopt one U.S. child. You paid $10,000 of qualified adoption expenses in an unsuccessful attempt to adopt a child. You later paid $8,000 of additional qualified adoption expenses in a successful adoption of a different child. Complete only the "Child 1" line because you made more than one attempt to adopt one eligible child.

Example 2. The facts are the same as in *Example 1* except that both attempts are unsuccessful and no adoption is ever finalized. Enter $18,000 ($10,000 + $8,000) on the "Child 1" line because you made more than one attempt to adopt one eligible child.

Example 3. You planned to adopt one U.S. child. You paid $9,000 in qualified adoption expenses in an unsuccessful attempt to adopt a child. You later successfully adopted twins, after paying an additional $24,000 in qualified adoption expenses ($12,000 per child). Enter $21,000 ($9,000 + $12,000) on the "Child 1" line because you made more than one attempt to adopt one eligible child. Enter $12,000 on the "Child 2" line because you made a successful attempt to adopt a second eligible child.

If you filed Form 8839 for a prior year in connection with this adoption, enter your 2014 information on the same line (Child 1, Child 2, or Child 3) that you used in the prior year.

More Than Three Eligible Children

If you adopted or tried to adopt more than three eligible children, fill in and attach as many Forms 8839 as you need to list them. Also, enter "See Attached" to the right of the *Caution* below line 1.

For Part II, fill in lines 2 through 6 and 10 and 11 for each child. But fill in lines 7 through 9 and 12 through 16 on only one Form 8839. The amount on line 12 of that Form 8839 should be the combined total of the amounts on line 11 of all Forms 8839.

For Part III, fill in lines 17 through 20, 22, 26, and 27 for each child. But fill in lines 21, 23 through 25, 28, and 29 on only one Form 8839. The amount on line 21 of that Form 8839 should be the combined total of the amounts on line 20 of all the Forms 8839. The amount on line 28 of that form should be the combined total of the amounts on line 27.

Column (c)

A disabled individual, one who is physically or mentally unable to care for himself or herself, is an eligible child regardless of his or her age at the time of adoption.

Column (d)

A child is a child with special needs if all three of the following statements are true.

1. The child was a citizen or resident of the United States or its possessions at the time the adoption effort began (U.S. child).

2. A state (including the District of Columbia) has determined that the child cannot or should not be returned to his or her parents' home.

3. The state has determined that the child will not be adopted unless assistance is provided to the adoptive parents. Factors used by states to make this determination include:

   a. The child's ethnic background and age,

   b. Whether the child is a member of a minority or sibling group, and

   c. Whether the child has a medical condition or a physical, mental, or emotional handicap.

The state must make a determination that a child has special needs before the child is considered to be a child with special needs. A child having a specific factor or condition is not enough to establish that the state has made a determination of special needs.

You may be able to claim an exclusion or credit for the adoption of a U.S. child with special needs even if you did not pay any qualified adoption expenses. See *Line 22* and the instructions for *Line 5*.

For more information, see Tax Topic 607 available at *www.irs.gov/taxtopics/tc607.html*.

Example 1. Agency A is the child welfare department of State V. Mark, Rachel, and Janet, brother and sisters, are U.S. children residing in State V. When Mark was 10, Rachel 8, and Janet 6, Agency A removed the children from the home of the biological parents.

After Agency A placed the children in foster care, Agency A determined it would be difficult to place the children for adoption without providing assistance to the adoptive family because of the ages and sibling relationship of the children. Agency A provided the adoptive parents with monthly subsidy payments on behalf of each child. The adoption assistance agreements entered into between Agency A and the adoptive parents are evidence that State V has determined that Mark, Rachel, and Janet are children with special needs and may be used to support the adoptive parents' claim to the adoption tax credit.

Mark, Rachel, and Janet are U.S. children who State V has removed from their biological parents. State V also has determined that each child has special needs. Their adoptive parents may claim an adoption tax credit for each child, even if the adoptive parents paid no qualifying adoption expenses, if all other requirements of the credit are met.

Example 2. Michael and Grace are born in State W and are members of a sibling group. Their biological mother places the siblings through a private adoption agency and voluntarily surrenders her parental rights. Membership in a sibling group is a factor that State W may use in determining that a child has special needs. State W also requires that adoptive parents requesting a state determination of special needs follow certain steps and make the request before the adoption is final. Michael and Grace's adoptive parents do not make a request or follow the required steps.

Michael and Grace are not children with special needs because State W did not remove them from their biological mother and did not make a determination of special needs. Although membership in a sibling group is a factor that State W may use in making a determination, State W did not make a determination that either Michael or Grace would not be adopted unless adoption assistance was provided to the adoptive parents. However, Michael and Grace's adoptive parents may claim adoption tax credits for the qualified adoption expenses they paid in connection with Michael and Grace's adoption, if all other requirements of the credit are met.

Example 3. Hannah is born in State X. Her biological parents place Hannah for adoption through a private adoption agency and voluntarily relinquish their parental rights. Hannah then is adopted. A medical exam performed shortly after Hannah's birth shows that Hannah has serious physical disabilities. Hannah is not a child with special needs because State X did not remove her from her biological parents and did not make a determination of special needs. However, Hannah's adoptive parents may claim the adoption tax credit for the qualified adoption expenses they paid in connection with Hannah's adoption, if all other requirements of the credit are met.

Example 4. Noah is born in Country Z and is diagnosed with serious physical and mental disabilities. Noah's adoptive parents, who are residents of State Y, adopt Noah in Country Z, bring him to the United States, and re-adopt him in State Y. Noah is not a child with special needs because he was not a citizen or resident of the United States when the adoption process began. Additionally, State Y did not remove him from the home of his biological parents and did not make a determination of special needs. However, Noah's adoptive parents may claim the adoption tax credit for the qualified adoption expenses they paid in connection with Noah's adoption, if all other requirements of the credit are met.

 If you check the box in column (d) indicating the child has special needs, be sure to keep evidence of the state's determination in your records.

Column (e)

A child is a foreign child if he or she was not a citizen or resident of the United States or its possessions at the time the adoption effort began.

Special rules. If you paid qualified adoption expenses in 2014 or any prior year in connection with the adoption of a foreign child and the adoption became final in 2014, you can use the

Exclusion of Prior Year Benefits Worksheet
(for the adoption of a foreign child that became final in 2014)

1. Enter the total employer-provided adoption benefits you received in **2014 and all prior years** for the adoption of the foreign child .... **1.** _____

2. Enter **$13,190**. If you and another person (other than your spouse if filing jointly) each received employer-provided adoption benefits in 2014 or any prior year to adopt the same child, see the instructions for line 2 at the end of this worksheet .... **2.** _____

3. Enter the **smaller** of line 1 or line 2 here and on Form 8839, line 17. If necessary, cross out the preprinted amount on line 17 and enter the result above the preprinted amount .... **3.** _____

Next:

- Enter -0- on Form 8839, line 18.
- Enter the amount from line 3 of this worksheet on Form 8839, line 19.
- On Form 8839, line 20, enter the total amount of employer-provided adoption benefits received in **2014 and all prior years.** On the dotted line next to line 20, enter "PYAB" and the total amount of benefits you received **before 2014.**
- Complete Form 8839 through line 28. Then, complete lines 4 through 9 of this worksheet to figure the amount of any prior year benefits you can exclude and the taxable benefits, if any, to enter on Form 8839, line 29.

4. Is the amount on your 2014 Form 8839, line 28, less than the amount on Form 8839, line 21?

   ☐ **No.** Skip lines 4 through 6 of this worksheet and go to line 7.

   ☐ **Yes.** Subtract Form 8839, line 28 from line 21 .... **4.** _____

5. Enter the total employer-provided adoption benefits you received **before 2014** included on Form 8839, line 20, for all children .... **5.** _____

6. **Taxable benefits.** Subtract line 5 of this worksheet from line 4. If zero or less, enter -0-. Enter the result here and on Form 8839, line 29. If more than zero, also include this amount on line 7 of Form 1040 or line 8 of Form 1040NR, and enter "AB" on the dotted line .... **6.** _____

7. Enter the amount from Form 8839, line 28 .... **7.** _____

8. Enter the total **2014** employer-provided adoption benefits included on Form 8839, line 20, for all children ...... **8.** _____

9. **Prior year excluded benefits.** Subtract line 8 of this worksheet from line 7. If zero or less, **stop;** you cannot exclude any of your prior year benefits .... **9.** _____

Next. Figure the total you would enter on line 7 of Form 1040 or line 8 of Form 1040NR **before** you exclude the amount from line 9 of this worksheet. Then, subtract the amount from line 9 of this worksheet from that total. Enter the result on line 7 of Form 1040 or line 8 of Form 1040NR. On the dotted line next to the line for wages, enter "PYAB" and the amount from line 9 of this worksheet.

Line 2. The maximum amount of employer-provided adoption benefits that can be excluded from income is $13,190 per child. If you and another person (other than your spouse if filing jointly) each received employer-provided adoption benefits to adopt the same child, the $13,190 limit must be divided between the two of you. You can divide it in any way you both agree. Enter your share of the $13,190 limit on line 2 of this worksheet.

---

total expenses you paid in 2014 and all prior years in determining the amount to enter on line 5. If you and another person (other than your spouse if filing jointly) each paid qualified adoption expenses to adopt the same child, the total qualified expenses must be divided between the two of you. You can divide it in any way you both agree.

If the adoption did not become final by the end of 2014, you cannot take the adoption credit for that child in 2014.

In general, the year of finality of a foreign adoption is determined either under Rev. Proc. 2005-31, I.R.B. 2005-31, 2005-26 1374, available at *www.irs.gov/irb/2005-26_IRB/ar14.html* (non-Hague adoptions) or under Rev. Proc. 2010-31, 2010-41 I.R.B. 413, available at *www.irs.gov/irb/2010-40_IRB/ar10.html* (Hague adoptions).

Non-Hague adoptions. In most non-Hague adoptions, there is an adoption proceeding in the foreign country (and the country is one that is not a party to the Hague Adoption Convention, discussed later) before the child is allowed to come to the United States. There may also be a re-adoption proceeding in the United States, either in the same year as the foreign adoption or in a later year. Rev. Proc. 2005-31 generally allows taxpayers to choose as the year of finality: (1) the year of the foreign-sending country adoption proceeding, or (2) the year of the re-adoption, if the re-adoption occurs in either the first or second year following the year of the foreign-country proceeding. The expenses of re-adoption are qualified adoption expenses in the year in which the expenses are paid, subject to the dollar limitation.

Example. Brian and Susan paid qualified adoption expenses of $7,000 in 2011, $8,000 in 2012, and $9,000 in 2013 in connection with the adoption of an eligible foreign child from Country X. Country X is a non-Hague country (a country not party to the Hague Adoption Convention). In 2013, Country X issued a final decree of adoption to Brian and Susan, who brought the child to the United States on an IR2, IR3, or IR4 visa. In 2014, Brian and Susan paid $1,000 in qualified adoption expenses in connection with re-adopting the child in their home state. Brian and Susan's modified gross income (MAGI) is less than the MAGI limitation in all years.

Under Rev. Proc. 2005-31, Brian and Susan may treat 2013 (the year of the adoption in Country X) or 2014 (the year of re-adoption in the United States) as the year of finality. If Brian and Susan choose 2013, then the $24,000 of aggregate qualified adoption expenses paid in 2011, 2012, and 2013 ($7,000 plus $8,000 plus $9,000) will be treated as paid in 2013. The credit will be limited to $12,970 (the dollar limitation for 2013).

Brian and Susan instead may choose to treat 2014 (the year of re-adoption in the United States) as the year of finality. If Brian and Susan choose 2014, then the $25,000 of aggregate qualified adoption expenses paid ($24,000 total from 2011, 2012, and 2013, plus the $1,000 of re-adoption expenses paid in 2014) will be treated as paid in 2014. The credit will be limited to $13,190 (the dollar limitation for 2014).

Hague adoptions. In Hague adoptions, there is usually an adoption proceeding in the sending country (and the country is one that is a party to the Hague Adoption Convention, discussed later) before the child is allowed to come to the United States. Rev. Proc. 2010-31 generally allows taxpayers to choose as the year of finality: (1) the year in which the sending country enters a final decree of adoption, or (2) the year in which the U.S. Secretary of State issues a certificate under section 301(a) of the Intercountry Adoption Act of 2000, 42 U.S.C. sections 14901 - 14954.

Custodial agreements followed by adoption in the United States. In a few cases, the sending country may allow the child to come to the United States under a custodial agreement. If so, the child will be adopted later in a state court in the United States. Both Rev. Proc. 2005-31 and Rev. Proc. 2010-31 allow the adoptive parent(s) to treat the year of the state-court adoption as the year of finality.

 The Hague Convention on Protection of Children and Co-operation in Respect of Intercountry Adoption (Hague Adoption Convention) entered into force for the United States on April 1, 2008. The Hague Adoption Convention applies if you adopted a child from a country that is party to the Hague Adoption Convention and you filed your application and petition (Forms I-800A and I-800) with the U.S. Citizenship and Immigration Service after March 31, 2008. See www.adoption.state.gov for more information on the Hague Adoption Convention, the application and petition, and a complete list of countries that are parties to the Convention.

If you received employer-provided adoption benefits in 2014 in connection with the adoption of a foreign child and the adoption did not become final by the end of 2014, you must include the benefits in the total entered on Form 1040, line 7, or Form 1040NR, line 8. Also, enter "AB" on the dotted line next to Form 1040, line 7, or Form 1040NR, line 8.

Exclusion of prior year benefits. If you received employer-provided adoption benefits before 2014 in connection with the adoption of a foreign child and the adoption became final in 2014, you may be able to exclude part or all of those benefits from your 2014 income. To find out if you can, complete the Exclusion of Prior Year Benefits Worksheet . You also must use that worksheet to complete Form 8839, Part III, and to figure any taxable benefits to enter on Form 8839, line 29.

If the adoption of more than one eligible foreign child became final in 2014, complete lines 1 through 3 of the Exclusion of Prior Year Benefits Worksheet separately for each foreign child and use the combined totals to complete lines 4 through 9 of the worksheet.

 If you check the box in column (e), you must also check the box in column (g), indicating the adoption was finalized in 2014 or earlier.

Column (f)

Enter the child's identifying number. This can be a social security number (SSN), an adoption taxpayer identification number (ATIN), or an individual taxpayer identification number (ITIN).

Enter the child's SSN if the child has an SSN or you will be able to get an SSN in time to file your tax return. Apply for an SSN using Form SS-5.

If you are in the process of adopting a child who is a U.S. citizen or resident alien but you cannot get an SSN for the child in time to file your return, apply for an ATIN using Form W-7A. However, if the child is not a U.S. citizen or resident alien, apply instead for an ITIN using Form W-7.

Column (g)

Check the box in column (g) if the adoption for each child became final in 2014 or earlier.

Part II—Adoption Credit
Line 2

The maximum adoption credit is $13,190 per child. If you and another person (other than your spouse if filing jointly) each paid qualified adoption expenses to adopt the same child, the $13,190 limit must be divided between the two of you. You can divide it in any way you both agree. Cross out the preprinted entry on line 2 and enter above line 2 your share of the $13,190 limit for that child.

Line 3

If you filed Form 8839 for a prior year for the same child, enter on line 3 the total of the amounts shown on lines 3 and 6 (or corresponding line) of the last form you filed for the child.

Line 5

 Special rules apply if you paid expenses in connection with the adoption of an eligible foreign child. See Column (e), earlier, for details.

Enter on line 5 the total qualified adoption expenses (as defined earlier) you paid in:
- 2013 if the adoption was not final by the end of 2014,
- 2013 and 2014 if the adoption became final in 2014, or
- 2014 if the adoption became final before 2014.

 Expenses reimbursed by your employer under a written qualified adoption assistance program are not qualified adoption expenses and must not be entered on line 5. See the examples following Employer-Provided Adoption Benefits, earlier.

Special needs adoption. If you adopted a U.S. child with special needs and the adoption became final in 2014, enter on line 5:
- $13,190, minus
- Any qualified adoption expenses you used to figure any adoption credit you claimed for the same child in a prior year. This is the amount you entered on line 3 of Form 8839 for this child.

If you did not claim any adoption credit for the child in a prior year, enter $13,190 on line 5 even if your qualified adoption expenses for the child were less than $13,190 (and even if you did not have any qualified adoption expenses for this child).

Form 8839 (2014)

Adoption Credit Carryforward Worksheet—Line 16

1. Enter the amount from Form 8839, line 12 . . . . **1.** _____

   Did you use the Adoption Credit Carryforward Worksheet—Line 16 in the 2013 Form 8839 instructions?

   ☐ **No.** Skip lines 2 and 3. Enter the amount from line 1 of this worksheet on line 4.

   ☐ **Yes.** Have that worksheet handy and go to line 2.

2. Enter any 2012 credit carryforward (line 5 of your 2013 worksheet) . . . . **2.** _____

3. Enter any 2013 credit carryforward (line 6 of your 2013 worksheet) . . . . **3.** _____

4. Add lines 1 through 3 . . . . **4.** _____

5. Enter the amount from Form 8839, line 16 . . . . **5.** _____

6. Subtract line 5 from line 4 . . . . **6.** _____

   Did you enter an amount on line 2 or 3 above?

   ☐ **No.** Enter the amount on line 6 on lines 11 and 12 below; skip all the other lines.

   ☐ **Yes.** Continue to line 7.

7. 2012 credit carryforward to 2015. Subtract line 5 from line 2. If zero or less, enter -0- . . . . **7.** _____

8. Subtract line 2 from line 5, If zero or less, enter -0- . . . . **8.** _____

9. 2013 credit carryforward to 2015. Subtract line 8 from line 3. If zero or less, enter -0- . . . . **9.** _____

10. Add lines 7 and 9 . . . . **10.** _____

11. 2014 credit carryforward to 2015. Subtract line 10 from line 6. If zero or less, enter -0- . . . . **11.** _____

12. Total credit carryforward to 2015. Add lines 10 and 11 . . . . **12.** _____

Unsuccessful adoption. If you paid qualified adoption expenses in an attempt to adopt a U.S. child and the attempt was unsuccessful, treat those expenses in the same manner as expenses you paid for adoptions not final by the end of the year.

Example. You paid $3,000 of qualified adoption expenses in 2013 in an attempt to adopt a U.S. child. You paid $2,000 in qualified adoption expenses early in 2014, However, the adoption attempt was unsuccessful. Enter $3,000 on line 5. The $2,000 paid in 2014 may qualify in 2015.

Line 7

Use the following chart to find your modified adjusted gross income to enter on line 7.

IF you file. . .	THEN enter on line 7 the amount from. . .

Form 1040	Form 1040, line 38, increased by the total of any:
	
	 • Exclusion of income from Puerto Rico and
	
	 • Amounts from–
	   • Form 2555, lines 45 and 50,
	   • Form 2555-EZ, line 18, and
	   • Form 4563, line 15.

Form 1040NR	Form 1040NR, line 37.

Line 15

Complete the credit limit worksheet to figure the limit of your nonrefundable adoption credit.

Credit Limit Worksheet—Line 15

1. Enter the amount from Form 8839, line 14 . . . . _____

2. Enter the amount from Form 1040, line 47, or Form 1040NR, line 45 . . . . _____

3. **1040 filers:** Enter the total of any amounts from Form 1040, lines 48 through 51; Form 5695, line 30; line 12 of the Line 11 Worksheet in Pub. 972; Form 8396, line 9; Form 8910, line 15; Form 8936, line 23; and Schedule R, line 22 . . . .

   1040NR filers: Enter the total of any amounts from Form 1040NR, lines 46 through 48; Form 5695, line 30; line 12 of the Line 11 Worksheet in Pub. 972; Form 8396, line 9; Form 8910, line 15; and Form 8936, line 23 . . . . _____

4. Subtract line 3 from line 2 . . . . _____

5. Enter the smaller of line 1 or line 4 here and on Form 8839, line 15 . . . . _____

 If you are not claiming the child tax credit for 2014, you do not need Pub. 972.

Line 16—Credit Carryforward to 2015

If Form 8839, line 15 is smaller than line 14, you may have an unused credit to carry forward to the next 5 years or until used, whichever comes first. Use the *Adoption Credit Carryforward Worksheet* to figure the amount of your credit carryforward. If you have any unused credit to carry forward to 2015, be sure you keep the worksheet. You will need it to figure your credit for 2015.

Part III—Employer-Provided Adoption Benefits
Line 17

The maximum amount that can be excluded from income for employer-provided adoption benefits is $13,190 per child. If you and another person (other than your spouse if filing jointly) each received employer-provided adoption benefits in connection with the adoption of the same eligible child, the $13,190 limit must be divided between the two of you. You can divide it in any way you both agree. Cross out the preprinted entry on line 17 and enter above line 17 your share of the $13,190 limit for that child.

Line 18

If you received employer-provided adoption benefits in a prior year for the same child, enter on line 18 the total of the amounts shown on lines 18 and 22 (or corresponding lines) of the last Form 8839 you filed for the child.

 Special rules apply if the prior year benefits were received in connection with the adoption of a foreign child and the adoption became final in 2014. See Exclusion of prior year benefits, *earlier.*

Line 22

If the child was a child with special needs and the adoption became final in 2014, enter the amount from line 19 only if your

employer has a qualified adoption assistance program, as defined earlier under *Employer-Provided Adoption Benefits.* This requirement applies whether or not you received any employer-provided adoption benefits under this plan.

If your employer has no qualified adoption assistance program, you must enter the smaller of line 19 or line 20.

Line 23

Use the following worksheet to figure your modified adjusted gross income.

 Your modified adjusted gross income (MAGI) for the adoption credit may not be the same as the MAGI figured in the following worksheet. If you are taking the credit, be sure to read Line 7 *before you enter an amount on that line.*

Modified Adjusted Gross Income (MAGI) Worksheet—Line 23   *Keep for Your Records*

Before you begin: ✓ If you file Form 1040, complete lines 8a through 21, 23 through 32, and 36 if they apply.
  ✓ If you file Form 1040NR, complete lines 9a through 21, 24 through 32, and 35 if they apply.

1. Enter the amount you would enter on line 7 of Form 1040 or line 8 of Form 1040NR if you could exclude the total amount on Form 8839, line 21 . . . .   **1.** _____

2. Enter the amount from Form 8839, line 21 . . . .   **2.** _____

3. **Form 1040 filers,** enter the total of lines 8a, 9a, 10 through 14, 15b, 16b, 17 through 19, 20b, and 21. **Form 1040NR filers,** enter the total of lines 9a, 10a, 11 through 15, 16b, 17b, and 18 through 21 . . . .   **3.** _____

4. Add lines 1, 2, and 3 . . . .   **4.** _____

5. **Form 1040 filers,** enter the total of lines 23 through 32, and any write-in adjustments entered on the dotted line next to line 36. **Form 1040NR filers,** enter the total of lines 24 through 32 and any write-in adjustments entered on the dotted line next to line 35 . . . .   **5.** _____

6. Subtract line 5 from line 4 . . . .   **6.** _____

Form 1040 filers, increase the amount on line 6 of this worksheet by the total of the following amounts. Enter the total on Form 8839, line 23.
  • Any amount from **Form 2555,** lines 45 and 50, **Form 2555-EZ,** line 18, and **Form 4563,** line 15, and
  • Any exclusion of income from Puerto Rico.

Form 1040NR filers, enter on Form 8839, line 23, the amount from line 6 of this worksheet.

Form 8839 (2014)

Form **8853**	**Archer MSAs and Long-Term Care Insurance Contracts**	OMB No. 1545-0074
Department of the Treasury Internal Revenue Service (99)	▶ Information about Form 8853 and its separate instructions is available at *www.irs.gov/form8853.* ▶ **Attach to Form 1040 or Form 1040NR.**	20**14** Attachment Sequence No. **39**

Name(s) shown on return

Social security number of MSA account holder. If both spouses have MSAs, see instructions ▶

Section A. Archer MSAs. If you have only a Medicare Advantage MSA, skip Section A and complete Section B.

Part I	**Archer MSA Contributions and Deductions.** See instructions before completing this part. If you are filing jointly and both you and your spouse have high deductible health plans with self-only coverage, complete a separate Part I for each spouse.

1 Total employer contributions to your Archer MSA(s) for 2014 . . . . | **1** |

2 Archer MSA contributions you made for 2014, including those made from January 1, 2015, through April 15, 2015, that were for 2014. Do not include rollovers (see instructions) . . . . . | **2** |

3 Limitation from the Line 3 Limitation Chart and Worksheet in the instructions . . . . | **3** |

4 Compensation (see instructions) from the employer maintaining the high deductible health plan. (If self-employed, enter your earned income from the trade or business under which the high deductible health plan was established.) . . . . | **4** |

5 **Archer MSA deduction.** Enter the **smallest** of line 2, 3, or 4 here. Also include this amount on Form 1040, line 36, or Form 1040NR, line 35. On the dotted line next to Form 1040, line 36, or Form 1040NR, line 35, enter "MSA" and the amount . . . . | **5** |

Caution: *If line 2 is more than line 5, you may have to pay an additional tax (see instructions).*

Part II	**Archer MSA Distributions**

6a Total distributions you and your spouse received in 2014 from all Archer MSAs (see instructions) . | **6a** |

   b Distributions included on line 6a that you rolled over to another Archer MSA or a health savings account. Also include any excess contributions (and the earnings on those excess contributions) included on line 6a that were withdrawn by the due date of your return (see instructions) . . . | **6b** |

   c Subtract line 6b from line 6a . . . . | **6c** |

7 Unreimbursed qualified medical expenses (see instructions) . . . . | **7** |

8 **Taxable Archer MSA distributions.** Subtract line 7 from line 6c. If zero or less, enter -0-. Also include this amount in the total on Form 1040, line 21, or Form 1040NR, line 21. On the dotted line next to line 21, enter "MSA" and the amount . . . . | **8** |

9a If any of the distributions included on line 8 meet any of the **Exceptions to the Additional 20% Tax** (see instructions), check here . . . . ▶ ☐ |

   b **Additional 20% tax** (see instructions). Enter 20% (.20) of the distributions included on line 8 that are subject to the additional 20% tax. Also include this amount in the total on Form 1040, line 62, or Form 1040NR, line 60. On the dotted line next to Form 1040, line 62, or Form 1040NR, line 60, enter "MSA" and the amount . . . . | **9b** |

Section B. Medicare Advantage MSA Distributions. If you are filing jointly and both you and your spouse received distributions in 2014 from a Medicare Advantage MSA, complete a separate Section B for each spouse (see instructions).

10 Total distributions you received in 2014 from all Medicare Advantage MSAs (see instructions) . . | **10** |

11 Unreimbursed qualified medical expenses (see instructions) . . . . | **11** |

12 **Taxable Medicare Advantage MSA distributions.** Subtract line 11 from line 10. If zero or less, enter -0-. Also include this amount in the total on Form 1040, line 21, or Form 1040NR, line 21. On the dotted line next to line 21, enter "Med MSA" and the amount . . . . | **12** |

13a If any of the distributions included on line 12 meet any of the **Exceptions to the Additional 50% Tax** (see instructions), check here . . . . ▶ ☐ |

   b **Additional 50% tax** (see instructions). Enter 50% (.50) of the distributions included on line 12 that are subject to the additional 50% tax. Also include this amount in the total on Form 1040, line 62, or Form 1040NR, line 60. On the dotted line next to Form 1040, line 62, or Form 1040NR, line 60, enter "Med MSA" and the amount . . . . | **13b** |

Name of policyholder (as shown on Form 1040)	Social security number of policyholder ▶

Section C. Long-Term Care (LTC) Insurance Contracts. See **Filing Requirements for Section C** in the instructions before completing this section.

If more than one Section C is attached, check here . . . . ▶ ☐

14a Name of insured ▶ _____ **b** Social security number of insured ▶ _____

15 In 2014, did anyone other than you receive payments on a per diem or other periodic basis under a qualified LTC insurance contract covering the insured or receive accelerated death benefits under a life insurance policy covering the insured? . . . . ☐ **Yes** ☐ **No**

16 Was the insured a terminally ill individual? . . . . ☐ **Yes** ☐ **No**
   Note: *If "Yes" and the **only** payments you received in 2014 were accelerated death benefits that were paid to you because the insured was terminally ill, skip lines 17 through 25 and enter -0- on line 26.*

17 Gross LTC payments received on a per diem or other periodic basis. Enter the total of the amounts from box 1 of all Forms 1099-LTC you received with respect to the insured on which the "Per diem" box in box 3 is checked **17**

   Caution: *Do not* *use lines 18 through 26 to figure the taxable amount of benefits paid under an LTC insurance contract that is not a **qualified** LTC insurance contract. Instead, if the benefits are not excludable from your income (for example, if the benefits are not paid for personal injuries or sickness through accident or health insurance), report the amount not excludable as income on Form 1040, line 21.*

18 Enter the part of the amount on line 17 that is from **qualified** LTC insurance contracts **18**

19 Accelerated death benefits received on a per diem or other periodic basis. Do not include any amounts you received because the insured was terminally ill (see instructions) **19**

20 Add lines 18 and 19 . . . . **20**
   Note: *If you checked "Yes" on line 15 above, see **Multiple Payees** in the instructions before completing lines 21 through 25.*

21 Multiply $330 by the number of days in the LTC period **21**

22 Costs incurred for qualified LTC services provided for the insured during the LTC period (see instructions) **22**

23 Enter the **larger** of line 21 or line 22 . . . . **23**

24 Reimbursements for qualified LTC services provided for the insured during the LTC period **24**
   Caution: *If you received any reimbursements from LTC contracts issued before August 1, 1996, see instructions.*

25 Per diem limitation. Subtract line 24 from line 23 . . . . **25**

26 **Taxable payments.** Subtract line 25 from line 20. If zero or less, enter -0-. Also include this amount in the total on Form 1040, line 21. On the dotted line next to line 21, enter "LTC" and the amount **26**

Form **8853** (2014)

Form **8863**	**Education Credits** **(American Opportunity and Lifetime Learning Credits)** ▶ Attach to Form 1040 or Form 1040A. ▶ **Information about Form 8863 and its separate instructions is at** *www.irs.gov/form8863.*	OMB No. 1545-0074 **2014**
Department of the Treasury Internal Revenue Service (99)		Attachment Sequence No. **50**

Name(s) shown on return	Your social security number

> ⚠️ **CAUTION**
>
> *Complete a separate Part III on page 2 for each student for whom you are claiming either credit before you complete Parts I and II.*

Part I — Refundable American Opportunity Credit

1	After completing Part III for each student, enter the total of all amounts from all Parts III, line 30 .	**1**	
2	Enter: $180,000 if married filing jointly; $90,000 if single, head of household, or qualifying widow(er)	**2**	
3	Enter the amount from Form 1040, line 38, or Form 1040A, line 22. If you are filing Form 2555, 2555-EZ, or 4563, or you are excluding income from Puerto Rico, see Pub. 970 for the amount to enter	**3**	
4	Subtract line 3 from line 2. If zero or less, **stop**; you cannot take any education credit	**4**	
5	Enter: $20,000 if married filing jointly; $10,000 if single, head of household, or qualifying widow(er)	**5**	
6	If line 4 is: • Equal to or more than line 5, enter 1.000 on line 6 . . . . • Less than line 5, divide line 4 by line 5. Enter the result as a decimal (rounded to at least three places)	**6**	.
7	Multiply line 1 by line 6. **Caution:** If you were under age 24 at the end of the year **and** meet the conditions described in the instructions, you **cannot** take the refundable American opportunity credit; skip line 8, enter the amount from line 7 on line 9, and check this box . . . . . ▶ ☐	**7**	
8	**Refundable American opportunity credit.** Multiply line 7 by 40% (.40). Enter the amount here and on Form 1040, line 68, or Form 1040A, line 44. Then go to line 9 below	**8**	

Part II — Nonrefundable Education Credits

9	Subtract line 8 from line 7. Enter here and on line 2 of the Credit Limit Worksheet (see instructions)	**9**	
10	After completing Part III for each student, enter the total of all amounts from all Parts III, line 31. If zero, skip lines 11 through 17, enter -0- on line 18, and go to line 19	**10**	
11	Enter the smaller of line 10 or $10,000	**11**	
12	Multiply line 11 by 20% (.20)	**12**	
13	Enter: $128,000 if married filing jointly; $64,000 if single, head of household, or qualifying widow(er)	**13**	
14	Enter the amount from Form 1040, line 38, or Form 1040A, line 22. If you are filing Form 2555, 2555-EZ, or 4563, or you are excluding income from Puerto Rico, see Pub. 970 for the amount to enter	**14**	
15	Subtract line 14 from line 13. If zero or less, skip lines 16 and 17, enter -0- on line 18, and go to line 19	**15**	
16	Enter: $20,000 if married filing jointly; $10,000 if single, head of household, or qualifying widow(er)	**16**	
17	If line 15 is: • Equal to or more than line 16, enter 1.000 on line 17 and go to line 18 • Less than line 16, divide line 15 by line 16. Enter the result as a decimal (rounded to at least three places)	**17**	.
18	Multiply line 12 by line 17. Enter here and on line 1 of the Credit Limit Worksheet (see instructions) ▶	**18**	
19	**Nonrefundable education credits.** Enter the amount from line 7 of the Credit Limit Worksheet (see instructions) here and on Form 1040, line 50, or Form 1040A, line 33	**19**	

For Paperwork Reduction Act Notice, see your tax return instructions.   Cat. No. 25379M   Form **8863** (2014)

Name(s) shown on return | Your social security number

 **CAUTION** *Complete Part III for each student for whom you are claiming either the American opportunity credit or lifetime learning credit. Use additional copies of Page 2 as needed for each student.*

| **Part III** | **Student and Educational Institution Information** |

See instructions.

20 Student name (as shown on page 1 of your tax return) | **21** Student social security number (as shown on page 1 of your tax return)

22 Educational institution information (see instructions)

a. Name of first educational institution | **b.** Name of second educational institution (if any)

(1) Address. Number and street (or P.O. box). City, town or post office, state, and ZIP code. If a foreign address, see instructions. | **(1)** Address. Number and street (or P.O. box). City, town or post office, state, and ZIP code. If a foreign address, see instructions.

(2) Did the student receive Form 1098-T from this institution for 2014? ☐ Yes ☐ No | **(2)** Did the student receive Form 1098-T from this institution for 2014? ☐ Yes ☐ No

(3) Did the student receive Form 1098-T from this institution for 2013 with Box 2 filled in and Box 7 checked? ☐ Yes ☐ No | **(3)** Did the student receive Form 1098-T from this institution for 2013 with Box 2 filled in and Box 7 checked? ☐ Yes ☐ No

If you checked "No" in **both (2)** and **(3)**, skip **(4)**. | If you checked "No" in **both (2)** and **(3)**, skip **(4)**.

(4) If you checked "Yes" in **(2) or (3)**, enter the institution's federal identification number (from Form 1098-T).

— — — — — — — — — | **(4)** If you checked "Yes" in **(2) or (3)**, enter the institution's federal identification number (from Form 1098-T).

— — — — — — — — —

23 Has the Hope Scholarship Credit or American opportunity credit been claimed for this student for any 4 tax years before 2014? | ☐ Yes — **Stop!** Go to line 31 for this student. | ☐ No — Go to line 24.

24 Was the student enrolled at least half-time for at least one academic period that began or is treated as having begun in 2014 at an eligible educational institution in a program leading towards a postsecondary degree, certificate, or other recognized postsecondary educational credential? (see instructions) | ☐ Yes — Go to line 25. | ☐ No — **Stop!** Go to line 31 for this student.

25 Did the student complete the first 4 years of post-secondary education before 2014? | ☐ Yes — **Stop!** Go to line 31 for this student. | ☐ No — Go to line 26.

26 Was the student convicted, before the end of 2014, of a felony for possession or distribution of a controlled substance? | ☐ Yes — **Stop!** Go to line 31 for this student. | ☐ No — Complete lines 27 through 30 for this student.

 **CAUTION** *You **cannot** take the American opportunity credit and the lifetime learning credit for the **same student** in the same year. If you complete lines 27 through 30 for this student, do not complete line 31.*

American Opportunity Credit

27 Adjusted qualified education expenses (see instructions). **Do not enter more than $4,000** . . . . | **27** |

28 Subtract $2,000 from line 27. If zero or less, enter -0-. . . . . | **28** |

29 Multiply line 28 by 25% (.25) . . . . | **29** |

30 If line 28 is zero, enter the amount from line 27. Otherwise, add $2,000 to the amount on line 29 and enter the result. Skip line 31. Include the total of all amounts from all Parts III, line 30 on Part I, line 1 . | **30** |

Lifetime Learning Credit

31 Adjusted qualified education expenses (see instructions). Include the total of all amounts from all Parts III, line 31, on Part II, line 10 . . . . | **31** |

2014

Department of the Treasury
Internal Revenue Service

Instructions for Form 8863

Education Credits (American Opportunity and Lifetime Learning Credits)

General Instructions

Section references are to the Internal Revenue Code unless otherwise noted.

Future Developments

For the latest information about developments related to Form 8863 and its instructions, such as legislation enacted after they were published, go to *www.irs.gov/form8863*.

What's New

Coordination with Pell grants and other scholarships or fellowship grants. Additional text is added to explain how choosing to include otherwise tax-free scholarships or fellowship grants in income can increase an education credit and lower your total tax or increase your refund. See *Coordination with Pell grants and other scholarships or fellowship grants* under *Adjusted Qualified Education Expenses.*

Limits on modified adjusted gross income (MAGI). The lifetime learning credit MAGI limit increases to $128,000 if you are filing married filing jointly ($64,000 if you are filing single, head of household, or qualifying widow(er)). The American opportunity credit MAGI limits remain unchanged. See Table 1 and the instructions for line 3 or line 14.

Purpose of Form

Use Form 8863 to figure and claim your education credits, which are based on adjusted qualified education expenses paid to an eligible educational institution (postsecondary). For 2014, there are two education credits.

* The American opportunity credit, part of which may be refundable.
* The lifetime learning credit, which is nonrefundable.

A **refundable** credit can give you a refund even if you owe no tax and are not otherwise required to file a tax return. A **nonrefundable** credit can reduce your tax, but any excess is not refunded to you.

Both of these credits have different rules that can affect your eligibility to claim a specific credit. These differences are shown in Table 1 below.

Who Can Claim an Education Credit

You may be able to claim an education credit if you, your spouse, or a dependent you claim on your tax return was a student enrolled at or attending an eligible educational

Table 1. Comparison of Education Credits for 2014

Caution. You can claim both the American opportunity credit and the lifetime learning credit on the same return but not for the same student.

	American Opportunity Credit	Lifetime Learning Credit
Maximum credit	Up to $2,500 credit per **eligible student**	Up to $2,000 credit per **return**
Limit on modified adjusted gross income (MAGI)	$180,000 if married filing jointly; $90,000 if single, head of household, or qualifying widow(er)	$128,000 if married filing jointly; $64,000 if single, head of household, or qualifying widow(er)
Refundable or nonrefundable	40% of credit may be refundable; the rest is nonrefundable	Nonrefundable—credit limited to the amount of tax you must pay on your taxable income
Number of years of postsecondary education	Available **ONLY** if the student had not completed the first 4 years of postsecondary education before 2014	Available for all years of postsecondary education and for courses to acquire or improve job skills
Number of tax years credit available	Available **ONLY** for **4** tax years per eligible student (including any year(s) Hope credit was claimed)	Available for an unlimited number of tax years
Type of program required	Student must be pursuing a program leading to a degree or other recognized education credential	Student does not need to be pursuing a program leading to a degree or other recognized education credential
Number of courses	Student must be enrolled at least half time for at least one academic period beginning during 2014 (or the first 3 months of 2015 if the qualified expenses were paid in 2014)	Available for one or more courses
Felony drug conviction	As of the end of 2014, the student had not been convicted of a felony for possessing or distributing a controlled substance	Felony drug convictions do not make the student ineligible
Qualified expenses	Tuition, required enrollment fees, and course materials that the student needs for a course of study whether or not the materials are bought at the educational institution as a condition of enrollment or attendance	Tuition and required enrollment fees (including amounts required to be paid to the institution for course-related books, supplies, and equipment)
Payments for academic periods	Payments made in 2014 for academic periods beginning in 2014 or beginning in the first 3 months of 2015	

institution. For 2014, the credits are based on the amount of adjusted qualified education expenses paid for the student in 2014 for academic periods beginning in 2014 or beginning in the first 3 months of 2015.

Academic period. An academic period is any quarter, semester, trimester, or any other period of study as reasonably determined by an eligible educational institution. If an eligible educational institution uses credit hours or clock hours and does not have academic terms, each payment period may be treated as an academic period. For details, see *Academic period* in chapters 2 and 3 of Pub. 970.

Who can claim a dependent's expenses. If a student is claimed as a dependent on another person's tax return, all qualified education expenses of the student are treated as having been paid by that person. Therefore, only that person can claim an education credit for the student. If a student is not claimed as a dependent on another person's tax return, only the student can claim a credit.

Expenses paid by a third party. Qualified education expenses paid on behalf of the student by someone other than the student (such as a relative) are treated as paid by the student. However, qualified education expenses paid (or treated as paid) by a student who is claimed as a dependent on your tax return are treated as paid by you. Therefore, you are treated as having paid expenses that were paid by the third party. For more information and an example, see *Who Can Claim a Dependent's Expenses* in Pub. 970, chapter 2 or 3.

Who cannot claim a credit. You cannot claim an education credit on a 2014 tax return if any of the following apply.

1. You are claimed as a dependent on another person's tax return, such as your parent's return.
2. Your filing status is married filing separately.
3. You (or your spouse) were a nonresident alien for any part of 2014 and did not elect to be treated as a resident alien for tax purposes.
4. Your modified adjusted gross income (MAGI) is:
   a. For the American opportunity credit: $180,000 or more if married filing jointly, or $90,000 or more if single, head of household, or qualifying widow(er) with dependent child.
   b. For the lifetime learning credit: $128,000 or more if married filing jointly, or $64,000 or more if single, head of household, or qualifying widow(er) with dependent child.

Generally, your MAGI is the amount on your Form 1040, line 38, or Form 1040A, line 22. However, if you are filing Form 2555, Foreign Earned Income; Form 2555-EZ, Foreign Earned Income Exclusion; or Form 4563, Exclusion of Income for Bona Fide Residents of American Samoa; or are excluding income from Puerto Rico; add to the amount on your Form 1040, line 38, or Form 1040A, line 22, the amount of income you excluded. For details, see Pub. 970.

American Opportunity Credit

You may be able to claim a credit of up to $2,500 for adjusted qualified education expenses (defined later) paid for each student who qualifies for the American opportunity credit. This credit equals 100% of the first $2,000 and 25% of the next $2,000 of adjusted qualified education expenses paid for each eligible student. The amount of your credit for 2014 is gradually reduced (phased out) if your MAGI is between $80,000 and $90,000 ($160,000 and $180,000 if you file a joint return). You

cannot claim a credit if your MAGI is $90,000 or more ($180,000 or more if you file a joint return).

 If you can claim the American opportunity credit for any student, you can choose between using that student's adjusted qualified education expenses for the American opportunity credit or for the lifetime learning credit. If you have this choice, the American opportunity credit will always be greater than the lifetime learning credit.

Student qualifications. Generally, you can claim the American opportunity credit for a student on a 2014 tax return only if **all** of the following four requirements are met.

1. As of the beginning of 2014, the student had not completed the first 4 years of postsecondary education (generally, the freshman through senior years of college), as determined by the eligible educational institution. For this purpose, do not include academic credit awarded solely because of the student's performance on proficiency examinations.

2. Neither the American opportunity credit nor the Hope scholarship credit has been claimed (by you or anyone else) for this student for any 4 tax years before 2014. If the American opportunity credit (and Hope scholarship credit) has been claimed for this student for any 3 or fewer tax years before 2014, this requirement is met.

Example 1. Sharon was eligible for the Hope scholarship credit for 2008 and for the American opportunity credit for 2009, 2011, and 2013. Her parents claimed the Hope scholarship credit for Sharon on their tax return for 2008 and claimed the American opportunity credit for Sharon on their 2009 and 2011 tax returns. Sharon claimed the American opportunity credit on her 2013 tax return. The American opportunity credit and Hope scholarship credit have been claimed for Sharon for 4 tax years before 2014. Therefore, the American opportunity credit **cannot** be claimed for Sharon for 2014. If Sharon were to file Form 8863 for 2014, she would check "Yes" for Part III, line 23, and would be eligible to claim only the lifetime learning credit.

Example 2. Wilbert was eligible for the American opportunity credit for 2010, 2011, 2012, and 2014. His parents claimed the American opportunity credit for Wilbert on their tax returns for 2010, 2011, and 2012. No one claimed an American opportunity credit or Hope scholarship credit for Wilbert for any other tax year. The American opportunity credit and Hope scholarship credit have been claimed for Wilbert for only 3 tax years before 2014. Therefore, Wilbert meets the second requirement to be eligible for the American opportunity credit. If Wilbert were to file Form 8863 for 2014, he would check "No" for Part III, line 23. If Wilbert meets all of the other requirements, he is eligible for the American opportunity credit.

3. For at least one academic period beginning or treated as beginning (see below) in 2014, the student both:
   a. Was enrolled in a program that leads to a degree, certificate, or other recognized educational credential; and
   b. Carried at least one-half the normal full-time workload for his or her course of study.

The standard for what is half of the normal full-time work load is determined by each eligible educational institution. However, the standard may not be lower than any of those established by the U.S. Department of Education under the Higher Education Act of 1965.

For 2014, treat an academic period beginning in the first 3 months of 2015 as if it began in 2014 if qualified education expenses for the student were paid in 2014 for that academic period. See *Prepaid Expenses,* later.

Example. Glenda enrolls on a full-time basis in a degree program for the 2015 Spring semester, which begins in January

2015. Glenda pays her tuition for the 2015 Spring semester in December 2014. Because the tuition Glenda paid in 2014 relates to an academic period that begins in the first 3 months of 2015, her eligibility to claim an American opportunity credit in 2014 is determined as if the 2015 Spring semester began in 2014. Therefore, Glenda satisfies this third requirement.

4. As of the end of 2014, the student had not been convicted of a federal or state felony for possessing or distributing a controlled substance.

 If the requirements above are not met for any student, you cannot claim the American opportunity credit for that student. You may be able to claim the lifetime learning credit for part or all of that student's qualified education expenses instead.

Lifetime Learning Credit

The lifetime learning credit equals 20% of adjusted qualified education expenses (defined later), up to a maximum of $10,000 of adjusted qualified education expenses per return. Therefore, the maximum lifetime learning credit you can claim on your return for the year is $2,000, regardless of the number of students for whom you paid qualified education expenses. The amount of your credit for 2014 is gradually reduced (phased out) if your MAGI is between $54,000 and $64,000 ($108,000 and $128,000 if you file a joint return). You cannot claim a credit if your MAGI is $64,000 or more ($128,000 or more if you file a joint return).

You cannot claim the lifetime learning credit for any student if you claim the American opportunity credit for that student for the same tax year.

Qualified Education Expenses

Generally, qualified education expenses are amounts paid in 2014 for tuition and fees required for the student's enrollment or attendance at an eligible educational institution. It does not matter whether the expenses were paid in cash, by check, by credit or debit card, or with borrowed funds.

For course-related books, supplies, and equipment only certain expenses qualify.
• American opportunity credit: Qualified education expenses include amounts spent on books, supplies, and equipment needed for a course of study, whether or not the materials are purchased from the educational institution as a condition of enrollment or attendance.
• Lifetime learning credit: Qualified education expenses include amounts for books, supplies, and equipment **only if** required to be paid to the institution as a condition of enrollment or attendance.

Qualified education expenses include nonacademic fees, such as student activity fees, athletic fees, or other expenses unrelated to the academic course of instruction, **only if** the fee must be paid to the institution as a condition of enrollment or attendance. However, fees for personal expenses (described below) are never qualified education expenses.

Qualified education expenses **do not** include amounts paid for:
• Personal expenses. This means room and board, insurance, medical expenses (including student health fees), transportation, and other similar personal, living, or family expenses.
• Any course or other education involving sports, games, or hobbies, or any noncredit course, unless such course or other education is part of the student's degree program or (for the lifetime learning credit only) helps the student acquire or improve job skills.

You may receive Form 1098-T, Tuition Statement, from the institution reporting either payments received in 2014 (box 1) or amounts billed in 2014 (box 2). However, the amount in box 1 or 2 of Form 1098-T may be different from the amount you paid (or are treated as having paid). In completing Form 8863, use only the amounts you actually paid (plus any amounts you are treated as having paid) in 2014 (reduced, as necessary, as described in *Adjusted Qualified Education Expenses,* later). See chapters 2 and 3 of Pub. 970 for more information on Form 1098-T.

Qualified education expenses paid on behalf of the student by someone other than the student (such as a relative) are treated as paid by the student. Qualified education expenses paid (or treated as paid) by a student who is claimed as a dependent on your tax return are treated as paid by you.

If you or the student takes a deduction for higher education expenses, such as on Schedule A or Schedule C (Form 1040), you cannot use those same expenses in your qualified education expenses when figuring your education credits.

 Any qualified expenses used to figure the education credits cannot be taken into account in determining the amount of a distribution from a Coverdell ESA or a qualified tuition program (section 529 plan) that is excluded from gross income. See Pub. 970, chapters 6 and 7, for more information.

Prepaid Expenses

Qualified education expenses paid in 2014 for an academic period that begins in the first 3 months of 2015 can be used in figuring an education credit for 2014 only. See *Academic period,* earlier. For example, if you pay $2,000 in December 2014 for qualified tuition for the 2015 winter quarter that begins in January 2015, you can use that $2,000 in figuring an education credit for 2014 only (if you meet all the other requirements).

 You cannot use any amount you paid in 2013 or 2015 to figure the qualified education expenses you use to figure your 2014 education credit(s).

Adjusted Qualified Education Expenses

For each student, reduce the qualified education expenses paid in 2014 by or on behalf of that student under the following rules. The result is the amount of adjusted qualified education expenses for each student.

Tax-free educational assistance. For tax-free educational assistance received in 2014, reduce the qualified educational expenses for each academic period by the amount of tax-free educational assistance allocable to that academic period. See *Academic period,* earlier.

Tax-free educational assistance includes:

1. The tax-free part of any scholarship or fellowship grant (including Pell grants),

2. The tax-free part of any employer-provided educational assistance,

3. Veterans' educational assistance, and

4. Any other educational assistance that is excludable from gross income (tax free), other than as a gift, bequest, devise, or inheritance.

 You may be able to increase the combined value of an education credit and certain educational assistance if the student includes some or all of the educational assistance in income in the year it is received.

Generally, any scholarship or fellowship grant is treated as tax-free educational assistance. However, a scholarship or fellowship grant is not treated as tax-free educational assistance to the extent the **student** includes it in gross income (the

student may or may not be required to file a tax return) for the year the scholarship or fellowship grant is received and either:
- The scholarship or fellowship grant (or any part of it) **must** be applied (by its terms) to expenses (such as room and board) other than qualified education expenses; or
- The scholarship or fellowship grant (or any part of it) **may** be applied (by its terms) to expenses (such as room and board) other than qualified education expenses.

Coordination with Pell grants and other scholarships or fellowship grants. You may be able to increase an education credit and reduce your total tax or increase your tax refund if the student (you, your spouse, or your dependent) chooses to include all or part of certain scholarships or fellowship grants in income. The scholarship or fellowship grant must be one that may qualify as a tax-free scholarship under the rules discussed in chapter 1 of Pub. 970. Also, the scholarship or fellowship grant must be one that may (by its terms) be used for expenses other than qualified education expenses (such as room and board).

The fact that the educational institution applies the scholarship or fellowship grant to qualified education expenses (such as tuition and related fees) does not prevent the student from choosing to apply certain scholarships or fellowship grants to other expenses (such as room and board). By choosing to do so, the student will include the part applied to other expenses (such as room and board) in gross income and may be required to file a tax return. But, this allows payments made in cash, by check, by credit or debit card, or with borrowed funds such as a student loan to be applied to qualified education expenses. These payments, unlike certain scholarships or fellowship grants, will not reduce the qualified education expenses available to figure an education credit. The result is generally a larger education credit that reduces your total tax or increases your tax refund.

Example 1. Last year, your child graduated from high school and enrolled in college for the fall semester. You and your child meet all other requirements to claim the American opportunity credit, and you need to determine adjusted qualified education expenses to figure the credit.

Your child has $5,000 of qualified education expenses and $4,000 of room and board. Your child received a $5,000 Pell grant and took out a $2,750 student loan to pay these expenses. You paid the remaining $1,250. The Pell grant by its terms may be used for any of these expenses.

If you and your child choose to apply the Pell grant to the qualified education expenses, it will qualify as a tax-free scholarship under the rules discussed in chapter 1 of Pub. 970. Your child will not include any part of the Pell grant in gross income. After reducing qualified education expenses by the tax-free scholarship you will have $0 ($5,000 - $5,000) of adjusted qualified education expenses available to figure your credit. Your credit will be $0.

Example 2. The facts are the same as in Example 1. If, unlike in Example 1, you and your child choose to apply only $1,000 of the Pell grant to the qualified education expenses and to apply the remaining $4,000 to room and board, only $1,000 will qualify as a tax-free scholarship.

Your child will include the $4,000 applied to room and board in gross income, and it will be treated as earned income for purposes of determining whether your child is required to file a tax return. If the $4,000 is your child's only income, your child will not be required to file a tax return.

After reducing qualified education expenses by the tax-free scholarship you will have $4,000 ($5,000 - $1,000) of adjusted qualified education expenses available to figure your credit. Your refundable American opportunity credit will be $1,000. Your

nonrefundable credit may be as much as $1,500 but depends on your tax liability.

If you are not otherwise required to file a tax return, you should file to get a refund of your $1,000 refundable credit but your tax liability and nonrefundable credit will be $0.

Note. The result may be different if your child has other income or if you are the student. If you are the student and you claim the earned income credit, choosing not to apply a Pell grant to qualified education expenses may decrease your earned income credit at certain income levels by raising your adjusted gross income. However, you generally need at least $2,000 of adjusted qualified education expenses to receive the maximum benefit of claiming both credits. For details and more examples, see Pub. 970.

 Unlike a scholarship or fellowship grant, a tax-free distribution from a Coverdell ESA or qualified tuition program (section 529 plan) can be applied to either qualified education expenses or certain other expenses (such as room and board) without creating a tax liability for the student. An education credit can be claimed in the same year the beneficiary takes a tax-free distribution from a Coverdell ESA or qualified tuition program, as long as the same expenses are not used for both benefits. For details, see Pub. 970, chapter 7 or 8.

Tax-free educational assistance treated as a refund. Some tax-free educational assistance received after 2014 may be treated as a refund of qualified education expenses paid in 2014. This tax-free educational assistance is any tax-free educational assistance received by you or anyone else after 2014 for qualified education expenses paid on behalf of a student in 2014 (or attributable to enrollment at an eligible educational institution during 2014).

If this tax-free educational assistance is received after 2014 but before you file your 2014 income tax return, see *Refunds received after 2014 but before your income tax return is filed,* later. If this tax-free educational assistance is received after 2014 and after you file your 2014 income tax return, see *Refunds received after 2014 and after your income tax return is filed,* later.

Refunds. A refund of qualified education expenses may reduce qualified education expenses for the tax year or may require you to repay (recapture) the credit that you claimed in an earlier year. Some tax-free educational assistance received after 2014 may be treated as a refund. See *Tax-free educational assistance treated as a refund,* earlier.

Refunds received in 2014. For each student, figure the adjusted qualified education expenses for 2014 by adding all the qualified education expenses paid in 2014 and subtracting any refunds of those expenses received from the eligible educational institution during 2014.

Refunds received after 2014 but before your income tax return is filed. If anyone receives a refund after 2014 of qualified education expenses paid on behalf of a student in 2014 and the refund is received before you file your 2014 income tax return, reduce the amount of qualified education expenses for 2014 by the amount of the refund.

Refunds received after 2014 and after your income tax return is filed. If anyone receives a refund after 2014 of qualified education expenses paid on behalf of a student in 2014 and the refund is received after you file your 2014 income tax return, you may need to repay some or all of the credit that you claimed. See *Credit recapture,* next.

Credit recapture. If any tax-free educational assistance for the qualified education expenses paid in 2014, or any refund of your qualified education expenses paid in 2014, is received after you file your 2014 income tax return, you must recapture (repay) any excess credit. You do this by refiguring the amount of your adjusted qualified education expenses for 2014 by reducing the expenses by the amount of the refund or tax-free educational assistance. You then refigure your education credit(s) for 2014 and figure the amount by which your 2014 tax liability would have increased if you had claimed the refigured credit(s). Include that amount as an additional tax for the year the refund or tax-free assistance was received.

Example. You paid $8,000 tuition and fees in December 2014 for your child's Spring semester beginning in January 2015. You filed your 2014 tax return on February 2, 2015, and claimed a lifetime learning credit of $1,600 ($8,000 qualified education expense paid x .20). You claimed no other tax credits. After you filed your return, your child withdrew from two courses and you received a refund of $1,400. You must refigure your 2014 lifetime learning credit using $6,600 ($8,000 qualified education expenses – $1,400 refund). The refigured credit is $1,320 and your tax liability increased by $280. You must include the difference of $280 ($1,600 credit originally claimed – $1,320 refigured credit) as additional tax on your 2015 income tax return. See the instructions for your 2015 income tax return to determine where to include this tax.

 If you paid qualified education expenses in both 2014 and 2015 for an academic period that begins in the first 3 months of 2015 and you receive tax-free educational assistance, or a refund, as described above, you may choose to reduce the qualified education expenses you paid in 2015 instead of reducing the qualified education expenses you paid in 2014.

Eligible Educational Institution

An eligible educational institution is generally any accredited public, nonprofit, or proprietary (private) college, university, vocational school, or other postsecondary institution. Also, the institution must be eligible to participate in a student aid program administered by the Department of Education. Virtually all accredited postsecondary institutions meet this definition.

An eligible educational institution also includes certain educational institutions located outside the United States that are eligible to participate in a student aid program administered by the Department of Education.

 The educational institution should be able to tell you if it is an eligible educational institution.

Additional Information

See Pub. 970, Tax Benefits for Education, chapters 2 and 3, for more information about these credits.

Specific Instructions

 You must complete a separate Part III on page 2 for each individual for whom you are claiming either credit before you complete Parts I and II.

Part I — Refundable American Opportunity Credit

Line 1

Enter the amount from Part III, line 30. If you are claiming the American opportunity credit for more than one student, add the amounts from each student's Part III, line 30, and enter the total for those students on line 1.

Line 3

Enter your modified adjusted gross income. Generally, your modified adjusted gross income is the amount on your Form 1040, line 38, or Form 1040A, line 22. However, if you are filing Form 2555, Form 2555-EZ, or Form 4563, or are excluding income from Puerto Rico, you must include on line 3 the amount of income you excluded. For details, see Pub. 970.

Line 7

If you were under age 24 at the end of 2014 and the conditions listed below apply to you, you **cannot** claim any part of the American opportunity credit as a refundable credit on your tax return. Instead, you can claim your allowed credit, figured in Part II, only as a nonrefundable credit to reduce your tax.

You do **not** qualify for a refundable American opportunity credit if 1 (a, b, or c), 2, and 3 below apply to you.

1. You were:
   a. Under age 18 at the end of 2014, **or**
   b. Age 18 at the end of 2014 **and** your earned income (defined later) was less than one-half of your support (defined later), **or**
   c. Over age 18 and under age 24 at the end of 2014 **and** a full-time student (defined later) **and** your earned income (defined later) was less than one-half of your support (defined later).
2. At least one of your parents was alive at the end of 2014.
3. You are not filing a joint return for 2014.

If you meet these conditions, check the box next to line 7, skip line 8, and enter the amount from line 7 on line 9. If these conditions do not apply to you, complete line 8.

You can answer the following questions to determine whether you qualify for a refundable American opportunity credit.

1. Were you under age 24 at the end of 2014?

   If no, stop here; you **do** qualify to claim part of the allowable American opportunity credit as a refundable credit.
   If yes, go to question 2.

2. Were you over age 18 at the end of 2014?

   If yes, go to question 3.
   If no, go to question 4.

3. Were you a full-time student (defined later) for 2014?

   If no, stop here; you **do** qualify to claim part of your allowable American opportunity credit as a refundable credit.
   If yes, go to question 5.

4. Were you age 18 at the end of 2014?

   If yes, go to question 5.
   If no, go to question 6.

5. Was your earned income (defined later) less than one-half of your support (defined later) for 2014?
   If no, stop here; you **do** qualify to claim part of your allowable American opportunity credit as a refundable credit.
   If yes, go to question 6.

6. Were either of your parents alive at the end of 2014?

   If no, stop here; you **do** qualify to claim part of your allowable American opportunity credit as a refundable credit.
   If yes, go to question 7.

7. Are you filing a joint return for 2014?

   If no, you **do not** qualify to claim part of your allowable American opportunity credit as a refundable credit.

If yes, you **do** qualify to claim part of your allowable American opportunity credit as a refundable credit.

Earned income. Earned income includes wages, salaries, professional fees, and other payments received for personal services actually performed. Earned income includes the part of any scholarship or fellowship grant that represents payment for teaching, research, or other services performed by the student that are required as a condition for receiving the scholarship or fellowship grant. Earned income does not include that part of the compensation for personal services rendered to a corporation which represents a distribution of earnings or profits rather than a reasonable allowance as compensation for the personal services actually rendered.

If you are a sole proprietor or a partner in a trade or business in which both personal services and capital are material income-producing factors, earned income also includes a reasonable allowance for compensation for personal services, but not more than 30% of your share of the net profits from that trade or business (after subtracting the deduction for one-half of self-employment tax). However, if capital is not an income-producing factor and your personal services produced the business income, the 30% limit does not apply.

Support. Your support includes food, shelter, clothing, medical and dental care, education and the like. Generally, the amount of an item of support will be the amount of expenses incurred by the one furnishing such item. If the item of support is in the form of property or lodging, measure the amount of such item of support by its fair market value. To figure your support, count support provided by you, your parents, and others. However, a scholarship received by you is not considered support if you were a full-time student (defined below) for 2014.

Full-time student. Solely for purposes of determining whether a scholarship is considered support, you were a full-time student for 2014 if during any part of any 5 calendar months during the year you were enrolled as a full-time student at an eligible educational institution (defined earlier), or took a full-time, on-farm training course given by such an institution or by a state, county, or local government agency.

Part II — Nonrefundable Education Credits

Line 9

Enter the amount from line 9 on line 2 of the Credit Limit Worksheet, later.

Line 10

Enter the amount from Part III, line 31. If you are claiming the lifetime learning credit for more than one student, add the amounts from each student's Part III, line 31, and enter the total for all those students on line 10.

Line 14

Generally, your modified adjusted gross income is the amount on your Form 1040, line 38, or Form 1040A, line 22. However, if you are filing Form 2555, Form 2555-EZ, or Form 4563, or are excluding income from Puerto Rico, you must include on line 14 the amount of income you excluded. For details, see Pub. 970.

Line 18

Enter the amount from line 18 on line 1 of the Credit Limit Worksheet, later.

Line 19

Enter the amount from line 7 of the Credit Limit Worksheet here and on Form 1040, line 50; or Form 1040A, line 33.

Credit Limit Worksheet
Complete this worksheet to figure the amount to enter on line 19.
1. Enter the amount from Form 8863, line 18 . . . .   **1.** _____
2. Enter the amount from Form 8863, line 9 . . . .   **2.** _____
3. Add lines 1 and 2 . . . .   **3.** _____
4. Enter the amount from: Form 1040, line 47; or Form 1040A, line 30 . . . .   **4.** _____
5. Enter the total of your credits from either: Form 1040, lines 48 and 49, and Schedule R, line 22; or Form 1040A, lines 31 and 32 . . . . . .   **5.** _____
6. Subtract line 5 from line 4 . . . .   **6.** _____
7. Enter the smaller of line 3 or line 6 here and on Form 8863, line 19 . . . .   **7.** _____

 You must complete Part III for each student for whom you are claiming either the American opportunity credit or lifetime learning credit before you complete either Part I or Part II. Use additional copies of page 2 as needed for each student.

Part III — Student and Educational Institution Information

Line 20

Enter the student's name as shown on page 1 of your tax return.

Line 21

Enter the student's taxpayer identification number as shown on page 1 of your tax return.

Line 22

If the student attended only one educational institution, enter the information about the institution and answer the questions about Form 1098-T in column (a). If the student attended a second educational institution, enter the information and answers for the second educational institution in column (b). If the student attended more than 2 educational institutions, attach an additional page 2 completed only through line 22.

If the educational institution has a foreign address, enter the foreign address here and do not abbreviate the country name. Follow the country's practice for entering the postal code and name of the province, country, or state.

Line 23

If the American opportunity credit has been claimed for this student for any 4 tax years before 2014 (including any year for which the Hope scholarship credit was claimed for the student), the American opportunity credit cannot be claimed for this student for 2014. Check "Yes" and go to line 31.

If the American opportunity and Hope scholarship credits have been claimed for this student for 3 or fewer prior tax years, check "No." See *Student qualifications,* earlier.

Line 24

Check "Yes" if the student enrolled at least half-time for at least one academic period that began or is treated as having begun (see below) in 2014 at an eligible educational institution in a program leading towards a postsecondary degree, certificate, or other recognized postsecondary educational credential. Otherwise, check "No."

If any qualified education expenses for the student were paid in 2014 for an academic period beginning in the first 3 months of 2015, treat that academic period as if it began in 2014. See *Student qualifications* and *Prepaid Expenses,* earlier.

If you checked "Yes," go to line 25. If you checked "No," the student is not eligible for the American opportunity credit; skip lines 25 through 30 and go to line 31.

Line 25

Check "Yes" if the student completed the first 4 years of postsecondary education before 2014. Otherwise, check "No."

A student has completed the first 4 years of postsecondary education before 2014 if the educational institution has awarded the student 4 years of academic credit at that institution for postsecondary coursework the student completed before 2014. Disregard any academic credit awarded solely on the basis of the student's performance on proficiency examinations.

If you checked "No," go to line 26. If you checked "Yes," the student is not eligible for the American opportunity credit; skip lines 26 through 30 and go to line 31.

Line 26

Check "Yes" if the student was convicted, before the end of 2014, of a federal or state felony for possession or distribution of a controlled substance.

If you checked "No," complete lines 27 through 30 for this student. If you checked "Yes," the student is not eligible for the American opportunity credit; skip lines 26 through 30 and go to line 31.

 *You **cannot** claim the American opportunity credit and the lifetime learning credit for the **same student** in the same year. If you complete lines 27 through 30 for this student, do not complete line 31.*

American Opportunity Credit

Line 27

Enter the student's adjusted qualified education expenses for line 27. See *Qualified Education Expenses,* earlier. Use the Adjusted Qualified Education Expenses Worksheet, later, to figure each student's adjusted qualified education expenses. Do not enter more than $4,000. Enter the total of all amounts from all Parts III, line 30, on Part I, line 1.

Lifetime Learning Credit

Line 31

Enter the student's adjusted qualified education expenses for line 31. See *Qualified Education Expenses,* earlier. Use the

Adjusted Qualified Education Expenses Worksheet, next, to figure each student's adjusted qualified education expenses. Enter the total of all amounts from Part III, line 31, on Part II, line 10.

Adjusted Qualified Education Expenses Worksheet

See *Qualified Education Expenses,* earlier, before completing.

Complete a separate worksheet for each student for each academic period beginning or treated as beginning (see below) in 2014 for which you paid (or are treated as having paid) qualified education expenses in 2014.

1.	Total qualified education expenses paid for or on behalf of the student in 2014 for the academic period	_____
2.	Less adjustments:	
	a. Tax-free educational assistance received in 2014 allocable to the academic period . . . . _____	
	b. Tax-free educational assistance received in 2015 (and before you file your 2014 tax return) allocable to the academic period . . . _____	
	c. Refunds of qualified education expenses paid in 2014 if the refund is received in 2014 or in 2015 before you file your 2014 tax return . . . . _____	
3.	Total adjustments (add lines 2a, 2b, and 2c)	_____
4.	Adjusted qualified education expenses. Subtract line 3 from line 1. If zero or less, enter -0-	_____

 If you are claiming an education credit for more than one student, complete a separate Part III for each student before returning to page 1 to complete Parts I and II.

If any qualified education expenses for the student were paid in 2014 for an academic period beginning in the first 3 months of 2015, treat that academic period as if it began in 2014. See *Student qualifications and Prepaid Expenses*, earlier.

Form **8949**	**Sales and Other Dispositions of Capital Assets**	OMB No. 1545-0074

Form **8949**

Department of the Treasury
Internal Revenue Service

Sales and Other Dispositions of Capital Assets

▶ Information about Form 8949 and its separate instructions is at *www.irs.gov/form8949.*
▶ File with your Schedule D to list your transactions for lines 1b, 2, 3, 8b, 9, and 10 of Schedule D.

OMB No. 1545-0074

20**14**

Attachment
Sequence No. **12A**

Name(s) shown on return	Social security number or taxpayer identification number

Before you check Box A, B, or C below, see whether you received any Form(s) 1099-B or substitute statement(s) from your broker. A substitute statement will have the same information as Form 1099-B. Either may show your basis (usually your cost) even if your broker did not report it to the IRS. Brokers must report basis to the IRS for most stock you bought in 2011 or later (and for certain debt instruments you bought in 2014 or later).

Part I **Short-Term.** Transactions involving capital assets you held 1 year or less are short term. For long-term transactions, see page 2.

Note. You may aggregate all short-term transactions reported on Form(s) 1099-B showing basis was reported to the IRS and for which no adjustments or codes are required. Enter the total directly on Schedule D, line 1a; you are not required to report these transactions on Form 8949 (see instructions).

You *must* check Box A, B, *or* C below. Check only one box. If more than one box applies for your short-term transactions, complete a separate Form 8949, page 1, for each applicable box. If you have more short-term transactions than will fit on this page for one or more of the boxes, complete as many forms with the same box checked as you need.

- ☐ **(A)** Short-term transactions reported on Form(s) 1099-B showing basis was reported to the IRS (see **Note** above)
- ☐ **(B)** Short-term transactions reported on Form(s) 1099-B showing basis was **not** reported to the IRS
- ☐ **(C)** Short-term transactions not reported to you on Form 1099-B

1 (a) Description of property (Example: 100 sh. XYZ Co.)	(b) Date acquired (Mo., day, yr.)	(c) Date sold or disposed (Mo., day, yr.)	(d) Proceeds (sales price) (see instructions)	(e) Cost or other basis. See the **Note** below and see *Column (e)* in the separate instructions	Adjustment, if any, to gain or loss. If you enter an amount in column (g), enter a code in column (f). See the separate instructions. (f) Code(s) from instructions	(g) Amount of adjustment	(h) Gain or (loss). Subtract column (e) from column (d) and combine the result with column (g)

2 Totals. Add the amounts in columns (d), (e), (g), and (h) (subtract negative amounts). Enter each total here and include on your Schedule D, **line 1b** (if **Box A** above is checked), **line 2** (if **Box B** above is checked), or **line 3** (if **Box C** above is checked) ▶

Note. If you checked Box A above but the basis reported to the IRS was incorrect, enter in column (e) the basis as reported to the IRS, and enter an adjustment in column (g) to correct the basis. See *Column (g)* in the separate instructions for how to figure the amount of the adjustment.

For Paperwork Reduction Act Notice, see your tax return instructions.   Cat. No. 37768Z   Form **8949** (2014)

Name(s) shown on return. Name and SSN or taxpayer identification no. not required if shown on other side	Social security number or taxpayer identification number

Before you check Box D, E, or F below, see whether you received any Form(s) 1099-B or substitute statement(s) from your broker. A substitute statement will have the same information as Form 1099-B. Either may show your basis (usually your cost) even if your broker did not report it to the IRS. Brokers must report basis to the IRS for most stock you bought in 2011 or later (and for certain debt instruments you bought in 2014 or later).

Part II   **Long-Term.** Transactions involving capital assets you held more than 1 year are long term. For short-term transactions, see page 1.

           Note. You may aggregate all long-term transactions reported on Form(s) 1099-B showing basis was reported to the IRS and for which no adjustments or codes are required. Enter the total directly on Schedule D, line 8a; you are not required to report these transactions on Form 8949 (see instructions).

You *must* check Box D, E, *or* F below. **Check only one box.** If more than one box applies for your long-term transactions, complete a separate Form 8949, page 2, for each applicable box. If you have more long-term transactions than will fit on this page for one or more of the boxes, complete as many forms with the same box checked as you need.

- ☐ **(D)** Long-term transactions reported on Form(s) 1099-B showing basis was reported to the IRS (see **Note** above)
- ☐ **(E)** Long-term transactions reported on Form(s) 1099-B showing basis was **not** reported to the IRS
- ☐ **(F)** Long-term transactions not reported to you on Form 1099-B

1 **(a)** Description of property (Example: 100 sh. XYZ Co.)	**(b)** Date acquired (Mo., day, yr.)	**(c)** Date sold or disposed (Mo., day, yr.)	**(d)** Proceeds (sales price) (see instructions)	**(e)** Cost or other basis. See the **Note** below and see *Column (e)* in the separate instructions	Adjustment, if any, to gain or loss. If you enter an amount in column (g), enter a code in column (f). See the separate instructions.		**(h)** Gain or (loss). Subtract column (e) from column (d) and combine the result with column (g)
					(f) Code(s) from instructions	**(g)** Amount of adjustment	
2 Totals. Add the amounts in columns (d), (e), (g), and (h) (subtract negative amounts). Enter each total here and include on your Schedule D, **line 8b** (if **Box D** above is checked), **line 9** (if **Box E** above is checked), or **line 10** (if **Box F** above is checked) ▶							

Note. If you checked Box D above but the basis reported to the IRS was incorrect, enter in column (e) the basis as reported to the IRS, and enter an adjustment in column (g) to correct the basis. See *Column (g)* in the separate instructions for how to figure the amount of the adjustment.

2014

Department of the Treasury
Internal Revenue Service

Instructions for Form 8949

Sales and Other Dispositions of Capital Assets

Section references are to the Internal Revenue Code unless otherwise noted.

Future Developments

For the latest information about developments related to Form 8949 and its instructions, such as legislation enacted after they were published, go to *www.irs.gov/form8949*.

What's New

Form 1099-B. Form 1099-B has been redesigned so that the information is reported in boxes that are numbered to match the corresponding line and column on Form 8949. A new box has also been added at the top of Form 1099-B to tell you which box to check when completing Form 8949. These changes will make it easier for you to complete Form 8949.

A Form 1099-B (or substitute statement) for transactions involving certain types of debt instruments acquired after 2013 will have more detailed information than a Form 1099-B (or substitute statement) for transactions involving debt instruments acquired before 2014. This is also true for a Form 1099-B (or substitute statement) for options granted or acquired after 2013 or securities futures contracts entered into after 2013. This additional information will help you complete Form 8949 and Schedule D.

General Instructions

File Form 8949 with the Schedule D for the return you are filing. This includes Schedule D of Forms 1040, 1041, 1065, 1065-B, 8865, 1120, 1120S, 1120-C, 1120-F, 1120-FSC, 1120-H, 1120-IC-DISC, 1120-L, 1120-ND, 1120-PC, 1120-POL, 1120-REIT, 1120-RIC, 1120-SF, and certain Forms 990-T.

Complete Form 8949 before you complete line 1b, 2, 3, 8b, 9, or 10 of Schedule D.

Purpose of Form

Use Form 8949 to report sales and exchanges of capital assets. Form 8949 allows you and the IRS to reconcile amounts that were reported to you and the IRS on Form 1099-B or 1099-S (or substitute statement) with the amounts you report on your return. If you receive Form 1099-B or 1099-S (or substitute statement), always report the proceeds (sales price) shown on that form (or statement) in column (d) of Form 8949. If Form 1099-B (or substitute statement) shows that the cost or other basis was reported to the IRS, always report the basis shown on that form (or statement) in column (e). If any correction or adjustment to these amounts is needed, make it in column (g). See *How To Complete Form 8949, Columns (f) and (g)*, later, for details about these adjustments.

If all Forms 1099-B you received (and all substitute statements) show basis was reported to the IRS and if no correction or adjustment is needed, you may not need to file Form 8949. See *Exception 1* under the instructions for line 1.

Individuals. Individuals use Form 8949 to report:
- The sale or exchange of a capital asset not reported on another form or schedule,
- Gains from involuntary conversions (other than from casualty or theft) of capital assets not held for business or profit,
- Nonbusiness bad debts, and
- Worthlessness of a security.

If you are filing a joint return, complete as many copies of Form 8949 as you need to report all of your and your spouse's transactions. You and your spouse may list your transactions on separate forms or you may combine them. However, you must include on your Schedule D the totals from all Forms 8949 for both you and your spouse.

Corporations and partnerships.
Corporations and partnerships use Form 8949 to report:
- The sale or exchange of a capital asset not reported on another form or schedule,
- Nonbusiness bad debts,
- Undistributed long-term capital gains from Form 2439, and
- Worthlessness of a security.

Corporations also use Form 8949 to report their share of gain or (loss) from a partnership, estate, or trust.

For corporations and partnerships meeting certain criteria, an exception to some of the normal requirements for completing Form 8949 has been provided. See *Special provision for certain corporations, partnerships, securities dealers, and other qualified entities* under the instructions for line 1.

Estates and trusts. Estates and trusts use Form 8949 to report:
- The sale or exchange of a capital asset not reported on another form or schedule,
- Nonbusiness bad debts, and
- Worthlessness of a security.

Schedule D. Use Schedule D for the following purposes.
- To figure the overall gain or loss from transactions reported on Form 8949.
- To report a gain from Form 6252 or Part I of Form 4797.
- To report a gain or loss from Form 4684, 6781, or 8824.
- To report capital gain distributions not reported directly on Form 1040, line 13 (or effectively connected capital gain distributions not reported directly on Form 1040NR, line 14).
- To report a capital loss carryover from the previous tax year to the current tax year.
- To report your share of a gain or (loss) from a partnership, S corporation, estate, or trust. (However, corporations report this type of gain or (loss) on Form 8949.)
- To report transactions reported to you on a Form 1099-B (or substitute statement) showing basis was reported to the IRS and for which you have no adjustments, as explained under *Exception 1*, later.

Individuals, estates, and trusts also use Schedule D to report undistributed long-term capital gains from Form 2439.

Additional information. See the instructions for the Schedule D you are filing for detailed information about other topics, including the following.
- Other forms you may have to file.
- The definition of capital asset.
- Reporting capital gain distributions, undistributed capital gains, the sale of a main home, the sale of capital assets held for personal use, or the sale of a partnership interest.
- Capital losses, nondeductible losses, and losses from wash sales.
- Traders in securities.
- Short sales.
- Gain or loss from options.
- Installment sales.
- Demutualization of life insurance companies.
- Exclusion or rollover of gain from the sale of qualified small business stock.
- Any other rollover of gain, such as gain from the sale of publicly traded securities.
- Exclusion of gain from the sale of DC Zone assets or qualified community assets.

- Certain other items that get special treatment.
- Special reporting rules for corporations, partnerships, estates, and trusts in certain situations.

For more information about reporting on Forms 6252, 4797, 4684, 6781, and 8824, see the instructions for those forms. See Pub. 544 and Pub. 550 for more details.

Basis and Recordkeeping

Basis is the amount of your investment in property for tax purposes. The basis of property you buy is usually its cost. You need to know your basis to figure any gain or loss on the sale or other disposition of the property. You must keep accurate records that show the basis and, if applicable, adjusted basis of your property. Your records should show the purchase price, including commissions; increases to basis, such as the cost of improvements; and decreases to basis, such as depreciation, nondividend distributions on stock, and stock splits.

For more information on basis, see *Column (e)—Cost or Other Basis*, later, and these publications.
- Pub. 550, Investment Income and Expenses (Including Capital Gains and Losses).
- Pub. 551, Basis of Assets.

If you lost or did not keep records to determine your basis in securities, contact your broker for help. If you receive a Form 1099-B (or substitute statement), your broker may have reported your basis for these securities in box 1e.

 The IRS partners with companies that offer Form 8949 software that can import trades from many brokerage firms and accounting software that can help you keep track of your adjusted basis in securities. To find out more, go to *www.irs.gov/efile*.

Short Term or Long Term

Separate your capital gains and losses according to how long you held or owned the property.

The holding period for short-term capital gains and losses is 1 year or less. Report these transactions on Part I of Form 8949 (or line 1a of Schedule D if you can use *Exception 1* under the instructions for Form 8949, line 1).

The holding period for long-term capital gains and losses is more than 1 year. Report these transactions on Part II of Form 8949 (or line 8a of Schedule D if you can use *Exception 1* under the instructions for Form 8949, line 1).

To figure the holding period, begin counting on the day after you received the property and include the day you disposed of it.

Generally, if you disposed of property that you acquired by inheritance, report the disposition as a long-term gain or loss regardless of how long you held the property.

A nonbusiness bad debt must be treated as a short-term capital loss. See Pub. 550 for what qualifies as a nonbusiness bad debt and how to enter it on Part I of Form 8949.

Form 1099-B. If you received a Form 1099-B (or substitute statement) for a transaction, box 2 may help you determine whether your gain or loss is short-term or long-term. If box 2 is blank and code X is in the "Applicable check box on Form 8949" box near the top of Form 1099-B, your broker doesn't know whether your gain or loss is short-term or long-term. Use your own records to determine whether your gain or loss is short-term or long-term.

Corporation's Gains and Losses from Partnerships, Estates, or Trusts

Report a corporation's share of capital gains and losses from investments in partnerships, estates, or trusts on the appropriate Part of Form 8949. Report a net short-term capital gain or (loss) on Part I (with box C checked) and a net long-term capital gain or (loss) on Part II (with box F checked). In column (a), enter "From Schedule K-1 (Form 1065)," "From Schedule K-1 (Form 1065-B)," or "From Schedule K-1 (Form 1041)," whichever applies; enter the gain or (loss) in column (h); and leave all other columns blank.

If more than one Schedule K-1 is received, report each on a separate row. Include additional identifying information, such as "Partnership X."

Rounding Off to Whole Dollars

You can round off cents to whole dollars on Form 8949. If you do round to whole dollars, round all amounts. To round, drop cent amounts under 50 cents and increase cent amounts over 49 cents to the next dollar. For example, $1.49 becomes $1 and $1.50 becomes $2.

Specific Instructions

Report short-term gains and losses on Part I. Report long-term gains and losses on Part II.

Line 1

Enter all sales and exchanges of capital assets, including stocks, bonds, and real estate (if not reported on line 1a or 8a of Schedule D or on Form 4684, 4797, 6252, 6781, or 8824). Include these transactions

even if you did not receive a Form 1099-B or 1099-S (or substitute statement) for the transaction. However, if the property you sold was your main home, see *Sale of Your Home* in the Instructions for Schedule D (Form 1040).

Enter the details of each transaction on a separate row (unless one of the *Exceptions to reporting each transaction on a separate row* described later applies to you).

Part I. Use a separate Part I for each type of short-term transaction described in the text for one of the boxes (A, B, or C) at the top of Part I. Include on each Part I only transactions described in the text for the box you check (A, B, or C). Check only one box on each Part I. For example, if you check box A in one Part I, include on that Part I only short-term transactions reported to you on a statement showing basis was reported to the IRS. Complete as many copies of Part I as you need to report all transactions of each type (A, B, or C).

If you received a Form 1099-B for a transaction, the "Applicable check box on Form 8949" box near the top of that form may help you determine which box to check on the Part I where you report that transaction.

Box A. Report on a Part I with box A checked all short-term transactions reported to you on Form 1099-B (or substitute statement) with an amount shown for cost or other basis **unless** the statement indicates that amount was not reported to the IRS. If your statement shows cost or other basis but indicates it was not reported to the IRS (for example, if box 3 of Form 1099-B is not checked), see *Box B*, below.

 If you do not need to make any adjustments to the basis or type of gain or loss (short-term or long-term) reported to you on Form 1099-B (or substitute statement) or to your gain or loss for any transactions for which basis has been reported to the IRS (normally reported on Form 8949 with box A checked), you do not have to include those transactions on Form 8949. Instead, you can report summary information for those transactions directly on Schedule D. For more information, see Exception 1, later.

Box B. Report on a Part I with box B checked all short-term transactions reported to you on Form 1099-B (or substitute statement) without an amount shown for cost or other basis or showing that cost or other basis was not reported to the IRS. If your statement shows cost or other basis for the transaction was reported to the IRS (for example, if box 3 of Form 1099-B is checked), see *Box A*.

Box C. Report on a Part I with box C checked all short-term transactions for which you cannot check box A or B because you did not receive a Form 1099-B (or substitute statement).

Part II. Use a separate Part II for each type of long-term transaction described in the text for one of the boxes (D, E, or F) at the top of Part II. Include on each Part II only transactions described in the text for the box you check (D, E, or F). Check only one box on each Part II. For example, if you check box D in one Part II, include on that Part II only long-term transactions reported to you on a statement showing basis was reported to the IRS. Complete as many copies of Part II as you need to report all transactions of each type (D, E, or F).

If you received a Form 1099-B for a transaction, the "Applicable check box on Form 8949" box near the top of that form may help you determine which box to check on the Part II where you report that transaction.

Box D. Report on a Part II with box D checked all long-term transactions reported to you on Form 1099-B (or substitute statement) with an amount shown for cost or other basis **unless** the statement indicates that amount was not reported to the IRS. If your statement shows cost or other basis but indicates it was not reported to the IRS (for example, if box 3 of Form 1099-B is not checked), see *Box E,* below.

 If you do not need to make any adjustments to the basis or type of gain or loss (short-term or long-term) reported to you on Form 1099-B (or substitute statement) or to your gain or loss for any transactions for which basis has been reported to the IRS (normally reported on Form 8949 with box D checked), you do not have to include those transactions on Form 8949. Instead, you can report summary information for those transactions directly on Schedule D. For more information, see Exception 1, later.

Box E. Report on a Part II with box E checked all long-term transactions reported to you on Form 1099-B (or substitute statement) without an amount shown for cost or other basis or showing that cost or other basis was not reported to the IRS. If your statement shows cost or other basis for the transaction was reported to the IRS (for example, if box 3 of Form 1099-B is checked), see *Box D,* above.

Box F. Report on a Part II with box F checked all long-term transactions for which you cannot check box D or E because you did not receive a Form 1099-B (or substitute statement).

You do not need to complete and file an entire copy of Form 8949 (Part I and Part II) if you can check a single box to describe all your transactions. In that case, complete and file either Part I or Part II and check the box that describes the transactions. Otherwise, complete a separate Part I or Part II for each category of your transactions, as described above.

Include on your Schedule D the totals from all your Parts I and Parts II. Form 8949 and Schedule D explain how to do this.

Exceptions to reporting each transaction on a separate row. There are exceptions to the rule that you must report each of your transactions on a separate row of Part I or Part II. Any taxpayer who qualifies can use *Exception 1* or *Exception 2*. Taxpayers who file Form 1120S, 1065, or 1065-B and other qualified entities should see *Special provision for certain corporations, partnerships, securities dealers, and other qualified entities,* later.

Exception 1. Form 8949 is not required for certain transactions. You may be able to aggregate those transactions and report them directly on either line 1a (for short-term transactions) or line 8a (for long-term transactions) of Schedule D. This option applies only to transactions (other than sales of collectibles) for which:
- You received a Form 1099-B (or substitute statement) that shows basis was reported to the IRS and does not show any adjustments in box 1g, and
- You do not need to make any adjustments to the basis or type of gain or loss (short-term or long-term) reported on Form 1099-B (or substitute statement), or to your gain or loss.

If you choose to report these transactions directly on Schedule D, you do not need to include them on Form 8949 and do not need to attach a statement. For more information, see the Schedule D instructions.

If you qualify to use *Exception 1* and also qualify to use *Exception 2*, you can use both. Report the transactions that qualify for *Exception 1* directly on either line 1a or 8a of Schedule D, whichever applies. Report the rest of your transactions as explained in *Exception 2*.

Exception 2. Instead of reporting each of your transactions on a separate row of Part I or Part II, you can report them on an attached statement containing all the same information as Parts I and II and in a similar format (i.e., description of property, dates of acquisition and disposition, proceeds, basis, adjustment and code(s), and gain or (loss)). Use as many attached statements as you need. Enter the combined totals from all your attached statements on Parts I and II with the appropriate box checked.

For example, report on Part I with box B checked all short-term gains and losses from transactions your broker reported to you on a statement showing basis was not reported to the IRS. Enter the name of the broker followed by the words "see attached statement" in column (a). Leave columns (b) and (c) blank. Enter "M" in column (f). If other codes also apply, enter all of them in column (f). Enter the totals that apply in columns (d), (e), (g), and (h). If you have statements from more than one broker, report the totals from each broker on a separate row.

Do not enter "Available upon request" and summary totals in lieu of reporting the details of each transaction on Part I or II or attached statements.

Special provision for certain corporations, partnerships, securities dealers, and other qualified entities. This special provision applies to certain corporations, partnerships, securities dealers, and nonprofit organizations. Individual taxpayers are not eligible except in rare circumstances.

You may enter summary totals instead of reporting the details of each transaction on a separate row of Part I or II or on attached statements if:

1. You file Form 1120S, 1065, or 1065-B or are a taxpayer exempt from receiving Form 1099-B, such as a corporation or exempt organization, under Regulations section 1.6045-1(c)(3)(i)(B), and

2. You must report more than five transactions for that Part.

If this provision applies to you, enter the summary totals on line 1. For short-term transactions, check box C at the top of Part I even if the summary totals include transactions described in the text for box A or B. For long-term transactions, check box F at the top of Part II even if the summary totals include transactions described in the text for box D or E. Enter "Available upon request" in column (a). Leave columns (b) and (c) blank. Enter "M" in column (f). If other codes also apply, enter all of them in column (f). Enter the totals that apply in columns (d), (e), (g), and (h).

Do not use a separate row for the totals from each broker. Instead, enter the summary totals from all brokers on a single row of Part I (with box C checked) or Part II (with box F checked).

E-file. If you e-file your return but choose not to report each transaction on a separate row on the electronic return, you must either (a) include Form 8949 as a PDF attachment to your return or (b) attach Form 8949 to Form 8453 (or the appropriate form in the Form 8453 series) and mail the forms to the IRS. (However, you cannot attach a paper Form 8949 to Form 8453-FE.) You can attach one or more statements containing all the same information as Form 8949, instead of attaching Form 8949, if the statements are in a format similar to Form 8949.

However, this does not apply to transactions that qualify for *Exception 1* or the *Special provision for certain corporations, partnerships, securities dealers, and other qualified entities*. In those cases, neither an attachment, a statement, nor Form 8453 is required.

Charitable gift annuity. If you are the beneficiary of a charitable gift annuity and receive a Form 1099-R showing an amount in box 3, report the box 3 amount on a Part II with box F checked. Enter "Form 1099-R" in column (a). Enter the box 3 amount in column (d). Also complete column (h).

Form 2438. Enter any net short-term capital gain from line 4 of Form 2438 on a Part I with box C checked. Enter "Net short-term capital gain from Form 2438, line 4" in column (a), enter the gain in column (h), and leave all other columns blank.

Enter any amount from line 12 of Form 2438 on a Part II with box F checked. Enter "Undistributed capital gains not designated (from Form 2438)" in column (a), enter the amount of the gain in column (h), and leave all other columns blank.

Form 2439. Corporations and partnerships report undistributed long-term capital gains from Form 2439 on a Part II with box F checked. Enter "From Form 2439" in column (a), enter the gain in column (h), and leave all other columns blank. Individuals report undistributed long-term capital gains from Form 2439 on line 11 of Schedule D (Form 1040). Estates and trusts report those amounts on line 11 of Schedule D (Form 1041).

NAV method for certain money market funds. If you have a capital gain or loss determined under the net asset value (NAV) method with respect to shares in a floating-NAV money market fund, enter the name of the fund followed by "(NAV)" in column (a) on a Part I with box C checked. Enter the net gain or loss in column (h). Leave all other columns blank. No long-term capital gain or loss can be entered under the NAV method.

Nondividend distributions. Distributions from a corporation that are a return of your cost (or other basis) are not taxed until you recover your cost (or other basis). Reduce your cost (or other basis) by these distributions, but not below zero. After you have recovered your entire cost (or other basis), any later nondividend distribution is taxable as a capital gain. Enter the name of the payer of any taxable nondividend distributions in column (a) on

a Part I with box C checked or Part II with box F checked (depending on how long you held the stock). Enter the taxable part of the distribution in columns (d) and (h). Each payer of a nondividend distribution should send you a Form 1099-DIV showing the amount of the distribution in box 3.

Other gains or losses where sales price or basis is not known. If you have another gain or loss for which you do not know the sales price or basis (such as a long-term capital gain from Form 8621), enter a description of the gain or loss in column (a) on a Part I with box C checked or Part II with box F checked (depending on how long you held the property). If you have a gain, enter it in columns (d) and (h). If you have a loss, enter it in columns (e) and (h). Complete any other columns you can.

Column (a)—Description of Property

For stock, include the number of shares. You can use stock ticker symbols or abbreviations to describe the property as long as they are based on the descriptions of the property as shown on Form 1099-B or 1099-S (or substitute statement).

If you inherited the property from someone who died in 2010 and the executor of the estate made the election to file Form 8939, also enter "INH-2010" in column (a).

Column (b)—Date Acquired

Enter in this column the date you acquired the property. Enter the trade date for stocks and bonds you purchased on an exchange or over-the-counter market. For a short sale, enter the date you acquired the property delivered to the broker or lender to close the short sale. For property you previously elected to treat as having been sold and reacquired on January 1, 2001 (or January 2, 2001, for readily tradeable stock), enter the date of the deemed sale and reacquisition.

If you received a Form 1099-B (or substitute statement), box 1b may help you determine when you acquired the property.

Inherited property. Generally, if you disposed of property that you acquired by inheritance, report the sale or exchange on a Part II with the appropriate box checked (D, E, or F). Enter "INHERITED" in column (b).

Stock acquired on various dates. If you sold a block of stock (or similar property) that you acquired through several different purchases, you may report the sale on one row and enter "VARIOUS" in column (b). However, you still must report the short-term gain or (loss) on the sale on

Part I and the long-term gain or (loss) on Part II.

Column (c)—Date Sold or Disposed

Enter in this column the date you sold or disposed of the property. Use the trade date for stocks and bonds traded on an exchange or over-the-counter market. For a short sale, enter the date you delivered the property to the broker or lender to close the short sale.

If you received a Form 1099-B (or substitute statement), box 1c may help you determine when you sold or disposed of the property.

Column (d)—Proceeds (Sales Price)

Follow the instructions below that apply to your transaction(s).

You did not receive a Form 1099-B or 1099-S (or substitute statement). If you did not receive a Form 1099-B or 1099-S (or substitute statement) for a transaction, enter in column (d) the net proceeds. The net proceeds equal the gross proceeds minus any selling expenses (such as broker's fees, commissions, and state and local transfer taxes). If you sold a call option and it was exercised, you must also adjust the sales price of the property sold under the option for any option premiums (as instructed in *Gain or Loss From Options* in the instructions for Schedule D (Form 1040)).

You received a Form 1099-B or 1099-S (or substitute statement). If you received a Form 1099-B or 1099-S (or substitute statement) for a transaction, enter in column (d) the proceeds shown on the form or statement you received. If there are any selling expenses or option premiums that are not reflected on the form or statement you received (by an adjustment to either the proceeds or basis shown), enter "E" in column (f) and the necessary adjustment in column (g). See the example under *Column (g)—Adjustments to Gain or Loss*, later.

If the proceeds you received were more than shown on Form 1099-B or 1099-S (or substitute statement), enter the correct proceeds in column (d). This might happen if, for example, box 4 on Form 1099-S is checked.

You should not have received a Form 1099-B (or substitute statement) for a transaction merely representing the return of your original investment in a nontransferable obligation, such as a savings bond or a certificate of deposit. But if you did, report the proceeds shown on Form 1099-B (or substitute statement) in both columns (d) and (e).

Column (e)—Cost or Other Basis

The basis of property you buy is usually its cost, including the purchase price and any costs of purchase, such as commissions. You may not be able to use the actual cost as the basis if you inherited the property, got it as a gift, or received it in a tax-free exchange or involuntary conversion or in connection with a "wash sale." If you do not use the actual cost, attach an explanation of your basis.

The basis of property acquired by gift is generally the basis of the property in the hands of the donor. The basis of inherited property is generally the fair market value at the date of death. See Pub. 551 for details. However, if you sold property that you inherited from someone who died in 2010 and the executor made the election to file Form 8939, see *Pub. 4895* (available at *www.irs.gov/publications/p4895*).

If you elected to recognize gain on property held on January 1, 2001, your basis in the property is its closing market price or fair market value, whichever applies, on the date of the deemed sale and reacquisition, whether the deemed sale resulted in a gain or an unallowed loss.

For more details, see Pub. 551 or Pub. 550.

Adjustments to basis. Before you can figure any gain or loss on a sale, exchange, or other disposition of property, you usually must make certain adjustments (increases and decreases) to the basis of the property. Increase the basis of your property by capital improvements. Decrease it by depreciation, amortization, and depletion.

If you sold stock, adjust your basis by subtracting all the nondividend distributions you received before the sale. Also adjust your basis for any stock splits. See Pub. 550 for details.

Increase the cost or other basis of an original issue discount (OID) debt instrument by the amount of OID that you have included in gross income for that instrument. See Pub. 550 for details.

If you elect to currently include in income the market discount on a bond, increase the basis of the bond by the market discount that has been included in income for that bond. See Pub. 550 for details.

If you elect to amortize bond premium on a taxable bond, reduce the basis of the bond by any bond premium amortization allowed as either an offset to interest income or as a deduction for that bond. See Pub. 550 for details. Reduce the basis of a tax-exempt bond by any bond premium amortization for that bond. See Pub. 550 for details.

If a charitable contribution deduction is allowable because of a bargain sale of property to a charitable organization, you must allocate your basis in the property between the part sold and the part contributed based on the fair market value of each. See Pub. 544 for details.

Average basis. You can use the average basis method to determine the basis of shares of stock if the shares are identical to each other, you acquired them at different prices and left them in an account with a custodian or agent, and either:

- They are shares in a mutual fund (or other regulated investment company);
- They are shares you hold in connection with a dividend reinvestment plan (DRP), and all the shares you hold in connection with the DRP are treated as covered securities (defined below); or
- You acquired them after 2011 in connection with a DRP.

Shares are identical if they have the same CUSIP number, except that shares of stock in a DRP are not identical to shares of stock that are not in a DRP, even if they have the same CUSIP number. If you are using the average basis method and received a Form 1099-B (or substitute statement) that shows an incorrect basis, enter "B" in column (f), enter the basis shown on Form 1099-B (or substitute statement) in column (e), and see *How To Complete Form 8949, Columns (f) and (g)*, later. For details on making the election and figuring average basis, see section 1012, Pub. 550, and Regulations section 1.1012-1(e).

Form 1099-B. If the property you sold was a covered security, its basis should be shown in box 1e of the Form 1099-B (or substitute statement) you received from your broker. Generally, a covered security is any of the following.

- Stock you acquired after 2010 (generally after 2011 if in a mutual fund or other regulated investment company, or acquired through a dividend reinvestment plan).
- Certain stock held in a mutual fund or in connection with a dividend reinvestment plan for which a single-account election is in effect.
- Certain debt instruments you acquired after 2013.
- Certain options, warrants, and stock rights you granted or acquired after 2013.
- A securities future contract you entered into after 2013.

For more information, see section 6045(g) and Regulations section 1.6045-1.

If box 5 on Form 1099-B is checked, the property sold was not a covered security.

Enter the basis shown on Form 1099-B (or substitute statement) in column (e). If the basis shown on Form 1099-B (or substitute statement) is not correct, see *How To Complete Form 8949, Columns (f) and (g)*, later, for the adjustment you must make.

If no basis is shown on Form 1099-B (or substitute statement), enter the correct basis of the property in column (e).

Column (f)—Code

In order to explain any adjustment to gain or loss in column (g), enter the appropriate code(s) in column (f). See *How To Complete Form 8949, Columns (f) and (g)*, later. If more than one code applies, enter all the codes that apply in alphabetical order (for example, "BOQ"). Do not separate the codes by a space or comma.

Column (g)—Adjustments to Gain or Loss

Enter in this column any necessary adjustments to gain or loss. Enter negative amounts in parentheses. Also enter a code in column (f) to explain the adjustment. See *How To Complete Form 8949, Columns (f) and (g)*, later.

More than one code. If you entered more than one code in column (f) on the same row, enter the net adjustment in column (g). For example, if one adjustment is $5,000 and another is ($1,000), enter $4,000 ($5,000 – $1,000).

Example. You sold your main home in 2014 for $320,000 and received a Form 1099-S showing the $320,000 gross proceeds. The home's basis was $100,000. You had selling expenses of $20,000. Under the tests described in *Sale of Your Home* in the Instructions for Schedule D (Form 1040), you can exclude the entire $200,000 gain from income. On Form 8949, Part II, check box F at the top. Complete columns (a), (b), and (c). Enter $320,000 in column (d) and $100,000 in column (e). Enter "EH" in column (f). In column (g), enter $220,000 ($20,000 selling expenses + $200,000 exclusion) as a negative number. Put it in parentheses to show it is negative. In column (h), enter -0- ($320,000 – $100,000 – $220,000). If this is your only transaction on this Part II, enter $320,000 in column (d) on line 10 of Schedule D (Form 1040), $100,000 in column (e), ($220,000) in column (g), and -0- in column (h).

How To Complete Form 8949, Columns (f) and (g)

For most transactions, you do not need to complete columns (f) and (g) and can leave them blank. You may need to complete columns (f) and (g) if you got a Form 1099-B or 1099-S (or substitute statement) that is incorrect, if you are excluding or postponing a capital gain, if you have a disallowed loss, or in certain other situations. Details are in the table below. If you enter more than one code in column (f), see *More than one code* in the instructions for column (g).

IF . . .	THEN enter this code in column (f) . . .	AND . . .
You received a Form 1099-B (or substitute statement) and the basis shown in box 1e is incorrect	B	• If box B is checked at the top of Part I or if box E is checked at the top of Part II, enter the correct basis in column (e), and enter -0- in column (g). • If box A is checked at the top of Part I or if box D is checked at the top of Part II, enter the basis shown on Form 1099-B (or substitute statement) in column (e), even though that basis is incorrect. Correct the error by entering an adjustment in column (g). To figure the adjustment needed, see the *Worksheet for Basis Adjustments in Column (g)*. Also see *Example 4—adjustment for incorrect basis* in the instructions for column (h).
You received a Form 1099-B (or substitute statement) and the type of gain or loss (short-term or long-term) shown in box 2 is incorrect	T	Enter -0- in column (g). Report the gain or loss on the correct **Part** of Form 8949.
You received a Form 1099-B or 1099-S (or substitute statement) as a nominee for the actual owner of the property	N	Report the transaction on Form 8949 as you would if you were the actual owner, but also enter any resulting gain as a negative adjustment (in parentheses) in column (g) or any resulting loss as a positive adjustment in column (g). As a result of this adjustment, the amount in column (h) should be zero. However, if you received capital gain distributions as a nominee, report them instead as described under *Capital Gain Distributions* in the Instructions for Schedule D (Form 1040).
You sold or exchanged your main home at a gain, must report the sale or exchange on Part II of Form 8949 (as explained in *Sale of Your Home* in the Instructions for Schedule D (Form 1040)), and can exclude some or all of the gain	H	Report the sale or exchange on Form 8949 as you would if you were not taking the exclusion. Then enter the amount of excluded (nontaxable) gain as a negative number (in parentheses) in column (g). See the example in the instructions for column (g).
You received a Form 1099-B showing accrued market discount in box 1g	D	Use the *Worksheet for Accrued Market Discount Adjustment in Column (g)*, later, to figure the amount to enter in column (g). However: • If you received a partial payment of principal on a bond, do not use the worksheet. Instead, enter the smaller of the accrued market discount or your proceeds in column (g). Also report it as interest on your tax return. • If you chose to include market discount in income currently, enter -0- in column (g). Before figuring your gain or loss, increase your basis in the bond by the market discount you have included in income for all years. See the instructions for code B, above. If the disposition of a market discount bond results in a loss subject to the wash sale rules, enter only "W" in column (f) and enter only the disallowed wash sale loss in column (g).
You sold or exchanged qualified small business stock and can exclude part of the gain	Q	Report the sale or exchange on Form 8949 as you would if you were not taking the exclusion and enter the amount of the exclusion as a negative number (in parentheses) in column (g). However, if the transaction is reported as an installment sale, see *Gain from an installment sale of QSB stock* in the Instructions for Schedule D (Form 1040).

IF . . .	THEN enter this code in column (f) . . .	AND. . .
You can exclude all or part of your gain under the rules explained in the Schedule D instructions for DC Zone assets or qualified community assets	X	Report the sale or exchange on Form 8949 as you would if you were not taking the exclusion. Then enter the amount of the exclusion as a negative number (in parentheses) in column (g).
You are electing to postpone all or part of your gain under the rules explained in the Schedule D instructions for any rollover of gain (for example, rollover of gain from QSB stock or publicly traded securities)	R	Report the sale or exchange on Form 8949 as you would if you were not making the election. Then enter the amount of postponed gain as a negative number (in parentheses) in column (g).
You have a nondeductible loss from a wash sale	W	Report the sale or exchange on Form 8949 and enter the amount of the nondeductible loss as a positive number in column (g). See the Schedule D instructions for more information about wash sales. If you received a Form 1099-B (or substitute statement) and the amount of nondeductible wash sale loss shown (box 1g with code W in box 1f of Form 1099-B) is incorrect, enter the correct amount of the nondeductible loss as a positive number in column (g). If the amount of the nondeductible loss is less than the amount shown on Form 1099-B (or substitute statement), attach a statement explaining the difference. If no part of the loss is a nondeductible loss from a wash sale transaction, enter -0- in column (g).
You have a nondeductible loss other than a loss indicated by code W	L	Report the sale or exchange on Form 8949 and enter the amount of the nondeductible loss as a positive number in column (g). See *Nondeductible Losses* in the Instructions for Schedule D (Form 1040).
You received a Form 1099-B or 1099-S (or substitute statement) for a transaction and there are selling expenses or option premiums that are not reflected on the form or statement by an adjustment to either the proceeds or basis shown	E	Enter in column (d) the proceeds shown on the form or statement you received. Enter in column (e) any cost or other basis shown on Form 1099-B (or substitute statement). In column (g), enter as a negative number (in parentheses) any selling expenses and option premium that you paid (and that are not reflected on the form or statement you received) and enter as a positive number any option premium that you received (and that is not reflected on the form or statement you received). For more information about option premiums, see *Gain or Loss From Options* in the Instructions for Schedule D (Form 1040).
You had a loss from the sale, exchange, or worthlessness of small business (section 1244) stock and the total loss is more than the maximum amount that can be treated as an ordinary loss	S	See *Small Business (Section 1244) Stock* in the Schedule D (Form 1040) instructions.
You disposed of collectibles (see the Schedule D instructions)	C	Enter -0- in column (g). Report the disposition on Form 8949 as you would report any sale or exchange.
You report multiple transactions on a single row as described in *Exception 2* or *Special provision for certain corporations, partnerships, securities dealers, and other qualified entities* under *Exceptions to reporting each transaction on a separate row*	M	See *Exception 2* and *Special provision for certain corporations, partnerships, securities dealers, and other qualified entities* under *Exceptions to reporting each transaction on a separate row*. Enter -0- in column (g) unless an adjustment is required because of another code.
You have an adjustment not explained earlier in this column	O	Enter the appropriate adjustment amount in column (g). See the instructions for column (g).
None of the other statements in this column apply	Leave columns (f) and (g) blank.	

Column (h)—Gain or (Loss)

Figure gain or loss on each row. First, subtract the cost or other basis in column (e) from the proceeds (sales price) in column (d). Then take into account any adjustments in column (g). Enter the gain or (loss) in column (h). Enter negative amounts in parentheses.

Example 1—gain. Column (d) is $6,000 and column (e) is $2,000. Enter $4,000 in column (h).

Example 2—loss. Column (d) is $6,000 and column (e) is $8,000. Enter ($2,000) in column (h).

Example 3—adjustment. Column (d) is $6,000, column (e) is $2,000, and column (g) is ($1,000). Enter $3,000 in column (h).

Example 4—adjustment for incorrect basis. You sold stock for $1,000. You had owned the stock for 3 months. Your correct basis for the stock is $100, but you receive a Form 1099-B that shows your basis is $900 and shows your broker reported that basis to the IRS. Enter $900 on line 1 of the *Worksheet for Basis Adjustments in Column (g)*. Enter $100 on line 2 of the worksheet. Since

line 1 is larger than line 2, leave line 3 blank and enter $800 ($900 – $100) as a positive number on line 4. Also enter $800 in column (g) of a Part I with box A checked at the top. Enter "B" in column (f). Enter $1,000 in column (d) and $900 in column (e). To figure your gain or loss, subtract $900 from $1,000. Combine the result, $100, with the $800 adjustment in column (g). Your gain is $900 ($100 + $800). Enter $900 in column (h).

Worksheet for Basis Adjustments in Column (g)

Keep for Your Records

If the basis shown on Form 1099-B (or substitute statement) is not correct, do the following.

- If the basis was not reported to the IRS, enter the correct basis in column (e) and enter -0- in column (g) (unless you must make an adjustment for some other reason).
- If the basis was reported to the IRS, enter the reported basis shown on Form 1099-B (or substitute statement) in column (e) and use this worksheet to figure the adjustment to include in column (g).

1.	Enter the cost or other basis shown on Form 1099-B (or substitute statement)	1. _____
2.	Enter the correct cost or other basis	2. _____
3.	If line 1 is larger than line 2, leave this line blank and go to line 4. If line 2 is larger than line 1, subtract line 1 from line 2. Enter the result here and in column (g) as a negative number (in parentheses)	3. _____
4.	If line 1 is larger than line 2, subtract line 2 from line 1. Enter the result here and in column (g) as a positive number	4. _____

Worksheet for Accrued Market Discount Adjustment in Column (g)

Keep for Your Records

If you received a Form 1099-B (or substitute statement) reporting the sale or retirement of a market discount bond, complete this worksheet to figure the amount to enter in column (g). If, in addition, any of the amounts shown on Form 1099-B (or substitute statement) are incorrect, see *How To Complete Form 8949, Columns (f) and (g)* for information on how to correct those amounts. Use the corrected amounts when completing this worksheet.

1.	Enter the proceeds from Form 1099-B, box 1d (or substitute statement)	1. _____
2.	Enter the basis from Form 1099-B, box 1e (or substitute statement)	2. _____
3.	Subtract line 2 from line 1. If zero or less, enter -0-	3. _____
4.	Enter the accrued market discount from Form 1099-B, box 1g (or substitute statement)	4. _____
5.	Enter the smaller of line 3 or line 4. If zero or less, enter -0-. This is the amount of your gain that is ordinary income. Enter it as a negative amount (in parentheses) in Form 8949, column (g). Also, report it as interest income on your tax return	5. _____

Line 2

The total of the amounts in column (h) of line 2 of all your Forms 8949 should equal the amount you get by combining columns (d), (e), and (g) on the corresponding line of Schedule D. For example, the total of the amounts in column (h) of line 2 of all your Forms 8949 with box A checked should equal the amount you get by combining columns (d), (e), and (g) on line 1b of Schedule D. The total of the amounts in column (h) of line 2 of all your Forms 8949 with box E checked should equal the amount you get by combining columns (d), (e), and (g) on line 9 of Schedule D.

Form **8960**

Department of the Treasury
Internal Revenue Service (99)

Net Investment Income Tax—
Individuals, Estates, and Trusts

▶ Attach to your tax return.
▶ **Information about Form 8960 and its separate instructions is at www.irs.gov/form8960.**

OMB No. 1545-2227

20**14**

Attachment
Sequence No. **72**

Name(s) shown on your tax return

Your social security number or EIN

Part I | Investment Income | ☐ Section 6013(g) election (see instructions)
☐ Section 6013(h) election (see instructions)
☐ Regulations section 1.1411-10(g) election (see instructions)

1	Taxable interest (see instructions)			**1**	
2	Ordinary dividends (see instructions)			**2**	
3	Annuities (see instructions)			**3**	
4a	Rental real estate, royalties, partnerships, S corporations, trusts, etc. (see instructions)	**4a**			
b	Adjustment for net income or loss derived in the ordinary course of a non-section 1411 trade or business (see instructions)	**4b**			
c	Combine lines 4a and 4b			**4c**	
5a	Net gain or loss from disposition of property (see instructions)	**5a**			
b	Net gain or loss from disposition of property that is not subject to net investment income tax (see instructions)	**5b**			
c	Adjustment from disposition of partnership interest or S corporation stock (see instructions)	**5c**			
d	Combine lines 5a through 5c			**5d**	
6	Adjustments to investment income for certain CFCs and PFICs (see instructions)			**6**	
7	Other modifications to investment income (see instructions)			**7**	
8	Total investment income. Combine lines 1, 2, 3, 4c, 5d, 6, and 7			**8**	

Part II | **Investment Expenses Allocable to Investment Income and Modifications**

9a	Investment interest expenses (see instructions)	**9a**			
b	State, local, and foreign income tax (see instructions)	**9b**			
c	Miscellaneous investment expenses (see instructions)	**9c**			
d	Add lines 9a, 9b, and 9c			**9d**	
10	Additional modifications (see instructions)			**10**	
11	Total deductions and modifications. Add lines 9d and 10			**11**	

Part III | **Tax Computation**

12	Net investment income. Subtract Part II, line 11 from Part I, line 8. Individuals complete lines 13–17. Estates and trusts complete lines 18a–21. If zero or less, enter -0-			**12**	
	Individuals:				
13	Modified adjusted gross income (see instructions)	**13**			
14	Threshold based on filing status (see instructions)	**14**			
15	Subtract line 14 from line 13. If zero or less, enter -0-	**15**			
16	Enter the smaller of line 12 or line 15			**16**	
17	Net investment income tax for individuals. Multiply line 16 by 3.8% (.038). **Enter here and include on your tax return** (see instructions)			**17**	
	Estates and Trusts:				
18a	Net investment income (line 12 above)	**18a**			
b	Deductions for distributions of net investment income and deductions under section 642(c) (see instructions)	**18b**			
c	Undistributed net investment income. Subtract line 18b from 18a (see instructions). If zero or less, enter -0-	**18c**			
19a	Adjusted gross income (see instructions)	**19a**			
b	Highest tax bracket for estates and trusts for the year (see instructions)	**19b**			
c	Subtract line 19b from line 19a. If zero or less, enter -0- . . .	**19c**			
20	Enter the smaller of line 18c or line 19c			**20**	
21	Net investment income tax for estates and trusts. Multiply line 20 by 3.8% (.038). **Enter here and include on your tax return** (see instructions)			**21**	

For Paperwork Reduction Act Notice, see your tax return instructions.

Cat. No. 59474M

Form **8960** (2014)

Instructions for Form 8960

Net Investment Income Tax—Individuals, Estates, and Trusts

Section references are to the Internal Revenue Code unless otherwise noted.

General Instructions

These instructions are based mostly on Regulations sections 1.1411-1 through 1.1411-10, which are effective for tax years beginning after 2013.

Future Developments

For the latest information about developments related to Form 8960 and its instructions, such as legislation enacted after they were published, go to *http://www.irs.gov/form8960*.

Who Must File

Attach Form 8960 to your return if Form 8960, line 17, is greater than zero (individuals) or line 21 is greater than zero (estates and trusts).

Purpose of Form

Use Form 8960 to figure the amount of your Net Investment Income Tax (NIIT).

Definitions

Controlled foreign corporation (CFC). Generally, a CFC is any foreign corporation if more than 50% of its voting power or stock value is owned or considered owned by US shareholders on any day during the tax year. Certain insurance companies are considered CFCs if more than 25% of their voting power or stock value is owned or considered owned by US shareholders on any day during the tax year. See section 953(c)(1)(B) and 957(a).

Excluded income. Excluded income means:
* Income excluded from gross income in IRC chapter 1,
* Income not included in net investment income, and
* Gross income and net gain specifically excluded by section 1411, related regulations, or other guidance published in the Internal Revenue Bulletin.

   Examples of excluded items are:
* Wages,
* Unemployment compensation,
* Alaska Permanent Fund Dividends,
* Alimony,
* Social Security benefits,
* Tax-exempt interest income,

* Income from certain qualified retirement plan distributions, and
* Income subject to self-employment taxes.

Net investment income. Generally, net investment income includes gross income from interest, dividends, annuities, royalties, and rents, unless they are derived from the ordinary course of a trade or business that is not (a) a passive activity or (b) a trade or business of trading in financial instruments or commodities. In addition, net investment income includes other gross income derived from a trade or business that is (a) a passive activity or (b) a trade or business of trading in financial instruments or commodities. Additionally, net investment income includes net gain (to the extent taken into account in computing taxable income) attributable to the disposition of property other than property held in a trade or business that is not (a) a passive activity or (b) a trade or business of trading in financial instruments or commodities. To arrive at net investment income, the above items are reduced by deductions allowed against the income tax which are properly allocable to those items of gross income or net gain. See section 1411(c) and Regulations sections 1.1411-4 and 1.1411-10(c).

Passive foreign investment company (PFIC). Generally, a PFIC is any foreign corporation if at least 75% of its gross income is passive income or an average of at least 50% of its assets produce passive income or are held for the production of passive income. See section 1297(a).

Qualified electing fund (QEF). Generally, a QEF is a PFIC for which the taxpayer has made an election under section 1295(b) and the PFIC complies with IRS requirements for determining ordinary earnings and net capital gain. See section 1295(a).

Section 1.1411-10(g) election. An election made under Regulations section 1.1411-10(g)(section 1.1411-10(g) election). See *Regulations Section 1.1411-10(g) Election*, later.

Section 1411 trade or business. Generally a trade or business that is either a passive activity for the taxpayer or is a trade or business of trading in financial instruments or commodities. See section

1411(c)(2) and Regulations section 1.1411-5(a).

Recordkeeping

For the NIIT, certain items of investment income and investment expense receive different treatment than for the regular income tax. Therefore, you need to keep all records and worksheets for the items you need to include on Form 8960. Keep all records for the entire life of the investment to show how you calculated basis. Also, you will need to know what you did in prior years if the investment was part of a carryback or carryforward.

Application to Individuals

U.S. citizens and residents. Individuals who have for the tax year (a) modified adjusted gross income (MAGI) that is over an applicable threshold amount, and (b) net investment income, must pay 3.8% of the smaller of (a) or (b) as their NIIT.

   The applicable threshold amount is based on your filing status:
* Married Filing Jointly or Qualifying Widower with Dependent Child is $250,000,
* Married Filing Separately is $125,000, or
* Single or Head of Household is $200,000.

Nonresidents. The NIIT does not apply to nonresident alien (NRA) individuals. If you are a U.S. citizen or resident married to an NRA, your filing status will be married filing separately for purposes of determining your MAGI, net investment income, and whether you are subject to the NIIT. However, see information later about certain elections to file jointly with NRA spouses.

Dual-resident individual. If you are a dual-resident individual, within the meaning of Regulations section 301.7701(b)-7(a)(1), generally you will be treated as a U.S. resident for purposes of the NIIT. However, you will be treated as an NRA for purposes of the NIIT if:
* You determine you would be treated as a resident of a foreign country for purposes of an income tax treaty between the United States and that foreign country,
* You elect to be treated as a resident of the foreign country for purposes of computing your U.S. income tax liability, and

- You file Form 1040NR, U.S. Nonresident Alien Income Tax Return, and Form 8833, Treaty-Based Return Position Return Disclosure Under Section 6114 or 7701(b), as provided in Regulations section 301.7701(b)-7(b).

Dual-status individual. If you were a dual-status individual — i.e., an individual who was a resident of the United States for part of the year and an NRA for the other part of the year — you are subject to the NIIT only for the portion of the year you were a U.S. resident. The relevant threshold amount is not reduced or prorated for a dual-status individual.

If you were a U.S. resident on the last day of the tax year, file Form 1040 and attach a statement showing your income for the part of the year you were a nonresident. You can use Form 1040NR as the statement.

If you were a nonresident on the last day of the tax year, file Form 1040NR and attach a statement showing your income for the part of the year you were a U.S. resident. You can use Form 1040 as the statement.

For more information, see Instructions for Form 1040NR and Pub. 519, Tax Guide for Aliens.

Election To File Jointly With Nonresident Spouse—Section 6013(g) or 6013(h)

If you and your spouse elect to file a joint return under section:
- 6013(g) (where an NRA is married to a U.S. citizen or resident at the end of the tax year); or
- 6013(h) (where at least one spouse was an NRA at the beginning of the tax year, but is a U.S. citizen or resident married to a U.S. citizen or resident at the end of the tax year);

you can also elect to apply the joint return election for NIIT purposes.

To make either election for NIIT purposes, use your combined items of income, gain, loss, and deduction from your joint return to figure your net investment income and MAGI; use the married filing joint return applicable threshold amount ($250,000); and check the appropriate check-box near the top of Form 8960, Part I.

Once you make either election, its duration and termination is governed by sections 6013(g) and 6013(h), respectively, and related regulations.

You can make either election on an amended return only if the tax year for which you are making the election, and all tax years affected by the election, are not closed by the period of limitations on assessments under section 6501.

If you elect to apply a section 6013(g) election for NIIT purposes and later determine that you did not meet the criteria for doing so in that tax year, your election for NIIT purposes will have no effect that year and for all future years. However, if, in a later year, you meet the criteria to elect to apply your section 6013(g) election for NIIT purposes, you will be treated as though you did elect to apply your section 6013(g) election in that later year unless you file (or amend) your return for that later year to report your NIIT without the election for NIIT purposes.

Application to Estates and Trusts

Domestic estates and trusts. The NIIT applies to estates and trusts that have undistributed net investment income and adjusted gross income (AGI) in excess of the threshold amount. The NIIT is 3.8% of the lesser of:
- the undistributed net investment income for the tax year, or
- the excess, if any, of AGI (as defined in section 67(e)) over the applicable threshold amount.

The applicable threshold amount is the dollar amount at which the highest tax bracket in section 1(e) begins for the tax year. See the instructions for Form 1041, Schedule G, line 1a and the instructions for Form 1041-QFT, line 13 for the dollar amount at which the highest tax bracket begins for the tax year.

Exception for certain domestic trusts. The following trusts are not subject to the NIIT:
- Trusts that are exempt from income taxes imposed by Subtitle A of the Internal Revenue Code:
    1. Charitable trusts and qualified retirement plan trusts exempt from tax under section 501, and
    2. Charitable Remainder Trusts exempt from tax under section 664;
- A trust or decedent's estate in which all of the unexpired interests are devoted to one or more of the purposes described in section 170(c)(2)(B);
- Trusts that are classified as "grantor trusts" under sections 671-679;
- Electing Alaska Native Settlement Funds (described in section 646);
- Perpetual Care (Cemetery) Trusts (described in section 642(i)); and
- Trusts that are not classified as "trusts" for federal income tax purposes. For example:
    1. Real Estate Investment Trusts, and
    2. Common Trust Funds.

Special computational rules for qualified funeral trusts (QFTs). The NIIT applies to the QFT (as defined in section

685) by treating each beneficiary's interest in that beneficiary's contract as a separate trust. Complete one consolidated Form 8960 for all beneficiary contracts subject to NIIT.

If a QFT has one or more beneficiary contracts that have net investment income in excess of the threshold amount:
- Complete Form 8960, lines 1-12, using only the sum of the net investment income of the beneficiary contracts that have net investment income in excess of the threshold amount, and
- On line 19b:
    1. Insert the number of beneficiary contracts that have net investment income in excess of the threshold amount next to the entry on the line, and
    2. Multiply the number of beneficiary contracts that have net investment income in excess of the threshold amount by the threshold amount for the year and enter that amount on line 19b.

Example. For 2014, a QFT has a beneficiary contract with $14,000 of interest income and another beneficiary contract with $13,000 of dividend income. Neither contract has any properly allocable deductions. The threshold amount for the 2014 tax year is $12,150. Therefore, the QFT has 2 beneficiary contracts with net investment income in excess of the threshold amount for the year.

The QFT will report $14,000 on line 1 (interest) and $13,000 on line 2 (dividends). Lines 12, 18a, and 19 would each be $27,000 ($14,000 plus $13,000). Enter "2" on the dotted line at the end of line 19b and enter $24,300 ($12,150 × 2) on the entry line for 19b. Lines 19c and 20 will be $2,700 ($27,000 less $24,300). On line 21, enter the NIIT liability of $102.60 ($2,700 × 3.8%).

Special computational rules for electing small business trusts (ESBTs). The NIIT has special computational rules for ESBTs. In general, ESBTs compute their NIIT in 3 steps:

1. The ESBT separately calculates the undistributed net investment income of the S portion and non-S portion according to the general rules for trusts under IRC chapter 1, and then combines the undistributed net investment income of the S portion and the non-S portion. In the case of an ESBT that has an S portion and a non-S portion, complete lines 1-11 of Form 8960 using the items from the non-S portion, and add undistributed net investment income of the S portion to net investment income on line 7.

2. The ESBT determines its AGI, solely for purposes of NIIT, by adding the net income or net loss from the S portion to the AGI of the non-S portion as a single

item of income or loss. See instructions to line 19a for more information.

3. To determine whether the ESBT is subject to NIIT, the ESBT compares the combined undistributed net investment income with the excess of its AGI over the section 1(e) threshold.

 For an ESBT with only S corporation income (no non-S portion), complete Form 8960 using the items from the S portion. For ESBTs with an S portion and a non-S portion, use Form 8960 as a worksheet for calculating the amounts to enter on line 7 and line 19a. On the S portion's Form 8960 worksheet, enter the S portion's net investment income on line 7 of the trust's Form 8960 and combine line 19a of the Form 8960 worksheet with the non-S portion's AGI to arrive at the amount on line 19a.

See Regulations section 1.1411-3(c) for more details and examples.

Special computational rules for bankruptcy estates of an individual. A bankruptcy estate of an individual debtor is treated as an individual for purposes of the NIIT. Regardless of the actual marital status of the debtor, the applicable threshold for purposes of determining the NIIT is the amount applicable for a married person filing separately.

Distributions from foreign estates and foreign trusts. If you are a U.S. person who receives a distribution of income from a foreign estate or foreign trust, generally, you must include the distribution in your net investment income calculation to the extent that the income is included in your AGI for regular income tax purposes. However, you do not need to include any distributions of accumulated income that you receive from a foreign trust.

Note. The NIIT does not apply directly to foreign estates or foreign trusts.

Passive Activity

General Rules

Net investment income generally includes income and gain from passive activities. A passive activity for purposes of net investment income has the same meaning as under section 469. A passive activity includes any trade or business in which you do not materially participate. A passive activity also includes any rental activity, regardless of whether you materially participate. There are limited exceptions for rentals. See the discussion on rentals later. For more details on passive activities, see the Instructions for Form 8582, Passive Activity Loss Limitations, and Pub. 925, Passive Activity and At-Risk Rules.

Trade or Business Activities

The definition of trade or business for NIIT purposes is limited to a trade or business within the meaning of section 162. This is more restrictive than the definition of a trade or business activity for purposes of the passive activity loss rules. For example, under the passive activity loss rules, a trade or business includes any activity conducted in anticipation of the commencement of a trade or business and any activity involving research or experimentation. In some cases, income from activities that are not passive activities under section 469 will be included in net investment income because the activity does not rise to the level of a trade or business within the meaning of section 162. The activity must be a trade or business within the meaning of section 162 and be nonpassive for purposes of section 469 before the income is excluded from the NIIT. If you own an interest in a pass-through entity, the determination of whether that is a trade or business is made at that entity's level.

Real Estate Professionals

If you are a real estate professional for purposes of section 469(c)(7), your rental income, or loss will not be passive if you materially participated in the rental real estate activity. For additional information on real estate professionals, see section 469(c)(7) and Pub. 925.

However, your rental income is included in net investment income if the income is not derived in the ordinary course of a trade or business. Qualifying as a real estate professional does not necessarily mean you are engaged in a trade or business with respect to the rental real estate activities. If your rental real estate activity is not a section 162 trade or business or you do not materially participate in the rental real estate activities, the rental income will be included in NIIT.

Safe Harbor for Real Estate Professionals

You qualify for the safe harbor if you are a real estate professional for purposes of section 469 and you:
• Participate in each rental real estate activity for more than 500 hours during the tax year, or
• Participated in a rental real estate activity for more than 500 hours in any 5 tax years (whether or not consecutive) during the 10 tax years immediately prior to this tax year.
If you qualify, your gross rental income from your rental real estate activity is treated as though derived in the ordinary course of a trade or business and is not included in your net investment income. If you qualify in the year you dispose of the

property used in the rental real estate activity, the amount of gain or loss from the disposition is also deemed to be derived from property used in the ordinary course of a trade or business and is not included in your net investment income.

Note. For real estate professionals with a Regulations section 1.469-9(g) election in effect, all of your rental real estate activities constitute a single activity for purposes of applying the 500-hour test described in *Safe Harbor for Real Estate Professionals*, earlier.

Note. If you are a real estate professional under section 469(c)(7), but you are unable to satisfy the qualifications for the safe harbor, you are not precluded from establishing that the gross income and gain or loss from the disposition of property associated with your rental real estate activity is not included in net investment income.

Special Rules for Certain Rental Income

For income tax purposes, Regulations section 1.469-2(f)(6) generally recharacterizes what otherwise would be passive rental income from a taxpayer's property as nonpassive where the taxpayer rents the property for use in a trade or business in which the taxpayer materially participates. Similarly, for income tax purposes, a rental activity that is properly grouped with a trade or business activity in which the taxpayer materially participates under Regulations section 1.469-4(d)(1) is a nonpassive activity. For purposes of calculating your net investment income, the gross rental income in both of these situations is treated as though it is derived in the ordinary course of a trade or business. Further, upon the disposition of the assets associated with the rental activity, any gain or loss is also treated as gain or loss attributable to the disposition of property held in a nonpassive trade or business and not included in your net investment income.

Treatment of Former Passive Activities

A former passive activity is any activity that was a passive activity in a prior tax year but it is not a passive activity in the current year. A prior tax year's unallowed loss from a former passive activity is allowed to the extent of current year income from the activity. For purposes of determining your net investment income, suspended losses from former passive activities are allowed as a properly allocable deduction, but only to the extent nonpassive income from the same activity is included in your net investment income in that year. For more information, see

Regulations section 1.1411-4(g)(8) and examples.

Disposition of Entire Interest

If you disposed of your entire interest in a passive activity or a former passive activity to an unrelated person in a fully taxable transaction, your losses allocable to the activity for that year are not limited by the passive activity loss rules for income tax purposes. A fully taxable transaction is a transaction in which you recognize all realized gain or loss. For purposes of calculating your net investment income, these losses may be properly allocable deductions, depending on the underlying character and origin of the losses.

Note. If you dispose of an activity that has always been a passive activity, the suspended passive losses from that activity are allowed in full as a properly allocable deduction.

Note. If you dispose of an activity that is a former passive activity, any suspended passive losses allowed in the year of disposition by reason of section 469(f)(1)(A) are included as properly allocable deductions, but only to the extent the gain on the disposition of the activity is included in net investment income (before taking into account any suspended losses). Any suspended passive losses that are allowed by reason of section 469(g) are allowed as additional properly allocable deductions.

Economic Grouping

You can treat one or more trade or business activities, or rental activities, as a single activity if those activities form an appropriate economic unit for measuring gain or loss under the passive activity loss rules. For additional information on passive activity grouping rules, see Pub. 925.

Regrouping rules. The passive activity grouping rules determine the scope of your trade or business and whether that trade or business is a passive activity for purposes of the NIIT. The proper grouping of a rental activity with a trade or business activity generally will not convert any gross income from rents into gross income derived from a trade or business.

Generally, you may not regroup activities unless your grouping was clearly inappropriate when originally made, or has become clearly inappropriate because of changed facts and circumstances. However, under the NIIT "fresh start" election you may regroup for the first tax year you are subject to the NIIT (without the effect of the regrouping). You may regroup only once under this election and that regrouping will apply to the tax year for which you regroup and all future tax years. If you are subject to the NIIT for

2013 and you do not regroup, you may make the election for the first tax year beginning after 2013 that you are subject to the NIIT.

You may regroup on an amended return, but only if you were not subject to the NIIT on your original return (or previously amended return), and if, because of a change to the original return, you owe NIIT for the year. For additional rules regarding regrouping on amended returns, see Regulations section 1.469-11(b)(3)(C).

Disclosure requirements. Regroupings under the NIIT "fresh start" are subject to the disclosure requirements of Rev. Proc. 2010-13.

Disposition of Partnership Interest or S Corporation Stock

In general, an interest in a partnership or S corporation is not property held for use in a trade or business and, therefore, gain or loss from the sale of a partnership interest or S corporation stock is included in your net investment income.

Adjustment

The amount of the gain or loss from the disposition for regular income tax purposes is included on Form 8960, line 5a, as a gain or loss. If you materially participated (as defined under the passive activity loss rules) in a trade or business activity of the partnership or S corporation (or one of its subsidiaries) and that trade or business activity is not the trade or business of trading in financial instruments or securities, then you must calculate the adjustment to report on line 5c. The adjustment described below only applies to dispositions of equity interests in partnerships and stock in S corporations and does not apply to gain or loss recognized on, for example, indebtedness owed to the taxpayer by a partnership or S corporation.

For more information on how to calculate the adjustment to report on line 5c, see the 2013 Proposed Regulations section 1.1411-7.

Note. If the tax basis of the interest in the partnership or S corporation for NIIT purposes is different than for regular income tax purposes due to certain adjustments associated with income from CFCs or QEFs, the amount of gain or loss may exceed the amount reported for regular income tax purposes.

Required statements. Attach a statement to your return for the year of disposition. Your statement must include:
- The name and taxpayer identification number of the partnership or S corporation of which the interest was transferred,

- The amount of the transferor's gain or loss on the disposition of the interest for regular income tax purposes included on line 5a,
- The information provided by the partnership or S corporation to the transferor relating to the disposition (if any), and
- The amount of adjustment to gain or loss due to basis adjustments attributable to ownership in certain CFCs and QEFs.

Deferred recognition sales (installment sales and private annuities). If you disposed of a partnership interest or S corporation stock in an installment sale transaction to which section 453 applies, you need to calculate your adjustment to net gain in the year of the disposition, even if the disposition occurred prior to 2013. The difference between the amount reported for regular income tax and NIIT will be taken into account when each payment is received. You must attach the statement described above to your return in the first year you are subject to NIIT. In subsequent years, attach a statement to your return that provides "Adjustment relates to a deferred recognition sale first reported on line 5c of the (enter year) return."

Regulations Section 1.1411-10(g) Election

In general, you may make the election provided in Regulations section 1.1411-10(g) if you own stock of a CFC or QEF. If a section 1.1411-10(g) election is in effect for stock of a CFC or QEF, generally, the amounts you include in income for regular income tax purposes under sections 951 and 1293 from the stock of the CFC or QEF are included in net investment income, and distributions from the stock of the CFC or QEF described in section 959(d) or 1293(c) are excluded from net investment income.

Your election applies only to the specific stock of the CFC or QEF for which it is made and stock of the CFC or QEF that you subsequently acquire. If you own a CFC or QEF through certain domestic pass-through entities, such as a domestic partnership, the entity may make the election for the stock of the CFC or QEF and you will be considered as having made the election with respect to the stock of the CFC or QEF owned or subsequently acquired by the pass-through entity. The election by the pass-through entity applies only to stock of the CFC or QEF held or subsequently acquired directly or indirectly by the pass-through entity. The pass-through entity's election does not apply to any stock of the CFC or QEF that you personally hold or subsequently acquire. If the entity does not make the election, you may make the election for the stock of the CFC or QEF owned through the entity.

Timing of election. Your election applies to the tax year for which it is made and later tax years, and applies to all interests in the CFC or QEF that you later acquire. You cannot revoke the election. In general, the election must be made no later than the first tax year beginning after 2013, in which you include an amount in income for regular income tax purposes under section 951(a) or 1293(a) for the stock of the CFC or QEF, and are subject to NIIT or would be subject to NIIT if you made the election for the stock of the CFC or QEF. The election may be made for a tax year beginning before 2014. The election can be made on an original or an amended return, provided that the tax year for which the election is made, and all tax years affected by the election, are not closed by the period of limitations on assessments under section 6501. For more information, see Regulations section 1.1411-10(g).

Example. If in 2014, a single individual acquires stock in a QEF, has a QEF inclusion of $5,000, and has MAGI of $150,000, the individual would not have to make a section 1.1411-10(g) election for 2014 because section 1411 is not applicable. If in 2015, the individual has MAGI in excess of 200,000, and the individual would like to take QEF inclusions into account for purposes of section 1411 in the same manner and in the same tax year as those amounts are taken into account for IRC chapter 1 purposes, the individual must make the section 1.1411-10(g) election for 2015 in the time and manner described in Regulations section 1.1411-10(g).

Content requirements of election. If you are making or made the election in a prior year, you must check the check-box for "Regulations section 1.1411-10(g) election" on the Form 8960 filed with your original or amended return. In addition, you must attach a statement to your return which includes the following:
• Your name and SSN (individuals) or EIN (estates and trusts),
• The following information for each CFC or PFIC for which an election is made:
   1. The name of the CFC or QEF, and
   2. Either the EIN of the CFC or QEF, or, if the CFC or QEF does not have an EIN, the reference ID number of the CFC or QEF.

In addition, list separately each CFC or QEF for which an election is being made for the first time with this return and include on the statement a declaration that you elect under Regulations section 1.1411-10(g) to apply the rules in section 1.1411-10(g).

Special Rule for Traders in Financial Instruments or Commodities

Gains and losses from your trade or business of trading in financial instruments or commodities are not subject to self-employment taxes. However, interest expense and other investment expenses are deducted by a trader on Schedule C (Form 1040), Profit or Loss From Business, if the expenses are from the trading business. A special rule may apply to a trader in financial instruments or commodities to reduce net investment income. The trader's interest and other investment expenses, to the extent the expenses are not used to reduce the trader's self-employment income, may be deductible for NIIT.

Specific Instructions

Part I—Investment Income

Elections for Investment Income

If you are making the section 6013(g) or 6013(h) election (see *Election To File Jointly With Nonresident Spouse—Section 6013(g) or 6013(h)*, earlier), check the corresponding check-box.

If you are making or have made a section 1.1411-10(g) election (see *Regulations Section 1.1411-10(g) Election*, earlier), check the corresponding check-box and attach a statement to your return as described earlier under *Content requirements of election*.

Line 1—Taxable Interest

Enter the amount of taxable interest received. Include the following amount from your return:
• Form 1040, line 8a;
• Form 1041, line 1;
• Form 1041-QFT, line 1a;
• Form 1040NR, taxable interest received for period of US residency shown on attached statement.

See *Special computational rules for qualified funeral trusts (QFTs)* and *Dual-status individual*, earlier.

Adjustments to interest. Interest income earned in the ordinary course of your non-section 1411 trade or business is excluded from net investment income. If this type of interest income is included in line 1, use line 7 to adjust your net investment income.

If line 1 includes self-charged interest income received from a partnership or S corporation that is a nonpassive activity (other than a trade or business of trading in financial instruments or commodities), see *Line 7—Other Modifications to Investment Income*, later, for a possible adjustment to net investment income.

Line 2—Ordinary Dividends

Enter the amount of ordinary dividends received. Include the following amount from your return:
• Form 1040, line 9a;
• Form 1041, line 2a;
• Form 1041-QFT, line 2a;
• Form 1040NR, ordinary dividends received for period of US residency shown on attached statement.

See *Special computational rules for qualified funeral trusts (QFTs)* and *Dual-status individual*, earlier.

Adjustments to dividends. If line 2 includes dividends from employer securities held in an employee stock ownership plan (ESOP) that are deductible under section 404(k) or Alaska Permanent Fund Dividends, include those amounts as negative modifications on line 7. See *Line 7—Other Modifications to Investment Income*, later.

Line 3—Annuities

Enter the gross income from all annuities, except annuities paid from the following:
• Section 401 - Qualified pension, profit-sharing, and stock bonus plans;
• Section 403(a) - Qualified annuity plans purchased by an employer for an employee;
• Section 403(b) - Annuities purchased by public schools or Section 501(c)(3) tax-exempt organizations;
• Section 408 - Individual Retirement Accounts (IRAs) or Annuities;
• Section 408A - Roth IRAs;
• Section 457(b) - Deferred compensation plans of a state and local government and tax-exempt organization; and
• Amounts paid in consideration for services (for example, distributions from a foreign retirement plan that are paid in the form of an annuity and include investment income that was earned by the retirement plan).

How your annuities are reported to you. Net investment income from annuities is reported to a recipient on Form 1099-R, Distributions From Pensions, Annuities, Retirement or Profit-Sharing Plans, IRAs, Insurance Contracts, etc. However, the amount reported on 1099-R may also include annuity payments from retirement plans that are exempt from NIIT. Amounts subject to NIIT should be identified with code "D" in box 7. If code "D" is shown in box 7 of Form 1099-R, include on Form 8960, line 3, the taxable amount reported on Form 1099-R, box 2a. However, if the payor checks box 2b indicating the taxable amount cannot be determined, you may need to calculate the taxable portion of your distribution. See Pub. 939, General Rule for Pensions and Annuities, and Pub. 575, Pension and Annuity Income, for details.

Line 4a—Rental Real Estate, Royalties, Partnerships, S Corporations, and Trusts

Enter the following amount from your properly completed return:
- Form 1040, line 17;
- Form 1041, line 5;
- Form 1041-QFT, the portion of line 4 that is income and loss that properly would be reported by a trust filing Form 1041 on Form 1041, line 5;
- Form 1040NR, the amount properly reported on the attachment to your Form 1040NR representing the amount that you would enter on Form 1040, line 17, if you were filing Form 1040 and including income and loss only for your period of US residency.

See *Special computational rules for qualified funeral trusts (QFTs)* and *Dual-status individual*, earlier.

Line 4b—Adjustment for Net Income or Loss Derived in the Ordinary Course of a Non-Section 1411 Trade or Business

Enter the net positive or net negative amount for the following items included in line 4a that are not included in determining net investment income:
- Net income or loss from a section 162 trade or business that is not a passive activity and is not engaged in a trade or business of trading financial instruments or commodities,
- Net income or loss from a section 1411 trade or business that is taken into account in determining self-employment income,
- Royalties derived in the ordinary course of a section 162 trade or business that is not a passive activity, and
- Passive losses of a former passive activity that are allowed as a deduction in the current year by reason of section 469(f)(1)(A).

In addition, use line 4b to adjust for certain types of nonpassive rental income or loss derived in the ordinary course of a section 162 trade or business. For example, line 4b includes the following items:
- Nonpassive net rental income or loss of a real estate professional where the rental activity rises to a section 162 trade or business.

- Net rental income or loss that is a nonpassive activity because it was grouped with a trade or business under Regulations section 1.469-4(d)(1). See *Special Rules for Certain Rental Income*, earlier.
- Other rental income or loss from a section 162 trade or business reported on Schedule K-1 (Form 1065), Partner's Share of Income, Deductions, Credits, etc., line 3, from a partnership, or Schedule K-1 (Form 1120S), Shareholder's Share of Income, Deductions, Credits, etc., line 3, from an S corporation, where the activity is not a passive activity.
- Net income that has been recharacterized as not from a passive activity under the section 469 passive loss rules and is derived in the ordinary course of a section 162 trade or business. For example:

1. Net rental income or loss from a rental that meets an exception under Regulations section 1.469-1T(e)(3)(ii), the activity rises to a section 162 trade or business, and you materially participated in the activity, or

2. Net income from property rented to a nonpassive activity. See *Special Rules for Certain Rental Income*, earlier.

Note. Any income from an estate or trust reported on Part III of Schedule E (Form 1040), Supplemental Income and Loss, that excluded net investment income is taken into account on line 7. Do not report those adjustments on line 4b.

 For line 4b adjustments, enter net positive amounts as a negative adjustment and enter net negative amounts as a positive adjustment.

Lines 5a-5d—Gains and Losses on the Dispositions of Property

Generally, net gain from the disposition of property not used in a trade or business and net gain or loss from the disposition of property held in a **section 1411 trade or business** is included in net investment income if included in taxable income.

Disposition usually means:
- Sale,
- Exchange,
- Transfer,
- Conversion,
- Cash settlement,
- Cancellation,
- Termination,
- Lapse,
- Expiration,
- Deemed disposition, for example under section 877A, or
- Other disposition.

Gains and losses that are not taken into account in computing taxable income are

not taken into account in computing net investment income. For example, gain that is not taxable by reason of section 121 (sale of a principal residence) or section 1031 (like-kind exchanges) is not included in net investment income.

See *Lines 5a-5d — Net Gains and Losses Worksheet*, later, for assistance in calculating net gain or loss includable in net investment income.

Line 5a—Net Gain or Loss From Disposition of Property

Calculate and enter the amount of net gain or loss from the disposition of property by combining the following amounts from your properly completed return:
- Form 1040, lines 13 and 14;
- Form 1041, lines 4 and 7;
- Form 1041-QFT, line 3 and the portion of line 4 attributed to ordinary gain/(loss);
- Form 1040NR, the amounts properly reported on the attachment to your Form 1040NR representing the amounts that you would enter on Form 1040, lines 13 and 14, if you were filing Form 1040 and including net gain or loss only for your period of US residency.

See *Dual-status individual* and *Special computational rules for qualified funeral trusts (QFTs)*, earlier.

Note. If you incur gain or loss from a disposition that is not reported as described in the previous paragraph, report it on line 7. See **Line 7—Other Modifications to Investment Income**, later.

Line 5b—Net Gain or Loss From Disposition of Property That Is Not Subject to Net Investment Income Tax

Use line 5b to adjust the amounts included on line 5a for gains and losses that are excluded from the calculation of net investment income. Enter the amount of gains (as a negative number) and losses (as a positive number) included on line 5a that are excluded from net investment income. For example, line 5b will include amounts such as:
- Gain or loss from the sale of property held in a non-section 1411 trade or business.

1. However, if the losses are attributable to formerly suspended passive losses of the non-section 1411 trade or business, such gains and losses are excluded from net investment income to the extent the nonpassive income from the non-section 1411 trade or business is excluded from net investment income. See Regulations section 1.1411-4(g)(8) for more information and examples.

Lines 5a-5d — Net Gains and Losses Worksheet

	(A) Capital gains/(losses) Form 1040, line 13; Form 1041, line 4; Form 1041-QFT, line 3; Form 1040NR, statement reflecting US residency portion of Form 1040, line 13	(B) Ordinary gains/(losses) Form 1040, line 14; Form 1041, line 7; Form 1041-QFT, portion of line 4 attributed to ordinary gain/(loss); Form 1040NR, statement reflecting US residency portion of Form 1040, line 14	Total of columns (A)+(B)
1. **Beginning net gains and losses**	_____	_____	**Enter this amount on line 5a** _____

2.   **Gains and losses excluded from net investment income.** *Use current year amounts for lines 2a-2g and 2i.*

	(A)	(B)	(A)+(B)
(a) Enter net gains from the disposition of property used in a non-section 1411 trade or business (enter as negative amounts): Name of Trade or Business Amount _____ (_____) _____ (_____)	(_____)	(_____)	
(b) Enter net losses from the disposition of property used in a non-section 1411 trade or business (enter as positive amounts): Name of Trade or Business Amount _____ ____ _____ ____	_____	_____	
(c) Enter net losses from a former passive activity (FPA) allowed by reason of section 469(f)(1)(A)	_____	_____	
(d) Gains recognized in the current year for payments received on an installment sale obligation or private annuity for the disposition of property used in a non-section 1411 trade or business	(_____)		
(e) Enter the net gain attributable to the net unrealized appreciation (NUA) in employer securities	(_____)		
(f) In the case of a QEF (other than a QEF held in a section 1411 trade or business) for which a section 1.1411-10(g) election is not in effect, enter the amount treated as long-term capital gain for regular income tax purposes under section 1293(a)(1)(B)	(_____)		
(g) Enter any other gains and losses included in net investment income that are not otherwise reported on Form 8960 and any other gains and losses excluded from net investment income reported on line 5a (enter excluded gains as a negative number and excluded losses as a positive number)	_____	_____	
(h) Enter the amount reported on line 2(i) of this worksheet from your prior tax year return calculations. Enter as a positive number	_____		
(i) If you do not have a capital loss carryover to next year, then skip this line and go to line 2(j). Otherwise, enter the lesser of (i)(1) or (i)(2) as a negative amount . . . . **(i)(1)** If the sum of the amounts entered on lines 2(a)-2(h) and line 3(d), column (A), is greater than zero, enter that amount here. Otherwise, enter -0- on line 2(i) and go to line 2(j) . . . . _____ **OR** **(i)(2)** The amount of capital loss carried over to next year (Schedule D (Form 1040), line 16, less the amount allowed as a current deduction on Schedule D (Form 1040), line 21) entered as a positive number . . . . _____	(_____)		
(j) Sum of lines 2(a) through 2(i)	_____	_____	**Enter this amount on line 5b** _____

		(A) Capital gains/(losses) Form 1040, line 13; Form 1041, line 4; Form 1041-QFT, line 3; Form 1040NR, statement reflecting US residency portion of Form 1040, line 13	(B) Ordinary gains/(losses) Form 1040, line 14; Form 1041, line 7; Form 1041-QFT, portion of line 4 attributed to ordinary gain/(loss); Form 1040NR, statement reflecting US residency portion of Form 1040, line 14	Total of columns (A)+(B)
3.	**Adjustment for gains and losses attributable to the disposition of interests in partnerships and S corporations**			
(a) **Net** **Gains**	(i) Enter the amount of net gain from the disposition of a partnership or S corporation included in line 5a to which section 1411(c)(4)(A) applies	_____	_____	
	(ii) Enter the amount of net gain included in net investment income after the application of Regulations section 1.1411-7. (The sum of columns A and B of line 3(a)(ii) must be less than, or equal to, the sum of columns A and B of line 3(a)(i).)	_____	_____	
	(iii) Enter the difference between line 3(a)(i) and line 3(a)(ii)	_____	_____	
(b) **Net** **Losses**	(i) Enter the amount of net loss from the disposition of a partnership or S corporation included in line 5a to which section 1411(c)(4)(B) applies	_____	_____	
	(ii) Enter the amount of net loss included in net investment income after the application of Regulations section 1.1411-7. (The sum of columns A and B of line 3(b)(ii) must be less than, or equal to, the sum of columns A and B of line 3(b)(i).)	_____	_____	
	(iii) Enter the difference between line 3(b)(i) and line 3(b)(ii)	_____	_____	
(c) **Deferred** **Sales**	(i) Enter the amount of gain recognized in the current year attributable payments received on an installment sale obligation or private annuity that was attributable to the disposition of an interest in a partnership or an S corporation in a year preceding the current year. Also report any gain or loss associated with section 736(b) payments on this line	_____	_____	
	(ii) Enter the amount of adjustment attributable to such gain	_____	_____	
	(iii) Subtract 3(c)(ii) from 3(c)(i)	_____	_____	
(d)	Combine the amounts on lines 3(a)(iii), 3(b)(iii), and 3(c)(iii)	_____	_____	Enter this amount on line 5c _____
4.	**Sum of items reported on lines 5a-5c**			
	Add lines 1, 2(j), and 3(d)	_____	_____	Enter this amount on line 5d _____

TIP *If the amount of gain for NIIT purposes is less than the amount of gain for regular income tax purposes, the entry on lines 3(a)(iii), 3(b)(iii), or 3(c)(iii) should be a negative number.*

If the amount of loss for NIIT purposes is less than the amount of loss for regular income tax purposes, the entry on lines 3(a)(iii), 3(b)(iii), or 3(c)(iii) should be a positive number.

2. Gain or loss from the sale of property held in a non-section 1411 trade or business does not include substantially appreciated property that is recharacterized as portfolio income. See *Substantially appreciated property*, later.

• Gain attributable to net unrealized appreciation (NUA) in employer securities held by a qualified plan. See *Net gain attributable to NUA in employer securities held by a qualified plan*, later.

• Adjustments to your capital loss carryforwards for items of excluded loss. See *Adjustments to your capital loss carryforwards*, later.

Substantially appreciated property. Generally, Regulations section 1.469-2(c)(2)(iii)(A) provides that if an interest in property previously used in a nonpassive activity but not used in a passive activity for more than 2 years prior to disposition is substantially appreciated at the time of disposition, any gain from the disposition is treated as not from a passive activity. The recharacterized gain may be taken into account under section 1411(c)(1)(A)(iii) if the gain is attributable to the disposition of property and recharacterized as portfolio income.

Net gain attributable to NUA in employer securities held by a qualified plan. Any gain attributable to NUA (within the meaning of section 402(e)(4)) that you realize on a disposition of employer securities held by a qualified plan is a distribution within the meaning of section 1411(c)(5) and is not included in net investment income. However, any gain realized on a disposition of employer securities attributable to appreciation in the value of your employer securities after the distribution from a qualified plan is not a distribution within the meaning of section 1411(c)(5) and is included in net investment income.

Shareholders of CFCs and QEFs without a section 1.1411-10(g) election. In the case of a QEF (other than a QEF held in a section 1411 trade or business) for which a section 1.1411-10(g) election is not in effect, enter the amount treated as long-term capital gain for regular income tax purposes under section 1293(a)(1)(B).

Also, in the case of a disposition of a CFC or QEF (other than a CFC or QEF held in a section 1411 trade or business) for which a section 1.1411-10(g) election is not in effect, enter the increase or decrease in the amount of gain or loss for NIIT purposes over the amount of gain or loss for regular income tax purposes. However, if the gain is higher (or the loss larger) for NIIT purposes compared to regular income tax purposes, in which case there is no impact to the adjustment for capital loss carryforwards for NIIT purposes, enter the difference on line 6.

Adjustments to your capital loss carryforwards. Starting in 2014, capital loss carryforwards must be adjusted if any sum of all capital gain or loss amounts excluded from net investment income on lines 5b and 5c was a net loss (the sum of all excluded capital losses was greater than the sum of all excluded capital gains). Generally, the annual adjustment to your capital losses carryforward is the lesser of:
• The amount of your capital loss carryforward from the previous year (the sum of carryforward amounts reflected on Schedule D (Form 1040), Capital Gains and Losses, lines 6 and 14, or
• The amount of excluded capital losses in excess of excluded capital gain in the previous year.
See *Lines 5a-5d — Net Gains and Losses Worksheet*, earlier, for assistance with the calculation of capital loss carryforwards. In addition, see the 2013 Proposed Regulations section 1.1411-4(d)(4)(iii) for more information and a comprehensive example of the application of this rule.

Pass-through entities. If you hold an interest in a pass-through entity, the determination of whether a trade or business exists is made at that entity's level.

Line 5c—Adjustment From Disposition of Partnership Interest or S Corporation Stock

Enter the amount from the worksheet for lines 5a-5d, Part II, line 3d. Attach a statement as described in *Required statements*, earlier, to your return for the year of the disposition.

Line 6—Adjustments to Investment Income for Certain CFCs and PFICs

If you own stock, directly or indirectly, in a CFC or a PFIC (other than certain CFCs and PFICs held in a section 1411 trade or business or PFICs marked to market under a provision of IRC chapter 1 other than section 1296), use line 6 for adjustments necessary to calculate your net investment income.

Income from investments in CFCs and PFICs is generally included in the calculation of net investment income and, in many cases, will be included (in whole or in part) on other lines of Form 8960. Generally, dividends from a CFC or a PFIC that are included in your regular income tax base are included on Form 8960, line 2, and gains and losses derived from the stock of a CFC or a PFIC that are included in your regular income tax base generally are included on Form 8960, line 5. Also, income derived from CFCs and certain PFICs you hold in a section

1411 trade or business is generally reported on Form 8960, line 4a.

Line 6 is used for adjustments that are the result of additional rules. These additional rules may apply when you own an interest in a CFC or PFIC and may require you to subtract or add amounts not otherwise included on Form 8960. These additional rules vary depending on the set of anti-deferral rules that apply to you for regular income tax purposes, and for CFCs and QEFs, and depending on whether you have a section 1.1411-10(g) election in effect for the CFC or QEF. For more information about determining the amount to report on line 6, see Regulations section 1.1411-10.

Section 1296 mark to market PFICs. Generally, if you are subject to the section 1296 mark to market rules for a PFIC, you will include in net investment income any amounts included in income for regular income tax purposes under section 1296(a)(1) and deduct from net investment income any amounts deducted from income for regular income tax purposes under section 1296(a)(2). Use line 6 to make increases or decreases to net investment income as a result of this rule (for items that are not otherwise reflected on Form 8960).

Section 1291 funds. If you are subject to the section 1291 rules for a PFIC, you will include in net investment income any "excess distributions that are dividends for NIIT purposes as well as any gains that are treated as excess distributions for regular income tax purposes." Use line 6 to make the increases to net investment income as a result of the application of this rule (for items that are not otherwise reflected on Form 8960).

CFCs and QEFs with a section 1.1411-10(g) election in effect. If you have a section 1.1411-10(g) election in effect for a CFC or QEF, you will include in net investment income any inclusions under section 951(a) or 1293(a) derived from the CFC or QEF. Inclusions under section 1293(a)(1)(B) may be reported elsewhere on Form 8960, such as on line 5a. Use line 6 to make the increases to net investment income as a result of the application of this rule (for items that are not otherwise reflected on Form 8960).

Note. If you included in income an amount under section 951(a) or section 1293(a) for a CFC or QEF in 2013 and made an election under Regulations section 1.1411-10(g) after 2013 for that CFC or QEF, special rules may apply to certain distributions of previously taxed income from the CFC or QEF that are not subject to regular income tax. For more information, see Regulations section 1.1411-10.

CFCs and QEFs without a section 1.1411-10(g) election in effect. If you do not have a section 1.1411-10(g) election in effect for a CFC or QEF, generally, you will include in net investment income certain distributions of previously taxed income from the CFC or QEF that are not subject to regular income tax. In addition, other special rules may apply, including rules that provide, as applicable, alternative basis calculations for your basis in the CFC or QEF, or your basis in a domestic partnership or S corporation that owns the interest in the CFC or QEF. Also, the amount of investment interest expense you take into account for NIIT purposes may be increased or decreased from the amount taken into account for regular income tax purposes. (For additional information on all of these rules, see Regulations section 1.1411-10.) As a result of these rules, you may need to include amounts in net investment income that aren't otherwise reported on Form 8960 or make adjustments to amounts reported elsewhere on Form 8960. For example, you may need to include distributions from a CFC or a QEF in net investment income. Use line 6 to make increases or decreases to net investment income as a result of the application of this rule (for items that are not otherwise reflected on Form 8960).

Note. Use line 5b to deduct inclusions under section 1293(a)(1)(B) that are allowed on line 5a, or to adjust the amount of gain or loss derived from the disposition of shares of a CFC or QEF. However, if the gain included in net investment income is higher than the amount reported for regular income tax (or the loss is greater), report the adjustment on line 6.

Note. Even if you do not have a section 1.1411-10(g) election in place for a CFC or QEF, there are certain instances in which distributions to you from the CFC or QEF may not be subject to NIIT. For example, if a prior holder of the CFC or QEF had made a section 1.1411-10(g) election for that CFC or QEF and you receive a distribution of earnings and profits which were previously included in the net investment income of the prior holder, you may not be subject to NIIT on that distribution. For more information, see Regulations section 1.1411-10.

Line 7—Other Modifications to Investment Income

Use line 7 to report additional net investment income modifications to net investment income that are not otherwise specified in lines 1-6. For example, use line 7 to report additions and modifications to net investment income such as

- Section 1411 net operating loss (NOL) (enter as a negative amount). See *Section 1411 NOL*, later.
- Any deductions described in section 62(a)(1) that are properly allocable to a passive activity or trading business, but are not taken into account on lines 4a or 5a (enter as a negative amount). See *Other section 62(a)(1) deductions*, later.
- Adjustments for distributions from Estates and Trusts. See *Distributions from estates and trusts*, later.
- Section 404(k) dividends reported on line 2 (enter as a negative amount). See *Line 2—Ordinary Dividends*, earlier.
- Interest income reported on line 1 received from certain nonpassive activities (entered as a negative amount). See *Self-charged interest*, later.
- Recoveries of deductions taken on a prior year's Form 8960. See *Deduction recoveries*, later.
- Other items of net investment income (or properly allocable deductions) not otherwise included on Form 8960 reported on Form 1040, line 21; Form 1041, line 8; Form 1041-QFT, lines 4 and 9; Form 1040NR, amount on statement reporting tax items for your period of US residency corresponding to Form 1040, line 21. For example, these items could include:

    1. Amounts reported on Form 8814, Parents' Election To Report Child's Interest and Dividends, line 12. See *Form 8814 election*, later;

    2. Substitute interest and dividend payments (generally reported on Form 1099-MISC, Miscellaneous Income); and

    3. Net positive periodic payments received from a notional principal contract (NPC) that is referenced to property (including an index) that produces (or would produce if the property were to produce income) interest, dividends, royalties, or rents. For example, an interest rate swap, cap, or floor and an equity swap would be treated as an NPC that produces net investment income.

- Gains and losses from the disposition of property not included on line 5a that are taken into account in computing taxable income. For example:

    1. Gain or loss from the disposition of an annuity or life insurance contract. See *Line 3—Annuities*, earlier.

    2. Casualty and theft losses reported on Schedule A (Form 1040), Itemized Deductions, line 20 (enter as a negative amount).

However, gains and losses attributable to assets held in a non-section 1411 trade or business are not included in net investment income. For more information, See *Line 5b—Net Gain or Loss From Disposition of Property That Is Not Subject to Net Investment Income Tax*, earlier.

Other section 62(a)(1) deductions. Use line 7 to report additional deductions attributable to a section 1411 trade or business that are not included on lines 4-6. Generally, these deductions are above-the-line deductions reported on Form 1040, lines 23-35.

Note. Expenses associated with the trade or business of trading in financial instruments or commodities that are reported on your Schedule C (Form 1040) are reported on Form 8960, line 10. See *Special rule for traders in financial instruments or commodities*, later.

Note. Early withdrawal penalty (Form 1040, line 30) is reported on Form 8960, line 10.

 Use line 7 to report the amount of your domestic production activities deduction from Form 1040, line 35, attributable to a section 1411 trade or business. Using Form 8903, Domestic Production Activities Deduction, as a worksheet, compute the domestic production activities deduction using only the information from your section 1411 trade or business. On line 7, enter the lesser of the amount on Form 1040, line 35 or the amount of the deduction reported on the recomputed Form 8903 worksheet. Keep the recomputed Form 8903 for your records; do not include it with your return.

Form 8814 election. Parents electing to include their child's dividends and capital gain distribution in their income by filing Form 8814 include on Form 8960, line 7, the amount on Form 8814, line 12, excluding Alaska Permanent Fund Dividends.

Distributions from estates and trusts. Enter the amount from Schedule K-1, Form 1041, Beneficiary's Share of Income, Deductions, Credits, etc., box 14, code "H."

Note. If the amount reported on Schedule K-1, Form 1041, box 14, with a code "H" is a positive number, enter it on Form 8960, line 7, and increase your MAGI on Form 8960, line 13 (or Form 8960, line 19a) by the same amount.

If the amount reported on Schedule K-1, Form 1041, box 14, with a code "H" is a negative number, and the trust has indicated some (or all) of the adjustment also requires a MAGI adjustment, enter it on Form 8960, line 7, and make the applicable increase or decrease to your MAGI on Form 8960, line 13 (or Form 8960, line 19a) as necessary.

Section 1411 NOL. If you have an NOL allowed under section 172 for purposes of determining your regular income tax, you

Example Calculation of Section 1411 NOL for NIIT

Assume an unmarried individual incurs the following NOLs:

NOL Origination Year	(A) Regular Income Tax NOL	(B) Section 1411 NOL	(C) Applicable Portion of NOL [Column B divided by Column A]
2012 Calendar Year	$150,000	None	0.00%
2013 Calendar Year	$100,000	$30,000	30.0%
2014 Calendar Year	$40,000	$40,000	100%
2015 Calendar Year	$120,000	$60,000	50.0%

Beginning in 2016, the unmarried individual begins to use the NOLs to offset his income:

Tax Year	NOL Origination Year	Regular Income	Applicable Portion	Section 1411 NOL
2016 Tax Year		$300,000		
	2012 NOL	($150,000)	0.00%	None
	2013 NOL	($100,000)	30.0%	($30,000)
	2014 NOL	($40,000)	100.0%	(40,000)
	2015 NOL	($10,000)	50.0%	($5,000)
Total Section 1411 NOL allowed as deduction against 2016 net investment income				($75,000)

In 2016, the regular income tax NOLs from 2012-2015 has caused the taxpayer's AGI ($0) to fall below the statutory threshold, therefore the individual is not subject to the NIIT.

Tax Year	NOL Origination Year	Regular Income	Applicable Portion	Section 1411 NOL
2017 Tax Year		$600,000		
	2015 NOL	($110,000)	50.0%	($55,000)
Total Section 1411 NOL allowed as deduction against 2017 net investment income				($55,000)

In 2017, the regular income tax NOL remaining from 2015 has reduced the taxpayer's income for regular income tax to $490,000. The individual is entitled to reduce his net investment income by $55,000 (entered as a negative on Form 8960, line 7).

may also be allowed to deduct some, or all, of the NOL in computing net investment income. Because NOLs are computed and carried over year by year, you must determine for each NOL year what portion of the NOL is attributable to net investment income. To determine how much of the accumulated NOL you can use in the current tax year as a deduction against your net investment income, you must first calculate your applicable portion of the NOL for each loss year. For more information and examples on the calculation of a section 1411 NOL and its use, see Regulations section 1.1411-4(h).

Note. No portion of an NOL incurred in a tax year beginning before 2013 is permitted to reduce net investment income.

Calculating your section 1411 NOL.
In any tax year in which a taxpayer incurs an NOL, the section 1411 NOL is the lesser of:
- The amount of the NOL for the loss year the taxpayer would incur if only items of gross income that are used to determine net investment income and only properly allocable deductions (other than a section 1411 NOL) are taken into account in determining the NOL under sections 172(c) and 172(d), or
- The amount of the taxpayer's NOL for the loss year.

 For purposes of calculating the section 1411 NOL, compute your NOL using Form 1045, Application for Tentative Refund, Schedule A—NOL, with only items of income, gain, loss, and deduction on Form 8960 for that year. If this amount is less

than your NOL computed for regular income tax purposes, then this amount is the applicable portion of your NOL. If this amount is equal to, or greater than, your NOL computed for regular income tax purposes, then your applicable portion is 100% of the regular income tax NOL (which means the entire NOL will be deductible in computing net investment income when the NOL is used for regular income tax purposes).

Using your section 1411 NOL.
When you deduct an NOL that originated in a previous year against the current year income, a portion of the NOL will be deductible in computing net investment income for that year, regardless of whether you are subject to the NIIT in that year without the NOL deduction. The amount of the regular income tax NOL used in calculating net investment income is called the "applicable portion." The applicable portion is the percentage of the regular income tax NOL that is a section 1411 NOL. Because NOLs are calculated on a year by year basis, the applicable portion of each NOL that is used in the current year may be different.

Note. If you incur an NOL in 2013 or 2014 and carry back that NOL to offset income in years preceding the imposition of the NIIT (for example, a carryback to calendar year 2011 and/or 2012), the amount of 1411 NOL that is included in the NOL carryback will be used (as an applicable portion) even though the NIIT was not in effect.

See *Example Calculation of Section 1411 NOL for NIIT*, later, for an illustration of the calculation and use of a section 1411 NOL for NIIT purposes.

Deduction recoveries. A recovery or refund of a previously deducted item increases net investment income in the year of the recovery. There are 2 exceptions to this general rule.

Generally, for purposes of determining the gross amount of the recovery, include the recovery of any amount that was deducted in a prior year, regardless of the application of the tax benefit rule (see section 111). For example, if a taxpayer receives a refund of state income taxes from a prior year, such a refund would be included in the taxpayer's gross income. However, if the taxpayer was subject to the alternative minimum tax in the year of the payment, the taxpayer may not have received any tax benefit under IRC chapter 1, and therefore section 111 may exclude some or all of the refund from gross income. However, the deductibility of state income taxes for NIIT is independent of the taxes for alternative minimum tax purposes. Therefore, the applicability of the recovery rule is determined without regard to whether the recovered amount was excluded from gross income by reason of section 111.

There are 2 exceptions to including recovered amounts in net investment income. The 2 exceptions apply the tax benefit rule of section 111 within the NIIT system, and therefore operate independently of the application of section 111 for IRC chapter 1 purposes. First, properly allocable deductions are not reduced in the year of the recovery if the amount deducted in the prior year did not reduce the amount of section 1411 liability. Second, properly allocable deductions are not reduced in the year of the recovery if the amount deducted in the prior year is included in net investment income.

Note. The total amount of recovery reported on Form 8960, line 7, cannot exceed the total amount of properly allocable deductions for the year.

[TIP] *If the recovered amount relates to a deduction taken in a tax year beginning before 2013, none of the recovery is included in net investment income in the year of recovery.*

[TIP] *If the recovered amount relates to a deduction taken in a tax year beginning after 2012 and you were not subject to the NIIT because your MAGI (see* Line 13—Modified Adjusted Gross Income (MAGI)*, later), was below the applicable threshold on line 14, then none of the recovery is included in net investment income in the year of recovery. However, this rule does not apply if you incurred an NOL in the year of the deduction, and a portion of your NOL is a section 1411 NOL.*

[TIP] *If the recovered amount is included in net investment income on line 1-6, none of the recovery is included in net investment income on line 7.*

See Regulations section 1.1411-4(g)(2) for more information and examples. See *Line 7—Deduction Recoveries Worksheet*, later, to determine the amount of any recovery to include on line 7.

[TIP] *In the case of multiple recoveries in a single year, complete this worksheet for each recovery. If multiple recoveries relate to a single deduction year, the amount reported on lines 8 and 9 of the first recovery worksheet will become lines 7 and 10, respectively, on the second recovery worksheet.*

Self-charged interest. The self-charged interest rules under section 469 (passive activity loss limitation) apply to lending transactions between a taxpayer and a pass-through entity in which the taxpayer

owns a direct or indirect interest, or between certain pass-through entities. The section 469 self-charged interest rules apply only to items of interest income and interest expense that are recognized in the same tax year. The self-charged interest rules:
• Treat certain interest income resulting from these lending transactions as passive activity income,
• Treat certain deductions for interest expense that are properly allocable to the interest income as passive activity deductions, and
• Allocate the passive activity gross income and passive activity deductions resulting from this treatment among the taxpayer's activities.

The rules for computing net investment income adopt a similar rule for self-charged interest. See Regulations section 1.1411-4(g)(5). Include on line 7 (as a negative amount) the amount of interest income you received that is equal to the amount of interest income that would have been considered passive income under the self-charged interest rules (Regulations section 1.469-7) had the nonpassive activity been considered a passive activity.

Note. This rule does not apply to interest received on loans made to a trade or business engaged in the trading of financial instruments or commodities.

Note. Do not include any adjustment for interest income on line 7 (as a negative amount) if the corresponding interest deduction is also taken into account in determining your self-employment income that is subject to tax under section 1401(b).

Part II—Investment Expenses Allocable to Investment Income and Modifications

Investment Expenses

Part II of Form 8960 includes deductions and modifications to net investment income that are not otherwise included in Part I. Generally, expenses associated with a passive activity trade or business, or the trade or business of trading in financial instruments or commodities conducted through a pass-through entity are already included on line 4a or on line 5a. Part II is used to report deductions that are, predominately, itemized deductions. For more information on what constitutes properly allocable deductions, see Regulations sections 1.1411-4(f)-(g).

Note. If you did not itemize your deductions for regular income tax purposes, you may not take any

deductions that would be reported on Schedule A (Form 1040) on your Form 8960.

Reasonable method allocations. To the extent that you have a properly allocable deduction that is allocable to both net investment income and excluded income, you may use any reasonable method to determine that portion of the deduction that is properly allocable to net investment income. The 3 items that may be allocated between net investment income and excluded income are:
• State, local, and foreign income taxes if properly deducted on your return when calculating your US regular income tax.
• All ordinary and necessary expenses paid or incurred during the tax year to determine, collect, or obtain a refund of any tax owed if properly deducted on your return when calculating your US regular income tax.
• Amounts paid or incurred by the fiduciary of an estate or trust on account of administration expenses, including fiduciaries' fees and expenses of litigation, which are ordinary and necessary in connection with the performance of the duties of administration if properly deducted on your return when calculating your US regular income tax.

If you have more than one of the deductions described above, you may use a different method of allocation for each one. The reasonable method of allocation may differ from year to year.

Examples of reasonable methods of allocation include, but are not limited to, an allocation of the deduction based on the ratio of the amount of a taxpayer's gross investment income (Form 8960, line 8) to the amount of the taxpayer's AGI (Form 1040, line 38). In the case of an estate or trust, an allocation of a deduction under Regulations section 1.652(b)-3(b), and in the case of ESBT, Regulations section 1.641(c)-1(h), is also a reasonable method.

Note. If an estate or trust allocates expenses for regular income tax purposes under Regulations section 1.652(b)-3(b) or 1.641(c)-1(h), any deviation from that allocation may not be a reasonable allocation method for NIIT purposes.

Items not deductible in calculating net investment income. Unless a deduction is specifically identified as properly allocable to net investment income in the section 1411 regulations, or in supplemental guidance issued by the IRS in the Internal Revenue Bulletin, the deduction is not permitted. For example, the following items are not deductible in computing net investment income:
• Deductions for moving expenses (Form 1040, line 26),

Line 7—Deduction Recoveries Worksheet
Keep for Your Records

1. Enter total amount of recovery included in gross income .... **1.** _____

   • Do not include recoveries of items that are included in net investment income in the year of recovery (included on lines 1-6).

   • Do not include recoveries of items if the amount relates to a deduction taken in a tax year beginning before 2013.

   • Do not include recoveries of items if the amount relates to a deduction taken in a tax year beginning after 2012, and you were not subject to the NIIT solely because your MAGI was below the applicable threshold.

   > ⚠️ **CAUTION** *This rule does not apply if you incurred a net operating loss (NOL) in such year, and a portion of such NOL constitutes a section 1411 NOL.*

2. Amount of the recovery that would have been included in gross income but for the application of the tax benefit rule under section 111 .... **2.** _____

3. Total amount of recovery (add lines 1 and 2) .... **3.** _____

4. Enter the percentage of the deduction allocated to net investment income in the prior year. (If the deduction was not allocated between investment income and non-investment income, enter 100%.) .... **4.** _____

5. Enter the lesser of (a) line 3 multiplied by line 4, or (b) the total amount deducted on the prior year Form 8960 attributable to item recovered (after any deduction limitations imposed by section 67 or 68) .... **5.** _____

Calculation of recoveries when the deduction is not taken into account in computing your section 1411 NOL.

6. Multiply line 5 by .038 .... **6.** _____

7. Enter the amount of net investment income in the year of the deduction (previous year's Form 8960, line 12, unless line 12 is zero, then previous year's Form 8960, line 8 minus line 11) .... **7.** _____

8. Add the amount of line 5 to line 7 .... **8.** _____

9. Using the previous year's Form 8960, recalculate the NIIT for the year of the deduction by replacing the amount reported on line 12 with the amount reported on line 8 of this worksheet (do not use the net investment income reported on that year's Form 8960, line 12). Enter your recalculated NIIT here .... **9.** _____

10. Enter the NIIT reported for the year of the deduction .... **10.** _____

11. Subtract line 10 from Line 9 .... **11.** _____

12. Enter the smaller of line 6 or Line 11 .... **12.** _____

13. Divide line 12 by 3.8% (line 12 ÷ .038). Enter the result here and include on Form 8960, line 7 .... **13.** _____

Calculation of recoveries when the deduction is taken into account in computing your section 1411 NOL

14. Enter the amount of the section 1411 NOL in the year of the deduction (entered as a positive number) .... **14.** _____

15. Enter the amount of the section 1411 NOL in the year of the deduction recomputed without the amount on line 5 (entered as a positive number, but not less than zero) .... **15.** _____

16. Subtract line 15 from line 14. Enter the result here and include on Form 8960, line 7 .... **16.** _____

- Expenses that are not deductible for regular income tax (for example, interest expense and investment expenses associated with investments in tax-exempt bonds),
- Deduction for alimony paid (Form 1040, line 31),
- Deduction for contributions to IRAs or other qualified plans,
- The standard deduction,
- Personal exemptions (Form 1040, line 42),
- Deductions for charitable contributions (Schedule A (Form 1040), line 19),
- Deductions for medical expenses (Schedule A (Form 1040), line 4),
- Deductions for mortgage interest expense (Schedule A (Form 1040), lines 10-13),
- Deductions for real estate taxes or personal property taxes that do not constitute investment expenses under section 163(d)(4)(C) and are reported on Form 4952, Investment Interest Expense Deduction, line 5 (Schedule A (Form 1040), lines 6-7), and
- Deductible contributions to Capital Contribution Funds under section 7518.

Line 9a—Investment Interest Expense

Enter on Form 8960, line 9a, interest expense you paid or accrued during the tax year entered on Schedule A (Form 1040), line 14. Estates and trusts enter amount from Form 4952, line 8 (if not required to file Form 4952, use the form as a worksheet). For individuals filing a Form 1040NR, include only the amount of investment interest expense deduction for your U.S. residency period.

Note. If Form 4952 includes investment interest expense that is deducted on Schedule E (Form 1040) and already taken into account on line 4a, do not include the same amount on line 9a.

Note. If you own a CFC or QEF for which a section 1.1411-10(g) election is not in effect, you may calculate your section 163(d) investment expense deduction for NIIT purposes differently than for regular income tax purposes. See Regulations section 1.1411-10(c)(5) for additional guidance. Any modification to your section 163(d) investment expense deduction for NIIT purposes is taken into account on line 6.

Line 9b—State, Local, and Foreign Income Tax

Include state, local and foreign income taxes you paid for the tax year that are attributable to net investment income. Form 1040NR filers include only taxes paid for the US residency period of the tax year. Sales taxes are not deductible in computing net investment income. You may not take a deduction for any foreign income taxes paid for the tax year if you took a credit for any portion of it. See section 275(a)(4).

You can determine the portion of your state, local, and foreign income taxes allocable to net investment income using any reasonable method. See *Reasonable method allocations*, earlier, and *Deductions subject to AGI limitations under section 67 or section 68*, later.

Note. Enter the amount of state, local, or foreign income taxes on Form 8960, line 9b, net of any deduction limitations imposed by section 68. See *Lines 9 and 10 — Application of Itemized Deduction Limitations on Deductions Properly Allocable to Investment Income Worksheet*, later, for assistance in figuring the amount to report on line 9b.

Line 9c—Miscellaneous Investment Expenses

Investment expenses you incur that are directly connected to the production of investment income are deductible expenses in determining your net investment income. Generally, these amounts are reported on Form 4952, line 5. See Form 4952 for the instructions for line 5 for more information. The amounts reported on line 9c are the amounts allowable after the application of the deduction limitations imposed by sections 67 and 68. See *Deductions subject to AGI limitations under section 67 or section 68*, later.

Note. Enter the amount of miscellaneous investment expenses on Form 8960, line 9c, net of any deduction limitations imposed by section 67 or section 68. See *Lines 9 and 10 — Application of Itemized Deduction Limitations on Deductions Properly Allocable to Investment Income Worksheet*, later, for assistance in figuring the amount to report on line 9c.

 Do not include expenses that have been deducted on other lines of the Form 8960, such as depletion or depreciation reported on Schedule E (Form 1040) and included on Form 8960, line 4a.

Dual-status individuals include only tax items related to their period of US residency. See *Dual-status individual*, earlier.

Lines 9 and 10 — Application of Itemized Deduction Limitations on Deductions Properly Allocable to Investment Income Worksheet

Keep for Your Records

Part I — Application of Section 67 to Deductions Properly Allocable to Investment Income

1. Enter the amount of Miscellaneous Itemized Deductions properly allocable to investment income before any itemized deduction limitations (Description and Form 8960 line number where they will be reported):

Description	Line	Amount
(a) _____	_____	_____
(b) _____	_____	_____

2. Enter the total of all items listed in line 1 . . . . **2.** _____

3. Enter the amount of all Miscellaneous Itemized Deductions after the application of the section 67 limitation (Schedule A (Form 1040), line 27) . . . . **3.** _____

4. Enter the lesser of the total reported on line 2 or line 3 . . . . **4.** _____

Part II — Application of Section 67 Limitation to Specific Deductions

(A) Reenter the amounts and descriptions from Part I, line 1.	(B) **IF** line 3 is less than line 2, **THEN** divide line 3 by line 2 **AND** enter the amount in column (B). **IF** amounts reported on Part I, lines 2 and 4 are equal, **THEN** enter 1.00 in column (B)	(C) Multiply the individual amounts in column (A) by the amount in column (B).

	Description	Line	Amount			
(a)	_____	_____	_____	×	_____	= _____
(b)	_____	_____	_____	×	_____	= _____

> **TIP**
>
> **Individuals** — Use the amounts in column (C) on Part III, line 1, to determine the amount of these deductions that are allowable after the application of the section 68 limitation.
>
> **Estates or trusts** — Enter the amounts in column (C) in the appropriate location on lines 9 and 10. Do not complete Parts III or IV of this worksheet.

Lines 9 and 10 — Application of Itemized Deduction Limitations on Deductions Properly Allocable to Investment Income Worksheet—*continued*

 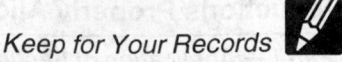

Part III — Application of Section 68 to deductions properly allocable to investment income (Individuals Only)

1. Enter the amount of Miscellaneous Itemized Deductions properly allocable to investment income from column (C) of Part II:

Description	Line	Amount
(a) _____	_____	_____
(b) _____	_____	_____

2. Enter the amount of state, local, and foreign income taxes that are properly allocable to investment income. . . . . **2.** _____

3. Enter the amounts of other Itemized Deductions subject to the section 68 limitation and properly allocable to investment income before any itemized deduction limitations (Description and Form 8960 line number):

Description	Line	Amount
(a) _____	_____	_____
(b) _____	_____	_____

4. Enter the total deductions properly allocable to investment income subject to the section 68 limitation. Enter the sum of lines 1 through 3 . . . . **4.** _____

5. Enter the amount of total itemized deductions reported on Form 1040, line 40 . . . . **5.** _____

6. Enter all other itemized deductions allowed but not subject to the section 68 deduction limitation:

    (a) Investment Interest Expense . . . . _____

    (b) Casualty Losses (other than losses described in section 165(c)(1)) . . . . _____

    (c) Medical Expenses . . . . _____

    (d) Gambling Losses . . . . _____

    (e) Total of lines 6(a) through 6(d) . . . . **6e.** _____

7. Subtract line 6e from line 5 . . . . **7.** _____

8. Enter the lesser of line 7 or line 4 . . . . **8.** _____

TIP *This is the amount of itemized deductions that are properly allocable to investment income after the application of the sections 67 and 68 deduction limitations. Use Part IV of this worksheet to reconcile this amount to the individual deduction amounts reported on Form 8960, lines 9 and 10.*

Lines 9 and 10 — Application of Itemized Deduction Limitations on Deductions Properly Allocable to Investment Income Worksheet—continued

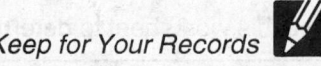 *Keep for Your Records*

Part IV — Reconciliation of Schedule A Deductions to Form 8960, lines 9 and 10 (Individuals Only)

(A) Reenter the amounts and descriptions from Part III, lines 1 – 3.	(B) IF Part III, line 8 is less than Part III, line 4, **THEN** divide line 8 by line 4 **AND** enter the amount in column (B). **IF** the amounts reported on Part III, lines 4 and 8 are equal, **THEN** enter 1.00 in column (B).	(C) Multiply the individual amounts in column (A) by the amount in column (B). Enter these amounts in the appropriate location on lines 9 and 10.

Miscellaneous Itemized Deductions properly allocable to investment income:

	Description	Line	Amount			
1. (a)	_____	_____	_____	×	_____	= _____
(b)	_____	_____	_____	×	_____	= _____
2. State, local, and foreign income taxes		_____		×	_____	= _____

Itemized Deductions Subject to Section 68 included on Line 3 of Part III:

3. (a)	_____		×	_____	= _____
(b)	_____		×	_____	= _____

Line 10—Additional Modifications

Use line 10 to report additional deductions and modifications to net investment income that are not otherwise reflected in lines 1-9. Enter amounts on line 10 as positive numbers.

Note. Enter the amount on line 10 after the application of section 67 or 68. See *Lines 9 and 10 — Application of Itemized Deduction Limitations on Deductions Properly Allocable to Investment Income Worksheet*, earlier, for assistance in figuring the amount to report on line 10.

You may use line 10 to report properly allocable deductions such as:
• The penalty paid for an early withdrawal of savings under section 62(a)(9) (Form 1040, line 30),
• The amount treated as an ordinary loss by a holder of a contingent payment debt instrument under Regulations section 1.1275-4(b) or an inflation-indexed debt instrument under Regulations section 1.1275-7(f)(1),
• Net negative periodic payments paid on a notional principal contract (NPC) that is referenced to property (including an index) that produces (or would produce if the property were to produce income) interest, dividends, royalties, or rents.
• Excess deductions allocated to a beneficiary upon the termination of an estate or trust under section 642(h)(2) that

would otherwise have been allowable but for the fact that the terminating trust or estate had negative net investment income upon termination. This amount may be some or all of the amount reported on Schedule K-1 (Form 1041), line 11a. See Regulations section 1.1411-4(g)(4)(iii),
• Certain amounts reported on Schedule A (Form 1040), line 28:

1. The amount of the deduction allowed to an annuitant for the annuitant's last tax year under section 72(b)(3), provided the income from the annuity (had the annuitant lived to receive such income) would have been included in net investment income and not otherwise excluded as a distribution from a qualified plan,

2. Deduction for payment of amounts under a claim of right if over $3,000, to the extent that such repayments relate to items of income included in net investment income in a preceding year that began after 2012. See Pub. 525, Taxable and Nontaxable Income, for details,

3. The amount of the deduction for estate taxes allowed by section 691(c) that is allocable to net investment income, except to the extent that the section 691(c) deduction is taken into account in computing net gain on line 5(a) (or line 7 if applicable), and

4. The amount of the deduction allowable under section 171(a)(1) for the amortizable bond premium on a taxable bond. Do not include the amount of bond premium amortization that is used to offset interest income under section 171(e) on your Schedule B (Form 1040A or 1040), Interest and Ordinary Dividends. This amount of bond premium amortization is already taken into account in computing interest income on Form 8960, line 1.

• If you are a partner in an Electing Large Partnership and receive a Schedule K-1 (Form 1065-B), Partner's Share of Income (Loss) From an Electing Large Partnership, and box 2 contains a loss, report this loss on line 10,
• To the extent these items are properly allocable to net investment income. See *Reasonable method allocations*, earlier,

1. All ordinary and necessary expenses paid or incurred during the tax year to determine, collect, or obtain a refund of any tax owed, but only to the extent the expenses are allocable to net investment income (Schedule A (Form 1040), line 22), and

2. Amounts paid or incurred by the fiduciary of an estate or trust on account of administration expenses, including fiduciaries' fees and expenses of litigation, which are ordinary and necessary in connection with the performance of the duties of administration.

Line 10—Worksheet for Traders in Financial Instruments That Maintain More Than One Trade or Business

Use this worksheet to determine the amount on line 10.

1 Enter the total amount from Schedule SE (Form 1040), line 3. .... **1**	_____
2 a If the amount on Schedule SE (Form 1040), line 3, is zero or greater, you cannot use the expenses from your trade or business to reduce your investment income. Stop here.	
b If the amount on Schedule SE (Form 1040), line 3, is a negative amount, enter your expenses from your trade or business of trading in financial instruments or commodities (entered as a positive amount). .... **2 b**	_____
3 Add line 1 to line 2b. **3**	_____
a If the amount on line 3 of this worksheet is zero or less, include the trade or business expenses (line 2b of the worksheet) on Form 8960, line 10.	
b If the amount on line 3 of this worksheet is a positive number, convert the amount from Schedule SE (Form 1040), line 3 (line 1 of this worksheet) into a positive number and include it on Form 8960, line 10.	

Special rule for traders in financial instruments or commodities. If your only business is trading in financial instruments or commodities, you may use the net loss amount on your Schedule C (Form 1040) as a deduction on line 10, and you do not need to complete Schedule SE (Form 1040), Self-Employment Tax.

If you have more than one trade or business, you must complete Schedule SE (Form 1040) to determine whether you can include some or all of the trading business Schedule C (Form 1040) expenses as a deduction on line 10. Complete the *Line 10—Worksheet for Traders in Financial Instruments That Maintain More Than One Trade or Business*.

Note. See the Instructions for Schedule SE (Form 1040) for who must file a Schedule SE (Form 1040). Retain a copy of the Schedule SE (Form 1040) and the worksheet used to determine the expenses included as a modification on line 10 with your records. Do not file the worksheet with Form 1040.

The amounts reported on line 10 are the amounts allowable after the application of the deduction limitations imposed by sections 67 and 68, as applicable. See *Deductions subject to AGI limitations under section 67 or section 68*, later.

Deductions subject to AGI limitations under section 67 or section 68. Any deduction allowed against net investment income that, for purposes of computing your regular income tax, is subject to either the 2% floor on miscellaneous itemized deductions (section 67) or the overall limitation on itemized deductions (section 68) is allowed in determining net investment income, but only to the extent

the items are deductible after application of both limitations.

Miscellaneous itemized deductions. The amount of your miscellaneous itemized deductions, after application of the 2% floor but before application of the overall limitation, used in determining your net investment income is the lesser of:
- That portion of your miscellaneous itemized deductions before the application of the 2% floor that is properly allocable to net investment income, or
- Your total miscellaneous itemized deductions allowed after the application of the 2% floor but before the application of the overall limitation on itemized deductions.

Itemized deductions. The amount of your itemized deductions allowed in determining your net investment income after applying both the 2% floor and overall limitation is the lesser of:
- The sum of:

  1. The amount of your miscellaneous itemized deductions allowed as a deduction against your net investment income (before application of the overall limitation), and

  2. The total amount of your itemized deductions that are not subject to the 2% floor and are properly allocable to items of income or net gain for purposes of determining your net investment income, or

- The total amount of your itemized deductions allowed after the application of both the 2% floor and the overall limitation on itemized deductions.

For more information and examples, see Regulations section 1.1411-4(f)(7).

Part III—Tax Computation

Individuals

Individuals complete lines 13-17.

Line 13—Modified Adjusted Gross Income (MAGI)

If you did not exclude any amounts from your gross income under section 911 and you do not own a CFC or PFIC, your MAGI is your AGI as reported on Form 1040, line 38. If you exclude amounts under section 911 or own certain CFCs or PFICs, your MAGI is your AGI as modified by certain rules described in Regulations section 1.1411-10(e)(1).

Section 911. If you exclude amounts from income under section 911, to calculate your MAGI, you must increase your AGI by the excess of the amount excluded from income under section 911(a)(1) over the amount of any deductions (taken into account in computing AGI) or exclusions disallowed under section 911(d)(6) for the amount excluded from income under section 911(a)(1). Use *Line 13 — MAGI Worksheet*, later, to compute your MAGI.

CFCs and PFICs. If you own, directly or indirectly, stock in a CFC or PFIC other than certain CFCs and PFICs held in a section 1411 trade or business or PFICs marked to market under section 1296 or any other provision, to calculate your MAGI, you may need to make certain adjustments to your AGI, as provided in Regulations section 1.1411-10(e)(1). Generally, these adjustments include:
- 1291 funds.

  1. Increase AGI by the amount of any excess distributions derived from a PFIC that are dividends included in MAGI but not included in gross income for regular income tax purposes, and

Line 13 — MAGI Worksheet

Keep for Your Records

1. **Enter your Adjusted Gross Income** .... 1. _____

2. **Foreign Earned Income Exclusion:**

   (a) Enter your Foreign Earned Income Exclusion (from Line 42 of Form 2555) .... _____

   (b) Enter the deductions reported on Line 44 of Form 2555 allocable to your Foreign Earned Income Exclusion .... (_____)

   (c) Combine Lines 2(a) and 2(b) .... 2. _____

3. **Adjustments for Certain CFCs and Certain PFICs** .... 3. _____

4. **Enter the sum of Line 1, Line 2(c), and Line 3. (Enter this amount on Form 8960, Line 13.)** .... 4. _____

---

2. Increase AGI by the amount of any gain treated as an excess distribution under section 1291 included in MAGI but not included in gross income for regular income tax purposes.

- CFCs and QEFs without a section 1.1411-10(g) election in effect.

1. Decrease AGI by the amount of any section 951(a) or 1293(a) inclusions,

2. Increase AGI by the amount of any distributions described in section 959(d) or 1293(c) included in your net investment income as a dividend,

3. Increase or decrease AGI (as appropriate) by the amount of any adjustment to gain or loss on the disposition of the CFC or QEF that results in an adjustment to your MAGI,

4. Increase or decrease AGI (as appropriate) by the amount of any adjustment to gain or loss on the disposition of an interest in a domestic partnership or S corporation that holds a CFC or QEF that results in an adjustment to your MAGI,

5. Increase or decrease AGI (as appropriate) by the amount of any adjustment to investment interest expense under Regulations section 1.1411-10(c)(5) that is taken into account in computing MAGI, and

6. Increase or decrease AGI (as appropriate) by the amount reported to you on Schedule K-1 (Form 1041) in box 14 with a code "H" that requires a MAGI adjustment.

- CFCs and QEFs held in a section 1411 trade or business or with a section 1.1411-10(g) election in effect.

Increase AGI by the amount of any distributions described in section 959(d) or 1293(c) included in your net investment income as a dividend (not applicable to tax years beginning before 2014).

TIP *If you do not own (directly or indirectly) any interests in CFCs or PFICs, and do not exclude any foreign earned income on Form 2555, Foreign Earned Income, enter your AGI from Form 1040, line 38 on line 13.*

Line 14—Threshold Based on Filing Status

The threshold amount is based on your filing status.

Filing Status	Threshold Amount
Married Filing Jointly	$250,000
Qualifying Widower with Dependent Child	$250,000
Married Filing Separately	$125,000
Single or Head of Household	$200,000

A bankruptcy estate of an individual enters $125,000 and uses Form 8960, lines 13-17, to compute the tax.

Line 17—Net Investment Income Tax for Individuals

- Form 1040 filers: Include this amount on Form 1040, line 62, and see the instructions there.
- Form 1040NR filers: Include this amount on the line of your US residency statement corresponding to Form 1040, line 62, and on Form 1040NR, line 60, and see the instructions there.

See *Dual-status individual*.

Estates and Trusts

Estates and trusts complete lines 18-21.

Line 18b—Deductions for Distributions of Net Investment Income and Deductions Under Section 642(c)

The undistributed net investment income of an estate or trust (reported on line 18c) equals its net investment income (reported on line 18a) reduced by the net investment income included in the distributions to beneficiaries deductible by the estate or trust under section 651 or 661, and by the net investment income for which the estate or trust was entitled to a section 642(c) deduction, in each case, as calculated under Regulations section 1.642(c)-2 and the allocation and ordering rules under Regulations section 1.662(b)-2. Regulations section 1.1411-3(e) applies the class system of income categorization, generally embodied in sections 651 through 663 and related regulations, to arrive at the trust's net investment income reduction in the case of distributions that are comprised of both net investment income and net excluded income items. See Regulations section 1.1411-3(e) for more information and examples on the calculation of undistributed net investment income.

Charitable deduction. Report the amount of net investment income distributed to beneficiaries of the estate or trust and the amount of net investment income allocated to distributions to charity pursuant to section 642(c). The amount of the deduction for net investment income distributed to charities under section 642(c) is the amount of the net investment income allocated to the charity in accordance with Regulations section 1.642(c)-2(b) and the allocation and ordering rules under Regulations section 1.662(b)-2.

TIP *Form 1041, Schedule A can be used as a worksheet to calculate the amounts of net investment* income allocable to charitable distributions by including on line 2 both tax-exempt income and the difference between adjusted total income and the trust's net investment income (Form 8960, line 18a).

 TIP *The amount of the deduction for net investment income distributed to beneficiaries should equal the sum of net investment income reported to the beneficiaries on their respective Schedules K-1 (Form 1041).*

Note. In general, the deduction for distributions of net investment income may not exceed the taxable income distributed to the beneficiary for regular income tax purposes. However, in the case of an estate or trust that owns an interest in certain CFCs or PFICs, the distribution of net investment income can exceed the distribution of taxable income when the amount of distributions exceed distributable net income for regular income tax purposes.

 TIP *Form 1041, Schedule B can be used as a worksheet to calculate the income distribution deduction for NIIT purposes by replacing line 1 with the trust's net investment income (Form 8960, line 18a) and including on line 2 both adjusted tax-exempt interest and the difference between line 1 and the trust's net investment income (Form 8960, line 18a).*

Line 18c—Undistributed Net Investment Income

Do not enter a negative number. If negative, enter zero.

Line 19a—Adjusted Gross Income (AGI)

If the estate or trust does not own a CFC or PFIC, enter it's AGI for regular income tax purposes. See the instructions for Form 1041, line 15c and Form 1041-QFT, line 10.

If the estate or trust owns a CFC or PFIC, it may need to make adjustments. See *Line 13—Modified Adjusted Gross Income (MAGI)*, earlier.

Line 19b—Highest Tax Bracket for Estates and Trusts

See the instructions for Form 1041, Schedule G, line 1a and the instructions for Form 1041-QFT, line 13 for the dollar amount at which the highest tax bracket begins for the tax year and enter that amount here.

In the case of a QFT, see *Special computational rules for qualified funeral trusts (QFTs)*, earlier, to determine the amount to report on Form 8960, line 19b.

Line 21—Net Investment Income Tax for Estates and Trusts

- Form 1041 filers: Include this amount on Form 1041, Schedule G, line 4 and see the instructions there.
- Form 1041-QFT filers: Include this amount on Form 1041-QFT, line 16, and see the instructions there.

Paperwork Reduction Act Notice. We ask for the information on this form to carry out the Internal Revenue laws of the United States. We need it to ensure that you are complying with these laws and to allow us to figure and collect the right amount of tax.

You are not required to provide the information requested on a form that is subject to the Paperwork Reduction Act unless the form displays a valid OMB control number. Books or records relating to a form or its instructions must be retained as long as their contents may become material in the administration of any internal revenue law. Generally, tax returns and return information are confidential, as required by section 6103.

The time needed to complete and file this form will vary depending on individual circumstances. The estimated average time is:

Recordkeeping	1 hr., 1 min.
Learning about the law or the form	6 hr., 4 min.
Preparing the form	1 hr., 47 min.
Copying, assembling, and sending the form to the IRS	20 min.

If you have comments concerning the accuracy of these time estimates or suggestions for making this form simpler, we would be happy to hear from you. You can write to us at *http://www.irs.gov/formspubs*, by clicking on "More Information," and then clicking on "Give us feedback." You can also send your comments to the Internal Revenue Service, Tax Products Coordinating Committee, SE:W:CAR:MP:T:T:SP, 1111 Constitution Ave. NW, IR-6526, Washington, DC 20224. **Do not send the form to this office.** Instead, include this form with your return, filing it according to the instructions for your return.

Form **8962**	**Premium Tax Credit (PTC)**	OMB No. 1545-0074
Department of the Treasury Internal Revenue Service	▶ Attach to Form 1040, 1040A, or 1040NR. ▶ Information about Form 8962 and its separate instructions is at *www.irs.gov/form8962*.	**20**14 Attachment Sequence No. **73**

Name shown on your return

Your social security number

Relief (see instructions) ☐

Part 1: Annual and Monthly Contribution Amount

1 Family Size: Enter the number of exemptions from Form 1040 or Form 1040A, line 6d, or Form 1040NR, line 7d . **1**

2a Modified AGI: Enter your modified AGI (see instructions) . . . . **2a** **b** Enter total of your dependents' modified AGI (see instructions) **2b**

3 Household Income: Add the amounts on lines 2a and 2b **3**

4 Federal Poverty Line: Enter the federal poverty amount as determined by the family size on line 1 and the federal poverty table for your state of residence during the tax year (see instructions). Check the appropriate box for the federal poverty table used. **a** ☐ Alaska **b** ☐ Hawaii **c** ☐ Other 48 states and DC **4**

5 Household Income as a Percentage of Federal Poverty Line: Divide line 3 by line 4. Enter the result rounded to a whole percentage. (For example, for 1.542 enter the result as 154, for 1.549 enter as 155.) (See instructions for special rules.) **5** %

6 Is the result entered on line 5 less than or equal to 400%? (See instructions if the result is less than 100%.)

  ☐ **Yes. Continue to line 7.**

  ☐ **No.** You are not eligible to receive PTC. If you received advance payment of PTC, see the instructions for how to report your Excess Advance PTC Repayment amount.

7 Applicable Figure: Using your line 5 percentage, locate your "applicable figure" on the table in the instructions . . **7**

8a Annual Contribution for Health Care: Multiply line 3 by line 7 . . . . **8a** **b** Monthly Contribution for Health Care: Divide line 8a by 12. Round to whole dollar amount **8b**

Part 2: Premium Tax Credit Claim and Reconciliation of Advance Payment of Premium Tax Credit

9 Did you share a policy with another taxpayer or get married during the year and want to use the alternative calculation? (see instructions)

  ☐ **Yes.** Skip to Part 4, Shared Policy Allocation, or Part 5, Alternative Calculation for Year of Marriage.   ☐ **No. Continue to line 10.**

10 Do all Forms 1095-A for your tax household include coverage for January through December with no changes in monthly amounts shown on lines 21–32, columns A and B?

  ☐ **Yes. Continue to line 11.** Compute your annual PTC. Skip lines 12–23 and continue to line 24.   ☐ **No. Continue to lines 12–23.** Compute your monthly PTC and continue to line 24.

Annual Calculation	**A.** Premium Amount (Form(s) 1095-A, line 33A)	**B.** Annual Premium Amount of SLCSP (Form(s) 1095-A, line 33B)	**C.** Annual Contribution Amount (Line 8a)	**D.** Annual Maximum Premium Assistance (Subtract C from B)	**E.** Annual Premium Tax Credit Allowed (Smaller of A or D)	**F.** Annual Advance Payment of PTC (Form(s) 1095-A, line 33C)
11 Annual Totals						

Monthly Calculation	**A.** Monthly Premium Amount (Form(s) 1095-A, lines 21–32, column A)	**B.** Monthly Premium Amount of SLCSP (Form(s) 1095-A, lines 21–32, column B)	**C.** Monthly Contribution Amount (Amount from line 8b or alternative marriage monthly contribution)	**D.** Monthly Maximum Premium Assistance (Subtract C from B)	**E.** Monthly Premium Tax Credit Allowed (Smaller of A or D)	**F.** Monthly Advance Payment of PTC (Form(s) 1095-A, lines 21–32, column C)
12 January						
13 February						
14 March						
15 April						
16 May						
17 June						
18 July						
19 August						
20 September						
21 October						
22 November						
23 December						

24 Total Premium Tax Credit: Enter the amount from line 11E or add lines 12E through 23E and enter the total here . **24**

25 Advance Payment of PTC: Enter the amount from line 11F or add lines 12F through 23F and enter the total here . **25**

26 Net Premium Tax Credit: If line 24 is greater than line 25, subtract line 25 from line 24. Enter the difference here and on Form 1040, line 69; Form 1040A, line 45; or Form 1040NR, line 65. If you elected the alternative calculation for marriage, enter zero. If line 24 equals line 25, enter zero. Stop here. If line 25 is greater than line 24, leave this line blank and continue to line 27 **26**

Part 3: Repayment of Excess Advance Payment of the Premium Tax Credit

27 Excess Advance Payment of PTC: If line 25 is greater than line 24, subtract line 24 from line 25. Enter the difference here **27**

28 Repayment Limitation: Using the percentage on line 5 and your filing status, locate the repayment limitation amount in the instructions. Enter the amount here **28**

29 Excess Advance Premium Tax Credit Repayment: Enter the smaller of line 27 or line 28 here and on Form 1040, line 46; Form 1040A, line 29; or Form 1040NR, line 44 . . . . **29**

For Paperwork Reduction Act Notice, see your tax return instructions.   Cat. No. 37784Z   Form **8962** (2014)

Part 4: Shared Policy Allocation
Complete the following information for up to four shared policy allocations. See instructions for allocation details.

Shared Policy Allocation 1

30	**a** Policy Number (Form 1095-A, line 2)	**b** SSN of taxpayer sharing allocation	**c** Allocation start month	**d** Allocation stop month
	Allocation percentage applied to monthly amounts	**e.** Premium Percentage	**f.** SLCSP Percentage	**g.** Advance Payment of the PTC Percentage

Shared Policy Allocation 2

31	**a** Policy Number (Form 1095-A, line 2)	**b** SSN of taxpayer sharing allocation	**c** Allocation start month	**d** Allocation stop month
	Allocation percentage applied to monthly amounts	**e.** Premium Percentage	**f.** SLCSP Percentage	**g.** Advance Payment of the PTC Percentage

Shared Policy Allocation 3

32	**a** Policy Number (Form 1095-A, line 2)	**b** SSN of taxpayer sharing allocation	**c** Allocation start month	**d** Allocation stop month
	Allocation percentage applied to monthly amounts	**e.** Premium Percentage	**f.** SLCSP Percentage	**g.** Advance Payment of the PTC Percentage

Shared Policy Allocation 4

33	**a** Policy Number (Form 1095-A, line 2)	**b** SSN of taxpayer sharing allocation	**c** Allocation start month	**d** Allocation stop month
	Allocation percentage applied to monthly amounts	**e.** Premium Percentage	**f.** SLCSP Percentage	**g.** Advance Payment of the PTC Percentage

34 Have you completed shared policy allocation information for all allocated Forms 1095-A?

☐ **Yes.** Multiply the amounts on Form 1095-A by the allocation percentages entered by policy. Add allocated amounts across all allocated policies with amounts for non-allocated policies from Forms 1095-A, if any, to compute a combined total for each month. Enter the combined total for each month on lines 12–23, columns A, B, and F. Compute the amounts for lines 12–23, columns C–E, and continue to line 24.

☐ **No.** See the instructions to report additional shared policy allocations.

Part 5: Alternative Calculation for Year of Marriage
Complete line(s) 35 and/or 36 to elect the alternative calculation for year of marriage. For eligibility to make the election, see the instructions for line 9. To complete line(s) 35 and/or 36 and compute the amounts for lines 12–23, see the instructions for this Part 5.

35	**Alternative entries for your SSN**	**a** Alternative family size	**b** Monthly contribution	**c** Alternative start month	**d** Alternative stop month
36	**Alternative entries for your spouse's SSN**	**a** Alternative family size	**b** Monthly contribution	**c** Alternative start month	**d** Alternative stop month

*Complete Form 8962 **only** for health insurance coverage in a <u>qualified health plan</u> (described later) purchased through a Health Insurance Marketplace (also known as an Exchange). This includes a qualified health plan purchased on <u>healthcare.gov</u> or through a State Marketplace.*

Future Developments

For the latest information about developments related to Form 8962 and its instructions, such as legislation enacted after they were published, go to *www.irs.gov/form8962*.

Reminder for 2015

Report changes in circumstances when you re-enroll in coverage and during the year. If <u>advance payments of the premium tax credit (APTC)</u> were made in 2014 or are made in 2015 for an individual in your <u>tax family</u> (described later) and you have had certain changes in circumstances (see the examples below), it is important that you report them to the Marketplace where you enroll. Reporting changes in circumstances promptly will allow the Marketplace to adjust your APTC to more accurately reflect the <u>premium tax credit (PTC)</u> you are estimated to be able to take on your tax return. Adjusting your APTC when you re-enroll in coverage and during the year can help you avoid owing tax when you file your tax return. Changes that you should report to the Marketplace include the following.

- Changes in <u>household income</u>.
- Moving to a different address.
- Gaining or losing eligibility for other health care coverage.
- Gaining, losing, or other changes to employment.
- Birth or adoption.
- Marriage or divorce.
- Other changes affecting the composition of your <u>tax family</u>.

General Instructions

Purpose of Form

Use Form 8962 to figure the amount of your <u>PTC</u> and reconcile it with any <u>APTC</u> paid.

What is the Premium Tax Credit (PTC)?

Premium tax credit (PTC). The PTC is a tax credit for certain people who enroll, or whose family member enrolls, in a <u>qualified health plan</u> offered through a Marketplace. The credit provides financial assistance to pay the premiums by reducing the amount of tax you owe, giving you a refund, or increasing your refund amount. You must file Form 8962 to compute and take the PTC on your tax return.

Advance payment of the premium tax credit (APTC). APTC is a payment made for coverage during the year to your insurance provider that pays for part or all of the premiums for the coverage of you or an individual in your <u>tax family</u>. Your APTC eligibility is based on the Marketplace's estimate of the PTC you will be able to take on your tax return. If APTC was paid for you or an individual in your tax family, you must file Form 8962 to reconcile (compare) this APTC with your PTC. If the APTC is more than your PTC, you have excess APTC and you must repay the excess, subject to certain limitations. If your PTC is more than the APTC, you can reduce your tax payment or increase your refund by the difference.

Note. The Marketplace determined your eligibility for 2014 APTC using projections of your income and your number of personal exemptions when you enrolled in a <u>qualified health plan</u>. If this information changed during 2014 and you did not promptly report it to the Marketplace, the amount of APTC paid may be substantially different from the amount of PTC you can take on your tax return. See *Report changes in circumstances when you re-enroll in coverage and during the year*, earlier, for changes that can affect the amount of your PTC.

Additional Information

You will need Form 1095-A, Health Insurance Marketplace Statement, to complete Form 8962. The Marketplace is required to provide or send Form 1095-A to the tax filer(s) identified in the enrollment application by January 31, 2015. If you are the tax filer expecting to receive Form 1095-A for a <u>qualified health plan</u> and you do not receive it by early February, contact the Marketplace.

Under certain circumstances, for example in the case of a divorce during the year, the Marketplace will provide Form 1095-A to one taxpayer, but another taxpayer will also need the information from that form to complete Form 8962. The recipient of Form 1095-A should provide a copy to other taxpayers as needed.

For additional information on the PTC, see Publication 974, Premium Tax Credit (PTC). You can also visit *www.irs.gov* and enter "premium tax credit" in the search box.

Self-employed health insurance deduction. If you are claiming the self-employed health insurance deduction for health insurance premiums, see Pub. 974.

Who Must File

You must file Form 8962 with your income tax return (Form 1040, Form 1040A, or Form 1040NR) if any of the following apply to you.

- You are taking the PTC.
- APTC was paid for you or another individual in your <u>tax family</u>.
- APTC was paid for an individual (including you) for whom you told the Marketplace you would claim a personal exemption and neither you nor anyone else claims a personal exemption for that individual. See *Individual you enrolled for whom no taxpayer will claim a personal exemption* under *Lines 12 through 23—Monthly Calculation*, later.

If any of the circumstances above apply to you, you must file an income tax return and attach Form 8962 even if you are not otherwise required to file. You must file Form 1040, Form 1040A, or Form 1040NR.

If you are claimed as a dependent, the person who claims you will file Form 8962 to take the PTC and, if necessary, repay excess APTC for your coverage. You do not need to file Form 8962.

If you are filing Form 8962, you cannot file Form 1040EZ, Form 1040NR-EZ, Form 1040-SS, or Form 1040-PR.

If someone else enrolled an individual in your tax family in coverage, and APTC was paid for that individual's coverage, you must file Form 8962 to reconcile the APTC. You need to obtain a copy of the Form 1095-A from the person who enrolled the individual.

Who Can Take the PTC

You can take the PTC for 2014 if you meet all of the conditions under (1) and (2) below.

1. For at least one month of the year, all of the following were true.

a. An individual in your tax family was enrolled in a qualified health plan offered through the Marketplace.

b. The individual was not eligible for minimum essential coverage, other than coverage in the individual market (see *Minimum essential coverage*, later).

c. The portion of the enrollment premiums for the month for which you are responsible was paid by the due date of your tax return (not including extensions).

2. You are an applicable taxpayer. To be an applicable taxpayer, you must meet all of the following requirements.

a. For 2014, your household income is at least 100% but no more than 400% of the Federal poverty line for your family size (see *Household income below 100% of the Federal poverty line*, later, for certain exceptions).

b. No one can claim you as a dependent on a tax return for 2014.

c. If you were married at the end of 2014, you must generally file a joint return. However, filing a separate return from your spouse will not disqualify you from being an applicable taxpayer if you meet certain requirements described under *Married taxpayers*, later.

You are not entitled to the PTC for your own health coverage for any period during which you are not lawfully present in the United States.

For additional requirements and more details, see *Applicable taxpayer*, later.

Terms You May Need to Know

Tax family. For purposes of the PTC, your tax family consists of the individuals for whom you claim a personal exemption on your tax return (generally you, your spouse with whom you are filing a joint return, and your dependents). Your personal exemptions are reported on your Form 1040 or Form 1040A, line 6d, or Form 1040NR, line 7d. Your family size equals the number of individuals in your tax family. If no one, including you, claims a personal exemption for you, and you indicated to the Marketplace when you enrolled that you would claim your own personal exemption, see Pub. 974 for instructions on completing Form 8962.

Household income. For purposes of the PTC, household income is the modified adjusted gross income (modified AGI) of you and your spouse (if filing a joint return) (see *Line 2a*, later) plus the modified AGI of each individual in your tax family whom you claim as a dependent and who is required to file a tax return because his or her income meets the income tax return filing threshold (see *Line 2b*, later). Household income does not include the modified AGI of those individuals whom you claim as dependents and who are filing a 2014 return only to claim a refund of withheld income tax or estimated tax. If your household income is less than zero, enter -0- on line 3.

Modified AGI. For purposes of the PTC, modified AGI is the AGI on your tax return plus certain income that is not subject to tax (foreign earned income, tax-exempt interest, and the portion of social security benefits that is not taxable). Use Worksheet 1-1 and Worksheet 1-2, later, to determine your modified AGI.

Taxpayer's tax return including income of a dependent child. A taxpayer who includes the gross income of a dependent child on the taxpayer's tax return must include in modified AGI the child's tax-exempt interest and the portion of social security benefits that is not taxable.

Monthly credit amount. The monthly credit amount is the amount of assistance in paying premiums for a month. Your PTC for the year is the sum of all of your monthly credit amounts. Your credit amount for each month is the lesser of:

- The enrollment premiums (described next) for the month for one or more qualified health plans in which you or any individual in your tax family enrolled; or
- The amount of the monthly premium for your applicable second lowest cost silver plan (SLCSP) (described below) less your monthly contribution amount (described below).

Enrollment premiums. The enrollment premiums are the total amount of the premiums for the month for one or more qualified health plans in which any individual in your tax family enrolled. Form 1095-A, Part III, column A, reports the enrollment premiums.

You are not allowed a monthly credit amount for the month if any part of the enrollment premiums for which you are responsible that month has not been paid by the due date of your tax return (not including extensions). Premiums another person pays on your behalf are treated as paid by you.

Premium for the applicable SLCSP. The premium for the applicable SLCSP is the second lowest cost silver plan premium offered through the Marketplace where you reside that applies to your coverage family (described below). The premium for the applicable SLCSP is not the same as your enrollment premium, unless you enroll in the applicable SLCSP. Form 1095-A, Part III, column B, generally reports the premium for the applicable SLCSP.

Monthly contribution amount. Your monthly contribution amount is the amount you would be required to pay as your share of premiums each month if you enrolled in the applicable SLCSP. Your monthly contribution amount is not based on the amount of premiums you paid out of pocket. You will compute your monthly contribution amount in Part 1 of Form 8962.

Termination for nonpayment of premiums. If you did not pay your premiums for three months and your policy was terminated, you are not allowed monthly credit amounts for those months. However, you continued to have coverage for at least the first month of nonpayment. If APTC was paid to your issuer you must repay it. See *Lines 12 through 23—Monthly Calculation*, later.

Coverage family. Your coverage family includes all individuals in your tax family who are enrolled in a qualified health plan and are not eligible for minimum essential coverage (other than coverage in the individual market). The individuals included in your coverage family may change from month to month. If individuals in your tax family are not enrolled in a qualified health plan, or are enrolled in a qualified health plan but are eligible for minimum essential coverage (other than coverage in the individual market), they are not part of your coverage family.

Your applicable SLCSP is the SLCSP that applies to your coverage family. As a result, your PTC is only available to help you pay for the coverage of the individuals included in your coverage family.

Child born or adopted or placed with you for adoption or foster care during the month. If you enroll a newborn child (or a child newly adopted or placed with you for adoption or foster care) in a qualified health plan, and the child's coverage is effective as of the date of birth, adoption, or placement, the child is treated as enrolled as of the first day of the month the child was born, adopted, or placed with you for adoption or foster care. The child is included in your coverage family for the month of birth, adoption, or placement for adoption or in foster care.

Qualified health plan. For purposes of the PTC, a qualified health plan is a health insurance plan or policy purchased through a Marketplace at the bronze, silver, gold, or platinum level. Plans sold as "catastrophic" coverage and plans purchased through the Small Business Health Options Program (SHOP) do not qualify a taxpayer to take the PTC. Throughout these instructions, a qualified health plan is also referred to as a policy.

Minimum essential coverage. Under the health care law, certain health coverage is called minimum essential coverage. Even if you have coverage purchased through a Marketplace, you cannot take the PTC for any individual in your tax family for any month when that individual is eligible for minimum essential coverage, other than coverage in the individual market. Types of minimum essential coverage include:
- Government-sponsored programs (including most Medicaid coverage, Medicare parts A or C, the Children's Health Insurance Program (CHIP), and Tricare).
- Employer-sponsored coverage, if the premiums are affordable and the deductibles and co-pays are no more than a certain amount, or if you enroll.
- Other health coverage the Department of Health and Human Services designates as minimum essential coverage.

Coverage purchased in the individual market outside the Marketplace is minimum essential coverage. Eligibility for this type of coverage does not prevent you from being eligible for the PTC for Marketplace coverage, but it does not qualify for the PTC.

For more details on eligibility for minimum essential coverage, including special eligibility rules, see *Minimum Essential Coverage* in Pub. 974. You can also check *www.irs.gov/uac/Individual-Shared-Responsibility-Provision* for future updates about types of coverage that are recognized as minimum essential coverage.

Example. You, your spouse, and your two children whom you claim as dependents were enrolled in a qualified health plan in 2014. Your children were eligible for coverage under CHIP. Your tax family size is four, consisting of you, your spouse, and your children. Your coverage family has only two members, you and your spouse. Your children are not part of the coverage family because they were eligible for CHIP, which is minimum essential coverage. As a result, although your children were enrolled in a qualified health plan, the PTC provides financial assistance only for the coverage of you and your spouse.

Applicable taxpayer. You must be an applicable taxpayer to take the PTC.

Generally, you are an applicable taxpayer if your household income for 2014 (described earlier) is at least 100% but not more than 400% of the Federal poverty line for your family size (provided in Tables 1-1, 1-2, and 1-3, later) and no one can claim you as a dependent for 2014. In addition, if you were married at the end of 2014, you must file a joint return to be an applicable taxpayer unless you meet one of the situations described in *Married taxpayers*, later.

For individuals with household income below 100% of the Federal poverty line, see *Household income below 100% of the Federal poverty line* under *Line 6*, later.

Individuals who are incarcerated. Individuals who are incarcerated (other than pending disposition of charges, for example awaiting trial) are not eligible to enroll in a qualified health plan through a Marketplace. However, these individuals may be applicable taxpayers and take the PTC for the coverage of individuals in their tax families who are eligible to enroll in a qualified health plan.

Individuals who are not lawfully present. Individuals who are not lawfully present in the United States are not eligible to enroll in a qualified health plan through a Marketplace. They also are not eligible for a PTC for their own coverage, and are not eligible for the repayment limitations in Table 5 for APTC paid for their own coverage. However, these individuals may be applicable taxpayers and take the PTC for the coverage of individuals in their tax families, such as their children, who are eligible to enroll in a qualified health plan. For more information about who is treated as lawfully present for this purpose, visit *healthcare.gov*. Also see Pub. 974 for more information.

Married taxpayers. If you are married, you generally must file a joint return with your spouse to take the PTC unless one of the two situations below applies to you. However, you are unmarried for all federal income tax purposes if you are divorced or legally separated according to your state law under a decree of divorce or separate maintenance. You are treated as unmarried and can file a separate return and take the PTC if *Situation 1* applies to you. If your filing status is married filing separately, you can take the PTC if *Situation 2* applies to you.

Situation 1. You are treated as unmarried for federal income tax purposes for 2014 if one of the following applies to you.
- You file a separate return from your spouse on Form 1040 or Form 1040A because you meet the requirements for *Married persons who live apart* under *Head of Household* in the instructions for Form 1040 or Form 1040A.
- You file as single on your Form 1040NR because you meet the requirements for *Married persons who live apart* under *Were You Single or Married?* in the instructions for Form 1040NR.

Situation 2. If you are a victim of domestic abuse or spousal abandonment, you can file a return as married filing separately and take the PTC if you meet all of the following.
- You are living apart from your spouse at the time you file your 2014 tax return.
- You are unable to file a joint return because you are a victim of domestic abuse (described next) or spousal abandonment (described below).
- You certify on your Form 8962 that you are a victim of domestic abuse or spousal abandonment.

Domestic abuse. Domestic abuse includes physical, psychological, sexual, or emotional abuse, including efforts to control, isolate, humiliate, and intimidate, or to undermine the victim's ability to reason independently. All the facts and circumstances are considered in determining whether an individual is abused, including the effects of alcohol or drug abuse by the victim's spouse. Depending on the facts and circumstances, abuse of the victim's child or other family member living in the household may constitute abuse of the victim.

Spousal abandonment. A taxpayer is a victim of spousal abandonment for a tax year if, taking into account all facts and circumstances, the taxpayer is unable to locate his or her spouse after reasonable diligence.

To certify that you are eligible for an exception to the requirement to file a joint return under Situation 2, check the **"Relief"** box in the top right-hand corner of Form 8962. Do not attach documentation of the abuse or abandonment to your tax return. Keep any documentation you may have with your tax return records. For examples of what documentation to keep, see Pub. 974.

Married filing separately. If you file as married filing separately and are not a victim of domestic abuse or spousal abandonment (see *Situation 2* under *Married taxpayers* above), then you are not an applicable taxpayer and you cannot take the PTC. You must generally repay all APTC paid for a qualified health plan that covered only individuals in your tax family, and one-half of the APTC paid for a policy that covered at least one individual in your tax family and at least one individual in your spouse's tax family. However, the amount of APTC you have to repay may be limited. See the instructions for line 28, later.

Specific Instructions

Name. Print or type your name exactly as you entered it on your tax return. If you are married and filing a joint return, enter the first name that appears on your return.

Social security number. The social security number on this form should match the social security number on your tax return. If you are married and filing a joint return, enter the first social security number that appears on your tax return.

Relief. Check this box if you are filing as married filing separately and you are a victim of domestic abuse or spousal abandonment (see *Situation 2* under *Married taxpayers*, earlier). By checking this box, you are certifying that you qualify for relief from filing a joint return with your spouse.

Married filing separately. If you do not qualify for relief from filing a joint return, you cannot take the PTC on a married filing separately return. You are not an applicable taxpayer and must repay some or all APTC. Complete lines 1 through 5 to figure your separate household income as a percentage of the Federal poverty line. Skip lines 6 through 8b and complete lines 9 and 10 (and Part 4, if applicable). When completing line 11 or lines 12 through 23, complete only column F. Then complete the rest of the form to determine how much you must repay.

Part 1—Annual and Monthly Contribution Amount

Line 1

Enter on line 1 the number of exemptions from your Form 1040 or Form 1040A, line 6d, or Form 1040NR, line 7d.

Line 2a

Enter your modified AGI on line 2a. Use the worksheet next to figure your modified AGI from your tax return.

Worksheet 1-1. **Taxpayer's Modified AGI—Line 2a**

1. Enter your adjusted gross income (AGI)* from Form 1040, line 38; Form 1040A, line 22; or Form 1040NR, line 37 . . . . 1._____
2. Enter any tax-exempt interest from Form 1040, line 8b; Form 1040A, line 8b; or Form 1040NR, line 9b . . . . 2._____
3. Enter any amounts from Form 2555, lines 45 and 50, and Form 2555-EZ, line 18 . . . . 3._____
4. Enter the excess, if any, of Form 1040, lines 20a over 20b; or Form 1040A, lines 14a over 14b . . . . 4._____
5. Add lines 2 through 4 . . . . 5._____
6. Add lines 1 and 5. Enter here and on Form 8962, line 2a . . . . 6._____

If you are filing Form 8814 and the amount on Form 8814, line 4, is more than $1,000, you must also include on line 1 of this worksheet the tax-exempt interest from Form 8814, line 1b; the lesser of Form 8814, line 4 or line 5; and any nontaxable social security benefits your child received.

Note. If the amount on line 6 of Worksheet 1-1 above is less than zero, see *Line 3*, later, before you enter an amount on Form 8962, line 3.

Line 2b

Enter the modified AGI for all of your dependents on line 2b. Use the worksheet next to figure the combined modified AGI for the dependents claimed as exemptions on your return. Only include the modified AGI of those dependents who are required to file a return. Do not include the modified AGI of dependents who are filing a tax return only to claim a refund of tax withheld or estimated tax.

Worksheet 1-2. **Dependents' Combined Modified AGI—Line 2b**

1. Enter the AGI for your dependents from Form 1040, line 38; Form 1040A, line 22; Form 1040EZ, line 3; and Form 1040NR, line 37 . . . . 1._____
2. Enter any tax-exempt interest for your dependents from Form 1040, line 8b; Form 1040A, line 8b; Form 1040EZ, the amount written to the left of the line 2 entry space; and Form 1040NR, line 9b . . . . 2._____
3. Enter any amounts for your dependents from Form 2555, lines 45 and 50, and Form 2555-EZ, line 18 . . . . 3._____
4. Enter for each of your dependents the excess, if any, of Form 1040, lines 20a over 20b; and Form 1040A, lines 14a over 14b . . . . 4._____
5. Add lines 2 through 4 . . . . 5._____
6. Add lines 1 and 5. Enter here and on Form 8962, line 2b . . . . 6._____

Note. If the amount on line 6 of Worksheet 1-2 above is less than zero, see *Line 3* next before you enter an amount on Form 8962, line 3.

Line 3

Combine lines 2a and 2b even if one or both of them are negative. If the total of lines 2a and 2b is less than zero, enter -0- on line 3.

Line 4

Enter on line 4 the amount from the table that represents the Federal poverty line for the family size you entered on line 1 of Form 8962. Use the table for your state of residence in 2014. If you moved at all during 2014 and you lived in Alaska and/or Hawaii, or you are filing jointly and you and your spouse lived in different states, use the table with the higher dollar amounts for your family size.

Table 1-1. **Federal Poverty Line for the 48 Contiguous States and the District of Columbia**

IF your Family Size* from Form 8962, line 1, was . . .	THEN enter the amount below on Form 8962, line 4 . . .
1	$11,490
2	$15,510
3	$19,530
4	$23,550
5	$27,570
6	$31,590
7	$35,610
8	$39,630

If your family size was more than 8 people, add $4,020 for each additional person. For example, if your family size is 11, you have 3 additional people. Multiply $4,020 by 3 and add the result of $12,060 to $39,630. Enter the result of $51,690 on Form 8962, line 4.

Table 1-2. Federal Poverty Line for Alaska

IF your Family Size* from Form 8962, line 1, was . . .	THEN enter the amount below on Form 8962, line 4 . . .
1	$14,350
2	$19,380
3	$24,410
4	$29,440
5	$34,470
6	$39,500
7	$44,530
8	$49,560

*If your family size was more than 8 people, add $5,030 for each additional person. For example, if your family size is 11, you have 3 additional people. Multiply $5,030 by 3 and add the result of $15,090 to $49,560. Enter the result of $64,650 on Form 8962, line 4.

Table 1-3. Federal Poverty Line for Hawaii

IF your Family Size* from Form 8962, line 1, was . . .	THEN enter the amount below on Form 8962, line 4 . . .
1	$13,230
2	$17,850
3	$22,470
4	$27,090
5	$31,710
6	$36,330
7	$40,950
8	$45,570

*If your family size was more than 8, add $4,620 for each additional person. For example, if your family size is 11, you have 3 additional people. Multiply $4,620 by 3 and add the result of $13,860 to $45,570. Enter the result of $59,430 on Form 8962, line 4.

Line 5

Divide the amount on line 3 by the amount on line 4 to figure your household income as a percentage of the Federal poverty line. Is the result between 1.00 and 3.99?

☐ **Yes.** Round up or down to the nearest whole percentage. For example, for 1.854, enter the result as 185; for 3.565, enter the result as 357.

☐ **No.** See *Special rounding rules* next.

Special rounding rules. If the result is less than 1.00 or more than 3.99, round the result as follows.
* For any amount less than 1.00, round **down** to the nearest whole percentage. For example, for .996, enter the result as 99.
* For any amount between 3.99 and 4.00, round **down** to 399. For example, for 3.998, enter the result as 399.
* For any amount more than 4.00 but no more than 9.99, round **up** to the nearest whole percentage. For example, for 4.004, enter the result as 401.
* For an amount more than 9.99, enter the result as 999. For example, for 10.456, enter the result as 999.

Line 6

If the amount on line 5 is at least 100 but no more than 400, check the **"Yes"** box on line 6 and continue to line 7. If the amount on line 5 is less than 100, see *Household income below 100% of the Federal poverty line* next to determine if you qualify

for the PTC. If the amount on line 5 is more than 400, you are not eligible for the PTC. Check the **"No"** box and see *Household income above 400% of the Federal poverty line* below for instructions on how to repay any APTC paid for your or your family's coverage.

Household income below 100% of the Federal poverty line. If the amount on line 5 is less than 100, you can take the PTC if you meet the requirements under *Estimated household income at least 100% of the Federal poverty line* next or *Alien lawfully present in the United States* below.

   Estimated household income at least 100% of the Federal poverty line. You may qualify for the PTC if your household income is less than 100% of the Federal poverty line and you meet all of the following requirements.
* You or an individual in your tax family enrolled in a qualified health plan through a Marketplace.
* The Marketplace estimated at the time of your enrollment that your household income would be between 100% and 400% of the Federal poverty line for your family size for 2014.
* APTC is paid for the coverage for one or more months during 2014.
* You otherwise qualify as an applicable taxpayer (without taking into account the Federal poverty line percentage).

   Alien lawfully present in the United States. Certain aliens with household income below 100% of the Federal poverty line are not eligible for Medicaid because of their immigration status. You may qualify for the PTC if your household income is less than 100% of the Federal poverty line if you meet all of the following requirements.
* You or an individual in your tax family enrolled in a qualified health plan through a Marketplace.
* The enrolled individual is lawfully present in the United States and is not eligible for Medicaid.
* You otherwise qualify as an applicable taxpayer (without taking into account the Federal poverty line percentage).

   If you meet all of the requirements under either *Estimated household income at least 100% of the Federal poverty line* or *Alien lawfully present in the United States*, check the **"Yes"** box on line 6 and continue to line 7.

   If your household income is less than 100% of the Federal poverty line and you did not meet the requirements under *Estimated household income at least 100% of the Federal poverty line* or *Alien lawfully present in the United States*, you are not an applicable taxpayer and you are not eligible to take the PTC. Check the **"No"** box on line 6, skip lines 7 and 8, and go to line 9. However, if no APTC was paid for any individuals in your tax family, **stop**; do not complete Form 8962.

Household income above 400% of the Federal poverty line. If the amount on line 5 is more than 400, you cannot take the PTC. You must repay all APTC paid for individuals in your tax family. Skip lines 7 and 8, and complete lines 9 and 10 (and Part 4, if applicable). When completing line 11 or lines 12 through 23, complete only column F. Then complete the rest of the form to determine how much you must repay. If no APTC was paid for any individuals in your tax family, **stop**; do not complete Form 8962.

   If you qualify for the alternative calculation for year of marriage (see the instructions for line 9, later), you may be able to reduce the amount of APTC you have to repay. If you enrolled an individual for whom another taxpayer will claim a personal exemption, the other taxpayer may be responsible to repay all or part of the APTC (see the instructions for line 9, later).

Line 7

Enter on line 7 the decimal number from <u>Table 2</u> next that applies to the amount you entered on line 5. This number is used to calculate your contribution amount.

Line 8a

Multiply line 3 by line 7 and enter the result on line 8a, rounded to the nearest whole dollar amount.

Table 2. Applicable Figure

 If the amount on line 5 is less than 133, your applicable figure is .0200. If the amount on line 5 is between 300 through 400, your applicable figure is .0950.

IF Form 8962, line 5 is . . .	ENTER on Form 8962, line 7 . . .	IF Form 8962, line 5 is . . .	ENTER on Form 8962, line 7 . . .	IF Form 8962, line 5 is . . .	ENTER on Form 8962, line 7 . . .	IF Form 8962, line 5 is . . .	ENTER on Form 8962, line 7 . . .
less than 133	0.0200	175	0.0515	218	0.0693	261	0.0837
133	0.0300	176	0.0520	219	0.0697	262	0.0840
134	0.0306	177	0.0524	220	0.0700	263	0.0843
135	0.0312	178	0.0529	221	0.0704	264	0.0846
136	0.0318	179	0.0533	222	0.0707	265	0.0849
137	0.0324	180	0.0538	223	0.0711	266	0.0851
138	0.0329	181	0.0543	224	0.0714	267	0.0854
139	0.0335	182	0.0547	225	0.0718	268	0.0857
140	0.0341	183	0.0552	226	0.0721	269	0.0860
141	0.0347	184	0.0556	227	0.0725	270	0.0863
142	0.0353	185	0.0561	228	0.0728	271	0.0866
143	0.0359	186	0.0566	229	0.0732	272	0.0869
144	0.0365	187	0.0570	230	0.0735	273	0.0872
145	0.0371	188	0.0575	231	0.0739	274	0.0875
146	0.0376	189	0.0579	232	0.0742	275	0.0878
147	0.0382	190	0.0584	233	0.0746	276	0.0880
148	0.0388	191	0.0589	234	0.0749	277	0.0883
149	0.0394	192	0.0593	235	0.0753	278	0.0886
150	0.0400	193	0.0598	236	0.0756	279	0.0889
151	0.0405	194	0.0602	237	0.0760	280	0.0892
152	0.0409	195	0.0607	238	0.0763	281	0.0895
153	0.0414	196	0.0612	239	0.0767	282	0.0898
154	0.0418	197	0.0616	240	0.0770	283	0.0901
155	0.0423	198	0.0621	241	0.0774	284	0.0904
156	0.0428	199	0.0625	242	0.0777	285	0.0907
157	0.0432	200	0.0630	243	0.0781	286	0.0909
158	0.0437	201	0.0634	244	0.0784	287	0.0912
159	0.0441	202	0.0637	245	0.0788	288	0.0915
160	0.0446	203	0.0641	246	0.0791	289	0.0918
161	0.0451	204	0.0644	247	0.0795	290	0.0921
162	0.0455	205	0.0648	248	0.0798	291	0.0924
163	0.0460	206	0.0651	249	0.0802	292	0.0927
164	0.0464	207	0.0655	250	0.0805	293	0.0930
165	0.0469	208	0.0658	251	0.0808	294	0.0933
166	0.0474	209	0.0662	252	0.0811	295	0.0936
167	0.0478	210	0.0665	253	0.0814	296	0.0938
168	0.0483	211	0.0669	254	0.0817	297	0.0941
169	0.0487	212	0.0672	255	0.0820	298	0.0944
170	0.0492	213	0.0676	256	0.0822	299	0.0947
171	0.0497	214	0.0679	257	0.0825	300 thru 400	0.0950
172	0.0501	215	0.0683	258	0.0828		
173	0.0506	216	0.0686	259	0.0831		
174	0.0510	217	0.0690	260	0.0834		

Part 2—Premium Tax Credit Claim and Reconciliation of Advance Payment of Premium Tax Credit

Line 9

If any of the following apply, see *Part 4* next and *Part 5* below. Otherwise, check the **"No"** box on line 9 and go to line 10.
- You got divorced during the year.
- You or an individual in your tax family were enrolled in a qualified health plan by someone not part of your tax family.
- You or an individual in your tax family enrolled someone not part of your tax family in a qualified health plan.
- You or an individual in your tax family were enrolled in a qualified health plan with another tax family and the applicable SLCSP premium for at least one tax family for at least one month

is different from the premium reported on Form 1095-A, Part III, column B.
- You got married during 2014.

Part 4. If you got divorced in 2014, or if for other reasons one policy covered at least one individual in your tax family and at least one individual not in your tax family, see Table 3. Shared Policy Allocation—Line 9 below to determine whether you must complete Part 4.

Part 5. If you got married during the year and APTC was paid for an individual in your tax family, you may be eligible to complete Part 5 to elect an optional calculation that may reduce the amount of excess APTC you would have to repay under the general rules. See Table 4. Alternative Calculation for Year of Marriage Eligibility, later, to determine whether you qualify for the alternative calculation.

Note. If both Part 4 and Part 5 apply to you, complete Part 4 first.

Table 3. Shared Policy Allocation—Line 9

Follow Steps 1–5 below to determine whether you need to complete *Part 4—Shared Policy Allocation*, later, for each qualified health plan that covers at least one individual in your tax family and at least one individual **not** in your tax family. For each shared policy, if your answer directs you to Part 4, skip directly to Part 4—you do not need to complete the remaining steps below. If your answers in Steps 1 through 4 do not direct you to Part 4 (or if you did not answer any questions in Steps 1 through 4), continue until you have completed Step 5.

STEP 1: Complete if You Divorced or Legally Separated from Your Spouse in 2014

1. Did the policy cover at least one individual in your tax family **AND** cover at least one individual in your former spouse's tax family?

   ☐ **Yes.** You must allocate the policy amounts. Check the **"Yes"** box on Form 8962, line 9, and skip to *Part 4—Shared Policy Allocation*.   ☐ **No.** Continue to Step 2.

STEP 2: Complete if You were Married at the End of 2014 but are Filing a Separate Return from Your Spouse*

2. Did the policy cover at least one individual in your tax family **AND** cover at least one individual in your spouse's tax family?

   ☐ **Yes.** You must allocate the policy amounts. Check the **"Yes"** box on Form 8962, line 9, and skip to *Part 4—Shared Policy Allocation*.   ☐ **No.** Continue to Step 3.

   *Also use this Step 2 if you meet the rules in *Situation 1* or *Situation 2* under *Married taxpayers*, earlier.

STEP 3: Complete if Another Taxpayer will Claim the Personal Exemption for an Individual You Enrolled in a Policy

3.a. Did the policy cover at least one individual in your tax family **AND** cover at least one individual whom you enrolled in the policy **but** who will be in another taxpayer's tax family*?

   ☐ **Yes.** Continue to question 3b.   ☐ **No.** Go to Step 4.

b. Did you indicate to the Marketplace at enrollment in the policy that you intended to claim the personal exemption(s) for the individual(s) in 3a above whom you enrolled but for whom another taxpayer will claim a personal exemption?

   ☐ **Yes.** You must allocate the policy amounts. Check the **"Yes"** box on Form 8962, line 9, and skip to *Part 4—Shared Policy Allocation*.   ☐ **No.** Continue to Step 4.

   *If no one claims the personal exemption for an individual you enrolled in a policy **and** you indicated to the Marketplace that you would claim the individual's personal exemption, you are responsible for reconciling any APTC paid on behalf of the individual. See *Individual you enrolled for whom no taxpayer will claim a personal exemption* under *Lines 12 through 23—Monthly Calculation*, later. You do not need to complete Part 4 for this policy. If you got married in 2014, continue to Table 4, later. Otherwise, check the **"No"** box on Form 8962, line 9, and continue to line 10.

STEP 4: Complete if You are Claiming the Personal Exemption for an Individual Another Taxpayer Enrolled in a Policy

4. Did the policy cover at least one individual in your tax family **but** whom another person enrolled in the policy **AND** cover at least one individual not in your tax family?

   ☐ **Yes.** You must allocate the policy amounts. Check the **"Yes"** box on Form 8962, line 9, and skip to *Part 4—Shared Policy Allocation*.   ☐ **No.** Continue to Step 5.

STEP 5: Complete for Other Allocation Scenarios

5.a. Did the policy cover at least one individual in your tax family **AND** cover at least one individual **not** in your tax family?

   ☐ **Yes.** Continue to question 5b.   ☐ **No. STOP.** You do not need to complete Part 4. If you got married in 2014, continue to Table 4, later. Otherwise, check the **"No"** box on Form 8962, line 9, and continue to line 10.

b. Does the information provided to the Marketplace at enrollment regarding who would claim the personal exemptions for covered individuals match who will claim the personal exemptions for those individuals for 2014 (answer **"Yes"** if you did not have to provide this information at enrollment)?

   ☐ **Yes.** Continue to question 5c.   ☐ **No.** You must allocate the policy amounts. Check the **"Yes"** box on Form 8962, line 9, and skip to *Part 4—Shared Policy Allocation*.

c. Did each tax family receive a separate Form 1095-A **AND** did each Form 1095-A have the correct applicable SLCSP premium for each tax family for each month in Part III, column B?

   ☐ **Yes. STOP.** You do not need to complete Part 4. If you got married in 2014, continue to Table 4, later. Otherwise, check the **"No"** box on Form 8962, line 9, and continue to line 10.   ☐ **No.** You may have to allocate the policy amounts. Check the **"Yes"** box on Form 8962, line 9, and skip to *Part 4—Shared Policy Allocation*.

Table 4. Alternative Calculation for Year of Marriage Eligibility

Answer questions 1–5 below to determine whether you may be eligible to elect the alternative calculation for year of marriage.

1   Were you married on December 31, 2014?

☐ **Yes.** Continue to the next question in this table.

☐ **No.** You are not eligible to elect the alternative calculation. Check the **"No"** box on Form 8962, line 9, and continue to line 10.

2   Are you filing a joint return with your spouse for 2014?

☐ **Yes.** Continue to the next question in this table.

☐ **No.** You are not eligible to elect the alternative calculation. Check the **"No"** box on Form 8962, line 9, and continue to line 10.

3   Were you and your spouse each unmarried on January 1, 2014?

☐ **Yes.** Continue to the next question in this table.

☐ **No.** You are not eligible to elect the alternative calculation. Check the **"No"** box on Form 8962, line 9, and continue to line 10.

4   Was anyone in your tax family enrolled in a qualified health plan before your first full month of marriage? (For example, if you got married on July 15, your first full month of marriage was August.)

☐ **Yes.** Continue to the next question in this table.

☐ **No.** You are not eligible to elect the alternative calculation. Check the **"No"** box on Form 8962, line 9, and continue to line 10.

5   Was APTC paid for anyone in your tax family during 2014?

☐ **Yes.** Continue to Worksheet 2 next to determine whether excess APTC was paid during 2014. If excess APTC was paid, you are eligible to elect the alternative calculation. If the amount you entered on Form 8962, line 5, is more than 400, do not complete Worksheet 2. See *Alternative Calculation for Year of Marriage* in Pub. 974 to determine if electing the alternative calculation reduces your repayment amount.

☐ **No.** You are not eligible to elect the alternative calculation. Do not complete Part 5. If you did not complete Part 4, check the **"No"** box on line 9 and continue to line 10. If you completed Part 4, check the **"No"** box on line 10, skip line 11, and continue to *Lines 12 through 23—Monthly Calculation*, later.

Worksheet 2. Alternative Calculation for Marriage Eligibility

Complete this worksheet to determine whether you received excess APTC in 2014.

⚠ *If* Part 4—Shared Policy Allocation *applies to you, do not complete this worksheet until you have completed Part 4.*

Monthly Calculation	A. Form(s) 1095-A, lines 21–32, column A*	B. Form(s) 1095-A, lines 21–32, column B**	C. Form 8962, line 8b	D. Subtract column C from column B	E. Smaller of column A or column D	F. Form(s) 1095-A, lines 21–32, column C***
1 January						
2 February						
3 March						
4 April						
5 May						
6 June						
7 July						
8 August						
9 September						
10 October						
11 November						
12 December						

13   **Totals:** Enter the total of column E, lines 1–12, and the total of column F, lines 1–12 . . . .

14   Is line 13, column E, less than line 13, column F?

☐ **Yes.** Excess APTC was paid in 2014. You are eligible to elect the alternative calculation. See *Alternative Calculation for Year of Marriage* in Pub. 974 to determine if electing the alternative calculation reduces your repayment amount.

☐ **No.** There was no excess APTC paid in 2014. You are not eligible to elect the alternative calculation. Do not complete Part 5.

• If you did not complete Part 4, check the **"No"** box on line 9 and continue to line 10. If you are required to use lines 12 through 23 of Form 8962, enter the amounts from lines 1 through 12 of this worksheet in the lines for the corresponding months and columns on Form 8962.

• If you completed Part 4, check the **"No"** box on line 10, skip line 11, and enter the amounts from lines 1 through 12 of this worksheet in the lines for the corresponding months and columns of lines 12 through 23 of Form 8962.

*See Column A under Lines 12 through 23—Monthly Calculation, *later, for instructions for the amounts to enter on lines 1 through 12, column A, of this worksheet. These are the amounts of the monthly premiums reported on Form(s) 1095-A, lines 21 through 32, column A.*

**See Column B under Lines 12 through 23—Monthly Calculation, *later, for instructions for the amounts to enter on lines 1 through 12, column B, of this worksheet. These are the amounts of the monthly premium for the applicable SLCSP reported on Form(s) 1095-A, lines 21 through 32, column B.*

***See Column F under Lines 12 through 23—Monthly Calculation, *later, for instructions for the amounts to enter on lines 1 through 12, column F, of this worksheet. These are the amounts of the monthly APTC reported on Form(s) 1095-A, lines 21 through 32, column C.*

Line 10

Full-year coverage with no changes on Form 1095-A, Part III, columns A or B. Check the "**Yes**" box on line 10 if all of the following apply for each Form 1095-A you received. Otherwise, check the "**No**" box.

- You had coverage for all 12 months during 2014 (January through December).
- The same amount is reported in column A, lines 21 through 32.
- The same amount is reported in column B, lines 21 through 32.
- Your coverage family did not change for any month in 2014. See *Exceptions* below if your coverage family changed during 2014 and you did not notify the Marketplace.

Note. If you got married during 2014, check the "**No**" box unless you got married in December.

Exceptions. If during 2014, your coverage family changed and you did not notify the Marketplace, the premium for the applicable SLCSP reported on your Form(s) 1095-A, Part III, column B, may not be accurate. Your coverage family and premium for the applicable SLCSP may change for any month and any following months that one of the following applies.

- You enroll an individual newly added to your tax family (for example, a newborn).
- An individual in your tax family is no longer enrolled in your qualified health plan.
- An individual included in your coverage family becomes eligible for or loses eligibility for employer coverage or other minimum essential coverage.
- You will claim the personal exemption for an individual, but you did not indicate to the Marketplace at enrollment that you would do so.
- You indicated to the Marketplace at enrollment that you would claim the personal exemption for an individual, but you will not claim a personal exemption for that individual.
- An individual enrolled in the coverage died but you did not remove the individual from the policy.
- You moved during the year.

If any of the above apply and you did not notify the Marketplace, you must determine the correct premium for the applicable SLCSP for the months affected. See Pub. 974 for information on determining the correct premium for the applicable SLCSP or, if you enrolled through the Federally-facilitated Marketplace, go to *www.healthcare.gov/taxes*. See the examples next.

If you checked the "**Yes**" box on line 10, complete line 11. If you checked the "**No**" box, complete lines 12–23.

Example 1. Mike and Susan enroll together in a qualified health plan through the Marketplace. They receive a Form 1095-A, which reports $800 for the enrollment premium in column A on lines 21 through 32 and $850 for the applicable SLCSP premium in column B on lines 21 through 32, for January through December. They check the "**Yes**" box on line 10 and complete line 11 because there is an amount for all 12 months and the amounts did not change for each of columns A and B.

Example 2. Same facts as *Example 1* above, but starting on August 1, Mike is eligible for Medicare and does not notify the Marketplace. Because Mike is eligible for other minimum essential coverage, their coverage family changed starting in August. As a result, Mike and Susan must update the premium for the applicable SLCSP reported in column B for the months of August through December (Form 1095-A, lines 28 through 32, column B). Since there will be a change for some months in column B, Mike and Susan must complete lines 12 through 23. Mike and Susan determine that the premium for the applicable

SLCSP for the coverage family of one (Susan) for August through December is $400 each month. Mike and Susan enter $850 in Form 8962, lines 12 through 18, column B, and $400 in lines 19 through 23, column B. Mike and Susan do not complete line 11.

Example 3. Lee receives a Form 1095-A, which reports in column A $1,000 on lines 21 through 32 for January through December and in column B $900 on lines 21 through 31 for January through November. However, column B reports $650 on line 32 because an individual included in Lee's coverage family was eligible for other minimum essential coverage for the entire month of December and Lee reported the change to the Marketplace. Lee checks the "**No**" box on line 10 and completes lines 12 through 23.

If you were enrolled in a qualified health plan for fewer than 12 months during 2014 (for example, you enrolled in January for coverage effective February 1), check the "**No**" box on line 10, and complete lines 12 through 23.

Line 11—Annual Calculation

If you checked the "**No**" box on line 6 or you are using filing status married filing separately and *Situation 2*, earlier, does not apply to you, skip columns A through E, and see *Column F*, later.

Column A. Enter the annual premiums from Form 1095-A, line 33, column A. If you have more than one Form 1095-A, add the amounts together and enter the total on Form 8962, line 11, column A. This amount is the total of your enrollment premiums for the year, including the portion paid by APTC.

 If you or a member of your tax family were enrolled in a stand-alone dental plan that provided pediatric benefits, the portion of the dental plan premiums for the pediatric benefits will be included in the amount on Form 1095-A, column A.

Column B. Enter the annual premium for the applicable SLCSP from Form 1095-A, line 33, column B. If you have more than one Form 1095-A, enter the following amount.

- If individuals in your coverage family enrolled in more than one policy in the same state you will receive a Form 1095-A for each policy. Enter the amount from column B of **only one** Form 1095-A. The Marketplace will enter the same SLCSP premium that applies to all members of your coverage family on each Form 1095-A. However, if you got married in December of 2014 and you and your spouse, or individuals in your and your spouse's tax families, were enrolled in separate qualified health plans, add the amounts from Form 1095-A, column B, for each plan (or plans) and enter the total.
- For individuals enrolled in qualified health plans in different states, add together the amounts from column B of the Forms 1095-A from each state and enter the total on Form 8962, line 11, column B.

If during 2014, your coverage family changed and you did not notify the Marketplace, or no APTC was paid, the premium for the applicable SLCSP reported on your Form(s) 1095-A may not be accurate (or may not be reported by the Marketplace). If you must determine a different premium for the applicable SLCSP than what is reported on Form 1095-A for any month, you cannot complete line 11. You must complete lines 12 through 23. See *Exceptions* under *Line 10* above to determine whether you must enter a different amount for the premium for the applicable SLCSP for any month reported on Form 1095-A.

Column C. Enter the amount from line 8a of Form 8962.

Column D. If column D is zero or less, enter -0-.

Column E. Enter the lesser of the amount in column A and the amount in column D.

Column F. Enter the APTC amount from Form 1095-A, line 33, column C. If you have more than one Form 1095-A, add the amounts together and enter the total on Form 8962, line 11, column F.

Not an applicable taxpayer. If you are not an applicable taxpayer because your household income is over 400% of the Federal poverty line or you are using filing status married filing separately and *Situation 2*, earlier, does not apply to you, you cannot take the PTC. You must repay the APTC entered on line 11, column F. To complete the rest of the form, skip lines 12 through 24, and enter the amount from line 11, column F, on lines 25 and 27. Then complete lines 28 (if it applies to you) and 29. Enter the amount from line 29 on your Form 1040, line 46; Form 1040A, line 29; or Form 1040NR, line 44.

Lines 12 through 23—Monthly Calculation

If you checked the **"No"** box on line 6 and you did not elect the alternative calculation for year of marriage **or** you are using filing status married filing separately and *Situation 2*, earlier, does not apply to you, skip columns A through E, and see *Column F*, later.

Column A. Enter on lines 12 through 23, column A, the amount of the monthly premiums reported on Form 1095-A, lines 21 through 32, column A, for the corresponding month. If you have more than one Form 1095-A affecting a particular month, add the amounts together for that month and enter the total on the appropriate line on Form 8962, column A. This amount is the total of your enrollment premiums for the month, including the portion paid by APTC.

If a -0- appears on Form 1095-A, on any of lines 21 through 32, column A, you are not entitled to a monthly credit amount for that month because enrollment premiums were not paid. Enter -0- on the appropriate line on Form 8962, column A.

If you completed Part 4—Shared Policy Allocation for any Form 1095-A, include only the monthly premium amounts allocated to you, if any, using the allocation percentage you entered on lines 30 through 33, column e, and combine those amounts with the monthly premiums for other policies that you did not allocate.

Column B. Enter on lines 12 through 23, column B, the amount of the monthly premium for the applicable SLCSP reported on Form 1095-A, lines 21 through 32, column B, for the corresponding month. If you have more than one Form 1095-A affecting a particular month, enter the following amounts on the appropriate line on Form 8962, column B, for that month.
- For individuals enrolled in separate policies in the same state, the Marketplace will report on each Form 1095-A issued the single applicable SLCSP premium that applies to all members of the 1095-A recipient's coverage family for coverage that same month. Enter this amount on Form 8962, lines 12 through 23, column B. See *Marriage in 2014*, later, if you got married during 2014.
- For individuals enrolled in qualified health plans in different states, add the amounts from column B of Forms 1095-A together and enter the total on Form 8962, lines 12 through 23, column B.
- If you completed Part 4—Shared Policy Allocation for any Form 1095-A, add the amounts of the premium for the applicable SLCSP allocated to you, if any, using the allocation percentage you entered on Form 8962, lines 30 through 33, column f, to the amount of the premium for your applicable SLCSP shown on the Form(s) 1095-A that you did not allocate.

If a -0- appears on Form 1095-A, on any of lines 21 through 32, column B, you are not entitled to a monthly credit amount for that month because enrollment premiums were not paid. Enter -0- on the appropriate line on Form 8962, column B.

If during 2014, your coverage family changed and you did not notify the Marketplace, the premium for the applicable SLCSP

reported on your Form(s) 1095-A may not be accurate. See *Exceptions* under *Line 10*, earlier, to determine whether you must enter a different amount for the premium for the applicable SLCSP for any month reported on Form 1095-A. If no APTC was paid, the Marketplace may not report a premium for the SLCSP (Form 1095-A, lines 21 through 32, column B, may be blank). You must determine the premium for your applicable SLCSP to take the PTC on your tax return. See Pub. 974 for information on determining the correct premium for the applicable SLCSP or, if you enrolled through the Federally-facilitated Marketplace, go to *www.healthcare.gov/taxes*.

Marriage in 2014. If you got married in 2014 and you and your spouse (or individuals in your tax family) were enrolled in separate qualified health plans during months prior to your first full month of marriage, add together the amounts from Form 1095-A, column B, for each plan (or plans) and enter the total. If you completed Part 5—Alternative Calculation for Year of Marriage, use the instructions in Pub. 974 for the entries to make for your pre-marriage months.

Column C. If you did not complete Part 5—Alternative Calculation for Year of Marriage, enter on lines 12 through 23, column C, your monthly contribution amount from line 8b. If columns A and B of any of lines 12 through 23 are blank, leave column C of the corresponding line blank.

If you completed Part 5—Alternative Calculation for Year of Marriage, see Pub. 974 for how to complete column C.

Column D. If an entry for column D is zero or less, enter -0-.

Column E. Generally, enter for each month the lesser of the amount in column A and the amount in column D for that month.

Column F. Enter on lines 12 through 23, column F, the amount of the monthly APTC reported on Form 1095-A, lines 21 through 32, column C. If you have more than one Form 1095-A affecting a particular month, add the amounts together for that month and enter the total on the appropriate line on Form 8962, column F.

If you completed Part 4—Shared Policy Allocation for any Form 1095-A, include only the amounts of the monthly APTC allocated to you, if any, using the allocation percentage you entered on lines 30 through 33, column g, and combine that amount with the amounts of the monthly APTC for other policies that you did not allocate.

Not an applicable taxpayer. If you are not an applicable taxpayer because your household income is over 400% of the Federal poverty line or you are using filing status married filing separately and *Situation 2*, earlier, does not apply to you, you must repay the total APTC entered on lines 12 through 23, column F (unless the alternative calculation for marriage rule applies to you and you are able to reduce your repayment amount). To complete the rest of the form, skip line 24, and enter the total of lines 12 through 23, column F, on lines 25 and 27. Then complete lines 28 (if it applies to you) and 29. Enter the amount from line 29 on your Form 1040, line 46; Form 1040A, line 29; or Form 1040NR, line 44.

Example. Melissa and Ryan were married at the beginning of 2014. They have no dependents. They were enrolled under the same qualified health plan through a Marketplace from January through April. Monthly APTC of $1,000 was paid for them, for a total of $4,000. They divorced April 10. Melissa enrolled in single coverage from May through December. Monthly APTC of $100 was paid for her, for a total of $800. Ryan did not enroll in coverage.

At the end of the year, Melissa or Ryan will receive a Form 1095-A reporting their coverage for January through April. The recipient of the Form 1095-A should provide a copy to the non-recipient. Melissa will receive a Form 1095-A reporting her coverage for May through December.

Instructions for Form 8962 (2014)

For 2014, Melissa's family size is one and her household income is 450% of the Federal poverty line. Ryan's family size is one and his household income is 410% of the Federal poverty line. Melissa and Ryan agree to allocate the APTC 60% to Melissa and 40% to Ryan. The allocation is only for the period of time Melissa and Ryan were married. The sum of the APTC allocated to Melissa is $2,400 ($1,000 x .6 x 4 months). Melissa must add this sum to her APTC of $800 for her single coverage. She enters the monthly amounts on lines 12–23, column F, and the total of $3,200 on Form 8962, lines 25, 27, and 29. Melissa enters the amount from line 29 on the applicable line of her tax return.

The sum of the APTC allocated to Ryan is $1,600 ($1,000 x .4 x 4 months). Ryan enters the monthly amounts on Form 8962, lines 12–23, column F, and the total of $1,600 on lines 25, 27, and 29. Ryan enters the $1,600 from line 29 on the applicable line of his tax return.

Individual you enrolled for whom no taxpayer will claim a personal exemption. If no taxpayer claims a personal exemption for an individual you enrolled in a qualified health plan (including yourself), you must report any APTC paid for the individual if you indicated to the Marketplace at enrollment that you would claim the individual's personal exemption. Follow the rules in *Column F*, earlier, to report this APTC.

Line 26

If line 24 is greater than line 25, subtract line 25 from line 24 and enter the result on line 26. This result is the amount of your PTC that is more than the APTC paid. This amount will reduce the amount of tax you must pay with your tax return or increase your refund. Also enter the result on your tax return as instructed on Form 8962, and skip lines 27 through 29. If line 24 is equal to line 25, enter -0- on line 26 and skip lines 27 through 29.

If you elected the alternative calculation for year of marriage, and line 24 is greater than line 25, enter -0- on line 26 and skip lines 27 through 29.

If line 25 is greater than line 24, skip line 26 and go to Part 3.

Part 3—Repayment of Excess Advance Payment of the Premium Tax Credit

Complete this part to figure the amount of excess APTC you must repay.

If one of the following applies, you must repay a portion or all of the APTC paid for you or a member of your tax family.
* You checked the **"No"** box on line 6. This means you entered a percentage of more than 400 on line 5 and you are not an applicable taxpayer eligible for the PTC. Enter the amount from Form 8962, line 25, on lines 27 and 29.
* Line 25 is greater than line 24. You have excess APTC. Go to line 27 of Form 8962 to figure the amount of your excess APTC.
* You are married at the end of 2014 but you are filing your return as married filing separately and did not check the **"Relief"** box because you are not a victim of domestic abuse or spousal abandonment.

Line 28

The excess APTC you must repay is limited to the amounts in Table 5 next. Enter the appropriate amount from Table 5 on line 28. If you were married at the end of 2014 but are filing separately from your spouse, the repayment limitation shown in Table 5 applies to you and your spouse separately based on the household income reported on each return.

If your entry on Form 8962, line 5, is 400 or more, there is no repayment limitation. You must repay the amount shown on

line 27. Leave line 28 blank and enter the amount from line 27 on line 29.

Table 5. **Repayment Limitation**

IF the amount on Form 8962, line 5 is . . .	ENTER on line 28 . . .	
	for a filing status of Single—	for any other filing status—
Less than 200	$300	$600
At least 200 but less than 300 . . .	$750	$1,500
At least 300 but less than 400 . . .	$1,250	$2,500
400 or more	leave line 28 blank	

Part 4—Shared Policy Allocation

You must complete Part 4 if both of the following apply.
* You checked the **"Yes"** box on line 9.
* Table 3 instructed you to allocate your policy amounts (one or more of the amounts in the columns in Part III of Form 1095-A) based on one of your answers to the questions in Steps 1 through 5 of the table.

To complete Part 4 for a qualified health plan, see *Specific Allocation Situations*, later, to find the situation (or situations) that applies to that policy. The instructions for each situation will describe the amounts you must allocate and your allocation options. Then see *Lines 30 through 33, columns a through g*, later, to use that information to complete the line(s) on Form 8962 that correspond to each qualified health plan.

Multiple allocations of one qualified health plan. You may have to allocate policy amounts from one qualified health plan among more than two tax families in the same month. You may also have to allocate amounts from one qualified health plan using more than one of the rules (either in the same month or in different months) under *Specific Allocation Situations*, later.

Multiple allocations in the same month. If one qualified health plan covers individuals from more than two tax families in the same month, use the worksheets and instructions necessary to allocate the amounts on Form 1095-A for that month that are in Pub. 974 under *Shared Policy Allocation*.

Example. One qualified health plan covers Bret, his spouse Maryanne, and their daughter Sophia from January through August. Bret and Maryanne divorce on August 26. Bret and Maryanne each file a tax return using a filing status of single. Sophia is claimed as a dependent by her grandfather, Mike. Bret, Maryanne, and Mike must allocate the amounts from Form 1095-A for the months of January through August on their tax returns using the worksheets and instructions in Pub. 974.

Multiple allocations in different months. If more than one of the allocation rules under *Specific Allocation Situations*, later, applies to the same qualified health plan for different months, you must use the rule (or rules if more than one rule applies in the same month – see *Multiple allocations in the same month* above) that applies for that month to allocate the amounts on Form 1095-A.

Example. Henry enrolled himself, his spouse, Cara, and their two dependent children, Heidi and Matt, in a policy for 2014. APTC was paid on behalf of each. The couple divorced on June 30, and Cara purchased different health insurance for July through December in which she enrolls with Heidi and Matt. Henry claims Heidi as a dependent on his tax return. Cara claims Matt as a dependent on her tax return. For the months Henry and Cara were married (January through June), they will allocate the amounts from the policy on line 30 using the rules under *Taxpayers divorced or legally separated in 2014*, later. For the months Henry and Cara were divorced (July through

Table 6. **Specific Allocation Situations Chart**

The steps in this chart refer to the steps in <u>Table 3</u>, earlier.
Step 1. If you answered **"Yes"** to question 1, see <u>Taxpayers divorced or legally separated in 2014</u> below.
Step 2. If you answered **"Yes"** to question 2, see <u>Taxpayers married at year end but filing separate returns</u> below.
Step 3. If you answered **"Yes"** to question 3b, see <u>Policy shared with an individual for whom another taxpayer claims a personal exemption</u>, later.
Step 4. If you answered **"Yes"** to question 4, see <u>Policy shared with an individual for whom another taxpayer claims a personal exemption</u>, later.
Step 5. If you answered **"No"** to question 5b, see <u>Policy shared by two or more tax families</u>, later.

If you answered **"No"** to question 5c, follow the bulleted item below that applies.
- If at enrollment, you enrolled an individual in a policy expecting to claim the personal exemption for the individual, but for 2014 another taxpayer will claim the personal exemption for that individual, see <u>Policy shared with an individual for whom another taxpayer claims a personal exemption</u>, later.
- If you and at least one other tax family enrolled in a single qualified health plan and a separate Form 1095-A was not issued to each tax family, or the correct applicable SLCSP premium for at least one tax family for at least one month is different than the amount reported on Form 1095-A, Part III, column B, see <u>Policy shared by two or more tax families</u>, later.

December), they will allocate the amounts from the policy on line 31 using the rules under <u>Policy shared with an individual for whom another taxpayer claims a personal exemption</u>, later.

Taxpayer allocated entire policy. Do not complete Part 4 if you agree to allocate all of the amounts shown on one Form 1095-A to one taxpayer under the rules of <u>Taxpayers divorced or legally separated in 2014</u> below or <u>Policy shared with an individual for whom another taxpayer claims a personal exemption</u>, later. If you are the taxpayer allocated one hundred percent of the amounts from Form 1095-A, use the general rules under <u>Line 11—Annual Calculation</u> or <u>Lines 12 through 23—Monthly Calculation</u>, earlier, to report the amounts. If you are the taxpayer allocated zero percent of the amounts from Form 1095-A, do not report anything on Form 8962, and do not file Form 8962 unless you are taking the PTC or reconciling APTC reported on another Form 1095-A.

Specific Allocation Situations

<u>Table 6</u> above will direct you to the instructions for allocating policy amounts.

Taxpayers divorced or legally separated in 2014. You and your former spouse must allocate policy amounts on your separate returns to figure your PTC if both of the following apply.
- You were married at some point during 2014 but were no longer married to that spouse at the end of 2014.
- You and your former spouse were enrolled in the same qualified health plan, or you or an individual in your tax family (as shown on your tax return) was enrolled in the same policy as your former spouse or as an individual in your former spouse's tax family at any time during 2014.

You will allocate with your former spouse a percentage of the total enrollment premiums, the premiums for the applicable SLCSP, and APTC for coverage under the plan during the months you were married. You will find these amounts on your Form(s) 1095-A, Part III, columns A, B, and C, respectively. You and your former spouse can allocate these amounts using any percentage you agree on between zero and one hundred percent, but you must allocate all amounts using the same percentage. If you do not agree on a percentage, you and your former spouse must allocate 50% of each of these amounts to you and 50% of each to your former spouse.

Example 1. Keith and Stephanie are married at the beginning of 2014 and have three children, Ben, Grace, and Max. In January, Keith enrolls Ben, Grace, and Max in a qualified health plan, with an effective coverage date of February 1. Keith and Stephanie divorce in July. The children become eligible for and enroll in government-sponsored health coverage and disenroll from the qualified health plan, effective August 1.

Keith claims Ben and Grace as dependents and Stephanie claims Max as a dependent for 2014. Keith and Stephanie agree to allocate the policy amounts 33% to Stephanie and 67% to Keith. Therefore, 33% of the enrollment premiums, the applicable SLCSP premiums, and APTC are allocated to Stephanie and 67% of these amounts are allocated to Keith. The allocation is only for the months Keith and Stephanie were married.

On her Form 8962, Part 4, line 30, Stephanie enters Keith's social security number in column b and enters "0.33" in columns e, f, and g. On his Form 8962, Part 4, line 30, Keith enters Stephanie's social security number in column b and enters "0.67" in columns e, f, and g. Stephanie and Keith both enter "02" in column c and "07" in column d.

Example 2. The facts are the same as in <u>Example 1</u> except that Keith and Stephanie cannot agree on an allocation percentage. Therefore, 50% of the enrollment premiums, the applicable SLCSP premiums, and APTC are allocated to each taxpayer. On their Forms 8962, Part 4, line 30, Keith and Stephanie each enter "0.50" in columns e, f, and g.

Taxpayers married at year end but filing separate returns. You may be able to take the PTC if you file a return as single or head of household (see <u>Situation 1</u> under <u>Married taxpayers</u>, earlier) or you file a return as married filing separately due to domestic abuse or spousal abandonment (see <u>Situation 2</u> under <u>Married taxpayers</u>, earlier). You cannot take the PTC if you are filing your return as married filing separately and Situation 2 does not apply. In any of these situations, on your separately filed returns, you and your spouse must equally allocate (50% to each spouse) certain policy amounts if both of the following apply.
- You are married at the end of 2014 but are filing a separate return from your spouse.
- You and your spouse were enrolled in the same qualified health plan, or you or an individual in your tax family was enrolled in the same policy as your spouse or an individual in your spouse's tax family, at any time during 2014.

If you must allocate policy amounts, see <u>Situation 1 or Situation 2</u> next, or if neither applies, see <u>Married filing separately (not in Situation 2)</u>, later.

If the policy covered individuals in only one spouse's tax family, the spouse whose tax family included the covered individual(s) must report all of the policy amounts (unless the policy must be allocated with another taxpayer).

Situation 1 or Situation 2. You and your spouse have separate tax families, as shown on your separate tax returns. Enter "0.50" in columns e and g of the appropriate line in Part 4 to allocate the enrollment premium and APTC. Leave column f blank because you do not allocate the premium for the applicable SLCSP. Instead, enter the applicable SLCSP premium for your coverage family on lines 12 through 23. See *Example 1* below and *Example 2*, later.

 If you enrolled in coverage in the Marketplace with your spouse or another individual who is not in your tax family, your coverage family and applicable SLCSP premium may be different from the coverage family and applicable SLCSP premium the Marketplace used to determine the amount of your APTC. In that case you must use a different applicable SLCSP premium to calculate your credit than the amount reported on Form 1095-A, Part III, column B. See Pub. 974 for information on determining the correct premium for the applicable SLCSP or, if you enrolled through the Federally-facilitated Marketplace, go to *www.healthcare.gov/taxes*.

Married filing separately (not in Situation 2). You and your spouse have separate tax families. Enter "0.50" in column g of the appropriate line in Part 4 to allocate the APTC. Leave columns e and f blank because you do not allocate the enrollment premium or premium for the applicable SLCSP. You must repay the APTC allocated to you subject to the limit on line 28 because you are not an applicable taxpayer. See *Example 3* and *Example 4* below.

Example 1. John and Carol are married at the end of 2014 and have one child, Mark. John and Carol enrolled in a qualified health plan for 2014. The plan covered John, Carol, and Mark, with an annual premium of $14,000 and APTC of $8,500, which applied to the coverage for all of the individuals. John moved out of the residence on May 15. Carol and Mark continued to reside at the residence. John and Carol file separate returns for 2014. Carol qualifies to file her return as head of household. John files his return as married filing separately. Carol claims Mark as her dependent. Because Carol and John are not filing a joint return, they each have their own tax families, which are different from the tax family they indicated to the Marketplace when they enrolled. Carol's family size reported on her tax return is now two because John is not in her tax family. Therefore, Carol's Federal poverty line percentage is determined using the modified AGI of her tax family. John's modified AGI is not included because he is not in Carol's tax family.

Carol's family size for 2014 for purposes of computing her contribution amount is two (Carol and her dependent Mark). Because John is not in Carol's tax family, he is not in her coverage family, which consists of Carol and her dependent Mark, for purposes of determining her applicable SLCSP premium. If neither John nor Carol notifies the Marketplace about the change in family circumstances, the Form 1095-A that Carol or John receives will report in column B the premium for the applicable SLCSP that covers Carol, Mark, and John, which will be incorrect. Carol must determine the correct premium for the applicable SLCSP covering Carol and Mark. Carol looks up her correct premium for the applicable SLCSP.

Carol takes into account $7,000 ($14,000 x .50) of the premiums of the plan in which she and Mark were enrolled in figuring her PTC. Carol must then reconcile $4,250 ($8,500 x .50) of the APTC for her coverage. Amounts from this policy are allocated for all months Carol and John were enrolled. On her Form 8962, Part 4, line 30, Carol enters John's social security number in column b and enters "0.50" in columns e and g. Column f is left blank. Instead of allocating the applicable SLCSP premium, Carol will enter the applicable SLCSP premium that applies to her and Mark.

Since John is filing his tax return as married filing separately and no exception to the married filing jointly requirement applies, he is not an applicable taxpayer and must repay the $4,250 APTC allocated to him, subject to the repayment limitations on line 28. On his Form 8962, Part 4, line 30, John enters Carol's social security number in column b and enters "0.50" in column g. John leaves columns e and f blank because he is not an applicable taxpayer and cannot take the PTC.

Example 2. Kevin and Nancy are married at the end of 2014 and have no dependents. Kevin and Nancy are enrolled in a qualified health plan for 2014 with an annual premium of $10,000 and APTC of $6,500. Nancy is a victim of domestic abuse and is unable to file a joint return under the rules outlined in *Situation 2* under *Married taxpayers*, earlier. Nancy files her return using the filing status married filing separately and checks the **"Relief"** box at the top of Form 8962.

Nancy's family size for 2014 for purposes of computing her monthly contribution is one (Nancy). Nancy's coverage family for purposes of determining her applicable SLCSP premium for 2014 also is one (Nancy). If neither Kevin nor Nancy notifies the Marketplace about the change in family circumstances, the Form 1095-A that Kevin or Nancy receives will report in column B the premium for the applicable SLCSP that covers Nancy and Kevin, which will be incorrect. Nancy must determine the correct premium for the applicable SLCSP covering only Nancy. Nancy looks up her correct premium for the applicable SLCSP.

Nancy's Federal poverty line percentage is determined using Nancy's modified AGI and her family size of one. Nancy takes into account $5,000 ($10,000 x .50) of the enrollment premiums in figuring her PTC. Nancy must reconcile $3,250 ($6,500 x .50) of the APTC for her coverage. On her Form 8962, Part 4, line 30, Nancy enters Kevin's social security number in column b and enters "0.50" in columns e and g. Column f is left blank. Instead of allocating the applicable SLCSP premium, Nancy will enter the applicable SLCSP premium that applies to Nancy. Nancy enters this amount on the applicable lines in column B, lines 12 through 23.

Example 3. For 2014, Michael and Colleen are married with no dependents and are enrolled in a qualified health plan. APTC of $8,700 is paid for them during 2014. Michael and Colleen each file their returns for 2014 as married filing separately and Situation 2 does not apply to either of them. Michael and Colleen are not applicable taxpayers and cannot take the PTC. They must allocate the APTC paid of $8,700, one-half (50%) to Michael and one-half (50%) to Colleen. On her Form 8962, Part 4, line 30, Colleen enters Michael's social security in column b and enters "0.50" in column g. On his Form 8962, Part 4, line 30, Michael enters Colleen's social security number in column b and enters "0.50" in column g.

Example 4. The facts are the same as *Example 3* except that only Colleen is covered under the policy. Colleen does not complete Part 4 of her Form 8962. She reports all of the APTC received on line 11 or lines 12 through 23, whichever applies. Michael does not file Form 8962 because he was not enrolled in a qualified health plan.

Policy shared with an individual for whom another taxpayer claims a personal exemption. If you or another person in your tax family was enrolled in a qualified health plan with an individual (for example, your child) for whom another taxpayer claims a personal exemption (for example, you are enrolled with your child but a former spouse claims your child's personal exemption), you must complete Part 4. The taxpayer claiming the personal exemption may be able to take the PTC for the individual's coverage. When you compute the PTC, you must allocate the enrollment premiums and the APTC for coverage of the individual. If you are required to allocate APTC, you also must allocate the applicable SLCSP premium. You also must do this allocation if, at enrollment, you indicated to the Marketplace that you would be a single tax family but are two or more tax families at filing, for example a child claims his or her own personal exemption.

You and the taxpayer claiming the personal exemption may agree on any allocation percentage between zero and one hundred percent. You may use the percentage you agreed on for every month during which this allocation rule applies, or you may agree on different percentages for different months. However, you must use the same allocation percentage for all policy amounts (enrollment premiums, applicable SLCSP premiums, and APTC) in a month. If you cannot agree on an allocation percentage, the allocation percentage is equal to the number of individuals enrolled by you for whom the other taxpayer claims a personal exemption for the tax year divided by the total number of individuals enrolled in the same policy as the individual. The allocation percentage is the percentage that applies to the amounts the taxpayer claiming the personal exemption must use to compute PTC and reconcile it with APTC. You must compute PTC and reconcile APTC using the remaining amounts.

 This allocation rule does not apply if you and one or more other tax families enrolled in a single qualified health plan as two or more tax families and remained two or more tax families for the year. Use Policy shared by two or more tax families, *later, for instructions on allocating in that situation.*

Note. If APTC is paid for coverage of an individual for whom no taxpayer claims a personal exemption, the taxpayer who attests to the Marketplace to the intention to claim a personal exemption for the individual is responsible for reporting and reconciling the APTC. See *Individual you enrolled for whom no taxpayer will claim a personal exemption* under *Lines 12 through 23—Monthly Calculation*, earlier.

Example 1. Joe and Alice have been divorced since January of 2013 and have two children, Chris and Jane. Joe enrolls in a qualified health plan covering Joe, Chris, and Jane for 2014. The premium for the plan is $13,000. Based on a family size and coverage family of three, and a premium for the applicable SLCSP of $12,000, Joe is approved for and receives APTC computed as follows: Joe's projected household income for 2014 is $58,590 (300% of the Federal poverty line for a family size of three). Joe's APTC for 2014 is $6,434 ($12,000 applicable SLCSP premiums less $5,566 contribution amount (household income $58,590 x applicable figure .095)). Joe's actual household income for 2014 is $58,988.

Jane lives with Alice for more than half of 2014 and Alice claims Jane as a dependent. Joe and Alice agree to an allocation percentage of 20% to determine how much of the total amounts related to the qualified health plan are for Jane's coverage. Therefore, 20% of the enrollment premiums, APTC, and the applicable SLCSP premiums are allocated to Alice and 80% are allocated to Joe.

In computing PTC, Joe takes into account $10,400 of enrollment premiums ($13,000 x .80). Joe must reconcile $5,147 of APTC ($6,434 x .80). Joe's tax family for 2014 includes only Joe and Chris, and Joe's household income of $58,988 is 380% of the Federal poverty line for a family size of two. Joe's applicable SLCSP premium for 2014 is $9,600 (the applicable SLCSP premium covering Joe, Chris, and Jane of $12,000, minus the amount allocated to Alice of $2,400 ($12,000 x .20)).

Joe's PTC for 2014 is $3,996 (the lesser of $3,996, the excess of Joe's applicable SLCSP premium of $9,600 minus the contribution amount of $5,604 ($58,998 x .095), and $10,400, Joe's enrollment premiums). Joe has excess APTC of $1,151 (the excess of the APTC of $5,147 over the PTC of $3,996).

When Joe completes Part 4 of Form 8962, he enters Alice's social security number on line 30, column b, and enters "0.80" in columns e, f, and g.

Alice is responsible for reconciling $1,287 ($6,434 x .20) of APTC for Jane's coverage. If Alice is eligible for the PTC, she will take into account $2,600 ($13,000 x .20) of the enrollment premiums for Jane and $2,400 ($12,000 x .20) of the applicable SLCSP premiums. Alice must compute her contribution amount using the Federal poverty line percentage for the household income and family size reported on her Form 8962.

Example 2. The facts are the same as in *Example 1* except that Joe and Alice do not agree on an allocation percentage. Therefore, the allocation percentage equals the number of individuals Joe enrolled in a qualified health plan for whom Alice claims a personal exemption (1, Jane), divided by the number of individuals enrolled in the plan (3, Joe, Chris, and Jane). The allocation percentage is 33%. Alice is allocated 33% of the enrollment premiums, APTC, and applicable SLCSP premiums and the remaining 67% of each is allocated to Joe.

Policy shared by two or more tax families. If you and one or more other tax families enrolled in a single qualified health plan as two or more tax families and remained two or more tax families for the year, you may have to allocate the enrollment premiums among the families. However, if a family that expects at enrollment to be a single tax family is two or more tax families at filing, for example as a result of a family member claiming his or her own personal exemption, see *Policy shared with an individual for whom another taxpayer claims a personal exemption*, earlier.

Each applicable taxpayer with at least one individual in his or her tax family covered by the plan can take the PTC, if otherwise allowable. PTC for each taxpayer is computed based on each taxpayer's household income, family size, and premium for the applicable SLCSP for the taxpayer's coverage family. However, because there is only one enrollment premium covering all tax families, a portion of the enrollment premiums must be allocated to each tax family. The Marketplace should report on Form 1095-A, Part III, only the amounts that apply to the tax family receiving that Form 1095-A, including in column A only that portion of the enrollment premiums allocated to that tax family. The enrollment premiums are allocated in proportion to the premiums for the applicable SLCSP for each taxpayer's coverage family. Therefore, you must complete Part 4 to allocate enrollment premiums only if:
• The Marketplace did not issue at least one Form 1095-A for each tax family (which may happen if no APTC is paid for any tax family), or
• The correct applicable SLCSP premium for at least one tax family for at least one month is different than the amount reported on Form 1095-A.

If the Marketplace furnishes only one Form 1095-A, the taxpayer receiving the Form 1095-A should provide a copy to the other taxpayers. You and the other taxpayer(s) must complete only column e on the appropriate line in Part 4 to allocate the enrollment premiums to each family.

Example. Gary and his 25-year-old nondependent son Jim enroll in a qualified health plan. Jim has no dependents. The policy covers Gary, Jim, and Gary's two young daughters who are Gary's dependents. No APTC is paid for this policy. The Form 1095-A furnished by the Marketplace to Gary shows an enrollment premium of $15,000 for the year and shows either an applicable SLCSP premium for a coverage family that incorrectly includes Gary, Gary's daughters, and Jim or does not report an applicable SLCSP premium. Gary and Jim determine that the premium for the applicable SLCSP covering Gary and his two dependents is $12,000 and the premium for the applicable SLCSP covering Jim is $6,000. Gary and Jim are applicable taxpayers and each can take the PTC.

Gary computes his credit using his household income and family size of three, and the applicable SLCSP premium for a coverage family of three of $12,000. Jim computes his credit using his household income and family size of one, and the applicable SLCSP premium for a coverage family of one of $6,000.

Gary and Jim must allocate the enrollment premium of $15,000 reported on the Form 1095-A, Part III, column A, in proportion to each taxpayer's applicable SLCSP premium as follows. Gary's allocated enrollment premium is $10,000 ($15,000 x $12,000/$18,000) (67% of the total premium of $15,000) and Jim's allocated enrollment premium is $5,000 ($15,000 x $6,000/$18,000) (33% of the total premium of $15,000).

Gary enters Jim's social security number on line 30, column b, and enters "0.67" in column e. Jim enters Gary's social security number on line 30, column b, and enters "0.33" in column e. Gary and Jim leave line 30, columns f and g, blank.

Lines 30 through 33, columns a through g

If you shared a policy with another taxpayer in one of the situations described in *Specific Allocation Situations*, earlier, complete line 30, columns a through g, as applicable. If you shared a policy with another taxpayer and you are not making an allocation in all three columns, e, f, and g, leave the column blank that does not apply.

If you shared multiple policies during the year or must do more than one allocation for a single policy, complete lines 31 through 33 for each separate allocation, as needed. For instructions on making more than four separate allocations, see *Line 34*, later.

Not an applicable taxpayer. If you are not an applicable taxpayer because your household income is over 400% of the Federal poverty line or you are using filing status married filing separately and *Situation 2*, earlier, does not apply to you, you cannot take the PTC. Unless you are electing the alternative calculation for year of marriage, do not enter any percentages in columns e or f when completing Part 4.

Lines 30 through 33, column a. Enter the Marketplace-assigned policy number from Form 1095-A, line 2. If the policy number of the Form 1095-A is more than 15 characters, enter only the last 15 characters.

Lines 30 through 33, column b. Enter the social security number of the taxpayer with whom you are allocating policy amounts. This social security number may or may not be reported on your Form 1095-A, depending on your relationship to the other taxpayer.

Lines 30 through 33, column c. Enter the first month you are allocating policy amounts. For example, if you were enrolled in a policy with your former spouse from January through June, enter "01" in column c.

Lines 30 through 33, column d. Enter the last month you are allocating policy amounts. For example, if you were enrolled in a policy with your former spouse from January through June, enter "06" in column d.

Lines 30 through 33, column e. If your allocation situation requires you to allocate the enrollment premiums on Form 1095-A, lines 21 through 32, column A, enter your allocation percentage for that policy in column e. Enter your allocation percentage as a decimal rounded to two places (for example, for 40%, enter 0.40). Otherwise, leave column e blank.

Lines 30 through 33, column f. If your allocation situation requires you to allocate the premium for the applicable SLCSP on Form 1095-A, lines 21 through 32, column B, enter your allocation percentage for that policy in column f. Enter your allocation percentage as a decimal rounded to two places (for example, for 67%, enter 0.67). You will enter an allocation percentage in column f, in the following two circumstances.

- You allocated the policy amounts under *Taxpayers divorced or legally separated in 2014*, earlier.
- You allocated the policy amounts under *Policy shared with an individual for whom another taxpayer claims a personal exemption*, earlier, **and** APTC was paid for an individual covered by the policy who was **not** in your tax family.

Leave column f blank in all other allocation situations because you do not allocate the premiums for the applicable SLCSP reported in those situations. Instead, you must determine the correct applicable SLCSP premium for your coverage family and enter that amount on Form 8962, lines 12 through 23, column B. See Pub. 974 for information on determining the correct premium for the applicable SLCSP or, if you enrolled through the Federally-facilitated Marketplace, go to *www.healthcare.gov/taxes*.

Lines 30 through 33, column g. If your allocation situation requires you to allocate the APTC on Form 1095-A, lines 21 through 32, column C, enter your allocation percentage for that policy in column g. Enter your allocation percentage as a decimal rounded to two places (for example, for 80%, enter 0.80). Otherwise, leave column g blank.

Line 34

If you have completed your required allocations of policy amounts shown on Forms 1095-A using lines 30 through 33, check the **"Yes"** box on line 34. If you must make more than four allocations of policy amounts shown on Forms 1095-A, check the **"No"** box on line 34 and attach a statement to your return providing the information shown on lines 30 through 33, columns a through g for each additional allocation.

If you got married in 2014 and APTC was paid for an individual in your tax family, see Table 4 under *Line 9* in the instructions for Part 2, earlier. Otherwise, check the "No" box on Form 8962, line 10, skip line 11, and continue to *Lines 12 through 23—Monthly Calculation* in the instructions for Part 2, earlier.

Part 5—Alternative Calculation for Year of Marriage

Complete Part 5 to elect the alternative calculation for your pre-marriage months. Electing the alternative calculation is optional, but may reduce the amount of excess APTC you must repay. To be eligible to make this election, you must meet either of the following conditions.
- You checked the **"No"** box on Form 8962, line 6, **and** you answered "Yes" to all 5 questions in Table 4, earlier.
- You checked the **"Yes"** box on Form 8962, line 6, **and** the **"Yes"** box on line 14 of Worksheet 2, earlier.

If you, your spouse, or any individual in your tax family had coverage under a qualified health plan for at least one month before your first full month of marriage, use the worksheets and instructions necessary to compute the alternative calculation that are in Pub. 974 under *Alternative Calculation for Year of Marriage*.

 Do not go to Pub. 974 until you have completed Table 4, earlier, to determine whether you meet the requirements to elect the alternative calculation.

Line 35. Complete line 35, columns a through d as indicated in Pub. 974 under *Alternative Calculation for Year of Marriage*.

Line 36. Complete line 36, columns a through d as indicated in Pub. 974 under *Alternative Calculation for Year of Marriage*.

Form **8965**

Department of the Treasury
Internal Revenue Service

Health Coverage Exemptions

▶ Attach to Form 1040, Form 1040A, or Form 1040EZ.
▶ **Information about Form 8965 and its separate instructions is at** *www.irs.gov/form8965*.

OMB No. 1545-0074

20**14**

Attachment
Sequence No. **75**

Name as shown on return

Your social security number

Complete this form if you have a Marketplace-granted coverage exemption or you are claiming a coverage exemption on your return.

Part I | **Marketplace-Granted Coverage Exemptions for Individuals:** If you and/or a member of your tax household have an exemption granted by the Marketplace, complete Part I.

	a Name of Individual	b SSN	c Exemption Certificate Number
1			
2			
3			
4			
5			
6			

Part II | **Coverage Exemptions for Your Household Claimed on Your Return:**

7a Are you claiming an exemption because your household income is below the filing threshold? . . . . ☐ Yes ☐ No

b Are you claiming a hardship exemption because your gross income is below the filing threshold? . . . . ☐ Yes ☐ No

Part III | **Coverage Exemptions for Individuals Claimed on Your Return:** If you and/or a member of your tax household are claiming an exemption on your return, complete Part III.

	a Name of Individual	b SSN	c Exemption Type	d Full Year	e Jan	f Feb	g Mar	h Apr	i May	j June	k July	l Aug	m Sept	n Oct	o Nov	p Dec
8																
9																
10																
11																
12																
13																

For Privacy Act and Paperwork Reduction Act Notice, see your tax return instructions. Cat. No. 37787G Form **8965** (2014)

2014

Department of the Treasury
Internal Revenue Service

Instructions for Form 8965

Health Coverage Exemptions
(and instructions for figuring your shared responsibility payment)

Future Developments

For the latest information about developments related to Form 8965 and its instructions, such as legislation enacted after they were published, go to *www.irs.gov/form8965*.

General Instructions

Purpose of Form

Beginning in 2014, individuals must have health care coverage, have a health coverage exemption, or make a shared responsibility payment with their tax return. Use Form 8965 to report a coverage exemption granted by the Marketplace (also called the "Exchange") or to claim a coverage exemption on your tax return. In addition, if for any month you or another member of your tax household had neither health care coverage nor a coverage exemption, these instructions provide the information you will need to calculate your shared responsibility payment.

Some coverage exemptions are available only from the Marketplace, others are available only by claiming them on your tax return, and others are available from either the Marketplace or by claiming them on your tax return. If you or another member of your tax household was granted a coverage exemption from the Marketplace, complete Part I of Form 8965. If you or another member of your tax household is claiming a coverage exemption on your tax return, complete Part II or Part III of Form 8965. Depending on your situation, you may need to complete one or more parts of the form.

These instructions also provide the information you will need to calculate your shared responsibility payment if, for any month, you or another member of your tax household did not have qualifying health care coverage (referred to as "minimum essential coverage") or a coverage exemption. Use the Shared Responsibility Payment Worksheet, later, to figure your payment, if any. You will report any payment amount on your tax return (Form 1040, line 61; Form 1040A, line 38; or Form 1040EZ, line 11).

Who Must File

If you are required to file a tax return, you do not have minimum essential coverage for yourself and everyone else in your tax household, and you want to report or claim a coverage exemption for yourself or another member of your tax household, file Form 8965 to report or claim coverage exemptions. Attach Form 8965 to your tax return (Form 1040, Form 1040A, or Form 1040EZ).

If you are unable to check the box on your Form 1040 series return indicating that every member of your tax household had minimum essential coverage in every month of 2014 (and therefore you are filing Form 8965 to report or claim a coverage exemption or

are making a shared responsibility payment), you do not need to take any action to indicate that some members of your tax household had minimum essential coverage for some or all months in 2014.

If you are not required to file a tax return, your tax household is exempt from the shared responsibility payment and you do not need to file a tax return to claim the coverage exemption. However, if you are not required to file a tax return but choose to file anyway, claim the coverage exemption on line 7a or 7b of Form 8965. (See the instructions under *Part II*, later.)

 Only one Form 8965 should be filed for each tax household. If you can be claimed as a dependent by another taxpayer, you do not need to file Form 8965 and do not owe a shared responsibility payment.

 Even if you do not need to report or claim a coverage exemption, you will need to use the Shared Responsibility Payment Worksheet included in these instructions to calculate the shared responsibility payment if you or another member of your tax household did not have minimum essential coverage or a coverage exemption for one or more months. Report any payment amount on your tax return but do not submit the Shared Responsibility Payment Worksheet to the IRS.

More Information

For more information on coverage exemptions, the shared responsibility payment, and other terms discussed in these instructions, including answers to Frequently Asked Questions and links to the final regulations issued by the Treasury Department and IRS, go to *www.irs.gov/uac/Individual-Shared-Responsibility-Provision*.

Types of Coverage Exemptions

The Types of Coverage Exemptions chart, later, shows the types of coverage exemptions available and whether the coverage exemption may be granted by the Marketplace, claimed on your tax return, or both. If you are claiming a coverage exemption in Part III, the right-hand column of the chart shows which code you should enter in column c to claim that particular coverage exemption.

 If you did not apply for a coverage exemption from the Marketplace during 2014, claim the coverage exemption on your tax return, if allowed. If the coverage exemption can be granted only by the Marketplace (for example, a coverage exemption based on membership in certain religious sects or certain other exemptions sometimes referred to as hardship exemptions), apply to the Marketplace for that coverage exemption before filing your tax return. If the Marketplace has not processed your application before you file your tax return, complete Part I and enter "pending" in column c for each individual listed.

Types of Coverage Exemptions

This chart shows all of the coverage exemptions available for 2014, including information about where the coverage exemptions can be obtained and the code for the coverage exemption that is to be used on Form 8965 when you claim the exemption. If your coverage exemption was granted by the Marketplace, enter the ECN (see the instructions for *Part I*).

Coverage Exemption	Granted by Marketplace	Claimed on tax return	Code for Exemption
Income below the filing threshold — Your gross income or your household income was less than your applicable minimum threshold for filing a tax return.			No Code See Part II
Coverage considered unaffordable — The minimum amount you would have paid for premiums is more than 8% of your household income.		✓	A
Short coverage gap — You went without coverage for less than 3 consecutive months during the year.		✓	B
Citizens living abroad and certain noncitizens — You were: • A U.S. citizen or resident who spent at least 330 full days outside of the U.S. during a 12–month period; • A U.S. citizen who was a bona fide resident of a foreign country or U.S. territory; • A resident alien who was a citizen of a foreign country with which the U.S. has an income tax treaty with a nondiscrimination clause, and you were a bona fide resident of a foreign country for the tax year; or • Not a U.S. citizen, not a U.S. national, and not an individual lawfully present in the U.S. For more information about who is treated as lawfully present for purposes of this coverage exemption, visit *healthcare.gov*.		✓	C
Members of a health care sharing ministry — You were a member of a health care sharing ministry.	✓	✓	D
Members of Indian tribes — You were either a member of a Federally-recognized Indian tribe, including an Alaska Native Claims Settlement Act (ANCSA) Corporation Shareholder (regional or village), or you were otherwise eligible for services through an Indian health care provider or the Indian Health Service.	✓	✓	E
Incarceration — You were in a jail, prison, or similar penal institution or correctional facility after the disposition of charges.	✓	✓	F
Aggregate self-only coverage considered unaffordable — Two or more family members' aggregate cost of self-only employer-sponsored coverage was more than 8% of household income, as was the cost of any available employer-sponsored coverage for the entire family.		✓	G
Gap in coverage at the beginning of 2014 — You had a coverage gap at the beginning of 2014 but were either enrolled in, or were treated as having enrolled in, coverage through the Marketplace or outside of the Marketplace with an effective date on or before May 1, 2014.		✓	G
Gap in CHIP coverage — You applied for CHIP coverage during the initial open enrollment period and were found eligible for CHIP based on that application but had a coverage gap at the beginning of 2014.		✓	G
Resident of a state that did not expand Medicaid — Your household income was below 138% of the federal poverty line for your family size and at any time in 2014 you resided in a state that did not participate in the Medicaid expansion under the Affordable Care Act.	✓	✓	G
Limited benefit Medicaid and TRICARE programs that are not minimum essential coverage — You were enrolled in certain types of Medicaid and TRICARE programs that are not minimum essential coverage. (Available only in 2014.)		✓	H
Employer coverage with non-calendar plan year beginning in 2013 — You were eligible, but did not purchase, coverage under an employer plan with a plan year that started in 2013 and ended in 2014. (Available only in 2014.)		✓	H
Members of certain religious sects — You are a member of a recognized religious sect.	✓		Need ECN See Part I
Determined ineligible for Medicaid in a state that did not expand Medicaid coverage — You were determined ineligible for Medicaid solely because the state in which you resided did not participate in Medicaid expansion under the Affordable Care Act.	✓		Need ECN See Part I
General hardship — You experienced a hardship that prevented you from obtaining coverage under a qualified health plan.	✓		Need ECN See Part I
Coverage considered unaffordable based on projected income — You did not have access to coverage that is considered affordable based on your projected household income.	✓		Need ECN See Part I
Unable to renew existing coverage — You were notified that your health insurance policy was not renewable and you considered the other plans available unaffordable.	✓		Need ECN See Part I
AmeriCorps coverage — You were engaged in service in AmeriCorps State and National, VISTA, or NCCC programs and were covered by short-term duration coverage or self-funded coverage provided by these programs.	✓		Need ECN See Part I

More Information

Definitions

Tax household. For purposes of Form 8965, your tax household generally includes you, your spouse (if filing a joint return), and any individual you claim as a dependent on your tax return. It also generally includes each individual you can, but do not, claim as a dependent on your tax return. To find out if you can claim someone as your dependent, see *Exemptions for Dependents* in Pub. 501,

Exemptions, Standard Deduction, and Filing Information, or *Line 6c—Dependents* in the instructions for Form 1040 or Form 1040A.

However, an individual is included in your tax household in a month only if he or she is alive for the full month. Also, if you adopt a child during the year, the child is included in your tax household only for the full months that follow the month in which the adoption occurs.

Dependents of more than one taxpayer. Your tax household does not include someone you can, but do not, claim as a dependent if the dependent is properly claimed on another taxpayer's return or can be claimed by a taxpayer with higher priority under the tie-breaker rules described in Pub. 501.

Household income. For purposes of Form 8965, your household income is your modified adjusted gross income (MAGI) plus the MAGI of each individual in your tax household whom you claim as a dependent and who is required to file his or her own tax return. Use the Filing Requirements for Children and Other Dependents chart to determine whether your dependent is required to file his or her own tax return. You will need to calculate your household income to determine if you can claim the exemption for unaffordable coverage or the exemption for individuals with household income below the filing threshold, and also if you owe a shared responsibility payment. For information on how to figure MAGI for this purpose, see *Modified adjusted gross income (MAGI)*, next.

Modified adjusted gross income (MAGI). For purposes of Form 8965, your MAGI is your adjusted gross income plus certain other items from your tax return.

If you file Form 1040. If you file Form 1040, figure your MAGI by adding the amounts reported on Form 1040, lines 8b and 37. If you claimed the foreign earned income exclusion, housing exclusion, or housing deduction, add the amount from Form 2555, lines 45 and 50, or Form 2555-EZ, line 18.

If you file Form 1040A. If you file Form 1040A, figure your MAGI by adding the amounts on Form 1040A, lines 8b and 21.

If you file Form 1040EZ. If you file Form 1040EZ, figure your MAGI by adding the amount on Form 1040EZ, line 4 and any tax-exempt interest reported in the space to the left of line 2.

Filing Requirements for Children and Other Dependents

This chart will help you determine whether your dependent is required to file his or her own tax return.

Single dependents. Was your dependent either age 65 or older or blind?

☐ **No.** Your dependent must file a return if **any** of the following apply.

- His or her unearned income was over $1,000.
- His or her earned income was over $6,200.
- His or her gross income was more than the **larger** of—
  - $1,000, or
  - His or her earned income (up to $5,850) plus $350.

☐ **Yes.** Your dependent must file a return if **any** of the following apply.

- His or her unearned income was over $2,550 ($4,100 if 65 or older **and** blind).
- His or her earned income was over $7,750 ($9,300 if 65 or older **and** blind).
- His or her gross income was more than the **larger** of—
  - $2,550 ($4,100 if 65 or older **and** blind), or
  - His or her earned income (up to $5,850) plus $1,900 ($3,450 if 65 or older **and** blind).

Married dependents. Was your dependent **either** age 65 or older **or** blind?

☐ **No.** Your dependent must file a return if **any** of the following apply.

- His or her unearned income was over $1,000.
- His or her earned income was over $6,200.
- His or her gross income was at least $5 and his or her spouse files a separate return and itemizes deductions.
- His or her gross income was more than the **larger** of—
  - $1,000, or
  - His or her earned income (up to $5,850) plus $350.

☐ **Yes.** Your dependent must file a return if **any** of the following apply.

- His or her unearned income was over $2,200 ($3,400 if 65 or older **and** blind).
- His or her earned income was over $7,400 ($8,600 if 65 or older **and** blind).
- His or her gross income was at least $5 and his or her spouse files a separate return and itemizes deductions.
- His or her gross income was more than the **larger** of—
  - $2,200 ($3,400 if 65 or older **and** blind), or
  - His or her earned income (up to $5,850) plus $1,550 ($2,750 if 65 or older **and** blind).

TIP In this chart, **unearned income** includes taxable interest, ordinary dividends, and capital gain distributions. It also includes unemployment compensation, taxable social security benefits, pensions, annuities, and distributions of unearned income from a trust. **Earned income** includes salaries, wages, tips, professional fees, and taxable scholarship and fellowship grants. **Gross income** is the total of your unearned and earned income.

Marketplace. A Marketplace, or Health Insurance Marketplace (also referred to as an "Exchange"), is a governmental agency or nonprofit entity that makes qualified health plans available to individuals. The term "Marketplace" refers to state Marketplaces, regional Marketplaces, subsidiary Marketplaces, and the Federally-facilitated Marketplace.

Minimum essential coverage. Minimum essential coverage is health coverage that satisfies the individual shared responsibility provision. Minimum essential coverage generally includes coverage under a government-sponsored program, coverage from your employer, a plan that you buy in the individual market, and certain other coverage. The Types of Minimum Essential Coverage chart provides more information about the plans and arrangements that are minimum essential coverage.

Timing. You are considered to have minimum essential coverage for a month if you have it for at least 1 day during that month. For example, if you start a new job on June 26 and are covered under your employer's plan starting on that day, you are treated as having coverage for the entire month of June.

Foreign coverage. In general, coverage provided by a foreign employer to its employees and related individuals is minimum essential coverage. Individuals with such coverage should see Pub. 974, Premium Tax Credit (PTC). However, coverage purchased directly from a foreign health insurance issuer or provided by the government of a foreign country does not qualify as minimum essential coverage unless recognized as minimum essential coverage by the Department of Health and Human Services (HHS). To find out if HHS has recognized particular forms of foreign coverage as minimum essential coverage, go to *www.irs.gov/uac/ Individual-Shared-Responsibility-Provision*.

Coverage for business owners. Minimum essential coverage includes coverage provided to a business owner (such as a partner or sole proprietor) under a plan that is eligible employer-sponsored coverage with respect to at least one employee.

Types of Minimum Essential Coverage

Employer-sponsored coverage:
- Group health insurance coverage for employees under—
    - A governmental plan, such as the Federal Employees Health Benefit program
    - A plan or coverage offered in the small or large group market within a state
    - A grandfathered health plan offered in a group market
- A self-insured health plan for employees
- COBRA coverage
- Retiree coverage

Individual health coverage:
- Health insurance you purchase directly from an insurance company
- Health insurance you purchase through the Marketplace
- Health insurance provided through a student health plan
- Health coverage provided through a student health plan that is self-funded by a university*

Coverage under government-sponsored programs:
- Medicare Part A coverage
- Medicare Advantage plans
- Most Medicaid coverage**
- Children's Health Insurance Program (CHIP)
- Most types of TRICARE coverage**
- Comprehensive health care programs offered by the Department of Veterans Affairs
- State high-risk health insurance pools*
- Health coverage provided to Peace Corps volunteers
- Department of Defense Nonappropriated Fund Health Benefits Program
- Refugee Medical Assistance

Other coverage:
- Certain foreign coverage
- Certain coverage for business owners

*This type of health coverage will not qualify as minimum essential coverage for plan years beginning after 2014 unless HHS recognizes it as minimum essential coverage under its own regulations.

**Medicaid and TRICARE programs that provide limited benefits generally do not qualify as minimum essential coverage; however, see *Limited benefit Medicaid or TRICARE programs that are not minimum essential coverage*, later.

Shared Responsibility Payment Worksheet

If you or another member of your tax household had neither minimum essential coverage nor a coverage exemption for any month during 2014, use the Shared Responsibility Payment Worksheet, below, to figure your shared responsibility payment. You will enter the amount from line 14 of the worksheet on Form 1040, line 61; Form 1040A, line 38; or Form 1040EZ, line 11.

Complete the monthly columns by placing "X's" in each month in which you or another member of your tax household had neither minimum essential coverage nor a coverage exemption.

Name	Jan	Feb	Mar	Apr	May	Jun	Jul	Aug	Sep	Oct	Nov	Dec
1. Total number of X's in a month. If 5 or more, enter 5												
2. Total number of X's in a month for individuals 18 or over*												
3. One-half the number of X's in a month for individuals under 18*												
4. Add lines 2 and 3 for each month												
5. Multiply line 4 by $95 for each month. If $285 or more, enter $285												

6. Sum of the monthly amounts entered on line 1 .... ____

7. Enter your household income (see *Household income*, earlier) .... ____

8. Enter your filing threshold (see *Filing Thresholds For Most People*, later) ..... ____

9. Subtract line 8 from line 7 .... ____

10. Multiply line 9 by 1% (.01) .... ____

11. Is line 10 more than $285?

  ☐ **Yes.** Multiply line 10 by the number of months for which line 1 is more than zero }
  ☐ **No.** Enter the amount from line 14 of the Flat Dollar Amount Worksheet } .... ____

12. Divide line 11 by 12.0 .... ____

13. Multiply line 6 by $204** .... ____

14. Enter the smaller of line 12 or line 13 here and on Form 1040, line 61; Form 1040A, line 38; or Form 1040EZ, line 11. This is your shared responsibility payment .... ____

*For purposes of figuring the shared responsibility payment, an individual is considered under 18 for an entire month if he or she did not turn 18 before the first day of the month. An individual turns 18 on the anniversary of the day the individual was born. For example, someone born on March 1, 1999, is considered age 18 on March 1, 2017, and, therefore, is not considered age 18 for purposes of the shared responsibility payment until April 2017.

**$204 is the 2014 national average premium for a bronze level health plan available through the Marketplace for one individual and should not be changed.

Flat Dollar Amount Worksheet

 Do not complete this worksheet unless the amount on line 10 of the Shared Responsibility Payment Worksheet is less than $285.

For each month, is the amount on line 5 of the Shared Responsibility Payment Worksheet less than the amount on line 10 of the Shared Responsibility Payment Worksheet?*	Yes	No
	Enter the amount from line 10	Enter the amount from line 5
1. January		
2. February		
3. March		
4. April		
5. May		
6. June		
7. July		
8. August		
9. September		
10. October		
11. November		
12. December		
13. Add the amounts in each column		
14. Add the amounts on line 13 of both columns. Enter the result on line 11 of the Shared Responsibility Payment Worksheet		

*If the amount on line 1 of the Shared Responsibility Payment Worksheet is -0- for any month, leave both columns of this worksheet blank for that month.

Filing Thresholds For Most People

If your filing status is:	And your age is:	Then you must file a tax return if your gross income is more than:
Single	Under 65	$10,150
	65 or older	$11,700
Head of Household	Under 65	$13,050
	65 or older	$14,600
Married Filing Jointly	Under 65 (both spouses)	$20,300
	65 or older (one spouse)	$21,500
	65 or older (both spouses)	$22,700
Married Filing Separately	Any age	$3,950
Qualifying Widow(er) with Dependent children	Under 65	$16,350
	65 or older	$17,550

 Gross income means all income you received in the form of money, goods, property, and services that is not exempt from tax, including any income from sources outside the United States or from the sale of your main home (even if you can exclude part or all of it). Include only the taxable part of social security benefits (Form 1040, line 20b; Form 1040A, line 14b). Also include gains, but not losses, reported on Form 8949 or Schedule D. Gross income from a business means, for example, the amount on Schedule C, line 7, or Schedule F, line 9. But, in figuring gross income, do not reduce your income by any losses, including any loss on Schedule C, line 7, or Schedule F, line 9.

Specific Instructions
Part I — Marketplace-Granted Coverage Exemptions for Individuals

If you or another member of your tax household has been granted one or more coverage exemptions from the Marketplace, or has an application for a coverage exemption pending with the Marketplace, complete Part I to report these exemptions. Complete a line for each individual who received or has a pending application for a Marketplace-granted coverage exemption. If an individual was granted or has a pending application for more than one coverage exemption from the Marketplace, complete a separate line for each coverage exemption for that individual. If your tax household was granted or has a pending application for more than six coverage exemptions from the Marketplace, attach a separate statement showing the information required in columns a through c for each additional coverage exemption.

Lines 1–6
Column a—Name of Individual

Enter the name of each person in your tax household who was granted a coverage exemption from the Marketplace or has an application for a coverage exemption pending with the Marketplace. If the individual is listed on page 1 of your tax return, enter the name exactly as it appears on your tax return.

Column b—Social Security Number (SSN)

Enter the SSN of the individual listed in column a. If the individual is listed on page 1 of your tax return, the SSN in this column should match the individual's SSN listed on your tax return.

Column c—Exemption Certificate Number (ECN)

Enter the ECN that you received from the Marketplace for the individual listed in column a. If you were granted a coverage exemption from the Marketplace, but did not receive an ECN, or do not know your ECN, contact the Marketplace to obtain your ECN. If the Marketplace has not processed your application before you file, enter "pending."

Members of certain religious sects (enter ECN). An individual may claim a coverage exemption for members of recognized religious sects only if the Marketplace has granted the individual an exemption. A recognized religious sect is a religious sect in existence since December 31, 1950, that is recognized by the Social Security Administration as conscientiously opposed to accepting any insurance benefits, including Medicare and social security.

 In addition to the coverage exemption for members of recognized religious sects, certain other exemptions sometimes referred to as hardship exemptions also may be granted only by the Marketplace. See the Types of Coverage Exemptions chart, earlier.

 Members of a health care sharing ministry, members of Federally-recognized Indian tribes, individuals eligible for services from an Indian health care provider, and incarcerated individuals may have been granted a coverage exemption from the Marketplace or may claim a coverage exemption on their tax return. If you received one of these coverage exemptions from the Marketplace, follow the instructions for Part I to report your exemption. If you did not receive a coverage exemption from the Marketplace and want to claim one of these exemptions on your tax return, see the instructions for Part III, later.

Part II — Coverage Exemptions for Your Household Claimed on Your Return

Use Part II to claim a coverage exemption on behalf of your tax household because your household income or your gross income is less than your filing threshold. See *Filing Thresholds For Most People*, earlier, to figure your filing threshold.

 If you are not required to file a tax return and do not wish to file a return, your tax household is exempt from the shared responsibility payment and you do not need to file a return or do anything else to claim the coverage exemption. If your gross income is less than your filing threshold but you file a tax return for any reason, see the instructions for lines 7a and 7b next.

Line 7a—Household Income Below Filing Threshold

You can claim a coverage exemption if your household income is less than your filing threshold. To claim this coverage exemption, you must first figure your household income (see *Household income*, under *Definitions*, earlier). Then compare your household income to the filing threshold that applies to you based on your filing status. If your household income is less than your filing threshold, check the box labeled "yes."

If you qualify for this coverage exemption, everyone in your tax household is exempt for the entire year.

Line 7b—Gross Income Below Filing Threshold

You can claim a coverage exemption if your gross income is less than your filing threshold. To claim this coverage exemption, you must first figure your gross income. Then compare your gross income to the filing threshold that applies to you based on your filing status. See *Filing Thresholds For Most People*, earlier. If your gross income is less than your filing threshold, check the box labeled "yes."

If you qualify for this coverage exemption, everyone in your tax household is exempt for the entire year.

Part III — Coverage Exemptions for Individuals Claimed on Your Return

Use Part III to claim a coverage exemption on your tax return for yourself or another member of your tax household. Complete a line for each individual for whom you are claiming a coverage exemption. If you are claiming more than one coverage exemption for any individual, you must generally complete a separate line for each coverage exemption. But if, for any individual, you are claiming two or more different types of coverage exemptions that have the same code listed in the Types of Coverage Exemptions chart, use a single line to claim those coverage exemptions. If you need more than six lines, attach an additional page showing the information required in columns a through p, as applicable, for each additional coverage exemption.

 Coverage exemptions that may be granted for less than a full tax year apply in all months in which an individual was eligible for the coverage exemption for at least one day in that month. For example, if an individual is incarcerated following the disposition of charges from June 28 to July 28, the individual is eligible for the coverage exemption for June and July.

Lines 8–13
Column a—Name of Individual

Enter the name of each person in your tax household for whom you are claiming a coverage exemption. If the individual is listed on page 1 of your tax return, enter the name exactly as it appears on your tax return.

Column b—Social Security Number (SSN)

Enter the SSN of the individual listed in column a. If the individual is listed on page 1 of your tax return, the SSN in this column should match the individual's SSN listed on your tax return.

IRS Individual Taxpayer Identification Number (ITIN) for Aliens. If the individual listed in column a does not have and is not eligible to get an SSN, enter the ITIN assigned to that person by the IRS. If the individual was placed with you for legal adoption and you do not know his or her SSN, enter the adoption taxpayer identification number (ATIN) assigned to that individual by the IRS.

No identification number. If the individual listed in column a does not have an SSN, ITIN, ATIN, or other identification number from the IRS, leave column b blank for that individual.

Column c—Exemption Type

Use column c to identify the type of coverage exemption you are claiming for yourself or another member of your tax household. Enter the code for the appropriate coverage exemption listed below and in the Types of Coverage Exemptions chart, earlier.

Coverage considered unaffordable (code "A"). You can claim a coverage exemption for yourself or another member of your tax household for any month when the lowest cost coverage through an employer sponsored plan or, if the individual does not have access to employer sponsored coverage, coverage in the Marketplace is unaffordable for the individual. Coverage is unaffordable if the individual's required contribution (described below) is more than 8% of household income.

Use the Affordability Worksheet, later, to determine whether this coverage exemption applies to you or another member of your tax household for one or months of the year.

To claim this coverage exemption, enter code "A" in Part III, column c, and identify the months to which the exemption applies as described under *Column d - p—Calendar Months*, later.

Your required contribution depends on the type of coverage you are eligible to purchase. If you or another member of your tax household is eligible for coverage under an employer plan, see *Determining an individual's required contribution—Individuals eligible for coverage under an employer plan*, later. If you or another member of your tax household is not eligible for coverage under an employer plan, see *Determining and individual's required contribution—Individuals not eligible for coverage under an employer plan*, later. An individual is eligible for coverage under an employer plan for a month if the individual could have enrolled in the plan and had coverage for any day that month, even if the individual is eligible for another type of minimum essential coverage. Individuals eligible for coverage under an employer plan for a month do not need to determine whether other coverage would be affordable for that month.

Household income adjustment. For purposes of determining whether this coverage exemption applies, increase household income by the amount that the wages of you or your tax household were reduced to pay all or a portion of the premiums for employer-sponsored coverage (a salary reduction arrangement).

Determining an individual's required contribution—Individuals eligible for coverage under an employer plan.

Employees eligible for self-only coverage from their employers. If you or another member of your tax household is an employee and is eligible for self-only coverage through his or her own employer, the employee's required contribution is the amount he or she would pay for the lowest cost self-only coverage in which he or she can enroll. For this purpose, the amount the employee would pay includes an amount that may be paid through a salary reduction arrangement.

Other family members eligible for employer coverage. If you or another member of your tax household is not eligible for coverage through his or her own employer (if any) but is eligible for family coverage under a plan offered by your employer or your spouse's employer if filing jointly (for example, a child who is eligible to enroll in family coverage offered by your employer), the individual's required contribution is the amount the employee would pay for the lowest cost family coverage that would cover everyone in the tax household:

- for whom a personal exemption deduction is claimed on your tax return,
- who is eligible for the coverage, and
- who does not qualify for another coverage exemption.

For this purpose, the amount the employee would pay includes amounts that may be paid through a salary reduction arrangement.

Example 1—unmarried employee with no dependents. Joyce is unmarried and has no dependents. Her household income is $60,000. During 2014, Joyce could purchase self-only coverage through her employer at a total cost to her of $5,000. As a result, Joyce can claim the exemption for unaffordable coverage because her required contribution ($5,000) is more than 8% of her household income ($4,800, which is $60,000 multiplied by .08).

Example 2—married employee with dependents. Susan and Lee are married and file a joint return for 2014. They have two children, Elizabeth and Emilee, whom they claim as dependents on their return. During 2014, Susan could purchase self-only coverage under a plan offered by her employer at a cost to her of $4,000. Susan could also purchase family coverage under the plan, which would cover her, Lee, Elizabeth, and Emilee, at a cost to her of $12,000. Their household income for 2014 is $90,000.

Susan is ineligible for the exemption for unaffordable coverage for 2014 because her required contribution ($4,000) is not more than 8% of her household income ($7,200, which is $90,000 multiplied by .08). The required contribution for Lee, Elizabeth, and Emilee is Susan's share of the cost for family coverage ($12,000), which is more than 8% of their household income ($7,200). As a result, Lee, Elizabeth, and Emilee are eligible for the exemption for unaffordable coverage for 2014.

Employer-sponsored coverage for part of the year. If you or another member of your tax household becomes unemployed or changes employers during the year, test the affordability of coverage for that individual separately for each employment period. Similarly, if the required contribution for any employer plan changes during the year (generally because one plan year ends and another one starts during the year), test the affordability of the coverage separately for each period.

Coverage under an employer plan is considered unaffordable for a part-year period if the annualized premium for self-only coverage (in the case of an employee) or family coverage (in the case of a related individual) under the plan for the part-year period is more than 8% of your household income.

You can use the Annualized Premium Worksheet to figure the annualized premium.

 If you or another member of your tax household was eligible for coverage under an employer plan with a plan year that started in 2013 and ended in 2014, see Non-calendar year employer plan beginning in 2013, later. You do not owe a shared responsibility payment for that individual for any month during that plan year (use code "H" to claim this coverage exemption). However, this exemption is not available for the months in 2014 that follow the last month included in the plan year that started in 2013 and ended in 2014.

Annualized Premium Worksheet

 Complete a separate worksheet for each part-year period.

1. Enter the premiums paid during the part-year period _____
2. Enter the number of full months in the part-year period _____
3. Divide line 1 by line 2 _____
4. Multiply line 3 by 12.0. This is your annualized premium _____

Example 3—plan year other than calendar year. Braden is unmarried and has no dependents. His household income is $60,000. Braden is eligible for coverage under his employer's plan, but the plan does not run on a calendar year. In June 2013, Braden could have purchased self-only coverage for the period from July 2013 through June 2014 at a total cost to him of $4,750. In June 2014, he could have purchased self-only coverage for the period from July 2014 through June 2015 at a total cost to him of $5,000. Braden can claim the coverage exemption for <u>non-calendar year employer plans from 2013</u>, explained later, for January 2014 through June 2014. Braden can claim the exemption for unaffordable coverage from July 2014 through December 2014 because his annualized required contribution for that period is $5,000 ($2,500 paid for premiums during the 6-month period divided by 6 and multiplied by 12), which is more than 8% of his household income ($4,800, which is $60,000 multiplied by .08).

Determining an individual's required contribution— Individuals not eligible for coverage under an employer plan. If you or another member of your tax household cannot purchase coverage under an employer plan, the individual's required contribution is based on the premium for the lowest cost bronze plan available through the Marketplace minus the maximum premium tax credit that you could have claimed if the individuals had enrolled in this plan. Use the <u>Marketplace Coverage Affordability Worksheet</u> to determine whether you or another member of your tax household is eligible for this coverage exemption.

For this purpose, use the lowest cost bronze plan available through the Marketplace that covers everyone in your tax household:
• for whom a personal exemption deduction is claimed on your tax return,
• who is not eligible for employer coverage, and
• who does not qualify for another coverage exemption.

For information on the lowest cost bronze plan you could have purchased for your tax household, visit *healthcare.gov* or contact the Marketplace serving your area. Subtract from the premium the maximum premium tax credit that you could have claimed if these individuals had enrolled in that plan. You can claim the exemption for unaffordable coverage for the individual if the result is more than 8% of your household income.

If the Marketplace serving the area where the individual resides does not offer a single bronze plan that would cover everyone in your tax household who may be eligible for the exemption for unaffordable coverage, add the premiums for the lowest cost bronze plans that are offered through the Marketplace where one or more of the members of your tax household who may be eligible for this exemption reside that would together cover all of these individuals.

For information about the premium tax credit, see the instructions for Form 8962 and Pub. 974.

Example 4—unmarried individual with no dependents and no employer coverage. Eastin is unmarried and has no dependents. His household income is $40,000. For each month in 2014, he is ineligible to enroll in employer coverage. The annual premium for the lowest cost bronze self-only plan in Eastin's rating area is $5,000 and the maximum premium tax credit that he could claim if he had enrolled in this coverage is $1,700. Eastin can claim the exemption for unaffordable coverage for 2014 because his required contribution is $3,300 ($5,000 minus $1,700), which is more than 8% of his household income ($3,200, which is $40,000 multiplied by .08).

Short coverage gap (code "B"). You generally can claim a coverage exemption for yourself or another member of your tax household for each month of a gap in coverage of less than 3 consecutive months. If an individual had more than one short coverage gap during the year, the individual is exempt only for the month(s) in the first gap. If an individual had a gap of 3 months or more, the individual is not exempt for any of those months. For

example, if an individual had coverage for every month in the year except February and March, the individual is exempt for those 2 months. However, if an individual had coverage for every month in the year except February, March, and April, the individual is not exempt for any of those months.

Example—short coverage gap. Fred has minimum essential coverage except for the period April 5 through July 25. An individual is treated as having coverage for any month in which he or she has coverage for at least 1 day of the month. As a result, Fred has minimum essential coverage in April and July and is eligible for the short coverage gap exemption for May and June.

To claim this coverage exemption, enter code "B" in Part III, column c, and identify the months to which the exemption applies as described under <u>Column d - p—Calendar Months</u>, later.

Citizens living abroad and certain noncitizens (code "C"). You can claim a coverage exemption for yourself or another member of your tax household to which any of the following apply.
• The individual is a U.S. citizen or resident who is physically present in a foreign country (or countries) for at least 330 full days within a 12-month period. You can claim the coverage exemption for any month during your tax year that is included in the 12-month period. For more information, see *Physical Presence Test* in Pub. 54, Tax Guide for U.S. Citizens and Resident Aliens Abroad.
• The individual is a U.S. citizen who is a bona fide resident of a foreign country (or countries) for an entire tax year. You can claim the coverage exemption for the entire year. For more information, see *Bona Fide Residence Test* in Pub. 54.
• The individual is a resident alien who is a citizen or national of a country with which the U.S. has an income tax treaty with an applicable nondiscrimination clause and who is a bona fide resident of a foreign country for an uninterrupted period that includes an entire tax year. You can claim the coverage exemption for the entire year. For more information, see *Bona Fide Residence Test* in Pub. 54.
• The individual is a bona fide resident of a U.S. territory. You can claim the coverage exemption for the entire year.
• The individual is not a U.S. citizen, not a U.S. national, and not an individual lawfully present in the U.S. For more information about who is treated as lawfully present for purposes of this coverage exemption, visit *healthcare.gov*.
• You file a Form 1040NR or Form 1040NR-EZ. Do not attach Form 8965 to your tax return.

To claim this coverage exemption, enter code "C" in Part III, column c, and identify the months to which the exemption applies as described under <u>Column d - p—Calendar Months</u>, later.

Members of a health care sharing ministry (code "D"). You can claim a coverage exemption for yourself or another member of your tax household for any month in which the individual was a member of a health care sharing ministry for at least 1 day in the month. Enter code "D" in Part III, column c, and identify the months to which the coverage exemption applies as described under <u>Column d - p—Calendar Months</u>, later.

In general, a health care sharing ministry is a tax-exempt organization whose members share a common set of ethical or religious beliefs and share medical expenses in accordance with those beliefs, even after a member develops a medical condition. The health care sharing ministry (or a predecessor) must have been in existence and sharing medical expenses continuously and without interruption since December 31, 1999. An individual who is unsure whether a ministry meets the requirements should contact the ministry for further information.

 If you or another member of your tax household was a member of a health care sharing ministry and was granted a coverage exemption by the Marketplace, see the instructions for <u>Part I</u>, *earlier, to claim the exemption.*

Members of Indian tribes or individuals otherwise eligible for services from an Indian health care provider (code "E"). You can claim a coverage exemption for yourself or another member of your tax household for any month in which the individual was a member of a Federally-recognized Indian tribe, including an Alaska Native Claims Settlement Act (ANCSA) Corporation Shareholder (regional or village), for at least 1 day in the month. The *list of Federally-recognized Indian tribes* is available at *www.bia.gov/ WhoWeAre/BIA/OIS/TribalGovernmentServices/TribalDirectory*. The list of village or regional corporations formed under ANCSA is available at *dnr.alaska.gov/mlw/trails/17b/corpindex.cfm*. You can also claim a coverage exemption for yourself or another member of

your tax household for any month in which the individual was eligible for services through an Indian health care provider or through the Indian Health Service.

To claim either of these coverage exemptions, enter code "E" in Part III, column c, and identify the months to which the exemption applies as described under *Column d - p—Calendar Months*, later.

 If you or another member of your tax household was a member of a Federally-recognized Indian tribe and was granted a coverage exemption by the Marketplace, see the instructions for Part I, earlier, to claim the exemption.

Affordability Worksheet

Use this worksheet to determine whether coverage for each individual in your tax household is unaffordable. If you or another member of your tax household is not eligible for employer-sponsored coverage, use the Marketplace Coverage Affordability Worksheet to figure the required contribution for that individual. An individual is exempt for any month in which (B), the Required Contribution, is more than (A), the Affordability Threshold.

(A) Affordability Threshold

Enter 8% of your household income (see *Household income*). For this purpose, increase household income by the amount of any premium that is paid through a salary reduction arrangement and excluded from gross income.

(B) Required Contribution Amount

For each member of your tax household, enter in the columns provided the annual premium for the first option below that applies to that person. If the monthly premium is the same for the whole year, enter the annual premium in the space for each month. If the premiums cover only part of the year, use the Annualized Premium Worksheet to determine what the annualized premium would be for each month. Once you have figured the annualized premium, enter it in the space for each month.

Options (use the first that applies to each member of your tax household, including you, for each month):
1. The lowest cost self-only policy offered to each member of your tax household by his or her employer.
2. The lowest cost family policy* offered by your employer or your spouse's employer (if you are filing a joint return).
3. The amount from the Marketplace Coverage Affordability Worksheet.

For each individual, coverage is unaffordable and the individual is exempt if (B), the Required Contribution Amount, is greater than (A), the Affordability Threshold.

Members of your tax household (enter one name per column):						
Premium for:						
January						
February						
March						
April						
May						
June						
July						
August						
September						
October						
November						
December						

*The policy must cover everyone in your tax household:

- for whom a personal exemption deduction is claimed on your tax return,
- who is not eligible for employer coverage, and
- who does not qualify for another coverage exemption.

Marketplace Coverage Affordability Worksheet

Use this worksheet to figure an individual's required contribution for any month in which the individual is not eligible for employer-sponsored coverage. Complete a separate worksheet for each part of the year in which either the individual resided in different geographic rating areas served by the Marketplace or for which the number of people in your tax household who are neither exempt nor eligible for employer-sponsored coverage was different.

Do not complete this worksheet unless you were instructed to do so in the Affordability Worksheet.

1. Enter the monthly premium for the lowest cost bronze plan that covers everyone in your tax household for whom a personal exemption deduction is claimed, who is not eligible for employer coverage, and who does not qualify for another coverage exemption for the month. To find the lowest cost bronze plan go to the Marketplace for your area . . . . _____

2. Enter your household income (see _Household income_) . . . . _____

3. Enter the total of all nontaxable social security benefits received by you, your spouse, and each claimed dependent who must file a tax return* . . . . _____

4. Add lines 2 and 3 . . . . _____

5. Enter the federal poverty line for the number of individuals in your tax household less any dependents not claimed. See the instructions for Form 8962, line 4 . . . . _____

6. Divide line 4 by line 5. If the result (without rounding) is less than 1.0 or more than 4.0, skip lines 7 though 10 and enter -0- on line 11. . . . . _____

7. Multiply line 6 by 100 and round to the nearest whole number. Enter the applicable figure for the result from the table in the instructions for Form 8962, line 7 . . . . _____

8. Multiply line 4 by line 7 . . . . _____

9. Divide line 8 by 12.0 . . . . _____

10. Enter the monthly premium for the second lowest cost silver plan premium that covers everyone in your tax household for whom a personal exemption deduction is claimed, who is not eligible for employer coverage, and who does not qualify for another coverage exemption for the month. To find the second lowest cost silver plan go the Marketplace for your area . . _____

11. Subtract line 9 from line 10 . . . . _____

12. Subtract line 11 from line 1. If zero or less, enter -0-. This is the individual's required contribution for the month . . . . . . _____

13. Is the individual eligible for this coverage for every month of the year?

☐ **Yes.** Multiply line 12 by 12.0. This is the annualized premium. Enter this amount in the space for every month on the Affordability Worksheet . . . . _____

☐ **No.** Use the Annualized Premium Worksheet to determine what the annualized premium would be for each month the individual was eligible for the coverage being tested. Enter the annualized premium in the space for the appropriate months on the Affordability Worksheet . . . . _____

*If the individual filed Form 1040, figure the nontaxable social security benefits received by that individual by subtracting Form 1040, line 20b from Form 1040, line 20a. If the individual filed Form 1040A, figure the nontaxable social security benefits received by that individual by subtracting Form 1040A, line 14b from Form 1040A, line 14a. If the individual filed Form 1040EZ, he or she should have received a Form SSA-1099 or Form RRB-1099 showing the social security benefits received by that individual, all of which were nontaxable.

Incarceration (code "F"). You can claim a coverage exemption for yourself or another member of your tax household for any month in which the individual was incarcerated for at least 1 day in the month. For this purpose, an individual is considered incarcerated if he or she was confined, after the disposition of charges, in a jail, prison, or similar penal institution or correctional facility. To claim this coverage exemption, enter code "F" in Part III, column c, and identify the months to which the exemption applies as described under _Column d - p—Calendar Months_, later.

TIP *If you or another member of your tax household was incarcerated and was granted a coverage exemption by the Marketplace, see the instructions for _Part I_, earlier, to claim the exemption.*

Aggregate self-only coverage considered unaffordable (code "G"). You and any other members of your tax household for whom you claim a personal exemption deduction can claim a coverage exemption for all months in 2014 if, for at least 1 month in 2014:

1. The cost of each self-only coverage through employers for two or more members of your tax household does not exceed 8% of household income when tested individually, and

2. The cost of family coverage that the members of your tax household described in condition 1 could enroll in through an employer exceeds 8% of household income, and

3. The combined cost of the self-only coverage identified in condition 1 exceeds 8% of household income.

Example 1—two offers of self-only coverage that together are unaffordable. Justin and Sally are married, have no dependents, and file a joint return. Justin is offered self-only coverage through his employer at a cost of 6% of the household income and is offered family coverage that would cover both Sally and him at a cost of 10% of the household income. Sally is offered self-only coverage through her employer at a cost of 5% of the household income but is not offered family coverage. Sally and Justin both may claim the coverage exemption for two or more members of a tax household whose combined cost of employer-sponsored coverage is considered unaffordable because the self-only coverage offered to Justin and Sally does not exceed 8% of the household income when tested individually, the cost of family coverage exceeds 8% of the household income, and the combined cost of the self-only coverage offered to Justin and Sally exceeds 8% of the household income.

Example 2—affordable family coverage. The facts are the same as in Example 1 except Justin's employer offers family coverage that would cover both Sally and him at a cost of 7% of the household income. Neither Justin nor Sally may claim the coverage exemption for two or more members of a tax household whose combined cost of employer-sponsored coverage is considered unaffordable, because the family coverage offered by Justin's employer covers both Justin and Sally and its cost does not exceed 8% of the household income.

Example 3—one spouse enrolls in coverage. The facts are the same as in Example 1 except Justin enrolls in the self-only coverage offered by his employer. Sally may claim the coverage exemption for two or more members of a tax household whose combined cost of employer-sponsored coverage is considered unaffordable.

To claim this coverage exemption, enter code "G" in Part III, column c, and check the box in column d.

Gap in coverage at the beginning of 2014 (code "G"). If you or another member of your tax household enrolled in coverage through the Marketplace and your coverage started on or before May 1, 2014, you can claim a coverage exemption for any month(s) prior to May 2014 that you (or another member of your tax household) did not have coverage.

In addition, if you or another member of your tax household enrolled in minimum essential coverage that started on or before May 1, 2014, from a source other than the Marketplace, you can claim a coverage exemption for that individual for any month(s) prior to May 2014 that you (or another member of your tax household) did not have coverage.

To claim this coverage exemption, enter code "G" in Part III, column c, and identify the months to which the exemption applies as described under *Column d - p—Calendar Months*, later. You can claim this exemption for any month prior to the effective date of the coverage.

 If you purchased insurance from the Marketplace on or after December 24, 2013, your insurance may not have been effective for 1 or more months during 2014. You can claim a coverage exemption for those months.

Gap in CHIP coverage (code "G"). If you or another member of your tax household applied for CHIP during the initial open enrollment period and, based on that application, was found eligible for CHIP, you can claim a coverage exemption for that individual for any month before the effective date of the individual's coverage. For most taxpayers, the initial open enrollment period began on October 1, 2013, and ended on March 31, 2014.

To claim this coverage exemption, enter code "G" in Part III, column c, and identify the months to which the exemption applies as described under *Column d - p—Calendar Months*, later.

Resident of a state that did not expand Medicaid (code "G"). You can claim a coverage exemption for yourself or another member of your tax household for 2014 if:
• Your household income is less than 138% of the federal poverty line for the number of individuals in your tax household, not including any dependents you did not claim; and
• At any time in 2014 the individual resided in Alabama, Alaska, Florida, Georgia, Idaho, Indiana, Kansas, Louisiana, Maine, Missouri, Mississippi, Montana, North Carolina, Nebraska, New Hampshire, Oklahoma, Pennsylvania, South Carolina, South Dakota, Tennessee, Texas, Utah, Virginia, Wyoming, or Wisconsin.

For purposes of this exemption, your household income is increased by the amount of any social security benefits that you received that were not included in your gross income. To see if your household income is less than 138% of the federal poverty line for the number of individuals in your tax household, not including any dependents you did not claim, see the instructions for Form 8962, line 4.

To claim this coverage exemption, enter code "G" in Part III, column c, and check the box in column d.

 Qualifying individuals can claim this exemption on their tax returns without visiting the Marketplace. However, if you applied to the Marketplace for the similar coverage exemption for individuals who resided in a state that did not expand Medicaid, see the instructions for Part I, earlier, to claim the exemption.

Limited benefit Medicaid or TRICARE programs that are not minimum essential coverage (code "H").
Government-sponsored programs that may provide only limited coverage generally do not qualify as minimum essential coverage; however, for 2014 only you can claim a coverage exemption with respect to an individual for any month during 2014 in which the individual is enrolled in one of the following programs:
• Family planning services Medicaid;
• Tuberculosis-related services Medicaid;
• Pregnancy-related Medicaid;
• Medicaid coverage only for emergency medical service;
• Coverage authorized under section 1115 of the Social Security Act;
• Medicaid for the medically needy, also known as Spend-down Medicaid or Share-of-cost Medicaid;
• Limited-benefit TRICARE coverage of space-available care; or
• Limited-benefit TRICARE coverage of line-of-duty care.

To claim this coverage exemption, enter code "H" in Part III, column c, and identify the months to which the exemption applies as described under *Column d - p—Calendar Months*, later.

 You should check www.irs.gov/uac/Individual-Shared-Responsibility-Provision for future updates about whether any of these programs are recognized as minimum essential coverage after 2014.

Non-calendar year employer plan beginning in 2013 (code "H"). If you or another member of your tax household was eligible for coverage under an employer plan with a plan year that started in 2013 and ended in 2014, you can claim a coverage exemption for that individual for any month during that plan year.

To claim this coverage exemption, enter code "H" in Part III, column c, and identify the months to which the exemption applies as described under *Column d - p—Calendar Months* next.

Columns d – p—Calendar Months

For each coverage exemption claimed in column a, check the appropriate box or boxes for the months for which the particular exemption applies. If the coverage exemption applies for the full year, check the box in column d and do not check the boxes in columns e – p.